JANE'S FIGHTING SHIPS

FOUNDED IN 1897 BY FRED T JANE

EDITED BY
Captain RICHARD SHARPE OBE RN

1992-93

ISBN 0 7106 0983 3

JANE'S DATA DIVISION
"Jane's" is a registered trade mark

In the USA and its dependencies
Jane's Information Group Inc, 1340 Braddock Place, Suite 300, Alexandria, VA 22314-1651, USA

British Library Cataloguing-in-Publication Data.
A catalogue record for this book is available from the British Library.

Printed and bound in Great Britain by Butler and Tanner Ltd, Frome and London.

SWAN HUNTER

Contents

Alphabetical list of advertisers

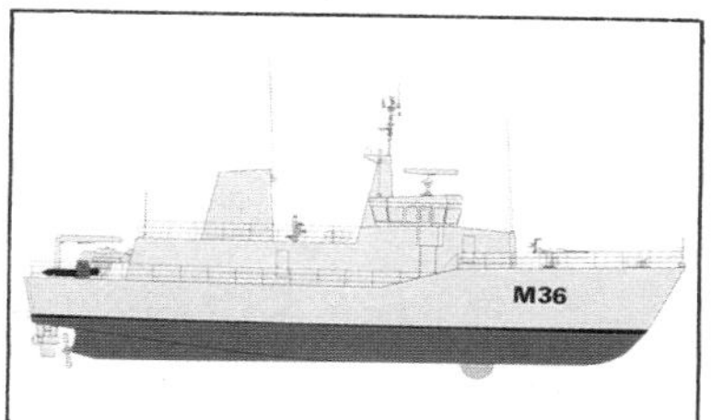

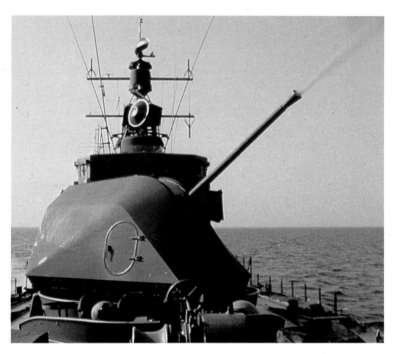

Royal Schelde
PO Box 16, 4380 AA, Vlissingen,
Holland .... [44]

S

Safare-Crouzet SA
98 avenue Saint-Lambert,
F-06105 Nice, Cedex 2
France .... [20]

Selenia Elsag Sistemi Navali
28/30 Via di S. Alessandro,
I-00131 Rome, Italy .... [13]

SEMT Pielstick
2 quai de Seine, I-93302 Saint-Denis,
France .... [70]

Sitep La Spezia
Via Vincinella loc.Ponzano,
I-19035 S. Stefano Magra, La Spezia,
Italy .... [38]

SMA SpA
PO Box 200, Florence,
Italy .... [14]

Societe Esercizio Cantieri (SEC)
Via Dei Pescatori 56, I-55049 Viareggio,
Italy .... [88]

Société Française Materiaux d'Armement (SOFMA)
17 Bd Malesherbes, F-75008 Paris,
France .... [68]

Sperry Marine Inc
1070 Seminole Trail,
Charlottesville, VA-22901,
USA .... [62]

Sulzer Escher Wyss
D-7980 Ravensburg,
Federal Republic of Germany .... [70]

Swedish Ordnance
S-691 80, Karlskoga, Sweden .... [9]

Swan Hunter Shipbuilders
Wallsend, Newcastle upon Tyne NE28 6EQ,
UK .... [2] & [3]

T

Teledyne INET
2750 West Lomita Boulevard,
Torrance, California 90505,
USA .... [46]

Thomson Sintra/ASM
525 route des Dolines, BP 138,
Parc Sophia Anitipolis, F-06561 Valbonne,
Cedex France .... [64]

Thyssen Nordseewerke GmbH
PO Box 2351, 2361 D-2970 Emden,
Federal Republic of Germany .... [104]

W

Wätsilä Diesel AB
Trollhätan, Sweden

Stork-Wärtsilä Diesel BV
Zwolle, The Netherlands .... [72]

Welse Consorzio Sistemi Subacque SpA
Via L Manara 2, I-16154 Genoa-Sestri,
Italy .... [41]

Whitehead SpA
Via Di Levante 48,
I-57128 Livorno, Italy .... [41]

Y

Yarrow (Shipbuilders) Ltd
South Street, Scotstoun, Glasgow G14 0XN,
Scotland .... [7]

Classified list of advertisers

The companies advertising in this publication have informed us that they are involved in the fields of manufacture indicated below:

Accelerometers
MagneTek Defense

AC Generators for electric systems, ships
MagneTek Defense
Netherlands Naval Industries Group
Wartsila Diesel

Acoustic sweeps
Thomson Sintra/ASM

Acoustic range equipment
Marconi Underwater
Safare-Crouzet
Thomson Sintra/ASM
WELSE
Whitehead

Acoustic transducers
Marconi Underwater
Safare-Crouzet
Selenia Elsag Sistemi Navali
Thomson Sintra/ASM
WELSE

Action information systems
Elbit Computers
NobelTech Systems

Action speed tactical trainers (ASTT)
Elbit Computers

Action information systems
Hollandse Signaalapparaten

Active Information Systems
NobelTech Systems

Air cushion vehicles
DCN
Hyundai Heavy Industries
Korea Tacoma Marine

Aircraft arresting gear
MacTaggart Scott

Aircraft carriers
DCN
Ingalls Shipbuilding
Melara Club Consortium
Swan Hunter

Aircraft ground support equipment (400 Hz power)
Teledyne INET

Aircraft ground support equipment (preconditioned air)
Teledyne INET

Air-sea rescue launches
FR Lürssen Werft

Ammunition
Empresa Nacional Bazan
Etienne Lacroix
OTO Melara
Swedish Ordnance
Whitehead

Ammunition fuzes
DCN
Etienne Lacroix
Matra Defense
NobelTech Electronics
OTO Melara
Swedish Ordnance

Ammunition hoists
DCN
MacTaggart Scott
OTO Melara

Amphibious ships
Hyundai Heavy Industries
Ingalls Shipbuilding
Korea Tacoma Marine
Royal Schelde
Swan Hunter
Yarrow Shipbuilders

Antennas
Elbit Computers
Elettronica
Hollandse Signaalapparaten
Selenia Elsag Sistemi Navali

Anti-aircraft missiles
Matra Defense
Swedish Ordnance

Anti-aircraft missiles (ship-launched)
Matra Defense
Selenia Elsag Sistemi Navali

Anti-ship missiles
Matra Defense
OTO Melara
Selenia Elsag Sistemi Navali

Anti-ship missile defence systems
Breda Meccanica Bresciana
Empresa Nacional Bazan
Hollandse Signaalapparaten
Matra Defense
OTO Melara
Selenia Elsag Sistemi Navali
Swedish Ordnance

Anti-ship missile (ship launched)
DCN
Matra Defense
OTO Melara
Selenia Elsag Sistemi Navali

Anti-submarine launchers
DCN
Loral Librascope
Matra Defense
OTO Melara
Whitehead

Anti-submarine rocket launchers
Creusot-Loire
DCN
Matra Defense

Anti-submarine systems
Loral Librascope
Marconi Underwater
Matra Defense
OTO Melara
Safare-Crouzet
Swedish Ordnance
Thomson Sintra/ASM
WELSE
Whitehead

Anti-submarine systems integration
Marconi Underwater
Safare-Crouzet
Selenia Elsag Sistemi Navali
Thomson Sintra/ASM
WELSE
Whitehead

Anti-submarine weapon systems, long-range
Loral Librascope
Marconi Underwater
Matra Defense
Mecanique Creusot-Loire
OTO Melara
Safare-Crouzet
Selenia Elsag Sistemi Navali
WELSE
Whitehead

Anti-tank missiles
Matra Defense
OTO Melara
Swedish Ordnance

Armour plates
Mecanique Creusot-Loire
OTO Melara

Armoured vehicles
Mecanique Creusot-Loire
OTO Melara
SOFMA
Swedish Ordnance

Artificial intelligence
DCN
Elbit Computers
Marconi Underwater
NEVESBU
Sperry Marine

Artillery
Empresa Nacional Bazan
OTO Melara
Swedish Ordnance

Assault craft
Crestitalia
Daewoo Shipbuilding & Heavy Machinery
FR Lürssen Werft
Hyundai Heavy Industries

Assault ships
Crestitalia
Daewoo Shipbuilding & Heavy Machinery
DCN
FR Lürssen Werft
Ingalls Shipbuilding
Melara Club Consortium
SOFMA
Swan Hunter
Yarrow Shipbuilders

ASW helicopter mission simulators
DCN
Whitehead

ASW weapon control systems
DCN
Hollandse Signaalapparaten
Marconi Underwater
NobelTech Systems
Safare-Crouzet
Thomson Sintra/ASM
WELSE
Whitehead

Automatic bus transfer switches
Teledyne INET

Automatic control systems
Riva Calzoni
Safare-Crouzet
Selenia Elsag Sistemi Navali
SEPA

Auxiliary machinery
DCN
Empresa Nacional Bazan
Wartsila Diesel

Auxiliary propulsion systems
Empresa Nacional Bazan
MacTaggart Scott
MagneTek Defense
Riva Calzoni
Wartsila Diesel

Auxiliary vessels
Bath Iron Works
Daewoo Shipbuilding & Heavy Machinery
DCN
Empresa Nacional Bazan
Fincantieri
FR Lürssen Werft
Hyundai Heavy Industries
Ingalls Shipbuilding
Melara Club Consortium
Swan Hunter
Yarrow Shipbuilders

Boilers
Daewoo Shipbuilding & Heavy Machinery
DCN
Empresa Nacional Bazan
Hyundai Heavy Industries

CLASSIFIED LIST OF ADVERTISERS

Bulk carriers
Daewoo Shipbuilding & Heavy Machinery
Fincantieri
Hyundai Heavy Industries

Cable-laying vessels
Daewoo Shipbuilding & Heavy Machinery
Fincantieri
Hyundai Heavy Industries
Swan Hunter

Cable looms
DCN
Marconi Underwater

Capstans and windlasses
MacTaggart Scott
Riva Calzoni

Car ferries
Daewoo Shipbuilding & Heavy Machinery
DCN
Fincantieri
Hyundai Heavy Industries
SEC
Swan Hunter

Cargo handling equipment
Hyundai Heavy Industries
MacTaggart Scott

Cargo ships
Daewoo Shipbuilding & Heavy Machinery
Fincantieri
Swan Hunter

Castings, aluminium-bronze
DCN
Netherlands Naval Industries Group

Castings, high-duty iron
DCN
Netherlands Naval Industries Group

Castings, non-ferrous
DCN
Netherlands Naval Industries Group

Castings, shell-moulded
DCN
Netherlands Naval Industries Group

Castings, SG iron
DCN
Netherlands Naval Industries Group

Castings, steel
DCN
Mecanique Creusot-Loire
Netherlands Naval Industries Group

Catamarans, multi-role, high-speed and workboats
Daewoo Shipbuilding & Heavy Machinery
DCN
Fincantieri
Hyundai Heavy Industries
SEC

Centralised & automatic control
Riva Calzoni
Safare-Crouzet
SEPA
Sperry Marine

Chaff
Etienne Lacroix
Swedish Ordnance

Chaff dispensers
Mecanique Creusot-Loire
Elbit Computers
Etienne Lacroix
Matra Defense
NobelTech Electronics

Chaff launchers
Breda Meccanica Bresciana
Etienne Lacroix
Loral Hycor
NobelTech Electronics
Selenia Elsag Sistemi Navali
Swedish Ordnance

Coast guard
Bath Iron Works
Fincantieri
Swan Hunter

Coast guard/patrol ships
Crestitalia
Daewoo Shipbuilding & Heavy Machinery
DCN
Empresa Nacional Bazan
Hyundai Heavy Industries
Korea Tacoma Marine
Netherlands Naval Industries Group
SEC
SOFMA
Swan Hunter
Yarrow Shipbuilders

Coast guard systems
FR Lürssen Werft
Safare-Crouzet

Coastal and inshore minesweepers
Crestitalia
DCN
FR Lürssen Werft
Netherlands Naval Industries Group
SOFMA
Swan Hunter
Yarrow Shipbuilders

Combat support boats
Crestitalia
Daewoo Shipbuilding & Heavy Machinery
FR Lürssen Werft
Hyundai Heavy Industries
Netherlands Naval Industries Group

Combat systems engineering
Bath Iron Works
C.I.S.DEG
DCN
Empresa Nacional Bazan
Hollandse Signaalapparaten
Loral Librascope
Melara Club Consortium

OTO Melara
Safare-Crouzet
Selenia Elsag Sistemi Navali
Yarrow Shipbuilders

Command/control/communications systems
Elbit Computers
Empresa Nacional Bazan
Hollandse Signaalapparaten
Loral Librascope
NobelTech Systems
Safare-Crouzet
Selenia Elsag Sistemi Navali
WELSE

Command/control real-time displays
Elbit Computers
Hollandse Signaalapparaten
Loral Librascope
NobelTech Systems
Sperry Marine
Thomson Sintra/ASM
WELSE

Communications systems
Elbit Computers
Loral Librascope
Marconi Underwater
Safare-Crouzet
Sperry Marine

Computer-assisted communications systems
Elbit Computers
Safare-Crouzet
Sperry Marine

Computer guidance
Marconi Underwater
WELSE

Computers
Hollandse Signaalapparaten
Marconi Underwater
Netherlands Naval Industries Group

Computer services
Marconi Underwater
NEVESBU
Swan Hunter

Construction, extension and modernisation
Empresa Nacional Bazan
Hyundai Heavy Industries
Swan Hunter

Container ships
Bath Iron Works
Daewoo Shipbuilding & Heavy Machinery
Fincantieri
Hyundai Heavy Industries
SEC
Swan Hunter

Control desks, electric
Netherlands Naval Industries Group

Corvettes
Daewoo Shipbuilding & Heavy Machinery
DCN
Empresa Nacional Bazan
Fincantieri
FR Lürssen Werft
Hyundai Heavy Industries
Ingalls Shipbuilding
Korea Tacoma Marine
Melara Club Consortium
Netherlands Naval Industries Group
SEC
Swan Hunter
Yarrow Shipbuilding

Countermeasures
Loral Librascope
MacTaggart Scott
MagneTek Defense
Marconi Underwater
Matra Defense
NobelTech Electronics
Safare-Crouzet
Sperry Marine
Swan Hunter
Thomson Sintra/ASM
WELSE
Whitehead

Craneships
Daewoo Shipbuilding & Heavy Machinery
Fincantieri
Hyundai Heavy Industries

Cruisers
Bath Iron Works
Fincantieri
Ingalls Shipbuilding
Melara Club Consortium
Swan Hunter

Cruise liners
Chantiers De l'Atlantique
Fincantieri
SEC
Swan Hunter

Current limiting devices
MagneTek Defense

Custom craft
Daewoo Shipbuilding & Heavy Machinery

Data links
Elbit Computers
Hollandse Signaalapparaten
Marconi Underwater
OTO Melara
WELSE

Data recording systems
Hollandse Signaalapparaten
Marconi Underwater

DC power supplies
MagneTek Defense
Teledyne INET
Wartsila Diesel

Deck machinery
DCN
Hyundai Heavy Industries
MacTaggart Scott
Riva Calzoni

Decoy systems (anti-ship missile)
Breda Meccanica Bresciana
Etienne Lacroix
NobelTech Electronics
Safare-Crouzet

Deep ocean survey
Marconi Underwater
Safare-Crouzet
Swan Hunter
Thomson Sintra/ASM

Defence contractors
Elbit Computers
Hollandse Signaalapparaten
MagneTek Defense
Marconi Underwater
Safare-Crouzet
Swan Hunter

Degaussing systems
MagneTek Defense
Thomson Sintra/ASM

Design of fast patrol boats/craft
Crestitalia
Daewoo Shipbuilding & Heavy Machinery
DCN
Empresa Nacional Bazan
Fincantieri
FR Lürssen Werft
Hyundai Heavy Industries
Korea Tacoma Marine
Swan Hunter

Design systems study and management services
Bath Iron Works
C.I.S.DEG
Empresa Nacional Bazan
Ingalls Shipbuilding
Marconi Underwater
NEVESBU
OTO Melara
Safare-Crouzet
Swan Hunter

Destroyers
Bath Iron Works
DCN
Empresa Nacional Bazan
Fincantieri
Hyundai Heavy Industries
Korea Tacoma Marine
Melara Club Consortium
Swan Hunter
Yarrow Shipbuilding

Diesel engines
CRM
Hyundai Heavy Industries
MTU
SEMT Pielstick
Wartsila Diesel

Diesel engines, auxiliary
Empresa Nacional Bazan
Fincantieri
Hyundai Heavy Industries
Netherlands Naval Industries Group
SEMT Pielstick
Wartsila Diesel

Diesel engines for locomotives
MTU
SEMT Pielstick

Diesel engines, main propulsion
Empresa Nacional Bazan
Fincantieri
Hyundai Heavy Industries
Netherlands Naval Industries Group
SEMT Pielstick
Wartsila Diesel

Diesel engine spare parts
Empresa Nacional Bazan
Fincantieri
Netherlands Naval Industries Group
SEMT Pielstick
Wartsila Diesel

Digital databus systems, shipborne
Elbit Computers
Hollandse Signaalapparaten
Marconi Underwater
Selenia Elsag Sistemi Navali
WELSE

Display systems
Elbit Computers
Hollandse Signaalapparaten
Marconi Underwater
Sperry Marine
Thomson Sintra/ASM

Distress beacon-submariner
Marconi Underwater
Safare-Crouzet
WELSE

Diver communications
Marconi Underwater
Safare-Crouzet
Thomson Sintra/ASM

Diving equipment
DCN
Safare-Crouzet

Diving systems
DCN
MacTaggart Scott
Mecanique Creusot-Loire
Safare-Crouzet

Diving vessels
Crestitalia
Daewoo Shipbuilding & Heavy Machinery
DCN
Hyundai Heavy Industries
Korea Tacoma Marine
Swan Hunter

Dock gates
DCN
MacTaggart Scott
Swan Hunter

Dredgers
Chantiers De l'Atlantique
Daewoo Shipbuilding & Heavy Machinery
DCN
Hyundai Heavy Industries
SEC
Swan Hunter

Dry cargo vessel
Chantiers De l'Atlantique
Daewoo Shipbuilding & Heavy Machinery
Fincantieri
Hyundai Heavy Industries
SEC
Swan Hunter

Dry-dock proprietors
Bath Iron Works
DCN
Empresa Nacional Bazan
Swan Hunter

Dynamic positioning
Riva Calzoni
SEPA
Thomson Sintra/ASM

Early warning systems
Hollandse Signaalapparaten
Safare-Crouzet
Selenia Elsag Sistemi Navali
Sperry Marine

Early warning systems, infa-red
Hollandse Signaalapparaten

Echo sounders
Safare-Crouzet
Thomson Sintra/ASM
WELSE

Electric-propulsion control panel on submarines
MagneTek Defense

Electrical auxiliaries
MagneTek Defense
Wartsila Diesel

Electrical equipment
MagneTek Defense
Wartsila Diesel

Electrical installations and repairs
Bath Iron Works
DCN
Netherlands Naval Industries Group
Wartsila Diesel

Electrical switchgear
Netherlands Naval Industries Group

Electrohydraulic auxiliaries
DCN
Hyundai Heavy Industries
MacTaggart Scott
Riva Calzoni

Electro-optics for airborne naval and ground defence
Barr & Stroud
Hollandse Signaalapparaten
Pilkington Optronics

Electronic countermeasures
Barr & Stroud
Loral Librascope
MagneTek Defense
Matra Defense
Pilkington Optronics
Safare-Crouzet
Sperry Marine
WELSE

Electronic engine room telegraph
Safare-Crouzet
SEPA

Electronic equipment
DCN
MagneTek Defense
Matra Defense
OTO Melara
Riva Calzoni
Safare-Crouzet
Sperry Marine

Electronic equipment refits
Bath Iron Works
DCN
MagneTek Defense
OTO Melara
Safare-Crouzet

Electronic power systems
MagneTek Defense
Safare-Crouzet
Teledyne INET

Electronic warfare (communications)
Safare-Crouzet

Electronic warfare evaluation systems
Safare-Crouzet
Sperry Marine

Engine monitors and data loggers
SEMT Pielstick

Engine parts, diesel
CRM
Empresa Nacional Bazan
Netherlands Naval Industries Group
SEMT Pielstick
Wartsila Diesel

Engine speed controls
MagneTek Defense

Engine start and shut-down controls
DCN
Hyundai Heavy Industries

Engines, diesel
Empresa Nacional Bazan
Fincantieri
Hyundai Heavy Industries
Netherlands Naval Industries Group
SEMT Pielstick
Wartsila Diesel

Engines, gas turbine
Empresa Nacional Bazan
Hyundai Heavy Industries

Engines, steam turbine
Empresa Nacional Bazan

Equipment for helicopters
DCN
Elbit Computers
Kaman Aerospace
OTO Melara

Exhibition organisers
DCN

Fast attack craft
Crestitalia
Daewoo Shipbuilding & Heavy Machinery
DCN
Fincantieri
FR Lürssen Werft
Hyundai Heavy Industries
Melara Club Consortium
SEC
Swan Hunter
Yarrow Shipbuilders

Fast patrol craft
Crestitalia
Daewoo Shipbuilding & Heavy Machinery
DCN
Empresa Nacional Bazan
Fincantieri
Hyundai Heavy Industries
Korea Tacoma Marine
Melara Club Consortium
SEC
Swan Hunter
Yarrow Shipbuilders

Fast strike craft
Crestitalia
Daewoo Shipbuilding & Heavy Machinery
DCN
FR Lürssen Werft
SEC
Swan Hunter
Yarrow Shipbuilders

Fast offshore patrol and attack craft
Crestitalia
Daewoo Shipbuilding & Heavy Machinery
DCN
Empresa Nacional Bazan
Fincantieri
FR Lürssen Werft
Korea Tacoma Marine
Netherlands Naval Industries Group
Royal Schelde
SEC
Swan Hunter
Yarrow Shipbuilders

Fast warship design service
Daewoo Shipbuilding & Heavy Machinery
DCN
Empresa Nacional Bazan
FR Lürssen Werft
Ingalls Shipbuilding
Korea Tacoma Marine
NEVESBU
Swan Hunter
Yarrow Shipbuilders

Ferries
Chantiers De l'Atlantique
Daewoo Shipbuilding & Heavy Machinery
DCN
Fincantieri
FR Lürssen Werft
Korea Tacoma Marine
SEC
Swan Hunter

Fibreglass vessels and other products
Crestitalia
Empresa Nacional Bazan

Fibre optics
Hollandse Signaalapparaten
Safare-Crouzet
Thomson Sintra/ASM

Fire control systems
Barr & Stroud
Elbit Computers
Hollandse Signaalapparaten
Loral Librascope
NobelTech Systems
OTO Melara
Pilkington Optronics
Thomson Sintra/ASM
WELSE

Fire control and gunnery equipment
Barr & Stroud
Hollandse Signaalapparaten
OTO Melara
Pilkington Optronics

Firefighting ships
Crestitalia
Daewoo Shipbuilding & Heavy Machinery
Empresa Nacional Bazan
FR Lürssen Werft
Korea Tacoma Marine
Swan Hunter

Fishery protection
Crestitalia
Empresa Nacional Bazan
FR Lürssen Werft
Swan Hunter

Fittings, ships
Empresa Nacional Bazan
Netherlands Naval Industries Group

Flares
Etienne Lacroix

Forgings, steel
Empresa Nacional Bazan
Mecanique Creusot-Loire

Frequency converters
MagneTek Defense
Teledyne INET

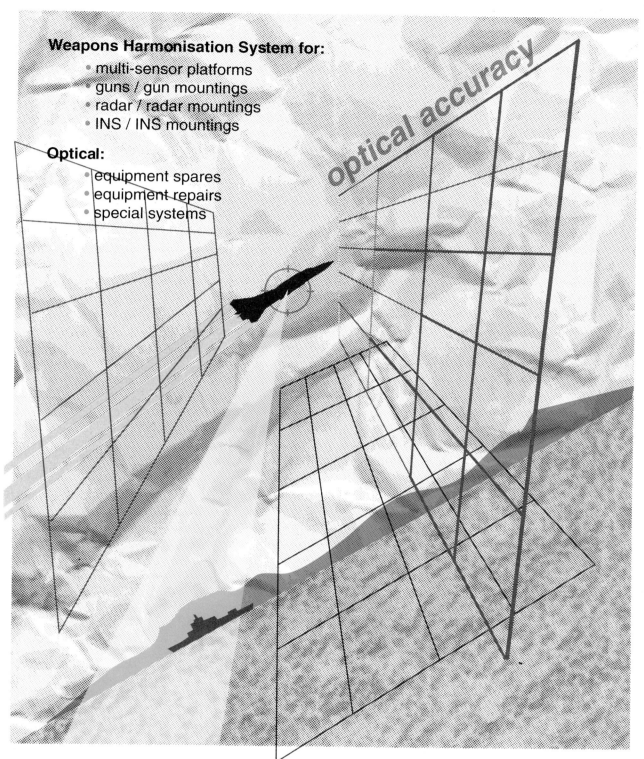

Frigates
Bath Iron Works
Chantiers De l'Atlantique
Daewoo Shipbuilding & Heavy Machinery
DCN
Empresa Nacional Bazan
Fincantieri
Hyundai Heavy Industries
Korea Tacoma Marine
Melara Club Consortium
Netherlands Naval Industries Group
Royal Schelde
Swan Hunter
Yarrow Shipbuilding

Frigates (light)
Daewoo Shipbuilding & Heavy Machinery
DCN
Empresa Nacional Bazan
FR Lürssen Werft
Hyundai Heavy Industries
Ingalls Shipbuilding
Melara Club Consortium
Netherlands Naval Industries Group
Royal Schelde
Swan Hunter
Yarrow Shipbuilding

Gas turbine boats
Empresa Nacional Bazan
FR Lürssen Werft
Swan Hunter

Gas turbines
Empresa Nacional Bazan

Generators, diesel
Netherlands Naval Industries Group
SEMT Pielstick
Wartsila Diesel

Generators, electric
MagneTek Defense
Netherlands Naval Industries Group

Glassfibre vessels and other products
DCN
Empresa Nacional Bazan
FR Lürssen Werft
Yarrow Shipbuilders

Guided missile launcher systems
FR Lürssen Werft
Matra Defense
OTO Melara

Guided missiles
Matra Defense
OTO Melara

Guided missile ships
Bath Iron Works
Daewoo Shipbuilding & Heavy Machinery
DCN
Ingalls Shipbuilding
Matra Defense
Swan Hunter

Gunnery equipment
Empresa Nacional Bazan
OTO Melara

Guns and mountings
Breda Meccanica Bresciana
DCN
Empresa Nacional Bazan
Mecanique Creusot-Loire
OTO Melara

Harbour defence vessels
Crestitalia
Daewoo Shipbuilding & Heavy Machinery
FR Lürssen Werft

Heat exchangers
Empresa Nacional Bazan

Heavy-duty mooring motorboats
Crestitalia
Mathiesen's Badebyggeri

Helicopter, anti-submarine patrol
Kaman Aerospace

Helicopter handling systems
MacTaggart Scott
Riva Calzoni
SOFMA

Helicopter, maritime reconnaissance
Kaman Aerospace

High energy laser systems
Barr & Stroud
Pilkington Optronics

Hydraulic equipment
DCN
MacTaggart Scott
Riva Calzoni

Hydraulic machinery
DCN
MacTaggart Scott
Riva Calzoni

Hydraulic plant
DCN
Riva Calzoni
Wartsila Diesel

Hydrofoils
DCN
Fincantieri
Hyundai Heavy Industries
Melara Club Consortium
Safare-Crouzet

Hydraulic survey equipment/vessels
Daewoo Shipbuilding & Heavy Machinery
FR Lürssen Werft
Hyundai Heavy Industries
Marconi Underwater

Hydrographic survey equipment/vessels
Crestitalia
Daewoo Shipbuilding & Heavy Machinery

2m
2m
1m
1m
brand.= -50
brand.= 50

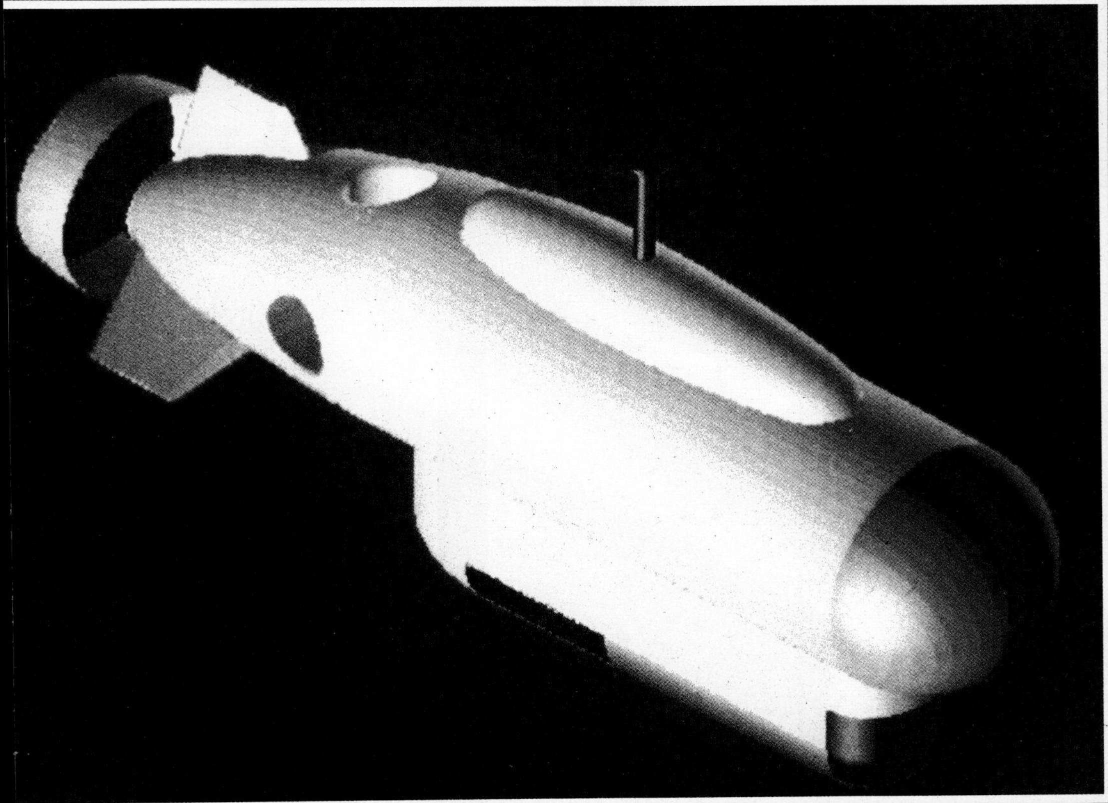

NAVAL INDUSTRIES GROUP

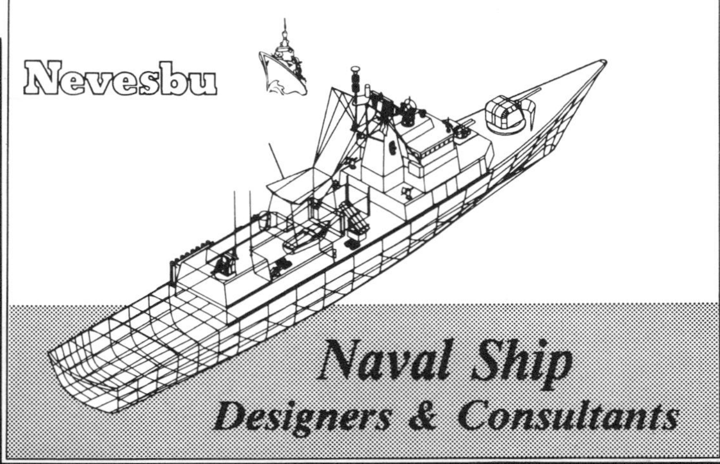

NEVESBU: THE NAVAL SHIP DESIGNERS

Surface vessels and submarines built in The Netherlands have proved themselves on the high seas in the past and today. They will continue to do so tomorrow!

The goal of the NNIG is to offer governments, naval forces and industries throughout the world the gateway to the members of the group.

Besides their specific fields of expertise to build high-technology naval ships the NNIG member companies cover also a wide range of general engineering technology with the capabilities to develop and supply advanced products and systems for civil as well as for defence markets.

For more information ask for the NNIG brochure.

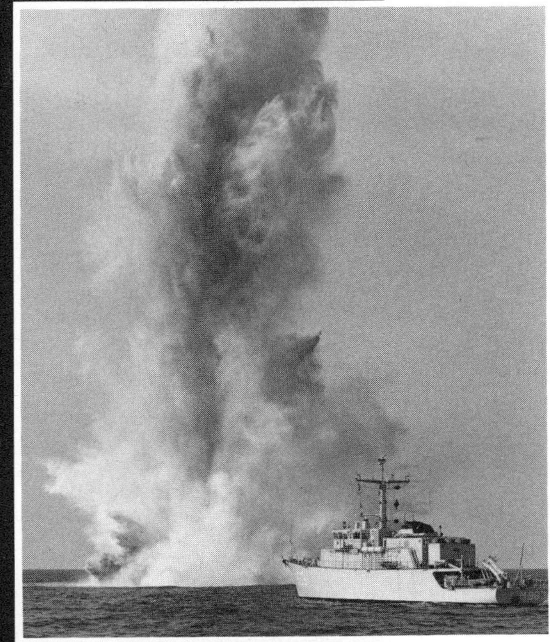

GNM's MINE HUNTER IN ACTION

R&H's CONTROL POSITION SCC M-CLASS FRIGATE

The Netherlands Naval Industries Group is ready to serve you

DCN
Empresa Nacional Bazan
MacTaggart Scott
Swan Hunter
Yarrow Shipbuilders

Hydrophones
Marconi Underwater
Thomson Sintra/ASM

Icebreakers
Ingalls Shipbuilding
Swan Hunter

IFF radar
Hollandse Signaalapparaten

Infra-red countermeasure systems
Etienne Lacroix
NobelTech Electronics

Infra-red materials
Barr & Stroud
Pilkington Optronics

Infra-red search & tracking systems
Barr & Stroud
Hollandse Signaalapparaten
Pilkington Optronics

Infra-red systems
Barr & Stroud
Hollandse Signaalapparaten
Pilkington Optronics

Instruments, electronic
Safare-Crouzet
Sperry Marine

Instruments, test equipment
Hollandse Signaalapparaten
Marconi Underwater
Safare-Crouzet

Integrated communications systems
Safare-Crouzet
Sperry Marine
WELSE

Integrated logistic support
Barr & Stroud
Bath Iron Works
Breda Meccanica Bresciana
C.I.S.DEG
Elbit Computers
Hollandse Signaalapparaten
Kaman Aerospace
MagneTek Defense
Marconi Underwater
Melara Club Consortium
OTO Melara
Pilkington Optronics
Royal Schelde
Safare-Crouzet
Swan Hunter
WELSE

Intercommunications systems
Safare-Crouzet
Sperry Marine

Interior design and furnishing for ships
DCN
Empresa Nacional Bazan
Swan Hunter

Inverters and battery chargers
MagneTek Defense
Whitehead

Landing craft
Crestitalia
Daewoo Shipbuilding & Heavy Machinery
DCN
Empresa Nacional Bazan
Fincantieri
FR Lürssen Werft
Hyundai Heavy Industries
Korea Tacoma Marine
Swan Hunter

Landing craft, logistics
Daewoo Shipbuilding & Heavy Machinery
Empresa Nacional Bazan
Fincantieri
FR Lürssen Werft
Hyundai Heavy Industries
Korea Tacoma Marine
Swan Hunter
Yarrow Shipbuilders

Landing ship tank
Daewoo Shipbuilding & Heavy Machinery
FR Lürssen Werft
Hyundai Heavy Industries
Korea Tacoma Marine
Melara Club Consortium
Yarrow Shipbuilders

Laser rangefinders
Barr & Stroud
Pilkington Optronics

Laser systems
Barr & Stroud
Pilkington Optronics

Launches, rescue
Crestitalia

Lifeboats/rescue
Crestitalia
Fincantieri

Lifts, hydraulic
MacTaggart Scott

Logistics management services
Bath Iron Works
C.I.S.DEG
Empresa Nacional Bazan
Hollandse Signaalapparaten
MagneTek Defense
Safare-Crouzet
Swan Hunter

Logistics support information systems
Bath Iron Works
C.I.S.DEG
Empresa Nacional Bazan
MagneTek Defense
Safare-Crouzet
SOFMA
Swan Hunter
Wartsila Diesel
Yarrow Shipbuilders

Logistics support vessels
Daewoo Shipbuilding & Heavy Machinery
DCN
Empresa Nacional Bazan
Hyundai Heavy Industries
Korea Tacoma Marine
Melara Club Consortium
Swan Hunter
Yarrow Shipbuilding

Machined parts, ferrous
DCN
Empresa Nacional Bazan

Machined parts, non-ferrous
DCN

Magnetic measurements facilities
MagneTek Defense

Maintenance and repair ships
DCN
Empresa Nacional Bazan
Ingalls Shipbuilding
Netherlands Naval Industries Group
Swan Hunter

Management services
Bath Iron Works
Hollandse Signaalapparaten

Marine architects
Bath Iron Works
Daewoo Shipbuilding & Heavy Machinery
DCN
NEVESBU
Swan Hunter

Marine consultants
Daewoo Shipbuilding & Heavy Machinery
NEVESBU
Safare-Crouzet
Swan Hunter

Marine electronic equipment
Netherlands Naval Industries Group
Safare-Crouzet
SEPA
Sperry Marine
Wartsila Diesel

Marine engine monitoring and data recording systems
Safare-Crouzet
SEPA
Wartsila Diesel

Merchant ships
Bath Iron Works
Daewoo Shipbuilding & Heavy Machinery
Hyundai Heavy Industries
Fincantieri
Royal Schelde
SEC
Swan Hunter

Microwave components
Hollandse Signaalapparaten
NobelTech Electronics

Microwave systems
Hollandse Signaalapparaten
Royal Schelde

Mines
DCN
Etienne Lacroix
Marconi Underwater
Swedish Ordnance

Mines (exercise)
DCN
Marconi Underwater
Swedish Ordnance
Thomson Sintra/ASM

Mines (naval)
DCN
Swedish Ordnance
Thomson Sintra/ASM
Whitehead

Mines and countermining charges
DCN
Swedish Ordnance
Whitehead

Mines countermeasure vessels
Crestitalia
DCN
FR Lürssen Werft
Swan Hunter
Yarrow Shipbuilders

Mine countermeasures
Consorzio SMIN
DCN
FR Lürssen Werft
MacTaggart Scott
MagneTek Defense
Thomson Sintra/ASM
WELSE

Minehunters
Crestitalia
DCN
Fincantieri
FR Lürssen Werft
Kaman Aerospace
Netherlands Naval Industries Group
SOFMA
Swan Hunter
Whitehead
Yarrow Shipbuilders

Minehunting support and training systems
FR Lürssen Werft
Marconi Underwater
Riva Calzoni
Thomson Sintra/ASM

Minelayers
Fincantieri
FR Lürssen Werft
Hyundai Heavy Industries

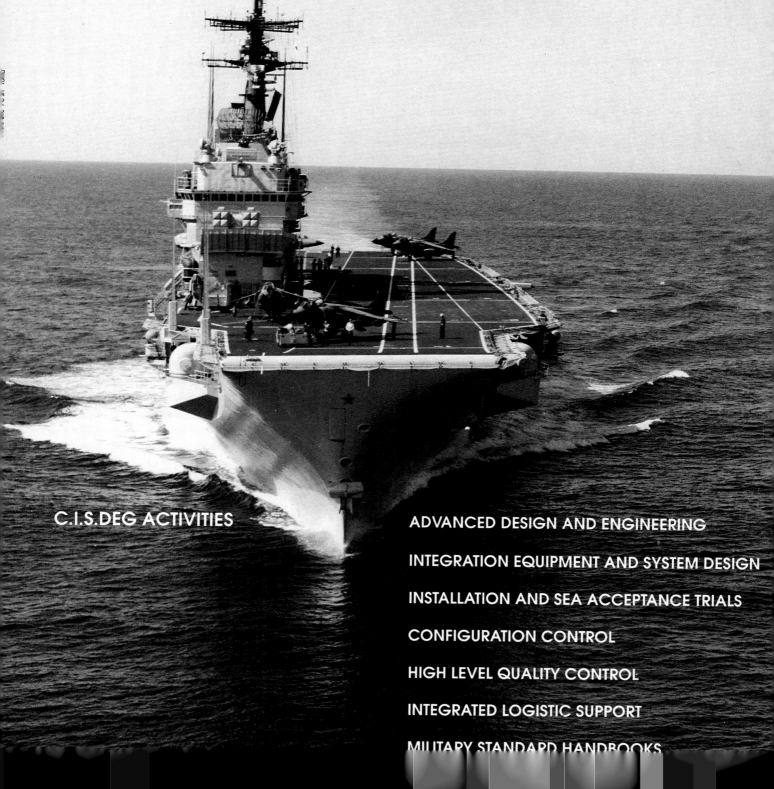

Swan Hunter
Yarrow Shipbuilders

Minesweepers
FR Lürssen Werft
Netherlands Naval Industries Group
SOFMA
Swan Hunter
Whitehead
Yarrow Shipbuilders

Minesweeping equipment
MacTaggart Scott
MagneTek Defense
Marconi Underwater
Safare-Crouzet
SOFMA
Swan Hunter
Thomson Sintra/ASM
Wartsila Diesel
Whitehead

Missile control systems
Hollandse Signaalapparaten
Matra Defense
OTO Melara

Missile installations
DCN
Hyundai Heavy Industries
Matra Defense
OTO Melara

Missile launching systems
DCN
Loral Librascope
Matra Defense
OTO Melara
Riva Calzoni

Missile ships
Bath Iron Works
Crestitalia
Daewoo Shipbuilding & Heavy Machinery
DCN
FR Lürssen Werft
Hyundai Heavy Industries
Ingalls Shipbuilding
Matra Defense
Yarrow Shipbuilders

Motor generators
Teledyne INET

Motors, hydraulic
DCN
Hyundai Heavy Industries
MacTaggart Scott
Riva Calzoni

Motor Torpedo boats
FR Lürssen Werft

Naval architects
DCN
Hyundai Heavy Industries
Ingalls Shipbuilding
Netherlands Naval Industries Group
NEVESBU
Royal Schelde
Yarrow Shipbuilders

Naval based design
Bath Iron Works
Daewoo Shipbuilding & Heavy Machinery
FR Lürssen Werft
Ingalls Shipbuilding
Wartsila Diesel

Naval guns
Breda Meccanica Bresciana
Empresa Nacional Bazan
Mecanique Creusot-Loire
OTO Melara
Swedish Ordnance

Naval patrol vessels
Bath Iron Works
Crestitalia
Daewoo Shipbuilding & Heavy Machinery
DCN
Empresa Nacional Bazan
Fincantieri
FR Lürssen Werft
Hyundai Heavy Industries
Ingalls Shipbuilding
Korea Tacoma Marine
Netherlands Naval Industries Group
SOFMA
Swan Hunter
Yarrow Shipbuilders

Naval radar
Hollandse Signaalapparaten
NobelTech Electronics
Sperry Marine

Naval systems, installation
Bath Iron Works
C.I.S.DEG
Empresa Nacional Bazan
Hollandse Signaalapparaten
Hyundai Heavy Industries
Ingalls Shipbuilding
Netherlands Naval Industries Group
NobelTech Systems
OTO Melara
Safare-Crouzet
Sperry Marine

Naval systems, planning and integration
Bath Iron Works
C.I.S.DEG
Elbit Computers
Ingalls Shipbuilding
NobelTech Systems
OTO Melara
Riva Calzoni
Safare-Crouzet
SITEP
Sperry Marine

Navigation aids
Sperry Marine

NBC protection equipment
Elbit Computers
Etienne Lacroix
SOFMA

Night vision systems
Barr & Stroud
Elbit Computers
Hollandse Signaalapparaten
Pilkington Optronics
Swedish Ordnance

Non hull penetrating masts
Barr & Stroud
MacTaggart Scott
Pilkington Optronics
Riva Calzoni
WELSE

Non-mganetic minesweepers
Crestitalia
FR Lürssen Werft
MacTaggart Scott
Netherlands Naval Industries Group
Yarrow Shipbuilders

Oceanographic instrumentation
Marconi Underwater
Thomson Sintra/ASM
Whitehead

Oceanographic survey ships
Crestitalia
Daewoo Shipbuilding & Heavy Machinery
DCN
Empresa Nacional Bazan
FR Lürssen Werft
Hyundai Heavy Industries
Korea Tacoma Marine
Melara Club Consortium
Royal Schelde
SEC
Swan Hunter
Yarrow Shipbuilders

Oceanographic systems integration
Marconi Underwater
Swan Hunter
Thomson Sintra/ASM

Offshore countermeasures
FR Lürssen Werft
Swan Hunter

Offshore patrol vessels
Chantiers De l'Atlantique
Crestitalia
Daewoo Shipbuilding & Heavy Machinery
DCN
Empresa Nacional Bazan
Fincantieri
FR Lürssen Werft
Hyundai Heavy Industries
Korea Tacoma Marine
Melara Club Consortium
Netherlands Naval Industries Group
Royal Schelde
SOFMA
Swan Hunter
Yarrow Shipbuilders

Oil drilling rigs
Daewoo Shipbuilding & Heavy Machinery
Hyundai Heavy Industries
Wartsila Diesel

Oil pollution control vessels
Daewoo Shipbuilding & Heavy Machinery
FR Lürssen Werft
Hyundai Heavy Industries

Oil rig supply vessels and work boats
Daewoo Shipbuilding & Heavy Machinery
Fincantieri
Hyundai Heavy Industries
Wartsila Diesel

Optical equipment
Hollandse Signaalapparaten

Optronics
Barr & Stroud
Hollandse Signaalapparaten
Matra Defense
Pilkington Optronics

Optronics masts
Barr & Stroud
MacTaggart Scott
Pilkington Optronics
Riva Calzoni
Sperry Marine
WELSE

Ordnance
Breda Meccanica Bresciana
Empresa Nacional Bazan
Netherlands Naval Industries Group
Swedish Ordnance

Parts for diesel engines
Empresa Nacional Bazan
Netherlands Naval Industries Group
SEMT Pielstick
Wartsila Diesel

Passenger ships
Crestitalia
Daewoo Shipbuilding & Heavy Machinery
DCN
Fincantieri
Korea Tacoma Marine
SEC
Swan Hunter

Patrol boats
Bath Iron Works
Crestitalia
Daewoo Shipbuilding & Heavy Machinery
DCN
Empresa Nacional Bazan
Fincantieri
FR Lürssen Werft
Hyundai Heavy Industries
SEC
SOFMA
Swan Hunter
Yarrow Shipbuilders

Patrol boats, launches
Crestitalia
DCN
FR Lürssen Werft
Hyundai Heavy Industries
Korea Tacoma Marine

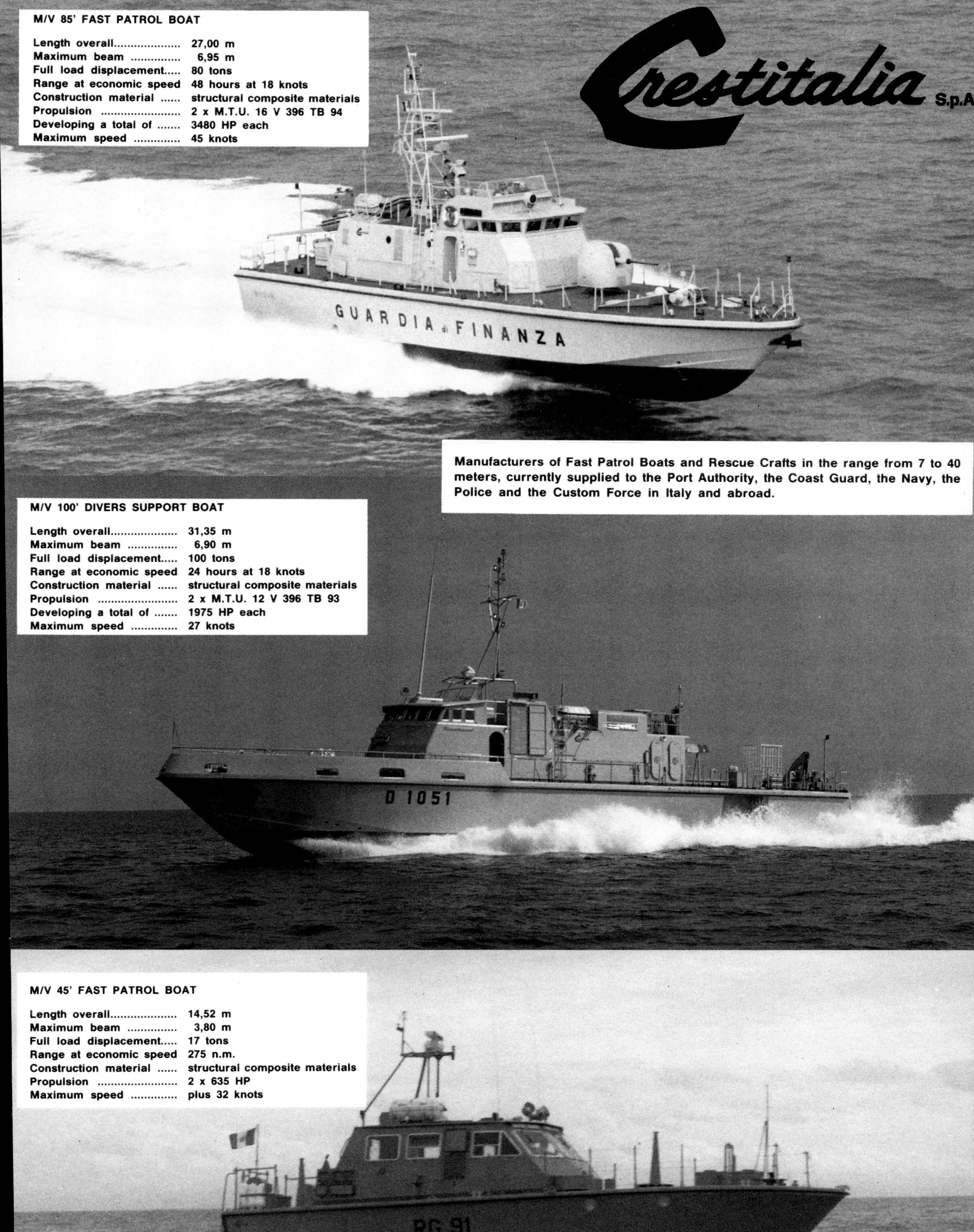
M/V 85' FAST PATROL BOAT
Length overall.................... 27,00 m
Maximum beam .... 6,95 m
Full load displacement..... 80 tons
Range at economic speed 48 hours at 18 knots
Construction material ...... structural composite materials
Propulsion .... 2 x M.T.U. 16 V 396 TB 94
Developing a total of .... 3480 HP each
Maximum speed .... 45 knots
Crestitalia S.p.A.
GUARDIA di FINANZA
Manufacturers of Fast Patrol Boats and Rescue Crafts in the range from 7 to 40 meters, currently supplied to the Port Authority, the Coast Guard, the Navy, the Police and the Custom Force in Italy and abroad.
M/V 100' DIVERS SUPPORT BOAT
Length overall.................... 31,35 m
Maximum beam .... 6,90 m
Full load displacement..... 100 tons
Range at economic speed 24 hours at 18 knots
Construction material ...... structural composite materials
Propulsion .... 2 x M.T.U. 12 V 396 TB 93
Developing a total of .... 1975 HP each
Maximum speed .... 27 knots
D 1051
M/V 45' FAST PATROL BOAT
Length overall.................... 14,52 m
Maximum beam .... 3,80 m
Full load displacement..... 17 tons
Range at economic speed 275 n.m.
Construction material ...... structural composite materials
Propulsion .... 2 x 635 HP
Maximum speed .... plus 32 knots
RG 91

THE TOTAL NAVAL DEFENCE SYSTEM

The major Italian Naval Industries, whose know-how and activities cover the complete field of Naval Products and Equipment, teamed to give comprehensive integrated responses to any naval requirement. Naval vessels, refittings, logistic support.

MELARA CLUB CONSORTIUM
11-6, Via Cesarea
16121 Genova, Italy
Phone + 39.10.585048
Fax + 39.10.566794
Telex 270009 CONMEC I

Patrol boats: launches, tenders and pinnacles
Castoldi
Crestitalia
Daewoo Shipbuilding & Heavy Machinery
DCN
FR Lürssen Werft
Hyundai Heavy Industries

Periscope fairings
Riva Calzoni
WELSE

Periscopes
Barr & Stroud
MacTaggart Scott
Pilkington Optronics
Sperry Marine
WELSE

Periscopes search
Barr & Stroud
MacTaggart Scott
Pilkington Optronics
Sperry Marine
WELSE

Periscopes attack
Barr & Stroud
MacTaggart Scott
Pilkington Optronics
Sperry Marine
WELSE

Pilot boats
Crestitalia
Hyundai Heavy Industries

Plotting and tracking systems
Hollandse Signaalapparaten

Plotting tables
Hollandse Signaalapparaten
Loral Librascope

Portable and containerised equipment
Hollandse Signaalapparaten

Portable testing equipment
Marconi Underwater
Hollandse Signaalapparaten

Power supplies
Hollandse Signaalapparaten
MagneTek Defense
Wartsila Diesel

Pressure vessels
Daewoo Shipbuilding & Heavy Machinery
Hyundai Heavy Industries

Project management
Bath Iron Works
DCN
Hollandse Signaalapparaten
Marconi Underwater
NEVESBU
Swan Hunter

Propeller shaft couplings, flexible
DCN
Wartsila Diesel

Propeller shafts
Bath Iron Works
DCN
Wartsila Diesel

Propeller shafts and intermediate shafts
DCN
Wartsila Diesel

Propellers, ship research
DCN
Wartsila Diesel

Propellers, ships
DCN
Hyundai Heavy Industries
Wartsila Diesel

Propulsion gearing
DCN
Hyundai Heavy Industries
The Cincinnati Gear Company
Wartsila Diesel

Propulsion machinery
DCN
Marconi Underwater
Riva Calzoni
Wartsila Diesel

Propulsion machinery control
DCN
Marconi Underwater
SEMT Pielstick
SEPA
Wartsila Diesel

Propulsion machinery surveillance
DCN
Empresa Nacional Bazan
SEMT Pielstick
Wartsila Diesel

Propulsion systems
DCN
Empresa Nacional Bazan
Fincantieri
MacTaggart Scott
MagneTek Defense
Marconi Underwater
Melara Club Consortium
SEMT Pielstick
Wartsila Diesel
Whitehead

Pumps
MacTaggart Scott
Netherlands Naval Industries Group

Radar antennas
Hollandse Signaalapparaten
NobelTech Electronics
SMA
Sperry Marine

Radar countermeasures
Etienne Lacroix
NobelTech Electronics

Radar for fire control
Hollandse Signaalapparaten
NobelTech Electronics
SMA

Radar subsystem units
Hollandse Signaalapparaten
NobelTech Electronics
SMA
Sperry Marine

Radar transponders
Hollandse Signaalapparaten

Radar, 360 maritime patrol
Hollandse Signaalapparaten
SMA

Radomes range-finders
DCN

Railcar diesel engines
MTU
SEMT Pielstick

Re-equipment, modernisation of naval vessels
Bath Iron Works
Wartsila Diesel

Remote level indicator equipment for submarine trim tanks
DCN

Remote power control systems
SEPA
Wartsila Diesel

Research ships
Daewoo Shipbuilding & Heavy Machinery
DCN
Empresa Nacional Bazan
FR Lürssen Werft
Hyundai Heavy Industries
Royal Schelde
Swan Hunter
Yarrow Shipbuilders

Reverse reduction gears, oil operated
Empresa Nacional Bazan
The Cincinnati Gear Company

Rocket launchers
Breda Meccanica Bresciana
Mecanique Creusot-Loire
DCN
Matra Defense

Salvage vessels
Crestitalia
Daewoo Shipbuilding & Heavy Machinery
Hyundai Heavy Industries
Korea Tacoma Marine
Swan Hunter

Search and rescue vessels
Crestitalia
Daewoo Shipbuilding & Heavy Machinery
Empresa Nacional Bazan
Hyundai Heavy Industries
SOFMA
Swan Hunter

Self-homing torpedo guidance head
Marconi Underwater
Thomson Sintra/ASM
Whitehead

Shipboard frequency converters
Teledyne INET

Ship design
Bath Iron Works
Hyundai Heavy Industries
Ingalls Shipbuilding
NEVESBU
Royal Schelde
Swan Hunter

Ship and repair yard design
Bath Iron Works
Daewoo Shipbuilding & Heavy Machinery
DCN
Empresa Nacional Bazan
FR Lürssen Werft
Ingalls Shipbuilding
Netherlands Naval Industries Group
NEVESBU
Swan Hunter

Ship and submarine design
Daewoo Shipbuilding & Heavy Machinery
DCN
Empresa Nacional Bazan
Fincantieri
Ingalls Shipbuilding
Netherlands Naval Industries Group
NEVESBU
Swan Hunter

Ship defence systems
Barr & Stroud
Breda Meccanica Bresciana
Empresa Nacional Bazan
Hollandse Signaalapparaten
MagneTek Defense
Marconi Underwater
Mecanique Creusot-Loire
Melara Club Consortium
NobelTech Systems
OTO Melara
Pilkington Optronics
Swan Hunter
Swedish Ordnance

Ship machinery
Empresa Nacional Bazan
MacTaggart Scott
Riva Calzoni
Wartsila Diesel

Ship repair/refit
Bath Iron Works
Daewoo Shipbuilding & Heavy Machinery
DCN
Empresa Nacional Bazan
Fincantieri
Ingalls Shipbuilding
Melara Club Consortium
Swan Hunter
Wartsila Diesel
Yarrow Shipbuilders

Ship stabilisers
Sperry Marine

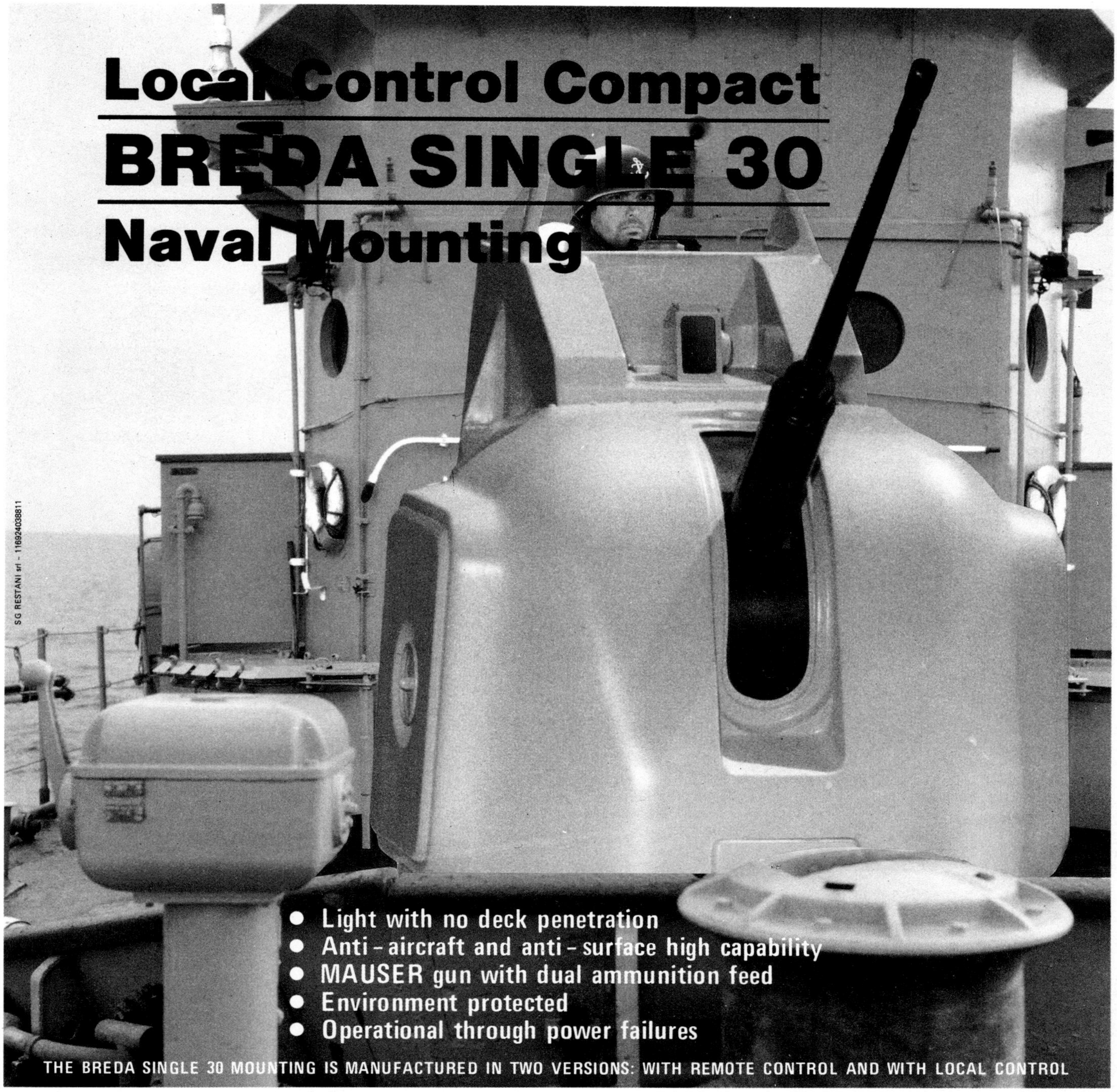

Local Control Compact
BREDA SINGLE 30
Naval Mounting

- Light with no deck penetration
- Anti-aircraft and anti-surface high capability
- MAUSER gun with dual ammunition feed
- Environment protected
- Operational through power failures

THE BREDA SINGLE 30 MOUNTING IS MANUFACTURED IN TWO VERSIONS: WITH REMOTE CONTROL AND WITH LOCAL CONTROL

SG RESTANI srl - 116924038811

▼BREDA SINGLE 30 COMPACT WITH REMOTE CONTROL▼

▲BREDA SINGLE 30 COMPACT WITH LOCAL CONTROL▲

BREDA MECCANICA BRESCIANA SpA

2 Via Lunga 25126 BRESCIA (Italy) Tel. 030/31911 Telex 300056 BREDAR I

GRUPPO EFIM

A Company of the OTO MELARA-BREDA MECCANICA BRESCIANA-OFFICINE GALILEO Consortium

CLASSIFIED LIST OF ADVERTISERS

Ship systems engineering
Bath Iron Works
DCN
Hollandse Signaalapparaten
Ingalls Shipbuilding
MacTaggart Scott
Melara Club Consortium
Swan Hunter
Wartsila Diesel

Simulators
DCN
Elbit Computers
Hollandse Signaalapparaten
Riva Calzoni
Thomson Sintra/ASM
Whitehead

Simulators hyperbaric
DCN

Software services
Bath Iron Works
DCN

Sonar decoys
Safare-Crouzet
Thomson Sintra/ASM

Sonar calibration equipment
Marconi Underwater
Safare-Crouzet
Thomson Sintra/ASM

Sonar equipment
Hollandse Signaalapparaten
MagneTek Defense
Marconi Underwater
Safare-Crouzet
Thomson Sintra/ASM

Sonar equipment (passive active-intercept)
Marconi Underwater
Safare-Crouzet
Thomson Sintra/ASM

Sonar equipment hull fittings and hydraulics
MacTaggart Scott
Marconi Underwater
Riva Calzoni
Safare-Crouzet
Thomson Sintra/ASM

Sonar interceptor direction-finder
Marconi Underwater
Safare-Crouzet
Thomson Sintra/ASM

Sonar rangers (design and installation)
Marconi Underwater
Safare-Crouzet
Thomson Sintra/ASM
WELSE

Sonobuoys
Safare-Crouzet
Thomson Sintra/ASM
Whitehead

Spare parts for diesel engines
Empresa Nacional Bazan
Netherlands Naval Industries Group
Wartsila Diesel

Speed boats
Daewoo Shipbuilding & Heavy Machinery
Mathiesen's Badebyggeri
Hyundai Heavy Industries
Korea Tacoma Marine

Stabilising equipment
DCN
Sperry Marine

Steam-raising plant, conventional
DCN

Steam-raising plant, nuclear
DCN

Steam turbines
Hyundai Heavy Industries

Steel alloy and special steel forgings, plates and section stampings
Empresa Nacional Bazan

Steering gear
MacTaggart Scott
Sperry Marine

Submarine control systems
Loral Librascope
NobelTech Systems
Riva Calzoni
Safare-Crouzet
SEPA
SOFMA
Sperry Marine
WELSE

Submarine distress buoy
Marconi Underwater
WELSE

Submarine fire control
Loral Librascope
NobelTech Systems
Thomson Sintra/ASM
WELSE
Whitehead

Submarine forward retractable hydroplanes
MacTaggart Scott

Submarine hull equipment
MacTaggart Scott
Netherlands Naval Industries Group
Riva Calzoni

Submarine inverters
MagneTek Defense

Submarine mast actuation
MacTaggart Scott
Riva Calzoni

Submarine snorkels
Riva Calzoni

Submarine team and attack trainers
Loral Librascope
Thomson Sintra/ASM
WELSE

Submarine winches
MacTaggart Scott
Riva Calzoni
Thomson Sintra/ASM

Submarines
Daewoo Shipbuilding & Heavy Machinery
DCN
Empresa Nacional Bazan
Fincantieri
Korea Tacoma Marine
Melara Club Consortium
Netherlands Naval Industries
SOFMA
Yarrow Shipbuilders

Submarines, conventional
Daewoo Shipbuilding & Heavy Machinery
DCN
Empresa Nacional Bazan
Fincantieri
Netherlands Naval Industries Group
Yarrow Shipbuilders

Submarines, external propelling systems
MacTaggart Scott
Netherlands Naval Industries Group

Submarines, unmanned submersibles
DCN
Marconi Underwater
Riva Calzoni
Safare-Crouzet
Thomson Sintra/ASM

Submarines, wet
DCN
Safare-Crouzet

Submersible search and recovery systems
DCN
Riva Calzoni
Thomson Sintra/ASM

Supply ships
Daewoo Shipbuilding & Heavy Machinery
DCN
Empresa Nacional Bazan
Fincantieri
Hyundai Heavy Industries
Melara Club Consortium
Swan Hunter

Support services
Daewoo Shipbuilding & Heavy Machinery
DCN
Ingalls Shipbuilding
Melara Club Consortium
Swan Hunter
Wartsila Diesel
Yarrow Shipbuilders

Support service vessels
DCN
FR Lürssen Werft
Hyundai Heavy Industries
Melara Club Consortium
Swan Hunter

Surface effect ships
DCN
Empresa Nacional Bazan
FR Lürssen Werft
Hyundai Heavy Industries
Royal Schelde
SEC
Swan Hunter

Surveillance craft
Crestitalia
Daewoo Shipbuilding & Heavy Machinery
FR Lürssen Werft
Swan Hunter

Tactical training simulators
DCN
WELSE
Whitehead

Tankers
Daewoo Shipbuilding & Heavy Machinery
DCN
Fincantieri
Korea Tacoma Marine
SEC
SOFMA
Swan Hunter

Tankers, small
Daewoo Shipbuilding & Heavy Machinery
DCN
Swan Hunter

Tanker, vessels
DCN
Fincantieri
Hyundai Heavy Industries
Swan Hunter

Technical co-operation
Daewoo Shipbuilding & Heavy Machinery
Hollandse Signaalapparaten
OTO Melara
Swan Hunter
Wartsila Diesel

Technical publications
C.I.S.DEG
Hollandse Signaalapparaten
Ingall Shipbuilding
Marconi Underwater
OTO Melara
Swan Hunter
Wartsila Diesel

Telecommunications equipment
Safare-Crouzet

Tender vessels
Crestitalia
Daewoo Shipbuilding & Heavy Machinery
FR Lürssen Werft
Hyundai Heavy Industries
Royal Schelde
Swan Hunter

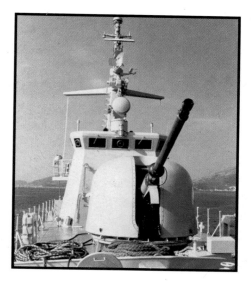

CLASSIFIED LIST OF ADVERTISERS

Test equipment for fire control systems
Barr & Stroud
DCN
Hollandse Signaalapparaten
Marconi Underwater
Pilkington Optronics
WELSE

Thermal imaging systems
Barr & Stroud
Elbit Computers
Pilkington Optronics
WELSE

Throughwater communications
Marconi Underwater
Safare-Crouzet

Thrusters
MagneTek Defense

Torpedo control systems
DCN
Loral Librascope
Marconi Underwater
Safare-Crouzet
SEPA
WELSE

Torpedo decoys
DCN
Etienne Lacroix
Loral Librascope
Marconi Underwater
Safare-Crouzet
Thomson Sintra/ASM
WELSE
Whitehead

Torpedo depth and roll recorders
Marconi Underwater
Whitehead

Torpedo handling systems
MacTaggart Scott
Riva Calzoni
Whitehead

Torpedo homing heads
Marconi Underwater
Thomson Sintra/ASM
Whitehead

Torpedo launching systems
DCN
Loral Librascope
OTO Melara
Thomson Sintra/ASM
Whitehead

Torpedo order and reflection control
Whitehead

Torpedo side-launchers
DCN
Korea Tacoma Marine
Whitehead

Torpedo-testing vessels
FR Lürssen Werft
Royal Schelde
Whitehead

Torpedo tubes
DCN
Whitehead

Torpedo workshops
DCN
Marconi Underwater
Whitehead

Torpedoes
DCN
Marconi Underwater
Whitehead

Towed array systems
DCN
MacTaggart Scott
Marconi Underwater
Thomson Sintra/ASM
Whitehead

Towed array systems integration
Marconi Underwater
Thomson Sintra/ASM
WELSE

Towed arrays
Marconi Underwater
Thomson Sintra/ASM
WELSE
Whitehead

Training equipment
DCN
Elbit Computers
Etienne Lacroix
Hollandse Signaalapparaten
Kaman Aerospace
Marconi Underwater
OTO Melara
Thomson Sintra/ASM
WELSE

Training programmes
Bath Iron Works
C.I.S.DEG
Empresa Nacional Bazan
Hollandse Signaalapparaten
Marconi Underwater
Melara Club Consortium
Sperry Marine
Swan Hunter
Wartsila Diesel

Training services
C.I.S.DEG
Hollandse Signaalapparaten
Marconi Underwater
Melara Club Consortium
Swan Hunter
Sperry Marine
Wartsila Diesel

Transducer arrays
Marconi Underwater
Safare-Crouzet
Thomson Sintra/ASM

Transducer calibration
Marconi Underwater
Safare-Crouzet

Transducers
MagneTek Defense
Marconi Underwater
Safare-Crouzet
Thomson Sintra/ASM

Trawlers
Mathiesen's Badebyggeri

Troop ships
Ingalls Shipbuilding
Korea Tacoma Marine
Swan Hunter

Tugs
Daewoo Shipbuilding & Heavy Machinery
DCN
Empresa Nacional Bazan
Hyundai Heavy Industries
Korea Tacoma Marine

Turbine gears
DCN

Turbines
DCN
Empresa Nacional Bazan

Turbines, gas marine
Empresa Nacional Bazan
Hyundai Heavy Industries

Turbines, steam marine
Empresa Nacional Bazan
DCN
Hyundai Heavy Industries

Ultra-fast attack boats
Crestitalia
FR Lürssen Werft
SEC
Swan Hunter

Ultra-fast patrol boats
Crestitalia
FR Lürssen Werft
SEC
Swan Hunter

Underwater acoustic systems
Marconi Underwater
Safare-Crouzet
Thomson Sintra/ASM
WELSE
Whitehead

Underwater communications
Marconi Underwater
Safare-Crouzet
Thomson Sintra/ASM
Whitehead

Underwater sonar towing systems
MacTaggart Scott
Marconi Underwater
Safare-Crouzet
Thomson Sintra/ASM
Whitehead

Underwater television equipment
Safare-Crouzet

Underwater warning systems
Marconi Underwater
Safare-Crouzet
Whitehead

Uninterruptible Power Supplies
Teledyne INET

VME cards and chassis
DY 4 Systems

Warship design
Bath Iron Works
Daewoo Shipbuilding & Heavy Machinery
DCN
Empresa Nacional Bazan
Fincantieri
FR Lürssen Werft
Hyundai Heavy Industries
Ingalls Shipbuilding
Korea Tacoma Marine
Melara Club Consortium
Netherlands Naval Industries Group
NEVESBU
Swan Hunter
Wartsila Diesel
Yarrow Shipbuilders

Warship design (systems engineering)
Bath Iron Works
DCN
FR Lürssen Werft
Ingalls Shipbuilding
Melara Club Consortium
Netherlands Naval Industries Group
NEVESBU
Swan Hunter
Yarrow Shipbuilders

Warship firefighting equipment and systems
DCN
Swan Hunter

Warship repairs
Bath Iron Works
Daewoo Shipbuilding & Heavy Machinery
DCN
Empresa Nacional Bazan
Fincantieri
FR Lürssen Werft
Hyundai Heavy Industries
Ingalls Shipbuilding
Netherlands Naval Industries Group
Swan Hunter

Warships
Bath Iron Works
Daewoo Shipbuilding & Heavy Machinery
Empresa Nacional Bazan
Fincantieri
FR Lürssen Werft
Hyundai Heavy Industries
Ingalls Shipbuilding
Melara Club Consortium
Royal Schelde

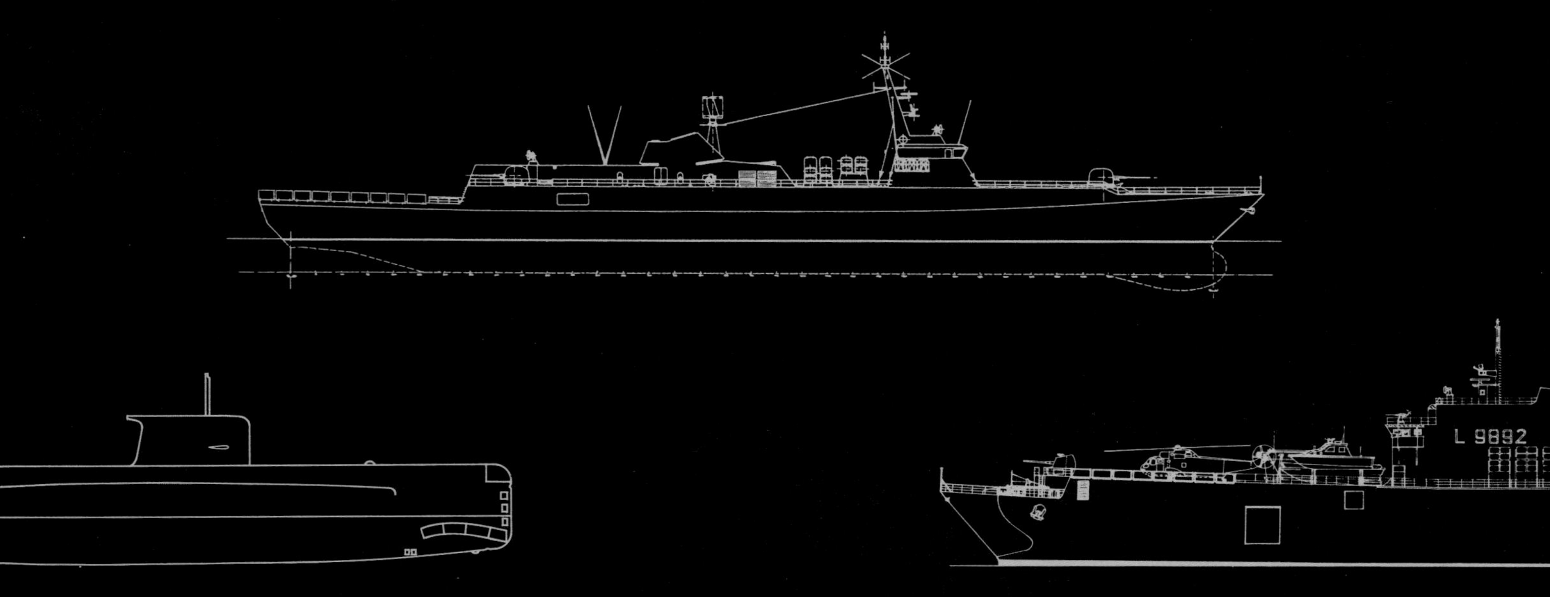
L 9892

SEC
Swan Hunter
Yarrow Shipbuilders

Waterjet propulsion systems
Castoldi
Riva Calzoni

Watertight doors
MacTaggart Scott
Netherlands Naval Industries Group

Weapon control systems
DCN
Empresa Nacional Bazan
Elbit Computers
Hollandse Signaalapparaten
Loral Librascope
NobelTech Electronics
NobelTech Systems
OTO Melara
Safare-Crouzet
Swedish Ordnance
Thomson Sintra/ASM
WELSE

Weapon systems
Bath Iron Works
Breda Meccanica Bresciana
Elbit Computers
Empresa Nacional Bazan
Loral Librascope
Marconi Underwater
Matra Defense
Mecanique Creusot-Loire
Melara Club Consortium
OTO Melara
Safare-Crouzet
Swedish Ordnance
Thomson Sintra/ASM
Whitehead

Weapon systems, engineering
DCN
Elbit Computers
Empresa Nacional Bazan
Hollandse Signaalapparaten
Loral Librascope
Marconi Underwater
Matra Defense
Melara Club Consortium
OTO Melara
Safare-Crouzet
Thomson Sintra/ASM

Weapon systems sonar component
DCN
Marconi Underwater
Safare-Crouzet
Thomson Sintra/ASM

Welding: arc, argon arc or gas
Bath Iron Works
DCN

X-ray work
DCN

Yachts, powered
DCN
FR Lürssen Werft

Solid-state Wind Sensor

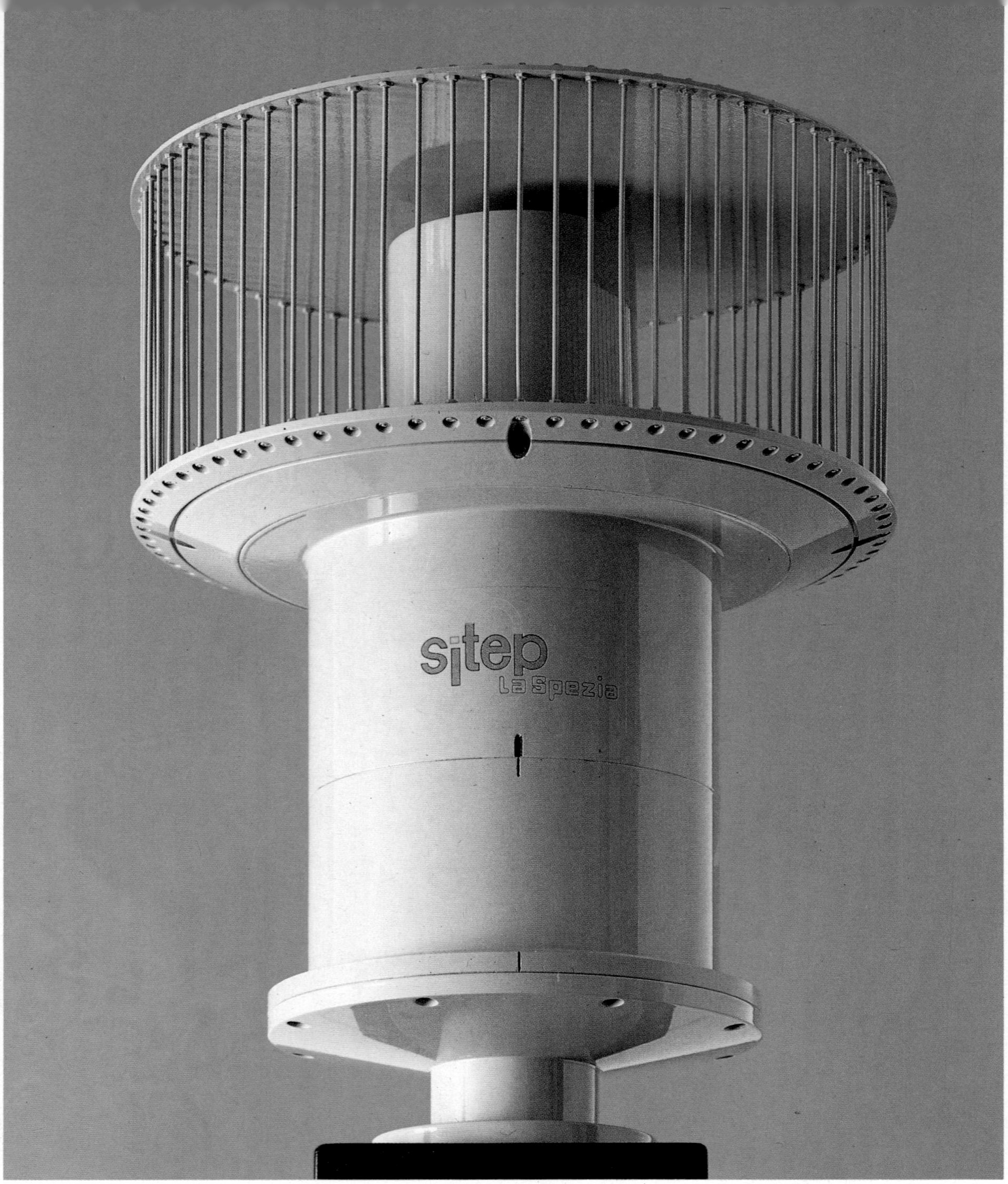

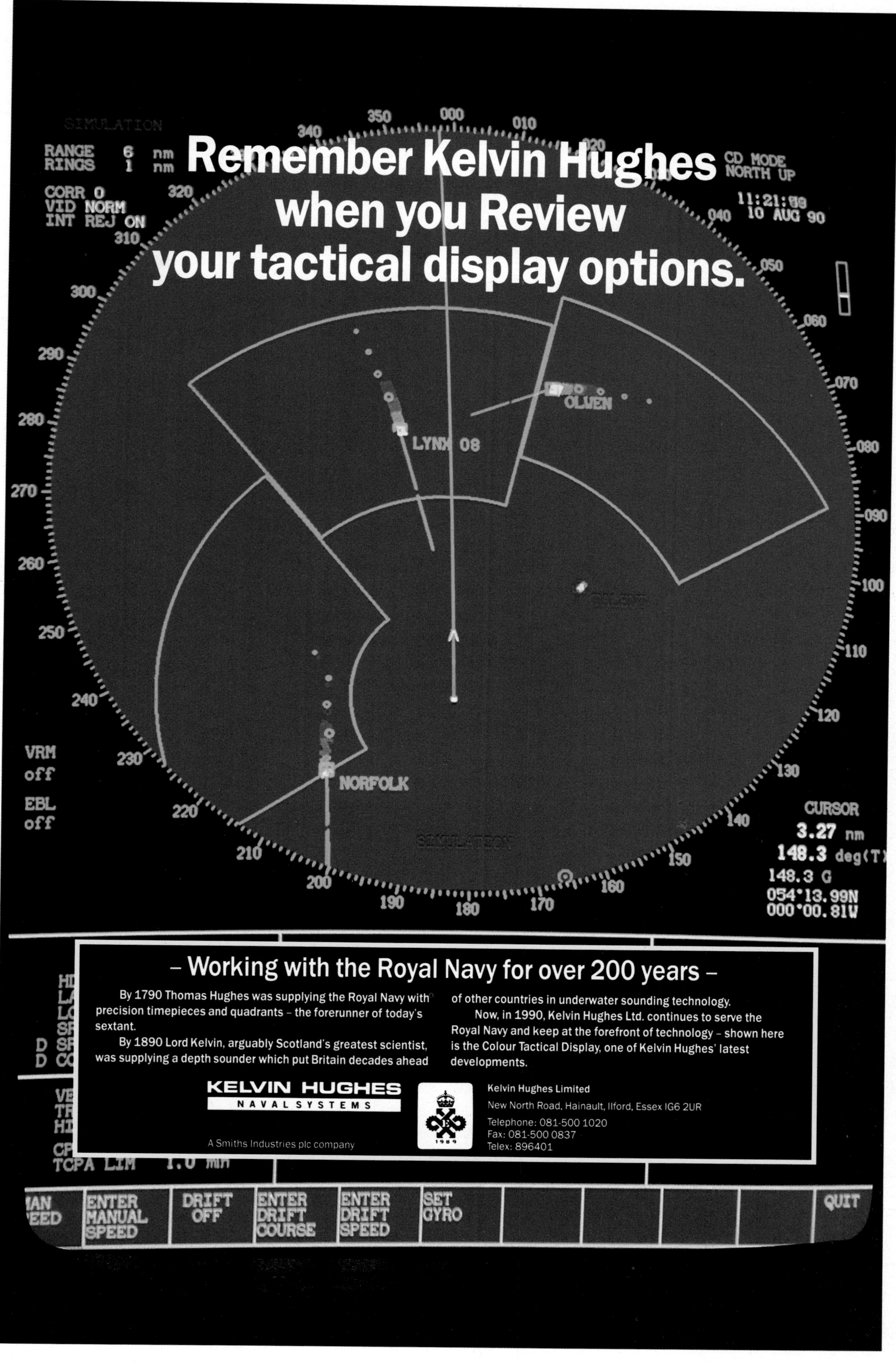

Remember Kelvin Hughes
when you Review
your tactical display options.
RANGE 6 nm
RINGS 1 nm
CORR 0
VID NORM
INT REJ ON
CD MODE
NORTH UP
11:21:00
10 AUG 90
LYNX 08
OLWEN
NORFOLK
VRM
off
EBL
off
CURSOR
3.27 nm
148.3 deg(T)
148.3 G
054°13.99N
000°00.81W
– Working with the Royal Navy for over 200 years –
By 1790 Thomas Hughes was supplying the Royal Navy with precision timepieces and quadrants – the forerunner of today's sextant.
By 1890 Lord Kelvin, arguably Scotland's greatest scientist, was supplying a depth sounder which put Britain decades ahead of other countries in underwater sounding technology.
Now, in 1990, Kelvin Hughes Ltd. continues to serve the Royal Navy and keep at the forefront of technology – shown here is the Colour Tactical Display, one of Kelvin Hughes' latest developments.
KELVIN HUGHES
NAVAL SYSTEMS
A Smiths Industries plc company
Kelvin Hughes Limited
New North Road, Hainault, Ilford, Essex IG6 2UR
Telephone: 081-500 1020
Fax: 081-500 0837
Telex: 896401
ENTER MANUAL SPEED
DRIFT OFF
ENTER DRIFT COURSE
ENTER DRIFT SPEED
SET GYRO
QUIT

THE TOTAL SYSTEM.
Whitehead
MISAR

WELSE
FIELD OF ACTIVITIES
● Submarine integrated systems
● Minisubmarine integrated systems
● ASW vessel integrated systems
● Integrated defence systems for: naval bases, harbours, straits and sea areas in general
● Underwater ranges
SISTEMI SUBACQUEI WELSE S.p.A. CONSORTILE
Via L. Manara, 2 - 16154 GENOVA SESTRI
Tel. (010) 6512283 - Fax (010) 6512147

The new Russian aircraft carrier Admiral Kuznetsov joining the Northern Fleet in January 1992. Coming or going?

JANE'S FIGHTING SHIPS 1992-93

Jane's Information Group Limited, Sentinel House, 163 Brighton Road, Coulsdon, Surrey CR5 2NH, UK
Jane's Information Group Inc, 1340 Braddock Place, Suite 300, Alexandria, VA 22314-1651, USA

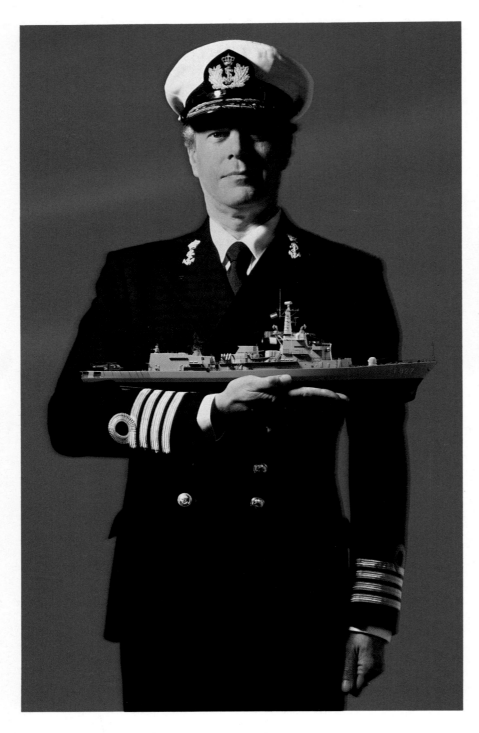

Foreword

"Everyone suddenly burst out singing."

There is no quotation that can do justice to the flood of events which has overwhelmed us in the last 12 months. It therefore seems appropriate to select one which was born in the long shadows of the earlier part of this century. Siegfried Sassoon's report of an unlikely outburst of exhilaration in the midst of the horrors of European trench warfare in 1916 is a timely reminder that one of the historical effects of the forceful resurrection of suppressed nationalism is war between neighbouring states.

The almost universal optimism which surrounded the aftermath of the ejection of Iraq from Kuwait in March last year, and five months later the overthrow of the military coup in Moscow, has led to much discussion of the dividends to be reaped from a new world order. To paraphrase Churchill - some new world, some new order.

If Soviet style communism has been the principal engine of repression and the main threat to civilised governments since 1945, it seems reasonable to suppose that its disintegration and defeat would lead to greater international stability. But the Soviet empire did more than just weld together the tribal factions that lived within its destructive embrace. It managed, in the aftermath of the Second World War, to forge through fear an Atlantic alliance and a Western European coalition underpinned by the military strength of the USA. In the Pacific, and to a lesser extent in the Indian Ocean, it generated bilateral defence arrangements, less structured than NATO, but sharing the same underlying assumption, which was the need to face up to the danger of further Soviet expansionism and the recognition that US power projection worldwide was the only guarantee of continuing independence. Under this umbrella, localised regional disputes could still flourish as long as there was a minimal risk of the horizontal escalation which ultimately might embrace both superpowers and lead to global nuclear war.

What we are now in the process of discovering is what happens when that fear, the cement of alliance, is removed. In reality of course not all the former Soviet capability has gone away and this is particularly true of what is now the Russian Navy. But in the short term at least, all those nuclear submarines at Murmansk and Vladivostok are not seen as threatening, and democratic governments react mostly to perceived short-term threats.

Furthermore, dependence on the US Navy, its communications, its intelligence, its sealift and its layered air and submarine defences is now an ingrained part of Western and Japanese maritime defence culture. Deprived of its superpower adversary, the only force native Americans had cause to fear, there is less obvious reason why the United States should continue to pay the bills for the regional maritime defence of the competitive economies of the European Community, or Japan, or anyone else.

The threat to the continuance of good order in international maritime affairs, on which economic prosperity depends, may therefore rest as much on the willingness of the US to go on deploying sufficient carrier battle groups worldwide as on the resurgence or otherwise of the Russian Navy.

This annual review must therefore be read in the light of the effect that events of the last 12 months have had, and will have, on both of the world's great navies; the Russian bear, maimed and sulking in its lair but still a formidable force, and the American eagle with wings clipped and in danger of being increasingly confined to its nest, thereby allowing the smaller predators greater freedom of manoeuvre. If that sounds too dramatic, a glance at the columns of this book which list the annual warship deletions in each of the major traditional blue water navies should serve to reinforce the point. For every new ship or submarine being ordered, on average three or four are being paid off, although that ratio is worse in some navies than in others. The table below illustrates the decline in the strength of the United States, UK and French navies since 1988 and there is every indication that this trend will continue. The figures given are for this year with 1988 in brackets.

	USA	UK	France
Strategic Submarines	25 (37)	4 (4)	5 (6)
Attack Submarines	83 (100)	19 (26)	13 (17)
Aircraft Carriers	12 (15)	3 (3)	2 (2)
Major Surface Warships	145 (204)	42 (48)	42 (43)
Major Amphibious Ships	60 (61)	7 (8)	4 (8)

Like all such tables it has its limitations not least in that a four-year snapshot ignores factors like the average age of the ships being deleted, or the quality and price of the new ships being built.

A similar table depicting the decline of Western-flagged merchant ships is beyond the scope of this book, but well chronicled reports from both sides of the Atlantic indicate that the point has long since passed when strategic contingencies can be met without the co-operation of flagged-out merchantmen. Hiring these ships on the open market may have its attractions but the problems start when they enter a war zone and come under attack.

None of this maritime decline would be surprising if international trade depended less on transport by sea than historically has been the case. But whether for commercial or military reasons, the sea remains the only way of shipping bulk cargo between continents, and the volume of that traffic is not going to reduce, at least until an alternative energy source emerges to replace fossil fuels. Since the end of the Second World War the only prolonged disruption to trade has been in the Persian Gulf where strong navies have been on hand to contain it. Similarly, and primarily because of the Cold War of the last four decades, there has been a Western naval presence to deter aggressive activity in the China Seas, the Caribbean, the eastern Mediterranean, or anywhere else where regional conflicts might spill over into maritime activity threatening world trade.

If anyone doubts the effectiveness of naval presence, the ill-timed announcement of the withdrawal of the British patrol ship from the South Atlantic in 1982 and the events which followed should still be a fresh enough example to be in the forefront of political consciousness. The trouble with successful deterrence is that it breeds complacency and nowhere is that more apparent than in the assumption that an indigenous merchant marine and the ability to defend it are no longer major imperatives for industrial nations dependent upon the sea for their economic well-being.

Not even a civilian airliner is as vulnerable as the large merchant ship. Its passage is slow, predictable and the antithesis of stealth. It offers a solid and unmistakeable radar and sonar target and, when fired on or boarded, it has inadequate numbers of people for effective damage control or self defence. Many of the major shipping routes pass through disputed territorial seas, not all of them bordered by enlightened democratic regimes. In addition, the merchant ship's cargo is usually of considerable value and increasingly the trend is towards multilingual, uncommitted and poorly paid ships' companies. Losses through piracy, poor maintenance and inadequate seamanship are a growing concern to the maritime insurance industry. But this is as nothing compared with the serious disruption of trade which could follow major curtailment of US naval activities worldwide. That Japan and Germany, two of the most powerful economic powers, remain committed to assist only in their own back yards is a vivid example of their implicit acceptance of dependency on the US Navy.

In the past decade we have seen warships used in hostile operations in the Gulf, the South Atlantic, the Indian Ocean, the China Seas, the Caribbean and the Mediterranean. These operations have been in support of major land/air warfare, in the destruction of coastal forces, for amphibious landings, in precision strikes against land targets, in mine clearance operations, in blockade, in the containment of a medium power navy and in air defence of high value units such as aircraft carriers and troop ships. In addition there have been numerous examples of effective naval presence and disaster relief. What we have not seen, other than in a very limited way during the Iran/Iraq war, are prolonged operations in defence of merchant shipping continually threatened by submarine or air attack. As usual it will take a major event of that sort to re-establish defence of economic trade as the first amongst equals of all naval tasks. Operations on land whether to contain military dictatorships or to honour post colonial defence treaties can always be dismissed as optional by the 'it will never happen that way again' and 'why should we get involved?' school of isolationist politics. On the other hand the capability to provide and to protect seaborne trade is not something which can be so readily dismissed. The signs are that it may need more than the exhortations of the maritime lobby to bring this message home.

Implicit dependence on US seapower

United States

You do not have to look very far for indications that with the defeat of their rival superpower Americans are less prepared to foot the bill as the world's maritime policeman. The scaling-down process is under way with withdrawal from some foreign bases, the placing in reserve of large numbers of ships, the cancellation of a few new construction shipbuilding and weapon development projects, and moves to go down-market on others. As this process is still in its early stages the bottom of the downward curve is still some way from being visible. It can be said with confidence that wherever the present trend leads, the descent in both deployment levels and in shipbuilding terms will not be as precipitate as that enveloping the Russian Navy. Perhaps more insidious is the potential effect on the morale of a service which has always had a crusading zeal in pursuit of its country's enemies. There is not a sailor alive in any navy who has not occasionally wondered what on earth he is doing flogging the ocean for months on end when he could be at home with his family. The introduction in ships of more women, some of them mothers, can only serve to reinforce that feeling. The antidote is a sense of purpose and the nation's strong support. Both demand an identifiable threat and a level of involvement necessary to contain it. To the professional the threat is still real enough, encapsulated both in Russian dormant capability and growing nationalist fervour in unstable countries, but with the disarmament lobby in full cry that may not be enough to maintain the level of popular support to which the Navy became accustomed in the days of the evil empire.

The other problem which has been looming on the horizon for many years is the increasing cost in real terms of new ships, submarines and naval aircraft, as the siren song of new technology has risen to an unsustainable crescendo. When the cost of a single submarine looks likely to absorb a third of the whole naval procurement budget, the time has come to pause for thought. No-one wants to equip their forces with less than the best available but the balance between quality and quantity has always required the wisdom of Solomon.

At the risk of offending both camps it needs saying that defence industries and defence journalists sometimes form an unholy alliance in extolling the virtues of new technologies with well publicised versions of selected or projected highlights. The military too are not immune from selling a particular form of combat by unbalanced presentations which ignore the frequent poor performances of those same systems.

With the concept of 'superior' Russian technology retreating with its tail between its legs, if not yet actually slain, the Seawolf programme has been an early casualty. Submariners are paragons of most virtues but they have one unfailing vice. Already enjoying an immunity from both detection and attack which by surface ship standards is remarkable, they seek the holy grail of total stealth. The trouble with the last five per cent of any capability is that it tends to cost as much as the previous 95 per cent.

On top of that there is the problem of magazine capacity. A submarine specialised in anti-submarine warfare can get away with a much smaller weapon load than one earmarked for operations against surface ships or for attacking land targets with cruise missiles, or even for minelaying. Against another submarine, one, or perhaps two, weapons per engagement ought to be sufficient, whereas for the other forms of warfare salvoes are more likely to be needed for a much greater number of targets. There is therefore a *prima facie* case for specialised submarines, particularly if reasonable force levels can be sustained. *Seawolf* herself may still be a remarkable ship but the price for too much new technology, too large a magazine and too many concurrent roles was ultimately over the top. Plans to develop a common hull and propulsion system with alternative weapon modules to be determined on build seems to be a more sensible way forward in a defence climate much different from the one in which *Seawolf* was conceived.

Immediate intentions for the strategic submarine force are not entirely clear. The goal seems to be 18 Ohio class by the end of the decade, but the numbers of Trident-equipped submarines to be maintained between now and then tend to vary with the release of successive policy statements. Poseidon-fitted ships were withdrawn from operational patrols last October and apart from two hulls which are to be converted for amphibious assault support operations, the remainder are in the process of being paid off. Together with the accelerated decommissioning of the older SSNs this must be putting quite a strain on reactor disposal facilities.

So far there remains a commitment to maintain 12 deployable aircraft carriers and 11 active air wings at least until 1995, but rumours persist of further reductions. Also uncertainty still surrounds the acquisition strategy for naval aircraft after the confusion caused by the cancellation of the A-12 and P-7A projects. It is intended to develop the AX attack aircraft as a replacement for the A-6E and an improved range F/A-18 looks probable. The follow-on to the ageing P-3C maritime patrol aircraft is being addressed as a matter of growing urgency.

The battleships have gone back into reserve, leaving a nasty hole in naval gunfire support for future amphibious operations. Finding alternatives for big gun firepower is a high priority programme. An equally high development priority is extending the range and improving the flight profile of the conventional warhead Tomahawk cruise missile, now that the nuclear warheads have been landed and placed in storage. All but a handful of shipborne tactical nuclear weapons of all types had been removed from active service by April 1992.

Those not yet convinced of the speed with which the so-called peace dividend is being taken up should compare the Proposed Shipbuilding Programme for FY 1993 with the table showing Ships Scheduled for Delivery during FY 1992. The deliveries this year number 22 vessels including an SSBN, two SSNs, an aircraft carrier, two cruisers, a destroyer, two major amphibious ships, two MCMVs, two survey ships and four oilers. The proposed request for FY 1993 includes just four destroyers and two minehunters.

Some of the more expensive technical options for the later ships of the Arleigh Burke class destroyer programme have been quietly shelved, but the requirement to include flight deck and helicopter hangar facilities has been given greater urgency as the regional conflict scenario takes precedence over deep water anti-submarine warfare. Frigate numbers are falling like a stone with the paying off to reserve of the whole Knox class apart from eight ships which will remain active with the Naval Reserve Force. In theory the ships in reserve can be reactivated (or reconstituted) in 180 days. Projected amphibious shipbuilding is inadequate to prevent the future block obsolescence of existing ships. After much Marine lobbying a sixth Wasp class LHD is now pencilled in and the new LX programme is up and running.

YOU
NEVER
KNOW
WHERE
DANGER
LURKS
BELIER ENTREPRISES · Meggs/Vloo

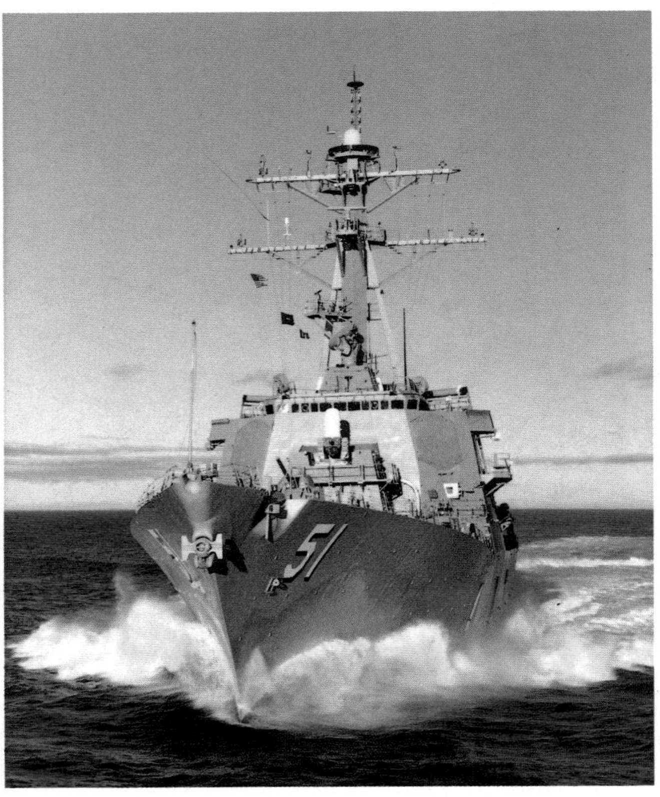

The only class of major warship in the FY 1993 Proposed Shipbuilding Programme *(Bath Iron Works)*

The Cinderella branch of mine warfare is being given another shot in the arm by the integration of all MCM assets and training under one operational commander. Two deployable groups are being formed comprising ocean-going vessels, Sea Dragon helicopters and clearance divers. The Marine Corps is also to take an active role. Two unmanned drones have been leased from Sweden for trials and also there is talk of acquiring dedicated support and heavy lift vessels. The plan to develop a common base has run into politically inspired home-porting objections which have still to be resolved. Perhaps the acid test of serious commitment will be whether the MCM Commander is given his own way on basing and other key issues. As a result of the Gulf War there is growing expertise in this difficult and dangerous task in a number of navies and the quickest way forward may be to exchange experiences with other nations.

The Sealift programme, around which more flak has flown for longer than almost any other, is now in danger of becoming a cuckoo's egg in the shipbuilding nest. The Navy is expected to both build and convert existing vessels to meet a requirement for 20 new Ro-Ro ships and two large container vessels by FY 1998. The first nine will be prepositioned with support equipment and the others will augment the existing fast sealift ships for rapid deployment.

Air defence takes priority in regional conflict *(Ingalls)*

Overall the strategic emphasis has moved decisively from fixed forward defence against a continental superpower, to flexible forward positioning in the event of regional instabilities affecting the United States and her allies. It is significant that in their combined annual statement in March this year the Secretary of the Navy and the Chief of Naval Operations raised again the spectre of the dangerously inadequate "hollow forces" that have resulted from defence cutbacks in the past. There is nothing hollow about the US Navy at the moment but the future looks decidedly more wobbly.

Russia and Associated States

What's in a name? The final dissolution of the former Soviet Union in December 1991 has caused more than a few difficulties as the international community looks for ways to describe an organisation featuring a number of semi-detached republics which, in one way or another, are less than fully independent of the old Moscow-based bureaucracies. The 'Unified' team graces the Olympic Games, but this is an acknowledged short-term expedient, and the 'Commonwealth of Independent States' neither sounds nor looks as though it has the stamina to survive for the long haul.

Fortunately for those reporting on maritime affairs, the Soviet Navy has always been predominantly Russian. Of the four Fleets only two have easy access to the world's oceans and those two have long been the home of all the nuclear submarines and a large proportion of the major surface units. As both the Northern and Pacific Fleets are also based wholly in Russian territory and officered predominantly by ethnic Russians, the transition to a Russian flag caused hardly a ripple on the surface of those bleak and inhospitable harbours in Kola and Kamchatka.

The Black Sea Fleet bases

The more obvious problems of the smaller Baltic and Black Sea Fleets have been well-publicised in the West, particularly while the Ukrainian leadership was overplaying its limited hand in seeking to control ships based in the Crimea. The only strategic role left for the Black Sea Fleet is to provide the main surface ship elements of the Mediterranean Squadron, and possibly to deploy ships in an emergency to the Indian Ocean via the Suez Canal. Otherwise Moscow seems content to hand over some of the coastal forces and probably the border guard ships to allow Ukraine control of its own seaward defences, while retaining the major units of what has become by Russian standards more of a Flotilla than a Fleet. Georgia also lays claim to its own patrol force, as does Azerbaijan in the Caspian Sea.

The status of the Crimea remains to be resolved with strong local feelings in favour either of independence or a return to the Russian republic, so reversing Kruschev's arbitrary gift to Ukraine in 1954. Ukrainian shipyards, particularly Nikolayev South with its aircraft carrier facilities, will go on building ships for whoever will pay for them, and that includes the Russian Navy, but with growing spare capacity in the White Sea, St Petersburg, Gorky and Komsomolsk, Ukrainian yards are not vital to the Navy's future.

In the Baltic, similar Coast Guard arrangements are being worked out with Lithuania, Latvia and Estonia. The Russian main base in the Kaliningrad/Baltysk complex remains accessible overland by special agreements with Byelorussia and Lithuania, and further north St Petersburg and Kronshtadt are also available as Russian ports, although with icing problems in Winter. The strategic significance of this Fleet has diminished, at least for the time being, even more than that in the Black Sea, and brown water Flotilla status seems inevitable if current trends continue.

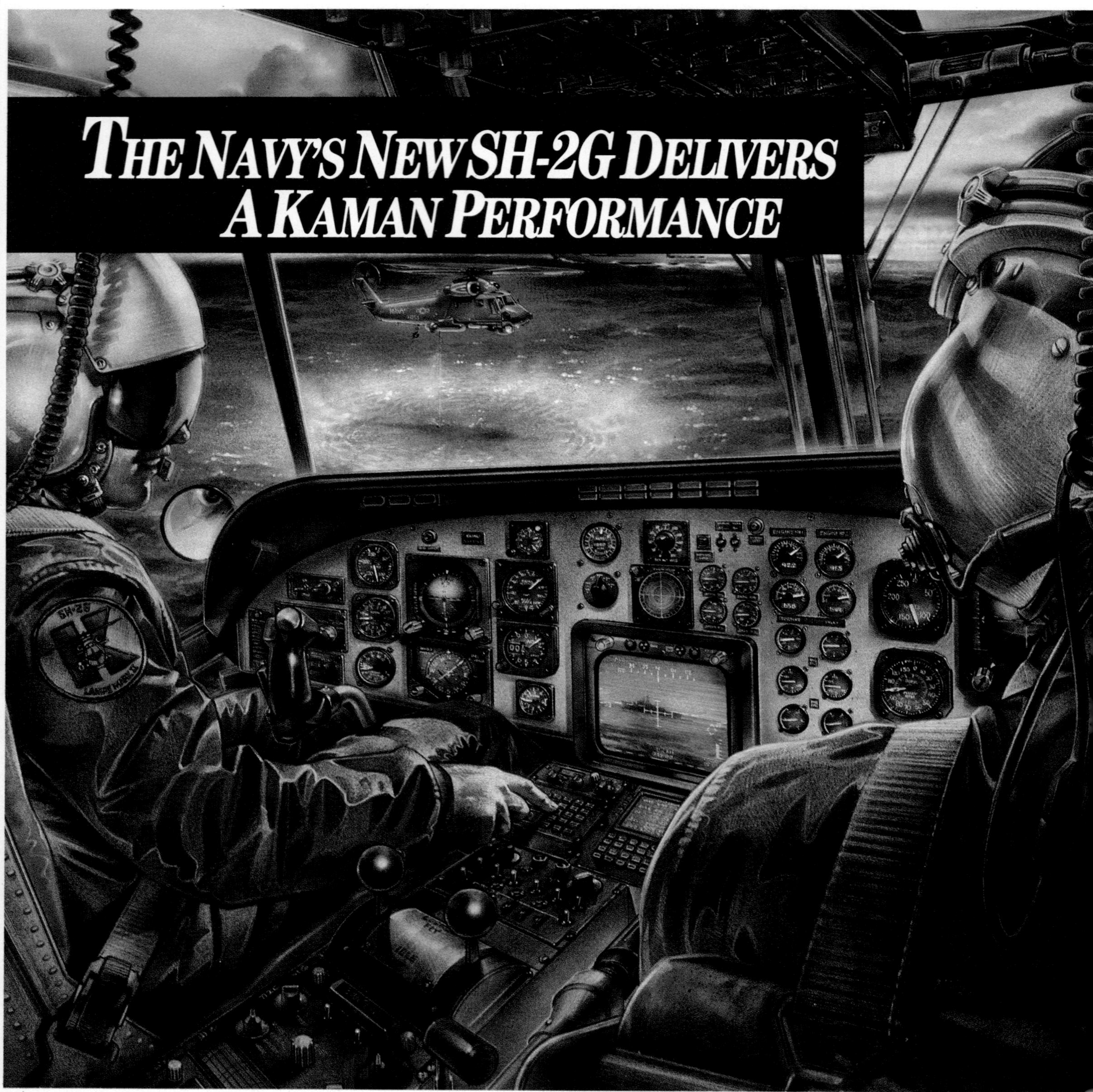
THE NAVY'S NEW SH-2G DELIVERS
A KAMAN PERFORMANCE

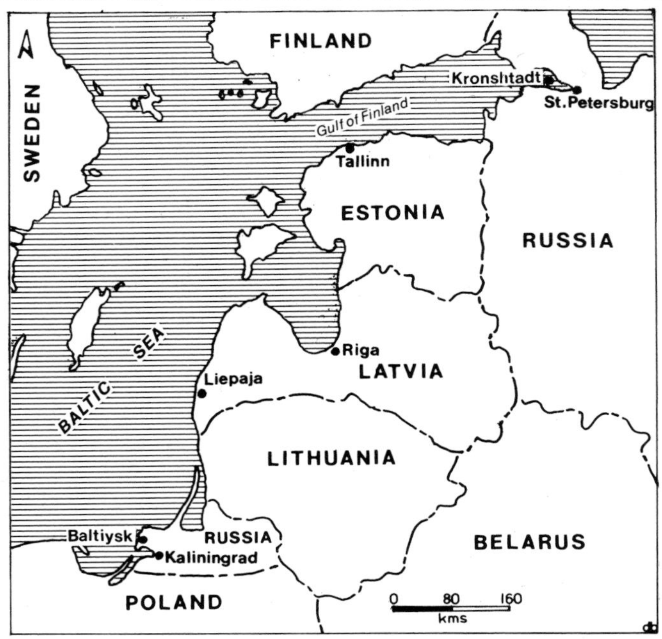

The Baltic Fleet bases

Operationally the last 12 months have seen a virtual cessation of Russian out-of-area surface ship activity with the Indian and South Atlantic Oceans deserted, the Cam Ranh Bay base abandoned by the last ship in January this year, and only occasional excursions to the Mediterranean. A few inter-Fleet transfers have taken place, the most notable being the sailing of the first truly fixed-wing aircraft carrier from the Black Sea to the Northern Fleet, on completion of builders' trials in December last year. As this period has coincided with the dissolution of the old union, a shortage of oil, currency destabilisation and chaos in some manufacturing industries, it would be premature to say the least to write off this great Navy as no longer being a potential player on the world stage. Activity in-area, exercises, weapon training and trials have continued at only a slightly reduced tempo and submarine operations have hardly been affected at all. This is far from being a Navy rotting at its moorings, and if spare parts are difficult to obtain and ship husbandry has declined from former standards, these are problems with which some Western navies are also familiar. An interesting pointer for the future is that oceanographic research work has continued, although at a much reduced level, in the Atlantic and northern seas, but not in the Pacific or Indian Oceans.

Attempts are being made to encourage a force comprising more volunteers. Coupled with the dropping off of non Russian-speaking conscripts from the republics of central Asia this could rapidly lead to much better motivated and trained ships' companies, which is a factor of greater significance by far than the state of the upper deck paintwork. Redundant political officers, many of them high quality people, have been retained for general morale and welfare work.

The latest aircraft carrier joins the Northern Fleet

Of the former 21 warship-building yards, nine have so far been declared surplus to requirements. Given the huge capacity of Severodvinsk on the White Sea, more redundancies could follow including Nikolayev North and Kerch, both in Ukraine. SSBN programmes have reached a temporary halt with the seventh and last Delta IV, but submarines continued to be launched in 1991 at the rate of three nuclear-powered SSNs and three Kilo class diesel-driven patrol boats. The nuclear attack Oscar, Akula and Sierra classes were still in series production in the Spring of 1992 but funding problems are increasingly severe and further cuts seem inevitable.

The principle difficulties facing the shipbuilders are that specialised component suppliers are spread around the Republics and many of these factories are trying to break into the more profitable commercial markets. In the old state-managed economy a monopoly source of, for example, marine gas turbines was no problem even if it happened to be in Kazakhstan. The merits of having available alternative sources of supply is a lesson being learned the hard way. Skilled workers are also moving to more profitable sectors of the economy and these will be even less easily replaced than the specialised supplier.

Major surface ship production also continues in spite of these difficulties. The second large aircraft carrier, the *Varyag*, is still expected to complete (although possibly only to be sold) but the future of the nuclear-powered *Ulyanovsk* now looks extremely doubtful, even though it would have been ready for launching by early 1993. Nonetheless two major fixed-wing carriers backed up by four smaller Kiev class could put to sea a formidable air wing, although in the case of the Kiev class, only if VSTOL development is allowed to continue. If it does not, the Kiev ships will revert to helicopter carriers once the Forgers have completed being withdrawn from service. The Flanker looks to be the favoured aircraft for the Kuznetsov class. The two elderly Moskva class helo carriers are destined for early scrapping.

Arctic tourists, courtesy of the Russian Navy

Sovremenny and Udaloy class destroyers remain in series production, although facing increasing difficulties in timely completions. An improved variant of the Udaloy is expected to launch this year. The last of the Krivak III class should also be completed soon and a surprise has been the sighting at sea of modified Krivak Is with improved electronics and sonar, and with the SS-N-25 Harpoonski fitted instead of the A/S mortars. Another surprise has been the emergence against the odds of a Kresta I from a six-year refit, which coincided with the scrapping of the only other two ships of the class still in commission. Doubts have been expressed over the continuance of the Kaliningrad-built frigates of the Neustrashimy class. This too would be surprising as it is the first helicopter-capable naval frigate. A possible explanation for the slowness of this programme is that the eight former KGB helicopter ships of the Krivak class are to be taken over by the Navy as opposed to being operated by the Border Guard. More major warships are expected to have their names changed to reflect the Russianisation of the fleet.

Corvettes, fast attack craft, patrol craft and minehunters are all still active programmes, with some being built for export, and it is likely that most of these new ships are available to anyone prepared to produce hard currency.

Any commentary on this Navy walks a thin dividing line between the twin concurrent forecasts of implosion and collapse if present political and industrial trends continue, or alternatively the resurgence of an aggressive politico-military Russian regime which may try to restore greater control and direction. The West may have lost its capacity to be surprised by events in the former Soviet Union and whatever happens next may only be the preliminary to what happens after that. In other words, assumptions based on the latest headlines may have no more substance than many that have been made in the last year. The only certainty for the harrassed strategic planner is not to assume that this massive naval capability is either ineffective or benign until every major modern warship and submarine has been consigned to the scrapyard, a prospect which still seems a very long way off. There is no historical precedent for a major military power losing a war without forfeiting most of its military effectiveness, either in battle or by unconditional surrender. What we are hoping to see is an equivalent voluntary surrender, but premature anticipation of the event would be an act of supreme irresponsibility.

United Kingdom

"In my view the course we should follow is that the British Army of the Rhine and our Air Force in Germany should be reduced to token forces and the three services given the opportunity to evolve on a tri-service basis to meet worldwide commitments which must remain with us for a great number of years to come. We should revert to our centuries-old tradition of mobility and flexibility, based on seapower, at the earliest opportunity."

By the end of the year no attack submarines will be under construction for the first time since 1901

Just the sort of thing you would expect from some crusty old Admiral pursuing vested interests, now that western Europe is no longer threatened by the Warsaw Pact and these islands are probably more secure from attack than at any time in their history? Well no! It is a quote from a letter to *The Times* by a General Murray when he was Commander-in-Chief Allied Forces Northern Europe in February 1968. Is his advice about to be taken some quarter of a century later? Well no, again, as an influential part of the Whitehall establishment continues to see the Armed Forces as an extension of a commitment to European unification, rather than as national forces equipped and ready to act in support of British interests wherever they may be threatened, and if necessary in coalition with like-minded nations.

It becomes depressing year after year to have to praise British naval competence in far-flung places while searching in vain in Defence White Papers for an acknowledgement that what sailors and marines have to spend their time doing is recognised as their primary purpose. Neither are there sufficient resources being allocated to allow the continuation of all the present tasks at the same level, or even the maintenance of the same high standards, although no-one in the Navy has yet stopped trying.

During the period since 1979 the Royal Navy has fought a war in the South Atlantic, conducted continuous patrols in the Gulf for the last 11 years (rising to a crescendo in 1990/91 and still continuing at a lower level), cleared mines in the Gulf and Red Sea and maintained almost constant patrols in the Caribbean, South Atlantic, Hong Kong and as part of NATO's Standing Naval Forces. It has also maintained a seaborne strategic nuclear deterrent. During that same decade destroyer and frigate numbers have been reduced by 42 per cent and submarines by 57 per cent, with further cutbacks still to come as the final part of the Options for Change salami slicing exercise is worked through in the next couple of years. Perhaps the worst example of the arbitrary nature of the cuts is the scrapping of the first of the Swiftsure class SSNs after less than 20 years' service. As in Canada, commensurate reductions in the size of the infrastructure and the civilian tail are delayed by political expediency, because closing down shore establishments attracts public attention in a way that paying off ships does not.

Order rates of new major surface ships and auxiliaries are down to a total of less than two a year, and between January 1986 and some unspecified time in the mid-1990s there are to be no submarine orders at all other than for Trident. The completion later this year of the last of the Upholder class will see the first break in attack submarine construction since the first Holland boat was launched in 1901. After five years of prevarication no-one is going to believe the latest political commitment to replacement amphibious ships until the contracts to build are placed, and that will not be for at least another year or more for the helicopter carrier, and much longer than that for the LPDs.

Treasury-led reductions on operational spending in the last year would have meant the end of the Antarctic patrol ship and the withdrawal of the Hong Kong Flotilla, had there not been direct and last minute Prime Ministerial intervention in both cases.

On the weapon systems side the news is slightly more encouraging with good progress in naval aircraft updates and replacements, and better radars, sonars and electronic warfare equipment entering service. Advances in new weapons are less impressive with continuing reliance on the obsolescent Sea Dart SAM system and the cancellation of some previously planned improvements to close-range hard-kill air defences in the aircraft carriers and destroyers. The critical destroyer capability of being able to defend high value units and merchant ships from air attack is not going to show any real progress until the introduction of the Type 42 replacement at the end of the decade.

The rolling out of the first of the majestic new Vanguard class SSBNs should not be allowed to obscure the unpalatable fact that this is now the only submarine construction programme, or that in the same week as the launch it was announced that the submarine squadron at Gosport is to be disbanded in 1993.

The passing of the major overland threat to western Europe and the uncertainties and potential instabilities of the new world order ought to have given a new focus to General Murray's contention that the UK's best contribution would take the form of the restoration of readily deployable Armed Forces based on the primacy of a maritime strategy. Whitehall's continuing antagonism to its Navy and Merchant Marine serves this country ill.

Europe

The Europe of the European Community is in transition and largely leaderless. Furthermore, whether the Community widens to embrace eastern European nations or deepens into a more federal structure of the existing countries, the leadership problem looks impossible to resolve. In February this year the annual European Community Security Policy conference in Munich heard the Secretary General of NATO reiterate that America was still indispensable to European security. The British Chief of the Defence Staff was reported as going even further, saying that Europe on its own would "Pretend to have a military capability and when the need arises we will find we haven't got a capability at all". Some countries of the European Community continue to put their faith in the long-term future of NATO. France is the strongest advocate of the Western European Union (WEU) as the

military arm of a federal Community, and a reunited and increasingly self-confident Germany has served notice that it is renewing its historical ties with central and eastern European countries which are neither members of NATO nor of the European Community. The other main institutional player in this mishmash of opportunistic nationalisms released from fear of the Red Army is the Conference on Security and Co-operation in Europe (CSCE), which may act as a forum to defuse conflict, but seems unlikely ever to develop beyond a useful talking shop. Its main advantage is that virtually every country is represented.

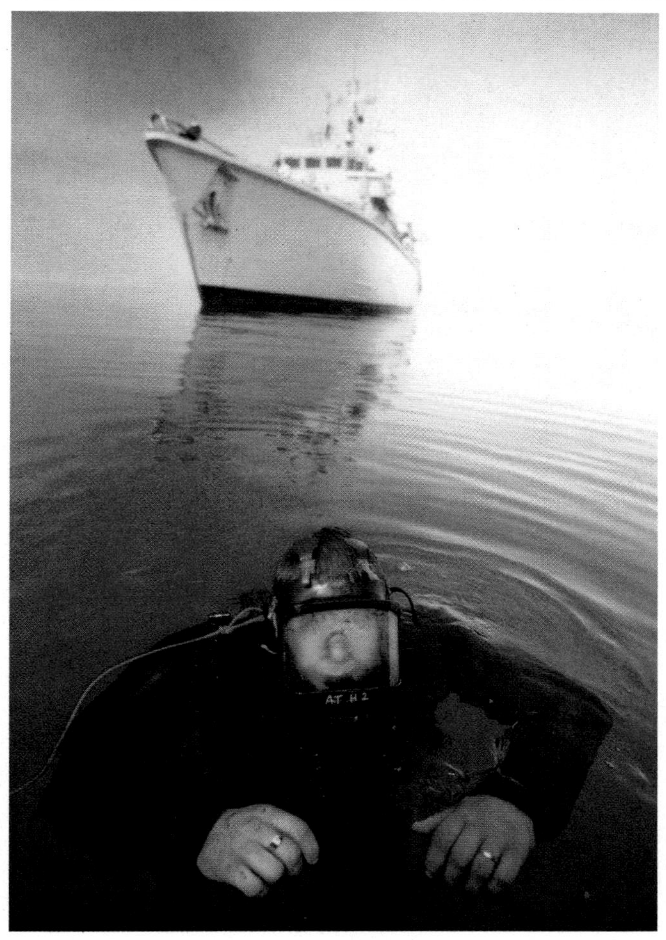

Some MCMV operations in the Gulf have been co-ordinated by the Western European Union

Whatever their reservations about autonomous defence, many northern and western European countries are united in reaping the peace dividend while protesting their commitment to strong defences. The combination of economic recession and public indifference to defence issues has encouraged cutbacks, and it seems certain there will be more unless something happens to disturb the current level of complacency.

In the Baltic both Sweden and Finland have benefited from reduced east/west tensions, but the fundamental roles of their navies have not been affected. Finland is concerned that Russian activity in the Gulf of Finland is growing as the major Baltic Fleet units withdraw from the ports of the newly independent Baltic states. Sweden remains highly sensitive to any intrusions into her vulnerable coastline and is building up amphibious battalions which will eventually cover the whole archipelago. Each battalion will have some 24 fast assault craft, which are now in series production, and about a dozen supply vessels. The Swedish Navy has also recently accepted into service a mini submarine to simulate covert penetration operations. Orders for three new air-independent propulsion submarines have been confirmed and new minelayers are being delivered this year.

Poland has nearly completed paying off its large force of Polnochny landing ships but is maintaining a sizeable Navy in other respects, although inevitably the shipyards are suffering from the end of Soviet orders. Denmark has acquired a fourth submarine of the Kobben class from Norway to be cannibalised to repair the salvaged *Saelen*. A sign of the times is the leasing of the new Thetis class frigate for three to four months a year for the next four years in order to conduct seismological surveys off Greenland. The strengthening of the Naval Home Guard with newer patrol craft may indicate growing concerns over the influx of illegal immigrants, something which is concerning all European Community nations.

Three air-independent propulsion submarines have been ordered by Sweden *(Horst Dehnst)*

Norway should commission the first of her twin-hulled minehunters this year, and has already completed the last of six new submarines. After the nine MCM vessels the priority will switch to replacing the fast attack craft. In December Norway was offered associate membership of the WEU which it seems likely she will accept.

Germany is the main banker of the European Community and is still faced with huge bills for assimilating and cleaning up East Germany, as well as paying reparations to Moscow for the early withdrawal of its forces from German soil. Given that background it is a measure of the economic strength of this country that it is also able to maintain sizeable armed forces. The latest Marine 2005 plan projects a balanced Fleet consisting of a minimum of 10 submarines, 16 frigates, 20 missile patrol craft, 20 MCMV and some 115 naval aircraft including Tornados, helicopters and LRMP. Six new depot ships and four task force supply ships will form the core of the auxiliary force. This means that all existing new construction programmes remain intact although some of the timescales have been expanded. Older ships are being paid off in large numbers.

German ships are confined to the NATO area *(Horst Dehnst)*

The key question is when will the constitution be amended to allow the frigates and supply ships to take their rightful place alongside allied blue water navies wherever they may be required? Many Germans were irritated by the criticism directed at them for failing to play a direct role in the Gulf War, particularly as they more than paid their way in indirect contributions. It would be surprising if this economically dominant continental power were to go on playing a similar low-key role for much longer.

The process of dismembering the former GDR Fleet has been completed. Not many ships have been bought on the open market, although there have been transfers of minesweepers to Uruguay and a few vessels have been sold in Europe for commercial use. A Tarantul class corvette is now running trials for the United States Navy, reflecting understandable interest in this ex-Soviet best seller, and other transfers are still possible before the remaining ships go to the breakers' yard.

There have been no changes of any great significance in the Dutch construction programmes, although delays and the premature retirements of some existing frigates remain a possibility. The Navy has been drawn into the drugs war in the Caribbean using ships and aircraft stationed in the Antilles.

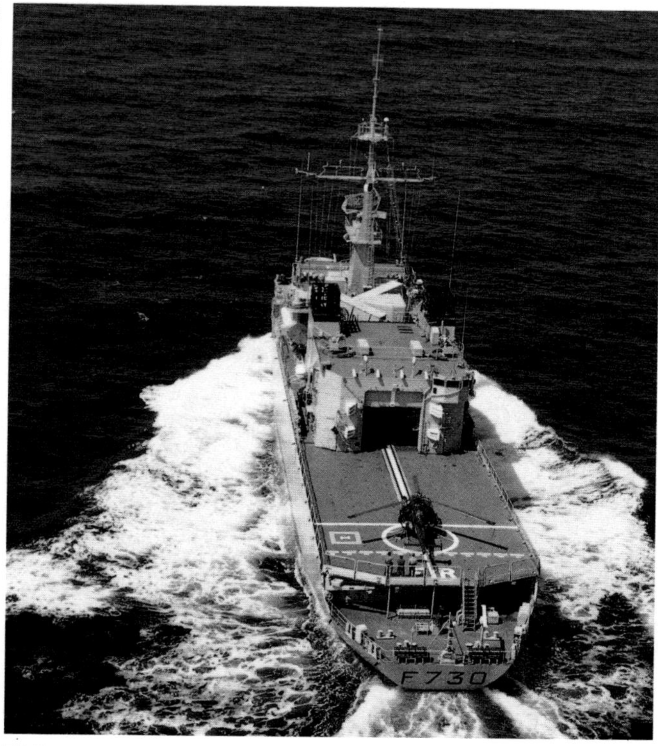

A new French light frigate

France has been busily absorbing the lessons learnt from her high profile involvement in coalition warfare in the Gulf. After years of self-imposed semi-autonomous isolation, the Navy inevitably found joint or co-ordinated operations something of a cultural shock. Shortcomings were revealed in command and communications interoperability, particularly with the US Navy and, as NATO navies have known for years, timely intelligence and airborne electronic warfare are now almost an American monopoly. Other major concerns are the lack of adequate air defence hard-kill systems, both medium- and short-range, and the unreliability and general obsolescence of the Crusader aircraft. Problems were also caused by the law preventing conscripts being allowed to serve in ships deployed away from French ports.

As in Britain, the government has been accused of cutting defence without a proper review of policy and more political blood will be spilt when the 'loi' or blueprint is published later this Spring. The Chief of Naval Staff has robustly voiced his concerns by saying the Navy cannot meet all its commitments on a shrinking budget and that there must be a reassessment of operational requirements. So far, the axe has fallen on the last SSN of the Amethyste class building programme and the SSBN construction schedule is being extended. In addition, a minehunter/sweeper project has been suspended, and not for the first time there is much sniping at the fixed-wing aircraft carrier programme, both in terms of replacement ships and the introduction of new aircraft.

France is dedicated to a more European defence alliance and in the last year the Navy has led a mixed Dutch and Belgian minesweeper force in the Gulf, under the auspices of the Western European Union. There is also enthusiasm for current collaboration with the UK over a future air defence ship to fill the vacuum left by the cancellation of the NATO frigate. The key SAM system is based on the French Aster missile, but whether there is sufficient commonality of other weapon requirements and shipbuilding programmes remains to be seen. Naval collaborative projects of this complexity have an unhappy history.

On the Iberian peninsula Portugal has commissioned the last of its three new frigates and may now team up with the Netherlands and Belgium for new minesweepers, although the patrol craft replacement programme seems to have the first priority. A new replenishment tanker is also needed.

Of all the European navies Spain probably has the most problems as a result of the current defence and economic climate. Routine repairs and maintenance are being delayed, fuel expenditure has been almost halved and every new construction programme is in trouble. The national shipyard Bazán is being forced to stop some work and reduce its labour force because of delayed payments by the Ministry of Defence. The plan Alta Mar is in real trouble.

Spain continues to move steadily towards greater military integration within NATO, and the defence of Spanish territory within the alliance operating area is now a NATO commitment. In spite of this, national sensibilities were disturbed when a frigate Captain indicated that for a time in the Gulf he had come under foreign operational control. This was immediately denied by the authorities. It will be a shame if the renewal of this competent Navy on Europe's dangerous southern flank is seriously impeded by financial problems.

The Mediterranean and Black Seas

As maritime regions where the presence of superpower alliances has helped suppress national enmities, the Mediterranean and Black Seas are self-evidently arenas for further conflicts. In an offshoot of the Conference for Security and Co-operation in Europe attempts are being made to form security groups at both the eastern and western ends of the Mediterranean.

Italy is involved in both and remains the pivotal link between them. The proposed new Italian Defence Model also recognises that the axis of threat to Italy may have shifted to the south and expenditure on the Navy might therefore have to be increased from the present 21 per cent to over 30 per cent of the defence budget. In spite of this, the Fleet will be reduced during the next decade to some 20 major surface warships and six submarines plus coastal, minehunter and support ship squadrons. On the manpower side there is to be a marked increase in the number of volunteers, but overall numbers of people will decline by about one-fifth.

Major Italian shipbuilders are suffering from a dearth of naval orders and the decision to take into the Navy the four Lupo class frigates originally built for Iraq has at least provided refurbishment work and compensated Fincantieri for some of the losses incurred in this ill-fated contract. With just one LPD training ship as the only major surface vessel under construction, these are dark days for the industry.

Operationally the Gulf War provided some much needed lengthy naval deployment experience which continued into 1991 with 16 ships involved and a total of 70 mines destroyed. The other highlight was the delivery of two Sea Harrier trainers, with the 18 fighters eagerly anticipated this year. A second Guiseppe Garibaldi carrier is now an obvious priority.

The Balkan cockpit

To the east of the Adriatic the ethnic cockpit of the Balkan states (Albania, Yugoslavia, Greece, Bulgaria, Romania and Turkey) needs reviewing with circumspection. This is historically a turbulent area, arguably now in a state of almost permanent instability. The breakup of Yugoslavia is already far advanced. As much of its coastline and the major ports and shipbuilding yards are all in Croatia, it is no surprise that some 20 warships of various types should now be in Croatian hands or that half the trained manpower of the Navy has gone with them. In fact it is questionable whether the old Federal Navy can even man its submarines. It seems inevitable that Croatia will develop as the predominant naval force. Gunboats, amphibious craft and minesweepers have all been active in the civil war and the callous bombardment from the sea of the old and beautiful town of Dubrovnik is one of the abiding media images of this campaign.

As the only one of the Balkan countries with membership of both NATO and the European Community (and therefore qualified for the Western European Union) Greece is in a position of responsibility and some power should she choose to exercise it. A defence co-operation agreement was signed with Bulgaria last December and there have been talks with Italy and Egypt over wider security issues in the eastern Mediterranean. Albania to the west, Macedonia to the north and Turkey across the Aegean remain overriding Greek defence preoccupations. The Navy has had a good year with new ships, helicopters and aircraft building or ordered and the introduction of a five-year volunteer engagement which can only improve professionalism within the service. Four Charles F Adams class destroyers are being delivered as part of the defence co-operation agreement signed with the USA in 1990, and new construction frigates and landing ships are commissioning later in the year. Up to three Knox class frigates are also scheduled to transfer within the next 12 months.

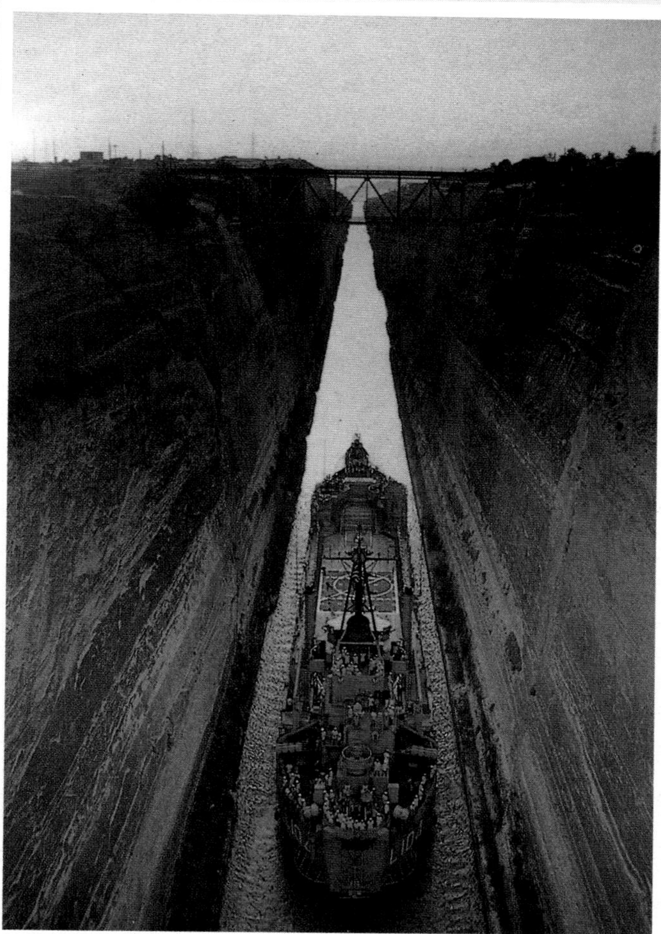

There continue to be tensions in the Aegean

Proposals for a Black Sea economic co-operation zone are one more example of the changing face of international relationships emerging from the ruins of the Soviet empire. This is a Turkish-led initiative with aspirations limited so far to trade agreements and pollution control. It embraces every country, including the former Soviet republics, with Black Sea ports, as well as Romania and Bulgaria, but not Greece which is still a long way from joining any venture sponsored by Turkey. Turkey's membership of the European Community will not be considered until 1993, but her role in the Gulf War and continuing strong support for NATO means that this country is as determined as ever to play its part in European security and maintain the balance of power on its eastern and southern flanks. The Navy has new submarines under construction, has ordered two new frigates which are marked improvements on the Yavuz Meko class recently commissioned, and it is planned to order new minehunters this year.

If Bulgaria has drawn closer to Greece, Romania is now seeking new accords with Russia and Ukraine. Both navies appear to be much more active than in the dying days of the Warsaw Pact. In particular, Romania acquired two more Tarantul missile corvettes earlier this year and has carried out some major structural improvements on the home-built Muntenia class destroyer.

Libyan ships are active in the central Mediterranean
(van Ginderen Collection)

On the eastern shore of the Mediterranean, Syria's military regime seems to be making the same mistake as Saddam Hussein in neglecting its Navy. Most of the submarines and patrol craft are 1970s vintage, and in spite of several rumours nothing new has been acquired since a training ship in 1987. As Syria has the resources there is clearly a maritime policy vacuum in Damascus. Lebanon's small Navy is once again back under national control and seeking to build up its patrol craft strength for offshore protection.

Not to be outdone in the proliferation of regional co-operation discussions, Israel has proposed co-ordinated naval search and rescue missions with some of its Arab neighbours as a way of building mutual trust. With two new submarines being built by Germany and three missile corvettes by the United States, indigenous shipyards are free to concentrate on improving existing attack craft and building faster gunboats.

In spite of the windfalls produced by co-operation with Saudi Arabia and its allies in the war with Iraq, Egypt has been surprisingly slow to take advantage by modernising the Navy. Adequate minehunting capability must be the first priority for the guardians of the most vulnerable part of the main trade route between East and West, and yet requirements and orders from a US shipyard have been surrounded by confusion and delay. Of the other North African navies, Libya is perhaps too easily discounted. The submarines may not go to sea but many of the surface warships are operational and often deployed. Camouflaged in various shades of green and black and white stripes, they are easily recognised on the high seas. Algeria continues to build its own corvettes and attack craft and is reported to be in the market for more Kilo class submarines and Chinese-built Coast Guard craft. Various attempts are being made to acquire Italian-built Iraqi corvettes or more Koni class frigates from Germany. The military aspirations of this potentially unstable country are a growing cause for concern.

Central and Southern Africa

In a world preoccupied by events in the northern hemisphere and with increasing funds being channelled into eastern Europe and the former Soviet republics, it is probably best to draw a discreet veil over the navies of the central and southern African continent. As well as being considered of lesser priority for financial aid, the present level of external financing available to these countries is under much closer scrutiny and disbursements are now based on the efficiency of domestic investment, not on the maintenance of prestige military projects.

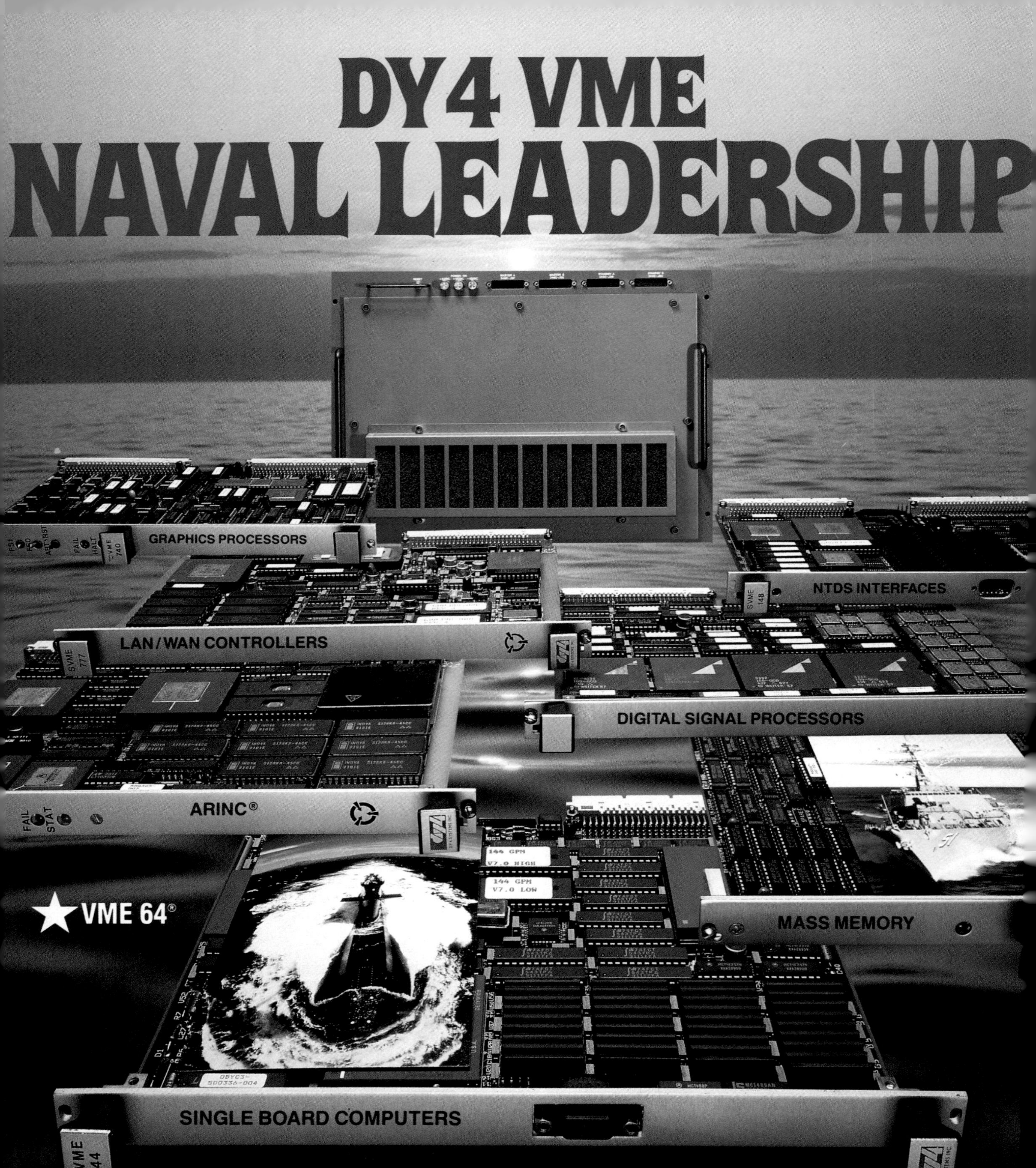

Added to that is the general level of political unrest and the realisation that non-alignment no longer has any real meaning. In those countries which have recently finished or are still enduring civil wars, the navies have been virtually destroyed. The extreme case is Somalia where every ship has been looted and stripped. Ethiopia ordered its Navy to Yemeni ports to prevent more of them falling into the hands of the Eritreans. The current situation is still confused but it seems likely that many of these vessels will not be returned. It is now far from clear which ships belong to Yemen, which to Ethiopia and which to the various Eritrean groupings. Not surprisingly the southern Red Sea and Gulf of Aden are areas of concern to merchant ship owners.

It is reported that South Africa has reached an accord with Namibia over Walvis Bay with a temporary joint administration until the sovereignty issue is resolved. Namibia has started to negotiate for its own patrol craft.

The once proud South African Navy has been reduced to a coastal force with a mission of providing 'seaward military services'. The process of contraction is not yet irreversible because although the frigates have finally been scrapped and the Marines disbanded, there is still a considerable infrastructure and, just as important, the residual expertise to redevelop an effective blue water Navy. What is missing is a national maritime policy with clearly defined objectives and perhaps a wider understanding in government of the contribution a Navy could make both to regional security and in redeveloping links with other industrial countries to ensure maritime stability.

Persian Gulf

Now that the dust has settled over Kuwait, the fires have been put out, and the oil slicks dispersed, superficially it seems that not a lot has changed in this region. Feudal barons and Muslim theocracies are still in charge and although there are Arabs who support the principles of democracy and political freedom, very few of them are in positions of much authority. In the aftermath of the war to expel Iraq from Kuwait, the Americans tried to set up an Arab multinational defence system to restrain Iraq from further aggression. Egypt and Syria refused to take part and the Gulf states were unwilling to exclude Iran which sees itself as the natural power broker in the region. The Gulf Co-operation Council formed in 1981 continues to be ineffective. This leaves a vacuum which, if stability is to be retained, can only be filled by bilateral arrangements with the still disliked but better respected western nations and with America in particular. A 10-year defence treaty with Kuwait was signed by the United States in September last year.

The port of Kuwait was reopened last September with warships from Australia, Denmark, Japan, Norway, Britain and the US in attendance. European shipyards are finalising contracts for new vessels up to frigate size for Oman and Saudi Arabia, and Kuwait is planning to rebuild its shattered Navy. As expected, Iraq has salvaged a few of its lesser combatant craft and support ships, but rigidly enforced United Nations embargoes are preventing any renewal of an operational status, and the rump of the Navy may even lose the port of Umm Qasr to Kuwait. Those few ships that escaped to Iran are unlikely ever to return.

Iran itself remains inimicable in its hostility to the West although unable to ignore the lessons of the demonstration of fire-power exercised against Iraq. The news that submarine crews are being trained in the Baltic, and that two or three Kilo class are scheduled for delivery, has been greeted by western governments as a particularly unhelpful example of a dangerous boost in weapon proliferation. But if Russia did not sell them, China or North Korea probably would, so there would still be a threat but perhaps of a lesser magnitude. The submarines are to be based outside the Gulf at Chah Bahar where they can menace the Straits of Hormuz. Submarine expertise is not acquired quickly but the prospect of Russian mercenaries being employed on board ought to dispel any tendency towards complacency by the West. Twelve Chinese-built missile craft are also on order.

Indian Ocean

Pakistan has finally made a decision to renew its MCMV capability with the early transfer of the last of the Éridan class built for the French Navy and the new construction of more of the same type. From being one of the principle recipients of FMS largesse the Pakistan Navy has had to live with its US supply lines cut off by Congress because of the nuclear proliferation issue. This abrupt change in US policy towards Pakistan appears to be an inelegant and inconsistent way of influencing regional affairs, and in spite of a new and active dialogue with India it seems unwise for the United States to drive Pakistan further towards its Chinese and Islamic connections.

With commendable pragmatism, India has abandoned its search for an elusive non-aligned status between the Soviet and Western camps, but not its championship of third world nations. Defence cuts have fallen less heavily on the Navy than the other two services but have still come at an unwelcome time when there are problems enough obtaining spare parts for the Soviet-built ships, and the Navy has been heavily criticised for inadequate routine maintenance and overlong refits. Although eight new vessels, of which six were built in India, have been commissioned in the last year, the next major warship to complete will probably be the new destroyer *Delhi* which is also suffering from late deliveries of Russian-built equipment. There is therefore a danger of block obsolescence and declining numbers of frigate-sized ships and above in the next few years.

It has emerged during the last 12 months that the Navy gave up its leased Soviet nuclear submarine with much reluctance and was disappointed not to receive a replacement. Emphasis is therefore being given to an indigenous SSN programme, probably based on the Charlie class hull, and this may have priority over the new aircraft carrier. Although it has taken a long time, the first home-built diesel submarine commissioned in February this year. Another of this class is still under construction but it is not yet clear whether more diesel boats will be built before the first SSN.

Plans for new aircraft carriers have been scaled down

Plans for a new large angle-deck carrier have been scaled back to a 15 000 ton design based on the Italian *Guiseppe Garibaldi* and capable of operating Sea Harriers and helicopters, but not fixed-wing fighters. It seems doubtful whether this new ship can be in service before the elderly *Vikrant* finally runs out of steam, and the possibility exists of buying second-hand from Russia.

After 30 years of almost obsessive isolation the Navy is at last beginning to encourage joint exercises with western alliance nations. An Australian frigate joined up with Indian ships off Port Blair in the Andaman Islands in November. British and French warships are to conduct exercises on passage and discussions have started on the prospects for combined operations with the USN as a result of a spate of high level exchange visits earlier this year. More Western technology transfers are also on the agenda after the scale of the inferiority of, for example, Soviet EW systems was revealed during the Gulf War.

The Indians would be very reluctant to admit it, but their championship of the non-aligned cause and their preference for Soviet ships and weapons has probably delayed naval progress by cutting them off from their natural allies. If that is about to change, it will be welcomed by like-minded nations and former close allies.

The Bangladesh Navy has attracted more than its fair share of problems in the last year. At least 12 ships were damaged and two

others sunk in the typhoon of April 1991, and then in August the new Jianghu class frigate *Osman* was struck by a merchant ship causing a gun mounting to be uprooted and SSM and RBU systems to be mis-aligned.

Burma continues to take advantage of the competing influences of China and India but this has not greatly affected its Navy which remains not much more than a riverine Flotilla.

The China Seas

From a maritime perspective this is always the most interesting part of the world, and its regional navies continue to be amongst the most dynamic. Not a single country has declared a peace dividend and none has reduced defence expenditure. From the Straits of Malacca in the west to the Philippines in the east, and from the Kuriles on the northern tip of Japan to the Timor Sea off Indonesia there are hosts of potential flashpoints fuelled by nationalist, religious and historical grievances of one sort or another. Although the Pentagon will fight a strong rearguard action, the decline in US presence is inevitable with the closure of the Subic Bay naval base and the diminishing Russian threat. That leaves China and Japan as the potential predominant powers and fear of both remains deep-rooted, should a power vacuum begin to become apparent. There is no shortage of discussion or of ideas for mutual security. An extended ASEAN free trade agreement to include a regional defence force has been proposed, but although parallels with Europe may stretch the imagination, the prospect of military alliance in this area of the world shares the same difficulty as Europe in not having a natural leader. At least there is less danger than in Europe of bureaucratic posturing being mistaken for genuine military capability.

Japan takes its place in the Gulf

In Japan the Navy finally found a way round its constitutional strait-jacket by deploying half a dozen minesweepers and support ships to the Gulf to assist in clearing the debris left over after the war to liberate Kuwait. The accompanying tanker was used to refuel coalition warships. A round-the-world cruise by three training ships also provided a rare opportunity to liaise with other navies on their home grounds, particularly in America and Europe. There remains in Japan an apparently unbridgeable divide between those who see the strict maintenance of the 1000 mile limit as an outdated and self-indulgent abrogation of wider defence responsibilities, and those who view any overseas deployment as the harbinger of reconstituted militarism. The result is a vibrant ship construction programme based on uncontentious destroyers, diesel submarines and minesweepers, but without the aircraft carriers or nuclear submarines which would follow from an unfettered defence policy.

Hopeful signs on the Korean peninsula include an agreement signed in December last year which aims at reconciliation and non-aggression but this has not stopped the remorseless buildup of arms by both North and South. In the North the naval emphasis is on amphibious capability, coastal patrol craft and submarines, while South Korea has now started building a new class of destroyers and its first German-built submarine is scheduled to enter service later this year. With the decline in support for the North from both Russia and China, prospects for the end of the civil war are better than for some time, although there would first have to be changes in the political regime. Should there be a genuine reconciliation in, say, five years time, the two navies combined could muster between them a force of 30 submarines, a dozen frigates, two dozen corvettes, 450 attack craft and 250 amphibious vessels, all of which would cause concern in both Japan and China.

China's Navy is beginning to show some tangible results from its lengthy association with western manufacturers. Improved SSN and diesel submarines are being built in reactivated construction programmes and last year saw the launch of a much more impressive looking destroyer than anything which has gone before. Surface-to-air missile systems are also beginning to be fitted in the larger ships, and patrol craft of more modern design are being built. Major exercises were carried out in the Pacific in 1991, a long way from mainland China, and these were probably designed to demonstrate long-range deployment capabilities in support of territorial claims to the disputed islands of the South China Sea. Nonetheless this remains a Navy more potent in image than in operational effectiveness, but there is no denying its ambition to join the major league.

Taiwan has a considerable lead over China in technology but not in numbers of vessels available should the mainland attempt either an amphibious assault or a blockade. Taiwan also suffers from the strength of China's clout in the international market place. This has most recently been demonstrated in the cancellation by the Netherlands Government of a potential life-saving order to Dutch shipyards for more submarines, although this decision may be reconsidered. New minesweepers have been acquired from Germany under cover of a commercial order for offshore patrol craft which have subsequently been converted in Taiwan. Submarines do not lend themselves to that sort of subterfuge. In spite of an active new frigate building programme, the older ships keep soldiering on, working for the Navy, Customs or Security Police as operational commitments dictate. The importance of naval defence was most recently reflected in the appointment of an admiral to be Chief of the Defence Staff.

The Philippines Navy is likely to feel more than a little naked when the last US ship leaves Subic Bay. There is a 10-year plan to provide more landing and attack craft for the Marine battalions deployed in the three Naval Districts, but the long-term neglect of the Navy is not going to be cheap or easy to remedy. Secure in the knowledge that the US presence was guard against external threats, most maritime effort has gone into internal security and policing tasks. The US Seventh Fleet will still be around even after 1992, but suddenly this archipelago with all its internal problems is looking increasingly vulnerable.

In one of the region's biggest political turnarounds, Vietnam is now looking for economic accords with its southern and western neighbours, and is even reported to be offering the facilities of Cam Ranh Bay to western navies, now that Russia has left.

Thailand is the region's strongest growing maritime force. The first four of the Chinese-built frigates have been delivered and taken into Bangkok Dockyard to be brought up to acceptable operational standards. Plans for a helicopter support ship received a setback when the contract with a German shipyard was not confirmed, but tenders were offered again and the ship has now been ordered from Bazán.

Relationships between Malaysia, Singapore and Indonesia continue to blow hot and cold. In spite of joint operations on a bilateral basis and some shared security concerns, it takes very little for traditional antagonisms to generate disproportionate heat. That Singapore has given a high priority to attracting the US Navy to its maintenance facilities says much for its real concern over regional instability. The Seventh Fleet Logistic Support Force will transfer from the Philippines before the end of the year. Malaysia has also offered Dockyard facilities.

By virtue of its size and potential wealth Indonesia sees itself as the natural leader of the ASEAN countries, but this role is far from being

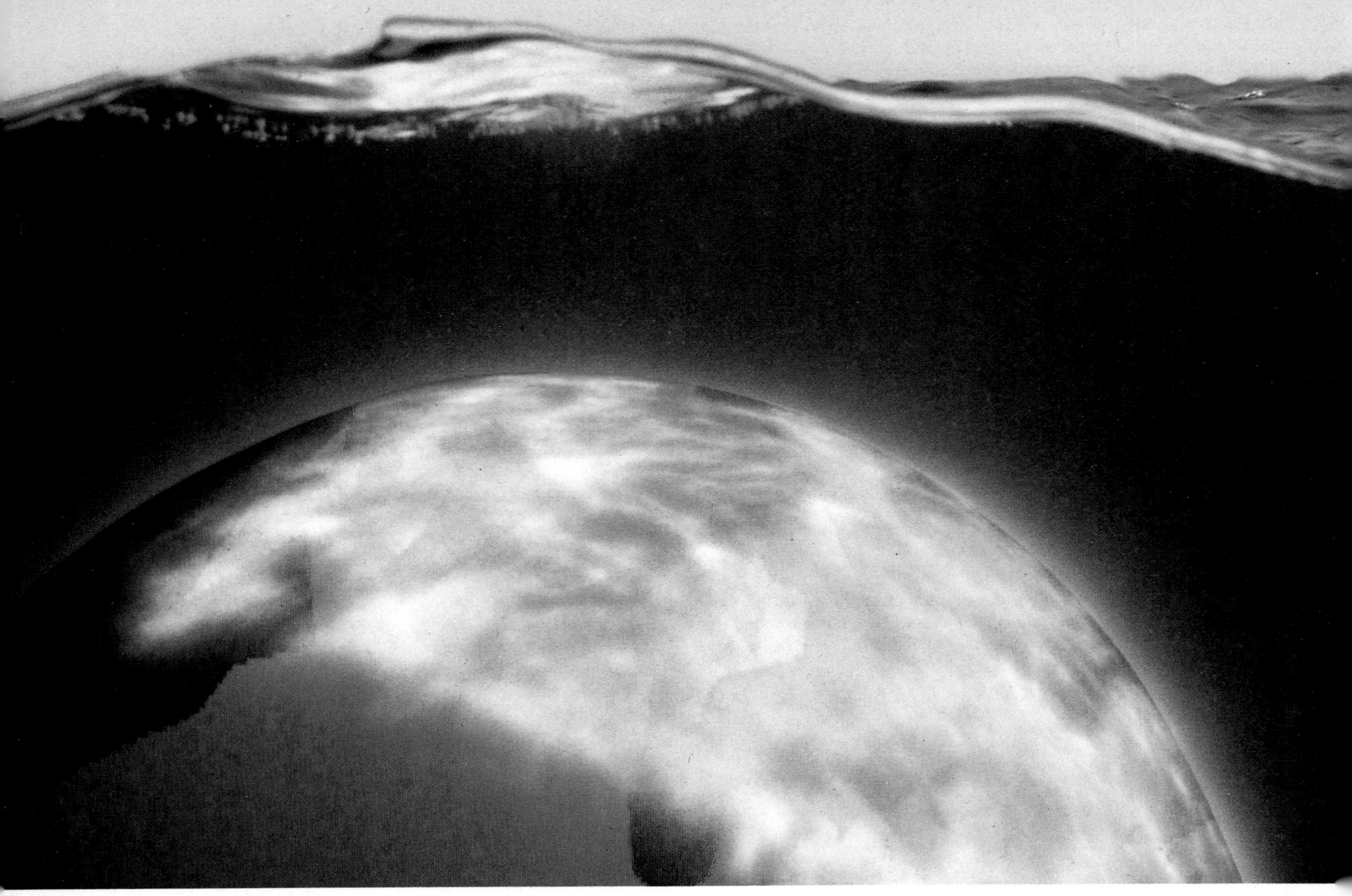

accepted by the others. Not helpful to mutual trust and confidence is Indonesia's belligerent policy of assuming control of a number of strategic international straits and waterways as part of the Archipelagic Concept that all the islands of Indonesia and their connecting waters are one indivisible sovereign country. Then there is the uneasy belief that much of the piracy and general lawlessness in the Malacca Straits is attributable to inadequate control being exercised by the Indonesian Navy. Counter claims include the accusation that Malaysia has assisted rebel forces in northern Sumatra, and there has been a strong protest over a recent Malaysian development on contested islets off Borneo which Indonesia maintained was a breach of a 30-year old understanding.

In spite of these tensions the Indonesian Navy is achieving only modest growth as there seems to be an unwillingness to translate ambitious plans for new submarines and frigates into actual orders. The most recent reports indicate both German and Chinese shipyards being involved in the latest round of negotiations. In general terms, it is Indonesia's inclination to engage in secret dialogue with China and her ruthlessness in suppressing internal dissent which combine to make the country an uneasy neighbour, both to the north and south, and an object of distrust to those trading nations whose ships have to pass within her territorial seas.

Australasia

To the question "Was he concerned with Australia's military reinforcement on its northern shores?" the Indonesian Armed Forces Commander replied that it made sense because only penguins could attack from the south. As a humorous answer to a debating point it could hardly have been bettered, and yet somehow the remark has an edge to it, if only for what he might have said, but did not, to reassure his questioner. In fact for the moment Indonesia has enough problems both internally and to the north not to be an immediate cause for concern to Australia.

It is perhaps one of the anachronisms of this region that the Five Power Defence Agreement signed in 1971 is still in operation because there has been nothing to replace it. Australia is now negotiating a range of bilateral agreements and, at least in academic forums, continues to argue for more local multinational arrangements.

Meanwhile the 1991 Forces Structure Review reinforced the commitment to existing submarine and frigate programmes and endorsed the requirement for at least four new minehunters to a proven design as a matter of urgency. Other projects include an upgrade of the Fremantle class patrol boats and their subsequent replacement, and a commitment to build a multi role helicopter support ship for training, disaster relief and air support operations. Whether all this will survive the latest cutback in defence spending remains to be seen.

In military terms the case for nuclear submarines is certainly as strong as Canada's. In both countries force mobility is a key factor if large and sparsely populated coastal regions and territorial seas are to be effectively patrolled and forces concentrated where they may be needed at short notice. It is questionable whether it is better to argue the case as Canada did, come to the right conclusion and then back off for political and economic reasons, or never publicly to acknowledge the requirement at all. With the defence budget in theory frozen for the next five years but already showing signs of stress, and a dynamic diesel submarine replacement programme in full swing, this is not the best time for the Australian Navy to resurrect the issue, but it is not going to go away.

If New Zealand was once again having doubts about its commitment to replacement frigates, resolve may well have been stiffened by the repeated suggestions of the Australian Defence Minister that a merging of the two countries' defences was inevitable within two decades. Interdependence is one thing, but an interchange of bases and personnel makes a mockery of nationhood, however well-intentioned (or clever) the proposal. The Defence Review of 1991 indicated that the Government was committed to rebuilding traditional defence alliances. Acquisition of a logistic support ship remains a high priority.

Latin America

To argue that as in central and southern Africa all the navies of this subcontinent are in decline is to overstate the case, and anyhow compared with Africa the force levels and general competence of the various Fleets is several orders of magnitude higher. The fact is though that there is very little progress in improving operational capabilities and many of the more ambitious naval projects are stalled by lack of adequate funds.

Argentina shows the most marked decline with its partially built German-designed frigates and submarines up for sale and its only aircraft carrier laid up now for some six years and unlikely to go to sea again. Pay and conditions of service are also a source of growing agitation. The Navy is now much less effective than it was in 1982. One battle that seems to have been won is that the Navy is to be given responsibility for policing the Economic Exclusion Zone out to 200 miles from shore, whereas the Coast Guard will be limited to operations within territorial limits out to 12 miles. This change came about because of the transfer of paramilitary organisations, including the Coast Guard, from Defence to the Ministry of the Interior. Relations between the two naval services have been increasingly bitter and the projected takeover by the Navy of the larger Coast Guard vessels has caused a major row. An ex-USN tanker is expected to be acquired later in the year.

Chile has the subcontinent's most active Navy

Chile has the highest ratio of coastline compared to surface area, and correspondingly the largest EEZ for its territorial size, than any other country in the world. It also has strong claims in Antarctica and a significant strategic role in the south-eastern Pacific. Not surprisingly it therefore maintains the region's most active and balanced Navy which is being modernised and kept up to date. There is a requirement for more submarines which it is hoped to build locally from a foreign design. Having bought one of the leading midget submarine production companies from Italy in 1991, this project may be less ambitious than has proved to be the case with other similar sized countries, which have embarked on submarine construction in the last decade and then run into technical difficulties.

Brazil has the largest Navy with an active helicopter carrier, a funded frigate upgrade programme and new submarines, frigates and patrol craft under construction. It also has an ambitious nuclear submarine project still at the design stage. On the down side there have been bankruptcies in defence industries and the country's huge international debt has so far restricted some further planned overseas acquisitions of, for instance, more destroyers from the United States. A confusion factor when reviewing this Navy is that a large number of support ships and auxiliaries appear to have been formally decommissioned and have had their pennant numbers removed. The problem stems from a cutback in officer numbers which means that these same ships are in fact still in service as tenders to naval establishments, but are now commanded by Warrant Officers.

Of the other South American navies Uruguay has acquired some ex-GDR minesweepers, Ecuador two Leander class frigates, and after many delays contracts are at last being awarded to update Venezuela's Lupo class frigates. Fast patrol craft are in great demand all along the northern coastline, as the navies of Venezuela, Colombia, Ecuador and even Peru become increasingly involved in the war against drug smugglers, supplementing the overstretched and inadequate resources of the law enforcement agencies.

If Colombia is situated in the heart of the narcotics departure zone, the Caribbean and Gulf of Mexico are astride the transit routes to the lucrative markets of North America. Mexico retains the region's largest Navy but all activity is geared towards coping with the drugs trade and the ageing Fleet has had some notable success. Unfortunately this specialised type of warfare is also absorbing the limited funds

available and the Navy no longer has the weapon systems capable of coping with a modern maritime threat.

The only other Navy of consequence is in Cuba and although Castro continues to defy gravity by maintaining political control, the Navy is falling into disrepair through lack of Russian assistance, spare parts, fuel and money.

Canada

As usual Canada's strong pacifist lobby has been casting doubts over virtually every defence commitment and equipment project. It must require a special kind of resilience to be a Canadian Serviceman, constantly bombarded with headlines like "Frigate Programme Hits Rocks Again", or "Minesweepers Could Sink in a Sea of Cuts", or even the comparatively mild "Canadian Defence in Shambles".

A Canadian commitment to maritime defence *(St John SB Ltd)*

Out of all this verbal wreckage the 12-ship new frigate programme sails steadily if still a bit noisily onwards, as does the Tribal class update, the MCDV programme and the commitment to replacement submarines. There are also plans for fast patrol corvettes and new shipborne helicopters. This puts the emphasis firmly on new equipment rather than continuing to maintain obsolete ships, and there is also a declared intention of closing some redundant bases at a politically expedient moment. All of which suggests that Vice Admiral Thomas's courageous resignation earlier last year was not in vain. It would be nice to think that his example might be taken up by Admirals in other countries who find themselves fundamentally in disagreement with defence policy, or lack of it, but sadly that kind of statement of strong commitment has gone out of fashion elsewhere.

The latest defence review shifts the maritime emphasis more towards the maintenance of a capability to conduct surveillance and control of Canadian waters including the Arctic, and away from the defence of sea lines of communication which are no longer seen as being under such severe threat. The Arctic role is to be met by seabed sonar arrays and it can be assumed that the new submarines will have air-independent propulsion systems to allow penetration under the ice.

If all this is not quite as exciting for the Navy as the 1987 Three Ocean Strategy, it could have been a lot worse. Should the pacifist lobby ever fall silent, Canadians will know that they have passed the defence of their country wholly to the United States, an event which happily still seems a long way off.

In Conclusion

As last year it is impossible to conclude this review without returning to the issue of coalition warfare.

Many influential people in the West seemed never to understand the dangers of Soviet imperialism, and even now believe that its collapse was somehow inevitable rather than the result of an expensive and at times dangerous political and military confrontation. The same apologists are now active in disclaiming the potential threat from those Islamic militants who fear and despise western values and whose beliefs are far more deep-rooted than were those of the disciples of Karl Marx.

"Western civilisation is the sick man of the modern world. It is destined for oblivion and will eventually take its place in the same dustbin of history that has already swallowed up Marxism. Islam alone is the antidote to a morally bankrupt and sick world." This was said by the leader of the British Muslim 'parliament' earlier this year, representing a view which is too easily ignored in the same way that Stalin dismissed the Pope as having no "battalions".

Both before and after the Gulf War there were two opposing views of the likely long-term effects of that conflict. One claimed that Arab

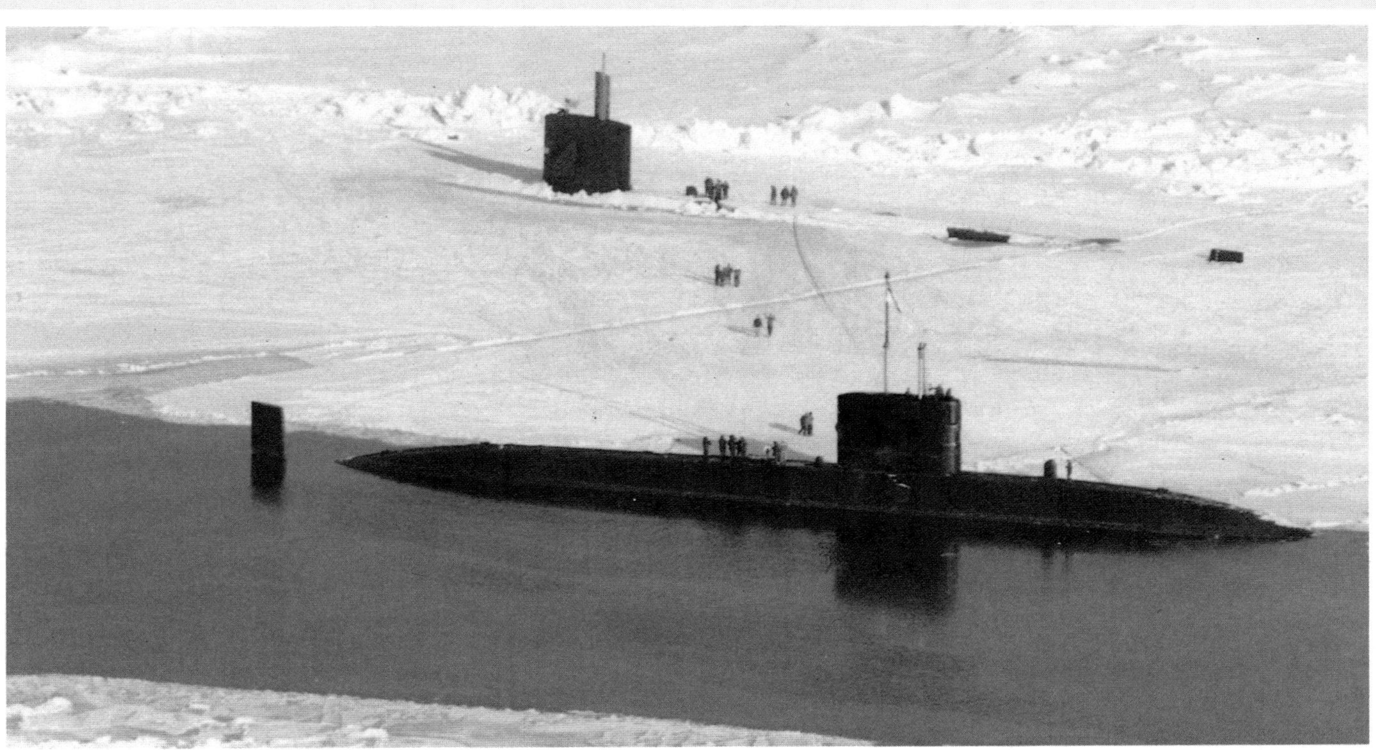

Nuclear submarines policing the Arctic Ocean

solidarity (always elusive but never insignificant) would be irreparably broken and that the clear advantage in military technology shown by the West would usher in a new spirit of realism and the spreading of democracy and human rights. The alternative view was that international terrorism would receive its biggest ever boost and pro-Western Arab governments would increasingly come under attack. As usual the truth lies mundanely between these two extremes. The early disengagement by Egypt and Syria from coalition forces in Saudi Arabia, and the preference shown by the Saudi rulers for an Iraq led by Sunni Muslims, even if that includes Saddam Hussein, are clear indicators for the future. A Shia majority in Iraq, under the influence of Iran, is the main fear of the Gulf states, and the rise in Iran's status seems to be inevitable as the predominantly Muslim southern republics of the former Soviet Union seek to build new regional alliances.

The Pope may still have no battalions, but all the way from Algeria to Indonesia, Islam most certainly does and in spite of the Gulf War there is a formidable concentration of military strength in the Middle East, as well as growing instability along the North African littoral. As was seen in the war against Iraq, none of this represents a military threat that cannot if necessary be contained by forces built up in the West primarily to deter the Soviet Union. The trouble is that those forces are now in the process of being run down with Europe triumphantly leading the way. In theory, a European Defence Community ought to be able to generate forces consistent with its economic muscle, but what Churchill foresaw in 1953 as a "sludgy amalgam, infinitely less effective than an alliance of national armies", looks ominously like developing. Coalition forces need clear leadership. It has emerged in the past year that during the Falklands campaign in 1982 the single decisive action which put the Argentine Navy out of the war only took place because the British Task Force Commander, in desperation to get a change in the rules of engagement, ordered an attack which exceeded his authority. The signal was intercepted in the Fleet Headquarters in the UK and the Commander-in-Chief then personally took the argument to the Prime Minister, who immediately agreed to the necessary change. Transpose that chain of events into the sort of political polyglot command and control processes which would be necessary in a European defence force and the difficulties are impossible to exaggerate.

Rapid reaction forces of a multinational nature are going to be essential in an uncertain and unstable international climate in which increasingly the authority of the United Nations is necessary if public support is to be guaranteed, even from within those nations doing the reacting. But once the force is dispatched it must have clear and decisive political and military leadership so that rapid decisions can be made and the confidence of those doing the fighting, and risking their lives, is sustained. Furthermore, those same people need to believe in the relevance of the cause to their own and their country's interest, and in the chain of command controlling their lives. A strong sense of identity is indispensable. The normal mechanisms of international bureaucracies are simply inadequate to take on this task. In other words, national leadership is critical to successful military action. In NATO and in the Gulf War with Iraq that leadership was, and still is, provided by the United States. The European reaction to the civil war in Yugoslavia demonstrated with great clarity what happens when the United States is not directly involved, although eventually single minded determination by Germany at least led to the recognition of Croatia by the European Community.

There is at present an apparently unbridgeable gap between the aspirations of the Brussels bureaucracy (and its fellow travellers in the capitals of western Europe) to create a European foreign and defence policy, and the political and practical difficulties of achieving decisive and unified politico-military command without the leadership of the United States. To continue to sacrifice national military capabilities in favour of this sludgy amalgam is to weaken and demoralise Europe's few effective Armed Forces. On the other hand, to support America in alliance under the banner of the United Nations still looks like the only sensible way forward, particularly for the declining navies of industrial countries, whether in Europe or anywhere else in the world, at least into the next century.

Everyone may have burst out singing but "The song was wordless; the singing will never be done".

April 1992 — Richard Sharpe

Everyone suddenly burst out singing

Acknowledgements

If last year's update was dominated by the Gulf War, the current primary source of change is the afterglow from the dissolution of the former Soviet Union. Coupled with the breakup of Yugoslavia this is creating half a dozen new navies as emerging republics in the Baltic, the Adriatic and the Black Seas form their own Coast Guards, either with the consent of the central authority, as in the Baltic States and Ukraine, or by defection which is what has happened in Croatia.

Reluctantly, we have had to move the old USSR section to a new heading under Russia and Associated States, which accurately reflects the new relationships with the former Soviet Navy and seems to have a greater chance of surviving current uncertainties than the new Commonwealth of Independent States. Unfortunately even a move from U to R will cause irritation to some of our regular users.

Just as important as the effect on Russia's own force levels and new construction programmes has been the reaction by Western governments and in particular the United States. The central theme of serious current debate on defence issues is that this is not the time to make any decisions with far-reaching consequences. The trouble is that economic recessions impose their own priorities and, if regional instability is now more likely, at least the risk of war between super-power alliances has for the time being been laid to rest. The result has been some fairly heavy deletions amongst the major navies and cutbacks on new construction.

The format used for ship entries continues to be driven by the twin requirements of simplicity in page layout for the seagoer in a hurry to identify a ship or its capabilities, and the growing market for easy data retrieval from compact disc.

Naval Attachés in London, government departments worldwide, and shipbuilders remain the most constant and the most reliable sources of detailed information. Individual photographers and other interested observers of the naval scene are also invaluable sources for keeping up with the rapid rate of change of most of the world's navies. If there is a choice to be made between two photographs of the same ship, our policy is to select the most recent one, even if the quality is not as good. Glossy pictures showing a structure or equipment which has since been modified are unhelpful to the professional user.

The Ministry of Defence in London and the US Navy Department in Washington deserve special mention. Sadly our former senior consultant, Captain Frans de Blocq van Kuffeler, has had to retire for family reasons, but Captain Vince Thomas, the editor of the US Navy League's *Seapower Almanac*, continues his major contribution, as does Ian Sturton with his uncluttered and accurate scale drawings. Many of the drawings have had significant revisions this year and most have had some changes, even if it is only to include the epidemic of satellite aerials. My thanks also to Arthur Wilcox for his work in rationalising the Main Machinery entries by including sustained maximum horsepower where it is known, and by adding power conversions. New information on Flags and Ensigns has been provided by the Flag Institute, Chester, England and put together by Keith Faulkner. James Pargiter has again done the Index and Pennant Lists. His inclusion of ship names and classes mentioned only in the Notes has been well received.

Amongst individuals who have sent photographs or information or both are Cdr Massimo Annati, Dr Giorgio Arra, Monsieur Guy de Bakker, Herr Ralf Bendfeldt, Herr Siegfried Breyer, Mr J L M van der Burg, Senor Camil Busquets i Vilanova, Senor Albert Campanera i Rovira, Senor Diego Quevedo Carmona, Senhor Mario Roberto Vaz Carneiro, Herr Harald Carstens, Mr Raymond Cheung, Dr Chien Chung, Signor Antonio O Ciampi, Senhor Sergio Baptista da Costa, Mr Gary Davies, Mr D M Dempsey, Mr Demetrios Dervissis, Herr Wilhelm Donko, Mr Kensuke Ebata, Herr Hartmut Ehlers, Mr Marko Enqvist, Cdr Aldo Fraccaroli, Mr Keith Franks, Senor Francisco Gámez Balcazar, Signor Giorgio Ghiglione, Mr Leo van Ginderen, Mr D G Glerean, Lt Col Werner Globke, Cdr James Goldrick, Capt Andres F Reina González-Novelles, Lt C T Gould, Cdr A W Grazebrook, Mr Helmoed-Römer Heitman, Cdr Ian Hewitt, Mr T B Hird, Mr P Humphries, Mr G Keith Jacobs, Mr Vic Jeffery, Rear Admiral F C Johnson, Lt Cdr P D Jones, Dr Manoj Joshi, Mr Ziro Kimata, Mr Yohei Kondoh, Herr G Koop, Mr Per Kornefeldt, Ldg Seaman B McBride, Flight Lt I M McKenzie, Mr C Douglas Maginley, Senor Antonio Moreno Garcia, Mr Erik Matzen Laursen, Mr Julio A Montes, Capt J E Moore, Mr John Mortimer, Mr James A Mulquin, Mr Hachiro Nakai, Mr P Neumann, Mr Gunnar Olsen, Mr P O'Keeffe, Cdr Nigel Overington, Mr A J R Risseeuw, Cdr L Robbins, Monsieur J Y Robert, Mr F Sadek, Mr Selim San, Mr W Sartori, Monsieur A Sheldon Duplaix, Herr N A Sifferlinger, Mr Adam Smigielski, Mr H M Steele, Senor X I Taibo, Messrs D and B Teague, Herr S Terzibaschitsch, Mr Guy Toremans, Mr Marek Twardowski, Mr Maurice Voss, Mr Eric Wang, Mr David J Warren, Dr Andre Wessels, Flight Lt C M Wright, Messrs Wright and Logan, Mr Cem D Yaylali, Mr John Young, Senor Luis Oscar Zunino.

From the *Jane's* catalogue, *All the World's Aircraft, High-Speed Marine Craft, Strategic Weapon Systems, Naval Weapon Systems, Radar and EW Systems* and *Underwater Warfare Systems* have all been consulted, as have the various contributors to the *Jane's* magazines, in particular *International Defense Review, Jane's Intelligence Review,* and *Jane's Defence Weekly.* My acknowledgements are due also to other international naval reference books including *Almanacco Navale* (Italy), *Flottes de Combat* (France) and *Weyers Flotten Taschenbuch* (Germany).

The main editorial load is borne by myself with invaluable assistance from my wife Joanna, but the transposition of 800 pages of detailed amendment into the database together with complex typesetting instructions is done by Ruth Simmance, Sarah Erskine and Christine Varndell, while the central computer is massaged by Alan Ricketts. All are indispensable to an accurate end product, as is Diana Burns who manages the various stages of book production, and Eddie Green's page composition team at Method Ltd which includes Jack Brenchley and Keith Biller.

Updating never stops so new information is welcome at any time, and modern technology allows changes to be made up to a few weeks before publication in May. However, because of the size of the book and the volume of change each year, major entries start to be made in October and regular contributors, particularly to the countries in the first half of the book, are asked to send in their first updates by then. The Fax machine is becoming a universal method of bypassing slow and not always reliable international mail services, but photographs must still be sent by post. Whichever method is selected to send material it will always be acknowledged within a few days of receipt.

My address is:

Captain Richard Sharpe, RN
Foundry House
Kingsley
Bordon
Hampshire GU35 9LY
United Kingdom

Fax number (UK) 0420 477833

Biographical note: The Editor
In 34 years in the Royal Navy the editor travelled all over the world. He has commanded nuclear and conventional submarines as well as a guided missile destroyer which was for some of the time the Flagship of NATO's Standing Naval Force Atlantic. He has also served in several appointments at the Ministry of Defence in London, including one in Naval Intelligence, and has been the Submarine Operations Officer on the staff of the UK Commander-in-Chief Fleet. In his last job before taking over as editor of *Jane's Fighting Ships* he was responsible for the selection of the next generation of RN officers.

Proven power
HERRERA

Glossary

(see also Type abbreviations at head of Pennant List)

AAW	Anti-air warfare
ACV	Air cushion vehicle
AEW	Airborne early warning
AGR	Radar picket ship
AIP	Air independent propulsion
ANV	Advanced naval vehicle
ARM	Anti-radiation missile
A/S, ASW	Anti-submarine (warfare)
ASM	Air-to-surface missile
BPDMS	Base point defence missile system
Cal	Calibre – the diameter of a gun barrel; also used for measuring length of the barrel eg a 6 in gun 50 calibres long (6 in/50) would be 25 ft long
CIWS	Close in weapon system
COD	Carrier onboard delivery
CODAG, CODOG, CODLAG, COGAG, COGOG, COSAG	Descriptions of mixed propulsion systems: combined diesel and gas turbine, diesel-electric and gas turbine, diesel or gas turbine, gas turbine and gas turbine, gas turbine or gas turbine, steam and gas turbine
CONAS	Combined nuclear and steam
cp	Controllable pitch (propellers)
DC	Depth charge
DCT	Depth charge thrower
DP	Dual purpose (gun) for surface or AA use
Displacement	Basically the weight of water displaced by a ship's hull when floating: (a) Light: without fuel, water or ammunition (b) Normal: used for Japanese MSA ships. Similar to 'standard' (c) Standard: as defined by Washington Naval Conference 1922 – fully manned and stored but without fuel or reserve feed-water (d) Full load: fully laden with all stores, ammunition, fuel and water
DSRV	Deep submergence recovery vessel
dwt	Deadweight tonnage
ECM	Electronic countermeasures eg jamming
ECCM	Electronic counter-countermeasures
EEZ	Exclusive economic zone
EHF	Extreme high frequency
ELF	Extreme low frequency radio
ELINT	Electronic intelligence eg recording radar, W/T etc
ESM	Electronic support measures eg intercept
EW	Electronic warfare
FAC	Fast attack craft
FLIR	Forward looking infra-red radar
FRAM	US Navy's 'Fleet rehabilitation and modernisation' programme
GFCS	Gun fire control system
GMLS	Guided missile launch system
GPS	Geographical positioning system
grt	Gross registered tonnage
GT	Geared turbine
GWS	Guided weapon system
Hedgehog	Spigot mortar for firing anti-submarine bombs
HF	High frequency
Horsepower (hp) or (hp(m))	Power developed or applied: (a) bhp: brake horsepower = power available at the crankshaft (b) shp: shaft horsepower = power delivered to the propeller shaft (c) ihp: indicated horsepower = power produced by expansion of gases in the cylinders of reciprocating steam engines (d) 1 kW = 1.341 hp = 1.360 metric hp 1 hp = 0.746 kW = 1.014 metric hp 1 metric hp = 0.735 kW = 0.968 hp
IFF	Identification friend/foe
kT	Kiloton
kW	Kilowatt
LAMPS	Light airborne multi-purpose system
LCM	Landing craft, mechanised
LCU	Landing craft, utility
LCVP/LCP	Landing craft, vehicles/personnel
Length	Expressed in various ways: (a) oa: overall = length between extremities (b) pp: between perpendiculars = between fore side of the stem and after side of the rudderpost (c) wl: water-line = between extremities on the water-line
LF	Low frequency
LMCR	Liquid metal cooled reactor
LRMP	Long-range maritime patrol
LSM	Landing ship, medium
MAD	Magnetic Anomaly Detector – for anti-submarine detection identifying a steel body in the earth's magnetic field
MAP	US Military Assistance Programme
MCMV	Mine countermeasures vessel
MDF	Maritime defence force
Measurement	See Tonnage
MF	Medium frequency
MFCS	Missile fire control system
MG	Machine gun
MIRV	Multiple, independently targetable re-entry vehicle
MRV	Multiple re-entry vehicle
MSA	Maritime safety agency
MSC	US Military Sealift Command
MSC	Coastal minesweeper
MSH	Minehunter
MW	Megawatt
NBC	Nuclear, biological and chemical (warfare)
net	Net registered tonnage
nm	Nautical miles
NTDS	Naval tactical data system
NTU	New Threat Upgrade
oa	Overall length
OPV	Offshore patrol vessel
OTC	Officer in Tactical Command
PDMS	Point defence missile system
PUFFS	Passive underwater fire control system
PWR	Pressurised water reactor
RAM	Radar absorbent material
RAS	Replenishment at sea
RBU	Anti-submarine rocket launcher
RIB	Rigid inflatable boat
Ro-flow	A ship able to embark smaller craft in a dock
Ro-ro	Roll-on/roll-off
ROV	Remote operated vehicle
rpm	Revolutions per minute of engines, propellers, radar aerials etc
SAM	Surface-to-air missile
SAR	Search and rescue
SATCOM	Satellite communications
SES	Surface effect ship
SHF	Super high frequency
SINS	Ship's inertial navigation system
SLBM	Submarine-launched ballistic missile
SLCM	Ship-launched cruise missile
SLEP	Service Life Extension Program
SNLE	Nuclear-powered ballistic missile submarine (French)
SRBOC	Super rapid blooming offboard chaff
SS	Attack submarine
SSAN	Auxiliary nuclear-powered submarine
SSBN	Nuclear-powered ballistic missile submarine
SSDE	Submerged signal and decoy ejector
SSG	Guided missile submarine
SSGN	Nuclear-powered guided missile submarine
SSM	Surface-to-surface missile
SSN	Nuclear-powered attack submarine
STIR	Surveillance Target Indicator Radar
Subroc/Asroc	Rocket-assisted torpedo part of whose range is in the air
SURTASS	Surface Towed Array Surveillance System
SUWN-1	Surface-to-underwater missile launcher
SWATH	Small waterplane area twin hull
TACAN	Tactical air navigation beacon
TACTASS	Tactical Towed Acoustic Sensor System
TAS	Target Acquisition System
TASS	Towed Array Surveillance System
Tonnage	Measurement tons, computed on capacity of a ship's hull rather than its 'displacement' (see above): (a) Gross: the internal volume of all spaces within the hull and all permanently enclosed spaces above decks that are available for cargo, stores and accommodation. The result in cubic feet divided by 100 = gross tonnage (b) Net: gross minus all those spaces used for machinery, accommodation etc ('non-earning' spaces) (c) Deadweight (dwt): the amount of cargo, bunkers, stores etc that a ship can carry at her load draught
UHF	Ultra-high frequency
VDS	Variable depth sonar which is lowered to best listening depth. Known as dunking sonar in helicopters.
Vertrep	Vertical replenishment
VLF	Very low frequency radio
VLS	Vertical launch system
VSTOL	Vertical or short take-off/landing
VTOL	Vertical take off/landing
WIG	Wing-in-ground effect
wl	Waterline length

Ensigns and Flags of the World's Navies

The following pictorial representations show each country's ensign where it has one or its national flag. In cases where countries do not have ensigns their warships normally fly the national flag.

Albania
National Flag and Ensign

Algeria
National Flag

Angola
National Flag

Antigua
National Flag

Argentina
National Flag and Ensign

Australia
Ensign

Austria
National Flag

Azerbaijan
National Flag

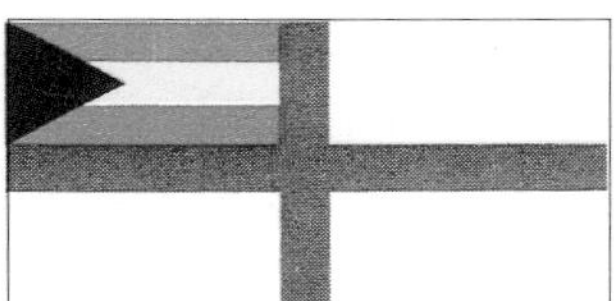

Bahamas
Ensign

Bahrain
National Flag

Bangladesh
National Flag

Barbados
Ensign

Belgium
Ensign

Belize
National Flag

Benin
National Flag

Bermuda
National Flag

Bolivia
Ensign

Brazil
National Flag and Ensign

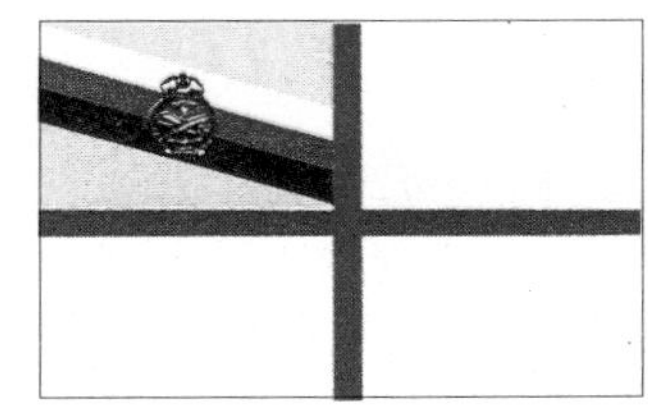

Brunei
Ensign

Bulgaria
Ensign

Burma
National Flag

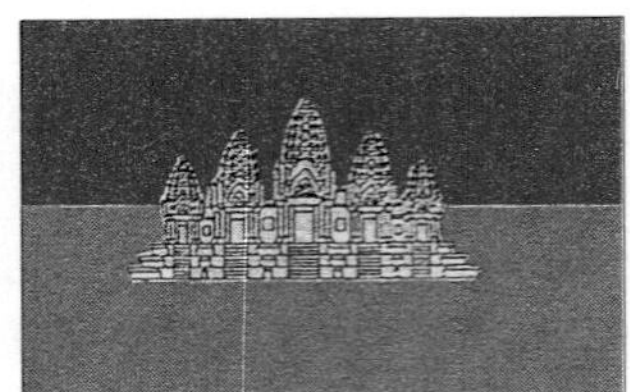
Cambodia
National Flag

Cameroon
National Flag

Canada
National Flag and Ensign

Cape Verde
National Flag

Chile
National Flag and Ensign

China, People's Republic
National Flag

Colombia
Ensign

Comoro Islands
National Flag

Congo
National Flag

Cook Islands
National Flag

Costa Rica
Ensign and Government Flag

Cote D'Ivoíre
National Flag

Croatia
National Flag

Cuba
National Flag and Ensign

Cyprus, Republic
National Flag

Cyprus, Turkish Republic
National Flag

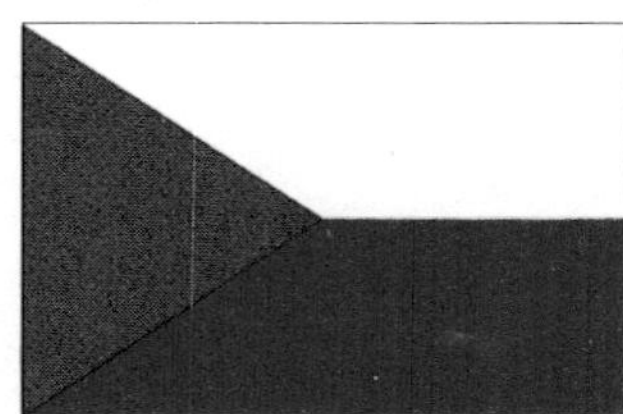
Czechoslovakia
National Flag

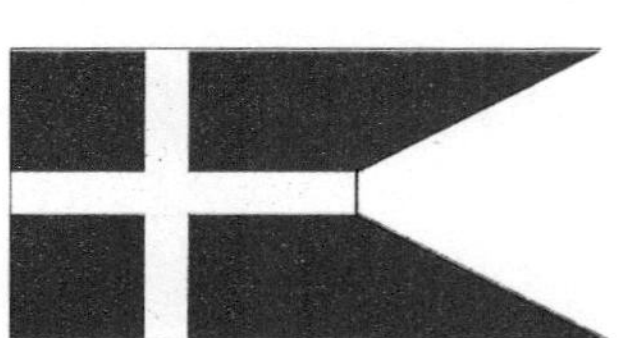
Denmark
Ensign

Djibouti
National Flag

Dominica
National Flag

Dominican Republic
Ensign

Ecuador
National Flag and Ensign

Egypt
Ensign

El Salvador
National Flag and Ensign

Equatorial Guinea
National Flag

Estonia
National Flag

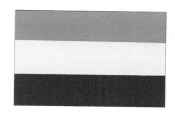

Ethiopia
National Flag

Faroes
The Islands Flag

Falkland Islands
Falkland Islands Flag

Fiji
Ensign

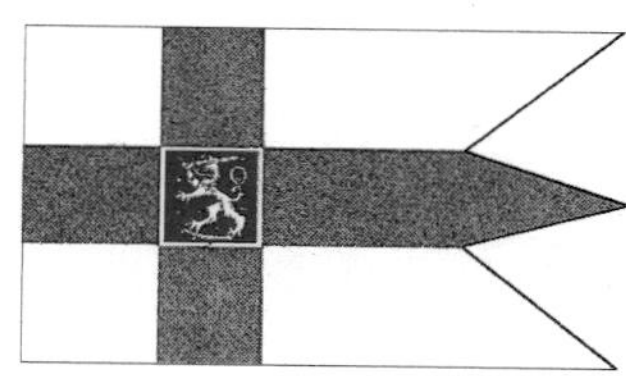

Finland
Ensign

France
Ensign

Gabon
National Flag

Gambia
National Flag

Georgia
National Flag

Germany
Ensign

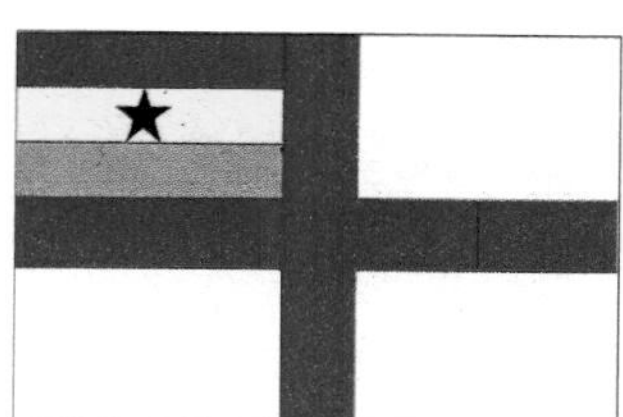

Ghana
Ensign

Greece
National Flag and Ensign

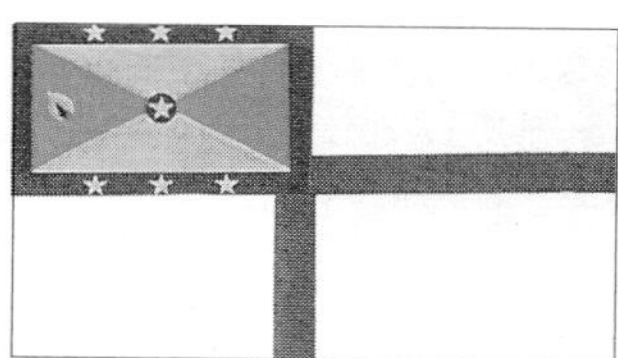

Grenada
Ensign

Guatemala
National Flag and Ensign

Guinea
National Flag

Guinea-Bissau
National Flag

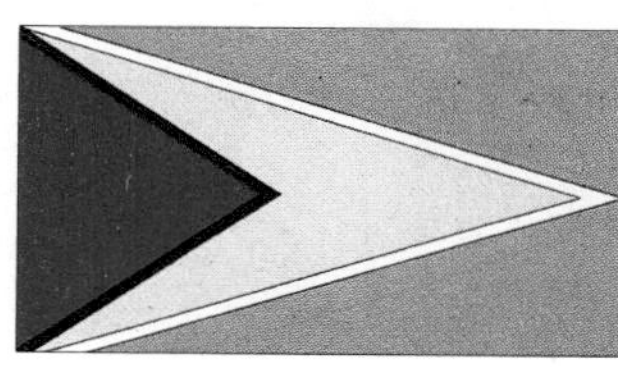

Guyana
National Flag

Haiti
State Flag and Ensign

Honduras
Ensign

Hong Kong
Hong Kong Flag

Hungary
National Flag

Iceland
Ensign

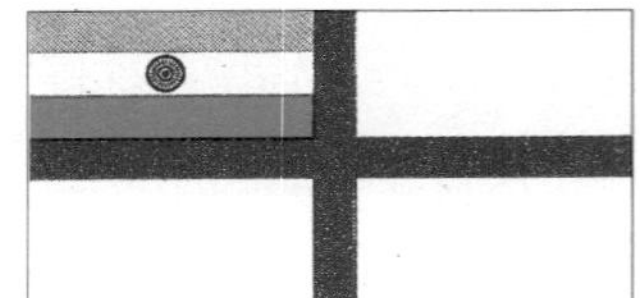

India
Ensign

Indonesia
National Flag and Ensign

Iran
National Flag

Iraq
National Flag

Ireland
National Flag and Ensign

Israel
Ensign

Italy
Ensign

Ivory Coast
National Flag

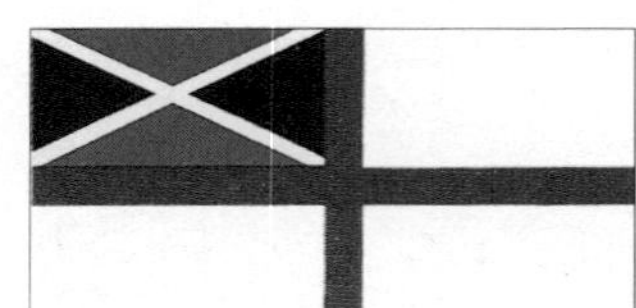

Jamaica
Ensign

Japan
Ensign

Jordan
Ensign

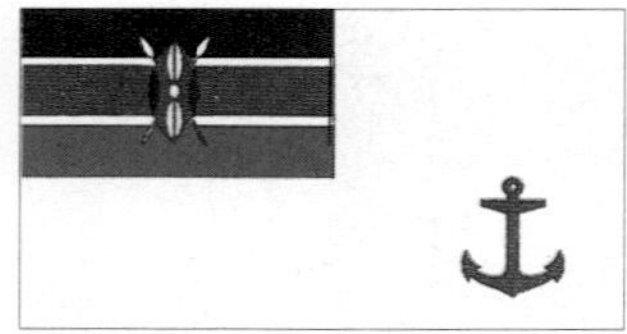

Kenya
Ensign

Korea, Democratic People's Republic (North)
National Flag

Korea, Republic (South)
Ensign

Kuwait
National Flag

Laos
National Flag

Latvia
National Flag

Lebanon
National Flag

Liberia
National Flag and Ensign

Libya
National Flag

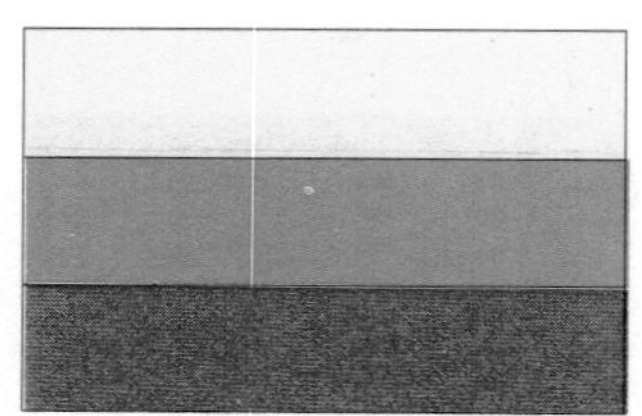

Lithuania
National Flag

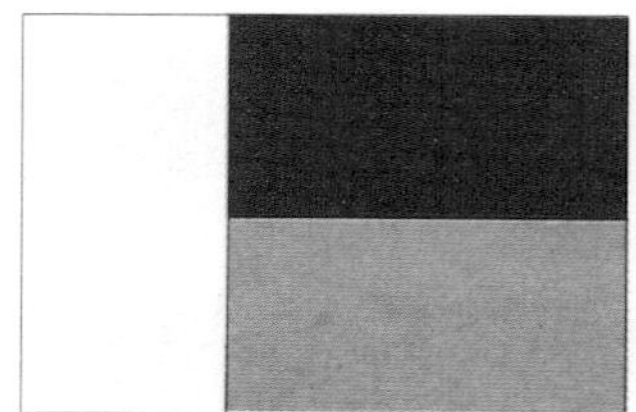

Madagascar
National Flag

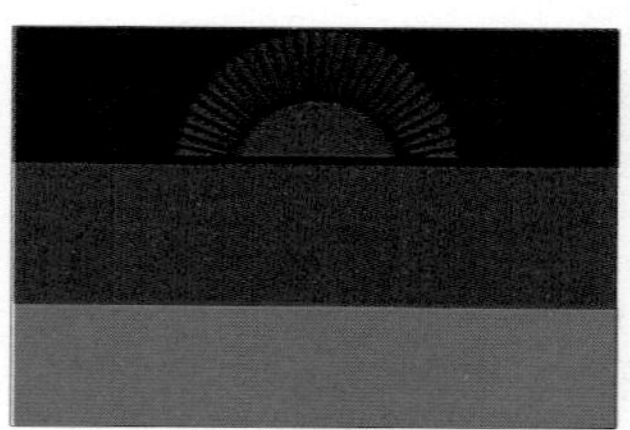

Malawi
National Flag

Malaysia
Ensign

Maldives
National Flag

Mali
National Flag

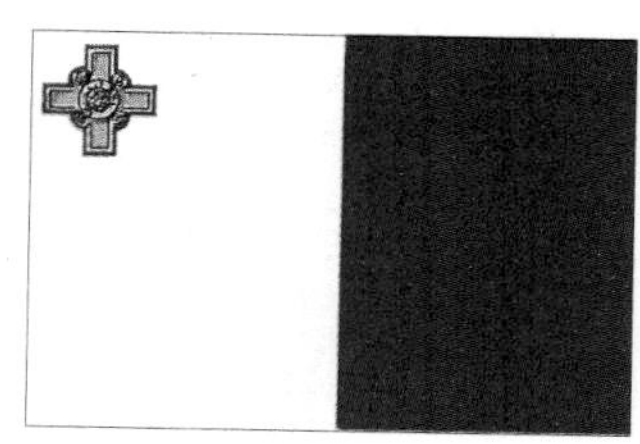

Malta
National Flag

Mauritania
National Flag

Mauritius
Ensign

Mexico
National Flag and Ensign

Monserrat
National Flag

Morocco
Ensign

Mozambique
National Flag

NATO
Flag of the North Atlantic Treaty Organization

Netherlands
National Flag and Ensign

New Zealand
Ensign

Nicaragua
National Flag and Ensign

Nigeria
Ensign

Norway
Ensign

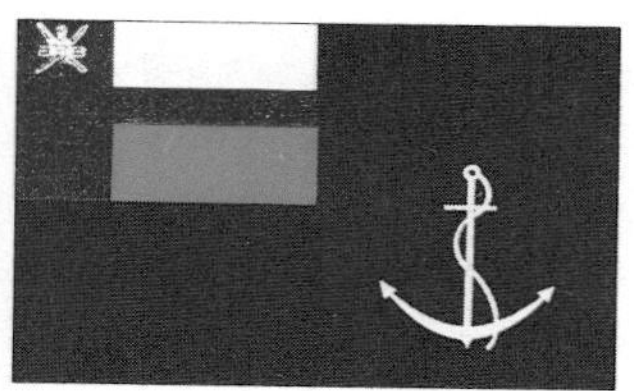

Oman
Ensign

Pakistan
Ensign

Panama
National Flag and Ensign

Papua New Guinea
Ensign

Paraguay
National Flag and Ensign

Paraguay
National Flag and Ensign (reverse)

Peru
Ensign

Philippines
National Flag

Poland
Ensign

Portugal
National Flag and Ensign

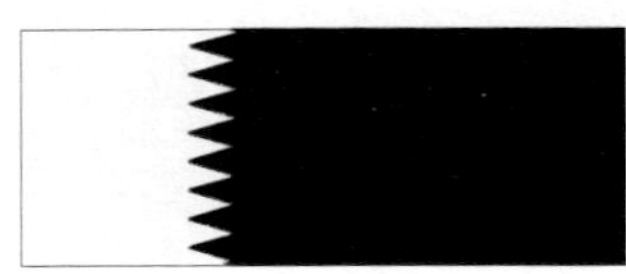
Qatar
National Flag

Romania
National Flag and Ensign

Russia
Ensign

St Kitts-Nevis
National Flag

St Lucia
National Flag

St Vincent
National Flag

Saudi Arabia
Ensign

Senegal
National Flag

Seychelles
National Flag

Sierre Leone
National Flag

Singapore
Ensign

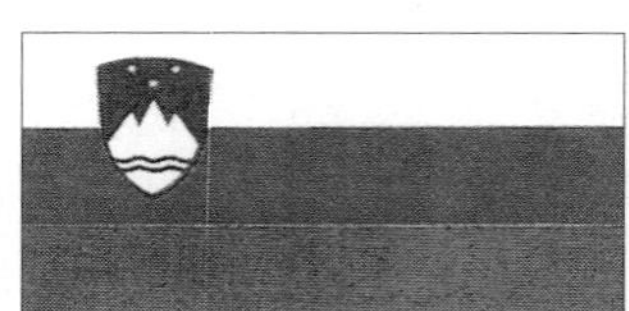
Slovenia
National Flag

Solomon Islands
National Flag

Somalia
National Flag

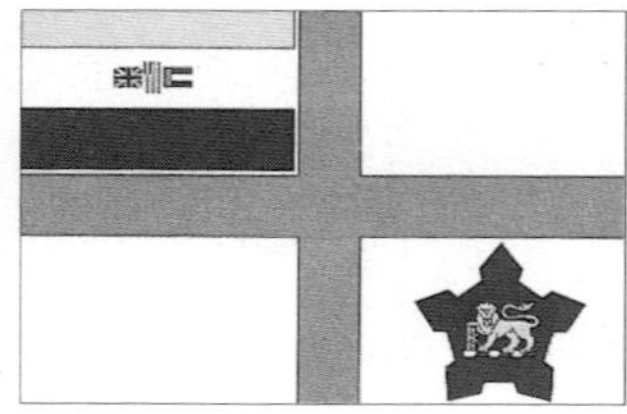
South Africa
Naval Ensign

Spain
National Flag and Ensign

Sri Lanka
Ensign

Sudan
National Flag

Surinam
National Flag

Sweden
Ensign and Jack

Switzerland
National Flag

Syria
National Flag

Taiwan
National Flag and Ensign

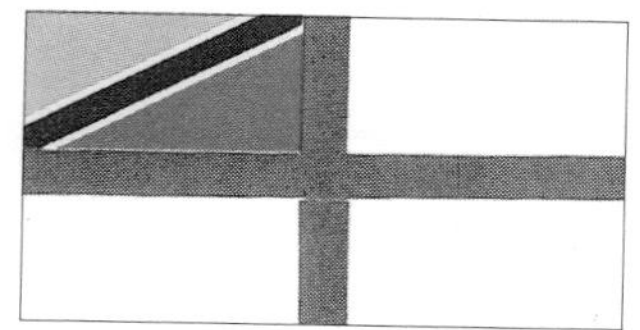

Tanzania
Ensign

Thailand
Ensign

Togo
National Flag

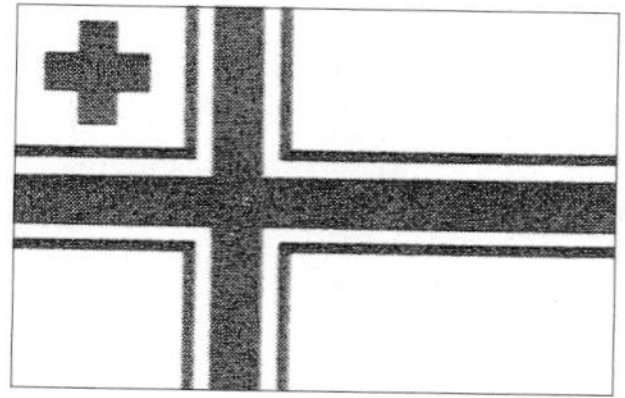

Tonga
Ensign

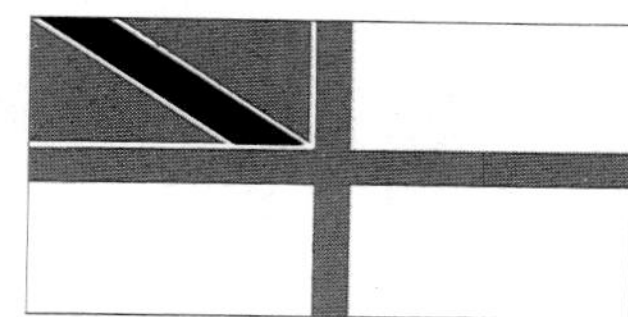

Trinidad and Tobago
Ensign

Tunisia
National Flag

Turkey
National Flag and Ensign

Turks and Caicos
National Flag

Uganda
National Flag

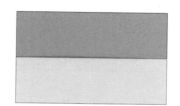

Ukraine
National Flag

Union of Soviet Socialist Republics (former)
Ensign

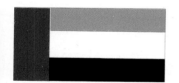

United Arab Emirates
National Flag

United Kingdom
White Ensign

United States of America
National Flag and Ensign

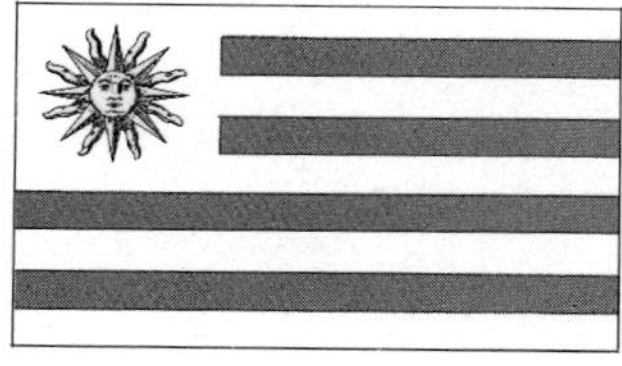

Uruguay
National Flag and Ensign

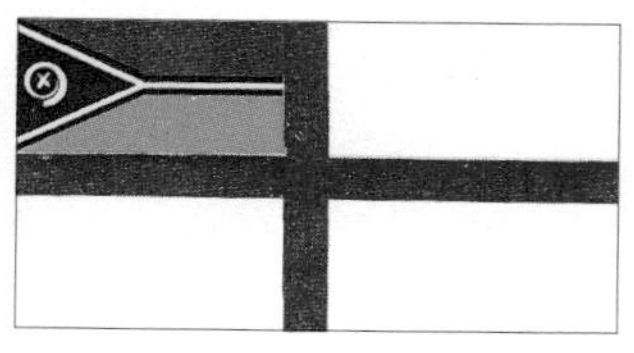

Vanuatu
Ensign

Venezuela
National Flag and Ensign

Vietnam
National Flag

Virgin Islands
National Flag

Western Samoa
National Flag

Yemen
National Flag

Yugoslavia
Ensign

Zaire
National Flag

Pennant list of major surface ships

Type abbreviations (for USA see page 725)

AD	Destroyer tender	BB	Battleship	FFL	Light frigate or corvette
AEFS	Fleet replenishment ship	CA	Gun cruiser	FFLG	Guided missile light frigate or corvette
AFS	Combat stores ship	CG	Guided missile cruiser	HSS	Helicopter support ship
AG	Miscellaneous	CGH	Guided missile/helicopter cruiser	LCC	Amphibious command ship
AG/FF	Frigate/FAC support ship	CGN	Guided missile cruiser (nuclear powered)	LHA	Amphibious assault ship (general purpose)
AGI	Auxiliary general intelligence	CL	Light cruiser	LHD	Amphibious assault ship (multi-purpose)
AGOR	Research ship	CLT	Light cruiser, training	LKA	Amphibious cargo ship
AGS	Surveying ship	CSL	Light cargo ship	LPD	Amphibious transport dock
AO	Oiler	CV	Multi-purpose aircraft carrier	LPH	Amphibious assault ship (helicopter)
AOE	Fast combat support ship	CVA	Attack aircraft carrier	LSD	Dock landing ship
AOF(L)	Large fleet tanker	CVH	Helicopter carrier	LSI	Landing ship, infantry
AOF(S)	Small fleet tanker	CVL	Light aircraft carrier	LSL	Landing ship, logistic
AOR	Replenishment oiler	CVN	Multi-purpose aircraft carrier (nuclear powered)	LST	Tank landing ship
AOS	Support tanker	CVS/CVSG	ASW aircraft carrier	MH	Minehunter
AP	Transport	DD	Destroyer	ML	Minelayer
APA	Amphibious transport	DDG	Guided missile destroyer (including surface-to-air missile)	MSC	Coastal minesweeper
AR	Repair ship	FF	Frigate	MSO	Ocean minesweeper
ARS	Salvage ship	FFG	Guided missile frigate (including surface-to-air missiles)	PV	Patrol vessel
AS	Submarine tender			TCD	Landing ship dock
ATS	Training support ship				
AVT	Auxiliary aircraft landing training ship				

Pennant numbers of major surface ships in numerical order

Number	Ship's name	Type	Country
A 00	Britannia	AG	UK
01	Adelaide	FFG	Australia
01	Pohjanmaa	ML	Finland
A 01	Ethiopia	AG	Ethiopia
A 01	Panuco	LST	Mexico
A 01	Contramaestre Casado	AP	Spain
B 01	Durango	FF	Mexico
C 01	Sebastian Jose Holzinger	PV	Mexico
G-01	Leandro Valle	PV	Mexico
GH 01	Cadete Virgilio Uribe	PV	Mexico
HL 01	Shoyo	AGS	Japan
HQ 01	Pham Ngu Lao	FFG	Vietnam
ID 01	Admirable class	PV	Mexico
LL 01	Tsushima	AG	Japan
S 01	Gladan	ATS	Sweden
1	Tachin	FF	Thailand
1	Longlom	FFL	Thailand
1	Rattanakosin	FFLG	Thailand
1	Thalang	MSC/AG	Thailand
1	Uruguay	FF	Uruguay
A 1	Comandante General Irigoyen	PV	Argentina
A 1	Al Mabrukah	PV/ATS	Oman
AFS 1	Mars	AFS	USA
AOE 1	Sacramento	AOE	USA
AOR 1	Wichita	AOR	USA
ATS 1	Edenton	ATS	USA
D 1	Hercules	DDG	Argentina
FM 1	Presidente Eloy Alfaro	FFG	Ecuador
L 1	Al Munassir	LSL	Oman
LHA 1	Tarawa	LHA	USA
LHD 1	Wasp	LHD	USA
LSV 1	General Frank S Besson Jr	LSL	USA
M 1	Neuquen	MSC	Argentina
MCM 1	Avenger	MSO	USA
MSF 1	Phosamton	ATS	Thailand
PC 1	Sarasin	PV	Thailand
PHM 1	Pegasus	PV	USA
Z 1	Baltyk	AO	Poland
02	Canberra	FFG	Australia
02	O'Higgins	CG	Chile
02	Hameenmaa	ML	Finland
A 02	Manzanillo	LST	Mexico
E 02	Cuitlahuac	DD	Mexico
FM 02	Moran Valverde	FFG	Ecuador
G-02	Guillermo Prieto	PV	Mexico
GA 02	Mitla	PV	Mexico
GH 02	Teniente José Azueta	PV	Mexico
HL 02	Takuyo	AGS	Japan
M 02	Älvsborg	ML/AS	Sweden
P 02	Nanawa	PV	Paraguay
S 02	Falken	ATS	Sweden
2	Khamronsin	FFL	Thailand
2	Prasae	FF	Thailand
2	Sukhothai	FFLG	Thailand
2	Bang Rachan	MH/MSC	Thailand
2	Chula	AOR	Thailand
2	General Artigas	FF	Uruguay
2/508	Al Hirasa	FF	Syria
A 2	Teniente Olivieri	AG	Argentina
AFS 2	Sylvania	AFS	USA
AOE 2	Camden	AOE	USA
AOR 2	Milwaukee	AOR	USA
ATS 2	Beaufort	ATS	USA
D 2	Santisima Trinidad	DDG	Argentina
L 2	Nasr Al Bahr	LSL	Oman
LHA 2	Saipan	LHA	USA
LHD 2	Essex	LHD	USA
LPH 2	Iwo Jima	LPH	USA
LST 2	Chang	LST	Thailand
LSV 2	CW 3 Harold C Clinger	LSL	USA
M 2	Rio Negro	MSC	Argentina
MCM 2	Defender	MSO	USA
PHM 2	Hercules	PV	USA
Q 2	Libertad	AG	Argentina
V 2	Veinticinco de Mayo	CVS	Argentina
03	Sydney	FFG	Australia
03	Turanmaa	FFL	Finland
E 03	Quetzalcoatl	DD	Mexico
G-03	Mariano Escobedo	PV	Mexico
GA 03	Peten PV	Mexico	
GH 03	Capitan de Fragata Pedro Sáinz de Baranda	PV	Mexico
HQ 03	Dai Ky	FFG	Vietnam
ID 03	Admirable class	PV	Mexico
M 03	Visborg	ML/AG	Sweden
P 03	Capitan Meza	PV	Paraguay
3	Pin Klao	FF	Thailand
3	Thayanchon	FFL	Thailand
3	Nongsarai	MH/MSC	Thailand
3	Maeklong	ATS	Thailand
A 3	Francisco de Gurruchaga	PV	Argentina
AFS 3	Niagara Falls	AFS	USA
AGF 3	La Salle	AG	USA
AOE 3	Seattle	AOE	USA
AOR 3	Kansas City	AOR	USA
ATS 3	Brunswick	ATS	USA
B 3	Canal Beagle	AP	Argentina
L 3	Fulk al Salamah	AP	Oman
LHA 3	Belleau Wood	LHA	USA
LHD 3	Kearsage	LHD	USA
LPH 3	Okinawa	LPH	USA

Number	Ship's name	Type	Country
LST 3	Pangan	LST	Thailand
LSV 3	General Brehon B Somervell	LSL	USA
M 3	Chubut	MSC	Argentina
MCM 3	Sentry	MSO	USA
PHM 3	Taurus	PV	USA
Z 3	Krab	AO	Poland
04	Darwin	FFG	Australia
04	Karjala	FFL	Finland
E 04	Netzahualcoyotl	DD	Mexico
GA 04	Anahuac	PV	Mexico
GH 04	Comodoro Carlos Castillo Bretón	PV	Mexico
HL 04	Tenyo	AGS	Japan
ID 04	Admirable class	PV	Mexico
M 04	Carlskrona	ML	Sweden
N 04	Aktion	ML	Greece
P 04	Teneinte Farina	PV	Paraguay
4	Sattahip	PV	Thailand
4	Montevideo	FF	Uruguay
AFS 4	White Plains	AFS	USA
AOE 4	Detroit	AOE	USA
AOR 4	Savannah	AOR	USA
B 4	Bahia San Blas	AP	Argentina
LHA 4	Nassau	LHA	USA
LPD 4	Austin	LPD	USA
LST 4	Lanta	LST	Thailand
LSV 4	Lt Gen William B Bunker	LSL	USA
M 4	Tierra del Fuego	MSC	Argentina
MCM 4	Champion	MSO	USA
PC 4	Phali	PV	Thailand
PHM 4	Aquila	PV	USA
05	Melbourne	FFG	Australia
05	Keihässalmi	ML	Finland
A 05	Vicente Guerrero	AG	Mexico
A 05	Tui	AGOR	New Zealand
G-05	Manuel Doblado	PV	Mexico
GH 05	Vicealmirante Othón Blanco	PV	Mexico
H 05	Altair	AGS	Mexico
ID 05	Admirable class	PV	Mexico
L 05	President El Hadj Omar Bongo	LCC	Gabon
N 05	Amvrakia	ML	Greece
R 05	Invincible	CVSG	UK
5	Tapi	FF	Thailand
5	Ladya	MSC	Thailand
5	Klongyai	PV	Thailand
AFS 5	Concord	AFS	USA
AOR 5	Wabash	AOR	USA
B 5	Cabo de Hornos	AP	Argentina
LHA 5	Peleliu	LHA	USA
LPD 5	Ogden	LPD	USA
LST 5	Prathong	LST	Thailand
LSV 5	Major General Charles P Gross	LSL	USA
M 5	Chaco	MH	Argentina
MCM 5	Guardian	MSO	USA
PC 5	Sukrip	PV	Thailand
PHM 5	Aries	PV	USA
Q 5	Almirante Irizar	AG	Argentina
06	Newcastle	FFG	Australia
06	Condell	FFG	Chile
A 06	Comodoro Manuel Azueta Azueta	FF	Mexico
A 06	Monowai	AGS	New Zealand
B 06	Usumacinta	FF	Mexico
G-06	Sebastian de la Tejada	PV	Mexico
GH 06	Contraalmirante Angel Ortiz Monasterio	PV	Mexico
R 06	Illustrious	CVSG	UK
6	Khirirat	FF	Thailand
6	Bangkeo	MSC	Thailand
6	Takbai	PV	Thailand
AFS 6	San Diego	AFS	USA
AOE 6	Supply	AOE	USA
AOR 6	Kalamazoo	AOR	USA
LPD 6	Duluth	LPD	USA
LST 6	Sichang	LST	Thailand
M 6	Formosa	MH	Argentina
MCM 6	Devastator	MSO	USA
PC 6	Tongpliu	PV	Thailand
PHM 6	Gemini	PV	USA
07	Lynch	FFG	Chile
A 07	Cuauhtemoc	AG	Mexico
B 07	Coahuila	FF	Mexico
G-07	Santos Degollado	PV	Mexico
HQ 07	Admirable class	FFL	Vietnam
P 07	Général d'Armée Ba Oumar	PV	Gabon
R 07	Ark Royal	CVSG	UK
7	Makut Rajakumarn	FF	Thailand
7	Tadindeng	MSC	Thailand
7	Kantang	PV	Thailand
AFS 7	San Jose	AFS	USA

Number	Ship's name	Type	Country
AOR 7	Roanoke	AOR	USA
C 7	Guanajuato	PV	Mexico
E 7	Inkadh	FF	Tunisia
FFG 7	Oliver Hazard Perry	FFG	USA
LPD 7	Cleveland	LPD	USA
LPH 7	Guadalcanal	LPH	USA
LST 7	Surin	LST	Thailand
MCM 7	Patriot	MSO	USA
PC 7	Liulom	PV	Thailand
08	Ministro Zenteno	FFG	Chile
A 08	Iguala	AP	Mexico
B 08	Chihuahua	FF	Mexico
G-08	Ignacio de la Llave	PV	Mexico
P 08	Colonel Djoue Dabany	PV	Gabon
8	Donchedi	MSC	Thailand
8	Thepha	PV	Thailand
AR 8	Jason	AR	USA
ARS 8	Preserver	ARS	USA
FFG 8	McInerney	FFG	USA
LPD 8	Dubuque	LPD	USA
MCM 8	Scout	MSO	USA
Q 8	Puerto Deseado	AGS	Argentina
Z 8	Medusa	AO	Poland
G-09	Juan N Alvares	PV	Mexico
9	Taimuang	PV	Thailand
A 9	Alferez Sobral	PV	Argentina
CGN 9	Long Beach	CGN	USA
FFG 9	Wadsworth	FFG	USA
LPD 9	Denver	LPD	USA
LPH 9	Guam	LPH	USA
MCM 9	Pioneer	MSO	USA
Z 9	Slimak	AO	Poland
A 10	Comodoro Somellera	PV	Argentina
D 10	Almirante Brown	DDG	Argentina
FFG 10	Duncan	FFG	USA
G-10	Manuel Gutierrez Zamora	PV	Mexico
L 10	Fearless	LPD	UK
LPD 10	Juneau	LPD	USA
LPH 10	Tripoli	LPH	USA
MCM 10	Warrior	MSO	USA
11	Smeli	FFG	Bulgaria
11	Prat	DDG	Chile
11	Mahamiru	MH	Malaysia
A 11	Minas Gerais	CVS	Brazil
A 11	Endeavour	AEFS	New Zealand
A 11	Mar del Norte	AOF(L)	Spain
AGF 11	Coronado	AG	USA
AGS 11	Chanthara	AGS	Thailand
BE 11	Simon Bolivar	ATS	Venezuela
BO 11	Punta Brava	AGS	Venezuela
CM 11	Esmeraldas	FFLG	Ecuador
D 11	La Argentina	DDG	Argentina
FFG 11	Clark	FFG	USA
G-11	Valentin G Farias	PV	Mexico
ID 11	Admirable class	PV	Mexico
K 11	Felinto Perry	ARS	Brazil
K 11	Stockholm	FFLG	Sweden
L 11	Velasco	LST	Spain
L 11	Intrepid	LPD	UK
LPH 11	New Orleans	LPH	USA
M 11	Galeb	ATS	Yugoslavia
MCM 11	Gladiator	MSO	USA
MUL 11	Kalvsund	ML	Sweden
R 11	Vikrant	CV	India
R 11	Principe de Asturias	CV	Spain
12	Druzki	FF	Bulgaria
12	Cochrane	DDG	Chile
12	Jerai	MH	Malaysia
CM 12	Manabi	FFLG	Ecuador
D 12	Heroina	DDG	Argentina
FFG 12	George Philip	FFG	USA
G-12	Ignacio Manuel Altamirano	PV	Mexico
ID 12	Admirable class	PV	Mexico
K12	Malmö	FFLG	Sweden
L 12	Martin Alvarez	LST	Spain
LPD 12	Shreveport	LPD	USA
LPH 12	Inchon	LPH	USA
MCM 12	Ardent	MSO	USA
MUL 12	Arkosund	ML	Sweden
PS 12	Spasilac	ARS	Yugoslavia
13	Bodri	FFG	Bulgaria
13	Ledang	MH	Malaysia
13	Democratia	FFL	Romania
ASR 13	Kittiwake	ASR	USA
CM 13	Los Rios	FFLG	Ecuador
D 13	Sarandi	DDG	Argentina
FFG 13	Samuel Eliot Morison	FFG	USA
G-13	Francisco Zarco	PV	Mexico
HQ 13	Admirable class	FFL	Vietnam
ID 13	Admirable class	PV	Mexico
LPD 13	Nashville	LPD	USA
MCM 13	Dexterous	MSO	USA

Number	Ship's name	Type	Country
MUL 13	Kalmarsund	ML	Sweden
14	Pauk class	FFLG	Bulgaria
14	Latorre	DDG	Chile
14	Kinabalu	MH	Malaysia
14	Descatusaria	FFL	Romania
CM 14	El Oro	FFLG	Ecuador
FFG 14	John H Sides	FFG	USA
G-14	Ignacio L Vallarta	PV	Mexico
ID 14	Admirable class	PV	Mexico
J 14	Nirupak	AGS	India
L 14	Ghorpad	LSM	India
LPD 14	Trenton	LPD	USA
MCM 14	Chief	MSO	USA
MUL 14	Alnösund	ML	Sweden
15	Blanco Encalada	DDG	Chile
15	Desrobirea	FFL	Romania
A 15	Nireehshak	AG	India
AD 15	Prairie	AD	USA
ASR 15	Sunbird	ASR	USA
CM 15	Los Galapagos	FFLG	Ecuador
DDG 15	Berkeley	DDG	USA
F 15	Abu Bakr	FF	Bangladesh
FFG 15	Estocin	FFG	USA
G-15	Jesus G Ortega	PV	Mexico
ID 15	Admirable class	PV	Mexico
J 15	Investigator	AGS	India
L 15	Kesari	LSM	India
LPD 15	Ponce	LPD	USA
M 15	Aratú	MSC	Brazil
MUL 15	Grundsund	ML	Sweden
V 15	Imperial Marinheiro	PV	Brazil
16	Ministro Zenteno	DD	Chile
16	Dreptatea	FFL	Romania
CG 16	Leahy	CG	USA
CM 16	Loja	FFLG	Ecuador
DE 16	Boyaca	PV	Colombia
F 16	Umar Farooq	FF	Bangladesh
FFG 16	Clifton Sprague	FFG	USA
G 16	Barroso Pereira	AP	Brazil
G-16	Melchor Ocampo	PV	Mexico
J 16	Jamuna	AGS	India
L 16	Shardul	LSM	India
M 16	Anhatomirim	MSC	Brazil
V 16	Iguatemi	PV	Brazil
CG 17	Harry E Yarnell	CG	USA
F 17	Ali Haider	FF	Bangladesh
ID 17	Admirable class	PV	Mexico
L 17	Sharabh	LSM	India
M 17	Atalaia	MSC	Brazil
MUL 17	Skramsösund	ML	Sweden
18	Almirante Riveros	DDG	Chile
AD 18	Sierra	AD	USA
AS 18	Orion	AS	USA
CG 18	Worden	CG	USA
F 18	Osman	FFG	Bangladesh
G-18	Juan Aldama	PV	Mexico
ID 18	Admirable class	PV	Mexico
L 18	Cheetah	LSM	India
M 18	Araçatuba	MSC	Brazil
MUL 18	Öresund	ML	Sweden
P 18	Armatolos	PV	Greece
V 18	Forte de Coimbra	PV	Brazil
19	Almirante Williams	DDG	Chile
AD 19	Yosemite	AD	USA
AS 19	Proteus	AS	USA
CG 19	Dale	CG	USA
FFG 19	John A Moore	FFG	USA
G-19	Hermenegildo Galeana	PV	Mexico
ID 19	Admirable class	PV	Mexico
J 19	Nirdeshak	AGS	India
L 19	Mahish	LSM	India
LCC 19	Blue Ridge	LCC	USA
M 19	Abrolhas	MSC	Brazil
MUL 19	Barösund	ML	Sweden
P 19	Navmachos	PV	Greece
PS 19	Miguel Malvar	FFL	Philippines
V 19	Caboclo	PV	Brazil
A 20	Moawin	AR	Pakistan
ASL 20	Cormorant	AG	Canada
CG 20	Richmond K Turner	CG	USA
F 20	Godavari	FFG	India
FFG 20	Antrim	FFG	USA
G 20	Custódio de Mello	AP	Brazil
L 20	Magar	LST	India
LCC 20	Mount Whitney	LCC	USA
M 20	Albardão	MSC	Brazil
MH 20	Henri Christophe	PV	Haiti
MUL 20	Furusund	ML	Sweden
P 20	Murature	PV	Argentina
P 20	Deirdre	PV	Ireland
PS 20	Magat Salamat	FFL	Philippines
U 20	Gastão Moutinho	AR	Brazil

Number	Ship's name	Type	Country
V 20	Angostura	PV	Brazil
21	Sour	PV	Lebanon
21	Musca class	MSC	Romania
A 21	Huasteco	AP	Mexico
AE 21	Suribachi	AEFS	USA
ASR 21	Pigeon	ASR	USA
CG 21	Gridley	CG	USA
F 21	Gomati	FFG	India
F 21	Mariscal Sucre	FFG	Venezuela
FFG 21	Flatley	FFG	USA
G 21	Ary Parreiras	AP	Brazil
H 21	Sirius	AGS	Brazil
K 21	Göteborg	FFLG	Sweden
L 21	Guldar	LSM	India
L 21	Castilla	AP	Spain
M 21	Jucar	MSC	Spain
P 21	King	PV	Argentina
P 21	Emer	PV	Ireland
P 21	Anaga	PV	Spain
V 21	Bahiana	PV	Brazil
22	Damour	PV	Lebanon
22	Musca class	MSC	Romania
A 22	Zapoteco	AP	Mexico
AE 22	Mauna Kea	AEFS	USA
ASR 22	Ortolan	ASR	USA
CG 22	England	CG	USA
F 22	Ganga	FFG	India
F 22	Almirante Brión	FFG	Venezuela
FFG 22	Fahrion	FFG	USA
G 22	Soares Dutra	AP	Brazil
H 22	Canopus	AGS	Brazil
K 22	Gälve	FFLG	Sweden
L 22	Kumbhir	LSM	India
L 22	Aragón	AP	Spain
M 22	Ebro	MSC	Spain
P 22	Aoife	PV	Ireland
P 22	Tagomago	PV	Spain
PS 22	Sultan Kudarat	FFL	Philippines
R 22	Viraat	CV	India
V 22	Mearim	PV	Brazil
23	Musca class	MSC	Romania
AE 23	Nitro	AEFS	USA
CG 23	Halsey	CG	USA
F 23	General Urdaneta	FFG	Venezuela
FFG 23	Lewis B Puller	FFG	USA
G 23	Almirante Gastão Motta	AOS	Brazil
K 23	Kalmar	FFLG	Sweden
L 23	Gharial	LST	India
M 23	Duero	MSC	Spain
P 23	Aisling	PV	Ireland
P 23	Marola	PV	Spain
PS 23	Datu Marikudo	FFL	Philippines
V 23	Purus	PV	Brazil
24	Rahmat	FF	Malaysia
24	Musca class	MSC	Romania
AE 24	Pyro	AEFS	USA
CG 24	Reeves	CG	USA
F 24	General Soublette	FFG	Venezuela
FFG 24	Jack Williams	FFG	USA
G 24	Belmonte	AR	Brazil
K 24	Sundsvall	FFLG	Sweden
M 24	Tajo	MSC	Spain
P 24	Mouro	PV	Spain
V 24	Solimões	PV	Brazil
25	Kasturi	FFLG	Malaysia
A 25	Tarasco	AFS	Mexico
AE 25	Haleakala	AEFS	USA
ARS 25	Chang Won	ARS	Korea, Republic
CGN 25	Bainbridge	CGN	USA
D 25	Marcilio Dias	DD	Brazil
F 25	General Salom	FFG	Venezuela
FFG 25	Copeland	FFG	USA
M 25	Genil	MSC	Spain
P 25	Grosa	PV	Spain
26	Lekir	FFLG	Malaysia
ARS 26	Gumi	ARS	Korea, Republic
CG 26	Belknap	CG	USA
D 26	Mariz E Barros	DD	Brazil
F 26	Almirante Garcia	FFG	Venezuela
FFG 26	Gallery	FFG	USA
G 26	Duque de Caxais	LST	Brazil
M 26	Odiel	MSC	Spain
P 26	Medas	PV	Spain
AE 27	Butte	AEFS	USA
CG 27	Josephus Daniels	CG	USA
D 27	Pará	FF	Brazil
FFG 27	Mahlon S Tisdale	FFG	USA
M 27	Sil	MSC	Spain
P 27	Izaro	PV	Spain
U 27	Brasil	AG	Brazil
AE 28	Santa Barbara	AEFS	USA
CG 28	Wainwright	CG	USA

Number	Ship's name	Type	Country
D 28	Paraíba	FF	Brazil
FFG 28	Boone	FFG	USA
M 28	Miño	MSC	Spain
P 28	Tabarca	PV	Spain
PS 28	Cebu	FFL	Philippines
29	Uribe	AG	Chile
AE 29	Mount Hood	AEFS	USA
CG 29	Jouett	CG	USA
D 29	Paraná	FF	Brazil
FFG 29	Stephen W Groves	FFG	USA
M 29	Brecon	MH/MSC	UK
P 29	Deva	PV	Spain
PS 29	Negros Occidental	FFL	Philippines
CG 30	Horne	CG	USA
D 30	Pernambuco	FF	Brazil
FFG 30	Reid	FFG	USA
G 30	Ceará	LSD	Brazil
M 30	Ledbury	MH/MSC	UK
P 30	Bergantin	PV	Spain
V 30	Inhaúma	FFG	Brazil
31	Drummond	FFG	Argentina
31	Iskir	MSC	Bulgaria
31	Poti class	FFL	Romania
A 31	Malaspina	AGOR	Spain
AS 31	Hunley	AS	USA
CG 31	Sterett	CG	USA
F 31	Descubierta	FFG	Spain
FFG 31	Stark	FFG	USA
G 31	Rio de Janeiro	LSD	Brazil
M 31	Cattistock	MH/MSC	UK
P 31	Eithne	FFL	Ireland
PS 31	Pangasinan	FFL	Philippines
Q 31	Piloto Alsina	AG	Argentina
V 31	Jaceguay	FFG	Brazil
VPB 31	Split	FFG	Yugoslavia
32	Guerrico	FFG	Argentina
32	Vanya class	MSC	Bulgaria
32	Poti class	FFL	Romania
A 32	Tofiño	AGOR	Spain
AE 32	Flint	AEFS	USA
AS 32	Holland	AS	USA
CG 32	William H Standley	CG	USA
F 32	Diana	FFG	Spain
FFG 32	John L Hall	FFG	USA
M 32	Cottesmore	MH/MSC	UK
PS 32	Iloilo	FFL	Philippines
V 32	Julio de Noronha	FFG	Brazil
VPB 32	Kopar	FFG	Yugoslavia
33	Granville	FFG	Argentina
33	Dobrotich	MSC	Bulgaria
33	Poti class	FFL	Romania
A 33	Hesperides	AGOR	Spain
AE 33	Shasta	AEFS	USA
AS 33	Simon Lake	AS	USA
CG 33	Fox	CG	USA
F 33	Nilgiri	FFG	India
F 33	Infanta Elena	FFG	Spain
FFG 33	Jarrett	FFG	USA
M 33	Brocklesby	MH/MSC	UK
P 33	Abhay	FFLG	India
PH 33	Andrija Mohorovičič	AGS	Yugoslavia
V 33	Frontin	FFG	Brazil
VPB 33	Kotor	FFG	Yugoslavia
34	Kirilminkov	MSC	Bulgaria
AE 34	Mount Baker	AEFS	USA
AS 34	Canopus	AS	USA
CG 34	Biddle	CG	USA
F 34	Himgiri	FFG	India
F 34	Infanta Cristina	FFG	Spain
FFG 34	Aubrey Fitch	FFG	USA
M 34	Middleton	MH/MSC	UK
P 34	Ajay	FFLG	India
VPB 34	Pula	FFG	Yugoslavia
35	Ekstati Kinarov	MSC	Bulgaria
AE 35	Kiska	AEFS	USA
CGN 35	Truxtun	CGN	USA
D 35	Sergipe	DD	Brazil
F 35	Udaygiri	FFG	India
F 35	Cazadora	FFG	Spain
M 35	Dulverton	MH/MSC	UK
P 35	Akshay	FFLG	India
36	Rang Dimiter Paskalev	MSC	Bulgaria
AS 36	L Y Spear	AS	USA
CGN 36	California	CGN	USA
D 36	Alagoas	DD	Brazil
F 36	Dunagiri	FFG	India
F 36	Vencedora	FFG	Spain
FFG 36	Underwood	FFG	USA
LSD 36	Anchorage	LSD	USA
M 36	Bicester	MH/MSC	UK
P 36	Agray	FFLG	India
37	Papudo	PV	Chile

Number	Ship's name	Type	Country
AD 37	Samuel Gompers	AD	USA
AS 37	Dixon	AS	USA
CGN 37	South Carolina	CGN	USA
D 37	Rio Grande do Norte	DD	Brazil
F 37	Beas	FF	India
FFG 37	Crommelin	FFG	USA
LSD 37	Portland	LSD	USA
M 37	Chiddingfold	MH/MSC	UK
38	Perth	DDG	Australia
AD 38	Puget Sound	AD	USA
ARS 38	Bolster	ARS	USA
CGN 38	Virginia	CGN	USA
D 38	Espirito Santo	DD	Brazil
FFG 38	Curts	FFG	USA
LSD 38	Pensacola	LSD	USA
M 38	Atherstone	MH/MSC	UK
39	Hobart	DDG	Australia
ARS 39	Conserver	ARS	USA
AS 39	Emory S Land	AS	USA
CGN 39	Texas	CGN	USA
DDG 39	MacDonough	DDG	USA
FFG 39	Doyle	FFG	USA
LSD 39	Mount Vernon	LSD	USA
M 39	Hurworth	MH/MSC	UK
ARS 40	Hoist	ARS	USA
AS 40	Frank Cable	AS	USA
CGN 40	Mississippi	CGN	USA
F 40	Niteroi	FFG	Brazil
F 40	Sirius	FFG	UK
FFG 40	Halyburton	FFG	USA
K 40	Veer	FFLG	India
LSD 40	Fort Fisher	LSD	USA
M 40	Berkeley	MH/MSC	UK
P 40	Graúna	PV	Brazil
41	Brisbane	DDG	Australia
41	Espora	FFG	Argentina
A 41	Dacca	AOR	Pakistan
AD 41	Yellowstone	AD	USA
ARS 41	Opportune	ARS	USA
AS 41	McKee	AS	USA
CGN 41	Arkansas	CGN	USA
F 41	Defensora	FFG	Brazil
F 41	Taragiri	FFG	India
FFG 41	McClusky	FFG	USA
H 41	Almirante Cãmara	AGS	Brazil
K 41	Nirbhik	FFLG	India
LSD 41	Whidbey Island	LSD	USA
M 41	Guadalete	MSO	Spain
M 41	Quorn	MH/MSC	UK
P 41	Goiana	PV	Brazil
P 41	Orla	PV	Ireland
PCE 41	Yan Taing Aung	FFL	Burma
42	Rosales	FFG	Argentina
AD 42	Acadia	AD	USA
ARS 42	Reclaimer	ARS	USA
DDG 42	Mahan	DDG	USA
F 42	Constituição	FFG	Brazil
F 42	Vindhyagiri	FFG	India
FFG 42	Klakring	FFG	USA
H 42	Barao de Teffé	AGS	Brazil
K 42	Nipat	FFLG	India
LSD 42	Germantown	LSD	USA
M 42	Guadalmedina	MSO	Spain
P 42	Grajaú	PV	Brazil
P 42	Ciara	PV	Ireland
PCE 42	Yan Gyi Aung	FFL	Burma
Q 42	Cabo San Antonio	LST	Argentina
43	Spiro	FFG	Argentina
43	Esmeralda	AG	Chile
AD 43	Cape Cod	AD	USA
ARS 43	Recovery	ARS	USA
DDG 43	Dahlgren	DDG	USA
F 43	Liberal	FFG	Brazil
F 43	Trishul	FFG	India
FFG 43	Thach	FFG	USA
H 43	Almirante Alvaro Alberto	AGS	Brazil
K 43	Nishank	FFLG	India
LSD 43	Fort McHenry	LSD	USA
M 43	Guadalquivir	MSO	Spain
N 43	Lindormen	ML	Denmark
P 43	Guaiba	PV	Brazil
44	Parker	FFG	Argentina
AD 44	Shenandoah	AD	USA
F 44	Independencia	FFG	Brazil
K 44	Nirghal	FFLG	India
LSD 44	Gunston Hall	LSD	USA
M 44	Guadiana	MSO	Spain
N 44	Lossen	ML	Denmark
P 44	Kirpan	FFLG	India
T 44	Puerto Cabello	AFS	Venezuela
45	Robinson	FFG	Argentina
45	Piloto Pardo	AG	Chile

Number	Ship's name	Type	Country
F 45	União	FFG	Brazil
FFG 45	De Wert	FFG	USA
K 45	Vibhuti	FFLG	India
LSD 45	Comstock	LSD	USA
46	Gomez Roca	FFG	Argentina
FFG 46	Rentz	FFG	USA
K 46	Vipul	FFLG	India
P 46	Kuthar	FFLG	India
LSD 46	Tortuga	LSD	USA
A 47	Nasr	AOR	Pakistan
AP 47	Aquiles	AP	Chile
CG 47	Ticonderoga	CG	USA
FFG 47	Nicholas	FFG	USA
LSD 47	Rushmore	LSD	USA
P 47	Khanjar	FFLG	India
CG 48	Yorktown	CG	USA
FFG 48	Vandegrift	FFG	USA
LSD 48	Ashland	LSD	USA
49	Derwent	FFG	Australia
CG 49	Vincennes	CG	USA
FFG 49	Robert G Bradley	FFG	USA
LSD 49	Harpers Ferry	LSD	USA
P 49	Khukri	FFLG	India
50	Swan	FFG	Australia
50	Al Manama	FFLG	Bahrain
A 50	Alster	AGI	Germany
A 50	Deepak	AOR	India
ARS 50	Safeguard	ARS	USA
CG 50	Valley Forge	CG	USA
FFG 50	Taylor	FFG	USA
L 50	Tobruk	LSH	Australia
P 50	Sukanya	PV	India
51	Al Muharraq	FFLG	Bahrain
51	Damavand	DDG	Iran
51	Chunji	AO	Korea, Republic
51	Shabab Oman	ATS	Oman
ARS 51	Grasp	ARS	USA
CG 51	Thomas S Gates	CG	USA
CM 51	Almirante Padilla	FFG	Colombia
D 51	Rajput	DDG	India
DDG 51	Arleigh Burke	DDG	USA
FFG 51	Gary	FFG	USA
FM 51	Meliton Carvajal	FFG	Peru
MHC 51	Osprey	MH	USA
P 51	Subhadra	PV	India
P 51	Nalón	PV	Spain
T 51	Amazonas	LST	Venezuela
52	Almirante Jorge Montt	AOF(L)	Chile
A 52	Oste	AGI	Germany
ARS 52	Salvor	ARS	USA
CG 52	Bunker Hill	CG	USA
CM 52	Caldas	FFG	Colombia
D 52	Rana	DDG	India
DDG 52	Barry	DDG	USA
F 52	Juno	ATS	UK
FFG 52	Carr	FFG	USA
FM 52	Manuel Villavicencio	FFG	Peru
MHC 52	Heron	MH	USA
N 52	Vidar	ML	Norway
P 52	Suvarna	PV	India
P 52	Ulla	PV	Spain
53	Torrens	FFG	Australia
53	Araucano	AOF(L)	Chile
A 53	Oker	AGI	Germany
ARS 53	Grapple	ARS	USA
CG 53	Mobile Bay	CG	USA
CM 53	Antioquia	FFG	Colombia
D 53	Ranjit	DDG	India
DDG 53	John Paul Jones	DDG	USA
FFG 53	Hawes	FFG	USA
FM 53	Montero	FFG	Peru
MHC 53	Pelican	MH	USA
N 53	Vale	ML	Norway
P 53	Savitri	PV	India
A 54	Amba	AS	India
CG 54	Antietam	CG	USA
CM 54	Independiente	FFG	Colombia
D 54	Ranvir	DDG	India
DDG 54	Curtis Wilbur	DDG	USA
FFG 54	Ford	FFG	USA
FM 54	Mariategui	FFG	Peru
P 54	Sarayu	PV	India
P 54	Turia	PV	Spain
CG 55	Leyte Gulf	CG	USA
D 55	Ranvijay	DDG	India
F 55	Waikato	FFG	New Zealand
FFG 55	Elrod	FFG	USA
FV 55	Indaw	PV	Burma
P 55	Sharada	PV	India
CG 56	San Jacinto	CG	USA
F 56	Argonaut	FFG	UK
FFG 56	Simpson	FFG	USA

Number	Ship's name	Type	Country
FV 56	Inma	PV	Burma
P 56	Sujatha	PV	India
A 57	Shakti	AOR	India
AL 57	Sierra Madre	LST	Philippines
CG 57	Lake Champlain	CG	USA
F 57	Andromeda	FFG	UK
FFG 57	Reuben James	FFG	USA
FV 57	Inya	PV	Burma
M 57	Arkö	MSC	Sweden
A 58	Rhein	AG	Germany
CG 58	Philippine Sea	CG	USA
FFG 58	Samuel B Roberts	FFG	USA
AVT 59	Forrestal	AVT	USA
CG 59	Princeton	CG	USA
FFG 59	Kauffman	FFG	USA
A 60	Gorch Fock	AG	Germany
CG 60	Normandy	CG	USA
CV 60	Saratoga	CV	USA
FFG 60	Rodney M Davis	FFG	USA
61	Babr	DDG	Iran
A 61	Elbe	AG	Germany
CG 61	Monterey	CG	USA
CV 61	Ranger	CV	USA
FFG 61	Ingraham	FFG	USA
M 61	Pondicherry	MSO	India
T 61	Hualcopo	LST	Ecuador
T 61	Capana	LST	Venezuela
62	Sonya class	MSC	Bulgaria
62	Palang	DDG	Iran
CG 62	Chancellorsville	CG	USA
CV 62	Independence	CV	USA
M 62	Porbandar	MSO	India
P 62	Niki	FFL	Greece
T 62	Esequibo	LST	Venezuela
63	Sonya class	MSC	Bulgaria
63	Sargento Aldea	PV	Chile
A 63	Main	AG	Germany
CG 63	Cowpens	CG	USA
CV 63	Kitty Hawk	CV	USA
M 63	Bedi	MSO	India
P 63	Doxa	FFL	Greece
T 63	Goajira	LST	Venezuela
64	Sonya class	MSC	Bulgaria
64	Yelcho	AGS	Chile
CG 64	Gettysburg	CG	USA
CV 64	Constellation	CV	USA
M 64	Bhavnagar	MSO	India
P 64	Thetis class	FFL	Greece
T 64	Los Llanos	LST	Venezuela
CG 65	Chosin	CG	USA
CVN 65	Enterprise	CVN	USA
F 65	Thetis class	FFL	Greece
M 65	Alleppey	MSO	India
CG 66	Hue City	CG	USA
CV 66	America	CV	USA
M 66	Ratnagiri	MSO	India
P 66	Thetis class	FFL	Greece
CG 67	Shiloh	CG	USA
CV 67	John F Kennedy	CV	USA
M 67	Karwar	MSO	India
M 67	Nämdo	MSC	Sweden
ATF 68	Leucoton	AG	Chile
CG 68	Anzio	CG	USA
CVN 68	Nimitz	CVN	USA
M 68	Cannanore	MSO	India
M 68	Blidö	MSC	Sweden
P 68	Arnala	FF	India
A 69	Donau	AG	Germany
CG 69	Vicksburg	DDG	USA
CVN 69	Dwight D Eisenhower	CVN	USA
F 69	Wellington	FFG	New Zealand
M 69	Cuddalore	MSO	India
P 69	Androth	FF	India
PS 69	Rizal	FFL	Philippines
70	Angamos	AS	Chile
CG 70	Lake Erie	CG	USA
CVN 70	Carl Vinson	CVN	USA
M 70	Kakinada	MSO	India
PS 70	Quezon	FFL	Philippines
71	Alvand	FFG	Iran
A 71	Juan Sebastian de Elcano	ATS	Spain
CG 71	Cape St George	CG	USA
CVN 71	Theodore Roosevelt	CVN	USA
F 71	Baleares	FFG	Spain
F 71	Scylla	FFG	UK
K 71	Vijay Durg	FFLG	India
M 71	Kozhikoda	MSO	India
M 71	Landsort	MH	Sweden
P 71	Serviola	PV	Spain
72	Alborz	FFG	Iran
A 72	Arosa	ATS	Spain
CVN 72	Abraham Lincoln	CVN	USA

Number	Ship's name	Type	Country
F 72	Andalucia	FFG	Spain
F 72	Ariadne	FFG	UK
K 72	Sindhu Durg	FFLG	India
M 72	Konkan	MSO	India
M 72	Arholma	MH	Sweden
P 72	Centinela	PV	Spain
RM 72	Pedro de Heredia	PV	Colombia
73	Sabalan	FFG	Iran
A 73	Moresby	AGS	Australia
A 73	Hispania	ATS	Spain
CVN 73	George Washington	CVN	USA
DM 73	Palacios	DDG	Peru
F 73	Cataluña	FFG	Spain
K 73	Hos Durg	FFLG	India
M 73	Koster	MH	Sweden
P 73	Anjadip	FF	India
P 73	Vigia	PV	Spain
RM 73	Sebastion de Belal Calzar	PV	Colombia
A 74	Aris	AG	Greece
A 74	La Graciosa	ATS	Spain
DM 74	Ferré	DDG	Peru
F 74	Asturias	FFG	Spain
M 74	Kullen	MH	Sweden
P 74	Atalaya	PV	Spain
RM 74	Rodrigo de Bastidas	PV	Colombia
F 75	Extremadura	FFG	Spain
M 75	Vinga	MH	Sweden
P 75	Amini	FF	India
76	Hang Tuah	FF	Malaysia
DD 76	Quiñones	DD	Peru
M 76	Ven	MH	Sweden
DD 77	Villar	DD	Peru
M 77	Ulvön	MH	Sweden
DD 78	Galvez	DD	Peru
P 78	Kadmath	FF	India
PF 78	Rajah Humabon	FF	Philippines
DD 79	Diez Canseco	DD	Peru
F 79	Lamine Sadji Kaba	PV	Guinea
N 80	Falster	ML	Denmark
81	Zhenghe	AT	China
81	Bayandor	FFL	Iran
A 81	Aka	ARS	Iraq
A 81	Brambleleaf	AOS	UK
CH 81	Almirante Grau	CG	Peru
F 81	Santa Maria	FFG	Spain
N 81	Fyen	ML	Denmark
82	Naghdi	FFL	Iran
F 82	Otobo	FFL	Nigeria
F 82	Victoria	FFG	Spain
N 82	Møen	ML	Denmark
F 83	Erinomi	FFLG	Nigeria
F 83	Numancia	FFG	Spain
N 83	Sjaelland	ML	Denmark
C 84	Babur	DDG	Pakistan
CH 84	Aguirre	CG	Peru
F 84	Enyimiri	FFLG	Nigeria
F 84	Reina Sofía	FFG	Spain
F 85	Cumberland	FFG	UK
A 86	Tir	AG	India
D 86	Birmingham	DDG	UK
F 86	Campbeltown	FFG	UK
LT 86	Zamboanga del Sur	LST	Philippines
D 87	Newcastle	DDG	UK
F 87	Obuma	FF	Nigeria
F 87	Chatham	FFG	UK
LT 87	Cotobato del Sur	LST	Philippines
AR 88	Narra	AR	Philippines
D 88	Glasgow	DDG	UK
F 88	Broadsword	FFG	UK
P 88	Victory	FFLG	Singapore
D 89	Exeter	DDG	UK
F 89	Aradu	FFG	Nigeria
F 89	Battleaxe	FFG	UK
P 89	Valour	FFLG	Singapore
D 90	Southampton	DDG	UK
F 90	Brilliant	FFG	UK
P 90	Vigilance	FFLG	Singapore
TK 90	Mactan	AG	Philippines
D 91	Nottingham	DDG	UK
F 91	Brazen	FFG	UK
HI 91	Orion	AGS	Ecuador
P 91	Valiant	FFLG	Singapore
R 91	Charles de Gaulle	CVN	France
D 92	Liverpool	DDG	UK
F 92	Boxer	FFG	UK
P 92	Vigour	FFLG	Singapore
F 93	Beaver	FFG	UK
P 93	Vengeance	FFLG	Singapore
F 94	Brave	FFG	UK
D 95	Manchester	DDG	UK
F 95	London	FFG	UK
D 96	Gloucester	DDG	UK

Number	Ship's name	Type	Country
F 96	Sheffield	FFG	UK
D 97	Edinburgh	DDG	UK
R 97	Jeanne d'Arc	CVH	France
D 98	York	DDG	UK
F 98	Coventry	FFG	UK
LT 98	Ilocos Norte	LST	Philippines
R 98	Clemenceau	CV	France
F 99	Cornwall	FFG	UK
R 99	Foch	CV	France
101	Anshan	DDG	China
101	Haibing class	AG	China
M 101	Sandown	MH	UK
N 101	Mordoğan	ML	Turkey
102	Fushun	DDG	China
102	Haibing class	AG	China
A 102	Agnadeen	AOR	Iraq
M 102	Mercury	MSC	Singapore
M 102	Inverness	MH	UK
103	Changchun	DDG	China
M 103	Cromer	MH	UK
104	Qingdao	DDG	China
F 104	Southland	FFG	New Zealand
L 104	Inouse	LST	Greece
M 104	Walney	MH	UK
N 104	Mersin	ML	Turkey
P 104	Bakassi	PVG	Cameroon
105	Jinan	DDG	China
M 105	Bridport	MH	UK
N 105	Mürefte	ML	Turkey
106	Xian	DDG	China
107	Yinchuan	DDG	China
108	Xining	DDG	China
D 108	Cardiff	DDG	UK
109	Kaifeng	DDG	China
A 109	Bayleaf	AOS	UK
110	Dalian	DDG	China
A 110	Orangeleaf	AOS	UK
MSA 110	Anticosti	MSC	Canada
N 110	Nusret	ML	Turkey
111	Luda class	DDG	China
111	Al Isar	MSO	Libya
A 111	Oakleaf	AOS	UK
P 111	Sultanhisar	PV	Turkey
112	Luhu	DDG	China
MSA 112	Moresby	MSC	Canada
P 112	Demirhisar	PV	Turkey
113	Al Tiyar	MSO	Libya
LKA 113	Charleston	LKA	USA
P 113	Yarhisar	PV	Turkey
LKA 114	Durham	LKA	USA
P 114	Akhisar	PV	Turkey
115	Ras al Hamman	MSO	Libya
DD 115	Asagumo	DD	Japan
LKA 115	Mobile	LKA	USA
N 115	Mehmetcik	ML	Turkey
P 115	Sivrihisar	PV	Turkey
DD 116	Minegumo	DD	Japan
L 116	Kos	LST	Greece
LKA 116	St Louis	LKA	USA
P 116	Koçhisar	PV	Turkey
117	Ras al Fulaijah	MSO	Libya
DD 117	Natsugumo	DD	Japan
LKA 117	El Paso	LKA	USA
DD 118	Murakumo	DD	Japan
119	Ras al Qula	MSO	Libya
DD 119	Aokumo	DD	Japan
DD 120	Akigumo	DD	Japan
NL 120	Bayraktar	LST	Turkey
121	Ras al Madwar	MSO	Libya
AG 121	Riverton	AGOR	Canada
DD 121	Yugumo	DD	Japan
J 121	Changxingdao	AS	China
NL 121	Sancaktar	LST	Turkey
A 122	Olwen	AOF (L)	UK
DD 122	Hatsuyuki	DDG	Japan
NL 122	Çakabey	LST	Turkey
123	Ras al Massad	MSO	Libya
A 123	Olna	AOF (L)	UK
DD 123	Shirayuki	DDG	Japan
NL 123	Sarucabey	LST	Turkey
A 124	Olmeda	AOF (L)	UK
DD 124	Mineyuki	DDG	Japan
NL 124	Karamürselbey	LST	Turkey
125	Ras al Hani	MSO	Libya
DD 125	Sawayuki	DDG	Japan
NL 125	Osman Gazi	LST	Turkey
DD 126	Hamayuki	DDG	Japan
DD 127	Isoyuki	DDG	Japan
DD 128	Haruyuki	DDG	Japan
DD 129	Yamayuki	DDG	Japan
A 130	Roebuck	AGS	UK
DD 130	Matsuyuki	DDG	Japan

Number	Ship's name	Type	Country
131	Nanjing	DDG	China
ATC 131	Ilo	AP	Peru
DD 131	Setoyuki	DDG	Japan
132	Hefei	DDG	China
132	Ibn Ouf	LST	Libya
A 132	Diligence	AR	UK
DD 132	Asayuki	DDG	Japan
133	Chongqing	DDG	China
A 133	Hecla	AGS	UK
DD 133	Shimayuki	DDG	Japan
134	Zunyi	DDG	China
134	Ibn Harissa	LST	Libya
A 135	Argus	AVT	UK
A 138	Herald	AGS	UK
139	Ropuchka class	LST	Yemen
DD 141	Haruna	DDG	Japan
DT 141	Paita	LST	Peru
DD 142	Hiei	DDG	Japan
DT 142	Pisco	LST	Peru
DD 143	Shirane	DDG	Japan
DT 143	Callao	LST	Peru
DD 144	Kurama	DDG	Japan
DT 144	Eten	LST	Peru
L 144	Siros	LST	Greece
ATP 150	Bayovar	AO	Peru
DD 151	Asagiri	DDG	Japan
M 151	Vukov Klanac	MH/MSC	Yugoslavia
152	Mutiara	AGS	Malaysia
ATP 152	Talara	AOR	Peru
DD 152	Yamagiri	DDG	Japan
M 152	Podgora	MH/MSC	Yugoslavia
DD 153	Yuugiri	DDG	Japan
L 153	Nafkratoussa	LSD	Greece
M 153	Blitvenica	MH/MSC	Yugoslavia
DD 154	Amagiri	DDG	Japan
L 154	Ikaria	LST	Greece
155	Providencia	AGS	Colombia
DD 155	Hamagiri	DDG	Japan
156	Malpelo	AGS	Colombia
ATP 156	Parinas	AOR	Peru
DD 156	Setogiri	DDG	Japan
DD 157	Sawagiri	DDG	Japan
L 157	Rodos	LST	Greece
ATP 158	Zorritos	AOS	Peru
DD 158	Umigiri	DDG	Japan
ATP 159	Lobitos	AOS	Peru
F 159	Tabuk	FFG	Pakistan
PB 159	Fundy	PV	Canada
160	Musytari	PV	Malaysia
D 160	Alamgir	DDG	Pakistan
M 160	Mahmood	MSC	Pakistan
PB 160	Chignecto	PV	Canada
161	Changsha	DDG	China
161	Marikh	PV	Malaysia
F 161	Badr	FFG	Pakistan
M 161	Gradac	MH/MSC	Yugoslavia
PB 161	Thunder	PV	Canada
162	Nanning	DDG	China
PB 162	Cowichan	PV	Canada
163	Nanchang	DDG	China
DD 163	Amatsukaze	DDG	Japan
F 163	Harbah	FFG	Pakistan
PB 163	Miramichi	PV	Canada
164	Guilin	DDG	China
D 164	Shahjahan	DDG	Pakistan
DD 164	Takatsuki	DDG	Japan
PB 164	Chaleur	PV	Canada
165	Sinan	DDG	China
DD 165	Kikuzuki	DDG	Japan
M 165	Mukhtar	MSC	Pakistan
166	Luda class	DDG	China
D 166	Taimur	DDG	Pakistan
D 167	Tughril	DDG	Pakistan
D 168	Tippu Sultan	DDG	Pakistan
DD 168	Tachikaze	DDG	Japan
DD 169	Asakaze	DDG	Japan
F 169	Hunain	FFG	Pakistan
F 169	Amazon	FFG	UK
DD 170	Sawakaze	DDG	Japan
AGOR 171	Endeavour	AGOR	Canada
DD 171	Hatakaze	DDG	Japan
F 171	Active	FFG	UK
L 171	Kriti	LST	Greece
AGOR 172	Quest	AGOR	Canada
DD 172	Shimakaze	DDG	Japan
F 172	Ambuscade	FFG	UK
DD 173	Kongo	DDG	Japan
F 173	Arrow	FFG	UK
L 173	Chios	LST	Greece
F 174	Alacrity	FFG	UK
L 174	Samos	LST	Greece
A 176	Polar Circle	PV	UK
L 176	Lesbos	LST	Greece
AO 177	Cimarron	AO	USA
AO 178	Monongahela	AO	USA
AO 179	Merrimack	AO	USA
AO 180	Willamette	AO	USA
D 181	Hamburg	DDG	Germany
D 182	Schleswig-Holstein	DDG	Germany
D 183	Bayern	DDG	Germany
A 185	Salmoor	ARS	UK
D 185	Lütjens	DDG	Germany
F 185	Avenger	FFG	UK
A 186	Salmaster	ARS	UK
AO 186	Platte	AO	USA
D 186	Mölders	DDG	Germany
A 187	Salmaid	ARS	UK
D 187	Rommel	DDG	Germany
192	Cheng Hai	LSD	Taiwan
O 195	Westralia	AOR	Australia
201	Captain 1st Rank Kiril Khalachev	AGS	Bulgaria
201	Chung Hai	LST	Taiwan
A 201	Orion	AGI	Sweden
L 201	Endurance	LST	Singapore
UAM 201	Creoula	ATS	Portugal
202	Mesar	AOS	Bulgaria
L 202	Excellence	LST	Singapore
M 202	Atalanti	MSC	Greece
203	Chung Ting	LST	Taiwan
GT 203	Jervis Bay	AG	Australia
L 203	Intrepid	LST	Singapore
204	Chung Hsing	LST	Taiwan
L 204	Resolution	LST	Singapore
P 204	Indépendencia	PV	Dominican Republic
205	Chung Chien	LST	Taiwan
L 205	Persistence	LST	Singapore
M 205	Antiope	MSC	Greece
P 205	Libertad	PV	Dominican Republic
206	Kapitan Dmitry Dobrev	AG	Bulgaria
206	Kiro	MSC	Fiji
206	Chung Chi	LST	Taiwan
M 206	Faedra	MSC	Greece
P 206	Restauracion	PV	Dominican Republic
207	Skeena	FF	Canada
F 207	Bremen	FFG	Germany
P 207	Cambiaso	FFL	Dominican Republic
208	Chung Shun	LST	Taiwan
F 208	Niedersachsen	FFG	Germany
P 208	Separacion	FFL	Dominican Republic
209	Chung Lien	LST	Taiwan
F 209	Rheinland-Pfalz	FFG	Germany
P 209	Calderas	FFL	Dominican Republic
210	Chung Yung	LST	Taiwan
D 210	Themistocles	DDG	Greece
F 210	Emden	FFG	Germany
M 210	Thalia	MSC	Greece
A 211	Belos	ARS	Sweden
D 211	Miaoulis	DDG	Greece
F 211	Köln	FFG	Germany
F 211	Dat Assawari	FFG	Libya
M 211	Alkyon	MSC	Greece
P 211	Meghna	PV	Bangladesh
D 212	Kanaris	DDG	Greece
F 212	Karlsruhe	FFG	Germany
F 212	Al Hani	FFG	Libya
P 212	Jamuna	PV	Bangladesh
D 213	Kountouriotis	DDG	Greece
F 213	Augsburg	FFG	Germany
F 213	Al Qirdabiyah	FFG	Libya
M 213	Klio	MSC	Greece
D 214	Sachtouris	DDG	Greece
F 214	Lübeck	FFG	Germany
M 214	Avra	MSC	Greece
D 215	Tompazis	DDG	Greece
DE 215	Chikugo	FF	Japan
216	Chung Kuang	LST	Taiwan
D 216	Apostolis	DDG	Greece
DE 216	Ayase	FF	Japan
217	Chung Suo	LST	Taiwan
D 217	Kriezis	DDG	Greece
DE 217	Mikuma	FF	Japan
D 218	Kimon	DDG	Greece
DE 218	Tokachi	FF	Japan
219	Kao Hsiung	AG	Taiwan
D 219	Nearchos	DDG	Greece
DE 219	Iwase	FF	Japan
D 220	Miltiadis	DDG	Greece
DE 220	Chitose	FF	Japan
221	Chung Chuan	LST	Taiwan
D 221	Konon	DDG	Greece
DE 221	Niyodo	FF	Japan

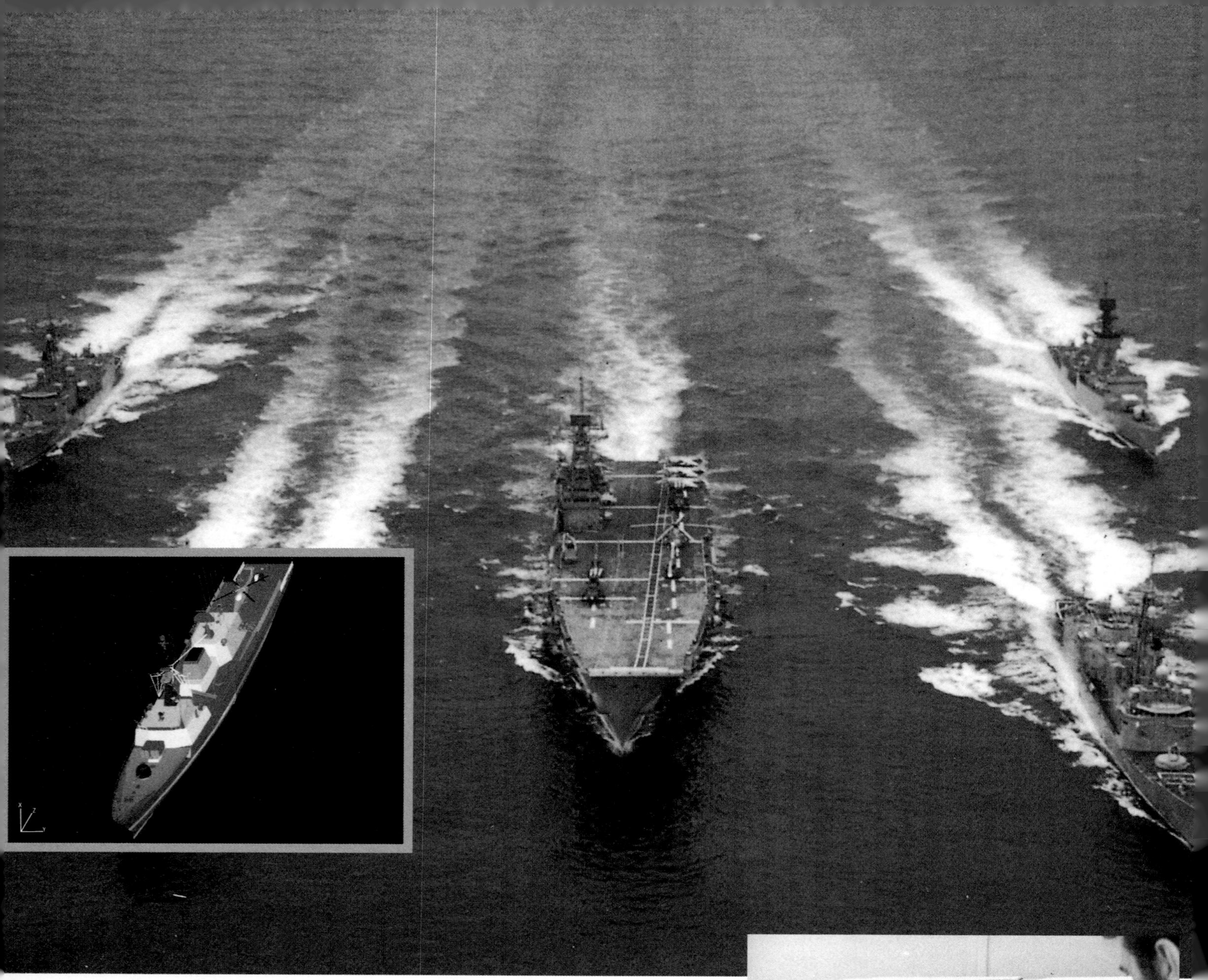

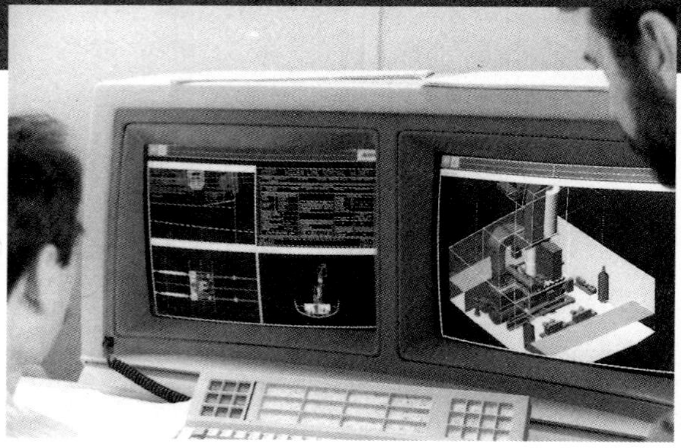

Number	Ship's name	Type	Country
222	Chung Sheng	LST	Taiwan
DE 222	Teshio	FF	Japan
223	Chung Fu	LST	Taiwan
DE 223	Yoshino	FF	Japan
DE 224	Kumano	FF	Japan
225	Chung Chiang	LST	Taiwan
DE 225	Noshiro	FF	Japan
226	Chung Chih	LST	Taiwan
DE 226	Ishikari	FFG	Japan
227	Chung Ming	LST	Taiwan
DE 227	Yubari	FFG	Japan
228	Chung Shu	LST	Taiwan
DE 228	Yubetsu	FFG	Japan
229	Ottawa	FF	Canada
229	Chung Wan	LST	Taiwan
DE 229	Abukuma	FFG	Japan
F 229	Lancaster	FFG	UK
230	Chung Pang	LST	Taiwan
DE 230	Jintsu	FFG	Japan
F 230	Norfolk	FFG	UK
231	Chung Yeh	LST	Taiwan
DE 231	Ohyodo	FFG	Japan
F 231	Argyll	FFG	UK
DE 232	Sendai	FFG	Japan
233	Fraser	FF	Canada
DE 233	Chikuma	FFG	Japan
F 233	Marlborough	FFG	UK
DE 234	Abukuma class	FFG	Japan
F 234	Iron Duke	FFG	UK
F 235	Monmouth	FFG	UK
236	Gatineau	FFG	Canada
F 236	Montrose	FFG	UK
F 237	Westminster	FFG	UK
P 239	Peacock	PV	UK
240	Kaszub	FFG	Poland
F 240	Yavuz	FFG	Turkey
M 240	Pleias	MSC	Greece
P 240	Plover	PV	UK
F 241	Turgutreis	FFG	Turkey
M 241	Kichli	MSC	Greece
P 241	Starling	PV	UK
F 242	Fatih	FFG	Turkey
M 242	Kissa	MSC	Greece
A 243	Tafelberg	AOR	South Africa
F 243	Yildirim	FFG	Turkey
M 246	Aigli	MSC	Greece
P 246	Sentinel	PV	UK
M 247	Dafni	MSC	Greece
M 248	Aedon	MSC	Greece
251	Wodnik	ATS	Poland
252	Gryf	ATS	Poland
M 254	Niovi	MSC	Greece
257	Restigouche	FFG	Canada
258	Kootenay	FFG	Canada
P 258	Leeds Castle	PV	UK
259	Terra Nova	FFG	Canada
P 259	Redpole	PV	UK
260	Tetal class	FF	Romania
P 260	Kingfisher	PV	UK
261	Mackenzie	FF	Canada
261	Kopernik	AGI	Poland
261	Tetal class	FF	Romania
P 261	Cygnet	PV	UK
262	Saskatchewan	FF	Canada
262	Nawigator	AGI	Poland
262	Tetal class	FF	Romania
F 262	Zulfiquar	FFG	Pakistan
263	Yukon	FF	Canada
263	Hydrograf	AGI	Poland
263	Tetal class	FF	Romania
F 263	Shamser	FFG	Pakistan
264	Qu'Appelle	FF	Canada
264	Tetal class	FF	Romania
F 264	Saif	FF	Pakistan
265	Annapolis	FF	Canada
265	Heweliusz	AGOR	Poland
F 265	Aslat	FF	Pakistan
P 265	Dumbarton Castle	PV	UK
266	Nipigon	FF	Canada
266	Arctowski	AGOR	Poland
F 266	Khaibar	FF	Pakistan
F 267	Siqqat	FF	Pakistan
A 269	Grey Rover	AOF (S)	UK
A 270	Blue Rover	AOF (S)	UK
271	Warszawa	DDG	Poland
271	Cosar class	ML	Romania
A 271	Gold Rover	AOF (S)	UK
A 273	Black Rover	AOF (S)	UK
274	Cosar class	ML	Romania
P 277	Anglesey	PV	UK
278	Cosar class	ML	Romania
P 278	Alderney	PV	UK
280	Iroquois	DDG	Canada
281	Huron	DDG	Canada
281	Piast	ARS	Poland
281	Constanta	AFS	Romania
282	Athabaskan	DDG	Canada
282	Lech	ARS	Poland
283	Algonquin	DDG	Canada
283	Croitor class	AFS	Romania
A 285	Auricula	AG	UK
P 295	Jersey	PV	UK
P 297	Guernsey	PV	UK
P 298	Shetland	PV	UK
P 299	Orkney	PV	UK
F 300	Oslo	FFG	Norway
P 300	Lindisfarne	PV	UK
301	General Vladimir Zaimov	AGS	Bulgaria
301	Shahrokh	MSC	Iran
A 301	Drakensberg	AOR	South Africa
F 301	Bergen	FFG	Norway
MSO 301	Yaeyama	MSO/MH	Japan
F 302	Trondheim	FFG	Norway
J 302	Chongmingdao	AS	China
MSO 302	Tsushima	MSO/MH	Japan
303	Karkas	MSC	Iran
F 303	Stavanger	FFG	Norway
F 304	Narvik	FFG	Norway
OR 304	Success	AOR	Australia
308	El Hahiq	PV	Morocco
309	Ettawfiq	PV	Morocco
310	L V Rabhi	PV	Morocco
F 310	Sleipner	FFL	Norway
311	Errachio	PV	Morocco
F 311	Aeger	FFL	Norway
312	El Akid	PV	Morocco
M 312	Sira	MSC	Norway
313	El Maher	PV	Morocco
M 313	Tana	MH	Norway
314	El Majid	PV	Morocco
M 314	Alta	MSC	Norway
315	El Bachir	PV	Morocco
316	El Hamiss	PV	Mexico
M 316	Vosso	MSC	Norway
317	El Karib	PV	Mexico
A 317	Bulldog	AGS	UK
M 317	Glomma	MSC	Norway
A 319	Beagle	AGS	UK
324	Ta Hu	ARS	Taiwan
A 324	Protea	AGS	South Africa
330	Halifax	FFG	Canada
F 330	Vasco da Gama	FFG	Portugal
331	Vancouver	FFG	Canada
331	Martha Kristina Tiyahahu	FFG	Indonesia
F 331	Alvares Cabral	FFG	Portugal
M 331	Tista	MSC	Norway
332	Ville de Québec	FFG	Canada
332	W Zakarias Yohannes	FFG	Indonesia
F 332	Corte Real	FFG	Portugal
M 332	Kvina	MSC	Norway
333	Toronto	FFG	Canada
333	Hasanuddin	FFG	Indonesia
334	Regina	FFG	Canada
M 334	Utla	MSC	Norway
336	Montreal	FFG	Canada
337	Fredericton	FFG	Canada
P 339	Bora	PV	Turkey
F 340	Beskytteren	FF	Denmark
M 340	Oksøy	MH	Norway
341	Samadikun	FF	Indonesia
342	Martadinata	FF	Indonesia
343	Monginsidi	FF	Indonesia
344	Ngurah Rai	FF	Indonesia
D 345	Yücetepe	DDG	Turkey
D 346	Alcitepe	DD	Turkey
D 347	Anittepe	DD	Turkey
D 348	Savaştepe	DDG	Turkey
D 349	Kiliç Ali Paşa	DDG	Turkey
350	Koni class	FFG	Cuba
D 350	Piyale Paşa	DDG	Turkey
V 350	Xiangyang Hong 09	AGS	China
351	Djebel Chinoise	FFL	Algeria
351	Ahmed Yani	FFG	Indonesia
D 351	M Fevzi Çakmak	DDG	Turkey
352	Slamet Riyadi	FFG	Indonesia
D 352	Gayret	DDG	Turkey
353	Koni class	FFG	Cuba
353	Yos Sudarso	FFG	Indonesia
D 353	Adatepe	DDG	Turkey
354	Oswald Siahann	FFG	Indonesia
D 354	Kocatepe	DDG	Turkey
F 354	Niels Juel	FFG	Denmark
355	Abdul Halim Perdana Kusuma	FFG	Indonesia

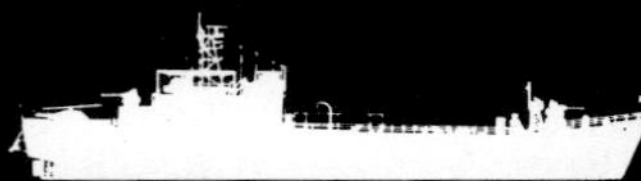

Number	Ship's name	Type	Country
F 355	Olfert Fischer	FFG	Denmark
356	Koni class	FFG	Cuba
356	Karel Satsuitubun	FFG	Indonesia
D 356	Zafer	DD	Turkey
F 356	Peter Tordenskiold	FFG	Denmark
DM 357	Muavenet	DD	Turkey
F 357	Thetis	FF	Denmark
D 358	Berk	FF	Turkey
F 358	Triton	FF	Denmark
AKL 359	Yung Kang	AGI	Taiwan
D 359	Peyk	FF	Turkey
F 359	Vaedderen	FF	Denmark
D 360	Gelibolu	FF	Turkey
F 360	Hvidbjørnen	FF	Denmark
361	Fatahillah	FFG	Indonesia
D 361	Gemlik	FF	Turkey
362	Malahayati	FFG	Indonesia
363	Nala	FFG	Indonesia
364	Hajar Dewantara	FFG	Indonesia
A 364	Whitehead	AG	UK
A 367	Newton	AG	UK
M 371	Ohue	MH/MSC	Nigeria
M 372	Maraba	MH/MSC	Nigeria
A 373	Hermis	AGI	Greece
A 377	Arethousa	AOS	Greece
A 378	Kinterbury	AG	UK
A 382	Arrochar	AG	UK
A 385	Fort Grange	AEFS	UK
A 386	Fort Austin	AEFS	UK
Y 386	Agdlek	PV	Denmark
A 387	Fort Victoria	AOR	UK
Y 387	Agpa	PV	Denmark
A 388	Fort George	AOR	UK
Y 388	Tulugaq	PV	Denmark
401	Admiral Branimir Ormanov	AGS	Bulgaria
L 401	Ertuğrul	LST	Turkey
M 401	São Roque	PV	Portugal
P 401	Cassiopea	PV	Italy
ASR 402	Fushimi	ARS	Japan
L 402	Serdar	LST	Turkey
M 402	Ribeira Grande	PV	Portugal
P 402	Libra	PV	Italy
P 403	Spica	PV	Italy
P 404	Vega	PV	Italy
405	Ad Dakhla	AFS	Morocco
AS 405	Chiyoda	AS	Japan
406	El Aigh	AFS	Morocco
407	Arrafiq	AP	Morocco
412	Assad Al Bihar	FFLG	Libya
MSC 412	Addriyah	MH/MSC	Saudi Arabia
413	Assad El Tougour	FFLG	Libya
414	Assad Al Khali	FFLG	Libya
A 414	Ariadni	AOS	Greece
MSC 414	Al Quysumah	MH/MSC	Saudi Arabia
415	Assad Al Hudud	FFLG	Libya
A 415	Evros	AG	Greece
416	Tariq Ibn Ziyad	FFLG	Libya
A 416	Ouranos	AO	Greece
MSC 416	Al Wadeeah	MH/MSC	Saudi Arabia
417	Ean Al Gazala	FFLG	Libya
A 417	Hyperion	AO	Greece
418	Ean Zara	FFLG	Libya
MSC 418	Safwa	MH/MSC	Saudi Arabia
420	Al Jawf	MSC	Saudi Arabia
421	Bandar Abbas	AFS	Iran
AOE 421	Sagami	AOE	Japan
F 421	Canterbury	FFG	New Zealand
422	Booshehr	AFS	Iran
422	Shaqra	MSC	Saudi Arabia
AOE 422	Towada	AOE	Japan
423	Yung Chou	MSC	Taiwan
AOE 423	Tokiwa	AOE	Japan
424	Al Kharj	MSC	Saudi Arabia
AOE 424	Hamana	AOE	Japan
426	Al Zahraa	AP	Iraq
MSO 427	Constant	MSO	USA
428	Khawla	AP	Iraq
429	Balqees	AP	Iraq
431	Kharg	AFS	Iran
432	Yung Ching	MSC	Taiwan
434	Gornik	FFLG	Poland
435	Hutnik	FFLG	Poland
436	Metalowiecz	FFLG	Poland
437	Rolnik	FFLG	Poland
MSO 439	Excel	MSO	USA
MSO 440	Exploit	MSO	USA
441	Chah Bahar	AR	Iran
441	Yung Cheng	MSC	Taiwan
441	Sonya class	MSC	Yemen
MSO 446	Fortify	MSO	USA
449	Yung An	MSC	Taiwan
F 450	Elli	FFG	Greece

Number	Ship's name	Type	Country
F 451	Mella	FF	Dominican Republic
F 451	Limnos	FFG	Greece
F 452	Hydra	FFG	Greece
BM 454	Prestol	FFL	Dominican Republic
455	Chao Phraya	FFG	Thailand
BM 455	Tortuguero	FFL	Dominican Republic
MSO 455	Implicit	MSO	USA
456	Bangpakong	FFG	Thailand
457	Yung Ju	MSC	Taiwan
457	Kraburi	FFG	Thailand
458	Saiburi	FFG	Thailand
462	Yung Sui	MSC	Taiwan
MST 462	Hayase	AG	Japan
A 464	Axios	AFS	Greece
469	Yung Lo	MSC	Taiwan
F 471	Antonio Enes	FF	Portugal
472	Kalaat Beni Hammad	LSL	Algeria
473	Kalaat Beni Rached	LSL	Algeria
F 475	João Coutinho	FF	Portugal
476	Yung Shan	MSC	Taiwan
F 476	Jacinto Candido	FF	Portugal
F 477	General Pereira d'Eça	FF	Portugal
A 478	Naftilos	AGS	Greece
479	Yung Nien	MSC	Taiwan
A 480	Resource	AEFS	UK
F 480	Comandante João Belo	FF	Portugal
F 481	Comandante Hermenegildo Capelo	FF	Portugal
482	Yung Fu	MSC	Taiwan
ARC 482	Muroto	AG	Japan
F 482	Comandante Roberto Ivens	FF	Portugal
F 483	Comandante Sacadura Cabral	FF	Portugal
F 484	Augusto de Castilho	FF	Portugal
485	Yung Jen	MSC	Taiwan
F 485	Honorio Barreto	FF	Portugal
A 486	Regent	AEFS	UK
F 486	Baptista de Andrade	FF	Portugal
F 487	João Roby	FF	Portugal
488	Yung Hsin	MSC	Taiwan
F 488	Afonso Cerqueira	FF	Portugal
MSO 488	Conquest	MSO	USA
A 489	Orion	AO	Greece
F 489	Oliveira E Carmo	FF	Portugal
MSO 489	Gallant	MSO	USA
A 490	Zeus	AO	Greece
MSO 492	Pledge	MSO	USA
P 495	Bambu	PV	Italy
P 496	Mango	PV	Italy
497	Yung Chi	MSC	Taiwan
P 497	Mogano	PV	Italy
498	Lana	AGS	Nigeria
P 500	Palma	PV	Italy
501	Nawarat	FFL	Burma
501	Xiaguan	FF	China
501	Gharbiya	MSO	Egypt
501	Teluk Langsa	LST	Indonesia
501	Lahav class	FFLG	Israel
501	Lieutenant Colonel Errhamani	FFG	Morocco
LT 501	Laguna	LST	Philippines
502	Nagakyay	FFL	Burma
502	Nanchong	FF	China
502	Teluk Bajur	LST	Indonesia
502	Lahav class	FFLG	Israel
AOTL 502	Dundurn	AOF(S)	Canada
HQ 502	Qui Nonh	LST	Vietnam
LT 502	Samar Oriental	LST	Philippines
503	Kaiyuan	FF	China
503	Teluk Amboina	LST	Indonesia
503	Lahav class	FFLG	Israel
HQ 503	Vung Tau	LST	Vietnam
504	Dongchuan	FF	China
504	Teluk Kau	LST	Indonesia
504	Hittin	MSO	Syria
LT 504	Lanao del Norte	LST	Philippines
505	Kunming	FFG	China
HQ 505	Da Nang	LST	Vietnam
506	Chengdu	FFG	China
J 506	Yongxingdao	AS	China
507	Pingxiang	FFG	China
507	Daqahliya	MSO	Egypt
507	Ibn Marjid	FF	Iraq
LT 507	Benguet	LST	Philippines
M 507	Seymen	MSC	Turkey
508	Xichang	FFG	China
508	Teluk Tomini	LST	Indonesia
AOR 508	Provider	AOR	Canada
M 508	Selçuk	MSC	Turkey
509	Chang De	FFG	China
509	Teluk Ratai	LST	Indonesia
AOR 509	Protecteur	AOR	Canada

The Experienced Builder of Naval Ships

The leading world shipbuilder, **Hyundai,** is also an experienced builder of naval ships that require specialized technology and expertise.

Our Special & Naval Shipbuilding Division is strategically poised to meet your needs for advanced naval defense. We have the technology and expertise to design and build a variety of naval ships including frigates, corvettes, fast strike boats, landing ships, logistic support vessels and other specialized naval support forces.

We know what advanced navies in the world require to reinforce defense system. **Hyundai** always aims to take initiative in complying with those requirements with Top Quality and Cost Efficiency.

HDF-2000 FRIGATE

HDC 1000 CORVETTE

HDA-8000 A.O.E

HDP-250 PATROL BOAT

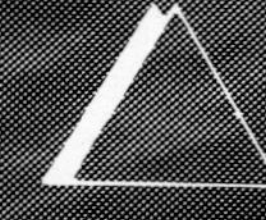

HYUNDAI

HEAVY INDUSTRIES CO., LTD.

Special & Naval Shipbuilding Division

1, Cheonha-dong, Ulsan, Korea Telex: K52220 Tel: Ulsan 32-1306-8 Seoul 741-1142 **Fax: (522) 32-4007**

Number	Ship's name	Type	Country
M 509	Seyhan	MSC	Turkey
510	Shaoxing	FFG	China
510	Teluk Saleh	LST	Indonesia
AOR 510	Preserver	AOR	Canada
LT 510	Samar del Norte	LST	Philippines
M 510	Samsun	MSC	Turkey
511	Nantong	FFG	China
511	Teluk Bone	LST	Indonesia
511	Hengam	LSL	Iran
A 511	Elbe	AG	Germany
M 511	Sinop	MSC	Turkey
MSO 511	Affray	MSO	USA
512	Wuxi	FFG	China
512	Teluk Semangka	LST	Indonesia
512	Larak	LSL	Iran
A 512	Mosel	AG	Germany
AOG 512	Wan Shou	AOS	Taiwan
LT 512	Tawi-Tawi	LST	Philippines
M 512	Surmene	MSC	Turkey
513	Huayin	FFG	China
513	Sinai	MSO	Egypt
513	Teluk Penju	LST	Indonesia
513	Tonb	LSL	Iran
A 513	Shahjalal	PV	Bangladesh
A 513	Rhein	AG	Germany
M 513	Seddulbahir	MSC	Turkey
514	Zhenjiang	FFG	China
514	Lavan	LSL	Iran
514	Teluk Mandar	LST	Indonesia
514	Chang Pei	AOS	Taiwan
A 514	Werra	AG	Germany
M 514	Silifke	MSC	Turkey
515	Xiamen	FFG	China
515	Teluk Sampit	LST	Indonesia
515	Lung Chuan	AOS	Taiwan
A 515	Khan Jahan Ali	AOS	Bangladesh
A 515	Main	AG	Germany
M 515	Saros	MSC	Turkey
516	Jiujiang	FFG	China
516	Assiout	MSO	Egypt
516	Teluk Banten	LST	Indonesia
516	Hsin Lung	AOS	Taiwan
A 516	Donau	AG	Germany
AE 516	Apayao	LST	Philippines
M 516	Sigacik	MSC	Turkey
517	Nanping	FFG	China
517	Teluk Ende	LST	Indonesia
AR 517	Yakal	AR	Philippines
M 517	Sapanca	MSC	Turkey
518	Jian	FFG	China
518	Yun Tai	AP	Taiwan
M 518	Sariyer	MSC	Turkey
519	Changzhi	FFG	China
520	Jianghu class	FFG	China
A 520	Sagres	ATS	Portugal
AP 520	Tai Wu	AP	Taiwan
M 520	Karamürsel	MSC	Turkey
521	Yu Tai	AR	Taiwan
M 521	Kerempe	MSC	Turkey
522	Tai Hu	AP	Taiwan
M 522	T 43 class	MSO	Algeria
M 522	Kilimli	MSC	Turkey
523	Yuen Feng	AP	Taiwan
M 523	Kozlu	MSC	Turkey
524	Yuen Feng class	YP	Taiwan
M 524	Kuşadasi	MSC	Turkey
525	Wu Kang	AP	Taiwan
M 525	Kemer	MSC	Turkey
526	Wu Kang class	AP	Taiwan
527	Wu Kang class	AP	Taiwan
A 527	Almeida Carvalho	AGS	Portugal
528	Wu Kang class	AP	Taiwan
529	Haikou	FF	China
529	Wu Kang class	AP	Taiwan
530	Aswan	MSO	Egypt
530	Wu Yi	AFS	Taiwan
A 530	Horten	AG	Norway
P 530	Trabzon	MSC/PV	Turkey
P 531	Terme	MSC/PV	Turkey
532	Yingtan	FFG	China
532	Sonya class	MSO	Syria
P 532	Tirebolu	MSC/PV	Turkey
533	Ningbo	FFG	China
533	Giza	MSO	Egypt
N 533	Norge	AG	Norway
534	Jinhua	FFG	China
535	Huangshi	FFG	China
536	Wu Hu	FFG	China
536	Qena	MSO	Egypt
537	Jianghu class	FFG	China
539	Jiangwei class	FFG	China
539	Sohag	MSO	Egypt

Number	Ship's name	Type	Country
540	Jiangwei class	FFG	China
A 540	Dannebrog	AG	Denmark
F 540	Pietro de Cristofaro	FFL	Italy
F 541	Umberto Grosso	FFL	Italy
543	Dandong	FFG	China
544	Siping	FFG	China
F 544	Alcione	FFL	Italy
545	Jianghu class	FFG	China
F 545	Airone	FFL	Italy
F 546	Licio Visintini	FFL	Italy
C 550	Vittorio Veneto	CGH	Italy
D 550	Ardito	DDG	Italy
F 550	Salvatore Todaro	FFL	Italy
P 550	Flyvefisken	PV	Denmark
551	Maoming	FFG	China
C 551	Giuseppe Garibaldi	CVL	Italy
D 551	Audace	DDG	Italy
F 551	Minerva	FFLG	Italy
MSC 551	Kum San	MSC	Korea, Republic
P 551	Hajen	PV	Denmark
PBR 551	Mornar	FFL	Yugoslavia
552	Yibin	FFG	China
F 552	Urania	FFLG	Italy
MSC 552	Ko Hung	MSC	Korea, Republic
P 552	Havkatten	PV	Denmark
PBR 552	Borac	FFL	Yugoslavia
553	Shaoguan	FFG	China
C 553	Andrea Doria	CGH	Italy
F 553	Danaide	FFLG	Italy
MSC 553	Kum Kok	MSC	Korea, Republic
P 553	Laxen	PV	Denmark
554	Anshun	FFG	China
F 554	Sfinge	FFLG	Italy
P 554	Makrelen	PV	Denmark
555	Jianghu class	FFG	China
F 555	Driade	FFLG	Italy
MSC 555	Nam Yang	MSC	Korea, Republic
P 555	Støren	PV	Denmark
556	Xiangtan	FFG	China
F 556	Chimera	FFLG	Italy
MSC 556	Ha Dong	MSC	Korea, Republic
P 556	Svaerdfisken	PV	Denmark
557	Jianghu class	FFG	China
F 557	Fenice	FFLG	Italy
MSC 557	Sam Kok	MSC	Korea, Republic
P 557	Glenten	PV	Denmark
F 558	Sibilla	FFLG	Italy
MSC 558	Yong Dong	MSC	Korea, Republic
P 558	Gribben	PV	Denmark
MSC 559	Ok Cheon	MSC	Korea, Republic
P 559	Lommen	PV	Denmark
D 560	Animoso	DDG	Italy
P 560	Raunen	PV	Denmark
561	Multatuli	AS	Indonesia
D 561	Ardimentoso	DDG	Italy
P 561	Skaden	PV	Denmark
P 562	Viben	PV	Denmark
AGS 563	Chiu Lien	AGS	Taiwan
F 564	Lupo	FFG	Italy
F 565	Sagittario	FFG	Italy
F 566	Perseo	FFG	Italy
F 567	Orsa	FFG	Italy
A 568	Rimfaxe	AOS	Denmark
A 569	Skinfaxe	AOS	Denmark
A 570	Taşkizak	AOS	Turkey
F 570	Maestrale	FFG	Italy
A 571	Yüzbaşi Tolunay	AOS	Turkey
F 571	Grecale	FFG	Italy
A 572	Albay Hakki Burak	AOS	Turkey
F 572	Libeccio	FFG	Italy
A 573	Binbaşi Saadettin Gürçan	AOS	Turkey
F 573	Scirocco	FFG	Italy
F 574	Aliseo	FFG	Italy
M 574	Grønsund	MSC	Denmark
A 575	Inebolu	AOS	Turkey
F 575	Euro	FFG	Italy
M 575	Guldborgsund	MSC	Denmark
X 575	Taicang	AOR	China
A 576	Derya	AD	Turkey
F 576	Espero	FFG	Italy
A 577	Sokullu Mehmet Paşa	ATS	Turkey
F 577	Zeffiro	FFG	Italy
M 578	Vilsund	MSC	Denmark
A 579	Cezayirli Gazi Hasan Pasa	ATS	Turkey
A 580	Akar	AOR	Turkey
F 580	Alpino	FF	Italy
A 581	Onaran	AR	Turkey
F 581	Carabiniere	FF	Italy
A 582	Başaran	AR	Turkey
A 584	Kurtaran	ARS	Turkey
A 585	Akin	ARS	Turkey
A 586	Ülkü	AS	Turkey

Number	Ship's name	Type	Country
A 588	Umur Bey	AS	Turkey
A 589	Işin	ARS	Turkey
A 590	Yunus	AGS	Turkey
A 601	Monge	AGOR	France
A 601	Tekirdag	MSC/AG	Turkey
P 601	Jayesagara	PV	Sri Lanka
D 602	Suffren	DDG	France
P 602	Sagarawardene	PV	Sri Lanka
D 603	Duquesne	DDG	France
A 607	Meuse	AOR	France
A 608	Var	AOR	France
D 609	Aconit	DDG	France
A 610	Ile d'Oléron	AG	France
D 610	Tourville	DDG	France
M 610	Ouistreham	MSO	France
D 611	Duguay-Trouin	DDG	France
612	Badr	FFLG	Saudi Arabia
D 612	De Grasse	DDG	France
M 612	Alençon	MSO	France
614	Al Yarmook	FFLG	Saudi Arabia
D 614	Cassard	DDG	France
A 615	Loire	AG	France
D 615	Jean Bart	DDG	France
X 615	Dongyun	AOR	China
616	Hitteen	FFLG	Saudi Arabia
616	Kormoran	MSO	Poland
A 617	Garonne	AG	France
618	Albatros	MSO	Poland
618	Tabuk	FFLG	Saudi Arabia
A 618	Rance	AG	France
619	Pelikan	MSO	Poland
620	Tukan	MSO	Poland
A 620	Jules Verne	AR	France
621	Flamingo	MSO	Poland
A 621	Rhin	AG	France
622	Rybitwa	MSO	Poland
A 622	Rhône	AG	France
623	Mewa	MSO	Poland
M 623	Baccarat	MSO	France
624	Czajka	MSO	Poland
625	Leniwka class	MSC	Poland
A 625	Papenoo	AOS	France
626	Leniwka class	MSC	Poland
A 629	Durance	AOR	France
630	Goplo	MSC	Poland
A 630	Marne	AOR	France
631	Gardno	MSC	Poland
A 631	Somme	AOR	France
632	Bukowo	MSC	Poland
A 632	Punaruu	AOS	France
633	Dabie class	MSC	Poland
634	Jamno	MSC	Poland
634	Natya class	MSO	Yemen
635	Mielno	MSC	Poland
636	Wicko	MSC	Poland
637	Resko	MSC	Poland
638	Sarbsko	MSC	Poland
639	Necko	MSC	Poland
640	Naklo	MSC	Poland
D 640	Georges Leygues	DDG	France
641	Druzno	MSC	Poland
641	Natya class	MSO	Yemen
D 641	Dupleix	DDG	France
M 641	Éridan	MH	France
642	Hancza	MSC	Poland
642	Natya class	PV	Syria
D 642	Montcalm	DDG	France
M 642	Cassiopée	MH	France
D 643	Jean de Vienne	DDG	France
M 643	Andromède	MH	France
A 644	Berry	AGOR	France
D 644	Primauguet	DDG	France
M 644	Pégase	MH	France
MSC 644	Oumi	MH/MSC	Japan
D 645	La Motte-Picquet	DDG	France
M 645	Orion	MH	France
MSC 645	Fukue	MH/MSC	Japan
A 646	Triton	AS	France
D 646	Latouche-Treville	DDG	France
M 646	Croix du Sud	MH	France
MSC 646	Okitsu	MH/MSC	Japan
M 647	Aigle	MH	France
MSC 647	Hashira	MH/MSC	Japan
M 648	Lyre	MH	France
MSC 648	Iwai	MH/MSC	Japan
M 649	Persée	MH	France
MSC 649	Hatsushima	MH/MSC	Japan
MSC 650	Ninoshima	MH/MSC	Japan
651	Singa	PV	Indonesia
MSC 651	Miyajima	MH/MSC	Japan
MSC 652	Enoshima	MH/MSC	Japan
653	Ajak	PV	Indonesia

Number	Ship's name	Type	Country
MSC 653	Ukishima	MH/MSC	Japan
MSC 654	Ooshima	MH/MSC	Japan
MSC 655	Niijima	MH/MSC	Japan
MSC 656	Yakushima	MH/MSC	Japan
MSC 657	Narushima	MH/MSC	Japan
MSC 658	Chichijima	MH/MSC	Japan
MSC 659	Torishima	MH/MSC	Japan
M 660	Narvik	MH/MSC	France
MSC 660	Hahajima	MH/MSC	Japan
MSC 661	Takashima	MH/MSC	Japan
MSC 662	Nuwajima	MH/MSC	Japan
MSC 663	Etajima	MH/MSC	Japan
MSC 664	Kamishima	MH/MSC	Japan
MSC 665	Himeshima	MH/MSC	Japan
MSC 666	Ogishima	MH/MSC	Japan
MSC 667	Moroshima	MH/MSC	Japan
MSC 668	Yurishima	MH/MSC	Japan
MSC 669	Hikoshima	MH/MSC	Japan
MSC 670	Awashima	MH/MSC	Japan
LST 671	Un Bong	LST	Korea, Republic
MSC 671	Sakushima	MH/MSC	Japan
MSC 672	Uwajima	MH/MSC	Japan
LST 673	Bi Bong	LST	Korea, Republic
MSC 673	Ieshima	MH/MSC	Japan
MSC 674	Hatsushima class	MH/MSC	Japan
LST 675	Kae Bong	LST	Korea, Republic
LST 676	Wee Bong	LST	Korea, Republic
LST 677	Su Yong	LST	Korea, Republic
LST 678	Buk Han	LST	Korea, Republic
LST 679	Hwa San	LST	Korea, Republic
P 681	Albatros	PV	France
P 682	L'Audacieuse	PV	France
P 683	La Boudeuse	PV	France
P 684	La Capricieuse	PV	France
P 685	La Fougueuse	PV	France
P 686	La Glorieuse	PV	France
P 687	La Gracieuse	PV	France
P 688	La Moqueuse	PV	France
P 689	La Railleuse	PV	France
P 690	La Rieuse	PV	France
P 691	La Tapageuse	PV	France
701	Pulau Rani	MSO	Indonesia
702	Pulau Ratewo	MSO	Indonesia
702	Madina	FFG	Saudi Arabia
704	Hofouf	FFG	Saudi Arabia
706	Abha	FFG	Saudi Arabia
708	Taif	FFG	Saudi Arabia
F 710	La Fayette	FFLG	France
711	Pulau Rengat	MH/MSC	Indonesia
711	Zeltin	AR	Libya
712	Pulau Rupat	MH/MSC	Indonesia
M 712	Cybèle	MH	France
M 713	Calliope	MH	France
M 714	Clio	MH	France
P 714	Abheetha	AG	Sri Lanka
M 715	Circé	MH	France
P 715	Edithara	AG	Sri Lanka
M 716	Cérès	MH	France
P 716	Wickrama	AG	Sri Lanka
722	Al Munjed	ARS	Libya
725	Sariwon class	PV	Korea, Democratic People's Republic
726	Sariwon class	PV	Korea, Democratic People's Republic
F 726	Commandant Bory	FFG	France
727	Sariwon class	PV	Korea, Democratic People's Republic
F 729	Balny	FF	France
F 730	Floreal	FFLG	France
F 731	Prairial	FFLG	France
F 732	Nivose	FFLG	France
A 733	Commandant Rivière	AG	France
F 733	Ventose	FFLG	France
F 734	Vendémiaire	FFG	France
F 749	Enseigne de Vaisseau Henry	FFG	France
751	Dong Hae	FFL	Korea, Republic
752	Su Won	FFL	Korea, Republic
753	Kang Reung	FFL	Korea, Republic
755	An Yang	FFL	Korea, Republic
756	Po Hang	FFLG	Korea, Republic
A 756	L'Espérance	AGS	France
757	Kun San	FFLG	Korea, Republic
A 757	D'Entrecasteaux	AGS	France
758	Kyong Ju	FFLG	Korea, Republic
759	Mok Po	FFLG	Korea, Republic
761	Kim Chon	FFLG	Korea, Republic
762	Chung Ju	FFLG	Korea, Republic
763	Jin Ju	FFLG	Korea, Republic
765	Yo Su	FFLG	Korea, Republic
766	An Dong	FFLG	Korea, Republic
767	Sun Chon	FFLG	Korea, Republic
768	Yee Ree	FFLG	Korea, Republic

Number	Ship's name	Type	Country
769	Won Ju	FFLG	Korea, Republic
771	Je Chon	FFLG	Korea, Republic
772	Chon An	FFLG	Korea, Republic
773	Song Nam	FFLG	Korea, Republic
775	Bu Chon	FFLG	Korea, Republic
775	Kadisia	MSC	Syria
776	Dae Chon	FFLG	Korea, Republic
776	Yarmuk	MSC	Syria
777	Jin Hae	FFLG	Korea, Republic
TP 777	Ang Pangulo	AG	Philippines
778	Sok Cho	FFLG	Korea, Republic
779	Yong Ju	FFLG	Korea, Republic
781	Nam Won	FFLG	Korea, Republic
F 781	D'Estienne d'Orves	FFG	France
782	Kwan Myong	FFLG	Korea, Republic
F 782	Amyot d'Inville	FFG	France
F 783	Drogou	FFG	France
F 784	Détroyat	FFG	France
F 785	Jean Moulin	FFG	France
F 786	Quartier Maître Anquetil	FFG	France
F 787	Commandant De Pimodan	FFG	France
F 788	Second Maître Le Bihan	FFG	France
F 789	Lieutenant de Vaisseau Le Hénaff	FFG	France
F 790	Lieutenant de Vaisseau Lavallée	FFG	France
A 791	Lapérouse	AGS	France
F 791	Commandant l'Herminier	FFG	France
A 792	Borda	AGS	France
F 792	Premier Maître L'Her	FFG	France
A 793	Laplace	AGS	France
F 793	Commandant Blaison	FFG	France
F 794	Enseigne de Vaisseau Jacoubet	FFG	France
A 795	Arago	AGS	France
F 795	Commandant Ducuing	FFG	France
F 796	Commandant Birot	FFG	France
F 797	Commandant Bouan	FFG	France
801	Rais Hamidou	FFLG	Algeria
801	Thu Tay Thi	AGS	Burma
801	Pandbong	PV	Indonesia
F 801	Tromp	FFG	Netherlands
802	Salah Rais	FFLG	Algeria
802	Sura	PV	Indonesia
M 802	Hoogezand	MSC	Netherlands
803	Rais Ali	FFLG	Algeria
F 806	De Ruyter	FFG	Netherlands
F 807	Kortenaer	FFG	Netherlands
F 808	Callenburgh	FFG	Netherlands
F 809	Van Kinsbergen	FFG	Netherlands
M 809	Naaldwijk	MSC	Netherlands
F 810	Banckert	FFG	Netherlands
M 810	Abcoude	MSC	Netherlands
811	Kakap	PV	Indonesia
F 811	Piet Heyn	FFG	Netherlands
812	Kerapu	PV	Indonesia
F 812	Jacob van Heemskerck	FFG	Netherlands
M 812	Drachten	MSC	Netherlands
813	Tongkol	PV	Indonesia
F 813	Witte de With	FFG	Netherlands
M 813	Ommen	MSC	Netherlands
814	Bervang	PV	Indonesia
815	Tien Shan	FF	Taiwan
M 815	Giethoorn	MSC	Netherlands
F 816	Abraham Crijnssen	FFG	Netherlands
M 817	Venlo	MSC	Netherlands
821	Lublin	LST	Poland
822	Gniezno	LST	Poland
823	Krakow	LST	Poland
F 823	Philips van Almonde	FFG	Netherlands
M 823	Naarden	MSC	Netherlands
824	Poznan	LST	Poland
F 824	Bloys van Treslong	FFG	Netherlands
825	Torun	LST	Poland
F 825	Jan van Brakel	FFG	Netherlands
F 826	Pieter Florisz	FFG	Netherlands
827	Pansio	ML	Finland
827	Tai Yuan	FF	Taiwan
F 827	Karel Doorman	FFG	Netherlands
M 827	Hoogeveen	MSC	Netherlands
828	Pansio class	ML	Finland
829	Pansio class	ML	Finland
F 829	Willem van der Zaan	FFG	Netherlands
F 830	Tjerk Hiddes	FFG	Netherlands
M 830	Sittard	MSC	Netherlands
F 831	Van Amstel	FFG	Netherlands
832	Yu Shan	FF	Taiwan
A 832	Zuiderkruis	AOE	Netherlands
F 832	Abraham van der Hulst	FFG	Netherlands
833	Hua Shan	FF	Taiwan
834	Wen Shan	FF	Taiwan
835	Fu Shan	FF	Taiwan
A 835	Poolster	AOE	Netherlands
836	Lu Shan	FF	Taiwan
837	Shou Shan	FF	Taiwan
838	Tai Shan	FF	Taiwan
841	Dadie class	AGI	China
M 841	Gemert	MSC	Netherlands
V 841	Beidiao	AGI	China
843	Chung Shan	FF	Taiwan
M 850	Alkmaar	MH	Netherlands
M 851	Delfzyl	MH	Netherlands
M 852	Dordrecht	MH	Netherlands
M 853	Haarlem	MH	Netherlands
M 854	Harlingen	MH	Netherlands
M 855	Scheveningen	MH	Netherlands
M 856	Maasluis	MH	Netherlands
V 856	Xing Fengshan	AGI	China
M 857	Makkum	MH	Netherlands
M 858	Middelburg	MH	Netherlands
M 859	Hellevoetsluis	MH	Netherlands
M 860	Schiedam	MH	Netherlands
M 861	Urk	MH	Netherlands
M 862	Zierikzee	MH	Netherlands
M 863	Vlaardingen	MH	Netherlands
M 864	Willemstad	MH	Netherlands
867	Ping Jin	FFL	Taiwan
884	Wu Sheng	FFL	Taiwan
U 891	Dagushan	AR	China
896	Chu Yung	FFL	Taiwan
A 900	Mercuur	AS	Netherlands
901	Murat Rais	FFG	Algeria
902	Rais Kellich	FFG	Algeria
902	Boraida	AOR	Saudi Arabia
902	Heng Yang	DDG	Taiwan
M 902	J E Van Haverbeke	MSO	Belgium
903	Rais Korfou	FFG	Algeria
903	Hua Yang	DDG	Taiwan
M 903	A F Dufour	MSO	Belgium
904	Yunbou	AOR	Saudi Arabia
M 904	De Brouwer	MSO	Belgium
905	Yuen Yang	DDG	Taiwan
906	Huei Yang	DDG	Taiwan
A 906	Tydeman	AGS	Netherlands
M 906	Breydel	MSO	Belgium
907	Fu Yang	DDG	Taiwan
908	Kwei Yang	DDG	Taiwan
M 908	G Truffaut	MSO	Belgium
909	Chiang Yang	DDG	Taiwan
M 909	F Bovesse	MSO	Belgium
F 910	Wielingen	FFG	Belgium
911	Sorong	AOR	Indonesia
911	Dang Yang	DDG	Taiwan
F 911	Westdiep	FFG	Belgium
912	Chien Yang	DDG	Taiwan
F 912	Wandelaar	FFG	Belgium
F 913	Westhinder	FFG	Belgium
914	Lo Yang	DDG	Taiwan
915	Han Yang	DDG	Taiwan
DD 915	Chung Buk	DDG	Korea, Republic
M 915	Aster	MH	Belgium
DD 916	Jeon Buk	DDG	Korea, Republic
M 916	Bellis	MH	Belgium
917	Nan Yang	DDG	Taiwan
DD 917	Dae Gu	DD	Korea, Republic
M 917	Crocus	MH	Belgium
918	An Yang	DDG	Taiwan
DD 918	Inchon	DD	Korea, Republic
M 918	Dianthus	MH	Belgium
919	Kun Yang	DDG	Taiwan
DD 919	Taejon	DDG	Korea, Republic
M 919	Fuchsia	MH	Belgium
920	Dazhi	AS	China
920	Lai Yang	DDG	Taiwan
M 920	Iris	MH	Belgium
921	El Fateh	DD	Egypt
921	Jaya Wijaya	AR	Indonesia
921	Liao Yang	DDG	Taiwan
DD 921	Kwang Ju	DDG	Korea, Republic
M 921	Lobelia	MH	Belgium
DD 922	Kang Won	DDG	Korea, Republic
M 922	Myosotis	MH	Belgium
923	Chen Yang	DDG	Taiwan
DD 923	Kyong Ki	DDG	Korea, Republic
M 923	Narcis	MH	Belgium
924	Kai Yang	DDG	Taiwan
M 924	Primula	MH	Belgium
925	Te Yang	DDG	Taiwan
DD 925	Jeon Ju	DDG	Korea, Republic
926	Shao Yang	DDG	Taiwan
927	Yun Yang	DDG	Taiwan
928	Shen Yang	DDG	Taiwan
929	Chao Yang	DDG	Taiwan
930	Lao Yang	DDG	Taiwan

Trendsetting Technology.
RENK TACKE Marine Gears.

Codad-type gears for corvettes.

In frigates, corvettes, fast vessels and other navy craft, RENK TACKE marine gears are successfully in action.

Navy vessels where top technology is called for have been equipped with RENK TACKE marine gears for years.
One of the specific properties of these gear units is the low noise development. This is the prerequisite for the successful fight against submarines.
RENK TACKE Codog-type gear units, particularly those of locked train design, are known for their low noise values.
RENK TACKE navy gears are high-technology special designs which consider the application profile of any vessel.

RENK TACKE supply complete gear systems.

Locked train gear units for modern NATO frigates.

RT 2.002 e1f

RENK TACKE GmbH · P.O. Box · D-8900 Augsburg · Telephone 0821/5700-0 · Telex 53781
Telefax 0821/5700-460

Number	Ship's name	Type	Country
931	Burujulasad	AGS	Indonesia
932	Dewa Kembar	AGS	Indonesia
933	Jalanidhi	AGOR	Indonesia
F 941	Abu Qir	FFG	Egypt
F 946	El Suez	FFG	Egypt
951	Najim al Zaffer	FFG	Egypt
951	Talaud	CSL	Indonesia
FF 951	Ulsan	FFG	Korea, Republic
MMC 951	Souya	ML	Japan
952	Nusa Telu	CSL	Indonesia
FF 952	Seoul	FFG	Korea, Republic
953	Natuna	CSL	Indonesia
FF 953	Chung Nam	FFG	Korea, Republic
FF 955	Masan	FFG	Korea, Republic
956	El Nasser	FFG	Egypt
956	Teluk Mentawai	CSL	Indonesia
FF 956	Kyong Buk	FFG	Korea, Republic
957	Karimundsa	CSL	Indonesia
FF 957	Chon Nam	FFG	Korea, Republic
FF 958	Che Ju	FFG	Korea, Republic
960	Karimata	CSL	Indonesia
A 960	Godetia	AG	Belgium
A 961	Zinnia	AG	Belgium
A 962	Belgica	AGOR	Belgium
DD 963	Spruance	DDG	USA
DD 964	Paul F Foster	DDG	USA
DD 965	Kinkaid	DDG	USA
DD 966	Hewitt	DDG	USA
DD 967	Elliott	DDG	USA
DD 968	Arthur W Radford	DDG	USA
DD 969	Peterson	DDG	USA
DD 970	Caron	DDG	USA
971	Tangung Pandan	AP	Indonesia
971	Tarantul class	FFLG	Yemen
DD 971	David R Ray	DDG	USA
972	Tanjung Oisina	AP	Indonesia
DD 972	Oldendorf	DDG	USA
DD 973	John Young	DDG	USA
DD 974	Comte de Grasse	DDG	USA
DD 975	O'Brien	DDG	USA
976	Taruntul class	FFLG	Yemen
DD 976	Merrill	DDG	USA
DD 977	Briscoe	DDG	USA
DD 978	Stump	DDG	USA
DD 979	Conolly	DDG	USA
DD 980	Moosbrugger	DDG	USA
DD 981	John Hancock	DDG	USA
DD 982	Nicholson	DDG	USA
DD 983	John Rodgers	DDG	USA
DD 984	Leftwich	DDG	USA
DD 985	Cushing	DDG	USA
DD 986	Harry W Hill	DDG	USA
DD 987	O'Bannon	DDG	USA
DD 988	Thorn	DDG	USA
DD 989	Deyo	DDG	USA
DD 990	Ingersoll	DDG	USA
DD 991	Fife	DDG	USA
DD 992	Fletcher	DDG	USA
DDG 993	Kidd	DDG	USA
DDG 994	Callaghan	DDG	USA
DDG 995	Scott	DDG	USA
DDG 996	Chandler	DDG	USA
DD 997	Hayler	DDG	USA
FF 1056	Connole	FF	USA
M 1059	Spica	MSC	Germany
M 1060	Weiden	MH	Germany
M 1061	Rottweil	MH	Germany
M 1062	Schütze	MSC	Germany
FF 1063	Reasoner	FF	USA
FF 1064	Lockwood	FF	USA
FF 1065	Stein	FF	USA
FF 1066	Marvin Shields	FF	USA
M 1066	Frankenthal	MH	Germany
FF 1067	Francis Hammond	FF	USA
FF 1068	Vreeland	FF	USA
FF 1070	Downes	FF	USA
M 1070	Göttingen	MH	Germany
M 1071	Koblenz	MH	Germany
M 1072	Lindau	MH	Germany
FF 1073	Robert E Peary	FF	USA
M 1073	Schleswig	MSC	Germany
FF 1074	Harold E Holt	FF	USA
M 1074	Tübingen	MH	Germany
FF 1075	Trippe	FF	USA
M 1075	Wetzlar	MH	Germany
FF 1076	Fanning	FF	USA
M 1076	Paderborn	MSC	Germany
FF 1077	Ouellet	FF	USA
M 1077	Weilheim	MH	Germany
FF 1078	Joseph Hewes	FF	USA
M 1078	Cuxhaven	MH	Germany
M 1079	Düren	MSC	Germany
FF 1079	Bowen	FF	USA
FF 1080	Paul	FF	USA
M 1080	Marburg	MH	Germany
FF 1081	Aylwin	FF	USA
M 1081	Konstanz	MSC	Germany
FF 1082	Elmer Montgomery	FF	USA
M 1082	Wolfsburg	MSC	Germany
FF 1083	Cook	FF	USA
M 1083	Ulm	MSC	Germany
FF 1084	McCandless	FF	USA
FF 1085	Donald B Beary	FF	USA
M 1085	Minden	MH	Germany
FF 1087	Kirk	FF	USA
FF 1089	Jesse L Brown	FF	USA
FF 1090	Ainsworth	FF	USA
M 1090	Pegnitz	MSC	Germany
M 1091	Kulmbach	MSC	Germany
FF 1092	Thomas C Hart	FF	USA
M 1092	Hameln	MSC	Germany
FF 1093	Capodanno	FF	USA
M 1093	Auerbach	MSC	Germany
FF 1094	Pharris	FF	USA
M 1094	Ensdorf	MSC	Germany
FF 1095	Truett	FF	USA
M 1095	Überherrn	MSC	Germany
M 1096	Passau	MSC	Germany
FF 1097	Moinester	FF	USA
M 1097	Laboe	MSC	Germany
M 1098	Siegburg	MSC	Germany
M 1099	Herten	MSC	Germany
1101	Cheng Kung	FFG	Taiwan
M 1114	Brinton	MH	UK
M 1116	Wilton	ATS	UK
M 1151	Iveston	MH	UK
M 1154	Kellington	MH	UK
M 1166	Nurton	MH	UK
LST 1179	Newport	LST	USA
LST 1180	Manitowoc	LST	USA
LST 1181	Sumter	LST	USA
M 1181	Sheraton	MH	UK
LST 1182	Fresno	LST	USA
LST 1183	Peoria	LST	USA
LST 1184	Frederick	LST	USA
LST 1185	Schenectady	LST	USA
LST 1186	Cayuga	LST	USA
LST 1187	Tuscaloosa	LST	USA
LST 1188	Saginaw	LST	USA
LST 1189	San Bernardino	LST	USA
LST 1190	Boulder	LST	USA
LST 1191	Racine	LST	USA
LST 1192	Spartanburg County	LST	USA
LST 1193	Fairfax County	LST	USA
LST 1194	La Moure County	LST	USA
LST 1196	Harlan County	LST	USA
LST 1197	Barnstable County	LST	USA
LST 1198	Bristol County	LST	USA
M 1210	Kimberley	MSC	South Africa
M 1214	Walvisbaai	MSC	South Africa
M 1215	East London	MSC	South Africa
LST 1312	Ambe	LST	Nigeria
LST 1313	Ofiom	LST	Nigeria
A 1407	Wittensee	AOS	Germany
A 1411	Lüneburg	AG	Germany
A 1413	Freiburg	AG	Germany
A 1414	Glücksburg	AG	Germany
A 1415	Saarburg	AG	Germany
A 1416	Nienburg	AG	Germany
A 1417	Offenburg	AG	Germany
A 1418	Meersburg	AG	Germany
A 1424	Walchensee	AOR	Germany
A 1425	Ammersee	AOR	Germany
1426	Tegernsee	AOR	Germany
A 1427	Westensee	AOR	Germany
A 1435	Westerwald	AG	Germany
A 1436	Odenwald	AG	Germany
A 1438	Steigerwald	AG	Germany
A 1442	Spessart	AOR	Germany
A 1443	Rhön	AOR	Germany
A 1450	Planet	AGOR	Germany
A1456	Alliance	AGOR	NATO
M 1498	Windhoek	MSC	South Africa
1501	Sri Banggi	LST	Malaysia
1502	Rajah Jarom	LST	Malaysia
1503	Sri Indera Sakti	LSL	Malaysia
1504	Mahawangsa	LSL	Malaysia
1616	Petya II class	FF	Ethiopia
1617	Petya II class	FF	Ethiopia
M 2003	Waveney	MSC	UK
M 2004	Carron	MSC	UK
M 2005	Dovey	MSC	UK
M 2006	Helford	MSC	UK
M 2007	Humber	MSC	UK

PENNANT LIST

Number	*Ship's name*	*Type*	*Country*
M 2008	Blackwater	MSC	UK
M 2009	Itchen	MSC	UK
M 2010	Helmsdale	MSC	UK
M 2011	Orwell	MSC	UK
M 2012	Ribble	MSC	UK
M 2013	Spey	MSC	UK
M 2014	Arun	MSC	UK
M 2670	Sömmerda	MSC	Germany
L 3004	Sir Bedivere	LSL	UK
L 3005	Sir Galahad	LSL	UK
L 3027	Sir Geraint	LSL	UK
L 3036	Sir Percivale	LSL	UK
TV 3501	Katori	ATS	Japan
L 3505	Sir Tristram	LSL	UK
TV 3506	Yamagumo	ATS	Japan
TV 3507	Makigumo	ATS	Japan
L 4001	Ardennes	LSL	UK
L 4003	Arakan	LSL	UK
LST 4101	Atsumi	LST	Japan
LST 4102	Motobu	LST	Japan
LST 4103	Nemuro	LST	Japan
LST 4151	Miura	LST	Japan
LST 4152	Ojika	LST	Japan
LST 4153	Satsuma	LST	Japan
ATS 4201	Azuma	ATS	Japan
ATS 4202	Kurobe	ATS	Japan
AGB 5002	Shirase	AG	Japan
AGS 5101	Akashi	AGS	Japan
AGS 5102	Futami	AGS	Japan
AGS 5103	Suma	AGS	Japan
AGS 5104	Wakasa	AGS	Japan
AOS 5201	Hibiki	AGS	Japan
AOS 5202	Harima	AGS	Japan
A 5206	São Gabriel	AOR	Portugal
A 5208	São Miguel	AFS	Portugal
A 5301	Pietro Cavezzale	AG	Italy
A 5303	Ammiraglio Magnaghi	AGS	Italy
A 5309	Anteo	ARS	Italy
A 5310	Proteo	ARS	Italy
A 5311	Palinuro	ATS	Italy
A 5312	Amerigo Vespucci	ATS	Italy
A 5327	Stromboli	AOR	Italy
A 5329	Vesuvio	AOR	Italy
M 5431	Storione	MSO	Italy
M 5433	Squalo	MSO	Italy
M 5504	Castagno	MH	Italy
M 5505	Cedro	MH	Italy
M 5509	Gelso	MH	Italy
M 5516	Platano	MH	Italy
M 5519	Mandorlo	MH	Italy
M 5550	Lerici	MH/MSC	Italy
M 5551	Sapri	MH/MSC	Italy
M 5552	Milazzo	MH/MSC	Italy
M 5553	Vieste	MH/MSC	Italy
M 5554	Gaeta	MH/MSC	Italy
M 5555	Termoli	MH/MSC	Italy
M 5556	Alghero	MH/MSC	Italy
M 5557	Numana	MH/MSC	Italy
M 5558	Crotone	MH/MSC	Italy
M 5559	Viareggio	MH/MSC	Italy
P 6053	Hermes	FFL	Germany
P 6055	Triton	FFL	Germany
P 6056	Theseus	FFL	Germany
JIP 6501	Muray	FFLG	United Arab Emirates
JIP 6502	Das	FFLG	United Arab Emirates
ASU 7010	Akizuki	AD	Japan
ASU 7012	Teruzuki	AS	Japan
ASU 7016	Kitikami	ATS	Japan
ASU 7017	Ooi	ATS	Japan
L 9011	Foudre	TCD	France
L 9021	Ouragan	TCD	France
L 9022	Orage	TCD	France
L 9030	Champlain	LST	France
L 9031	Francis Garnier	LST	France
L 9032	Dumont D'Urville	LST	France
L 9033	Jacques Cartier	LST	France
L 9034	La Grandière	LST	France
L 9077	Bougainville	TCD	France
L 9892	San Giorgio	LPD	Italy
L 9893	San Marco	LPD	Italy

Ship Reference Section

(See also Glossary)

1. Details of major warships are grouped under six separate non-printable headings. These are:-

(a) **Number and Class Name**. Totals of vessels per class are listed as 'active + building + ordered (proposed)'.

(b) **Building Programme**. This includes builders' names and key dates. In general the 'laid down' column reflects keel laying but modern shipbuilding techniques are making it increasingly difficult to be specific about the start date of actual construction. In this edition any date after March 1992 is projected or estimated and therefore liable to change.

(c) **Hull**. This section tends to have only specification and performance parameters and contains little free text. Hull related details such as **Military lift** and **Cargo capacity** may be included when appropriate. **Displacement** and **Measurement** tonnages, **Dimensions**, **Horsepower** etc are defined in the Glossary. Throughout the life of a ship its displacement tends to creep upwards as additional equipment is added and redundant fixtures and fittings are left in place. For the same reasons, ships of the same class, active in different navies, frequently have different displacements and other dissimilar characteristics. Unless otherwise stated the lengths given are overall. Sustained maximum horsepower is given where the information is available.

(d) **Weapon Systems**. This section contains operational details and some free text on weapons and sensors which are laid out in a consistent order using the same sub-headings throughout the book. The titles are:- **Missiles** (sub-divided into SLBM, SSM, SAM, A/S); **Guns** (numbers of barrels are given and the rate of fire is 'per barrel' unless stated otherwise); **Torpedoes**; **A/S Mortars**; **Depth Charges**; **Mines**; **Countermeasures**; **Combat Data Systems**; **Fire control**; **Radars**; **Sonars**. The Fire control heading is used for weapons' direction equipment. In most cases the performance specifications are those of the manufacturer and may therefore be considered to be at the top end of the spectrum of effective performance. So-called 'operational effectiveness' is difficult to define, depends upon many variables and in the context of range may be considerably less than the theoretical maximum. Numbers inserted in the text refer to similar numbers included on line drawings.

(e) **Aircraft**. Only the types and numbers are included here. Where appropriate each country has a separate section listing overall numbers and operational parameters of frontline shipborne and land-based maritime aircraft, normally included after the Frigate section. The main exception to this is that in the countries which only have Light Forces the aircraft details will be towards the end of the warship section.

(f) **General Comments**. A maximum of six sub-headings are used to sweep up the variety of additional information which is available but has no logical place in the other sections. These headings are: **Programmes**; **Modernisation**; **Structure**; **Operational**; **Sales** and **Opinion**. The last of these allows the Editor free rein for informed comment.

2. Minor or less important ship entries follow the same format except that there is often much less detail in the first four headings and all additional remarks are put together under the single heading of **Comment**. The distinction between major and minor depends upon editorial judgement and is primarily a function of firepower. The age of the ship or class and its relative importance within the Navy concerned is also taken into account.

3. The space devoted to frontline maritime aircraft reflects the importance of air power as an addition to the naval weapon systems armoury, but the format used is necessarily brief and covers only numbers, roles and operational characteristics. Greater detail can be found in *Jane's All the World's Aircraft* and the appropriate volume of the *Jane's Weapon Systems* series.

4. Other than for coastal navies, tables are included at the front of each country section with such things as strength of the Fleet, senior appointments, personnel numbers, bases etc. There is also a list of pennant numbers and a Deletions column covering the previous three years. If you can't find your favourite ship, always look in the Deletions list first.

5. No addenda is included because modern typesetting technology allows changes to the main text to be made up to a few weeks before publication.

6. Shipbuilding companies and weapons manufacturers frequently change their names by merger or takeover. As far as possible the published name shows the title when the ship was completed or weapon system installed. It is therefore historically accurate.

7. Like many descriptive terms in international naval nomenclature, differences between Coast Guards, Armed Police craft, Customs and other paramilitary maritime forces are often indistinct and particular to an individual nation. Such vessels are usually included if they have a military function.

8. Where major defence industries build a speculative or demonstrator vessel, it is usually mentioned in a **Note**. Full details are only given if the ship is commissioned into the Navy.

9. When selecting photographs for inclusion, priority is given to those that have been taken most recently.

10. The Ship Reference section is geared to the professional user who needs to be able to make an assessment of the fighting characteristics of a Navy or class of ship without having to cross refer to other Navies and sections of the book. Much effort has also been made to prevent entries spilling across from one page to another.

ALBANIA

Personnel

(a) 1992: 2000 including 400 coastal defence
(b) Ratings on 3 years' military service

Bases

Durazzo (Durresi), Valona (Vlorë), Sazan Island (Gulf of Vlorë), Sarande, Shingjin, Paşa Liman.

Operational

Having lost the support of both the Soviet Union and China, some units have to be used to provide spares for others. No modern equipment has been fitted for several years.

Pennant Numbers

Pennant numbers are changed at intervals.

Mercantile Marine

Lloyd's Register of Shipping:
24 vessels of 59 060 tons gross

DELETIONS

1988-89 3 Huchuan class, 3 PO 2 class

SUBMARINES

2 Ex-SOVIET WHISKEY CLASS

422 442

Displacement, tons: 1080 surfaced; 1350 dived
Dimensions, feet (metres): 249.3 × 21.3 × 16.1 *(76 × 6.5 × 4.9)*
Main machinery: Diesel-electric; 2 Type 37-D diesels; 4000 hp(m) *(2.94 MW)*; 2 motors; 2700 hp(m) *(1.98 MW)*; 2 shafts
Speed, knots: 18 surfaced; 14 dived; 7 snorting
Range, miles: 8500 at 10 kts surfaced
Complement: 54

Torpedoes: 6—21 in *(533 mm)* tubes (4 bow, 2 stern). 12 obsolescent Soviet Type 53; dual purpose; pattern active/passive homing up to 20 km *(10.8 nm)* at up to 45 kts; warhead 400 kg.
Mines: 24 instead of torpedoes.
Radars: Surface search: Snoop Plate; I band.
Sonars: Tamir; passive; high frequency.

Programmes: Two transferred from USSR in 1960 and two others acquired from the USSR in mid-1961.
Structure: Diving depth, 150 m *(500 ft)*.
Operational: A third submarine of the class is used as a harbour training boat and charging station. The fourth has been deleted. All are based at Sazan.

LIGHT FORCES

Note: (i) 12 P4 patrol craft still have limited operational status.
(ii) A number of small patrol boats are stationed on the lakes bordering Greece and Yugoslavia.

2 Ex-SOVIET KRONSHTADT CLASS (LARGE PATROL CRAFT)

Displacement, tons: 303 standard; 335 full load
Dimensions, feet (metres): 170.9 × 21.3 × 6.9 *(52.1 × 6.5 × 2.1)*
Main machinery: 3 Kolumna Type 9-D-8 diesels; 3300 hp(m) *(2.4 MW)*; 3 shafts
Speed, knots: 18. **Range, miles:** 1400 at 12 kts
Complement: 51 (4 officers)

Guns: 1—3.5 in *(85 mm)*/52; 85° elevation; 18 rounds/minute to 15.5 km *(8.5 nm)*; weight of shell 9.5 kg.
2—37 mm/63; 85° elevation; 160 rounds/minute to 4 km *(2.2 nm)*; weight of shell 0.7 kg.
6—12.7 mm (3 vertical twin) MGs.
A/S mortars: 2 RBU 1200 five-tubed rocket launchers; range 2 km; warhead 34 kg.
Depth charges: 2 projectors; 2 racks.
Mines: 2 rails; approx 8 mines.
Radars: Surface search: Ball Gun; E/F band; range 37 km *(20 nm)*.
Navigation: Neptun; I band.
IFF: High Pole.

Programmes: Four were transferred from the USSR in 1958. Albania sent two for A/S updating in 1960 and two others in 1961. Two subsequently deleted, and the effectiveness of the survivors is in doubt.

KRONSHTADT Class *1989*

6 Ex-CHINESE SHANGHAI II CLASS (FAST ATTACK CRAFT—GUN)

Displacement, tons: 113 standard; 131 full load
Dimensions, feet (metres): 127.3 × 17.7 × 5.6 *(38.8 × 5.4 × 1.7)*
Main machinery: 2 Type L12-180 diesels; 2400 hp(m) *(1.76 MW)* (forward)
2 Type 12-D-6 diesels; 1820 hp(m) *(1.34 MW)* (aft); 4 shafts
Speed, knots: 30. **Range, miles:** 700 at 16.5 kts
Complement: 34

Guns: 4 China 37 mm/63 (2 twin); 85° elevation; 180 rounds/minute to 8.5 km *(4.6 nm)*; weight of shell 1.42 kg.
4 USSR 25 mm/60 (2 twin); 85° elevation; 270 rounds/minute to 3 km *(1.6 nm)*; weight of shell 0.34 kg.
Depth charges: 2 projectors; 8 depth charges.
Mines: Rails can be fitted; probably only 10 mines.
Radars: Surface search/fire control: Skin Head; I band; range 37 km *(20 nm)*.
Sonars: Hull-mounted set probably fitted.

Comment: Four transferred in mid-1974 and two in 1975. Doubtful operational status.

29 Ex-CHINESE HUCHUAN CLASS (FAST ATTACK HYDROFOIL—TORPEDO)

Displacement, tons: 39 standard; 45 full load
Dimensions, feet (metres): 71.5 × 20.7 × 11.8 (hullborne) *(21.8 × 6.3 × 3.6)*
Main machinery: 3 Type M 50F-12 diesels; 2550 hp(m) *(1.9 MW)* sustained; 2 shafts
Speed, knots: 50 foilborne. **Range, miles:** 500 at 30 kts
Complement: 11

Guns: 4—14.5 mm (2 twin) MGs.
Torpedoes: 2—21 in *(533 mm)* tubes. Obsolescent Soviet Type 53.
Radars: Surface search/fire control: Skin Head; I band; range 37 km *(20 nm)*.

Programmes: Built in Shanghai and transferred as follows; six in 1968, 15 in 1969, two in 1970, seven in 1971, two in June 1974. Three deleted.
Structure: Have foils forward while the stern planes on the surface.
Operational: Not all are seaworthy. One escaped to Italy in May 1991 and was seized by the Italian authorities.

HUCHUAN Class *1983*

3 Ex-SOVIET PO 2 CLASS (COASTAL PATROL CRAFT)

Displacement, tons: 56 full load
Dimensions, feet (metres): 70.5 × 11.5 × 3.3 *(21.5 × 3.5 × 1)*
Main machinery: 1 diesel; 300 hp(m) *(220 kW)*; 1 shaft
Speed, knots: 12
Complement: 8
Guns: 1—12.7 mm MG.

Comment: At least three have survived from a total of 11 transferred 1957-60. Previous minesweeping gear has been removed and the craft are used for utility roles.

P02 Class *10/1990*

4 ARCOR 25 CLASS (HARBOUR PATROL CRAFT)

Displacement, tons: 2.1 full load
Dimensions, feet (metres): 25.3 × 9.8 × 2.6 *(7.7 × 3 × 0.8)*
Speed, knots: 35
Complement: 2
Guns: 1—7.62 mm MG.

Comment: Delivered in November 1990. Four more may be acquired in due course.

ARCOR 25 *1990 Arcor*

MINE WARFARE FORCES

2 Ex-SOVIET T 43 CLASS (MINESWEEPERS—OCEAN)

Displacement, tons: 500 standard; 580 full load
Dimensions, feet (metres): 190.2 × 27.6 × 6.9 *(58 × 8.4 × 2.1)*
Main machinery: 2 Kolumna Type 9-D-8 diesels; 2200 hp(m) *(1.6 MW)*; 2 shafts
Speed, knots: 15. **Range, miles:** 3000 at 10 kts; 2000 at 14 kts
Complement: 65

Guns: 2—37 mm/63 (twin); 85° elevation; 160 rounds/minute to 9 km *(5 nm)*; weight of shell 0.7 kg. 8—12.7 mm MGs.
Depth charges: 2 projectors.
Mines: 16.
Radars: Air/surface search: Ball End; E/F band.
Navigation: Neptun; I band.
Sonars: Hull-mounted set probably fitted.

Programmes: Transferred in 1960. Both in reserve.

4 Ex-SOVIET T 301 CLASS (MINESWEEPERS—INSHORE)

Displacement, tons: 146 standard; 160 full load
Dimensions, feet (metres): 124.7 × 16.7 × 5.2 *(38 × 5.1 × 1.6)*
Main machinery: 3—6-cyl diesels; 1440 hp(m) *(1.06 MW)*; 3 shafts
Speed, knots: 12. **Range, miles:** 2200 at 9 kts
Complement: 25
Guns: 2—37 mm/63; 160 rounds/minute to 8.5 km *(5 nm)*; weight of shell 0.7 kg. 4—12.7 mm (2 twin) MGs.
Mines: Mine rails fitted.

Comment: Transferred from the USSR—two in 1957, two in 1959 and two in 1960. Two marginally operational since 1979; two in reserve; two deleted.

T 43 Class

TANKERS

2 Ex-SOVIET KHOBI CLASS (SUPPORT TANKERS)

PATOS **SEMANI**

Displacement, tons: 700 light; 1500 full load
Measurement, tons: 1600 dwt
Dimensions, feet (metres): 206.6 × 33 × 14.8 *(63 × 10.1 × 4.5)*
Main machinery: 2 diesels; 1600 hp(m) *(1.12 MW)*; 2 shafts
Speed, knots: 13. **Range, miles:** 2500 at 12 kts
Complement: 35
Cargo capacity: 500 tons; oil fuel
Radars: Navigation: Neptun; I band.

Comment: Launched in 1956. Transferred from the USSR in September 1958 and February 1959. *Semani* is civilian manned.

1 Ex-SOVIET TOPLIVO I CLASS (YARD TANKER)

TOMB

Displacement, tons: 425 full load
Dimensions, feet (metres): 115 × 22 × 9.6 *(34.5 × 6.5 × 3)*
Main machinery: 1 diesel; 1 shaft
Speed, knots: 10. **Range, miles:** 400 at 7 kts
Complement: 16
Cargo capacity: 200 tons oil fuel

Comment: Transferred from the USSR in March 1960. Similar to Khobi class in appearance though smaller.

TOPLIVO Class *3/1991, Erik Laursen*

TUGS

2 Ex-SOVIET TUGUR CLASS

MUJOULQINAKU +1

Displacement, tons: 300 full load
Dimensions, feet (metres): 100.7 × 25.3 × 7.5 *(30.7 × 7.7 × 2.3)*
Main machinery: Boilers; 2 triple expansion reciprocating; 500 ihp(m) *(376 kW)*; 1 shaft
Speed, knots: 10

Comment: Built in Finland for the USSR in the 1950s. Two other small tugs are employed in local duties or harbour service.

TUGUR Class *7/1991, Erik Laursen*

AUXILIARIES

Note: There are reported to be a dozen or so harbour and port tenders including a Duna class floating power barge, a water carrier and a barrack ship. The Atrek class submarine tender transferred from the USSR in 1961 as a depot ship was converted into a merchant ship.

2 Ex-SOVIET SHALANDA I CLASS

SERANDE **SAZAN**

Comment: Civilian freighters transferred in early 1960s. One used as AKL and one as YF.

SHALANDA Class *3/1991, Erik Laursen*

1 Ex-SOVIET SEKSTAN CLASS (DEGAUSSING SHIP)

SHENJIN

Displacement, tons: 280 standard; 400 full load
Dimensions, feet (metres): 133.8 × 30.5 × 14.1 *(40.8 × 9.3 × 4.3)*
Main machinery: 1 diesel; 400 hp(m) *(294 kW)*; 1 shaft
Speed, knots: 11. **Range, miles:** 1000 at 11 kts
Complement: 24
Cargo capacity: 115 tons

Comment: Built in Finland in 1956. Transferred from the USSR in 1960.

1 Ex-SOVIET POLUCHAT I CLASS

SKENDERBEU

Displacement, tons: 70 standard; 100 full load
Dimensions, feet (metres): 97.1 × 19 × 4.8 *(29.6 × 5.8 × 1.5)*
Main machinery: 2 Type M 50-F-12 diesels; 1700 hp(m) *(1.25 MW)* sustained; 2 shafts
Speed, knots: 20. **Range, miles:** 1500 at 10 kts
Complement: 15
Guns: 2—14.5 mm MGs.

Comment: Used for torpedo recovery. Transferred in 1958.

1 Ex-SOVIET NYRYAT 1 CLASS (DIVING TENDER)

SQIPETARI

Displacement, tons: 120 full load
Dimensions, feet (metres): 93 × 18 × 5.5 *(28.4 × 5.5 × 1.7)*
Main machinery: Diesel; 450 hp(m) *(330 kW)*; 1 shaft
Speed, knots: 12.5. **Range, miles:** 1600 at 10 kts
Complement: 15

Comment: Built about 1955.

ALGERIA

Senior Officer

Commander of the Navy:
Colonel Abdelmadjid Taright

Personnel

(a) 1992: Total 6700 (Navy); 580 (Coast Guard)
(b) Voluntary service

Bases

Algiers, Annaba, Mers-el-Kebir

Strength of the Fleet

Type	*Active*	*Building*
Submarines	2	2
Frigates	3	—
Corvettes	4	2
Fast Attack Craft (Missile)	11	—
Fast Attack Craft (Gun)	12	3
Minesweepers—Ocean	1	—
LSLs	2	—
LCT	1	—
Miscellaneous	6	—
Coast Guard	38	1

Mercantile Marine

Lloyd's Register of Shipping:
148 vessels of 921 342 tons gross

DELETIONS

1989 2 Romeo class
1 Osa I class
1 Zhuk class

SUBMARINES

2 + 2 SOVIET KILO CLASS

Displacement, tons: 2325 surfaced; 3076 dived
Dimensions, feet (metres): 243.8 × 32.8 × 21.7 *(74.3 × 10 × 6.6)*
Main machinery: Diesel-electric; 2 diesels; 3650 hp(m) *(2.68 MW)*; 2 generators; 1 motor; 5900 hp(m) *(4.34 MW)*; 1 shaft
Speed, knots: 17 dived; 10 surfaced; 9 snorting
Range, miles: 20 000 at 11 kts surfaced; 6000 at 8 kts dived
Complement: 45

Torpedoes: 6—21 in *(533 mm)* tubes. 18 Soviet Type 53; dual purpose; pattern active/passive homing up to 20 km *(10.8 nm)* at up to 45 kts; warhead 400 kg.
Mines: 36 in lieu of torpedoes.
Countermeasures: ESM: Brick Group; radar warning.
Radars: Surface search: Snoop Tray; I band.
Sonars: Sharks Teeth; hull-mounted; passive/active search and attack; medium frequency.
Mouse Roar; active attack; high frequency.

Programmes: New construction hulls; first one delivered in October 1987, second in January 1988 as replacements for the Romeo class. Two more expected in due course.
Structure: Diving depth, 300 m *(985 ft)*.

KILO Class *1987*

FRIGATES

3 SOVIET KONI CLASS (TYPE II)

Name	*No*	*Builders*	*Commissioned*
MOURAD RAIS	901	Zelenodolsk Shipyard	Dec 1980
RAIS KELLICH	902	Zelenodolsk Shipyard	Apr 1982
RAIS KORFOU	903	Zelenodolsk Shipyard	Jan 1985

Displacement, tons: 1440 standard; 1900 full load
Dimensions, feet (metres): 316.3 × 41.3 × 11.5 *(96.4 × 12.6 × 3.5)*
Main machinery: CODAG; 1 SGW, Nikolayev, M8B gas turbine (centre shaft); 18 000 hp(m) *(13.25 MW)* sustained; 2 Russki B-68 diesels; 15 820 hp(m) *(11.63 MW)* sustained; 3 shafts
Speed, knots: 27 gas; 22 diesel. **Range, miles:** 1800 at 14 kts
Complement: 130

Missiles: SAM: SA-N-4 Gecko twin launcher ❶; semi-active radar homing to 15 km *(8 nm)* at 2.5 Mach; height envelope 9-3048 m *(29.5-10 000 ft)*; warhead 50 kg; 20 missiles. Some anti-surface capability.
Guns: 4—3 in *(76 mm)*/60 (2 twin) ❷; 80° elevation; 90 rounds/minute to 15 km *(8 nm)*; weight of shell 6.8 kg.
4—30 mm/65 (2 twin) ❸; 85° elevation; 500 rounds/minute to 5 km *(2.7 nm)*; weight of shell 0.54 kg.
A/S mortars: 2—12-barrelled RBU 6000 ❹; range 6000 m; warhead 31 kg.
Depth charges: 2 racks.
Mines: Rails; capacity 22.
Countermeasures: Decoys: 2—16-barrelled Chaff launchers.
ESM: Watch Dog. Cross Loop D/F.

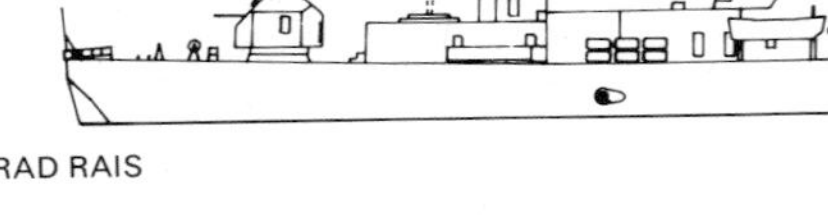

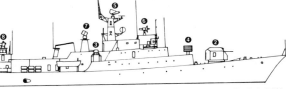

MOURAD RAIS *(Scale 1 : 900), Ian Sturton*

Radars: Air/surface search: Strut Curve ❺; F band; range 110 km *(60 nm)* for 2 m² target.
Navigation: Don 2; I band.
Fire Control: Hawk screech ❻; I band; range 27 km *(15 nm)* (for guns).
Drum tilt ❼; H/I band (for search and acquisition).
Pop Group ❽; F/H/I band (for missile control).
IFF: High Pole B. Two Square Head.
Sonars: Hull-mounted; active search and attack; medium frequency.

Programmes: New construction ships with hull numbers 5, 7 and 10 in sequence. Others of the class built for Cuba, Yugoslavia, East Germany and Libya. Interest was shown in ex-GDR ships in 1991 but sale was rejected by the German Government.
Structure: The deck house aft in Type II Konis is thought to house air-conditioning machinery. No torpedo tubes.

RAIS KELLICH *5/1986*

CORVETTES

3 SOVIET NANUCHKA II CLASS (MISSILE CORVETTES)

RAIS HAMIDOU 801 **SALAH RAIS** 802 **RAIS ALI** 803

Displacement, tons: 850 full load
Dimensions, feet (metres): 194.5 × 38.7 × 8.5 *(59.3 × 11.8 × 2.6)*
Main machinery: 3 Type M 507 diesels; 26 000 hp(m) *(19 MW)* sustained; 3 shafts
Speed, knots: 36. **Range, miles:** 2500 at 12 kts; 900 at 31 kts
Complement: 70 (12 officers)

Missiles: SSM: 4 SS-N-2B; active radar or IR homing to 46 km *(25 nm)* at 0.9 Mach; warhead 513 kg. Preset altitude up to 300 m.
SAM: SA-N-4 Gecko twin launcher; semi-active radar homing to 15 km *(8 nm)* at 2.5 Mach; height envelope 9-3048 m *(29.5-10 000 ft)*; warhead 50 kg; 20 missiles. Some anti-surface capability.
Guns: 2—57 mm/80 (twin); 85° elevation; 120 rounds/minute to 6 km *(3.3 nm)*; weight of shell 2.8 kg.
Countermeasures: Decoys: 2—16-barrelled Chaff launchers.
ESM: Bell Tap. Cross Loop; D/F.
Radars: Surface search: Square Tie (Radome); I band; range 73 km *(40 nm)* or limits of radar horizon.
Navigation: Don 2; I band.
Fire control: Pop Group; F/H/I band (SAN-4). Muff Cob; G/H band.
IFF: Square Head. High Pole.

Programmes: Delivered 4 July 1980, 9 February 1981, 8 May 1982 from Baltic. New construction.
Modernisation: Plans to re-engine with new diesels.

RAIS ALI *1982, Ralf Bendfeldt*

1 + 2 DJEBEL CHINOISE CLASS (CORVETTE)

DJEBEL CHINOISE 351 **352** **353**

Displacement, tons: 496 standard; 540 full load
Dimensions, feet (metres): 191.6 × 27.9 × 8.5 *(58.4 × 8.5 × 2.6)*
Main machinery: 3 MTU 20V 538 TB92 diesels; 12 800 hp(m) *(9.4 MW)*; 3 shafts
Speed, knots: 31
Complement: 52 (6 officers)

Guns: 1 OTO Melara 3 in *(76 mm)*/62; 85° elevation; 85 rounds/minute to 16 km *(9 nm)* anti-surface; 12 km *(6.5 nm)* anti-aircraft; weight of shell 6 kg.
2 Breda 40 mm/70 (twin); 85° elevation; 300 rounds/minute to 12.5 km *(6.8 nm)*; weight of shell 0.96 kg.
4 USSR 23 mm (2 twin).
Fire control: Optronic director for 76 mm.
Radars: Surface search: Racal Decca 1226; I band.

Programmes: Ordered July 1983. Project 802 is a class of corvette building at ECRN, Mers-el-Kebir with Bulgarian assistance. First one launched 3 February 1985 and completed trials in 1988. Second launched in early 1990 but progress has been very slow due to shipyard debt problems.
Structure: Hull size suggests narrow Nanuchka derivative without the missiles.

DJEBEL CHINOISE (without 76 mm gun or optronic director) *11/1988, French Navy*

MINE WARFARE FORCES

1 Ex-SOVIET T 43 CLASS (MINESWEEPERS—OCEAN)

M 522

Displacement, tons: 500 standard; 580 full load
Dimensions, feet (metres): 190.2 × 27.6 × 6.9 *(58 × 8.4 × 2.1)*
Main machinery: 2 Kolumna Type 9-D-8 diesels; 2200 hp(m) *(1.6 MW)*; 2 shafts
Speed, knots: 15. **Range, miles:** 3000 at 10 kts
Complement: 65

Guns: 2—45 mm/85; 90° elevation; 75 rounds/minute to 9 km *(5 nm)*; weight of shell 2.2 kg.
A/S mortars: 2 projectors.
Mines: Can carry 16.
Radars: Navigation: Neptun; I band.

Programmes: Two transferred in 1968. One cannibalised for spares.

LIGHT FORCES

9 Ex-SOVIET OSA II and 2 OSA I CLASS (FAST ATTACK CRAFT—MISSILE)

OSA II—644-652
OSA I—642-643

Displacement, tons: 171 standard; 210 full load (Osa I); 245 full load (Osa II)
Dimensions, feet (metres): 110.2 × 24.9 × 8.8 *(33.6 × 7.6 × 2.7)*
Main machinery: 3 M504 diesels; 15 000 hp(m) *(11 MW)*; 3 shafts (Osa II)
3 M503A diesels; 12 000 hp(m) *(8.8 MW)*; 3 shafts (Osa I)
Speed, knots: 35 (Osa I); 37 (Osa II). **Range, miles:** 400 at 34 kts (Osa I); 500 at 35 kts (Osa II)
Complement: 30

Missiles: SSM: 4 SS-N-2A Styx (Osa I) or 2B (Osa II); active radar or IR homing to 46 km *(25 nm)* at 0.9 Mach; warhead 513 kg.
Guns: 4—30 mm/65 (2 twin); 85° elevation; 500 rounds/minute to 5 km *(2.7 nm)*; weight of shell 0.54 kg.
Radars: Surface search: Square Tie; I band.
Fire Control: Drum Tilt; H/I band.
IFF: Two Square Head. High Pole B.

Programmes: One Osa I was delivered by the USSR on 7 October 1967. Two others transferred later in same year. Osa II transferred 1976-77 (four), fifth in September 1978, sixth in December 1978, next pair in 1979 and one from the Black Sea on 7 December 1981. Osa II No 643 was rebuilt after an explosion in 1981.
Modernisation: Plans to re-engine had still not been started by early 1992.

OSA 652 *1989*

12 + 3 KEBIR CLASS (FAST ATTACK CRAFT—GUN)

EL YADEKH 341 **EL KECHEF** 343 **EL RASSED** 345 **347-349**
EL MOURAKEB 342 **EL MOUTARID** 344 **EL DJARI** 346 **360-365**

Displacement, tons: 166 standard; 200 full load
Dimensions, feet (metres): 123 × 22.6 × 5.6 *(37.5 × 6.9 × 1.7)*
Main machinery: 2 MTU 12V 538 TB92 diesels; 8530 hp(m) *(6.3 MW)*; 2 shafts (see *Structure*)
Speed, knots: 27. **Range, miles:** 3300 at 12 kts; 2600 at 15 kts
Complement: 27 (3 officers)

Guns: 1 OTO Melara 3 in *(76 mm)*/62 compact (in first five); 85° elevation; 85 rounds/minute to 16 km *(9 nm)* anti-surface; 12 km *(6.5 nm)* anti-aircraft; weight of shell 6 kg.
4 USSR 25 mm/60 (2 twin) (remainder); 85° elevation; 270 rounds/minute to 3 km *(1.6 nm)*; weight of shell 0.34 kg.
2 USSR 23 mm (twin).
Fire control: Lawrence Scott optronic director.
Radars: Surface search: Racal Decca 1226; I band.

Programmes: Design and first pair ordered from Brooke Marine in June 1981. First left for Algeria without armament in September 1982, second arrived Algiers 12 June 1983. The remainder assembled or built at ECRN, Mers-el-Kebir with assistance from Vosper Thornycroft. 346 commissioned 10 November 1985. *347-349* ordered June 1986, and delivered in 1988-89; *360-362* ordered in August 1989 and in service by the end of 1991. *363-365* were still under construction in early 1992.
Structure: Same hull as Barbados *Trident*. There are some variations in armament and *363-365* are reported as having lower powered engines.
Operational: Six of the class may have been transferred temporarily to the Coast Guard.

EL MOURAKEB and EL YADEKH *5/1990*

AMPHIBIOUS FORCES

2 LANDING SHIPS (LOGISTIC)

Name	No	Builders	Commissioned
KALAAT BENI HAMMAD	472	Brooke Marine, Lowestoft	Apr 1984
KALAAT BENI RACHED	473	Vosper Thornycroft Ltd	Oct 1984

Displacement, tons: 2450 full load
Dimensions, feet (metres): 305 × 50.9 × 8.1 *(93 × 15.5 × 2.5)*
Main machinery: 2 MTU 16V 11 63 TB82 diesels; 8880 hp(m) *(6.5 MW)* sustained; 2 shafts
Speed, knots: 15. **Range, miles:** 3000 at 12 kts
Complement: 81
Military lift: 240 troops; 7 MBTs and 380 tons other cargo; 2 ton crane with athwartships travel

Guns: 2 Breda 40 mm/70 (twin); 85° elevation; 300 rounds/minute to 12.5 km *(6.8 nm)*; weight of shell 0.96 kg.
Countermeasures: Decoys: Wallop Barricade double layer Chaff launchers.
Fire control: CSEE Naja optronic.
Radars: Navigation: Racal Decca TM 1226; I band.

Helicopters: Platform only.

Programmes: First ordered in June 1981, and launched 18 May 1983; second ordered 18 October 1982 and launched 15 May 1984. Similar hulls to Omani *Nasr El Bahr*.
Structure: These ships have a through tank deck closed by bow and stern ramps. The forward ramp is of two sections measuring length 18 m (when extended) × 5 m breadth, and the single section stern ramp measures 4.3 × 5 m with the addition of 1.1 m finger flaps. Both hatches can support a 60 ton tank, and are winch operated. In addition, side access doors are provided on each side forward. The tank deck side bulkheads extend 2.25 m above the upper deck between the forecastle and the forward end of the superstructure, and provide two hatch openings to the tank deck below.

KALAAT BENI RACHED *1985, Vosper Thornycroft*

1 Ex-SOVIET POLNOCHNY B CLASS (LCT)

471

Displacement, tons: 760 standard; 860 full load
Dimensions, feet (metres): 242.7 × 27.9 × 5.8 *(74 × 8.5 × 1.8)*
Main machinery: 2 Type 40-D diesels; 5000 hp(m) *(3.67 MW)*; 2 shafts
Speed, knots: 19. **Range, miles:** 1000 at 18 kts
Complement: 40
Military lift: 180 troops; 350 tons including up to 6 tanks

Guns: 2—30 mm/65 (twin); 85° elevation; 500 rounds/minute to 5 km *(2.7 nm)*; weight of shell 0.54 kg.
2—140 mm 18-tubed rocket launchers; shore bombardment; range 9 km *(5 nm)*.
Radars: Navigation: Don 2; I band.
Fire Control: Drum Tilt; H/I band.
IFF: Square Head. High Pole A.

Programmes: Class built in Poland 1968-70. Transferred in August 1976.

POLNOCHNY 471 *1990, van Ginderen Collection*

LAND-BASED MARITIME AIRCRAFT

Numbers/Type: 2 Beechcraft Super King Air 200T.
Operational speed: 282 kts *(523 km/h)*.
Service ceiling: 35 000 ft *(10 670 m)*.
Range: 2030 nm *(3756 km)*.
Role/Weapon systems: Operated by air force for close-range EEZ operations. Sensors: Weather radar only. Weapons: Unarmed.

Numbers/Type: 8 Fokker F27-400/600.
Operational speed: 250 kts *(463 km/h)*.
Service ceiling: 25 000 ft *(7620 m)*.
Range: 2700 nm *(5000 km)*.
Role/Weapon systems: Visual reconnaissance duties in support of EEZ, particularly offshore platforms. Sensors: Weather radar and visual means only. Weapons: Limited armament.

MISCELLANEOUS

1 Ex-SOVIET POLUCHAT I CLASS (TRV)

A 641

Displacement, tons: 70 standard; 100 full load
Dimensions, feet (metres): 97.1 × 19 × 4.8 *(29.6 × 5.8 × 1.5)*
Main machinery: 2 Type M 50F-12 diesels; 1700 hp(m) *(1.25 MW)* sustained; 2 shafts
Speed, knots: 20. **Range, miles:** 1500 at 10 kts
Complement: 15

1 Ex-SOVIET NYRYAT CLASS (DIVING TENDER)

YAVDEZAN VP 650

Displacement, tons: 120 full load
Dimensions, feet (metres): 93 × 18 × 5.5 *(28.4 × 5.5 × 1.7)*
Main machinery: Diesel; 450 hp(m) *(3.3 MW)*; 1 shaft
Speed, knots: 12.5. **Range, miles:** 1600 at 10 kts
Complement: 15

Comment: Delivered in 1965.

1 SURVEY SHIP

EL IDRISSI A 673

Displacement, tons: 540 full load
Complement: 28 (6 officers)

Comment: Built by Matsukara, Japan and delivered 17 April 1980.

EL IDRISSI *9/1990*

2 SURVEY CRAFT

RAS TARSA **ALIDADE**

Comment: Both of about 18 tons acquired in the early 1980s.

1 HARBOUR TUG

KADER A 210

Displacement, tons: 265 full load
Dimensions, feet (metres): 85.3 × 21.7 × 9.2 *(26 × 6.6 × 2.8)*
Main machinery: 2 diesels; 1900 hp(m) *(1.4 MW)*; 2 shafts
Speed, knots: 11

Comment: Acquired in 1989.

KADER *7/1989, van Ginderen Collection*

COAST GUARD

Note: Six Kebir class have been transferred temporarily from the Navy.

1 CHINESE SUPPORT SHIP

GC 261

Displacement, tons: 600 full load
Dimensions, feet (metres): 193.6 × 27.6 × 6.9 *(59 × 8.4 × 2.1)*
Main machinery: 2 diesels; 2200 hp(m) *(1.6 MW)*; 2 shafts
Speed, knots: 14
Complement: 60

Comment: Delivered by transporter ship in April 1990. The design appears to be a derivative of the T43 minesweeper but with a stern gantry.

GC 261 *7/1991*

6 + 1 CHINESE CHUI-E CLASS

GC 251 GC 252 GC 253 GC 254 GC 255 GC 256

Displacement, tons: 380 full load
Dimensions, feet (metres): 190.3 × 23.3 × 6.6 *(58 × 7.1 × 2)*
Main machinery: 2 diesels; 2 shafts
Speed, knots: 24
Complement: 42
Guns: 2 China 37 mm/63 (twin).

Comment: Two delivered by transporter ship in April 1990 and described as training vessels. Two more acquired in January 1991 and the last pair in July 1991. One more expected in 1992.

GC 251 *8/1990, van Ginderen Collection*

6 MANGUSTA CLASS

OMBRINE GC 323 **REQUIN** GC 331 **MARSOUIN** GC 333
DORADE GC 324 **ESPADON** GC 332 **MURÈNE** GC 334

Displacement, tons: 91 full load
Dimensions, feet (metres): 98.4 × 19 × 7.2 *(30 × 5.8 × 2.2)*
Main machinery: 3 MTU diesels; 4000 hp(m) *(2.94 MW)*; 3 shafts
Speed, knots: 32.5. **Range, miles:** 800 at 24 kts
Complement: 14 (3 officers)
Guns: Can carry 1 Breda Bofors 40 mm/70 and 1 Oerlikon 20 mm.
Radars: Navigation: SMA 3 RM; I band; range 73 km *(40 nm)*.

Comment: First delivered early 1977 by Baglietto, Varazze, Italy. Some may have been scrapped.

12 FISHERY PROTECTION CRAFT

JEBEL ANTAR **JEBEL HANDA** +10

Displacement, tons: 18

Comment: Completed 1982/83 at Mers-el-Kebir.

10 BAGLIETTO TYPE 20 GC

GC 100 GC 113 GC 221 GC 235 GC 237
GC 112 GC 114 GC 222 GC 236 GC 329

Displacement, tons: 44 full load
Dimensions, feet (metres): 66.9 × 17.1 × 5.5 *(20.4 × 5.2 × 1.7)*
Main machinery: 2 CRM 18DS diesels; 2660 hp(m) *(2 MW)*; 2 shafts
Speed, knots: 36. **Range, miles:** 445 at 20 kts
Complement: 11 (3 officers)
Guns: 1 Oerlikon 20 mm.

Comment: The first pair delivered by Baglietto, Varazze in August 1976 and the remainder in pairs at two monthly intervals. Fitted with three radar sets and optical fire control. Some may have been scrapped.

BAGLIETTO 20 GC CRAFT *1978, Baglietto*

3 CHINESE SAR CRAFT

GC 231-GC 233

Comment: 25 m SAR craft delivered by transporter ship which arrived in Algiers in April 1990. Unarmed.

3 SAR CRAFT (with GC 251, 252 and 261) *2/1990, 92 Wing RAAF*

CUSTOMS SERVICE

3 P 1200 CLASS

BOUZAGZA **DJURDJURA** **HODNA**

Displacement, tons: 39 full load
Dimensions, feet (metres): 68.2 × 18.4 × 5.2 *(20.8 × 5.6 × 1.6)*
Main machinery: 2 MAN D2540 diesels; 1300 hp(m) *(955 kW)*; 2 shafts
Speed, knots: 33. **Range, miles:** 300 at 22 kts
Complement: 4
Guns: 2—7.62 mm MGs.

Comment: Ordered from Watercraft Ltd, Shoreham, England in late 1984. Completed 21 November 1985. GRP construction.

2 P 802 CLASS

AURES **HOGGAR**

Comment: Ordered from Watercraft Ltd, Shoreham, England in late 1984. 8 m craft with two Volvo AQAD 40 inboard/outboard diesels for speed of 30+ kts. Completed 21 November 1985.

ANGOLA

Headquarters' Appointment

Commander of the Navy and Vice Minister of Defence:
Major General Antonio Jose Condessa de Carvalho

Personnel

(a) 1992: 1500
(b) Voluntary service

Mercantile Marine

Lloyd's Register of Shipping:
111 vessels of 93 144 tons gross

General

Peace Agreement signed in May 1991. There are plans to expand the Navy to a personnel strength of 4000 men but this will take a long time to achieve. At the end of 1991 most of the listed vessels were in various states of disrepair and decay but all, in theory, could be recovered. The priority is for new craft. The Portuguese are involved in the training of the new Navy.

Ports and Bases

Luanda, Lobito, Namibe. (There are other good harbours available on the 1000 mile coastline.) Naval HQ at Luanda on Ila de Luanda is fortified, as is Namibe.

LIGHT FORCES

Note: A contract was proposed at the end of 1989 with Bazán, Spain for three Cormoran class fast attack craft with OTO Melara 76 mm guns and six high speed craft with 20 mm guns. By early 1992 the only firm contract was for four patrol craft.

6 Ex-SOVIET OSA II CLASS (FAST ATTACK CRAFT—MISSILE)

Displacement, tons: 245 full load
Dimensions, feet (metres): 110.2 × 24.9 × 8.8 *(33.6 × 7.6 × 2.7)*
Main machinery: 3 Type M 504 diesels; 15 000 hp(m) *(11 MW)*; 3 shafts
Speed, knots: 37. **Range, miles:** 800 at 30 kts; 500 at 35 kts
Complement: 30

Missiles: SSM: 4 SS-N-2B Styx; active radar or IR homing to 46 km *(25 nm)* at 0.9 Mach; warhead 513 kg.
Guns: 4—30 mm/65 (2 twin); 85° elevation; 500 rounds/minute to 5 km *(2.7 nm)*; weight of shell 0.54 kg.
Radars: Surface search: Square Tie; I band.
Fire Control: Drum Tilt; H/I band.
IFF: Square Head. High Pole B.

Programmes: Transferred 29 September 1982 (first pair), 29 December 1982 (second pair), and 1 November 1983 (third pair). All virtually derelict at the end of 1991.

OSA II Class

4 Ex-SOVIET SHERSHEN CLASS (FAST ATTACK CRAFT—TORPEDO)

Displacement, tons: 145 standard; 170 full load
Dimensions, feet (metres): 113.8 × 22 × 4.9 *(34.7 × 6.7 × 1.5)*
Main machinery: 3 Type M 503A diesels; 12 000 hp(m) *(8.8 MW)*; 3 shafts
Speed, knots: 45. **Range, miles:** 850 at 30 kts; 460 at 42 kts
Complement: 23

Guns: 4—30 mm/65 (2 twin); 85° elevation; 500 rounds/minute to 5 km *(2.7 nm)*; weight of shell 0.54 kg.
Torpedoes: 4—21 in *(533 mm)* tubes. Obsolescent Soviet Type 53.
Depth charges: 12.
Mines: Capacity for 6.
Radars: Surface search: Pot Drum; H/I band.
Fire control: Drum Tilt; H/I band.
IFF: High Pole A. Square Head.

Programmes: Built in late 1960s. First transferred December 1977, one more in December 1978, one in May 1981 and the fourth in early 1983. Unlikely that more than one is operational.

SHERSHEN Class

4 Ex-PORTUGUESE ARGOS CLASS (LARGE PATROL CRAFT)

Name	*No*	*Builders*	*Commissioned*
Ex-**ORION**	P 362	Estaleiros Navais de Viano do Castelo	1964
Ex-**ESCORPIAO**	P 375	Arsenal do Alfeite, Lisbon	1964
Ex-**PEGASO**	P 379	Estaleiros Navais de Viano do Castelo	1963
Ex-**CENTAURO**	P 1130	Arsenal do Alfeite, Lisbon	1965

Displacement, tons: 180 standard; 210 full load
Dimensions, feet (metres): 136.8 × 20.5 × 7 *(41.6 × 6.2 × 2.2)*
Main machinery: 2 Maybach MTU diesels; 1200 hp(m) *(882 kW)*; 2 shafts
Speed, knots: 17. **Range, miles:** 4000 at 12 kts
Complement: 24 (2 officers)
Guns: 2 Bofors 40 mm/70; 90° elevation; 300 rounds/minute to 12 km *(6.5 nm)*; weight of shell 0.96 kg.

Comment: *Argos* and *Dragao* of same class transferred, reportedly, for spares. All probably non-operational.

ARGOS Class *Portuguese Navy*

1 Ex-SOVIET ZHUK CLASS (COASTAL PATROL CRAFT)

Displacement, tons: 50 full load
Dimensions, feet (metres): 75.4 × 17 × 6.2 *(23 × 5.2 × 1.9)*
Main machinery: 2 Type M 50F-12 diesels; 1700 hp(m) *(1.25 MW)* sustained; 2 shafts
Speed, knots: 30. **Range, miles:** 1100 at 15 kts
Complement: 17
Guns: 2—14.5 mm (twin, aft) MGs.

Comment: Transferred 23 January 1977. Two more may have been acquired in the late 1980s.

ZHUK Class

2 Ex-SOVIET POLUCHAT I CLASS (COASTAL PATROL CRAFT)

Displacement, tons: 70 standard; 100 full load
Dimensions, feet (metres): 97.1 × 19 × 4.8 *(29.6 × 5.8 × 1.5)*
Main machinery: 2 Type M 50F-12 diesels; 1700 hp(m) *(1.25 MW)* sustained; 2 shafts
Speed, knots: 20. **Range, miles:** 1500 at 10 kts
Complement: 15
Guns: 2—14.5 mm MGs.
Radars: Navigation: Spin Trough; I band.

Comment: Transferred December 1979.

POLUCHAT I Class

MINE WARFARE FORCES

2 Ex-SOVIET YEVGENYA CLASS

Displacement, tons: 77 standard; 90 full load
Dimensions, feet (metres): 80.4 × 18 × 4.6 *(24.5 × 5.5 × 1.4)*
Main machinery: 2 Type 3-D-12 diesels; 400 hp(m) *(300 kW)*; 2 shafts
Speed, knots: 11. **Range, miles:** 300 at 10 kts
Complement: 10
Guns: 2 USSR 25 mm/80 (twin).
Radars: Navigation: Don 2; I band.
Sonars: VDS (lifted over stern on crane); minehunting; high frequency.

Comment: Both transferred in September 1987.

YEVGENYA Class *1988, P. D. Jones*

AMPHIBIOUS FORCES

Note: (a) In addition to those below there are four derelict ex-Soviet T-4 class originally transferred in 1976. Also four out of nine ex-Portuguese LDM 400 class and three LDP 200 are in service but in very poor condition.
(b) Two new LCUs may be built by Bazán, Spain, if a contract being negotiated in late 1989 eventually goes ahead.
(c) 14 ex-GDR Frosch class acquired in 1991 for 'civilian' use.

1 Ex-PORTUGUESE ALFANGE CLASS (LCT)

Name	*No*	*Builders*	*Commissioned*
Ex-ALFANGE	LDG 101	Estaleiros Navais do Mondego	1965

Displacement, tons: 500
Dimensions, feet (metres): 187 × 39 × 6.2 *(57 × 12 × 1.9)*
Main machinery: 2 diesels; 1000 hp(m) *(735 kW)*; 2 shafts
Speed, knots: 11
Complement: 20 (plus 35 troops)

Ex-ALFANGE *Portuguese Navy*

3 Ex-SOVIET POLNOCHNY B CLASS (LCT)

Displacement, tons: 760 standard; 860 full load
Dimensions, feet (metres): 242.7 × 27.9 × 5.8 *(74 × 8.5 × 1.8)*
Main machinery: 2 Type 40-D diesels; 5000 hp(m) *(3.67 MW)*; 2 shafts
Speed, knots: 19. **Range, miles:** 1000 at 18 kts
Complement: 40
Military lift: 180 troops; 350 tons including up to 6 tanks

Guns: 4—30 mm/65 (2 twin); 85° elevation; 500 rounds/minute to 5 km *(2.7 nm)*; weight of shell 0.54 kg.
2—140 mm 18-tubed rocket launchers; shore bombardment; range 9 km *(5 nm)*.
Radars: Navigation: Don 2 or Spin Trough; I band.
Fire control: Drum Tilt; H/I band.
IFF: Square Head.

Programmes: First transferred November 1977, the second 10 February 1979 and the third 11 December 1979.

POLNOCHNY Class (Group B)

LAND-BASED MARITIME AIRCRAFT

Note: Two Aviocar C-218-300N to be delivered in 1993. Four more ordered in 1991.

Numbers/Type: 2 Embraer EMB-111 Bandeirante.
Operational speed: 194 kts *(360 km/h)*.
Service ceiling: 25 500 ft *(7770 m)*.
Range: 1590 nm *(2945 km)*.
Role/Weapon systems: Armed MR and coastal patrol delivered in 1988. Sensors: APS-128 radar, limited EW. Weapons: ASV; 70 mm or 127 mm pods or rockets.

Numbers/Type: 4 Aerospatiale SA 365F Dauphin.
Operational speed: 140 kts *(260 km/h)*.
Service ceiling: 15 000 ft *(4575 m)*.
Range: 410 nm *(758 km)*.
Role/Weapon systems: ASV reconnaissance seems most likely role. Sensors: Possible radar fit.

Numbers/Type: 1 Fokker F27-600.
Operational speed: 250 kts *(46.3 km/h)*.
Service ceiling: 25 000 ft *(7620 m)*.
Range: 2700 nm *(5000 km)*.
Role/Weapon systems: Visual/radar reconnaissance. Sensors: Litton 360° radar. Weapons: None.

MISCELLANEOUS

1 FLOATING DOCK

Comment: Capacity 4500 tons. Delivered from USSR in 1982.

ANGUILLA

Marine Police

Elliot Mc N Richardson CPM, JP, Commissioner of Police.

Mercantile Marine

Lloyd's Register of Shipping:
17 vessels of 4966 tons gross

DELETIONS

1991 *Mapleleaf*, 1 Interceptor class

1 HALMATIC M160 CLASS (INSHORE PATROL CRAFT)

DOLPHIN

Displacement, tons: 18 light
Dimensions, feet (metres): 52.5 × 15.4 × 4.6 *(16 × 4.7 × 1.4)*
Main machinery: 2 Detroit Diesels 6V-92TA; 510 hp *(380 kW)* sustained; 2 shafts
Speed, knots: 27. **Range, miles:** 500 at 17 kts
Complement: 8

Comment: Built by Halmatic and delivered 22 December 1989. Identical craft to Montserrat and Turks and Caicos Islands. GRP hulls. Rigid inflatable boat launched by gravity davit.

2 INSHORE PATROL CRAFT

LAPWING **ANGUILLETTA**

Comment: *Lapwing* is a 28 ft launch acquired in 1974 from Fairey Marine. *Anguilletta* is the survivor of two craft built locally in 1984. She has two Evinrude outboard engines and is 32 ft in length.

DOLPHIN *1989, Halmatic*

ANTIGUA and BARBUDA

Headquarters' Appointments

Commanding Officer, Coastguard:
Lieutenant Commander A J Gilmour

Port

St John's (capital).

Mercantile Marine

Lloyd's Register of Shipping:
241 vessels of 485 344 tons gross

PATROL FORCES

1 SWIFT 65 ft CLASS

Name	*No*	*Builders*	*Commissioned*
LIBERTA	P 01	Swiftships, Morgan City	30 Apr 1984

Displacement, tons: 31.7 full load
Dimensions, feet (metres): 65.5 × 18.4 × 5 *(20 × 5.6 × 1.5)*
Main machinery: 2 Detroit Diesel 12V-71TA diesels; 840 hp *(616 kW)* sustained; 2 shafts
Speed, knots: 22. **Range, miles:** 250 at 18 kts
Complement: 9
Guns: 1—12.7 mm MG. 2—7.62 mm MGs.
Radars: Surface search: Furuno; I band.

Comment: Ordered in November 1983. Aluminium construction.

LIBERTA *1991, Antigua Coastguard*

ARGENTINA

Headquarters' Appointments

Chief of Defence Staff:
Admiral Emilio Osses
Chief of Naval General Staff:
Admiral Jorge Osvaldo Ferrer
Deputy Commander-in-Chief Navy:
Vice Admiral Juan Carlos Bott
Commander Fleet:
Vice Admiral Enrique Molina Pico
Naval Area South:
Rear Admiral Ismael Jorge Garcia
Naval Area Puerto Belgrano:
Rear Admiral Daniel Antonio Fusari
Naval Area Fluvial:
Captain Ricardo Angel Franzosi

Diplomatic Representation

Naval Attaché in Spain:
Captain Raul Pueyrredon
Naval Attaché in Japan:
Captain Luis A Garcia Bourimborde
Naval Attaché in Italy:
Captain Fernando Sola
Naval Attaché in Germany and Holland:
Captain Rodolfo Hasenbal
Naval Attaché in France:
Captain Roberto O Roscoe
Naval Attaché in Brazil:
Captain Arturo Massat
Naval Attaché in Chile:
Captain Luis Posse
Naval Attaché in London:
Captain Alberto C Secchi
Naval Attaché in USA and Canada:
Rear Admiral Horacio Reyser

Personnel

(a) 1992: 27 500 (4000 officers, 17 500 petty officers and ratings and 6000 conscripts)
Marine Corps: 6000 officers and men
(b) Volunteers plus 12 months' national service (being phased out)

Organisation

Naval Area Centre (HQ Puerto Belgrano) covers area from River Plate to Valdes Peninsula.
Naval Area South (HQ Ushuaia) covers coastal area from Valdes Peninsula to Drake Passage.
Naval Area Fluvial (HQ Buenos Aires) covers coast of River Plate.
Naval Area Antarctica (HQ Buenos Aires) covers Antarctica.

Naval Bases

Buenos Aires (Dársena Norte): Dockyard, 2 dry docks, 4 floating docks, 1 floating crane, 1 synchrolift, schools.
Rio Santiago (La Plata): Schools, naval shipbuilding yard (AFNE), 1 slipway, 1 floating crane.
Mar del Plata: Submarine base with slipway.
Puerto Belgrano: Main naval base, schools, 2 dry docks, 1 floating dock.
Ushuaia, Deseado: Small naval bases.

Naval Building Yards (being privatised)

(a) Astilleros y Fábricas Navales del Estado (AFNE), Rio Santiago.
(b) Tandanor, Dársena Norte (Planta 1) and Dársena Este (Planta 2); 88.8 per cent naval owned and 11.2 per cent by Adm Gen de Puertos.
Planta 1 has two dry docks and two floating docks. Planta 2 has two floating docks (A and B) and a synchrolift of 185 × 32 m.
(c) Astillero Domecq Garcia, Buenos Aires. Submarine building yard.

Coast Guard

In 1991 it was proposed that the Coast Guard should be limited to operations inside the 12 mile territorial seas. If this happens some patrol ships may be transferred to the Navy.

Prefix to Ships' Names

ARA (Armada Republica Argentina)

Naval Aviation

Personnel: 2500
1st Naval Air Wing (Punta del Indio Naval Air Base): Naval Aviation School with Beech T-34Cs and Beech King Airs.
2nd Naval Air Wing (Comandante Espora Naval Air Base): Anti Submarine Squadron with Grumman S-2E Trackers; 2nd Naval Helicopter Squadron with Agusta/Sikorsky SH-3D and S-61D.
3rd Naval Air Wing (Comandante Espora Naval Air Base): 2nd Naval Fighter/Attack Squadron with Super Etendards; 1st Naval Helicopter Squadron with Alouette III.
4th Naval Air Wing (Punta Indio Naval Air Base): 1st Naval Attack Squadron with Macchi MB 326B, MB 339A and Embraer EMB 326 Xavantes; Naval Aerophotographic Squadron with Beech Queen Airs and Beech King Air 200s.
5th Naval Air Wing (Ezeiza Naval Air Base): 1st Naval Logistic Support Squadron with Lockheed Electra; 2nd Naval Logistic Support Squadron with Fokker F28s.
6th Naval Air Wing (Almirante Zar Naval Air Base): Naval Reconnaissance Squadron with Beech Queen Airs and Lockheed Electra L-188E.
Approximately half the aircraft, including most of the Super Etendards, were reported out of service due to shortage of spare parts at the beginning of 1991. There had been no improvement by early 1992.

Marine Corps

Organisation and Deployment

1st Marine Infantry Force (HQ Río Gallegos)
1st Marine Infantry Brigade (Baterías)
Amphibious Support Group (Puerto Belgrano)

1st Marine Infantry Battalion (HQ Baterías)
2nd Marine Infantry Battalion (Baterías)
3rd Marine Infantry Battalion (La Plata)
4th Marine Infantry Battalion (Río Gallegos)
5th Marine Infantry Battalion (Río Grande)

Marine Field Artillery Battalion (Puerto Belgrano)
Logistics Support Battalion (Baterías)
Amphibious Vehicles Battalion (Baterías)
Communications Battalion (Puerto Belgrano)
Marine A/A Battalion (Puerto Belgrano)
Scout Company (Baterías)
Marine A/T Company (Baterías)
Amphibious Engineers Company (Puerto Belgrano)
Amphibious Commandos Company (Baterías)
Navy Chief of Staff Security Battalion (Buenos Aires)
Puerto Belgrano Security Battalion (Puerto Belgrano)
There are Marine Security Companies in Buenos Aires, Rio Santiago, Punta Indio, Azul, Mar del Plata, Comandante Espora Naval Air Base, Zárate, Ezeiza, Trelew, Ushuaia and Rio Grande.

Strength of the Fleet

Type	*Active*	*Building (Planned)*
Patrol Submarines	4	2
Destroyers	6	—
Frigates	7	2
Patrol Ships	7	—
Fast Attack Craft (Gun)	2	—
Coastal Patrol Craft	4	—
Minesweepers (Coastal)	4	—
Minehunters	2	—
Landing Ship (Tank)	1	—
Minor Landing Craft	20	—
Survey/Oceanographic Ships	3	—
Survey Launches	2	—
Transports	4	(1)
Training Ships	2	—
Tugs	13	—
Floating Docks	5	—
Sail Training Ships	4	—

Mercantile Marine

Lloyd's Register of Shipping:
490 vessels of 1 708 565 tons gross

DELETION

Transports

1989 *Bahia Paraiso* (sunk)

PENNANT LIST

Submarines

S 31	Salta
S 32	San Luis
S 41	Santa Cruz
S 42	San Juan
S 43	Santa Fé (bldg)
S 44	Santiago del Estero (bldg)

Aircraft Carrier

V 2	Veinticinco de Mayo (reserve)

Destroyers

D 1	Hercules
D 2	Santisima Trinidad
D 10	Almirante Brown
D 11	La Argentina
D 12	Heroina
D 13	Sarandi

Frigates

31	Drummond
32	Guerrico
33	Granville
41	Espora
42	Rosales
43	Spiro
44	Parker
45	Robinson (bldg)
46	Gomez Roca (bldg)

Patrol Ships

A 1	Com G Irigoyen
A 2	Teniente Olivieri
A 3	Francisco de Gurruchaga
A 9	Alferez Sobral
A 10	Comodoro Somellera
P 20	Murature
P 21	King

Light Forces

P 61	Baradero
P 62	Barranqueras
P 63	Clorinda
P 64	Concepcion del Uruguay
P 85	Intrepida
P 86	Indomita

Amphibious Force

Q 42	Cabo San Antonio

Mine Warfare Forces

M 1	Neuquen
M 2	Rio Negro
M 3	Chubut
M 4	Tierra del Fuego
M 5	Chaco
M 6	Formosa

Miscellaneous

A 8	Sanaviron
B 3	Canal Beagle
B 4	Bahia San Blas
B 5	Cabo de Hornos
Q 2	Libertad
Q 5	Almirante Irizar
Q 8	Puerto Deseado
Q 11	Comodoro Rivadavia
Q 15	Cormoran
Q 16	Petrel
Q 25	Fortuna I
Q 26	Fortuna II
Q 31	Piloto Alsina
Q 72	Tequara
Q 73	Itati II
R 1	Huarpe
R 2	Querandi
R 3	Tehuelche
R 4	Mataco
R 5	Mocovi
R 6	Calchaqui
R 7	Ona
R 8	Toba
R 10	Chulupi
R 16	Capayan
R 18	Chiquillan
R 19	Morcoyan

SUBMARINES

2 + 2 TR 1700 TYPE

Name	*No*	*Builders*	*Laid down*	*Launched*	*Commissioned*
SANTA CRUZ	S 41	Thyssen Nordseewerke	6 Dec 1980	28 Sep 1982	18 Oct 1984
SAN JUAN	S 42	Thyssen Nordseewerke	18 Mar 1982	20 June 1983	19 Nov 1985
SANTA FÈ	S 43	Astilleros Domecq Garcia	4 Oct 1983	—	—
SANTIAGO DEL ESTERO	S 44	Astilleros Domecq Garcia	5 Aug 1985	—	—

Displacement, tons: 2116 surfaced; 2264 dived
Dimensions, feet (metres): 216.5 × 23.9 × 21.3 *(66 × 7.3 × 6.5)*
Main machinery: Diesel-electric; 4 MTU 16V 652 MB 81 diesels; 6720 hp(m) *(4.94 MW)* sustained; 4 alternators; 4.4 MW; 1 motor; 8000 hp(m) *(5.9 MW)*; 1 shaft
Speed, knots: 15 surfaced; 15 snorting; 25 dived
Range, miles: 12 000 at 8 kts surfaced; 20 at 25 kts; 460 at 6 kts dived
Complement: 26 plus 6 spare berths

Torpedoes: 6—21 in *(533 mm)* bow tubes. 22 AEG SST 4; wire-guided; active/passive homing to 12/28 km *(6.5/15 nm)* at 35/23 kts; warhead 260 kg; automatic reload in 50 seconds. Swim-out discharge. US Mk 37 are also carried.
Mines: Capable of carrying ground mines.
Countermeasures: ESM: Sea Sentry III; Radar warning.
Fire control: Signaal Sinbads; can handle 5 targets and 3 torpedoes simultaneously.
Radars: Navigation: Thomson-CSF Calypso IV; I band.
Sonars: Krupp Atlas CSU 3/4; active/passive search and attack; medium frequency.
Thomson Sintra DUUX 5; passive ranging.

SANTA CRUZ *5/1987, van Ginderen Collection*

Programmes: Contract signed 30 November 1977 with Thyssen Nordseewerke for two submarines to be built at Emden with parts and overseeing for four more boats to be built in Argentina by Astilleros Domecq Garcia, Buenos Aires. At the start of 1991 it was reported that completion of numbers three and four would depend on the acquisition of foreign sales money. No further progress had been made by early 1992 and plans for numbers five and six have been shelved.
Structure: Diving depth, 270 m *(890 ft)*.
Operational: Maximum endurance is 70 days.
Sales: The Government of the FGR has financially guaranteed the project and in 1986 it gave permission for the Argentine Navy to sell the locally built submarines if it could find a buyer.

2 SALTA CLASS (209 CLASS—1200 TYPE)

Name	*No*	*Builders*	*Laid down*	*Launched*	*Commissioned*
SALTA	S 31	Howaldtswerke, Kiel	30 Apr 1970	9 Nov 1972	7 Mar 1974
SAN LUIS	S 32	Howaldtswerke, Kiel	1 Oct 1970	3 Apr 1973	24 May 1974

Displacement, tons: 1248 surfaced; 1440 dived
Dimensions, feet (metres): 183.4 × 20.5 × 17.9 *(55.9 × 6.3 × 5.5)*
Main machinery: Diesel-electric; 4 MTU 12V493 AZ80 diesels; 2400 hp(m) *(1.76 MW)* sustained; 4 alternators; 1.7 MW; 1 motor; 4600 hp(m) *(3.36 MW)*; 1 shaft
Speed, knots: 10 surfaced; 22 dived; 11 snorting
Range, miles: 6000 at 8 kts surfaced; 230 at 8 kts; 400 at 4 kts dived
Complement: 32

Torpedoes: 8—21 in *(533 mm)* bow tubes. 14 AEG SST 4; wire-guided; active/passive homing to 12/28 km *(6.5/15 nm)* at 35/23 kts; warhead 260 kg or US Mk 37; wire-guided; active/passive homing to 8 km *(4.4 nm)* at 24 kts; warhead 150 kg. Swim-out discharge.
Mines: Capable of carrying ground mines.
Countermeasures: ESM: DR 2000; radar warning.
Fire control: Signaal M8 digital; computer-based; up to 3 targets engaged simultaneously.
Radars: Navigation: Thomson-CSF Calypso II.
Sonars: Krupp Atlas CSU 3 (AN 526/AN 5039/41); active/passive search and attack; medium frequency.
Thomson Sintra DUUX 2C and DUUG 1D; passive ranging.

Programmes: Ordered in 1968. Built in sections by Howaldtswerke Deutsche Werft AG, Kiel from the IK 68 design of Ingenieurkontor, Lübeck. Sections were shipped to Argentina for assembly at Tandanor, Buenos Aires.
Modernisation: *Salta* is undergoing a mid-life modernisation at the Domecq Garcia Shipyard. New engines, weapons and electrical systems are being fitted and the last 15 m of the hull have been separated from the main hull to allow work in the main engineering section. Work was suspended in May 1990 for lack of funds. By October 1991 *San Luis* was also being refitted and work had restarted on *Salta*.
Structure: Diving depth, 250 m *(820 ft)*.
Sales: Modernisation progress may depend upon both submarines being sold. Indonesia is a possible buyer.

SALTA *1988*

SALTA *1982, Argentine Navy*

AIRCRAFT CARRIER

1 Ex-BRITISH COLOSSUS CLASS

Name	*No*	*Builders*	*Laid down*	*Launched*	*Commissioned*
VEINTICINCO DE MAYO	V 2	Cammell Laird & Co Ltd, Birkenhead	3 Dec 1942	30 Dec 1943	17 Jan 1945

(ex-HrMs *Karel Doorman*, ex-HMS *Venerable*)

Displacement, tons: 15 892 standard; 19 896 full load
Dimensions, feet (metres): 630 pp; 693.2 oa × 80 × 25 *(192; 211.3 × 24.4 × 7.6)*
Flight deck, feet (metres): 697.7 × 133.4 *(212.6 × 40.6)*
Main machinery: Parsons geared turbines; 40 000 shp; 2 shafts. (see *Modernisation*)
Speed, knots: 24. **Range, miles:** 12 000 at 14 kts; 6200 at 23 kts
Complement: 1000 plus up to 500 air crew

Guns: 9 Bofors 40 mm/70; 85° elevation; 300 rounds/minute to 12 km *(6.5 nm)* anti-surface; 4 km *(2.2 nm)* anti-aircraft; weight of shell 0.96 kg.
Combat data systems: Signaal SEWACO; Link 10.
Radars: Air search: Signaal LW 08; D band.
Surface/Air search: Signaal DA 08; F band.
Height finder: VI/SGR-109.
Surface search: Signaal LW 02; E/F band.
Navigation: Signaal ZW 01; I/J band.
Racal Decca 1226; I band.
CCA: Selenia MM/SPN 720; I band.
Tacan: URN 20.

Fixed wing aircraft: 12 Super Etendards and 6 S-2E Trackers (see *Shipborne Aircraft* section).
Helicopters: 4 SH-3D Sea King ASW and 1 A 103 Alouette III.

Programmes: Purchased from the UK on 1 April 1948 and commissioned in the Royal Netherlands Navy on 28 May 1948. Damaged by boiler fire on 29 April 1968. Sold to Argentina on 15 October 1968 and refitted at Rotterdam by N V Dok en Werf Mij Wilton-Fijenoord, being fitted with new turbines from HMS *Leviathan*. Commissioned in the Argentine Navy on 12 March 1969. Completed refit on 22 August 1969 and sailed for Argentina on 3 September 1969.
Modernisation: In 1980-81 her flight deck area was increased allowing for two extra aircraft in the deck-park and at the same time all necessary modifications, including lengthening and strengthening of catapult, were made to allow for operation of Super Etendards. In 1983 Plessey CAAIS was replaced by a SEWACO system compatible with the Meko 360 class. Major refit was planned to start in 1988 for modifications to main engines, flight deck, electrical systems, NBCD and the bridge. At that stage alternative main engine plans included COSAG (new boilers plus GT boost) or CODOG (4 Sulzer diesels plus GT boost). In June 1990 Fincantieri won an initial contract to give technical assistance to AFNE, Santiago, to replace the Parsons turbines with GE/Fiat Aviazione LM 2500 gas turbines, vp propellers, and a DMD power generation system. However in October 1991 it was announced that the ship was still being maintained but would not be refitted and would probably be sold.

VEINTICINCO DE MAYO — *1987, Argentine Navy*

Structure: Hangar dimensions, feet (metres): 455 × 52 × 17.5 *(138.7 × 15.8 × 5.3)*. Modified bridge superstructure, tripod radar mast and tall raked funnel are distinctive changes from the original Colossus class.
Operational: The ship has not been fully operational since 1985 and remains at Rio Santiago.

DESTROYERS

4 MEKO 360 TYPE

Name	*No*	*Builders*	*Laid down*	*Launched*	*Commissioned*
ALMIRANTE BROWN	D 10	Blohm and Voss, Hamburg	8 Sep 1980	28 Mar 1981	26 Jan 1983
LA ARGENTINA	D 11	Blohm and Voss, Hamburg	30 Mar 1981	25 Sep 1981	4 May 1983
HEROINA	D 12	Blohm and Voss, Hamburg	24 Aug 1981	17 Feb 1982	31 Oct 1983
SARANDI	D 13	Blohm and Voss, Hamburg	9 Mar 1982	31 Aug 1982	16 Apr 1984

Displacement, tons: 2900 standard; 3360 full load
Dimensions, feet (metres): 413.1 × 46 × 19 (screws) *(125.9 × 14 × 5.8)*
Main machinery: COGOG; 2 RR Olympus TM3B gas turbines; 43 000 hp *(32 MW)* sustained
2 RR Type RM1C gas turbines; 10 680 hp *(8 MW)* sustained; 2 shafts; cp props
Speed, knots: 30.5; 20.5 cruising. **Range, miles:** 4500 at 18 kts
Complement: 200 (26 officers)

Missiles: SSM: 8 Aerospatiale MM 40 Exocet (2 quad) launchers ❶; inertial cruise; active radar homing to 70 km *(40 nm)*; warhead 165 kg; sea-skimmer.
SAM: Selenia/Elsag Albatros octuple launcher ❷; 24 Aspide; semi-active homing to 13 km *(7 nm)* at 2.5 Mach; height envelope 15-5000 m *(49.2-16 405 ft)*; warhead 30 kg.
Guns: 1 OTO Melara 5 in *(127 mm)*/54 automatic ❸; 85° elevation; 45 rounds/minute to 16 km *(8.7 nm)* anti-surface; 7 km *(3.6 nm)* anti-aircraft; weight of shell 32 kg; ready ammunition 69 rounds using 3 loading drums; also fires Chaff and illuminants.
8 Breda/Bofors 40 mm/70 (4 twin) ❹; 85° elevation; 300 rounds/minute to 12.6 km *(6.8 nm)* anti-surface; 4 km *(2.2 nm)* anti-aircraft; weight of shell 0.96 kg; ready ammunition 736 (or 444) using AP Tracer, impact or proximity fuzing.
Torpedoes: 6—324 mm ILAS 3 (2 triple) tubes ❺. Whitehead A 244; anti-submarine; active/passive homing to 7 km *(3.8 nm)* at 33 kts; warhead 34 kg (shaped charge); 18 reloads.
Countermeasures: Decoys: CSEE Dagaie double mounting; Graseby G1738 towed torpedo decoy system.
2 Breda 105 mm SCLAR Chaff rocket launchers; 20 tubes per launcher; can be trained and elevated; Chaff to 5 km *(2.7 nm)*; illuminants to 12 km *(6.6 nm)*.
ESM/ECM: Sphinx/Scimitar.
Combat data systems: Signaal SEWACO; Link 10/11. SATCOMs can be fitted.
Fire control: 2 Signaal LIROD radar/optronic systems each controlling 2 twin 40 mm mounts ❻. Signaal WM 25 FCS ❼.
Radars: Air/surface search: Signaal DA 08A ❽; F band; range 204 km *(110 nm)* for 2 m² target.
Surface search: Signaal ZW 06; I band.
Navigation: Decca 1226; I band.
Fire control: Signaal STIR ❾; I/J/K band; range 140 km *(76 nm)* for 1 m² target.
Sonars: Krupp Atlas 80; hull-mounted; active search and attack; medium frequency.
DSQS 21BZ.

Helicopters: 2 SA 319B Alouette III ❿

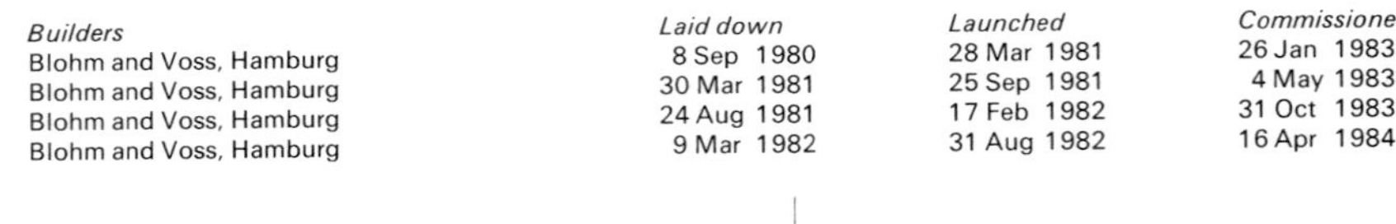
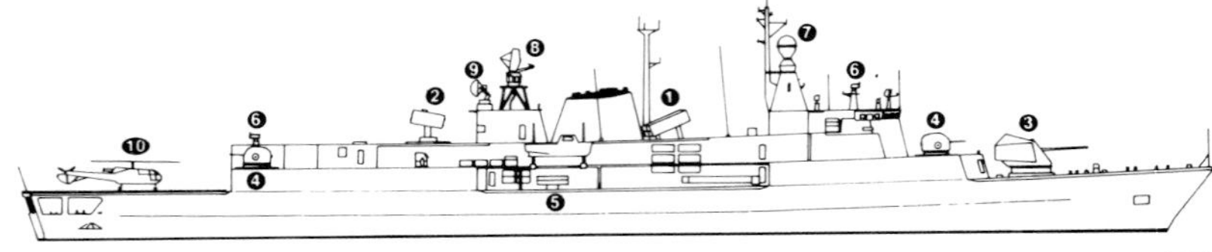

ALMIRANTE BROWN — *(Scale 1 : 1200), Ian Sturton*

ALMIRANTE BROWN — *11/1990*

Programmes: Six were originally ordered in 1978, but later restricted to four when Meko 140 frigates were ordered in 1979.
Structure: Pennant numbers are displayed without the D prefix.
Operational: High operational availability was reflected in decision to send one of the class to take part in allied Gulf operations in late 1990.
Opinion: Currently deficient in ASW capability with obsolete helicopter equipment after order for Lynx cancelled in 1982. AB 212ASW was selected but acquisition not funded. Suitable helicopters are being sought in the United States who may provide Kaman SH-2 in due course.

2 BRITISH TYPE 42

Name	No	Builders	Laid down	Launched	Commissioned
HERCULES	D 1 (ex-28)	Vickers, Barrow	16 June 1971	24 Oct 1972	12 July 1976
SANTISIMA TRINIDAD	D 2	AFNE, Rio Santiago	11 Oct 1971	9 Nov 1974	July 1981

Displacement, tons: 3150 standard; 4100 full load
Dimensions, feet (metres): 412 × 47 × 19 (screws) *(125.6 × 14.3 × 5.8)*
Main machinery: COGOG; 2 RR Olympus TM3B gas turbines; 43 000 hp *(32 MW)* sustained
2 RR Type RM1A gas turbines; 8500 hp *(6.3 MW)* sustained; 2 shafts; cp props
Speed, knots: 29. **Range, miles:** 4000 at 18 kts
Complement: 300

Missiles: SSM: 4 Aerospatiale MM 38 Exocet ❶; inertial cruise; active homing to 42 km *(23 nm)* at 0.9 Mach; warhead 165 kg; sea-skimmer.
SAM: British Aerospace Sea Dart Mk 30 twin launcher ❷; semi-active radar homing to 40 km *(21.5 nm)* at 2 Mach; height envelope 100-18 300 m *(328-60 042 ft)*; 22 missiles; limited anti-ship capability.
Guns: 1 Vickers 4.5 in *(115 mm)*/55 Mk 8 automatic ❸; 25 rounds/minute to 22 km *(12 nm)*; weight of shell 21 kg; also fires Chaff and illuminants.
2 Oerlikon 20 mm Mk 7 ❹.
Torpedoes: 6—324 mm ILAS 3 (2 triple) tubes ❺. Whitehead A 244/S; anti-submarine; active/passive homing to 7 km *(3.8 nm)* at 33 kts; warhead 34 kg (shaped charge).
Countermeasures: Decoys; Graseby GI 738 towed torpedo decoy. Knebworth Corvus 8-tubed trainable launchers for Chaff ❻.
ESM: Racal RDL 257; FH5 DF; radar intercept and DF.
ECM: Racal RCM 2 (*Hercules* only); jammer.
Combat data systems: Plessey-Ferranti ADAWS-4; Link 10.
Radars: Air search: Marconi Type 965P with double AKE2 array and 1010/1011 IFF ❼; A band.
Surface search: Marconi Type 992Q ❽; E/F band.
Navigation, HDWS and helicopter control: Kelvin Hughes Type 1006; I band.
Fire control: Two Marconi Type 909 ❾; I/J band (for Sea Dart missile control).
Sonars: Graseby Type 184M; hull-mounted; active search and attack; medium frequency 6-9 kHz.
Kelvin Hughes Type 162M classification set; sideways looking; active; high frequency.

Helicopters: 1 SA 319B Alouette III ❿.

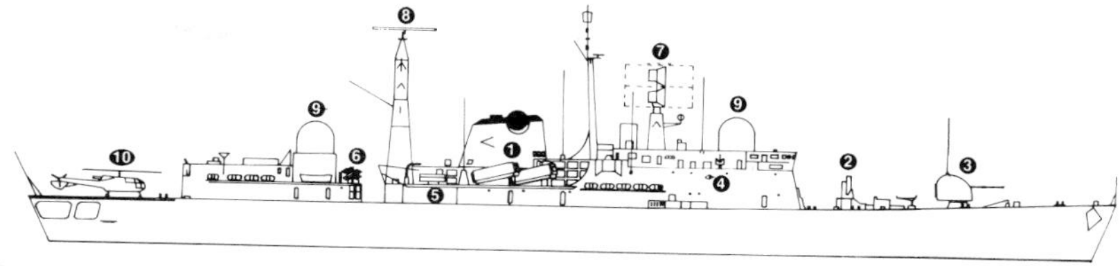

HERCULES
(Scale 1 : 1 200), Ian Sturton

HERCULES
1982, Argentine Navy

Programmes: Contract signed 18 May 1970 between the Argentine Government and Vickers Ltd. This provided for the construction of these two ships, one to be built at Barrow-in-Furness and the second at Rio Santiago with British assistance and overseeing. *Santisima Trinidad* was sabotaged on 22 August 1975 whilst fitting-out and subsequently placed in floating-dock at AFNE. Began trials early 1981.
Structure: Pennant numbers are displayed without the D prefix.
Operational: Although laid up for some time between 1983 and 1986 both ships were at sea for short periods in 1987 and back with the Fleet from 1988.

FRIGATES

4 + 2 MEKO 140 TYPE

Name	No	Builders	Laid down	Launched	Commissioned
ESPORA	41	AFNE, Rio Santiago	3 Oct 1980	23 Jan 1982	5 July 1985
ROSALES	42	AFNE, Rio Santiago	1 July 1981	4 Mar 1983	14 Nov 1986
SPIRO	43	AFNE, Rio Santiago	4 Jan 1982	24 June 1983	24 Nov 1987
PARKER	44	AFNE, Rio Santiago	2 Aug 1982	31 Mar 1984	17 Apr 1990
ROBINSON	45	AFNE, Rio Santiago	6 June 1983	15 Feb 1985	—
GOMEZ ROCA	46	AFNE, Rio Santiago	1 Dec 1983	14 Nov 1986	—

Displacement, tons: 1470 standard; 1790 full load
Dimensions, feet (metres): 299.1 × 36.4 × 11.2 *(91.2 × 11.1 × 3.4)*
Main machinery: 2 SEMT-Pielstick 16 PC2-5V400 diesels; 20 400 hp(m) *(15 MW)* sustained; 2 shafts
Speed, knots: 27. **Range, miles:** 4000 at 18 kts
Complement: 93 (11 officers)

Missiles: SSM: 4 Aerospatiale MM 38 Exocet ❶ or 8 MM 40; inertial cruise; active radar homing to 42 km *(23 nm)* (MM 38); 70 km *(40 nm)* (MM 40); warhead 165 kg; sea-skimmer. Intention is to convert to 8 MM 40 and *Espora* was first to be fitted.
Guns: 1 OTO Melara 3 in *(76 mm)*/62 compact ❷; 85° elevation; 85 rounds/minute to 16 km *(8.7 nm)* anti-surface; 12 km *(6.5 nm)* anti-aircraft; weight of shell 6 kg; also fires Chaff and illuminants.
4 Breda 40 mm/70 (2 twin) ❸; 85° elevation; 300 rounds/minute to 12.5 km *(6.8 nm)*; weight of shell 0.96 kg; ready ammunition 736 (or 444) using AP tracer, impact or proximity fuzing.
2—12.7 mm MGs.
Torpedoes: 6—324 mm ILAS 3 (2 triple) tubes ❹. Whitehead A 244/S; anti-submarine; active/passive homing to 7 km *(3.8 nm)* at 33 kts; warhead 34 kg (shaped charge).
Countermeasures: Decoys: CSEE Dagaie double mounting; 10 or 6 replaceable containers; trainable; Chaff to 12 km *(6.5 nm)*; illuminants to 4 km *(2.2 nm)*; decoys in H-J bands.
ESM: Racal RQN-3B; radar warning.
ECM: Racal TQN-2X; jammer.
Combat data systems: Signaal SEWACO.
Fire control: Signaal WM 22/41 integrated system; 1 LIROD 8 optronic director ❺ (plus 2 sights—one on each bridge wing).
Radars: Air/surface search: Signaal DA 05 ❻; E/F band; range 137 km *(75 nm)* for 2 m² target.
Navigation: Decca TM 1226; I band.
Fire Control: Signaal WM 28 ❼; I/J band; range 46 km *(25 nm)*.
IFF: Mk 10.
Sonars: Krupp Atlas ASQ 4; hull-mounted; active search and attack; medium frequency.

Helicopters: 1 SA 319B Alouette III.

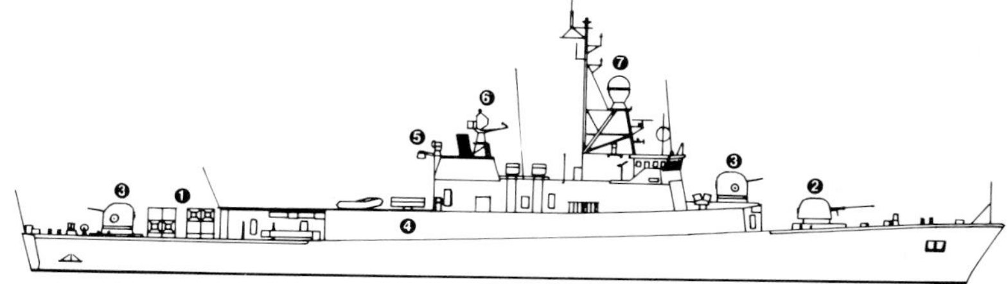

ESPORA
(Scale 1 : 900), Ian Sturton

SPIRO
12/1990

Programmes: A contract was signed with Blohm & Voss on 1 August 1979 for this group of ships which are scaled down Meko 360s. All six have been fabricated in AFNE, Rio Santiago. *Parker* flooded while fitting out which delayed commissioning. Completion of the last pair depends upon funds from foreign sales.
Structure: *Parker* and later ships fitted with a telescopic hangar which will be retro-fitted in first three. Fitted with stabilisers.
Operational: Mostly used for offshore patrol and fishery protection duties but *Spiro* and *Rosales* sent to the Gulf in 1990/91.
Sales: Venezuela has shown interest in acquiring the two which are for sale.

3 FRENCH TYPE A 69

Name	No	Builders	Laid down	Launched	Completed
DRUMMOND (ex-*Good Hope*, ex-*Lieutenant de Vaisseau le Hénaff* F 789)	31	Lorient Naval Dockyard	12 Mar 1976	5 Mar 1977	Mar 1978
GUERRICO (ex-*Transvaal*, ex-*Commandant l'Herminier* F 791)	32	Lorient Naval Dockyard	1 Oct 1976	13 Sep 1977	Oct 1978
GRANVILLE	33	Lorient Naval Dockyard	1 Dec 1978	28 June 1980	22 June 1981

Displacement, tons: 950 standard; 1170 full load
Dimensions, feet (metres): 262.5 × 33.8 × 9.8; 18 (sonar) *(80 × 10.3 × 3; 5.5)*
Main machinery: 2 SEMT-Pielstick 12 PC2.2 V400 diesels; 12 000 hp(m) *(8.82 MW)* sustained; 2 shafts; cp props
Speed, knots: 24. **Range, miles:** 4500 at 15 kts; 3000 at 18 kts
Complement: 93 (10 officers)

Missiles: SSM: 4 Aerospatiale MM 38 Exocet (2 twin) launchers ❶; inertial cruise; active radar homing to 42 km *(23 nm)*; warhead 165 kg; sea-skimmer.
Guns: 1 Creusot Loire 3.9 in *(100 mm)*/55 ❷; 80° elevation; 60-80 rounds/minute to 17 km *(9 nm)* anti-surface; 8 km *(4.4 nm)* anti-aircraft; weight of shell 13.5 kg.
2 Breda 40 mm/70 (twin) ❸; 300 rounds/minute to 12.5 km *(6.8 nm)*; weight of shell 0.96 kg; ready ammunition 736 (or 444) using AP tracer, impact or proximity fuzing.
2 Oerlikon 20 mm ❹; 1000 rounds/minute.
Torpedoes: 6—324 mm Mk 32 (2 triple) tubes ❺. Whitehead A 244; anti-submarine; active/passive homing to 7 km *(3.8 nm)* at 33 kts; warhead 34 kg.
Countermeasures: Decoys: CSEE Dagaie double mounting; 10 or 6 replaceable containers; trainable; Chaff to 12 km *(6.5 nm)*; illuminants to 4 km *(2.2 nm)*; decoys in H-J bands.
ESM: DR 2000/DALIA 500; radar warning.
ECM: Thomson-CSF Alligator; jammer.
Fire control: CSEE Naja optronics director for 40 mm in *Granville*. *Drummond* and *Guerrico* have CSEE Panda Mk 2 optical director ❻.
Radars: Air/surface search: Thomson-CSF DRBV 51A ❼ with UPX12 IFF; G band.
Navigation: Decca 1226; I band.
Fire control: Thomson-CSF DRBC 32E ❽; I/J band (for 100 mm gun).
Sonars: Thomson Sintra Diodon; hull-mounted; active search and attack; selectable 11, 12 or 13 kHz.

Programmes: The first pair was originally built for the French Navy and sold to the South African Navy in 1976 while under construction. As a result of a UN embargo on arms sales to South Africa this sale was cancelled. Purchased by Argentina in autumn 1978. Both arrived in Argentina 2 November 1978 (third ship being ordered some time later) and all have proved very popular ships in the Argentine Navy.

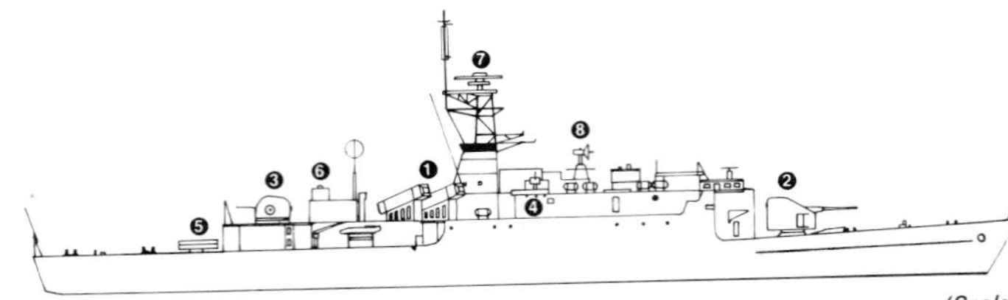

DRUMMOND *(Scale 1 : 900), Ian Sturton*

DRUMMOND *2/1988*

Modernisation: *Drummond* has had her armament updated to the same standard as the other two, replacing the Bofors 40/60.

Operational: Endurance, 15 days. Very economical in fuel consumption.

SHIPBORNE AIRCRAFT

Notes: (i) New ASW helicopters are the highest procurement priority, with 6-8 Kaman Seasprite the most likely purchase.
(ii) Fixed wing aircraft fly once a year from USN aircraft carriers.

Numbers/Type: 5 Aerospatiale SA 319B Alouette III.
Operational speed: 113 kts *(210 km/h)*.
Service ceiling: 10 500 ft *(3200 m)*.
Range: 290 nm *(540 km)*.
Role/Weapon systems: ASW Helicopter; used for liaison in peacetime; wartime role includes commando assault and ASW/ASVW. Reported that there is a requirement for 12 Kaman SH-2G in due course as replacements. Sensors: Nose-mounted search radar. Weapons: ASW; 2 × Mk 44 torpedoes. ASV; 2 × AS12 missiles.

ALOUETTE III *1988, Argentine Navy*

Numbers/Type: 7 Agusta-Sikorsky ASH-3H Sea King.
Operational speed: 120 kts *(222 km/h)*.
Service ceiling: 12 205 ft *(3720 m)*.
Range: 630 nm *(1165 km)*.
Role/Weapon systems: ASW Helicopter; carrier or land-based for ASW with limited surface search capability. Sensors: Search radar, Bendix sonar. Weapons: ASW; up to 4 × A 244 torpedoes or 4 × depth bombs.

SEA KING *1990, Argentine Navy*

Numbers/Type: 12 Dassault-Breguet Super Etendard.
Operational speed: Mach 1.
Service ceiling: 44 950 ft *(13 700 m)*.
Range: 920 nm *(1700 km)*.
Role/Weapon systems: Strike Fighter with anti-shipping ability proved in South Atlantic; carrier-borne strike, air defence and ASV roles, can also be land-based. All except one were in reserve in early 1990. Hi-lo-hi combat radius 460 nm *(850 km)*. Sensors: Agave multi-mode radar, ECM. Weapons: Strike; 2.1 tons of 'iron' bombs. ASVW; 1 × Exocet or 1 × Martin Pescador missiles. Self-defence; 2 × Magic AAMs. Standard; 2 × 30 mm cannon.

SUPER ETENDARD *1985, Argentine Navy*

Numbers/Type: 5 Grumman S-2E Tracker.
Operational speed: 130 kts *(241 km/h)*.
Service ceiling: 25 000 ft *(7620 m)*.
Range: 1350 nm *(2500 km)*.
Role/Weapon systems: Carrier-borne medium-range ASW aircraft; also used for shore-based MR and EEZ patrol. One shipped to Israel in 1989 for Garrett turboprop installation. Possi' le prototype for fleet conversion but progress delayed by lack of funds. Sensors: Search radar up to 32 sonobuoys, echo-ranging depth charges. Weapons: ASW; torpedoes, bombs and depth charges.

TRACKER *1985, Argentine Navy*

LAND-BASED MARITIME AIRCRAFT (FRONT LINE)

Numbers/Type: 9 Aermacchi MB 326GB.
Operational speed: 468 kts *(867 km/h)*.
Service ceiling: 47 000 ft *(14 325 m)*.
Range: 1320 nm *(2446 km)*.
Role/Weapon systems: Light Attack; supplements anti-shipping/strike; also has training role. Weapons: ASV; 1.8 tons of 'iron' bombs. Strike; 6 × rockets. Recce; underwing camera pod.

Numbers/Type: 14 Aermacchi MB-339A.
Operational speed: 485 kts *(898 km/h)*.
Service ceiling: 48 000 ft *(14 630 m)*.
Range: 650 nm *(1200 km)*.
Role/Weapon systems: Limited anti-shipping support; aircraft equip one squadron only, all aircraft in store. Weapons: ASV; 1.8 tons of 'iron' bombs. Strike; 2 × 30 mm and 6 × rockets. Self-defence; 2 × Magic AAMs.

Numbers/Type: 4 Lockheed L-188E Electra.
Operational speed: 389 kts *(721 km/h)*.
Service ceiling: 28 400 ft *(8655 m)*.
Range: 3000 nm *(5570 km)*.
Role/Weapon systems: Converted from transport aircraft for overwater Elint/EW role and long-range MR with South Atlantic. Sensors: Various EW systems including Elisra ESM. Weapons: Unarmed.

Numbers/Type: 5 Beechcraft Queen Air.
Operational speed: 260 kts *(482 km/h)*.
Service ceiling: 25 000 ft *(7620 m)*.
Range: 2000 nm *(3705 km)*.
Role/Weapon systems: Naval reconnaissance for protection of port installations; also has training role. Sensors: Bendix search radar. Weapons: Unarmed.

PATROL SHIPS

2 KING CLASS

Name	*No*	*Builders*	*Commissioned*
MURATURE	P 20	Base Nav Rio Santiago	12 Apr 1945
KING	P 21	Base Nav Rio Santiago	28 July 1946

Displacement, tons: 913 standard; 1000 normal; 1032 full load
Dimensions, feet (metres): 252.7 × 29.5 × 13.1 *(77 × 9 × 4)*
Main machinery: 2 Werkspoor diesels; 2500 hp(m) *(1.8 MW)*; 2 shafts
Speed, knots: 18. **Range, miles:** 9000 at 12 kts
Complement: 130
Guns: 3 Vickers 4 in *(105 mm)*/45; 80° elevation; 16 rounds/minute to 19 km *(10 nm)*; weight of shell 16 kg.
4 Bofors 40 mm/60 (1 twin, 2 single); 80° elevation; 120 rounds/minute/barrel to 10 km *(5.5 nm)*; weight of shell 0.89 kg.
5—12.7 mm MGs.
Depth charges: 4 projectors.
Radars: Surface search: Racal Decca 1226; I band.

Comment: Named after Captain John King, an Irish follower of Admiral Brown, who distinguished himself in the war with Brazil, 1826-28; and Captain Jose Murature, who performed conspicuous service against the Paraguayans at the Battle of Cuevas in 1865. *King* laid down June 1938, launched 3 November 1943. *Murature* laid down March 1940, launched July 1943. Used for cadet training.

MURATURE *1988, Argentine Navy*

2 Ex-US CHEROKEE CLASS

Name	*No*	*Builders*	*Commissioned*
COMANDANTE GENERAL IRIGOYEN (ex-USS *Cahuilla*)	A 1	Charleston S B and D D Co	10 Mar 1945
FRANCISCO DE GURRUCHAGA (ex-USS *Luiseno* ATF 156)	A 3	Charleston S B and D D Co	16 June 1945

Displacement, tons: 1235 standard; 1731 full load
Dimensions, feet (metres): 205 × 38.5 × 17 *(62.5 × 11.7 × 5.2)*
Main machinery: Diesel-electric; 4 GM 12-278 diesels; 4400 hp *(3.28 MW)*; 4 generators; 1 motor; 3000 hp *(2.24 MW)*; 1 shaft
Speed, knots: 16. **Range, miles:** 6500 at 15 kts; 15 000 at 8 kts
Complement: 85
Guns: 4 Bofors 40 mm/60 (1 twin; 2 single); 80° elevation; 120 rounds/minute to 10 km *(5.5 nm)* anti-surface; 3 km *(1.6 nm)* anti-aircraft; weight of shell 0.89 kg.
2 Oerlikon 20 mm (mounted only in *Comandante General Irigoyen*); 800 rounds/minute to 2 km.
Radars: Surface search: Racal Decca 626; I band.
Navigation: Racal Decca 1230; I band.

Comment: Fitted with powerful pumps and other salvage equipment. *Comandante General Irigoyen* transferred by sale to Argentina at San Diego, California, on 9 July 1961. Classified as a tug until 1966 when she was re-rated as patrol vessel. *Francisco De Gurruchaga* transferred on 1 July 1975 by sale.

GURRUCHAGA *1989, Argentine Navy*

2 Ex-US SOTOYOMO CLASS

Name	*No*	*Builders*	*Commissioned*
ALFEREZ SOBRAL (ex-USS *Salish* ATA 187)	A 9	Levingstone S B Co, Orange	9 Sep 1944
COMODORO SOMELLERA (ex-USS *Catawba* ATA 210)	A 10	Levingstone S B Co, Orange	7 Dec 1944

Displacement, tons: 800 full load
Dimensions, feet (metres): 143 × 33.9 × 13 *(43.6 × 10.3 × 4)*
Main machinery: Diesel-electric; 2 GM 12-278A diesels; 2200 hp *(1.64 MW)*; 2 generators; 1 motor; 1500 hp *(1.12 MW)*; 1 shaft
Speed, knots: 12.5. **Range, miles:** 16 500 at 8 kts
Complement: 49

Comment: Former US ocean tugs transferred on 10 February 1972. *Sanaviron* (A 8) operates as a tug. *Alferez Sobral* was paid off in 1987 but is now back in service.

COMODORO SOMELLERA *1986, Argentine Navy*

1 OLIVIERI CLASS

Name	*No*	*Builders*	*Commissioned*
TENIENTE OLIVIERI (ex-*Marsea 10*)	A 2	Quality SB, Louisiana	Dec 1987

Displacement, tons: 1640 full load
Dimensions, feet (metres): 184.8 × 40 × 14 *(56.3 × 12.2 × 4.3)*
Main machinery: 2 GM/EMD 16-645 E6; 3900 hp *(2.9 MW)*; 2 shafts
Speed, knots: 16
Complement: 15 (4 officers)
Guns: 2—12.7 mm MGs.

Comment: Built by Quality Shipyards, New Orleans, as a large tug but rated as an Aviso. Acquired from US Maritime Administration in December 1987.

LIGHT FORCES

2 TYPE TNC 45 (FAST ATTACK CRAFT—GUN)

Name	*No*	*Builders*	*Commissioned*
INTREPIDA	P 85	Lürssen, Bremen	20 July 1974
INDOMITA	P 86	Lürssen, Bremen	12 Dec 1974

Displacement, tons: 268 full load
Dimensions, feet (metres): 147.3 × 24.3 × 7.9 *(44.9 × 7.4 × 2.4)*
Main machinery: 4 MTU MD872 diesels; 12 000 hp(m) *(8.82 MW)*; 4 shafts
Speed, knots: 38. **Range, miles:** 1450 at 20 kts
Complement: 39 (2 officers)
Guns: 1 OTO Melara 3 in *(76 mm)*/62 compact; 85 rounds/minute to 16 km *(9 nm)* anti-surface; 12 km *(6.5 nm)* anti-aircraft; weight of shell 6 kg.
2 Bofors 40 mm/70; 330 rounds/minute to 12 km *(6.5 nm)* anti-surface; 4 km *(2.2 nm)* anti-aircraft; weight of shell 0.89 kg.
2 Oerlikon 81 mm rocket launchers for illuminants.
Torpedoes: 2—21 in *(533 mm)* launchers. AEG SST-4; wire-guided; active/passive homing to 28 km *(15 nm)* at 23 kts.
Countermeasures: ESM: Racal RDL 1; radar warning.
Fire control: Signaal WM22 optronic for guns. Signaal M11 for torpedo guidance and control.
Radars: Surface search: Decca 626; I band.

Comment: These two vessels were ordered in 1970. *Intrepida* launched on 2 December 1973, *Indomita* on 8 April 1974.

INDOMITA *1986, van Ginderen Collection*

4 DABUR CLASS (COASTAL PATROL CRAFT)

Name	*No*	*Builders*	*Commissioned*
BARADERO	P 61	Israel Aircraft Industries	1978
BARRANQUERAS	P 62	Israel Aircraft Industries	1978
CLORINDA	P 63	Israel Aircraft Industries	1978
CONCEPCIÓN DEL URUGUAY	P 64	Israel Aircraft Industries	1978

Displacement, tons: 33.7 standard; 39 full load
Dimensions, feet (metres): 64.9 × 18 × 5.8 *(19.8 × 5.5 × 1.8)*
Main machinery: 2 GM 12V-71TA diesels; 840 hp *(627 kW)*; 2 shafts
Speed, knots: 19. **Range, miles:** 450 at 13 kts
Complement: 9
Guns: 2 Oerlikon 20 mm. 4—12.7 mm (2 twin) MGs.
Depth charges: 2 portable rails.
Radars: Navigation: Decca 101; I band.

Comment: Of all aluminium construction. Employed from 1991 as part of the UN Central American peace keeping force.

DABUR Class *1978, RAMTA*

MINE WARFARE FORCES

6 Ex-BRITISH TON CLASS (4 MINESWEEPERS—COASTAL and 2 MINEHUNTERS)

Name	*No*	*Builders*	*Launched*
NEUQUEN (ex-HMS *Hickleton*)	M 1	Thornycroft	26 Jan 1955
RIO NEGRO (ex-HMS *Tarlton*)	M 2	Doig	10 Nov 1954
CHUBUT (ex-HMS *Santon*)	M 3	Fleetlands	18 Aug 1955
TIERRA DEL FUEGO (ex-HMS *Bevington*)	M 4	Whites	17 Mar 1953
CHACO (ex-HMS *Rennington*)	M 5	Richards	27 Nov 1958
FORMOSA (ex-HMS *Ilmington*)	M 6	Camper, Nicholson	8 Mar 1954

Displacement, tons: 360 standard; 440 full load
Dimensions, feet (metres): 153 × 28.9 × 8.2 *(46.6 × 8.8 × 2.5)*
Main machinery: 2 Paxman Deltic/Mirrlees JVSS-12 diesels; 3000 hp *(2.24 MW)*; 2 shafts
Speed, knots: 15. **Range, miles:** 2500 at 12 kts
Complement: Minesweepers 27; Minehunters 36

Guns: 1 or 2 Bofors 40 mm/60 (in some); 80° elevation; 120 rounds/minute to 10 km *(5.5 nm)* anti-surface; 3 km *(1.6 nm)* anti-aircraft; weight of shell 0.89 kg.
Radars: Navigation: Decca 45; I band. Type 955 IFF transponder.
Sonars: Plessey Type 193 (in minehunters); active minehunting; 100/300 kHz.

Programmes: Former British coastal minesweepers of the Ton class. Purchased in 1967.
Modernisation: In 1968 *Chaco* and *Formosa* were converted into minehunters in HM Dockyard, Portsmouth, and the other four were refitted and modernised as minesweepers by the Vosper Thornycroft Group with Vosper activated-fin stabiliser equipment. Of composite wooden and non-magnetic metal construction.
Operational: All were active in 1991.

NEUQUEN *1988, Argentine Navy*

AMPHIBIOUS FORCES

Note: Plans for a 4000 ton LST have been shelved.

1 LANDING SHIP (TANK)

Name	*No*	*Builders*	*Commissioned*
CABO SAN ANTONIO	Q 42	AFNE, Rio Santiago	1971

Displacement, tons: 4164 light; 8000 full load
Dimensions, feet (metres): 472.3 × 68.9 × 9.8 *(144 × 21 × 3)*
Main machinery: 6 diesels; 13 700 hp *(10.2 MW)*; 2 shafts
Speed, knots: 16
Complement: 124
Military lift: 700 troops; 23 medium tanks; 8 LCVPs each capable of carrying 36 troops or 3.5 tons
Guns: 12 Bofors 40/60 mm (3 quad); 120 rounds/minute to 10 km *(5.5 nm)* anti-surface; 3 km *(1.6 nm)* anti-aircraft; weight of shell 0.89 kg.
4 Oerlikon 20 mm (2 twin).
Fire control: 3 US Mk 5 Mod 2 optical GFCS.
Radars: Navigation: Plessey AWS-1; E/F band; has some air search capability.
Helicopters: Capable of operating up to CH-47 Chinook transport helicopter cross-deck.

Comment: Modified US De Soto County class—principal difference being the fitting of 60 tons Stülcken heavy-lift gear and different armament.

CABO SAN ANTONIO *1978, Argentine Navy*

4 Ex-US LCM 6 CLASS

EDM 1, 2, 3, 4

Displacement, tons: 56 full load
Dimensions, feet (metres): 56 × 14 × 3.9 *(17.1 × 4.3 × 1.2)*
Main machinery: 2 Gray 64 HN9 diesels; 330 hp *(246 kW)* sustained; 2 shafts
Speed, knots: 11. **Range, miles:** 130 at 10 kts
Military lift: 30 tons
Guns: 2—12.7 mm MGs.

Comment: Acquired in June 1971.

8 Ex-US LCVPs

EDVP 30-37

Displacement, tons: 13 full load
Dimensions, feet (metres): 35.8 × 10.5 × 3.6 *(10.9 × 3.2 × 1.1)*
Main machinery: 1 Gray 64 HN9 diesel; 165 hp *(123 kW)* sustained; 1 shaft
Speed, knots: 9. **Range, miles:** 110 at 9 kts
Military lift: 3.5 tons or 36 troops

Comment: Acquired in May 1970.

8 ARGENTINIAN LCVPs

Displacement, tons: 7.5
Dimensions, feet (metres): 35.8 × 10.5 × 1.6 *(10.9 × 3.2 × 0.5)*
Main machinery: Fiat diesel; 200 hp(m) *(147 kW)*; 1 shaft
Speed, knots: 9

Comment: Built by AFNE and El Tigre since 1971.

SURVEY AND OCEANOGRAPHIC SHIPS

1 PUERTO DESEADO CLASS

Name	*No*	*Builders*	*Commissioned*
PUERTO DESEADO	Q 8	Astarsa, San Fernando	26 Feb 1979

Displacement, tons: 2133 standard; 2400 full load
Dimensions, feet (metres): 251.9 × 51.8 × 21.3 *(76.8 × 15.8 × 6.5)*
Main machinery: 2 Fiat-GMT diesels; 3600 hp(m) *(2.65 MW)*; 1 shaft
Speed, knots: 15. **Range, miles:** 12 000 at 12 kts
Complement: 61 (12 officers) plus 20 scientists
Radars: Navigation: I band.

Comment: Laid down on 17 March 1976 for Consejo Nacional de Investigaciones Tecnicas y Scientificas. Launched on 4 December 1976. For survey work fitted with: four Hewlett-Packard 2108-A, gravimeter, magnetometer, seismic systems, geological laboratory. Omega and NAVSAT equipped.

1 RESEARCH SHIP

Name	*No*	*Builders*	*Commissioned*
COMODORO RIVADAVIA	Q 11	Mestrina, Tigre	6 Dec 1974

Displacement, tons: 609 standard; 700 full load
Dimensions, feet (metres): 171.2 × 28.9 × 8.5 *(52.2 × 8.8 × 2.6)*
Main machinery: 2 Stork Werkspoor RHO-218K diesels; 1160 hp(m) *(853 kW)*; 2 shafts
Speed, knots: 12. **Range, miles:** 6000 at 12 kts
Complement: 33 (5 officers)
Helicopters: Provision for SA 319B Alouette III helicopter.

Comment: Laid down on 17 July 1971 and launched on 2 December 1972.

COMODORO RIVADAVIA *8/1988, van Ginderen Collection*

1 COASTAL SURVEY LAUNCH

Name	*No*	*Builders*	*Commissioned*
CORMORAN	Q 15	AFNE, Rio Santiago	20 Feb 1964

Displacement, tons: 102 full load
Dimensions, feet (metres): 83 × 16.4 × 5.9 *(25.3 × 5 × 1.8)*
Main machinery: 2 diesels; 440 hp(m) *(323 kW)*; 2 shafts
Speed, knots: 11
Complement: 19 (3 officers)

Comment: Launched 10 August 1963.

1 COASTAL SURVEY LAUNCH

Name	*No*	*Builders*	*Commissioned*
PETREL	Q 16	Cadenazzi, Tigre	1965

Displacement, tons: 50 full load
Dimensions, feet (metres): 64.8 × 14.8 × 5.6 *(19.7 × 4.5 × 1.7)*
Main machinery: 2 diesels; 340 hp(m) *(250 kW)*; 2 shafts
Speed, knots: 9
Complement: 9 (2 officers)

Comment: Built using hull of EM 128 transferred from Prefectura Naval.

PETREL *1986, van Ginderen Collection*

TRANSPORTS

Note: There are plans for a large fleet replenishment ship to replace the *Punta Medanos* deleted in 1987. A lease from the USN seems the most likely way of meeting the requirement although the Navy would prefer a derivative of the Spanish *Mar del Norte*.

3 COSTA SUR CLASS

Name	*No*	*Builders*	*Commissioned*
CANAL BEAGLE	B 3	Astillero Principe y Menghi SA	29 Apr 1978
BAHIA SAN BLAS	B 4	Astillero Principe y Menghi SA	27 Nov 1978
CABO DE HORNOS (ex-*Bahia Camarones*)	B 5	Astillero Principe y Menghi SA	28 June 1979

Measurement, tons: 5800 dwt; 4600 gross
Dimensions, feet (metres): 390.3 × 57.4 × 21 *(119 × 17.5 × 6.4)*
Main machinery: 2 AFNE-Sulzer diesels; 6400 hp(m) *(4.7 MW)*; 2 shafts
Speed, knots: 15

Comment: Ordered December 1975. Laid down 10 January 1977, 11 April 1977 and 29 April 1978. Launched 19 October 1977, 29 April 1978 and 4 November 1978. Used to supply offshore research installations in Naval Area South.

CANAL BEAGLE *1988, Argentine Navy*

1 ICEBREAKER

Name	*No*	*Builders*	*Commissioned*
ALMIRANTE IRIZAR	Q 5	Wärtsilä, Helsinki	15 Dec 1978

Displacement, tons: 14 900 full load
Dimensions, feet (metres): 392 × 82 × 31.2 *(119.3 × 25 × 9.5)*
Main machinery: Diesel-electric; 4 Wärtsilä-SEMT-Pielstick 8PC2.5L diesels; 18 720 hp(m) *(13.77 MW)* sustained; 4 generators; 2 motors; 16 200 hp(m) *(11.9 MW)*; 2 shafts
Speed, knots: 16.5
Complement: 133 ship's company plus 100 passengers
Guns: 2 Bofors 40 mm/70; 300 rounds/minute to 12 km *(6.5 nm)* anti-surface; 4 km *(2.2 nm)* anti-aircraft; weight of shell 0.96 kg.
Radars: Air/surface search: Plessey AWS 2; E/F band.
Navigation: Two Decca; I band.
Helicopters: 2 ASH-3H Sea King.

Comment: Fitted for landing craft with two 16 ton cranes, fin stabilisers, Wärtsilä bubbling system and a 60 ton towing winch. Red hull with white upperworks and red funnel. Designed for Antarctic support operations and able to remain in polar regions throughout the winter with 210 people aboard. Used as a transport to South Georgia in December 1981 and as a hospital ship during the Falklands campaign April to June 1982. Currently used as the Patagonian supply ship.

ALMIRANTE IRIZAR *1988, Argentine Navy*

PRESIDENTIAL YACHT

1 YACHT

Name	No	Builders	Commissioned
TEQUARA	Q 72	—	1936

Displacement, tons: 195 full load
Dimensions, feet (metres): 124.7 × 22.3 × 5.2 *(38 × 6.8 × 1.6)*
Complement: 7 (2 officers)

Comment: Based on the River Lujan. Can be used as a Hospital Ship.

TEQUARA *1989, Argentine Navy*

TRAINING SHIPS

Note: There are also three small yachts: *Itati II* (Q 73), *Fortuna I* (Q 25) and *Fortuna II* (Q 26).

Name	No	Builders	Commissioned
LIBERTAD	Q 2	AFNE, Rio Santiago	28 May 1963

Displacement, tons: 3025 standard; 3765 full load
Dimensions, feet (metres): 262 wl; 301 oa × 45.3 × 21.8 *(79.9; 91.7 × 13.8 × 6.6)*
Main machinery: 2 Sulzer diesels; 2400 hp(m) *(1.76 MW)*; 2 shafts
Speed, knots: 13.5 under power. **Range, miles:** 12 000
Complement: 220 crew plus 150 cadets
Guns: 1—3 in *(76 mm)* and 4—40 mm (fitted for but not with). 4—47 mm saluting guns.
Radars: Navigation: Decca; I band.

Comment: Launched 30 May 1956. She set up record for crossing the North Atlantic under sail in 1966, a record which still stands. Sail area, 27 265 sq m.

LIBERTAD *8/1990, G. Toremans*

Name	No	Builders	Commissioned
PILOTO ALSINA (ex-MV *Ciudad de Formosa*)	Q 31	U N Levante, Spain	1963

Displacement, tons: 2800 full load
Measurement, tons: 720 dwt; 3986 gross
Dimensions, feet (metres): 346 × 57.1 × 26.9 *(105.5 × 17.4 × 8.2)*
Main machinery: 3 Maquinista/B&W diesels; 4500 hp(m) *(3.3 MW)*; 1 shaft
Speed, knots: 14

Comment: Commissioned in Navy 17 March 1981. Former ferry.

PILOTO ALSINA *4/1991, Luis Oscar Zunino*

TUGS

Name	No	Builders	Commissioned
SANAVIRON (ex-US ATA 228)	A 8	Levingstone S B Co, Orange	5 Aug 1947

Comment: Details as for Sotoyomo class under *Patrol Ships*.

SANAVIRON *8/1989, van Ginderen Collection*

Name	No	Builders	Commissioned
QUERANDI	R 2	Ast Vicente Forte, Buenos Aires	22 Aug 1978
TEHUELCHE	R 3	Ast Vicente Forte, Buenos Aires	2 Nov 1978

Displacement, tons: 270 full load
Dimensions, feet (metres): 110.2 × 27.6 × 9.8 *(33.6 × 8.4 × 3)*
Main machinery: 2 MAN diesels; 1320 hp(m) *(970 kW)*; 2 shafts
Speed, knots: 12. **Range, miles:** 1100 at 12 kts
Complement: 30
Radars: Navigation: Decca; I band.

Comment: Ordered 1973. Launched 20 December 1977.

Name	No	Name	No
HUARPE	R 1	**ONA**	R 7
MATACO	R 4	**TOBA**	R 8

Displacement, tons: 208 full load
Dimensions, feet (metres): 99.4 × 27.6 × 10.5 *(30.3 × 8.4 × 3.2)*
Main machinery: 2 MAN diesels; 830 hp(m) *(610 kW)*; 1 shaft
Speed, knots: 12
Complement: 10 (2 officers)

Comment: Transferred from the River Flotilla to the Navy in 1988.

Name	No	Name	No
MOCOVI	R 5 (ex-US YTL 441)	**CAPAYAN**	R 16 (ex-US YTL 443)
CALCHAQUI	R 6 (ex-US YTL 445)	**CHIQUILLAN**	R 18 (ex-US YTL 444)
CHULUPI	R 10 (ex-US YTL 426)	**MORCOYAN**	R 19 (ex-US YTL 448)

Displacement, tons: 70
Dimensions, feet (metres): 63 × 16.4 × 7.2 *(19.2 × 5 × 2.2)*
Main machinery: 1 Hoover-Owens-Rentscheer diesel; 310 hp(m) *(228 kW)*; 1 shaft
Speed, knots: 10
Complement: 5

Comment: YTL Type built in USA and transferred on lease in March 1965 (R 16, 18, 19), remainder in March 1969. All purchased on 16 June 1977.

FLOATING DOCKS

Number	Dimensions, feet (metres)	Capacity, tons
Y 1 (ex-ARD 23)	492 × 88.6 × 56 *(150 × 27 × 17.1)*	3500
2	300.1 × 60 × 41 *(91.5 × 18.3 × 12.5)*	1500
—	215.8 × 46 × 45.5 *(65.8 × 14 × 13.7)*	750
A	565.8 × 85.3 *(172.5 × 26)*	12 000
B	360.8 × 59 *(110 × 18)*	2800
—	623.4 × 78.7 *(190 × 24)*	12 000

Comment: First one is at Mar del Plata naval base, the second at Dársena Norte, Buenos Aires, the third at Puerto Belgrano and last two at Dársena Este. No 2 was built in 1913, A in 1957-58 and B in 1956. Another 12 000 ton dock was built in 1987 at Rio Santiago Shipyard. There are also at least four floating cranes.

ARMY WATERCRAFT

Comment: Several LCPs (BDPs) are operated by Batallón de Ingenieros Anfibios 601 at Santa Fé. Built by Ast Vicente Forte. Ferries for crossing Rio Paraña include two built in 1969. In addition there are over 1000 Ferramar 'Asalto' and 'Comando' inflatable craft.

FERRAMAR ASALTO *1990, Ferramar*

PREFECTURA NAVAL ARGENTINA (COAST GUARD)

Headquarters' Appointments

Commander:
Prefecto General Jorge H Maggi
Vice Commander:
Prefecto General Jorge A Gentiluomo

Senior Appointments

Director of Navigation Police and Safety:
Prefecto General Juan C Babich
Director of Prefectura's Zones:
Prefecto General Raimundo Pelinsky
Director of Materiel:
Prefecto General Andres R Lorenzo
Director of Administration:
Prefecto General Carlos J Leyes
Director of Judicial Police:
Prefecto Mayor Juan M Redón
Director of Personnel:
Prefecto General Fortunato C Benasulin
Director of Pilot Services:
Prefecto General Pedro L Bustamante

Personnel

1992: 13 500 (1280 officers) including 950 civilians

Tasks

Under the General Organisation Act the PNA is charged with:
(a) Enforcement of Federal Laws on the high seas and waters subject to the Argentine Republic.
(b) Enforcement of environmental protection laws in Federal waters.
(c) Search and Rescue.
(d) Security of waterfront facilities and vessels in port.
(e) Operations of certain Navaids.
(f) Operation of Pilot Services.
(g) Management and operation of Aviation Department, Coastguard Vessels, Salvage, Fire and Anti-Pollution Service, National Diving School and several Fire Brigades.

Organisation

Formed in 10 districts; High Paraña River, Upper Paraña and Paraguay Rivers, Lower Paraña River, Upper Uruguay River, Lower Uruguay River, Delta, River Plate, Northern Argentine Sea, Southern Argentine Sea, Lakes and Comahue.

History

The Spanish authorities in South America established similar organisations to those in Spain. In 1756 the Captainship of the Port came into being in Buenos Aires—in 1810 the Ship Registry office was added to this title. On 29 October 1896 the title of Capitania General de Puertos was established by Act of Congress, the beginning of the PNA. Today, as a security and safety force, it has responsibilities throughout the rivers of Argentina, the ports and harbours as well as within territorial waters out to the 12 mile limit.

Identity markings

Two unequal blue stripes with, superimposed, crossed white anchors followed by the title Prefectura Naval.

Strength of Prefectura

Patrol Ships	6
Large Patrol Craft	4
Coastal Patrol Craft	53
Training Ships	3
Pilot Craft	23

PENNANT LIST

Prefectura Naval Argentina

GC 13	Delfin
GC 21	Lynch
GC 22	Toll
GC 24	Mantilla
GC 25	Azopardo
GC 26	Thompson
GC 27	Prefecto Pique
GC 28	Prefecto Derbes
GC 43	Mandubi
GC 47	Tonina
GC 48-61	Patrol Craft
GC 64	Mar del Plata
GC 65	Martin Garcia
GC 66	Rio Lujan
GC 67	Rio Uruguay
GC 68	Rio Paraguay
GC 69	Rio Parana
GC 70	Rio de la Plata
GC 71	La Plata
GC 72	Buenos Aires
GC 73	Cabo Corrientes
GC 74	Rio Quequen
GC 75	Bahia Blanca
GC 76	Ingeniero White
GC 77	Golfo San Matias
GC 78	Madryn
GC 79	Rio Deseado
GC 80	Ushuaia
GC 81	Canal de Beagle
GC 88-95	Patrol Craft
GC 101	Dorado
GC 102-114	Patrol Craft

PATROL FORCES

Note: In addition to the ships and craft listed below the PNA operates 450 craft, including floating cranes, runabouts and inflatables of all types including LS 11201-3, LS 11001-4, LS 9500-9, LS 6301-17, LS 6801-12, LS 5801-5865, SB9.

1 PATROL SHIP

Name	*No*	*Builders*	*Completed*
DELFIN	GC 13	Ijsselwerf, Netherlands	14 May 1957

Displacement, tons: 700 standard; 1000 full load
Dimensions, feet (metres): 193.5 × 29.8 × 13.8 *(59 × 9.1 × 4.2)*
Main machinery: 2 MAN diesels; 2300 hp(m) *(1.69 MW)*; 2 shafts
Speed, knots: 15. **Range, miles:** 6720 at 10 kts
Complement: 27
Guns: 1 Oerlikon 20 mm. 2—12.7 mm Browning MGs.
Radars: Navigation: Decca; I band.

Comment: Whaler acquired for PNA in 1969. Commissioned 23 January 1970.

DELFIN *1988, Reinaldo Carrera*

5 HALCON CLASS (B 119)

Name	*No*	*Builders*	*Commissioned*
MANTILLA	GC 24	Bazán, El Ferrol	20 Dec 1982
AZOPARDO	GC 25	Bazán, El Ferrol	28 Apr 1983
THOMPSON	GC 26	Bazán, El Ferrol	20 June 1983
PREFECTO PIQUE	GC 27	Bazán, El Ferrol	29 July 1983
PREFECTO DERBES	GC 28	Bazán, El Ferrol	20 Nov 1983

Displacement, tons: 910 standard; 1084 full load
Dimensions, feet (metres): 219.9 × 34.4 × 13.8 *(67 × 10.5 × 4.2)*
Main machinery: 2 Bazán-MTU 16V 956 TB91 diesels; 7500 hp(m) *(5.52 MW)* sustained; 2 shafts
Speed, knots: 20. **Range, miles:** 5000 at 18 kts
Complement: 33 (10 officers)
Guns: 1 Breda 40 mm/70; 300 rounds/minute to 12.5 km *(7 nm)*; weight of shell 0.96 kg. 2—12.7 mm MGs.
Radars: Navigation: Decca 1226; I band.
Helicopters: 1 HB 350B Esquilo (see *Comment*).

Comment: Ordered in 1979 from Bazán, El Ferrol, Spain. All have helicopter hangar and Magnavox MX 1102 SATNAV. Hospital with four beds. Carry one rigid rescue craft (*6.1 m*) with Perkins outboard and a capacity of 12 and two inflatable craft (*4.1 m*) with Evinrude outboard. Esquilo helicopters were to have replaced the Alouettes loaned from the Navy but as this acquisition has been delayed until at least 1993, helicopters are currently no longer carried.

MANTILLA *6/1989, Ernesto I. Portela*

2 LYNCH CLASS (LARGE PATROL CRAFT)

Name	*No*	*Builders*	*Commissioned*
LYNCH	GC 21	AFNE, Rio Santiago	20 May 1964
TOLL	GC 22	AFNE, Rio Santiago	7 July 1966

Displacement, tons: 100 standard; 117 full load
Dimensions, feet (metres): 98.4 × 21 × 5.6 *(30 × 6.4 × 1.7)*
Main machinery: 2 MTU Maybach diesels; 2700 hp(m) *(1.98 MW)*; 2 shafts
Speed, knots: 22. **Range, miles:** 2000
Complement: 11
Guns: 1 Oerlikon 20 mm.

TOLL *1990, Prefectura Naval Argentina*

1 LARGE PATROL CRAFT

Name	*No*	*Builders*	*Commissioned*
MANDUBI	GC 43	Base Naval Rio Santiago	1940

Displacement, tons: 270 full load
Dimensions, feet (metres): 108.9 × 20.7 × 6.2 *(33.2 × 6.3 × 1.9)*
Main machinery: 2 MAN G6V-23.5/33 diesels; 500 hp(m) *(367 kW)*; 1 shaft
Speed, knots: 14. **Range, miles:** 800 at 14 kts; 3400 at 10 kts
Complement: 12
Guns: 2—12.7 mm Browning MGs.

Comment: Since 1986 has acted as training craft for PNA Cadets School carrying 20 cadets.

MANDUBI *1990, Prefectura Naval Argentina*

1 RIVER PATROL SHIP

Name	*No*	*Builders*	*Commissioned*
TONINA	GC 47	SANYM SA San Fernando, Argentina	30 June 1978

Displacement, tons: 103 standard; 153 full load
Dimensions, feet (metres): 83.8 × 21.3 × 10.1 *(25.5 × 6.5 × 3.3)*
Main machinery: 2 GM 16V-71TA diesels; 1380 hp *(1.03 MW)*; 2 shafts
Speed, knots: 10. **Range, miles:** 2800 at 10 kts
Complement: 11 (3 officers)
Guns: 1 Oerlikon 20 mm.
Radars: Navigation: Decca 1226; I band.

Comment: Served as training ship for PNA Cadets School until 1986. Now acts as salvage ship with salvage pumps and recompression chamber. Capable of operating divers and underwater swimmers.

TONINA *1989, Prefectura Naval Argentina*

18 BLOHM & VOSS Z-28 TYPE (COASTAL PATROL CRAFT)

MAR DEL PLATA GC 64	**LA PLATA** GC 71	**MADRYN** GC 78
MARTIN GARCIA GC 65	**BUENOS AIRES** GC 72	**RIO DESEADO** GC 79
RIO LUJAN GC 66	**CABO CORRIENTES** GC 73	**USHUAIA** GC 80
RIO URUGUAY GC 67	**RIO QUEQUEN** GC 74	**CANAL DE BEAGLE** GC 81
RIO PARAGUAY GC 68	**BAHIA BLANCA** GC 75	
RIO PARAÑA GC 69	**INGENIERO WHITE** GC 76	
RIO DE LA PLATA GC 70	**GOLFO SAN MATIAS** GC 77	

Displacement, tons: 81 full load
Dimensions, feet (metres): 91.8 × 17.4 × 5.2 *(28 × 5.3 × 1.6)*
Main machinery: 2 MTU 8V 331 TC 92 diesels; 1770 hp(m) *(1.3 MW)* sustained; 2 shafts
Speed, knots: 22. **Range, miles:** 1200 at 12 kts; 780 at 18 kts
Complement: 14 (3 officers)
Guns: 1 Oerlikon 20 mm. 2—12.7 mm Browning MGs.
Radars: Navigation: Decca 1226; I band.

Comment: Ordered 24 November 1978. First delivered mid-1979 and then at monthly intervals. Steel hulls. GC 82 and 83 were captured by the British Forces in 1982.

CANAL DE BEAGLE *1989, Luis Oscar Zunino*

1 COASTAL PATROL CRAFT

Name	*No*	*Builders*	*Commissioned*
DORADO	GC 101	Base Naval, Rio Santiago	17 Dec 1939

Displacement, tons: 43 full load
Dimensions, feet (metres): 69.5 × 14.1 × 4.9 *(21.2 × 4.3 × 1.5)*
Main machinery: 2 GM 6071-6A diesels; 360 hp *(268 kW)*; 1 shaft
Speed, knots: 12. **Range, miles:** 1550
Complement: 7 (1 officer)

DORADO *11/1988, Prefectura Naval Argentina*

34 SMALL PATROL CRAFT

GC 48-61 **GC 88-95** **GC 102-108** **GC 110-114**

Displacement, tons: 15 full load
Dimensions, feet (metres): 41 × 11.8 × 3.6 *(12.5 × 3.6 × 1.1)*
Main machinery: 2 GM diesels; 514 hp *(383 kW)*; 2 shafts
Speed, knots: 20. **Range, miles:** 400 at 18 kts
Complement: 3
Guns: 12.7 mm Browning MG.

Comment: First delivered September 1978. First 14 built by Cadenazzi, Tigre 1977-79, remainder by Ast Belen de Escobar 1984-86. GC 102-114 are slightly smaller.

GC 52 *11/1988, Prefectura Naval Argentina*

23 PILOT CRAFT

ALUMINE SP 14
TRAFUL SP 15
COLHUE SP 16
MASCARDI SP 17
ARGENTINO SP 18
NAHUEL HUAPI SP 19
VIEDMA SP 20
SAN MARTIN SP 21
BUENOS AIRES SP 22
FAGNANO SP 23
RECALDO (ex-*Lacar*) SP 24
CARDIEL SP 25
MUSTERS SP 26
QUILLEN SP 27
ROCA SP 28
PUELO SP 29
FUTALAUFQUEN SP 30
FALKNER SP 31
FONTANA SP 32
COLHUE HUAPI SP 33
HUECHULAFQUEN SP 34
YEHUIN SP 35

(All names preceded by **LAGO**)

Comment: There are five different types of named pilot craft. SP 14-15 of 33.7 tons built in 1981; SP 16-18 of 47 tons built since 1981; SP 19-23 of 51 tons built since 1981; SP 24-27 of 20 tons built in 1981; SP 28-30 of 16.5 m built in 1983; SP31-35 of 7 tons built in 1986-1991. Most built by Damen SY, Netherlands. No armament. In 1991 SP 24 was converted into a navigation tender.

LAGO VIEDMA *1988, Prefectura Naval Argentina*

3 TRAINING SHIPS

ESPERANZA **ADHARA II** **TALITA II**

Displacement, tons: 33.5 standard
Dimensions, feet (metres): 62.3 × 14.1 × 8.9 *(19 × 4.3 × 2.7)*
Main machinery: 1 VM diesel; 90 hp(m) *(66 kW)*; 1 shaft
Speed, knots: 6; 15 sailing
Complement: 6 plus 6 cadets

Comment: Details given are for *Esperanza* built by Ast Central de la PNA. Launched and commissioned 20 December 1968 as a sail training ship. In addition there are two 30 ton training craft *Adhara II* and *Talita II* of similar dimensions.

6 HARBOUR TUGS

CANAL EMILIO MITRE SB 8 +**SB 3, 4, 5** and **10**

Comment: *Canal Emilio Mitre* is of 53 tons full load and has a speed of 10 kts and was built by Damen Shipyard, Netherlands in 1982.

CANAL EMILIO MITRE *1986, van Ginderen Collection*

LAND-BASED MARITIME AIRCRAFT

Note: 10 Helibras Esquilo shipborne helicopters (planned to replace Alouettes loaned from the Navy) will not now be acquired until at least 1993.

Numbers/Type: 2 Aerospatiale SA 330 Super Puma.
Operational speed: 151 kts *(279 km/h)*.
Service ceiling: 15 090 ft *(4600 m)*.
Range: 335 nm *(620 km)*.
Role/Weapon systems: Support and SAR helicopter for Patrol work. Sensors: Possible Omera search radar. Weapons: Can carry pintle-mounted machine guns but are usually unarmed.

Numbers/Type: 5 CASA C-212 Aviocar.
Operational speed: 190 kts *(353 km/h)*.
Service ceiling: 24 000 ft *(7315 m)*.
Range: 1650 nm *(3055 km)*.
Role/Weapon systems: Two acquired in 1989, three more in 1990. Medium-range reconnaissance and coastal surveillance duties in EEZ. Sensor: Bendix RDS 32 surface search radar. Omega Global GNS-500. Weapons: ASW; can carry torpedoes, depth bombs or mines. ASV; 2 × rockets or machine gun pods not normally fitted.

AUSTRALIA

Headquarters' Appointments

Chief of Naval Staff:
Vice Admiral I D G MacDougall, AO
Deputy Chief of Naval Staff:
Rear Admiral R G Taylor, AM
Assistant Chief of Naval Staff (Personnel):
Rear Admiral D B Chalmers
Assistant Chief of Naval Staff (Materiel):
Rear Admiral A L Hunt, AO

Senior Appointments

Maritime Commander, Australia:
Rear Admiral R A K Walls, AM
Flag Officer Naval Support Command:
Rear Admiral D G Holthouse, AO
Commodore Flotillas:
Commodore R A Christie, AM
Commodore Training:
Commodore G A Morton

Diplomatic Representation

Head of Australia Defence Staff, Washington:
Rear Admiral A M Carwardine, AO
Naval Attaché in Jakarta:
Captain K J Jordan
Assistant Defence Attaché in Kuala Lumpur:
Commander M Adams
Naval Adviser in London:
Captain P J Parkins
Defence Adviser in New Delhi:
Captain R G Dagworthy
Defence Attaché in Peking:
Captain I E Pfenningwerth
Naval Attaché in Washington and Ottawa:
Commodore T A A Roach, AM
Defence Attaché in Bonn/Berlin:
Captain J G J Newman
Naval Adviser in Honiara:
Commander K R Eglen

Personnel

1992: 15 000 officers and sailors
4500 Reserves (active and inactive)

RAN Reserve

The Naval Reserve is integrated into the Permanent Force. Personnel are either Active Reservists with regular commitments or Inactive Reservists with periodic or contingent duty. The missions undertaken by the Reserve include Naval Control of Shipping, Aviation, MCM, Intelligence, Clearance Diving and patrol boat/landing craft operations. In addition, members of the Ready Reserve (a component of the Active Reserve) are shadow posted to selected major fleet units.

Navy Estimates

A$
1989-90: 1 921 748 000
1990-91: 2 198 700 000
1991-92: 2 593 000 000

Shore Establishments

Sydney: Maritime Headquarters Australia, Fleet Base East (Garden Island), *Platypus* (Submarines), *Waterhen* (Mine warfare), *Watson* (Warfare Training), *Penguin* (Diving, NBCD, Hospital, Staff College), *Kuttabul* (Administration), *Nirimba* (Apprentice training).
Jervis Bay Area: *Albatross* (Air Station), *Creswell* (Naval College and Fleet Support), Jervis Bay Range Facility.
Cockburn Sound (WA): Headquarters NOCWA, Fleet Base West, *Stirling* (Administration and Maintenance Support), Submarine School.
Darwin: Headquarters NOCNA, Minor warship base, *Coonawarra* (Communications Station).
Cairns: Headquarters Patrol Boat Force, *Cairns* (Minor warship base).
Canberra: Navy Office, *Harman* (Communications Station).
Westernport: *Cerberus* (Major training facility, minor warship base).
Brisbane: *Moreton* (Reserve training/minor warship base).
Adelaide: *Encounter* (Reserve training/minor warship base).
Hobart: *Huon* (Reserve training/minor warship base).
North West Cape: Harold E Holt Communications Station.

Fleet Deployment 1992

Fleet Base East (and other Sydney bases): 3 SS, 3 DDG, 4 FFG, 1 AOR, 1 GT, 1 LSH, 1 ASR, 2 MHI, 4 MSA, 1 PTF, 2 LCH.
Fleet Base West: 2 SS, 1 FFG, 3 DE, 1 AO, 1 AGS, 2 PTF, 1 PC.
Darwin Naval Base: 6 PTF, 1 LCH.
Cairns: 5 PTF, 2 LCH, 5 AGS.
Westernport, Hobart, Adelaide: 1 PTF/PC each.
Brisbane: 1 LCH.

Fleet Air Arm (see *Shipborne Aircraft* section).

Squadron	*Aircraft*
HC-723	Squirrel AS 350B, utility, FFG embarked flights, SAR HS 748, Fixed wing, EW operations and training Bell 206B, survey support
HS-817	Sea King Mk 50, ASW
HS-816	Seahawk S-70B-2, ASW, ASST

Prefix to Ships' Names

HMAS. Her Majesty's Australian Ship

Strength of the Fleet

Type	*Active (Reserve)*	*Building (Projected)*
Patrol Submarines (SS)	5	6
Destroyers (DDG)	3	—
Frigates (FFG)	5	1 (8)
Destroyer Escorts (DE)	3	—
Minehunters (Coastal)	—	(4 + 2)
Minehunters (Inshore)	2	—
Minesweepers (Auxiliary)	4	(1)
Offshore Patrol Vessels (OPV)	—	(12)
Large Patrol Craft (PTF)	15 (2 RANR)	—
Coastal Patrol Craft (PC)	3 (RANR)	—
Amphibious Heavy Lift Ship (LSH)	1	—
Heavy Landing Craft (LCH)	3 (2 RANR) (1)	—
Marine Science Ships (AGS)	6	(3-5)
Replenishment Ships (AO)	2	—
Training Ship (AGT)	1	(1)
Trials and Safety Ship (ASR)	1	—
Tugs (AT)	5	—
Torpedo Recovery Vessels (TRV)	3	—

Surface Ship Development Plan

The surface combatant force is being developed under a two Tier concept. Tier One are destroyers and frigates, while Tier Two are offshore patrol vessels. A force of 16 Tier One and 12 Tier Two ships is envisaged.

Mercantile Marine

Lloyd's Register of Shipping:
714 vessels of 2 571 867 tons gross

DELETIONS

Submarines

1992 *Oxley*

Frigates

1991 *Parramatta* (January)
Stuart (June)

Destroyer Tender

1989 *Stalwart* (December; sold as Greek cruise ship)

Minesweepers

1990 *Curlew* (April)
1991 *Wave Rider* (March: returned to civilian use)
1992 *Salvatore V* (Feb)

Miscellaneous

1989 *NP 0801, SDB 1325*
1990 *Cook* (October)
1991 TB 1536 (sold)
1992 *Adroit*

PENNANT LIST

Submarines

59	Otway
60	Onslow
61	Orion
62	Otama
70	Ovens
71	Collins (bldg)
72	Farncomb (bldg)
73	Waller (bldg)
74	Dechaineux (bldg)
75	Sheean (bldg)
76	Rankin (bldg)

Destroyers

38	Perth
39	Hobart
41	Brisbane

Frigates

01	Adelaide
02	Canberra
03	Sydney
04	Darwin
05	Melbourne
06	Newcastle (bldg)
49	Derwent
50	Swan
53	Torrens

Mine Warfare Vessels

M 80	Rushcutter
M 81	Shoalwater
Y 298	Bandicoot
Y 299	Wallaroo

Training Ships

GT 203	Jervis Bay
P 225	Argus (RANR)

Large Patrol Craft

87	Ardent (RANR)
91	Aware (RANR)
203	Fremantle (RANR)
204	Warrnambool (RANR)
205	Townsville
206	Wollongong
207	Launceston
208	Whyalla
209	Ipswich
210	Cessnock
211	Bendigo
212	Gawler
213	Geraldton
214	Dubbo
215	Geelong
216	Gladstone
217	Bunbury

Amphibious Heavy Lift Ship

L 50	Tobruk

Landing Craft

L 126	Balikpapan (RANR)
L 127	Brunei
L 128	Labuan (RANR)
L 129	Tarakan
L 130	Wewak
L 133	Betano

Survey Ships

A 73	Moresby
A 312	Flinders
A 01	Paluma
A 02	Mermaid
A 03	Shepparton
A 04	Benalla

Replenishment Ships

O 195	Westralia
OR 304	Success

Trials and Safety Ship

ASR 241	Protector

General Purpose Ships

A 244	Banks
A 247	Bass (RANR)

Torpedo Recovery Vessels

TRV 801	Tuna
TRV 802	Trevally
TRV 803	Tailor

SUBMARINES

0 + 3 + 3 COLLINS CLASS

Name	*No*	*Builders*	*Laid down*	*Launched*	*Commissioned*
COLLINS	71	Australia Submarine Corp, Adelaide	14 Feb 1990	1994	1995
FARNCOMB	72	Australia Submarine Corp, Adelaide	1 Mar 1991	1994	1996
WALLER	73	Australia Submarine Corp, Adelaide	1992	1995	1997
DECHAINEUX	74	Australia Submarine Corp, Adelaide	1993	1996	1998
SHEEAN	75	Australia Submarine Corp, Adelaide	1994	1997	1999
RANKIN	76	Australia Submarine Corp, Adelaide	1995	1998	2000

Displacement, tons: 2500 surfaced; 3298 dived
Dimensions, feet (metres): 254 × 25.6 × 23 *(77.5 × 7.8 × 7)*
Main machinery: Diesel-electric; 3 Hedemora/Garden Island V 18B 210 diesels; 6000 hp(m) *(4.41 MW)*; Jeumont Schneider motor; 1 shaft
Speed, knots: 10 surfaced; 10 snorting; 20 dived
Range, miles: 9000 at 10 kts
Complement: 42 plus 5 trainees

Missiles: SSM: McDonnell Douglas Sub Harpoon.
Torpedoes: 6—21 in *(533 mm)* fwd tubes. Air turbine pump discharge. Total of 23 weapons including Mk 48 and Sub Harpoon.
Mines: In lieu of torpedoes. The Swedish external attachment is an option.
Countermeasures: Decoys: 2 SSDE.
ESM: Argo; radar warning.
Fire control: Librascope weapons control system.
Radars: Navigation: GEC Marconi; I band.
Sonars: Thomson Sintra Scylla bow and flank arrays. Kariwara retractable passive towed array.

COLLINS (model) — *1989, Kockums*

Programmes: Contract signed on 2 June 1987 for construction of six Swedish designed Kockums Type 471. Fabrication work started in June 1989; bow and stern sections of the first submarine are being built in Sweden. The option on two additional boats, recommended by the Navy, was not taken up.

Structure: Air independent propulsion (AIP) developments will be monitored but acquisition is a low priority. Scylla is an updated Eledone sonar suite. Diving depth, 300 m *(985 ft)*.
Operational: All will be based at Fleet Base West with one or two deploying regularly to the east coast. A 'two crew' cycle is being considered.

5 OBERON CLASS

Name	*No*	*Builders*	*Laid down*	*Launched*	*Commissioned*
OTWAY	59	Scotts' Shipbuilding & Eng Co Ltd, Greenock	29 June 1965	29 Nov 1966	23 Apr 1968
ONSLOW	60	Scotts' Shipbuilding & Eng Co Ltd, Greenock	4 Dec 1967	3 Dec 1968	22 Dec 1969
ORION	61	Scotts' Shipbuilding & Eng Co Ltd, Greenock	6 Oct 1972	16 Sep 1974	15 June 1977
OTAMA	62	Scotts' Shipbuilding & Eng Co Ltd, Greenock	25 May 1973	3 Dec 1975	27 Apr 1978
OVENS	70	Scotts' Shipbuilding & Eng Co Ltd, Greenock	17 June 1966	4 Dec 1967	18 Apr 1969

Displacement, tons: 1610 standard; 2030 surfaced; 2410 dived
Dimensions, feet (metres): 295.2 × 26.5 × 18 *(90 × 8.1 × 5.5)*
Main machinery: Diesel-electric; 2 ASR 16 VVS-ASR1 diesels; 3680 hp *(2.74 MW)*; 2 AEI motors; 6000 hp *(4.48 MW)*; 2 shafts
Speed, knots: 12 surfaced; 17 dived; 11 snorting
Range, miles: 9000 at 12 kts surfaced
Complement: 64 (8 officers)

Missiles: SSM: McDonnell Douglas Sub Harpoon; active radar homing to 130 km *(70 nm)* at 0.9 Mach; warhead 227 kg.
Torpedoes: 6—21 in *(533 mm)* bow tubes (HP air discharge). Gould Mk 48 Mod 4; dual purpose; wire-guided; active/passive homing to 38 km *(21 nm)* at 55 kts; 50 km *(27 nm)* at 40 kts; warhead 267 kg. Combined total of 20 SSM and torpedoes carried.
Countermeasures: Decoys: 2 SSDE.
ESM: MEL Manta; radar warning.
Fire control: Singer Librascope SFCS Mk 1 data handling and fire control system.
Radars: Surface search: Kelvin Hughes Type 1006; I band.
Sonars: Krupp Atlas Type CSU3-41; bow array; active/passive; medium frequency; has intercept and UWT capability.
BAC Type 2007; flank array; passive; long range; low frequency.
Sperry BQQ 4 micropuffs; passive; range-finding.

OVENS — *11/1991, John Mortimer*

Programmes: In 1963 an order was placed for four submarines of the Oberon class to be built in British shipyards. Subsequently two more were ordered in October 1971 for delivery in 1975-76 later extended to 1977-78. Scheduled deletion dates for the last five are *Otway* 1993, *Ovens* 1994, *Orion* 1996, *Onslow* 1997 and *Otama* 1998.
Modernisation: Between October 1977 and October 1985 all submarines of the class were given a mid-life modernisation at Vickers, Cockatoo. Trials are continuing on one submarine for the Kariwara towed array but this is not yet an operational system and may not be until 1994. Sub Harpoon fitted in 1985-86. The two short stern tubes have been removed.
Operational: 1st Submarine Squadron is based at *Platypus*, Neutral Bay, Sydney. *Orion* is based at *Stirling* in Western Australia. A 'two crew' trial in *Otway*, working a three month rotation cycle, is a possible precursor for the Collins class.

DESTROYERS

3 MODIFIED US DDG-2 CLASS (DDGs)

Name	*No*	*Builders*	*Laid down*	*Launched*	*Commissioned*
PERTH	38	Defoe Shipbuilding Co, Bay City, Michigan	21 Sep 1962	26 Sep 1963	17 July 1965
HOBART	39	Defoe Shipbuilding Co, Bay City, Michigan	26 Oct 1962	9 Jan 1964	18 Dec 1965
BRISBANE	41	Defoe Shipbuilding Co, Bay City, Michigan	15 Feb 1965	5 May 1966	16 Dec 1967

Displacement, tons: 3370 standard; 4618 full load
Dimensions, feet (metres): 440.8 × 47.1 × 20.1 *(134.3 × 14.3 × 6.1)*
Main machinery: 4 Foster-Wheeler boilers; 1200 psi *(84.37 kg/cm sq)*, 950°F *(510°C)*; 2 GE turbines; 70 000 hp *(52 MW)*; 2 shafts
Speed, knots: 30+. **Range, miles:** 6000 at 15 kts; 2000 at 30 kts
Complement: 325 (25 officers)

Missiles: SSM: McDonnell Douglas Harpoon (fitted for but not with).
SAM: 40 GDC Pomona Standard SM-1MR; Mk 13 Mod 6 launcher ❶; command guidance; semi-active radar homing to 46 km *(25 nm)* at 2 Mach; height 45.7-18 288 m *(150-60 000 ft)*.
Guns: 2 FMC 5 in *(127 mm)*/54 Mk 42 Mod 10 automatic ❷; 85° elevation; 40 rounds/minute to 24 km *(13 nm)* anti-surface; 14 km *(8 nm)* anti-aircraft; weight of shell 32 kg.
2 GE/GDC 20 mm Mk 15 Vulcan Phalanx ❸; 6 barrels per mounting; 3000 rounds/minute combined to 1.5 km. Mountings rotated between ships.
Up to 6—12.7 mm MGs.
Torpedoes: 6—324 mm Mk 32 Mod 5 (2 triple) tubes ❹. Honeywell Mk 46; anti-submarine; active/passive homing to 11 km *(5.9 nm)* at 40 kts; warhead 44 kg. Some obsolete Mk 44 torpedoes still in service.
Countermeasures: Decoys: 2 Loral Hycor SRBOC 6-barrelled fixed Mk 36; Chaff and IR flares to 1-4 km *(0.6-2.2 nm)*.
SLQ 25; towed torpedo decoy.
ESM/ECM: WLR-1H; intercept.
Combat data systems: NCDS with NTDS consoles and Univac UYK-7 computers; Link 11. OE-2 SATCOM ❺.
Fire control: GFCS Mk 68. Missile control Mk 74. Electro-optic sights may be fitted.
Radars: Air search: Hughes SPS 52C ❻; E/F band; range 439 km *(240 nm)*.
Lockheed SPS 40C ❼; E/F band; range 320 km *(175 nm)*.
Surface search: Norden SPS 67V ❽; G band.
Fire control: Two Raytheon SPG 51C ❾; G/I band (for Standard missile system).
Western Electric SPG 53 ❿; I/J band (for guns).
IFF: AIMS Mk 12.
Tacan: URN 20.
Sonars: Sangamo SQS 23KL; hull-mounted; active; medium frequency; with limited bottom bounce capability.

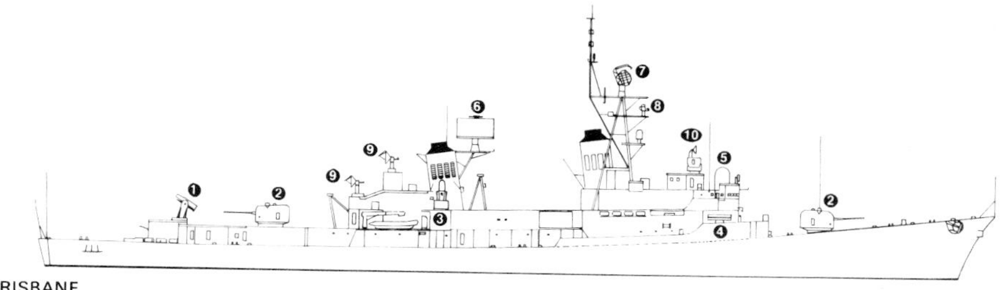

BRISBANE (Scale 1 : 1 200), *Ian Sturton*

PERTH *10/1991, John Mortimer*

Modernisation: *Perth* was first modernised in 1974 in the USA with the installation of Standard missiles, replacement gun mountings, new combat data system and modern radars. *Hobart* and *Brisbane* were brought to the same standard in 1978 and 1979 at the Garden Island Dockyard in Sydney. A second modernisation programme: *Brisbane* completed 1987; *Perth* completed 1989; *Hobart* completed 1991. Major equipment upgraded: search radars, naval combat data system, gun systems, the Mk 13 missile launcher. Missile modernisation included decoy and improved ECM equipment; three-dimensional radar SPS 52B upgraded to SPS 52C. In 1990/91 all ships were fitted for Phalanx CIWS, although the mountings are rotated in a fleet pool system. To accommodate Phalanx the ship's boats have been replaced by RIBs. Ikara launchers have been removed.

Structure: Generally similar to the US Charles F Adams class, but they differ by the addition of a broad deckhouse between the funnels which was the magazine for the now deleted Ikara system. In *Hobart* this space has been modified to include Flag accommodation.

Operational: Operational deployments include communications enhancements and portable RAM panels.

BRISBANE (with Phalanx) *8/1991, Bill McBride, RAN*

FRIGATES

5 +1 US FFG 7 CLASS

Name	No	Builders	Laid down	Launched	Commissioned
ADELAIDE	01	Todd Pacific Shipyard Corporation, Seattle, USA	29 July 1977	21 June 1978	15 Nov 1980
CANBERRA	02	Todd Pacific Shipyard Corporation, Seattle, USA	1 Mar 1978	1 Dec 1978	21 Mar 1981
SYDNEY	03	Todd Pacific Shipyard Corporation, Seattle, USA	16 Jan 1980	26 Sep 1980	29 Jan 1983
DARWIN	04	Todd Pacific Shipyard Corporation, Seattle, USA	3 July 1981	26 Mar 1982	21 July 1984
MELBOURNE	05	Australian Marine Eng (Consolidated), Williamstown	12 July 1985	5 May 1989	15 Feb 1992
NEWCASTLE	06	Australian Marine Eng (Consolidated), Williamstown	21 July 1989	21 Feb 1992	Nov 1993

Displacement, tons: 3962 (4000 *Melbourne*, 4100 *Newcastle*) full load
Dimensions, feet (metres): 453 × 45 × 24.5 (sonar); 14.8 (keel) *(138.1 × 13.7 × 7.5; 4.5)*
Main machinery: 2 GE LM 2500 gas turbines; 44 000 hp *(33 MW)* sustained; 1 shaft; cp prop; 2 auxiliary electric retractable propulsors fwd; 650 hp *(490 kW)*.
Speed, knots: 29 (4 on propulsors). **Range, miles:** 4500 at 20 kts
Complement: 184 (15 officers)

Missiles: SSM: 8 McDonnell Douglas Harpoon; active radar homing to 130 km *(70 nm)* at 0.9 mach; warhead 227 kg. *Canberra* carried out RAN's first Harpoon firing at hulk of USS *Stoddart*. A hit was registered at over 40 nm.
SAM: GDC Pomona Standard SM-1MR; Mk 13 Mod 4 launcher for both SAM and SSM systems ❶; command guidance; semi-active radar homing to 46 km *(25 nm)* at 2 mach; height 45.7-18 288 m *(150-60 000 ft)*; 40 missiles (combined SSM and SAM).
Guns: 1 OTO Melara 3 in *(76 mm)*/62 US Mk 75 compact ❷; 85° elevation; 85 rounds/minute to 16 km *(9 nm)* anti-surface; 12 km *(6.5 nm)* anti-aircraft; weight of shell 6 kg. Guns for 05 and 06 manufactured in Australia.
1 General Electric/GDC 20 mm Mk 15 Vulcan Phalanx ❸; anti-missile system with 6 barrels; 3000 rounds/minute combined to 1.5 km. Retrofitted in 01 and 02 in 1985; 03-06 fitted on completion.
Up to 6—12.7 mm MGs.
Torpedoes: 6—324 mm Mk 32 (2 triple) tubes ❹. Honeywell Mk 46; anti-submarine; active/passive homing to 11 km *(5.9 nm)* at 40 kts; warhead 44 kg. Some Mk 44 torpedoes are still in service.
Countermeasures: Decoys: 2 Loral Hycor SRBOC Mk 36 Chaff and IR decoy launchers; fixed 6-barrelled system; range 1-4 km. The Nulka hovering rocket may be retrofitted in all.
SLQ 25; towed torpedo decoy.
ESM/ECM: Raytheon SLQ-32C; intercept; J band.
Combat data systems: NCDS using NTDS consoles and Sperry Univac UYK 7 computers. OE-2 SATCOM; Link 11.
Fire control: Sperry Mk 92 Mod 2 gun and missile control (HSA derivative). Electro-optic sights.
Radars: Air search: Raytheon SPS 49 ❺; C/D band; range 457 km *(250 nm)*.
Surface search/navigation: ISC Cardion SPS 55 ❻; I/J band.
Fire control: Lockheed SPG 60 ❼; I/J band; range 110 km *(60 nm)*; Doppler search and tracking.
Sperry Mk 92 (Signaal WM 28) ❽; I/J band; range 46 km *(25 nm)*.
IFF: AIMS Mk XII.
Tacan: URN-25.
Sonars: Raytheon SQS 56; hull-mounted; active; medium frequency. Commercial derivative of DE 1160 series. 05 and 06 will have EMI/Honeywell Mulloka system instead of SQS 56. Kariwara towed passive array in due course.

Helicopters: 2 Sikorsky S-70B-2 Seahawks ❾ or 1 Seahawk and 1 Squirrel (see *Shipborne Aircraft* section).

Programmes: US numbers: *Adelaide* FFG 17; *Canberra* FFG 18; *Sydney* FFG 35; *Darwin* FFG 44.

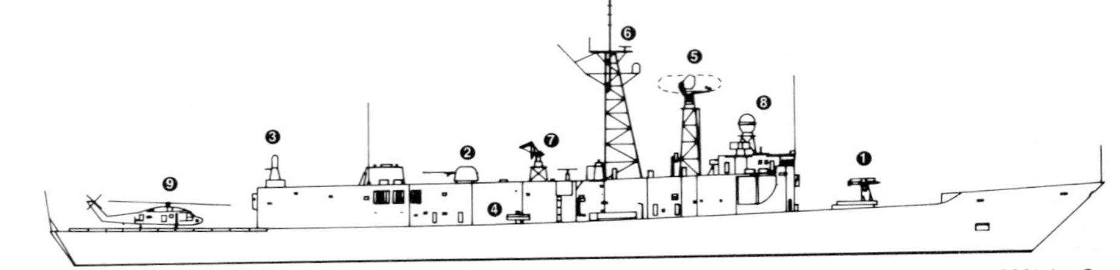
ADELAIDE (Scale 1 : 1 200), *Ian Sturton*

ADELAIDE *4/1991, Bill McBride, RAN*

Modernisation: *Adelaide* in November 1989, *Sydney* February 1989 and *Canberra* December 1991 completed a 12 month Helicopter Modification Programme to allow operation of Seahawk helicopters. The modification, fitted to *Darwin* during construction, involved angling the transom (increasing the ship's overall length by 8 ft) and fitting the RAST helo recovery system. *Melbourne* and *Newcastle* fitted during construction which also includes longitudinal strengthening and buoyancy upgrades. A mid-life modernisation is being considered—to include SM2 missiles, towed array sonars and improved torpedoes.
Operational: *Adelaide* based at Fleet Base West by October 1992 and she will be followed by another FFG by the mid-1990s. The remainder are based at Fleet Base East. For operational tasks ships are fitted with enhanced communications, electro-optical sights, rigid inflatable boats and portable RAM panels.

DARWIN (with SATCOM aerials) *11/1991, John Mortimer*

3 RIVER CLASS

Name	No	Builders	Laid down	Launched	Commissioned
DERWENT	49	HMA Naval Dockyard, Melbourne	16 June 1958	17 Apr 1961	30 Apr 1964
SWAN	50	HMA Naval Dockyard, Melbourne	18 Aug 1965	16 Dec 1967	20 Jan 1970
TORRENS	53	Cockatoo Island Dockyard, Sydney	18 Aug 1965	28 Sep 1968	19 Jan 1971

Displacement, tons: 2100 standard; 2700 full load
Dimensions, feet (metres): 360 wl; 370 oa × 41 × 17.3 (screws) *(109.8; 112.8 × 12.5 × 5.3)*
Main machinery: 2 B&W boilers; 550 psi *(38.7 kg/cm sq)*; 850°F *(450°C)*; 2 steam turbines; 30 000 hp *(22.4 MW)*; 2 shafts
Speed, knots: 30. **Range, miles:** 3400 at 12 kts
Complement: 234 (20 officers); 224 (21 officers) (in 49)

Guns: 2 Vickers 4.5 in *(114 mm)*/45 Mk 6 (twin) ❶; 80° elevation; 20 rounds/minute to 19 km *(10 nm)* anti-surface; 6 km *(3 nm)* anti-aircraft; weight of shell 25 kg.
4—12.7 mm MGs.
Torpedoes: 6—324 mm (2 triple) Mk 32 tubes ❷. Honeywell Mk 46; anti-submarine; active/passive homing to 11 km *(5.9 nm)* at 40 kts; warhead 44 kg. Some US Mk 44 torpedoes still in service.
Countermeasures: Decoys: SLQ 25 (50 and 53) and Type 182 (49) towed torpedo decoy.
ESM: ELT 901.
Radars: Air search: Signaal LW 02 ❸; D band; range 183 km *(100 nm)*.
Surface search: ISC Cardion SPS 55 (in 49) ❹; I/J band.
Krupp Atlas 8600 ARPA (in 50 and 53); I band.
Fire control: Signaal M 22 ❺; I/J band; range 46 km *(25 nm)*.
IFF: AIMS Mk XII.
Sonars: EMI/Honeywell Mulloka; hull-mounted; active search and attack; medium frequency.
Kelvin Hughes Type 162 M; sideways looking classification; 50 kHz.

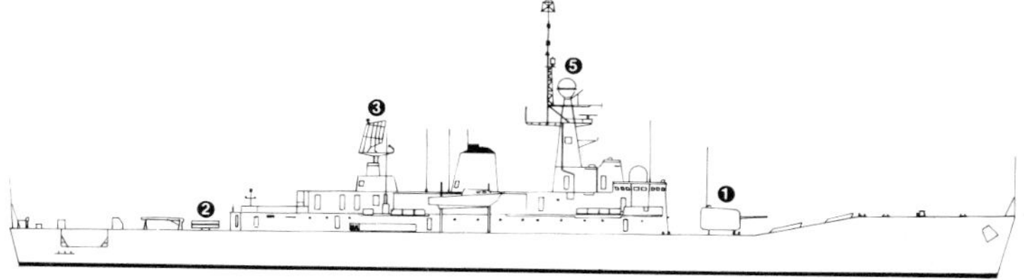

TORRENS
(Scale 1 : 1 200), Ian Sturton

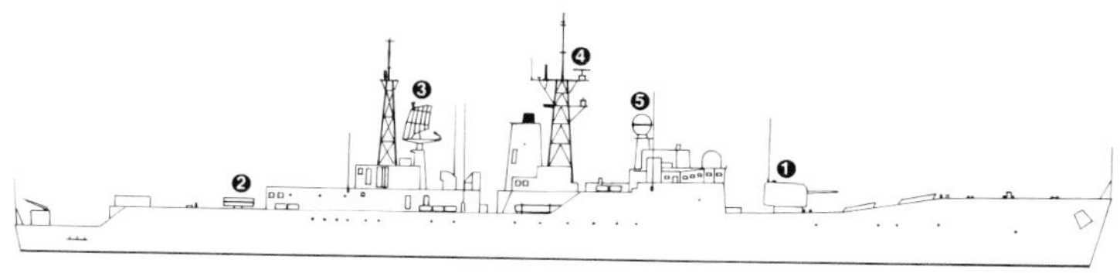

DERWENT
(Scale 1 : 1 200), Ian Sturton

Modernisation: *Derwent* half-life modernisation completed December 1985. This programme included improved accommodation consequent on reduction in complement, installation of M22 system, the fitting of Australian Mulloka sonar, the conversion of the boilers to burn diesel fuel, installation of Mk 32 torpedo tubes in lieu of Mk 10 mortar and new navigation radar. *Swan* and *Torrens* had a half-life refit which completed in September 1985. This refit included installation of Mulloka sonar, Mk 32 torpedo tubes in lieu of Mk 10 mortar and a torpedo decoy. Seacat and Ikara deleted from operational service in 1991.
Structure: The design of *Derwent* is basically similar to that of British Type 12 (now deleted), the other pair to that of the Leander frigates. Note difference in silhouette between *Swan/Torrens* and *Derwent*, the former pair having a straight-run upper deck.
Operational: Classified as Destroyer Escorts. Based at Fleet Base West as part of the deployment of the fleet as a 'Two Ocean Navy'. An RBS 70 missile detachment can be embarked if required.

SWAN (no Ikara or Seacat)
8/1991, P. Steele, RAN

DERWENT (no Ikara or Seacat)
10/1991, S. Connolly, RAN

0 + 1 + 7 ANZAC CLASS

Name	*No*	*Builders*	*Laid down*	*Launched*	*Commissioned*
—	07	Amecon	1992	Mar 1994	Oct 1995
—	08	Amecon	1994	Jan 1996	Nov 1997

Displacement, tons: 3600 full load
Dimensions, feet (metres): 387.1 oa; 357.6 wl × 48.6 × 14.3 *(118; 109 × 14.8 × 4.35)*
Main machinery: CODOG; 1 GE LM 2500 gas turbine; 23 000 hp *(17.2 MW)* sustained; 2 MTU 12V 1163 TB83 diesels; 8840 hp(m) *(6.5 MW)* sustained; 2 shafts; cp props
Speed, knots: 27. **Range, miles:** 6000 at 18 kts
Complement: 163

Missiles: SAM: Raytheon Sea Sparrow RIM-7P; Mk 41 Mod 4 octuple vertical launcher ❶; 16 missiles total.
Guns: 1 FMC 5 in (127 mm)/54 Mk 45 Mod 2 ❷. 2—12.7 mm MGs.
Torpedoes: 6—324 mm Mk 32 (2 triple tubes) to be fitted for but not with.
Countermeasures: Decoys: Loral Hycor Mk 36 Chaff launchers ❸ for SRBOC.
SLQ-25 Nixie towed torpedo decoy (probably).
ESM: THORN EMI modified Sceptre A; radar intercept.
Combat data systems: NobelTech 9LV 453 Mk 3. Link 11.
Fire control: NobelTech Sea Viking optronic director. Raytheon CW Mk 73 (for SAM).
Radars: Air search: Raytheon SPS 49(V)8 ANZ ❹; C/D band.
Air/surface search: Ericsson/Bofors Sea Giraffe 150 HC ❺; G/H band.
Navigation: Krupp Atlas 8600 ARPA; I band.
Fire control: NobelTech 9LV 200 ❻; I/J band.
IFF: Cossor AIMS Mk XII.
Sonars: Thomson Sintra Spherion B; hull-mounted; active search and attack; medium frequency. Provision for Kariwara towed array; passive search; very low frequency.

Helicopters: 1 S-70B Seahawk size ❼.

Programmes: Contract signed with Australian Marine Engineering Consolidated on 19 November 1989 to build eight Blohm & Voss designed MEKO 200 ANZ frigates for Australia and two for New Zealand, which has an option for two more. Modules are being constructed at Newcastle and shipped to Melbourne for assembly. The second and fourth ships are for New Zealand. It is possible that a stretched version of this class may be ordered in due course as replacements for the DDGs.
Structure: The helicopter eventually selected may be cheaper and smaller than the Seahawk, but the ship is to be Seahawk capable. 'Space and weight' reserved for a CIWS, Harpoon SSM, an additional octuple VLS, second channel of fire for VLS, towed array sonar, offboard active ECM, extended ESM frequency coverage, Helo data link and SATCOM. Stealth features are incorporated in the design. All steel construction. Fin stabilisers. Torpedo tubes may be taken from the River class. Indal RAST helicopter recovery system.

ANZAC (Artist's impression) *1990, RAN*

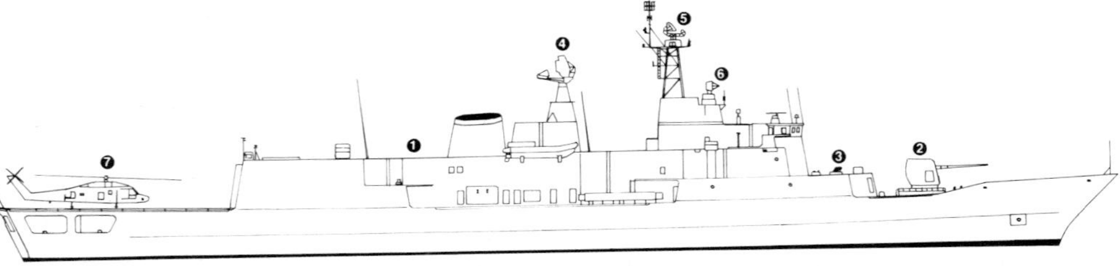

ANZAC *(Scale 1 : 900), Ian Sturton*

SHIPBORNE AIRCRAFT

Note: Six maritime utility helicopters are to be ordered in the mid-1990s.

Numbers/Type: 16 Sikorsky S-70B-2 Seahawk.
Operational speed: 135 kts *(250 km/h)*.
Service ceiling: 12 000 ft *(3810 m)*.
Range: 600 nm *(1110 km)*.
Role/Weapon systems: Sixteen Seahawk derivative aircraft designed by Sikorsky to meet RAN specifications for ASW and ASST operations. Eight assembled by ASTA in Victoria. Helicopters embarked in FFG-7 and may be utilised in ANZAC frigates. Sensors: MEL Surface surveillance radar, CDC Sonobuoy Processor and Barra Side Processor, and CAE Magnetic Anomaly Detector Set controlled by a versatile Tactical Display/Management System. Weapons: ASW; two Mk 46 torpedoes. ASV; two Mag 58 MGs.

SEAHAWK *3/1991, RAN*

Numbers/Type: 6 Aerospatiale AS 350B Squirrel.
Operational speed: 125 kts *(232 km/h)*.
Service ceiling: 10 000 ft *(3050 m)*.
Range: 390 nm *(720 km)*.
Role/Weapon systems: Support helicopter for operational training of naval personnel on new FFG-7 frigates prior to delivery of S-70B, then for utility tasks and training duties. Sensors: None. Weapons: ASV; two Mag 58 MGs.

SQUIRREL *8/1990, RAN*

Numbers/Type: 6 Westland Sea King HAS 50/50A.
Operational speed: 125 kts *(230 km/h)*.
Service ceiling: 10 500 ft *(3200 m)*.
Range: 630 nm *(1165 km)*.
Role/Weapon systems: ASW and Utility helicopter; land-based since 1982 for ASW but embarked periodically for operations from Afloat Support Ships. Sensors: MEL 5955 radar, Bendix ASQ-13A/B dipping sonar. Weapons: ASW; up to 4 × Mk 44 or Mk 46 torpedoes or depth bombs.

SEA KING *1988, RAN*

LAND-BASED MARITIME AIRCRAFT

Numbers/Type: 2 British Aerospace HS 748.
Operational speed: 140 kts *(259 km/h)*.
Service ceiling: 25 000 ft *(7620 m)*.
Range: 2675 nm *(4950 km)*.
Role/Weapon systems: ELINT aircraft operated by Squadron RAN HC 723 specially equipped by Sanders Associates, USA. Sensors: Complete EW suite classified.

Numbers/Type: 22 General Dynamics F-111C.
Operational speed: 793 kts *(1469 km/h)*.
Service ceiling: 60 000 ft *(18 290 m)*.
Range: 2540 nm *(4700 km)*.
Role/Weapon systems: Royal Australian Air Force operates the F-111 for anti-shipping strike and its small force of RF-111 for coastline surveillance duties using EW/ESM and photographic equipment underwing. Sensors: GE AN/APG-144, podded EW. Weapons: ASV; 4 × Harpoon missiles. Strike; 4 × Snakeye bombs. Self-defence; 2 × AIM-9P.

Numbers/Type: 19 Lockheed P-3C/Update II Orion.
Operational speed: 410 kts *(760 km/h)*.
Service ceiling: 28 300 ft *(8625 m)*.
Range: 4000 nm *(7410 km)*.
Role/Weapon systems: Operated by air force for long-range ocean surveillance and ASW. Sensors: APS-115 radar, AQS-901 processor, AQS-81 MAD, ECM, Elta/IAI, ESM, 80 × BARRA sonobuoys. Weapons: ASW; 8 × Mk 44 or Mk 46 torpedoes, Mk 25 mines, 8 × Mk 54 depth bombs. ASV; up to six Harpoon.

ORION *1991, RAAF*

Numbers/Type: 72 McDonnell Douglas F-18 Hornet.
Operational speed: 1032 kts *(1910 km/h)*.
Service ceiling: 50 000 ft *(15 240 m)*.
Range: 1000 nm *(1829 km)*.
Role/Weapon systems: Air defence and strike aircraft operated by RAAF but with fleet defence and anti-shipping secondary roles. Sensors: APG-65 attack radar, AAS-38 FLIR/ALR-67 radar warning receiver. Weapons: ASV; 4 × Harpoon missiles. Strike; 1 × 20 mm cannon, up to 7.7 tons of 'iron' bombs. Fleet defence; 4 × AIM-7 Sparrow and 4 × AIM-9L Sidewinder.

LIGHT FORCES

Note: The plan is to build 12 Tier Two Offshore Patrol Vessels starting in 1997. The class will have better seakeeping, endurance, weapons and sensors than the Fremantle class.

15 FREMANTLE CLASS (LARGE PATROL CRAFT)

Name	*No*	*Builders*	*Commissioned*
FREMANTLE	203	Brooke Marine, Lowestoft	17 Mar 1980
WARRNAMBOOL	204	NQEA Australia, Cairns	14 Mar 1981
TOWNSVILLE	205	NQEA Australia, Cairns	18 July 1981
WOLLONGONG	206	NQEA Australia, Cairns	28 Nov 1981
LAUNCESTON	207	NQEA Australia, Cairns	1 Mar 1982
WHYALLA	208	NQEA Australia, Cairns	3 July 1982
IPSWICH	209	NQEA Australia, Cairns	13 Nov 1982
CESSNOCK	210	NQEA Australia, Cairns	5 Mar 1983
BENDIGO	211	NQEA Australia, Cairns	28 May 1983
GAWLER	212	NQEA Australia, Cairns	27 Aug 1983
GERALDTON	213	NQEA Australia, Cairns	10 Dec 1983
DUBBO	214	NQEA Australia, Cairns	10 Mar 1984
GEELONG	215	NQEA Australia, Cairns	2 June 1984
GLADSTONE	216	NQEA Australia, Cairns	8 Sep 1984
BUNBURY	217	NQEA Australia, Cairns	15 Dec 1984

Displacement, tons: 211 full load
Dimensions, feet (metres): 137.1 × 23.3 × 5.9 *(41.8 × 7.1 × 1.8)*
Main machinery: 2 MTU 16V 538 TB91 diesels; 6120 hp(m) *(4.5 MW)*
1 Dorman diesel on centre line for cruising; 3 shafts
Speed, knots: 30; 8 on cruising diesel. **Range, miles:** 1450 at 30 kts; 4800 cruising
Complement: 22 (3 officers)

Guns: 1 Bofors AN 4—40 mm/60; 120 rounds/minute to 10 km *(5.5 nm)*. The 40 mm mountings were designed by Australian Government Ordnance Factory and although the guns are of older manufacture, this mounting gives greater accuracy particularly in heavy weather.
1—81 mm mortar. 2—12.7 mm MGs.
Radars: Navigation: Kelvin Hughes Type 1006; I band.

Programmes: The decision to buy these PCF 420 class patrol craft was announced in September 1977. The design is by Brooke Marine Ltd, Lowestoft which built the lead ship.
Modernisation: A life extension programme, including sensor upgrade, will be given to keep these craft in service until OPV replacements are built.
Operational: Bases: Cairns—P 205, 208, 209, 211, 216. Darwin—P 206, 207, 210, 212, 214, 215. Sydney—P 203 (reserve training). Melbourne—P 204 (reserve training). W Australia—P 213, 217.

GERALDTON *8/1991, S. Connolly, RAN*

2 ATTACK CLASS (LARGE PATROL CRAFT)

Name	*No*	*Builders*	*Commissioned*
ARDENT	87	Evans Deakin Ltd	26 Oct 1968
AWARE	91	Evans Deakin Ltd	21 June 1968

Displacement, tons: 146 full load
Dimensions, feet (metres): 107.5 × 20 × 7.3 *(32.8 × 6.1 × 2.2)*
Main machinery: 2 Paxman Ventura 16 YJCM diesels; 4000 hp *(2.98 MW)*; 2 shafts
Speed, knots: 24. **Range, miles:** 1220 at 13 kts
Complement: 19 (3 officers)

Guns: 1 Bofors 40 mm/70 Mk 7; 85° elevation; 300 rounds/minute to 12 km *(6.5 nm)*; weight of shell 0.96 kg.
2—7.62 mm MGs.
Radars: Navigation: Racal Decca RM 916; I band.

Programmes: Steel construction. First ordered in November 1965.
Operational: Bases are: Adelaide PD—91 (Reserve Training). Hobart PD—87 (Reserve Training). In addition *Bayonet* is an unarmed training platform at *Cerberus* but is still seagoing and in good condition.
Sales: *Bandolier* transferred to Indonesia 1973; *Archer* 1974. *Aitape, Ladava, Lae, Madang,* and *Samarai* transferred to Papua New Guinea Defence Force 1975. *Barricade* to Indonesia 1982; *Acute, Bombard* 1983; *Barbette, Assail, Attack* 1985; *Buccaneer* disposed of in 1984 and sunk as a target in October 1988. *Advance* to National Maritime Museum.

ATTACK Class (old number) *6/1991, Vic Jeffery, RAN*

MINE WARFARE FORCES

Note: (1) Four (possibly six) MCMV of a proven design are to be ordered as a matter of priority. Requests for tenders are expected to be issued to chosen contractors by Autumn 1992. It is planned to have the first vessel in service in 1994.
(2) Of the four vessels involved in the COOP programme, *Wave Rider* and *Salvatore V* have been returned to their owners and a replacement for the latter is planned to be bought in mid-1992. The full programme involves having equipment available for large numbers of earmarked fishing vessels.

2 BAY CLASS (MINEHUNTERS—INSHORE)

Name	*No*	*Builders*	*Commissioned*
RUSHCUTTER	M 80	Carrington Slipways	1 Nov 1986
SHOALWATER	M 81	Carrington Slipways	10 Oct 1987

Displacement, tons: 170 approx
Dimensions, feet (metres): 101.7 × 29.5 × 6.6 *(30.9 × 9 × 2)*
Main machinery: 2 Poyaud/Grossel diesel generator sets; 2 Schottel hydraulic transmission and steering systems (one to each hull)
Speed, knots: 10. **Range, miles:** 1200 at 10 kts
Complement: 14 (3 officers)

Guns: 4—12.7 mm MGs.
Countermeasures: MCM system is containerised allowing for rapid replacement or removal. Four subsystems are located in the container—sonar, tactical data, precision navigation and mine disposal weapon control. The latter operates a remote-controlled ECA 38 system using two PAP 104 vehicles.
Radars: Navigation: Kelvin Hughes Type 1006; I band.
Sonars: Krupp Atlas or Thomson Sintra; minehunting; high frequency.

Programmes: Tenders for two prototypes of this new concept of minehunters were sought in April 1981. Ordered January 1983. First launched 3 May 1986; second 20 June 1987. Follow-on units will not now be built.
Structure: The catamaran hull form was chosen as it provides stability, a large deck area, greater manoeuvrability than a mono-hull and reduction in signatures by placing heavy machinery high in the ship. Each hull is 3 m beam with 3 m space between. Foam sandwich construction was adopted and a policy of repair by replacement.
Operational: Due to performance deficiencies of the MWS 80 minehunting weapon system, comparative trials are being conducted between the Krupp Atlas MWS 80-4 and the Thomson Sintra Ibis V Mk 2 systems. Subject to satisfactory conclusion of the trials, the two ships will be based in Sydney and used for training and operations in confined waters.

RUSHCUTTER *10/1990, van Ginderen Collection*

2 MINESWEEPERS AUXILIARY (TUGS) (MSA(T))

BANDICOOT (ex-*Grenville VII*) Y 298 **WALLAROO** (ex-*Grenville V*) Y 299

Displacement, tons: 242 full load
Dimensions, feet (metres): 95.8 × 28 × 11.3 *(29.6 × 8.5 × 3.4)*
Main machinery: 2 Stork Werkspoor diesels; 2400 hp(m) *(1.76 MW)*; 2 shafts
Speed, knots: 11. **Range, miles:** 6300 at 10 kts
Complement: 10
Radars: Navigation: Furuno 7040D; I band.

Comment: Built in Singapore 1982 and operated by Maritime (PTE) Ltd. Purchased by the RAN and refurbished prior to delivery 11 August 1990. Initially being used for minesweeping trials towing large influence and mechanical sweeps. No side scan sonar. Also used as berthing tugs. Bollard pull, 30 tons.

WALLAROO *5/1991, van Ginderen Collection*

1 MINESWEEPER AUXILIARY (SMALL) (MSA(S))

BROLGA (ex-*Lumen*)

Displacement, tons: 268 full load
Dimensions, feet (metres): 93.2 × 26.6 × 11.5 *(28.4 × 8.1 × 3.5)*
Main machinery: 1 Mirrlees Blackstone diesel; 540 hp *(403 kW)*; 1 shaft; cp prop
Speed, knots: 10.5
Complement: 8 (1 officer)

Comment: Acquired from the Department of Transport on 10 February 1988 for the COOP programme. The COOP tow a magnetic body and acoustic noise makers for influence minesweeping, a mechanical sweep to counter moored mines and a Klein side scan sonar for route surveillance.

BROLGA *11/1988, John Mortimer*

1 MINESWEEPER AUXILIARY (SMALL) (MSA(S))

KORAAGA (ex-*Grozdana 'A'*)

Displacement, tons: 119 full load
Dimensions, feet (metres): 71.9 × 21 × 9.8 *(21.9 × 6.4 × 3)*
Main machinery: 1 Caterpillar D346 diesel; 1 shaft
Speed, knots: 11
Complement: 8 (1 officer)

Comment: Acquired 16 February 1989 for the COOP programme.

KORAAGA *7/1989, John Mortimer*

AMPHIBIOUS FORCES

1 AMPHIBIOUS HEAVY LIFT SHIP (LSH)

Name	*No*	*Builders*	*Laid down*	*Launched*	*Commissioned*
TOBRUK	L 50	Carrington Slipways Pty Ltd	7 Feb 1978	1 Mar 1980	23 Apr 1981

Displacement, tons: 3300 standard; 5700 full load
Dimensions, feet (metres): 417 × 60 × 16 *(127 × 18.3 × 4.9)*
Main machinery: 2 Mirrlees Blackstone KDMR8 diesels; 9600 hp *(7.2 MW)*; 2 shafts
Speed, knots: 18. **Range, miles:** 8000 at 15 kts
Complement: 144 (13 officers)
Military lift: 350-500 troops; 1300 tons cargo; 70 tons capacity derrick; 2—4.25 ton cranes; 2 LCVP; 2 LCM

Guns: 2 Bofors 40 mm/60; dual purpose; 80° elevation; 120 rounds/minute to 10 km *(5.5 nm)* anti-surface.
2—12.7 mm MGs.
Radars: Surface search: Kelvin Hughes Type 1006; I band.
Navigation: Racal Decca RM 916; I band.

Helicopters: Platform only for up to 4 Sea King.

Structure: The design is an update of the British Sir Bedivere class and provides facilities for the operation of helicopters, landing craft, amphibians or side-carried pontoons for ship-to-shore movement. A special feature is the ship's heavy lift derrick system for handling heavy loads. The LSH is able to embark a squadron of Leopard tanks plus a number of wheeled vehicles and artillery in addition to its troop lift. Bow and stern ramps are fitted. Carries two 20 kt waterjet LCVPs at davits. Fitted for side-carrying two NLE pontoons. Two LCM 8 carried on deck. Helicopters can be operated from the well deck or the after platform.
Operational: A comprehensive communication fit and minor hospital facilities are provided. Can operate all in-service helicopters. Based at Sydney.

TOBRUK *1990, RAN*

6 LANDING CRAFT (HEAVY) (LCH)

Name	*No*	*Builders*	*Commissioned*
BALIKPAPAN	L 126	Walkers Ltd, Queensland	8 Dec 1971
BRUNEI	L 127	Walkers Ltd, Queensland	5 Jan 1973
LABUAN	L 128	Walkers Ltd, Queensland	9 Mar 1973
TARAKAN	L 129	Walkers Ltd, Queensland	15 June 1973
WEWAK	L 130	Walkers Ltd, Queensland	10 Aug 1973
BETANO	L 133	Walkers Ltd, Queensland	8 Feb 1974

Displacement, tons: 310 light; 503 full load
Dimensions, feet (metres): 146 × 33 × 6.5 *(44.5 × 10.1 × 2)*
Main machinery: 2 GM 6-71 diesels; 360 hp *(268 kW)* sustained; 2 shafts
Speed, knots: 10. **Range, miles:** 3000 at 10 kts
Complement: 13 (2 officers)
Military lift: 3 medium tanks or equivalent
Guns: 2—7.62 mm MGs.
Radars: Navigation: Racal Decca RM 916; I band.

Comment: Originally this class was ordered for the Army with which *Balikpapan* remained until June 1974, being commissioned for naval service on 27 September 1974. The remainder were built for the Navy. *Brunei* and *Betano* act as diving tenders. *Labuan* at Brisbane and *Balikpapan* at Darwin for reserve training. *Wewak* in operational reserve at Cairns but could be made operational quickly. *Tarakan* operates from Cairns in a survey ship role and for general duties. All are available for amphibious duties and the plan is to base more of them in the north. *Buna* and *Salamaua* transferred to Papua New Guinea Defence Force in November 1974.

BRUNEI *5/1991, John Mortimer*

OCEANOGRAPHIC AND SURVEY SHIPS (MARINE SCIENCE FORCE)

Note: (i) In addition to the ships listed below there are four civilian survey vessels; *Icebird, Franklin, Rig Seismic* and *Lady Franklin*. Also an arctic supply ship *Aurora Australis* started operating in the Antarctic in 1990; this vessel carries 70 scientists and has a helicopter hangar.
(ii) The need for replacement hydrographic and oceanographic vessels has been reviewed; the plan is to acquire at least three ships, one for oceanography and two for hydrography.

Name	*No*	*Builders*	*Commissioned*
MORESBY	A 73	Dockyard, Newcastle	6 Mar 1964

Displacement, tons: 1714 standard; 2351 full load
Dimensions, feet (metres): 314 × 42 × 15 *(95.7 × 12.8 × 4.6)*
Main machinery: Diesel-electric; 3 diesel generators; 2 motors; 3990 hp *(2.9 MW)*; 2 shafts
Speed, knots: 19
Complement: 138 (12 officers)
Guns: 2 Bofors 40 mm (removed).
Radars: Navigation: Racal Decca TM 916C; I band.
Sonars: Simrad SU2; high definition; retractable dome.
Helicopters: 1 Bell 206B.

Comment: The RAN's first specifically designed survey ship. Launched 7 September 1963. During refit in 1973 *Moresby's* funnel was heightened, her 40 mm guns removed and an exhaust outlet fitted on her forecastle. Three new survey launches with jet drive embarked in 1982. Has Qubit Hydlaps data logging and processing system. Based at *Stirling* (Cockburn Sound WA).

MORESBY *1/1992, S. Connolly, RAN*

Name	*No*	*Builders*	*Commissioned*
FLINDERS	A 312	HMA Dockyard, Williamstown	27 Apr 1973

Displacement, tons: 750
Dimensions, feet (metres): 161 × 33 × 12 *(49.1 × 10 × 3.7)*
Main machinery: 2 Paxman Ventura 8CM diesels; 2000 hp *(1.5 MW)* sustained; 2 shafts; cp props
Speed, knots: 13.5. **Range, miles:** 5000 at 9 kts
Complement: 43 (5 officers)
Radars: Navigation: Racal Decca TM 916C; I band.
Sonars: Simrad SU2; high definition; retractable dome.

Comment: Launched 29 July 1972. Similar in design to *Atyimba* built for the Philippines. New survey launch with jet drive embarked in 1982. Has Qubit Hydlaps data logging and processing system. The ship is based at Cairns, with primary responsibility in the Barrier Reef area. A commercial vessel may be leased as a replacement.

FLINDERS *10/1986, John Mortimer*

4 PALUMA CLASS (SURVEY SHIPS)

Name	*No*	*Builders*	*Commissioned*
PALUMA	A 01	Eglo, Adelaide	27 Feb 1989
MERMAID	A 02	Eglo, Adelaide	4 Dec 1989
SHEPPARTON	A 03	Eglo, Adelaide	24 Jan 1990
BENALLA	A 04	Eglo, Adelaide	20 Mar 1990

Displacement, tons: 320 full load
Dimensions, feet (metres): 118.9 × 45.3 × 6.2 *(36.6 × 13.8 × 1.9)*
Main machinery: 2 Detroit 12V-92TA diesels; 1020 hp *(760 kW)* sustained; 2 shafts
Speed, knots: 12. **Range, miles:** 3500 at 11 kts
Complement: 12 (2 officers)
Radars: Navigation: JRC JMA-3710-6; I band.
Sonars: Skipper S113; hull-mounted; active; high frequency. ELAC LAZ 72; hull-mounted side scan; active; high frequency.

Comment: Catamaran design based on Prince class Ro-Ro passenger ferries. Steel hulls and aluminium superstructure. Contract signed in November 1987. Although she commissioned in February 1989, *Paluma* was not accepted into service until September 1989 because of noise problems. As a result other members of the class were about six months late completing. Qubit Hydlaps data logging and processing system fitted. All are based at Cairns and are fitted out for operations in shallow waters of Northern Australia. Normally operate in pairs.

MERMAID *5/1990, John Mortimer*

PALUMA *6/1990, RAN*

SERVICE FORCES

Note: Project Definition for a new helicopter-capable training ship is due to complete in 1993. The plan is to order the ship in 1995 (possible merchant conversion) and bring it into service to relieve *Jervis Bay* (and in part *Tobruk*) in 1997/98. The vessel will be able to embark at least six helicopters and be available for use in disaster relief operations.

1 LEAF CLASS (UNDERWAY REPLENISHMENT TANKER)

Name	*No*	*Builder*	*Laid down*	*Launched*	*Commissioned*
WESTRALIA (ex-*Hudson Cavalier*, ex-*Appleleaf)*	O 195 (ex-A 79)	Cammell Laird, Birkenhead	1974	24 July 1975	Nov 1979

Displacement, tons: 40 870 full load
Measurement, tons: 20 761 gross; 10 851 net; 33 595 dwt
Dimensions, feet (metres): 560 × 85 × 38.9 *(170.7 × 25.9 × 11.9)*
Main machinery: 2 SEMT-Pielstick 14 PC 2.2 V400 diesels; 14 000 hp(m) *(10.3 MW)* sustained; 1 shaft
Speed, knots: 16 (11 on one engine). **Range, miles:** 7260 at 15 kts

Complement: 61 (8 officers) plus 9 spare berths
Cargo capacity: 22 000 tons dieso; 3800 tons aviation fuel
Radars: Navigation: 2 Kelvin Hughes ARPA; I and E/F bands.

Comment: Part of an order by the Hudson Fuel and Shipping Co which was subsequently cancelled. Leased by the RN from 1979 until transferred on 9 October 1989 on a five year lease to the RAN, arriving in Fremantle 20 December 1989. Option to purchase in 1994. Has three 3 ton cranes and two 5 ton derricks. Hospital facilities. Two beam and one stern replenishment stations. Based at *Stirling*. RBS 70 SAM systems (with Army detachment) and 4—12.7 mm MGs may be embarked for operations. Also modified to provide a large Vertrep platform aft.

WESTRALIA *1/1991, Vic Jeffery, RAN*

1 DURANCE CLASS (UNDERWAY REPLENISHMENT TANKER)

Name	*No*	*Builders*	*Laid down*	*Launched*	*Commissioned*
SUCCESS	OR 304	Cockatoo Dockyard	9 Aug 1980	3 Mar 1984	19 Feb 1986

Displacement, tons: 17 933 full load
Dimensions, feet (metres): 515.7 × 69.5 × 38.4 *(157.2 × 21.2 × 10.8)*
Main machinery: 2 SEMT-Pielstick 16 PC 2.5 V400 diesels; 20 800 hp(m) *(15.3 MW)* sustained; 2 shafts; cp props
Speed, knots: 20. **Range, miles:** 9000 at 15 kts
Complement: 205 (26 officers)
Cargo capacity: 10 088 tons: 8220 dieso; 1300 Avcat; 259 distilled water; 183 victuals; 250 munitions including SM1 missiles and Mk 46 torpedoes; 45 naval stores and spares

Guns: 3 Bofors 40 mm (2 fwd, 1 aft). 4—12.7 mm MGs.
Radars: Navigation. Two Kelvin Hughes Type 1006; I band.
Helicopters: 1 AS 350B Squirrel.

Comment: Based on French Durance class design. Replenishment at sea from four beam positions (two having heavy transfer capability) and vertrep. Carries an LCVP.

SUCCESS *3/1991, van Ginderen Collection*

1 HELICOPTER AND LOGISTIC SUPPORT SHIP

Name	*No*	*Builders*	*Laid down*	*Launched*	*Commissioned*
JERVIS BAY (ex-*Australian Trader)*	GT 203	State Dockyard, Newcastle, NSW	18 Aug 1967	17 Feb 1969	17 June 1969

Displacement, tons: 8915 full load
Dimensions, feet (metres): 445.1 × 70.6 × 20.1 *(135.7 × 21.5 × 6.1)*
Main machinery: 2 Crossley Pielstick 16 PC 2.2 V400 diesels; 16 000 hp(m) *(11.8 MW)* sustained; 2 shafts; bow thruster
Speed, knots: 19.5
Complement: 177 (14 officers) plus 76 trainees

Guns: 2—12.7 mm MGs.
Radars: Surface search: Kelvin Hughes Type 1006; I band. Navigation: Krupp Atlas 8600; I band.
Helicopters: Platform only for 1 Sea King.

Comment: Classified as a Helicopter, Logistic Support and Training Ship, the former roll-on roll-off vessel commissioned in the RAN on 25 August 1977. For the training role a navigation bridge was added in 1978. In 1987 the deckhouse was removed and the after deck strengthened for a Sea King sized helicopter. More ambitious plans to carry up to six aircraft were shelved. Based at Sydney.

JERVIS BAY *11/1990, John Mortimer*

GENERAL PURPOSE VESSELS

Name	*No*	*Builders*	*Commissioned*
BANKS	AG 244	Walkers, Maryborough, Queensland	16 Feb 1960
BASS	AG 247	Walkers, Maryborough, Queensland	25 May 1960

Displacement, tons: 207 standard; 255 and 260 full load respectively
Dimensions, feet (metres): 90 pp; 101 oa × 22 × 8 *(27.5; 30.8 × 6.7 × 2.4)*
Main machinery: 2 diesels; 260 hp *(190 kW)*; 2 shafts
Speed, knots: 10
Complement: 12 (2 officers)
Radars: Navigation: Racal Decca 916; I band.

Comment: Explorer class; all steel construction. *Banks* was fitted for fishery surveillance and *Bass* for surveying. *Bass* has a black funnel top. *Banks* based in Sydney. *Bass* moved to Sydney from Darwin in May 1990 for RANR duties.

BANKS *10/1990, van Ginderen Collection*

TUGS

Note: In addition the two MSA(L) ships are used as tugs. Details under Mine Warfare Forces.

TAMMAR DT 2601

Displacement, tons: 265
Dimensions, feet (metres): 84.3 × 26.9 × 6.6 *(25.7 × 8.2 × 2)*
Main machinery: 2 diesels; 2800 hp *(2.09 MW)*; 2 shafts
Speed, knots: 11. **Range, miles:** 1450 at 11 kts
Complement: 6

Comment: Built by Australian Shipbuilding Industries, South Coogee, WA. Launched 10 March 1984 for service at *Stirling*, Cockburn Sound, completed 15 March 1984. Bollard pull 35 tons.

TAMMAR *11/1991, S. Connolly, RAN*

QUOKKA DT 1801

Displacement, tons: 110
Dimensions, feet (metres): 59.4 × 19.4 × 7.9 *(18.1 × 5.9 × 2.4)*
Main machinery: 2 Detroit 6V-53 diesels; 296 hp *(220 kW)* sustained; 2 shafts
Speed, knots: 9
Complement: 4

Comment: Built by Shoreline Engineering Pty Ltd, Portland, Victoria. Launched October 1983 for service at *Stirling*, Cockburn Sound. Bollard pull 8 tons.

QUOKKA *3/1991, Vic Jeffery, RAN*

BRONZEWING HTS 501
CURRAWONG HTS 502
MOLLYMAWK HTS 504

Displacement, tons: 47.5
Dimensions, feet (metres): 50 × 15 × 6.2 *(15.2 × 4.6 × 1.9)*
Main machinery: 2 GM diesels; 340 hp *(250 kW)*; 2 shafts
Speed, knots: 8
Complement: 3

Comment: First pair with bipod mast funnel built by Stannard Bros, Sydney in 1969 and second pair (including 503) with conventional funnel by Perrin Engineering, Brisbane in 1972. Bollard pull 5 tons. 503 transferred to Papua New Guinea in 1974.

BRONZEWING *11/1991, John Mortimer*

TORPEDO RECOVERY VESSELS

3 FISH CLASS

TUNA TRV 801 **TREVALLY** TRV 802 **TAILOR** TRV 803

Displacement, tons: 91.6
Dimensions, feet (metres): 88.5 × 20.9 × 4.5 *(27 × 6.4 × 1.4)*
Main machinery: 3 GM diesels; 890 hp *(664 kW)*; 3 shafts
Speed, knots: 13
Complement: 9

Comment: All built at Williamstown completed between January 1970 and April 1971. Can transport eight torpedoes.

TAILOR *1/1991, Vic Jeffery, RAN*

AUXILIARIES

1 TRIALS AND SAFETY VESSEL

Name	*No*	*Builders*	*Commissioned*
PROTECTOR (ex-*Blue Nabilla*)	ASR 241	Stirling Marine Services, WA	1984

Displacement, tons: 670 full load
Dimensions, feet (metres): 140.1 × 31.2 × 9.8 *(42.7 × 9.5 × 3)*
Main machinery: 2 Detroit 12V-92TA diesels; 1020 hp *(760 kW)* sustained; 2 Heimdal cp props
Speed, knots: 11.5. **Range, miles:** 10 000 at 11 kts
Complement: 13
Radars: Navigation: JRC 310; I band. Decca RM 970BT; I band.
Sonars: Klein; side scan; high frequency.
Helicopters: Platform for one light.

Comment: A former National Safety Council of Australia vessel commissioned in November 1990 to be used to support contractor's sea trials of the Collins class submarines, and for mine warfare trials and diving operations. Rescue capability down to 300 m (PC1804 manned submersible), LIPS dynamic positioning, two ROVs, recompression chamber and helicopter deck.

PROTECTOR *5/1991, John Mortimer*

1 RESERVE TRAINING CRAFT

ARGUS P 225

Displacement, tons: 8.8 full load
Dimensions, feet (metres): 34.1 × 11.2 × 3.3 *(10.4 × 3.4 × 1)*
Main machinery: 2 Volvo TAMD 60C diesels; 304 hp(m) *(223 kW)* sustained; 2 shafts
Speed, knots: 25. **Range, miles:** 400
Complement: 3
Radars: Navigation: FCR 1411; I band.

Comment: Former Federal Police craft built by Stebercraft in 1984 and commissioned into the Navy 8 June 1990. GRP construction. Based at Thursday Island and used for Reserve Port Division training.

4 SELF-PROPELLED LIGHTERS

WARRIGAL WFL 8001
WALLABY WFL 8002
WOMBAT WFL 8003
WYULDA WFL 8004

Displacement, tons: 265 light; 1206 full load
Dimensions, feet (metres): 124.6 × 33.5 × 12.5 *(38 × 10.2 × 3.8)*
Main machinery: 2 Harbourmaster outdrives (1 fwd, 1 aft)

Comment: First three were laid down at Williamstown in 1978. The fourth, for HMAS *Stirling*, was ordered in 1981 from Williamstown Dockyard. Total cost A$7 million. Used for water/fuel transport. Steel hulls with twin, swivelling, outboard propellers. Based at Jervis Bay and Cockburn Sound (WFL 8001, 8004), other pair at Garden Island, Sydney.

WYULDA *9/1991 van Ginderen Collection*

4 LIGHTERS—CATAMARAN

WATTLE CSL 01 **BORONIA** CSL 02 **TELOPEA** CSL 03 **AWL 304**

Comment: 175 ton self-propelled lighters used for general cargo duties.

WATTLE *9/1988, Hachiro Nakai*

1 RANGE CLEARANCE VESSEL

RCV 0701

Comment: GRP catamaran hull of 23 ft *(7 m)* with top speed of 27 kts. Entered service early 1981. At Jervis Bay.

SAIL TRAINING VESSELS

Note: In addition to *Young Endeavour* there are five Fleet class. Of 36.1 ft *(11 m)*. GRP yachts named *Charlotte of Cerberus, Friendship of Leeuwin, Scarborough of Cerberus, Lady Penrhyn of Nirimba* and *Alexander of Cresswell*. The names are a combination of Australia's first colonising fleet and the training base to which each yacht is allocated.

YOUNG ENDEAVOUR

Displacement, tons: 200
Dimensions, feet (metres): 144 × 26 × 13 *(44 × 7.8 × 4)*
Main machinery: 2 Perkins diesels; 334 hp *(294 kW)*; 1 shaft
Speed, knots: 14 sail; 7 diesel. **Range, miles:** 1500 at 7 kts
Complement: 32 (8 RAN crew, 24 youth crew)

Comment: Built to Lloyds 100 AI LMC yacht classification. Sail area, 5500 sq ft *(510 m)*. Presented to Australia by UK Government 25 January 1987 as a Bicentennial gift. Operated by RAN as a tender to HMAS *Waterhen* for benefit of Australian youth.

YOUNG ENDEAVOUR *1988, John Mortimer*

WORK BOATS

OTTER NWBD 1281
WALRUS NWBD 1282
BEAVER NWBD 1283
GRAMPUS NWBD 1285
DOLPHIN NWBD 1286
DUGONG NWBD 1287
TURTLE NWBD 1292
AWB 400-445

Comment: Of 12 tons and 39.3 ft *(12 m)* long. Built by North Queensland Engineers and Agents, Cairns of aluminium with varying superstructures. There are also four hydrofoil Cheetah remote-controlled surface targets capable of 35 kts.

WALRUS *11/1991, John Mortimer*

ARMY WATERCRAFT

Note: (i) Operated by Royal Australian Army Corps of Transport. Personnel: 300-400 as required.
(ii) In addition to the craft listed below there are some 150 assault boats 16.4 ft *(5 m)* in length and capable of 30 kts. Can carry 12 troops or 1200 kg of equipment.

16 US LCM(8) CLASS

AB 1050-1053, 1055, 1056, 1058-1067

Displacement, tons: 116 full load
Dimensions, feet (metres): 73.5 × 21 × 5.2 *(22.4 × 6.4 × 1.6)*
Main machinery: 2 GM 12V-71 diesels; 680 hp *(508 kW)* sustained; 2 shafts
Speed, knots: 10. **Range, miles:** 480 at 10 kts
Complement: 3-5

Comment: Built by North Queensland Engineers, Cairns and Dillinghams, Fremantle to US design. Based at Sydney, Darwin, Fremantle and Brisbane (some in dry storage). More are to be based at Darwin in 1992. Can carry 55 tons of cargo. Three of these craft carry names: 1050 *Coconut Queen;* 1052 *Reluctant Lady* and 1053 *Sea Widow*. AB 1057 transferred to Tonga 1982.

AB 1058 *9/1985, E. Pitman RAN*

2 TUGS

JOE MANN AT 2700 **THE LUKE** AT 2701

Displacement, tons: 60
Dimensions, feet (metres): 60.5 × 17.3 × 5.5 *(18.4 × 5.3 × 1.7)*
Main machinery: 2 GM 6-71 diesels; 348 hp *(260 kW)* sustained; 2 shafts
Speed, knots: 10.5. **Range, miles:** 5060 at 10 kts

Comment: Built in 1962. Fitted for firefighting, the first at Sydney, the second at Brisbane.

JOE MANN *1983, Graeme Andrews*

7 WORK BOATS

OOLAH AM 417 **KEWOL** 418 **SEA HORSE ONE** 419 **BOONGAREE** AM 420
MENA II 421 **AKUNA** 422 **GABINGA** 423

Comment: Similar to naval NWBD 1280 type. Based at Sydney, Melbourne, Brisbane, Townsville. Have poor handling qualities.

BOONGAREE *7/1989, John Mortimer*

6 SHARK CAT CLASS

AM 215-220

Comment: Multi-hulled craft with twin Johnson engines from 175-200 hp. Length 27.2 ft *(8.3 m)*. Speed, 35 kts. Operated by Army Safety Organisation.

AM 215 *11/1983, van Ginderen Collection*

P SERIES

CASTOR 201 **POLLUX** 202

Comment: Self-propelled lighters; speed, 7 kts; load capacity 90 tons; based at Sydney.

RAAF

WARANA 016-100

Comment: Of 76 ft *(23 m)*, 49 tons standard, 18 kts, range 400 nm. Deployed in support of RAAF Townsville.

2 SHARK CAT CLASS

AIR EAGLE 08-002 **AIR CONDOR** 08-003

Comment: Sisters to the Army Shark Cats. Based at Townsville for range safety, and rescue. Two others deleted.

AIR EAGLE *10/1983, Royal Australian Air Force*

1 STEBER 36 CLASS

AIR HAWK 011-001

Comment: Replaced one of the Shark Cats in October 1989. Twin diesels 750 hp *(560 kW)* giving 27 kts. Length 36 ft *(11 m)*. Has a crew of eight. Based at Crook Point.

AIR HAWK *1989, Dennis Hersey*

NON-NAVAL PATROL CRAFT

Comment: Various State and Federal agencies, including some fishery departments, have built offshore patrol craft up to 25 m and 26 kts.
Cocos Island patrol carried out by *Sir Zelman Cowan* of 47.9 × 14 ft *(14.6 × 4.3 m)* with two Cummins diesels; 20 kts, range 400 nm at 17 kts, complement 13 (3 officers). Operated by West Australian Department of Harbours and Lights.

AUSTRIA

Ministerial

Minister of Defence:
Dr Werner Fasslabend

Commanding Officer

Major Ing Friedrich Hegna

Diplomatic Representation

Defence Attaché in London:
Brigadier H Lerider

Personnel

(a) 1992: 32 (cadre personnel and national service), plus a small shipyard unit
(b) 6 months' national service plus 2 months a year for 12 years

Base

Marinekaserne Tegetthof, Wien-Kuchelau (under command of Austrian School of Military Engineering)

Mercantile Marine

Lloyd's Register of Shipping:
32 vessels of 139 347 tons gross

RIVER PATROL CRAFT

Name	*No*	*Builders*	*Commissioned*
NIEDERÖSTERREICH	A 604	Korneuberg Werft AG	16 Apr 1970

Displacement, tons: 75 full load
Dimensions, feet (metres): 96.8 × 17.8 × 3.6 *(29.4 × 5.4 × 1.1)*
Main machinery: 2 MWM V16 diesels; 1600 hp(m) *(1.18 MW)*; 2 shafts
Speed, knots: 22
Complement: 9 (1 officer)
Guns: 1 Oerlikon 20 mm SPz Mk 66; 50° elevation; 800 rounds/minute to 2 km. 1—12.7 mm MG. 1—7.62 mm MG. 1—84 mm PAR 66 'Carl Gustav' AT mortar.

Comment: Fully welded. Only one built of a projected class of 12. Re-engined in 1985.

NIEDERÖSTERREICH *7/1991, Austrian Government*

Name	*No*	*Builders*	*Commissioned*
OBERST BRECHT	A 601	Korneuberg Werft AG	14 Jan 1958

Displacement, tons: 10 full load
Dimensions, feet (metres): 40.3 × 8.2 × 2.5 *(12.3 × 2.5 × 0.75)*
Main machinery: 2 MAN 6-cyl diesels; 290 hp(m) *(213 kW)*; 2 shafts
Speed, knots: 10
Complement: 5
Guns: 1—12.7 mm MG. 1—84 mm PAR 66 Carl Gustav AT mortar.

OBERST BRECHT *7/1990, Austrian Government*

10 M-BOOT 80 PATROL CRAFT

Displacement, tons: 4.7 full load
Dimensions, feet (metres): 24.6 × 8.2 × 2 *(7.5 × 2.5 × 0.6)*
Main machinery: 1 Klöckner-Humboldt-Deutz V diesel; 1 shaft
Speed, knots: 14

Comment: Built by Schottel-Werft, Spay, West Germany. Unarmed, they are general-purpose work boats.

M-BOOT 80 Class *1984, Austrian Government*

BAHAMAS

Senior Officers

Commander Royal Bahamas Defence Force:
Commodore L L Smith, RBDF
Base Commander:
Captain C A Snell, RBDF

Base

HMBS *Coral Harbour*, New Providence Island

Personnel

1992: 870

Prefix to Ships' Names

HMBS

Mercantile Marine

Lloyd's Register of Shipping:
973 vessels of 17 541 196 tons gross

DELETION

1990 *Fort Charlotte* (old)

PATROL CRAFT

3 PROTECTOR CLASS

YELLOW ELDER P 03
SAMANA P 05
PORT NELSON P 04

Displacement, tons: 110 standard; 180 full load
Dimensions, feet (metres): 108.3 × 22 × 6.9 *(33 × 6.7 × 2.1)*
Main machinery: 3 Detroit 16V-149 TIB diesels; 4398 hp *(3.28 MW)* sustained; 3 shafts
Speed, knots: 30. **Range, miles:** 300 at 24 kts; 600 at 14 kts on 1 engine
Complement: 20 plus 5 spare berths
Guns: 1 Rheinmetall 20 mm. 3—7.62 mm MGs.

Comment: Ordered December 1984 from Fairey Marine Ltd, Cowes, delivered in November 1986. All commissioned 20 November 1986.

PORT NELSON *8/1986, RBDF*

6 Ex-USCG CAPE CLASS

Name	No	Name	No
FENRICK STURRUP (ex-*Shoalwater*)	P 06	**EDWARD WILLIAMS** (ex-*York*)	P 09
DAVID TUCKER (ex-*Upright*)	P 07	**SAN SALVADOR II** (ex-*Fox*)	P 10
AUSTIN SMITH (ex-*Current*)	P 08	**FORT FINCASTLE** (ex-*Morgan*)	P 11

Displacement, tons: 98 standard; 148 full load
Dimensions, feet (metres): 95 × 20.2 × 6.6 *(28.9 × 6.2 × 2)*
Main machinery: 2 Detroit 16V-149 TI diesels; 2480 hp *(1.85 MW)* sustained; 2 shafts
Speed, knots: 20. **Range, miles:** 2500 at 10 kts
Complement: 18 (2 officers)
Guns: 2—12.7 mm MGs.
Radars: Navigation: Raytheon SPS 64; I band.

Comment: Built at the Coast Guard Yard, Maryland between 1953 and 1959 and modernised 1977-81. Modernisation included new engines, electronics and improved habitability. P 06, 07, 09 and 10 commissioned into the Bahamian Navy in February 1989 and the remaining two in November 1989. Designed for port security and search and rescue, they are a formidable addition to the surveillance capabilities of the RBDF.

AUSTIN SMITH *12/1989, Giorgio Arra*

1 VOSPER TYPE

Name	No	Builders	Commissioned
MARLIN	P 01	Vosper Thornycroft	23 May 1978

Displacement, tons: 96 standard; 109 full load
Dimensions, feet (metres): 103 × 19.8 × 5.5 *(31.4 × 6 × 1.7)*
Main machinery: 2 Paxman Ventura 12 CM diesels; 3000 hp *(2.24 MW)* sustained; 2 shafts
Speed, knots: 25. **Range, miles:** 2000 at 13 kts
Complement: 19 (3 officers)
Guns: 1 Rheinmetall 20 mm. 2 MGs. 2 flare launchers.
Radars: Surface Search: Racal Decca; I band.

Comment: *Marlin* laid down 22 November 1976, launched 20 June 1977. Sister ship *Flamingo* sunk by Cuban aircraft on 11 May 1980.

MARLIN *1984, RBDF*

5 KEITH NELSON TYPE

Name	No	Builders	Commissioned
ELEUTHERA	P 22	Vosper Thornycroft	5 Mar 1971
ANDROS	P 23	Vosper Thornycroft	5 Mar 1971
ABACO	P 25	Vosper Thornycroft	10 Dec 1977
EXUMA	P 26	Vosper Thornycroft	10 Dec 1977
INAGUA	P 27	Vosper Thornycroft	10 Dec 1977

Displacement, tons: 30 standard; 37 full load
Dimensions, feet (metres): 60 × 15.8 × 4.6 *(18.3 × 4.8 × 1.4)*
Main machinery: 2 Detroit 12V-71 diesels (P 22-23); 680 hp *(508 kW)*
2 Caterpillar 3408 TA diesels (P 25-27); 940 hp *(700 kW)*; 2 shafts
Speed, knots: 20. **Range, miles:** 650 at 16 kts
Complement: 11
Guns: 3—7.62 mm MGs.
Radars: Surface Search: Racal Decca; I band.

Comment: The first two were the original units of the Bahamas Police Marine Division. With air-conditioned living spaces, these craft are designed for patrol among the many islands of the Bahamas Group. Light machine guns mounted in sockets either side of the bridge. Main engines replaced in the first pair in 1990.

ABACO *1984, RBDF*

10 LAUNCHES

P30-P33 **P101-P106**

Displacement, tons: 8 standard (P30—33)
Dimensions, feet (metres): 28.9 × 10 × 2.3 *(8.8 × 3 × 0.7)* (P30—33)
Main machinery: 2 Volvo TAMD 40A diesels; 91 hp(m) *(67 kW)* sustained; 2 shafts
Speed, knots: 24+. **Range, miles:** 350 at 21 kts
Complement: 4
Guns: 2—7.62 mm MGs.

Comment: P30-33 are GRP launches built by Phoenix Marine, Florida and commissioned in 1981-82. P101-106 are between 28 and 40 ft in length; P102 and 104 have Mercruises inboard engines, the remainder Mercury, Johnson or Yamaha twin outboards.

P33 *1982, RBDF*

4 Ex-FISHING VESSELS

P 34—(ex-*Lady Hero*)
P 35—(ex-*Carey*)
P 36—Hatteras 45 ft motor yacht
P 37—(ex-*Maria Mercedes II*)

Comment: P 34, P 35 and P 37 have a single GM diesel; 12 kts. P 36 has twin diesels; 15 kts.

SUPPORT CRAFT

FORT CHARLOTTE A02 (ex-YFU 97, ex-LCU 1611)

Displacement, tons: 339 full load
Dimensions, feet (metres): 134.9 × 29 × 6.1 *(41.1 × 8.8 × 1.9)*
Main machinery: 2 Detroit 12V-71 diesels; 896 hp *(668 kW)* sustained; 2 shafts
Speed, knots: 11. **Range, miles:** 1200 at 10 kts
Complement: 15 (2 officers)
Guns: 2—7.62 mm MGs.
Radars: Navigation: Raytheon AN/SPS-66; I band.

Comment: Constructed by the Christy Corporation, Sturgeon Bay, in 1958; later converted and assigned to AUTEC in 1978 as harbour utility craft. Commissioned in the RBDF on 19 June 1991. Large cargo capacity and main deck area. Used primarily as a supply ship and mobile support platform.

FORT CHARLOTTE *6/1991, RBDF*

FORT MONTAGUE A 01

Displacement, tons: 90 full load
Dimensions, feet (metres): 94 × 23 × 6 *(28.6 × 7 × 1.8)*
Main machinery: 2 Detroit 12V-71 diesels; 896 hp *(668 kW)* sustained; 2 shafts
Speed, knots: 13. **Range, miles:** 3000 at 10 kts
Complement: 16
Guns: 2—7.62 mm MGs.
Radars: Navigation: Racal Decca; I band.

Comment: Acquired 6 August 1980. Used as a supply ship.

FORT MONTAGUE *1984, RBDF*

BAHRAIN

Ministerial

Minister of Defence:
Major General Shaikh Mohamad Ibn Khalifa Ibn Hamid Al Khalifa

Senior Officers

Chief of Naval Staff:
Brigadier Shaikh Abdullah Bin Salman Bin Khalid Al Khalifa
Commander of Navy:
Major Yousaf Al Mulalaha

Personnel

(a) 1992: 650 (Navy), 250 (Coast Guard—seagoing)
(b) Voluntary service

Coast Guard

This unit is under the direction of the Ministry of the Interior and not Defence.

Director of Coast Guard:
Colonel Abdul-Aziz Attiyatullah Al Khalifa

Mercantile Marine

Lloyd's Register of Shipping:
93 vessels of 211 297 tons gross

DELETION

1990 *Dera'a 2* (old)

MISSILE CORVETTES

2 LÜRSSEN FPB 62 TYPE (FAST ATTACK CRAFT)

Name	*No*	*Builders*	*Commissioned*
AL MANAMA	50	Lürssen	14 Dec 1987
AL MUHARRAQ	51	Lürssen	3 Feb 1988

Displacement, tons: 632 full load
Dimensions, feet (metres): 206.7 × 30.5 × 9.5 *(63 × 9.3 × 2.9)*
Main machinery: 4 MTU 20V 538 TB 93 diesels; 18 740 hp(m) *(13.78 MW)* sustained; 4 shafts
Speed, knots: 32. **Range, miles:** 4000 at 16 kts
Complement: 43 (7 officers)

Missiles: SSM: 4 Aerospatiale MM 38 Exocet launchers (2 twin); inertial cruise; active radar homing to 42 km *(23 nm)* at 0.9 Mach; warhead 165 kg; sea-skimmer.
Guns: 1 OTO Melara 3 in *(76 mm)*/62 compact; 85° elevation; 85 rounds/minute to 16 km *(8.7 nm)* anti-surface; 12 km *(6.5 nm)* anti-aircraft; weight of shell 6 kg.
2 Breda 40 mm/70 (twin); 85° elevation; 300 rounds/minute to 12.5 km *(6.8 nm)*; weight of shell 0.96 kg.
2 Oerlikon GAM-BO1 20 mm/93.
Countermeasures: Decoys: CSEE Dagaie; Chaff and IR flares.
ESM/ECM: Racal Decca Cutlass/Cygnus; intercept and jammer.
Fire control: CSEE Panda Mk 2 optical director. Philips TV/IR optronic director.
Radars: Air/surface search: Philips Sea Giraffe; G band.
Navigation: Racal Decca 1226; I band.
Fire control: Philips 9LV 331; J band.

Helicopters: 1 SA 365F Dauphin 2.

Programmes: Ordered February 1984.
Structure: Similar to Abu Dhabi and Singapore designs. Steel hull, aluminium superstructure. Fitted with a helicopter platform which incorporates a lift to lower the aircraft into the hangar.
Operational: SA 365F armed with Aerospatiale AS 15TT anti-ship missiles, eight of which are carried on board ship.

AL MANAMA *2/1991, van Ginderen Collection*

4 LÜRSSEN FPB 45 TYPE (FAST ATTACK CRAFT—MISSILE)

Name	*No*	*Builders*	*Commissioned*
AHMAD EL FATEH	20	Lürssen	5 Feb 1984
AL JABIRI	21	Lürssen	3 May 1984
ABDUL RAHMAN AL FADEL	22	Lürssen	10 Sep 1986
AL TAWEELAH	23	Lürssen	25 Mar 1989

Displacement, tons: 228 half load; 259 full load
Dimensions, feet (metres): 147.3 × 22.9 × 8.2 *(44.9 × 7 × 2.5)*
Main machinery: 4 MTU 16V 538 TB92 diesels; 12 820 hp(m) *(9.42 MW)* sustained; 4 shafts
Speed, knots: 40. **Range, miles:** 1600 at 16 kts
Complement: 36 (6 officers)

Missiles: SSM: 4 Aerospatiale MM 40 Exocet (2 twin); inertial cruise; active radar homing to 70 km *(40 nm)* at 0.9 Mach; warhead 165 kg; sea-skimmer.
Guns: 1 OTO Melara 3 in *(76 mm)*/62; dual purpose; 85° elevation; 85 rounds/minute to 16 km *(8.7 nm)* anti-surface; 12 km *(6.5 nm)* anti-aircraft; weight of shell 6 kg.
2 Breda 40 mm/70 (twin); 85° elevation; 300 rounds/minute to 12.5 km *(6.8 nm)*; weight of shell 0.96 kg.
3—7.62 mm MGs.
Countermeasures: Decoys: CSEE Dagaie launcher; trainable mounting; 10 containers firing Chaff decoys and IR flares.
ESM: RDL 2 ABC; radar warning.
ECM: Racal Cygnus (not in 20 and 21); jammer.
Fire control: 1 Panda optical director for 40 mm guns.
Radars: Surface search/fire control: Philips LV223; J band.
Navigation: Racal Decca 1226; I band.

Programmes: First pair ordered in 1979, second pair in 1985. Rumours of a third pair were not confirmed.

ABDUL RAHMAN AL FADEL *9/1991*

PATROL FORCES

2 LÜRSSEN FPB 38 TYPE (FAST ATTACK CRAFT—GUN)

Name	*No*	*Builders*	*Commissioned*
AL RIFFA	10	Lürssen	Aug 1981
HAWAR	11	Lürssen	Nov 1981

Displacement, tons: 188 half load; 205 full load
Dimensions, feet (metres): 126.3 × 22.9 × 7.2 *(38.5 × 7 × 2.2)*
Main machinery: 2 MTU 16V 538 TB92 diesels; 6410 hp(m) *(4.7 MW)* sustained; 2 shafts
Speed, knots: 32. **Range, miles:** 1100 at 16 kts
Complement: 27 (3 officers)
Guns: 2 Breda 40 mm/70 (twin); dual purpose; 85° elevation; 300 rounds/minute to 12 km *(6.5 nm)* anti-surface; 4 km *(2.2 nm)*; weight of shell 0.96 kg.
1—57 mm Starshell rocket launcher.
Mines: Mine rails fitted.
Fire control: CSEE Lynx optical director with Philips 9LV 100 optronic system.
Radars: Surface search: Philips 9GR 600; I band.
Navigation: Racal Decca 1226; I band.

Comment: Ordered in 1979. *Al Riffa* launched April 1981. *Hawar* launched July 1981.

HAWAR *8/1990*

2 SWIFT FPB 20 TYPE (FAST ATTACK CRAFT—GUN)

AL JARIM 30 **AL JASRAH** 31

Displacement, tons: 33 full load
Dimensions, feet (metres): 63 × 18.4 × 6.5 *(19.2 × 5.6 × 2)*
Main machinery: 2 Detroit 12V-71TA diesels; 840 hp(m) *(627 kW)* sustained; 2 shafts
Speed, knots: 30. **Range, miles:** 1200 at 18 kts
Guns: 1 Oerlikon 20 mm.
Radars: Navigation: Decca 110; I band.

Comment: Built by Swiftships, Morgan City, USA. Both commissioned in February 1982. Aluminium hulls.

SUPPORT SHIP

AJEERA 41

Displacement, tons: 420 full load
Dimensions, feet (metres): 129.9 × 36.1 × 5.9 *(39.6 × 11 × 1.8)*
Main machinery: 2 Detroit 16V-71N diesels; 896 hp *(668 kW)* sustained; 2 shafts
Speed, knots: 13. **Range, miles:** 1500 at 10 kts
Complement: 21

Comment: Built by Swiftships, Morgan City, USA. Commissioned in October 1982. Used as a general purpose cargo ship and can carry up to 200 tons of fuel and water. Built to an LCU design with a bow ramp and 15 ton crane.

AJEERA *9/1990*

SHIPBORNE AIRCRAFT

Numbers/Type: 2 Aerospatiale SA 365F Dauphin.
Operational speed: 140 kts *(260 km/h)*.
Service ceiling: 15 000 ft *(4575 m)*.
Range: 410 nm *(758 km)*.
Role/Weapon systems: A requirement for these helicopters, equipped with the Thomson-CSF Agrion radar and armed with AS 15TT anti-ship missiles, was reported in September 1988.

COAST GUARD

Note: In addition to the craft listed below about ten motorised Dhows are used for patrol duties.

1 WASP 30 METRE CLASS

AL MUHARRAQ

Displacement, tons: 90 standard; 103 full load
Dimensions, feet (metres): 98.5 × 21 × 5.5 *(30 × 6.4 × 1.6)*
Main machinery: 2 Detroit 16V-149 TI diesels; 2790 hp *(2.1 MW)* sustained; 2 shafts
Speed, knots: 25. **Range, miles:** 500 at 22 kts
Complement: 9
Guns: 1—30 mm. 2—7.62 mm MGs.

Comment: Ordered from Souters, Cowes, Isle of Wight in 1984. Laid down November 1984, launched August 1985, shipped 21 October 1985. GRP hull.

4 HALMATIC 20 METRE CLASS

DERA'A 2, 6, 7 and **8**

Displacement, tons: 31.5 full load
Dimensions, feet (metres): 65.9 × 17.3 × 5.1 *(20.1 × 5.3 × 1.5)*
Main machinery: 2 Detroit 12V-71TA diesels; 820 hp *(626 kW)* sustained; 2 shafts
Speed, knots: 25. **Range, miles:** 500 at 20 kts
Complement: 7
Guns: 2—7.62 mm MG.

Comment: Three delivered in late 1991, the last in early 1992. GRP hulls.

DERA'A 6 *1991, Bahrain Coast Guard*

2 WASP 20 METRE

DERA'A 4 and **5**

Displacement, tons: 36.3 full load
Dimensions, feet (metres): 65.6 × 16.4 × 4.9 *(20 × 5 × 1.5)*
Main machinery: 2 Detroit 12V-71TA diesels; 820 hp *(626 kW)* sustained; 2 shafts
Speed, knots: 24.5. **Range, miles:** 500 at 20 kts
Complement: 8
Guns: 2—7.62 mm MGs.

Comment: Built by Souters, Cowes, Isle of Wight. Delivered 1983. GRP hulls.

DERA'A 4 and 5 *1983, Beken of Cowes Ltd*

3 WASP 11 METRE CLASS

SAHAM 1, 2 and **3**

Displacement, tons: 7.25 full load
Dimensions, feet (metres): 36.1 × 10.5 × 2 *(11 × 3.2 × 0.6)*
Main machinery: 2 Perkins diesels; 612 hp *(462 kW)*; 2 waterjets
Speed, knots: 24
Guns: 1—7.62 mm MG.

Comment: Built by Souters, Cowes, Isle of Wight. Delivered 1983.

SAHAM 1 *1983, Beken of Cowes Ltd*

2 TRACKER CLASS

DERA'A 1 and **3**

Displacement, tons: 31 full load
Dimensions, feet (metres): 64 × 16 × 5 *(19.5 × 4.9 × 1.5)*
Main machinery: 2 General Motors diesels; 1120 hp *(823 kW)*; 2 shafts
Speed, knots: 29
Guns: 1 Oerlikon 20 mm.

Comment: All built by Fairey Marine Ltd. The first purchased in 1974, the other two in 1980. One deleted in 1990.

1 CHEVERTON TYPE

Name	*No*	*Builders*	*Commissioned*
MASHTAN	6	Cheverton Ltd, Isle of Wight	1976

Displacement, tons: 17.3 full load
Dimensions, feet (metres): 50 × 14.7 × 4.5 *(15.2 × 4.5 × 1.4)*
Main machinery: 2 GM 8V-71 diesels; 460 hp *(344 kW)* sustained; 2 shafts
Speed, knots: 22. **Range, miles:** 660 at 12 kts

Comment: GRP hull.

3 COASTAL PATROL CRAFT

AL-BAYNEH **JUNNAN** **QUAIMAS**

Displacement, tons: 6.3 full load
Dimensions, feet (metres): 36.4 × 10.7 × 2.9 *(11.1 × 3.3 × 0.9)*
Main machinery: 1 Sabre diesel; 210 hp *(156 kW)*; 1 shaft
Speed, knots: 27

Comment: Built by Vosper Private Ltd, Singapore in 1977.

6 HALMATIC 14 METRE CLASS

SAIF 5, 6, 7, 8, 9 and **10**

Displacement, tons: 17 full load
Dimensions, feet (metres): 47.2 × 12.8 × 3.9 *(14.4 × 3.9 × 1.2)*
Main machinery: 2 Detroit 6V-92TA diesels; 510 hp *(380 kW)* sustained; 2 shafts
Speed, knots: 27. **Range, miles:** 500 at 22 kts
Complement: 4

Comment: Delivered in 1990/91. GRP hulls. More could be ordered for delivery in 1992.

SAIF 9 *1991, Bahrain Coast Guard*

4 FAIREY SWORD CLASS

SAIF 1, 2, 3 and **4**

Displacement, tons: 15
Dimensions, feet (metres): 44.9 × 13.4 × 4.3 *(13.7 × 4.1 × 1.3)*
Main machinery: 2 GM 8V-71 diesels; 460 hp *(344 kW)* sustained; 2 shafts
Speed, knots: 28
Complement: 6

Comment: Purchased in 1980. Built by Fairey Marine Ltd.

SAIF 1 *1982, Bahrain Coast Guard*

1 HARBOUR TUG

Displacement, tons: 12
Main machinery: 1 GM 6V-71 diesel; 174 hp *(130 kW)* sustained; 1 shaft

Comment: Purchased in 1981.

3 CHEVERTON TYPE

Name	*No*	*Builders*	*Commissioned*
NOON	15	Cheverton Ltd, Isle of Wight	1977
ASKAR	16	Cheverton Ltd, Isle of Wight	1977
SUWAD	17	Cheverton Ltd, Isle of Wight	1977

Displacement, tons: 3.5 full load
Dimensions, feet (metres): 27 × 9 × 2.8 *(8.2 × 2.7 × 0.8)*
Main machinery: 2 diesels; 150 hp *(111 kW)*; 2 shafts
Speed, knots: 15

Comment: Purchased 1976.

1 SUPPORT CRAFT

Name	*No*	*Builders*	*Commissioned*
SAFRA 3	—	Halmatic, Havant	1992

Displacement, tons: 165 full load
Dimensions, feet (metres): 85 × 25.9 × 5.2 *(25.9 × 7.9 × 1.6)*
Main machinery: 2 Detroit 16V-92 diesels; 2480 hp *(1.85 MW)*; 2 shafts
Speed, knots: 13. **Range, miles:** 700 at 12 kts
Complement: 6

Comment: Delivered in early 1992. General purpose workboat.

1 LANDING CRAFT

Name	*No*	*Builders*	*Commissioned*
SAFRA 2	40	Fairey Marine Ltd	1981

Displacement, tons: 150 full load
Measurement, tons: 90 dwt
Dimensions, feet (metres): 73.9 × 24.9 × 4 *(22.5 × 7.5 × 1.2)*
Main machinery: 2 Detroit 12V-71 diesels; 680 hp *(508 kW)* sustained; 2 shafts
Speed, knots: 8
Complement: 8

1 60 ft LOADMASTER

Name	*No*	*Builders*	*Commissioned*
SAFRA 1	7	Cheverton Ltd, Isle of Wight	Dec 1977

Displacement, tons: 90 full load
Dimensions, feet (metres): 60 × 20 × 3.5 *(18.3 × 6.1 × 1.1)*
Main machinery: 2 diesels; 348 hp *(260 kW)*; 2 shafts
Speed, knots: 9
Complement: 13
Military lift: 45 tons of equipment

1 TIGER CLASS HOVERCRAFT

Displacement, tons: 4.5 full load
Dimensions, feet (metres): 26.2 × 12.5 × 7.5 *(7.97 × 3.8 × 2.26)*
Main machinery: 1 AMC 5900 cc petrol driven; 180 hp *(134 kW)*
Speed, knots: 35

Comment: Built by AVL Cowes.

BANGLADESH

Headquarters' Appointments

Chief of Naval Staff:
Rear Admiral Muyhammad Muhaiminul Islam
Assistant Chief of Naval Staff (Personnel):
Commodore A Z Nizam
Assistant Chief of Naval Staff (Logistics):
Commodore F Ahmed
Assistant Chief of Naval Staff (Material):
Captain Z Ali

Senior Appointments

Naval Administrative Authority (Dhaka):
Commodore M M Islam
Commodore Commanding Chittagong:
Commodore M M Rahman
Commodore Commanding BN Flotilla:
Commodore S S Nizam

Naval Bases

Chittagong (BNS *Issa Khan*, BN Dockyard Complex and Naval Academy), Dhaka (BNS *Haji Mohsin*), Khulna (BNS *Titumir* and *Mongla*), Kaptai (BNS *Shaheed Moazzam*)

Personnel

(a) 1992: 8000 (650 officers)
(b) Voluntary service

General

Two ships were sunk and 12 others badly damaged in the April 1991 typhoon. Most of these may be recoverable but it will take a long time.

Prefix to Ships' Names

BNS

Mercantile Marine

Lloyd's Register of Shipping:
308 vessels of 456 268 tons gross

Strength of the Fleet

Type	*Active*
Frigates	4
Fast Attack Craft (Missile)	8
Fast Attack Craft (Torpedo)	4
Fast Attack Craft (Patrol)	2
Fast Attack Craft (Gun)	8
Large Patrol Craft	7
Coastal Patrol Craft	1
Riverine Patrol Craft	5
Training Ship	1
Repair Ship	1
Tanker	1
Coastal Survey Craft	2
Landing Craft	7

DELETIONS

1989 4 Type 123K (P 4 class)

PENNANT LIST

Frigates

F 15	Abu Bakr
F 16	Umar Farooq
F 17	Ali Haider
F 18	Osman

Light Forces

P 111	Pabna
P 112	Noakhali
P 113	Patuakhali
P 114	Rangamati
P 115	Bogra
P 211	Meghna
P 212	Jamuna
P 311	Bishkhali
P 312	Padma
P 313	Surma
P 314	Karnaphuli (reserve)
P 315	Tista
P 411	Shaheed Daulat
P 412	Shaheed Farid
P 413	Shaheed Mohibullah
P 414	Shaheed Akhtaruddin
P 611	Tawheed
P 612	Tawfiq
P 613	Tawjeed
P 614	Tanveer
P 811	Durjoy
P 812	Nirbhoy
P 8111	Durbar
P 8112	Duranta
P 8113	Durvedya
P 8114	Durdam
P 8125	Durdharsha
P 8126	Durdanta
P 8127	Durnibar
P 8128	Dordanda
A 513	Shahjalal

Auxiliaries

A 511	Shaheed Ruhul Amin
A 512	Shahayak
A 515	Khan Jahan Ali
A 581	Darshak
A 582	Tallashi
A 721	Khadem
L 900	Shahamanat

FRIGATES

1 + 1 CHINESE JIANGHU I CLASS (TYPE 053 H1)

Name	*No*	*Builders*	*Laid down*	*Launched*	*Commissioned*
OSMAN	F18	Hutong SY, Shanghai	—	—	4 Nov 1989

Displacement, tons: 1425 standard; 1702 full load
Dimensions, feet (metres): 338.6 × 35.4 × 10.2 *(103.2 × 10.7 × 3.1)*
Main machinery: 2 Type 12 PA6 280 BTC (Type 12 E 390V) diesels; 14 400 hp(m) *(10.6 MW)* sustained; 2 shafts
Speed, knots: 26. **Range, miles:** 4000 at 18 kts
Complement: 300 (27 officers)

Missiles: SSM: 4 Hai Ying 2 (2 twin) launchers ❶; active radar or IR homing to 80 km *(43.2 nm)* at 0.9 Mach; warhead 513 kg.
Guns: 4 China 3.9 in *(100 mm)*/56 (2 twin) ❷; 85° elevation; 18 rounds/minute to 22 km *(12 nm)*; weight of shell 15.9 kg.
8 China 37 mm/76 (4 twin) ❸; 85° elevation; 180 rounds/minute to 8.5 km *(4.6 nm)* anti-aircraft; weight of shell 1.42 kg.
A/S mortars: 2 RBU 1200 5-tubed fixed launchers ❹; range 1200 m; warhead 34 kg.
Depth charges: 2 BMB-2 projectors; 2 racks.
Mines: Can carry up to 60.
Countermeasures: Decoys: 2 Loral Hycor SRBOC Mk 36 6-barrelled Chaff launchers.
ESM: Watchdog; radar warning.
Radars: Air/surface search: MX 902 Eye Shield (922-1) ❺; possible E band.
Surface search/fire control: Square Tie (254) ❻; I band.

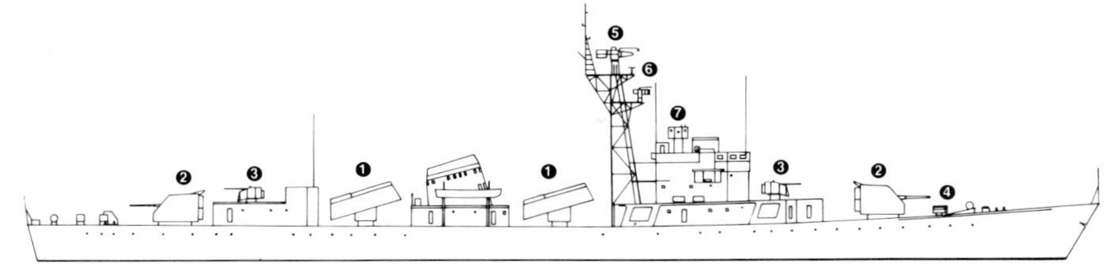

OSMAN *(Scale 1 : 900), Ian Sturton*

Navigation: Fin Curve (352); I band.
Fire control: Wok Won (752A) ❼.
IFF: High Pole A.
Sonars: Echo Type 5; hull-mounted; active search and attack; medium frequency.

Programmes: First transferred 26 September 1989, arrived Bangladesh 8 October 1989. Second expected in 1991 but has either been postponed or cancelled.

Structure: This is a Jianghu Type I (version 4) hull with twin 100 mm guns (vice the 57 mm in the ships sold to Egypt), Wok Won fire control system, and a rounded funnel.
Operational: Damaged in collision with a merchant ship in August 1991. One 37 mm mounting uprooted and SSM and RBU mountings misaligned.

OSMAN *6/1990, G. Jacobs*

1 Ex-BRITISH SALISBURY CLASS (TYPE 61)

Name	*No*	*Builders*	*Laid down*	*Launched*	*Commissioned*
UMAR FAROOQ (ex-HMS *Llandaff*)	F 16	Hawthorn Leslie Ltd	27 Aug 1953	30 Nov 1955	11 Apr 1958

Displacement, tons: 2170 standard; 2408 full load
Dimensions, feet (metres): 339.8 × 40 × 15.5 (screws) *(103.6 × 12.2 × 4.7)*
Main machinery: 8 VVS ASR 1 diesels; 12 380 hp *(9.2 MW)* sustained; 2 shafts
Speed, knots: 24. **Range, miles:** 2300 at full power; 7500 at 16 kts
Complement: 237 (14 officers)

Guns: 2 Vickers 4.5 in *(115 mm)*/45 (twin) Mk 6 ❶; dual purpose; 80° elevation; 20 rounds/minute to 19 km *(10 nm)* anti-surface; 6 km *(3.3 nm)* anti-aircraft; weight of shell 25 kg.
2 Bofors 40 mm/60 Mk 9 ❷; 80° elevation; 120 rounds/minute to 3 km *(1.6 nm)* anti-aircraft; 10 km *(5.5 nm)* maximum.
A/S mortars: 1 triple-barrelled Squid Mk 4 ❸; fires pattern of 3 depth charges to 300 m ahead of ship.
Fire control: 1 Mk 6M gun director.
Radars: Air search: Marconi Type 965 with double AKE 2 array ❹; A band.
Air/surface search: Plessey Type 993 ❺; E/F band.

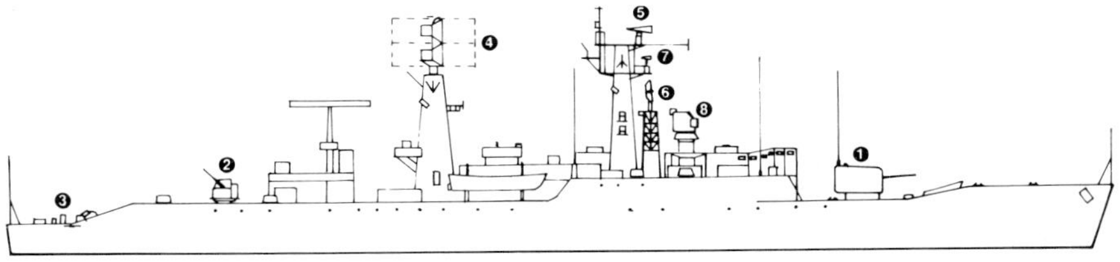

UMAR FAROOQ *(Scale 1 : 900), Ian Sturton*

Height finder: Type 278M ❻; E band.
Surface search: Kelvin Hughes Type 1007 ❼; I/J band.
Navigation: Decca Type 978; I band.
Fire control: Type 275 ❽; F band.
Sonars: Type 174; hull-mounted; active search; medium frequency.
Graseby Type 170B; hull-mounted; active attack; 15 kHz.

Programmes: Transferred to Bangladesh at Royal Albert Dock, London 10 December 1976.
Operational: Suffered major machinery accident in 1985 but is now fully operational. The radar Type 982 aerial is still retained on the after mast but the set is non-operational.

UMAR FAROOQ *6/1990, G. Jacobs*

2 Ex-BRITISH LEOPARD CLASS (TYPE 41)

Name	*No*	*Builders*	*Laid down*	*Launched*	*Commissioned*
ABU BAKR (ex-HMS *Lynx*)	F 15	John Brown & Co Ltd, Clydebank	13 Aug 1953	12 Jan 1955	14 Mar 1957
ALI HAIDER (ex-HMS *Jaguar*)	F 17	Wm Denny & Bros Ltd, Dumbarton	2 Nov 1953	30 July 1957	12 Dec 1959

Displacement, tons: 2300 standard; 2520 full load
Dimensions, feet (metres): 339.8 × 40 × 15.5 (screws) *(103.6 × 12.2 × 4.7)*
Main machinery: 8 VVS ASR 1 diesels; 12 380 hp *(9.2 MW)* sustained; 2 shafts
Speed, knots: 24. **Range, miles:** 2300 at full power; 7500 at 16 kts
Complement: 235 (15 officers)

Guns: 4 Vickers 4.5 in *(115 mm)*/45 (2 twin) Mk 6 ❶; dual purpose; 80° elevation; 20 rounds/minute to 19 km *(10 nm)* anti-surface; 6 km *(3.3 nm)* anti-aircraft; weight of shell 25 kg.
1 Bofors 40 mm/60 Mk 9 ❷; 80° elevation; 120 rounds/minute to 3 km *(1.6 nm)* anti-aircraft; 10 km *(5.5 nm)* maximum.
Countermeasures: ESM: Radar warning.
Fire control: Mk 6M gun director.
Radars: Air search: Marconi Type 965 with single AKE 1 array ❸; A band.
Air/surface search: Plessey Type 993 ❹; E/F band.
Navigation: Decca Type 978; Kelvin Hughes 1007; I band.
Fire control: Type 275 ❺; F band.

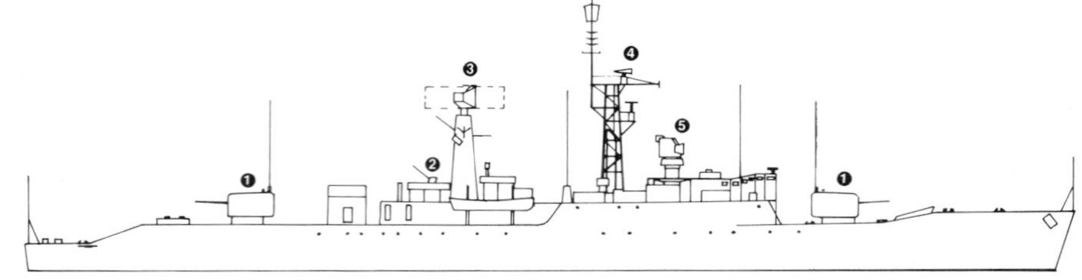

ABU BAKR (Scale 1 : 900), *Ian Sturton*

Programmes: *Ali Haider* transferred 16 July 1978 and *Abu Bakr* on 12 March 1982. *Ali Haider* refitted at Vosper Thornycroft August-October 1978. *Abu Bakr* extensively refitted in 1982.
Structure: All welded. Fitted with stabilisers. Sonars removed while still in service with RN. Fuel tanks have a water compensation system to improve stability.
Operational: Designed as air-defence ships.

ALI HAIDER *5/1990, John Mortimer*

LIGHT FORCES

4 TYPE 021 (CHINESE HUANGFEN CLASS) (FAST ATTACK CRAFT—MISSILE)

DURDHARSHA P 8125
DURDANTA P 8126
DURNIBAR P 8127
DORDANDA P 8128

Displacement, tons: 171 standard; 205 full load
Dimensions, feet (metres): 110.2 × 24.9 × 8.9 *(33.6 × 7.6 × 2.7)*
Main machinery: 3 Type 42-160 diesels; 12 000 hp(m) *(8.8 MW)*; 3 shafts
Speed, knots: 35. **Range, miles:** 800 at 30 kts
Complement: 65 (5 officers)
Missiles: SSM: 4 Hai Ying 2; active radar or IR homing to 80 km *(43.2 nm)* at 0.9 Mach; warhead 513 kg.
Guns: 4 USSR 30 mm/69 (2 twin); 85° elevation; 1000 rounds/minute to 3 km *(1.6 nm)* anti-aircraft.
Radars: Surface search: Square Tie; I band.
IFF: High Pole A.

Comment: Commissioned in Bangladesh Navy on 10 November 1988. Chinese equivalent of the Soviet Osa class which started building in 1985. All four damaged in April 1991 typhoon.

DURDHARSHA *6/1990, G. Jacobs*

4 TYPE 024 (CHINESE HEGU CLASS) (FAST ATTACK CRAFT—MISSILE)

DURBAR P 8111
DURANTA P 8112
DURVEDYA P 8113
DURDAM P 8114

Displacement, tons: 68 standard; 79.2 full load
Dimensions, feet (metres): 88.6 × 20.7 × 4.3 *(27 × 6.3 × 1.3)*
Main machinery: 4 Type L-12V-180 diesels; 4800 hp(m) *(3.53 MW)*; 4 shafts
Speed, knots: 37.5. **Range, miles:** 400 at 30 kts
Complement: 17 (4 officers)
Missiles: SSM: 2 Hai Ying 2; active radar or IR homing to 80 km *(43.2 nm)* at 0.9 Mach; warhead 513 kg.
Guns: 2—25 mm/80 (twin); dual purpose; 85° elevation; 270 rounds/minute to 3 km *(1.6 nm)*; weight of shell 0.34 kg.
Radars: Surface search: Square Tie; I band; range 73 km *(40 nm)* or limits of radar horizon.

Comment: First pair commissioned in Bangladesh Navy on 6 April 1983, second pair on 10 November 1983. Two badly damaged in April 1991 typhoon.

DURANTA *6/1990, G. Jacobs*

4 TYPE 026 (CHINESE HUCHUAN CLASS) (FAST ATTACK CRAFT—TORPEDO)

TB 8235-TB 8238

Displacement, tons: 46 full load
Dimensions, feet (metres): 73.8 × 16.4 × 6.9 (foil) *(22.5 × 5 × 2.1)*
Main machinery: 3 Type L-12V-180 diesels; 3600 hp(m) *(2.64 MW)*; 3 shafts
Speed, knots: 50. **Range, miles:** 500 cruising
Complement: 23 (3 officers)
Guns: 4 China 14.5 mm (2 twin); 85° elevation; 600 rounds/minute to 7 km *(3.8 km)*.
Torpedoes: 2—21 in *(533 mm)*; anti-ship; active/passive homing; warhead 380 kg.
Radars: Surface search: Skin Head; I band.

Comment: This is the newer version of the Huchuan class with some minor differences. All commissioned on 1 March 1988. Two damaged in April 1991 typhoon.

TB 8235 — *4/1988, Bangladesh Navy*

TB 8237 — *6/1990, G. Jacobs*

2 CHINESE HAINAN CLASS (FAST ATTACK CRAFT—PATROL)

DURJOY P 811 **NIRBHOY** P 812

Displacement, tons: 375 standard; 392 full load
Dimensions, feet (metres): 192.8 × 23.6 × 6 *(58.8 × 7.2 × 2.2)*
Main machinery: 4 PCR/Kolumna Type 9-D-8 diesels; 4400 hp(m) *(3.2 MW)*; 4 shafts
Speed, knots: 30.5. **Range, miles:** 1300 at 15 kts
Complement: 70
Guns: 4 China 57 mm/70 (2 twin); 85° elevation; 120 rounds/minute to 12 km *(6.5 nm)* anti-aircraft; weight of shell 6.31 kg.
4—25 mm (2 twin); 85° elevation; 270 rounds/minute to 3 km *(1.6 nm)* anti-aircraft.
A/S mortars: 4 RBU 1200 fixed 5-barrelled launchers; range 1200 m; warhead 34 kg.
Depth charges: 2 racks; 2 throwers.
Mines: Fitted with rails.
Radars: Surface search: Pot Head (Skin Head in some); I band.
IFF: High Pole.
Sonars: Tamir II; hull-mounted; short range attack; high frequency.

Comment: First transferred and commissioned in BN 10 September 1982 and the second 1 December 1985. Form part of Escort Squadron 81 at Chittagong. Some previous confusion over numbers of this class. Both damaged in April 1991 typhoon.

DURJOY — *1984, Bangladesh Navy*

8 Ex-CHINESE SHANGHAI II CLASS (FAST ATTACK CRAFT—GUN)

SHAHEED DAULAT P 411
SHAHEED FARID P 412
SHAHEED MOHIBULLAH P 413
SHAHEED AKHTARUDDIN P 414
TAWHEED P 611
TAWFIQ P 612
TAWJEED P 613
TANVEER P 614

Displacement, tons: 113 standard; 131 full load
Dimensions, feet (metres): 127.3 × 17.7 × 5.6 *(38.8 × 5.4 × 1.7)*
Main machinery: 4 Type M 50F-12 diesels; 3400 hp(m) *(2.5 MW)* sustained; 4 shafts
Speed, knots: 30. **Range, miles:** 800 at 16.5 kts
Complement: 36
Guns: 4—37 mm/63 (2 twin); 85° elevation; 180 rounds/minute to 8.5 km *(4.6 nm)*; weight of shell 1.4 kg.
4—25 mm/80 (2 twin); 85° elevation; 270 rounds/minute to 3 km *(1.6 nm)* anti-aircraft.
Depth charges: 2 throwers; 8 charges.
Mines: 10 can be carried.
Radars: Surface search: Skin Head/Pot Head; I band.
Sonars: Hull-mounted; active; short range; high frequency. Some reported to have VDS.

Comment: First four transferred March 1980, remainder in 1982. Different engine arrangement to Chinese craft. Four based at Chittagong form Patrol Squadron 41.

SHAHEED FARID — *1984, Bangladesh Navy*

TAWJEED — *6/1990, G. Jacobs*

2 Ex-YUGOSLAV KRALJEVICA CLASS (LARGE PATROL CRAFT)

Name	*No*	*Builders*	*Commissioned*
KARNAPHULI (ex-*PBR 502*)	P 314	Yugoslavia	1956
TISTA (ex-*PBR 505*)	P 315	Yugoslavia	1956

Displacement, tons: 195 standard; 245 full load
Dimensions, feet (metres): 141.4 × 20.7 × 5.7 *(43.1 × 6.3 × 1.8)*
Main machinery: 2 MAN V8V 30/38 diesels; 3300 hp(m) *(2.42 MW)*; 2 shafts
Speed, knots: 19. **Range, miles:** 1500 at 12 kts
Complement: 44 (4 officers)
Guns: 2 Bofors 40 mm/70. 4 Oerlikon 20 mm. 2—128 mm rocket launchers (5 barrels per mounting).
Depth charges: 2 racks; 2 Mk 6 projectors.
Radars: Surface search: Decca 45; I band.
Sonars: QCU 2; hull-mounted; active; high frequency.

Comment: Transferred and commissioned 6 June 1975. *Karnaphuli* placed in Class III reserve in 1988.

KARNAPHULI — *1984, Bangladesh Navy*

2 Ex-INDIAN AKSHAY CLASS (LARGE PATROL CRAFT)

Name	*No*	*Builders*	*Commissioned*
PADMA (ex-INS *Akshay*)	P 312	Hooghly D & E Co, Calcutta	1962
SURMA (ex-INS *Ajay*)	P 313	Hooghly D & E Co, Calcutta	1962

Displacement, tons: 120 standard; 150 full load
Dimensions, feet (metres): 117.2 × 20 × 5.5 *(35.7 × 6.1 × 1.7)*
Main machinery: 2 Paxman YHAXM diesels; 1100 hp *(820 kW)*; 2 shafts
Speed, knots: 18
Complement: 35 (3 officers)
Guns: 8 Oerlikon 20 mm (2 quad).
Radars: Surface search: Racal Decca; I band.

Comment: Generally similar to the Royal Navy's former Ford class. Transferred and commissioned 12 April 1973 and 26 July 1974 respectively. *Surma* refitted in 1983.

PADMA — *1984, Bangladesh Navy*

2 MEGHNA CLASS (LARGE PATROL CRAFT)

MEGHNA P 211 **JAMUNA** P 212

Displacement, tons: 410 full load
Dimensions, feet (metres): 152.5 × 24.6 × 6.6 *(46.5 × 7.5 × 2)*
Main machinery: 2 Paxman Valenta 12CM diesels; 5000 hp *(3.73 MW)* sustained; 2 shafts
Speed, knots: 20. **Range, miles:** 2000 at 16 kts
Complement: 47 (3 officers)
Guns: 1 Bofors 57 mm/70 Mk 1; 75° elevation; 200 rounds/minute to 17 km *(9.3 nm)*; weight of shell 2.4 kg.
1 Bofors 40 mm/70; 90° elevation; 300 rounds/minute to 12 km *(6.5 nm)*; weight of shell 0.96 kg.
2—7.62 mm MGs; launchers for illuminants on the 57 mm gun.
Fire control: Selenia NA 18 B optronic system.
Radars: Surface search: Decca 1229; I band.

Comment: Built by Vosper Private Ltd, Singapore for EEZ work under the Ministry of Agriculture. *Meghna* launched 19 January 1984, *Jamuna* 19 March 1984. Both completed late 1984. Reported that MTU diesels may have been fitted giving a top speed of 24 kts. Both damaged in April 1991 typhoon.

MEGHNA *6/1990, G. Jacobs*

1 RIVER CLASS (LARGE PATROL CRAFT)

Name	*No*	*Builders*	*Commissioned*
BISHKHALI (ex-PNS *Jessore*)	P 311	Brooke Marine Ltd	20 May 1965

Displacement, tons: 115 standard; 143 full load
Dimensions, feet (metres): 107 × 20 × 6.9 *(32.6 × 6.1 × 2.1)*
Main machinery: 2 MTU 12V 538 TB 90 diesels; 3000 hp(m) *(2.2 MW)* sustained; 2 shafts
Speed, knots: 24
Complement: 30
Guns: 2 Breda 40 mm/70; 85° elevation; 300 rounds/minute to 12.5 km *(6.8 nm)*; weight of shell 0.96 kg.
Radars: Surface search: Racal Decca; I band.

Comment: PNS *Jessore*, which was sunk during the 1971 war, was salvaged and extensively repaired at Khulna Shipyard and recommissioned as *Bishkhali* on 23 November 1978.

BISHKHALI *1984, Bangladesh Navy*

5 PABNA CLASS (RIVERINE PATROL CRAFT)

Name	*No*	*Builders*	*Commissioned*
PABNA	P 111	DEW Narayangonj, Dhaka	12 June 1972
NOAKHALI	P 112	DEW Narayangonj, Dhaka	8 July 1972
PATUAKHALI	P 113	DEW Narayangonj, Dhaka	7 Nov 1974
RANGAMATI	P 114	DEW Narayangonj, Dhaka	11 Feb 1977
BOGRA	P 115	DEW Narayangonj, Dhaka	15 July 1977

Displacement, tons: 69.5
Dimensions, feet (metres): 75 × 20 × 3.5 *(22.9 × 6.1 × 1.1)*
Main machinery: 2 Cummins diesels; 2 shafts
Speed, knots: 10.8. **Range, miles:** 700 at 8 kts
Complement: 33 (3 officers)
Guns: 1 Bofors 40 mm/60; 80° elevation; 120 rounds/minute to 10 km *(5.5 nm)*; weight of shell 0.89 kg.

Comment: The first indigenous naval craft built in Bangladesh. Form River Patrol Squadron 11 at Mongla.

RANGAMATI *1984, Bangladesh Navy*

1 COASTAL PATROL CRAFT

SHAHJALAL A 513

Displacement, tons: 600 full load
Dimensions, feet (metres): 131.8 × 29.7 × 12.6 *(40.2 × 9.1 × 3.8)*
Main machinery: 1 V-16 cyl Type diesel; 1 shaft
Speed, knots: 12. **Range, miles:** 7000 at 12 kts
Complement: 55 (3 officers)
Guns: 2 Oerlikon 20 mm.

Comment: Ex-Thai fishing vessel SMS *Gold 4*. Probably built in Tokyo. Commissioned into BN on 15 January 1987 and used as a patrol craft in spite of its A pennant number.

SHAHJALAL *8/1987, Bangladesh Navy*

AUXILIARIES

1 TRAINING SHIP

SHAHEED RUHUL AMIN (ex-MV *Anticosti*) A 511

Displacement, tons: 710 full load
Dimensions, feet (metres): 155.8 × 36.5 × 10 *(47.5 × 11.1 × 3.1)*
Main machinery: 1 Caterpillar diesel; 1 shaft
Speed, knots: 11.5. **Range, miles:** 4000 at 10 kts
Complement: 80 (8 officers)
Guns: 1 Bofors 40 mm/60.

Comment: Built by Atlantic Shipbuilding Co, Montreal. Laid down 1956, completed March 1957. Sold to India as MV *Anticosti*. After use in relief work was handed over to BN in 1972, modified at Khulna and commissioned 10 December 1974 as a training ship.

SHAHEED RUHUL AMIN *6/1990, G. Jacobs*

1 TANKER

KHAN JAHAN ALI A 515

Displacement, tons: 2900 full load
Measurement, tons: 1343 gross
Dimensions, feet (metres): 250.8 × 37.5 × 18.4 *(76.4 × 11.4 × 5.6)*
Main machinery: 1 diesel; 1350 hp(m) *(992 kW)*; 1 shaft
Speed, knots: 12
Complement: 26 (3 officers)
Cargo capacity: 1500 tons

Comment: Completed in Japan in 1983.

KHAN JAHAN ALI *6/1987, Gilbert Gyssels*

1 REPAIR SHIP

SHAHAYAK A 512

Displacement, tons: 477 full load
Dimensions, feet (metres): 146.6 × 26.2 × 6.6 *(44.7 × 8 × 2)*
Main machinery: 1 Type 12 VTS 6 diesel; 1 shaft
Speed, knots: 11.5. **Range, miles:** 3800 at 11.5 kts
Complement: 45 (1 officer)
Guns: 1 Oerlikon 20 mm.

Comment: Re-engined and modernised at Khulna Shipyard and commissioned in 1978 to act as repair vessel.

SHAHAYAK *1984, Bangladesh Navy*

1 OCEAN TUG

KHADEM A 721

Displacement, tons: 1472 full load
Dimensions, feet (metres): 197.5 × 38 × 16.1 *(60.2 × 11.6 × 4.9)*
Main machinery: 2 diesels; 2 shafts
Speed, knots: 14. **Range, miles:** 7200 at 14 kts
Complement: 56 (7 officers)
Guns: 2—12.7 mm MGs.

Comment: Commissioned 6 May 1984.

KHADEM *6/1990, G. Jacobs*

2 Ex-CHINESE YUCH'IN CLASS (TYPE 069)

DARSHAK A 581 **TALLASHI** A 582

Displacement, tons: 83 full load
Dimensions, feet (metres): 79.1 × 17.1 × 4.3 *(24.1 × 5.2 × 1.3)*
Main machinery: 2 Type 12V 150 diesels; 600 hp(m) *(440 kW)*; 2 shafts
Speed, knots: 11.5. **Range, miles:** 700 at 11.5 kts
Complement: 26 (1 officer)

Comment: Transferred from China in 1983 and used as coastal survey craft.

TALLASHI *1984, Bangladesh Navy*

1 LANDING CRAFT LOGISTIC (LSL)

SHAHAMANAT L 900

Displacement, tons: 366 full load
Dimensions, feet (metres): 154.2 × 34.1 × 8 *(47 × 10.4 × 2.4)*
Main machinery: 2 Caterpillar D343 diesels; 360 hp *(268 kW)*; 2 shafts
Speed, knots: 9.5
Complement: 31 (3 officers)

Comment: One of two Danyard built LSLs delivered in 1988 for civilian use and transferred to the Navy in 1990. The second may also be taken over by the Navy in due course.

SHAHAMANAT *6/1990, Bangladesh Navy*

4 Ex-CHINESE YUCH'IN CLASS (TYPE 068)

LCT 101-LCT 104 **A 584-587**

Displacement, tons: 85 full load
Dimensions, feet (metres): 81.2 × 17.1 × 4.3 *(24.8 × 5.2 × 1.3)*
Main machinery: 2 Type 12V 150 diesels; 600 hp(m) *(440 kW)*; 2 shafts
Speed, knots: 11.5. **Range, miles:** 450 at 11.5 kts
Complement: 23
Military lift: Up to 150 troops
Guns: 4 China 14.5 mm (2 twin) MGs.

Comment: First two transferred 4 May 1986; second pair 1 July 1986. Probably built in the late 1960s. Two badly damaged in April 1991 typhoon.

A 586 *6/1990, G. Jacobs*

3 LCVP

LCVP 011, 012, 013

Displacement, tons: 83 full load
Dimensions, feet (metres): 69.9 × 17.1 × 4.9 *(21.3 × 5.2 × 1.5)*
Main machinery: 2 Cummins diesels; 365 hp *(272 kW)*; 2 shafts
Speed, knots: 12.
Complement: 10 (1 officer)

Comment: First two built at Khulna Shipyard and *013* at DEW Narayangong; all completed in 1984.

LCVP 012 *1984, Bangladesh Navy*

1 Ex-FISHING VESSEL

MFV 66

Displacement, tons: 96 full load
Dimensions, feet (metres): 91.9 × 19.7 × 5.9 *(28 × 6 × 1.8)*
Main machinery: 1 diesel; 1 shaft
Speed, knots: 8. **Range, miles:** 750 at 8 kts
Complement: 24 (1 officer)
Guns: 1 Oerlikon 20 mm.

Comment: Ex-Thai steel hulled fishing vessel. Confiscated and taken into naval service.

MFV 66 *1989, Bangladesh Navy*

SANKET

Displacement, tons: 80 full load
Dimensions, feet (metres): 96.5 × 20 × 5.9 *(29.4 × 6.1 × 1.8)*
Main machinery: 2 Deutz Sea diesels; 1215 hp(m) *(893 kW)*; 2 shafts
Speed, knots: 18. **Range, miles:** 1000 at 16 kts
Complement: 24 (1 officer)
Guns: 1 Oerlikon 20 mm.

Comment: Acquired in 1989. Used for general harbour duties.

1 FLOATING DOCK and 1 FLOATING CRANE

Comment: Floating Dock (*Sundarban*) acquired from Brodogradiliste Joso Lozovina-Mosor, Trogir, Yugoslavia in 1980; capacity 3500 tons. Floating crane (*Balaban*) is self-propelled at 9 kts and has a lift of 70 tons; built at Khulna Shipyard and commissioned 18 May 1988.

SUNDARBAN *1984, Bangladesh Navy*

BALABAN *1990, Bangladesh Navy*

BARBADOS

Ministerial

Minister of Defence:
Hon Erskine L Sandiford, Prime Minister

Headquarters' Appointments

Chief of Staff, Barbados Defence Force:
Brigadier Rudyard E C Lewis

Commanding Officer Coast Guard Squadron

Lieutenant Commander C V C Belle

Personnel

(a) 1992: 107 (12 officers)
(b) Voluntary service

Coast Guard

This was formed early in 1973. In 1979 it became the naval arm of the Barbados Defence Force.

Base

Bridgetown (HMBS *Willoughby Fort*)

Headquarters

St Ann's Fort, Garrison, St Michael

Prefix to Ships' Names

HMBS

Mercantile Marine

Lloyd's Register of Shipping:
35 vessels of 7745 tons gross

PATROL FORCES

1 KEBIR CLASS (LARGE PATROL CRAFT)

Name	*No*	*Builders*	*Commissioned*
TRIDENT	P 01	Brooke Marine Ltd	Nov 1981

Displacement, tons: 155.5 standard; 190 full load
Dimensions, feet (metres): 123 × 22.6 × 5.6 *(37.5 × 6.9 × 1.7)*
Main machinery: 2 Paxman Valenta 12 RP200 diesels; 5000 hp *(3.73 MW)* sustained; 2 shafts
Speed, knots: 29. **Range, miles:** 3000 at 12 kts
Complement: 28
Guns: 2—12.7 mm MGs.
Radars: Surface search: Racal Decca TM 1226C; I band.

Comment: Launched 14 April 1981. Similar to Algerian vessels. Refitted by Bender Shipyard in 1990.

TRIDENT *11/1990, Bob Hanlon*

3 GUARDIAN II CLASS (COASTAL PATROL CRAFT)

Name	*No*	*Builders*	*Commissioned*
T T LEWIS	P 04	Halmatic/Aquarius UK	Dec 1973
COMMANDER MARSHALL	P 05	Halmatic/Aquarius UK	Dec 1973
J T C RAMSEY	P 06	Halmatic/Aquarius UK	Nov 1974

Displacement, tons: 11
Dimensions, feet (metres): 41 × 12.1 × 3.3 *(12.5 × 3.7 × 1)*
Main machinery: 2 Caterpillar Mk 334 TA diesels; 580 hp *(432 kW)*; 2 shafts
Speed, knots: 24
Complement: 4
Guns: 1—7.62 mm MG (fitted for but not with).

Comment: GRP hulls. Designed for coastal patrol/SAR duties by T T Boat Designs Ltd. Fitted out by Aquarius Boat Co Ltd, Christchurch.

COMMANDER MARSHALL *1988, BDF*

1 ENTERPRISE CLASS (OFFSHORE PATROL CRAFT)

Name	*No*	*Builders*	*Commissioned*
EXCELLENCE	P 03	Desco Marine	Dec 1981

Displacement, tons: 87 full load
Dimensions, feet (metres): 73.7 × 22 × 9 *(22.5 × 6.7 × 2.7)*
Main machinery: 1 Caterpillar diesel; 1 shaft
Speed, knots: 9.5
Complement: 9
Guns: 1—12.7 mm MG.
Radars: Surface search: Racal Decca TM 1229C; I band.

Comment: Shrimp boat converted for patrol duties by Swan Hunter (Trinidad) in 1980-81.

EXCELLENCE *11/1990, Bob Hanlon*

3 INSHORE PATROL CRAFT

Comment: One Arctic 22 ft craft for SAR duties; speed 30 kts; commissioned November 1985. Two Boston Whalers 22 ft craft for law enforcement role; speed 40 kts; commissioned early 1989.

ARCTIC 22 *1988, BDF*

BELGIUM

Headquarters' Appointments

Chief of Naval Staff:
Vice Admiral J de Wilde
Deputy Chief of Naval Staff:
Captain J L Barbieux

Diplomatic Representation

Naval, Military and Air Attaché in Bonn:
Colonel R Heyman (Army)
Naval, Military and Air Attaché in Kinshasa:
Colonel F Pettiaux (Army)
Naval, Military and Air Attaché in London:
Captain G Busard (Navy)
Naval, Military and Air Attaché in Madrid:
Colonel P Tancre (Army)
Naval, Military and Air Attaché in Paris:
Colonel M Derycker (Air)
Naval, Military and Air Attaché in Washington:
Commodore J Ceux (Navy)
Naval, Military and Air Attaché in Moscow:
Colonel C Buze (Army)
Naval, Military and Air Attaché in Riyadh:
Colonel R Reynders (Army)
Naval, Military and Air Attaché in Bangkok:
Colonel A Bertram (Air)

Personnel

(a) 1992: 3985 (1016 national service)
(b) 10 months' national service

Note: 70 per cent of junior ratings are regulars.

Strength of the Fleet

Type	*Active*	*Building*
Frigates	4	—
Minehunters (Ocean)	6	—
Minehunters (Coastal)	10	(6)
Command and Support Ships	2	—
Training Ship	1	—
Research Ships	1	—
Auxiliary and Service Craft	10	—

Bases

Zeebrugge: Frigates, MCMV, Reserve Units.
Ostend: Clearance Diving.
Koksijde: Naval aviation.

Mercantile Marine

Lloyd's Register of Shipping:
268 vessels of 314 198 tons gross

DELETIONS

Mine Warfare Vessels

1989 *Kortrijk, Oudenaarde*
1990 *Seraing, Huy*
1991 *Andenne, Turnhout, Tongeren, Merksem, Herstal, Vise, Ougrée, Dinant, Heist, Rochefort, Nieuwport, Koksijde*

PENNANT LIST

Frigates

F 910 Wielingen
F 911 Westdiep
F 912 Wandelaar
F 913 Westhinder

Mine Warfare Forces

M 902 Van Haverbeke
M 903 Dufour
M 904 De Brouwer
M 906 Breydel
M 908 Truffaut
M 909 Bovesse
M 915 Aster
M 916 Bellis
M 917 Crocus
M 918 Dianthus
M 919 Fuchsia
M 920 Iris
M 921 Lobelia
M 922 Myosotis
M 923 Narcis
M 924 Primula

River Patrol Craft

P 902 Liberation

Support Ships

A 960 Godetia
A 961 Zinnia

Research Ships

A 962 Belgica

Training Ships

A 958 Zenobe Gramme

Auxiliary and Service Craft

A 950 Valcke
A 951 Hommel
A 953 Bij
A 954 Zeemeeuw
A 956 Krekel
A 963 Spa
A 997 Spin
A 998 Ekster

WESTHINDER *11/1991, van Ginderen Collection*

FRIGATES

4 WIELINGEN CLASS (E-71)

Name	No	Builders	Laid down	Launched	Commissioned
WIELINGEN	F 910	Boelwerf, Temse	5 Mar 1974	30 Mar 1976	20 Jan 1978
WESTDIEP	F 911	Cockerill, Hoboken	2 Sep 1974	8 Dec 1975	20 Jan 1978
WANDELAAR	F 912	Boelwerf, Temse	28 Mar 1975	21 June 1977	27 Oct 1978
WESTHINDER	F 913	Cockerill, Hoboken	8 Dec 1975	28 Jan 1977	27 Oct 1978

Displacement, tons: 1940 light; 2430 full load
Dimensions, feet (metres): 349 × 40.3 × 18.4 *(106.4 × 12.3 × 5.6)*
Main machinery: CODOG; 1 RR Olympus TM3B gas turbine; 21 500 hp *(16 MW)* sustained; 2 Cockerill CO-240 V-12 diesels; 6000 hp(m) *(4.4 MW)*; 2 shafts; cp props
Speed, knots: 26; 15 on 1 diesel; 20 on 2 diesels
Range, miles: 4500 at 18 kts; 6000 at 15 kts
Complement: 159 (13 officers)

Missiles: SSM: 4 Aerospatiale MM 38 Exocet (2 twin) launchers ❶; inertial cruise; active radar homing to 42 km *(23 nm)* at 0.9 Mach; warhead 165 kg; sea-skimmer.
SAM: Raytheon Sea Sparrow Mk 29 octuple launcher ❷; semi-active radar homing to 14.6 km *(8 nm)* at 2.5 Mach; warhead 39 kg.
Guns: 1 Creusot Loire 3.9 in *(100 mm)*/55 Mod 68 ❸; 80° elevation; 60-80 rounds/minute to 17 km *(9 nm)* anti-surface; 8 km *(4.4 nm)* anti-aircraft; weight of shell 13.5 kg.
Torpedoes: 2—21 in *(533 mm)* launchers. ECAN L5 Mod 4; anti-submarine; active/passive homing to 9.5 km *(5 nm)* at 35 kts; warhead 150 kg; depth to 550 m *(1800 ft)*.
A/S Mortars: 1 Creusot Loire 375 mm 6-barrelled trainable launcher ❹; Bofors rockets to 1600 m; warhead 107 kg.
Countermeasures: Decoys: 2 Tracor MBA SRBOC 6-barrelled Mk 36 launchers; Chaff decoys and IR flares to 4 km *(2.2 nm)*. Nixie SLQ 25; towed anti-torpedo decoy.
ESM: CSF DR 2000; radar warning.
Combat data systems: Signaal SEWACO IV action data automation; Link 11. SATCOM may be fitted.
Fire control: 2 CSEE optical directors.
Radars: Air/surface search: Signaal DA 05 ❺; E/F band; range 137 km *(75 nm)* for 2 m² target.
Surface search/fire control: Signaal WM 25 ❻; I/J band; range 46 km *(25 nm)*.
Navigation: Raytheon TM 1645/9X; I/J band.
IFF: Mk X11.
Sonars: Westinghouse SQS 505A; hull-mounted; active search and attack; medium frequency.

Programmes: This compact, well-armed class of frigate is the first class fully designed by the Belgian Navy and built in Belgian yards. The programme was approved on 23 June 1971 and design studies completed July 1973. An order was placed in October 1973 and F 910 and F 911 were first delivered in December 1976 and returned to the yard for engine overhaul which was completed a year later.

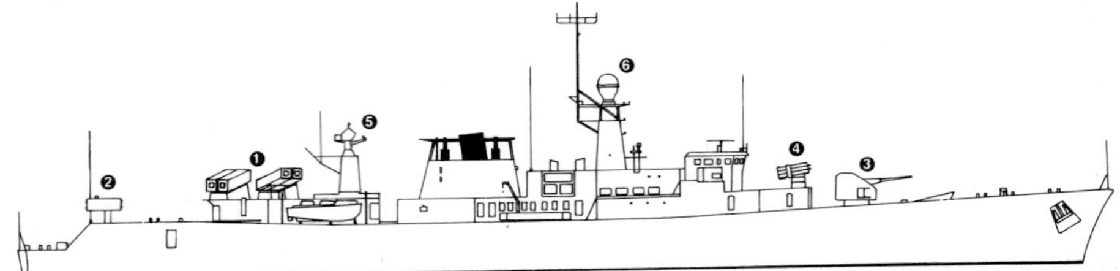

WIELINGEN *(Scale 1 : 900), Ian Sturton*

WESTDIEP *6/1991, Gilbert Gyssels*

Modernisation: Plans to fit Goalkeeper and new ESM have been shelved but Sea Sparrow has been updated and L5 Mod 4 torpedoes acquired.

Structure: Fully air-conditioned. Fin stabilisers fitted.
Operational: Based at Zeebrugge.

MINE WARFARE FORCES

Note: Memorandum of Understanding signed 6 April 1989 for a joint Belgium/Netherlands minesweeper project. Design contract awarded November 1990 to Van de Giessen de Noord Marinebouw in a joint venture with Beliard Polyship NV, to be completed in June 1992 with orders of up to six vessels for Belgium and eight for the Netherlands; first to be laid down in 1993 and all to complete by 1999. Displacement 610 tons approx; the ships are to have dimensions of 52 × 10 × 3 m, a range of 3000 miles at a sweep speed of 10 kts and a complement of between 25 and 30. The requirement is to be able to sweep bottom mines which have sunk so far into the soft sand of the Southern North Sea that they are not detected by hunters.

10 TRIPARTITE MINEHUNTERS (COASTAL)

Name	No	Builders	Laid down	Launched	Commissioned
ASTER	M 915	Beliard S.Y., Ostend and Rupelmonde	26 Apr 1983	6 June 1985	17 Dec 1985
BELLIS	M 916	Beliard S.Y., Ostend and Rupelmonde	9 Feb 1984	14 Feb 1986	14 Aug 1986
CROCUS	M 917	Beliard S.Y., Ostend and Rupelmonde	9 Oct 1984	6 Aug 1986	5 Feb 1987
DIANTHUS	M 918	Beliard S.Y., Ostend and Rupelmonde	4 Apr 1985	26 Feb 1987	17 Aug 1987
FUCHSIA	M 919	Beliard S.Y., Ostend and Rupelmonde	31 Oct 1985	23 Sep 1987	18 Feb 1988
IRIS	M 920	Beliard S.Y., Ostend and Rupelmonde	23 May 1986	21 Apr 1987	6 Oct 1988
LOBELIA	M 921	Beliard S.Y., Ostend and Rupelmonde	4 Dec 1986	6 Jan 1988	9 May 1989
MYOSOTIS	M 922	Beliard S.Y., Ostend and Rupelmonde	6 July 1987	4 Aug 1988	14 Dec 1989
NARCIS	M 923	Beliard S.Y., Ostend and Rupelmonde	25 Feb 1988	30 Mar 1990	27 Sep 1990
PRIMULA	M 924	Beliard S.Y., Ostend and Rupelmonde	10 Nov 1988	17 Dec 1990	29 May 1991

Displacement, tons: 562 standard; 595 full load
Dimensions, feet (metres): 168.9 × 29.2 × 8.2 *(51.5 × 8.9 × 2.5)*
Main machinery: 1 Brons/Werkspoor A-RUB 215X-12 diesel; 1860 hp(m) *(1.37 MW)* sustained; 1 shaft; Lips cp prop; 2 motors; 240 hp(m) *(176 kW)*; 2 active rudders; 2 bow thrusters
Speed, knots: 15. **Range, miles:** 3000 at 12 kts
Complement: 46 (5 officers)

Guns: 1 DCN 20 mm/20; 60° elevation; 720 rounds/minute to 10 km *(5.5 nm)*. 1—12.7 mm MG.
Countermeasures: MCM: 2 PAP 104 remote controlled mine locators; 39 charges.
Mechanical sweep gear (medium depth).
Radars: Navigation: Racal Decca 1229; I band.
Sonars: Thomson Sintra DUBM 21A; hull-mounted; active minehunting; 100 KHz ± 10 KHz.

Programmes: Developed in co-operation with France and the Netherlands. A 'ship factory' for the hulls was built at Ostend and the hulls were towed to Rupelmonde for fitting out. Each country built its own hulls but for all 35 ships France provided MCM gear and electronics, Belgium electrical installation and the Netherlands the engine room equipment.
Structure: GRP hull fitted with active tank stabilisation, full NBC protection and air-conditioning. Has automatic pilot and buoy tracking.
Operational: A 5 ton container can be carried, stored for varying tasks—HQ support, research, patrol, extended diving, drone control. The ship's company varies from 23-46 depending on the assigned task. Six divers are carried when minehunting. All of the class are based at Zeebrugge.

PRIMULA *6/1991, Guy Toremans*

6 Ex-US AGGRESSIVE CLASS (MINEHUNTERS/SWEEPERS — OCEAN)

Name	*No*	*Builders*	*Laid down*	*Launched*	*Commissioned*
J E VAN HAVERBEKE (ex-MSO 522)	M 902	Peterson Builders Inc, Sturgeon Bay, Wisc.	2 Mar 1959	29 Oct 1959	7 Nov 1960
A F DUFOUR (ex-*Lagen* M 950, ex-MSO 498, ex-AM 498)	M 903	Bellingham Shipyard Inc, Wash.	11 Feb 1954	13 Aug 1954	27 Sep 1955
DE BROUWER (ex-*Namsen* M 951, ex-MSO 499, ex-AM 499)	M 904	Bellingham Shipyard Inc, Wash.	25 Apr 1954	15 Oct 1954	1 Nov 1955
BREYDEL (ex-MSO 504, ex-AM 504)	M 906	Tacoma Boatbuilding Co, Tacoma, Wash.	25 Nov 1954	25 Mar 1955	24 Jan 1956
G TRUFFAUT (ex-MSO 515, ex-AM 515)	M 908	Tampa Marine Co Inc, Tampa, Fla.	1 Feb 1955	1 Nov 1955	21 Sep 1956
F BOVESSE (ex-MSO 516, ex-AM 516)	M 909	Tampa Marine Co Inc, Tampa, Fla.	1 Apr 1954	8 Feb 1956	21 Dec 1956

Displacement, tons: 720 standard; 780 full load
Dimensions, feet (metres): 172.5 × 35.1 × 14.1 *(52.6 × 10.7 × 4.3)*
Main machinery: 2 GM 8-268A diesels; 1760 hp *(1.3 MW)*; 2 shafts; cp props
Speed, knots: 14. **Range, miles:** 2400 at 12 kts; 3000 at 10 kts
Complement: 40 (3 officers)

Guns: 2 Oerlikon 20 mm (twin). 2—12.7 mm MGs (M 906 and M 908).
Radars: Navigation: Racal Decca 1229; I band.
Sonars: GE SQQ 14; VDS; minehunting; high frequency.

Programmes: Transfer dates; M 902 9 December 1960, M 903 14 April 1966, M 904 14 April 1966, M 906 15 February 1956, M 908 12 October 1956, M 909 25 January 1957. M 903 and M 904 originally served in Royal Norwegian Navy (1955-66).

Structure: Wooden hulls and non-magnetic structure. Capable of sweeping mines of all types. Diesels of non-magnetic stainless steel alloy. LIPS cp propellers.
Operational: Based at Zeebrugge.

PAP 104 *3/1991, van Ginderen Collection*

BREYDEL *10/1991, W. Sartori*

SHIPBORNE AIRCRAFT

Numbers/Type: 3 Aerospatiale SA 316B Alouette III.
Operational speed: 113 kts *(210 km/h)*.
Service ceiling: 10 500 ft *(3200 m)*.
Range: 290 nm *(540 km)*.
Role/Weapon systems: CG helicopter; used for close-range search and rescue and support for commando forces. Sensors: Carries French-design search radar. Weapons: Unarmed. One SA 319B is used for transport on shore.

ALOUETTE III *3/1991, van Ginderen Collection*

LAND-BASED MARITIME AIRCRAFT

Numbers/Type: 5 Westland Sea King Mk 48.
Operational speed: 140 kts *(260 km/h)*.
Service ceiling: 10 500 ft *(3200 m)*.
Range: 630 nm *(1165 km)*.
Role/Weapon systems: SAR helicopter; operated by air force; used for surface search and combat rescue tasks. Sensors: MEL ARI 5955 search radar. Weapons: Unarmed.

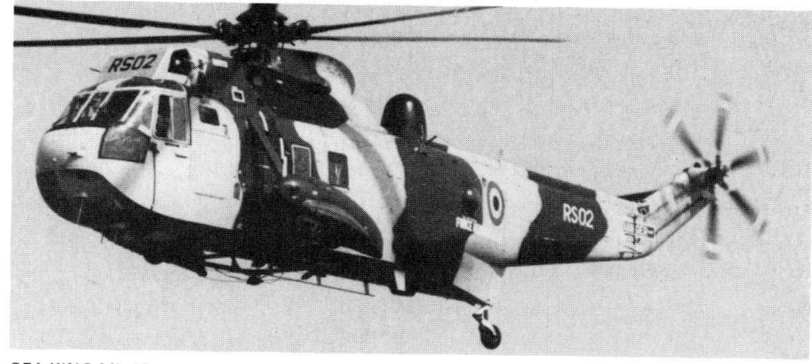

SEA KING Mk 48 *1989, Paul Beaver*

LIGHT FORCES

Note: A new fast patrol craft is planned probably to be funded by the Ministry of Agriculture but naval manned. Could be built in 1992/93 and in service in 1994.

1 RIVER PATROL CRAFT

Name	*No*	*Builders*	*Commissioned*
LIBERATION	P 902	Hitzler, Regensburg	4 Aug 1954

Displacement, tons: 275 full load
Dimensions, feet (metres): 85.5 × 13.1 × 3.2 *(26.1 × 4 × 1)*
Main machinery: 2 diesels; 440 hp(m) *(323 kW)*; 2 shafts
Speed, knots: 19
Complement: 7
Guns: 2—12.7 mm MGs.
Radars: Navigation: Racal Decca; I band.

Comment: Paid off in June 1987 but overhauled and put back in active service in March 1990.

LIBERATION *6/1991, van Ginderen Collection*

AUXILIARIES

1 AMMUNITION TRANSPORT

Name	*No*	*Builders*	*Commissioned*
SPA	A 963 (ex-M 9 953 271-78)	Boel and Zonen, Temse	10 Mar 1955

Displacement, tons: 390 full load
Dimensions, feet (metres): 144.3 × 27.9 × 8.9 *(44 × 8.5 × 2.7)*
Main machinery: 2 GM 8-268A diesels; 880 hp *(656 kW)*; 2 shafts
Speed, knots: 13.5. **Range, miles:** 3000 at 10 kts
Complement: 36 (4 officers)
Radars: Navigation: Racal Decca 1229; I band.

Comment: Ex-MSC converted in 1978 to Ammunition Transport for guided missiles. Based at Zeebrugge.

SPA *4/1989, Gilbert Gyssels*

COMMAND AND SUPPORT SHIPS

Note: Also serve as Royal Yachts when required.

Name	*No*	*Builders*	*Commissioned*
ZINNIA	A 961	Cockerill, Hoboken	22 Sep 1967

Displacement, tons: 1705 light; 2620 full load
Dimensions, feet (metres): 324.7 × 45.9 × 11.8 *(99 × 14 × 3.6)*
Main machinery: 2 Cockerill Ougree V 12 RT 240 CO diesels; 5000 hp(m) *(3.68 MW)*; 1 shaft; cp prop
Speed, knots: 18. **Range, miles:** 14 000 at 12.5 kts
Complement: 125 (13 officers)
Guns: 3 Bofors 40 mm/60.
Radars: Surface search: Racal Decca 1229; I band.
Helicopters: 1 Alouette III.

Comment: Laid down 8 November 1966, launched on 6 May 1967. Design includes a telescopic hangar. Rated as Command and Logistic Support Ship with an oil fuel capacity of 500 tons. Fitted with Chaff launchers for prolonged operations. Based at Zeebrugge.

ZINNIA *11/1991, Antonio Moreno*

Name	*No*	*Builders*	*Commissioned*
GODETIA	A 960	Boelwerf, Temse	3 June 1966

Displacement, tons: 2000 standard; 2260 full load
Dimensions, feet (metres): 301 × 46 × 11.5 *(91.8 × 14 × 3.5)*
Main machinery: 4 ACEC-MAN diesels; 5400 hp(m) *(3.97 MW)*; 2 shafts; cp props
Speed, knots: 19. **Range, miles:** 8700 at 12.5 kts
Complement: 100 (10 officers) plus 35 spare billets
Guns: 1 Bofors 40 mm/60. 2 midships sponsons for 12.7 mm MGs.
Radars: Surface search: Racal Decca 1229; I band.

Comment: Laid down 15 February 1965 and launched 7 December 1965. Rated as Command and Logistic Support Ship. Refit (1979-80) and mid-life conversion (1981-82) included helicopter hangar and replacement cranes. Minesweeping cables fitted either side of helo deck.

GODETIA *2/1990, Guy Toremans*

RESEARCH SHIP

Name	*No*	*Builders*	*Commissioned*
BELGICA	A 962	Boelwerf, Temse	5 July 1984

Displacement, tons: 1085
Dimensions, feet (metres): 167 × 32.8 × 14.4 *(50.9 × 10 × 4.4)*
Main machinery: 1 ABC 6M DZC diesel; 1600 hp(m) *(1.18 MW)*; 1 Kort nozzle prop
Speed, knots: 13.5. **Range, miles:** 5000 at 12 kts
Complement: 26 (11 civilian)
Radars: Navigation: Racal Decca 1229; I band.

Comment: Ordered 1 December 1982. Laid down 17 October 1983, launched 6 January 1984. Used for hydrography, oceanography, meteorology and fishery control. Based at Zeebrugge. Painted white.

BELGICA *11/1991, van Ginderen Collection*

TRAINING SHIP

Name	*No*	*Builders*	*Commissioned*
ZENOBE GRAMME	A 958	Boel and Zonen, Temse	1962

Displacement, tons: 149
Dimensions, feet (metres): 92 × 22.5 × 7 *(28 × 6.8 × 2.1)*
Main machinery: 1 MWM diesel; 200 hp(m) *(147 kW)*; 1 shaft
Speed, knots: 10
Complement: 14

Comment: Auxiliary sail ketch. Laid down 7 October 1960 and launched 23 October 1961. Designed for scientific research but now only used as a training ship.

ZENOBE GRAMME *8/1990, G. Toremans*

TUGS and MISCELLANEOUS

2 COASTAL TUGS

VALCKE (ex-*Steenbank*, ex-*Astroloog*) A 950
EKSTER (ex-*Schouwenbank*, ex-*Astronoom*) A 998

Displacement, tons: 183
Dimensions, feet (metres): 99.7 × 24.9 × 11.8 *(30.4 × 7.6 × 3.6)*
Main machinery: Diesel-electric; 2 Deutz diesel generators; 1240 hp(m) *(911 kW)*; 1 shaft
Speed, knots: 12
Complement: 12

Comment: Originally Netherlands civilian tugs built by H H Bodewes, Millingen in 1960. Bought by Belgian Navy in April 1980. Based at Zeebrugge.

VALCKE *12/1990, van Ginderen Collection*

BIJ A 953 **KREKEL** A 956

Comment: Harbour tugs with firefighting facilities. Of 71 tons and twin shafts; 400 hp(m) *(294 kW)* with Voith-Schneider propellers; 10 kts. A 953 built at Akerboom, Lisse 1959 and based at Ostend, A 956 by Scheepswerf van Rupelmonde at Rupelmonde 1961 and based at Antwerp.

KREKEL *8/1990, G. Toremans*

ZEEMEEUW A 954

Displacement, tons: 220
Dimensions, feet (metres): 91.8 × 23.6 × 11.8 *(28 × 7.2 × 3.6)*
Speed, knots: 10

Comment: Ex-civilian tug (same name) built in 1971 at Hemiksem, acquired in December 1981. Based at Zeebrugge.

ZEEMEEUW 5/1991, van Ginderen Collection

HOMMEL A 951

Comment: Harbour tug of 22 tons, 300 hp(m) *(220 kW)* diesels with Voith-Schneider propellers. Built by Clausen, Remagen-Oberwinter in 1953. Based at Ostend.

SPIN A 997

Comment: Harbour launch of 32 tons built in Netherlands 1958. Based at Ostend.

BELIZE

Headquarters' Appointment

Officer Commanding Defence Force Maritime Wing:
Maritime Wing Major H H Cain

Personnel

(a) 1992: 50 (8 officers)
(b) The Maritime Wing of the Belize Defence Force comprises volunteers from the Army.

Bases

Belize, Placencia.

Mercantile Marine

Lloyd's Register of Shipping:
3 vessels of 620 tons gross

2 WASP 20 METRE (COASTAL PATROL CRAFT)

DANGRIGA PB 01 **TOLEDO** PB 02

Displacement, tons: 36.3 full load
Dimensions, feet (metres): 65.6 × 16.4 × 4.9 *(20 × 5 × 1.5)*
Main machinery: 2 Detroit 16V-71N diesels; 896 hp *(668 kW)* sustained; 2 shafts
Speed, knots: 18
Complement: 10 (2 officers)
Guns: 1—12.7 mm MG. 2—7.62 mm MGs.

Comment: Built by Souters, Cowes, Isle of Wight. Completed August 1983 and commissioned 19 September 1984. GRP hulls. It is reported that these vessels have too great a draught for the shallow waters frequented by smugglers.

DANGRIGA 8/1983, W. Sartori

8 INSHORE PATROL CRAFT

Comment: The BDFMW has two Mexican Skiffs and two Avon type boats. The Police Maritime Wing has three armed Seacraft (P1-P3) with two outboard motors capable of 35 kts; one 12.7 mm MG. Also one Mexican Skiff.

POLICE CRAFT 7/1989, BDFMW

LAND-BASED MARITIME AIRCRAFT

Numbers/Type: 2 Pilatus Britten-Norman Defender.
Operational speed: 150 kts *(280 km/h)*.
Service ceiling: 18 900 ft *(5760 m)*.
Range: 1500 nm *(2775 km)*.
Role/Weapon systems: Coastal patrol, EEZ protection and anti-drug operations. Sensors: Nose-mounted search radar, underwing searchlight. Weapons: Underwing rocket and gun pods possible.

BENIN

Ministerial

Minister of Defence:
Nicephore Soglo

General

In 1978 a decision was taken to found a naval force. As the coastline of Benin is no more than 75 miles long the Patrol Craft can cover the whole coast in a little over two hours. The four Zhuk patrol craft still exist but are unlikely to go to sea again.

Base

Cotonou

Personnel

1992: 150

Mercantile Marine

Lloyd's Register of Shipping:
12 vessels of 1666 tons gross

DELETIONS

1988-89: 2 P4; 4 Zhuk

PATROL FORCES

1 PR 360T COASTAL PATROL CRAFT

PATRIOTE

Displacement, tons: 70 full load
Dimensions, feet (metres): 124.7 × 22.3 × 4.3 *(38 × 6.8 × 1.3)*
Main machinery: 3 Baudouin 12 P15-2SR7 diesels; 3600 hp(m) *(2.65 MW)*; 3 waterjets
Speed, knots: 35. **Range, miles:** 1500 at 16 kts
Complement: 23
Guns: 1 Oerlikon 20 mm. 2—12.7 mm MGs.

Comment: Laid down by Société Bretonne de Construction Navale (Loctudy) in October 1986. Launched January 1988 and completed 15 May 1988. Has a wood/epoxy resin composite hull. Endurance 10 days. The craft was damaged shortly after delivery and had still not been repaired fully by mid-1991.

1 COASTAL TUG

KONDO

Displacement, tons: 350
Main machinery: Deutz diesel; 2000 hp(m) *(1.47 MW)*; 1 shaft
Speed, knots: 12.5

Comment: Ordered from Oelkers, West Germany, in February 1984. Completed late 1985.

BERMUDA

General

A small group operated by the Bermuda Police under the charge of Inspector P J Every.

Base

Hamilton

Mercantile Marine

Lloyd's Register of Shipping:
100 vessels of 3 036 987 tons gross

BLUE HERON

Comment: Delivered 22 May 1978 by Harris Boat, Newburyport, Massachusetts, USA. Of 7 tons, 36 ft *(10.9 m)* with two GM 8 2 Y diesels; 420 hp *(313 kW)*. Complement three.

BLUE HERON *1982, Bermuda Police*

RESCUE I **RESCUE II**

Comment: First one delivered September 1986 and second May 1988 by Osborne Rescue Boats Ltd. An 'Arctic' rigid hull inflatable. Of 1.45 tons, 24 ft *(7.3 m)* with twin Yamaha 115 hp(m) *(84.5 kW)* outboard engines. Complement three.

RESCUE II *1991, Bermuda Police*

HERON I **HERON II** **HERON III**

Comment: *Heron III* delivered in October 1987, *Heron II* in December 1988 and *Heron I* in August 1991. All are Boston Whaler type craft of 1.5 tons, 22 ft *(6.7 m)* and have twin Yamaha 115 hp(m) *(84.5 kW)* outboard engines.

2 TUGS

POWERFUL **FAITHFUL**

Displacement, tons: 450 full load
Dimensions, feet (metres): 100.1 × 30.5 × 15.4 *(30.5 × 9.3 × 4.7)*
Main machinery: 2 Ruston 6RK 270M diesels; 3780 hp *(2.8 MW)*; 2 shafts
Speed, knots: 12. **Range, miles:** 6000 at 12 kts
Complement: 8

Comment: Ordered from Cochrane, Selby in April 1987. First completed in May 1988, second in April 1989. Both have firefighting and pollution control capabilities.

POWERFUL *1991, Bermuda Police*

BOLIVIA

Headquarters' Appointments

Commander Armada Boliviana:
Vice Admiral Anibal Gutierrez Chavez
Chief of Staff:
Rear Admiral Rolando Herrera

General

A small navy, Armada Boliviana, used for patrolling Lake Titicaca and the Beni, Madre de Dios, Mamoré and Paraguay river systems was founded in 1963, receiving its present name in 1982. These rivers cover over 10 000 miles. Most of the advanced training of officers and senior ratings is carried out in friendly countries. The junior ratings are almost entirely converted soldiers. The vessels listed were those operational at the end of 1991, all the others have been deleted.

Personnel

(a) 1992: 5000 officers and men
(b) 12 months' selective military service

Organisation

The country is divided into five naval districts, each with one flotilla.
1st Naval District (HQ Riberalta). Patrol craft and two BTL logistic vessels on the Beni/Mamoré river system.
2nd Naval District (HQ Trinidad). Patrol craft and two BTL logistic vessels on the northern portion of Lake Titicaca.
3rd Naval District (HQ Puerto Guayaramerin). Four patrol craft and two BTL logistic vessels on the Madre de Dios river.
4th Naval District (HQ Tiquina). Patrol craft and the hospital ship on the southern portion of Lake Titicaca.
5th Naval District (HQ Puerto Quijarro). Three patrol craft and one BTL logistic vessel on the upper Paraguay river.

Marine Corps

Infanteria de Marina of 600 men based at Tiquina (Almirante Grau battalion)
Equipment: light infantry weapons and Unimos trucks

Prefix to Ships' Names

ARB

Mercantile Marine

Lloyd's Register of Shipping:
1 vessel of 9610 tons gross

PATROL FORCES

9 RIVER/LAKE PATROL CRAFT

Name	*No*	*Tonnage*
COMANDO	LP-01	10
TACTICA	LP-02	10
INTI	LP-04	10
MALLCU	LP-05	10
AUXILIAR	LP-08	10
SANTA CRUZ DE LA SIERRA	PR-51	50
TAMENGO	LP-502	10
SUAREZ ARANA	LP-510	10
MARISCAL SANTA CRUZ	LP-512	10

Comment: In addition to the above, four Boston Whalers were acquired from the US in late 1989 and 11 more in early 1991. A 55 ft craft *General Banzer* was launched in September 1990 and was fitting out in 1991.

17 LOGISTIC SUPPORT and PATROL CRAFT

Name	*No*	*Tonnage*
GENERAL PANDO	BTL-01	40
NICOLAS SUAREZ	BTL-02	40
MARISCAL CRUZ	BTL-03	40
MAX PAREDES	BTL-04	40
V A H UGARTECHE	BTL-06	45
MANURIPI	BTL-07	40
ALMIRANTE GRAU	M-101	20
COMANDANTE ARANDIA	M-103	20
LIBERTADOR	M-223	20
TRINIDAD	M-224	20
LITORAL	M-18	20
J CHAVEZ SUAREZ	M-225	20
ING PALACIOS	M-315	20
ITENEZ	M-322	20
BRUNO RACUA	M-329	20
TF R RIOS V	M-331	20
ING GUMUCIO	M-341	70

Comment: The craft with BTL numbers have a liquid cargo capacity of 250 000 litres.

4 AUXILIARIES

Name	*No*	*Tonnage*
JULIAN APAZA	AH 01	150
GENERAL BELGRANO	LT 01	30
PIONERA	LH 01	30
CENTAURO	LH 03	30

Comment: AH 01 is a hospital ship given by the USA in 1972. LT 01 is a transport vessel and LH 01 and LH 03 are survey ships.

LAND-BASED MARITIME AIRCRAFT

Numbers/Type: 8 Helibras (Aerospatiale) SA 315B Gavião (Lama).
Operational speed: 124 kts *(230 km/h)*.
Service ceiling: 7710 ft *(2350 m)*.
Range: 390 nm *(720 km)*.
Role/Weapon systems: Support helicopter for SAR/commando forces. Sensors: Visual reconnaissance. Weapons: Unarmed.

Numbers/Type: 1 Cessna 402-C.
Operational speed: 210 kts *(389 km/h)*.
Service ceiling: 27 000 ft *(9000 m)*.
Range: 1080 nm *(2000 km)*.
Role/Weapon systems: Fixed-wing MR for short-range operations. Sensors: Visual reconnaissance. Weapons: Unarmed.

BRAZIL

Headquarters' Appointments

Chief of Naval Staff:
Admiral Renalto de Miranda Monteiro
Chief of Naval Operations:
Admiral José do Cabo Teixeira de Carvalho
Chief of Naval Personnel:
Admiral Ivan da Silveira Serpa
Commandant General Brazilian Marines:
Admiral Coaraciara Bricio Godinho
Vice Chief of Naval Staff:
Vice Admiral Augusto Cesar da Silva Carvalhedo

Senior Officer

Flag Officer Commanding Fleet:
Vice Admiral Jelcias Baptista da Silva Castro

Diplomatic Representation

Naval Attaché in Bolivia:
Captain Ronaldo da Silva
Naval Attaché in England, Sweden and Norway:
Captain Jorge de Carvalho Lopes
Defence Attaché in Spain:
Captain Léo Teixeira Cuiabano
Naval Attaché in Uruguay:
Captain Sergio Oliveira de Araújo
Naval Attaché in France:
Captain Francisco Jose de Oliveira Lima
Naval Attaché in Italy:
Captain Luiz Fernando Coelho Pinto de Almeida
Defence Attaché in Japan and Korea:
Captain Heitor Wegmann da Silva
Naval Attaché in Paraguay:
Captain Frederico Felix Antonio Bullaty
Naval Attaché in Germany and Netherlands:
Captain Roberio da Cunha Coutinho
Naval Attaché in Argentina:
Captain Fernando Sergio Nogueira de Araujo
Naval Attaché in Venezuela:
Captain Francisco Paulo Valente Miranda Chaves
Naval Attaché in Peru:
Captain Helio Pereira Celidônio
Naval Attaché in Portugal:
Captain José Roberto Paulon Silva
Naval Attaché in Chile:
Captain Luiz Costa Albernaz
Naval Attaché in USA and Canada:
Rear Admiral Luiz Paulo Aguiar Reguffe
Head of Brazilian Naval Commission in Europe:
Captain Manoel Rodrigues de Amaral
Head of Brazilian Naval Commission in Washington:
Captain João Matriciano Filho

Personnel

(a) 1992: 50 000 (5700 officers)
Figures include 14 600 marines and also auxiliary corps
(b) 1 year's national service

Naval Bases

Arsenal de Marinha do Rio de Janeiro - Rio de Janeiro (Naval shipyard with three dry docks and one floating dock with graving docks of up to 70 000 tons capacity)
Base Naval do Rio de Janeiro - Rio de Janeiro (Main Naval Base with two dry docks)
Base Almirante Castro e Silva - Rio de Janeiro (Naval Base for submarines)
Base Naval de Aratu - Bahia (Naval Base and repair yard with one dry dock and synchrolift)
Base Naval de Val-de-Cães - Pará (Naval River and repair yard with one dry dock)
Base Naval Almirante Ary Parreiras - Rio Grande do Norte (Small Naval Base and repair yard with one floating dock)
Base Fluvial de Ladário - Mato Grosso do Sul (Small Naval River Base and repair yard with one dry dock)
Base Aérea Naval de São Pedro d'Aldeia - Rio de Janeiro (Naval Air Station)
Estação Naval do Rio Negro - Amazonas (Small Naval River Station and repair yard with one floating dock)

Organisation

Naval Districts as follows:
I Naval District (HQ Rio de Janeiro)
II Naval District (HQ São Salvador)
III Naval District (HQ Natal)
IV Naval District (HQ Belém)
V Naval District (HQ Rio Grande)
VI Naval District (HQ Ladário)
VII Naval District (HQ Manaus)
Comando Naval de Brasilia (Brasilia)

Naval Aviation

A Fleet Air Arm was formed on 26 January 1965.
Squadrons: HA-1 Lynx; HS-1 Sea King; HI-1 Jet Ranger; HU-1 Ecureuil; HU-2 Super Puma.

Coast Guard

Plans to form a Coast Guard have been dropped.

Prefix to Ships' Names

These vary, indicating the type of ship for example, N Ae L = Aircraft Carrier; CT = Destroyer.

Pennant Numbers

Ships which lose their pennant numbers are formally decommissioned from the Navy as a result of cuts in Officer numbers. They are then retained in service as tenders to Naval establishments and are commanded by Warrant Officers.

Marines (Corpo de Fuzileiros Navais)

14 600 officers and men.

Headquarters at Fort São José, Rio de Janeiro
Divisão Anfibia: 1 Command Batallion, 3 Infantry Batallions (Riachuelo, Humaita and Paissandu), 1 Artillery group.
Comando de Reforço: 1 Special Forces Batallion (Tonelero). Transport, engineer and medical units.
Gruppo Regional: One security group in each naval district.

Divisão Anfibia and Comando de Reforço form together the Forca de Fuzileiros da Esquadra stationed at Rio de Janeiro, other units called Grupamentos Regionais are stationed at or near naval installations in the rest of the country.

Strength of the Fleet

Type	*Active*	*Building (Planned)*
Submarines (Patrol)	4	2 (1)
Aircraft Carrier (light)	1	—
Destroyers	6	(2)
Frigates	12	2
Coastal Patrol Ships	9	—
Landing Ships	3	—
Landing Craft	39	—
River Monitor	1	—
River Patrol Ships	5	—
Large Patrol Craft	7	3 (4)
Coastal Patrol Craft	4	—
Minesweepers (Coastal)	6	—
Survey Ships	9	(1)
Survey Launches	7	—
Buoy Tenders	9	—
S/M Rescue Ship	1	—
Repair and Support Ships	2	—
Large Tanker	1	—
Small Tanker	1	—
Training Ships	7	—
Transports	16	—
Tugs—Ocean	5	—

Mercantile Marine

Lloyd's Register of Shipping:
669 vessels of 5 882 528 tons gross

DELETIONS

Submarines

1990 *Goias, Bahia* (training only until Dec 1992)
1992 *Amazonas*

Destroyers

1989 *Piaui*
1990 *Maranhão, Mato Grosso*

Amphibious Forces

1989 *Garcia D'Ávila*

Miscellaneous

1991 *Marajó, Almirante Saldanha, Rio Doce*

PENNANT LIST

Submarines

S 20	Humaitá
S 21	Tonelero
S 22	Riachuelo
S 30	Tupi
S 31	Tamoio (bldg)
S 32	Timbira (bldg)
S 33	Tapajós (planned)

Aircraft Carrier

A 11	Minas Gerais

Destroyers

D 25	Marcílio Dias
D 26	Mariz E Barros
D 27	Pará
D 28	Paraiba
D 29	Paraná
D 30	Pernambuco
D 35	Sergipe
D 36	Alagoas
D 37	Rio Grande do Norte
D 38	Espírito Santo

Frigates

F 40	Niteroi
F 41	Defensora
F 42	Constituição
F 43	Liberal
F 44	Independência
F 45	União
V 30	Inhaúma
V 31	Jaceguay
V 32	Julio de Noronha (bldg)
V 33	Frontin (bldg)

Amphibious Forces

G 26	Duque de Caxais
G 30	Ceará
G 31	Rio de Janeiro
(ex-L10)	Guarapari
(ex-L11)	Tambaú
(ex-L12)	Camboriú

Patrol Forces

V 15	Imperial Marinheiro
V 16	Iguatemi

Patrol Forces

V 18	Forte De Coimbra
V 19	Caboclo
V 20	Angostura
V 21	Bahiana
V 22	Mearim
V 23	Purus
V 24	Solimões
P 10	Piratini
P 11	Pirajá
P 12	Pampeiro
P 13	Parati
P 14	Penedo
P 15	Poti
P 20	Pedro Teixeira
P 21	Raposo Tavares
P 30	Roraima
P 31	Rondônia
P 32	Amapá
P 40	Graúna
P 41	Goiana
P 42	Grajaú (bldg)
P 43	Guaiba (bldg)
P 44	Guajará (planned)
P 45	Guaporé (planned)
P 46	Gurupá (planned)
P 47	Gurupi (planned)

Mine Warfare Forces

M 15	Aratú
M 16	Anhatomirim
M 17	Atalaia
M 18	Araçatuba
M 19	Abrolhos
M 20	Albardão

Oceanographic Vessels and Tenders

(ex-H 11)	Paraibano
(ex-H 12)	Rio Branco
H 13	Mestre João dos Santos
(ex-H 14)	Nogueira da Gama
(ex-H 15)	Itacurussá
(ex-H 16)	Camocim
(ex-H 17)	Caravelas
H 18	Comandante Varella
H 19	Tenente Castelo
H 20	Comandante Manhães
H 21	Sirius
H 22	Canopus
H 24	Castelhanos
H 25	Tenente Boanerges
H 26	Faroleiro Mário Seixas
H 27	Faroleiro Areas
H 30	Faroleiro Nascimento
H 31	Argus
H 32	Orion
H 33	Taurus
H 34	Almirante Graça Aranha
H 40	Antares
H 41	Almirante Câmara
H 42	Barão de Teffé
H 43	Almirante Alvaro Alberto

Miscellaneous

G 15	Paraguassú
G 16	Barroso Pereira
G 17	Potengi
G 20	Custódio de Mello
G 21	Ary Parreiras
G 22	Soares Dutra
G 23	Almirante Gastao Motta
G 24	Belmonte
K 11	Felinto Perry
(ex-R 15)	Comandante Marroig
(ex-R 16)	Comandante Didier
(ex-R 17)	Tenente Magalhães
(ex-R 18)	Cabo Schramm
R 21	Tritão
R 22	Tridente
R 23	Triunfo
R 24	Almirante Guilhem
R 25	Almirante Guillobel
U 10	Aspirante Nascimento
U 11	Guarda Marinha Jensen
U 12	Guarda Marinha Brito
(ex-U 15)	Suboficial Oliveira
U 16	Trindade
U 17	Parnaiba
U 18	Oswaldo Cruz
U 19	Carlos Chagas
U 20	Gastão Moutinho
U 27	Brasil
U 29	Piraim
(ex-U 30)	Almirante Hess

SUBMARINES

Notes: (a) Plans for the construction of nuclear powered submarines are advancing with a prototype nuclear reactor being built at São Paulo. A uranium enrichment plant was inaugurated at Ipero in April 1988. The prototype SSN (S-NAC-2) to be about 2800 tons and have a power plant developing 50 MW for a speed of 25 kts. In spite of delays in the diesel submarine programme, the SSN has a very high priority.

(b) Ex-Guppy II class *Bahia* (S 12) is still used for alongside training but is to be scrapped in December 1992.

1 + 2 (1) TUPI CLASS (209 TYPE 1400)

Name	No	Builders	Laid down	Launched	Commissioned
TUPI	S 30	Howaldtswerke-Deutsche Werft (Kiel)	8 Mar 1985	28 Apr 1987	6 May 1989
TAMOIO	S 31	Arsenal de Marinha, Rio de Janeiro	15 July 1986	Oct 1992	1993
TIMBIRA	S 32	Arsenal de Marinha, Rio de Janeiro	15 Sep 1987	June 1993	1994
TAPAJÓS	S 33	Arsenal de Marinha, Rio de Janeiro	—	—	—

Displacement, tons: 1260 surfaced; 1440 dived
Dimensions, feet (metres): 200.1 × 20.3 × 18 *(61 × 6.2 × 5.5)*
Main machinery: Diesel-electric; 4 MTU 12V 493 AZ80 GA31L diesels; 2400 hp(m) *(1.76 MW)*; 4 alternators; 1.7 MW; 1 Siemens motor; 4600 hp(m) *(3.36 MW)* sustained; 1 shaft
Speed, knots: 11 surfaced/snorting; 21.5 dived
Range, miles: 8200 at 8 kts surfaced; 400 at 4 kts dived
Complement: 30

Torpedoes: 8—21 in *(533 mm)* bow tubes. 16 Marconi Mk 24 Tigerfish Mod 1; wire-guided; active homing to 13 km *(7 nm)* at 35 kts; passive homing to 29 km *(15.7 nm)* at 24 kts; warhead 134 kg. Swim-out discharge.
Countermeasures: ESM: Thomson-CSF DR-4000; electronic warfare suite.
Fire control: Ferranti KAFS-A10 action data automation. Sperry Mk 29 inertial navigation. 2 Kollmorgen Mod 76 periscopes.
Radars: Navigation: Thomson-CSF Calypso III; I band.
Sonars: Krupp Atlas CSU-83/1; hull-mounted; passive/active search and attack; medium frequency.

Programmes: Contract signed with Howaldtswerke in February 1984. Financial negotiations were completed with the West German Government in October 1984. Original plans included building four followed by two improved Tupis for a total of six by the end of the 1990s. The last two would be to a Brazilian design for a stretched version of the Type 209, to be called S-NAC-1. A 2420 ton design was submitted by the Naval Engineering Directorate in January 1990. *Tapajós* may be cancelled in favour of the first S-NAC-1 which could be laid down in late 1992.
Structure: Diving depth, 250 m *(820 ft)*.

TUPI *5/1990, Mário R. V. Carneiro*

3 BRITISH OBERON CLASS

Name	No	Builders	Laid down	Launched	Commissioned
HUMAITÁ	S 20	Vickers, Barrow	3 Nov 1970	5 Oct 1971	18 June 1973
TONELERO	S 21	Vickers, Barrow	18 Nov 1971	22 Nov 1972	10 Dec 1977
RIACHUELO	S 22	Vickers, Barrow	26 May 1973	6 Sep 1975	12 Mar 1977

Displacement, tons: 1610 standard; 2030 surfaced; 2410 dived
Dimensions, feet (metres): 295.2 × 26.5 × 18 *(90 × 8.1 × 5.5)*
Main machinery: Diesel-electric; 2 ASR 16 VVS-ASR1 diesels; 3680 hp *(2.74 MW)*; 2 AEI motors; 6000 hp *(4.48 MW)*; 2 shafts
Speed, knots: 12 surfaced; 17 dived. **Range, miles:** 9000 surfaced at 12 kts
Complement: 70 (6 officers)

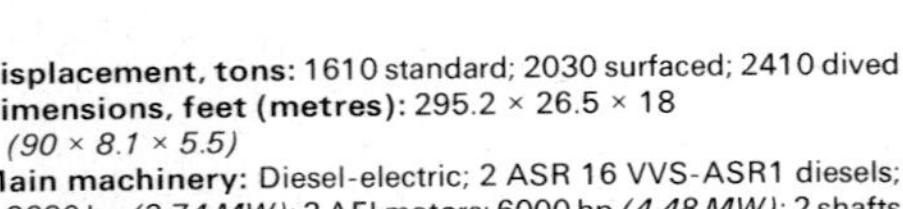

Torpedoes: 8—21 in *(533 mm)* (6 bow, 2 stern) tubes. 22 Marconi Mk 24 Tigerfish Mod 1; wire-guided; active homing to 13 km *(7 nm)* at 35 kts; passive homing to 29 km *(15.7 nm)* at 24 kts; warhead 134 kg.
4 Honeywell Mk 37 Mod 2 (stern tubes); wire-guided; active/passive homing to 8 km *(4.4 nm)* at 24 kts; warhead 150 kg.
Some Mk 8 Mod 4 anti-ship torpedoes (4.5 km at 45 kts) are still in service.
Countermeasures: ESM: Radar warning.
Fire control: Ferranti DCH tactical data system.
Radars: Navigation: Kelvin Hughes Type 1006; I band.
Sonars: Thorn-EMI Type 187; hull-mounted; search and attack; medium frequency.
BAC Type 2007; flank array; passive search; low frequency.

Programmes: Two ordered from Vickers in 1969, the third in 1972. Completion of *Tonelero* was much delayed by a serious fire on board originating in the cabling. It was this fire which resulted in re-cabling of all Oberon class under construction.

TONELERO *6/1989, Mário R. V. Carneiro*

Modernisation: The previously planned modernisation programme was finally cancelled in 1990.

Operational: Two short torpedo tubes aft reported as not operational, are in fact still in service.

AIRCRAFT CARRIER

1 Ex-BRITISH COLOSSUS CLASS

Name	*No*	*Builders*	*Laid down*	*Launched*	*Commissioned*
MINAS GERAIS (ex-HMS *Vengeance*)	A 11	Swan, Hunter & Wigham Richardson, Ltd, Wallsend on Tyne	16 Nov 1942	23 Feb 1944	15 Jan 1945

Displacement, tons: 15 890 standard; 17 500 normal; 19 890 full load (13 190 standard; 18 010 full load before reconstruction)
Dimensions, feet (metres): 695 × 80 × 24.5 *(211.8 × 24.4 × 7.5)*
Flight deck, feet (metres): 690 × 119.6 *(210.3 × 36.4)*
Main machinery: 4 Admiralty boilers; 400 psi *(28.1 kg/cm sq)*, 700°F *(371°C)*; 2 Parsons turbines; 40 000 hp *(30 MW)*; 2 shafts
Speed, knots: 24. **Range, miles:** 12 000 at 14 kts; 6200 at 23 kts
Complement: 1300 (300 aircrew)

Guns: 10 Bofors 40 mm/60 (2 quad Mk 2, 1 twin Mk 1); 330 rounds/minute to 3 km *(1.6 nm)* anti-aircraft; weight of shell 0.89 kg.
2—47 mm saluting guns.
Countermeasures: Decoys: Plessey Shield Chaff launcher.
ESM: SLR-2; radar warning.
Combat data systems: Ferranti Link system compatible with CAAIS fitted ships. SATCOM.
Fire control: 2 Mk 63 GFCS. 1 Mk 51 Mod 2 GFCS.
Radars: Air search: Lockheed SPS 40B; E/F band; range 320 km *(175 nm)*.
Surface search: Signaal ZW 06; I band.
Navigation: Scanter Mil; I band.
Fire control: Two SPG 34; I/J band.
CCA: Terma GSA; I band.

Fixed wing aircraft: 6 Grumman S-2G Trackers.
Helicopters: 4-6 Agusta SH-3A Sea Kings; 2 Aerospatiale UH-13 Ecureuil II; 3 Aerospatiale UH-14 Super Puma.

Programmes: Served in the Royal Navy from 1945 onwards. Fitted out 1948-49 for experimental cruise to the Arctic. Lent to the RAN early in August 1953, returned to the Royal Navy in 1955. Purchased by the Brazilian Government on 14 December 1956 and commissioned in the Brazilian Navy on 6 December 1960.
Modernisation: During reconstruction in 1957-60 at Rotterdam the steam capacity was increased when the boilers were retubed. New lifts were installed; also included were one MacTaggart-Scott single track steam catapult for launching, and arrester wires for recovering 30 000 lb aircraft at 60 kts. The conversion and overhaul also included the installation of the 8¼ degrees angled deck, mirror-sight deck landing system, armament fire control, a new island and radar equipment. Completed refit in 1981 but further modernisation was postponed until 1991 when new search and CCA radars were fitted. Improved propulsion is also planned.
Structure: Hangar dimensions: length, 135.6 m *(445 ft)*; width, 15.8 m *(52 ft)*; clear depth, 5.3 m *(17.5 ft)*. Aircraft lifts: 13.7 × 10.4 m *(45 × 34 ft)*. The ship's overall length quoted does not include the catapult spur.
Opinion: Plans delayed but still under consideration for a new 35 000-40 000 ton ship. It is reported that she will, if built, have a speed of 28 kts with two steam catapults, carry 30-40 aircraft and have modern anti-aircraft defences.

MINAS GERAIS *6/1990*

MINAS GERAIS *5/1990, Mário R. V. Carneiro*

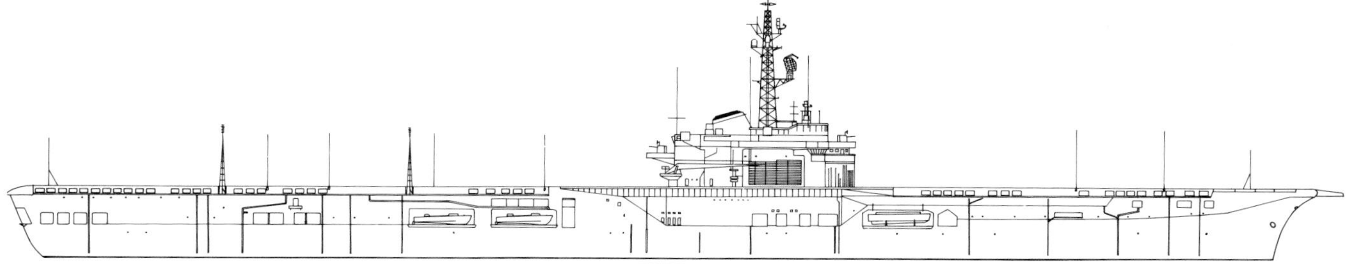
MINAS GERAIS *(Scale 1 : 1 200), Ian Sturton*

MINAS GERAIS *1988, Brazilian Navy*

DESTROYERS

Note: There are provisional plans to acquire up to four ex-USN Charles F Adams class.

2 Ex-US GEARING (FRAM I) CLASS

Name	No	Builders	Laid down	Launched	Commissioned
MARCILIO DIAS (ex-USS *Henry W Tucker* DD 875)	D 25	Consolidated Steel	29 May 1944	8 Nov 1944	12 Mar 1945
MARIZ E BARROS (ex-USS *Brinkley Bass* DD 887)	D 26	Consolidated Steel	20 Dec 1944	26 May 1945	1 Oct 1945

Displacement, tons: 2425 standard; 3500 full load
Dimensions, feet (metres): 390.5 × 41.2 × 19 *(119 × 12.6 × 5.8)*
Main machinery: 4 Babcock & Wilcox boilers; 600 psi *(43.3 kg/cm sq)*; 850°F *(454°C)*; 2 GE turbines; 60 000 hp *(45 MW)*; 2 shafts
Speed, knots: 32. **Range, miles:** 5800 at 15 kts
Complement: 274 (14 officers)

Missiles: A/S: Honeywell ASROC Mk 116 octuple launcher ❶. Not operational.
Guns: 4—5 in *(127 mm)*/38 (2 twin) Mk 38 ❷; 15 rounds/minute to 17 km *(9.2 nm)* anti-surface; 11 km *(5.9 nm)* anti-aircraft; weight of shell 25 kg.
Torpedoes: 6—324 mm Mk 32 (2 triple) tubes ❸. Honeywell Mk 46 Mod 5; anti-submarine; active/passive homing to 11 km *(5.9 nm)* at 40 kts; warhead 44 kg.
Countermeasures: ESM: WLR 3; radar warning.
ECM: VLQ 6; jammer.
Fire control: Mk 37 GFCS.

MARCILIO DIAS

(Scale 1 : 1 200), Ian Sturton

Radars: Air search: Lockheed SPS 40 ❹; E/F band; range 320 km *(175 nm)*.
Surface search: Raytheon/Sylvania SPS 10 ❺; G band.
Fire control: Western Electric Mk 25 ❻; I/J band.
Sonars: Sangamo SQS 23; hull-mounted; active search and attack; medium frequency; with bottom bounce.

Helicopters: 1 Bell JetRanger III ❼.

Programmes: Transferred 8 December 1973.
Operational: Plans for new engines and re-arming have been dropped. JetRanger helicopter has replaced the deleted Wasp. ASROC is not operational.

MARCILIO DIAS *7/1990*

4 Ex-US ALLEN M SUMNER (FRAM II) CLASSES

Name	No	Builders	Laid down	Launched	Commissioned
SERGIPE (ex-USS *James C Owens* DD 776)	D 35	Bethlehem Steel Co (San Pedro)	9 Apr 1944	1 Oct 1944	17 Feb 1945
ALAGOAS (ex-USS *Buck* DD 761)	D 36	Bethlehem Steel Co (San Francisco)	1 Feb 1944	11 Mar 1945	28 June 1946
RIO GRANDE DO NORTE (ex-USS *Strong* DD 758)	D 37	Bethlehem Steel Co (San Francisco)	25 July 1943	23 Apr 1944	8 Mar 1945
ESPIRITO SANTO (ex-USS *Lowry* DD 770)	D 38	Bethlehem Steel Co (San Pedro)	1 Aug 1943	6 Feb 1944	23 July 1944

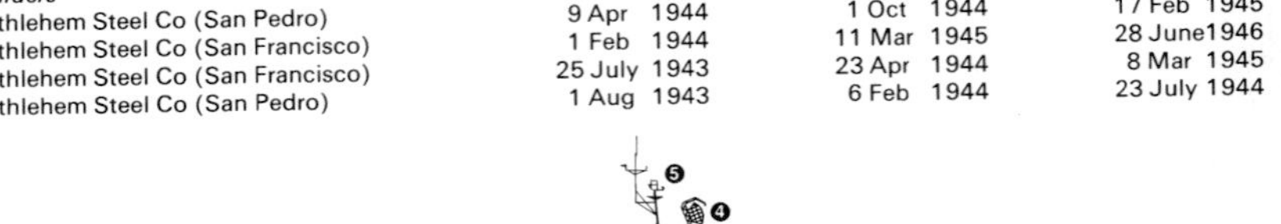

Displacement, tons: 2200 standard; 3320 full load
Dimensions, feet (metres): 376.5 × 40.9 × 19 *(114.8 × 12.5 × 5.8)*
Main machinery: 4 Babcock & Wilcox boilers; 600 psi *(43.3 kg/cm sq)*; 850°F *(454°C)*; 2 GE turbines; 60 000 hp *(45 MW)*; 2 shafts
Speed, knots: 34. **Range, miles:** 4600 at 15 kts; 1260 at 30 kts
Complement: 274 (15 officers)

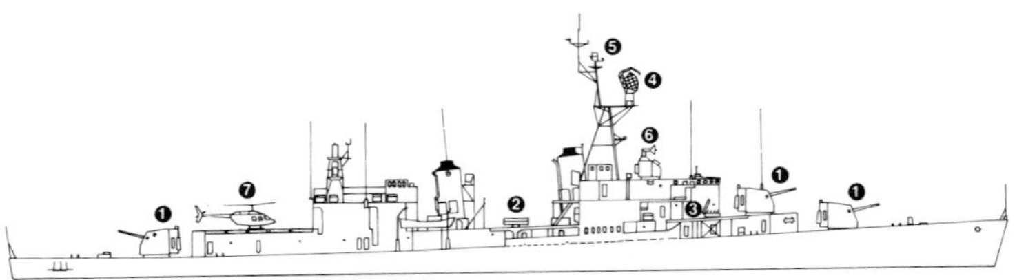

ALAGOAS

(Scale 1 : 1 200), Ian Sturton

Guns: 6—5 in *(127 mm)*/38 (3 twin) Mk 38 ❶; 15 rounds/minute to 17 km *(9.2 nm)* anti-surface; 11 km *(5.9 nm)* anti-aircraft; weight of shell 25 kg.
Torpedoes: 6—324 mm Mk 32 (2 triple) tubes ❷. Honeywell Mk 46 Mod 5; anti-submarine; active/passive homing to 11 km *(5.9 nm)* at 40 kts; warhead 44 kg.
A/S mortars: 2 Hedgehogs ❸; 24 manually loaded rockets; range 350 m.
Countermeasures: ESM: WLR 3; radar warning.
ECM: ULQ-6 *(Espirito Santo)*; jammer.
Fire control: Mk 37 GFCS.
Radars: Air search: Westinghouse SPS 29 *(Espirito Santo)*; B/C band; range 457 km *(250 nm)*.
Lockheed SPS 40 (others) ❹; E/F band; range 320 km *(175 nm)*.
Surface search: Raytheon/Sylvania SPS 10 ❺; G band.
Fire control: Western Electric Mk 25 ❻; I/J band
Sonars: SQS 40; hull-mounted; active search and attack; medium frequency.

Helicopters: 1 Bell JetRanger ❼.

Programmes: Transferred to Brazil by sale as follows: *Sergipe* and *Alagoas* 16 July 1973, *Espirito Santo* 29 October 1973 and *Rio Grande do Norte* 31 October 1973.
Operational: *Sergipe* VDS removed.

ESPIRITO SANTO *5/1990, Brazilian Navy*

FRIGATES

Note: A cheaper corvette design is likely to follow the Inhaúma class in 1992/93.

6 NITEROI CLASS

Name	*No*	*Builders*	*Laid down*	*Launched*	*Commissioned*
NITEROI	F 40	Vosper Thornycroft Ltd	8 June 1972	8 Feb 1974	20 Nov 1976
DEFENSORA	F 41	Vosper Thornycroft Ltd	14 Dec 1972	27 Mar 1975	5 Mar 1977
CONSTITUIÇÃO	F 42*	Vosper Thornycroft Ltd	13 Mar 1974	15 Apr 1976	31 Mar 1978
LIBERAL	F 43*	Vosper Thornycroft Ltd	2 May 1975	7 Feb 1977	18 Nov 1978
INDEPENDÊNCIA	F 44	Arsenal de Marinha do Rio de Janeiro	11 June 1972	2 Sep 1974	3 Sep 1979
UNIÃO	F 45	Arsenal de Marinha do Rio de Janeiro	11 June 1972	14 Mar 1975	12 Sep 1980

***GP design.**

Displacement, tons: 3200 standard; 3707 full load
Dimensions, feet (metres): 424 × 44.2 × 18.2 (sonar) *(129.2 × 13.5 × 5.5)*
Main machinery: CODOG; 2 RR Olympus TM3B gas turbines; 43 000 hp *(32 MW)* sustained; 4 MTU 16V 956 TB91 diesels; 15 000 hp(m) *(11 MW)* sustained; 2 shafts; cp props
Speed, knots: 30 gas; 22 diesels. **Range, miles:** 5300 at 17 kts on 2 diesels; 4200 at 19 kts on 4 diesels; 1300 at 28 kts on gas
Complement: 209 (22 officers)

Missiles: SSM: 4 Aerospatiale MM 40 Exocet (2 twin) launchers ❶; inertial cruise; active radar homing to 70 km *(40 nm)* at 0.9 Mach; warhead 165 kg; sea-skimmer.
SAM: 2 Short Bros Seacat triple launchers ❷; optical/radar guidance to 5 km *(2.7 nm)*; warhead 10 kg; 60 missiles.
A/S: 1 Ikara launcher (Branik standard) (A/S version) ❸; command radio/radar guidance to 24 km *(13 nm)* at 0.8 Mach; 10 missiles; payload Mk 46 torpedoes.
Guns: 2 Vickers 4.5 in *(115 mm)*/55 Mk 8 (GP version) ❹; 55° elevation; 25 rounds/minute to 22 km *(12 nm)* anti-surface; 6 km *(3.2 nm)* anti-aircraft; weight of shell 21 kg. A/S version only has 1 mounting.
2 Bofors 40 mm/70 ❺; 90° elevation; 300 rounds/minute to 12 km *(6.5 nm)* anti-surface; 4 km *(2.2 nm)* anti-aircraft; weight of shell 0.96 kg.
Torpedoes: 6—324 mm Plessey STWS-1 (2 triple) tubes ❻. Honeywell Mk 46 Mod 5; anti-submarine; active/passive homing to 11 km *(5.9 nm)* at 40 kts; warhead 44 kg.
A/S mortars: 1 Bofors 375 mm trainable rocket launcher (twin-tube) ❼; automatic loading; range 1600 m.
Depth charges: 1 rail; 5 charges (GP version).
Countermeasures: Decoys: 2 Plessey Shield Chaff launchers.
ESM: SDR-2 and SDR-7; radar warning. FH5 HF/DF.
Combat data systems: Ferranti CAAIS 400 with FM 1600B computers.
Fire control: Ikara tracker (A/S version).
Radars: Air/surface search: Plessey AWS 2 with Mk 10 IFF ❽; E/F band; range 110 km *(60 nm)*.
Surface search: Signaal ZW 06 ❾; I band; range 26 km *(14 nm)*.
Fire control: Two Selenia Orion RTN 10X ❿; I/J band; range 40 km *(22 nm)*.
Sonars: EDO 610E; hull-mounted; active search and attack; medium frequency.
EDO 700E VDS (F 40 and 41); active search and attack; medium frequency.

Helicopters: 1 Westland Lynx SAH-11 ⓫.

Programmes: A contract announced on 29 September 1970 was signed between the Brazilian Government and Vosper Thornycroft for the design and building of six Vosper Thornycroft Mark 10 frigates.
Modernisation: The latest modernisation plan in late 1991 included replacing Seacat/RTN 10X by VL Seawolf/Marconi 1802SW, Plessey AWS 2 radar by AWS 5, ZW 06 radar by Kelvin Hughes Type 1007, updating the Bofors gun and fitting the same SAAB Optronic FCS, Plessey Shield countermeasures and Racal Cutlass ESM equipment as the Inhaúma class. ESM systems are being developed by the Instituto de Pesquisas da Marinas. By early 1992 contracts were expected for the first two (probably the GP versions) but alternative proposals by Selenia Elsag for an Albatros SAM system, and RAN 20S and RTN 30X radars, were also being studied.
Structure: F 40, 41, 44 and 45 are of the A/S configuration. F 42 and 43 are General Purpose design. Materials, equipment and lead-yard services supplied by Vosper Thornycroft at Navyard, Rio de Janeiro. Fitted with retractable stabilisers. Seventh ship with differing armament was ordered from Navyard, Rio de Janeiro in June 1981 and is used as a training ship.

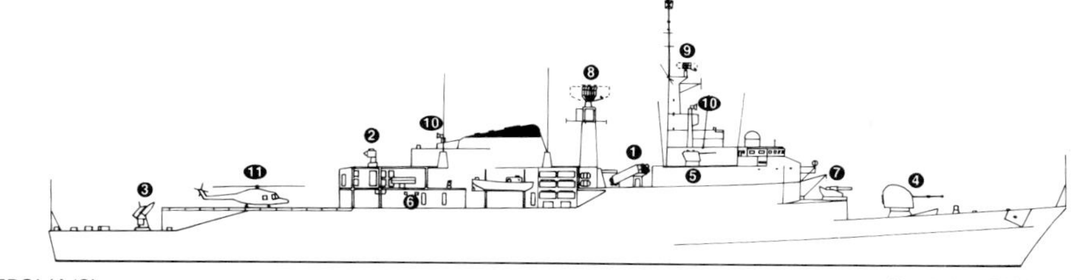

NITEROI (A/S) *(Scale 1 : 1 200), Ian Sturton*

DEFENSORA *6/1990*

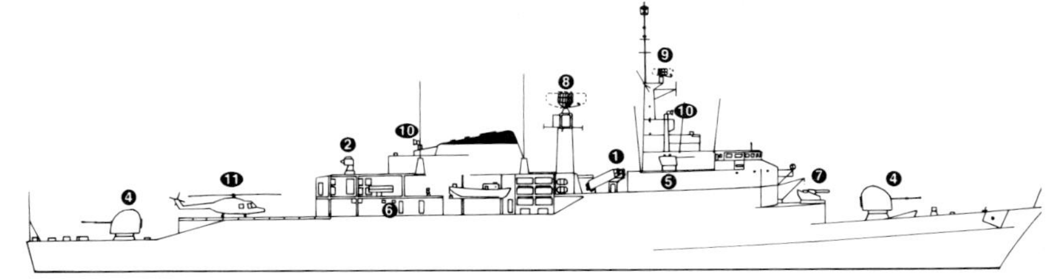

CONSTITUIÇÃO (GP) *(Scale 1 : 1 200), Ian Sturton*

Operational: At the time they were built these ships were economical in personnel, amounting to a 50 per cent reduction of manpower in relation to previous warships of this size and complexity. Endurance, 45 days' stores, 60 days' provisions. Oil fuel, 530 tons. The helicopter has Sea Skua ASM.

CONSTITUIÇÃO *7/1988, Orlando Gallardo*

4 Ex-US GARCIA CLASS

Name	No	Builders	Laid down	Launched	Commissioned	Recommissioned
PARÁ (ex-*Albert David*)	D 27 (ex-FF 1050)	Lockheed S B & Construction Co	29 Apr 1964	19 Dec 1964	19 Oct 1968	18 Sep 1989
PARAÍBA (ex-*Davidson*)	D 28 (ex-FF 1045)	Avondale Shipyards	20 Sep 1963	2 Oct 1964	7 Dec 1965	25 July 1989
PARANÁ (ex-*Sample*)	D 29 (ex-FF 1048)	Lockheed S B & Construction Co	19 July 1963	28 Apr 1964	23 Mar 1968	24 Aug 1989
PERNAMBUCO (ex-*Bradley*)	D 30 (ex-FF 1041)	Bethlehem Steel, San Francisco	17 Jan 1963	26 Mar 1964	15 May 1965	25 Sep 1989

Displacement, tons: 2620 standard; 3403 full load
Dimensions, feet (metres): 414.5 × 44.2 × 24 sonar; 14.5 keel *(126.3 × 13.5 × 7.3; 4.4)*
Main machinery: 2 Foster-Wheeler boilers; 1200 psi *(83.4 kg/cm sq)*; 950°F *(510°C)*; 1 Westinghouse or GE turbine; 35 000 hp *(26 MW)*; 1 shaft
Speed, knots: 27.5. **Range, miles:** 4000 at 20 kts
Complement: 270 (18 officers)

Missiles: A/S: Honeywell ASROC Mk 112 octuple launcher (1); inertial guidance to 1.6-10 km *(1-5.4 nm)*; payload Mk 46 torpedo. *Pará* and *Paraná* have automatic ASROC reload system.
Guns: 2 USN 5 in *(127 mm)*/38 Mk 30 (2); 85° elevation; 15 rounds/minute to 17 km *(9.3 nm)*; weight of shell 25 kg.
Torpedoes: 6—324 mm Mk 32 (2 triple) tubes (3). 14 Honeywell Mk 46 Mod 5; anti-submarine; active/passive homing to 11 km *(5.9 nm)* at 40 kts; warhead 44 kg.
Countermeasures: Decoys: 2 Loral Hycor Mk 33 RBOC 6 tubed Chaff launchers. T-Mk 6 Fanfare; torpedo decoy system. Prairie/Masker; hull/blade rate noise suppression.
ESM: WLR-1; WLR-6; radar warning.
ECM: ULQ-6; jammer.
Fire control: Mk 56 GFCS. Mk 114 ASW FCS.
Radars: Air search: Lockheed SPS 40 (4); E/F band; range 320 km *(175 nm)*.
Surface search: Raytheon SPS 10 (5); G band.
Navigation: Marconi LN 66; I band.
Fire control: General Electric Mk 35 (6); I/J band.
Tacan: SRN 15.
Sonars: EDO/General Electric SQS 26 AXR (D 29 and 30) or SQS 26B; bow-mounted; active search and attack; medium frequency.

Helicopters: Westland Lynx SAH-11 (7).

Programmes: First three transferred by five year lease 15 April 1989 and last one 1 October 1989. All arrived in Brazil on 13 December 1989.
Structure: All four have the enlarged hangar capable of taking a Sea King size helicopter but in USN service *Pará* and *Paraná* had the flight deck area converted to take SQR 15 towed array which was removed on transfer.

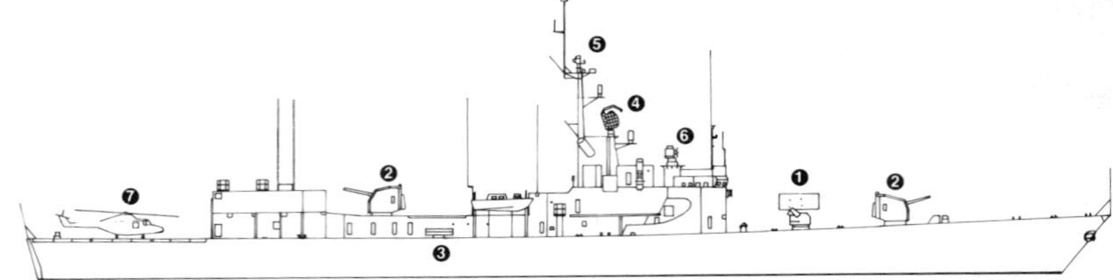

PARAIBA (Scale 1 : 1 200), Ian Sturton

PARÁ 5/1990, Brazilian Navy

2 + 2 INHAÚMA CLASS

Name	No	Builders	Laid down	Launched	Commissioned
INHAÚMA	V 30	Arsenal de Marinha do Rio de Janeiro	23 Sep 1983	13 Dec 1986	12 Dec 1989
JACEGUAY	V 31	Arsenal de Marinha do Rio de Janeiro	15 Oct 1984	8 June 1987	2 Apr 1991
JULIO DE NORONHA	V 32	Verolme, Angra dos Reis/Arsenal de Marinha	8 Dec 1986	15 Dec 1989	1992
FRONTIN	V 33	Verolme, Angra dos Reis/Arsenal de Marinha	14 May 1987	1992	1993

Displacement, tons: 1600 standard; 1970 full load
Dimensions, feet (metres): 314.2 × 37.4 × 12.1; 17.4 (sonar) *(95.8 × 11.4 × 3.7; 5.3)*
Main machinery: CODOG; 1 GE LM2500 gas turbine; 23 000 hp *(17.2 MW)* sustained; 2 MTU 16V 396 TB94 diesels; 5080 hp(m) *(3.73 MW)* sustained; 2 shafts; cp props
Speed, knots: 27. **Range, miles:** 4000 at 15 kts
Complement: 162 (19 officers)

Missiles: SSM: 4 Aerospatiale MM 40 Exocet (1); inertial cruise; active radar homing to 70 km *(40 nm)* at 0.9 Mach; warhead 165 kg; sea-skimmer.
Guns: 1 Vickers 4.5 in *(115 mm)* Mk 8 (2); 55° elevation; 25 rounds/minute to 22 km *(12 nm)* anti-surface; 6 km *(3.3 nm)* anti-aircraft, weight of shell 21 kg.
2 Bofors 40 mm/70 (3); 90° elevation; 300 rounds/minute to 12 km *(6.5 nm)* anti-surface; 4 km *(2.2 nm)* anti-aircraft; weight of shell 0.96 kg.
Torpedoes: 6—324 mm Mk 32 (2 triple) tubes (4). Honeywell Mk 46 Mod 5; anti-submarine; active/passive homing to 11 km *(5.9 nm)* at 40 kts; warhead 44 kg.
Countermeasures: Decoys: 2 Plessey Shield Chaff launchers (5); fires Chaff and IR flares in distraction, decoy or centroid patterns.
ESM/ECM: IPqM SDR-2 (V 30) or Racal Cygnus B1 (V 31 and 32) radar intercept (6) and IPqM jammer (7).
Combat data systems: Ferranti CAAIS 450.
Fire control: Saab EOS-400 missile and gun FCS with optronic (8) director and two optical (9) directors.
Radars: Surface search: Plessey ASW 4 (10); E/F band; range 101 km *(55 nm)*.
Navigation: Kelvin Hughes Type 1007; I/J band.
Fire control: Selenia Orion RTN 10X (11); I/J band; range 40 km *(22 nm)*.
Sonars: Krupp Atlas ASO 4 Mod 2; hull-mounted; active; medium frequency.

Helicopters: 1 Westland Lynx (12).

Programmes: Designed by Brazilian Naval Design Office with advice from West German private Marine Technik design company. Signature of final contract on 1 October 1981. First pair ordered on 15 February 1982 and second pair 9 January 1986. In mid-1986 the government approved in principle construction of a total of 16 ships but it now seems likely that only four will be completed and a cheaper corvette design will follow on in 1992/93. The bankruptcy of Verolme in 1991 means that the last two ships are being completed by Arsenal de Marinha after considerable delays.
Structure: The plan was that later ships might carry Brazilian made Barracuda instead of Exocet, eight Avibras SSAI-N anti-submarine rocket launchers, an Avibras FILA 20 mm anti-air gun system in place of the Bofors 40 mm and a Vulcan Phalanx CIWS, but all of this has been cancelled probably because the design has topweight problems. A single tube SAM may be fitted on the stern in due course.

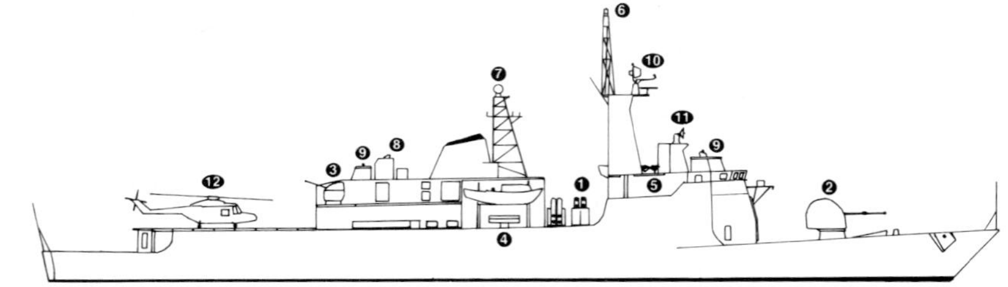

INHAÚMA (Scale 1 : 900), Ian Sturton

INHAÚMA 6/1990, Mário R. V. Carneiro

JACEGUAY

10/1990, Mário R. V. Carneiro

SHIPBORNE AIRCRAFT (FRONT LINE)

Note: Up to 7 Super Lynx may be acquired in 1992/93.

Numbers/Type: 7 Aerospatiale UH-12 (AS 350B Ecureuil).
Operational speed: 120 kts *(222 km/h)*.
Service ceiling: 10 000 ft *(3050 m)*.
Range: 240 nm *(445 km)*.
Role/Weapon systems: Support helicopters for Fleet liaison and Marine Corps transportation. Sensors: None. Weapons: 1 axial MG or 1 lateral MG or 2 rocket pods.

UH-12

1990, Brazilian Navy

Numbers/Type: 5 Aerospatiale UH-14 (AS 332F1 Super Puma).
Operational speed: 100 kts *(182 km/h)*.
Service ceiling: 20 000 ft *(6100 m)*.
Range: 345 nm *(635 km)*.
Role/Weapon systems: SAR, troop transport and ASVW. Sensors: Search radar. Weapons: None. Total of 15 planned.

UH-14

1989, Brazilian Navy

Numbers/Type: 12 Grumman S-2G P16 Tracker (Air Force).
Operational speed: 229 kts *(426 km/h)*.
Service ceiling: 25 000 ft *(7620 m)*.
Range: 799 nm *(1480 km)*.
Role/Weapon systems: Air Force operated; carrier-borne surveillance and medium-range ASW aircraft re-engined with PT6A-67-CF turbos; supplemented by Sea King; land-based for coastal and EEZ surveillance. Sensors: Thomson-CSF Varan Search radar, MAD. Weapons: ASW; various internally stored bombs, mines or depth bombs, rockets on wings.

Numbers/Type: 10 Aerospatiale UH-13 (AS 355F2 Ecureuil 2).
Operational speed: 121 kts *(224 km/h)*.
Service ceiling: 11 150 ft *(3400 m)*.
Range: 240 nm *(445 km)*.
Role/Weapon systems: SAR, liaison and utility in support of Marine Corps. Sensors: Search radar. Weapons: 2 axial MGs or 1 lateral MG or 2 rocket pods.

UH-13

1990, Brazilian Navy

Numbers/Type: 4/3 Agusta/Sikorsky SH 3A/SH 3D Sea King.
Operational speed: 100 kts *(182 km/h)*.
Service ceiling: 12 200 ft *(3720 m)*.
Range: 400 nm *(740 km)*.
Role/Weapon systems: ASW helicopter; carrier-borne and shore-based for medium-range ASW, ASVW and SAR. Sensors: 1 APS-705(V)II Search radar. Weapons: ASW; up to 4 × Mk 44/46 torpedoes, or 4 × depth bombs. ASVW; 4 × AM 39 Exocet missiles.

SEA KING

1991, Brazilian Navy

Numbers/Type: 16 UH-6B (Bell JetRanger III).
Operational speed: 115 kts *(213 km/h)*.
Service ceiling: 20 000 ft *(6100 m)*.
Range: 368 nm *(682 km)*.
Role/Weapon systems: Utility and training helicopters. Sensors: None. Weapons: 2 MGs or 2 rocket pods.

UH 6B

1991, Brazilian Navy

Numbers/Type: 7 Westland Lynx SAH-11 (HAS 21).
Operational speed: 125 kts *(232 km/h)*.
Service ceiling: 12 000 ft *(3650 m)*.
Range: 160 nm *(296 km)*.
Role/Weapon systems: ASW helicopter; embarked in Niteroi, Inhaúma and Pará classes for ASW patrol and support; additional ASVW role from 1988. May be upgraded in due course to Super Lynx standard with Mk 3 radar and Racal Kestrel EW suite. Sensors: Sea Spray Mk 1 radar. Weapons: ASW; 2 × Mk 44 or Mk 46 torpedoes, or depth bombs. ASV; 4 × Sea Skua missiles.

LYNX *1989, Brazilian Navy*

LAND-BASED MARITIME AIRCRAFT (FRONT LINE)

Numbers/Type: 10 Bandeirante P-95 (EMB-111(A)).
Operational speed: 194 kts *(360 km/h)*.
Service ceiling: 25 500 ft *(7770 m)*.
Range: 1590 nm *(2945 km)*.
Role/Weapon systems: Air Force operated for coastal surveillance role by three squadrons in 7 Group. Sensors: AN/APS-128 search radar, ECM, searchlight pod on starboard wing. Weapons: ASW; various internally stored bombs, mines or depth bombs, rockets on wings.

Numbers/Type: 10 Bandeirante P-95B (EMB-111(B)).
Operational speed: 194 kts *(360 km/h)*.
Service ceiling: 25 500 ft *(7770 m)*.
Range: 1590 nm *(2945 km)*.
Role/Weapon systems: Air Force operated for coastal surveillance role by three squadrons in 7 Group. Sensors: MEL sea search radar, ECM, searchlight pod on starboard wing, EFIS-74 (electronic flight instrumentation) and Collins APS-65 (autopilot); ESM Thomson-CSF DR2000A/Dalia 1000A Mk II, Marconi Canada CMA-771 Mk III (Omega navigation system). Weapons: Strike; 6 or 8 × 127 mm rockets, or up to 28 × 70 mm rockets.

Numbers/Type: 16 Xavante AT-26 (EMB-326GB).
Operational speed: 468 kts *(867 km/h)*.
Service ceiling: 47 000 ft *(14 325 m)*.
Range: 1320 nm *(2446 km)*.
Role/Weapon systems: Air Force operated for light attack; supplements anti-shipping/strike; also has reconnaissance role by 3/10 Group. Sensors: None. Weapons: ASV; 1.8 tons of bombs. Strike; 28 × 70 mm rockets. Recce; underwing camera pod.

Numbers/Type: 8 Tucano AT-27 (EMB-312).
Operational speed: 270 kts *(500 km/h)*.
Service ceiling: 30 000 ft *(9150 m)*.
Range: 995 nm *(1844 km)*.
Role/Weapon systems: Air Force operated for liaison and attack by 2 ELO. Sensors: None. Weapons: 6 or 8 × 127 mm rockets or bombs and 1 MG pod in each wing.

AMPHIBIOUS FORCES

2 Ex-US THOMASTON CLASS (LSD)

Name	*No*	*Builders*	*Laid Down*	*Launched*	*Commissioned*	*Recommissioned*
CEARÁ (ex-*Hermitage*)	G 30 (ex-LSD 34)	Ingalls, Pascagoula	11 April 1955	12 June 1956	14 Dec 1956	28 Nov 1989
RIO DE JANEIRO (ex-*Alamo*)	G 31 (ex-LSD 33)	Ingalls, Pascagoula	11 Oct 1954	20 Jan 1956	24 Aug 1956	21 Nov 1990

Displacement, tons: 6880 light; 12 150 full load
Dimensions, feet (metres): 510 × 84 × 19 *(155.5 × 25.6 × 5.8)*
Main machinery: 2 Babcock & Wilcox boilers; 580 psi *(40.8 kg/cm sq)*; 2 GE turbines; 24 000 hp *(17.9 MW)*; 2 shafts
Speed, knots: 22.5. **Range, miles:** 10 000 at 18 kts
Complement: 345 (20 officers)
Military lift: 340 troops; 21 LCM 6s or 3 LCUs and 6 LCMs or 50 LVTs; 30 LVTs on upper deck
Guns: 6 USN 3 in *(76 mm)*/50 (3 twin) Mk 33; 85° elevation; 50 rounds/minute to 12.8 km *(7 nm)*; weight of shell 6 kg.
Radars: Air search: Westinghouse SPS 6C; D band (in G 30).
Surface search: Raytheon SPS 10; G band.
Navigation: CRP 3100; I band.
Helicopters: Platform (over docking well).

Programmes: The original plan to build a 4500 ton LST was overtaken by the acquisition of these two LSDs.
Structure: Have two 50 ton capacity cranes and a docking well of 391 × 48 ft *(119.2 × 14.6 m)*. Phalanx guns removed before transfer. *Rio de Janeiro* has been fitted with a more modern air search radar.

CEARÁ *1990, Brazilian Navy*

1 Ex-US DE SOTO COUNTY CLASS (LST)

Name	*No*	*Builders*	*Commissioned*
DUQUE DE CAXAIS (ex-USS *Grant County* LST 1174)	G 26	Avondale, New Orleans	8 Nov 1957

Displacement, tons: 4164 light; 7804 full load
Dimensions, feet (metres): 445 × 62 × 17.5 *(135.6 × 18.9 × 5.3)*
Main machinery: 4 Fairbanks-Morse 38D 8 1/8-12 diesels; 8500 hp *(6.34 MW)* sustained; 2 shafts; cp props
Speed, knots: 16.5. **Range, miles:** 13 000 at 10 kts
Complement: 175 (11 officers)
Military lift: 575 troops
Guns: 6 FMC 3 in *(76 mm)*/50 (3 twin) Mk 33; 85° elevation; 50 rounds/minute to 12.8 km *(6.9 nm)*; weight of shell 6 kg.
Fire control: 1 Mk 51 Mod 5 GFCS.
Radars: Surface search: Raytheon SPS 21; G/H band; range 22 km *(12 nm)*.

Comment: Launched 12 October 1956 and transferred 15 January 1973, purchased 11 February 1980. Now has Stülcken 60 tons heavy-lift gear fitted. Four LCVPs carried on davits; helicopter platform. Probably to be paid off in 1992.

DUQUE DE CAXAIS *1987, Brazilian Navy*

3 US LCU 1610 TYPE (EDCG)

GUARAPARI (ex-L 10) **TAMBAÚ** (ex-L 11) **CAMBORIÚ** (ex-L 12)

Displacement, tons: 390 full load
Dimensions, feet (metres): 134.5 × 27.6 × 6.6 *(41 × 8.4 × 2.0)*
Main machinery: 2 GM 12V-71 diesels; 680 hp *(508 kW)*; 2 shafts; cp props
Speed, knots: 11. **Range, miles:** 1200 at 8 kts
Military lift: 172 tons
Guns: 3—12.7 mm MGs.
Radars: Navigation: Racal Decca; I band.

Comment: All built at AMRJ, Rio de Janeiro. *Guarapari* launched 16 June 1977, *Tambaú* on 14 September 1977. Both commissioned 27 March 1978. *Camboriú* laid down 27 March 1978 and commissioned 6 January 1981. Status changed in 1991 when all of the class were reclassified EDCG (landing craft) and lost their pennant numbers having been decommissioned from the Navy. They remain in service as support vessels to establishments.

CAMBORIÚ *1985, Ronaldo S. Olive*

6 EDVM (LCM)

301-306

Dimensions, feet (metres): 55.8 × 14.4 × 3.9 *(17 × 4.4 × 1.2)*
Main machinery: 2 Saab Scania diesels; 470 hp(m) *(345 kW)*; 2 shafts
Speed, knots: 9
Military lift: 80 troops plus 31 tons equipment

EDVM 301 — *1985, Ronaldo S. Olive*

30 EDVP (LCP)

501-530

Displacement, tons: 13 full load
Dimensions, feet (metres): 35.8 × 9.8 × 3 *(10.9 × 3 × 0.9)*
Main machinery: Saab Scania diesel; 235 hp(m) *(173 kW)*; 1 shaft
Speed, knots: 10
Military lift: 3.7 tons or 36 men

Comment: GRP hulls built in Brazil in 1971-73. Some in Mato Grosso flotilla at Ladario.

EDVP 512 — *1985, Ronaldo S. Olive*

PATROL FORCES

Note: The *Porto Esperança* (P 8) River Patrol Craft project was cancelled in 1990.

9 IMPERIAL MARINHEIRO CLASS (COASTAL PATROL SHIPS)

Name	*No*	*Builders*	*Commissioned*
IMPERIAL MARINHEIRO	V 15	Smit, Kinderdijk, Netherlands	8 June 1955
IGUATEMI	V 16	Smit, Kinderdijk, Netherlands	17 Sep 1955
FORTE DE COIMBRA	V 18	Smit, Kinderdijk, Netherlands	26 July 1955
CABOCLO	V 19	Smit, Kinderdijk, Netherlands	5 Apr 1955
ANGOSTURA	V 20	Smit, Kinderdijk, Netherlands	21 May 1955
BAHIANA	V 21	Smit, Kinderdijk, Netherlands	27 June 1955
MEARIM	V 22	Smit, Kinderdijk, Netherlands	3 Aug 1955
PURUS	V 23	Smit, Kinderdijk, Netherlands	17 Apr 1955
SOLIMÕES	V 24	Smit, Kinderdijk, Netherlands	3 Aug 1955

Displacement, tons: 911 standard; 960 full load
Dimensions, feet (metres): 184 × 30.5 × 11.7 *(56 × 9.3 × 3.6)*
Main machinery: 2 Sulzer diesels; 2160 hp(m) *(1.59 MW)*; 2 shafts
Speed, knots: 16
Complement: 60
Guns: 1—3 in *(76 mm)*/50 Mk 33; 85° elevation; 50 rounds/minute to 12.8 km *(6.9 nm)*; weight of shell 6 kg.
2 or 4 Oerlikon 20 mm; 55° elevation; 800 rounds/minute to 2 km.

Comment: Fleet tugs classed as corvettes. Equipped for firefighting. *Imperial Marinheiro* has acted as a submarine support ship but gave up the role in 1990.

IMPERIAL MARINHEIRO — *1989, Brazilian Navy*

1 + 3 (4) GRAÚNA CLASS (LARGE PATROL CRAFT)

Name	*No*	*Builders*	*Commissioned*
GRAÚNA	P 40	Estaleiro Mauá, Niteroi	Apr 1992
GOIANA	P 41	Estaleiro Mauá, Niteroi	Nov 1992
GRAJAÚ	P 42	Estaleiro Mauá, Niteroi	1993
GUAIBA	P 43	Estaleiro Mauá, Niteroi	1993

Displacement, tons: 410 full load
Dimensions, feet (metres): 152.6 × 24.6 × 7.5 *(46.5 × 7.5 × 2.3)*
Main machinery: 2 MTU 16 V 396 TB 94 diesels; 5800 hp(m) *(4.26 MW)* sustained; 2 shafts
Speed, knots: 22. **Range, miles:** 2000 at 12 kts
Complement: 25 (4 officers)
Guns: 1 Bofors 40 mm/70. 2 Oerlikon 20 mm.
Radars: Surface search: Racal Decca 1290A; I band.

Comment: Two ordered in late 1987 to a Vosper QAF design similar to Bangladesh Meghna class. Technology transfer in February 1988 and construction started in December 1988 for the first pair. Second pair ordered in September 1990. Used for patrol duties and diver support. Four more to be built in due course but progress is very slow. Second batch of names allocated: *Guajará* P44, *Guaporé* P 45, *Gurupá* P 46 and *Gurupi* P 47.

VOSPER TYPE (larger gun) — *1988, Vosper QAF*

3 RORAIMA CLASS (RIVER PATROL SHIPS)

Name	*No*	*Builders*	*Commissioned*
RORAIMA	P 30	Maclaren, Niteroi	21 Feb 1975
RONDÔNIA	P 31	Maclaren, Niteroi	3 Dec 1975
AMAPÁ	P 32	Maclaren, Niteroi	12 Jan 1976

Displacement, tons: 340 standard; 365 full load
Dimensions, feet (metres): 151.9 × 27.9 × 4.6 *(46.3 × 8.5 × 1.4)*
Main machinery: 2 MAN V6 V16/18TL diesels; 1920 hp(m) *(1.41 MW)*; 2 shafts
Speed, knots: 14. **Range, miles:** 6000 at 12 kts
Complement: 40 (9 officers)
Guns: 1 Bofors 40 mm/60; 90° elevation; 300 rounds/minute to 12 km *(6.5 nm)* anti-surface; 4 km *(2.2 nm)* anti-aircraft; weight of shell 0.89 kg.
2—81 mm mortars. 6—12.7 mm MGs.
Radars: Surface search: 2 Racal Decca; I band.

Comment: *Roraima* launched 2 November 1972, *Rondônia* 10 January, *Amapá* 9 March 1973. Carry two armed LCVPs. Belong to Amazon Flotilla.

RONDÔNIA — *1989, Brazilian Navy*

2 PEDRO TEIXEIRA CLASS (RIVER PATROL SHIPS)

Name	*No*	*Builders*	*Commissioned*
PEDRO TEIXEIRA	P 20	Arsenal de Marinha, Rio de Janeiro	17 Dec 1973
RAPOSO TAVARES	P 21	Arsenal de Marinha, Rio de Janeiro	17 Dec 1973

Displacement, tons: 690 standard
Dimensions, feet (metres): 208.7 × 31.8 × 5.6 *(63.6 × 9.7 × 1.7)*
Main machinery: 2 MAN V6 V16/18 TL diesels; 1920 hp(m) *(1.41 MW)*; 2 shafts
Speed, knots: 16. **Range, miles:** 6800 at 13 kts
Complement: 60 (6 officers)
Guns: 1 Bofors 40 mm/60; 90° elevation; 300 rounds/minute to 12 km *(6.5 nm)* anti-surface; 4 km *(2.2 nm)* anti-aircraft; weight of shell 0.89 kg.
6—12.7 mm MGs. 2—81 mm Mk 2 mortars.
Radars: Surface search: 2 Racal Decca; I band.
Helicopters: 1 Bell JetRanger.

Comment: *Pedro Teixeira* launched 14 October 1970, *Raposo Tavares* 11 June 1972. Belong to Amazon Flotilla. Can carry two armed LCVPs.

RAPOSO TAVARES *1988*

1 THORNYCROFT TYPE (RIVER MONITOR)

Name	*No*	*Builders*	*Commissioned*
PARNAIBA	U 17 (ex-P 2)	Arsenal de Marinha, Rio de Janeiro	6 Nov 1938

Displacement, tons: 620 standard; 720 full load
Dimensions, feet (metres): 180.5 × 33.3 × 5.1 *(55 × 10.1 × 1.6)*
Main machinery: 2 Thornycroft triple expansion; 1300 ihp *(970 kW)*; 2 shafts
Speed, knots: 12. **Range, miles:** 1350 at 10 kts
Complement: 90
Guns: 1—3 in *(76 mm)*/50 Mk 33; 85° elevation; 50 rounds/minute to 12.8 km *(6.9 nm)*; weight of shell 6 kg.
2 Bofors 40 mm/60 (twin). 6 Oerlikon 20 mm.

Comment: Laid down 11 June 1936. Launched 2 September 1937. In Mato Grosso Flotilla. Re-armed with new guns in 1960. 3 in *(76 mm)* side armour and partial deck protection. Oil fuel, 70 tons. Was to have been replaced by *Porto Esperança* in 1991 but will now run on until 1994.

PARNAIBA *1985, Brazilian Navy*

6 PIRATINI CLASS (LARGE PATROL CRAFT)

Name	*No*	*Builders*	*Commissioned*
PIRATINI (ex-PGM 109)	P 10	Arsenal de Marinha, Rio de Janeiro	Nov 1970
PIRAJÁ (ex-PGM 110)	P 11	Arsenal de Marinha, Rio de Janeiro	Mar 1971
PAMPEIRO (ex-PGM 118)	P 12	Arsenal de Marinha, Rio de Janeiro	May 1971
PARATI (ex-PGM 119)	P 13	Arsenal de Marinha, Rio de Janeiro	July 1971
PENEDO (ex-PGM 120)	P 14	Arsenal de Marinha, Rio de Janeiro	Sep 1971
POTI (ex-PGM 121)	P 15	Arsenal de Marinha, Rio de Janeiro	Oct 1971

Displacement, tons: 105 standard
Dimensions, feet (metres): 95 × 19 × 6.5 *(29 × 5.8 × 2)*
Main machinery: 4 Cummins VT-12M diesels; 1100 hp *(820 kW)*; 2 shafts
Speed, knots: 17. **Range, miles:** 1700 at 12 kts
Complement: 15 (2 officers)
Guns: 1 Oerlikon 20 mm. 2—12.7 mm MGs.

Comment: Built under offshore agreement with the USA. 81 mm mortar removed in 1988.

POTI *1988, Van Boeijin*

4 TRACKER II CLASS (COASTAL PATROL CRAFT)

P 8002 **P 8003** **P 3004** **P 3005**

Displacement, tons: 37 full load
Dimensions, feet (metres): 68.6 × 17 × 4.8 *(20.9 × 5.2 × 1.5)*
Main machinery: 2 MTU 8 V 396 TB 83 diesels; 2100 hp(m) *(1.54 MW)*; 2 shafts
Speed, knots: 27. **Range, miles:** 600 at 15 kts
Complement: 12 (4 officers)
Guns: 2—12.7 mm MGs.
Radars: Racal Decca RM 1070A.

Comment: First four ordered in February 1987 to a Fairey design and built at Astreleiros Shipyard, Porto Alegre. National input is 60 per cent increasing to 70 per cent in later hulls. It was planned to build two a year, but the timing has suffered from budgetary constraints. First of class completed building 22 February 1990. First four entered service in May 1991; plans for more were postponed in 1991. Designed for EEZ patrol.

P 8002 *1991, Brazilian Navy*

MINE WARFARE FORCES

6 ARATÚ CLASS (MINESWEEPERS—COASTAL)

Name	*No*	*Builders*	*Commissioned*
ARATÚ	M 15	Abeking & Rasmussen	5 May 1971
ANHATOMIRIM	M 16	Abeking & Rasmussen	30 Nov 1971
ATALAIA	M 17	Abeking & Rasmussen	13 Dec 1972
ARAÇATUBA	M 18	Abeking & Rasmussen	13 Dec 1972
ABROLHOS	M 19	Abeking & Rasmussen	25 Feb 1976
ALBARDÃO	M 20	Abeking & Rasmussen	25 Feb 1976

Displacement, tons: 230 standard; 280 full load
Dimensions, feet (metres): 154.9 × 23.6 × 6.9 *(47.2 × 7.2 × 2.1)*
Main machinery: 4 MTU Maybach diesels; 4500 hp(m) *(3.3 MW)*; 2 shafts; 2 Escher-Weiss cp props
Speed, knots: 24. **Range, miles:** 710 at 20 kts
Complement: 39 (4 officers)
Guns: 1 Bofors 40 mm/70.
Radars: Surface search: Signaal ZW 06; I band.

Comment: Wooden hulled. First four ordered in April 1969 and last pair in November 1973. Same design as West German Schütze class. Can carry out wire, magnetic and acoustic sweeping. Modernisation expected in the 1990s.

ATALAIA *1988, Brazilian Navy*

OCEANOGRAPHIC AND SURVEY SHIPS

0 + (1) ANTARCTIC SURVEY SHIP

Displacement, tons: 6000
Dimensions, feet (metres): 328 oa; 305 wl × 65.6 × 23 *(100; 93 × 20 × 7)*
Main machinery: 2 diesels; 10 000 hp(m) *(7.35 MW)*; 2 motors; 1300 kW; 2 pumpjets
Speed, knots: 17 (diesels); 3 (motors). **Range, miles:** 20 000 at 13 kts
Complement: 95 (22 officers) plus 40 scientists
Helicopters: 2 light.

Comment: Replacement for *Barão de Teffé* to be built by Caneco, Rio de Janeiro to a Cleaver and Walkinshaw (Vancouver) design. Six laboratories (seismic, meteorology, oceanography, geology, geophysical and marine biology) are planned. Cost (1987 prices) US $36 million for the ship and probably as much again for the equipment. Originally ordered in September 1987 but the project was still suspended at the beginning of 1992 for lack of funds.

Name	*No*	*Builders*	*Commissioned*
BARÃO DE TEFFÉ (ex-*Thala Dan*)	H 42	Aalborg Vaerft	1957

Measurement, tons: 2183 gross
Dimensions, feet (metres): 246.6 × 45.2 × 20.8 *(75.2 × 14.2 × 6.3)*
Main machinery: 1 Burmeister & Wain diesel; 1970 hp(m) *(1.45 MW)*; 1 shaft; cp prop
Speed, knots: 12
Complement: 46 (11 officers)
Helicopters: 2 Aerospatiale UH-13 Ecureuil 2.

Comment: A Danish polar supply ship acquired in 1982 and commissioned on 28 September 1982. Strengthened for ice. SATCOM fitted. This ship has a red/pale brown hull.

BARÃO DE TEFFÉ *10/1982, Michael D. J. Lennon*

Name	*No*	*Builders*	*Commissioned*
ANTARES (ex-M/V *Lady Harrison*)	H 40	Mjellem and Karlsen A/S, Bergen	1984

Displacement, tons: 855 light
Dimensions, feet (metres): 180.3 × 33.8 × 14.1 *(55 × 10.3 × 4.3)*
Main machinery: 1 Burmeister & Wain Alpha diesel; 1860 hp(m) *(1.37 MW)*; 1 shaft; bow thruster
Speed, knots: 13.5. **Range, miles:** 10 000 at 12 kts
Complement: 49 (9 officers)

Comment: Research vessel acquired from Racal Energy Resources. Used for seismographic survey. Recommissioned 6 June 1988. Painted white with orange masts and funnels.

ANTARES *1989, Brazilian Navy*

1 Ex-US ROBERT D CONRAD CLASS

Name	*No*	*Builders*	*Commissioned*
ALMIRANTE CÂMARA (ex-USNS *Sands* T-AGOR 6)	H 41	Marietta Co, Point Pleasant, West Va.	8 Feb 1965

Displacement, tons: 1200 standard; 1380 full load
Dimensions, feet (metres): 208.9 × 40 × 15.3 *(63.7 × 12.2 × 4.7)*
Main machinery: 2 Caterpillar D-378 diesels; 1000 hp *(735 kW)*; 1 shaft; bow thruster
Speed, knots: 13.5. **Range, miles:** 12 000 at 12 kts
Complement: 36 (7 officers) plus 15 scientists
Radars: Navigation: RCA CRM-NIA-75; I/J band.

Comment: Built specifically for oceanographic research. Equipped for gravimetric, magnetic and geological research. 10 ton crane and 620 hp gas turbine for providing 'quiet power'. Transferred 1 July 1974. Has a white hull and orange superstructure.

ALMIRANTE CAMARA *1989, Brazilian Navy*

2 SIRIUS CLASS

Name	*No*	*Builders*	*Commissioned*
SIRIUS	H 21	Ishikawajima Co Ltd, Tokyo	1 Jan 1958
CANOPUS	H 22	Ishikawajima Co Ltd, Tokyo	15 Mar 1958

Displacement, tons: 1463 standard; 1800 full load
Dimensions, feet (metres): 255.7 × 39.3 × 12.2 *(78 × 12.1 × 3.7)*
Main machinery: 2 Sulzer 7T6-36 diesels; 2700 hp(m) *(1.98 MW)*; 2 shafts; cp props
Speed, knots: 15.7. **Range, miles:** 12 000 at 11 kts
Complement: 116 (16 officers) plus 14 scientists
Helicopters: 1 Bell JetRanger.

Comment: Laid down 1955-56. Painted white with orange funnels and masts. Special surveying apparatus, echo sounders, Raydist equipment, sounding machines installed, and landing craft (LCVP), jeep, and survey launches carried. All living and working spaces are air-conditioned.

CANOPUS *1987, Brazilian Navy*

3 ARGUS CLASS

Name	*No*	*Builders*	*Commissioned*
ARGUS	H 31	Arsenal de Marinha, Rio de Janeiro	29 Jan 1959
ORION	H 32	Arsenal de Marinha, Rio de Janeiro	11 June 1959
TAURUS	H 33	Arsenal de Marinha, Rio de Janeiro	23 Apr 1959

Displacement, tons: 250 standard; 343 full load
Dimensions, feet (metres): 146.7 × 21.3 × 9.2 *(44.7 × 6.5 × 2.8)*
Main machinery: 2 Caterpillar DT 379 diesels; 1200 hp *(895 kW)*; 2 shafts
Speed, knots: 15. **Range, miles:** 3000 at 15 kts
Complement: 42 (6 officers)
Guns: 2 Oerlikon 20 mm (removed).
Radars: Navigation: Racal Decca; I band.
Helicopters: 1 Bell JetRanger (when carried).

Comment: All laid down in 1955 and launched between December 1957—February 1958. *Orion* re-engined in 1974. Replacement ships are needed.

ORION *1985, Brazilian Navy*

Name	*No*	*Builders*	*Commissioned*
ALMIRANTE ALVARO ALBERTO (ex-M V *Grant Mariner*)	H 43	Burton S B Co, Texas	1973

Displacement, tons: 1517 light; 2180 full load
Dimensions, feet (metres): 217.1 × 44 × 15.4 *(66.2 × 13.4 × 4.7)*
Main machinery: 3 Fairbanks-Morse diesels; 7200 hp *(5.37 MW)*; 3 shafts; bow thruster
Speed, knots: 13.5
Complement: 48 (10 officers)
Radars: Navigation: 2 Racal Decca; I band.

Comment: Supply vessel acquired in October 1987 from Grant Norfac (USA). Recommissioned 6 June 1988 as a seismic survey ship. Has a platform for one light helicopter.

ALVARO ALBERTO *1989, Brazilian Navy*

1 LIGHTHOUSE TENDER

Name	*No*	*Builders*	*Commissioned*
ALMIRANTE GRAÇA ARANHA	H 34	Elbin, Niteroi	9 Sep 1976

Displacement, tons: 2390 full load
Dimensions, feet (metres): 245.3 × 42.6 × 13.8 *(74.8 × 13 × 4.2)*
Main machinery: 1 diesel; 2440 hp(m) *(1.8 MW)*; 1 shaft; bow thruster
Speed, knots: 14
Complement: 95 (13 officers)
Radars: Navigation: 2 Racal Decca; I band.
Helicopters: 1 Bell JetRanger.

Comment: Laid down in 1971 and launched 23 May 1974. Fitted with telescopic hangar, 10 ton crane, two landing craft, GP launch and two Land Rovers. Omega navigation system.

ALMIRANTE GRAÇA ARANHA *5/1990, Mario R. V. Carneiro*

4 BUOY TENDERS

Name	*No*	*Builders*	*Commissioned*
COMANDANTE VARELLA	H 18	AMRJ, Rio de Janeiro	20 May 1982
TENENTE CASTELO	H 19	Estanave, Manaus	15 Aug 1984
COMANDANTE MANHÃES	H 20	Estanave, Manaus	15 Dec 1983
TENENTE BOANERGES	H 25	Estanave, Manaus	29 Mar 1985

Displacement, tons: 440 full load
Dimensions, feet (metres): 123 × 28.2 × 8.5 *(37.5 × 8.6 × 2.6)*
Main machinery: 2—8-cyl diesels; 1300 hp(m) *(955 kW)*; 2 shafts
Speed, knots: 12. **Range, miles:** 2880 at 10 kts
Complement: 28 (2 officers)

Comment: Dual purpose minelayers. *Tenente Castelo* is based at Santana, *Tenente Boanerges* at Sao Luiz.

COMANDANTE VARELLA *1987, Brazilian Navy*

5 BUOY TENDERS

MESTRE JOÃO DOS SANTOS H 13
CASTELHANOS H 24
FAROLEIRO MÁRIO SEIXAS H 26
FAROLEIRO AREAS H 27
FAROLEIRO NASCIMENTO H 30

Displacement, tons: 195 (H 13); 110 (H 24, 27 and 30); 242 (H 26)
Complement: 17 (1 or 2 officers)

Comment: First four taken over 1973—H 26 on 21 January 1984. H 13 launched in 1950 and H 26 in 1962; remainder 1954-57.

SURVEY LAUNCHES

PARAIBANO (ex-H 11)
RIO BRANCO (ex-H 12)
NOGUEIRA DA GAMA (ex-*Jaceguai*) (ex-H 14)
ITACURUSSÁ (ex-H 15)
CAMOCIM (ex-H 16)
CARAVELAS (ex-H 17)

Displacement, tons: 32 standard; 50 full load
Dimensions, feet (metres): 52.5 × 15.1 × 4.3 *(16 × 4.6 × 1.3)*
Main machinery: 2 GM diesels; 330 hp *(246 kW)*; 2 shafts
Speed, knots: 11. **Range, miles:** 600 at 11 kts
Complement: 10 (1 officer)

Comment: First pair commissioned 7 November 1969, second pair 8 March 1971 and last two 22 September 1972. Built by Bormann, Rio de Janeiro. Majority work in Amazon Flotilla. Wooden hulls. All decommissioned in 1991 but retained in service as support to naval establishments and reclassified AvHi (inshore survey craft).

PARAIBANO *1985, Brazilian Navy*

SUBOFICIAL OLIVEIRA (ex-U 15)

Displacement, tons: 170 full load
Dimensions, feet (metres): 116.4 × 22 × 15.7 *(35.5 × 6.7 × 4.8)*
Main machinery: 2 diesels; 740 hp(m) *(544 kW)*; 2 shafts
Speed, knots: 8. **Range, miles:** 1400 at 8 kts
Complement: 10 (2 officers)

Comment: Commissioned at Fortaleza for Naval Research Institute on 6 May 1981. Decommissioned in 1991 but retained in service as an AvPqOc (ocean survey craft).

SUBOFICIAL OLIVEIRA *1990, Brazilian Navy*

SUBMARINE RESCUE SHIP

Name	*No*	*Builders*	*Commissioned*
FELINTO PERRY (ex-*Holger Dane*, ex-*Wildrake*)	K 11	Stord Verft, Norway	1979

Displacement, tons: 1380 full load
Dimensions, feet (metres): 256.6 × 57.4 × 15.1 *(78.2 × 17.5 × 4.6)*
Main machinery: Diesel-electric; 2 BMK KVG B12 and 2 KVGB 16 diesels; 11 400 hp(m) *(8.4 MW)*; 2 motors; 7000 hp(m) *(5.15 MW)*; 2 shafts; cp props; 2 bow thrusters; 2 stern thrusters
Speed, knots: 14.5
Complement: 65 (9 officers)
Helicopters: Platform only.

Comment: Former oilfield support ship acquired 28 December 1988. Has an octagonal heliport (62.5 ft diameter) above the bridge. Has replaced *Gastão Moutinho* as the submarine rescue ship.

FELINTO PERRY *11/1988, W. Sartori*

REPAIR SHIPS

Name	No	Builders	Commissioned
BELMONTE (ex-USS *Helios* ARB 12, ex-LST 1127)	G 24	Maryland D D Co, Baltimore	26 Feb 1945

Displacement, tons: 1625 light; 2030 standard; 4100 full load
Dimensions, feet (metres): 328 × 50 × 11 *(100 × 15.2 × 3.4)*
Main machinery: 2 GM 12-567A diesels; 1800 hp *(1.34 MW)*; 2 shafts
Speed, knots: 11.6. **Range, miles:** 6000 at 9 kts
Guns: 8 Bofors 40 mm/60 (2 quad); 90° elevation; 300 rounds/minute to 12 km *(6.5 nm)* anti-surface; 4 km *(2.2 nm)* anti-aircraft; weight of shell 0.89 kg.

Comment: Former US battle damage repair ship (ex-LST). Laid down 23 November 1944. Launched 14 February 1945. Transferred by lease to Brazil by USA 16 April 1963 under MAP and purchased 28 December 1977. Oil fuel, 1000 tons.

BELMONTE *1985, Brazilian Navy*

Name	No	Builders	Launched
GASTÃO MOUTINHO (ex-USS *Skylark* ASR 20)	U 20 (ex-K 10)	Charleston S B & D D Co	19 Mar 1946

Displacement, tons: 1653 standard; 2320 full load
Dimensions, feet (metres): 251.5 × 44 × 16 *(76.7 × 13.4 × 4.9)*
Main machinery: Diesel-electric; 4 GM 12-278A diesel generators; 4400 hp *(3.58 MW)*; 1 motor; 3000 hp *(2.2 MW)*; 1 shaft
Speed, knots: 15. **Range, miles:** 15 000 at 8 kts
Complement: 85
Guns: 2 Oerlikon 20 mm.
Radars: Surface search: Westinghouse SPS 5; G/H band.

Comment: Fitted with special pumps, compressors and submarine rescue chamber in 1947. Transferred 30 June 1973 and used as the submarine rescue ship until replaced by *Felinto Perry*. Now employed as a tender for the MCMV force at Aratu naval base.

GASTÃO MOUTINHO (old number) *1988, Brazilian Navy*

HOSPITAL SHIPS

Name	No	Builders	Commissioned
OSWALDO CRUZ	U 18	AMRJ, Rio de Janeiro	29 May 1984
CARLOS CHAGAS	U 19	AMRJ, Rio de Janeiro	7 Dec 1984

Displacement, tons: 500 full load
Dimensions, feet (metres): 154.2 × 26.9 × 5.9 *(47.2 × 8.5 × 1.8)*
Main machinery: 2 diesels; 714 hp(m) *(525 kW)*; 2 shafts
Speed, knots: 9. **Range, miles:** 4000 at 9 kts
Complement: 46 (4 officers) plus 21 medical (6 doctors/dentists)
Radars: Navigation: Racal Decca; I band.
Helicopters: 1 Helibras HB-350B.

Comment: *Oswaldo Cruz* launched 11 July 1983, and *Carlos Chagas* 16 April 1984. Have two sick bays, dental surgery, a laboratory, two clinics and X-ray centre. The design is a development of the Roraima class with which they operate in the Amazon Flotilla.

CARLOS CHAGAS *12/1984, Mário R. V. Carneiro*

TRANSPORTS

Name	No	Builders	Commissioned
PARAGUASSU (ex-*Guarapunava*)	G 15	Amsterdam Drydock	1951

Displacement, tons: 285 full load
Dimensions, feet (metres): 131.2 × 23 × 6.6 *(40 × 7 × 2)*
Main machinery: 3 diesels; 2505 hp(m) *(1.84 MW)*; 1 shaft
Speed, knots: 13. **Range, miles:** 2500 at 10 kts
Complement: 43 (4 officers)
Military lift: 178 troops

Comment: Passenger ship converted into a troop carrier in 1957 and acquired in 1971.

PARAGUASSU *1989, Brazilian Navy*

4 BARROSO PEREIRA CLASS

Name	No	Builders	Commissioned
BARROSO PEREIRA	G 16	Ishikawajima Co Ltd, Tokyo	22 Mar 1955
CUSTÓDIO DE MELLO	G 20 (ex-U 26)	Ishikawajima Co Ltd, Tokyo	8 Feb 1955
ARY PARREIRAS	G 21	Ishikawajima Co Ltd, Tokyo	6 Mar 1957
SOARES DUTRA	G 22	Ishikawajima Co Ltd, Tokyo	27 May 1957

Displacement, tons: 4800 standard; 7300 full load
Measurement, tons: 4200 dwt; 4879 gross (Panama)
Dimensions, feet (metres): 362 pp; 391.8 oa × 52.5 × 20.5 *(110.4; 119.5 × 16 × 6.3)*
Main machinery: 2 Ishikawajima boilers and turbines; 4800 hp(m) *(3.53 MW)*; 2 shafts
Speed, knots: 15
Complement: 127
Military lift: 1972 troops (overload); 497 troops (normal)
Cargo capacity: 425 m³ refrigerated cargo space; 4000 tons
Guns: 2—3 in *(76 mm)* Mk 33; 85° elevation; 50 rounds/minute to 12.8 km *(6.9 nm)* anti-aircraft; weight of shell 6 kg.
2 or 4 Oerlikon 20 mm; 55° elevation; 800 rounds/minute to 2 km.
Radars: Navigation: SPS 4 (*Custódio de Mello* only). Two unknown types (others).

Comment: Transports and cargo vessels. Helicopter landing platform aft except in *Custódio de Mello* and *Barroso Pereira*. Medical, hospital and dental facilities. Working and living quarters are mechanically ventilated with partial air-conditioning. Refrigerated cargo space 15 500 cu ft. *Custódio de Mello* was classified as a training ship in July 1961, replaced by *Brasil* in 1987 and has now reverted to being a transport. All operate commercially from time to time.

BARROSO PEREIRA *8/1987, van Ginderen Collection*

TANKERS/SUPPLY SHIPS

Name	*No*	*Builders*	*Commissioned*
ALMIRANTE GASTÃO MOTTA	G 23	Ishibras, Rio de Janeiro	26 Nov 1991

Measurement, tons: 10 300 dwt
Dimensions, feet (metres): 442.9 × 62.3 × 24.6 *(135 × 19 × 7.5)*
Main machinery: Diesel electric; 2 Wärtsilä 12V32 diesel generators; 11 700 hp(m) *(8.57 MW)* sustained; 1 motor; 1 shaft
Speed, knots: 18. **Range, miles:** 10 000 at 15 kts
Complement: 121 (13 officers)
Cargo capacity: 5000 tons liquid; 200 tons dry

Comment: Ordered March 1987 to replace *Marajó*. Launched 11 December 1989. Fitted for abeam and stern refuelling. Probably armed with light guns.

ALMIRANTE GASTÃO MOTTA (artist's impression) *1988, Brazilian Navy*

Name	*No*	*Builders*	*Commissioned*
POTENGI	G 17	Papendrecht, Netherlands	28 June 1938

Displacement, tons: 600 full load
Dimensions, feet (metres): 178.8 × 24.5 × 6 *(54.5 × 7.5 × 1.8)*
Main machinery: 2 diesels; 550 hp(m) *(404 kW)*; 2 shafts
Speed, knots: 10. **Range, miles:** 600 at 8 kts
Complement: 19
Cargo capacity: 450 tons

Comment: Employed in the Mato Grosso Flotilla on river service.

POTENGI *1985, Brazilian Navy*

Name	*No*	*Builders*	*Commissioned*
TRINDADE (ex-*Nobistor*)	U 16	Lavenburg	1969

Displacement, tons: 590 light; 1308 full load
Dimensions, feet (metres): 176.1 × 20 × 6.9 *(53.7 × 6.1 × 2.1)*
Speed, knots: 12.7 kts

Comment: Ex-Panamanian tug seized for smuggling in 1989 and commissioned in the Navy 31 January 1990. Used for target towing.

TRINDADE *1990, Mário R. V. Carneiro*

TRAINING SHIPS

1 MODIFIED NITEROI CLASS

Name	*No*	*Builders*	*Commissioned*
BRASIL	U 27	A de M, Rio de Janeiro	21 Aug 1986

Displacement, tons: 2380 light; 3400 full load
Dimensions, feet (metres): 430.7 × 44.3 × 13.8 *(131.3 × 13.5 × 4.2)*
Main machinery: 2 Pielstick/Ishikawajima (Brazil) 6 PC 2.5 L400 diesels; 7020 hp(m) *(5.17 MW)* sustained; 2 shafts
Speed, knots: 18. **Range, miles:** 7000 at 15 kts
Complement: 221 (27 officers) plus 200 midshipmen
Guns: 2 Bofors 40 mm. 4 saluting guns.
Countermeasures: ESM: Racal RDL; radar intercept.
Fire control: Saab Scania TVT 300 optronic director.
Radars: Surface search: Racal Decca RMS 1230C; E/F band.
Navigation: Racal Decca TM 1226C; I band.
Helicopters: Platform for 2 Sea King.

Comment: A modification of the Vosper Thornycroft Mk 10 Frigate design ordered in June 1981. Laid down 18 September 1981, launched 23 September 1983. Designed to carry midshipmen and other trainees from the Naval and Merchant Marine Academies. Minimum electronics as required for training.

BRASIL *9/1991, Camil Busquets i Vilanova*

ASPIRANTE NASCIMENTO U 10 **GUARDA MARINHA BRITO** U 12
GUARDA MARINHA JENSEN U 11

Displacement, tons: 108.5 standard; 130 full load
Dimensions, feet (metres): 91.8 × 21.3 × 5.9 *(28 × 6.5 × 1.8)*
Main machinery: 2 MWM D232V12 diesels; 650 hp(m) *(478 kW)*; 2 shafts
Speed, knots: 10. **Range, miles:** 700 at 10 kts
Complement: 12
Guns: 1—12.7 mm MG.
Radars: Navigation: Racal Decca; I band.

Comment: *A Nascimento* completed December 1980, other pair completed 1981. Can carry 24 trainees overnight. All of the class are attached to the Naval Academy.

GUARDA MARINHA JENSEN *1985, Ronaldo S. Olive*

ROSCA FINA (ex-U 31) **VOGA PICADA** (ex-U 32) **LEVA ARRIBA** (ex-U 33)

Displacement, tons: 50
Dimensions, feet (metres): 61 × 15.4 × 3.9 *(18.6 × 4.7 × 1.2)*
Main machinery: 1 diesel; 650 hp(m) *(477 kW)*; 1 shaft
Speed, knots: 11. **Range, miles:** 200
Complement: 5 plus trainees
Radars: Navigation: Racal Decca; I band.

Comment: Built by Carbrasmar, Rio de Janeiro. All commissioned 21 February 1984 and attached to the Naval College. Pennant numbers removed in 1989. In addition the former American fishing vessel *Night Hawk* is in use for training at Centro de Instrucao Almirante Braz de Aguiar.

VOGA PICADA (old pennant number) *1984, Brazilian Navy*

8 SAIL TRAINING VESSELS

SARGACO BL 177
SITIO FORTE BL 1130
ALBATROZ (ex-*Cisne Branco*)
ITAPOA (ex-*Cri-Cri*)
BREKELE (ex-*Carro Chefe*) BL 898
VENDAVAL
CISNE BRANCO (ex-*Ondine*) BL 810
JACANA II

Comment: Some are used for civilian training as well.

TUGS

Note: In addition to the vessels listed below there are three harbour tugs: *Wandenkolk* (R 20), *Antonio Joao* (R 26) and *Etchebarne* (R 28).

2 ALMIRANTE GUILHEM CLASS (FLEET OCEAN TUGS)

Name	*No*	*Builders*	*Launched*	*Commissioned*
ALMIRANTE GUILHEM (ex-*Superpesa 4*)	R 24	Sumitomo Heavy Industry, Japan	1976	22 Jan 1981
ALMIRANTE GUILLOBEL (ex-*Superpesa 5*)	R 25	Sumitomo Heavy Industry, Japan	1976	22 Jan 1981

Displacement, tons: 1200 dwt
Dimensions, feet (metres): 207 × 44 × 14.8 *(63.2 × 13.4 × 4.5)*
Main machinery: 2 GM EMD 20-645 F7B diesels; 7200 hp *(5.37 MW)* sustained; 2 shafts; cp props; bow thruster
Speed, knots: 14
Complement: 40

Comment: Originally built as civilian tugs. Bollard pull, 84 tons.

ALMIRANTE GUILLOBEL *1985, Mário R. V. Carneiro*

3 TRITÃO CLASS (FLEET OCEAN TUGS)

Name	*No*	*Builders*	*Commissioned*
TRITÃO (ex-*Sarandí*)	R 21	Estanave, Manaos	19 Feb 1987
TRIDENTE (ex-*Sambaiba*)	R 22	Estanave, Manaos	8 Oct 1987
TRIUNFO (ex-*Scrocaba*)	R 23	Estanave, Manaos	5 July 1986

Displacement, tons: 840 standard; 1480 full load
Dimensions, feet (metres): 181.8 × 38.1 × 11.2 *(55.4 × 11.6 × 3.4)*
Main machinery: 2 diesels; 2480 hp(m) *(1.82 MW)*; 2 shafts
Speed, knots: 12
Complement: 49
Guns: 2 Oerlikon 20 mm.
Radars: Navigation: Racal Decca; I band.

Comment: All acquired from National Oil Company of Brazil and converted for naval use. Assumed names of previous three ships of Sotoyomo class. Fitted to act both as tugs and patrol vessels. Bollard pull, 23.5 tons. Firefighting capability. Endurance, 45 days.

TRIUNFO *1987, Brazilian Navy*

4 COASTAL TUGS

COMANDANTE MARROIG (ex-R 15)
COMANDANTE DIDIER (ex-R 16)
TENENTE MAGALHÃES (ex-R 17)
CABO SCHRAMM (ex-R 18)

Displacement, tons: 115 standard
Dimensions, feet (metres): 65 × 23 × 6.5 *(19.8 × 7 × 2)*
Main machinery: 2 GM diesels; 900 hp(m) *(661 kW)*; 2 shafts
Complement: 6

Comment: Built by Turn-Ship Limited, USA. First pair commissioned 30 April 1981, second pair 14 September 1982. *Comandante Marroig* sank in 1990 in an incident with *Ceará* but has been salvaged and was active again in 1991. Decommissioned in 1991 but retained in service as support ships to naval establishments and designated Rb.

CABO SCHRAMM *6/1989, Mário R. V. Carneiro*

2 COASTAL TUGS

LAHMEYER **D.N.O.G.**

Comment: Both commissioned in 1972. Of 100 tons and 105 ft *(32 m)* long. Based at Aratu naval base.

AUXILIARIES

Note: In addition to the vessels listed below there are (1) three 485 ton water tankers *Dr Gondim* (R 38), *Itapura* (R 42) and *Paulo Afonso* (R 43); (2) two general purpose auxiliaries *Guairia* (R 40) and *Iguacu* (R 41); (3) six river patrol launches *Arenque* (R 55), *Atum* (R 56), *Acara* (R 57), *Agulha* (R 58), *Aruana* (R 59) and *Argentina* (R 60).

9 RIO DOCE and RIO PARDO CLASSES

RIO DAS CONTAS (ex-U 21)
RIO FORMOSO (ex-U 22)
RIO REAL (ex-U 23)
RIO TURVO (ex-U 24)
RIO VERDE (ex-U 25)
RIO PARDO (ex-U 40)
RIO NEGRO (ex-U 41)
RIO CHUI (ex-U 42)
RIO OIAPOQUE (ex-U 43)

Displacement, tons: 150 full load
Dimensions, feet (metres): 120 × 21.3 × 6.2 *(36.6 × 6.5 × 1.9)*
Main machinery: 2 Sulzer 6-TD24; 900 hp(m) *(661 kW)*; 2 shafts
Speed, knots: 14. **Range, miles:** 700 at 14 kts
Complement: 10

Comment: Can carry 600 passengers. The first five were built by Holland Nautic, commissioned in 1954 and the second group by Inconav de Niteroi in 1975/76. Pennant numbers removed in 1989. *Rio Doce* (ex-U 20) sold for civilian use in 1986.

SARGENTO BORGES (ex-R 47)

Displacement, tons: 108.5
Dimensions, feet (metres): 91.8 × 21.3 × 4.9 *(28 × 6.5 × 1.5)*
Main machinery: 2 diesels; 650 hp(m) *(478 kW)*; 2 shafts
Speed, knots: 10. **Range, miles:** 400 at 10 kts
Complement: 10

Comment: Built by Ebrasa, Itajai. Launched 29 August 1974. Can carry 106 passengers. Pennant number removed in 1989.

1 RIVER TRANSPORT

PIRAIM U 29

Displacement, tons: 91.5 full load
Dimensions, feet (metres): 82.0 × 18.0 × 3.2 *(25.0 × 5.5 × 0.97)*
Main machinery: 2 MWM diesels; 400 hp(m) *(294 kW)*; 2 shafts
Speed, knots: 7. **Range, miles:** 700 at 7 kts
Complement: 17 (2 officers)

Comment: Built by Estaleiro SNBP, Mato Grosso. Commissioned 10 March 1982.

TORPEDO TRANSPORTS/TRV

ALMIRANTE HESS (ex-U 30)

Displacement, tons: 91 full load
Dimensions, feet (metres): 77.4 × 19.7 × 6.6 *(23.6 × 6 × 2)*
Speed, knots: 13

Comment: Built by Inace S/A, Ceará and commissioned 2 December 1983. Attached to Trem da Esquadra. Can transport up to four torpedoes. Decommissioned in 1991 but retained in service as an AvPpCo (coast support craft).

FLOATING DOCKS

CIDADE DE NATAL (ex-AFDL 39) G 27
AFONSO PENA (ex-*Ceara*, ex-ARD14) G 25
ALMIRANTE SCHIECK
JERONIMO GONÇALVES (ex-*Goiaz* AFDL 4) G 26

Comment: The first three are floating docks loaned to Brazil by US Navy in the mid-1960s and purchased 11 February 1980. Ship lifts of 2800 tons, 1800 tons and 1000 tons respectively. *Almirante Schieck* was built by AMRJ, Rio de Janeiro and commissioned 12 October 1989. There are also two Floating Cranes, *Campos Salles* and *Atlas* of 100 tons and 30 tons capacity respectively.

BRUNEI

Commanding Officer

Lieutenant Colonel Mohammad Shahri bin Haji Ali

Personnel

(a) 1992: 681 (57 officers)
This total includes Special Combat Squadron and River Division
(b) Voluntary service

Base

Flotilla Base—Muara

Prefix to Ships' Names

KDB (Kapal Di-Raja Brunei)

General

Tentera Laut Diraja Brunei (Royal Brunei Navy).

Mercantile Marine

Lloyd's Register of Shipping:
48 vessels of 360 766 tons gross

DELETIONS

1991 *Abadi, Penang*

CORVETTES

Note: Order placed in October 1989 for three Vosper Vigilance class was not confirmed. Tenders re-opened but further delays have been caused by priority being given to the purchase of Hawk aircraft. An order for two vessels is expected in 1992.

LIGHT FORCES

3 WASPADA CLASS (FAST ATTACK CRAFT—MISSILE)

Name	*No*	*Builders*	*Commissioned*
WASPADA	P 02	Vosper (Singapore)	1978
PEJUANG	P 03	Vosper (Singapore)	1979
SETERIA	P 04	Vosper (Singapore)	1979

Displacement, tons: 206 full load
Dimensions, feet (metres): 121 × 23.5 × 6 *(36.9 × 7.2 × 1.8)*
Main machinery: 2 MTU 20V 538 TB91 diesels; 9000 hp(m) *(6.6 MW)*; 2 shafts
Speed, knots: 32. **Range, miles:** 1200 at 14 kts
Complement: 24 (4 officers)

Missiles: SSM: 2 Aerospatiale MM 38 Exocet; inertial cruise; active radar homing to 42 km *(23 nm)* at 0.9 Mach; warhead 165 kg.
Guns: 2 Oerlikon 30 mm GCM-B01 (twin); 85° elevation; 650 rounds/minute to 10 km *(5.5 nm)*; weight of shell 1 kg.
2—7.62 mm MGs. 2 MOD(N) 2 in launchers for illuminants.
Countermeasures: ESM: Decca RDL; radar intercept.
Fire control: Sea Archer system with Sperry Co-ordinate Calculator and 1412A digital computer.
Radars: Surface search: Racal Decca TM 1629AC; I band.

Programmes: *Waspada* launched in August 1977, the remaining two in March and June 1978 respectively.
Modernisation: Started in 1988 and includes improved gun fire control and ESM equipment.
Structure: Welded steel hull with aluminium alloy superstructure. *Waspada* has an enclosed upper bridge for training purposes.

WASPADA *5/1990, John Mortimer*

3 PERWIRA CLASS (COASTAL PATROL CRAFT)

Name	*No*	*Builders*	*Commissioned*
PERWIRA	P 14	Vosper (Singapore)	9 Sep 1974
PEMBURU	P 15	Vosper (Singapore)	17 June 1975
PENYERANG	P 16	Vosper (Singapore)	24 June 1975

Displacement, tons: 38 full load
Dimensions, feet (metres): 71 × 20 × 5 *(21.7 × 6.1 × 1.2)*
Main machinery: 2 MTU MB 12V 331 TC81 diesels; 2450 hp(m) *(1.8 MW)*; 2 shafts
Speed, knots: 32. **Range, miles:** 600 at 22 kts; 1000 at 16 kts
Complement: 14 (2 officers)
Guns: 2 Hispano Suiza 20 mm; 720 rounds/minute to 10 km *(5.5 nm)*.
2—7.62 mm MGs.
Radars: Surface search: Racal Decca RM 1290; I band.

Comment: *Perwira* launched May 1974, other two in January and March 1975 respectively. Of all wooden construction on laminated frames. Fitted with enclosed bridges—modified July 1976.

PENYERANG *6/1990, James Goldrick*

24 FAST ASSAULT BOATS

Comment: Rigid Raider type with one 140 hp *(103 kW)* outboard mostly 16.4-19.7 ft *(5-6 m)* long. One 7.62 mm MG. Operated in rivers and estuaries by River Division for Infantry Battalions.

2 CHEVERTON LOADMASTERS

Name	*No*	*Builders*	*Commissioned*
DAMUAN	L 31	Cheverton Ltd, Isle of Wight	May 1976
PUNI	L 32	Cheverton Ltd, Isle of Wight	Feb 1977

Displacement, tons: 60; 64 *(Puni)*
Dimensions, feet (metres): 65 × 20 × 3.6 *(19.8 × 6.1 × 1.1)* (length 74.8 *(22.8) Puni*)
Main machinery: 2 Detroit 6V-71 diesels; 348 hp *(260 kW)* sustained; 2 shafts
Speed, knots: 9. **Range, miles:** 1000 at 9 kts
Complement: 8
Military lift: 32 tons
Radars: Navigation: Racal Decca RM 1216; I band.

DAMUAN *1988, Royal Brunei Armed Forces*

3 ROTORK TYPE (INSHORE PATROL CRAFT)

S 24, 25, 26

Displacement, tons: 8.8 full load
Dimensions, feet (metres): 41.5 × 10.5 × 4.8 *(12.7 × 3.2 × 1.5)*
Main machinery: 2 Ford Mermaid diesels; 430 hp *(320 kW)*; 2 Castoldi 06 waterjets
Speed, knots: 27 light; 12 heavy. **Range, miles:** 100 at 12 kts
Complement: 3
Guns: 3—7.62 mm MGs.
Radars: Navigation: Decca 60; I band.

Comment: Rotork Marine FPB 512 type. S 24 was delivered in November 1980 for patrol and transport duties. S 25 and 26 delivered May 1981.

S 26 *1982, Royal Brunei Armed Forces*

2 UTILITY CRAFT

BURONG NURI

Displacement, tons: 23 full load
Dimensions, feet (metres): 58.4 × 14.1 × 4.9 *(17.8 × 4.3 × 1.5)*
Main machinery: 2 diesels; 400 hp *(298 kW)*; 2 shafts
Speed, knots: 12
Complement: 5

Comment: Built by Cheverton in 1982. Serves as tug, tender or anti-pollution vessel.

BURONG NURI *6/1990, James Goldrick*

NORAIN

Displacement, tons: 25
Dimensions, feet (metres): 62 × 16 × 4.5 *(18.9 × 4.8 × 1.4)*
Main machinery: 2 diesels; 1250 hp *(932 kW)*; 2 shafts
Speed, knots: 26
Complement: 5

Comment: Built by Cheverton in 1982. Serves as SAR vessel or tender and as VIP transport.

NORAIN *6/1990, James Goldrick*

LAND-BASED MARITIME AIRCRAFT

Numbers/Type: 3 ASA/IPTN CN-235.
Operational speed: 240 kts *(445 km/h)*.
Service ceiling: 26 600 ft *(8110 m)*.
Range: 669 nm *(1240 km)*.
Role/Weapon systems: Long-range maritime patrol for surface surveillance and ASW; order announced in 1989 for operational service in due course. Sensors: Search radar: Litton AN/APS 504(V)5; MAD; acoustic processors; sonobuoys. Weapons; Mk 46 torpedoes (in due course).

MARINE POLICE

Note: In addition to the vessels listed below there are two 36 ft launches with Sabre engines, some 30 GRP patrol boats of 19 ft with outboard engines, and 17 miscellaneous small craft.

7 COASTAL PATROL CRAFT

PDB 12-18

Displacement, tons: 20 full load
Dimensions, feet (metres): 47.7 × 13.9 × 3.9 *(14.5 × 4.2 × 1.2)*
Main machinery: 2 MAN D 2840 LE diesels; 1270 hp(m) *(933 kW)*; 2 shafts
Speed, knots: 30. **Range, miles:** 310 at 22 kts
Complement: 7
Guns: 1—7.62 mm MG

Comment: Built by Singapore Shipbuilding and Engineering Ltd. First three handed over in October 1987, remainder in 1988. Aluminium hulls.

PDB 13 *10/1987, Royal Brunei Police Force*

3 + 4 COASTAL PATROL CRAFT

BENDEHARU P 21
MAHARAJALELA P 22
KEMAINDERA P 23
+ **P 24-27**

Displacement, tons: 68 full load
Dimensions, feet (metres): 91.8 × 17.7 × 5.9 *(28.5 × 5.4 × 1.7)*
Main machinery: 2 MTU diesels; 2260 hp(m) *(1.6 MW)*; 2 shafts
Complement: 19
Guns: 1—12.7 mm MG.

Comment: Reported ordered for the Police from PT Pal Surabaya, Indonesia in 1989. Three delivered in 1991, remainder to follow. Details are not confirmed.

BULGARIA

Headquarters' Appointments

Commander-in-Chief, Navy:
Admiral V G Yanakiev
Deputy Commander-in-Chief, Navy:
Rear Admiral Stefan Damianov
Chief of Staff Navy:
Rear Admiral D Uzunov
Head of Naval Political Directorate:
Rear Admiral Valcho Gelev

Diplomatic Representation

Naval, Military and Air Attaché in London:
Lieutenant Colonel S I Tzonkov

Personnel

(a) 1992: 8800 officers and ratings (2100 afloat, 2200 coastal defence, 1800 training, 2500 shore support, 200 naval aviation)
(b) 18 months' national service

Pennant Numbers

In some cases these appear to change with ships' tasks.

Bases

Varna; Naval HQ, Fleet HQ, Air Station
Burgas; Naval Base, Air Station
Sozopol; Naval Base
Vidin; Danube Flotilla HQ
Atiya; Danube Base
Balchik; Danube Base
Higher Naval School *(Nikola Yonkov Vaptsarov)* and PO's School *(Anton Ivanov)* at Varna. Missile, gun, radar and signal stations on Black Sea coast under Coastal Defence command.

Strength of the Fleet

Type	*Active*
Patrol Submarines	3
Frigates	2
Corvettes	9
Fast Attack Craft (Missile)	3
Fast Attack Craft (Torpedo)	5
Coastal Patrol Craft	8
Minesweepers (Coastal)	10
Minesweepers (Inshore)	3
Minesweeping Boats	15
Landing Craft	14
Surveying Ships	5
Support Tankers	2

Mercantile Marine

Lloyd's Register of Shipping:
226 vessels of 1 366 792 tons gross

DELETIONS

Submarine

1989 *Slava*

Frigates

1990 *Smeli* (old), *Krabri, Strogi, Bodri* (old)

Minesweepers

1991 1 T 43, 3 PO 2

Light Forces

1988 4 SOI
1990 2 SOI, Shershen 117
1991 3 OSA I

Amphibious Forces

1991 4 MFP D-3 Type

Miscellaneous

1990 *Vessletz*
1991 *Nikola Vaptzarov* (civilian), *Perun* (civilian)

SUBMARINES (PATROL)

Note: It is reported that a Kilo class submarine is to be acquired in due course.

3 Ex-SOVIET ROMEO CLASS

POBEDA 81 —83 —84

Displacement, tons: 1475 surfaced; 1830 dived
Dimensions, feet (metres): 251.3 × 22 × 16.1 *(76.6 × 6.7 × 4.9)*
Main machinery: Diesel-electric; 2 Type 37-D diesels; 4000 hp(m) *(2.94 MW)*; 2 motors; 2700 hp(m) *(1.98 MW)*; 2 creep motors; 2 shafts
Speed, knots: 16 surfaced; 13 dived. **Range, miles:** 9000 at 9 kts surfaced
Complement: 54

Torpedoes: 8—21 in *(533 mm)* tubes (6 bow, 2 stern). 14 Soviet Type 53; dual purpose; pattern active/passive homing up to 20 km *(10.8 nm)* at up to 45 kts; warhead 400 kg.
Mines: Can carry up to 28 in lieu of torpedoes.
Radars: Surface search: Snoop Plate; I band.
Sonars: Hull-mounted; active/passive search and attack; high frequency.

Programmes: Built between 1958 and 1961. First pair transferred in 1972-73, one of which was scrapped in 1989. A third transferred during 1985 and a fourth in 1986.
Operational: In 1991 all three were again fully operational.

POBEDA and 84 *1989, S. S. Breyer*

FRIGATES

1 Ex-SOVIET KONI CLASS

SMELI (ex-*Delfin*) 11

Displacement, tons: 1440 standard; 1900 full load
Dimensions, feet (metres): 316.3 × 41.3 × 11.5 *(96.4 × 12.6 × 3.5)*
Main machinery: CODAG; 1 SGW, Nikayev M8B gas turbine (centre shaft); 18 000 hp(m) *(13.25 MW)* sustained; 2 Russki B-68 diesels; 15 820 hp(m) *(11.63 MW)* sustained; 3 shafts
Speed, knots: 27 gas; 22 diesel. **Range, miles:** 1800 at 14 kts
Complement: 110

Missiles: SAM: SA-N-4 Gecko twin launcher ❶; semi-active radar homing to 15 km *(8 nm)* at 2.5 Mach; warhead 50 kg; altitude 9.1-3048 m *(30-10 000 ft)*; 20 missiles.
Guns: 4—3 in *(76 mm)*/60 (2 twin) ❷; 80° elevation; 60 rounds/minute to 15 km *(8 nm)*; weight of shell 7 kg.
4—30 mm/65 (2 twin) ❸; 85° elevation; 500 rounds/minute to 5 km *(2.7 nm)*; weight of shell 0.54 kg.
A/S mortars: 2 RBU 6000 12-tubed trainable ❹; range 6000 m; warhead 31 kg.
Depth charges: 2 racks.
Mines: Capacity for 22.
Countermeasures: Decoys: 2—16-tubed Chaff launchers.
ESM: 2 Watch Dog.
Radars: Air search: Strut Curve ❺; F band; range 110 km *(60 nm)* for 2 m² target.
Surface search: Don 2; I band.
Fire control: Hawk Screech ❻; I band (for 76 mm). Drum Tilt ❼; H/I band (for 30 mm). Pop Group ❽; F/H/I band (for SA-N-4).
IFF: High Pole B.
Sonars: Hull-mounted; active search and attack; medium frequency.

Programmes: First reported in the Black Sea in 1976. Type I retained by the USSR for training foreign crews but transferred in February 1990 when the Koni programme terminated. Others of the class acquired by the former East German Navy, Yugoslavia, Algeria, Cuba and Libya.

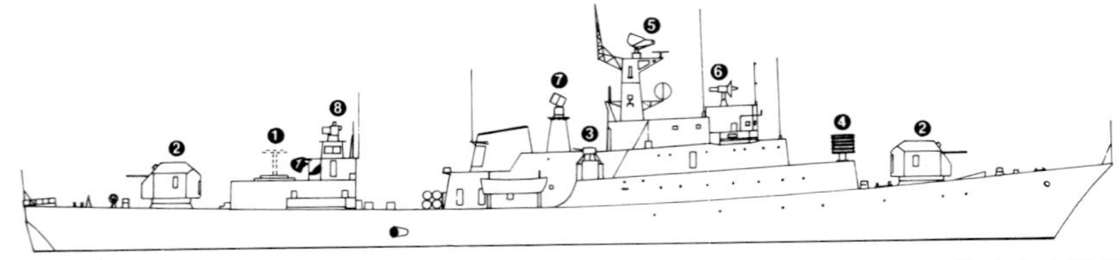
KONI Class *(Scale 1 : 900), Ian Sturton*

SMELI (old number) *5/1982*

1 Ex-SOVIET RIGA CLASS

DRUZKI 12

Displacement, tons: 1260 standard; 1510 full load
Dimensions, feet (metres): 300.1 × 33.1 × 10.5 *(91.5 × 10.1 × 3.2)*
Main machinery: 2 boilers; 2 turbines; 20 000 hp(m) *(14. MW)*; 2 shafts
Speed, knots: 30. **Range, miles:** 2000 at 13 kts
Complement: 175

Guns: 3 USSR 3.9 in *(100 mm)*/56 ❶; 40° elevation; 15 rounds/minute to 16 km *(8.7 nm)*; weight of shell 13.5 kg.
4—37 mm/63 (2 twin) ❷; 80° elevation; 160 rounds/minute to 9 km *(5 nm)*; weight of shell 0.7 kg.
2—25 mm (twin).
Torpedoes: 3—21 in *(533 mm)* tubes ❸. Soviet Type 53; active/passive homing up to 20 km *(10.8 nm)* at up to 45 kts; warhead 400 kg.
A/S mortars: 4 RBU 1200 5-tubed fixed launchers ❹; range 1200 m; warhead 34 kg.
Depth charges: 4 projectors.
Mines: 28.
Countermeasures: ESM: Watch Dog; radar intercept.
Radars: Surface search: Slim Net ❺; E/F band.
Navigation: Neptun; I band.
Fire control: Wasp Head/Sun Visor B ❻; G/H/I band.
IFF: High Pole. Square Head.
Sonars: Hull-mounted; active search and attack; high frequency.

Programmes: Transferred in November 1985. The last of three of the class, the other two being scrapped in 1990 at a Turkish Shipyard.
Operational: Pennant number varies with deployment.

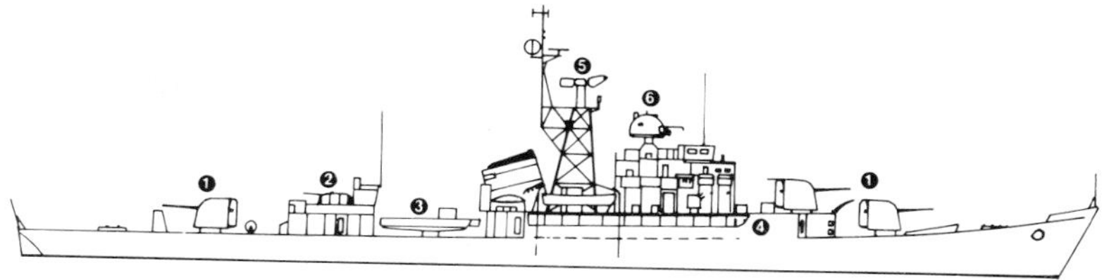
DRUZKI

(Scale 1 : 900), Ian Sturton

DRUZKI (out of area number)

6/1986, G. Jacobs

LAND-BASED MARITIME AIRCRAFT (FRONT LINE)

Numbers/Type: 12 Mil Mi-14PL ('Haze A').
Operational speed: 120 kts *(222 km/h)*.
Service ceiling: 15 000 ft *(4570 m)*.
Range: 240 nm *(445 km)*.
Role/Weapon systems: Primary role as inshore/coastal ASW and Fleet support helicopter; coastal patrol and surface search. Up to nine are probably non-operational. Sensors: Search radar, MAD, sonobuoys, dipping sonar. Weapons: ASW; up to 2 × torpedoes, or mines, or depth bombs.

CORVETTES

1 Ex-SOVIET TARANTUL II CLASS

101

Displacement, tons: 385 standard; 455 full load
Dimensions, feet (metres): 184.1 × 37.7 × 8.2 *(56.1 × 11.5 × 2.5)*
Main machinery: COGOG; 2 NK-12MV gas turbines; 24 000 hp(m) *(17.6 MW)*; 2 gas turbines with reversible gearbox; 8000 hp(m) *(5.9 MW)*; 2 shafts
Speed, knots: 36 on 4 turbines. **Range, miles:** 400 at 36 kts; 2000 at 20 kts
Complement: 34 (5 officers)

Missiles: SSM: 4 SS-N-2C Styx (2 twin) launchers; active radar or IR homing to 83 km *(45 nm)* at 0.9 Mach; warhead 513 kg; sea-skimmer at end of run.
SAM: SA-N-5 Grail quad launcher; manual aiming; IR homing to 6 km *(3.2 nm)* at 1.5 Mach; altitude to 2500 m *(8000 ft)*; warhead 1.5 kg.
Guns: 1—3 in *(76 mm)*/60; 85° elevation; 120 rounds/minute to 7 km *(3.8 nm)*; weight of shell 7 kg.
2—30 mm/65; 6 barrels per mounting; 3000 rounds/minute to 2 km.
Countermeasures: Decoys: 2—16-barrelled Chaff launchers.
ESM: 2 receivers.
Fire control: Hood Wink optronic director.
Radars: Air/surface search: Plank Shave (also for missile control); E band.
Navigation: Spin Trough; I band.
Fire control: Bass Tilt; H/I band.
IFF: Square Head. High Pole.

Programmes: Built at Volodarski, Rybinsk. Transferred in March 1990.

2 Ex-SOVIET PAUK I CLASS

BODRI 13 — 14

Displacement, tons: 440 full load
Dimensions, feet (metres): 195.2 × 33.5 × 11.2 *(59.5 × 10.2 × 3.4)*
Main machinery: 2 diesels; 20 800 hp(m) *(15.3 MW)*; 2 shafts
Speed, knots: 32. **Range, miles:** 2300 at 18 kts
Complement: 32

Missiles: SAM: SA-N-5 Grail quad launcher; manual aiming; IR homing to 6 km *(3.2 nm)* at 1.5 Mach; altitude to 2500 m *(8000 ft)*; warhead 1.5 kg; 8 missiles.
Guns: 1—3 in *(76 mm)*/60; 85° elevation; 120 rounds/minute to 7 km *(3.8 nm)*; weight of shell 7 kg.
1—30 mm/65; 6 barrels; 3000 rounds/minute combined to 2 km.
Torpedoes: 4—16 in *(406 mm)* tubes. Type 40; anti-submarine; active/passive homing up to 15 km *(8 nm)* at up to 40 kts; warhead 100-150 kg.
A/S mortars: 2 RBU 1200 5-tubed fixed; range 1200 m; warhead 34 kg.
Depth charges: 2 racks (12).
Countermeasures: Decoys: 2—16-barrelled Chaff launchers.
ESM: Passive receivers.
Radars: Air/surface search: Peel Cone; E band.
Surface search: Spin Trough; I band.
Fire control: Bass Tilt; H/I band.
Sonars: Rat Tail VDS (mounted on transom); active attack; high frequency.

Programmes: *Bodri* transferred in September 1989, second one in December 1990.

PAUK I Class

1990, S. Breyer

TARANTUL II Class (Russian number)

5/1990

6 Ex-SOVIET POTI CLASS

41 42 43 44 45 46

Displacement, tons: 400 full load
Dimensions, feet (metres): 196.8 × 26.2 × 6.6 *(60 × 8 × 2)*
Main machinery: CODAG; 2 gas turbines; 30 000 hp(m) *(22 MW)*; 2 M503A diesels; 8000 hp(m) *(2.94 MW)*; 2 shafts
Speed, knots: 38. **Range, miles:** 4500 at 10 kts; 500 at 37 kts
Complement: 80

Guns: 2 USSR 57 mm/80 (twin); 85° elevation; 120 rounds/minute to 6 km *(3 nm)*; weight of shell 2.8 kg.
Torpedoes: 4—16 in *(406 mm)* tubes. Soviet Type 40; anti-submarine; active/passive homing up to 15 km *(8 nm)* at up to 40 kts; warhead 100-150 kg.
A/S mortars: 2 RBU 6000 12-tubed trainable launchers; automatic loading; range 6000 m; warhead 31 kg.
Countermeasures: ESM: Watch Dog; radar warning.
Radars: Air search: Strut Curve; F band; range 110 km *(60 nm)* for 2 m² target.
Surface search: Don; I band.
Fire control: Muff Cob; G/H band.
IFF: Square Head. High Pole.
Sonars: Hull-mounted; active search and attack; high frequency.

Programmes: Series built between 1961 and 1968. Three transferred December 1975. The fourth probably transferred at the end of 1986 and the last two in 1990.

POTI 14 (old number) *1988, S. Breyer*

LIGHT FORCES

5 Ex-SOVIET SHERSHEN CLASS (FAST ATTACK CRAFT—TORPEDO)

113 114 115 116 118

Displacement, tons: 145 standard; 170 full load
Dimensions, feet (metres): 113.8 × 22 × 4.9 *(34.7 × 6.7 × 1.5)*
Main machinery: 3 M503A diesels; 12 000 hp(m) *(8.8 MW)*; 3 shafts
Speed, knots: 45. **Range, miles:** 850 at 30 kts; 460 at 42 kts
Complement: 23
Guns: 4 USSR 30 mm/65 (2 twin); 85° elevation; 500 rounds/minute to 5 km *(2.7 nm)*; weight of shell 0.54 kg.
Torpedoes: 4—21 in *(533 mm)* tubes. Soviet Type 53; dual purpose; pattern active/passive homing up to 20 km *(10.8 nm)* at up to 45 kts; warhead 400 kg.
Depth charges: 12; warheads up to 150 kg.
Mines: Capacity 6.
Radars: Surface search: Pot Drum; H/I band.
Fire control: Drum Tilt; H/I band.
IFF: High Pole A. Two Square Head.

Comment: Six transferred from the USSR in 1970. Series built 1962 to 1974.

SHERSHEN Class *10/1989, Gilbert Gyssels*

3 Ex-SOVIET OSA II CLASS (FAST ATTACK CRAFT—MISSILE)

102 104 111

Displacement, tons: 245 full load
Dimensions, feet (metres): 110.2 × 24.9 × 8.8 *(33.6 × 7.6 × 2.7)*
Main machinery: 3 M504 diesels; 15 000 hp(m) *(11 MW)*; 3 shafts
Speed, knots: 37. **Range, miles:** 500 at 35 kts
Complement: 30
Missiles: SSM: 4 SS-N-2 Styx B; active radar/IR homing to 46 km *(25 nm)* at 0.9 Mach; warhead 513 kg.
Guns: 4 USSR 30 mm/65 (2 twin); 85° elevation; 500 rounds/minute to 5 km *(2.7 nm)*; weight of shell 0.54 kg.
Radars: Surface search/fire control: Square Tie; I band; range 73 km *(40 nm)*.
Fire control: Drum Tilt; H/I band.
IFF: High Pole. Square Head.

Comment: Built between 1965 and 1970. First one transferred in 1978, one in 1982 and one in late 1984.

8 Ex-SOVIET ZHUK CLASS (COASTAL PATROL CRAFT)

512, 522, 523, 527, 530, 531, 532, 533

Displacement, tons: 50 full load
Dimensions, feet (metres): 75.4 × 17 × 6.2 *(23 × 5.2 × 1.9)*
Main machinery: 2 Type M50F-12 diesels; 1700 hp(m) *(1.25 MW)* sustained; 2 shafts
Speed, knots: 30. **Range, miles:** 1100 at 15 kts
Complement: 17
Guns: 4 USSR 14.5 mm (2 twin) MGs.
Radars: Surface search: Spin Trough; I band.

Comment: Transferred 1980-81.

ZHUK Class *1988, S. Breyer*

MINE WARFARE FORCES

6 Ex-SOVIET VANYA CLASS (MINESWEEPERS—COASTAL)

ISKIR 31
— 32
DOBROTICH 33
KIRILMINKOV 34
EKSTATI KINAROV 35
RANG DIMITER PASKALEV 36

Displacement, tons: 260 full load
Dimensions, feet (metres): 131.2 × 23.9 × 5.9 *(40 × 7.3 × 1.8)*
Main machinery: 2 Type 9D8 diesels; 2200 hp(m) *(1.6 MW)*; 2 shafts
Speed, knots: 16. **Range, miles:** 2400 at 10 kts
Complement: 30
Guns: 2 USSR 30 mm/65 (twin); 85° elevation; 500 rounds/minute to 5 km *(2.7 nm)*; weight of shell 0.54 kg.
Mines: Can carry 8.
Radars: Surface search: Don 2; I band.

Comment: Built 1961 to 1973. Transferred from the USSR—two in 1970, two in 1971 and two in 1985. Can act as minehunters.

ISKIR *1989, S. S. Breyer*

4 Ex-SOVIET SONYA CLASS (MINESWEEPERS—COASTAL)

61 62 63 64

Displacement, tons: 450 full load
Dimensions, feet (metres): 157.4 × 28.9 × 6.6 *(48 × 8.8 × 2)*
Main machinery: 2 Kolumna Type 9D8 diesels; 2200 hp(m) *(1.6 MW)*; 2 shafts
Speed, knots: 15. **Range, miles:** 1500 at 14 kts
Complement: 43
Guns: 2 USSR 30 mm/65 (twin); 85° elevation; 500 rounds/minute to 5 km *(2.7 nm)*; weight of shell 0.54 kg.
2 USSR 25 mm/60 (twin); 85° elevation; 270 rounds/minute to 3 km *(1.6 nm)* anti-aircraft; weight of shell 0.34 kg.
Mines: 5.
Radars: Surface search/navigation: Don 2; I band.
IFF: Two Square Head. High Pole B.

Comment: Wooden hulled ships transferred in 1981-84.

SONYA 61 *1984*

3 Ex-SOVIET YEVGENYA CLASS (MINESWEEPERS—INSHORE)

53 56 58

Displacement, tons: 77 standard; 90 full load
Dimensions, feet (metres): 80.4 × 18 × 4.6 *(24.5 × 5.5 × 1.4)*
Main machinery: 2 Type 3D12 diesels; 400 hp(m) *(294 kW)*; 2 shafts
Speed, knots: 11. **Range, miles:** 300 at 10 kts
Complement: 10
Guns: 2—14.5 mm MGs.
Radars: Navigation: Spin Trough; I band.
IFF: High Pole.

Comment: GRP hulls built at Kolpino. Transferred 1977.

YEVGENYA Class

3 Ex-SOVIET OLYA CLASS (MINESWEEPERS—INSHORE)

51 52 54

Displacement, tons: 66 full load
Dimensions, feet (metres): 74.8 × 14.8 × 4.6 *(22.8 × 4.5 × 1.4)*
Main machinery: 2 Type 3D12 diesels; 400 hp(m) *(294 kW)*; 2 shafts
Speed, knots: 12. **Range (miles):** 500 at 10 kts
Complement: 15
Guns: 2—25 mm/80 (twin).
Radars: Surface search: Spin Trough; I band.

Comment: Transferred in 1977 with the three Yevgenya class.

15 PO 2 CLASS (MSB)

Displacement, tons: 56 full load
Dimensions, feet (metres): 70.5 × 11.5 × 3.3 *(21.5 × 3.5 × 1)*
Main machinery: 1 diesel; 300 hp(m) *(220 kW)*; 1 shaft
Speed, knots: 12
Complement: 8

Comment: Built in Bulgaria—first units completed in early 1950s and last in early 1960s. Originally a class of 24. Numbers are in 400 and 600 series. Belong to Danube flotilla. Occasionally carry a 12.7 mm MG. Doubtful operational status.

SURVEY SHIPS

3 SURVEY SHIPS (AGS)

CAPTAIN 1st RANK KIRIL KHALACHEV 201 **ADMIRAL BRANIMIR ORMANOV** 401
GENERAL VLADIMIR ZAIMOV 301

Displacement, tons: 1580 full load (201 and 401)
Dimensions, feet (metres): 240.5 × 36.8 × 12.8 *(73.3 × 11.2 × 3.9)* (201 and 401)
Main machinery: 2 Skoda-Sulzer 6TD48 diesels; 3300 hp(m) *(2.43 MW)* sustained; 2 shafts
Speed, knots: 17. **Range, miles:** 9000 at 12 kts
Complement: 37 (5 officers)
Radars: Navigation: Two Don-2; I band.

Comment: Details given are for 201 built in Bulgaria in 1983 and 401 built in Poland in 1977; both are Moma class. 301 is a Varna class of about 600 tons built in 1973.

1 Ex-SOVIET T 43 CLASS (AGS)

N I VAPTSAROV 421

Comment: Built 1948 to 1957. The survivor of three transferred from the USSR in 1953, this is now the only short-hulled, low bridge, tripod mast T 43 in commission. Used as a survey ship.

1 COASTAL SURVEY VESSEL

Displacement, tons: 114 full load
Dimensions, feet (metres): 86.9 × 19 × 9.5 *(26.5 × 5.8 × 2.9)*
Main machinery: 2 Type 3D-12A diesels; 600 hp(m) (441 kw); 2 shafts
Speed, knots: 12. **Range, miles:** 600 at 10 kts
Complement: 9

Comment: Built in Bulgaria in the early 1980s.

231 *1991, S. Breyer*

AMPHIBIOUS FORCES

2 Ex-SOVIET POLNOCHNY A CLASS

IVAN ZAGUBANSKI 701 — 702

Displacement, tons: 750 standard; 800 full load
Dimensions, feet (metres): 239.5 × 27.9 × 5.8 *(73 × 8.5 × 1.8)*
Main machinery: 2 Type 40-D diesels; 5000 hp(m) *(3.67 MW)*; 2 shafts
Speed, knots: 19. **Range, miles:** 1000 at 18 kts
Complement: 40
Military lift: 350 tons including 6 tanks; 180 troops
Guns: 2 USSR 30 mm (twin). 2—140 mm 18-barrelled rocket launchers.
Radars: Navigation: Spin Trough; I band.

Comment: Built 1963 to 1968. Transferred 1986/87. Apparently not fitted either with the SA-N-5 Grail SAM system or with Drum Tilt fire control radars.

IVAN ZAGUBANSKI *9/1989, S. S. Breyer*

12 Ex-SOVIET VYDRA CLASS

602 603 605 609 612
704 705 707-711

Displacement, tons: 425 standard; 550 full load
Dimensions, feet (metres): 179.7 × 25.3 × 6.6 *(54.8 × 7.7 × 2)*
Main machinery: 2 diesels; 1000 hp(m) *(730 kW)*; 2 shafts
Speed, knots: 12. **Range, miles:** 2500 at 10 kts
Complement: 20
Military lift: 200 tons or 100 troops or 3 MBTs
Radars: Navigation: Spin Trough; I band.
IFF: High Pole.

Comment: Built 1963 to 1969. Ten transferred from the USSR in 1970, eight in 1979 and two in 1980. Two deleted in 1987, six more in 1990/91. Pennant numbers are not consecutive.

VYDRA 705 *11/1989, S. S. Breyer*

AUXILIARIES

Note: Training ship *Nikola Vaptzarov* and sail training ship *Kaliakra* deleted as both belong to the Merchant Marine.

2 SUPPORT TANKERS

MESAR (ex-*Anlene*) 202 **DIMITRI A DIMITROV** —

Displacement, tons: 3500 full load
Dimensions, feet (metres): 319.8 × 43.3 × 16.4 *(97.5 × 13.2 × 5)*
Main machinery: 2 diesels; 12 000 hp(m) *(8.82 MW)*; 2 shafts
Speed, knots: 20
Guns: 4 USSR 30 mm/65 (2 twin).

Comment: *Mesar* built in Bulgaria in 1979-80. Second delivered in 1987. Abeam fuelling to port and astern fuelling. Mount 1.5 ton crane amidships. Also carry dry stores. Support ships for Mediterranean naval excursions.

MESAR *1981*

1 BOLVA CLASS (BARRACK SHIP)

SALGIR

Comment: Used for refit crews. Five other smaller barrack ships reported.

1 DIVING TENDER

GEORGIY DIMITROV

Dimensions, feet (metres): 91.5 × 17.1 × 7.2 *(27.9 × 5.2 × 2.2)*
Main machinery: Diesel electric; 2 MCK 83-4 diesel generators; 1 motor; 300 hp(m) (220 kw); 1 shaft
Speed, knots: 10
Complement: 13

Comment: Built in Bulgaria in mid 1980s.

1 BEREZA CLASS

KAPITAN DMITRY DOBREV 206

Displacement, tons: 2000 full load
Dimensions, feet (metres): 229.6 × 40.7 × 10.8 *(70 × 12.4 × 3.3)*
Main machinery: 2 Skoda-Sulzer diesels; 3000 hp(m) *(2.2 MW)*; 2 shafts; cp props
Speed, knots: 15
Complement: 70
Radars: Navigation: Kivach; I band.

Comment: New construction built in Poland and transferred July 1988. Used as a degaussing ship.

1 SALVAGE TUG

JUPITER 221

Displacement, tons: 792 full load
Dimensions, feet (metres): 146.6 × 35.1 × 12.7 *(44.7 × 10.7 × 3.9)*
Main machinery: 2—12 KVD 21 diesels; 1760 hp(m) *(1.3 MW)*; 2 shafts
Speed, knots: 12.5. **Range, miles:** 3000 at 12 kts
Complement: 39 (6 officers)
Guns: 4—25 mm/70 (2 twin) automatic.

Comment: Bollard pull, 16 tons. Former DDR Type 700.

10 AUXILIARIES

231, 331, 333, 337

Comment: Ten or more other auxiliaries, probably including TRVs, water boats and diving vessels. 231 and 331 are 100 ton craft built in 1986 and 1988 respectively.

BORDER GUARD

Comment: Total of 60 small craft including 12 ex-Soviet PO2 class.

BURMA

General

The title used by the current government is Myanmar.

Headquarters' Appointments

Vice-Chief of Staff, Defence Services (Navy):
Vice Admiral Maung Maung Khin
Chief of Staff, Navy:
Rear Admiral Than Nyunt

Bases

Bassein, Mergui, Moulmein, Rangoon, Seikyi, Sittwe (Akyab), Sinmalaik.

Personnel

(a) 1992: 12 000
(b) Voluntary service

Strength of the Fleet

Type	*Active*	*Building*
Corvettes	3 (1)	—
Offshore Patrol Vessels	3	—
Fast Attack Craft (Gun)	—	2
Coastal Patrol Craft	22	—
River Patrol Craft and Gunboats	64	—
Amphibious Vessels	15	—
Survey Vessels	3	—

Mercantile Marine

Lloyd's Register of Shipping:
154 vessels of 1 046 029 tons gross

CORVETTES

Note: All Corvettes come under the Major War Vessels Command.

1 Ex-US PCE 827 CLASS

Name	*No*	*Builders*	*Commissioned*
YAN TAING AUNG (ex-USS *Farmington* PCE 894)	PCE 41	Willamette Iron & Steel Co, Portland, Oregon	10 Aug 1943

Displacement, tons: 640 standard; 903 full load
Dimensions, feet (metres): 184 × 33 × 9.5 *(56 × 10.1 × 2.9)*
Main machinery: 2 GM 12-567A diesels; 1800 hp *(1.34 MW)*; 2 shafts
Speed, knots: 15
Complement: 72

Guns: 1 US 3 in *(76 mm)*/50 Mk 26; 85° elevation; 20 rounds/minute to 12 km *(6.6 nm)*; weight of shell 6 kg.
2 Bofors 40 mm/60 (twin). 8 Oerlikon 20 mm (4 twin).
A/S mortars: 1 Hedgehog Mk 10; 24 rockets; manual loading; range 350 m; warhead 26 kg.
Depth charges: 2 racks. 2 Mk 6 projectors; range 160 m; warhead 150 kg.
Radars: Surface search: Raytheon SPS 5; G/H band; range 37 km *(20 nm)*.
Sonars: RCA QCU-2; hull-mounted; active attack; high frequency.

Programmes: Laid down on 7 December 1942 and launched on 15 May 1943. Transferred on 18 June 1965.
Operational: In poor condition in 1991 but still operational.

YAN TAING AUNG *1987*

1 Ex-US ADMIRABLE CLASS

Name	*No*	*Builders*	*Commissioned*
YAN GYI AUNG (ex-USS *Creddock* MSF 356)	PCE 42	Willamette Iron & Steel Co, Portland, Oregon	1944

Displacement, tons: 650 standard; 945 full load
Dimensions, feet (metres): 184.5 × 33 × 9.8 *(56.2 × 10.1 × 3)*
Main machinery: 2 Busch-Sulzer BS-539 diesels; 1500 hp(m) *(1.1 MW)*; 2 shafts
Speed, knots: 14.8. **Range, miles:** 4300 at 10 kts
Complement: 73

Guns: 1 US 3 in *(76 mm)*/50 Mk 26; 85° elevation; 20 rounds/minute to 12 km *(6.6 nm)*; weight of shell 6 kg.
4 Bofors 40 mm/60 (2 twin). 4 Oerlikon 20 mm (2 twin).
A/S mortars: 1 Hedgehog Mk 10; 24 rockets; manual loading; range 350 m; warhead 26 kg.
Depth charges: 2 racks. 2 Mk 6 projectors; range 160 m; warhead 150 kg.
Radars: Surface search: Raytheon SPS 5; G/H band; range 37 km *(20 nm)*.
Sonars: RCA QCU-2; hull-mounted; active attack; high frequency.

Programmes: Laid down on 10 November 1943 and launched on 22 July 1944. Transferred at San Diego on 31 March 1967.
Operational: Minesweeping gear removed. Fully operational in 1991.

YAN GYI AUNG 12/1991

2 NAWARAT CLASS

Name	*No*	*Builders*	*Commissioned*
NAWARAT	501	Government Dockyard, Dawbon, Rangoon	26 Apr 1960
NAGAKYAY	502	Government Dockyard, Dawbon, Rangoon	3 Dec 1960

Displacement, tons: 400 standard; 450 full load
Dimensions, feet (metres): 163 × 26.8 × 5.8 *(49.7 × 8.2 × 1.8)*
Main machinery: 2 Paxman Ricardo diesels; 1160 hp(m) *(865 kW)*; 2 shafts
Speed, knots: 12
Complement: 43
Guns: 2—25 pdr (88 mm) QF. 2 Bofors 40 mm.

Comment: In spite of their size, these vessels are used mostly for river patrols.

NAWARAT

OFFSHORE PATROL VESSELS

3 OSPREY CLASS

INDAW FV 55 **INMA** FV 56 **INYA** FV 57

Displacement, tons: 385 standard; 505 full load
Dimensions, feet (metres): 164 × 34.5 × 9 *(50 × 10.5 × 2.8)*
Main machinery: 2 Burmeister and Wain Alpha diesels; 4640 hp(m) *(3.4 MW)*; 2 shafts
Speed, knots: 20. **Range, miles:** 4500 at 16 kts
Complement: 20 (5 officers) (accommodation for 35)
Guns: 1 Bofors 40 mm/60. 2 Oerlikon 20 mm.

Comment: *Indaw* completed 30 May 1980 by Frederikshavn Dockyard, Denmark, *Inma* and *Inya* 25 March 1982. Operated by Burmese Navy for the People's Pearl and Fishery Department. Helicopter deck with hangar in *Indaw*. Carry David Still craft capable of 25 kts.

INYA 1990

LIGHT FORCES

0 + 2 FAST ATTACK CRAFT (GUN)

Displacement, tons: 213 full load
Dimensions, feet (metres): 147.3 × 23 × 8.2 *(45 × 7 × 2.5)*
Main machinery: 2 Mercedes Benz diesels; 2 shafts
Speed, knots: 30+
Complement: 34 (7 officers)
Guns: 2 Bofors 40 mm/60.

Comment: Reported as being under construction in 1991.

6 CHINESE HAINAN CLASS (COASTAL PATROL CRAFT)

Name	*No*	*Name*	*No*
YAN SIT AUNG	43	**YAN KHWIN AUNG**	46
YAN MYAT AUNG	44	**YAN MIN AUNG**	47
YAN NYEIN AUNG	45	**YAN YE AUNG**	48

Displacement, tons: 375 standard; 392 full load
Dimensions, feet (metres): 192.8 × 23.6 × 6 *(58.8 × 7.2 × 2.2)*
Main machinery: 4 diesels; 8800 hp(m) *(6.4 MW)*; 4 shafts
Speed, knots: 30.5. **Range, miles:** 1300 at 15 kts
Complement: 69
Guns: 4 China 57 mm/70 (2 twin); dual purpose; 120 rounds/minute to 12 km *(6.5 nm)*; weight of shell 6.31 kg.
4 USSR 25 mm/60 (2 twin); 85° elevation; 270 rounds/minute to 3 km *(1.6 nm)* anti-aircraft; weight of shell 0.34 kg.
A/S mortars: 4 RBU 1200 5-tubed fixed launchers; range 1200 m; warhead 34 kg.
Depth charges: 2 BMB-2 projectors; 2 racks.
Mines: Rails fitted.
Radars: Surface search: Pot Head; I band.
Navigation: Raytheon Pathfinder; I band.
IFF: High Pole.
Sonars: Hull-mounted; active search and attack; high frequency.

Comment: Later variant of this class with tripod masts. Delivered in January 1991.

YAN SIT AUNG 1991

3 YUGOSLAV PB 90 CLASS (COASTAL PATROL CRAFT)

336 337 338

Displacement, tons: 80 standard
Dimensions, feet (metres): 89.9 × 21.5 × 7.2 *(27.4 × 6.6 × 2.2)*
Main machinery: 3 diesels; 4290 hp(m) *(3.15 MW)*; 3 shafts
Speed, knots: 32. **Range, miles:** 400 at 25 kts
Complement: 17
Guns: 8—20 mm M75 (two quad). 1—128 mm launcher for illuminants.
Radars: Navigation: I band.

Comment: Built by Brodotechnika, Yugoslavia for an African country and completed in 1986-87. Laid up when the sale did not go through and shipped to Burma arriving in October 1990.

PB 90 Class 1990, Yugoslav FDSP

4 PGM TYPE (COASTAL PATROL CRAFT)

PGM 412-PGM 415

Displacement, tons: 128 full load
Dimensions, feet (metres): 110 × 22 × 6.5 *(33.5 × 6.7 × 2)*
Main machinery: 2 Deutz SBA 16 MB 816 LLKR diesels; 2720 hp(m) *(2 MW)*; 2 shafts
Speed, knots: 16. **Range, miles:** 1400 at 14 kts
Complement: 17
Guns: 2 Bofors 40 mm/60.

Comment: First two completed 1983. Two more built in Burma Naval Dockyard.

PGM 412 *1991*

6 Ex-US PGM TYPE (COASTAL PATROL CRAFT)

PGM 401-PGM 406

Displacement, tons: 141 full load
Dimensions, feet (metres): 101 × 21.1 × 7.5 *(30.8 × 6.4 × 2.3)*
Main machinery: 8 GM 6-71 diesels; 1920 hp *(1.43 MW)* sustained; 2 shafts
Speed, knots: 17. **Range, miles:** 1000 at 15 kts
Complement: 17
Guns: 2 Bofors 40 mm/60. 2 Oerlikon 20 mm (twin). 2—12.7 mm MGs.
Radars: Navigation: Raytheon 1500 (PGM 405-406).
EDO 320 (PGM 401-404); I/J band.

Comment: Built by the Marinette Marine Corporation, USA in 1959-61. Ex-US PGM 43-46, 51 and 52 respectively.

3 SWIFT TYPE PGM (COASTAL PATROL CRAFT)

121 122 123

Displacement, tons: 111 full load
Dimensions, feet (metres): 103.3 × 23.8 × 6.9 *(31.5 × 7.2 × 3.1)*
Main machinery: 2 MTU 12V 331 TC81 diesels; 2 shafts
Speed, knots: 27. **Range, miles:** 1800 at 18 kts
Complement: 25
Guns: 2 Bofors 40 mm. 2 Oerlikon 20 mm. 2—12.7 mm MGs.

Comment: Swiftships construction completed in 1979. Acquired 1980 through Vosper, Singapore.

SWIFT PGM *1979, Swiftships*

2 IMPROVED Y 301 CLASS (RIVER GUNBOATS)

Y 311 Y 312

Displacement, tons: 250 full load
Dimensions, feet (metres): 121.4 × 24 × 3.9 *(37 × 7.3 × 1.2)*
Main machinery: 2 Mercedes-Benz diesels; 1000 hp(m) *(735 kW)*; 2 shafts
Speed, knots: 12
Complement: 37
Guns: 2 Bofors 40 mm. 4 Oerlikon 20 mm.

Comment: Built at Simmilak in 1969 and based on similar Yugoslav craft.

Y311 *1987*

10 Y 301 CLASS (RIVER GUNBOATS)

Y 301-Y 310

Displacement, tons: 120 full load
Dimensions, feet (metres): 104.8 × 24 × 3 *(32 × 7.3 × 0.9)*
Main machinery: 2 Mercedes-Benz MTU diesels; 1000 hp(m) *(735 kW)*; 2 shafts
Speed, knots: 13
Complement: 29
Guns: 2 Bofors 40 mm/60 or 1 Bofors 40 mm/60 and 1—2 pdr.

Comment: All of these boats were completed in 1958 at the Uljanik Shipyard, Pula, Yugoslavia.

Y304 *1991*

4 RIVER GUNBOATS (Ex-TRANSPORTS)

SAGU SEINMA SHWETHIDA SINMIN

Displacement, tons: 98 full load
Dimensions, feet (metres): 94.5 × 22 × 4.5 *(28.8 × 6.7 × 1.4)*
Main machinery: 1 Crossley ERL-6 cyl diesel; 160 hp *(119 kW)*; 1 shaft
Speed, knots: 12
Complement: 32
Guns: 1—40 mm/60 *(Sagu)*. 1—20 mm (3 in *Sagu*).

Comment: Built in mid-1950s. *Sinmin, Seinma* and *Shwethida* have a roofed in upper deck with a 20 mm gun forward of the funnel. *Sagu* has an open upper deck aft of the funnel but with a 40 mm gun forward and mountings for 20 mm aft on the upper deck and midships either side on the lower deck. Four other ships of the same type are probably unarmed and are listed under *Miscellaneous*.

SINMIN *1989*

SAGU *1990*

2 Ex-US CGC TYPE (RIVER GUNBOATS)

MGB 102 MGB 110

Displacement, tons: 49 standard; 66 full load
Dimensions, feet (metres): 83 × 16 × 5.5 *(25.3 × 4.9 × 1.7)*
Main machinery: 4 GM diesels; 800 hp *(596 kW)*; 2 shafts
Speed, knots: 11
Complement: 16
Guns: 1 Bofors 40 mm. 1 Oerlikon 20 mm.

Comment: Ex-USCG type cutters with new hulls built in Burma. Completed in 1960.

MGB 110

4 RIVER PATROL CRAFT

Displacement, tons: 37
Guns: 3—12.7 mm MGs (1 twin, 1 single).

Comment: 60 ft craft built by the Naval Engineering Depot. First one commissioned 11 April 1990.

5 RIVER PATROL CRAFT

RPC 11 12 13 14 15

Displacement, tons: 30
Dimensions, feet (metres): 50 × 14 × 3.5 *(15.2 × 4.3 × 1.1)*
Main machinery: 2 Thornycroft RZ 6 diesels; 250 hp *(186 kW)*; 2 shafts
Speed, knots: 10. **Range, miles:** 400 at 8 kts
Complement: 8
Guns: 1 Oerlikon 20 mm.

Comment: Probably built locally in mid-1980s.

RIVER PATROL CRAFT (unidentified) *1990*

6 RIVER PATROL CRAFT

PBR 211-216

Displacement, tons: 9 full load
Dimensions, feet (metres): 32 × 11 × 2.6 *(9.8 × 3.4 × 0.8)*
Main machinery: 2 GM 6V-53N diesels; 320 hp *(238 kW)* sustained; 2 waterjets
Speed, knots: 25. **Range, miles:** 180 at 20 kts
Complement: 4 or 5
Guns: 2—12.7 mm (twin, fwd) MGs. 1—7.9 mm LMG (aft).

Comment: Acquired in 1978. Built by Uniflite, Washington.

25 YUGOSLAV-BUILT RIVER PATROL CRAFT

001-025

Comment: Small craft, 52 ft *(15.8 m)* long, acquired from Yugoslavia in 1965.

6 CARPENTARIA CLASS (RIVER PATROL CRAFT)

01-06

Displacement, tons: 26 full load
Dimensions, feet (metres): 51.5 × 15.7 × 4.3 *(15.7 × 4.8 × 1.3)*
Main machinery: 2 diesels; 1360 hp *(1.01 MW)*; 2 shafts
Speed, knots: 29. **Range, miles:** 950 at 18 kts
Complement: 10
Guns: 1—12.7 mm MG.

Comment: Built by De Havilland Marine, Sydney. First two delivered 1979, remainder in 1980.

CARPENTARIA Class *1991*

SHIPBORNE AIRCRAFT

Numbers/Type: 10 Aerospatiale SA 316B Alouette III.
Operational speed: 113 kts *(210 km/h)*.
Service ceiling: 10 500 ft *(3200 m)*.
Range: 290 nm *(540 km)*.
Role/Weapon systems: Embarked in offshore patrol craft for support duties. Sensors: None. Weapons: Possible 7.62 mm machine gun mountings.

LAND-BASED MARITIME AIRCRAFT

Numbers/Type: 10 Kawasaki-Bell 47G-3.
Operational speed: 74 kts *(137 km/h)*.
Service ceiling: 13 200 ft *(4023 m)*.
Range: 261 nm *(483 km)*.
Role/Weapon systems: Light liaison and utility tasks. Sensors: None. Weapons: Unarmed, but possible single 7.62 mm mounting has been supplied.

Numbers/Type: 3 Fokker F27M.
Operational speed: 250 kts *(463 km/h)*.
Service ceiling: 25 000 ft *(7620 m)*.
Range: 2700 nm *(5000 km)*.
Role/Weapon systems: Long-range patrol of coastlines. Sensors: Bendix weather radar, wingtip searchlight. Weapons: Unarmed.

AMPHIBIOUS FORCES

Note: As well as the vessels listed below there are at least three Army Landing Craft (001-003).

LCM 003 *1991*

4 LCUs

AIYAR MAI 604
AIYAR MAUNG 605
AIYAR MINTHAMEE 606
AIYAR MIN THAR 607

Displacement, tons: 250 full load
Dimensions, feet (metres): 125.6 × 29.8 × 4.6 *(38.3 × 9.1 × 1.4)*
Main machinery: 2 diesels; 600 hp(m) *(441 kW)*; 2 shafts
Speed, knots: 10
Complement: 10
Military lift: 100 tons

Comment: All built at Yokohama in 1969.

AIYAR MAUNG *1991*

1 LCU

AIYAR LULIN 603

Displacement, tons: 360 full load
Dimensions, feet (metres): 119 × 34 × 6 *(36.3 × 10.4 × 1.8)*
Main machinery: 2 diesels; 600 hp *(448 kW)*; 2 shafts
Speed, knots: 10
Complement: 14
Military lift: 168 tons

Comment: Built in Rangoon in 1966.

AIYAR LULIN *1990*

10 Ex-US LCM 3 TYPE

LCM 701-710

Displacement, tons: 52 full load
Dimensions, feet (metres): 50 × 14 × 4 *(15.2 × 4.3 × 1.2)*
Main machinery: 2 Gray Marine diesels; 450 hp *(335 kW)*; 2 shafts
Speed, knots: 9
Guns: 2 Oerlikon 20 mm.

Comment: US-built LCM type landing craft. Used as local transports for stores and personnel. Cargo capacity, 30 tons.

SURVEY VESSELS

Note: In addition to the two ships listed below there is a third survey vessel of undetermined size.

1 OCEAN SURVEY SHIP

Name	*No*	*Builders*	*Commissioned*
THU TAY THI	801	Brodogradiliste 'Tito', Belgrade, Yugoslavia	1965

Displacement, tons: 1059 standard
Dimensions, feet (metres): 204 × 36 × 11.8 *(62.2 × 11 × 3.6)*
Main machinery: 2 MB820 Db diesels; 1710 hp(m) *(1.26 MW)*; 2 shafts
Speed, knots: 15
Complement: 99 (7 officers)
Guns: 1 Bofors 40 mm. 2 Oerlikon 20 mm (twin) can be fitted.

Comment: Fitted with helicopter platform and two surveying motor boats.

THU TAY THI

1 Ex-RESEARCH TRAWLER

Name	*No*	*Builders*	*Commissioned*
— (ex-*Changi*)	802	Miho Shipyard, Shimizu	20 June 1969

Measurement, tons: 387 gross; 118 dwt
Dimensions, feet (metres): 154.2 × 28.6 × 11.9 *(47 × 8.7 × 3.6)*
Main machinery: 1 Niigata diesel; 1 shaft
Speed, knots: 13
Complement: 35

Comment: A fishery research ship of Singapore origin, arrested and taken into service as a survey vessel in about 1981. Stern trawler type.

802 *1990*

MISCELLANEOUS

Note: As well as the ships listed below there is a small coastal oil tanker, a harbour tug and several harbour launches and personnel carriers.

1 DIVING SUPPORT VESSEL

YAN LON AUNG 200

Comment: Light forces support diving ship of 520 tons, acquired from Japan in 1967. Has a crew of 88 and carries a Bofors 40 mm gun.

YAN LON AUNG

4 TRANSPORT VESSELS

SABAN SETHAYA SHWEPAZUN SETYAHAT

Displacement, tons: 98 full load
Dimensions, feet (metres): 94.5 × 22 × 4.5 *(28.8 × 6.7 × 1.4)*
Main machinery: 1 Crossley ERL-6 cyl diesel; 160 hp *(119 kW)*; 1 shaft
Speed, knots: 12
Complement: 30

Comment: These are sister ships to the armed gunboats shown under *Light Forces*. It is possible that a 20 mm gun may be mounted on some occasions.

SHWEPAZUN *1991*

HSAD DAN

Displacement, tons: 706 full load
Dimensions, feet (metres): 130.6 × 37.1 × 8.9 *(39.8 × 11.3 × 2.7)*
Main machinery: 2 Deutz SBA 8M816R diesels; 2 shafts
Speed, knots: 10
Complement: 23

Comment: Built by Italthai in 1986. Buoy tender operated by the Rangoon Port Authority.

1 TRANSPORT VESSEL

PYI DAW AYE

Measurement, tons: 700 dwt
Dimensions, feet (metres): 160 × 27 × 11 *(48.8 × 8.2 × 3.4)*
Main machinery: 2 diesels; 600 hp *(447 kW)*; 2 shafts
Speed, knots: 11
Complement: 12

Comment: Completed in about 1975. Dimensions are approximate. Naval manned.

PYI DAW AYE *1991*

1 PRESIDENTIAL YACHT

YADANABON

Comment: Built in Burma and used for VIP cruises on the Irrawaddy river and in coastal waters. Armed with 2—7.62 mm MGs and manned by the Navy.

PRESIDENT'S YACHT *1990*

4 MFVs

901, 906, 520, 523

Comment: Armed vessels of approximately 200 tons (901) and 80 tons (remainder) with a 12.7 mm MG mounted above the bridge.

MFV 906 *1990*

CAMBODIA

Ministerial

Defence Minister:
Tea Banh

General

The Marine Royale Khmer was established on 1 March 1954 and became Marine Nationale Khmer (MNK) on 9 October 1970. Originally Cambodia, became known as the Khmer Republic, then The People's Republic of Kampuchea and is now back to being Cambodia again.

Personnel

(a) 1992: 950
(b) 18 months' national service

Bases

Kompongson, Phumi, Phoar, Ream

Operational

The operational state of this force is still uncertain as is the number and types of craft. There are large numbers of armed fishing boats used by the Navy.

Mercantile Marine

Lloyd's Register of Shipping:
3 vessels of 3558 tons gross

PATROL FORCES

Note: Two Swift class patrol boats previously thought sunk may still be operational and there is one LCU of undetermined type.

2 Ex-SOVIET TURYA CLASS (FAST ATTACK CRAFT—HYDROFOIL)

Displacement, tons: 190 standard; 250 full load
Dimensions, feet (metres): 129.9 × 24.9 (41 foils) × 5.9 (13.1 foils) *(39.6 × 7.6 (12.5) × 1.8 (4))*
Main machinery: 3 diesels; 12 000 hp(m) *(8.8 MW)* sustained; 3 shafts
Speed, knots: 40 foils. **Range, miles:** 600 at 35 kts foils; 1450 at 14 kts hull
Complement: 30
Guns: 2—57 mm (twin). 2—25 mm (twin).
Radars: Search: Pot Drum.
Fire control: Muff Cob; G/H band.
IFF: High Pole B. Square Head.

Comment: Transferred March 1984 and February 1985 without torpedo tubes and dipping sonars. Probably non-operational in early 1992.

TURYA Class *1987*

4 Ex-SOVIET SHMEL CLASS (RIVER PATROL CRAFT)

Displacement, tons: 85 full load
Dimensions, feet (metres): 91.8 × 14.1 × 3.6 *(28 × 4.3 × 1.1)*
Main machinery: 2 M50-F4 diesels; 2400 hp(m) *(1.76 MW)*; 2 shafts
Speed, knots: 22. **Range, miles:** 600 at 12 kts
Complement: 12
Guns: 1—3 in *(76 mm)*. 2—25 mm (twin). 5—7.62 mm MGs.
Mines: 9.
Radars: Spin Trough; I band

Comment: Two transferred March 1984, two in January 1985.

SHMEL Class *1990*

2 Ex-SOVIET T 4 CLASS (LCVPs)

Displacement, tons: 70 full load
Dimensions, feet (metres): 62.3 × 14 × 3.3 *(19 × 4.3 × 1)*
Main machinery: 2 diesels; 400 hp(m) *(294 kW)*; 2 shafts
Speed, knots: 10
Complement: 4

Comment: Transferred January 1985. Only one may be operational.

2 Ex-SOVIET MODIFIED STENKA CLASS (FAST ATTACK CRAFT—PATROL)

Displacement, tons: 170 standard; 210 full load
Dimensions, feet (metres): 127.9 × 25.6 × 5.9 *(39 × 7.8 × 1.8)*
Main machinery: 3 M503A diesels; 12 000 hp(m) *(8.8 MW)*; 3 shafts
Speed, knots: 36. **Range, miles:** 800 at 24 kts; 500 at 35 kts
Complement: 30
Guns: 4—30 mm/65 (2 twin).
Radars: Search: Pot Drum.
Fire control: Muff Cob; G/H band.
IFF: High Pole. Two Square Head.

Comment: Transferred in November 1987. Both are the export model without torpedo tubes and sonar. Replaced two others which are used for spares. Probably non-operational in early 1992.

STENKA Class *US Navy*

1 SOVIET ZHUK CLASS (RIVER PATROL CRAFT)

Displacement, tons: 50 full load
Dimensions, feet (metres): 75.4 × 17 × 6.2 *(23 × 5.2 × 1.9)*
Main machinery: 2 M50-F4 diesels; 2400 hp(m) *(1.76 MW)*; 2 shafts
Speed, knots: 30. **Range, miles:** 1100 at 15 kts
Complement: 17
Guns: 2—14.5 mm (twin, fwd) MGs. 1—12.7 mm (aft) MG.
Radars: Surface search: Spin Trough; I band.

Comment: Transferred via Vietnam between 1985 and 1987. There may have been two more of the class but this appears to be the sole survivor.

CAMEROON

Headquarters' Appointments

Chief of Naval Staff:
Commander Guillaume Ngouah Ngally

Diplomatic Representation

Naval Attaché in London:
Lieutenant Commander E Babou

Personnel

1992: 1400 officers and men

Bases

Douala, Limbe, Kribi

Mercantile Marine

Lloyd's Register of Shipping:
45 vessels of 34 453 tons gross

DELETIONS

Light Forces

1989 2 Rotork Craft
1990 *Quartier Maître Alfred Motto*

LIGHT FORCES

1 P 48S TYPE (MISSILE PATROL CRAFT)

Name	*No*	*Builders*	*Commissioned*
BAKASSI	P 104	SFCN, Villeneuve-La-Garenne	9 Jan 1984

Displacement, tons: 308 full load
Dimensions, feet (metres): 172.5 × 23.6 × 7.9 *(52.6 × 7.2 × 2.4)*
Main machinery: 2 SACM 195V16 CZSHR diesels; 5790 hp(m) *(4.26 MW)* sustained; 2 shafts
Speed, knots: 25. **Range, miles:** 2000 at 16 kts
Complement: 39 (6 officers)

Missiles: SSM: 8 Aerospatiale MM 40 Exocet (2 quad) launchers; inertial cruise; active radar homing to 70 km *(40 nm)* at 0.9 Mach; warhead 165 kg; sea-skimmer.
Guns: 2 Bofors 40 mm/70; 85° elevation; 300 rounds/minute to 12.8 km *(7 nm)*; weight of shell 0.96 kg.
Fire control: Two Naja optronic systems. Racal Decca Cane 100 command system.
Radars: Navigation/surface search: Two Racal Decca 1226; I band.

Programmes: Ordered January 1981. Laid down 16 December 1981. Launched 22 October 1982.
Modernisation: Radars have been updated.

BAKASSI *1984, SFCN*

1 PR 48 TYPE (LARGE PATROL CRAFT)

Name	*No*	*Builders*	*Commissioned*
L'AUDACIEUX	P 103	Soc Française de Construction Naval	11 May 1976

Displacement, tons: 250 full load
Dimensions, feet (metres): 157.5 × 23.3 × 7.5 *(48 × 7.1 × 2.3)*
Main machinery: 2 SACM 195 V12 CZSHR diesels; 3600 hp(m) *(2.65 MW)* sustained; 2 shafts; cp props
Speed, knots: 23. **Range, miles:** 2000 at 16 kts
Complement: 25 (4 officers)
Missiles: SSM: Fitted for 8 Aerospatiale SS 12M; wire-guided to 5.5 km *(3 nm)* subsonic; warhead 30 kg.
Guns: 2 Bofors 40 mm/70; 85° elevation; 300 rounds/minute to 12.8 km *(7 nm)*; weight of shell 0.96 kg.

Comment: *L'Audacieux* ordered in September 1974. Laid down on 10 February 1975, launched on 31 October 1975. Similar to Bizerte class in Tunisia. Planned to be modernised, probably in France.

4 RIVER PATROL CRAFT

Displacement, tons: 8 full load
Dimensions, feet (metres): 36.4 × 11.5 × 3.3 *(11.1 × 3.5 × 1)*
Main machinery: 2 diesels; 900 hp(m) *(661 kW)*; 2 shafts
Speed, knots: 30
Complement: 6
Guns: 1—7.62 mm MG.

Comment: Simmoneau SM 36 type delivered in early 1991.

30 RIVER PATROL CRAFT

PR 01-30

Displacement, tons: 12 full load
Dimensions, feet (metres): 38 × 12.5 × 3.2 *(11.6 × 3.8 × 1)*
Main machinery: 2 Stewart and Stevenson 6V-92 MTAB diesels; 880 hp *(656 kW)* sustained; 2 shafts
Speed, knots: 32. **Range, miles:** 210 at 20 kts
Complement: 4
Guns: 2—12.7 mm MGs. 2—7.62 mm MGs.

Comment: Built by Swiftships and supplied under the US Military Assistance Programme. First 10 delivered in March 1987, second 10 in September 1987 and the remainder by the end of 1987. Ten of the craft are used by the gendarmerie.

LAND-BASED MARITIME AIRCRAFT

Numbers/Type: 3 Dornier Do 128-6MPA.
Operational speed: 165 kts *(305 km/h)*.
Service ceiling: 32 600 ft *(9335 m)*.
Range: 790 nm *(1460 km)*.
Role/Weapon systems: Sole MR assets with short-range EEZ protection and coastal surveillance. Sensors: MEL Marec radar. Weapons: Unarmed.

MISCELLANEOUS

2 LCMs

BETIKA **BIBUNDI**

Comment: *Betika* built by Carena, Abidjan, Ivory Coast and refitted in 1987. *Bibundi* built by Tanguy Marine, France in 1982/83. Both are 56 ft *(17.1 m)* in length and have a speed of 10 kts.

5 LCVP

INDÉPENDANCE **REUNIFICATION** **SOUELLABA** **MACHTIGAL** **MANOKA**

Comment: Built by Ateliers et Chantiers de l'Afrique Equatoriale, Libreville, Gabon except *Souellaba* at A.C.R.E., Libreville. Of 11 tons and 10 kts.

3 RAIDER CRAFT

Comment: Supplied by Napco Int in 1987. 19.7 or 23 ft *(6 or 7 m)* in length Boston Whaler Type with twin 140 hp *(104 kW)* outboards giving a speed of 40 kts and a range in excess of 200 miles. Fitted for two 12.7 mm machine guns.

1 TUG

GRAND BATANGA

Comment: Completed by La Manche Dieppe 30 October 1985. Of 96.4 × 29.5 × 12.1 ft *(29.4 × 9 × 3.7 m)*. Fitted with 2 Sacha AGO diesels; 2000 hp(m) *(1.47 MW)*. Speed 12.8 kts.

8 AUXILIARIES

Comment: *Tornade* and *Ouragan*—built in 1966. *St Sylvestre*—built in 1967. *Mungo* operated by Transport Ministry. *Dr Jamot* operated by Health Ministry. *Sanaga* and *Bimbia* harbour launches. *Nyong* at 218 grt buoy tender was built by Cassens, Emden and delivered in December 1990.

CANADA

Headquarters' Appointments

Chief of Defence Staff:
General A J G D de Chastelain, CMM
Deputy Chief of Defence Staff:
Vice Admiral R E George, CMM
Chief of Maritime Doctrine and Operations:
Rear Admiral L Mason
Assistant Deputy Minister (Policy):
Rear Admiral L E Murray, OMM

Senior Appointments

Commander, Maritime Command:
Vice Admiral J R Anderson, CMM
Chief of Staff, Maritime Command:
Rear Admiral R C Waller, OMM
Commander, Maritime Forces, Pacific:
Rear Admiral P W Cairns

Diplomatic Representation

Naval Adviser, London:
Captain (N) E E Davie
Naval Attaché, Moscow:
Commander R M Williams
Naval Attaché, Washington:
Commodore Eion E Lawder

Establishment

The Royal Canadian Navy (RCN) was officially established on 4 May 1910, when Royal Assent was given to the Naval Service Act. On 1 February 1968 the Canadian Forces Reorganisation Act unified the three branches of the Canadian Forces and the title 'Royal Canadian Navy' was dropped.

Personnel

(a) 1992: 17 100 (Maritime Forces)
(b) 4000 reserves

Prefix to Ships' Names

HMCS

Bases

Halifax and Esquimalt

Fleet Deployment

Atlantic:
1st Destroyer Squadron (Operational East Coast ships)
5th Destroyer Squadron (Ships under refit, trials and work up)
3 Oberon class submarines
Protecteur, Preserver
Diving Support Vessel *Cormorant*

Pacific:
2nd Destroyer Squadron (2 Improved Restigouche class, 1 Annapolis class and 1 Tribal)
4th Destroyer Squadron (4 Mackenzie class)
Provider

Strength of the Fleet

Type	*Active*	*Building (Projected)*
Submarines (Patrol)	3 (1)	(6)
Destroyers	4	—
Frigates	15	10
MCM Vessels	2	12
Operational Support Ships	3	—
Diving Support Ship	1	—
Patrol Vessels	7	—
Gate Vessels	5	—
Yacht	1	—
Research Vessels	3	—
Transport Oiler, small	1	—
Tenders	8	—
Tugs	11	—
Torpedo and Ship Ranging Vessels	4	—
Naval Reserve Unit Tenders	17	(2)

Mercantile Marine

Lloyd's Register of Shipping:
1204 vessels of 2 684 614 tons gross

Maritime Air Group (MAG)

Commander MAG (Chief of Staff (Air) Marcom)—based in Halifax

Squadron/ Unit	*Base*	*Aircraft*	*Function*
VU 32	Shearwater, NS	Silver Star, Twin Huey	Utility
VU 33	Comox, BC	Silver Star	MR/Utility
MP 404	Greenwood, NS	Aurora/ Arcturus	LRMP/ Training
MP 405	Greenwood, NS	Aurora	LRMP
HT 406	Shearwater, NS	Sea King	Training
MP 407	Comox, BC	Aurora	LRMP
MP 415	Greenwood, NS	Aurora	LRMP
HS 423	Shearwater, NS	Sea King	ASW
HS 443	Shearwater, NS	Sea King	ASW
HOTEF	Shearwater, NS	Sea King	Test
MPEU	Greenwood, NS	Aurora	Test

Notes

(a) Detachments from HS 423 and HS 443 meet ships' needs.

(b) No 420 ARS is an Air Reserve Group (ARG) formation under the operational control of Maritime Air Group.

(c) In addition there are the maritime search and rescue squadrons (nos 413, 442) and units (No 103) of Air Transport Group (ATG).

(d) The Silver Star is a Canadair-built T-33.

(e) The Department of National Defence is currently in contract with European Helicopter Industries (Canada) for the replacement of the Sea King fleet with EH 101s.

(f) HS 443 provides a four helicopter detachment in support of Pacific Fleet operations.

DELETIONS

Frigates

1989 *Assiniboine* (harbour training ship)
1990 *Saguenay*
1992 *Margaree*

Research Vessels

1990 *Bluethroat*

Tenders

1990 *Wildwood*
1991 *Songhee, Nimpkish, Ehkoli,* YPT 4

PENNANT LIST

Submarines

SS 72	Ojibwa
SS 73	Onondaga
SS 74	Okanagan

Destroyers

DDH 280	Iroquois
DDH 281	Huron
DDH 282	Athabaskan
DDH 283	Algonquin

Frigates

DDH 207	Skeena
DDH 229	Ottawa
DDH 233	Fraser
DD 236	Gatineau
DD 257	Restigouche
DD 258	Kootenay
DD 259	Terra Nova
DD 261	Mackenzie
DD 262	Saskatchewan
DD 263	Yukon
DD 264	Qu'Appelle
DDH 265	Annapolis
DDH 266	Nipigon
FFH 330	Halifax
FFH 331	Vancouver
FFH 332	Ville de Québec (building)
FFH 333	Toronto (building)
FFH 334	Regina (building)
FFH 335	Calgary (building)
FFH 336	Montreal (building)
FFH 337	Fredericton (building)
FFH 338	Winnipeg (building)
FFH 339	Charlottetown (building)
FFH 340	St John's (building)
FFH 341	Ottawa (building)

Operational Support Ships

AOR 508	Provider
AOR 509	Protecteur
AOR 510	Preserver

Diving Support Ship

ASL 20	Cormorant

Patrol Vessels

PB 140	Fort Steele
PB 159	Fundy
PB 160	Chignecto
PB 161	Thunder
PB 162	Cowichan
PB 163	Miramichi
PB 164	Chaleur

Minesweepers

MSA 110	Anticosti
MSA 112	Moresby

Gate Vessels

YNG 180	Porte St Jean
YNG 183	Porte St Louis
YNG 184	Porte de la Reine
YNG 185	Porte Quebec
YNG 186	Porte Dauphine

Sail Training Ship

YAC 3	Oriole

Research Vessels

AGOR 171	Endeavour
AGOR 172	Quest
AG 121	Riverton

Transport Oiler

AOTL 502	Dundurn

Tenders

YDT	6, 8, 9, 10, 11, 12
YTR 561	Firebird
YTR 562	Firebrand

Tugs

ATA 531	Saint Anthony
ATA 533	Saint Charles
YTB 640	Glendyne
YTB 641	Glendale
YTB 643	Glenbrook
YTL 583	Beamsville
YTL 590	Lawrenceville
YTL 591	Parksville
YTL 592	Listerville
YTL 593	Merrickville
YTL 594	Marysville

TSRVs

YPT 610	Sechelt
YPT 611	Sikanni
YPT 612	Sooke
YPT 613	Stikine

Naval Reserve Unit Tenders

YDT 2	Caribou
PB 141	Rally
PB 142	Rapid
PB 191	Adversus
PB 193	Captor
PB 194	Acadian
PB 195	Sydney
PB 196	Nicholson
PB 197	Crossbow
PB 198	Service
PB 199	Standoff
YFL 104	Pogo
YTL 578	Cavalier
YTL 582	Burrard
YTL 586	Queensville
YTL 587	Plainsville
YTL 588	Youville
YTL 589	Loganville

SUBMARINES

Note: (a) The revised schedule for replacement submarines is to contract out Project Definition in late 1992, with a start being made on construction in 1996 and an in service date of 2001. Air independent propulsion is being investigated.

(b) Ex-British *Olympus* was purchased in August 1989 and is used for alongside training in Halifax.

3 OBERON CLASS (PATROL SUBMARINES)

Name	*No*	*Builders*	*Laid down*	*Launched*	*Commissioned*
OJIBWA (ex-*Onyx*)	72	HM Dockyard, Chatham	27 Sep 1962	29 Feb 1964	23 Sep 1965
ONONDAGA	73	HM Dockyard, Chatham	18 June 1964	25 Sep 1965	22 June 1967
OKANAGAN	74	HM Dockyard, Chatham	25 Mar 1965	17 Sep 1966	22 June 1968

Displacement, tons: 2030 surfaced; 2410 dived
Dimensions, feet (metres): 295.2 × 26.5 × 18 *(90 × 8.1 × 5.5)*
Main machinery: Diesel-electric; 2 ASR 16 VVS-ASR1 diesels; 3680 hp *(2.74 MW)*; 2 AEI motors; 6000 hp *(4.48 MW)*; 2 shafts
Speed, knots: 12 surfaced; 17 dived; 10 snorting
Range, miles: 9000 surfaced at 12 kts
Complement: 65 (7 officers)

Torpedoes: 6—21 in *(533 mm)* bow tubes. 20 Gould Mk 48 Mod 4; dual purpose; active/passive homing to 50 km *(27 nm)*/38 km *(21 nm)* at 40/55 kts; warhead 267 kg.
Countermeasures: ESM: Radar warning.
Fire control: Singer Librascope TFCS with Sperry UYK 20 computer.
Radars: Navigation: Kelvin Hughes Type 1006; I band.
Sonars: Plessey Triton Type 2051 or Type 187C *(Ojibwa)*; hull-mounted; passive/active search and attack; medium frequency.
BAC Type 2007; flank array; passive search; long range; low frequency.
BQG 501 Sperry Micropuffs; passive ranging.
Hermes Electronics/MUSL towed arrays to be fitted from 1993.

Programmes: In 1962 the Ministry of National Defence announced that Canada was to buy three Oberon class submarines in the UK. The first of these patrol submarines was obtained by the Canadian Government from the Royal Navy construction programme. She was laid down as *Onyx* but launched as *Ojibwa*. The other two were Canadian orders. There were some design changes to meet specific new needs including installation of RCN communications equipment and increase of air-conditioning capacity to meet the wide extremes of climate encountered in Canadian operating areas. All are to have their service lives extended until the end of the century.

ONANDAGA (new bow sonar) 5/1991

Modernisation: All underwent SOUP (Submarine Operational Update Project) with more modern sonar and fire control equipment fitted. *Ojibwa* 1980-82, *Onondaga* 1982-84 and *Okanagan* 1984-86. Starting in 1987 weapon launching and fire control systems were upgraded to take the US Mk 48 torpedo which replaced the Mk 37. Plessey Triton Type 2051 sonar purchased in 1989 and is being fitted to replace Type 187C. Trials have been done with towed array sonars in *Onondaga* and it is intended to fit all three submarines starting with *Okanagan* in 1993.
Structure: Diving depth, 200 m *(656 ft)*. Stern tubes have been blanked off.

DESTROYERS

4 TRIBAL CLASS

Name	*No*	*Builders*	*Laid down*	*Launched*	*Commissioned*
IROQUOIS	280	Marine Industries Ltd, Sorel	15 Jan 1969	28 Nov 1970	29 July 1972
HURON	281	Marine Industries Ltd, Sorel	15 Jan 1969	3 Apr 1971	16 Dec 1972
ATHABASKAN	282	Davie S B Co, Lauzon	1 June 1969	27 Nov 1970	30 Nov 1972
ALGONQUIN	283	Davie S B Co, Lauzon	1 Sep 1969	23 Apr 1971	30 Sep 1973

Displacement, tons: 5100 full load (4700 *Huron*)
Dimensions, feet (metres): 398 wl; 426 oa × 50 × 15.5 keel/21.5 screws *(121.4; 129.8 × 15.2 × 4.7/6.6)*
Main machinery: COGOG; 2 Pratt & Whitney FT4A2 gas turbines; 50 000 hp *(37 MW)*; 2 Pratt & Whitney FT12AH3 *(Huron)*; 7400 hp *(5.5 MW)*; 2 GM Allison 570-KF gas turbines (remainder); 12 700 hp *(9.5 MW)* sustained; 2 shafts; cp props
Speed, knots: 29+. **Range, miles:** 4500 at 20 kts
Complement: 255 (23 officers) plus aircrew 30 (11 officers); 245 *(Huron)* (20 officers) plus aircrew 40 (7 officers)

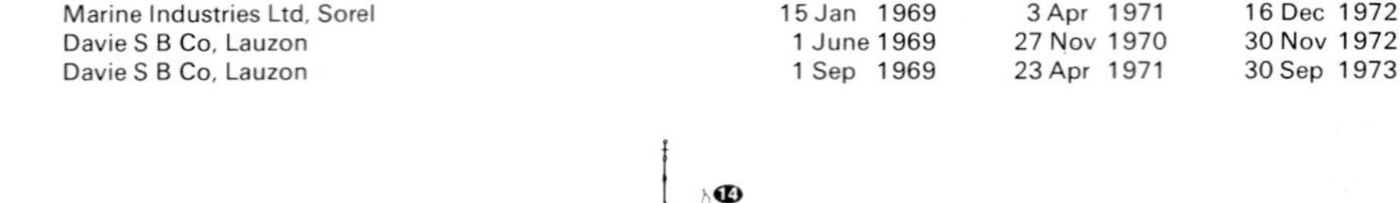

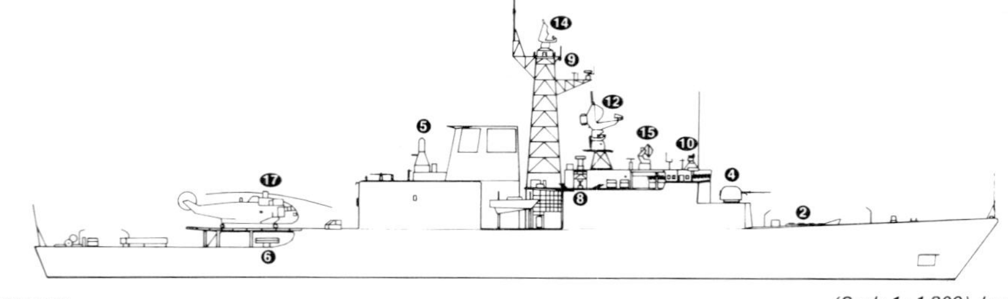

ALGONQUIN *(Scale 1 : 1 200), Ian Sturton*

Missiles: SAM: 2 Raytheon Sea Sparrow quad launchers *(Huron)* ❶; semi-active radar homing to 14.6 km *(8 nm)* at 2.5 Mach; warhead 39 kg; 32 missiles.
1 Martin Marietta Mk 41 VLS ❷ for 29 GDC Standard SM-2MR (remainder); command/inertial guidance; semi active radar homing to 73 km *(40 nm)* at 2 Mach.
Guns: 1 OTO Melara 5 in *(127 mm)*/54 *(Huron)* ❸; 85° elevation; 45 rounds/minute to 16 km *(8.7 nm)*; weight of shell 32 kg.
1 OTO Melara 3 in *(76 mm)*/62 Super Rapid (remainder) ❹; 85° elevation; 120 rounds/minute to 16 km *(8.7 nm)*; weight of shell 6 kg.
1 General Electric/General Dynamics 20 mm/76 6-barrelled Vulcan Phalanx Mk 15 ❺; 3000 rounds/minute combined to 1.5 km.
Torpedoes: 6—324 mm Mk 32 (2 triple) tubes ❻. Honeywell Mk 46; anti-submarine; active/passive homing to 11 km *(5.9 nm)* at 40 kts; warhead 44 kg.
Countermeasures: Decoys: 2 Vickers Knebworth Corvus 8-tubed trainable launchers *(Huron)* ❼. Plessey P4 Chaff rockets fired in distraction or centroid modes.
2 Plessey Shield 6-tubed trainable launchers (remainder) ❽. SLQ 25 Nixie; torpedo decoy.
ESM: MEL SLQ 504 Canews ❾; radar warning.
ECM: ULQ-6; jammer.
Combat data systems: Litton CCS 280 *(Huron)*. SHINPADS (remainder), automated data handling with UYQ-504 and UYK-505 processors. Links 11 and 14. WSC-IV and SSR-1 SATCOM.
Fire control: GFCS Mk 60 *(Huron)*. Signaal WM 25 (remainder) including LIROD 8 ❿ optronic director. SAR-8 IRSTD may be fitted in due course.
Radars: Air search: SPS 501 (LW 03 antenna) *(Huron)* ⓫; D band.
Signaal LW 08 (remainder) ⓬; D band.
Surface search/navigation: SMA SPQ 2D *(Huron)* ⓭; I band.
Signaal DA 08 (remainder) ⓮; E/F band.
Fire control: Two Signaal WM 22 *(Huron)* ⓯; I/J band.
Two Signaal STIR 1.8 (remainder) ⓰; I/J band.
Tacan: URN 25.
Sonars: Westinghouse SQS 505; combined VDS and hull-mounted; active search and attack; 7 kHz.
Westinghouse SQS 501; hull-mounted; bottom target classification; high frequency.

Helicopters: 2 CH-124A Sea King ASW ⓱ (see *Operational*).

ALGONQUIN (post TRUMP) *7/1991, Canadian Forces*

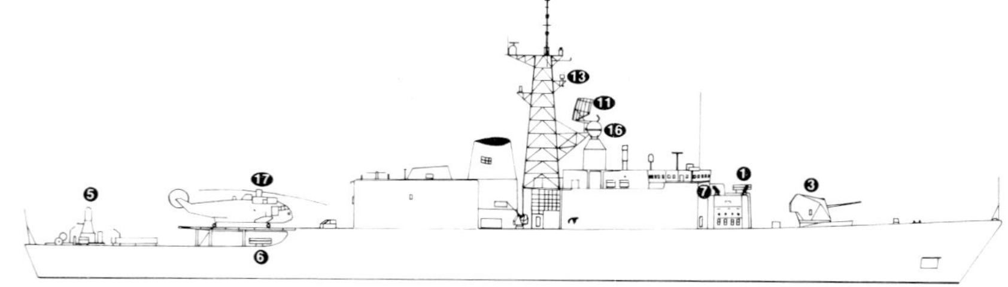

HURON *(Scale 1 : 1 200), Ian Sturton*

Modernisation: A contract for the Tribal Class Update and Modernisation Project (TRUMP) was awarded to Litton Systems Canada Limited in June 1986. The modernisation gives the ships an area air defence capability provided by Standard SM-2 (MR) missiles fired from a Mk 41 Vertical Launch System (VLS). Other equipment fitted includes: OTO Melara 76 mm Super Rapid gun; Phalanx CIWS; Signaal WM 25 FCS including LIROD 8 optronic director, ATMS automatic tracking and management system (SHINPADS) and two STIR tracking radars; LW-08 and DA-08 radars; inertial navigation; and, an infra-red suppression device fitted in the new single funnel. EW systems include new Plessey Shield Chaff and IR launch systems and MEL Canews ESM. The ASW capability provided by two helicopters and shipboard torpedoes is retained with a new sonobuoy processor system but towed arrays are not fitted. Some machinery noise suppression improvements are made. The new equipment reflects the changing role of the ship and replaces systems that did not meet the air defence requirement. *Algonquin* started modernisation in November 1987 at Mil Davie, Quebec, and completed 11 October 1991, followed by *Iroquois*, started November 1988, and should complete in 1992. *Athabaskan* entered the yard on 30 September 1991 and is scheduled to complete in mid-1994. *Huron* is planned to start in mid-1992. The Navy took over as prime contractor for the TRUMP programme on 30 September 1991.
Structure: These ships are also fitted with a landing deck equipped with double hauldown and Beartrap, flume type anti-rolling tanks to stabilise the ships at low speed, pre-wetting system to counter radio-active fallout, enclosed citadel, and bridge control of machinery. The flume type anti-roll tanks are replaced during modernisation with a water displaced fuel system.
Operational: *Huron* is the only unmodernised ship still in commission in early 1992 and she still has the Gulf fit which includes the Limbo mortar replaced by Phalanx CIWS and Blowpipe and Shorts Javelin SAM systems in both shoulder-launched and lightweight versions. Additionally both helicopters can carry 12.7 mm MGs and ESM instead of ASW gear.

HURON *7/1991, 92 Wing RAAF*

FRIGATES

2 + 10 HALIFAX CLASS (FFH)

Name	*No*	*Builders*	*Laid down*	*Launched*	*Completed*	*Commissioned*
HALIFAX	330	St John S B Ltd, New Brunswick	19 Mar 1987	30 Apr 1988	28 June 1991	July 1992
VANCOUVER	331	St John S B Ltd, New Brunswick	19 May 1988	8 July 1989	June 1992	1992
VILLE DE QUÉBEC	332	Marine Industries Ltd, Sorel	17 Jan 1989	16 May 1991	Mar 1993	1993
TORONTO	333	St John S B Ltd, New Brunswick	24 Apr 1989	18 Dec 1990	Dec 1992	1992
REGINA	334	Marine Industries Ltd, Sorel	6 Oct 1989	May 1992	Dec 1993	1993
CALGARY	335	Marine Industries Ltd, Sorel	15 June 1991	May 1993	Sep 1994	1994
MONTREAL	336	St John S B Ltd, New Brunswick	8 Feb 1991	28 Feb 1992	Sep 1993	1993
FREDERICTON	337	St John S B Ltd, New Brunswick	29 Apr 1992	Nov 1992	May 1994	1994
WINNIPEG	338	St John S B Ltd, New Brunswick	Nov 1992	Aug 1993	Jan 1995	1995
CHARLOTTETOWN	339	St John S B Ltd, New Brunswick	Aug 1993	Apr 1994	Sep 1995	1995
ST JOHN'S	340	St John S B Ltd, New Brunswick	Apr 1994	Dec 1994	Mar 1996	1996
OTTAWA	341	St John S B Ltd, New Brunswick	Dec 1994	Aug 1995	Sep 1996	1997

Displacement, tons: 5235 full load
Dimensions, feet (metres): 440 oa; 408.5 pp × 53.8 × 16.1 *(134.1; 124.5 × 16.4 × 4.9)*
Main machinery: CODOG; 2 GE LM 2500 gas turbines; 46 000 hp *(34.3 MW)* sustained
1 SEMT-Pielstick 20 PA6-V280 diesel; 8000 hp(m) *(5.9 MW)* sustained; 2 shafts; cp props
Speed, knots: 28. **Range, miles:** 7100 at 15 kts (diesel); 4500 at 15 kts (gas)
Complement: 225

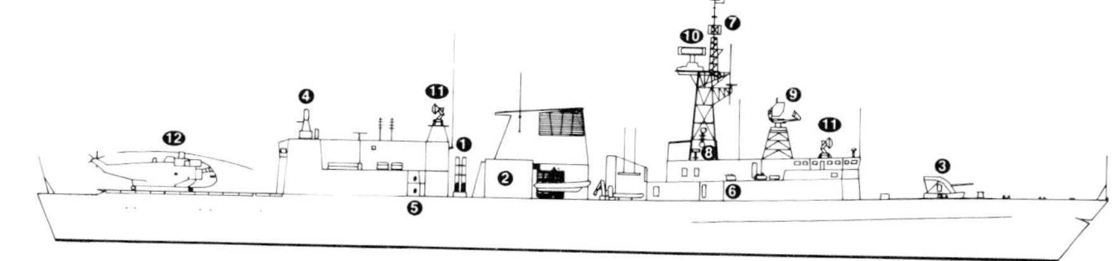

HALIFAX

(Scale 1 : 1 200), Ian Sturton

Missiles: SSM: 8 McDonnell Douglas Harpoon Block 1C (2 quad) launchers ❶; active radar homing to 130 km *(70 nm)* at 0.9 Mach; warhead 227 kg.
SAM: 2 Raytheon Sea Sparrow Mk 48 octuple vertical launchers ❷; semi-active radar homing to 14.6 km *(8 nm)* at 2.5 Mach; warhead 39 kg; 28 missiles (16 normally carried).
Guns: 1 Bofors 57 mm/70 Mk 2 ❸; 77° elevation; 220 rounds/minute to 17 km *(9 nm)*; weight of shell 2.4 kg.
1 GE/GDC 20 mm Vulcan Phalanx Mk 16 Mod 1 ❹; anti-missile; 3000 rounds/minute (6 barrels combined) to 1.5 km.
8—12.7 mm MGs.
Torpedoes: 4—324 mm Mk 32 Mod 9 (2 twin) tubes ❺. 24 Honeywell Mk 46 Mod I or Mod 5; anti-submarine; active/passive homing to 11 km *(5.9 nm)* at 40 kts; warhead 44 kg.
Countermeasures: Decoys: 4 Plessey Shield decoy launchers ❻; triple mountings; fires P8 Chaff and P6 IR flares in distraction, decoy or centroid modes.
Nixie SLQ 25; towed acoustic decoy.
ESM: MEL/Lockheed Canews SLQ 504 ❼; radar intercept; (0.5-18 GHz).
ECM: MEL/Lockheed Ramses SLQ 503 ❽; jammer.
Combat data systems: SHINPADS action data automation with UYQ-504 and UYK-505 or 507 (336-341) processors. Links 11 and 14.
Fire control: Spar Aerospace SAR 8 IRSTD (infra red search and target designation) to be fitted in due course. SWG-1(V) for Harpoon. CDC UYS 503(V); sonobuoy processing system.
Radars: Air search: Raytheon SPS 49(V)5 ❾; C/D band; range 457 km *(250 nm)*.
Air/surface search: Ericsson Sea Giraffe HC 150 ❿; G band; range 40 km *(21.6 nm)* against missiles in clear conditions.
Fire control: Two Signaal VM 25 STIR ⓫; K/I band; range 140 km *(76 nm)* for 1 m² target.
Navigation: Sperry Mk 340; I band.
Tacan: URN 25. IFF Mk XII.
Sonars: Westinghouse SQS 505(V)6; hull-mounted; active search and attack; medium frequency.
CDC SQR 501 CANTASS towed array (uses part of Martin Marietta SQR 19 TACTASS).

Helicopters: 1 CH 124A Sea King ASW ⓬ or 1 EH 101.

HALIFAX

9/1991, Giorgio Arra

Programmes: On 29 June 1983 St John Shipbuilding Ltd won the long running competition for the first six of a new class of patrol frigates to be assisted by Paramax Electronics Inc of Montreal, a subsidiary of Unisys Co (formerly Sperry). Three were subcontracted to Marine Industries Ltd in Lauzon and Sorel. On 18 December 1987 six additional ships of the same design were ordered from St John S.B. Ltd with delivery by 1997. Sometimes referred to as the City class. *Halifax* started sea trials 6 August 1990. There have been problems keeping to the planned construction programme. Legal action taken by SJSL to cancel the MIL contract in 1991.
Structure: Plans to lengthen some of the class to increase SAM capacity and improve accommodation have been shelved which means there is limited reserve for mid-life modernisation. Much effort has gone into stealth technology. Gas turbine engines are raft mounted. Female accomodation is provided. It is claimed there is more equipment per cubic volume of space than in any other comparable NATO frigate.
Operational: Problems on first of class trials have included higher than designed radiated noise levels which are reported as speed associated.

HALIFAX

9/1991, Giorgio Arra

2 ANNAPOLIS CLASS

Name	*No*	*Builders*	*Laid down*	*Launched*	*Commissioned*
ANNAPOLIS	265	Halifax Shipyards Ltd, Halifax	July 1960	27 Apr 1963	19 Dec 1964
NIPIGON	266	Marine Industries Ltd, Sorel	Apr 1960	10 Dec 1961	30 May 1964

Displacement, tons: 2400 standard; 2930 full load
Dimensions, feet (metres): 371 × 42 × 14.4 *(113.1 × 12.8 × 4.4)*
Main machinery: 2 Babcock & Wilcox boilers; 600 psi *(43.3 kg/cm sq)*; 850°F *(454°C)*; 2 English Electric turbines; 30 000 hp *(22.4 MW)*; 2 shafts
Speed, knots: 28 (30 on trials). **Range, miles:** 4570 at 14 kts
Complement: 210 (11 officers)

Guns: 2 FMC 3 in *(76 mm)*/50 Mk 33 (twin) ❶; 85° elevation; 50 rounds/minute to 12.8 km *(7 nm)*; weight of shell 6 kg.
Torpedoes: 6—324 mm Mk 32 (2 triple) tubes ❷. Honeywell Mk 46; anti-submarine; active/passive homing to 11 km *(5.9 nm)* at 40 kts; warhead 44 kg.
Countermeasures: Decoys: 4 Loral Hycor SRBOC; Chaff and IR flares to 4 km *(2.2 nm)*.
ESM: MEL Canews; radar warning; 0.5-18 GHz.
Combat data systems: Litton ADLIPS automated tactical data handling; Links 11 and 14.
Fire control: GFCS Mk 60.
Radars: Air/surface search: Marconi SPS 503 (CMR 1820) ❸; E/F band; range 128 km *(70 nm)*.
Surface search: Raytheon/Sylvania SPS 10 ❹; G band.
Fire control: Bell SPG 48 ❺; I/J band.
Tacan: URN 25.
Sonars: Westinghouse SQS 505; hull-mounted; active search and attack; 7 kHz.
SQS 501; hull-mounted; bottom target classification; high frequency.
CDC SQR 501 CANTASS; trials towed array; passive; very low frequency. Uses part of SQR-19.

Helicopters: 1 CH-124A Sea King ASW ❻.

Programmes: Officially classified as DDH. These two ships represented the logical development of the original St Laurent class, through the Restigouche and Mackenzie designs.
Modernisation: A full Delex (Destroyer Life Extension Programme) took place in 1982-85 including new air radar, GFC, communications, sonar and EW equipment. Extension until 1994-96. Both ships fitted with a trials CANTASS vice VDS in 1987/88.
Operational: *Annapolis* is based in the Pacific Fleet.

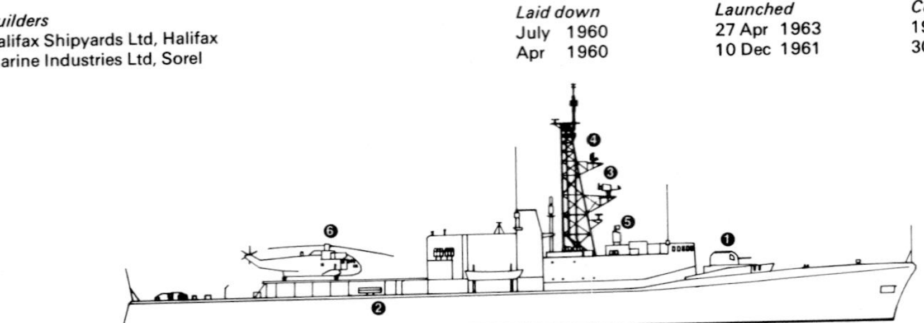
ANNAPOLIS (Towed Array) *(Scale 1 : 1 200), Ian Sturton*

NIPIGON *11/1991, Harald Carstens*

4 MACKENZIE CLASS

Name	*No*	*Builders*	*Laid down*	*Launched*	*Commissioned*
MACKENZIE	261	Canadian Vickers Ltd, Montreal	15 Dec 1958	25 May 1961	6 Oct 1962
SASKATCHEWAN	262	Victoria Machinery (and Yarrows Ltd)	16 July 1959	1 Feb 1961	16 Feb 1963
YUKON	263	Burrard Dry Dock & Shipbuilding	25 Oct 1959	27 July 1961	25 May 1963
QU'APPELLE	264	Davie Shipbuilding & Repairing	14 Jan 1960	2 May 1962	14 Sep 1963

Displacement, tons: 2380 standard; 2880 full load
Dimensions, feet (metres): 366 × 42 × 13.5 *(111.6 × 12.8 × 4.1)*
Main machinery: 2 Babcock & Wilcox boilers; 600 psi *(43.3 kg/cm sq)*; 850°F *(454°C)*; 2 English Electric turbines; 30 000 hp *(22.4 MW)*; 2 shafts
Speed, knots: 28. **Range, miles:** 4750 at 14 kts
Complement: 210 (11 officers)

Guns: 2 Vickers 3 in *(76 mm)*/70 Mk 6 mounting (twin) (not in *Qu'Appelle*) ❶; 90° elevation; 90 rounds/minute to 17 km *(9 nm)*; weight of shell 7 kg.
2 FMC 3 in *(76 mm)*/50 Mk 33 mounting (twin) (second mounting fwd in *Qu'Appelle*) ❷; 85° elevation; 50 rounds/minute to 12.8 km *(7 nm)*; weight of shell 6 kg.
Torpedoes: 6—324 mm Mk 32 (2 triple) tubes ❸. Honeywell Mk 46; anti-submarine; active/passive homing to 11 km *(5.9 nm)* at 40 kts; warhead 44 kg.
Countermeasures: ESM: WLR 1; radar warning.
Combat data systems: Litton ADLIPS; automated tactical data handling; Links 11 and 14.
Fire control: GFCS Mk 69. GFCS Mk 63.

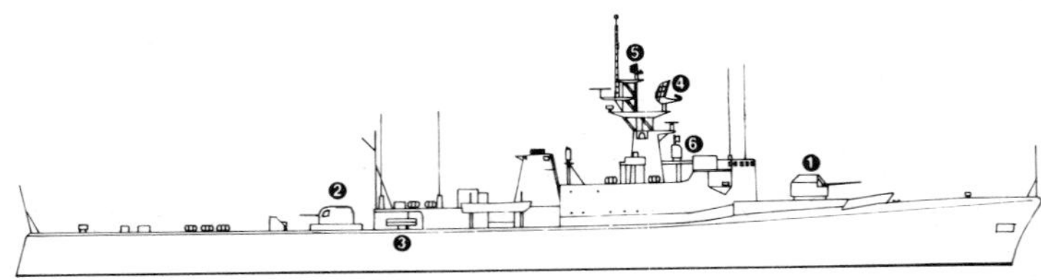
MACKENZIE *(Scale 1 : 1 200), Ian Sturton*

Radars: Air search: RCA SPS 12 ❹; D band; range 119 km *(65 nm)*.
Surface search: Raytheon SPS 10 ❺; G band.
Fire control: SPG 48 ❻; I/J band.
SPG 34; I/J band.
Sonars: Westinghouse SQS 505; combined VDS and hull-mounted; active search and attack; medium frequency.
SQS 501; hull-mounted; bottom target classification; high frequency.

Programmes: Officially classified as DD.
Modernisation: All modernised at Esquimalt by Burrard/Yarrow Inc under Delex (Destroyer Life Extension Programme) 1982-85 including improved sonar and communications, and modifications to SPS 12 radar. Extension until 1993 but may be further extended.
Operational: All based in the Pacific Fleet.

SASKATCHEWAN *10/1991, John Mortimer*

4 IMPROVED RESTIGOUCHE CLASS

Name	No	Builders	Laid down	Launched	Commissioned
GATINEAU	236	Davie Shipbuilding & Repairing	30 Apr 1953	3 June 1957	17 Feb 1959
RESTIGOUCHE	257	Canadian Vickers, Montreal	15 July 1953	22 Nov 1954	7 June 1958
KOOTENAY	258	Burrard Dry Dock & Shipbuilding	21 Aug 1952	15 June 1954	7 Mar 1959
TERRA NOVA	259	Victoria Machinery Depot Co	14 Nov 1952	21 June 1955	6 June 1959

Displacement, tons: 2390 standard; 2900 full load
Dimensions, feet (metres): 371 × 42 × 14.1 *(113.1 × 12.8 × 4.3)*
Main machinery: 2 Babcock & Wilcox boilers; 600 psi *(43.3 kg/cm sq)*; 850°F *(454°C)*; 2 English Electric turbines; 30 000 hp *(22.4 MW)*; 2 shafts
Speed, knots: 28. **Range, miles:** 4750 at 14 kts
Complement: 214 (13 officers)

Missiles: SSM: 8 McDonnell Douglas Harpoon 2 quad launchers ❶ (*Terra Nova* and *Restigouche*); active radar homing to 130 km *(70 nm)* at 0.9 Mach; warhead 227 kg.
A/S: Honeywell ASROC Mk 112 octuple launcher ❷ (*Gatineau* and *Kootenay*); 8 reloads; inertial guidance to 1.6-10 km *(1-5.4 nm)*; payload Mk 46 torpedo. Replaced by 8 Harpoon during Gulf deployments.
Guns: 2 Vickers 3 in *(76 mm)*/70 (twin) Mk 6 ❸; dual purpose; 90° elevation; 90 rounds/minute to 17 km *(9 nm)*; weight of shell 7 kg.
1 GE/GD 20 mm/76 6-barrelled Vulcan Phalanx Mk 15 (modified) ❹ (*Terra Nova* and *Restigouche*); 3000 rounds/minute combined to 1.5 km.
2 Bofors 40 mm/60 ❺ (*Terra Nova* and *Restigouche*).
Torpedoes: 6—324 mm Mk 32 (2 triple) tubes ❻. Honeywell Mk 46; anti-submarine; active/passive homing to 11 km *(5.9 nm)* at 40 kts; warhead 44 kg.
A/S mortars: 1 Limbo Mk 10 (3 tubed) ❼ (*Gatineau* and *Kootenay*); range 1000 m; warhead 92 kg.
Countermeasures: Decoys: 4 Loral Hycor SRBOC Mk 36 ❽; 4 launchers with 4 fixed barrels firing Chaff decoys and IR flares to 4 km *(2.2 nm)*. Plessey Shield Chaff launchers (*Terra Nova* and *Restigouche*).
ESM: Canews ❾; radar warning.
ECM: ULQ-6; jammer.
Combat data systems: Litton ADLIPS; automated data handling; Links 11 and 14. SATCOM ❿ (*Terra Nova* and *Restigouche*).
Fire control: GFCS Mk 69.
Radars: Air search: Marconi SPS 503 (CMR 1820) ⓫; E/F band; range 128 km *(70 nm)*.
Surface search: Raytheon SPS 10 ⓬; G band.
Navigation: Decca 127E; I band.
Fire control: Bell SPG 48 ⓭; I/J band.
Tacan: URN 25.
Sonars: Westinghouse SQS 505; combined VDS and hull-mounted; active search and attack; 7 kHz.
C-Tech mine avoidance active.
SQS 501; hull-mounted; bottom target classification; high frequency.

Programmes: Officially classified as DD.

Modernisation: These four ships were first refitted with ASROC aft and lattice foremast. Work included removing the after 3 in/50 twin gun mounting and one Limbo A/S Mk 10 triple mortar, to make way for ASROC and variable depth sonar. Refits also included improvements to communications fit and completed 1968-73. Three other ships of the class were paid off without being refitted. All four modernised again under Delex programme 1983-86 with new air radar, GFCS, communications and EW equipment. The Bofors rocket launcher replaced by Super RBOC and Tacan fitted on a pole mast replacing the top section of the lattice mast. Triple Mark 32 torpedo tubes fitted. For operational deployments *Terra Nova* and *Restigouche* have had the ASROC launcher replaced by 8 Harpoon SSM, the Limbo Mk 10 by Phalanx, and the ships boats by two single Bofors 40 mm/60.

Operational: *Restigouche* and *Kootenay* based in the Pacific Fleet. *Columbia* (paid off in 1974) is used as a harbour training ship at Esquimalt. Additional 12.7 mm MGs can be carried plus Blowpipe and Javelin shoulder-launched SAM.

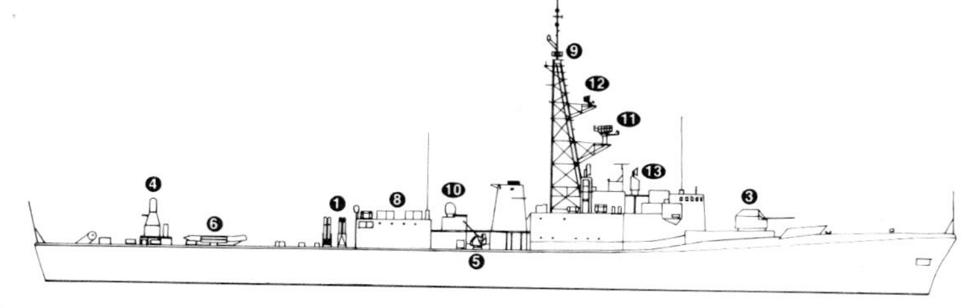

TERRA NOVA (Scale 1 : 1 200), Ian Sturton

RESTIGOUCHE 7/1991, Guy Toremans

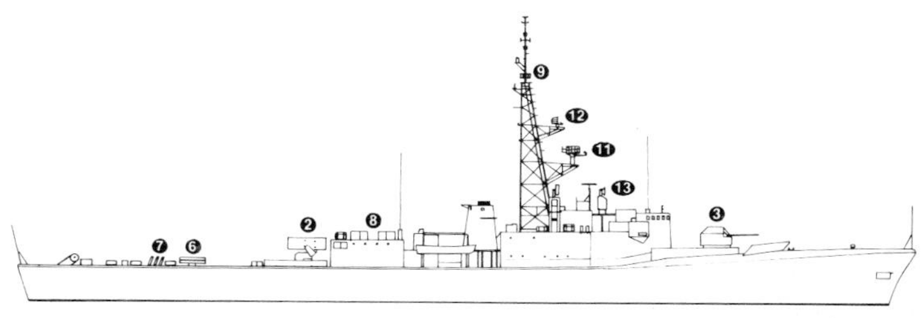

GATINEAU (Scale 1 : 1 200), Ian Sturton

GATINEAU 11/1990, J. L. M. van der Burg

3 ST LAURENT CLASS

Name	No	Builders	Laid down	Launched	Commissioned
SKEENA	207	Burrard Dry Dock & Shipbuilding	1 June 1951	19 Aug 1952	30 Mar 1957
OTTAWA	229	Canadian Vickers Ltd, Montreal	8 June 1951	29 Apr 1953	10 Nov 1956
FRASER	233	Yarrows Ltd, Esquimalt, BC	11 Dec 1951	19 Feb 1953	28 June1957

Displacement, tons: 2260 standard; 3051 full load (after conversion)
Dimensions, feet (metres): 366 × 42 × 14 (hull) *(111.6 × 12.8 × 5.4)*
Main machinery: 2 Babcock & Wilcox boilers; 600 psi *(43.3 kg/cm sq)*; 850°F *(454°C)*; 2 English Electric turbines; 30 000 hp *(22.4 MW)*; 2 shafts
Speed, knots: 27. **Range, miles:** 4570 at 12 kts
Complement: 213 (16 officers) plus 20 aircrew (7 officers)

Guns: 2 FMC 3 in *(76 mm)*/50 Mk 33 (twin) ❶; dual purpose; 85° elevation; 50 rounds/minute to 12.8 km *(7 nm)*; weight of shell 6 kg.
Torpedoes: 6—324 mm Mk 32 (2 triple) tubes ❷. Honeywell Mk 46; anti-submarine; active/passive homing to 11 km *(5.9 nm)* at 40 kts; warhead 44 kg. A few Mk 44 torpedoes are still in service.
A/S mortars: 1 Limbo Mk 10 (3 tubed) ❸; automatic loading; range 1000 m; warhead 92 kg (see *Structure*).
Countermeasures: ESM: WLR 1; radar warning.
Fire control: GFCS Mk 63.
Radars: Air search: RCA SPS 12 ❹; D band; range 119 km *(65 nm)*.
Surface search: Raytheon SPS 10 ❺; G band.
Fire control: Bell SPG 48; I/J band.
Navigation: Sperry Mk II; I band.
Tacan: URN 20 ❻.
Sonars: SQS 503; hull-mounted; active search and attack; medium frequency.
SQS 504; VDS; active search; medium frequency; or SQR 19 (wet end only in *Fraser*) towed array.
SQS 502; hull-mounted; active attack (mortar control); high frequency.
SQS 501; hull-mounted; bottom target classification; high frequency.

Helicopters: 1 CH-124A Sea King ASW ❼.

Programmes: Officially classified as DDH. The first major warships to be designed in Canada.
Modernisation: All modernised under Delex programme 1979-84 although no new sensors were included. Towed array sonar fitted to *Fraser* in 1988.
Structure: Twin funnels were fitted to permit fwd extension of the helicopter hangar. Fitted with fin stabilisers. Gunhouses are of glass fibre. In providing helicopter platforms and hangars it was possible to retain only one 3-barrelled Limbo mortar although this is inoperative when towed array is carried. *Fraser* has lattice radar-mast between the funnels for Tacan aerial. All other ships have this aerial on a pole mast.
Operational: *Assiniboine* paid off in 1989 and is used as a harbour training ship at Halifax. *Margaree* decommissioned in mid-1992 and the remaining ships of the class are planned to decommission in the early 1990s.

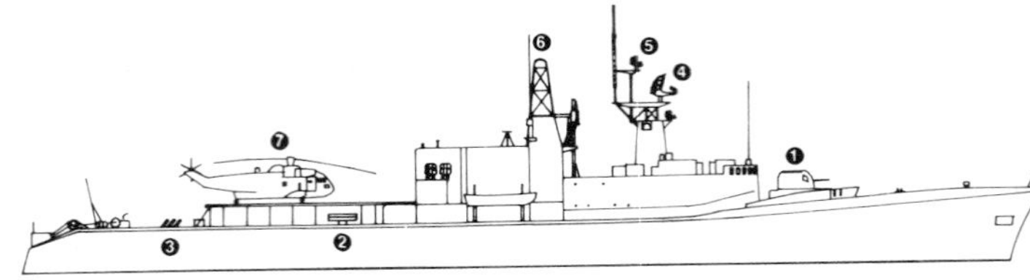
FRASER *(Scale 1 : 1 200), Ian Sturton*

FRASER *10/1988, Maritime Photographic*

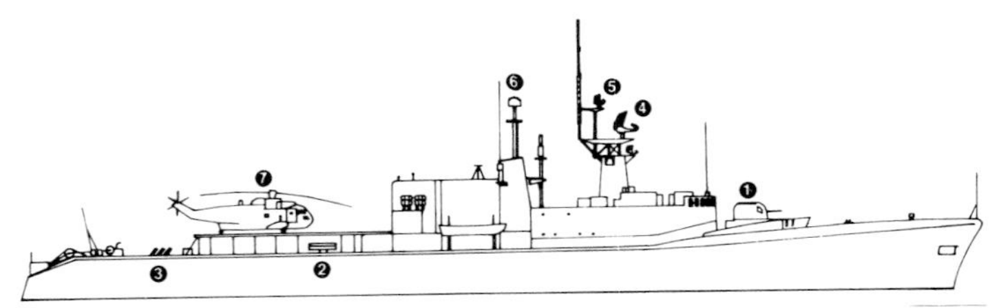
OTTAWA *(Scale 1 : 1 200), Ian Sturton*

SKEENA *9/1990, van Ginderen Collection*

OPERATIONAL SUPPORT SHIPS

ame	No	Builders	Laid down	Launched	Commissioned
ROTECTEUR	AOR 509	St John Dry Dock Co Ltd, NB	17 Oct 1967	18 July 1968	30 Aug 1969
RESERVER	AOR 510	St John Dry Dock Co Ltd, NB	17 Oct 1967	29 May 1969	30 July 1970

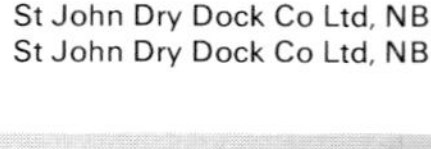

isplacement, tons: 8380 light; 24 700 full load
imensions, feet (metres): 564 × 76 × 30 *(171.9 × 23.2 × 9.1)*
lain machinery: 2 boilers; 1 GE Canada turbine; 21 000 hp *(15.7 MW)*; 1 shaft; bow thruster
peed, knots: 21. Range, miles: 4100 at 20 kts; 7500 at 11.5 kts
omplement: 290 (28 officers)
argo capacity: 13 700 tons fuel; 400 tons aviation fuel; 1048 tons dry cargo; 1250 tons ammunition; 2 cranes (15 ton lift)
uns: 2 FMC 3 in *(76 mm)*/50 Mk 33 (twin). Mounted in the bow and under local control it was removed from both ships in 1983 but replaced in *Protecteur* in 1990 and *Preserver* in 1992.
2 Vulcan Phalanx and 2 Bofors 40/60 fitted in *Protecteur* in 1990 and *Preserver* in 1992.
ountermeasures: Decoys: 4 Plessey Shield Chaff launchers.
SM: Racal Kestrel SLQ 504; radar warning.
ombat data systems: ADLIPS with Link 11; SATCOM WSC-3(V).
adars: Surface search: SPS 502 with Mk XII IFF.
avigation: Sperry Mk II. Racal Decca TM 969; I band.
acan: URN 20.
onars: Westinghouse SQS 505; hull-mounted; active search; 7 kHz.
C-Tech mine avoidance for Gulf.
elicopters: 3 CH-124A Sea King ASW (see *Comment*).

PROTECTEUR *8/1990, G. Toremans*

omment: An improved design based on the prototype *Provider*. Four replenishment positions. Both have been used as Flagships and troop carriers. They can carry anti-submarine helicopters, military vehicles and bulk equipment for sealift purposes; also four LCVPs. Both for, and as a result of, Gulf deployments, the 76 mm gun was replaced, two Vulcan Phalanx and two Bofors 40/60 guns fitted and 4 Plessey Shield Chaff launchers and ESM equipment provided. Additionally all helicopters carried 12.7 mm MGs and ESM equipment instead of ASW gear. The positioning of the weapon systems may be changed in *Preserver* (completed refit in early 1992) and in *Protecteur* during her next refit which starts in late 1992.

ame	No	Builders	Laid down	Launched	Commissioned
ROVIDER	AOR 508	Davie Shipbuilding Ltd, Lauzon	1 May 1961	5 July 1962	28 Sep 1963

isplacement, tons: 7300 light; 22 000 full load
imensions, feet (metres): 555 × 76 × 32 *(169.2 × 23.2 × 9.8)*
lain machinery: 2 boilers; 1 GE Canada steam turbine; 21 000 hp *(15.7 MW)*; 1 shaft
peed, knots: 21. Range, miles: 3600 at 20 kts
omplement: 166 (15 officers)
argo capacity: 12 000 tons fuel; 900 tons aviation fuel; 250 tons dry cargo
ountermeasures: ESM: Racal Kestrel SLQ 504; radar warning.
ombat data systems: ADLIPS with Link 11; SATCOM WSC-3(V).
adars: Navigation: Racal Decca TM 969; I band.
elicopters: 3 CH-124A Sea King ASW.

omment: The flight deck can receive the largest and heaviest helicopters. A total of 20 electro-hydraulic winches are fitted on deck for ship-to-ship movements of cargo and supplies, as well as shore-to-ship requirements when alongside. Based in the Pacific Fleet. Can be fitted with Bofors and Vulcan Phalanx guns, Chaff and ESM if sent on operational deployments.

PROVIDER *10/1991, John Mortimer*

DUN CLASS TANKER

UNDURN AOTL 502 (ex-AOC 502)

isplacement, tons: 950 light; 1500 full load
imensions, feet (metres): 178.8 × 32.2 × 13 *(54.5 × 9.8 × 3.9)*
lain machinery: 1 Fairbanks-Morse 38D8-1/8-4 diesel; 708 hp *(528 kW)*; 1 shaft
peed, knots: 10
omplement: 24
argo capacity: 790 tons fuel; 25 tons dry cargo

omment: Small tanker, classed as fleet auxiliary.

UNDURN *1985, Sgt John Smith CF*

FLEET DIVING SUPPORT SHIP

Name	No	Builder	Commissioned
CORMORANT (ex-*Aspa Quarto*)	ASL 20	Marelli, Italy	10 Nov 1978 (CAF)

Displacement, tons: 2350 full load
Dimensions, feet (metres): 245 × 39 × 16.5 *(74.7 × 11.9 × 5)*
Main machinery: Diesel-electric; 3 Marelli-Deutz ACR 12456 EV diesels; 1800 hp(m) *(1.32 MW)*; 1 shaft; cp prop
Speed, knots: 14. **Range, miles:** 13 000 at 12 kts
Complement: 74
Radars: Navigation: Two Decca 1229; I band.

Comment: Ex-Italian stern trawler bought in 1975 which underwent maintenance and design modification until 1977. She was then taken in hand for conversion by Davie Shipbuilding Ltd, Lauzon, returning to Halifax a year later to commission. She carries two SDL-1 submersibles in a heated hangar and is capable of conducting mixed gas diving operations to 328.1 ft *(100 m)*. The SDL-1 is a manned untethered craft capable of operations to 2001.4 ft *(610 m)* with a lock-out compartment for divers. Several high frequency sonic devices are fitted. This was the first RCN ship to carry women crew members in 1980.

CORMORANT *1990, van Ginderen Collection*

SHIPBORNE AIRCRAFT

Numbers/Type: 32 Sikorsky CH-124A Sea King.
Operational speed: 125 kts *(230 km/h)*.
Service ceiling: 10 500 ft *(3200 m)*.
Range: 630 nm *(1165 km)*.
Role/Weapon systems: ASW and Support helicopter; carried by larger ASW escorts; 280 class has 2 × CH-124A embarked for ASW and surface search. Update being carried out for those earmarked for Halifax class. To be replaced by EH 101 in due course; contract expected in 1991-92. Sensors: APS 503 search radar, sonobuoys, ASQ-13 dipping sonar. Some modified for Jez. Six modified for Gulf operations including FLIR, APR-39, ALE 37 Chaff dispenser, ALQ144 IR countermeasures. Weapons: ASW; up to 4 × Mk 46 torpedoes or 4 × Mk 11 depth bombs.

SEA KING *(Nipigon)* *8/1991, Antonio Moreno*

LAND-BASED MARITIME AIRCRAFT (FRONT LINE)

Numbers/Type: 18/3 Lockheed CP-140 Aurora/P-3C Arcturus.
Operational speed: 410 kts *(760 km/h)*.
Service ceiling: 28 300 ft *(8625 m)*.
Range: 4000 nm *(7410 km)*.
Role/Weapon systems: Aurora operated for long-range maritime surveillance on Atlantic and Pacific Oceans; roles include ASW/ASV and SAR; three Arcturus ordered 1989 for unarmed High Arctic patrol. Sensors: APS-116 radar, IFF, ESM, ECM, DIFAR processor, ASQ-81 MAD, OL 5004 processor.

MINE WARFARE FORCES

2 MINESWEEPERS AUXILIARY (MSA)

Name	*No*	*Builders*	*Commissioned*
ANTICOSTI (ex-*Jean Tide*)	MSA 110	Allied SB, Vancouver	Sep 1973
MORESBY (ex-*Joyce Tide*)	MSA 112	Allied SB, Vancouver	Apr 1973

Displacement, tons: 2205 full load
Dimensions, feet (metres): 191 × 43 × 17 *(58.2 × 13.1 × 5.2)*
Main machinery: 4 Nohab Polar SF 16RS diesels; 4600 hp(m) *(3.38 MW)*; 2 shafts; Gil Jet bow thruster; 575 hp *(429 kW)*
Speed, knots: 13.5. **Range, miles:** 12 000 at 13 kts
Complement: 18 (5 officers)
Guns: 2—7.62 mm MGs.
Countermeasures: MCM: BAJ Mk 9 mechanical sweep with WSMF (monitoring equipment).
Radars: Navigation: 2 Racal Decca; I band.
Sonars: Side scan towed VDS; high frequency.

Comment: Former offshore towing/supply vessels Ice class 3, suitable for navigation in light ice. Purchased in March 1988 and commissioned 7 May 1989. Mechanical sweeps, sonar, Hyperfix and PINS 9000 navigation system completed fitting in mid-1991. Mixed crews of Regulars and Reservists. They will operate until the MCDV vessels start to enter service in 1995.

MORESBY *8/1991, Canadian Forces*

0 + 12 MARITIME COASTAL DEFENCE VESSELS (MCDV)

Displacement, tons: 962 full load
Dimensions, feet (metres): 180.4 × 37.1 × 11.2 *(55 × 11.3 × 3.4)*
Main machinery: Diesel-electric; 3000 hp(m) *(2.2 MW)*; 2 shafts; 2 azimuth thrusters
Speed, knots: 15. **Range, miles:** 5000 at 12 kts
Complement: 37
Guns: 1 Bofors 40 mm/60. 2—12.7 mm MGs.
Countermeasures: MCM: Mechanical, acoustic and magnetic sweep gear. 2 ROVs.
Radars: Surface search: E/F band.
Navigation: I band.
Sonars: Towfish sidescan; high frequency; for route survey.

Comment: Tenders requested 31 August 1988. Contract awarded to Fenco Engineers on 2 Octob 1991. The design is by German Marine, Dartmouth and the ships are to be built b Halifax-Dartmouth Industries starting in 1993 for a first of class delivery in 1995. Thomson-CSF a to provide combat system support. The vessels are to combine MCM capabilities with gener patrol duties and will be stationed on both coasts and in the St Lawrence. Reserve manpower is be increased from 6500 to 8500 to allow continuous operation on both coasts.

MCDV (artist impression) *1991, Canadian Forc*

SAIL TRAINING SHIP

Name	*No*	*Builders*	*Launched*
ORIOLE	YAC 3	Owens	4 June 1921

Displacement, tons: 78.2 full load
Dimensions, feet (metres): 102 × 19 × 9 *(31.1 × 5.8 × 2.7)*
Main machinery: 1 Cummins diesel; 165 hp *(123 kW)*; 1 shaft
Speed, knots: 8
Complement: 24 (2 officers)

Comment: Commissioned in the Navy in 1948 and based at Esquimalt. Sail area (with spinnake 11 000 sq ft. Height of mainmast 94 ft *(28.7 m)*, mizzen 55.2 ft *(16.8 m)*. Usually cruises with 1 trainee officers at a time.

PATROL VESSELS

Note: There are plans for a new 46 m coastal patrol vessel.

1 FORT CLASS PATROL VESSEL (PB)

Name	*No*	*Builders*	*Commissione*
FORT STEELE	PB 140	Canadian S B and Eng Co	Nov 1955

Displacement, tons: 85
Dimensions, feet (metres): 118 × 21 × 7 *(36 × 6.4 × 2.1)*
Main machinery: 2 Paxman Ventura 12 YJCM diesels; 3000 hp *(2.24 MW)*; 2 shafts; KaMeWa c props
Speed, knots: 18. **Range, miles:** 1200 at 16 kts
Complement: 16

Comment: Steel hull aluminium superstructure. Twin rudders. Acquired by DND in 1973 fro RCMP—acts as Reserve Training ship based at Halifax.

FORT STEELE *11/1989, van Ginderen Collectio*

6 BAY CLASS Ex-MSC (PB)

Name	No	Builders	Commissioned
FUNDY	PB 159	Davie Shipbuilding Co, Lauzon	27 Nov 1956
CHIGNECTO	PB 160	Davie Shipbuilding Co, Lauzon	1 Aug 1957
THUNDER	PB 161	Port Arthur S B Co	3 Oct 1957
COWICHAN	PB 162	Yarrows Ltd, Esquimalt	19 Dec 1957
MIRAMICHI	PB 163	Victoria Machinery Depot Co	28 Oct 1957
CHALEUR	PB 164	Marine Industries Ltd, Sorel	12 Sep 1957

Displacement, tons: 370 standard; 470 full load
Dimensions, feet (metres): 164 × 30.2 × 9.2 *(50 × 9.2 × 2.8)*
Main machinery: 2 GM 12-278A diesels; 2400 hp *(1.79 MW)*; 2 shafts
Speed, knots: 15. **Range, miles:** 4500 at 11 kts
Complement: 35 (4 officers)
Guns: 1 Bofors 40 mm/60 (fitted for but not with).
Radars: Surface Search: Racal Decca; I band.

Comment: Wooden hulls with aluminium frames and decks. There were originally 20 vessels of this class of which six were transferred to France, four to Turkey and four sold commercially. Named after Canadian straits and bays. Designation changed from AMC to MCB in 1954. They were redesignated as Patrol Escorts (small) (PF) in 1972, being used as training ships and PB from 1979.

THUNDER *7/1987, van Ginderen Collection*

5 PORTE CLASS (GATE VESSELS)

Name	No	Builders	Commissioned
PORTE ST JEAN	YNG 180	Geo T Davie, Lauzon	4 June 1952
PORTE ST LOUIS	YNG 183	Geo T Davie, Lauzon	28 Aug 1952
PORTE DE LA REINE	YNG 184	Victoria Machinery	19 Sep 1952
PORTE QUEBEC	YNG 185	Burrard Dry Dock	7 Oct 1952
PORTE DAUPHINE	YNG 186	Ferguson Ind.	12 Dec 1952

Displacement, tons: 429 full load
Dimensions, feet (metres): 125.5 × 26.3 × 13 *(38.3 × 8 × 4)*
Main machinery: Diesel-electric; 1 Fairbanks-Morse 38D8-1/8-6 diesel generator; 724 kW; 1 shaft
Speed, knots: 11. **Range, miles:** 4000 at 10 kts
Complement: 23 (3 officers)
Radars: Navigation: Racal Decca; I band.

Comment: Of trawler design. Multi-purpose vessels used for operating gates in A/S booms, fleet auxiliaries, anti-submarine netlayers for entrances to defended harbours. Can be fitted for minesweeping. First four used during summer for training Reserves. *Porte Dauphine* was re-acquired from DOT in 1974 and employed on West Coast with *Porte de la Reine* and *Porte Quebec*.

PORTE DE LA REINE *1989, van Ginderen Collection*

RESEARCH VESSELS

Name	No	Builders	Commissioned
QUEST	AGOR 172	Burrard Dry Dock Co, Vancouver	21 Aug 1969

Displacement, tons: 2130
Dimensions, feet (metres): 235 × 42 × 15.5 *(71.6 × 12.8 × 4.6)*
Main machinery: Diesel-electric; 4 Fairbanks-Morse 38D8-1/8-9 diesel generators; 4.36 MW; 2 shafts; cp props
Speed, knots: 16. **Range, miles:** 10 000 at 12 kts
Complement: 55
Helicopters: Platform only.

Comment: Built for the Naval Research Establishment of the Defence Research Board for acoustic, hydrographic and general oceanographic work. Capable of operating in heavy ice in the company of an icebreaker. Launched on 9 July 1968. Based at Halifax and does line array acoustic research in the straits of the northern archipelago.

QUEST *1986, Canadian Forces*

Name	No	Builders	Commissioned
ENDEAVOUR	AGOR 171	Yarrows Ltd, Esquimalt, BC	9 Mar 1965

Displacement, tons: 1560
Dimensions, feet (metres): 236 × 38.5 × 13 *(71.9 × 11.7 × 4)*
Main machinery: Diesel-electric; 4 Fairbanks-Morse 38D8-1/8-9 diesel generators; 4.36 MW; 2 shafts; cp props
Speed, knots: 16. **Range, miles:** 10 000 at 12 kts
Complement: 50 (10 officers, 13 scientists, 2 aircrew)
Helicopters: 1 light.

Comment: A naval research ship designed primarily for anti-submarine research. Flight deck 48 × 31 ft *(14.6 × 9.4 m)*. Stiffened for operating in ice-covered areas. Able to turn in 2.5 times her own length. Two 9 ton Austin-Weston telescopic cranes are fitted. There are two oceanographical winches each holding 5000 fathoms of wire, two bathythermograph winches and a deep-sea anchoring and coring winch. She has acoustic insulation in her machinery spaces.

ENDEAVOUR *1990, Canadian Forces*

Name	No	Builders	Commissioned
RIVERTON (ex-*Smit-Lloyd* 112)	AG 121	De Waal, Netherlands	1975

Displacement, tons: 2563 full load
Dimensions, feet (metres): 209 × 43.5 × 16.5 *(63.9 × 13.3 × 5.1)*
Main machinery: 2 6TM-410 Stork-Werkspoor diesels; 10 100 hp(m) *(17.42 MW)*; 2 shafts; Koort nozzle bow thrusters
Speed, knots: 15.5. **Range, miles:** 13 000 at 12 kts
Complement: 10 (5 officers) plus 16 scientists

Comment: An offshore supply and support vessel acquired 3 March 1989 for conversion to a general purpose auxiliary research and support ship. Replaced *Bluethroat* in mid-1990 and used for the CPF first of class trials.

RIVERTON *1991, Canadian Forces*

SUPPORT VESSELS AND TENDERS

8 NAVAL RESERVE TENDERS

RALLY	PB 141	**ACADIAN**	PB 194
RAPID	PB 142	**SYDNEY**	PB 195
ADVERSUS	PB 191	**NICHOLSON**	PB 196
CAPTOR	PB 193	**STANDOFF**	PB 199

Displacement, tons: 48 full load (191-195); 85 (196 and 199); 105 (141-142)
Main machinery: 2 Paxman YJCM diesels; 2800 hp *(2.1 MW)*; 2 shafts
Speed, knots: 16. **Range, miles:** 900 at 13 kts
Complement: 18

Comment: 141 and 142 are R class described in Coast Guard section and based in Halifax. Sister ships *Racer* and *Ready* were deleted from the Coast Guard in 1991 but there has been no confirmation that they have been taken on by the Navy. 191 to 195, completed by Smith and Rhulorel, Lunenburg, NS in 1968 transferred from RCMP in 1975 and 196 and 199 in 1976 and 1980 respectively.

CAPTOR *1991, van Ginderen Collection*

4 TORPEDO AND SHIP RANGING VESSELS (TSRV)

Name	*No*	*Builders*	*Commissioned*
SECHELT	YPT 610	West Coast Manly	10 Nov 1990
SIKANNI	YPT 611	West Coast Manly	10 Nov 1990
SOOKE	YPT 612	West Coast Manly	10 Nov 1990
STIKINE	YPT 613	West Coast Manly	10 Nov 1990

Displacement, tons: 290 full load
Dimensions, feet (metres): 108.5 × 27.8 × 7.8 *(33.1 × 8.5 × 2.4)*
Main machinery: 2 Caterpillar 3412 diesels; 1342 hp *(1.1 MW)* sustained; 2 shafts
Speed, knots: 12.5
Complement: 4

Comment: Based at the Nanoose Bay Maritime Experimental and Test Range. Replaced the 1940s vintage TRVs.

SECHELT *1991, Canadian Forces*

7 VILLE CLASS (OLD)

Name	*No*	*Builders*	*Commissioned*
CAVALIER (ex-*Listerville*)	YTL 578	Russel Bros	12 Oct 1944
BURRARD (ex-*Lawrenceville*)	YTL 582	Russel Bros	8 Jan 1944
BEAMSVILLE	YTL 583	Russel Bros	16 Jan 1944
QUEENSVILLE	YTL 586	Russel Bros	5 Dec 1944
PLAINSVILLE	YTL 587	Russel Bros	23 Nov 1944
YOUVILLE	YTL 588	Russel Bros	5 Dec 1944
LOGANVILLE	YTL 589	Russel Bros	13 Dec 1944

Dimensions, feet (metres): 40 × 10.5 × 4.8 *(12.2 × 3.2 × 1.5)*
Main machinery: Diesel; 150 hp *(112 kW)*; 1 shaft

Comment: Small harbour tugs. All except *Beamsville* used for Reserve training.

6 DIVING TENDERS

YDT 6, 8, 9, 10, 11, 12

Displacement, tons: 70; 110 (YDT 11-12)
Main machinery: 2 GM diesels; 165 hp *(123 kW)* (228 hp *(170 kW)* in YDT 11-12); 2 shafts
Speed, knots: 11
Complement: 23 (3 officers)

Comment: Can operate four divers at a time to 75 m. Recompression chamber. Ex-Diving Tender YDT 2 *Caribou* of 46 ft *(14 m)* is used for sea-cadet training.

TUGS

2 SAINT CLASS

Name	*No*	*Builders*	*Commissioned*
SAINT ANTHONY	ATA 531	St John Dry Dock Co	22 Feb 1957
SAINT CHARLES	ATA 533	St John Dry Dock Co	7 June 1957

Displacement, tons: 840
Dimensions, feet (metres): 151.5 × 33 × 17 *(46.2 × 10 × 5.2)*
Main machinery: Diesel; 1920 hp *(1.43 MW)*; 1 shaft
Speed, knots: 14
Complement: 21

Comment: Ocean tugs. Authorised under the 1951 Programme. Originally class of three. There are plans to replace them in the mid-1990s with two 1500 ton support vessels.

3 GLEN CLASS (HARBOUR/COASTAL)

Name	*No*	*Builders*	*Commissioned*
GLENDYNE	YTB 640	Yarrows, Esquimalt	8 Aug 1975
GLENDALE	YTB 641	Yarrows, Esquimalt	16 Sep 1975
GLENBROOK	YTB 643	Georgetown S Y, PEI	16 Dec 1976

Displacement, tons: 255
Dimensions, feet (metres): 92.5 × 28 × 14.5 *(28.2 × 8.5 × 4.4)*
Main machinery: 2 diesels; 1300 hp *(970 kW)*; 2 Voith-Schneider props
Speed, knots: 11.5
Complement: 6

Comment: Two of the class sold to McKiel Workboats in late 1980s.

5 VILLE CLASS (NEW)

Name	*No*	*Builders*	*Commissioned*
LAWRENCEVILLE	YTL 590	Vito Steel & Barge Co	17 Jan 1974
PARKSVILLE	YTL 591	Vito Steel & Barge Co	17 Jan 1974
LISTERVILLE	YTL 592	Georgetown S Y, PEI	31 July 1974
MERRICKVILLE	YTL 593	Georgetown S Y, PEI	11 Sep 1974
MARYSVILLE	YTL 594	Georgetown S Y, PEI	11 Sep 1974

Displacement, tons: 70 full load
Dimensions, feet (metres): 64 × 15.5 × 9 *(19.5 × 4.7 × 2.7)*
Main machinery: 1 Diesel; 365 hp *(272 kW)*; 1 shaft
Speed, knots: 9.8

Comment: Small harbour tugs employed at Esquimalt and Halifax.

MISCELLANEOUS

MISCELLANEOUS SERVICE CRAFT AND LAUNCHES

CROSSBOW PB 197
SERVICE PB 198
POGO YFL 104
FIREBIRD YTR 561
FIREBRAND YTR 562

Comment: The two YTRs are 130 ton firefighting craft.

COAST GUARD

Administration

Commissioner Canadian Coast Guard/Associate Deputy Minister Transport:
R A Quail

Ships

The Canadian Coast Guard comprises 122 ships and craft of all types, operating in the Atlantic and Pacific coastal waters and from the head of the Great Lakes to the northernmost reaches of Canada's Arctic. The Fleet is composed of icebreakers of various sizes, buoy tenders and lighthouse resupply vessels, specialised vessels for tasks such as search and rescue, oil pollution clean-up, submarine communication cable laying and repair, channel sounding and shallow-draught operations in areas such as the Mackenzie River system and Lake Winnipeg. In addition, the Fleet is supplemented by a wide variety of small craft such as shore-based workboats, landing craft and inflatable boats, used on all navigable waterways within Canadian waters.

Establishment

In January 1962 all ships owned and operated by the Federal Department of Transport, with the exception of pilotage and canal craft, were amalgamated into the Canadian Coast Guard Fleet. The Canadian Coast Guard is a civilian organisation and its members are public servants. Its Headquarters are in Ottawa while field operations are administered from five regional offices located in Vancouver, British Columbia; Toronto, Ontario; Quebec, Quebec; Dartmouth, Nova Scotia; and St John's, Newfoundland. The principal bases for the ships and aircraft are: St John's, Newfoundland; Dartmouth, NS; Saint John, NB; Charlottetown, PEI; Quebec and Sorel, Quebec; Prescott, Amherstburg and Parry Sound, Ontario; Victoria and Prince Rupert, BC; and Hay River, Northwest Territories.

Flag and Identity Markings

The Canadian Coast Guard has its own distinctive jack, a red maple leaf on a white ground at the hoist and two gold dolphins on a blue ground at the fly.
Canadian Coast Guard vessels have red hulls with white superstructures. The funnel is white with a red maple leaf on each side. A white diagonal stripe extends aft on the hull below the bridge on both sides. The words 'Coast Guard — Garde Côtière' appear aft of the stripe preceded by a stylised Canadian flag. The markings include the word 'Canada' on each side of the vessel near the stern. Search and Rescue vessels' superstructures are international yellow in colour.

Missions

The Canadian Coast Guard carries out the following missions:
(a) Icebreaking and Escort. Icebreaking and escort of commercial ships is carried out in waters off the Atlantic seaboard, in the Gulf of St Lawrence, St Lawrence River and the Great Lakes in winter and in Arctic waters in summer.
(b) Aids to Navigation. Installation, supply and maintenance of fixed and floating aids to navigation in Canadian waters.
(c) Organise and provide icebreaker escort to commercial shipping in support of the annual Northern Sealift which supplies bases and settlements in the Canadian Arctic, Hudson Bay and Foxe Basin.
(d) Provide and operate a wide range of marine search and rescue vessels.
(e) Provide and operate hydrographic survey and sounding vessels for the St Lawrence River Ship Channel.
(f) Provide and operate a vessel for the laying, maintenance and repair of submarine communication cables.
(g) Operate a fleet of one fixed wing aircraft and 35 helicopters primarily used for aids to navigation, ice reconnaissance when based in icebreakers, and pollution control work.

Strength of the Fleet

Type	*Active*
Heavy Icebreakers	6 + 1 (leased)
Heavy Icebreaker/Cable Ship	1
Light Icebreaker/Navaids Tenders	11
Ice Strengthened Navaids Tenders	9
Small Navaids Tenders	8
Small River Navaids Tenders	5
Offshore and Intermediate SAR Cutter	3
Ice Strengthened Offshore SAR Cutters	2
Small SAR Cutters	7
SAR Lifeboats	17
Small Ice Strengthened SAR Cutters	2
Small SAR Utility Craft	10
Training Vessel	1
Survey and Sounding Vessel	1
Total	83 + 1

(plus approximately 35 Inshore Rescue Craft)

Note: This list does not include lifeboats, surfboats, self-propelled barges and other small craft which are carried on board the larger vessels. Also excluded are shore-based workboats, floating oil spill boats, oil slick-lickers or any of the small boats which are available for use at the various Canadian Coast Guard Bases and lighthouse stations.

DELETIONS

1989 *Skidegate, Eckaloo* (old), *Alexander Mackenzie, Beauport*
1990 *William, Montmorency*
1991 *Thomas Carleton, George E Darby, Ready, Racer, John A MacDonald, Kenoki, Jackman*

HEAVY ICEBREAKERS

1 GULF CLASS (Type 1300)

Name	*No*	*Builders*	*Commissioned*
LOUIS S ST LAURENT	—	Canadian Vickers Ltd, Montreal	Oct 1969

Displacement, tons: 13 800 full load
Measurement, tons: 10 908 gross; 5370 net
Dimensions, feet (metres): 392.7 × 80.1 × 32.2 *(119.7 × 24.4 × 9.8)*
Main machinery: Diesel-electric; 5 diesel generators; 40 000 hp *(29.8 MW)*; 3 motors; 3 shafts
Speed, knots: 18
Complement: 56
Helicopters: 2 light type, such as BO 105CBS.

Comment: Launched on 3 December 1966. Larger than any of the former Coast Guard icebreakers. Helicopter hangar fitted below the flight deck, with an elevator to raise the two helicopters to the deck when required. Two 49.2 ft *(15 m)* landing craft embarked. Mid-life modernisation July 1988 to late 1992 includes replacing main engines with a diesel-electric system, adding a more efficient *Henry Larsen* type ice breaking bow (adds 8 m to length) with an air bubbler system and improving helicopter facilities with a new fixed hangar. In addition the complement is reduced to 56. Based in the Maritimes.

LOUIS S ST LAURENT *11/1990, Hemlon*

3 R CLASS (Type 1200)

Name	*No*	*Builders*	*Commissioned*
PIERRE RADISSON	—	Burrard D D Co Ltd, Vancouver, BC	June 1978
SIR JOHN FRANKLIN	—	Burrard D D Co Ltd, Vancouver, BC	Mar 1979
DES GROSEILLIERS	—	Port Weller D D Co Ltd, Ontario	Aug 1983

Displacement, tons: 6400 standard; 8180 (7594, *Des Groseilliers*) full load
Measurement, tons: 5910 gross; 1678 net
Dimensions, feet (metres): 322 × 64 × 23.6 *(98.1 × 19.5 × 7.2)*
Main machinery: Diesel-electric; 6 Montreal Loco 251V-16F diesels; 17 580 hp *(13.1 MW)*; 6 GEC generators; 11.1 MW sustained; 2 motors; 13 600 hp *(10 MW)*; 2 shafts
Speed, knots: 16. **Range, miles:** 15 000 at 13.5 kts
Complement: 59
Helicopters: 1 Bell 212.

Comment: First two ordered on 1 May 1975. *Pierre Radisson* launched on 3 June 1977, *Franklin* on 10 March 1978 and *Des Groseilliers* on 20 February 1982. *Franklin* is based at Newfoundland, the other two in the Laurentides.

PIERRE RADISSON *2/1989, van Ginderen Collection*

1 MODIFIED R CLASS (Type 1200)

Name	*No*	*Builders*	*Commissioned*
HENRY LARSEN	—	Versatile Pacific S Y, Vancouver, BC	29 June 1988

Displacement, tons: 5798 light; 8290 full load
Measurement, tons: 6172 gross; 1741 net
Dimensions, feet (metres): 327.3 × 64.6 × 24 *(99.8 × 19.7 × 7.3)*
Main machinery: Diesel-electric; 3 Wärtsilä Vasa 16V32 diesel generators; 17.13 MW/60 Hz sustained; 3 motors; 20 100 hp(m) *(14.8 MW)*; 3 shafts
Speed, knots: 16. **Range, miles:** 15 000 at 13.5 kts
Complement: 52 (15 officers) plus 20 spare berths
Helicopters: 1 Bell 212.

Comment: Contract date 25 May 1984, laid down 23 August 1985, launched 3 January 1987; she is officially designated as 'Medium Gulf/River Icebreaker'. Although similar in many ways to the R class she has a different hull form particularly at the bow and a very different propulsion system. Fitted with Wärtsilä air bubbling system which is also in the *Sir Humphrey Gilbert*. Based at Dartmouth for operations in the Maritimes.

HENRY LARSEN *3/1989, Doug Maginley*

Name	*No*	*Builders*	*Commissioned*
TERRY FOX	—	Burrard Yarrow, Vancouver	1983

Measurement, tons: 4233 gross; 1955 net
Dimensions, feet (metres): 288.7 × 58.7 × 27.2 *(88 × 17.9 × 8.3)*
Main machinery: 2 diesels; 2 shafts
Speed, knots: 15

Comment: Leased for two years from Gulf Canada Resources during the completion of *Louis S St Laurent* conversion. Commissioned in Coast Guard colours 1 November 1991. Based in the Maritimes.

Name	*No*	*Builders*	*Commissioned*
NORMAN McLEOD ROGERS	—	Canadian Vickers Ltd, Montreal	Oct 1969

Displacement, tons: 6320 full load
Measurement, tons: 4179 gross; 1847 net
Dimensions, feet (metres): 294.9 × 62.5 × 20 *(89.9 × 19.1 × 6.1)*
Main machinery: CODLAG; 4 Fairbanks-Morse 38D8-1/8-12 diesels; 8296 hp *(6.2 MW)* sustained
2 GE W-41G diesel generators; 2 gas turbine generators; 2 motors; 12 000 hp *(8.95 MW)*; 2 shafts
Speed, knots: 15. **Range, miles:** 12 000 at 12 kts
Complement: 56
Helicopters: 1 light type, such as BO 105CBS.

Comment: Type 1200 based on the West Coast.

NORMAN McLEOD ROGERS *3/1988, van Ginderen Collection*

HEAVY ICEBREAKER/CABLE SHIP

Name	*No*	*Builders*	*Commissioned*
JOHN CABOT	—	Canadian Vickers Ltd, Montreal	July 1965

Displacement, tons: 6375 full load
Measurement, tons: 5234 gross; 2069 net
Dimensions, feet (metres): 291 × 60 × 22 *(88.7 × 18.3 × 6.7)*
Main machinery: Diesel-electric; 4 Fairbanks-Morse 38D8-1/8-12 diesel generators; 5.8 MW sustained; 2 motors; 2 shafts
Speed, knots: 15. **Range, miles:** 10 000 at 12 kts
Complement: 76
Helicopters: 1 light type, such as Bell 206L.

Comment: Launched on 15 April 1964. Combination cable repair ship and icebreaker. Designed to repair and lay cable over the bow only. For use in East Coast and Arctic waters. Bow waterjet reaction manoeuvring system, heeling tanks and Flume stabilisation system. Three circular storage holds handle a total of 400 miles of submarine cable. Type 1200 based in Newfoundland.

JOHN CABOT *11/1989, van Ginderen Collection*

LIGHT ICEBREAKERS/NAVAIDS TENDERS

6 TYPE 1100

Name	No	Builders	Commissioned
MARTHA L BLACK	—	Versatile Pacific, Vancouver, BC	30 Apr 1986
GEORGE R PEARKES	—	Versatile Pacific, Vancouver, BC	17 Apr 1986
EDWARD CORNWALLIS	—	Marine Industries Ltd, Tracy, Quebec	14 Aug 1986
SIR WILLIAM ALEXANDER	—	Marine Industries Ltd, Tracy, Quebec	13 Feb 1987
SIR WILFRID LAURIER	—	Canadian Shipbuilding Ltd, Collingwood, Ontario	15 Nov 1986
ANN HARVEY	—	Halifax Industries Ltd, Halifax, NS	29 June 1987

Displacement, tons: 4662
Measurement, tons: 3818 (*Martha L Black*); 3809 (*George R Pearkes*); 3812 (*Sir Wilfrid Laurier*); 3727 (remainder) gross
Dimensions, feet (metres): 272.2 × 53.1 × 18.9 *(83 × 16.2 × 5.8)*
Main machinery: Diesel-electric; 3 Bombadier/Alco 12V-251 diesels; 8019 hp *(6 MW)* sustained; 3 Canadian GE generators; 6 MW; 2 Canadian GE motors; 8450 hp *(6.3 MW)*; 2 shafts; bow thrusters
Speed, knots: 15.5. **Range, miles:** 6500 at 15 kts
Complement: 40 plus 12 spare berths; 28 *(Ann Harvey, Edward Cornwallis)*
Helicopters: 1 light type, such as Bell 206L.

Comment: *Black, Laurier* and *Pearkes* based in the Laurentides, *Cornwallis* and *Alexander* in the Maritimes and *Ann Harvey* in Newfoundland.

SIR WILLIAM ALEXANDER *1990, Canadian Coast Guard*

ANN HARVEY *1989, R. Cotie*

2 TYPE 1050

Name	No	Builders	Commissioned
SAMUEL RISLEY	—	Vito Construction Ltd, Delta, BC	4 July 1985
EARL GREY	—	Pictou Shipyards Ltd, Pictou, NS	30 May 1986

Displacement, tons: 2935 full load
Measurement, tons: 1988 gross *(Grey)*; 1967 gross *(Risley)*; 642 net *(Grey)*; 649.5 net *(Risley)*
Dimensions, feet (metres): 228.7 × 44.9 × 17.4 *(69.7 × 13.7 × 5.3)*
Main machinery: Diesel-electric; 4 diesel generators; 2 motors; 8800 hp *(6.56 MW) (Earl Grey)*; 8970 hp *(6.7 MW) (Samuel Risley)*; 2 shafts
Speed, knots: 14.5
Complement: 24

Comment: *Risley* based in the Central Region, *Grey* in the Maritimes.

SAMUEL RISLEY *5/1990, van Ginderen Collection*

Name	No	Builders	Commissioned
GRIFFON	—	Davie Shipbuilding Ltd, Lauzon	Dec 1970

Displacement, tons: 3096
Measurement, tons: 2212 gross; 752 net
Dimensions, feet (metres): 233.9 × 49 × 15.5 *(71.3 × 14.9 × 4.7)*
Main machinery: Diesel-electric; 4 Fairbanks-Morse 38D8-1/8-12 diesel generators; 5.8 MW sustained; 2 motors; 2 shafts
Speed, knots: 14. **Range, miles:** 5500 at 10 kts
Complement: 40
Helicopters: Platform for 1 light type, such as Bell 206L.

Comment: Type 1100 based in the Central Region.

GRIFFON *1989, M. Willis*

Name	No	Builders	Commissioned
J E BERNIER	—	Davie Shipbuilding Ltd, Lauzon	Aug 1967

Displacement, tons: 3096
Measurement, tons: 2457 gross; 705 net
Dimensions, feet (metres): 231 × 49 × 16 *(70.5 × 14.9 × 4.9)*
Main machinery: Diesel-electric; 2 diesel generators; 4250 hp *(3.17 MW)*; 2 motors; 2 shafts
Speed, knots: 13.5. **Range, miles:** 8000 at 11 kts
Complement: 38
Helicopters: 1 Bell 206L/L-1.

Comment: Type 1100 based in Newfoundland.

J E BERNIER *12/1984, van Ginderen Collection*

Name	No	Builders	Commissioned
SIR HUMPHREY GILBERT	—	Davie Shipbuilding Ltd, Lauzon	June 1959

Displacement, tons: 3000 full load
Measurement, tons: 2152 gross; 728 net
Dimensions, feet (metres): 228 × 48 × 16.3 *(69.5 × 14.6 × 5)*
Main machinery: Diesel-electric; 2 diesel generators; 4250 hp *(3.17 MW)*; 2 motors; 2 shafts
Speed, knots: 13. **Range, miles:** 10 000 at 11 kts
Complement: 41
Helicopters: 1 Bell 206L/L-1.

Comment: First Canadian Coast Guard vessel to be fitted with an air-bubbling system. In 1984-85 completed a major refit which included a diesel-electric a/c-a/c propulsion system, the fitting of a new bow and a new derrick. Type 1100 based at Newfoundland.

SIR HUMPHREY GILBERT *1989, B. Briggs*

ICE STRENGTHENED NAVAIDS TENDERS

Name	*No*	*Builders*	*Commissioned*
TUPPER	—	Marine Industries Ltd, Sorel	Dec 1959
SIMON FRASER	—	Burrard Dry Dock Co Ltd, Vancouver	Feb 1960

Displacement, tons: 1375 full load
Measurement, tons: 1358 gross; 419 net
Dimensions, feet (metres): 204.5 × 42 × 15.1 *(62.4 × 12.8 × 4.6)*
Main machinery: Diesel-electric; 2 diesel generators; 2900 hp *(2.16 MW)*; 2 motors; 2 shafts
Speed, knots: 13.5. **Range, miles:** 5000 at 10 kts
Complement: 37; 25 (*Simon Fraser*)
Helicopters: Platform for 1 Bell 206L/L-1.

Comment: *Simon Fraser* is a Type 600 used primarily for SAR in the Maritimes and is more properly counted as an Offshore SAR Cutter. *Tupper* is a Type 1000 based in the Maritimes.

TUPPER *1989, R. Cotie*

Name	*No*	*Builders*	*Commissioned*
NARWHAL	—	Canadian Vickers Ltd, Montreal	July 1963

Displacement, tons: 2220 full load
Measurement, tons: 2064 gross; 935 net
Dimensions, feet (metres): 259.8 × 42 × 12.5 *(79.2 × 12.8 × 3.8)*
Main machinery: 2 Cooper-Bessemer diesels; 2000 hp *(1.49 MW)*; 2 shafts
Speed, knots: 12. **Range, miles:** 9500 at 10 kts
Complement: 38
Helicopters: 1 light type, such as BO 105CBS.

Comment: Re-engined in 1985. Helicopter deck and hangar added. Type 1000 based on the West Coast.

NARWHAL *7/1987, C. D. Maginley*

Name	*No*	*Builders*	*Commissioned*
TRACY	—	Port Weller Drydocks, Ontario	1968

Displacement, tons: 1300
Measurement, tons: 963 gross; 290 net
Dimensions, feet (metres): 181.1 × 38 × 12.1 *(55.2 × 11.6 × 3.7)*
Main machinery: Diesel-electric; 2 Fairbanks-Morse 38D8-1/8-8 diesel generators; 1.94 MW sustained; 2 motors; 2 shafts
Speed, knots: 13. **Range, miles:** 5000 at 11 kts
Complement: 30

Comment: Type 1000 based in Laurentides.

TRACY *1984, Canadian Coast Guard*

Name	*No*	*Builders*	*Commissioned*
BARTLETT	—	Marine Industries, Sorel	1969
PROVO WALLIS	—	Marine Industries, Sorel	1969

Displacement, tons: 1620
Measurement, tons: 1317 gross; 491 net
Dimensions, feet (metres): 189.3; 209 *(Provo Wallis)* × 42.5 × 19 *(57.7; 63.7 × 13 × 5.8)*
Main machinery: 2 diesels; 1760 hp *(1.3 MW)*; 2 shafts; cp props
Speed, knots: 12.5. **Range, miles:** 3300 at 11 kts
Complement: 31

Comment: Both Type 1000. *Bartlett* based in Central Region, *Wallis* in the Maritimes. *Bartlett* was modernised in 1988 and *Wallis* completed one year modernisation at Marystown, Newfoundland at the end of 1990. Work included lengthening the hull by 6 m, installing new equipment and improving accommodation.

BARTLETT *1988, Larry Ferris*

PROVO WALLIS *4/1991 Canadian Coast Guard*

Name	*No*	*Builders*	*Commissioned*
SIMCOE	—	Canadian Vickers Ltd, Montreal	1962

Displacement, tons: 1300 full load
Measurement, tons: 961 gross; 361 net
Dimensions, feet (metres): 179.1 × 38 × 12.5 *(54.6 × 11.6 × 3.8)*
Main machinery: Diesel-electric; 2 diesel generators; 2000 hp *(1.49 MW)*; 2 motors; 2 shafts
Speed, knots: 13. **Range, miles:** 5000 at 10 kts
Complement: 32

Comment: Type 1000 based in Central Region.

SIMCOE *10/1989, van Ginderen Collection*

Name	*No*	*Builders*	*Commissioned*
SIR JAMES DOUGLAS	—	Burrard Dry Dock Co Ltd	Nov 1956

Measurement, tons: 564 gross; 173 net
Dimensions, feet (metres): 149.6 × 30.8 × 10.5 *(45.6 × 9.4 × 3.2)*
Main machinery: 2 diesels; 850 hp *(634 kW)*; 2 shafts
Speed, knots: 12
Complement: 31

Comment: Type 900 based in the Central Region. Probably in reserve.

Name	*No*	*Builders*	*Commissioned*
MONTMAGNY	—	Russel Bros, Owen Sound, Ontario	May 1963

Displacement, tons: 565 full load
Measurement, tons: 497 gross; 195 net
Dimensions, feet (metres): 148 × 28.9 × 8.5 *(45.1 × 8.8 × 2.6)*
Main machinery: Diesel; 1000 hp *(746 kW)*; 2 shafts
Speed, knots: 12
Complement: 23

Comment: Type 900 based in Laurentides. To be paid off in April 1994.

MONTMAGNY *6/1986, van Ginderen Collection*

SHIPBORNE AIRCRAFT

Numbers/Type: 6 Bell 206B JetRanger.
Operational speed: 115 kts *(213 km/h)*.
Service ceiling: 13 500 ft *(4115 m)*.
Range: 368 nm *(682 km)*.
Role/Weapon systems: Liaison and limited SAR helicopter. Sensors: None. Weapons: None.

Numbers/Type: 5/2 Bell 206L/206L-1 LongRanger.
Operational speed: 108 kts *(200 km/h)*.
Service ceiling: 19 000 ft *(5795 m)*.
Range: 304 nm *(563 km)*.
Role/Weapon systems: Liaison and limited SAR. Sensors: None. Weapons: None.

Numbers/Type: 5 Bell 212.
Operational speed: 100 kts *(185 km/h)*.
Service ceiling: 13 200 ft *(4023 m)*.
Range: 224 nm *(415 km)*.
Role/Weapon systems: Liaison and medium support helicopter. Sensors: None. Weapons: None.

Numbers/Type: 16 MBB BO 105CBS.
Operational speed: 110 kts *(204 km/h)*.
Service ceiling: 20 000 ft *(6090 m)*.
Range: 278 nm *(515 km)*.
Role/Weapon systems: Liaison, SAR and shipborne reconnaissance duties; replaces older single-engined types. Sensors: None. Weapons: None.

BO 105 *1991*

Numbers/Type: 1 Sikorsky S-61N.
Operational speed: 121 kts *(224 km/h)*.
Service ceiling: 12 500 ft *(3810 m)*.
Range: 440 nm *(815 km)*.
Role/Weapon systems: Based on West Coast for long-range SAR and navigational aids. Sensors: Bendix search radar. Weapons: None.

OFFSHORE AND INTERMEDIATE SEARCH AND RESCUE CUTTER

Name	*No*	*Builders*	*Commissioned*
ALERT	—	Davie Shipbuilding Ltd, Lauzon	1969

Displacement, tons: 2025
Measurement, tons: 1752 gross; 495 net
Dimensions, feet (metres): 234.3 × 39.7 × 16.1 *(71.4 × 12.1 × 4.9)*
Main machinery: Diesel-electric; 2 diesel generators; 7874 hp *(5.9 MW)*; 2 shafts
Speed, knots: 18.5
Complement: 25
Helicopters: 1 light type, such as BO 105CBS.

Comment: Type 600 Offshore cutter based in the Maritimes Region. To be paid off in April 1994.

ALERT *1983, Canadian Coast Guard*

Name	*No*	*Builders*	*Commissioned*
GORDON REID	—	Versatile Pacific, Vancouver	Oct 1990
JOHN JACOBSON	—	Versatile Pacific, Vancouver	Nov 1990

Displacement, tons:X
Measurement, tons: 836 gross
Dimensions, feet (metres): 163.9 × 36.1 × 13.1 *(49.9 × 11 × 4)*
Main machinery: 4 Deutz SBV-6M-628 diesels; 4732 hp(m) *(3.48 MW)*; 2 shafts; bow thruster; 500 hp *(373 kW)*
Speed, knots: 17. **Range, miles:** 2500 at 15 kts
Complement: 13 plus 5 spare

Comment: Type 500 Intermediate cutters. Designed for long-range patrols along the British Columbian coast out to 200 mile limit. They have a stern ramp for launching rigid inflatables in up to Sea State 6. Both based in the Western Region.

GORDON REID (with RACER [deleted 1991]) *1990, Canadian Coast Guard*

SPECIAL RIVER NAVAIDS TENDERS (Type 700)

Note: All based on the Hay River, North West Territories.

Name	*No*	*Builders*	*Commissioned*
NAHIDIK	—	Allied Shipbuilders Ltd, N Vancouver	1974

Measurement, tons: 856 gross; 392 net
Dimensions, feet (metres): 175.2 × 49.9 × 6.6 *(53.4 × 15.2 × 2)*
Main machinery: 2 diesels; 4290 hp *(3.2 MW)*; 2 shafts
Speed, knots: 14
Complement: 15

NAHIDIK *1991, Canadian Coast Guard*

Name	No	Builders	Commissioned
DUMIT	—	Allied Shipbuilders Ltd, N Vancouver	1979

Measurement, tons: 569 gross; 176 net
Dimensions, feet (metres): 160.1 × 40 × 5.2 *(48.8 × 12.2 × 1.6)*
Main machinery: 2 diesels; 839 hp *(626 kW)*; 2 shafts
Speed, knots: 12
Complement: 10

Name	No	Builders	Commissioned
TEMBAH	—	Allied Shipbuilders Ltd, N Vancouver	1963

Measurement, tons: 189 gross; 58 net
Dimensions, feet (metres): 123 × 25.9 × 3 *(37.5 × 7.9 × 0.9)*
Main machinery: 2 diesels; 500 hp *(373 kW)*; 2 shafts
Speed, knots: 13
Complement: 9

Comment: In reserve in 1991.

TEMBAH *1978, Canadian Coast Guard*

Name	No	Builders	Commissioned
ECKALOO	—	Vancouver S Y Ltd	July 1988

Displacement, tons: 534
Measurement, tons: 661 gross; 213 net
Dimensions, feet (metres): 160.8 × 44 × 4 *(49 × 13.4 × 1.2)*
Main machinery: 2 Caterpillar 3512TA; 2120 hp *(1.6 MW)* sustained; 2 shafts
Speed, knots: 13
Complement: 9
Helicopters: Platform for 1 Bell 206L/L-1.

Comment: Replaced vessel of the same name. Similar design to *Dumit*.

ECKALOO *7/1988, Murray McLellan Photo*

Name	No	Builders	Commissioned
MISKINAW	—	Allied Shipbuilders Ltd, N Vancouver	1958

Measurement, tons: 104 gross; 47 net
Dimensions, feet (metres): 64 × 19.7 × 3.9 *(19.5 × 6 × 1.2)*
Main machinery: 2 diesels; 358 hp *(267 kW)*; 2 shafts
Speed, knots: 10
Complement: 8

SMALL NAVAIDS TENDERS

Name	No	Builders	Commissioned
COVE ISLE	—	Canadian D and D, Kingston, Ontario	1980
GULL ISLE	—	Canadian D and D, Kingston, Ontario	1980

Measurement, tons: 80 gross; 33 net
Dimensions, feet (metres): 65.6 × 19.7 × 4.6 *(20 × 6 × 1.4)*
Main machinery: 2 diesels; 373 hp *(278 kW)*; 2 shafts
Speed, knots: 10
Complement: 5

Comment: Type 800 based in Central Region.

Name	No	Builders	Commissioned
NAMAO	—	Riverton Boat Works, Manitoba	1975

Displacement, tons: 380
Measurement, tons: 318 gross; 107 net
Dimensions, feet (metres): 110 × 28 × 7 *(33.5 × 8.5 × 2.1)*
Main machinery: 2 diesels; 1350 hp *(1 MW)*; 2 shafts
Speed, knots: 12
Complement: 11

Comment: Type 900 based in the Central Region on Lake Winnipeg.

Name	No	Builders	Commissioned
PARTRIDGE ISLAND	—	Breton Industries, Port Hawkesbury, N S	31 Oct 1985
ILE DES BARQUES	—	Breton Industries, Port Hawkesbury, N S	26 Nov 1985
ILE SAINT-OURS	—	Breton Industries, Port Hawkesbury, N S	15 May 1986
CARIBOU ISLE	—	Breton Industries, Port Hawkesbury, N S	16 June 1986

Measurement, tons: 92 gross; 36 net
Dimensions, feet (metres): 75.5 × 19.7 × 4.4 *(23 × 6 × 1.4)*
Main machinery: 2 diesels; 475 hp *(354 kW)*; 2 shafts
Speed, knots: 11
Complement: 5

Comment: Type 800. *Partridge Island* based in the Maritimes, *Caribou Isle* in the Central Region and the other two in the Laurentides.

CARIBOU ISLE *5/1986, Gilbert Gyssels*

Name	No	Builders	Commissioned
ROBERT FOULIS	—	St John Drydock, NB	1969

Displacement, tons: 260
Measurement, tons: 258 gross; 29 net
Dimensions, feet (metres): 104 × 25 × 7.9 *(31.7 × 7.6 × 2.4)*
Main machinery: 2 diesels; 960 hp *(716 kW)*; 2 shafts
Speed, knots: 12
Complement: 12

Comment: Type 900 based in the Maritimes.

ROBERT FOULIS *1984, Canadian Coast Guard*

ICE STRENGTHENED OFFSHORE SEARCH AND RESCUE CUTTERS

Note: Plans to build two Type 600 replacements were cancelled in 1990.

Name	No	Builders	Commissioned
MARY HICHENS	—	Marystown Shipyard Ltd, Newfoundland	1983

Displacement, tons: 3262
Measurement, tons: 1684 gross; 696 net
Dimensions, feet (metres): 210 × 45 × 19.7 *(64 × 13.8 × 6)*
Main machinery: 2 Burmeister & Wain Alpha 18 V 28/32-VO diesels; 10 800 hp(m) *(7.94 MW)* sustained; 2 shafts; 2 Kort nozzle cp props; bow thrusters
Speed, knots: 15
Complement: 18

Comment: Type 600 based in the Maritimes Region.

MARY HICHENS *1986, Canadian Coast Guard*

Name	*No*	*Builders*	*Commissioned*
SIR WILFRED GRENFELL	—	Marystown S Y, Newfoundland	1987

Displacement, tons: 3753
Measurement, tons: 2403 gross; 664.5 net
Dimensions, feet (metres): 224.7 × 49.2 × 16.4 *(68.5 × 15 × 5)*
Main machinery: Diesel-electric; 4 diesel generators; 12 860 hp *(9.6 MW)*; 2 shafts
Speed, knots: 16
Complement: 20

Comment: Built on speculation in 1984/85. Modified to include an 85 tonne towing winch and additional SAR accommodation and equipment; replaced *Grenfell* in December 1987. Type 600 large SAR cutter and based at St John's, Newfoundland.

SIR WILFRED GRENFELL *1989, Canadian Coast Guard*

SMALL SEARCH AND RESCUE CUTTERS

Name	*No*	*Builders*	*Commissioned*
SPINDRIFT	—	Cliff Richards Boats, Meaford, Ontario	1965
SPRAY	—	J J Taylor & Sons Ltd, Toronto	1964
SPUME	—	Crew Ltd, Prescott, Ontario	1963

Measurement, tons: 56 gross; 17 net
Dimensions, feet (metres): 69.9 × 16.7 × 4.6 *(21.3 × 5.1 × 1.4)*
Main machinery: 2 diesels; 1064 hp *(794 kW)*; 2 shafts
Speed, knots: 12.5
Complement: 4

Comment: Employed on Great Lakes Patrol in the Central Region.

SPINDRIFT *1986, Canadian Coast Guard*

Name	*No*	*Builders*	*Commissioned*
POINT HENRY	—	Breton Industrial and Machinery	1980
ISLE ROUGE	—	Breton Industrial and Machinery	1980
POINT RACE	—	Pt Hawkesbury, NS	1982
CAPE HURD	—	Pt Hawkesbury, NS	1982

Displacement, tons: 49
Measurement, tons: 57 gross; 14 net
Dimensions, feet (metres): 70.8 × 18 × 5.6 *(21.6 × 5.5 × 1.7)*
Main machinery: 2 MTU 8V 396 TC82 diesels; 1740 hp(m) *(1.28 MW)* sustained; 2 shafts
Speed, knots: 20
Complement: 5

Comment: Aluminium alloy hulls. *Point Henry* based in Western Region, *Cape Hurd* in Central Region, and the other two in the Laurentides.

POINT HENRY (old number) *1982, Canadian Coast Guard*

SAR SELF-RIGHTING LIFEBOATS

Name	*No*	*Builders*	*Commissioned*
BICKERTON	—	Halmatic, Havant	Aug 1989

Measurement, tons: 34 gross
Dimensions, feet (metres): 52 × 17.5 × 4.6 *(15.9 × 5.3 × 1.5)*
Main machinery: 2 Caterpillar 3408BTA diesels; 1170 hp *(872 kW)* sustained; 2 shafts
Speed, knots: 18

Comment: Arun Type 300. Final total has not been decided. To replace up to 10 Westport class.

BICKERTON *7/1989, J. Carte*

Name	*Builders*	*Commissioned*
WESTPORT	Paspediac, Quebec	1969
BAMFIELD	McKay Cormack Ltd, Victoria, BC	1970
TOFINO	McKay Cormack Ltd, Victoria, BC	1970
BULL HARBOUR	McKay Cormack Ltd, Victoria, BC	1970
BURIN	Georgetown Shipyard, Georgetown, PEI	1973
TOBERMORY	Georgetown Shipyard, Georgetown, PEI	1974
WESTFORT (ex-*Thunder Bay*)	Georgetown Shipyard, Georgetown, PEI	1974
BURGEO	Georgetown Shipyard, Georgetown, PEI	1974
SHIPPEGAN	Eastern Equipment, Montreal, Quebec	1975
CLARK'S HARBOUR	Eastern Equipment, Montreal, Quebec	1975
SAMBRO	Eastern Equipment, Montreal, Quebec	1975
LOUISBOURG	Eastern Equipment, Montreal, Quebec	1975
PORT MOUTON	Georgetown Shipyard, Georgetown, PEI	1982
CAP AUX MEULES	Georgetown Shipyard, Georgetown, PEI	1982
SOURIS	Hike Metal Products Ltd, Wheatley, Ontario	1985
CAP GOÉLANDS	Hike Metal Products Ltd, Wheatley, Ontario	1985

Measurement, tons: 10 gross
Dimensions, feet (metres): 44.1 × 12.7 × 3.4 *(13.5 × 3.9 × 1)*
Main machinery: 2 diesels; 485 hp *(362 kW)*; 2 shafts
Speed, knots: 12.5
Complement: 3 or 4

Comment: Eight based in the Maritimes, three Western, two Central, two Newfoundland and one in Laurentides.

CAP GOÉLANDS *1986, Canadian Coast Guard*

SMALL ICE STRENGTHENED SAR CUTTERS

Name	*No*	*Builders*	*Commissioned*
HARP	—	Georgetown SY, Georgetown, PEI	12 Dec 1986
HOOD	—	Georgetown SY, Georgetown, PEI	12 Dec 1986

Displacement, tons: 225
Measurement, tons: 179 gross; 69 net
Dimensions, feet (metres): 80.4 × 27.6 × 7.9 *(24.5 × 8.5 × 2.4)*
Main machinery: 2 diesels; 850 hp *(634 kW)*; 2 shafts
Speed, knots: 10. **Range, miles:** 500 at 10 kts
Complement: 7 plus 10 spare berths

Comment: Ordered 26 April 1985 and launched in September and November 1986. Type 200 based in Newfoundland.

SMALL SAR CRAFT

Name	*Builders*	*Commissioned*
MALLARD	Matsumoto Shipyard, Vancouver, B C	1985
SKUA	Matsumoto Shipyard, Vancouver, B C	1986
OSPREY	Matsumoto Shipyard, Vancouver, B C	1986
STERNE	Matsumoto Shipyard, Vancouver, B C	1987

Measurement, tons: 15 gross
Dimensions, feet (metres): 40.8 × 13.2 × 4.2 *(12.4 × 4.1 × 1.3)*
Main machinery: 2 diesels; 637 hp *(475 kW)*; 2 shafts
Speed, knots: 26
Complement: 3

Comment: Type 100 utility craft.

Name	*Measurement, tons*	*Speed, knots*	*Built*
CGR 100	9.2 gross	26	1986
BITTERN	20 gross	26	1982
SORA	20 gross	12	1968
SWIFT	5 gross	36	1981
CG 119	20 gross	18	1973
AVOCET (ex-*Sterne*)	20 gross	15	1973

Comment: The most recent craft *CGR 100* is a Type 300 Medina self-righting liftboat based in Central Region.

BITTERN *1986, Canadian Coast Guard*

INSHORE RESCUE CRAFT *1989, Canadian Coast Guard*

CCG COLLEGE CADET SEA TRAINING VESSELS

Note: In addition to *Mikula* there are three 10.5 m craft, *Mink, Martin* and *Muskrat*.

Name	*No*	*Builders*	*Commissioned*
MIKULA (ex-*Lurcher*)	—	Kingston S Y, Ontario	1959

Displacement, tons: 617
Measurement, tons: 526 gross; 135 net
Dimensions, feet (metres): 128 × 30.5 × 11 *(39 × 9.3 × 3.4)*
Main machinery: 1 diesel; 372 hp *(277 kW)*; 1 shaft
Speed, knots: 10
Complement: 6 plus 21 cadets

Comment: Former Lightship.

MIKULA *1986, R. Allan*

SURVEY AND SOUNDING VESSELS

Name	*No*	*Builders*	*Commissioned*
NICOLET	—	Collingwood S Y, Ontario	1966

Displacement, tons: 935 full load
Measurement, tons: 887 gross; 147 net
Dimensions, feet (metres): 169.6 × 36.4 × 10.2 *(51.7 × 11.1 × 3.1)*
Main machinery: 2 diesels; 1237 hp *(923 kW)*; 2 shafts; cp props
Speed, knots: 13
Complement: 27

Comment: Based in Laurentides. To be paid off in 1994.

NICOLET *1986, Canadian Coast Guard*

HOVERCRAFT

3 SR.N6 TYPE

CG 039 **CG 045** **CG 086**

Displacement, tons: 10.9 full load
Dimensions, feet (metres): 48.5 × 23 × 3.9 (skirt) *(14.8 × 7 × 1.2)*
Main machinery: 1 RR Gnome 1050 gas turbine; 1050 hp *(783 kW)*
Speed, knots: 60. **Range, miles:** 170 at 54 kts
Complement: 3

Comment: Built in 1968 and 1977. Based at Vancouver and Parksville, B C. Can carry up to 6 tons of equipment.

SR.N6 Type *1986, Canadian Coast Guard*

AP.I-88/200 TYPE

Name	*No*	*Builders*	*Commissioned*
WABAN-AKI	—	Westland Aerospace	15 July 1987

Displacement, tons: 47.6 light
Dimensions, feet (metres): 80.4 × 36.7 × 19.6 *(24.5 × 11.2 × 6.6)* (height on cushion)
Main machinery: 4 diesels
Speed, knots: 50; 35 cruising
Complement: 3
Cargo capacity: 12 tons

Comment: Based at Quebec and capable of year round operation as a Navaid Tender for flood control operations in the St Lawrence. Fitted with a hydraulic crane. The name means People of the Dawn.

WABAN-AKI *1989, Canadian Coast Guard*

DEPARTMENT OF FISHERIES AND OCEANS

Senior Appointment

Director, Ship Branch:
Commodore J M Cutts

General

The department has two separate fleets. The hydrographic, oceanographic and fishery research vessels are painted white with buff masts and buff funnels with black tops. They are based on the East Coast at the Bedford Institute of Oceanography, Dartmouth NS and at St Johns, Newfoundland; on the West Coast at the Pacific Institute of Ocean Sciences, Sidney, BC; and in the Great Lakes at the Canada Centre for Inland Waters at Burlington, Ontario.

The fishery patrol vessels are painted grey with the departmental crest on the funnel. They are based in their respective patrol areas. These vessels are armed with machine guns and carry armed boarding parties.

Apart from the major vessels whose details are given below there are some 700 medium and small patrol craft.

FISHERY RESEARCH VESSELS

Name	*Commissioned*	*Based*	*Complement*
ALFRED NEEDLER	1982	Nova Scotia	37 (15 scientists)
WILFRED TEMPLEMAN	1982	Nova Scotia	37 (15 scientists)
E E PRINCE	1966	Nova Scotia	20 (6 scientists)
W E RICKER (ex-*Callistratus*)	1978	West Coast	36 (12 scientists)

ALFRED NEEDLER *1989, DFO*

E E PRINCE *1990, DFO*

FISHERY PATROL VESSELS

Name	*Builders*	*Commissioned*
CYGNUS	Marystown Shipyard, Nfld	1981
CAPE ROGER	Ferguson Industries, Pictou NS	1977

Measurement, tons: 1255 grt
Dimensions, feet (metres): 205 × 40 × 13 *(62.5 × 12.2 × 4.1)*
Main machinery: 2 Nohab diesels, 2400 hp(m) *(1.76 MW)*; 1 shaft
Speed, knots: 16. **Range, miles:** 2450 at 10 kts
Complement: 19
Guns: 2—12.7 mm MGs.
Helicopters: Capability for one light.

Comment: *Cygnus* based in Nova Scotia, *Cape Roger* in Newfoundland. Two crews per ship work a 14 day patrol cycle.

CYGNUS *1989, DFO*

Name	*Builders*	*Commissioned*
LEONARD J COWLEY	Manly Shipyard, RivTow Ind, Vancouver BC	1985

Measurement, tons: 2244 grt
Dimensions, feet (metres): 236.2 × 45.9 × 16.1 *(72 × 14 × 4.9)*
Main machinery: 2 Nohab diesels; 2325 hp(m) *(1.71 MW)*; 1 shaft
Speed, knots: 14. **Range, miles:** 12 000 at 14 kts
Complement: 19
Guns: 2—12.7 mm MGs.
Helicopters: Capability for one light.

Comment: Based in Newfoundland.

Name	*Builders*	*Commissioned*
JAMES SINCLAIR	Manly Shipyard, RivTow Ind, Vancouver BC	1981

Measurement, tons: 323 grt
Dimensions, feet (metres): 124 × 27.5 × 12 *(37.8 × 8.4 × 3.7)*
Main machinery: 2 MTU diesels; 4600 hp(m) *(3.38 MW)*; 2 shafts
Speed, knots: 16.5
Complement: 14
Guns: 2—12.7 mm MGs.

Comment: Based in British Columbia.

Name	*Builders*	*Commissioned*
CHEBUCTO	Ferguson Industries, Pictou NS	1966

Measurement, tons: 751 grt
Dimensions, feet (metres): 179 × 31 × 15 *(54.6 × 9.4 × 3.6)*
Main machinery: 2 Fairbanks-Morse diesels; 2560 hp *(1.91 MW)*; 2 shafts
Speed, knots: 14. **Range, miles:** 7320 at 10 kts
Complement: 21
Guns: 2—12.7 mm MGs.

Comment: Based in Nova Scotia. Mid-life refit in 1987. Operates a two crew system changing every 14 days.

CHEBUCTO *1989, DFO*

Name	*Builders*	*Commissioned*
TANU	Yarrows Ltd, Victoria BC	1968

Measurement, tons: 746 grt
Dimensions, feet (metres): 179.5 × 32.8 × 10.8 *(54.7 × 10 × 3.3)*
Main machinery: 1 diesel; 2624 hp *(1.96 MW)*; 1 shaft
Speed, knots: 12.
Complement: 18
Guns: 2—12.7 mm MGs.

Comment: Based in British Columbia.

TANU *1990, van Ginderen Collection*

Name	*Builders*	*Commissioned*
LOUISBOURG	Breton Industries, Pt Hawkesbury NS	1977

Measurement, tons: 295 grt
Dimensions, feet (metres): 125 × 27 × 7.8 *(38.1 × 8.3 × 2.5)*
Main machinery: 2 MTU diesels; 4500 hp(m) *(3.3 MW)*; 2 shafts
Speed, knots: 19. **Range, miles:** 4380 at 12.5 kts
Complement: 14
Guns: 2—12.7 mm MGs (not carried).

Comment: Stationed in Nova Scotia. Disarmed in 1991.

LOUISBOURG *1989, DFO*

HYDROGRAPHIC AND OCEANOGRAPHIC VESSELS

Note: *Baffin* and *Dawson* deleted in 1991.

Name	*Commissioned*	*Based*	*Complement*
HUDSON	1963	East Coast	65 (25 scientists)
MATTHEW	1990	East Coast	—
F C G SMITH	1986	East Coast	11 (4 scientists)
MAXWELL	1962	East Coast	19 (7 scientists)
JOHN P TULLY	1985	West Coast	36 (15 scientists)
PARIZEAU	1967	East Coast	45 (13 scientists)

Name	*Commissioned*	*Based*	*Complement*
VECTOR	1967	West Coast	25 (8 scientists)
LOUIS M LAUZIER (ex-*Cape Harrison*)	1977	St Lawrence	14 (6 scientists)
LIMNOS	1968	St Lawrence	30 (14 scientists)
BAYFIELD (ex-*Hildur*)	1966	St Lawrence	16 (6 scientists)
R B YOUNG	1990	West Coast	11 (5 scientists)

HUDSON *1989, DFO*

LIMNOS *1989, DFO*

CAPE VERDE

Personnel

1992: 200

Bases

Praia, main naval base.
Porto Grande (Isle de Sao Vicente), naval repair yard built with Soviet assistance.

Mercantile Marine

Lloyd's Register of Shipping:
41 vessels of 21 777 tons gross

3 Ex-SOVIET ZHUK CLASS (COASTAL PATROL CRAFT)

Displacement, tons: 50
Dimensions, feet (metres): 75.4 × 17 × 6.2 *(23 × 5.2 × 1.9)*
Main machinery: 2 Type M50F-12 diesels; 2400 hp(m) *(1.76 MW)*; 2 shafts
Speed, knots: 30. **Range, miles:** 1100 at 15 kts
Complement: 17
Guns: 4—14.5 mm (2 twin) MGs.
Radars: Surface search: Spin Trough; I band.

Comment: Transferred 1980. Only one was operational in 1991.

1 Ex-SOVIET BIYA CLASS (SURVEY SHIP)

5th JULY A 450

Displacement, tons: 750 full load
Dimensions, feet (metres): 180.4 × 32.1 × 8.5 *(55 × 9.8 × 2.6)*
Main machinery: 2 diesels; 1200 hp(m) *(88.2 kW)*; 2 shafts; cp props
Speed, knots: 13. **Range, miles:** 4700 at 11 kts
Complement: 25

Comment: Transferred in 1979. Class built in Poland 1972-76. Probably non-operational.

2 Ex-SOVIET SHERSHEN CLASS (FAST ATTACK CRAFT)

451 **452**

Displacement, tons: 145 standard; 170 full load
Dimensions, feet (metres): 113.8 × 22 × 4.9 *(34.7 × 6.7 × 1.5)*
Main machinery: 3 M503A diesels; 12 000 hp(m) *(8.8 MW)*; 3 shafts
Speed, knots: 45. **Range, miles:** 460 at 42 kts; 850 at 30 kts
Complement: 23
Guns: 4 USSR 30 mm/65 (2 twin); 85° elevation; 500 rounds/minute to 5 km *(2.7 nm)*; weight of shell 0.54 kg.
Depth charges: 12.
Radars: Surface search: Pot Head; I band; range 37 km *(20 nm)*.
Fire control: Drum Tilt; H/I band.

Comment: Supplied without the usual four torpedo tubes. Delivered March and July 1979. Class built in period 1962-74.

1 LANDING CRAFT LOGISTIC

ILHEN RASO

Comment: A 28.5 m craft built by Sürken, West Germany and delivered in October 1988. Probably a civilian manned Ro-Ro.

SHERSHEN 451 and 452 *1991, van Ginderen Collection*

CHILE

Headquarters' Appointments

Commander-in-Chief:
Admiral Jorge Martinez
Chief of the Naval Staff:
Rear Admiral Jorge Arancibia Reyes
Flag Officer, Fleet:
Vice Admiral Juan Mackay
Flag Officer, Submarines:
Rear Admiral Eduardo Oelckers
Flag Officer, Naval Aviation:
Rear Admiral Ariel Rosas
Flag Officer, Marines:
Rear Admiral Miguel Alvarez
Flag Officer, Maritime Territory:
Vice Admiral Carlos Toledo de la Maza
Flag Officer, 1st Naval Zone:
Rear Admiral Jorge Arancibia
Flag Officer, 2nd Naval Zone:
Vice Admiral Jorge Llorente
Flag Officer, 3rd Naval Zone:
Rear Admiral Hugo Bruna
Flag Officer, 4th Naval Zone:
Rear Admiral Roman Fritis

Diplomatic Representation

Naval Attaché in London, The Hague and Stockholm:
Rear Admiral Eduardo Berardi
Naval Attaché in Washington:
Rear Admiral Arturo Oxley
Naval Attaché in Paris:
Captain Carlos Valderrama
Naval Attaché in Buenos Aires:
Captain Rodolfo Camacho
Naval Attaché in Brasilia:
Captain Christian de Bonnafos
Naval Attaché in Quito:
Captain Juan Wichmann
Naval Attaché in Tel Aviv:
Commander Daniel Arellano
Naval Attaché in Pretoria:
Captain Fernando Gaete
Naval Attaché in Lima:
Captain Enrique Mayer-Rechnitz
Naval Attaché in Madrid:
Captain Pedro Veas Diabuno

Personnel

(a) 1992: 24 500 (excluding Marines) (2000 officers)
(b) 2 years' national service

Command Organisation

1st Naval Zone. HQ at Valparaiso. From 26°S to Topocalma Point (33°S).
2nd Naval Zone. HQ at Talcahuano. From Topocalma Point to 47°S.
3rd Naval Zone. HQ at Punta Arenas. From 47°S to South Pole including Beagle Naval District.
4th Naval Zone. HQ at Iquique. From Peruvian frontier to 26°S.

Naval Air Stations and Organisation

Having won the battle to own all military aircraft flying over the sea, a fixed wing squadron of about 20 CASA/ENAER Halcón is envisaged when finances permit.
Viña del Mar (Valparaiso); *Almirante Von Schroeders* (Punta Arenas); *Guardiamarina Zañartu* (Puerto Williams).
Four Squadrons: VP1 (MP) Bandeirante; HS1 (Helicopters) Alouette III, Super Puma, Dauphin; VC1 (GP) Bandeirante, Aviocar, JetRangers; VT1 (Training) Pilatus PC-7.

Infanteria de Marina

Personnel: 5200.
Organisation: 4 detachments each comprising Amphibious Warfare, Coast Defence and Local Security. Also embarked are detachments of commandos, engineering units and a logistic battalion.
1st Marine Infantry Detachment 'Patricio Lynch'. At Iquique.
2nd Marine Infantry Detachment 'Miller'. At Viña del Mar.
3rd Marine Infantry Detachment 'Sargento Aldea'. At Talcahuano.
4th Marine Infantry Detachment 'Cochrane'. At Punta Arenas.
51 Commando Group. At Valparaiso.
Some embarked units, commando and engineering units and a logistics battalion.
Equipment: Infantry personnel and support weapons; LVTP 5 amphibious assault vehicles; MOWAG Roland APCs; light field artillery.

Naval Bases

Valparaiso. Main naval base, schools, repair yard. HQ 1st Naval Zone. Air station.
Talcahuano. Naval base, schools, major repair yard (two dry docks, three floating docks), two floating cranes. HQ 2nd Naval Zone. Submarine Base.
Punta Arenas. Naval base. Dockyard with slipway having building and repair facilities. HQ 3rd Naval Zone. Air station.
Iquique. Small naval base. HQ 4th Naval Zone.
Puerto Montt. Small naval base.
Puerto Williams (Beagle Channel). Small naval base. Air station.
Dawson Island (Magellan Straits). Small naval base.

Strength of the Fleet

Type	*Active*	*Projected*
Patrol Submarines	4	(4)
Cruiser	1	—
Destroyers	6	—
Frigates	3	1
Patrol Ships	2	(5)
Landing Ships (Tank)	3	—
Landing Craft	2	—
Fast Attack Craft (Missile)	4	—
Fast Attack Craft (Torpedo)	4	—
Large Patrol Craft	1	—
Coastal Patrol Craft	6	—
Survey Ship	1	—
Training Ships	3	—
Transports	3	—
Tankers	3	—
Tugs/Supply Ships	4	—
Submarine Support Ship	1	—
Coast Guard	37	(6)

Mercantile Marine

Lloyd's Register of Shipping:
387 vessels of 618 188 tons gross

DELETIONS

Cruisers

1992 *O'Higgins*

Destroyers

1990 *Ministro Zenteno* (old), *Ministro Portales*

Patrol Forces

1990 *Lautaro* (old)

Miscellaneous

1990 *Grumete Perez*

PENNANT LIST

Note: Chilean naval vessels no longer carry visible pennant numbers.

Submarines

20	Thomson
21	Simpson
22	O'Brien
23	Hyatt

Cruisers

02	O'Higgins

Destroyers/Frigates

06	Condell
07	Lynch
08	Ministro Zenteno
11	Prat
12	Cochrane
14	Latorre
15	Blanco Encalada
18	Almirante Riveros
19	Almirante Williams

Patrol Forces

45	Piloto Pardo
63	Sargento Aldea

Light Forces

30	Casma
31	Chipana
32	Iquique
33	Covadonga
37	Papudo
80	Guacolda
81	Fresia
82	Quidora
83	Tegualda
1814	Grumete Diaz
1815	Grumete Bolados
1816	Grumete Salinas
1817	Grumete Tellez
1818	Grumete Bravo
1819	Grumete Campos

Survey Ship

64	Yelcho

Training Ships

29	Uribe
43	Esmeralda

Submarine Support Ship

70	Angamos

Amphibious Forces

90	Elicura
91	Maipo
92	Rancagua
93	Chacabuco
94	Orompello

Transports

AP 47	Aquiles
AP 48	Aguila
YFB 110	Meteoro

Tankers

52	Almirante Jorge Montt
53	Araucano
YOG 101	Guardian Brito

Tugs/Supply Ships

ATF 65	Janequeo
ATF 66	Galvarino
ATF 67	Lautaro
ATF 68	Leucoton

SUBMARINES

Note: Up to four new submarines are required. The Equipment fit has been decided and an order for a new class of about 1400 tons may be placed in 1992/93. First to be built abroad, remainder by ASMAR.

2 OBERON CLASS

Name	*No*	*Builders*	*Laid down*	*Launched*	*Commissioned*
O'BRIEN	22	Scott-Lithgow	17 Jan 1971	21 Dec 1972	15 Apr 1976
HYATT (ex-*Condell*)	23	Scott-Lithgow	10 Jan 1972	26 Sep 1973	27 Sep 1976

Displacement, tons: 1610 standard; 2030 surfaced; 2410 dived
Dimensions, feet (metres): 295.2 × 26.5 × 18.1 *(90 × 8.1 × 5.5)*
Main machinery: Diesel-electric; 2 ASR 16 VVS-ASR1 diesels; 3680 hp *(2.74 MW)*; 2 AEI motors; 6000 hp *(4.48 MW)*; 2 shafts
Speed, knots: 12 surfaced; 17 dived
Complement: 65 (7 officers)

Torpedoes: 8—21 in *(533 mm)* tubes (6 bow, 2 stern). 22 AEG SUT; wire-guided; active homing to 12 km *(6.5 nm)* at 35 kts; passive homing to 28 km *(15 nm)* at 23 kts; warhead 250 kg.
Radars: Navigation: Kelvin Hughes Type 1006; I band.
Sonars: BAC Type 2007; flank array; passive; long range; low frequency.
EMI Type 187; bow-mounted; passive/active search and attack; medium frequency.
Programmes: Ordered from Scott's Shipbuilding & Engineering Co Ltd, Greenock, late 1969. Both suffered delays in fitting out due to re-cabling and a minor explosion in *Hyatt* in January 1976.

O'BRIEN *1991, Chilean Navy*

Modernisation: Both will be refitted with new sonar and fire control systems in 1992/93.

Operational: Stern tubes may no longer be used.

2 TYPE 209 CLASS (TYPE 1300)

Name	No	Builders	Laid down	Launched	Commissioned
THOMSON	20	Howaldtswerke	1 Nov 1980	28 Oct 1982	31 Aug 1984
SIMPSON	21	Howaldtswerke	15 Feb 1982	29 July 1983	18 Sep 1984

Displacement, tons: 1260 surfaced; 1390 dived
Dimensions, feet (metres): 195.2 × 20.3 × 18 *(59.5 × 6.2 × 5.5)*
Main machinery: Diesel-electric; 4 MTU 12V 493 AZ80 GA31L diesels; 2400 hp(m) *(1.76 MW)* sustained; 4 Piller alternators; 1.7 MW; 1 Siemens motor; 4600 hp(m) *(3.38 MW)* sustained; 1 shaft
Speed, knots: 11 surfaced; 21.5 dived
Range, miles: 400 at 4 kts surfaced; 16 at 21.5 kts dived; 8200 at 8 kts snorkel
Complement: 32 (5 officers)

Torpedoes: 8—21 in *(533 mm)* bow tubes. 14 AEG SUT; wire-guided; active homing to 12 km *(6.5 nm)* at 35 kts; passive homing to 28 km *(15 nm)* at 23 kts; warhead 250 kg.
Radars: Surface search: Thomson-CSF Calypso II; I band.
Sonars: Krupp Atlas CSU 3; hull-mounted; active/passive search and attack; medium frequency.

Programmes: Ordered from Howaldtswerke, Kiel in 1980. Two more projected in 1988 five year plan but this has been overtaken by the requirement for a new class of four of similar displacement.
Modernisation: *Thomson* refit completed at Talcahuano in late 1990, *Simpson* in 1991. Refit duration about 10 months each.
Structure: Fin and associated masts lengthened by 50 cm to cope with wave size off Chilean coast.

THOMSON (with Marines) *1991, Chilean Navy*

SIMPSON *2/1990 Maritime Photographic*

CRUISER

1 Ex-US BROOKLYN CLASS

Name	No	Builders	Laid down	Launched	Commissioned
O'HIGGINS (ex-USS *Brooklyn* CL 40)	02	New York Navy Yard	12 Mar 1935	30 Nov 1936	30 Sep 1937

Displacement, tons: 10 000 standard; 13 500 full load
Dimensions, feet (metres): 608.3 × 69 × 24 *(185.4 × 21 × 7.3)*
Main machinery: 8 Babcock & Wilcox boilers; 400 psi *(28 kg/cm sq)*; 650°F *(342°C)*; 4 Parsons turbines; 100 000 hp *(75 MW)*; 4 shafts
Speed, knots: 32.5. **Range, miles:** 7600 at 15 kts
Complement: 888 to 975

Guns: 15—6 in *(152 mm)*/47 (5 triple) Mk 16; 10 rounds/minute to 23.5 km *(13 nm)*; weight of shell 46.5 kg.
8—5 in *(127 mm)*/25 Mk 27; 22 rounds/minute to 16.5 km *(9 nm)*; weight of shell 25 kg.
28 Bofors 40 mm/60 (4 quad, 6 twin Mk 2 and Mk 1); 80° elevation; 120 rounds/minute to 10 km *(5.5 nm)*; weight of shell 0.89 kg.
24 Oerlikon 20 mm/80 (single, twin).

Fire control: 2 Mk 34 directors for 6 in armament; 2 Mk 57; 6 Mk 51.
Radars: Air search: RCA SPS 12; D band; range 119 km *(65 nm)*.
Surface search: Raytheon SPS 10; G band.
Fire control: 4 Raytheon Mk 28; I band.

Helicopters: 1 Bell 206B JetRanger.

Programmes: Former cruiser of the US Brooklyn class. Purchased from the USA in 1951 at a price representing 10 per cent of original cost ($37 million) plus the expense of reconditioning. Again refitted in USA 1957-58. Damaged by grounding on 12 August 1974. She was subsequently used as an alongside accommodation ship and was no longer considered operational. However, after a very expensive refit in 1977/78 she was again recommissioned.

Structure: Hangar: The hangar in the hull right aft could accommodate six aircraft if necessary together with engine spares and duplicate parts, though four aircraft is the normal capacity. Above the hangar two catapults were mounted as far outboard as possible but have been removed and a revolving crane was placed at the stern extremity overhanging the aircraft hatch.
Armour, inches (mm): Belt 4—1¼ *(102—38)*; Decks 3—2 *(76—51)*; Turrets 5—3 *(127—76)*; Conning tower 8 *(203)*.
Operational: The ship is in good condition and went to sea two or three times a year with a reduced crew. To be paid off in 1992 and may become a museum ship or alternatively be sold for scrap. After 65 years' service she deserves her place in this book for one more year.

O'HIGGINS *1989, Chilean Navy*

DESTROYERS

4 Ex-BRITISH COUNTY CLASS

Name	No	Builders	Laid down	Launched	Commissioned
PRAT (ex-HMS *Norfolk*)	11	Swan Hunter, Wallsend	15 Mar 1966	16 Nov 1967	7 Mar 1970
COCHRANE (ex-HMS *Antrim*)	12	Fairfield S.B. & Eng Co Ltd, Govan	20 Jan 1966	19 Oct 1967	14 July 1970
LATORRE (ex-HMS *Glamorgan*)	14	Vickers (Shipbuilding) Ltd, Newcastle-upon-Tyne	13 Sep 1962	9 July 1964	11 Oct 1966
BLANCO ENCALADA (ex-HMS *Fife*)	15	Fairfield S.B. & Eng Co Ltd, Govan	1 June 1962	9 July 1964	21 June1966

Displacement, tons: 5440 standard; 6200 full load
Dimensions, feet (metres): 520.5 × 54 × 20.5 *(158.7 × 16.5 × 6.3)*
Main machinery: COSAG; 2 Babcock & Wilcox boilers; 700 psi *(49.2 kg/cm sq)*; 950°F *(510°C)*; 2 AEI steam turbines; 30 000 hp *(22.4 MW)*; 4 English Electric G6 gas turbines; 30 000 hp *(22.4 MW)*; 2 shafts
Speed, knots: 30. **Range, miles:** 3500 at 28 kts
Complement: 470 (36 officers)

BLANCO ENCALADA

(Scale 1 : 1 500), Ian Sturton

Missiles: SSM: 4 Aerospatiale MM 38 Exocet ❶; inertial cruise; active radar homing to 42 km *(23 nm)* at 0.9 Mach; warhead 165 kg; sea-skimmer.
SAM: Short Bros Seaslug Mk 2 (11 and 14 only) ❷; range 45 km *(25 nm)* at 2 Mach; warhead HE; beam riding. Limited anti-surface role.
2 Shorts Seacat quad launchers (not in 14) ❸; optical/radar guidance to 5 km *(2.7 nm)*; warhead 10 kg. To be replaced by Israeli Barak I in due course.
Guns: 2 Vickers 4.5 in *(115 mm)* Mk 6 semi-automatic (twin) ❹; 80° elevation; 20 rounds/minute to 19 km *(10.3 nm)* anti-surface; 6 km *(3.2 nm)* anti-aircraft; weight of shell 25 kg.
2 or 4 Oerlikon 20 mm Mk 9 ❺; 55° elevation; 800 rounds/minute to 2 km.
2 Bofors 40 mm/60 (14 only).
12.7 mm (single or twin) MGs.
Torpedoes: 6—324 mm Mk 32 (2 triple) tubes ❻; Honeywell Mk 44 Mod 1; active homing to 5.5 km *(3 nm)* at 30 kts; warhead 34 kg.
Countermeasures: Decoys: 2 Corvus 8-barrelled trainable Chaff launchers; distraction or centroid patterns to 1 km.
2 Wallop Barricade double layer Chaff launchers; 6 sets triple-barrelled with four modes of fire.
ESM: UA 8/9; radar warning.
Combat data systems: ADAWS-1. A decision on a new command and control system is still expected.
Fire control: Gunnery MRS 3 system. Seacat 2 GWS 22 systems (not in 14).
Radars: Air search: Marconi Type 965 M ❼ or 966 (14 and 15); A band.
Admiralty Type 277 M ❾; E band. For height finding.
Surface search: Marconi Type 992 Q or R ❽; E/F band; range 55 km *(30 nm)*.
Navigation: Decca Type 978/1006; I band.
Fire control: Gunnery; Plessey Type 903 ❿; I band.
Seaslug; Marconi Type 901 (in 11 and 14) ⓫; G/H band.
Seacat; Two Plessey Type 904 (not in 14) ⓬; I band.

BLANCO ENCALADA

1991, Chilean Navy

Sonars: Kelvin Hughes Type 162 M; hull-mounted; sideways looking classification; high-frequency.
Graseby Type 184 M or Type 184 S (15); hull-mounted; active search and attack; medium range; 7-9 kHz.

Helicopters: 1 Aerospatiale SA 319B Alouette III or SA 365F Dauphin (11 and 14) ⓭. 2 NAS 332F Super Puma (12 and 15) ⓮.

Programmes: Transferred 6 April 1982 *(Prat)*, 22 June 1984 *(Cochrane)*, 3 October 1986 *(Latorre)* and 12 August 1987 *(Blanco Encalada)*. Extensive refits carried out after transfer. *Glamorgan* renamed *Latorre* after the Swedish built cruiser which paid off in 1986. Although all are named after senior officers, the titles Almirante and Capitan are not used.

Modernisation: *Blanco Encalada* converted at Talcahuano into helicopter carrier for two Super Pumas completed May 1988; *Cochrane* undergoing similar conversion with planned completion in 1992. The remaining two will serve as Flagships. All of the class to get PDMS, probably the Israeli Barak I and new command, control and communications, optronic directors and ECM equipment. VDS sonars and torpedo decoys are also a possibility. *Latorre* was transferred with 40 mm guns in lieu of Seacats (damaged in the Falklands War).

Structure: *Blanco Encalada* and *Cochrane* are now markedly different in appearance from their two half-sisters with a greatly enlarged flight deck continued right aft to accommodate two large helicopters simultaneously, making them effectively flush-decked. The hangar has also been completely rebuilt and resembles that of the fleet oiler *Montt*.

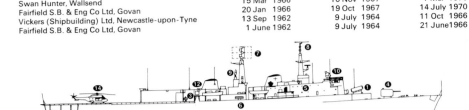

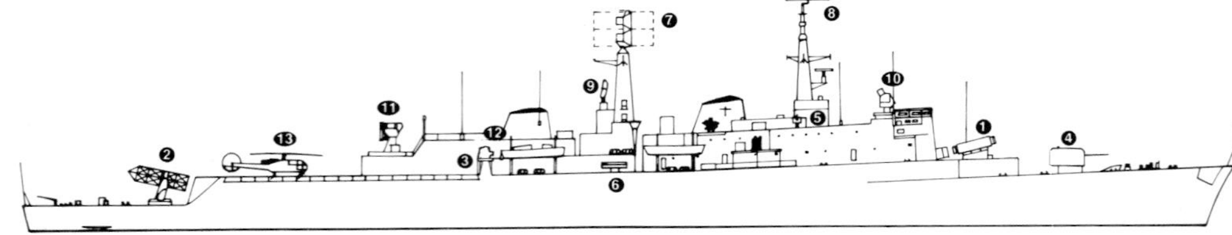

PRAT

(Scale 1 : 1 200), Ian Sturton

PRAT

1991, Chilean Navy

2 ALMIRANTE CLASS

Name	No	Builders	Laid down	Launched	Commissioned
ALMIRANTE RIVEROS	18	Vickers-Armstrong Ltd, Barrow	12 Apr 1957	12 Dec 1958	31 Dec 1960
ALMIRANTE WILLIAMS	19	Vickers-Armstrong Ltd, Barrow	20 June 1956	5 May 1958	26 Mar 1960

Displacement, tons: 2730 standard; 3300 full load
Dimensions, feet (metres): 402 × 43 × 13.3 *(122.5 × 13.1 × 4)*
Main machinery: 2 Babcock & Wilcox boilers; 600 psi *(43.3 kg/cm sq)*; 850°F *(454°C)*; 2 Parsons Pametrada turbines; 54 000 hp *(40 MW)*; 2 shafts
Speed, knots: 34.5. **Range, miles:** 6000 at 16 kts
Complement: 266 (17 officers)

Missiles: SSM: 4 Aerospatiale MM 38 Exocet ❶; inertial cruise; active radar homing to 42 km *(23 nm)* at 0.9 Mach; warhead 165 kg; sea-skimmer.
SAM: 2 Short Bros Seacat quad launchers ❷; optical/radar guidance to 5 km *(2.7 nm)*; warhead 10 kg; 16 reloads.
Guns: 3 or 4 Vickers 4 in *(102 mm)*/60 Mk(N)R ❸; 75° elevation; 40 rounds/minute to 18 km *(10 nm)* anti-surface; 12 km *(6.5 nm)* anti-aircraft; weight of shell 16 kg.
4 Bofors 40 mm/70 ❹; 90° elevation; 300 rounds/minute to 12 km *(6.5 nm)* anti-surface; 4 km *(2.2 nm)* anti-aircraft; weight of shell 2.4 kg.
Torpedoes: 6—324 mm Mk 32 (2 triple) tubes ❺. Honeywell Mk 44 Mod 1; active homing to 5.5 km *(3 nm)* at 30 kts; warhead 34 kg.
A/S mortars: 2 Admiralty Squid DC mortars (3-barrelled) ❻; range 800 m; warhead 52 kg.
Countermeasures: ESM: 1 WLR-1; radar warning (new aerial in *Almirante Riveros*).
Combat data systems: Ferranti action data with autonomous displays.
Fire control: 2 Signaal M-4 directors for Seacat SAMs
Radars: Air search: Plessey AWS 1 ❼; range 110 km *(60 nm)*.
Air/surface search: Marconi SNW 10 ❽; E/F band.
Navigation: Racal Decca 1629; I band.
Fire control: Two SGR 102 ❾; Signaal M4/3 ❿; I/J band.
Sonars: Graseby Type 184 B; hull-mounted; active search and attack; medium frequency (6/9 kHz).
Type 170; hull mounted; active attack; high frequency (15 kHz).

Programmes: Ordered in May 1955. Layout and general arrangements are conventional.
Modernisation: Both modernised by Swan Hunter in co-operation with Plessey: *Almirante Williams* in 1971-74 and *Almirante Riveros* in 1973-75. In the late 1980s both were given a further extensive refit with the addition of modern electronic equipment including Netherlands M4 fire control radars. Israeli Barak I may replace Seacat but these ships have a lower priority than the County and Leander classes. New ESM fitted in 1990.
Operational: 4 in guns were removed one at a time for refurbishment in 1986-88 and ships operated minus one or two turrets each while the work was done.

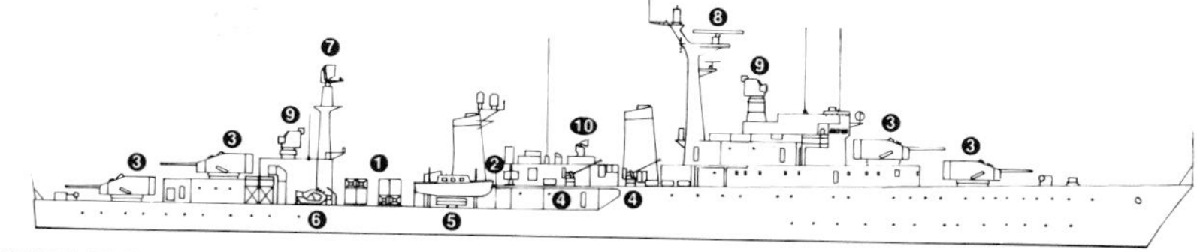

ALMIRANTE RIVEROS *(Scale 1 : 1 200), Ian Sturton*

ALMIRANTE RIVEROS *1991, Chilean Navy*

ALMIRANTE RIVEROS *2/1990, Maritime Photographic*

FRIGATES

3 + 1 BRITISH LEANDER CLASS

Name	*No*	*Builders*	*Laid down*	*Launched*	*Commissioned*
CONDELL	06	Yarrow & Co, Scotstoun	5 June 1971	12 June 1972	21 Dec 1973
LYNCH	07	Yarrow & Co, Scotstoun	6 Dec 1971	6 Dec 1972	25 May 1974
MINISTRO ZENTENO (ex-*Achilles*)	08	Yarrow & Co, Scotstoun	1 Dec 1967	21 Nov 1968	9 July 1970

Displacement, tons: 2500 standard; 2962 full load
Dimensions, feet (metres): 372 oa; 360 wl × 43 × 18 (screws) *(113.4; 109.7 × 13.1 × 5.5)*
Main machinery: 2 Babcock & Wilcox boilers; 550 psi *(38.7 kg/cm sq)*; 850°F *(450°C)*; 2 White/English Electric turbines; 30 000 hp *(22.4 MW)*; 2 shafts
Speed, knots: 29. **Range, miles:** 4500 at 12 kts
Complement: 263 (20 officers)

Missiles: SSM: 4 Aerospatiale MM 40 Exocet (07, 08) ❶; 4 Aerospatiale MM 38 Exocet (06) ❷; inertial cruise; active radar homing to 70 km *(40 nm)* (MM 40), 42 km *(23 nm)* (MM 38) at 0.9 Mach; warhead 165 kg; sea-skimmer.
SAM: Short Bros Seacat GWS 22 quad launcher ❸; optical/radar guidance to 5 km *(2.7 nm)*; warhead 10 kg; 16 reloads. Being replaced by Israeli Barak I vertical launch canisters.
Guns: 2 Vickers 4.5 in *(115 mm)*/45 Mk 6 (twin) semi-automatic ❹; 80° elevation; 20 rounds/minute to 19 km *(10 nm)* anti-surface; 6 km *(3.2 nm)* anti-aircraft; weight of shell 45 kg.
2 Oerlikon 20 mm Mk 9 ❺; 55° elevation; 800 rounds/minute to 2 km.
Torpedoes: 6—324 mm Mk 32 (2 triple) tubes ❻. Honeywell Mk 44 Mod 1; active homing to 5.5 km *(3 nm)* at 30 kts; warhead 34 kg. To be replaced by Murene in due course.
Countermeasures: Decoys: 2 Corvus 8-barrelled trainable Chaff rocket launchers ❼; distraction or centroid patterns to 1 km. Wallop Barricade double layer Chaff launchers.
ESM: UA 8/9; radar intercept. FH12 HF/DF. Elta IR sensor.
Fire control: MRS 3 system for gunnery. GWS 22 system for Seacat.
Radars: Air search: Marconi Type 965/966 ❽; A band.
Surface search: Marconi Type 992 Q ❾; Plessey Type 994 (08); E/F band; range 55 km *(30 nm)*.
Navigation: Kelvin Hughes Type 1006; I band.
Fire control: Plessey Type 903 ❿; I band (for guns).
Plessey Type 904 ⓫; I band (for Seacat). Both radars may be replaced by IAI/Elta in due course.
Sonars: Graseby Type 184 M; hull-mounted; active search and attack; medium frequency (6/9 kHz).
Graseby Type 170 B; hull-mounted; active attack; high frequency (15 kHz).
Kelvin Hughes Type 162 M; hull-mounted; sideways looking classification; high frequency.

Helicopters: 1 Aerospatiale SA 319B Alouette III or SA 365F Dauphin ⓬. Platform for Super Puma (after modernisation).

Programmes: First two ordered from Yarrow & Co Ltd, Scotstoun in the late 1960s. Third ship purchased in September 1990 and transported to Chile in December. One more Batch 3 Leander to follow, probably *Ariadne* in 1992 (plus *Cleopatra*?).
Modernisation: In 1989 *Lynch* was considerably modified at Talcahuano Dockyard with two twin MM 40 Exocet launchers being mounted on each side of the hangar (instead of the MM 38 aft) and by moving the torpedo tubes down one deck. The enlarged flight deck can now take a Super Puma aircraft. Other modifications include Barak VLS canisters to replace Seacat in due course, improvements to the fire control radars and Israeli made EW systems. *Ministro Zenteno* was being similarly modified in 1991 with *Condell* to follow.

Structure: *Condell* and *Lynch* have slightly taller foremasts than British Leander class.

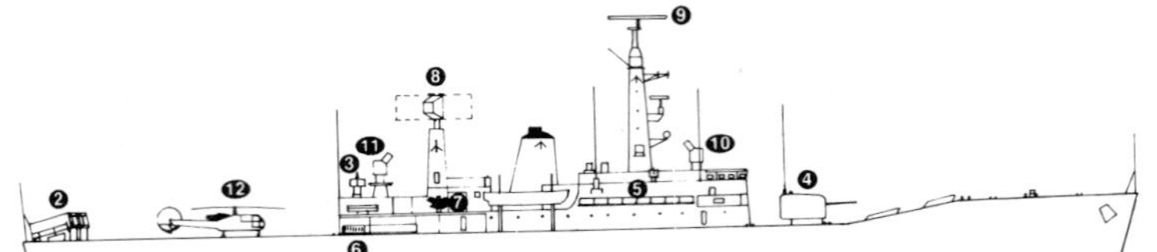
CONDELL *(Scale 1 : 1 200), Ian Sturton*

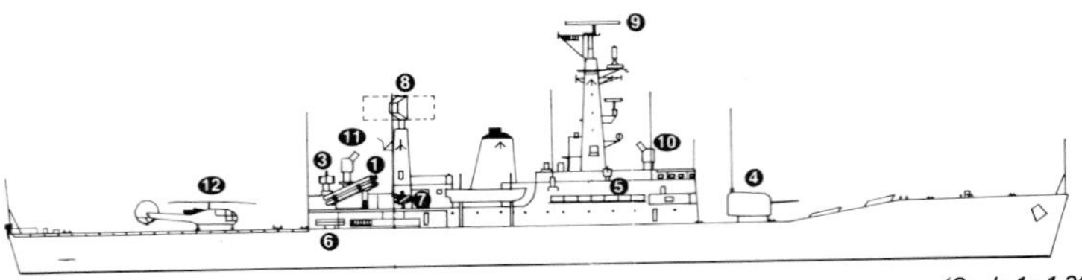
LYNCH *(Scale 1 : 1 200), Ian Sturton*

LYNCH (with MM40 and new EW) *2/1990, Maritime Photographic*

CONDELL (with SSM on stern) *1989, Pedro del Fierro Carmona*

SHIPBORNE AIRCRAFT

Numbers/Type: 7 Aerospatiale SA 319B Alouette III.
Operational speed: 113 kts *(210 km/h)*.
Service ceiling: 10 500 ft *(3200 m)*.
Range: 290 nm *(540 km)*.
Role/Weapon systems: Operated as standard shipborne helicopter and being replaced by Dauphin SA 365F; some shore-based in similar ASW role and for SAR utility duties. Sensors: Omera search radar, hand-mounted FLIR. Weapons: ASW; 1 × Mk 44 torpedo.

Numbers/Type: 4 Aerospatiale SA 365F Dauphin.
Operational speed: 140 kts *(260 km/h)*.
Service ceiling: 15 000 ft *(4575 m)*.
Range: 410 nm *(758 km)*.
Role/Weapon systems: ASW helicopters for escorts to replace SA 319B Alouette IIIs ordered in October 1988 and delivered in 1991. More may be acquired. Sensors: Thomson-CSF Agrion 15 radar. Weapons: 2 × Mk 44 torpedoes (to be replaced by Murene).

Numbers/Type: 7 Bell 206B JetRanger.
Operational speed: 115 kts *(213 km/h)*.
Service ceiling: 13 500 ft *(4115 m)*.
Range: 368 nm *(682 km)*.
Role/Weapon systems: Some tasks and training carried out by torpedo-armed liaison helicopter; emergency war role for ASW. Weapons: ASW; 1 × Mk 44 torpedo.

ALOUETTE III *2/1990, Maritime Photographic*

Numbers/Type: MBB BO 105C.
Operational speed: 113 kts *(210 km/h)*.
Service ceiling: 9845 ft *(3000 m)*.
Range: 407 nm *(754 km)*.
Role/Weapon systems: Coastal patrol helicopter for patrol, training and liaison duties; SAR as secondary role. Sensors: Bendix search radar. Weapons: Unarmed.

BO 105C *1991, Chilean Navy*

Numbers/Type: 4 Nurtanio (Aerospatiale) NAS 332SC Super Puma.
Operational speed: 151 kts *(279 km/h)*.
Service ceiling: 15 090 ft *(4600 m)*.
Range: 335 nm *(620 km)*.
Role/Weapon systems: ASV/ASW helicopters for DLG conversions; surface search and SAR secondary roles. Sensors: Thomson-CSF radar and Alcatel dipping sonar. Weapons: ASW; 2 × Mk 46 torpedoes (to be replaced by Murene) or depth bombs. ASV; 1 or 2 × AM 39 Exocet anti-ship missile.

SUPER PUMA *1991, Chilean Navy*

LAND-BASED MARITIME AIRCRAFT (FRONT LINE)

Numbers/Type: 6 Embraer EMB-111 Bandeirante.
Operational speed: 194 kts *(360 km/h)*.
Service ceiling: 25 500 ft *(7770 m)*.
Range: 1590 nm *(2945 km)*.
Role/Weapon systems: Designated EMB-111N for peacetime EEZ and wartime MR. Sensors: Eaton-AIL AN/APS-128 search radar, ECM/ESM, searchlight. Weapons: Strike; 6 × 127 mm or 28 × 70 mm rockets.

Numbers/Type: 10 Pilatus PC-7 Turbo-Trainer.
Operational speed: 270 kts *(500 km/h)*.
Service ceiling: 32 000 ft *(9755 m)*.
Range: 1420 nm *(2630 km)*.
Role/Weapon systems: Training includes simulated attacks to exercise ships' AA defences; emergency war role for strike operations. Sensors: None. Weapons: 4 × 127 mm or similar rockets and machine gun pods.

Numbers/Type: 2 Dassault-Breguet Gardian.
Operational speed: 470 kts *(870 km/h)*.
Service ceiling: 45 000 ft *(13 715 m)*.
Range: 2425 nm *(4490 km)*.
Role/Weapon systems: Maritime reconnaissance role with limited strike capability. Sensors: Thomson-CSF Varan radar. Omega navigation. ESM/ECM pods. Weapons: ASV; can carry 4 × AM 39 Exocet or podded guns or rocket launchers.

PATROL FORCES

Note: Five new patrol vessels are to be ordered in 1992. 70 m in length with a helo deck and light gun. It is possible that this requirement may be met by acquiring ex-GDR Kondor II minesweepers as patrol craft.

1 Ex-US CHEROKEE CLASS

Name	*No*	*Builders*	*Commissioned*
SARGENTO ALDEA (ex-USS *Arikara* ATF 98)	63	Charleston S.B. & D.D. Co	5 Jan 1944

Displacement, tons: 1235 standard; 1640 full load
Dimensions, feet (metres): 205 × 38.5 × 17 *(62.5 × 11.7 × 5.2)*
Main machinery: Diesel-electric; 4 Busch-Sulzer BS-539 diesels; 4 generators; 1 motor; 3000 hp *(2.24 MW)*; 1 shaft
Speed, knots: 16. **Range, miles:** 7000 at 15 kts; 15 000 at 8 kts
Complement: 85
Guns: 1 USN 3 in *(76 mm)*/50 Mk 26; 85° elevation; 20 rounds/minute to 12 km *(6.5 nm)* anti-surface; 9 km *(5 nm)* anti-aircraft; weight of shell 6 kg.
2 Oerlikon 20 mm; 55° elevation; 800 rounds/minute to 2 km.
Radars: Surface search: Westinghouse SPS 5; G/H band; range 37 km *(20 nm)*.

Comment: Launched on 22 June 1943. Transferred on 1 July 1971 by sale.

SARGENTO ALDEA *1991, Chilean Navy*

1 ANTARCTIC PATROL SHIP

Name	*No*	*Builders*	*Commissioned*
PILOTO PARDO	45	Haarlemsche Scheepsbouw, Netherlands	Aug 1958

Displacement, tons: 1250 light; 2750 full load
Dimensions, feet (metres): 269 × 39 × 1 *(82 × 11.9 × 4.6)*
Main machinery: Diesel-electric; 2000 hp(m) *(1.47 MW)*; 1 shaft
Speed, knots: 14. **Range, miles:** 6000 at 10 kts
Complement: 56 (8 officers)
Military lift: 24 troops
Guns: 1—3 in *(76 mm)* (not always embarked).
Helicopters: 1 Aerospatiale SA 319B Alouette III.

Comment: Antarctic patrol ship, transport and research vessel with reinforced hull to navigate in ice. Launched on 11 June 1958. Also listed as a survey ship by the International Hydrographic Bureau. Possible replacement being sought together with an Icebreaker Tug.

PILOTO PARDO *1991, Chilean Navy*

LIGHT FORCES

2 ISRAELI SAAR 4 CLASS (FAST ATTACK CRAFT—MISSILE)

Name	*No*	*Builders*	*Commissioned*
CASMA (ex-*Romah*)	30	Haifa Shipyard	Mar 1974
CHIPANA (ex-*Keshet*)	31	Haifa Shipyard	Oct 1973

Displacement, tons: 415 standard; 450 full load
Dimensions, feet (metres): 190.6 × 25 × 8 *(58 × 7.8 × 2.4)*
Main machinery: 4 MTU 16V538 TB82 diesels; 11 880 hp(m) *(8.74 MW)* sustained; 4 shafts
Speed, knots: 32. **Range, miles:** 1650 at 30 kts; 4000 at 17.5 kts
Complement: 45

Missiles: SSM: 4 IAI Gabriel I; radar or optical guidance; semi-active radar homing to 20 km *(10.8 nm)* at 0.7 Mach; warhead 75 kg HE.
Guns: 2 OTO Melara 3 in *(76 mm)*/62 compact; 85° elevation; 85 rounds/minute to 16 km *(8.7 nm)* anti-surface; 12 km *(6.5 nm)* anti-aircraft; weight of shell 6 kg.
2 Oerlikon 20 mm; 55° elevation; 800 rounds/minute to 2 km.
Countermeasures: Decoys: 4 Rafael LRCR Chaff decoy launchers.
Radars: Surface search: Thomson-CSF THD 1040 Neptune; E/F band; range 110 km *(60 nm)*.
Fire control: Elta Electronics M 2221; I/J band; range 40 km *(22 nm)*.

Programmes: One transferred late 1979 and second in February 1981 for refit and deployment to Beagle Channel.

CASMA *1988, Chilean Navy*

2 ISRAELI SAAR 3 CLASS (FAST ATTACK CRAFT—MISSILE)

Name	*No*	*Builders*	*Commissioned*
IQUIQUE (ex-*Hamit*)	32	CMN Cherbourg	1969
COVADONGA (ex-*Hefz*)	33	CMN Cherbourg	1969

Displacement, tons: 220 standard; 250 full load
Dimensions, feet (metres): 147.6 × 23 × 8.2 *(45 × 7 × 2.5)*
Main machinery: 4 MTU MD 871 diesels; 10 000 hp(m) *(7.35 MW)* sustained; 4 shafts
Speed, knots: 40+. **Range, miles:** 2500 at 15 kts; 1600 at 20 kts; 1000 at 30 kts
Complement: 35-40 (5 officers)

Missiles: SSM: 6 IAI Gabriel II; active radar or optical TV guidance; semi-active radar homing to 36 km *(20 nm)* at 0.7 Mach; warhead 75 kg.
Guns: 1 OTO Melara 3 in *(76 mm)*/62 DP; 85° elevation; 65 rounds/minute to 8 km *(4.4 nm)*; weight of shell 6 kg.
2—12.7 mm MGs.
Countermeasures: Decoys: 6—24 tube, 4 single tube Chaff launchers.
ESM: Elta Electronics MN-53; intercept.
ECM: Jammer.
Radars: Air/surface search: Thomson-CSF TH-D 1040 Neptune; G band; range 33 km *(18 nm)* for 2 m² target.
Fire control: Selenia Orion RTN 10X; I/J band; range 40 km *(22 nm)*.

Programmes: Both acquired from Israel in December 1988 and commissioned into the Chilean Navy 3 May 1989. There are no immediate plans to transfer any more of the class.

IQUIQUE *1991, Chilean Navy*

4 LÜRSSEN TYPE (FAST ATTACK CRAFT—TORPEDO)

Name	*No*	*Builders*	*Commissioned*
GUACOLDA	80	Bazán, San Fernando	30 July 1965
FRESIA	81	Bazán, San Fernando	9 Dec 1965
QUIDORA	82	Bazán, San Fernando	28 Mar 1966
TEGUALDA	83	Bazán, San Fernando	1 July 1966

Displacement, tons: 134 full load
Dimensions, feet (metres): 118.1 × 18.4 × 7.2 *(36 × 5.6 × 2.2)*
Main machinery: 2 MTU Mercedes-Benz 839Bb diesels; 4800 hp(m) *(3.53 MW)* sustained; 2 shafts
Speed, knots: 32. **Range, miles:** 1500 at 15 kts
Complement: 20
Guns: 2 Bofors 40 mm/70.
Torpedoes: 4—21 in *(533 mm)* tubes for heavyweight anti-ship torpedoes.
Radars: Navigation: Decca 505; I band.

Comment: Built to West German Lürssen design from 1963 to 1966. First launched 1964.

FRESIA *1989, Chilean Navy*

1 US PC-1638 CLASS (LARGE PATROL CRAFT)

Name	*No*	*Builders*	*Commissioned*
PAPUDO (ex-US *PC 1646*)	37	Asmar, Talcahuano	27 Nov 1971

Displacement, tons: 412 full load
Dimensions, feet (metres): 173.7 × 23 × 10.2 *(53 × 7 × 3.1)*
Main machinery: 2 GM 16—567 diesels; 2800 hp *(2.1 MW)*; 2 shafts
Speed, knots: 19. **Range, miles:** 5000 at 10 kts
Complement: 69 (4 officers)
Guns: 1 Bofors 40 mm/60; 90° elevation; 300 rounds/minute to 12 km *(6.5 nm)* anti-surface; 4 km *(2.2 nm)* anti-aircraft; weight of shell 0.89 kg.
4 Oerlikon 20 mm; 50° elevation; 800 rounds/minute to 2 km.
Depth charges: 2 K-type throwers; 4 racks.

Comment: Of similar design to the Turkish Hisar class built to the US PC plan. Hedgehog mortar has been removed.

PAPUDO *1990, Chilean Navy*

6 ISRAELI DABUR CLASS (COASTAL PATROL CRAFT)

GRUMETE DIAZ 1814
GRUMETE BOLADOS 1815
GRUMETE SALINAS 1816
GRUMETE TELLEZ 1817
GRUMETE BRAVO 1818
GRUMETE CAMPOS 1819

Displacement, tons: 35 full load
Dimensions, feet (metres): 65 × 18 × 5.9 *(19.8 × 5.5 × 1.8)*
Main machinery: 2 Detroit 12V-71 diesels; 1920 hp *(1.4 MW)*; 2 shafts
Speed, knots: 22. **Range, miles:** 600 at 13 kts
Complement: 8 (2 officers)
Guns: 2 Oerlikon 20 mm. 2—12.7 mm MGs.
Radars: Surface search: Racal Decca Super 101 Mk 3; I band.

Comment: Transferred from Israel and commissioned 3 January 1991. A fast inflatable boat is carried on the stern. Deployed in the Fourth Naval Zone.

GRUMETE TELLEZ *1991, Chilean Navy*

AMPHIBIOUS FORCES

3 BATRAL CLASS (LSTs)

Name	*No*	*Builders*	*Launched*	*Commissioned*
MAIPO	91	Asmar, Talcahuano	26 Sep 1981	1 Jan 1982
RANCAGUA	92	Asmar, Talcahuano	6 Mar 1982	8 Aug 1983
CHACABUCO	93	Asmar, Talcahuano	16 July 1985	15 Apr 1986

Displacement, tons: 873 standard; 1409 full load
Dimensions, feet (metres): 260.4 × 42.7 × 8.2 *(79.4 × 13 × 2.5)*
Main machinery: 2 SACM Type 195 V12 CSHR diesels; 3600 hp(m) *(2.65 MW)* sustained; 2 shafts; cp props
Speed, knots: 16. **Range, miles:** 3500 at 13 kts
Complement: 49
Military lift: 180 troops; 350 tons
Guns: 1 Bofors 40 mm/60. 1 Oerlikon 20 mm. 2—81 mm mortars.
Radars: Navigation: Decca; I/J band.
Helicopters: Platform for 1 Super Puma.

Comment: First pair laid down in 1980 to standard French design with French equipment. Reported that only two are operational.

RANCAGUA *1990, Chilean Navy*

2 CHILEAN LANDING CRAFT

Name	No	Builders	Commissioned
ELICURA	90	Talcahuano	10 Dec 1968
OROMPELLO	94	Dade Dry Dock Co, Miami	15 Sep 1964

Displacement, tons: 290 light; 750 full load
Dimensions, feet (metres): 145 × 34 × 12.8 *(44.2 × 10.4 × 3.9)*
Main machinery: 2 Cummins VT-17-700M diesels; 900 hp *(660 kW)*; 2 shafts
Speed, knots: 10.5. **Range, miles:** 2900 at 9 kts
Complement: 20
Military lift: 350 tons
Guns: 3 Oerlikon 20 mm (can be carried).
Radars: Navigation: Raytheon 1500B; I/J band.

Comment: Two of similar class operated by Chilean Shipping Co. Oil fuel, 77 tons.

ELICURA *1991, Chilean Navy*

SURVEY SHIP

Note: *Piloto Pardo* also listed—see *Patrol Forces*.

1 Ex-US CHEROKEE CLASS

Name	No	Builders	Commissioned
YELCHO (ex-USS *Tekesta* ATF 93)	64	Commercial Iron Works, Portland, Oregon	16 Aug 1943

Displacement, tons: 1235 standard; 1640 full load
Dimensions, feet (metres): 205 × 38.5 × 17 *(62.5 × 11.7 × 5.2)*
Main machinery: Diesel-electric; 4 GM 12-278A diesels; 4400 hp *(3.28 MW)*; 4 generators; 1 motor; 3000 hp *(2.24 MW)*; 1 shaft
Speed, knots: 16. **Range, miles:** 7000 at 15 kts; 15 000 at 8 kts
Complement: 72 (7 officers)
Guns: 1—3 in *(76 mm)* Mk 26; 85° elevation; 20 rounds/minute to 12 km *(6 nm)* anti-surface; 9 km *(5 nm)* anti-aircraft; weight of shell 6 kg.
2 Oerlikon 20 mm; 55° elevation; 800 rounds/minute to 2 km.

Comment: Was fitted with powerful pumps and other salvage equipment although these were removed on conversion for surveying. Laid down on 7 September 1942, launched on 20 March 1943 and loaned to Chile by the USA on 15 May 1960. Employed as Antarctic research ship and surveying vessel. Similar to *Sargento Aldea* listed under *Patrol Forces*.

YELCHO *1987, Pedro del Fierro Carmona*

TRAINING SHIPS

Note: There is also a small training yacht *Blanca Estela* which can carry a crew of 14 cadets.

Name	No	Builders	Commissioned
URIBE (ex-USS *Daniel Griffin*, APD38)	29	Bethlehem, Hingham	9 June 1943

Displacement, tons: 2130 full load
Dimensions, feet (metres): 306 × 37 × 12.6 *(93.3 × 11.3 × 3.8)*
Main machinery: Turbo-electric; 2 Foster-Wheeler boilers; 435 psi *(30.6 kg/cm sq)*; 750°F *(399°C)*; 2 GE turbo-generators; 12 000 hp *(9 MW)*; 2 motors; 2 shafts
Speed, knots: 22. **Range, miles:** 5000 at 15 kts
Complement: 209
Guns: 1—5 in *(127 mm)*/38 Mk 30. 6 Bofors 40 mm/60 (2 twin).
Radars: Surface search: SPS 4; E/F band.

Comment: Ex-US Charles Lawrence class converted transport transferred 1 December 1966. Paid off in 1984 but was back in commission again in 1988 as a training and general purpose vessel based at Talcahuano.

URIBE *1991, Chilean Navy*

Name	No	Builders	Commissioned
ESMERALDA (ex-*Don Juan de Austria*)	43	Bazán, Cadiz	15 June1954

Displacement, tons: 3420 standard; 3754 full load
Dimensions, feet (metres): 269.2 pp; 360 oa × 44.6 × 23 *(82; 109.8 × 13.1 × 7)*
Main machinery: 1 Fiat diesel; 1400 hp(m) *(1.03 MW)*; 1 shaft
Speed, knots: 11. **Range, miles:** 8000 at 8 kts
Complement: 271 plus 80 cadets
Guns: 2—37 mm saluting guns.

Comment: Four-masted schooner originally intended for the Spanish Navy. Near sister ship of *Juan Sebastian de Elcano* in the Spanish Navy. Refitted Saldanha Bay, South Africa, 1977. Sail area, 26 910 sq ft.

ESMERALDA *7/1990, Maritime Photographic*

TRANSPORTS

Name	No	Builders	Commissioned
AQUILES	AP 47	Asmar, Talcahuano	15 July 1988

Displacement, tons: 2767 light; 4550 full load
Dimensions, feet (metres): 337.8 × 55.8 × 18 *(103 × 17 × 5.5 (max))*
Main machinery: 2 MAK 8 M453B diesels; 7200 hp(m) *(5.29 MW)*; 1 shaft
Speed, knots: 18
Complement: 80
Military lift: 250 troops
Helicopters: Platform for up to Super Puma size.

Comment: Ordered 4 October 1985, launched 4 December 1987. Can be converted rapidly to act as hospital ship. Has replaced the old *Aquiles* (ex-*Tjaldur*).

AQUILES *1988, Pedro del Fierro Carmona*

Name	*No*	*Builders*	*Commissioned*
AGUILA (ex-*Australgas*)	AP 48	Suendborg, Denmark	1957

Displacement, tons: 735 full load
Dimensions, feet (metres): 168.3 × 28.5 × 11.8 *(51.3 × 8.7 × 3.6)*
Main machinery: 1 Burmeister & Wain Alpha diesel; 480 hp(m) *(353 kW)*; 1 shaft
Speed, knots: 9. **Range, miles:** 6000 at 9 kts
Complement: 13
Guns: 3 Oerlikon 20 mm.

Comment: Acquired in 1984 and commissioned into the Navy in 1985. Former commercial liquid gas carrier, now used as a transport.

AGUILA *1990, Chilean Navy*

Name	*No*	*Builders*	*Commissioned*
METEORO	YFB 110	Asmar, Talcahuano	1967

Displacement, tons: 205 full load
Dimensions, feet (metres): 80 × 22 × 8.5 *(24.4 × 6.7 × 2.6)*
Main machinery: 1 diesel; 1 shaft
Speed, knots: 8
Military lift: 220 troops

Comment: Transferred to Seaman's School as harbour transport.

METEORO *1990, Chilean Navy*

TANKERS

Name	*No*	*Builders*	*Commissioned*
ALMIRANTE JORGE MONTT (ex-RFA *Tidepool*)	52	Hawthorn Leslie, Hebburn	28 June 1963

Displacement, tons: 8531 light; 27 400 full load
Measurement, tons: 18 900 dwt; 14 130 gross
Dimensions, feet (metres): 583 × 71 × 32 *(177.6 × 21.6 × 9.8)*
Main machinery: 2 Babcock & Wilcox boilers; 850 psi *(60 kg/cm sq)*; 950°F *(510°C)*; Pametrada turbines; 15 000 hp *(11.2 MW)*; 1 shaft
Speed, knots: 18.3
Complement: 110
Cargo capacity: 18 000 tons liquids
Guns: 4 Oerlikon 20 mm Mk 9; 4 Browning 12.7 mm (2 twin) MGs.
Radars: Navigation: Kelvin Hughes 14/12; I band.
Helicopter Control: Kelvin Hughes 14/16; I band.
Helicopters: Platform for up to 3 Super Puma.

Comment: Eventually transferred August 1982, after being delayed by the British in April 1982 for use in the Falklands' campaign.

ALMIRANTE JORGE MONTT *2/1990, Maritime Photographic*

Name	*No*	*Builders*	*Commissioned*
ARAUCANO	53	Burmeister & Wain, Copenhagen	10 Jan 1967

Displacement, tons: 17 300
Dimensions, feet (metres): 497.6 × 74.9 × 28.8 *(151.7 × 22.8 × 8.8)*
Main machinery: 1 Burmeister & Wain Type 62 VT 2BF140 diesel; 10 800 hp(m) *(7.94 MW)*; 1 shaft
Speed, knots: 17. **Range, miles:** 12 000 at 15.5 kts
Cargo capacity: 21 126 m³ liquid; 1444 m³ dry
Guns: 8 Bofors 40 mm/70 (4 twin); 80° elevation; 120 rounds/minute to 10 km *(5 nm)* anti-surface; 3 km *(1.6 nm)* anti-aircraft; weight of shell 0.89 kg.

Comment: Launched on 21 June 1966.

ARAUCANO *1988, Chilean Navy*

Name	*No*	*Builders*	*Commissioned*
GUARDIAN BRITO (ex-M.S. *Sylvia*)	YOG 101	Marco Chilena Sa-Iquique	1966

Displacement, tons: 482 full load
Dimensions, feet (metres): 129.9 × 23.9 × 10.8 *(39.6 × 7.3 × 3.3)*
Main machinery: 1 MWM diesel; 400 hp(m) *(294 kW)*; 1 shaft
Speed, knots: 10. **Range, miles:** 3000 at 8 kts
Complement: 8 (1 officer)

Comment: Small former commercial tanker. Enlarged for naval service at Asmar, Talcahuano after acquisition 13 January 1983.

GUARDIAN BRITO *1990, Chilean Navy*

SUBMARINE SUPPORT VESSEL

Note: *Huascar*, completed 1865, previously Peruvian monitor, now harbour Flagship at Talcahuano and open to the public as a museum.

Name	*No*	*Builders*	*Commissioned*
ANGAMOS (ex-M/V *Puerto Montt*, ex-M/V *Kobenhavn*)	70	Orenstein & Koppel, West Germany	1966

Measurement, tons: 4616 gross
Dimensions, feet (metres): 308.2 × 53.2 × 13.6 *(93.9 × 16.2 × 4.1)*
Main machinery: 2 Lind-Pielstick diesels; 6500 hp(m) *(4.78 MW)*; 2 shafts
Speed, knots: 17

Comment: Acquired from Chilean state shipping company early 1977 for conversion to submarine support vessel. Entered service early 1979. Former Chilean and Danish ferry.

ANGAMOS *2/1990, Maritime Photographic*

TUGS/SUPPLY VESSELS

Note: Small harbour tugs *Caupolican, Reyes, Galvez* and *Cortés*, and the small personnel transport *Sobenes* are also in commission.

SOBENES *1991, Chilean Navy*

3 VERITAS CLASS (TUG/SUPPLY VESSELS)

Name	*No*	*Builders*	*Commissioned*
JANEQUEO (ex-*Maersk Transporter*)	ATF 65	Salthammex Batbyggeri, Vestness	1974
GALVARINO (ex-*Maersk Traveller*)	ATF 66	Aukra Bruk, Aukra	1974
LAUTARO	ATF 67	—	—

Displacement, tons: 941 light; 2380 full load
Dimensions, feet (metres): 191.3 × 41.4 × 12.8 *(58.3 × 12.6 × 3.9)*
Main machinery: 2 MAK 8M 453AK diesels; 6400 hp(m) *(4.7 MW)*; 2 shafts; cp props; bow thruster
Speed, knots: 14
Complement: 11 plus 12 spare berths
Cargo capacity: 1400 tons
Radars: Navigation: Terma Pilot 7T-48; Furuno FR 240; I band.

Comment: Delivered from Maersk and commissioned into Navy 26 January 1988. Bollard pull, 70 metric tons; towing winch, 100 tons. Fully air-conditioned. Designed for towing large semi-submersible platform in extreme weather conditions. Ice strengthened.

JANEQUEO *1990, Chilean Navy*

Name	*No*	*Builders*	*Commissioned*
LEUCOTON (ex-*Smit Lloyd* 44)	ATF 68	de Waal, Zaltbommel	1972

Displacement, tons: 1750 full load
Dimensions, feet (metres): 174.2 × 39.4 × 14.4 *(53.1 × 12 × 4.4)*
Main machinery: 2 Burmeister & Wain Alpha diesels; 4000 hp(m) *(2.94 MW)*; 2 shafts
Speed, knots: 13

Comment: Acquired in February 1991. Modified at Punta Arenas and now used mainly as a supply ship.

FLOATING DOCKS

Name	*No*	*Lift*	*Commissioned*
INGENIERO MERY (ex-*ARD 25*)	131	3000 tons	1944 (1973)
MUTILLA (ex-*ARD 32*)	132	3000 tons	1944 (1960)
MARINERO GUTIERREZ	—	1200 tons	1991

COAST GUARD

2 BUOY TENDERS

Name	*No*	*Builders*	*Commissioned*
MARINERO FUENTEALBA	75	Asmar, Talcahuano	22 July 1966
CABO ODGER	76	Asmar, Talcahuano	21 Apr 1967

Displacement, tons: 215
Dimensions, feet (metres): 80 × 21 × 9 *(24.4 × 6.4 × 2.7)*
Main machinery: 1 Cummins diesel; 340 hp *(254 kW)*; 1 shaft
Speed, knots: 9. **Range, miles:** 2600 at 9 kts
Complement: 19
Guns: 1 Oerlikon 20 mm. 3 Browning 12.7 mm MGs.

MARINERO FUENTEALBA *1991, Chilean Navy*

2 + (6) PROTECTOR CLASS

ALACALUFE LEP 1603 **HALLEF** LEP 1604

Displacement, tons: 107 full load
Dimensions, feet (metres): 107.3 × 22 × 6.6 *(32.7 × 6.7 × 2)*
Main machinery: 2 MTU diesels; 5200 hp(m) *(3.82 MW)*; 2 shafts
Speed, knots: 20. **Range, miles:** 1000 at 15 kts
Complement: 16

Comment: Built under licence from FBM at Asmar, Talcahuano, in conjunction with FBM Marine. First commissioned 24 June 1989; options on six more. Manned by the Navy for patrol and Pilot Service duties in the Magellan Straits.

ALACALUFE *2/1991, Maritime Photographic*

1 PATROL VESSEL

CASTOR WPC 113

Displacement, tons: 149 full load
Dimensions, feet (metres): 70.8 × 20.7 × 10.5 *(21.6 × 6.3 × 3.2)*
Main machinery: 1 Cummins diesel; 365 hp *(272 kW)*; 1 shaft
Speed, knots: 8
Complement: 14
Guns: 2 Oerlikon 20 mm. 2 Browning 12.7 mm MGs.

Comment: Built in 1968 and commissioned into the Coast Guard in 1975.

10 COASTAL PATROL CRAFT

PILLAN GC 1801
TRONADOR GC 1802
RANO KAU GC 1803
VILLARRICA GC 1804
CORCOVADO GC 1805
LLAIMA GC 1806
ANTUCO GC 1807
OSORNO GC 1808
CHOSHUENCO GC 1809
COPAHUE GC 1810

Displacement, tons: 43 full load
Dimensions, feet (metres): 61 × 17.3 × 5.6 *(18.6 × 5.3 × 1.7)*
Main machinery: 2 MTU 8V331 TC 82 diesels; 1740 hp(m) *(1.28 MW)* sustained; 2 shafts
Speed, knots: 30. **Range, miles:** 700 at 15 kts
Guns: 2 Oerlikon 20 mm; 85° elevation; 800 rounds/minute.
Depth charges: 2 racks.

Comment: Built by Maclaren, Niteroi, Brazil. Ordered 1977. GRP hulls. *Pillan* commissioned August 1979 (approx); *Tronador*, August 1980 (approx); *Rano Kau* and *Villarrica*, November 1980; *Corcovado*, 6 March 1981; *Llaima*, 10 April 1981; *Choshuenco* and *Copahue*, 16 April 1982.

CORCOVADO *1991, Chilean Navy*

2 COASTAL PATROL CRAFT

ONA LEP 1601 **YAGAN** LEP 1602

Displacement, tons: 79 full load
Dimensions, feet (metres): 80.7 × 17.4 × 9.5 *(24.6 × 5.3 × 2.9)*
Main machinery: 2 MTU 6V 331 TC82 diesels; 1300 hp(m) *(960 kW)* sustained; 2 shafts
Speed, knots: 22
Complement: 5
Guns: 2—12.7 mm MGs.

Comment: Built by Asenav and commissioned in 1980.

2 COASTAL PATROL CRAFT

KIMITAHI LPC 1701 **GUALE** LPC 1811

Comment: Details not known.

1 INSHORE PATROL CRAFT

BELLATRIX

Dimensions, feet (metres): 31.8 × 10.2 × 3 *(9.7 × 3.1 × 0.9)*
Main machinery: 2 Volvo diesels; 500 hp(m) *(367 kW)*; 1 shaft
Speed, knots: 24

Comment: Built in 1953.

1 SAR CRAFT

Displacement, tons: 10 full load
Dimensions, feet (metres): 41.7 × 12.8 × 1.6 *(12.7 × 3.9 × 0.5)*
Main machinery: 2 Volvo Penta TAMD-41A diesels; 300 hp(m) *(220 kW)*; 2 waterjets
Speed, knots: 25
Complement: 4 + 32 survivors
Guns: 1—7.62 mm MG.

Comment: Built at Asmar, Talcahuano and completed 8 August 1991. GRP hull.

15 INSHORE PATROL CRAFT

MAULE LPM 1901
LAUCA LPM 1902
ACONCAGUA LPM 1903
RAPEL LPM 1904
ISLUGA LPM 1905
LOA LPM 1906
MAULIN LPM 1907
COPIAPO LPM 1908
CAU-CAU LPM 1909
PUDETO LPM 1910
RIO RINIHUE LPM 1911
CHADMO LPM 1912
CASPANA LPM 1914
PETROHUE LPM 1916
RIO BUENO LPM 1917

Displacement, tons: 14 full load
Dimensions, feet (metres): 43.3 × 11.5 × 3.5 *(13.2 × 3.5 × 1.1)*
Main machinery: 2 MTU 6V 331 TC82 diesels; 1300 hp(m) *(960 kW)* sustained; 2 shafts
Speed, knots: 18
Guns: 1 Browning 12.7 mm MG.

Comment: LPM 1901-1910 ordered in August 1981. Completed by Asenav 1982-83. Remainder built in the late 1980s.

MAULE *1990, Chilean Navy*

1 HOSPITAL SHIP

Name	*No*	*Builders*	*Commissioned*
CIRUJANO VIDELA	GC 111	Asmar, Talcahuano	1964

Displacement, tons: 140 full load
Dimensions, feet (metres): 101.7 × 21.3 × 6.6 *(31 × 6.5 × 2)*
Main machinery: 2 Cummins VT-12-700M diesels; 1400 hp *(1.05 MW)*; 2 shafts
Speed, knots: 14

Comment: Hospital and dental facilities are fitted. A modified version of US PGM 59 design with larger superstructure and less power. Manned by Ministry of Health and operated by Coast Guard.

CIRUJANO VIDELA *1991, Chilean Navy*

LYNCH *2/1990, Maritime Photographic*

CHINA, People's Republic

Note: Chinese names are transliterated in Pin Yin.

Headquarters' Appointments

Commander-in-Chief of the Navy:
Vice Admiral Zhang Lianzhong
Political Commissar of the Navy:
Vice Admiral Wei Jinshan
Deputy Commanders-in-Chief of the Navy:
Vice Admiral Li Jing (naval aviation)
Vice Admiral Zhang Xusan (Chief of Staff)
Vice Admiral Chen Mingshan

Fleet Commanders

North Sea Fleet:
Vice Admiral Qu Zhenmou
East Sea Fleet:
Vice Admiral Nie Kuiju
South Sea Fleet:
Vice Admiral Gao Zhenjia

Personnel

(a) 1992: 260 000 officers and men, including 25 000 naval air force, 6000 marines (28 000 in time of war) and 28 000 for coastal defence
(b) 4 years' national service for sailors afloat; 3 years for those in shore service. Some stay on for up to 15 years.

General

The Soviet involvement with China after 1949 included plans to develop a Sino-Soviet naval presence in the Pacific. These fell apart in the early 1960s as the rift between the two countries deepened but, when Lin Biao was in charge of defence, there was a resurgence of naval programmes. With Lin's death in 1971 these again suffered an eclipse which was intensified in the later years of the Cultural Revolution. The results of this national disaster were the swingeing cuts made in scientific and industrial improvements which delayed any notable advance in naval architecture or weapons systems development. It was only by the mid-1980s that there were signs that this dead period had been put aside and the naval export market was probing beyond the transfer of current designs to Bangladesh, Egypt and Pakistan. New designs of submarines, frigates and patrol craft were advertised and assistance was actively sought from Western Defence industries. Unfortunately the events of 1989 caused a check in co-operation with the West but an active market was maintained in Thailand and Algeria. In 1992 foreign sales efforts are continuing but improved submarine and destroyer designs for the Chinese Navy are being completed and interest in helicopter carriers remains high.

Bases

North Sea Fleet: Qingdao (HQ), Lushun, Weihai Wei, Qingshan, Luda, Huludao, Xiaopingdao, Lien Yun, Ling Shan, Ta Ku Shan, Changshandao, Liuzhuang, Dayuanjiadun
East Sea Fleet: Ningbo (HQ), Zhoushan, Zhenjiangguan, Wusong, Xinxiang, Wenzhou, Sanduao, Xiamen, Xingxiang, Quandou, Wen Zhou SE, Wuhan
South Sea Fleet: Zhanjiang (HQ), Yulin, Haikou, Huangfu, Guangzhou (Canton), Shantou, Humen, Kuanchuang, Tsun, Kuan Chung, Mawai, Beihai, Ping Tan, San Chou Shih, Tang-Chiah Huan, Longmen, Bailong, Dongcun, Baimajing, Xiachuandao, Zhanjiang
(The fleet is split with the main emphasis on the North Sea Fleet).

Training

The main training centres are:

Dalian: First Surface Vessel Academy, Political School
Canton: Second Surface Vessel Academy
Qingdao: Submarine Academy, Aviation School
Wuhan: Engineering College
Jinxi: Aviation School, Artillery (Missile Academy)
Taiyuan: Electronic Engineering College
Nanjing: Naval Staff College, Medical School

Naval Air Force

With 25 000 officers and men and over 700 aircraft, this is a considerable naval air force primarily land-based and with a defensive role. There is also some ASW capability. Interest has been shown in the possibility of an aircraft carrier either in the form of a new construction ship of some 48 000 tons or as a Ro-Ro conversion of an existing vessel.

Strength of the Fleet

Type	*Active (Reserve)*	*Building (Planned)*
SSBN	1	(1)
SSB	(1)	—
Fleet Submarines (SSN)	5	1
Cruise Missile Submarine (SSG)	1	—
Patrol Submarines	43 (60)	2
Destroyers (DDG)	17 (4)	2 (2)
Frigates	38	3 (2)
Fast Attack Craft (Missile)	215	3
Fast Attack Craft (Gun)	370+	?10
Fast Attack Craft (Torpedo)	150 (70)	?
Fast Attack Craft (Patrol)	83	3
Large Patrol Craft	12	?
Coastal Patrol Craft	?	?
River Patrol Craft	69	?
Minesweepers (Ocean)	41	—
Minesweepers (Coastal)	93	2
Mine Warfare Drones	50+	—
Minelayer	1	?
Hovercraft	?	?
Troop Transports	9	—
LSTs	16	?
LSMs	54	—
LSILs	4	—
LCMs—LCUs	370+	—
Submarine Support Ships	11	—
Salvage Ships	21+	—
Survey & Research Ships	60	—
Supply Ships	28+	3
Tankers	33+	—
Boom Defence Vessels	5+	—
Icebreakers	4	—
Repair Ships	2	—
Degaussing Ships	10	—
Miscellaneous	600+	—

Mercantile Marine

Lloyd's Register of Shipping:
2382 vessels of 14 298 912 tons gross

DELETIONS

Note: Where alterations of numbers occur this is as a result of more up-to-date information as well as the normal replacement of older hulls.

PENNANT LIST

Destroyers

101	Anshan
102	Fushun
103	Changchun
104	Qingdao
105	Jinan
106	Xian
107	Yinchuan
108	Xining
109	Kaifeng
110	Dalian
111	—
112	Luhu
131	Nanjing
132	Hefei
133	Chongqing
134	Zunyi
161	Changsha
162	Nanning
163	Nanchang
164	Guilin
165	Sinan
166	—

Frigates

501	Xiaguan
502	Nanchong
503	Kaiyuan
504	Dongchuan
505	Kunming
506	Chengdu
507	Pingxiang
508	Xichang
509	Chang De
510	Shaoxing
511	Nantong
512	Wuxi
513	Huayin
514	Zhenjiang
515	Xiamen
516	Jiujiang
517	Nanping
518	Jian
519	Changzhi
520	—
529	Haikou
531	Yingtan
532	—
533	Ningbo
534	Jinhua
535	Huangshi
536	Wu Hu
537	—
539	—
540	—
543	Dandong
544	Siping
545	—
551	Maoming
552	Yibin
553	Shaoguan
554	Anshun
555	—
556	Xiangtan
557	—

Principal Support Ships

81	Zhenghe
920	Dazhi
J 121	Changxingdao
J 302	Chongmingdao
J 506	Yongxingdao
U 891	Dagushan
X 575	Taicang
X 615	Dongyun

SUBMARINES

Note: The force comprises about 100 hulls of which probably less than half are fully operational. The nuclear propulsion programme is once again proceeding after a pause to try and improve propulsion plant reliability.

Strategic Missile Submarines

1 SOVIET GOLF CLASS (SSB)

200

Displacement, tons: 2350 surfaced; 2950 dived
Dimensions, feet (metres): 321.5 × 28.2 × 21.7 *(98 × 8.6 × 6.6)*
Main machinery: Diesel-electric; 3 Type 73-D diesels; 6000 hp(m) *(4.41 MW)*; 3 motors; 5500 hp(m) *(4 MW)*; 3 shafts
Speed, knots: 17 surfaced; 13 dived
Range, miles: 6000 surfaced at 15 kts
Complement: 86 (12 officers)

Missiles: SLBM: 2 CSS-N-3; two stage solid fuel; inertial guidance to 2700 km *(1460 nm)*; warhead nuclear 2 MT.
Torpedoes: 10—21 in *(533 mm)* tubes (6 bow, 4 stern). 12 Soviet Type 53; dual purpose; pattern active/passive homing up to 20 km *(10.8 nm)* at up to 45 kts; warhead 400 kg.
Radars: Navigation: Snoop Plate; I band.

Programmes: Ballistic missile submarine similar but not identical to the Soviet Golf class. Built at Dalian and launched in 1964.
Structure: Two Missile tubes only because the Chinese missile is reported as having a larger diameter than the Soviet SS-N-5.
Operational: This was the trials submarine for the CSS-N-3 ballistic missile which was successfully launched to 1800 km in October 1982. As the missile is now operational it is probable that the submarine is in reserve but still available if needed.

GOLF Class *1988*

1 XIA CLASS (TYPE 092) (SSBN)

XIA 406

Displacement, tons: 8000 dived
Dimensions, feet (metres): 393.6 × 33 × 26.2
(120 × 10 × 8)
Main machinery: Nuclear; turbo-electric; 1 PWR; 90 MW; 1 shaft
Speed, knots: 22 dived
Complement: 84

Missiles: SLBM: 12 CSS-N-3; two stage solid fuel; inertial guidance to 2700 km *(1460 nm)*; warhead single nuclear 2 MT. An improved version called CSS-NX-4 is being developed.
Torpedoes: 6—21 in *(533 mm)* bow tubes.

Programmes: First laid down in 1978 at Huludao Shipyard and launched 30 April 1981; finally became operational in 1987. A second of class was reported launched in 1982 but it now seems likely that this was not correct and considerable doubts exist about the status of the second hull. A new design Type 094 is being developed with a longer range missile.
Modernisation: CSS-N-3 may be replaced by CSS-NX-4 possibly with MIRV but not until sometime in the mid-1990s.
Structure: Diving depth about 300 m *(985 ft)*.
Operational: First test launch of the two stage CSS-NX-3 missile took place on 30 April 1982 from a submerged pontoon near Huludao (Yellow Sea). Range 1800 km. Second launched on 12 October 1982, from a Golf class trials submarine. The first firing from Xia was in 1985 and was unsuccessful (delaying final acceptance into service of the submarine) and it was not until September 1988 that a satisfactory launch took place.
Opinion: To maintain one submarine on continuous patrol takes a minimum of three and, to be absolutely safe, an optimum number of five hulls. Because of this known requirement there has been a tendency in the West to exaggerate the Chinese SSBN programme both in terms of numbers and timescales.

XIA *1987, Xinhua*

XIA *1987, Xinhua*

XIA *1988, Chinese Gazette*

Attack Submarines

5 + 1 HAN CLASS (SSN)

401 402 403 404 405

Displacement, tons: 5000 dived
Dimensions, feet (metres): 330; 356 (403 onwards) × 36 × 27.9 approx
(100; 108 × 11 × 8.5)
Main machinery: Nuclear; turbo-electric; 1 PWR; 90 MW; 1 shaft
Speed, knots: 25 dived
Complement: 75

Missiles: SSM (403 onwards); Ying Ji (Eagle Strike); inertial cruise; active radar homing to 40 km *(22 nm)* at 0.9 Mach; warhead 165 kg; sea-skimmer.
Torpedoes: 6—21 in *(533 mm)* bow tubes.
Sonars: May include French DUUX-5, some having been delivered in 1985.

HAN Class *1989, CSSC*

Programmes: These are the first Chinese nuclear submarines. With an Albacore hull the first of this class was laid down about 1968 in Huludao shipyard. Her construction may have been delayed as problems were encountered with the power plant, but she appears to have been launched in 1972 and ran trials in 1974. Second Han class was launched in 1977, third in 1983, the fourth in 1987 and the fifth on 8 April 1990.
Structure: From 403 onwards the hull has been extended by some 8 m and Ying Ji SSM tubes fitted aft of the fin.
Operational: In North Sea Fleet. The first pair are probably non-operational and may even have been laid up for scrap.
Sales: Unconfirmed reports suggest Pakistan has been showing an interest.
Opinion: Rumours persist of an improved design at some time in the future and public statements by Chinese Admirals have affirmed that submarine construction and modernisation will remain the top priority to the end of the century.

Patrol Submarines

1 MODIFIED ROMEO CLASS (SSG)

351

Displacement, tons: 1650 surfaced; 2100 dived
Dimensions, feet (metres): 251.3 × 22 × 17.1
(76.6 × 6.7 × 5.2)
Main machinery: Diesel-electric; 2 Type 37-D diesels; 4000 hp(m) *(2.94 MW)*; 2 motors; 2700 hp(m) *(1.98 MW)*; 2 creep motors; 2 shafts
Speed, knots: 13 dived; 15 surfaced; 10 snorting
Complement: 54 (10 officers)

Missiles: SSM: 6 Ying Ji (Eagle Strike); three launchers either side of fin; inertial cruise; active radar homing to 40 km *(22 nm)* at 0.9 Mach; warhead 165 kg; sea-skimmer.
Torpedoes: 8—21 in *(533 mm)* (6 bow, 2 stern) tubes. 16 Soviet Type 53; dual purpose; pattern active/passive homing up to 20 km *(10.8 nm)* at up to 45 kts; warhead 400 kg.
Mines: 20 in lieu of torpedoes.
Radars: Surface search: Snoop Plate and Snoop Tray; I band.
Sonars: Hercules or Tamir 5; hull-mounted; active/passive search and attack; high frequency.

MOD ROMEO 351 (firing Ying Ji) *1987, Xinhua*

Programmes: This design, designated ES5G, is a modified Romeo (Wuhan) rebuilt as a trials SSM platform. Others may be converted in due course.
Structure: The six missile tubes are built into the casing abreast the fin and elevate to fire much as in the Soviet Juliett class. To provide target acquisition an additional radar mast (Snoop Tray) is mounted between the two periscopes.
Operational: Has to surface to fire missiles.

8 + 2 MING CLASS (TYPE 035)

232 233 342 353 356 + 3

Displacement, tons: 1584 surfaced; 2113 dived
Dimensions, feet (metres): 249.3 × 24.9 × 16.7
(76 × 7.6 × 5.1)
Main machinery: Diesel-electric; 2 diesels; 5200 hp(m) *(3.82 MW)*; 2 shafts
Speed, knots: 15 surfaced; 18 dived; 10 snorting
Range, miles: 8000 at 8 kts snorting; 330 at 4 kts dived
Complement: 57 (12 officers)

Torpedoes: 8—21 in *(533 mm)* (6 fwd, 2 aft) tubes. Soviet Type 53; dual purpose; pattern active/passive homing up to 20 km *(10.8 nm)* at up to 45 kts; warhead 400 kg. Total of 16.
Mines: 32 in lieu of torpedoes.
Radars: Surface search: Snoop Plate or Snoop Tray; I band.
Sonars: Hercules/Feniks; hull-mounted; active/passive search and attack; high frequency.

MING 353 *1991*

Programmes: First three completed between 1971 and 1979 one of which was scrapped after a fire. These were Type ES5C/D. Building resumed in 1987 at the rate of more than one per year to a modified design ES5E. This design is probably to be superseded by Type 039 of which the first of class may be laid down in 1992 at Wuzhang Shipyard.
Structure: Diving depth, 300 m *(985 ft)*.
Operational: Active in the East Sea Fleet. Fitted with Magnavox Satnav.

30 + 50 RESERVE SOVIET and CHINESE ROMEO CLASS (TYPE 033)

Displacement, tons: 1475 surfaced; 1830 dived
Dimensions, feet (metres): 251.3 × 22 × 17.1
(76.6 × 6.7 × 5.2)
Main machinery: Diesel-electric; 2 Type 37-D diesels; 4000 hp(m) *(2.94 MW)*; 2 motors; 2700 hp(m) *(1.98 MW)*; 2 creep motors; 2 shafts
Speed, knots: 15.2 surfaced; 13 dived; 10 snorting
Range, miles: 9000 at 9 kts surfaced
Complement: 54 (10 officers)

Torpedoes: 8—21 in *(533 mm)* (6 bow, 2 stern) tubes. 14 Soviet Type 53; dual purpose; pattern; active/passive homing up to 20 km *(10.8 nm)* at up to 45 kts; warhead 400 kg.
Mines: 28 in lieu of torpedoes.
Radars: Surface search: Snoop Plate or Snoop Tray; I band.
Sonars: Hercules or Tamir 5; hull-mounted; active/passive search and attack; high frequency. Thomson Sintra DUUX 5 in some of the class.

ROMEO 250 *12/1989, G. Jacobs*

Programmes: The Chinese continued to construct their own submarines to the Soviet Romeo design up until the end of 1984. The first boats of this class were built at Jiangnan SY, Shanghai in mid-1962 with Wuzhang being used later. The basic Romeo class design is at least 30 years old and has evolved from the Type 031 (ES3B). Construction stopped around 1987 with the resumption of the Ming Class programme.
Modernisation: Battery refits are being done and the more modern boats have French passive ranging sonar; Italian torpedoes have also been reported but not confirmed.
Structure: Diving depth, 300 m *(984 ft)*. There are probably some dimensional variations between newer and older ships of the class.
Operational: Operational numbers are difficult to assess. Of the original 84, at least 50 are in various states of non-operational reserve. ASW capability is virtually non-existent.
Sales: Seven to North Korea in 1973-75. Two to Egypt February/March 1982, two in 1984. All new construction.

5 + 10 (RESERVE) SOVIET WHISKEY V CLASS

Displacement, tons: 1080 surfaced; 1350 dived
Dimensions, feet (metres): 249.3 × 21.3 × 16.1
(76 × 6.5 × 4.9)
Main machinery: Diesel-electric; 2 Type 37-D diesels; 4000 hp(m) *(2.94 MW)*; 2 motors 2700 hp(m) *(1.98 MW)*; 2 shafts
Speed, knots: 18 surfaced; 14 dived
Range, miles: 8500 at 10 kts surfaced
Complement: 54

Guns: 2—25 mm (twin) in some at base of fin.
Torpedoes: 6—21 in *(533 mm)* (4 bow, 2 stern) tubes. 12 Soviet Type 53 or 24 mines.
Radars: Surface search: Snoop Plate; I band.
Sonars: Hull-mounted; active/passive attack; high frequency.

Programmes: Built in China in the 1960s.
Operational: Several have paid off but a few of the remaining 15 have limited operational capability while others are in reserve. Little time is spent at sea.

DESTROYERS

17 LUDA (TYPE 051) CLASS (DDG)

Name	No
JINAN	105 (Type II)
XIAN	106
YINCHUAN	107
XINING	108
KAIFENG	109
DALIAN	110
—	111
NANJING	131
HEFEI	132
CHONGQING	133 (? Type II)
ZUNYI	134
CHANGSHA	161
NANNING	162
NANCHANG	163
GUILIN	164
SINAN	165 (Type III)
—	166 (Type III)

Displacement, tons: 3250 standard; 3670 full load
Dimensions, feet (metres): 433.1 × 42 × 15.1 *(132 × 12.8 × 4.6)*
Main machinery: 2 boilers; 2 turbines; 72 000 hp(m) *(53 MW)*; 2 shafts
Speed, knots: 32. **Range, miles:** 2970 at 18 kts
Complement: 220 (27 officers)

Missiles: SSM: 6 HY-2 (2 triple) launchers ❶; (Types I and II); active radar or IR homing to 80 km *(43.2 nm)* at 0.9 Mach; warhead 513 kg.
4 Ying Ji (Eagle Strike) (quad) launchers (Type III); active radar homing to 40 km *(22 nm)* at 0.9 Mach; warhead 165 kg; sea-skimmer.
SAM: Thomson-CSF Crotale octuple launcher (Type III); fitted forward of bridge; line of sight guidance to 13 km *(7 nm)* at 2.4 Mach; warhead 14 kg.
Guns: 4 (Type I) or 2 (Type II) USSR 5.1 in *(130 mm)*/58 (2 twin) (Type I) ❷; 85° elevation; 17 rounds/minute to 29 km *(16 nm)*; weight of shell 33.4 kg.
2 China 3.9 in *(100 mm)*/56 (twin) (Type III); 85° elevation; 18 rounds/minute to 22 km *(12 nm)*; weight of shell 15.9 kg.
8 China 57 mm/70 (4 twin) ❸; 85° elevation; 120 rounds/minute to 12 km *(6.5 nm)*; weight of shell 6.31 kg. These guns are fitted in some of the class, the others have 37 mm.
6 or 8 China 37 mm/63 (3 or 4 twin) (3 twin in Types II and III); 85° elevation; 180 rounds/minute to 8.5 km *(4.6 nm)*; weight of shell 1.42 kg.
8 USSR 25 mm/60 (4 twin) ❹; 85° elevation; 270 rounds/minute to 3 km *(1.6 nm)* anti-aircraft; weight of shell 0.34 kg.
A/S mortars: 2 FQF 2500 12-tubed fixed launchers ❺; 120 rockets; range 1200 m; warhead 34 kg. Similar in design to the Soviet RBU 1200.
Depth charges: 2 or 4 projectors; 2 or 4 racks.
Mines: 38.
Countermeasures: Decoys: Chaff launchers (fitted to some).
ESM: Jug Pair (RW-23-1); 2-18 GHz; radar warning.
Combat data systems: Thomson-CSF TAVITAC with Vega FCS (Type III).
Radars: Air search: Knife Rest or Cross Slot; A band or Bean Sticks or Pea Sticks ❻; E/F band.
Rice Screen (on mainmast in some); 3D; G band. Similar to Hughes SPS-39A.
Surface search: Eye Shield ❼; E band or Thomson-CSF Sea Tiger (Type III); E/F band.
Square Tie (not in all); I band; range 73 km *(40 nm)* or limits of radar horizon.
Navigation: Fin Curve; I band.
Fire control: Wasp Head (series 1). Also known as Wok Won.
Sun Visor B (series 2) ❽; G/H band.
2 Rice Lamp (series 2) ❾; I band (for 57 mm guns).
IFF: High Pole.
Sonars: Pegas 2M and Tamir 2; hull-mounted; active search and attack; high frequency.
VDS (Type III); active attack.
Helicopters: 2 Harbin Z-9A (Dauphin) ❿ (Type II).

Programmes: The first Chinese-designed destroyers of such a capability to be built. First of class completed in 1971. 105-111 built at Luda; 131-134 at Shanghai and 161-166 at Guangzhou. Similar to the deleted Soviet Kotlin class. The programme was much retarded after 1971 by drastic cuts in the defence budget. In early 1977 building of series two of this class was put in hand and includes those after 109, all but one of which commissioned in the 1980s with the latest 164 in April 1987, 165 in early 1990 and 166 and 111 in 1992. The order of completion was 105, 160 (scrapped), 106, 161, 107, 162, 131, 108, 132, 109, 163, 110, 133, 134, 164, 165, 111 and 166.
Modernisation: First of class 105 completed a major refit in 1987 as a Type II trials ship, with the after armament replaced by a twin helicopter hangar and deck. Other candidates for helo conversions include *Chongqing*.
Structure: Electronics vary in later ships. Some ships have 57 mm guns, others 37 mm. *Jinan* may have Alcatel 'Safecopter' landing aid. 165 and 166 are Type III with a quadruple trainable Ying Ji launcher between the funnels and a twin 100 mm mounting (similar to those in the Jiangdong class). Thomsea combat data system including Vega FCS has been installed with Crotale CIWS and Sea Tiger search radar.
Operational: Capable of foreign deployment, although command and control is limited. Underway refuelling is practised. Deployment; 105 series in North and East Sea Fleets; 131 series in East Sea Fleet; 161 series in South Sea Fleet. 160 was damaged by an explosion in 1978, and was scrapped. 105 completed helicopter trials in December 1987 following modifications made by the China Design and Research Institute for shipborne operations.

LUDA Class (with Rice Screen) *1990, CSSC*

HEFEI *8/1991*

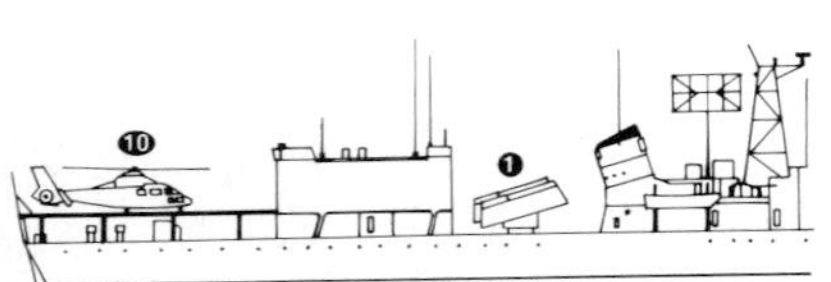

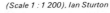

TYPE II *(Scale 1 : 1 200), Ian Sturton*

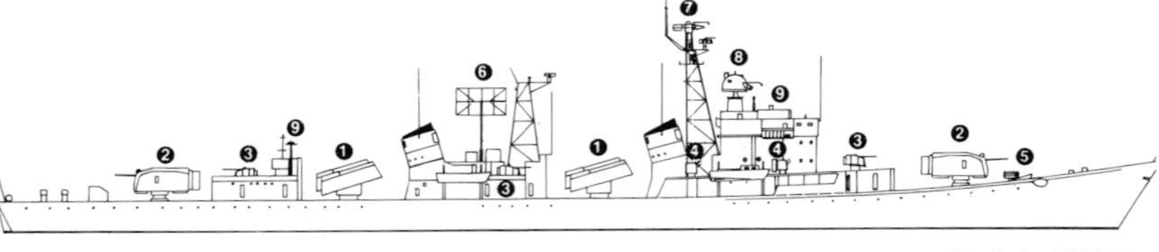
TYPE I *(Scale 1 : 1 200), Ian Sturton*

JINAN *1991*

HEFEI 1/1990

0 + 1 + 1 (2) LUHU (TYPE 052) CLASS (DDG)

Name	*No*	*Builders*	*Laid down*	*Launched*	*Commissioned*
LUHU	112	Jiangnan Shipyard	1988	June 1991	1993

Displacement, tons: 4200 standard
Measurement, tons: 492 × 52.5 × 16.4
(150 × 16 × 5)
Main machinery: CODOG; 2 GE LM 2500 gas turbines; 44 000 hp *(33 MW)* sustained; 2 MTU 12V 1163 TB83 diesels; 8840 hp(m) *(6.5 MW)*; 2 shafts; cp props
Speed, knots: 30
Complement: 300

Missiles: SSM: 8 Ying Ji (Eagle Strike) ❶.
SAM: HQ-61 or Crotale ❷.
Guns: 1—3.9 in *(100 mm)*/56 ❸.
8—37 mm/63 (4 twin) ❹.
Torpedoes: 6—324 mm Whitehead B515 (2 triple) tubes ❺. Whitehead A 244S; anti-submarine.
A/S mortars: 2 FQF 2500 ❻ 12-tubed fixed launchers.
Countermeasures: Decoys: 2 SRBOC Mk 33; 6-barrelled Chaff launchers. 2 China 26-barrelled Chaff launchers.
ESM/ECM: Intercept and jammer.
Combat data systems: Thomson-CSF TAVITAC; action data automation.
Radars: Air search: Rice Screen ❼; 3D; G band.
Air/surface search: Thomson-CSF Sea Tiger type ❽; E/F band.
Surface search: Eye Shield ❾; E band.
Navigation: I band.
Fire control: Type 343 Sun Visor ❿; I band (for SSM and 100 mm).
Two type 347G ⓫; I band (for 37 mm).
Sonars: Hull-mounted; active search and attack; medium frequency.
VDS; active attack; medium frequency.
Helicopters: 2 Harbin Z9A (Dauphin) ⓬.

Programmes: First of a new class expected for some years but delayed by priority being given to export orders for Thailand. Now in series production probably replacing the Luda class. Sea trials expected in mid-1992.
Structure: Weapon systems not all installed by early 1992 so a SAM or Crotale PDMS is a possibility. Many of the other details listed are to some extent also speculative.
Opinion: By Chinese standards this is an impressive looking ship and the assiduous wooing of Western manufacturers has achieved a major step forward in operational capabilities.

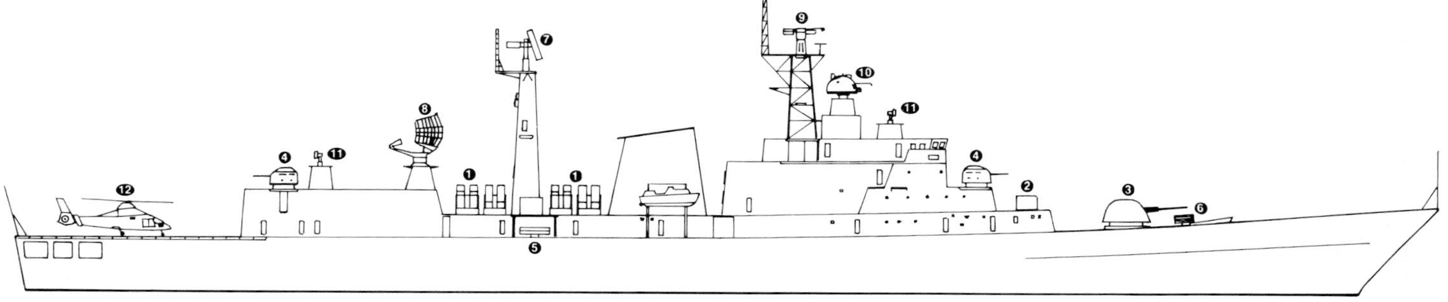
LUHU (impression) *(Not to scale), Ian Sturton*

4 (RESERVE) GORDY (TYPE 07) CLASS (DDG)

Name	*No*	*Builders*	*Laid down*	*Launched*	*Commissioned*
ANSHAN (ex-*Razyaschy*)	101	Nikolayev-Dalzavod	1935	1938	1940
FUSHUN (ex-*Rezky*)	102	Nikolayev-Komsomolsk	1935	1939	1942
CHANGCHUN (ex-*Reshiteleny*)	103	Nikolayev-Dalzavod	1935	1939	1941
QINGDAO (ex-*Retivy*)	104	Nikolayev-Komsomolsk	1936	1939	1942

Displacement, tons: 1660 standard; 2040 full load
Dimensions, feet (metres): 370 × 33.5 × 13
(112.8 × 10.2 × 4)
Main machinery: 3 boilers; 2 Tosi turbines; 48 000 hp(m) *(35 MW)*; 2 shafts
Speed, knots: 32. **Range, miles:** 2670 at 19 kts; 850 at 32 kts
Complement: 205 (15 officers)

Missiles: SSM: 4 HY-2 (2 twin) launchers ❶; active radar or IR homing to 80 km *(43.2 m)* at 0.9 Mach; warhead 513 kg.
Guns: 4 USSR 5.1 in *(130 mm)*/50 ❷; 45° elevation; 12 rounds/minute to 25 km *(13.6 nm)*; weight of shell 33.4 kg.
8 China 37 mm/63 (4 twin) ❸; 85° elevation; 180 rounds/minute to 8.5 km *(4.6 nm)* anti-aircraft; weight of shell 1.42 kg.
Depth charges: 2 Projectors; 2 racks.
Mines: Can carry 60.
Fire control: Mina GFCS. Four Eyes optronic director ❹.
Radars: Air search: Cross Bird ❺; A band.
Air/surface search: High Sieve ❻; E/F band.
Surface search: Square Tie ❼; I band; range 73 km *(40 nm)* or limits of radar horizon.
Ball End ❽; E/F band; range 37 km *(20 nm)*.
Navigation: Neptun or Fin Curve; I band.
IFF: Yard Rake.
Sonars: Pegas-2M; hull-mounted; active search and attack; high frequency.

Programmes: Gordy Type 7 of Odero-Terni-Orlando design assembled in the Pacific Fleet yards from kits supplied by Nikolayev. Two transferred in December 1954 and two in July 1955.
Modernisation: Converted between 1971 and 1974. The alterations consist of the replacement of the torpedo tubes by a pair of twin Hai Ying 2 launchers and the fitting of twin 37 mm mounts in place of the original singles.
Operational: Held in operational reserve but unlikely to go to sea again.

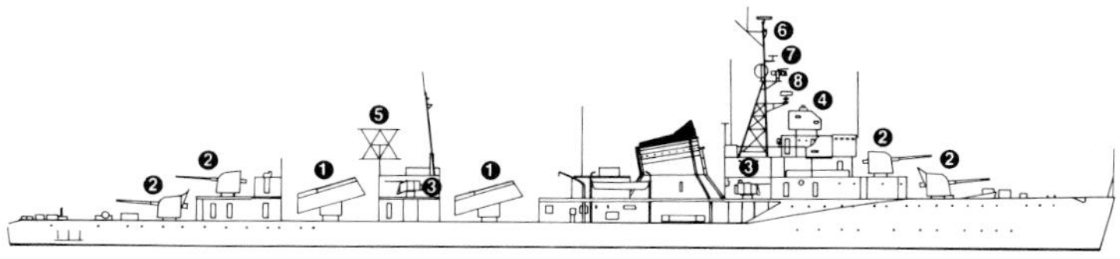

ANSHAN *(Scale 1 : 1 200), Ian Sturton*

ANSHAN *1986, G. Jacobs*

FRIGATES

27 JIANGHU (TYPE 053) CLASS (FFG)

Name	No	Name	No	Name	No
CHANG DE	509	**JIAN**	518	**SIPING**	544 (Type II)
SHAOXING	510	**CHANGZHI**	519	—	545
NANTONG	511	—	520	**MAOMING**	551
WUXI	512	**NINGBO**	533	**YIBIN**	552
HUAYIN	513	**JINHUA**	534	**SHAOGUAN**	553
ZHENJIANG	514	**HUANGSHI**	535 (Type III)	**ANSHUN**	554 (Type III)
XIAMEN	515	**WU HU**	536 (Type III)	—	555
JIUJIANG	516	—	537 (Type III)	**XIANGTAN**	556
NANPING	517	**DANDONG**	543	—	557

Displacement, tons: 1425 standard; 1702, 1820 (Type II), 1924 (Type III) full load
Dimensions, feet (metres): 338.5 × 35.4 × 10.2 *(103.2 × 10.8 × 3.1)*
Main machinery: 2 SEMT-Pielstick 12 PA6 BTC diesels; 14 400 hp(m) *(10.6 MW)* sustained; 2 shafts
Speed, knots: 26. **Range, miles:** 4000 at 15 kts; 2700 at 18 kts
Complement: 185 (25 officers)

Missiles: SSM: 4 HY-2 (2 twin) launchers (2 in Type II, none in Type III) ❶; active radar or IR homing to 80 km *(43.2 nm)* at 0.9 Mach; warhead 513 kg.
8 Ying Ji (Eagle Strike) (Type III) ❷; active radar homing to 40 km *(22 nm)* at 0.9 Mach; warhead 165 kg; sea-skimmer. May be replaced by YJ-2 in due course. This improved version has a range of 85 km *(45.9 nm)*.
Guns: 2 or 4 China 3.9 in *(100 mm)*/56 ❸ (1 or 2 twin), none in Type II); 85° elevation; 18 rounds/minute to 22 km *(12 nm)*; weight of shell 15.9 kg.
1 Creusot Loire 3.9 in *(100 mm)*/55 ❹ (Type II); 85° elevation; 60-80 rounds/minute to 17 km *(9.3 nm)*; weight of shell 13.5 kg.
12 China 37 mm/63 (6 twin) ❺ (8 (4 twin), in some Type I, II and III); 85° elevation; 180 rounds/minute to 8.5 km *(4.6 nm)* anti-aircraft; weight of shell 1.42 kg.
Torpedoes: 6—324 mm ILAS (2 triple) tubes ❻ (Type II). Whitehead A 244S; anti-submarine.
A/S mortars: 2 RBU 1200 5-tubed fixed launchers (4 in some) ❼; range 1200 m; warhead 34 kg.
Depth charges: 2 BMB-2 projectors; 2 racks.
Mines: Can carry up to 60.
Countermeasures: Decoys: 2 SRBOC Mk 33 6-barrelled Chaff launchers (in some). 2 China 26-barrelled launchers (in remainder).
ESM: Jug Pair or Watchdog or Elettronica Newton (Type III); radar warning.
ECM: Elettronica 929 (Type III); jammers.
Fire control: Naja optronic director (Type II) for 100 mm gun.
Radars: Air/surface search: MX 902 Eye Shield ❽; possible E band.
Surface search/fire control: Square Tie ❾; I band; range 73 km *(40 nm)*.
Navigation: Don 2 or Fin Curve; I band.
Fire control: Wok Won (in Types I and II) ❿.
Sun Visor (Type III and some Type I) ⓫; I band.
Rice Lamp ⓬ (in Type III and some Type I).
IFF: High Pole A. Yard Rake or Square Head.
Sonars: Echo Type 5; hull-mounted; active search and attack; medium frequency.

Helicopters: Harbin Z-9A (Dauphin) (in Type II) ⓭.

Programmes: A modification of Jiangdong class with SSM in place of SAM. Pennant numbers changed in 1979. All built in Shanghai starting in the mid 1970s at the Hudong and Jiangnan shipyards and still continuing with priority being given to export orders.
Modernisation: Fire control and electronics equipment is being modernised. Sun Visor and Rice Lamp have been seen on newly refitted Type Is.
Structure: All of the class have the same hull dimensions. Previously reported Type numbers have been superseded by the following designations:
Type I has four versions. Version 1 has an oval funnel and square bridge wings; version 2 a square funnel with bevelled bridge face; version 3 an octagonal funnel and version 4 reverts back to the oval funnel.
Type II (No 544) has a hangar and flight deck and only two Hai Ying (twin) SSM and is referred to as 053HT(H). Has CSEE Naja optronic director and Alcatel 'Safecopter' landing aid. A candidate for the second conversion is 511 seen in September 1990 with its after superstructure stripped to deck level.
Type III (Nos 535 and 536) are referred to as New Missile Frigates (053HT) and have an increased displacement, eight Ying Ji SSMs, four 100 mm (two twin), eight 37 mm (four twin) guns, Rice Lamp fire control radar and Italian EW equipment. Also the main deck is higher in the midships section and the lower part of the mast is solid. Torpedo tubes may be fitted in due course.

Sales: Two have been transferred to Egypt, one in September 1984, the other in March 1985, and two to Bangladesh, the first in November 1989. Four more being built for Thailand (2 Type II and 2 Type III). Thailand has also ordered two much larger ships of 2900 tons (full load) and 119 m in length.

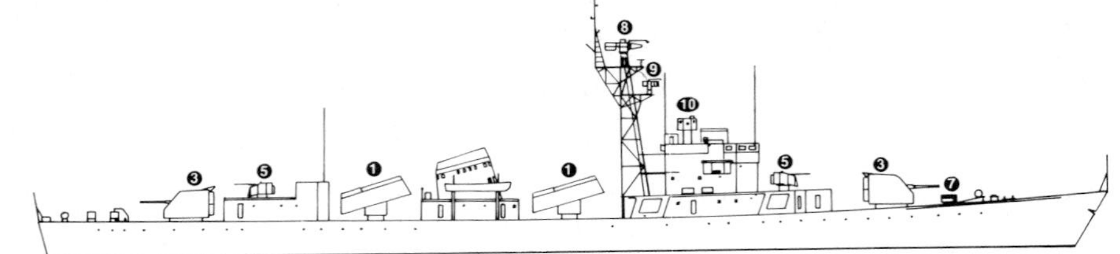

JIANGHU Type I (053) *(Scale 1 : 900), Ian Sturton*

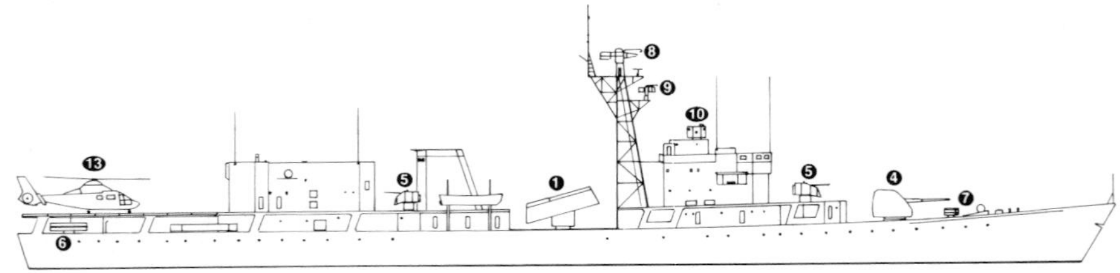

JIANGHU Type II (053HT(H)) *(Scale 1 : 900), Ian Sturton*

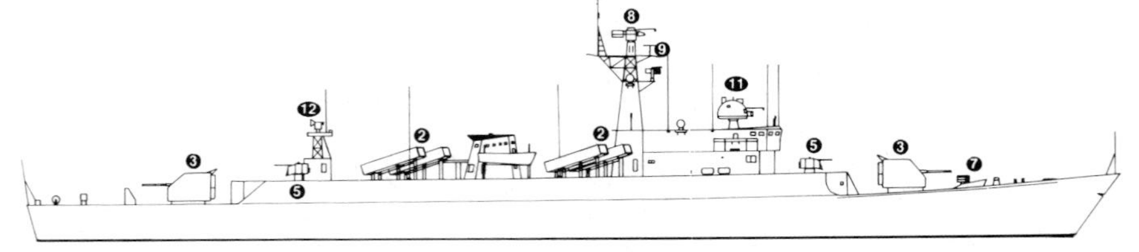

JIANGHU Type III (053HT) *(Scale 1 : 900), Ian Sturton*

CHANGZHI *1988*

XIANGTAN *1988*

DANDONG *1991*

NANTONG (alongside Zhenjiang) *7/1991*

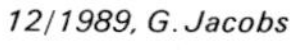
WU HU *12/1989, G. Jacobs*

WU HU *1989*

SIPING *1990*

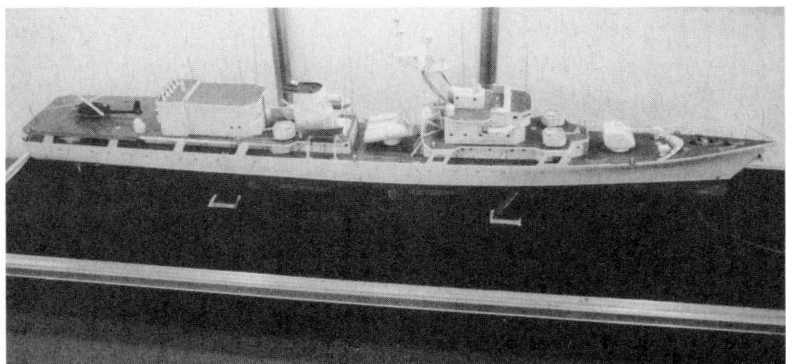

SIPING (model) *1990*

0 + 2 + 1 (2) JIANGWEI CLASS (FFG)

Name	No	Builders	Laid down	Launched	Commissioned
—	539	Huangzhou Shipyard	1988	1990	1992
—	540	Hudong Shipyard	1989	1990	1992
—	—	Huangzhou Shipyard	1990	1992	1993

Displacement, tons: 2250 standard
Dimensions, feet (metres): 377.3 × 45.9 × 13.1 *(115 × 14 × 4)*
Main machinery: 2 SEMT-Pielstick 12 PA6 BTC diesels; 14 400 hp(m) *(10.6 MW)* sustained; 2 shafts
Speed, knots: 25
Complement: 200

Missiles: SSM: 4 Ying Ji (Eagle Strike) may be fitted.
SAM: 8 HQ-61 M (CSA-N-1) VLS/canister launch system.
Thomson-CSF Crotale octuple launcher (539) (in B gun position).
Guns: 2 China 3.9 in *(100 mm)*/56 (twin).
4 or 8 China 37 mm/63 (2 or 4 twin).
Countermeasures: 2 SRBOC Mk 33 6-barrelled Chaff launchers.
2 China 26-barrelled Chaff launchers.
Radars: Air search: Rice Screen; G band.
Surface search: Square Tie; I band.
Fire control: 2 Rice Lamp.
Navigation: Fin Curve; I band.
Sonars: Echo Type 5; hull-mounted; active search and attack; medium frequency.

Helicopters: 1 Harbin Z9A (Dauphin).

Programmes: There has been ineviatable confusion between this programme, the Jianghu Type IIs and the Thai frigates. It is possible this is just another variation of the Jianghu design. First one conducted sea trials in 1991. In series production.
Structure: Some of the details listed are speculative. The Crotale SAM system is reported as fitted forward in the first of class. An operational SAM system is long overdue and this may be instead of the SSM launchers.

JIANGWEI Class *1991*

2 JIANGDONG (TYPE 053K) CLASS (FFG)

YINGTAN 531 — 532

Displacement, tons: 1674 standard; 1924 full load
Dimensions, feet (metres): 338.5 × 35.1 × 10.2 *(103.2 × 10.7 × 3.1)*
Main machinery: 2 SEMT-Pielstick 12 PA6 280 BTC diesels; 14 400 hp(m) *(10.6 MW)* sustained; 2 shafts
Speed, knots: 26. **Range, miles:** 4000 at 15 kts; 1800 at 25 kts
Complement: 185

Missiles: SAM: 2 CSA-NX-2 (HQ 61) twin arm launchers ❶; command guidance; semi-active radar homing to 10 km *(5.5 nm)* at 3 Mach; height 50-8000 m *(164-26 250 ft)*.
Guns: 4 China 3.9 in *(100 mm)*/56 (2 twin) ❷; 85° elevation; 18 rounds/minute to 22 km *(12 nm)*; weight of shell 15.9 kg.
8 China 37 mm/63 (4 twin) ❸; 85° elevation; 180 rounds/minute to 8.5 km *(4.6 nm)* anti-aircraft; weight of shell 1.42 kg.
A/S mortars: 2 RBU 1200 5-tubed fixed launchers ❹; range 1200 m; warhead 34 kg.
Depth charges: 2 BMB-2 projectors; 2 racks.
Countermeasures: ESM: 2 Jug Pair.
Fire control: Fog Lamp FCS fitted in 531 in 1985. System may be used in new construction.
Radars: Air search: Rice Screen ❺; 3D; G band.
Surface search: Square Tie ❻; I band; range 73 km *(40 nm)* or limits of radar horizon.
Navigation: Fin Curve; I band.
Fire control: Sun Visor B ❼; G/H/I band (for 57 mm guns).
2 Fog Lamp ❽; H/I band (for SAM).
Rice Lamp ❾; I band (for 37 mm guns).
IFF: Ski Pole. Yard Rake.
Sonars: Probably Pegas-2M and Tamir 2; hull-mounted; active search and attack; medium/high frequency.

Programmes: *Yingtan* was laid down at Hudong, Shanghai in 1970 and commissioned in 1977. The second of class (532) built two years later at Jiuxin, Shanghai has not been reported since it was photographed in 1982 without SAM systems. Jiangdong class is called an 'Anti-Air Missile Frigate'.
Structure: First SAM armed Chinese ship(s). Rice Screen is also the first modern air search radar to be fitted.
Operational: The SAM system has a long history of problems and may still not be fully operational.

YINGTAN *12/1988, G. Jacobs*

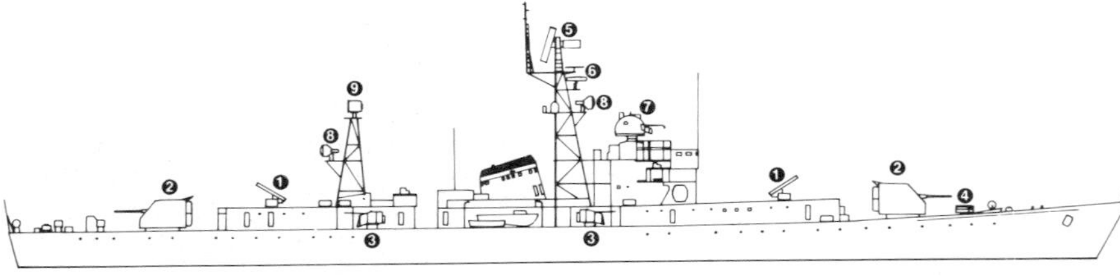

YINGTAN *(Scale 1 : 900), Ian Sturton*

5 JIANGNAN (TYPE 065) CLASS (FF)

XIAGUAN	501	KAIYUAN	503	HAIKOU	529
NANCHONG	502	DONGCHUAN	504		

Displacement, tons: 1350 standard; 1600 full load
Dimensions, feet (metres): 300.1 × 33.1 × 10.5 *(91.5 × 10.1 × 3.2)*
Main machinery: 2 SEMT-Pielstick 12 PA6 280 BTC diesels; 14 400 hp(m) *(10.6 MW)* sustained; 2 shafts
Speed, knots: 28. **Range, miles:** 3000 at 10 kts; 900 at 26 kts
Complement: 180 (15 officers)

Guns: 3 China 3.9 in *(100 mm)*/56 (1 fwd, 2 aft) ❶; 85° elevation; 18 rounds/minute to 22 km *(12 nm)*; weight of shell 15.9 kg.
8 China 37 mm/63 (4 twin) ❷; 85° elevation; 180 rounds/minute to 8.5 km *(4.6 nm)*; weight of shell 1.42 kg.
4 China 14.5 mm/93 (2 twin); 85° elevation; 600 rounds/minute to 7 km *(3.8 nm)*.
A/S mortars: 2 RBU 1200 5-tubed fixed launchers ❸; range 1200 m; warhead 34 kg.
Depth charges: 4 BMB-2 projectors; 2 racks.
Mines: Can carry up to 60.
Radars: Surface search: Ball End ❹; E/F band; range 37 km *(20 nm)*.
Navigation: Neptun or Fin Curve; I band.
Fire control: Twin Eyes ❺.
Sonars: Pegas-2M and Tamir 2; hull-mounted; active search and attack; medium/high frequency.

Programmes: The Chinese Navy embarked on a new building programme in 1965 of which this class was the first. All five built at Guangzhou and commissioned in 1967-68. Development of Soviet Riga class. All had major refits since 1974.
Operational: Four with South Sea Fleet and one with East Sea Fleet. One may have been used as an early trials ship for the HY 2 SSM.

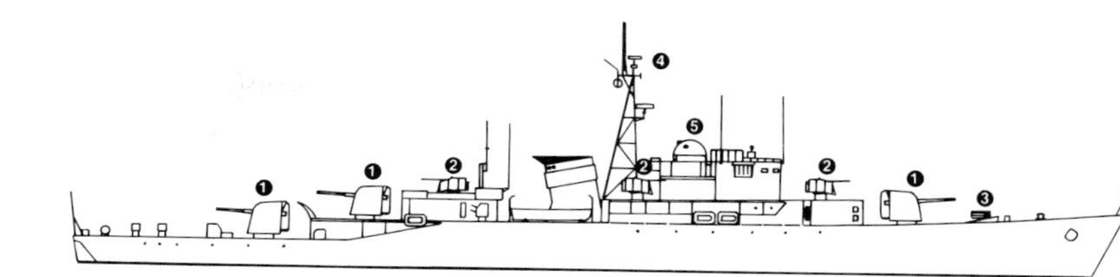

JIANGNAN Class *(Scale 1 : 900), Ian Sturton*

KAIYUAN *1986*

4 CHENGDU (TYPE 01) CLASS (FFG)

Name	*No*	*Builders*	*Laid down*	*Launched*	*Commissioned*
KUNMING	505	Hutong, Shanghai	1955	26 Sep 1956	1958
CHENGDU	506	Guangzhou	1955	1957	1959
PINGXIANG	507	Hutong, Shanghai	1955	28 Apr 1956	1958
XICHANG	508	Guangzhou	1955	1957	1959

Displacement, tons: 1240 standard; 1460 full load
Dimensions, feet (metres): 300.1 × 33.1 × 10.5 *(91.5 × 10.1 × 3.2)*
Main machinery: 2 boilers; 2 turbines; 20 000 hp(m) *(14.7 MW)*; 2 shafts
Speed, knots: 28. **Range, miles:** 2000 at 10 kts
Complement: 170 (16 officers)

Missiles: SSM: 2 HY-2 (twin) launcher ❶; active radar or IR homing to 80 km *(43.2 nm)* at 0.9 Mach; warhead 513 kg.
Guns: 2 or 3 China 3.9 in *(100 mm)*/56 ❷; 85° elevation; 18 rounds/minute to 22 km *(12 nm)*; weight of shell 15.9 kg.
4 China 37 mm/63 (2 twin) ❸; 85° elevation; 180 rounds/minute to 8.5 km *(4.6 nm)* anti-aircraft; weight of shell 1.42 kg.
4 China 14.5 mm/93 (2 twin) ❹; 85° elevation; 600 rounds/minute to 7 km *(3.8 nm)*.
Depth charges: 4 BMB-2 projectors; 2 racks.
Mines: Can be carried.
Radars: Air/surface search: Slim Net ❺; E/F band.
Navigation: Neptun; I band.
Fire control: Sun Visor B ❻; G/H/I band (for guns).
Square Tie ❼; I or G/H band (for missiles).
IFF: High Pole A.
Sonars: Hull-mounted; active search and attack; medium/high frequency.

Programmes: Similar to the Soviet Riga class and assembled from Soviet components. Designated 'Old Missile Frigates'.
Modernisation: Two started conversion in 1971 for the replacement of the torpedo tubes by a twin SS-N-2 launcher. All converted at Hudong SY. In 1978-79 additional 37 mm and 14.5 mm guns added.
Structure: All had light tripod mast and high superstructure, but later converted with heavier mast and larger bridge. Two were redesigned with modified superstructure and not all have the after 100 mm gun.
Operational: All stationed in South Sea Fleet.

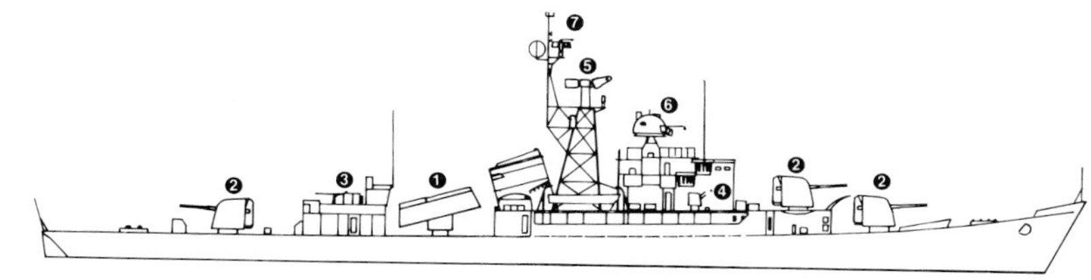

CHENGDU Class *(Scale 1 : 900) Ian Sturton*

PINGXIANG *1986*

SHIPBORNE AIRCRAFT

Numbers/Type: 10/2 Aerospatiale SA 321G/Zhi-8 Super Frelon.
Operational speed: 134 kts *(248 km/h)*.
Service ceiling: 10 000 ft *(3100 m)*.
Range: 440 nm *(815 km)*.
Role/Weapon systems: ASW helicopter; SA 321G delivered from France but now being supplemented by locally built Zhi-8, of which the first operational aircraft was delivered in late 1991. Plans to fit Thomson Sintra HS-12 in three SA 321Gs completed for SSBN escort role. Sensors: Early dipping sonar and processor, some have French-built search radar. Weapons: ASW; probably Whitehead A244 torpedo carried.

Numbers/Type: 50 Harbin Z-9A Haitun (Dauphin 2).
Operational speed: 140 kts *(260 km/h)*.
Service ceiling: 15 000 ft *(4575 m)*.
Range: 410 nm *(758 km)*.
Role/Weapon systems: New doctrine being developed for these licence-built helicopters, which are embarked in latest Chinese escorts. China has an option to continue building after these first 50 have been produced. Not all are naval. Sensors: Thomson-CSF Agrion; HS-12 dipping sonar; Crouzet MAD. Weapons: ASV; up to 4 × locally built radar-guided anti-ship missiles and Whitehead A244 torpedoes or locally built Mk 46 Mod 2.

HAITUN *1991*

LAND-BASED MARITIME AIRCRAFT (FRONT LINE)

Note: Naval versions of the Hongzhaji B7 and F-8-II Finback strike aircraft are being developed.

Numbers/Type: 1 Sukhoi Su-27 Flanker.
Operational speed: 1345 kts *(2500 km/h)*.
Service ceiling: 59 000 ft *(18 000 m)*.
Range: 2160 nm *(4000 km)*.
Role/Weapon systems: Air defence fighter acquired in 1991 for trials. Sensors: Doppler radar. Weapons: 1 × 30 mm cannon; 10 × AAMs.

Numbers/Type: 10 Beriev Be-6 ('Madge').
Operational speed: 224 kts *(415 km/h)*.
Service ceiling: 20 000 ft *(6100 m)*.
Range: 2645 nm *(4900 km)*.
Role/Weapon systems: Flying-boat of obsolescent design now thought to be operated by one squadron only. Weapons: ASW/ASV; up to 4 tons of bombs and other weapons. Standard; 5 × 23 mm cannon.

Numbers/Type: 3 Hanzhong Y-8MPA.
Operational speed: 351 kts *(650 km/h)*.
Service ceiling: 34 120 ft *(10 400 m)*.
Range: 3020 nm *(5600 km)*.
Role/Weapon systems: Maritime patrol version of Y-8 (AN-12) transport; first flown 1985; now being evaluated to replace Be-6 for ASW and AEW roles. Sensors: Litton APSO-504(V)3 search radar in undernose radome. 2 Litton LTN 72R INS and Omega/Loran. Weapons: No weapons carried.

Numbers/Type: 70 Harbin H-5 (Il-28 'Beagle').
Operational speed: 487 kts *(902 km/h)*.
Service ceiling: 40 350 ft *(12 300 m)*.
Range: 1175 nm *(2180 km)*.
Role/Weapon systems: Overwater strike aircraft with ASW/ASVW roles; some recently moved into second line roles such as target towing and ECM training. Weapons: ASW; 2 × torpedoes or 4 × depth bombs. ASVW; 1 × torpedo + mines. Standard; 4 × 23 mm cannon.

Numbers/Type: 40 Harbin Z-5 (Mi-4 'Hound').
Operational speed: 113 kts *(210 km/h)*.
Service ceiling: 18 000 ft *(5500 m)*.
Range: 217 nm *(400 km)*.
Role/Weapon systems: ASW and SAR helicopter; normally shore-based but some have been embarked for short periods, mainly for SAR. Sensors: Search radar only. Weapons: ASW; 1 × ASW torpedo.

Numbers/Type: 80 Shenyang J-8-II Finback.
Operational speed: 701 kts *(1300 km/h)*.
Service ceiling: 65 620 ft *(20 000 m)*.
Range: 1187 nm *(2200 km)*.
Role/Weapon systems: Dual role, all weather fighter introduced into service in 1990. Weapons: 23 mm twin barrel cannon; AAM; 90 mm ASM.

Numbers/Type: 75 Nanchang Q-5 ('Fantan').
Operational speed: 643 kts *(1190 km/h)*.
Service ceiling: 52 500 ft *(16 000 m)*.
Range: 650 nm *(1188 km)*.
Role/Weapon systems: Strike aircraft developed from Shenyang J-6; operated by Chinese People's Naval Aviation Arm (CPNAA) in the beachhead and coastal shipping attack role. Q-5I version adapted to carry 2 torpedoes or C801 ASM. Weapons: 2 × 23 mm cannon, 2 × cluster bombs, 1 or 2 × air-to-air missiles. Capable of carrying 1 ton warload.

Numbers/Type: 110 Shenyang J-5 (MiG-17F 'Fresco').
Operational speed: 618 kts *(1145 km/h)*.
Service ceiling: 54 450 ft *(16 600 m)*.
Range: 755 nm *(1400 km)*.
Role/Weapon systems: Coastal strike and inshore Fleet support fighter; some aircraft modified for limited all-weather defence role. Weapons: Strike; 1 × 37 mm and 2 × 23 mm cannon, 32 rockets, or 500 kg of bombs underwing.

Numbers/Type: 240 Shenyang J-6 (MiG-19 'Farmer').
Operational speed: 831 kts *(1540 km/h)*.
Service ceiling: 58 725 ft *(17 900 m)*.
Range: 1187 nm *(2200 km)*.
Role/Weapon systems: Strike fighter operated by CPNAA (supported by Air Force of PLA) for Fleet air defence and anti-shipping strike; no reliable inventory figures available. Weapons: Fleet air defence role; 4 × AA-1 ('Alkali') beam-riding missiles. Attack; some 1000 kg of underwing bombs or depth charges, PL-2 missile has anti-ship capability.

Numbers/Type: 30 Xian H-6 (Tu-16 'Badger').
Operational speed: 535 kts *(992 km/h)*.
Service ceiling: 40 350 ft *(12 300 m)*.
Range: 2605 nm *(4800 km)*.
Role/Weapon systems: Bomber and maritime reconnaissance aircraft. Sensors: Search/attack radar. Weapons: ASV; 2 × underwing anti-shipping missiles of local manufacture, including C-601. Self-protection; ECM, up to 5 × 23 mm cannon.

Numbers/Type: 180 Xian J-7 (MiG-21 'Fishbed').
Operational speed: 1175 kts *(2175 km/h)*.
Service ceiling: 61 680 ft *(18 800 m)*.
Range: 804 nm *(1490 km)*.
Role/Weapon systems: Land-based Fleet air defence fighter with limited strike role against enemy shipping or beachhead. Sensors: Search attack radar, some ECM. Weapons: Strike; 500 kg bombs or 36 × rockets. Standard; 2 × 30 mm cannon. AD; 2 × 'Atoll' AAMs.

LIGHT FORCES

1 + 2 HUANG (TYPE 520) CLASS (FAST ATTACK CRAFT—MISSILE)

Name	*No*	*Builders*	*Commissioned*
—	770	Zhejaing Shipyard	July 1991

Displacement, tons: 520 standard
Dimensions, feet (metres): 214.6 × 27.6 × 7.9 *(65.4 × 8.4 × 2.4)*
Main machinery: 3 SEMT-Pielstick 12 PA6V 280 MPC; 17 300 hp(m) *(12.7 MW)*
Speed, knots: 32. **Range, miles:** 1800 at 18 kts
Complement: 75

Missiles: SSM: 6 Ying Ji (Eagle Strike) (2 triple); inertial cruise; active radar homing to 40 km *(22 nm)* at 0.9 Mach.
Guns: 1 OTO Melara 76 mm/62 compact; 85° elevation; 85 rounds/minute to 16 km *(8.7 nm)* anti-surface; 12 km *(6.6 nm)* anti-aircraft; weight of shell 6 kg.
4—30 mm/65 (2 twin); 500 rounds/minute to 5 km *(2.7 nm)*; weight of shell 0.54 kg.
Countermeasures: ESM/ECM: Intercept and jammer.
Radars: Surface search: Square Tie; I band.
Fire control: Rice Lamp; I band.

Programmes: Probably laid down in 1989 and built in a very short time probably with the export market in mind. An obvious replacement class for the ageing Huangfen class.
Structure: Some of the details are not confirmed.

HUANG 770 *1991*

1 + 1 HOUXIN CLASS (FAST ATTACK CRAFT—MISSILE)

Name	*No*	*Builders*	*Commissioned*
—	62	Quixin Shipyard	1991

Displacement, tons: 430 full load
Dimensions, feet (metres): 203.4 × 23.6 × 7.5 *(62 × 72 × 2.3)*
Main machinery: 4 diesels; 13 200 hp(m) *(9.7 MW)* 4 shafts
Speed, knots: 32. **Range, miles:** 750 at 18 kts
Complement: 60

Missiles: SSM: 4 Ying Ji (Eagle Strike) (2 twin); active radar homing to 40 km *(22 nm)* at 0.9 Mach; warhead 165 kg; sea skimmer.
Guns: 4—37 mm/63 (2 twin); 180 rounds/minute to 8.5 km *(4.6 nm)* anti-aircraft; weight of shell 1.42 kg
4—14.5 mm (2 twin); 600 rounds/minute to 7 km *(3.8 nm)*.
Countermeasures: ESM/ECM: Intercept and jammer.
Radars: Surface search: Square Tie; I band.
Fire control: Rice Lamp; I band.

Programmes: First seen in 1991. Probable follow-on class to outdated Hegu or Hoku class.
Structure: Some of the details are not confirmed.

HOUXIN Class 1991, CSSC

108 CHINESE HUANGFEN (TYPE 021) (OSA I TYPE) and 1 HOLA CLASS (FAST ATTACK CRAFT—MISSILE)

215, 218, 3103, 3113, 3114, 3115, 3128-3131, 5100, 7100 et al

Displacement, tons: 171 standard; 205 full load
Dimensions, feet (metres): 110.2 × 24.9 × 8.9 *(33.6 × 7.6 × 2.7)*
Main machinery: 3 M503A diesels; 12 000 hp(m) *(8.8 MW)*; 3 shafts
Speed, knots: 35. **Range, miles:** 800 at 30 kts
Complement: 28

Missiles: SSM: 6 or 8 Ying Ji (Eagle Strike); inertial cruise; active radar homing to 40 km *(22 nm)* at 0.9 Mach; warhead 165 kg; sea-skimmer.
4 Hai Ying 2 (twin) launchers (still fitted in some).
Guns: 4 USSR 25 mm/60 (2 twin); 85° elevation; 270 rounds/minute to 3 km *(1.6 nm)* anti-aircraft. Being replaced in some by 4 Soviet 30 mm/65 (2 twin); 85° elevation; 500 rounds/minute to 5 km *(2.7 nm)*; weight of shell 0.54 kg.
Radars: Surface search: Square Tie; I band; range 73 km *(40 nm)* or limits of radar horizon.
Fire control: Round Ball (in 30 mm boats); H/I band.
IFF: 2 Square Head; High Pole A.

Programmes: Most of the original Osas transferred in the 1960s have been scrapped and replaced by a rolling programme of Huangfens, which was first reported in 1985.
Modernisation: The Ying Ji missile is slowly replacing the Hai Yings. With its launcher being half the weight of the Hai Ying 2 this means the doubling of the original missile armament of this class.
Structure: The only boat of the Hola class has a radome aft, four launchers, no guns, slightly larger dimensions (137.8 ft *(42 m)* long) and a folding mast. This radome is also fitted in others which carry 30 mm guns. Pennant numbers: Hola, 5100 and the remainder 200, 1100 and 3100/7100 series.
Operational: China credits this class with a speed of 41 kts. 215, 3128-3131 in reserve at Shanghai.
Sales: Four to Pakistan in 1984. Four to Bangladesh in 1988.

HUANGFEN 3115 *1990*

102 CHINESE HEGU or HOKU (TYPE 024) and 1 HEMA CLASS (FAST ATTACK CRAFT—MISSILE)

Displacement, tons: 68 standard; 79.2 full load
Dimensions, feet (metres): 88.6 × 20.7 × 4.3 *(27 × 6.3 × 1.3) (28.6 m*—Hema class)
Main machinery: 4 Type L-12V-180 diesels; 4800 hp(m) *(3.53 MW)*; 4 shafts
Speed, knots: 37.5. **Range, miles:** 400 at 30 kts
Complement: 17 (2 officers)

Missiles: SSM: 4 Ying Ji (Eagle Strike); inertial cruise; active radar homing to 40 km *(22 nm)* at 0.9 Mach; warhead 165 kg; sea-skimmer.
2 Hai Ying 2 (still fitted in some).
Guns: 2 USSR 25 mm/60 (twin) (4 (2 twin) in Hema class); 85° elevation; 270 rounds/minute to 3 km *(1.6 nm)* anti-aircraft; weight of shell 0.34 kg.
Radars: Surface search: Square Tie; I band; range 73 km *(40 nm)* or limits of radar horizon.
IFF: High pole A.

Programmes: The Komars delivered from the USSR in the 1960s have been deleted. A building programme of ten a year is assumed of the Hegu class, a Chinese variant of the Komar with a steel hull instead of wooden. Pennant numbers; 1100 and 3100 series as some of the Huangfen class.
Modernisation: Ying Ji missile is progressively replacing the Hai Yings. At half the weight, the number of launchers is double that of the original armament.
Structure: The chief external difference is the siting of the launchers clear of the bridge and further inboard, eliminating sponsons and use of pole instead of lattice mast. A hydrofoil variant, the Hema class, has a semi-submerged foil fwd. The extra 6 ft length allows for the mounting of a second twin 25 mm abaft the missile launchers.
Sales: Four to Pakistan, 1981; four to Bangladesh, February 1983; six to Egypt, 1984; ten to Iran in 1992.

HEGU Class (Egyptian with Hai Ying 2) *4/1988, A. Sheldon Duplaix*

12 KRONSHTADT CLASS (TYPE 04) (LARGE PATROL CRAFT)

251-258 (North Sea Fleet); **262-3, 630, 633-5** (East Sea Fleet); **651-6** (South Sea Fleet) (eight of these deleted)

Displacement, tons: 303 standard; 335 full load
Dimensions, feet (metres): 170.9 × 21.3 × 6.9 *(52.1 × 6.5 × 2.1)*
Main machinery: 3 Kolumna Type 9-D-8 diesels; 3300 hp(m) *(2.4 MW)*; 3 shafts
Speed, knots: 18. **Range, miles:** 1400 at 12 kts
Complement: 51 (4 officers)

Guns: 1 USSR 3.5 in *(85 mm)*/52; dual purpose; 85° elevation; 18 rounds/minute to 15 km *(8 nm)*; weight of shell 9.6 kg.
2 China 37 mm/63; 180 rounds/minute to 8.5 km *(4.6 nm)* anti-aircraft; weight of shell 1.42 kg.
6 China 14.5 mm/93 (3 twin); 85° elevation; 600 rounds/minute to 7 km *(3.8 nm)* anti-aircraft.
A/S mortars: 2 RBU 1200 5-tubed fixed launchers; range 1200 m; warhead 34 kg.
Depth charges: 2 racks.
Mines: 2 rails for 8-10 mines.
Radars: Surface search/navigation: Ball End or Fin Curve; E/F band.
IFF: Dead Duck. Ski Pole.
Sonars: Tamir II; hull-mounted; active search and attack; high frequency.

Programmes: Six built in 1950-53 were received from USSR in July 1955. Remainder were built at Shanghai and Guangzhou, with 12 completed in 1956. The last was completed in 1957. Eight deleted since 1986.
Operational: North Sea Fleet ships based at Qingdao and Lushun, East Sea Fleet in Chou Shan Islands and South Sea Fleet ships at Yulin and Hainan.

KRONSHTADT 253 *1986*

4 HAIJUI CLASS (FAST ATTACK CRAFT—PATROL)

688 + 3

Displacement, tons: 430 standard
Dimensions, feet (metres): 203.4 × 23.6 × 7.2 *(62 × 7.2 × 2.2)*
Main machinery: 4 diesels; 8800 hp(m) *(6.47 MW)*; 4 shafts
Speed, knots: 28. **Range, miles:** 750 at 18 kts
Complement: 72
Guns: 4 China 57 mm/70 (2 twin); dual purpose; 85° elevation; 120 rounds/minute to 12 km *(6.5 nm)*; weight of shell 6.31 kg.
4 USSR 30 mm/65 (2 twin); 85° elevation; 500 rounds/minute to 5 km *(2.7 nm)* anti-aircraft; weight of shell 0.54 kg.
A/S mortars: 4 RBU 1200 5-tubed fixed launchers; range 1200 m; warhead 34 kg.
Depth charges: 2 rails.
Radars: Surface search: Pot Head; I band.
Fire control: I band.

Comment: A lengthened version of the Hainan class. Probably mainly used for trials. 688 seen in 1989 with a Thomson Sintra SS 12 VDS Sonar and again in 1990 with twin missile tubes replacing the forward 57 mm gun. A second of class appears to have no funnel.

HAIJUI Class *1986*

HAIJUI Class *4/1990, John Mapletoft*

HAINAN 686 *4/1988*

76 HAINAN CLASS (TYPE 037) (FAST ATTACK CRAFT—PATROL)

Nos 267-285, 290, 302, 305, 609, 610, 641, 642, 649, 661-70, 677, 678, 680, 686, 687, 690 et al

Displacement, tons: 375 standard; 392 full load
Dimensions, feet (metres): 192.8 × 23.6 × 6 *(58.8 × 7.2 × 2.2)*
Main machinery: 4 PCR/Kolumna Type 9-D-8 diesels; 4400 hp(m) *(3.2 MW)*; 4 shafts
Speed, knots: 30.5. **Range, miles:** 1300 at 15 kts
Complement: 69

Missiles: Can be fitted with four Ying Ji launchers in lieu of the after 57 mm gun.
Guns: 4 China 57 mm/70 (2 twin); dual purpose; 120 rounds/minute to 12 km *(6.5 nm)*; weight of shell 6.31 kg.
4 USSR 25 mm/60 (2 twin); 85° elevation; 270 rounds/minute to 3 km *(1.6 nm)* anti-aircraft; weight of shell 0.34 kg.
A/S mortars: 4 RBU 1200 5-tubed fixed launchers; range 1200 m; warhead 34 kg.
Depth charges: 2 BMB-2 projectors; 2 racks.
Mines: Rails fitted.
Radars: Surface search: Pot Head or Skin Head; I band.
IFF: High Pole.
Sonars: Hull-mounted; active search and attack; high frequency.
Thomson Sintra SS 12 (on at least two of the class); VDS.

Programmes: A larger Chinese built version of Soviet SO 1. Low freeboard. Programme started 1963-64 and continues with new hulls replacing the first ships of the class.
Structure: Later ships have a tripod foremast in place of a pole and a short stub mainmast. Two trials SS 12 sonars fitted in 1987.
Sales: Eight to Bangladesh; eight to Egypt; six to North Korea; four to Pakistan; eight to Burma.

320+ SHANGHAI CLASS (TYPE 062) (FAST ATTACK CRAFT—GUN)

E 277, 321 N 1121, 1127, 3215, 3313, 4301 et al

Displacement, tons: 113 standard; 131 full load
Dimensions, feet (metres): 127.3 × 17.7 × 5.6 *(38.8 × 5.4 × 1.7)*
Main machinery: 2 Type L12-180 diesels; 2400 hp(m) *(1.76 MW)* (forward); 2 Type 12-D-6 diesels; 1820 hp(m) *(1.34 MW)* (aft); 4 shafts
Speed, knots: 30. **Range, miles:** 700 at 16.5 kts on one engine
Complement: 34

Guns: 4 China 37 mm/63 (2 twin); 85° elevation; 180 rounds/minute to 8.5 km *(4.6 nm)*; weight of shell 1.42 kg.
4 USSR 25 mm/60 (2 twin); 85° elevation; 270 rounds/minute to 3 km *(1.6 nm)* anti-aircraft; weight of shell 0.34 kg.
Some are fitted with a twin 57 mm/70 and some have a twin 75 mm Type 56 recoilless rifle mounted fwd.
Depth charges: 2 projectors; 8 weapons.
Mines: Mine rails can be fitted for 10 mines.
Radars: Surface search: Skin Head or Pot Head; I band.
IFF: High Pole.
Sonars: It is reported that a hull-mounted set is fitted, with VDS in some.

Programmes: Construction began in 1961 and continues at Shanghai and other yards at rate of about ten a year.
Structure: The five versions of this class vary slightly in the outline of their bridges. A few of the class have been reported as fitted with RBU 1200 anti-submarine mortars. Displacement and dimensions are for the Shanghai II class.
Sales: Eight to North Vietnam in May 1966, plus Romanian craft of indigenous construction. Seven to Tanzania in 1970-71, six to Guinea, twelve to North Korea, twelve to Pakistan, five to Sri Lanka in 1972, six to Albania, one to Angola, eight to Bangladesh in 1980-82, three to Congo, four to Egypt in 1984 and three to Sri Lanka in 1991. Many of these have since been deleted.

SHANGHAI II Class *6/1987*

SHANGHAI II Class *9/1984*

3 + 3 HULUDAO TYPE 206 CLASS (FAST ATTACK CRAFT—PATROL)

65 77

Displacement, tons: 180 full load
Dimensions, feet (metres): 147.6 × 21 × 5.6 *(45 × 6.4 × 1.7)*
Main machinery: 3 MWM TBD 604B V12 diesels; 4944 hp(m) *(3.64 MW)*; 3 shafts
Speed, knots: 29. **Range, miles:** 1000 at 15 kts
Complement: 24 (6 officers)
Guns: 2 China 14.5 mm Type 82 (twin); 85° elevation; 600 rounds/minute to 7 km *(3.8 nm)*; weight of shell 1.42 kg.

Comment: New class of EEZ patrol craft first seen at Wuxi Shipyard in 1988. Fourth and fifth of class reported ordered in May 1991. May be more heavily armed with more than one 14.5 mm mounting. The craft looks like a scaled down version of the Pakistan Barkat class.

HULUDAO Class *1991, CSSC*

50 SHANTOU CLASS (FAST ATTACK CRAFT—GUN)

Displacement, tons: 60 standard; 80 full load
Dimensions, feet (metres): 83.5 × 19 × 6.5 *(25.5 × 5.8 × 2)*
Main machinery: 2 Type 3-D-12 diesels; 616 hp(m) *(4.52 kW)* sustained; 2 Type M50L diesels; 2400 hp(m) *(1.76 MW)*; 4 shafts
Speed, knots: 28. **Range, miles:** 500 at 28 kts; 750 at 15 kts
Complement: 17

Guns: 4 China 37 mm/63 (2 twin); 85° elevation; 180 rounds/minute to 8.5 km *(4.6 nm)*; weight of shell 1.42 kg.
2—12.7 mm MGs (some boats mount a twin 75 mm recoilless rifle fwd).
Depth charges: 8.
Radars: Surface search: Skin Head; I band; range 37 km *(20 nm)*.

Programmes: From 1958 constructed at Luda, Guangzhou and Shanghai. A steel-hulled version of Soviet P 6. Previously Swatow class.
Operational: 20 in East Sea Fleet, 16 in South Sea Fleet, 14 in North Sea Fleet. Many are in reserve.
Sales: Eight to North Korea, 14 to North Vietnam, two to Equitorial Guinea.

SHANTOU Class *1987*

120+ HUCHUAN CLASS (TYPE 025/026) (FAST ATTACK CRAFT—TORPEDO)

205, 207-209, 248, 3206, 3214, 6218, 7230 et al

Displacement, tons: 39 standard; 45.8 full load
Dimensions, feet (metres): 71.5 × 20.7 oa × 11.8 (hullborne) *(21.8 × 6.3 × 3.6 (max))*
Main machinery: 3 Type M50F-12 diesels; 2550 hp(m) *(1.9 MW)* sustained; 2 shafts
Speed, knots: 50 foilborne. **Range, miles:** 500 cruising
Complement: 11

Guns: 4 China 14.5 mm (2 twin); 85° elevation; 600 rounds/minute to 7 km *(3.8 nm)*.
Torpedoes: 2—21 in *(533 mm)* tubes. Probably fires older Soviet Type 53.
Radars: Surface search: Skin Head (some variations); I band.

Programmes: Hydrofoils designed and built by China, in the Hutong yard, Shanghai. Construction started in 1966. Previously Hu Chwan class. Construction discontinued in 1988-89.
Structure: Of all-metal construction with a bridge well fwd and a low superstructure extending aft. Fwd pair of foils can apparently be withdrawn into recesses in the hull. There are two variants. Older boats have a twin mounting amidships and one aft with the front of the bridge well fwd of the lips of the tubes. Newer versions have the front of the bridge in line with the lips of the tubes and the first mounting on the fo'c'sle and have differences in their electronics. Not all are hydrofoil fitted.
Sales: 32 to Albania, four to Pakistan, four to Tanzania, three to Romania plus additional craft of indigenous construction. Four to Bangladesh in 1989.

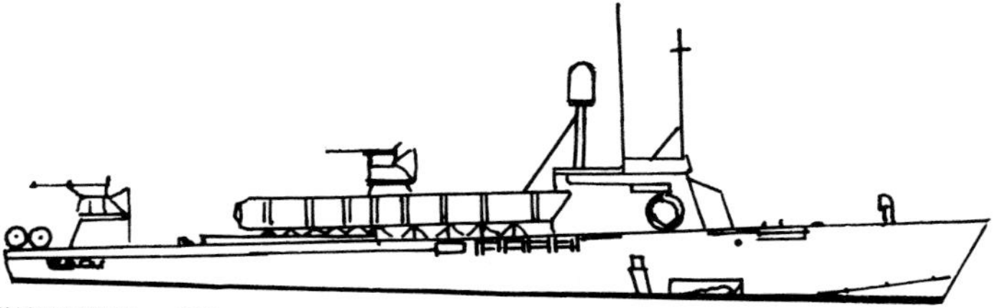
HUCHUAN Class. Older version

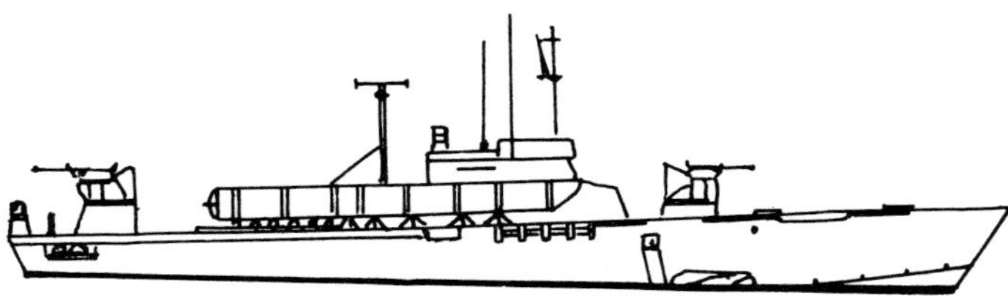
HUCHUAN Class. Newer version

HUCHUAN Class 1978

60 P 4 CLASS (FAST ATTACK CRAFT—TORPEDO)

Displacement, tons: 22.5 standard; 25 full load
Dimensions, feet (metres): 62.3 × 10.8 × 3.3 *(19 × 3.3 × 1)*
Main machinery: 2 Type M50 diesels; 2400 hp(m) *(1.76 MW)*; 2 shafts
Speed, knots: 50. **Range, miles:** 410 at 30 kts
Complement: 12
Guns: 2 China 14.5 mm (twin) (some carry 2 twin mountings); 85° elevation; 600 rounds/minute to 7 km *(3.8 nm)*.
Torpedoes: 2—18 in *(457 mm)* tubes.
Depth charges: 8.

Comment: This class has aluminium hulls. Many in reserve. Six transferred to Albania, four to Bangladesh in 1984.

P 4 Class 1980

40 P 6 CLASS (TYPE 083) (FAST ATTACK CRAFT—TORPEDO)

Displacement, tons: 64 standard; 73 full load
Dimensions, feet (metres): 85.3 × 20 × 4.9 *(26 × 6.1 × 1.5)*
Main machinery: 4 Type M50F-12 diesels; 3400 hp(m) *(2.5 MW)* sustained; 4 shafts
Speed, knots: 41. **Range, miles:** 450 at 30 kts; 600 at 15 kts
Complement: 15
Guns: 4 USSR 25 mm/60 (2 twin); 85° elevation; 270 rounds/minute to 3 km *(1.6 nm)*.
Torpedoes: 2—21 in *(533 mm)* tubes (or mines or 12 DCs); anti-surface.
Depth charges: Up to 12.
Mines: Can be carried.
Radars: Surface search: Skin Head; I band; range 37 km *(20 nm)*.
IFF: High Pole.

Comment: This class has wooden hulls. Some were constructed in Chinese yards largely at Shanghai. Most built prior to 1966. Pennant numbers; in 5200 series. Six sold to North Vietnam in 1967. Some already deleted, most of the remainder are in reserve.

P 6 Class 1980

1 IMPROVED BEIHAI CLASS (COASTAL PATROL CRAFT)

Displacement, tons: 56 full load
Dimensions, feet (metres): 83.6 × 16.4 × 3.3 *(25 × 5 × 1)*
Main machinery: 3 diesels; 3600 hp(m) *(2.65 MW)*; 3 shafts
Speed, knots: 37. **Range, miles:** 490 at 25 kts
Complement: 20
Guns: 4 USSR 25 mm/60 (2 twin); 85° elevation; 270 rounds/minute to 3 km *(1.6 nm)*.

Comment: Replacement for Beihai class, begun in early 1980s but programme abandoned. All remaining Beihai class have been deleted.

YINGKOU CLASS (COASTAL PATROL CRAFT)

Displacement, tons: 35 full load
Dimensions, feet (metres): 70 × 12 × 3 *(21.3 × 3.7 × 0.9)*
Main machinery: 2 diesels; 600 hp(m) *(441 kW)*; 2 shafts
Speed, knots: 16
Guns: 2—12.7 mm MGs.

Comment: Built in early 1960s. Numbers not known. Used by South China militia.

YINGKOU Class 1975

45 HUANGPU CLASS (RIVER PATROL CRAFT)

Displacement, tons: 42 standard; 50 full load
Dimensions, feet (metres): 88.6 × 13 × 5 *(27 × 4 × 1.5)*
Main machinery: 2 diesels; 1000 hp(m) *(735 kW)*; 2 shafts
Speed, knots: 14. **Range, miles:** 400 at 9 kts
Complement: 25
Guns: 2 or 4 USSR 25 mm/60 (1 or 2 twin); 85° elevation; 270 rounds/minute to 3 km *(1.6 nm)*. Recently rearmed.
Radars: Surface search: Skin Head; I band; range 37 km *(20 nm)*.

Comment: Armament varies—above is the most common fit. Built in Guangzhou and Shanghai 1950-55 probably for riverine duties. Underpowered with low freeboard although some have been modified for greater crew safety. Previously Whampoa class. 30 in East Sea Fleet, six in North Sea Fleet and nine in South Sea Fleet.

HUANGPU Class 1989

4 HUXIN CLASS (RIVER PATROL CRAFT)

Comment: This is a class of modified Huangpu design with a greater freeboard and a slightly larger displacement. First seen in 1989.

HUXIN Class *1989, P. D. Jones*

20 YULIN CLASS (RIVER PATROL CRAFT)

Displacement, tons: 9.8 full load
Dimensions, feet (metres): 42.6 × 9.5 × 3.5 *(13 × 2.9 × 1.1)*
Main machinery: 1 PRC Type 12150 diesel; 300 hp(m) *(220 kW)*; 1 shaft
Speed, knots: 24
Complement: 10
Guns: 2 China 14.5 mm/93 (twin); 85° elevation; 600 rounds/minute to 7 km *(3.8 nm)*.
2—12.7 mm (twin) MGs.

Comment: Up to 100 were probably built in Shanghai 1964-68. Being phased out. Four sold to Congo (1966), three to Cambodia, four to Tanzania.

MINE WARFARE FORCES

Note: There are also some 60 auxiliary minesweepers of various types including trawlers and motor-driven junks.

1 BELEIJAN CLASS (MINELAYER)

814

Comment: First of a new class probably built at Shanghai and completed successful sea trials in 1988. Displacement about 1000 tons, 93 × 14 m.

41 SOVIET T 43 CLASS (TYPE 010) (MINESWEEPERS—OCEAN)

124, 364-6, 377-9, 386-9, 396-9, 801-3, 807-9, 821-3, 829-832, 853-4, 994-6 et al

Displacement, tons: 520 standard; 590 full load (Chinese built)
Dimensions, feet (metres): 196.8 × 27.6 × 6.9 *(60 × 8.8 × 2.3)*
Main machinery: 2 PCR/Kolumna Type 9-D-8 diesels; 2200 hp(m) *(1.62 MW)*; 2 shafts
Speed, knots: 14. **Range, miles:** 3000 at 10 kts
Complement: 70 (10 officers)

Guns: 2 or 4 China 37 mm/63 (1 or 2 twin) (3 of the class have a 65 mm/52 forward instead of one twin 37 mm/63); dual purpose; 85° elevation; 180 rounds/minute to 8.5 km *(4.6 nm)*; weight of shell 1.42 kg.
4 USSR 25 mm/60 (2 twin); 85° elevation; 270 rounds/minute to 3 km *(1.6 nm)*.
4 China 14.5 mm/93 (2 twin); 85° elevation; 600 rounds/minute to 7 km *(3.8 nm)*.
Some ships also carry 1—85 mm/52 Mk 90K; 18 rounds/minute to 15 km *(8 nm)*; weight of shell 9.6 kg.
Depth charges: 2 BMB-2 projectors; 20 depth charges.
Mines: Can carry 12-16.
Countermeasures: MCMV; MPT-1 paravanes; MPT-3 mechanical sweep; acoustic and magnetic gear.
Radars: Surface search: Ball End; E/F band; range 37 km *(20 nm)*.
Navigation: Fin Curve or Neptun; I band.
IFF: High Pole or Yard Rake.
Sonars: Tamir II; hull-mounted; active search and attack; high frequency.

Programmes: Four were acquired from USSR in 1954-55, one being returned 1960; 26 more were built in Chinese shipyards, the first two in 1956. The construction of T 43 class fleet minesweepers started again in mid-1980s at Wuzhang and at Guangzhou.
Structure: Displacement figures are for Chinese built ships. Three (Soviet ships) converted for surveying, three transferred as civilian research ships.
Operational: Seven in North Sea Fleet (364-6, 801-3, 807), nine in East Sea Fleet (821, 829, 830, 832, 853-4, 994-6) and eight in South Sea Fleet (386-9, 396-9). Remainder not known. Some are used as patrol ships with sweep gear removed. Three units reported as having a 65 mm/52 gun forward.

T43 831 *5/1991*

T43 Class *12/1989, G. Jacobs*

3 + 2 WOSAO CLASS (MINESWEEPER—COASTAL)

4422 +2

Displacement, tons: 310 full load
Dimensions, feet (metres): 147 × 20.3 × 7.5 *(44.8 × 6.2 × 2.3)*
Main machinery: 2 diesels; 2000 hp(m) *(1.47 MW)*; 2 shafts
Speed, knots: 15.5. **Range, miles:** 500 at 15 kts
Complement: 25
Guns: 4 China 25 mm/60 (2 twin); 85° elevation; 270 rounds/minute to 3 km *(1.6 nm)*.
Countermeasures: Acoustic, magnetic and mechanical sweeps.

Comment: Building programme started in 1986. First of class commissioned in 1988. Steel hull with low magnetic properties.

WOSAO Class *1990, CSSC*

10 FUSHUN CLASS (MINESWEEPERS—COASTAL)

Displacement, tons: 275
Dimensions, feet (metres): 131.2 × 18 × 9.8 *(40 × 5.5 × 3)*
Main machinery: 2 Type M 50F-12 diesels; 1700 hp(m) *(1.25 MW)* sustained; 2 Type 12-D-6 diesels; 1820 hp(m) *(1.34 MW)*; *4 shafts*
Speed, knots: 18. **Range, miles:** 750 at 16 kts
Guns: 2 USSR 25 mm/60 (twin); forward.
4 China 14.5 mm/9 (2 twin); midships.

Comment: A modification of the Shanghai II class fast attack craft fitted with minesweeping winch and two davits. Several have been deleted.

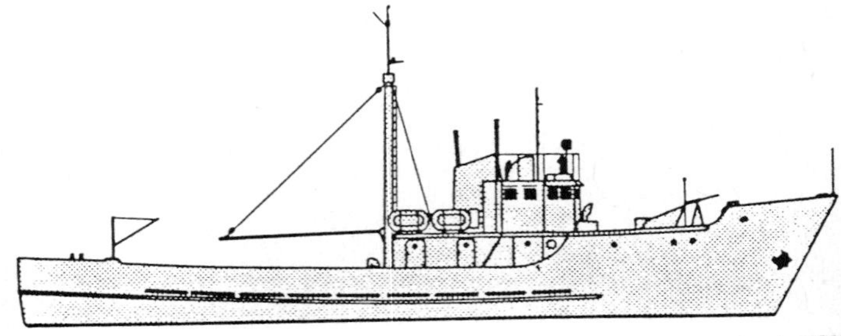

FUSHUN Class *1986*

80 LIENYUN CLASS (MINESWEEPERS—COASTAL)

Displacement, tons: 400
Dimensions, feet (metres): 131.2 × 26.2 × 11.5 *(40 × 8 × 3.5)*
Main machinery: 1 diesel; 400 hp(m) *(294 kW)*; 1 shaft
Speed, knots: 8
Guns: 2—12.7 mm MGs.

Comment: Built to a converted trawler design with steel hulls. Have a minesweeping winch and davits aft.

LIENYUN Class *1990*

50+ TYPE 312 DRONE MINESWEEPERS

Displacement, tons: 47 standard
Dimensions, feet (metres): 68.6 × 12.8 × 6.9 *(20.9 × 3.9 × 2.1)*
Main machinery: Diesel-electric; 1 Type 12V150C diesel; 300 hp(m) *(220 kW)*; 1 motor; cp prop
Speed, knots: 12. **Range, miles:** 144 at 12 kts
Complement: 3

Comment: A large number of these craft, similar to the German Troikas, have been built since the early 1970s. Fitted to carry out magnetic and acoustic sweeping under remote control up to 5 km *(2.7 nm)* from shore control station.

DRONE *1988, CSSC*

AMPHIBIOUS WARFARE FORCES

Note: (i) In addition to the ships listed below there are up to 500 minor LCM/LCVP types used to transport stores and personnel. There is also a 67 ton DAGU class research hovercraft designed by Shanghai SB R&D Institute.
(ii) A Ro-Ro conversion to an aviation support ship is being actively studied as one option to improve amphibious capability out of range of shore based aircraft. If taken up the Navy may introduce STOVL aircraft to the Fleet. The alternative of a 48 000 ton fixed wing carrier is also under consideration. The Ministry of Communications ship *Huayuankou* has been mentioned as a possible candidate for conversion.

9 QIONSHA (7 AP + 2 AH) CLASS

Y 831, Y 832, Y833 + 6

Displacement, tons: 2150 full load
Dimensions, feet (metres): 282.1 × 44.3 × 13.1 *(86 × 13.5 × 4)*
Main machinery: 3 SKL 8 NVD 48 A-2U diesels; 3960 hp(m) *(2.91 MW)* sustained; 3 shafts
Speed, knots: 16
Complement: 59
Military lift: 400 troops; 350 tons cargo
Guns: 8 China 14.5/93 mm (4 twin); 85° elevation; 600 rounds/minute to 7 km *(3.8 nm)*.

Comment: Personnel attack transports begun about 1980 at Guangzhou. All South Sea Fleet. Have four sets of davits, light cargo booms serving fwd and aft. No helicopter pad. Twin funnels. Carry a number of LCAs. Construction now ceased. Two converted to Hospital Ships (AH) and painted white.

QIONSHA Class *1985, G. Jacobs*

QIONSHA 832 (Hospital ship alongside YUKAN class) *12/1988, G. Jacobs*

3 YUKAN CLASS (TYPE 072) (LST)

927 928 929

Displacement, tons: 3110 standard
Dimensions, feet (metres): 393.6 × 50 × 9.5 *(120 × 15.3 × 2.9)*
Main machinery: 2 SEMT-Pielstick 12PA 6V 280 diesels; 9600 hp(m) *(7.1 MW)* sustained; 2 shafts
Speed, knots: 18. **Range, miles:** 3000 at 14 kts
Complement: 109
Military lift: 200 troops; 10 tanks; 2 LCVP
Missiles:X
Guns: 8 China 57 mm/50 (4 twin) (some carry 4—57 mm (2 twin) and 4—37 mm (2 twin)); 85° elevation; 120 rounds/minute to 12 km *(6.5 nm)*; weight of shell 6.31 kg.
4—25 mm/60 (2 twin) (some also have 4—25 mm (2 twin) mountings amidships above the tank deck); 85° elevation; 270 rounds/minute to 3 km *(1.6 nm)*.
Radars: Navigation: 2 Neptun; I band.

Comment: First completed in 1980. Bow and stern ramps fitted. Carry two LCVPs. Some reports indicate up to 14 of this class may be completed with 10 earmarked for the South Fleet and four for the East Fleet. At least two of the class were active off the Spratley Islands in 1989. Bow ramp maximum load 50 tons, stern ramp 20 tons.

YUKAN 927 *9/1990, John Mapletoft*

YUKAN 929 *9/1990, John Mapletoft*

13 Ex-US 1-511 (SHAN) CLASS (LST)

351, 355, 902-3, 905-7, 921-6

Displacement, tons: 1653 standard; 4080 full load
Dimensions, feet (metres): 328 × 50 × 14 *(100 × 15.3 × 4.3)*
Main machinery: 2 GM 12-567A diesels; 1500 hp(m) *(1.12 MW)*; 2 shafts
Speed, knots: 11
Military lift: 165 troops; 2100 tons cargo; 2 LCVP
Guns: 2—76 mm/50; dual purpose; 85° elevation; 18 rounds/minute to 12.8 km *(7 nm)*; weight of shell 5.92 kg.
9 China 37 mm/63 (3 twin, 3 single); 180 rounds/minute to 8.5 km *(4.6 nm)*; weight of shell 1.42 kg.
Mines: All capable of minelaying.

Comment: Two transferred to North Vietnam as tankers. Some other ex-US LSTs are in the merchant service or used as tenders. Some armed with rocket launchers. All built between 1942 and 1945. Five (902-3, 905-7) in North Sea Fleet at Luda, six (921-6) in East Sea Fleet at Shanghai and two (351, 355) in South Sea Fleet at Guangzhou.

SHAN 926 *1/1990*

35 YULIANG CLASS (TYPE 079) and 1 YULING CLASS (LSM)

Displacement, tons: 800 standard; 1600 full load
Dimensions, feet (metres): 236.2 × 45.3 × 10.8 *(72 × 13.8 × 3.3)*
Main machinery: 2 diesels; 2 shafts
Military lift: 3 tanks
Guns: 4 China 37 mm/63 (2 twin) (Type I only); 85° elevation; 180 rounds/minute to 8.5 km *(4.6 nm)*; weight of shell 1.42 kg.
4—25 mm/60 (2 twin); 85° elevation; 270 rounds/minute to 3 km *(1.6 nm)*.
2 BM 21 MRL rocket launchers; range about 9 km *(5 nm)*.

Comment: Yuling started in China in 1971. Stationed at Qingdao. Yuliang class is a variation of what may have been a prototype. Data is similar but there are variations in the superstructure. Series production started in 1980 in three or four smaller shipyards (Shantou etc).

YULIANG 1122 *4/1989, G. Jacobs*

4 YUDAO CLASS (LSM)

Displacement, tons: 1460 full load
Dimensions, feet (metres): 285.4 × 41.3 × 10.2 *(87 × 12.6 × 3.1)*
Guns: 8—25 mm/60 (2 quad); 85° elevation; 270 rounds/minute to 3 km *(1.6 nm)*.

Comment: Probably first entered service in early 1980s. In South Fleet.

YUDAO Class *12/1988, G. Jacobs*

320 YUNNAN CLASS (TYPE 067) (LCU)

Displacement, tons: 128 full load
Dimensions, feet (metres): 93.8 × 17.7 × 4.6 *(28.6 × 5.4 × 1.4)*
Main machinery: 2 diesels; 600 hp(m) *(441 kW)*; 2 shafts
Speed, knots: 12. **Range, miles:** 500 at 10 kts
Complement: 12
Military lift: 46 tons
Guns: 2—12.7 mm MGs.

Comment: Built in China 1968-72 although a continuing programme was reported in 1982. Pennant numbers in 3000 series (3313, 3321, 3344 seen). 5000 series (5526 seen) and 7000 series (7566 and 7568 seen). Numbers split evenly between the three fleets. One to Sri Lanka in 1991.

YUNNAN Class *4/1980, Andrew Li*

40-50 YUCH'IN CLASS (LCU/LCP)

Displacement, tons: 58 standard; 85 full load
Dimensions, feet (metres): 81.2 × 17.1 × 4.3 *(24.8 × 5.2 × 1.3)*
Main machinery: 2 12V 150 diesels; 600 hp(m) *(441 kW)*; 2 shafts
Speed, knots: 11.5. **Range, miles:** 450 at 11.5 kts
Military lift: Up to 150 troops
Guns: 4—14.5 mm (2 twin) MGs.

Comment: Built in Shanghai 1962-72. Smaller version of Yunnan class with a shorter tank deck and longer poop deck. Primarily intended for personnel transport.

YUCH'IN Class *1987*

14 Ex-US LSM (HUA) TYPE

352-4, 393, 511, 809-811, 931-6

Displacement, tons: 743 beaching; 1095 full load
Dimensions, feet (metres): 203.5 × 34.2 × 8.3 *(62.1 × 10.4 × 2.5)*
Main machinery: 2 Fairbanks-Morse 38D8-1/8-9 or GM 16-278A diesels; 3000 hp *(2.24 MW)*; 2 shafts
Speed, knots: 13. **Range, miles:** 2500 at 12 kts
Complement: 60
Guns: 4 China 37 mm/63 (2 twin). 4—25 mm (2 twin).

Comment: Built in USA in 1944-45. Some were converted for minelaying and as support ships. Three in North Sea Fleet (809-811), seven in East Sea Fleet (511, 931-6) and four in South Sea Fleet (352-4, 393). Armament varies.

LSM 936 *1980*

20 YUCHAI CLASS (LCMs)

Displacement, tons: 35 standard; 92 full load
Dimensions, feet (metres): 65.6 × 14.1 × 3.3 *(20 × 4.3 × 1)*
Main machinery: 2 diesels; 600 hp(m) *(441 kW)*; 2 shafts
Military lift: 50 tons or 125 troops
Guns: 4—14.5 mm (2 twin) MGs.

Comment: Built in 1960s at Shanghai, similar to Soviet T 4 class. Carry conspicuous kedge anchor on centre-line at stern.

4 Ex-US LSIL (MIN) TYPE

231, 232, 371, 372

Displacement, tons: 230 light; 387 full load
Dimensions, feet (metres): 157 × 23 × 6 *(47.9 × 7 × 1.8)*
Main machinery: 2 diesels; 1320 hp *(985 kW)*; 2 shafts
Speed, knots: 14
Guns: 4—25 mm.

Comment: Built in USA in 1943-45. Reported to be fitted with rocket launchers. Some are fitted as minesweepers. Two in East Sea Fleet (Shanghai) (371-2) and two in South Sea Fleet (Zhanjiang) (231-2). Armament varies. See also *Salvage Ships*.

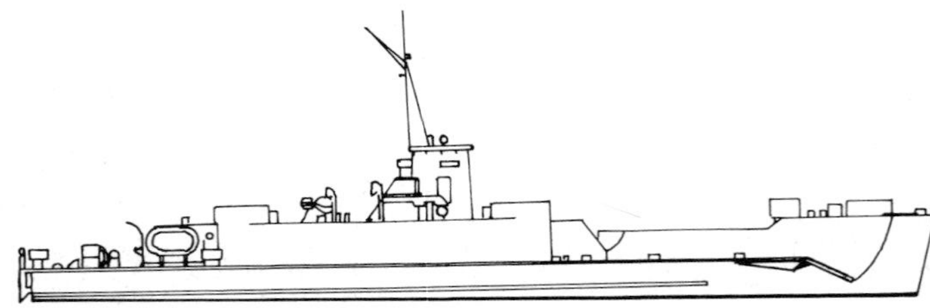

Ex-US LSIL Type

JINGSAH CLASS (HOVERCRAFT)

Displacement, tons: 70
Dimensions, feet (metres): 72.2 × 26.2 *(22 × 8)*
Main machinery: 2 propulsion motors; 2 lift motors
Speed, knots: 55
Military lift: 15 tons

Comment: Built at Dagu in 1979. Unknown number built—probably more in production.

PAYI CLASS (HOVERCRAFT)

Dimensions, feet (metres): 49.2 × 23 *(15 × 7)*
Speed, knots: 55
Military lift: 15 tons

Comment: An unknown number already built possibly with more in production. First seen at Wusung in 1970.

TRAINING SHIP

1 DAXIN CLASS

ZHENGHE 81

Displacement, tons: 4500 standard
Dimensions, feet (metres): 390.4 × 51.8 × 15.7 *(119 × 15.8 × 4.8)*
Main machinery: 2 diesels; 7800 hp(m) *(5.73 MW)*; 2 shafts
Speed, knots: 15
Complement: 170 plus 30 instructors plus 200 Midshipmen
Guns: 4 China 57 mm/70 (2 twin). 4—37 mm/63 (2 twin). 4—12.7 mm MGs.
A/S mortars: 2 FQF 2500 fixed 12 tubed launchers.
Radars: Navigation: 2 Racal Decca; I band.
Helicopters: Platform only.

Comment: Built at Qiuxin SY, Shanghai. Launched 12 July 1986, commissioned 27 April 1987. Resembles a small cruise liner. Subordinate to the Naval Academy and replaced *Huian*.

ZHENGHE *4/1990, G. Jacobs*

SUBMARINE SUPPORT SHIPS

3 DAJIANG CLASS

CHANGXINGDAO J 121 **YONGXINGDAO** J 506
CHONGMINGDAO J 302

Displacement, tons: 10 975 full load
Dimensions, feet (metres): 511.7 × 67.2 × 22.3 *(156 × 20.5 × 6.8)*
Main machinery: 2 MAN K9Z60/105E diesels; 9000 hp(m) *(6.6 MW)*; 2 shafts
Speed, knots: 20
Guns: Light MGs. Can carry 6—37 mm (3 twin).
Radars: Surface search: Eye Shield; E band.
Navigation: Two Fin Curve; I band.
Helicopters: 2 Aerospatiale SA 321 G Super Frelon.

Comment: Submarine support and salvage ships built at Shanghai. First launched in mid-1973, operational in 1976. *Yongxingdao* has a smoke deflector on funnel and appears to have been fitted with a new foremast. Provision for DSRV on fwd well deck aft of launching crane. A fourth and fifth of the class are listed under *Research Ships*. A new type of DSRV was tested in 1986. Its dimensions are 15 × 4 × 2.6 m and it can dive to 600 m at a speed of 4 kts. With a crew of 4 it has underwater TV, a manipulator arm and a high frequency sonar. Rescue capacity is 22 people per trip. New foremast on *Yongxingdao* suggests possible conversion to research ship role with long range communications similar to Russian *Fedor Vidyaev*.

CHANGXINGDAO *1991*

YONGXINGDAO (with new foremast) *7/1989*

1 DA DONG CLASS AND 1 DADAO CLASS

J 304 + 1

Displacement, tons: 2500 approx
Dimensions, feet (metres): 269 × 36.1 × 8.9 *(82 × 11 × 2.7)*

Comment: J304 reported to have been built at Hudung in late 1970s. Has a large and conspicuous crane aft. A second ship of approximately same dimensions and designed for the same duties was launched at Huludao shipyard and commissioned 12 January 1986 possibly with a civilian crew. Principal role is wreck location and salvage.

DADAO Class *1989, Gilbert Gyssels*

2 DALANG and 1 DONGXIU CLASS

J 503 J504 U911

Displacement, tons: 3700 standard; 4300 full load (est)
Dimensions, feet (metres): 367 × 47.9 × 14.1 *(111.9 × 14.6 × 4.3)*
Main machinery: 2 diesels; 4000 hp(m) *(2.94 MW)*; 2 shafts
Speed, knots: 16. **Range, miles:** 8000 at 14 kts
Guns: 8 China 37 mm/63 (4 twin). 4 or 8 China 14.5 mm (2 or 4 twin) MGs.
Radars: Navigation: Fin Curve; I band.

Comment: First two built at Guangzhou Shipyard. First one commissioned November 1975, second in 1986. The Dongxiu class ship (U 911) is slightly larger and was built at Wuhu shipyard, commissioning in late 1986. Bulbous bow with notable rake to funnel amidships.

1 DAZHI CLASS

DAZHI 920

Displacement, tons: 5600 full load
Dimensions, feet (metres): 350 × 50 × 20 *(106.7 × 15.3 × 6.1)*
Main machinery: 2 diesels; 3500 hp(m) *(2.57 MW)*; 2 shafts
Speed, knots: 14. **Range, miles:** 6000 at 14 kts
Complement: 290
Cargo capacity: 500 tons dieso
Guns: 4 China 37 mm/63 (2 twin). 4—25 mm/60 (2 twin).
Radars: Navigation: Fin Curve; I band.

Comment: Built at Hudung, Shanghai 1963-65. Has four electro-hydraulic cranes. Carries large stock of torpedoes and stores.

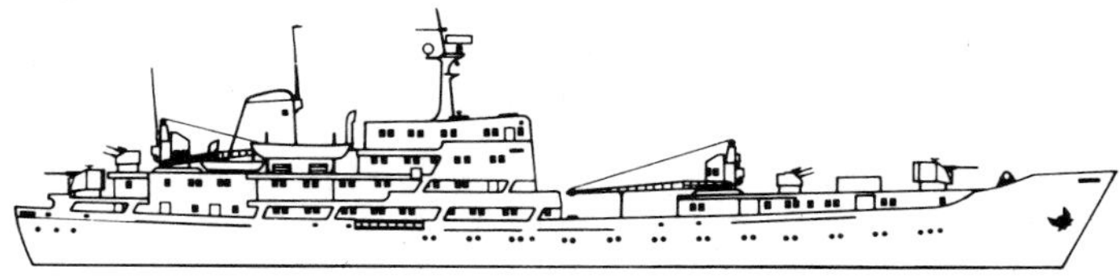

DAZHI

1 HUDUNG CLASS (ASR)

HAIJUI 512 (ex-J 301) **HAIJUI** 403

Displacement, tons: 4500 standard (est); 4900+ full load (est)
Dimensions, feet (metres): 308.5 × 55.8 × 15.1 *(94 × 17 × 4.6)*
Main machinery: 2 diesels; 3600 hp(m) *(2.64 MW)*; 2 shafts
Speed, knots: 16. **Range, miles:** 5000 at 12 kts
Complement: 225 (est)
Guns: 6 China 37 mm/63 (3 twin).
Radars: Navigation: Fin Curve; I band.

Comment: Both built at Hudung Shipyard, Shanghai. Laid down 1965, launched 1967. Design revised before completion. 512 has two bow and two stern anchors. Two 5 ton booms and stern gantry for submarine rescue bell. 403 may be slightly smaller.

HAIJUI 512 *1987*

SALVAGE SHIPS

Note: There are at least two DRSVs used for submarine rescue or salvage. 14.9 m in length capable of 'wet' rescue at 200 m and diving to 600 m. Capacity six survivors. Speed 4 kts or 20 hours at 2 kts.

DSRV *1991, CSSC*

4 YEN TING CLASS (ARS)

HAI LAO 456, 520, 523, 666

Displacement, tons: 260-275 standard
Dimensions, feet (metres): 103.3 × 23 × 8.2 *(31.5 × 7 × 2.5)*
Main machinery: 1 Type 3D-12 diesel; 315 hp(m) *(231 kW)* sustained; 1 shaft
Speed, knots: 10
Complement: 18
Guns: 2 China 14.5 mm/93 (twin).

Comment: Trawler-type hull, similar to enlarged FT series. Built in 1972-74.

YEN TING 666 *12/1989, G. Jacobs*

1 KANSHA CLASS

Displacement, tons: 1325
Dimensions, feet (metres): 229.3 × 34.4 × 11.8 *(69.9 × 10.5 × 3.6)*
Main machinery: 2 Type 8300 ZC diesels; 2200 hp(m) *(1.62 MW)*; 2 shafts
Speed, knots: 13.5. **Range, miles:** 2400 at 13 kts

Comment: Built at Chunghua SY, Shanghai in 1980-81. Trials July 1981. Designed by Chinese Marine Design and Research Institute. Carries one French SM-358-S DSRV (deep submergence recovery vehicle), 7 m long with a crew of five and an operating depth of 985 ft *(300 m)*. Ship has one 5 ton crane fwd and a 2 ton crane aft. Based in East China Sea.

3 Ex-US LSIL TYPE

HAI LAO 441, 821, 698

Comment: Converted from LSIL—see *Amphibious Warfare Forces* section for details.

3 DING HAI CLASS

HAI LAO 446, 447, 511

Displacement, tons: 375 full load (approx)
Dimensions, feet (metres): 123 × 23 × 11.5 *(37.5 × 7 × 3.5)*
Main machinery: 1 Type 3-D-12 diesel; 315 hp(m) *(231 kW)*; 1 shaft
Speed, knots: 12
Complement: 30 max
Guns: 4 China 14.5 mm/93 (2 twin, fwd and aft).

Comment: Coastal salvage ships built 1964-66. Have small cargo hatch aft.

10+ LUNG MA CLASS

Displacement, tons: 115
Dimensions, feet (metres): 83.7 × 18 × 4.9 *(25.5 × 5.5 × 1.5)*

Comment: Diving tenders for coastal and river work.

REPAIR SHIPS

1 Ex-US ACHELOUS CLASS

DAGUSHAN (ex-*Hsiang An*, ex-USS *Achilles* ARL 41, ex-LST 455) U 891

Displacement, tons: 1625 light; 4325 full load
Dimensions, feet (metres): 328 × 50 × 14 *(100 × 15.2 × 4.3)*
Main machinery: 2 GM 12-567A diesels; 1800 hp *(1.34 MW)*; 2 shafts
Speed, knots: 12
Complement: 270
Guns: 12 China 37 mm/63 (6 twin). 4 China 14.5 mm/93 (2 twin).
Radars: Navigation: Fin Curve; I band.

Comment: Launched on 17 October 1942. Transferred to Nationalist China as *Hsiang An* in September 1947. Burned and grounded in 1949, salvaged and refitted. Has 60 ton A-frame and 25 ton crane. Mostly alongside in Shanghai.

DAGUSHAN *7/1985, Fischer/Donko*

1 DA LIANG CLASS (AR)

HAI WU 809

Comment: Built in 1968-69 possibly as a repair ship for small craft.

RESEARCH AND SURVEY SHIPS

Notes: (a) In addition to naval ships listed the following ships work for the Hydrographic Bureau of the Ministry of Communications and therefore act as AGIs: *Sui Hang Biao No 1, Hu Hang Biao No 3* and *Jin Hang Biao No 1* (all of 1400 tons) and *Sui Hang CE Nos 1* and *2, Hu Hang CE Nos 11-15*, and *Jin Hang CE Nos 1* and *2* (all of 300 tons).
(b) *Qionsha* H 263 is a survey ship which is armed with 2—37 mm twins and 2—25 mm twins. This is probably an adaptation of the class of same name listed in *Amphibious Warfare Forces* section as an AP.

1 RESEARCH SHIP

JI DI HAO

Displacement, tons: 1050 full load
Dimensions, feet (metres): 164 × 34 × 16.4 *(50 × 10.4 × 5)*
Main machinery: 1 Burmeister and Wain Alpha L23/30 diesel; 2200 hp(m) *(1.62 MW)* sustained; 1 shaft
Speed, knots: 14. **Range, miles:** 12 000 at 11 kts
Complement: 26 plus 15 scientists

Comment: Ordered from Mjellem and Karlsen, Bergen, Norway in 1983. Laid down 15 November 1983. Similar to civilian research ships built for Mexico.

2 DAJIANG CLASS (RESEARCH SHIPS)

R 327 YUAN WANG 3

Displacement, tons: 10 975 full load
Dimensions, feet (metres): 511.7 × 67.2 × 37.7 *(156 × 20.5 × 11.5)*
Main machinery: 2 MAN K9Z60/105E diesels; 9000 hp(m) *(6.6 MW)*; 2 shafts
Speed, knots: 20
Helicopters: 2 Aerospatiale SA 321G Super Frelon (*R 237* only).

Comment: Built at Hutong, Shanghai. Completed 1981-82. Sisters of submarine support and salvage ships and operate for Academy of Sciences.

R 327 *1980, RNZAF*

YUAN WANG 3 *1984*

2 SPACE EVENT SHIPS

YUAN WANG 1 and **2**

Displacement, tons: 17 100 standard; 21 000 full load
Dimensions, feet (metres): 623.2 × 74.1 × 24.6 *(190 × 22.6 × 7.5)*
Main machinery: 1 diesel; 1 shaft
Speed, knots: 20

Comment: Built by Shanghai Jiangnan Yard. Probably commissioned in 1979. Have helicopter platform but no hangar. New communications, SATNAV and meteorological equipment fitted in Jiangnan SY in 1986-87. Both being refitted in 1991.

YUAN WANG 2 *9/1988*

1 SHIH YEN CLASS (AGOR)

SHIH YEN (ex-*Kim Guam)*

Displacement, tons: 2500 full load
Dimensions, feet (metres): 213.3 × 38.1 × 16.4 *(65 × 11.6 × 5)*
Main machinery: 2 UK Polar diesels; 1200 hp *(895 kW)*; 2 shafts
Speed, knots: 11 (est)
Radars: Navigation: Fin Curve or Japan OKI NXE-12c; I band.

Comment: Former coastal steamer purchased by China from Quan Quan Shipping Ltd (Singapore) about 1973. Cargo holds forward and amidships. Believed rebuilt in late 1970s for oceanographic duties. Operated by one of China's research academies or China Institute of Oceanography. Painted white.

2 SHIJIAN CLASS (AGOR)

SHIJIAN **KEXUEYIHAO**

Displacement, tons: 3700 full load
Dimensions, feet (metres): 311.6 × 46 × 16.4 *(95 × 14 × 5)*
Main machinery: 2 Type 6 ESDZ 48/82 diesels; 4000 hp(m) *(2.94 MW)*; 2 shafts
Speed, knots: 15. **Range, miles:** 10 000 at 12 kts
Complement: 125 approx
Guns: 8 China 14.5 mm/93 (4 twin).
Radars: Navigation: Fin curve; I band.

Comment: *Shijian* built at Shanghai in 1965-68 as enlarged unit of Dong Fang Hong class AGOR. Electronics updated in 1991. Operates in East China Sea area under civil authority of the State Bureau of Oceanography and with scientists of the Chinese Academy of Sciences. Twelve labs on board. Painted white. *Kexueyihao* was first seen in late 1989 and is a slightly modified version.

SHIJIAN *1989, Ships of the World*

1 DADIE CLASS (AGI)

841

Displacement, tons: 2300 standard
Dimensions, feet (metres): 308.4 × 37.1 × 13.1 *(94 × 11.3 × 4)*
Main machinery: 2 diesels; 2 shafts
Speed, knots: 17
Complement: 170 (18 officers)
Guns: 4 China 37 mm/63 (2 twin).

Comment: Built at Wuhan shipyard, Wuchang and commissioned in 1986. North Sea Fleet and seen regularly in Sea of Japan and East China Sea.

841 *1991, Ships of the World*

2 HAI YING CLASS (AGOR)

KE XUE YIHAO 1 **KE XUE YIHAO** 2

Displacement, tons: 4500 standard
Dimensions, feet (metres): 412 × 51 × 24 *(125.6 × 15.5 × 7.3)*
Main machinery: 2 PRC ESDZ diesels; 2 shafts
Speed, knots: 22
Complement: 148 (20 officers)
Radars: Navigation: 2 Fin Curve.

Comment: Successor design to Xiangyang Hong 9 series of civilian research ship. Believed to have been built in 1987-89. Fitted with deep sea cable reel on stern. Observed in East China Sea in March and September 1990 and Sea of Japan in 1991.

KE XUE YIHAO *12/1990, G. Jacobs*

1 KAN CLASS (AGOR)

KAN 102

Displacement, tons: 2300 standard
Dimensions, feet (metres): 225 × 22.5 × 9 *(68.6 × 6.9 × 2.7)*
Main machinery: 2 diesels; 2 shafts
Speed, knots: 18
Radars: Navigation: Fin Curve; I band.

Comment: Believed built in 1985-87, possibly at Shanghai. Large open stern area. Aft main deck area covered and may have cable reel system. Operated in East China Sea and Sea of Japan during 1991.

KAN 102 *9/1990, G. Jacobs*

1 XING FENGSHAN CLASS (AGI)

XING FENGSHAN V 856

Displacement, tons: 5500

Comment: Launched in June 1987. Similar to Dalang class.

XING FENGSHAN *1987, Ships of the World*

XIANGYANG HONG 01

Displacement, tons: 1100 standard; 1150 full load
Dimensions, feet (metres): 219.8 × 32.8 × 13.1 *(67 × 10 × 4)*
Main machinery: 2 diesels; 2 shafts
Guns: 2 China 37 mm/63 (twin). 8 China 14.5 mm/93 (2 quad).
Radars: Navigation: Fin Curve; I band.

Comment: The generic name Xiangyang Hong means 'The East is Red'. Initial vessel built either at Jiangnan or Tsingdao about 1970. Commissioned in 1971 and employed as research vessel but painted grey as if naval subordinated. Weapons not normally included on vessels subordinated to the Chinese Academy of Sciences.

XIANGYANG HONG 04, 06

Displacement, tons: 2000
Speed, knots: 15

Comment: Research ships built 1971-73.

XIANGYANG HONG 04 *1980, USN*

XIANGYANG HONG 02, 03, 08

Displacement, tons: 800 standard; 1000 full load
Dimensions, feet (metres): 236.2 × 26.2 × 8.2 *(72 × 8 × 2.5)*
Main machinery: 2 diesels; 2 shafts
Speed, knots: 14
Radars: Navigation: Fin Curve; I band.

Comment: Built in 1971-73 at Guangzhou. Operated by Chinese Academy of Sciences for coastal survey. Painted white.

XIANGYANG HONG 05

Displacement, tons: 14 500 full load
Dimensions, feet (metres): 500 × 64 × 28.9 *(152.5 × 19.5 × 8.8)*
Main machinery: 2 diesels; 2 shafts
Speed, knots: 16. **Range, miles:** 12-15 000
Radars: Navigation: Square Tie; I band.

Comment: Built as Polish B41 Type *(Francesco Nullo)* in 1967. Purchased by China and rebuilt 1970-72 in Guangzhou. Stationed at Guangzhou. Acts as environmental research ship. Four sister ships in Chinese mercantile fleet. Operated by Academy of Science. The goal post with a parabolic aerial has been removed from its position aft.

XIANGYANG HONG 05 *1980, RNZAF*

XIANGYANG HONG 09 (ex-*21*) V 350

Displacement, tons: 4435 standard
Dimensions, feet (metres): 400.3 × 49.9 × 23.6 *(122 × 15.2 × 7.2)*
Main machinery: 2 PRC ESDZ 43/82B diesels; 9000 hp(m) *(6.6 MW)*; 2 shafts
Speed, knots: 22. **Range, miles:** 11 000 at 15 kts
Complement: 145 (20 officers)
Radars: Navigation: Type 756; I band.

Comment: Originally built as Xiang Yang Hong 21 (AGOR) at Hudong Shipyard, Shanghai, in 1978. Conversion to AGI completed about 1986 and has since been observed monitoring US-ROK 'Team Spirit' military exercises in Sea of Japan and Yellow Sea. Prominent 5 ton cargo boom aft and two forward kingposts with extensive electronics mounted. Painted dark grey. Operated in East China Sea in 1989.

XIANGYANG HONG 09 *6/1988, G. Jacobs*

XIANGYANG HONG 10

Displacement, tons: 10 975
Dimensions, feet (metres): 512.3 × 67.6 × 22.3 *(156.2 × 20.6 × 6.8)*
Main machinery: 2 diesels; 2 shafts
Speed, knots: 20
Helicopters: 1 Aerospatiale SA 321G Super Frelon.

Comment: Built at Jiangnan Shipyard, Shanghai in 1979. Operates in conjunction with the Academy of Science.

XIANGYANG HONG 10 *1980, USN*

XIANGYANG HONG 11-16

Measurement, tons: 2894 grt (14 and 16)
Dimensions, feet (metres): 364.2 × 49.9 × 23.3 *(111 × 15.2 × 7.1)*
Main machinery: 2 diesels; 2 shafts

Comment: A series of research ships of varying dimensions but similar appearance. 14 and 16 built in 1981.

XIANGYANG HONG 14 (alongside XIANGYANG HONG 10) *9/1990, John Mapletoft*

XIANGYANG HONG 12 *7/1987*

1 YEN HSI CLASS (AGM)

HSUN 701

Displacement, tons: 930 standard; 1200 full load
Dimensions, feet (metres): 196.86 × 35.3 × 11.48 *(60 × 11 × 3.5)*
Main machinery: 2 diesels; 1800 hp(m) *(1.32 MW)*; 2 shafts
Speed, knots: 16 max; 11 cruise. **Range, miles:** 4500 at 11 kts
Complement: 110
Guns: 2 China 37 mm/63 (twin). 4 China 14.5 mm (2 twin) MGs.
Radars: Navigation: Fin Curve; I band.

Comment: Built in Shanghai in 1968-70. Has pronounced flare fwd and bow bulwark. Appearance is that of Hsiang Yang Hung 02-series of AGORs, though lighter in displacement and may have originally been planned as an AGOR/AGS unit.

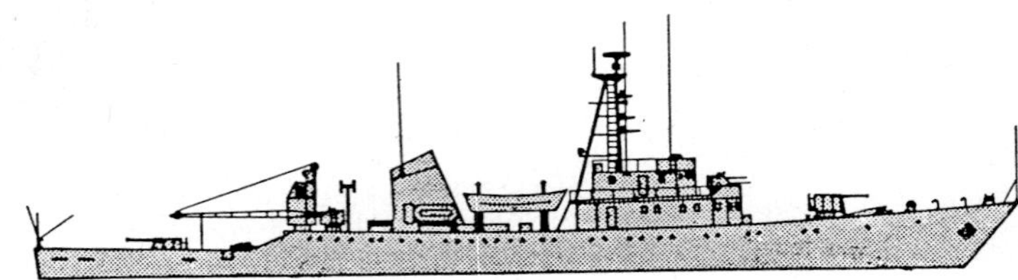

3 GEOPHYSICAL RESEARCH SHIPS

NAN HAI 502 **BIN HAI** 511 —

Measurement, tons: 697 dwt; 1257 gross
Dimensions, feet (metres): 215.5 × 36.9 × 13.5 *(65.7 × 11.2 × 4.1)*
Main machinery: 2 Yanmar CG-ST diesels; 2000 hp(m) *(1.47 MW)*; 1 shaft; cp prop
Speed, knots: 15
Complement: 50 (31 plus 19 scientists)

Comment: Built by Mitsubishi Heavy Industries in 1979. Designed for bathymetric and seismic research using satellite and terrestrial fixing. 511 modified in 1983 to include a helicopter deck. Arrays up to 3600 m can be towed.

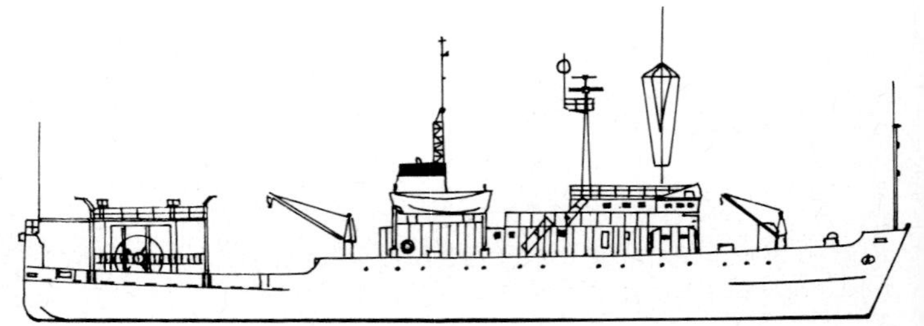

NAN HAI

3 SHUGUANG CLASS (ex T-43) (AGOR/AGH)

SHUGUANG 1, 2 and 3

Displacement, tons: 500 standard; 570 full load
Dimensions, feet (metres): 190.3 × 28.9 × 11.5 *(58 × 8.8 × 3.5)*
Main machinery: 2 PRC/Kolumna Type 9-D-8 diesels; 2200 hp(m) *(1.62 MW)*; 2 shafts
Speed, knots: 15. **Range, miles:** 5300 at 8 kts
Complement: 55-60

Comment: Converted from ex-Soviet T43 Minesweepers in late 1960s. All painted white. One used for hydro-acoustic work in the East Sea Fleet has the number S994.

SHUGUANG 3 *1980*

5 SHUGUANG 04 CLASS (AGOR)

SHUGUANG 04, 05, 06, 07, 08

Displacement, tons: 1700 standard; 2400 full load
Dimensions, feet (metres): 214.9 × 32.8 × — *(65.5 × 10 × —)*
Main machinery: 2 diesels; 2 shafts
Speed, knots: 16
Guns: 2 China 37 mm/63 (twin). 4 China 25 mm/80 (2 twin).
Radars: Navigation: Fin Curve; I band.

Comment: Built at Guangzhou from 1970 to about 1975, based on modified design of *Hsiang Yan Hung 1* AGOR. Units differ slightly in superstructure appearance. At least three units subordinated to the Chinese Academy of Sciences and are without armament. Operated in East China and South China Seas.

SHUGUANG 04 Class *9/1990, John Mapletoft*

5 YENLAI CLASS (AGS)

K 200 226 426 427 943

Displacement, tons: 1100 full load
Dimensions, feet (metres): 229.6 × 32.1 × 9.7 *(70 × 9.8 × 3)*
Main machinery: 2 PRC/Kolumna Type 9-D-8 diesels; 2200 hp(m) *(1.62 MW)*; 2 shafts
Speed, knots: 16. **Range, miles:** 4000 at 14 kts
Complement: 100
Guns: 4 China 37 mm/63 (2 twin). 4—25 mm/60 (2 twin).
Radars: Navigation: Fin Curve; I band.

Comment: Built at Zhonghua Shipyard, Shanghai in early 1970s. Carry four survey motor boats.

YENLAI 427 *1987, G. Jacobs*

1 YENLUN CLASS (AGS) + 2 Ex-US ARMY (AGS)

HAITSE 583 **HAITSE** 502 **HAITSE** 601

Displacement, tons: 1250 standard; 2000 full load (583)
Dimensions, feet (metres): 229.7 × 65.6 × 9.8 *(70 × 20 × 3)* (583)
Main machinery: 2 PRC/Kolumna Type 9-D-8 diesels; 2200 hp(m) *(1.62 MW)*; 2 shafts
Speed, knots: 17
Guns: 4—25 mm/60 (2 twin).
Radars: Navigation: Fin Curve; I band.

Comment: 583 has prominent twin funnels amidships. First twin-hulled vessel built by PRC, with open well deck aft for supporting diving equipment and deep ocean survey work. Two small cranes aft. 502 and 601 are smaller ex-US Army craft of about 800 tons.

2 HAI YANG CLASS (AGOR)

HAI YANG 01 **HAI YANG 02**

Displacement, tons: 3300 standard; 4500 full load
Dimensions, feet (metres): 341.2 × 42.7 × 14.8 *(104 × 13 × 4.5)*
Main machinery: 2 diesels; 8000 hp(m) *(5.9 MW)*; 2 shafts
Speed, knots: 21. **Range, miles:** 10 000 at 18 kts
Complement: 150 including scientists
Guns: 4 China 37 mm/63 (2 twin).
Radars: Navigation: Fin Curve; I band.

Comment: Built at Shanghai during 1969-71. *Hai Yang 01* commissioned in 1972; *Hai Yang 02* in 1973 or 1974. Funnel amidships. Subordinated to Chinese Academy of Sciences. Painted white.

HAI YANG Class *7/1989, G. Jacobs*

1 DONG FANG HONG CLASS (AGOR)

Displacement, tons: 3000 full load
Dimensions, feet (metres): 282.2 × 37.7 × 14.8 *(86 × 11.5 × 4.5)*
Main machinery: 2 diesels; 2 shafts
Speed, knots: 14
Radars: Navigation: Fin Curve; I band.

Comment: Built at Hutong, Shanghai 1964-66.

DONG FANG HONG *1988*

1 HAI CLASS (AGOR)

HAI 521

Displacement, tons: 550 full load
Dimensions, feet (metres): 164 × 32.8 × 11.5 *(50 × 10 × 3.5)*
Main machinery: 2 Niigata Type 6M26KHHS diesels; 1600 hp(m) *(1.18 MW)*; 2 shafts; bow thruster
Speed, knots: 14. **Range, miles:** 5000 at 11 kts
Complement: 15 (7 officers) plus 25 scientists
Radars: Navigation: Japanese AR-M31; I band.

Comment: Built by Niigata Engineering Co., Niigata (Japan) in 1974-75. Launched 10 March 1975. Commissioned July 1975. First operated by the China National Machinery Export-Import Corp. on oceanographic duties. Operates on East and South China research projects but based in North China. For small vessel, has unique cruiser stern with raked bow, and small funnel well aft. Capability to operate single DSRV and the Chinese Navy has a number of Japanese-built KSWB-300 submersibles. Painted white.

2 DING HAI CLASS and 1 KAIBOBAN CLASS (AGS)

HAI SHENG 701, 702 and 623

Displacement, tons: 330 full load (701, 702)
Dimensions, feet (metres): 128 × 24.6 × 11.5 *(39 × 7.5 × 3.5)* (701, 702)
Main machinery: 1 PRC/Soviet Type 3-D-12 diesel; 315 hp *(232 kW)* sustained; 1 shaft
Speed, knots: 13
Guns: 4—14.5 mm/93 (2 twin).

Comment: Coastal trawler design. Naval subordinated. 701 and 702 are South Sea Fleet units. 623 is a larger craft of 67.5 m assigned to the North Sea Fleet.

1 GANZHU CLASS (AGS)

K 420

Displacement, tons: 850 standard; 1000 full load
Dimensions, feet (metres): 213.2 × 29.5 × 9.7 *(65 × 9 × 3)*
Main machinery: 4 diesels; 4400 hp(m) *(3.23 MW)*; 2 shafts
Speed, knots: 20
Complement: 125 (est)
Guns: 4—37 mm/63 (2 twin). 4—25 mm/60 (2 twin).

Comment: Built in Zhu Zhiang 1973-75. Frigate-type bridge. Prominent raked funnel.

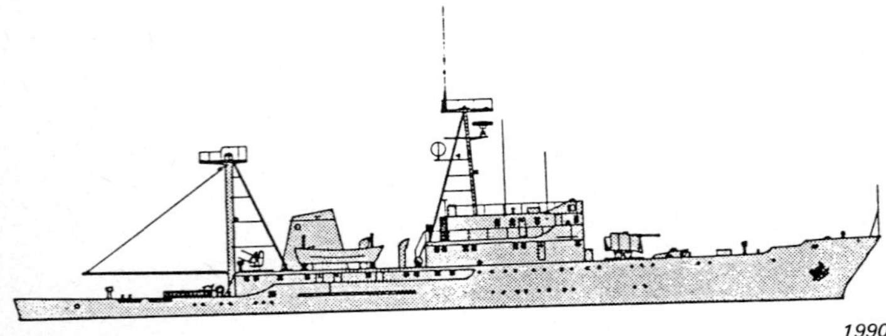

GANZHU Class 1990

1 YANXI CLASS (AGS)

V 201

Displacement, tons: 1150 standard
Dimensions, feet (metres): 213.9 × 34.4 × 10.8 *(65.2 × 10.5 × 3.3)*
Main machinery: 2 diesels; 4000 hp(m) *(2.9 MW)*; 2 shafts
Speed, knots: 16
Guns: 4 China 37 mm/63 Type 61/74 (2 twin); 4 China 25 mm/80 Type 61 (2 twin).

Comment: Built 1968-69; commissioned 1970. Outfitted initially to provide electronic monitoring support for China's SLBM missile tests.

2 YANNAN CLASS (AGS)

K 982 983

Displacement, tons: 1750 standard
Dimensions, feet (metres): 237.2 × 38.7 × 13.1 *(72.3 × 11.8 × 4)*
Main machinery: 1 diesel; 500 hp(m) *(367 kW)*; 1 shaft
Complement: 95

Comment: Built 1978-79; commissioned 1980.

CABLE SHIPS

Note: Several classes of cable layers are in service. These carry 'B' pennant numbers while similar ships with 'H' numbers act as buoy tenders and those with 'N' numbers are based at Nanjing. Examples are B 873, H 263 and N 2304, all of the same class.

1 WULAI CLASS (ARC)

230

Displacement, tons: 500 full load
Dimensions, feet (metres): 177.1 × 28.9 × 7.5 *(54 × 8.8 × 2.3)*
Complement: 50 approx
Guns: 4—25 mm/60 (2 twin).
Radars: Navigation: Skin Head; I band.

Comment: Built at Guangzhou in 1968-69 as coastal cable repair ship. Has noticeable davits aft. Fitted with bow sheaves. Also acts as salvage ship in South Sea Fleet.

BOOM DEFENCE VESSELS

Note: There are several classes of vessel including Yen Tai, Yen Bai, Yen Kuan, Hang Feng and some trawler conversions. Most are armed with at least 14.5 mm MGs.

5 Ex-US AILANTHUS CLASS

Displacement, tons: 560 standard; 805 full load
Dimensions, feet (metres): 194.5 × 34.5 × 14.8 *(59.3 × 10.5 × 4.5)*
Main machinery: Diesel-electric; 1200 hp(m) *(895 kW)*
Speed, knots: 14
Complement: 55
Guns: 1—14.5 mm MG.

Comment: Probably now used as service vessels.

SUPPLY SHIPS

Note: In addition to the following there may be another 12 coastal merchant ships operating under naval control as well as several 450 ton cargo ships wearing 'N' numbers.

1 CHANDOU CLASS (AF)

HAIYUN 126

Measurement, tons: 3200 dwt; 9796 gross
Dimensions, feet (metres): 499.3 × 71 × 28.6 *(151.8 × 21.6 × 8.7)*
Main machinery: 2 diesels; 2 shafts
Speed, knots: 13. **Range, miles:** 3500 at 12 kts
Cargo capacity: 2600 tons
Radars: Navigation: Fin Curve; I band.

Comment: Chinese-built in 1959-60. Six 3-5 ton booms. Serves in North Sea Fleet. Two sister ships converted to civilian salvage ships. Similar to Chan Tou class merchant ships.

2 GALATI CLASS (AK)

HAIYUN 318 HAIJIU 600

Displacement, tons: 5300
Dimensions, feet (metres): 328 × 45.6 × 21.6 *(100 × 13.9 × 6.6)*
Main machinery: 1 Sulzer 5TAD56 diesel; 2500 hp(m) *(1.84 MW)*; 1 shaft
Speed, knots: 12.5. **Range, miles:** 5000 at 12 kts
Complement: 50
Cargo capacity: 3750 tons; 20 ton; 3-5 ton cranes

Comment: Built at Santieral Shipyard, Galati, Romania in 1960s. Nine ships purchased of which these two were converted to AKs in early 1970s. Both reported operating in South Sea Fleet.

4 DANLIN CLASS (AK)

HAI LENG L 191, L 201 HAI YUN L 790, L 795

Displacement, tons: 900 standard; 1290 full load
Dimensions, feet (metres): 198.5 × 29.5 × 13.1 *(60.5 × 9 × 4)*
Main machinery: 1 Soviet/PRC Type 6DRN 30/50 diesel; 750 hp(m) *(551 kW)*; 1 shaft
Speed, knots: 15
Complement: 35
Cargo capacity: 750-800 tons
Guns: 4—25 mm/80 (2 twin).
Radars: Navigation: Fin Curve or Skin Head; I band.

Comment: Built in China in early 1960-62. Have a refrigerated stores capability. Two serve in each of South and East Sea Fleets. Two or more in civilian service.

4 HONGQI CLASS (AK)

Y 433 Y 443 Y 528 Y 771

Displacement, tons: 1600 full load
Dimensions, feet (metres): 203.4 × 39.4 × 14.4 *(62 × 12 × 4.4)*
Main machinery: 1 diesel; 1 shaft
Speed, knots: 14. **Range, miles:** 2500 at 11 kts
Guns: 4 China 25/80 (2 twin).

Comment: Used to support offshore military garrisons. A further ship, L 202, appears to be similar but carries no armament.

1 DAMEN CLASS (AK)

Y 529

Displacement, tons: 1050 standard; 1400 full load
Dimensions, feet (metres): 205.1 × 30.8 × 11.8 *(62.5 × 9.4 × 3.6)*
Complement: 30
Cargo capacity: 450 tons

Comment: Built at CSSC Shipyard, Xiamen in 1983.

2 Ex-US ARMY FS 381 TYPE

HAIYUN 300 (Ex-US Army FS 146, ex-*Clover*)
HAIYUN 315 (Ex-US Army FS 155, ex-*Violet*)

Displacement, tons: 935 full load
Dimensions, feet (metres): 180 × 32 × 10 *(54.9 × 9.8 × 3)*
Main machinery: 2 GM diesels; 1000 hp *(746 kW)*; 2 shafts
Speed, knots: 12. **Range, miles:** 4000 at 10 kts
Complement: 25
Guns: 14.5 mm MGs but variable.
Radars: Navigation: Skin Head; I band.

Comment: Built in USA in 1944-45. Reported to be employed as support ships for fast attack craft. With South Sea Fleet. A third of the class may be with the North Sea Fleet.

2 Ex-US LSILs

HAI SHUI 352 +1

Comment: At Shanghai supporting island garrisons. (See *Amphibious* section for details.)

3 LEIZHOU CLASS (WTL)

HAI SHUI 412, 555, 558

Comment: Details under same class in *Tankers* section. Two in South Sea and one in East Sea Fleets.

9 FUZHOU CLASS (WTL)

HAI SHUI 416, HAI SHUI 419, HAI SHUI 556, HAI SHUI 557, HAI SHUI 608 et al

Displacement, tons: 1100
Dimensions, feet (metres): 196.8 × 29.5 × 11.5 *(60 × 9 × 3.5)*
Main machinery: 1 diesel; 600 hp(m) *(441 kW)*; 1 shaft
Speed, knots: 12
Complement: 35
Guns: 4—25 mm (2 twin). 4—12.7 mm (2 twin) (not in all).

Comment: Built in Shanghai 1964-70. Large water carriers. Four in North Sea Fleet, two in East Sea Fleet, two in South Sea Fleet. Fourteen of same class in Tanker section.

FUZHOU 608 *7/1989*

TANKERS

Note: In addition to the ships listed below there are some elderly coastal tankers of the Kuangzhou (X 624, X 627), Fuzhi and Mettawge classes.

2 FUQING CLASS (AOR)

TAICANG X 575 **DONGYUN** (ex-*Fenfcang*) X 615

Displacement, tons: 7500 standard; 21 750 full load
Dimensions, feet (metres): 552 × 71.5 × 30.8 *(168.2 × 21.8 × 9.4)*
Main machinery: 1 Sulzer 8RL B66 diesel; 15 000 hp(m) *(11 MW)* sustained; 1 shaft
Speed, knots: 18. **Range, miles:** 18 000 at 14 kts
Complement: 130 (24 officers)
Cargo capacity: 10 550 tons fuel; 1000 tons dieso; 200 tons feed water; 200 tons drinking water; 4 small cranes
Guns: 8—37 mm (4 twin) (fitted for but not with).
Radars: Navigation: Two Fin Curve; I band.

Comment: Operational in late 1979. This is the first class of ships built for underway replenishment in the Chinese Navy. Helicopter platform but no hangar. No armament. All built at Talien. Two liquid replenishment positions each side with one solid replenishment position each side by the funnel. X 615 has a rounded funnel vice the square shape of the X 575. A third of the class *Hongcang* (X 950) was converted to merchant use in 1989 and renamed *Hai Lang*, registered at Dalian. A fourth (X 350) was sold to Pakistan in 1987.

DONGYUN *4/1990, G. Jacobs*

2 SHENGLI CLASS (AOT)

X 620 **X 621**

Displacement, tons: 3300 standard; 4950 full load
Dimensions, feet (metres): 331.4 × 45.3 × 18 *(101 × 13.8 × 5.5)*
Main machinery: 1 PRC 6 ESDZ 43 diesel; 2600 hp(m) *(1.91 MW)*; 1 shaft
Speed, knots: 14. **Range, miles:** 2400 at 11 kts
Cargo capacity: 3400 tons dieso
Guns: 2—57 mm (twin). 2—25 mm (twin).

Comment: Built at Hudong SY, Shanghai in late 1970s. Others of the class in commercial service.

SHENGLI 620 *7/1989*

3 JINYOU CLASS (AOT)

X 622 **X 625** **X 675**

Displacement, tons: 2500 standard; 4800 full load
Dimensions, feet (metres): 324.8 × 45.3 × 18.7 *(99 × 31.8 × 5.7)*
Main machinery: 1 SEMT-Pielstick 8PC2.2L diesel; 4000 hp(m) *(2.94 MW)* sustained; 1 shaft
Speed, knots: 15. **Range, miles:** 4000 at 9 kts

Comment: Built at Kanashashi SY, Japan.

JINYOU 625 *9/1990, John Mapletoft*

7 FULIN CLASS

X 583 **X 606** **X 607** **X 609** **X 628** **X 629** **X 633**

Displacement, tons: 2300 standard
Dimensions, feet (metres): 216.5 × 42.6 × 13.1 *(66 × 13 × 4)*
Main machinery: 1 diesel; 600 hp(m) *(441 kW)*; 1 shaft
Speed, knots: 10. **Range, miles:** 1500 at 8 kts
Complement: 30
Guns: 4—25 mm/80 (2 twin).
Radars: Navigation: Fin Curve; I band.

Comment: A total of 20 of these ships built at Hutong, Shanghai, beginning 1972. Thirteen in civilian service. Naval ships painted dark grey. Some having single underway replenishment rig. One in South Sea Fleet.

14 FUZHOU CLASS (AOT)

X 573 **X 580** **X 606** **X 629** **et al**

Cargo capacity: 600 tons fuel

Comment: Details under same class in Supply Ships. Built in Hudung SY, Shanghai 1964-70. Prominent bridge and funnel aft. Five in South Sea Fleet.

FUZHOU 606 *7/1989*

5 LEIZHOU CLASS (AOTL)

Displacement, tons: 900 standard
Dimensions, feet (metres): 173.9 × 32.2 × 10.5 *(53 × 9.8 × 3.2)*
Main machinery: 1 diesel; 500 hp(m) *(367 kW)*; 1 shaft
Speed, knots: 12. **Range, miles:** 1200 at 10 kts
Complement: 25-30
Cargo capacity: 450 tons
Guns: 4—37 mm (2 twin).
Radars: Navigation: Skin Head; I band.

Comment: Built in late 1960s probably at Qingdao or Wutong.

LEIZHOU 1101 *1990*

DEGAUSSING SHIPS

Note: In addition to the vessels listed below four ex-US LSIL conversions, *Hai Dzu 741, 742, 804* and *821* act as degaussing ships.

2 YEN PAI CLASS (ADG)

HAI DZU 746 **DONG QIN 863**

Displacement, tons: 746 standard
Dimensions, feet (metres): 213.3 × 29.5 × 8.5 *(65 × 9 × 2.6)*
Main machinery: Diesel-electric; 2 12VE 230ZC diesels; 2200 hp(m) *(1.62 MW)*; 2 ZDH-99/57 motors; 2 shafts
Speed, knots: 16. **Range, miles:** 800 at 15 kts
Complement: 55 (est)
Guns: 4—37 mm/63 (2 twin). 4—25 mm/80 (2 twin).

Comment: Enlarged version of T 43 MSF with larger bridge and funnel amidships. Reels on quarterdeck for degaussing function. Not all the guns are embarked.

HAI DZU *1991, CSSC*

2 YENKA CLASS (ADG)

HAI DZU 745 +1

Displacement, tons: 395 full load
Dimensions, feet (metres): 154.2 × 24.6 × 7.2 *(47 × 7.5 × 2.2)*
Main machinery: 2 PRC/Kolumna 9-D-8 diesels; 2200 hp(m) *(1.62 MW)*; 2 shafts
Speed, knots: 18. **Range, miles:** 3000 at 11 kts
Complement: 50
Guns: 2—37 mm/63 (twin). 2 or 4—14.5 mm/93 (1 or 2 twin) MGs.

Comment: Built at Chunghua Shipyard, Shanghai about 1966-68. Modified trawler hull. Prominent angled funnel and transom stern.

2 YEN FANG CLASS (ADG)

HAI DZU 950 **HAI DZU 951**

Displacement, tons: 110 standard; 125 full load
Dimensions, feet (metres): 101.7 × 20 × 5.9 *(31 × 6.1 × 1.8)*
Main machinery: 2 Soviet/PRC Type 3-D-6 diesels; 316 hp(m) *(232 kW)*; 2 shafts
Speed, knots: 9
Complement: 14-16

Comment: Trawler hull conversion. Cable reels on stern. Converted mid-1960s.

ICEBREAKERS

2 HAIBING CLASS (AGB)

101 (ex-*C723*) **102** (ex-*C721*)

Displacement, tons: 2900 standard; 3400 full load
Dimensions, feet (metres): 275 × 50 × 16.4 *(83.8 × 15.3 × 5)*
Main machinery: Diesel-electric; 2 diesel generators; 5250 hp(m) *(3.86 MW)*; 1 motor; 1 shaft
Speed, knots: 16
Complement: 90-95
Guns: 8—37 mm/63 (4 twin). 4 or 8—25 mm/80 (2 or 4 twin).
Radars: Navigation: Fin Curve; I band.

Comment: Built in 1969-73 at Chiu Hsin SY, Shanghai. Employed as icebreaking tugs in Bo Hai Gulf for port clearance. Sometimes deployed as AGIs.

102 *1982, G. Jacobs*

1 MOD YANHA CLASS (AGB)

723

Displacement, tons: 4000 full load
Dimensions, feet (metres): 310 × 56 × 19.5 *(94.5 × 17.1 × 5.9)*
Main machinery: Diesel-electric; 2 diesels; 2 shafts
Speed, knots: 17.5
Complement: 95
Guns: 8—37 mm/63 Type 61/74 (4 twin).
Radars: Navigation: Fin Curve; I band.

Comment: Enlarged version of Yanha class icebreaker, with greater displacement, longer and wider hull, added deck level and curved upper funnel. In October 1990, painted white while operating in Sea of Japan.

723 *1991, Ships of the World*

1 YANHA CLASS (AGB)

519

Displacement, tons: 3400 full load
Dimensions, feet (metres): 290 × 53 × 17 *(88.4 × 16.2 × 5.2)*
Main machinery: Diesel-electric; 2 diesels; 1 shaft
Speed, knots: 17.5
Complement: 90
Guns: 8—37 mm/63 Type 61/74 (4 twin); 4—25 mm/80 Type 61.
Radars: Navigation: Fin Curve; I band.

Comment: Commissioned in 1989. Similar to Haibing class with minor differences. Painted in PLAN grey colour. Operated in East China Sea in late 1990.

519 *10/1991, G. Jacobs*

SERVICE CRAFT

Note: There are probably over 500 armed motor junks, launches and miscellaneous service craft.

TUGS

Note: The vessels below represent a small cross-section of the craft available.

1 YAN JIU CLASS (ATA)

YAN JIU 14

Comment: Probably one of a series with dual military civilian use.

YAN JIU 14 *9/1991, G. Jacobs*

5 YUNG GANG CLASS (ATA)

Displacement, tons: 320
Dimensions, feet (metres): 87 × 31.4 × 10.8 *(26.5 × 9.6 × 3.3)*
Main machinery: 2 Daihatsu 6DLM-24 diesels; 3000 hp(m) *(2.2 MW)* sustained; 2 shafts
Speed, knots: 15

Comment: *Yung Gang 16* launched 29 July 1981 at Ishikawajima, built in Japan. It is not known whether these are for naval or civilian use.

16 GROMOVOY CLASS (ATA)

HAITO 210, 221, 230, 231, 235, 319, T 147, T 716, T 802, T 814 +6

Displacement, tons: 795 standard; 890 full load
Dimensions, feet (metres): 149.9 × 31.2 × 15.1 *(45.7 × 9.5 × 4.6)*
Main machinery: 2 diesels; 1300 hp(m) *(956 kW)*; 2 shafts
Speed, knots: 11. **Range, miles:** 7000 at 7 kts
Complement: 25-30 (varies)
Guns: 4—14.5 mm (2 twin) or 12.7 mm (2 twin) MGs.
Radars: Navigation: Fin Curve or Oki X-NE-12 (Japanese); I band.

Comment: Built at Luda Shipyard and Shanghai International, 1958-62. Nine in North Sea Fleet and seven in East Sea Fleet. Oil fuel, 175 tons.

GROMOVOY 802 *6/1987*

3 HUJIU CLASS (ATA)

T 155 **T 711** **T 867**

Displacement, tons: 750 full load
Dimensions, feet (metres): 160.8 × 31.2 × 12.1 *(49 × 9.5 × 3.7)*
Main machinery: 2 LVP 24 diesels; 1800 hp(m) *(1.32 MW)*; 2 shafts
Speed, knots: 13.5. **Range, miles:** 2200 at 13 kts

Comment: Built in 1980s; may be more to follow.

4 ROSLAVL CLASS (ARS)

J 120, HAITO 302, 403 + 1

Displacement, tons: 670 full load
Dimensions, feet (metres): 149.9 × 31 × 15.1 *(45.7 × 9.5 × 4.6)*
Main machinery: 2 diesels; 1500 hp(m) *(1.1 MW)*; 2 shafts
Speed, knots: 12. **Range, miles:** 6000 at 11 kts
Complement: 28
Guns: 4—14.5 mm (2 twin) MGs.

Comment: First ship (*302*) transferred by the USSR late 1950s. Remainder built in China in mid-1960s. One carries diving bell and submarine rescue gear on stern. Fuel, 90 tons.

1 JIN JIAN XUN 05 CLASS (ARS)

Displacement, tons: 559 standard
Dimensions, feet (metres): 196.9 × 24.3 × 8.5 *(60 × 7.4 × 2.6)*
Main machinery: 2 Niigata 6M2 6BGT diesels; 1700 hp(m) *(1.25 MW)* sustained; 2 shafts
Speed, knots: 18.4

Comment: Built by Osaka Shipyard, Niigata, Japan in early 1986. Commissioned November 1986. Identified as a rescue ship and towing vessel.

4 TUZHONG CLASS (ATR)

T 154 **T 710** **T 830** **T 890**

Displacement, tons: 3600 full load
Dimensions, feet (metres): 278.5 × 46 × 18 *(84.9 × 14 × 5.5)*
Main machinery: 2 PRC 10 ESDZ 43/82B diesels; 8600 hp(m) *(6.32 MW)*; 2 shafts
Speed, knots: 18.5
Radars: Navigation: Fin Curve; I band.

Comment: Built in late 1970s. Can be fitted with twin 37 mm AA armament and at least one of the class has been fitted with a Square Tie radar. 35 ton towing winch.

TUZHONG Class *6/1987, G. Jacobs*

HARBOUR TUGS

HARBOUR TUG *1990*

MARITIME MILITIA (M.B.D.F.)

Note: In the early 1950s certain ships of the deep-sea and coastal fishing fleets were formed into the Maritime Militia. These ships, under the control of the local branch of the party, act in support or as cover for naval forces. Their normal task is reconnaissance and surveillance but, on occasions, they have been armed with machine guns. About 100 ex-Soviet T 4 LCMs are used by the M.B.D.F. Some Fuzhou class coastal tankers are operated by M.B.D.F. to support East Sea Fleet island garrisons.

MBDF 136 *12/1991, 92 Wing RAAF*

COLOMBIA

Headquarters' Appointments

Fleet Commander:
Admiral Gustavo Adolfo Angel Mejia
Deputy Fleet Commander and Chief of Operations:
Vice Admiral Alberto Sandoval Solano
Commander, Pacific Force:
Vice Admiral Hernando Garcia Ramirez
Commander, Atlantic Force:
Vice Admiral Holdan Delgado Villamil

Personnel

(a) 1992: 14 000 (including 6800 marines)
(b) 2 years' national service (few conscripts in the Navy)

Organisation

Atlantic Coast Command: HQ at Cartagena.
Pacific Coast Command: HQ at Bahia Malaga.
Naval Force South: HQ at Puerto Leguizamo.
River Forces Command: HQ at Bogota.

Bases

Cartagena, ARC *Bolivar*: Main naval base (floating dock, 1 slipway), schools.
ARC *Bahia Malaga*: Major Pacific base.
ARC *Barranquilla*: Minor naval base.
Puerto Leguizamo: Putumayo River base.
Leticia: Meta River base.
Puerto Orocué, Puerto Carreño: River bases.

Naval and Maritime Air

A Fleet Air Arm has been established with one fixed wing squadron and one helicopter squadron.
The Colombian Air Force with 50 helicopters and a number of attack/reconnaissance aircraft provides support including Type A 37B.

Cuerpo de Infanteria de Marina

Organisation: Atlàntico Brigade: 1st Battalion (Cartagena).
5th Battalion (Coveñas also has Amphibious Warfare School).
Paćifico Brigade: 2nd Battalion (Tumaco).
3rd Battalion (Buenaventura).
4th (Jungle) Battalion, subordinate to Western River Forces Command (Puerto Leguizamo).

Prefix to Ships' Names

ARC (Armada Republica de Colombia)

DIMAR

Naval authority in charge of hydrography, pilotage, navigational aids and port authorities.

Customs

The Coast Guard was established in 1979 but has now given way to the Customs Service. Some of the former CG vessels transferred to the Navy, others have been retained by Customs.

Strength of the Fleet

Type	*Active*
Patrol Submarines	2
Midget Submarines	2
Frigates	4
Patrol Ships	4
Fast Attack Craft (Gun)	2
Coastal/River Patrol Craft	20
Gunboats	3
Survey/Research Vessels	4
Transports	16+
Training Ship	1
Tugs	15

Mercantile Marine

Lloyd's Register of Shipping:
100 vessels of 313 000 tons gross

DELETIONS

Auxiliaries

1989 *Ciudad De Quibdo*
1990 *Jurado, Mario Serpa*

Customs

1990 *Rodriguez, Nito Restrepo*

PENNANT LIST

Submarines

SS 20	Intrepido
SS 21	Indomable
SS 28	Pijao
SS 29	Tayrona

Frigates

CM 51	Almirante Padilla
CM 52	Caldas
CM 53	Antioquia
CM 54	Independiente

Patrol Ships

DE 16	Boyaca
RM 72	Pedro de Heredia
RM 73	Sebastion de Belal Calzar
RM 74	Rodrigo de Bastidas

Light Forces

111	Albuquerque
112	Quita Sueno
CF 135	Riohacha
CF 136	Leticia
CF 137	Arauca
GC 100	Espartana
GC 101	Capitan R D Binney
GC 102	Rafael del Castillo y Rada
GC 103	Jose Maria Palas
GC 104	Medardo Monzon
GC 105	Jaime Gomez
GC 106	Nepomuceno Peña
LR I	Rio Magdalena
LR II	Rio Cauca
LR III	Rio Sinu
LR IV	Rio Atrato
LR V	Rio San Jorge
LR 122	Juan Lucio
LR 123	Alfonso Vargas
LR 124	Fritz Hagale
LR 126	Humberto Cortes
LR 127	Calibio
LR 128	Carlos Galindo

Survey Vessels

155	Providencia
156	Malpelo
BO 153	Quindio
BO 161	Gorgona

Auxiliaries

BD 33	Socorro
BD 35	Hernando Gutierrez
RR 73	Teniente Sorzano
RM 76	Josué Alvarez
RR 81	Capitan Castro
RR 84	Capitan Alvaro Ruiz
RR 86	Capitan Rigoberto Giraldo
RR 87	Capitan Vladimir Valek
RR 88	Teniente Luis Bernal
RR 89	Teniente Miguel Silva
RR 90	Néstor Orpina
RM 93	Segeri
RR 96	Inirida
TM 42	Turbo
TM 44	Tolú
TM 45	Serranilla
TM 47	Bahia Cupica
TM 60	San Andres
LR 92	Igaraparana
LR 95	Manacasias
NF 141	Filogonio Hichamón
170	Mayor Jaime Arias

SUBMARINES

2 209 CLASS (TYPE 1200) PATROL SUBMARINES

Name	*No*	*Builders*	*Laid down*	*Launched*	*Commissioned*
PIJAO	SS 28	Howaldtswerke, Kiel	1 Apr 1972	10 Apr 1974	18 Apr 1975
TAYRONA	SS 29	Howaldtswerke, Kiel	1 May 1972	16 July 1974	16 July 1975

Displacement, tons: 1180 surfaced; 1285 dived
Dimensions, feet (metres): 183.4 × 20.5 × 17.9 *(55.9 × 6.3 × 5.4)*
Main machinery: Diesel-electric; 4 MTU 12V 493 AZ80 diesels; 2400 hp(m) *(1.76 MW)* sustained; 4 AEG alternators; 1.7 MW; 1 Siemens motor; 4600 hp(m) *(3.38 MW)* sustained; 1 shaft
Speed, knots: 22 dived; 11 surfaced
Range, miles: 8000 at 8 kts surfaced; 4000 at 4 kts dived
Complement: 34 (7 officers)

Torpedoes: 8—21 in *(533 mm)* bow tubes. 14 AEG SUT; dual purpose; wire-guided; active/passive homing to 12 km *(6.5 nm)* at 35 kts; 28 km *(15 nm)* at 23 kts; warhead 250 kg. Swim-out discharge.
Fire control: Signaal M8/24 action data automation.
Radars: Surface search: Thomson-CSF Calypso II; I band.
Sonars: Krupp Atlas CSU 3-2; hull-mounted; active/passive search and attack; medium frequency.
Krupp Atlas PRS 3-4; passive ranging; integral with CSU 3.

TAYRONA *8/1991, Foto Flite*

Programmes: Ordered in 1971. Two more are required but money is not available. Both refitted by HDW at Kiel; *Pijao* completed refit in July 1990 and *Tayrona* in September 1991. Main batteries were replaced.

Structure: Diving depth, 820 ft *(250 m)*.

2 MIDGET SUBMARINES

Name	*No*	*Builders*	*Commissioned*
INTREPIDO	SS 20	Cosmos, Livorno	1972
INDOMABLE	SS 21	Cosmos, Livorno	1972

Displacement, tons: 40 surfaced; 70 dived
Dimensions, feet (metres): 75.5 × 13.1 *(23 × 4)*
Speed, knots: 11 surfaced; 6 dived
Range, miles: 1200 surfaced; 60 dived
Complement: 4

Comment: Similar to those in service with Pakistan Navy. They can carry eight swimmers with 2 tons of explosive as well as two swimmer delivery vehicles (SDVs).

INDOMABLE *10/1990, Hartmut Ehlers*

FRIGATES

4 TYPE FS 1500

Name	*No*	*Builders*	*Laid down*	*Launched*	*Commissioned*
ALMIRANTE PADILLA	CM 51	Howaldtswerke, Kiel	17 Mar 1981	6 Jan 1982	31 Oct 1983
CALDAS	CM 52	Howaldtswerke, Kiel	14 June 1981	23 Apr 1982	14 Feb 1984
ANTIOQUIA	CM 53	Howaldtswerke, Kiel	22 June 1981	28 Aug 1982	30 Apr 1984
INDEPENDIENTE	CM 54	Howaldtswerke, Kiel	22 June 1981	21 Jan 1983	24 July 1984

Displacement, tons: 1500 standard; 2100 full load
Dimensions, feet (metres): 325.1 × 37.1 × 12.1 *(99.1 × 11.3 × 3.7)*
Main machinery: 4 MTU 20V 1163 TB92 diesels; 23 400 hp(m) *(17.2 MW)* sustained; 2 shafts; cp props
Speed, knots: 27; 18 on 2 diesels. **Range, miles:** 7000 at 14 kts; 5000 at 18 kts
Complement: 94

Missiles: SSM: 8 Aerospatiale MM 40 Exocet ❶; inertial cruise; active radar homing to 70 km *(40 nm)* at 0.9 Mach; warhead 165 kg; sea-skimmer.
SAM: ❷ To be fitted forward of the bridge when funds become available.
Guns: 1 OTO Melara 3 in *(76 mm)*/62 compact ❸; 85° elevation; 85 rounds/minute to 16 km *(8.7 nm)*; weight of shell 6 kg.
2 Breda 40 mm/70 (twin) ❹; 85° elevation; 300 rounds/minute to 12.5 km *(6.8 nm)* anti-surface; weight of shell 0.96 kg.
4 Oerlikon 30 mm/75 Mk 74 (2 twin); 85° elevation; 650 rounds/minute to 10 km *(5.5 nm)*; 950 ready use rounds.
Torpedoes: 6—324 mm Mk 32 (2 triple) tubes ❺; anti-submarine.
Countermeasures: Decoys: 1 CSEE Dagaie double mounting; IR flares and Chaff decoys (H-J band).
ESM: AC672; radar warning.
ECM: Scimitar; jammer.
Combat data systems: Thomson-CSF TAVITAC action data automation. Possibly Link Y fitted.
Fire control: 2 Canopus optronic directors. Thomson-CSF Vega II GFCS.
Radars: Combined search: Thomson-CSF Sea Tiger ❻; E/F band; range 110 km *(60 nm)* for 2 m² target.
Fire control: Castor II B ❼; I/J band; range 15 km *(8 nm)* for 1 m² target.
IFF: Mk 10.
Sonars: Krupp Atlas ASO 4-2; hull-mounted; active attack; medium frequency.

Helicopters: 1 MBB BO 105 CB, ASW ❽.

Programmes: Order placed late 1980. *Almirante Padilla* started trials July 1982. Near sisters to Malaysian frigates.
Structure: No confirmation yet of SAM fit. Albatros/Aspide, Crotale and Barak have all been mentioned.

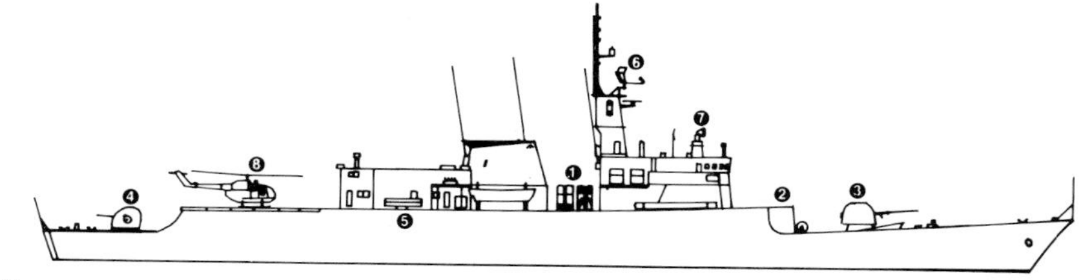

FS 1500 *(Scale 1 : 900), Ian Sturton*

INDEPENDIENTE *11/1990, Hartmut Ehlers*

ANTIOQUIA *11/1990, Hartmut Ehlers*

PATROL SHIPS

1 Ex-US COURTNEY CLASS

Name	*No*	*Builders*	*Commissioned*
BOYACA (ex-USS *Hartley*)	DE 16	New York SB	26 Jan 1957

Displacement, tons: 1450 standard; 1914 full load
Dimensions, feet (metres): 314.5 × 36.8 × 13.6 *(95.9 × 11.2 × 4.1)*
Main machinery: 2 Foster-Wheeler boilers; 300 psi *(42 kg/cm sq)*; 950°F *(510°C)*; 1 De Laval turbine; 20 000 hp *(15 MW)*; 1 shaft
Speed, knots: 24. **Range, miles:** 4500 at 15 kts
Complement: 161 (11 officers)

Guns: 2 USN 3 in (76 mm)/50 Mk 33 (twin); 85° elevation; 50 rounds/minute to 12.8 km *(7 nm)*; weight of shell 6 kg.
Torpedoes: 6—324 mm Mk 32 (2 triple tubes); anti-submarine.
Depth charges: 1 rack.
Fire control: Mk 63 GFCS.
Radars: Surface search: Raytheon SPS 10; G band.
Fire control: Western Electric SPG 34; I/J band.
Sonars: Sangamo SQS 23; hull-mouunted active search and attack; medium frequency.

Helicopters: Platform only.

Programmes: Transferred 8 July 1972; paid off into reserve in 1983. Brought out of retirement in 1988 for use mostly as a Headquarters ship.

BOYACA *11/1990, Hartmut Ehlers*

3 Ex-US CHEROKEE CLASS

Name	No	Builders	Commissioned
PEDRO DE HEREDIA (ex-*Choctaw*)	RM 72	Charleston SB & DD Co	21 Apr 1943
SEBASTION DE BELAL CALZAR (ex-*Carib*)	RM 73	Charleston SB & DD Co	24 July 1943
RODRIGO DE BASTIDAS (ex-*Hidatsa*)	RM 74	Charleston SB & DD Co	25 Apr 1944

Displacement, tons: 1235 standard; 1640 full load
Dimensions, feet (metres): 205 × 38.5 × 17 *(62.5 × 11.7 × 5.2)*
Main machinery: Diesel-electric; 4 GM 12-278 diesels; 4400 hp *(3.28 MW)*; 4 generators; 1 motor; 3000 hp *(2.24 MW)*; 1 shaft
Speed, knots: 15
Complement: 75
Guns: 1 USN 3 in *(76 mm)*/50 Mk 22.

Comment: Transferred by sale on 15 March 1979 and paid off in 1987. Reactivated in 1990. Originally built as tugs but used as patrol ships.

PEDRO DE HEREDIA *11/1990, Hartmut Ehlers*

SHIPBORNE AIRCRAFT

Numbers/Type: 4 MBB BO 105CB.
Operational speed: 113 kts *(210 km/h)*.
Service ceiling: 9854 ft *(3000 m)*.
Range: 407 nm *(754 km)*.
Role/Weapon systems: Shipborne surface search and limited ASW helicopter. Sensors: Search/weather radar. Weapons: ASW; provision to carry depth bombs. ASV; light attack role with machine gun pods.

BO 105 *1990, Colombian Navy*

LIGHT FORCES

Note: Reported that at least one 106 ft *(32 m)* patrol craft is to be acquired from Bender Marine, Mobile, Alabama in 1992. Possibly US funding.

2 Ex-US ASHEVILLE CLASS (FAST ATTACK CRAFT—GUN)

Name	No	Builders	Commissioned
ALBUQUERQUE (ex-USS *Welch*)	111	Peterson Builders	8 Sep 1969
QUITA SUENO (ex-USS *Tacoma*)	112	Tacoma Boat Building	14 July 1969

Displacement, tons: 225 standard; 245 full load
Dimensions, feet (metres): 164.5 × 23.8 × 9.5 *(50.1 × 7.3 × 2.9)*
Main machinery: CODOG; 2 Cummins VT12-875M diesels; 1450 hp *(1.08 MW)*; 1 GE LM-1500 gas turbine; 13 300 hp *(9.92 MW)*; 2 shafts; cp props
Speed, knots: 40. **Range, miles:** 1700 at 16 kts on diesels; 325 at 37 kts
Complement: 24
Guns: 1 US 3 in *(76 mm)*/50 Mk 34; 85° elevation; 50 rounds/minute to 12.8 km *(7 nm)*; weight of shell 6 kg.
1 Bofors 40 mm/56; 45° elevation; 160 rounds/minute to 11 km *(5.9 nm)* anti-aircraft; weight of shell 0.96 kg.
2—12.7 mm (twin) MGs.
Fire control: Mk 63 GCFS.
Radars: Surface search: Marconi LN 66/LP; I band.
Fire control: Western Electric SPG 50; I/J band.

Comment: Decommissioned in US Navy 30 September 1981. Transferred by lease 16 May 1983.

QUITA SUENO *11/1990, Hartmut Ehlers*

3 ARAUCA CLASS RIVER GUNBOATS

Name	No	Builders	Commissioned
RIOHACHA	CF 135 (ex-35)	Union Industrial de Barranquilla	1956
LETICIA	CF 136 (ex-36)	Union Industrial de Barranquilla	1956
ARAUCA	CF 137 (ex-37)	Union Industrial de Barranquilla	1956

Displacement, tons: 184 full load
Dimensions, feet (metres): 163.5 × 23.5 × 2.8 *(49.9 × 7.2 × 0.9)*
Main machinery: 2 Caterpillar diesels; 916 hp *(683 kW)*; 2 shafts
Speed, knots: 14. **Range, miles:** 1890 at 14 kts
Complement: 43; 39 plus 6 orderlies (*Leticia*)
Guns: 2 USN 3 in *(76 mm)*/50. 4 Oerlikon 20 mm.

Comment: Launched in 1955. *Leticia* has been equipped as a hospital ship with six beds and reported as disarmed.

ARAUCA *1991, Colombian Navy*

1 LARGE PATROL CRAFT

Name	No	Builders	Commissioned
ESPARTANA	GC 100	Ast Naval, Cartagena	1950

Displacement, tons: 50
Dimensions, feet (metres): 96 × 13.5 × 4 *(29.3 × 4.1 × 1.2)*
Main machinery: 2 diesels; 300 hp *(224 kW)*; 2 shafts
Speed, knots: 13.5
Guns: 1 Oerlikon 20 mm.

Comment: May be decommissioned in 1992.

2 SWIFT 110 ft CLASS (LARGE PATROL CRAFT)

Name	No	Builders	Commissioned
JOSE MARIA PALAS	GC 103	Swiftships Inc, Berwick	Sep 1989
MEDARDO MONZON	GC 104	Swiftships Inc, Berwick	July 1990

Displacement, tons: 95 full load
Dimensions, feet (metres): 109.9 × 24.6 × 6.6 *(33.5 × 7.5 × 2)*
Main machinery: 2 MTU diesels; 2 shafts
Speed, knots: 25. **Range, miles:** 2250 at 15 kts
Complement: 19 (3 officers)
Guns: 1 Bofors 40 mm/60. 1—12.7 mm MG. 2—7.62 mm MGs.

JOSE MARIA PALAS *1990, Colombian Navy*

1 SWIFT 105 ft CLASS (LARGE PATROL CRAFT)

Name	No	Builders	Commissioned
RAFAEL DEL CASTILLO Y RADA	GC 102 (ex-AN 102)	Swiftships Inc, Berwick	Feb 1983

Displacement, tons: 103 full load
Dimensions, feet (metres): 105 × 22 × 7 *(31.5 × 6.7 × 2.1)*
Main machinery: 4 MTU 12V331 TC 92 diesels; 5320 hp(m) *(3.97 MW)*; 4 shafts
Speed, knots: 25. **Range, miles:** 1200 at 18 kts
Complement: 19 (3 officers)
Guns: 1 Bofors 40 mm/60. 2—12.7 mm MGs.

Comment: Second of two delivered in the early 1980s. The other craft was badly damaged in 1986 but is now back in service with the Customs. *Castillo y Rada* transferred to the Navy in 1989.

RAFAEL DEL CASTILLO Y RADA *1988*

1 COASTAL PATROL CRAFT

Name	*No*	*Builders*	*Commissioned*
CAPITAN R D BINNEY	GC 101	Ast Naval, Cartagena	1947

Displacement, tons: 23 full load
Dimensions, feet (metres): 67 × 10.7 × 3.5 *(20.4 × 3.3 × 1.1)*
Main machinery: 2 Diesels; 115 hp(m) *(85 kW)*; 2 shafts
Speed, knots: 13

Comment: Buoy and lighthouse inspection boat. Named after first head of Colombian Naval Academy, Lieutenant Commander Ralph Douglas Binney, RN.

CAPITAN R. D. BINNEY *1991, Colombian Navy*

2 Ex-US Mk III PBs (COASTAL PATROL CRAFT)

JAIME GOMEZ GC 105 **NEPOMUCENO PEÑA** GC 106

Displacement, tons: 34 full load
Dimensions, feet (metres): 64.9 × 18 × 5.1 *(19.8 × 5.5 × 1.6)*
Main machinery: 3 Detroit 8V-71 diesels; 690 hp *(515 kW)* sustained; 3 shafts
Speed, knots: 28. **Range, miles:** 450 at 26 kts
Complement: 7 (1 officer)
Guns: 2—12.7 mm MGs. 2—7.62 mm MGs. 1 Mk 19 Grenade launcher.

Comment: Swiftships 65 ft type delivered in 1990. Original 40 mm and 20 mm guns replaced by lighter armament.

JAIME GOMEZ *1990, Colombian Navy*

6 RIVER PATROL CRAFT

Name	*No*	*Builders*	*Commissioned*
JUAN LUCIO	LR 122	Ast Naval, Cartagena	1953
ALFONSO VARGAS	LR 123	Ast Naval, Cartagena	1952
FRITZ HAGALE	LR 124	Ast Naval, Cartagena	1952
HUMBERTO CORTES	LR 126	Ast Naval, Cartagena	1953
CALIBIO	LR 127	Ast Naval, Cartagena	1953
CARLOS GALINDO	LR 128	Ast Naval, Cartagena	1954

Displacement, tons: 33 full load
Dimensions, feet (metres): 76 × 12 × 2.8 *(23.2 × 3.7 × 0.8)*
Main machinery: 2 GM diesels; 280 hp *(209 kW)*; 2 shafts
Speed, knots: 13
Complement: 10
Guns: 2 Oerlikon 20 mm or 1 Oerlikon and 4 mortars.

Comment: Some may be unserviceable.

JUAN LUCIO *1991, Colombian Navy*

5 RIO CLASS (RIVER PATROL CRAFT)

RIO MAGDALENA LR I
RIO CAUCA LR II
RIO SINU LR III
RIO ATRATO LR IV
RIO SAN JORGE LR V

Displacement, tons: 9 full load
Dimensions, feet (metres): 31 × 11.1 × 2 *(9.8 × 3.5 × 0.6)*
Main machinery: 2 Detroit 6V53N diesels; 296 hp *(221 kW)* sustained; 2 waterjets
Speed, knots: 24. **Range, miles:** 150 at 22 kts
Complement: 4
Guns: 2—12.7 mm (twin) MGs. 1—7.62 mm MG. 1—60 mm mortar.
Radars: Surface search: Raytheon 1900; I band.

Comment: Acquired in 1989-90. Ex-US PBR Mk II built by Uniflite. GRP hulls. May be numbered 176-180.

RIO SAN JORGE *11/1990, Hartmut Ehlers*

2 ROTORK CRAFT

MANUELA SAENZ **JAMIE ROOK**

Displacement, tons: 9 full load
Dimensions, feet (metres): 41.7 × 10.5 × 2.3 *(12.7 × 3.2 × 0.7)*
Main machinery: 2 Caterpillar diesels; 240 hp *(179 kW)*; 2 shafts
Speed, knots: 25
Complement: 4
Military lift: 4 tons
Guns: 1—12.7 mm MG. 2—7.62 mm MGs.

Comment: Acquired in 1989-90. Capable of transporting eight fully equipped marines.

ROTORK Craft *1990, Colombian Navy*

1 ADMIRAL'S YACHT

CONTRALMIRANTE BELL SALTER

Comment: Could be used as a patrol craft in an emergency.

CONTRALMIRANTE BELL SALTER *10/1990, Hartmut Ehlers*

SURVEY VESSELS

Name	*No*	*Builders*	*Commissioned*
PROVIDENCIA	155	Martin Jansen SY, Leer	24 July 1981
MALPELO	156	Martin Jansen SY, Leer	24 July 1981

Displacement, tons: 1040 full load
Measurement, tons: 830 gross
Dimensions, feet (metres): 164.3 × 32.8 × 13.1 *(50.3 × 10 × 4)*
Main machinery: 1 MAN-Augsburg diesel; 1570 hp(m) *(1.15 MW)*; 1 shaft; bow thruster
Speed, knots: 13. **Range, miles:** 15 000 at 12 kts
Complement: 21 (5 officers) plus 6 scientists

Comment: Both launched in January 1981. *Malpelo* employed on fishery research and *Providencia* on geophysical research. Both are operated by DIMAR, the naval authority in charge of hydrographic, pilotage, navigational and ports services. Painted white.

PROVIDENCIA *1991, Colombian Navy*

Name	*No*	*Builders*	*Commissioned*
GORGONA	BO 161 (ex-FB 161)	Lidingoverken, Sweden	1955

Displacement, tons: 574 full load
Dimensions, feet (metres): 135 × 29.5 × 9.3 *(41.2 × 9 × 2.8)*
Main machinery: 2 diesels; 910 hp(m) *(669 kW)*; 2 shafts
Speed, knots: 13
Complement: 45

Comment: Paid off in 1982 but is undergoing a complete overhaul at Cartagena naval base and is expected to be back in service in 1992.

Name	*No*	*Builders*	*Commissioned*
QUINDIO (ex-US YFR 443)	BO 153	Niagara S.B. Corporation	11 Nov 1943

Displacement, tons: 380 light; 600 full load
Dimensions, feet (metres): 131 × 29.8 × 9 *(40 × 9.1 × 2.7)*
Main machinery: 2 Union diesels; 300 hp *(224 kW)*; 2 shafts
Speed, knots: 10
Complement: 17 (2 officers)

Comment: Transferred by lease in July 1964 and by sale on 31 March 1979.

QUINDIO *11/1990, Hartmut Ehlers*

TRANSPORTS

Name	*No*	*Builders*	*Commissioned*
SAN ANDRES (ex-*Philip P*)	TM 60 (ex-BO 154)	H Rancke, Hamburg	1956

Measurement, tons: 680 dwt
Dimensions, feet (metres): 170.3 × 27.6 × 11.5 *(51.9 × 8.4 × 3.5)*
Main machinery: 1 diesel; 300 hp(m) *(220 kW)*; 1 shaft
Speed, knots: 9

Comment: Former Honduran coaster confiscated for smuggling and commissioned in the Navy in 1986. Used as a transport ship.

SAN ANDRES *10/1990, Hartmut Ehlers*

Name	*No*	*Builders*	*Commissioned*
HERNANDO GUTIERREZ	BD 35 (ex-TF 52)	Ast Naval, Cartagena	1955
SOCORRO (ex-*Alberto Gomez)*	BD 33	Ast Naval, Cartagena	1956

Displacement, tons: 70
Dimensions, feet (metres): 82 × 18 × 2.8 *(25 × 5.5 × 0.9)*
Main machinery: 2 GM diesels; 260 hp *(194 kW)*; 2 shafts
Speed, knots: 9. **Range, miles:** 650 at 9 kts
Complement: 12 plus berths for 48 troops and medical staff
Guns: 2—12.7 mm MGs.

Comment: River transports. Named after Army officers. *Socorro* was converted in July 1967 into a floating surgery. *Hernando Gutierrez* was converted into a dispensary ship in 1970.

HERNANDO GUTIERREZ *10/1990, Hartmut Ehlers*

TURBO TM 42
TOLÚ TM 44
SERRANILLA TM 45
BAHIA CUPICA TM 47
FILOGONIO HICHAMÓN NF 141

Comment: Captured drug running vessels of various characteristics and now 'poachers turned gamekeepers'. There are probably many more of this type. *Tolú* is used as a diving tender.

TURBO *10/1990, Hartmut Ehlers*

TOLÜ *10/1990, Hartmut Ehlers*

8 LCU 1466A CLASS

Displacement, tons: 360 full load
Dimensions, feet (metres): 119 × 34 × 6 *(36.3 × 10.4 × 1.8)*
Main machinery: 3 Gray Marine 64 YTL diesels; 675 hp *(504 kW)*; 3 shafts
Speed, knots: 10
Complement: 14

Comment: Former US Army craft built in the 1950s and transferred in 1991. Used as inshore transports.

FLOATING DOCKS

Note: It is reported that the 6700 ton *Rodriguez Zamora* (ex-ARD 28), the small floating dock *Manuel Lara*, the floating workshop *Mantilla* (ex-YR 66) purchased April 1979 and the repair craft *Victor Cubillos* (ex-USS YFND 6) purchased on 31 March 1978, are in use by Compania Colombiana de Astilleros Limitada (CONASTIL), Cartagena which is the former naval dockyard still owned by the Navy.

MAYOR JAIME ARIAS 170

Displacement, tons: 700

Comment: Capacity of 165 tons, length 140 ft *(42.7 m)*. Used as a non self-propelled depot ship for the midget submarines.

MAYOR JAIME ARIAS *10/1990, Hartmut Ehlers*

TUGS

CAPITAN CASTRO RR 81
CAPITAN ALVARO RUIZ RR 84
CAPITAN RIGOBERTO GIRALDO RR 86
CAPITAN VLADIMIR VALEK RR 87
TENIENTE LUIS BERNAL RR 88

Displacement, tons: 50
Dimensions, feet (metres): 63 × 14 × 2.5 *(19.2 × 4.3 × 0.8)*
Main machinery: 2 GM diesels; 260 hp *(194 kW)*; 2 shafts
Speed, knots: 9

TENIENTE SORZANO (ex-USS YTL 231) RR 73

Displacement, tons: 54
Dimensions, feet (metres): 65.7 × 17.5 × 9 *(20 × 5.3 × 2.7)*
Main machinery: 6-cyl diesel; 240 hp(m) *(176 kW)*; 1 shaft
Speed, knots: 9

Comment: Formerly on loan—purchased on 31 March 1978. Dockyard tug at CONASTIL, Cartagena.

IGARAPARANA LR 92 **MANACASIAS** LR 95

Displacement, tons: 104 full load
Dimensions, feet (metres): 102.4 × 23.6 × 2.8 *(31.2 × 7.2 × 0.9)*
Main machinery: 2 Detroit 4-71 diesels; 230 hp *(172 kW)*; 2 shafts
Speed, knots: 7. **Range, miles:** 1600 at 7 kts
Complement: 7 (1 officer)

Comment: River tugs built by Servicio Naviero Armada R. de Colombia at Puerto Leguizamo. Completed June 1985 (LR 92) and June 1986 (LR 95). Used to transport materials to places difficult to reach by road.

MANACASÍAS *1988, Juan Mazuero*

TENIENTE MIGUEL SILVA RR 89 **NÉSTOR ORPINA** RR 90

Dimensions, feet (metres): 73.3 × 17.5 × 3 *(22.4 × 5.3 × 0.9)*
Main machinery: 2 diesels; 260 hp *(194 kW)*; 2 shafts
Speed, knots: 9

Comment: River tugs built by Union Industrial (UNIMAL), Barranquilla.

SEGERI RM 93
MITU RR —
INIRIDA RR 96
CALIMA RM —
JOSUÉ ALVAREZ RM 76

Comment: Probably captured drug running vessels. Characteristics unknown.

SAIL TRAINING SHIP

Name	*No*	*Builders*	*Commissioned*
GLORIA	—	A T Celaya, Bilbao	May 1969

Displacement, tons: 1150 full load
Dimensions, feet (metres): 249.3 oa; 211.9 wl; × 34.8 × 21.7 *(76; 64.6 × 10.6 × 6.6)*
Main machinery: 1 auxiliary diesel; 530 hp(m) *(389 kW)*; 1 shaft
Speed, knots: 10.5
Complement: 51 (10 officers) plus 88 trainees

Comment: Sail training ship. Barque rigged. Hull is entirely welded. Sail area, 1675 sq yards *(1400 sq m)*. Endurance, 60 days.

GLORIA *11/1990, Hartmut Ehlers*

CUSTOMS (ADUANAS)

Note: Pennant numbers are in the 200 series. When the Coast Guard was abolished, its assets were divided between the Navy and Customs services.

Name	*No*	*Builders*	*Commissioned*
OLAYA HERRERA	AN 201	Swiftships, Berwick	16 Oct 1981

Displacement, tons: 103 full load
Dimensions, feet (metres): 105 × 22 × 7 *(31.5 × 6.7 × 2.1)*
Main machinery: 4 MTU 12V 331 TC92 diesels; 5320 hp *(3.97 MW)*; 4 shafts
Speed, knots: 25. **Range, miles:** 1200 at 18 kts
Complement: 19
Guns: 1 Bofors 40 mm/60. 2—12.7 mm MGs.

Comment: Badly damaged in 1986 but repaired and brought back into service in 1991. Sister craft transferred to the Navy.

Name	*No*	*Builders*	*Commissioned*
CARLOS ALBAN	AN 208	Rauma Repola, Finland	1971

Displacement, tons: 130 full load
Dimensions, feet (metres): 108 × 18 × 5.9 *(33 × 5.5 × 1.8)*
Main machinery: 2 MTU diesels; 2500 hp(m) *(1.84 MW)*; 2 shafts; cp props
Speed, knots: 17
Complement: 20
Guns: 2 Oerlikon 20 mm.

Comment: Similar to Finnish Ruissalo class. Acquired in 1980. Second of class deleted in 1990.

CARLOS ALBAN

COMORO ISLANDS

General

Three of the four main islands of this group joined in a unilateral Declaration of Independence in July 1975. This has been legitimised by France.

Base

Moroni.

Mercantile Marine

Lloyd's Register of Shipping:
7 vessels of 2621 tons gross

PATROL FORCES

2 JAPANESE YAMAYURI CLASS

Name	*No*	*Builders*	*Commissioned*
KARTHALA	—	Ishihara Dockyard Co Ltd	Oct 1981
NTRINGUI	—	Ishihara Dockyard Co Ltd	Oct 1981

Displacement, tons: 26.5 standard; 41 full load
Dimensions, feet (metres): 59 × 14.1 × 3.6 *(18 × 4.3 × 1.1)*
Main machinery: 2 Nissan RD10TA06 diesels; 900 hp(m) *(661 kW)*; 2 shafts
Speed, knots: 20
Complement: 6
Guns: 2—12.7 mm (twin) MGs.

Comment: These two patrol vessels of the 18M type (steel-hulled) supplied under Japanese Government co-operation plan.

KARTHALA *10/1981, Ishihara D. Y.*

CONGO

Senior Officer

Head of the Navy:
Captain Jean-Felix Ongouya

General

The People's Republic of Congo became independent on 15 August 1960 and formed a naval service.

Personnel

(a) 1992: 350 officers and men
(b) Voluntary service

Base

Pointe-Noire.

Mercantile Marine

Lloyd's Register of Shipping:
22 vessels of 8598 tons gross

DELETIONS

1988-89 1 Shershen class
1989-90 4 Yulin class
1990-91 3 Shanghai II class

PATROL FORCES

3 SPANISH PIRAÑA CLASS (FAST ATTACK CRAFT—PATROL)

Name	*No*	*Builders*	*Completed*
MARIEN N'GOUABI (ex-*L'Intrepide*)	P 601	Bazán, Cadiz	Nov 1982
LES TROIS GLORIEUSES (ex-*Le Vaillant*)	P 602	Bazán, Cadiz	Jan 1983
LES MALOANGO (ex-*Le Terrible*)	P 603	Bazán, Cadiz	Mar 1983

Displacement, tons: 140 full load
Dimensions, feet (metres): 107.3 × 20.2 × 5.1 *(32.7 × 6.2 × 1.6)*
Main machinery: 2 MTU 12V 538 TB 92 diesels; 5110 hp(m) *(3.76 MW)* sustained; 2 shafts
Speed, knots: 28. **Range, miles:** 700 at 17 kts
Complement: 19 (3 officers)
Guns: 1 Breda 40 mm/70; 85° elevation; 300 rounds/minute to 12.5 km *(6.8 nm)*; weight of shell 0.96 kg.
1 Oerlikon 20 mm. 2—12.7 mm MGs.
Fire control: CSEE Panda optronic director.
Radars: Navigation: Decca; I band.

Comment: Ordered in 1980. Steel hulls. Derivative of Barcelo class. All were officially commissioned on arrival at Pointe-Noire 3 April 1983. Only one serviceable in late 1991.

MARIEN N'GOUABI *1983, Bazán*

4 ARCO RIVER PATROL CRAFT

Comment: Two of 42.6 ft *(13 m)* and two of 37.4 ft *(11.4 m)* with Volvo Penta diesels. Delivered 1982. Used for River patrols together with a number of small boats with outboard motors.

1 TUG

HINDA

Displacement, tons: 200 full load
Dimensions, feet (metres): 96.8 × — × 12.5 *(29.5 × — × 3.8)*
Main machinery: 1 MGO diesel; 900 hp(m) *(661 kW)*; 1 shaft
Speed, knots: 11
Complement: 16

Comment: Ordered from La Manche, St Malo. Laid down 16 February 1981, launched 31 March 1981, completed 3 October 1981.

3 Ex-SOVIET ZHUK CLASS

301 302 303

Displacement, tons: 50 full load
Dimensions, feet (metres): 75.4 × 17 × 6.2 *(23 × 5.2 × 1.9)*
Main machinery: 2 M50-F4 diesels; 2400 hp(m) *(1.76 MW)*; 2 shafts
Speed, knots: 30. **Range, miles:** 1100 at 15 kts
Complement: 17
Guns: 4—14.5 mm (2 twin) MGs.

Comment: Transferred in 1982. Three more were expected in 1984 but did not materialise.

ZHUK *1987*

COOK ISLANDS

eneral

group of islands which are self governing in free association with ›w Zealand. Defence is the responsibility of New Zealand in nsultation with the islands' Government.

PACIFIC FORUM TYPE
.ARGE PATROL CRAFT)

me	*Builders*	*Commissioned*
KUKUPA	Australian Shipbuilding Industries	1 Sep 1989

splacement, tons: 162 full load
mensions, feet (metres): 103.3 × 26.6 × 6.9 *(31.5 × 8.1 × 2.1)*
ain machinery: 2 Caterpillar 3516 TA diesels; 2820 hp *(2.1 MW)*; 2 shafts
eed, knots: 20. **Range, miles:** 2500 at 12 kts
mplement: 17 (3 officers)
dars: Surface search: Furuno 1011; I band.

mment: Laid down 16 May 1988 and launched 27 January 1989. Cost, training and support provided by Australia under Defence Co-operation. Acceptance date was 9 March 1989 but he handover was deferred another six months because of the hange in local government. Has Furuno D/F equipment, SATNAV and a seaboat with a 40 hp outboard engine.

TE KUKUPA *10/1991, John Mortimer*

COSTA RICA

adquarters' Appointment

ad of Maritime Civil Guard:
Commander Carlos M Solano

Personnel

(a) 1992: 160 officers and men
(b) Voluntary service

Ports

Golfito, Puntarenas, Puerto Limon

Mercantile Marine

Lloyd's Register of Shipping:
29 vessels of 14 392 tons gross

PATROL FORCES

Ex-USCG CAPE CLASS (LARGE PATROL CRAFT)

me	*No*	*Builders*	*Commissioned*
TRONAUTA FRANKLIN CHANG (ex-*Cape Henlopen*)	95-1	Coast Guard Yard, Curtis Bay	5 Dec 1958

splacement, tons: 98 standard; 148 full load
nensions, feet (metres): 94.8 × 20.3 × 6.6 *(28.9 × 6.2 × 2)*
in machinery: 2 Detroit 16V-149TI diesels; 2070 hp *(1.54 MW)* sustained; 2 shafts
eed, knots: 20. **Range, miles:** 2500 at 10 kts
mplement: 14 (1 officer)
ns: 2—12.7 mm MGs.
dars: Surface search: Raytheon SPS 64(V)1; I band.

mment: Transferred from US Coast Guard 28 September 1989 after a refit by Bender SB and Repair Co. Painted white.

TRONAUTA FRANKLIN CHANG *1989, Bender SB & R Co.*

SWIFT 105 ft CLASS (FAST PATROL CRAFT)

A DEL COCO 1055

placement, tons: 118 full load
nensions, feet (metres): 105 × 23.3 × 7.2 *(32 × 7.1 × 2.2)*
in machinery: 3 MTU 12V-1163 TC 92 diesels; 10 530 hp(m) *(7.74 MW)*; 3 shafts
eed, knots: 33. **Range, miles:** 1200 at 18 kts; 2000 at 12 kts
nplement: 21 (3 officers)
ns: 1—12.7 mm MG. 4—7.62 mm (2 twin) MGs. 1—60 mm mortar.
dars: Navigation: Decca RM 916; I band.

nment: Built by Swiftships, Morgan City in 1978. Refitted in 1985-86 under FMS funding. The win MGs are fitted abaft the bridge and the mortar is on the stern.

ISLA DEL COCO *2/1989*

4 SWIFT 65 ft CLASS (COASTAL PATROL CRAFT)

CABO VELAS 656
ISLA UVITA 657
CABO BLANCO 658
PUNTA BURICA 659

Displacement, tons: 35 full load
Dimensions, feet (metres): 65.5 × 18.4 × 6.6 *(20 × 5.6 × 2)*
Main machinery: 2 MTU 8V 331 TC 92 diesels; 1770 hp(m) *(1.3 MW)*; 2 shafts
Speed, knots: 23. **Range, miles:** 500 at 18 kts
Complement: 7 (2 officers)
Guns: 1—12.7 mm MG. 4—7.62 mm (2 twin) MGs. 1—60 mm mortar.
Radars: Navigation: Decca RM 916; I band.

Comment: Built by Swiftships, Morgan City in 1979. Refitted 1985-86 under FMS funding.

ISLA UVITA *12/1987*

1 SWIFT 42 ft CLASS (INSHORE PATROL CRAFT)

DONNA MARGARITA (ex-*Puntarena*) 421

Displacement, tons: 11 full load
Dimensions, feet (metres): 42 × 14.1 × 3 *(12.8 × 4.3 × 0.9)*
Main machinery: 2 Detroit 8V-92TA diesels; 700 hp *(522 kW)*; 2 shafts
Speed, knots: 33. **Range, miles:** 300 at 30 kts; 450 at 18 kts.
Complement: 4 (1 officer)

Comment: Built by Swiftships, Morgan City in 1986. The original name has been changed and she is now used as a hospital ship with armament removed.

DONNA MARGARITA *1989*

8 BOSTON WHALERS

181-188

Comment: The survivors of 13 delivered in 1983. Craft of 18 ft with 70 hp *(52 kW)* outboard engines.

2 SWIFT 36 ft CLASS (INSHORE PATROL CRAFT)

TELAMANCA 361 **CARIARI** 362

Displacement, tons: 11 full load
Dimensions, feet (metres): 36 × 10 × 2.6 *(11 × 3.1 × 0.8)*
Main machinery: 2 Detroit 8240 MT diesels; 500 hp *(373 kW)*; 2 shafts
Speed, knots: 24. **Range, miles:** 250 at 18 kts
Complement: 4 (1 officer)
Guns: 1—12.7 mm MG. 1—60 mm mortar.

Comment: Built by Swiftships, Morgan City in 1986.

CARIARI *199*

CROATIA

General

In January 1992 the independence of the former Yugoslav state was recognised by the European Community. As most of the old Yugoslav coastline and the major shipyards are within Croatian territory, a new Navy or Coast Guard is being formed, initially using vessels captured during the war with Serbia.

In early 1992 insufficient details of this new force are available, but according to the Croatian Maritime Commander, Admiral Letica, the order of battle is 2 missile corvettes (possibly Kobra class still building), 4 Shershen class FAC(T), 10 attack cra including Osa, Koncar and Mirna classes, 20 amphibious vesse (mainly small landing craft) and 5 support tenders. Details of the ships can be found under the Yugoslavia section.

CUBA

Headquarters' Appointments

Chief of the Navy:
Vice Admiral Pedro Perez Betancourt

Personnel

(a) 1992: 13 500 (8500 conscripts) including 1000 marines
(b) 2 years' national service

Command Organisation

Territorial:
Western Naval District (HQ Cabanas).
Central Naval District (HQ Cienfuegos).
Eastern Naval District (HQ Holguin).
Operational:
Missile Boat Flotilla, Torpedo Boat Flotilla, ASW Flotilla, Mine Warfare Division. These are deployed in whole or part amongst the Territorial Flotillas. Submarine Flotilla is based at Cienfuegos. Guard Flotilla consists of 1000 marines.

General

Cuba still has the highest estimated annual defence expenditure in Central America and the Caribbean. The Navy is the smallest of the three services and has the reputation of having a reasonable level of tactical and material efficiency.

Naval Establishments

Naval Academy:
At Punta Santa Ana, for officers and cadets.
Naval School:
At Playa Del Salado, for petty officers and men.
Naval Bases:
Cabanas, Nicaro, Cienfuegos, Havana, Mariel, Punta Ballenatos, Varadero, Canasi.

Mercantile Marine

Lloyd's Register of Shipping:
401 vessels of 770 197 tons gross

Strength of the Fleet

Type	*Active*
Submarines	3
Frigates	3
Corvette	1
Fast Attack Craft (Missile)	18
Fast Attack Craft (Patrol)	12
Minesweepers	16
LSMs	2
LCPs	2
Survey Vessels	7
Border Guard	34

DELETIONS

1989 2 Zhuk class, 2 Nyryat-I class
1990 2 SO 1 class, 2 T 4 class

SUBMARINES

725 727 729

Displacement, tons: 1950 surfaced; 2475 dived
Dimensions, feet (metres): 299.5 × 24.6 × 19.7 *(91.3 × 7.5 × 6)*
Main machinery: Diesel-electric; 3 Type 37D diesels; 5956 hp(m) *(4.3 MW)*; 3 motors; 5400 hp(m) *(3.97 MW)*; 3 shafts
Speed, knots: 16 surfaced; 15 dived; 9 snorting
Range, miles: 16 000 at 8 kts surfaced
Complement: 75

Torpedoes: 10—21 in *(533 mm)* (6 bow, 4 stern) tubes. 22 Soviet Type 53; dual purpose; pattern active/passive homing up to 20 km *(10.8 nm)* at up to 45 kts; warhead 400 kg.
Mines: 44 in lieu of torpedoes.
Radars: Surface search: Snoop Tray; I band.
Sonars: Herkules/Feniks hull-mounted; active/passive search and attack; high frequency.

Programmes: First arrived Cuba 7 February 1979, second in January 1980 and third on 7 February 1984.
Structure: Diving depth, 250 m *(820 ft)*.

FOXTROT 729 *19*

Operational: An ex-Soviet Whiskey class is used as a non-operational charging station and training submarine. *725* started a five year refit in Havana in March 1986 which had not completed by the end of 1991. *727* started a similar refit in Ju 1989.

FRIGATES

3 SOVIET KONI CLASS

350 353 356

Displacement, tons: 1440 standard; 1900 full load
Dimensions, feet (metres): 316.3 × 41.3 × 11.5 *(96.4 × 12.6 × 3.5)*
Main machinery: CODAG; 1 SGW, Nikolayev, M8B gas turbine (centre shaft); 18 000 hp(m) *(13.25 MW)* sustained; 2 Russki B-68 diesels; 15 820 hp(m) *(11.63 MW)* sustained; 3 shafts
Speed, knots: 27 gas; 22 diesel. **Range, miles:** 1800 at 14 kts
Complement: 110

Missiles: SAM: SA-N-4 Gecko twin launcher ❶; semi-active radar homing to 15 km *(8 nm)* at 2.5 Mach; height envelope 9-3048 m *(29.5-10 000 ft)*; warhead 50 kg; magazine silo holds missiles. Some anti-surface capability.
Guns: 4 USSR 3 in *(76 mm)*/60 (2 twin) ❷; 80° elevation; 90 rounds/minute to 15 km *(8 nm)*; weight of shell 6.8 kg.
4 USSR 30 mm/65 (2 twin) (353 and 356) ❸; 85° elevation; 500 rounds/minute to 5 km *(2.7 nm)* anti-aircraft; weight of shell 0.54 kg.
2—6-barrelled Gatlings (350 only); 3000 rounds/minute combined to 2 km anti-missile.
A/S mortars: 2 RBU 6000 12-tubed trainable launchers ❹; range 6000 m; warhead 31 kg.
Depth charges: 2 rails.
Mines: Can lay 22 mines.
Countermeasures: Decoys: 2—16-barrelled Chaff launchers.
ESM: Watch Dog; radar warning.
Radars: Air search: Strut Curve ❺; F band; range 110 km *(60 nm)* for 2 m² target.
Navigation: Don 2; I band.
Fire control: Hawk Screech ❻; I band; range 27 km *(15 nm)*.
Drum Tilt ❼; H/I band.
Pop Group ❽; F/H/I band (for SAM).
IFF: Two Square Head. High Pole A.
Sonars: Hull-mounted; active search and attack; medium frequency.

Programmes: First transferred 24 September 1981; second 8 February 1984; third 10 April 1988. These ships have no names; two are based at Mariel.
Structure: Similar to the Algerian Konis.

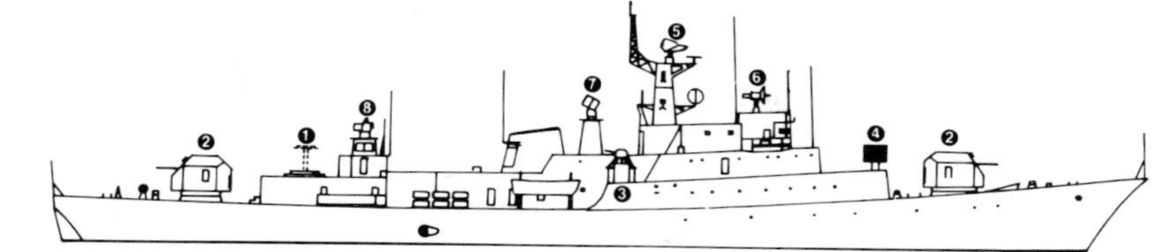

KONI Class *(Scale 1 : 900), Ian Sturton*

KONI 353 *3/1988, van Boeijen*

CORVETTE

1 SOVIET PAUK II CLASS

321

Displacement, tons: 520 full load
Dimensions, feet (metres): 195.2 × 33.5 × 11.2 *(59.5 × 10.2 × 3.4)*
Main machinery: 2 diesels; 21 000 hp(m) *(15.3 MW)*; 2 shafts
Speed, knots: 32. **Range, miles:** 2200 at 18 kts
Complement: 32

Missiles: SAM: SA-N-5 quad launcher; manual aiming, IR homing to 10 km *(5.4 nm)* at 1.5 Mach; warhead 1.1 kg.
Guns: 1 USSR 76 mm/60; 85° elevation; 120 rounds/minute to 7 km *(3.8 nm)*; weight of shell 16 kg.
1—30 mm/65; 6 barrels; 3000 rounds/minute combined to 2 km.
Torpedoes: 4—21 in *(533 mm)* (2 twin) tubes. Soviet type 53; active/passive homing up to 20 km *(11 nm)* at up to 45 kts; warhead 400 kg.
A/S mortars: 2 RBU 1200 5-tubed fixed; range 1200 m; warhead 34 kg.
Countermeasures: 2—16-tubed Chaff launchers.
Radars: Air/surface search: Cross Sword; E/F band.
Navigation: Pechora; I band.
Fire control: Bass Tilt; H/I band.
Sonars: Rat Tail; VDS (on transom); attack; high frequency.

Programmes: Built at Yaroslav Shipyard and transferred in May 1990. Similar to the ships building for India.
Structure: Has a longer superstructure than the Pauk I and new electronics with a radome similar to the Parchim II class.

PAUK II Class (Indian number) *1989*

LIGHT FORCES

5 Ex-SOVIET OSA I and 13 OSA II CLASS
(FAST ATTACK CRAFT—MISSILE)

251-255 (Osa I)
212, 225, 256-262, 267, 268, 271, 274 (Osa II)

Displacement, tons: 171 standard; 210 full load (Osa I); 245 full load (Osa II)
Dimensions, feet (metres): 110.2 × 24.9 × 8.8 *(33.6 × 7.6 × 2.7)*
Main machinery: 3 M503A diesels; 12 000 hp(m) *(8.8 MW)* (Osa I); 3 M504 diesels; 15 000 hp(m) *(11 MW)*; 3 shafts (Osa II)
Speed, knots: 35 (Osa I); 37 (Osa II)
Range, miles: 400 at 34 kts (Osa I); 500 at 35 kts (Osa II)
Complement: 30
Missiles: SSM: 4 SS-N-2 Styx; active radar or IR homing to 46 km *(25 nm)* at 0.9 Mach; warhead 513 kg.
Guns: 4—30 mm/65 (2 twin); 80° elevation; 500 rounds/minute to 5 km *(2.7 nm)*; weight of shell 0.54 kg.
Radars: Surface search: Square Tie; I band.
Fire control: Drum Tilt; H/I band.
IFF: Square Head. High Pole A (Osa I). High Pole B (Osa II).

Comment: Two boats of Osa I class were transferred to Cuba from the USSR in January 1972 and three in 1973. These were followed by one Osa I and one Osa II in mid-1976, one Osa II in January 1977 and one Osa II in March 1978. Further two Osa II delivered in December 1978, one in April 1979, one in October 1979, two from Black Sea November 1981, four in February 1982. One Osa I deleted in 1981.

OSA I 252 *1988*

9 Ex-SOVIET TURYA CLASS
(FAST ATTACK CRAFT—HYDROFOIL)

101 102 108 112 130
165 178 180 193

Displacement, tons: 190 standard; 250 full load
Dimensions, feet (metres): 129.9 × 24.9 (41 over foils) × 5.9 (13.1 over foils) *(39.6 × 7.6 (12.5) × 1.8 (4))*
Main machinery: 3 M504 diesels; 15 000 hp(m) *(11 MW)*; 3 shafts
Speed, knots: 40 foilborne. **Range, miles:** 600 at 35 kts foilborne; 1450 at 14 kts
Complement: 30
Missiles: SAM: SA-N-5 Grail; IR homing to 6 km *(3.2 nm)* at 1.5 Mach; warhead 1.5 kg.
Guns: 2—57 mm/80 (twin, aft); 85° elevation; 120 rounds/minute to 6 km *(3.3 nm)*; weight of shell 2.8 kg.
2—25 mm/80 (twin, fwd); 85° elevation; 270 rounds/minute to 3 km *(1.6 nm)*; weight of shell 0.34 kg.
Torpedoes: 4—21 in *(533 mm)* tubes (some). 4 Soviet Type 53; dual purpose; pattern active/passive homing up to 20 km *(10.8 nm)* at up to 45 kts; warhead 400 kg.
Radars: Surface search: Pot Drum; H/I band.
Fire control: Muff Cob; G/H band.
IFF: High Pole. Square Head.
Sonars: May have helicopter type VDS.

Comment: Transferred February 1979 (first pair); February 1980 (second pair); from the Pacific 17 February 1981 (third pair); 9 January 1983 (fourth pair); 13 November 1983 (single craft).

TURYA 102 *1988*

LAND-BASED MARITIME AIRCRAFT

Numbers/Type: 4 Mil Mi-14 ('Haze A').
Operational speed: 120 kts *(222 km/h)*.
Service ceiling: 15 000 ft *(4572 m)*.
Range: 240 nm *(445 km)*.
Role/Weapon systems: Fleet defence helicopter; shore-based for coastal duties; possibly operated by Soviet crews in support of Soviet naval forces. Sensors: Search radar, dipping sonar, MAD. Weapons: ASW; 2 × torpedoes, depth bombs or mines.

Numbers/Type: 4 Kamov Ka-28 ('Helix A').
Operational speed: 135 kts *(250 km/h)*.
Service ceiling: 19 685 ft *(6000 m)*.
Range: 432 nm *(800 km)*.
Role/Weapon systems: Probably intended as replacements for the Haze. Delivered in 1988. Sensors: Search radar, dipping sonar, sonobuoys, MAD, ECM. Weapons: 3 torpedoes, depth bombs, mines.

Numbers/Type: 6 Mikoyan MiG-29 Fulcrum.
Operational speed: 1320 kts *(1520 mph)*.
Service ceiling: 56 000 ft *(17 000 m)*.
Range: 1130 nm *(2100 km)*.
Role/Weapon systems: Air force manned air defence or Ground Attack fighters acquired with two training aircraft in 1989. Sensors: Pulse Doppler radar, IR scanner, laser rangefinder. Weapons: 1 × 30 mm cannon; 6 × AA-10 or AA-11.

MINE WARFARE FORCES

4 Ex-SOVIET SONYA CLASS (MINESWEEPERS/HUNTERS)

560 561 571 578

Displacement, tons: 400 full load
Dimensions, feet (metres): 157.4 × 28.9 × 6.6 *(48 × 8.8 × 2)*
Main machinery: 2 diesels; 2000 hp(m) *(1.47 MW)*; 2 shafts
Speed, knots: 15. **Range, miles:** 3000 at 10 kts
Complement: 43
Guns: 2—30 mm/65 (twin); 85° elevation; 500 rounds/minute to 5 km *(2.7 nm)*; weight of shell 0.54 kg.
2—25 mm/80 (twin); 85° elevation; 270 rounds/minute to 3 km *(1.6 nm)*.
Mines: Can carry 8.
Radars: Navigation: Don 2; I band.
IFF: Two Square Head. High Pole B.

Comment: Transferred August, December 1980, January and December 1985.

SONYA (German number) *5/1990*

12 Ex-SOVIET YEVGENYA CLASS (MINEHUNTERS—INSHORE)

501-504 507 509 510-514 538

Displacement, tons: 77 standard; 90 full load
Dimensions, feet (metres): 80.7 × 18 × 4.9 *(24.6 × 5.5 × 1.5)*
Main machinery: 2 diesels; 400 hp(m) *(294 kW)*; 2 shafts
Speed, knots: 11. **Range, miles:** 300 at 10 kts
Complement: 10
Guns: 2—14.5 mm (twin) MGs.
Countermeasures: Minehunting gear is lowered on a crane at the stern.
Radars: Navigation: Don 2; I band.

Comment: First pair transferred in November 1977, one in September 1978, two in November 1979, two in December 1980, two from the Baltic on 10 December 1981, one in October 1982 and four on 1 September 1984. There are two squadrons, one central and one west.

AMPHIBIOUS FORCES

2 POLNOCHNY B CLASS (LSM)

690 691

Displacement, tons: 760 standard; 800 full load
Dimensions, feet (metres): 242.7 × 27.9 × 5.8 *(74 × 8.5 × 1.8)*
Main machinery: 2 Type 40D diesels; 5000 hp(m) *(3.67 MW)*; 2 shafts
Speed, knots: 19. **Range, miles:** 1000 at 18 kts
Complement: 40
Military lift: 350 tons including 6 tanks and 200 troops
Guns: 4—30 mm/65 (2 twin); 85° elevation; 500 rounds/minute to 5 km *(2.7 nm)*; weight of shell 0.54 kg.
2—140 mm rocket launchers; 18 tubes; range 9 km *(5 nm)*.
Radars: Navigation: Don 2 or Spin Trough; I band.
Fire control: Drum Tilt; H/I band.

Comment: Transferred September/December 1982.

2 Ex-POLISH EICHSTADEN CLASS (LCPs)

Displacement, tons: 30 full load
Dimensions, feet (metres): 53.1 × 11.5 × 3.3 *(16.2 × 3.5 × 1)*
Main machinery: 2 diesels; 300 hp(m) *(220 kW)*; 2 shafts
Speed, knots: 15
Complement: 3
Military lift: 20 troops

Comment: Acquired from Poland in 1990 possibly to replace the last of the T 4 class.

SURVEY VESSELS

1 Ex-SOVIET BIYA CLASS (AGS)

GUAMA H 103

Displacement, tons: 750 full load
Dimensions, feet (metres): 180.4 × 32.1 × 8.5 *(55 × 9.8 × 2.6)*
Main machinery: 2 diesels; 1200 hp(m) *(882 kW)*; 2 shafts; cp props
Speed, knots: 13. **Range, miles:** 4700+ at 11 kts
Complement: 25
Radars: Navigation: Don 2; I band.

Comment: Has laboratory facilities, one survey launch and a five ton crane. Built in Poland in 1970s. Subordinate to Institute of Hydrography.

BIYA Class *1976*

SIBONEY H 101

Displacement, tons: 530
Dimensions, feet (metres): 138.5 × 27.2 × 8.5 *(42.2 × 8.3 × 2.6)*
Main machinery: 2 diesels; 910 hp(m) *(669 kW)*; 2 shafts
Speed, knots: 11

Comment: An ex-fishing trawler/buoy tender also used for cadet training.

TAINO H 102

Displacement, tons: 1100
Dimensions, feet (metres): 173.9 × 34.1 × 11.5 *(53 × 10.4 × 3.5)*
Main machinery: 2 diesels; 1550 hp(m) *(1.14 MW)*; 2 shafts
Speed, knots: 12

Comment: Mostly used as a buoy tender.

4 Ex-SOVIET NYRYAT-1 CLASS

H 93-96

Displacement, tons: 120 full load
Dimensions, feet (metres): 93 × 18 × 5.5 *(28.4 × 5.5 × 1.7)*
Speed, knots: 12.5
Complement: 15

Comment: Mostly used for surveying. Two (*H 91-92*) deleted so far and the remainder may be scrapped soon.

MISCELLANEOUS

Note: Tanker *Las Guasimas* of 8300 tons is capable of alongside refuelling. Civilian manned.

2 Ex-SOVIET POLUCHAT 1 CLASS

RT 81 **RT 83**

Displacement, tons: 100 full load
Dimensions, feet (metres): 97.1 × 19 × 4.8 *(29.6 × 5.8 × 1.5)*
Main machinery: 2 Type M 50 diesels; 1700 hp(m) *(1.25 MW)*; 2 shafts
Speed, knots: 20. **Range, miles:** 1500 at 10 kts
Complement: 15
Guns: 4—14.7 mm (2 twin) MGs.

Comment: Used as torpedo recovery vessels.

4 TRAINING SHIPS

XX ANIVERSARIO (ex-*Oranje Nassau*)
VIETNAM HERIOCO
JOSE MARTI
GAVIOTA PRIMERO

Comment: Different types of ships. *Gaviota Primero* is used for sail training.

1 ARMINZA CLASS (AGI)

ISLA DE LA JUVENTUD

Measurement, tons: 1556 gross
Dimensions, feet (metres): 230 × 41.3 × 17.7 *(70 × 12.6 × 5.4)*
Main machinery: 1 diesel; 2200 hp(m) *(1.62 MW)*; 1 shaft
Speed, knots: 13

Comment: Ex-trawler used as an intelligence collection ship since 1982.

ISLA DE LA JUVENTUD *7/1984, US Navy*

1 Ex-SOVIET PELYM CLASS (DEGAUSSING SHIP)

Displacement, tons: 1300 full load
Dimensions, feet (metres): 214.8 × 38 × 11.2 *(65.5 × 11.6 × 3.4)*
Main machinery: 2 diesels; 4000 hp(m) *(2.94 MW)*; 2 shafts
Speed, knots: 14
Complement: 70

Comment: Built in USSR in mid-1970s. Transferred in 1982.

1 Ex-SOVIET YELVA CLASS (DIVING TENDERS)

015

Displacement, tons: 300 full load
Dimensions, feet (metres): 134.2 × 26.2 × 6.6 *(40.9 × 8 × 2)*
Main machinery: 2 Type 3 D12 A diesels; 630 hp(m) *(463 kW)*; 2 shafts
Speed, knots: 12.5
Complement: 30
Radars: Navigation: Spin Trough; I band.

Comment: Built in early 1970s, transferred 1973. Two 1.5 ton cranes.

YELVA Class *1973*

1 Ex-SOVIET OKHTENSKY CLASS (OCEAN TUG)

CARIBE

Displacement, tons: 930 full load
Dimensions, feet (metres): 156.1 × 34 × 13.4 *(47.6 × 10.4 × 4.1)*
Main machinery: 2 BM diesel generators; 2 motors; 1500 hp(m) *(1.1 MW)*; 1 shaft
Speed, knots: 13. **Range, miles:** 6000 at 13 kts
Complement: 34
Guns: 1—3 in *(76 mm)*/60. 2—25 mm/80 (twin).

Comment: Transferred in 1976 to replace *Diez de Octubre*. Name taken from deleted corvette.

BORDER GUARD

Note: Operates under the Ministry of the Interior. Pennant numbers painted in red.

31 Ex-SOVIET ZHUK CLASS (FAST ATTACK CRAFT—PATROL)

Displacement, tons: 50 full load
Dimensions, feet (metres): 75.4 × 17 × 6.2 *(23 × 5.2 × 1.9)*
Main machinery: 2 M50 F-4 diesels; 2400 hp(m) *(1.76 MW)*; 2 shafts
Speed, knots: 30. **Range, miles:** 1100 at 15 kts
Complement: 17
Guns: 4—14.5 mm (2 twin) MGs.
Radars: Surface search: Spin Trough; I band.

Comment: A total of 40 acquired since 1971. Last batch of two arrived December 1989. Some transferred to Nicaragua. The total has been reduced to allow for wastage.

ZHUK Class *1990*

3 Ex-SOVIET STENKA CLASS (FAST ATTACK CRAFT—PATROL)

Displacement, tons: 170 standard; 210 full load
Dimensions, feet (metres): 127.9 × 25.6 × 5.9 *(39 × 7.8 × 1.8)*
Main machinery: 3 M503A diesels; 12 000 hp(m) *(8.8 MW)*; 3 shafts
Speed, knots: 36. **Range, miles:** 800 at 24 kts; 500 at 35 kts
Complement: 30
Guns: 4—30 mm/65 (2 twin); dual purpose; 85° elevation; 500 rounds/minute to 5 km *(2.7 nm)*; weight of shell 0.54 kg.
Radars: Surface search: Pot Drum; H/I band.
Fire control: Muff Cob; G/H band.
IFF: High Pole. Square Head.

Comment: Similar to class operated by KGB with torpedo tubes and sonar removed. Transferred in February 1985 (two) and August 1985 (one).

STENKA Class *1990*

CYPRUS, Republic

Senior Officer

Chief of Navy:
Captain J Vragalis, HN

Personnel

1992: 330

Mercantile Marine

Lloyd's Register of Shipping:
1359 vessels of 20 297 661 tons gross

COASTAL PATROL CRAFT

Notes: (1) In addition to the craft listed below two smaller Yugoslavian craft were delivered in August 1991; names *Adonis* and *Kiniris*.
(2) Two more craft may be acquired from Germany in 1992. Possible names are *Agathos* and *Panagos*.

Name	*No*	*Builders*	*Commissioned*
SALAMIS	P 01	C N de l'Esterel	1982

Displacement, tons: 94.5 full load
Dimensions, feet (metres): 105.3 × 21.3 × 3 *(32.1 × 6.5 × 0.9)*
Main machinery: 2 SACM UD33 V12 M5 diesels; 4000 hp(m) *(2.94 MW)*; 2 shafts
Speed, knots: 30. **Range, miles:** 1500 at 15 kts
Guns: 1 Breda 40 mm/70; 85° elevation; 300 rounds/minute to 12.5 km *(6.8 nm)* anti-surface; weight of shell 0.96 kg.
1—12.7 mm MG.

Comment: Laid down in December 1981, completed in 1982 for Naval Command of National Guard.

SALAMIS *10/1991*

Name	*No*	*Builders*	*Commissioned*
APHRODITE	PL 1	C N de l'Esterel	1982
KIMON	PL 2	C N de l'Esterel	1982

Main machinery: 2 MTU diesels; 2 shafts

Comment: Of 58.1 ft *(17.7 m)*. Controlled by Cyprus Maritime Police.

Name	*No*	*Builders*	*Commissioned*
EVAGORAS	PV 20	Brodotehnika SY, Yugoslavia	21 Nov 1991
POSIDON	PV 21	Brodotehnika SY, Yugoslavia	21 Nov 1991

Displacement, tons: 60 full load
Dimensions, feet (metres): 80.7 × 17.4 × 3.9 *(24.6 × 5.3 × 1.2)*
Main machinery: 2 diesels; 3560 hp(m) *(2.62 MW)*; 2 KaMeWa waterjets
Speed, knots: 45. **Range, miles:** 400 at 40 kts
Guns: 1 Oerlikon 20 mm; ISBRS rocket launcher

Comment: Designated as FAC-23 Jets.

EVAGORAS *11/1991*

LAND-BASED MARITIME AIRCRAFT

Numbers/Type: 1 Pilatus Britten-Norman Maritime Defender.
Operational speed: 150 kts *(280 km/h)*.
Service ceiling: 18 900 ft *(5760 m)*.
Range: 1500 nm *(2775 km)*.
Role/Weapon systems: Operated around Greek-Cypriot coastline to prevent smuggling and terrorist activity. Sensors: Search radar, searchlight mounted on wings. Weapons: ASV; various machine gun pods and rockets.

CYPRUS, Turkish Republic (North)

General

An independent Republic declared in November 1983 but recognised only by Turkey.

Base

Girne.

Turkish Navy

The Turkish naval patrol craft *Caner Gönyeli* (P 145) is permanently based at Girne (see *Turkey* section for details).

COASTAL PATROL CRAFT

RAIF DENKTAS 74

Displacement, tons: 10
Dimensions, feet (metres): 38 × 11.5 × — *(11.6 × 3.5 × —)*
Main machinery: 2 Volvo Aquamatic AQ 200F diesels; 400 hp(m) *(294 kW)*; 2 shafts
Speed, knots: 28. **Range, miles:** 250 at 25 kts
Complement: 6
Guns: 1—12.7 mm MG.
Radars: Surface search: Raytheon; I band.

Comment: Built by Profilo Holdings' Protekson Shipyard, Istanbul. Transferred from Turkish Coast Guard 23 September 1988. Can be equipped with a rocket launcher and is to be used for anti-smuggling patrols.

RAIF DENKTAS *9/1988, Selçuk Emre*

102 **103**

Displacement, tons: 25 full load
Dimensions, feet (metres): 47.9 × 11.5 × 3.6 *(14.6 × 3.5 × 1.1)*
Main machinery: 2 diesels; 700 hp(m) *(514 kW)*; 2 shafts
Speed, knots: 18
Complement: 6
Guns: 1—12.7 mm MG.

Comment: Built at Taskizak Yard in Turkey as part of an order, some of which are for the Turkish Coast Guard. First one delivered in August 1990, second in July 1991.

102 *8/1990, Selçuk Emre*

CZECHOSLOVAKIA

General

Although a navy as such does not exist there is a river patrol force of some 18 craft manned by personnel from the Border Guard wearing naval-type uniforms. The River Patrol is organised as a Battalion and is about 160 strong.

Base

Headquarters is at Bratislava.

Mercantile Marine

Lloyd's Register of Shipping:
24 vessels of 360 733 tons gross

DENMARK

Headquarters' Appointments

Flag Officer Denmark:
Rear Admiral K E J Borck

Diplomatic Representation

Defence Attaché, Bonn:
Colonel S S Jensen (Army)
Defence Attaché, London:
Captain S Lund
Defence Attaché, Stockholm:
Commander (S G) N Friis
Defence Attaché, Warsaw:
Colonel J G Hjort (Army)
Defence Attaché, Washington and Ottawa:
Brigadier K D Andersen (Air Force)
Defence Attaché, Paris:
Colonel M Christensen (Air Force)

Personnel

(a) 1992: 1150 officers, 3050 regular ratings,
1000 national service ratings.
Reserves: 5700.
Naval Home Guard: 4000.
(b) 9 months' national service

Naval Bases

Copenhagen (being phased out), Korsør (Corvettes, FACs, Stanflex), Frederikshavn (Submarines, MCMV, Fishery Protection Ships), Grønnedal (Greenland)

Naval Air Arm

Naval helicopters owned and operated by Navy in naval squadron based at Värlöse near Copenhagen. All servicing and maintenance by air force. LRMP are flown by the Air Force.

Coast Defence

There are forts at Stevns and Langeland (on southern approaches to Sound and Great Belt) armed with 150 mm and 40 mm guns. Six radar stations and a number of coast watching stations in the area. There are also two mobile batteries planned to be operational in 1994. Linked by a Terma command and control system they will each consist of three trailers, one for command and two for carrying Harpoon missiles taken from deleted frigates.

Command and Control

It was originally the intention to have all government vessels under The Directorate of Waters (Farvandsdirektoratet). However the Ministry of Trade and Shipping now runs the icebreakers and some training ships (the icebreakers are maintained by the Navy and are based at Frederikshavn in the Summer) while the Ministry of the Environment (Miljøministeriet) controls two environmental protection divisions based at Copenhagen (being phased out) and Korsør (both manned and maintained by the Navy). Survey ships are run by the Farvandsdirektoratet Nautisk Afdeling (Administration of Navigation and Hydrography) under the Ministry of Defence and the Ministry of Fisheries has four rescue vessels and an Osprey class.

Appearance

Ships are painted in 6 different colours as follows:
Grey: Frigates, corvettes and patrol frigates.
Olive-green: FACs and tankers.
Black: Submarines.
Orange: Survey Vessels.
White: The Royal Yacht and the Sail Training Yawls.
Black/yellow: Service Vessels, tugs and ferryboats.

Prefix to Ships' Names

HDMS

Mercantile Marine

Lloyd's Register of Shipping:
1290 vessels of 5 870 589 tons gross

Strength of the Fleet

Type	*Active*	*Building (Projected)*
Submarines (Coastal)	5	—
Frigates	7	1
Fast Attack Craft (Missile)	10	—
Large Patrol Craft	23	7 (3)
Coastal Patrol Craft	3	—
Naval Home Guard	39	5 (12)
Minelayers	6	—
Minesweepers (Coastal)	3	—
Minesweepers (Drones)	2	(10)
Support Ship	1	—
Tankers (Small)	2	—
Icebreakers	4	—
Royal Yacht	1	—
Tugs	2	—
TRVs	3	—
Survey and Training Craft	8	—
Environment Craft	6	—

DELETIONS

Submarines

1990 *Spaekhuggeren, Springeren* (old)

Frigates

1990 *Peder Skram, Herluf Trolle*
1991 *Fylla*
1992 *Ingolf, Vaedderen* (old), *Hvidbjørnen* (old)

Light Forces

1989 *Neptun, Rota*
1990 *Søløven, Søridderen, Søbjørnen, Søhesten, Søhunden, Søulven, Daphne, Ran, Havfruen*

Miscellaneous

1990 SKB 3

PENNANT LIST

Submarines

S 320	Narhvalen
S 321	Nordkaperen
S 322	Tumleren
S 323	Saelen
S 324	Springeren (new)

Frigates

F 340	Beskytteren
F 354	Niels Juel
F 355	Olfert Fischer
F 356	Peter Tordenskiold
F 357	Thetis
F 358	Triton
F 359	Vaedderen
F 360	Hvidbjørnen (building)

Light Forces

P 531	Dryaden
P 534	Najaden
P 535	Nymfen
P 540	Bille
P 541	Bredal
P 542	Hammer
P 543	Huitfeld
P 544	Krieger
P 545	Norby
P 546	Rodsteen
P 547	Sehested
P 548	Suenson
P 549	Willemoes
P 550	Flyvefisken
P 551	Hajen
P 552	Havkatten
P 553	Laxen
P 554	Makrelen
P 555	Støren
P 556	Svaerdfisken (building)
P 557	Glenten (building)
P 558	Gribben (building)
P 559	Lommen (building)
P 560	Raunen (building)
P 561	Skaden (building)
P 562	Viben (building)
Y 300	Barsø
Y 301	Drejø
Y 302	Romsø
Y 303	Samsø
Y 304	Thurø
Y 305	Vejrø
Y 306	Farø
Y 307	Laesø
Y 308	Rømø
Y 343	Lunden
Y 384	Maagen
Y 385	Mallemukken
Y 386	Agdlek
Y 387	Agpa
Y 388	Tulugaq

Mine Warfare Forces

N 43	Lindormen
N 44	Lossen
N 80	Falster
N 81	Fyen
N 82	Møen
N 83	Sjaelland
M 574	Grønsund
M 575	Guldborgsund
M 578	Vilsund

Auxiliaries

A 540	Dannebrog
A 559	Sleipner
A 568	Rimfaxe
A 569	Skinfaxe
TO 8	Hugin
TO 9	Munin
TO 10	Mimer

SUBMARINES

3 TUMLEREN (ex-KOBBEN) CLASS (TYPE 207)

Name	*No*	*Builders*	*Laid down*	*Launched*	*Commissioned*	*Recommissioned*
TUMLEREN (ex-*Utvaer*)	S 322	Rheinstahl-Nordseewerke, Emden	24 Mar 1965	30 July 1965	1 Dec 1965	20 Oct 1989
SAELEN (ex-*Uthaug*)	S 323	Rheinstahl-Nordseewerke, Emden	31 May 1965	3 Oct 1965	16 Feb 1966	5 Oct 1990
SPRINGEREN (ex-*Kya*)	S 324	Rheinstahl-Nordseewerke, Emden	26 May 1963	20 Feb 1964	15 Jan 1964	10 Oct 1991

Displacement, tons: 459 surfaced; 524 dived
Dimensions, feet (metres): 155.5 × 15 × 14 *(47.4 × 4.6 × 4.3)*
Main machinery: Diesel-electric; 2 MTU 12V 493 AZ80 diesels; 1200 hp(m) *(880 kW)*; 1 motor; 1700 hp(m) *(1.25 MW)*; 1 shaft
Speed, knots: 12 surfaced; 18 dived
Range, miles: 5000 at 8 kts snorting
Complement: 18 (5 officers)

Torpedoes: 8—21 in *(533 mm)* bow tubes. FFV Type 61; anti-surface; wire-guided; passive homing to 25 km *(13.7 nm)* at 45 kts; warhead 240 kg.
Countermeasures: ESM: Racal; radar warning.
Fire control: Terma TFCS.
Radars: Surface search: Terma; I band.
Sonars: Reson Systems; passive search and attack; medium frequency.

Programmes: First two acquired from Norway in 1986 for modernisation; the third in late 1989. Have replaced Delfinen class.

Modernisation: Work done at Urivale Shipyard, Bergen between 1987 and 1991 included lengthening by 5.2 ft *(1.6 m)* (which has increased displacement) and new communications, navigation and fire control equipment.
Structure: Diving depth, 200 m *(650 ft)*.
Operational: *Saelen* sank in the Kattegat while unmanned and under tow in late 1990. Salvaged and docked, there are plans to repair the damage using spares taken from the ex-Norwegian *Kaura*, which has been purchased for cannibalisation.

SPRINGEREN *11/1991, Hartmut Ehlers*

2 NARHVALEN CLASS

Name	*No*	*Builders*	*Laid down*	*Launched*	*Commissioned*
NARHVALEN	S 320	Royal Dockyard, Copenhagen	16 Feb 1965	10 Sep 1968	27 Feb 1970
NORDKAPEREN	S 321	Royal Dockyard, Copenhagen	4 Mar 1966	18 Dec 1969	22 Dec 1970

Displacement, tons: 420 surfaced; 450 dived
Dimensions, feet (metres): 145.3 × 15 × 13.8 *(44.3 × 4.6 × 4.2)*
Main machinery: Diesel-electric; 2 MTU 12V 493 TY7; 2250 hp(m) *(1.62 MW)*; 1 motor; 1200 hp(m) *(882 kW)*; 1 shaft
Speed, knots: 12 surfaced; 17 dived
Complement: 21 (4 officers)

Torpedoes: 8—21 in *(533 mm)* bow tubes. Combination of FFV Type 61; wire-guided; passive homing to 25 km *(13.7 nm)* anti-surface at 45 kts; warhead 240 kg and FFV Type 41; anti-submarine; passive homing to 20 km *(10.8 nm)* at 25 kts; warhead 45 kg; no reloads.
Fire control: Signaal M8.
Radars: Surface search: Thomson-CSF Calypso; I band.
Sonars: Krupp Atlas CSU 3-2; hull-mounted; active/passive search and attack; medium frequency.
PRS 3-4; passive ranging; part of CSU 3.

Programmes: These coastal submarines are similar to the West German Improved Type 205 and were built under licence at the Royal Dockyard, Copenhagen with modifications for Danish needs.

Modernisation: A programme has been approved for an equipment update similar to the Tumleren class to enable both submarines to serve until the end of the decade. Work starts on *Narhvalen* in 1993 and *Nordkaperen* in 1995 and includes new periscopes, ESM, radar and sonar.

NARHVALEN *10/1990, Maritime Photographic*

FRIGATES

3 NIELS JUEL CLASS

me	*No*	*Builders*	*Laid down*	*Launched*	*Commissioned*
ELS JUEL	F 354	Aalborg Vaerft	20 Oct 1976	17 Feb 1978	26 Aug 1980
FERT FISCHER	F 355	Aalborg Vaerft	6 Dec 1978	10 May 1979	16 Oct 1981
TER TORDENSKIOLD	F 356	Aalborg Vaerft	3 Dec 1979	30 Apr 1980	2 Apr 1982

splacement, tons: 1320 full load
nensions, feet (metres): 275.5 × 33.8 × 10.2 *84 × 10.3 × 3.1)*
in machinery: CODOG; 1 GE LM 2500 gas turbine; 22 000 p *(16.4 MW)* sustained; 1 MTU 20 V 956 TB82 diesel; 5210 p(m) *(3.83 MW)* sustained; 2 shafts
eed, knots: 28 (gas); 20 (diesel). **Range, miles:** 2500 at 18 ts
mplement: 98 (18 officers)

ssiles: SSM: 8 McDonnell Douglas Harpoon (2 quad) unchers ❶; active radar homing to 130 km *(70 nm)* at 0.9 lach; warhead 227 kg.
M: Raytheon NATO Sea Sparrow Mk 29 octuple launcher ❷; emi-active radar homing to 14.6 km *(8 nm)* at 2.5 Mach; arhead 39 kg; 8 missiles.
ns: 1 OTO Melara 3 in *(76 mm)*/62 compact ❸; 85° elevation; 5 rounds/minute to 16 km *(8.7 nm)* anti-surface; 12 km *6.6 nm)* anti-aircraft; weight of shell 6 kg.
Oerlikon 20 mm (one each side of the funnel and two abaft the ast) ❹.
oth charges: 1 rack.
ntermeasures: Decoys: 2 THORN EMI Sea Gnat 6-barrelled haff launchers ❺.
M: Racal Cutlass; radar warning.

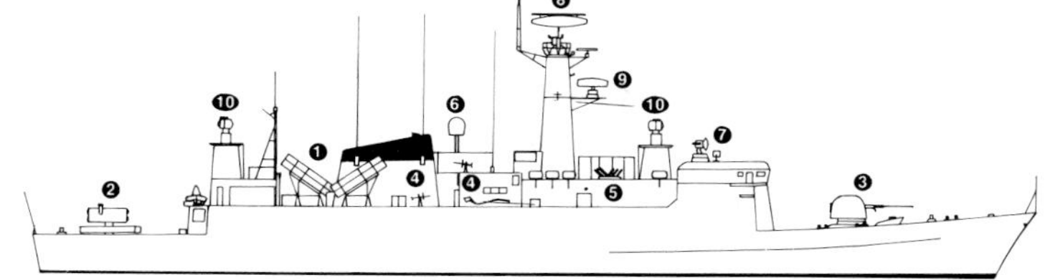

NIELS JUEL Class *(Scale 1 : 900), Ian Sturton*

Combat data systems: Ericsson EPLO action data automation; Link 11. SATCOMs ❻.
Fire control: Philips 9LV 200 Mk 2 GFCS with TV tracker ❼. Raytheon Mk 91 Mod 1 MFCS with two directors. Harpoon to 1A(V) standard.
Radars: Air search: Plessey AWS 5 ❽; 3D; E/F band; range 155 km *(85 nm)* for 4 m² target.
Surface search: Philips 9GR 600 ❾; I band.
Fire control: Two Selenia RTN 10 ❿; I/J band.
Navigation: Burmeister & Wain Elektronik Scanter Mil 009; E/I band.

Sonars: Plessey PMS 26; hull-mounted; active search and attack; 10 kHz.

Programmes: YARD Glasgow designed the class to Danish order.
Modernisation: A mid-life update is planned including 2 RAM launchers and new combat data and communications systems. The seaboat was replaced by a rigid inflatable type in 1989.

ER TORDENSKIOLD *8/1991, Gunnar Olsen*

ERT FISCHER *3/1991, Royal Danish Navy*

3 + 1 THETIS CLASS

Name	*No*	*Builders*	*Laid down*	*Launched*	*Commissione*
THETIS	F 357	Svenborg Vaerft	10 Oct 1988	14 July 1989	1 July 1991
TRITON	F 358	Svenborg Vaerft	27 June 1989	16 Mar 1990	2 Dec 1991
HVIDBJØRNEN	F 360	Svenborg Vaerft	2 Jan 1991	11 Oct 1991	Mar 1993
VAEDDEREN	F 359	Svenborg Vaerft	19 Mar 1990	21 Dec 1990	May 1992

TRITON *7/1991, Erik Laursen*

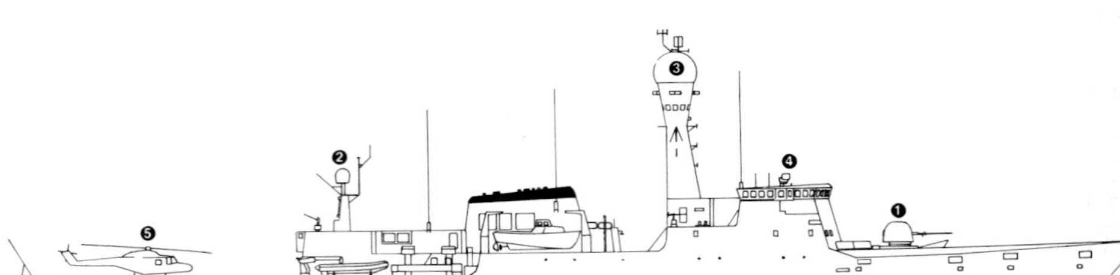

THETIS *(Scale 1 : 900), Ian Sturt*

Displacement, tons: 2600 standard; 3500 full load
Dimensions, feet (metres): 369.1 oa; 327.4 wl × 47.2 × 19.7 *(112.5; 99.8 × 14.4 × 6.0)*
Main machinery: 3 MAN/Burmeister & Wain Alpha 12V 28/32A diesels; 10 800 hp(m) *(7.94 MW)* sustained; 1 shaft; cp prop; bow and azimuth thrusters; 880 hp(m) *(647 kW)*, 1100 hp(m) *(800 kW)*

Speed, knots: 20; 8 on thrusters. **Range, miles:** 8500 at 15.5 kts
Complement: 61 (11 officers) plus 12 spare berths
Guns: 1 OTO Melara 3 in *(76 mm)*/62; Super Rapid ❶; dual purpose; 85° elevation; 120 rounds/minute to 16 km *(8.7 nm)*; weight of shell 6 kg.
1 or 2 Oerlikon 20 mm.
Depth charges: 2 Rails (door in stern).
Countermeasures: ESM: Racal Cutlass; radar warning.
Combat data systems: Terma TDS; SATCOM ❷.
Fire control: Bofors 9LV 200 Mk 3 optronic director.
Radars: Air/surface search: Plessey AWS 6 ❸; G band; range 88 km *(48 nm)*.
Navigation: Terma Scanter Mil ❹; I band.
Fire control: Bofors Electronic 9LV 200; I/J band.
Sonars: Thomson Sintra TSM 2640 Salmon; hull-mounted and VDS; active search and attack; medium frequency.

Helicopters: 1 Westland Lynx Mk 80/91 ❺.

Programmes: Preliminary study by YARD in 1986 led to Dwinger Marine Consultants being awarded a contract for a detailed design completed in mid-1987. All four ordered in October 1987.

Structure: The hull is some 30 m longer than the Hvidbjørn class to improve sea-keeping qualities and allow considera extra space for additional armament. The design allows the u of containerised equipment to be shipped depending on r and there is some commonality with the Flex 300 ships. So sensors have been transferred from the Hvidbjørnen class as t latter paid off. The hull is ice strengthened to enable penetrati of 1 m thick ice and efforts have been made to incorporate stea technology, for instance by putting anchor equipment, bolla and winches below the upper deck. There is a double skin up 2 m below the waterline. The flight deck (28 × 14 m) strengthened to take Sea King or Merlin helicopters. A ri inflatable boarding craft plumbed by a hydraulic crane is fitt alongside the fixed hangar.
Operational: Primary role is fishery protection. *Thetis* employed for 3-4 months a year doing seismological surveys the Greenland EEZ. A 4000 m towed array is used to rece signals generated by pneumatic noise guns towed 800 m aste
Opinion: It seems likely that the built-in flexibility of the desi may allow the development of a fully armed frigate in d course. The following systems have been considered: Harpo VLS Sea Sparrow, triple torpedo tubes, RAM PDMS, SRBOC Sea Gnat decoys, Nixie, fire control radars and passive so towed array.

THETIS *1991, Royal Danish N*

1 MODIFIED HVIDBJØRNEN CLASS

Name	*No*	*Builders*	*Laid down*	*Launched*	*Commission*
BESKYTTEREN	F 340	Aalborg Vaerft	11 Dec 1974	29 May 1975	27 Feb 1976

Displacement, tons: 1970 full load
Dimensions, feet (metres): 245 × 40 × 17.4 *(74.7 × 12.2 × 5.3)*
Main machinery: 3 MAN/Burmeister & Wain Alpha diesels; 7440 hp(m) *(5.47 MW)*; 1 shaft; cp prop
Speed, knots: 18. **Range, miles:** 4500 at 16 kts on 2 engines; 6000 at 13 kts on 1 engine
Complement: 67 (8 officers)

Guns: 1 USN 3 in *(76 mm)*/50; dual purpose.
Countermeasures: Decoys: THORN EMI Sea Gnat 6-barrelled Chaff launchers.
ESM: Racal Cutlass; radar warning.
Combat data systems: Terma TDS; SATCOM.
Radars: Air/surface search: Plessey AWS 6; G band.
Navigation: Burmeister & Wain Elektronik Scanter Mil 009; E/I band.
Sonars: Plessey PMS 26; hull-mounted; active search and attack; 10 kHz.

Helicopters: 1 Westland Lynx Mk 80/91.

Modernisation: May be modernised in due course.
Structure: Strengthened for ice operations.
Operational: Used for similar fishery protection duties.

BESKYTTEREN *2/1991, Royal Danish N*

SHIPBORNE AIRCRAFT

Numbers/Type: 8/2 Westland Lynx Mk 80/91.
Operational speed: 125 kts *(232 km/h)*.
Service ceiling: 12 500 ft *(3810 m)*.
Range: 320 nm *(593 km)*.
Role/Weapon systems: Shipborne helicopter for EEZ and surface search tasks. Sensors: Bendix weather radar to be replaced by Ferranti Seaspray; Kestrel ESM. Weapons: Unarmed.

LYNX *1989, Royal Danish Navy*

LAND-BASED MARITIME AIRCRAFT

Numbers/Type: 3 Gulfstream Aerospace SMA-3 Gulfstream III.
Operational speed: 500 kts *(926 km/h)*.
Service ceiling: 45 000 ft *(13 720 m)*.
Range: 3940 nm *(7300 km)*.
Role/Weapon systems: MR and liaison aircraft; flown on EEZ patrol around Greenland coast and in Danish sea areas in Baltic; EW work undertaken. Sensors: APS-127 surveillance radar. Weapons: Unarmed.

Numbers/Type: 7 Sikorsky S-61A-1 Sea King.
Operational speed: 118 kts *(219 km/h)*.
Service ceiling: 14 700 ft *(4480 m)*.
Range: 542 nm *(1005 km)*.
Role/Weapon systems: Land-based SAR helicopter for peacetime search and rescue; wartime combat rescue and surface search. Sensors: Bendix weather radar; GEC Avionics FLIR to be fitted. Weapons: Unarmed.

SEA KING *5/1991, Gunnar Olsen*

LIGHT FORCES

10 WILLEMOES CLASS (FAST ATTACK CRAFT—MISSILE)

Name	*No*	*Builders*	*Commissioned*
BILLE	P 540	Frederikshavn V and F	1 Oct 1976
BREDAL	P 541	Frederikshavn V and F	21 Jan 1977
HAMMER	P 542	Frederikshavn V and F	1 Apr 1977
HUITFELD	P 543	Frederikshavn V and F	15 June 1977
KRIEGER	P 544	Frederikshavn V and F	22 Sep 1977
NORBY	P 545	Frederikshavn V and F	22 Nov 1977
RODSTEEN	P 546	Frederikshavn V and F	16 Feb 1978
SEHESTED	P 547	Frederikshavn V and F	19 May 1978
SUENSON	P 548	Frederikshavn V and F	10 Aug 1978
WILLEMOES	P 549	Frederikshavn V and F	21 June 1976

Displacement, tons: 260 full load
Dimensions, feet (metres): 151 × 24 × 8.2 *(46 × 7.4 × 2.5)*
Main machinery: CODOG; 3 Rolls-Royce Proteus 52M/544 gas turbines; 12 750 hp *(9.51 MW)*; 2 GM 8V-71 diesels for cruising on wing shafts; 460 hp *(343 kW)* sustained; 3 shafts; cp props
Speed, knots: 38 (12 on diesels)
Complement: 25 (5 officers)

Missiles: SSM: 4 or 8 McDonnell Douglas Harpoon; active radar homing to 130 km *(70 nm)* at 0.9 Mach; warhead 227 kg.
Numbers carried depend on task and numbers of torpedoes.
Guns: 1 OTO Melara 3 in *(76 mm)*/62 compact; 85° elevation; 85 rounds/minute to 16 km *(8.7 nm)*; weight of shell 6 kg.
2 triple 103 mm illumination rocket launchers.
Torpedoes: 2 or 4—21 in *(533 mm)* tubes. FFV Type 61; wire-guided; passive homing to 25 km *(13.7 nm)* at 45 kts; warhead 240 kg.
Countermeasures: ESM: Racal Cutlass; radar warning.
Combat data systems: EPLO action data automation. Being replaced by Terma.
Radars: Air/surface search: 9GA 208; E/F band.
Navigation: Terma Elektronik 20T 48 Super; E/I band.
Fire control: Philips 9LV 200; J band.

Programmes: Designed by Lürssen to Danish order. Very similar to Swedish Spica II class (also Lürssen). Original order to Frederikshavn for four boats, increased to eight and finally ten. *Willemoes* (prototype) laid down in July 1974.
Modernisation: *Norby* has conducted trials with a Simbad light SAM system fitted on the platform aft of the mast. Sea Gnat decoy launchers may be fitted, otherwise there are no further modernisation plans.
Operational: Patrols do not normally exceed 36 hours. The mix of weapons varies.

HAMMER *5/1991, Erik Laursen*

HUITFELD *1991, Royal Danish Navy*

6 + 7 (3) FLYVEFISKEN CLASS (LARGE PATROL CRAFT)

Name	No	Builders	Commissioned
FLYVEFISKEN	P 550	Danyard A/S, Aalborg	19 Dec 1989
HAJEN	P 551	Danyard A/S, Aalborg	19 July 1990
HAVKATTEN	P 552	Danyard A/S, Aalborg	1 Nov 1990
LAXEN	P 553	Danyard A/S, Aalborg	22 Mar 1991
MAKRELEN	P 554	Danyard A/S, Aalborg	1 Oct 1991
STØREN	P 555	Danyard A/S, Aalborg	June 1992
SVAERDFISKEN	P 556	Danyard A/S, Aalborg	Dec 1992
GLENTEN	P 557	Danyard A/S, Aalborg	June 1993
GRIBBEN	P 558	Danyard A/S, Aalborg	Dec 1993
LOMMEN	P 559	Danyard A/S, Aalborg	June 1994
RAUNEN	P 560	Danyard A/S, Aalborg	Dec 1994
SKADEN	P 561	Danyard A/S, Aalborg	June 1995
VIBEN	P 562	Danyard A/S, Aalborg	Dec 1995

Displacement, tons: 300 standard
Dimensions, feet (metres): 177.2 × 29.5 × 8.2 *(54 × 9 × 2.5)*
Main machinery: CODAG; 1 GE LM 500 gas turbine (centre shaft); 5450 hp *(4.1 MW)* sustained; 1 GM 12V-71 diesel; 340 hp *(254 kW)* sustained (centre shaft) (also powers the hydraulic drive); 2 MTU 16V 396 TB94 diesels (outer shafts); 5800 hp(m) *(4.26 MW)* sustained; 3 shafts; cp props on outer shafts; bow thruster
Speed, knots: 30; 20 on diesels; 6 on electric propulsion
Complement: 15-18 plus 10 spare berths
Missiles: SSM: 8 McDonnell Douglas Harpoon; active radar homing to 130 km *(70 nm)* at 0.9 Mach; warhead 227 kg.
Guns: 1 OTO Melara 3 in *(76 mm)*/62 Super Rapid; dual purpose; 85° elevation; 120 rounds/minute to 16 km *(8.7 nm)*; weight of shell 6 kg.
2—12.7 mm MGs.
Torpedoes: 2—21 in *(533 mm)* tubes; FFV Type 613; wire-guided passive homing.
Mines: Can be carried.
Countermeasures: MCMV: Ibis 43 minehunting system with Thomson Sintra 2061 tactical system and 2054 sidescan sonar in a towed body.
Decoys: 1 Sea Gnat 6-barrelled launcher for Chaff.
ESM: Racal Mermaid; radar warning.
Combat data systems: Terma system primarily for control of MCMV robot drones.
Fire control: Bofors Electronic 9LV Mk 3 optronic director. Harpoon to 1A(V) standard.
Radars: Air/surface search: Plessey AWS 6; G band; range 88 km *(48 nm)*.
Navigation: Terma Pilot; E/I band.
Fire control: Philips 9LV 200; J band.
Sonars: Thomson Sintra TSM 2640 hull-mounted and VDS; active search and attack; medium frequency.

Programmes: Standard Flex 300 design to replace Daphne (seaward defence craft), Søløven (fast attack craft torpedo) and Sund (MCM) classes. First batch of seven with option on a further nine contracted with Danyard on 27 July 1985. Second batch of six ordered 14 June 1990. The last three are to be funded in FY 1992-94. Building rate is two per year completing in 1997.
Structure: GRP hulls. Positions prepared to plug in armament and operations rooms containers, extra guns, up to four SSMs, one SAM system, two 533 mm torpedo tubes, ASW and MCM equipment. As MCMVs these ships operate a tethered underwater vehicle for classification and control two surface 'robot' boats each with a Thomson Sintra TSM 2054 sidescan sonar. Details of the robots can be found in the *Mine Warfare Forces* section under SAV class.
Operational: Seven to be used chiefly for surveillance and MCM, remaining nine mainly as FAC with SSM and PDMS but the overall design will allow ships to change roles as required. Requirement is to be able to change within 48 hours.

FLYVEFISKEN *1990, Royal Danish Navy*

HAJEN (with SSM and TT) *1990, Royal Danish Navy*

LAXEN *3/1991, Hartmut Ehlers*

MRF 1 ROBOT (see Mine Warfare section) *4/1991, Royal Danish Navy*

3 DAPHNE CLASS (SEAWARD DEFENCE CRAFT)

Name	*No*	*Builders*	*Commissioned*
DRYADEN	P 531	R Dockyard, Copenhagen	4 Apr 1961
NAJADEN	P 534	R Dockyard, Copenhagen	26 Apr 1963
NYMFEN	P 535	R Dockyard, Copenhagen	4 Oct 1963

Displacement, tons: 170
Dimensions, feet (metres): 121.3 × 20 × 8.5 *(37 × 6.8 × 2.6) (Dryaden)*
Main machinery: 2 Maybach 12-cyl diesels; 2600 hp(m) *(1.9 MW)*; 1 Foden FD-6 diesel; 100 hp *(74 kW)*; 2 shafts
Speed, knots: 20
Complement: 23
Guns: 1 Bofors 40 mm/70. 1 Oerlikon 20 mm.
Depth charges: 2 racks.
Radars: Surface search: Terma 20T 48 Super; E/I band; range 88 km *(48 nm)*.
Sonars: Plessey PMS 26; hull-mounted; active search and attack; 10 kHz.

Comment: Four were built under US offshore programme. Five were given a service life extension starting in 1983. The hulls are now painted grey rather than olive green as previously. *Dryaden* has a rounded stern and *Najaden* and *Nymfen* have a straight stern. These last three of the class are due to be phased out and replaced by Flyvefisken class.

NAJADEN *4/1990, Gunnar Olsen*

3 AGDLEK CLASS (LARGE PATROL CRAFT)

Name	*No*	*Builders*	*Commissioned*
AGDLEK	Y 386	Svendborg Vaerft	12 Mar 1974
AGPA	Y 387	Svendborg Vaerft	14 May 1974
TULUGAQ	Y 388	Svendborg Vaerft	26 June 1979

Displacement, tons: 300; 330 (Y 388)
Dimensions, feet (metres): 103 × 25.3 × 11.2 *(31.4 × 7.7 × 3.4)*
Main machinery: 1 Burmeister & Wain Alpha A08-26 VO diesel; 800 hp(m) *(588 kW)*; 1 shaft
Speed, knots: 12
Complement: 14
Guns: 2 Oerlikon 20 mm.
Radars: Surface search: Terma 20T 48 Super; E/I band; range 88 km *(48 nm)*.
Navigation: Skanter 009; I band.

Comment: Designed for service off Greenland. Ice strengthened. Sometimes SATCOM fitted.

TULUGAQ *1990, Royal Danish Navy*

2 MAAGEN CLASS (LARGE PATROL CRAFT)

Name	*No*	*Builders*	*Commissioned*
MAAGEN	Y 384	Helsingør Dockyard	19 May 1960
MALLEMUKKEN	Y 385	Helsingør Dockyard	19 May 1960

Displacement, tons: 190
Dimensions, feet (metres): 88.5 × 22.9 × 9.8 *(27 × 7 × 3)*
Main machinery: 1 diesel; 385 hp(m) *(283 kW)*; 1 shaft
Speed, knots: 10
Complement: 14
Guns: 2 Oerlikon 20 mm (not mounted).
Radars: Surface search: Terma 20T 48 Super; E/I band; range 88 km *(48 nm)*.
Navigation: Skanter 009; I band.

Comment: Of steel construction. Laid down on 15 January 1960.

MAAGEN *1988, Royal Danish Navy*

9 Ø CLASS (LARGE PATROL CRAFT)

Name	*No*	*Builders*	*Commissioned*
BARSØ	Y 300	Svendborg Vaerft	13 June 1969
DREJØ	Y 301	Svendborg Vaerft	1 July 1969
ROMSØ	Y 302	Svendborg Vaerft	21 July 1969
SAMSØ	Y 303	Svendborg Vaerft	15 Aug 1969
THURØ	Y 304	Svendborg Vaerft	12 Sep 1969
VEJRØ	Y 305	Svendborg Vaerft	17 Oct 1969
FARØ	Y 306	Svendborg Vaerft	17 May 1973
LAESØ	Y 307	Svendborg Vaerft	23 July 1973
ROMØ	Y 308	Svendborg Vaerft	3 Sep 1973

Displacement, tons: 155
Dimensions, feet (metres): 84 × 19.7 × 9.2 *(25.6 × 6 × 2.8)*
Main machinery: 1 diesel; 385 hp(m) *(283 kW)*; 1 shaft
Speed, knots: 11
Complement: 20
Guns: 2 Oerlikon 20 mm (not always fitted). 1—12.7 mm MG.
Radars: Navigation: Skanter 009; I band.

Comment: Rated as patrol cutters. *Laesø* acts as diver support ship with a recompression chamber. The last three have a wheelhouse which extends over the full beam.

FARØ *1988, Royal Danish Navy*

2 LARGE BOTVED TYPE (COASTAL PATROL CRAFT)

Y 375 **Y 376**

Displacement, tons: 12 (Y 376); 13.5 (Y 375)
Dimensions, feet (metres): 43.6 × 14.8 × 3.7 *(13.3 × 4.5 × 1.1)*
Main machinery: 2 diesels; 680 hp(m) *(500 kW)*; 2 shafts
Speed, knots: 26
Guns: 1—7.62 mm MG
Radars: Navigation: NWS 3; I band.

Comment: Built in 1974 by Botved Boats. Y 375 is 45.9 ft *(14 m)* in length overall having a stern ladder extension for divers.

Y376 *1988, Royal Danish Navy*

1 Y TYPE (COASTAL PATROL CRAFT)

LUNDEN Y 343

Displacement, tons: 71.5
Dimensions, feet (metres): 64.6 × 17.7 × 9.2 *(19.7 × 5.4 × 2.8)*
Speed, knots: 8
Guns: 1—7.62 mm MG.

Comment: Cutter of a similar type to trawlers MHV 51 and 76, built in 1941.

LUNDEN *1988, Royal Danish Navy*

NAVAL HOME GUARD

Note: In addition to the vessels listed below there are two elderly motor vessels, *Aldebaran* (MHV 1) and *Andromeda* (MHV 15).

13 KUTTER CLASS (COASTAL PATROL CRAFT)

ANTARES MHV 51
APOLLO MHV 56
ARIES MHV 60
BETELGEUSE MHV 61
CARINA MHV 62
CASSIOPEIA MHV 63
CRUX MHV 64
DUBHE MHV 66
GEMINI MHV 67
HERCULES MHV 73
JUPITER MHV 74
LUNA MHV 75
LYRA MHV 76 (ex-Y 339)

Displacement, tons: 35 *(Gemini)*
Dimensions, feet (metres): 60.4 × 17.1 × 7.5 *(18.4 × 5.2 × 2.3)*
Speed, knots: 9
Guns: 2—7.62 mm MGs.

Comment: Built between 1922 and 1941. Details above apply only to *Gemini* but the rest are similar. Apart from *Hercules* all are veterans of the Second World War.

BETELGEUSE *8/1991, Gunnar Olsen*

1 + 5 (12) MHV 800 CLASS

MHV 800-805

Displacement, tons: 83 full load
Dimensions, feet (metres): 77.8 × 18.4 × 6.6 *(23.7 × 5.6 × 2)*
Main machinery: 2 diesels; 900 hp(m) *(661 kW)*; 2 shafts
Speed, knots: 13. **Range, miles:** 990 at 11 kts
Complement: 12
Guns: 2—7.62 mm MGs. 2—20 mm (can be fitted).

Comment: A new class of Home Guard patrol craft. First six ordered in April 1991 from Søby Shipyard, Aero Island. First of class commissioned in May 1992, with the remainder planned to follow at approximately six month intervals, to a final total of 25. Steel hulls with a moderate ice capability.

MHV 801 (model) *1989, Royal Danish Navy*

6 MHV 90 CLASS (COASTAL PATROL CRAFT)

BOPA MHV 90
BRIGADEN MHV 91
HOLGER DANSKE MHV 92
HVIDSTEN MHV 93
RINGEN MHV 94
SPEDITØREN MHV 95

Displacement, tons: 85
Dimensions, feet (metres): 64.9 × 18.7 × 8.2 *(19.8 × 5.7 × 2.5)*
Main machinery: 1 Burmeister & Wain diesel; 400 hp(m) *(294 kW)*; 1 shaft
Speed, knots: 11
Guns: 2—7.62 mm MGs.
Radars: Navigation: RM 1290S; I band.

Comment: Built between 1973 and 1975.

BOPA *6/1991, van Ginderen Collection*

7 MHV 80 CLASS (COASTAL PATROL CRAFT)

Name	*No*	*Builders*	*Commissioned*
FAENØ (ex-MHV 69, ex-MS 6)	MHV 80	Denmark	July 1941
ASKØ (ex-Y 386, ex-M 560, ex-MS 2)	MHV 81	Denmark	1 Aug 1941
ENØ (ex-Y 388, ex-M 562, ex-MS 5)	MHV 82	Denmark	18 Aug 1941
MANØ (ex-Y 391, ex-M 566, ex-MS 9)	MHV 83	Denmark	30 Oct 1941
BAAGØ (ex-Y 387, ex-M 561, ex-MS 3)	MHV 84	Denmark	9 Aug 1941
HJORTØ (ex-Y 389, ex-M 564, ex-MS 7)	MHV 85	Denmark	24 Sep 1941
LYØ (ex-Y 390, ex-M 565, ex-MS 8)	MHV 86	Denmark	22 Oct 1941

Displacement, tons: 80
Dimensions, feet (metres): 80.1 × 15.1 × 5.2 *(24.4 × 4.6 × 1.6)*
Main machinery: Diesel; 350 hp(m) *(257 kW)*; 1 shaft
Speed, knots: 11
Guns: 2—7.62 mm MGs.
Radars: Navigation: RM 1290S; I band.

Comment: Of wooden construction. All launched in 1941. Former inshore minesweepers.

HJORTØ *8/1991, Gunnar Olsen*

3 MHV 70 CLASS (COASTAL PATROL CRAFT)

SATURN MHV 70 **SCORPIUS** MHV 71 **SIRIUS** MHV 72

Displacement, tons: 76
Dimensions, feet (metres): 64 × 16.7 × 8.2 *(19.5 × 5.1 × 2.5)*
Main machinery: 1 diesel; 200 hp(m) *(147 kW)*; 1 shaft
Speed, knots: 10
Guns: 2—7.62 mm MGs.
Radars: Navigation: RM 1290S; I band.

Comment: Patrol boats and training craft for the Naval Home Guard. Built in the Royal Dockyard, Copenhagen and commissioned in 1958. Formerly designated DMH, but allocated MHV numbers in 1969.

SIRIUS *6/1989, Jean M. Otten*

6 MHV 20 CLASS (COASTAL PATROL CRAFT)

BAUNEN MHV 20 **BUDSTIKKEN** MHV 21 **KUREREN** MHV 22 **PARTISAN** MHV 23 **PATRIOTEN** MHV 24 **SABOTØREN** MHV 25

Displacement, tons: 60 full load
Dimensions, feet (metres): 54.1 × 13.8 × 4.9 *(16.5 × 4.2 × 1.5)*
Main machinery: 2 MTU diesels; 500 hp(m) *(367 kW)*; 2 shafts
Speed, knots: 15
Complement: 9
Guns: 2—7.62 mm MGs.
Radars: Navigation: Terma 9T48/9; I band.

Comment: Built of GRP by Ejvinds Plastikbodevaerft, Svendborg between 1978 and 1982. Used for patrols in The Sound.

SABATØREN *8/1991, Gunnar Olsen*

MINE WARFARE FORCES

Note: See also Flyvefisken class under *Light Forces*.

2 LINDORMEN CLASS (COASTAL MINELAYERS)

Name	*No*	*Builders*	*Commissioned*
LINDORMEN	N 43	Svendborg Vaerft	16 Feb 1978
LOSSEN	N 44	Svendborg Vaerft	14 June 1978

Displacement, tons: 570
Dimensions, feet (metres): 146 × 29.5 × 8 *(44.5 × 9 × 2.6)*
Main machinery: 2 Frichs diesels; 1600 hp(m) *(1.2 MW)*; 2 shafts
Speed, knots: 14
Complement: 30
Guns: 3 Oerlikon 20 mm.
Mines: 50-60 (depending on type).
Radars: NWS 3; I band.

Comment: Controlled Minelayers. *Lindormen* laid down on 2 February 1977, launched on 7 June 1977 and *Lossen* laid down on 9 July 1977, launched on 11 October 1977.

LOSSEN *7/1991, Antonio Moreno*

4 FALSTER CLASS (MINELAYERS)

Name	*No*	*Builders*	*Commissioned*
FALSTER	N 80	Nakskov Skibsvaerft	7 Nov 1963
FYEN	N 81	Frederikshavn Vaerft	18 Sep 1963
MØEN	N 82	Frederikshavn Vaerft	29 Apr 1964
SJAELLAND	N 83	Nakskov Skibsvaerft	7 July 1964

Displacement, tons: 1880 full load
Dimensions, feet (metres): 252.6 × 42 × 11.8 *(77 × 12.8 × 3.6)*
Main machinery: 2 GM/EMD 16-567D3 diesels; 4800 hp *(3.58 MW)*; 2 shafts
Speed, knots: 17
Complement: 133 (10 officers)

Guns: 4 US 3 in *(76 mm)*/50 Mk 33 (2 twin); 85° elevation; 25 rounds/minute to 12.8 km *(7 nm)*; weight of shell 6 kg. May be replaced by Creusot Loire 100 mm in due course.
4 Oerlikon 20 mm.
Mines: 4 rails; 400.
Countermeasures: Decoys: 2—57 mm multiple Chaff launchers.
Combat data systems: Terma TDS (after modernisation).
Fire control: Contraves.
Radars: Air/surface search: CWS 2; E/F band.
Fire control: CGS 1; I band.
Surface search: NWS 2; I band.
Navigation: Terma Pilot; E/I band.

Programmes: Ordered in 1960-61 and launched 1962-63. All are named after Danish islands. Similar to Turkish *Nusret*. *Sjaelland* converted in 1976 to act as depot ship for submarines and FAC but retains minelaying capability.
Modernisation: Being refitted to allow them to serve until late 1990s; includes Terma command and control system and possibly a light SAM in due course. First completed in 1990 and work is progressing at one ship per year. Mine stocks being updated in collaboration with Germany.
Structure: The steel hull is flush-decked with a raking stem, a full stern and a prominent knuckle fwd. The hull has been specially strengthened for ice navigation. In 1987 *Sjaelland* after mast was raised; *Falster* and *Fyen* similarly modified in 1989-91, *Møen* planned in 1992.
Operational: *Møen* and sometimes *Fyen* employed on midshipmen's training.

SJAELLAND *10/1991, Erik Laursen*

3 Ex-US BLUEBIRD CLASS (SUND CLASS) (Ex-AMS) (MINESWEEPERS—COASTAL)

GRØNSUND (ex-MSC 256) M 574
GULDBORGSUND (ex-MSC 257) M 575
VILSUND (ex-MSC 264) M 578

Displacement, tons: 350 standard; 376 full load
Dimensions, feet (metres): 147.6 × 27.9 × 8.5 *(45 × 8.5 × 2.6)*
Main machinery: 2 GM 8-268A diesels; 880 hp *(656 kW)*; 2 shafts
Speed, knots: 13. **Range, miles:** 3000 at 10 kts
Complement: 35
Guns: 1 Bofors 40 mm/60.
Radars: Navigation: Terma Pilot; E/I band.

Comment: MSC (ex-AMS) 60 class NATO coastal minesweepers all built in USA. Completed in 1954-56. *Grønsund* on 21 September 1956, *Guldborgsund* on 11 November 1956, and *Vilsund* on 15 November 1956. *Guldborgsund* and *Grønsund* have been fitted with a charthouse between bridge and funnel and have been employed on surveying duties. *Vilsund* has a deckhouse abaft the bridge after modernisation in 1985. All will be replaced by Flyvefisken class.

GRØNSUND *12/1990, Hartmut Ehlers*

2 + (10) SAV CLASS (MINESWEEPER—DRONES)

MRF 1 **MRF 2**

Displacement, tons: 32 full load
Dimensions, feet (metres): 59.7 × 15.6 × 3.9 *(18.2 × 4.8 × 1.2)*
Main machinery: 1 Schottel pump jet propulsor
Speed, knots: 12
Combat data systems: Terma link to Flyvefisken class (in MCMV configuration).
Radars: Navigation: Furuno; I band.
Sonars: Thomson Sintra TSM 2054 sidescan; high frequency active.

Comment: Being built by Danyard with GRP hulls. First one completed in March 1991, second in December 1991. Trials should complete by the end of 1992. Robot drones (or Surface Auxiliary Vessels (SAV)) operated in pairs by the Flyvefisken class in MCMV configuration. Hull is based on the Hugin class TRVs with low noise propulsion. The towfish with sidescan sonar is lowered and raised from the stern-mounted gantry.

MRF 1 *4/1991, Royal Danish Navy*

SERVICE FORCES

Note: There is a road-borne support unit (MOBA) for the Fast Attack Craft with two sections. The first, of eight vehicles with radar, W/T and control offices is MOBA (Ops) and the second, of 25 vehicles for stores, fuel, provisions, torpedoes and workshops is MOBA (Log).

Name	*No*	*Builders*	*Commissioned*
SLEIPNER	A 559	Åbenrå Vaerft og A/S	18 July 1986

Displacement, tons: 150 full load
Dimensions, feet (metres): 119.6 × 24.9 × 8.8 *(36.5 × 7.6 × 2.7)*
Main machinery: 1 Callesen diesel; 1 shaft
Speed, knots: 11
Complement: 6
Cargo capacity: 150 tons

SLEIPNER *5/1990, Gilbert Gyssels*

2 Ex-US YO 65 CLASS (TANKERS)

Name	*No*	*Builders*	*Commissioned*
RIMFAXE (ex-US YO 226)	A 568	Jefferson Bridge & Machine Co, USA	2 Nov 1945
SKINFAXE (ex-US YO 229)	A 569	Jefferson Bridge & Machine Co, USA	7 Dec 1945

Displacement, tons: 1400 full load
Dimensions, feet (metres): 174 × 32.9 × 13.3 *(53.1 × 10 × 4.1)*
Main machinery: 1 GM diesel; 560 hp *(418 kW)*; 1 shaft
Speed, knots: 10
Complement: 19
Cargo capacity: 900 tons fuel
Guns: 1 Oerlikon 20 mm.

Comment: Transferred from the USA on 2 August 1962. Act as tenders for the Willemoes class.

RIMFAXE *1990, Royal Danish Navy*

1 ROYAL YACHT

Name	*No*	*Builders*	*Commissioned*
DANNEBROG	A 540	R Dockyard, Copenhagen	20 May 1932

Displacement, tons: 1130
Dimensions, feet (metres): 246 × 34 × 12.1 *(75 × 10.4 × 3.7)*
Main machinery: 2 Burmeister & Wain Alpha T23L-KVO diesels; 1800 hp(m) *(1.32 MW)*; 2 shafts; cp props
Speed, knots: 14
Complement: 55
Guns: 2—37 mm saluting guns.

Comment: Laid down 2 January 1931, launched on 10 October 1931. Major refit 1980 included new engines and electrical gear.

DANNEBROG *4/1990, Gunnar Olsen*

2 HARBOUR TUGS

BALDER **HERMOD**

Dimensions, feet (metres): 39 × 13.1 × 3.9 *(11.9 × 4 × 1.2)*
Main machinery: 1 GM diesel; 300 hp *(224 kW)*; 1 shaft
Speed, knots: 8.5

Comment: Berthing tugs based at Holmen Naval Base, Copenhagen. Built in 1983 at Assens.

HERMOD *8/1991, Gunnar Olsen*

3 HUGIN CLASS (TORPEDO RECOVERY VESSELS)

HUGIN TO 8 **MUNIN** TO 9 **MIMER** TO 10

Displacement, tons: 23 full load
Dimensions, feet (metres): 53.1 × 13.8 × 3.9 *(16.2 × 4.2 × 1.2)*
Main machinery: 1 MWM diesel; 450 hp(m) *(330 kW)*; 1 shaft
Speed, knots: 15

Comment: Built by Ejvinds, Svenborg. The same hull, slightly lengthened, is the basis of the robot boats for MCM systems.

MUNIN *1988, Royal Danish Navy*

ICEBREAKERS

Note: Icebreakers, once controlled by the Ministry of Trade and Shipping are being transferred to the Navy but will continue to have a combined naval and civilian crew. Maintenance is done at Frederikshavn in Summer. During Summer period one icebreaker may be employed on surveying duties in Danish waters for the Administration of Navigation and Hydrography.

Name	*No*	*Builders*	*Commissioned*
THORBJØRN	—	Svendborg Vaerft	1981

Displacement, tons: 2344 full load
Dimensions, feet (metres): 221.4 × 50.2 × 15.4 *(67.5 × 15.3 × 4.7)*
Main machinery: Diesel-electric; 4 Burmeister & Wain Alpha diesels; 6800 hp(m) *(5 MW)*; 2 motors; 2 shafts
Speed, knots: 16.5
Complement: 29 (8 officers)

Comment: No bow thruster. Side rolling tanks. Fitted for surveying duties in non-ice periods.

THORBJØRN *7/1990, A. Sheldon Duplaix*

Name	*No*	*Builders*	*Commissioned*
DANBJØRN	—	Lindø Vaerft, Odense	1965
ISBJØRN	—	Lindø Vaerft, Odense	1966

Displacement, tons: 3685
Dimensions, feet (metres): 252 × 56 × 20 *(76.8 × 17.1 × 6.1)*
Main machinery: Diesel-electric; 2 diesel generators; 10 500 hp(m) *(7.72 MW)*; 2 shafts
Speed, knots: 14
Complement: 34

ISBJØRN *6/1990, van Ginderen Collection*

Name	*No*	*Builders*	*Commissioned*
ELBJØRN	—	Frederikshavn Vaerft	1966

Displacement, tons: 893 standard; 1400 full load
Dimensions, feet (metres): 156.5 × 40.3 × 14.5 *(47 × 12.1 × 4.4)*
Main machinery: Diesel-electric; 2 diesel generators; 3600 hp(m) *(2.64 MW)*; 2 shafts
Speed, knots: 12

ELBJØRN *7/1990, A. Sheldon Duplaix*

FISHERY PROTECTION

1 OSPREY TYPE FV 710

Name	*No*	*Builders*	*Commissioned*
HAVØRNEN	—	Frederikshavn Vaerft	July 1979

Displacement, tons: 505 full load
Dimensions, feet (metres): 164 × 34.5 × 9 *(50 × 10.5 × 2.8)*
Main machinery: 2 Burmeister & Wain Alpha 16V23L diesels; 4640 hp(m) *(3.41 MW)*; 2 shafts; cp props
Speed, knots: 20
Complement: 15 plus accommodation for 35
Radars: Navigation: Furuno Type FRM 64; I band.

Comment: Built to Det Norske Veritas classification. One completed for Burma in 1980, two more in 1982. One delivered to Senegambia in June 1987 and two to Morocco in 1987-88 and two more in 1990. Also two built in Greece in 1990 with two more to be delivered in 1993. A helicopter flight deck can handle a Westland Lynx. There is space allowed for a hangar. The Pacific 22 inflatable craft is launched from a slipway in the stern. Civilian manned.

HAVØRNEN *3/1990, Erik Laursen*

4 RESCUE VESSELS

NORDJYLLAND **NORDSØEN** **VESTKYSTEN** **JENS VAEVER**

Displacement, tons: 475; 657 (*Vestkysten*); 141 (*Jens Vaever*)
Dimensions, feet (metres): 134.5 × 32.8 × 13 *(41 × 10 × 4)*
163.7 × 32.8 × 10.8 *(49.9 × 10 × 3.3) (Vestkysten)*
95.1 × 19.7 × 9.8 *(29 × 6 × 3) (Jens Vaever)*

Comment: Three for the North Sea, one for the Baltic. *Jens Vaever* commissioned 1960; *Nordjylland* 1967 and *Nordsøen* 1968. *Vestkysten* commissioned in 1987 and replaced the old ship of the same name.

VESTKYSTEN *1987, Royal Danish Navy*

TRAINING AND SURVEY VESSELS

Note: *Thorbjorn* also used as a survey ship.

SKB 1 SKB 2 SKB 4

Displacement, tons: 27
Speed, knots: 9

Comment: Built 1958-68. Length 42.7 ft *(13 m)*. Training vessels.

SKB 1 *7/1991, Antonio Moreno*

SKB 4 *1990, Royal Danish Navy*

SKA 11 12 13 14 15 16

Displacement, tons: 52
Dimensions, feet (metres): 65.6 × 17.1 × 6.9 *(20 × 5.2 × 2.1)*
Main machinery: 1 GM diesel; 540 hp *(403 kW)*; 1 shaft
Speed, knots: 12
Complement: 6 (1 officer)

Comment: GRP hulls. Built 1981-84. Have red hulls. Survey motor launches.

SKA 11 *1989, Royal Danish Navy*

ENVIRONMENT CRAFT

2 POLLUTION CONTROL CRAFT

MILJØ 101 and **102**

Displacement, tons: 16
Dimensions, feet (metres): 53.8 × 14.4 × 7.1 *(16.2 × 4.2 × 2.2)*
Main machinery: 1 MWM TBD 232 V12 diesel; 454 hp(m) *(334 kW)*; 1 shaft
Speed, knots: 15. **Range, miles:** 350 at 8 kts
Complement: 3

Comment: Built by Ejvinds Plastikbodevaerft, Svendborg. Carry derricks and booms for framing oil slicks and dispersant fluids. Naval manned. Delivered 1 November and 1 December 1977.

MILJØ 102 *1987, Royal Danish Navy*

2 SEA TRUCKS

METTE MILJØ MARIE MILJØ

Displacement, tons: 157
Dimensions, feet (metres): 97.7 × 26.2 × 5.2 *(29.8 × 8 × 1.6)*
Main machinery: 2 Grenaa diesels; 660 hp(m) *(485 kW)*; 2 shafts
Speed, knots: 10
Complement: 8

Comment: Built by Carl B Hoffmann A/S, Esbjerg and Søren Larsen & Sønners Skibsvaerft A/S, Nykøbing Mors. Delivered 22 February 1980. Have orange and yellow superstructure.

METTE MILJØ *5/1991, Gunnar Olsen*

2 OIL POLLUTION CRAFT

GUNNAR THORSON GUNNAR SEIDENFADEN

Displacement, tons: 750
Dimensions, feet (metres): 183.7 × 40.3 × 12.8 *(56 × 12.3 × 3.9)*
Main machinery: 2 Burmeister and Wain Alpha diesels; 2320 hp(m) *(1.7 MW)*; 2 shafts
Speed, knots: 12.5
Complement: 17

Comment: Built by Ørnskov Stålskibsvaerft, Frederikshavn. Delivered May and July 1981 respectively. *G Thorson* at Copenhagen, *G Seidenfaden* at Korsør. Carry firefighting equipment. Large hydraulic crane fitted in 1988 for the secondary task of buoy tending. Orange painted hulls.

GUNNAR SEIDENFADEN (with crane) *1988, Royal Danish Navy*

DJIBOUTI

Headquarters' Appointment

Chief of Staff:
Major General Ali Meidal Wais

Personnel

1992: 90

Mercantile Marine

Lloyd's Register of Shipping:
8 vessels of 3404 tons gross

LIGHT FORCES

1 TECIMAR CLASS (COASTAL PATROL CRAFT)

ZENA

Displacement, tons: 30 full load
Dimensions, feet (metres): 43.6 × 13.8 × 3.6 *(13.3 × 4.2 × 1.1)*
Main machinery: 2 GM diesels; 240 hp *(179 kW)*; 2 shafts
Speed, knots: 25
Guns: 1—12.7 mm MG. 1—7.62 mm MG.

Comment: Built in 1974 and transferred by France after Declaration of Independence in 1977.

3 SEA RIDERS

Comment: Rigid inflatable craft acquired from UK 25 October 1988. It is also reported that five 36 ft fibreglass patrol boats were acquired from Iraq in 1990 but this is not confirmed.

2 PLASCOA CLASS (COASTAL PATROL CRAFT)

MOUSSA ALI P 10 **MONT ARREH** P 11

Displacement, tons: 35 full load
Dimensions, feet (metres): 75.5 × 18 × 4.9 *(23 × 5.5 × 1.5)*
Main machinery: 2 SACM Poyaud diesels; 1700 hp(m) *(1.25 MW)*; 2 shafts
Speed, knots: 25. **Range, miles:** 750 at 12 kts
Complement: 15
Guns: 1 GIAT 20 mm. 1 Browning 12.7 mm MG.
Radars: Navigation: Decca; I band.

Comment: Completed by Plascoa, Cannes on 8 June 1985 (P 10) and 16 February 1986 (P 11) as gift from France. GRP hulls.

DOMINICA

Senior Appointments

Commissioner of Police:
D Blanchard
Head of Coast Guard:
Sergeant Frederick

Personnel

1992: 40

General

An independent island in the British Commonwealth situated north of Martinique.

Ports

Roseau, Portsmouth, Ange-de-Mai

Mercantile Marine

Lloyd's Register of Shipping:
7 vessels of 2107 tons gross

1 SWIFT 65 ft CLASS

MELVILLE D 4

Displacement, tons: 33
Dimensions, feet (metres): 64.9 × 18.4 × 6.6 *(19.8 × 5.6 × 2)*
Main machinery: 2 Detroit diesels; 1300 hp *(970 kW)*; 2 shafts
Speed, knots: 23. **Range, miles:** 500 at 18 kts
Complement: 10
Radars: Navigation: Furuno; I/J band.

Comment: Ordered from Swiftships, Morgan City in November 1983. Commissioned 1 May 1984. Similar craft supplied to Antigua and St Lucia.

MELVILLE *1989, Dominica CG*

2 PATROL CRAFT

VIGILANCE **OBSERVER**

Displacement, tons: 2.4 full load
Dimensions, feet (metres): 27 × 8.4 × 1 *(8.2 × 2.6 × 0.3)*
Main machinery: 1 Johnson outboard motor; 155 hp *(116 kW)*
Speed, knots: 25
Complement: 3

Comment: Boston Whalers acquired in 1988 to replace the Brooke Marine and ex-Canadian craft.

VIGILANCE *1989, Dominica CG*

DOMINICAN REPUBLIC

Headquarters' Appointments

Chief of Naval Staff:
Vice Admiral José Santos Sánchez
Vice-Chief of Naval Staff:
Rear Admiral Victor F Garcia Alecont

Personnel

(a) 1992: 4400 officers and men (including naval infantry)
(b) Selective military service

General

Not all the ships listed are operational. Some of the older vessels are seaworthy but of questionable fighting capability.

Naval Bases

27 de Febrero, Santo Domingo: HQ of CNS, Naval School. Supply base.
Las Calderas: Las Calderas, Bañi: Naval dockyard, 700 ton synchrolift. Training centre. Supply base.
Haina: Dockyard facility. Supply base.
Puerto Plata. Small naval base.

Mercantile Marine

Lloyd's Register of Shipping:
29 vessels of 12 263 tons gross

Strength of the Fleet

Type	*Active (Reserve)*
Frigate	1
Corvettes	5
Large Patrol Craft	4 (3)
Coastal Patrol Craft	5
LCU	1
Survey Craft	1
Tanker (Small)	1
Tugs (Large)	5
Tugs (Harbour)	3
Training Ship and Tenders	11
Floating Dock	1

DELETIONS

1989 *Capitan W Arvelo* (sunk), *Isabela*
1990 *Atlantida*

FRIGATE

1 Ex-CANADIAN RIVER CLASS

Name	*No*	*Builders*	*Laid down*	*Launched*	*Commissioned*
MELLA (ex-*Presidente Trujillo*, ex-HMCS *Carlplace*)	F 451	Davie S B & Repairing Co, Lauzon, Canada	30 Nov 1943	6 July 1944	13 Dec 1944

Displacement, tons: 1445 standard; 2125 full load
Dimensions, feet (metres): 304 × 37.5 × 12.5 *(92.7 × 11.4 × 4.1)*
Main machinery: 2 boilers; 2 triple expansion reciprocating engines; 5500 ihp *(4.1 MW)*; 2 shafts
Speed, knots: 20. **Range, miles:** 7200 at 12 kts
Complement: 195 (15 officers, 50 midshipmen)
Guns: 1 Vickers 4 in *(102 mm)*/45 Mk 23; 80° elevation; 16 rounds/minute to 19 km *(10.4 nm)*; weight of shell 16 kg.
Fitted for 2—40 mm (twin) and 4—20 mm but these are not all always carried.
2—47 mm saluting guns.
Radars: Navigation: Raytheon SPS 64; I band.

Programmes: Transferred to the Dominican Navy in 1946. Pennant number as a frigate was F 101, but now carries pennant number 451 as flagship of Dominican naval forces. Renamed *Mella* in 1962.
Structure: Modified for use as Presidential yacht with extra accommodation and deckhouses built up aft in place of some armament.
Operational: Used by staff in naval operations and as a cadet training ship.

MELLA *11/1990, Hartmut Ehlers*

CORVETTES

3 Ex-US COHOES CLASS

Name	*No*	*Builders*	*Commissioned*
CAMBIASO (ex-USS *Etlah* AN 79)	P 207	Marietta Manufacturing Co	16 Apr 1945
SEPARACION (ex-USS *Passaconaway* AN 86)	P 208	Marine S B Co	27 Apr 1945
CALDERAS (ex-USS *Passaic* AN 87)	P 209	Leatham D Smith S B Co	6 Mar 1945

Displacement, tons: 650 standard; 855 full load
Dimensions, feet (metres): 162.3 × 33.8 × 11.7 *(49.5 × 10.3 × 3.6)*
Main machinery: Diesel-electric; 2 Busch-Sulzer BS-539 diesels; 1500 hp(m) *(1.1 MW)*; 1 shaft
Speed, knots: 12
Complement: 64 (5 officers)
Guns: 2—3 in *(76 mm)*. 3 Oerlikon 20 mm.

Comment: Ex-netlayers in reserve in USA by 1963. Transferred by sale on 29 September 1976. Now used for patrol duties. P 207 and 208 modified in 1980 with the removal of the bow horns. P209 has only one 76 mm gun and is used as a survey ship.

SEPARACION *6/1989, Hartmut Ehlers*

2 Ex-US ADMIRABLE CLASS

Name	*No*	*Builders*	*Commissioned*
PRESTOL (ex-*Separacion*, ex-USS *Skirmish* MSF 303)	BM 454	Associated SB	16 Aug 1943
TORTUGUERO (ex-USS *Signet* MSF 302)	BM 455	Associated SB	16 Aug 1943

Displacement, tons: 650 standard; 900 full load
Dimensions, feet (metres): 184.5 × 33 × 14.4 *(56.3 × 10.1 × 4.4)*
Main machinery: 2 Cooper-Bessemer GSB8 diesels; 1710 hp *(1.28 MW)*; 2 shafts
Speed, knots: 15. **Range, miles:** 4300 at 10 kts
Complement: 90 (8 officers)
Guns: 1—3 in *(76 mm)*/50. 2 Bofors 40 mm/60. 6 Oerlikon 20 mm.
Radars: Surface search: SPS 69; I band.

Comment: Former US fleet minesweepers. Purchased on 13 January 1965. BM 454 renamed early 1976. Sweep-gear removed. Classified as Cañoneros.

PRESTOL *11/1990, Hartmut Ehlers*

LIGHT FORCES

3 (RESERVE) Ex-USCG ARGO CLASS (LARGE PATROL CRAFT)

Name	*No*	*Builders*	*Commissioned*
INDÉPENDENCIA (ex-USCGC *Icarus*)	P 204 (ex-P 105)	Bath Iron Works	1932
LIBERTAD (ex-*Rafael Atoa*, ex-USCGC *Thetis*)	P 205 (ex-P 106)	Bath Iron Works	1931
RESTAURACION (ex-USCGC *Galatea*)	P 206 (ex-P 104)	John H Mathis & Co, Camden, NJ	1933

Displacement, tons: 337 standard
Dimensions, feet (metres): 165 × 25.2 × 9.5 *(50.3 × 7.7 × 2.9)*
Main machinery: 2 diesels; 1280 hp *(955 kW)*; 2 shafts
Speed, knots: 15. **Range, miles:** 1300 at 15 kts
Complement: 49 (5 officers)
Guns: 1—3 in *(76 mm)*. 1 Bofors 40 mm/60. 2 Oerlikon 20 mm.

Comment: Ex-US Coast Guard Cutters. Rebuilt in 1975. In reserve and may not go to sea again.

INDÉPENDENCIA *1982, Dominican Navy*

1 LARGE PATROL CRAFT

Name	*No*	*Builders*	*Commissioned*
CAPITAN ALSINA (ex-*RL 101*)	GC 105	—	1944

Displacement, tons: 100 standard
Dimensions, feet (metres): 104.8 × 19.2 × 5.8 *(32 × 5.9 × 1.8)*
Main machinery: 2 GM diesels; 1000 hp *(746 kW)*; 2 shafts
Speed, knots: 17
Complement: 20
Guns: 2 Oerlikon 20 mm.

Comment: Former US SAR craft of wooden construction. Launched in 1944. Renamed in 1957. Rebuilt 1977 and used as a training vessel.

CAPITAN ALSINA

1 US PGM 71 CLASS (LARGE PATROL CRAFT)

Name	*No*	*Builders*	*Commissioned*
BETELGEUSE (ex-US *PGM 77*)	GC 102	Peterson, USA	1966

Displacement, tons: 130 standard; 145 full load
Dimensions, feet (metres): 101.5 × 21 × 5 *(30.9 × 6.4 × 1.5)*
Main machinery: 2 Caterpillar D-348TA diesels; 1450 hp *(1.08 MW)*; 2 shafts
Speed, knots: 21. **Range, miles:** 1500 at 10 kts
Complement: 20
Guns: 1 Oerlikon 20 mm. 2—12.7 mm MGs.

Comment: Built in the USA and transferred to the Dominican Republic under the Military Aid Programme on 14 January 1966.

2 SWIFTSHIPS 110 FT CLASS (LARGE PATROL CRAFT)

Name	*No*	*Builders*	*Commissioned*
CANOPUS	GC 107	Swiftships, Morgan City	June 1984
ORION	GC 109	Swiftships, Morgan City	Aug 1984

Displacement, tons: 93.5 full load
Dimensions, feet (metres): 109.9 × 23.9 × 5.9 *(33.5 × 7.3 × 1.8)*
Main machinery: 3 Detroit 12V 92TA diesels; 1530 hp *(1.14 MW)* sustained; 3 shafts
Speed, knots: 23. **Range, miles:** 1500 at 12 kts
Complement: 19 (3 officers)
Guns: 1 Bofors 40 mm/60. 2—12.7 mm MGs.

Comment: Built of aluminium.

ORION *9/1989*

4 BELLATRIX CLASS (COASTAL PATROL CRAFT)

Name	*No*	*Builders*	*Commissioned*
PROCION	GC 103	Sewart Seacraft Inc, Berwick, La.	1967
ALDEBARÁN	GC 104	Sewart Seacraft Inc, Berwick, La.	1972
BELLATRIX	GC 106	Sewart Seacraft Inc, Berwick, La.	1967
CAPELLA	GC 108	Sewart Seacraft Inc, Berwick, La.	1968

Displacement, tons: 60
Dimensions, feet (metres): 85 × 18 × 5 *(25.9 × 5.5 × 1.5)*
Main machinery: 2 GM 16V-71N diesels; 896 hp *(668 kW)* sustained; 2 shafts
Speed, knots: 18.7. **Range, miles:** 800 at 15 kts
Complement: 12
Guns: 3—12.7 mm MGs.

Comment: Transferred to the Dominican Navy by the USA.

ALDEBARÁN *6/1989, Hartmut Ehlers*

1 COASTAL PATROL CRAFT

LUPERON GC 110

Comment: This is not a Swiftships 110 ft class as previously listed. Length about 60 ft *(18 m)*.

LAND-BASED MARITIME AIRCRAFT (FRONT LINE)

Numbers/Type: 2 Aerospatiale SA 316B Alouette III.
Operational speed: 113 kts *(210 km/h)*.
Service ceiling: 10 500 ft *(3200 m)*.
Range: 290 nm *(540 km)*.
Role/Weapon systems: Operated by air force liaison and SAR tasks. Sensors: None. Weapons: Possibly 7.62 mm machine gun.

Numbers/Type: 7 Cessna T-41D.
Operational speed: 102 kts *(188 km/h)*.
Service ceiling: 13 100 ft *(3995 m)*.
Range: 535 nm *(990 km)*.
Role/Weapon systems: Inshore/coastal reconnaissance reporting role; also used for training. Sensors: Hand-held cameras only. Weapons: Unarmed.

AMPHIBIOUS FORCES

1 LCU

Name	*No*	*Builders*	*Commissioned*
SAMANA (ex-*LA 2*)	LDM 302	Ast Navales Dominicanos	1958

Displacement, tons: 150 standard; 310 full load
Dimensions, feet (metres): 119.5 × 36 × 3 *(36.4 × 11 × 0.9)*
Main machinery: 3 GM 6X4NY diesels; 441 hp *(329 kW)*; 3 shafts
Speed, knots: 8
Complement: 17
Guns: 1—12.7 mm MG.

Comment: Similar characteristics to US LCT 5 type although slightly larger. Oil fuel, 80 tons.

SAMANA *1972, Dominican Navy*

SURVEY CRAFT

Note: *Atlantida* BA 08 is unlikely to go to sea again.

Name	*No*	*Builders*	*Commissioned*
NEPTUNO (ex-*Toro*)	BA 10	John H Mathis, New Jersey	Feb 1954

Displacement, tons: 72 full load
Dimensions, feet (metres): 64 × 18.1 × 8 *(19.5 × 5.7 × 2.4)*
Main machinery: 1 GM 6-71 diesel; 174 hp *(130 kW)* sustained; 1 shaft
Speed, knots: 10
Complement: 7 (1 officer)

Comment: Deleted in error in 1989. Also used as a buoy tender.

NEPTUNO *11/1990, Hartmut Ehlers*

TANKERS

1 Ex-US OIL BARGE

Name	*No*	*Builders*	*Commissioned*
CAPITAN BEOTEGUI (ex-US *YO 215*)	BT 5	Ira S Bushey, Brooklyn	17 Dec 1945

Displacement, tons: 422 light; 1400 full load
Dimensions, feet (metres): 174 × 32.9 × 13.3 *(53.1 × 10 × 4.1)*
Main machinery: 1 Union diesel; 525 hp *(392 kW)*; 1 shaft
Speed, knots: 8
Complement: 23
Cargo capacity: 6570 barrels
Guns: 2 Oerlikon 20 mm.

Comment: Former US self-propelled fuel oil barge. Lent by the USA in April 1964. Lease renewed 31 December 1980. Sister ship sank 21 February 1989.

CAPITAN BEOTEGUI (with COJINOA) *6/1989, Hartmut Ehlers*

TRAINING SHIPS AND TENDERS

Note: In addition to those listed below there are various tenders mostly acquired 1986-88: *Cojinoa* BA 01, *Bonito* BA 02, *Beata* BA 14, *Albacora* BA 18, *Salinas* BA 19, *Carey* BA 20.

4 COASTAL PATROL CRAFT

Name	*No*	*Builders*	*Commissioned*
CARITE	BA 3	Ast Navales Dominicanos	1975
ATÚN	BA 6	Ast Navales Dominicanos	1975
PICÚA	BA 9	Ast Navales Dominicanos	1975
JUREL	BA 15	Ast Navales Dominicanos	1975

Displacement, tons: 24
Dimensions, feet (metres): 45 × 13 × 6.6 *(13.7 × 4 × 1.9)*
Main machinery: 1 GM diesel; 101 hp *(75 kW)*; 1 shaft
Speed, knots: 9
Complement: 4
Guns: 1—7.62 mm MG.

Comment: Auxiliary sailing craft with a sail area of 750 sq ft and a cargo capacity of 7 tons. Used for training. There may be more of this class.

NUBE DEL MAR BA 7

Displacement, tons: 40
Dimensions, feet (metres): 42 × 12 × 1 *(12.8 × 3.6 × 0.3)*
Main machinery: 1 Volvo Pentax 21A; 75 hp *(55 kW)*; 1 shaft
Speed, knots: 10

Comment: Auxiliary yacht used for sail training at the Naval School. Completed 1979.

TUGS

1 Ex-US CHEROKEE CLASS

Name	*No*	*Builders*	*Commissioned*
MACORIX (ex-USS *Kiowa* ATF 72)	RM 21	Charleston S B and D D Co	7 June 1943

Displacement, tons: 1235 standard; 1675 full load
Dimensions, feet (metres): 205 × 38.5 × 15.5 *(62.5 × 11.7 × 4.7)*
Main machinery: Diesel-electric; 4 GM 12-278 diesels; 4400 hp *(3.28 MW)*; 4 generators; 1 motor; 3000 hp *(2.24 MW)*; 1 shaft
Speed, knots: 16.5
Complement: 85
Guns: 1 US 3 in *(76 mm)*/50. 1 Oerlikon 20 mm.
Radars: Navigation: Raytheon SPS 5D; G/H band.

Comment: Carries additional salvage equipment. Transferred on 6 October 1972. Lease renewed 31 December 1980.

MACORIX *1975, Dominican Navy*

2 Ex-US SOTOYOMO CLASS

Name	*No*	*Builders*	*Commissioned*
CAONABO (ex-USS *Sagamore* ATA 208)	RM 18	Gulfport Boiler and Welding Works	19 Mar 1945
ENRIQUILLO (ex-USS *Stallion* ATA 193)	RM 22	Levington S B Co, Orange, Texas	26 Feb 1945

Displacement, tons: 534 standard; 860 full load
Dimensions, feet (metres): 143 × 33.9 × 13 *(43.6 × 10.3 × 4)*
Main machinery: Diesel-electric; 2 GM 12-278A diesels; 2200 hp *(1.64 MW)*; 2 generators; 1 motor; 1500 hp *(1.12 MW)*; 1 shaft
Speed, knots: 13
Complement: 45
Guns: 1 US 3 in *(76 mm)* (RM 18). 2 Oerlikon 20 mm (RM 22).
Radars: Surface search: Raytheon SPS 5D; G/H band.

Comment: RM 18 transferred on lease 1 February 1972 and RM 22 transferred by sale 30 October 1980.

ENRIQUILLO *6/1989, Hartmut Ehlers*

ENRIQUILLO *11/1990, Hartmut Ehlers*

2 HERCULES CLASS

Name	*No*	*Builders*	*Commissioned*
HERCULES (ex-*R 2*)	RP 12	Ast Navales Dominicanos	1960
GUACANAGARIX (ex-*R 5*)	RP 13	Ast Navales Dominicanos	1960

Displacement, tons: 200 approx
Dimensions, feet (metres): 70 × 15.6 × 9 *(21.4 × 4.8 × 2.7)*
Main machinery: 1 Caterpillar motor; 500 hp *(373 kW)*; 1 shaft
Complement: 8

1 LCU TUG

Name	*No*	*Builders*	*Commissioned*
OCOA	LDP 303	Ast Navales Dominicanos	1976

Displacement, tons: 50 full load
Dimensions, feet (metres): 56.2 × 14 × 3.9 *(17.1 × 4.3 × 1.2)*
Main machinery: 2 GM 6-71 diesels; 360 hp *(268 kW)* sustained; 2 shafts
Speed, knots: 9. **Range, miles:** 130 at 9 kts
Complement: 5
Cargo capacity: 30 tons

Comment: Converted for use as a tug, retaining bow ramp.

OCOA *1979, Dominican Navy*

2 HARBOUR TUGS

BOHECHIO (ex-US *YTL 600*) RP 16 **CAYACCA** RP 19

Comment: Small tugs for harbour and coastal use. Not of uniform type and dimensions. RP 16 transferred January 1971. Lease extended 31 December 1980.

FLOATING DOCKS

1 FLOATING DOCK

ENDEAVOR DF 1 (ex-AFDL 1)

Comment: Lift, 1000 tons. Commissioned in 1943. Transferred on loan 8 March 1986.

ENDEAVOR *11/1988*

ECUADOR

Headquarters' Appointments

Commander-in-Chief of the Navy:
Admiral Hugo Unda
Chief of Naval Operations:
Vice Admiral Thelmo Delgado
Chief of Naval Staff:
Vice Admiral German Jepez
Chief of Naval Personnel:
Vice Admiral Vicente Jaramillo
Chief of Naval Materiel:
Captain Hugo Cañarte

Diplomatic Representation

Naval Attaché in Rome and Bonn:
Captain Victor E Garces
Naval Attaché in London and Paris:
Captain Hector Ruilova
Naval Attaché in Washington:
Captain Galo P Aleman

Personnel

(a) 1992: Total 5000 including 1900 marines
(b) 2 years' selective national service

Naval Bases

Guayaquil (main naval base), Jaramijo, Salinas, Esmeraldas. San Lorenzo and Galapagos Islands (small bases).

Establishments

The Naval Academy, Naval War College and Merchant Navy Academy in Guayaquil.

Naval Aviation

Naval Aviation wing is based at Guayaquil Air Base. Annual budget comprises 5-7.5 per cent of naval budget.
Personnel: 35 pilots, 75 aircrew, and 200 enlisted maintenance/other rating. Pilot training is conducted at foreign flight training facilities.

Naval Infantry

A force of naval infantry is based at Guayaquil, on the Galapagos Islands and at Oriente (Esmeraldas Manta).

Coast Guard

Small force formed in 1980.

Prefix to Ships' Names

BAE

Strength of the Fleet

Type	*Active*
Patrol Submarines	2
Frigates	2
Corvettes	6
Fast Attack Craft (Missile)	6
LST	1
Depot Ship	1
Survey Vessels	2
Tugs	9
Floating Docks	2
Sail Training Ship	1
Coast Guard Craft	27

Mercantile Marine

Lloyd's Register of Shipping:
158 vessels of 383 839 tons gross

DELETION

1989 *Morán Valverde* (old)
1991 *Presidente Eloy Alfaro* (old)

PENNANT LIST

Submarines

S 101 Shyri
S 102 Huancavilca

Frigates

FM 1 Presidente Eloy Alfaro (new)
FM 02 Moran Valverde (new)

Corvettes

CM 11 Esmeraldas
CM 12 Manabi
CM 13 Los Rios
CM 14 El Oro
CM 15 Los Galapagos
CM 16 Loja

Light Forces

LM 21 Quito
LM 23 Guayaquil
LM 24 Cuenca
LM 25 Manta
LM 26 Tulcan
LM 27 Nuevo Rocafuerte

Amphibious Forces

T 61 Hualcopo

Survey/Research Vessels

HI 91 Orion
LH 92 Rigel

Tugs

R 710 Chimborazo
R 711 Cayambe
R 720 Sangay
R 721 Cotopaxi
R 722 Tungurahua
R 723 Antizana
R 724 Sirius
R 725 Altar
R 726 Quilotoa

Miscellaneous

T 63 Atahualpa
T 66 Taurus
BE 51 Guayas
BT 84 Putumayo
DF 81 Amazonas
DF 82 Napo
UT 111 Isla de la Plata
UT 112 Isla Puná

Coast Guard

LGC 31 25 de Julio
LGC 32 24 de Mayo
LGC 33 10 de Agosto
LGC 35 3 de Noviembre
LGC 39 9 de Octubre
LGC 40 Rio Puyango
LGC 41 Rio Matage
LGC 42 Rio Zarumilla
LGC 43 Rio Chone
LGC 44 Rio Daule
LGC 45 Rio Babahoyo

SUBMARINES

2 TYPE 209 CLASS (TYPE 1300)

Name	*No*	*Builders*	*Laid down*	*Launched*	*Commissioned*
SHYRI	S 101 (ex-S 11)	Howaldtswerke, Kiel	5 Aug 1974	6 Oct 1976	5 Nov 1977
HUANCAVILCA	S 102 (ex-S 12)	Howaldtswerke, Kiel	2 Jan 1975	15 Mar 1977	16 Mar 1978

Displacement, tons: 1285 surfaced; 1390 dived
Dimensions, feet (metres): 195.1 × 20.5 × 17.9 *(59.5 × 6.3 × 5.4)*
Main machinery: Diesel-electric; 4 MTU 12V 493 AZ80 GA31L diesels; 2400 hp(m) *(1.76 MW)* sustained; 4 Siemens alternators; 1.7 MW; 1 Siemens motor; 4600 hp(m) *(3.38 MW)* sustained; 1 shaft
Speed, knots: 11 surfaced/snorting; 21.5 dived
Complement: 33 (5 officers)

Torpedoes: 8—21 in *(533 mm)* bow tubes. 14 AEG SUT; dual purpose; wire-guided; active/passive homing to 28 km *(15 nm)* at 23 kts; 12 km *(6.5 nm)* at 35 kts; warhead 250 kg.
Fire control: Signaal M8 Mod 24.
Radars: Surface search: Thomson-CSF Calypso; I band.
Sonars: Krupp Atlas CSU 3; hull-mounted; active/passive search and attack; medium frequency.
Thomson Sintra DUUX 2; passive ranging.

Programmes: Ordered in March 1974. *Shyri* underwent major refit in West Germany in 1983; *Huancavilca* in 1984. Second refits being planned for 1992/93.
Operational: Based at Guayaquil.

HUANCAVILCA *9/1981, USN*

FRIGATES

2 Ex-BRITISH LEANDER CLASS

Name	No	Builders	Laid down	Launched	Commissioned
PRESIDENTE ELOY ALFARO (ex-*Penelope*)	FM 1 (ex-F 127)	Vickers Armstrong, Newcastle	14 Mar 1961	17 Aug 1962	31 Oct 1963
MORAN VALVERDE (ex-*Danae*)	FM 02 (ex-F 47)	HM Dockyard, Devonport	16 Dec 1964	31 Oct 1965	7 Sep 1967

Displacement, tons: 2450 standard; 3200 full load
Dimensions, feet (metres): 360 wl; 372 oa × 41 × 14.8 (keel); 19 (screws) *(109.7; 113.4 × 12.5 × 4.5; 5.8)*
Main machinery: 2 Babcock & Wilcox boilers; 38.7 kg/cm sq; 850°F *(450°C)*; 2 English Electric/White turbines; 30 000 hp *(22.4 MW)*; 2 shafts
Speed, knots: 28. **Range, miles:** 4000 at 15 kts
Complement: 248 (20 officers)

Missiles: SSM: 4 Aerospatiale MM 38 Exocet ❶; inertial cruise; active radar homing to 42 km *(23 nm)* at 0.9 Mach; warhead 165 kg.
SAM: 3 Shorts Seacat GWS 22 quad launchers ❷; radar guidance to 5 km *(2.7 nm)*; warhead HE; sea-skimmer; anti-ship capability.
Guns: 2 Bofors 40 mm/60 Mk 9 ❸; 80° elevation; 120 rounds/minute to 10 km *(5.4 nm)* anti-surface; 3 km *(1.6 nm)* anti-aircraft; weight of shell 0.89 kg.
2 Oerlikon/BMARC 20 mm GAM-BO1 can be fitted midships or aft.
Countermeasures: Decoys: Graseby Type 182; towed torpedo decoy.
2 Vickers Corvus 8-barrelled trainable launchers ❹; Chaff to 1 km.
ESM: UA-8/9; radar warning.
ECM: Type 667/668; jammer.
Combat data systems: CAAIS action data automation. Links 10 and 14 (receive).
Fire control: GWS 50.
Radars: Air search: Marconi Type 966 ❺; A band.
Surface search: Plessey Type 994 ❻; E/F band.
Navigation: Kelvin Hughes Type 1006; I band.
Fire control: Two Plessey Type 903/904 (for Seacat) ❼.
Sonars: Kelvin Hughes Type 162M; hull-mounted; bottom classification; 50 kHz.
Graseby Type 184P; hull-mounted; active search and attack; 7-9 kHz.

Helicopters: 1 Bell 206 B ❽.

Programmes: Both ships acquired 25 April 1991 and sailed for Ecuador after working up in July and August respectively.
Structure: These are Batch 2 Exocet conversions completed in 1980 and 1982. Torpedo tubes were subsequently removed in 1988/89. The ships were transferred without Exocet or Seacat ammunition.

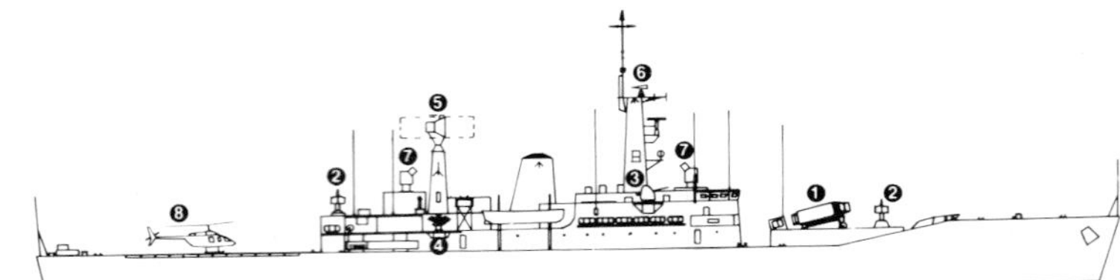

MORAN VALVERDE *(Scale 1 : 1 200), Ian Sturton*

PRESIDENTE ELOY ALFARO *6/1991, D & B Teague*

CORVETTES

6 ESMERALDAS CLASS (CORVETTES)

Name	No	Builders	Laid down	Launched	Commissioned
ESMERALDAS	CM 11	Fincantieri Muggiano	27 Sep 1979	1 Oct 1980	7 Aug 1982
MANABI	CM 12	Fincantieri Ancona	19 Feb 1980	9 Feb 1981	21 June 1983
LOS RIOS	CM 13	Fincantieri Muggiano	5 Dec 1979	27 Feb 1981	9 Oct 1983
EL ORO	CM 14	Fincantieri Ancona	20 Mar 1980	9 Feb 1981	11 Dec 1983
LOS GALAPAGOS	CM 15	Fincantieri Muggiano	4 Dec 1980	4 July 1981	26 May 1984
LOJA	CM 16	Fincantieri Ancona	25 Mar 1981	27 Feb 1982	26 May 1984

Displacement, tons: 685 full load
Dimensions, feet (metres): 204.4 × 30.5 × 8 *(62.3 × 9.3 × 2.5)*
Main machinery: 4 MTU 20V 956 TB 92 diesels; 22 140 hp(m) *(16.27 MW)* sustained; 4 shafts
Speed, knots: 37. **Range, miles:** 4400 at 14 kts
Complement: 51

Missiles: SSM: 6 Aerospatiale MM 40 Exocet (2 triple) launchers ❶; inertial cruise; active radar homing to 70 km *(40 nm)* at 0.9 Mach; warhead 165 kg; sea-skimmer.
SAM: Selenia Elsag Albatros quad launcher ❷; Aspide; semi-active radar homing to 13 km *(7 nm)* at 2.5 Mach; height envelope 15-5000 m *(49.2-16 405 ft)*; warhead 30 kg.
Guns: 1 OTO Melara 3 in *(76 mm)*/62 compact ❸; 85° elevation; 85 rounds/minute to 16 km *(8.7 nm)*; weight of shell 6 kg.
2 Breda 40 mm/70 (twin) ❹; 85° elevation; 300 rounds/minute to 12.5 km *(6.8 nm)* anti-surface; weight of shell 0.96 kg.
Torpedoes: 6—324 mm ILAS-3 (2 triple) tubes ❺; Whitehead Motofides A244; anti-submarine; self adaptive patterns to 6 km *(3.3 nm)* at 30 kts; warhead 34 kg.
Countermeasures: Decoys: 1 Breda 105 mm SCLAR launcher; Chaff to 5 km *(2.7 nm)*; illuminants to 12 km *(6.6 nm)*.
ESM/ECM: Elettronika Gamma ED; radar intercept and jammer.
Combat data systems: Selenia IPN 10 action data automation.
Fire control: 2 Selenia NA21 with C03 directors.
Radars: Air/surface search: Selenia RAN 10S ❻; E/F band; range 155 km *(85 nm)*.
Navigation: SMA 3 RM 20; I band; range 73 km *(40 nm)*.
Fire control: 2 Selenia Orion 10X ❼; I/J band; range 40 km *(22 nm)*.
Sonars: Thomson Sintra Diodon; hull-mounted; active search and attack; 11, 12 or 13 kHz.

Helicopters: 1 Bell 206B can be embarked (platform only).

Programmes: Ordered in 1979. *El Oro* out of commission for two years from mid-1985 after a bad fire.
Structure: Similar to Libyan and Iraqi corvettes, with a helicopter deck and larger engines.

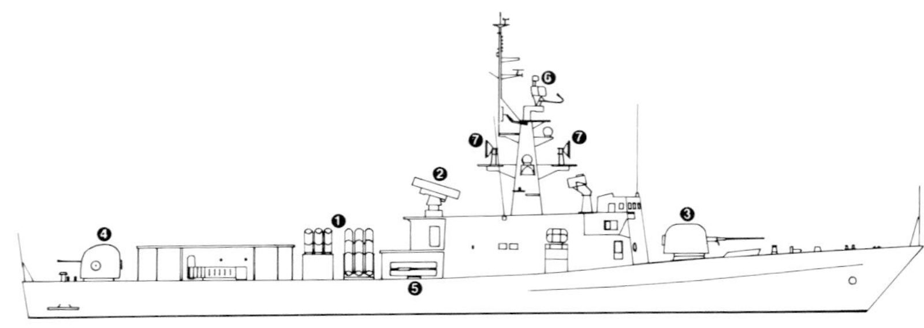

ESMERALDAS *(Scale 1: 600), Ian Sturton*

ESMERALDAS *1985*

SHIPBORNE AIRCRAFT

Numbers/Type: 3 Bell 206B JetRanger.
Operational speed: 115 kts *(213 km/h)*.
Service ceiling: 13 500 ft *(4115 m)*.
Range: 368 nm *(682 km)*.
Role/Weapon systems: Support helicopter for afloat reconnaissance and SAR. Sensors: None. Weapons: None.

JETRANGER *1989, Textron*

LAND-BASED MARITIME AIRCRAFT (FRONT LINE)

Numbers/Type: 3 Beech T-34C-1 Turbo-Mentor.
Operational speed: 250 kts *(404 km/h)*.
Service ceiling: 30 000 ft *(9145 m)*.
Range: 650 nm *(1205 km)*.
Role/Weapon systems: Operated for training and surveillance tasks. Sensors: None. Weapons: Underwing pylons for rockets, cannon and bombs.

Numbers/Type: 1 Beech Super King 200T.
Operational speed: 282 kts *(523 km/h)*.
Service ceiling: 35 000 ft *(10 670 m)*.
Range: 2030 nm *(3756 km)*.
Role/Weapon systems: Maritime reconnaissance and drug interdiction. Sensors: Weather radar only. Weapons: Unarmed.

LIGHT FORCES

3 LÜRSSEN 45 CLASS (FAST ATTACK CRAFT—MISSILE)

Name	*No*	*Builders*	*Commissioned*
QUITO	LM 21	Lürssen, Vegesack	13 July 1976
GUAYAQUIL	LM 23	Lürssen, Vegesack	22 Dec 1977
CUENCA	LM 24	Lürssen, Vegesack	17 July 1977

Displacement, tons: 255
Dimensions, feet (metres): 147.6 × 23 × 8.1 *(45 × 7 × 2.5)*
Main machinery: 4 MTU 16V 538 TB 91 diesels; 12 240 hp(m) *(9.11 MW)* sustained; 4 shafts
Speed, knots: 40. **Range, miles:** 700 at 40 kts; 1800 at 16 kts
Complement: 35

Missiles: SSM: 4 Aerospatiale MM 38 Exocet; inertial cruise; active radar homing to 42 km *(23 nm)* at 0.9 Mach; warhead 165 kg; sea-skimmer.
Guns: 1 OTO Melara 3 in *(76 mm)*/62 compact; 85° elevation; 85 rounds/minute to 16 km *(8.7 nm)*; weight of shell 6 kg.
2 Oerlikon 35 mm/90 (twin); 85° elevation; 550 rounds/minute to 6 km *(3.3 nm)*; weight of shell 1.55 kg.
Fire control: Thomson-CSF Vega system.
Radars: Air/surface search: Thomson-CSF Triton; G band; range 33 km *(18 nm)* for 2 m² target.
Fire control: Thomson-CSF Pollux; I/J band; range 31 km *(17 nm)* for 2 m² target.
Navigation: Racal Decca; I band.

Programmes: Launched—*Quito* on 20 November 1975; *Guayaquil* on 5 April 1976; *Cuenca* in December 1976.

QUITO *9/1981, USN*

3 MANTA CLASS (FAST ATTACK CRAFT—MISSILE)

Name	*No*	*Builders*	*Commissioned*
MANTA	LM 25	Lürssen, Vegesack	11 June 1971
TULCAN	LM 26	Lürssen, Vegesack	2 Apr 1971
NUEVO ROCAFUERTE	LM 27	Lürssen, Vegesack	23 June 1971

Displacement, tons: 119 standard; 134 full load
Dimensions, feet (metres): 119.4 × 19.1 × 6 *(36.4 × 5.8 × 1.8)*
Main machinery: 3 Mercedes-Benz diesels; 9000 hp(m) *(6.61 MW)*; 3 shafts
Speed, knots: 42. **Range, miles:** 700 at 30 kts; 1500 at 15 kts
Complement: 19

Missiles: SSM: 4 IAI Gabriel II; radar or optical guidance; semi-active radar homing to 36 km *(19.4 nm)* at 0.7 Mach; warhead 75 kg.
Guns: 2 Emerson Electric 30 mm (twin); 80° elevation; 1200 rounds/minute combined to 6 km *(3.3 nm)*; weight of shell 0.35 kg.
Fire control: Thomson-CSF Vega system.
Radars: Fire control: Thomson-CSF Pollux; I/J band; range 31 km *(17 nm)* for 2 m² target.
Navigation: I band.

Modernisation: Rearmed in 1980 with new electronic fit and missiles. Torpedo tubes have been removed.
Structure: Similar design to the Chilean Guacolda class with an extra diesel, 3 kts faster.
Operational: Missiles are not carried when used on EEZ surveillance.

AMPHIBIOUS SHIPS

1 Ex-US 512-1152 SERIES (LST)

Name	*No*	*Builders*	*Commissioned*
HUALCOPO (ex-USS *Summit County* LST 1146)	T 61	Chicago Bridge and Iron Co	9 June 1945

Displacement, tons: 1653 standard; 4080 full load
Dimensions, feet (metres): 328 × 50 × 14 *(100 × 16.1 × 4.3)*
Main machinery: 2 GM 12-567A diesels; 1800 hp *(1.34 MW)*; 2 shafts
Speed, knots: 11.6. **Range, miles:** 7200 at 10 kts
Complement: 119
Military lift: 147 troops
Guns: 8 Bofors 40 mm. 2 Oerlikon 20 mm.

Comment: Purchased on 14 February 1977. Commissioned in November 1977 after extensive refit. May still have the ice strengthened bow fitted in the early 1950s. Plans for replacement not yet realised.

HUALCOPO *10/1984, R. E. Parkinson*

6 ROTORK CRAFT

LF 91-96

Displacement, tons: 9 full load
Dimensions, feet (metres): 41.5 × 10.5 × 3 *(12.6 × 3.2 × 0.9)*
Main machinery: 2 Volvo AQD 40A diesels; 220 hp(m) *(162 kW)* sustained; 2 shafts
Speed, knots: 26
Complement: 4
Military lift: 4 tons

Comment: Purchased 1979 from UK.

SURVEY/RESEARCH VESSELS

Name	*No*	*Builders*	*Commissioned*
RIGEL	LH 92	Halter Marine	1975

Displacement, tons: 50
Dimensions, feet (metres): 64.5 × 17.1 × 3.6 *(19.7 × 5.2 × 1.1)*
Main machinery: 2 diesels; 2 shafts
Speed, knots: 10
Complement: 10 (2 officers)

Comment: Used for inshore oceanographic work.

Name	No	Builders	Commissioned
ORION (ex-*Dometer*)	HI 91 (ex-HI 92)	Ishikawajima, Tokyo	10 Nov 1982

Measurement, tons: 1105 gross
Dimensions, feet (metres): 210.6 pp × 35.1 × 11.8 *(64.2 × 10.7 × 3.6)*
Main machinery: Diesel-electric; 3 Detroit 16V 92TA diesels; 2070 hp *(1.54 MW)* sustained; 2 motors; 1900 hp *(1.42 MW)*; 1 shaft
Speed, knots: 12.6. **Range, miles:** 6000 at 12 kts
Complement: 45 (6 officers) plus 14 civilians
Radars: Navigation: Two Decca; I band.

Comment: Research vessel for oceanographic, hydrographic and meteorological work.

ORION *3/1990, T. J. Gander*

TUGS

2 Ex-US CHEROKEE CLASS

Name	No	Builders	Commissioned
CAYAMBE (ex-USS *Cusabo* ATF 155)	R 711 (ex-R 101, ex-R 51, ex-R 01)	Charleston S B & D D Co	28 Apr 1945
CHIMBORAZO (ex-USS *Chowanoc* ATF 100)	R 710 (ex-R 71, ex-R 105)	Charleston S B & D D Co	21 Feb 1945

Displacement, tons: 1235 standard; 1640 full load
Dimensions, feet (metres): 205 × 38.5 × 17 *(62.5 × 11.7 × 5.2)*
Main machinery: Diesel-electric; 4 GM 12-278 diesels; 4400 hp *(3.28 MW)*; 4 generators; 1 motor; 3000 hp *(2.24 MW)*; 1 shaft (R 711)
Diesel-electric; 4 Busch-Sulzer BS-539 diesels; 4 generators; 1 motor; 3000 hp *(2.24 MW)*; 1 shaft (R 710)
Speed, knots: 16.5. **Range, miles:** 7000 at 15 kts
Complement: 85
Guns: 1—3 in *(76 mm)*. 2 Bofors 40 mm. 2 Oerlikon 20 mm (not all fitted).

Comment: *Cayambe* launched on 26 February 1945. Fitted with powerful pumps and other salvage equipment. Transferred to Ecuador by lease on 2 November 1960 and renamed *Los Rios*. Again renamed *Cayambe* in 1966 and purchased on 30 August 1978. *Chimborazo* transferred 1 October 1977.

CAYAMBE (old number) *1970, Equadorian Navy*

Name	No	Builders	Commissioned
SANGAY (ex-*Loja*)	R 720 (ex-R 102, ex-R 53)	—	1952

Displacement, tons: 295 light; 390 full load
Dimensions, feet (metres): 107 × 26 × 14 *(32.6 × 7.9 × 4.3)*
Main machinery: 1 Fairbanks-Morse diesel; 1 shaft
Speed, knots: 12

Comment: Acquired in 1964. Renamed in 1966.

Name	No	Builders	Commissioned
COTOPAXI (ex-USS *R T Ellis*)	R 721 (ex-R 103, ex-R 52)	Equitable Building Corporation	1945

Displacement, tons: 150
Dimensions, feet (metres): 82 × 21 × 8 *(25 × 6.4 × 2.4)*
Main machinery: 1 Diesel; 650 hp *(478 kW)*; 1 shaft
Speed, knots: 9

Comment: Purchased from the USA in 1947.

TUNGURAHUA	R 722	**ALTAR**	R 725
ANTIZANA	R 723	**QUILOTOA**	R 726
SIRIUS	R 724		

Displacement, tons: 490
Dimensions, feet (metres): 100.4 × — × 8.2 *(30.6 × — × 2.5)*
Speed, knots: 8

MISCELLANEOUS

Note: It is reported that the 2000 ton ex-UK RMAS *Throsk* may be acquired in 1992 as an armament stores carrier.

1 Ex-GDR DARSS CLASS (DEPOT SHIP)

— (ex-*Jasmund*)

Displacement, tons: 2292 full load
Dimensions, feet (metres): 250.3 × 39.7 × 13.8 *(76.3 × 12.1 × 4.2)*
Main machinery: 1 Type 40 DM diesel; 2000 hp(m) *(1.47 MW)*; 1 shaft; cp prop
Speed, knots: 12. **Range, miles:** 1000 at 12 kts
Complement: 60
Cargo capacity: 650 tons dry stores; 200 tons dieso; 25 ton crane
Guns: Fitted for 6 USSR 25 mm/70 (3 twin) automatic; 85° elevation; 270 rounds/minute to 3 km *(1.6 nm)*; weight of shell 0.34 kg.
Radars: Navigation: TSR 333; I band.

Comment: Acquired in 1991. Ex-GDR ship built by Peenewerft, Wolgast. First launched 27 February 1982. Does not have underway replenishment capability but refuelling can be done on either side or on the stern. Used as an AGI by the GDR Navy so additional accommodation has been fitted.

DARSS Class *1/1991, Reinhard Kramer*

1 Ex-US YW CLASS WATER CARRIER

Name	No	Builders	Commissioned
ATAHUALPA (ex-US *YW 131*)	T 63 (ex-T 62, ex-T 33, ex-T 41, ex-A 01)	Leatham D Smith S B Co	1945

Displacement, tons: 415 light; 1235 full load
Dimensions, feet (metres): 174 × 32 × 15 *(53.1 × 9.8 × 4.6)*
Main machinery: 2 GM 8-278A diesels; 1500 hp *(1.12 MW)*; 2 shafts
Speed, knots: 11.5

Comment: Acquired by the Ecuadorian Navy on 2 May 1963. Purchased on 1 December 1977. Paid off in 1988 but back in service in 1990.

1 TANKER

Name	No	Builders	Commissioned
TAURUS	T 66	Astinave, Guayaquil	1985

Measurement, tons: 1175 dwt; 1110 gross
Dimensions, feet (metres): 174.2 × 36 × 14.4 *(53.1 × 11 × 4.4)*
Main machinery: 1 GM diesel; 1050 hp *(783 kW)*; 1 shaft
Speed, knots: 11

Comment: Acquired for the Navy in 1987.

1 TRAINING SHIP

Name	No	Builders	Commissioned
GUAYAS	BE 51 (ex-BE 01)	Ast Celaya, Spain	23 July 1977

Measurement, tons: 234 dwt; 934 gross
Dimensions, feet (metres): 264 × 33.5 × 13.4 *(80 × 10.2 × 4.2)*
Main machinery: 1 GM 12V-149T diesel; 875 hp *(652 kW)* sustained; 1 shaft
Speed, knots: 11.3

Comment: Three masted sail training ship. Launched 23 September 1976. Has accommodation for 180.

GUAYAS *1988, John Mortimer*

1 ARMAMENT STORES CARRIER (AKF)

Name	*No*	*Builders*	*Commissioned*
CALICUCHIMA (ex-*Throsk*)	(ex-A 379)	Cleland S B Co, Wallsend	20 Sep 1977

Displacement, tons: 2207 full load
Dimensions, feet (metres): 231.2 × 39 × 15 *(70.5 × 11.9 × 4.6)*
Main machinery: 2 Mirrlees-Blackstone diesels; 3000 hp *(2.2 MW)*; 1 shaft
Speed, knots: 14.5. **Range, miles:** 4000 at 11 kts
Complement: 24 (8 officers)

Comment: Acquired from the UK in November 1991.

CALICUCHIMA (old number) *8/1982, M. Lennon*

1 WATER CLASS

Name	*No*	*Builders*	*Commissioned*
QUISQUIS (ex-*Waterside*)	(ex-Y 20)	Drypool Engineering & Drydock Co, Hull	1968

Measurement, tons: 285 gross
Dimensions, feet (metres): 131.5 × 24.8 × 8 *(40.1 × 7.5 × 2.4)*
Main machinery: 1 Lister-Blackstone ERS-8-MCR diesel; 660 hp *(492 kW)*; 1 shaft
Speed, knots: 11
Complement: 8

Comment: Acquired from the UK in November 1991.

QUISQUIS (old number) *1989*

2 Ex-US YP TYPE

ISLA DE LA PLATA UT 111 **ISLA PUNA** UT 112

Displacement, tons: 11
Dimensions, feet (metres): 42 × 11.5 × 3.9 *(12.8 × 3.5 × 1.2)*

Comment: Transferred 1962. Ex US Coast Guard utility boats.

1 Ex-US YR TYPE

Name	*No*	*Builders*	*Commissioned*
PUTUMAYO (ex-US *YR 34*)	BT 84 (ex-BT 123, ex-BT 62)	New York Navy Yard	—

Displacement, tons: 770 full load

Comment: Repair barge leased July 1962. Purchased on 1 December 1977.

2 Ex-US ARD 12 CLASS FLOATING DOCK

Name	*No*	*Builders*	*Commissioned*
AMAZONAS (ex-US *ARD 17*)	DF 81 (ex-DF 121)	USA	1944
NAPO (ex-US *ARD 24*)	DF 82	USA	1944

Dimensions, feet (metres): 492 × 81 × 17.7 *(150 × 24.7 × 5.4)*

Comment: *Amazonas* leased in 1961 and bought outright in 1982; *Napo* bought in 1988. Suitable for docking ships up to 3200 tons. A repair barge *Rio Putumayo* is a companion craft to the Floating Docks.

COAST GUARD

2 US PGM-71 CLASS (LARGE PATROL CRAFT)

Name	*No*	*Builders*	*Commissioned*
25 DE JULIO (ex-*Quito*)	LGC 31 (ex-LC 71)	Peterson, USA	30 Nov 1965
24 DE MAYO (ex-*Guayaquil*)	LGC 32 (ex-LC 72)	Peterson, USA	30 Nov 1965

Displacement, tons: 130 standard; 146 full load
Dimensions, feet (metres): 101.5 × 21 × 5 *(30.9 × 6.4 × 1.5)*
Main machinery: 4 diesels; 880 hp *(656 kW)*; 2 shafts
Speed, knots: 21. **Range, miles:** 1000 at 12 kts
Complement: 15
Guns: 1 Bofors 40 mm/60. 4 Oerlikon 20 mm (2 twin). 2—12.7 mm MGs.

Comment: Transferred to the Navy under MAP on 30 November 1965 and then to the Coast Guard in 1980. Paid off into reserve in 1983 and deleted from the order of battle. Refitted with new engines in 1988-89 and now back in service with new pennant numbers.

3 COASTAL PATROL CRAFT

Name	*No*	*Builders*	*Commissioned*
10 DE AGOSTO	LC 33	Schurenstedt, Bardenfleth	Aug 1954
9 DE OCTUBRE	LC 39	Schurenstedt, Bardenfleth	Aug 1954
3 DE NOVIEMBRE	LC 35	Schurenstedt, Bardenfleth	1955

Displacement, tons: 45 standard; 64 full load
Dimensions, feet (metres): 76.8 × 13.5 × 6.2 *(23.4 × 4.6 × 1.9)*
Main machinery: 2 Bohn & Kähler diesels; 1200 hp(m) *(882 kW)*; 2 shafts
Speed, knots: 22. **Range, miles:** 550 at 16 kts
Complement: 9
Guns: 1 or 2—7.62 mm MGs.

Comment: Ordered in 1954.

6 RIO PUYANGO CLASS (COAST GUARD PATROL CRAFT)

Name	*No*	*Builders*	*Commissioned*
RIO PUYANGO	LGC 40	Halter Marine, New Orleans	June 1986
RIO MATAGE	LGC 41	Halter Marine, New Orleans	June 1986
RIO ZARUMILLA	LGC 42	Astinave, Guayaquil	11 Mar 1988
RIO CHONE	LGC 43	Astinave, Guayaquil	11 Mar 1988
RIO DAULE	LGC 44	Astinave, Guayaquil	17 June 1988
RIO BABAHOYO	LGC 45	Astinave, Guayaquil	17 June 1988

Displacement, tons: 17
Dimensions, feet (metres): 44 × 13.5 × 3.5 *(13.4 × 4.1 × 1.1)*
Main machinery: 2 Detroit 8V 71 TA diesels; 460 hp *(343 kW)* sustained; 2 shafts
Speed, knots: 26. **Range, miles:** 500 at 18 kts
Complement: 5 (1 officer)
Guns: 1—12.7 mm MG. 2—7.62 mm MGs.
Radars: Surface search: Furuno 2400; I band.

Comment: Two delivered by Halter Marine in June 1986. Four more ordered in February 1987; assembled under licence at Astinave shipyard, Guayaquil. Manned by the Coast Guard and used mainly for drug interdiction.

RIO PUYANGO *1/1988, Halter Marine*

2 ESPADA CLASS (LARGE PATROL CRAFT)

Name	*No*	*Builders*	*Commissioned*
5 DE AGOSTO	—	Moss Point Marine, Escatawpa	May 1991
27 DE FEBRERO	—	Moss Point Marine, Escatawpa	Nov 1991

Displacement, tons: 190 full load
Dimensions, feet (metres): 112 × 22.5 × 7 *(34.1 × 6.9 × 2.1)*
Main machinery: 2 Detroit 16V 149 TI diesels; 2790 hp *(2.08 MW)*; 1 Detroit 16V 92 TA; 690 hp *(514 kW)*; 3 shafts
Speed, knots: 27
Complement: 19 (5 officers)
Guns: 1 Bofors 40 mm/60. 2—12.7 mm MGs.
Radars: Surface search: Racal Decca; I band.

Comment: Steel hulls and aluminium superstructure. Accommodation is air-conditioned. Carry a 10 man RIB and launching crane on the stern.

5 DE AGOSTO (gun not fitted) *1991, Trinity Marine*

14 US 40 ft BAYCRAFT (COASTAL PATROL CRAFT)

Comment: Modified civilian sporting craft purchased in 1980.

EGYPT

Headquarters' Appointment

Commander of Naval Forces:
Vice Admiral Ahmed Ali Fadel

Diplomatic Representation

Naval Attaché in London:
Captain M Draz

Personnel

(a) 1992: 19 500 officers and men, including the Coast Guard (Reserves of about 15 000)
(b) 3 years' national service

Bases

Alexandria, Port Said, Mersa Matru, Abu Qir, Suez. Safaqa and Hurghada on the Red Sea.
Naval Academy: Abu Qir.

Coastal Defences

The Samlet, Otomat and modified CSS-N-1 Styx missiles employed for Coastal Defence by the Border Guard are naval-manned.

Maritime Air

Although the navy has no air arm the Air Force has a number of E2Cs, ASW Sea Kings and Gazelles with an ASM capability (see *Land-based Maritime Aircraft* section). The Sea Kings are controlled by the Anti-Submarine Brigade and have naval sensor operators.

Prefix to Ships' Name

ENS

Strength of the Fleet

Type	*Active*	*Building (Projected)*
Submarines (Patrol)	8	(2)
Destroyer	1	—
Frigates	4 (+ 1)	—
Fast Attack Craft (Missile)	22	—
Fast Attack Craft (Torpedo)	2	—
Fast Attack Craft (Gun)	8	—
Fast Attack Craft (Patrol)	8 (+ 5 P6)	—
LSMs	3	—
LCUs	9	—
Minesweepers (Ocean)	8	—
Minehunters (Inshore)	—	2 (4)
Support Ships	20	—
Coast Guard	78	—

Mercantile Marine

Lloyd's Register of Shipping:
444 vessels of 1 256 641 tons gross

DELETIONS

Submarines

1989 2 Romeo class

Light Forces

1988-89 3 Osa class, 2 October class

Amphibious Forces

1991 2 SMB 1 class, 3 Winchester Hovercraft

Mine Warfare Forces

1991 *El Fayoum, El Manufieh*

Miscellaneous

1990 *Rashid*
1991 1 Nyryat class

Coast Guard

1990 *Nimr, Nur, Al Bahr*

SUBMARINES

Note: After several attempts to buy second-hand had come to nothing, a request for quotation on two new construction submarines was made in September 1991. The German-built 209 or Dolphin class seem to be the most likely candidates.

4 Ex-SOVIET and 4 Ex-CHINESE ROMEO CLASS

831, 840, 843, 846—ex-Soviet
849, 852, 855, 858—ex-Chinese

Displacement, tons: 1475 surfaced; 1830 dived
Dimensions, feet (metres): 251.3 × 22 × 16.1 *(76.6 × 6.7 × 4.9)*
Main machinery: Diesel-electric; 2 Type 37-D diesels; 4000 hp(m) *(2.94 MW)*; 2 motors; 2700 hp(m) *(1.98 MW)*; 2 creep motors; 2 shafts
Speed, knots: 16 surfaced; 13 dived
Range, miles: 9000 at 9 kts surfaced
Complement: 54

Torpedoes: 8—21 in *(533 mm)* tubes (6 bow, 2 stern). 14 Soviet Type 53; dual purpose; pattern active/passive homing up to 20 km *(10.8 nm)* at up to 45 kts; warhead 400 kg.
Mines: 28 in lieu of torpedoes.
Countermeasures: ESM: Racal; radar warning
Fire control: Singer Librascope Mk 2 (in 4).
Radars: Surface search: Snoop Plate; I band.
Sonars: Hull-mounted; active/passive; high frequency.

Programmes: One Romeo class was transferred to Egypt by the USSR in 1966. Two more replaced Whiskey class in May 1966 and another pair was delivered later that year. The sixth boat joined in 1969. Two transferred from China 22 March 1982. Second pair arrived 3 January 1984, commissioned 21 May 1984.
Modernisation: The ex-Soviet submarines have been refitted with limited up-date to bridge the gap until completion of a full modernisation programme of the four ex-Chinese vessels. In early 1988 a five year contract was signed with Tacoma, Washington to retrofit the ex-Chinese submarines with Harpoon, and convert them to fire Mk 37 wire-guided torpedoes; weapon systems improvements to include Loral active sonar, Krupp Atlas passive sonar and either Ferranti or Singer Librascope FCS. The US Congress did not give approval to start work until July 1989 and the first submarine is unlikely to complete before late 1993.
Operational: Two Soviet submarines deleted in 1989 and of the remaining four Soviet type, only one was operating regularly in 1991.

ROMEO Class (ex-Chinese) (old number) *1984*

ROMEO Class (old number) *1987*

DESTROYER

1 Ex-BRITISH Z CLASS

Name	No	Builders	Laid down	Launched	Commissioned
EL FATEH (ex-HMS *Zenith*, ex-HMS *Wessex*)	921	Wm Denny & Bros, Dumbarton	19 May 1942	5 June 1944	22 Dec 1944

Displacement, tons: 1730 standard; 2575 full load
Dimensions, feet (metres): 362.8 × 35.7 × 16 *(110.6 × 10.9 × 4.9)*
Main machinery: 2 Admiralty boilers; 2 Parsons turbines; 40 000 hp *(30 MW)*; 2 shafts
Speed, knots: 31. **Range, miles:** 2800 at 20 kts
Complement: 186

Guns: 4 Vickers 4.5 in *(115 mm)*/45 hand loaded Mk 5 mounting; 50° elevation; 14 rounds/minute to 17 km *(9.3 nm)*; weight of shell 25 kg.
6 China 37 mm/63 (3 twin); 180 rounds/minute to 8.5 km *(4.6 nm)*; weight of shell 1.42 kg.
Torpedoes: 4—21 in *(533 mm)* (quad) tubes. Probably Soviet anti-surface Type 53.
Depth charges: 4 projectors.
Fire control: Fly 4 director.
Radars: Air search: Marconi SNW 10; probably D band.
Surface search: Racal Decca 916; I band.
Fire control: Marconi Type 275; F band.

Programmes: Purchased from the UK in 1955. Before being taken over by Egypt, *El Fateh* was refitted by John I. Thornycroft & Co Ltd, Woolston, Southampton in July 1956, subsequently modernised by J S White & Co Ltd, Cowes, completed in July 1964.
Modernisation: Bofors replaced by Chinese 37 mm guns. Sonars removed.
Operational: Is still being used for sea training.

EL FATEH *5/1985, van Ginderen Collection*

FRIGATES

Note: The old Black Swan class frigate *Tariq* was once again seen conducting sea training days in 1991.

2 DESCUBIERTA CLASS

Name	No	Builders	Laid down	Launched	Commissioned
ABU QIR (ex-*Serviola*)	F 941	Bazán	28 Feb 1979	20 Dec 1979	27 Oct 1984
EL SUEZ (ex-*Centinela*)	F 946	Bazán	31 Oct 1978	6 Oct 1979	21 May 1984

Displacement, tons: 1233 standard; 1479 full load
Dimensions, feet (metres): 291.3 × 34 × 12.5 *(88.8 × 10.4 × 3.8)*
Main machinery: 4 MTU-Bazán 16V 956 TB 91 diesels; 15 000 hp(m) *(11 MW)* sustained; 2 shafts; cp props
Speed, knots: 25.5; 28 trials. **Range, miles:** 4000 at 18 kts
Complement: 116

Missiles: SSM: 8 McDonnell Douglas Harpoon (2 quad) launchers ❶; active radar homing to 130 km *(70 nm)* at 0.9 Mach; warhead 227 kg.
SAM: Selenia Elsag Albatros octuple launcher ❷; 24 Aspide; semi-active radar homing to 13 km *(7 nm)* at 2.5 Mach; height envelope 15-5000 m *(49.2-16 405 ft)*; warhead 30 kg.
Guns: 1 OTO Melara 3 in *(76 mm)*/62 compact ❸; 85° elevation; 85 rounds/minute to 16 km *(8.7 nm)*; weight of shell 6 kg.
2 Bofors 40 mm/70 ❹; 85° elevation; 300 rounds/minute to 12.5 km *(6.8 nm)*; weight of shell 0.96 kg.
Torpedoes: 6—324 mm Mk 32 (2 triple) tubes ❺. MUSL Stingray; anti-submarine; active/passive homing to 11 km *(5.9 nm)* at 45 kts; warhead 35 kg (shaped charge); depth to 750 m *(2460 ft)*.
A/S mortars: 1 Bofors 375 mm twin-barrelled trainable launcher ❻; automatic loading; range 1600 m or 3600 m depending on type of rocket.

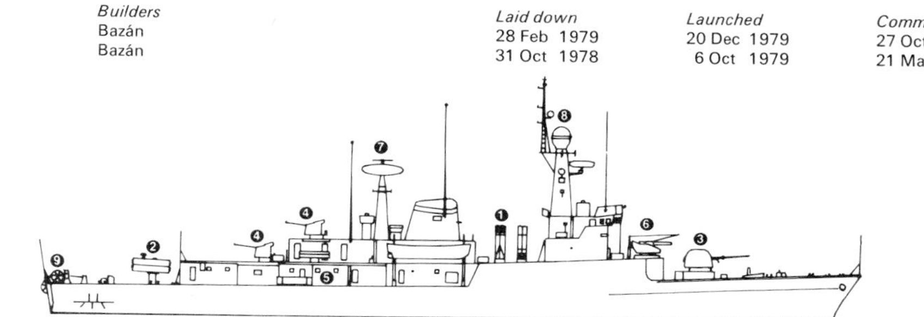
EL SUEZ *(Scale 1 : 900), Ian Sturton*

Countermeasures: ESM: Elettronica SpA Beta; radar intercept. Prairie Masker; acoustic signature suppression.
Combat data systems: Signaal SEWACO action data automation. Link Y.
Radars: Air/surface search: Signaal DA 05 ❼; E/F band; range 137 km *(75 nm)* for 2 m² target.
Navigation: Signaal ZW 06; I band.
Fire control: Signaal WM 25 ❽; I/J band; range 46 km *(25 nm)*.
Sonars: Raytheon 1160B; hull-mounted; active search and attack; medium frequency.
Raytheon 1167 ❾; VDS; active search; 12-7.5 kHz.

Programmes: Ordered September 1982 from Bazán, Spain. The two Spanish ships *Centinela* and *Serviola* were sold to Egypt prior to completion and transferred after completion at Ferrol and modification at Cartagena. *El Suez* completed 28 February 1984 and *Abu Qir* on 31 July 1984.
Operational: Stabilisers fitted. Modern noise insulation of main and auxiliary machinery.

EL SUEZ *10/1991*

2 CHINESE JIANGHU I CLASS

Name	No	Builders	Commissioned
NAJIM AL ZAFFER	951	Hutong, Shanghai	27 Oct 1984
EL NASSER	956	Hutong, Shanghai	16 Apr 1985

Displacement, tons: 1425 standard; 1702 full load
Dimensions, feet (metres): 338.5 × 35.4 × 10.2 *(103.2 × 10.8 × 3.1)*
Main machinery: 2 SEMT-Pielstick 12 PA6 280 BTC diesels; 14 400 hp(m) *(10.6 MW)* sustained; 2 shafts
Speed, knots: 26. **Range, miles:** 4000 at 15 kts
Complement: 195

Missiles: SSM: 4 Hai Ying 2 (Flying Dragon) (2 twin) ❶; active radar or passive IR homing to 80 km *(43.2 nm)* at 0.9 Mach; warhead 513 kg.
Guns: 4 China 57 mm/70 (2 twin) ❷; 85° elevation; 120 rounds/minute to 12 km *(6.5 nm)*; weight of shell 6.31 kg.
12 China 37 mm/63 (6 twin) ❸; 85° elevation; 180 rounds/minute to 8.5 km *(4.6 nm)*; weight of shell 1.42 kg.
A/S mortars: 2 RBU 1200 5-tubed fixed launchers ❹; range 1200 m; warhead 34 kg.
Depth charges: 2 projectors; 2 racks.
Mines: Up to 60.
Countermeasures: ESM: Elettronica SpA Beta; radar intercept.
Radars: Air search: Type 765 ❺.
Surface search: Eye Shield ❻; E band.
Surface search/gun direction: Square Tie; I band; range 73 km *(40 nm)*.
Navigation: Decca; I band.
Sonars: Hull-mounted; active search and attack; high frequency.

Programmes: Ordered in 1982. This is a Jianghu I class modified with 57 mm guns vice the standard 100 mm.
Modernisation: Combat data system to be fitted together with optronic fire control directors. There are also plans to remove the after superstructure and guns and build a flight deck for a LAMPS helicopter.
Structure: The funnel is the rounded type of the Jianghu class.

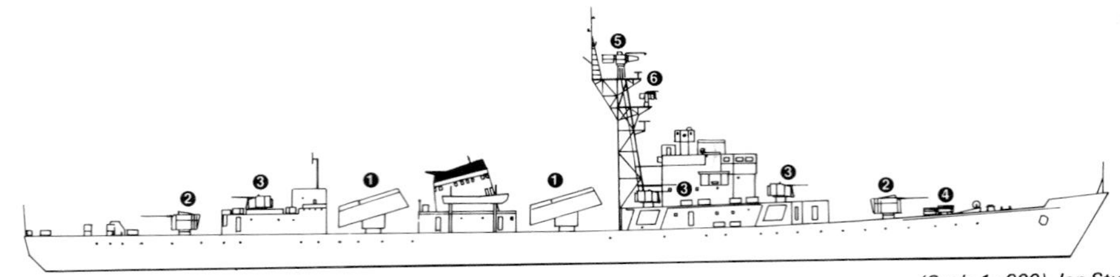

NAJIM AL ZAFFER *(Scale 1 : 900), Ian Sturton*

EL NASSER *6/1991, Campanera i Rovira*

NAJIM AL ZAFFER *12/1990*

LAND-BASED MARITIME AIRCRAFT (FRONT LINE)

Note: All Badger and Beagle aircraft non-operational by late 1991.

Numbers/Type: 12 Aerospatiale SA 342L Gazelle.
Operational speed: 142 kts *(264 km/h)*.
Service ceiling: 14 105 ft *(4300 m)*.
Range: 407 nm *(755 km)*.
Role/Weapon systems: Land-based helicopter for coastal anti-shipping strike, particularly against FAC and insurgents. Sensors: SFIM sight. Weapons: ASV; 2 × AS-12 wire-guided missiles.

Numbers/Type: 5 Grumman E-2C Hawkeye.
Operational speed: 269 kts *(499 km/h)*.
Service ceiling: 30 800 ft *(9390 m)*.
Range: 1350 nm *(2500 km)*.
Role/Weapon systems: Airborne early warning and control tasks; capable of handling up to 30 tracks over water or land. Sensors: APS-125 search/warning radar, various ESM/ECM systems. Weapons: Unarmed.

Numbers/Type: 15 Westland Sea King Mk 47.
Operational speed: 112 kts *(208 km/h)*.
Service ceiling: 14 700 ft *(4480 m)*.
Range: 664 nm *(1230 km)*.
Role/Weapon systems: Shore-based helicopter for ASW and surface search; secondary role as SAR helicopter; may be embarked in due course. Airframe and engine refurbishment in 1990 for first five. Sensors: MEL search radar. Weapons: ASW; 4 × Mk 46 or Stingray torpedoes or depth bombs. ASV; Otomat.

Numbers/Type: 2 Beechcraft 1900C.
Operational speed: 267 kts *(495 km/h)*.
Service ceiling: 25 000 ft *(7620 m)*.
Range: 1569 nm *(2907 km)*.
Role/Weapon systems: Two (of six) Air Force aircraft acquired in 1988 and used for maritime surveillance. Sensors: Litton search radar; Motorola multi-mode SLAMMR radar; Singer S-3075 ESM; Data Link Y. Weapons: Unarmed.

LIGHT FORCES

Note: 1. Five modified ex-Soviet P 6 class (Fast Attack Craft—Patrol) with BM 21 rocket launchers were active in 1991 (pennant numbers 201, 243, 246, 251, 253).
2. Two Komar class were also brought out of reserve in 1991.

6 RAMADAN CLASS (FAST ATTACK CRAFT—MISSILE)

Name	*No*	*Builders*	*Laid down*	*Launched*	*Commissioned*
RAMADAN	670	Vosper Thornycroft	22 Sep 1978	6 Sep 1979	20 July 1981
KHYBER	672	Vosper Thornycroft	23 Feb 1979	31 Jan 1980	15 Sep 1981
EL KADESSAYA	674	Vosper Thornycroft	24 Apr 1979	19 Feb 1980	6 Apr 1982
EL YARMOUK	676	Vosper Thornycroft	15 May 1979	12 June 1980	18 May 1982
BADR	678	Vosper Thornycroft	29 Sep 1979	17 June 1981	17 June1982
HETTEIN	680	Vosper Thornycroft	29 Feb 1980	25 Nov 1980	28 Oct 1982

Displacement, tons: 307 full load
Dimensions, feet (metres): 170.6 × 25 × 7.5 *(52 × 7.6 × 2.3)*
Main machinery: 4 MTU 20V 538 TB91 diesels; 15 360 hp(m) *(11.29 MW)* sustained; 4 shafts
Speed, knots: 40. **Range, miles:** 1600 at 18 kts
Complement: 30 (4 officers)

Missiles: SSM: 4 OTO Melara/Matra Otomat Mk 1; active radar homing to 80 km *(43.2 nm)* at 0.9 Mach; warhead 210 kg.
Guns: 1 OTO Melara 3 in *(76 mm)* compact; 85° elevation; 85 rounds/minute to 16 km *(8.7 nm)*; weight of shell 6 kg.
2 Breda 40 mm/70 (twin); 85° elevation; 300 rounds/minute to 12.5 km *(6.8 nm)* anti-surface; weight of shell 0.96 kg.
Countermeasures: Decoys: 4 Protean fixed launchers each with 4 magazines containing 36 Chaff decoy and IR flare grenades.
ESM: Racal Cutlass; radar intercept.
ECM: Racal Cygnus; jammer.
Combat data systems: Ferranti CAAIS action data automation.
Fire control: Marconi Sapphire System with 2 radar/TV and 2 optical directors.
Radars: Air/surface search: Marconi S 820; E/F band; range 73 km *(40 nm)*.
Navigation: Marconi S 810; I band; range 48 km *(25 nm)*.
Fire control: Two Marconi ST 802; I band.

Programmes: The contract was carried out at the Porchester yard of Vosper Thornycroft Ltd with some hulls built at Portsmouth Old Yard, being towed to Porchester for fitting out.
Modernisation: The intention is to double the SSM capability with eight lightweight Otomat or Harpoon.
Operational: Portable SAM SA-N-5 sometimes carried.

HETTEIN *10/1991*

4 Ex-SOVIET OSA I CLASS (FAST ATTACK CRAFT—MISSILE)

633 637 641 643

Displacement, tons: 171 standard; 210 full load
Dimensions, feet (metres): 110.2 × 24.9 × 8.9 *(33.6 × 7.6 × 2.7)*
Main machinery: 3 MTU diesels; 12 000 hp(m) *(8.82 MW)*; 3 shafts
Speed, knots: 35. **Range, miles:** 400 at 34 kts
Complement: 30

Missiles: SSM: 4 SS-N-2A Styx; active radar or IR homing to 46 km *(25 nm)* at 0.9 Mach; altitude pre-set up to 300 m *(984.3 ft)*; warhead 513 kg.
SAM: SA-N-5 Grail; manual aiming; IR homing to 6 km *(3.2 nm)* at 1.5 Mach; altitude to 2500 m *(8000 ft)*; warhead 1.5 kg.
Guns: 4 USSR 30 mm/65 (2 twin); 85° elevation; 500 rounds/minute to 5 km *(2.7 nm)* anti-aircraft; weight of shell 0.54 kg.
2—12.7 mm MGs.
Countermeasures: ESM: Radar warning.
Radars: Air/surface search: Kelvin Hughes; I band.
Navigation: Racal Decca 916; I band.
Fire control: Drum Tilt; H/I band.
IFF: High Pole. Square Head.

Programmes: Thirteen reported to have been delivered to Egypt by the Soviet Navy in 1966-68 but some were sunk in war with Israel, October 1973. Four of the remaining seven were derelict in 1989 but one more was back in service in 1991.
Modernisation: Refitted with MTU diesels and two machine guns.

OSA 633 *1986*

6 EGYPTIAN OCTOBER CLASS (FAST ATTACK CRAFT—MISSILE)

781 783 785 787 789 791

Displacement, tons: 82 full load
Dimensions, feet (metres): 84 × 20 × 5 *(25.5 × 6.1 × 1.3)*
Main machinery: 4 CRM 18V-12D/55 YE diesels; 5400 hp(m) *(3.97 MW)*; 4 shafts
Speed, knots: 40. **Range, miles:** 400 at 30 kts
Complement: 20

Missiles: SSM: 2 OTO Melara/Matra Otomat Mk 1; active radar homing to 80 km *(43.2 nm)* at 0.9 Mach; warhead 210 kg.
Guns: 4 BMARC/Oerlikon 30 mm/75 (2 twin); 85° elevation; 650 rounds/minute to 10 km *(5.5 nm)* anti-surface; 3 km *(1.6 nm)* anti-aircraft; weight of shell 1 kg and 0.36 kg mixed.
Countermeasures: Decoys: 2 Protean fixed launchers each with 4 magazines containing 36 Chaff decoy and IR flare grenades.
ESM: Matilda; radar warning.
Fire control: Marconi Sapphire radar/TV system.
Radars: Air/surface search: Marconi S 810; range 48 km *(25 nm)*.
Fire control: Marconi/ST 802; I band.

Programmes: Built in Alexandria 1975-76. Hull of same design as Soviet Komar class. Refitted by Vosper Thornycroft, completed 1979-81. 791 was washed overboard on return trip, recovered and returned to Portsmouth for refit. Left UK after repairs on 12 August 1982.

OCTOBER Class *7/1980, Wright and Logan*

6 CHINESE HEGU CLASS (FAST ATTACK CRAFT—MISSILE)

609 611 613 615 617 619

Displacement, tons: 68 standard; 79.2 full load
Dimensions, feet (metres): 88.6 × 20.7 × 4.3 *(27 × 6.3 × 1.3)*
Main machinery: 4 Type L-12V-180 diesels; 4800 hp(m) *(3.53 MW)*; 4 shafts
Speed, knots: 37.5. **Range, miles:** 400 at 30 kts
Complement: 17 (2 officers)

Missiles: SSM: 2 Fei Lung 2 (Flying Dragon); active radar or passive IR homing to 95 km *(51 nm)* at 0.9 Mach; warhead 513 kg.
Guns: 2—23 mm (twin); locally constructed to fit 25 mm mounting.
Radars: Air/surface search: Square Tie; I band; range 73 km *(40 nm)* (mounted in radome).
IFF: High Pole A.

Programmes: All commissioned in Egypt on 27 October 1984. Reported that two may be non-operational.

HEGU 615 *4/1988, A. Sheldon Duplaix*

8 Ex-CHINESE HAINAN CLASS (FAST ATTACK CRAFT—PATROL)

AL NOUR 430 **AL HADY** 433 **AL HAKIM** 436 **AL WAKIL** 439
AL QATAR 442 **AL SADDAM** 445 **AL SALAM** 448 **AL RAFIA** 451

Displacement, tons: 375 standard; 392 full load
Dimensions, feet (metres): 192.8 × 23.6 × 6 *(58.8 × 7.2 × 2.2)*
Main machinery: 4 PRC/Kolumna Type 9-D-8 diesels; 4400 hp *(3.23 MW)*; 4 shafts
Speed, knots: 30.5. **Range, miles:** 1300 at 15 kts
Complement: 69

Guns: 4 China 57 mm/70 (2 twin); 85° elevation; 120 rounds/minute to 12 km *(6.5 nm)*; weight of shell 6.31 kg.
4—23 mm (2 twin); locally constructed to fit the 25 mm mountings.
A/S mortars: 4 RBU 1200 fixed 5-tubed launchers; range 1200 m; warhead 34 kg.
Depth charges: 2 projectors; 2 racks.
Mines: Rails fitted.
Radars: Surface search: Pot Head; I band; range 37 km *(20 nm)*.
Navigation: Decca; I band.
IFF: High Pole.
Sonars: Hull-mounted; active search and attack; high frequency.

Programmes: First pair transferred to Egypt in October 1983, next three in February 1984 (commissioned 21 May 1984) and last three late 1984.
Modernisation: Two to be fitted with 6—324 mm (2 triple) tubes for MUSL Stingray torpedoes and with Singer Librascope fire control in due course. If successful the remainder of the class may follow.

6 Ex-SOVIET SHERSHEN CLASS (FAST ATTACK CRAFT—2 TORPEDO, 4 GUN)

751 753 755 757 759 761

Displacement, tons: 145 standard; 170 full load
Dimensions, feet (metres): 113.8 × 22 × 4.9 *(34.7 × 6.7 × 1.5)*
Main machinery: 3 M503A diesels; 12 000 hp(m) *(8.8 MW)*; 3 shafts
Speed, knots: 45 kts. **Range, miles:** 850 at 30 kts
Complement: 23

Missiles: SAM: SA-N-5 Grail *(755-761)*; manual aiming; IR homing to 6 km *(3.2 nm)* at 1.5 Mach; warhead 1.5 kg.
Guns: 4 USSR 30 mm/65 (2 twin); 85° elevation; 500 rounds/minute to 5 km *(2.7 nm)*; weight of shell 0.54 kg.
2 USSR 122 mm rocket launchers *(755-761* in lieu of torpedo tubes); 20 barrels per launcher; range 9 km *(5 nm)*.
Torpedoes: 4—21 in *(533 mm)* tubes *(751* and *753)*. Soviet Type 53; dual purpose; pattern active/passive homing up to 20 km *(10.8 nm)* at up to 45 kts; warhead 400 kg.
Depth charges: 12.
Radars: Surface search: Pot Drum; H/I band.
Fire control: Drum Tilt, H/I band.
IFF: High Pole.

Programmes: Five delivered from USSR in 1967 and two more in 1968. One deleted. 753 completed an extensive refit at Ismailia in 1987; 751 in 1988.
Structure: The last four have had their torpedo tubes removed to make way for multiple BM21 rocket-launchers and one SA-N-5 Grail.

SHERSHEN (with SA-N-5) *6/1990*

4 Ex-CHINESE SHANGHAI II CLASS (FAST ATTACK CRAFT—GUN)

793 795 797 799

Displacement, tons: 113 standard; 131 full load
Dimensions, feet (metres): 127.3 × 17.7 × 5.6 *(38.8 × 5.4 × 1.7)*
Main machinery: 2 Type L12-180 diesels; 2400 hp(m) *(1.76 MW)* (forward); 2 Type L12-180Z diesels; 1820 hp(m) *(1.34 MW)* (aft); 4 shafts
Speed, knots: 30. **Range, miles:** 700 at 16.5 kts
Complement: 34

Guns: 4 China 37 mm/63 (2 twin); 85° elevation; 180 rounds/minute to 8.5 km *(4.6 nm)*; weight of shell 1.42 kg.
4—23 mm (2 twin); locally constructed to fit the 25 mm mountings.
Mines: Rails can be fitted for 10 mines.
Radars: Surface search: Pot Head; I band; range 37 km *(20 nm)*.
IFF: High Pole.

Programmes: Transferred in 1984.
Structure: Painted black.

SHANGHAI II 793 *3/1987*

AMPHIBIOUS FORCES

Note: There are plans to build landing craft locally, probably to a Chinese design. There is also the possibility of leasing an LST/LSM from the US.

10 SEAFOX TYPE (SWIMMER DELIVERY CRAFT)

21-30

Displacement, tons: 11.3 full load
Dimensions, feet (metres): 36.1 × 9.8 × 2.6 *(11 × 3 × 0.8)*
Main machinery: 2 GM 6V-92TA diesels; 520 hp *(388 kW)*; 2 shafts
Speed, knots: 30
Complement: 3
Guns: 2—12.7 mm MGs. 2—7.62 mm MGs.

Comment: Ordered from Uniflite, Washington in 1982. GRP construction painted black. There is a strong underwater team in the Egyptian Navy who are also known to use commercial two-man underwater chariots.

3 Ex-SOVIET POLNOCHNY A CLASS (LSMs)

Displacement, tons: 800 full load
Dimensions, feet (metres): 239.5 × 27.9 × 5.8 *(73 × 8.5 × 1.8)*
Main machinery: 2 Type 40D diesels; 5000 hp(m) *(3.68 MW)*; 2 shafts
Speed, knots: 19. **Range, miles:** 1000 at 18 kts
Complement: 40
Military lift: 6 tanks; 350 tons
Guns: 2 USSR 30 mm/65 (twin); 85° elevation; 500 rounds/minute to 5 km *(2.7 nm)*; weight of shell 0.54 kg.
2—140 mm rocket launchers; 18 barrels to 9 km *(4.9 nm)*.
Radars: Surface search: Don 2; I band.
Fire control: Drum Tilt; H/I band.

Comment: Transferred 1973-74. All used for Gulf logistic support in 1990-91.

POLNOCHNY A 1987

9 Ex-SOVIET VYDRA CLASS (LCUs)

330 332 334 336 338
340 342 344 346

Displacement, tons: 425 standard; 600 full load
Dimensions, feet (metres): 179.7 × 25.3 × 6.6 *(54.8 × 7.7 × 2)*
Main machinery: 2—3D 12 diesels; 630 hp(m) *(463 kW)*; 2 shafts
Speed, knots: 11. **Range, miles:** 2500 at 10 kts
Complement: 20
Military lift: 200 troops; 250 tons.

Comment: Built in late 1960s, transferred 1968-69. For a period after the Israeli war of October 1973 several were fitted with rocket launchers and two 37 or 40 mm guns, all of which have now been removed. At least two are in reserve.

VYDRA Class (old number) 1989

MINE WARFARE FORCES

Ex-SOVIET T 43 CLASS (MINESWEEPERS—OCEAN)

ASSIOUT 516 SINAI 513 GHARBIYA 501 DAQAHLIYA 507

Displacement, tons: 580 full load
Dimensions, feet (metres): 190.2 × 27.6 × 6.9 *(58 × 8.4 × 2.1)*
Main machinery: 2 Kolumna Type 9-D-8 diesels; 2200 hp(m) *(1.62 MW)*; 2 shafts
Speed, knots: 15. **Range, miles:** 3000 at 10 kts
Complement: 65
Guns: 4—37 mm/63 (2 twin); 85° elevation; 160 rounds/minute to 9 km *(5 nm)*; weight of shell 0.7 kg.
8—12.7 mm MGs.
Mines: Can carry 20.

Comment: Delivered in the early 1970s. Others of the class have been sunk or used as targets or cannibalised for spares. The plan to fit them with VDS sonars and ROVs may have been shelved in favour of new minehunters.

ASSIOUT 10/1987, W. Donko

4 Ex-SOVIET YURKA CLASS (MINESWEEPERS—OCEAN)

GIZA 533 ASWAN 530 QENA 536 SOHAG 539

Displacement, tons: 460 full load
Dimensions, feet (metres): 170.6 × 30.8 × 8.5 *(52 × 9.4 × 2.6)*
Main machinery: 2 diesels; 5500 hp(m) *(4 MW)*; 2 shafts
Speed, knots: 17. **Range, miles:** 1500 at 12 kts
Complement: 60
Guns: 4 USSR 30 mm/65 (2 twin); 85° elevation; 500 rounds/minute to 5 km *(2.7 nm)*; weight of shell 0.54 kg.
Mines: Can lay 10.
Radars: Navigation: Don; I band.

Comment: Steel-hulled minesweepers transferred from the USSR in 1969. Built 1963-69. Egyptian Yurka class do not carry Drum Tilt radar and have a number of ship's-side scuttles. The plan to equip them with VDS sonar and ROVs may have been shelved in favour of new minehunters.

ASWAN 10/1986

0 + 2 (4) INSHORE MINEHUNTERS

Displacement, tons: 175 full load
Dimensions, feet (metres): 110 × 27 × 5.5 *(33.5 × 8.2 × 1.7)*
Main machinery: 2 MTU diesels; 1034 hp(m) *(760 kW)*; 2 shafts
Speed, knots: 12.4
Complement: 17

Comment: Route survey vessels with GRP hulls ordered from Swiftships in June 1991 with FMS funding. These are very small ships with limited MCMV capability and it is reported that the operational requirement is being reviewed in favour of larger vessels of about 500 tons.

SAFAGA 610 ABU EL GHOSON 613

Displacement, tons: 20
Complement: 18 (4 officers)

Comment: Launched in 1968. Route survey vessels belonging to the Minesweeper flotilla.

SUPPORT SHIPS

6 SOVIET TOPLIVO 2 CLASS (YARD TANKERS)

MARYUT ATBARAH 214 AYEDA 3 216 + 4

Displacement, tons: 1200 full load
Dimensions, feet (metres): 178.1 × 30.8 × 11.2 *(54.3 × 9.4 × 3.4)*
Main machinery: 1 diesel; 600 hp(m) *(441 kW)*; 1 shaft
Speed, knots: 10. **Range, miles:** 400 at 7 kts
Complement: 16
Cargo capacity: 500 tons diesel (some used for water)

Comment: Built in Egypt in 1972-77.

1 Ex-SOVIET NYRYAT I CLASS

Displacement, tons: 120 full load
Dimensions, feet (metres): 93 × 18 × 5.5 *(28.4 × 5.5 × 1.7)*
Main machinery: 1 diesel; 450 hp(m) *(330 kW)*; 1 shaft
Speed, knots: 12
Complement: 15

Comment: Diving support ship transferred in 1964.

2 Ex-SOVIET POLUCHAT I CLASS

Displacement, tons: 100 full load
Dimensions, feet (metres): 97.1 × 19 × 4.8 *(29.6 × 5.8 × 1.5)*
Main machinery: 2 M 50 diesels; 1700 hp(m) *(1.25 MW)*; 2 shafts
Speed, knots: 20
Complement: 15

Comment: Torpedo recovery craft.

6 Ex-SOVIET OKHTENSKY CLASS (TUGS)

AL MEKS 103
AL AGAMI 105
ANTAR 107
AL DIKHILA 109
AL ISKANDARANI 111
— 113

Displacement, tons: 930 full load
Dimensions, feet (metres): 156.1 × 34 × 13.4 *(47.6 × 10.4 × 4.1)*
Main machinery: Diesel-electric; 2 diesel generators; 1 motor; 1500 hp(m) *(1.1 MW)*; 1 shaft
Speed, knots: 13. **Range, miles:** 6000 at 13 kts
Complement: 38

Comment: Two transferred to the Egyptian Navy in 1966, others assembled in Egypt.

AL AGAMI *5/1991, F. Sadek*

AMIRA RAMA

Comment: An ex-trawler used as a lighthouse tender and acquired by the Navy in 1987.

5 TRAINING SHIPS

Comment: *Al Kousser* is a 1000 ton vessel belonging to the Naval Academy. *Intishat* is a 500 ton training ship. Pennant number 160 is a USSR Sekstan class used as a cadet training ship. Two YSB training craft acquired from the USA in 1989. A 3300 ton training ship *Aida IV* presented by Japan in 1988 for delivery in March 1992 belongs to the Arab Maritime Transport Academy.

COAST GUARD

10 SWIFTSHIPS 93 ft CLASS

335-343 **346**

Displacement, tons: 102 full load
Dimensions, feet (metres): 93.2 × 18.7 × 4.9 *(28.4 × 5.7 × 1.5)*
Main machinery: 2 MTU 12V 331 TC92 diesels; 2660 hp(m) *(1.96 MW)* sustained; 2 shafts
Speed, knots: 27. **Range, miles:** 900 at 12 kts
Complement: 14 (2 officers)
Guns: 2 Oerlikon 20 mm.

Comment: Ordered November 1983. First three built in USA, remainder assembled in Egypt. First four commissioned 16 April 1985.

SWIFTSHIPS 93ft Class *10/1986*

3 NISR CLASS (LARGE PATROL CRAFT)

NISR 713 **THAR** +1

Displacement, tons: 110 full load
Dimensions, feet (metres): 102 × 18 × 4.9 *(31 × 5.2 × 1.5)*
Main machinery: 2 Maybach diesels; 3000 hp(m) *(2.2 MW)*; 2 shafts
Speed, knots: 24
Guns: 1 Oerlikon 20 mm.

Comment: Built by Castro, Port Said. First three launched in May 1963, two of which have been scrapped. Two more completed 1983.

12 TIMSAH CLASS (LARGE PATROL CRAFT)

01-12

Displacement, tons: 100
Dimensions, feet (metres): 101.8 × 17 × 4.8 *(30.5 × 5.2 × 1.5)*
Main machinery: 2 MTU 8V 331 TC92 diesels; 1770 hp *(1.3 MW)* sustained; 2 shafts (first 6); 2 MTU 12V 331 TC92 diesels; 2660 hp(m) *(1.96 MW)* sustained; 2 shafts (second 6)
Speed, knots: 25
Complement: 13
Guns: 2 Oerlikon 30 mm (twin) or 2 Oerlikon 20 mm.

Comment: First three completed December 1981, second three December 1982 at Timsah SY, Ismailia. Further six ordered in January 1985 and completed in 1988-89 with a different type of engine and with waterline exhaust vice a funnel.

TIMSAH Class *9/1987, F. Sadek*

6 CRESTITALIA 70 ft CLASS (COASTAL PATROL CRAFT)

Displacement, tons: 36 full load
Dimensions, feet (metres): 68.9 × 17.4 × 3 *(21 × 5.3 × 0.9)*
Main machinery: 2 MTU 12V 331 TC92 diesels; 2660 hp(m) *(1.96 MW)* sustained; 2 shafts
Speed, knots: 35. **Range, miles:** 500 at 32 kts
Guns: 2 Oerlikon 30 mm A32 (twin). 1 Oerlikon 20 mm.

Comment: Ordered 1980—GRP hulls. Naval manned, employed on Coast Guard duties.

CRESTITALIA 70 ft *1980, Crestitalia*

6 SMALL PATROL CRAFT

Displacement, tons: 10
Main machinery: 1 diesel; 1 shaft

Comment: Ordered from Canal Naval Construction, Port Fuad on 12 December 1983. Two more delivered for port service in Alexandria in October 1989.

7 BERTRAM TYPE (COASTAL PATROL CRAFT)

702-708

Displacement, tons: 3
Dimensions, feet (metres): 28 × — × — *(8.5 × — × —)*
Main machinery: 2 Mercury diesels; 340 hp *(254 kW)*; 2 shafts
Speed, knots: 36
Guns: 2—7.62 mm MGs.

Comment: GRP hulls. Built in Miami, Florida in 1973. Armament changed on transfer. One of the original 20 craft is part of a permanent military Panorama Exhibition in Cairo.

BERTRAM Type *10/197-*

30 DC 35 TYPE

Displacement, tons: 4
Dimensions, feet (metres): 35.1 × 11.5 × 2.6 *(10.7 × 3.5 × 0.8)*
Main machinery: 2 diesels; 390 hp *(287 kW)*; 2 shafts
Speed, knots: 25
Complement: 4

Comment: Built by Dawncraft, Wroxham, UK, 1982.

4 DAMEN TYPE TUGS

KHOUFAN **KHAFRA** **RAMSES** **KARIR**

Comment: Delivered by Damen, Netherlands in 1982.

EL SALVADOR

Ministerial

Minister of Defence and Public Security:
General Rene Emilio Ponce

Senior Officer

Commander of the Navy:
Captain Fernando Menjivar Campos

Personnel

(a) 1992: 2200 (including 700 Marines and 650 Commandos)
(b) Voluntary service

Ports

Acajutla, La Libertad, El Triunfo y La Union

Mercantile Marine

Lloyd's Register of Shipping:
12 vessels of 1529 tons gross

DELETIONS

1988-90 *GC 1, GC 5* (sunk)

3 CAMCRAFT TYPE

GC 6, GC 7, GC 8

Displacement, tons: 100 full load
Dimensions, feet (metres): 100 × 21 × 4.9 *(30.5 × 6.4 × 1.5)*
Main machinery: 3 Detroit 12V-71TA diesels; 2325 hp *(1.73 MW)*; 3 shafts
Speed, knots: 25. **Range, miles:** 780 at 24 kts
Complement: 10
Guns: 1 Oerlikon 20 mm or 1—12.7 mm MG. 2—7.62 mm MGs.
Radars: Surface search: Racal Decca; I band.

Comment: Delivered October, November, December 1975. Refitted in 1986. Sometimes carry a combined 12.7 mm MG/81 mm mortar mounting in the stern.

GC 6 and 7 *1984*

1 SWIFTSHIPS 77 ft CLASS

GC 11

Displacement, tons: 48 full load
Dimensions, feet (metres): 77.1 × 20 × 4.9 *(23.5 × 6.1 × 1.5)*
Main machinery: 3 Detroit 12V-71TA diesels; 2325 hp *(1.73 MW)*; 3 shafts
Speed, knots: 26
Guns: 2—12.7 mm MGs. Aft MG combined with 81 mm mortar.
Radars: Surface search: Furuno; I band.

Comment: Aluminium hull. Delivered by Swiftships, Morgan City in June 1985.

GC11 *1986, Swiftships*

6 PIRANHA CLASS

LOF 1-6

Displacement, tons: 8.2 full load
Dimensions, feet (metres): 36 × 10.1 × 1.6 *(11 × 3.1 × 0.5)*
Main machinery: 2 Caterpillar 3208 TA diesels; 680 hp *(507 kW)* sustained; 2 shafts
Speed, knots: 26
Complement: 5
Guns: 2—12.7 mm (twin) MGs. 2—7.62 mm (twin) MGs.
Radars: Surface search: Furuno 3600; I band.

Comment: Riverine craft with Kevlar hulls. Completed in March 1987 by Lantana Boatyard, Florida. Same type supplied to Honduras.

PIRANHA Class *1988, Julio Montes*

1 SWIFTSHIPS 65 ft CLASS

GC 10

Displacement, tons: 36 full load
Dimensions, feet (metres): 65.6 × 18.3 × 5 *(20 × 6 × 1.5)*
Main machinery: 2 Detroit 12V-71TA diesels; 1550 hp *(1.15 MW)*; 2 shafts
Speed, knots: 23. **Range, miles:** 600 at 18 kts
Complement: 6
Guns: 1 Oerlikon 20 mm. 1 or 2—12.7 mm MGs.
Radars: Surface search: Furuno; I band.

Comment: Aluminium hull. Delivered by Swiftships, Morgan City in June 1984. Was laid up for a time in 1989/90 but became operational again in 1991.

GC10 *1986, Julio Montes*

10 PROTECTOR CLASS

LP 03 1-10

Displacement, tons: 9 full load
Dimensions, feet (metres): 40.4 × 13.4 × 1.4 *(12.3 × 4 × 0.4)*
Main machinery: 2 Caterpillar 3208 TA diesels; 680 hp *(507 kW)* sustained; 2 shafts
Speed, knots: 28. **Range, miles:** 350 at 20 kts
Complement: 4
Guns: 2—12.7 mm MGs. 2—7.62 mm MGs.
Radars: Navigation: Furuno 3600; I band.

Comment: Ordered in December 1987 from SeaArk Marine (ex-MonArk). Five delivered in December 1988 and the remainder in February and March 1989.

PROTECTOR Class *1989, SeaArk Marine*

10 MERCOUGAR RIVERINE CRAFT

LP 04 1-5 LOF 7-11

Comment: Five 40 ft monohulls *(LP 04)* and five 35 ft catamarans *(LOF)* completed by Mercougar, Miami in 1988-89. Both types are powered by two Ford Merlin diesels, 600 hp *(448 kW)*, giving speeds up to 40 kts. The 40 ft craft have a range of 556 km *(300 nm)* which extends to 741 km *(400 nm)* in the 35 ft version. One 40 ft craft is equipped as a hospital vessel.

1 TUG

LIBERTAD

Dimensions, feet (metres): 85.3 × 25.9 × 13.1 *(26 × 7.9 × 4)*
Main machinery: 1 Crepelle diesel; 1400 hp(m) *(1.03 MW)*; 1 shaft
Speed, knots: 11.5

Comment: Built by A C de la Manche, St Malo. Completed 2 April 1981. Bollard pull, 21.45 tons. Civilian manned in Acajutla port.

3 LCMs

Comment: One LCM 6 (LD 1) and two LCM 8s (LD 2-3) transferred by the USA in April 1986 and January 1987 respectively.

EQUATORIAL GUINEA

Personnel

1992: 120 officers and men

Ports

Malabo (Fernando Po), Bata (Rio Muni)

Mercantile Marine

Lloyd's Register of Shipping:
2 vessels of 6412 tons gross

2 EX-CHINESE SHANTOU CLASS

Displacement, tons: 60 standard; 80 full load
Dimensions, feet (metres): 83.5 × 19 × 6.5 *(25.5 × 5.8 × 2)*
Main machinery: 2 Type 3-D-12 diesels; 616 hp(m) *(460 kW)* sustained; 2 Type M502 diesels; 2400 hp(m) *(1.76 MW)*; 4 shafts
Speed, knots: 28. **Range, miles:** 500 at 28 kts
Complement: 17
Guns: 4—37 mm/63 (2 twin). 2—12.7 mm MGs.
Radars: Surface search: Skin Head; I band; range 37 km *(20 nm)*.

Comment: Transferred in 1983. Doubtful operational status but seen alongside in 1991.

1 LANTANA TYPE

ISLA DE BIOKO

Displacement, tons: 33 full load
Dimensions, feet (metres): 68.8 × 18 × 4 *(21 × 5.5 × 1.5)*
Main machinery: 2 Detroit 8V-92TA diesels; 1270 hp *(947 kW)* sustained; 2 shafts
Speed, knots: 24. **Range, miles:** 800 at 15 kts
Guns: 2—12.7 mm MGs. 2—7.62 mm MGs.
Radars: Surface search: Furuno; I band.

Comment: Completed in July 1988 by Lantana Boatyard, Florida, and paid for by USA.

1 VAN MILL TYPE

RIOWELE (ex-*P 220*)

Displacement, tons: 45 full load
Dimensions, feet (metres): 66.3 × 17.4 × 5.9 *(20.2 × 5.3 × 1.8)*
Main machinery: 2 MTU diesels; 2200 hp(m) *(1.62 MW)*; 2 shafts
Speed, knots: 35. **Range, miles:** 950 at 25 kts
Complement: 12 (2 officers)
Guns: 1 Rheinmetall 20 mm. 2—7.62 mm MGs.

Comment: Built by Van Mill, Netherlands in 1986 and transferred from Nigeria. This was one of the second group of three fitted with MTU diesels vice the GM type of the first batch.

ISLA DE BIOKO *1987, Lantana Boatyard*

ETHIOPIA

Headquarters' Appointments

Commander of the Navy:
Rear Admiral Yehuwalashet Girma
Director Naval Operations:
Commodore Telahoun Makonnen

Personnel

(a) 1991: 4000
(b) Volunteers (Navy)

General

Some of the ships listed below were damaged during an assault on Massawa in March 1990 by the Eritrean PLP using 35 ft patrol boats. When the civil war ended in May 1991 much of the Navy sailed to Yemen ports. The drydock at Dahlak Island has been sunk.

Naval Bases

Main: Massawa, Assab
Forward: Dahlak Island
Marines: Debrebrehan

Mercantile Marine

Lloyd's Register of Shipping:
27 vessels of 69 481 tons gross

DELETIONS

1989-90 A 04 (Wildervank class), *GB 21-24* (Sewart class), *LTC 1035* (Edic class), *Ras Dedgen* (transport)

FRIGATES

2 Ex-SOVIET PETYA II CLASS

F 1616 F 1617

Displacement, tons: 950 standard; 1180 full load
Dimensions, feet (metres): 268.3 × 29.9 × 9.5 *(81.8 × 9.1 × 2.9)*
Main machinery: CODAG; 1 Type 61V-3 diesel on centre shaft; 6000 hp(m) *(4.41 MW)*; 2 gas turbines on outer shafts; 30 000 hp(m) *(22 MW)*; 3 shafts; cp prop on centre shaft
Speed, knots: 32. **Range, miles:** 4870 at 10 kts; 450 at 29 kts
Complement: 98 (8 officers)

Guns: 4 USSR 3 in *(76 mm)*/60 (2 twin) ❶; 80° elevation; 90 rounds/minute to 15 km *(8 nm)*; weight of shell 6.8 kg.
1 Multi Barrelled Rocket Launcher (MBRL) is mounted on the stern ❷.
1—12.7 mm MG.
Torpedoes: 5—16 in *(406 mm)* (1 quin) tubes ❸. Soviet Type 40; anti-submarine; active/passive homing up to 15 km *(8 nm)* at up to 40 kts; warhead 100-150 kg.
A/S mortars: 2 RBU 6000 12-tubed trainable mountings ❹; range 6000 m; warhead 31 kg.
Depth charges: 2 racks.
Mines: 22.
Countermeasures: ESM: Watch Dog; radar warning.
Radars: Air search: Strut Curve ❺; F band; range 110 km *(60 nm)* for 2 m² target.
Navigation: Don 2; I band.
Fire control: Hawk Screech ❻; I band; range 27 km *(15 nm)*.
IFF: High Pole B.
Sonars: Hull-mounted; active search and attack; medium frequency.

Programmes: First transferred 21 July 1983; second 19 March 1984. Both were towed to Massawa by Soviet warships. F 1616 was named *Zerai Deres* but this had been expunged by 1990.
Structure: This is the standard armament except that one MBRL replaces the after quintuple torpedo tubes.

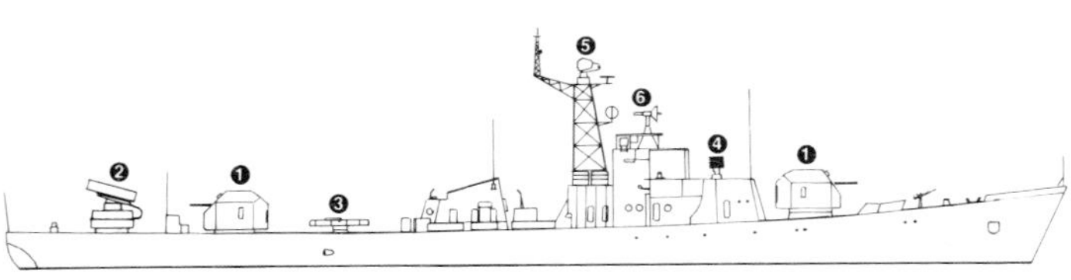

F 1616 *(Scale 1 : 900), Ian Sturton*

F1616 *1990, Ethiopean Navy*

TRAINING SHIP

Ex-US BARNEGAT CLASS

ame	No	Builders	Commissioned
THIOPIA (ex-USS *Orca* AVP 49)	A 01	Lake Washington SY	23 Jan 1944

isplacement, tons: 1766 standard; 2800 full load
imensions, feet (metres): 310.8 × 41 × 13.5 *(94.7 × 12.5 × 4.1)*
ain machinery: 2 Fairbanks-Morse 38D8-1/8-10 diesels; 3540 hp *(2.64 MW)* sustained; 2 shafts
peed, knots: 18.2
omplement: 215
uns: 1 US 5 in *(127 mm)*/38; 85° elevation; 15 rounds/minute to 17 km *(9.3 nm)*; weight of shell 25 kg.
5 Bofors 40 mm/56 (2 twin, 1 single); 45° elevation; 160 rounds/minute to 6 km *(3.3 nm)* anti-aircraft; weight of shell 0.9 kg.
adars: Air search: RCA SPS 12; D band; range 119 km *(65 nm)*.
avigation: I band.
ire control: RCA/GE Mk 26; I/J band.

omment: Former US small seaplane tender. Laid down on 18 July 1942 and launched on 4 October 1942. Transferred from the US Navy on loan in 1962 and by sale March 1976.

THIOPIA *Ethiopian Navy*

LIGHT FORCES

Ex-SOVIET OSA II CLASS (FAST ATTACK CRAFT—MISSILE)

MB 160 FMB 161 FMB 162 FMB 163

isplacement, tons: 245 full load
imensions, feet (metres): 110.2 × 24.9 × 8.8 *(33.6 × 7.6 × 2.7)*
ain machinery: 3 M504 diesels; 15 000 hp(m) *(11 MW)*; 3 shafts
peed, knots: 37. **Range, miles:** 800 at 30 kts
omplement: 30

issiles: SSM: 4 SS-N-2A Styx; active radar or IR homing to 46 km *(25 nm)* at 0.9 Mach; warhead 513 kg.
uns: 4—30 mm/65 (2 twin); 85° elevation; 500 rounds/minute to 5 km *(2.7 nm)* anti-aircraft; weight of shell 0.54 kg.
adars: Surface search: Square Tie; I band.
ire control: Drum Tilt; H/I band.
F: Square Head. High Pole B.

rogrammes: First delivered January 1978, the second in September 1980 and two on 13 January 1981. Three more transferred from PDRY in June 1986 but were returned in 1987 after the PDRY lost two of their own—sunk.

MB 163 *1991*

Ex-SOVIET TURYA CLASS (FAST ATTACK CRAFT—HYDROFOIL)

TB 112 HTB 113

isplacement, tons: 190 standard; 250 full load
imensions, feet (metres): 129.9 × 24.9 (41 over foils) × 5.9 (13.1 over foils) *(39.6 × 7.6 (12.5) × 1.8 (4))*
ain machinery: 3 M504 diesels; 15 000 hp(m) *(11 MW)* (foilborne); 3 shafts
peed, knots: 40 foilborne. **Range, miles:** 600 at 35 kts foilborne; 1450 at 14 kts hull
omplement: 30

uns: 2—57 mm/80 (twin, aft); 85° elevation; 120 rounds/minute to 6 km *(3.3 nm)*; weight of shell 2.8 kg.
2—25 mm/80 (twin, fwd); 85° elevation; 270 rounds/minute to 3 km *(1.6 nm)* anti-aircraft; weight of shell 0.34 kg.
orpedoes: 4—21 in *(533 mm)* tubes. Soviet Type 53; dual purpose; pattern active/passive homing up to 20 km *(10.8 nm)* at up to 45 kts; warhead 400 kg.
epth charges: 2 racks.
adars: Surface search: Pot Drum; H/I band.
ire control: Muff Cob; G/H band.
F: High Pole B. Square Head.

rogrammes: First transferred March 1985, second in March 1986.
tructure: Has an Osa type hull.
perational: As in the transfers of Stenka class to Cuba, the sonar has been removed and therefore it is probable that depth charges are not carried.

TURYA Class *1989*

2 Ex-SOVIET MOL CLASS (FAST ATTACK CRAFT—TORPEDO)

FTB 110 FTB 111

Displacement, tons: 160 standard; 200 full load
Dimensions, feet (metres): 127.9 × 26.6 × 5.9 (*39 × 8.1 × 1.8*)
Main machinery: 3 M504 diesels; 15 000 hp(m) *(11 MW)*; 3 shafts
Speed, knots: 36. **Range, miles:** 1250 at 14 kts
Complement: 25 (3 officers)
Guns: 4—30 mm/65 (2 twin); 85° elevation; 500 rounds/minute to 5 km *(2.7 nm)*; weight of shell 0.54 kg.
Torpedoes: 4—21 in *(533 mm)* tubes. Soviet Type 53; dual purpose; pattern active/passive homing up to 20 km *(10.8 nm)* at up to 45 kts; warhead 400 kg.
Depth charges: 12.
Radars: Surface search: H/I band.
Fire control: Drum Tilt; H/I band.
IFF: Square Head. High Pole B.

Comment: Transferred January 1978. It is not certain whether the torpedo tubes are shipped.

MOL Class (without torpedo tubes)

3 SWIFTSHIPS 105 ft CLASS (LARGE PATROL CRAFT)

P 201 P 203 P 204

Displacement, tons: 118 full load
Dimensions, feet (metres): 105 × 23.6 × 6.5 *(32 × 7.2 × 2)*
Main machinery: 2 MTU MD 16V 538 TB90 diesels; 6000 hp(m) *(4.41 MW)* sustained; 2 shafts
Speed, knots: 30. **Range, miles:** 1200 at 18 kts
Complement: 21
Guns: 4 Emerlec 30 mm (2 twin); 80° elevation; 600 rounds/minute to 6 km *(3.3 nm)*; weight of shell 0.35 kg.
2—23 mm (twin) (201). 2—12.7 mm (twin) (203, 204).
Radars: Surface search: Decca RM 916; I band.

Comment: Six ordered in 1976 of which four were delivered in April 1977 before the cessation of US arms sales to Ethiopia. Built by Swiftships, Louisiana. One deserted to Somalia and served in that Navy for a time.

4 BOGHAMMAR TYPE (INSHORE PATROL CRAFT)

Displacement, tons: 13.5 full load
Dimensions, feet (metres): 46.9 × 12.1 × 3.9 *(14.3 × 3.7 × 1.2)*
Main machinery: 2 MTU 12V 183 TE 91 diesels; 1200 hp(m) *(882 kW)*; 2 shafts
Speed, knots: 40. **Range, miles:** 300 at 40 kts
Complement: 8
Guns: 1—12.7 mm MG. 1 Rocket launcher.
Radars: Surface search: Racal Decca 85; I band

Comment: Fast assault boats acquired in 1990 for 'Ethiopian Shipping Lines'.

BOGHAMMAR craft *1991*

4 Ex-SOVIET ZHUK CLASS (COASTAL PATROL CRAFT)

P 205 (ex-*PC 16*) **P 206** (ex-*PC 17*) **P 207** **P 208**

Displacement, tons: 50 full load
Dimensions, feet (metres): 75.4 × 17 × 6.2 *(23 × 5.2 × 1.9)*
Main machinery: 2 M50 diesels; 2400 hp(m) *(1.76 MW)*; 2 shafts
Speed, knots: 30. **Range, miles:** 1100 at 15 kts
Complement: 17
Guns: 2—14.5 mm (twin) MGs.
Radars: Surface search: Spin Trough; I band.

Comment: First two delivered 9 October 1982 in Fizik Korchatov. Second pair arrived in Assad on 9 June 1990.

P 206 *1987*

AMPHIBIOUS FORCES

1 FRENCH EDIC CLASS

LTC 1036

Displacement, tons: 250 standard; 670 full load
Dimensions, feet (metres): 193.5 × 39.2 × 4.2 *(59 × 12 × 1.3)*
Main machinery: 2 SACM MGO 175 V12 diesels; 1200 hp(m) *(882 kW)* sustained; 2 shafts
Speed, knots: 12. **Range, miles:** 1800 at 8 kts
Complement: 16 (1 officer)
Military lift: 5 heavy vehicles or 11 personnel carriers
Guns: 2 DCN 20 mm (twin).

Comment: Two of the class completed by SFCN, Villeneuve la Garenne, France in May 1977. Cargo deck space 28.5 × 5 m *(93.5 × 16.4 ft)*. One deleted in 1990.

LTC 1036 *1990, Ethiopian Navy*

2 Ex-SOVIET POLNOCHNY B CLASS

LTC 1037 **LTC 1038**

Displacement, tons: 760 standard; 800 full load
Dimensions, feet (metres): 242.7 × 27.9 × 5.8 *(74 × 8.5 × 1.8)*
Main machinery: 2 Type 40D diesels; 5000 hp(m) *(3.67 MW)*; 2 shafts
Speed, knots: 19. **Range, miles:** 1000 at 18 kts
Complement: 40
Military lift: 350 tons including 6 tanks; 180 troops
Guns: 4—30 mm (2 twin). 2—140 mm rocket launchers; range 9 km *(4.9 nm)*.
Radars: Surface search: Don 2; I band.
Fire control: Drum Tilt; H/I band.

Comment: First transferred under tow from USSR 9 November 1981, second 8 January 1983.

POLNOCHNY 1038 *199*

2 CHAMO CLASS (LCL)

CHAMO **ZIWAY**

Displacement, tons: 995 full load
Dimensions, feet (metres): 196.9 × 39 × 4.9 *(60 × 11.9 × 1.5)*
Main machinery: 2 diesels; 1300 hp(m) *(955 kW)*; 2 shafts
Speed, knots: 10
Military lift: 60 tons

Comment: Built by Seebeckwerft, Bremerhaven and completed in November and December 198 respectively. Similar to Edic class. Delivered to Ethiopian Shipping Lines for use by the Ministry o Transport. Civilian manned but have obvious naval potential.

CHAMO *12/1988, Seebeckwerf*

4 Ex-SOVIET T 4 CLASS (LCVP)

Displacement, tons: 70 full load
Dimensions, feet (metres): 62.3 × 14 × 3.3 *(19 × 4.3 × 1)*
Main machinery: 2 diesels; 400 hp(m) *(294 kW)*; 2 shafts
Speed, knots: 10
Complement: 4

Comment: First transferred in September 1978 and three in September 1979.

SUPPORT SHIP

1 COASTAL TANKER

A 502

Displacement, tons: 1029 full load
Dimensions, feet (metres): 176.2 × 31.8 × 10.5 *(53.7 × 9.7 × 3.2)*
Main machinery: 1 6DR 30/50-5 diesel; 600 hp(m) *(441 kW)*; 1 shaft
Speed, knots: 10.5
Complement: 23
Guns: 2—12.7 mm MGs.
Radars: Navigation: Don; I band.

Comment: Acquired in 1989-90.

A 502 *199*

FAEROES

COAST GUARD

1 PATROL CRAFT

TJALDRID

Displacement, tons: 650 full load
Dimensions, feet (metres): 146 × 33.1 × 10.5 *(44.5 × 10.1 × 3.2)*
Main machinery: 2 MWM diesels; 2400 hp(m) *(1.76 MW)*; 2 shafts
Speed, knots: 14.5
Complement: 18
Guns: 1—57 mm of late 19th century vintage can be carried.

Comment: Originally a commercial tug built in 1976 by Svolvaer, Verksted and acquired by the local government in 1987. Although Denmark retains control of defence the Coast Guard and Fisheries come under the Landsstyri which is the islands' local government. The ship is based at Tórshavn on the island of Streymoy.

TJALDRID *6/1987, Gunnar Olsen*

FALKLAND ISLANDS

General

A dependent territory of the United Kingdom. The capital and principle town is at Stanley. In 1987 Britain declared a fishing zone off the Falklands within which only licensed ships may work. On 26 December 1990 a further outer zone was declared, extending the original zones. No fishing is allowed in this outer area. Both zones are patrolled by two vessels throughout the year. Both ships have red hulls and white superstructures. There are also two Pilatus Britten-Norman Defender unarmed maritime surveillance aircraft.

Mercantile Marine

Lloyd's Register of Shipping:
7 vessels of 9838 tons gross

DELETIONS

1989-90 *Falkland Right* (ex-*Lancella*), *Beaulieu* (sold to Chile), *Blakeney* (sunk)
1991 *Falkland Sound* (civilian), *Mount Kent* (civilian)

FALKLAND DESIRE (ex-*Southella*)

Measurement, tons: 1496 grt
Dimensions, feet (metres): 229 × 41.6 × 15.1 *(69.6 × 12.7 × 4.6)*
Main machinery: 1 Mirrlees KMR8 diesel; 2880 hp *(2.15 MW)*; 1 shaft; cp prop; Jetsam bow thruster; 250 hp *(186 kW)*
Speed, knots: 15
Complement: 40 + 21 spare

Comment: Research Vessel Ice Class III built in 1969, refitted in 1981 and again in 1987.

FALKLAND PROTECTOR (ex-*Falkland Right*, ex-*G A Reay*, ex-*Arctic Privateer*)

Measurement, tons: 1878 grt
Dimensions, feet (metres): 227 × 39.4 × 16.4 *(69.2 × 12 × 5)*
Main machinery: 1 diesel; 2500 hp(m) *(1.84 MW)*; 1 shaft
Speed, knots: 14.5
Complement: 23 plus 6 spare

Comment: Ex-trawler built at Gdynia, Poland and first leased in February 1987. The ship returned to Gdynia to refit in 1989-90, being replaced by the ex-*Lancella* which was also called *Falkland Right*. Refit completed in March 1990 and returned to station in September 1990, now named *Falkland Protector*.

FALKLAND DESIRE *1991, Government House*

FALKLAND PROTECTOR *1991, Government House*

FIJI

Commanding Officers

Fiji Military Forces:
Brigadier E G Ganilau MC, MSD
Fiji Navy:
Commander Josaia Voreqe Bainimarama

Personnel

1992: 276

Base

FNS *Viti*, at Togalevu (Training).
Operation base at Walu Bay, Suva.

General

On 12 June 1975 the then Royal Fiji Military Forces were authorised to raise a Naval Division to carry out Fishery Protection, Surveillance, Hydrographic Surveying and Coast Guard duties. On 14 May 1987 a military coup overthrew the government and Fiji became a Republic on 10 October 1987. The Fiji Navy comes under the authority of the Minister of Home Affairs, and has been accountable to the CinC Military Forces since June 1989.

Prefix to Ships' Names

FNS

Mercantile Marine

Lloyd's Register of Shipping:
62 vessels of 52 273 tons gross

DELETIONS

1990 *Kula*
1991 *Kikau*

1 Ex-US REDWING CLASS (MINESWEEPER—COASTAL)

Name	*No*	*Builders*	*Commissioned*
KIRO (ex-USS *Warbler*, MSC 206)	206	Bellingham SY, USA	23 July 1955

Displacement, tons: 370 full load
Dimensions, feet (metres): 144 × 28 × 8.5 *(43.9 × 8.5 × 2.5)*
Main machinery: 2 GM 8-268A diesels; 880 hp *(656 kW)*; 2 shafts
Speed, knots: 12
Complement: 28
Guns: 1 Oerlikon 20 mm. 2—12.7 mm MGs.

Comment: Transferred in June 1976. Retained in 1991 as a training ship. *Kula* (deleted in 1990) was the only one of the class to have a helicopter platform.

REDWING Class (deleted) *1984, FMF*

2 COASTAL PATROL CRAFT

LEVUKA 101 **LAUTOKA** 102

Displacement, tons: 97 full load
Dimensions, feet (metres): 110 × 24 × 5 *(33.8 × 7.4 × 1.5)*
Main machinery: 4 GM 12V 71 TI diesels; 1680 hp *(1.25 MW)*; 4 shafts
Speed, knots: 12
Guns: 1—12.7 mm MG.

Comment: Built in 1979-80 by Beaux's Bay Craft Inc, Louisiana as oil rig support craft. Purchased in September 1987 and commissioned on 22 and 28 October 1987 respectively. All aluminium construction.

LAUTOKA *10/1987, Fiji Navy*

4 Ex-ISRAEL DABUR CLASS (COASTAL PATROL CRAFT)

VAI 301 **SAKU** 303
OGO 302 **SAQA** 304

Displacement, tons: 39 full load
Dimensions, feet (metres): 64.9 × 18 × 5.8 *(19.8 × 5.5 × 1.8)*
Main machinery: 2 GM 12V-71 TI diesels; 840 hp *(627 kW)* sustained; 2 shafts
Speed, knots: 19. **Range, miles:** 450 at 13 kts
Complement: 9
Guns: 2 Oerlikon 20 mm. 2—12.7 mm MGs.
Torpedoes: 2—324 mm tubes (may have been removed).
Radars: Surface search: Decca 101; I band.

Comment: Built in mid-1970s by Israeli Aircraft Industries and commissioned in the Fiji Navy 22 November 1991.

DABUR Class *1989, Rupert Pengelly*

1 HYDROGRAPHIC SURVEY SHIP

TOVUTO (ex-*Babale*, ex-*Eugene McDermott II*)

Displacement, tons: 920 full load
Dimensions, feet (metres): 171 × 38 × 11 *(52.6 × 11.7 × 3.4)*
Main machinery: 2 Caterpillar 399; 2 shafts
Speed, knots: 12. **Range, miles:** 9400 at 10 kts
Complement: 41 (5 officers)

Comment: Originally a commercial exploration vessel launched by Carrington Slipways in 1971. Delivered April 1987. Transferred 9 December 1989 to the Marine Department of the Ministry of Transport, then later to the Ministry of Works and Communications. Civilian manned.

TOVUTO *1987, Fiji Navy*

1 TRAINING VESSEL

VANIDORO

Comment: Presidential yacht taken over in March 1991 and now used as a training ship. Has a crew of 20.

FINLAND

Headquarters' Appointments

Commander-in-Chief Defence Forces:
Admiral Jan Klenberg
Commander-in-Chief Finnish Navy:
Rear Admiral Sakari Visa
Chief Engineer Defence Forces:
Rear Admiral (E) Auvo Vappula
Chief of Staff:
Captain Seppo Lintula

Diplomatic Representation

Defence Attaché in London:
Commander Juhani Kaskeala
Defence Attaché in Moscow:
Colonel Kalevi Rissanon
Defence Attaché in Paris:
Lieutenant Colonel Harri Vilkuna
Defence Attaché in Washington:
Captain Kari Savolainen
Defence Attaché in Bonn:
Lieutenant Colonel Matti Lehtonen

Treaty Limitations

The Treaty of Paris (1947) limited the Navy to 10 000 tons of ships and 4500 personnel with submarines and torpedo boats prohibited. In September 1990 the government 'disengaged' from parts of the Treaty so allowing a reappraisal of defence requirements, including submarines.

Personnel

(a) 1992: 1800 (200 officers, 500 POs and 1100 conscripts)
(b) 11 months' national service
(c) 600 Frontier Guards

Fleet Organisation

Turku: Gunboat Squadron; (Turunmaa, Nuoli and Tuima classes).
Missile Squadron; *(Karjala*, Helsinki class).
Mine Warfare Squadron; minelayers and sweepers.
Helsinki: Patrol Squadron.
Not all ships are fully manned all the time but all are rotated on a regular basis.

Coastal Artillery

The following vessels are used by the Coastal Artillery: *Vahakari, Vaarlahti, Vänö, Kampela 1* and *2*, 6 Hauki class, 2 Loki class, *Askeri, Parainen, Träskö*.

Strength of the Fleet

Type	*Active*	*Building (Planned)*
Corvettes	2	—
Fast Attack Craft (Missile)	11	1
Fast Attack Craft (Gun)	6	—
Large Patrol Craft	5	—
Coastal Patrol Craft	1	—
Minelayers	4	3
Minesweepers, Inshore	13	—
Tugs	2	—
Command Craft	11	—
Transports (Landing Craft)	26	—
Cable Ship	1	—
Icebreakers	8	—
Support and Transport Ships	14	2

Bases

Helsinki (Naval Staff, training establishments).
Turku (main Fleet Base).

Frontier Guard

All Frontier Guard vessels come under the Ministry of the Interior.

Type	*Active*	*Building*
Large Patrol Craft	8	(2)
Coastal Patrol Craft	53	5

Hydrographic Department

This office and the survey ships come under the Ministry of Trade and Industry.

Icebreakers

All these ships work for the Board of Navigation.

Mercantile Marine

Lloyd's Register of Shipping:
266 vessels of 1 052 980 tons gross

DELETIONS

1989 *Aranda* (old)
1990 *Kave 1-4, 6, Pyhäranta*
1991 *Pansio* (old), *Porkkala*

PENNANT LIST

Corvettes

03	Turunmaa
04	Karjala

Light Forces

11	Tuima
12	Tuisku
14	Tuuli
15	Tyrsky
30	Hurja
35, 38, 40-43	Nuoli class
51	Rihtniemi
52	Rymättylä
53	Ruissalo
54	Raisio
55	Röytta
60	Helsinki
61	Turku
62	Oulu
63	Kotka
70	Rauma
71	Raahe
72	Porvoo

Mine Warfare Forces

01	Pohjanmaa
02	Hämeenmaa
05	Keihässalmi
21-26	Kuha class
521-527	Kiiski class
876	Pansio (new)

Support Ships and Miscellaneous

91	Viiri
92	Putsaari
93	Kemio
97	Valas
98	Mursu
99	Kustaanmiekka
121	Vahakari
133	Havouri
222	Vaarlahti
232	Hauki
235	Hirsala
237	Hila
238	Harun
241	Askeri
251	Lohi
272	Kampela 2
323	Vänö
334	Hankoniemi
372	Kala 2
420	Parainen
431	Hakuni
436	Houtskar
452	Lohm
471	Kampela 1
511	Vinha
521	Raju
531	Syöksy
541	Vihuri
557	Kampela 3
731	Haukipää
773	Kala 3
776	Kala 6
799	Hylje
826	Isku
831	Kallanpää
871	Kala 1
874	Kala 4
875	Kala 5
899	Halli
992	Träskö

CORVETTES

2 TURUNMAA CLASS

Name	*No*	*Builders*	*Laid down*	*Launched*	*Commissioned*
TURUNMAA	03	Wärtsilä, Helsinki	Mar 1967	11 July 1967	29 Aug 1968
KARJALA	04	Wärtsilä, Helsinki	Mar 1967	16 Aug 1967	21 Oct 1968

Displacement, tons: 660 standard; 770 full load
Dimensions, feet (metres): 243.1 × 25.6 × 7.9 *(74.1 × 7.8 × 2.4)*
Main machinery: CODOG; 1 RR Olympus TM1A gas turbine; 15 000 hp *(11.2 MW)*; 3 Mercedes-Benz MTU diesels; 3000 hp(m) *(2.2 MW)*; 3 shafts; cp props
Speed, knots: 35; 17 diesel. **Range, miles:** 2500 at 14 kts
Complement: 70

Guns: 1 Bofors 4.7 in *(120 mm)*/46 ❶; 80° elevation; 80 rounds/minute to 18.5 km *(10 nm)*; weight of shell 21 kg. 6—103 mm rails for illuminants are fitted on the side of the mounting.
2 Bofors 40 mm/70 ❷; 90° elevation; 300 rounds/minute to 12 km (6.6 nm); weight of shell 0.96 kg.
4 USSR 23 mm/87 (2 twin) ❸.
A/S mortars: 2 RBU 1200 5-tubed fixed launchers ❹ (mounted inside main deck superstructure abaft the pennant number); range 1200 m; warhead 34 kg.
Depth charges: 2 racks.
Countermeasures: Decoys: Wallop Barricade double Chaff launcher.
SM: Argo ❺; radar intercept.
ire control: SAAB EOS-400 optronic director ❻.
Radars: Surface search: Terma 20T 48 Super ❼; E/F band.
ire control: Signaal WM 22 ❽; I/J band; range 46 km *(25 nm)*.
Navigation: Raytheon ARPA; I band.
Sonars: Hull-mounted; active search and attack; high frequency. Optimised for operations in archipelago waters.

rogrammes: Ordered on 18 February 1965.
Modernisation: Both completed refit at the Wärtsilä Shipyard, Turku in 1986. New equipment included radar, EW and sonar.
tructure: Flush decked. Fitted with Vosper Thornycroft fin stabiliser equipment. The exhaust system is trunked on either side of the quarter-deck, the two plumes coalescing some 50 ft abaft the stern.

KARJALA

9/1990, Antonio Moreno

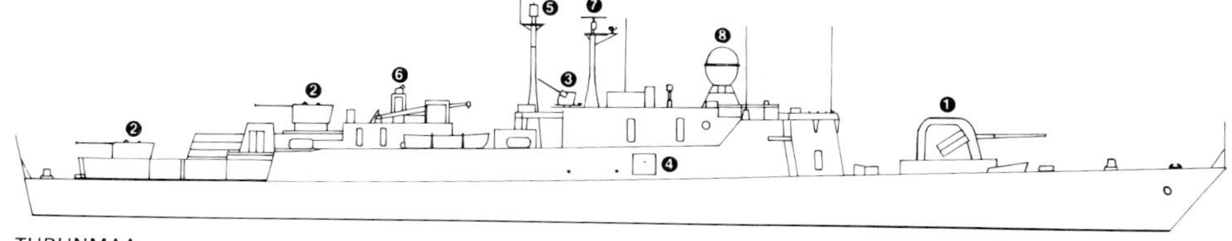

TURUNMAA

(Scale 1 : 600), Ian Sturton

RUNMAA (firing RBU)

1991, Finnish Navy

LIGHT FORCES

4 HELSINKI CLASS (FAST ATTACK CRAFT—MISSILE)

Name	No	Builders	Commissioned
HELSINKI	60	Wärtsilä, Helsinki	1 Sep 1981
TURKU	61	Wärtsilä, Helsinki	3 June 1985
OULU	62	Wärtsilä, Helsinki	1 Oct 1985
KOTKA	63	Wärtsilä, Helsinki	16 June 1986

Displacement, tons: 280 standard; 300 full load
Dimensions, feet (metres): 147.6 × 29.2 × 9.9 *(45 × 8.9 × 3)*
Main machinery: 3 MTU 16V 538 TB92 diesels; 10 230 hp(m) *(7.52 MW)* sustained; 3 shafts
Speed, knots: 30
Complement: 30

Missiles: SSM: 8 Saab RBS 15; inertial guidance; active radar homing to 70 km *(37.8 nm)* at 0.8 Mach; warhead 150 kg; sea-skimmer.
Guns: 1 Bofors 57 mm/70; 75° elevation; 200 rounds/minute to 17 km *(9.3 nm)*; weight of shell 2.4 kg. 6—103 mm rails for rocket illuminants.
4 USSR 23 mm/87 (2 twin). Being replaced (see *Modernisation*).
Depth charges: 2 rails.
Countermeasures: Decoys: Philax Chaff and IR flare launcher.
ESM: Argo; radar intercept.
Fire control: Saab EOS 400 optronic.
Radars: Surface search: 9GA 208; I band.
Fire control: Philips 9LV 225; J band.
Sonars: Simrad Marine SS 304; high resolution active scanning.

Programmes: *Helsinki* was launched 5 November 1980. Next three ordered to a revised design on 13 January 1983.
Modernisation: *Helsinki's* bridge and armament have been modified and are now the same as the other three of the class. 23 mm guns to be replaced by a *Kotka* type barbet which can take either twin 23 mm guns or six Mistral missiles. A decision to fit a SAM system had not been taken by the end of 1991.
Structure: The light armament can be altered to suit the planned role. Hull and superstructure of light alloy.

KOTKA (new 23mm gun casing) *10/1990, Antonio Moreno*

OULU *9/1990, Antonio Moreno*

KOTKA (left) and HELSINKI *6/1991, Harald Carstens*

3 + 1 RAUMA CLASS (FAST ATTACK CRAFT—MISSILE)

Name	No	Builders	Commissioned
RAUMA	70	Hollming, Rauma	May 1990
RAAHE	71	Hollming, Rauma	Aug 1991
PORVOO	72	Hollming, Rauma	Apr 1992
—	73	Hollming, Rauma	Aug 1992

Displacement, tons: 215 standard; 248 full load
Dimensions, feet (metres): 157.5 × 26.2 × 4.5 *(48 × 8 × 1.5)*
Main machinery: 2 MTU 16V538 TB 93 diesels; 7510 hp(m) *(5.52 MW)* sustained; 2 Riva Calzoni waterjets
Speed, knots: 30
Complement: 19 (5 officers)

Missiles: SSM: 6 Saab RBS 15SF (could embark 8); active radar homing to 150 km *(80 nm)* at 0.8 Mach; warhead 200 kg.
SAM: Matra Sadral sextuple launcher; Mistral; IR homing to 4 km *(2.2 nm)*; warhead 3 kg.
Guns: Bofors 40 mm/70; 90° elevation; 300 rounds/minute to 12 km *(6.6 nm)*; weight of shell 96 kg. 6—103 mm rails for rocket illuminants.
2 USSR 23 mm/87 (twin); can be fitted instead of Sadral on the after mounting.
A/S mortars: 4 Saab Elma LLS-920 9-tubed launchers; range 300 m; warhead 4.2 kg shaped charge.
Depth charges: 1 rail.
Countermeasures: Decoys: Philax Chaff and IR flares.
ESM: MEL Matilda; radar intercept.
Fire control: Bofors Electronic 9LV200 Mk 3 optronic director with TV camera; infra-red and laser telemetry.
Radars: Surface search: 9GA 208; I band.
Fire control: Bofors Electronic 9LV 225; J band.
Navigation: Raytheon ARPA; I band.
Sonars: Simrad Subsea toadfish sonar; search and attack; high frequency.

Programmes: Four ordered 27 August 1987. Another eight of these craft are planned for the future, but further orders are uncertain.
Structure: Hull and superstructure of light alloy. SAM and 23 mm guns are interchangeable within the same barbet.
Operational: Primary function is the anti-ship role but there is some ASW capability and mention is also made of a secondary role in mine warfare, as it is in all Finnish war vessels.

RAUMA *1991, Finnish Nav*

4 TUIMA CLASS (FAST ATTACK CRAFT—MISSILE)

TUIMA 11 **TUISKU** 12 **TUULI** 14 **TYRSKY** 15

Displacement, tons: 210 standard; 245 full load
Dimensions, feet (metres): 110.2 × 24.9 × 8.8 *(33.6 × 7.6 × 2.7)*
Main machinery: 3 M504 diesels; 15 000 hp(m) *(11 MW)*; 3 shafts
Speed, knots: 37. **Range, miles:** 500 at 35 kts
Complement: 30

Missiles: SSM: 4 SS-N-2B Styx; active radar or IR homing to 46 km *(25 nm)* at 0.9 Mach; warhea 513 kg.
Guns: 4 USSR 30 mm/65 (2 twin); 85° elevation; 500 rounds/minute to 5 km *(2.7 nm)*; weight c shell 0.54 kg.
Radars: Surface search: Square Tie; I band.
Fire control: Drum Tilt; H/I band.
Navigation: Racal Decca; I band.

Programmes: Ex-Soviet Osa II class purchased from the USSR 1974-75.
Modernisation: New construction but with Finnish electronics and Western navigational rada *Tuisku* to be converted in 1992 to a minelayer with the missile system removed. The others may als be converted in due course.

TUULI *1991, Finnish Nav*

NUOLI CLASS (FAST ATTACK CRAFT—GUN)

ame	No	Builders	Commissioned
UOLI 5, 8, 10—13	35, 38, 40—43	Laivateollisuus, Turku	1961-66

isplacement, tons: 40 standard
imensions, feet (metres): 72.2 × 21.7 × 5 *(22 × 6.6 × 1.5)*
ain machinery: 3 Type M50 diesels; 3600 hp(m) *(2.65 MW)*; 3 shafts
peed, knots: 40
omplement: 15
uns: 1 Bofors 40 mm/70 or 2 USSR 23 mm/87 (twin, aft). 1 Oerlikon 20 mm or 12.7 mm (fwd) MG.
epth charges: 4
adars: Surface search: Decca; I band.

omment: Delivery dates—6 July 1962, 22 August 1962, 5 May 1964, 5 May 1964, 30 November 1964, 12 October 1966. This class is split into two: *Nuoli 1* (5 and 8) and *Nuoli 2* (10-13). The main difference is a lower superstructure in *Nuoli 2*. These six were modernised under the 1979 estimates, the remainder used for target practice.

UOLI 13 (with 40 mm gun) *1991, Finnish Navy*

UOLI 5 (with 23 mm gun) *1988, Finnish Navy*

RUISSALO CLASS (LARGE PATROL CRAFT)

ame	No	Builders	Commissioned
UISSALO	53	Laivateollisuus, Turku	11 Aug 1959
AISIO	54	Laivateollisuus, Turku	12 Sep 1959
ÖYTTA	55	Laivateollisuus, Turku	14 Oct 1959

isplacement, tons: 110 standard; 130 full load
imensions, feet (metres): 108.9 × 18.5 × 5.9 *(33 × 5.6 × 1.8)*
ain machinery: 2 Mercedes-Benz MTU diesels; 2500 hp(m) *(1.84 MW)*; 2 shafts
peed, knots: 17
omplement: 20
uns: 4 USSR 23 mm/87 (2 twin).
/S mortars: 2 RBU 1200 fixed 5-tubed launchers; range 1200 m; warhead 34 kg.
ines: Can lay mines.
adars: Navigation: Decca; I band.
onars: Hull-mounted; active search and attack; high frequency.

omment: Ordered in January 1958. Launched on 16 June, 2 July and 2 June 1959. *Ruissalo* was modernised in 1976, other pair in 1980.

AISIO *1988, Finnish Navy*

2 RIHTNIEMI CLASS (LARGE PATROL CRAFT)

Name	No	Builders	Commissioned
RIHTNIEMI	51	Rauma-Repola, Rauma	21 Feb 1957
RYMÄTTYLÄ	52	Rauma-Repola, Rauma	20 May 1957

Displacement, tons: 90 standard; 110 full load
Dimensions, feet (metres): 101.7 × 18.7 × 5.9 *(31 × 5.6 × 1.8)*
Main machinery: 2 Mercedes-Benz MTU diesels; 2500 hp(m) *(1.84 MW)*; 2 shafts; cp props
Speed, knots: 18
Complement: 20
Guns: 4 USSR 23 mm/87 (2 twin).
A/S mortars: 2 RBU 1200 fixed 5-tubed launchers; range 1200 m; warhead 34 kg.
Mines: Can lay mines.
Radars: Navigation: Decca; I band.
Sonars: Hull-mounted; active search and attack; high frequency.

Comment: Ordered in June 1955, launched in 1956. Both modernised for A/S work—further modernisation completed 1981.

RIHTNIEMI *1990, van Ginderen Collection*

1 TRIALS SHIP

Name	No	Builders	Commissioned
ISKU	826 (ex-16)	Reposaaron Konepaja	1970

Displacement, tons: 180 standard
Dimensions, feet (metres): 108.5 × 28.5 × 5.9 *(33 × 8.7 × 1.8)*
Main machinery: 4 Type M50 diesels; 4800 hp(m) *(3.53 MW)*; 4 shafts
Speed, knots: 18
Complement: 25
Radars: Navigation: Raytheon ARPA; I band

Comment: Formerly a missile experimental craft, now used for various equipment trials. Modernised in 1989-90 by Uusikaupunki Shipyard and lengthened by 7 metres. Can quickly be converted to a minelayer.

ISKU *1990, Finnish Navy*

1 EXPERIMENTAL COASTAL PATROL CRAFT

HURJA 30

Displacement, tons: 30
Dimensions, feet (metres): 72.2 × 16.4 × 6.6 *(22 × 5 × 2)*
Main machinery: 3 diesels; 3800 hp(m) *(2.2 MW)*; 3 waterjets
Speed, knots: 30
Complement: 10

Comment: Built by Fiskars, Turun, Turku. Completed 1981. GRP hull. Probably did not come up to expectations and is now used as trials craft.

HURJA *1991, Finnish Navy*

MINE WARFARE FORCES

Note: *Tuisku* (see *Light Forces*) being converted in 1992 to a fast minelayer.

1 + 1 HÄMEENMAA CLASS (MINELAYER)

Name	*No*	*Builders*	*Laid down*	*Launched*	*Commissioned*
HÄMEENMAA	02	Hollming, Rauma	2 Apr 1991	11 Nov 1991	Apr 1992
—	—	Hollming, Rauma	12 Nov 1991	June1992	Sep 1992

Displacement, tons: 1000 standard
Dimensions, feet (metres): 249.3 × 38.1 × 9.8 *(76 × 11.6 × 3)*
Main machinery: 2 Wärtsilä 16V-22 MD diesels; 6300 hp(m) *(4.63 MW)* sustained; 2 shafts; bow thruster
Speed, knots: 19
Complement: 70

Missiles: SAM: Matra Sadral sextuple launcher; Mistral; IR homing to 4 km *(2.2 nm)*; warhead 3 kg.
Guns: 2 Bofors 40 mm/70. 4 or 6—23 mm/87 (2 or 3 twin) (the third mounting is interchangeable with Sadral launcher).
Mines: 100-150.
Countermeasures: Decoys: 2 ML/Wallop Superbarricade multi-Chaff launchers.
ESM: Radar warning.
Fire control: Radamec System 2400 optronic director; 2 Galileo optical directors.
Radars: Surface search and Navigation: Three Selesmar ARPA; I band.
Sonars: Hull-mounted high frequency mine detection set.

Programmes: First one ordered 29 December 1989 from Hollming after the original order in July from Wärtsilä had been cancelled. Second ordered 13 February 1991. Dual role as a transport and support ship.

HAMEENMAA *11/1991, Hollming*

Structure: Steel hull and alloy superstructure. Ramps in bow and stern. The Sadral launcher is mounted at the stern. The after 40 mm gun is on the after end of the superstructure. SAM system can be replaced by a third twin 23 mm mounting within the same barbet.

1 MINELAYER

Name	*No*	*Builders*	*Laid down*	*Launched*	*Commissioned*
POHJANMAA	01	Wärtsilä, Helsinki	4 May 1978	28 Aug 1978	8 June 1979

Displacement, tons: 1000 standard; 1100 full load
Dimensions, feet (metres): 255.8 × 37.7 × 9.8 *(78.2 × 11.6 × 3)*
Main machinery: 2 Wärtsilä Vasa 16V22B diesels; 5850 hp(m) *(4.3 MW)* sustained; 2 shafts; cp props; bow thruster
Speed, knots: 19. **Range, miles:** 3500 at 15 kts
Complement: 90

Guns: 1 Bofors 4.7 in *(120 mm)*/46; 80° elevation; 80 rounds/minute to 18.5 km *(10 nm)*; weight of shell 21 kg. 6—103 mm launchers for illuminants fitted to the mounting.
2 Bofors 40 mm/70; 90° elevation; 300 rounds/minute to 12 km *(6.6 nm)*; weight of shell 0.96 kg.
8 USSR 23 mm/87 (4 twin).
A/S mortars: 2 RBU 1200 fixed 5-tubed launchers; range 1200 m; warhead 34 kg.
Depth charges: 2 rails.
Mines: 120 including UK Stonefish.
Countermeasures: Decoys: Philax Chaff and IR flare launcher.
ESM: Argo; radar intercept.
Radars: Air search: Signaal DA 05; E/F band; range 137 km *(75 nm)* for 2 m² target.
Fire control: Phillips 9LV 200; J band.
Navigation: I band.
Sonars: Hull-mounted; active search and attack; high frequency. Bottom classification; search; high frequency.

POHJANMAA *7/1991, Camil Busquets i Vilanova*

Programmes: Design completed 1976. Ordered late 1977.
Modernisation: The plan to fit Sadral SAM in 1991 appears to have been cancelled.
Operational: Also serves as training ship. Carries 70 trainees accommodated in Portakabins on the mine deck. Helicopter area on quarter-deck but no hangar.

1 MINELAYER

Name	*No*	*Builders*	*Commissioned*
KEIHÄSSALMI	05	Valmet, Helsinki	1957

Displacement, tons: 360
Dimensions, feet (metres): 184.8 × 25.4 × 6.6 *(56 × 7.7 × 2)*
Main machinery: 2 Wärtsilä diesels; 1600 hp(m) *(1.18 MW)*; 2 shafts
Speed, knots: 15
Complement: 60
Guns: 4 USSR 30 mm/65 (2 twin). 2 Oerlikon 20 mm.
Mines: Up to 100.
Radars: Navigation: Decca; I band.
Fire control: Drum Tilt; H/I band.

Comment: Contract dated June 1955. Launched on 16 March 1957. Armament modified in 1972. Will probably remain in service after Minelayer 90 has commissioned.

KEIHÄSSALMI *1991, Finnish Navy*

1 + 2 PANSIO CLASS (MINELAYERS—LCU TYPE)

Name	*No*	*Builders*	*Commissioned*
PANSIO	876	Olkiluoto Shipyard	Aug 1991
—	877	Olkiluoto Shipyard	Aug 1992
—	878	Olkiluoto Shipyard	Nov 1992

Displacement, tons: 450 standard
Dimensions, feet (metres): 144.3 × 32.8 × 6.6 *(44 × 10 × 2)*
Main machinery: 2 MTU 12V 183 diesels; 1500 hp(m) *(1.1 MW)*; 2 shafts; bow thruster
Speed, knots: 10
Complement: 12
Guns: 4 USSR 23 mm/87 (2 twin).
Mines: 50.
Radars: Navigation: Raytheon ARPA; I band.

Comment: Ordered in May 1990. Used for inshore minelaying and transport with a capacity of 100 tons. Ice strengthened with ramps in bow and stern.

PANSIO *1991, Finnish Navy*

2 MINELAYING BARGES

721 **821**

Displacement, tons: 130 full load
Dimensions, feet (metres): 49.2 × 23 × 4.9 *(15 × 7 × 1.5)*

Comment: Built by Lehtinen, Rauma in 1987. Dumb barges used to transport and lay mines in port approaches.

6 KUHA CLASS (MINESWEEPERS—INSHORE)

Name	*No*	*Builders*	*Commissioned*
KUHA 21—26	21—26	Laivateollisuus, Turku	1974-75

Displacement, tons: 90 full load
Dimensions, feet (metres): 87.2 × 22.7 × 6.6 *(26.6 × 6.9 × 2)*
Main machinery: 2 Cummins MT-380M diesels; 600 hp(m) *(448 kW)*; 1 shaft; cp prop; active rudder
Speed, knots: 12
Complement: 15
Guns: 2 USSR 23 mm/60 (twin). 1—12.7 mm MG.
Radars: Navigation: Decca; I band.

Comment: All ordered 1972. *Kuha 21* completed 28 June 1974, *Kuha 26* in late 1975. Fitted for magnetic, acoustic and pressure-mine clearance. Hulls are of GRP.

KUHA 25 — *6/1988, Stefan Terzibaschitsch*

7 KIISKI CLASS (MINESWEEPERS—INSHORE)

521-527

Displacement, tons: 20
Dimensions, feet (metres): 49.9 × 13.4 × 3.3 *(15.2 × 4.1 × 1.2)*
Main machinery: 2 Valmet 611 CSMP diesels; 340 hp(m) *(250 kW)*; 2 waterjets
Speed, knots: 11
Complement: 4

Comment: Ordered January 1983 from Fiskars, Turun, Turku. All completed by 24 May 1984. GRP hull. Built to be used with Kuha class for unmanned teleguided sweeping, but this was not successful and they are now used for manned sweeping operations with crew of four.

KIISKI 522 — *1987, Finnish Navy*

ICEBREAKERS

Note: Controlled by Board of Navigation which also operates 14 transport ships and 9 oil recovery vessels. There is also the German owned, Finnish manned, icebreaker *Hansa*, of the Karhu class (since deleted), completed on 25 November 1966, which operates off Germany in winter and off Finland at other times.

HANSA — *8/1988, Gilbert Gyssels*

2 KARHU 2 CLASS

OTSO **KONTIO**

Measurement, tons: 9200 dwt
Dimensions, feet (metres): 324.7 × 79.4 × 26.2 *(99 × 24.2 × 8)*
Main machinery: Diesel-electric; 4 Wärtsilä Vasa 16V32 diesel generators; 31.26 MW; 2 motors; 17 700 hp(m) *(13 MW)*; 2 shafts
Speed, knots: 18.5
Complement: 28
Helicopters: 1 light.

Comment: First ordered from Wärtsilä 29 March 1984, completed 30 January 1986. Second ordered 29 November 1985, delivered 29 January 1987.

KONTIO — *1/1987, Wärtsilä*

2 URHO CLASS

URHO **SISU**

Displacement, tons: 7800 *Urho* (7900, *Sisu*) standard; 9500 full load
Dimensions, feet (metres): 343.1 × 78.1 × 27.2 *(104.6 × 23.8 × 8.3)*
Main machinery: Diesel-electric; 5 Wärtsilä-SEMT-Pielstick diesels; 25 000 hp(m) *(18.37 MW)*; 4 motors; 22 000 hp(m) *(16.2 MW)*; 4 shafts (2 fwd, 2 aft)
Speed, knots: 18
Complement: 47
Helicopters: 1 light.

Comment: Built by Wärtsilä and commissioned on 5 March 1975 and 28 January 1976 respectively. Fitted with two screws aft, taking 60 per cent of available power and two fwd, taking the remainder. Sisters to Swedish Atle class.

URHO and SISU — *6/1988, A. Sheldon Duplaix*

3 TARMO CLASS

TARMO **VARMA** **APU**

Displacement, tons: 4890
Dimensions, feet (metres): 281 × 71 × 23.9 *(85.7 × 21.7 × 7.3)*
Main machinery: Diesel-electric; 4 Wärtsilä-Sulzer diesels; electric drive; 12 000 hp(m) *(8.82 MW)*; 4 shafts (2 screws fwd, 2 aft)
Speed, knots: 17
Helicopters: 1 light.

Comment: Built by Wärtsilä and commissioned in 1963, 1968 and 1970 respectively.

TARMO — *1989, Finnish Navy*

1 VOIMA CLASS

VOIMA

Displacement, tons: 4415
Dimensions, feet (metres): 274 × 63.7 × 23 *(83.6 × 19.4 × 7)*
Main machinery: Diesel-electric; 6 Wärtsilä Vasa 16 V 22 diesel generators; 16.8 MW sustained; 4 motors; 13 600 hp(m) *(10 MW)*; 4 shafts (2 fwd, 2 aft)
Speed, knots: 16.5

Comment: Launched in 1953. Modernised in 1978-79 with new main machinery and a remodelled superstructure and living quarters by Wärtsilä. This has given her a life expectancy until 1994. *Voima* when built was sister to the Soviet Kapitan Belousov class and the Swedish *Oden* (since deleted).

VOIMA — *1991, van Ginderen Collection*

SUPPORT SHIPS

2 COMMAND SHIPS

KEMIÖ 93 **KUSTAANMIEKKA** (ex-*Valvoja III*) 99

Displacement, tons: 340 full load
Dimensions, feet (metres): 118.1 × 29.5 × 9.8 *(36 × 9 × 3)*
Main machinery: 1 diesel; 670 hp(m) *(492 kW)*; 1 shaft
Speed, knots: 11
Complement: 10
Guns: 2 USSR 23 mm/60 (twin).

Comment: *Kemiö* completed in 1958. *Kustaanmiekka* in 1963. Former buoy tenders transferred from Board of Navigation and converted by Hollming, Rauma in 1983 and 1989 respectively. Bofors 40 mm gun replaced in 1988.

KEMIÖ (old gun) — *1987, Finnish Navy*

3 KAMPELA CLASS (LCU TRANSPORTS)

Name	*No*	*Builders*	*Commissioned*
KAMPELA 1	471	Enso Gutzeit	29 July 1976
KAMPELA 2	272	Enso Gutzeit	21 Oct 1976
KAMPELA 3	557 (ex-77)	Finnmekano	23 Oct 1979

Displacement, tons: 90 light; 260 full load
Dimensions, feet (metres): 106.6 × 26.2 × 4.9 *(32.5 × 8 × 1.5)*
Main machinery: 2 Scania diesels; 460 hp(m) *(338 kW)*; 2 shafts
Speed, knots: 9
Complement: 10
Guns: 2 or 4 USSR 23 mm/60 (1 or 2 twin).
Mines: About 20 can be carried.

Comment: Can be used as amphibious craft, transports, minelayers or for shore support. Armament can be changed to suit role. *Kampela 1* and *2* are used by the Coastal Artillery.

KAMPELA Class — *1988, Finnish Navy*

5 VALAS CLASS (GP TRANSPORTS)

VALAS 97 **MURSU** 98 **VAHAKARI** 121 **VAARLAHTI** 222 **VANO** 323

Displacement, tons: 300 full load
Dimensions, feet (metres): 100.4 × 26.5 × 10.4 *(30.6 × 8.1 × 3.2)*
Main machinery: 1 Wärtsilä Vasa 22 diesel; 1450 hp(m) *(1.07 MW)*; 1 shaft
Speed, knots: 12
Complement: 11
Military lift: 35 tons
Guns: 2—23 mm/60 (twin). 1—12.7 mm MG.
Mines: 28 can be carried.

Comment: Completed 1979-80. *Mursu* acts as a diving tender; *Vahakari, Vaarlahti* and *Vano* are used by the Coastal Artillery. Funnel is offset to starboard. Can be used as minelayers or transport/cargo carriers and are capable of breaking thin ice.

VAARLAHTI — *10/1990, van Ginderen Collectior*

6 KALA CLASS (LCU TRANSPORTS)

KALA 1 871 **KALA 3** 773 **KALA 5** 875
KALA 2 372 **KALA 4** 874 **KALA 6** 776

Displacement, tons: 60 light; 200 full load
Dimensions, feet (metres): 88.6 × 26.2 × 6 *(27 × 8 × 1.8)*
Main machinery: 2 Valmet diesels; 360 hp(m) *(265 kW)*; 2 shafts
Speed, knots: 9
Complement: 10
Guns: 1 Oerlikon 20 mm (not in all).
Mines: 34.

Comment: Completed between 20 June 1956 *(Kala 1)* and 4 December 1959 *(Kala 6)*. Can be usec as transports, amphibious craft, minelayers or for shore support. Armament can be changed to sui role. Pennant numbers changed in 1990.

KALA Class — *7/1988, A. Sheldon Duplai*

6 HAUKI CLASS (TRANSPORTS)

HAVOURI 133 **HIRSALA** 235 **HAKUNI** 431
HAUKI 232 **HANKONIEMI** 334 **HOUTSKÄR** 436

Displacement, tons: 45 full load
Dimensions, feet (metres): 47.6 × 15.1 × 7.2 *(14.5 × 4.6 × 2.2)*
Main machinery: 2 Valmet 611 CSM diesels; 586 hp(m) *(431 kW)*; 1 shaft
Speed, knots: 12
Complement: 4
Cargo capacity: 6 tons or 40 passengers

Comment: Completed 1979. Ice strengthened; two serve isolated island defences. Four convertec in 1988 as tenders to the Marine War College, but from 1990 back in service as light transports. Al used by the Coastal Artillery.

HIRSALA — *1991, Finnish Nav*

2 + 2 HILA CLASS (TRANSPORTS)

HILA 237 **HARUN** 238

Displacement, tons: 50 full load
Dimensions, feet (metres): 49.2 × 13.1 × 5.9 *(15 × 4 × 1.8)*
Main machinery: 2 diesels; 416 hp(m) *(306 kW)*; 2 shafts
Speed, knots: 12
Complement: 4

Comment: Ordered from Kotkan Telakka in August 1990. Ice strengthened. All for use by Coastal Artillery.

HILA *10/1991, Finnish Navy*

2 LOHI CLASS (LCU TRANSPORTS)

LOHI 251 **LOHM** 452

Displacement, tons: 38 full load
Dimensions, feet (metres): 65.6 × 19.7 × 3 *(20 × 6 × 0.9)*
Main machinery: 2 WMB diesels; 1200 hp(m) *(882 kW)*; 2 waterjets
Speed, knots: 20. **Range, miles:** 240 at 20 kts
Complement: 4
Guns: 2 USSR 23 mm/60 (twin). 1—14.5 mm MG.

Comment: Commissioned September 1984. Used as troop carriers and for light cargo by the Coastal Artillery. Guns not always carried.

LOHM *7/1988, A. Sheldon Duplaix*

2 TRANSPORT and COMMAND LAUNCHES

ASKERI 241 **VIIRI** 91

Displacement, tons: 20
Dimensions, feet (metres): 52.6 × 14.5 × 4.5 *(16 × 4.4 × 1.4)*
Speed, knots: 20

Comment: Closely resemble Spanish PVC II class. *Askeri* is used by the Coastal Artillery.

VIIRI *1991, Finnish Navy*

7 VIHURI CLASS (COMMAND LAUNCHES)

VIHURI 541 **RAJU** 521 **TRÄSKÖ** 992
VINHA 511 **SYÖKSY** 531 + **2**

Displacement, tons: 13 full load
Dimensions, feet (metres): 42.7 × 13.1 × 3 *(13 × 4 × 0.9)*
Main machinery: 2 diesels; 772 hp(m) *(567 kW)*; 2 waterjets
Speed, knots: 30

Comment: First four commissioned in 1991 as Command launches for the Coastal Fleet Squadrons. Last three commissioned in 1991/92 and are used as fast transports for the Coastal Artillery.

VIHURI *1988, Finnish Navy*

15 MERIUISKO CLASS (LCAs)

Displacement, tons: 9.8 full load
Dimensions, feet (metres): 36 × 11.5 × 2.9 *(11 × 3.5 × 0.9)*
Main machinery: 2 Volvo TAMD 70E diesels; 418 hp(m) *(307 kW)*; 2 waterjets
Speed, knots: 36; 30 full load
Military lift: 48 troops

Comment: First 11 completed by Alumina Varvet from 1983 to 1986. Last four ordered in 1989. Constructed of light alloy. Two of the class equipped with cable handling system for boom defence work.

MERIUISKO Class *1988, Finnish Navy*

1 SUPPORT SHIP

PARAINEN (ex-*Pellinki*, ex-*Meteor*) 420 (ex-210)

Displacement, tons: 404
Dimensions, feet (metres): 126.3 × 29.5 × 14.8 *(38.5 × 9 × 4.5)*
Main machinery: 1 diesel; 1800 hp(m) *(1.32 MW)*; 1 shaft
Speed, knots: 13
Complement: 17
Guns: 1 Madsen 20 mm.

Comment: Built as a tug in 1960. Acquired late 1980 from Oy Neptun Ab and modernised in 1987 by Teijon Telakka. Used by the Coastal Artillery.

PARAINEN *9/1988, Antonio Moreno*

MISCELLANEOUS

Note: In addition to the vessels listed below there is a fuel/water barge PA3 of 540 tons, self-propelled at 2 kts (normally towed). Built in 1979.

1 CABLE SHIP

PUTSAARI 92

Displacement, tons: 45
Dimensions, feet (metres): 149.5 × 28.6 × 8.2 *(45.6 × 8.7 × 2.5)*
Main machinery: 1 Wärtsilä diesel; 510 hp(m) *(375 kW)*; 1 shaft; active rudder; bow thruster
Speed, knots: 10
Complement: 20

Comment: Built by Rauma Repola, Rauma and commissioned in 1966. Modernised by Wärtsilä in 1987. Fitted with two 10 ton cable winches. Strengthened for ice operations.

PUTSAARI *1988, Finnish Navy*

POLLUTION CONTROL VESSELS

HYLJE 799 **HALLI** 899

Displacement, tons: 1500
Dimensions, feet (metres): 164 × 41 × 9.8 *(50 × 12.5 × 3)*
Main machinery: 2 Saab diesels; 680 hp(m) *(500 kW)*; 2 shafts; active rudders; bow thruster
Speed, knots: 7

Comment: Painted grey. Strengthened for ice. Owned by Board of Navigation, civilian manned but operated by Navy from Turku. *Hylje* commissioned 3 June 1981, *Halli* in January 1987. Capacity is about 1400 cu m of contaminated seawater. The ships have slightly different superstructure lines aft.

HALLI *1987, Finnish Navy*

2 HARBOUR TUGS

HAUKIPÄÄ 731 **KALLANPÄÄ** 831

Displacement, tons: 38
Dimensions, feet (metres): 45.9 × 16.4 × 7.5 *(14 × 5 × 2.3)*
Main machinery: 2 diesels; 360 hp(m) *(265 kW)*; 2 shafts
Speed, knots: 9
Complement: 2

Comment: Delivered by Teijon Telakka Oy in December 1985. Similar to Hauki class.

KALLANPÄÄ *1988, Finnish Navy*

SURVEYING AND RESEARCH VESSELS

Note: Controlled by Ministry of Trade and Industry

Name	*Displacement*	*Launched*	*Complement*
PRISMA	1080 tons	1978	50 (12)
KALLA	920 tons	1963	50 (12)
SAARISTO	537 tons	1965	32 (7)
LINSSI	444 tons	1979	29 (6)
AIRISTO	350 tons	1972	13 (6)
TAUVO	187 tons	1963	13 (4)
SESTA	119 tons	1979	11 (2)

Plus 36 surveying launches.

1 RESEARCH SHIP

ARANDA

Displacement, tons: 1800 full load
Dimensions, feet (metres): 193.6 × 44.6 × 15.7 *(59 × 13.6 × 4.8)*
Main machinery: 1 Wärtsilä diesel; 2720 hp(m) *(2 MW)*; 1 shaft; bow and stern thrusters
Speed, knots: 12
Complement: 12 plus 12-25 research staff
Helicopters: Platform only.

Comment: Ordered from Laivateollisuus, Turku, to a Wärtsilä design in February 1988 and delivered in Spring 1989. Has 270 square metres of laboratory space. Replacement for old *Aranda* whose conversion in 1985 was not satisfactory.

ARANDA *1991, van Ginderen Collection*

ARANDA *1989, Finnish Navy*

FRONTIER GUARD

Note: Controlled by Ministry of the Interior.

2 TURSAS CLASS (LARGE PATROL CRAFT)

TURSAS **UISKO**

Displacement, tons: 700
Dimensions, feet (metres): 149 × 34.1 × 13.1 *(45.4 × 10.4 × 4)*
Main machinery: 2 Wärtsilä Vasa 8R22 diesels; 3152 hp(m) *(2.32 MW)* sustained; 2 shafts
Speed, knots: 16
Guns: 2 USSR 23 mm/60 (twin).
Sonars: Simrad SS105; active scanning; 14 kHz.

Comment: First ordered from Rauma-Repola on 21 December 1984. Launched 31 January 1986. Delivered June 1986. Second ordered 20 March 1986. Delivered 27 January 1987. Operate as offshore patrol craft and can act as salvage tugs. Ice strengthened.

TURSAS *1991, Finnish Frontier Guard*

1 IMPROVED VALPAS CLASS (LARGE PATROL CRAFT)

TURVA

Displacement, tons: 550
Dimensions, feet (metres): 159.1 × 28 × 12.8 *(48.5 × 8.6 × 3.9)*
Main machinery: 2 Wärtsilä diesels; 2000 hp(m) *(1.47 MW)*; 1 shaft
Speed, knots: 15
Guns: 1 Oerlikon 20 mm.
Sonars: Simrad SS105; active scanning; 14 kHz.

Comment: Built by Laivateollisuus, Turku and commissioned 15 December 1977.

TURVA *1991, Finnish Frontier Guard*

1 VALPAS CLASS (LARGE PATROL CRAFT)

VALPAS

Displacement, tons: 545
Dimensions, feet (metres): 159.1 × 27.9 × 12.5 *(48.5 × 8.5 × 3.8)*
Main machinery: 1 Werkspoor diesel; 2000 hp(m) *(1.47 MW)*; 1 shaft
Speed, knots: 15
Complement: 22
Guns: 1 Oerlikon 20 mm.
Sonars: Simrad SS105; active scanning; 14 kHz.

Comment: An improvement on the *Silmä* design. Built by Laivateollisuus, Turku, and commissioned 21 July 1971. Ice strengthened.

VALPAS *1/1990, van Ginderen Collection*

1 SILMÄ CLASS (LARGE PATROL CRAFT)

SILMÄ

Displacement, tons: 530
Dimensions, feet (metres): 158.5 × 27.2 × 14.1 *(48.3 × 8.3 × 4.3)*
Main machinery: 1 Werkspoor diesel; 1800 hp(m) *(1.32 MW)*; 1 shaft
Speed, knots: 15
Complement: 22
Guns: 1 Oerlikon 20 mm.
Sonars: Simrad SS105; active scanning; 14 kHz.

Comment: Built by Laivateollisuus, Turku and commissioned 19 August 1963.

SILMÄ *4/1990, van Ginderen Collection*

2 + (2) KIISLA CLASS

KIISLA **KURKI**

Displacement, tons: 270 full load
Dimensions, feet (metres): 158.5 × 28.9 × 7.2 *(48.3 × 8.8 × 2.2)*
Main machinery: 2 MTU 16V 538 TB93 diesels; 9370 hp(m) *(6.9 MW)* sustained; 2 KaMeWa waterjets
Speed, knots: 25
Complement: 22
Guns: 2 USSR 23 mm/60 (twin) or 1 Madsen 20 mm.
Sonars: Simrad SS304 hull-mounted and VDS; active search; high frequency.

Comment: First ordered from Hollming on 23 November 1984 and commissioned 25 May 1987 after lengthy trials. Three more of an improved type ordered 22 November 1988; the first of which was laid down 3 August 1989 and commissioned in late 1990. Work on the last pair has been postponed. To replace Koskelo class. The design allows for rapid conversion to attack craft, ASW craft, minelayer, minesweeper or minehunter. A central telescopic crane over the engine room casing is used to launch a 5.7 m rigid inflatable sea boat. A fire monitor is mounted in the bows. The KaMeWa steerable waterjets extend the overall hull length by 2 m.

KIISLA *1991, Finnish Frontier Guard*

KURKI *1991, van Ginderen Collection*

1 LARGE PATROL CRAFT

VIIMA

Displacement, tons: 135
Dimensions, feet (metres): 118.1 × 21.7 × 7.5 *(36 × 6.6 × 2.3)*
Main machinery: 3 Mercedes-Benz MTU diesels; 4050 hp(m) *(2.98 MW)*; 3 shafts; cp props
Speed, knots: 25
Complement: 13
Guns: 1 Oerlikon 20 mm.

Comment: Built by Laivateollisuus, Turku and commissioned in 1964.

VIIMA *1991, Finnish Frontier Guard*

4 LOKKI CLASS (COASTAL PATROL CRAFT)

LOKKI **TIIRA** **KAJAVA** **KIHU**

Displacement, tons: 59 *(Lokki)*; 64 (remainder)
Dimensions, feet (metres): 87.9 × 18 × 6.2 *(26.8 × 5.5 × 1.9)*
87.9 × 17.1 × 8.5 *(26.8 × 5.2 × 2.1) (Lokki)*
Main machinery: 2 MTU 8V 396 TB 82 diesels; 1740 hp(m) *(1.28 MW)* sustained (*Lokki*)
2 MTU 8V 396 TB 84 diesels; 2100 hp(m) *(1.54 MW)* sustained (remainder); 2 shafts
Speed, knots: 25
Complement: 8

Comment: Under a contract signed on 12 May 1980 Valmet/Laivateollisuus Oy (Turku) built the prototype craft *Lokki* which completed in autumn 1981. *Tiira* completed 1 November 1985, *Kajava* 28 August 1986 and *Kihu* in December 1986. Built in light metal alloy. *Lokki* has a V-shaped hull.

KIHU *1991, Ships of the World*

RV 38 *1978, Finnish Frontier Guard*

9 + 5 COASTAL PATROL CRAFT

PV 11, 12, 104, 108, 205, 209, 210, 306, 307

Displacement, tons: 10
Speed, knots: 28
Complement: 2

Comment: Built by Fiskars, Turku. All launched by June 1983, first (209) completed September 1984. Five more ordered in 1989 from Waterman-Teiso, to replace older craft.

PV 306 *1988, Finnish Frontier Guard*

4 TELKKÄ/KOSKELO CLASS (COASTAL PATROL CRAFT)

KUIKKA* **TAVI*** **KURKI*** **TELKKÄ**

(*Koskelo class)

Displacement, tons: 95; 92 (*Telkkä*) full load
Dimensions, feet (metres): 95.1 × 16.4 × 4.9 *(29 × 5 × 1.5)*
Main machinery: 2 Mercedes-Benz MTU diesels; 2700 hp(m) *(1.98 MW)*; 2 shafts
Speed, knots: 23
Complement: 11
Guns: 1 Oerlikon 20 mm. 1 Bofors 40 mm (fitted for but not always embarked).

Comment: Built of steel, between 1955 and 1960 *(Tavi)*. Originally of much lower horsepower. *Telkkä* modernised in 1970 and Koskelo class in 1972-74 by Laivateollisuus. New internal arrangements, new decking and new engines increased their speed by 8 kts. *Telkkä* modified for use as training vessel. Being replaced by Kiisla class and at least two are to pay off in 1992.

KUIKKA *1991, Finnish Frontier Guard*

TELKKÄ *1989, van Ginderen Collection*

7 COASTAL PATROL CRAFT

RV 37-41 **RV 142** **RV 243**

Displacement, tons: 20
Dimensions, feet (metres): 46.9 × 11.8 × 5.2 *(14.3 × 3.6 × 1.6)*
Main machinery: 1 Mercedes-Benz MTU diesel; 300 hp(m) *(220 kW)*; 1 shaft
Speed, knots: 12

Comment: Built by Hollming Oy, Rauma. Two completed January 1978, the third 1 September 1978, two more in early 1984 and the last two in 1985. For patrol, towing and salvage.

COASTAL PATROL CRAFT

Class	*Total*	*Tonnage*	*Speed*	*Commissioned*
RV 1 (ex-RV 41)	1	17	10	1965
RV 8	1	10	10	1958
RV 9	9	12	10	1959-60
RV 10	11	18	10	1961-63
RV 30	7	19	10	1973-74
TENDERS	2	6	13	1986

TENDER *6/1988, A. Sheldon Duplaix*

LAND-BASED MARITIME AIRCRAFT

Note: Both Mi-8s transferred to the Air Force in 1990.

Numbers/Type: 2 Agusta AB 412 Griffon.
Operational speed: 122 kts *(226 km/h)*.
Service ceiling: 14 200 ft *(4330 m)*.
Range: 227 nm *(420 km)*.
Role/Weapon systems: Operated by Coast Guard/Frontier force for patrol and SAR. Sensors: Possible radar. Weapons: Unarmed at present but possible mountings for machine guns.

Numbers/Type: 2 Aerospatiale AS 332B Super Puma.
Operational speed: 151 kts *(279 km/h)*.
Service ceiling: 15 090 ft *(4600 m)*.
Range: 335 nm *(620 km)*.
Role/Weapon systems: Coastal patrol, surveillance and SAR helicopters. Sensors: Surveillance radar, tactical navigation systems and SAR equipment. Weapons: Unarmed.

Numbers/Type: 3 Agusta AB 206B JetRanger.
Operational speed: 116 kts *(215 km/h)*.
Service ceiling: 13 500 ft *(4120 m)*.
Range: 311 nm *(576 km)*.
Role/Weapon systems: Coastal patrol and inshore surveillance helicopters. Sensors: Visual means only. Weapons: Unarmed.

Numbers/Type: 2 Piper PA-31 Navajo.
Operational speed: 220 kts *(410 km/h)*.
Service ceiling: 27 200 ft *(8290 m)*.
Range: 755 nm *(1400 km)*.
Role/Weapon systems: Medium range maritime patrol aircraft. Sensors: Weather/search radar. Weapons: Unarmed.

FRANCE

Headquarters' Appointments

Chief of the Naval Staff:
Amiral Coatanea
Inspector General of the Navy:
Amiral J M E Merveilleux du Vignaux
Director of Personnel:
Vice-Amiral d'escadre Calmon
Major General of the Navy:
Vice-Amiral Turcat

Senior Appointments

C-in-C Atlantic Theatre (CECLANT):
Vice-Amiral d'escadre R Merveilleux du Vignaux
C-in-C Mediterranean Theatre (CECMED):
Vice-Amiral d'escadre Tripier
Flag Officer French Forces Polynesia:
Vice-Amiral Quérat
Flag Officer Atlantic Squadron:
Contre-Amiral Rouyer
Flag Officer Mediterranean Squadron:
Vice-Amiral Merlo
Flag Officer Indian Ocean:
Contre-Amiral Gazzano
Flag Officer (Submarines):
Vice-Amiral Orsini
Flag Officer (Naval Air):
Vice-Amiral Deramond
Flag Officer (Aircraft Carriers):
Contre-Amiral Wild

Commandant Marines:
Capitaine de Vaisseau Delbrel

Diplomatic Representation

Naval Attaché in London:
Vice-Amiral Garibal
Naval Attaché in Washington:
Contre-Amiral Sassy
Military Attaché in Saudi Arabia:
Contre-Amiral Lacaille
Military Attaché to SACLANT:
Contre-Amiral Gachot
Military Attaché to CINC South:
Contre-Amiral Desgrées du Lou

Personnel

(a) 1992: 66 600 (4716 officers)
(b) 10 months' national service (19 100)

Bases

Cherbourg: Channel Command base. Prémar Un (comes under Atlantic Maritime command)
Brest: Main Atlantic base. SSBN base. Prémar Deux
Lorient: Atlantic submarine base
Toulon: Mediterranean Command base. Prémar Trois
Papeete (Tahiti): Refitting base with 3800 ton capacity floating docks, 23 ton floating crane and earth stations for Syracuse communications
Fort-de-France (Martinique): Small base; Syracuse communications
Nouméa (New Caledonia): Small base
Degrad des Cannes (French Guiana): Small base
Saint Denis (La Réunion): Small base; Syracuse communications.
From 6 July 1990 there are only two 'territorial' commands in mainland France: (a) Atlantic Command (Zone Maritime Atlantique) with HQ in Brest and subordinate commands in Cherbourg (Channel) and Lorient. (b) Mediterranean Command with HQ in Toulon.

Shipyards (Naval)

Cherbourg: Submarines and Fast Attack Craft (private shipyard)
Brest: Major warships and refitting
Lorient: Destroyers and Frigates, MCMVs, Patrol Craft
Toulon: Major warships and refits.

Submarine Service

SSBN *(SNLE)* force based at Ile Longue near Brest with a training base at Roche-Douvres and VLFW/T station at Rosnay. Known as Force Océanique Stratégique (FOST) with headquarters at Houilles near Paris. Patrol submarines are based at Lorient and Toulon, nuclear fleet submarines at Toulon.

New Construction

There is a legal requirement for all the major ships of the French Navy to be built in naval shipyards whilst ships built for export must be built in private yards. However, under Clause 29, suitable export ships may be built on spec. with a guarantee that, if not otherwise sold, they will be purchased by the Navy. This clause has been invoked to maintain some yards in existence when threatened with closure eg the Batral *La Grandière*, survey ship *Arago*, BTS *Bougainville* and the fifth of the Durance class, *Somme*.

Dates

Armement pour essais: After launching when the ship is sufficiently advanced to allow a crew to live on board, and the commanding officer has joined. From this date the ship hoists the French flag and is ready to undertake her first harbour trials.
Armement définitif: On this date the ship has received her full complement and is able to undergo sea trials.
Clôture d'armement: Trials are completed and the ship is now able to undertake her first endurance cruise.
Croisière de longue durée or traversée de longue durée: The endurance cruise follows the clôture d'armement and lasts until the ship is accepted with all systems fully operational.
Admission au service actif: Commissioning date.

Reserve

A ship in 'Reserve Normale' has no complement but is available at short notice. 'Reserve Speciale' means that a refit will be required before the ship can go to sea again. 'Condamnation' is the state before being broken up or sold; at this stage a Q number is allocated.

Strength of the Fleet

Type	*Active (Reserve)*	*Building (Projected)*
Submarines (Ballistic Missile)	5	2 (3)
Submarines (Fleet)	5	2
Submarines (Patrol)	8	—
Aircraft Carriers	2	1 (1)
Helicopter Carrier	1	—
Destroyers	15	—
Frigates	26	6 (4)
Public Service Force	3	—
Fast Attack Craft (Patrol)	10	—
Large Patrol Craft	1	—
LSDs	4	(2)
LCTs	12	—
LCMs	25	—
Minesweepers	3	—
Minehunters	14	2 (5)?
Diving Support Ships	4	—
Surveying Ships	6	—
Tankers (URs)	5	—
Tankers (Support)	2	—
Maintenance Ship	1	—
Depot Ships	5	—
Trials Ships	9	(1)
Boom Defence Vessels	7	—
Supply Tenders	9	—
Transports	15	—
Tenders	15	—
Tugs	102	—
Training Ships	14	2

Prefix

FS is used in NATO communications but is not official.

Mercantile Marine

Lloyd's Register of Shipping:
910 vessels of 3 988 072 tons gross

Fleet Air Arm Bases

Base/Squadron No	*Aircraft*	*Task*
Embarked Squadrons (68 fixed wing aircraft; 40 helicopters)		
Lann Bihoué/4F	Alizé (modernised)	Safety
Nîmes Garons/6F	Alizé (modernised)	Safety
Landivisiau/11F	Super Etendard	Assault
Landivisiau/12F	F-8E(FN) Crusader	Fighters
Landivisiau/14F	Super Etendard	Assault
Landivisiau/16F	Etendard IVP	Reconnaissance
St Mandrier/31F	Lynx	ASW
Lanvéoc-Poulmic/32F	Super Frelon	Support
St Mandrier/33F	Super Frelon	Support
Lanvéoc-Poulmic/34F	Lynx	ASW
J d'Arc, Lanvéoc-Poulmic/35F	Lynx/Alouette II/III	Training
Support Squadrons		
Lann Bihoué/2S	Xingu/Nord 262 A/E	Support Atlantic Region
Hyères/3S	Falcon 10 MER/ Nord 262 A/E	Support Mediterranean Region
St Raphael/10S	Alizé (mod) Nord 262/Xingu Alouette II/III Super Frelon/Lynx	Trials CEPA
Dugny-Le-Bourget/11S	Nord 262A/Xingu	Support
Lanvéoc-Poulmic/22S	Alouette III	Support Atlantic Region, SAR
St Mandrier/23S	Alouette II/III Dauphin	Support Mediterranean Region, SAR
Landivisiau/57S	Falcon 10 MER/Paris	Support
Maritime Patrol Squadrons		
Nîmes-Garons/21F	Atlantic Mk 1 (NATO)	MP
Nîmes-Garons/22F	Atlantique Mk 2	MP
Lann Bihoué/23F	Atlantique Mk 2	MP
Lann Bihoué/24F	Atlantique Mk 1 (converting to Mk 2)	MP
Training Squadrons		
Lann Bihoué/52S	Xingu	Flying School
Nimes Garons/56S	Nord 262E/Navajo	Flying School
Hyères/59S	Super Etendard/ Zéphyr	Fighter School
Lanvéoc-Poulmic/SOS	MS 880 Rallye	Naval School Recreational
Dax/SME Dax	Alouette II	Helicopter School
Rochefort/51S	CAP 10/MS 880 Rallye	Initial Flying School
Overseas Detachments		
Tontouta/9S	Gardian	MP
Faaa (Papeete)/12S	Gardian Alouette III	MP Support

In addition, Atlantique Mk 1 aircraft are permanently deployed to Dakar, Fort-de-France and Djibouti.

Approximate Fleet Dispositions (not including refits) on 1 December 1991

Type	*Mediterranean*	*Atlantic*	*Area* *Channel*	*Indian Ocean*	*Pacific*	*Antilles*
Carrier	2	1 (Helo)	—	—	—	—
SSN	5	—	—	—	—	—
SS	2	6	—	—	—	—
DDG/DD	8	8	—	—	—	—
FF	5	6	3	5	3	—
MCMV (incl Tenders)	6	10	6	—	—	—
Light forces (nil GM large)	3	12	3	4	4	2
Amphibious forces	2	6	—	2	6	1

Note: (1) CEP Nuclear Test Range Pacific: *Bougainville*; EDICs, L 9051; L 9072; L 9074;
Supply Tenders, *Taape, Tapatai, Chamois, Rari, Revi;* Tugs, *Maroa, Maito, Manini.*

(2) In addition to permanent deployments, there is usually a DD/DDG and an FF in the Indian Ocean, and an FF in the Antilles as reinforcements.

DELETIONS

Submarines

1989 *Daphné, Flore*
1990 *Vénus*
1991 *Le Redoutable, Galatée*

Cruisers

1991 *Colbert*

Destroyers

1990 *La Galissonnière*
1991 *Du Chayla*
1992 *Duperré*

Frigates

1990 *Commandant Bourdais, Amiral Charner* (both to Uruguay)
1991 *Doudart de Lagrée*
1992 *Protet*

Light Forces

1991 *Mercure*

Mine Warfare Forces

1989 *Garigliano, Cantho, Berlaimont*
1992 *Phénix, Sagittaire* (sold to Pakistan)

Amphibious Forces

1989 *Trieux*
1990 L 9092, L 9096, LCM 1055-56
1991 L 9094, CTM 5

Survey Ships

1990 *Boussole, Corail*
1991 *L'Estafette*
1992 *L'Archéonaute, Henri Poincaré*

Service Forces

1989 *Pelican, Aber Wrach, Vendres* (lease expired September)
1990 *Palangrin, Dahlia, Abeille Supporter*
1991 *Engageante, Vigilante*

Tugs

1990 *Okoume, Aigrette, Héron*
1991 *Hercule, Balsa, Geyser*

Gendarmerie

1992 *La Combattante*

PENNANT LIST

Submarines

S 601 Rubis
S 602 Saphir
S 603 Casabianca
S 604 Emeraude
S 605 Amethyste
S 606 Perle (bldg)
S 607 Turquoise (bldg)
S 610 Le Foudroyant
S 612 Le Terrible
S 613 L'Indomptable
S 614 Le Tonnant
S 615 L'Inflexible
S 616 Le Triomphant (bldg)
S 617 Le Téméraire (bldg)
S 620 Agosta
S 621 Bévéziers
S 622 La Praya
S 623 Ouessant
S 633 Dauphin (trials)
S 643 Doris
S 648 Junon
S 650 Psyché
S 651 Sirène

Aircraft and Helicopter Carriers

R 91 Charles de Gaulle (bldg)
R 97 Jeanne d'Arc
R 98 Clemenceau
R 99 Foch

Destroyers

D 602 Suffren
D 603 Duquesne
D 609 Aconit
D 610 Tourville
D 611 Duguay-Trouin
D 612 De Grasse
D 614 Cassard
D 615 Jean Bart
D 640 Georges Leygues
D 641 Dupleix
D 642 Montcalm
D 643 Jean de Vienne
D 644 Primauguet
D 645 La Motte-Picquet
D 646 Latouche-Tréville

Frigates

F 710 La Fayette (bldg)
F 711 Surcouf (bldg)
F 712 Courbet (bldg)
F 726 Commandant Bory
F 729 Balny
F 730 Floréal
F 731 Prairial
F 732 Nivôse
F 733 Ventôse (bldg)
F 734 Vendémiaire (bldg)
F 735 Germinal (bldg)
F 749 Enseigne de Vaisseau Henry
F 781 D'Estienne d'Orves
F 782 Amyot d'Inville
F 783 Drogou
F 784 Détroyat
F 785 Jean Moulin
F 786 Quartier Maître Anquetil
F 787 Commandant de Pimodan
F 788 Second Maître Le Bihan
F 789 Lieutenant de Vaisseau le Hénaff
F 790 Lieutenant de Vaisseau Lavallée
F 791 Commandant l'Herminier
F 792 Premier Maître l'Her
F 793 Commandant Blaison
F 794 Enseigne de Vaisseau Jacoubet
F 795 Commandant Ducuing
F 796 Commandant Birot
F 797 Commandant Bouan

Mine Warfare Forces

M 610 Ouistreham
M 611 Vulcain
M 612 Alençon
M 614 Styx
M 622 Pluton
M 623 Baccarat
M 641 Éridan
M 642 Cassiopée
M 643 Andromède
M 644 Pégase
M 645 Orion
M 646 Croix du Sud
M 647 Aigle
M 648 Lyre
M 649 Persée
M 660 Narvik (bldg)
M 712 Cybèle
M 713 Calliope
M 714 Clio
M 715 Circé
M 716 Cérès

Light Forces

P 670 Trident GM
P 671 Glaive GM
P 672 Épée GM
P 673 Pertuisane GM
P 679 Grèbe
P 680 Sterne
P 681 Albatros
P 682 L'Audacieuse
P 683 La Boudeuse
P 684 La Capricieuse
P 685 La Fougueuse
P 686 La Glorieuse
P 687 La Gracieuse
P 688 La Moqueuse
P 689 La Railleuse
P 690 La Rieuse
P 691 La Tapageuse
P 696 Iris

Amphibious Forces

L 9011 Foudre
L 9021 Ouragan
L 9022 Orage
L 9030 Champlain
L 9031 Francis Garnier
L 9032 Dumont D'Urville
L 9033 Jacques Cartier
L 9034 La Grandière
L 9051 EDIC
L 9052 EDIC
L 9061 CDIC
L 9062 CDIC
L 9070 EDIC
L 9072 EDIC
L 9074 EDIC
L 9077 Bougainville
L 9090 Gapeau

Auxiliaries Survey and Support Ships

A 601 Monge
A 607 Meuse
A 608 Var
A 610 Ile d'Oléron
A 613 Achéron
A 615 Loire
A 617 Garonne
A 618 Rance
A 620 Jules Verne
A 621 Rhin
A 622 Rhône
A 625 Papenoo
A 629 Durance
A 630 Marne
A 631 Somme
A 632 Punaruu
A 633 Taape
A 634 Rari
A 635 Revi
A 636 Maroa
A 637 Maito
A 638 Manini
A 644 Berry
A 646 Triton
A 649 L'Étoile
A 650 La Belle Poule
A 652 Mutin
A 653 La Grande Hermine
A 664 Malabar
A 669 Tenace
A 671 Le Fort
A 672 Utile
A 673 Lutteur
A 674 Centaure
A 675 Fréhel
A 676 Saire
A 677 Armen
A 678 La Houssaye
A 679 Sicie
A 680 Lardier
A 685 Robuste
A 686 Actif
A 687 Laborieux
A 688 Valeureux
A 692 Travailleur
A 693 Acharné
A 694 Efficace
A 695 Bélier
A 696 Buffle
A 697 Bison
A 702 Girelle
A 712 Athos
A 713 Aramis
A 714 Tourmaline
A 722 Poséidon
A 731 La Tianée
A 733 Commandant Rivière
A 743 Denti
A 748 Léopard
A 749 Panthère
A 750 Jaguar
A 751 Lynx
A 752 Guépard
A 753 Chacal
A 754 Tigre
A 755 Lion
A 756 L'Espérance
A 757 D'Entrecasteaux
A 767 Chamois
A 768 Élan
A 774 Chevreuil
A 775 Gazelle
A 776 Isard
A 779 Tapatai
A 785 Thétis
A 786 Agnes 200
A 790 Coralline
A 791 Lapérouse
A 792 Borda
A 793 Laplace
A 795 Arago

Auxiliaries

GFA 1-6 Floating Cranes
Y 601 Acajou
Y 604 Ariel
Y 611 Bengali
Y 613 Faune
Y 617 Mouette
Y 618 Cascade
Y 620 Chataigner
Y 621 Mésange
Y 623 Charme
Y 624 Chêne
Y 625 Cigogne
Y 628 Colibri
Y 629 Cormier
Y 630 Bonite
Y 632 Cygne
Y 634 Rouget
Y 636 Martinet
Y 637 Fauvette
Y 644 Frêne
Y 645 Gave
Y 648 Goéland
Y 654 Hêtre
Y 655 Hévéa
Y 661 Korrigan
Y 662 Dryade
Y 663 Latanier
Y 666 Manguier
Y 667 Tupa
Y 668 Méléze
Y 669 Merisier
Y 670 Merle
Y 671 Morgane
Y 673 Moineau
Y 675 Martin Pêcheur
Y 684 Oued
Y 686 Palétuvier
Y 687 Passereau
Y 688 Peuplier
Y 689 Pin
Y 691 Pinson
Y 692 Telenn Mor
Y 694 Pivert
Y 695 Platane
Y 696 Alphée
Y 698 Calmar
Y 700 Nereide
Y 701 Ondine
Y 702 Naiade
Y 706 Chimère
Y 708 Saule
Y 709 Sycomore
Y 710 Sylphe
Y 711 Farfadet
Y 717 Ébène
Y 718 Érable
Y 719 Olivier
Y 720 Santal
Y 721 Alouette
Y 722 Vanneau
Y 723 Engoulevent
Y 724 Sarcelle
Y 725 Marabout
Y 726 Toucan
Y 727 Macreuse
Y 728 Grand Duc
Y 729 Eider
Y 730 Ara
Y 732 DGV—S de D No 3
Y 735 Merlin
Y 736 Mélusine
Y 738 Maronnier
Y 739 Noyer
Y 740 Papayer
Y 741 Elfe
Y 745 Aiguière
Y 746 Embrun
Y 747 Loriot
Y 748 Gélinotte
Y 749 La Prudente
Y 750 La Persévérante
Y 751 La Fidèle
Y 790-799 Tenders

GM = Gendarmerie Maritime

SUBMARINES

Strategic Missile Submarines (Sous-Marins Nucléaires Lanceurs d'Engins (SNLE))

0 + 2 + 1 (2) LE TRIOMPHANT CLASS (SNLE-NG)

Name	No	Builders	Laid down	Launched	Operational
LE TRIOMPHANT	S 616	Cherbourg Naval Dockyard	9 June 1989	1993	July 1995
LE TÉMÉRAIRE	S 617	Cherbourg Naval Dockyard	1991	1995	July 1997
—	S 618	Cherbourg Naval Dockyard	1993	1997	1999

Displacement, tons: 12 640 surfaced; 14 120 dived
Dimensions, feet (metres): 453 × 41 × 41 *(138 × 12.5 × 12.5)*
Main machinery: Nuclear; turbo-electric; 1 PWR Type K15 (enlarged CAS 48); 150 MW; 2 turbo-alternators; 1 motor; 41 500 hp(m) *(30.5 MW)*; diesel-electric auxiliary propulsion; 1 shaft; pump jet propulsor
Speed, knots: 25 dived
Complement: 110 (14 officers) (2 crews)

Missiles: SLBM: 16 Aerospatiale M45/TN 71; three stage solid fuel rockets; inertial guidance to 5300 km *(2860 nm)*; thermonuclear warhead with 6 MRV each of 150 kT. (To be replaced by M5/TN 75 which has a planned range of 11 000 km *(6000 nm)* and 10-12 MRVs).
SSM: Aerospatiale SM 39 Exocet; launched from 21 in *(533 mm)* torpedo tubes; inertial cruise; active radar homing to 50 km *(27 nm)* at 0.9 Mach; warhead 165 kg.
Torpedoes: 4—21 in *(533 mm)* tubes. ECAN L5 Mod 3; dual purpose; active/passive homing to 9.5 km *(5.1 nm)* at 35 kts; warhead 150 kg; depth to 550 m *(1800 ft)*; total of 18 torpedoes and SSM carried in a mixed load.
Countermeasures: ESM: Warning.
Fire control: SAD (Système d'Armes de Dissuasion) tactical data system; DLA 4A weapon control system.
Radars: Search: Dassault; I band.
Sonars: Thomson Sintra DMUX 80 'multi-function' passive bow and flank arrays.
DUUX 5; passive ranging and intercept; low frequency.
DSUV 61; towed array.

Programmes: First of class ordered 10 March 1986 with building decision taken 18 June 1987. Second of class ordered in 1990 and third in 1992. Class of six originally planned but this is now reduced to a total of five. Trials of *Le Triomphant* planned to start in 1994. Will replace the Redoutable class. SNLE-NG (Sous-Marins Nucléaires Lanceurs Engins Nouvelle Génération).
Modernisation: The M5 missile development was first funded in the 1988 budget and the programme has been brought forward to start in 1992/93, which is two years earlier than planned. Hull No 3 will be the first to commission with M5, the others being back fitted in due course. Only four sets of missiles will be ordered.

LE TRIOMPHANT (artist's impression) *1990, DCN*

Structure: Later versions may be longer, up to 170 m. Diving depth greater than 300 m *(984 ft)*.

5 L'INFLEXIBLE CLASS (SNLE)

Name	No	Builders	Laid down	Launched	Operational
LE FOUDROYANT	S 610	Cherbourg Naval Dockyard	12 Dec 1969	4 Dec 1971	6 June 1974
LE TERRIBLE	S 612	Cherbourg Naval Dockyard	24 June 1967	12 Dec 1969	1 Dec 1973
L'INDOMPTABLE	S 613	Cherbourg Naval Dockyard	4 Dec 1971	17 Aug 1974	31 Dec 1976
LE TONNANT	S 614	Cherbourg Naval Dockyard	17 Oct 1974	17 Sep 1977	3 May 1980
L'INFLEXIBLE	S 615	Cherbourg Naval Dockyard	16 Mar 1979	23 June 1982	1 Apr 1985

Displacement, tons: 8080 surfaced; 8920 dived
Dimensions, feet (metres): 422.1 × 34.8 × 32.8 *(128.7 × 10.6 × 10)*
Main machinery: Nuclear; turbo-electric; 1 PWR; 2 turbo-alternators; 1 Jeumont Schneider motor; 16 000 hp(m) *(11.76 MW)*; twin SEMT-Pielstick/Jeumont Schneider 8PA4 185 diesel-electric auxiliary propulsion; 1.5 MW; 1 emergency motor; 1 shaft
Speed, knots: 25 dived; 20 surfaced
Range, miles: 5000 at 4 kts on auxiliary propulsion only
Complement: 2 alternating crews each of 114 (14 officers)

Missiles: SLBM: 16 Aerospatiale M4; three stage solid fuel rockets; inertial guidance to 5300 km *(2860 nm)*; thermonuclear warhead with 6 MRV each of 150 kT.
SSM: Aerospatiale SM 39 Exocet; launched from 21 in *(533 mm)* torpedo tubes; inertial cruise; active radar homing to 50 km *(27 nm)* at 0.9 Mach; warhead 165 kg (to be carried in all in due course).
Torpedoes: 4—21 in *(533 mm)* tubes. ECAN L5 Mod 3; dual purpose; active/passive homing to 9.5 km *(5.1 nm)* at 35 kts; warhead 150 kg; depth to 550 m *(1800 ft)*; and ECAN F17 Mod 2; wire-guided; active/passive homing to 20 km *(10.8 nm)* at 40 kts; warhead 250 kg; depth 600 m *(1970 ft)*; total of 18 torpedoes and SSM carried in a mixed load.
Countermeasures: ESM: Intercept.
Fire control: SAD (Système d'Armes de Dissuasion) tactical data system; DLA 1A weapon control system.
Radars: Navigation: Thomson-CSF DRUA 33; I band.
Sonars: Thomson Sintra DSUX 21 'multi-function' passive bow and flank arrays.
DUUX 5; passive ranging and intercept; low frequency.
DSUV 61; towed array.

Programmes: With the paying off of *Le Redoutable* in December 1991, the remaining submarines of the class are now known as L'Inflexible class SNLE M4.
Modernisation: All are fitted with M4 missiles. *Le Tonnant* recommissioned 10 October 1987; *L'Indomptable* 10 May 1989; *Le Terrible* 15 May 1990. *Le Foudroyant* started refit in September 1990 and is due to complete in February 1993. As well as replacing the missile system, work included an improved reactor core, noise reduction efforts, updating sonar and other equipment to the same standard as *L'Inflexible* on build.
Structure: Diving depth, 250 m *(820 ft)* approx. Improved streamlining of M4 conversion submarines changes the silhouette so that they resemble *L'Inflexible*.

L'INFLEXIBLE *1990, DCN*

Operational: First operational launch of M4 by *Le Tonnant* on 15 September 1987 in the Atlantic.

Attack Submarines (Sous-Marins Nucléaires d'Attaque (SNA))

5 + 2 RUBIS CLASS (SNA 72)

Name	*No*	*Builders*	*Laid down*	*Launched*	*Operational*
RUBIS	S 601	Cherbourg Naval Dockyard	11 Dec 1976	7 July 1979	23 Feb 1983
SAPHIR	S 602	Cherbourg Naval Dockyard	1 Sep 1979	1 Sep 1981	6 July 1984
CASABIANCA	S 603	Cherbourg Naval Dockyard	19 Sep 1979	22 Dec 1984	21 Apr 1987
EMERAUDE	S 604	Cherbourg Naval Dockyard	1 Mar 1983	12 Apr 1986	16 Sep 1988
AMETHYSTE	S 605	Cherbourg Naval Dockyard	11 Oct 1984	14 May 1988	Mar 1992
PERLE	S 606	Cherbourg Naval Dockyard	27 Mar 1987	22 Sep 1990	Dec 1993
TURQUOISE	S 607	Cherbourg Naval Dockyard	1992	1995	1997

Displacement, tons: 2385 (2410, S 605 onwards) surfaced; 2670 dived
Dimensions, feet (metres): 236.5 (241.5, S 605 onwards) × 24.9 × 21 *(72.1 (73.6) × 7.6 × 6.4)*
Main machinery: Nuclear; turbo-electric; 1 PWR CAS 48; 48 MW; 2 turbo-alternators; 1 motor; 9500 hp(m) *(7 MW)*; twin SEMT-Pielstick/Jeumont Schneider 8 PA4 185 diesel-electric auxiliary propulsion; 1.5 MW; 1 emergency motor; 1 shaft
Speed, knots: 25
Complement: 2 alternating crews each of 70 (8 officers)

Missiles: SSM: Aerospatiale SM 39 Exocet; launched from 21 in *(533 mm)* torpedo tubes; inertial cruise; active radar homing to 50 km *(27 nm)* at 0.9 Mach; warhead 165 kg.
Torpedoes: 4—21 in *(533 mm)* tubes. ECAN L5 Mod 3; dual purpose; active/passive homing to 9.5 km *(5.1 nm)* at 35 kts; warhead 150 kg; depth to 550 m *(1800 ft)*; and ECAN F17 Mod 2; wire-guided; active/passive homing to 20 km *(10.8 nm)* at 40 kts; warhead 250 kg; depth 600 m *(1970 ft)*. Total of 18 torpedoes and missiles carried in a mixed load.
Mines: Up to 32 FG 29 in lieu of torpedoes.
Countermeasures: ESM: ARUR, ARUD; intercept and warning.
Fire control: SAT (Système d'Armes Tactique) or SAD tactical data handling. DLA 2B or 3 weapon control system.
Radars: Search: Thomson-CSF DRUA 33; I band.
Sonars: Thomson Sintra DSUV 22 or DMUX 20 multi-function (S 605 onwards, S 602, S 601 and remainder after modernisation); passive search; low frequency.
DUUA 2B; active; medium frequency; 8 kHz.
DUUX 2 or DUUX 5; passive ranging and intercept.
DSUV 62 or DSUV 62C (S 605 onwards, S 602 and remainder after modernisation); towed passive array; very low frequency.

EMERAUDE *7/1991, J. Y. Robert*

CASABIANCA *6/1991, van Ginderen Collection*

Programmes: *Perle* starts trials in 1992. The programme has been slowed down by defence economies with the eighth of class *Diamant* being cancelled and *Turquoise* delayed. SNA No 8 (displacement: 4000 tons) will be of a new and improved class with VLS SSM and may be proposed for 1995.
Modernisation: Between 1989 and 1995 the first four boats of this class are being converted under operation Améthyste (AMÉlioration Tactique HYdrodynamique Silence Transmission Ecoute) to bring them to the same standard of ASW efficiency as the later boats rather than that required for the original anti-surface ship role. *Saphir* recommissioned 1 July 1991, and will be followed at 18 month intervals by *Rubis*, *Casabianca* and *Emeraude*.
Structure: Diving depth, 300 m *(984 ft)*. As this is the smallest class of SSNs ever designed except for the 400 ton NR-1 of the US Navy there has clearly been a marked reduction in the size of the reactor compared with the Le Redoutable class. S 605 and onwards have had their length increased to 241.5 ft (73.6 m) and are being built to a modified design. This includes a new bow form, Syracuse 2 SATCOM System, a new design sonar DMUX 20 in place of DSUV 22, a new DSUV 62C towed array sonar, a major silencing programme, a streamlining of the superstructure as well as new tactical and attack systems and improved electronics.
Operational: Two squadrons of these submarines are forecast to be based at Toulon and probably Lorient. The first five are all based at Toulon. Endurance up to 60 days.

AMETHYSTE *1991, DCN*

Patrol Submarines (Sous-Marins d'Attaque)

4 AGOSTA CLASS

Name	No	Builders	Laid down	Launched	Commissioned
AGOSTA	S 620	Cherbourg Naval Dockyard	1 Nov 1972	19 Oct 1974	28 July 1977
BÉVÉZIERS	S 621	Cherbourg Naval Dockyard	17 May 1973	14 June 1975	27 Sep 1977
LA PRAYA	S 622	Cherbourg Naval Dockyard	1974	15 May 1976	9 Mar 1978
OUESSANT	S 623	Cherbourg Naval Dockyard	1974	23 Oct 1976	27 July 1978

Displacement, tons: 1230 standard; 1510 surfaced; 1760 dived
Dimensions, feet (metres): 221.7 × 22.3 × 17.7 *(67.6 × 6.8 × 5.4)*
Main machinery: Diesel-electric; 2 SEMT-Pielstick 16 PA4 V185 VG diesels; 3600 hp(m) *(2.65 MW)*; 2 alternators; 1.7 MW; 1 motor; 4600 hp(m) *(3.4 MW)*; 1 cruising motor; 31 hp(m) *(23 kW)*; 1 shaft
Speed, knots: 12 surfaced; 20 dived
Range, miles: 8500 at 9 kts snorting; 350 at 3.5 kts dived
Complement: 58 (7 officers)

Missiles: SSM: Aerospatiale SM 39 Exocet; launched from 21 in *(533 mm)* tubes; inertial cruise; active radar homing to 50 km *(27 nm)* at 0.9 Mach; warhead 165 kg.
Torpedoes: 4—21 in *(533 mm)* bow tubes. ECAN L5 Mod 3; dual purpose; active/passive homing to 9.5 km *(5.1 nm)* at 35 kts; warhead 150 kg; depth to 550 m *(1800 ft)* and ECAN F17 Mod 2; wire-guided; active/passive homing to 20 km *(10.8 nm)* at 40 kts; warhead 250 kg; depth 600 m *(1970 ft)*. Total of 20 torpedoes and missiles carried in a mixed load.
Mines: Up to 36 in lieu of torpedoes.
Countermeasures: ESM: ARUR, ARUD; intercept and warning.
Fire control: DLA 2A weapon control system.
Radars: Search: Thomson-CSF DRUA 33; I band.
Sonars: Thomson Sintra DSUV 22; passive search; medium frequency.
DUUA 2D; active search and attack; 8 kHz.
DUUA 1D; active search. DUUX 2; passive ranging.
DSUV 62; passive towed array; very low frequency.

Programmes: Building of this class was announced in 1970 under the third five-year new construction plan 1971-75. Considerable efforts have been made to improve noise reduction, including a clean casing and the damping of internal noise. Service lives: *Ouessant* 2003, remainder 2002 but these dates may be extended.
Modernisation: Included fitting of SM 39 Exocet and better torpedo discharge and reloading. Completed in 1987.
Structure: First diesel submarines in the French Navy to be fitted with 21 in *(533 mm)* tubes. Diving depth, 320 m *(1050 ft)*. Has twice the battery capacity of the Daphne class.
Operational: All based at Lorient. Endurance, 45 days. Torpedoes can be fired at all speeds and down to full diving depth. Rapid reloading gear fitted.
Sales: Four built at Cartagena for Spanish Navy and two for Pakistan by Dubigeon.

LA PRAYA *5/1991, D & B Teague*

QUESSANT *7/1989, Wright & Logan*

4 DAPHNÉ CLASS

Name	No	Builders	Laid down	Launched	Commissioned
DORIS	S 643	Cherbourg Naval Dockyard	Sep 1958	14 May 1960	26 Aug 1964
JUNON	S 648	Cherbourg Naval Dockyard	July 1961	11 May 1964	25 Feb 1966
PSYCHÉ	S 650	Brest Naval Dockyard	May 1965	28 June 1967	1 July 1969
SIRÈNE	S 651	Brest Naval Dockyard	May 1965	28 June 1967	1 Mar 1970

Displacement, tons: 860 surfaced; 1038 dived
Dimensions, feet (metres): 189.6 × 22.3 × 15.1 *(57.8 × 6.8 × 4.6)*
Main machinery: Diesel-electric; 2 SEMT-Pielstick 12 PA1 diesels (S 643 and 648); 2 SEMT-Pielstick 12 PA4 V 185 diesels (S 650 and 651); 2450 hp(m) *(1.8 MW)*; 2 Jeumont Schneider alternators; 900 kW; 2 motors; 2600 hp(m) *(1.9 MW)*; 2 shafts
Speed, knots: 13.5 surfaced; 16 dived
Range, miles: 2700 at 12.5 kts; 10 000 at 7 kts surfaced; 4500 at 5 kts; 3000 at 7 kts snorting
Complement: 53 (7 officers)

Torpedoes: 12—21.7 in *(550 mm)* (8 bow, 4 stern) tubes. 12 ECAN E15; dual purpose; passive homing to 12 km *(6.6 nm)* at 25 kts; warhead 300 kg. Larger version of shorter range E14. Submarine target must be cavitating; no reloads.
Fire control: DLT D3 torpedo control.
Radars: Search: Thomson-CSF Calypso; I/J band.
Sonars: Thomson Sintra DSUV 2; passive search; medium frequency.
DUUA 2; active search and attack.
DUUX 2; passive ranging.

Programmes: Service lives have been extended as SSN completion rate is slower than planned. *Flore* paid off in 1989 and is used as a training submarine.
Modernisation: Carried out between 1971 and 1981.
Structure: Diving depth, 300 m *(984 ft)*; crushing at 575 m *(1886 ft)*.
Operational: *Doris* and *Junon* based at Toulon, *Psyché* and *Sirène* at Lorient.
Sales: South Africa (1967) (3), Pakistan (1966) (3), (1 from Portugal later), Portugal (1964) (4), Spain (built in Spain) (1965) (4).

JUNON *1/1988, Gilbert Gyssels*

AIRCRAFT CARRIERS (Porte-Avions)

0 + 1 + (1) NUCLEAR-PROPELLED AIRCRAFT CARRIERS (Porte-Avions Nucléaires PAN) (CVN)

Name	*No*	*Builders*	*Laid down*	*Launched*	*Commissioned*
CHARLES DE GAULLE	R 91	Brest Naval Dockyard	24 Apr 1989	Apr 1994	Dec 1998

Displacement, tons: 35 500 standard; 39 680 full load
Dimensions, feet (metres): 780.8 wl; 857.7 oa × 103.3 wl; 211.3 oa × 27.8 *(238; 261.5 × 31.5; 64.4 × 8.5)*
Flight deck, feet (metres): 857.9 × 211.3 *(261.5 × 64.4)*
Main machinery: Nuclear; 2 PWR Type K15; 300 MW; 2 turbines; 83 000 hp(m) *(61 MW)*; 2 shafts
Speed, knots: 27
Complement: 1150 ship's company plus 550 aircrew plus 50 Flag Staff; (accommodation for 1950) (plus temporary 800 marines)

Missiles: SAM: 4 Thomson-CSF SAAM VLS octuple launchers ❶; Aerospatiale ASTER 15; anti-missile system with inertial guidance and midcourse update; active radar homing to 15 km *(8.1 nm)*; warhead 3 kg.
2 Matra Sadral PDMS sextuple launchers ❷; Mistral; IR homing to 4 km *(2.2 nm)*; warhead 3 kg; anti-sea-skimmer; able to engage targets down to 10 ft above sea level.
Guns: 8 GIAT 20F2 20 mm; 60° elevation; 720 rounds/minute to 8 km *(4.3 nm)*; weight of shell: 0.25 kg.
Countermeasures: Decoys: 4 CSEE Sagaie 10-barrelled trainable launchers ❸; medium range; Chaff to 8 km *(4.3 nm)*; IR flares to 3 km *(1.6 nm)*.
ESM: ARBR 17; radar warning. DIBV 1A Vampir ❹; IR detector.
ECM: 2 ARBB 33 ❺; jammers.
Combat data systems: SENIT; Links 11 and 14 (later Link 16). Syracuse 2 SATCOM ❻. AIDCOMER command support system.
Radars: Air search: Thomson-CSF DRBJ 11D/E ❼; 3D; E/F band; range 366 km *(200 nm)*.
Thomson-CSF DRBV 27 ❽; D band; range 183 km *(100 nm)* for 2 m² target.
Air/surface search: Thomson-CSF DRBV 15C ❾; E/F band; range 50 km *(27 nm)*.
Navigation: Two Racal 1229; I band.
Fire control: Arabel ❿; I/J band (for SAAM).
Tacan: NRBP 20A ⓫.
Sonars: To include SLAT torpedo attack warning.

Fixed wing aircraft: 35-40 capacity including Rafale.

CHARLES DE GAULLE (model) *1990, DCN*

Programmes: On 23 September 1980 the Defence Council decided to build two nuclear-propelled carriers to replace *Clemenceau* in 1996 and *Foch* some years later. First of class ordered 4 February 1986, first metal cut 24 November 1987. Second ship, if built, will probably be called *Clemenceau* and was to have been ordered in 1992 but this may be postponed until 1994. Funds for preliminary work at Brest provided in 1984 estimates and for the construction and trials of the nuclear-power plant at Cadarache in the 1982-83 estimates. A 19.8 m *(65 ft)* long one-twelfth scale model has been built. Constructed of light alloy, and with a crew of three, it is used for hydrodynamic trials. Building programme delayed two years due to 1989 defence budget cuts but second launch date of April 1994 is forecast with sea trials starting in March 1997.
Structure: Two lifts 62.3 × 41 ft *(19 × 12.5 m)* of 36 tons capacity. Hangar for 20-25 aircraft; dimensions 454.4 × 96.5 × 20 ft *(138.5 × 29.4 × 6.1 m)*. Angled deck 8.5°. Catapults: 2 USN Type C13; length 75 m *(246 ft)* for Super Etendards and up to 22 tonne aircraft. Enhanced weight capability of flight deck to allow operation of AEW aircraft. Island placed well fwd so that both lifts can be abaft it and thus protected from the weather. MLS system for deck approach.
Operational: Five years continuous steaming at 25 kts available before refuelling (same reactors as *Le Triomphant*).

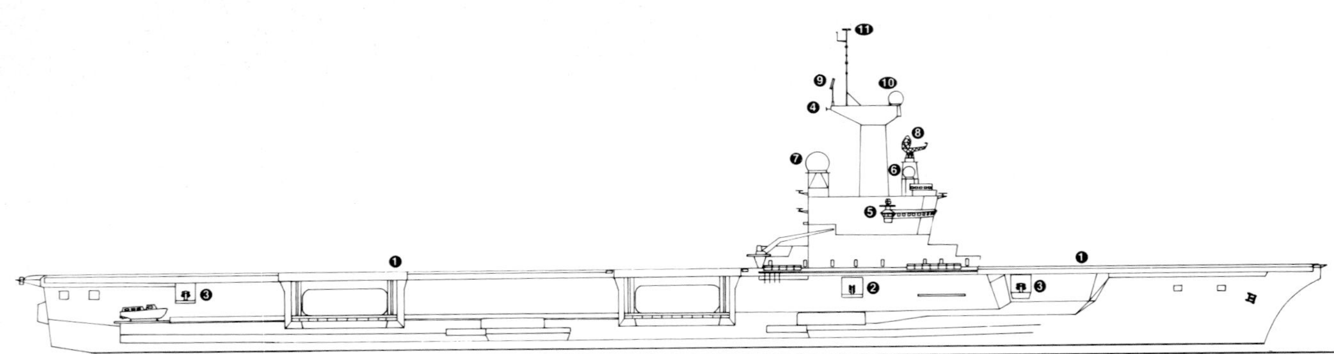
CHARLES DE GAULLE *(Scale 1 : 1 500), Ian Sturton*

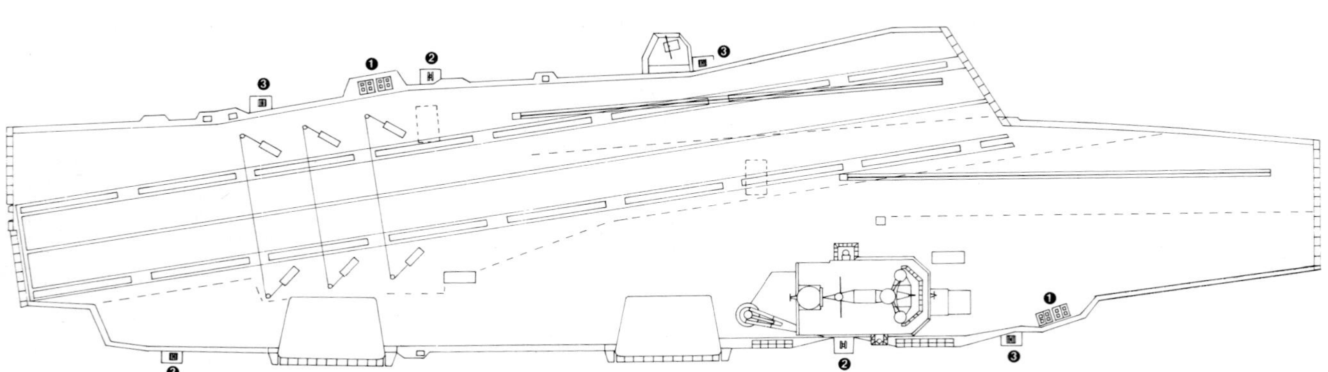
CHARLES DE GAULLE *(Scale 1 : 1 500), Ian Sturton*

2 CLEMENCEAU CLASS (CV)

Name	*No*	*Builders*	*Laid down*	*Launched*	*Commissioned*
CLEMENCEAU	R 98	Brest Naval Dockyard	Nov 1955	21 Dec 1957	22 Nov 1961
FOCH	R 99	Chantiers de l'Atlantique, St. Nazaire	Feb 1957	28 July 1960	15 July 1963

Displacement, tons: 27 307 standard; 32 780 full load
Dimensions, feet (metres): 869.4 × 104.1 hull (168 oa) × 28.2 *(265 × 31.7 (51.2) × 8.6)*
Flight deck, feet (metres): 543 × 96.8 *(165.5 × 29.5)*
Main machinery: 6 boilers; 640 psi *(45 kg/cm sq)*; 840°F *(450°C)*; 2 Parsons turbines; 126 000 hp(m) *(93 MW)*; 2 shafts
Speed, knots: 32. **Range, miles:** 7500 at 18 kts; 4800 at 24 kts; 3500 at full power
Complement: 1017 (47 officers) plus 672 aircrew

Missiles: SAM: 2 Thomson-CSF Crotale EDIR octuple launchers ❶; 18 missiles per magazine; radar and IR line of sight guidance to 13 km *(7 nm)* at 2.4 Mach; warhead 14 kg. Replaced 4 of the 100 mm guns.
Guns: 4 DCN 3.9 in *(100 mm)*/55 Mod 1953 automatic ❷; 80° elevation; 60 rounds/minute to 17 km *(9 nm)* anti-surface; 8 km *(4.4 nm)* anti-aircraft; weight of shell 13.5 kg. Several M2 12.7 mm MGs.
Countermeasures: Decoys: 2 CSEE Sagaie 10-barrelled trainable launchers ❸; medium range decoy rockets; Chaff to 8 km *(4.3 nm)*; IR flares to 3 km *(1.6 nm)*.
ESM: ARBR 16; radar warning.
ECM: ARBX 10; jammer.
Combat data systems: SENIT 2 tactical data automation system; Links 11 and 14 (later 16); Syracuse 1 SATCOM. AIDCOMER command support system.
Radars: Air search: Thomson-CSF DRBV 23B ❹; D band; range 201 km *(110 nm)*.
Air/surface search: Two DRBI 10 ❺; E/F band; range 256 km *(140 nm)*.
DRBV 15 ❻; E/F band.
Navigation: Racal Decca 1226; I band.
Fire control: Two DRBC 32A ❼; I band; two Crotale; I band.
Tacan: SRN-6.
Landing approach control: NRBA 51 ❽; I band.
Sonars: Westinghouse SQS 505; hull-mounted; active search; medium frequency; 7 kHz.

Fixed wing aircraft: 18 Super Etendard; 4 Etendard IVP; 8 Crusaders; 7 Alizé.
Helicopters: 2 SA 365F Dauphin 2.

Programmes: First aircraft carriers designed as such and built from the keel to be completed in France. Authorised in 1953 and 1955 respectively. Under current plans *Clemenceau* is due to pay off (when *Charles de Gaulle* commissions) in 1998 and *Foch* in 2004.
Modernisation: *Clemenceau* refitted in 1978 to accommodate Super Etendard aircraft and tactical nuclear weapons. *Foch* had a similar refit to *Clemenceau*'s in 1980-81. *Clemenceau* started a refit 1 September 1985, ended October 1986. This included the replacement of four of the 100 mm guns by two Crotale EDIR, retubing of boilers and other major engine overhauls, fitting of stronger aircraft lifts and catapults, modernisation of communications (including Syracuse 1 SATCOM) and electronics, fitting of Sagaie, new long range air warning radar and passive radar detection system, and modernised combat data system. *Foch* similarly modified in her 1987-88 refit, which also included a trial CSEE Dallas (Deck Approach and Landing Laser System), and a capability to accommodate ASMP nuclear missiles for Super Etendard. *Foch* to have a 'Rafale capability' refit in 1992.
Structure: Flight deck, island superstructure and bridges, hull (over machinery spaces and magazines) are all armour plated. There are 3 bridges: Flag, Command and Aviation.
2 Mitchell-Brown steam catapults; Mk BS 5; able to launch 20 ton aircraft at 110 kts. The flight deck is angled at 8 degrees. Two lifts 52.5 × 36 ft *(16 × 10.97 m)* one of which is on the starboard deck edge. Dimensions of the hangar are 590.6 × 78.7 × 23 ft *(180 × 24 × 7 m)*. Positions of DRBV 23 and DRBV 15 radars in *Foch* were the reverse of those in *Clemenceau* but *Clemenceau* has been retrofitted as *Foch* in 1989. *Clemenceau* mainmast shortened in 1990. *Foch* is getting a mini ski jump (10 × 0.02 m high) for deck trials of Rafale aircraft in 1992.
Operational: Oil fuel capacity is 3720 tons. Flight deck letters: F = *Foch*, U = *Clemenceau*. The aircraft complement for the helicopter carrier role includes between 30 and 40 with a mixture of Super Frelon, Lynx, Super Puma, Puma and Gazelle (the last three types being army owned). Crusaders are being refitted to be able to fly until 1995. *Clemenceau* classified as an Attack Carrier, *Foch* as Helicopter and Amphibious Support Carrier. Deck trials of Rafale M aircraft scheduled for 1993.

CLEMENCEAU *7/1991, J. Y. Robert*

CLEMENCEAU *6/1991, van Ginderen Collection*

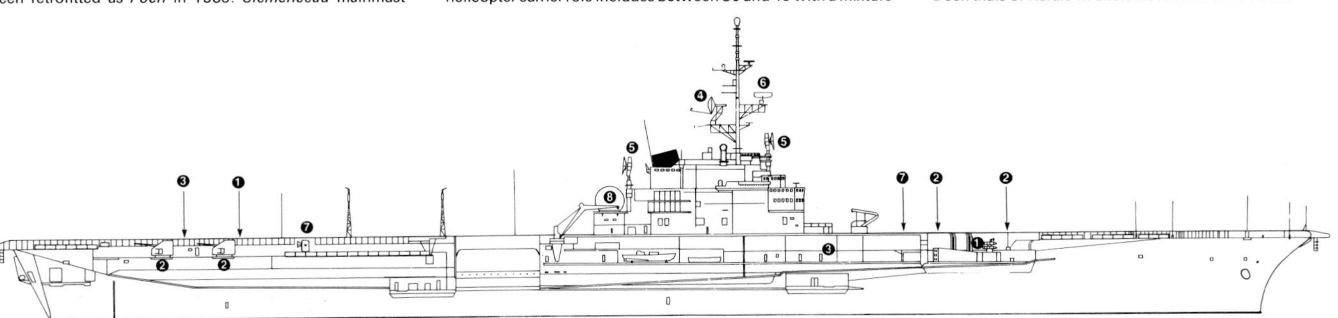

CLEMENCEAU *(Scale 1 : 1 500), Ian Sturton*

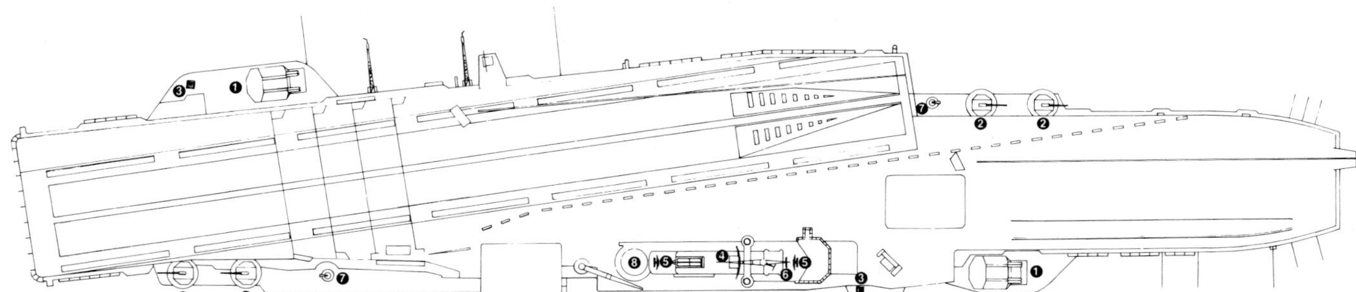

CLEMENCEAU *(Scale 1 : 1 500), Ian Sturton*

HELICOPTER CARRIER (Porte-Hélicoptères) (CVH)

Name	*No*	*Builders*	*Laid down*	*Launched*	*Commissioned*
JEANNE D'ARC (ex-*La Résolue*)	R 97	Brest Naval Dockyard	7 July 1960	30 Sep 1961	16 July 1964

Displacement, tons: 10 000 standard; 13 270 full load
Dimensions, feet (metres): 597.1 × 78.7 hull × 24 *(182 × 24 × 7.3)*
Flight deck, feet (metres): 203.4 × 68.9 *(62 × 21)*
Main machinery: 4 boilers; 640 psi *(45 kg/cm sq)*; 840°F *(450°C)*; 2 Rateau-Bretagne turbines; 40 000 hp(m) *(29.4 MW)*; 2 shafts
Speed, knots: 26.5. **Range, miles:** 6000 at 15 kts
Complement: 626 (30 officers) plus 140 cadets

Missiles: SSM: 6 Aerospatiale MM 38 Exocet ❶; inertial cruise; active radar homing to 42 km *(23 nm)* at 0.9 Mach; warhead 165 kg; sea-skimmer.
Guns: 4 DCN 3.9 in *(100 mm)*/55 Mod 1964 CADAM automatic ❷; 80° elevation; 80 rounds/minute to 17 km *(9 nm)* anti-surface; 8 km *(4.4 nm)* anti-aircraft; weight of shell 13.5 kg.
Countermeasures: Decoys: 2 CSEE/VSEL Syllex 8-barrelled trainable launchers; Chaff to 1 km in distraction and centroid patterns depending on threat.
ESM: ARBR 16; radar warning.
Radars: Air search: Thomson-CSF DRBV 22D ❸; D band; range 366 km *(200 nm)*.
Air/surface search: DRBV 51 ❹; G band.
Navigation: DRBN 32; I band.
Fire control: Three DRBC 32A ❺; I band.
Tacan: SRN-6.
Sonars: Thomson Sintra DUBV 24; hull-mounted; active search; medium frequency; 5 kHz.

Helicopters: 4 Alouette III (to be replaced by Dauphin). War inventory includes 8 Super Puma and Lynx.

Programmes: Due to pay off after 2005.
Modernisation: Long refits in the Summers of 1989 and 1990 have allowed equipment to be updated to enable the ship to continue well into the next century. SENIT 2 combat data system was to have been fitted but this was cancelled as a cost saving measure. DRBV 51 radar fitted in 1992.
Structure: Flight deck lift has a capacity of 12 tons. Some of the hangar space is used to accommodate officers under training. The ship is almost entirely air-conditioned. Carries two LCVPs.
Operational: Used for training officer cadets in peacetime. In wartime, after rapid modification, she would be used as a commando ship, helicopter carrier or troop transport with commando equipment and a battalion of 700 men. Operates with the Training Squadron for an autumn/spring cruise with summer refit. Belongs to Atlantic Fleet.

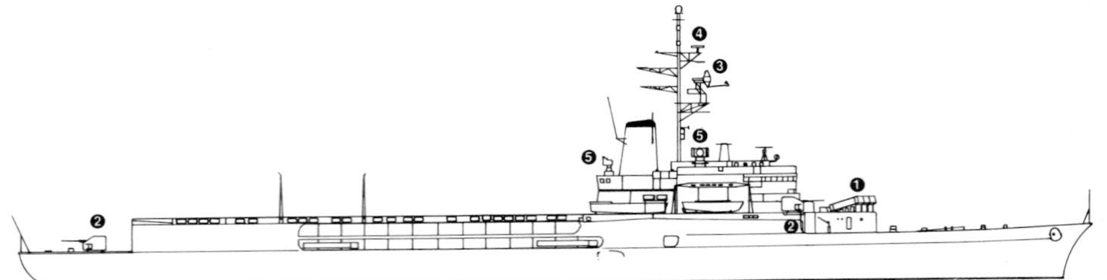
JEANNE D'ARC *(Scale 1 : 1500), Ian Sturton*

JEANNE D'ARC *5/1991, Hartmut Ehlers*

DESTROYERS (Frégates or Escorteurs d'Escadres)

2 SUFFREN CLASS

Name	*No*	*Builders*	*Laid down*	*Launched*	*Commissioned*
SUFFREN	D 602	Lorient Naval Dockyard	Dec 1962	15 May 1965	20 July 1967
DUQUESNE	D 603	Brest Naval Dockyard	Nov 1964	12 Feb 1966	1 Apr 1970

Displacement, tons: 5090 standard; 6910 full load
Dimensions, feet (metres): 517.1 × 50.9 × 20 *(157.6 × 15.5 × 6.1)*
Main machinery: 4 boilers; 640 psi *(45 kg/cm sq)*; 842°F *(450°C)*; 2 Rateau turbines; 72 500 hp(m) *(53 MW)*; 2 shafts
Speed, knots: 34. **Range, miles:** 5100 at 18 kts; 2400 at 29 kts
Complement: 355 (23 officers)

Missiles: SSM: 4 Aerospatiale MM 38 Exocet ❶; inertial cruise; active radar homing to 42 km *(23 nm)* at 0.9 Mach; warhead 165 kg; sea-skimmer.
SAM: ECAN Ruelle Masurca twin launcher ❷; Mk 2 Mod 3 semi-active radar homers; range 55 km *(30 nm)*; warhead 98 kg; 48 missiles.
A/S: Latecoere Malafon ❸; range 13 km *(7 nm)* at 450 kts; payload L4 acoustic homing torpedo; warhead 100 kg; 13 missiles.
Guns: 2 DCN 3.9 in *(100 mm)*/55 Mod 1964 CADAM automatic ❹; 80° elevation; 80 rounds/minute to 17 km *(9 nm)* anti-surface; 8 km *(4.4 nm)* anti-aircraft; weight of shell 13.5 kg.
4 or 6 Oerlikon 20 mm; 720 rounds/minute to 10 km *(5.5 nm)*.
Torpedoes: 4 launchers (2 each side) ❺. 10 ECAN L5; anti-submarine; active/passive homing to 9.5 km *(5.1 nm)* at 35 kts; warhead 150 kg; depth to 550 m *(1800 ft)*.
Countermeasures: Decoys: 2 CSEE Sagaie 10-barrelled trainable launchers; Chaff to 8 km *(4.4 nm)* and IR flares to 3 km *(1.6 nm)*. 2 Dagaie launchers ❻.
ESM: ARBR 17; intercept.
ECM: ARBB 33; jammer.
Combat data systems: SENIT 2 action data automation; Links 11 and 14. Syracuse 1 SATCOM ⓬.
Fire control: DIBC-1A Piranha IR tracker; DCN CTMS optronic control system. 2 Sagem DMA optical directors.
Radars: Air search (radome): DRBI 23 ❼; D band.
Air/surface search: DRBV 15A ❽; E/F band.
Navigation: Racal Decca 1226; I band.
Fire control: Two DRBR 51 ❾; G/I band (for Masurca).
DRBC 33A ❿ (for guns).
Tacan: URN 20.
Sonars: Thomson Sintra DUBV 23; hull-mounted; active search and attack; 5 kHz.
DUBV 43 ⓫; VDS; medium frequency 5 kHz; tows at up to 24 kts at 200 m *(656 ft)*.

Programmes: Ordered under the 1960 programme. Service lives: Both extended to over 2000.
Modernisation: MM 38 Exocet fitted in 1977 *(Duquesne)* and 1979 *(Suffren)*; Masurca modernised in 1984-85 *(Duquesne)* and 1988-89 *(Suffren)*, with new computers. DRBV 15A radars replaced DRBV 50. *Suffren* had a major refit from May 1988 to September 1989 and *Duquesne* from June 1990 to March 1991: modernisation of the DRBI-23 radar; new computers for the SENIT combat data system; new CTMS fire control system for 100 mm guns fitted (with DRBC-33A radar, TV camera and DIBC-1A Piranha IR tracker). New ESM/ECM suite: ARBR 17 radar interceptor, ARBB 33 jammer and Sagaie decoy launchers. Two 20 mm guns fitted either side of DRBC 33A.
Structure: Equipped with gyro-controlled stabilisers operating three pairs of non-retractable fins. NBC citadel fitted during modernisation. Air-conditioning of accommodation and operational areas. Excellent sea boats and weapon platforms.
Operational: Both ships operate in the Mediterranean. Officially frégates lance-missiles (FLM).

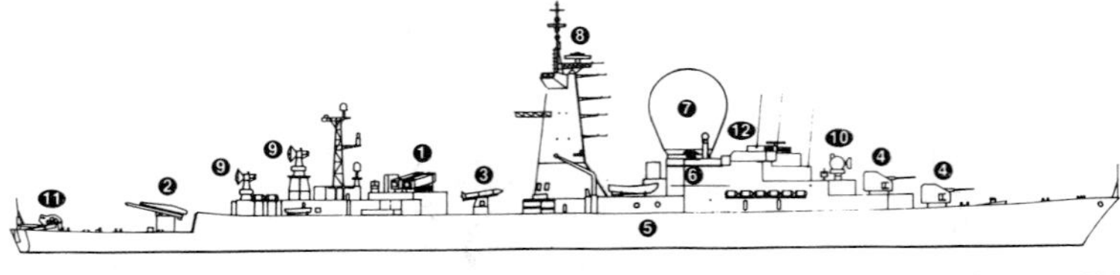
DUQUESNE *(Scale 1 : 1 500), Ian Sturton*

DUQUESNE *6/1991, van Ginderen Collection*

7 GEORGES LEYGUES CLASS (TYPE F 70 (ASW))

Name	*No*	*Builders*	*Laid down*	*Launched*	*Commissioned*
GEORGES LEYGUES	D 640	Brest Naval Dockyard	16 Sep 1974	17 Dec 1976	10 Dec 1979
DUPLEIX	D 641	Brest Naval Dockyard	17 Oct 1975	2 Dec 1978	13 June 1981
MONTCALM	D 642	Brest Naval Dockyard	5 Dec 1975	31 May 1980	28 May 1982
JEAN DE VIENNE	D 643	Brest Naval Dockyard	26 Oct 1979	17 Nov 1981	25 May 1984
PRIMAUGUET	D 644	Brest Naval Dockyard	19 Nov 1981	17 Mar 1984	7 Nov 1986
LA MOTTE-PICQUET	D 645	Brest Naval Dockyard/Lorient	12 Feb 1982	6 Feb 1985	18 Feb 1988
LATOUCHE-TRÉVILLE	D 646	Brest Naval Dockyard/Lorient	15 Feb 1984	19 Mar 1988	16 July 1990

Displacement, tons: 3830 standard; 4300 (D 640-643); 4490 (D 644-646) full load
Dimensions, feet (metres): 455.9 × 45.9 × 18.7 *(139 × 14 × 5.7)*
Main machinery: CODOG; 2 RR Olympus TM3B gas turbines; 43 000 hp *(32 MW)* sustained; 2 SEMT-Pielstick 16PA6 V280 diesels; 12 800 hp(m) *(9.41 MW)* sustained; 2 shafts; cp props
Speed, knots: 30; 21 on diesels. **Range, miles:** 8500 at 18 kts on diesels; 2500 at 28 kts
Complement: 218 (16 officers) plus 16 spare billets

Missiles: SSM: 4 Aerospatiale MM 38 Exocet (MM 40 in D 642-646) ❶; inertial cruise; active radar homing to 42 km *(23 nm)* at 0.9 Mach (MM 38); active radar homing to 70 km *(40 nm)* at 0.9 Mach (MM 40); warhead 165 kg; sea-skimmer. 4 additional Exocet missiles can be carried as a warload (D 644-646).
SAM: Thomson-CSF Crotale Navale EDIR octuple launcher ❷; radar guidance; line of sight guidance to 13 km *(7 nm)* at 2.4 Mach; warhead 14 kg; 26 missiles.
Guns: 1—3.9 in *(100 mm)*/55 Mod 68 CADAM automatic ❸; dual purpose; 80° elevation; 78 rounds/minute to 17 km *(9 nm)* anti-surface; 8 km *(4.4 nm)* anti-aircraft; weight of shell 13.5 kg.
2 Oerlikon 20 mm ❹; 720 rounds/minute to 10 km *(5.5 nm)*.
4 M2HB 12.7 mm MGs.
Torpedoes: 2 fixed launchers. 10 ECAN L5; anti-submarine; active/passive homing to 9.5 km *(5.1 nm)* at 35 kts; warhead 150 kg; depth to 550 m *(1800 ft)*. 12 Honeywell Mk 46 for helicopters.
Countermeasures: Decoys: 2 CSEE Dagaie 10-barrelled double trainable launcher (replacing Syllex) ❺; Chaff and IR flares; H-J band.
ESM: ARBR 17 ❻; radar warning. DIBV 1A Vampir; IR detector (D 644-646).
ECM: ARBB 32 B; jammer.
Combat data systems: SENIT 4 action data automation; Links 11 and 14. SLASM integrated ASW (to be fitted in due course). Syracuse 1 SATCOM ❼.
Fire control: CSEE Panda optical director for 3.9 in *(100 mm)* gun. Thomson-CSF Vega (D 640-643) and CTMS (D 644-646) optronic systems. DIBC 1A Piranha IR tracker for 100 mm (D 644-646; integrated to CTMS FCS). DLT L4 (D 640-643) and DLT L5 (D 644-646) torpedo control system.
Radars: Air search: DRBV 26 (not in D 644-646) ❽; D band; range 182 km *(100 nm)* for 2 m² target.
Air/surface search: Thomson-CSF DRBV 51C (DRBV 15A in D 644-646) ❾; G band; range 120 km *(65 nm)* for 2 m² target.
Navigation: Two Decca 1226; I band (one for close-range helicopter control).
Fire control: Thomson-CSF Vega with DRBC 32E (D 640-643) ❿; I band; DCN CTMS with DRBC 33A (D 644-646) ⓫; I band.
Sonars: Thomson Sintra DUBV 23D (DUBV 24C in D 644-646); bow-mounted; active search and attack; 5 kHz.
DUBV 43B (43C in D 643-646) ⓬; VDS; search; medium frequency; paired with DUBV 23D/24; tows at 24 kts down to 200 m *(650 ft)*, (700 m *(3000 ft)* for 43C). Length of tow 600 m *(2000 ft)*; being upgraded to 43C.
DSBV 61B (in D 644 onward); passive linear towed array; low frequency; 365 m *(1200 ft)*. DSBV 62C may be fitted in first four during mid-life refits in early 1990s.

Helicopters: 2 Lynx Mk 4 ⓭.

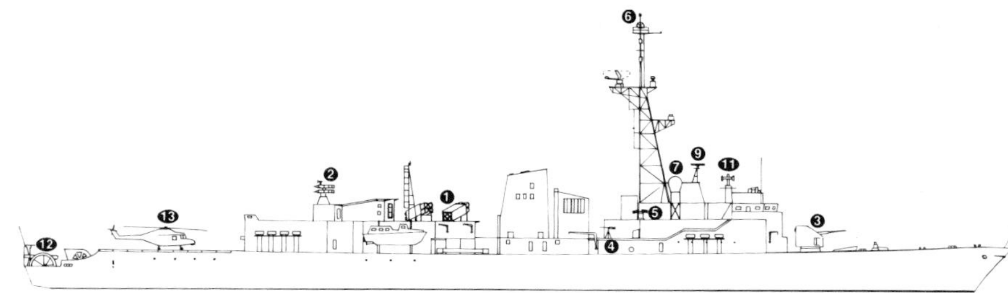

PRIMAUGUET *(Scale 1 : 1 200), Ian Sturton*

JEAN DE VIENNE (low bridge; DRBV 26) *6/1991, van Ginderen Collection*

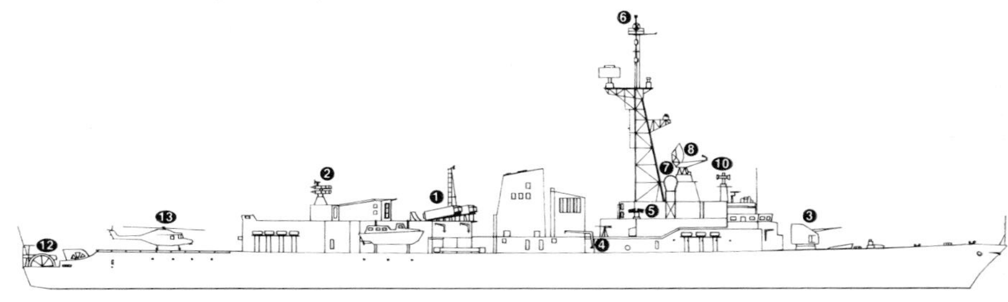

GEORGES LEYGUES *(Scale 1 : 1 200), Ian Sturton*

Programmes: First three were in the 1971-76 new construction programme, fourth in 1978 estimates, fifth in 1980 estimates, sixth in 1981 estimates, seventh in 1983 estimates. D 645 and 646 were towed from Brest to Lorient for completion. Service lives: *Georges Leygues*, 2004; *Dupleix* and *Montcalm*, 2006; *Jean de Vienne*, 2008; *Primauguet*, 2011; *La Motte-Picquet*, 2012; *Latouche-Tréville*, 2014. Re-rated F 70 'frégates anti-sous-marines (FASM)' (ex-C 70) on 6 June 1988.
Modernisation: The class is to receive the new OTO Melara/Matra ASW missile Milas. The projected SLASM update from 1997 includes a new bow sonar and a VLF towed active sonar with separate passive array. The first four may be back fitted with towed arrays in mid-life refits in early 1990s.
Structure: Bridge raised one deck in the last three of the class.
Operational: First four deployed to Mediterranean, remainder to Atlantic. The ships' helicopters are dual roled, either carrying sonar or sonobuoy dispenser and ASW weapons or AS 12 anti-ship missiles.

LATOUCHE-TREVILLE (high bridge) *1990, DCN*

2 CASSARD CLASS (TYPE F 70 (A/A))

Name	*No*	*Builders*	*Laid down*	*Launched*	*Commissioned*
CASSARD	D 614	Lorient Naval Dockyard	3 Sep 1982	6 Feb 1985	28 July 1988
JEAN BART	D 615	Lorient Naval Dockyard	12 Mar 1986	19 Mar 1988	21 Sep 1991

Displacement, tons: 4230 standard; 4668 full load
Dimensions, feet (metres): 455.9 × 45.9 × 21.3 (sonar) *(139 × 14 × 6.5)*
Main machinery: 4 SEMT-Pielstick 18PA6 280 BTC diesels; 43 200 hp(m) *(31.75 MW)*; 2 shafts
Speed, knots: 29.5. **Range, miles:** 8200 at 17 kts; 4800 at 24 kts
Complement: 244 (22 officers) accommodation for 251

Missiles: SSM: 8 Aerospatiale MM 40 Exocet ❶; inertial cruise; active radar homing to 70 km *(40 nm)* at 0.9 Mach; warhead 165 kg; sea-skimmer.
SAM: 40 GDC Pomona Standard SM-1MR; Mk 13 Mod 5 launcher ❷; semi-active radar homing to 46 km *(25 nm)* at 2 Mach; height envelope 45-18 288 m *(150-60 000 ft)*. Launchers taken from T 47 (DDG) ships.
2 Matra Sadral PDMS sextuple launchers ❸; Mistral; IR homing to 4 km *(2.2 nm)*; warhead 3 kg; anti-sea-skimmer; able to engage targets down to 10 ft above sea level.
Guns: 1 DCN 3.9 in *(100 mm)*/55 Mod 68 CADAM automatic ❹; 80° elevation; 80 rounds/minute to 17 km *(9 nm)* anti-surface; 8 km *(4.4 nm)* anti-aircraft; weight of shell 13.5 kg.
2 Oerlikon 20 mm ❺; 720 rounds/minute to 10 km *(5.5 nm)*.
4—12.7 mm MGs.
Torpedoes: 2 fixed launchers model KD 59E ❻. 10 ECAN L5 Mod 4; anti-submarine; active/passive homing to 9.5 km *(5.1 nm)* at 35 kts; warhead 150 kg; depth to 550 m *(1800 ft)*. Honeywell Mk 46 torpedoes for the helicopter.
Countermeasures: Decoys: 2 CSEE Dagaie ❼ and 2 Sagaie 10-barrelled trainable launchers ❽; fires a combination of Chaff and IR flares. Nixie; towed torpedo decoy.
ESM: ARBR 17B ❾; radar warning. DIBV 1A Vampir ❿; IR detector (integrated with search radar for active/passive tracking in all weathers). Saigon radio intercept at masthead.
ECM: ARBB 33; jammer; H, I and J bands.
Combat data systems: SENIT 6 action data automation; Links 11 and 14 (later 16). Syracuse 1 SATCOM ⓫.
Fire control: DIBC 1A Piranha II IR tracker; DCN CTMS optronic control system; CSEE Najir secondary director.
Radars: Air search: Thomson-CSF DRBJ 11B ⓬; 3D; range 366 km *(200 nm)*.
Air/surface search: DRBV 26C ⓭; D band; range 182 km *(100 nm)*.
Navigation: Two Racal Decca 1229; I band (one for close-range helicopter control ⓮); to be replaced by DRBN 34.
Fire control: DRBC 33A ⓯; I band.
Two Raytheon SPG 51C ⓰; G/I band (for missiles).
Sonars: Thomson Sintra DUBA 25A; hull-mounted; active search and attack; medium frequency. May be fitted later with DSBV 62 passive towed array; very low frequency.

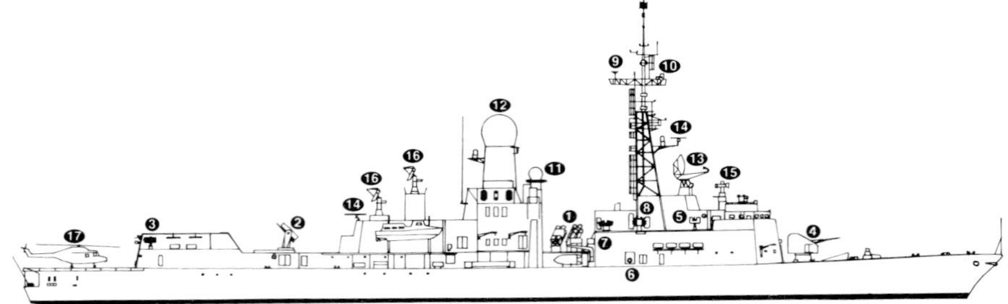
JEAN BART *(Scale 1 : 1 200), Ian Sturton*

JEAN BART *5/1991, Foto Flite*

Helicopters: 1 Lynx Mk 4 ⓱.

Programmes: On the same hull as the F 70 (A/S) a very different armament and propulsion system has been introduced. Funds for the first ship allotted in 1978 estimates, for the second in 1979 estimates (ordered 27 September 1979), and for the third and fourth in 1983 estimates. Third and fourth ships ordered 27 February 1984, but then cancelled. The building programme has been considerably slowed down by finance problems and doubts about the increasingly obsolescent Standard SM 1 missile system, and the SM 2 is reported as being too expensive. Service lives: First, 2013; second, 2015. Re-rated F 70 (ex-C 70) on 6 June 1988, officially 'frégates anti-aériennes (FAA)'.
Structure: Samahe 210 helicopter handling system. It is reported that both ships are to be fitted with Aster SAM during their first refits. *Cassard* fitted with DRBJ 11B radar (replacing DRBV 15) in 1992.
Operational: Helicopter used for third party targeting for the SSM. Both ships are in the Mediterranean Fleet.

JEAN BART *2/1991, 92 Wing RAAF*

3 TOURVILLE CLASS (TYPE F 67)

Name	*No*	*Builders*	*Laid down*	*Launched*	*Commissioned*
TOURVILLE	D 610	Lorient Naval Dockyard	16 Mar 1970	13 May 1972	21 June 1974
DUGUAY-TROUIN	D 611	Lorient Naval Dockyard	25 Feb 1971	1 June 1973	17 Sep 1975
DE GRASSE	D 612	Lorient Naval Dockyard	June 1972	30 Nov 1974	1 Oct 1977

Displacement, tons: 4580 standard; 5950 full load
Dimensions, feet (metres): 501.6 × 52.4 × 18.7 *(152.8 × 16 × 5.7)*
Main machinery: 4 boilers; 640 psi *(45 kg/cm sq)*; 840°F *(450°C)*; 2 Rateau turbines; 58 000 hp(m) *(43 MW)*; 2 shafts
Speed, knots: 32. **Range, miles:** 5000 at 18 kts
Complement: 301 (21 officers)

Missiles: SSM: 6 Aerospatiale MM 38 Exocet ❶; inertial cruise; active radar homing to 42 km *(23 nm)* at 0.9 Mach; warhead 165 kg; sea-skimmer.
SAM: Thomson-CSF Crotale Navale EDIR octuple launcher ❷; radar and IR line of sight guidance to 13 km *(7 nm)* at 2.4 Mach; warhead 14 kg.
A/S: Latecoere Malafon (to be replaced by Milas from 1997) ❸; range 13 km *(7 nm)* at 450 kts; payload L4 acoustic homing torpedo; warhead 100 kg; 13 missiles.
Guns: 2 DCN 3.9 in *(100 mm)*/55 Mod 68 CADAM automatic ❹; dual purpose; 80° elevation; 80 rounds/minute to 17 km *(9 nm)* anti-surface; 8 km *(4.4 nm)* anti-aircraft; weight of shell 13.5 kg.
2 Oerlikon 20 mm ❺; 720 rounds/minute to 10 km *(5.5 nm)*.
Torpedoes: 2 launchers ❻. 10 ECAN L5; anti-submarine; active/passive homing to 9.5 km *(5.1 nm)* at 35 kts; warhead 150 kg; depth to 550 m *(1800 ft)*. Honeywell Mk 46 torpedoes for helicopters.
Countermeasures: Decoys: 2 CSEE/VSEL Syllex 8-barrelled trainable launcher (to be replaced by 2 Dagaie systems) ❼; Chaff to 1 km in centroid and distraction patterns.
ESM: ARBR 16; radar warning.
ECM: ARBB 32; jammer (ARBB 33 in due course).
Combat data systems: SENIT 3 action data automation; Links 11 and 14. Syracuse 1 SATCOM ⓭. AIDCOMER command support system (*Duguay-Trouin*).

TOURVILLE *(Scale 1 : 1 200), Ian Sturton*

Radars: Air search: DRBV 26 ❽; D band; range 182 km *(100 nm)* for 2 m² target.
Air/surface search: Thomson-CSF DRBV 51B ❾; G band; range 29 km *(16 nm)*.
Navigation: Two Racal Decca Type 1226; I band (one for helicopter control).
Fire control: DRBC 32D ❿; I band.
Sonars: Thomson Sintra DUBV 23; bow-mounted; active search and attack; 5 kHz.
DUBV 43C ⓫; VDS; medium frequency; tows at up to 24 kts at 200 m.
DSBV 62C; passive linear towed array; low frequency.

Helicopters: 2 WG 13 Lynx ASW ⓬.

Programmes: Developed from the Aconit design. Originally rated as corvettes but reclassified as 'frégates anti-sous-marins (FASM)' on 8 July 1971 and given D pennant numbers like destroyers. *De Grasse* completed major refit September 1981, *Duguay-Trouin* in 1984-85.
Service lives: *Tourville*, 2000; *Duguay-Trouin*, 2001; *De Grasse*, 2003. These will probably be extended.
Modernisation: Planned to complete *Tourville* 1994, *De Grasse* 1995, *Duguay-Trouin* 1996; to include new bow sonar plus VLF towed active sonar with separate towed passive array (SLASM), Murene torpedoes launched from (a) helicopter (b) ships' tubes and (c) using OTO Melara/Matra Milas vice Malafon as stand off delivery vehicle. Passive towed arrays fitted to all three ships in 1990.
Operational: All based in the Atlantic; *Duguay-Trouin* as Flagship.

TOURVILLE *1/1991, van Ginderen Collection*

1 TYPE F 65 (ASW)

Name	*No*	*Builders*	*Laid down*	*Launched*	*Commissioned*
ACONIT	D 609 (ex-*F 703*)	Lorient Naval Dockyard	Jan 1966	7 Mar 1970	30 Mar 1973

Displacement, tons: 3500 standard; 3900 full load
Dimensions, feet (metres): 416.7 × 44 × 18.9 *(127 × 13.4 × 5.8)*
Main machinery: 2 boilers; 640 psi *(45 kg/cm sq)*; 842°F *(450°C)*; 1 Rateau turbine; 28 650 hp(m) *(21 MW)*; 1 shaft
Speed, knots: 27. **Range, miles:** 5000 at 18 kts
Complement: 228 (15 officers)

Missiles: SSM: 8 Aerospatiale MM 40 Exocet ❶; inertial cruise; active radar homing to 70 km *(40 nm)* at 0.9 Mach; warhead 165 kg; sea-skimmer.
SAM: 2 Matra Simbad twin launchers for Mistral (can be fitted on 20 mm gun pedestals).
A/S: Latecoere Malafon ❷; range 13 km *(7 nm)* at 450 kts; payload L4 acoustic homing torpedo; warhead 100 kg; 13 missiles.
Guns: 2 DCN 3.9 in *(100 mm)*/55 Mod 68 CADAM automatic ❸; 80° elevation; 80 rounds/minute to 17 km *(9 nm)* anti-surface; 8 km *(4.4 nm)* anti-aircraft; weight of shell 13.5 kg.
2 Oerlikon 20 mm or SAM.
Torpedoes: 2 launchers. 10 ECAN L5; anti-submarine; active/passive homing to 9.5 km *(5.1 nm)* at 35 kts; warhead 150 kg; depth to 550 m *(1800 ft)*.
Countermeasures: Decoys: 2 CSEE/VSEL Syllex 8-barrelled trainable launchers; Chaff to 1 km in distraction and centroid patterns. Nixie; towed torpedo decoy.
ESM: ARBR 16; radar warning.
ECM: ARBB 32; jammer.
Combat data systems: SENIT 3 action data automation; Links 11 and 14.
Radars: Air search: DRBV 22A ❹; D band.
Air/surface search: Thomson-CSF DRBV 15A ❺; E/F band.
Navigation: DRBN 32 (Decca 1226); I band.
Fire control: DRBC 32D ❻; I band (for guns).
Sonars: Thomson Sintra DUBV 23; bow-mounted; active search and attack; 5 kHz.
DUBV 43C ❼; VDS; medium frequency 5 kHz; tows at up to 24 kts at 200 m.
DSBV 62C; passive linear towed array; low frequency.

Programmes: Forerunner of the F 67 Type. A one-off class ordered under 1965 programme. Due to pay off in 2004.

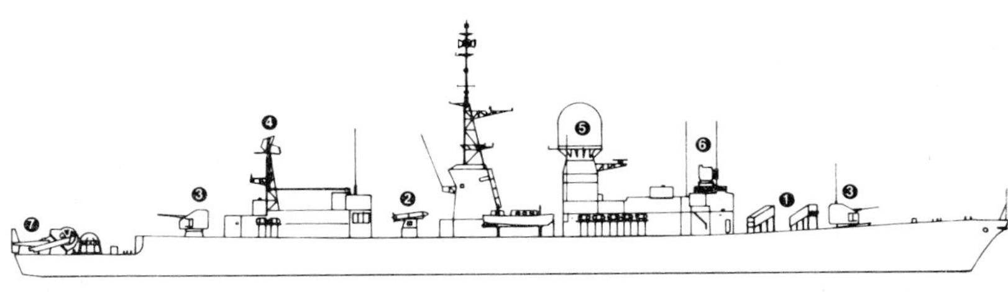

ACONIT *(Scale 1 : 1 200), Ian Sturton*

ACONIT *4/1989, Gilbert Gyssels*

Modernisation: A second quadruple Exocet launcher has been fitted. DSBV 62 passive sonar towed array fitted in 1991. A lightweight DRBC 32D fire control radar has replaced the 32B barrel-shaped director.

Operational: Atlantic Squadron.

FRIGATES (Frégates, Avisos-escorteurs, Avisos)

3 + 3 FLORÉAL CLASS (PATROL FRIGATES)

Name	No	Builders	Laid down	Launched	Commissioned
FLORÉAL	F 730	Chantiers de L'Atlantique, St Nazaire	2 Apr 1990	6 Oct 1990	May 1992
PRAIRIAL	F 731	Chantiers de L'Atlantique, St Nazaire	11 Sep 1990	23 Mar 1991	June 1992
NIVÔSE	F 732	Chantiers de L'Atlantique, St Nazaire	16 Jan 1991	10 Aug 1991	Oct 1992
VENTÔSE	F 733	Chantiers de L'Atlantique, St Nazaire	28 June 1991	14 Mar 1992	Jan 1993
VENDÉMIAIRE	F 734	Chantiers de L'Atlantique, St Nazaire	17 Jan 1992	Aug 1992	June 1993
GERMINAL	F 735	Chantiers de L'Atlantique, St Nazaire	Oct 1992	Mar 1993	Dec 1993

Displacement, tons: 2600 standard; 2950 full load
Dimensions, feet (metres): 306.8 × 45.9 × 14.1 *(93.5 × 14 × 4.3)*
Main machinery: CODAD; 4 SEMT-Pielstick 6PA 6L280 diesels; 9600 hp(m) *(7.1 MW)* sustained; 2 shafts; cp props; bow thruster; 340 hp(m) *(250 kW)*
Speed, knots: 20. **Range, miles:** 10 000 at 15 kts
Complement: 81 (7 officers) plus 42 spare

Missiles: SSM: 2 Aerospatiale MM 38 Exocet ❶; inertial cruise; active radar homing to 42 km *(23 nm)* at 0.9 Mach; warhead 165 kg; sea-skimmer.
SAM: 2 Matra Simbad twin launchers to replace 20 mm guns in due course.
Guns: 1 DCN 3.9 in *(100 mm)*/55 Mod 68 CADAM ❷; 80° elevation; 80 rounds/minute to 17 km *(9 nm)*; weight of shell 13.5 kg.
2 GIAT 20 F2 20 mm ❸; 720 rounds/minute to 10 km *(5.5 nm)*.
Countermeasures: Decoys: 2 CSEE Dagaie II; 10-barrelled trainable launchers ❹; Chaff and IR flares.
ESM: Thomson-CSF ARBR 17 ❺; radar intercept.
Fire control: CSEE Najir optronic director ❻. Syracuse 2 SATCOM ❼.
Radars: Air/surface search: Thomson-CSF Mars DRBV 24 ❽; D band.
Navigation: 2 Racal Decca 1226; I band (one for helicopter control ❾).

Helicopters: 1 AS 332F Super Puma ❿ or 1 Dauphin or 1 NFH-90.

Programmes: Officially described as 'Frégates de Surveillance' or 'Ocean capable patrol vessel' and designed to operate in the offshore zone in low intensity operations. First two ordered on 20 January 1989; built at Chantiers de L'Atlantique, St Nazaire, with weapon systems fitted by DCAN Lorient. Second pair ordered 9 January 1990; third pair in January 1991. Named after the months of the Revolutionary calendar.
Structure: Built to merchant passenger marine standards with stabilisers and air-conditioning. New funnel design improves airflow over the flight deck. Has one freight bunker aft for about 100 tons cargo. Second-hand Exocet MM 38 has been fitted instead of planned MM 40.
Operational: Endurance, 50 days. Range proved to be better than expected during sea trials. Able to operate a helicopter up to seastate 5. *Prairial* armed for trials 11 September 1991. Stations planned as follows: *Floreal* in South Indian Ocean, *Ventose* in Antilles, *Germinal* tender to *Jeanne d'Arc*, remainder in the Pacific.

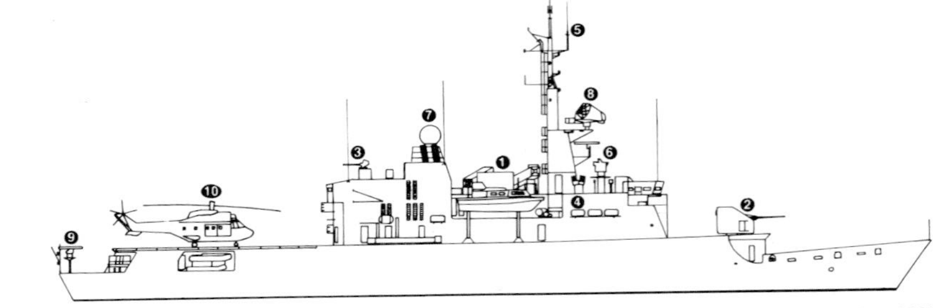

FLOREAL *(Scale 1 : 900), Ian Sturton*

FLOREAL *8/1991, 92 Wing RAAF*

FLOREAL *8/1991, 92 Wing RAAF*

3 COMMANDANT RIVIÈRE CLASS (Avisos Escorteurs)

Name	*No*	*Builders*	*Laid down*	*Launched*	*Commissioned*
COMMANDANT BORY	F 726	Lorient Naval Dockyard	Mar 1958	Oct 1958	5 Mar 1964
BALNY	F 729	Lorient Naval Dockyard	Mar 1960	Mar 1962	1 Feb 1970
ENSEIGNE DE VAISSEAU HENRY	F 749	Lorient Naval Dockyard	Sep 1962	Dec 1963	1 Jan 1965

Displacement, tons: 1750 standard; 2250 full load
1650 standard; 1950 full load *(Balny)*
Dimensions, feet (metres): 336.9 × 38.4 × 14.1
(102.7 × 11.7 × 4.3)
Main machinery: 4 SEMT-Pielstick 12PC series diesels; 16 000 hp(m) *(11.8 MW)*; 2 shafts *(Enseigne de Vaisseau Henry)*
CODAG; 2 SEMT-Pielstick 16-cyl diesels; 1 TG Turbomeca M38; 1 shaft; cp prop *(Balny)*
2 SEMT-Pielstick 12 PC2-V400 diesels; 12 000 hp(m) *(8.2 MW)*; 2 shafts; cp props *(Commandant Bory)*
Speed, knots: 25. **Range, miles:** 7500 at 15 kts; 8000 at 12 kts *(Balny)*
Complement: 159 (9 officers)

Missiles: SSM: 4 Aerospatiale MM 38 Exocet (not fitted in *Balny*) ❶; active radar homing to 42 km *(23 nm)* at 0.9 Mach; warhead 165 kg; sea-skimmer.
Guns: 2 DCN 3.9 in *(100 mm)*/55 Mod 1953 automatic ❷; dual purpose; 80° elevation; 60 rounds/minute to 17 km *(9 nm)* anti-surface; 8 km *(4.4 nm)* anti-aircraft; weight of shell 13.5 kg.
2 Hispano Suiza 30 mm/70 or 2 Bofors 40/60 ❸.
Torpedoes: 6—21.7 in *(550 mm)* (2 triple) tubes ❹. ECAN L3; anti-submarine; active homing to 5.5 km *(3 nm)* at 25 kts; warhead 200 kg; depth to 300 m *(985 ft)*.
A/S mortars: 1 Mortier 305 mm 4-barrelled launcher ❺; automatic loading; range 2700 m; warhead 227 kg.
Countermeasures: Decoys: 2 CSEE Dagaie 10-barrelled trainable launchers ❻; Chaff and IR flares; H-J band.
ESM: ARBR 16; radar warning.
Radars: Air/surface search: Thomson-CSF DRBV 22A ❼; D band.
Surface search: Racal Decca 1226 ❽; I band.
Fire control: DRBC 32C ❾; I band.
Sonars: EDO SQS 17; hull-mounted; active search; medium frequency.
Thomson Sintra DUBA 3; active attack; high frequency.

Programmes: *Commandant Rivière* is now a trials ship. (See *Trials/Research ships* section). *Balny* was made the CODAG trials ship in 1964 but later again became fully operational.
Service lives: 1995. To be replaced by new classes of Light Frigates.
Operational: Can carry a senior officer and staff. If necessary a force of 80 soldiers can be embarked as well as two 30 ft *(9 m)* LCPs with a capacity of 25 men at 11 kts. Pacific, one ship; Indian Ocean, one ship. *Enseigne de Vaisseau Henry* acts as tender to *Jeanne d'Arc*.
Sales: *Victor Schoelcher* sold to Uruguay 30 September 1988, *Commandant Bourdais* and *Amiral Charner*, 14 March 1990.

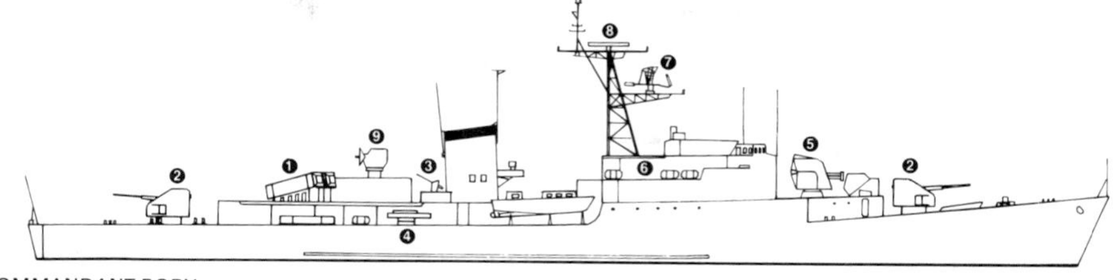

COMMANDANT BORY *(Scale 1 : 900), Ian Sturton*

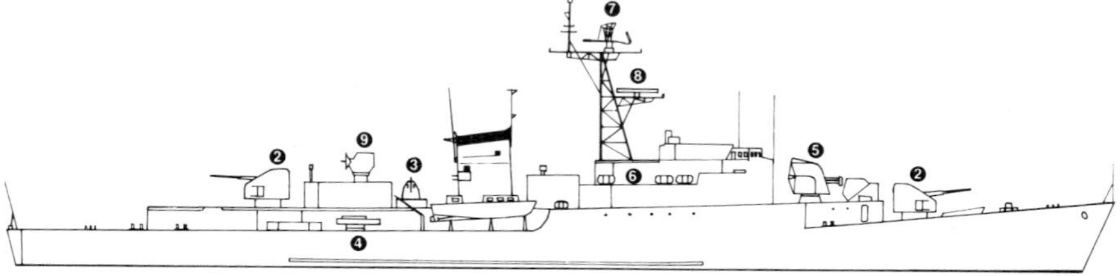

BALNY *(Scale 1 : 900), Ian Sturton*

BALNY *6/1991, John Mortimer*

ENSEIGNE DE VAISSEAU HENRY *6/1991, Harald Carstens*

17 D'ESTIENNE D'ORVES (TYPE A 69) CLASS

Name	No	Builders	Laid down	Launched	Commissioned
D'ESTIENNE D'ORVES	F 781	Lorient Naval Dockyard	1 Sep 1972	1 June 1973	10 Sep 1976
AMYOT D'INVILLE	F 782	Lorient Naval Dockyard	Sep 1973	30 Nov 1974	13 Oct 1976
DROGOU	F 783	Lorient Naval Dockyard	1 Oct 1973	30 Nov 1974	30 Sep 1976
DÉTROYAT	F 784	Lorient Naval Dockyard	15 Dec 1974	31 Jan 1976	4 May 1977
JEAN MOULIN	F 785	Lorient Naval Dockyard	15 Jan 1975	31 Jan 1976	11 May 1977
QUARTIER MAÎTRE ANQUETIL	F 786	Lorient Naval Dockyard	1 Aug 1975	7 Aug 1976	4 Feb 1978
COMMANDANT DE PIMODAN	F 787	Lorient Naval Dockyard	1 Sep 1975	7 Aug 1976	20 May 1978
SECOND MAÎTRE LE BIHAN	F 788	Lorient Naval Dockyard	1 Nov 1976	13 Aug 1977	7 July 1979
LIEUTENANT DE VAISSEAU LE HÉNAFF	F 789	Lorient Naval Dockyard	21 Mar 1977	16 Sep 1978	13 Feb 1980
LIEUTENANT DE VAISSEAU LAVALLÉE	F 790	Lorient Naval Dockyard	1 Nov 1977	29 May 1979	16 Aug 1980
COMMANDANT L'HERMINIER	F 791	Lorient Naval Dockyard	29 May 1979	7 Mar 1981	22 Feb 1986
PREMIER MAÎTRE L'HER	F 792	Lorient Naval Dockyard	24 July 1979	28 June 1980	5 Dec 1981
COMMANDANT BLAISON	F 793	Lorient Naval Dockyard	15 Nov 1979	7 Mar 1981	28 Apr 1982
ENSEIGNE DE VAISSEAU JACOUBET	F 794	Lorient Naval Dockyard	June 1980	28 Sep 1981	23 Oct 1982
COMMANDANT DUCUING	F 795	Lorient Naval Dockyard	1 Oct 1980	28 Sep 1981	17 Mar 1983
COMMANDANT BIROT	F 796	Lorient Naval Dockyard	23 Mar 1981	22 May 1982	14 Mar 1984
COMMANDANT BOUAN	F 797	Lorient Naval Dockyard	12 Oct 1981	23 Apr 1983	1 Nov 1984

Displacement, tons: 950 standard; 1170 (1250, later ships) full load
Dimensions, feet (metres): 262.5 × 33.8 × 18 (sonar) *(80 × 10.3 × 5.5)*
Main machinery: 2 SEMT-Pielstick 12PC2-V400 diesels; 12 000 hp(m) *(8.82 MW)*; 2 shafts; cp props
2 SEMT-Pielstick 12 PA6 280 BTC diesels; 28 800 hp(m) *(21.2 MW)* sustained; 2 shafts; cp props *(Commandant L'Herminier)*
Speed, knots: 23. **Range, miles:** 4500 at 15 kts
Complement: 90 (7 officers)

Missiles: SSM: 4 Aerospatiale MM 40 (or 2 MM 38) Exocet ❶; inertial cruise; active radar homing to 70 km *(40 nm)* (or 42 km *(23 nm)*) at 0.9 Mach; warhead 165 kg; sea-skimmer. Most will get dual fit capability ITL in due course (see *Modernisation*) but a few only have MM 38 capability (ITS) and some none at all.
Guns: 1 DCN 3.9 in *(100 mm)*/55 Mod 68 CADAM automatic ❷; 80° elevation; 80 rounds/minute to 17 km *(9 nm)* anti-surface; 8 km *(4.4 nm)* anti-aircraft; weight of shell 13.5 kg.
2 Oerlikon 20 mm ❸; 720 rounds/minute to 10 km *(5.5 nm)*.
Torpedoes: 4 fixed tubes ❹. ECAN L3; anti-submarine; active homing to 5.5 km *(3 nm)* at 25 kts; warhead 200 kg; depth to 300 m *(985 ft)* and ECAN L5; dual purpose; active/passive homing to 9.5 km *(5.1 nm)* at 35 kts; warhead 150 kg; depth to 550 m *(1800 ft)*.
A/S mortars: 1 Creusot Loire 375 mm Mk 54 6-tubed trainable launcher ❺; range 1600 m; warhead 107 kg.
Countermeasures: Decoys: 2 CSEE Dagaie 10-barrelled trainable launchers (fitted from F 792 onwards; remainder being fitted at refit) ❻; Chaff and IR flares; H-J band.
Nixie torpedo decoy.
ESM: ARBR 16; radar warning.
Fire control: Thomson-CSF Vega system.
Radars: Air/surface search: Thomson-CSF DRBV 51A ❼; G band; range 29 km *(16 nm)*.
Navigation: Racal Decca 1226; I band.
Fire control: DRBC 32E ❽; I band.
Sonars: Thomson Sintra DUBA 25; hull-mounted; search and attack; medium frequency.

Programmes: Classified as 'Avisos'. Service lives: The first three due to pay off in 1996 and then regularly until *Commandant Bouan* in 2004.
Modernisation: In 1985 *Commandant L'Herminier*, F 791, fitted with 12PA6 BTC Diesels Rapides as trial for Type F 70. Most have dual MM 38/MM 40 ITL (Installation de Tir Légère) capability. Weapon fit depends on deployment and operational requirement. Those without ITL are being retrofitted with ITS (Installation de Tir Standard) as Commandant Rivière class pay off.
Operational: Endurance, 30 days and primarily intended for coastal A/S operations. Also available for overseas patrols. Deployment: 1st Division d'Avisos, Cherbourg (3 ships); 2nd Division d'Avisos, Brest (suspended); 3rd Division d'Avisos, Toulon (3 ships); 4th Division d'Avisos, Brest (4 ships); 5th Division d'Avisos, Toulon (3 ships). Some ships deployed overseas pending the delivery of new frigates. *Commandant Ducuing* transferred to the Indian Ocean until 1992, *Commandant Birot* and *Lieutenant de Vaisseau Lavallée* to the Pacific until 1993. The Second Division has been temporarily disbanded until 1993 as most of its ships are overseas. Any remaining have transferred to the Fourth Division.
Sales: The original *Lieutenant de Vaisseau Le Hénaff* and *Commandant l'Herminier* sold to South Africa in 1976 while under construction. As a result of the UN embargo on arms sales to South Africa, they were sold to Argentina in September 1978 followed by a third, specially built.

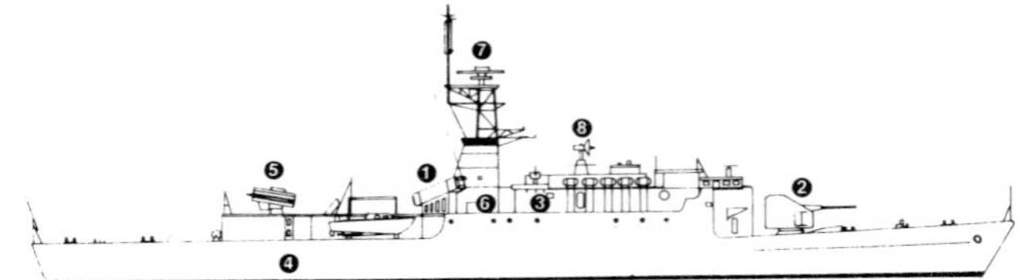

TYPE A 69 *(Scale 1 : 900), Ian Sturton*

D'ESTIENNE D'ORVES *6/1991, van Ginderen Collection*

DROGOU *10/1990, Selim San*

0 + 3 + 3 (4) LA FAYETTE CLASS (LIGHT FRIGATES)

Name	*No*	*Builders*	*Laid down*	*Launched*	*Commissioned*
LA FAYETTE	F 710	Lorient Naval Dockyard	15 Dec 1990	1992	June 1994
SURCOUF	F 711	Lorient Naval Dockyard	June 1992	1994	July 1995
COURBET	F 712	Lorient Naval Dockyard	May 1993	1996	Jan 1997

Displacement, tons: 3500 full load
Dimensions, feet (metres): 410.1 oa; 377.3 pp × 50.5 × 13.1 *(125; 115 × 15.4 × 4)*
Main machinery: CODAD; 4 SEMT-Pielstick 12 PA 6V 280 BTC; diesels; 28 800 hp(m) *(21.2 MW)* sustained; 2 shafts
Speed, knots: 25. **Range, miles:** 7000 at 15 kts; 9000 at 12 kts
Complement: 139 (15 officers) plus 25 spare

Missiles: SSM: 8 Aerospatiale MM 40 Exocet ❶; inertial cruise; active radar homing to 70 km *(40 nm)* at 0.9 Mach; warhead 165 kg; sea-skimmer.
SAM: Thomson-CSF Crotale NG (nouvelle generation) octuple launcher ❷; radar guidance; line of sight radar and IR guidance to 13 km *(7 nm)* at 3.5 Mach; warhead 14 kg. Replaced by SAAM VLS ❸ with 16 Aster 15 missiles in second three.
Guns: 1 DCN 3.9 in *(100 mm)*/55 Mod 68 CADAM ❹; 80° elevation; 80 rounds/minute to 17 km *(9 nm)*; weight of shell 13.5 kg.
2 GIAT 20F2 20 mm ❺; 720 rounds/minute to 10 km *(5.5 nm)*.
2—12.7 mm MGs.
Countermeasures: Decoys: 2 CSEE Dagaie ❻ 10-barrelled trainable launchers; Chaff and IR flares. SLAT anti-wake homing torpedoes system (when available).
ESM: Thomson-CSF DR 3000-S ARBR 17 ❼; radar intercept.
DIBV 10 Vampir ❽; IR detector.
ECM: ARBB 33; jammer.
Combat data systems: Thomson-CSF TAVITAC 2000. Syracuse 2 SATCOM ❾.
Fire control: Thomson-CSF CTM system.
Radars: Air/surface search: Thomson-CSF Sea Tiger (DRBV 15C) ❿; E/F band.
Navigation: Racal Decca 1226 ⓫; I band. A second set may be fitted for helicopter control.
Fire control: Castor II ⓬; I band; range 15 km *(8 nm)* for 1 m^2 target.
Arabel for SAAM (for second three).

Helicopters: 1 Dauphin ⓭ or 1 NFH 90.

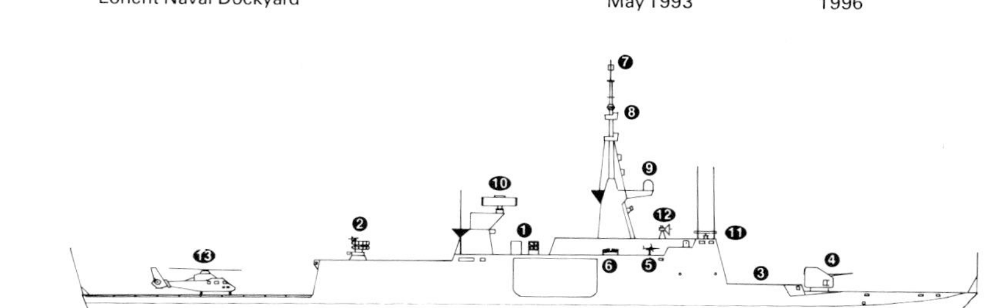

LA FAYETTE (Scale 1 : 1 200), Ian Sturton

LA FAYETTE (artist's impression) 1990, DCN

Programmes: Officially described as 'Frégates Légères'. First three ordered 25 July 1988; three more authorised for orders in 1992 with a planned total of up to 10. The programme was delayed by up to one year by the 1989 defence budget. First steel cut for each hull about 14 months before the keel is laid.
Structure: Space left for a SAAM launcher forward of the bridge which will replace Crotale in the second three of the class on build and the first three at refit. This might mean putting the Arabel fire control radar on top of a more solid looking foremast once Crotale is removed. Superstructure inclines at 10° to the vertical to reduce radar echoing area. External equipment such as capstans, bollards etc either 'hidden' or installed as low as possible. Radar absorbent paint is used extensively. Sensitive areas are armour plated. SLAT anti-torpedo system may be fitted when available. Magazine for AM 39 Exocet and AS 15 for the NFH-90 helicopter.
Operational: *La Fayette* planned to start trials in April 1993, *Surcouf* in April 1994 and *Courbet* in October 1995. These frigates are designed for out of area operations on overseas stations.
Sales: Three of an improved design to Saudi Arabia and a possible 16 to Taiwan of which the first six are to be built in France.
Opinion: Plans to fit sonar have apparently been dropped but in the future an ASW version of the ship could be built with hull and towed array sonars, lightweight torpedo launchers, and an ASW configured helicopter.

SHIPBORNE AIRCRAFT

Note: Rafale ACM to start deck trials in 1993.

Numbers/Type: 13 Aerospatiale SA 319B Alouette III.
Operational speed: 113 kts *(210 km/h)*.
Service ceiling: 10 500 ft *(3200 m)*.
Range: 290 nm *(540 km)*.
Role/Weapon systems: General purpose helicopter; replaced by Lynx for ASW; now used for trials, surveillance and training tasks. Sensors: Some radar. Weapons: Unarmed.

ALOUETTE III 1988, French Navy

Numbers/Type: 4 (15) Aerospatiale SA 365F/AS 565MA Dauphin 2.
Operational speed: 140 kts *(260 km/h)*.
Service ceiling: 15 000 ft *(4575 m)*.
Range: 410 nm *(758 km)*.
Role/Weapon systems: Replace Alouette III for carrier-borne SAR and one in English Channel. 15 more ordered in several batches for light and patrol frigates, pending delivery of NFH 90. More of these aircraft are operated for SAR duties on behalf of the Navy. May be armed with AS 15 if NFH 90 is delayed. Sensors: Agrion search radar. Weapons: Unarmed.

DAUPHIN 2 8/1990, J. Y. Robert

Numbers/Type: 26 Bréguet Br 1050 Alizé (modernised).
Operational speed: 254 kts *(470 km/h)*.
Service ceiling: 26 250 ft *(8000 m)*.
Range: 1350 nm *(2500 km)*.
Role/Weapon systems: ASW and strike aircraft embarked in CVLs for surface search, ASV and ASW roles; updated 1985-86 for 1990s role. Sensors: Thomson-CSF Iguane surveillance radar, sonobuoys, ECM/ESM. Weapons: ASW; 1 × torpedo or 3 × 160 kg depth bombs or 1 × nuclear depth bomb. ASV; 2 × AS12 missiles and 6 × rockets.

ALIZÉ 1987, Breguet

Numbers/Type: 11 Dassault Etendard IV-P.
Operational speed: Mach 1.02.
Service ceiling: 49 000 ft *(15 000 m)*.
Range: 1520 nm *(2817 km)*.
Role/Weapon systems: Primary role is photo-reconnaissance and overwater surveillance; armed IV-M version is retained for training; carrier-borne and land-based depending on needs. Sensors: Up to 5 × Omera cameras. Weapons: Unarmed.

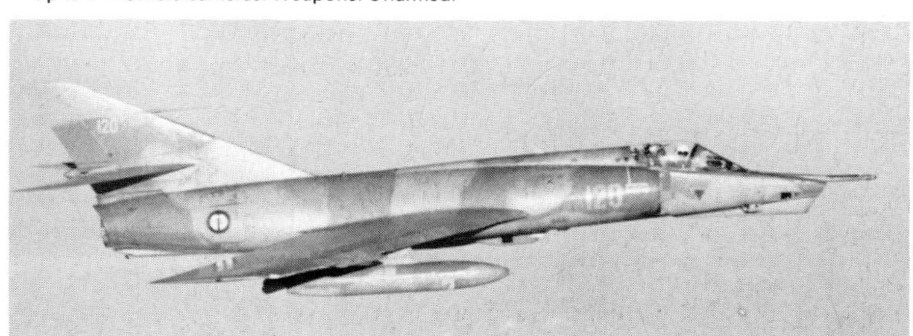

ETENDARD IV-P 1988, French Navy

Numbers/Type: 59 Dassault-Bréguet Super Etendard.
Operational speed: Approx Mach 1.
Service ceiling: 45 000 ft *(13 700 m)*.
Range: 920 nm *(1682 km)*.
Role/Weapon systems: Carrier-borne strike fighter with limited air defence role with nuclear strike. 50-55 to be modernised at 12 per year 1992-97 to keep 38 operational. New Anémone ESD radar and AS 30L laser-guided weapon to be fitted. Sensors: Thomson-CSF Agave radar, ECM/ESM. Weapons: Strike; 1 × Aerospatiale ASMP stand-off weapon; range 300 km; nuclear warhead, 2.1 tons of underwing stores including AM 39 Exocet. Defence; 2 × Magic AAM and drop tanks. Self protection; 2 × 30 mm DEFA cannon. 56 are to be modernised from 1990 (first two aircraft to be delivered in 1992): new radar (Dassault Electronique Anémone), new computer (SAGEM UAT 90), new displays, new ESM/ECM and AS 30L (laser) missile.

SUPER ETENDARD (with ASMP) *1988, Aerospatiale*

Numbers/Type: 19 LTV F-8E(FN) Crusader.
Operational speed: 868 kts *(1610 km/h)*.
Service ceiling: 50 000 ft *(15 240 m)*.
Range: 740 nm *(1370 km)*.
Role/Weapon systems: Carrier-borne air defence fighter modified for French needs. 17 to be refurbished to last until 1997/98 when they will be replaced by Rafale. Sensors: Search/attack radar, ECM. Weapons: AD; 2 × Magic AAM or 2 × R530 AAM. Self protection; 4 × 20 mm cannon.

CRUSADER *1984*

Numbers/Type: 35 Westland Lynx Mk 4 (FN).
Operational speed: 125 kts *(232 km/h)*.
Service ceiling: 12 500 ft *(3810 m)*.
Range: 320 nm *(593 km)*.
Role/Weapon systems: Sole French ASW helicopter, all now of the Mk 4 variant; embarked in destroyers and deployed on training tasks. Sensors: Omera 31 search radar, Alcatel (HS-12 in Mk 2, DUAV 4 in Mk 4) dipping sonar, sonobuoys. Weapons: ASV; 4 × AS12 missiles/SFIM M335 sight. ASW; 2 × Mk 46 Mod 1 (or MU 90 in due course) torpedoes, or depth charges.

LYNX (with MU 90 Impact torpedo) *1987, Thomson Sintra*

Numbers/Type: 17 Aerospatiale SA 321G Super Frelon.
Operational speed: 148 kts *(275 km/h)*.
Service ceiling: 10 170 ft *(3100 m)*.
Range: 442 nm *(820 km)*.
Role/Weapon systems: Formerly ASW helicopter; now used for assault and support tasks embarked on carriers and LSDs; possible update for ASV not proceeded with but radar updated; provision for 27 passengers. Sensors: Omera ORB search radar. Weapons: Provision for 20 mm gun.

SUPER FRELON *1990, French Navy*

LAND-BASED MARITIME AIRCRAFT (FRONT LINE)

Numbers/Type: 28 Bréguet Atlantic (NATO) Mk 1.
Operational speed: 355 kts *(658 km/h)*.
Service ceiling: 32 800 ft *(10 000 m)*.
Range: 4855 nm *(8995 km)*.
Role/Weapon systems: Maritime reconnaissance carried out in Atlantic and Mediterranean; may be deployed to Pacific. Primarily ASW but useful ASV role; being replaced by Atlantique 2. Sensors: Thomson-CSF radar, ECM/ESM, MAD, sonobuoys. Weapons: ASW; 9 × torpedoes (including Mk 46) or depth bombs and mines. ASV; 3/4 Martel ARM.

Numbers/Type: 6 Dassault-Bréguet Falcon 10MER.
Operational speed: 492 kts *(912 km/h)*.
Service ceiling: 35 500 ft *(10 670 m)*.
Range: 1920 nm *(3560 km)*.
Role/Weapon systems: Primary aircrew/ECM training role in peacetime but also has overwater surveillance role in wartime; France sole user. Sensors: Search radar. Weapons: Unarmed.

Numbers/Type: 13 Dassault Aviation Atlantique Mk 2.
Operational speed: 355 kts *(658 km/h)*.
Service ceiling: 32 800 ft *(10 000 m)*.
Range: 8 hours patrol at 1000 nm from base; 4 hours patrol at 1500 nm from base.
Role/Weapon systems: Maritime reconnaissance. ASW, ASV, COMINT/ELINT roles. 28 ordered by early 1992 with 13 delivered and 7 more expected in 1992. Total requirement 42 reduced to 28. Sensors: Thomson-CSF Iguane radar, ARAR 13 ESM, ECM, FLIR, MAD, sonobuoys (with DSAX-1 Thomson-CSF Sadang processing equipment). Link 11 (in due course). COMINT/ELINT equipment optional. Integrated sensor/weapon system built around a CIMSA 15/125X computer. Weapons: 2 × AM 39 Exocet ASMs in ventral bay, or up to eight lightweight torpedoes (Mk 46 and later MU 90), or depth charges, mines or bombs.

Numbers/Type: 5 Dassault-Bréguet Gardian.
Operational speed: 470 kts *(870 km/h)*.
Service ceiling: 45 000 ft *(13 715 m)*.
Range: 2425 nm *(4490 km)*.
Role/Weapon systems: Maritime reconnaissance role in French Pacific area. Sensors: Thomson-CSF Varan radar, Omega navigation, ECM/ESM pods. Weapons: Unarmed.

AMPHIBIOUS FORCES

1 BOUGAINVILLE CLASS (BTS)

Name	*No*	*Builders*	*Laid down*	*Launched*	*Commissioned*
BOUGAINVILLE	L 9077	Chantier Dubigeon, Nantes	28 Jan 1986	3 Oct 1986	June 1988

Displacement, tons: 4876 standard; 5100 full load
Dimensions, feet (metres): 372.3; 344.4 wl × 55.8 × 14.1 *(113.5; 105 × 17 × 4.3)*
Flight deck, feet (metres): 85.3 × 55.8 *(26 × 17)*
Main machinery: 2 SACM AGO 195 V12 RVR diesels; 4410 hp(m) *(3.24 MW)* sustained; 2 shafts; cp props; bow thruster; 400 hp(m) *(294 kW)*
Speed, knots: 15. **Range, miles:** 6000 at 12 kts
Complement: 53 (5 officers) plus 10 staff
Military lift: 500 troops for 8 days; 1180 tons cargo; 2 LCU in support or 10 LCP plus 2 LCM for amphibious role

Guns: 2—12.7 mm MGs.
Radars: Navigation: Two Decca 1226; I band.

Helicopters: Platform for 2 AS 332B Super Puma.

BOUGAINVILLE *1988, Alsthom*

Programmes: Ordered November 1984 for the Direction du Centre d'Experimentations Nucléaires (DIRCEN). As Chantier Dubigeon closed down after her launch she was completed by Chantier de l'Atlantique of the Alsthom group. Bâtiment de Transport et de Soutien (BTS).
Structure: Well size is 78 × 10.2 m *(256 × 33.5 ft)*. It can receive tugs and one BSR or two CTMs, a supply tender of the Chamois class, containers, mixed bulk cargo. Has extensive repair workshops and repair facilities for helicopters. Can act as mobile crew accommodation and has medical facilities. Storerooms for spare parts, victuals and ammunition. Hull to civilian standards. Carries a 37 ton crane.

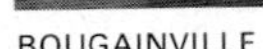

Operational: Completed sea trials 25 February 1988. Based in the Pacific Squadron for use at the nuclear test base. Can dock a 400 ton ship.

1 FOUDRE CLASS (LANDING SHIPS (DOCK)) (TYPE TCD 90)

Name	*No*	*Builders*	*Laid down*	*Launched*	*Commissioned*
FOUDRE	L 9011	Brest Naval Dockyard	26 Mar 1986	19 Nov 1988	7 Dec 1990

Displacement, tons: 8190 light; 11 900 full load
Dimensions, feet (metres): 551 × 77.1 × 17 (30.2 flooded) *(168 × 23.5 × 5.2 (9.2))*
Main machinery: 2 SEMT-Pielstick 16 PC 2.5 V400 diesels; 15 300 hp(m) *(11.24 MW)* sustained; 2 shafts; cp props; bow thruster; 1000 hp(m) *(735 kW)*
Speed, knots: 21. **Range, miles:** 11 000 at 15 kts
Complement: 210 (13 officers)
Military lift: 470 troops plus 1810 tons load; 2 CDIC or 10 CTM or 1 P 400 patrol craft

Missiles: SAM: 2 Matra Sadral sextuple launchers ❶ (to be replaced by 2 twin Simbad launchers in late 1992); Mistral; IR homing to 4 km *(2.2 nm)*; warhead 3 kg.
Guns: 1 Bofors 40 mm/60 ❷. 2 GIAT 20F2 20 mm guns ❸. 4—12.7 mm MGs.
Combat data systems: Syracuse SATCOM ❹.
Radars: Air/surface search: Thomson-CSF Rodeo (Army type) ❺.
Surface search: Racal Decca 2459 ❻; I band.
Navigation: 2 Racal Decca RM 1229; I band (1 for helo control ❼).

Helicopters: 4 AS 332F Super Puma ❽.

Programmes: First ordered 5 November 1984. Second and third (L 9012 and 9013) orders postponed until 1994. Transports de Chalands de Débarquement (TCD).

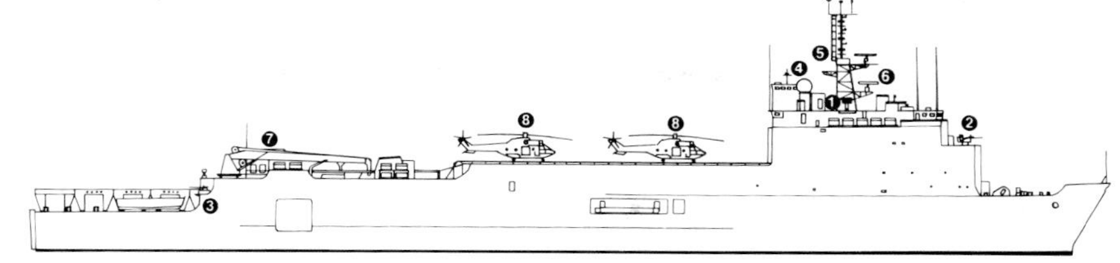
FOUDRE *(Scale 1 : 1 500), Ian Sturton*

Structure: Designed to take a mechanised regiment of the Rapid Action Force and act as a logistic support ship. Extensive command and hospital facilities include two operating theatres and 47 beds. Sadral SAM to be replaced in late 1992 by two lightweight Simbad SAMs either side of bridge. Hangar capacity: two Super Frelons or four Super Pumas. Well dock 122 × 14.2 × 7.7 m. Lift of 52 tons capacity. Flight deck 1450 m² with Samahe haul down system. Flume stabilisation to be fitted in 1993.
Operational: Two landing spots on flight deck plus one on deck well rolling cover. Can operate up to seven Super Puma helicopters. Could carry up to 1600 troops in emergency. Endurance, 30 days (with 700 persons aboard). A 400 ton ship can be docked. Based at Toulon.

FOUDRE *5/1991, J. Y. Robert*

FOUDRE *1990, Ships of the World*

2 OURAGAN CLASS (LANDING SHIPS (DOCK) (TCDs))

Name	*No*	*Builders*	*Laid down*	*Launched*	*Commissioned*
OURAGAN	L 9021	Brest Naval Dockyard	June 1962	9 Nov 1963	1 June 1965
ORAGE	L 9022	Brest Naval Dockyard	June 1966	22 Apr 1967	1 Apr 1968

Displacement, tons: 5800 light; 8500 full load; 15 000 when fully docked down
Dimensions, feet (metres): 488.9 × 75.4 × 17.7 (28.5 flooded) *(149 × 23 × 5.4 (8.7))*
Main machinery: 2 SEMT-Pielstick diesels; 8600 hp(m) *(6.32 MW)*; 2 shafts; cp props
Speed, knots: 17. **Range, miles:** 9000 at 15 kts
Complement: 213 (10 officers)
Military lift: 343 troops (plus 129 short haul only); 2 LCTs (EDIC) with 11 light tanks each or 8 loaded CTMs; logistic load 1500 tons; 2 cranes (35 tons each)

Guns: 2—4.7 in *(120 mm)* mortars; 42 rounds/minute to 20 km *(10.8 nm)*; weight of shell 24 kg.
4 Bofors 40 mm; 300 rounds/minute to 12 km *(6.5 nm)*.
Radars: Navigation: Racal Decca 1226; I band.
Sonars: EDO SQS-17 *(Ouragan)*; search; medium frequency.

Helicopters: 4 SA 321G Super Frelon or Super Pumas or 10 SA 319B Alouette III.

Programmes: Service lives will be extended until L 9012 and L 9013 are commissioned.
Structure: Normal helicopter platform for operating three Super Frelon or 10 Alouette III plus a portable platform for a further one Super Frelon or three Alouette III. Bridge is on the starboard side. Three LCVPs can also be carried. Extensive workshops.
Operational: Typical loads—18 Super Frelon or 80 Alouette III helicopters or 120 AMX 13 tanks or 84 DUKWs or 340 Jeeps or 12—50 ton barges. A 400 ton ship can be docked. Command facilities for directing amphibious and helicopter operations. Both ships in Atlantic Fleet although they regularly deploy worldwide.

OURAGAN *5/1991, A. Campanera i Rovira*

2 CDIC CLASS (LCT)

L 9061 **L 9062**

Displacement, tons: 380 light; 710 full load
Dimensions, feet (metres): 194.9 × 39 × 5.9 *(59.4 × 11.9 × 1.8)*
Main machinery: 2 SACM Uni Diesel UD 30 V12 M1 diesels; 1200 hp(m) *(882 kW)* sustained; 2 shafts
Speed, knots: 10.5. **Range, miles:** 1000 at 10 kts
Complement: 12 (1 officer)
Military lift: 336 tons
Guns: 2 GIAT 20F2 20 mm. 2—12.7 mm MGs.

Comment: First laid down September 1987 at SFCN, Villeneuve la Garenne. Commissioned 19 October 1988 and 2 March 1989 respectively. CDIC (Chaland de Débarquement d'Infanterie et de Chars) designed to replace the EDICs and specially built to work with Foudre class. The wheelhouse can be lowered to facilitate docking manoeuvres in the LPDs. More of the class may be ordered.

L 9062 *6/1991, van Ginderen Collection*

5 BATRAL TYPE (LIGHT TRANSPORTS and LANDING SHIPS)

Name	No	Builders	Commissioned
CHAMPLAIN	L 9030	Brest Naval Dockyard	5 Oct 1974
FRANCIS GARNIER	L 9031	Brest Naval Dockyard	21 June 1974
DUMONT D'URVILLE	L 9032	CMN, Cherbourg	5 Feb 1983
JACQUES CARTIER	L 9033	CMN, Cherbourg	29 Sep 1983
LA GRANDIÈRE	L 9034	CMN, Cherbourg	21 Jan 1987

Displacement, tons: 750 standard; 1330 (1400, second pair) full load
Dimensions, feet (metres): 262.4 × 42.6 × 7.9 *(80 × 13 × 2.4)*
Main machinery: 2 SACM AGO 195 V12 diesels; 3600 hp(m) *(2.65 MW)* sustained; 2 shafts; cp props
Speed, knots: 16. **Range, miles:** 4500 at 13 kts
Complement: 39 (3 officers)
Military lift: 138 troops (180 in second pair); 12 vehicles; 350 tons load; 10 ton crane

Guns: 2 Bofors 40 mm/60 (L 9030, L 9031). 2 GIAT 20F2 20 mm (L 9032, L 9033). 1—81 mm mortar. 2—12.7 mm MGs.
Radars: Navigation: DRBN 32; I band.
Sonars: Two; hull-mounted.

Helicopters: 1 SA 319B Alouette III.

Programmes: Classified as Batral 3F. Bâtiments d'Assaut et de TRAnsport Légers (BATRAL). First two launched 17 November 1973. *Dumont D'Urville* floated out 27 November 1981. *Jacques Cartier* launched 28 April 1982 and *La Grandière* 15 December 1985.
Structure: 40 ton bow ramp; stowage for vehicles above and below decks. One LCVP and one LCPS carried. Helicopter landing platform. Last three of class have bridge one deck higher.
Operational: Deployment: *La Grandière*, Indian Ocean; *F Garnier*, Antilles/French Guiana; *D D'Urville*, Papeete; *J Cartier*, New Caledonia; *Champlain*, Lorient.
Sales: Ships of this class built for Chile, Gabon, Ivory Coast and Morocco. *La Grandière* was also built for Gabon under Clause 29 arrangements but funds were not available.

FRANCIS GARNIER — *6/1989, Hartmut Ehlers*

2 EDIC 700 CLASS (LCT)

L 9051 **L 9052**

Displacement, tons: 736 full load
Dimensions, feet (metres): 193.6 × 38.1 × 5.8 *(59 × 11.6 × 1.7)*
Main machinery: 2 SACM Uni Diesel UD 30 V12 M1 diesels; 1200 hp(m) *(882 kW)* sustained; 2 shafts
Speed, knots: 12. **Range, miles:** 1800 at 12 kts
Complement: 17
Military lift: 350 tons
Guns: 2 GIAT 20F2 20 mm. 2—12.7 mm MGs.

Comment: Ordered 10 March 1986 from SFCN, Villeneuve la Garenne. Commissioned on 13 June 1987 and 19 December 1987 respectively. Rated as Engins de Débarquement d'Infanterie et Chars (EDIC III). Based at the Pacific Test Centre (*L 9051*) and Djibouti (*L 9052*).

L 9052 — *4/1991, Guy Toremans*

3 EDIC CLASS (LCT)

L 9070 (29 Mar 1967) **L 9074** (7 Feb 1970)
L 9072 (1968)

Displacement, tons: 635 (L 9070)
Dimensions, feet (metres): 193.5 × 39.2 × 4.5 *(59 × 12 × 1.3)*
Main machinery: 2 SACM MGO 175 V12 diesels; 1000 hp(m) *(753 kW)* sustained; 2 shafts
Speed, knots: 8. **Range, miles:** 1800 at 8 kts
Complement: 17
Military lift: 5 LVTs or 11 lorries
Guns: 2 Oerlikon 20 mm.

Comment: *L 9095* to Senegal 1 July 1974 as *La Falence*. *L 9082* transferred to Madagascar in 1985 and renamed *Aina Vao Vao*. Of the remainder *L 9072* is deployed to the Pacific Test Range, *L 9070* is at Lorient and *L 9074* at Toulon. Being replaced by the CDICs.

L 9074 — *8/1990, J. Y. Robert*

23 CTMs (LCMs)

CTM 2, 3, 9-10, 12-30

Displacement, tons: 56 standard; 150 full load
Dimensions, feet (metres): 78 × 21 × 4.2 *(23.8 × 6.4 × 1.3)*
Main machinery: 2 Poyaud 520 V8 diesels; 225 hp(m) *(165 kW)*; 2 shafts
Speed, knots: 9.5. **Range, miles:** 350 at 8 kts
Complement: 6
Military lift: 90 tons (maximum); 48 tons (normal)

Comment: First series of 16 built 1966-70 and so far seven have been deleted. Second series built at CMN, Cherbourg 1982-89. All have a bow ramp but the second series has a different shaped pilot house. Chalands de Transport de Matériel (CTM).

CTM 12 — *8/1990, J. Y. Robert*

2 LCM 6s

1057 **1058**

Comment: Of 52 tons full load and 8 kts. Built in Réunion for service at Mayotte Naval Base. Completed March 1983. Some others operated by French Army overseas.

LIGHT FORCES

1 THOMSON-CSF TYPE (LARGE PATROL CRAFT)

Name	No	Builders	Commissioned
IRIS	P 696	Chantier Naval de L'Esterel	15 Aug 1990

Displacement, tons: 210 standard; 227 full load
Dimensions, feet (metres): 150.3 × 27.2 × 7.2 *(45.8 × 8.3 × 2.2)*
Main machinery: 2 MTU 16V 396 TB 83 diesels; 4200 hp(m) *(3.09 MW)*; 2 shafts
Speed, knots: 23. **Range, miles:** 3000 at 13 kts
Complement: 7 (2 officers) plus 11 spare berths
Missiles: SAM: Thomson-CSF Crotale Modulaire octuple launcher.
SATCP Mistral launcher.
Guns: 2 Oerlikon 35 mm (twin).
Radars: Fire control: Thomson-CSF DRBC 32D; I/J band.

Comment: Built by Thomson-CSF as a demonstrator but naval controlled and manned and will probably transfer to the Navy in due course. Hull is 'Deep V' as in *Grebe*. Armament modules including missiles and guns can be changed within 24 hours.

IRIS — *2/1991, 92 Wing RAAF*

L'AUDACIEUSE (twin funnels) *6/1991, Foto Flite*

10 P 400 CLASS (FAST ATTACK CRAFT—PATROL)

Name	*No*	*Builders*	*Commissioned*
L'AUDACIEUSE	P 682	CMN, Cherbourg	18 Sep 1986
LA BOUDEUSE	P 683	CMN, Cherbourg	15 Jan 1987
LA CAPRICIEUSE	P 684	CMN, Cherbourg	13 Mar 1987
LA FOUGUEUSE	P 685	CMN, Cherbourg	13 Mar 1987
LA GLORIEUSE	P 686	CMN, Cherbourg	18 Apr 1987
LA GRACIEUSE	P 687	CMN, Cherbourg	17 July 1987
LA MOQUEUSE	P 688	CMN, Cherbourg	18 Apr 1987
LA RAILLEUSE	P 689	CMN, Cherbourg	16 May 1987
LA RIEUSE	P 690	CMN, Cherbourg	13 June 1987
LA TAPAGEUSE	P 691	CMN, Cherbourg	11 Feb 1988

Displacement, tons: 406 standard; 454 full load
Dimensions, feet (metres): 178.6 × 26.2 × 8.5 *(54.5 × 8 × 2.5)*
Main machinery: 2 SEMT-Pielstick 16PA4 200 VGDS diesels; 8000 hp(m) *(5.88 MW)* sustained; 2 shafts; cp props
Speed, knots: 24.5. **Range, miles:** 4200 at 15 kts
Complement: 26 (3 officers) plus 20 passengers

Guns: 1 Bofors 40 mm/60; 1 GIAT 20F2 20 mm; 2—12.7 mm MGs.
Radars: Surface search: Racal Decca 1226; I band.

Programmes: First six ordered in May 1982, with further four in March 1984. The original engines of this class were unsatisfactory. Replacements were ordered and construction was slowed. Those completed were laid up at Lorient until new engines became available. This class relieved the Patra fast patrol craft which have all transferred to the Gendarmerie.
Structure: Steel hull and superstructure protected by an upper deck bulwark. Design modified from original missile craft configuration. Now capable of transporting personnel with appropriate store-rooms. Of more robust construction than previously planned—to be used as overseas transports. Can be converted for missile armament (MM 38) with dockyard assistance and Sadral PDMS has been considered. *L'Audacieuse* has done trials with a VDS-12 sonar. Twin funnels replaced the unsatisfactory submerged diesel exhausts in 1990/91.
Operational: Deployments: Antilles/French Guiana; P 684, 685. Noumea; P 686, 688. Mayotte (Indian Ocean); P 683, 690. Tahiti; P 687, 689, 691. Cherbourg; P 682. Endurance, 15 days with 45 people aboard.

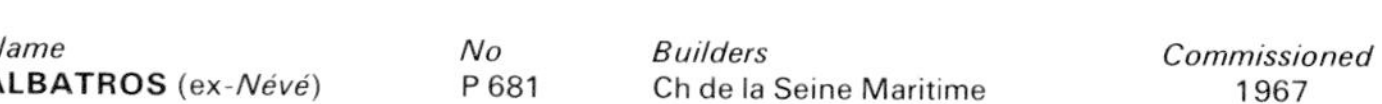

Name	*No*	*Builders*	*Commissioned*
ALBATROS (ex-*Névé*)	P 681	Ch de la Seine Maritime	1967

Displacement, tons: 2800 full load
Dimensions, feet (metres): 278.1 × 44.3 × 18.4 *(84.8 × 13.5 × 5.6)*
Main machinery: Diesel-electric; 2 Uni Diesel UD 33 V12 M6 diesels; 4410 hp(m) *(3.24 MW)* sustained; 2 motors; 3046 hp(m) *(2.24 MW)*; 1 shaft
Speed, knots: 15
Complement: 46 (5 officers) plus 16 passengers
Guns: 1 Bofors 40 mm/60. 2—12.7 mm MGs.
Helicopters: Platform for Alouette III.

Comment: Former trawler bought in April 1983 from Compagnie Nav. Caennaise for conversion into a patrol ship. Commissioned 19 May 1984. Conducts patrols from Réunion to Kerguelen, Crozet, St Paul and Amsterdam Islands with occasional deployments to South Pacific. Can carry 200 tons cargo, has extensive sick berth arrangements and VIP accommodation. Major refit in Lorient from June 1990 to March 1991 which included new diesel-electric propulsion. Service life: 2015.

ALBATROS *1986, French Navy*

FORCE DE SURFACE A MISSIONS CIVILES—FSMC

Note: This designation is applied to a programme of ships and craft designed for offshore and coastal patrol, fishery protection, maritime traffic surveillance, anti-pollution duties and search and rescue, all being manned by the Navy.

Name	*No*	*Builders*	*Commissioned*
STERNE	P 680	La Perrière, Lorient	25 Oct 1980

Displacement, tons: 380 full load
Dimensions, feet (metres): 160.7 × 24.6 × 9.2 *(49 × 7.5 × 2.8)*
Main machinery: 2 SACM 195 V12 CZSHR diesels; 4340 hp(m) *(3.19 MW)* sustained; electrohydraulic auxiliary propulsion on starboard shaft; 150 hp(m) *(110 kW)*; 2 shafts
Speed, knots: 20; 6 on auxiliary propulsion. **Range, miles:** 4900 at 12 kts; 1500 at 20 kts
Complement: 18 (3 officers); 2 crews
Guns: 2—12.7 mm MGs.
Radars: Navigation: Racal Decca; I band.

Comment: *Sterne* was the first ship for the FSMC. Has active tank stabilisation. Paid for by shipping owners but manned and operated by navy. A second of class may be ordered in 1991—it will be 53 m in length and have a stern dock.

STERNE *8/1986, A. Toremans*

Name	*No*	*Builders*	*Commissioned*
GRÈBE	P 679	SFCN, Villeneuve La Garenne	6 Apr 1991

Displacement, tons: 410 full load
Dimensions, feet (metres): 170.6 × 32.2 × 9 *(52 × 9.8 × 2.8)*
Main machinery: 2 Uni Diesel UD 33 V12 M6 diesels; 4410 hp(m) *(3.24 MW)*; diesel-electric auxiliary propulsion; 2 shafts; cp props
Speed, knots: 23; 7.5 on auxiliary propulsion. **Range, miles:** 4500 at 12 kts
Complement: 19 (4 officers); accommodation for 24; 2 crews
Guns: 2—12.7 mm MGs.
Radars: Navigation: Racal Decca; I band.

Comment: Type Espadon 50 ordered 17 July 1988 and launched 16 November 1989; 'Deep V' hull; stern ramp for craft handling. Large deck area (8 × 8 m) for Vertrep operations. Pollution control equipment and remotely operated waterjet gun for firefighting. A larger 1100 ton ship with the same deep V hull is being designed. Based at Lorient.

GRÈBE *6/1990, Giorgio Arra*

MINE WARFARE FORCES

0 + 1 + (5) NARVIK CLASS (MINEHUNTER/SWEEPER)

NARVIK M 660 **BIR HAKEIM** **GARIGLIANO**
AUTUN **COLMAR** **BERLAIMONT**

Displacement, tons: 905 full load
Dimensions, feet (metres): 170.6 oa; 152.9 wl × 48.6 × 11.8 *(52; 46.6 × 14.8 × 3.6)*
Main machinery: 2 diesels; 2700 hp(m) *(1.98 MW)*; 2 shafts; cp props; auxiliary propulsion: diesel-electric; 500 kW; bow thruster; 204 hp(m) *(150 kW)*
Speed, knots: 15. **Range, miles:** 5000 at 10 kts
Complement: 46

Guns: 1 GIAT 20 mm F2. 2—12.7 mm MGs.
Countermeasures: MCM: Will carry one or two remote controlled minehunting PAP Mk 5 with DUBM 60 sonar and television. Mechanical, magnetic and acoustic (DCN AP4) sweeps.
Sonars: Thomson Sintra DUBM 42; towed; active; high frequency; can be towed at 10 kts down to 300 m *(984 ft)*.

Programmes: Designed by DCN; to be built by Lorient Naval Dockyard. BAMO (Bâtiment Anti-Mines Océanique). The programme has been badly affected by budget cuts and may be cancelled. *Narvik* launched 22 March 1991 and should be in service in 1994. Construction rate of one every nine months was planned if the programme is not abandoned. Weapon systems to be tested in *Thétis*.
Structure: GRP hulls with a catamaran design. This type of hull offers a larger working area than a monohull of equivalent displacement. Other claimed advantages include seakeeping, stability and manoeuvrability. May also have a hull-mounted sonar set. A Matra Simbad twin-launcher SAM may be fitted on the 20 mm gun mounting.

BAMO Type (model) *8/1988, J. Y. Robert*

9 + 1 ÉRIDAN (TRIPARTITE) CLASS (MINEHUNTERS)

Name	*No*	*Laid down*	*Launched*	*Commissioned*
ÉRIDAN	M 641	20 Dec 1977	2 Feb 1979	16 Apr 1984
CASSIOPÉE	M 642	26 Mar 1979	28 Sep 1981	5 May 1984
ANDROMÈDE	M 643	6 Mar 1980	22 May 1982	18 Oct 1984
PÉGASE	M 644	22 Oct 1980	23 Apr 1983	30 May 1985
ORION	M 645	17 Aug 1981	6 Feb 1985	14 Jan 1986
CROIX DU SUD	M 646	22 Apr 1982	6 Feb 1985	14 Nov 1986
AIGLE	M 647	2 Dec 1982	8 Mar 1986	1 July 1987
LYRE	M 648	14 Oct 1983	15 Nov 1986	16 Dec 1987
PERSÉE	M 649	30 Oct 1984	19 Apr 1988	4 Nov 1988

Displacement, tons: 562 standard; 595 full load
Dimensions, feet (metres): 168.9 × 29.2 × 8.2 *(51.5 × 8.9 × 2.5)*
Main machinery: 1 Brons Werkspoor A-RUB 215X-12 diesel; 1860 hp(m) *(1.37 MW)* sustained; 1 shaft; Lips cp prop
Auxiliary propulsion; 2 motors; 240 hp(m) *(179 kW)*; 2 active rudders; 2 bow thrusters
Speed, knots: 15; 7 on auxiliary propulsion. **Range, miles:** 3000 at 12 kts
Complement: 46 (5 officers)

Guns: 1 GIAT 20F2 20 mm; 1—12.7 mm MG.
Countermeasures: MCM: 2 PAP 104 systems; mechanical sweep gear. AP-4 acoustic sweep.
Radars: Navigation: Racal Decca 1229; I band.
Sonars: Thomson Sintra DUBM 21B; hull-mounted; active; high frequency; 100 kHz (±10 kHz).

Programmes: All built in Lorient. Belgium, France and the Netherlands each agreed to build 15 (10 in Belgium with option on five more). Subsequently the French programme was cut to 10. Each country provided people to man a joint bureau de programme in Paris and built its own GRP hulls to a central design. Belgium provided all the electrical installations, France all the minehunting gear and some electronics and the Netherlands the propulsion systems.
Structure: GRP hull. Equipment includes: autopilot and hovering; automatic radar navigation; navigation aids by Loran and Syledis; Evec data system; Decca Hifix.
Operational: Minehunting, minesweeping, patrol, training, directing ship for unmanned minesweeping, HQ ship for diving operations and pollution control. Pre-packed 5 ton modules of equipment to be embarked for separate tasks. M 641-646 based at Brest, remainder at Toulon. Chasseurs de Mines Tripartites (CMT).
Sales: The tenth ship of the class, completed in 1989, was sold to Pakistan in January 1992 as part of an order for three; the second to be built in Lorient, the third in Karachi. A replacement will be built for the French Navy.

CROIX DU SUD *10/1990, Harald Carstens*

5 CIRCÉ CLASS (MINEHUNTERS)

Name	*No*	*Builders*	*Commissioned*
CYBÈLE	M 712	CMN, Cherbourg	28 Sep 1972
CALLIOPE	M 713	CMN, Cherbourg	28 Sep 1972
CLIO	M 714	CMN, Cherbourg	18 May 1972
CIRCÉ	M 715	CMN, Cherbourg	18 May 1972
CÉRÈS	M 716	CMN, Cherbourg	8 Mar 1973

Displacement, tons: 460 standard; 495 normal; 510 full load
Dimensions, feet (metres): 167 × 29.2 × 11.2 *(50.9 × 8.9 × 3.4)*
Main machinery: 1 MTU diesel; 1800 hp(m) *(1.32 MW)*; 2 active rudders; 1 shaft
Speed, knots: 15. **Range, miles:** 3000 at 12 kts
Complement: 48 (5 officers)

Guns: 1 Oerlikon 20 mm.
Countermeasures: MCM: The 9 ft *(2.74 m)* long PAP is propelled by two electric motors at 6 kts and is wire-guided to a maximum range of 500 m. Fitted with a television camera, this machine detects the mine and lays its 100 kg charge nearby. This is then detonated by an ultra-sonic signal. These ships carry no normal minesweeping equipment.
Radars: Navigation: Racal Decca 1229; I band.
Sonars: Thomson Sintra DUBM 20B; hull-mounted; active search; high frequency.

Programmes: Ordered in 1968. Due for deletion 1991-93 but will be retained until BAMOs come into service.
Modernisation: Programmes completed 1989 included computer-aided sonar classification.
Operational: All based at Cherbourg.

CYBÈLE *11/1991, van Ginderen Collection*

3 Ex-US AGGRESSIVE CLASS (MINESWEEPERS)

OUISTREHAM (ex-MSO 513) M 610 **BACCARAT** (ex-MSO 505) M 623
ALENÇON (ex-MSO 453) M 612

Displacement, tons: 700 standard; 780 full load
Dimensions, feet (metres): 172 × 36 × 13.6 *(52.4 × 11 × 4.1)*
Main machinery: 2 GM 8-268A diesels; 1760 hp *(1.31 MW)*; 2 shafts; cp props
Speed, knots: 13.5. **Range, miles:** 3000 at 10 kts
Complement: 58 (5 officers)

Guns: 1 Bofors 40 mm/60; 2—12.7 mm MGs.
Countermeasures: MCM: Mechanical minesweeping capabilities; AP 4 acoustic sweep.
Radars: Navigation: Racal Decca 1229; I band.
Sonars: DUBM 41B; towed; side scanning; active search; high frequency.

Programmes: The USA transferred these MSOs to France in three batches during 1953. Four paid off in 1987 and three more in 1989.
Modernisation: Modernised with improved DUBM 41 and AP 4 acoustic sweep.
Structure: *Alençon* has a shorter funnel than the others.

OUISTREHAM *2/1991, van Ginderen Collection*

MCM DIVING TENDERS

4 MCM DIVING SUPPORT SHIPS

Name	*No*	*Builders*	*Commissioned*
VULCAIN	M 611	La Perrière, Lorient	11 Oct 1986
PLUTON	M 622	La Perrière, Lorient	10 Dec 1986
ACHÉRON	A 613	CMN, Cherbourg	21 Apr 1987
STYX	M 614	CMN, Cherbourg	22 July 1987

Displacement, tons: 375 standard; 505 full load
Dimensions, feet (metres): 136.5 × 24.6 × 12.5 *(41.6 × 7.5 × 3.8)*
Main machinery: 2 SACM MGO 175 V16 ASHR diesels; 2200 hp(m) *(1.62 MW)*; 2 shafts; bow thruster; 70 hp(m) *(51 kW)*
Speed, knots: 13.7. **Range, miles:** 2800 at 13 kts; 7400 at 9 kts
Complement: 14 (1 officer) plus 12 divers
Guns: 1—12.7 mm MG.
Radars: Navigation: Decca 1226; I band.

Comment: First pair ordered in December 1984. Second pair ordered July 1985. Designed to act as support ships for clearance divers. (Bâtiments Bases pour Plongeurs Démineurs - BBPD). *Vulcain* launched 17 January 1986, based at Cherbourg. *Pluton* launched 13 May 1986, based at Toulon. *Achéron* launched 9 November 1986, based at Toulon as a diving school tender and *Styx* launched 3 March 1987, based at Brest. Modified Chamois (BSR) class design. 5 ton hydraulic crane.

STYX *5/1989, Maritime Photographic*

OCEANOGRAPHIC AND SURVEY SHIPS

Notes: (a) These ships are painted white.
(b) A total of about 100 officers and technicians with oceanographic and hydrographic training is employed in addition to the ships' companies listed here. They occupy the extra billets marked as 'scientists'.

4 BH2 CLASS (Bâtiments Hydrographiques de 2e classe)

Name	*No*	*Builders*	*Commissioned*
LAPÉROUSE	A 791	Lorient Naval Dockyard	20 Apr 1988
BORDA	A 792	Lorient Naval Dockyard	18 June 1988
LAPLACE	A 793	Lorient Naval Dockyard	5 Oct 1989
ARAGO	A 795	Lorient Naval Dockyard	9 July 1991

Displacement, tons: 970 standard; 1100 full load
Dimensions, feet (metres): 193.5 × 35.8 × 11.9 *(59 × 10.9 × 3.6)*
Main machinery: 2 SACM MGO 175 V12 RVR diesels; 2500 hp(m) *(1.84 MW)*; 2 cp props; bow thruster
Speed, knots: 15. **Range, miles:** 6000 at 12 kts
Complement: 27 (2 officers) plus 11 scientists plus 7 spare berths
Radars: Navigation: Decca 1226; I band.
Sonars: Thomson-Sintra DUBM 42 or DUBM 21C (A 791); active search; high frequency.

Comment: Have replaced L'Espérance and L'Astrolabe classes. Ordered under 1982 and 1986 estimates, first pair on 24 July 1984, third 22 January 1986 and fourth 12 April 1988.
Two variants: BH2A (A 791)—Carry Thomson Sintra DUBM 21C sonar for detection of underwater obstacles. Based at Brest; BH2C (remainder)—Carry two VH8 survey launches for hydrographic work. A 793 sailed for the Pacific 9 October 1989, joined by A 795 on 1 October 1991. A 792 based at Brest. *Borda* has the TSM 5260 Lennermor multi-path echo sounder.

LAPEROUSE *10/1991, van Ginderen Collection*

Name	*No*	*Builders*	*Commissioned*
D'ENTRECASTEAUX	A 757	Brest Naval Dockyard	10 Oct 1970

Displacement, tons: 2400 full load
Dimensions, feet (metres): 292 × 42.7 × 14.4 *(89 × 13 × 4.4)*
Main machinery: Diesel-electric; 2 diesel generators; 2720 hp(m) *(2 MW)*; 2 motors; 2 shafts; cp props
Auxiliary propulsion; 2 Schottel trainable and retractable props
Speed, knots: 15. **Range, miles:** 10 000 at 12 kts
Complement: 88 (6 officers) plus 38 scientific staff
Radars: Navigation: Two Racal Decca 1226; I band.
Helicopters: 1 SA 319B Alouette III.

Comment: This ship was specially designed for oceanographic surveys capable of working to 6000 m *(19 686 ft)*. Bâtiment Océanographique (BO). Carries one LCP and three survey launches. Telescopic hangar. Serves in the Mediterranean.

D'ENTRECASTEAUX *7/1991, J. Y. Robert*

Name	*No*	*Builders*	*Commissioned*
L'ESPÉRANCE (ex-*Jacques Coeur*)	A 756	Gdynia	12 July 1969

Displacement, tons: 956 standard; 1360 full load
Dimensions, feet (metres): 208.3 × 32.1 × 19.4 *(63.5 × 9.8 × 5.9)*
Main machinery: 2 MAN diesels; 1850 hp(m) *(1.36 MW)*; 2 shafts
Speed, knots: 15. **Range, miles:** 7500 at 13 kts
Complement: 32 (3 officers) plus 14 scientists

Comment: Former trawler built in 1962 at Gdynia and purchased in 1968-69. Adapted as survey ship. Based in Atlantic. Has a TSM 5260 Lennermor multi-path echo sounder.

L'ESPÉRANCE *1/1989, van Ginderen Collection*

SERVICE FORCES

Note: The support tankers *Vendres, Penhors* and *Mascarin* (included in 1988-89 edition) are fitted for replenishment at sea and are available but no longer on loan to the Navy.

2 SUPPORT TANKERS

PAPENOO (ex-*Bow Queen*) A 625
PUNARUU (ex-*Bow Cecil*) A 632

Displacement, tons: 1195 standard; 4050 full load
Dimensions, feet (metres): 272.2 × 45.6 × 19 *(83 × 13.9 × 5.8)*
Main machinery: 2 NORMO LSMC-8 diesels; 2050 hp(m) *(1.51 MW)*; 1 shaft; cp prop; bow thruster
Speed, knots: 12. **Range, miles:** 8000 at 11 kts
Complement: 24 (2 officers)

Comment: Two small Norwegian-built tankers added to the Navy. Commissioned 9 and 16 November 1971 respectively. Capacity 2500 cu m (10 tanks). Have replenishment at sea facility astern. Serve in Pacific. Due for deletion in 1994.

PAPENOO *5/1990, van Ginderen Collection*

5 DURANCE CLASS (UNDERWAY REPLENISHMENT TANKERS)

Name	No	Builders	Laid down	Launched	Commissioned
MEUSE	A 607	Brest Naval Dockyard	2 June 1977	2 Dec 1978	21 Nov 1980
VAR	A 608	Brest Naval Dockyard	8 May 1979	1 June 1981	29 Jan 1983
DURANCE	A 629	Brest Naval Dockyard	12 Dec 1973	6 Sep 1975	1 Dec 1976
MARNE	A 630	Brest Naval Dockyard	4 Aug 1982	2 Feb 1985	16 Jan 1987
SOMME	A 631	Normed, la Seyne	3 May 1985	3 Oct 1987	7 Mar 1990

Displacement, tons: 17 800 full load
Dimensions, feet (metres): 515.9 × 69.5 × 38.5 *(157.3 × 21.2 × 10.8)*
Main machinery: 2 SEMT-Pielstick 16 PC 2.5 V400 diesels; 20 800 hp(m) *(15.3 MW)* sustained; 2 shafts; cp props
Speed, knots: 19. **Range, miles:** 9000 at 15 kts
Complement: 164 (18 officers)
Cargo capacity: 7500 tons FFO; 1500 diesel; 500 TR5 Avcat; 140 distilled water; 170 victuals; 150 munitions; 50 naval stores *(Durance)*. 5000 tons FFO; 3200 diesel; 1800 TR5 Avcat; 130 distilled water; 170 victuals; 150 munitions; 50 naval stores *(Meuse)*. 5090 tons FFO; 3310 diesel; 1090 TR5 Avcat; 260 distilled water; 180 munitions; 15 stores *(Var* and *Marne)*
Guns: 2 Bofors 40 mm/60 *(Durance)*. 1 Bofors 40 mm/60. 2 Oerlikon 20 mm (remainder). 4—12.7 mm MGs.
Radars: Navigation: 2 Racal Decca 1226; I band.

Helicopters: 1 Lynx Mk 2/4.

Programmes: Classed as Pétrolier Ravitailleur d'Escadre (PRE). Fifth ship ordered 24 January 1984 and intended for export but has been taken over by the Navy under Clause 29.
Structure: Four beam transfer positions and two astern, two of the beam positions having heavy transfer capability. *Var, Marne* and *Somme* differ from the others in several respects. The bridge extends further aft, boats are located either side of the funnel and a crane is located between the gantries.
Operational: *Var, Marne* and *Somme* are designed to carry a Maritime Zone staff or Commander of a Logistic Formation and a commando unit of up to 45 men. Capable of accommodating 250 men. Also fitted with Syracuse SATCOM system. Deployment: Mediterranean, *Marne* and *Meuse*; Atlantic, *Somme* and *Durance*; Indian Ocean, *Var*.
Sales: One to Australia built locally; two of similar but smaller design to Saudi Arabia.

SOMME *5/1991, Foto Flite*

5 RHIN CLASS (DEPOT and SUPPORT SHIPS)

Name	No	Builders	Commissioned
LOIRE	A 615	Lorient Naval Dockyard	10 Oct 1967
GARONNE	A 617	Lorient Naval Dockyard	1 Sep 1965
RANCE	A 618	Lorient Naval Dockyard	5 Feb 1966
RHIN	A 621	Lorient Naval Dockyard	1 Mar 1964
RHÔNE	A 622	Lorient Naval Dockyard	1 Dec 1964

Displacement, tons: 2075 (2320, *Garonne* and *Loire)* standard; 2445 full load
Dimensions, feet (metres): 331.5 × 43 × 12.1 *(101.1 × 13.1 × 3.7)*
Main machinery: 2 SEMT-Pielstick 16PA2V diesels (*Rhin* and *Rhône*); 3300 hp(m) *(2.43 MW)*; 1 shaft
2 SEMT-Pielstick 12PA4V diesels (*Rance, Loire* and *Garonne*); 4000 hp(m) *(2.94 MW)*; 1 shaft
Speed, knots: 16.5; 13 *(Rance)*. **Range, miles:** 13 000 at 13 kts
Complement: 165 (11 officers) (*Rhin* and *Rhône*); 120 (7 officers) and about 118 passengers *(Rance)*; 167 (19 officers) *(Garonne)*; 156 (12 officers) *(Loire)*
Guns: 3 Bofors 40 mm/60 (*Loire, Rhin* and *Rhône*). 1 Bofors 40 mm/60. 2 Oerlikon 20 mm (*Garonne*). None in *Rance*. 3—12.7 mm MGs.
Radars: Air search: DRBV 23C (in *Rance* in addition).
Air/surface search: Thomson-CSF DRBV 50; D band.
Helicopters: 1-3 SA 310B Alouette III (except *Garonne)*. Platform only *(Rhône)*.

Comment: Designed for supporting various classes of ships. Have a 5 ton crane, carry two LCPs and have a helicopter platform (except *Garonne)*. *Rhin* has a hangar and carries two helicopters; *Rance* has two platforms and carries three in her hangar; *Loire* has a hangar for one. *Garonne* is designed as a Repair Workshop, *Loire* for minesweeper support, *Rhin* for electronic maintenance and *Rhône* for submarines. *Rance* has been converted as a command and medical support ship for La Force d'Assistance Rapide with several modifications, and is also used as flagship of the Fleet Training Centre (Mediterranean). *Rhône* operates in the Atlantic, *Garonne* in the Indian Ocean/Pacific, *Loire* at Brest and *Rhin* in the Indian Ocean. Another ship (Bâtiment de Soutien Logistique—BSL) was to have been ordered in 1992 but this has been postponed.

GARONNE *10/1991, Bill McBride, RAN*

RHÔNE *7/1990, Giorgio Arra*

RANCE *6/1991, van Ginderen Collection*

1 MAINTENANCE and REPAIR SHIP

Name	No	Builders	Commissioned
JULES VERNE (ex-*Achéron*)	A 620	Brest Naval Dockyard	1 June 1976

Displacement, tons: 6485 standard; 10 250 full load
Dimensions, feet (metres): 482.2 × 70.5 × 21.3 *(147 × 21.5 × 6.5)*
Main machinery: 2 SEMT-Pielstick 18 PC 2.2 V diesels; 18 000 hp(m) *(13.2 MW)* sustained; 2 shafts
Speed, knots: 18. **Range, miles:** 9500 at 18 kts
Complement: 294 (15 officers)
Guns: 2 Bofors 40 mm/60. Several 12.7 mm MGs.
Helicopters: 2 SA 319B Alouette III.

Comment: Ordered in 1961 budget, originally as an Armament Supply Ship. Role and design changed whilst building—now rated as Engineering and Electrical Maintenance Ship. Launched 30 May 1970. Serves in Indian Ocean, providing general support for all ships. Carries stocks of torpedoes and ammunition. Refit in France November 1988-June 1989.

JULES VERNE *9/1989, Photo Sami*

7 CHAMOIS CLASS (SUPPLY TENDERS)

Name	*No*	*Builders*	*Commissioned*
TAAPE	A 633	La Perrière, Lorient	2 Nov 1983
CHAMOIS	A 767	La Perrière, Lorient	24 Sep 1976
ÉLAN	A 768	La Perrière, Lorient	7 Apr 1978
CHEVREUIL	A 774	La Perrière, Lorient	7 Oct 1977
GAZELLE	A 775	La Perrière, Lorient	13 Jan 1978
ISARD	A 776	La Perrière, Lorient	15 Dec 1978
TAPATAI (ex-*Silver Fish*)	A 779	La Perrière, Lorient	27 Mar 1981

Displacement, tons: 495 (500, *Taape*) full load
Dimensions, feet (metres): 136.1 × 24.6 × 10.5 *(41.5 × 7.5 × 3.2)*
Main machinery: 2 SACM AGO 175 V16 diesels; 2700 hp(m) *(1.98 MW)*; 2 shafts; cp props; bow thruster
Speed, knots: 14.2. **Range, miles:** 6000 at 12 kts
Complement: 10 plus 10 spare berths
Radars: Navigation: Racal Decca 1226; I band.

Comment: Similar to the standard Fish oil rig support ships. Can act as tugs, oil pollution vessels, salvage craft (two 30 ton and two 5 ton winches), coastal and harbour controlled minelaying, torpedo recovery, diving tenders and a variety of other tasks. Can carry 100 tons of stores on deck or 125 tons of fuel and 40 tons of water or 65 tons of fuel and 120 tons of water. *Taape* ordered in March 1982 from La Perrière—of improved design but basically similar with bridge one deck higher. *Tapatai* launched in 1971 but taken up from trade by the Navy for use at Centre d'Expérimentation du Pacifique with *Taape* and *Chamois*. Remainder based in France. *Isard* serves as a special diving support ship with an extra deckhouse.

SARD 6/1991, *van Ginderen Collection*

AZELLE 5/1991, *J. Y. Robert*

APE (high bridge) 1990, *van Ginderen Collection*

RR 4000 TYPE (SUPPLY TENDERS)

me	*No*	*Builders*	*Commissioned*
RI	A 634	Breheret	21 Feb 1985
VI	A 635	Breheret	9 Mar 1985

splacement, tons: 900 light; 1450 full load
mensions, feet (metres): 167.3 × 41.3 × 13.1 *(51 × 12.6 × 4)*
ain machinery: 2 SACM AGO 195 V12 diesels; 4410 hp(m) *(3.24 MW)*; 2 shafts; cp props; bow hruster
eed, knots: 14.5. **Range, miles:** 6000 at 12 kts
mplement: 22 plus 18 passengers

mment: Two 'remorqueurs ravitailleurs' for le Centre d'Expérimentation du Pacifique. Can carry 00 tons of cargo on deck.

RARI 8/1985, *J. Y. Robert*

1 TRANSPORT LANDING SHIP

Name	*No*	*Builders*	*Commissioned*
GAPEAU	L 9090	Chantier Serra, la Seyne	2 Oct 1987

Displacement, tons: 509 standard; 1058 full load
Dimensions, feet (metres): 216.5 × 40 × 11.2 *(66 × 12.2 × 3.4)*
Main machinery: 2 diesels; 2 shafts
Speed, knots: 10
Complement: 6 + 30 scientists
Cargo capacity: 460 tons

Comment: Supply ship with bow doors. Operates for Centre d'Essais de la Mediterranée, Levant Island (missile range).

GAPEAU 5/1991, *Giorgio Ghiglione*

TRIALS/RESEARCH SHIPS

Note: (a) In addition to the ships listed below there is a civilian manned 25 m trawler *L'Aventurière II* (launched July 1986) operated by GESMA, Brest for underwater research which comes under DCN.
(b) A new *Berry* is to be ordered as soon as possible as a purpose-built Electronics intelligence gathering ship.

Name	*No*	*Builders*	*Commissioned*
DAUPHIN (trials)	S 633	Cherbourg Naval Dockyard	1 Aug 1958

Displacement, tons: 1320 standard; 1635 surfaced; 1910 dived
Dimensions, feet (metres): 255.8 × 23.6 × 18 *(78 × 7.2 × 5.5)*
Main machinery: Diesel-electric; 3 SEMT-Pielstick 12 PA 4 diesels; 6012 hp(m) *(4.42 MW)* sustained; 3 generators; 2 motors; 2400 hp(m) *(1.76 MW)*; 2 shafts
Speed, knots: 15 surfaced; 18 dived
Range, miles: 15 000 at 8 kts snorting
Complement: 43 (4 officers)

Torpedoes: 6—21.7 in *(550 mm)* bow tubes. Can carry 20 torpedoes but see *Operational* note.
Radars: Navigation: Thomson-CSF DRUA 33; I band.
Sonars: Thomson Sintra DUUA 2A; active/passive search and attack.
Various sonars for trials.

Programmes: Improved version based on the West German Type XXI launched 17 September 1955. Survivor of a class of six. Refitted in 1990 and stays in service until the end of 1992.
Structure: Diving depth, 200 m *(656 ft)*; crushing at 400 m *(1312 ft)*.
Operational: Acts as a trials boat for equipment under development for new construction. Based at Toulon. To be paid off in December 1992.

DAUPHIN 7/1991, *J. Y. Robert*

MONGE 5/1991, Giorgio Arra

Name	No	Builders	Commissioned
MONGE	A 601	Chantiers de l'Atlantique, St Nazaire	Dec 1992

Displacement, tons: 21 040 full load
Dimensions, feet (metres): 740.2 × 81.4 × 25.3 *(225.6 × 24.8 × 7.7)*
Main machinery: 2 SEMT-Pielstick 8 PC 2.5 L 400 diesels; 9360 hp(m) *(6.88 MW)* sustained; 1 shaft; bow thruster
Speed, knots: 16. **Range, miles:** 15 000 at 15 kts
Complement: 188 plus 100 technicians (military and civilians)
Guns: 2 GIAT F2 20 mm.
Radars: Air search: Thomson-CSF DRBV 15C; E/F band.
Missile tracking: One L band (new model); one Gascogne; two Armor; one Savoie; two Antares.
Navigation: Two Racal Decca (one for helo control); I band.
Helicopters: 2 Super Frelon.

Comment: Ordered 25 November 1988. Rated as a BEM (Bâtiment d'Essais et de Mesures). Laid down 26 March 1990, and launched 6 October 1990. Delivered in February 1991 and having completed contractors' sea trials sailed to Brest in March 1991. First sea cruise 12 April to 25 May 1991. She has 14 telemetry antennas; optronic tracking unit. LIDAR. Syracuse SATCOM. Flume tank stabilisation restricts the ship to a maximum of 9° roll at slow speed in Sea State 6. Takes over as Flagship of the Trials Squadron in late 1992. Replacing *Henri Poincaré* which is unable to track M45 and M5 missiles.

MONGE 3/1991, Chantiers de l'Atlantique

Name	No	Builders	Commissioned
ILE D'OLÉRON (ex-*München*, ex-*Mür*)	A 610	Weser, Bremen	1939

Displacement, tons: 5500 standard; 6500 full load
Dimensions, feet (metres): 378 × 50 × 21.3 *(115.2 × 15.2 × 6.5)*
Main machinery: 2 MAN 6-cyl diesels; 3500 hp(m) *(2.57 MW)*; 1 shaft
Speed, knots: 14.5. **Range, miles:** 7200 at 12 kts
Complement: 195 (12 officers)
Radars: Various, according to experiments (DRBV 22C, DRBI 10, DRBV 50).
Navigation: Racal Decca 1226; I band.
Helicopters: Platform only for Alouette III.

Comment: Taken as a war prize. Commissioned in French Navy 29 August 1945. Formerly rated as a transport. Converted to experimental guided missile ship in 1957-58 by Chantiers de Provence and l'Arsenal de Toulon. Commissioned early in 1959. Fitted with one launcher for target planes. Has been fitted with various equipment and weapon systems for trials: Masurca, Crotale, Otomat, MM 40 Exocet, Sadral, 100 mm gun with CTMS fire control system, Crotale Modulaire, Sagaie, Simbad. Fitted for sea trials of Milas in 1992 (ASW torpedo delivery missile with a range of 50 km). Also trials continue on prototype Sylver launchers for VLS Aster 15 PDMS and Aster 30 Area SAM. Operated by the Centre d'Etudes Pratiques du Matériel et Armes Navales (CEPMAN) in Toulon.

ILE D'OLERON 5/1991, Camil Busquets i Vilanova

ILE D'OLERON 9/1991, J.Y.Robert

Name	No	Builders	Commissioned
BERRY (ex-M/S *Médoc*)	A 644	Roland Werft, Bremen	26 Nov 1964

Displacement, tons: 1148 standard; 2700 full load
Dimensions, feet (metres): 284.5 × 38 × 15 *(86.7 × 11.6 × 4.6)*
Main machinery: 2 MWM diesels; 2400 hp(m) *(1.76 MW)*; 1 shaft
Speed, knots: 13. **Range, miles:** 7000 at 15 kts
Guns: 2—12.7 mm MGs.
Radars: Navigation: Racal Decca 1226; I band.

Comment: Launched on 10 May 1958. In 1976-77 converted at Toulon from victualling stores ship to Mediterranean electronic trials ship. Recommissioned February 1977. Deleted in error in 1991. It is planned to replace her as soon as possible, her performance having been inadequate in the Gulf in 1991.

BERRY 6/1991, van Ginderen Collection

Name	*No*	*Builders*	*Commissioned*
COMMANDANT RIVIÈRE	A 733	Lorient	4 Dec 1962

Displacement, tons: 2100 full load
Dimensions, feet (metres): 337.9 × 41 × 14.1 *(103 × 12.5 × 4.3)*
Main machinery: 4 SEMT-Pielstick 12 PC diesels; 16 000 hp(m) *(11.76 MW)*; 2 shafts
Speed, knots: 24
Complement: 115 (9 officers) plus 37 passengers
Guns: 1 Bofors 40 mm/60 (B position). 2—12.7 mm MGs.
Radars: Air/surface search: Thomson-CSF DRBV 22A; D band.
Navigation: 2 Racal Decca 1226; I band.

Comment: Frigate converted into sonar and trials ship. Quarter-deck widened. Fitted with DUBV-24 TASS sonar (towed array) and DUBV 43 VDS system to which is attached a VLF active transmitter. Operated by Centre d'Etudes Pratiques du Matériel et Armes Navales (CEPMAN) in Toulon. Has retained three torpedo tubes.

COMMANDANT RIVIÈRE *6/1991, van Ginderen Collection*

Name	*No*	*Builders*	*Commissioned*
THÉTIS (ex-*Nereide*)	A 785	Lorient Naval Dockyard	9 Nov 1988

Displacement, tons: 720 standard; 1000 full load
Dimensions, feet (metres): 185.4 × 35.8 × 11.8 *(56.5 × 10.9 × 3.6)*
Main machinery: 2 Uni Diesel UD 30 V16 M4 diesels; 2710 hp(m) *(1.99 MW)* sustained; 1 shaft; cp prop
Speed, knots: 15. **Range, miles:** 6000
Complement: 36 (2 officers) plus 7 passengers
Guns: 2—12.7 mm MGs.
Radars: Navigation: Racal Decca 1226; I band.
Sonars: VDS; Thomson Sintra DUBM 42 and DUBM 60A; active search; high frequency.

Comment: Same hull as Laperouse class. Classified as Bâtiment Experimental Guerre de Mines (BEGM). Operated by the Centre d'Etudes, d'Instruction et d'Entraînement de la Guerre des Mines (CETIEGM) in Brest. Launched 19 March 1988. Renamed to avoid confusion with Y 700. Equipped to conduct trials on all underwater weapons and sensors for mine warfare. Can lay mines. Can support six divers. Fitted with the Thomson Sintra mine warfare combat system designed for the delayed or cancelled BAMO. This uses DUBM 42 and DUBM 60A in a towed body.

THETIS *3/1991, Foto Flite*

Name	*No*	*Builders*	*Commissioned*
TRITON	A 646	Lorient	20 Jan 1972

Displacement, tons: 1410 standard; 1510 full load
Dimensions, feet (metres): 242.7 × 38.9 × 12 *(74 × 11.8 × 3.7)*
Main machinery: 2 MGO V12 diesels; 1800 hp(m) *(1.32 MW)*; 1 Voith-Schneider screw (aft); 2 motors; 800 kW; 1 Voith-Schneider screw (fwd)
Speed, knots: 13. **Range, miles:** 4000 at 13 kts
Complement: 54 (5 officers) plus 5 officers and 12 men for diving
Radars: Navigation: Racal Decca 1226; I band.

Comment: Launched on 7 March 1970. Support ship for the two-man submarine *Griffon*. Painted white. Operated by Groupe d'Intervention sous la Mer (GISMER) for trials of submarines and deep-sea diving equipment. Underwater TV, recompression chamber, four-man diving bell of 13.5 tons and laboratories are fitted. Available as submarine rescue ship. Also carries a number of diving saucers. Special sonar equipment is fitted and there is a helicopter platform. The midget submarine *Griffon* is carried amidships on the starboard side of *Triton*. She is 25 ft *(7.8 m)* long, displaces 16 tons and is driven by an electric motor. Her diving depth is 600 m *(2000 ft)* and her endurance 24 miles at 4 kts. Can be used for deep recovery operations. Fitted with manipulating arm.

TRITON *11/1990, Maritime Photographic*

Name	*No*	*Builders*	*Commissioned*
DENTI	A 743	DCAN Toulon	15 July 1976

Displacement, tons: 170 full load
Dimensions, feet (metres): 113.8 × 21.6 × 7.5 *(34.7 × 6.6 × 2.3)*
Main machinery: 2 Baudouin DP8 diesels; 960 hp(m) *(706 kW)*; 2 shafts; cp props
Speed, knots: 12. **Range, miles:** 800 at 12 kts
Complement: 6 (2 officers)

Comment: Launched 7 October 1975. Employed on ammunition trials off Toulon.

DENTI *6/1991, van Ginderen Collection*

Name	*No*	*Builders*	*Commissioned*
AGNES 200	A 786	CMN, Cherbourg	1992

Displacement, tons: 259.4 full load
Dimensions, feet (metres): 162.7 × 42.7 × 9.8 (3.6 (SES)) *(49.6 × 13 × 3 (1.1))*
Main machinery: 2 MTU 16V 538 TB93 diesels; 7510 hp(m) *(5.52 MW)* sustained; 2 MTU 8V 396 TB 83 (lift) diesels; 1780 hp(m) *(1.31 MW)* sustained; 2 KaMeWa waterjets
Speed, knots: 40+ (SES); 15 (hull). **Range, miles:** 1200 at 14 kts (hull); 750 at 25 kts (SES)
Complement: 22 (5 officers) plus 12 passengers

Comment: Ordered 18 February 1988 from CMN, Cherbourg as a result of European industrial co-operation. Partially funded by the French MoD. Laid down September 1988, launched 2 July 1990 and started trials in October 1990 at Lorient. Surface Effect catamaran design with a 200 m² helicopter deck aft and a troop carrying capacity of 50. Armament depends on role but the craft could carry a 30 mm gun forward, and four MM 40 Exocet plus SADRAL SAM aft or a Dauphin SA 365 F helicopter. The two smaller 'lift' diesels can drive the hydrojets when the fans are disengaged. This is an experimental platform for developing escort ships to replace the A 69 class in the 2000s. One full year of military experiments to the end of 1991. Main French naval interest is in the helicopter version.

AGNES 200 *1990, DCN*

BOOM AND MOORING VESSELS

TUPA Y 667 **TELENN MOR** Y 692

Comment: 292 tons with 210 hp(m) *(154 kW)* diesel. *Tupa* commissioned 16 March 1974, *Telenn Mor* on 16 January 1986. Mooring vessels. *Tupa* based at Papeete.

TELENN MOR *8/1988, J. Y. Robert*

Name	*No*	*Builders*	*Commissioned*
LA PRUDENTE	Y 749	AC Manche	27 July 1969
LA PERSÉVÉRANTE	Y 750	AC La Rochelle	3 Mar 1969
LA FIDÈLE	Y 751	AC Manche	10 June 1969

Displacement, tons: 626 full load
Dimensions, feet (metres): 142.8 × 32.8 × 9.2 *(43.5 × 10 × 2.8)*
Main machinery: Diesel-electric; 2 Baudouin diesels; 620 hp(m) *(441 kW)*; 1 shaft
Speed, knots: 10. **Range, miles:** 4000 at 10 kts
Complement: 30 (1 officer)

Comment: Net layers and tenders. Launched on 13 May 1968 *(La Prudente)*, 14 May 1968 *(La Persévérante)* and 26 August 1968 *(La Fidèle)*. Have a 25 ton lift. Based at Brest, Toulon and Cherbourg respectively.

LA PRUDENTE *8/1988, J. Y. Robert*

Name	*No*	*Builders*	*Commissioned*
LA TIANÉE	A 731	Arsenal de Brest	8 July 1975

Displacement, tons: 842 standard; 905 full load
Dimensions, feet (metres): 178.1 × 34.8 × 11.2 *(54.3 × 10.6 × 3.4)*
Main machinery: Diesel-electric; 2 diesel generators; 1300 hp(m) *(960 kW)*; 1 motor; 1200 hp(m) *(880 kW)*; 1 shaft
Speed, knots: 12. **Range, miles:** 5200 at 12 kts
Complement: 37 (1 officer)

Comment: Launched 17 November 1973. Fitted with lateral screws in bow tunnel. Refitted early 1985, based at Toulon.

LA TIANÉE *10/1991, Aldo Fraccaroli*

CALMAR Y 698

Comment: A 270 ton harbour tug converted for raising moorings. One diesel engine. Commissioned 12 August 1970. Based at Lorient.

CALMAR *8/1990, J. Y. Robert*

TRANSPORTS

ARIEL Y 604
FAUNE Y 613
KORRIGAN Y 661
DRYADE Y 662
ALPHÉE Y 696
NEREIDE Y 700
ONDINE Y 701
NAIADE Y 702
ELFE Y 741

Displacement, tons: 195 standard; 225 full load
Dimensions, feet (metres): 132.8 × 24.5 × 10.8 *(40.5 × 7.5 × 3.3)*
Main machinery: 2 SACM MGO or Poyaud diesels; 1640 hp(m) *(1.21 MW)* or 1730 hp(m) *(1.2 MW)*; 2 shafts
Speed, knots: 15.3. **Range, miles:** 940 at 14 kts
Complement: 9

Comment: All built by Société Française de Construction Naval (ex-Franco-Belge) except f *Nereide, Ondine* and *Naiade* by DCAN Brest. *Ariel* in service 1964, *Elfe* in 1980; the remainder approximately two year intervals. Can carry 400 passengers (250 seated). *Naiade* based with CE Toulon.

FAUNE *8/1990, J. Y. Robe*

SYLPHE Y 710

Displacement, tons: 171 standard; 189 full load
Dimensions, feet (metres): 126.5 × 22.7 × 8.2 *(38.5 × 6.9 × 2.5)*
Main machinery: 1 SACM MGO diesel; 833 hp(m) *(612 kW)*; 1 shaft
Speed, knots: 12
Complement: 9

Comment: Small transport for passengers, built by Chantiers Franco-Belge in 1959-60. In reserve Brest since 1981.

SYLPHE *8/1982, J. Y. Robe*

TREBERON

Comment: Commissioned at Brest 26 November 1979.

TREBERON *8/1988, J. Y. Robe*

MORGANE Y 671 **MERLIN** Y 735 **MÉLUSINE** Y 736

Displacement, tons: 170 full load
Dimensions, feet (metres): 103.3 × 23.2 × 7.9 *(31.5 × 7.1 × 2.4)*
Main machinery: 2 SACM MGO diesels; 940 hp(m) *(691 kW)*; 2 shafts
Speed, knots: 11

Comment: Small transports for 400 passengers built by Chantiers Navals Franco-Belge at Chalo sur Saône *(Mélusine* and *Merlin)* and Ars. de Mourillon *(Morgane)*. Commissioned in June 196 Based at Toulon.

MORGANE *6/1987, A. Torema*

TENDERS

POSÉIDON A 722

Displacement, tons: 220 full load
Dimensions, feet (metres): 132.9 × 23.6 × 7.3 *(40.5 × 7.2 × 2.2)*
Main machinery: 1 diesel; 600 hp(m) *(441 kW)*; 1 shaft
Speed, knots: 13
Complement: 42

Comment: Base ship for assault swimmers. Completed 6 August 1975.

POSEIDON *6/1991, van Ginderen Collection*

TOURMALINE A 714

Displacement, tons: 45
Dimensions, feet (metres): 88 × 16.8 × 4.8 *(26.8 × 5.1 × 1.5)*
Main machinery: 2 diesels; 1120 hp(m) *(823 kW)*; 2 shafts
Speed, knots: 27

Comment: Commissioned 14 February 1974. Built by Chantiers Navals de L'Esterel. Attached to Mediterranean Test Range, Port Pothau, Toulon.

TOURMALINE *6/1985, Giorgio Arra*

ATHOS A 712 **ARAMIS** A 713

Displacement, tons: 100 full load
Dimensions, feet (metres): 105.3 × 21.3 × 6.2 *(32.1 × 6.5 × 1.9)*
Main machinery: 2 SACM diesels; 4400 hp(m) *(3.23 MW)*; 2 shafts
Speed, knots: 32. **Range, miles:** 1500 at 15 kts
Complement: 12 plus 6 passengers
Guns: 1 Oerlikon 20 mm. 2—12.7 mm MGs.
Radars: Navigation: Racal Decca 1226; I band.

Comment: Built by Chantiers Navals de l'Esterel for Missile Trials Centre of Les Landes (CEL). Based at Bayonne, forming Groupe des Vedettes de l'Adour. Commissioned 1980.

ATHOS *9/1983, van Ginderen Collection*

Y 732

Comment: Built in Lorient. Commissioned 3 March 1979. Based at Brest. Designated 'Station de Démagnétisation No 3'.

732 *8/1990, J. Y. Robert*

CORALLINE A 790 **Y 790-798**

Displacement, tons: 44 full load
Dimensions, feet (metres): 68.9 × 14.8 × 3.6 *(21 × 4.5 × 1.1)*
Main machinery: 2 diesels; 264 hp(m) *(194 kW)*; 2 shafts
Speed, knots: 13
Complement: 4 plus 14 divers

Comment: Diving tenders building at Lorient. First one delivered in February 1990. *Coralline* is used for radioactive monitoring in Cherbourg.

Y 790 *6/1991, van Ginderen Collection*

TRAINING SHIPS

Note: Two trawler type vessels are building by SOCAREM, Boulogne. Names are *Glycine* and *Eglantine*. To commission in 1992 for navigation training.

8 LÉOPARD CLASS

Name	*No*	*Builders*	*Commissioned*
LÉOPARD	A 748	ACM, St Malo	4 Dec 1982
PANTHÈRE	A 749	ACM, St Malo	4 Dec 1982
JAGUAR	A 750	ACM, St Malo	18 Dec 1982
LYNX	A 751	La Perrière, Lorient	18 Dec 1982
GUÉPARD	A 752	ACM, St Malo	1 July 1983
CHACAL	A 753	ACM, St Malo	10 Sep 1983
TIGRE	A 754	La Perrière, Lorient	1 July 1983
LION	A 755	La Perrière, Lorient	10 Sep 1983

Displacement, tons: 463 full load
Dimensions, feet (metres): 141 × 27.1 × 10.5 *(43 × 8.3 × 3.2)*
Main machinery: 2 SACM MGO 175 V16 ASHR diesels; 2200 hp(m) *(1.62 MW)*; 2 shafts
Speed, knots: 15. **Range, miles:** 4100 at 12 kts
Complement: 14 plus 21 trainees
Guns: 2 Oerlikon 20 mm.
Radars: Navigation: Racal Decca 1226; I band.

Comment: First four ordered May 1980. Further four ordered April 1981. Form 20ème Divec (Training division) for shiphandling training and occasional EEZ patrols.

TIGRE *12/1991, van Ginderen Collection*

CHIMÈRE Y 706 **FARFADET** Y 711

Displacement, tons: 100
Main machinery: 1 diesel; 200 hp(m) *(147 kW)*; 1 shaft
Speed, knots: 11

Comment: Built at Bayonne in 1971. Tenders to the Naval School.

LA GRANDE HERMINE (ex-*La Route Est Belle*, ex-*Ménestral*) A 653

Comment: Ex-sailing fishing boat built in 1932. Purchased in 1964 as the Navigation School (EOR) training ship. Length 46 ft *(14.02 m)*.

MUTIN A 652

Comment: A 57 ton coastal tender built in 1927 by Chaffeteau, Les Sables d'Olonne. Auxiliary diesel and sails. Attached to the Navigation School.

L'ÉTOILE A 649 **LA BELLE POULE** A 650

Displacement, tons: 227
Dimensions, feet (metres): 105.9 × 22.9 × 10.5 *(32.3 × 7 × 3.2)*
Main machinery: Sulzer diesel; 125 hp(m) *(92 kW)*; 1 shaft
Speed, knots: 6

Comment: Auxiliary sail vessels. Built by Chantiers de Normandie (Fécamp) in 1932. Accommodation for three officers, 30 cadets, 5 petty officers, 12 men. Attached to Naval School.

L'ÉTOILE *6/1991, Guy Toremans*

TUGS

OCEAN TUGS (Remorqueurs de Haute Mer RHM)

MALABAR A 664 **TENACE** A 669 **CENTAURE** A 674

Displacement, tons: 1080 light; 1454 full load
Dimensions, feet (metres): 167.3 × 37.8 × 18.6 *(51 × 11.5 × 5.7)*
Main machinery: 2 MAK 9 M US2 AK diesels; 4600 hp(m) *(3.38 MW)*; 1 shaft; Kort nozzles
Speed, knots: 15. **Range, miles:** 9500 at 15 kts
Complement: 42

Comment: *Malabar* and *Tenace* built by J. Oelkers, Hamburg, *Centaure* built at La Pallice. *Tenace* commissioned 15 November 1973, *Centaure* on 15 November 1974 and *Malabar* on 7 October 1975. All based at Brest with one operating as Fishery Protection ship off US coast. Carry firefighting equipment. Bollard pull, 60 tons.

CENTAURE *8/1990, Photo Sami*

COASTAL TUGS (Remorqueurs Côtiers RC)

BÉLIER A 695 **BUFFLE** A 696 **BISON** A 697

Displacement, tons: 500 standard; 800 full load
Dimensions, feet (metres): 104.9 × 28.9 × 10.5 *(32 × 8.8 × 3.2)*
Main machinery: 2 SACM AGO 195 V8 CSHR diesels; 2600 hp(m) *(1.91 MW)*; 2 Voith-Schneider props
Speed, knots: 11
Complement: 12

Comment: Built at Cherbourg. *Bélier* commissioned 10 July 1980, *Buffle* on 19 July 1980, *Bison* on 16 April 1981. All based at Toulon. Bollard pull, 25 tons.

BÉLIER *6/1991, van Ginderen Collection*

MAROA A 636 **MAITO** A 637 **MANINI** A 638

Displacement, tons: 245 full load
Dimensions, feet (metres): 90.5 × 27.2 × 11.5 *(27.6 × 8.9 × 3.5)*
Main machinery: 2 SACM diesels; 1280 hp(m) *(941 kW)*; 2 Voith-Schneider props
Speed, knots: 11. **Range, miles:** 1200 at 10 kts
Complement: 10

Comment: Built by SFCN and Villeneuve La Garonne (A 638) for CEP Nuclear Test Range. *Maito* commissioned 25 July 1984, *Maroa* 28 July 1984, *Manini* 12 September 1985. Bollard pull, 12 tons.

LE FORT A 671 (12 July 1971)
UTILE A 672 (8 Apr 1971)
LUTTEUR A 673 (19 July 1963)
ROBUSTE A 685 (4 Apr 1960)
ACTIF A 686 (11 July 1963)
LABORIEUX A 687 (14 Aug 1963)
VALEUREUX A 688 (17 Oct 1960)
TRAVAILLEUR A 692 (11 July 1963)
ACHARNÉ A 693 (5 July 1974)
EFFICACE A 694 (17 Oct 1974)

Displacement, tons: 230 full load
Dimensions, feet (metres): 92 × 26 × 13 *(28.1 × 7.9 × 4)*
Main machinery: 1 SACM MGO diesel; 1050 hp(m) *(773 kW)* or 1450 hp(m) *(1.07 MW)* (later ships); 1 shaft
Speed, knots: 11. **Range, miles:** 2400 at 10 kts
Complement: 15

Comment: Commissioning dates in brackets. Bollard pull, 13 tons.

ACHARNÉ *6/1990, Gilbert Gysse*

FREHEL A 675
SAIRE A 676
ARMEN A 677
LA HOUSSAYE A 678
SICIE A 679
LARDIER A 680

Displacement, tons: 259 full load
Dimensions, feet (metres): 82 × 27.6 × 11.2 *(25 × 8.4 × 3.4)*
Main machinery: 2 diesels; 1280 hp(m) *(941 kW)*; 2 Voith-Schneider props
Speed, knots: 10. **Range, miles:** 800 at 10 kts
Complement: 8

Comment: Building at La Perrière Shipyard, Lorient. *Frehel* in service 23 May 1989 at Lorient; *Saire* 16 October 1989 at Cherbourg. Remainder delayed until 1992/93 by changes to the propulsion system. Bollard pull, 12 tons. Replacing older tugs.

FREHEL *8/1990, J. Y. Robe*

HARBOUR TUGS (Remorqueurs de port)

25—105 TON TYPE

Acajou Y 601, *Chataigner* Y 620, *Charme* Y 623, *Chêne* Y 624, *Cormier* Y629, *Frêne* Y 644, *Hêtre* Y 654, *Hevea* Y 655, *Latanier* Y 663, *Manguier* Y 666, *Méléze* Y 668, *Merisier* Y 669, *Paletuvier* Y 686, *Peuplier* Y 688, *Pin* Y 689, *Platane* Y 695, *Saule* Y 708, *Sycomore* Y 709, *Ébène* Y 71?, *Érable* Y 718, *Olivier* Y 719, *Santal* Y 720, *Maronnier* Y 738, *Noyer* Y 739, *Papayer* Y 740.

Comment: Of 105 tons, 10 ton bollard pull with 700 hp(m) *(514 kW)* diesel and maximum speed of 11 kts.

ACAJOU *5/1991, J. Y. Robe*

2—93 TON TYPE

Bonite Y 630 *Rouget* Y 634

Comment: Of 93 tons, 7 ton bollard pull with 380 hp(m) *(279 kW)* and maximum speed of 10 kts.

ROUGET and BONITE *8/1990, J. Y. Robert*

27—65 TON TYPE

Bengali Y 611, *Mouette* Y 617, *Mésange* Y 621, *Cigogne* Y 625, *Colibri* Y 628, *Cygne* Y 632, *Martinet* Y 636, *Fauvette* Y 637, *Goéland* Y 648, *Merle* Y 670, *Moineau* Y 673, *Martin Pêcheur* Y 675, *Passereau* Y 687, *Pinson* Y 691, *Pivert* Y 694, *Alouette* Y 721, *Vanneau* Y 722, *Engoulevent* Y 723, *Sarcelle* Y 724, *Marabout* Y 725, *Toucan* Y 726, *Macreuse* Y 727, *Grand Duc* Y 728, *Eider* Y 729, *Ara* Y 730, *Loriot* Y 747, *Gélinotte* Y 748.

Comment: Of 65 tons, 3.5 ton bollard pull with 250 hp(m) *(184 kW)* diesel and maximum speed of 9 kts. *Ibis* Y 658 loaned to Senegambia.

ALOUETTE *8/1990, J. Y. Robert*

22 WATER TRACTORS

P 1-22

Displacement, tons: 24
Dimensions, feet (metres): 37.7 × 14.1 × 4.6 *(11.5 × 4.3 × 1.4)*
Main machinery: 2 SACM Poyaud 520 V8M diesels; 440 hp(m) *(323 kW)*; 2 shafts
Speed, knots: 9.2

Comment: Pusher-tugs built by Ch et A de La Perrière. First of the second series *(P13)* delivered 23 December 1980, *P20* in service 2 May 1989. *P 21* in service December 1990, *P 22* January 1991. Bollard push, 4 tons.

P 16 *5/1991, J. Y. Robert*

5 FIREFIGHTING TUGS

CASCADE Y 618 **OUED** Y 684 **EMBRUN** Y 746
GAVE Y 645 **AIGUIÈRE** Y 745

Displacement, tons: 85 full load
Dimensions, feet (metres): 78.1 × 17.4 × 5.6 *(23.8 × 5.3 × 1.7)*
Main machinery: 2 SACM Poyaud diesels; 410 hp(m) *(301 kW)*; 2 shafts
Speed, knots: 11.3

Comment: Have red hulls and white superstructure. Beginning to be paid off.

AIGUIÈRE *4/1989, van Ginderen Collection*

MISCELLANEOUS

1 FLOATING DOCK

Comment: Of 3800 tons capacity, built at Brest in 1975. Based at Papeete for use by Centre Expérimentation du Pacifique. 150 × 33 m.

6 FLOATING CRANES

GFA 1-6

Comment: With lifts of 7.5-15 tons. One in Cherbourg, three in Brest, two in Toulon. Self-propelled. Grue Flottante Automotrice (GFA).

18 HARBOUR SUPPORT CRAFT

CHA 8 19 23-38

Comment: Of 20 tons based at Cherbourg, Brest, Lorient, Toulon, Rochefort. Used as harbour craft. *CHA 27-34* in service 1988, 35-38 in service 1989.

CHA 27 *8/1988, J. Y. Robert*

FLOTTE AUXILIAIRE OCCASIONNELLE (FAO)

Note: The ships listed below were on the 'taken up from trade' list at the beginning of 1992.

ABEILLE FLANDRE (ex-*Neptun Suecia*) **ABEILLE LANGUEDOC** (ex-*Neptun Gothia*)
ABEILLE BRETAGNE

Displacement, tons: 1577
Dimensions, feet (metres): 208 × 48.2 × 2.9 *(63.4 × 14.7 × 0.9)*
Main machinery: 4 Atlas diesels; 23 000 hp(m) *(16.9 MW)*; 2 shafts
Speed, knots: 17

Comment: Details given are for *Abeille Flandre* and *Abeille Languedoc*. *Abeille Bretagne* is of 670 tons and 43.7 m. Built by Ulstein Hatlo in Norway in 1978. *Abeille Flandre* based at Brest, *Abeille Languedoc* at Cherbourg, and *Abeille Bretagne* at Tahiti. Used as salvage tugs.

ABEILLE FLANDRE *7/1990, M. Voss*

ALBACORE (ex-*Beryl Fish*) **MÉROU** (ex-*King Fish*)
GIRELLE (ex-*Moon Fish*) A 702

Comment: All of about 55 m in length and capable of 12 kts. *Mérou* and *Girelle* built in the Netherlands in 1981-82 and based in Toulon. *Albacore* on loan from Feronica International and also based in the Mediterranean. Used as supply ships.

ALBACORE 10/1990, J. Y. Robert/M. Pouget

MEROU 6/1991, van Ginderen Collection

AILETTE (ex-*Cyrus*) **ALCYON** (ex-*Bahram*)

Displacement, tons: 1500 full load
Dimensions, feet (metres): 173.9 × 43.6 × 14.8 *(53 × 13.3 × 4.5)*
Main machinery: 2 diesels; 5200 hp(m) *(3.8 MW)*; 2 shafts
Speed, knots: 12
Complement: 7

Comment: Built in 1981/82. Replaced deleted boom defence vessels. Bollard pull, 62 tons. Fitted with a 30 ton stern gantry. Have green hulls and white superstructures.

LANGEVIN (ex-*Percy Navigator*, ex-*Martin Fish*)

Displacement, tons: 1650 full load
Dimensions, feet (metres): 222.1 × 44 × 16.1 *(67.7 × 13.4 × 4.9)*
Main machinery: Diesel-electric; 3 GM 16V 149 TI diesels; 2 motors; 3600 hp(m) *(2.6 MW)*; 2 shafts
Speed, knots: 12

Comment: Built in 1980 by Halter Marine. Leased in May 1990 by DCN for use as an SNLE trials support ship.

GOVERNMENT MARITIME FORCES

GENDARMERIE MARITIME

Note: These ships are operated and maintained by the Navy but are manned by Gendarmes.

4 PATRA CLASS (FAST PATROL CRAFT)

Name	*No*	*Builders*	*Commissioned*
TRIDENT	P 670	Auroux, Arcachon	17 Dec 1976
GLAIVE	P 671	Auroux, Arcachon	2 Apr 1977
ÉPÉE	P 672	CMN, Cherbourg	9 Oct 1976
PERTUISANE	P 673	CMN, Cherbourg	20 Jan 1977

Displacement, tons: 115 standard; 147.5 full load
Dimensions, feet (metres): 132.5 × 19.4 × 5.2 *(40.4 × 5.9 × 1.6)*
Main machinery: 2 SACM AGO 195 V12 diesels; 4410 hp(m) *(3.24 MW)*; 2 shafts; cp props
Speed, knots: 26. **Range, miles:** 1750 at 10 kts; 750 at 20 kts
Complement: 18 (1 officer)
Guns: 1 Bofors 40 mm/60. 1 or 2—12.7 mm MGs.
Radars: Surface search: Racal Decca 1226; I band.

Comment: P 672 transferred to Gendarmerie in February 1986, P 670 in June 1987, P 671 in September 1987 and P 673 in November 1987. The class proved to be too small for their intended naval role. SS-12 SSM removed. P 670 and 672 based at Lorient, the other two at Toulon.

ÉPÉE 6/1989, Gilbert Gyssels

P 772 **P 774**

Comment: Tecimar Volte 43 class of 14 tons with 2 MGs and 25 kts. Commissioned in 1975 and based at Brest; *P 770* deleted in November 1991.

P 772 (with P 791) 8/1990, J. Y. Robert

P 703-705	**P 775**	**Y 753-754**	**Y 779**
P 760-761	**P 778-781**	**Y 762-763**	**Y 781**
P 764	**P 789-792**	**Y 776-777**	**Y 786-791**

Displacement, tons: 30 full load
Dimensions, feet (metres): 81.7 × 17.4 × 5.2 *(24.9 × 5.3 × 1.6)*
Main machinery: 2 Detroit 8V-71 diesels; 460 hp *(343 kW)* sustained; 2 shafts
Speed, knots: 24
Complement: 4
Guns: 1—12.7 mm MG (not in all).

Comment: Type V 14 (SC) or V 14 (Y numbers with Navy crews). Unofficial names: *Gyane* P 780 and *Karukera* P 781 in Antilles/French Guiana; P 779 at Papeete; Y 754 and Y 786 at the Pacific nuclear test centre; P 760 at New Caledonia. Details given are for older craft only.

Y 776 6/1991, van Ginderen Collection

Y 781 6/1991, J. Y. Robert

AFFAIRES MARITIMES

Note: A force of some 30 patrol ships and craft of varying sizes. The vessels are unarmed and manned by civilians on behalf of the Préfectures Maritimes. Their duties mainly involve navigation and pilotage supervision as well as search and rescue. All have PM numbers painted on the bow and Préfectures Maritime written on the superstructure in the vicinity of the bridge.

ANCELLE (Préfectures) *8/1989, Hartmut Ehlers*

DOUANES FRANÇAISES

Note: The French customs service has a number of tasks not normally associated with such an organisation. In addition to the usual duties of dealing with ships entering either its coastal area or ports it also has certain responsibilities for rescue at sea, control of navigation, fishery protection and pollution protection. For these purposes 650 officers and men operate a number of craft of various dimensions: Class I of 30 m, 24 kts and a range of 1200 miles; Class II of 27 m, 24 kts and with a range of 900 miles; Class III of 17-20 m, 24 kts and a range of 400 miles; Class IV of 12-17 m, 24 kts and a range of 400 miles. In addition it operates a number of helicopters and fixed wing aircraft. All vessels have DF numbers painted on the bow.

TRAMONTANA (Customs) *7/1989, A. Sheldon Duplaix*

GABON

Senior Officer

Commanding Officer of the Navy:
Captain Jean-Leonard Mbini

Bases

Port Gentil, Mayumba

Personnel

(a) 1992: 470 officers and men

Coast Guard

Has a number of small inshore patrol launches. Three named *N'Djolé, N'Gombé* and *Omboué* are of doubtful operational status but a number of smaller 'vedettes' are in regular service.

Mercantile Marine

Lloyd's Register of Shipping:
28 vessels of 24 817 tons gross

DELETIONS

1989 *N'Guene, President A B Bongo* (ex-*Colonel D Dabany*)

LIGHT FORCES

2 FRENCH P 400 CLASS (FAST ATTACK CRAFT—PATROL)

Name	*No*	*Builders*	*Commissioned*
GÉNÉRAL d'ARMÉE BA OUMAR	P 07	CMN, Cherbourg	27 June 1988
COLONEL DJOUE DABANY	P 08	CMN, Cherbourg	14 Sep 1990

Displacement, tons: 446 full load
Dimensions, feet (metres): 179 × 26.2 × 8.5 *(54.6 × 8 × 2.5)*
Main machinery: 2 SACM UD 33 V16 M7 diesels; 8000 hp(m) *(5.88 MW)* sustained; 2 shafts; cp props
Speed, knots: 24. **Range, miles:** 4200 at 15 kts
Complement: 32 (4 officers)
Military lift: 20 troops

Guns: 1 Bofors 57 mm/70 SAK 57 Mk 2 (P 07); 75° elevation; 220 rounds/minute to 17 km *(9 nm)*; weight of shell 2.4 kg. Not in P 08 which has a second Oerlikon 20 mm.
2 GIAT F2 20 mm (twin) (P 08).
Fire control: CSEE Naja optronic director (P 07).
Radars: Navigation: Racal Decca 1226C; I band.

Programmes: Contract signed May 1985 with CMN Cherbourg. First laid down 2 July 1986, launched 18 December 1987 and arrived in Gabon 6 August 1988 for a local christening ceremony. Second ordered in February 1989 and launched 29 March 1990.
Structure: There is space on the quarterdeck for two MM 40 Exocet surface-to-surface missiles. These craft are similar to the French vessels but with different engines.

1 FAST ATTACK CRAFT (MISSILE)

Name	*No*	*Builders*	*Commissioned*
GENERAL NAZAIRE BOULINGUI (ex-*President Omar Bongo)*	P 10	Chantiers Navals de l'Estérel	7 Aug 1978

Displacement, tons: 150 full load
Dimensions, feet (metres): 138 × 25.3 × 6.5 *(42 × 7.7 × 1.9)*
Main machinery: 3 SACM 195 V12 CSHR diesels; 5400 hp(m) *(3.97 MW)*; 3 shafts
Speed, knots: 32. **Range, miles:** 1500 at 15 kts
Complement: 20 (3 officers)

Missiles: SSM: 4 Aerospatiale SS 12M; wire-guided to 5.5 km *(3 nm)* subsonic; warhead 30 kg.
Guns: 1 Bofors 40 mm/60; 90° elevation; 300 rounds/minute to 12 km *(6.5 nm)* anti-surface; 4 km *(2.2 nm)* anti-aircraft; weight of shell 0.89 kg.
1 DCN 20 mm; 50° elevation; 800 rounds/minute to 2 km; weight of shell 0.24 kg.
Radars: Navigation: Racal Decca RM1226; I band.

Programmes: Launched 21 November 1977. Engines changed in 1985.
Structure: Triple skinned mahogany hull.

GENERAL NAZAIRE BOULINGUI *1978, Chantiers Navals de l'Esterel*

GÉNÉRAL d'ARMÉE BA OUMAR *1988, CMN Cherbourg*

AMPHIBIOUS FORCES

Note: The Gendarmerie has a number of Simmoneau 6.8 m LCVPs and small patrol craft.

1 BATRAL TYPE

Name	*No*	*Builders*	*Commissioned*
PRESIDENT EL HADJ OMAR BONGO	L 05	CMN, Cherbourg	3 Nov 1984

Displacement, tons: 1336 full load
Dimensions, feet (metres): 262.4 × 42.6 × 7.9 *(80 × 13 × 2.4)*
Main machinery: 2 SACM Type 195 V12 CSHR diesels; 3600 hp(m) *(2.65 MW)*; 2 shafts; cp props
Speed, knots: 16. **Range, miles:** 4500 at 13 kts
Complement: 39
Military lift: 188 troops; 12 vehicles; 350 tons cargo
Guns: 1 Bofors 40 mm; 90° elevation; 300 rounds/minute to 12 km *(6.5 nm)* anti-surface; 4 km *(2.2 nm)* anti-aircraft; weight of shell 0.89 kg.
2 Oerlikon 20 mm; 50° elevation; 800 rounds/minute to 2 km; weight of shell 0.24 kg.
2—81 mm mortars. 2 Browning 12.7 mm MGs. 1—7.62 mm MG.
Radars: Navigation: Racal Decca 1226; I band.
Helicopters: Capable of operating up to SA 330 Puma size.

Comment: Sister to French *La Grandière*. Carries one LCVP and one LCP.

BATRAL Type (French number) *6/1989, Hartmut Ehlers*

1 LCM

Name	*No*	*Builders*	*Commissioned*
MANGA	—	DCAN, Dakar	11 May 1976

Displacement, tons: 150 full load
Dimensions, feet (metres): 78.8 × 21 × 4.2 *(24 × 6.4 × 1.3)*
Main machinery: 2 Poyaud V8-250 diesels; 480 hp(m) *(353 kW)*; 2 shafts
Speed, knots: 8. **Range, miles:** 600 at 5 kts
Complement: 10
Guns: 2 Browning 12.7 mm MGs.
Radars: Navigation: Racal Decca 110; I band.

Comment: Fitted with bow doors.

2 SEA TRUCKS

Comment: Built by Tanguy Marine, Le Havre in 1985. One of 12.2 m with two 165 hp(m) *(121 kW)* engines and one of 10.2 m with one engine.

LAND-BASED MARITIME AIRCRAFT

Numbers/Type: 1 Embraer EMB-111 Bandeirante.
Operational speed: 194 kts *(360 km/h)*.
Service ceiling: 25 500 ft *(7770 m)*.
Range: 1590 nm *(2945 km)*.
Role/Weapon systems: Coastal surveillance and EEZ protection tasks are primary roles but operational status is doubtful. Sensors: APS-128 search radar, limited ECM, searchlight. Weapons: ASV; 8 × 127 mm rockets or 28 × 70 mm rockets.

THE GAMBIA

Political

On 1 February 1982 the two countries of Senegal and Gambia united to form the confederation of Senegambia, which included merging the armed forces. Confederation was cancelled on 30 September 1989 and the forces are once again national and independent of each other.

General

The patrol craft come under the Marine Unit of the National Army.

Personnel

(a) 1992: 60 officers and men
(b) Voluntary service

Bases

Banjul

Mercantile Marine

Lloyd's Register of Shipping:
9 vessels of 2823 tons gross

2 Ex-CHINESE SHANGHAI II CLASS (FAST ATTACK CRAFT—GUN)

GONJUR 101 **BRUFUT** 102

Displacement, tons: 113 standard; 131 full load
Dimensions, feet (metres): 127.3 × 17.4 × 5.2 *(38.8 × 5.3 × 1.6)*
Main machinery: 2 L12-180 diesels (fwd); 2400 hp(m) *(1.76 MW)*; 2 L12-180Z diesels (aft); 2000 hp(m) *(1.47 MW)*; 4 shafts
Speed, knots: 26. **Range, miles:** 700 at 16 kts (on 2 diesels)
Complement: 34
Guns: 6—25 mm/80 (3 twin).
Radars: Surface search: Furuno 1505; I band.

Comment: Built in May 1979 and refitted in China in mid 1988. Delivered as a gift from the PLA(N) on 2 February 1989 and commissioned in May 1989. The 37 mm gun normally mounted aft in this class has been replaced by a boat davit.

GONJUR *1/1990, E. Grove*

1 FAIREY MARINE TRACKER 2 CLASS (COASTAL PATROL CRAFT)

Name	*No*	*Builders*	*Commissioned*
JATO	P 12	Fairey Marine, UK	1978

Displacement, tons: 31.5 full load
Dimensions, feet (metres): 65.7 × 17 × 4.8 *(20 × 5.2 × 1.5)*
Main machinery: 2 GM 12V-71TA diesels; 840 hp *(617 kW)* sustained; 2 shafts
Speed, knots: 29. **Range, miles:** 650 at 20 kts
Complement: 11
Guns: 1 Oerlikon 20 mm. 2—7.62 mm MGs.
Radars: Surface search: Racal Decca; I band.

Comment: Hull and superstructure of GRP. Air-conditioned accommodation. The other two of the class returned to Senegal in 1989.

JATO *1/1990, E. Grove*

1 FAIREY MARINE LANCE CLASS (COASTAL PATROL CRAFT)

Name	*No*	*Builders*	*Commissioned*
SEA DOG	P 11	Fairey Marine, UK	28 Oct 1976

Displacement, tons: 17 full load
Dimensions, feet (metres): 48.7 × 15.3 × 4.3 *(14.8 × 4.7 × 1.3)*
Main machinery: 2 GM 8V-71TA diesels; 650 hp *(485 kW)* sustained; 2 shafts
Speed, knots: 24. **Range, miles:** 500 at 16 kts
Complement: 9
Guns: 2—7.62 mm MGs (not carried).
Radars: Surface search: Racal Decca 110; I band.

Comment: Delivered 28 October 1976. Unarmed and used for training.

SEA DOG *1/1990, E. Grove*

GERMANY

Headquarters' Appointments

Chief of Naval Staff:
Vice Admiral Hein-Peter Weyher
Chief of Staff:
Rear Admiral Hans-Rudolf Bohmer

Commander-in-Chief

Commander-in-Chief, Fleet:
Vice Admiral Dieter Franz Braun
Deputy Commander-in-Chief, Fleet:
Rear Admiral Hans-Jochen Meyer Höper

Diplomatic Representation

Defence and Naval Attaché in London:
Rear Admiral Karlheinz Reichert
Naval Assistant in London:
Commander U P Stickdorn

Personnel

(a) 1992: 32 190 (4990 officers) (includes Naval Air Arm)
(b) 12 months' national service (8670)

Squadron Allocations

Lütjens class, 1st DS; Hamburg class, 2nd DS; 4 Bremen class, 2nd FS; 4 Bremen class, 4th FS.

Naval Air Arm

MFG (Marine Flieger Geschwader)
MFG 1 (Fighter Bomber Wing at Schleswig-Jagel)
PA 200 Tornado
MFG 2 (Fighter Bomber and Reconnaissance Wing at Eggebek)
PA 200 Tornado
MFG 3 'Graf Zeppelin' (LRMP Wing at Nordholz)
Breguet Atlantic of which 5 converted for Sigint, Sea Lynx (landbase for embarkation and maintenance)
MFG 5 (SAR and Liaison Wing at Kiel)
Sea King Mk 41, Do 28D-2 Skyservant of which 2 converted for pollution control plus 1 Dornier Do 228
MF Hubschraubergruppe (SAR and Liaison Wing at Parow/Stralsund)
Mi-8 Hip, Mi-14 Haze

Volksmarine

The former GDR Navy ceased to exist after reunification on 3 October 1990. Most of the warships organised into a Coastal Guard Squadron subordinate to the District Command at Rostock were paid off in 1991, although a few auxiliaries have been retained.

Bases

C-in-C Fleet: Glücksburg. Flag Officer Naval Command: Rostock.
Baltic: Kiel, Olpenitz, Flensburg*, Eckernförde*, Neustadt*, Warnemunde.
North Sea: Wilhelmshaven, Borkum*, Emden*.
Naval Arsenal: Wilhelmshaven, Kiel.
Training (other than in Bases above): Bremerhaven, Brake*, Glückstaat, List/Sylt, Plön, Grossenbrode*, Stralsund.
The administration of the bases is vested in the Naval Support Command at Wilhelmshaven. Those marked with an asterisk are to close by 2005.

Prefix to Ships' Names

Prefix FGS is used in communications.

Strength of the Fleet

Type	*Active*	*Building (Projected)*
Submarines—Patrol	22	(12)
Destroyers	6	—
Frigates	8	4 (4)
Corvettes	3	—
Fast Attack Craft—Missile	40	—
LCUs	10	—
LCMs	17	—
Minehunters	9	10
Minesweepers—Coastal	20	—
Minesweepers—Inshore	14	—
Minesweepers-Drones	18	—
Diver Support Vessels	1	—
Tenders	4	6
Support Ships	7	(4)
Replenishment Tankers	6	(2)
Support Tankers	3	—
Accommodation Ships	7	—
Ammunition Transports	2	—
Mine Transports	1	—
Water Boats	2	—
Tugs—Salvage	5	—
Tugs—Icebreaking	2	—
Tugs—Coastal/Harbour	20	(6)
Surveillance Ships	3	—
Training Ships	4	—
Sail Training Ships	2	—
TRVs	4	—
Trials Ships	16+	(5)
Miscellaneous	25	(2)
Non-naval Vessels		
Coast Guard Patrol Craft	34	—
Police Patrol Craft	17+	—
Fishery Protection Ships	8+	—
Research and Survey Ships	14	—
Army craft	43	—

Future Projects

Building:
12 submarines to replace the Type 205 and unmodernised Type 206 in late 1990s. Type 212
4 frigates to replace the Hamburg class in 1994-96. Type 123
4 frigates to replace the Type 103 destroyers from 2004 onwards. Type 124
10 minehunters 1991-95. Type 332
4 combat store ships in early 2000s. Type 702
6 tenders to replace the Rhein class in 1992-94. Type 404
1 multi-purpose boat-medium to replace *Walther von Ledebur* in mid-1990s. Type 748
2 multi-purpose boats-large to replace *Heinz Roggenkamp* and *Hans Bürckner* in 1990s. Type 749
1 trials craft-fast (SES with 50 kts). Type 751
1 research ship (SWATH) to replace *Planet*. Type 752
1 floating dock to replace *Schwimmdock B*
6 tugs to replace Type 724 until 1994. Type 725

Naval Aviation:
12 LRAACA to replace the BR 1150 Atlantic not before 1997
Helicopters to replace Sea King and Sea Lynx after 2000

Weapons:
New SSMs 'Anti-Navire Supersonique' (ANS) for Type 143B, 143A and 123 in late 1990s
262 ASMs 'Kormoran 2' for PA 200 Tornado in early 1990s
New SAM systems for frigates
58 RAM launchers with 1923 SAMs in 1992-96
4432 SAMs 'Fliegerfaust 2' in 1989-98
New torpedoes for modernised submarines
New influence mines 'SGM 80' in 1990-96
New projectile mines against air cushion vehicles

Modernisation

10 FAC Type 143 in mid 1990s including new SSMs
RAM-ASDM launcher for Types 103(2), 122(2), 123(2), 143(1) 1991-96
Light SAMs 'Fliegerfaust 2' (similar to USSR SA-N-5, with Stinger-SAM) for support ships and minor combatants

Hydrographic Service

This service, under the direction of the Ministry of Transport, is civilian manned with HQ at Hamburg. Survey ships are listed at the end of the section.

Mercantile Marine

Lloyd's Register of Shipping:
1522 vessels of 5 971 254 tons gross

DELETIONS

Submarines

1991 *U 1* (TNSW trials)
1992 *U 2*

Destroyers

1990 *Hessen*

Frigates

1989 *Braunschweig* (sold to Turkey)
1990 *Berlin* (ex-GDR)
1991 *Rostock* (ex-GDR), *Halle* (ex-GDR)

Corvettes

1990 11 Parchim I class (ex-GDR), 4 Tarantul I class (ex-GDR)
1991 *Grevesmühlen, Gadebusch, Teterow, Lübz, Wismar, Hiddensee* (all ex-GDR)
Thetis, Najade (both to Greece)

Light Forces

1990 6 Shershen class (ex-GDR), 14 Libelle class (ex-GDR), 12 Osa I class (ex-GDR)

Mine Warfare Vessels

1989 *Widder, Fische, Deneb, Jupiter, Neptun*
1990 *Rigel, Skorpion, Sirius, Regulus,* 23 Kondor II class (ex-GDR) (one to Uruguay)
1991 *Castor, Flensburg, Tangerhütte, Bitterfeld, Eisleben, Bernau, Eilenburg* (last five ex-GDR, last three to Uruguay)
1992 *Pollux, Mars, Fulda, Völklingen, Ariadne, Vineta, Amazone, Gazelle, Hansa*

Landing Craft

1990 12 Frosch I class (ex-GDR), 2 Frosch II class (ex-GDR)
1991 *LCM 1-11* (to Greece), *Barbe, Delphin, Dorsch, Felchen, Forelle, Makrele*
1992 *Rochen, Schlei, Brasse, Muräne*

Auxiliaries

1989 *Lech, Neckar*
1990 *Deutschland, Mosel,* 4 Support Ships (ex-GDR) (*Jasmund* to Ecuador)
1991 *Saar, Lahn, Werra, Sachsenwald, Odin, Wotan, Wittow, Mönchgut, Darss, Kühlung, Werdau* (last five ex-GDR), *Coburg* (to Greece)
1992 *Eifel, Harz*

Miscellaneous

1989 *Alster* (old) (to Turkey), TF 104, TF 107 (to Turkey), *Otto Meycke*
1990 TF 106 and TF 108 (to Greece), TF 4 (to Greece), *Mellum* (to Greece), *Trischen* (to Greece), *Knechtsand* (old) (to Greece), *Scharhörn* (old) (to Greece), *Hans Bürckner, Lütje Hörn* (old) (to Greece)
30+ Tugs and Miscellaneous (ex-GDR)
1991 EF 3, *FW 4* (to Turkey), *FW 6* (to Greece), *Kollicker Ort* (ex-GDR), *KW 3, Otto Von Guericke* (to Uruguay), *Zingst* (to Uruguay), *TF 6* (to Greece)
1992 *H 13*

Coast Guard

1990 *Uelzen,* 9 Kondor I class (ex-GDR)

PENNANT LIST

Submarines

S 170	U 21
S 171	U 22
S 172	U 23
S 173	U 24
S 174	U 25
S 175	U 26
S 176	U 27
S 177	U 28
S 178	U 29
S 179	U 30
S 188	U 9
S 189	U 10
S 190	U 11
S 191	U 12
S 192	U 13
S 193	U 14
S 194	U 15
S 195	U 16
S 196	U 17
S 197	U 18
S 198	U 19
S 199	U 20

Destroyers

D 181	Hamburg
D 182	Schleswig-Holstein
D 183	Bayern
D 185	Lütjens
D 186	Mölders
D 187	Rommel

Frigates

F 207	Bremen
F 208	Niedersachsen
F 209	Rheinland-Pfalz
F 210	Emden
F 211	Köln
F 212	Karlsruhe
F 213	Augsburg
F 214	Lübeck
F 215	Brandenburg

Corvettes

P 6053	Hermes
P 6055	Triton
P 6056	Theseus

Light Forces

P 6111	S 61 Albatros
P 6112	S 62 Falke
P 6113	S 63 Geier
P 6114	S 64 Bussard
P 6115	S 65 Sperber
P 6116	S 66 Greif
P 6117	S 67 Kondor
P 6118	S 68 Seeadler
P 6119	S 69 Habicht
P 6120	S 70 Kormoran
P 6121	S 71 Gepard
P 6122	S 72 Puma
P 6123	S 73 Hermelin
P 6124	S 74 Nerz
P 6125	S 75 Zobel

P 6126	S 76 Frettchen
P 6127	S 77 Dachs
P 6128	S 78 Ozelot
P 6129	S 79 Wiesel
P 6130	S 80 Hyäne
P 6141	S 41 Tiger
P 6142	S 42 Iltis
P 6143	S 43 Luchs
P 6144	S 44 Marder
P 6145	S 45 Leopard
P 6146	S 46 Fuchs
P 6147	S 47 Jaguar
P 6148	S 48 Löwe
P 6149	S 49 Wolf
P 6150	S 50 Panther
P 6151	S 51 Häher
P 6152	S 52 Storch
P 6153	S 53 Pelikan
P 6154	S 54 Elster
P 6155	S 55 Alk
P 6156	S 56 Dommel
P 6157	S 57 Weihe
P 6158	S 58 Pinguin
P 6159	S 59 Reiher
P 6160	S 60 Kranich

Mine Warfare Forces

M 1050	TB 1
M 1053	Stier
M 1059	Spica
M 1060	Weiden (bldg)
M 1061	Rottweil (bldg)
M 1062	Schütze (old)
M 1062	Sulzbach-Rosenberg (bldg) (new)
M 1063	Waage (old)
M 1063	Bad Bevensen (bldg)
M 1064	Grömitz (bldg)
M 1065	Dillingen (bldg)
M 1066	Frankenthal (bldg)
M 1067	Bad Rappenau (bldg)
M 1068	Datteln (bldg)
M 1069	Homburg (bldg)
M 1070	Göttingen
M 1071	Koblenz
M 1072	Lindau
M 1073	Schleswig
M 1074	Tübingen
M 1075	Wetzlar
M 1076	Paderborn
M 1077	Weilheim
M 1078	Cuxhaven
M 1079	Düren
M 1080	Marburg
M 1081	Konstanz
M 1082	Wolfsburg
M 1083	Ulm
M 1084	Flensburg
M 1085	Minden
M 1086	Fulda
M 1087	Völklingen
M 1090	Pegnitz
M 1091	Kulmbach
M 1092	Hameln
M 1093	Auerbach
M 1094	Ensdorf
M 1095	Überherrn
M 1096	Passau
M 1097	Laboe
M 1098	Siegburg
M 1099	Herten
M 2651	Freya
M 2653	Hertha
M 2654	Nymphe
M 2655	Nixe
M 2658	Frauenlob
M 2659	Nautilus
M 2660	Gefion
M 2661	Medusa
M 2662	Undine
M 2663	Minerva
M 2664	Diana
M 2665	Loreley
M 2666	Atlantis
M 2667	Acheron
M 2670	Sömmerda

Amphibious Forces

L 760	Flunder
L 761	Karpfen
L 762	Lachs
L 763	Plötze
L 766	Stör
L 767	Tümmler
L 768	Wels
L 769	Zander
LCM12	Sprotte
LCM13	Sardine
LCM14	Sardelle
LCM15	Hering
LCM16	Orfe
LCM16	Maräne
LCM18	Saibling
LCM19	Stint
LCM20	Aesche
L 780	LCM 21 Hummer
L 781	LCM 22 Krill
L 782	LCM 23 Krabbe
L 783	LCM 24 Auster
L 784	LCM 25 Muschel
L 785	LCM 26 Koralle
L 786	LCM 27 Garnele
L 787	LCM 28 Languste
L 788	Butt
L 795	Inger

Support Ships and Auxiliaries

A 50	Alster
A 52	Oste
A 53	Oker
A 58	Rhein
A 60	Gorch Fock
A 61	Elbe (old)
A 63	Main
A 69	Donau
A 511	Elbe (new)
A 1400	Holnis
A 1401	Eisvogel
A 1402	Eisbär
A 1403	FW 1
A 1405	FW 5
A 1407	Wittensee
A 1408	SP 1
A 1409	Wilhelm Pullwer
A 1410	Walther von Ledebur
A 1411	Lüneburg
A 1413	Freiburg
A 1414	Glücksburg
A 1415	Saarburg
A 1416	Nienburg
A 1417	Offenburg
A 1418	Meersburg
A 1424	Walchensee
A 1425	Ammersee
A 1426	Tegernsee
A 1427	Westensee
A 1435	Westerwald
A 1436	Odenwald
A 1438	Steigerwald
A 1439	Baltrum
A 1440	Juist
A 1441	Langeoog
A 1442	Spessart
A 1443	Rhön
A 1450	Planet
A 1451	Wangerooge
A 1452	Spiekeroog
A 1455	Norderney
A 1457	Helgoland
A 1458	Fehmarn
Y 811	Knurrhahn
Y 812	Lütje Hörn
Y 814	Knechtsand
Y 815	Scharhorn
Y 816	Vogelsand
Y 817	Nordstrand
Y 819	Langeness
Y 820	Sylt
Y 821	Föhr
Y 822	Amrum
Y 823	Neuwerk
Y 827	KW 15
Y 830	KW 16
Y 832	KW 18
Y 834	Nordwind
Y 842	Schwimmdock A
Y 844	Barbara
Y 845	KW 17
Y 846	KW 20
Y 851	TF 1
Y 852	TF 2
Y 853	TF 3
Y 855	TF 5
Y 857	H 11
Y 860	Schwedeneck
Y 861	Kronsort
Y 862	Helmsand
Y 863	Stollergrund
Y 864	Mittelgrund
Y 865	Kalkgrund
Y 866	Breitgrund
Y 867	Bant
Y 871	Heinz Roggenkamp
Y 875	Hiev
Y 876	Griep
Y 879	Schwimmdock B
Y 890	Vogtland
Y 891	Altmark
Y 892	Havelland
Y 893	Uckermark
Y 894	Borde
Y 895	Wische
Y 1641	Förde
Y 1642	Jade
Y 1643	Bottsand
Y 1644	Eversand
Y 1650	Ummanz
Y 1651	Koos
Y 1652	Kölpinsee
Y 1654	Havel
Y 1656	Wustrow
Y 1657	Fleesensee
Y 1658	Dranske
Y 1659	Oder
Y 1660	Saale
Y 1670	MT-Boot
Y 1671	AK 1
Y 1672	AK 3
Y 1673	AK 5
Y 1674	AM 6
Y 1675	AM 8
Y 1676	MA 2
Y 1677	MA 3
Y 1679	AM 7
Y 1680	Neuende
Y 1681	Heppens
Y 1682	Ellerbek
Y 1683	AK 6
Y 1684	Peter Bachmann
Y 1686	AK 2
Y 1687	Borby
Y 1689	Bums
Y 1690	LP 3

SUBMARINES

4 TYPE 205

Name	*No*	*Builders*	*Laid down*	*Launched*	*Commissioned*
U 9	S 188	Howaldtswerke, Kiel	10 Dec 1964	20 Oct 1966	11 Apr 1967
U 10	S 189	Howaldtswerke, Kiel	15 July 1965	5 June 1967	28 Nov 1967
U 11	S 190	Howaldtswerke, Kiel	1 Apr 1966	9 Feb 1968	21 June 1968
U 12	S 191	Howaldtswerke, Kiel	1 Sep 1966	10 Sep 1968	14 Jan 1969

Displacement, tons: 419 surfaced; 450 dived
Dimensions, feet (metres): 144 × 15.1 × 14.1 *(43.9 × 4.6 × 4.3)*
Main machinery: Diesel-electric; 2 MTU 12V 493 AZ80 GA 31L diesels; 1200 hp(m) *(882 kW)* sustained; 2 alternators; 810 kW; 1 Siemens motor; 1800 hp(m) *(1.32 MW)* sustained; 1 shaft
Speed, knots: 10 surfaced; 17 dived
Complement: 22 (4 officers)

Torpedoes: 8—21 in *(533 mm)* tubes. AEG Seeal; wire-guided; active homing to 13 km *(7 nm)* at 35 kts; passive homing to 28 km *(15 nm)* at 23 kts; warhead 260 kg; no reloads.
Mines: 16 in place of torpedoes.
Countermeasures: ESM: Radar warning.
Fire control: Signaal Mk 8.
Radars: Surface search: Thompson-CSF Calypso II; I band; range 31 km *(17 nm)* for 10 m² target.
Sonars: Krupp Atlas SRS M1H; passive/active search and attack; high frequency.

Programmes: All built in floating docks. First submarines designed and built by West Germany since the end of the Second World War. Hulls of steel alloys with non-magnetic properties. No plans for modernisation but some are modified for trials of new equipment.
Structure: Diving depth, 159 m *(490 ft)*. *U 1* was lengthened by 3.8 m *(12.5 ft)* and was fitted with an air-independent propulsion system (fuel cell) for trials which completed successfully in May 1990 after nine months, when the fuel cell equipment was removed. The submarine was paid off in January 1992. *U 11* (Type 205A) converted as a padded target in 1988; *U 12* (Type 205B) acts as a sonar trials platform.
Operational: The boats are trimmed by the stern to load through the bow caps.
Sales: *U 1* decommissioned 29 November 1991 and is on loan to TNSW for trials of a 250 kW closed cycle diesel developed by Carlton Deep Sea Systems (Cosworth) and TNSW.

U 12 — *6/1991, Stefan Terzibaschitsch*

U 11 — *6/1991, Stefan Terzibaschitsch*

0 + (12) TYPE 212

Displacement, tons: 1280 surfaced; 1800 dived
Dimensions, feet (metres): 167.3 × 22.6 × 21 *(51 × 6.9 × 6.4)*
Main machinery: Diesel-electric; 1 MTU 16V 396 diesel; 1 Siemens Permasyn motor; 1 shaft; HDW fuel cell (AIP); Sodium Sulphide high energy batteries
Complement: 22 + 5 training

Torpedoes: 6—21 in *(533 mm)* bow tubes; water ram discharge; DMT (formerly AEG) Seeal 3 or Seehecht.
Mines: Abeking & Rasmussen external belt.
Countermeasures: ESM: TST FL 1800U; radar warning.
Fire control: NFT (formerly Kongsberg) MFI-90U weapons control system.
Sonars: Krupp Atlas bow and flank arrays. Ferranti FMS 52; high frequency; active.
Krupp Atlas clip-on towed passive array (for use outside Baltic).

Programmes: Design phase completed in 1990 by IKL in conjunction with HDW and TNSW. The HDW/TNSW consortium expects to contract the building of the first batch of four in 1995. First of class to enter service in 1999.
Structure: Primarily equipped for Baltic and North Sea operations with a hybrid fuel cell/battery propulsion based on the HDW prototype successfully evaluated in *U1* in 1988-89. This prototype had 16 fuel cells each generating 25 kW of power. It is hoped to achieve a five-fold increase in power by replacing the liquid electrolyte with solid polymer technology. The submarine is designed with a partial double hull which has a larger diameter forward. This is joined to the after end by a short conical section which houses the fuel cell plant. Two LOX tanks and 38 Hydrogen cylinders are carried around the circumference of the smaller hull section.

TYPE 212 (artist's impression) *1990, HDW*

6 TYPE 206 and 12 TYPE 206A

Name	*No*	*Builders*	*Laid down*	*Launched*	*Commissioned*
U 13	S 192	Howaldtswerke, Kiel	15 Nov 1969	28 Sep 1971	19 Apr 1973
U 14	S 193	Rheinstahl Nordseewerke, Emden	1 Mar 1970	1 Feb 1972	19 Apr 1973
U 15*	S 194	Howaldtswerke, Kiel	1 June 1970	15 June 1972	17 July 1974
U 16*	S 195	Rheinstahl Nordseewerke, Emden	1 Nov 1970	29 Aug 1972	9 Nov 1973
U 17*	S 196	Howaldtswerke, Kiel	1 Oct 1970	10 Oct 1972	28 Nov 1973
U 18*	S 197	Rheinstahl Nordseewerke, Emden	1 Apr 1971	31 Oct 1972	19 Dec 1973
U 19	S 198	Howaldtswerke, Kiel	5 Jan 1971	15 Dec 1972	9 Nov 1973
U 20	S 199	Rheinstahl Nordseewerke, Emden	3 Sep 1971	16 Jan 1973	24 May 1974
U 21	S 170	Howaldtswerke, Kiel	15 Apr 1971	9 Mar 1973	16 Aug 1974
U 22*	S 171	Rheinstahl Nordseewerke, Emden	18 Nov 1971	27 Mar 1973	26 July 1974
U 23*	S 172	Rheinstahl Nordseewerke, Emden	5 Mar 1973	25 May 1974	2 May 1975
U 24*	S 173	Rheinstahl Nordseewerke, Emden	20 Mar 1972	26 June 1973	16 Oct 1974
U 25*	S 174	Howaldtswerke, Kiel	1 July 1971	23 May 1973	14 June 1974
U 26*	S 175	Rheinstahl Nordseewerke, Emden	14 July 1972	20 Nov 1973	13 Mar 1975
U 27	S 176	Howaldtswerke, Kiel	1 Oct 1971	21 Aug 1973	16 Oct 1974
U 28*	S 177	Rheinstahl Nordseewerke, Emden	4 Oct 1972	22 Jan 1974	18 Dec 1974
U 29*	S 178	Howaldtswerke, Kiel	10 Jan 1972	5 Nov 1973	27 Nov 1974
U 30*	S 179	Rheinstahl Nordseewerke, Emden	5 Dec 1972	26 Mar 1974	13 Mar 1975

* **Type 206A (see** *Modernisation*)

Displacement, tons: 450 surfaced; 498 dived
Dimensions, feet (metres): 159.4 × 15.1 × 14.8 *(48.6 × 4.6 × 4.5)*
Main machinery: Diesel-electric; 2 MTU 12V 493 AZ80 GA 31L diesels; 1200 hp(m) *(882 kW)* sustained; 2 alternators; 810 kW; 1 Siemens motor; 1800 hp(m) *(1.32 MW)* sustained; 1 shaft
Speed, knots: 10 surfaced; 17 dived
Range, miles: 4500 at 5 kts surfaced
Complement: 22 (4 officers)

Torpedoes: 8—21 in *(533 mm)* bow tubes. AEG Seeschlenge (Type 206); wire-guided; active homing to 6 km *(3.3 nm)* at 35 kts; passive homing to 14 km *(7.6 nm)* at 23 kts; warhead 100 kg.
DMT (ex-AEG) Seeal 3 (Type 206A); wire-guided; active homing to 13 km *(7 nm)* at 35 kts; passive homing to 28 km *(15 nm)* at 23 kts; warhead 260 kg.

Mines: GRP container secured outside hull each side. Each container holds 12 mines, carried in addition to the normal torpedo or mine armament (16 in place of torpedoes).
Countermeasures: ESM: Radar warning.
Fire control: Signaal Mk 8 (Type 206). CSU 83 (Type 206A).
Radars: Surface search: Thomson-CSF Calypso II; I band; range 31 km *(17 nm)* for 10 m² target.
Sonars: Thomson Sintra DUUX 2; passive ranging.
Krupp Atlas 410 A4 (Type 206); Krupp Atlas DBQS-21D (Type 206A); passive/active search and attack; medium frequency.

Programmes: Authorised on 7 June 1969 from Howaldtswerke Deutsche Werft (8) and Rheinstahl Nordseewerke, Emden (10).
Modernisation: Mid-life conversion of 12 of the class (Type 206A) was a very extensive one, including the installation of new sensors (sonar DBQS-21D with training simulator STU-5), periscopes, weapon control system (LEWA), weapons (torpedo Seeal), GPS navigation, and a comprehensive refitting of the propulsion system, as well as habitability improvements. Conversion work was shared between Thyssen Nordseewerke *(U 23, 30, 22, 27, 15, 26)* at Emden and HDW *(U 29, 16, 25, 28, 17, 18)* at Kiel. The work started in mid-1987 and completed in February 1992.
Structure: Type 206 hulls are built of high-tensile non-magnetic steel. In this the West German submarines are unique. Modernised Type 206A submarines have a slight difference in superstructure shape.
Operational: First squadron *(Meersburg)*: four Type 205; six unmodernised Type 206; based at Kiel.
Third squadron: 12 Type 206A; based at Eckernförde. *U 27* was in a collision in 1991 and may be paid off early.

U 14 *3/1991, van Ginderen Collection*

U 30 *1991, Horst Dehnst*

DESTROYERS

3 Ex-US MODIFIED CHARLES F ADAMS CLASS (TYPE 103B) (DDGs)

Name	No	Builders	Laid down	Launched	Commissioned
LÜTJENS (ex-US DDG 28)	D 185	Bath Iron Works Corporation	1 Mar 1966	11 Aug 1967	22 Mar 1969
MÖLDERS (ex-US DDG 29)	D 186	Bath Iron Works Corporation	12 Apr 1966	13 Apr 1968	20 Sep 1969
ROMMEL (ex-US DDG 30)	D 187	Bath Iron Works Corporation	22 Aug 1967	1 Feb 1969	2 May 1970

Displacement, tons: 3370 standard; 4500 full load
Dimensions, feet (metres): 437 × 47 × 20 *(133.2 × 14.3 × 6.1)*
Main machinery: 4 Combustion Engineering boilers; 1200 psi *(84.4 kg/cm sq)*; 900°F *(500°C)*; 2 turbines; 70 000 hp *(52.2 MW)*; 2 shafts
Speed, knots: 32. **Range, miles:** 4500 at 20 kts
Complement: 337 (19 officers)

Missiles: SSM: McDonnell Douglas Harpoon; active radar homing to 130 km *(70 nm)* at 0.9 Mach; warhead 227 kg. Combined Mk 13 single-arm launcher with SAM system ❶.
SAM: GDC Pomona Standard SM-1MR; Mk 13 Mod 0 launcher; command guidance; semi-active radar homing to 46 km *(25 nm)* at 2 Mach; 40 missiles—combined SSM and SAM.
2 RAM 21 cell Mk 49 launchers to be fitted 1992-95.
A/S: Honeywell ASROC Mk 112 octuple launcher ❷; inertial guidance to 1.6-10 km *(1-5.4 nm)*; payload Mk 46 torpedo.
Guns: 2 FMC 5 in *(127 mm)*/54 Mk 42 Mod 10 automatic ❸; 65° elevation; 20 rounds/minute to 23 km *(12.4 nm)* anti-surface; 15 km *(8 nm)* anti-aircraft; weight of shell 32 kg.
Torpedoes: 6—324 mm US Mk 32 (2 triple) tubes ❹. Honeywell Mk 46; anti-submarine; active/passive homing to 11 km *(5.9 nm)* at 40 kts; warhead 44 kg.
Depth charges: 1 projector ❺.
Countermeasures: Decoys: Loral Hycor Mk 36 SRBOC 6-barrelled Chaff launcher; range 1-4 km *(0.6-2.2 nm)*.
ESM/ECM: AEG FL-1800S; radar intercept and jammer.
Combat data systems: SATIR 1 action data automation; Link 11. SATCOM to be fitted.
Fire control: Mk 86 GFCS. Mk 74 MFCS.
Radars: Air search: Lockheed SPS 40 ❻; E/F band; range 320 km *(175 nm)*.
Hughes SPS 52 ❼; 3D; E/F band; range 439 km *(240 nm)*.
Surface search: Raytheon/Sylvania SPS 10 ❽; G band.
Fire control: Two Raytheon SPG 51 ❾; G/I band (for missiles).
Lockheed SPQ 9 ❿; I/J band; range 37 km *(20 nm)*.
Lockheed SPG 60 ⓫; I/J band; range 110 km *(60 nm)*.
Tacan: URN 20 ⓬.
Sonars: Krupp Atlas DSQS 21B; hull-mounted; active search and attack; medium frequency.

Programmes: Modified to suit West German requirements and practice. 1965 contract.
Modernisation: The Type 103B modernisation and other modifications included:
(a) Installation of one single-arm Mk 13 launcher for Standard SAM and Harpoon SSM.
(b) Improved fire control with digital in place of analogue computers.
(c) Higher superstructure abaft bridge with SPG 60 and SPQ 9 on a mast platform.

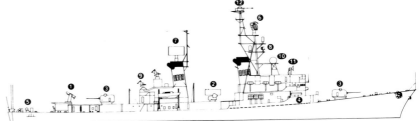

MÖLDERS (Scale 1 : 1 200), *Ian Sturton*

MÖLDERS *6/1991, Stefan Terzibaschitsch*

Carried out by Naval Arsenal, Kiel and Howaldtswerke, Kiel: *Mölders* completed 29 March 1984, *Rommel* 26 July 1985, *Lütjens* 16 December 1986. RAM launchers are to be fitted in front of the bridge and aft of the Mk 13 launcher between 1992 and 1995.

Structure: Some differences from Charles F Adams in W/T aerials and general outline, particularly the funnels.
Operational: These ships are planned to have a life of at least 30 years.

3 HAMBURG CLASS (TYPE 101A)

Name	No	Builders	Laid down	Launched	Commissioned
HAMBURG	D 181	H C Stülcken Sohn, Hamburg	29 Jan 1959	26 Mar 1960	23 Mar 1964
SCHLESWIG-HOLSTEIN	D 182	H C Stülcken Sohn, Hamburg	20 Aug 1959	20 Aug 1960	12 Oct 1964
BAYERN	D 183	H C Stülcken Sohn, Hamburg	14 Sep 1960	14 Aug 1962	6 July 1965

Displacement, tons: 3340 standard; 4680 full load
Dimensions, feet (metres): 438.5 × 44 × 20.3 *(133.7 × 13.4 × 6.2)*
Main machinery: 4 Wahodag boilers; 910 psi *(64 kg/cm sq)*; 860°F *(460°C)*; 2 Wahodag turbines; 68 000 hp *(51 MW)*; 2 shafts
Speed, knots: 34. **Range, miles:** 6000 at 13 kts; 920 at 34 kts
Complement: 268 (19 officers)

Missiles: SSM: 4 Aerospatiale MM 38 Exocet (2 twin) launchers ❶; inertial cruise; active radar homing to 42 km *(23 nm)* at 0.9 Mach; warhead 165 kg; sea-skimmer.
Guns: 3 DCN 3.9 in *(100 mm)*/55 Mod 1954 ❷; 80° elevation; 60-80 rounds/minute to 17 km *(9 nm)* anti-surface; 8 km *(4.4 nm)* anti-aircraft; weight of shell 13.5 kg.
8 Breda 40 mm/70 (4 twin) ❸; 85° elevation; 300 rounds/minute to 12.5 km *(6.8 nm)*; weight of shell 0.96 kg.
Torpedoes: 4—21 in *(533 mm)* single tubes ❹.
A/S mortars: 2 Bofors 375 mm 4-barrelled trainable mortars ❺; automatic loading; range 1600 m.
Depth charges: 2 projectors ❻; DC rails.
Mines: Can lay mines.
Countermeasures: Decoys: 2 Breda 105 mm SCLAR; 20 barrels per launcher; Chaff to 5 km *(2.7 nm)*; illuminants to 12 km *(6.6 nm)*.
ESM: WLR-6; radar warning.
Fire control: Signaal M 45 series.
Radars: Air search: Signaal LW 04 ❼; D band; range 219 km *(120 nm)* for 2 m² target.
Air/surface search: Signaal DA 08 ❽; F band; range 204 km *(110 nm)* for 2 m² target.
Surface search: Signaal ZW 01 ❾; I/J band.
Navigation: Kelvin Hughes 14/9; I band.
Fire control: Three Signaal M 45 ❿; I/J band; short range.
Sonars: Krupp Atlas ELAC 1BV; hull-mounted; active search and attack; medium frequency.

Modernisation: Replacement of 100 mm gun by four MM 38 Exocet, 40 mm Breda/Bofors guns and LW 02 radar by LW 04. Two extra A/S torpedo tubes were also added. *Hamburg* completed modernisation mid-1976; *Schleswig-Holstein* February 1977 and *Bayern* November 1977. During refit bridges were re-modelled. There are no plans to fit RAM and further limited modernisation has been shelved. Due to be replaced by the Type 123 class.

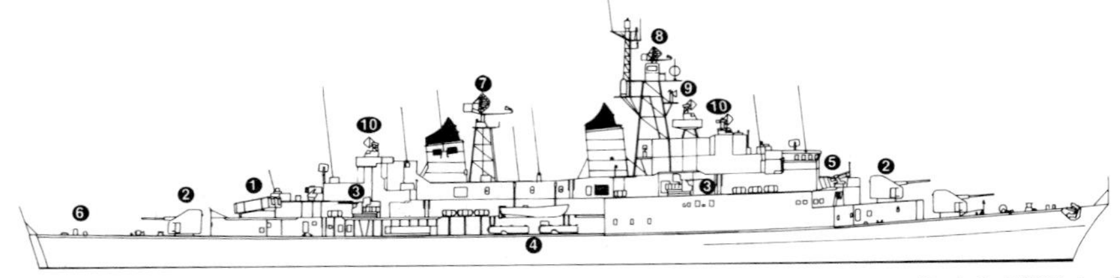

HAMBURG Class *(Scale 1 : 1 200), Ian Sturton*

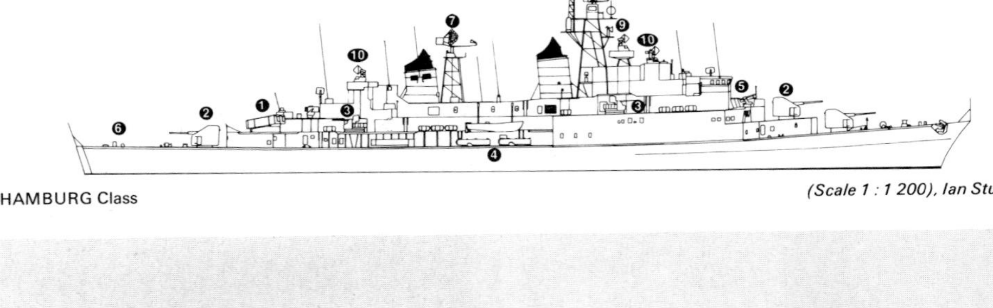

SCHLESWIG-HOLSTEIN *7/1991, Guy Toremans*

FRIGATES

Note: Four Type 124 air defence ships will be needed from 2004 onwards to replace the Lütjens class. Design is likely to be based on the Type 123 with a possible joint venture with the Netherlands.

8 BREMEN CLASS (TYPE 122)

Name	*No*	*Builders*	*Laid down*	*Launched*	*Commissioned*
BREMEN	F 207	Bremer Vulkan	9 July 1979	27 Sep 1979	7 May 1982
NIEDERSACHSEN	F 208	AG Weser/Bremer Vulkan	9 Nov 1979	9 June 1980	15 Oct 1982
RHEINLAND-PFALZ	F 209	Blohm & Voss/Bremer Vulkan	29 Sep 1979	3 Sep 1980	9 May 1983
EMDEN	F 210	Thyssen Nordseewerke, Emden/Bremer Vulkan	23 June 1980	17 Dec 1980	7 Oct 1983
KÖLN	F 211	Blohm & Voss/Bremer Vulkan	16 June 1980	29 May 1981	19 Oct 1984
KARLSRUHE	F 212	Howaldtswerke, Kiel/Bremer Vulkan	10 Mar 1981	8 Jan 1982	19 Apr 1984
AUGSBURG	F 213	Bremer Vulkan	4 Apr 1987	17 Sep 1987	3 Oct 1989
LÜBECK	F 214	Thyssen Nordseewerke, Emden/Bremer Vulkan	1 June 1987	15 Oct 1987	19 Mar 1990

Displacement, tons: 3600 full load
Dimensions, feet (metres): 426.4 × 47.6 × 21.3 *(130 × 14.5 × 6.5)*
Main machinery: CODOG; 2 GE LM 2500 gas turbines; 44 000 hp *(33 MW)* sustained; 2 MTU 20V 956 TB92 diesels; 11 070 hp(m) *(8.14 MW)* sustained; 2 shafts; cp props
Speed, knots: 30; 20 on diesels. **Range, miles:** 4000 at 18 kts
Complement: 207 (aircrew 18)

Missiles: SSM: 8 McDonnell Douglas Harpoon (2 quad) launchers ❶; active radar homing to 130 km *(70 nm)* at 0.9 Mach; warhead 227 kg.
SAM: 16 Raytheon NATO Sea Sparrow; Mk 29 octuple launcher ❷; semi-active radar homing to 14.6 km *(8 nm)* at 2.5 Mach; warhead 39 kg.
2 GDC RAM 21 cell point-defence systems (to be fitted on hangar roof 1993-96) ❸; passive IR/anti-radiation homing to 9.6 km *(5.2 nm)* at 2 Mach; warhead 9.1 kg. Goalkeeper fitted as a contingency in three of the class in 1991.
Guns: 1 OTO Melara 3 in *(76 mm)*/62 Mk 75 ❹; 85° elevation; 85 rounds/minute to 16 km *(8.6 nm)* anti-surface; 12 km *(6.5 nm)* anti-aircraft; weight of shell 6 kg.
Torpedoes: 4—324 mm Mk 32 (2 twin) tubes ❺. 8 Honeywell Mk 46 Mod 1; anti-submarine; active/passive homing to 11 km *(5.9 nm)* at 40 kts; warhead 44 kg.
Countermeasures: Decoys: 4 Loral Hycor SRBOC ❻ 6-barrelled fixed Mk 36; Chaff and IR flares to 4 km *(2.2 nm)*.
SLQ 25 Nixie; towed torpedo decoy. Prairie bubble noise reduction.
ESM/ECM: AEG FL 1800 ❼; radar warning and jammers.
Combat data systems: SATIR action data automation; Link 11; SCOT 1A SATCOM ❽ (in some).
Fire control: Signaal WM 25/STIR.
Radars: Air/surface search: Signaal DA 08 ❾; F band; range 204 km *(110 nm)* for 2 m² target.
Navigation: SMA 3 RM 20; I band; range 73 km *(40 nm)*.
Fire control: Signaal WM 25 ❿; I/J band; range 46 km *(25 nm)*.
Signaal STIR ⓫; I/J/K band; range 140 km *(76 nm)* for 1 m² target.
Sonars: Krupp Atlas DSQS 21 BZ (BO); hull-mounted; active search and attack; medium frequency.

Helicopters: 2 Westland Sea Lynx Mk 88 ⓬.

Programmes: Approval given in early 1976 for first six of this class, a modification of the Netherlands Kortenaer class. Replaced the deleted Fletcher and Köln classes. Equipment ordered February 1986 after order placed 6 December 1985 for last pair. Hulls and some engines are provided in the five building yards. Ships are then towed to the prime contractor Bremer Vulkan where weapon systems and electronics are fitted and trials conducted. The three names for F210-212 were changed from the names of Länder to take the well known town names of the Köln class as they were paid off.
Operational: Form 2nd and 4th Frigate Squadrons. Three containerised SCOT 1A terminals acquired in 1988 and when fitted are mounted on the hangar roof. Dutch Goalkeeper CIWS was installed on the port side of the hangar roof in F 207, 208 and 212 as a short-term contingency in 1991.

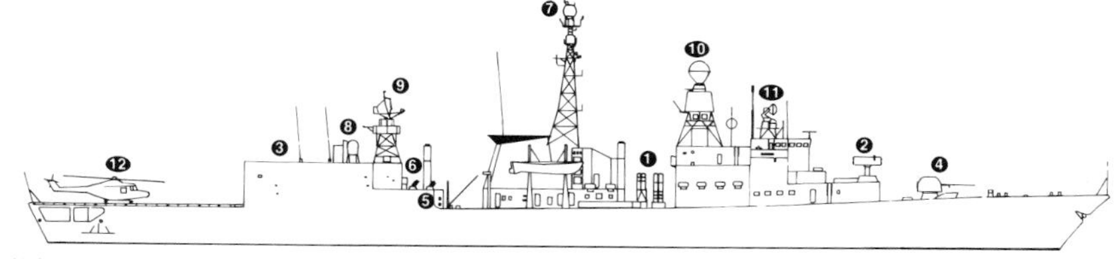

BREMEN Class *(Scale 1 : 1 200), Ian Sturton*

LÜBECK *4/1991, W. Sartori*

KÖLN *11/1991, Harald Carstens*

0 + 4 BRANDENBURG CLASS (TYPE 123)

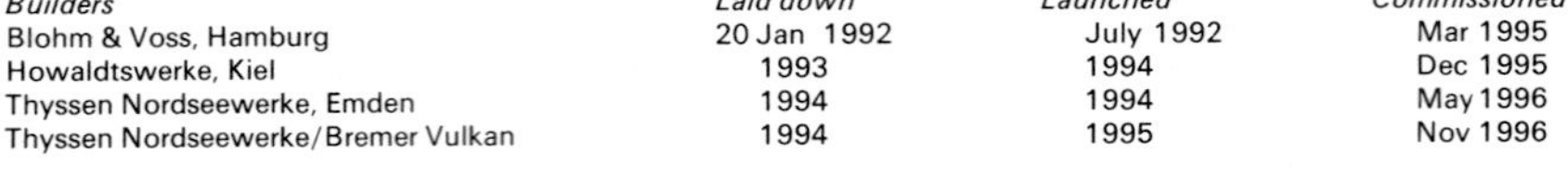

Name	*No*	*Builders*	*Laid down*	*Launched*	*Commissioned*
BRANDENBURG	F 215	Blohm & Voss, Hamburg	20 Jan 1992	July 1992	Mar 1995
SCHLESWIG-HOLSTEIN	F 216	Howaldtswerke, Kiel	1993	1994	Dec 1995
BAYERN	F 217	Thyssen Nordseewerke, Emden	1994	1994	May 1996
MECKLENBURG-VORPOMMERN	F 218	Thyssen Nordseewerke/Bremer Vulkan	1994	1995	Nov 1996

Displacement, tons: 4490 full load
Dimensions, feet (metres): 455.7 oa; 417.7 wl × 54.8 × 14.4 *(138.9; 126.1 × 16.7 × 4.4)*
Main machinery: CODOG; 2 GE LM 2500 gas turbines; 46 000 hp *(34.3 MW)* sustained; 2 MTU 20V 956 TB92 diesels; 11 070 hp(m) *(8.14 MW)* sustained; 2 shafts; cp props
Speed, knots: 29; 18 on diesels. **Range, miles:** 4000 at 18 kts
Complement: 197 plus 22 aircrew

Missiles: SSM: 4 Aerospatiale MM 38 Exocet ❶ (from Type 101A); later ANS.
SAM: Martin Marietta VLS Mk 41 ❷ for 16 NATO Sea Sparrow. 2 RAM 21 cell Mk 49 launchers ❸.
Guns: 1 OTO Melara 76 mm/62 ❹.
Torpedoes: 4—324 mm Mk 32 (2 twin) tubes ❺; anti-submarine. Honeywell Mk 46; anti-submarine.
Countermeasures: Decoys: 2 Breda SCLAR ❻.
ESM/ECM: TST FL 1800S; intercept and jammers.
Combat data systems: SATIR action data automation with Unisys UYK 43 computer; Link 11.
Fire control: Signaal MWCS.
Radars: Air search: Signaal LW 08 ❼; D band.
Air/Surface search ❽: Signaal SMART; 3D; F band.
Fire control: Two Signaal STIR 180 trackers ❾.
Navigation: Two Raypath; I band.
Sonars: Krupp Atlas DSQS 23BZ; hull-mounted; medium frequency.
Towed array (provision only).

Helicopters: 2 Sea Lynx Mk 88 ❿.

Programmes: Four ordered 28 June 1989. Developed by Blohm & Voss whose design was selected in October 1988. To replace Hamburg class. First metal cut 5 February 1991.
Structure: The design is a mixture of MEKO and improved serviceability Type 122 having the same propulsion as the Type 122. Contemporary stealth features. All steel. Fin stabilisers.

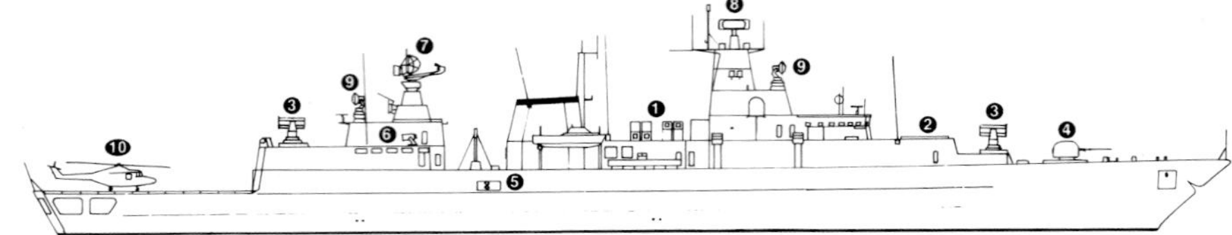

BRANDENBURG *(Scale 1 : 1 200), Ian Sturton*

BRANDENBURG (artist's impression) *1988, Jochen Sachse*

SHIPBORNE AIRCRAFT

Numbers/Type: 19 Westland Sea Lynx Mk 88.
Operational speed: 125 kts *(232 km/h)*.
Service ceiling: 12 500 ft *(3010 m)*.
Range: 320 nm *(593 km)*.
Role/Weapon systems: Shipborne ASW/ASV role in support of coastal defence roles and North/Baltic Seas anti-submarine warfare. Sensors: Ferranti Sea Spray Mk 1 radar, ECM and Bendix AQS-18 dipping sonar. Weapons: ASW; up to 2 × Mk 46 torpedoes or depth charges. ASV; possible update.

SEA LYNX *1991, German Navy*

LAND-BASED MARITIME AIRCRAFT (FRONT LINE)

Note: 13 Mi-8 Hip and 17 Mi-14 Haze retained for SAR and liaison duties until due next major inspection (latest 1994).

HAZE *7/1991, Hartmut Ehlers*

HIP *6/1991, Hartmut Ehlers*

Numbers/Type: 22 Westland Sea King Mk 41 KWS.
Operational speed: 140 kts *(260 km/h)*.
Service ceiling: 10 500 ft *(3200 m)*.
Range: 630 nm *(1165 km)*.
Role/Weapon systems: Role change from primary combat rescue helicopter to ASV started in 1988 with new camouflage appearance and an update programme by MBB with BAe/Ferranti support which completes in 1992. Sensors: Ferranti Sea Spray Mk 3 radar, Link 11, ECM. Weapons: ASW; limited ability with torpedoes and depth charges. ASV; 4 × Sea Skua missiles.

SEA KING *11/1989, Ralf Bendfeldt*

Numbers/Type: 16 Breguet Atlantic 1.
Operational speed: 355 kts *(658 km/h)*.
Service ceiling: 32 800 ft *(10 000 m)*.
Range: 4850 nm *(8990 km)*.
Role/Weapon systems: Long-range/endurance MR tasks carried out in North and Baltic Seas, also Atlantic Ocean; five aircraft also allocated to Elint/SIGINT tasks in Baltic Sea area; to be replaced in the late 1990s. Sensors: Thomson-CSF radar, Loral ESM/ECM, MAD, sonobuoys. Weapons: ASW; 9 × torpedoes (including Mk 46) or mines or depth bombs. ASV; 2 × AS30 missiles.

Numbers/Type: 20 Dornier Do 28D-2.
Operational speed: 156 kts *(290 km/h)*.
Service ceiling: 20 700 ft *(6300 m)*.
Range: 667 nm *(1235 km)*.
Role/Weapon systems: Short-range surveillance tasks flown; SAR and EEZ protection. Two converted for pollution control. Sensors: Weather radar; converted aircraft also have SLAR, IR/UR scanner, microwave radiometer and LLL TV camera. Weapons: Unarmed.

Numbers/Type: 107 Panavia Tornado IDS.
Operational speed: Mach 2.2.
Service ceiling: 80 000 ft *(24 385 m)*.
Range: 1500 nm *(2780 km)*.
Role/Weapon systems: Swing-wing strike and recce; shore-based for fleet air defence and ASV strike primary roles; two wings have been equipped for North and Baltic Sea defence; update with Kormoran 2 and Texas Instruments HARM; 35 are to be transferred to the Air Force. Sensors: Texas Instruments nav/attack system. Weapons: ASV; 4 × Kormoran missiles. Fleet AD; 2 × 27 mm cannon, 4 × AIM-9L Sidewinder.

CORVETTES

Notes: (a) Remainder of Parchim I and Tarantul I classes paid off 31 December 1991. For transfers see *Deletions*.
(b) Sassnitz class transferred to the BGS (Coastguard) in 1991.

3 THETIS CLASS (TYPE 420)

Name	*No*	*Builders*	*Commissioned*
HERMES	P 6053	Rolandwerft, Bremen	16 Dec 1961
TRITON	P 6055	Rolandwerft, Bremen	10 Nov 1962
THESEUS	P 6056	Rolandwerft, Bremen	15 Aug 1963

Displacement, tons: 575 standard; 732 full load
Dimensions, feet (metres): 229.7 × 26.9 × 8.6 *(70 × 8.2 × 2.7)*
Main machinery: 2 MAN V84V diesels; 6800 hp(m) *(5 MW)*; 2 shafts
Speed, knots: 19.5. **Range, miles:** 2760 at 15 kts
Complement: 64 (4 officers)

Guns: 2 Breda 40 mm/70 (twin); 85° elevation; 300 rounds/minute to 12.5 km *(6.7 nm)*; weight of shell 0.96 kg.
Torpedoes: 4—324 mm single tubes. 4 Honeywell Mk 46 Mod 1; active/passive homing to 11 km *(5.9 nm)* at 40 kts; warhead 44 kg.
A/S mortars: 1 Bofors 375 mm 4-barrelled trainable launcher; automatic loading; range 1600 m; 20 rockets.
Depth charges: 2 rails.
Fire control: Signaal Mk 9 TFCS.
Radars: Surface search: Thomson-CSF TRS 3001; E/F band.
Navigation: Kelvin Hughes 14/9; I band.
Sonars: Krupp Atlas ELAC 1BV; hull-mounted; active search and attack; high frequency.

Structure: Torpedo tubes have liners effectively reducing their diameter to 324 mm.
Sales: Two of the class transferred to Greece 6 September 1991. Remainder are planned to follow in the second half of 1992.

HERMES *8/1991, Foto Flite*

LIGHT FORCES

Note: Vessels in this section now have an 'S' number as part of their name as well as a 'P' pennant number. The 'S' number is shown in the Pennant List at the front of this country.

10 GEPARD CLASS (TYPE 143 A) (FAST ATTACK CRAFT—MISSILE)

Name	*No*	*Builders*	*Commissioned*
GEPARD	P 6121	AEG/Lürssen	13 Dec 1982
PUMA	P 6122	AEG/Lürssen	24 Feb 1983
HERMELIN	P 6123	AEG/Kröger	5 May 1983
NERZ	P 6124	AEG/Lürssen	14 July 1983
ZOBEL	P 6125	AEG/Kröger	25 Sep 1983
FRETTCHEN	P 6126	AEG/Lürssen	15 Dec 1983
DACHS	P 6127	AEG/Kröger	22 Mar 1984
OZELOT	P 6128	AEG/Lürssen	3 May 1984
WIESEL	P 6129	AEG/Lürssen	12 July 1984
HYÄNE	P 6130	AEG/Lürssen	13 Nov 1984

Displacement, tons: 391 full load
Dimensions, feet (metres): 190 × 25.6 × 8.5 *(57.6 × 7.8 × 2.6)*
Main machinery: 4 MTU MA16V 956 SB80 diesels; 13 200 hp(m) *(9.7 MW)* sustained; 4 shafts
Speed, knots: 40. **Range, miles:** 2600 at 16 kts; 600 at 33 kts
Complement: 34 (4 officers)

Missiles: SSM: 4 Aerospatiale MM 38 Exocet; inertial cruise; active radar homing to 42 km *(23 nm)* at 0.9 Mach; warhead 165 kg; sea-skimmer. To be replaced by ANS in due course.
SAM: GDC RAM 21 cell point defence system (to be fitted behind Exocet 1992-95); passive IR/anti-radiation homing to 9.6 km *(5.2 nm)* at 2 Mach; warhead 9.1 kg.
Guns: 1 OTO Melara 3 in *(76 mm)*/62 compact; 85° elevation; 85 rounds/minute to 16 km *(8.6 nm)* anti-surface; 12 km *(6.5 nm)* anti-aircraft; weight of shell 6 kg.
Mines: Can lay mines.
Countermeasures: Decoys: Buck-Wegmann Hot Dog/Silver Dog; IR/Chaff dispenser.
ESM/ECM: AEG FL 1800s; radar intercept and jammer.
Combat data systems: AEG AGIS action data automation; Link 11.
Radars: Surface search/fire control: Signaal WM 27; I/J band; range 46 km *(25 nm)*.
Navigation: SMA 3 RM 20; I band; range 73 km *(40 nm)*.

Programmes: Ordered mid-1978 from AEG-Telefunken with sub-contracting to Lürssen (P 6121, 6122, 6124-6128) and Kröger (P 6123, 6129, 6130). First of class laid down 11 July 1979.
Structure: Wooden hulls on aluminium frames.
Operational: Form 7th Squadron based at Kiel on tender *Elbe*.

NERZ (and 3 others) *6/1991, Antonio Moreno*

OZELOT *8/1991, Maritime Photographic*

10 ALBATROS CLASS (TYPE 143/143B) (FAST ATTACK CRAFT—MISSILE)

Name	No	Builders	Commissioned
ALBATROS	P 6111	Lürssen, Vegesack	1 Nov 1976
FALKE	P 6112	Lürssen, Vegesack	13 Apr 1976
GEIER	P 6113	Lürssen, Vegesack	2 June 1976
BUSSARD	P 6114	Lürssen, Vegesack	14 Aug 1976
SPERBER	P 6115	Kröger, Rendsburg	27 Sep 1976
GREIF	P 6116	Lürssen, Vegesack	25 Nov 1976
KONDOR	P 6117	Kröger, Rendsburg	17 Dec 1976
SEEADLER	P 6118	Lürssen, Vegesack	28 Mar 1977
HABICHT	P 6119	Kröger, Rendsburg	23 Dec 1977
KORMORAN	P 6120	Lürssen, Vegesack	29 July 1977

Displacement, tons: 398 full load
Dimensions, feet (metres): 189 × 25.6 × 8.5 *(57.6 × 7.8 × 2.6)*
Main machinery: 4 MTU 16V956 TB91 diesels; 17 700 hp(m) *(13 MW)* sustained; 4 shafts
Speed, knots: 40. **Range, miles:** 1300 at 30 kts
Complement: 40 (4 officers)

Missiles: SSM: 4 Aerospatiale MM 38 Exocet (2 twin) launchers; inertial cruise; active radar homing to 42 km *(23 nm)* at 0.9 Mach; warhead 165 kg; sea-skimmer.
Guns: 2 OTO Melara 3 in *(76 mm)*/62 compact; 85° elevation; 85 rounds/minute to 16 km *(8.6 nm)* anti-surface; 12 km *(6.5 nm)* anti-aircraft; weight of shell 6 kg.
Torpedoes: 2—21 in *(533 mm)* aft tubes. AEG Seeal; wire-guided; active homing to 13 km *(7 nm)* at 35 kts; passive homing to 28 km *(15 nm)* at 23 kts; warhead 260 kg.
Countermeasures: Decoys: Buck-Wegmann Hot Dog/Silver Dog; IR/Chaff dispenser.
ESM/ECM: Thomson-CSF DR 2000 (radar warning) or Racal Octopus (Cutlass intercept, Scorpion jammer).
Combat data systems: Fully automatic data processing command and fire control system; Link 11.
Fire control: ORG7/3 optronics GFCS.
Radars: Surface search/fire control: Signaal WM 27; I/J band; range 46 km *(25 nm)*.
Navigation: SMA 3 RM 20; I band; range 73 km *(40 nm)*.

Programmes: AEG-Telefunken main contractor with construction by sub-contractors. Ordered in 1972.
Modernisation: *Habicht* started trials with RAM-ASDM mounting in 1983. Plans for major modernisation have been reduced to fitting a new EW system, Racal Octopus, starting in 1992. Then to be classified Type 143B.
Structure: Wooden hulled craft.
Operational: Form 2nd Squadron at Olpenitz. Tender *Donau*.

HABICHT (with GD RAM-ASDM SAM aft) *5/1983, Michael D. J. Lennon*

GREIF *10/1991, van Ginderen Collection*

GEIER *6/1990, van Ginderen Collection*

20 TIGER CLASS (TYPE 148) (FAST ATTACK CRAFT—MISSILE)

Name	No	Builders	Commissioned
TIGER	P 6141	CMN, Cherbourg	30 Oct 1972
ILTIS	P 6142	CMN, Cherbourg	8 Jan 1973
LUCHS	P 6143	CMN, Cherbourg	9 Apr 1973
MARDER	P 6144	CMN, Cherbourg	14 June 1973
LEOPARD	P 6145	CMN, Cherbourg	21 Aug 1973
FUCHS	P 6146	CMN, Cherbourg	17 Oct 1973
JAGUAR	P 6147	CMN, Cherbourg	13 Nov 1973
LÖWE	P 6148	CMN, Cherbourg	9 Jan 1974
WOLF	P 6149	CMN, Cherbourg	26 Feb 1974
PANTHER	P 6150	CMN, Cherbourg	27 Mar 1974
HÄHER	P 6151	CMN, Cherbourg	12 June 1974
STORCH	P 6152	CMN, Cherbourg	17 July 1974
PELIKAN	P 6153	CMN, Cherbourg	24 Sep 1974
ELSTER	P 6154	CMN, Cherbourg	14 Nov 1974
ALK	P 6155	CMN, Cherbourg	7 Jan 1975
DOMMEL	P 6156	CMN, Cherbourg	12 Feb 1975
WEIHE	P 6157	CMN, Cherbourg	3 Apr 1975
PINGUIN	P 6158	CMN, Cherbourg	22 May 1975
REIHER	P 6159	CMN, Cherbourg	24 June 1975
KRANICH	P 6160	CMN, Cherbourg	6 Aug 1975

Displacement, tons: 234 standard; 265 full load
Dimensions, feet (metres): 154.2 × 23 × 8.9 *(47 × 7 × 2.7)*
Main machinery: 4 MTU MD 16V 538 TB90 diesels; 12 000 hp(m) *(8.82 MW)* sustained; 4 shaft
Speed, knots: 36. **Range, miles:** 570 at 30 kts; 1600 at 15 kts
Complement: 30 (4 officers)

Missiles: SSM: 4 Aerospatiale MM 38 Exocet (2 twin) launchers; inertial cruise; active radar homin to 42 km *(23 nm)* at 0.9 Mach; warhead 165 kg; sea-skimmer.
Guns: 1 OTO Melara 3 in *(76 mm)*/62 compact; 85° elevation; 85 rounds/minute to 16 km *(8.6 nm* anti-surface; 12 km *(6.5 nm)* anti-aircraft; weight of shell 6 kg.
1 Bofors 40 mm/70; 80° elevation; 330 rounds/minute to 12 km *(6.5 nm)* anti-surface; 4 kr *(2.2 nm)* anti-aircraft; weight of shell 0.96 kg; fitted with GRP dome (1984) (see *Modernisation*)
Mines: Laying capability.
Countermeasures: Decoys: Wolke Chaff launcher.
ESM/ECM: Racal Octopus (Cutlass B1 radar intercept and Scorpion jammer).
Combat data systems: PALIS and Link 11.
Fire control: CSEE Panda optical director. Thomson-CSF Vega PCET system, controlling missile and guns.
Radars: Air/surface search: Thomson-CSF Triton; G band; range 33 km *(18 nm)* for 2 m² target.
Navigation: SMA 3 RM 20; I band; range 73 km *(40 nm)*.
Fire control: Thomson-CSF Castor; I/J band.

Programmes: Ordered in December 1970 from DTCN as main contractors. Eight hulls contracted t Lürssen (P 6146, 6148, 6150, 6152, 6154, 6156, 6158, 6160) but all fitted out in France.
Modernisation: New Triton search and Castor fire control radars fitted to the whole class; also Rac EW systems as part of a mid-life update. *Dommel* had the 40 mm/70 gun replaced by a Maus Vierling Taifun CIWS for trials in September 1991. The gun has four 27 mm barrels and a combine rate of fire of 6800 rounds/minute.
Structure: Steel-hulled craft. Similar to Combattante II craft.
Operational: 3rd Sqn: P 6141-6150 based at Flensburg. May pay off to reserve by 1994. Tend *Rhein*.
5th Sqn: P 6151-6160 based at Olpenitz. Tender *Main*.

LUCHS *7/1991, Hartmut Ehle*

AMPHIBIOUS FORCES

Note: As with Light Forces, most LCMs now have an LCM number as part of their name. Thes numbers are in the Pennant List. The exceptions are LCMs 12-20 which have no L pennant numbe

10 TYPE 520 (LCUs)

FLUNDER L 760 **KARPFEN** L 761 **LACHS** L 762 **PLOTZE** L 763 **STÖR** L 766 **TÜMMLER** L 767 **WELS** L 768 **ZANDER** L 769 **BUTT** L 788 **INGER** L 795

Displacement, tons: 400 full load
Dimensions, feet (metres): 131.2 × 28.9 × 7.2 *(40 × 8.8 × 2.2)*
Main machinery: 2 MWM 12-cyl diesels; 1020 hp(m) *(750 kW)*; 2 shafts
Speed, knots: 12
Complement: 17
Military lift: 160 tons
Guns: 2 Oerlikon 20 mm; 55° elevation; 800 rounds/minute to 2 km; weight of shell 0.24 kg.

Comment: Similar to the US LCU (Landing Craft Utility) type. Provided with bow and stern ram Built by Howaldtswerke, Hamburg, 1965-66. *Inger* employed for seamanship training at Borku Two sold to Greece in November 1989. All other units at Kiel - Stickenhörn. Five more to pay off the end of 1992.

INGER *9/1991, Hartmut Ehl*

17 TYPE 521 (LCMs)

SPROTTE LCM 12
SARDINE LCM 13
SARDELLE LCM 14
HERING LCM 15
ORFE LCM 16
MARÄNE LCM 17
SAIBLING LCM 18
STINT LCM 19
AESCHE LCM 20
HUMMER L 780
KRILL L 781
KRABBE L 782
AUSTER L 783
MUSCHEL L 784
KORALLE L 785
GARNELE L 786 (ex-A 1406)
LANGUSTE L 787 (ex-A 1410)

Displacement, tons: 168 full load
Dimensions, feet (metres): 77.4 × 20.9 × 4.9 *(23.6 × 6.4 × 1.5)*
Main machinery: 2 MWM 8-cyl diesels; 685 hp(m) *(503 kW)*; 2 shafts
Speed, knots: 10.5
Complement: 7
Military lift: 60 tons or 50 troops

Comment: Built by Rheinwerft, Walsam (first two of class by Blohm & Voss). Completed in 1964-67 and later placed in reserve. LCM 21-28 recommissioned 4 September 1980. The design is similar to US LCM 8—LCM 12-20 have a derrick and can be used for carrying 18 torpedoes. All craft were allocated names in August 1986 and most now have navigational radar. Those with L pennant numbers have their own crews; others are rated as 'floating equipment' without crews and have LCM numbers only on the bows in small characters. LCM 1-11 sold to Greece in April 1991. Deployments: Kiel; LCM 12, LCM 16, L 780-L 785. Flensburg; LCM 13. Wilhelmshaven; LCM 1-11 (reserve), LCM 14. Borkum; LCM 15, LCM 17. Olpenitz; LCM 18. Neustadt; LCM 19. Eckernförde; LCM 20. Coastal Services School, Grossenbrode; L 786-L 787.

GARNELE *7/1991, Hartmut Ehlers*

MINE WARFARE FORCES

Note: Squadrons

Minesweeper Squadron 1 (Flensburg) (deletion 1993)	3 Schütze class *Steigerwald* (mine transport)
Minesweeper Squadron 2 (forms in 1993)	10 Frankenthal class
Minesweeper Squadron 3 (Kiel) (deletion 1992)	4 Ariadne class
Minesweeper Squadron 4 (Wilhelmshaven)	9 Lindau class
Minesweeper Squadron 5 (Olpenitz)	10 Hameln class
Minesweeper Squadron 6 (Wilhelmshaven) (deletion 1996)	6 Lindau class 18 Seehund class
Minesweeper Squadron 7 (Neustadt)	10 Frauenlob class
Clearance Diver Company (Eckernförde)	*Stier* (diver support ship)

3 SCHÜTZE CLASS (TYPE 340-341) (MINESWEEPERS—COASTAL)

Name	*No*	*Builders*	*Commissioned*
SPICA	M 1059	Abeking & Rasmussen	1961
SCHÜTZE	M 1062	Abeking & Rasmussen	1959
WAAGE	M 1063	Abeking & Rasmussen	1962

Displacement, tons: 305 full load
Dimensions, feet (metres): 155.5 × 22.9 × 7.2 *(47.4 × 7 × 2.2)*
Main machinery: 2 Maybach diesels; 4500 hp(m) *(3.31 MW)*; 2 shafts
Speed, knots: 24. **Range, miles:** 2000 at 13 kts
Complement: 36 (4 officers)

Guns: Bofors 40 mm/70; 90° elevation; 330 rounds/minute to 12 km *(5.6 nm)* anti-surface; 4 km *(2.2 nm)* anti-aircraft; weight of shell 0.96 kg.
Radars: Navigation: Krupp Atlas TRS N; I band.

Programmes: Thirty originally built between 1959 and 1964. The design is a development of the R boats of the Second World War. Formerly classified as inshore minesweepers, but re-rated as fast minesweepers in 1966. *Capella, Pluto, Neptun, Krebs, Orion, Steinbock* and *Uranus* transferred to Deutscher Marinebund. The class is being replaced by the Hameln class and the last three are to be deleted in late 1992.
Operational: *Stier* is clearance diver support vessel. *Widder* is a training hulk at Borkum.

WAAGE *6/1991, Stefan Terzibaschitsch*

15 LINDAU CLASS (TYPE 331, MINEHUNTERS (9); TYPE 351, TROIKA (6)) (MINESWEEPERS—COASTAL and MINEHUNTERS)

Name	*No*	*Builders*	*Commissioned*
GÖTTINGEN	M 1070	Burmester, Bremen	31 May 1958
KOBLENZ	M 1071	Burmester, Bremen	8 July 1958
LINDAU	M 1072	Burmester, Bremen	24 Apr 1958
SCHLESWIG*	M 1073	Burmester, Bremen	30 Oct 1958
TÜBINGEN	M 1074	Burmester, Bremen	25 Sep 1958
WETZLAR	M 1075	Burmester, Bremen	20 Aug 1958
PADERBORN*	M 1076	Burmester, Bremen	16 Dec 1958
WEILHEIM	M 1077	Burmester, Bremen	28 Jan 1959
CUXHAVEN	M 1078	Burmester, Bremen	11 Mar 1959
DÜREN*	M 1079	Burmester, Bremen	22 Apr 1959
MARBURG	M 1080	Burmester, Bremen	11 June 1959
KONSTANZ*	M 1081	Burmester, Bremen	23 July 1959
WOLFSBURG*	M 1082	Burmester, Bremen	8 Oct 1959
ULM*	M 1083	Burmester, Bremen	7 Nov 1959
MINDEN	M 1085	Burmester, Bremen	22 Jan 1960

* Troika control ships

Displacement, tons: 463 full load (Hunters); 465 full load (Troika)
Dimensions, feet (metres): 154.5 × 27.2 × 9.8 (9.2 Troika) *(47.1 × 8.3 × 3) (2.8)*
Main machinery: 2 Maybach MTU diesels; 4000 hp(m) *(2.94 MW)*; 2 shafts (Hunters)
2 MTU MD 16V 538 TB90 diesels; 5000 hp(m) *(3.68 MW)*; 2 shafts
Speed, knots: 16.5. **Range, miles:** 850 at 16.5 kts
Complement: 43 (5 officers) (Hunters); 44 (4 officers) (Troika)

Guns: 1 Bofors 40 mm/70; 90° elevation; 330 rounds/minute to 12 km *(6.5 nm)* anti-surface; 4 km *(2.2 nm)* anti-aircraft; weight of shell 0.96 kg.
Radars: Navigation: Kelvin Hughes 14/9; I band or Krupp Atlas TRS N. Being replaced by Raytheon.
Sonars: Krupp Atlas DSQS 11; minehunting; high frequency or Plessey 193 m; minehunting; high frequency (100/300 kHz).

Programmes: *Lindau*, first West German-built vessel for the Navy since the Second World War, launched on 16 February 1957.
Modernisation: Minehunter conversions: (Type 331) Completion dates: *Lindau* 10 Feb 1978, *Tübingen* 20 Mar 1978, *Minden* 31 May 1978, *Koblenz* 21 June 1978, *Wetzlar* 6 Oct 1978, *Weilheim* 17 Nov 1978, *Göttingen* 19 June 1978, *Cuxhaven* 6 June 1979, *Marburg* 28 June 1979. This conversion involved the fitting of Plessey 193M sonar and ECA/PAP 105 disposal vehicles. Prime contractor was VFW-Fokker.
Troika conversions: (Type 351) The six ships *(Düren, Konstanz, Paderborn, Ulm, Schleswig* and *Wolfsburg)* not being converted to minehunters but converted as guidance ships for Troika. Each guide three of these unmanned minesweeping vehicles as well as maintaining their moored minesweeping capabilities. *Schleswig* completed 27 May 1981, *Paderborn* 17 September 1981, *Ulm* 17 November 1981, *Wolfsburg* 4 March 1982, *Konstanz* 24 May 1982 and *Düren* 7 November 1983. *Göttingen, Koblenz, Lindau, Schleswig, Tübingen* and *Wetzlar* were modified with lower bridges in 1958-59. All were lengthened by 6.8 ft *(2.07 m)* in 1960-64.
Structure: The hull is of wooden construction, laminated with plastic glue. The engines are of non-magnetic materials.

GÖTTINGEN (Hunter) *8/1990, Maritime Photographic*

DÜREN *6/1991, Hartmut Ehlers*

WEILHEIM (Hunter) *1/1992, van Ginderen Collection*

18 TROIKA (MINESWEEPERS—DRONES)

SEEHUND 1-18

Displacement, tons: 99
Dimensions, feet (metres): 88.5 × 15 × 4.5 *(26.9 × 4.6 × 1.4)*
Main machinery: 1 Deutz MWM D602 diesel; 446 hp(m) *(328 kW)*; 1 shaft
Speed, knots: 10. **Range, miles:** 520 at 9 kts
Complement: 3 (passage crew)

Comment: Built by MaK, Kiel and Blohm & Voss, Hamburg between August 1980 and May 1982. Commissioned in groups of three with the converted parent vessels. Remote control using magnetic and acoustic sweeping gear.

SEEHUND 4 *10/1990, G. Toremans*

1 KONDOR II CLASS (MINESWEEPER—COASTAL)

SÖMMERDA M 2670 (ex-311)

Displacement, tons: 414 standard
Dimensions, feet (metres): 186 × 24.6 × 7.9 *(56.7 × 7.5 × 2.4)*
Main machinery: 2 Type 40D diesels; 5000 hp(m) *(3.68 MW)*; 2 shafts; cp props
Speed, knots: 21
Complement: 40
Guns: 6—25 mm (3 twin) automatic (4—25 mm (2 twin) in some); 85° elevation; 270 rounds/minute to 3 km *(1.6 nm)*; weight of shell 0.34 kg.
Mines: 2 rails.
Radars: Navigation: TSR 333; I band.
Sonars: Probably fitted with high frequency active search for mine detection.

Comment: Ex-GDR built by Peenewerft, Wolgast in the 1970s. The remainder paid off in 1991 but *Sömmerda* has been retained for trials at Eckernförde. Four of the class sold to Uruguay in October 1991.

SÖMMERDA *5/1991, Hartmut Ehlers*

4 ARIADNE CLASS (TYPE 393) (MINESWEEPERS—INSHORE)

Name	*No*	*Builders*	*Commissioned*
FREYA	M 2651	Krögerwerft, Rendsburg	6 Jan 1962
HERTHA	M 2653	Krögerwerft, Rendsburg	7 June 1962
NYMPHE	M 2654	Krögerwerft, Rendsburg	8 May 1963
NIXE	M 2655	Krögerwerft, Rendsburg	29 June 1963

Displacement, tons: 252 full load
Dimensions, feet (metres): 124.6 × 25.3 × 7.2 *(38 × 7.7 × 2.2)*
Main machinery: 2 MTU MB 12V 439 diesels; 2200 hp(m) *(1.62 MW)* sustained; 2 shafts
Speed, knots: 14. **Range, miles:** 740 at 14 kts
Complement: 25 (2 officers)
Guns: 1 Bofors 40 mm/70; 90° elevation; 330 rounds/minute to 12 km *(6.5 nm)* anti-surface; 4 km *(2.2 nm)* anti-aircraft; weight of shell 0.96 kg.
Mines: Laying capability.
Radars: Navigation: I band.

Comment: Formerly classified as patrol boats but re-rated as inshore minesweepers in 1966. These last four are to be paid off in mid-1992.

FREYA *11/1991, Hartmut Ehlers*

10 FRAUENLOB CLASS (TYPE 394) (MINESWEEPERS—INSHORE)

Name	*No*	*Builders*	*Commissioned*
FRAUENLOB	M 2658	Krögerwerft, Rendsburg	27 Sep 1966
NAUTILUS	M 2659	Krögerwerft, Rendsburg	26 Oct 1966
GEFION	M 2660	Krögerwerft, Rendsberg	17 Feb 1967
MEDUSA	M 2661	Krögerwerft, Rendsburg	17 Feb 1967
UNDINE	M 2662	Krögerwerft, Rendsburg	20 Mar 1967
MINERVA	M 2663	Krögerwerft, Rendsburg	16 June 1967
DIANA	M 2664	Krögerwerft, Rendsburg	21 Sep 1967
LORELEY	M 2665	Krögerwerft, Rendsburg	29 Mar 1968
ATLANTIS	M 2666	Krögerwerft, Rendsburg	29 Mar 1968
ACHERON	M 2667	Krögerwerft, Rendsburg	10 Feb 1969

Displacement, tons: 246 full load
Dimensions, feet (metres): 124.6 × 26.9 × 6.6 *(38 × 8.2 × 2)*
Main machinery: 2 MTU MB 12V 493 diesels; 2200 hp(m) *(1.62 MW)* sustained; 2 shafts
Speed, knots: 12+. **Range, miles:** 700 at 14 kts
Complement: 25 (2 officers)

Guns: 1 Bofors 40 mm/70; 90° elevation; 330 rounds/minute to 12 km *(6.5 nm)* anti-surface; 4 km *(2.2 nm)* anti-aircraft; weight of shell 0.96 kg.
Mines: Laying capability.
Radars: Navigation: I band.

Programmes: Launched in 1965-67. Originally designed coast guard boats with W numbers. Rated as inshore minesweepers in 1968 with the M numbers. All subsequently allocated Y numbers and later re-allocated M numbers.
Operational: 7th MCM Squadron.

NAUTILUS *1991, Horst Dehnst*

0 + 10 FRANKENTHAL CLASS (TYPE 332) (MINEHUNTERS—COASTAL)

Name	*No*	*Builders*	*Commissioned*
FRANKENTHAL	M 1066	Lürssenwerft	Dec 1992
WEIDEN	M 1060	Abeking & Rasmussen	Mar 1993
ROTTWEIL	M 1061	Krögerwerft	July 1993
BAD BEVENSEN	M 1063	Lürssenwerft	Dec 1993
BAD RAPPENAU	M 1067	Abeking & Rasmussen	Apr 1994
GRÖMITZ	M 1064	Krögerwerft	Aug 1994
DATTELN	M 1068	Lürssenwerft	Dec 1994
DILLINGEN	M 1065	Abeking & Rasmussen	Apr 1995
HOMBURG	M 1069	Krögerwerft	Aug 1995
SULZBACH-ROSENBERG	M 1062	Lürssenwerft	Dec 1995

Displacement, tons: 650 full load
Dimensions, feet (metres): 178.8 × 30.2 × 8.5 *(54.5 × 9.2 × 2.6)*
Main machinery: 2 MTU 16V 396 TB 84 diesels; 4200 hp(m) *(3.09 MW)* sustained; 2 shafts; cp props. 1 motor (minehunting)
Speed, knots: 18
Complement: 40 (5 officers)

Missiles: SAM: 2 Stinger quad launchers.
Guns: 1 Bofors 40 mm/70; 90° elevation; 330 rounds/minute to 12 km *(6.5 nm)* anti-surface; 4 km *(2.2 nm)* anti-aircraft; weight of shell 0.96 kg.
Radars: Navigation: Raytheon; I band.
Sonars: Krupp Atlas DSQS-11M; hull-mounted; high frequency.

Programmes: Ordered in September 1988 with MBB as main contractor. First of class laid down at Lürssen 6 December 1989 and launched January 1992.
Structure: Same hull, similar superstructure and high standardisation as Type 343. Built of amagnetic steel. Two MBB-Pinguin-B3 drones with sonar and TV cameras but not Troika control and minelaying capabilities. Fitted with Krupp Atlas MWS 80-4 minehunting control system.
Operational: To form 2nd Minesweeper Squadron.

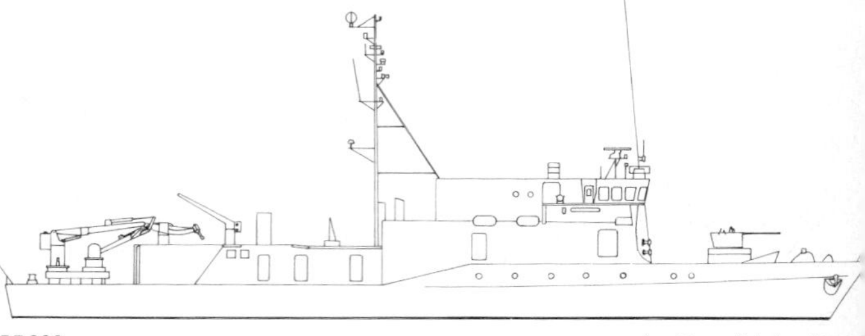

TYPE 332 *(not to scale), Ian Sturton*

10 HAMELN CLASS (TYPE 343) (MINESWEEPERS—COASTAL)

Name	*No*	*Builders*	*Launched*	*Commissioned*
HAMELN	M 1092	Lürssenwerft	15 Mar 1988	29 June 1989
ÜBERHERRN	M 1095	Abeking & Rasmussen	30 Aug 1988	19 Sep 1989
LABOE	M 1097	Krögerwerft	13 Sep 1988	7 Dec 1989
PEGNITZ	M 1090	Lürssenwerft	14 Mar 1989	8 Mar 1990
KULMBACH	M 1091	Abeking & Rasmussen	20 June 1989	23 May 1990
SIEGBURG	M 1098	Krögerwerft	18 Apr 1989	26 July 1990
ENSDORF	M 1094	Lürssenwerft	14 Dec 1989	14 Oct 1990
PASSAU	M 1096	Abeking & Rasmussen	13 Mar 1990	18 Dec 1990
HERTEN	M 1099	Krögerwerft	21 Dec 1989	26 Mar 1991
AUERBACH	M 1093	Lürssenwerft	23 Aug 1990	7 May 1991

Displacement, tons: 635 full load
Dimensions, feet (metres): 178.5 × 30.2 × 8.2 *(54.4 × 9.2 × 2.5)*
Main machinery: 2 MTU 16V 538 TB 91 diesels; 6120 hp(m) *(4.5 MW)* sustained; 2 shafts; cp props
Speed, knots: 18
Complement: 37 (4 officers)

Missiles: SAM: 2 Stinger quad launchers may be added.
Guns: 2 Bofors 40 mm/70; 90° elevation; 330 rounds/minute to 12 km *(6.5 nm)* anti-surface; 4 km *(2.2 nm)* anti-aircraft; weight of shell 0.96 kg.
Mines: 60.
Countermeasures: Decoys: 2 Silver Dog Chaff rocket launchers.
ESM: Thomson-CSF DR 2000; radar warning.
Radars: Surface Search/fire control: Signaal WM 20/2; I/J band; range 46 km *(25 nm)*.
Navigation: Raytheon SPS 64; I band.
Sonars: Krupp Atlas DSQS-11M; hull-mounted; high frequency (being fitted).

Programmes: On 3 January 1985 an MBB headed consortium (ARGE SM-343) was awarded the order. The German designation of 'Schnelles Minenkampfboot' was changed in 1989 to 'Minensuchboot'.
Structure: Ships built of amagnetic steel adapted from submarine construction. Signaal M 20 System removed from the deleted Zobel class fast attack craft. PALIS active link. M 1095, 1091 and 1097 fitted with sonars by early 1992; the remainder to be back fitted. The MWS 80 minehunting control system may also be fitted in due course.
Operational: 5th MCM squadron at Olpenitz. Primary tasks are minesweeping and Troika control. Replacing the Schütze class.

PASSAU — *9/1991, Harald Carstens*

1 TRIALS SHIP (TYPE 740) (Ex-MINESWEEPER)

Name	*No*	*Builders*	*Commissioned*
HOLNIS	A 1400 (ex-A 836)	Abeking & Rasmussen	31 Mar 1966

Displacement, tons: 150 standard; 180 full load
Dimensions, feet (metres): 116.8 × 24.3 × 6.9 *(35.6 × 7.4 × 2.1)*
Main machinery: 2 MTU MB 12V 493 diesels; 2200 hp(m) *(1.62 MW)* sustained; 2 shafts
Speed, knots: 14.5
Complement: 21

Comment: Now serving for trials and evaluation. *Holnis* was launched on 22 May 1965 as the prototype of a new design projected as a class of 20 such vessels but she is the only unit of this type, the other 19 boats having been cancelled. Hull number changed from M 2651 to Y 836 in 1970, to A 836 in 1985 and to A 1400 in 1987.

HOLNIS — *6/1989, Hartmut Ehlers*

1 SCHÜTZE CLASS (TYPE 732) (DIVER—SUPPORT SHIP)

Name	*No*	*Builders*	*Commissioned*
STIER	M 1053 (ex-Y 849)	Abeking & Rasmussen	1961

Comment: Details as for Schütze class with deckhouse and recompression chamber added. Original pennant number M 1061. Operates clearance divers.

STIER — *4/1989, Hartmut Ehlers*

1 SACHSENWALD CLASS (TYPE 762) (MINE TRANSPORT)

Name	*No*	*Builders*	*Commissioned*
STEIGERWALD	A 1438	Blohm & Voss, Hamburg	20 Aug 1969

Displacement, tons: 3380 full load
Dimensions, feet (metres): 363.8 × 45.6 × 12.5 *(110.9 × 13.9 × 3.8)*
Main machinery: 2 Maybach MD 874 diesels; 5600 hp(m) *(4.1 MW)*; 2 shafts
Speed, knots: 17.8. **Range, miles:** 3500 at 14 kts
Complement: 65
Guns: 4 Bofors 40 mm/70 (2 twin); 80° elevation; 300 rounds/minute to 12 km *(6.5 nm)* anti-surface; 4 km *(2.2 nm)* anti-aircraft; weight of shell 0.96 kg.
Mines: Laying capacity.

Comment: Built as a mine transport. Mine ports in the stern and can be used as a minelayer. Part of 1st MCM squadron.

STEIGERWALD — *1/1991, MoD Bonn*

SERVICE FORCES

Notes: (a) Four KSV 90 combat support ships (Type 702) are projected for completion not before 2003. Of 15 000 tons for underway replenishment of fuel, ammunition and solids. Will carry helicopters for VERTREP.
(b) The six ex-GDR Darss class were sold in 1991 to a Norwegian company.

4 RHEIN CLASS (TYPE 401) (TENDERS)

Name	*No*	*Builders*	*Commissioned*
RHEIN	A 58	Schliekerwerft, Hamburg	6 Nov 1961
ELBE	A 61	Schliekerwerft, Hamburg	17 Apr 1962
MAIN	A 63	Lindenau, Kiel	29 June 1963
DONAU	A 69	Schlichting, Travemünde	23 May 1964

Displacement, tons: 2940 full load
Dimensions, feet (metres): 322.1 × 38.8 × 14.4/19.7 *(98.2 × 11.8 × 4.4/6)*
Main machinery: 6 Maybach diesels; 14 400 hp(m) *(10.58 MW)*; 2 shafts
Speed, knots: 20.5. **Range, miles:** 1625 at 15 kts
Complement: 153; 163 *(Elbe)*

Guns: 2 DCN 3.9 in *(100 mm)*; 80° elevation; 60-80 rounds/minute to 17 km *(9.2 nm)* anti-surface; 8 km *(4.4 nm)* anti-aircraft; weight of shell 13.5 kg.
2 or 4 Bofors 40 mm/70 (2 singles or 2 twin); 90° elevation; 300 rounds/minute to 12 km *(6.5 nm)* anti-surface; 4 km *(2.2 nm)* anti-aircraft; weight of shell 0.96 kg.
Fire control: 2 Signaal M 45 GFCS for gunnery.
Radars: Surface search: Signaal ZW 01; I/J band.
Signaal DA 02; E/F band; range 73 km *(40 nm)*.
Navigation: Kelvin Hughes 14/9; I band.
Fire control: Two Signaal M 45; I/J band; short range for gunnery.
Sonars: Krupp Atlas; hull-mounted; active search; medium frequency.

Programmes: Originally a class of 13. The survivors are rated as tenders for fast attack craft.
Operational: *Donau*, 2nd FPB Squadron; *Rhein*, 3rd FPB Squadron; *Main*, 5th FPB Squadron; *Elbe*, 7th FPB Squadron; *Rhein* and *Elbe* are expected to pay off in June and December 1992 respectively and the last pair in 1994. All to be relieved by Type 404 ships.
Sales: *Weser* to Greece 1975. *Ruhr* to Turkey 1976, *Isar* to Turkey October 1982.

ELBE — *6/1991, Antonio Moreno*

0 + 6 ELBE CLASS (TYPE 404) (TENDERS)

Name	No	Builders	Commissioned
ELBE	A 511	Bremer Vulkan	Dec 1992
MOSEL	A 512	Bremer Vulkan	July 1993
RHEIN	A 513	Flensburger Schiffbau	Oct 1993
WERRA	A 514	Flensburger Schiffbau	Dec 1993
MAIN	A 515	Lürssen/Krögerwerft	July 1994
DONAU	A 516	Lürssen/Krögerwerft	Nov 1994

Displacement, tons: 3586 full load
Dimensions, feet (metres): 329.7 oa; 285.4 wl × 49.2 × 13.5 *(100.5; 87 × 15 × 4.1)*
Main machinery: 1 Deutz MWM diesel; 3335 hp(m) *(2.45 MW)*; 1 shaft; bow thruster
Speed, knots: 15. **Range, miles:** 2000 at 15 kts
Complement: 40 (4 officers) plus 12 squadron staff plus 50 maintainers
Cargo capacity: 450 tons dieso; 150 tons water; 11 tons luboil; 130 tons ammunition
Missiles: SAM: 2 Stinger (Fliegerfaust 2) quad launchers.

Comment: Funds released in November 1990 for the construction of six ships to replace the Rhein class. Fitted with helicopter platform and containers for maintenance and repairs, spare parts and supplies for fast attack craft and minesweepers. Waste disposal capacity: 270 cu m liquids, 60 cu m solids. The use of the Darss class (all sold in 1991) was investigated as an alternative but rejected on the grounds of higher long-term costs because of the age of the ships.

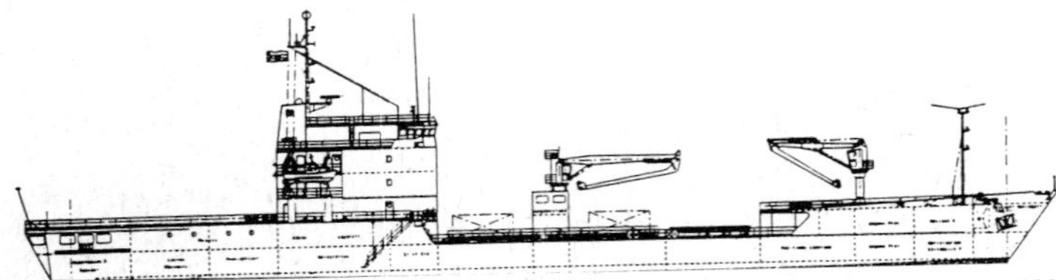
TYPE 404 *1990*

2 REPLENISHMENT TANKERS (TYPE 704)

Name	No	Builders	Commissioned
SPESSART (ex-*Okapi*)	A 1442	Kröger, Rendsburg	1974
RHÖN (ex-*Okene*)	A 1443	Kröger, Rendsburg	1974

Displacement, tons: 14 169 full load
Measurement, tons: 6103 grt; 10 800 dwt
Dimensions, feet (metres): 427.1 × 63.3 × 26.9 *(130.2 × 19.3 × 8.2)*
Main machinery: 1 MAK 12-cyl diesel; 8000 hp(m) *(5.88 MW)*; 1 shaft
Speed, knots: 16. **Range, miles:** 7400 at 16 kts
Complement: 42
Cargo capacity: 11 000 cu m fuel; 400 cu m water

Comment: Completed for Terkol Group as tankers. Acquired in 1976 for conversion *(Spessart* at Bremerhaven, *Rhön* at Kröger*)*. The former commissioned for naval service on 5 September 1977 and the latter on 23 September 1977. Unarmed and civilian manned.

SPESSART *8/1991, Antonio Moreno*

4 WALCHENSEE CLASS (TYPE 703) (REPLENISHMENT TANKERS)

Name	No	Builders	Commissioned
WALCHENSEE	A 1424	Lindenau, Kiel	29 June 1966
AMMERSEE	A 1425	Lindenau, Kiel	2 Mar 1967
TEGERNSEE	A 1426	Lindenau, Kiel	23 Mar 1967
WESTENSEE	A 1427	Lindenau, Kiel	6 Oct 1967

Displacement, tons: 2191
Dimensions, feet (metres): 235.8 × 36.7 × 13.5 *(71.9 × 11.2 × 4.1)*
Main machinery: 2 MWM 12-cyl diesels; 1370 hp(m) *(1 MW)*; 2 shafts
Speed, knots: 12.6. **Range, miles:** 3250 at 12 kts
Complement: 21

Comment: Civilian manned.

TEGERNSEE *9/1991, van Ginderen Collection*

7 LÜNEBURG CLASS (TYPE 701) (SUPPORT SHIPS)

Name	No	Builders	Commissioned
LÜNEBURG	A 1411	Flensburger Schiffbau/Bremer Vulkan	31 Jan 1966
FREIBURG*	A 1413	Blohm & Voss	27 May 1968
GLÜCKSBURG*	A 1414	Bremer Vulkan/Flensburger Schiffbau	9 July 1968
SAARBURG*	A 1415	Blohm & Voss	30 July 1968
NIENBURG	A 1416	Bremer Vulkan/Flensburger Schiffbau	1 Aug 1968
OFFENBURG	A 1417	Blohm & Voss	27 May 1968
MEERSBURG*	A 1418	Bremer Vulkan/Flensburger Schiffbau	25 June 1968

*conversions

Displacement, tons: 3483; 3709 (conversions); 3900 *Freiburg*
Dimensions, feet (metres): 341.2 × 43.3 × 13.8 *(104 × 13.2 × 4.2)* (374.9 ft *(114.3 m)* for conversions; 388.1 ft *(118.3 m)* for *Freiburg*)
Main machinery: 2 Maybach MTU MD 872 diesels; 5600 hp(m) *(4.1 MW)*; 2 shafts; cp props; bow thruster
Speed, knots: 17. **Range, miles:** 3200 at 14 kts
Complement: 71
Cargo capacity: 1100 tons
Guns: 4 Bofors 40 mm/70 (2 twin) (cocooned in most).

Comment: Four of this class were lengthened in 1975-76 by 33.7 ft *(10.3 m)* and modernised to serve the missile installations of the new classes of fast attack craft and converted destroyers, including MM 38 Exocet maintenance. *Freiburg* was lengthened in 1984 by 46.9 ft *(14.3 m)*, has a helicopter deck, portside larger crane and will act as support ship for Bremen class carrying nine spare Harpoons. Most serve as support ships for fast attack craft or MCM squadrons. *Meersburg* replaced *Lahn* as depot ship for 1st Submarine Squadron and *Nienburg* replaced *Werra* in 1991. In 1988 *Offenburg* was fitted with rectangular bridge windows and also has two Selenia SCLAR Chaff launchers. *Coburg* transferred to Greece 25 September 1991.

GLUCKSBURG *4/1991, Guy Toremans*

MEERSBURG *6/1991, Guy Toremans*

FREIBURG (with helo deck) *6/1989, Gilbert Gyssels*

2 GUSTAV KÖNIGS CLASS (HARBOUR TANKERS)

Name	No
KÖLPINSEE	Y 1652 (ex-C 11)
FLEESENSEE	Y 1657 (ex-C 40)

Displacement, tons: 1010 full load
Dimensions, feet (metres): 219.8 × 26.9 × 7.2 *(67 × 8.2 × 2.2)*
Main machinery: 1 R8DV 148 diesel; 420 hp(m) *(308 kW)*; 1 shaft
Speed, knots: 8

Comment: Ex-GDR built by VEB/Rosslau-Elbe. Able to pass under river bridges.

FLEESENSEE *6/1991, Hartmut Ehler*

1 TYPE 763 (SUPPORT TANKER)

Name	*No*	*Builders*	*Commissioned*
WITTENSEE (ex-*Sioux*)	A 1407	Lindenau, Kiel	26 Mar 1959

Displacement, tons: 1854 full load
Dimensions, feet (metres): 221.4 × 32 × 14.1 *(67.5 × 9.8 × 4.3)*
Main machinery: 1 MAK diesel; 1050 hp(m) *(772 kW)*; 1 shaft
Speed, knots: 12
Complement: 21

Comment: Civilian manned. *Bodensee* sold to Turkey in 1977.

WITTENSEE *6/1990, Stefan Terzibaschitsch*

6 OHRE CLASS (ACCOMMODATION SHIPS)

VOGTLAND Y 890 (ex-H 71)
ALTMARK Y 891 (ex-H 11)
HAVELLAND Y 892 (ex-H 51)
UCKERMARK Y 893 (ex-H 91)
BÖRDE Y 894 (ex-H 72)
WISCHE (ex-*Harz*) Y 895 (ex-H 31)

Displacement, tons: 1320 full load
Dimensions, feet (metres): 231 × 39.4 × 5 *(70.4 × 12 × 1.6)*

Comment: Ex-GDR-built by Peenewerft, Wolgast. One hydraulic 8 ton crane fitted. First commissioned 1985. Classified as 'Schwimmende Stuetzpunkte'. Propulsion and armament is being removed and they are used as non self-propelled accommodation ships for crews of vessels in refit. Civilian manned.

UCKERMARK *6/1991, Hartmut Ehlers*

2 WESTERWALD CLASS (TYPE 760) (AMMUNITION TRANSPORTS)

Name	*No*	*Builders*	*Commissioned*
WESTERWALD	A 1435	Orenstein and Koppel, Lübeck	11 Feb 1967
ODENWALD	A 1436	Orenstein and Koppel, Lübeck	23 Mar 1967

Displacement, tons: 3460 standard; 4042 full load
Dimensions, feet (metres): 344.4 × 46 × 12.2 *(105 × 14 × 3.7)*
Main machinery: 2 Maybach MTU MD 872 diesels; 5600 hp(m) *(4.1 MW)*; 2 shafts; cp props
Speed, knots: 17. **Range, miles:** 3500 at 17 kts
Complement: 60 *(Westerwald)*; 31 *(Odenwald)* (civilian manned)
Cargo capacity: 1080 tons ammunition
Guns: 4 Bofors 40 mm/70 (2 twin) (cocooned in *Odenwald*).

Comment: *Odenwald* based at Wilhelmshaven; *Westerwald* at Flensburg.

WESTERWALD *1990, van Ginderen Collection*

2 TYPE 705 (WATER BOATS)

FW 1 A 1403 (ex-Y 864) **FW 5** A 1405 (ex-Y 868)

Displacement, tons: 626 full load
Dimensions, feet (metres): 144.4 × 25.6 × 8.2 *(44.1 × 7.8 × 2.5)*
Main machinery: 1 MWM diesel; 230 hp(m) *(169 kW)*; 1 shaft
Speed, knots: 9.5
Complement: 6
Cargo capacity: 340 tons

Comment: Originally class of six built in pairs by Schiffbarges, Unterweser, Bremerhaven; H. Rancke, Hamburg and Jadewerft, Wilhelmshaven, in 1963-64. *FW 2* (3 December 1975) and *FW 4* (12 April 1991) to Turkey; *FW 3* (22 April 1976) and *FW 6* (5 March 1991) to Greece.

FW 5 *6/1991, Stefan Terzibaschitsch*

1 KNURRHAHN CLASS (TYPE 730) (ACCOMMODATION SHIP)

Name	*No*	*Builders*	*Commissioned*
KNURRHAHN	Y 811	Sietas/Norderwerft	Nov 1989

Displacement, tons: 1424 full load
Dimensions, feet (metres): 157.5 × 45.9 × 5.9 *(48 × 14 × 1.8)*

Comment: Based at Bremerhaven. Accommodation for 230 people.

KNURRHAHN *4/1991, G. Koop*

3 BATTERY CHARGING CRAFT (TYPE 718)

Name	*No*	*Builders*	*Commissioned*
LP 1	—	Jadewerft, Wilhelmshaven	18 Feb 1964
LP 2	—	Oelkers, Hamburg	17 Apr 1964
LP 3	Y 1690	Jadewerft, Wilhelmshaven	12 Sep 1974

Displacement, tons: 234 (267 *LP 3*) full load
Dimensions, feet (metres): 90.6 × 23 × 5.2 *(27.6 × 7.0 × 1.6)*
Main machinery: 1 MTU MB diesel; 250 hp(m) *(184 kW)*; 1 shaft
Speed, knots: 9
Complement: 6

Comment: Have diesel charging generators for submarine batteries. *LP 3* is 1.6 ft *(0.5 m)* more in beam than the first two.

LP 2 *6/1991, Stefan Terzibaschitsch*

5 TOWING LAUNCHES (TYPE 946)

AK 1 Y 1671	**MA 2** Y 1676	**BORBY** Y 1687
AK 3 Y 1672	**MA 3** Y 1677	

Dimensions, feet (metres): 39.4 × 12.8 × 6.2 *(12.0 × 3.9 × 1.9)*
Main machinery: 1 MAN D 2540 MTE diesel; 366 hp(m) *(269 kW)*; 1 shaft

Comment: Built by Hans Boost, Trier. All completed in 1985.

AK 1 — *6/1991, Antonio Moreno*

12 OIL BARGES (TYPE 737)

Comment: Numbered Ölschute 1-12 and completed in 1986-87. 65.6 ft *(20 m)* dumb barges with 150 tons capacity.

AUXILIARY AND TRIALS SHIPS

Note: In addition to those listed below there are two SES trials craft:
(a) *Corsair* which is owned by Blohm & Voss and has a 57 mm Bofors.
(b) *Moses* completed by Lürssen in October 1990 with two Tohatsu outboard engines giving a speed of 25 kts. This is a scaled down version of the Type 751 below.

CORSAIR — *1991, van Ginderen Collection*

0 + (1) SES TRIALS CRAFT (TYPE 751)

Displacement, tons: 720 full load
Dimensions, feet (metres): 219.8 × 52.8 × 9.4 (hullborne) *(67.0 × 16.1 × 2.8)*
Main machinery: 4 Allison 571 KF gas turbines, 29 920 hp(m) *(22 MW)*; 2 KaMeWa waterjets
Speed, knots: 50+

Comment: MTG Marinetechnik Hamburg has been contracted to design a craft characterised by a top speed of 50 knots for construction in the 1990s.
Prior to construction of the full scale SES a manned and self-propelled model in scale 1:6.3 has been built at Lürssen and completed on 21 Aug 1990.

3 OSTE CLASS (TYPE 423) (AGI)

Name	*No*	*Builders*	*Commissioned*
ALSTER	A 50	Schiffsbaugesellschaft, Flensburg	5 Oct 1989
OSTE	A 52	Schiffsbaugesellschaft, Flensburg	30 June 1988
OKER	A 53	Schiffsbaugesellschaft, Flensburg	10 Nov 1988

Displacement, tons: 3200 full load
Dimensions, feet (metres): 273.9 × 47.9 × 13.8 *(83.5 × 14.6 × 4.2)*
Main machinery: 2 Deutz-MWM BV 16M 628 diesels; 8980 hp(m) *(6.6 MW)* sustained; 1 shaft; 1 motor (for slow speed)
Speed, knots: 19
Complement: 40 plus 40 specialists (2 crews)

Comment: Three new vessels ordered in March 1985 and December 1986 and have replaced the Radar Trials Ships of the same name (old *Oker* and *Alster* transferred to Greece and Turkey respectively). *Oste* launched 15 May 1987, *Oker* 24 September 1987, *Alster* 4 November 1988. Carry Krupp Atlas passive sonar and optical ELAM and electronic surveillance equipment. Particular attention has been given to accommodation standards.

ALSTER — *8/1991, Antonio Moreno*

1 TRIALS SHIP (TYPE 742)

Name	*No*	*Builders*	*Commissioned*
WALTHER VON LEDEBUR	A 1410 (ex-Y 841)	Burmester, Bremen	21 Dec 1967

Displacement, tons: 775 standard; 825 full load
Dimensions, feet (metres): 206.6 × 34.8 × 8.9 *(63 × 10.6 × 2.7)*
Main machinery: 2 Maybach MTU 16-cyl diesels; 5200 hp(m) *(3.82 MW)*; 2 shafts
Speed, knots: 19
Complement: 11 plus 10 trials party

Comment: Wooden hulled vessel. Launched on 30 June 1966 as a prototype minesweeper but completed as a trials ship. To be replaced in 1995 by fourth Type 748.

WALTHER VON LEDEBUR — *6/1990, Gilbert Gyssels*

3 + (1) SCHWEDENECK CLASS (TYPE 748) (MULTI-PURPOSE)

Name	*No*	*Builders*	*Commissioned*
SCHWEDENECK	Y 860	Krögerwerft, Rendsburg	20 Oct 1987
KRONSORT	Y 861	Elsflether Werft	2 Dec 1987
HELMSAND	Y 862	Krögerwerft, Rendsburg	4 Mar 1988

Displacement, tons: 1018 full load
Dimensions, feet (metres): 185.3 × 35.4 × 17 *(56.5 × 10.8 × 5.2)*
Main machinery: Diesel-electric; 3 MTU 6V 396 TB 53 diesel generators; 1485 kW sustained; 1 motor; 1 shaft
Speed, knots: 13. **Range, miles:** 2400 at 13 kts
Complement: 13 plus 10 trials parties
Radars: Navigation: Two Raytheon; I band.

Comment: Order for first three placed in mid-1985. One more planned after 1995 to replace *Walther von Ledebur*.

HELMSAND — *9/1991, Hartmut Ehlers*

5 + (2) STOLLERGRUND CLASS (TYPE 745) (MULTI-PURPOSE)

Name	*No*	*Builders*	*Commissioned*
STOLLERGRUND	Y 863	Krögerwerft	31 May 1989
MITTELGRUND	Y 864	Elsflether Werft	23 Aug 1989
KALKGRUND	Y 865	Krögerwerft	23 Nov 1989
BREITGRUND	Y 866	Elsflether Werft	19 Dec 1989
BANT	Y 867	Krögerwerft	28 May 1990

Displacement, tons: 450 full load
Dimensions, feet (metres): 126.6 × 30.2 × 10.5 *(38.6 × 9.2 × 3.2)*
Main machinery: 1 Deutz-MWM BV 6M 628 diesel; 2075 hp(m) *(1.24 MW)* sustained; 1 shaft
Speed, knots: 12. **Range, miles:** 1000 at 12 kts.
Complement: 7 plus 6 trials personnel

Comment: Five ordered from Lürssen in November 1987; two subcontracted to Elsflether. Equipment includes two I band radars and an intercept sonar. The first four are based at the Armed Forces Technical Centre; *Bant* at Wilhelmshaven. Two more planned for the mid-1990s.

BANT *6/1991, van Ginderen Collection*

0 + (2) TYPE 749 (MULTI-PURPOSE)

Displacement, tons: 1750 approx
Dimensions, feet (metres): 246 × 41.3 × 12.5 *(75 × 12.6 × 3.8)*

Comment: Planned to relieve *Hans Bürckner* and *Heinz Roggenkamp* in the 1990s but the former paid off earlier than expected in October 1990 because of an asbestos insulation problem. Type 749A for torpedo trials and Type 749B for sonar trials.

1 RESEARCH SHIP (TYPE 750)

Name	*No*	*Builders*	*Commissioned*
PLANET	A 1450	Norderwerft, Hamburg	15 Apr 1967

Displacement, tons: 1943 full load
Dimensions, feet (metres): 263.8 × 41.3 × 13.1 *(80.4 × 12.6 × 4)*
Main machinery: Diesel-electric; 4 MWM diesel generators; 1 motor; 1390 hp(m) *(1.02 MW)*; 1 shaft; bow thruster
Speed, knots: 13. **Range, miles:** 9400 at 13 kts
Complement: 39 plus 22 scientists
Radars: Navigation: Two Raytheon; I band.
Sonars: Hull-mounted; high frequency search.
Helicopters: 1 Bell 206B or MBB BO105CB can be embarked.

Comment: Weapons research ship launched 23 September 1965. Planned to be replaced by SWATH type ship (Type 751).

PLANET *1991, van Ginderen Collection*

1 TRIALS SHIP (TYPE 740)

Name	*No*	*Builders*	*Commissioned*
HEINZ ROGGENKAMP	Y 871	Weser, Bremerhaven	30 Dec 1952

Displacement, tons: 996 full load
Dimensions, feet (metres): 187.7 × 29.5 × 10.2 *(57.2 × 9 × 3.1)*
Main machinery: 1 Klockner-Humboldt-Deutz diesel; 1145 hp(m) *(841 kW)*; 1 shaft
Speed, knots: 12
Complement: 19

Comment: Built as a trawler and converted in 1964 as a torpedo trials ship with both 533 mm and 324 mm tubes.

HEINZ ROGGENKAMP *6/1991, Stefan Terzibaschitsch*

2 TRIALS SHIPS (TYPE 741)

Name	*No*	*Builders*	*Commissioned*
SP 1	A 1408 (ex-A 837)	Schürenstadt, Bardenfleth	29 June 1967
WILHELM PULLWER	A 1409 (ex-Y 838)	Schürenstadt, Bardenfleth	22 Dec 1967

Displacement, tons: 160 full load
Dimensions, feet (metres): 103.3 × 24.6 × 7.2 *(31.5 × 7.5 × 2.2)*
Main machinery: 2 MB diesels; 700 hp(m) *(514 kW)*; 2 Voith-Schneider props
Speed, knots: 12.5
Complement: 17

Comment: Wooden hulled trials ships for barrage systems. *SP 1* works for the Naval Service Test Command.

SP 1 *6/1991, Stefan Terzibaschitsch*

1 DIVING TENDER (TYPE 732)

Name	*No*	*Builders*	*Commissioned*
TB 1	M 1050	Burmeister, Bremen	21 June 1972

Displacement, tons: 70 full load
Dimensions, feet (metres): 91.2 × 19 × 6.2 *(27.8 × 5.8 × 1.9)*
Main machinery: 1 MWM diesel; 950 hp(m) *(698 kW)*; 1 shaft
Speed, knots: 17
Complement: 6 plus divers

Comment: Similar to Type 430 TRVs.

TB 1 *6/1991, van Ginderen Collection*

1 TRIALS PLATFORM

BARBARA Y 844

Comment: Artillery testing ship of 3500 tons and 170.9 ft *(52.1 m)*. Commissioned in June 1964. No propulsion. Named after the patron saint of artillery.

BARBARA *1990, van Ginderen Collection*

5 FLOATING DOCKS (TYPES 712-715) and 2 CRANES (TYPE 711)

SCHWIMMDOCKS A Y 842
SCHWIMMDOCKS B Y 879
C, 2 and **3**
HIEV Y 875
GRIEP Y 876

Comment: Dock lift capacity: 3 (8000 tons); B (4500 tons); A and 2 (1000 tons). C is used for submarine pressure tests; Cranes (100 tons).

Y 879 *6/1991, Stefan Terzibaschitsch*

2 TANK CLEANING VESSELS (TYPE 710)

FÖRDE Y 1641 **JADE** Y 1642

Displacement, tons: 1830 full load
Dimensions, feet (metres): 191.9 × 34.1 × 13.5 *(58.5 × 10.4 × 4.1)*
Main machinery: 1 MWM diesel; 390 hp(m) *(287 kW)*; 1 shaft
Speed, knots: 8
Complement: 16

Comment: Built in 1967 by Deutsche Werft, Hamburg.

JADE *7/1991, Hartmut Ehlers*

SAIL TRAINING SHIPS

Note: In addition to the two listed below there are 54 other sail training vessels (Types 910-915)

Name	*No*	*Builders*	*Commissioned*
GORCH FOCK	A 60	Blohm & Voss, Hamburg	17 Dec 1958

Displacement, tons: 1760 standard; 1870 full load
Dimensions, feet (metres): 293 × 39.2 × 16.1 *(89.3 × 12 × 4.9)*
Main machinery: Auxiliary 1 Deutz MWM SBV 6M 628 diesel; 1660 hp(m) *(1.22 MW)*; 1 shaft; KaMeWa cp prop
Speed, knots: 11 power; 15 sail. **Range, miles:** 1990 at 10 kts
Complement: 206 (10 officers, 140 cadets)

Comment: Sail training ship of the improved Horst Wessel type. Barque rig. Launched on 23 August 1958. Sail area, 21 141 sq ft. Major modernisation in 1985 at Howaldtswerke. Second major refit in 1991 at Motorenwerke, Bremerhaven included a new propulsion engine and three diesel generators.

GORCH FOCK *6/1991, Stefan Terzibaschitsch*

Name	*No*	*Builders*	*Commissioned*
NORDWIND	Y 834	—	1944

Displacement, tons: 110
Dimensions, feet (metres): 78.8 × 21 × 8.2 *(24 × 6.4 × 2.5)*
Main machinery: 1 Demag diesel; 150 hp(m) *(110 kW)*; 1 shaft
Speed, knots: 8. **Range, miles:** 1200 at 7 kts
Complement: 10

Comment: Ketch rigged. Sail area, 2037.5 sq ft. Ex-Second World War patrol craft. Taken over from Border Guard in 1956.

NORDWIND *6/1990, Stefan Terzibaschitsch*

MISCELLANEOUS

Note: The trials submarine *Jonas* (ex-Swedish *Valen*) is a hulk without propulsion machinery at Eckernförde.

1 TRIAL BOAT (TYPE 740)

Name	*No*	*Builders*	*Commissioned*
BUMS	Y 1689	Howaldtswerke, Kiel	—

Dimensions, feet (metres): 86.6 × 22.3 × 4.9 *(26.4 × 6.8 × 1.5)*

Comment: Single diesel engine. Originally an MTB from Second World War. Has a 3 ton crane.

BUMS *1983, Ralf Bendfeldt*

8 GENERAL SERVICE LAUNCHES (TYPES 740, 743, 744, 744A)

MT-BOOT Y 1670
AK 5 Y 1673
AM 6 Y 1674
AM 8 Y 1675
AM 7 Y 1679
AK 6 Y 1683
PETER BACHMANN Y 1684
AK 2 Y 1686

Dimensions, feet (metres): 52.5 × 13.1 × 3.9 *(16 × 4 × 1.2)* approx
Main machinery: 1 or 2 diesels

Comment: For personnel transport and trials work. Types 744 and 744A *(AK 2)* are radio calibration craft; Type 740 *(AK 5)* is a radar trials craft.

AK 6 — *6/1991, Antonio Moreno*

AK 5 — *6/1990, van Ginderen Collection*

6 RANGE SAFETY CRAFT (5 TYPE 369, 1 TYPE 909)

KW 15 Y 827
KW 16 Y 830
KW 17 Y 845
KW 18 Y 832
KW 20 Y 846
H 11 Y 857

Displacement, tons: 70 full load
Dimensions, feet (metres): 93.5 × 15.4 × 4.9 *(28.9 × 4.7 × 1.5)*
Main machinery: 2 Mercedes-Benz diesels; 2000 hp(m) *(1.47 MW)*; 2 shafts
Speed, knots: 25
Complement: 17

Comment: Built in 1951-53 for Weser river patrol. Can be fitted with two Oerlikon 20 mm. For Todendorf AAW range. One paid off in early 1992.

KW 15 — *6/1991, Stefan Terzibaschitsch*

2 TWIN HULL OIL RECOVERY SHIPS (TYPE 738)

Name	*No*	*Builders*	*Commissioned*
BOTTSAND	Y 1643	Lühring, Brake	24 Jan 1985
EVERSAND	Y 1644	Lühring, Brake	11 June 1988

Measurement, tons: 500 gross; 650 dwt
Dimensions, feet (metres): 151.9 × 39.4 (137.8, bow opened) × 10.2 *(46.3 × 12 (42) × 3.1)*
Main machinery: 1 Deutz BA 12M 816 diesel; 2010 hp(m) *(1.48 MW)* sustained; 2 shafts
Speed, knots: 10
Complement: 6

Comment: Built with two hulls which are connected with a hinge in the stern. During pollution clearance the bow will be opened. Ordered by Ministry of Transport but taken over by West German Navy. Normally used as tank cleaning vessels. Civilian manned. *Bottsand* based at Olpenik, *Eversand* at Wilhelmshaven. A third of class *Thor* belongs to the Ministry of Transport.

BOTTSAND — *8/1991, Antonio Moreno*

4 TORPEDO RECOVERY VESSELS (TYPE 430A)

TF 1-3 Y 851-853 **TF 5** Y 855

Comment: All built in 1966 of approximately 56 tons. Provided with stern ramp for torpedo recovery. One sold to the Turkish Navy, two to Greece in 1989 and two more in 1991 (*TF 4* and *TF 6*). Being replaced by Type 745 multi-purpose vessels.

TF 2 — *6/1990, Stefan Terzibaschitsch*

TUGS

2 HELGOLAND CLASS (TYPE 720) (SALVAGE TUGS)

Name	*No*	*Builders*	*Commissioned*
HELGOLAND	A 1457	Unterweser, Bremerhaven	8 Mar 1966
FEHMARN	A 1458	Unterweser, Bremerhaven	1 Feb 1967

Displacement, tons: 1310 standard; 1643 full load
Dimensions, feet (metres): 223.1 × 41.7 × 14.4 *(68 × 12.7 × 4.4)*
Main machinery: Diesel-electric; 4 MWM 12-cyl diesel generators; 2 motors; 3300 hp(m) *(2.43 MW)*; 2 shafts
Speed, knots: 17. **Range, miles:** 6400 at 16 kts
Complement: 34
Guns: 2 Bofors 40 mm/70 (twin) (cocooned or removed)
Mines: Laying capacity.
Radars: Navigation: Raytheon; I band.
Sonars: High definition, hull-mounted for wreck search.

Comment: Launched on 25 November 1965 and 9 April 1965. Carry firefighting equipment and have an ice strengthened hull. *Fehmarn* (Type 720B) modernised and employed as safety ship for the submarine training group.

HELGOLAND — *6/1991, Guy Toremans*

6 WANGEROOGE CLASS (3 TYPE 722 and 3 TYPE 754)

Name	No	Builders	Commissioned
WANGEROOGE	A 1451	Schichau, Bremerhaven	9 Apr 1968
SPIEKEROOG	A 1452	Schichau, Bremerhaven	14 Aug 1968
NORDERNEY	A 1455	Schichau, Bremerhaven	15 Oct 1970
BALTRUM	A 1439	Schichau, Bremerhaven	8 Oct 1968
JUIST	A 1440	Schichau, Bremerhaven	1 Oct 1971
LANGEOOG	A 1441	Schichau, Bremerhaven	14 Aug 1968

Displacement, tons: 854 standard; 1024 full load
Dimensions, feet (metres): 170.6 × 39.4 × 12.8 *(52 × 12.1 × 3.9)*
Main machinery: Diesel-electric; 4 MWM 16-cyl diesel generators; 2 motors; 2400 hp(m) *(1.76 MW)*; 2 shafts
Speed, knots: 14. **Range, miles:** 5000 at 10 kts
Complement: 24 plus 33 trainees (A 1439-1441)
Guns: 1 Bofors 40 mm/70 (cocooned in some, not fitted in all).

Comment: First three are salvage tugs with firefighting equipment and ice strengthened hulls. *Wangerooge* sometimes used for pilot training and *Spiekeroog* and *Norderney* as submarine safety ships. The second three were converted 1974-78 to training ships with *Baltrum* and *Juist* being used as diving training vessels with recompression chambers.

BALTRUM *5/1991, Hartmut Ehlers*

4 HARBOUR TUGS (TYPE 724)

Name	No	Builders	Commissioned
SYLT	Y 820	Schichau, Bremerhaven	1962
FÖHR	Y 821	Schichau, Bremerhaven	1962
AMRUM	Y 822	Schichau, Bremerhaven	1963
NEUWERK	Y 823	Schichau, Bremerhaven	1963

Displacement, tons: 244 standard; 266 full load
Dimensions, feet (metres): 100.7 × 24.6 × 13.1 *(30.6 × 7.5 × 4)*
Main machinery: 1 Deutz MAK 8-cyl diesel; 1000 hp(m) *(735 kW)*; 1 shaft
Speed, knots: 12
Complement: 10

Comment: Launched in 1961. Civilian manned. Carry firefighting equipment.

NEUWERK *11/1991, Hartmut Ehlers*

3 HARBOUR TUGS (TYPE 724)

Name	No	Builders	Commissioned
NEUENDE	Y 1680	Schichau, Bremerhaven	27 Oct 1971
HEPPENS	Y 1681	Schichau, Bremerhaven	17 Dec 1971
ELLERBEK	Y 1682	Schichau, Bremerhaven	26 Nov 1971

Displacement, tons: 232
Dimensions, feet (metres): 87.2 × 24.3 × 8.5 *(26.6 × 7.4 × 2.6)*
Main machinery: 1 MWM 8-cyl diesel; 800 hp(m) *(588 kW)*; 1 shaft
Speed, knots: 12
Complement: 6

ELLERBEK *6/1991, Stefan Terzibaschitsch*

6 + (6) HARBOUR TUGS (TYPE 725)

Name	No	Builders	Commissioned
VOGELSAND	Y 816	Orenstein und Koppel, Lübeck	14 Apr 1987
NORDSTRAND	Y 817	Orenstein und Koppel, Lübeck	20 Jan 1987
LANGENESS	Y 819	Orenstein und Koppel, Lübeck	5 Mar 1987
LÜTJE HORN	Y 812	Husumer Schiffswerft	31 May 1990
KNECHTSAND	Y 814	Husumer Schiffswerft	16 Nov 1990
SCHARHÖRN	Y 815	Husumer Schiffswerft	1 Oct 1990

Displacement, tons: 445
Dimensions, feet (metres): 99.3 × 29.8 × 8.5 *(30.3 × 9.1 × 2.6)*
Main machinery: 2 Deutz MWM BV 6M 628 diesels; 4159 hp(m) *(3.06 MW)* sustained; 2 Voith-Schneider props
Speed, knots: 12
Complement: 10

Comment: Bollard pull, 23 tons. Second batch of three (Y 812, 814-815) have retained the same names and pennant numbers of the Type 723 tugs they replaced. Six more to complete by 1994, to replace Type 724.

LÜTJE HORN *6/1991, Antonio Moreno*

3 HARBOUR TUGS (TYPE 414)

KOOS (ex-*Delphin*) Y 1651 (ex-A 08)
WUSTROW (ex-*Zander*) Y 1656 (ex-A 45)
DRANKSE (ex-*Kormoran*) Y 1658 (ex-A 68)

Displacement, tons: 320 full load
Dimensions, feet (metres): 96.1 × 27.2 × 12.1 *(29.3 × 8.3 × 3.7)*
Main machinery: 2 diesels; 1200 hp(m) *(882 kW)*; 2 shafts
Speed, knots: 11. **Range, miles:** 1800 at 11 kts
Complement: 3

Comment: Ex-GDR vessels being retained in service.

KOOS *3/1991, Hartmut Ehlers*

4 HARBOUR TUGS

UMMANZ Y 1650 (ex-A 10)
HAVEL Y 1654 (ex-A 442)
ODER Y 1659 (ex-A 661)
SAALE Y 1660 (ex-A 662)

Comment: All ex-GDR of about 250 tons. *Ummanz* is an ex-Soviet Prometey class to be paid off at the end of 1992. The other three are Type 270. *Zingst* was sold to Uruguay in 1991.

ODER *4/1991, Hartmut Ehlers*

ICEBREAKERS

Note: *Polarstern*, *Hanse* and *Max Waldeck* do not belong to the Navy.

Name	*No*	*Builders*	*Commissioned*
EISVOGEL	A 1401	J G Hitzler, Lauenburg	11 Mar 1961
EISBÄR	A 1402	J G Hitzler, Lauenburg	1 Nov 1961

Displacement, tons: 560 standard
Dimensions, feet (metres): 125.3 × 31.2 × 15.1 *(38.2 × 9.5 × 4.6)*
Main machinery: 2 Maybach 12-cyl diesels; 2400 hp(m) *(1.76 MW)*; 2 shafts
Speed, knots: 13
Complement: 16

Comment: Launched on 28 April and 9 June 1960 respectively. Icebreaking tugs of limited capability. Civilian manned. Fitted for but not with one Bofors 40 mm/70.

EISBAR *3/1991, van Ginderen Collection*

RIVER ENGINEERS (ARMY)

Note: Four companies are located along the River Rhine at Krefeld, Koblenz, Neuwied and Wiesbaden. Each company is provided with Landing Craft (Mannheim 59 or Bodan class), River Patrol Craft and one River Tug and each has its own numbered series: 80101-31, 80111-31, 85011-31, 85111-31.

14 MANNHEIM 59 CLASS (RIVER LANDING CRAFT) (LCMs)

Displacement, tons: 89 standard
Dimensions, feet (metres): 89.9 × 23.6 × 3.9 *(27.4 × 7.2 × 1.2)*
Main machinery: 2 MWM RHS 518 A diesels; 432 hp(m) *(317 kW)*; 2 shafts
Speed, knots: 9
Complement: 9
Guns: 4—7.62 mm MGs.

Comment: Ordered in April 1959 and built by Schiffs und Motorenwerke AG, Mannheim. Normal load 70 tons but can carry 90 tons. One transferred to Tonga in 1989. Eight paid off for sale in August 1991.

LCM 85131 *9/1991, van Ginderen Collection*

12 RIVER PATROL CRAFT

Displacement, tons: 255 full load
Dimensions, feet (metres): 82 × 12.5 × 3.3 *(25 × 3.8 × 1)*
Main machinery: 2 MWM RHS 418 A diesels; 440 hp(m) *(323 kW)*; 2 shafts
Speed, knots: 20.5
Complement: 7
Guns: 4—12.7 mm Browning MGs.

Comment: Resemble the Belgian river patrol craft *Liberation*.

S 80102 *1991, van Ginderen Collection*

13 BODAN CLASS (RIVER LANDING CRAFT) (LCMs)

Dimensions, feet (metres): 98.4 × 19 *(30 × 5.8)* (loading area)
Main machinery: 4 diesels; 596 hp(m) *(438 kW)*; 4 Schottel props
Guns: 1 Oerlikon 20 mm.

Comment: Built of 12 pontoons, provided with bow and stern ramp. Can carry 90 tons.

LCM 85012 *11/1991, van Ginderen Collection*

4 RIVER TUGS

T 80001 T 80101 T 85001 T 85101

Dimensions, feet (metres): 91.8 × 19.4 × 3.9 *(28 × 5.9 × 1.2)*
Main machinery: 2 KHD SBF 12 M 716 diesels; 760 hp(m) *(559 kW)*; 2 shafts
Speed, knots: 11
Complement: 7
Guns: 2—7.62 mm MGs.

T 80101 *8/1984, Gunnar Olsen*

COAST GUARD VESSELS

(Bundesgrenzschutz—See)

Notes: (a) This paramilitary force consists of about 1000 men who operate the craft below as well as Bell UH-1D and Puma SA 330 helicopters. Headquarters is at Neustadt.
(b) A maritime section of the anti-terrorist force GSG 9 attached to the Bundesgrenzschutz.
(c) Craft have blue hulls and white superstructures.

9 KONDOR I CLASS (MINESWEEPER/PATROL CRAFT)

Name	*No*	*Name*	*No*
ÜCKERMÜNDE	GS 01 (ex-G 411)	**TEMPLIN**	BG31 (ex-GS06,ex-G442)
DEMMIN	GS 02 (ex-G 422)	**KÜHLUNGSBORN**	BG32 (ex-GS07,ex-G445)
MALCHIN	GS 03 (ex-G 441)	**AHRENSHOOP**	BG33 (ex-GS08,ex-G415)
ALTENTREPTOW	GS 04 (ex-G 414)	**BOLTENHAGEN**	GS 09 (ex-G 443)
PASEWALK	GS 05 (ex-G 423)		

Displacement, tons: 327 standard; 377 full load
Dimensions, feet (metres): 171.3 × 22.6 × 7.2 *(52.2 × 6.9 × 2.2)*
Main machinery: 2—40DM diesels; 5000 hp(m) *(3.68 MW)*; 2 shafts; cp props
Speed, knots: 18
Complement: 30
Guns: 2—25 mm (twin) automatic.
Mines: 2 rails
Radars: Navigation: TSR-333; I band.
Sonars: Hull-mounted; active search; high frequency.

Comment: Built by Peenewerft, Wolgast in 1969-71. Ex-GDR Grenzebrigade Küste (GBK) originally taken over from the Navy. Not all are active and some may be sold.

KÜHLUNGSBORN *6/1991, Hartmut Ehlers*

1 BREDSTEDT CLASS (LARGE PATROL CRAFT)

Name	*No*	*Builders*	*Commissioned*
BREDSTEDT	BG 21	Elsflether Werft	24 May 1989

Displacement, tons: 673 full load
Dimensions, feet (metres): 214.6 × 30.2 × 10.5 *(65.4 × 9.2 × 3.2)*
Main machinery: 1 MTU 20V 1163TB 93 diesel; 8325 hp(m) *(6.12 MW)* sustained; 1 shaft; bow thruster; 1 auxiliary diesel generator; 1 motor
Speed, knots: 25 (12 on motor). **Range, miles:** 2000 at 25 kts; 7000 at 10 kts
Complement: 13 plus 9 spare berths
Guns: 1 Bofors 40 mm/70.
Helicopters: Platform only.

Comment: Ordered 27 November 1987, laid down 3 March 1988 and launched 18 December 1988. An Avon Searider rigid inflatable craft can be lowered by a stern ramp. A second RIB on the port side is launched by crane. Based in the German Bight.

BREDSTEDT *6/1991, Hartmut Ehlers*

3 SASSNITZ CLASS

Name	*No*	*Builders*	*Commissioned*
SASSNITZ	— (ex-P 6165, ex-591)	Peenewerft	31 July 1990
SELLIN	— (ex-592)	Peenewerft	2 Oct 1990
BINZ	— (ex-593)	Peenewerft	23 Dec 1990

Displacement, tons: 369 full load
Dimensions, feet (metres): 160.4 oa; 147.6 wl × 28.5 × 7.2 *(48.9; 45 × 8.7 × 2.2)*
Main machinery: 3 M 520 diesels; 14 670 hp(m) *(10.78 MW)*; 3 shafts
Speed, knots: 28. **Range, miles:** 2400 at 20 kts
Complement: 33 (7 officers)

Guns: 1 USSR 3 in *(76 mm)*/66 automatic; 85° elevation; 120 rounds/minute to 15 km *(8 nm)*; weight of shell 7 kg.
1—30 mm/65 ADG; 6 barrels; 3000 rounds/minute combined to 2 km.
Radars: Air/surface search: Plank Shave; E band.
Fire control: Bass Tilt; H/I band.

Programmes: Ex-GDR designated Balcom 10 and seen for the first time in the Baltic in August 1988. The original intention was to build up to 50 for the USSR, Poland and the GDR. By August 1990 the first five hulls were afloat and five more were in various stages of production. In 1991 the first three were transferred to the Border Guard, based at Neustadt.
Structure: Being fitted with German engines and electronics in 1992.
Sales: Three hulls transferred to Poland for completion at Gdynia.

SASSNITZ (old number) *5/1991, Hartmut Ehlers*

7 NEUSTADT CLASS (LARGE PATROL CRAFT)

Name	*No*	*Name*	*No*
NEUSTADT	BG 11	**ALSFELD**	BG 16
BAD BRAMSTEDT	BG 12	**BAYREUTH**	BG 17
DUDERSTADT	BG 14	**ROSENHEIM**	BG 18
ESCHWEGE	BG 15		

Displacement, tons: 218 full load
Dimensions, feet (metres): 127.1 × 23 × 5 *(38.5 × 7 × 2.2)*
Main machinery: 2 Maybach MTU diesels; 6000 hp(m) *(4.41 MW)*; 1 MWM diesel; 685 hp(m) *(500 kW)*; 3 shafts
Speed, knots: 30. **Range, miles:** 450 at 27 kts
Complement: 24
Guns: 1 or 2 Bofors 40 mm/70. After mounting removed in some of the class.

Comment: All built between 1969 and late 1970 by Lürssen, Vegesack. Form two flotillas: BG 11-14 the first and BG 15-18 the second. BG 13 was sold to Mauritania in February 1990.

DUDERSTADT *6/1991, Hartmut Ehlers*

4 RIVER PATROL CRAFT

SCHLUTUP +1 **BG 6** **BG 7**

Comment: *Schlutup* and sister ship of 7 m and 20 kts completed in 1988 and were used for border patrol in the Lübeck area. *BG 6* and *BG 7* of 15 m and 6 kts are former river engineers craft acquired in the 1970s.

BG 7 *10/1991, Hartmut Ehlers*

9 BREMSE CLASS (HARBOUR PATROL CRAFT)

GS 23 **GS 30-32** **GS 40-42** **GS 51-52**

Displacement, tons: 25 full load
Dimensions, feet (metres): 74 × 16.4 × 3.6 *(23 × 5 × 1.1)*
Main machinery: 2 DM diesels; 600 hp(m) *(441 kW)*; 2 shafts
Speed, knots: 14
Guns: 2—14.5 mm (twin) MGs can be carried.
Radars: Navigation: TSR 333; I band.

Comment: Built in 1971-72 for the ex-GDR GBK. Based at Warnemunde. Not all are active.

GS 31 *4/1991, Hartmut Ehlers*

1 ICEBREAKING TUG (TYPE 724)

Name	*No*	*Builders*	*Commissioned*
RETTIN	BG 5	Mützelfeldwerft	3 Dec 1976

Measurement, tons: 120 grt
Dimensions, feet (metres): 73.8 × 21.7 × 9.5 *(22.5 × 6.6 × 2.9)*
Main machinery: 2 MWM diesels; 590 hp(m) *(434 kW)*; 2 Voith-Schneider props
Speed, knots: 9
Complement: 4

Comment: Launched 29 October 1976. Bollard pull, 7.5 tons. Carries firefighting equipment.

RETTIN *7/1991, Hartmut Ehlers*

FISHERY PROTECTION AND RESEARCH SHIPS

(Operated by Ministry of Agriculture and Fisheries)

WARNEMUNDE of 377 tons and 18 kts. Ex-Kondor I class refitted October 1991
FRITHJOF of 2150 tons and 16 kts. Completed September 1968
MEERKATZE of 2250 tons and 15 kts. Completed December 1977
SEEFALKE of 1820 tons gross and 20 kts. Completed August 1981
SOLEA of 340 tons and 12 kts. Completed May 1974
UTHÖRN of 200 tons and 10 kts. Completed June 1982
WALTHER HERWIG of 2500 tons and 15 kts. Completed October 1972
HEINCKE of 1322 tons gross and 13 kts. Completed in June 1990

Comment: First four are Fishery Protection ships serving the fleet in the North Atlantic. *Seefalcke* has a helicopter platform. The remainder are research ships carrying scientists.

WARNEMUNDE (ex-Bergen) *6/1991, Hartmut Ehler*

SURVEY AND RESEARCH SHIPS

Note: The following ships operate for the Bundesamt für Seeschiff-fahrt und Hydrographie (BSH), under the Ministry of Transport or for the Ministry of Research and Technology.

ATAIR, ALKOR, WEGA 1050 tons, diesel-electric, 11.5 kts. Complement 16 plus 6 scientists. Built by Krögerwerft, completed 3 August 1987, 2 May 1990 and 26 October 1990 respectively
METEOR (research ship) 97.5 × 16.5 × 4.8 m, diesel-electric, 14 kts, range 10 000 nm. Complement 33 plus 29 research staff. Completed by Schlichting, Travemünde 15 March 1986
KOMET (survey and research) 1535 grt, speed 15 kts. Complement 42 plus 4 scientists. Completed 26 August 1969
GAUSS (survey and research) 1813 grt, completed 6 May 1980, speed 13.5 kts, complement 19 + 12 scientists. Modernised 1985
CARL FR GAUSS, DENEB, POLARSTERN, POSEIDON, SONNE.

METEOR *1991, Harald Carstens*

ALKOR *6/1991, Antonio Moreno*

CUSTOMS SERVICE

Note: (a) Operated by Ministry of Finance with a total of over 100 craft. Green hulls with grey superstructure and sometimes carry machine guns.
(b) Seaward patrol craft include *Hamburg, Bremerhaven, Schleswig-Holstein, Emden, Kniepsand, Alte Liebe, Priwall, Glückstadt, Helgoland, Oldenburg, Laboe, Ner Darchau* and *Hohwacht*.

PRIWALL *8/1991, Maritime Photographic*

POLICE

Note: (a) Under the control of regional governments. Blue hulls with white superstructure.
(b) There are 10 seaward patrol craft: *Wasserschutzpolizei 5, WSP 1* and *4, Bremen 2* and *3, Helgoland, Sylt, Fehmarn, Birknack* and *Falshöft*.
(c) Harbour craft include *Dithmarchen, Probstei, Schwansen, Vossbrook, Angela, Brunswick, Habicht*.

WSP 4 *11/1991, Antonio Moreno*

WATER AND NAVIGATION BOARD

Note: (a) Comes under the Ministry of Transport. Most ships have black hulls with black/red/yellow stripes.
(b) Three icebreakers: *Polarstern, Hanse* and *Max Waldeck*.
(c) Eight buoy tenders: *Walter Körte, Kurt Burkowitz, Otto Treplin, Gustav Meyer, Bruno Illing, Konrad Meisel, Barsemeister Brehme, J G Repsold*.
(d) Five oil recovery ships: *Scharhörn, Oland, Nordsee, Mellum, Kiel*.

MELLUM *5/1988, Hartmut Ehlers*

GHANA

Administration

Commander, Navy:
Captain Tom Kwesi Annan

Personnel

(a) 1992: 950
(b) Voluntary service

Naval Bases

Sekondi (Western Naval Command)
Tema, near Accra (Eastern Naval Command)

Mercantile Marine

Lloyd's Register of Shipping:
160 vessels of 134 865 tons gross

DELETIONS

1988-89 *Kromantse, Keta, Dela, Sahene,* 2 Spear 2 class, 2 Rotork craft

2 LÜRSSEN PB 57 CLASS (FAST ATTACK CRAFT—GUN)

Name	*No.*	*Builders*	*Commissioned*
ACHIMOTA	P 28	Lürssen, Vegesack	27 Mar 1981
YOGAGA	P 29	Lürssen, Vegesack	27 Mar 1981

Displacement, tons: 389 full load
Dimensions, feet (metres): 190.6 × 25 × 9.2 *(58.1 × 7.6 × 2.8)*
Main machinery: 3 MTU 16V538 TB91 diesels; 9180 hp(m) *(6.75 MW)* sustained; 3 shafts
Speed, knots: 30
Complement: 45 plus 2 VIPs
Guns: 1 OTO Melara 3 in *(76 mm)* compact; 85° elevation; 85 rounds/minute to 16 km *(8.6 nm)* anti-surface; 12 km *(6.5 nm)* anti-air; weight of shell 6 kg; 250 rounds.
1 Breda 40 mm/70; 85° elevation; 300 rounds/minute to 12.5 km *(6.8 nm)* anti-surface; weight of shell 0.96 kg; 750 rounds.
Fire control: LIOD optronic director.
Radars: Surface search/fire control: Thomson-CSF Canopus B; I/J band.
Navigation: Decca TM 1226C; I band.

Comment: Ordered in 1977. *Yogaga* completed a major overhaul at Swan Hunter's Wallsend, Tyneside yard 8 May 1989. *Achimota* started a similar refit at CMN Cherbourg in May 1991 and was joined by *Yogaga* for repairs in late 1991. Employed on Fishery Protection duties.

YOGAGA *5/1989, Swan Hunter*

2 LÜRSSEN FPB 45 CLASS (FAST ATTACK CRAFT—GUN)

Name	*No.*	*Builders*	*Commissioned*
DZATA	P 26	Lürssen, Vegesack	4 Dec 1979
SEBO	P 27	Lürssen, Vegesack	2 May 1980

Displacement, tons: 269 full load
Dimensions, feet (metres): 147.3 × 23 × 8.9 *(44.9 × 7 × 2.7)*
Main machinery: 2 MTU 16V538 TB91 diesels; 6120 hp(m) *(4.5 MW)* sustained; 2 shafts
Speed, knots: 27. **Range, miles:** 1800 at 16 kts; 700 at 25 kts
Complement: 55 (5 officers)
Guns: 2 Breda 40 mm/70; 80° elevation; 300 rounds/minute to 12.5 km *(6.8 nm)*; weight of shell 0.96 kg.
Fire control: LIOD optronic director.
Radars: Surface search/fire control: Thomson-CSF Canopus B; I/J band.
Navigation: Decca Type 978; I band.

Comment: Ordered in 1976. *Dzata* completed a major overhaul at Swan Hunter's Wallsend, Tyneside yard on 8 May 1989. *Sebo* started a similar refit at CMN Cherbourg in May 1991. Employed in Fishery Protection role.

DZATA *5/1989, Swan Hunter*

LAND-BASED MARITIME AIRCRAFT

Numbers/Type: 2 Fokker F27 400M.
Operational speed: 250 kts *(463 km/h)*.
Service ceiling: 25 000 ft *(7 620 m)*.
Range: 2 700 nm *(5 000 km)*.
Role/Weapon systems: Operated for coastal surveillance, SAR and shipping control tasks. Sensors: Weather radar. Weapons: Unarmed.

GREECE

Headquarters' Appointments

Chief of the Hellenic Navy:
Vice Admiral E Lagaras
Deputy Chief of the Hellenic Navy:
Rear Admiral G Demestihas
Deputy Chief, National Defence Staff:
Vice Admiral I Paloubis

Fleet Command

Commander of the Fleet:
Vice Admiral I Theophilopoulos
Chief of Staff, Fleet HQ:
Rear Admiral I Panagiotopoulos

Senior Appointments

Commander, Navy Training Command:
Rear Admiral N Fostieris
Commander, Navy Logistics Command:
Rear Admiral H Drikos

Diplomatic Representation

Naval Attaché in Ankara:
Commander K Mayatis
Naval Attaché in Bonn:
Captain E Rapatzikos
Naval Attaché in Cairo:
Captain D Lioumis
Naval Attaché in London:
Captain M Zevelakis
Naval Attaché in Paris:
Captain D Hatzidakis
Naval Attaché in Washington:
Captain A Kopitsas

Personnel

(a) 1992: 19 500 (2600 officers)
(b) Between 19 and 23 months' national service depending on location

Naval Bases

Salamis and Suda Bay

Naval Commands

Commander of the Fleet has under his flag all combatant ships. Navy Logistic Command is responsible for the bases at Salamis and Suda Bay, the Supply Centre and all auxiliary ships. Navy Training Command is in charge of the Naval Officers' Academy, Petty Officers' School, three training centres and a training ship.

Naval Districts

Aegean, Ionian and Northern Greece

Naval Aviation

Alouette III helicopters (No 1 Squadron).
AB 212ASW helicopters (No 2 and 3 Squadrons).
HU-16B Albatros are operated under naval command by mixed Air Force and Navy crews.

Prefix to Ships' Names

HS (Hellenic Ship)

Strength of the Fleet

Type	*Active (Reserve)*	*Building (Planned)*
Patrol Submarines	10	—
Destroyers	12	—
Frigates	2	(4)
Corvettes	2	(3)
Fast Attack Craft—Missile	14	—
Fast Attack Craft—Torpedo	10	—
Fast Attack Craft—Patrol	2	2
Large Patrol Craft	2	—
Coastal Patrol Craft	5	—
Major Landing Ships	12	4
LCUs	6	(6)
LCTs	2	—
Minor Landing Craft	77	—
Minelayers—Coastal	2	—
Minesweepers—Coastal	14	—
Survey and Research Vessels	6	—
Support Ship	1	—
Training Ship	1	—
Support Tankers	2	—
Harbour Tankers	4	—
Lighthouse Tenders	2	—
Tugs	17	—
Netlayer	1	—
Water Boats	8	—
Auxiliary Transports	2	—
Ammunition Ship	1	—

Mercantile Marine

Lloyd's Register of Shipping:
1863 vessels of 22 752 919 tons gross

)ELETIONS

ote: Many of the deleted ships are in unmaintained reserve in ıchorages.

estroyers

991 *Aspis, Velos, Lonchi, Sfendoni*

Frigates

1991 *Aetos, Ierax* (training hulk), *Leon* (training hulk)
1992 *Panthir*

Light Forces

1989 *Agathos*
1990 *N I Goulandris 1*
1991 *E Panagopoulos 1*

Amphibious Forces

1990 *I Tournas, Kea, Skopelos*
1991 *Lesbos* (old), *Kassos, Karpathos*

Miscellaneous

1989 *Vivies*
1990 *Minotaurus, Perseus*
1991 *Argo* (sold), *Aegeon, Arhikelefstis Stassis*

PENNANT LIST

ubmarines

S 110 Glavkos
S 111 Nereus
S 112 Triton
S 113 Proteus
S 114 Papanikolis
S 115 Katsonis
S 116 Posydon
S 117 Amphitrite
S 118 Okeanos
S 119 Pontos

estroyers

D 210 Themistocles
D 211 Miaoulis
D 212 Kanaris
D 213 Kountouriotis
D 214 Sachtouris
D 215 Tompazis
D 216 Apostolis
D 217 Kriezis
D 218 Kimon
D 219 Nearchos
D 220 Miltiadis
D 221 Konon

igates

F 450 Elli
F 451 Limnos
F 452 Hydra (bldg)
F 453 Spetsai (bldg)
F 454 Psara (bldg)
F 455 Salamis (bldg)

rvettes

P 62 Niki
P 63 Doxa

ght Forces

P 14 Anthipoploiarhos Anninos
P 15 Ipoploiarhos Arliotis
P 16 Ipoploiarhos Konidis
P 17 Ipoploiarhos Batsis
P 18 Armatolos
P 19 Navmachos
P 20 Antiploiarhos Laskos
P 21 Plotarhis Blessas
P 22 Ipoploiarhos Mikonios
P 23 Ipoploiarhos Troupakis
P 24 Simeoforos Kavaloudis
P 25 Anthipoploiarhos Kostakos
P 26 Ipoploiarhos Deyiannis
P 27 Simeoforos Xenos
P 28 Simeoforos Simitzopoulos
P 29 Simeoforos Starakis
P 50 Hesperos
P 52 Kentauros
P 53 Kyklon
P 54 Lelaps
P 55 Skorpios
P 56 Tyfon
P 70 E Panagopoulos 2
P 96 E Panagopoulos 3
P 196 Andromeda
P 198 Kyknos
P 199 Pigasos
P 228 Toxotis
P 229 Tolmi
P 230 Ormi
P 266 Adamidis
P 267 Dilos
P 268 Knossos
P 269 Lindos
P 286 Diopos Antoniou
P 287 Kelefstis Stamou

Amphibious Forces

L 104 Inouse
L 116 Kos
L 144 Siros
L 147 Kimolos
L 149 Kithnos
L 150 Sifnos
L 152 Skiathos
L 153 Nafkratoussa
L 154 Ikaria (old)
L 157 Rodos (old)
L 161 I Grigoropoulos
L 163 I Daniolos
L 164 I Roussen
L 165 I Krystalidis
L 171 Kriti
L 173 Chios
L 174 Samos
L 175 Ikaria (bldg)
L 176 Lesbos (new) (bldg)
L 177 Rodos (new) (bldg)
L 178 Naxos
L 179 Paros
L 185 Kithera
L 189 Milos

Minelayers

N 04 Aktion
N 05 Amvrakia

Minesweepers

M 202 Atalanti
M 205 Antiopi
M 206 Faedra
M 210 Thalia
M 211 Alkyon
M 213 Klio
M 214 Avra
M 240 Pleias
M 241 Kichli
M 242 Kissa
M 246 Aigli
M 247 Dafni
M 248 Aedon
M 254 Niovi

Service Forces

A 74 Aris
A 307 Thetis
A 373 Hermis
A 377 Arethousa
A 407 Antaios
A 408 Atlas
A 409 Acchileus
A 410 Atromitos
A 411 Adamastos
A 412 Aias
A 413 Pilefs
A 414 Ariadni
A 415 Evros
A 416 Ouranos
A 417 Hyperion
A 419 Pandora
A 420 Pandrosos
A 422 Kadmos
A 423 Heraklis
A 424 Iason
A 425 Odisseus
A 426 Kiklops
A 427 Danaos
A 428 Nestor
A 430 Pelops
A 431 Titan
A 432 Gigas
A 433 Kerkini
A 434 Prespa
A 435 Kekrops
A 436 Minos
A 437 Pelias
A 438 Aegeus
A 460 Evrotas
A 461 Arachthos
A 462 Strymon
A 463 Nestos
A 464 Axios
A 465 Yliki
A 466 Trichonis
A 467 Doirani
A 468 Kalliroe
A 469 Stynfalia
A 470 Kastoria
A 474 Pytheas
A 475 Doris
A 476 Strabon
A 478 Naftilos
A 479 I Karavoyiannos Theophilopoulos
A 481 St Likoudis
A 489 Orion
A 490 Zeus

SUBMARINES

8 GLAVKOS CLASS (209 TYPES 1100 and 1200)

me	*No*	*Builders*	*Laid down*	*Launched*	*Commissioned*
.AVKOS	S 110	Howaldtswerke, Kiel	1 Sep 1968	15 Sep 1970	6 Sep 1971
EREUS	S 111	Howaldtswerke, Kiel	15 Jan 1969	7 June 1971	10 Feb 1972
ITON	S 112	Howaldtswerke, Kiel	1 June 1969	14 Oct 1971	8 Aug 1972
ROTEUS	S 113	Howaldtswerke, Kiel	1 Oct 1969	1 Feb 1972	8 Aug 1972
)SYDON	S 116	Howaldtswerke, Kiel	15 Jan 1976	21 Mar 1978	22 Mar 1979
MPHITRITE	S 117	Howaldtswerke, Kiel	26 Apr 1976	14 June 1978	14 Sep 1979
KEANOS	S 118	Howaldtswerke, Kiel	1 Oct 1976	16 Nov 1978	15 Nov 1979
)NTOS	S 119	Howaldtswerke, Kiel	25 Jan 1977	21 Mar 1979	29 Apr 1980

splacement, tons: 1100 surfaced; 1210 (1285, second four) dived
mensions, feet (metres): 178.4; 183.4 (116-119) × 20.3 × 17.9 *(54.4; 55.9 × 6.2 × 5.5)*
ain machinery: Diesel-electric; 4 MTU 12V 493 AZ 80 diesels; 2400 hp(m) *(1.76 MW)* sustained; 4 Siemens alternators; 1.7 MW; 1 Siemens motor; 4600 hp(m) *(3.38 MW)* sustained; 1 shaft
eed, knots: 11 surfaced; 21.5 dived
omplement: 31 (6 officers)

issiles: McDonnell Douglas Sub Harpoon (after modernisation); active radar homing to 130 km *(70 nm)* at 0.9 Mach; warhead 258 kg.
rpedoes: 8—21 in *(533 mm)* bow tubes. 14 probably AEG SST 4; wire-guided; active homing to 13 km *(7 nm)* at 35 kts; passive homing to 28 km *(15 nm)* at 23 kts; warhead 260 kg. Swim-out discharge. Probably to be replaced by AEG SEEAL 3.
untermeasures: ESM: radar warning.
re control: Kanaris (unmodernised). Signaal (S 116-S 119). Unisys (after modernisation)
adars: Surface search: Thomson-CSF Calypso II; I band; range 31 km *(17 nm)* for 10 m² target.
onars: Krupp Atlas CSU 3-2 (unmodernised); hull-mounted; active/passive search and attack; medium frequency.
Krupp Atlas PRS-3-4; passive ranging.
Krupp Atlas CSU 83-90 (DBQS-21) (after modernisation)
Krupp Atlas CSU-3-4 (S 112, 116-119); hull-mounted; active/passive search and attack; medium frequency.
Thomson Sintra DUUX 2; passive ranging.

ogrammes: Designed by Ingenieurkontor, Lübeck for construction by Howaldtswerke, Kiel and sale by Ferrostaal, Essen all acting as a consortium.

AMPHITRITE *1987, van Ginderen Collection*

Modernisation: Contract signed 5 May 1989 with HDW and Ferrostaal to implement a Neptune update programme to bring first four up to the same standard as the others and along the same lines as the German S 206A class. Also to include Sub Harpoon. *Triton* completed refit at Kiel in March 1992, remainder are being done at Salamis between 1991 and 1996. A quarter of the cost is covered by German Military Aid.

Structure: A single-hull design with two ballast tanks and fwd and after trim tanks. Fitted with snort and remote machinery control. The single screw is slow revving. Very high capacity batteries with GRP lead-acid cells and battery cooling—by Wilh Hagen and VARTA. Diving depth, 250 m *(820 ft)*. Fitted with two periscopes.
Operational: Endurance, 50 days.

1 Ex-US GUPPY III CLASS

Name	No	Builders	Laid down	Launched	Commissioned
KATSONIS (ex-USS *Remora* SS 487)	S 115	Portsmouth Navy Yard	5 Mar 1945	12 July 1945	3 Jan 1946

Displacement, tons: 1975 standard; 2450 dived
Dimensions, feet (metres): 326.5 × 27 × 17 *(99.4 × 8.2 × 5.2)*
Main machinery: Diesel-electric; 4 Fairbanks-Morse 38D8 1/8-10 diesels; 6000 hp *(4.48 MW)*; 2 motors; 5600 hp *(4.18 MW)*; 2 shafts
Speed, knots: 20 surfaced; 15 dived
Range, miles: 12 000 at 10 kts surfaced
Complement: 85

Torpedoes: 10—21 in *(533 mm)* tubes (6 bow, 4 stern). 24 probably Honeywell Mk 37 Mod 1; wire-guided; active/passive homing to 8 km *(4.4 nm)* at 24 kts; warhead 150 kg.
Countermeasures: ESM: WLR-1; radar warning.
Radars: Surface search: I band.
Sonars: EDO BQR 2B; hull-mounted; passive; medium frequency.
Sperry/Raytheon BQG 4; fire control; hull-mounted; passive; medium frequency.

Programmes: Transferred 29 October 1973 by sale.
Operational: Training boat.

KATSONIS — *1989, Hellenic Navy*

1 Ex-US GUPPY IIA CLASS

Name	No	Builders	Laid down	Launched	Commissioned
PAPANIKOLIS (ex-USS *Hardhead* SS 365)	S 114	Manitowoc SB Co	7 July 1943	12 Dec 1943	Apr 1944

Displacement, tons: 1840 standard; 2445 dived
Dimensions, feet (metres): 306 × 27 × 17 *(93.2 × 8.2 × 5.2)*
Main machinery: Diesel-electric; 3 GM 16-278A diesels; 4500 hp *(3.36 MW)*; 2 motors; 5400 hp *(4.3 MW)*; 2 shafts
Speed, knots: 17 surfaced; 15 dived
Range, miles: 12 000 at 10 kts surfaced
Complement: 84

Torpedoes: 10—21 in *(533 mm)* tubes (6 bow, 4 stern). 24 probably Honeywell Mk 37 Mod 1; wire-guided; active/passive homing to 8 km *(4.3 nm)* at 24 kts; warhead 150 kg.
Countermeasures: ESM: WLR-1; radar warning.
Radars: Surface search: I band.
Sonars: EDO BQR 2B; hull-mounted; passive search; medium frequency.

Programmes: Transferred 26 July 1972 by sale.
Operational: Training boat.

PAPANIKOLIS — *1990, Hellenic Navy*

DESTROYERS

4 Ex-US CHARLES F ADAMS CLASS

Name	No	Builders	Laid down	Launched	Commissioned	Recommiss
KIMON (ex-*Semmes*)	D 218 (ex-DDG 18)	Avondale Marine Ways	18 Aug 1960	20 May 1961	10 Dec 1962	12 Sep 1
NEARCHOS (ex-*Byrd*)	D 219 (ex-DDG 23)	Todd Shipyards	12 Apr 1961	6 Feb 1962	7 Mar 1964	13 May 1
MILTIADIS (ex-*Strauss*)	D 220 (ex-DDG 16)	New York Shipbuilding	27 Dec 1960	9 Dec 1961	20 Apr 1963	27 Aug 1
KONON (ex-*Waddell*)	D 221 (ex-DDG 24)	Todd Shipyards	6 Feb 1962	26 Feb 1963	28 Aug 1964	15 Sep 1

*Planned dates

Displacement, tons: 3370 standard; 4825 full load
Dimensions, feet (metres): 437 × 47 × 15.6; 21 (sonar) *(133.2 × 14.3 × 4.8; 6.4)*
Main machinery: 4 boilers (Foster-Wheeler in D 219, 221, Combustion Engineering in D 218, 220); 2 turbines (General Electric in D 218, 220, Westinghouse in D 219, 221); 70 000 hp *(52.2 MW)*; 2 shafts
Speed, knots: 30. **Range, miles:** 6000 at 15 kts; 1600 at 30 kts
Complement: 340 (22 officers)

Missiles: SSM: 6 McDonnell Douglas Harpoon; active radar homing to 130 km *(70 nm)* at 0.9 Mach; warhead 227 kg.
SAM: 34 GDC Standard SM-1MR; command guidance; semi-active radar homing to 46 km *(25 nm)* at 2 Mach; height 150-60 000 ft (45.7-18 288 m).
1 single Mk 13 launcher ❶; can load, direct, and fire about 6 missiles per minute. There are 40 missiles carried. 6 Harpoons are stored in the magazines as part of the load.
A/S: Honeywell ASROC Mk 16 octuple launcher ❷; inertial guidance to 1.6-10 km *(1-5.4 nm)*; payload Mk 46 Mod 5.
Guns: 2 FMC 5 in *(127 nm)*/54 Mk 42 ❸; 85° elevation; 20-40 rounds/minute to 24 km *(13 nm)*; weight of shell 32 kg.
4—12.7 mm MGs.
Torpedoes: 6—324 mm Mk 32 (2 triple) tubes ❹. Honeywell Mk 46; anti-submarine; active/passive homing to 11 km *(5.9 nm)* at 40 kts; warhead 44 kg.
Countermeasures: Decoys: 4 Loral Hycor SRBOC 6-barrelled fixed Mk 36; IR flares and Chaff to 4 km *(2.2 nm)*.
T—Mk-6 Fanfare; torpedo decoy.
ESM/ECM: SLQ 32V(2); radar warning.
Combat data systems: NTDS. Link 14 receive only. SATCOM.
Fire control: Mk 68 GFCS. Mk 4 WDS. Mk 70 MFCS. Mk 114 FCS ASW. SYS-1 IADT.
Radars: Air search: Hughes SPS 52B/C ❺; 3D; E/F band; range 439 km *(240 nm)*.
Lockheed SPS 40B/D ❻; E/F band; range 320 km *(175 nm)*.
Surface search: Raytheon SPS 10D/F ❼; G band.
Navigation: Marconi LN 66; I band.
Fire control: Two Raytheon SPG 51D ❽; G/I band.
Lockheed SPG 53A ❾; K band.
Tacan: URN 25/SRN 6. IFF Mk XII.
Sonars: Sangamo SQS 23D; hull-mounted (bow-mounted SQQ 23 Pair in D 219, 221); active search and attack; medium frequency.

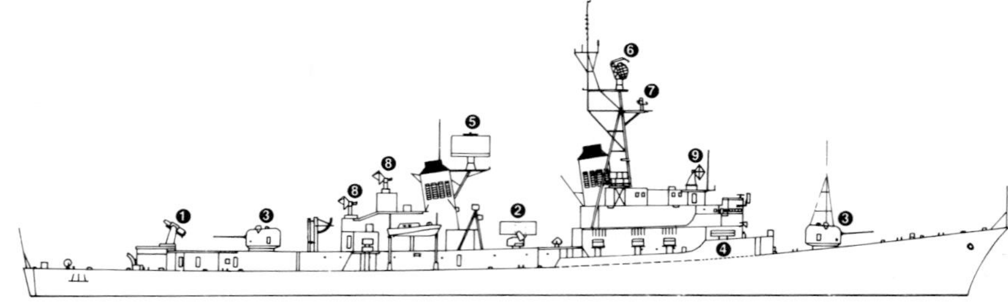

KIMON — *(Scale 1 : 1 200), Ian Sturton*

KIMON (old number) — *6/1990, Giorgio Ar*

Programmes: Leased as part of the Defence Co-operation Agreement signed with the USA on 8 July 1990. Planned transfer dates are shown in the Recommissioned column for the last three ships.

Structure: *Nearchos* and *Konon* have stern anchors because c the sonar Pair arrangement.

1 Ex-US GEARING (FRAM II) and 6 Ex-US GEARING (FRAM I) CLASSES

Name	No	Builders	Laid down	Launched	Commissioned
THEMISTOCLES (ex-USS *Frank Knox* DD 742)	D 210	Bath Iron Works	8 May 1944	17 Sep 1944	11 Dec 1944
KANARIS (ex-USS *Stickell* DD 888)	D 212	Consolidated Steel Corporation	5 Jan 1945	16 June 1945	26 Sep 1945
KOUNTOURIOTIS (ex-USS *Rupertus* DD 851)	D 213	Bethlehem (Quincy)	2 May 1945	21 Sep 1945	8 Mar 1946
SACHTOURIS (ex-USS *Arnold J Isbell* DD 869)	D 214	Bethlehem (Staten Island)	14 Mar 1945	6 Aug 1945	5 Jan 1946
TOMPAZIS (ex-USS *Gurke* DD 783)	D 215	Todd Pacific Shipyards	Oct 1944	15 Feb 1945	12 May 1945
APOSTOLIS (ex-USS *Charles P Cecil* DD 835)	D 216	Bath Iron Works	2 Dec 1944	22 Apr 1945	29 June 1945
KRIEZIS (ex-USS *Corry* DD 817)	D 217	Consolidated Steel Corporation	5 Apr 1945	28 July 1945	26 Feb 1946

Displacement, tons: 2425 standard; 3500 full load
Dimensions, feet (metres): 390.5 × 41.2 × 19 *(119 × 12.6 × 5.8)*
Main machinery: 4 Babcock & Wilcox boilers; 600 psi *(43.3 kg/cm sq)*; 850°F *(454°C)*; 2 Westinghouse turbines; 60 000 hp *(45 MW)*; 2 shafts
Speed, knots: 32.5. **Range, miles:** 4800 at 15 kts
Complement: 269 (16 officers)

Missiles: SSM: 4 McDonnell Douglas Harpoon (not in D 210, D 216-217) ❶; active radar homing to 130 km *(70 nm)* at 0.9 Mach; warhead 227 kg.
SAM: Portable Redeye; shoulder-launched; short range.
A/S: Honeywell ASROC Mk 112 octuple launcher (not in D 210) ❷; inertial guidance to 10 km *(5.4 nm)*. Mk 46 torpedo; active/passive homing to 11 km *(5.9 nm)* at 40 kts; warhead 45 kg.
Guns: 4 USN 5 in *(127 mm)*/38 (2 twin) Mk 38 (D 210 has 3 twin mountings) ❸; 85° elevation; 15 rounds/minute to 17 km *(9 nm)* anti-surface; 11 km *(5.9 nm)* anti-aircraft; weight of shell 25 kg.
1 OTO Melara 3 in *(76 mm)*/62 compact aft (D 212-217) ❹; 85° elevation; 85 rounds/minute to 16 km *(8.6 nm)* anti-surface; 12 km *(6.5 nm)* anti-aircraft; weight of shell 6 kg.
1 Bofors 40 mm/70 (D 216-217); 90° elevation; 300 rounds/minute to 12 km *(6.5 nm)*; weight of shell 2.4 kg.
4 Rheinmetall 20 mm/20 Mk 20 (D 210 amidships) ❺; 55° elevation; 1000 rounds/minute to 2 km.
2—12.7 mm MGs (all).
Torpedoes: 6—324 mm Mk 32 (2 triple) tubes ❻. Honeywell Mk 46; anti-submarine; active/passive homing to 11 km *(5.9 nm)* at 40 kts; warhead 44 kg.
A/S mortars: 2 USN Mk 10 Hedgehog 24-barrelled rocket launchers (D 210); manual loading; range 350 m; warhead 26 kg.
Depth charges: 2 racks (not in D 210).
Countermeasures: Decoys: 2 Loral-Hycor SRBOC fixed triple 6-barrelled Chaff launchers; range 1-4 km *(0.6-2.2 nm)*.
ESM: WLR-1; radar warning.
ECM: ULQ-6; jammer.
Fire control: Mk 37 GFCS. Elsag NA 21/30.
Radars: Air search: Westinghouse SPS 37 (D 212, D 215, D 216) ❼; B/C band; range 556 km *(300 nm)*.
Lockheed SPS 40 (remainder) ❼; E/F band; range 320 km *(175 nm)*.
Surface search: Raytheon/Sylvania SPS 10 ❽; G band.
Navigation: Decca; I band.
Fire control: Western Electric Mk 25 ❾; I/J band.
Selenia RTN 10X (not in D 210) ❿; I/J band; range 40 km *(22 nm)*.
Sonars: Sangamo SQS 23 or DE 1191; hull-mounted; active search and attack; medium frequency.
Litton SQA 10 (D 210); VDS; active search; medium frequency.

Helicopters: 1 AB 212ASW (D 210) ⓫.

Programmes: From USA: D 214, 4 Dec 1973 (sold 11 July 1978); D 212, 1 July 1972; D 213, 10 July 1973 (sold 11 July 1978); D 210, 30 Jan 1971; D 215, by sale 17 Mar 1977, commissioned 20 Mar 1977; D 216 and ex-USS *Myles C Fox* 2 August 1980. D 217 and ex-USS *Dyess* DD 880 transferred 27 February 1981 by sale. *(Myles C Fox* and *Dyess* transferred for spares but scrapped in 1991.) D 210 was a FRAM II Radar Picket conversion, remainder are FRAM I DD conversions.
Modernisation: Major modernisation programme in 1987-88 for all except D 210. Included Harpoon, OTO Melara 76 mm/62 gun placed aft and a new FCS (NA-30 or NA-21). D 216 and D 217 completed in 1987 without Harpoon but with a forward Bofors 40 mm/70 mounted between the torpedo tubes. D 210, refitted in the Eleusis Shipyard, received a telescopic hangar for a larger helicopter (AB 212). Harpoon is not always carried. SQS 23 being replaced by DE 1191 hull-mounted sonar in at least three of the class. Further planned modifications have been cancelled because of the acquisition of newer ships.

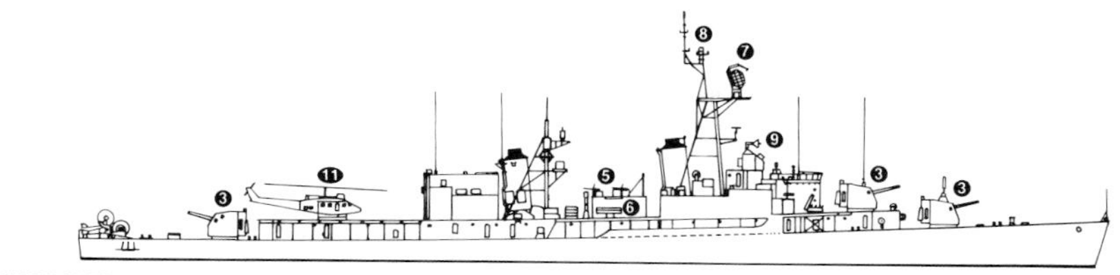

THEMISTOCLES *(Scale 1 : 1 200), Ian Sturton*

THEMISTOCLES *10/1991, D. Dervissis*

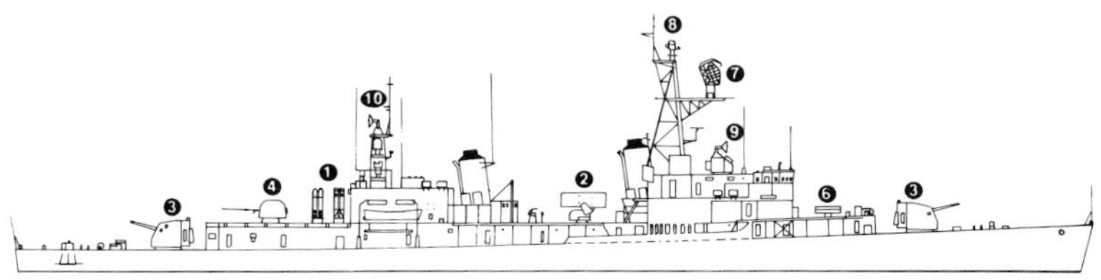

KANARIS *(Scale 1 : 1 200), Ian Sturton*

KOUNTOURIOTIS *9/1991, van Ginderen Collection*

KANARIS (Flagship Navocformed) *10/1990, Hellenic Navy*

1 Ex-US ALLEN M SUMNER (FRAM II) CLASS

Name	No	Builders	Laid down	Launched	Commissioned
MIAOULIS (ex-USS *Ingraham* DD 694)	D 211	Federal SB & DD Co	4 Aug 1943	16 Jan 1944	10 Mar 1944

Displacement, tons: 2200 standard; 3320 full load
Dimensions, feet (metres): 376.5 × 40.9 × 19 *(114.8 × 12.5 × 5.8)*
Main machinery: 4 Babcock & Wilcox boilers; 600 psi *(43.3 kg/cm sq)*; 850°F *(454°C)*; 2 turbines; 60 000 hp *(45 MW)*; 2 shafts
Speed, knots: 34. **Range, miles:** 4600 at 15 kts
Complement: 269 (16 officers)

Missiles: SAM: Portable Redeye; shoulder-launched; short range.
Guns: 6 USN 5 in *(127 mm)*/38 (3 twin) Mk 38 ❶; 85° elevation; 15 rounds/minute to 17 km *(9.2 nm)* anti-surface; 11 km *(5.9 nm)* anti-aircraft; weight of shell 25 kg.
2 Rheinmetall 20 mm/20 Mk 20; 55° elevation; 1000 rounds/minute to 2 km.
2—12.7 mm MGs.
Torpedoes: 6—324 mm Mk 32 (2 triple) tubes ❷. Honeywell Mk 46; anti-submarine; active/passive homing to 11 km *(5.9 nm)* at 40 kts; warhead 44 kg.
A/S mortars: 2 USN Hedgehog Mk 10 24-barrelled rocket launchers ❸; manual loading; range 350 m; warhead 26 kg.
Countermeasures: Decoys: 2 triple Loral-Hycor 6-barrelled Chaff launchers; range 1-4 km *(0.6-2.2 nm)*.
ESM: WLR-1; radar warning.
Fire control: Mk 37 GFCS.
Radars: Air search: Lockheed SPS 40 ❹; E/F band; range 320 km *(175 nm)*.
Surface search: Raytheon/Sylvania SPS 10 ❺; G band.
Navigation: Decca; I band.
Fire control: Western Electric Mk 25 Mod 3 ❻; I/J band.
Sonars: DE 1191; hull-mounted; active search and attack; medium frequency.

Helicopters: 1 AB 212ASW ❼.

Programmes: Former fleet destroyer of the Allen M Sumner class which had been modernised under the FRAM II programme. Transferred by USA 16 July 1971 by sale.
Modernisation: Work carried out at the Eleusis Shipyards during 1986-87. Improvements included a new telescopic hangar to accommodate larger helicopter and a telescopic crane. At the same time the VDS was removed. SQS 29 sonar probably replaced by DE 1191 in 1991.

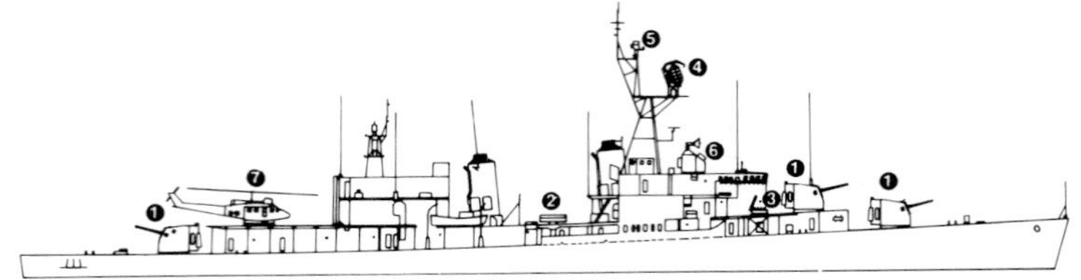

MIAOULIS *(Scale 1 : 1 200), Ian Sturton*

MIAOULIS *1990, Hellenic Navy*

FRIGATES

Notes: (1) Two ex-US Knox class are planned to be transferred in late 1992 or early 1993. It is also intended to acquire two more ex-Dutch Kortenaer class in due course.
(2) The Cannon class *Leon* (D 54) and *Ierax* (D 31) are used by the Training Command. D 54 may occasionally be at sea during the day but D 31 is permanently moored.

0 + 4 HYDRA CLASS (MEKO 200HN)

Name	No	Builders	Laid down	Launched	Commissioned
HYDRA	F 452	Blohm & Voss, Hamburg	17 Dec 1990	25 June 1991	Oct 1992
SPETSAI	F 453	Hellenic Shipyards, Skaramanga	2 Dec 1991	Oct 1992	Apr 1995
PSARA	F 454	Hellenic Shipyards, Skaramanga	Apr 1993	Jan 1994	July 1996
SALAMIS	F 455	Hellenic Shipyards, Skaramanga	May 1994	Mar 1995	June 1997

Displacement, tons: 2710 light; 3200 full load
Dimensions, feet (metres): 383.9; 357.6 (wl) × 48.6 × 13.5 *(117; 109 × 14.8 × 4.1)*
Main machinery: CODOG; 2 GE LM 2500 gas turbines; 46 000 hp *(34.3 MW)* sustained; 2 MTU 20V 956 TB82 diesels; 11 070 hp(m) *(8.14 MW)* sustained; 2 shafts; cp props
Speed, knots: 31 gas; 20 diesel. **Range, miles:** 4100 at 16 kts
Complement: 173 plus 16 flag staff

Missiles: SSM: 8 McDonnell Douglas Harpoon Block 1C; 2 quad launchers ❶; active radar homing to 130 km *(70 nm)* at 0.9 Mach; warhead 227 kg.
SAM: Raytheon NATO Sea Sparrow Mk 48 Mod 2A vertical launcher ❷; 16 missiles; semi-active radar homing to 14.6 km *(8 nm)* at 2.5 Mach; warhead 39 kg.
Guns: 1 FMC Mk 45 Mod 2A 5 in *(127 mm)*/54 ❸; dual purpose.
2 GD/GE Vulcan Phalanx 20 mm Mk 15 Mod 12 ❹; 6 barrels per mounting; 3000 rounds/minute combined to 1.5 km.
Torpedoes: 6—324 mm Mk 32 Mod 5 (2 triple) tubes ❺. Honeywell Mk 46; anti-submarine; active/passive homing to 11 km *(5.9 nm)* at 40 kts; warhead 44 kg.
Countermeasures: Decoys: 4 Mk 36 Mod 2 SRBOC Chaff launchers ❻.
SLQ-25 Nixie; torpedo decoy.
ESM: Argo AR 700; Telegon 10; intercept.
ECM: Argo APECS II; jammer.
Combat data systems: Signaal STACOS Mod 2; Links 11 and 14.
Fire control: Two Signaal Mk 73 Mod 1 (for SAM). Vesta Helo transponder with data link for OTHT. SAR-8 IR search. SWG 1 A(V) Harpoon LCS.
Radars: Air search: Signaal MW 08 ❼; 3D; F/G band.
Air Surface search: Signaal/Magnavox; DA 08 ❽, F band.
Navigation: Racal Decca 2690 BT; I band.
Fire Control: 2 Signaal STIR ❾; I/J/K band.
IFF: Mk XII Mod 4.
Sonars: Raytheon SQS-56/DE 1160; hull-mounted and VDS.

Helicopters: 1 Sikorsky S-70B6 Seahawk ❿.

Programmes: Decision to buy four Meko 200 Mod 3HN announced on 18 April 1988. West German Government offset of tanks and aircraft went with the sale, and the electronics and some of the weapon systems secured through US FMS credits. The first ship ordered 10 February 1989 built by Blohm & Voss, Hamburg and the remainder ordered 10 May 1989 at Hellenic Shipyards, Skaramanga, with German technical assistance. They will replace the deleted Fletcher class. Programme may be delayed by financial problems at Hellenic Shipyards in early 1992.

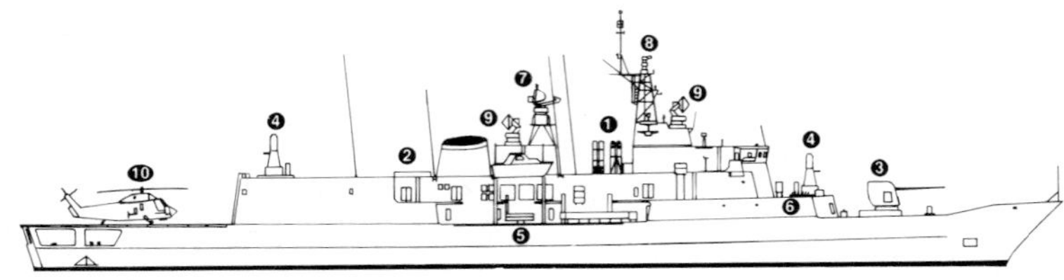

HYDRA *(Scale 1 : 1 200), Ian Sturton*

HYDRA (artist's impression) *1991, Hellenic Navy*

Structure: The design follows the Portuguese Vasco da Gama class. All steel fin stabilisers.

2 + (2) NETHERLANDS KORTENAER CLASS

Name	No	Builders	Laid down	Launched	Commissioned
ELLI (ex-*Pieter Florisz* F 812)	F 450	Koninklijke Maatschappij de Schelde, Flushing	1 July 1977	15 Dec 1979	10 Oct 1981
LIMNOS (ex-*Witte de With* F 813)	F 451	Koninklijke Maatschappij de Schelde, Flushing	13 June 1978	27 Oct 1979	18 Sep 1982

Displacement, tons: 3050 standard; 3630 full load
Dimensions, feet (metres): 428 × 47.9 × 20.3 (screws) *(130.5 × 14.6 × 6.2)*
Main machinery: COGOG; 2 RR Olympus TM3B gas turbines; 43 000 hp *(32 MW)* sustained; 2 RR Tyne RM1C gas turbines; 10 680 hp *(8 MW)* sustained; 2 shafts; cp props
Speed, knots: 30. **Range, miles:** 4700 at 16 kts
Complement: 176 (17 officers)

Missiles: SSM: 8 McDonnell Douglas Harpoon (2 quad) launchers ❶; active radar homing to 130 km *(70 nm)* at 0.9 Mach; warhead 227 kg; 16 missiles.
SAM: Raytheon NATO Sea Sparrow ❷; 24 missiles; semi-active radar homing to 14.6 km *(8 nm)* at 2.5 Mach; warhead 39 kg.
Portable Redeye; shoulder-launched; short range.
Guns: 2 OTO Melara 3 in *(76 mm)*/62 compact ❸; 85° elevation; 85 rounds/minute to 16 km *(8.6 nm)* anti-surface; 12 km *(6.5 nm)* anti-aircraft; weight of shell 6 kg.
2 GE/GD Vulcan Phalanx 20 mm Mk 15 6-barrelled ❹; 90° elevation; 3000 rounds/minute combined to 1.5 km.
Torpedoes: 4—324 mm Mk 32 (2 twin) tubes ❺. 16 Honeywell Mk 46 Mod 1/2; anti-submarine; active/passive homing to 11 km *(5.9 nm)* at 40 kts; warhead 44 kg.
Countermeasures: Decoys: 2 Loral Hycor Mk 36 SRBOC Chaff launchers.
ESM: Elettronika Sphinx; radar warning.
ECM: Jammer.
Combat data systems: SEWACO II action data automation; Links 10 and 11.
Radars: Air search: Signaal LW 08 ❻; D band; range 264 km *(145 nm)* for 2 m² target.
Surface search: Signaal ZW 06 ❼; I band; range 26 km *(14 nm)*.
Fire control: Signaal WM 25 ❽; I/J band; range 46 km *(25 nm)*.
Signaal STIR ❾; I/J/K band; range 140 km *(76 nm)* for 1 m² target.
Sonars: Canadian Westinghouse SQS 505; hull-mounted; active search and attack; 7 kHz.

Helicopters: 2 AB 212ASW ❿.

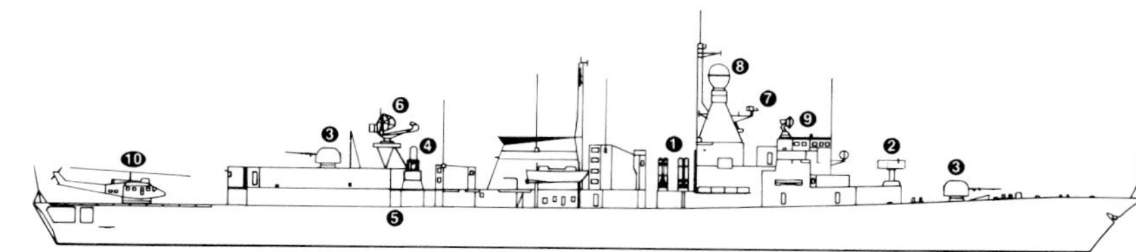

ELLI (Scale 1 : 1 200), *Ian Sturton*

LIMNOS (with Gulf fit) *9/1990, Photo Sami*

Programmes: A contract was signed with the Netherlands on 15 September 1980 for the purchase of one of the Kortenaer class building for the Netherlands' Navy, and an option on a second of class, which was taken up 7 June 1981.
Modernisation: The original plan was to fit one Phalanx CIWS in place of the after 76 mm gun but for Gulf deployments in 1990-91 the gun was retained and two Phalanx fitted on the deck above the torpedo tubes. Corvus Chaff launchers replaced by SRBOC (fitted either side of the bridge).
Structure: Hangar is 2 m longer than in Netherlands' ships to accommodate AB 212ASW helicopters.
Opinion: If the Netherlands Navy continues with the planned early retirement of four of its Kortenaer class, the Hellenic Navy may seek to acquire two of them.

SHIPBORNE AIRCRAFT

Numbers/Type: 5 Sikorsky S-70B6 Seahawk.
Operational speed: 135 kts *(250 km/h)*.
Service ceiling: 10 000 ft *(3050 m)*.
Range: 600 nm *(1110 km)*.
Role/Weapon systems: Ordered 25 July 1991 with an option for 7 more. To be used on the Hydra class. Sensors and weapons not yet confirmed.

Numbers/Type: 4 Aerospatiale SA 319B Alouette III.
Operational speed: 113 kts *(210 km/h)*.
Service ceiling: 10 500 ft *(3200 m)*.
Range: 290 nm *(540 km)*.
Role/Weapon systems: Shipborne ASW/SAR role on older escorts; thought to be limited to daylight operations only. Sensors: None. Weapons: ASW; 1 or 2 × Mk 44/46 torpedoes.

Numbers/Type: 12 Agusta AB 212ASW.
Operational speed: 106 kts *(196 km/h)*.
Service ceiling: 14 200 ft *(4330 m)*.
Range: 230 nm *(425 km)*.
Role/Weapon systems: Shipborne ASW/Elint and surface search role from new escorts. Sensors: Selenia APS-705 radar, AQS-18 dipping sonar. Weapons: ASW; 2 × Mk 46 or 2 × A244/S homing torpedoes.

AB 212ASW *1987, Hellenic Navy*

LAND-BASED MARITIME AIRCRAFT

Numbers/Type: 12 Grumman HU-16B Albatross.
Operational speed: 130 kts *(241 km/h)*.
Service ceiling: 25 000 ft *(7620 m)*.
Range: 2480 nm *(4590 km)*.
Role/Weapon systems: Aegean Sea reconnaissance amphibian; update programme abandoned in favour of procurement of 6 P-3A Orion replacement aircraft by 1992. Sensors: Search radar. Weapons: ASW; 6 × torpedoes or depth bombs or mines.

Numbers/Type: 12 Lockheed P-3A Orion.
Operational speed: 410 kts *(760 km/h)*.
Service ceiling: 28 300 ft *(8625 m)*.
Range: 4000 nm *(7410 km)*.
Role/Weapon systems: Maritime reconnaissance aircraft transferred from the USN in 1992 as part of the Defence Co-operation Agreement signed in July 1990; 4 to be kept in reserve. Sensors: APS 115 radar; sonobuoys; ESM. Weapons: ASW; Mk 44/46 torpedoes, depth bombs and mines.

CORVETTES

2 + 3 EX-GERMAN THETIS CLASS

Name	No	Commissioned	Recommissioned
NIKI (ex-*Thetis*)	P 62 (ex-P 6052)	1 July 1961	6 Sep 1991
DOXA (ex-*Najade*)	P 63 (ex-P 6054)	12 May 1962	6 Sep 1991
— (ex-*Triton*)	P 64 (ex-P 6055)	10 Nov 1962	June 1992
— (ex-*Hermes*)	P 65 (ex-P 6053)	16 Dec 1961	Sep 1992
— (ex-*Theseus*)	P 66 (ex-P 6056)	15 Aug 1963	Nov 1992

Displacement, tons: 575 standard; 732 full load
Dimensions, feet (metres): 229.7 × 26.9 × 8.6 *(70 × 8.2 × 2.7)*
Main machinery: 2 MAN V84V diesels; 6800 hp(m) *(5 MW)*; 2 shafts
Speed, knots: 19.5. **Range, miles:** 2760 at 15 kts
Complement: 64 (4 officers)

Guns: 2 Breda 40 mm/70 (twin); 85° elevation; 300 rounds/minute to 12.5 km *(6.7 nm)*; weight of shell 0.96 kg.
Torpedoes: 4—324 mm single tubes. 4 Honeywell Mk 46; active/passive homing to 11 km *(5.9 nm)* at 40 kts; warhead 44 kg.
A/S mortars: 1 Bofors 375 mm 4-barrelled trainable launcher; automatic loading; range 1600 m; 20 rockets.
Depth charges: 2 rails.
Fire control: Signaal Mk 9 TFCS.
Radars: Surface search: Thomson-CSF TRS 3001; E/F band.
Navigation: Kelvin Hughes 14/9; I band.
Sonars: Krupp Atlas ELAC 1 BV; hull-mounted; active search and attack; high frequency.

Programmes: All built by Rolandwerft, Bremen. Transfer dates for the last three are estimates only.
Structure: *Doxa* has a deckhouse before bridge for sick bay. Torpedo tubes have liners effectively reducing their diameter to 324 mm.

NIKI (old number) *6/1991, Stefan Terzibaschitisch*

LIGHT FORCES

0 + 2 HELLENIC 56 class (FAST ATTACK CRAFT – PATROL)

Displacement, tons: 550 full load
Dimensions, feet (metres): 185.4 × 32.8 × 8.9 *(56.5 × 10 × 2.7)*
Main machinery: 2 Wärtsilä 16 V 25 diesels; 9200 hp(m) *(6.76 MW)* sustained; 2 shafts
Speed, knots: 25. **Range, miles:** 2200 at 15 kts; 800 at 25 kts
Complement: 36 plus 23 spare
Guns: 1 Bofors 40 mm/70. 2 Rheinmetall 20 mm.
Mines: 2 rails.
Fire control: Selenia Elsag NA 21.
Radars: Surface search: Thomson-CSF Triton; I band.

Comment: Ordered from Hellenic Shipyards 20 February 1990. This is a new design by Hellenic which uses the modular concept so that weapons and sensors can be changed as required. First of class to be delivered in late 1992. Alternative guns + 2 Harpoon SSM can be fitted.

2 OSPREY 55 CLASS (FAST ATTACK CRAFT—PATROL)

Name	*No*	*Builders*	*Commissioned*
ARMATOLOS	P 18	Hellenic Shipyards, Skaramanga	27 Mar 1990
NAVMACHOS	P 19	Hellenic Shipyards, Skaramanga	15 July 1990

Displacement, tons: 515 full load
Dimensions, feet (metres): 179.8; 166.7 (wl) × 34.4 × 8.5 *(54.8; 50.8 × 10.5 × 2.6)*
Main machinery: 2 MTU 16V 1163 TB 63 diesels; 10 000 hp(m) *(7.3 MW)* sustained; 2 shafts; cp props
Speed, knots: 25. **Range, miles:** 500 at 25 kts
Complement: 36 plus 25 spare
Missiles: SSM: 4 McDonnell Douglas Harpoon (not carried).
Guns: 1 OTO Melara 3 in *(76 mm)*/62 compact; 85° elevation; 85 rounds/minute to 16 km *(8.6 nm)* anti-surface; 12 km *(6.6 nm)* anti-aircraft; weight of shell 6 kg.
2 Rheinmetall 20 mm.
Mines: Rails.
Fire control: Selenia Elsag NA 21.
Radars: Surface search: Thomson-CSF Triton; G band.
Fire control: Selenia RTNX; I/J band.

Comment: Built in co-operation with Danyard A/S. Ordered in March 1988. First one laid down 8 May 1989 and launched 19 December 1989. Second laid down 9 November 1989 and launched 16 May 1990. The original armament has been modified with Harpoon fitted for but not with, and Rheinmetall 20 mm guns although there is also space for a 40 mm/70 (twin). Armament is of modular design and therefore can be changed. Options on more of the class were shelved in favour of a modified Hellenic design.

NAVMACHOS *5/1991, Erik Laursen*

4 LA COMBATTANTE II CLASS (FAST ATTACK CRAFT—MISSILE)

Name	*No*	*Builders*	*Commissioned*
ANTHIPOPLOIARHOS ANNINOS (ex-*Navsithoi*)	P 14	CMN Cherbourg	June 1972
IPOPLOIARHOS ARLIOTIS (ex-*Evniki*)	P 15	CMN Cherbourg	Apr 1972
IPOPLOIARHOS KONIDIS (ex-*Kymothoi*)	P 16	CMN Cherbourg	July 1972
IPOPLOIARHOS BATSIS (ex-*Calypso*)	P 17	CMN Cherbourg	Dec 1971

Displacement, tons: 234 standard; 255 full load
Dimensions, feet (metres): 154.2 × 23.3 × 8.2 *(47 × 7.1 × 2.5)*
Main machinery: 4 MTU MD 16V 538 TB 90 diesels; 12 000 hp(m) *(8.82 MW)* sustained; 4 shafts
Speed, knots: 36.5. **Range, miles:** 850 at 25 kts
Complement: 40 (4 officers)

Missiles: SSM: 4 Aerospatiale MM 38 Exocet; inertial cruise; active radar homing to 42 km *(23 nm)* at 0.9 Mach; warhead 165 kg; sea-skimmer.
Guns: 4 Oerlikon 35 mm/90 (2 twin); 85° elevation; 550 rounds/minute to 6 km *(3.2 nm)* anti-surface; 5 km *(2.7 nm)* anti-aircraft; weight of shell 1.55 kg.
Torpedoes: 2—21 in *(533 mm)* tubes. AEG SST-4; wire-guided; active homing to 12 km *(6.5 nm)* at 35 kts; passive homing to 28 km *(15 nm)* at 23 kts; warhead 250 kg.
Fire control: Thomson-CSF Vega system.
Radars: Surface search: Thomson-CSF Triton; G band; range 33 km *(18 nm)* for 2 m² target.
Navigation: Decca 1226C; I band.
Fire Control: Thomson-CSF Pollux; I/J band; range 31 km *(17 nm)* for 2 m² target.
IFF: Plessey Mk 10.

Programmes: Ordered in 1969. P 15 launched 8 September 1971; P 14 on 20 December 1971; P 17 on 27 April 1971; P 16 on 26 January 1972.
Modernisation: Plans to modernise include updating the fire control system.

IPOPLOIARHOS BATSIS *1989, Hellenic Navy*

10 LA COMBATTANTE III CLASS (FAST ATTACK CRAFT—MISSILE)

Name	*No*	*Builders*	*Commissioned*
ANTIPLOIARHOS LASKOS	P 20	CMN Cherbourg	20 Apr 1977
PLOTARHIS BLESSAS	P 21	CMN Cherbourg	7 July 1977
IPOPLOIARHOS MIKONIOS	P 22	CMN Cherbourg	10 Feb 1978
IPOPLOIARHOS TROUPAKIS	P 23	CMN Cherbourg	8 Nov 1977
SIMEOFOROS KAVALOUDIS	P 24	Hellenic Shipyards, Skaramanga	14 July 1980
ANTHIPOPLOIARHOS KOSTAKOS	P 25	Hellenic Shipyards, Skaramanga	9 Sep 1980
IPOPLOIARHOS DEYIANNIS	P 26	Hellenic Shipyards, Skaramanga	Dec 1980
SIMEOFOROS XENOS	P 27	Hellenic Shipyards, Skaramanga	31 Mar 1981
SIMEOFOROS SIMITZOPOULOS	P 28	Hellenic Shipyards, Skaramanga	June 1981
SIMEOFOROS STARAKIS	P 29	Hellenic Shipyards, Skaramanga	12 Oct 1981

Displacement, tons: 359 standard; 425 full load (P 20-23)
329 standard; 429 full load (P 24-29)
Dimensions, feet (metres): 184 × 26.2 × 7 *(56.2 × 8 × 2.1)*
Main machinery: 4 MTU 20V538 TB 92 diesels; 17 060 hp(m) *(12.54 MW)* sustained; 4 shafts (P 20-23)
4 MTU 20V538 TB 91 diesels; 15 360 hp(m) *(11.29 MW)* sustained; 4 shafts (P 24-29)
Speed, knots: 36 (P 20-23); 32.5 (P 24-29). **Range, miles:** 700 at 32 kts; 2700 at 15 kts
Complement: 42 (5 officers)

Missiles: SSM: 4 Aerospatiale MM 38 Exocet (P 20-P 23); inertial cruise; active radar homing to 42 km *(23 nm)* at 0.9 Mach; warhead 165 kg.
6 Kongsberg Penguin Mk 2 (P 24-P 29); inertial/IR homing to 27 km *(15 nm)* at 0.8 Mach; warhead 120 kg.
Guns: 2 OTO Melara 3 in *(76 mm)*/62 compact; 85° elevation; 85 rounds/minute to 16 km *(8.6 nm)* anti-surface; 12 km *(6.5 nm)* anti-aircraft; weight of shell 6 kg.
4 Emerson Electric 30 mm (2 twin); multi-purpose; 80° elevation; 1200 rounds/minute combined to 6 km *(3.2 nm)*; weight of shell 0.35 kg.
Torpedoes: 2—21 in *(533 mm)* aft tubes. AEG SST-4; anti-surface; wire-guided; active homing to 12 km *(6.5 nm)* at 35 kts; passive homing to 28 km *(15 nm)* at 23 kts; warhead 250 kg.
Fire control: 2 CSEE Panda optical directors for 30 mm guns. Thomson-CSF Vega I or II system.
Radars: Surface search: Thomson-CSF Triton; G band; range 33 km *(18 nm)* for 2 m² target.
Navigation: Decca 1226C; I band.
Fire control: Thomson-CSF Castor II; I/J band; range 31 km *(17 nm)* for 2 m² target.
Thomson-CSF Pollux; I/J band; range 31 km *(17 nm)* for 2 m² target.

Programmes: First four ordered in September 1974. Second group of six ordered 1978.
Structure: First four fitted with SSM Exocet; remainder have Penguin.

PLOTARHIS BLESSAS (with Exocet) *1988, Hellenic Navy*

IPOPLOIARHOS DEYIANNIS (with Penguin) *1988, Hellenic Navy*

6 Ex-FDR JAGUAR CLASS (FAST ATTACK CRAFT—TORPEDO)

Name	*No*	*Builders*	*Commissioned*
HESPEROS (ex-*Seeadler* P 6068)	P 50	Lürssen, Vegesack	29 Aug 1958
KENTAUROS (ex-*Habicht* P 6075)	P 52	Krogerwerft, Rendsburg	15 Nov 1958
KYKLON (ex-*Greif* P 6071)	P 53	Lürssen, Vegesack	3 Mar 1959
LELAPS (ex-*Kondor* P 6070)	P 54	Lürssen, Vegesack	24 Feb 1959
SKORPIOS (ex-*Kormoran* P 6077)	P 55	Krogerwerft, Rendsburg	9 Nov 1959
TYFON (ex-*Geier* P 6073)	P 56	Lürssen, Vegesack	3 June 1959

Displacement, tons: 160 standard; 190 full load
Dimensions, feet (metres): 139.4 × 23.6 × 7.9 *(42.5 × 7.2 × 2.4)*
Main machinery: 4 MTU MD 16V 538 TB 90 diesels; 12 000 hp(m) *(8.82 MW)* sustained; 4 shafts
Speed, knots: 42. **Range, miles:** 500 at 40 kts; 1000 at 32 kts
Complement: 39
Guns: 2 Bofors 40 mm/70; 90° elevation; 300 rounds/minute to 12 km *(6.5 nm)* anti-surface; 4 km *(2.2 nm)* anti-aircraft; weight of shell 2.4 kg.
Torpedoes: 4—21 in *(533 mm)* tubes. Probably AEG SST-4; anti-surface; wire-guided; passive homing to 28 km *(15.3 nm)* at 23 kts; active homing to 12 km *(6.6 nm)* at 35 kts; warhead 260 kg.
Mines: 2 in lieu of each torpedo.

Comment: Transferred 1976-77. P 53 and P 56 commissioned in Hellenic Navy 12 December 1976. P 50 and P 54 on 24 March 1977, P 52 and P 55 on 22 May 1977. Three others (ex-*Albatros*, ex-*Bussard*, and ex-*Sperber*) transferred at same time for spares.

HESPEROS *1989, Hellenic Navy*

4 Ex-NASTY CLASS (FAST ATTACK CRAFT—TORPEDO)

Name	No	Builders	Commissioned
ANDROMEDA	P 196	Mandal, Norway	Nov 1966
KYKNOS	P 198	Mandal, Norway	Feb 1967
PIGASOS	P 199	Mandal, Norway	Apr 1967
TOXOTIS	P 228	Mandal, Norway	May 1967

Displacement, tons: 72 full load
Dimensions, feet (metres): 80.4 × 24.6 × 6.9 *(24.5 × 7.5 × 2.1)*
Main machinery: 2 MTU 12V 331 TC 92 diesels; 2660 hp(m) *(1.96 MW)* sustained; 2 shafts
Speed, knots: 40. **Range, miles:** 676 at 17 kts
Complement: 20
Guns: 1 Bofors 40 mm/70. 1 Rheinmetall 20 mm.
Torpedoes: 4—21 in *(533 mm)* tubes.
Radars: Navigation: I band.

Comment: Six of the class acquired from Norway in 1967 and paid off into reserve in the early 1980s. Four re-engined and brought back into service in 1988.

KYKNOS *1988, Hellenic Navy*

2 Ex-US ASHEVILLE CLASS (LARGE PATROL CRAFT)

Name	No	Builders	Commissioned
TOLMI (ex-*Green Bay*)	P 229	Peterson, Wisconsin	5 Dec 1969
ORMI (ex-*Beacon*)	P 230	Peterson, Wisconsin	21 Nov 1969

Displacement, tons: 225 standard; 245 full load
Dimensions, feet (metres): 164.5 × 23.8 × 9.5 *(50.1 × 7.3 × 2.9)*
Main machinery: 2 Cummins VT12-875 diesels; 1450 hp *(1.07 MW)*; 2 shafts
Speed, knots: 16. **Range, miles:** 1700 at 16 kts
Complement: 24 (3 officers)
Missiles: SSM: 4 Aerospatiale SS 12M; wire-guided to 5.5 km *(3 nm)* subsonic; warhead 30 kg.
Guns: 1 USN 3 in *(76 mm)*/50 Mk 34; 85° elevation; 50 rounds/minute to 12.8 km *(7 nm)*; weight of shell 6 kg.
1 Bofors 40 mm/56 Mk 10. 4—12.7 mm (2 twin) MGs.
Fire control: Mk 63 GFCS.
Radars: Surface search: Sperry SPS 53; I/J band.
Fire control: Western Electric SPG 50; I/J band.

Comment: Transferred from the USN in mid-1990 after a refit. Both were in reserve from April 1977 having originally been built for the Cuban crisis. Similar craft in Turkish, Colombian and South Korean navies. Gas turbine propulsion engine removed prior to transfer.

TOLMI *1990, Hellenic Navy*

2 FAST ATTACK CRAFT (PATROL)

Name	No	Builders	Commissioned
DIOPOS ANTONIOU	P 286	Ch N de l'Esterel	4 Dec 1975
KELEFSTIS STAMOU	P 287	Ch N de l'Esterel	28 July 1975

Displacement, tons: 115 full load
Dimensions, feet (metres): 105 × 19 × 5.3 *(32 × 5.8 × 1.6)*
Main machinery: 2 MTU 12V 331 TC 81 diesels; 2610 hp(m) *(1.92 MW)* sustained; 2 shafts
Speed, knots: 30. **Range, miles:** 1500 at 15 kts
Complement: 17
Missiles: SSM: 4 Aerospatiale SS 12M; wire-guided to 5.5 km *(3 nm)* subsonic; warhead 30 kg.
Guns: 1 Rheinmetall 20 mm. 1—12.7 mm MG.

Comment: Originally ordered for Cyprus, later transferred to Greece. Wooden hulls.

DIOPOS ANTONIOU *1990, Hellenic Navy*

3 DILOS CLASS (COASTAL PATROL CRAFT)

DILOS P 267 **KNOSSOS** P 268 **LINDOS** P 269

Displacement, tons: 74.5 standard; 86 full load
Dimensions, feet (metres): 95.1 × 16.2 × 5.6 *(29 × 5 × 1.7)*
Main machinery: 2 MTU 12V 331 TC92 diesels; 2660 hp(m) *(1.96 MW)* sustained; 2 shafts
Speed, knots: 27. **Range, miles:** 1600 at 24 kts
Complement: 15
Guns: 2 Rheinmetall 20 mm.
Radars: Surface search: Racal Decca 1226C; I band.

Comment: Ordered from Hellenic Shipyards, Skaramanga in May 1976 to a design by Abeking & Rasmussen. The Navy uses these craft for air-sea rescue duties. Based at the National SAR centre. Four more of this class serve in Coast Guard and three in Customs service. *Adamidis* (P 266), the survivor of a class of five similar craft commissioned in 1956 is used for training alongside.

KNOSSOS *7/1989, D. Dervissis*

2 COASTAL PATROL CRAFT

Name	No	Builders	Commissioned
E PANAGOPOULOS 2	P 70	Hellenic Shipyards, Skaramanga	1980
E PANAGOPOULOS 3	P 96	Hellenic Shipyards, Skaramanga	1981

Displacement, tons: 35 full load
Dimensions, feet (metres): 75.5 × 16.4 × 3.3 *(23 × 5 × 1)*
Main machinery: 2 MTU 12V 331 TC 92 diesels; 2660 hp(m) *(1.96 MW)* sustained; 2 shafts
Speed, knots: 38
Complement: 6
Guns: 2—6-barrelled 106 mm rocket launchers. 1—12.7 mm MG.
Radars: Navigation: Decca; I band.

Comment: Officially classified as 'pursuit vessels'. Have aluminium hulls. The first of class paid off in 1991.

E PANAGOPOULOS 3 *5/1990, Erik Laursen*

AMPHIBIOUS FORCES

Note: There are a number of paid off LSTs and LSMs in unmaintained reserve at Salamis.

1 Ex-US CABILDO CLASS (LSD)

Name	No	Builders	Commissioned
NAFKRATOUSSA (ex-USS *Fort Mandan* LSD 21)	L 153	Boston Navy Yard	31 Oct 1945

Displacement, tons: 4790 light; 9357 full load
Dimensions, feet (metres): 457.8 × 72.2 × 18 *(139.6 × 22 × 5.5)*
Main machinery: 2 boilers; 435 psi *(30.6 kg/cm sq)*; 750° *(393°C)*; 2 turbines; 7000 hp *(5.22 MW)*; 2 shafts
Speed, knots: 15.4. **Range, miles:** 8000 at 12 kts
Complement: 250
Military lift: 18 LCMs; 2—35 ton cranes
Guns: 12 Bofors 40 mm/60 (2 quad and 2 twin); 90° elevation; 300 rounds/minute to 12 km *(6.5 nm)* anti-surface; 4 km *(2.2 nm)* anti-aircraft; weight of shell 0.89 kg.
Radars: Air search: Bendix SPS 6; D band; range 146 km *(80 nm)*.
Surface search: Westinghouse SPS 5; G/H band; range 37 km *(20 nm)*.
Helicopters: Platform for 1 light.

Comment: Laid down on 2 January 1945. Launched on 22 May 1945. Taken over on lease from USA in 1971, acquired by sale 5 February 1980. Headquarters ship for Captain Landing Forces.

NAFKRATOUSSA *7/1988, D. Dervissis*

1 + 4 JASON CLASS (LST)

Name	No	Builders	Commissioned
CHIOS	L 173	Eleusis Shipyard	May 1992
SAMOS	L 174	Eleusis Shipyard	Oct 1992
LESBOS	L 176	Eleusis Shipyard	Mar 1993
IKARIA	L 175	Eleusis Shipyard	Aug 1993
RODOS	L 177	Eleusis Shipyard	Jan 1994

Displacement, tons: 4400 full load
Dimensions, feet (metres): 380.5 × 50.2 × 11.3 *(116 × 15.3 × 3.4)*
Main machinery: 2 Wärtsilä Nohba 16V 25 diesels; 10 000 hp(m) *(7.36 MW)*; 2 shafts
Speed, knots: 16
Military lift: 300 troops plus vehicles; 4 LCVPs
Guns: 1 OTO Melara 76 mm/62 Mod 9 compact; 85° elevation; 100 rounds/minute to 16 km *(8.6 nm)* anti-surface; 12 km *(6.5 nm)* anti-aircraft; weight of shell 6 kg.
4 Breda 40 mm/70 (2 twin) compact Fast 40; 85° elevation; 900 rounds/minute to 12 km *(6.5 nm)*; weight of shell 2.4 kg.
4 Rheinmetall 20 mm (2 twin).
Fire control: 1 CSEE Panda optical director. Thomson-CSF Canopus GFCS.
Radars: Thomson-CSF Triton; G band.
Fire control: Thomson-CSF Pollux; I/J band.
Navigation: Kelvin Hughes Type 1007; I band.
Helicopters: Platform for one.

Comment: Contract for construction of five LSTs by Eleusis Shipyard signed 15 May 1986. Bow and stern ramps, drive through design. First laid down 18 April 1987, second in September 1987, third in May 1988, fourth April 1989 and fifth November 1989. First launched 16 December 1988, second 6 April 1989, third 5 July 1990. Completion of all five delayed by shipyard financial problems.

CHIOS (model) *1989, Eleusis Shipyard*

2 Ex-US TERREBONNE PARISH CLASS (LSTs)

Name	No	Builders	Commissioned
INOUSE (ex-USS *Terrell County* LST 1157)	L 104	Bath Iron Works Corporation	19 Mar 1953
KOS (ex-USS *Whitfield County* LST 1169)	L 116	Christy Corporation	14 Sep 1954

Displacement, tons: 2590 light; 5800 full load
Dimensions, feet (metres): 384 × 55 × 17 *(117.1 × 16.8 × 5.2)*
Main machinery: 4 GM 16-278A diesels; 6000 hp *(4.48 MW)*; 2 shafts; cp props
Speed, knots: 15
Complement: 115
Military lift: 400 troops; 4 LCVPs
Guns: 6 USN 3 in *(76 mm)*/50 Mk 21 (3 twin); 85° elevation; 20 rounds/minute to 12 km *(6.5 nm)* anti-surface; 9 km *(4.9 nm)* anti-aircraft; weight of shell 6 kg.
3 Rheinmetall 20 mm S 20.
Fire control: 2 Mk 63 GFCS.
Radars: Surface search: Raytheon/Sylvania SPS 10; G band.
Fire control: Two Western Electric Mk 34; I/J band.

Comment: Part of class of 16 of which these two were transferred 17 March 1977 by sale.

KOS *1988, Hellenic Navy*

4 Ex-US 511—1152 and 1—510 CLASSES (LSTs)

Name	No	Builders	Commissioned
IKARIA (ex-USS *Potter County* LST 1086)	L 154	AM Bridge Co	14 Mar 1945
KRITI (ex-USS *Page County* LST 1076)	L 171	Bethlehem Steel Co, Hingham	1 May 1945
SIROS (ex-USS LST 325)	L 144	Philadelphia Navy Yard	1 Feb 1943
RODOS (ex-USS *Bowman County LST 391)*	L 157	Newport News	3 Dec 1942

Displacement, tons: 1653 standard; 2366 beaching; 4080 full load
Dimensions, feet (metres): 328 × 50 × 14 *(100 × 15.3 × 4.3)*
Main machinery: 2 GM 12-567A diesels; 1800 hp *(1.34 MW)*; 2 shafts
Speed, knots: 11.6. **Range, miles:** 9500 at 9 kts
Complement: 93 (8 officers)
Military lift: 2100 tons; 4 LCVPs
Guns: 8 Bofors 40 mm/60 (2 twin, 4 single) (10 in L 157).
4 Oerlikon 20 mm/2 Rheinmetall 20 mm S 20.
Radars: Navigation: I band.

Comment: Former US tank landing ships. L 154 and 171 are 511—1152 class and L 144 and 157 are 1—510 class. L 157 and 154 were transferred to the Hellenic Navy in May 1960 and August 1960 respectively. L 144 was transferred on 29 May 1964, L 171 in March 1971. To be replaced by the Jason class.

LST I-150 Class (old number) *5/1990, Gilbert Gyssels*

4 Ex-US LSM 1 CLASS

Name	No	Builders	Commissioned
IPOPLOIARHOS GRIGOROPOULOS (ex-USS *LSM 45*)	L 161	Brown SB Co, Houston	3 July 1944
IPOPLOIARHOS DANIOLOS (ex-USS *LSM 227*)	L 163	Dravo Corp, Wilmington	5 Oct 1944
IPOPLOIARHOS ROUSSEN (ex-USS *LSM 399*)	L 164	Charleston Navy Yard	13 Aug 1945
IPOPLOIARHOS KRYSTALIDIS (ex-USS *LSM 541*)	L 165	Brown SB Co, Houston	7 Dec 1945

Displacement, tons: 743 beaching; 1095 full load
Dimensions, feet (metres): 203.5 × 34.2 × 8.3 *(62.1 × 10.4 × 2.5)*
Main machinery: 2 Fairbanks-Morse 38D8-1/8-10 diesels; 3540 hp *(2.64 MW)*; 2 shafts (L 161, 163 and 165); 4 GM 16-278A diesels; 3000 hp *(2.24 MW)*; 2 shafts (L 164)
Speed, knots: 13. **Range, miles:** 4900 at 12 kts
Complement: 60
Guns: 2 Bofors 40 mm/60 (twin). 8 Oerlikon 20 mm.

Comment: *LSM 541* was handed over to Greece at Salamis on 30 October 1958 and *LSM 45, LSM 227* and *399* at Portsmouth, Virginia on 3 November 1958. All were renamed after naval heroes killed during the Second World War.

I GRIGOROPOULOS *5/1990, Erik Laursen*

2 Ex-BRITISH LCTs

Name	No	Builders	Commissioned
KITHERA (ex-*LCT 1198*)	L 185	UK	1945
MILOS (ex-*LCT 1300*)	L 189	UK	1945

Displacement, tons: 400 full load
Dimensions, feet (metres): 187.2 × 38.7 × 4.3 *(57 × 11.8 × 1.3)*
Main machinery: 2 Paxman diesels; 1000 hp *(746 kW)*; 2 shafts
Speed, knots: 7. **Range, miles:** 3000 at 7 kts
Complement: 12
Military lift: 350 tons
Guns: 2 Oerlikon 20 mm.

Comment: The survivors of a class of 12 acquired in 1946.

KITHNOS *9/1987, van Ginderen Collection*

2 Ex-GERMAN LCUs (TYPE 520)

NAXOS (ex-*Renke*) L 178 **PAROS** (ex-*Salm*) L 179

Displacement, tons: 400 full load
Dimensions, feet (metres): 131.2 × 28.9 × 7.2 *(40 × 8.8 × 2.2)*
Main machinery: 2 MWM 12-cyl diesels; 1020 hp(m) *(750 kW)*; 2 shafts
Speed, knots: 12
Complement: 17
Military lift: 160 tons
Guns: 2 Oerlikon 20 mm.

Comment: Transferred 16 November 1989. Built by HDW, Hamburg in 1966. Bow and stern ramps similar to US Type. Six more to be transferred in 1992.

LCU TYPE 520 (old number) *5/1988, Hartmut Ehlers*

4 Ex-US LCU 501 CLASS (Ex-LCT 6)

Name	*No*	*Builders*	*Commissioned*
KIMOLOS (ex-*LCU 971*)	L 147	Mare Island Naval Yard	1 Feb 1944
KITHNOS (ex-*LCU 763*)	L 149	Missouri Valley Bridge and Iron Co	24 Dec 1944
SIFNOS (ex-*LCU 677*)	L 150	Pidgeon-Thomas Iron Co	11 Mar 1944
SKIATHOS (ex-*LCU 827*)	L 152	Kansas City Steel	10 Apr 1944

Displacement, tons: 143 standard; 309 full load
Dimensions, feet (metres): 119 × 32.7 × 5 *(36.3 × 10 × 1.5)*
Main machinery: 3 GM 6-71 diesels; 522 hp *(389 kW)* sustained; 3 shafts
Speed, knots: 8
Complement: 13
Guns: 2 Oerlikon 20 mm.

Comment: Former US Utility Landing Craft of the LCU (ex-LCT 6) type acquired 1959-1962.

KITHNOS *9/1987, van Ginderen Collection*

1 Ex-GERMAN LCMs (TYPE 521)

isplacement, tons: 168 full load
imensions, feet (metres): 77.4 × 20.9 × 4.9 *(23.6 × 6.4 × 1.5)*
ain machinery: 1 MWM 8-cyl diesel; 685 hp(m) *(503 kW)*; 2 shafts
peed, knots: 10.5
omplement: 7
ilitary lift: 60 tons or 50 troops

omment: Built in 1964-67 but spent much of their time in reserve. Transferred in April 1991 and numbered ABM 20-30.

CM Type (German Flag) *6/1991, van Ginderen Collection*

1 Ex-US LCMs

isplacement, tons: 56 full load
imensions, feet (metres): 56 × 14.4 × 3.9 *(17 × 4.4 × 1.2)*
ain machinery: 2 Gray Marine 64HN9 diesels; 330 hp *(264 kW)*; 2 shafts
peed, knots: 10. **Range, miles:** 130 at 10 kts
ilitary lift: 30 tons

mment: Transferred from the USA in 1956-58.

4 Ex-US LCVPs + 14 LCPs + 7 LCAs

isplacement, tons: 13 full load
eed, knots: 6-9
ilitary lift: 36 troops or 3 tons equipment

mment: LCVPs transferred from the USA between 1956-71, LCPs built in Greece in 1977 and LCAs in 1981.

MINE WARFARE FORCES

9 US MSC 294 CLASS (MINESWEEPERS—COASTAL)

Name	*No*	*Builders*	*Commissioned*
ALKYON (ex-*MSC 319*)	M 211	Peterson Builders	3 Dec 1968
KLIO (ex-*Argo*, ex-*MSC 317*)	M 213	Peterson Builders	7 Aug 1968
AVRA (ex-*MSC 318*)	M 214	Peterson Builders	3 Oct 1968
PLEIAS (ex-*MSC 314*)	M 240	Peterson Builders	22 June 1967
KICHLI (ex-*MSC 308*)	M 241	Peterson Builders	14 July 1964
KISSA (ex-*MSC 309*)	M 242	Peterson Builders	1 Sep 1964
AIGLI (ex-*MSC 299*)	M 246	Tacoma, California	4 Jan 1965
DAFNI (ex-*MSC 307*)	M 247	Peterson Builders	23 Sep 1964
AEDON (ex-*MSC 310*)	M 248	Peterson Builders	13 Oct 1964

Displacement, tons: 320 standard; 370 full load
Dimensions, feet (metres): 144 × 28 × 8.2 *(43.3 × 8.5 × 2.5)*
Main machinery: 2 GM Waukesha L-1616 diesels (being replaced); 1200 hp *(882 kW)*; 2 shafts
Speed, knots: 13. **Range, miles:** 2500 at 10 kts
Complement: 39 (4 officers)
Guns: 2 Oerlikon 20 mm (twin).
Radars: Navigation: I band.
Sonars: UQS 1D; active; high frequency.

Comment: Built in the USA for Greece, wooden hulls. *Doris* acts as survey ship. Modernisation programme started in 1990 with replacement main engines and navigation radar. New sonar under consideration.

AEDON *6/1987, Gilbert Gyssels*

5 Ex-US ADJUTANT CLASS (MINESWEEPERS—COASTAL)

Name	*No*
ATALANTI (ex-Belgian *St Truiden* M 919, ex-USS *MSC 169*)	M 202
ANTIOPI (ex-Belgian *Herve* M 921, ex-USS *MSC 153*)	M 205
FAEDRA (ex-Belgian *Malmedy* M 922, ex-USS *MSC 154*)	M 206
THALIA (ex-Belgian *Blankenberge* M 923, ex-USS *MSC 170*)	M 210
NIOVI (ex-Belgian *Laroche* M 924, ex-USS *MSC 171*)	M 254

Displacement, tons: 330 standard; 402 full load
Dimensions, feet (metres): 145 × 27.9 × 8 *(44.2 × 8.5 × 2.4)*
Main machinery: 2 GM 8-268A diesels; 880 hp *(656 kW)*; 2 shafts
Speed, knots: 14. **Range, miles:** 2500 at 10 kts
Complement: 38 (4 officers)
Guns: 1 Oerlikon 20 mm.

Comment: Originally supplied to Belgium under MDAP. All built in 1954 in the USA—M202, M210 and M 254 by Consolidated SB Corp, Morris Heights and the other pair by Hodgson Bros, Goudy and Stevens, East Booth Bay. Subsequently returned to the USA and simultaneously transferred to Greece as follows: 29 July 1969 *(Herve* and *St Truiden)* and 26 September 1969 *(Laroche, Malmedy* and *Blankenberge)*.

ATALANTI *1989, Hellenic Navy*

4 MINESWEEPING LAUNCHES

Displacement, tons: 21 full load
Dimensions, feet (metres): 49.9 × 13.1 × 4.3 *(15.2 × 4 × 1.3)*
Main machinery: 1 diesel; 60 hp(m) *(44 kW)*; 1 shaft
Speed, knots: 8
Complement: 6

Comment: Transferred from USA in 1971 on loan and bought in 1981.

2 COASTAL MINELAYERS

Name	*No*	*Builders*	*Commissioned*
AKTION (ex-*LSM 301*, ex-*MMC 6*)	N 04	Charleston Naval Shipyard	1 Jan 1945
AMVRAKIA (ex-*LSM 303*, ex-*MMC 7*)	N 05	Charleston Naval Shipyard	6 Jan 1945

Displacement, tons: 720 standard; 1100 full load
Dimensions, feet (metres): 203.5 × 34.5 × 8.3 *(62.1 × 10.5 × 2.5)*
Main machinery: 2 GM 16-278A diesels; 3000 hp *(2.24 MW)*; 2 shafts
Speed, knots: 12.5. **Range, miles:** 3000 at 12 kts
Complement: 65
Guns: 8 Bofors 40 mm/60 (4 twin). 6 Oerlikon 20 mm.
Mines: Capacity 100-130; 2 rails.
Fire control: 4 Mk 51 optical directors for 40 mm guns.
Radars: Navigation: I band.

Comment: Former US LSM 1 class. N 04 was launched on 1 January 1945 and N 05 on 14 November 1944. Converted in the USA into minelayers for the Hellenic Navy. Underwent extensive rebuilding from the deck up. Twin rudders. Transferred on 1 December 1953.

AKTION *9/1987, van Ginderen Collection*

SERVICE FORCES

1 TRAINING SHIP

Name	*No*	*Builders*	*Commissioned*
ARIS	A 74	Salamis	Jan 1980

Displacement, tons: 2400 standard; 2630 full load
Dimensions, feet (metres): 328 × 48.2 × 14.8 *(100 × 14.7 × 4.5)*
Main machinery: 2 MAK diesels; 10 000 hp(m) *(7.35 MW)*; 2 shafts
Speed, knots: 18
Complement: 500 (21 officers, up to 370 cadets)
Guns: 2 US 3 in *(76 mm)* Mk 26; 85° elevation; 50 rounds/minute to 12 km *(6.5 nm)*; weight of shell 6 kg.
2 Bofors 40 mm/70 (twin); 90° elevation; 300 rounds/minute to 12 km *(6.5 nm)* anti-surface; 4 km *(2.2 nm)* anti-aircraft; weight of shell 0.96 kg.
4 Rheinmetall 20 mm.
Radars: Surface search: Two Racal Decca 1226C; I band.
Helicopters: 1 Aerospatiale SA 319B Alouette III.

Comment: Laid down October 1976 at Salamis. Launched 4 October 1978. Hangar reactivated in 1986. The 76 mm guns are mounted on sponsons forward of the funnel. Can be used as transport or hospital ship. SATCOM fitted.

ARIS *7/1991, W. Sartori*

Ex-GERMAN LÜNEBURG CLASS (SUPPORT SHIP)

Name	*No*	*Builders*	*Commissioned*	*Recommissioned*
AXIOS (ex-*Coburg*)	A464 (ex-A 1412)	Bremer Vulcan	9 July 1968	30 Sep 1991

Displacement, tons: 3709 full load
Dimensions, feet (metres): 374.9 × 43.3 × 13.8 *(114.3 × 13.2 × 4.2)*
Main machinery: 2 Maybach MTU MD 872 diesels; 5600 hp(m) *(4.1 MW)*; 2 shafts; cp props; bow thruster
Speed, knots: 17. **Range, miles:** 3200 at 14 kts
Complement: 71
Cargo capacity: 1100 tons
Guns: 4 Bofors 40 mm/70 (2 twin); 90° elevation; 300 rounds/minute to 12 km *(6.5 nm)*; weight of shell 0.96 kg.

Comment: Lengthened by 33.7 ft *(10.3 m)* and modified in 1975. Serves as a depot ship for fast attack craft and is capable of servicing all weapons including missiles. Has replaced *Aegeon*.

AXIOS (old number) *6/1991, Wright & Logan*

2 Ex-US PATAPSCO CLASS (SUPPORT TANKERS)

Name	*No*	*Builders*	*Commissioned*
ARETHOUSA (ex-USS *Natchaug* AOG 54)	A 377	Cargill Inc, Savage, Minn	11 June 1945
ARIADNI (ex-USS *Tombigbee* AOG 11)	A 414	Cargill Inc, Savage, Minn	12 July 1944

Displacement, tons: 1850 light; 4335 full load
Measurement, tons: 2575 dwt
Dimensions, feet (metres): 292 wl; 310.8 oa × 48.5 × 15.7 *(89.1; 94.8 × 14.8 × 4.8)*
Main machinery: 2 GM 16-278A diesels; 3000 hp *(2.24 MW)*; 2 shafts
Speed, knots: 14
Complement: 43 (6 officers)
Cargo capacity: 2040 tons
Guns: 1 USN 3 in *(76 mm)*/50; 85° elevation; 20 rounds/minute to 12 km *(6.6 nm)*; weight of shell 6 kg.
2 Oerlikon 20 mm/85; 55° elevation; 800 rounds/minute to 2 km.
Fire control: 1 Mk 26 system for guns.
Radars: Surface search: Westinghouse SPS 5; G/H band; range 37 km *(20 nm)*.
Navigation: Decca; I band.

Comment: Former US petrol carriers. A 377 laid down on 15 August 1944. Launched on 16 December 1944. Transferred from the USA to Greece under the Mutual Defense Assistance Program in July 1959 and A 414 transferred 7 July 1972 (sold 11 July 1978), both at Pearl Harbour.

ARETHOUSA *1988, Hellenic Navy*

1 AMMUNITION SHIP

Name	*No*	*Builders*	*Commissioned*
EVROS (ex-FDR *Schwarzwald A 1400, ex-Amalthee*)	A 415	Ch Dubigeon Nantes	1957

Displacement, tons: 2400
Measurement, tons: 1667 gross
Dimensions, feet (metres): 263.1 × 39 × 15.1 *(80.2 × 11.9 × 4.6)*
Main machinery: 1 Sulzer 6-SD-60 diesel; 3000 hp(m) *(2.2 MW)*; 1 shaft
Speed, knots: 15
Guns: 4 Bofors 40 mm/60.

Comment: Bought by FDR from Société Navale Caënnaise in February 1960. Transferred to Greece 6 June 1976.

EVROS *1987, Hellenic Navy*

4 HARBOUR TANKERS

Name	*No*	*Builders*	*Commissioned*
OURANOS	A 416	Kinosoura Shipyard	27 Jan 1977
HYPERION	A 417	Kinosoura Shipyard	27 Apr 1977
ORION	A 489	Hellenic Shipyards	5 May 1989
ZEUS	A 490	Hellenic Shipyards	21 Feb 1989

Displacement, tons: 1900 full load
Dimensions, feet (metres): 219.8; 198.2 (wl) × 32.8 × 13.8 *(67; 60.4 × 10 × 4.2)*
Main machinery: 1 MAN-Burmeister & Wain 12V 20/27 diesel; 1632 hp(m) *(1.2 MW)* sustained; 1 shaft
Speed, knots: 12
Complement: 28
Cargo capacity: 1323 cu m
Guns: 2 Rheinmetall 20 mm.

Comment: First two are oil tankers. The last pair were ordered from Hellenic Shipyards, Skaramanga in December 1986 and are used as petrol tankers. There are some minor superstructure differences between the first two and the last pair which have a forward crane.

ZEUS *1989, Hellenic Shipyards*

OURANOS *1983, D. Dervissis*

SURVEY AND RESEARCH VESSELS

Name	*No*	*Builders*	*Commissioned*
NAFTILOS	A 478	Annastadiades Tsortanides (Perama)	3 Apr 1976

Displacement, tons: 1400
Dimensions, feet (metres): 207 × 38 × 13.8 *(63.1 × 11.6 × 4.2)*
Main machinery: 2 Burmeister & Wain SS28LM diesels; 2640 hp(m) *(1.94 MW)*; 2 shafts
Speed, knots: 15
Complement: 74 (8 officers)

Comment: Launched 19 November 1975. Of similar design to the two lighthouse tenders.

NAFTILOS *1989, Hellenic Navy*

Name	*No*	*Builders*	*Commissioned*
HERMIS (ex-*Oker*, ex-*Hoheweg*)	A 373	Unterweser, Bremen	19 Oct 1960

Displacement, tons: 1497 full load
Dimensions, feet (metres): 237.8 × 34.4 × 16.1 *(72.5 × 10.5 × 4.9)*
Main machinery: Diesel-electric: 1 Klöckner-Deutz diesel; 1800 hp(m) *(1.32 MW)* 1 Klöckner-Deutz auxiliary diesel; 400 hp(m) *(294 kW)*; 1 shaft
Speed, knots: 15
Complement: 30

Comment: First converted in 1972 to serve as an AGI in the West German Navy. Transferred 12 February 1988 and now based at Suda Bay. Serves as an AGI.

HERMIS *9/1989, Hellenic Navy*

Name	*No*	*Builders*	*Commissioned*
PYTHEAS	A 474	Annastadiades Tsortanides (Perama)	Dec 1983

Displacement, tons: 670 standard; 840 full load
Dimensions, feet (metres): 164.7 × 31.5 × 21.6 *(50.2 × 9.6 × 6.6)*
Main machinery: 2 Detroit 12V-92TA diesels; 1380 hp *(1.03 MW)* sustained; 2 shafts
Speed, knots: 14
Complement: 58 (8 officers)

Comment: *Pytheas* ordered in May 1982. Launched 19 September 1983. A similar ship, *Aigeo*, was constructed to Navy specification in 1985 but belongs to the National Maritime Research Centre.

PYTHEAS *10/1987, D. Dervissis*

Name	*No*	*Builders*	*Commissioned*
STRABON	A 476	Emanuil-Maliris, Perama	27 Feb 1989

Displacement, tons: 252 full load
Dimensions, feet (metres): 107.3 × 20 × 8.2 *(32.7 × 6.1 × 2.5)*
Main machinery: 1 MAN D2842LE; 707 hp(m) *(520 kW)* sustained; 1 shaft
Speed, knots: 12.5
Complement: 20 (2 officers)

Comment: Ordered in 1987, launched September 1988.

STRABON (Pytheas behind) *1991, Hellenic Navy*

Name	*No*	*Builders*	*Commissioned*
DORIS (ex-*MSC 298*)	A 475 (ex-M 245)	Tacoma, California	9 Nov 1964

Comment: Of same details as MSC 294 class in *Mine Warfare* section except that her displacement is now 383 tons full load and complement 35 (3 officers).

OLYMPIAS

Dimensions, feet (metres): 121.4 × 17.1 × 4.9 *(37 × 5.2 × 1.5)*
Main machinery: 170 oars (85 each side in three rows)
Speed, knots: 9-12
Complement: 180

Comment: Construction started in 1985 and completed in 1987. Made of Oregon pine. Built for historic research and as a reminder of the naval hegemony of ancient Greeks. Part of the Hellenic Navy.

OLYMPIAS *1988, Hellenic Navy*

MISCELLANEOUS

1 NETLAYER

Name	No	Builders	Commissioned
THETIS (ex-USS *AN 103*)	A 307	Kröger, Rendsburg	Apr 1960

Displacement, tons: 680 standard; 805 full load
Dimensions, feet (metres): 169.5 × 33.5 × 11.8 *(51.7 × 10.2 × 3.6)*
Main machinery: Diesel-electric; 1 MAN GTV-40/60 diesel generator; 1 motor; 1470 hp(m) *(1.08 MW)*; 1 shaft
Speed, knots: 12. **Range, miles:** 6500 at 10 kts
Complement: 48 (5 officers)
Guns: 1 Bofors 40 mm/60. 3 Rheinmetall 20 mm.

Comment: US offshore order. Launched in 1959. Some guns not always embarked.

THETIS *1988, Hellenic Navy*

2 AUXILIARY TRANSPORTS

Name	No	Builders	Commissioned
PANDORA	A 419	Perama Shipyard	26 Oct 1973
PANDROSOS	A 420	Perama Shipyard	1 Dec 1973

Displacement, tons: 390 full load
Dimensions, feet (metres): 153.5 × 27.2 × 6.2 *(46.8 × 8.3 × 1.9)*
Main machinery: 2 diesels; 2 shafts
Speed, knots: 12
Military lift: 500 troops

Comment: Launched 1972 and 1973.

PANDROSOS *6/1986, van Ginderen Collection*

4 Ex-GERMAN TORPEDO RECOVERY VESSELS (TYPE 430A)

EVROTAS (ex-*TF 106*) A 460 (ex-Y 872)
ARACHTHOS (ex-*TF 1088*) A 461 (ex-Y 874)
STRYMON (ex-*TF 6*) A 462 (ex-Y 856)
NESTOS (ex-*TF 4*) A 463 (ex-Y 854)

Comment: First two acquired on 16 November 1989, second pair on 5 March 1991. Of about 56 tons with stern ramps for torpedo recovery. Built in 1966.

EVROTAS (old number) *5/1989, Ralf Bendfeldt*

1 FLOATING DOCK and 5 FLOATING CRANES

Comment: The floating dock is 45 m *(147.6 ft)* in length and has a 6000 ton lift. Built at Eleusis with Swedish assistance and launched 5 May 1988; delivered 1989. The cranes were all built in Greece.

2 LIGHTHOUSE TENDERS

Name	No	Builders	Commissioned
I KARAVOYIANNOS THEOPHILOPOULOS	A 479	Perama Shipyard	17 Mar 1976
ST LIKOUDIS	A 481	Perama Shipyard	2 Jan 1976

Displacement, tons: 1450 full load
Dimensions, feet (metres): 207.3 × 38 × 13.1 *(63.2 × 11.6 × 4)*
Main machinery: 1 MWM TBD 500 8UD diesel; 2400 hp(m) *(1.76 MW)*; 1 shaft
Speed, knots: 15
Complement: 40
Radars: Navigation: Racal Decca; I band.
Helicopters: Platform for 1 light.

I. KARAVOYIANNOS THEOPHILOPOULOS *5/1991, Erik Laursen*

18 HARBOUR TUGS

Name	No	Commissioned
ANTAIOS (ex-USS *Busy* YTM 2012)	A 407	1947
ATLAS (ex-HMS *Mediator*)	A 408	1944
ACCHILEUS (ex-USS *Confident*)	A 409	1947
ATROMITOS	A 410	1968
ADAMASTOS	A 411	1968
AIAS (ex-USS *Ankachak* YTM 767)	A 412	1972
PILEFS (ex-German)	A 413	1991
KADMOS (ex-US)	A 422	1989
KIKLOPS	A 426	1947
DANAOS (ex-US)	A 427	1989
NESTOR (ex-US)	A 428	1989
PELOPS	A 430	1989
TITAN	A 431	1962
GIGAS	A 432	1961
KEKROPS	A 435	1989
MINOS (ex-German)	A 436	1991
PELIAS (ex-German)	A 437	1991
AEGEUS (ex-German)	A 438	1991

ACCHILEUS *1982*

3 COASTAL TUGS

HERAKLIS A 423 **IASON** A 424 **ODISSEUS** A 425

Displacement, tons: 345 full load
Dimensions, feet (metres): 98.5 × 26 × 11.3 *(30 × 7.9 × 3.4)*
Main machinery: 1 MWM diesel; 1200 hp(m) *(882 kW)*; 1 shaft
Speed, knots: 12

Comment: Laid down 1977 at Perama Shipyard. Commissioned 6 April, 6 March and 28 June 1978 respectively.

8 WATER BOATS

KERKINI (ex-German *FW 3*) A 433
PRESPA A 434
YLIKI A 465
TRICHONIS (ex-German *FW 6*) A 466
DOIRANI A 467
KALLIROE A 468
STYNFALIA A 469
KASTORIA A 470

Comment: All built between 1964 and 1972. Capacity, 600 tons except A 433 and A 466 which can carry 300 tons.

DOIRANI *6/1986, van Ginderen Collection*

COAST GUARD (Limenikon Soma)

Senior Officers

Commander-in-Chief:
Vice Admiral G Vasopoulos
Deputy Commander-in-Chief:
Rear Admiral N Hasiotis

Bases

HQ: Piraeus
Main bases: Piraeus, Eleusis, Thessalonika, Volos, Patra, Corfu, Rhodes, Mytilene, Heraklion (Crete), Chios, Kavala, Chalcis
Minor bases: Every port and island of Greece

Ships and Craft

In general very similar in appearance to naval ships, being painted grey. Since 1990 pennant numbers have been painted white and on both sides of the hull they carry a blue and white band with two crossed anchors. In addition to the Coast Guard vessels about 20 very similar craft are operated by the Customs Service's Anti-Smuggling Flotilla.

Personnel

1992: 4300 (850 officers). Includes about 230 women.

General

This force consists of some 158 patrol craft and anti-pollution vessels made up of four offshore patrol craft, 33 coastal craft of 45 ft *(13.7 m)*, 108 up to 27.5 ft *(8.4 m)* plus 18 inflatables for the 48 man Underwater Missions Squad and 12 anti-pollution vessels. There is also a special SAR ship. Administration in peacetime is by the Ministry of Merchant Marine. In wartime it would be transferred to naval command.
Officers are trained at the Naval Academy and ratings at two special schools.
The Abeking & Rasmussen class of four craft (details of same class in main section under *Light Forces*), pennant numbers 80-83, are the largest currently in use. The pennant numbers are all preceded as in the accompanying photographs by Greek 'Lambda Sigma' for Limenikon Soma. New plans include 8 more 45 ft craft.
Three more Abeking & Rasmussen craft are operated by the Customs Service.

Duties

The policing of all Greek harbours, coasts and territorial waters, navigational safety, SAR operations, anti-pollution surveillance and operations, supervision of port authorities, merchant navy training, inspection of Greek merchant ships world-wide.

Coast Guard Air Service

In October 1981 the Coast Guard acquired two Cessna Cutlass 172 RG aircraft and in July 1988 two Socata TB 20s. Maintenance and training by the Air Force. Based at Dekelia air base. New plans include larger aircraft.

Coast Guard Craft (new colours) *1990, Greek Coast Guard*

Coast Guard Craft *5/1991, Erik Laursen*

GRENADA

Headquarters' Appointment

Coast Guard Commander
Inspector Charles

Personnel

1992: 36

Ports

St George, Grenville, Hillsborough

General

Grenada was granted self-government, in association with the UK (which was responsible for its defence) on 3 March 1967. Independence was achieved in February 1974. Coast Guard craft are operated under the direction of the Commissioner of Police.

Mercantile Marine

Lloyd's Register of Shipping:
3 vessels of 623 tons gross

DELETIONS

1988-89 2 Spear class
1990 1 Brooke Marine class (PB 02), 1 Spear class

PATROL FORCES

1 GUARDIAN CLASS (COASTAL PATROL CRAFT)

Name	*No*	*Builders*	*Commissioned*
TYRREL BAY	PB 01	Lantana, Florida	21 Nov 1984

Displacement, tons: 90 full load
Dimensions, feet (metres): 105 × 20.6 × 7 *(32 × 6.3 × 2.1)*
Main machinery: 3 Detroit 12V 71TA diesels; 1260 hp *(939 kW)* sustained; 3 shafts
Speed, knots: 24. **Range, miles:** 1500 at 18 kts
Complement: 15 (2 officers)
Guns: 3—12.7 mm MGs. 2—7.62 mm MGs.
Radars: Surface search: Furuno 1411 Mk II; I band.

Comment: Similar to Jamaican and Honduras vessels.

TYRREL BAY *11/1990, Bob Hanlon*

2 BOSTON WHALERS

Displacement, tons: 1.3 full load
Dimensions, feet (metres): 22.3 × 7.4 × 1.2 *(6.7 × 2.3 × 0.4)*
Main machinery: 2 outboards; 240 hp *(179 kW)*
Speed, knots: 40+
Complement: 4
Guns: 1—12.7 mm MG.

Comment: Acquired in 1988-89.

BOSTON WHALER *11/1990, Bob Hanlon*

GUATEMALA

Senior Appointments

Commander Atlantic Naval Base:
Captain Edgar Abdiel Villanueva Vargas
Commander Pacific Naval Base:
Captain Anibel Ruben Giron Arriola

Personnel

(a) 1992: 1230 (125 officers) including 700 Marines (2 battalions) (mostly volunteers)
(b) 2½ years' national service

Note: With army logistic support the total employed on naval work is about 1500 (including 900 conscripts).

Bases

Santo Tomás de Castillas (Atlantic); Sipacate and Puerto Quetzal (Pacific)

Mercantile Marine

Lloyd's Register of Shipping:
7 vessels of 1479 tons gross

PATROL FORCES

Note: (a) There is also a naval manned Ferry *Orca* (T 691).
(b) Still trying to acquire new patrol craft possibly with assistance from the USA. Three 32 m patrol boats reportedly ordered from CMN Cherbourg in February 1990 were cancelled.

1 BROADSWORD CLASS (COASTAL PATROL CRAFT)

Name	*No*	*Builder*	*Commissioned*
KUKULKÁN	P 1051	Halter Marine	4 Aug 1976

Displacement, tons: 90.5 standard; 110 full load
Dimensions, feet (metres): 105 × 20.4 × 6.3 *(32 × 6.2 × 1.9)*
Main machinery: 2 GM 16V 149 TI diesels; 3105 hp *(2.32 MW)* sustained; 2 shafts
Speed, knots: 32. **Range, miles:** 1150 at 20 kts
Complement: 20 (5 officers)
Guns: 1—75 mm recoilless. 2 Oerlikon 20 mm. 2—7.62 mm MGs.
Radars: Surface search: Racal Decca; I band.

Comment: As the flagship she used to rotate between Pacific and Atlantic bases every two years but remained in the Pacific from 1989 to 1991. Rearmed with 20 mm guns in 1989.

KUKULKÁN *5/1985*

2 SEWART CLASS (COASTAL PATROL CRAFT)

Name	*No*	*Builders*	*Commissioned*
UTATLAN	P 851	Sewart, Louisiana	May 1967
SUBTENIENTE USORIO SARAVIA	P 852	Sewart, Louisiana	Nov 1972

Displacement, tons: 43 standard; 54 full load
Dimensions, feet (metres): 85 × 18.7 × 7.2 *(25.9 × 5.7 × 2.2)*
Main machinery: 2 GM 16V 71 TI diesels; 2200 hp *(1.64 MW)*; 2 shafts
Speed, knots: 23. **Range, miles:** 400 at 12 kts
Complement: 17 (4 officers)
Guns: 2—75 mm recoilless. 2 Oerlikon 20 mm. 2—7.62 mm MGs.
Radars: Surface search: Racal Decca; I band.

Comment: Aluminium superstructure. P 852 may be non-operational. P 851 rearmed with 20 mm guns in 1989.

UTATLAN *8/1987*

6 US CUTLASS CLASS (5 COASTAL PATROL CRAFT AND 1 SURVEY CRAFT)

Name	*No*	*Builders*	*Commissioned*
TECUNUMAN	P 651	Halter Marine	26 Nov 1971
KAIBIL BALAM	P 652	Halter Marine	8 Feb 1972
AZUMANCHE	P 653	Halter Marine	8 Feb 1972
ITZACOL	P 654	Halter Marine	10 Mar 1976
BITOL	P 655	Halter Marine	4 Aug 1976
GUCUMAZ	BH 656	Halter Marine	15 May 1981

Displacement, tons: 45 full load
Dimensions, feet (metres): 64.5 × 17 × 3 *(19.7 × 5.2 × 0.9)*
Main machinery: 2 GM 12V 71 diesels; 680 hp *(507 kW)* sustained; 2 shafts
Speed, knots: 25. **Range, miles:** 400 at 15 kts
Complement: 10 (2 officers)
Guns: 2 Oerlikon 20 mm or 2—12.7 mm MGs. 3—7.62 mm (triple) MGs.
Radars: Surface search: Racal Decca; I band.

Comment: *Gucumaz* used for Survey duties. All reported in 1991 rearmed with 20 mm guns.

BITOL *1987*

2 MACHETE CLASS (TROOP CARRIERS)

Name	*No*	*Builders*	*Commissioned*
PICUDA	D 361	Halter Marine	4 Aug 1976
BARRACUDA	D 362	Halter Marine	4 Aug 1976

Displacement, tons: 8.3 full load
Dimensions, feet (metres): 36 × 12.5 × 2 *(11 × 3.8 × 0.6)*
Main machinery: 2 GM 6V-53PI; 296 hp *(221 kW)* sustained; 2 waterjets
Speed, knots: 36
Complement: 2
Military lift: 20 troops

Comment: Armoured, open deck, aluminium craft.

BARRACUDA *1986*

RIVER PATROL CRAFT

KOCHAB	**PAMPANU**	**SPICA**	**PAMPANO**
ALIOTH	**PROCYON**	**SCHEDAR**	**ESCUINTLA**
SIRIES	**VEGA**	**STELLA MARIS**	**MAZATENANGO**
MERO	**POLUX**	**SARDINA**	**RETALHULEU**
			LAGO DE ATITLAN

Dimensions, feet (metres): 29.8 × 12.1 × 2 *(9.1 × 3.7 × 0.6)*
Main machinery: 1 diesel; 150 hp *(112 kW)* (series 1); 300 hp *(224 kW)* (series 2); 1 shaft
Speed, knots: 19 (series 1); 28 (series 2)
Guns: 2—7.62 mm (twin) MGs.

Comment: Built by Trabejos Baros SY in 1979. Wooden hulls. Two series. Some have L pennant numbers. Some of those listed have been replaced by aluminium hulled craft which may have been given the same names. Numbers are uncertain.

GUINEA

Senior Appointment

Commander of the Navy:
Lieutenant Commander Amara Bangoura

General

Some of the craft listed below are probably non-operational.

Personnel

(a) 1992: 400 officers and men
(b) 2 years' conscript service

Bases

Conakry, Kakanda

Mercantile Marine

Lloyd's Register of Shipping:
26 vessels of 9062 tons gross

DELETIONS

1989-90 6 Shanghai II class, 3 Shershen class

PATROL FORCES

1 Ex-SOVIET T 58 CLASS (PATROL SHIP)

LAMINE SADJI KABA F 79

Displacement, tons: 790 standard; 860 full load
Dimensions, feet (metres): 229.9 × 29.5 × 7.9 *(70.1 × 9 × 2.4)*
Main machinery: 2 diesels; 4000 hp(m) *(2.94 MW)*; 2 shafts
Speed, knots: 17. **Range, miles:** 2500 at 13 kts
Complement: 82
Guns: 4—57 mm/70 (2 twin); 85° elevation; 120 rounds/minute to 8 km *(4.4 nm)*; weight of shell 2.8 kg.
4—25 mm/60 (2 twin); 85° elevation; 270 rounds/minute to 3 km *(1.6 nm)*; weight of shell 0.34 kg.
Mines: Laying capability.
Radars: Surface search: Don 2; I band.
Fire control: Muff Cob; G/H band.

Comment: Transferred May 1979. MCM equipment removed. Refitted in Luanda 1984. Not in good condition and last reported at sea in 1989.

3 SOVIET BOGOMOL CLASS (FAST ATTACK CRAFT—GUN)

Displacement, tons: 245 full load
Dimensions, feet (metres): 127.9 × 25.6 × 5.9 *(39 × 7.8 × 1.8)*
Main machinery: 3 M 504 diesels; 15 000 hp(m) *(11 MW)*; 3 shafts
Speed, knots: 37. **Range, miles:** 500 at 35 kts
Complement: 30
Guns: 1 USSR 3 in *(76 mm)*/66; 85°elevation; 120 rounds/minute to 15 km *(8 nm)*; weight of shell 7 kg.
2 USSR 30 mm/65 (twin); 85° elevation; 500 rounds/minute to 5 km *(2.7 nm)*; weight of shell 0.54 kg.
Radars: Surface search: Pot Head; H/I band.
Fire control: Bass Tilt; H/I band.

Comment: Built by Isora (Kolpino) in the Pacific and completed in April 1989. A Soviet export model with an Osa hull and machinery. Possibly two more delivered in 1990/91.

BOGOMOL (in transporter) *1989, G. Jacobs*

1 SWIFTSHIPS 77 FT CLASS

Name	*No*	*Builders*	*Commissioned*
INTREPIDE	P 328	Swiftships, Morgan City	Feb 1987

Displacement, tons: 47.5 full load
Dimensions, feet (metres): 77.1 × 20 × 4.9 *(23.5 × 6.1 × 1.5)*
Main machinery: 3 Detroit 12V-71TA diesels; 1260 hp *(993 kW)* sustained; 3 shafts
Speed, knots: 26. **Range, miles:** 600 at 18 kts
Complement: 10
Guns: 2 Browning 12.7 mm MGs. 2—7.62 mm MGs.

Comment: Ordered in July 1985 and completed 18 December 1986. Aluminium hull.

1 COASTAL PATROL CRAFT

Name	*No*	*Builder*	*Commissioned*
ALMAMY BOCAR BIRO BARRY	P 400	Chantiers Navals d l'Esterel	Aug 1979

Displacement, tons: 56 full load
Dimensions, feet (metres): 91.8 × 17.1 × 5.2 *(28 × 5.2 × 1.6)*
Main machinery: 2 MTU 12V331 TC82 diesels; 2605 hp(m) *(1.91 MW)* sustained; 2 shafts
Speed, knots: 35. **Range, miles:** 750 at 15 kts
Complement: 13
Guns: 1—12.7 mm MG.

Comment: Two more of the class were expected in 1987 but the order was cancelled.

1 SWIFTSHIPS 65 FT CLASS

Name	*No*	*Builders*	*Commissioned*
VIGILANTE	P 300	Swiftships, Morgan City	6 Jan 1986

Displacement, tons: 36.5
Dimensions, feet (metres): 64.9 × 18.4 × 5.2 *(19.8 × 5.6 × 1.6)*
Main machinery: 2 Detroit 12V-71TA diesels; 840 hp *(627 kW)* sustained; 2 shafts
Speed, knots: 24. **Range, miles:** 500 at 18 kts
Complement: 10
Guns: 2 Browning 12.7 mm MGs. 2—7.62 mm MGs.

Comment: Ordered in October 1984. Aluminium hull.

VIGILANTE *1985, Swiftships*

2 Ex-SOVIET ZHUK CLASS (COASTAL PATROL CRAFT)

Displacement, tons: 50
Dimensions, feet (metres): 75.4 × 17 × 6.2 *(23 × 5.2 × 1.9)*
Main machinery: 2 M50 F4 diesels; 2400 hp(m) *(1.76 MW)*; 2 shafts
Speed, knots: 30. **Range, miles:** 1100 at 15 kts
Complement: 17
Guns: 2—14.5 mm (twin) MGs. 1—12.7 mm MG.

Comment: Transferred July 1987 after refurbishment.

2 STINGER CLASS

P 30 **P 35**

Displacement, tons: 2.9 full load
Dimensions, feet (metres): 26.3 × 11.1 × 1.5 *(8 × 3.4 × 0.5)*
Main machinery: 2 MC outboards; 310 hp *(231 kW)*
Speed, knots: 35
Complement: 4
Guns: 2—12.7 mm MGs.
Radars: Navigation: Raytheon 1200; I band.

Comment: Coastal/river patrol craft delivered in 1986 by SeaArk Marine (ex-MonArk).

STINGER Class *1987, MonArk Boats*

GUINEA-BISSAU

Personnel

(a) 1992: 300 officers and men
(b) Voluntary service

Base

Bissau

General

A Cessna 337 patrol aircraft is used for offshore surveillance. Several small craft including some ex-Soviet and Chinese LCU types may still be in service. There are also unconfirmed reports of an ex-German Kondor class minesweeper being acquired in 1991.

Mercantile Marine

Lloyd's Register of Shipping:
19 vessels of 4380 tons gross

DELETIONS

1989 2 Shantou class
1990 2 Poluchat class, *Cabo Roxo, Ilha de Poilao*
1991 4 Bazán type

PATROL FORCES

3 SOVIET BOGOMOL CLASS (FAST ATTACK CRAFT—GUN)

Displacement, tons: 245 full load
Dimensions, feet (metres): 127.9 × 25.6 × 5.9 *(39 × 7.8 × 1.8)*
Main machinery: 3 M 504 diesels; 15 000 hp(m) *(11 MW)*; 3 shafts
Speed, knots: 37. **Range, miles:** 500 at 35 kts
Complement: 30
Guns: 1 USSR 3 in *(76 mm)*/66; 85° elevation; 120 rounds/minute to 15 km *(8 nm)*; weight of shell 7 kg.
2 USSR 30 mm/65 (twin); 85° elevation; 500 rounds/minute to 5 km *(2.7 nm)*; weight of shell 0.54 kg.
Radars: Surface search: Pot Head; H/I band.
Fire control: Bass Tilt; H/I band.

Comment: Built in the Pacific by Isora (Kolpino). Soviet export model with an Osa hull and machinery. First one delivered in early 1988, second in June 1990 from Vladivostock. Possibly one more in 1991.

BOGOMOL (in transporter) *1989, G. Jacobs*

2 Ex-CHINESE SHANTOU CLASS

Displacement, tons: 80 full load
Dimensions, feet (metres): 83.3 × 19 × 6.5 *(25.5 × 5.8 × 2)*
Main machinery: 2 Type 3-D-12 diesels; 616 hp(m) *(453 kW)*; 2 Type M50L diesels; 2400 hp(m) *(1.76 MW)*; 4 shafts
Speed, knots: 28. **Range, miles:** 500 at 28 kts
Complement: 36
Guns: 4—37 mm/63 (2 twin); 85° elevation; 160 rounds/minute to 8.5 km *(4.6 nm)*; weight of shell 1.46 kg.
2—12.7 mm MGs.
Depth charges: 8.
Radars: Surface search: Skin Head; I band; range 37 km *(20 nm)*.

Comment: Two delivered in 1983, two more in March 1986. First two used to provide spares for the others.

0 + 2 COASTAL PATROL CRAFT

Displacement, tons: 47 light
Dimensions, feet (metres): 64.6 × 19 × 10.6 *(19.7 × 5.8 × 3.2)*
Main machinery: 3 MTU 12V183TE92 diesels; 1000 hp(m) *(735 kW)*; 3 waterjets
Speed, knots: 28
Complement: 9 (1 officer)
Radars: Navigation, Furuno FR 2010

Comment: Ordered from Arsenal do Alfeite in 1991 for delivery by 1993.

3 COASTAL PATROL CRAFT

Displacement, tons: 21.2 full load
Dimensions, feet (metres): 52.2 × 14.4 × 4.3 *(15.9 × 4.4 × 1.3)*
Main machinery: 2 Baudouin DNP-8 M1R diesels; 768 hp(m) *(564 kW)*; 2 shafts
Speed, knots: 25.7. **Range, miles:** 430 at 18 kts
Complement: 5
Guns: 1—12.7 mm MG.

Comment: Three ordered from Bazán, Ferrol in 1978. Four more ordered in September 1981. At least four deleted.

GUYANA

Senior Appointment

Commanding Officer Coast Guard:
Lieutenant Colonel Cecil Austin

General

In 1991 every vessel was either sunk or destroyed. Two Tugs and two Boston Whalers acquired in late 1991 were the only operational vessels at the beginning of 1992. Some of the sunken ships may be recoverable.

Personnel

(a) 1992: 100 members of Guyana Defence Force
(b) Voluntary

Bases

Georgetown, New Amsterdam

Prefix to Ships' Names

GDFS

Mercantile Marine

Lloyd's Register of Shipping:
81 vessels of 15 620 tons gross

DELETIONS

1991 *Peccari, Eereku, Waitipu, Maipuri, Hymara, Houri, Pirai, Kimbia*

HAITI

Headquarters' Appointments

Commander-in-Chief Armed Forces:
Lieutenant General Raoul Cedras
Commander of the Coast Guard:
Captain Ambroise Seide
Deputy Commander:
Commander Charles A André

Personnel

(a) 1992: 340 (Total Armed Forces 7000)
(b) Voluntary service

Base

Port Au Prince

Mercantile Marine

Lloyd's Register of Shipping:
3 vessels of 711 tons gross

State Yacht

Also reported, though not confirmed, that *Sans Souci* has been retained as a state yacht.

DELETIONS

1990 *MH 22, MH 23*

PATROL FORCES

1 Ex-US SOTOYOMO CLASS

Name	*No*	*Builders*	*Commissioned*
HENRI CHRISTOPHE (ex-USS *Samoset* ATA 190)	MH 20	Levingston S B Co, Orange, Texas	1 Jan 1945

Displacement, tons: 534 standard; 860 full load
Dimensions, feet (metres): 143 × 33.9 × 13 *(43.6 × 10.3 × 4)*
Main machinery: Diesel-electric; 2 GM 12-278A diesels; 2200 hp *(1.64 MW)*; 2 generators; 1 motor; 1500 hp *(1.12 MW)*; 1 shaft
Speed, knots: 13. **Range, miles:** 16 500 at 9 kts
Complement: 49
Guns: 2 Bofors 40 mm. 2—12.7 mm (twin) MGs.

Comment: Transferred by sale 16 October 1978.

HENRI CHRISTOPHE *1988, van Ginderen Collection*

US 3812-VCF CLASS (COASTAL PATROL CRAFT)

E MAROON MH 11
GE MH 12
HAVANNES MH 13
APOIS MH 14
AUKMAN MH 15
MAKANDAL MH 16
CHARLEMAGNE PERRAULT MH 17
SONTHONAX MH 18
BOIS ROND TONNERRE MH 19

isplacement, tons: 15
imensions, feet (metres): 40.8 × 13.3 × 1.4 *(12.4 × 4.1 × 0.4)*
lain machinery: 2 Detroit 6V-71N diesels; 348 hp *(260 kW)* sustained; 2 shafts
peed, knots: 25. **Range, miles:** 350 at 20 kts
omplement: 4
uns: 1 Browning 12.7 mm MG. 2 FN Herstal 7.62 mm (twin) MGs.

omment: Built by MonArk, Monticello, Arkansas in 1981. Three used for spares; six only operational in 1991.

CHAVANNES *1988, van Ginderen Collection*

HONDURAS

enior Appointments

hief of the Armed Forces:
Brigadier Luis Discua Elvir
ommander of Honduran Navy:
Colonel Reynaldo Andino Flores

ersonnel

a) 1992: 900 (95 officers)
b) 24 months' conscript service

Bases

Puerto Cortés, Amapala, Puerto Castilla, La Ceiba, Puerto Trujillo

General

Two ex-Polish Polnochny class LCTs were seen flying the Honduran flag at Kiel in April 1990. These ships had been bought commercially for scrapping in a Spanish shipyard, and not to be transferred to the Honduran Navy.

Mercantile Marine

Lloyd's Register of Shipping:
846 vessels of 815 916 tons gross

PATROL FORCES

SWIFT 105 FT CLASS (FAST ATTACK CRAFT—GUN)

UAYMURAS FNH 101 **HONDURAS** FNH 102 **HIBUERAS** FNH 103

isplacement, tons: 103 full load
imensions, feet (metres): 105 × 20.6 × 7 *(32 × 6.3 × 2.1)*
ain machinery: 2 MTU diesels; 7000 hp(m) *(5.15 MW)*; 2 shafts
peed, knots: 30. **Range, miles:** 1200 at 18 kts
omplement: 17 (3 officers)
uns: 1 General Electric Sea Vulcan 20 mm Gatling (FNH 101-102). 2—12.7 mm MGs.
6 Hispano-Suiza 20 mm (2 triple) (FNH 103).

omment: First delivered by Swiftships, Morgan City in April 1977 and last two in March 1980. Gatling guns acquired in 1987 with HSV-20NCS fire control system.

IBUERAS *12/1987*

GUARDIAN CLASS (COASTAL PATROL CRAFT)

OPAN FNH 106 **TEGUCIGALPA** FNH 107

isplacement, tons: 94 full load
imensions, feet (metres): 106 × 20.6 × 7 *(32.3 × 6.3 × 2.1)*
lain machinery: 3 Detroit 16V-92TA diesels; 2070 hp *(1.54 MW)*; 3 shafts
peed, knots: 30. **Range, miles:** 1500 at 18 kts
omplement: 17 (3 officers)
uns: 1 General Electric Sea Vulcan 20 mm Gatling.
3 Hispano Suiza 20 mm (1 triple). 2—12.7 mm MGs.
adars: Navigation: Furuno; I band.

omment: Delivered by Lantana Boatyard, Florida in January 1983 and August 1986. A third of the class, completed in May 1984, became the Jamaican *Paul Bogle*.

OPAN *7/1986, Giorgio Arra*

1 COASTAL PATROL CRAFT

CHAMELECON FN 8501

Displacement, tons: 50 full load
Dimensions, feet (metres): 85.3 × 19 × 3.3 *(26 × 5.8 × 1)*
Main machinery: 2 GM 12V 71 TI diesels; 840 hp *(627 kW)* sustained; 2 shafts
Speed, knots: 23. **Range, miles:** 780 at 18 kts
Complement: 10 (2 officers)
Guns: 1 Oerlikon 20 mm. 2—12.7 mm MGs.

Comment: Built by Swiftships, Morgan City in 1967. Ex-*Rio Kuringuras* defected from Nicaragua in 1979.

CHAMELECON and GOASCORAN *1988*

5 SWIFT 65 FT CLASS (COASTAL PATROL CRAFT)

NACAOME (ex-*Aguan*, ex-*Gral*) FNH 6501
GOASCORAN (ex-*General J T Cabanas*) FNH 6502
CHOLUTECA FNH 6505
PETULA FNH 6503
ULUA FNH 6504

Displacement, tons: 33 full load
Dimensions, feet (metres): 69.9 × 17.1 × 5.2 *(21.3 × 5.2 × 1.6)*
Main machinery: 2 GM 12V 71 TI diesels; 840 hp *(627 kW)*; 2 shafts (FNH 6501-2)
2 MTU 8V96 TB93 diesels; 2180 hp(m) *(1.6 MW)*; 2 shafts (FNH 6503-5)
Speed, knots: 25 (FNH 6501-2); 36 (FNH 6503-5). **Range, miles:** 2000 at 22 kts (FNH 6501-2)
Complement: 9 (2 officers)
Guns: 1 Oerlikon 20 mm. 2 Browning 12.7 mm (twin) MGs.

Comment: First pair built by Swiftships, Morgan City originally for Haiti. Contract cancelled and Honduras bought the two which had been completed in 1973-74. Delivered in 1977. Last three ordered in 1979 and delivered 1980.

7 PIRANHA CLASS (RIVER PATROL CRAFT)

Displacement, tons: 8.2
Dimensions, feet (metres): 36 × 10 × 1.6 *(11 × 3.1 × 0.5)*
Main machinery: 2 Caterpillar diesels; 630 hp *(470 kW)*; 2 shafts
Speed, knots: 26
Complement: 5
Guns: 2—12.7 mm MGs. 2—7.62 mm MGs.

Comment: Eight built by Lantana Boatyard, Florida, and delivered on 3 February 1986. Also supplied to El Salvador. One reported sunk in September 1988 in a clash with Nicaraguan craft. More of this class may be acquired.

PIRANHA Class *1988, Honduras Navy*

10 OUTRAGE CLASS (RIVER PATROL CRAFT)

Displacement, tons: 2.2
Dimensions, feet (metres): 24.9 × 7.9 × 1.3 *(7.6 × 2.4 × 0.4)*
Main machinery: 2 Evinrude outboards; 300 hp *(224 kW)*
Speed, knots: 30. **Range:** 200 at 30 kts
Complement: 4
Guns: 1—12.7 mm MG. 2—7.62 mm MGs.

Comment: Built by Boston Whaler in 1982.

1 Ex-US HOLLYHOCK CLASS (BUOY TENDER)

YOJOA (ex-USS *Walnut*) FNH 252

Displacement, tons: 989 full load
Dimensions, feet (metres): 175.2 × 34.1 × 12.1 *(53.4 × 10.4 × 3.7)*
Main machinery: 2 diesels; 1350 hp *(1 MW)*; 2 shafts
Speed, knots: 12
Complement: 40 (4 officers)

Comment: Transferred in July 1982. Built by Moore Drydock Co in 1939.

YOJOA *8/1989*

1 LANDING CRAFT (LCU)

PUNTA CAXINAS FNH 1491

Displacement, tons: 625 full load
Dimensions, feet (metres): 149 × 33 × 6.5 *(45.4 × 10 × 2)*
Main machinery: 3 Caterpillar 3412 diesels; 1821 hp *(1.4 MW)*; 3 shafts
Speed, knots: 14. **Range:** 3500 at 12 kts
Complement: 18 (3 officers)
Military lift: 100 tons equipment or 50 000 gallons dieso plus 4 standard containers

Comment: Ordered in 1986 from Lantana, Florida, and commissioned 12 January 1988.

PUNTA CAXINAS *1988, Honduras Navy*

9 TRANSPORT CRAFT

In addition to the above, three old ex-US LCM 8 (*Warunta* FNH 7401, *Tansin* FNH 7402, *Caratasca* FNH 7403) transferred in 1987, and six ex-Fishing Boats (*Juliana* FNH 7501, *San Rafael* FNH 7502, *Carmen* FNH 7503, *Mairy* FNH 7504, *Yosuro* FNH 7505, *Gregori* FNH 7506) are used as transport vessels.

LCM 8 *8/1989*

LAND-BASED MARITIME AIRCRAFT

Numbers/Type: 2 Embraer EMB-III Bandeirante.
Operational speed: 194 kts *(360 km/h)*.
Service ceiling: 25 500 ft *(7770 m)*.
Range: 1590 nm *(2945 km)*.
Role/Weapon systems: Armed MR and coastal patrol against insurgents. Air Force manned. Sensors: APS-128 radar. Weapons: ASV; up to 28 × 70 mm rockets or 6 or 8—127 mm rockets.

HONG KONG

General

All the listed craft are operated by the Marine Region of the Royal Hong Kong Police Force (RHKP). This is a Coast Guard Force responsible for the territorial waters of Hong Kong including the colony's 244 islands. The four main tasks are the prevention of illegal immigration from China, the detention of Vietnamese boat people, the prevention of smuggling by water between Hong Kong and mainland China and SAR operations.

Senior Officers

Regional Commander:
B J Deegan, QPM, CPM
Deputy Regional Commander:
Lim Sak-Yeung

Organisation

Marine Police Regional HQ, Tsim Sha Tsui, Kowloon
Bases at Ma Liu Shui, Tui Min Hoi, Tai Lam Chung, Aberdeen, Sai Wan Ho

Personnel

(a) 1992: 2600
(b) Voluntary service

Mercantile Marine

Lloyd's Register of Shipping:
355 vessels of 5 875 825 tons gross

2 COMMAND VESSELS

SEA PANTHER PL 3   **SEA HORSE** PL 4

Displacement, tons: 420
Dimensions, feet (metres): 131.2 × 28.2 × 10.5 *(40 × 8.6 × 3.2)*
Main machinery: 2 Caterpillar 3512 diesels; 2350 hp *(1.75 MW)* sustained; 2 shafts
Speed, knots: 14. **Range, miles:** 1500 at 14 kts
Complement: 33
Guns: 2—12.7 mm MGs.
Radars: Surface search: Two Racal Decca; I band.

Comment: Built by Hong Kong SY, PL 3 completed 27 July 1987, PL 4 on 29 September 1987. Both commissioned 1 February 1988. Steel hulls. Both have a Racal Cane command system.

SEA PANTHER *1987, RHKP*

PATROL FORCES

2 COMMAND VESSELS

SEA LION PL 1 **SEA TIGER** PL 2

Displacement, tons: 222.5
Dimensions, feet (metres): 111.3 × 24 × 10.5 *(33.9 × 7.3 × 3.2)*
Main machinery: 2 Lister Blackstone ER6 MGR diesels; 674 hp *(503 kW)*; 2 shafts
Speed, knots: 11.8. **Range, miles:** 1800 at 11.5 kts
Complement: 27
Guns: 1 Browning 12.7 mm MG.
Radars: Surface search: Racal Decca; I band.

Comment: Built at Taikoo 1965 (now Hong Kong United Dockyard). Can carry two platoons in addition to complement. To be paid off in 1993.

SEA LION *11/1986, Giorgio Arra*

15 DAMEN Mk III (PATROL CRAFT)

KING LAI PL 70 **KING YEE** PL 71 **KING LIM** PL 72 **KING HAU** PL 73 **KING DAI** PL 74 **KING CHUNG** PL 75 **KING SHUN** PL 76 **KING TAK** PL 77 **KING CHI** PL 78 **KING TAI** PL 79 **KING KWAN** PL 80 **KING MEI** PL 81 **KING YAN** PL 82 **KING YUNG** PL 83 **KING KAN** PL 84

Displacement, tons: 95
Dimensions, feet (metres): 87 × 19 × 6 *(26.5 × 5.8 × 1.8)*
Main machinery: 2 MTU 12V396 TC82 diesels; 2610 hp(m) *(1.92 MW)* sustained; 2 shafts
1 Mercedes-Benz OM-424A 12V diesel; 374 hp(m) *(275 kW)* sustained; 1 KaMeWa waterjet
Speed, knots: 26 on 3 diesels; 8 on waterjet and cruising diesel. **Range, miles:** 600 at 14 kts
Complement: 17
Guns: 1 Browning 12.7 mm MG.
Radars: Surface search: Racal Decca.

Comment: Steel hulled craft constructed by Chung Wah SB & Eng Co Ltd 1984/85.

KING CHUNG *1988, RHKP*

9 DAMEN CLASS (PATROL CRAFT)

PL 60-68

Displacement, tons: 86
Dimensions, feet (metres): 85.9 × 19.4 × 5.9 *(26.2 × 5.9 × 1.8)*
Main machinery: 2 MTU 12V396 TC82 diesels; 2610 hp(m) *(1.92 MW)* sustained; 2 shafts
1 MAN D 2566 diesel; 195 hp(m) *(143 kW)*; Schottel prop (centre line)
Speed, knots: 23 MTU; 6 MAN. **Range, miles:** 600 at 14 kts
Complement: 14
Guns: 1 Browning 12.7 mm MG.
Radars: Surface search: Racal Decca; I band.

Comment: Designed by Damen SY, Netherlands. Steel hulled craft built by Chung Wah SB & Eng Co Ltd. Delivered February 1980 to January 1981.

PL 65 *11/1985, Giorgio Arra*

0 + 6 ASI 315 CLASS (PATROL CRAFT)

Displacement, tons: 170 full load
Dimensions, feet (metres): 107 × 26.9 × 5.2 *(32.6 × 8.2 × 1.6)*
Main machinery: 2 Caterpillar 3516 diesels; 2820 hp *(2.1 MW)*; 2 shafts; 1 Caterpillar 3412 DITA Hamilton jet (centre line); 764 hp *(570 kW)*
Speed, knots: 24. **Range, miles:** 600 at 18 kts
Complement: 18
Guns: 1 Browning 12.7 mm MG.
Radars: Surface search: 2 Racal Decca; I band.

Comment: Ordered from Australian Shipbuilding Industries in August 1991 for delivery by the end of 1992. As well as patrol work, the craft provide command platforms for Divisional commanders.

ASI 315 Class *1988, John Mortimer*

7 PATROL CRAFT

SEA CAT PL 50 **SEA PUMA** PL 51 **SEA LEOPARD** PL 52 **SEA EAGLE** PL 53 **SEA HAWK** PL 54 **SEA LYNX** PL 55 **SEA FALCON** PL 56

Displacement, tons: 80 (vary)
Dimensions, feet (metres): 78.5 × 17.2 × 5.6 *(23.9 × 5.2 × 1.7)*
Main machinery: 2 Cummins diesels; 1500 hp *(1.12 MW)*; 2 shafts
Speed, knots: 20.7. **Range, miles:** 400 at 20 kts
Complement: 12
Guns: 1 Browning 12.7 mm MG.
Radars: Surface search: Racal Decca; I band.

Comment: Steel hulled craft built by Thornycroft, Singapore. Delivered May 1972 to May 1973. To be paid off in 1992/93.

SEA LYNX *1979, Giorgio Arra*

3 SHALLOW WATER PATROL CRAFT (JET)

JETSTREAM PL 6 **SWIFTSTREAM** PL 7 **TIDESTREAM** PL 8

Displacement, tons: 24
Dimensions, feet (metres): 53.8 × 14.8 × 2.8 *(16.4 × 4.5 × 0.8)*
Main machinery: 2 Daimler-Benz OM 422A 8V diesels; 455 hp(m) *(334 kW)*; 2 Hamilton 421 waterjets
Speed, knots: 18. **Range, miles:** 300 at 15 kts
Complement: 8

Comment: Fibreglass hull built by Choy Lee Shipyards Limited. Completed April 1986 *(Jetstream)*, May 1986 *(Swiftstream)*, and June 1986 *(Tidestream)*.

JETSTREAM *1986, RHKP*

7 HARBOUR PATROL CRAFT

PETREL PL 11
AUK PL 12
GULL PL 13
TERN PL 14
SKUA PL 15
PUFFIN PL 16
GANNET PL 17

Displacement, tons: 36
Dimensions, feet (metres): 52.5 × 15.1 × 4.9 *(16 × 4.6 × 1.5)*
Main machinery: 2 Cummins NTA 855M diesels; 680 hp *(507 kW)*; 2 waterjets
Speed, knots: 12
Complement: 7

Comment: Built by Chung Wah SB & Eng Co Ltd in 1986-87. Replaced old patrol craft some of which had the same names.

3 DAMEN LOGISTIC CRAFT

MERCURY PL 57 **VULCAN** PL 58 **CERES** PL 59

Displacement, tons: 86
Dimensions, feet (metres): 85.9 × 19.4 × 5.9 *(26.2 × 5.9 × 1.8)*
Main machinery: 2 MTU 12V396 TC82 diesels; 2610 hp(m) *(1.92 MW)*; 2 shafts
1 Daimler-Benz OM 422 8V diesel; 208 hp(m) *(153 kW)*; 1 Hamilton 421 waterjet
Speed, knots: 23+ MTU; 7 waterjet and cruising diesels. **Range, miles:** 600 at 14 kts
Complement: 5 (10 for patrol work)
Military lift: 2 platoons of troops
Guns: 1 Browning 12.7 mm MG.
Radars: Navigation: Decca 150; I band.

Comment: Modified PL 60 design by Damen SY, Netherlands. Built by Chung Wah SB & Eng Co Ltd. Completed 26 January 1982 *(Mercury)*, 22 March 1982 *(Vulcan)*, 29 March 1982 *(Ceres)*. To be converted to patrol craft in 1992/93.

CERES *1987, Giorgio Arra*

0 + 4 SEASPRAY LOGISTIC CRAFT

Displacement, tons: 37.4 × 13.8 × 4.3 *(11.4 × 4.2 × 1.3)*
Main machinery: 2 Caterpillar 3208 TA diesels; 700 hp *(522 kW)*; 2 shafts
Speed, knots: 30
Complement: 4

Comment: Built by Seaspray Boats, Fremantle. First to be delivered in mid-1992.

9 FAIREY ALLDAY MARINE SPEAR CLASS

PL 37-45

Displacement, tons: 4.3
Dimensions, feet (metres): 29.8 × 9 × 2.9 *(9.1 × 2.8 × 0.9)*
Main machinery: 2 Perkins T63 544 diesels; 360 hp *(269 kW)*; 2 shafts
Speed, knots: 26. **Range, miles:** 250 at 25 kts
Complement: 4

Comment: Operational 1981. Inshore patrol craft. To be paid off in 1992.

PL 41 *1982, RHKP*

0 + 11 SEASPRAY INSHORE PATROL CRAFT

Displacement, tons: 32.5 × 13.8 × 4.3 *(9.9 × 4.2 × 1.3)*
Main machinery: 2 Caterpillar 3208 TA diesels; 700 hp *(522 kW)*; 2 shafts
Speed, knots: 35
Complement: 4

Comment: Being built by Seaspray Boats, Fremantle. First three to be delivered in mid-1992.

2 SHARK CAT INTERCEPTORS

PL 20-21

Displacement, tons: 4.5
Dimensions, feet (metres): 27 × 9.2 × 1.6 *(8.3 × 2.8 × 0.5)*
Main machinery: 2 outboards; 540 hp *(403 kW)*
Speed, knots: 40+
Complement: 4

Comment: Catamaran construction. Commissioned in October 1988.

PL 20 *10/1988, RHKP*

7 WIN CLASS POLICE MOTOR BOATS

PL 35, 36, PL 85-89

Comment: Built by Choy Lee SY in 1970. Of 4.8 tons and 20 kts with a range of 160 miles at full speed.

WIN Class *1987, RHKP*

29 HIGH SPEED INTERCEPTORS

PV 10-11 **PV 14-17** **PV 30-37** **PV 90-98** **+6**

Comment: Typhoon rigid inflatables (*PV 10-11, PV 30-37*); Tempest rigid inflatables (*PV 14-17*); Sillinger inflatables (*PV 90-98*). All operated as a Small Boat Unit. Six more Typhoons acquired in 1990.

CUSTOMS SERVICE

Note: Among other craft three Damen 26 metre Sector command launches were completed in 1986 by Chung Wah SB & Eng Co Ltd, Kowloon. In all essentials these craft are sisters of the 15 operated by the Royal Hong Kong Police with the exception of the latter's slow speed waterjet. Names: *Sea Glory* (Customs 6), *Sea Guardian* (Customs 5), *Sea Leader* (Customs 2).

LAND-BASED MARITIME AIRCRAFT

Note: Eight S-76A helicopters on order for SAR/transport duties.

Numbers/Type: 1 Cessna 404 Titan.
Operational speed: 258 kts *(478 km/h)*.
Service ceiling: 30 200 ft *(9200 m)*.
Range: 1485 nm *(2748 km)*.
Role/Weapon systems: Coastal surveillance for smugglers and 'boat people'. Sensors: Weather radar and cameras. Weapons: Unarmed.

Numbers/Type: 1 Pilatus Britten-Norman Islander.
Operational speed: 150 kts *(280 km/h)*.
Service ceiling: 18 900 ft *(5760 m)*.
Range: 1500 nm *(2775 km)*.
Role/Weapon systems: Supports RHKP in inter-island surveillance and against smugglers. Sensors: Weather radar and cameras. Weapons: Unarmed.

HUNGARY

Headquarters' Appointment

Chief of General Staff:
Lieutenant General Laszlo Borsits

Diplomatic Representation

Defence Attaché in London:
Colonel Peter Szücs

Personnel

(a) 1992: 400 officers and men
(b) 12 months' national service

General

The Navy was dissolved by 1968 but a maritime wing of the Army is still active on the Danube in the form of an independent maritime brigade. The total number of craft operated is about 13 and the rest are held in reserve. Based in Budapest.

Mercantile Marine

Lloyd's Register of Shipping:
17 vessels of 103 854 tons gross

6 Ex-YUGOSLAV NESTIN CLASS (RIVER MINESWEEPERS)

ÚJPEST AM 11
BAJA AM 12
SZASZHALOMBATTA AM 21
ÓBUDA AM 22
DUNAÚJVÁROS AM 31
DUNAFOLDVAR AM 32

Displacement, tons: 65 full load
Dimensions, feet (metres): 88.6 × 20.7 × 5.2 *(27 × 6.3 × 1.6)*
Main machinery: 2 diesels; 520 hp(m) *(382 kW)*; 2 shafts
Speed, knots: 15. **Range, miles:** 860 at 11 kts
Complement: 17
Guns: 5 Hispano 20 mm (1 triple fwd, 2 single aft).
Mines: 24 ground mines.
Radars: Navigation: Decca; I band.

Comment: Built by Brodotehnika, Belgrade in 1979-80. Full magnetic/acoustic and wire sweeping capabilities. Two more, *AM 14* and *AM 24* are in reserve.

SZASZHALOMBATTA *9/1990, Per Kornefeldt*

SERVICE FORCES

Several troop transports of up to 1000 tons.
Five small LCUs.
A number of tugs.
Several river icebreakers.
Two transport barges (511-001, 002) which can double as landing craft (one tank) or bridging elements.

45 AN-2 CLASS MINE WARFARE/PATROL CRAFT

542-001 to **542-053**

Displacement, tons: 11.5
Dimensions, feet (metres): 44 × 12.5 × 2 *(13.4 × 3.8 × 0.6)*
Main machinery: 2 diesels; 220 hp(m) *(162 kW)*; 2 shafts
Speed, knots: 9
Complement: 6
Guns: 2—12.7 mm (twin) MGs.
Mines: Can lay ground mines.

Comment: Aluminium hulls. Act as MCMV/patrol craft. Mostly in reserve.

542-051 *9/1990, Per Kornefeldt*

LST 002 *1989, S. Breyer*

ICELAND

Senior Officer

Director of Coast Guard:
Gunnar K Bergsteinsson

Duties

The Coast Guard Service deals with fishery protection, salvage, rescue, hydrographic research, surveying and lighthouse duties. All ships have at least double the number of berths required for the complement.

Personnel

1992: 125 officers and men

Colours

In 1990 all vessels were marked with red, white and blue diagonal stripes on the ships' side and the Coast Guard name (Landhelgisgaeslan).

Base

Reykjavik

Research Ships

A number of Government Research Ships bearing RE pennant numbers operate off Iceland.

Mercantile Marine

Lloyd's Register of Shipping:
392 vessels of 167 592 tons gross

COAST GUARD VESSELS

Name	*No*	*Builders*	*Commissioned*
AEGIR	—	Aalborg Vaerft, Denmark	1968
TYR	—	Dannebrog Vaerft, Denmark	15 Mar 1975

Displacement, tons: 1200 (1300 *Tyr*) standard; 1500 full load
Dimensions, feet (metres): 229.6 × 33 × 14.8 *(70 × 10 × 4.6)*
Main machinery: 2 MAN/Burmeister & Wain R8V 40/54 diesels; 8000 hp(m) *(5.88 MW)*; 2 shafts
Speed, knots: 19 *(Aegir)*; 20 *(Tyr)*
Complement: 22
Guns: 1 Bofors 40 mm/60.
Radars: Navigation: Two sets.
Sonars: Hull-mounted; active search; high frequency (*Tyr*).
Helicopters: 1 light reconnaissance type.

Comment: Similar ships but *Tyr* has a slightly improved design and *Aegir* has no sonar. The hangar is between the funnels. The old 57 mm gun has been replaced.

TYR *1990, Iceland Coast Guard*

Name	*No*	*Builders*	*Commissioned*
BALDUR	—	Vélsmiöja Seyöisfjaröar	8 May 1991

Displacement, tons: 54 full load
Dimensions, feet (metres): 65.6 × 17.1 × 8.6 *(20 × 5.2 × 2.7)*
Main machinery: 2 Caterpillar diesels; 320 hp *(240 kW)*; 2 shafts
Speed, knots: 12
Complement: 5
Radars: Navigation: One set.

Comment: Built in an Icelandic Shipyard. Used for survey work.

BALDUR *5/1991, Iceland Coast Guard*

Name	*No*	*Builders*	*Commissioned*
ODINN	—	Aalborg Vaerft, Denmark	Jan 1960

Displacement, tons: 1200 full load
Dimensions, feet (metres): 210 × 33 × 13 *(64 × 10 × 4)*
Main machinery: 2 MAN/Burmeister & Wain diesels; 5050 hp(m) *(3.71 MW)*; 2 shafts
Speed, knots: 18
Complement: 22
Guns: 1 Bofors 40 mm/60.
Radars: Navigation: Two sets.
Helicopters: 1 light reconnaissance can be carried.

Comment: Refitted in Denmark by Aarhus Flydedock AS late 1975. Has twin funnels and helicopter hangar. A large crane was fitted in 1989 on the starboard side at the forward end of the flight deck. The old 57 mm gun has been replaced.

ODINN *1991, Iceland Coast Guard*

LAND-BASED MARITIME AIRCRAFT

Note: In addition there is the single engined Ecureil A8 350B helicopter.

Numbers/Type: 1 Aerospatiale SA 365N Dauphin 2.
Operational speed: 140 kts *(260 km/h)*.
Service ceiling: 15 000 ft *(4575 m)*.
Range: 410 nm *(758 km)*.
Role/Weapon systems: Coast Guard SAR and surveillance helicopter with no armed role. Sensors: Flir weather radar. Weapons: Unarmed.

Numbers/Type: 1 Fokker F27 Friendship.
Operational speed: 250 kts *(463 km/h)*.
Service ceiling: 25 000 ft *(7620 m)*.
Range: 2700 nm *(5000 km)*.
Role/Weapon systems: Longer-range surveillance, especially fisheries patrol and SAR operations. Sensors: Bendix 1500B search radar. Weapons: Unarmed.

INDIA

Headquarters' Appointments

Chief of the Naval Staff:
Admiral L Ramdas, AVSM, Vr C, VSM
Vice Chief of Naval Staff:
Vice Admiral S P Govil
Deputy Chief of Naval Staff:
Vice Admiral B Guha, AVSM
Chief of Personnel:
Vice Admiral V L Koppikar, AVSM
Chief of Materiel:
Vice Admiral I C Rao
Chief of Logistics Support:
Vice Admiral A C Bhatia
Assistant Chief of Naval Staff (Policy and Plans):
Rear Admiral A R Tandon, AVSM
Assistant Chief of Naval Staff (Operations):
Rear Admiral S Khanna
Assistant Chief of Naval Staff (Materials):
Rear Admiral A P Revi

Senior Appointments

Flag Officer C-in-C Western Naval Command:
Vice Admiral H Johnson, VSM
Flag Officer C-in-C Eastern Naval Command:
Vice Admiral V S Shekhawat, AVSM
Flag Officer C-in-C Southern Naval Command:
Vice Admiral K A S Z Raju, AVSM
Flag Officer Commanding Western Fleet:
Rear Admiral K K Kohli
Flag Officer Commanding Eastern Fleet:
Rear Admiral V Bhagwat
Fortress Commander, Andaman and Nicobar Islands:
Vice Admiral S K Chand
Flag Officer, Naval Aviation and Goa area (at Goa):
Rear Admiral P Debrass, AVSM
Flag Officer, Submarines (Vishakapatnam):
Rear Admiral R N Ganesh

Personnel

(a) 1992: 55 000 officers and ratings (including 5000 Naval Air Arm)
(b) Voluntary service
(c) A regiment of 1000 Marines was formed in 1986; second regiment reported planned.

Naval Air Arm

Squadron	*Aircraft*	*Role*
300 (Goa)	Sea Harrier FRS Mk 51	Fighter/Strike
	Sea Harrier T Mk 60	Trainer
312 (Goa)	Tu-142M 'Bear F'	LRMP/ASW
315 (Goa)	Il-38 May	LRMP/ASW
318 (Goa)	PBN Defender	Utility
321 (Goa)	HAL Chetak	Utility/SAR (Flight)
330 (Cochin)	Sea King Mk 42/42A	ASW
331 (Cochin)	HAL Chetak	Utility/SAR
333 (ships) (Goa)	Kamov Ka-25 'Hormone'	ASW
	Kamov Ka-28 'Helix'	ASW
336 (Cochin)	Sea King Mk 42/42A	ASW
339 (Bombay)	Sea King 42B	ASW/ASVW
550 (Vishwanath)	Tu-142M 'Bear F' Mod 3	LRMP/ASW (Flight)
551 (Goa)	HAL HJT-16 Kiran	Training (OCU)
561 (Cochin)	HAL Chetak	Training
562 (Cochin)	Hughes 300, Chetak	Training
	HAL Jaguar	Strike

Air Stations

Name	*Location*	*Role*
INS *Garuda*	Wellington Island, Cochin	Training, helicopter
INS *Hansa*	Goa	HQ Flag Officer Naval Air Stations, LRMP, Strike/Fighter
INS *Sea Bird*	Karwar	Fleet Support (mid-1990s)
INS *Utkrosh*	Port Blair, Andaman Isles	Maritime Patrol
	Uchipuli, Tamil Nadu	Maritime Patrol
	Ramanathuram	Maritime Patrol
	Vishakapatnam	Fleet support and maritime patrol
	Tiruchirapalli	building
	Arakkonam	building
	Bangalore	LRMP building
		Naval Air Technical School

Prefix to Ships' Names

INS

Naval Bases and Establishments

New Delhi, HQ (INS *India*)
Bombay, C-in-C **Western Command**, barracks and main Dockyard; with two 'Carrier' docks. New submarine pens being built. Supply school (INS *Hamla*). The region includes Mazagon and Goa shipyards.
Vishakapatnam, C-in-C **Eastern Command**, submarine base (INS *Virbahu*), submarine school (INS *Satyavahana*) and major dockyard built with Soviet support and being extended. Naval Air Station (INS *Dega*). New entry training (INS *Chilka*). At Vijayaraghavapuram is the submarine VLF W/T station completed in September 1986. Facilities at Madras and Calcutta. The region includes Hindustan and Garden Reach shipyards.
Cochin, C-in-C **Southern Command**, Naval Air Station, and professional schools (INS *Venduruthy*) (all naval Training now comes under Southern Command). Ship repair yard. Trials establishment (INS *Dronacharya*).
Goa is HQ Flag Officer Naval Air Stations.
Karwar (near Goa) has been selected as the site for a new naval base; first phase due for completion in 1993. Alongside berthing for Aircraft Carriers and a naval air station are planned. At Lakshadweep in the Laccadive Islands there is a patrol craft base. There are also limited support facilities including a floating dock at Andaman and Nicobar bases.
Naval Academy at Goa to move to Ezhimala in 1992, new base called INS *Jawarhalal Nehru*. A college of naval warfare has been established at Karanja.
Shipbuilding: Bombay (submarines, destroyers, frigates, corvettes); Calcutta (frigates, corvettes, LSTs, auxiliaries); Goa (patrol craft, LCU, MCMV facility planned).

Weapons and Sensors

Indian developments include:
SSM: Prithvi test fired in 1987; range 240 km; warhead 1000 kg. Similar to Skud.
SAM: Agri, Akash and Trishul; all being developed, at least one for the Navy. Trishul has a reported range of 10 km and is to be in service in 1991.
NST 58 surface ship launched A/S torpedo and APSOH active sonar already at sea.
Medium range Chaff decoy rocket.

Strength of the Fleet

Type	*Active*	*Building (Projected)*
Patrol Submarines	18	1 (8)
Attack Carriers (Medium)	2	(2)
Destroyers	5	2 (2)
Frigates	16	3
Corvettes	18	16 (4)
Patrol Ships	6	4
Fast Attack Craft—Missile	8	—
Fast Attack Craft—Patrol/Torpedo	12	1
Fast Patrol Boats	—	24
Landing Ships	9	1
LCUs	7	—
Minesweepers—Ocean	12	—
Minesweepers—Inshore	10	—
Minehunters	—	(6)
Survey Ships	9	1 (1)
Training Ships	1	1
Submarine Tender	1	—
Diving Support/Rescue Ships	1	2
Replenishment Tankers	2	1
Support Tankers	4	—
Tugs	11	—
Coast Guard	47	3 (10)

Mercantile Marine

Lloyd's Register of Shipping:
890 vessels of 6 516 780 tons gross

DELETIONS

Submarines

1991 *Chakra, Kanderi*

Frigates

1990 *Andaman* (sunk)
1991 *Kamorta, Betwa*

Light Forces

1989 *Katchal, Nipat*
1990 *Vinash, Vidyut, Vijeta, Nashat, Nirghat*

Service Forces

1989 *Nistar, Darshak*
1990 *Desh Deep*

PENNANT LIST

Submarines

S 20	Kursura
S 21	Karanj
S 23	Kalvari
S 40	Vela
S 41	Vagir
S 42	Vagli
S 43	Vagsheer
S 44	Shishumar
S 45	Shankush
S 46	Shalki
S 47	Shankul
S 55	Sindhughosh
S 56	Sindhudhvaj
S 57	Sindhuraj
S 58	Sindhuvir
S 59	Sindhuratna
S 60	Sindhukesari
S 61	Sindhukiri
S 62	Sindhuvijay

Aircraft Carriers

R 11	Vikrant
R 22	Viraat

Destroyers

—	Delhi (bldg)
—	Mysore (bldg)
D 51	Rajput
D 52	Rana
D 53	Ranjit
D 54	Ranvir
D 55	Ranvijay

Frigates

F 20	Godavari
F 21	Gomati
F 22	Ganga
F 33	Nilgiri
F 34	Himgiri
F 35	Udaygiri
F 36	Dunagiri
F 37	Beas
F 41	Taragiri
F 42	Vindhyagiri
F 43	Trishul
P 68	Arnala
P 69	Androth
P 73	Anjadip
P 75	Amini
P 78	Kadmath

Corvettes

P 33	Abhay
P 34	Ajay
P 35	Akshay
P 36	Agray
P 44	Kirpan
P 46	Kuthar
P 47	Khanjar
P 49	Khukri
K 40	Veer
K 41	Nirbhik
K 42	Nipat
K 43	Nishank
K 44	Nirghat
K 45	Vibhuti
K 46	Vipul
K 47	Vinash
K 71	Vijay Durg
K 72	Sindhu Durg
K 73	Hos Durg

Patrol Ships

P 50	Sukanya
P 51	Subhadra
P 52	Suvarna
P 53	Savitri
P 54	Sarayu
P 55	Sharada
P 56	Sujatha

Light Forces

K 90	Prachand
K 91	Pralaya
K 92	Pratap
K 93	Prabal
K 94	Chapal
K 95	Chamak
K 96	Chatak
K 97	Charag

Mine Warfare Forces

M 61	Pondicherry
M 62	Porbandar
M 63	Bedi
M 64	Bhavnagar
M 65	Alleppey
M 66	Ratnagiri
M 67	Karwar
M 68	Cannanore
M 69	Cuddalore
M 70	Kakinada
M 71	Kozhikoda
M 72	Konkan
M 83	Mahé
M 84	Malvan
M 85	Mangalore
M 86	Malpe
M 87	Mulki
M 88	Magdala
M 89	Bulsar
M 90	Bhatkal
M 2705	Bimlipitan
M 2707	Bassein

Amphibious Forces

L 14	Ghorpad
L 15	Kesari
L 16	Shardul
L 17	Sharabh
L 18	Cheetah
L 19	Mahish
L 20	Magar
L 21	Guldar
L 22	Kumbhir
L 23	Gharial
L 34	Vasco da Gama
L 38	Midhur
L 39	Mangala

Service Forces

A —	Rajaba Gan Palan
A 15	Nireekshak
A 50	Deepak
A 51	Gaj
A 54	Amba
A 57	Shakti
A 86	Tir
J —	Sandhayak
J 14	Nirupak
J 15	Investigator
J 16	Jamuna
J 17	Sutlej
J 19	Nirdeshak
J 33	Makar
J 34	Mithun
J 35	Meen
J 36	Mesh

SUBMARINES

Notes: 1. The ex-Soviet Charlie class nuclear-powered submarine *Chakra* was leased for three years from January 1988. The lease was not extended and she returned to Vladivostock in January 1991. The plan now is to build a nuclear propelled submarine in India. For this purpose there is an R&D project called the Advanced Technology Vessel which is reasonably well funded and has facilities in Delhi, Hyderabad, Vishakapatnam and Kalpakkam. A Navy-Defence Research and Development Organisation (DRDO) runs the project and since the mid-1980s has had a Vice Admiral in charge. The submarine will have a single reactor of the PWR type and will be a development of the Charlie I. The reactor will be of Indian design. This project has priority over the new aircraft carrier.

2. It is probable that India has acquired at least three midget submarines including two of the Italian Cosmos SX-756 type, which displace 80 tons dived and were bought commercially in 1988. The third may be slightly larger at 110 tons. There may be additional units together with a number of two man chariot underwater vehicles.

3 + 1 209 CLASS (TYPE 1500)

Name	*No*	*Builders*	*Laid down*	*Launched*	*Commissioned*
SHISHUMAR	S 44	Howaldtswerke, Kiel	1 May 1982	13 Dec 1984	22 Sep 1986
SHANKUSH	S 45	Howaldtswerke, Kiel	1 Sep 1982	11 May 1984	20 Nov 1986
SHALKI	S 46	Mazagon SY, Bombay	5 June 1984	30 Sep 1989	7 Feb 1992
SHANKUL	S 47	Mazagon SY, Bombay	3 Sep 1989	1992	1994

Displacement, tons: 1450 standard; 1660 surfaced; 1850 dived
Dimensions, feet (metres): 211.2 × 21.3 × 19.7 *(64.4 × 6.5 × 6)*
Main machinery: Diesel-electric; 4 MTU 12V 493 AZ 80 GA31L diesels; 2400 hp(m) *(1.76 MW)* sustained; 4 alternators; 1.8 MW; 1 Siemens motor; 4600 hp(m) *(3.38 MW)* sustained; 1 shaft
Speed, knots: 11 surfaced; 22 dived
Range, miles: 8000 snorting at 8 kts; 13 000 surfaced at 10 kts
Complement: 40 (8 officers)

Torpedoes: 8—21 in *(533 mm)* tubes. 14 AEG SUT; wire-guided; active/passive homing to 28 km *(15.3 nm)* at 23 kts; 12 km *(6.6 nm)* at 35 kts; warhead 250 kg.
Mines: External 'strap-on' type.
Countermeasures: ESM: Phoenix II; radar warning.
Fire control: Singer Librascope Mk 1.
Radars: Surface search: Thomson-CSF Calypso; I band.
Sonars: Krupp Atlas CSU 83; active/passive search and attack; medium frequency.
Thomson Sintra DUUX-5 (S 46 and 47); passive ranging and intercept.

SHANKUSH *2/1991*

Programmes: After several years of discussion Howaldtswerke concluded an agreement with the Indian Navy on 11 December 1981. This was in four basic parts: the building in West Germany of two Type 1500 submarines; the supply of 'packages' for the building of two more boats at Mazagon SY, Bombay; training of various groups of specialists for the design and construction of the Mazagon pair; logistic services during the trials and early part of the commissions as well as consultation services in Bombay. The first two sailed for India February 1987. The second two delayed by assembly problems caused by faulty welding.
In 1984 it was announced that a further two submarines would be built at Mazagon for a total of six but this was overtaken by events in 1987-88 and the agreement with HDW terminated at four. The medium term plan is for an indigenous design of 2000 tons to be built at Bombay after the 209 class programme is completed and Western designs have been evaluated.

Structure: The Type 1500 has a central bulkhead and an IKL designed integrated escape sphere which can carry the full crew of up to 40 men, has an oxygen supply for eight hours, and can withstand pressures at least as great as those that can be withstood by the submarine's pressure hull. Diving depth 260 m *(853 ft)*. DUUX-5 sonar will be back fitted to the first pair in the mid-1990s.
Operational: *Shalki* started sea trials in October 1991.

8 SOVIET KILO CLASS

Name	*No*	*Builders*	*Commissioned*
SINDHUGHOSH	S 55	Sudomekh, Leningrad	30 Apr 1986
SINDHUDHVAJ	S 56	Sudomekh, Leningrad	12 June 1987
SINDHURAJ	S 57	Sudomekh, Leningrad	20 Oct 1987
SINDHUVIR	S 58	Sudomekh, Leningrad	26 Aug 1988
SINDHURATNA	S 59	Sudomekh, Leningrad	16 Feb 1989
SINDHUKESARI	S 60	Sudomekh, Leningrad	10 Mar 1989
SINDHUKIRI	S 61	Sudomekh, Leningrad	4 Mar 1990
SINDHUVIJAY	S 62	Sudomekh, Leningrad	8 Mar 1991

Displacement, tons: 2325 surfaced; 3076 dived
Dimensions, feet (metres): 243.8 × 32.8 × 21.7 *(74.3 × 10 × 6.6)*
Main machinery: Diesel-electric; 2 diesels; 3650 hp(m) *(2.68 MW)*; 2 generators; 1 motor; 5900 hp(m) *(4.34 MW)*; 1 shaft
Speed, knots: 10 surfaced; 17 dived
Range, miles: 6000 at 7 kts surfaced; 400 at 3 kts dived
Complement: 60

Missiles: SAM; SA-N-8/14 (S 58 onwards, but not confirmed).
Torpedoes: 6—21 in *(533 mm)* tubes. 18 Indian (based on Type 53); pattern; active/passive homing up to 20 km *(10.8 nm)* at up to 45 kts; warhead 400 kg.
Mines: 36 in lieu of torpedoes.
Countermeasures: ESM: Stop Light; radar warning. Quad Loop D/F.
Radars: Navigation: Snoop Tray; I band.
Sonars: Shark Teeth; hull-mounted; active/passive search and attack; medium frequency.
Whale series; passive search; low frequency.

SINDHUKIRI *1/1991*

Programmes: The Kilo class was launched in the Soviet Navy in 1979 and although India was the first country to acquire one they have since been transferred to Algeria, Poland and Romania. Because of the slowness of the S 209 programme and its early termination, the original order in 1983 for six Kilo class expanded to ten but was then cut back again to eight. Plans to manufacture the class under licence in India have been shelved for the time being but design drawings are held should this project be resurrected. More of the class may still be acquired from Russia.
Structure: Diving depth, 350 m *(1150 ft)*. Reported that from *Sindhuvir* onwards these submarines have an SA-N-8/14 SAM capability.
Operational: Based at Vishakapatnam and Bombay.

7 SOVIET FOXTROT CLASS

KURSURA S 20
KARANJ S 21
KALVARI S 23
VELA S 40
VAGIR S 41
VAGLI S 42
VAGSHEER S 43

Displacement, tons: 1952 surfaced; 2475 dived
Dimensions, feet (metres): 299.5 × 24.6 × 19.7 *(91.3 × 7.5 × 6)*
Main machinery: Diesel-electric; 3 diesels; 5956 hp(m) *(4.3 MW)*; 3 motors; 5400 hp(m) *(3.97 MW)*; 3 shafts
Speed, knots: 16 surfaced; 15 dived
Range, miles: 20 000 at 8 kts surfaced; 380 at 2 kts dived
Complement: 75 (8 officers)

Torpedoes: 10—21 in *(533 mm)* (6 fwd, 4 aft) tubes. 22 Soviet Type 53; pattern active/passive homing up to 20 km *(10.8 nm)* at up to 45 kts; warhead 400 kg.
Mines: 44 in lieu of torpedoes.
Countermeasures: ESM: Stop Light; radar warning.
Radars: Surface search: Snoop Tray; I band.
Sonars: Bow-mounted; passive search and attack; medium frequency.
Bow-mounted; active search and attack; high frequency.

VAGLI *11/1987, G. Jacobs*

Programmes: *Kalvari* arrived in India on 16 July 1968, *Karanj* in October 1970, *Kursura* in December 1970, *Vela* November 1973, *Vagir* December 1973, *Vagli* September 1974, *Vagsheer* December 1975. All new construction. At least two have been refitted in the USSR.
Structure: Diving depth 250 m *(820 ft)*.
Operational: First one paid off in 1990 and has been cannibalised for spares. At least six of the others were operational in 1991, two as training ships.

AIRCRAFT CARRIERS

Note: The plan announced in 1989 was to build two new aircraft carriers, the first to replace *Vikrant* in 1997. A design study contract was signed with DCN (France) for a ship of about 28 000 tons and with a speed in excess of 30 kts. Size restricted by available construction dock capacity. Options included Ski Jump and CTOL. The Indian Naval Design Organisation was to translate the design study into the production model with construction to start at Cochin in 1993. However in mid-1991 the Committee on Defence Expenditure told the Navy to abandon plans for large carriers, and design effort has shifted to smaller 14 000 ton ASW ships probably to an Italian design. The whole project takes second priority to the nuclear submarine effort.

1 Ex-BRITISH HERMES CLASS

Name	*No*	*Builders*	*Laid down*	*Launched*	*Commissioned*
VIRAAT (ex-HMS *Hermes)*	R 22	Vickers Shipbuilding Ltd, Barrow-in-Furness	21 June 1944	16 Feb 1953	18 Nov 1959

Displacement, tons: 23 900 standard; 28 700 full load
Dimensions, feet (metres): 685 wl; 744.3 oa × 90; 160 oa × 28.5 *(208.8; 226.9 × 27.4; 48.8 × 8.7)*
Main machinery: 4 Admiralty boilers; 400 psi *(28 kg/cm sq)*; 700°F *(370°C)*; 2 Parsons geared turbines; 76 000 hp *(57 MW)*; 2 shafts
Speed, knots: 28
Complement: 1350 (143 officers)

Missiles: SAM: 2 Shorts Seacat quad launchers; radar guidance to 5 km *(3.3 nm)*.
Guns: Some 30 mm/65 6-barrelled ADGs may be fitted.
Countermeasures: Decoys: 2 Knebworth Corvus Chaff launchers.
ESM: Radar intercept and jamming.
Combat data systems: CAAIS action data automation; Link 10.
Fire control: GWS 22 for SAM.

Radars: Air search: Marconi Type 996; E/F band with IFF 1010.
Air/surface search: Plessey Type 994; E/F band.
Navigation: Two Racal Decca 1006; I band.
Fire control: Two Plessey Type 904; I/J band.
Tacan: FT 13-S/M.
Sonars: Graseby Type 184M; hull-mounted; active search and attack; 6-9 kHz.

Fixed wing aircraft: 12 Sea Harriers FRS Mk 51 (capacity for 30).
Helicopters: 7 Sea King Mk 42B/C ASW/ASV/Vertrep and Ka-25 Hormone.

Programmes: Purchased in May 1986 for £50 million thence to an extensive refit in Devonport Dockyard costing £15 million. Life extension of at least 10 years. Commissioned in Indian Navy 20 May 1987.

Modernisation: Devonport refit included new fire control equipment, navigation radars, and deck landing aids. Boilers were converted to take distillate fuel and the ship was given improved NBC protection. Seacat launchers removed but subsequently replaced. It is reported that a Soviet CIWS is to be fitted during further modernisation.
Structure: Fitted with 12° ski jump. Reinforced flight deck (0.75 in); 1-2 inches of armour over magazines and machinery spaces. Four LCVP on after davits. Magazine capacity includes 80 lightweight torpedoes.
Operational: The Sea Harrier complement will normally be no more than 12 or 18 aircraft leaving room for a greater mix of Sea King and Hormone helicopters (see *Shipborne Aircraft* section).

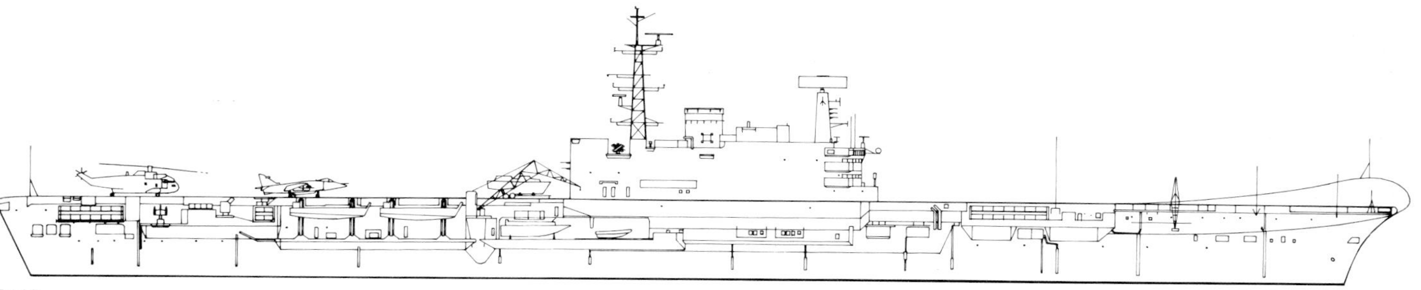

VIRAAT *(Scale 1 : 1 200), Ian Sturton*

VIRAAT *6/1987*

VIRAAT *3/1990*

VIRAAT *1989, Indian Navy*

1 Ex-BRITISH MAJESTIC CLASS

Name	No	Builders	Laid down	Launched	Commissioned
VIKRANT (ex-HMS *Hercules*)	R 11	Vickers-Armstrong Ltd, Tyne	14 Oct 1943	22 Sep 1945	4 Mar 1961

Displacement, tons: 16 000 standard; 19 500 full load
Dimensions, feet (metres): 700 × 80; 128 oa × 24 *(213.4 × 24.4; 39 oa × 7.3)*
Flight deck, feet (metres): 690 × 112 *(210 × 34)*
Main machinery: 4 Admiralty boilers; 400 psi *(28 kg/cm sq)*; 700°F *(370°C)*; 2 Parsons turbines; 40 000 hp *(30 MW)*; 2 shafts
Speed, knots: 24.5
Range, miles: 12 000 at 14 kts; 6200 at 23 kts
Complement: 1075 peace; 1345 war

Guns: 7 Bofors 40 mm/70; 90° elevation; 300 rounds/minute to 12 km *(6.6 nm)* anti-aircraft; weight of shell 2.4 kg. Some may have been replaced by 30 mm/65 6-barrelled ADGs.
Combat data systems: Selenia IPN-10 action data automation.
Radars: Air search: Signaal LW 08; D band; range 264 km *(145 nm)* for 2 m² target.
Air/surface search: Signaal DA 05; E/F band; range 137 km *(75 nm)* for 2 m² target.
Navigation: Signaal ZW 06; I band.
Sonars: Graseby 750; hull-mounted; active search and attack; medium frequency.

Fixed wing aircraft: 6 Sea Harriers FRS Mk 51.
Helicopters: 9 Sea Kings Mk 42 ASW/ASV. 1 Chetak SAR.

VIKRANT (modified ski jump) *1991*

Programmes: Acquired from the UK in January 1957 after having been suspended in May 1946 when structurally almost complete and 75% fitted out. Taken in hand by Harland & Wolff Ltd, Belfast, in April 1957 for completion in 1961. Commissioned on 4 March 1961 and renamed *Vikrant*.
Modernisation: Major two-year refit began in January 1979. Re-entered service 3 January 1982. Second major refit in 1983. Third refit in 1987-89 (recommissioned 12 February 1989) to increase life expectancy to 1997 at least; ski jump fitted and possible improvements made to CIWS.
Structure: Flight deck: Two electrically operated lifts. 9.75° ski-ramp to take '150 ton lift' installed during 1987-89 modernisation; steam catapults removed. The original ski jump structure was not strong enough for a fully loaded Sea Harrier and further modifications were made in 1990/91.
Operational: Total capacity for 22 aircraft.

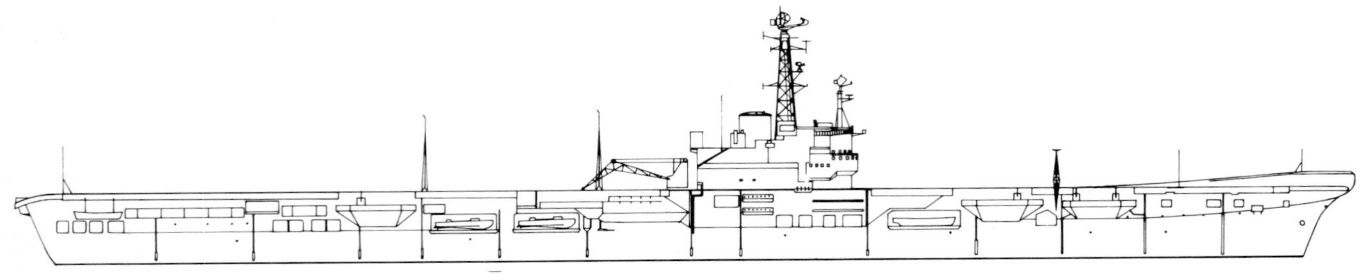
VIKRANT *(Scale 1 : 1 200), Ian Sturton*

DESTROYERS

5 SOVIET KASHIN II CLASS

Name	No	Builders	Commissioned
RAJPUT	D 51	Kommuna, Nikolayev	30 Sep 1980
RANA	D 52	Kommuna, Nikolayev	28 June 1982
RANJIT	D 53	Kommuna, Nikolayev	24 Nov 1983
RANVIR	D 54	Kommuna, Nikolayev	28 Aug 1986
RANVIJAY	D 55	Kommuna, Nikolayev	15 Jan 1988

Displacement, tons: 3950 standard; 4950 full load
Dimensions, feet (metres): 480.5 × 51.8 × 15.7 *(146.5 × 15.8 × 4.8)*
Main machinery: 4 gas turbines; 72 000 hp(m) *(53 MW)*; 2 shafts
Speed, knots: 35. **Range, miles:** 4500 at 18 kts; 2600 at 30 kts
Complement: 320 (35 officers)

Missiles: SSM: 4 SS-N-2C Styx ❶; active radar or IR homing to 83 km *(45 nm)* at 0.9 Mach; warhead 513 kg; sea-skimmer at end of run.
SAM: 2 SA-N-1 Goa twin launchers ❷; command guidance to 31.5 km *(17 nm)* at 2 Mach; height 91-22 860 m *(300-75 000 ft)*; warhead 60 kg; 44 missiles. Some SSM capability.
Guns: 2—3 in *(76 mm)*/60 (twin, fwd) ❸; 80° elevation; 90 rounds/minute to 15 km *(8 nm)*; weight of shell 6.8 kg.
8—30 mm/65 (4 twin) *(Rajput, Rana* and *Ranjit)* ❹; 85° elevation; 500 rounds/minute to 5 km *(2.7 nm)*; weight of shell 0.54 kg.
4—30 mm/65 (6-barrels per mounting) (*Ranvir* and *Ranvijay*); 85° elevation; 3000 rounds/minute combined to 2 km.
Torpedoes: 5—21 in *(533 mm)* (quin) tubes ❺. Probably Soviet Type 53; pattern active/passive homing up to 20 km *(10.8 nm)* at up to 45 kts; warhead 400 kg.
A/S mortars: 2 RBU 6000 12-tubed trainable ❻; range 6000 m; warhead 31 kg.
Countermeasures: 4—16-barrelled Chaff launchers for radar decoy and distraction.
ESM: Two Watch Dog. Two Top Hat A and B; radar warning.
Radars: Air search: Big Net A ❼; C band; range 183 km *(100 nm)* for 2 m² target.
Air/surface search: Head Net C ❽; 3D; E band; range 128 km *(70 nm)*.
Navigation: Two Don Kay; I band.
Fire control: Two Peel Group ❾; H/I band; range 73 km *(40 nm)* for 2 m² target.
Owl Screech ❿; G band.
Two Drum Tilt ⓫ or Two Bass Tilt (*Ranvir* and *Ranvijay*); H/I band.
IFF: Two High Pole B.
Sonars: Hull-mounted and VDS; active search and attack; medium frequency.

Helicopters: 1 Ka-25 Hormone B or 1 Ka-28 Helix (*Ranvir* and *Ranvijay*) (to be retrofitted in earlier ships) ⓬.

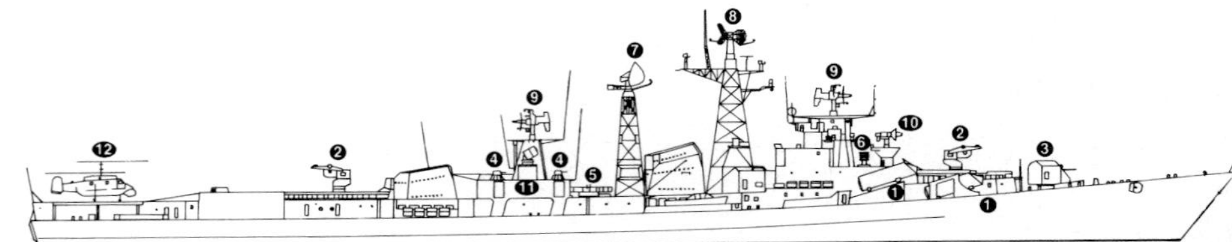
RANA *(Scale 1 : 1 200), Ian Sturton*

RAJPUT *198*

RANJIT *199*

Programmes: First batch of three ordered in the mid-1970s. *Ranvir* was the first of the second batch ordered on 20 December 1982.
Structure: All built as new construction for India at Nikolayev with considerable modifications to the Soviet design. Helicopter hangar, which is reached by a lift from the flight deck, replaces after 76 mm twin mount and the SS-N-2C launchers are sited forward of the bridge. *Ranvir* and *Ranvijay* differ from previous ships in class by being fitted with ADGM-630 30 mm guns, two Bass Tilt fire control radars and possibly infra-red attachment t SS-N-2C missile launchers. It is possible that an Italian comba data system is installed.

0 + 2 + (2) DELHI CLASS (DDG)

Name	No	Builders	Laid down	Launched	Commissioned
DELHI	—	Mazagon, Bombay	14 Nov 1987	1 Feb 1991	1995
MYSORE	—	Mazagon, Bombay	2 Feb 1991	1994	1998

Displacement, tons: 5900 standard
Dimensions, feet (metres): 524.9 × 55.8 × 21.3 *(160 × 17 × 6.5)*
Main machinery: CODAG; 2 AM-50 Soviet gas turbines (GE/HAL LM 2500 in later ships); 54 000 hp(m) *(49 MW)*; 2 Bergen/Garden Reach KVM-18 diesels; 9920 hp(m) *(7.73 MW)* sustained; 2 shafts
Speed, knots: 28

Missiles: SSM: 4 SS-N-22.
SAM: SA-N-7 twin launcher (aft of the 76 mm gun) and/or 2 Trishul.
Guns: 1 USSR 3 in *(76 mm)*/60 (on the forecastle).
4 USSR 30 mm/65; 6 barrels per mounting (2 each side).
Torpedoes: 6 Whitehead 324 mm (2 triple tubes)
Depth charges: 2 rails.
Countermeasures: ESM/ECM DRDO EW equipment
Radars: Air search: Bharat/Signaal RALW (LW 08); D band.
Surface search: Indra; E band.
Sonars: Thomson Sintra TSM 2633 Spherion; hull-mounted; active search; medium frequency.
Indian developed VDS or linear towed array.

Helicopters: 2 Westland Sea Kings Mk 42B or 2 Hindustan Aeronautics ALH.

DELHI 2/1991

Programmes: Being built with Russian assistance. *Delhi* ordered in March 1986. *Mysore* ordered in 1990 and laid down as soon as *Delhi* was launched. Programme is called Project 15.

Structure: The design is described as a 'stretched *Rajput*' with some *Godavari* features. Soviet gas turbines have been fitted in *Delhi* (and may be in *Mysore*), later ships will have LM 2500 built in India by HAL under licence. A combination of Soviet and Indian weapon systems is being fitted, with decisions still to be made on some of the systems.

FRIGATES

6 BRITISH LEANDER CLASS

Name	No	Builders	Laid down	Launched	Commissioned
NILGIRI	F 33	Mazagon Docks Ltd, Bombay	Oct 1966	23 Oct 1968	3 June 1972
HIMGIRI	F 34	Mazagon Docks Ltd, Bombay	1967	6 May 1970	23 Nov 1974
UDAYGIRI	F 35	Mazagon Docks Ltd, Bombay	Jan 1973	9 Mar 1974	5 May 1977
DUNAGIRI	F 36	Mazagon Docks Ltd, Bombay	14 Sep 1970	24 Oct 1972	18 Feb 1976
TARAGIRI	F 41	Mazagon Docks Ltd, Bombay	1974	25 Oct 1976	16 May 1980
VINDHYAGIRI	F 42	Mazagon Docks Ltd, Bombay	1975	12 Nov 1977	8 July 1981

Displacement, tons: 2682 standard; 2962 full load
Dimensions, feet (metres): 372 × 43 × 18 *(113.4 × 13.1 × 5.5)*
Main machinery: 2 Babcock & Wilcox boilers; 550 psi *(38.7 kg/cm sq)*; 850°F *(450°C)*; 2 turbines; 30 000 hp *(22.4 MW)*; 2 shafts
Speed, knots: 27; 28 (*Taragiri* and *Vindhyagiri*). **Range, miles:** 4500 at 12 kts
Complement: 267 (17 officers)

Missiles: SSM: 4 SSN-2B Styx (*Taragiri* and *Vindhyagiri*); not always embarked.
SAM: 1 or 2 Short Bros Seacat quad launchers ❶; optical radar guidance to 5 km *(2.7 nm)*; warhead 10 kg; 32 missiles. *Nilgiri* and *Himgiri* have 1 Seacat with GWS22 control. Remainder have 2 Seacat with 2 Dutch M44 directors.
Guns: 2 Vickers 4.5 in *(114 mm)*/45 (twin) Mk 6 ❷; 80° elevation; 20 rounds/minute to 19 km *(10.4 nm)* anti-surface; 6 km *(3.3 nm)* anti-aircraft; weight of shell 25 kg.
2 Oerlikon 20 mm/70 ❸; 800 rounds/minute to 2 km.
Torpedoes: 6—324 mm ILAS 3 (2 triple) tubes (*Taragiri* and *Vindhyagiri*) ❹. Whitehead A244S or Indian NST 58 version; anti-submarine; active/passive homing to 7 km *(3.8 nm)* at 33 kts; warhead 34 kg (shaped charge).
A/S mortars: 1 Bofors 375 mm twin-tubed launcher (*Taragiri* and *Vindhyagiri*) ❺; range 1600 m.
1 Limbo MK 10 triple-tubed launcher (remainder) ❻; range 1000 m; warhead 92 kg.
Countermeasures: Decoys: Graseby G 738; towed torpedo decoy; effective against both active and passive torpedoes.
ESM: Racal UA 8/9; radar intercept. FH5 Telegon D/F.
ECM: Type 667; jammer.
Fire control: 2 M44 MFCS. 1 GWS 22 *(Nilgiri)*. MRS 3 GFCS (*Nilgiri*).
Radars: Air search: Signaal LW 08 ❼; D band; range 265 km *(145 nm)* for 2 m² target.
Marconi Type 965M *(Nilgiri)* ❽; A band.
Surface search: Signaal ZW 06 ❾; I band; range 26 km *(14 nm)*.
RN Type 993 *(Nilgiri)* ❿; E/F band.
Navigation: Decca 978; I band.
Fire control: Two Signaal M44 (not in *Nilgiri* and *Himgiri*) ⓫; I/J band (for Seacat).
Plessey Type 904 (*Nilgiri* and *Himgiri*) ⓬; I band (for Seacat).
Signaal M 45 ⓭; I/J band.
Plessey Type 903 ⓮ (*Nilgiri* and *Himgiri*); I band.
IFF: Type 944; 954M.
Sonars: Graseby 750 (APSOH fitted in *Himgiri* as trials ship); hull-mounted; active search and attack; medium frequency.
Type 170; active attack; high frequency.
EMI Type 199 or Westinghouse VDS (first four only); active; medium frequency. Thomson Sintra VDS in *Taragiri* and *Vindhyagiri*. Type 162M; bottom classification; high frequency.

Helicopters: 1 Chetak (in first 4) ⓯.
1 Sea King Mk 42 (in *Taragiri* and *Vindhyagiri*) ❻.

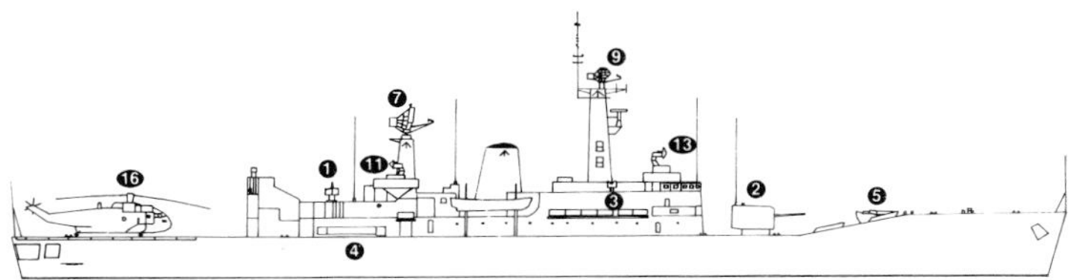

TARAGIRI *(Scale 1 : 1 200), Ian Sturton*

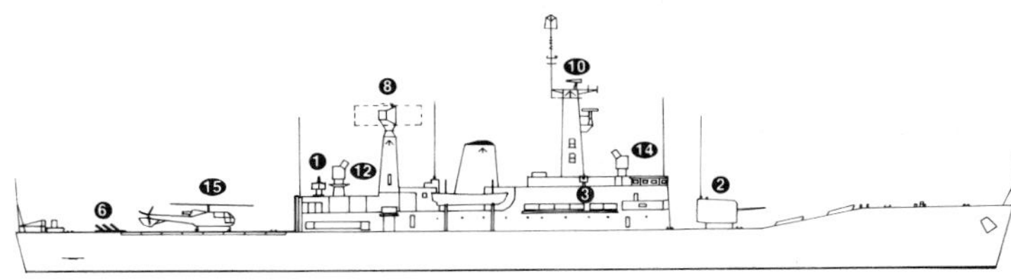

NILGIRI *(Scale 1 : 1 200), Ian Sturton*

DUNAGIRI *1985*

Programmes: The first major warships built in Indian yards with a 60% indigenous component.
Modernisation: At future refits earlier ships are to have their armament brought into line with later ships. *Taragiri* and *Vindhyagiri* are fitted for two SSN-2 Styx launchers; these may have come from Osa class. Westinghouse has supplied the Indian Navy with ASW sonar systems, two hull-mounted arrays and three variable depth sonar (VDS) arrays for Leander class frigates. The VDS arrays are installed inside towed bodies built by Fathom Oceanology Ltd of Canada. The transducer elements in both cases are identical.
Structure: Of similar design to the Broad-beam Leanders but with several differences. In the first four the hangar was provided with telescopic extension to take the Alouette III helicopter while in the last pair, a much-changed design, the Mk 10 Mortar has been removed as well as VDS and the aircraft space increased to make way for a Sea King helicopter with a telescopic hangar and Canadian Beartrap haul-down gear. In these two an open deck has been left below the flight deck for handling mooring gear and there is a cut-down to the stern.
Operational: It is reported that *Vindhyagiri* and *Taragiri* have more powerful engines than the remainder. Form 14th Frigate Squadron. Oil fuel, 382 tons plus 10 tons avgas.

3 + 3 GODAVARI CLASS

Name	No	Builders	Laid down	Launched	Commissioned
GODAVARI	F 20	Mazagon Docks Ltd, Bombay	2 June 1978	15 May 1980	10 Dec 1983
GOMATI	F 21	Mazagon Docks Ltd, Bombay	1981	19 Mar 1984	16 Apr 1988
GANGA	F 22	Mazagon Docks Ltd, Bombay	1980	21 Oct 1981	30 Dec 1985
—	—	Garden Reach, Calcutta	1989	1992	1994

Displacement, tons: 3600 standard; 4000 full load
Dimensions, feet (metres): 414.9 × 47.6 × 14.8 (29.5 sonar) *(126.5 × 14.5 × 4.5 (9))*
Main machinery: 2 Babcock & Wilcox boilers; 550 psi *(38.7 kg/cm sq)*; 850°F *(450°C)*; 2 turbines; 30 000 hp *(22.4 MW)*; 2 shafts
Speed, knots: 27. **Range, miles:** 4500 at 12 kts
Complement: 313 (40 officers including 13 aircrew)

Missiles: SSM: 4 SS-N-2C Styx (1); active radar or IR homing to 83 km *(45 nm)* at 0.9 Mach; warhead 513 kg; sea-skimmer at end of run. Indian designation P 20 or P 21.
SAM: SA-N-4 Gecko twin launcher (2); semi-active radar homing to 15 km *(8 nm)* at 2.5 mach; height 9.1-3048 m *(130-10 000 ft)*; warhead 50 kg; limited surface-to-surface capability; 20 missiles. System called 'Osa-M'.
Guns: 2—57 mm/70 (twin) (3); 90° elevation; 120 rounds/minute to 8 km *(4.4 nm)*; weight of shell 2.8 kg.
8—30 mm/65 (4 twin) (4); 85° elevation; 500 rounds/minute to 5 km *(2.7 nm)*; weight of shell 0.54 kg.
Torpedoes: 6—324 mm ILAS 3 (2 triple) tubes (5). Whitehead A244S; anti-submarine; active/passive homing to 7 km *(3.8 nm)* at 33 kts; warhead 34 kg (shaped charge). *Godavari* has tube modifications for the Indian NST 58 version of A244S.
Countermeasures: Decoys: 2 Chaff launchers. Graseby G738 towed torpedo decoy.
ESM/ECM: Selenia INS-3; intercept and jammer.
Combat data systems: Selenia IPN-10 action data automation. Inmarsat communications (JRC) (6).
Fire control: MR 301 MFCS. MR 103 GFCS.
Radars: Air search: Signaal LW 08 (7); D band; range 264 km *(145 nm)* for 2 m² target.
Air/surface search: Head Net C (8); 3D; E band; range 128 km *(70 nm)*.
Navigation/helo control: 2 Signaal ZW 06 (9); I band.
Fire control: Two Drum Tilt (10); H/I band (for 30 mm).
Pop Group (11); F/H/I band (for SA-N-4).
Muff Cob (12); G/H band (for 57 mm).
Sonars: Graseby 750 *(Godavari)*; Bharat APSOH *(Ganga* and *Gomati)*; hull-mounted; active panoramic search and attack; medium frequency.
Fathoms Oceanic VDS (not in *Godavari*).
Type 162M; bottom classification; high frequency.

Helicopters: 2 Sea King or 1 Sea King and 1 Chetak (13).

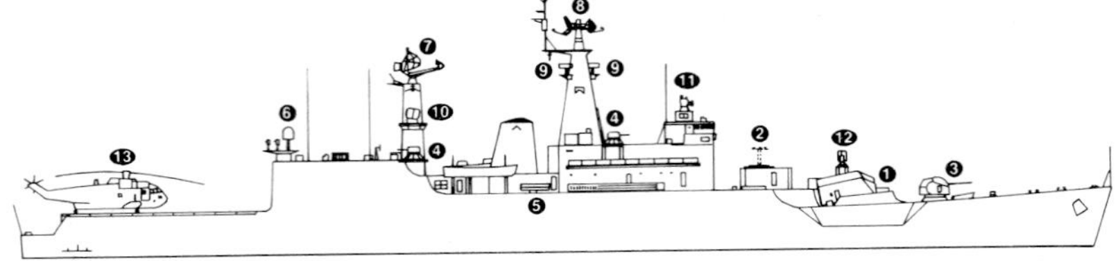

GODAVARI (Scale 1 : 1 200), *Ian Sturton*

GANGA 5/1990, *John Mortimer*

Programmes: The second batch of three ordered from Garden Reach, Calcutta. This is Project 16A, indicating an improved Godavari design but probably with the same hull. Work is proceeding very slowly and hull number 5 is unlikely to be laid down until 1992.
Structure: The first three were a further modification of the original Leander design with an indigenous content of 72% and a larger hull. Poor welding is noticeable in *Godavari*. *Gomati* is the first Indian ship to have digital electronics in her combat data system. The second three may have more Western weapon systems equipment and other structural modifications based on lessons learned from the first of class.
Operational: French helicopter handling equipment is fitted. Usually only one helo is carried with more than one crew. The first three have a unique mixture of Soviet, Western and Indian weapon systems which has inevitably led to some equipment compatibility problems.

GANGA 5/1990, *92 Wing RAAF*

5 SOVIET PETYA II CLASS

ARNALA P 68
ANDROTH P 69
ANJADIP P 73
AMINI P 75
KADMATH P 78

Displacement, tons: 950 standard; 1100 full load
Dimensions, feet (metres): 270 × 29.9 × 10.5 *(82.3 × 9.1 × 3.2)*
Main machinery: CODOG; 2 gas turbines; 30 000 hp(m) *(22 MW)*; 1 Type 61-V3 diesel (centre shaft); 6000 hp(m) *(4.41 MW)*; 3 shafts
Speed, knots: 32. **Range, miles:** 4000 at 20 kts
Complement: 98

Guns: 4 USSR 3 in *(76 mm)*/60 (2 twin) ❶; 80° elevation; 90 rounds/minute to 15 km *(8 nm)*; weight of shell 6.8 kg.
Torpedoes: 3—21 in *(533 mm)* (triple) tubes ❷. Probably Soviet Type 53; pattern active/passive homing up to 20 km *(10.8 nm)* at up to 45 kts; warhead 400 kg.
A/S mortars: 4 RBU 2500 16-tubed trainable launchers ❸; range 2500 m; warhead 21 kg.
Depth charges: 2 racks.
Mines: 2 rails.
Radars: Surface search: Slim Net ❹; E/F band.
Navigation: Don 2; I band.
Fire control: Hawk Screech ❺; I band; range 27 km *(15 nm)*.
IFF: High Pole B.
Sonars: Hercules; hull-mounted; active search and attack; medium/high frequency.

Programmes: An export version of Petya II class with simplified communications.
Transfers: *Kadmath* (originally built for Egypt) February 1969; *Arnala* and *Androth* August 1972; *Anjadip* (built at Khabarovsk) February 1973; *Amini* (built at Khabarovsk) March 1974.
Operational: Form 31st and 32nd Frigate Squadrons. *Andaman* (P 74) sank in heavy weather in the Bay of Bengal 22 August 1990. Fourteen of the crew were lost. Four deleted so far, last one in October 1991.

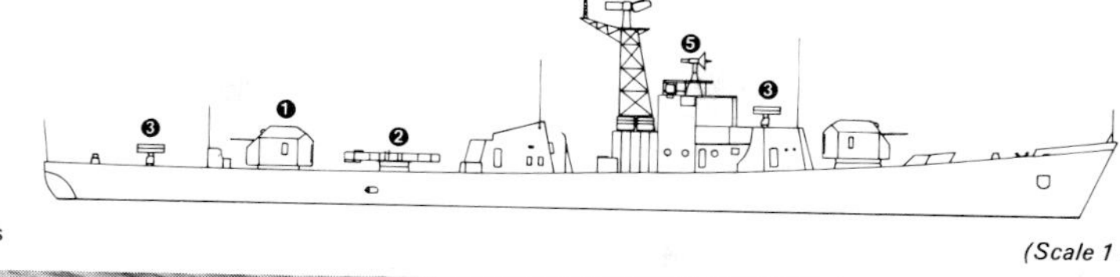

PETYA II Class *(Scale 1 : 900), Ian Sturton*

PETYA II Class (old number) *7/1987, G. Jacobs*

1 BRITISH WHITBY CLASS (TYPE 12)

Name	*No*	*Builders*	*Laid down*	*Launched*	*Commissioned*
TRISHUL	F 43	Harland & Wolff Ltd, Belfast	1957	18 June 1959	Jan 1960

Displacement, tons: 2144 standard; 2545 *(Talwar)*, 2557 *(Trishul)* full load
Dimensions, feet (metres): 369.8 × 41 × 17.8 (screws) *(112.7 × 12.5 × 5.4)*
Main machinery: 2 Babcock & Wilcox boilers; 550 psi *(38.7 kg/cm sq)*; 850°F *(450°C)*; 2 turbines; 30 000 hp *(22.4 MW)*; 2 shafts
Speed, knots: 30. **Range, miles:** 4500 at 12 kts
Complement: 231 (11 officers)

Missiles: SSM: 3 SS-N-2A Styx ❶; active radar or IR homing to 46 km *(25 nm)* at 0.9 Mach; warhead 513 kg.
Guns: 4 USSR 30 mm/65 (2 twin) ❷; 85° elevation; 500 rounds/minute to 5 km *(2.7 nm)*; weight of shell 0.54 kg.
A/S mortars: 1 Limbo Mk 10 launcher ❸; range 1000 m.
Countermeasures: Decoys: 2 UK Mk 5 Chaff launchers. Graseby G738; towed torpedo decoy.
ESM: Telegon IV D/F.
Radars: Air/surface search: Signaal DA 05 ❹; E/F band; range 137 km *(75 nm)* for 2 m² target.
Surface search: Square Tie ❺; I band; range 73 km *(40 nm)* or limits of radar horizon.
Navigation: Signaal ZW 06 ❻; I band.
Fire control: Two Drum Tilt ❼; H/I band (for 30 mm).
Sonars: Graseby Type 177; hull-mounted; active search; 7-9 kHz.
Graseby Type 170B; hull-mounted; active search; 15 kHz.
Type 162M; bottom classification; high frequency.

Helicopters: 1 Chetak ❽.

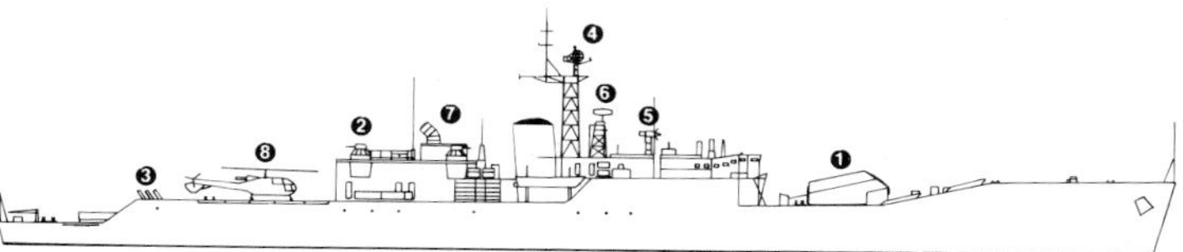

TRISHUL *(Scale 1 : 1 200), Ian Sturton*

TRISHUL *1989*

Modernisation: SS-N-2 missile launchers from an Osa class were fitted in place of the 4.5 in gun in 1977-78. *Trishul* reconstructed at Mazagon SY, Bombay, 1982-83. Rebuilt after section included construction of helicopter deck and hangar and Bofors guns were replaced by Soviet 30 mm.

Structure: Generally similar to the British frigates of the deleted Whitby class, but modified to suit Indian conditions.

1 BRITISH LEOPARD CLASS

Name	*No*	*Builders*	*Laid down*	*Launched*	*Commissioned*
BEAS	F 37	Vickers-Armstrong Ltd, Tyne	1957	9 Oct 1958	24 May 1960

Displacement, tons: 2320 standard; 2555 full load
Dimensions, feet (metres): 339.8 × 40 × 16 *(103.6 × 12.2 × 4.9)*
Main machinery: 8 VVS-ASR1 diesels; 12 380 hp *(9.2 MW)*; 2 shafts
Speed, knots: 24. **Range, miles:** 6000 at 15 kts
Complement: 228 (15 officers)

Guns: 2 Vickers 4.5 in *(114 mm)*/45 (twin) Mk 6; dual purpose; 80° elevation; 20 rounds/minute to 19 km *(10.4 nm)* anti-surface; 6 km *(3.3 nm)* anti-aircraft; weight of shell 25 kg.
2 Bofors 40 mm/60; 120 rounds/minute to 10 km *(5.5 nm)* anti-aircraft; weight of shell 0.89 kg.
A/S mortars: 1 Squid 3-tubed launcher.
Countermeasures: Decoys: 2 UK Mk 5 Chaff launchers.
ESM: Telegon IV D/F.
Radars: Surface search: RN Type 293Q; E/F band.
Navigation: Decca Type 978; I band.
Fire control: Type 275; F band.
Sonars: Graseby Type 177; hull-mounted; active search and attack; 7-9 kHz.
Kelvin Hughes Type 162; classification; 50 kHz.

Structure: Generally similar to the British frigates of the discarded Leopard class, but modified to suit Indian conditions. Has a deckhouse in place of after turret.
Operational: Formed part of the Training Squadron at Cochin but replaced by the Tir class (see *Service Forces*).

LEOPARD Class (old number) *11/1984, G. Jacobs*

CORVETTES

4 + 4 (4) KHUKRI CLASS (PROJECT 25)

Name	No	Builders	Laid down	Launched	Commissioned
KHUKRI	P 49	Mazagon, Bombay	27 Sep 1985	3 Dec 1986	23 Aug 1989
KUTHAR	P 46	Mazagon, Bombay	13 Sep 1986	15 Apr 1989	7 June 1990
KIRPAN	P 44	Garden Reach, Calcutta	1987	16 Aug 1988	12 Jan 1991
KHANJAR	P 47	Garden Reach, Calcutta	1987	16 Aug 1988	22 Oct 1991
—	—	Garden Reach, Calcutta	1990	1992	—
—	—	Garden Reach, Calcutta	1990	1992	—

Displacement, tons: 1350 full load
Dimensions, feet (metres): 298.6 × 34.4 × 8.2 *(91 × 10.5 × 2.5)*
Main machinery: 2 SEMT-Pielstick 18PA6 V280 diesels; 14 400 hp(m) *(10.58 MW)* sustained; 2 shafts; cp props
Speed, knots: 25. **Range, miles:** 4000 at 16 kts
Complement: 79 (10 officers)

Missiles: SSM: 2 or 4 SS-N-2C Styx (1 or 2 twin) launchers ❶; active radar or IR homing to 83 km *(45 nm)* at 0.9 Mach; warhead 513 kg; sea-skimmer at end of run.
SAM: SA-N-5 Grail ❷; manual aiming; IR homing to 6 km *(3.2 nm)* at 1.5 Mach; altitude to 2500 m *(8000 ft)*; warhead 1.5 kg.
Guns: 1 USSR AK 176 3 in *(76 mm)*/60 ❸; 85° elevation; 120 rounds/minute to 15 km *(8 nm)*; weight of shell 7 kg.
2—30 mm/65 (twin) AK 630 ❹; 85° elevation; 500 rounds/minute to 5 km *(2.7 nm)*; weight of shell 0.54 kg.
Countermeasures: Decoys: 2—16-barrelled Chaff launchers ❺. NPOL (Cochin); towed torpedo decoy.
ESM: Bharat Ajanta P; radar warning.
Combat data systems: Selenia system *(Khukri)*; Bharat Vympal system (remainder).
Radars: Air search: Positive E/Cross Sword ❻; E/F band; range 130 km *(70 nm)*.
Air/surface search: Plank Shave ❼; I band.
Fire control: Bass Tilt ❽; H/I band.
Navigation: Bharat 1245; I band.

Helicopters: Platform only ❾ for Chetak (to be replaced by Hindustan Aeronautics ALH in due course).

Programmes: First two ordered December 1983; two more ordered in 1985 and the next batch of four from Garden Reach/Mazagon in April 1990. Total of 12 planned. The diesels are assembled in India under licence by Kirloskar. Indigenous content of the whole ship is about 65 per cent. This class is replacing the Petyas. The follow-on class will be an upgraded version.

Structure: SA-N-4 may be fitted in the second batch of four. The reported plan was to make the first four ASW ships, and the remainder anti-aircraft or general purpose. However *Khukri* has neither torpedo tubes nor a sonar (apart from a Krupp Atlas echo sounder), so if the plan is correct these ships will rely on an ALH helicopter which will have dunking sonar and ASW torpedoes and depth charges. All have fin stabilisers and full air-conditioning.
Operational: Based in Bombay. The advanced light helicopter (ALH) to have Sea Eagle SSM, torpedoes and dipping sonar.

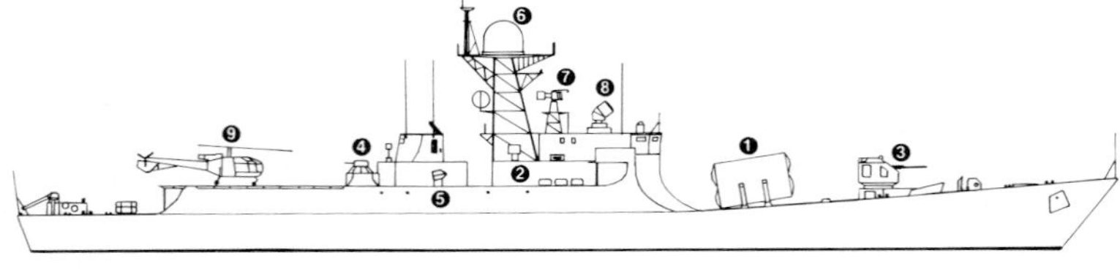

KHUKRI *(Scale 1 : 900), Ian Sturton*

KHUKRI *5/1990, 92 Wing RAAF*

4 + 1 ABHAY (PAUK) CLASS

Name	No	Builders	Commissioned
ABHAY	P 33	Volodarski, Rybinsk	Mar 1989
AJAY	P 34	Volodarski, Rybinsk	24 Jan 1990
AKSHAY	P 35	Volodarski, Rybinsk	Dec 1990
AGRAY	P 36	Volodarski, Rybinsk	Feb 1991

Displacement, tons: 520 full load
Dimensions, feet (metres): 195.2 × 33.5 × 10.8 *(59.5 × 10.2 × 3.3)*
Main machinery: 2 diesels; 21 000 hp(m) *(15.3 MW)*; 2 shafts
Speed, knots: 32. **Range, miles:** 2200 at 18 kts
Complement: 32

Missiles: SAM: SA-N-5 Grail quad launcher; manual aiming, IR homing to 6 km *(3.2 nm)* at 1.5 Mach; warhead 1.5 kg.
Guns: 1 USSR 3 in *(76 mm)*/60; 85° elevation; 120 rounds/minute to 15 km *(8 nm)*; weight of shell 7 kg.
1—30 mm/65; 6 barrels; 3000 rounds/minute combined to 2 km.
Torpedoes: 4—21 in *(533 mm)* (2 twin) tubes. Soviet type 53; active/passive homing up to 20 km *(11 nm)* at up to 45 kts; warhead 400 kg.
A/S mortars: 2 RBU 1200 5-tubed fixed; range 1200 m; warhead 34 kg.
Countermeasures: 2—16-tubed Chaff launchers.
Radars: Air/Surface search: Positive E/Cross Sword; E/F band.
Navigation: Pechora; I band.
Fire Control: Bass Tilt; H/I band.
Sonars: Rat Tail VDS (on transom); attack; high frequency.

ABHAY *1989, Indian Navy*

Programmes: Modified Pauk II class built in the USSR for export. Original order in late 1983 but completion of the first delayed by lack of funds and the order for the others was not reinstated until 1987. Names associated with former coastal patrol craft. One of the same class has been acquired by Cuba.

Structure: Has a longer superstructure than the Pauk I and new electronics with a radome similar to the Parchim II class.

7 + 11 VEER (TARANTUL I) CLASS

Name	No	Builders	Laid down	Launched	Commissioned
VEER	K 40	Volodarski, Rybinsk	—	—	May 1987
NIRBHIK	K 41	Volodarski, Rybinsk	—	—	Jan 1988
NIPAT	K 42	Volodarski, Rybinsk	—	—	Jan 1989
NISHANK	K 43	Volodarski, Rybinsk	—	—	Sep 1989
NIRGHAT	K 44	Volodarski, Rybinsk	—	—	Feb 1990
VIBHUTI	K 45	Mazagon, Bombay	Mar 1988	26 Apr 1990	3 June 1991
VIPUL	K 46	Mazagon, Bombay	July 1988	3 Jan 1991	Jan 1992
VINASH	K 47	Mazagon, Bombay	June 1990	24 Jan 1992	1993
—	K 48-59	Mazagon, Goa/Garden Reach	—	—	—

Displacement, tons: 385 standard; 450 full load
Dimensions, feet (metres): 184.1 × 37.7 × 8.2 *(56.1 × 11.5 × 2.5)*
Main machinery: COGOG; 2 Type NK-12 MV gas turbines; 24 000 hp(m) *(17.6 MW)*; 2 gas turbines with reversible gear box; 8000 hp(m) *(5.9 MW)*; 2 shafts (K40-44)
CODOG; 1 GE LM 2500 gas turbine; 23 000 hp *(17.16 MW)* sustained; 2 MTU 12V 538 TB 92 diesels; 5610 hp(m) *(3.76 MW)* sustained; 2 shafts (K45 onwards)
Speed, knots: 36. **Range, miles:** 2000 at 20 kts; 400 at 36 kts
Complement: 41 (5 officers)

Missiles: SSM: 4 SS-N-2C Styx; active radar or IR homing to 83 km *(45 nm)* at 0.9 Mach; warhead 513 kg; sea-skimmer at end of run.
SAM: SA-N-5 Grail quad launcher; manual aiming; IR homing to 6 km *(3.2 nm)* at 1.5 Mach; warhead 1.5 kg.
Guns: 1 USSR 3 in *(76 mm)*/60; 85° elevation; 120 rounds/minute to 15 km *(8 nm)*; weight of shell 7 kg.
2—30 mm/65; 85° elevation; 500 rounds/minute to 5 km *(2.7 nm)*; weight of shell 0.54 kg.
Fire control: Hood Wink optronic director.
Radars: Air/surface search: Plank Shave; E band.
Navigation: Pechora; I Band.
Fire Control: Bass tilt: H/I band.
IFF: Salt Pot, Square Head A.

Programmes: First five are Soviet Tarantul I class built for export. Remainder of this type are building in India.
Structure: Variations in the Indian built ships include CODOG propulsion (with one gas turbine and two diesels) and improved countermeasures equipment.

NIRGHAT *1991*

VIBHUTI *1991*

3 Ex-SOVIET NANUCHKA II CLASS

Name	No	Builders	Commissioned
VIJAY DURG	K 71	Petrovskiy, Leningrad	Apr 1976
SINDHU DURG	K 72	Petrovskiy, Leningrad	Sep 1977
HOS DURG	K 73	Petrovskiy, Leningrad	Apr 1978

Displacement, tons: 850 full load
Dimensions, feet (metres): 194.5 × 38.7 × 8.5 *(59.3 × 11.8 × 2.6)*
Main machinery: 3 Type M507 diesels; 26 000 hp(m) *(19 MW)*; 3 shafts
Speed, knots: 34. **Range, miles:** 2500 at 12 kts; 900 at 31 kts
Complement: 60

Missiles: SSM: 4 SS-N-2B Styx; active radar or IR homing to 46 km *(25 nm)* at 0.9 Mach; warhead 513 kg.
SAM: SA-N-4 Gecko twin launcher; semi-active radar homing to 15 km *(8 nm)* at 2.5 Mach; height envelope 9-3048 m *(29.5-10 000 ft)*; warhead 50 kg; 20 missiles.
Guns: 2 USSR 57 mm/80 (twin); 90° elevation; 120 rounds/minute to 8 km *(4.4 nm)*; weight of shell 2.8 kg.
Countermeasures: 2—16-barrelled Chaff launchers.
ESM: Radar warning.
Radars: Air/surface search: Square Tie; I band; range 73 km *(40 nm)* (mounted in radome).
Fire control: Pop Group; F/H/I band (for SAN-4).
Muff Cob; G/H band.
Navigation: Don 2; I band.
IFF: High Pole. Two Square Head.

Structure: The radome is mounted lower than in Soviet ships of this class due to the absence of Fish Bowl because of the use of SS-N-2 missiles in place of SS-N-9.

VIJAY DURG *1990*

PATROL SHIPS

6 + 4 SUKANYA CLASS (OFFSHORE PATROL SHIPS)

Name	*No*	*Builders*	*Launched*	*Commissioned*
SUKANYA	P 50	Korea Tacoma, Masan	1989	31 Aug 1989
SUBHADRA	P 51	Korea Tacoma, Masan	1989	25 Jan 1990
SUVARNA	P 52	Korea Tacoma, Masan	22 Aug 1990	1991
SAVITRI	P 53	Hindustan SY, Vishakapatnam	23 May 1989	27 Nov 1990
SARAYU	P 54	Hindustan SY, Vishakapatnam	16 Oct 1989	1991
SHARADA	P 55	Hindustan SY, Vishakapatnam	22 Aug 1990	27 Oct 1991
SUJATHA	P 56	Hindustan SY, Vishakapatnam	25 Oct 1991	1992
—	P 57-59	Mazagon, Goa	—	—

Displacement, tons: 1890 full load
Dimensions, feet (metres): 334.6 oa; 315 wl × 37.7 × 11.2 *(102; 96 × 11.5 × 3.4)*
Main machinery: 2 SEMT-Pielstick 16 PA 6V 280 diesels; 12 800 hp(m) *(9.41 MW)* sustained; 2 shafts
Speed, knots: 21. **Range, miles:** 7000 at 15 kts
Complement: 145 (12 officers)

Guns: 1 Oerlikon 20 mm.
Radars: Surface search: Selenia; I band.
Navigation: Racal Decca; I band.
Helicopters: 1 Chetak.

Comment: First three ordered in March 1987 from Korea Tacoma to an Ulsan class design. Second four ordered in August 1987. The Korean built ships commissioned at Masan and then sailed for India where the armament was fitted. Three more reported ordered from Goa in April 1990. Lightly armed and able to 'stage' helicopters, they are fitted out for offshore patrol work only but have the capacity to be much more heavily armed. Fin stabilisers fitted. Firefighting pump on hangar roof aft. These are naval ships (not Coast Guard) used for harbour defence, protection of offshore installations and patrol of the EEZ. Potential for role change is considerable (see Ulsan class under *South Korea*). Inmarsat can be fitted on the hangar roof.

SAVITRI *6/1991*

SHIPBORNE AIRCRAFT

Note: Naval versions of the Advanced Light Aircraft are being developed.

Numbers/Type: HAL Advanced Light Helicopter (ALH).
Operational speed: 156 kts *(290 km/h)*.
Service ceiling: 9850 ft *(3000 m)*.
Range: 216 nm *(400 km)*.
Role/Weapon systems: Full production expected from 1993. Sensors and weapons not yet known.

Numbers/Type: 9 Aerospatiale (HAL) SA 319B Chetak (Alouette III).
Operational speed: 113 kts *(210 km/h)*.
Service ceiling: 10 500 ft *(3200 m)*.
Range: 290 nm *(540 km)*.
Role/Weapon systems: Several helicopter roles still performed including embarked ASW and carrier-based SAR, utility and support to commando forces. Sensors: Some helicopters have search radar. Weapons: ASW; 2 × Whitehead A244S torpedoes.

Numbers/Type: 23 British Aerospace Sea Harrier FRS Mk 51 (plus 3 Mk 60 trainers).
Operational speed: 640 kts *(1186 km/h)*.
Service ceiling: 51 200 ft *(15 600 m)*.
Range: 800 nm *(1480 km)*.
Role/Weapon systems: Fleet air defence, strike and reconnaissance STOVL fighter with future ASV role with Sea Eagle missiles; mid-life update planned after 1995; seven on order. Sensors: Ferranti Blue Fox air interception radar, limited ECM/RWR. Weapons: Air defence; 2 × Magic AAMs, 2 × 30 mm Aden cannon. Strike; 2 × Sea Eagle missiles or 3.6 tons of 'iron' bombs.

Numbers/Type: 5 Kamov Ka-25 ('Hormone').
Operational speed: 104 kts *(193 km/h)*.
Service ceiling: 11 500 ft *(3500 m)*.
Range: 217 nm *(400 km)*.
Role/Weapon systems: ASW helicopter embarked in Soviet-built Kashin class destroyers for ASW tasks. Sensors: Search radar, dipping sonar, sonobuoys. Weapons: ASW; 2 × torpedoes or 4 × depth bombs.

KAMOV KA 25 *1989, Indian Navy*

Numbers/Type: 18 Kamov Ka-27 (Helix A).
Operational speed: 110 kts *(204 km/h)*.
Service ceiling: 12 000 ft *(3660 m)*.
Range: 270 nm *(500 km)*.
Role/Weapon systems: ASW helicopter embarked in new generation/updated Soviet-designed escorts. Total of 18 ordered; will replace Ka-25. Sensors: Search radar, dipping sonar, sonobuoys. Weapons: ASW; 2 × Whitehead A244S torpedoes or 4 × depth bombs.

Numbers/Type: 7 Westland Sea King Mks 42/42A.
Operational speed: 112 kts *(208 km/h)*.
Service ceiling: 11 500 ft *(3500 m)*.
Range: 664 nm *(1230 km)*.
Role/Weapon systems: Primary ASW helicopter for large escorts and CVL; some are shore-based for training and surface search. Sensors: MEL search radar, Alcatel dipping sonar. Weapons: ASW; 4 × Whitehead A244S torpedoes, BAe Mk 11 depth bombs or mines.

Numbers/Type: 20/5/5 Westland Sea King Mks 42B/42C/42D.
Operational speed: 112 kts *(208 km/h)*.
Service ceiling: 11 500 ft *(3500 m)*.
Range: 664 nm *(1230 km)*.
Role/Weapon systems: Advanced shipborne helicopter for embarked and shore-based role; Mk 42B has primary ASV capability; Mk 42C for commando assault/vertrep; Mk 42D for AEW up to five bought. Intention is to buy up to nine more. Sensors: MEL Super Searcher radar, Thomson Sintra H/S-12 dipping sonar, AQS 902B acoustic processor; Marconi Hermes ESM (Mk 42B); Bendix weather radar (Mk 42C); Thorn EMI Searchwater radar, Racal MIR-2 (Mk 42D). Weapons: ASW; 2 Whitehead A244S torpedoes; Mk 11 depth bombs, mines (Mk 42B only). ASV; 2 × Sea Eagle (Mk 42B only). Unarmed (Mk 42C/D).

SEA KING 42B *11/1987, Paul Beaver*

LAND-BASED MARITIME AIRCRAFT (FRONT LINE)

Numbers/Type: 36 Dornier 228.
Operational speed: 200 kts *(370 km/h)*.
Service ceiling: 28 000 ft *(8535 m)*.
Range: 940 nm *(1740 km)*.
Role/Weapon systems: Coastal surveillance and EEZ protection duties for Navy and Coast Guard. Sensors: MEL Marec 2 search radar, cameras and searchlight. Weapons: Unarmed, but will carry anti-ship missiles eventually, type unknown.

Numbers/Type: 6 Ilyushin Il-38 (May).
Operational speed: 347 kts *(645 km/h)*.
Service ceiling: 32 800 ft *(10 000 m)*.
Range: 3887 nm *(7200 km)*.
Role/Weapon systems: Shore-based long-range ASW reconnaissance into Indian Ocean. Sensors: Search radar, MAD, sonobuoys, ESM. Weapons: ASW; various torpedoes, mines and depth bombs.

Numbers/Type: 18 Pilatus Britten-Norman Maritime Defender.
Operational speed: 150 kts *(280 km/h)*.
Service ceiling: 18 900 ft *(5760 m)*.
Range: 1500 nm *(2775 km)*.
Role/Weapon systems: Coastal and short-range reconnaissance tasks undertaken in support of Navy (5) and Coast Guard. Sensors: Search radar, camera. Weapons: Unarmed.

Numbers/Type: 10 Tupolev Tu-142M (Bear F).
Operational speed: 500 kts *(925 km/h)*.
Service ceiling: 45 000 ft *(13 720 m)*.
Range: 6775 nm *(12 550 km)*.
Role/Weapon systems: First entered service in April 1988 for long-range surface surveillance and ASW. Air Force manned. Sensors: Search and attack radars, MAD, cameras. Active and passive sonobuoys. Weapons: ASW; 12 × torpedoes, depth bombs. ASV; 2 × 23 mm cannon (no AS-4 ASM).

Numbers/Type: 2 Fokker F-27 Friendship.
Operational speed: 250 kts *(463 km/h)*.
Service ceiling: 29 500 ft *(8990 m)*.
Range: 2700 nm *(5000 km)*.
Role/Weapon systems: Operated by Coast Guard for long-range patrol. Sensors: Search radar only. Weapons: Unarmed.

Numbers/Type: 12 SEPECAT/HAL Jaguar International.
Operational speed: 917 kts *(1699 km/h)* (max).
Service ceiling: 36 000 ft *(11 000 m)*.
Range: 760 nm *(1408 km)*.
Role/Weapon systems: A maritime strike squadron. Sensors: Thomson-CSF Agave radar. Weapons: ASV; 2 BAe Sea Eagle anti-ship missiles underwing; 2 DEFA 30 mm cannon or up to 8—1000 lb bombs. Can carry two air-to-air missiles overwing.

LIGHT FORCES

Note: 24 patrol boats were reported in 1991 as ordered from American Body Armor and Equipment nc. This report was not correct.

8 OSA II CLASS (FAST ATTACK CRAFT—MISSILE)

PRACHAND K 90
PRALAYA K 91
PRATAP K 92
PRABAL K 93
CHAPAL K 94
CHAMAK K 95
CHATAK K 96
CHARAG K 97

Displacement, tons: 245 full load
Dimensions, feet (metres): 110.2 × 24.9 × 8.6 *(33.6 × 7.6 × 2.7)*
Main machinery: 3 M504 diesels; 15 000 hp(m) *(11 MW)*; 3 shafts
Speed, knots: 37. **Range, miles:** 800 at 25 kts
Complement: 30

Missiles: SSM: 4 SS-N-2A or B Styx; active radar or IR homing to 46 km *(25 nm)* at 0.9 Mach; warhead 513 kg.
Guns: 4 USSR 30 mm/65 (2 twin); 85° elevation; 500 rounds/minute to 5 km *(2.7 nm)*; weight of shell 0.54 kg.
Radars: Surface search: Square Tie; I band.
Fire control: Drum Tilt; H/I band.
IFF: High Pole. Square Head.

Programmes: Eight Osa II class delivered January 1976-September 1977. Being replaced by Tarantul class and beginning to be paid off. Some are in reserve.

CHAPAL — *2/1989, G. Jacobs*

SDB Mk 2 CLASS (FAST ATTACK CRAFT—PATROL)

Displacement, tons: 203 full load
Dimensions, feet (metres): 123 × 24.6 × 5.9 *(37.5 × 7.5 × 1.8)*
Main machinery: 2 Paxman Deltic 18-42K diesels; 6240 hp *(4.66 MW)*; 2 shafts. Auxiliary propulsion; 1 Kirloskar-Cummins diesel; 165 hp *(123 kW)*
Speed, knots: 29; 4 on auxiliary diesel
Range, miles: 1400 at 14 kts
Complement: 28 (4 officers)
Guns: 1 Bofors 40 mm/60; 80° elevation; 120 rounds/minute to 10 km *(5.5 nm)*; weight of shell 0.89 kg.
1—7.62 mm MG.
Depth charges: 18 Mk 7; 10 Mk 12.
Sonars: Hull-mounted; active attack; high frequency.

Comment: First three commissioned in 1977-78; last two in 1984. All built by Garden Reach SY, Calcutta. Reported that problems delayed launchings of the first group. This might be due to use of GRP hulls. All with Eastern Naval Command. Same class built for Coast Guard.

SDB Mk 3 CLASS (FAST ATTACK CRAFT—PATROL)

Displacement, tons: 210 full load
Dimensions, feet (metres): 124 × 24.6 × 6.2 *(37.8 × 7.5 × 1.9)*
Main machinery: 2 MTU 16V 538 TB92 diesels; 6820 hp(m) *(5 MW)*; 2 shafts
Speed, knots: 30
Complement: 32
Guns: 2 Bofors 40 mm/60; 80° elevation; 120 rounds/minute to 10 km *(5.5 nm)*; weight of shell 0.89 kg.

Comment: First pair and Nos 4 and 5 ordered from Garden Reach SY, Calcutta, remainder from Mazagon, Goa. First three completed in 1984, remainder in 1985-86.

SDB Mk 3 — *1989, G. Jacobs*

0 + 1 FAST ATTACK CRAFT (TORPEDO)

Displacement, tons: 90 full load
Dimensions, feet (metres): 84.6 × 22.6 × 3.9 *(25.8 × 6.9 × 1.2)*
Main machinery: 2 diesels; 5000 hp *(3.73 MW)*; 2 shafts
Speed, knots: 30. **Range, miles:** 400 at 20 kts
Complement: 7 (3 officers)
Guns: 2—12.7 mm MGs.
Torpedoes: 2—21 in *(533 mm)* tubes; anti-surface.
Radars: Surface search: I band.

Comment: A Mazagon design reported building for the Indian Navy. Numbers not known.

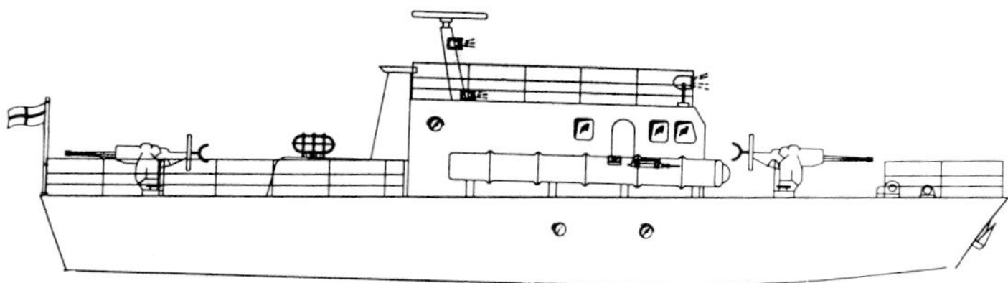
FAST ATTACK CRAFT — *1990, Mazagon Dock*

AMPHIBIOUS FORCES

Note: An agreement has been reached for the production of US LCAs in India. Project definition started 1 April 1990 and full production is expected by 1995.

8 SOVIET POLNOCHNY C and D CLASS (LSMs)

GHORPAD L 14
KESARI L 15
SHARDUL L 16
SHARABH L 17
CHEETAH L 18
MAHISH L 19
GULDAR L 21
KUMBHIR L 22

Displacement, tons: 1120 standard; 1150 full load
Dimensions, feet (metres): 269 × 32.8 × 6.6 *(82 × 10 × 2)*
Main machinery: 2 diesels; 5000 hp(m) *(3.68 MW)*; 2 shafts
Speed, knots: 18. **Range, miles:** 2000 at 12 kts
Complement: 60
Military lift: 350 tons; 140 troops
Guns: 4—30 mm (2 twin). 2—140 mm 18-tubed rocket launchers.
Radars: Navigation: Don 2 or Krivach (SRN 745); I band.
Fire control: Drum Tilt; H/I band (in D class).
Helicopters: Platform only (in D class).

Comment: All new construction direct from Poland. *Ghorpad* and *Kesari* transferred in March 1975, *Shardul* and *Sharabh* in February 1976, *Cheetah* in February 1985, *Mahish* in July 1985, *Guldar* in March 1986 and *Kumbhir* in November 1986. The last four are Polnochny Ds with the flight deck forward of the bridge and different radars. At least two are in reserve.

CHEETAH — *1988*

7 Mk 3 LANDING CRAFT (LCU)

VASCO DA GAMA L 34
MIDHUR L 38
MANGALA L 39
L 35-37, L 40

Displacement, tons: 500 full load
Dimensions, feet (metres): 188.6 oa; 174.5 pp × 26.9 × 5.2 *(57.5; 53.2 × 8.2 × 1.6)*
Main machinery: 3 Kirloskar-MAN V8V 17.5/22 AMAL diesels; 1686 hp(m) *(1.24 MW)*; 3 shafts
Speed, knots: 11. **Range, miles:** 1000 at 8 kts
Complement: 287 including troops
Military lift: 250 tons; 2 PT 76 or 2 APC
Guns: 2 Bofors 40 mm/60 (aft).
Mines: Can be embarked.

Comment: First two built by Hooghly D and E Co and remainder at Goa SY (subsidiary of Mazagon Docks Ltd). First craft *(Vasco da Gama)* launched 29 November 1978 and the last one commissioned 25 March 1987.

MIDHUR — *2/1989, G. Jacobs*

2 MAGAR CLASS (LST)

Name	No	Builders	Commissioned
MAGAR	L 20	Garden Reach, Calcutta	15 July 1987
GHARIAL	L 23	Hindustan/Garden Reach	Mar 1992

Displacement, tons: 5655 full load
Dimensions, feet (metres): 409.4 oa; 393.7 wl × 57.4 × 13.1 *(124.8; 120 × 17.5 × 4)*
Main machinery: 2 SEMT-Pielstick 8 PC 2V 400 Mk 3 diesels; 8560 hp(m) *(6.29 MW)* sustained; 2 shafts
Speed, knots: 15. **Range, miles:** 3000 at 14 kts
Complement: 136 (16 officers)
Guns: 4 Bofors 40 mm/60. 2 multi-barrel rocket launchers in the bow.
Helicopters: 1 Sea King 42C; platform for 2.

Comment: A new *Magar*, maintaining the name of the deleted ex-British LST 3 and based on the *Sir Lancelot* design, was launched on 7 November 1984. *Gharial* ordered in 1985, launched 1 April 1991 at Hindustan Shipyard but is fitting out at Garden Reach. Carries four LCVPs on davits. Bow door. Can beach on gradients 1 in 40 or more. Original plan was for eight of the class.

MAGAR *10/1990, 92 Wing RAAF*

MINE WARFARE FORCES

Note: A need for at least 10 minehunters has been accepted with the lead vessels to be built overseas and the remainder at Goa. An alternative is to build all 10 to a Soviet design. Hulls to be of GRP. In 1990 it was reported that six (M 89-M 94) were to be ordered from Goa Shipyard which is installing GRP facilities. Progress is slow.

12 SOVIET NATYA I CLASS (MINESWEEPERS—OCEAN)

PONDICHERRY M 61
PORBANDAR M 62
BEDI M 63
BHAVNAGAR M 64
ALLEPPEY M 65
RATNAGIRI M 66
KARWAR M 67
CANNANORE M 68
CUDDALORE M 69
KAKINADA M 70
KOZHIKODA M 71
KONKAN M 72

Displacement, tons: 770 full load
Dimensions, feet (metres): 200.1 × 31.8 × 8.9 *(61 × 9.7 × 2.7)*
Main machinery: 2 diesels; 8000 hp(m) *(5.88 MW)*; 2 shafts
Speed, knots: 19. **Range, miles:** 4000 at 10 kts
Complement: 58

Guns: 4—30 mm/65 (2 twin); 85° elevation; 500 rounds/minute to 5 km *(2.7 nm)*; weight of shell 0.54 kg.
4—25 mm/70 (2 twin); 85° elevation; 270 rounds/minute to 3 km *(1.6 nm)*.
A/S mortars: 2 RBU 1200 5-tubed fixed; range 1200 m; warhead 34 kg.
Mines: Can carry 10.
Radars: Navigation: Don 2; I band.
Fire control: Drum Tilt; H/I band.
IFF: Two Square Head. High Pole B.
Sonars: Hull-mounted; active mine detection; high frequency.

Programmes: Built for export at Isora Yard, Leningrad. First pair transferred April 1978, second pair July 1979, third pair August 1980, one in October 1986, one in June 1987, one in December 1987, one in May 1988, one in November 1988 and the last in early 1989. Last six have been delivered out of pennant number order.
Structure: Steel hulls but do not have stern ramp as in Soviet class.
Operational: Some are fitted with two quad SA-N-5 systems. All are capable of magnetic, acoustic and mechanical sweeping. *Pondicherry* was painted white and used as the Presidential yacht for the Indian Fleet Review by President R Venkataramen on 15 February 1989; she reverted to her normal role and colour on completion. One serves as an AGI.

CANNANORE *1989, van Ginderen Collection*

4 HAM CLASS (MINESWEEPERS—INSHORE)

Name	No	Builders	Commissioned
BULSAR	M 89	Mazagon Docks Ltd, Bombay	1970
BHATKAL	M 90	Mazagon Docks Ltd, Bombay	1968
BIMLIPITAN (ex-HMS *Hildersham*)	M 2705	Vosper, Portsmouth	1954
BASSEIN (ex-HMS *Littleham*)	M 2707	Brooke Marine, Lowestoft	1954

Displacement, tons: 120 standard; 159 full load
Dimensions, feet (metres): 107.5 × 22 × 5.8 *(32.8 × 6.7 × 1.8)*
Main machinery: 2 Paxman YHAZM diesels; 1100 hp *(821 kW)*; 2 shafts
Speed, knots: 14; 9 sweeping
Complement: 15 (2 officers)
Guns: 1 Oerlikon 20 mm.
Radars: Decca 978; I band.

Comment: Of wooden construction; two were built for the Royal Navy but transferred from the U to the Indian Navy in 1955. *Bassein* was launched on 4 May 1954, *Bimlipitan* on 5 February 195 *Bhatkal* in April 1967, and *Bulsar* on 17 May 1969.

6 SOVIET YEVGENYA CLASS (MINESWEEPERS—INSHORE)

MAHÉ M 83
MALVAN M 84
MANGALORE M 85
MALPE M 86
MULKI M 87
MAGDALA M 88

Displacement, tons: 77 standard; 90 full load
Dimensions, feet (metres): 80.7 × 18 × 4.9 *(24.6 × 5.5 × 1.5)*
Main machinery: 2 diesels; 400 hp(m) *(294 kW)*; 2 shafts
Speed, knots: 11. **Range, miles:** 300 at 10 kts
Complement: 10
Guns: 2 USSR 25 mm/80 (twin).
Radars: Navigation: Don 2; I band.
Sonars: A small transducer streamed over the stern on a crane.

Comment: First three delivered as deck cargo 16 May 1983 and second three on 3 February 1984. mid-1960s design with GRP hulls built at Kolpino. All based at Cochin.

MANGALORE *5/198*

SURVEY AND OCEANOGRAPHIC SHIPS

Note: The National Institute of Oceanography operates several research and survey ships includin *Sagar Kanya, Samudra Manthan, Sagar Sampada, Samudra Sarvekshak, Samudra Nidhi* an *Samudra Sandhari*. A new acoustic research ship *Mars* was launched in May 1991 at Garden Reac Calcutta.

5 + 1 (1) SANDHAYAK CLASS (SURVEY SHIPS)

Name	No	Builders	Commissioned
SANDHAYAK	—	Garden Reach DY, Calcutta	1 Mar 1981
NIRDESHAK	J 19	Garden Reach DY, Calcutta	4 Oct 1982
NIRUPAK	J 14	Garden Reach DY, Calcutta	14 Aug 1985
INVESTIGATOR	J 15	Garden Reach DY, Calcutta	11 Jan 1990
JAMUNA	J 16	Garden Reach DY, Calcutta	31 Aug 1991
SUTLEJ	J 17	Garden Reach DY, Calcutta	July 1992

Displacement, tons: 1929 full load
Dimensions, feet (metres): 281.3 × 42 × 11 *(85.8 × 12.8 × 3.3)*
Main machinery: 2 GRSE MAN G8V 30/45 ATL diesels; 3860 hp(m) *(2.84 MW)*; 2 shafts; activ rudder
Speed, knots: 16. **Range, miles:** 6000 at 14 kts; 14 000 at 10 kts
Complement: 189 (14 officers) plus 30 scientists
Guns: 1 Bofors 40 mm/60.
Countermeasures: ESM: Telegon IV HF D/F.
Radars: Navigation: Racal Decca 1629; I band.
Helicopters: 1 Alouette III.

Comment: *Investigator* launched 8 August 1987 and *Jamuna* in September 1989. *Sutlej* laid dow in 1990. Total of seven planned. Telescopic hangar. Fitted with three echo sounders, extensivel equipped laboratories, and carries four GRP survey launches on davits amidships. Painted whi with yellow funnels. An active rudder with a DC motor gives speeds of up to 5 kts.

NIRUPAK *1987, Gilbert Gysse*

4 MAKAR CLASS (SURVEY CRAFT)

MAKAR J 33
MITHUN J 34
MEEN J 35
MESH J 36

Displacement, tons: 210 full load
Dimensions, feet (metres): 123 × 24.6 × 6.2 *(37.5 × 7.5 × 1.9)*
Main machinery: 2 diesels; 1124 hp(m) *(826 kW)*; 2 shafts
Speed, knots: 12. **Range, miles:** 1500 at 12 kts
Complement: 36 (4 officers)
Guns: 1 Bofors 40 mm/60.

Comment: Launched at Goa in 1981-82. Similar hulls to SDB Mk 2 class but with much smaller engines.

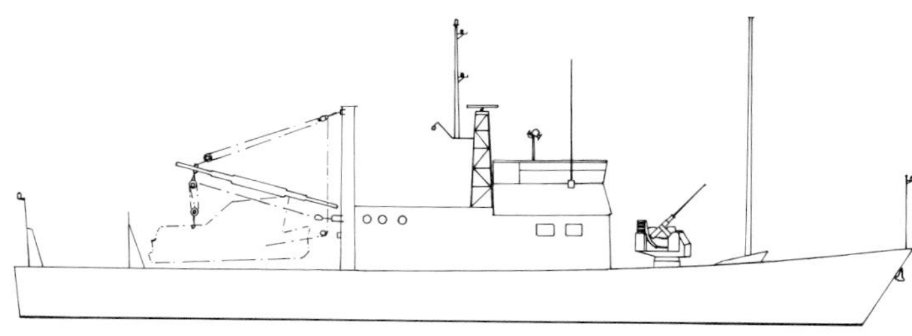

MAKAR Class *1990 (not to scale), Ian Sturton*

SERVICE FORCES

1 + 1 TIR CLASS (TRAINING SHIPS)

Name	*No*	*Builders*	*Commissioned*
TIR	A 86	Mazagon Dock, Bombay	21 Feb 1986

Displacement, tons: 2400 full load
Dimensions, feet (metres): 347.4 × 43.3 × 15.7 *(105.9 × 13.2 × 4.8)*
Main machinery: 2 Crossley-Pielstick 8 PC 2V Mk 2 diesels; 8000 hp(m) *(5.88 MW)* sustained; 2 shafts
Speed, knots: 18. **Range, miles:** 6000 at 12 kts
Complement: 239 (35 officers) plus 120 cadets
Guns: 2 Bofors 40 mm/60 (twin) with launchers for illuminants. 4 saluting guns.
Countermeasures: ESM: Telegon IV D/F.
Radars: Navigation: Two Indian design.
Helicopters: Platform for Alouette III.

Comment: First launched 15 April 1983. Second reported ordered May 1986. Built to commercial standards. Decca collision avoidance plot and SATNAV. Can carry up to 120 cadets and 20 instructors. Some doubt exists over the status of the second of class.

TIR *5/1991, 92 Wing RAAF*

1 Ex-SOVIET UGRA CLASS (SUBMARINE TENDER)

AMBA A 54

Displacement, tons: 6750 standard; 9650 full load
Dimensions, feet (metres): 462.6 × 57.7 × 23 *(141 × 17.6 × 7)*
Main machinery: Diesel-electric; 4 Kolumna Type diesel generators; 2 motors; 8000 hp(m) *(5.88 MW)*; 2 shafts
Speed, knots: 17. **Range, miles:** 21 000 at 10 kts
Complement: 400
Guns: 4 USSR 3 in *(76 mm)*/60 (2 twin); 80° elevation; 90 rounds/minute to 15 km *(8 nm)*; weight of shell 6.8 kg.
Radars: Air/surface search: Slim Net; E/F band.
Fire control: Two Hawk Screech; I band.
Navigation: Don 2; I band.
IFF: Two Square Head. High Pole A.

Comment: Acquired from the USSR in 1968. Provision for helicopter. Can accommodate 750. Two cranes, one of 6 tons and one of 10 tons. Differs from others of the class by having 76 mm guns.

AMBA *1991*

1 DIVING SUPPORT SHIP

Name	*No*	*Builders*	*Commissioned*
NIREEKSHAK	A 15	Mazagon Docks, Bombay	8 June 1989

Displacement, tons: 3600 full load
Dimensions, feet (metres): 231.3 × 57.4 × 16.4 *(70.5 × 17.5 × 5)*
Main machinery: 2 Bergen KRM-8 diesels; 4410 hp(m) *(3.24 MW)* sustained; 2 shafts; cp props; 2 bow thrusters; 2 stern thrusters; 990 hp(m) *(727 kW)*
Speed, knots: 12
Complement: 63 (15 officers)

Comment: Laid down in August 1982 and launched January 1984. Acquired on three year lease with an option for purchase. The vessel was built for offshore support operations but has been modified for naval requirements. Two DSRV, capable of taking 12 men to 300 m, are carried together with two six-man recompression chambers and one three man bell. Kongsberg ADP-503 Mk II. Dynamic positioning system. The ship will be used for submarine SAR until the purpose-built ships are completed.

NIREEKSHAK *1991*

0 + 2 SUPPORT AND RESCUE SHIPS

Displacement, tons: 7000 full load
Dimensions, feet (metres): 334 × 298.6 × 28.5 *(101.8 × 91 × 8.7)*
Main machinery: Diesel-electric; 5 diesel generators; 11.6 MW; 2 motors; 1 shaft; cp prop; 2 bow thrusters; 4020 hp(m) *(2.95 MW)*; 2 stern thrusters; 4830 hp(m) *(3.5 MW)*
Speed, knots: 13. **Range, miles:** 19 500 at 12 kts
Complement: 84 (28 officers) plus 26 spare berths

Comment: Reported authorised in mid-1990 to a Rauma Repola design for delivery of the first in the mid-1990s. Kongsberg ADP 503 Mk II dynamic positioning system. One 120 ton crane. Two DSRVs for 12 men to 300 m. Helicopter platform forward. Two hospitals. One might be used by the Coast Guard as an SAR and pollution control ship.

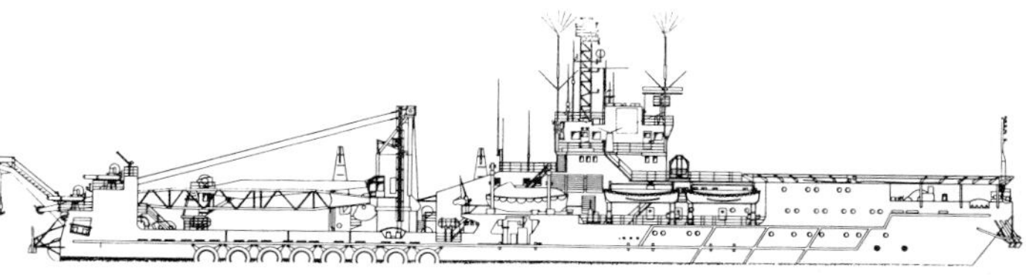

SUPPORT SHIP *1990, Mazagon Dock*

2 DEEPAK CLASS (REPLENISHMENT TANKERS)

Name	*No*	*Builders*	*Commissioned*
DEEPAK	A 50	Bremer-Vulkan	20 Nov 1967
SHAKTI	A 57	Bremer-Vulkan	31 Dec 1975

Displacement, tons: 6785 light; 15 828 full load
Measurement, tons: 12 013 gross
Dimensions, feet (metres): 552.4 × 75.5 × 30 *(168.4 × 23 × 9.2)*
Main machinery: 2 Babcock & Wilcox boilers; 1 BV/BBC steam turbine; 16 500 hp(m) *(12.13 MW)*; 1 shaft
Speed, knots: 18.5. **Range, miles:** 5500 at 16 kts
Complement: 169
Cargo capacity: 1280 tons diesel; 12 624 tons FFO; 1495 tons avcat; 812 tons FW
Guns: 4 Bofors 40 mm/60. 2 Oerlikon 20 mm.
Countermeasures: ESM: Telegon IV HF D/F.
Radars: Navigation: Decca Type 1006; I band.
Helicopters: 1 Chetak.

Comment: *Deepak* on charter to Indian Navy from Mogul Lines which paid for the construction when the Navy could not afford the expense. Automatic tensioning fitted to replenishment gear. Heavy and light jackstays. Stern fuelling as well as alongside. DG fitted.

SHAKTI *1991*

0 + 1 MODIFIED DEEPAK CLASS (REPLENISHMENT AND REPAIR SHIP)

Name	*No*	*Builders*	*Commissioned*
RAJABA GAN PALAN	—	Garden Reach, Calcutta	1993

Displacement, tons: 22 000 full load
Dimensions, feet (metres): 564.3 × 75.5 × 29.9 *(172 × 23 × 9.1)*
Main machinery: 2 diesels; 24 000 hp(m) *(17.6 MW)*; 1 shaft; bow thruster
Speed, knots: 20. **Range, miles:** 10 000 at 16 kts
Complement: 191 plus 6 spare berths
Cargo capacity: 14 200 cu m diesel and avcat; 2250 cu m water; 2170 cu m ammunition and stores
Guns: 3 Bofors 40 mm/60.
Helicopters: 1 Chetak.

Comment: Ordered in July 1987 to a Bremer-Vulkan design. Lengthened version of Deepak class but with a multi-purpose workshop. The bridge and accommodation superstructure are towards the stern, with the helicopter platform right aft. Fully air-conditioned. A second one may follow in due course.

2 POSHAK CLASS (SUPPORT TANKERS)

POSHAK **PURAN**

Displacement, tons: 600 full load
Dimensions, feet (metres): 119.1 × 24.9 × 7.9 *(36.3 × 7.6 × 2.4)*
Main machinery: 1 diesel; 225 hp(m) *(165 kW)*; 1 shaft
Speed, knots: 9
Cargo capacity: 200 tons

Comment: Built at Mazagon, Bombay. *Poshak* completed April 1982, and *Puran* in November 1988.

2 PRADHAYAK CLASS (SUPPORT TANKERS)

PRADHAYAK **PURAK**

Displacement, tons: 960 full load
Dimensions, feet (metres): 163 × 26.2 × 9.8 *(49.7 × 8 × 3)*
Main machinery: 1 diesel; 560 hp(m) *(412 kW)*; 1 shaft
Speed, knots: 9
Cargo capacity: 376 tons

Comment: Built at Rajabagan Yard, Calcutta. *Pradhayak* completed February 1978, *Purak* June 1977.

1 HOSPITAL SHIP

LAKSHADWEEP

Dimensions, feet (metres): 171 × 29.5 × 10.5 *(52 × 9 × 3.2)*
Main machinery: 2 diesels; 900 hp(m) *(661 kW)*; 2 shafts
Speed, knots: 12
Complement: 35 (including 16 medical)

Comment: Ordered from Hindok, Calcutta in 1980. Launched 28 August 1981. Has accommodation for 90 patients.

1 SAIL TRAINING SHIP

VARUNA

Displacement, tons: 105

Comment: Completed in April 1981 by Alcock-Ashdown, Bhavnagar. Can carry 26 cadets.

VARUNA *1/1988, van Ginderen Collection*

2 TUGS (OCEAN)

GAJ A 51 **MATANGA**

Displacement, tons: 1465 (*Gaj*); 1600 (*Matanga*) full load
Dimensions, feet (metres): 216.5 × 37.7 × 13.1 *(66 × 11.5 × 4) (Gaj)*
Main machinery: 2 GRSE/MAN G7V diesels; 3920 hp(m) *(2.88 MW)*; 2 shafts
Speed, knots: 15. **Range, miles:** 8000 at 12 kts.

Comment: Built by Garden Reach SY. *Gaj* completed September 1973, *Matanga* launched 29 October 1977. The largest tugs so far built in India with a bollard pull of 40 tons and capable of towing a 20 000 ton ship at 8 kts. *Matanga* is 3 m longer and 1 m broader.

1 TUG (COASTAL)

RAJAJI

Displacement, tons: 428
Dimensions, feet (metres): 100 × 31.3 × 12.5 *(30.5 × 9.5 × 3.8)*
Main machinery: 2 GRSE-MAN diesels; 2120 hp(m) *(1.56 MW)*; 2 shafts; Kort nozzles
Speed, knots: 12.5

Comment: Built by Garden Reach SY. Completed July 1982.

8 HARBOUR TUGS

AGARAL **ARJUN** **BALSHIL** **+ 5**

Comment: First three built by Mazagon DY, Bombay in 1973-74. Five more delivered in 1988-89.

3 WATER CARRIERS

AMBUDA **COCHIN** **+1**

Displacement, tons: 200
Dimensions, feet (metres): 108.3 × — × 8 *(32 × — × 2.4)*
Speed, knots: 9

Comment: First laid down Rajabagan Yard 18 January 1977. Second and third built at Mazagon Docks Ltd, Bombay.

3 TORPEDO RECOVERY VESSELS

A 71 **A 72** **ASTRAVAHINI**

Displacement, tons: 110
Dimensions, feet (metres): 93.5 × 20 × 4.6 *(28.5 × 6.1 × 1.4)*
Main machinery: 2 Kirloskar V12 diesels; 720 hp(m) *(529 kW)*; 2 shafts
Speed, knots: 11
Complement: 13

Comment: Details above apply only to *A 71* and *A 72*. First completed early 1980, second 1981 at Goa Shipyard. *Astravahini* completed in 1984 at Vishakapatnam.

TRV A72 *2/1989, G. Jacobs*

3 DIVING TENDERS

Displacement, tons: 36
Dimensions, feet (metres): 48.9 × 14.4 × 3.9 *(14.9 × 4.4 × 1.2)*
Main machinery: 2 diesels; 130 hp(m) *(96 kW)*; 2 shafts
Speed, knots: 12

Comment: Built at Cleback Yard. First completed 1979; second and third in 1984.

COAST GUARD

Administration

Director General:
Vice Admiral S W Lakhkar, NM, VSM
Deputy Director General:
Inspector General A K Sharma, NM, PTM

Personnel

1992: 5280 (660 officers)

General

An Interim Coast Guard Force started operations as a part of the Indian Navy on 1 February 1977. It was constituted as an independent paramilitary service on 19 August 1978 with the passing of the Coast Guard Act, 1978 by the Indian Parliament. It functions under the Ministry of Defence but with the budget met by the Department of Revenue.

Its responsibilities include:

(a) Ensuring the safety and protection of artificial islands, offshore terminals and other installations in the Maritime Zones.
(b) Measures for the safety of life and property at sea including assistance to mariners in distress.
(c) Measures to preserve and protect the marine environment and control marine pollution.
(d) Assisting the Customs and other authorities in anti-smuggling operations.
(e) Enforcing the provisions of enactments in force in the Maritime Zones.

Bases

The Headquarters of the Coast Guard is located in Delhi with Regional Headquarters in Bombay, Madras and Port Blair. District Headquarters established at Bombay, Haldia, Porbandar, Cochin, Vishakhapatnam, Campbell Bay and Diglipur. Stations at Vadinar, Mandapam and Ohma.

Coast Guard Air Squadron 800 with 3 Chetak helicopters was commissioned at Goa on 22 May 1982 and now has six helos. CGAS 700 at Calcutta with 2 F 27-200 aircraft. CGAS 744 at Madras commissioned 26 April 1991 with four Dornier 228 and two helicopters and expects to get six more Dorniers by 1996. A further 25 aircraft are planned.

Future plans

Future plans include the following total strength by 2000: 24 OPVs, six for each region and six for offshore oil platform protection; 36 IPVs for regional work; six Deep Sea Patrol Vessels for deep water surveillance; four specialised pollution control vessels; six medium range surveillance aircraft; 36 light surveillance aircraft; six twin engined helicopters for SAR and 30 light helicopters for shipborne operations.

9 VIKRAM CLASS (OFFSHORE PATROL VESSELS TYPE P 957)

Name	*No*	*Builders*	*Commissioned*
VIKRAM	33	Mazagon Dock, Bombay	20 Dec 1983
VIJAYA	34	Mazagon Dock, Bombay	12 Apr 1985
VEERA	35	Mazagon Dock, Bombay	3 May 1986
VARUNA	36	Mazagon Dock, Bombay	27 Feb 1988
VAJRA	37	Mazagon Dock, Bombay	22 Dec 1988
VIVEK	38	Mazagon Dock, Bombay	19 Aug 1989
VIGRAHA	39	Mazagon Dock, Bombay	12 Apr 1990
VARAD	40	Goa Shipyard	19 July 1990
VARAHA	41	Goa Shipyard	Mar 1992

Displacement, tons: 1224 full load
Dimensions, feet (metres): 243.1 × 37.4 × 10.5 *(74.1 × 11.4 × 3.2)*
Main machinery: 2 SEMT-Pielstick 16 PA6 280 diesels; 12 800 hp(m) *(9.41 MW)* sustained; 2 shafts; cp props
Speed, knots: 22. **Range, miles:** 4000 at 16 kts
Complement: 96 (11 officers)
Guns: 1 or 2 Bofors 40 mm/60. 2—7.62 mm MGs.
Fire control: Lynx optical sights.
Radars: Navigation: Two Decca 1226; I band.
Helicopters: 1 HAL (Aerospatiale) Chetak or 1 Sea King.

Comment: Owes something to a NEVESBU (Netherlands) design, being a stretched version of its 750 ton offshore patrol vessels. Ordered in 1979. Fin stabilisers. Diving equipment. 4.5 ton deck crane. External firefighting pumps. Has one GRP boat and two inflatable craft. Reported that this class is considered too small for its required task and the next class to be built is up to 1800 tons displacement.

VAJRA *12/1988, Indian Coast Guard*

8 + 3 JIJA BAI MOD I CLASS (INSHORE PATROL CRAFT)

TARA BAI 71
AHALYA BAI 72
LAKSHMI BAI 73
AKKA DEVI 74
NAIKI DEVI 75
GANGA DEVI 76
PRIYADARSINI 221
RAZIA SULTANA 222
ANNIE BESANT 223
KAMLA DEVI 224
AMRIT KAUR 225

Displacement, tons: 215 full load
Dimensions, feet (metres): 150.9 × 24.6 × 6.9 *(46 × 7.5 × 2.1)*
Main machinery: 2 MTU 12V 538 TB82 diesels; 5940 hp(m) *(4.37 MW)* sustained; 2 shafts
Speed, knots: 23. **Range, miles:** 2400 at 12 kts
Complement: 34 (7 officers)
Guns: 1 Bofors 40 mm/60. 2—7.62 mm MGs.
Radars: Surface search: Racal Decca 1226 or BEL 1245/6X; I band.

Comment: Two ordered in June 1986 from Singapore Shipbuilding and Engineering Ltd and built at Singapore to a Lürssen 45 design; completed May and July 1987. Four more laid down in 1987 at Garden Reach, Calcutta, first completed in April 1989, *Akka Devi* in September 1989, and the last two December 1989 and April 1990 respectively. A further batch of five are following on with *Priyadarsini* commissioned in January 1992 at Garden Reach, and the others at approximately six month intervals. This is a 'follow-on' class to the Type 956 and is known as the Jija Bai Mod I class.

TARA BAI *5/1987, Singapore SB & E Ltd*

0 + 3 SAMAR CLASS (OFFSHORE PATROL VESSELS)

Name	*No*	*Builders*	*Commissioned*
SAMAR	42	Goa Shipyard	1994
SANGRAM	43	Goa Shipyard	1995
SARANG	44	Goa Shipyard	1996

Comment: Ordered in 1991. With an 1800 ton displacement these will be the largest Coast Guard vessels built so far.

7 JIJA BAI CLASS (INSHORE PATROL CRAFT TYPE 956)

JIJA BAI 64
CHAND BIBI 65
KITTUR CHINNAMA 66
RANI JINDAN 67
HABBAKHATUN 68
RAMADEVI 69
AVVAYAR 70

Displacement, tons: 181 full load
Dimensions, feet (metres): 144.3 × 24.3 × 7.5 *(44 × 7.4 × 2.3)*
Main machinery: 2 MTU 12V 538 TB82 diesels; 5940 hp(m) *(4.37 MW)* sustained; 2 shafts
Speed, knots: 25. **Range, miles:** 2375 at 14 kts
Complement: 34 (7 officers)
Guns: 1 Bofors 40 mm/60. 2—7.62 mm MGs.
Radars: Surface search: Racal Decca 1226; I band.

Comment: The first three were completed by Sumidagawa and subsequent four craft built at Garden Reach, Calcutta. First of class commissioned 20 June 1983 and the last on 19 October 1985.

AVVAYAR *1985, Indian Coast Guard*

0 + 10 INSHORE PATROL CRAFT

Displacement, tons: 49 full load
Dimensions, feet (metres): 68.2 × 19 × 4.9 *(20.8 × 5.8 × 1.5)*
Main machinery: 2 MWM TBD 234 V12 diesels; 1644 hp(m) *(1.21 MW)*; 1 MWM TBD 234 V8 diesel; 550 hp(m) *(404 kW)*; 3 waterjets
Speed, knots: 25. **Range, miles:** 600 at 15 kts
Complement: 10 (4 officers)
Guns: 1 Oerlikon 20 mm. 1—7.62 mm MG.
Radars: Navigation: I band.

Comment: Ordered from Anderson Marine, Goa in September 1990 to a P-2000 design. GRP hull. First one should be delivered by the end of 1992. Official description is 'Interceptor Boats'.

8 INSHORE PATROL CRAFT

C 01-08

Displacement, tons: 32 full load
Dimensions, feet (metres): 65.6 × 15.4 × 5 *(20 × 4.7 × 1.5)*
Main machinery: 2 Detroit 12V-71TA diesels; 840 hp *(627 kW)* sustained; 2 shafts
Speed, knots: 20. **Range, miles:** 400 at 20 kts
Complement: 8
Guns: 1—7.62 mm MG.
Radars: Navigation: I band.

Comment: Built by Swallow Craft Co, Pusan, South Korea. Six commissioned 24 September 1980, and two on 22 May 1982 having been taken over from India Oil Corporation.

SOUTH KOREAN TYPE *1983, Indian Coast Guard*

5 SDB Mk 2 RAJ CLASS (INSHORE PATROL CRAFT)

RAJHANS 56 **RAJKIRAN** 59 **RAJKAMAL** 61
RAJTARANG 57 **RAJSHREE** 60

Displacement, tons: 203 full load
Dimensions, feet (metres): 123 × 24.6 × 5.9 *(37.5 × 7.5 × 1.8)*
Main machinery: 2 Paxman Deltic 18-42K diesels; 6240 hp *(4.66 MW)*; 2 shafts. Auxiliary propulsion; 1 Kirloska-Cummins diesel; 165 hp *(123 kW)*
Speed, knots: 29; 4 auxiliary. **Range, miles:** 1400 at 14 kts
Complement: 28
Guns: 2 Bofors 40 mm/60.

Comment: Built by Garden Reach SY, Calcutta. Commissioned—*Rajhans*, 23 December 1980; *Rajtarang*, 25 November 1981; *Rajkiran* March 1984; *Rajshree* September 1984 and *Rajkamal* September 1986. All other previously reported vessels of this class belong to the Navy.

RAJKAMAL *1989, Indian Coast Guard*

INDONESIA

Administration

Chief of the Naval Staff:
Vice Admiral Mohammad Arifin
Deputy Chief of the Naval Staff (Operations):
Rear Admiral Soemartono
Deputy Chief of the Naval Staff (Logistics):
Rear Admiral Nyoman Suharta
Deputy Chief of the Naval Staff (Personnel):
Rear Admiral Ketut Wiresata
Inspector General of the Navy:
Major General Aminullah Ibrahim

Fleet Command

Commander-in-Chief Western Fleet (Barat):
Rear Admiral Yusuf Effendi
Commander-in-Chief Eastern Fleet (Timur):
Rear Admiral Tanto Kuswanto
Commandant of Navy Marine Corps:
Major General Baroto Sardadi
Commander Military Sealift Command:
Rear Admiral Oentoeng Sarwono

Diplomatic Representation

Naval Attaché in London:
Colonel Kav Johnny P Mandas

Personnel

(a) 1992: 41 000 including 12 000 Marine Commando Corps and 1000 Naval Air Arm
(b) Selective national service

Bases

Tanjung Priok (Jakarta), Ujung (Surabaya), Sabang, Medan (Sumatra), Makasar (Celebes), Balikpapan (East Borneo), Biak (New Guinea), Tanjung Pinang, Manado (Celebes), Teluk Ratai (South Sumatra). Naval Air Arm at Ujung, Biak and Pekan Baru. Ujung (Surabaya) is concerned with building, particularly naval patrol craft, and is the main naval dockyard as well as housing Eastern Command. New base to be built at Teluk Ratai in Lampung.

Command Structure

Eastern Command (Surabaya)
Western Command (Teluk Ratai)
Training Command
Military Sea Communications Command (Maritime Security Agency)
Military Sealift Command (Logistic Support)

Strength of the Fleet

Type	*Active (Reserve)*	*Building (Projected)*
Patrol Submarines	2	(2)
Frigates	17	(19)
Fast Attack Craft—Missile	4	—
Large Patrol Craft	18	1
Coastal Patrol Craft	18	—
Hydrofoils	5	6
LSTs	14	—
LCM/LCU	45+	—
MCMV	4	(10)
Survey Ships	6	—
Submarine Tender	1	—
Repair Ship	1	—
Replenishment Tanker	1	—
Harbour Tankers	2	—
Transports	2	—
Cable Ship	1	—
Tugs	4	—
Sail Training Ship	1	—

Future Plans

Indonesia, now having nine shipbuilding yards, is in a position to build its own ships up to frigate standard. Tenders were called for from 13 firms for design for 2300/2800 ton frigates, details to be submitted in 1989. In 1990 no decision was taken although talks continued with European shipyards and Chinese Type 25T of the sort building for Thailand were also discussed. The latest plan in early 1992 is reported as having scaled the requirement down to 19 corvettes of German design, the first to be built in the successful designer's yard, the remainder at P T Pal, Surabaya over the next 30 years. Frigate requirements may be met either from China or by buying more second hand from the Netherlands. There is also an intention to acquire at least two more submarines by 1995.

Prefix to Ships' Names

KRI (Kapal di Republik Indonesia)

Mercantile Marine

Lloyd's Register of Shipping:
1991 vessels of 2 336 880 tons gross

DELETIONS

Submarines

1990 *Pasopati*

Light Forces

1989 *Hiu* (target)

Survey Ship

1990 *Bimasakti* (civilian)

Auxiliaries

1990 *Ratulangi*

PENNANT LIST

Submarines

401 Cakra
402 Nanggala

Frigates

331 Martha Kristina Tiyahahu
332 W Zakarias Yohannes
333 Hasanuddin
341 Samadikun
342 Martadinata
343 Monginsidi
344 Ngurah Rai
351 Ahmed Yani
352 Slamet Riyadi
353 Yos Sudarso
354 Oswald Siahann
355 Abdul Halim Perdana Kusuma
356 Karel Satsiutubun
361 Fatahillah
362 Malahayati
363 Nala
364 Hajar Dewantara

Light Forces

621 Mandau
622 Rencong
623 Badik
624 Keris
651 Singa
653 Ajak
801 Pandbong
802 Sura
811 Kakap
812 Kerapu
813 Tongkol
814 Bervang
819 Lajang
822 Dorang
823 Todak
829 Tohok
830 Sembilang
847 Sibarau
848 Siliman
851 Samadar
852 Sasila
853 Sabola
854 Sawangi
855 Sadarin
856 Salmaneti
857 Sigalu
858 Silea
859 Siribua
862 Siada
863 Sikuda
864 Sigurot

Amphibious Forces

501 Teluk Langsa
502 Teluk Bajur
503 Teluk Amboina
504 Teluk Kau
508 Teluk Tomini
509 Teluk Ratai
510 Teluk Saleh
511 Teluk Bone
512 Teluk Semangka
513 Teluk Penju
514 Teluk Mandar
515 Teluk Sampit
516 Teluk Banten
517 Teluk Ende
580 Dore
581 Amurang
582 Kupang
583 Dili
584 Nusantara

Mine Warfare Forces

701 Pulau Rani
702 Pulau Retewo
711 Pulau Rengat
712 Pulau Rupat

Support Ship

561 Multatuli

Service Forces

901 Balikpapan
909 Pakan Baru
911 Sorong
921 Jaya Wijaya
922 Rakata
934 Lampo Batang
935 Tambora
936 Bromo
951 Talaud
952 Nusa Telu
953 Natuna
956 Teluk Mentawai
957 Karimundsa
960 Karimata
971 Tangung Pandan
972 Tangung Oisina

Survey Ships

931 Burujulasad
932 Dewa Kembar
933 Jalanidhi

SUBMARINES

2 TYPE 209 CLASS (1300 TYPE)

Name	*No*	*Builders*	*Laid down*	*Launched*	*Commissioned*
CAKRA	401	Howaldtswerke, Kiel	25 Nov 1977	10 Sep 1980	19 Mar 1981
NANGGALA	402	Howaldtswerke, Kiel	14 Mar 1978	10 Sep 1980	6 July 1981

Displacement, tons: 1285 surfaced; 1390 dived
Dimensions, feet (metres): 195.2 × 20.3 × 17.9 *(59.5 × 6.2 × 5.4)*
Main machinery: Diesel-electric; 4 MTU 12V 493 AZ80 GA31L diesels; 2400 hp(m) *(1.76 MW)* sustained; 4 Siemens alternators; 1.7 MW; 1 Siemens motor; 4600 hp(m) *(3.38 MW)* sustained; 1 shaft
Speed, knots: 11 surfaced; 21.5 dived
Range, miles: 8200 at 8 kts
Complement: 34 (6 officers)

Torpedoes: 8—21 in *(533 mm)* bow tubes. 14 AEG SUT; dual purpose; wire-guided; active/passive homing to 12 km *(6.5 nm)* at 35 kts; 28 km *(15 nm)* at 23 kts; warhead 250 kg.
Fire control: Signaal Sinbad system.
Radars: Surface search: Thomson-CSF Calypso; I band.
Sonars: Krupp Atlas CSU 3-2; active/passive search and attack; medium frequency.
PRS-3/4; (integral with CSU) passive ranging.

Programmes: First pair ordered on 2 April 1977. Designed by Ingenieurkontor, Lübeck for construction by Howaldtswerke, Kiel and sale by Ferrostaal, Essen—all acting as a consortium. Orders for two more planned but now abandoned as the design is said to be out of date.
Modernisation: Major refits at HDW spanning three years from 1986 to 1989. These refits were expensive, and lengthy, and may have discouraged further orders until they were completed.
Structure: Have high capacity batteries with GRP lead-acid cells and battery cooling supplied by Wilhelm Hagen AG. Diving depth, 240 m *(790 ft)*.
Operational: Endurance, 50 days.

NANGGALA — *9/1991, 92 Wing RAAF*

FRIGATES

Note: See comment under *Future Plans* at the beginning of the section.

3 FATAHILLAH CLASS

Name	*No*	*Builders*	*Laid down*	*Launched*	*Commissioned*
FATAHILLAH	361	Wilton Fijenoord, Schiedam	31 Jan 1977	22 Dec 1977	16 July 1979
MALAHAYATI	362	Wilton Fijenoord, Schiedam	28 July 1977	19 June 1978	21 Mar 1980
NALA	363	Wilton Fijenoord, Schiedam	27 Jan 1978	11 Jan 1979	4 Aug 1980

Displacement, tons: 1200 standard; 1450 full load
Dimensions, feet (metres): 276 × 36.4 × 10.7 *(84 × 11.1 × 3.3)*
Main machinery: CODOG; 1 RR Olympus TM3B gas turbine; 21 500 hp *(16 MW)* sustained; 2 MTU 20V 956 TB 92 diesels; 11 070 hp(m) *(8.14 MW)* sustained; 2 shafts; LIPS cp props
Speed, knots: 30. **Range, miles:** 4250 at 16 kts
Complement: 89 (11 officers)

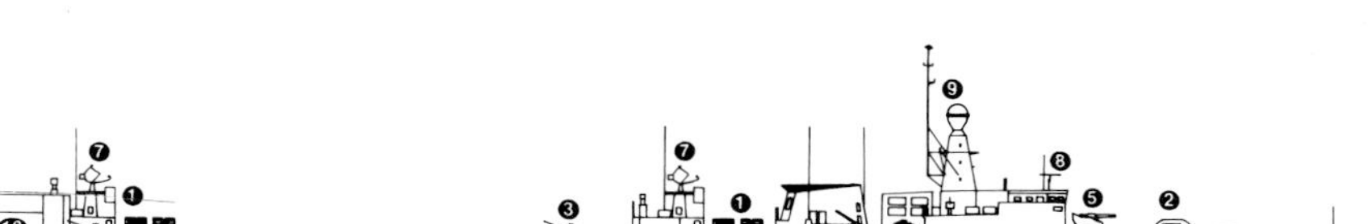
NALA   FATAHILLAH — *(Scale 1 : 1 200), Ian Sturton*

Missiles: SSM: 4 Aerospatiale MM 38 Exocet ❶; inertial cruise; active radar homing to 42 km *(23 nm)* at 0.9 Mach; warhead 165 kg; sea-skimmer.
Guns: 1 Bofors 4.7 in *(120 mm)*/46 ❷; 80° elevation; 80 rounds/minute to 18.5 km *(10 nm)*; weight of shell 21 kg.
1 or 2 Bofors 40 mm/70 (2 in *Nala*) ❸; 90° elevation; 300 rounds/minute to 12 km *(6.6 nm)*; weight of shell 0.96 kg.
2 Rheinmetall 20 mm; 55° elevation; 1000 rounds/minute to 2 km anti-aircraft; weight of shell 0.24 kg.
Torpedoes: 6—324 mm Mk 32 or ILAS 3 (2 triple) tubes (none in *Nala*) ❹. 12 Mk 46 (or A244S); anti-submarine; active/passive homing to 11 km *(5.9 nm)* at 40 kts; warhead 44 kg.
A/S mortars: 1 Bofors 375 mm twin-barrelled trainable ❺; 54 Erika; range 1600 m and Nelli; range 3600 m.
Countermeasures: Decoys: 2 Knebworth Corvus 8-tubed trainable Chaff launchers ❻; radar distraction or centroid modes to 1 km. 1 T-Mk 6; torpedo decoy.
ESM: MEL Susie 1; radar intercept.
Combat data systems: Signaal SEWACO-RI action data automation.
Fire control: GFCS has Signaal LIROD laser/TV directors.
Radars: Air/surface search: Signaal DA 05 ❼; E/F band; range 137 km *(75 nm)* for 2 m² target.
Surface search: Racal Decca AC 1229 ❽; I band.
Fire control: Signaal WM 28 ❾; I/J band; range 46 km *(25 nm)*.
Sonars: Signaal PHS 32; hull-mounted; active search and attack; medium frequency.

Helicopters: 1 Westland Wasp (*Nala* only) ❿.

Programmes: Ordered August 1975. Officially rated as Corvettes.
Structure: NEVESBU design. *Nala* is fitted with a folding hangar/landing deck.

FATAHILLAH — *9/1991, 92 Wing RAAF*

6 Ex-NETHERLANDS VAN SPEIJK CLASS

Name	*No*	*Builders*	*Laid down*	*Launched*	*Commissioned*
AHMED YANI (ex-*Tjerk Hiddes*)	351	Nederlandse Dok en Scheepsbouw Mij, Amsterdam	1 June 1964	17 Dec 1965	16 Aug 1967
SLAMET RIYADI (ex-*Van Speijk*)	352	Nederlandse Dok en Scheepsbouw Mij, Amsterdam	1 Oct 1963	5 Mar 1965	14 Feb 1967
YOS SUDARSO (ex-*Van Galen*)	353	Koninklijke Maatschappij de Schelde, Flushing	25 July 1963	19 June 1965	1 Mar 1967
OSWALD SIAHANN (ex-*Van Nes*)	354	Koninklijke Maatschappij de Schelde, Flushing	25 July 1963	26 Mar 1966	9 Aug 1967
ABDUL HALIM PERDANA KUSUMA (ex-*Evertsen*)	355	Koninklijke Maatschappij de Schelde, Flushing	6 July 1965	18 June 1966	21 Dec 1967
KAREL SATSUITUBUN (ex-*Isaac Sweers*)	356	Nederlandse Dok en Scheepsbouw Mij, Amsterdam	5 May 1965	10 Mar 1967	15 May 1968

Displacement, tons: 2225 standard; 2835 full load
Dimensions, feet (metres): 372 × 41 × 13.8 *(113.4 × 12.5 × 4.2)*
Main machinery: 2 Babcock & Wilcox boilers; 550 psi *(38.7 kg/cm sq)*; 850°F *(450°C)*; 2 Werkspoor/English Electric turbines; 30 000 hp *(22.4 MW)*; 2 shafts
Speed, knots: 28.5. **Range, miles:** 4500 at 12 kts
Complement: 180

Missiles: SSM: 8 McDonnell Douglas Harpoon ❶; active radar homing to 130 km *(70 nm)* at 0.9 Mach; warhead 227 kg.
SAM: 2 Short Bros Seacat quad launchers ❷; optical/radar guidance to 5 km *(2.7 nm)*; warhead 10 kg.
Guns: 1 OTO Melara 3 in *(76 mm)*/62 compact ❸; 85° elevation; 85 rounds/minute to 16 km *(8.7 nm)* anti-surface; 12 km *(6.6 nm)* anti-aircraft; weight of shell 6 kg.
Torpedoes: 6—324 mm Mk 32 (2 triple) tubes ❹. Honeywell Mk 46; anti-submarine; active/passive homing to 11 km *(5.9 nm)* at 40 kts; warhead 44 kg.
Countermeasures: Decoys: 2 Knebworth Corvus 8-tubed trainable; radar distraction or centroid Chaff to 1 km.
ESM: UA 8/9; UA 13 (355 and 356); radar warning. FH5 D/F.
Combat data systems: SEWACO V action data automation and Daisy data processing.
Fire control: Signaal LIROD optronic director.
Radars: Air search: Signaal LW 03 ❺; D band; range 219 km *(120 nm)* for 2 m² target.
Air/surface search: Signaal DA 05 ❻; E/F band; range 137 km *(75 nm)* for 2 m² target.
Navigation: Racal Decca 1229; I band.
Fire control: Signaal M 45 ❼; I/J band (for 76 mm gun).
2 Signaal M 44 ❽; I/J band (for Seacat).
Sonars: Signaal CWE 610; hull-mounted; active search and attack; medium frequency. VDS; medium frequency.

Helicopters: 1 Westland Wasp ❾.

Programmes: On 11 February 1986 agreement signed for transfer of two of this class with an option on two more *(Van Galen, Van Nes)*. Transfer dates:—*Tjerk Hiddes*, 31 October 1986; *Van Speijk*, 1 November 1986; *Van Galen*, 2 November 1987; *Van Nes*, 31 October 1988. Contract of sale for the last two of the class signed 13 May 1989. *Evertsen* transferred 1 November 1989 and *Isaac Sweers* 1 November 1990. Ships provided with all spare parts but not towed arrays or helicopters.
Modernisation: This class underwent mid-life modernisation at Rykswerf Den Helder from 1976. This included replacement of 4.5 in turret by 76 mm, A/S mortar by torpedo tubes, new electronics and electrics, updating combat data system, improved communications, extensive automation with reduction in complement, enlarged hangar for Lynx and improved habitability. Update on transfer included LIROD optronic director. Harpoon for first two only initially because there was no FMS funding for the others. However the USN then provided sufficient SWG 1A panels for all of the class to be retrofitted again with Harpoon missiles.

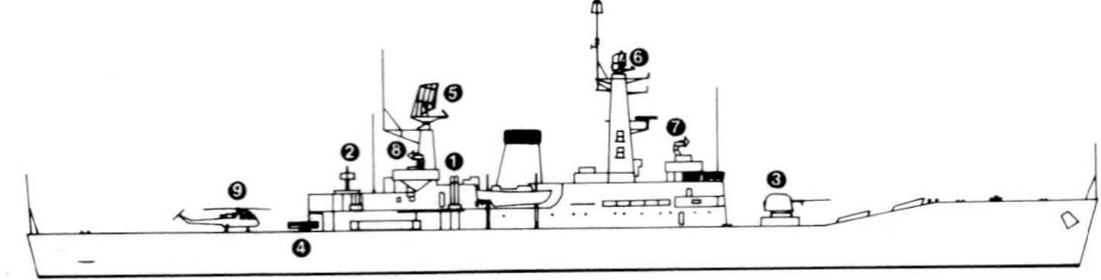

AHMED YANI *(Scale 1 : 1 200), Ian Sturton*

YOS SUDARSO *10/1991, 92 Wing RAAF*

AHMED YANI *8/1991, L. P. Duane, RAN*

3 Ex-BRITISH TRIBAL CLASS

Name	No	Builders	Laid down	Launched	Commissioned
MARTHA KRISTINA TIYAHAHU (ex-HMS *Zulu*)	331	Alex Stephen & Sons Ltd, Govan	13 Dec 1960	3 July 1962	17 Apr 1964
WILHELMUS ZAKARIAS YOHANNES (ex-HMS *Gurkha*)	332	J I Thornycroft Ltd, Woolston	3 Nov 1958	11 July 1960	13 Feb 1963
HASANUDDIN (ex-HMS *Tartar*)	333	HM Dockyard, Devonport	22 Oct 1959	19 Sep 1960	26 Feb 1962

Displacement, tons: 2300 standard; 2700 full load
Dimensions, feet (metres): 350 wl; 360 oa × 42.5 × 18 (screws), 12.5 (keel) *(106.7; 109.7 × 13 × 5.5, 3.8)*
Main machinery: COSAG; 1 Babcock & Wilcox boiler; 550 psi *(38.7 kg/cm sq)*; 850°F *(450°C)*; 1 Parsons Metrovick turbine; 12 500 hp *(9.3 MW)*; 2 Yarrow/AEI G-6 gas turbines; 7500 hp *(5.6 MW)*; 1 shaft; cp prop
Speed, knots: 25; 17 gas turbines. **Range, miles:** 5400 at 12 kts
Complement: 250 (19 officers)

Missiles: SAM: 2 Short Bros Seacat quad launchers ❶; optical/radar guidance to 5 km *(2.7 nm)*; warhead 10 kg.
Guns: 2 Vickers 4.5 in *(114 mm)* ❷; 50° elevation; 14 rounds/minute to 17 km *(9.3 nm)*; weight of shell 25 kg.
2 Oerlikon 20 mm ❸; 55° elevation; 800 rounds/minute to 2 km anti-aircraft.
2—12.7 mm MGs.
A/S mortars: 1 Limbo 3-tubed Mk 10 ❹; range 1000 m; warhead 92 kg.
Countermeasures: Decoys: 2 Knebworth Corvus 8-tubed Chaff launchers; distraction or centroid modes to 1 km.
ESM: Radar warning.
Fire control: MRS 3 (for guns). 2 GWS 21 ❽ optical directors (for SAM).
Radars: Air search: Marconi Type 965 ❺; A band.
Surface search: Type 993 ❻; E/F band.
Navigation: Decca 978; I band.
Fire control: Plessey Type 903 ❼; I band (for guns).
Sonars: Graseby Type 177; hull-mounted; active search; 7-9 kHz.
Graseby Type 170 B; hull-mounted; active attack; 15 kHz.
Kelvin Hughes Type 162; classification; 50 kHz.

Helicopters: 1 Westland Wasp ❾.

Programmes: Refitted by Vosper Thornycroft Ltd. 331 commissioned in Indonesian Navy on 2 May 1985, 332 on 16 October 1985 and 333 on 3 April 1986.
Structure: Helicopter descends by flight deck lift and is covered by portable panels. MGs fitted just aft of the GWS 21 directors.

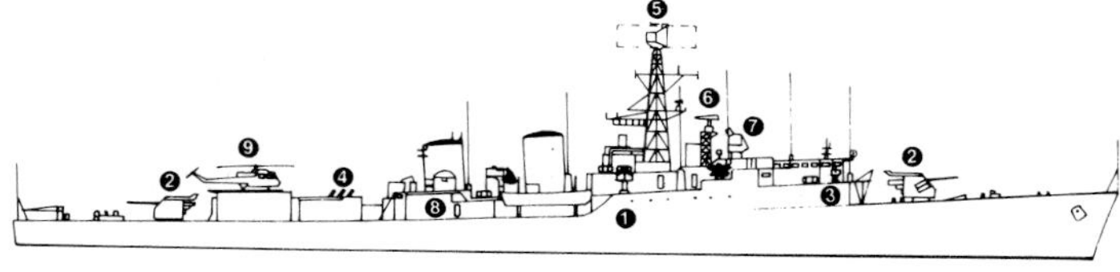

HASANUDDIN *(Scale 1 : 1 200), Ian Sturton*

WILHELMUS ZAKARIAS YOHANNES *7/1991, 92 Wing RAAF*

4 Ex-US CLAUD JONES CLASS

Name	No	Builders	Laid down	Launched	Commissioned
SAMADIKUN (ex-USS *John R Perry* DE 1034)	341	Avondale Marine Ways	1 Oct 1957	29 July 1958	5 May 1959
MARTADINATA (ex-USS *Charles Berry* DE 1035)	342	American S B Co, Toledo, Ohio	29 Oct 1958	17 Mar 1959	25 Nov 1959
MONGINSIDI (ex-USS *Claud Jones* DE 1033)	343	Avondale Marine Ways	1 June 1957	27 May 1958	10 Feb 1959
NGURAH RAI (ex-USS *McMorris* DE 1036)	344	American S B Co, Toledo, Ohio	5 Nov 1958	26 May 1959	4 Mar 1960

Displacement, tons: 1720 standard; 1968 full load
Dimensions, feet (metres): 310 × 38.7 × 18 *(95 × 11.8 × 5.5)*
Main machinery: 2 Fairbanks-Morse 38ND 8-1/8-12 diesels (or 2 GM 16V 71 in 343); 7000 hp *(5.2 MW)* sustained; 1 shaft
Speed, knots: 22. **Range, miles:** 3000 at 18 kts
Complement: 171 (12 officers)

Guns: 1 US 3 in *(76 mm)*/50 Mk 34 ❶; 85° elevation; 50 rounds/minute to 12.8 km *(7 nm)*; weight of shell 6 kg.
2 USSR 37 mm/63 (twin) ❷; 80° elevation; 160 rounds/minute to 9 km *(5 nm)*; weight of shell 0.7 kg.
2 USSR 25 mm/80 (twin) ❸; 85° elevation; 270 rounds/minute to 3 km *(1.6 nm)*; weight of shell 0.34 kg.
Torpedoes: 6—324 mm Mk 32 (2 triple) tubes ❹. Probably fires Honeywell Mk 46; anti-submarine; active/passive homing to 11 km *(5.9 nm)* at 40 kts; warhead 44 kg.
A/S mortars: 2 Hedgehog 24-tubed launchers ❺; range 350 m; warhead 26 kg.
Countermeasures: ESM: WLR-1C (except *Samadikun*); radar warning.
Fire control: Mk 70 for guns. Mk 105 for A/S weapons.
Radars: Air search: Westinghouse SPS 6E ❻; D band; range 146 km *(80 nm)* (for fighter).
Surface search: Raytheon SPS 5D ❼; G/H band; range 37 km *(20 nm)*.
Raytheon SPS 4 *(Ngurah Rai)*; G/H band.
Navigation: Racal Decca 1226; I band.
Fire control: Lockheed SPG 52 ❽; K band.
Sonars: EDO *(Samadikun)*; SQS 45V *(Martadinata)*; SQS 39V *(Monginsidi)*; SQS 42V *(Ngurah Rai)*; hull-mounted; active search and attack; medium/high frequency.

Programmes: *Samadikun* transferred 20 February 1973; *Martadinata*, 31 January 1974; *Monginsidi* and *Ngurah Rai*, 16 December 1974. All refitted at Subic Bay 1979-82.
Operational: Replaced by Van Speijk class and all are reported to be in reserve in 1992.

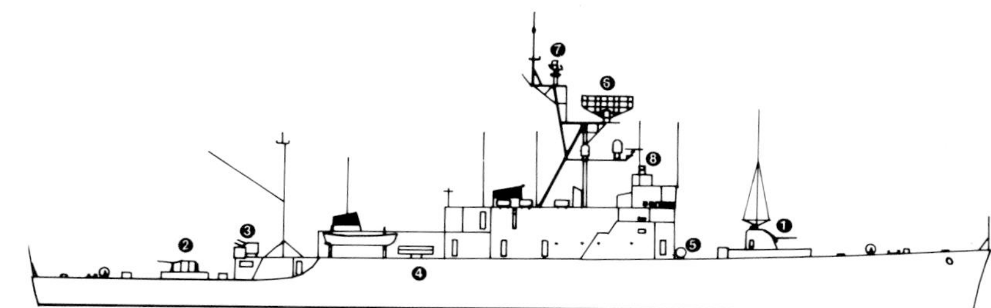

MARTADINATA *(Scale 1 : 900), Ian Sturton*

MARTADINATA *6/1989, 92 Wing RAAF*

1 HAJAR DEWANTARA CLASS

Name	*No*	*Builders*	*Laid down*	*Launched*	*Commissioned*
HAJAR DEWANTARA	364	Split SY, Yugoslavia	11 May 1979	11 Oct 1980	31 Oct 1981

Displacement, tons: 1850 full load
Dimensions, feet (metres): 317.3 × 36.7 × 15.7 *(96.7 × 11.2 × 4.8)*
Main machinery: CODOG; 1 RR Olympus TM3B gas turbine; 21 500 hp *(16 MW)* sustained; 2 MTU 16V 956 TB 92 diesels; 11 070 hp(m) *(8.14 MW)* sustained; 2 shafts; cp props
Speed, knots: 26 gas; 20 diesels. **Range, miles:** 4000 at 18 kts; 1150 at 25 kts
Complement: 191 (11 officers) including 14 instructors and 100 cadets

Missiles: SSM: 4 Aerospatiale MM 38 Exocet; inertial cruise; active radar homing to 42 km *(23 nm)* at 0.9 Mach; warhead 165 kg; sea-skimmer.
Guns: 1 Bofors 57 mm/70; 75° elevation; 200 rounds/minute to 17 km *(9.3 nm)*; weight of shell 2.4 kg.
4 Rheinmetall 20 mm (2 twin); anti-aircraft.
Torpedoes: 2—21 in *(533 mm)* tubes. AEG SUT; dual purpose; wire-guided; active/passive homing to 28 km *(15 nm)* at 23 kts; 12 km *(6.5 nm)* at 35 kts; warhead 250 kg.
Depth charges: 1 projector/mortar.
Countermeasures: Decoys: 2—128 mm twin-tubed flare launchers.
ESM: Susie; radar intercept.
Fire control: Signaal SEWACO-RI action data automation.
Radars: Surface search: Racal Decca 1229; I band.
Fire control: Signaal WM 28; I/J band; range 46 km *(25 nm)*.
Sonars: Signaal PHS 32; hull-mounted; active search and attack; medium frequency.

Helicopters: Platform for 1 NBO 105 helicopter.

Programmes: First ordered 14 March 1978 from Split SY, Yugoslavia where the hull was built and engines fitted. Armament and electronics fitted in the Netherlands and Indonesia. Near sister to Iraqi *Ibn Khaldoum*. Second reported ordered in 1983 but was cancelled.
Structure: Two LCVPs on davits either side of the funnel.
Operational: Used for training and troop transport. War roles include escort, ASW and troop transport. This ship is rarely seen outside the Indonesian archipelago.

HAJAR DEWANTARA *1982*

SHIPBORNE AIRCRAFT

Numbers/Type: 2 Aerospatiale SA 316B Alouette III.
Operational speed: 113 kts *(210 km/h)*.
Service ceiling: 10 500 ft *(3200 m)*.
Range: 290 nm *(540 km)*.
Role/Weapon systems: Embarked for support duties. Sensors: None. Weapons: Unarmed.

Numbers/Type: 4 Bell 47J.
Operational speed: 74 kts *(137 km/h)*.
Service ceiling: 13 200 ft *(4025 m)*.
Range: 261 nm *(483 km)*.
Role/Weapon systems: Embarked for survey ship liaison duties. Sensors: None. Weapons: Unarmed.

Numbers/Type: 30 Nurtanio (Aerospatiale) NAS-332 Super Puma.
Operational speed: 151 kts *(279 km/h)*.
Service ceiling: 15 090 ft *(4600 m)*.
Range: 335 nm *(620 km)*.
Role/Weapon systems: ASW and assault operations with secondary role in utility and SAR; ASVW development possible with Exocet or similar. Sensors: Thomson-CSF Omera radar and Alcatel dipping sonar in some. Weapons: ASW; 2 × Mk 46 torpedoes or depth bombs. ASV; planned for future.

Numbers/Type: 6 Nurtanio (MBB) NBO 105C.
Operational speed: 113 kts *(210 km/h)*.
Service ceiling: 9845 ft *(3000 m)*.
Range: 407 nm *(754 km)*.
Role/Weapon systems: Embarked for liaison and support duties. Numbers are increasing slowly. Sensors: None. Weapons: Unarmed.

NBO 105C *11/1990*

Numbers/Type: 14 Westland Wasp (HAS Mk 1).
Operational speed: 96 kts *(177 km/h)*.
Service ceiling: 12 200 ft *(3720 m)*.
Range: 263 nm *(488 km)*.
Role/Weapon systems: Shipborne ASW helicopter weapons carrier and reconnaissance; SAR and utility as secondary roles. Preferred replacement is Westland Navy Lynx. Sensors: None. Weapons: ASW; 2 × Mk 44 or 1 × Mk 46 torpedoes, depth bombs or mines.

LAND-BASED MARITIME AIRCRAFT (FRONT LINE)

Numbers/Type: 3 Boeing 737-200 Surveiller.
Operational speed: 462 kts *(856 km/h)*.
Service ceiling: 50 000 ft *(15 240 m)*.
Range: 2530 nm *(4688 km)*.
Role/Weapon systems: Land-based for long-range maritime surveillance roles. Sensors upgraded in 1991 to include IFF. Sensors: 2 × Motorola APS-135(v) SLAM MR radars, various specialist radars. Weapons: Unarmed.

Numbers/Type: 12/6 GAF Searchmaster B/L.
Operational speed: 168 kts *(311 km/h)*.
Service ceiling: 21 000 ft *(6400 m)*.
Range: 730 nm *(1352 km)*.
Role/Weapon systems: Short-range maritime patrol, EEZ protection and anti-smuggler duties. Nomad type built in Australia. Sensors: Nose-mounted search radar. Weapons: Unarmed.

Numbers/Type: 4 Grumman HU-16B Albatross.
Operational speed: 205 kts *(379 km/h)*.
Service ceiling: 21 000 ft *(6400 m)*.
Range: 2850 nm *(3280 km)*.
Role/Weapon systems: Peacetime role as SAR amphibian; in wartime could operate for ASW, surface search and combat rescue tasks. Sensors: Search radar. Weapons: Generally unarmed but can carry depth bombs or 'iron' bombs.

Numbers/Type: 1 Lockheed C-130H-MP Hercules.
Operational speed: 325 kts *(602 km/h)*.
Service ceiling: 33 000 ft *(10 060 m)*.
Range: 4250 nm *(7876 km)*.
Role/Weapon systems: Long-range maritime reconnaissance role; two extra on order. Sensors: Search/weather radar. Weapons: Unarmed.

Numbers/Type: 16 Northrop F-5E Tiger II.
Operational speed: 940 kts *(1740 km/h)*.
Service ceiling: 51 800 ft *(15 790 m)*.
Range: 300 nm *(556 km)*.
Role/Weapon systems: Fleet air defence and strike fighter, formed 'naval co-operation unit'. Sensors: AI radar. Weapons: AD; 2 × AIM-9 Sidewinder, 2 × 20 mm cannon. Strike; 3175 tons of underwater stores.

Numbers/Type: 6 CASA/Nurtanio CN-235 MPA
Operational speed: 240 kts *(445 km/h)*.
Service ceiling: 26 600 ft *(8110 m)*.
Range: 669 nm *(1240 km)*.
Role/Weapon systems: Medium-range maritime reconnaissance role; 12 transport variants also in service. Sensors: Search/weather radar. Weapons: ASV; may have ASMs.

LIGHT FORCES

Note: It is reported that two ex-Soviet Kronshtadt class patrol craft (*Tohok* 829 and *Sembilang* 830) were resurrected in 1988 and still in service in 1990. Two patrol craft similar to the Attack class and with pennant numbers 860 and 861 have also been reported.

4 DAGGER CLASS (FAST ATTACK CRAFT—MISSILE)

Name	*No*	*Builders*	*Commissioned*
MANDAU	621	Korea Tacoma, Masan	20 July 1979
RENCONG	622	Korea Tacoma, Masan	20 July 1979
BADIK	623	Korea Tacoma, Masan	Feb 1980
KERIS	624	Korea Tacoma, Masan	Feb 1980

Displacement, tons: 270 full load
Dimensions, feet (metres): 164.7 × 23.9 × 7.5 *(50.2 × 7.3 × 2.3)*
Main machinery: CODOG; 1 GE LM 2500 gas turbine; 23 000 hp *(17.16 MW)* sustained; 2 MTU 12V 331 TC81 diesels; 2240 hp(m) *(1.65 MW)* sustained; 2 shafts; cp props
Speed, knots: 41 gas; 17 diesel. **Range, miles:** 2000 at 17 kts
Complement: 43 (7 officers)

Missiles: SSM: 4 Aerospatiale MM 38 Exocet; inertial cruise; active radar homing to 42 km *(23 nm)* at 0.9 Mach; warhead 165 kg; sea-skimmer.
Guns: 1 Bofors 57 mm/70 Mk 1; 75° elevation; 200 rounds/minute to 17 km *(9.3 nm)*; weight of shell 0.96 kg. Launchers for illuminants on each side.
1 Bofors 40 mm/70; 90° elevation; 300 rounds/minute to 12 km *(6.6 nm)*; weight of shell 2.4 kg.
2 Rheinmetall 20 mm.
Countermeasures: ESM (in 623 and 624).
Fire Control: Selenia NA-18 optronic director.
Radars: Surface search: Racal Decca 1226; I band.
Fire control: Signaal WM 28; I/J band; range 46 km *(25 nm)*.

Programmes: PSMM Mk 5 type craft ordered in 1975.
Structure: Shorter in length and smaller displacement than South Korean units. *Mandau* has a different shaped mast with a tripod base.

KERIS *7/1991, James Goldrick, RAN*

4 LÜRSSEN PB 57 CLASS (NAV I and II) (LARGE PATROL CRAFT)

Name	*No*	*Builders*	*Commissioned*
SINGA	651	Lürssen/PT Pal Surabaya	Apr 1988
AJAK	653	Lürssen/PT Pal Surabaya	5 Apr 1989
PANDBONG	801	PT Pal Surabaya	1990
SURA	802	PT Pal Surabaya	1991

Displacement, tons: 447 full load (NAV I); 428 full load (NAV II)
Dimensions, feet (metres): 190.6 × 25 × 9.2 *(58.1 × 7.6 × 2.8)*
Main machinery: 2 MTU 16V 956 TB 92 diesels; 8850 hp(m) *(6.5 MW)* sustained; 2 shafts
Speed, knots: 27. **Range, miles:** 6100 at 15 kts; 2200 at 27 kts
Complement: 42 (6 officers)

Guns: 1 Bofors SAK 57 mm/70 Mk 2; 75° elevation; 220 rounds/minute to 14 km *(7.6 nm)*; weight of shell 2.4 kg.
1 Bofors SAK 40 mm/70; 90° elevation; 300 rounds/minute to 12 km *(6.6 nm)*; weight of shell 0.96 kg.
2 Rheinmetall 20 mm (NAV II).
Torpedoes: 2—21 in *(533 mm)* Toro tubes (NAV I). AEG SUT; anti-submarine; wire-guided; active/passive homing to 12 km *(6.6 nm)* at 35 kts; 28 km *(15 nm)* at 23 kts; warhead 250 kg.
Countermeasures: Decoys: CSEE Dagaie single trainable launcher; automatic dispenser for IR flares and Chaff; H/J band.
ESM: DR 2000 S3 with Dalia analyser; radar intercept. Telegon VIII D/F.
Fire control: Signaal LIOD 73 Ri optronic director. Signaal WM 22 72 Ri WCS.
Radars: Surface search: Racal Decca 2459; I band.
Fire control: Signaal WM 22; I/J band; range 46 km *(25 nm)*.
Sonars: Signaal PMS 32 (NAV I); active search and attack; medium frequency.

Comment: Class ordered from Lürssen in 1982. First launched and shipped incomplete to P T Pal Surabaya for fitting out in January 1984. Second shipped July 1984. The first two are NAV I ASW versions with torpedo tubes and sonars. The second pair are NAV II AAW versions with an augmented gun armament but without torpedo tubes and sonars.

SINGA *5/1990, van Ginderen Collection*

AJAK *5/1990, 92 Wing RAAF*

3 + 1 LÜRSSEN PB 57 CLASS (NAV III and IV) (LARGE PATROL CRAFT)

Name	*No*	*Builders*	*Commissioned*
KAKAP	811	Lürssen/PT Pal Surabaya	Oct 1988
KERAPU	812	Lürssen/PT Pal Surabaya	5 Apr 1989
TONGKOL	813	PT Pal Surabaya	1991
BERVANG	814	PT Pal Surabaya	1992

Displacement, tons: 423 full load
Dimensions, feet (metres): 190.6 × 25 × 9.2 *(58.1 × 7.6 × 2.8)*
Main machinery: 2 MTU 16V 956 TB 92 diesels; 8850 hp(m) *(6.5 MW)* sustained; 2 shafts
Speed, knots: 27. **Range, miles:** 6100 at 15 kts; 2200 at 27 kts
Complement: 40 plus 17 spare berths

Guns: 1 Bofors 40 mm/60. 90° elevation; 240 rounds/minute to 12.6 km *(6.8 nm)*; weight of shell 0.96 kg. 2—12.7 mm MGs.
Radars: Surface search: Racal Decca 2459; I band.
Navigation: KH 1007; I band.
Helicopters: Platform for 1 NBO 105 or Wasp.

Comment: Ordered in 1982. First pair shipped from West Germany and completed at P T Pal Surabaya. Second pair assembled at Surabaya. The first pair are NAV III SAR versions and by comparison with NAV I are very lightly armed and have a 13 × 7.1 m helicopter deck in place of the after guns and torpedo tubes. The ship can be used for Patrol purposes as well as SAR, and can transport two rifle platoons. There is also a fast seaboat with launching crane at the stern and two water guns for firefighting. The NAV IV version has some minor variations. There is some doubt over whether there is a fourth of the class (814). These are naval craft not Maritime Security Agency as previously indicated.

KAKAP *5/1990, John Mortimer*

3 Ex-YUGOSLAV KRALJEVICA CLASS (LARGE PATROL CRAFT)

LAJANG (ex-*PBR 515*) 819
DORANG (ex-*PBR 514*) 822
TODAK (ex-*PBR 518*) 823

Displacement, tons: 195 standard; 245 full load
Dimensions, feet (metres): 141.4 × 20.7 × 5.5 *(43.1 × 6.3 × 1.7)*
Main machinery: 2 MAN/Burmeister & Wain V8V 30/38 diesels; 3300 hp(m) *(2.43 MW)*; 2 shafts
Speed, knots: 19. **Range, miles:** 1500 at 12 kts
Complement: 52 (4 officers)

Guns: 1 US 3 in *(76 mm)*/50; 85° elevation; 20 rounds/minute to 12 km *(6.6 nm)*; weight of shell 6 kg.
1 Bofors 40 mm/60. 4—12.7 mm (2 twin) MGs.
A/S mortars: 2—24-tubed Hedgehogs; range 350 m; warhead 26 kg.
Depth charges: 2 racks.
Radars: Surface search: Decca 974; I band.
Sonars: US QCU 2; hull-mounted; active attack; high frequency.

Comment: Purchased and transferred March-April 1959. All built at Tito SY. All in reserve and soon to be scrapped.

TODAK *7/1983, P. D. Jones*

8 Ex-AUSTRALIAN ATTACK CLASS (LARGE PATROL CRAFT)

Name	*No*	*Builders*	*Commissioned*
SIBARAU (ex-HMAS *Bandolier*)	847	Walkers, Australia	14 Dec 1968
SILIMAN (ex-HMAS *Archer*)	848	Walkers, Australia	15 May 1968
SIGALU (ex-HMAS *Barricade*)	857	Walkers, Australia	26 Oct 1968
SILEA (ex-HMAS *Acute*)	858	Evans Deakin	24 Apr 1968
SIRIBUA (ex-HMAS *Bombard*)	859	Walkers, Australia	5 Nov 1968
SIADA (ex-HMAS *Barbette*)	862	Walkers, Australia	16 Aug 1968
SIKUDA (ex-HMAS *Attack*)	863	Evans Deakin	17 Nov 1967
SIGUROT (ex-HMAS *Assail*)	864	Evans Deakin	12 July 1968

Displacement, tons: 146 full load
Dimensions, feet (metres): 107.5 × 20 × 7.3 *(32.8 × 6.1 × 2.2)*
Main machinery: 2 Davey-Paxman Ventura 16CM diesels; 4000 hp *(2.98 MW)* sustained; 2 shafts
Speed, knots: 21. **Range, miles:** 1220 at 13 kts
Complement: 19 (3 officers)
Guns: 1 Bofors 40 mm/60. 1—12.5 mm MG.
Radars: Surface search: Decca 916; I band; range 88 km *(48 nm)*.

Comment: Transferred from RAN after refit—*Bandolier* 16 November 1973, *Archer* in 1974, *Barricade* March 1982, *Acute* 6 May 1983, *Bombard* September 1983, *Attack* 22 February 1985 (recommissioned 24 May 1985), *Barbette* February 1985, *Assail* February 1986. All carry rocket/flare launchers.

SIADA *4/1990, 92 Wing RAAF*

18 KAL KANGEAN CLASS (COASTAL PATROL CRAFT)

Displacement, tons: 44.7 full load
Dimensions, feet (metres): 80.4 × 14.1 × 3.3 *(24.5 × 4.3 × 1)*
Main machinery: 2 diesels; 2 shafts
Speed, knots: 18
Guns: 2 USSR 25 mm/80 (twin). 2 USSR 14.5 mm (twin) MGs.

Comment: Ordered from PT Kabrick Kapal in about 1984 and completed between 1987 and 1990.

KAL KANGEAN 1112 *10/1988, Trevor Brown*

5 + 6 BOEING JETFOILS

BIMA SAMUDERA 1 +4

Displacement, tons: 117 full load
Dimensions, feet (metres): 102 × 30 × 17.5/7.8 *(31 × 9.1 × 5.3/2.4)*
Main machinery: 2 Allison 501-K20A gas turbines; 7560 hp *(5.64 MW)*; 2 shafts; 2 Detroit 8V-92TA diesels; 700 hp *(522 kW)* sustained; 2 waterjets
Speed, knots: 48. **Range, miles:** 900 at 40 kts; 1500 at 15 kts
Complement: 12
Military lift: 100 troops
Guns: Combinations of 1 Bofors 40 mm/60. 1 Rheinmetall 20 mm. 2—12.7 mm MGs.
Radars: Navigation: Decca; I band.

Comment: First ordered for evaluation in sundry naval and civilian roles including gunboat and troop transporter. Launched 22 October 1981, arrived Indonesia January 1982 for start of trials in March. In 1983 further four ordered from Boeing for delivery in 1984, 1985 and 1986 and six more ordered in 1985. Plans to increase the total to 47 seem to have been abandoned and it is doubtful if the last six have been delivered.

BOEING JETFOIL *1987*

AMPHIBIOUS FORCES

Note: This section includes some vessels of the Military Sealift Command—Kolinlamil.

7 Ex-US LST 1-511 and 512-1152 CLASSES

Name	*No*	*Builders*	*Commissioned*
TELUK LANGSA (ex-USS *LST 1128*)	501	Chicago Bridge and Iron Works	9 Mar 1945
TELUK BAJUR (ex-USS *LST 616*)	502	Chicago Bridge and Iron Works	29 May 1944
TELUK KAU (ex-USS *LST 652*)	504	Chicago Bridge and Iron Works	1 Jan 1945
TELUK TOMINI (ex-MV *Inagua Crest*, ex-MV *Brunei*, ex-USS *Bledsoe County, LST 356*)	508	Charleston NY	22 Dec 1942
TELUK RATAI (ex-Liberian *Inagua Shipper*, ex-USS *Presque Isle*, APB 44, ex-*LST 678*, ex-*Teluk Sindoro*)	509	American Bridge Co, Pennsylvania	30 June 1944
TELUK SALEH (ex-USS *Clark County, LST 601*)	510	Chicago Bridge and Iron Works	25 Mar 1944
TELUK BONE (ex-USS *Iredell County, LST 839*)	511	American Bridge Co, Pennsylvania	6 Dec 1944

Displacement, tons: 1653 standard; 4080 full load
Dimensions, feet (metres): 328 × 50 × 14 *(100 × 15.2 × 4.3)*
Main machinery: 2 GM 12-567A diesels; 1800 hp *(1.34 MW)*; 2 shafts
Speed, knots: 11.6. **Range, miles:** 11 000 at 10 kts
Complement: 119 (accommodation for 266)
Military lift: 2100 tons

Guns: 7—40 mm. 2—20 mm *(Teluk Langsa)*. 6—37 mm (remainder).
Older units and previously unarmed ships now fitted with ex-Soviet 37 mm guns.
Radars: Surface search: SPS 21 *(Teluk Tomini, Teluk Sindoro)*.
SPS 53 *(Teluk Saleh, Teluk Bone)*. SO-1 *(Teluk Kau)*. SO-6 *(Teluk Langsa)*.

Programmes: *Teluk Bajur, Teluk Saleh* and *Teluk Bone* transferred in June 1961 (and purchased 22 February 1979). *Teluk Kau* and *Teluk Langsa* in July 1970.
Operational: *Teluk Bajur* and *Teluk Tomini* in Military Sealift Command and are classified as LCCs.

TELUK KAU *3/1991, 92 Wing RAAF*

1 JAPANESE TYPE LST

Name	*No*	*Builders*	*Commissioned*
TELUK AMBOINA	503	Sasebo, Japan	17 Mar 1961

Displacement, tons: 2378 standard; 4200 full load
Dimensions, feet (metres): 327 × 50 × 15 *(99.7 × 15.3 × 4.6)*
Main machinery: 2 MAN V6V 22/30 diesels; 3425 hp(m) *(2.52 MW)*; 2 shafts
Speed, knots: 13.1. **Range, miles:** 4000 at 13.1 kts
Complement: 88
Military lift: 212 troops; 2100 tons

Guns: 6—37 mm; anti-aircraft.

Programmes: Launched on 17 March 1961 and transferred in June 1961.
Structure: A faster copy of US LST 511 class with 30 ton crane forward of bridge.
Operational: Military Sealift Command.

TELUK AMBOINA *10/1988, Trevor Brown*

2 LCU TYPE

DORE 580 **AMURANG** 581

Displacement, tons: 182 standard; 275 full load
Dimensions, feet (metres): 125.7 × 32.8 × 5.9 *(38.3 × 10 × 1.8)*
Main machinery: 2 diesels; 600 hp(m) *(441 kW)*; 2 shafts
Speed, knots: 8
Complement: 17
Military lift: 4 light tanks or 9 trucks
Guns: 1—12.7 mm MG.

Comment: Military Sealift Command. Built by Korneuberg SY, Austria in 1968. Two of same class are civilian operated in West Irian.

6 TACOMA TYPE LST

Name	*No*	*Builders*	*Commissioned*
TELUK SEMANGKA	512	Korea-Tacoma, Masan	20 Jan 1981
TELUK PENJU	513	Korea-Tacoma, Masan	20 Jan 1981
TELUK MANDAR	514	Korea-Tacoma, Masan	July 1981
TELUK SAMPIT	515	Korea-Tacoma, Masan	June 1981
TELUK BANTEN	516	Korea-Tacoma, Masan	May 1982
TELUK ENDE	517	Korea-Tacoma, Masan	2 Sep 1982

Displacement, tons: 3750 full load
Dimensions, feet (metres): 328 × 47.2 × 13.8 *(100 × 14.4 × 4.2)*
Main machinery: 2 diesels; 6860 hp(m) *(5.04 MW)*; 2 shafts
Speed, knots: 15. **Range, miles:** 7500 at 13 kts
Complement: 90 (13 officers)
Military lift: 1800 tons (including 17 MBTs); 2 LCVPs; 200 troops

Guns: 2—40 mm/60. 2 Rheinmetall 20 mm.
Radars: Navigation: Racal Decca; I band.

Helicopters: 1 Westland Wasp; 3 NAS-332 Super Pumas can be carried in last pair.

Programmes: First four ordered in June 1979, last pair June 1981.
Structure: No hangar in *Teluk Semangka* and *Teluk Mandar*. Two hangars in *Teluk Ende*. First four ordered June 1979, last pair June 1981. The last pair differ in silhouette having drowned exhausts in place of funnels and having their LCVPs carried forward of the bridge.
Operational: Battalion of marines can be embarked if no tanks are carried. One of the class is fitted out as a hospital ship and the last pair act as Command ships.

TELUK SAMPIT *8/1991, James Goldrick, RAN*

TELUK SEMANGKA *1/1991, 92 Wing RAAF*

TELUK ENDE (no funnel) *10/1988, Trevor Brown*

3 LCUs

KUPANG 582 **DILI** 583 **NUSANTARA** 584

Displacement, tons: 400 full load
Dimensions, feet (metres): 140.7 × 29.9 × 4.6 *(42.9 × 9.1 × 1.4)*
Main machinery: 2 diesels; 2 shafts
Speed, knots: 12. **Range, miles:** 700 at 11 kts
Complement: 17
Military lift: 200 tons

Comment: Built at Naval Training Centre, Surabaya in 1978-80. Military Sealift Command.

40+ LCMs

Displacement, tons: 62
Main machinery: 2 Gray Marine 64 HN 9 diesels; 330 hp *(264 kW)*; 2 shafts
Speed, knots: 8

Comment: A programme which has continued since 1960 although some of the details may have changed. Some may have come from Taiwan.

MINE WARFARE FORCES

2 + (10) TRIPARTITE TYPE (MINE WARFARE VESSELS)

Name	*No*	*Builders*	*Commissioned*
PULAU RENGAT	711	Van der Giessen-de-Noord	26 Mar 1988
PULAU RUPAT	712	Van der Giessen-de-Noord	26 Mar 1988

Displacement, tons: 502 standard; 568 full load
Dimensions, feet (metres): 168.9 × 29.2 × 8.2 *(51.5 × 8.9 × 2.5)*
Main machinery: 2 MTU 12V 396 TC 82 diesels; 2610 hp(m) *(1.92 MW)* sustained; 2 shafts; auxiliary propulsion; 3 Turbomeca gas turbine generators; 2 motors; 2400 hp(m) *(1.76 MW)*; 2 retractable Schottel propulsors; 2 bow thrusters; 150 hp(m) *(110 kW)*
Speed, knots: 15; 7 auxiliary propulsion. **Range, miles:** 3000 at 12 kts
Complement: 46 plus 4 spare berths

Guns: 2 Rheinmetall 20 mm. An additional short range missile system may be added for patrol duties or a third 20 mm gun.
Countermeasures: MCM: OD3 Oropesa mechanical sweep gear; Fiskars F-82 magnetic and SA Marine AS 203 acoustic sweeps; Ibis V minehunting system; 2 PAP 104 Mk 4 minehunting vehicles.
Combat data systems: Signaal SEWACO-RI action data automation.
Radars: Navigation: Racal Decca AC 1229C; I band.
Sonars: Thomson Sintra TSM 2022; active minehunting; high frequency.

Programmes: First ordered on 29 March 1985, laid down 22 July 1985 and launched 23 July 1987. Second ordered 30 August 1985, laid down 15 December 1985 and launched 27 August 1987. More were to have been built in Indonesia up to a total of 12 but this programme has been suspended by lack of funds.
Structure: There are differences in design between these ships and the European Tripartites, apart from their propulsion. Deck-houses and general layout are different as they will be required to act as minehunters, minesweepers and patrol ships. Hull construction is GRP shock proven Tripartite design.
Operational: Endurance, 15 days. Automatic operations, navigation and recording systems, Thomson-CSF Naviplot TSM 2060 tactical display. A 5 ton container can be shipped, stored for varying tasks—research; patrol; extended diving; drone control.

PULAU RENGAT *6/1988, Gilbert Gyssels*

2 Ex-SOVIET T 43 CLASS (MINESWEEPERS—OCEAN)

PULAU RANI 701 **PULAU RATEWO** 702

Displacement, tons: 580 full load
Dimensions, feet (metres): 190.2 × 27.6 × 6.9 *(58 × 8.4 × 2.1)*
Main machinery: 2 Kolumna 9-D-8 diesels; 2200 hp(m) *(1.62 MW)*; 2 shafts
Speed, knots: 15. **Range, miles:** 3000 at 10 kts
Complement: 77
Guns: 4—37 mm/63 (2 twin). 8—12.7 mm (4 twin) MGs.
Depth charges: 2 projectors.
Radars: Navigation: Decca 110; I band.
Sonars: Hull-mounted; active search and attack; high frequency.

Comment: Transferred in 1964. Mostly used as patrol craft.

SURVEY SHIPS

1 Ex-BRITISH HECLA CLASS

Name	*No*	*Builders*	*Commissioned*
DEWA KEMBAR (ex-HMS *Hydra*)	932	Yarrow and Co., Blythswood	5 May 1966

Displacement, tons: 1915 light; 2733 full load
Dimensions, feet (metres): 260.1 × 49.1 × 15.4 *(79.3 × 15 × 4.7)*
Main machinery: Diesel electric; 3 Paxman Ventura 12CZ diesels; 3780 hp *(2.82 MW)*; 3 generators; 1 motor; 2000 hp(m) *(1.49 MW)*; 1 shaft; bow thruster
Speed, knots: 14. **Range, miles:** 12 000 at 11 kts
Complement: 123 (14 officers)
Radars: Navigation: Kelvin Hughes Type 1006; I band.
Helicopters: 1 Westland Wasp.

Comment: Transferred 18 April 1986 for refit. Commissioned in Indonesian Navy 10 September 1986. SATCOM fitted. Two survey launches on davits.

DEWA KEMBAR *9/1986, W. Sartori*

3 HYDROGRAPHIC/RESEARCH SHIPS

Name	*No*	*Builders*	*Commissioned*
BARUNAJAYA I	—	CMN, Cherbourg	15 Sep 1989
BARUNAJAYA II	—	CMN, Cherbourg	Dec 1989
BARUNAJAYA III	—	CMN, Cherbourg	Apr 1990

Displacement, tons: 1180 full load
Dimensions, feet (metres): 198.2 × 38 × 13.8 *(60.4 × 11.6 × 4.2)*
Main machinery: 2 Niigata/SEMT-Pielstick 5 PA 5-L 255 diesels; 2990 hp(m) *(2.2 MW)* sustained; 2 shafts; cp props
Speed, knots: 14. **Range, miles:** 7500 at 12 kts
Complement: 24 plus 26 scientists

Comment: Ordered from La Manche, Dieppe in February 1985 by the office of Technology, Ministry of Industry and Research. Badly delayed by the closing down of the original shipbuilders (ACM, Dieppe) and construction taken over by CMN at St Malo. *Barunajaya 1* is employed entirely on hydrography, the second on oceanography and the third combines both tasks.

BARUNAJAYA II *1989, CMN, Cherbourg*

Name	*No*	*Builders*	*Commissioned*
BURUJULASAD	931	Schlichting, Lübeck-Travemünde	1967

Displacement, tons: 2165 full load
Dimensions, feet (metres): 269.5 × 37.4 × 11.5 *(82.2 × 11.4 × 3.5)*
Main machinery: 4 MAN V6V 22/30 diesels; 6850 hp(m) *(5.03 MW)*; 2 shafts
Speed, knots: 19.1. **Range, miles:** 14 500 at 15 kts
Complement: 108 (15 officers) plus 28 scientists
Guns: 1—37 mm. 4—12.7 mm (2 twin) MGs.
Radars: Surface search: Decca TM 262; I band.
Helicopters: 1 Bell 47J.

Comment: *Burujulasad* was launched in August 1965; her equipment includes laboratories for oceanic and meteorological research and a cartographic room. Carries one LCVP and three surveying motor boats.

BURUJULASAD *5/1991, 92 Wing RAAF*

Name	*No*	*Builders*	*Commissioned*
JALANIDHI	933	Sasebo Heavy Industries	12 Jan 1963

Displacement, tons: 985 full load
Dimensions, feet (metres): 176.8 × 31.2 × 14.1 *(53.9 × 9.5 × 4.3)*
Main machinery: 1 MAN G6V 30/42 diesel; 1000 hp(m) *(735 kW)*; 1 shaft
Speed, knots: 11.5. **Range, miles:** 7200 at 10 kts
Complement: 87 (13 officers) plus 26 scientists
Radars: Navigation: Nikkon Denko; I band.

Comment: Launched in 1962. Oceanographic research ship with hydromet facilities. Three ton boom aft. Operated by Hydrographic Office.

JALANIDHI *1990, Indonesian Navy*

COMMAND AND SUPPORT SHIPS

1 SUBMARINE TENDER

Name	*No*	*Builders*	*Commissioned*
MULTATULI	561	Ishikawajima-Harima Heavy Industries Co Ltd	Aug 1961

Displacement, tons: 3220 standard; 6741 full load
Dimensions, feet (metres): 365.3 × 52.5 × 23 *(111.4 × 16 × 7)*
Main machinery: 1 Burmeister & Wain diesel; 5500 hp(m) *(4.04 MW)*; 1 shaft
Speed, knots: 18.5. **Range, miles:** 6000 at 16 kts
Complement: 130

Guns: 6 USSR 37 mm/63 (2 twin, 2 single); 85° elevation; 160 rounds/minute to 9 km *(5 nm)*; weight of shell 0.7 kg.
8—12.7 mm MGs.
Radars: Surface search: Ball End; E/F band; range 37 km *(20 nm)*.
Navigation: I band.

Helicopters: Platform for Alouette size.

Programmes: Built as a submarine tender. Launched on 15 May 1961. Delivered to Indonesia August 1961.
Modernisation: Original after 76 mm mounting replaced by helicopter deck.
Structure: Living and working spaces air-conditioned.
Operational: Capacity for replenishment at sea (fuel oil, fresh water, provisions, ammunition, naval stores and personnel). Medical and hospital facilities. Now used as fleet flagship (Eastern Force) and is fitted with ICS-3 communications.

MULTATULI *9/1988, 92 Wing RAAF*

SERVICE FORCES

1 Ex-US ACHELOUS CLASS (REPAIR SHIP)

Name	*No*	*Builders*	*Commissioned*
JAYA WIJAYA (ex-USS *Askari*, ex-*ARL 30*, ex-*LST 1131*)	921	Chicago Bridge and Iron Co.	15 Mar 1945

Displacement, tons: 1625 light; 4325 full load
Dimensions, feet (metres): 328 × 50 × 14 *(100 × 15.3 × 4.3)*
Main machinery: 2 GM 12-567A diesels; 1800 hp *(1.34 MW)*; 2 shafts
Speed, knots: 12. **Range, miles:** 17 000 at 7 kts
Complement: 180 (11 officers)
Cargo capacity: 300 tons; 60 ton crane

Guns: 8 Bofors 40 mm/56 (2 quad); 45° elevation; 160 rounds/minute to 11 km *(5.9 nm)*; weight of shell 0.9 kg.
Radars: Air/surface search: Sperry SPS 53; I/J band.
Navigation: Raytheon 1900; I/J band.
IFF: UPX 12B.

Programmes: In reserve from 1956-66. She was recommissioned and reached Vietnam in 1967 to support River Assault Flotilla One. She was used by the US Navy and Vietnamese Navy working up the Mekong in support of the Cambodian operations in May 1970. Transferred on lease to Indonesia at Guam on 31 August 1971 and purchased 22 February 1979.
Structure: Bow doors welded shut. Carries two LCVPs.

JAYA WIJAYA *9/1988, 92 Wing RAAF*

1 REPLENISHMENT TANKER

Name	*No*	*Builders*	*Commissioned*
SORONG	911	Trogir SY, Yugoslavia	Apr 1965

Measurement, tons: 5100 dwt; 4090 gross
Dimensions, feet (metres): 367.4 × 50.5 × 21.6 *(112 × 15.4 × 6.6)*
Main machinery: 1 diesel; 1 shaft
Speed, knots: 15
Cargo capacity: 4200 tons fuel; 300 tons water
Guns: 4—12.7 mm (2 twin) MGs.
Radars: Navigation: Don; I band.

Comment: Has limited under way replenishment facilities.

SORONG *5/1989, 92 Wing RAAF*

0 + 1 Ex-BRITISH ROVER CLASS

Name	*No*	*Builders*	*Commissioned*
(ex-*Green Rover*)	—	Swan Hunter, Tyneside	15 Aug 1969

Displacement, tons: 4700 light; 11 522 full load
Dimensions, feet (metres): 461 × 63 × 24 *(140.6 × 19.2 × 7.3)*
Main machinery: 2 SEMT-Pielstick 16PA4 diesels; 15 360 hp(m) *(11.46 MW)*; 1 shaft; cp prop; bow thruster
Speed, knots: 19. **Range, miles:** 15 000 at 15 kts
Complement: 49
Cargo capacity: 6600 tons fuel
Guns: 2 Oerlikon 20 mm
Radars: Navigation: Kelvin Hughes Type 1006; I band
Helicopters: Platform for Westland Sea King type

Comment: Small fleet tanker designed to replenish ships at sea with fuel, fresh water, limited dry cargo and refrigerated stores under all conditions while under way. No hangar but helicopter landing platform is served by a stores lift, to enable stores to be transferred at sea by 'vertical lift'. Capable of HIFR. Planned to transfer in 1992 after a refit at Swan Hunter.

ROVER Class (old number) *11/1990, J. L. M. van der Burg*

2 Ex-SOVIET KHOBI CLASS (COASTAL TANKERS)

BALIKPAPAN 901 **PAKAN BARU** (ex-*Aragua*) 909

Displacement, tons: 1525 full load
Dimensions, feet (metres): 206.6 × 33 × 14.8 *(63 × 10.1 × 4.5)*
Main machinery: 2 diesels; 1600 hp(m) *(1.12 MW)*; 2 shafts
Speed, knots: 13. **Range, miles:** 2500 at 12 kts
Complement: 37 (4 officers)
Cargo capacity: 550 tons dieso
Guns: 4—12.7 mm (2 twin) MGs.
Radars: Navigation: Neptun; I band.

Comment: Transferred 1959.

BALIKPAPAN *6/1990, 92 Wing RAAF*

MISCELLANEOUS

6 TISZA CLASS (AKL)

TALAUD 951 **NATUNA** 953 **KARIMUNDSA** 957
NUSA TELU 952 **TELUK MENTAWAI** 956 **KARIMATA** 960

Displacement, tons: 2400 full load
Dimensions, feet (metres): 258.4 × 35.4 × 15.1 *(78.8 × 10.8 × 4.6)*
Main machinery: 1 MAN diesel; 1000 hp(m) *(735 kW)*; 1 shaft
Speed, knots: 12. **Range, miles:** 3000 at 11 kts
Complement: 26
Cargo capacity: 875 tons dry; 11 tons liquid
Guns: 4—12.7 mm (2 twin) MGs.
Radars: Navigation: Spin Trough; I band.

Comment: Built in Hungary. All transferred in 1963-64. Military Sealift Command since 1978.

2 TRANSPORTS

TANJUNG PANDAN 971 **TANJUNG OISINA** 972

Measurement, tons: 8000 grt

Comment: Passenger liners built in the 1940s and purchased in 1978. Ex-Mecca pilgrim transports now used for troop transfers between islands. Unarmed. Military Sealift Command.

TANJUNG OISINA *4/1989, 92 Wing RAAF*

1 SAIL TRAINING SHIP

Name	*No*	*Builders*	*Commissioned*
DEWARUTJI	—	H C Stülcken & Sohn, Hamburg	9 July 1953

Displacement, tons: 810 standard; 1500 full load
Dimensions, feet (metres): 136.2 pp; 191.2 oa × 31.2 × 13.9 *(41.5; 58.3 × 9.5 × 4.2)*
Main machinery: 1 MAN diesel; 600 hp(m) *(441 kW)*; 1 shaft
Speed, knots: 10.5
Complement: 110 (includes 78 midshipmen)

Comment: Barquentine of steel construction. Sail area, 1305 sq yards *(1091 sq m)*. Launched on 24 January 1953.

DEWARUTJI *5/1990, Guy Toremans*

1 CABLE SHIP

Name	*No*	*Builders*	*Commissioned*
BIDUK	—	J & K Smit, Kinderijk	30 July 1952

Displacement, tons: 1250 standard
Dimensions, feet (metres): 213.2 × 39.5 × 11.5 *(65 × 12 × 3.5)*
Main machinery: 2 boilers; 1 triple expansion engine; 1600 ihp(m) *(1.12 MW)*; 1 shaft
Speed, knots: 12
Complement: 66

Comment: Launched on 30 October 1951. Cable layer, lighthouse tender, and multi-purpose auxiliary.

2 BUOY TENDERS

MAJANG **MIZAN**

Displacement, tons: 2150 full load
Dimensions, feet (metres): 255.9 × 44.9 × 13.1 *(7.8 × 13.7 × 4)*
Complement: 70

Comment: Have three 20 ton derricks and a survey launch.

FLOATING DOCKS

Comment: There are three large floating docks in Surabaya which are used for naval purposes.

TUGS

Note: Two BIMA VIII class of 423 tons completed in 1991 are not naval.

1 Ex-US CHEROKEE CLASS

RAKATA (ex-USS *Menominee* ATF 73) 922

Displacement, tons: 1235 standard; 1640 full load
Dimensions, feet (metres): 205 × 38.5 × 17 *(62.5 × 11.7 × 5.2)*
Main machinery: Diesel-electric; 4 GM 12-278 diesels; 4400 hp *(3.28 MW)*; 4 generators; 1 motor; 3000 hp *(2.24 MW)*; 1 shaft
Speed, knots: 15. **Range, miles:** 6500 at 15 kts
Complement: 67
Guns: 1 US 3 in *(76 mm)*/50. 2 Bofors 40 mm/60 aft. 4—25 mm (2 twin) (bridge wings).
Radars: Surface search: Raytheon SPS 5B; G/H band; range 37 km *(20 nm)*.

Comment: Launched on 14 February 1942 by United Eng. Alameda. Commissioned 25 September 1942. Transferred at San Diego in March 1961.

Name	*No*	*Builders*	*Commissioned*
LAMPO BATANG	934	Ishikawajima-Harima	Sep 1961

Displacement, tons: 154 light; 280 full load
Dimensions, feet (metres): 92.3 × 23.2 × 11.3 *(28.2 × 7.1 × 3.4)*
Main machinery: 2 MAN diesels; 600 hp(m) *(441 kW)*; 2 shafts
Speed, knots: 11. **Range, miles:** 1000 at 11 kts
Complement: 13

Comment: Ocean tug. Launched in April 1961.

Name	*No*	*Builders*	*Commissioned*
TAMBORA (Army)	935	Ishikawajima-Harima	June 1961
BROMO	936	Ishikawajima-Harima	Aug 1961

Displacement, tons: 150 light; 250 full load
Dimensions, feet (metres): 79 × 21.7 × 9.7 *(24.1 × 6.6 × 3)*
Main machinery: 2 MAN diesels; 600 hp(m) *(441 kW)*; 2 shafts
Speed, knots: 10.5. **Range, miles:** 690 at 10.5 kts
Complement: 15

Comment: Harbour tugs.

CUSTOMS PATROL CRAFT

17 COASTAL PATROL CRAFT

BC 1001-1010 **BC 3001-3007**

Displacement, tons: 55 (1001 class); 62 (3001 class)
Dimensions, feet (metres): 92.5 × 17 × 5.3 *(28.2 × 5.2 × 1.6)*
Main machinery: 2 MTU 12V 331 TC 81 diesels; 2610 hp(m) *(1.92 MW)* sustained; 2 shafts
Speed, knots: 34. **Range, miles:** 750 at 15 kts
Complement: 18
Guns: 1—20 mm (BC 3001 class). 1—12.7 mm MG (BC 1001 class).

Comment: Built by Chantiers Navals de l'Esterel. BC 1001-3 commissioned April, June and November 1975, BC 3001-2 and BC 1004-6 in 1979, BC 3003-3005 and 1007-9 in 1980, BC 3006-7 7 January 1981 and BC 1010 in April 1981.

BC 3006 *10/1986, van Ginderen Collection*

7 COASTAL PATROL CRAFT

BC 2001-2007

Displacement, tons: 70.3 full load
Dimensions, feet (metres): 93.5 × 17.7 × 5.5 *(28.5 × 5.4 × 1.7)*
Main machinery: 2 MTU 12V 331 TC 92 diesels; 2660 hp(m) *(1.96 MW)* sustained; 2 shafts
Speed, knots: 29.7
Guns: 1—12.7 mm MG.

Comment: Built CMN Cherbourg to Lürssen design. Ordered in January 1979. Last two commissioned 7 November 1980 (2006) and 10 February 1981 (2007).

BC 2007 *1/1990, 92 Wing RAAF*

48 LÜRSSEN 28 METRE TYPE

BC 4001-3, 5001-3, 6001-24, 7001-6, 8001-6, 9001-6

Displacement, tons: 68 full load
Dimensions, feet (metres): 91.8 × 17.7 × 5.9 *(28 × 5.4 × 1.8)*
Main machinery: 2 Deutz diesels; 2720 hp(m) *(2 MW)*; or 2 MTU diesels; 2260 hp(m) *(1.66 MW)*; 2 shafts
Speed, knots: 30. **Range, miles:** 1100 at 15 kts; 860 at 28 kts
Complement: 19 (6 officers)
Guns: 1—12.7 mm MG.

Comment: Replacements for the deleted BT series. Lürssen design, some built by Fulton Marine and Scheepswerven van Langebrugge of Belgium, some by Lürssen Vegesack and some by PT Pal Surabaya (which also assembled most of them). Programme started in 1980 and continues into the 1990s.

BC 8003 *8/1991, 92 Wing RAAF*

BC 5003 *8/1991, 92 Wing RAAF*

MARITIME SECURITY AGENCY

Note: Established in 1978 to control the 200 mile EEZ and to maintain navigational aids. Comes under the Military Sea Communications Command.

5 SAR CRAFT

KUJANG 201 **CELURIT** 203 **BELATI** 205
PARANG 202 **CUNDRIK** 204

Displacement, tons: 162 full load
Dimensions, feet (metres): 125.6 × 19.6 × 6.8 *(38.3 × 6 × 2.1)*
Main machinery: 2 AGO SACM 195 V12 CZ SHR T5 diesels; 4410 hp(m) *(3.24 MW)*; 2 shafts
Speed, knots: 28. **Range, miles:** 1500 at 18 kts
Complement: 18
Guns: 1—12.7 mm MG.

Comment: Built by SFCN, Villeneuve la Garenne. Completed April 1981 *(Kujang* and *Parang)*, August 1981 *(Celurit)*, October 1981 *(Cundrik)*, December 1981 *(Belati)*.

KUJANG *8/1988, 92 Wing RAAF*

SAR CRAFT

OLOK 206 — **PANAN** 207 — **PEDANG** 208 — **KAPAK** 209

isplacement, tons: 190 full load
imensions, feet (metres): 123 pp × 23.6 × 6.6 *(37.5 × 7.2 × 2)*
lain machinery: 2 MTU 16V 652 TB91 diesels; 4610 hp(m) *(3.39 MW)* sustained; 2 shafts
peed, knots: 25. **Range, miles:** 1500 at 18 kts
omplement: 18
uns: 1 Rheinmetall 20 mm.

omment: All launched 5 November 1981. First pair completed 12 March 1982. Last pair completed 12 May 1982. Built by Deutsche Industrie Werke, Berlin. Fitted out by Schlichting, Travemünde.

PAT CLASS

AT 01 — **PAT 02** — **PAT 03** — **PAT 04** — **PAT 05** — **PAT 06**

isplacement, tons: 12 full load
imensions, feet (metres): 40 × 14.1 × 3.3 *(12.2 × 4.3 × 1)*
ain machinery: 1 diesel; 260 hp(m) *(191 kW)*; 1 shaft
oeed, knots: 14
uns: 1—7.62 mm MG.

omment: Built at Tanjung Priok Shipyard 1978-79.

ARMY CRAFT

ote: The Army (ADRI) craft have mostly been transferred to the Military Sealift Command (Logistic ıpport). More LSLs are reported to be planned.

8 LANDING CRAFT LOGISTICS

DRI XXXI-ADRI LVIII

splacement, tons: 580 full load
mensions, feet (metres): 137.8 × 35.1 × 5.9 *(42 × 10.7 × 1.8)*
ain machinery: 2 Detroit 6-71 diesels; 348 hp(m) *(260 kW)* sustained; 2 shafts
eed, knots: 10. **Range, miles:** 1500 at 10 kts
mplement: 15
ilitary lift: 122 tons equipment

mment: Built in Tanjung Priok Shipyard 1979-82.

AIR FORCE CRAFT

ote: AURI operates six 600 ton cargo ships (all with bow doors) built in the mid-1960s.

POLICE CRAFT

ote: The police operates a number of craft of varying sizes including 14 Bango class of 194 tons and Hamilton waterjet craft of 7.9 m, 234 hp giving a speed of 28 kts. The Carpentaria class have been nsferred from the Navy, and the Lürssen type (619-623) are identical to Customs craft.

LICE 622 — *7/1991, James Goldrick, RAN*

10 COASTAL PATROL CRAFT

DKN 504-DKN 513

Displacement, tons: 440 full load
Dimensions, feet (metres): 157.8 × 24.6 × 9.5 *(48.1 × 7.5 × 2.9)*
Main machinery: 2 MAN V8V 22/30 diesels; 1400 hp(m) *(1.03 MW)*; 2 shafts
Speed, knots: 15. **Range, miles:** 2700 at 14 kts
Complement: 35
Guns: 1 Rheinmetall 20 mm. 2—12.7 mm MGs.

Comment: Built in Japan in the early 1960s. Can carry 70 tons equipment.

9 COASTAL PATROL CRAFT

DKN 908-DKN 916

Displacement, tons: 159 full load
Dimensions, feet (metres): 137.8 × 21.3 × 5.9 *(42 × 6.5 × 1.8)*
Main machinery: 2 MTU MD 655 diesels; 3000 hp(m) *(2.2 MW)*; 2 shafts
Speed, knots: 24.5. **Range, miles:** 1500 at 18 kts
Complement: 22
Guns: 4 Rheinmetall 20 mm.

Comment: Built by Baglietto and Riva Trigosa 1961-64.

DKN 916 — *7/1983*

6 CARPENTARIA CLASS (COASTAL PATROL CRAFT)

Name	*No*	*Builders*	*Commissioned*
SAMADAR	851	Hawker-De Havilland Australia	Aug 1976
SASILA	852	Hawker-De Havilland Australia	Sep 1976
SABOLA	853	Hawker-De Havilland Australia	Oct 1976
SAWANGI	854	Hawker-De Havilland Australia	Nov 1976
SADARIN	855	Hawker-De Havilland Australia	Jan 1977
SALMANETI	856	Hawker-De Havilland Australia	Jan 1977

Displacement, tons: 27
Dimensions, feet (metres): 51.5 × 15.7 × 4.3 *(15.7 × 4.8 × 1.3)*
Main machinery: 2 MTU 8V 331 TC 92 diesels; 2660 hp(m) *(1.96 MW)* sustained; 2 shafts
Speed, knots: 29. **Range, miles:** 950 at 18 kts
Complement: 10
Guns: 2—12.7 mm MGs.
Radars: Surface search: Decca; I band.

Comment: First delivered June 1976. Endurance, 4-5 days. Transferred from the Navy in the mid-1980s and probably have new numbers.

SAWANGI — *1980, P. D. Jones*

IRAN

adquarters' Appointments

mmander of the Iranian Navy:
Rear Admiral Ali Shamkhani
puty Commander:
Commodore Abbas Mohtaj
mmander of the Pasdaran Naval Forces:
Hussein Alai

rsonnel

1992: 14 500 officers and men (Navy)
) 2 years' national service

ses

rsian Gulf: Bandar Abbas (MHQ), Boushehr (also a Dockyard), arg Island, Khorramshar (Light Forces)
dian Ocean: Chah Bahar
spian Sea: Bandar—Pahlavi (Training)

Strength of the Fleet

Type	*Active*	*Building*
Submarines	—	2 (1)
Midget Submarines	2	1
Destroyers	3	—
Frigates	3	—
Corvettes	2	—
Fast Attack Craft—Missile	10	10
Fast Attack Craft—Gun	3	—
Large Patrol Craft	6	—
Hovercraft	13	—
Landing Ships (Logistic)	4	—
Landing Craft (Tank)	6	—
LCU	6	—
Minesweepers—Coastal	2	—
Minesweeper—Inshore	1	—
Replenishment Ship	1	—
Supply Ships	2	—
Repair Ship	1	—
Support Ships	7	—
Water Tankers	2	—
Service Craft	57	—
Tugs	15	—
Ex-Yacht	2	—
Floating Dock	2	—
Customs Craft	2	—
Patrol Craft	172+	—

Prefix to Ships' Names

IS

Mercantile Marine

Lloyd's Register of Shipping:
401 vessels of 4 583 179 tons

PENNANT LIST

Destroyers

51	Damavand
61	Babr
62	Palang

Frigates

71	Alvand
72	Alborz
73	Sabalan

Corvettes

81	Bayandor
82	Naghdi

Light Forces

01-08	Winchester class hovercraft
101-105	Wellington class hovercraft
201	Kaivan
202	Azadi
204	Mahvan
211	Parvin
212	Bahram
213	Nahid
P 221	Kaman
P 222	Zoubin
P 223	Khadang
P 226	Falakhon
P 227	Shamshir
P 228	Gorz
P 229	Gardouneh
P 230	Khanjar
P 231	Neyzeh
P 232	Tabarzin

Mine Warfare Forces

301	Shahrokh
303	Karkas
312	Riazi

Service and Auxiliary Forces

21	LCT
22	LCT
23	LCT
24	LST
25	LST
26	LST
101	Foque
411	Kangan
412	Taheri
421	Bandar Abbas
422	Boushehr
431	Kharg
441	Chah Bahar
511	Hengam
512	Larak
513	Tonb
514	Lavan

SUBMARINES

0 + 2 (1) KILO CLASS

Displacement, tons: 2356 surfaced; 3076 dived
Dimensions, feet (metres): 243.8 × 32.8 × 21.7 *(74.3 × 10 × 6.6)*
Main machinery: Diesel-electric; 2 diesels; 3650 hp(m) *(2.68 MW)*; 2 generators; 1 motor; 5900 hp(m) *(4.34 MW)*; 1 shaft
Speed, knots: 17 dived; 9 snorting; 10 surfaced
Range, miles: 6000 at 7 kts surfaced; 400 at 3 kts dived
Complement: 45

Torpedoes: 6—2 in *(533 mm)* tubes; 18 Type 53; dual purpose; pattern active/passive homing up to 20 km *(10.8 nm)* at up to 45 kts; warhead 400 kg.
Mines: In lieu of torpedoes.
Countermeasures: ESM: Squid Head or Brick Pulp; radar warning. Quad Loop D/F.
Radars: Surface search; Snoop Tray; I band.
Sonars: Sharks Teeth; hull-mounted; passive/active search and attack; medium frequency.
Mouse Roar; active attack; high frequency.

Programmes: The CinC Navy revealed in 1990 that sailors were being trained at Riga with the aim of establishing a submarine force. Starting from scratch this will be a lengthy process and handing over the first submarine to an all Iranian crew could take a long time.
Structure: Diving depth, 300 m *(985 ft)*.
Operational: The plan is to base these submarines at Chah Bahar which is outside the Persian Gulf on the northern shore of the Gulf of Oman.

KILO Class 199

Opinion: This sale would represent major naval force proliferation to a potentially hostile country. For the transfer to go ahead the Russians would have to resist intense Western pressure t cancel the order.

2 MIDGET SUBMARINES

Displacement, tons: 27 surfaced; 30 dived
Dimensions, feet (metres): 51.3 × 5.7 × 5.7 *(15.6 × 1.7 × 1.7)*
Main machinery: Diesel; 1 shaft
Speed, knots: 6.5 surfaced; 6 dived
Range, miles: 1200 at 6 kts
Complement: 5

Mines: Two side cargoes each of 2 tons or 14 limpets.

Programmes: Initial submarine constructed in Iran and assembled at Bandar Abbas, combining Japanese and German Second World War design drawings with locally available fabrication and imported equipment. Initially completed in May 1987 but shipped to Tehran in late 1988 for modifications, as diving tests were unsuccessful. Second midget submarine of North Korean (DPRK) design delivered in June 1988. Although the programme has not so far been successful, developments continue in 1992 with the possibility of a Pakistan model.

Structure: The listed characteristics are based on a Second Wor War design which observers report the first submarine close resembles, but this one has a more powerful engine and larg diesel exhaust. Diving depth, approx 300 ft *(90 m)*. There is 'wet and dry' compartment for divers.
Operational: Based at Boushehr. Side cargoes can be release from inside the hull but limpet mines require a diver to ex attach the mines to the target and then re-enter.

DESTROYERS

1 Ex-BRITISH BATTLE CLASS

Name	*No*	*Builders*	*Laid down*	*Launched*	*Commissione*
DAMAVAND (ex-HMS *Sluys* D 60, ex-*Artemiz)*	51	Cammell Laird & Co Ltd, Birkenhead	24 Nov 1943	28 Feb 1945	30 Sep 1946

Displacement, tons: 2288 standard; 3404 full load
Dimensions, feet (metres): 379 × 40.3 × 17.1 (screws) *(115.5 × 12.3 × 5.2)*
Main machinery: 2 Admiralty boilers; 2 Parsons turbines; 50 000 hp *(37 MW)*; 2 shafts
Speed, knots: 31. **Range, miles:** 3200 at 20 kts; 4400 at 12 kts
Complement: 270

Missiles: SAM: 4 GDC Pomona Standard SM-1MR box launchers ❶; command guidance; semi-active radar homing to 46 km *(25 nm)* at 2 Mach; height envelope 45.7-18 288 m *(150-60 000 ft)*; 4 missiles.
Guns: 4 Vickers 4.5 in *(114 mm)*/45 (2 twin, fwd) ❷; 80° elevation; 15 rounds/minute to 18 km *(10 nm)* anti-surface; 8 km *(4.4 nm)* anti-aircraft; weight of shell 25 kg.
2 Bofors 40 mm/60 ❸; 80° elevation; 120 rounds/minute to 10 km *(5.5 nm)*; weight of shell 0.89 kg.
4 USSR 23 mm/80 (2 twin) ❹; (one replaced Seacat launcher and one mounted forward of bridge).
A/S mortars: 1 Mk 4 3-tubed Squid ❺; range 350 m.
Countermeasures: ESM: Decca RDL 1. Racal FH 5-HF/DF.
Fire control: US Mk 25 for 4.5 in guns and MR SAM. MCS 2 for Squid.
Radars: Air/surface search: Plessey AWS 1 ❻; E/F band; range 110 km *(60 nm)*.
Surface search: Decca 629 ❼; I band.
Fire control: Contraves Sea Hunter Mk 4 ❽; I/J band.
IFF: UK Mk 10.
Sonars: Plessey PMS 26; hull-mounted; lightweight; active search and attack; 10 kHz.

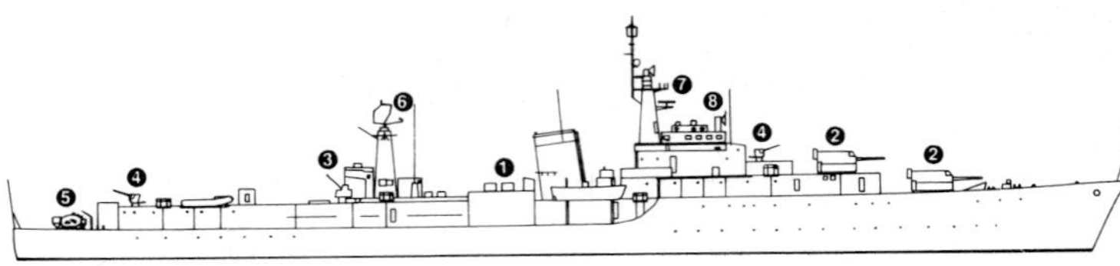

DAMAVAND *(Scale 1 : 1 200), Ian Sturto*

DAMAVAND 3/198

Programmes: Transferred to Iran at Southampton on 26 January 1967, and handed over to the Imperial Iranian Navy after a three-year modernisation refit by the Vosper Thornycroft Group. Refitted again in South Africa 1976.

Operational: Standard SAM has some surface-to-surfa capability. Seacat has been removed except for the optic director and two twin 23 mm guns are mounted. Regularly se at sea in 1989, but not much since then.

2 Ex-US ALLEN M SUMNER (FRAM II) CLASS

Name	No	Builders	Laid down	Launched	Commissioned
BABR (ex-USS *Zellers* DD 777)	61	Todd Pacific Shipyards	24 Dec 1943	19 July 1944	25 Oct 1944
PALANG (ex-USS *Stormes* DD 780)	62	Todd Pacific Shipyards	15 Apr 1944	4 Nov 1944	27 Jan 1945

Displacement, tons: 2388 standard; 3254 full load
Dimensions, feet (metres): 376.5 × 41 × 21.4 *(114.8 × 12.5 × 6.5)*
Main machinery: 2 Babcock & Wilcox and 2 Foster-Wheeler boilers; 600 psi *(43.3 kg/cm sq)*; 850°F *(454°C)*; 2 turbines; 60 000 hp *(45 MW)*; 2 shafts
Speed, knots: 34. **Range, miles:** 3740 at 12.5 kts
Complement: 290 (14 officers)

Missiles: SAM: 4 GDC Pomona Standard SM-1MR box launchers ❶; command guidance; semi-active radar homing to 46 km *(25 nm)* at 2 Mach; height envelope 45.7-18 288 m *(150-60 000 ft)*; 8 missiles.
Guns: 4 US 5 in *(127 mm)*/38 (2 twin) Mk 38 ❷; 85° elevation; 15 rounds/minute to 17 km *(9.3 nm)* anti-surface; 11 km *(5.9 nm)* anti-aircraft; weight of shell 25 kg.
2 USSR 23 mm/80 (twin) ❸; (replaced VDS right aft).
Torpedoes: 6—324 mm Mk 32 (2 triple) tubes ❹. Possibly Honeywell Mk 44 or 46.
Countermeasures: ESM: WLR-1; radar warning.
ECM: ULQ/6; jammers.
Fire control: Mk 37 GFCS. Mk 105 TFCS.
Radars: Air search: Westinghouse SPS 29C ❺; B/C band; range 457 km *(250 nm)*.
Surface search: Raytheon SPS 10B ❻; G band.
Navigation: LN 66; I band.
Fire control: Western Electric Mk 25 ❼; I/J band.
IFF: UPX-1/UPX-12.
Sonars: SQS 43 (*Babr*), SQS 44 (*Palang*); hull-mounted; active search and attack; medium/high frequency.

Helicopters: 1 Agusta AB 204AS ❽.

Programmes: Two FRAM II conversion destroyers of the Allen M Sumner class transferred to Iran from the US Navy 19 March 1971 and 16 February 1972 respectively, both by sale.
Modernisation: Both ships received a full refit as well as conversion at Philadelphia NSY before sailing for Iran. This included a much-improved air-conditioning layout, the removal of B gun-mount with its magazine, altered accommodation, the fitting of a Canadian telescopic hangar, the siting of the four Standard missile launchers athwartships beside the new torpedo stowage between the funnels, the rigging of VDS and fitting of Hedgehogs in B position. VDS and Hedgehogs subsequently removed and a 23 mm gun fitted right aft.
Operational: Both ships reported doing regular patrols in 1991. The pennant numbers have the second digit painted out.

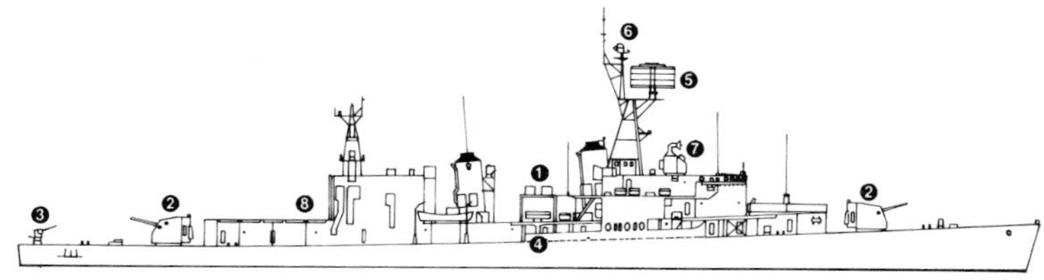
BABR (*Scale 1 : 1 200*), *Ian Sturton*

PALANG 7/1988

FRIGATES

3 VOSPER MARK 5 CLASS

Name	No	Builders	Laid down	Launched	Commissioned
ALVAND (ex-*Saam*)	71	Vosper Thornycroft, Woolston	22 May 1967	25 July 1968	20 May 1971
ALBORZ (ex-*Zaal*)	72	Vickers, Barrow	3 Mar 1968	4 Mar 1969	1 Mar 1971
SABALAN (ex-*Rostam*)	73	Vickers, Newcastle & Barrow	10 Dec 1967	4 Mar 1969	June 1972

Displacement, tons: 1100 standard; 1350 full load
Dimensions, feet (metres): 310 × 36.4 × 14.1 (screws) *(94.5 × 11.1 × 4.3)*
Main machinery: CODOG; 2 RR Olympus TM 3A gas turbines; 44 000 hp *(33 MW)* sustained; 2 Paxman Ventura 16CM diesels; 3800 hp *(2.83 MW)* sustained; 2 shafts
Speed, knots: 39 gas; 18 diesel. **Range, miles:** 3650 at 18 kts; 550 at 36 kts
Complement: 125 (accommodation for 146)

Missiles: SSM: 1 Sistel Sea Killer II quin launcher ❶; beam rider radio command or optical guidance to 25 km *(13.5 nm)* at 0.8 Mach; warhead 70 kg. May have been modified by removal of top row of cassettes to incorporate a BM-21 MRL.
Guns: 1 Vickers 4.5 in *(114 mm)*/55 Mk 8 ❷; 55° elevation; 25 rounds/minute to 22 km *(12 nm)* anti-surface; 6 km *(3.3 nm)* anti-aircraft; weight of shell 21 kg.
2 Oerlikon 35 mm/90 (twin) ❸; 85° elevation; 550 rounds/minute to 6 km *(3.3 nm)*; weight of shell 1.55 kg.
3 Oerlikon GAM-B01 20 mm ❹ (replaced 23 mm and both seaboats).
2—12.7 mm MGs.
A/S mortars: 1—3-tubed Limbo Mk 10 ❺; automatic loading; range 1000 m; warhead 92 kg.
Countermeasures: Decoys: 2 UK Mk 5 rocket flare launchers.
ESM: Decca RDL 2AC; radar warning. Racal FH 5-HF/DF.
Radars: Air/surface search: Plessey AWS 1 ❻; E/F band; range 110 km *(60 nm)*.
Surface search: Racal Decca 1226 ❼; I band.
Navigation: Decca 629; I band.
Fire control: Two Contraves Sea Hunter ❽; I/J band.
IFF: UK Mk 10.
Sonars: Graseby 174; hull-mounted; active search; medium/high frequency.
Graseby 170; hull-mounted; active attack; 15 kHz.

Programmes: It was announced on 25 August 1966 that Vosper Ltd, Portsmouth, had received an order for four Mark 5 frigates for the Iranian Navy, two of which were to be built by Vickers. *Sabalan* was towed to Barrow for completion.
Modernisation: *Alvand* and *Alborz* taken in hand by HM Dockyard Devonport July/August 1975 for major refit including replacement of Mk 5 4.5 in gun by Mk 8. Completed 1977. Modifications in 1988 included replacing Seacat with a 23 mm gun and boat davits with minor armaments. By 1990 the 23 mm and both boats had been replaced by GAM-B01 20 mm guns.
Structure: Air-conditioned throughout. Fitted with Vosper stabilisers.
Operational: *Sahand* sunk by USN on 18 April 1988. *Sabalan* had her back broken by a laser-guided bomb in the same skirmish but was out of dock by the end of 1990 and was operational again in late 1991.

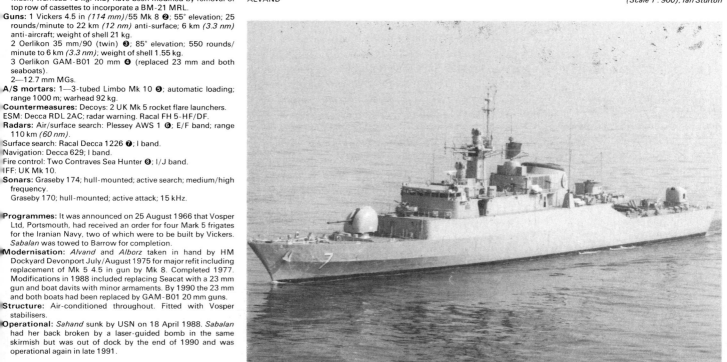

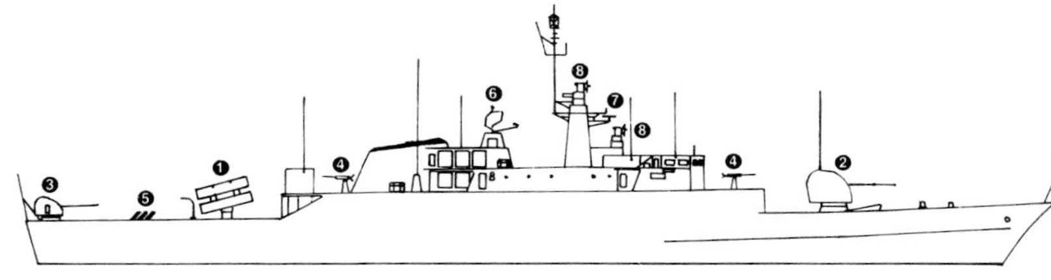
ALVAND (*Scale 1 : 900*), *Ian Sturton*

ALBORZ 1/1991

CORVETTES

2 Ex-US PF 103 CLASS

Name	*No*	*Builders*	*Laid down*	*Launched*	*Commissioned*
BAYANDOR (ex-US *PF 103*)	81	Levingstone Shipbuilding Co, Orange, Texas	20 Aug 1962	7 July 1963	18 May 1964
NAGHDI (ex-US *PF 104*)	82	Levingstone Shipbuilding Co, Orange, Texas	12 Sep 1962	10 Oct 1963	22 July 1964

Displacement, tons: 900 standard; 1135 full load
Dimensions, feet (metres): 275.6 × 33.1 × 10.2 *(84 × 10.1 × 3.1)*
Main machinery: 2 Fairbanks-Morse 38 TD 8-1/8-9 diesels; 5250 hp *(3.92 MW)* sustained; 2 shafts
Speed, knots: 20. **Range, miles:** 2400 at 18 kts; 4800 at 12 kts
Complement: 140

Guns: 2 US 3 in *(76 mm)*/50 Mk 34 ❶; 85° elevation; 50 rounds/minute to 12.8 km *(7 nm)*; weight of shell 6 kg.
2 Bofors 40 mm/60 (twin) ❷; 80° elevation; 120 rounds/minute to 10 km *(5.5 nm)*; weight of shell 0.89 kg.
2 Oerlikon GAM-B01 20 mm ❸. 2—12.7 mm MGs.
Fire control: Mk 63 for 76 mm gun. Mk 51 for 40 mm gun.
Radars: Air/surface search: Westinghouse SPS 6C ❹; D band; range 146 km *(80 nm)* (for fighter).
Navigation: Raytheon 1650 ❺; I/J band.
Fire control: Western Electric Mk 36 ❻; I/J band.
IFF: UPX-12B.
Sonars: EDO SQS 17A; hull-mounted; active attack; high frequency.

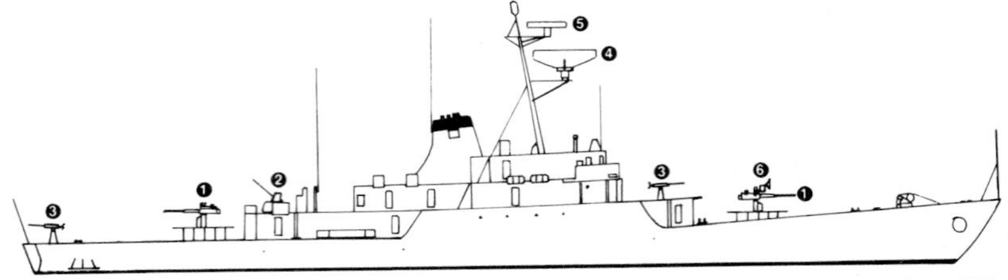

BAYANDOR *(Scale 1 : 900), Ian Sturton*

Programmes: Transferred from the USA to Iran under the Mutual Assistance programme in 1964.
Modernisation: *Naghdi* change of engines and reconstruction of accommodation completed in mid-1988. 23 mm gun and depth charge racks replaced by 20 mm guns in 1990.

Operational: *Milanian* and *Khanamuie* sunk in 1982 during war with Iraq.

BAYANDOR *9/1990*

SHIPBORNE AIRCRAFT

Numbers/Type: 9 Agusta AB 204ASW.
Operational speed: 104 kts *(193 km/h)*.
Service ceiling: 11 500 ft *(3505 m)*.
Range: 332 nm *(615 km)*.
Role/Weapon systems: Only small ship helicopter in service, mainly engaged in ASV operations in defence of oil installations. Sensors: APS 705 search radar, dipping sonar (if carried). Weapons: ASW; 2 × torpedoes. ASV; 2 × AS 12 missiles.

LAND-BASED MARITIME AIRCRAFT (FRONT LINE)

Numbers/Type: 6 Agusta-Sikorsky ASH-3D Sea King.
Operational speed: 120 kts *(222 km/h)*.
Service ceiling: 12 200 ft *(3720 m)*.
Range: 630 nm *(1165 km)*.
Role/Weapon systems: Shore-based ASW helicopter to defend major port and oil installations. Sensors: Selenia search radar, dipping sonar. Weapons: ASW; 4 × A244/S torpedoes or depth bombs.

Numbers/Type: 2 Lockheed P-3F Orion.
Operational speed: 410 kts *(760 km/h)*.
Service ceiling: 28 300 ft *(8625 m)*.
Range: 4000 nm *(7410 km)*.
Role/Weapon systems: One of the remaining aircraft used for early warning and control duties for strikes. Sensors: Search radar, sonobuoys. Weapons: ASW; various weapons can be carried.

Numbers/Type: 5 Sikorsky RH-53D.
Operational speed: 125 kts *(232 km/h)*.
Service ceiling: 11 100 ft *(3385 m)*.
Range: 405 nm *(750 km)*.
Role/Weapon systems: Mine clearance and surface search helicopter. Sensors: Weather radar. Weapons: Unarmed.

Numbers/Type: 5 Lockheed C-130H-MP Hercules.
Operational speed: 325 kts *(602 km/h)*.
Service ceiling: 33 000 ft *(10 060 m)*.
Range: 4250 nm *(7876 km)*.
Role/Weapon systems: Long-range maritime reconnaissance role. Sensors: Search/weather radar. Weapons: Unarmed.

LIGHT FORCES

Note: In addition to the vessels listed Iran has at least one Osa II and one Bogomol class patrol craft from Iraq, refugees from the Gulf War in 1991. It is unlikely they will be returned.

3 Ex-NORTH KOREA CHAHO CLASS (FAST ATTACK CRAFT—GUN)

Displacement, tons: 70 standard; 82 full load
Dimensions, feet (metres): 85.3 × 19 × 6.6 *(26 × 5.8 × 2)*
Main machinery: 4 diesels; 4 shafts
Speed, knots: 40
Complement: 17
Guns: 2 USSR 23 mm/80 (twin) (aft). 2—14.5 mm (twin) MG (forward). 1 BM-21 40-barrelled rocket launcher (MRL).
Radars: Surface search: Racal Decca; I band.

Comment: Built in North Korea. Transferred to Iran in April 1987 and re-engined (type unknown) so top speed may be reduced. Called the Zafar class by the Iranians. Hull based on Soviet P6 class.

CHAHO Class *4/1988*

10 COMBATTANTE II (KAMAN) CLASS (FAST ATTACK CRAFT—MISSILE)

Name	No	Builders	Commissioned
KAMAN	P 221	CMN, Cherbourg	12 Aug 1977
ZOUBIN	P 222	CMN, Cherbourg	12 Sep 1977
KHADANG	P 223	CMN, Cherbourg	15 Mar 1978
FALAKHON	P 226	CMN, Cherbourg	31 Mar 1978
SHAMSHIR	P 227	CMN, Cherbourg	31 Mar 1978
GORZ	P 228	CMN, Cherbourg	22 Aug 1978
GARDOUNEH	P 229	CMN, Cherbourg	11 Sep 1978
KHANJAR	P 230	CMN, Cherbourg	1 Aug 1981
NEYZEH	P 231	CMN, Cherbourg	1 Aug 1981
TABARZIN	P 232	CMN, Cherbourg	1 Aug 1981

Displacement, tons: 249 standard; 275 full load
Dimensions, feet (metres): 154.2 × 23.3 × 6.2 *(47 × 7.1 × 1.9)*
Main machinery: 4 MTU 16V 538 TB 91 diesels; 12 280 hp(m) *(9.03 MW)* sustained; 4 shafts
Speed, knots: 37.5. **Range, miles:** 2000 at 15 kts; 700 at 33.7 kts
Complement: 31

Missiles: SSM: 4 McDonnell Douglas Harpoon or Chinese C 801.
Guns: 1 OTO Melara 3 in *(76 mm)*/62 compact; 85° elevation; 85 rounds/minute to 16 km *(8.7 nm)* anti-surface; 12 km *(6.6 nm)* anti-aircraft; weight of shell 6 kg; 320 rounds.
1 Breda Bofors 40 mm/70; 90° elevation; 300 rounds/minute to 12 km *(6.6 nm)*; weight of shell 0.96 kg; 900 rounds.
Countermeasures: ESM: TMV 433 Dalia; radar intercept
ECM: Alligator; jammer.
Radars: Surface search/fire control: Signaal WM 28; I/J band.
Navigation: Racal Decca 1226; I band.
IFF: UPZ 27N/APX 72.

Programmes: Ordered in February 1974. The transfer of the last three craft was delayed by the French Government after the Iranian revolution. On 12 July 1981 France decided to hand them over. This took place on 1 August—on 2 August they sailed and soon after *Tabarzin* was seized by a pro-Royalist group off Cadiz. After the latter surrendered to the French in Toulon further problems were prevented by sending all three to Iran in a merchant ship.
Structure: The last three were not fitted with Harpoon tubes on delivery. Portable SA-7 launchers may be embarked in some. Harpoon may have been replaced by Chinese SSM.
Operational: *Peykan* was sunk in 1980 by Iraq; *Joshan* in April 1988 by the USN.

KAMAN Class *11/1987*

0 + 10 Ex-CHINESE HEGU CLASS (FAST ATTACK CRAFT—MISSILE)

Displacement, tons: 68 standard; 79.2 full load
Dimensions, feet (metres): 88.6 × 20.7 × 4.3 *(27 × 6.3 × 1.3)*
Main machinery: 4 Type L-12V-180 diesels; 4800 hp(m) *(3.53 MW)*; 4 shafts
Speed, knots: 37.5. **Range, miles:** 400 at 30 kts
Complement: 17 (2 officers)

Missiles: SSM: 4 Ying Ji (Eagle Strike); inertial cruise; active radar homing to 40 km *(22 nm)* at 0.9 Mach; warhead 165 kg; sea-skimmer.
Guns: 2 USSR 25 mm/60 (twin); 85° elevation; 270 rounds/minute to 3 km *(1.6 nm)* anti-aircraft; weight of shell 0.34 kg.
Radars: Surface search: Square Tie; I band
IFF: High Pole A.

Programmes: Chinese variant of the Komar class with a steel hull which has been building since the late 1970s. Sometimes called the Hoku class. Negotiations for sale started in late 1991; the date of transfer may depend on whether these vessels are new or second hand. Similar craft transferred to Bangladesh, Pakistan and Egypt.

3 US COAST GUARD CAPE CLASS (LARGE PATROL CRAFT)

Name	No	Builders	Commissioned
KAIVAN	201	USA	14 Jan 1956
AZADI (ex-*Tiran*)	202	US Coast Guard, Curtis Bay, Maryland	1957
MAHVAN	204	USA	1959

Displacement, tons: 98 standard; 148 full load
Dimensions, feet (metres): 95 × 20.2 × 6.6 *(28.9 × 6.2 × 2)*
Main machinery: 4 Cummins NYHMS-1200 diesels; 2120 hp *(1.58 MW)*; 2 shafts
Speed, knots: 21. **Range, miles:** 460 at 20 kts; 2324 at 8 kts
Complement: 15
Guns: 1 Bofors 40 mm/60. 2 USSR 23 mm/80 (twin). 2—12.7 mm MGs.
Depth charges: 2 racks; 8—136 kg charges.
Sonars: Hull-mounted; active attack; high frequency (probably not operational).

Comment: *Mehran* (203) destroyed during war with Iraq. *Kaivan* and *Mahvan* damaged but have been made operational again. The Mk 22 Mousetrap was replaced by the USSR ZU 23 mm/80 twin mounting which may in turn have been replaced by an Oerlikon 20 mm.

3 IMPROVED PGM-71 CLASS (LARGE PATROL CRAFT)

Name	No	Builders	Commissioned
PARVIN (ex-US *PGM 103*)	211	Peterson Builders Inc	1967
BAHRAM (ex-US *PGM 112*)	212	Peterson Builders Inc	1969
NAHID (ex-US *PGM 122*)	213	Peterson Builders Inc	1970

Displacement, tons: 98 standard; 148 full load
Dimensions, feet (metres): 101 × 21.3 × 8.3 *(30.8 × 6.5 × 2.5)*
Main machinery: 8 GM 6-71 diesels; 1392 hp *(1.04 MW)* sustained; 2 shafts
Speed, knots: 22. **Range, miles:** 1140 at 17 kts

Complement: 20
Guns: 1 Bofors 40 mm/60. 2 Oerlikon 20 mm. 2—12.7 mm MGs.
Depth charges: 4 racks (8 US Mk 6).
Radars: Surface search: Decca 303; I band.
Sonars: SQS 17B; hull-mounted active attack; high frequency.

Comment: The heavier 40 mm gun is mounted aft and the 20 mm forward to compensate for the large SQS 17B sonar dome under the bows.

5 WELLINGTON (BH.7) CLASS (HOVERCRAFT)

101-105

Displacement, tons: 53.8 full load
Dimensions, feet (metres): 78.3 × 45.6 × 5.6 (skirt) *(23.9 × 13.9 × 1.7)*
Main machinery: 1 RR Proteus 15 M/541 gas turbine; 4250 hp *(3.17 MW)*
Speed, knots: 70; 30 in sea state 5 or more. **Range, miles:** 620 at 66 kts
Guns: 2 Browning 12.7 mm MGs.
Radars: Surface search: Decca 1226; I band.

Comment: First pair are British Hovercraft Corporation 7 Mk 4 commissioned in 1970-71 and the next four are Mk 5 craft commissioned in 1974-75. Mk 5 craft fitted for, but not with Standard missiles. Some refitted in UK in 1984. Can embark troops and vehicles or normal support cargoes. Two probably operational, three in refit/reserve. One was sunk during the war with Iraq.

WELLINGTON Hovercraft 103 *9/1985, Michael D. J. Lennon*

8 WINCHESTER (SR.N6) CLASS (HOVERCRAFT)

01-08

Displacement, tons: 10.9 full load
Dimensions, feet (metres): 48.5 × 23 × 3.9 (skirt) *(14.8 × 7 × 1.2)*
Main machinery: 1 RR Gnome Model 1050 gas turbine; 1050 hp *(783 kW)*
Speed, knots: 60. **Range, miles:** 170 at 54 kts
Complement: 3
Guns: 1 or 2—12.7 mm MGs.
Radars: Surface search: Decca 202; I band.

Comment: Ordered 1970-72 and commissioned 1973-75. First three were Mk 3, remainder Mk 4. Some refitted in UK in 1984. Can carry 20 troops and 5 tons of cargo. Can also be fitted with four 500 kg mines on the side decks. Probably only half are operational.

WINCHESTER Hovercraft 03 *1971*

MINE WARFARE FORCES

1 US CAPE CLASS (MINESWEEPER—INSHORE)

Name	No	Builders	Commissioned
RIAZI (ex-*MSI 13*)	312	Tacoma Boatbuilding Co	15 Oct 1964

Displacement, tons: 239 full load
Dimensions, feet (metres): 111 × 23 × 7.9 *(33.9 × 7 × 2.4)*
Main machinery: 4 Type 2490 8V diesels; 1300 hp *(970 kW)*; 2 shafts
Speed, knots: 13. **Range, miles:** 1200 at 12 kts; 3500 at 8 kts
Complement: 21 (5 officers)
Guns: 1—12.7 mm MG.
Radars: Surface search: Decca 303N; I band

Comment: Delivered to Iran under MAP. Laid down on 1 February 1963, and transferred at Seattle, Washington, on 15 October 1964. *Riazi* is still operational with mechanical, acoustic and magnetic sweep gear.

RIAZI (old pennant number) *1975, Imperial Iranian Navy*

2 Ex-US MSC 292 and 268 CLASS (MINESWEEPERS—COASTAL)

Name	No	Builders	Commissioned
SHAHROKH (ex-USS *MSC 276*)	301	Bellingham Shipyards Co	1960
KARKAS (ex-USS *MSC 292*)	303	Peterson Builders Inc	1959

Displacement, tons: 376 (*Shahrokh*); 384 (*Karkas*) full load
Dimensions, feet (metres): 145.8 × 28 × 8.3 *(44.5 × 8.5 × 2.5)*
Main machinery: 2 GM 8-268A diesels (*Shahrokh*); 880 hp *(656 kW)*; 2 shafts
4 GM diesels (*Karkas*); 890 hp *(664 kW)*; 2 shafts
Speed, knots: 13. **Range, miles:** 2400 at 10 kts
Complement: 40 (6 officers)
Guns: 2 Oerlikon 20 mm (twin).
Radars: Surface search: Decca; I band.

Comment: Originally class of four. Of wooden construction with mechanical, acoustic and magnetic sweeps. Transferred from the USA to Iran under MAP. *Shahrokh* now in the Caspian Sea as a training ship. *Karkas* still active but rarely seen at sea.

AMPHIBIOUS FORCES

4 HENGAM CLASS (LSL)

Name	No	Builders	Commissioned
HENGAM	511	Yarrow (Shipbuilders) Ltd, Clyde	12 Aug 1974
LARAK	512	Yarrow (Shipbuilders) Ltd, Clyde	12 Nov 1974
TONB	513	Yarrow (Shipbuilders) Ltd, Clyde	21 Feb 1985
LAVAN	514	Yarrow (Shipbuilders) Ltd, Clyde	16 Jan 1985

Displacement, tons: 2540 full load
Dimensions, feet (metres): 305 × 49 × 7.3 *(93 × 15 × 2.4)*
Main machinery: 4 Paxman Ventura 12 CM diesels *(Hengam, Larak)*; 3000 hp *(2.24 MW)* sustained; 2 shafts
4 MTU 16V 652 TB 81 diesels *(Tonb, Lavan)*; 4600 hp(m) *(3.38 MW)* sustained; 2 shafts
Speed, knots: 14.5. **Range, miles:** 4000+ at 12 kts
Complement: 80
Military lift: Up to 9 tanks depending on size; 600 tons cargo; 227 troops; 10 ton crane

Guns: 4 Bofors 40 mm/60 (*Hengam* and *Larak*). 8 USSR 23 mm/80 (4 twin) (*Tonb* and *Lavan*). 2—12.7 mm MGs.
1 BM-21 multiple rocket launcher.
Countermeasures: Decoys: 2 UK Mk 5 rocket flare launchers.
Radars: Navigation: Racal Decca 1229; I band.
IFF: SSR 1520 (*Hengam* and *Larak*).
Tacan: URN 25.

Helicopters: Can embark 1 medium.

Programmes: Named after islands in the Gulf. First two ordered 25 July 1972. Four more ordered 20 July 1977. The material for the last two ships of the second order had been ordered by Yarrows when the order was cancelled in early 1979. *Tonb* carried out trials in October 1984 followed by *Lavan* later in the year and both were released by the UK in 1985 as 'Hospital Ships'.
Structure: Smaller than British *Sir Lancelot* design with no through tank deck.
Operational: Two LCVPs and a number of small landing craft can be carried. Can act as Depot Ships for MCMV and small craft and have been used to ferry Pasdaran small craft around the Gulf.

LAVAN — *2/1991, 92 Wing RAAF*

2 IRAN AJR CLASS (LSTs)

IRAN ASIR (ex-*Arya Akian*) **IRAN GHAYDR** (ex-*Arya Sahand*)

Displacement, tons: 2274 full load
Measurement, tons: 1691 gross
Dimensions, feet (metres): 176 × 35.4 × 9.9 *(53.7 × 10.8 × 3)*
Main machinery: 2 diesels; 2200 hp(m) *(1.62 MW)*; 2 shafts
Speed, knots: 12.5
Complement: 30
Military lift: 650 tons
Guns: 2—12.7 mm MGs.

Comment: Five built by Teraoka, Japan in 1978-79. Ro-Ro landing craft acquired by the Iranian Navy in 1980 primarily for minelaying. The *Iran Ajr* was captured and scuttled by the US Navy in September 1987 and two others of the class were sunk by Iraq in 1980.

3 IRAN HORMUZ 24 CLASS (LSTs)

24-26

Displacement, tons: 2014 full load
Dimensions, feet (metres): 239.8 × 46.6 × 8.2 *(73.1 × 14.2 × 2.5)*
Main machinery: 2 Daihatsu 6DLM-22 diesels; 2400 hp(m) *(1.76 MW)*; 2 shafts
Speed, knots: 12
Complement: 30 plus 110 berths
Military lift: 9 tanks, 140 troops

Comment: Built by Inchon, South Korea in 1985-86 and as with the Iran Hormuz class officially classed as Merchant Ships. Large bow doors. Have been used to support Pasdaran activities.

3 IRAN HORMUZ 21 CLASS (LCT)

21-23

Displacement, tons: 1400 full load
Measurement, tons: 750 dwt
Dimensions, feet (metres): 213.3 × 39.4 × 8.5 *(65 × 12 × 2.6)*
Main machinery: 2 MAN V12V-12.5/14 diesels; 730 hp(m) *(537 kW)*; 2 shafts
Speed, knots: 9
Complement: 28
Military lift: 600 tons

Comment: Officially ordered for 'civilian use' and built by Ravenstein, Netherlands in 1984-85. Similar but slightly smaller than the Iran Ajr class. No 21 is operational but the others are in a poor state of repair.

1 FOQUE CLASS (LSLs)

FOQUE 101

Displacement, tons: 250 full load
Dimensions, feet (metres): 124.6 × 33.5 × 5.9 *(38 × 10.2 × 1.8)*
Military lift: 120 tons

Comment: Launched at the Nuh-e Nabi shipyard, Bandar Abbas on 17 June 1988. More of the class to follow but apparently these are 'civilian' ships.

6 ROTORK CRAFT (LCU)

Displacement, tons: 9 full load
Dimensions, feet (metres): 41.7 × 10.5 × 3 *(12.7 × 3.2 × 0.9)*
Main machinery: 2 Volvo Penta diesels; 240 hp(m) *(176 kW)*; 2 shafts
Speed, knots: 28
Military lift: 30 troops
Guns: Up to 4—7.62 mm MGs.

Comment: Some are used by the Coast Guard. Many of these craft have been deleted.

SERVICE FORCES

2 FLEET SUPPLY SHIPS

Name	No	Builders	Commissioned
BANDAR ABBAS	421	C Lühring Yard, Brake, West Germany	Apr 1974
BOUSHEHR	422	C Lühring Yard, Brake, West Germany	Nov 1974

Displacement, tons: 4673 full load
Measurement, tons: 3250 dwt; 3186 gross
Dimensions, feet (metres): 354.2 × 54.4 × 14.8 *(108 × 16.6 × 4.5)*
Main machinery: 2 MAN 6L 52/55 diesels; 12 060 hp(m) *(8.86 MW)* sustained; 2 shafts
Speed, knots: 20. **Range, miles:** 3500 at 16 kts
Complement: 59
Guns: 2 USSR 23 mm/80 (twin). 2 Oerlikon 20 mm. 8—14.5 mm (2 quad) MGs.
Radars: Navigation: Two Decca 1226; I band.
Helicopters: 1 light reconnaissance.

Comment: *Bandar Abbas* launched 11 August 1973, *Boushehr* launched 23 March 1974. Combined tankers and store-ships carrying victualling, armament and general stores. Telescopic hangar for Bell UH-1N size helicopter. Both carry 2 SA-7 portable SAM and 20 mm guns have been fitted alongside the hangar.

BOUSHEHR — *2/1990*

1 Ex-US AMPHION CLASS (REPAIR SHIP)

Name	No	Builders	Commissioned
CHAH BAHAR (ex-USS *Amphion*, ex-*AR 13*)	441	Tampa Shipbuilding Co	30 Jan 1946

Displacement, tons: 8941 standard; 14 803 full load
Dimensions, feet (metres): 492 × 69.6 × 27.5 *(150.1 × 21.2 × 8.4)*
Main machinery: 2 Foster-Wheeler boilers; 2 Westinghouse turbines; 8560 hp *(6.39 MW)*; 1 shaft
Speed, knots: 18. **Range, miles:** 13 950 at 11.5 kts
Complement: 880

Comment: Launched on 15 May 1945. Transferred on loan to the Iran Navy on 2 October 1971. Purchased 1 March 1977. Non-operational and based at Bandar Abbas as permanent repair facility. Two US 3 in (76 mm)/50 guns have been removed but navigational radar (SPS 4) is retained.

CHAH BAHAR (old pennant number) — *1972, Imperial Iranian Navy*

1 REPLENISHMENT SHIP

Name	*No*	*Builders*	*Commissioned*
KHARG	431	Swan Hunter Ltd, Wallsend	5 Oct 1984

Displacement, tons: 11 064 light; 33 014 full load
Measurement, tons: 9367 dwt; 18 582 gross
Dimensions, feet (metres): 679 × 86.9 × 30 *(207.2 × 26.5 × 9.2)*
Main machinery: 2 Babcock & Wilcox boilers; 2 Westinghouse turbines; 26 870 hp *(19.75 MW)*; 1 shaft
Speed, knots: 21.5
Complement: 248
Guns: 1 OTO Melara 76 mm/62 compact. 4 USSR 23 mm/80 (2 twin).
Radars: Navigation: Two Decca 1229; I band.
IFF: 955M.
Helicopters: Three can be embarked (twin hangar).

Comment: Ordered October 1974. Laid down 27 January 1976. Launched 3 February 1977. Ship handed over to Iranian crew on 25 April 1980 but remained in UK. In 1983 Iranian Government requested this ship's transfer. The British Government delayed approval until January 1984. On 10 July 1984 began refit at Tyne Ship Repairers. Trials began 4 September 1984 and ship was then delivered without guns which have now been fitted. A design incorporating some of the features of the British Ol class but carrying ammunition and dry stores in addition to fuel. Inmarsat fitted.

KHARG *3/1987, Michael D. J. Lennon*

2 KANGAN CLASS (WATER TANKERS)

Name	*No*	*Builders*	*Commissioned*
KANGAN	411	Mazagon Dock, Bombay	1978
TAHERI	412	Mazagon Dock, Bombay	1979

Displacement, tons: 12 000 full load
Measurement, tons: 9430 dwt
Dimensions, feet (metres): 485.6 × 70.5 × 16.4 *(148 × 21.5 × 5)*
Main machinery: 1 MAN 7L52/55A diesel; 7385 hp(m) *(5.43 MW)* sustained; 1 shaft
Speed, knots: 15
Complement: 14
Cargo capacity: 9000 cu m of water
Guns: 2 USSR 23 mm/80 (twin). 2—12.7 mm MGs.
Radars: Navigation: Decca 1229; I band.

Comment: Accommodation is air-conditioned. These are two of the largest water tankers afloat and are used to supply remote coastal towns and islands.

TAHERI *5/1989*

7 DELVAR CLASS (SUPPORT SHIPS)

CHARAK **CHIROO** **DELVAR** **DILIM**
SOURU **SIRJAN** **DAYER**

Measurement, tons: 890 gross; 765 dwt
Dimensions, feet (metres): 210 × 34.4 × 10.9 *(64 × 10.5 × 3.3)*
Main machinery: 2 MAN G6V 23.5/33ATL diesels; 1560 hp(m) *(1.15 MW)*; 2 shafts
Speed, knots: 11
Guns: 2 USSR 23 mm/80 (twin).
Radars: Navigation: Decca 1226; I band.

Comment: All built by Karachi SY in 1980-82. *Delvar* and *Sirjan* are ammunition ships, *Dayer* and *Dilim* water carriers and the other three are general cargo ships. The water carriers have only one crane (against two on the other types), and have rounded sterns (as opposed to transoms).

1 TUG

YORKSHIREMAN

Comment: Of 686 tons, acquired in 1987.

1 BUOY TENDER

Comment: Of 2400 grt, built by Iran Marine and launched on 29 January 1987.

14 HARBOUR TUGS

No 1 (ex-West German *Karl*) **MENAB** **SEFID-RUD**
No 2 (ex-West German *Ise*) **HARI-RUD** **ATRAK**
HAAMOON **ARAS** **+5** (YTM class)
HIRMAND

Comment: All between 70 and 90 ft in length. All but the first two (which were built in the early 1960s and acquired in June 1974) built in 1984-85.

6 HENDIJAN CLASS (TENDERS)

HENDIJAN **KONARAK** **SIRIK**
KALAT **GENAVEH** **SAVATAR**

Measurement, tons: 445 grt
Dimensions, feet (metres): 154.3 × 28.1 × 11.5 *(47 × 8.6 × 3.5)*
Main machinery: 2 diesels; 2 shafts

Comment: Built by Damen, Netherlands 1988-90.

KONORAK *6/1989, Gilbert Gyssels*

4 UTILITY CRAFT

1701 **1702** **BAKHTARAN** **KORAMSHAHR**

Comment: 1701 and 1702 of 213 ft *(65 m)* and built by Karachi SY and Eng Works. Completed 1977-78. *Bakhtaran* and *Koramshahr* of 166.5 ft *(50.8 m)* and built by Scheepswerf Damen in 1985.

45+ BARGES AND SERVICE CRAFT

Comment: Many built in Karachi 1976-79 the largest being a 260 ft *(79.2 m)* self-propelled lighter. The latest to be delivered from Iran Marine is of 1000 grt and was launched on 2 March 1987.

2 FLOATING DOCKS

400 (ex-US *ARD 29*, ex-*FD 4*) **DOLPHIN**

Dimensions, feet (metres): 487 × 80.2 × 32.5 *(149.9 × 24.7 × 10) (400)*
786.9 × 172.1 × 58.4 *(240 × 52.5 × 17.8) (Dolphin)*

Comment: *400* is an ex-US ARD 12 class built by Pacific Bridge, California and transferred in 1977; lift 3556 tons. *Dolphin* built by MAN-GHH Nordenham, West Germany and completed in November 1985; lift 28 000 tons.

EX-YACHTS

Name	*No*	*Builders*	*Commissioned*
HAMZEH (ex-*Shahsavar*)	155	NV Boele, Bolnes, Netherlands	1936

Displacement, tons: 530
Dimensions, feet (metres): 176 × 25.3 × 10.5 *(53.7 × 7.7 × 3.2)*
Main machinery: 2 Werkspoor-Stork diesels; 1318 hp(m) *(969 kW)*; 2 shafts
Speed, knots: 15
Complement: 25

Comment: Transported by floating dock through the Soviet canal system to Bandar Anjali on the Caspian Sea. Refitted in 1956 by Muggiano, La Spezia. No military value but manned by the Navy.

KISH

Displacement, tons: 178 full load
Dimensions, feet (metres): 122 × 24.9 × 7.3 *(37.2 × 7.6 × 2.2)*
Main machinery: 2 MTU diesels; 2920 hp(m) *(2.15 MW)*; 2 shafts
Speed, knots: 20
Complement: 20
Radars: Navigation: I band

Comment: Completed in 1970 by Yacht und Bootswerft, West Germany. Refitted in Bandar Abbas and used for training.

ABNEGAR (ex-*Glimmer*)

Displacement, tons: 85 full load
Dimensions, feet (metres): 67.9 × 19.4 × 7.5 *(20.7 × 5.9 × 2.3)*
Main machinery: 1 Kelvin T8 diesel; 240 hp *(179 kW)*; 1 shaft

Comment: Built at Malahide Shipyard, Dublin in 1972 as a yacht. Acquired by the Navy in 1974 and used as survey ship.

COASTAL PATROL CRAFT

11 US Mk III CLASS (COASTAL PATROL CRAFT)

Displacement, tons: 41.6 full load
Dimensions, feet (metres): 65 × 18.1 × 6 *(19.8 × 5.5 × 1.8)*
Main machinery: 3 GM 8V 71 TI diesels; 690 hp *(515 kW)* sustained; 3 shafts
Speed, knots: 30. **Range, miles:** 500 at 28 kts
Complement: 5
Guns: 3—12.7 mm (1 twin, 1 single) MGs.
Radars: Surface search: RCA LN-66; I band

Comment: Twenty ordered from Marinette Marine Corp, Wisconsin, USA; the first delivered in December 1975 and the last in December 1976. A further 50 were ordered in 1976 to be shipped out and completed in Iran. It is not known how many were finally assembled. Six lost in the Gulf war, others have been scrapped.

US Mk III *1991*

6 US Mk II CLASS (COASTAL PATROL CRAFT)

Displacement, tons: 22.9 full load
Dimensions, feet (metres): 49.9 × 15.1 × 4.3 *(15.2 × 4.6 × 1.3)*
Main machinery: 2 GM 8V-71 TI diesels; 460 hp *(343 kW)* sustained; 2 shafts
Speed, knots: 28. **Range, miles:** 750 at 26 kts
Complement: 6
Guns: 4—12.7 mm (2 twin) MGs.
Radars: Surface search: SPS 6; I band.

Comment: Twenty-six ordered from Peterson, USA in 1976-77. Six were for the Navy and the remainder for the Imperial Gendarmerie. All were built in association with Arvandan Maritime Corporation, Abadan. The six naval units operate in the Caspian sea. Of the remaining 20, six were delivered complete and the others were only 65 per cent assembled on arrival in Iran. Some were lost when the Iraqi army captured Kormansaar. Others have been lost at sea.

70 PBI TYPE (COASTAL PATROL CRAFT)

Displacement, tons: 20.1 full load
Dimensions, feet (metres): 50 × 15 × 4 *(15.2 × 4.6 × 1.2)*
Main machinery: 2 GM 8V-71 TI diesels; 460 hp *(343 kW)* sustained; 2 shafts
Speed, knots: 28. **Range, miles:** 750 at 26 kts
Complement: 5 (1 officer)
Missiles: SSM: Tigercat; range 6 km *(3.2 nm)*.
Guns: 2—12.7 mm MGs.
Radars: Surface search: I band.

Comment: Ordered by Iranian Arvandan Maritime Company. First 19 completed by Petersons and remainder shipped as kits for completion in Iran. The SSM is crude and unguided.

PBI Type *1991*

12 ENFORCER TYPE

Displacement, tons: 4.7 full load
Dimensions, feet (metres): 30.5 × 11.2 × 3 *(9.3 × 3.4 × 0.9)*
Main machinery: 2 GM 6V-53 diesels; 296 hp *(221 kW)* sustained; 2 shafts
Speed, knots: 28. **Range, miles:** 146 at 16 kts
Complement: 4
Guns: 1—12.7 mm MG.
Radars: Surface search: Apelco AD7-7; I band.

Comment: Built by Bertram Yacht, Miami in 1972. Thirty-six units delivered; so far twenty-four deleted.

3 SEWART TYPE (COASTAL PATROL CRAFT)

MAHNAVI-HAMRAZ **MAHNAVI-VAHEDI** **MAHNAVI-TAHERI**

Displacement, tons: 9.1 full load
Dimensions, feet (metres): 40 × 12.1 × 3.3 *(12.2 × 3.7 × 1)*
Main machinery: 2 GM 6-71 diesels; 348 hp *(260 kW)* sustained; 2 shafts
Speed, knots: 31
Complement: 6
Guns: 1—12.7 mm MG.

Comment: Small launches for port duties of Sewart (USA) standard 40 ft type. Six transferred in 1970 and six in 1986. *Mardjan, Morvarid* and *Sadaf* given to Sudan in December 1975, remainder deleted.

35 BOGHAMMAR CRAFT

Displacement, tons: 6.4 full load
Dimensions, feet (metres): 41.2 × 8.6 × 2.3 *(13 × 2.7 × 0.7)*
Main machinery: 2 Volvo Penta TAMD 71A diesels; 714 hp(m) *(525 kW)*; or 2 Seatek 6-4V-9 diesels; 1160 hp *(853 kW)*; 2 shafts
Speed, knots: 46. **Range, miles:** 500 at 40 kts
Complement: 5/6
Guns: 1—12.7 mm MG. 1 RPG-7 rocket launcher or 106 mm recoilless rifle. 1—12-barrelled 107 mm rocket launcher (MRL)
Radars: Surface search: Decca 170; I band

Comment: Ordered in 1983 and completed in 1984-85 for Customs Service. Total of 51 delivered. Used extensively by the Pasdaran (Islamic Revolutionary Guard) for operations against merchant vessels in the Persian Gulf. Maximum payload 450 kg. Speed is dependent on load carried. They can be transported by Amphibious Lift Ships and can operate from bases at Farsi, Sirri and Abu Musa Islands with a main base at Bandar Abbas. Being re-engined with Seatek diesels from 1991. There are also a further 10—11 Metre craft with similar characteristics. Known as TAREQ or TORAGH boats.

BOGHAMMAR *1988*

35 BOSTON WHALER CRAFT (TYPE 1)

Displacement, tons: 1.3 full load
Dimensions, feet (metres): 22.3 × 7.4 × 1.2 *(6.7 × 2.3 × 0.4)*
Main machinery: 2 outboards; 240 hp *(179 kW)*
Speed, knots: 40+
Complement: 4
Guns: Various, but can include 1—12-barrelled 107 mm MRL or 1—12.7 mm MG.

Comment: Designed for coastal law enforcement by Boston Whaler Inc, USA. GRP hulls. Numerous indigenously constructed hulls.

BOSTON WHALER *1988*

RIVER ROADSTEAD PATROL AND HOVERCRAFT

Comment: Numerous craft used by the Revolutionary Guard include:
Type 2: Dimensions, feet (metres): 22.0 × 7.2 *(6.7 × 2.2)*; single outboard engine; 1—12.7 mm MG.
Type 3: Dimensions, feet (metres): 16.4 × 5.2 *(5.0 × 1.6)*; single outboard engine; small arms.
Type 4: Dimensions, feet (metres): 13.1-26.2 × 7.9 *(4-8 × 1.6)*; two outboard engines; small arms.
Type 5: Dimensions, feet (metres): 24.6 × 9.2 *(7.5 × 2.8)*; Damen assault craft.
Type 6: Dimensions, feet (metres): 30.9 × 11.8 *(9.4 × 3.6)*; single outboard engine; 1—12.7 mm MG.
Dhows: Dimensions, feet (metres): 77.1 × 20 *(23.5 × 6.1)*; single diesel engine; mine rails.
Yunus: Dimensions, feet (metres): 27.6 × 9.8 *(8.4 × 3)*; speed 32 kts.

YUNUS *1989*

IRAQ

Administration

Commander-in-Chief:
Rear Admiral Abd Muhammad Abdullah
Chief of Staff:
Commander Samad Sat Al Mufti

Bases

Basra, Umm Qasr, Az Zubayr

Mercantile Marine

Lloyd's Register of Shipping:
138 vessels of 930 535 tons

General

As expected some of the minor war vessels were recoverable after Operation Desert Storm in February/March 1991. The operational status of the survivors is questionable due to battle damage and the shortage of spare parts. Some captured Kuwaiti vessels were still held in late 1991.

DELETIONS

Note: Captured Kuwaiti vessels destroyed in 1991 are shown in *Kuwait* section.

Frigates

1992 *Hittin, Thi Qar, Al Qadisiya, Al Yarmouk* (all retained in Italian ports)

Corvettes

1992 *Mussa Ben Nussair, Tariq Ibn Ziad, Abdulla Ben Abi Sarh, Khalid Ibn Al Walid, Saad Ibn Abi Waccade, Salah Ad Deen Al Ayoori* (all retained in Italian ports until sold)

Patrol Forces

1991 2 Osa I, 5 Osa II (one to Iran), 6 P6, 3 SO1, 1 Poluchat I, 3 Zhuk, 8 PO2, 1 Bogomol (to Iran), 3 PB 90, 5 Winchester Hovercraft, 6 Rotork Type 412

Mine Warfare Forces

1991 1 Yevgenya, 2 T43

Amphibious Forces

1991 3 Polnochny

FRIGATES

Note: 1. Four Modified Lupo class frigates and six Assad class corvettes completed between 1985 and 1988 were not transferred and remained laid up in Italian ports in early 1992 (see *Italian* section for details). The frigates have been taken up by the Italian Navy, the corvettes are for sale.

2. Two Jianghu class frigates were to have been acquired from China in 1991 and this contract may be honoured in due course.

1 YUGOSLAV TYPE

Name	*No*	*Builders*	*Laid down*	*Launched*	*Commissioned*
IBN MARJID (ex-*Ibn Khaldoum*)	507	Uljanic, Yugoslavia	1977	1978	20 Mar 1980

Displacement, tons: 1850 full load
Dimensions, feet (metres): 317.3 × 36.7 × 14.8 *(96.7 × 11.2 × 4.5)*
Main machinery: CODOG; 1 RR Olympus TM 3B gas turbine; 21 500 hp *(16 MW)* sustained; 2 MTU 16V 956 TB 91 diesels; 7500 hp(m) *(5.5 MW)* sustained; 2 shafts
Speed, knots: 26 gas; 20 diesels. **Range, miles:** 4000 at 20 kts
Complement: 93 plus 100 trainees

Missiles: Can carry 4 Aerospatiale SSM Exocet ❶ (but not fitted).
Guns: 1 Bofors 57 mm/70 ❷. 1 Bofors 40 mm/70 ❸. 8 Oerlikon 20 mm (4 twin) ❹.
Torpedoes: Fitted for 2—21 in *(533 mm)* tubes.
Depth charges: 1 rail.
Countermeasures: ESM/ECM: Radar intercept and jammer.
Radars: Surface search/navigation: Two Racal Decca 1229 ❺; I band.
Fire control: Philips Elektronik 9LV200 Mk 2 ❻; J band.

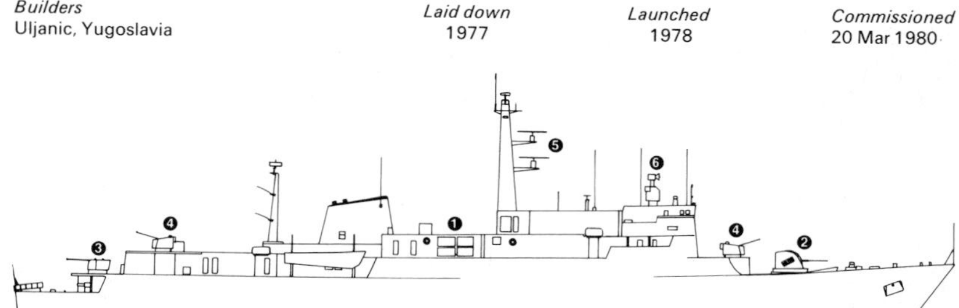

IBN MARJID *(Scale 1 : 900), Ian Sturton*

Sonars: Hull-mounted; active search and attack; medium frequency.

Structure: Near sister to Indonesian *Hajar Dewantara* but with no helicopter deck. Training ship with frigate capability.

Operational: Mainly used as a training ship and transport during war with Iran. Subsequently used mostly as an accommodation and supply ship and is unlikely to become operational again as a frigate.

LIGHT FORCES

Note: 1. In addition to the vessels listed, one Osa II and one Bogomol are held in Iranian ports.
2. A number of ex-Kuwaiti Vosper patrol craft and five ex-Kuwaiti Seagull class craft were still held by Iraq in late 1991.

1 BOGOMOL CLASS (COASTAL PATROL CRAFT)

Displacement, tons: 245 full load
Dimensions, feet (metres): 127.9 × 25.6 × 5.9 *(39 × 7.8 × 1.8)*
Main machinery: 3 diesels; 15 000 hp(m) *(11 MW)*; 3 shafts
Speed, knots: 37. **Range, miles:** 500 at 35 kts
Complement: 30
Guns: 1 USSR 3 in *(76 mm)*/66; 85° elevation; 120 rounds/minute to 15 km *(8 nm)*; weight of shell 7 kg.
2 USSR 30 mm/65 (twin); 85° elevation; 500 rounds/minute to 5 km *(2.7 nm)*; weight of shell 0.54 kg.
Radars: Surface search: Pot Head; H/I band.
Fire control: Bass Tilt; H/I band.

Comment: Delivered in March 1990. Similar to craft delivered to Guinea-Bissau. Another of this class held in an Iranian port in early 1992.

1 Ex-SOVIET POLUCHAT I CLASS (LARGE PATROL CRAFT)

Displacement, tons: 70 standard; 100 full load
Dimensions, feet (metres): 97.1 × 19 × 4.8 *(29.6 × 5.8 × 1.5)*
Main machinery: 2 diesels; 1700 hp(m) *(1.25 MW)*; 2 shafts
Speed, knots: 20. **Range, miles:** 1500 at 10 kts
Complement: 20
Guns: 2—14.5 mm (twin) MGs.
Radars: Surface search: Spin Trough; I band.

Comment: Transferred by the USSR in late 1960s. Also used for torpedo recovery.

2 Ex-SOVIET ZHUK CLASS (COASTAL PATROL CRAFT)

Displacement, tons: 50 full load
Dimensions, feet (metres): 75.4 × 17 × 6.2 *(23 × 5.2 × 1.9)*
Main machinery: 2 diesels; 2400 hp(m) *(1.76 MW)*; 2 shafts
Speed, knots: 30. **Range, miles:** 1100 at 15 kts
Complement: 17
Guns: 4—14.5 mm (2 twin) MGs. 1—12.7 mm MG.
Radars: Surface search: Spin Trough; I band.
IFF: High Pole B.

Comment: Transferred in 1975. Survivors of a class of five.

6 PB 90 CLASS (COASTAL PATROL CRAFT)

Displacement, tons: 90
Dimensions, feet (metres): 100 × 19.5 × 10 *(30.5 × 5.9 × 3.1)*
Main machinery: 3 diesels; 4350 hp(m) *(3.2 MW)*; 3 shafts
Speed, knots: 27. **Range, miles:** 800 at 20 kts
Complement: 17
Guns: 1 Bofors 40 mm/70. 4 Oerlikon 20 mm (quad). 2 twin 128 mm MRL.
Countermeasures: Decoys: 2 twin-barrelled Chaff launchers.
Radars: Surface search: Decca 1226; I band.

Comment: Built by Tito, Yugoslavia. Four of the class delivered via Kuwait in July 1984 and the remainder in 1985. Six sunk in war with Iran, and three more in Desert Storm.

1 SRN 6 MK 6 WINCHESTER CLASS (HOVERCRAFT)

Displacement, tons: 10.9 full load
Dimensions, feet (metres): 48.4 × 23 × 3.9 (skirt) *(14.8 × 7 × 1.2)*
Main machinery: 1 RR Gnome Model GT; 1050 hp *(783 kW)*
Speed, knots: 60. **Range, miles:** 170 at 54 kts
Complement: 3
Guns: 1—12.7 mm MG.

Comment: Six built by British Hovercraft, Cowes in 1981. Can carry five tons of cargo plus 20 troops. The sole survivor is probably non-operational.

SAWARI CLASS (INSHORE PATROL BOATS)

Comment: This is a range of Iraqi-built boats, the largest types being Sawari 4 of 11 m and 22 kts and Sawari 6 of 12.5 m and 25 kts. Most have outboard engines and are capable of 25 kts in calm conditions. Used as patrol boats and landing craft armed with MGs and rocket launchers.

MINE WARFARE FORCES

2 Ex-SOVIET YEVGENYA CLASS (MINEHUNTERS—INSHORE)

Displacement, tons: 90 full load
Dimensions, feet (metres): 80.7 × 18 × 4.9 *(24.6 × 5.5 × 1.5)*
Main machinery: 2 diesels; 400 hp(m) *(294 kW)*; 2 shafts
Speed, knots: 11. **Range, miles:** 300 at 10 kts
Complement: 10
Guns: 2—25 mm/80 (twin).
Radars: Navigation: Spin Trough; I band.
IFF: High Pole.
Sonars: Helo type VDS (on stern); minehunting; high frequency.

Comment: GRP hulls. Delivered in January 1975 under cover-name of 'oceanographic craft'. One sunk in Desert Storm; these two damaged but may have been repaired.

2 YUGOSLAV NESTIN CLASS (MINESWEEPERS—INSHORE)

Displacement, tons: 72 full load
Dimensions, feet (metres): 88.6 × 21.3 × 3.9 *(27 × 6.5 × 1.2)*
Main machinery: 2 diesels; 520 hp(m) *(382 kW)*; 2 shafts
Speed, knots: 12. **Range, miles:** 860 at 11 kts
Complement: 17
Guns: 3 Hispano 20 mm (triple).
Mines: Can lay 24.

Comment: Built Brodotehnika, Belgrade. Transferred 1979-80. Have magnetic, acoustic and explosive sweep gear. One deleted in 1989.

SERVICE FORCES

Note: In addition to the vessels listed below there were about six captured Kuwaiti LCUs, including three Cheverton Loadmasters still in Iraqi hands in late 1991.

3 TRANSPORT SHIPS

Name	*No*	*Builders*	*Commissioned*
AL ZAHRAA	426	Helsingør SY	21 Apr 1983
KHAWLA	428	Helsingør SY	July 1983
BALQEES	429	Helsingør SY	Oct 1983

Displacement, tons: 5800 full load
Measurement, tons: 3681 gross
Dimensions, feet (metres): 347.8 × 61.7 × 17.4 *(106 × 18.8 × 5.3)*
Main machinery: 2 MTU 12V1163 TB82 diesels; 6600 hp(m) *(4.85 MW)* sustained; 2 shafts
Speed, knots: 15.5
Complement: 35
Military lift: 250 troops; 16 tanks

Comment: Fitted with helicopter deck. A Ro-Ro design based on civilian requirements and therefore cannot beach. Fitted with a stern ramp capable of handling 55 ton tanks to shore and launching amphibious 41 ton tanks. 55 ton lift between decks. A 1200 ton trim arrangement allows the embarkation of small landing craft. At least one of the class sails under Iraqi Line colours.

BALQEES *4/1990, 92 Wing RAAF*

1 STROMBOLI CLASS (REPLENISHMENT TANKER)

Name	*No*	*Builders*	*Commissioned*
AGNADEEN	A 102	Castellamare di Stabia, Naples	29 Oct 1984

Displacement, tons: 3556 light; 8706 full load
Dimensions, feet (metres): 423.1 × 59 × 21.3 *(129 × 18 × 6.5)*
Main machinery: 2 GMT A 420.8 H diesels; 9400 hp(m) *(6.91 MW)* sustained; 1 shaft
Speed, knots: 18.5. **Range, miles:** 5080 at 18.5 kts
Complement: 115

Guns: 1 OTO Melara 3 in *(76 mm)*/62; 85° elevation; 60 rounds/minute to 16 km *(8.7 nm)* anti-surface; 5 km *(2.7 nm)* anti-aircraft; weight of shell 6 kg.
Radars: Navigation: SMA 3 RM; I band; range 73 km *(40 nm)*.
Fire control: Selenia RTN 10X; I/J band; range 40 km *(22 nm)*.

Programmes: Ordered 1 February 1981. Laid down 29 January 1982 under sub-contract from Fincantieri, Muggiano. Launched 22 October 1982. Completed 20 December 1983.
Structure: Underway replenishment facilities on both sides of the ship.
Operational: Laid up in Alexandria since 1986.

1 SPASILAC CLASS (SALVAGE SHIP)

Name	*No*	*Builders*	*Commissioned*
AKA	A 81 (ex-A 51)	Tito SY, Belgrade	1978

Displacement, tons: 1600 full load
Dimensions, feet (metres): 182 × 37.6 × 12.2 *(55.5 × 11.5 × 3.8)*
Main machinery: 2 diesels; 4340 hp(m) *(3.19 MW)*; 2 shafts; cp props
Speed, knots: 15. **Range, miles:** 1700 at 12 kts
Complement: 50
Guns: 4—14.5 mm MGs.
Radars: Navigation: Racal Decca; I band.

Comment: Similar to Libyan and Yugoslav naval ships. Can carry 750 tons of equipment and liquids. Has facilities for divers. Damaged in Desert Storm but may have been repaired.

AKA *1989, Peter Jones*

1 Ex-SOVIET POZHARNY (FIRE BOAT)

A 82

Displacement, tons: 180 full load
Dimensions, feet (metres): 114.5 × 20 × 6 *(34.9 × 6.1 × 1.8)*
Main machinery: 2 diesels; 1800 hp(m) *(1.32 MW)*; 2 shafts
Speed, knots: 10

Comment: Built in the mid-1950s. Survived Desert Storm.

A 82 *1989, Peter Jones*

1 PRESIDENTIAL YACHT

QADISSIYAT SADDAM

Displacement, tons: 1660 full load
Dimensions, feet (metres): 269 × 42.8 × 10.8 *(82 × 13 × 3.3)*
Main machinery: 2 MTU 12V 1163 TB82 diesels; 6600 hp(m) *(4.85 MW)*; 2 shafts
Speed, knots: 19

Comment: Built by Helsingør SY, Denmark. Completed September 1981. Helicopter deck. Accommodation for 56 passengers.

AGNADEEN *7/1988*

IRELAND

Senior Appointment

Flag Officer Commanding Naval Service:
Commodore J A Deasy

Naval Bases

Haulbowline Island (Cork), Headquarters' naval base and dockyard, sea-going replacement section, ship support and maintenance and communications section. Haulbowline Naval Base and Ballincollig Barracks, Cork, are the centres for all recruit and continuation training. A new training establishment is to be set up at Ringaskiddy in Cork Harbour.

Naval Requirement

If the EEZ is to be policed effectively, the OPV requirement is for 12 vessels (two at 2000 tons, six at 1000 tons and four at 500 tons).

Personnel

Establishment: 1266 (158 officers, 568 petty officers, 540 ratings)
(a) 1992: Currently under strength at 995 (125 officers)
(b) Voluntary service

Operational

All seven ships are in full commission in 1992.

Prefix to Ships' Names

L.É (Long Éirennach = Irish Ship)

Mercantile Marine

Lloyd's Register of Shipping:
187 vessels of 195 111 tons gross

1 P 31 CLASS (CORVETTE)

Name	*No*	*Builders*	*Laid down*	*Launched*	*Commissioned*
EITHNE	P 31	Verolme, Cork	15 Dec 1982	19 Dec 1983	7 Dec 1984

Displacement, tons: 1760 standard; 1910 full load
Dimensions, feet (metres): 265 × 39.4 × 14.1 *(80.8 × 12 × 4.3)*
Main machinery: 2 Ruston Paxman 12RKC diesels; 6800 hp *(5.07 MW)* sustained; 2 shafts
Speed, knots: 20+; 19 normal. **Range, miles:** 7000 at 15 kts
Complement: 85 (9 officers)

Guns: 1 Bofors 57 mm/70 Mk 1; 75° elevation; 200 rounds/minute to 17 km *(9.3 nm)*; weight of shell 2.4 kg.
2 Rheinmetall 20 mm/20.
2 Wallop 57 mm launchers for illuminants.
Fire control: Signaal LIOD system.
Radars: Air/surface search: Signaal DA 05 Mk 4; E/F band; range 137 km *(75 nm)* for 2 m² target.
Navigation: Two Racal Decca; I band.
Tacan: MEL RRB transponder.
Sonars: Plessey PMS 26; hull-mounted; lightweight; active search and attack; 10 kHz.

Helicopters: 1 SA 365F Dauphin 2.

EITHNE *1991, T. Smith, Irish Navy*

Programmes: Ordered 23 April 1982 from Verolme, Cork, this was the last ship to be built at this yard. It is reported that a second of class is being considered with EC assistance but this is not confirmed by the Navy.

Structure: Fitted with retractable stabilisers. Closed circuit TV for flight deck operations. Satellite navigation and communications.

Operational: Manpower problems have made it difficult to operate the helicopter but progress is being made with naval aircrew training.

4 P 21 and DEIRDRE CLASSES (PATROL VESSELS)

Name	*No*	*Builders*	*Commissioned*
DEIRDRE	P 20	Verolme, Cork	19 June 1972
EMER	P 21	Verolme, Cork	16 Jan 1978
AOIFE	P 22	Verolme, Cork	29 Nov 1979
AISLING	P 23	Verolme, Cork	21 May 1980

Displacement, tons: 972 *(Deirdre)*; 1019.5 (remainder)
Dimensions, feet (metres): 184.3 pp × 34.1 × 14.4 *(56.2 × 10.4 × 4.4) (Deirdre)*
213.7 × 34.4 × 14 *(65.2 × 10.5 × 4.4)* (remainder)
Main machinery: 2 British Polar SF112 VS-F diesels; 4200 hp *(3.13 MW)*; 1 shaft *(Deirdre)*
2 SEMT-Pielstick 6 PA6L-280 diesels; 4800 hp *(3.53 MW)*; 1 shaft (remainder)
Speed, knots: 17. **Range, miles:** 4000 at 17 kts; 6750 at 12 kts
Complement: 46 (5 officers)

Guns: 1 Bofors 40 mm/60; may be uprated from 120 to 180 rounds/minute.
2 GAMB-01 20 mm (except *Deirdre*); 60° elevation; 900 rounds/minute to 2 km.
2—12.7 mm MGs *(Deirdre)*.
Radars: Surface search: Selesmar/Selescan 1024; I band.
Navigation: Racal Decca RM 1229; I band.
Sonars: Simrad Marine; hull-mounted; active search; 34 kHz.

Programmes: *Deirdre* was the first vessel ever built for the Naval Service in Ireland.
Structure: All of Nevesbu design. Stabilisers fitted. *Aoife* and *Aisling* are of similar construction to *Emer* with the addition of a bow thruster and KaMeWa four-bladed skewed propeller. Satellite navigation and communications.
Operational: Decca Mk 53 Navigator and SATNAV. The practice of keeping one in reserve and rotating every six months was stopped at the end of 1990 and all have been operational since then.

AISLING *6/1989, Bram Risseeuw*

DEIRDRE *6/1991, Stefan Terzibaschitsch*

2 P 41 PEACOCK CLASS (PATROL VESSEL)

Name	*No*	*Builders*	*Commissioned*
ORLA (ex-HMS *Swift*)	P 41	Hall Russell, Aberdeen	3 May 1985
CIARA (ex-HMS *Swallow*)	P 42	Hall Russell, Aberdeen	17 Oct 1984

Displacement, tons: 712 full load
Dimensions, feet (metres): 204.1 × 32.8 × 8.9 *(62.6 × 10 × 2.7)*
Main machinery: 2 Crossley SEMT-Pielstick 18 PA6V 280 diesels; 14 400 hp(m) *(10.58 MW)* sustained; 2 shafts; auxiliary drive; Schottel prop; 181 hp(m) *(133 kW)*
Speed, knots: 25. **Range, miles:** 2500 at 17 kts
Complement: 39 (6 officers)

Guns: 1—3 in (76 mm)/62 OTO Melara compact; 85° elevation; 85 rounds/minute to 16 km *(8.6 nm)*; weight of shell 6 kg.
2—12.7 mm MGs. 4—7.62 mm MGs.
Fire control: BAe Sea Archer (for 76 mm).
Radars: Surface search: Kelvin Hughes Type 1006; I band.

Programmes: *Orla* launched 11 September 1984 and *Ciara* 31 March 1984. Both served in Hong Kong from mid-1985 until early 1988. Acquired by the Irish Navy and commissioned 21 November 1988. There is interest in buying more of this class as they become available.
Structure: Can carry Sea Rider craft. Have loiter drive. Displacement increased by the addition of more electronic equipment including Satellite navigation and communications.
Operational: Sprint speed is nearly 30 kts. Complement augmented by boarding party personnel.

CIARA *1991, T. Smith, Irish Navy*

SHIPBORNE AIRCRAFT

Numbers/Type: 5 Aerospatiale SA 365F Dauphin 2.
Operational speed: 140 kts *(260 km/h)*.
Service ceiling: 15 000 ft *(4575 m)*.
Range: 410 nm *(758 km)*.
Role/Weapon systems: Embarked helicopter for MR/SAR tasks in *Eithne*; some shore land-based training by Army Air Corps and SAR. Sensors: Bendix RDR 1500 radar. Weapons: Unarmed.

DAUPHIN

LAND-BASED MARITIME AIRCRAFT

Note: 2 civilian operated Sikorsky S-61 helicopters provide long-range SAR services.

Numbers/Type: 2 Beechcraft Super King Air 200T.
Operational speed: 282 kts *(523 km/h)*.
Service ceiling: 35 000 ft *(10 670 m)*.
Range: 2030 nm *(3756 km)*.
Role/Weapon systems: SAR and EEZ protection. Flown by the Army Air Corps. Being replaced by Casa 235. Sensors: Weather/search radar. Weapons: Unarmed.

Numbers/Type: 1 Casa 235.
Operational speed: 210 kts *(384 km/h)*.
Service ceiling: 24 000 ft *(7315 m)*.
Range: 2000 nm *(3218 km)*.
Role/Weapon systems: EEZ surveillance. Delivered in 1991 with two more to follow in 1993/94 to replace the Beechcraft. Sensors: Search radar Bendix APS 504(V)5; FLIR. Weapons: Unarmed.

CASA 235 *1991, John Daly*

MISCELLANEOUS

Note: In addition there are a number of mostly civilian manned auxiliaries including: *Seabhac* a small tug acquired in 1983; *Fainleog, David F* (built in 1962) and *Fiachdubh* passenger craft, the last two taken over after lease in 1988 and the first in 1983; *Colleen II* a service launch at Haulbowline built in 1972; *Tailte* a Dufour 35 ft sail training yacht bought in 1979. *Gray Seal* (ex-*Seaforth Clansman*) is a lighthouse tender operated by the Commissioners of Irish Lights.

FAINLEOG *6/1989, Bram Risseeuw*

ISRAEL

Headquarters' Appointment

Commander-in-Chief of the Israeli Navy:
Rear Admiral Ami Ayalon

Personnel

(a) 1992: 9000 (1000 officers and 8000 men, of whom 3000 are conscripts. Includes a Naval Commando)
(b) 3 years' national service for Jews and Druses

Note: An additional 1000 Reserves available on mobilisation.

Bases

Haifa, Ashdod, Eilat
(The repair base at Eilat has a synchrolift)

Prefix to Ships' Names

INS (Israeli Naval Ship)

Deployment

About 7 Dabur class and some smaller vessels are based at Eilat. Remainder of fleet in the Mediterranean.

Strength of the Fleet

Type	*Active*	*Building (Planned)*
Patrol Submarines	3	2 (1)
Corvettes	0	3
Fast Attack Craft—Missile	19 (1)	—
Fast Attack Craft—Gun	12	6
Hydrofoils	2 (1)	—
Coastal Patrol Craft	14	—
LCTs	3	(2)
LCPs	1	—
Support Ships	1	—

Mercantile Marine

Lloyd's Register of Shipping:
58 vessels of 603 799 tons gross

DELETIONS

Light Forces

1990 *Saar, Gaash, Herev*, 9 Yatush class
1991 1 Dvora, 10 Super Dvora (6 to Chile, 4 to Fiji)

Amphibious Forces

1990 2 LCPs
1991 *Etzion Geuber, Shiqmona, Kessaraya*

Support Ship

1991 *Ma'oz*

SUBMARINES

0 + 2 (1) DOLPHIN CLASS

Displacement, tons: 1550 surfaced; 1720 dived
Dimensions, feet (metres): 187 × 22.3 × 20.3 *(57 × 6.8 × 6.2)*
Main machinery: 3 MTU 16V 396 SE diesels; 2910 hp(m) *(2.14 MW)* sustained; 1 Siemens motor; 2850 hp(m) *(2.09 MW)* sustained; 1 shaft
Speed, knots: 20 dived; 11 snorting
Complement: 35

Torpedoes: 10—21 in *(533 mm)* bow tubes.
Countermeasures: ESM: Radar warning.
Fire control: Krupp Atlas or Litton TCS.
Radars: Surface search.
Sonars: Krupp Atlas; hull-mounted; passive/active search and attack.

Programmes: In mid-1988 Ingalls Shipbuilding Division of Litton Corporation was chosen as the prime contractor for two IKL-designed Dolphin class submarines to be built in West Germany with FMS funds by HDW in conjunction with Thyssen Nordseewerke. Funds approved in July 1989 with an effective contract date of January 1990 but the project was cancelled in November 1990 due to pressures on defence funds. After the Gulf War in April 1991 the contract was resurrected, this time with German funding for two submarines with an option on a third. First steel cut in March and April 1992 with projected delivery dates in 1997. One building at Kiel by HDW, the other at Emden by TNSW.
Structure: Diving depth at least 250 m *(820 ft)*. Similar to German Type 212 in design but with a 'wet and dry' compartment for underwater swimmers, and a greater torpedo capacity.
Operational: Endurance, 30 days. To be used for interdiction and special boat operations.

3 IKL/VICKERS TYPE 540

Name	No	Builders	Laid down	Launched	Commissioned
GAL	—	Vickers Ltd, Barrow	1973	2 Dec 1975	Jan 1977
TANIN	—	Vickers Ltd, Barrow	1974	25 Oct 1976	June 1977
RAHAV	—	Vickers Ltd, Barrow	1974	1977	Dec 1977

Displacement, tons: 420 surfaced; 600 dived
Dimensions, feet (metres): 146.7 × 15.4 × 12 *(45 × 4.7 × 3.7)*
Main machinery: Diesel-electric; 2 MTU 12V 483 AZ80 GA31L diesels; 1200 hp(m) *(882 kW)* sustained; 2 alternators; 810 kW; 1 motor; 1800 hp(m) *(1.32 MW)* sustained; 1 shaft
Speed, knots: 11 surfaced; 17 dived
Complement: 22

Missiles: SSM: McDonnell Douglas Sub Harpoon launched from torpedo tubes; active radar homing to 130 km *(70 nm)* at 0.9 Mach; warhead 227 kg.
Torpedoes: 8—21 in *(533 mm)* bow tubes. Honeywell NT 37E; active/passive homing to 20 km *(10.8 nm)* at 35 kts; warhead 150 kg. Total of 10 missiles and torpedoes can be embarked.
Countermeasures: ESM: Elisra NS 9034; radar warning.
Fire control: Tios System.
Radars: Surface search: Plessey; I band.
Sonars: Plessey; hull-mounted; passive search and attack; medium/high frequency.

RAHAV *1988*

Programmes: A contract was signed by Vickers in April 1972.
Modernisation: Sub Harpoon and associated fire control equipment installed in 1983 and the NT 37E torpedoes replaced the obsolete Mk 37 in 1987-88. A local contract has been let to update sensors and fire control equipment starting in 1994. Krupp Atlas is the most likely supplier of equipment.

CORVETTES

0 + 3 LAHAV (SAAR 5) CLASS

501 **502** **503**

Displacement, tons: 1075 standard; 1200 full load
Dimensions, feet (metres): 280.8 oa; 251.3 wl × 39 × 10.5 *(85.6; 76.6 × 11.9 × 3.2)*
Main machinery: CODOG; 1 GE LM 2500 gas turbine; 23 000 hp *(17.16 MW)* sustained; 2 MTU 12V 1163 TB82 diesels; 6600 hp(m) *(4.85 MW)* sustained; 2 shafts; KaMeWa cp props
Speed, knots: 33 gas; 20 diesels. **Range, miles:** 3500 at 17 kts
Complement: 64 (16 officers) plus 10 (4 officers) aircrew

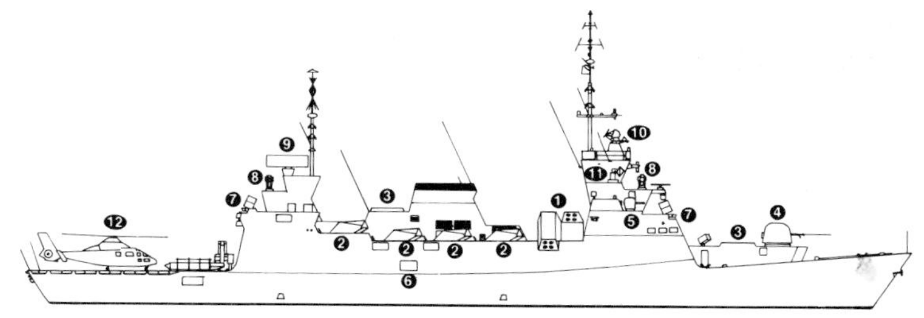

LAHAV *(Scale 1 : 900), Ian Sturton*

Missiles: SSM: 8 McDonnell Douglas Harpoon (2 quad) launchers ❶; active radar homing to 130 km *(70 nm)* at 0.9 Mach; warhead 227 kg.
8 IAI Gabriel II ❷; radar or optical guidance; semi-active homing to 36 km *(19.4 nm)* at 0.7 Mach; warhead 75 kg.
SAM: 2 Israeli Industries Barak I (vertical launch) ❸; 2 × 32 cells; command line of sight radar or optical guidance to 10 km *(5.5 nm)* at 2 Mach; warhead 22 kg.
Guns: OTO Melara 3 in *(76 mm)*/62 compact ❹; 85° elevation; 85 rounds/minute to 16 km *(8.7 nm)*; weight of shell 6 kg. Interchangeable with a Bofors 57 mm gun or Vulcan Phalanx CIWS.
2 Sea Vulcan 25 mm CIWS ❺; range 1 km.
Torpedoes: 6—324 mm Mk 32 (2 triple) tubes ❻. Honeywell Mk 46; anti-submarine.
Countermeasures: Decoys: 4 Chaff launchers ❼; Nixie SLQ 25 towed torpedo decoy
ESM/ECM: Elisra NS 9000 series; intercept and jammer.
Combat data systems: Possibly ELBIT NTCCS. Data link.
Fire control: 3 Elop optronic directors ❽.

Radars: Air search ❾.
Air/surface search ❿.
Navigation.
Fire control: 2 Elta EL/M 2221 GM STGR; I/K band ⓫.
Sonars: Hull-mounted; search and attack; medium frequency.
VDS or towed array; active and passive search; medium/low frequency.

Helicopters: 1 Dauphin SA 366G ⓬ or SH-2F or Hellstar RPV.

Programmes: A new design (QU-09-35) prepared by Israeli Shipyards, Haifa in conjunction with Ingalls Shipbuilding Division of Litton Corporation which was authorised to act as main contractor using FMS funding. Ships building at Pascagoula with some final fitting out in Israel. Contract awarded 8 February 1989. First ship started fabrication 3 October 1991 and is scheduled for delivery in October 1993, second in April 1994 and third in October 1994. An option for a fourth is unlikely to be taken up.
Structure: Steel hull. Stealth features including resilient mounts for main machinery, and Prairie Masker Bubbler system.
Operational: Endurance, 20 days. The main role will be to counter threats in main shipping routes.
Opinion: The Israeli Navy wanted eight in two batches of four so unless more are subsequently ordered, updated versions of the Saar 4 class will be needed to replace some of the other FAC hulls.

LIGHT FORCES

Note: The *Shaldag* was launched by Israeli Shipyards on 25 December 1989. This is a 55 ton, 50 kt fast patrol boat demonstrator, which is unlikely to be taken into service by the Navy.

3 US FLAGSTAFF 2 CLASS (HYDROFOILS)

SHIMRIT M 161 **LIVNIT** M 162 **SNAPIRIT** M 163

Displacement, tons: 105 full load
Dimensions, feet (metres): 84 × 24 × 5 *(25.6 × 7.3 × 1.6)*
Main machinery: 2 Allison 501KF gas turbines; 9570 hp *(7.14 MW)*; 2 shafts
Speed, knots: 48. **Range, miles:** 2600 at 8 kts hullborne; 1000 at 42 kts foilborne
Complement: 15

Missiles: SSM: 2 McDonnell Douglas Harpoon; active radar homing to 130 km *(70 nm)* at 0.9 Mach; warhead 227 kg.
2 IAI Gabriel III; active radar plus anti-radiation homing to 36 km *(19.4 nm)* at 0.7 Mach; warhead 75 kg.
Guns: 2 MBT/Oerlikon TCM 30; 85° elevation; 650 rounds/minute to 10 km *(5.5 nm)* anti-surface; 3 km *(1.6 nm)* anti-aircraft; weight of shell 1 kg or 0.36 kg.
2—12.7 mm MGs.
Countermeasures: ESM/ECM: Intercept/jammer.
Fire control: Probable data link system.
Radars: Navigation: I band.

Programmes: *Shimrit* was ordered in the USA from Grumman Lantana Yard, Florida with *Livnit* and possibly 10 more to be built in Israel. *Shimrit* launched 27 May 1981. Subsequently there were considerable teething troubles but *Shimrit* was eventually accepted in mid-1982. *Snapirit*, completed June 1985, is now third and last of originally planned class of 12. This might be due to dissatisfaction with the design for the tasks assigned.
Structure: Aluminium superstructure. Radome conceals fire control and countermeasures aerials.
Operational: Two reported still operational in 1991 but all could be paid off at any time.

SHIMRIT *1982, Grumman*

5 ALIYA/ROMAT/HETZ (SAAR 4.5) CLASS (FAST ATTACK CRAFT—MISSILE)

Name	*Builders*	*Launched*	*Commissioned*
ALIYA	Haifa Shipyard	11 July 1980	Aug 1980
GEOULA	Haifa Shipyard	Oct 1980	31 Dec 1980
ROMAT	Haifa Shipyard	30 Oct 1981	Oct 1981
KESHET	Haifa Shipyard	Oct 1982	Nov 1982
HETZ (ex-*Nirit*)	Haifa Shipyard	Oct 1990	Feb 1991

Displacement, tons: 488 full load
Dimensions, feet (metres): 202.4 × 24.9 × 8.2 *(61.7 × 7.6 × 2.5)*
Main machinery: 4 MTU/Bazán 16V 956 TB 91 diesels; 15 000 hp(m) *(11.03 MW)* sustained; 4 shafts
4 MTU 16V 538 TB 93 diesels; 16 600 hp(m) *(12.2 MW)*; 4 shafts *(Hetz)*
Speed, knots: 31. **Range, miles:** 3000 at 17 kts; 1500 at 30 kts
Complement: 53 (*Aliya, Hetz* and *Geoula*); 45 (*Romat* and *Keshet*)

Missiles: SSM: McDonnell Douglas Harpoon; active radar homing to 130 km *(70 nm)* at 0.9 Mach; warhead 227 kg.
IAI Gabriel II or III; radar or optical guidance; semi-active radar plus anti-radiation homing (III) to 36 km *(19.4 nm)* at 0.7 Mach; warhead 75 kg.
4 Harpoon (2 twin) plus 4 Gabriel (*Aliya* and *Geoula*).
8 Harpoon (2 quad) plus 6 or 8 Gabriel (*Romat, Keshet* and *Hetz)*.
SAM: Israeli Industries Barak I (vertical launch) *(Hetz)*; 32 cells in three silos; command line-of-sight radar or optical guidance to 10 km *(5.5 m)* at 2 Mach; warhead 22 kg.
Guns: 1 OTO Melara 3 in *(76 mm)*/62 (*Romat, Keshet* and *Hetz*); 85° elevation; 85 rounds/minute to 16 km *(8.7 nm)*; weight of shell 6 kg.
2 Oerlikon 20 mm; 55° elevation; 800 rounds/minute to 2 km.
1 General Electric/General Dynamics Vulcan Phalanx 6-barrelled 20 mm Mk 15; 3000 rounds/minute combined to 1.5 km anti-missile.
2 or 4—12.7 mm (twin or quad) MGs.
Countermeasures: Decoys: 1—45 tube, 4—24 tube, 4 single tube Chaff launchers.
ESM/ECM: Elisra EW suite.
Combat data systems: IAI Reshet data link.
Radars: Air/surface search: Thomson-CSF TH-D 1040 Neptune; G band; range 33 km *(18 nm)* for 2 m² target.
Fire control: Selenia Orion RTN-10X; I/J band; range 40 km *(22 nm)*.
Elta EL/M-2221 GM STGR *(Hetz)*; I/K band

Helicopters: 1 SA 366G Dauphin reconnaissance for OTH targeting (*Aliya* and *Geoula*). Can be replaced by Hellstar RPV.

Programmes: *Hetz* started construction in 1984 as the fifth of the class but was not completed, as an economy measure. Taken in hand again in 1989 and fitted out as the trials ship for some of the systems to be fitted in the Saar 5 class.
Modernisation: It is reported that *Romat* and *Keshet* and perhaps the other pair are to be fitted with Barak VLS and new fire control radar in due course.
Structure: In the second pair the hangar was replaced by a 76 mm gun aft and four additional Gabriel launchers. The CIWS is mounted in the eyes of the ship in all cases replacing the 40 mm gun. The fifth of the class has a Barak VLS system fitted aft in place of two of the Gabriel launchers and a quite different mast to house the various new sensors being tested for the Saar 5 class, including the fire control system for Barak, which is to be fitted on the platform aft of the bridge on the port side. *Hetz* also has more powerful engines.

KESHET *1990*

ALIYA *1991*

8 RESHEF (SAAR 4) CLASS (FAST ATTACK CRAFT—MISSILE)

Name	*Builders*	*Launched*	*Commissioned*
RESHEF	Haifa Shipyard	19 Feb 1973	Apr 1973
KIDON	Haifa Shipyard	4 July 1974	Sep 1974
TARSHISH	Haifa Shipyard	17 Jan 1975	Mar 1975
YAFFO	Haifa Shipyard	3 Feb 1975	Apr 1975
NITZHON	Haifa Shipyard	10 July 1978	Sep 1978
ATSMOUT	Haifa Shipyard	3 Dec 1978	Feb 1979
MOLEDET	Haifa Shipyard	22 Mar 1979	May 1979
KOMEMIUT	Haifa Shipyard	19 July 1978	Aug 1980

Displacement, tons: 415 standard; 450 full load
Dimensions, feet (metres): 190.6 × 25 × 8 *(58 × 7.8 × 2.4)*
Main machinery: 4 MTU/Bazán 16V 956 TB 91 diesels; 15 000 hp(m) *(11.03 MW)* sustained; 4 shafts
Speed, knots: 32. **Range, miles:** 1650 at 30 kts; 4000 at 17.5 kts
Complement: 45

Missiles: SSM: 2-4 McDonnell Douglas Harpoon (twin or quad) launchers; active radar homing to 130 km *(70 nm)* at 0.9 Mach; warhead 227 kg.
4-6 Gabriel II or III; radar or TV optical guidance; semi-active radar plus anti-radiation (III) homing to 36 km *(20 nm)* at 0.7 Mach; warhead 75 kg.
Harpoons fitted with Israeli homing systems. The Gabriel II system carries a TV camera which can transmit a homing picture to the firing ship beyond the radar horizon. This has now been superseded in operational boats by Gabriel III. The missile fit currently varies in training boats—2 Harpoon, 5 Gabriel II.
Guns: 1 or 2 OTO Melara 3 in *(76 mm)*/62 compact; 85° elevation; 85 rounds/minute to 16 km *(8.7 nm)*; weight of shell 6 kg. Adapted for shore bombardment.
2 Oerlikon 20 mm; 55° elevation; 800 rounds/minute to 2 km.
1 General Electrics/General Dynamics Vulcan Phalanx 6-barrelled 20 mm Mk 15 (fitted fwd of the bridge); 3000 rounds/minute combined to 1.5 km anti-missile.
2—12.7 mm MGs.
Countermeasures: Decoys: 1—45 tube, 4 or 6—24 tube, 4 single tube Chaff launchers.
ESM: Elta MN-53; intercept.
ECM: Jammer.
Combat data systems: IAI Reshet data link.
Radars: Air/surface search: Thomson-CSF TH-D 1040 Neptune; G band; range 33 km *(18 nm)* for 2 m² target.
Fire control: Selenia Orion RTN 10X; I/J band; range 40 km *(22 nm)*.
Sonars: EDO 780; VDS; occasionally fitted in some of the class.

Helicopters: *Tarshish* had her after 76 mm gun removed to make way for a helicopter platform, a temporary trial in 1979, but there is an option for replacing the after gun with a Hellstar RPV.

Modernisation: It is planned to replace Vulcan Phalanx by the Barak SAM system. VDS sonars can be fitted.
Operational: This very interesting class has a long range at cruising speed, two pairs having made the passage from Israel to the Red Sea via the Strait of Gibraltar and Cape of Good Hope, relying only on refuelling at sea. This is a tribute not only to their endurance but also to their seakeeping qualities. All now deployed in Mediterranean.
Sales: Eight of this class built for South Africa in Haifa and Durban. One *(Romat)* transferred to Chile late 1979 and one *(Keshet)* in February 1981.

SAAR 4 *1985*

HETZ *1991, Israeli Shipyards*

6 MIVTACH (SAAR 2) and 1 SAAR (SAAR 3) CLASSES (FAST ATTACK CRAFT—MISSILE)

Name	No	Builders	Commissioned
Saar 2			
MIVTACH	311	CMN, Cherbourg	1968
MIZNAG	312	CMN, Cherbourg	1968
MIFGAV	313	CMN, Cherbourg	1968
EILATH	321	CMN, Cherbourg	1968
HAIFA	322	CMN, Cherbourg	1968
AKKO	323	CMN, Cherbourg	1968
Saar 3			
SOUFA	332	CMN, Cherbourg	1969

Displacement, tons: 220 standard; 250 full load
Dimensions, feet (metres): 147.6 × 23 × 8.2 *(45 × 7 × 2.5)*
Main machinery: 4 MTU MD 16V 538 TB 90 diesels; 12 000 hp(m) *(8.82 MW)* sustained; 4 shafts
Speed, knots: 40+. **Range, miles:** 2500 at 15 kts; 1600 at 20 kts; 1000 at 30 kts
Complement: 35-40 (5 officers)

Missiles: SSM: 2 or 4 McDonnell Douglas Harpoon; active radar homing to 130 km *(70 nm)* at 0.9 Mach; warhead 227 kg. Harpoon is replacing Gabriel to reduce top weight.
6 or 3 IAI Gabriel II; active radar or optical guidance; semi-active radar homing to 36 km *(19.4 nm)* at 0.7 Mach; warhead 75 kg.
Guns: 1 OTO Melara 3 in *(76 mm)*/62 DP; 85° elevation; 65 rounds/minute to 8 km *(4.4 nm)*; weight of shell 6 kg.
1-3 Breda 40 mm/70; 85° elevation; 300 rounds/minute to 4 km *(2.2 nm)* anti-aircraft; weight of shell 0.96 kg (see *Operational*).
2 or 4—12.7 mm MGs.
Torpedoes: 2 or 4—324 mm Mk 32 tubes (Saar 2 class only and not fitted in all). Honeywell Mk 46; anti-submarine; active/passive homing to 11 km *(5.9 nm)* at 40 kts; warhead 44 kg.
Countermeasures: Decoys: 6—24 tube, 4 single tube Chaff launchers.
ESM: Elta MN-53; intercept.
ECM: Jammer.
Combat data systems: IAI Reshet data link.
Radars: Air/surface search: Thomson-CSF TH-D 1040 Neptune; G band; range 33 km *(18 nm)* for 2 m^2 target.
Fire control: Selenia Orion RTN 10X; I/J band; range 40 km *(22 nm)*.
Sonars: EDO 780 (Saar 2 class only and not fitted in all); VDS; active search and attack; 13.7 and 5 kHz.

Programmes: Built from designs by Lürssen Werft of Bremen. Political problems caused their building in France instead of West Germany. Two batches: the first six being ordered in 1965, the second six in 1966. Five of these ships were delivered to Israel after the 1969 French arms embargo and two *(Akko* and *Saar)* made the journey on completion of local trials. The last five arrived off Haifa in January 1970 after a much-publicised passage which began on Christmas Eve off the west coast of France and proved the remarkable endurance of this class.
Structure: Steel hulls and light alloy superstructure. The class suffers from top weight problems, being alleviated to some extent by substituting Harpoon for Gabriel.
Operational: Saar 2 can mount an armament varying from one 40 mm gun and Harpoon or Gabriel missiles to three 40 mm guns and four A/S torpedo tubes plus VDS. Saar 3 can mount Harpoon and Gabriel missiles as well as the 76 mm gun forward but does not have sonar. The plan was for Saar 2 to concentrate on ASW and to pay off Saar 3 as Saar 5 are commissioned, but by early 1991 all but one of the Saar 3 were already paid off and by early 1992 even that one was permanently moored.
Sales: *Hanit* and *Hetz* (Saar 3 class) transferred to Chile in 1988; more may follow if funds become available.

SAAR 2 (with VDS) *1990*

SAAR 2 (with torpedo tubes) *1989*

12 + 6 SUPER DVORA CLASS (FAST ATTACK CRAFT—GUN)

810-821

Displacement, tons: 54 full load
Dimensions, feet (metres): 71 × 18 × 5.9 screws *(21.6 × 5.5 × 1.8)*
Main machinery: 2 MTU 12V 396 TB 93 diesels; 3260 hp(m) *(2.4 MW)* sustained; 2 shafts (Mk I)
2 Detroit 16V-92TA diesels; 2800 hp *(2.1 MW)*; 2 shafts (Mk II)
3 Detroit 16V-92TA diesels; 4200 hp *(3.13 MW)*; 3 shafts (Mk III)
Speed, knots: 36 or 46 (Mk III). **Range, miles:** 1200 at 17 kts
Complement: 9 (1 officer)

Guns: 2 Oerlikon 20 mm/80. 2—12.7 or 7.62 mm MGs. 1—84 mm rocket launcher.
Depth charges: 2 racks.
Fire control: Elop optronic director.
Radars: Surface search: Raytheon; I band.

Programmes: A further improvement on the Dabur design ordered in March 1987 from Israeli Aircraft Industries (RAMTA). First started trials in November 1988, and first two commissioned in June 1989. Remainder following at two to four per year.
Structure: All gun armament and improved speed and endurance compared with the prototype Dvora. SSM, depth charges, torpedoes or a 130 mm MRL can be fitted if required. The first 10 are probably Mk I and II with the much faster Mk III version coming in at about hull number 11.

SUPER DVORA *1989, Israeli Aircraft Industries*

SUPER DVORA 811 *5/1989, Rupert Pengelley*

14 DABUR CLASS (COASTAL PATROL CRAFT)

Displacement, tons: 39 full load
Dimensions, feet (metres): 64.9 × 18 × 5.8 *(19.8 × 5.5 × 1.8)*
Main machinery: 2 GM 12V-71 TI diesels; 840 hp *(627 kW)* sustained; 2 shafts
About 6 have more powerful GE engines.
Speed, knots: 19; 30 (GE engines). **Range, miles:** 450 at 13 kts
Complement: 6/9 depending on armament

Guns: 2 Oerlikon 20 mm; 55° elevation; 800 rounds/minute to 2 km.
2—12.7 mm MGs. Carl Gustav 84 mm portable rocket launchers.
Torpedoes: 2—324 mm tubes. Honeywell Mk 46; anti-submarine; active/passive homing to 11 km *(5.9 nm)* at 40 kts; warhead 44 kg.
Depth charges: 2 racks in some.
Fire control: Elop optronic director.
Radars: Surface search: Decca Super 101 Mk 3; I band.
Sonars: Active search and attack; high frequency.

Programmes: Twelve built by Sewart Seacraft USA and remainder by Israel Aircraft Industries (RAMTA) between 1973 and 1977. Final total of 34.
Structure: Aluminium hull. Several variations in the armament. Six of the class are fitted with more powerful General Electric engines to increase speed to 30 kts.
Operational: Deployed in the Mediterranean and Red Sea, these craft have been designed for overland transport. Good rough weather performance. Portable rocket launchers are carried for anti-terrorist purposes. Not considered fast enough to cope with modern terrorist speedboats and are being sold as more Super Dvoras are commissioned.
Sales: Four to Argentina in 1978; four to Nicaragua in 1978; two to Sri Lanka in 1984; four to Fiji and six to Chile in 1991. Five also given to Lebanon Christian Militia in 1976 but these were returned.

DABUR 882 — *5/1989, Rupert Pengelley*

SHIPBORNE AIRCRAFT

Numbers/Type: 2 Aerospatiale SA 366G Dauphin.
Operational speed: 140 kts *(260 km/h)*.
Service ceiling: 15 000 ft *(4575 m)*.
Range: 410 nm *(758 km)*.
Role/Weapon systems: SAR/MR helicopter embarked for trials; primarily SAR/MR but growing submarine threat could mean upgrading; 20 more on order in 1987. Sensors: Israeli designed radar/FLIR systems. Weapons: Unarmed at present but plans for ASV/ASW.

DAUPHIN — *1986, Ofer Karni*

Numbers/Type: IAI/Mata Hellstar.
Operational speed: 55 kts *(102 km/h)*.
Service ceiling: 15 000 ft *(4575 m)*.
Range: 245 nm *(454 km)*.
Role/Weapons systems: Unmanned reconnaissance and surveillance helicopter, started trials in July 1990. Sensors: Israeli designed radar/FLIR systems with data link; Elop optronic trackers. Weapons: ASV/ASW in due course.

HELLSTAR — *1991, IAI*

Numbers/Type: 6 Agusta AB 206B JetRanger.
Operational speed: 115 kts *(213 km/h)*.
Service ceiling: 13 500 ft *(4115 m)*.
Range: 368 nm *(682 km)*.
Role/Weapon systems: Liaison and limited SAR helicopter. Sensors: None. Weapons: Unarmed.

LAND-BASED MARITIME AIRCRAFT

Note: Army helicopters can be used including Cobras.

Numbers/Type: 25 Bell 212.
Operational speed: 100 kts *(185 km/h)*.
Service ceiling: 13 200 ft *(4025 m)*.
Range: 224 nm *(415 km)*.
Role/Weapon systems: SAR and coastal helicopter surveillance tasks undertaken. Sensors: IAI EW systems. Weapons: Unarmed except for self-defence machine guns.

Numbers/Type: 4 Grumman E-2C Hawkeye.
Operational speed: 269 kts *(499 km/h)*.
Service ceiling: 30 800 ft *(9390 m)*.
Range: 1350 nm *(2500 km)*.
Role/Weapon systems: Airborne early warning and control aircraft; operated for air defence and strike direction by the Air Force. Sensors: APS-125 radar, various EW systems. Weapons: Unarmed.

Numbers/Type: 3 IAI 1124 Sea Scan.
Operational speed: 471 kts *(873 km/h)*.
Service ceiling: 45 000 ft *(13 725 m)*.
Range: 2500 nm *(4633 km)*.
Role/Weapon systems: Coastal surveillance tasks with long endurance; used for intelligence gathering. Sensors: Include radar, IFF, MAD and various EW systems of IAI manufacture.

AMPHIBIOUS FORCES

Note: Two new construction landing ships are planned by the Navy to transport large numbers of troops. No funds available. A Ro-Ro ship may be in use for research and development.

3 ASHDOD CLASS (LCTs)

Name	*No*	*Builders*	*Commissioned*
ASHDOD	61	Israel Shipyards, Haifa	1966
ASHKELON	63	Israel Shipyards, Haifa	1967
ACHZIV	65	Israel Shipyards, Haifa	1967

Displacement, tons: 400 standard; 730 full load
Dimensions, feet (metres): 205.5 × 32.8 × 5.8 *(62.7 × 10 × 1.8)*
Main machinery: 3 MWM diesels; 1900 hp(m) *(1.4 MW)*; 3 shafts
Speed, knots: 10.5
Complement: 20
Guns: 2 Oerlikon 20 mm.

Comment: At least one has a helicopter deck aft. *Ashdod* was an early trials ship for Barak VLS.

ASHDOD Class — *1989*

1 Ex-US LCP TYPE

Displacement, tons: 24 full load
Dimensions, feet (metres): 52.5 × 14.4 × 5.6 *(16 × 4.4 × 1.7)*
Main machinery: 2 Saturn gas turbines; 2000 hp *(1.49 MW)*; 2 shafts
Speed, knots: 35
Complement: 8
Military lift: 22 troops; 1 ton equipment

Comment: The survivor of four transferred in 1968. Used for swimmer operations.

SUPPORT SHIP

1 BAT SHEVA CLASS (TRANSPORT)

Name	*No*	*Builders*	*Commissioned*
BAT SHEVA	—	Netherlands	1967

Displacement, tons: 1150 full load
Dimensions, feet (metres): 311.7 × 36.7 × 26.9 *(95.1 × 11.2 × 8.2)*
Main machinery: 2 diesels; 2 shafts
Speed, knots: 10
Complement: 26
Guns: 4 Oerlikon 20 mm. 4—12.7 mm MGs.

Comment: Purchased from South Africa in 1968.

ITALY

eadquarters' Appointments

hief of Naval Staff:
Admiral Guido Venturoni
ce Chief of Naval Staff:
Admiral Mario Angeli
hief of Naval Personnel:
Admiral Alfeo Battelli
hief of Procurement and Technical Support:
Engineer Admiral Antonio Carloni

rincipal Commands

ommander, Allied Naval Forces, Southern Europe (Naples) and Commander-in-Chief Basso Tirreno:
Admiral Carlo Alberto Vandini
ommander-in-Chief of Fleet (and Comedcent):
Admiral Angelo Mariani
ommander-in-Chief Alto Tirreno (La Spezia):
Admiral Mario Strigini
ommander-in-Chief Adriatico (Ancona):
Vice Admiral Frigerio Bonvicino
ommander-in-Chief dello Jonio e Canale d'Otranto (Taranto):
Admiral Luciano Monego
ommander Sicilian Naval Area (Messina):
Vice Admiral Giovanni Iannucci
ommander Sardinian Naval Area (La Maddalena):
Vice Admiral Egidio Alberti
ommander Submarine Force:
Captain Francesco Ricci
t Naval Division:
Rear Admiral Leandro Papa
d Naval Division:
Rear Admiral Benito Maggio
d Naval Division:
Rear Admiral Paolo Alberto Timossi
val Commandos and Special Naval Group:
Rear Admiral Mario de Feo
ne Countermeasures Force:
Captain Alessandro Valentini
val Training Command:
Rear Admiral Gianfranco Coviello

plomatic Representation

val Attaché in Bonn:
Captain Claudio de Polo
val Attaché in London:
Captain Antonio Giungato
val Attaché in Moscow:
Captain Franco Paoli
val Attaché in Paris:
Captain Gianluca Assettati
val Attaché in Washington:
Captain Bruno Branciforte

ganisation

me	*Base*	*Units*
st Division	La Spezia	Major warships
cond Division	Taranto	Major warships
rd Division	Brindisi	Amphibious ships; Hydrofoils
bmarine Command	Taranto	Submarines
ne Countermeasures Command	La Spezia	MCMVs

In addition there is a 'Special Force and Underwater Swimmers (COMSUBIN)' including Commandos plus support and minor craft; located near La Spezia. The former Auxiliary Force has been disbanded.

Bases

Main—La Spezia (Alto Tirreno), Taranto (Jonio e Canale d'Otranto)
Regional—Ancona (Adriatico), Naples (Basso Tirreno)
Secondary—Brindisi, Augusta, Messina, La Maddalena, Cagliari, Venice

New Construction Plans

Short term programme (already financed) includes a new LPD, 18 VTOL aircraft and 12 EH 101 helicopters.
Medium term plan (already defined projects) calls for 2 S-90 submarines, 4 ocean minehunters/sweepers, 2 other Vespri class minehunters, an OPV (the 5th of the class), an MCM support vessel, 2 survey vessels, a water tanker, a replenishment tanker, a Commando-Deep Divers Support ship, 30 EH 101 Helos.
Long term plans envisage a second aircraft carrier, two more DDGs, 6 frigates, 4 S-90 submarines. All the units of the Long Term Plan are expected to be laid down not earlier than 1995-96.

Strength of the Fleet

Type	*Active*	*Building (Planned)*
Submarines	8	2 (2)
Light Aircraft Carrier	1	(1)
Cruisers	1	—
Destroyers	3	1
Frigates	14	4
Corvettes	14	(4)
Offshore Patrol Vessels	8	—
Hydrofoils—Missile	6	—
LPDs	2	1
Minehunters/sweepers—Ocean	5	7
Minesweepers—Ocean	2	—
Minesweepers/hunters—Coastal	5	—
Survey/Research Vessels	3	2
Replenishment Tankers	2	(1)
Harbour Tankers	7	—
Experimental Ships	4	—
Fleet Support Ship	1	—
Coastal Transports	10	—
Commando Support Craft	2	—
Transports (MTM/MTP/MEN)	41	—
Sail Training Ships	6	—
Training Ships	6	—
Lighthouse Tenders	5	—
Salvage Ships	2	—
Repair Craft	5	—
Large Water Carriers	11	—
Tugs	51	—
Floating Docks	14	—

Naval Air Arm—Planned strength and deployment

2 LRMP Squadrons—Bréguet Atlantique (No 41, Catania; No 30, Cagliari/Elmas); operated by Navy with Air Force support and maintenance
2 SH-3D/H helicopter squadrons (1st and 3rd based at Luni and Catania respectively)
3 AB-212 helicopter squadrons (2nd, 4th and 5th based at Luni, Taranto and Catania respectively)
1 AV-8B Harrier II squadron at Grottaglie, Taranto (2 TAV-8B plus 16 AV-8B from 1993)

Personnel

(a) 1992: 49 500 (6050 officers) plus 1900 Naval Air Arm and 3500 marines
(b) 1 year's national service
(c) 23 000 of the Navy are conscripts

Marines

San Marco Battalion became a Group in late 1990 absorbing the Security and Base Defence Units and the related School formerly held at the Special Forces Command (COMSUBIN).
The Italian Army also operates an autonomous 'Amphibious Command' composed of an Amphibious Assault Battalion and an Amphibious and Marine Crafts Battalion, both operating in the Venice Lagoons area.

Mercantile Marine

Lloyd's Register of Shipping:
1652 vessels of 8 121 595 tons gross

DELETIONS

Submarines

1991 *Attilio Bagnolini, Enrico Toti*

Cruisers

1990 *Caio Duilio*
1992 *Andrea Doria*

Destroyers

1991 *Intrepido, Impavido*

Frigates

1989 *Carlo Margottini*
1990 *Virginio Fasan*

Corvettes

1992 *Aquila*

Light Forces

1991 *Sparviero*

Minesweepers

1989 *Agave, Ebano, Sandalo*
1990 *Salmone, Sgombro, Gelsomino, Giaggiolo*
1991 *Alloro, Frassino, Timo, Vischio*
1992 *Loto*

Amphibious Forces

1989 *Caorle*
1990 *Grado*

Miscellaneous

1989 *MTF 1301-1303, Mesco* (tug), *Ercole* (tug), *Montecristo* (tug), *Adige* (water carrier), *MTC 1004-5, MTC 1007-10*
1990 *Vigoroso* (tug), *Ustica* (tug), *Panaria* (tug), *Albenga* (tug), *San Benedetto* (tug)
1991 *Arzachena* (tug), *Ustica* (tug), *Quarto, Alicudi, MOC 1207*

PENNANT LIST

bmarines

13	Enrico Dandolo
14	Lazzaro Mocenigo
18	Nazario Sauro
19	Fecia di Cossato
20	Leonardo da Vinci
21	Guglielmo Marconi
22	Salvatore Pelosi
23	Giuliano Prini
24	Primo Longobardo (bldg)
25	Gazzana Priaroggia (bldg)

ght Aircraft Carrier

51	Giuseppe Garibaldi

uisers

50	Vittorio Veneto

stroyers

50	Ardito
51	Audace
60	Animoso
61	Ardimentoso (bldg)

gates

64	Lupo
65	Sagittario
66	Perseo
67	Orsa
70	Maestrale
71	Grecale
72	Libeccio
73	Scirocco
74	Aliseo
75	Euro
76	Espero
77	Zeffiro
80	Alpino
81	Carabiniere

Corvettes

F 540	Pietro de Cristofaro
F 541	Umberto Grosso
F 544	Alcione
F 545	Airone
F 546	Licio Visintini
F 550	Salvatore Todaro
F 551	Minerva
F 552	Urania
F 553	Danaide
F 554	Sfinge
F 555	Driade
F 556	Chimera
F 557	Fenice
F 558	Sibilla

Offshore Patrol Vessels

P 401	Cassiopea
P 402	Libra
P 403	Spica
P 404	Vega
P 495	Bambù
P 496	Mango
P 497	Mogano
P 500	Palma

Light Forces

P 421	Nibbio
P 422	Falcone
P 423	Astore
P 424	Grifone
P 425	Gheppio
P 426	Condor
P 492	Barbara

Minesweepers/Hunters

M 5431	Storione
M 5433	Squalo
M 5504	Castagno*
M 5505	Cedro*
M 5509	Gelso*
M 5516	Platano*
M 5519	Mandorlo*
M 5550	Lerici*
M 5551	Sapri*
M 5552	Milazzo*
M 5553	Vieste*
M 5554	Gaeta
M 5555	Termoli (bldg)
M 5556	Alghero (bldg)
M 5557	Numana (bldg)
M 5558	Crotone (bldg)
M 5559	Viareggio (bldg)
M 5560	Chioggia (bldg)
M 5561	Rimini (bldg)

* Hunters

Amphibious Forces

L 9892	San Giorgio
L 9893	San Marco
L 9894	Cristoforo Colombo

Service Forces

A 5301	Pietro Cavezzale
A 5302	Caroly
A 5303	Ammiraglio Magnaghi
A 5304	Alicudi
A 5305	Murena
A 5306	Mirto
A 5307	Pioppo
A 5308	Alloro
A 5309	Anteo
A 5310	Proteo
A 5311	Palinuro
A 5312	Amerigo Vespucci
A 5313	Stella Polare
A 5315	Raffaele Rossetti
A 5316	Corsaro II
A 5317	Atlante
A 5318	Prometeo
A 5319	Ciclope
A 5320	Vincenzo Martellotta
A 5324	Titano
A 5325	Polifemo
A 5327	Stromboli
A 5328	Gigante
A 5329	Vesuvio
A 5330	Saturno
A 5331-5	MOC 1201-5
A 5341	MTC 1001
A 5346	MTC 1006
A 5347	Gorgona
A 5348	Tremiti
A 5349	Caprera
A 5351	Pantelleria
A 5352	Lipari
A 5353	Capri
A 5354	Piave
A 5356	Basento
A 5357	Bradano
A 5358	Brenta
A 5359	Bormida
A 5364	Ponza
A 5365	Tenace
A 5366	Levanzo
A 5367	Palmaria
A 5368	Tavolara
A 5370-3	MCC 1101-4
A 5374	Mincio
A 5375	Simeto
A 5378	Aragosta
A 5379	Astice
A 5380	Mitilo
A 5381	Polipo
A 5382	Porpora
A 5383	Procida
Y 413	Porto Fossone
Y 416	Porto Torres
Y 417	Porto Corsini
Y 421	Porto Empedocle
Y 422	Porto Pisano
Y 423	Porto Conte
Y 425	Portoferraio
Y 426	Portovenere
Y 428	Porto Salvo
Y 436	Porto d'Ischia
Y 443	Riva Trigoso
Y 498	Mario Marino
Y 499	Alcide Pedretti

SUBMARINES

0 + (2) TYPE S 90 CLASS

Displacement, tons: 2500 surfaced; 2780 dived
Dimensions, feet (metres): 228.7 × 26.9 × 20.1 (69.7 × 8.2 × 6.3)
Main machinery: Diesel-electric; 3 Fincantieri GMT 210.16 SM diesels; 6400 hp(m) *(4.7 MW)*; 1 motor; 6000 hp(m) *(4.41 MW)*; 1 shaft
Speed, knots: 20 dived; 11 surfaced
Range, miles: 6000 at 6 kts dived
Complement: 50 (8 officers)

Torpedoes: 6—21 in *(533 mm)* (2 triple) bow tubes. Total of 24 missiles, guided and unguided torpedoes.

Programmes: The programme is uncertain because of the possibility that overall submarine numbers may be cut from 10 to eight. The characteristics shown above are still subject to the completion of Project Definition but the first of class should be ordered in 1993 to commission in 1998, if not further delayed by defence cutbacks.

Structure: Diving depth is expected to be about 400 m *(1300 ft)*. This is to be a high performance conventional submarine an although gaseous storage toroidal designs have been tested i midget submarines built by Maritalia and the concept could b applied to larger (2800 or 1400 ton) submarines, th technology will not be incorporated in the S 90.

2 + 2 IMPROVED SAURO CLASS

Name	*No*	*Builders*	*Laid down*	*Launched*	*Commissioned*
SALVATORE PELOSI	S 522	Fincantieri, Monfalcone	24 May 1984	29 Dec 1986	14 July 1988
GIULIANO PRINI	S 523	Fincantieri, Monfalcone	30 May 1985	12 Dec 1987	11 Nov 1989
PRIMO LONGOBARDO	S 524	Fincantieri, Monfalcone	28 July 1988	Apr 1992	Feb 1993
GAZZANA PRIAROGGIA	S 525	Fincantieri, Monfalcone	28 July 1988	Oct 1992	Sep 1994

Displacement, tons: 1476 (1653, S 524-5) surfaced; 1662 (1862, S 524-5) dived
Dimensions, feet (metres): 211.2 (217.8 S 524-5) × 22.3 × 18.4 *(64.4 (66.4) × 6.8 × 5.6)*
Main machinery: Diesel-electric; 3 Fincantieri GMT 210.16 SM diesels; 6400 hp(m) *(4.7 MW)* sustained; 3 alternators; 2.16 MW; 1 motor; 4270 hp(m) *(3.14 MW)*; 1 shaft
Speed, knots: 11 surfaced; 19 dived; 12 snorting
Range, miles: 11 000 at 11 kts surfaced; 250 at 4 kts dived
Complement: 45 (7 officers)

Missiles: Capability to launch Harpoon being considered.
Torpedoes: 6—21 in *(533 mm)* bow tubes. 12 Whitehead A184; dual purpose; wire-guided; active/passive homing to 25 km *(13.7 nm)* at 24 kts; 17 km *(9.2 nm)* at 38 kts; warhead 250 kg. Swim-out discharge.
Countermeasures: ESM: Elettronica MM/BLD-727; radar warning; 2 aerials—1 on a mast, second in search periscope.
Fire control: SMA BSN 716(V)2; SACTIS including Link 11 (receive only).
Radars: Search/navigation: SMA BPS 704; I band; also periscope radar for attack ranging.
Sonars: Selenia Elsag IPD 70/S; linear passive array; 200 Hz-7.5 kHz; active and UWT transducers in bow (15 kHz).
Selenia Elsag MD 100S; passive ranging.

Programmes: The first two were ordered in March 1983 and the second pair in July 1988.

GIULIANO PRINI *1991, van Ginderen Collectio*

Structure: Pressure hull of HY 80 steel with a central bulkhead for escape purposes. Diving depth, 300 m *(985 ft)* (test) and 600 m *(1970 ft)* (crushing). The second pair have a slightly longer hull. Periscopes: Kollmorgen; S 76 Mod 322 with laser rangefinder and ESM—attack; S 76 Mod 323 with radar rangefinder and ESM—search. Wave contour snort head has a very low rad profile.
Operational: Litton Italia PL 41 inertial navigation; Ferrar autopilot Omega and Transit. Endurance, 45 days possib increased in second pair.

4 SAURO CLASS (1081 TYPE)

Name	*No*	*Builders*	*Laid down*	*Launched*	*Commissioned*
NAZARIO SAURO	S 518	Italcantieri, Monfalcone	27 June 1974	9 Oct 1976	12 Feb 1980
FECIA DI COSSATO	S 519	Italcantieri, Monfalcone	15 Nov 1975	16 Nov 1977	5 Nov 1979
LEONARDO DA VINCI	S 520	Italcantieri, Monfalcone	8 June 1978	20 Oct 1979	23 Oct 1981
GUGLIELMO MARCONI	S 521	Italcantieri, Monfalcone	23 Oct 1979	20 Sep 1980	11 Sep 1982

Displacement, tons: 1456 surfaced; 1631 dived
Dimensions, feet (metres): 210 × 22.5 × 18.9 *(63.9 × 6.8 × 5.7)*
Main machinery: Diesel-electric; 3 Fincantieri GMT 210.16 NM diesels; 3350 hp(m) *(2.46 MW)*; 3 alternators; 2.16 MW; 1 motor; 3210 hp(m) *(2.36 MW)*; 1 shaft
Speed, knots: 11 surfaced; 19 dived; 12 snorting.
Range, miles: 11 000 surfaced at 11 kts; 250 dived at 4 kts
Complement: 45 (7 officers) plus 4 trainees

Torpedoes: 6—21 in *(533 mm)* bow tubes. 12 Whitehead A184; dual purpose; wire-guided; active/passive homing to 25 km *(13.7 nm)* at 24 kts; 17 km *(9.2 nm)* at 38 kts; warhead 250 kg. Swim-out discharge.
Countermeasures: ESM: Elettronica BLD 727; radar warning.
Fire control: SMA BSN 716(V)1; SACTIS data processing and computer-based TMA. CCRG FCS.
Radars: Search/navigation: SMA BPS 704; I band.
Sonars: Selenia Elsag IPD 70/S; linear passive array; 200 Hz-7.5 kHz; active and UWT transducers in bow (15 kHz).
Selenia Elsag MD 100; passive ranging.

LEONARDO DA VINCI *9/1991, van Ginderen Collectio*

Programmes: Two of this class were originally ordered in 1967 but were cancelled in the following year. Reinstated in the building programme in 1972. Second pair provided for in Legge Navale and ordered 12 February 1976.
The discrepancy in commissioning dates of *N Sauro* and *F di Cossato* was due to problems over the main batteries. *F di Cossato* was provided with a new CGA battery which was satisfactory. *N Sauro* was then similarly fitted.
Modernisation: All being modernised. *Fecia di Cossato* started in 1990, *Nazario Sauro* in 1991. All to complete by 1995. Ne batteries have greater capacity, some auxiliary machine replaced and habitability improved.
Structure: Diving depth, 300 m *(985 ft)* (max) and 250 *(820 ft)* (normal).
Operational: Endurance, 35 days. Reliability improved by th mid-life modernisation programme.

2 TOTI CLASS (1075 TYPE)

Name	*No*	*Builders*	*Laid down*	*Launched*	*Commissioned*
ENRICO DANDOLO	S 513	Italcantieri, Monfalcone	10 Mar 1967	16 Dec 1967	25 Sep 1968
LAZZARO MOCENIGO	S 514	Italcantieri, Monfalcone	12 June 1967	20 Apr 1968	11 Jan 1969

Displacement, tons: 460 standard; 524 surfaced; 582 dived
Dimensions, feet (metres): 151.5 × 15.4 × 13.1 *(46.2 × 4.7 × 4)*
Main machinery: Diesel-electric; 2 Fiat/MTU 12V 493 TY7 diesels; 2200 hp(m) *(1.62 MW)*; 2 alternators; 1.08 MW; 1 motor; 2200 hp(m) *(1.62 MW)*; 1 shaft
Speed, knots: 14 surfaced; 15 dived. **Range, miles:** 3000 at 5 kts surfaced
Complement: 26 (4 officers)

Torpedoes: 4—21 in *(533 mm)* bow tubes. 6 Whitehead A184; dual purpose; wire-guided; active/passive homing to 25 km *(13.7 nm)* at 24 kts; 17 km *(9.2 nm)* at 38 kts; warhead 250 kg.
Countermeasures: ESM: BPR-2; radar warning.
Fire control: Selenia IPD 64 TFCS.
Radars: Search/navigation: SMA 3RM 20A/SMG; I band.
Sonars: Selenia Elsag IPD 64; passive/active search and attack; medium frequency.
Selenia Elsag MD 64; passive ranging.

LAZZARO MOCENIGO *7/1991, van Ginderen Collectio*

Programmes: Italy's first indigenously built submarines since the Second World War. First of class paid off to reserve in July 1990, second in late 1991. The remainder may be deleted earlier than expected if the overall size of the submarine force is reduced.

Structure: Diving depth, 180 m *(600 ft)*.

LIGHT AIRCRAFT CARRIER

ne	*No*	*Builders*	*Laid down*	*Launched*	*Commissioned*
SEPPE GARIBALDI	C 551	Italcantieri, Monfalcone	26 Mar 1981	4 June 1983	9 Aug 1987

placement, tons: 10 100 standard; 13 370 full load
nensions, feet (metres): 591 × 110.2 × 22
80 × 33.4 × 6.7)
ht deck, feet (metres): 570.2 × 99.7 *(173.8 × 30.4)*
in machinery: COGAG; 4 Fiat/GE LM 2500 gas turbines; 3 000 hp *(66 MW)* sustained; 2 shafts
ed, knots: 30. **Range, miles:** 7000 at 20 kts
nplement: 550 ship plus 230 air group (accommodation for 25 including Flag and staff)

ssiles: SSM: 4 OTO Melara Teseo Mk 2 (TG 2) ❶; active radar oming to 180 km *(98.4 nm)* at 0.9 Mach; warhead 210 kg; ea-skimmer for last 4 km *(2.2 nm)*.
M: 2 Selenia Elsag Albatros octuple launchers ❷; 48 Aspide; emi-active radar homing to 13 km *(7 nm)* at 2.5 Mach; height nvelope 15-5000 m *(49.2-16 405 ft)*; warhead 30 kg.
ns: 6 Breda 40 mm/70 (3 twin) MB ❸; 85° elevation; 300 ounds/minute to 12.5 km *(6.8 nm)* anti-surface; 4 km *(2.2 nm)* nti-aircraft; weight of shell 0.96 kg.
pedoes: 6—324 mm B-515 (2 triple) tubes ❹. Honeywell Mk 6; anti-submarine; active/passive homing to 11 km *(5.9 nm)* at 0 kts; warhead 44 kg. Being replaced by new A 290.
untermeasures: Decoys: AN/SLQ 25 Nixie; noisemaker.
Breda SCLAR 105 mm 20-barrelled launchers; trains and levates; Chaff to 5 km *(2.7 nm)*; illuminants to 12 km *(6.6 nm)*.
M/ECM: Elettronica Nettuno SLQ 732; integrated intercept and amming system.
mbat data systems: IPN 20 (SADOC 2) action data utomation including Links 11 and 14.
e control: 3 NA 30 electro-optical backup for SAM. 3 Dardo JA21 for guns.
dars: Long range air search: Hughes SPS 52C ❺; 3D; E/F and; range 440 km *(240 nm)*.
search: Selenia SPS 768 (RAN 3L) ❻; D band; range 220 km *120 nm)*.
SMA SPN 728; I band; range 73 km *(40 nm)*; TV indicator.
/surface search: Selenia SPS 774 (RAN 10S) ❼; E/F band; ange 155 km *(85 nm)*.
face search/target indication: SMA SPS 702 UPX; 718 beacon; band.
vigation: SMA SPN 749; I band.
e control: Three Selenia SPG 75 (RTN 30X) ❽; I/J band; range 5 km *(8 nm)* (for Albatros).
Three Selenia SPG 74 (RTN 20X) ❾; I/J band; range 13 km *7 nm)* (for Dardo).
: Mk XII.
can: SRN-15A.
nars: Raytheon DE 1160 LF; bow-mounted; active search; medium frequency.

ked wing aircraft: 16 AV-8B Harrier II (1993).

GIUSEPPE GARIBALDI *8/1991, Giorgio Arra*

Helicopters: 18 SH-3D Sea King helicopters (12 in hangar, 6 on deck). The total capacity is either 16 Harriers or 18 helicopters. In practice a combination will be embarked.

Programmes: Contract awarded 21 November 1977. The design was changed considerably. Design work completed February 1980 and engineering work began in March 1980. Started sea trials 3 December 1984. Refitted late 1986-January 1987. A sister ship, *Giuseppe Mazzini*, was to replace *Vittorio Veneto* in the mid-1990s. This project was suspended in 1990 but may be revived in 1992.
Structure: Six decks with 13 vertical watertight bulkheads. Fitted with 6.5° ski-jump and VSTOL operating equipment. Two 15 ton lifts 18 × 10 m *(59 × 32.8 ft)*. Hangar size 110 × 15 × 6 m *(361 × 49.2 × 19.7 ft)*. Has a slightly narrower flight deck than UK Invincible class. Two MEN class fast personnel launches (capacity 250) can be embarked for amphibious operations or disaster relief.
Operational: Fleet Flagship. The long-standing dispute between the Navy and the Air Force concerning the former's operation of fixed-wing aircraft (dating back to pre-World War II legislation) was finally resolved by legislation passed on 29 January 1989. Embarked aircraft are operated by the Navy with the Air Force providing evaluation and maintenance and any additional pilots required. Two trainer TAV-8B aircraft acquired in early 1991. First operational aircraft to be embarked in 1993.

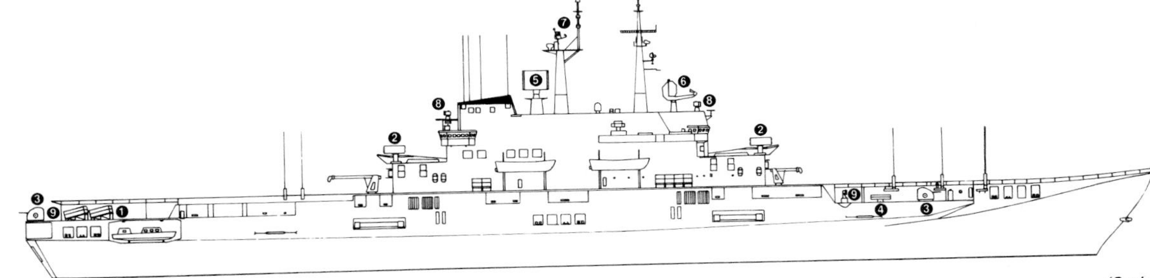
IUSEPPE GARIBALDI *(Scale 1 : 1 200), Ian Sturton*

GIUSEPPE GARIBALDI *8/1991, Giorgio Arra*

CRUISERS

Name	*No*	*Builders*	*Laid down*	*Launched*	*Commissione*
VITTORIO VENETO	C 550	Italcantieri, Castellammare	10 June 1965	5 Feb 1967	12 July 1969

Displacement, tons: 7500 standard; 9500 full load
Dimensions, feet (metres): 589 × 63.6 × 19.7 *(179.6 × 19.4 × 6)*
Flight deck, feet (metres): 131 × 61 *(40 × 18.6)*
Main machinery: 4 Foster-Wheeler boilers (Ansaldo); 700 psi *(50 kg/cm sq)*; 850°F *(450°C)*; 2 Tosi turbines; 73 000 hp(m) *(54 MW)*; 2 shafts
Speed, knots: 32. **Range, miles:** 5000 at 17 kts
Complement: 550 (53 officers)

Missiles: SSM: 4 OTO Melara Teseo Mk 2 (TG 2) ❶; inertial cruise; active radar homing to 180 km *(98.4 nm)* at 0.9 Mach; warhead 210 kg; sea-skimmer.
SAM: GDC Pomona Standard SM-1ER; Aster twin Mk 10 Mod 9 launcher ❷; capacity for 60 missiles (including ASROC) on 3 drums; command guidance; semi-active radar homing to 64 km *(35 nm)* at 2.5 Mach.
A/S: Honeywell ASROC; inertial guidance to 1.6-10 km *(1-5.4 nm)*; payload Mk 46 torpedo.
Guns: 8 OTO Melara 3 in *(76 mm)*/62 MMK ❸; 85° elevation; 55-65 rounds/minute to 8 km *(4.4 nm)*; weight of shell 6 kg.
6 Breda 40 mm/70 (3 twin) ❹; 85° elevation; 300 rounds/minute to 12.5 km *(6.8 nm)* anti-surface; 4 km *(2.2 nm)* anti-aircraft; weight of shell 0.96 kg.
Torpedoes: 6—324 mm US Mk 32 (2 triple) tubes ❺. Honeywell Mk 46; anti-submarine; active/passive homing to 11 km *(5.9 nm)* at 40 kts; warhead 44 kg.
Countermeasures: Decoys: 2 Breda SCLAR 105 mm 20-barrelled trainable ❻; Chaff to 5 km *(2.7 nm)*; illuminants to 12 km *(6.6 nm)*. SLQ 25 Nixie; towed torpedo decoy.
ESM: SLR 4; intercept.
ECM: 3 SLQ-B; 2 SLQ-C; jammers.
Combat data systems: SADOC 1 action data automation; Link 11.
Fire control: 4 Argo 10 systems for 76 mm guns. 2 Dardo systems for 40 mm guns.
Radars: Long range air search: Hughes SPS 52C ❼; 3D; E/F band; range 440 km *(240 nm)*.
Air search: Selenia SPS 768 (RAN 3L) ❽; D band; range 220 km *(120 nm)*.
Surface search/target indication: SMA SPS 702 ❾; I band.
Navigation: SMA SPS 748; I band; range 73 km *(40 nm)*.
Fire control: Four Selenia SPG 70 (RTN 10X) ❿; I/J band; range 40 km *(22 nm)* (for Argo).

VITTORIO VENETO *1991, Camil Busquets i Vilanov*

Two Selenia SPG 74 (RTN 20X) ⓫; I/J band; range 13 km *(7 nm)* (for Dardo).
Two Sperry/RCA SPG 55C ⓬; G/H band; range 51 km *(28 nm)* (for Standard).
IFF: Mk XII. Tacan: SRN-15A.
Sonars: Sangamo SQS 23G; bow-mounted; active search and attack; medium frequency.

Helicopters: 6 AB 212ASW ⓭.

Programmes: Projected under the 1959-60 New Constructio Programme, but her design was recast several times. Starte trials 30 April 1969. Defined as a Guided Missile Helicopte Cruiser.
Modernisation: In hand from 1981 to early 1984 for modernis ation which included the four Teseo launchers and the thre twin Breda compact 40 mm.
Structure: Developed from the Andrea Doria class but wit much larger helicopter squadron and improved facilities fc anti-submarine operations. Fitted with two sets of stabilisers.

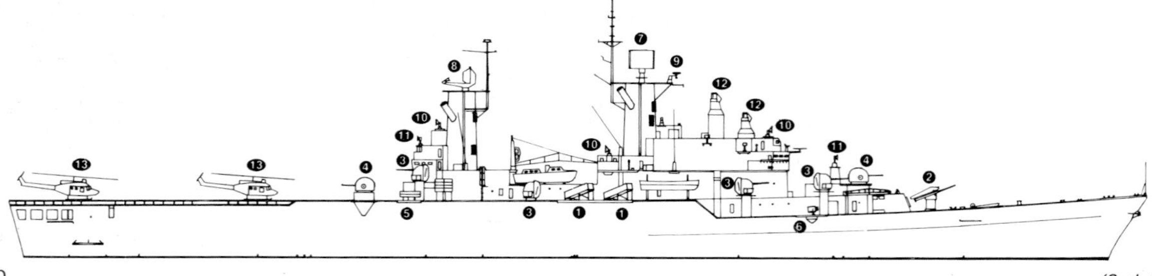
VITTORIO VENETO *(Scale 1 : 1 200), Ian Sturto*

VITTORIO VENETO *3/1990, Aldo Fraccaro*

DESTROYERS

1 + 1 ANIMOSO CLASS (DDG)

Name	*No*	*Builders*	*Laid down*	*Launched*	*Commissioned*
ANIMOSO	D 560	Fincantieri, Riva Trigoso/Muggiano	20 Jan 1988	29 Oct 1989	July 1992
ARDIMENTOSO	D 561	Fincantieri, Riva Trigoso/Muggiano	15 Nov 1989	13 Apr 1991	Feb 1993

Displacement, tons: 4330 standard; 5400 full load
Dimensions, feet (metres): 487.4 × 52.8 × 16.5 *(147.7 × 16.1 × 5)*
Flight deck, feet (metres): 78.7 × 42.7 *(24 × 13)*
Main machinery: CODOG; 2 Fiat/GE LM2500 gas turbines; 44 000 hp *(33 MW)* sustained; 2 GMT BL 230.20 DVM diesels; 12 600 hp(m) *(9.3 MW)* sustained; 2 shafts; cp props
Speed, knots: 31.5. **Range, miles:** 7000 at 18 kts
Complement: 400 approx (35 officers)

Missiles: SSM: 4 or 8 OTO Melara/Matra Teseo Mk 2 (TG 2) (2 or 4 twin) ❶; mid-course guidance; active radar homing to 180 km *(98.4 nm)* at 0.9 Mach; warhead 210 kg; sea-skimmer. 4 SSM may be replaced by 4 Milas A/S launchers.
SAM: 40 GDC Pomona Standard SM-1MR; Mk 13 Mod 4 launcher ❷; command guidance; semi-active radar homing to 46 km *(25 nm)* at 2 Mach.
Selenia Albatros Mk 2 octuple launcher for Aspide ❸; semi-active radar homing to 13 km *(7 nm)* at 2.5 Mach; 16 missiles. Automatic reloading.
Guns: 1 OTO Melara 5 in *(127 mm)*/54 ❹; 85° elevation; 45 rounds/minute to 16 km *(8.7 nm)*; weight of shell 32 kg.
3 OTO Melara 3 in *(76 mm)*/62 Super Rapid ❺; 85° elevation; 120 rounds/minute to 16 km *(8.7 nm)*; weight of shell 6 kg.
Torpedoes: 6—324 mm B-515 (2 triple) tubes ❻. Whitehead A 290; anti-submarine.
Countermeasures: Decoys: 2 CSEE Sagaie Chaff launchers. 1 Elmer anti-torpedo system.
ESM/ECM: SLQ 732 Nettuno; integrated intercept and jamming system.
Combat data systems: Selenia Elsag IPN 20; Links 11 and 14.
Fire control: 4 Dardo E systems (3 channels for Aspide). Milas TFCS.
Radars: Long range air search: Hughes SPS 52C; 3D ❼; E/F band; range 440 km *(240 nm)*.
Air search: Selenia SPS 768 (RAN 3L) ❽; D band; range 220 km *(120 nm)*.
Air/surface search: Selenia SPS 774 (RAN 10S) ❾; E/F band; range 155 km *(85 nm)*.
Surface search: SMA SPS 702 ❿; I band.
Fire control: Four Selenia SPG 76 (RTN 30X) ⓫; I/J band (for Dardo).
Two Raytheon SPG 51D ⓬; G/I band (for SAM).
Navigation: SMA SPN 748 (3 RM 20); I band; range 73 km *(40 nm)*.
IFF: Mk XII. Tacan: SRN-15A.
Sonars: Raytheon/Elsag DE 1167LF and DE 1164; integrated hull and VDS; active search and attack; medium frequency.

Helicopters: 2 AB 212ASW ⓭; EH 101 capable.

Programmes: Order placed 9 March 1986 with Riva Trigoso. To replace the Impavido class. Two more to follow in due course. All ships built at Riva Trigoso are completed at Muggiano after launching.

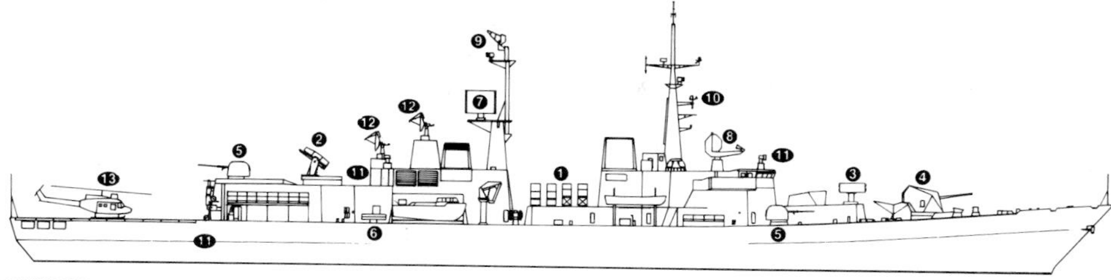

ANIMOSO *(Scale 1 : 1 200), Ian Sturton*

ARDIMENTOSO *4/1991, Giorgio Ghiglione*

Structure: Kevlar armour fitted. Prairie Masker noise suppression system. The 127 mm guns are ex-Audace class B turrets. Fully stabilised. Hangar is 18.5 m in length.

Operational: GPS and Meteosat receivers fitted. The three Super Rapid 76 mm guns are to be used as a combined medium range anti-surface armament and CIWS against missiles.

ANIMOSO *9/1991, Milpress*

2 AUDACE CLASS (DDG)

Name	*No*	*Builders*	*Laid down*	*Launched*	*Commissioned*
ARDITO	D 550	Italcantieri, Castellammare	19 July 1968	27 Nov 1971	5 Dec 1972
AUDACE	D 551	Fincantieri, Riva Trigoso/Muggiano	27 Apr 1968	2 Oct 1971	16 Nov 1972

Displacement, tons: 3600 standard; 4400 full load
Dimensions, feet (metres): 448 × 46.6 × 15.1 *(136.6 × 14.2 × 4.6)*
Main machinery: 4 Foster-Wheeler boilers; 600 psi *(43 kg/cm sq)*; 850°F *(450°C)*; 2 turbines; 73 000 hp(m) *(54 MW)*; 2 shafts
Speed, knots: 34. **Range, miles:** 3000 at 20 kts
Complement: 380 (30 officers)

Missiles: SSM: 8 OTO Melara/Matra Teseo Mk 2 (TG 2) (4 twin) ❶; mid-course guidance; active radar homing to 180 km (98.4 nm) at 0.9 Mach; warhead 210 kg; sea-skimmer.
SAM: 40 GDC Pomona Standard SM-1MR; Mk 13 Mod 4 launcher ❷; command guidance; semi-active radar homing to 46 km *(25 nm)* at 2 Mach; height envelope 45.7-18 288 m *(150-60 000 ft)*.
Selenia Albatros octuple launcher for Aspide ❸; semi-active radar homing to 13 km *(7 nm)* at 2.5 Mach.
Guns: 1 OTO Melara 5 in *(127 mm)*/54 ❹; 85° elevation; 45 rounds/minute to 16 km *(8.7 nm)* anti-surface; 7 km *(3.8 nm)* anti-aircraft; weight of shell 32 kg.
3 OTO Melara 3 in *(76 mm)*/62 Compact (*Ardito*) and 1 (*Ardito*) or 4 (*Audace*) Super Rapid ❺; 85° elevation; 85 rounds/minute (Compact) or 120 rounds/minute (Super Rapid) to 16 km *(8.7 nm)* anti-surface; 12 km *(6.6 nm)* anti-aircraft; weight of shell 6 kg.
Torpedoes: 6—324 mm US Mk 32 (2 triple) tubes ❻. Honeywell Mk 46; anti-submarine; active/passive homing to 11 km *(5.9 nm)* at 40 kts; warhead 44 kg. Transom tubes have been removed.
Countermeasures: Decoys: 2 Breda 105 mm SCLAR 20-barrelled trainable; Chaff to 5 km *(2.7 nm)*; illuminants to 12 km *(6.6 nm)*. SLQ 25 Nixie; towed torpedo decoy.
ESM: SLR-4; intercept.
ECM: 3 SLQ-B, 2 SLQ-C; jammers.
Combat data systems: Selenia Elsag IPN-20 action data automation; Links 11 and 14. SATCOM.
Fire control: 3 Dardo E FCS (3 channels for Aspide). Selenia NA 30 optronic director.
Radars: Long range air search: Hughes SPS 52C ❼; 3D; E/F band; range 440 km *(240 nm)*.
Air search: Selenia SPS 768 (RAN 3L) ❽; D band; range 220 km *(120 nm)*.
Air/surface search: Selenia SPS 774 (RAN 10S) ❾; E/F band; range 155 km *(85 nm)*.
Surface search: SMA SPQ 2D ❿; I band.
Navigation: SMA SPN 748; I band.
Fire control: Three Selenia SPG 76 (RTN 30X) ⓫; I/J band; range 40 km *(22 nm)* (for Dardo E).
Two Raytheon SPG 51 ⓬; G/I band (for Standard).
IFF: Mk XII.
Tacan: SRN-15A.
Sonars: CWE 610; hull-mounted; active search and attack; medium frequency.

Helicopters: 2 AB 212ASW ⓭.

Programmes: It was announced in April 1966 that two new guided missile destroyers would be built. They are basically similar to, but an improvement in design on, that of the Impavido class.

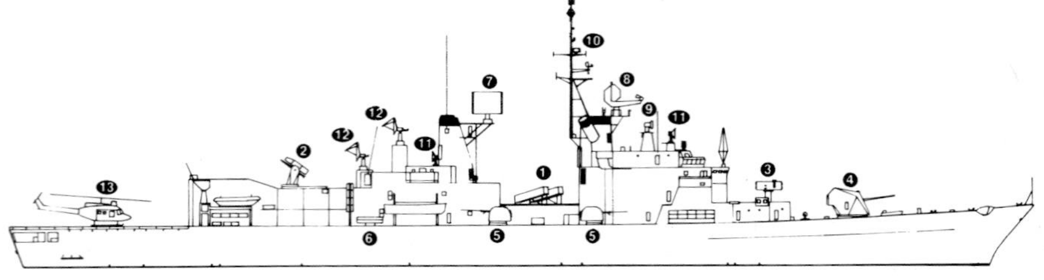

AUDACE *(Scale 1 : 1 200), Ian Sturton*

ARDITO *6/1991, Barbara Fraccaroli*

Modernisation: B gun has been replaced by Albatros PDMS. Stern torpedo tubes removed. *Audace* fitted with four and *Ardito* one Super Rapid guns vice the 76 mm Compacts. *Ardito* should get three more by 1994. *Ardito* completed modernisation in March 1988 and *Audace* in early 1991.
Structure: Both fitted with stabilisers.

AUDACE *7/1991, Giorgio Ghiglione*

FRIGATES

8 MAESTRALE CLASS

Name	No	Builders	Laid down	Launched	Commissioned
MAESTRALE	F 570	Fincantieri, Riva Trigoso	8 Mar 1978	2 Feb 1981	6 Mar 1982
GRECALE	F 571	Fincantieri, Muggiano	21 Mar 1979	12 Sep 1981	5 Feb 1983
LIBECCIO	F 572	Fincantieri, Riva Trigoso	1 Aug 1979	7 Sep 1981	5 Feb 1983
SCIROCCO	F 573	Fincantieri, Riva Trigoso	26 Feb 1980	17 Apr 1982	20 Sep 1983
ALISEO	F 574	Fincantieri, Riva Trigoso	10 Aug 1980	29 Oct 1982	7 Sep 1983
EURO	F 575	Fincantieri, Riva Trigoso	15 Apr 1981	25 Apr 1983	24 Jan 1984
ESPERO	F 576	Fincantieri, Riva Trigoso	29 July 1982	19 Nov 1983	4 May 1984
ZEFFIRO	F 577	Fincantieri, Riva Trigoso	15 Mar 1983	19 May 1984	4 May 1985

Displacement, tons: 2500 standard; 3200 full load
Dimensions, feet (metres): 405 × 42.5 × 15.1 *(122.7 × 12.9 × 4.6)*
Flight deck, feet (metres): 89 × 39 *(27 × 12)*
Main machinery: CODOG; 2 Fiat/GE LM 2500 gas turbines; 44 000 hp *(33 MW)* sustained; 2 GMT BL 230.20 DVM diesels; 12 600 hp(m) *(9.3 MW)* sustained; 2 shafts; cp props
Speed, knots: 32 gas; 21 diesels. **Range, miles:** 6000 at 16 kts
Complement: 232 (24 officers)

Missiles: SSM: 4 OTO Melara Teseo Mk 2 (TG 2) ❶; mid-course guidance; active radar homing to 180 km *(98.4 nm)*; warhead 210 kg; sea-skimmer.
SAM: Selenia Albatros octuple launcher; 16 Aspide ❷; semi-active homing to 13 km *(7 nm)* at 2.5 Mach; height envelope 15-5000 m *(49.2-16 405 ft)*; warhead 30 kg.
Guns: 1 OTO Melara 5 in *(127 mm)*/54 automatic ❸; 85° elevation; 45 rounds/minute to 16 km *(8.7 nm)* anti-surface; 7 km *(3.8 nm)* anti-aircraft; weight of shell 32 kg; fires Chaff and illuminants.
4 Breda 40 mm/70 (2 twin) compact ❹; 85° elevation; 300 rounds/minute to 12.5 km *(6.8 nm)* anti-surface; 4 km *(2.2 nm)* anti-aircraft; weight of shell 0.96 kg.
2 Oerlikon 20 mm fitted for Gulf deployments in 1990-91.
Torpedoes: 6—324 mm US Mk 32 (2 triple) tubes ❺. Honeywell Mk 46; anti-submarine; active/passive homing to 11 km *(5.9 nm)* at 40 kts; warhead 44 kg.
2—21 in *(533 mm)* B516 tubes in transom ❻. Whitehead A184; dual purpose; wire-guided; active/passive homing to 17 km *(9.2 nm)* at 38 kts; 25 km *(13.7 nm)* at 24 kts; warhead 250 kg.
Countermeasures: Decoys: 2 Breda 105 mm SCLAR 20-tubed trainable Chaff rocket launchers ❼; Chaff to 5 km *(2.7 nm)*; illuminants to 12 km *(6.6 nm)*. 2 Dagaie Chaff launchers being fitted in all.
SLQ 25; towed torpedo decoy. Prairie Masker; noise suppression system.
ESM: SLR-4; intercept.
ECM: 2 SLQ-D; jammers.
Combat data systems: IPN 20 (SADOC 2) action data automation; Link 11. SATCOM ❽.
Fire control: NA 30 for Albatros and 5 in guns. 2 Dardo for 40 mm guns.
Radars: Air/surface search: Selenia SPS 774 (RAN 10S) ❾; E/F band; range 155 km *(85 nm)*.
Surface search: SMA SPS 702 ❿; I band.
Navigation: SMA SPN 703; I band.
Fire control: Selenia SPG 75 (RTN 30X) ⓫; I/J band (for Albatros and 12.7 mm gun).
Two Selenia SPG 74 (RTN 20X) ⓬; I/J band; range 15 km *(8 nm)* (for Dardo).
IFF: Mk XII.
Sonars: Raytheon DE 1164; hull-mounted; VDS; active/passive attack; medium frequency. VDS can be towed at up to 28 kts. Maximum depth 300 m.

Helicopters: 2 AB 212ASW ⓭.

Programmes: First six ordered December 1976 and last pair in October 1980. All Riva Trigoso ships completed at Muggiano after launch.
Structure: There has been a notable increase of 34 ft in length and 5 ft in beam over the Lupo class to provide for the fixed hangar and VDS, the result providing more comfortable accommodation but a small loss of top speed. Fittted with stabilisers.
Operational: A towed passive LF array may be attached to the VDS body. F 574 fitted with an Oerlikon Breda 25 mm gun for evaluation in 1991.

MAESTRALE *(Scale 1 : 1 200) Ian Sturton*

ESPERO *10/1991*

LIBECCIO *5/1990, 92 Wing RAAF*

4 + 4 LUPO CLASS

Name	No	Builders	Laid down	Launched	Commissioned
LUPO	F 564	Fincantieri, Riva Trigoso	11 Oct 1974	29 July 1976	12 Sep 1977
SAGITTARIO	F 565	Fincantieri, Riva Trigoso	4 Feb 1976	22 June 1977	18 Nov 1978
PERSEO	F 566	Fincantieri, Riva Trigoso	28 Feb 1977	12 July 1978	1 Mar 1980
ORSA	F 567	Fincantieri, Muggiano	1 Aug 1977	1 Mar 1979	1 Mar 1980
— (ex-*Hittin*)	(ex-F 14)	Fincantieri, Ancona	31 Mar 1982	27 July 1983	1992
— (ex-*Thi Qar*)	(ex-F 15)	Fincantieri, Ancona	3 Sep 1982	19 Dec 1984	1992
— (ex-*Al Qadisiya*)	(ex-F 16)	Fincantieri, Ancona	1 Dec 1983	1 June 1985	1992
— (ex-*Al Yarmouk*)	(ex-F 17)	Fincantieri, Riva Trigoso	12 Mar 1984	18 Apr 1985	1992

Displacement, tons: 2208 standard; 2500 full load
Dimensions, feet (metres): 371.3 × 37.1 × 12.1 *(113.2 × 11.3 × 3.7)*
Main machinery: CODOG; 2 Fiat/GE LM 2500 gas turbines; 44 000 hp *(33 MW)* sustained; 2 GMT BL 230.20M diesels; 10 000 hp(m) *(7.3 MW)*; 2 shafts; cp props
Speed, knots: 35 turbines; 21 diesels. **Range, miles:** 4350 at 16 kts on diesels
Complement: 185 (16 officers)

Missiles: SSM: 8 OTO Melara Teseo Mk 2 (TG 2) ❶; mid-course guidance; active radar homing to 180 km *(98.4 nm)* at 0.9 Mach; warhead 210 kg; sea-skimmer.
SAM: Raytheon NATO Sea Sparrow Mk 29 octuple launcher ❷; semi-active radar homing to 14.6 km *(8 nm)* at 2.5 Mach; warhead 39 kg. 8 reloads. Updated for RIM-7H so cannot now fire Aspide.
Guns: 1 OTO Melara 5 in *(127 mm)*/54 ❸; 85° elevation; 45 rounds/minute to 16 km *(8.7 nm)* anti-surface; 7 km *(3.8 nm)* anti-aircraft; weight of shell 32 kg.
4 Breda 40 mm/70 (2 twin) compact ❹; 85° elevation; 300 rounds/minute to 12.5 km *(6.8 nm)* anti-surface; 4 km *(2.2 nm)* anti-aircraft; weight of shell 0.96 kg.
2 Oerlikon 20 mm can be fitted.
Torpedoes: 6—324 mm US Mk 32 tubes ❺. Honeywell Mk 46; anti-submarine; active/passive homing to 11 km *(5.9 nm)* at 40 kts; warhead 44 kg.
Countermeasures: Decoys: 2 Breda 105 mm SCLAR 20-tubed trainable ❻; Chaff to 5 km *(2.7 nm)*; illuminants to 12 km *(6.6 nm)*.
SLQ 25 Nixie; towed torpedo decoy.
ESM: SLR-4; intercept.
ECM: 2 SLQ-D; jammers.
Combat data systems: IPN 20 (SADOC 2) action data automation; Link 11. SATCOM.
Fire control: Argo NA10 Mod 2 for missiles and 5 in gun. 2 Dardo for 40 mm guns.
Radars: Air search: Selenia SPS 774 (RAN 10S) ❼; E/F band; range 155 km *(85 nm)* (see *Structure*).
Surface search: SMA SPQ2 F ❽; I band.
Navigation: SMA SPN 748; I band.
Fire control: Selenia SPG 70 (RTN 10X) ❾; I/J band; range 40 km *(22 nm)* (for Argo).
Two Selenia SPG 74 (RTN 20X) ❿; I/J band; range 15 km *(8 nm)* (for Dardo).
US Mk 95 Mod 1 (for SAM) ⓫; I band.
IFF: Mk XII.
Sonars: Raytheon DE 1160B; hull-mounted; active search and attack; medium frequency.

Helicopters: 1 AB 212ASW ⓬.

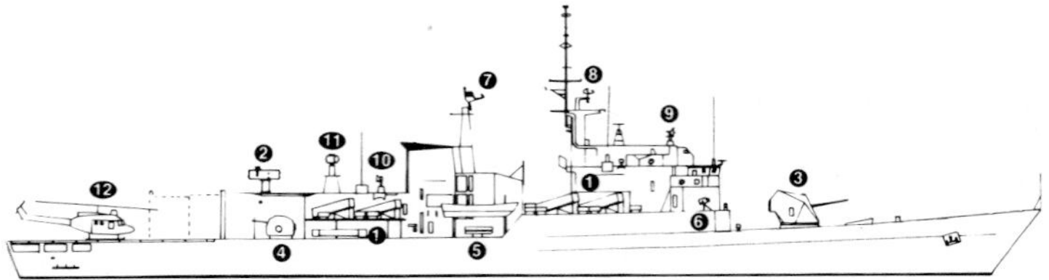

LUPO (Scale 1 : 1 200), *Ian Sturton*

PERSEO *1990, Italian Navy*

Programmes: In February 1992 it was decided to transfer the four ships built for Iraq to the Italian Navy. No major upgrade was foreseen because the ships have been kept in good condition by Fincantieri after their completion in 1986/87. The original sale to Iraq was first delayed by payment problems and then cancelled in 1990 when UN embargoes were placed on military sales to Iraq. The ships should enter service as offshore patrol vessels in late 1992 after a minor refit.

Structure: 14 watertight compartments; fixed-fin stabilisers; telescopic hangar. *Sagittario* has a white radome covering an experimental low altitude search radar. The Iraqi ships are not identical having some radar and electronic differences but these systems may be updated to Italian standards.
Sales: Similar ships built for Peru (4) and Venezuela (6).
Operational: Ships deploying to the Gulf in 1991 had SATCOM fitted above the bridge.

2 ALPINO CLASS

Name	No	Builders	Laid down	Launched	Commissioned
ALPINO (ex-*Circe*)	F 580	Fincantieri, Riva Trigoso	27 Feb 1963	10 June 1967	14 Jan 1968
CARABINIERE (ex-*Climene*)	F 581	Fincantieri, Riva Trigoso	9 Jan 1965	30 Sep 1967	28 Apr 1968

Displacement, tons: 2400 standard; 2700 full load
Dimensions, feet (metres): 371.7 × 43.6 × 12.7 *(113.3 × 13.3 × 3.9)*
Main machinery: CODAG; 2 Metrovick gas turbines; 15 000 hp(m) *(11.2 MW)*; 4 Tosi OTV-320 diesels; 16 800 hp(m) *(12.35 MW)*; 2 shafts
Speed, knots: 20 diesel; 28 diesel and gas. **Range, miles:** 3500 at 18 kts
Complement: 163 (13 officers)

Missiles: SAM: VLS for Aster 15 trials *(Carabiniere)*.
Guns: 6 OTO Melara 3 in *(76 mm)*/62 ❶ *(Alpino)*; 85° elevation; 60 rounds/minute to 16 km *(8.7 nm)*; weight of shell 6 kg.
Torpedoes: 6—324 mm US Mk 32 (2 triple) tubes ❷. Honeywell Mk 46; anti-submarine; active/passive homing to 11 km *(5.9 nm)* at 40 kts; warhead 44 kg.
A/S mortars: 1 Whitehead K 113 single-barrelled automatic *(Alpino)* ❸; range 900 m; warhead 160 kg. MILAS launchers *(Carabiniere)*.
Countermeasures: Decoys: 2 Breda 105 mm SCLAR 20-tubed trainable ❹; Chaff to 5 km *(2.7 nm)*; illuminants to 12 km *(6.6 nm)*.
ESM/ECM: Selenia SLQ 747; integrated intercept and jammer.
Fire control: 2 Argo 'O' for 3 in guns.
Radars: Air search: RCA SPS 12 ❺; D band; range 120 km *(65 nm)*.
Surface search: SMA SPS 702 ❻; I band.
Navigation: SMA SPN 748; I band.
Fire control: Two Selenia SPG 70 (RTN 10X) ❼; I/J band; range 40 km *(22 nm)* (for Argo).
Sonars: Raytheon DE 1164; integrated hull and VDS; active search and attack; medium frequency.

Helicopters: 1 AB 212ASW ❽.

Modernisation: Both have been updated with new sonar, CCIC and EW. *Carabiniere* has been modified to replace *Quarto* as a trials ship. B gun turret and the Whitehead mortar have been replaced by MILAS launchers, and the two after 76 mm guns by the VLS for the Aster 15 SAM system.
Structure: Stabilisers fitted.
Operational: *Alpino* is likely to pay off in 1992.

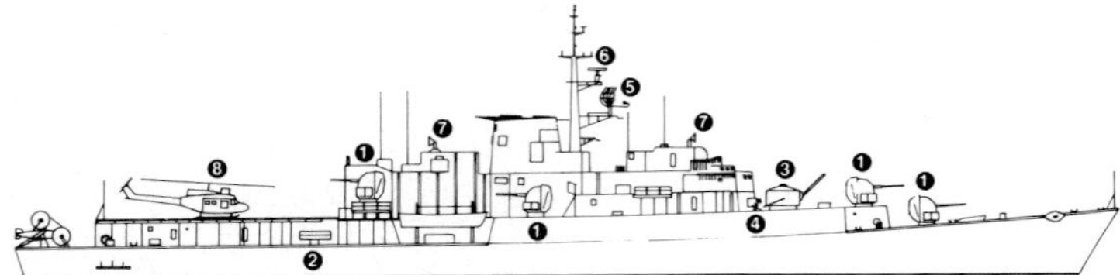

ALPINO (Scale 1 : 1 200), *Ian Sturton*

CARABINIERE (modified for SAM trials) *5/1991, Giorgio Ghiglione*

CORVETTES

8 + (4) MINERVA CLASS

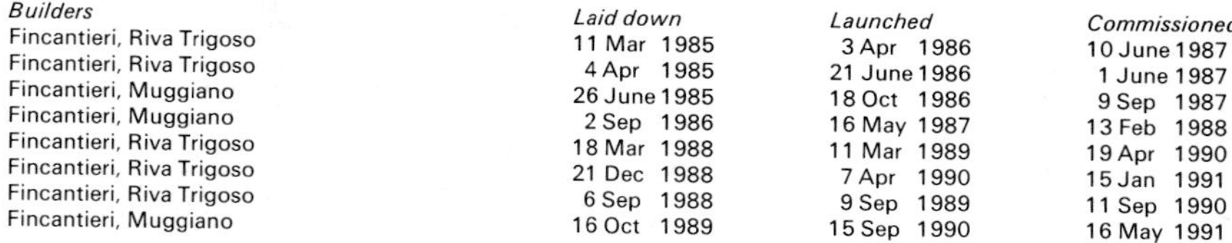

Name	*No*	*Builders*	*Laid down*	*Launched*	*Commissioned*
MINERVA	F 551	Fincantieri, Riva Trigoso	11 Mar 1985	3 Apr 1986	10 June 1987
URANIA	F 552	Fincantieri, Riva Trigoso	4 Apr 1985	21 June 1986	1 June 1987
DANAIDE	F 553	Fincantieri, Muggiano	26 June 1985	18 Oct 1986	9 Sep 1987
SFINGE	F 554	Fincantieri, Muggiano	2 Sep 1986	16 May 1987	13 Feb 1988
DRIADE	F 555	Fincantieri, Riva Trigoso	18 Mar 1988	11 Mar 1989	19 Apr 1990
CHIMERA	F 556	Fincantieri, Riva Trigoso	21 Dec 1988	7 Apr 1990	15 Jan 1991
FENICE	F 557	Fincantieri, Riva Trigoso	6 Sep 1988	9 Sep 1989	11 Sep 1990
SIBILLA	F 558	Fincantieri, Muggiano	16 Oct 1989	15 Sep 1990	16 May 1991

Displacement, tons: 1029 light; 1285 full load
Dimensions, feet (metres): 284.1 × 34.5 × 10.5 *(86.6 × 10.5 × 3.2)*
Main machinery: 2 Fincantieri GMT BM 230.20 DVM diesels; 12 600 hp(m) *(9.26 MW)* sustained; 2 shafts; cp props
Speed, knots: 24. **Range, miles:** 3500 at 18 kts
Complement: 123 (10 officers)

Missiles: SSM: Fitted for but not with 4 or 6 Teseo Otomat between the masts.
SAM: Selenia Elsag Albatros octuple launcher ❶; 8 Aspide; semi-active radar homing to 13 km *(7 nm)* at 2.5 Mach; height envelope 15-5000 m *(49.2-16 405 ft)*; warhead 30 kg. Capacity for larger magazine.
Guns: 1 OTO Melara 3 in *(76 mm)*/62 Super Rapid ❷; 85° elevation; 120 rounds/minute to 16 km *(8.7 nm)* anti-surface; 12 km *(6.6 nm)* anti-aircraft; weight of shell 6 kg.
Torpedoes: 6—324 mm Whitehead B 515 (2 triple) tubes ❸. Honeywell Mk 46; active/passive homing to 11 km *(5.9 nm)* at 40 kts; warhead 44 kg. Being replaced by Whitehead A 290.
Countermeasures: Decoys: 2 Wallop Barricade double layer launchers for Chaff and IR flares. SLQ 25 Nixie; towed torpedo decoy.
ESM/ECM: Selenia SLQ 747 intercept and jammer.

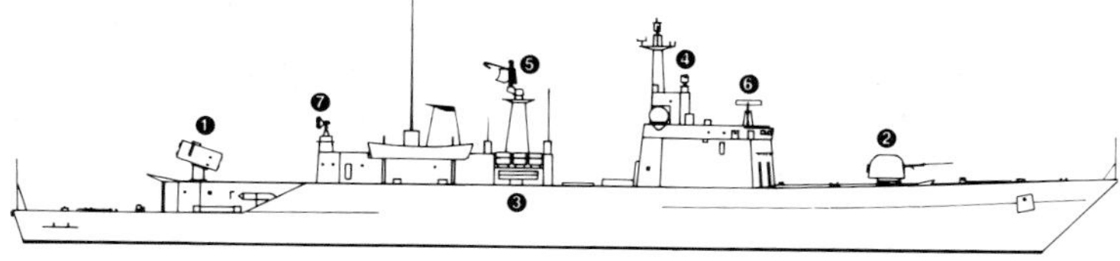

MINERVA

(Scale 1 : 900), Ian Sturton

Combat data systems: Selenia IPN 10 Mini SADOC action data automation; Link 11.
Fire control: 1 Elsag Dardo E system. Selenia/Elsag NA 18L Pegaso optronic director ❹. Elmer TLC system.
Radars: Air/surface search: Selenia SPS 774 (RAN 10S) ❺; E/F band; range 155 km *(85 nm)*.
Navigation: SMA SPN 728 ❻; I band.
Fire control: Selenia SPG 76 (RTN 30X) ❼; I/J band (for Albatros and gun).
Sonars: Raytheon/Elsag DE 1167; hull-mounted; active search and attack; 7.5-12 kHz.

Programmes: First four ordered in November 1982, second four in January 1987. A third four are planned, allowing all other corvette classes to be scrapped.
Structure: The funnels remodelled to reduce turbulence and IR signature. Two fin stabilisers.
Operational: Omega transit fitted. Intended for a number of roles including EEZ patrol, fishery protection and Commanding Officers training. First four based at Augusta, Sicily.

MINERVA

6/1991, Antonio Moreno

4 DE CRISTOFARO CLASS

Name	*No*	*Builders*	*Laid down*	*Launched*	*Commissioned*
PIETRO DE CRISTOFARO	F 540	Cantieri Navali Riuniti, Riva Trigoso	30 Apr 1963	29 May 1965	19 Dec 1965
UMBERTO GROSSO	F 541	Cantieri Ansaldo, Leghorn	21 Oct 1962	12 Dec 1964	25 Apr 1966
LICIO VISINTINI	F 546	CRDA, Monfalcone	30 Sep 1963	30 May 1965	25 Aug 1966
SALVATORE TODARO	F 550	Cantieri Ansaldo, Leghorn	21 Oct 1962	24 Oct 1964	25 Apr 1966

Displacement, tons: 850 standard; 1020 full load
Dimensions, feet (metres): 263.2 × 33.7 × 9 *(80.2 × 10.3 × 2.7)*
Main machinery: 2 Fiat 3012 RSS diesels; 8400 hp(m) *(6.17 MW)*; 2 shafts
Speed, knots: 23. **Range, miles:** 4000 at 16 kts
Complement: 131 (8 officers)

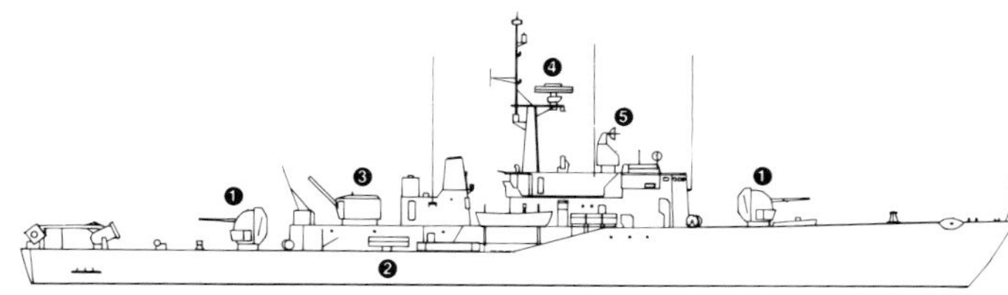

UMBERTO GROSSO

(Scale 1 : 900), Ian Sturton

Guns: 2 OTO Melara 3 in *(76 mm)*/62 ❶; 85° elevation; 60 rounds/minute to 16 km *(8.7 nm)*; weight of shell 6 kg.
Torpedoes: 6—324 mm US Mk 32 (2 triple) tubes ❷. Honeywell Mk 46; anti-submarine; active/passive homing to 11 km *(5.9 nm)*; warhead 44 kg.
A/S mortars: 1 Whitehead K 113 single-barrelled automatic ❸; range 900 m; warhead 160 kg.
Countermeasures: ESM: Elettronica SPR; intercept.
Fire control: OG3 director for guns. DLB 1 for A/S weapons.
Radars: Air/surface search: SMA SPQ 2B ❹; I band.
Navigation: BX 732; I band.
Fire control: Selenia Orion 7 ❺; I/J band (for OG3); range 73 km *(40 nm)*.
Sonars: EDO SQS 36; hull-mounted and VDS; active search and attack; medium frequency.

Structure: The design is an improved version of the Albatros class.
Operational: *De Cristofaro* converted for other duties—VDS, EW systems and A/S mortar removed. To start paying off in 1992.

LICIO VISINTINI

7/1991, van Ginderen Collection

2 ALBATROS CLASS

Name	No	Builders	Laid down	Launched	Commissioned
ALCIONE	F 544	Navalmeccanica, Castellammare	1953	19 Sep 1954	23 Oct 1955
AIRONE	F 545	Navalmeccanica, Castellammare	1953	21 Nov 1954	29 Dec 1955

Displacement, tons: 800 standard; 950 full load
Dimensions, feet (metres): 250.3 × 31.5 × 9.2 *(76.3 × 9.6 × 2.8)*
Main machinery: 2 Fiat M 409 diesels; 5200 hp(m) *(3.82 MW)*; 2 shafts
Speed, knots: 19. **Range, miles:** 5000 at 18 kts
Complement: 99 (6 officers)

Guns: 3 Bofors 40 mm/70; 90° elevation; 300 rounds/minute to 12 km *(6.6 nm)*; weight of shell 2.4 kg.
Torpedoes: 6—324 mm US Mk 32 (2 triple) tubes (not in all).
A/S mortars: 2—24-tubed Hedgehogs *(Airone)*; range 350 m; warhead 26 kg.
Depth charges: 2 projectors; 1 rack *(Airone)*.
Radars: Air/surface search: SMA SPQ 2; I band.
Navigation: BX 732; I band.
Sonars: QCU 2; hull-mounted; active search and attack; high frequency.

Programmes: Eight ships of this class were built in Italy under US offshore MDAP orders; three for Italy, four for Denmark (since deleted) and one for the Netherlands. Being replaced by Minerva class.
Operational: Used only for target towing and target drone control. The last two to be paid off in 1992.

ALBATROS Class (old number) *1988, Aldo Fraccaroli*

OFFSHORE PATROL VESSELS (OPV)

4 CASSIOPEA CLASS

Name	No	Builders	Laid down	Launched	Commissioned
CASSIOPEA	P 401	Fincantieri, Muggiano	16 Dec 1987	20 July 1988	6 July 1989
LIBRA	P 402	Fincantieri, Muggiano	17 Dec 1987	27 July 1988	28 Nov 1989
SPICA	P 403	Fincantieri, Muggiano	5 Sep 1988	27 May 1989	3 May 1990
VEGA	P 404	Fincantieri, Muggiano	20 June 1989	24 Feb 1990	25 Oct 1990

Displacement, tons: 1002 standard; 1475 full load
Dimensions, feet (metres): 261.8 × 38.7 × 11.5 *(79.8 × 11.8 × 3.5)*
Flight deck, feet (metres): 72.2 × 26.2 *(22 × 8)*
Main machinery: 2 Fincantieri/GMT BL 230.16 M diesels; 7940 hp(m) *(5.84 MW)* sustained; 2 shafts
Speed, knots: 20. **Range, miles:** 3300 at 17 kts
Complement: 78 (8 officers)

Guns: 1 OTO Melara 3 in *(76 mm)*/62; 85° elevation; 60 rounds/minute to 16 km *(8.7 nm)*; weight of shell 6 kg.
2—12.7 mm MGs.
Fire control: Argo NA 10.
Radars: Surface search: SMA SPS 702; I band.
Navigation: SMA SPN 748; I band.
Fire control: Selenia SPG 70 (RTN 10X); I/J band.

Helicopters: 1 AB 212ASW.

Programmes: Ordered in December 1986 for operations in EEZ. Officially 'pattugliatori marittimi'. Funded by the Ministry of the Merchant Navy but all operated by the Navy. The projected fifth of the class was cancelled in 1991.
Structure: Fitted for firefighting, rescue and supply tasks. Telescopic hangar. The guns and fire control radars are old stock taken from Bergamini class. There is a 500 cu m tank for storing oil polluted water.

VEGA *12/1990, Giorgio Ghiglione*

4 AGAVE CLASS

BAMBU P 495 (ex-M 5521) **MOGANO** P 497 (ex-M 5524)
MANGO P 496 (ex-M 5523) **PALMA** P 500 (ex-M 5525)

Displacement, tons: 375 standard; 405 full load
Dimensions, feet (metres): 144 × 25.6 × 8.5 *(43 × 7.8 × 2.6)*
Main machinery: 2 GM 8-268A diesels; 880 hp *(656 kW)*; 2 shafts
Speed, knots: 13.5. **Range, miles:** 2500 at 10 kts
Complement: 38 (5 officers)
Guns: 2 Oerlikon 20 mm (twin).
Radars: Navigation: SPN 750; I band.

Comment: Non-magnetic minesweepers of composite wooden and alloy construction similar to those transferred from the USA but built in Italian yards; all completed November 1956-April 1957. Originally class of 19. *Mirto* now used for surveying and *Alloro* as training ship for Petty Officers' School, La Maddalena. These four were converted for patrol duties with UN force in Red Sea and carry P numbers.

AGAVE Class (old number) *1/1990, Giorgio Ghiglione*

AMPHIBIOUS FORCES

2 + 1 SAN GIORGIO CLASS (LPDs)

Name	*No*	*Builders*	*Laid down*	*Launched*	*Commissioned*
SAN GIORGIO	L 9892	Fincantieri, Riva Trigoso	27 June 1985	25 Feb 1987	9 Oct 1987
SAN MARCO	L 9893	Fincantieri, Riva Trigoso	28 June 1986	21 Oct 1987	18 Mar 1988
CRISTOFORO COLOMBO	L 9894	Fincantieri, Riva Trigoso	Oct 1991	Jan 1993	June1993

Displacement, tons: 6687 standard; 7665 full load
Dimensions, feet (metres): 437.2 × 67.3 × 17.4 *(133.3 × 20.5 × 5.3)*
Flight deck, feet (metres): 328.1 × 67.3 *(100 × 20.5)*
Main machinery: 2 Fincantieri GMT A420.12 diesels; 16 800 hp(m) *(12.35 MW)* sustained; 2 shafts; cp props
Speed, knots: 21. **Range, miles:** 7500 at 16 kts; 4500 at 20 kts
Complement: 170
Military lift: Battalion of 400 plus 30-36 APCs or 30 medium tanks. 3 LCMs in stern docking well. 3 LCVPs on upper deck

Guns: 1 OTO Melara 3 in *(76 mm)*/62; 85° elevation; 60 rounds/minute to 16 km *(8.7 nm)*; weight of shell 6 kg.
2 Oerlikon 20 mm. 2—12.7 mm MGs.
Countermeasures: ESM: SRL 730.
Combat data systems: Selenia IPN 20 in due course.
Fire control: Elsag NA 21.
Radars: Surface search: SMA SPS 702; I band.
Navigation: SMA SPN 748; I band.
Fire control: Selenia SPG 70 (RTN 10X); I/J band; range 40 km *(22 nm)*.

Helicopters: Up to 5 CH-47C Chinook size.

Programmes: *San Giorgio* ordered 26 November 1983, *San Marco* on 5 March 1984 and *Cristoforo Colombo* 1 March 1991. Launching dates of the first two are slightly later than the 'official' launching ceremony because of poor weather.
Structure: Aircraft carrier type flight deck with island to starboard. Three landing spots. Bow ramp for amphibious landings. Stern docking well 20.5 × 7 m. Fitted with a 30 ton lift and two 40 ton travelling cranes for LCMs. *Cristoforo Colombo* is 300 tons heavier, of similar design except for more accommodation, a slightly longer island and different LCVP davit arrangement. Also no bow doors and therefore no beaching capability.
Operational: *San Giorgio* replaced *Caio Duilio* for midshipmen training and amphibious squadron but will be relieved by *Cristoforo Colombo* in 1994. *San Marco*, being run in conjunction with and paid for by the Ministry of Civil Protection, is specially fitted for disaster relief but will be transferred to the Navy in a crisis. Both are based at Brindisi and assigned to the Third Naval Division.
Opinion: An imaginative but cheap and versatile design which has applications in Amphibious, ASW support or disaster relief operations. Being studied by a number of other navies.

SAN GIORGIO *1991, Milpress*

SHIPBORNE AIRCRAFT

Numbers/Type: 1 Westland/Agusta EH 101 Merlin.
Operational speed: 160 kts *(296 km/h)*.
Service ceiling: —
Range: 550 nm *(1019 km)*.
Role/Weapon systems: Primary anti-submarine role with secondary anti-surface and troop carrying capabilities. Up to 30 planned in due course. Sensors: Radar, dipping sonar, sonobuoy acoustic processor, ESM, ECM. Weapons: ASW; 4 Whitehead torpedoes. ASV; 4 Sea Killer or replacement, capability for guidance of ship-launched SSM.

MERLIN *1991, Italian Navy*

Numbers/Type: 16/2 AV-8B/TAV-8B Harrier II Plus.
Operational speed: 562 kts *(1041 km/h)*.
Service ceiling: 50 000 ft *(15 240 m)*.
Range: 800 nm *(1480 km)*.
Role/Weapon systems: Two trainers delivered in July 1991 plus 16 front line aircraft to be delivered from 1993. Sensors: Radar derived from APG-65, FLIR and ECM. Weapons: Strike and AD missiles, bombs and cannon.

SEA HARRIER *1991, Italian Navy*

Numbers/Type: 57/5 Agusta-Bell 212ASW/EW.
Operational speed: 106 kts *(196 km/h)*.
Service ceiling: 17 000 ft *(5180 m)*.
Range: 360 nm *(667 km)*.
Role/Weapon systems: ASW/ECM helicopter; mainly deployed to escorts, but also shore-based for ASW support duties. Sensors: Selenia APS 705 search/attack radar, AQS-13B dipping sonar or GUFO ESM/ECM. Weapons: ASW; 2 × Mk 46 torpedoes.

AB 212 *1990, Camil Busquets i Vilanova*

Numbers/Type: 36 Agusta-Sikorsky SH-3D/H Sea King.
Operational speed: 120 kts *(222 km/h)*.
Service ceiling: 12 200 ft *(3720 m)*.
Range: 630 nm *(1165 km)*.
Role/Weapon systems: ASW helicopter; embarked in larger ASW ships, including CVL; also shore-based for medium ASV-ASW in Mediterranean Sea; several sub-variants operated. Sensors: Selenia APS 705 search radar, AQS-13B dipping sonar, sonobuoys. Weapons: ASW; 4 × Mk 46 torpedoes. ASV; 2 × Marte 2/Sea Killer missiles.

SEA KING *1989, Aldo Fraccaroli*

LAND-BASED MARITIME AIRCRAFT

Numbers/Type: 18 Bréguet Atlantique 1.
Operational speed: 355 kts *(658 km/h)*.
Service ceiling: 22 800 ft *(10 000 m)*.
Range: 4855 nm *(8995 km)*.
Role/Weapon systems: Shore-based for long-range MR and shipping surveillance; wartime role includes ASW support to helicopters. Sensors: Thomson-CSF radar, ECM/ESM, MAD, sonobuoys. Weapons: ASW; 9 × torpedoes (including Mk 46 torpedoes) or depth bombs or mines.

Numbers/Type: 18 Panavia Tornado IDS.
Operational speed: Mach 2.2.
Service ceiling: 80 000 ft *(24 385 m)*.
Range: 1500 nm *(2780 km)*.
Role/Weapon systems: Swing wing strike and recce; part of a force of a total of 100 aircraft of which 18 are used for maritime operations based near Bari. Sensors: Texas instruments nav/attack systems. Weapons: ASV; 4 Kormoran missiles; 2 × 27 mm cannon. AD; 4 AIM-9L Sidewinder.

LIGHT FORCES

Note: 1. *Saettia* (P 920) is a private Fincantieri venture and will not be bought by the Italian Navy. 2. A 23 m Fast Patrol Craft called the Aliscarfi class is being planned to replace the Sparviero class.

6 SPARVIERO CLASS (HYDROFOIL—MISSILE)

Name	*No*	*Builders*	*Commissioned*
NIBBIO	P 421	Fincantieri, Muggiano	6 Mar 1982
FALCONE	P 422	Fincantieri, Muggiano	6 Mar 1982
ASTORE	P 423	Fincantieri, Muggiano	5 Feb 1983
GRIFONE	P 424	Fincantieri, Muggiano	5 Feb 1983
GHEPPIO	P 425	Fincantieri, Muggiano	20 Jan 1983
CONDOR	P 426	Fincantieri, Muggiano	18 Jan 1984

Displacement, tons: 60.6 full load
Dimensions, feet (metres): 80.7 × 23.1 × 14.4 *(24.6 × 7 × 4.4)* (length and beam foils extended, draught hullborne); 75.4 × 22.9 × 5.2 *(23 × 7 × 1.6)* (hull size)
Main machinery: Foilborne; 1 RR Proteus 15M560 gas turbine; 4500 hp *(3.36 MW)*; 1 waterjet Hullborne; 1 Isotta Fraschini ID 38 N 6V diesel; 290 hp(m) *(213 kW)* sustained; 1 retractable prop
Speed, knots: 48; 8 hullborne on diesel. **Range, miles:** 400 at 45 kts; 1200 at 8 kts
Complement: 10 (2 officers)

Missiles: SSM: 2 OTO Melara/Matra Otomat Teseo Mk 2 (TG 1); active radar homing to 80 km *(43.2 nm)* at 0.9 Mach; warhead 210 kg; sea-skimmer.
Guns: 1 OTO Melara 3 in *(76 mm)*/62 compact; 85° elevation; 85 rounds/minute to 16 km *(8.7 nm)* anti-surface; 12 km *(6.6 nm)* anti-aircraft; weight of shell 6 kg.
Fire control: Elsag NA 10 Mod 3.
Radars: Surface search: SMA SPQ 701 (3 RM 7-250 in P 420); I band; range 73 km *(40 nm)*; IFF. Fire control: Selenia SPG 70 (RTN 10X); I/J band; range 40 km *(22 nm)*.

Modernisation: Plans to change to a more powerful GT engine have been postponed but a new diesel has been fitted.
Structure: Aluminium hull and superstructure. Payload equal to 25 per cent of displacement.
Operational: Day running capability—no sleeping accommodation. Prototype paid off in October 1991.
Sales: Up to 12 of the class being built under licence in Japan.

GHEPPIO *1990, Camil Busquets i Vilanova*

MINE WARFARE FORCES

2 Ex-US AGGRESSIVE CLASS (MINESWEEPERS—OCEAN)

Name	*No*	*Builders*	*Commissioned*
STORIONE (ex-*MSO 506*)	M 5431	Martinolich S B Co	23 Feb 1956
SQUALO (ex-*MSO 518*)	M 5433	Tampa Marine Co	20 June 1957

Displacement, tons: 665 standard; 720 full load
Dimensions, feet (metres): 172 × 36 × 13.6 *(52.4 × 11 × 4.1)*
Main machinery: 2 GM 8-278 ANW diesels; 1500 hp *(1.12 MW)*; 2 shafts; cp props
Speed, knots: 14. **Range, miles:** 2400 at 10 kts
Complement: 62 (4 officers)
Guns: 1 US/Bofors 40 mm/56.
Radars: Navigation: SMA SPN 703; I band; range 73 km *(40 nm)*.
Sonars: GE UQS-1; active mine detection; high frequency.

Comment: Plans to convert the last two of this class to patrol craft may not survive.

STORIONE *1990, van Ginderen Collection*

4 LERICI AND 1 + 7 GAETA CLASS (MINEHUNTERS/SWEEPERS)

Name	*No*	*Builders*	*Commissioned*
LERICI	M 5550	Intermarine, Sarzana	22 Mar 1985
SAPRI	M 5551	Intermarine, Sarzana	4 June 1985
MILAZZO	M 5552	Intermarine, Sarzana	6 Aug 1985
VIESTE	M 5553	Intermarine, Sarzana	2 Dec 1985
GAETA	M 5554	Intermarine, Sarzana	Apr 1992
TERMOLI	M 5555	Intermarine, Sarzana	Sep 1992
ALGHERO	M 5556	Intermarine, Sarzana	Oct 1992
NUMANA	M 5557	Intermarine, Sarzana	Feb 1993
CROTONE	M 5558	Intermarine, Sarzana	July 1993
VIAREGGIO	M 5559	Intermarine, Sarzana	Dec 1993
CHIOGGIA	M 5560	Intermarine, Sarzana	May 1994
RIMINI	M 5561	Intermarine, Sarzana	Oct 1994

Displacement, tons: 485 standard; 502 (672, *Gaeta* onwards) full load
Dimensions, feet (metres): 164 (167.3 *Gaeta*) × 31.5 × 8.6 *(50 (51) × 9.6 × 2.6)*
Main machinery: 1 Fincantieri GMT BL230.8 M diesel (passage); 1985 hp(m) *(1.46 MW)* sustained; 1 shaft; cp prop; 3 Isotta Fraschini ID 36 SS 6V diesels (hunting); 1481 hp(m) *(1.1 MW)* sustained; 3 hydraulic thrust props (1 fwd, 2 aft)
Speed, knots: 15; 7 hunting. **Range, miles:** 2500 at 12 kts
Complement: 47 (4 officers) including 7 divers

Guns: 1 Oerlikon 20 mm/70 or 2 Oerlikon 20 mm/70 (twin) (*Gaeta* onwards). 2 additional 20 mm guns added for deployments.
Countermeasures: MCM; Motorola MRS III/GPS Eagle precision navigation system with Datamat SMA SSN-714V(2) automatic plotting and radar indicator IP-7113; 1 Min 77 Mk 2 ROV; 1 Pluto mine destruction systems; diving equipment and recompression chamber. Minesweeping—Oropesa Mk 4 wire sweep.
Radars: Navigation: SMA SPN 728V(3); I band; range 73 km *(40 nm)*.
Sonars: FIAR SQQ 14(IT) VDS (lowered from keel fwd of bridge); classification and route survey; high frequency.

Programmes: First four ordered 7 January 1978 under Legge Navale. Next six ordered from Intermarine 30 April 1988 and two more in 1991. From No 5 onwards ships are 1 m longer and are of an improved design with a better minehunting sonar which has been retrofitted in the first four in 1991. Construction of first three Gaetas started in 1988, with *Gaeta* launched 28 July 1990, *Termoli* 15 December 1990, *Alghero* 11 May 1991, and the last three scheduled in 1992.
Structure: Of heavy GRP throughout hull, decks and bulkheads, with frames eliminated. All machinery is mounted on vibration dampers and main engines made of amagnetic material. Fitted with Galeazzi 2 man compression chambers and a telescopic crane for launching Callegari frogmen boats.
Operational: Endurance, 12 days. For long passages passive roll-stabilising tanks can be used for extra fuel increasing range to 4000 miles at 12 kts.
Sales: Four to Malaysia, two to Nigeria and some of a modified design being built by the USA.

VIESTE *1990, Camil Busquets i Vilanova*

NUMANA *10/1991, Giorgio Ghiglione*

5 Ex-US ADJUTANT CLASS (MINEHUNTERS—COASTAL)

CASTAGNO M 5504
CEDRO M 5505
GELSO M 5509
PLATANO M 5516
MANDORLO M 5519

Displacement, tons: 378 (360, *Mandorlo*) standard; 390 full load
Dimensions, feet (metres): 144 × 27.9 × 8 *(43.9 × 8.5 × 2.4)*
Main machinery: 2 GM 8-268A diesels; 880 hp *(656 kW)*; 2 shafts
Speed, knots: 13.5. **Range, miles:** 3000 at 10 kts
Complement: 41 (3 officers)
Guns: 2 Oerlikon 20 mm (twin) (in some).
Countermeasures: Pluto remote control system (minehunting).
Radars: Navigation: SMA 3 RM 20R (SPN 703); I band; range 73 km *(40 nm)*.
Sonars: GE SQQ 14; VDS; mine detection; high frequency.

Comment: Wooden hulled and constructed throughout of anti-magnetic materials. All commissioned August 1953-December 1954 and transferred by the USA in 1953-54. Originally class of 18. *Pioppo* used for surveying (see *Survey Vessels*). Minehunting conversion: *Mandorlo* completed 1975, *Platano* in 1979, *Cedro* in 1982, *Castagno* in 1983 and *Gelso* in 1984.

GELSO *9/1991, van Ginderen Collection*

SURVEY VESSELS

Note: Two 300 ton 38 m GRP hulls to be built by Intermarine, Sarzana. These ships are planned to replace *Mirto* and *Pioppo* in due course if the contract goes ahead, which is doubtful.

Name	*No*	*Builders*	*Commissioned*
AMMIRAGLIO MAGNAGHI	A 5303	Fincantieri, Riva Trigoso	2 May 1975

Displacement, tons: 1700 full load
Dimensions, feet (metres): 271.3 × 44.9 × 11.5 *(82.7 × 13.7 × 3.5)*
Main machinery: 2 GMT B 306 SS diesels; 3000 hp(m) *(2.2 MW)*; 1 shaft; cp prop; auxiliary motor; 240 hp(m) *(176 kW)*; bow thruster
Speed, knots: 16. **Range, miles:** 6000 at 12 kts (1 diesel); 4200 at 16 kts (2 diesels)
Complement: 148 (14 officers, 15 scientists)
Guns: 1 Breda 40 mm/70 (not fitted).
Radars: Navigation: SMA 3 RM 20; I band; range 73 km *(40 nm)*.
Helicopters: Platform only.

Comment: Ordered under 1972 programme. Laid down 13 June 1973. Launched 11 October 1974. Full air-conditioning, bridge engine controls, flume-type stabilisers. Equipped for oceanographical studies including laboratories and underwater TV. Carries six surveying motor boats.

AMMIRAGLIO MAGNAGHI *5/1991, Giorgio Ghiglione*

Name	*No*	*Builders*	*Commissioned*
MIRTO	A 5306	Breda, Porta Marghera	4 Aug 1956
PIOPPO	A 5307	Bellingham SY, Seattle	31 July 1954

Comment: *Mirto* of the Agave class and *Pioppo* of the Adjutant class (see *OPV* and *Mine Warfare* sections for details) have been converted for surveying duties with complement of four officers and 36 men. To be replaced by two new construction ships in due course.

MIRTO *9/1989, Marina Fraccaroli*

SERVICE FORCES

0 + (1) ETNA CLASS (REPLENISHMENT TANKER)

Displacement, tons: 11 810 full load
Dimensions, feet (metres): 433 × 68.9 × 22.3 *(132 × 21 × 6.8)*
Flight deck, feet (metres): 92 × 68.9 *(28 × 21)*
Main machinery: 2 GMT A 420.16 H diesels; 22 400 hp(m) *(16.46 MW)* sustained; 2 shafts
Speed, knots: 22. **Range, miles:** 6300 at 22 kts
Complement: 230
Cargo capacity: 5000 tons gas oil; 500 tons JP5; 2000 m³ ammunition and stores
Guns: 1 OTO Melara 76 mm/62. 2 Breda 40 mm/70 (twin).
Helicopters: 1 light.

Comment: Details are for a class of four ships. The order for the first one has been suspended because of budget cuts. There is a possibility that the Iraqi tanker *Agnadeen* stopped in Alexandria may be re-sold to the Italian Navy. This proposal is not supported by the Navy.

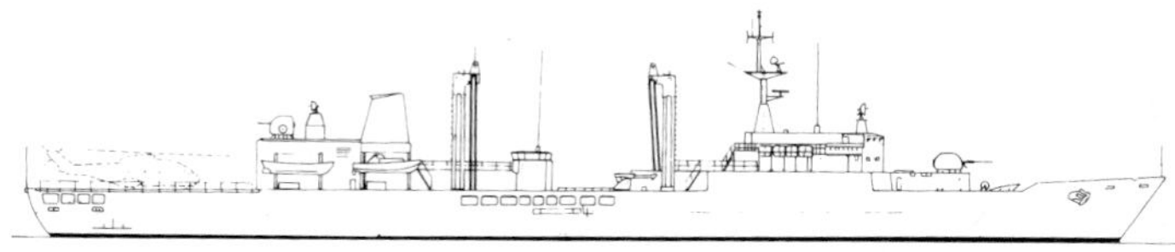

ETNA *Lieut Comdr Erminio Bagnasco*

2 STROMBOLI CLASS (REPLENISHMENT TANKERS)

Name	*No*	*Builders*	*Commissioned*
STROMBOLI	A 5327	Fincantieri, Riva Trigoso	20 Nov 1975
VESUVIO	A 5329	Fincantieri, Muggiano	18 Nov 1978

Displacement, tons: 3556 light; 8706 full load
Dimensions, feet (metres): 423.1 × 59 × 21.3 *(129 × 18 × 6.5)*
Main machinery: 2 GMT C428 SS diesels; 9600 hp(m) *(7.06 MW)*; 1 shaft; Lips cp prop
Speed, knots: 18.5. **Range, miles:** 5080 at 18 kts
Complement: 115 (9 officers)
Cargo capacity: 3000 tons FFO; 1000 tons dieso; 400 tons JP5; 300 tons other stores
Guns: 1 OTO Melara 3 in *(76 mm)*/62.
2 Breda 40 mm/70 (not fitted).
4 Oerlikon 20 mm (2 twin) fitted for Gulf deployments 1987-91.
Fire control: Argo NA 10 system.
Radars: Surface search: SMA SPQ 2; I band.
Navigation: SMA SPN 748; I band.
Fire control: Selenia SPG 70 (RTN 10X); I/J band; range 40 km *(22 nm)*.
Helicopters: Flight deck but no hangar.

Comment: *Stromboli* launched 20 February 1975, *Vesuvio* 4 June 1977. *Vesuvio* was the first large ship to be built at Muggiano (near La Spezia) since the war and the first with funds under Legge Navale 1975. Beam and stern refuelling stations for fuel and stores. Also Vertrep. The two ships have different midships crane arrangements. Similar ship built for Iraq and laid up in Alexandria since 1986.

VESUVIO *9/1991, van Ginderen Collection*

4 EXPERIMENTAL SHIPS

Name	*No*	*Builders*	*Commissioned*
RAFFAELE ROSSETTI	A 5315	Picchiotti, Viareggio	20 Dec 1986

Displacement, tons: 320 full load
Dimensions, feet (metres): 146.3 × 25.9 × 6.9 *(44.6 × 7.9 × 2.1)*
Main machinery: 2 Fincantieri Isotta Fraschini ID 36 N12V diesels; 1200 hp(m) *(882 kW)*; 2 shafts; bow thruster
Speed, knots: 17.5. **Range, miles:** 700 at 15 kts
Complement: 17 (1 officer, 8 technicians)

Comment: Launched on 12 July 1986. Five different design torpedo tubes fitted for above and underwater testing and trials. Other equipment for research into communications, surface and air search as well as underwater weapons. There is a stern doorway which is partially submerged and the ship has a set of 96 batteries to allow 'silent' propulsion. Operated by the Permanent Commission for Experiments of War Materials at La Spezia.

RAFFAELE ROSSETTI *7/1987, Marina Fraccaroli*

Name	*No*	*Builders*	*Commissioned*
VINCENZO MARTELLOTTA	A 5320	Picchiotti, Viareggio	22 Dec 1990

Displacement, tons: 340 full load
Dimensions, feet (metres): 146.3 × 25.9 × 7.5 *(44.6 × 7.9 × 2.3)*
Main machinery: 2 Fincantieri Isotta Fraschini ID 36 SS 16V diesels; 3520 hp(m) *(2.59 MW)*; 2 shafts; bow thruster
Speed, knots: 17. **Range, miles:** 700 at 15 kts
Complement: 17 (1 officer)

Comment: Launched on 28 May 1988. Has one 21 in *(533 mm)* and three 12.75 in *(324 mm)* torpedo tubes and acoustic equipment to operate a 3D tracking range for torpedoes or underwater vehicles. Like *Rossetti* she is operated by the Commission at La Spezia.

V MARTELLOTTA *6/1990, Aldo Fraccaroli*

BARBARA P 492

Displacement, tons: 195 full load
Dimensions, feet (metres): 98.4 × 20.7 × 4.9 *(30 × 6.3 × 1.5)*
Main machinery: 2 diesels; 600 hp(m) *(441 kW)*; 2 shafts
Speed, knots: 12

Comment: Built by Castracani, Ancona. A fishing vessel purchased and converted for research work in 1975. Converted in 1986 to Coastal Patrol Boat. Operates under the Technical and Scientific Council of Defence for missile testing at Perdasdefogu, Sardinia.

BARBARA *1989, Aldo Fraccaroli*

MURENA (ex-*Scampo*) A 5305

Displacement, tons: 188 full load
Dimensions, feet (metres): 106 × 21 × 6 *(32.5 × 6.4 × 1.8)*
Main machinery: 2 Fiat/MTU MB 12V 493 TY7 diesels; 2200 hp(m) *(1.62 MW)* sustained; 2 shafts
Speed, knots: 14. **Range, miles:** 2000 at 9 kts
Complement: 16 (4 officers)

Comment: Built in 1957. Converted Aragosta class MSI used as a torpedo launching and support vessel.

MURENA *11/1990, Giorgio Ghiglione*

2 Ex-GERMAN MFP TYPE (COASTAL TRANSPORT)

MTC 1001 A 5341 **MTC 1006** A 5346

Displacement, tons: 240 full load
Dimensions, feet (metres): 154.2 × 21.3 × 3.6 *(47 × 6.5 × 1.1)*
Main machinery: 3 diesels; 450 hp(m) *(331 kW)*; 3 shafts
Speed, knots: 10
Complement: 16 (1 officer)
Cargo capacity: 150 tons
Guns: 2 Oerlikon 20 mm.
Radars: Navigation: BX 732; I band.

Comment: MTC *(Moto-Trasporti Costieri)*. Ex-German vessels built in 1943-44.

MTC 1001 *9/1991, van Ginderen Collection*

1 Ex-US BARNEGAT CLASS (SUPPORT SHIP)

Name	*No*	*Builders*	*Commissioned*
PIETRO CAVEZZALE (ex-USS *Oyster Bay*, ex-AGP 6, AVP 28)	A 5301	Lake Washington Shipyard	17 Nov 1943

Displacement, tons: 1766 standard; 2800 full load
Dimensions, feet (metres): 310.8 × 41 × 13.5 *(94.7 × 12.5 × 4.1)*
Main machinery: 2 Fairbanks-Morse 38 D8-1/8-10 diesels; 3540 hp *(2.64 MW)* sustained; 2 shafts
Speed, knots: 16. **Range, miles:** 10 000 at 11 kts
Complement: 114 (7 officers)
Guns: 1 US 3 in *(76 mm)*/50. 2 US/Bofors 40 mm/56.
Radars: Air search: Westinghouse SPS 6C; D band; range 146 km *(80 nm)* against fighter aircraft.
Surface search: SMA SPN 748; I band.

Comment: Former US seaplane tender (subsequently motor torpedo boat tender). Launched on 7 September 1942. Transferred to the Italian Navy on 23 October 1957. Was to have been paid off in 1991 but this has been delayed.

PIETRO CAVEZZALE *9/1991, van Ginderen Collection*

6 MTC 1011 CLASS (RAMPED TRANSPORTS)

Name	*No*	*Builders*	*Commissioned*
GORGONA (1011)	A 5347	C N Mario Marini	23 Dec 1986
TREMITI (1012)	A 5348	C N Mario Marini	2 Mar 1987
CAPRERA (1013)	A 5349	C N Mario Marini	10 Apr 1987
PANTELLERIA (1014)	A 5351	C N Mario Marini	26 May 1987
LIPARI (1015)	A 5352	C N Mario Marini	10 July 1987
CAPRI (1016)	A 5353	C N Mario Marini	16 Sep 1987

Displacement, tons: 631 full load
Dimensions, feet (metres): 186 × 32.8 × 8.2 *(56.7 × 10 × 2.5)*
Main machinery: 2 CRM 12D/SS diesels; 1760 hp(m) *(1.29 MW)*; 2 shafts
Speed, knots: 14.5. **Range, miles:** 1500 at 14 kts
Complement: 32 (4 officers)
Guns: 1 Oerlikon 20 mm (fitted for). 2—7.62 mm MGs.
Radars: Navigation: SMA SPN 748; I band.

Comment: As well as transporting stores, oil or water they can act as support ships for Light Forces, salvage ships or minelayers. 1015 and 1016 are attached to the Italian Naval Academy at Livorno, 1011 based at La Spezia, 1012 at Ancona, 1013 at La Maddalena and 1014 at Taranto.

GORGONA *1/1990, Giorgio Ghiglione*

2 PEDRETTI CLASS (COMMANDO SUPPORT CRAFT)

Name	*No*	*Builders*	*Commissioned*
ALCIDE PEDRETTI	Y 499 (ex-MEN 213)	Crestitalia-Ameglia	23 Oct 1984
MARIO MARINO	Y 498 (ex-MEN 214)	Crestitalia-Ameglia	21 Dec 1984

Displacement, tons: 75.4 *(Alcide Pedretti)*, 69.5 *(Mario Marino)* full load
Dimensions, feet (metres): 86.6 × 22.6 × 3.3 *(26.4 × 6.9 × 1)*
Main machinery: 2 Isotta Fraschini ID 36 SS 12V diesels; 2640 hp(m) *(1.94 MW)* sustained; 2 shafts
Speed, knots: 25. **Range, miles:** 450 *(Alcide Pedretti)*, 250 *(Mario Marino)* at 23 kts
Complement: 6

Comment: Both laid down 8 September 1983. For use by assault swimmers of COMSUBIN. Both have decompression chambers. *Alcide Pedretti* has a floodable dock aft and is used for combat swimmers and special operations, while *Mario Marino* is fitted for underwater work and rescue missions. Based at Varignano, La Spezia. A similar but more heavily equipped vessel serves with the UAE coastguard.

ALCIDE PEDRETTI *9/1987, Aldo Fraccaroli*

2 MEN 215 CLASS (LCVP)

MEN 215 **MEN 216**

Displacement, tons: 82 full load
Dimensions, feet (metres): 89.6 × 23 × 3.6 *(27.3 × 7 × 1.1)*
Main machinery: 2 Isotta Fraschini ID 36 SS 12V diesels; 2640 hp(m) *(1.94 MW)* sustained; 2 shafts
Speed, knots: 28. **Range, miles:** 250 at 14 kts
Complement: 4

Comment: Fast personnel launches completed in June 1986 by Crestitalia. Usually attached to *G Garibaldi* and can transport 250 men. Can also be used for amphibious operations or disaster relief.

MEN 215 *1987, Crestitalia*

1 SAR CRAFT

Name	*No*	*Builders*	*Commissioned*
PAOLUCCI	—	Picchiotti, Viareggio	12 Sep 1970

Displacement, tons: 70 full load
Dimensions, feet (metres): 90.9 × 24.3 × 3.3 *(27.7 × 7.4 × 1)*
Speed, knots: 21
Complement: 8 (1 officer)

Comment: Used as an air/sea rescue and ambulance craft.

PAOLUCCI *1991, Italian Navy*

1 MEN 212 CLASS (TRV)

MEN 212

Displacement, tons: 32 full load
Dimensions, feet (metres): 58.4 × 16.7 × 3.3 *(17.8 × 5.1 × 1)*
Main machinery: 2 HP diesels; 1380 hp(m) *(1.01 MW)*; 2 shafts
Speed, knots: 22. **Range, miles:** 250 at 20 kts
Complement: 4

Comment: Torpedo Recovery Vessel completed in October 1983 by Crestitalia. GRP construction with a stern ramp.

MEN 212 (and assorted harbour launches) *9/1991, Nikolaus Sifferlinger*

15 Ex-US LCMs

MTM 542-556 (9908-9922)

Displacement, tons: 56 full load
Dimensions, feet (metres): 56.1 × 14.4 × 3.9 *(17.1 × 4.4 × 1.2)*
Main machinery: 2 Gray Marine 64 NH9 diesels; 330 hp *(264 kW)*; 2 shafts
Speed, knots: 11. **Range, miles:** 130 at 10 kts
Cargo capacity: 30 tons
Guns: 2—12.7 mm MGs.

Comment: Transferred in 1953.

MTM 545 *11/1988, Aldo Fraccaroli*

11 MTM 217 CLASS (LCMs)

MTM 217-227 (9923-9933)

Displacement, tons: 64.6 full load
Dimensions, feet (metres): 60.7 × 16.7 × 3 *(18.5 × 5.1 × 0.9)*
Speed, knots: 9. **Range, miles:** 300 at 9 kts
Complement: 3
Cargo capacity: 30 tons

Comment: Built at Muggiano, La Spezia by Fincantieri. Three completed 9 October 1987 for *San Giorgio*, three completed 8 March 1988 for *San Marco*. Two commissioned in 1989. Three more ordered in March 1991 from a different shipyard.

MTM 220 *9/1991, van Ginderen Collection*

6 US LCVP TYPE

MTP 9726	**MTP 9748**	**MTP 9750**
MTP 9731	**MTP 9749**	**MTP 9751**

Displacement, tons: 11 full load
Dimensions, feet (metres): 36.5 × 10.8 × 3 *(11.1 × 3.3 × 0.9)*
Main machinery: 1 Gray Marine 64 HN 9 diesel; 165 hp *(123 kW)*; 1 shaft
Speed, knots: 10. **Range, miles:** 110 at 9 kts
Guns: 2—12.7 mm MGs.

Comment: Italian construction but built to a basic US design. Pennant numbers in the 523-539 series.

12 MTP 96 CLASS (LCVP)

MTP 96-107 (9755-9766)

Displacement, tons: 14.3 full load
Dimensions, feet (metres): 44.9 × 12.5 × 2.3 *(13.7 × 3.8 × 0.7)*
Main machinery: 2 diesels; 700 hp(m) *(515 kW)*; 2 shafts
Speed, knots: 22. **Range, miles:** 100 at 12 kts
Complement: 3

Comment: Built by Crestitalia 1987 (three) and 1988 (five). Can carry 45 men or 4.5 tons of cargo. Speed reduced to 9 kts fully laden. Four more delivered in 1991. These craft have Kevlar armour.

HARBOUR TANKERS

GRS TYPE

Displacement, tons: 500 approx

Comment: Have GRS numbers. The old 170 series is being replaced by the 1010 series.

GRS Type *3/1991, Giorgio Ghiglione*

TRAINING SHIPS

Note: In addition to the ships listed *San Giorgio* is used in the training role until *Cristoforo Colombo* takes over.

Name	*No*	*Builders*	*Commissioned*
AMERIGO VESPUCCI	A 5312	Castellammare	15 May 1931

Displacement, tons: 3543 standard; 4146 full load
Dimensions, feet (metres): 229.5 pp; 270 oa hull; 330 oa bowsprit × 51 × 22 *(70; 82.4; 100 × 15.5 × 7)*
Main machinery: Diesel-electric; 2 Fiat B 306 ESS diesel generators; 2 Marelli motors; 2000 hp(m) *(1.47 MW)*; 1 shaft
Speed, knots: 10. **Range, miles:** 5450 at 6.5 kts
Complement: 243 (13 officers)
Radars: Navigation: Two SMA SPN 748; I band.

Comment: Launched on 22 March 1930. Hull, masts and yards are of steel. Sail area, 22 604 sq ft. Extensively refitted at La Spezia Naval Dockyard in 1973 and again in 1984. Used for Naval Academy Summer cruise.

AMERIGO VESPUCCI *8/1991, Maritime Photographic*

Name	*No*	*Builders*	*Commissioned*
PALINURO (ex-*Commandant Louis Richard*)	A 5311	Ch Dubigeon, Nantes	1934

Displacement, tons: 1042 standard; 1450 full load
Measurement, tons: 858 gross
Dimensions, feet (metres): 193.5 × 32.8 × 15.7 *(59 × 10 × 4.8)*
Main machinery: 1 diesel; 450 hp(m) *(331 kW)*; 1 shaft
Speed, knots: 7.5. **Range, miles:** 5390 at 7.5 kts
Complement: 47

Comment: Barquentine launched in 1934. Purchased in 1951. Rebuilt in 1954-55 and commissioned in Italian Navy on 1 July 1955. Sail area, 1152 sq ft. She was one of the last two French Grand Bank cod-fishing barquentines. Owned by the Armement Glâtre she was based at St Malo until bought by Italy. Used for seamanship basic training.

PALINURO *5/1990, van Ginderen Collection*

ARAGOSTA A 5378
ASTICE A 5379
MITILO A 5380
POLIPO A 5381
PORPORA A 5382

Displacement, tons: 188 full load
Dimensions, feet (metres): 106 × 21 × 6 *(32.5 × 6.4 × 1.8)*
Main machinery: 2 Fiat-MTU 12V 493 TY7 diesels; 2200 hp(m) *(1.62 MW)* sustained; 2 shafts
Speed, knots: 14. **Range, miles:** 2000 at 9 kts
Complement: 15 (2 officers)
Radars: Navigation: BX 732; I band.

Comment: Builders: CRDA, Monfalcone: *Aragosta, Astice*. Picchiotti, Viareggio: *Mitilo*. Costaguta, Voltri: *Polipo, Porpora*.
Similar to the late British Ham class. All constructed to the order of NATO in 1955-57. Designed armament of one 20 mm gun not mounted. Originally class of 20. Remaining five converted for training 1986. *Polipo* and *Porpora* used by the Naval Academy. *Aragosta* has large deckhouse aft as support ship for frogmen. Others of the class include *Murena* the experimental ship and GLS 501-502 ferries.

ASTICE *9/1991, van Ginderen Collection*

ALLORO A 5308 (ex-M 5532)

Displacement, tons: 405 full load
Dimensions, feet (metres): 144 × 25.6 × 8.5 *(43 × 7.8 × 2.6)*
Main machinery: 2 Fiat diesels; 1200 hp(m) *(882 kW)*; 2 shafts
Speed, knots: 13.5. **Range, miles:** 2500 at 10 kts
Complement: 38 (5 officers)
Guns: 2 Oerlikon 20 mm.
Radars: Navigation: SPN 750; I band.

Comment: Agave class minesweeper built in 1957. Used by the Petty Officers training school at La Maddalena.

Name	*No*	*Builders*	*Commissioned*
CAROLY	A 5302	Baglietto, Varazze	1948
STELLA POLARE	A 5313	Sangermani, Chiavari	7 Oct 1965
CORSARO II	A 5316	Costaguta, Voltri	5 Jan 1961
CRISTOFORO COLOMBO II	—	Sai Ambrosini	Oct 1991

Comment: The first three are sail training ships of between 40 and 60 tons with a crew including trainees of about 16. *C Colombo II* built for the 1992 regatta to commemorate the 500th anniversary of the discovery of America. She displaces 82 tons and has a crew of 20. Sail area of 9900 sq ft.

SALVAGE SHIPS

Name	*No*	*Builders*	*Commissioned*
PROTEO (ex-*Perseo*)	A 5310	Cantieri Navali Riuniti, Ancona	24 Aug 1951

Displacement, tons: 1865 standard; 2147 full load
Dimensions, feet (metres): 248 × 38 × 21 *(75.6 × 11.6 × 6.4)*
Main machinery: 2 Fiat diesels; 4800 hp(m) *(3.53 MW)*; 1 shaft
Speed, knots: 16. **Range, miles:** 7500 at 13 kts
Complement: 122 (8 officers)
Guns: 3 Oerlikon 20 mm.
Radars: Navigation: SMA SPN 748; I band.

Comment: Laid down at Cantieri Navali Riuniti, Ancona, in 1943. Suspended in 1944. Seized by Germans and transferred to Trieste. Construction re-started at Cantieri Navali Riuniti, Ancona, in 1949. Formerly mounted one 3.9 in gun and two 20 mm.

PROTEO *1985, Milpress*

Name	*No*	*Builders*	*Commissioned*
ANTEO	A 5309	C N Breda-Mestre	31 July 1980

Displacement, tons: 3200 full load
Dimensions, feet (metres): 322.8 × 51.8 × 16.7 *(98.4 × 15.8 × 5.1)*
Main machinery: 2 GMT A-230.12 diesels; 5000 hp(m) *(3.68 MW)*; 2 motors; 6000 hp(m) *(4.41 MW)*; 1 shaft; 2 bow thrusters; 1000 hp(m) *(735 kW)*
Speed, knots: 20. **Range, miles:** 4000 at 14 kts
Complement: 121 (including salvage staff)
Guns: 2 Oerlikon 20 mm fitted during deployments.
Radars: Surface search: SMA SPN 751; I band.
Navigation: SMA SPN 748; I band.
Helicopters: 1 AB 212.

Comment: Ordered mid-1977, launched 11 November 1978. Comprehensively fitted with flight deck and hangar, extensive salvage gear, including rescue bell, and recompression chambers. Carries four lifeboats of various types. Three firefighting systems. Full towing equipment. Carries midget submarine, *Usel*, of 13.2 tons dived with dimensions 26.2 × 6.2 × 8.9 ft *(8 × 1.9 × 2.7 m)*. Carries two men and can dive to 600 m. Endurance, 120 hours at 5 kts. Also has a McCann rescue chamber.

ANTEO *7/1990, J. Y. Robert*

USEL *6/1987, Aldo Fraccaroli*

LIGHTHOUSE TENDERS

5 PONZA CLASS

Name	*No*	*Builders*	*Commissioned*
PONZA	A 5364	Morini Yard, Ancona	9 Dec 1988
LEVANZO	A 5366	Morini Yard, Ancona	24 Jan 1989
TAVOLARA	A 5368	Morini Yard, Ancona	12 Apr 1989
PALMARIA	A 5367	Morini Yard, Ancona	12 May 1989
PROCIDA	A 5383	Morini Yard, Ancona	14 Nov 1990

Displacement, tons: 608 full load
Dimensions, feet (metres): 186 × 35.4 × 8.2 *(56.7 × 10.8 × 2.5)*
Main machinery: 2 Fincantieri Isotta Fraschini ID 36 SS 8V diesels; 1760 hp(m) *(1.29 MW)* sustained; 2 shafts
Speed, knots: 14.5. **Range, miles:** 1500 at 14 kts
Complement: 34
Guns: 2—7.62 mm MGs.

Comment: MTF 1304-1308. Similar to MTC 1011 class.

TAVOLARA *9/1991, van Ginderen Collection*

REPAIR CRAFT

5 Ex-BRITISH LCT 3 TYPE

MOC 1201 A 5331 **MOC 1203** A 5333 **MOC 1205** A 5335
MOC 1202 A 5332 **MOC 1204** A 5334

Displacement, tons: 350 standard; 640 full load
Dimensions, feet (metres): 192 × 31 × 7 *(58.6 × 9.5 × 2.1)*
Main machinery: 2 diesels; 1000 hp *(746 kW)*; 2 shafts
Speed, knots: 8
Complement: 24 (3 officers)
Guns: 2 Bofors 40 mm/70. 2 Oerlikon 20 mm.
2 ships have 2—40 mm and 1 ship has 3—20 mm.

Comment: Built in 1943. Originally converted as repair craft. Other duties have been taken over—*MOC 1201* is used for torpedo trials and *MOC 1203* is the minesweepers support ship.

MOC 1203 *1990, Milpress*

MOC 1201 *8/1991, Aldo Fraccaroli*

FERRIES

TARANTOLA

Comment: Based at La Spezia. Has replaced *GLS 502*.

TARANTOLA *9/1991, van Ginderen Collection*

WATER CARRIERS

Name	*No*	*Builders*	*Commissioned*
BASENTO	A 5356	Inma di La Spezia	19 July 1971
BRADANO	A 5357	Inma di La Spezia	29 Dec 1971
BRENTA	A 5358	Inma di La Spezia	18 Apr 1972

Displacement, tons: 1914 full load
Dimensions, feet (metres): 225.4 × 33.1 × 12.8 *(68.7 × 10.1 × 3.9)*
Main machinery: 2 Fiat LA 230 diesels; 1730 hp(m) *(1.27 MW)*; 2 shafts
Speed, knots: 13. **Range, miles:** 1650 at 12 kts
Complement: 24 (3 officers)
Cargo capacity: 1200 tons
Guns: 2 Oerlikon 20 mm (not fitted in all ships).

BRADANO *9/1989, Marina Fraccaroli*

Name	No	Builders	Commissioned
PIAVE	A 5354	Orlando, Leghorn	23 May 1973

Displacement, tons: 4973 full load
Dimensions, feet (metres): 320.8 × 44 × 19.4 *(97.8 × 13.4 × 5.9)*
Main machinery: 2 diesels; 2560 hp(m) *(1.88 MW)*; 2 shafts
Speed, knots: 13. **Range, miles:** 1500 at 12 kts
Complement: 55 (7 officers)
Cargo capacity: 3500 tons
Guns: 4 Breda 40 mm/70 (2 twin) (not mounted).
Radars: Navigation: SMA SPN 748; I band.

PIAVE *1989, Aldo Fraccaroli*

MINCIO A 5374

Displacement, tons: 645
Dimensions, feet (metres): 141.4 × 26.2 × 9.8 *(43.1 × 8 × 3)*
Speed, knots: 6
Complement: 19 (1 officer)

Comment: Launched in 1929.

BORMIDA (ex-*GGS 1011*) A 5359

Displacement, tons: 736
Dimensions, feet (metres): 131.9 × 23.6 × 10.5 *(40.2 × 7.2 × 3.2)*
Complement: 11 (1 officer)
Cargo capacity: 260 tons

Comment: Converted at La Spezia in 1974. To be paid off in 1992.

BORMIDA *9/1991, van Ginderen Collection*

GGS 185, 186, 500, 501, 502, 503, 507, 1009

Displacement, tons: 200

Comment: 185 and 502 at Taranto, 500 and 501 at Naples, 503 and 1009 at La Maddalena, 507 at Brindisi, 186 at La Spezia. GGS indicates water carriers.

GGS 186 *9/1991, van Ginderen Collection*

Name	No	Builders	Commissioned
SIMETO	A 5375	Cinet, Molfitta	9 July 1988

Displacement, tons: 1858 full load
Dimensions, feet (metres): 224 × 32.8 × 12.8 *(68.3 × 10 × 3.9)*
Main machinery: 2 GMT B 230.6 diesels; 2700 hp(m) *(1.98 MW)* sustained; 2 shafts
Speed, knots: 13. **Range, miles:** 1650 at 12 kts
Complement: 27 (2 officers)
Cargo capacity: 1200 tons

Comment: A second of the class may be built.

MCC 1101 A 5370
MCC 1102 A 5371
MCC 1103 A 5372
MCC 1104 A 5373

Displacement, tons: 898 full load
Dimensions, feet (metres): 155.2 × 32.8 × 10.8 *(47.3 × 10 × 3.3)*
Main machinery: 2 Fincantieri Isotta Fraschini ID 36 SS 6V diesels; 1320 hp(m) *(970 kW)* sustained; 2 shafts
Speed, knots: 13. **Range, miles:** 1500 at 12 kts
Complement: 12
Cargo capacity: 550 tons

Comment: Built by Ferrari, La Spezia and completed one in 1986, two in May 1987, one in May 1988.

MCC 1101 *9/1991, van Ginderen Collection*

TUGS

Name	No	Builders	Commissioned
ATLANTE	A 5317	Visentini-Donada	14 Aug 1975
PROMETEO	A 5318	Visentini-Donada	14 Aug 1975

Displacement, tons: 750 full load
Dimensions, feet (metres): 127.9 × 32.1 × 13.4 *(39 × 9.6 × 4.1)*
Main machinery: 1 Tosi QT 320/8 SS diesel; 2670 hp(m) *(1.96 MW)*; 1 shaft; cp prop
Speed, knots: 13.5. **Range, miles:** 4000 at 12 kts
Complement: 25

PROMETEO *1990, van Ginderen Collection*

CICLOPE A 5319
TITANO A 5324
POLIFEMO A 5325
GIGANTE A 5328
SATURNO A 5330
TENACE A 5365

Displacement, tons: 658 full load
Dimensions, feet (metres): 127.6 × 32.5 × 12.1 *(38.9 × 9.9 × 3.7)*
Main machinery: 2 GMT B 230.8 M diesels; 3600 hp(m) *(2.65 MW)* sustained; 2 shafts
Speed, knots: 14.5. **Range, miles:** 3000 at 14 kts
Complement: 12

Comment: Built by C N Ferrari, La Spezia. Completed *Ciclope*, 5 September 1985; *Titano*, 7 December 1985; *Polifemo*, 21 April 1986; *Gigante*, 18 July 1986; *Saturno* 5 April 1988 and *Tenace* 9 July 1988. All fitted with firefighting equipment and two portable submersible pumps. Bollard pull 45 tons.

TENACE *9/1991, van Ginderen Collection*

9 COASTAL TUGS

PORTO EMPEDOCLE Y 421
PORTO PISANO Y 422
PORTO CONTE Y 423
PORTO FERRAIO Y 425
PORTO VENERE Y 426
PORTO SALVO Y 428
PORTO FOSSONE Y 413
PORTO TORRES Y 416
PORTO CORSINI Y 417

Displacement, tons: 412 full load
Measurement, tons: 122 dwt
Dimensions, feet (metres): 106.3 × 27.9 × 10.8 *(32.4 × 8.5 × 3.3)*
Main machinery: 2 GMT B 230.8 M diesels; 3600 hp(m) *(2.65 MW)* sustained; 2 shafts
Speed, knots: 12.7. **Range, miles:** 4000 at 12 kts
Complement: 13
Radars: Navigation: GEM BX 132; I band.
Sonars: Honeywell/Elac Type LAZ-50.

Comment: Six ordered from CN De Poli (Pallestrina) and further three from Ferbex (Naples) in 1986.
Delivery dates *Porto Salvo* (13 Sep 1985), *Porto Pisano* (22 Oct 1985), *Porto Ferraio* (20 July 1985), *Porto Conte* (21 Nov 1985), *Porto Empedocle* (19 Mar 1986), *Porto Venere* (16 May 1989), *Porto Fossone* (24 Sep 1990), *Porto Torres* (16 Jan 1991) and *Porto Corsini* (4 Mar 1991).
Fitted for firefighting and anti-pollution. Carry a 1 ton telescopic crane. Based at Taranto, La Spezia, Augusta and La Maddalena.

PORTO SALVO *12/1991, Giorgio Ghiglione*

PORTO D'ISCHIA Y 436 **RIVA TRIGOSO** Y 443

Displacement, tons: 296 full load
Dimensions, feet (metres): 89.5 × 23.3 × 10.8 *(27.3 × 7.1 × 3.3)*
Main machinery: Diesel; 850 hp(m) *(625 kW)*; 1 shaft; cp prop
Speed, knots: 12.1

Comment: Both launched in September 1969 by CNR, Riva Trigoso. *Porto d'Ischia* commissioned 1970, *Riva Trigoso*, 1969.

RIVA TRIGOSO *9/1991, van Ginderen Collection*

32 HARBOUR TUGS

RP 101 Y 403 (1972)
RP 102 Y 404 (1972)
RP 103 Y 406 (1974)
RP 104 Y 407 (1974)
RP 105 Y 408 (1974)
RP 106 Y 410 (1974)
RP 108 Y 452 (1975)
RP 109 Y 456 (1975)
RP 110 Y 458 (1975)
RP 111 Y 460 (1975)
RP 112 Y 462 (1975)
RP 113 Y 463 (1978)
RP 114 Y 464 (1980)
RP 115 Y 465 (1980)
RP 116 Y 466 (1980)
RP 118 Y 468 (1980)
RP 119 Y 470 (1980)
RP 120 Y 471 (1980)
RP 121 — (1984)
RP 122 Y 473 (1981)
RP 123 Y 467 (1981)
RP 124 Y 477 (1981)
RP 125 Y 478 (1983)
RP 126 Y 479 (1983)
RP 127 Y 480 (1984)
RP 128 Y 481 (1984)
RP 129 Y 482 (1984)
RP 130 Y 483 (1985)
RP 131 Y 484 (1985)
RP 132 Y 485 (1985)
RP 133 Y 486 (1985)
RP 134 Y 487 (1985)

Comment: *RP 126* by Cantieri Navali Vittoria of Adria and *RP 121* by Baia, Naples. *RP 127-131* and *134* built by Ferrari Yard, La Spezia. *RP 132* and *133* built by CINET Yard, Molfetta. *RP 113-126* are of slightly larger dimensions and differ somewhat in appearance. *RP 127-134* are larger and slower.

RP 121 *10/1991, Aldo Fraccaroli*

FLOATING DOCKS

Number	*Date*	*Capacity-tons*
GO 1	1942	1000
GO 5	1893	100
GO 8	1904	3800
GO 10	1900	2000
GO 11	1920	2700
GO 17	1917	500
GO 18A	1920	800
GO 18B	1920	600
GO 20	1935	1600
GO 22	1935	1000
GO 23	1935	1000
GO 51	1971	2000
GO 52	1988	6000
GO 53	1991	6000

Comment: Stationed at La Spezia (*GS 52*) and Augusta (*GS 53*).

ITALIAN ARMY, AMPHIBIOUS COMMAND

Note: The following units are operated by the 'Sile Amphibious Battalion' in the Venice Lagoons area. EIG means Italian Army Craft and is part of the hull number. Four LCM (EIG 29, 30, 31, 32), 60 tons; two LCVP (EIG 26, 27), 13 tons; four recce craft (EIG 3, 48, 49, 206), 5 tons; two command craft (EIG 208, 210), 21.5 tons; one rescue tug (EIG 209), 45 tons; one inshore tanker (EIG 44), 95 tons; one ambulance and rescue craft (EIG 28) and 15 minor craft (ferries, barges, rigid inflatable raiders).

GOVERNMENT MARITIME FORCES

GUARDIA COSTIERA—CAPITANERIE DI PORTO (COAST GUARD)

Note: This is a force of 130 craft which is affiliated with the Marina Militare under whose command it would be placed in an emergency. The Coast Guard denomination was given after the Sea Protection Law in 1988. All vessels now have a red diagonal stripe painted on the hull. There are some 4700 naval personnel including 770 officers of which 2550 are doing national service.
SAR craft; 8 CP 400 class of 100 tons. *Michelle Fiorillo* CP 307 (84 tons); *Bruno Gregoretti* CP 312 (65 tons); *Dante Novaro* CP 313; CP 314-315 (43 tons); CP 301-306, 308-311 (29 tons), CP 303-304 (18 tons).
Fast patrol craft; CP 239-245 (25 tons), CP 254-256 (22.5 tons), CP 246-253 (21.5 tons), CP 226-30 (18-20 tons), CP 231-238 (14 tons), CP 257-258 (24 tons).
Coastal patrol craft; CP 2069-2081 (13 tons), CP 2049-2051, 2053-2058, 2060-2068 (12.5 tons), CP 2043-2047 (12.4 tons), CP 2033-2035 (12 tons), CP 2010-2017 (10 tons), CP 2001-2005 (9 tons), CP 207 (8 tons), CP 502-505 (6.6 tons), CP 1001-1006 (5.2 tons), CP 501, 601-605 (3 tons).
In addition there are five patrol craft of the CP 100 designation, 50 of the CP 5000 class with a speed of 25-30 kts, six inflatable rescue craft and 12 Crestitalia small patrol craft CP 6001-6012. Several of the larger craft are armed.
Aircraft include 12 Piaggio P 166 DL3 maritime patrol. Four Griffon AB 412 helicopters in service in 1992.

CP 406 *5/1991, Giorgio Ghiglione*

CP 244 *9/1991, van Ginderen Collection*

SERVIZIO NAVALE CARABINIERI

Note: The Carabinieri established its maritime force in 1969. This currently numbers 163 craft which operate in coastal waters within the three-mile limit and in inshore waters. The following are typical of the craft concerned;
8—700 class of 22 tons; 25—600 class of 12 tons; 30 N 500 class of 6 tons; 3 S 500 class of 7 tons; 23—500 class of 2.6 tons; 54—400 class of 1.4 tons.
All but the 500 and 400 classes are equipped with radar and all but the N 500 class (18 kts) are capable of 20-25 kts. 18 Rio 630 class ordered in mid-1989.

500 Class *11/1991, van Ginderen Collection*

SERVIZIO NAVALE GUARDIA DI FINANZA

Notes: 1. This force is operated by the Ministry of Finance but in time of war would come under the command of the Marina Militare. It is divided into 16 areas, 20 operational sectors and 28 squadrons. Their task is to patrol ports, lakes and rivers. The total manpower is 5300 operating 445 craft. Nearly all the larger craft are armed with a 20 mm gun or a machine gun. The first P-166 patrol aircraft was delivered by Piaggio in early 1991. A total of 10 has been ordered.

2. Patrol craft, 2 of 210 tons; Offshore patrol craft, *Genna* G 96 (120 tons); 4 of 57 tons G 72, 75, 77, 79; 2 of 54 tons G 70-71; 56 of 40 tons G 10-G 37, G 39-G 44, G 46-G 66; Coastal patrol craft, 2 of 20.4 tons building by Intermarine, 18 of 16.4 tons GL 314-331; 2 of 13.3 tons GL 432-433; 2 of 7.1 tons GL 103, 106; Local patrol craft; 34 of 15 tons V 5800-5833; 2 of 10.5 tons V 5901-5902; 81 of 7.8 tons V 5500-5581; 15 of 6.9 tons V 4000-4014; 3 of 5.1 tons V 5300-5302; 3 of 4.9 tons V 2911-2913; 1 of 2.9 tons V 3000; 1 of 1.8 tons V 2901; Training craft, *Giorgio Cini* of 800 tons; *Gian Maria Paolini* G 95 of 348 tons.
In addition 210 small craft operate on Italian lakes and rivers.

GIAN MARIA PAOLINI *9/1991, van Ginderen Collection*

2 + (4) ANTONIO ZARA CLASS

ANTONIO ZARA P 01 **VIZZARI** P 02

Displacement, tons: 320 full load
Dimensions, feet (metres): 167 × 24.6 × 6.2 *(51 × 7.5 × 1.9)*
Main machinery: 2 GMT BL 230.12 diesels; 5956 hp(m) *(4.38 MW)* sustained; 2 shafts
Speed, knots: 28. **Range, miles:** 2700 at 15 kts
Complement: 30 (1 officer)
Guns: 2 Breda 30 mm (twin). 2—7.62 mm MGs.
Fire control: Selenia Pegaso optronic director.

Comment: Built by Fincantieri at Muggiano, La Spezia. Similar to the Ratcharit class built for Thailand in 1976-79. Ordered in August 1987. *Antonio Zara* delivered 23 February 1990, *Vizzari* 27 April 1990. Plans for four more of the class have been suspended. This is a second attempt by the Customs Service to create a force of high capability craft able to control the EEZ. Many years ago two 300 ton patrol boats were built and rejected as not meeting the operational requirement.

ANTONIO ZARA *1/1990, Giorgio Ghiglione*

2 + 10 CORRUBIA and 2 + 6 BIGLIANI CLASSES

BIGLIANI G 80 **CORRUBIA** G 90
CAVAGLIA G 81 **GIUDICE** G 91

Displacement, tons: 80 full load
Dimensions, feet (metres): 86.6 × 23 × 3.6 *(26.4 × 7 × 1.1)*
Main machinery: 2 MTU 16 V396 TB 94 diesels; 5800 hp(m) *(4.26 MW)* sustained; 2 shafts
Speed, knots: 40-45. **Range, miles:** 700 at 25 kts
Complement: 11
Guns: 1 Breda 30 mm. 2—7.62 mm MGs.
Fire control: Elsag Medusa optronic director.

Comment: Details given are for the Bigliani class (G 80 and G 81) built by Crestitalia and delivered October 1987 at La Spezia. G 90 and G 91 built by Cantieri Navale, Gaeta and delivered in 1990. Six more Corrubia class are now building at Crestitalia and should complete in 1992, and ten more Bigliani class are building at Gaeta. The Corrubia class displace 81 tons and are capable of only 40 kts having slightly less powerful engines.

BIGLIANI *7/1987, Crestitalia*

IVORY COAST

Headquarters' Appointment

Chief of Naval Staff
Capitaine de Vaisseau C V Timité Lassana

Senior Officers

Capitaine de Vaisseau Fako Kone
Capitaine de Frégate Dakoury Gnagrah

Bases

Use made of ports at Abidjan, Sassandra, Tabou and San-Pédro

General

This force is primarily concerned, in conjunction with aircraft, with offshore, riverine and coastal protection. Particular emphasis is placed on environmental protection, anti-pollution operations and dealing with fires. There are also some Halter and Arcoa craft which are non-naval.

Personnel

1992: 700 (70 officers)

Mercantile Marine

Lloyd's Register of Shipping:
51 vessels of 82 084 tons gross

PATROL FORCES

2 PATRA CLASS (FAST ATTACK CRAFT—MISSILE)

Name	*No*	*Builders*	*Commissioned*
L'ARDENT	—	Auroux, Arcachon	6 Oct 1978
L'INTRÉPIDE	—	Auroux, Arcachon	6 Oct 1978

Displacement, tons: 147.5 full load
Dimensions, feet (metres): 132.5 × 19.4 × 5.2 *(40.4 × 5.9 × 1.6)*
Main machinery: 2 SACM AGO 195 V12 CZSHR diesels; 4340 hp(m) *(3.19 MW)* sustained; 2 shafts
Speed, knots: 26. **Range, miles:** 1750 at 10 kts; 750 at 20 kts
Complement: 19 (2 officers)
Missiles: SSM: 4 Aerospatiale SS 12M; wire-guided to 5.5 km *(3 nm)* subsonic; warhead 30 kg.
Guns: 1 Breda 40 mm/70. 1 Oerlikon 20 mm. 2—7.62 mm MGs.
Radars: Surface search: Racal Decca 1226; I band.

Comment: Of similar design to French Patra class. Laid down 7 July 1977 *(Intrépide)* and 7 May 1977 *(Ardent)*. Both launched 21 July 1978. Patrol endurance of five days.

2 FRANCO-BELGE TYPE

Name	*No*	*Builders*	*Commissioned*
LE VIGILANT	—	SFCN, Villeneuve	1968
LE VALEUREUX	—	SFCN, Villeneuve	25 Oct 1976

Displacement, tons: 235 standard; 250 full load
Dimensions, feet (metres): 155.8 × 23.6 × 7.5 *(47.5 × 7 × 2.3)*
Main machinery: 2 AGO diesels; 4220 hp(m) *(3 MW)*; 2 shafts *(Valeureux)*
2 MGO diesels; 2400 hp(m) *(1.76 MW)*; 2 shafts *(Vigilant)*
Speed, knots: 22 *(Valeureux)*; 18.5 *(Vigilant)*. **Range, miles:** 2000 at 15 kts
Complement: 34 (4 officers)
Guns: 2 Breda 40 mm/70. 2—12.7 mm MGs.
Radars: Surface search: Racal Decca; I band.

Comment: *Le Vigilant* laid down in February 1967; launched on 23 May 1967. *Le Valeureux*, laid down 20 October 1975; launched 8 March 1976. Have been reported as Exocet fitted but this is not confirmed. *Le Valeureux* received new engines in 1987.

1 BATRAL TYPE (LIGHT TRANSPORT)

Name	*No*	*Builders*	*Commissioned*
L'ÉLÉPHANT	—	A Français de l'Ouest, Grand Queville	2 Feb 1977

Displacement, tons: 750 standard; 1330 full load
Dimensions, feet (metres): 262.4 × 42.6 × 7.9 *(80 × 13 × 2.4)*
Main machinery: 2 SACM Type 195 V12 diesels; 3600 hp(m) *(2.65 MW)*; 2 shafts; cp props
Speed, knots: 16. **Range, miles:** 4500 at 13 kts
Complement: 47 (5 officers)
Military lift: 180 troops; 12 vehicles; 350 tons cargo
Guns: 2 Breda 40 mm/70. 2—81 mm mortars.
Helicopters: Platform only.

Comment: Ordered 20 August 1974. Laid down 1975.

2 LCVPs

Displacement, tons: 9 full load
Dimensions, feet (metres): 34.4 × 10.5 × 3.3 *(10.5 × 3.2 × 1.0)*
Main machinery: 1 Baudouin diesel; 1 shaft
Speed, knots: 9
Guns: 1—12.7 mm MG.

Comment: Built by DCAN, Cherbourg in 1976.

3 ROTORK TYPE 412

Displacement, tons: 9 full load
Dimensions, feet (metres): 41.7 × 10.5 × 3 *(12.7 × 3.2 × 0.9)*
Main machinery: 2 Volvo Penta diesels; 240 hp(m) *(176 kW)*; 2 shafts
Speed, knots: 28
Military lift: 30 troops

Comment: One fast assault boat supplied in 1980. Two others supplied for civilian use at the same time have now been taken over.

9 ARCOR TYPE

Displacement, tons: 5 full load
Dimensions, feet (metres): 31 × 11.5 × 2.6 *(9.5 × 3.5 × 0.8)*
Main machinery: 2 Baudouin diesels; 320 hp(m) *(235 kW)*; 2 shafts
Speed, knots: 20
Military lift: 30 troops

Comment: Delivered between 1982 and 1985.

JAMAICA

Defence Force Coast Guard

Jamaica, which became independent within the Commonwealth on 6 August 1962, formed the Sea Squadron on 25 August 1963 as the Maritime Arm of the Defence Force. The squadron was renamed the Defence Force Coast Guard on 1 January 1966.

Administration

Commanding Officer Jamaica Defence Force Coast Guard:
Commander H M Lewin

Personnel

1992: 180 (18 officers)
(Coast Guard Reserve: 46 (12 officers))

Training

(a) Officers: JDF Training depot, BRNC Dartmouth and other RN Establishments, RCN and Canadian Coast Guard, USN and US Coast Guard.
(b) Ratings: JDF Training depot, RN, RCN and Canadian Coast Guard, US Coast Guard and MTU Engineering Germany.

Bases

HMJS *Cagway*, Port Royal. Discovery Bay CG station

Mercantile Marine

Lloyd's Register of Shipping:
12 vessels of 14 433 tons gross

PATROL FORCES

1 FORT CLASS

Name	*No*	*Builders*	*Commissioned*
FORT CHARLES	P 7	Sewart Seacraft Inc, Berwick, La, USA	Sep 1974

Displacement, tons: 130 full load
Dimensions, feet (metres): 115 × 24 × 7 *(34.5 × 7.3 × 2.1)*
Main machinery: 2 MTU 16V 538 TB90 diesels; 6000 hp(m) *(4.41 MW)* sustained; 2 shafts
Speed, knots: 32. **Range, miles:** 1500 at 18 kts
Complement: 20 (4 officers)
Guns: 1 Oerlikon 20 mm. 2—12.7 mm MGs.

Comment: Of all-aluminium construction, launched July 1974. Underwent refit at Jacksonville, Fla, in 1980-81 which included extensive modifications to the bow resulting in increased length. Accommodation for 18 soldiers and may be used as 18-bed mobile hospital in an emergency.

FORT CHARLES *10/1990, JDFCG*

1 HERO CLASS

Name	*No*	*Builders*	*Commissioned*
PAUL BOGLE	P 8	Lantana Boatyard Inc, Fla, USA	17 Sep 1985

Displacement, tons: 93 full load
Dimensions, feet (metres): 105 × 20.6 × 7 *(32 × 6.3 × 2.1)*
Main machinery: 3 MTU 8V 396 TB93 diesels; 3270 hp(m) *(2.4 MW)* sustained; 3 shafts
Speed, knots: 30+
Complement: 20 (4 officers)
Guns: 1 Oerlikon 20 mm. 2—12.7 mm MGs.
Radars: Surface search: Furuno; I band.

Comment: Of all-aluminium construction, launched in 1984. *Paul Bogle* was originally intended for Honduras as the third of the Guardian class. Similar to patrol craft in Honduras and Grenada navies.

PAUL BOGLE *10/1990, JDFCG*

3 BAY CLASS

Name	*No*	*Builders*	*Commissioned*
DISCOVERY BAY	P 4	Sewart Seacraft Inc, Berwick, La, USA	3 Nov 1966
HOLLAND BAY	P 5	Sewart Seacraft Inc, Berwick, La, USA	4 Apr 1967
MANATEE BAY	P 6	Sewart Seacraft Inc, Berwick, La, USA	9 Aug 1967

Displacement, tons: 72 full load
Dimensions, feet (metres): 85 × 18 × 6 *(25.9 × 5.7 × 1.8)*
Main machinery: 3 MTU 8V 396 TC82 diesels; 2610 hp(m) *(1.92 MW)* sustained; 3 shafts
Speed, knots: 25. **Range, miles:** 800 at 15 kts
Complement: 14 (3 officers)
Guns: 3—12.7 mm MGs.

Comment: All-aluminium construction. *Discovery Bay*, the prototype, was launched in August 1966. *Holland Bay* and *Manatee Bay* were supplied under the US Military Assistance programme. All three boats were extensively refitted and modified in 1972-73 by the builders with General Motors 12V 71 turbo-injected engines to give greater range, speed and operational flexibility. They were again re-engined and refitted at Swiftships, Louisiana, 1975-77. Between 1981 and 1984 a third engine change to MTU 396 diesels was done by Atlantic Dry Docks at Jacksonville.

DISCOVERY BAY *10/1990, JDFCG*

MANATEE BAY *10/1990, JDFCG*

0 + 7 FAST PATROL CRAFT

Comment: Two SeaArk Marine (Montecello) 41 ft, three Offshore Marine Performance (Miami) 33 ft and two Boston Whaler 27 ft craft are projected. The first 41 ft and 33 ft craft are expected to be delivered in mid-1992.

JAPAN (MSDF)
MARITIME SELF-DEFENCE FORCE

Naval Board

Chief of Staff, Maritime Self-Defence Force:
Admiral Fumio Okabe
Commander-in-Chief, Self-Defence Fleet:
Vice Admiral Tatsuji Ito
Director, Administration, Maritime Staff Office:
Rear Admiral Akira Sugimoto

Senior Appointments

Commander Fleet Escort Force
Vice Admiral Koutarou Uchida
Commander Submarine Force
Vice Admiral Makotu Satou

Diplomatic Representation

Defence (Naval) Attaché in London:
Captain Osamu Iizuka
Defence Attaché in Paris:
Colonel Tadashi Yoshida
Naval Attaché in Washington:
Captain Kazunari Michiie

Personnel

1992: 46 520 (including Naval Air) plus 3978 civilians

Organisation of the Major Surface Units of Japan (MSDF)

Four escort flotillas each consisting of DDH (Flagship); two Air Defence ships and three or so ASW/general purpose Divisions of up to three ships each.

Escort Fleet (Yokosuka)
Murakumo (DD 118) Flagship

Escort Flotilla 1 (Yokosuka)
Shirane (DDH 143)
48th Destroyer Division
Umigiri (DD 158)
Hamagori (DD 155)
Setogiri (DD 156)
46th Destroyer Division
Yuugiri (DD 153)
Amagiri (DD 154)
61st Destroyer Division
Asakaze (DDG 169)
Hatakaze (DDG 171)

Escort Flotilla 3 (Maizuru)
Haruna (DDH 141)
42nd Destroyer Division
Mineyuki (DD 124)
Hamayuki (DD 126)
45th Destroyer Division
Setoyuki (DD 131)
Asayuki (DD 132)
Shimayuki (DD 133)
63rd Destroyer Division
Amatsukaze (DDG 163)
Shimakaze (DD 172)

Escort Flotilla 2 (Sasebo)
Kurama (DDH 144)
47th Destroyer Division
Asagiri (DD 151)
Yamagiri (DD 152)
Sawagiri (DD 157)
44th Destroyer Division
Yamayuki (DD 129)
Matsuyuki (DD 130)
62nd Destroyer Division
Tachikaze (DDG 168)
Sawakaze (DDG 170)

Escort Flotilla 4 (Yokosuka)
Hiei (DDH 142)
1st Destroyer Division
Takatsuki (DD 164)
Kikuzuki (DD 165)
41st Destroyer Division
Hatsuyuki (DD 122)
Shirayuki (DD 123)
Sawayuki (DD 125)
43rd Destroyer Division
Isoyuki (DD 127)
Haruyuki (DD 128)

District Flotillas

In addition to the Escort Fleet there are 2 Submarine Flotillas (Kure and Yokosuka), 2 MCM Flotillas (Kure and Yokosuka) and 5 District Flotillas (Yokosuka, Maizuru, Oominato, Sasebo and Kure).

Bases

Naval—Yokosuka, Kure, Sasebo, Maizuru, Oominato
Naval Air—Atsugi, Hachinohe, Iwakuni, Kanoya, Komatsujima, Naha, Ozuki, Oominato, Omura, Shimofusa, Tateyama, Tokushima

Strength of the Fleet

Type	*Active (Auxiliary)*	*Building (Projected)*
Submarines—Patrol	15 (3)	2 (2)
Destroyers	39 (4)	3 (7)
Frigates	18 (2)	2
Fast Attack Hydrofoil—Missile	0	2 (1)
Fast Attack Craft—Torpedo	2	—
Patrol Craft—Coastal	9	—
LSTs	6	(1)
LSUs	2	—
Landing Craft (LCU/LSM/LCVP)	32	1
M/S Support Ships	3	(2)
Minehunters—Ocean	0	3 (3)
Minesweepers—Coastal	30	2 (3)
MSBs	4	—
Training Ships	1*	1
Training Support Ships	2	—
S/M Rescue Vessels	2	—
Fleet Support Ships	4	—
Tenders	12	—
Harbour Tankers	34	1
Icebreaker	1	—
Survey Ships	4	—
Cable Layer	1	—
Experimental Ships	1	1
Surtass Ships	2	(3)

* *not including conversions*

New Construction Programme

1988 1—7200 ton DDG, 1—2400 ton SS, 2—490 ton MSC.
1989 2—1900 ton DE, 1—2400 ton SS, 2—1000 ton MSO, 1—2800 ton AOS.
1990 1—7200 ton DDG, 1—2400 ton SS, 1—1000 ton MSO, 1—490 ton MSC, 2—50 ton PG, 1—2800 ton AOS, 1—420 ton LCU.
1991 1—7200 ton DDG, 1—4400 ton DD, 1—2400 ton SS, 1—490 ton MSC.
1992 1—4400 ton DD, 1—2500 ton SS, 3—490 ton MSC, 1—50 ton PG, 1—4000 ton TV, 1—4200 ton ASE.

Mercantile Marine

Lloyd's Register of Shipping:
10 063 vessels of 26 406 930 tons gross

Fleet Air Arm

16 Air ASW Sqns: P-3C, P-2J, HSS-2
6 Air Training Sqns: P-3C, YS-11, TC-90, B-65, KM-2, Mentor, OH-6, HSS-2, U-36A, SH-60J
1 Transport Sqn: YS-11
1 MCM Sqn: MH-53E
Air Wings at Kanoya (Wing 1), Hachinohe (Wing 2), Atsugi (Wing 4), Naha (Wing 5), Tateyama (Wing 21), Omura (Wing 22), Iwakuni (Wing 31)
The 1991-95 procurement plan includes 8 P-3C, 3 EP-3, 36 SH-60J, 8 UH-60J and 1 MH-53E

DELETIONS and CONVERSIONS

Submarines

1990 *Narushio* (converted May)
1991 *Kuroshio* (converted March), *Takashio* (converted July)
1991 *Isoshio* (Mar)

Destroyers

1989 *Takaname* (Mar), *Harusame* (May)
1990 *Oonami* (Mar), *Makinami* (Mar)
1991 *Yamagumo, Makigumo* (both converted June)
1992 *Mochizuki, Nagatsuki*

Frigates

1990 *Ooi* (converted Jan), *Kitakami* (converted Jan)
1991 *Mogami* (June)
1992 *Isuzu* (Mar)

Light Forces

1990 *Ash 6* (Mar), *PT 811* (Nov)
1991 *PT 812-813* (Oct)

Mine Warfare Forces

1989 2 MSC (638, 639) (converted Nov)
1990 2 MSC (640, 641) (converted Nov)
1992 2 MSC (642, 643) (converted Mar), 2 MSB (707, 708) (Mar)

Support Ships

1989 ASU 7011 *(Chihaya)*, ASU 65 *(Kumataka)*, ASU 66 *(Shiratori)*, YAS 77 *(Amami)*, YAS 80 *(Ibuki)*, YAS 78 *(Urume)*, YAS 67 *(Mikura)*
1990 ASU 7001 *(Tsugaru)*, YAS 79 *(Minase)*, YAS 81 *(Katsura)*
1991 YAS 82 *(Takami)*, YO 5, YW 1-2, YW 7-9, YO 7-8, YT 35
1992 YT 34-35

PENNANT LIST

Submarines—Patrol

SS 572 Yaeshio
SS 573 Yuushio
SS 574 Mochishio
SS 575 Setoshio
SS 576 Okishio
SS 577 Nadashio
SS 578 Hamashio
SS 579 Akishio
SS 580 Takeshio
SS 581 Yukishio
SS 582 Sachishio
SS 583 Harushio
SS 584 Natsushio
SS 585 Hayashio

Submarines—Auxiliary

ATSS 8002 Narushio
ATSS 8003 Kuroshio
ATSS 8004 Takashio

Destroyers

DD 115 Asagumo
DD 116 Minegumo
DD 117 Natsugumo
DD 118 Murakumo
DD 119 Aokumo
DD 120 Akigumo
DD 121 Yugumo
DD 122 Hatsuyuki
DD 123 Shirayuki
DD 124 Mineyuki
DD 125 Sawayuki
DD 126 Hamayuki
DD 127 Isoyuki
DD 128 Haruyuki
DD 129 Yamayuki
DD 130 Matsuyuki
DD 131 Setoyuki
DD 132 Asayuki
DD 133 Shimayuki
DD 141 Haruna
DD 142 Hiei
DD 143 Shirane
DD 144 Kurama
DD 151 Asagiri
DD 152 Yamagiri
DD 153 Yuugiri
DD 154 Amagiri
DD 155 Hamagiri
DD 156 Setogiri
DD 157 Sawagiri
DD 158 Umigiri
DD 163 Amatsukaze
DD 164 Takatsuki
DD 165 Kikuzuki
DD 168 Tachikaze
DD 169 Asakaze
DD 170 Sawakaze
DD 171 Hatakaze
DD 172 Shimakaze
DD 173 Kongo (bldg)

Frigates

DE 215 Chikugo
DE 216 Ayase
DE 217 Mikuma
DE 218 Tokachi
DE 219 Iwase
DE 220 Chitose
DE 221 Niyodo
DE 222 Teshio
DE 223 Yoshino
DE 224 Kumano
DE 225 Noshiro
DE 226 Ishikari
DE 227 Yubari
DE 228 Yubetsu
DE 229 Abukuma
DE 230 Jintsu
DE 231 Ohyodo
DE 232 Sendai
DE 233 Chikuma (bldg)
DE 234 Tone (bldg)

Light Forces

PT 814-815 PT 14-15
PB 919-927 PB 19-27
PG 821-822 PG 21-22 (bldg)

Minehunters/Sweepers—Ocean

MSO 301 Yaeyama (bldg)
MSO 302 Tsushima (bldg)

Minesweepers—Coastal

MSC 644 Oumi
MSC 645 Fukue
MSC 646 Okitsu
MSC 647 Hashira
MSC 648 Iwai
MSC 649 Hatsushima
MSC 650 Ninoshima
MSC 651 Miyajima
MSC 652 Enoshima
MSC 653 Ukishima
MSC 654 Ooshima
MSC 655 Niijima
MSC 656 Yakushima
MSC 657 Narushima
MSC 658 Chichijima
MSC 659 Torishima
MSC 660 Hahajima
MSC 661 Takashima
MSC 662 Nuwajima
MSC 663 Etajima
MSC 664 Kamishima
MSC 665 Himeshima
MSC 666 Ogishima
MSC 667 Moroshima
MSC 668 Yurishima
MSC 669 Hikoshima
MSC 670 Awashima
MSC 671 Sakushima
MSC 672 Uwajima
MSC 673 Ieshima

Minesweeping Boats

709 Kyuu-Go
710 Jyuu-Go
711 Jyuu-Ichi-Go
712 Jyuu-Ni-Go

MCM Support Ships

MMC 951 Souya
MST 462 Hayase
MST 475 Utone

Amphibious Forces

LST 4101	Atsumi
LST 4102	Motobu
LST 4103	Nemuro
LST 4151	Miura
LST 4152	Ojika
LST 4153	Satsuma
LSU 4171	Yura
LSU 4172	Noto
LCU 2001	Yusotei-Ichi-Go
LCU 2002	Yusotei-Ni-Go

Submarine Depot/Rescue Ships

AS 405	Chiyoda
ASR 402	Fushimi

Fleet Support Ships

AOE 421	Sagami
AOE 422	Towada
AOE 423	Tokiwa
AOE 424	Hamana

Training Ships

TV 3501	Katori
TV 3506	Yamagumo
TV 3507	Makigumo

Training Support Ship

ATS 4201	Azuma
ATS 4202	Kurobe

Cable Layer

ARC 482	Muroto

Icebreaker

AGB 5002	Shirase

Surveying Ships

AGS 5101	Akashi
AGS 5102	Futami
AGS 5103	Suma
AGS 5104	Wakasa

Surtass Ships

AOS 5201	Hibiki
AOS 5202	Harima

Tenders

ASE 6101	Kurihama
ASU 81-85	
ASY 92	Hiyodori
ASU 7010	Akizuki
ASU 7012	Teruzuki
ASU 7016	Kitakami
ASU 7017	Ooi
YAS 83	Iou
YAS 84	Miyake
YAS 85	Awaji
YAS 86	Toushi
YAS 87	Teuri
YAS 88	Murotsu
YAS 89	Tashiro
YAS 90	Miyato
YAS 91	Takane
YAS 92	Muzuki
YAS 93	Yokoze
YAS 94	Sakate

SUBMARINES

Note: Operational numbers are to be maintained at 14-16 hulls.

3 + 2 + 1 (1) HARUSHIO CLASS

Name	*No*	*Builders*	*Laid down*	*Launched*	*Commissioned*
HARUSHIO	SS 583	Mitsubishi, Kobe	21 Apr 1987	26 July 1989	30 Nov 1990
NATSUSHIO	SS 584	Kawasaki, Kobe	8 Apr 1988	20 Mar 1990	20 Mar 1991
HAYASHIO	SS 585	Mitsubishi, Kobe	9 Dec 1988	17 Jan 1991	Mar 1992
—	SS 586	Kawasaki, Kobe	8 Jan 1990	Mar 1992	Mar 1993
—	SS 587	Mitsubishi, Kobe	12 Dec 1990	Jan 1993	Mar 1994
—	SS 588	Kawasaki, Kobe	Jan 1992	1994	1995
—	SS 589	Mitsubishi, Kobe	1992	1994	1995

Displacement, tons: 2450 standard; 2750 dived
Dimensions, feet (metres): 262.5 × 35.4 × 25.6 *(80 × 10.8 × 7.8)*
Main machinery: Diesel-electric; 2 Kawasaki 12V 25/25S diesels; 5520 hp(m) *(4.1 MW)*; 2 Kawasaki alternators; 3.7 MW; 1 Fuji motor; 7200 hp(m) *(5.3 MW)*; 1 shaft
Speed, knots: 12 surfaced; 20+ dived
Complement: 75 (10 officers)

Missiles: SSM: McDonnell Douglas Sub-Harpoon; active radar homing to 130 km *(70 nm)* at 0.9 Mach; warhead 227 kg (fired from torpedo tubes).
Torpedoes: 6—21 in *(533 mm)* tubes. Japanese Type 89; high speed active homing.
Countermeasures: ESM: ZLR 3-6; radar warning.
Radars: Surface search: JRC ZPS 6; I band.
Sonars: Hughes/Oki ZQQ 5B; hull-mounted; active/passive search and attack; medium/low frequency.
ZQR 1 towed array similar to BQR 15; passive search; very low frequency.

Programmes: First approved in 1986 estimates and one per year since then. Total of six is likely.
Structure: The slight growth in all dimensions suggests a natural evolution from the Yuushio class. Anechoic coating.
Opinion: The 1992 request is for an Improved Harushio class of 2500 tons. As a Sterling closed cycle engine was purchased in 1990 it is possible that SS 589 may be the first to be fitted with air-independent propulsion.

HARUSHIO *2/1991, Hachiro Nakai*

10 YUUSHIO CLASS

Name	*No*	*Builders*	*Laid down*	*Launched*	*Commissioned*
YUUSHIO	SS 573	Mitsubishi, Kobe	3 Dec 1976	29 Mar 1979	26 Feb 1980
MOCHISHIO	SS 574	Kawasaki, Kobe	9 May 1978	12 Mar 1980	5 Mar 1981
SETOSHIO	SS 575	Mitsubishi, Kobe	17 Apr 1979	10 Feb 1981	17 Mar 1982
OKISHIO	SS 576	Kawasaki, Kobe	17 Apr 1980	5 Mar 1982	1 Mar 1983
NADASHIO	SS 577	Mitsubishi, Kobe	16 Apr 1981	27 Jan 1983	6 Mar 1984
HAMASHIO	SS 578	Kawasaki, Kobe	8 Apr 1982	1 Feb 1984	5 Mar 1985
AKISHIO	SS 579	Mitsubishi, Kobe	15 Apr 1983	22 Jan 1985	5 Mar 1986
TAKESHIO	SS 580	Kawasaki, Kobe	3 Apr 1984	9 Feb 1986	3 Mar 1987
YUKISHIO	SS 581	Mitsubishi, Kobe	11 Apr 1985	23 Jan 1987	11 Mar 1988
SACHISHIO	SS 582	Kawasaki, Kobe	11 Apr 1986	17 Feb 1988	24 Mar 1989

Displacement, tons: 2200; 2250 (SS 574 and 577-582); 2300 (SS 576) standard; 2450 dived
Dimensions, feet (metres): 249.3 × 32.5 × 24.3 *(76 × 9.9 × 7.4)*
Main machinery: Diesel-electric; 2 Kawasaki-MAN V8V24-30 ATL diesels; 3400 hp(m) *(2.5 MW)*; 1 motor; 7200 hp(m) *(5.3 MW)*; 1 shaft
Speed, knots: 12 surfaced; 20+ dived
Complement: 75 (10 officers)

Missiles: SSM: McDonnell Douglas Sub-Harpoon (SS 574, SS 577-582, others may be back fitted); active radar homing to 130 km *(70 nm)* at 0.9 Mach; warhead 227 kg; fired from torpedo tubes.
Torpedoes: 6—21 in *(533 mm)* tubes amidships. Probably a combination of Japanese Type 89 and US Mk 37C.
Countermeasures: ESM: ZLR 3-6; radar warning.
Radars: Surface search: JRC ZPS 6; I band.
Sonars: Hughes/Oki ZQQ 4 (or 5 in some) (modified BQS 4); bow-mounted; passive/active search and attack; medium/low frequency.
ZQR 1 towed array similar to BQR 15 (in some of the class); passive search; very low frequency.

Programmes: SS 573 approved in FY 1975, SS 574 in FY 1977, SS 575 in FY 1978, SS 576 in FY 1979, SS 577 in FY 1980, SS 578 in FY 1981, SS 579 in FY 1982, SS 580 in FY 1983, SS 581 in FY 1984 and SS 582 in FY 1985.

YUUSHIO *2/1991, Hachiro Nakai*

Modernisation: Towed sonar array fitted in *Okishio* in 1987 and now back fitted to others in the class including *Akishio* and *Sachishio*. ZQQ 5 is also being retrofitted.
Structure: An enlarged version of the Uzushio class with improved diving depth to 275 m *(900 ft)*. Double hull construction. Probably carries 18 torpedoes and missiles. The towed array is stowed in a conduit on the starboard side of the casing.
Operational: In July 1988 *Nadashio* on the surface collided with a fishing boat which caused much loss of life.

4 UZUSHIO CLASS

Name	*No*	*Builders*	*Laid down*	*Launched*	*Commissioned*
NARUSHIO	ATSS 8002 (ex-SS 569)	Mitsubishi, Kobe	8 May 1971	22 Nov 1972	28 Sep 1973
KUROSHIO	ATSS 8003 (ex-SS 570)	Kawasaki, Kobe	5 July 1972	22 Feb 1974	27 Nov 1974
TAKASHIO	ATSS 8004 (ex-SS 571)	Mitsubishi, Kobe	6 July 1973	30 June 1975	30 Jan 1976
YAESHIO	SS 572	Kawasaki, Kobe	14 Apr 1975	19 May 1977	7 Mar 1978

Displacement, tons: 1850 standard; 1900 surfaced; 2430 dived
Dimensions, feet (metres): 236.2 × 32.5 × 24.6 *(72 × 9.9 × 7.5)*
Main machinery: Diesel-electric; 2 Kawasaki-MAN V8V24 ATL diesels; 3400 hp(m) *(2.5 MW)*; 1 motor; 7200 hp(m) *(5.3 MW)*; 1 shaft
Speed, knots: 12 surfaced; 20 dived
Complement: 80 (10 officers); 70 plus 20 trainees (ATSS)

Torpedoes: 6—21 in *(533 mm)* tubes amidships. Japanese Type 89 high speed active homing.
Countermeasures: ESM: ZLR 3-6; radar warning.
Radars: Surface search: JRC ZPS 4; I band.
Sonars: Hughes/Oki ZQQ 2 (SS 572 has ZQQ 3 in lieu); bow-mounted; passive/active search and attack; medium/low frequency.

Programmes: Being paid off at one a year as new constructions commission.
Structure: Diving depth, 200 m *(656 ft)*. Double-hull construction and 'tear-drop' form, built of high tensile steel to increase diving depth.
Operational: *Narushio* became an auxiliary training submarine in June 1990; *Kuroshio* in May 1991 and *Takashio* in June 1992. One of the class may have been fitted with a Sterling engine for trials starting in late 1991.

KUROSHIO *4/1991, Hachiro Nakai*

DESTROYERS

0 + 2 + 1 (1) KONGO CLASS

Name	*No*	*Builders*	*Laid down*	*Launched*	*Commissioned*
KONGO (ex-*Yukikaze*)	DD 173	Mitsubishi, Nagasaki	8 May 1990	26 Sep 1991	Mar 1993
—	DD 174	Mitsubishi, Nagasaki	May 1992	Sep 1993	Mar 1995
—	DD 175	Mitsubishi, Nagasaki	May 1993	1994	Mar 1996

Displacement, tons: 7200 standard; 9485 full load
Dimensions, feet (metres): 528.2 × 68.9 × 20.3 *(161 × 21 × 6.2)*
Main machinery: COGAG; 4 GE LM 2500 gas turbines; 92 000 hp *(68.6 MW)* sustained; 2 shafts; cp props
Speed, knots: 30. **Range, miles:** 4500 at 20 kts
Complement: 300

Missiles: SSM: 8 McDonnell Douglas Harpoon (2 quad) ❶ launchers.
SAM: GDC Pomona Standard SM-2MR. Martin Marietta Mk 41 VLS (61 cells) aft; FMC Mk 41 (29 cells) forward ❷. Total of 90 Standard and ASROC weapons.
A/S: Vertical launch ASROC.
Guns: 1 OTO Melara 5 in *(127 mm)*/54 Compatto ❸. 2—20 mm/76 Mk 15 Vulcan Phalanx ❹.
Torpedoes: 6—324 mm (2 triple) tubes ❺. Honeywell Mk 46.
Countermeasures: Decoys: 4 Mk 36 SRBOC; towed torpedo decoy.
ESM: Melko NOLQ 2; intercept.
ECM: Fujitsu OLT-3; jammer.
Combat data systems: Aegis NTDS with Links 11 and 14; Link 16 in due course.
Fire control: 3 Mk 99 Mod 1 MFCS. Type 2-21 GFCS. Mk 116 Mod 7 for ASW.

KONGO *(Scale 1 : 1 500), Ian Sturton*

Radars: Air search: RCA SPY 1D ❻; 3D.
Surface search: JRC OPS 28D ❼.
Navigation: JRC OPS 20.
Fire control: 3 SPG 62 ❽; 1 Mk 2/21 ❾.
Tacan: UPX 29.
Sonars: Nec OQS 102 (SQS 53B/C) hull-mounted; active search and attack.
Oki OQR 2 (SQR 19A (V)) TACTASS; towed array.

Helicopters: Platform ❿ and fuelling facilities for SH-60J Seahawk.

Programmes: Proposed in the FY 1987 programme; first one accepted in FY 1988 estimates, second in FY 1990, third in FY 1991; one more to be ordered probably in FY 1993.
Structure: This is an enlarged and improved version of the USN *Arleigh Burke* with a lightweight version of the Aegis system. There are two missile magazines. OQS 102 plus OQR 2 towed array is the equivalent of SQQ 89.
Opinion: The combination of cost and US Congressional reluctance to release Aegis technology slowed the programme down but the plan is to complete all four by the end of 1998.

KONGO *9/1991, Hachiro Nakai*

2 HATAKAZE CLASS

Name	*No*	*Builders*	*Laid down*	*Launched*	*Commissioned*
HATAKAZE	DD 171	Mitsubishi, Nagasaki	20 May 1983	9 Nov 1984	27 Mar 1986
SHIMAKAZE	DD 172	Mitsubishi, Nagasaki	13 Jan 1985	30 Jan 1987	23 Mar 1988

Displacement, tons: 4600 (4650, DD 172) standard; 5500 full load
Dimensions, feet (metres): 492 × 53.8 × 15.7 *(150 × 16.4 × 4.8)*
Main machinery: COGAG; 2 RR Olympus TM3B gas turbines; 43 000 hp *(32 MW)* sustained; 2 RR Spey SM1A gas turbines; 29 500 hp *(22 MW)* sustained; 2 shafts; cp props
Speed, knots: 30
Complement: 260

Missiles: SSM: 8 McDonnell Douglas Harpoon ❶; active radar homing to 130 km *(70 nm)* at 0.9 Mach; warhead 227 kg HE.
SAM: 40 GDC Pomona Standard SM-1MR; Mk 13 Mod 4 launcher ❷; command guidance; semi-active radar homing to 46 km *(25 nm)* at 2 Mach; height envelope 45-18 288 m *(150-60 000 ft)*.
A/S: Honeywell ASROC Mk 112 octuple launcher ❸; inertial guidance to 1.6-10 km *(1-5.4 nm)* at 0.9 Mach; payload Mk 46 Mod 5 Neartip. Reload capability.
Guns: 2 FMC 5 in *(127 mm)*/54 Mk 42 automatic ❹; 85° elevation; 20-40 rounds/minute to 24 km *(13 nm)* anti-surface; 14 km *(7.6 nm)* anti-aircraft; weight of shell 32 kg.
2 General Electric/General Dynamics 20 mm Phalanx Mk 15 CIWS ❺; 6 barrels per mounting; 3000 rounds/minute combined to 1.5 km.
Torpedoes: 6—324 mm Type 68 (2 triple) tubes ❻. Honeywell Mk 46 Mod 5 Neartip; anti-submarine; active/passive homing to 11 km *(5.9 nm)* at 40 kts; warhead 44 kg.
Countermeasures: Decoys: 2 Loral Hycor SRBOC 6-barrelled Mk 36 Chaff launchers; range 4 km *(2.2 nm)*.
ESM: Melco NOLQ 1; intercept.
ECM: Fujitsu OLT 3; jammer.
Combat data systems: OYQ-4 Mod 1 action data automation; Links 11 and 14. SATCOM.
Fire control: Type 2-21C for 127 mm guns. General Electric Mk 74 Mod 13 for Standard.
Radars: Air search: Hughes SPS 52C ❼; 3D; E/F band; range 439 km *(240 nm)*.
Melco OPS 11C ❽.
Surface search: JRC OPS 28 B ❾; G/H band.
Fire control: Two Raytheon SPG 51C ❿; G/I band.
Melco 2-21 ⓫; I/J band.
Type 2-12 ⓬; I band.
Tacan: Nec ORN-6.

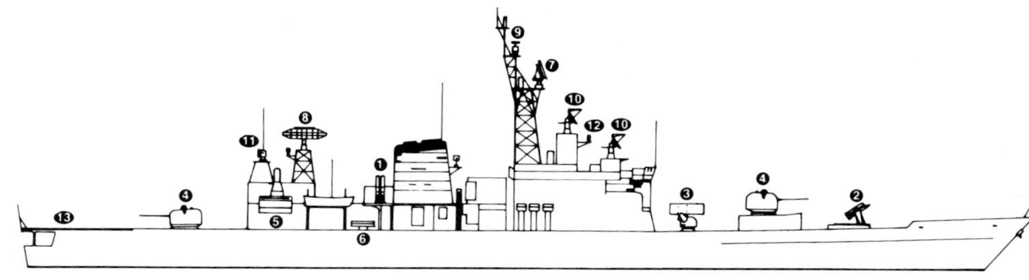
HATAKAZE *(Scale 1 : 1 200), Ian Sturton*

SHIMAKAZE *4/1991, Hachiro Nakai*

Sonars: Nec OQS 4; hull-mounted; active search and attack; medium frequency.
Helicopters: Platform for 1 Mitsubishi HSS-2B Sea King ⓭.

Programmes: DD 171 provided for in 1981 programme. DD 172 provided for in 1983 programme, ordered 29 March 1984.

2 SHIRANE CLASS

Name	*No*	*Builders*	*Laid down*	*Launched*	*Commissioned*
SHIRANE	DD 143	Ishikawajima Harima, Tokyo	25 Feb 1977	18 Sep 1978	17 Mar 1980
KURAMA	DD 144	Ishikawajima Harima, Tokyo	17 Feb 1978	20 Sep 1979	27 Mar 1981

Displacement, tons: 5200 standard
Dimensions, feet (metres): 521.5 × 57.5 × 17.5 *(159 × 17.5 × 5.3)*
Main machinery: 2 boilers; 850 psi *(60 kg/cm sq)*; 900°F *(480°C)*; 2 turbines; 70 000 hp(m) *(51.5 MW)*; 2 shafts
Speed, knots: 32
Complement: 350; 360 *(Kurama)*

Missiles: SAM: Raytheon Sea Sparrow Mk 29 octuple launcher ❶; semi-active radar homing to 14.6 km *(8 nm)* at 2.5 Mach; warhead 39 kg; 24 missiles.
A/S: Honeywell ASROC Mk 112 octuple launcher ❷; inertial guidance to 10 km *(5.4 nm)* at 0.9 Mach; payload Mk 46 Mod 5 Neartip.
Guns: 2 FMC 5 in *(127 mm)*/54 Mk 42 automatic ❸; 85° elevation; 20-40 rounds/minute to 24 km *(13 nm)* anti-surface; 14 km *(7.6 nm)* anti-aircraft; weight of shell 32 kg.
2 General Electric/General Dynamics 20 mm Phalanx Mk 15 CIWS ❹; 6 barrels per mounting; 3000 rounds/minute combined to 1.5 km.
Torpedoes: 6—324 mm Type 68 (2 triple) tubes ❺. Honeywell Mk 46 Mod 5 Neartip; anti-submarine; active/passive homing to 11 km *(5.9 nm)* at 40 kts; warhead 44 kg.
Countermeasures: ESM: Melco NOLQ 1; intercept.
ECM: Fujitsu OLR-9B; jammer.
Prairie Masker; blade rate suppression system.

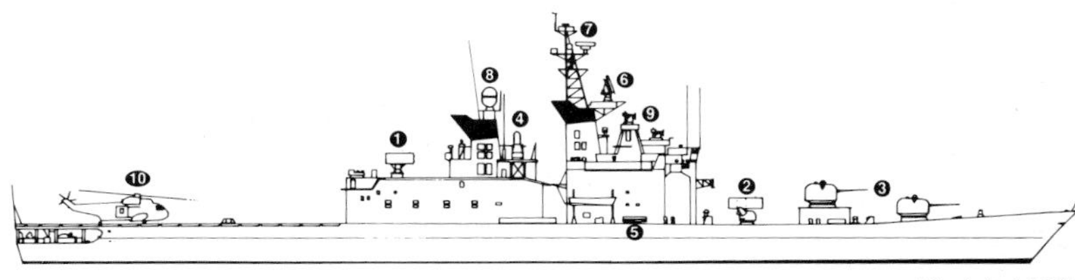
KURAMA *(Scale 1 : 1 500), Ian Sturton*

Combat data systems: OYQ-6; Links 11 and 14. SATCOM.
Fire control: Singer Mk 114 for ASROC system. Type 72-1A GFCS.
Radars: Air search: Nec OPS 12 ❻; 3D; D band; range 119 km *(65 nm)*.
Surface search: JRC OPS 28 ❼; G/H band.
Navigation: Koden OPN-11; I band.
Fire control: Signaal WM 25 ❽; I/J band; range 46 km *(25 nm)*.
Two Type 72-1A FCS ❾; I/J band.
Tacan: ORN-6.
Sonars: EDO/Nec SQS 35(J); VDS; active/passive search; medium frequency.
Nec OQS 101; hull-mounted; low frequency.
EDO/Nec SQR 18A; towed array; passive; very low frequency.

Helicopters: 3 Mitsubishi HSS-2B Sea King ❿ or SH-60J Sea Hawk.

Programmes: One each in 1975 and 1976 programmes.
Modernisation: DD 143 refit in 1989-90. Both fitted with CIWS and towed array sonars by mid-1990.
Structure: Fitted with Vosper Thornycroft fin stabilisers. The after funnel is set to starboard and the forward one to port. The crane is on the starboard after corner of the hangar.

SHIRANE *4/1991, Hachiro Nakai*

2 HARUNA CLASS

Name	No	Builders	Laid down	Launched	Commissioned
HARUNA	DD 141	Mitsubishi, Nagasaki	19 Mar 1970	1 Feb 1972	22 Feb 1973
HIEI	DD 142	Ishikawajima, Tokyo	8 Mar 1972	13 Aug 1973	27 Nov 1974

Displacement, tons: 4950 (4700, DD 142) standard
Dimensions, feet (metres): 502 × 57.4 × 17.1 *(153 × 17.5 × 5.2)*
Main machinery: 2 boilers; 850 psi *(60 kg/cm sq)*; 900°F *(480°C)*; 2 GE/Ishikawajima turbines; 70 000 hp *(51.5 MW)*; 2 shafts
Speed, knots: 31
Complement: 370 (360, DD 142) (36 officers)

Missiles: SAM: Raytheon Sea Sparrow Mk 29 octuple launcher ❶; semi-active radar homing to 14.6 km *(8 nm)* at 2.5 Mach; warhead 39 kg; 24 missiles.
A/S: Honeywell ASROC Mk 112 octuple launcher ❷; inertial guidance to 1.6-10 km *(1-5.4 nm)* at 0.9 Mach; payload Mk 46 Mod 5 Neartip.
Guns: 2 FMC 5 in *(127 mm)*/54 Mk 42 automatic ❸; 85° elevation; 20-40 rounds/minute to 24 km *(13 nm)* anti-surface; 14 km *(7.6 nm)* anti-aircraft; weight of shell 32 kg.
2 General Electric/General Dynamics 20 mm Phalanx Mk 15 CIWS ❹; 6 barrels per mounting; 3000 rounds/minute combined to 1.5 km.
Torpedoes: 6—324 mm Type 68 (2 triple) tubes ❺. Honeywell Mk 46 Mod 5 Neartip; anti-submarine; active/passive homing to 11 km *(5.9 nm)* at 40 kts; warhead 44 kg.
Countermeasures: Decoys: 4 Loral Hycor SRBOC Mk 36 multi-barrelled Chaff launchers.
ESM: Melco NOLQ 1; intercept.
ECM: Fujitsu OLR 9; jammer.

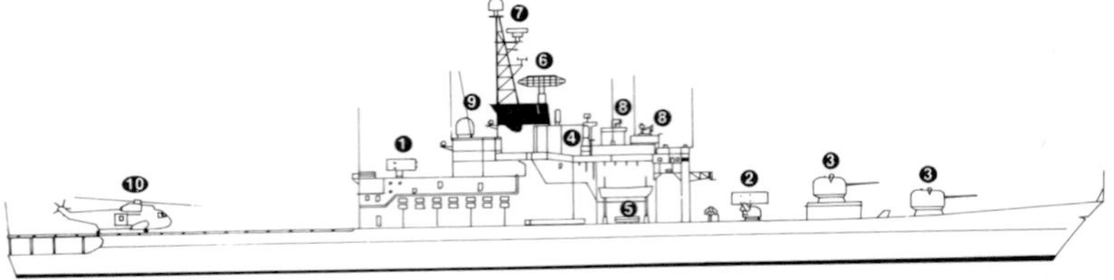

HARUNA

(Scale 1 : 1 500), Ian Sturton

Combat data systems: OYQ-6 action data automation; Links 11 and 14. SATCOM.
Fire control: 2 Type 2-12 FCS (one for guns, one for SAM).
Radars: Air search: Melco OPS 11C ❻; D band.
Surface search: JRC OPS 28 ❼; G/H band.
Fire control: One Type 1A ❽; I/J band (guns).
One Type 2-12 ❾; I/J band (SAM).
IFF: US Mk 10.
Tacan: Nec ORN-6.
Sonars: Sangamo/Mitsubishi OQS 3; hull-mounted; active search and attack; low frequency with bottom bounce.

Helicopters: 3 Mitsubishi HSS-2B Sea King ❿.

Programmes: Ordered under the third five-year defence programme (from 1967-71).
Modernisation: DD 141 taken in hand from 31 March 1986 to 31 October 1987 for FRAM at Mitsubishi, Nagasaki; DD 142 received FRAM from 31 August 1987 to 30 March 1989 at IHI, Tokyo; included Sea Sparrow, two CIWS and Chaff launchers.
Structure: The funnel is offset slightly to port. Fitted with fin stabilisers. A heavy crane has been fitted on the top of the hangar, starboard side.
Operational: Fitted with Canadian Beartrap hauldown gear.

HARUNA

4/1991, Hachiro Nakai

0 + 1 + 1 (6) TAKAO CLASS

Name	No	Builders	Laid down	Launched	Commissioned
TAKAO (?)	—	Ishikawajima Harima, Yokohama	May 1993	Dec 1994	Mar 1996

Displacement, tons: 4400 full load
Main machinery: COGAG; 2 GE LM 2500 gas turbines; 46 000 hp *(34.3 MW)* sustained; 2 RR Spey SM1C gas turbines; 41 630 hp *(31 MW)* sustained; 2 shafts
Speed, knots: 30
Complement: 160

Missiles: SSM: 8 SSM-1B ❶ or Harpoon.
SAM: Raytheon Mk 48 VLS ❷ Sea Sparrow.
A/S: VL ASROC.
Guns: 1 OTO Melara 76 mm/62 ❸; 2 Vulcan Phalanx 20 mm ❹.
Torpedoes: 6—324 mm Type 68 (2 triple) tubes ❺.
Radars: Air search: OPS 24 ❻.
Surface search: OPS 28C ❼.
Fire control: Two Type 2-21 ❽.

Helicopters: 1 SH-60J Seahawk ❾.

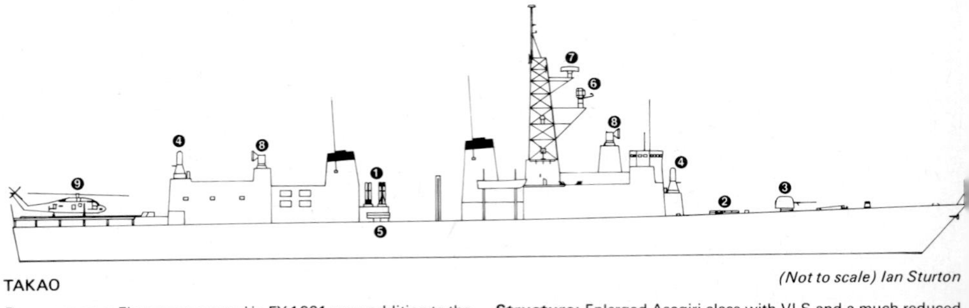

TAKAO

(Not to scale) Ian Sturton

Programmes: First one approved in FY 1991 as an addition to the third Aegis type destroyer. Second approved in FY 1992. A total of eight is to be built and named after previous cruisers.

Structure: Enlarged Asagiri class with VLS and a much reduced complement. Some of the weapons systems have still to be decided.

8 ASAGIRI CLASS

Name	*No*	*Builders*	*Laid down*	*Launched*	*Commissioned*
ASAGIRI	DD 151	Ishikawajima Harima, Tokyo	13 Feb 1985	19 Sep 1986	17 Mar 1988
YAMAGIRI	DD 152	Mitsui, Tamano	5 Feb 1986	8 Oct 1987	25 Jan 1989
YUUGIRI	DD 153	Sumitomo, Uraga	25 Feb 1986	21 Sep 1987	28 Feb 1989
AMAGIRI	DD 154	Ishikawajima Harima, Tokyo	3 Mar 1986	9 Sep 1987	17 Mar 1989
HAMAGIRI	DD 155	Hitachi, Maizuru	20 Jan 1987	4 June 1988	31 Jan 1990
SETOGIRI	DD 156	Sumitomo, Uraga	9 Mar 1987	12 Sep 1988	14 Feb 1990
SAWAGIRI	DD 157	Mitsubishi, Nagasaki	14 Jan 1987	25 Nov 1988	6 Mar 1990
UMIGIRI	DD 158	Ishikawajima Harima, Tokyo	31 Oct 1988	9 Nov 1989	12 Mar 1991

Displacement, tons: 3500 standard; 4200 full load
Dimensions, feet (metres): 449.4 × 48 × 14.6 *(137 × 14.6 × 4.5)*
Main machinery: COGAG; 4 RR Spey SM1A gas turbines; 59 000 hp *(44 MW)* sustained; 2 shafts; cp props
Speed, knots: 30+
Complement: 220

Missiles: SSM: 8 McDonnell Douglas Harpoon (2 quad) launchers ❶; active radar homing to 130 km *(70 nm)* at 0.9 Mach; warhead 227 kg.
SAM: Raytheon Sea Sparrow Mk 29 octuple launcher ❷; semi-active radar homing to 14.6 km *(8 nm)* at 2.5 Mach; warhead 39 kg; 20 missiles.
A/S: Honeywell ASROC Mk 112 octuple launcher ❸; inertial guidance to 1.6-10 km *(1-5.4 nm)* at 0.9 Mach; payload Mk 46 Mod 5 Neartip. Reload capability.
Guns: 1 OTO Melara 3 in *(76 mm)*/62 compact ❹; 85° elevation; 85 rounds/minute to 16 km *(8.6 nm)* anti-surface; 12 km *(6.5 nm)* anti-aircraft; weight of shell 6 kg.
2 General Electric/General Dynamics 20 mm Phalanx Mk 15 CIWS ❺; 6 barrels per mounting; 3000 rounds/minute combined to 1.5 km.
Torpedoes: 6—324 mm Type 68 (2 triple) HOS 301 tubes ❻. Honeywell Mk 46 Mod 5 Neartip; anti-submarine; active/passive homing to 11 km *(5.9 nm)* at 40 kts; warhead 44 kg.
Countermeasures: Decoys: 2 Loral Hycor SRBOC 6-barrelled Mk 36 Chaff launchers ❼; range 4 km *(2.2 nm)*.
1 SLQ 51 Nixie; towed anti-torpedo decoy.
ESM: Nec NOLR 6C ❽; intercept.
ECM: Fujitsu OLT-3; jammer.
Combat data systems: OYQ-6 action data automation; Link 11. SATCOM. Helicopter datalink ❾ for SH-60J.
Radars: Air search: Melco OPS 14C (DD 151-154) ❿.
Melco OPS 24 (DD 155-158) ⓫; 3D; D band.
Surface search: JRC OPS 28C ⓬; G/H band.
Fire control: Type 2-22 (for guns) ⓭. Type 2-12E (for SAM) ⓮ (DD 151-154); Type 2-12G (for SAM) ⓯ (DD 155-158).
Tacan: ORN-6.
Sonars: Mitsubishi OQS 4A (II); hull-mounted; active search and attack; low frequency.
OQR-1; towed array; passive search; very low frequency (being fitted to all).

Helicopters: 1 Mitsubishi HSS-2B Sea King ⓰ or SH-60J Sea Hawk ⓱.

Programmes: DD 151 in 1983 estimates, DD 152-154 in 1984, DD 155-157 in 1985 and DD 158 in 1986.
Modernisation: The last four have been fitted on build with improved air search radar, updated fire control radars and a helicopter datalink. *Umigiri* also commissioned with a sonar towed array which is being fitted to the rest of the class, as are the other improvements in due course. Sea Hawk helos are replacing the Sea Kings.
Structure: Because of the enhanced IR signature and damage to electronic systems on the mainmast caused by after funnel gases there have been modifications to help contain the problem. The mainmast is now slightly higher than originally designed and in *Asagiri* the mast was moved to port. In the others of the class the mast has retained its central position but the after funnel has been offset to starboard. The hangar structure is asymmetrical extending to the after funnel on the starboard side but only to the mainmast to port. SATCOM is fitted at the after end of the hangar roof.
Operational: Beartrap helicopter hauldown system.

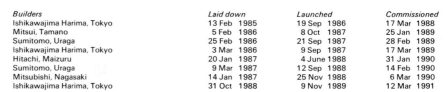

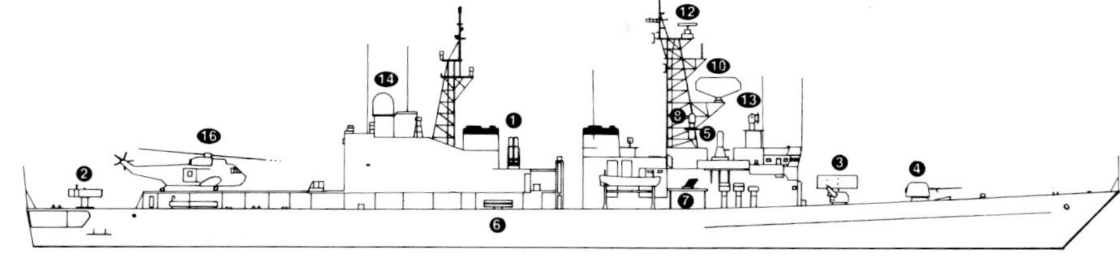
ASAGIRI *(Scale 1 : 1 200), Ian Sturton*

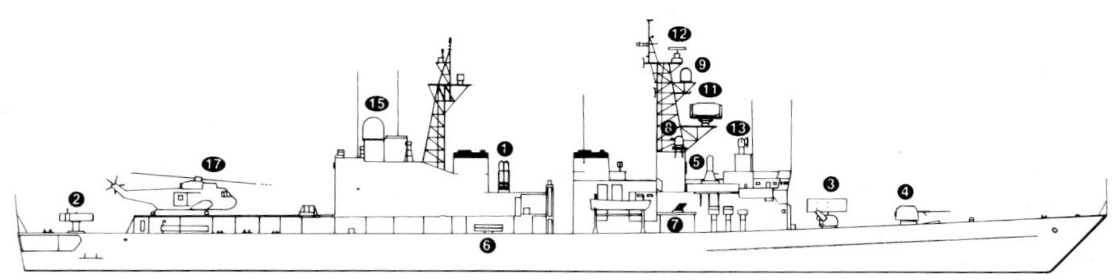
UMIGIRI *(Scale 1 : 1 200), Ian Sturton*

HAMAGIRI (with OPS-24, helodatalink and SATCOM) *4/1991, Hachiro Nakai*

YUUGIRI *7/1991, Hachiro Nakai*

12 HATSUYUKI CLASS

Name	*No*	*Builders*	*Laid down*	*Launched*	*Commissioned*
HATSUYUKI	DD 122	Sumitomo, Uraga	14 Mar 1979	7 Nov 1980	23 Mar 1982
SHIRAYUKI	DD 123	Hitachi, Maizuru	3 Dec 1979	4 Aug 1981	8 Feb 1983
MINEYUKI	DD 124	Mitsubishi, Nagasaki	7 May 1981	19 Oct 1982	26 Jan 1984
SAWAYUKI	DD 125	Ishikawajima Harima, Tokyo	22 Apr 1981	21 June 1982	15 Feb 1984
HAMAYUKI	DD 126	Mitsui, Tamano	4 Feb 1981	27 May 1982	18 Nov 1983
ISOYUKI	DD 127	Ishikawajima Harima, Tokyo	20 Apr 1982	19 Sep 1983	23 Jan 1985
HARUYUKI	DD 128	Sumitomo, Uraga	11 Mar 1982	6 Sep 1983	14 Mar 1985
YAMAYUKI	DD 129	Hitachi, Maizuru	25 Feb 1983	10 July 1984	3 Dec 1985
MATSUYUKI	DD 130	Ishikawajima Harima, Tokyo	7 Apr 1983	25 Oct 1984	19 Mar 1986
SETOYUKI	DD 131	Mitsui, Tamano	26 Jan 1984	3 July 1985	11 Dec 1986
ASAYUKI	DD 132	Sumitomo, Uraga	22 Dec 1983	16 Oct 1985	20 Feb 1987
SHIMAYUKI	DD 133	Mitsubishi, Nagasaki	8 May 1984	29 Jan 1986	17 Feb 1987

Displacement, tons: 2950 (3050 from DD 129 onwards) standard; 3700 (3800) full load
Dimensions, feet (metres): 426.4 × 44.6 × 13.8 (14.4 from 129 onwards) *(130 × 13.6 × 4.2) (4.4)*
Main machinery: COGOG; 2 Kawasaki-RR Olympus TM3B gas turbines; 43 000 hp *(32 MW)* sustained; 2 RR Type RM1C gas turbines; 10 680 hp *(8 MW)* sustained; 2 shafts; cp props
Speed, knots: 30
Complement: 195 (200, DD 124 onwards)

Missiles: SSM: 8 McDonnell Douglas Harpoon (2 quad) launchers ❶; active radar homing to 130 km *(70 nm)* at 0.9 Mach; warhead 227 kg.
SAM: Raytheon Sea Sparrow Type 3 (A-1) launcher ❷; semi-active radar homing to 14.6 km *(8 nm)* at 2.5 Mach; warhead 39 kg; 12 missiles.
A/S: Honeywell ASROC Mk 112 octuple launcher ❸; inertial guidance to 1.6-10 km *(1-5.4 nm)* at 0.9 Mach; payload Mk 46 Mod 5 Neartip.
Guns: 1 OTO Melara 3 in *(76 mm)*/62 compact ❹; 85° elevation; 85 rounds/minute to 16 km *(8.6 nm)* anti-surface; 12 km *(6.5 nm)* anti-aircraft; weight of shell 6 kg.
2 General Electric/General Dynamics 20 mm Phalanx Mk 15 CIWS (DDG 123 onwards) ❺; 6 barrels per mounting; 3000 rounds/minute combined to 1.5 km.
Torpedoes: 6—324 mm Type 68 (2 triple) tubes ❻. Honeywell Mk 46 Mod 5 Neartip; anti-submarine; active/passive homing to 11 km *(5.9 nm)* at 40 kts; warhead 44 kg.
Countermeasures: Decoys: 2 Loral Hycor SRBOC 6-barrelled Mk 36 Chaff launchers; range 4 km *(2.2 nm)*.
ESM: Nec NOLR 6C; intercept.
ECM: Fujitsu OLT 3; jammer.
Combat data systems: OYQ-5 action data automation; Link 14 (receive only).
Radars: Air search: Melco OPS 14B ❼.
Surface search: JRC OPS 18 ❽; G/H band.
Fire control: Type 2-12 A ❾; I/J band (for SAM).
Two Type 2-21/21A ❿; I/J band (for guns).
Tacan: URN 25.
Sonars: Nec OQS 4A (II) (SQS 23 type); hull-mounted; active search and attack; low frequency.
OQR 1 TACTASS (being fitted in all).

Helicopters: 1 Mitsubishi HSS-2B Sea King ⓫.

Modernisation: *Shirayuki* retrofitted with Phalanx in early 1992, *Hatsuyuki* to follow in 1993. *Matsuyuki* first to get sonar towed array in 1990; the others are being fitted.
Structure: Fitted with fin stabilisers. Steel in place of aluminium alloy for bridge etc after DD 129 which increased displacement.
Operational: Canadian Beartrap helicopter landing aid. Improved ECM equipment in the last three of the class.

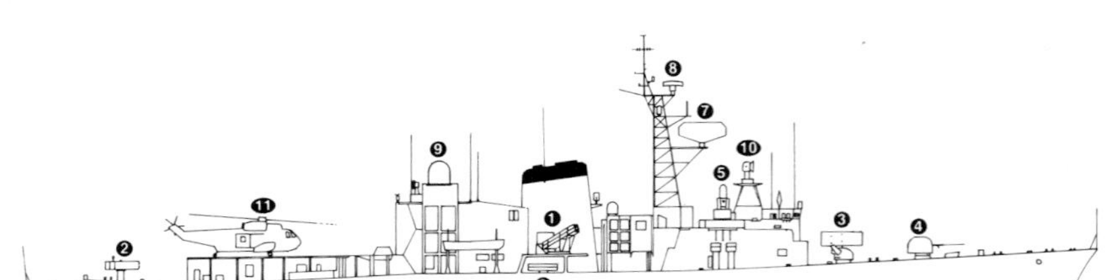

MINEYUKI *(Scale 1 : 1 200), Ian Sturton*

YAMAYUKI *11/1991, 92 Wing RAAF*

HATSUYUKI (without Phalanx) *8/1991, Wright & Logan*

3 TACHIKAZE CLASS

Name	*No*	*Builders*	*Laid down*	*Launched*	*Commissioned*
TACHIKAZE	DD 168	Mitsubishi, Nagasaki	19 June 1973	17 Dec 1974	26 Mar 1976
ASAKAZE	DD 169	Mitsubishi, Nagasaki	27 May 1976	15 Oct 1977	27 Mar 1979
SAWAKAZE	DD 170	Mitsubishi, Nagasaki	14 Sep 1979	4 June 1981	30 Mar 1983

Displacement, tons: 3850 (3950, DD 170) standard
Dimensions, feet (metres): 469 × 47 × 15.4
(143 × 14.3 × 4.7)
Main machinery: 2 boilers; 600 psi *(60 kg/cm sq)*; 850°F *(454°C)*; 2 Mitsubishi turbines; 70 000 hp(m); *(51.5 MW)*; 2 shafts
Speed, knots: 32
Complement: 250; 255 (D 170)

Missiles: SSM: 8 McDonnell Douglas Harpoon; active radar homing to 130 km *(70 nm)* at 0.9 Mach; warhead 227 kg HE.
SAM: GDC Pomona Standard SM-1MR; Mk 13 Mod 3 or 4 launcher ❶; command guidance; semi-active radar homing to 46 km *(25 nm)* at 2 Mach; height envelope 45-18 288 m *(150-60 000 ft)*; 40 missiles (SSM and SAM combined).
A/S: Honeywell ASROC Mk 112 octuple launcher ❷; inertial guidance to 1.6-10 km *(1-5.4 nm)* at 0.9 Mach; payload Mk 46 Mod 5 Neartip. Reloads in DD 170 only.
Guns: 2 FMC 5 in *(127 mm)*/54 Mk 42 automatic ❸; 85° elevation; 20-40 rounds/minute to 24 km *(13 nm)* anti-surface; 14 km *(7.6 nm)* anti-aircraft; weight of shell 32 kg.
2 General Electric/General Dynamics 20 mm Phalanx CIWS Mk 15 ❹; 6 barrels per mounting; 3000 rounds/minute combined to 1.5 km.
Torpedoes: 6—324 mm Type 68 (2 triple) tubes ❺. Honeywell Mk 46 Mod 5 Neartip; anti-submarine; active/passive homing to 11 km *(5.9 nm)* at 40 kts; warhead 44 kg.
Countermeasures: Decoys: 4 Loral Hycor SRBOC Mk 36 multi-barrelled Chaff launchers.
ESM: Nec NOLR 6 (DD 168); Nec NOLQ 1 (others); intercept.
ECM: Fujitsu OLT 3; jammer.
Combat data systems: OYQ-5 action data automation; Link 14.
Fire control: 2 Mk 74 Mod 13 missile control directors. US Mk 114 ASW control. GFCS-2 for gun (DD 170). GFCS-1A for gun (others).
Radars: Air search: Melco OPS 11 ❻.
Hughes SPS 52C ❼; 3D; E/F band; range 439 km *(240 nm)*.
Surface search: JRC OPS 16 ❽; D band.
JRC OPS 28 (DD 170); G/H band.
Fire control: Two Raytheon SPG 51 ❾; G/I band.
Type 2 FCS ❿; I/J band.
IFF: US Mk 10.
Sonars: Nec ORS-3 (DD 168); Nec OQS-3A (DD 169-170); hull-mounted; active search and attack; low frequency.

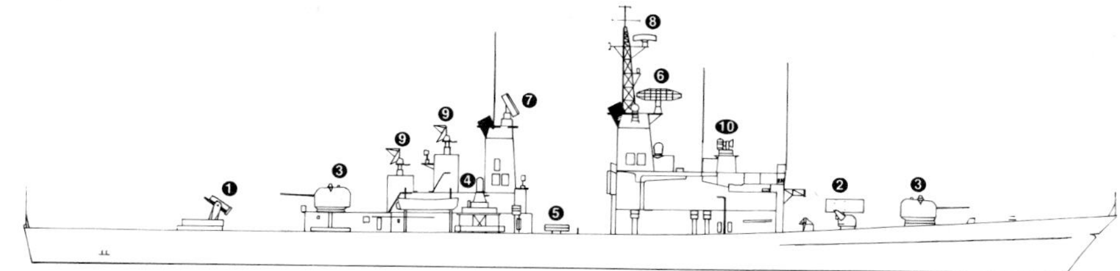
TACHIKAZE *(Scale 1 : 1 200), Ian Sturton*

SAWAKAZE *4/1991, Hachiro Nakai*

Modernisation: Harpoon and CIWS added to DD 168 in 1983, DD 169 and 170 in 1987.

2 TAKATSUKI CLASS

Name	*No*	*Builders*	*Laid down*	*Launched*	*Commissioned*
TAKATSUKI	DD 164	Ishikawajima Harima, Tokyo	8 Oct 1964	7 Jan 1966	15 Mar 1967
KIKUZUKI	DD 165	Mitsubishi, Nagasaki	15 Mar 1966	25 Mar 1967	27 Mar 1968

Displacement, tons: 3250 standard
Dimensions, feet (metres): 446.1 × 44 × 14.8
(136 × 13.4 × 4.5)
Main machinery: 2 boilers; 600 psi *(60 kg/cm sq)*; 850°F *(454°C)*; 2 Mitsubishi turbines; 70 000 hp(m); *(51.5 MW)*; 2 shafts
Speed, knots: 31. **Range, miles:** 7000 at 20 kts
Complement: 260

Missiles: SSM: 8 McDonnell Douglas Harpoon (2 quad) launchers ❶; active radar homing to 130 km *(70 nm)* at 0.9 Mach; warhead 227 kg.
SAM: Raytheon Sea Sparrow Mk 29 octuple launcher ❷; semi-active radar homing to 14.6 km *(8 nm)* at 2.5 Mach; warhead 39 kg; 16 missiles.
A/S: Honeywell ASROC Mk 112 octuple launcher ❸; inertial guidance to 10 km *(5.4 nm)* at 0.9 Mach; payload Mk 46 Mod 5 Neartip.
Guns: 1 FMC 5 in *(127 mm)*/54 Mk 42 automatic ❹; 85° elevation; 20-40 rounds/minute to 24 km *(13 nm)* anti-surface; 14 km *(7.6 nm)* anti-aircraft; weight of shell 32 kg.
1 General Electric/General Dynamics 20 mm Phalanx CIWS Mk 15 ❺; 6 barrels per mounting; 3000 rounds/minute combined to 1.5 km.
Torpedoes: 6—324 mm Type 68 (2 triple) tubes ❻. Honeywell Mk 46 Mod 5 Neartip; anti-submarine; active/passive homing to 11 km *(5.9 nm)* at 40 kts; warhead 44 kg.
A/S mortars: 1—375 mm Bofors Type 71 4-barrelled trainable rocket launcher ❼; automatic loading; range 1.6 km.
Countermeasures: Decoys: 2 Loral Hycor SRBOC 6-barrelled Mk 36 Chaff launchers; range 4 km *(2.2 nm)*.
ESM: Nec NOLR 6C (NOLR 9 in *Kikuzuki*); intercept.
ECM: Fujitsu OLT 3; jammer.
Combat data systems: OYQ-5 action data automation; Link 14.
Fire control: US Mk 56 or GFCS-1 for 127 mm guns. US Type 2-12B for Sea Sparrow system.
Radars: Air search: Melco OPS 11B ❽.
Surface search: JRC OPS 17 ❾; G/H band.
Fire control: Type 2-12B ❿; I/J band.
General Electric Mk 35 ⓫; I/J band.
Sonars: Nec SQS 35J; hull-mounted; active search and attack; low frequency.
EDO SQR 18 TACTASS; passive; low frequency.

Modernisation: From 1 April 1984 to 31 October 1985 DD 164 taken in hand for modifications to include removal of after 5 in gun and Dash hangar, fitting of Harpoon and Sea Sparrow, removal of VDS and its replacement by TASS, installation of FCS-2, and fittings for one 20 mm Phalanx mounting on after superstructure. Similar alterations carried out in DD 165 from May 1985 to December 1986. Phalanx not fitted in DD 164 until 1989. NOLR 9 installed in DD 165 for trials in 1991/92.
Operational: Two unmodified ships of the class paid off in 1992.

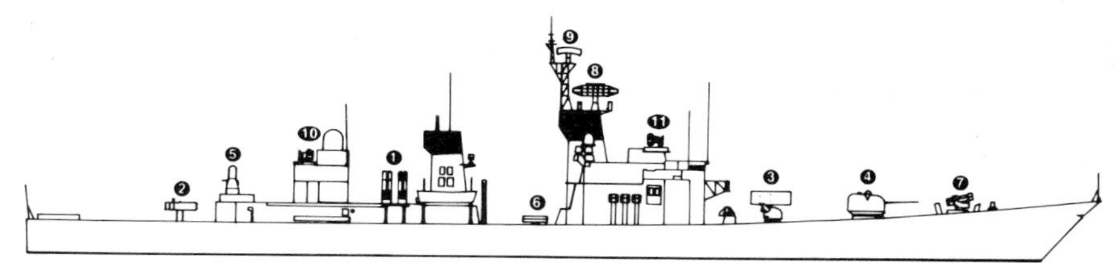
TAKATSUKI *(Scale 1 : 1 200), Ian Sturton*

TAKATSUKI *7/1991, Hachiro Nakai*

4 YAMAGUMO CLASS

Name	*No*	*Builders*	*Laid down*	*Launched*	*Commissioned*
ASAGUMO	DD 115	Hitachi, Maizuru	24 June 1965	25 Nov 1966	29 Aug 1967
AOKUMO	DD 119	Sumitomo, Uraga	2 Oct 1970	30 Mar 1972	25 Nov 1972
AKIGUMO	DD 120	Sumitomo, Uraga	7 July 1972	23 Oct 1973	24 July 1974
YUGUMO	DD 121	Sumitomo, Uraga	4 Feb 1976	31 May 1977	24 Mar 1978

Displacement, tons: 2150 standard
Dimensions, feet (metres): 377.2 × 38.7 × 13.1 *(114.9 × 11.8 × 4)*
Main machinery: 6 Mitsubishi 12UEV30/40N diesels; 21 600 hp(m) *(15.9 MW)* sustained; 2 shafts
Speed, knots: 27. **Range, miles:** 7000 at 20 kts
Complement: 210 (19 officers)

Missiles: A/S: Honeywell ASROC Mk 112 octuple launcher ❶; inertial guidance to 1.6-10 km *(1-5.4 nm)* at 0.9 Mach; payload Mk 46 Mod 5 Neartip.
Guns: 4 USN 3 in *(76 mm)*/50 Mk 33 (2 twin) ❷; 85° elevation; 50 rounds/minute to 12.8 km *(6.9 nm)*; weight of shell 6 kg.
Torpedoes: 6—324 mm Type 68 (2 triple) tubes ❸. Honeywell Mk 46 Mod 5 Neartip; anti-submarine; active/passive homing to 11 km *(5.9 nm)* at 40 kts; warhead 44 kg.
A/S mortars: 1 Bofors 375 mm Type 71 4-barrelled trainable rocket launcher ❹; automatic loading; range 1.6 km.
Countermeasures: ESM: Nec NOLR 5 (DD 119-121); Nec NOLR 1B (DD 115); radar intercept.
Fire control: US Mk 56 or 63 for 76 mm guns (DD 115, 119). Japanese GFCS-1 for 76 mm guns (DD 120, 121).
Radars: Air search: Melco OPS 11 ❺.
Surface search: JRC OPS 17 ❻; G/H band.
Fire control: Two General Electric Mk 35 ❼; I/J band.
IFF: US Mk 10.
Sonars: Sangamo SQS 23 (DD 115); hull mounted; active search and attack; low frequency.
Nec OQS 3A (DD 119, 120, 121); hull mounted; active search and attack.
EDO SQS 35(J) (DD 120, 121); VDS; active/passive search; medium frequency.

Structure: DD 115 has a tripod mainmast and the remainder lattice mainmasts.
Operational: The first two of the class were converted to Training Ships on 20 June 1991.

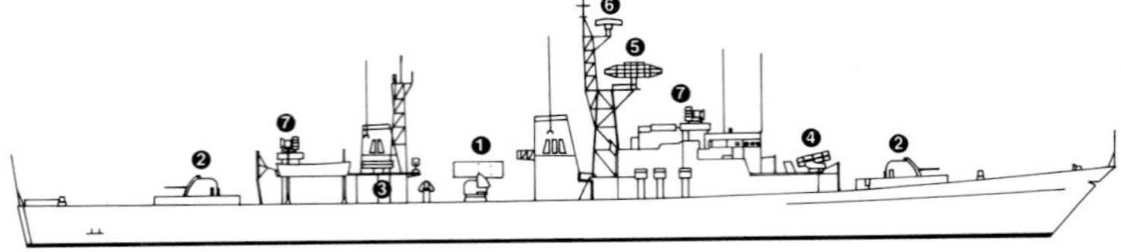
YUGUMO (Scale 1 : 1 200), *Ian Sturton*

AKIGUMO *3/1991, Hachiro Nakai*

3 MINEGUMO CLASS

Name	*No*	*Builders*	*Laid down*	*Launched*	*Commissioned*
MINEGUMO	DD 116	Mitsui, Tamano	14 Mar 1967	16 Dec 1967	31 Aug 1968
NATSUGUMO	DD 117	Uraga	30 June 1967	25 July 1968	15 May 1969
MURAKUMO	DD 118	Maizuru	19 Oct 1968	15 Nov 1969	21 Aug 1970

Displacement, tons: 2100 (2150, DD 118) standard
Dimensions, feet (metres): 373.9 (377.2, DD 118) × 38.7 × 13.1 *(114 (115) × 11.8 × 4)*
Main machinery: 6 Mitsubishi 12UEV 30/40N diesels; 21 600 hp(m) *(15.9 MW)* sustained; 2 shafts
Speed, knots: 27. **Range, miles:** 7000 at 20 kts
Complement: 210 (220, DD 118) (19 officers)

Missiles: A/S: Honeywell ASROC Mk 112 octuple launcher ❶; inertial guidance to 1.6-10 km *(1-5.4 nm)* at 0.9 Mach; payload Mk 46 Mod 5 Neartip.
Guns: 4 USN 3 in *(76 mm)*/50 Mk 33 (2 twin) (only 2 in DD 118) ❷; 85° elevation; 50 rounds/minute to 12.8 km *(6.9 nm)*; weight of shell 6 kg.
1 FMC/OTO Melara 3 in *(76 mm)*/62 Mk 75 compact (DD 118 only) ❸; 85° elevation; 50 rounds/minute to 16 km *(8.6 nm)* anti-surface; 12 km *(6.5 nm)* anti-aircraft; weight of shell 6 kg.
Torpedoes: 6—324 mm Type 68 (2 triple) tubes ❹. Honeywell Mk 46 Mod 5 Neartip; anti-submarine; active/passive homing to 11 km *(5.9 nm)* at 40 kts; warhead 44 kg.
A/S mortars: 1 Bofors 375 mm Type 71 4-barrelled trainable rocket launcher ❺; automatic loading; range 1.6 km.
Countermeasures: ESM: Nec NOLR 5; intercept.

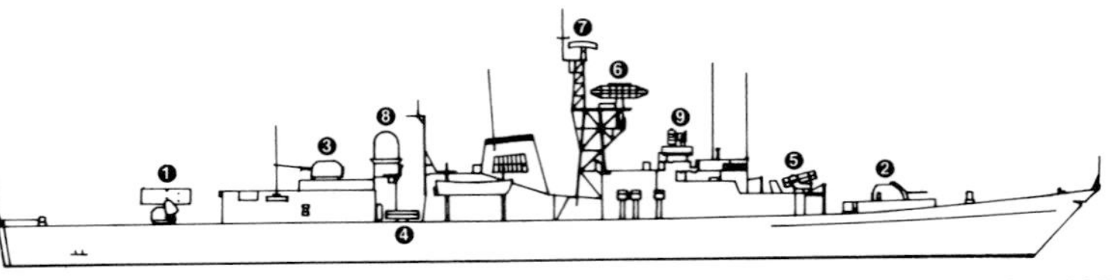
MURAKUMO (Scale 1 : 1 200), *Ian Sturton*

Fire control: Japanese Type 2 for guns.
Radars: Air search: Melco OPS 11 ❻.
Surface search: JRC OPS 17 ❼; G/H band.
Fire control: Type 2-12B ❽; I/J band.
Western Electric SPG 34 (DD 118 only).
Type 1A FCS ❾.
IFF: US Mk 10.
Sonars: Nec OQS 3; hull-mounted; active/passive; low frequency.
EDO SQS 36(J) (DD 118); VDS; active/passive search; medium frequency.

Programmes: As completed the three Minegumo class had the same basic characteristics as the early Yamagumo.
Modernisation: ASROC replaced the Dash ASW helicopter. In 1978 DD 118 was rearmed with an OTO Melara 76 mm replacing one USN Mk 33 mounting.

NATSUGUMO *7/1991, Hachiro Nakai*

1 AMATSUKAZE CLASS

Name	*No*	*Builders*	*Laid down*	*Launched*	*Commissioned*
AMATSUKAZE	DD 163	Mitsubishi, Nagasaki	29 Nov 1962	5 Oct 1963	15 Feb 1965

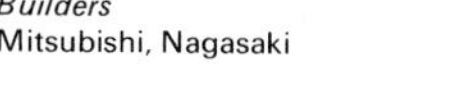

Displacement, tons: 3050 standard; 4000 full load
Dimensions, feet (metres): 429.8 × 44 × 13.8 *(131 × 13.4 × 4.2)*
Main machinery: 2 boilers 540 psi *(38 kg/cm sq)*; 820°F *(438°C)*; 2 Ishikawajima turbines; 60 000 hp(m) *(44 MW)*; 2 shafts
Speed, knots: 33. **Range, miles:** 7000 at 18 kts
Complement: 290

Missiles: SAM: 40 GDC Pomona Standard SM-1MR; Mk 13 Mod 0 launcher ❶; command guidance; semi-active radar homing to 46 km *(25 nm)* at 2 Mach; height envelope 45-18 288 m *(150-60 000 ft)*.
A/S: Honeywell ASROC Mk 112 octuple launcher ❷; inertial guidance to 1.6-10 km *(1-5.4 nm)* at 0.9 Mach; payload Mk 46 Mod 5 Neartip.
Guns: 4 USN 3 in *(76 mm)*/50 Mk 33 (2 twin) ❸; 85° elevation; 50 rounds/minute to 12.8 km *(6.9 nm)*; weight of shell 6 kg. To be replaced by OTO Melara 76 mm. Vulcan Phalanx CIWS to be fitted.
Torpedoes: 6—324 mm Type 68 (2 triple) tubes ❹. Honeywell Mk 46 Mod 5 Neartip; anti-submarine; active/passive homing to 11 km *(5.9 nm)* at 40 kts; warhead 44 kg.
A/S mortars: 2 USN Hedgehog Mk 15 trainable rocket launchers; manually loaded; range 350 m; warhead 26 kg.
Countermeasures: ESM: Nec NOLR 6; intercept.
ECM: Fujitsu OLT 3; jammer.
Fire control: Japanese Type 2-21 system for 76 mm guns.
Radars: Air search: Hughes SPS 39 ❺; 3D; E/F band.
Westinghouse SPS 29A ❻; B/C band; range 457 km *(250 nm)*.
Surface search: JRC OPS 17 ❼; G/H band.
Fire control: Two Raytheon SPG 51C ❽; G/I band (for Standard).
SPG 34 Mod 16 ❾; I/J band.
Sonars: Sangamo SQS 23G; hull-mounted; active search and attack; low frequency.

Programmes: Ordered under the 1960 programme.
Modernisation: Refitted in 1967 when A/S tubes and new sonar were fitted. In 1968 equipped with ASROC launcher between funnels. Further planned modernisation (life extension programme) to include OTO Melara 76 mm guns and Phalanx CIWS may have been cancelled and it is reported that the ship will pay off in 1993.

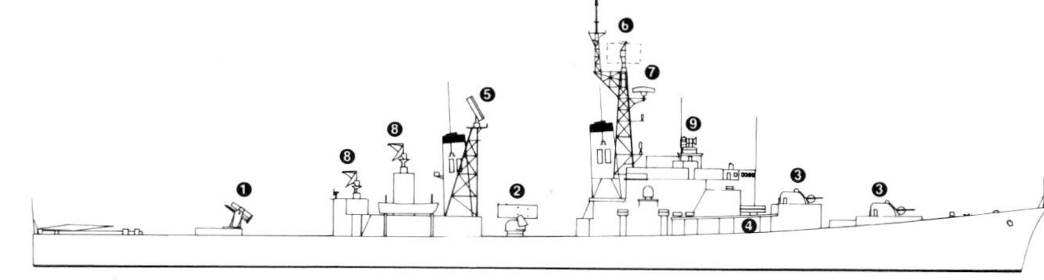

AMATSUKAZE *(Scale 1 : 1 200), Ian Sturton*

AMATSUKAZE *11/1989, Hachiro Nakai*

FRIGATES

4 + 2 ABUKUMA CLASS

Name	*No*	*Builders*	*Laid down*	*Launched*	*Commissioned*
ABUKUMA	DE 229	Mitsui, Tamano	17 Mar 1988	21 Dec 1988	12 Dec 1989
JINTSU	DE 230	Hitachi, Maizuru	14 Apr 1988	31 Jan 1989	28 Feb 1990
OHYODO	DE 231	Mitsui, Tamano	8 Mar 1989	19 Dec 1989	23 Jan 1991
SENDAI	DE 232	Sumitomo, Uraga	14 Apr 1989	26 Jan 1990	15 Mar 1991
CHIKUMA	DE 233	Hitachi, Kobe	14 Feb 1991	22 Jan 1992	Mar 1993
TONE	DE 234	Sumitomo, Uraga	8 Feb 1991	6 Dec 1991	Feb 1993

Displacement, tons: 2050 standard; 2550 full load
Dimensions, feet (metres): 357.6 × 44 × 12.5 *(109 × 13.4 × 3.8)*
Main machinery: CODOG; 2 RR Spey SM1A gas turbines; 29 500 hp *(22 MW)* sustained; 2 Mitsubishi S 12 U-MTK diesels; 6000 hp(m) *(4.4 MW)*; 2 shafts
Speed, knots: 27
Complement: 115

Missiles: SSM: 8 McDonnell Douglas Harpoon (2 quad) launchers ❶; active radar homing to 130 km *(70 nm)* at 0.9 Mach; warhead 227 kg.
A/S: Honeywell ASROC Mk 112 octuple launcher ❷; inertial guidance to 1.6-10 km *(1-5.4 nm)* at 0.9 Mach; payload Mk 46 Mod 5 Neartip.
Guns: 1 OTO Melara 3 in *(76 mm)*/62 compact ❸; 85° elevation; 85 rounds/minute to 16 km *(8.6 nm)* anti-surface; 12 km *(6.5 nm)* anti-aircraft; weight of shell 6 kg.
1 General Electric/General Dynamics 20 mm Phalanx CIWS Mk 15 ❹; 6 barrels per mounting; 3000 rounds/minute combined to 1.5 km.
Torpedoes: 6—324 mm Type 68 (2 triple) tubes ❺. Honeywell Mk 46 Mod 5 Neartip; anti-submarine; active/passive homing to 11 km *(5.9 nm)* at 40 kts; warhead 44 kg.
Countermeasures: Decoys: 2 Loral Hycor SRBOC 6-barrelled Mk 36 Chaff launchers.
ESM: Nec NOLQ-6C; intercept.
ECM: Fujitsu OLT-3; jammer.
Combat data systems: OYQ action data automation.
Fire control: Type 2-21; GFCS.
Radars: Air search: Melco OPS 14C ❻.
Surface search: JRC OPS 28 ❼; G/H band.
Fire control: Mk 2-21 ❽.
Sonars: Hitachi OQS-8 (DE 1167); hull-mounted; active search and attack; medium frequency.
SQR 19A towed passive array in due course.

Programmes: First pair of this class approved in 1986 estimates, ordered March 1987; second pair in 1987 estimates, ordered February 1988; last two in 1989 estimates, ordered 24 January 1989. The name of the first of class was last used for a light cruiser which was sunk in the battle of Leyte Gulf in October 1944.
Structure: Stealth features include non-vertical and rounded surfaces. German RAM PDMS may be fitted later and space has been left for a towed sonar array.

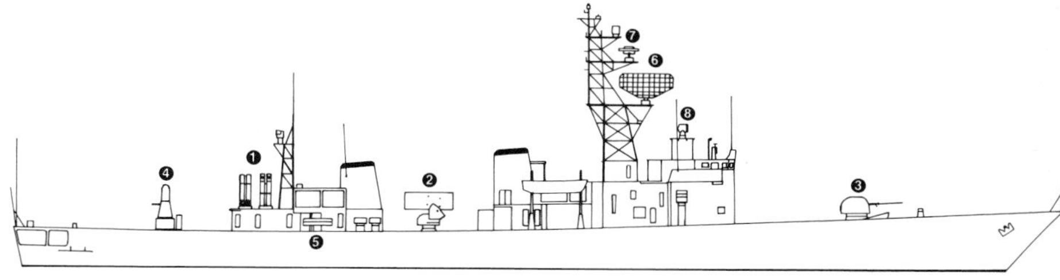

ABUKUMA *(Scale 1 : 900), Ian Sturton*

OHYODO *9/1991, Hachiro Nakai*

2 YUBARI CLASS

Name	*No*	*Builders*	*Laid down*	*Launched*	*Commissioned*
YUBARI	DE 227	Sumitomo, Uraga	9 Feb 1981	22 Feb 1982	18 Mar 1983
YUBETSU	DE 228	Hitachi, Maizuru	14 Jan 1982	25 Jan 1983	14 Feb 1984

Displacement, tons: 1470 standard; 1690 full load
Dimensions, feet (metres): 298.5 × 35.4 × 11.8 *(91 × 10.8 × 3.6)*
Main machinery: CODOG; 1 Kawasaki/RR Olympus TM3B gas turbine; 21 500 hp *(16 MW)* sustained; 1 Mitsubishi/MAN 6DRV diesel; 4700 hp(m) *(3.45 MW)*; 2 shafts; cp props
Speed, knots: 25
Complement: 95

Missiles: SSM: 8 McDonnell Douglas Harpoon (2 quad) launchers ❶; active radar homing to 130 km *(70 nm)* at 0.9 Mach; warhead 227 kg.
Guns: 1 OTO Melara 3 in *(76 mm)*/62 compact ❷; 85° elevation; 85 rounds/minute to 16 km *(8.6 nm)* anti-surface; 12 km *(6.5 nm)* anti-aircraft; weight of shell 6 kg.
1 General Electric/General Dynamics 20 mm Phalanx CIWS Mk 15 (not yet fitted) ❸; 6 barrels per mounting; 3000 rounds/minute combined to 1.5 km.
Torpedoes: 6—324 mm Type 68 (2 triple) tubes ❹. Honeywell Mk 46 Mod 5 Neartip; anti-submarine; active/passive homing to 11 km *(5.9 nm)* at 40 kts; warhead 44 kg.
A/S mortars: 1—375 mm Bofors Type 71 4-6-barrelled trainable rocket launcher ❺; automatic loading; range 1.6 km.
Countermeasures: Decoys: 2 Loral Hycor SRBOC 6-barrelled Mk 36 Chaff launchers ❻; range 4 km *(2.2 nm)*.
ESM: Nec NOLQ 6C ❼; intercept.
ECM: Fujitsu OLT 3; jammer.
Combat data systems: OYQ action data automation.
Fire control: Type 2-21 system for 76 mm guns.
Radars: Surface search: JRC OPS 28C ❽; G/H band.
Navigation: Fujitsu OPS 19B; I band.
Fire control: Type 2-21 ❾; I/J band.
Sonars: Nec SQS 36J; hull-mounted; active/passive; medium frequency.

Programmes: The *Yubari* design is based on experience with *Ishikari* (DE 226).

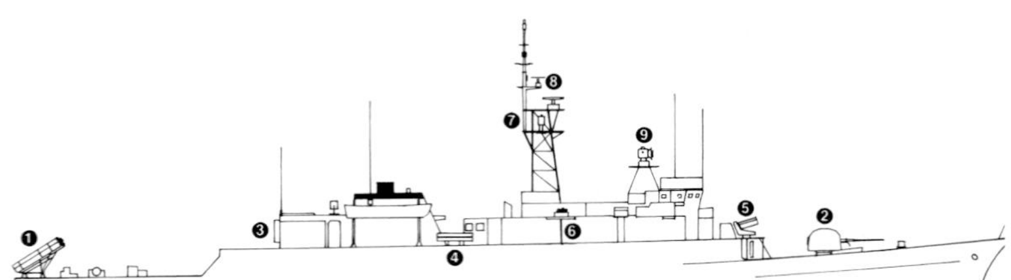
YUBARI *(Scale 1 : 900), Ian Sturton*

YUBARI (Phalanx not fitted) *11/1989, W. Donko*

Structure: The increased space for the same weapons systems as *Ishikari* has meant improved accommodation and an increase in fuel oil carried.

11 CHIKUGO CLASS

Name	*No*	*Builders*	*Laid down*	*Launched*	*Commissioned*
CHIKUGO	DE 215	Mitsui, Tamano	9 Dec 1968	13 Jan 1970	31 July 1970
AYASE	DE 216	Ishikawajima Harima	5 Dec 1969	16 Sep 1970	20 May 1971
MIKUMA	DE 217	Mitsui, Tamano	17 Mar 1970	16 Feb 1971	26 Aug 1971
TOKACHI	DE 218	Mitsui, Tamano	11 Dec 1970	25 Nov 1971	17 May 1972
IWASE	DE 219	Mitsui, Tamano	6 Aug 1971	29 June 1972	12 Dec 1972
CHITOSE	DE 220	Hitachi, Maizuru	7 Oct 1971	25 Jan 1973	31 Aug 1973
NIYODO	DE 221	Mitsui, Tamano	20 Sep 1972	28 Aug 1973	8 Feb 1974
TESHIO	DE 222	Hitachi, Maizuru	11 July 1973	29 May 1974	10 Jan 1975
YOSHINO	DE 223	Mitsui, Tamano	28 Sep 1973	22 Aug 1974	6 Feb 1975
KUMANO	DE 224	Hitachi, Maizuru	29 May 1974	24 Feb 1975	19 Nov 1975
NOSHIRO	DE 225	Mitsui, Tamano	27 Jan 1976	23 Dec 1976	30 June 1977

Displacement, tons: 1470 (DE 215, 217-219 and 221); 1480 (DE 216, 220); 1500 (DE 222 onwards) standard
Dimensions, feet (metres): 305 × 35.5 × 11.5 *(93 × 10.8 × 3.5)*
Main machinery: 4 Mitsubishi-Burmeister & Wain UEV 30/40 diesels; 16 000 hp(m) *(11.8 MW)* (Mitsui ships)
4 Matsui 228 V 3BU-38V diesels; 16 000 hp(m) *(11.8 MW)* (Hitachi ships); 2 shafts
Speed, knots: 25. **Range, miles:** 10 900 at 12 kts
Complement: 160 (12 officers)

Missiles: A/S: Honeywell ASROC Mk 112 octuple launcher ❶; inertial guidance to 1.6-10 km *(1-5.4 nm)* at 0.9 Mach; payload Mk 46 Mod 5 Neartip.
Guns: 2 USN 3 in *(76 mm)*/50 Mk 33 (twin) ❷; 85° elevation; 50 rounds/minute to 12.8 km *(6.9 nm)*; weight of shell 6 kg.
2 Bofors 40 mm/60 Mk 1 (twin) ❸; 80° elevation; 120 rounds/minute to 10 km *(5.4 nm)* anti-surface; 3 km *(1.6 nm)* anti-aircraft; weight of shell 0.89 kg.
Torpedoes: 6—324 mm Type 68 (2 triple) tubes ❹. Honeywell Mk 46 Mod 5 Neartip; anti-submarine; active/passive homing to 11 km *(5.9 nm)* at 40 kts; warhead 44 kg.

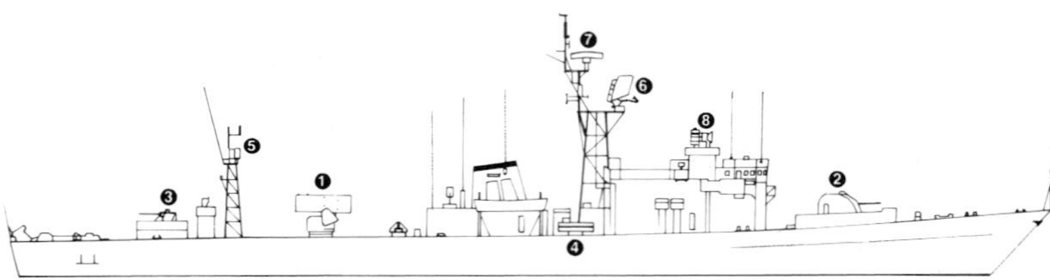
TESHIO *(Scale 1 : 900), Ian Sturton*

Countermeasures: ESM: Nec NORL 5 ❺; intercept.
Fire control: GFCS-1 for 76 mm gun. Mk 51 GFCS for 40 mm gun.
Radars: Air search: Melco OPS 14 ❻.
Surface search: JRC OPS 16 ❼; D band.
Fire control: Type 1B ❽; I/J band.
IFF: US Mk 10.

Sonars: Hitachi OQS 3A; hull-mounted; active search and attack; medium frequency.
EDO SPS 35(J) (in last five ships only); VDS; active/passive search; medium frequency.

Structure: These are the smallest warships in the world to mount ASROC.

NIYODO *7/1991, Hachiro Nakai*

1 ISHIKARI CLASS

Name	*No*	*Builders*	*Laid down*	*Launched*	*Commissioned*
ISHIKARI	DE 226	Mitsui, Tamano	17 May 1979	18 Mar 1980	28 Mar 1981

Displacement, tons: 1290 standard; 1450 full load
Dimensions, feet (metres): 278.8 × 34.7 × 11.5 *(85 × 10.6 × 3.5)*
Main machinery: CODOG; 1 Kawasaki/RR Olympus TM3B gas turbine; 21 500 hp *(16 MW)*; 1 Mitsubishi/MAN 6DRV diesel; 4700 hp(m) *(3.45 MW)*; 2 shafts; cp props
Speed, knots: 25
Complement: 90

Missiles: SSM: 8 McDonnell Douglas Harpoon (2 quad) launchers ❶; active radar homing to 130 km *(70 nm)* at 0.9 Mach; warhead 227 kg.
Guns: 1 OTO Melara 3 in *(76 mm)*/62 compact ❷; 85° elevation; 85 rounds/minute to 16 km *(8.6 nm)* anti-surface; 12 km *(6.5 nm)* anti-aircraft; weight of shell 6 kg.
Torpedoes: 6—324 mm Type 68 (2 triple) tubes ❸. Honeywell Mk 46 Mod 5 Neartip; anti-submarine; active/passive homing to 11 km *(5.9 nm)* at 40 kts; warhead 44 kg.
A/S mortars: 1—375 mm Bofors Type 71 4-barrelled trainable rocket launcher ❹; automatic loading; range 1.6 km.
Countermeasures: Decoys: 1 Loral Hycor SRBOC 6-barrelled Mk 36 Chaff launcher ❺; range 4 km *(2.2 nm)*.
ESM: Nec NOLQ 6C ❻; intercept.
ECM: Fujitsu OLT 2; jammer.
Fire control: Type 2-21 system for 76 mm gun.
Radars: Surface search: JRC OPS 28 ❼; G/H band.
Navigation: Fujitsu OPS 19B; I band.
Fire control: Type 2-21 FCS ❽; I/J band.
Sonars: Nec SQS 36D(J); hull-mounted; active/passive; low frequency.

Programmes: The Japanese had not constructed a frigate since the Chikugo class, which was designed in the mid-1960s. The development of so many new systems since that time probably dictated the need for a prototype.
Modernisation: To be fitted with Vulcan Phalanx when available.

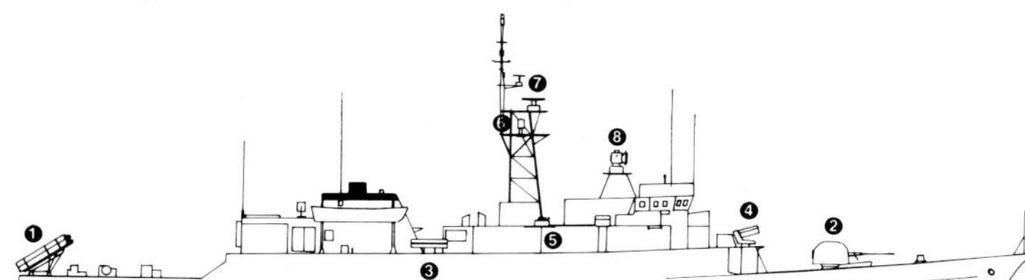
ISHIKARI *(Scale 1 : 900), Ian Sturton*

ISHIKARI *11/1987, Hachiro Nakai*

SHIPBORNE AIRCRAFT

Numbers/Type: 71 Mitsubishi SH-3A (HSS-2B) Sea King.
Operational speed: 120 kts *(222 km/h)*.
Service ceiling: 12 200 ft *(3720 m)*.
Range: 630 nm *(1165 km)*.
Role/Weapon systems: Shipborne ASW helicopter and surface search. Production completed in 1990. Sensors: Search radar, ESM ALR 66(V)1, Bendix AQS-13 dipping sonar. Weapons: ASW; 4 × Mk 46 torpedoes or depth bombs.

SEA KING (Yamayuki) *1991, 92 Wing RAAF*

Numbers/Type: 14 Sikorsky/Mitsubishi SH-60J Seahawk.
Operational speed: 135 kts *(250 km/h)*.
Service ceiling: 12 500 ft *(3810 m)*.
Range: 600 nm *(1110 km)*.
Role/Weapon systems: ASW and ASV helicopter; selected to replace SH-3A/HSS-2 from July 1991; being built in Japan; prototypes fitted by Mitsubishi with Japanese avionics and mission equipment. Total of 41 authorised by the end of 1991. Plans include up to 100 plus 18 UH-60J for SAR. Sensors: Search radar; sonobuoys plus datalink; Bendix AQS 18/Nippon HQS 103 dipping sonar, ECM, HLR 108 ESM. Weapons: ASW; 2 × Mk 46 torpedoes or depth bombs. ASV; possible missile armament.

SEAHAWK *1989, Ships of the World*

LAND-BASED MARITIME AIRCRAFT (FRONT LINE)

Numbers/Type: 78/2 Kawasaki P-3C/EP3B Update II Orion.
Operational speed: 410 kts *(760 km/h)*.
Service ceiling: 28 300 ft *(8625 m)*.
Range: 4000 nm *(7410 km)*.
Role/Weapon systems: Long-range MR/ASW and surface surveillance and attack to supplement and replace P-2Js; four EW version EP-3 being acquired. The aim is a total of 91 by 1993. Sensors: APS-115 radar, ASQ-81 MAD, AQA 7 processor, AQS-114 computer, IFF, ECM, ALQ 78, ESM, ALR 66, sonobuoys. Weapons: ASW; 8 × Mk 46 torpedoes, depth bombs or mines, 10 underwing stations for Harpoon and other systems.

ORION *4/1990, Hachiro Nakai*

Numbers/Type: 6 Kawasaki P-2J.
Operational speed: 217 kts *(402 km/h)*.
Service ceiling: 30 000 ft *(9150 m)*.
Range: 2400 nm *(4450 km)*.
Role/Weapon systems: Long-range MR/ASW being phased out. Only one squadron left in mid-1991. Sensors: APS-80 search radar, ESM, ALQ 101, MAD, smoke detector, Tacan and sonobuoy processor, EW, some aircraft equipped for Elint. Weapons: ASW; Mk 46 torpedoes, depth bombs or mines.

Numbers/Type: 7 Shin Meiwa US-1A.
Operational speed: 295 kts *(546 km/h)*.
Service ceiling: 29 500 ft *(9000 m)*.
Range: 2060 nm *(3817 km)*.
Role/Weapon systems: Long-range patrol and SAR amphibian aircraft. Sensors: Search radar, MAD, sonobuoys, ECM. Weapons: ASW; Mk 46 torpedoes, depth bombs, mines, life rafts and flares.

Numbers/Type: 7 Sikorsky/Mitsubishi S-80M-1 Sea Dragon (MH53E).
Operational speed: 170 kts *(315 km/h)*.
Service ceiling: 18 500 ft *(5640 m)*.
Range: 1120 nm *(2000 km)*.
Role/Weapon systems: Improved, three-engined AMCM helicopter with mechanical, magnetic and acoustic sweep equipment; self-deployed if necessary. 11 authorised by the end of 1991 with one more to come. Sensors: None. Weapons: 2 × 12.7 mm guns for self-defence.

LIGHT FORCES

0 + 2 + 1 (3) ITALIAN SPARVIERO TYPE (PG) (FAST ATTACK HYDROFOIL—MISSILE)

Name	*No*	*Builders*	*Commissioned*
PG 21	821	Sumitomo, Uraga	Mar 1993
PG 22	822	Sumitomo, Uraga	Mar 1993

Displacement, tons: 50 standard
Dimensions, feet (metres): 75.4 × 22.9 × 5.6 *(23 × 7 × 1.7)* (hull)
80.7 × 23.1 × 14.4 *(24.6 × 7 × 4.4)* (foilborne)
Main machinery: 1 GE/IHI LM 500 gas turbine; 4020 hp *(2.95 MW)* 1 pumpjet (foilborne); 1 diesel; 1 retractable prop (hullborne)
Speed, knots: 40+; 8 (diesel). **Range, miles:** 400 at 45 kts; 1200 at 8 kts
Complement: 10 (2 officers)
Missiles: SSM: 4 Mitsubishi SSM-1B ❶ (derivative of land-based system); range 150 km *(81 nm)*.
Guns: 1 GE 20 mm/76 Sea Vulcan ❷; 3 barrels per mounting; 55° elevation; 1500 rounds/minute combined to 4 km *(2.2 nm)*.
Countermeasures: Decoys: 2 Loral Hycor Mk 36 SRBOC Chaff launchers ❸.
ESM/ECM: intercept and jammer.
Combat data systems: Link 11.
Radars: Surface search ❹; I band.

Comment: First two approved in FY 1990 and both laid down 25 March 1991 and planned to be launched in July 1992. One more approved in FY 1992. Being built with Italian assistance from Fincantieri. Final total expected to be six. Planned to improve the Navy's interceptor capabilities, this is an ambitious choice of vessel bearing in mind the falling popularity of the hydrofoil in the few navies (US, Italy and USSR) that have built them up to now.

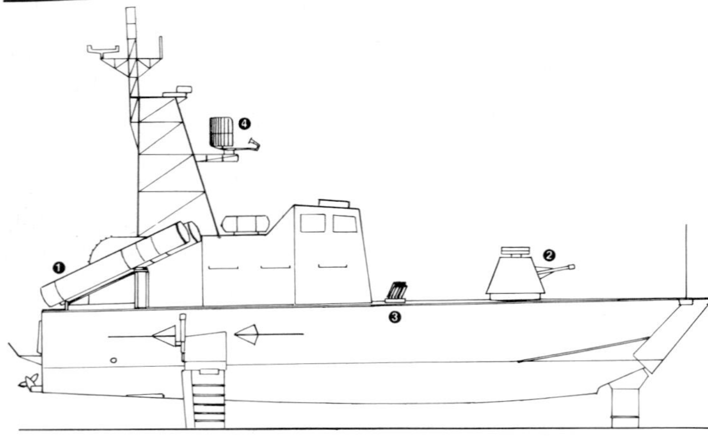

PG 21 *(Not to scale), Ian Sturton*

2 FAST ATTACK CRAFT—TORPEDO

Name	*No*	*Builders*	*Commissioned*
PT 14	PT 814	Mitsubishi, Shimonoseki	15 Feb 1974
PT 15	PT 815	Mitsubishi, Shimonoseki	10 July 1975

Displacement, tons: 100 standard; 125 full load
Dimensions, feet (metres): 114.8 × 30.2 × 3.9 *(35 × 9.2 × 1.2)*
Main machinery: CODAG; 2 IHI IM-300 gas turbines; 11 000 hp(m) *(8.08 MW)*; 2 Mitsubishi 24 WZ-31MC diesels; 3 shafts
Speed, knots: 40. **Range, miles:** 1000 at 18 kts; 300 at 40 kts
Complement: 26-28
Guns: 2 Bofors 40 mm/70 Mk 3; 90° elevation; 300 rounds/minute to 12 km *(6.5 nm)* anti-surface; 4 km *(2.2 nm)* anti-aircraft; weight of shell 0.96 kg.
Torpedoes: 4—21 in *(533 mm)* tubes; anti-surface.
Radars: Surface search: Fujitsu OPS 19; G/H band.

Comment: Deployed to Yoichi, Hokkaido.

PT 14 *10/1991, Hachiro Nakai*

9 COASTAL PATROL CRAFT

Name	*No*	*Builders*	*Commissioned*
PB 19	PB 919	Ishikawajima, Yokohama	31 Mar 1971
PB 20	PB 920	Ishikawajima, Yokohama	31 Mar 1971
PB 21	PB 921	Ishikawajima, Yokohama	31 Mar 1971
PB 22	PB 922	Ishikawajima, Yokohama	31 Mar 1971
PB 23	PB 923	Ishikawajima, Yokohama	31 Mar 1972
PB 24	PB 924	Ishikawajima, Yokohama	31 Mar 1972
PB 25	PB 925	Ishikawajima, Yokohama	29 Mar 1973
PB 26	PB 926	Ishikawajima, Yokohama	29 Mar 1973
PB 27	PB 927	Ishikawajima, Yokohama	29 Mar 1973

Displacement, tons: 18 standard
Dimensions, feet (metres): 55.8 × 14.1 × 2.3 *(17 × 4.3 × 0.7)*
Main machinery: 2 Isuzu V170T diesels; 760 hp(m) *(560 kW)*; 2 shafts
Speed, knots: 20. **Range, miles:** 400 at 20 kts
Complement: 6
Guns: 1 USN 20 mm/80 Mk 10; 55° elevation; 800 rounds/minute to 2 km; weight of shell 0.24 kg.
Radars: Navigation: Koden OPS 29.

Comment: GRP hulls. Some of the class have a 12.7 mm MG instead of the 20 mm gun.

PB 24 *8/1989, Hachiro Nakai*

AMPHIBIOUS FORCES

Note: A 5500 ton LSD was requested but not approved in the 1989 or 1990 estimates. The published design resembled the Italian San Giorgio with a large flight deck and a stern dock. Clearly a candidate for operating Sea Harriers perhaps as an interim step towards building an aircraft carrier. No request in FY 1991 or 1992 but the five-year construction plan (1991-95) now includes an 8500 ton LST.

3 MIURA CLASS (LSTs)

Name	*No*	*Builders*	*Commissioned*
MIURA	LST 4151	Ishikawajima Harima, Tokyo	29 Jan 1975
OJIKA	LST 4152	Ishikawajima Harima, Tokyo	22 Mar 1976
SATSUMA	LST 4153	Ishikawajima Harima, Tokyo	17 Feb 1977

Displacement, tons: 2000 standard
Dimensions, feet (metres): 321.4 × 45.9 × 9.8 *(98 × 14 × 3)*
Main machinery: 2 Kawasaki-MAN V8V 22/30 ATL diesels; 4400 hp(m) *(3.23 MW)*; 2 shafts
Speed, knots: 14
Complement: 115
Military lift: 200 troops; 2 LCMs; 2 LCVPs; 10 Type 74 main battle tanks
Guns: 2 USN 3 in *(76 mm)*/50 Mk 33 (twin); 85° elevation; 50 rounds/minute to 12.8 km *(6.9 nm)*; weight of shell 6 kg.
2 Bofors 40 mm/70 (twin) (LST 4151-4152); 90° elevation; 300 rounds/minute to 12 km *(6.5 nm)* anti-surface; 4 km *(2.2 nm)* anti-aircraft; weight of shell 0.96 kg.
Fire control: Type 72-1B for 76 mm guns *(Miura)*; US Mk 63 for 76 mm guns (remainder). US Mk 51 for 40 mm guns.
Radars: Air search: Melco OPS 14.
Surface search: JRC OPS 16 *(Miura)*; JRS OPS 18 (remainder); D/G/H band.

Comment: Reported to be used primarily for logistic support.

OJIKA *9/1990, Hachiro Nakai*

3 ATSUMI CLASS (LSTs)

Name	*No*	*Builders*	*Commissioned*
ATSUMI	LST 4101	Sasebo Heavy Industries	27 Nov 1972
MOTOBU	LST 4102	Sasebo Heavy Industries	21 Dec 1973
NEMURO	LST 4103	Sasebo Heavy Industries	27 Oct 1977

Displacement, tons: 1480 (LST 4101), 1550 (LST 4102-4103) standard
Dimensions, feet (metres): 291.9 × 42.6 × 8.9 *(89 × 13 × 2.7)*
Main machinery: 2 Kawasaki-MAN V8V 22/30 ATL diesels; 4400 hp(m) *(3.23 MW)*; 2 shafts
Speed, knots: 13 (LST 4102-4103); 14 (LST 4101). **Range, miles:** 9000 at 12 kts
Complement: 100 (LST 4101); 95 (LST 4102-4103)
Military lift: 130 troops; 400 tons cargo including 5 Type 74 tanks; 2 LCVPs
Guns: 4 Bofors 40 mm/70 Mk 1 (2 twin); 90° elevation; 300 rounds/minute to 12 km *(6.5 nm)*; weight of shell 0.96 kg.
Fire control: 2 US Mk 51 for 40 mm guns.
Radars: Navigation: Fujitsu OPS 9; I band.

Comment: *Nemuro* has an electric crane at the after end of the cargo deck.

MOTOBU *9/1991, Hachiro Nakai*

2 YURA CLASS (LSU)

Name	*No*	*Builders*	*Commissioned*
YURA	4171	Sasebo Heavy Industries	27 Mar 1981
NOTO	4172	Sasebo Heavy Industries	27 Mar 1981

Displacement, tons: 590 standard
Dimensions, feet (metres): 190.2 × 31.2 × 5.6 *(58 × 9.5 × 1.7)*
Main machinery: 2 Fuji 6L-27.5XF diesels; 3000 hp(m) *(2.21 MW)*; 2 shafts; 2 cp props
Speed, knots: 12
Complement: 30
Military lift: 70 troops
Guns: 1 GE 20 mm/76 Sea Vulcan 20; 3 barrels per mounting; 55° elevation; 1500 rounds/minute combined to 4 km *(2.2 nm)*.

Comment: Both laid down 23 April 1980. LST 4171 launched 15 October 1980 and LST 4172 on 12 November 1980.

YURA *8/1989, Hachiro Nakai*

2 YUSOTEI CLASS (LCU)

Name	*No*	*Builders*	*Commissioned*
YUSOTEI-ICHI-GO	2001	Sasebo Heavy Industries	17 Mar 1988
YUSOTEI-NI-GO	2002	Sasebo Heavy Industries	Mar 1992

Displacement, tons: 420 standard
Dimensions, feet (metres): 170.6 × 28.5 × 5.2 *(52 × 8.7 × 1.6)*
Main machinery: 2 S16-MTK Mitsubishi diesels; 3040 hp(m) *(3.23 MW)*; 2 shafts
Speed, knots: 12
Complement: 28
Guns: 1 GE 20 mm/76 Sea Vulcan; 3 barrels per mounting; 1500 rounds/minute combined to 4 km *(2.2 nm)*.

Comment: First approved in 1986 estimates, laid down 11 May 1987, launched 9 October 1987. Second approved in FY 1990 estimates, laid down 15 May 1991, launched 7 October 1991; plans for a third have been scrapped.

YUSOTEI-ICHI-GO *8/1989, Hachiro Nakai*

9 + 1 LCM TYPE

YF 2075 **2097-98** **2121** **2124-25** **2127-29**

Displacement, tons: 25 standard
Dimensions, feet (metres): 56.2 × 14 × 3.9 *(17.1 × 4.3 × 1.2)*
Main machinery: 2 Isuzu E120-MF6R diesels; 480 hp(m) *(353 kW)*; 2 shafts
Speed, knots: 10. **Range, miles:** 130 at 9 kts
Complement: 3
Military lift: 34 tons or 80 troops

Comment: Built in Japan. These are in addition to the six LCMs carried in the Miura class which do not have pennant numbers.

YF 2125 *10/1991, Hachiro Nakai*

21 LCVP TYPE

YF 2066-74 **2078-81** **2083-87** **2091** **2110** **2116**

Displacement, tons: 12 full load
Dimensions, feet (metres): 35.8 × 10.5 × 3.3 *(10.9 × 3.2 × 1)*
Main machinery: 1 Yanmar 6CH-DTE diesel; 190 hp(m) *(140 kW)*; 1 shaft
Speed, knots: 9
Complement: 3
Military lift: 40 troops

Comment: Built in Japan with wooden hulls. In addition to these there are 12 more carried in the LSTs which have no pennant numbers.

LCVP *1990, Ships of the World*

MINE WARFARE FORCES

Note: Two 3000 ton new conversion Minesweeper Support Ships are in the 1991-95 ship construction plan.

1 SOUYA CLASS (MINELAYER/SUPPORT SHIP)

Name	*No*	*Builders*	*Commissioned*
SOUYA	MMC 951	Hitachi, Maizuru	30 Sep 1971

Displacement, tons: 2150 standard; 3300 full load
Dimensions, feet (metres): 324.8 × 49.5 × 13.9 *(99 × 15 × 4.2)*
Main machinery: 4 Kawasaki-MAN V6V 22/30 ATL diesels; 6400 hp(m) *(4.7 MW)*; 2 shafts
Speed, knots: 18. **Range, miles:** 7500 at 14 kts
Complement: 185

Guns: 2 USN 3 in *(76 mm)*/50 Mk 33 (twin); 85° elevation; 50 rounds/minute to 12.8 km *(6.9 nm)*; weight of shell 6 kg.
2 GE 20 mm/76 Sea Vulcan; 3 barrels per mounting; 1500 rounds/minute combined to 4 km *(2.2 nm)*.
Torpedoes: 6—324 mm Type 68 (2 triple) tubes. Honeywell Mk 46 Mod 5 Neartip; anti-submarine; active/passive homing to 11 km *(5.9 nm)* at 40 kts; warhead 44 kg.
Mines: 6 internal plus 2 external rails; 460 buoyant.
Fire control: GFCS-1 for 76 mm guns.
Radars: Air search: Melco OPS 14.
Surface search: JRC OPS 16; D band.
IFF: US Mk 10.
Sonars: SQS 11A; hull-mounted; active search and attack; medium frequency.
ZQS 1B; bow-mounted; active search and attack; high frequency.

Helicopters: Platform for one Sea Dragon.

Operational: Dual purpose ship used as minelayer with a minesweeper support capability and acts at times as command ship for MCM forces.

SOUYA *2/1990, Hachiro Nakai*

1 HAYASE CLASS (MINESWEEPER SUPPORT SHIP)

Name	No	Builders	Commissioned
HAYASE	MST 462	Ishikawajima, Harima	6 Nov 1971

Displacement, tons: 2000 standard
Dimensions, feet (metres): 324.8 × 47.6 × 13.8 *(99 × 14.5 × 4.2)*
Main machinery: 2 Kawasaki-MAN V6V 22/30 ATL diesels; 6400 hp(m) *(4.7 MW)*; 2 shafts
Speed, knots: 18
Complement: 180

Guns: 2 USN 3 in *(76 mm)*/50 Mk 33 (twin); 85° elevation; 50 rounds/minute to 12.8 km *(6.9 nm)*; weight of shell 6 kg.
2 GE 20 mm/76 Sea Vulcan; 3 barrels per mounting; 1500 rounds/minute combined to 4 km *(2 nm)*.
Torpedoes: 6—324 mm Type 68 (2 triple) tubes. Honeywell Mk 46 Mod 5 Neartip; anti-submarine; active/passive homing to 11 km *(5.9 nm)* at 40 kts; warhead 44 kg.
Mines: 5 internal rails; 116 buoyant mines.
Fire control: US Mk 63 for 76 mm guns.
Radars: Air search: Melco OPS 14.
Surface search: JRC OPS 16; D band.
Fire control: Western Electric Mk 34; I/J band.
Sonars: SQS 11A; hull-mounted; active search and attack; medium frequency.

Helicopters: Platform for 1 Sea Dragon.

Operational: Flagship of historic Gulf deployment in 1991.

HAYASE (return from Gulf) *10/1991, 92 Wing RAAF*

5 TAKAMI CLASS (MINE HUNTERS/SWEEPERS—COASTAL)

Name	No	Builders	Commissioned
OUMI	MSC 644	Hitachi, Kanagawa	18 Nov 1976
FUKUE	MSC 645	Nippon Steel Tube Co	18 Nov 1976
OKITSU	MSC 646	Hitachi, Kanagawa	20 Sep 1977
HASHIRA	MSC 647	Nippon Steel Tube Co	28 Mar 1978
IWAI	MSC 648	Hitachi, Kanagawa	28 Mar 1978

Displacement, tons: 380 standard; 530 full load
Dimensions, feet (metres): 170.6 × 28.9 × 7.9 *(52 × 8.8 × 2.4)*
Main machinery: 2 Mitsubishi YV12ZC-15/20 diesels; 1440 hp(m) *(1.06 MW)*; 2 shafts
Speed, knots: 14
Complement: 45

Guns: 1 GE 20 mm/76 Sea Vulcan 20; 3 barrels per mounting; 55° elevation; 1500 rounds/minute combined to 4 km *(2.2 nm)*.
Radars: Surface search: Fujitsu OPS 9; I band.
Sonars: Nec/Hitachi ZQS 2 (Type 193M); hull-mounted; minehunting; high frequency.

Programmes: Numbers gradually being reduced (converted to auxiliaries) as Hatsushima class complete.
Operational: Fitted with wire and acoustic minesweeping gear. Also carry four clearance divers.

OKITSU *2/1991, Hachiro Nakai*

25 + 2 + (3) HATSUSHIMA CLASS (MINEHUNTERS/SWEEPERS—COASTAL)

Name	No	Builders	Commissioned
HATSUSHIMA	MSC 649	Nippon Steel Tube Co (Tsurumi)	30 Mar 1979
NINOSHIMA	MSC 650	Hitachi, Kanagawa	19 Dec 1979
MIYAJIMA	MSC 651	Nippon Steel Tube Co (Tsurumi)	29 Jan 1980
ENOSHIMA	MSC 652	Nippon Steel Tube Co (Tsurumi)	25 Dec 1980
UKISHIMA	MSC 653	Hitachi, Kanagawa	27 Nov 1980
OOSHIMA	MSC 654	Hitachi, Kanagawa	26 Nov 1981
NIIJIMA	MSC 655	Nippon Steel Tube Co (Tsurumi)	26 Nov 1981
YAKUSHIMA	MSC 656	Nippon Steel Tube Co (Tsurumi)	17 Dec 1982
NARUSHIMA	MSC 657	Hitachi, Kanagawa	17 Dec 1982
CHICHIJIMA	MSC 658	Hitachi, Kanagawa	16 Dec 1983
TORISHIMA	MSC 659	Nippon Steel Tube Co (Tsurumi)	16 Dec 1983
HAHAJIMA	MSC 660	Nippon Steel Tube Co (Tsurumi)	18 Dec 1984
TAKASHIMA	MSC 661	Hitachi, Kanagawa	18 Dec 1984
NUWAJIMA	MSC 662	Hitachi, Kanagawa	12 Dec 1985
ETAJIMA	MSC 663	Nippon Steel Tube Co (Tsurumi)	12 Dec 1985
KAMISHIMA	MSC 664	Nippon Steel Tube Co (Tsurumi)	16 Dec 1986
HIMESHIMA	MSC 665	Hitachi, Kanagawa	16 Dec 1986
OGISHIMA	MSC 666	Hitachi, Kanagawa	17 Dec 1987
MOROSHIMA	MSC 667	Nippon Steel Tube Co (Tsurumi)	17 Dec 1987
YURISHIMA	MSC 668	Nippon Steel Tube Co (Tsurumi)	15 Dec 1988
HIKOSHIMA	MSC 669	Hitachi, Kanagawa	15 Dec 1988
AWASHIMA	MSC 670	Hitachi, Kanagawa	13 Dec 1989
SAKUSHIMA	MSC 671	Nippon Steel Tube Co (Tsurumi)	13 Dec 1989
UWAJIMA	MSC 672	Nippon Steel Tube Co (Tsurumi)	19 Dec 1990
IESHIMA	MSC 673	Hitachi, Kanagawa	19 Dec 1990
—	MSC 674	Hitachi, Kanagawa	Mar 1993
—	MSC 675	Nippon Steel Tube Co (Tsurumi)	Mar 1994

Displacement, tons: 440 (490, MSC 670 onwards) standard; 510 full load
Dimensions, feet (metres): 180.4 (189.3, MSC 670 onwards) × 30.8 × 7.9 *(55 (57.7) × 9.4 × 2.4)*
Main machinery: 2 Mitsubishi YV122C-15/20 diesels (MSC 649-665); 1440 hp(m) *(1.06 MW)*; 2 Mitsubishi 6NMU-TAI diesels (MSC 666 onwards); 2400 hp(m) *(1.76 MW)*; 2 shafts
Speed, knots: 14
Complement: 45

Guns: 1 GE 20 mm/76 Sea Vulcan 20; 55° elevation; 3 barrels per mounting; 1500 rounds/minute combined to 4 km *(2.2 nm)*.
Radars: Surface search: Fujitsu OPS 9; I band.
Sonars: Nec/Hitachi ZQS 2B or ZQS 3 (MSC 672 onwards); hull-mounted; minehunting; high frequency.

Programmes: First ordered in 1976. MSC 674 laid down 27 May 1991 and to be launched July 1992. MSC 675 laid down May 1992. One more approved in FY 1991 and three in FY 1992.
Structure: From MSC 670 onwards the hull is lengthened by 2.7 m in order to improve the sleeping accommodation from three tier to two tier bunks.
Operational: Fitted with new S4 (S7 from MSC 672 onwards) mine detonating equipment, a remote-controlled counter-mine charge. MSC 668, 669, 670 and 671 formed the Minesweeper Squadron to deploy to the Gulf in 1991.

IESHIMA *5/1991, Hachiro Nakai*

HIKOSHIMA (return from Gulf) *10/1991, 92 Wing RAAF*

0 + 3 + (3) YAEYAMA CLASS (MINEHUNTER/SWEEPER—OCEAN)

Name	*No*	*Builders*	*Commissioned*
YAEYAMA	MSO 301	Hitachi, Kanagawa	Mar 1993
TSUSHIMA	MSO 302	Nippon Steel Tube Co, Tsurumi	Mar 1993
—	MSO 303	Nippon Steel Tube Co, Tsurumi	Mar 1994

Displacement, tons: 1000 approx
Dimensions, feet (metres): 219.8 × 38.7 × 10.2 *(67 × 11.8 × 3.1)*
Main machinery: 2 Mitsubishi 6NMU-TAI diesels; 2400 hp(m) *(1.76 MW)*; 2 shafts
Speed, knots: 14
Complement: 60
Guns: 1 GE 20 mm/76 Sea Vulcan; 3 barrels per mounting; 1500 rounds/minute combined to 4 km *(2.2 nm)*.
Radars: Surface search: Fujitsu OPS 9; I band.
Sonars: Raytheon SQQ 32 (for Hunters); high frequency; active.

Comment: First two approved in 1989 estimates, third in 1990. First laid down 30 August 1990 and launched 29 August 1991; second laid down 20 July 1990 and launched 20 September 1991; third laid down 17 May 1991 and to be launched in September 1992. Wooden hulls. Probable class of six. Fitted with S 7 deep sea minehunting system and S 8 deep sea moored minesweeping equipment.

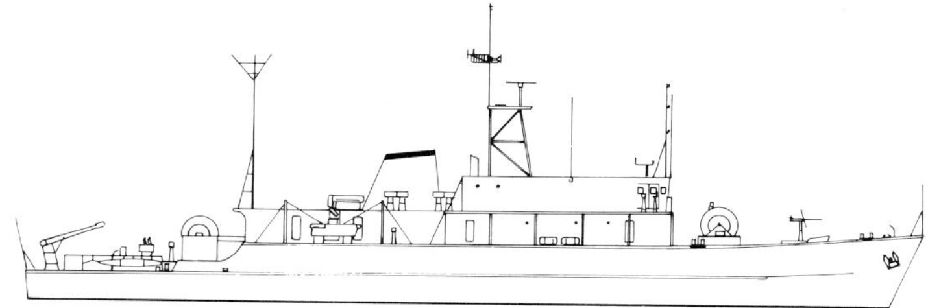

YAEYAMA *(Not to scale), Ian Sturton*

YAEYAMA (artist's impression) *1991, Ships of the World*

4 NANA-GO CLASS (MSBs)

Name	*No*	*Builders*	*Commissioned*
KYUU-GO	709	Nippon Steel Tube Co	28 Mar 1974
JYUU-GO	710	Nippon Steel Tube Co	29 Mar 1974
JYUU-ICHI-GO	711	Hitachi, Kanagawa	10 May 1975
JYUU-NI-GO	712	Nippon Steel Tube Co	22 Apr 1975

Displacement, tons: 58 standard
Dimensions, feet (metres): 73.8 × 17.7 × 3.3 *(22.5 × 5.4 × 1)*
Main machinery: 2 Mitsubishi 4 ZV20M diesels; 480 hp(m) *(353 kW)*; 2 shafts
Speed, knots: 11
Complement: 10
Radars: Navigation: Koden OPS 29D.

Comment: Wooden hulls. *Utone* is the depot ship. Two deleted in March 1992.

JYUU-ICHI-GO *4/1991, Hachiro Nakai*

1 MCM SUPPORT SHIP

Name	*No*	*Builders*	*Commissioned*
UTONE	MST 475 (ex-*MSC 633*)	Hitachi, Kanagawa	3 Sep 1970

Displacement, tons: 380 standard; 530 full load
Dimensions, feet (metres): 170.6 × 28.9 × 7.9 *(52 × 8.8 × 2.4)*
Main machinery: 2 Mitsubishi YV 12ZC-15/20 diesels; 1440 hp(m) *(1.06 MW)* 2 shafts
Speed, knots: 14
Complement: 38
Guns: 1 GE 20 mm/76 Sea Vulcan 20; 55° elevation; 3 barrels per mounting; 1500 rounds/minute combined to 4 km *(2.2 nm)*.
Radars: Surface search: Fujitsu OPS 9.
Sonars: Nec/Hitachi ZQS 2; hull-mounted; minehunting.

Comment: Takami class; minesweeping gear removed and fitted as MCM command ship, recommissioned 16 Dec 1986. Used as tender for Nana-Go class MSBs.

UTONE *5/1987, Hachiro Nakai*

SERVICE FORCES AND AUXILIARIES

2 AKIZUKI CLASS

Name	*No*	*Builders*	*Commissioned*
AKIZUKI	ASU 7010 (ex-DD 161)	Mitsubishi, Nagasaki	13 Feb 1960
TERUZUKI	ASU 7012 (ex-TV 3504) (ex-DD 162)	Shin Mitsubishi, Kobe	29 Feb 1960

Displacement, tons: 2350 standard; 2890 full load
Dimensions, feet (metres): 387.2 × 39.4 × 13.1 *(118 × 12 × 4)*
Main machinery: 4 boilers; 2 Mitsubishi turbines; 45 000 hp(m) *(33 MW)*; 2 shafts
Speed, knots: 32
Complement: 310; 190 (TV 3504)
Guns: 2 or 3 USN 5 in *(127 mm)*/54 Mk 39; 80° elevation; 15 rounds/minute to 22 km *(12 nm)* anti-surface; 13 km *(7 nm)* anti-aircraft; weight of shell 32 kg. Originally mounted in US Midway class.
4 USN 3 in *(76 mm)*/50 Mk 33 (2 twin); 85° elevation; 50 rounds/minute to 12.8 km *(6.9 nm)*; weight of shell 6 kg.
Torpedoes: 6—324 mm Type 68 (2 triple) tubes. Honeywell Mk 46 Mod 5 Neartip; anti-submarine; active/passive homing to 11 km *(5.9 nm)* at 40 kts; warhead 44 kg.
A/S mortars: 1 Bofors 375 mm Type 71 4-barrelled trainable rocket launcher; automatic loading; range 1.6 km.
Fire control: US Mk 63 for 127 mm guns. US Mk 57 for 76 mm guns.
Radars: Air search: Melco OPS 1; G band.
Surface search: JRC OPS 15; D band; range 146 km *(80 nm)*.
Fire control: Western Electric Mk 34; I/J band (for Mk 63 system).
IFF: US Mk 10.
Sonars: Sangamo SQS 23; hull-mounted; active search and attack; medium frequency.
Towed array for trials *(Akizuki)*.

Comment: Built under the 1957 Military Aid Programme as destroyers. *Akizuki* converted to ASU in 1985 and *Teruzuki* 27 Mar 1986. *Teruzuki* transferred to training duties 1 July 1987 and back again to ASU 20 June 1991 as a submarine depot ship. Both have had 21 in torpedo tubes and VDS removed and *Akizuki* had Y gun turret replaced by a trials towed sonar array in 1989.

TERUZUKI *7/1991, Hachiro Nakai*

0 + 1 TRAINING SHIP

Displacement, tons: 4200 standard
Main machinery: 2 gas turbines; 2 shafts
Speed, knots: 27
Complement: 370
Missiles: SSM and SAM.
Guns: 1 OTO Melara 76 mm/62.

Comment: Approved in FY 1991 as a dedicated training ship to replace *Katori* but the project postponed to FY 1992 as a budget saving measure. Probable commissioning date is 1995.

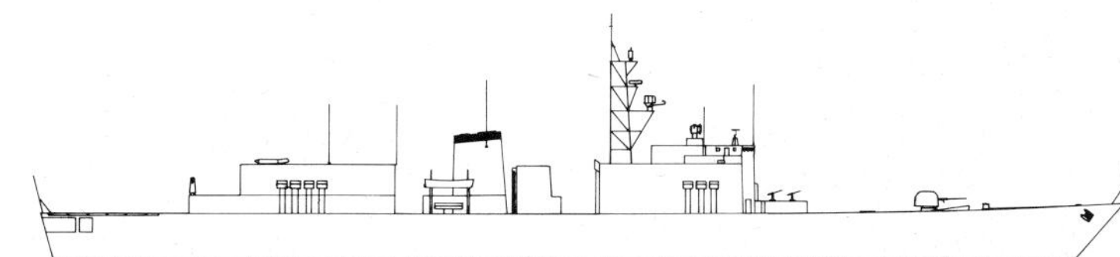

TRAINING SHIP *(Not to scale), Ian Sturton*

2 YAMAGUMO CLASS

Name	*No*	*Builders*	*Commissioned*
YAMAGUMO	TV 3506 (ex-DD 113)	Mitsui, Tamano	29 Jan 1966
MAKIGUMO	TV 3507 (ex-DD 114)	Sumitomo, Uraga	19 Mar 1966

Displacement, tons: 2050 standard
Dimensions, feet (metres): 373.9 × 38.7 × 13.1 *(114 × 11.8 × 4)*
Main machinery: 6 Mitsubishi 12UEV30/40N diesels 21 600 hp(m) *(15.9 MW)* sustained; 2 shafts
Speed, knots: 27. **Range, miles:** 7000 at 20 kts
Complement: 210 (19 officers)
Missiles: A/S: Honeywell ASROC Mk 112 octuple launcher; inertial guidance to 1.6-10 km *(1-5.4 nm)* at 0.9 Mach; payload Mk 46 Mod 5 Neartip.
Guns: 4 USN 3 in *(76 mm)*/50 Mk 33 (2 twin); 85° elevation; 50 rounds/minute to 12.8 km *(6.9 nm)*; weight of shell 6 kg.
Torpedoes: 6—324 mm Type 68 (2 triple) tubes. Honeywell Mk 46 Mod 5 Neartip; anti-submarine; active/passive homing to 11 km *(5.9 nm)* at 40 kts; warhead 44 kg.
A/S mortars: 1 Bofors 375 mm Type 71 4-barrelled trainable rocket launcher; automatic loading; range 1.6 km.
Countermeasures: ESM: Nec NOLR 1B; radar intercept.
Fire control: US Mk 56 or 63 for 76 mm guns.
Radars: Air search: Melco OPS 11.
Surface search: JRC OPS 17; G/H band.
Fire control: Two GE Mk 35; I/J band.
IFF: US Mk 10.
Sonars: Sangamo SQS 23; hull-mounted; active search and attack; low frequency.
EDO SQS 35(J); VDS; active/passive search; medium frequency.

Comment: Converted as training ships on 24 October 1991. Lecture room added under ASROC, chart room on the signal deck and accommodation for 16 women.

MAKIGUMO *10/1991, Hachiro Nakai*

2 ISUZU CLASS

Name	*No*	*Builders*	*Commissioned*
KITAKAMI	ASU 7016 (ex-DE 213)	Ishikawajima Harima, Tokyo	27 Feb 1964
OOI	ASU 7017 (ex-DE 214)	Hitachi, Maizuru	22 Jan 1964

Displacement, tons: 1490 standard; 1788 full load
Dimensions, feet (metres): 308.3 × 34.2 × 11.5 *(94 × 10.4 × 3.5)*
Main machinery: 4 Mitsubishi 12 UEV 30/40 diesels; 14 400 hp(m) *(10.6 MW)* or 4 Mitsui diesels *(Ooi)*; 16 000 hp(m) *(11.76 MW)*; 2 shafts
Speed, knots: 25
Complement: 160
Guns: 4 USN 3 in *(76 mm)*/50 Mk 33 (2 twin); 85° elevation; 50 rounds/minute to 12.8 km *(6.9 nm)*; weight of shell 6 kg.
A/S mortars: 1—375 mm Bofors Type 71 4-barrelled trainable rocket launchers; automatic loading; range 1.6 km.
Depth charges: 1 Y-gun projector*(Ooi)*; 1 rack.
Countermeasures: ESM: BLR-1; intercept.
Fire control: 2 US Mk 63 for 76 mm guns. US Mk 105 for ASW.
Radars: Air search: Melco OPS 1; G band.
Surface search: JRC OPS 16; D band.
Navigation: ORD 1; I band.
Fire control: Two Western Electric Mk 34; I/J band.
IFF: US Mk 10.
Sonars: SQS 29; hull-mounted; active search and attack; medium frequency.

Comment: Both converted 31 January 1990 to training role with lecture hall replacing torpedo tubes and VDS removed.

ISUZU Class (old number) *9/1990, Hachiro Nakai*

1 TRAINING SHIP

Name	*No*	*Builders*	*Commissioned*
KATORI	TV 3501	Ishikawajima Harima, Tokyo	10 Sep 1969

Displacement, tons: 3350 standard
Dimensions, feet (metres): 419.8 × 49.2 × 14.1 *(128 × 15 × 4.3)*
Flight deck, feet (metres): 98.4 × 42.6 *(30 × 13)*
Main machinery: 2 Ishikawajima boilers; 610 psi *(43 kg/cm sq)*; 850°F *(454°C)*; 2 Ishikawajima geared turbines; 20 000 hp(m) *(14.7 MW)*; 2 shafts; 454°C
Speed, knots: 25. **Range, miles:** 7000 at 18 kts
Complement: 463 (165 trainees)
Guns: 4 USN 3 in *(76 mm)*/50 Mk 33 (2 twin); 85° elevation; 50 rounds/minute to 12.8 km *(6.9 nm)*; weight of shell 6 kg.
Torpedoes: 6—324 mm Type 68 (2 triple) tubes. Honeywell Mk 46 Mod 5 Neartip; anti-submarine; active/passive homing to 11 km *(5.9 nm)* at 40 kts; warhead 44 kg.
A/S mortars: 1—375 mm Bofors Type 71 4-barrelled trainable rocket launcher; automatic loading; range 1.6 km.
Countermeasures: ESM: Nec NOLR 1B; radar warning.
Radars: Air search: RCA SPS 12; D band; range 119 km *(65 nm)*.
Air/surface search: JRC OPS 17; D band.
Navigation: JRC OPS 20; I band.
Sonars: Sangamo/General Electric SQS 4; hull-mounted; active; short-range; high frequency.

Comment: Provided with a large auditorium amidships and an open deck space aft which is used as a parade ground. Used for training officers.

KATORI *8/1991, Wright & Logan*

KATORI *5/1990, G. Toremans*

1 AZUMA CLASS (TRAINING SUPPORT SHIP)

Name	*No*	*Builders*	*Commissioned*
AZUMA	ATS 4201	Hitachi, Maizuru	26 Nov 1969

Displacement, tons: 1950 standard
Dimensions, feet (metres): 321.5 × 42.7 × 12.5 *(98 × 13 × 3.8)*
Main machinery: 2 Kawasaki-MAN V8V 22/30 ATL diesels; 4000 hp(m) *(2.94 MW)*; 2 shafts
Speed, knots: 18
Complement: 185
Guns: 1 USN 3 in *(76 mm)*/50; 85° elevation; 50 rounds/minute to 12.8 km *(6.9 nm)*; weight of shell 6 kg.
Torpedoes: 2—483 mm Mk 4 tubes. USN Mk 32; active/passive homing to 8 km *(4.4 nm)* at 12 kts; warhead 49 kg.
Fire control: US Mk 51 Mod 2 for 76 mm gun system.
Radars: Air/Surface search: JRC OPS 16; D band; range 146 km *(80 nm)*.
Lockheed SPS 40; E/F band; range 320 km *(175 nm)*.
Fire control: Target control and tracking system (TCATS) (for drones).
Sonars: SQS 11A; hull-mounted; active search and attack.

Comment: Drone hangar amidships and catapult on flight deck. Can operate towed target. In 1982 target control and tracking system (TCATS) fitted to work with high-speed drones. Carries 10 Northrop KD2R-5 and 4 BQM-34-AJ Chaca II drones. Training support ship for AA gunnery.

AZUMA *7/1986, Hachiro Nakai*

1 KUROBE CLASS (TRAINING SUPPORT SHIP)

Name	*No*	*Builders*	*Commissioned*
KUROBE	ATS 4202	Nippon Steel Tube Co, Tsurumi	23 Mar 1989

Displacement, tons: 2270 standard; 3200 full load
Dimensions, feet (metres): 331.4 × 54.1 × 13.1 *(101 × 16.5 × 4)*
Main machinery: 4 Fuji 8L 27.5XF diesels; 8800 hp(m) *(6.47 MW)*; 2 shafts
Speed, knots: 20
Complement: 156
Guns: 1 FMC/OTO Melara 3 in *(76 mm)*/62 Mk 75; 85° elevation; 85 rounds/minute to 16 km *(8.6 nm)* anti-surface; 12 km *(6.5 nm)* anti-aircraft; weight of shell 6 kg.
Radars: Air search: Melco OPS 14.
Surface search: JRC OPS 18.

Comment: Approved under 1986 estimates, laid down 31 July 1987, launched 23 May 1988. Carries four BQM-34AJ high speed drones and four Northrop Chukar II drones with two stern launchers. Used for training crews in anti-aircraft operations and evaluating the effectiveness and capability of ships' anti-aircraft missile systems.

KUROBE *2/1990, Hachiro Nakai*

6 TAKAMI CLASS (EOD TENDERS)

MIYAKE (ex-*MSC 632*) YAS 84
AWAJI (ex-*MSC 634*) YAS 85
TEURI (ex-*MSC 636*) YAS 87
TASHIRO (ex-*MSC 638*) YAS 89
MIYATO (ex-*MSC 639*) YAS 90
YOKOSE (ex-*MSC 642*) YAS 93

Displacement, tons: 380 standard; 510 full load
Dimensions, feet (metres): 170.6 × 28.9 × 7.9 *(52 × 8.8 × 2.4)*
Main machinery: 2 Mitsubishi YV 122 C-15/20 diesels; 1440 hp(m) *(1.06 MW)*; 2 shafts
Speed, knots: 14
Complement: 43
Guns: 1 Oerlikon 20 mm.

Comment: Transferred after conversion to Explosive Ordnance Disposal (EOD) Unit (Mine Hunting Diver) duties which includes removal of minesweeping gear to provide for divers' room and equipment.

MIYATO *9/1991, Hachiro Nakai*

1 CHIYODA CLASS (SUBMARINE DEPOT AND RESCUE SHIP)

Name	*No*	*Builders*	*Commissioned*
CHIYODA	AS 405	Mitsui, Tamano	27 Mar 1985

Displacement, tons: 3650 standard; 4450 full load
Dimensions, feet (metres): 370.6 × 57.7 × 15.1 *(113 × 17.6 × 4.6)*
Main machinery: 2 Mitsui 8LV2M diesels; 11 500 hp(m) *(8.45 MW)*; 2 shafts; cp props; bow and stern thrusters
Speed, knots: 17
Complement: 120
Helicopters: Platform for up to Sea King size.

Comment: Laid down 19 January 1983, launched 7 December 1983. Carries a Deep Submergence Rescue Vehicle (DSRV), built by Kawasaki Heavy Industries, Kobe, of 40 tons, 40.7 × 10.5 × 14.1 ft *(12.4 × 3.2 × 4.3 m)* with a 30 hp(m) *(22 kW)* electric motor and speed of 4 kts, it has space for 12 people. Based at Yokosuka.

CHIYODA *9/1990, Hachiro Nakai*

1 SUBMARINE RESCUE SHIP

Name	*No*	*Builders*	*Commissioned*
FUSHIMI	ASR 402	Sumitomo, Uraga	10 Feb 1970

Displacement, tons: 1430 standard
Dimensions, feet (metres): 249.5 × 41 × 12.5 *(76 × 12.5 × 3.8)*
Main machinery: 2 Kawasaki-MAN V6V 22/30 ATL diesels; 3200 hp(m) *(2.35 MW)*; 1 shaft
Speed, knots: 16
Complement: 100
Radars: Surface search: Fujitsu OPS 9; I band.
IFF: US Mk 10.
Sonars: SQS 11A; hull-mounted.

Comment: Laid down on 5 November 1968, launched 10 September 1969. Equipped with rescue chamber and two recompression chambers.

FUSHIMI *7/1991, Hachiro Nakai*

3 TOWADA CLASS (FLEET SUPPORT SHIP)

Name	*No*	*Builders*	*Commissioned*
TOWADA	AOE 422	Hitachi, Maizuru	24 Mar 1987
TOKIWA	AOE 423	Ishikawajima, Tokyo	12 Mar 1990
HAMANA	AOE 424	Hitachi, Maizuru	29 Mar 1990

Displacement, tons: 8150 standard; 15 850 full load
Dimensions, feet (metres): 547.8 × 72.2 × 26.9 *(167 × 22 × 8.2)*
Main machinery: 2 Mitsui 16V 42MA diesels; 26 000 hp(m) *(19.1 MW)*; 2 shafts
Speed, knots: 22
Complement: 140
Cargo capacity: 5700 tons
Radars: Surface search: JRC OPS 18; I band.
Helicopters: Platform for 1 Sea King size.

Comment: First approved under 1984 estimates, laid down 17 April 1985, launched 25 March 1986. Second and third of class in 1987 estimates. AOE 423 laid down 12 May 1988, launched 23 March 1989. AOE 424 laid down 8 July 1988, launched 18 May 1989. Two replenishment at sea positions on each side (one fuel only, one fuel or stores).

TOKIWA (return from Gulf) *10/1991, 92 Wing RAAF*

1 FLEET SUPPORT SHIP

Name	*No*	*Builders*	*Commissioned*
SAGAMI	AOE 421	Hitachi, Maizuru	30 Mar 1979

Displacement, tons: 5000 standard; 11 600 full load
Dimensions, feet (metres): 478.9 × 62.3 × 24 *(146 × 19 × 7.3)*
Main machinery: 2 Type 12 DRV diesels; 18 000 hp(m) *(13.23 MW)*; 2 shafts
Speed, knots: 22. **Range, miles:** 9500 at 18 kts
Complement: 130
Cargo capacity: 5000 tons
Radars: Surface search: JRC OPS 18; D band.
Helicopters: Platform for 1 Sea King size.

Comment: Merchant type hull. Ordered December 1976. Laid down 28 September 1977, launched 4 September 1978. Two fuel stations each side. No armament but can be fitted.

SAGAMI *2/1990, Hachiro Nakai*

34 + 1 HARBOUR TANKERS

Comment: There are: 12 of 490 tons (YO 9, 14, 21-27, 29-31); three of 310 tons (YW 17-19); four of 290 tons (YO 10-13); eight of 270 tons (YO 19, 28 and YG 201-206); five of 160 tons (YW 12-16); two of 100 tons (YO 18 and YW 10). One more of 490 tons approved in FY 1992.

YW 13 — *10/1991, Hachiro Nakai*

YG 205 — *1990, Ships of the World*

1 CABLE LAYER

Name	*No*	*Builders*	*Commissioned*
MUROTO	ARC 482	Mitsubishi, Shimonoseki	27 Mar 1980

Displacement, tons: 4544 standard
Dimensions, feet (metres): 436.2 × 57.1 × 18.7 *(133 × 17.4 × 5.7)*
Main machinery: 4 Mitsubishi-MTU V8V 22/30 diesels; 8800 hp(m) *(6.47 MW)*; 2 shafts; cp props; bow thruster
Speed, knots: 18
Complement: 135

Comment: Ocean survey capability. Laid down 28 November 1978, launched 25 July 1979.

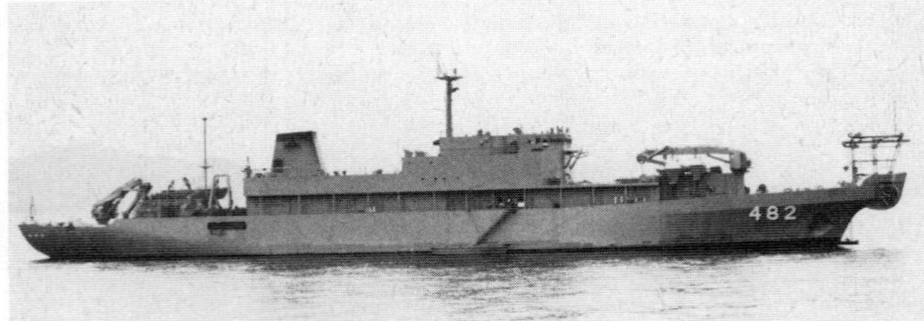

MUROTO — *10/1991, Hachiro Nakai*

TENDERS

5 81-GO CLASS

Name	*Laid down*	*Launched*	*Commissioned*
ASU 81	21 Oct 1967	18 Jan 1968	30 Mar 1968
ASU 82	25 Sep 1968	20 Dec 1968	31 Mar 1969
ASU 83	2 Apr 1971	24 May 1971	30 Sep 1971
ASU 84	4 Feb 1972	15 June 1972	13 Sep 1972
ASU 85	20 Feb 1973	16 July 1973	19 Sep 1973

Displacement, tons: 500 (ASU 85), 490 (ASU 82-84), 480 (ASU 81) standard
Dimensions, feet (metres): 170.6 × 32.8 × 8.3 *(52 × 10 × 2.5)*
Main machinery: 2 Akasaka UH-27-42 diesels; 1600 hp(m) *(1.18 MW)*; 2 shafts
Speed, knots: 14
Complement: 25; 35 (ASU 81-83)
Radars: Navigation: Fujitsu OPS 19 (ASU 84/85). Oki OPS 10 (others).

Comment: Training support and rescue. The after deck crane is able to lift a helicopter. *ASU 82* and *ASU 83* can launch propeller driven drones by catapult.

ASU 84 — *2/1991, Hachiro Nakai*

1 MIZUTORI CLASS

Name	*No*	*Builders*	*Commissioned*
HIYODORI	ASY 92 (ex-PC 320)	Sasebo	28 Feb 1966

Displacement, tons: 390 standard
Dimensions, feet (metres): 197 × 23.3 × 8.3 *(60 × 7.1 × 2.5)*
Main machinery: 2 Kawasaki-MAN V8V 22/30 ATL diesels; 4000 hp(m) *(2.94 MW)*; 2 shafts
Speed, knots: 20
Complement: 35 (90 passengers)

Comment: Built under FY 1964 programme as large patrol craft. Reconstructed as Auxiliary Special Service Yacht (ASY) at Yokohama Yacht Co Ltd, completed 27 April 1987.

HIYODORI — *5/1987, Hachiro Nakai*

6 Ex-TAKAMI CLASS

Name	*No*	*Builders*	*Commissioned*
IOU	YAS 83 (ex-MSC 631)	Nippon Steel Tube Co	22 Jan 1970
TOUSHI	YAS 86 (ex-MSC 635)	Nippon Steel Tube Co	18 Mar 1971
MUROTSU	YAS 88 (ex-MSC 637)	Hitachi, Kanagawa	30 Mar 1972
TAKANE	YAS 91 (ex-MSC 640)	Nippon Steel Tube Co	28 Aug 1974
MUZUKI	YAS 92 (ex-MSC 641)	Hitachi, Kanagawa	28 Aug 1974
SAKATE	YAS 94 (ex-MSC 643)	Nippon Steel Tube Co	15 Dec 1975

Comment: Details as for Takami class under Mine Warfare Forces. YAS 83 converted 27 March 1986, YAS 86 24 March 1987, YAS 88 23 March 1988, YAS 91 and 92 in December 1990 and YAS 94 in 1991.

TOUSHI — *3/1990, Hachiro Nakai*

SURVEY AND EXPERIMENTAL SHIPS

Note: The SES trials ship *Merguro* does not belong to the MSDF.

2 + (3) HIBIKI CLASS (AOS)

Name	*No*	*Builders*	*Commissioned*
HIBIKI	AOS 5201	Mitsui, Tamano	30 Jan 1991
HARIMA	AOS 5202	Mitsui, Tamano	Mar 1992

Displacement, tons: 2850 standard
Dimensions, feet (metres): 219.8 × 98.1 × 24.6 *(67 × 29.9 × 7.5)*
Main machinery: Diesel-electric; 4 Mitsubishi S6U diesels; 6000 hp(m) *(4.4 MW)*; 4 generators; 2 motors; 3000 hp(m) *(2.2 MW)*; 2 shafts
Speed, knots: 11 (3 towing). **Range, miles:** 3800 at 10 kts
Complement: 40
Radars: Navigation: JRC OPS 16; I band.
Sonars: UQQ 2 SURTASS; passive surveillance.
Helicopters: Platform only.

Comment: First authorised 24 January 1989, laid down 28 November 1989 and launched 27 July 1990. Second approved in FY 1990, laid down 26 December 1990 and launched 11 September 1991. Total of five planned. Auxiliary Ocean Surveillance (AOS) ships to a SWATH design similar to USN TAGOS-19 class; the first of class embarks US civilians. A data collection station is based at Yokosuka Bay using WSC-6 satellite data relay to the AOS.

HIBIKI — *1/1991, Hachiro Nakai*

1 SUMA CLASS (AGS)

Name	No	Builders	Commissioned
SUMA	AGS 5103	Hitachi, Maizuru	30 Mar 1982

Displacement, tons: 1180 standard
Dimensions, feet (metres): 236.2 × 42 × 11.1 *(72 × 12.8 × 3.4)*
Main machinery: 2 Fuji 6L-27.5XF diesels; 3300 hp(m) *(2.43 MW)*; 2 shafts; cp props; bow thruster
Speed, knots: 15
Complement: 64

Comment: Laid down 24 September 1980, launched 1 September 1981. Carries an 11 m launch for surveying work.

SUMA *10/1987, Hachiro Nakai*

2 FUTAMI CLASS (AGS)

Name	No	Builders	Commissioned
FUTAMI	AGS 5102	Mitsubishi, Shimonoseki	27 Feb 1979
WAKASA	AGS 5104	Hitachi Zosen, Maizuru	25 Feb 1986

Displacement, tons: 2050 standard; 3175 full load
Dimensions, feet (metres): 318.2 × 49.2 × 13.8 *(97 × 15 × 4.2)*
Main machinery: 2 Kawasaki-MAN V8V-22/30 ATL diesels; 4000 hp(m) *(2.94 MW)* (AGS 5102); 2 Fuji 6L-27.5XF diesels; 3300 hp(m) *(2.43 MW)* (AGS 5104); 2 shafts; cp props; bow thruster
Speed, knots: 16
Complement: 105
Radars: Navigation: JRC OPS 18; I band.

Comment: AGS 5102 laid down 20 January 1978. Launched 9 August 1978. AGS 5104 laid down 21 August 1984, launched 21 May 1985. Built to merchant marine design. Carry an RCV-22 remote controlled rescue/underwater survey submarine. *Wakasa* has a slightly taller funnel.

FUTAMI *5/1987, Hachiro Nakai*

1 AKASHI CLASS (AGS)

Name	No	Builders	Commissioned
AKASHI	AGS 5101	Nippon Steel Tube Co	25 Oct 1969

Displacement, tons: 1420 standard
Dimensions, feet (metres): 242.7 × 42.2 × 14.2 *(74 × 13 × 4.3)*
Main machinery: 2 Kawasaki-MAN V6V 22/30 ATL diesels; 4000 hp(m) *(2.94 MW)*; 2 shafts; bow thruster
Speed, knots: 16. **Range, miles:** 16 500 at 14 kts
Complement: 65 plus 10 scientists
Countermeasures: ESM: Nec NOLR-5; radar intercept.
Radars: Navigation: Fujitus OPS 9; I band.

Comment: Has a large number of electronic intercept aerials.

AKASHI *1990, JMSDF*

1 KURIHAMA CLASS (ASE)

Name	No	Builders	Commissioned
KURIHAMA	ASE 6101	Sasebo H.I.	8 Apr 1980

Displacement, tons: 959 standard
Dimensions, feet (metres): 223 × 37.9 × 9.8 (screws) *(68 × 11.6 × 3)*
Main machinery: 2 Fuji 6S 30B diesels; 5200 hp(m) *(3.82 MW)*; 2 shafts; 2 cp props; bow thruster
Speed, knots: 15
Complement: 40 plus 12 scientists

Comment: Experimental ship built for the Technical Research and Development Institute and used for testing underwater weapons and sensors.

KURIHAMA *12/1984, Hachiro Nakai*

0 + 1 ASE

Displacement, tons: 4200 standard
Main machinery: 2 gas turbines; 2 shafts
Speed, knots: 27
Complement: 170 plus 100 scientists

Comment: Included in the FY 1992 programme. For experimental and weapon systems testing.

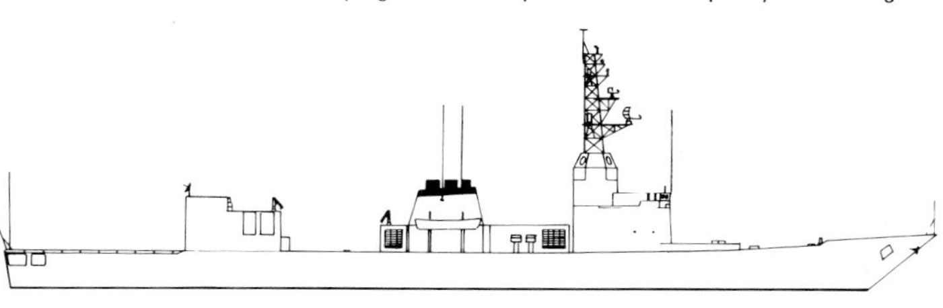
ASE *(not to scale) Ian Sturton*

TUGS

13 OCEAN TUGS

YT 58 **YT 63-74**

Displacement, tons: 260 standard
Dimensions, feet (metres): 93 × 28 × 8.2 *(28.4 × 8.6 × 2.5)*
Main machinery: 2 Niigata 6L25B diesels; 1800 hp(m) *(1.32 MW)*; 2 shafts
Speed, knots: 11
Complement: 10

Comment: YT 58 entered service on 31 October 1978, YT 63 on 27 September 1982, YT 64 on 30 September 1983, YT 65 on 20 September 1984, YT 66 on 20 September 1985, YT 67 on 4 September 1986, YT 68 on 9 September 1987, YT 69 on 16 September 1987, YT 70 on 2 September 1988, YT 71 on 28 July 1989, YT 72 on 27 July 1990, YT 73 on 31 July 1991 and YT 74 on 30 September 1991. All built by Yokohama Yacht.

YT 65 *3/1989, Hachiro Nakai*

4 COASTAL TUGS

YT 53, 55-57

Displacement, tons: 190 standard
Dimensions, feet (metres): 84.8 × 23 × 7.5 *(25.7 × 7 × 2.3)*
Main machinery: 2 Kubota M6D20BUCS diesels; 1500 hp(m) *(1.1 MW)*; 2 shafts
Speed, knots: 11
Complement: 10

Comment: YT 53 entered service on 8 March 1975, YT 55 on 22 August 1975, YT 56 on 13 July 1976, YT 57 on 22 August 1977. Similar in appearance to the YT 58 class.

7 COASTAL TUGS

YT 37, YT 40-41, YT 44-46, YT 48

Displacement, tons: 100 standard
Dimensions, feet (metres): 78.1 × 17.7 × 7.9 *(23.8 × 5.4 × 2.4)*
Main machinery: 1 diesel; 400 hp(m) *(294 kW)*; 1 shaft
Speed, knots: 10

YT 45 *8/1990, Hachiro Nakai*

13 HARBOUR TUGS

YT 36, YT 38-39, YT 42-43, YT 47, YT 49, YT 51, YT 54, YT 59-62

Comment: Of varying sizes from 26-35 tons.

HARBOUR CRAFT

Comment: Large numbers of harbour craft fly the naval ensign.

HARBOUR CRAFT *3/1990, Hachiro Nakai*

ICEBREAKER

Name	*No*	*Builders*	*Commissioned*
SHIRASE	AGB 5002	Nippon Steel Tube Co, Tsurumi	12 Nov 1982

Displacement, tons: 11 600 standard; 17 600 full load
Dimensions, feet (metres): 439.5 × 91.8 × 30.2 *(134 × 28 × 9.2)*
Main machinery: Diesel-electric; 6 Mitsui-MAN 12V 42M diesel generators; 3 motors; 30 000 hp(m) *(22 MW)*; 3 shafts
Speed, knots: 19. **Range, miles:** 25 000 at 15 kts
Complement: 174 (37 officers) plus 60 scientists
Cargo capacity: 1000 tons
Helicopters: 2 Mitsubishi S-61A; 1 Kawasaki OH-6J.

Comment: Laid down 5 March 1981 and launched 11 December 1981. Fully equipped for marine and atmospheric research. Stabilised.

SHIRASE *8/1990, Hachiro Nakai*

MARITIME SAFETY AGENCY

(KAIJO HOANCHO)

Commandant of the MSA

Haruki Miyamoto

Establishment

Established in May 1948 as an external organisation of the Ministry of Transport to carry out patrol and rescue duties as well as hydrographic and navigation aids services. Since then a very considerable organisation with HQ in Tokyo has been built up. The Academy for the Agency is in Kure and the School in Maizuru.
The main operational branches are the Guard and Rescue, the Hydrographic and the Aids to Navigation Departments. Regional Maritime Safety offices control the 11 districts with their location as follows (air bases in brackets): RMS 1—Otaru (Chitose, Hakodate, Kushiro); 2—Shiogama (Sendai); 3—Yokohama (Haneda); 4—Nagoya (Ise); 5—Kobe (Yao); 6—Hiroshima (Hiroshima); 7—Kitakyushu (Fukuoka); 8—Maizuru (Miho); 9—Niigata (Niigata); 10—Kagoshima (Kagoshima); 11—Naha (Naha, Ishigaki). This organisation includes, as well as the RMS HQ, 66 MS offices, 57 MS stations, 26 MS detachments, 14 MS air stations, 9 district communication centres, 3 traffic advisory service centres, 4 hydrographic observatories and 119 aids to navigation offices.

Personnel

1992: 12 300 (2600 officers)

Strength of the Fleet

Type	*Active*	*Building*
GUARD AND RESCUE SERVICE		
Patrol Vessels:		
Large with helicopter (PLH)	10	1
Large (PL)	37	1
Medium (PM)	47	1
Small (PS)	19	1
Firefighting Vessels (FL)	5	—
Patrol Craft:		
Patrol Craft (PC)	60	—
Patrol Craft (CL)	165	7
Firefighting Craft (FM)	10	—
Special Service Craft:		
Monitoring Craft (MS)	4	—
Guard Boats (GS)	2	—
Surveillance Craft (SS)	34	—
Oil Recovery Craft (OR)	5	—
Oil Skimming Craft (OS)	3	—
Oil Boom Craft (OX)	19	—
Miscellaneous (NO)	3	—
HYDROGRAPHIC SERVICE		
Surveying Vessels:		
Large (HL)	4	1
Medium (HM)	1	—
Small (HS)	16	—

Type	*Active*	*Building*
AIDS TO NAVIGATION SERVICE		
Aids to Navigation Research Vessel (LL)	1	—
Buoy Tenders:		
Large (LL)	3	—
Medium (LM)	1	—
Aids to Navigation Tenders:		
Medium (LM)	11	—
Small (LS)	62	1

DELETIONS

1989 *Nojima* PL 11 (old), *Seiun* LM 110 (old), *Haruhikari* LS 201, *Setohikari* LS 203, *Akiyoshi* PS 37
1990 *Takanawa* PS 36, *Takahikari* LS 202, *Sekihikari* LS 156, *Meiyo* HL 03 (old)
1991 *Ojika* PL 12 (old), *Rokko* PS 35, *Hamashio* HS 01, *Sekiun* LM 105, *Houn* LM 111

LARGE PATROL VESSELS

1 SHIKISHIMA CLASS

Name	*No*	*Builders*	*Commissioned*
SHIKISHIMA	PLH 31	Ishikawajima Harima, Tokyo	Apr 1992

Displacement, tons: 6500 standard
Dimensions, feet (metres): 492.1 × 55.8 × 19.7 *(150 × 17 × 6)*
Main machinery: 2 SEMT-Pielstick 16PC2.5V 400; 20 800 hp(m) *(15.29 MW)*; 2 shafts
Speed, knots: 25. **Range, miles:** 20 000 at 18 kts
Guns: 4 Oerlikon 35 mm/90 (2 twin). 2 JM-61 MB 20 mm Gatling.
Helicopters: 2 Super Puma.

Comment: Authorised in the FY 1989 programme in place of the third Mizuho class. Laid down 24 August 1990 and launched 27 June 1991. Will be used to escort the plutonium transport ship but both the armament and the command and control systems are barely adequate for escort duties.

SHIKISHIMA *6/1991, Ships of the World*

YASHIMA 5/1991, Hachiro Nakai

2 MIZUHO CLASS

Name	No	Builders	Commissioned
MIZUHO	PLH 21	Mitsubishi, Nagasaki	19 Mar 1986
YASHIMA	PLH 22	Nippon Kokan, Tsurumi	1 Dec 1988

Displacement, tons: 4900 standard; 5204 full load
Dimensions, feet (metres): 426.5 × 50.9 × 17.7 *(130 × 15.5 × 5.4)*
Main machinery: 2 SEMT-Pielstick 14PC2.5V 400 diesels; 18 200 hp(m) *(13.38 MW)* sustained; 2 shafts; cp props; bow thruster
Speed, knots: 23. **Range, miles:** 8500 at 22 kts
Complement: 100 plus 30 aircrew
Guns: 1 Oerlikon 35 mm/90; 85° elevation; 550 rounds/minute to 6 km *(3.2 nm)* anti-surface; 5 km *(2.7 nm)* anti-aircraft; weight of shell 1.55 kg.
1 JM-61 MB 20 mm Gatling.
Radars: Navigation: Two sets.
Helicopter control: One set.
Helicopters: 2 Sikorsky S-62 Seaguard or Fuji-Bell 212.

Comment: PLH 21 ordered under the FY 1983 programme laid down 27 August 1984 and launched 5 June 1985. PLH 22 in 1986 estimates, laid down 3 October 1987 and launched 20 January 1988. Two sets of fixed electric fin stabilisers that have a lift of 26 tons × 2 and reduce rolling by 90 per cent at 18 kts. Employed in search and rescue beyond 200 miles from the base line.

8 SOYA CLASS

Name	No	Builders	Commissioned
SOYA	PLH 01	Nippon Kokan, Tsurumi	22 Nov 1978
TSUGARU	PLH 02	IHI, Tokyo	17 Apr 1979
OOSUMI	PLH 03	Mitsui Tamano	18 Oct 1979
URAGA	PLH 04	Hitachi, Maizuru	5 Mar 1980
ZAO	PLH 05	Mitsubishi, Nagasaki	19 Mar 1982
CHIKUZEN	PLH 06	Kawasaki, Kobe	28 Sep 1983
SETTSU	PLH 07	Sumitomo, Oppama	27 Sep 1984
ECHIGO	PLH 08	Mitsui Tamano	28 Feb 1990

Displacement, tons: 3562 (PLH 01), 3744 (others) standard
Dimensions, feet (metres): 323.4 × 51.2 × 17.1 *(98.6 × 15.6 × 5.2)* (PLH 01)
345.8 × 47.9 × 15.7 *(105.4 × 14.6 × 4.8)*
Main machinery: 2 SEMT-Pielstick 12PC2.5V 400 diesels; 15 604 hp(m) *(11.47 MW)* sustained; 2 shafts; cp props; bow thruster
Speed, knots: 21 (PLH 01); 22 (others). **Range, miles:** 5700 at 18 kts
Complement: 71 (PLH 01-04); 69 (others)
Guns: 1 Bofors 40 mm or Oerlikon 35 mm. 1 Oerlikon 20 mm (PLH 01, 02, 05-07).
Radars: Navigation: Two sets.
Helicopter control: CCA Type.
Helicopters: 1 Fuji-Bell 212.

Comment: PLH 01 has an icebreaking capability while the other ships are only ice strengthened. Fitted with both fin stabilisers and anti-rolling tanks of 70 tons capacity. The fixed electric hydraulic fins have a lift of 26 tons × 2 at 18 kts which reduces rolling by 90 per cent at that speed. At slow speed the reduction is 50 per cent, using the tanks.

CHIKUZEN 5/1991, Hachiro Nakai

0 + 1 TYPE 2650 TON CLASS

Name	No	Builders	Commissioned
—	—	Hitachi, Maizuru	May 1993

Displacement, tons: 2650 normal
Dimensions, feet (metres): 377.3 × 45.9 × 16.4 *(115 × 14 × 5)*
Main machinery: 2 diesels; 8000 hp(m) *(5.9 MW)*; 2 shafts
Speed, knots: 18. **Range, miles:** 7000 at 15 kts
Complement: 118
Guns: 1 Oerlikon 35 mm/90. 1—20 mm. 1—12.7 mm MG.

Comment: Authorised in the FY 1990 programme and ordered in March 1991.

2 IZU CLASS

Name	No	Builders	Commissioned
IZU	PL 31	Hitachi Mukaishima	31 July 1967
MIURA	PL 32	Maizuru	15 Mar 1969

Displacement, tons: 2081 normal
Dimensions, feet (metres): 313.3 × 38 × 12.8 *(95.5 × 11.6 × 3.9)*
Main machinery: 2 SEMT-Pielstick 12PC2.5V 400 diesels; 15 604 hp(m) *(11.47 MW)* sustained; 2 shafts; cp props; bow thruster
Speed, knots: 20. **Range, miles:** 6000 at 18.8 kts
Complement: 72
Guns: 1 Bofors 40 mm/70.
Radars: Navigation: Two sets.

Comment: PL 31 was laid down in August 1966, launched in January 1967. PL 32 was laid down in May 1968, launched in October 1968. Equipped with various types of marine instruments. Ice strengthened hull. Armament may be removed depending on employment. Based at Yokohama and employed in long-range rescue and patrol duties.

MIURA 12/1990, Hachiro Nakai

4 ERIMO and DAIO CLASSES

Name	No	Builders	Commissioned
ERIMO	PL 13	Hitachi, Mukaishima	30 Nov 1965
SATSUMA	PL 14	Hitachi, Mukaishima	30 July 1966
DAIO	PL 15	Hitachi, Maizuru	28 Sep 1973
MUROTO	PL 16	Naikai	30 Nov 1974

Displacement, tons: 1010 (1206, PL 15-16) normal
Dimensions, feet (metres): 251.3 × 30.2 × 9.9 *(76.6 × 9.2 × 3)* (PL 13-14)
251.3 × 31.5 × 10.7 *(76.6 × 9.6 × 3.3)* (PL 15-16)
Main machinery: 2 Burmeister & Wain 635V 2BV45 diesels (PL 13-14); 4800 hp(m) *(3.53 MW)*; 2 Fuji 8S40B44A diesels (PL 15-16); 7000 hp(m) *(5.15 MW)*; 2 shafts; cp props
Speed, knots: 20. **Range, miles:** 5000 at 18 kts (PL 13-14); 4400 at 18 kts (PL 15-16)
Complement: 72 (PL 13-14); 50 (PL 15-16)
Guns: 1 Oerlikon 20 mm. 1 Bofors 40 mm (PL 15-16). 1 Oerlikon 20 mm (PL 13-14).
Radars: Navigation: JMA 1576.
JMA 1596.

Comment: PL 13's structure is strengthened against ice. Based at Kamaishi (PL 13); Kagoshima (PL 14); Kushiro (PL 15); Aburatsu (PL 16).

SATSUMA 1990, Ships of the World

28 SHIRETOKO CLASS

Name	*No*	*Builders*	*Commissioned*
SHIRETOKO	PL 101	Mitsui Tamano	8 Nov 1978
ESAN	PL 102	Sumitomo	16 Nov 1978
WAKASA	PL 103	Kawasaki, Kobe	29 Nov 1978
YAHIKO	PL 104	Mitsubishi, Shimonoseki	16 Nov 1978
MOTOBU	PL 105	Sasebo	29 Nov 1978
RISHIRI	PL 106	Shikoku	12 Sep 1979
MATSUSHIMA	PL 107	Tohoku	14 Sep 1979
IWAKI	PL 108	Naikai	10 Aug 1979
SHIKINE	PL 109	Usuki	20 Sep 1979
SURUGA	PL 110	Kurushima	28 Sep 1979
REBUN	PL 111	Narasaki	21 Nov 1979
CHOKAI	PL 112	Nihonkai	30 Nov 1979
ASHIZURI	PL 113	Sanoyasu	31 Oct 1979
OKI	PL 114	Tsuneishi	16 Nov 1979
NOTO	PL 115	Miho	30 Nov 1979
YONAKUNI	PL 116	Hayashikane	31 Oct 1979
KUDAKA (ex-*Daisetsu*)	PL 117	Hakodate	31 Jan 1980
SHIMOKITA	PL 118	Ishikawajima, Kakoki	12 Mar 1980
SUZUKA	PL 119	Kanazashi	7 Mar 1980
KUNISAKI	PL 120	Kouyo	29 Feb 1980
GENKAI	PL 121	Oshima	31 Jan 1980
GOTO	PL 122	Onomichi	29 Feb 1980
KOSHIKI	PL 123	Kasado	25 Jan 1980
HATERUMA	PL 124	Osaka	12 Mar 1980
KATORI	PL 125	Tohoku	21 Oct 1980
KUNIGAMI	PL 126	Kanda	17 Oct 1980
ETOMO	PL 127	Naikai	17 Mar 1982
MASHU	PL 128	Shiikoku	12 Mar 1982

Displacement, tons: 974 normal; 1360 full load
Dimensions, feet (metres): 255.8 × 31.5 × 10.5 *(78 × 9.6 × 3.2)*
Main machinery: 2 Fuji 8S40B or 2 Niigata 8MA 40 diesels; 7000 hp(m) *(5.15 MW)*; 2 shafts; cp props
Speed, knots: 20. **Range, miles:** 4400 at 17 kts
Complement: 41
Guns: 1 Bofors 40 mm or 1 Oerlikon 35 mm. 1 Oerlikon 20 mm (PL 101-105, 127 and 128).
Radars: Navigation: One set.

Comment: Average time from launch to commissioning was about four to five months. Designed for EEZ patrol duties. PL 117 changed her name on 1 April 1988.

KUDAKA *9/1991, Hachiro Nakai*

2 NOJIMA and OJIKA CLASSES

Name	*No*	*Builders*	*Commissioned*
NOJIMA	PL 01	Ishikawajima Harima, Tokyo	21 Sep 1989
OJIKA	PL 02	Mitsui, Tamano	31 Oct 1991

Displacement, tons: 950 normal (PL 01); 1200 normal (PL 02)
Dimensions, feet (metres): 285.4; 300 (PL 02) × 34.4 × 11.5 *(87; 91.4 × 10.5 × 3.5)*
Main machinery: 2 Fuji 8S40B diesels; 7000 hp(m) *(5.15 MW)*; 2 shafts
Speed, knots: 19
Guns: 1—20 mm JM-61B Gatling.
Radars: Navigation.
Helicopters: Platform for 1 light.

Comment: *Nojima* laid down 16 August 1988 and launched 30 May 1989. *Ojika* which is slightly larger was launched 23 April 1991. Both equipped as surveillance and rescue command ships.

NOJIMA *5/1990, Hachiro Nakai*

1 KOJIMA CLASS

Name	*No*	*Builders*	*Commissioned*
KOJIMA	PL 21	Kure	20 May 1964

Displacement, tons: 1201 normal
Dimensions, feet (metres): 228.3 × 33.8 × 10.5 *(69.6 × 10.3 × 3.2)*
Main machinery: 1 Uraga-Sulzer 7MD 51 diesel; 2600 hp(m) *(1.91 MW)*; 1 shaft
Speed, knots: 15. **Range, miles:** 6000 at 13 kts
Complement: 60 (17 officers) plus 47 trainees
Guns: 1 Bofors 40 mm Mk 3. 1 USN 20 mm/80 Mk 10. 1 Browning 12.7 mm MG.
Radars: Navigation: Two MM-5A.

Comment: Maritime Safety Academy training ship.

KOJIMA *5/1991, Hachiro Nakai*

SHIPBORNE AIRCRAFT

Numbers/Type: 36 Bell 212.
Operational speed: 100 kts *(185 km/h)*.
Service ceiling: 10 000 ft *(3048 m)*.
Range: 412 nm *(763 km)*.
Role/Weapon systems: Liaison, medium range support and SAR. Sensors: Search radar. Weapons: Unarmed.

BELL 212 *7/1990, Hachiro Nakai*

LAND-BASED MARITIME AIRCRAFT (FRONT LINE)

Numbers/Type: 16 Beech Super King Air 200T.
Operational speed: 245 kts *(453 km/h)*.
Service ceiling: 35 000 ft *(10 670 m)*.
Range: 1460 nm *(2703 km)*.
Role/Weapon systems: Visual reconnaissance in support of EEZ. Sensors: Weather/search radar. Weapons: Unarmed.

Numbers/Type: 3 Bell 206B JetRanger.
Operational speed: 115 kts *(213 km/h)*.
Service ceiling: 10 000 ft *(3048 m)*.
Range: 312 nm *(577 km)*.
Role/Weapon systems: Liaison and training. Sensors: None. Weapons: Unarmed.

Numbers/Type: 5 NAMC YS-11A.
Operational speed: 230 kts *(425 km/h)*.
Service ceiling: 21 600 ft *(6580 m)*.
Range: 1960 nm *(3629 km)*.
Role/Weapon systems: Maritime surveillance and associated tasks. Sensors: Weather/search radar. Weapons: Unarmed.

Numbers/Type: 2 Shorts Skyvan 3.
Operational speed: 175 kts *(324 km/h)*.
Service ceiling: 10 000 ft *(3048 m)*.
Range: 847 nm *(1568 km)*.
Role/Weapon systems: Coastal patrol and support aircraft. Sensors: Weather radar. Weapons: Unarmed.

Numbers/Type: 2 Falcon 900.
Operational speed: 428 kts *(792 km/h)*.
Service ceiling: 51 000 ft *(15 544 m)*.
Range: 4170 nm *(7722 km)*.
Role/Weapon systems: Maritime surveillance. Sensors: Weather/search radar. Weapons: Unarmed.

MEDIUM PATROL VESSELS

14 TESHIO CLASS

Name	*No*	*Builders*	*Commissioned*
TESHIO	PM 01	Shikoku	30 Sep 1980
OIRASE	PM 02	Naikai	29 Aug 1980
ECHIZEN	PM 03	Usuki	30 Sep 1980
TOKACHI	PM 04	Narazaki	24 Mar 1981
HITACHI	PM 05	Tohoku	19 Mar 1981
OKITSU	PM 06	Usuki	17 Mar 1981
ISAZU	PM 07	Naikai	18 Feb 1982
CHITOSE	PM 08	Shikoku	15 Mar 1983
KUWANO	PM 09	Naikai	10 Mar 1983
SORACHI	PM 10	Tohoku	30 Aug 1984
YUBARI	PM 11	Usuki	28 Nov 1985
MOTOURA	PM 12	Shikoku	21 Nov 1986
KANO	PM 13	Naikai	13 Nov 1986
SENDAI	PM 14	Shikoku	1 June 1988

Displacement, tons: 630 normal; 670 full load
Dimensions, feet (metres): 222.4 × 25.9 × 6.6 *(67.8 × 7.9 × 2.7)*
Main machinery: 2 Fuji 6-S32F diesels; 3000 hp(m) *(2.21 MW)*; 2 shafts
Speed, knots: 18. **Range, miles:** 3200 at 16 kts
Complement: 33
Guns: 1 JN-61B 20 mm Gatling.
Radars: Navigation: Two JMA 159B; I band.

Comment: First three built under FY 1979 programme and second three under FY 1980, seventh under FY 1981, PM 08-09 under FY 1982, PM 10 under FY 1983, PM 11 under FY 1984, PM 12-13 under FY 1985, PM 14 under FY 1987.

ISAZU *5/1991, Hachiro Nakai*

20 BIHORO CLASS (350-M4 TYPE)

Name	*No*	*Builders*	*Commissioned*
BIHORO	PM 73	Tohoku	28 Feb 1974
KUMA	PM 74	Usuki	28 Feb 1974
FUJI	PM 75	Usuki	7 Feb 1975
KABASHIMA	PM 76	Usuki	25 Mar 1975
SADO	PM 77	Tohoku	7 Feb 1975
ISHIKARI	PM 78	Tohoku	13 Mar 1976
ABUKUMA	PM 79	Tohoku	30 Jan 1976
ISUZU	PM 80	Naikai	10 Mar 1976
KIKUCHI	PM 81	Usuki	6 Feb 1976
KUZURYU	PM 82	Usuki	18 Mar 1976
HOROBETSU	PM 83	Tohoku	27 Jan 1977
SHIRAKAMI	PM 84	Tohoku	24 Mar 1977
SAGAMI	PM 85	Naikai	30 Nov 1976
TONE	PM 86	Usuki	30 Nov 1976
YOSHINO	PM 87	Usuki	28 Jan 1977
KUROBE	PM 88	Shikoku	15 Feb 1977
CHIKUGO	PM 90	Naikai	27 Jan 1978
YAMAKUNI	PM 91	Usuki	26 Jan 1978
KATSURA	PM 92	Shikoku	15 Feb 1978
SHINANO	PM 93	Tohoku	23 Feb 1978

Displacement, tons: 615 normal; 636 full load
Dimensions, feet (metres): 208 × 25.6 × 8.3 *(63.4 × 7.8 × 2.5)*
Main machinery: 2 Niigata 6M 31 EX diesels; 3000 hp(m) *(2.21 MW)*; 2 shafts; cp props
Speed, knots: 18. **Range, miles:** 3200 at 16 kts
Complement: 34
Guns: 1 USN 20 mm/80 Mk 10.
Radars: Navigation: JMA 1596 and JMA 1576; I band.

Comment: Average time from launch to commissioning, four months. Fitted with Loran.

ISUZU *1990, Ships of the World*

2 TAKATORI CLASS

Name	*No*	*Builders*	*Commissioned*
TAKATORI	PM 89	Naikai	24 Mar 1978
KUMANO	PM 94	Namura	23 Feb 1979

Displacement, tons: 634 normal
Dimensions, feet (metres): 152.5 × 30.2 × 9.3 *(46.5 × 9.2 × 2.9)*
Main machinery: 2 Niigata 6M31 EX diesels; 3000 hp(m) *(2.21 MW)*; 2 shafts; cp props
Speed, knots: 15. **Range, miles:** 700 at 14 kts
Complement: 34

Comment: SAR vessels equipped for salvage and firefighting.

KUMANO *7/1990, Hachiro Nakai*

7 KUNASHIRI CLASS (350-M3 TYPE)

Name	*No*	*Builders*	*Commissioned*
KUNASHIRI	PM 65	Maizuru	28 Mar 1969
MINABE	PM 66	Maizuru	28 Mar 1970
SAROBETSU	PM 67	Maizuru	30 Mar 1971
KAMISHIMA	PM 68	Usuki	31 Jan 1972
MIYAKE	PM 70	Tohoku	25 Jan 1973
AWAJI	PM 71	Usuki	25 Jan 1973
YAEYAMA	PM 72	Usuki	20 Dec 1972

Displacement, tons: 498 normal
Dimensions, feet (metres): 190.4 × 24.3 × 7.9 *(58 × 7.4 × 2.4)*
Main machinery: 2 Niigata 6MF32H diesels; 2600 hp(m) *(1.91 MW)*; 2 shafts
Speed, knots: 17. **Range, miles:** 3000 at 16 kts
Complement: 40
Guns: 1 USN 20 mm Mk 10.
Radars: Navigation: JMA 1576 or 1596 (PM 70-72).

Comment: The last three have slightly more powerful 6M31EX diesels giving 3000 hp and a top speed of 18 kts.

KUNASHIRI *1988, JMSA*

3 MATSUURA CLASS (350-M2 TYPE)

Name	*No*	*Builders*	*Commissioned*
AMAMI	PM 62	Hitachi, Mukaishima	29 Mar 1965
NATORI	PM 63	Hitachi, Mukaishima	20 Jan 1966
KARATSU	PM 64	Hitachi, Mukaishima	29 Mar 1967

Displacement, tons: 455 normal
Dimensions, feet (metres): 181.4 × 23 × 7.5 *(55.3 × 7 × 2.3)*
Main machinery: 2 Ikegai 6MSB3HS diesels (PM 62-63); 1800 hp(m) *(1.32 MW)*; 2 Ikegai 6MA31X diesels (PM 64); 2600 hp(m) *(1.91 MW)*; 2 shafts
Speed, knots: 17. **Range, miles:** 3500 at 13 kts
Complement: 40
Guns: 1 USN 20 mm Mk 10.
Radars: Navigation: One set.

NATORI *1990, Ships of the World*

1 YAHAGI CLASS (350 TYPE)

Name	*No*	*Builders*	*Commissioned*
MISASA (ex-*Okinawa*)	PM 69	Usuki	23 Oct 1970

Displacement, tons: 376 normal
Dimensions, feet (metres): 164.9 × 24 × 7.4 *(50.3 × 7.3 × 2.3)*
Main machinery: 2 diesels; 1400 hp(m) *(1.03 MW)*; 2 shafts
Speed, knots: 15.5. **Range, miles:** 2900 at 14 kts
Complement: 44
Guns: 1 USN 20 mm Mk 10.
Radars: Navigation: One set.

Comment: Transferred to MSA in 1972. Changed her name 1 April 1988.

MISASA *1988, JMSA*

SMALL PATROL VESSELS

4 MIHASHI CLASS (180 TYPE)

Name	*No*	*Builders*	*Commissioned*
MIHASHI	PS 01	Mitsubishi, Shimonoseki	9 Sep 1988
SAROMA	PS 02	Hitachi, Kanagawa	24 Nov 1989
INASA	PS 03	Mitsubishi, Shimonoseki	31 Jan 1990
KIRISHIMA	PS 04	Hitachi, Kanagawa	22 Mar 1991

Displacement, tons: 180 normal; 195 full load
Dimensions, feet (metres): 141.1 × 24.6 × 5.6 *(43 × 7.5 × 1.7)*
Main machinery: 2 Mitsubishi S12V diesels; 6400 hp(m) *(4.7 MW)*; 2 shafts
1 Mitsubishi S8V diesel; 2500 hp(m) *(1.84 MW)*; KaMeWa waterjet
Speed, knots: 35. **Range, miles:** 650 at 34 kts
Complement: 34
Guns: 1—12.7 mm MG.

Comment: First one launched 28 June 1988, second 28 June 1989 and third 20 October 1989. Fourth laid down 10 May 1990. Capable of 15 kts on the waterjet alone.

KIRISHIMA *5/1991, Hachiro Nakai*

7 AKAGI CLASS

Name	*No*	*Builders*	*Commissioned*
AKAGI	PS 101	Sumidagawa	26 Mar 1980
TSUKUBA	PS 102	Sumidagawa	24 Feb 1982
KONGOU	PS 103	Ishihara	16 Mar 1987
KATSURAGI	PS 104	Ishihara	24 Mar 1988
HIROMINE	PS 105	Yokohama Yacht	24 Mar 1988
SHIZUKI	PS 106	Sumidagawa	24 Mar 1988
TAKACHIHO	PS 107	Sumidagawa	24 Mar 1988

Displacement, tons: 115 full load
Dimensions, feet (metres): 114.8 × 20.7 × 4.3 *(35 × 6.3 × 1.3)*
Main machinery: 2 Pielstick 16PA 4V.185 diesels; 5344 hp(m) *(3.93 MW)* sustained; 2 shafts
Speed, knots: 28. **Range, miles:** 500 at 20 kts
Complement: 22
Guns: 1 Browning 12.7 mm MG.
Radars: Navigation: One set.

Comment: Carry a 25-man inflatable rescue craft. The last four were ordered on 31 August 1987 and commissioned less than seven months later.

KONGOU *5/1991, Hachiro Nakai*

0 + 1 TYPE 230 TON CLASS

Displacement, tons: 230 normal
Dimensions, feet (metres): 183.7 × 24.6 × 6.6 *(56 × 7.5 × 2)*
Main machinery: 2 Fuji 8S40B diesels; 7000 hp(m) *(5.15 MW)*; 2 shafts
Speed, knots: 25
Guns: 1 Gatling 20 mm.

Comment: Authorised in the FY 1991 programme.

0 + 1 TYPE 115 TON CLASS

Displacement, tons: 115 normal
Dimensions, feet (metres): 114.8 × 22 × 4.3 *(35 × 6.7 × 1.3)*
Main machinery: 2 diesels; 5200 hp(m) *(3.82 MW)*; 2 KaMeWa waterjets
Speed, knots: 35
Guns: 1—12.7 mm MG.

Comment: Authorised in the FY 1991 programme.

7 HIDAKA CLASS

Name	*No*	*Builders*	*Commissioned*
KUNIMI	PS 38	Hayashikane	15 Feb 1965
TAKATSUKI	PS 39	Kurushima	30 Mar 1965
KAMUI	PS 41	Hayashikane	15 Feb 1966
ASHITAKA	PS 43	Usuki	10 Feb 1967
KURAMA	PS 44	Usuki	28 Feb 1967
IBUKI	PS 45	Usuki	5 Mar 1968
TOUMI	PS 46	Usuki	20 Feb 1968

Displacement, tons: 169 normal
Dimensions, feet (metres): 104 × 20.8 × 5.5 *(31.7 × 6.3 × 1.7)*
Main machinery: 1 Ikegai 6MSB31A diesel; 700 hp(m) *(515 kW)*; 1 shaft
Speed, knots: 12.5. **Range, miles:** 1000 at 12 kts
Complement: 17
Radars: Navigation: One set.

Comment: Occasionally carry a 12.7 mm MG. Beginning to be paid off.

KURAMA *4/1991, Hachiro Nakai*

1 BIZAN CLASS

Name	*No*	*Builders*	*Commissioned*
SHIRAMINE	PS 48	Mitsubishi, Shimonoseki	15 Dec 1969

Displacement, tons: 42 full load
Dimensions, feet (metres): 85.3 × 18.3 × 2.8 *(26 × 5.6 × 0.9)*
Main machinery: 2 MTU diesels; 2200 hp(m) *(1.62 MW)*; 2 shafts
Speed, knots: 25. **Range, miles:** 250 at 25 kts
Complement: 14
Radars: Navigation: MD 808.

Comment: Aluminium alloy construction. Soon to be paid off.

SHIRAMINE *10/1991, Hachiro Nakai*

COASTAL PATROL CRAFT

23 MURAKUMO CLASS

Name	No	Builders	Commissioned
MURAKUMO	PC 201	Mitsubishi, Shimonoseki	24 Mar 1978
KITAGUMO	PC 202	Hitachi, Kanagawa	17 Mar 1978
YUKIGUMO	PC 203	Hitachi, Kanagawa	27 Sep 1978
ASAGUMO	PC 204	Mitsubishi, Shimonoseki	21 Sep 1978
HAYAGUMO	PC 205	Mitsubishi, Shimonoseki	30 Jan 1979
AKIGUMO	PC 206	Hitachi, Kanagawa	28 Feb 1979
YAEGUMO	PC 207	Mitsubishi, Shimonoseki	16 Mar 1979
NATSUGUMO	PC 208	Hitachi, Kanagawa	22 Mar 1979
YAMAGIRI	PC 209	Hitachi, Kanagawa	29 June 1979
KAWAGIRI	PC 210	Hitachi, Kanagawa	27 July 1979
TERUZUKI	PC 211	Mitsubishi, Shimonoseki	26 June 1979
NATSUZUKI	PC 212	Mitsubishi, Shimonoseki	26 July 1979
MIYAZUKI	PC 213	Hitachi, Kanagawa	13 Mar 1980
NIJIGUMO	PC 214	Mitsubishi, Shimonoseki	29 Jan 1981
TATSUGUMO	PC 215	Mitsubishi, Shimonoseki	19 Mar 1981
HAMAYUKI	PC 216	Hitachi, Kanagawa	27 Feb 1981
ISONAMI	PC 217	Mitsubishi, Shimonoseki	19 Mar 1981
NAGOZUKI	PC 218	Hitachi, Kanagawa	29 Jan 1981
YAEZUKI	PC 219	Hitachi, Kanagawa	19 Mar 1981
YAMAYUKI	PC 220	Hitachi, Kanagawa	16 Feb 1982
KOMAYUKI	PC 221	Mitsubishi, Shimonoseki	10 Feb 1982
UMIGIRI	PC 222	Hitachi, Kanagawa	17 Feb 1983
ASAGIRI	PC 223	Mitsubishi, Shimonoseki	23 Feb 1983

Displacement, tons: 85 normal
Dimensions, feet (metres): 98.4 × 20.7 × 7.2 *(30 × 6.3 × 2.2)*
Main machinery: 2 Ikegai MTU 16V 652 TB71 diesels; 4610 hp(m) *(3.39 MW)* sustained; 2 shafts
Speed, knots: 30. **Range, miles:** 350 at 28 kts
Complement: 13
Guns: 1 Browning 12.7 mm MG.

HAMAYUKI *5/1991, Hachiro Nakai*

15 AKIZUKI CLASS

Name	No	Builders	Commissioned
AKIZUKI	PC 64	Mitsubishi, Shimonoseki	28 Feb 1974
SHINONOME	PC 65	Mitsubishi, Shimonoseki	25 Mar 1974
URAYUKI	PC 72	Mitsubishi, Shimonoseki	31 May 1975
ISEYUKI	PC 73	Mitsubishi, Shimonoseki	31 July 1975
HATAGUMO	PC 75	Mitsubishi, Shimonoseki	21 Feb 1976
MAKIGUMO	PC 76	Mitsubishi, Shimonoseki	19 Mar 1976
HAMAZUKI	PC 77	Mitsubishi, Shimonoseki	29 Nov 1976
ISOZUKI	PC 78	Mitsubishi, Shimonoseki	18 Mar 1977
SHIMANAMI	PC 79	Mitsubishi, Shimonoseki	23 Dec 1977
YUZUKI	PC 80	Mitsubishi, Shimonoseki	22 Mar 1979
HANAYUKI	PC 81	Mitsubishi, Shimonoseki	27 Mar 1981
AWAGIRI	PC 82	Mitsubishi, Shimonoseki	24 Mar 1983
SHIMAGIRI	PC 83	Hitachi, Kanagawa	7 Feb 1985
SETOGIRI	PC 84	Hitachi, Kanagawa	22 Mar 1985
HAYAGIRI	PC 85	Mitsubishi, Shimonoseki	22 Feb 1985

Displacement, tons: 77 normal
Dimensions, feet (metres): 85.3 × 20.7 × 6.9 *(26 × 6.3 × 2.1)*
Main machinery: 3 Mitsubishi 12DM20MTK diesels; 3000 hp(m) *(2.21 MW)*; 3 shafts
Speed, knots: 22. **Range, miles:** 220 at 21.5 kts
Complement: 10
Radars: Navigation: FRA 10 Mk 2.

Comment: Aluminium hulls.

HANAYUKI *8/1990, Hachiro Nakai*

1 MATSUNAMI CLASS

Name	No	Builders	Commissioned
MATSUNAMI	PC 53	Hitachi, Kanagawa	30 Mar 1971

Displacement, tons: 59 normal
Dimensions, feet (metres): 82 × 19.7 × 3.6 *(25 × 6 × 1.1)*
Main machinery: 2 Mercedes-Benz MTU 12V 493 TY7 diesels; 2200 hp(m) *(1.62 MW)* sustained; 2 shafts
Speed, knots: 20. **Range, miles:** 270 at 18 kts
Complement: 30

Comment: Used for Oceanographic survey and specially fitted out for the Emperor.

MATSUNAMI *1990, Ships of the World*

17 SHIKINAMI CLASS

Name	No	Builders	Commissioned
SHIKINAMI	PC 54	Mitsubishi, Shimonoseki	25 Feb 1971
TOMONAMI	PC 55	Mitsubishi, Shimonoseki	20 Mar 1971
WAKANAMI	PC 56	Mitsubishi, Shimonoseki	30 Oct 1971
ISENAMI	PC 57	Hitachi, Kanagawa	29 Feb 1972
TAKANAMI	PC 58	Mitsubishi, Shimonoseki	30 Nov 1971
MUTSUKI	PC 59	Hitachi, Kanagawa	18 Dec 1972
MOCHIZUKI	PC 60	Hitachi, Kanagawa	18 Dec 1972
HARUZUKI	PC 61	Mitsubishi, Shimonoseki	30 Nov 1972
KIYOZUKI	PC 62	Mitsubishi, Shimonoseki	18 Dec 1972
URAZUKI	PC 63	Hitachi, Kanagawa	30 Jan 1973
URANAMI	PC 66	Hitachi, Kanagawa	22 Dec 1973
TAMANAMI	PC 67	Mitsubishi, Shimonoseki	25 Dec 1973
MINEGUMO	PC 68	Mitsubishi, Shimonoseki	30 Nov 1973
KIYONAMI	PC 69	Mitsubishi, Shimonoseki	30 Oct 1973
OKINAMI	PC 70	Hitachi, Kanagawa	8 Feb 1974
WAKAGUMO	PC 71	Hitachi, Kanagawa	25 Mar 1974
ASOYUKI	PC 74	Hitachi, Kanagawa	16 June 1975

Displacement, tons: 46 normal
Dimensions, feet (metres): 69 × 17.4 × 3.3 *(21 × 5.3 × 1)*
Main machinery: 2 Mercedes-Benz MTU 12V 493 TY7 diesels; 2200 hp(m) *(1.62 MW)* sustained; 2 shafts
Speed, knots: 26. **Range, miles:** 230 at 23.8 kts
Complement: 10
Radars: Navigation: MD 806.

Comment: Built completely of light alloy.

URANAMI *7/1990, Hachiro Nakai*

2 HAMAGIRI CLASS

Name	No	Builders	Commissioned
HAMAGIRI	PC 48	Sumidagawa	19 Mar 1970
HAMANAMI	PC 52	Sumidagawa	22 Mar 1971

Displacement, tons: 51 normal
Dimensions, feet (metres): 69 × 16.6 × 3.3 *(21 × 5.1 × 1)*
Main machinery: 2 Mercedes-Benz MTU 12V 493 TY7 diesels (PC 52); 2200 hp(m) *(1.62 MW)* 2 Mitsubishi 12DHTK diesels (PC 48); 1140 hp(m) *(838 kW)*; 2 shafts
Speed, knots: 14.6 (PC 48); 21.8 (PC 52). **Range, miles:** 300 at 9 kts (PC 52); 270 at 13 kts (PC 48)
Complement: 10
Guns: 1 Browning 12.7 mm MG.
Radars: Navigation: MD 808.

Comment: Steel hulls.

165 COASTAL PATROL AND RESCUE CRAFT

CL 01-04, 50-51, 53-55, 65-156, 201-264

Displacement, tons: 27 normal
Dimensions, feet (metres): 59 × 14.1 × 4.3 *(18 × 4.3 × 1.3)*
Main machinery: 2 Mitsubishi DH24AK diesels; 900 hp(m) *(661 kW)*; 2 shafts
Speed, knots: 20. **Range, miles:** 180 at 19 kts
Complement: 6

Comment: This total includes five similar classes—Isokaze, Yakaze, Chiyokaze, Nogekaze and Yamayuri, the latter being the largest. Data for Yamayuri class. Some (Yamayuri class of 66) have firefighting capability. Built by Shigi, Ishihana and Sumidagawa and Yokohama Yacht Co, CL 44, 50 to 98 are of 24 tons and 49.2 ft *(15 m)*, capable of 18 kts. *Isokaze* (CL 01) and *Hayakaze* (CL 02) completed 23 March 1989, *Nadakaze* (CL 03) and *Kotokaze* (CL 04) completed 15 March 1991. For coastal patrol and rescue duties. Built of high tensile steel.

NADAKAZE *7/1991, Hachiro Nakai*

SHIRAGIKU *7/1990, Hachiro Nakai*

2 NATSUGIRI CLASS

Name	*No*	*Builders*	*Commissioned*
NATSUGIRI	PC 86	Sumidagawa, Tokyo	29 Jan 1990
SUGANAMI	PC 87	Sumidagawa, Tokyo	29 Jan 1990

Displacement, tons: 54 normal
Dimensions, feet (metres): 88.6 × 18.4 × 3.9 *(27 × 5.6 × 1.2)*
Main machinery: 2 diesels; 3000 hp(m) *(2.21 MW)*; 2 shafts
Speed, knots: 26.5

Comment: Built under FY 1988 programme. Steel hulls.

SUGANAMI *5/1990, Hachiro Nakai*

0 + 7 TYPE 20 METRE CLASS

Displacement, tons: 48 normal
Dimensions, feet (metres): 65.6 × 16.4 × 3.3 *(20 × 5 × 1)*
Main machinery: 2 diesels; 1820 hp(m) *(1.34 MW)*; 2 shafts
Speed, knots: 30

Comment: Authorised in FY 1991 programme.

HYDROGRAPHIC SERVICE

Name	*No*	*Builders*	*Commissioned*
TAKUYO	HL 02	Nippon Kokan, Tsurumi	31 Aug 1983

Displacement, tons: 3000 normal
Dimensions, feet (metres): 314.9 × 46.6 × 15.1 *(96 × 14.2 × 4.6)*
Main machinery: 2 Fuji 6S40B diesels; 5200 hp(m) *(3.82 MW)*; 2 shafts; cp props
Speed, knots: 17. **Range, miles:** 12 000 at 16 kts
Complement: 60 (24 officers)
Radars: Navigation: Two sets.

Comment: Laid down on 14 April 1982, launched on 24 March 1983. Based at Tokyo.

TAKUYO *5/1990, Hachiro Nakai*

Name	*No*	*Builders*	*Commissioned*
SHOYO	HL 01	Hitachi, Maizuru	26 Feb 1972

Displacement, tons: 2200 normal
Dimensions, feet (metres): 268 × 41.3 × 13.8 *(81.7 × 12.6 × 4.2)*
Main machinery: 2 Fuji 12VM32 H2F diesels; 4800 hp(m) *(3.53 MW)*; 1 shaft
Speed, knots: 17. **Range, miles:** 11 000 at 14 kts
Complement: 58 (23 officers)
Radars: Navigation: Two sets.

Comment: Launched 18 September 1971. Fully equipped for all types of hydrographic and oceanographic work. Carries MX702 SATNAV and Loran. Based at Tokyo.

SHOYO *5/1990, Hachiro Nakai*

Name	*No*	*Builders*	*Commissioned*
TENYO	HL 04	Sumitomo, Oppama	27 Nov 1986

Displacement, tons: 770 normal
Dimensions, feet (metres): 183.7 × 32.2 × 9.5 *(56 × 9.8 × 2.9)*
Main machinery: 2 Akasaka diesels; 1300 hp(m) *(955 kW)*; 2 shafts
Speed, knots: 13. **Range, miles:** 5400 at 12 kts
Complement: 43 (18 officers)

Comment: Laid down 11 April 1986, launched 5 August 1986. Based at Tokyo.

TENYO *1986, Maritime Safety Agency*

Name	No	Builders	Commissioned
MEIYO	HL 03	Kawasaki, Kobe	24 Oct 1990
—	HL 05	Kawasaki, Kobe	1993

Displacement, tons: 550 normal
Dimensions, feet (metres): 196.9 × 34.4 × 10.2 *(60 × 10.5 × 3.1)*
Main machinery: 2 Daihatsu 6 DLM-24 diesels; 3000 hp(m) *(2.2 MW)*; 2 shafts; bow thruster
Speed, knots: 15. **Range, miles:** 5280 at 11 kts
Complement: 25 + 13 scientists

Comment: *Meiyo* laid down 24 July 1989 and launched 29 June 1990; second of class authorised in FY 1991 programme. Have anti-roll tanks and resiliently mounted main machinery. A large survey launch is carried on the port side.

MEIYO *10/1990, Hachiro Nakai*

Name	No	Builders	Commissioned
KAIYO	HM 06	Nagoya	14 Mar 1964

Displacement, tons: 380 normal
Dimensions, feet (metres): 106 × 26.5 × 7.8 *(44.5 × 8.1 × 2.4)*
Main machinery: 1 Sumiyoshi Tekko S6 NBS diesel; 450 hp(m) *(331 kW)*; 1 shaft; cp prop
Speed, knots: 10
Complement: 35 (13 officers)

Comment: Flume tanks fitted.

KAIYO *1990, Ships of the World*

SURVEYING CRAFT

10 ISESHIO CLASS

ISESHIO HS 02
SETOSHIO HS 03
UZUSHIO HS 04
HAYASHIO HS 05
ISOSHIO HS 06
TAKASHIO HS 07
WAKASHIO HS 08
YUKISHIO HS 09
OYASHIO HS 10
KUROSHIO HS 11

Displacement, tons: 6
Dimensions, feet (metres): 32.8 *(10)* long
Main machinery: 1 Nissan MTU UD326 diesel; 90 hp(m) *(66 kW)*; 1 shaft
Speed, knots: 8.8
Complement: 7

Comment: Completed 1969-72. GRP hulls. One carried in *Shoyo* (HL 01).

WAKASHIO *4/1991, Hachiro Nakai*

5 AKASHI CLASS

AKASHI HS 31
KERAMA HS 32
HAYATOMO HS 33
KURIHAMA HS 34
KURUSHIMA HS 35

Displacement, tons: 21
Dimensions, feet (metres): 49.2 *(15)* long
Main machinery: 1 Nissan UD 626 diesel; 180 hp(m) *(132 kW)*; 1 shaft
Speed, knots: 9. **Range, miles:** 400 at 9 kts
Complement: 7

Comment: Completed 1973-77. Steel hulls.

KURIHAMA *5/1991, Hachiro Nakai*

1 HAMASHIO CLASS

HAMASHIO HS 21

Displacement, tons: 27
Dimensions, feet (metres): 68.9 × 14.8 × 3.9 *(21 × 4.5 × 1.2)*
Main machinery: 3 diesels; 1015 hp(m) *(746 kW)*; 3 shafts
Speed, knots: 15
Complement: 3

Comment: Built by Yokohama Yacht and completed 25 March 1991.

HAMASHIO *6/1991, Ships of the World*

AIDS TO NAVIGATION SERVICE

Name	No	Builders	Commissioned
TSUSHIMA	LL 01	Mitsui, Tamano	9 Sep 1977

Displacement, tons: 1950 normal
Dimensions, feet (metres): 246 × 41 × 13.8 *(75 × 12.5 × 4.2)*
Main machinery: 1 Fuji-Sulzer 85 40C diesel; 4200 hp(m) *(3.09 MW)*; 1 shaft; cp prop; bow thruster
Speed, knots: 15.5. **Range, miles:** 10 000 at 15 kts
Complement: 54

Comment: Lighthouse Supply Ship. Fitted with tank stabilisers. Equipped with modern electronic instruments for carrying out research on electronic aids to navigation.

TSUSHIMA *5/1990, Hachiro Nakai*

3 HOKUTO CLASS

Name	No	Builders	Commissioned
HOKUTO	LL 11	Sasebo	29 June 1979
KAIO	LL 12	Sasebo	11 Mar 1980
GINGA	LL 13	Kawasaki, Kobe	18 Mar 1980

Displacement, tons: 700 normal
Dimensions, feet (metres): 180.4 × 34.8 × 8.7 *(55 × 10.6 × 2.7)*
Main machinery: 2 Asakasa MH23 diesels; 1400 hp(m) *(1.03 MW)*; 2 shafts
Speed, knots: 12. **Range, miles:** 3900 at 12 kts
Complement: 31

KAIO *8/1990, Hachiro Nakai*

Name	No	Builders	Commissioned
MYOJO	LM 11	Nippon Kokan, Tsurumi	25 Mar 1974

Displacement, tons: 303 normal
Dimensions, feet (metres): 88.6 × 39.4 × 8.8 *(27 × 12 × 2.7)*
Main machinery: 2 Niigata 6M9 16HS diesels; 600 hp(m) *(441 kW)*; 2 shafts; cp props
Speed, knots: 10.5. **Range, miles:** 1360 at 10.5 kts
Complement: 18

Comment: Catamaran type buoy tender, this ship is employed in maintenance and position adjustment service to floating aids to navigation.

MYOJO *10/1991, Hachiro Nakai*

AIDS TO NAVIGATION TENDERS

11 MEDIUM TENDERS

Name	No	Builders	Commissioned
ZUIUN	LM 101	Usuki	27 July 1983
REIUN	LM 102	Kanto Kogyo	27 Nov 1971
HAKUUN	LM 106	Sumidagawa	28 Feb 1978
TOUN	LM 107	Sumidagawa	14 Mar 1979
AYABANE	LM 112	Shimoda	25 Dec 1972
GENUN	LM 113	Izumi	23 Mar 1973
TOKUUN	LM 114	Yokohama Yacht	23 Mar 1981
SHOUN	LM 201	Sumidagawa	26 Mar 1986
SEIUN	LM 202	Sumidagawa	22 Feb 1989
SEKIUN	LM 203	Ishihara	12 Mar 1991
HOUUN	LM 204	Ishihara	22 Mar 1991

Comment: There are four classes of Medium Tenders of different characteristics—Zuiun, Hakuun, Ayabane, Shoun.

Details of *Zuiun* as follows:

Displacement, tons: 370 normal
Dimensions, feet (metres): 146.3 × 24.6 × 7.2 *(44.6 × 7.5 × 2.2)*
Main machinery: 2 Mitsubishi-Asakasa MH23 series diesels; 1300 hp(m) *(955 kW)*; 2 shafts; cp props
Speed, knots: 13.5. **Range, miles:** 1000 at 13 kts
Complement: 20

ZUIUN *1988, JMSA*

Details of *Hakuun* as follows:

Displacement, tons: 58 full load
Dimensions, feet (metres): 75.5 × 19.7 × 3.3 *(23 × 6 × 1)*
Main machinery: 2 GM 12V71 TI diesels; 840 hp *(627 kW)* sustained; 2 shafts
Speed, knots: 14. **Range, miles:** 250 at 14 kts
Complement: 9

SEKIUN *6/1991, Ships of the World*

62 + 1 SMALL TENDERS

Details of LS 204 class as follows:

HATSUHIKARI LS 204, LS 205-221

Displacement, tons: 25 full load
Dimensions, feet (metres): 54.4 × 14.1 × 2.6 *(17.5 × 4.3 × 0.9)*
Main machinery: 2 diesels; 560 hp(m) *(412 kW)*; 2 shafts
Speed, knots: 15. **Range, miles:** 230 at 14.5 kts
Complement: 8

Comment: Others include: Shitoko class, LS 184-195. Built by Haruna, Yokohama, last two completed 1987. Kaiko class, LS 152-170, last one completed 1987. LS 204 class, last one completed 31 January 1990 and one new type authorised in FY 1991. Others with varying characteristics.

LS 213 *7/1990, Hachiro Nakai*

FIREFIGHTING VESSELS AND CRAFT

5 HIRYU CLASS

Name	No	Builders	Commissioned
HIRYU	FL 01	Nippon Kokan, Tsurumi	4 Mar 1969
SHORYU	FL 02	Nippon Kokan, Tsurumi	4 Mar 1970
NANRYU	FL 03	Nippon Kokan, Tsurumi	4 Mar 1971
KAIRYU	FL 04	Nippon Kokan, Tsurumi	18 Mar 1977
SUIRYU	FL 05	Yokohama Yacht Co	24 Mar 1978

Displacement, tons: 215 normal
Dimensions, feet (metres): 90.2 × 34.1 × 7.2 *(27.5 × 10.4 × 2.2)*
Main machinery: 2 Ikegai/Mercedes-Benz MTU 12V 493 TY7 diesels; 2200 hp(m) *(1.62 MW)* sustained; 2 shafts
Speed, knots: 13.2. **Range, miles:** 300 at 13 kts
Complement: 14

Comment: Catamaran type fire boats designed and built for firefighting services to large tankers.

HIRYU *5/1990, Hachiro Nakai*

10 NUNOBIKI CLASS

Name	No	Builders	Commissioned
NUNOBIKI	FM 01	Yokohama Yacht Co	25 Feb 1974
YODO	FM 02	Sumidagawa	30 Mar 1975
OTOWA	FM 03	Yokohama Yacht Co	25 Dec 1974
SHIRAITO	FM 04	Yokohama Yacht Co	25 Feb 1975
KOTOBIKI	FM 05	Yokohama Yacht Co	31 Jan 1976
NACHI	FM 06	Sumidagawa	14 Feb 1976
KEGON	FM 07	Yokohama Yacht Co	29 Jan 1977
MINOO	FM 08	Sumidagawa	27 Jan 1978
RYUSEI	FM 09	Yokohama Yacht Co	24 Mar 1980
KIYOTAKI	FM 10	Sumidagawa	25 Mar 1981

Displacement, tons: 89 normal
Dimensions, feet (metres): 75.4 × 19.7 × 5.2 *(23 × 6 × 1.6)*
Main machinery: 1 Mercedes-Benz MTU 12V 493 TY7 diesel; 1100 hp(m) *(810 kW)* sustained; 1 shaft
2 Nissan diesels; 500 hp(m) *(515 kW)*; 3 shafts
Speed, knots: 14. **Range, miles:** 180 at 13.5 kts
Complement: 12
Radars: Navigation: FRA 10.

Comment: Equipped for chemical firefighting.

NUNOBIKI 12/1989, *Hachiro Nakai*

MISCELLANEOUS

3 + 1 MONITORING CRAFT

KINUGASA MS 01 **SAIKAI** MS 02 **KATSUREN** MS 03

Comment: First two 10 m catamaran craft, MS 03 of 16 m. One more authorised in 1991.

SAIKAI 3/1990, *Hachiro Nakai*

3 OIL SKIMMERS

OS 01-03

Comment: Completed 1974-75 by Lockheed.

2 GUARD BOATS

HAYATE GS 01 **INAZUMA** GS 02

Displacement, tons: 7.9 full load
Dimensions, feet (metres): 39 × 10.5 × 4.9 *(11.9 × 3.2 × 1.5)*
Main machinery: 2 Mitsubishi S 6M2 diesels; 580 hp(m) *(426 kW)*; 2 shafts
Speed, knots: 30. **Range, miles:** 150 at 28 kts

Comment: Built by Yokohama Yacht and commissioned 21 December 1987.

HAYATE 7/1991, *Hachiro Nakai*

34 SURVEILLANCE CRAFT

SS 01, 02, 04-35

Comment: Craft of 6 m completed between 1972-79. SS 15 is equipped with waterjet. SS 35 of 7 m completed 1984.

5 OIL RECOVERY CRAFT

SHIRASAGI OR 01 **MIZUNANGI** OR 03 **ISOSHIGI** OR 05
SHIRATORI OR 02 **CHIDORI** OR 04

Displacement, tons: 153 normal
Dimensions, feet (metres): 72.3 × 21 × 2.6 *(22 × 6.4 × 0.9)*
Main machinery: 2 Nissan UD 626 diesels; 360 hp(m) *(265 kW)*; 2 shafts
Speed, knots: 6. **Range, miles:** 160 at 6 kts
Complement: 7

Comment: Completed by Sumidagawa (OR 01), Shigi (OR 02 and 04) and Ishihara (OR 03 and 05) between 31 January 1977 and 23 March 1979.

SHIRASAGI 5/1990, *Hachiro Nakai*

JORDAN

Headquarters' Appointment

Chief of Staff:
Major General Abu Taleb

Diplomatic Representation

Defence Attaché in London:
Brigadier H Al Russan

Coastal Guard

The Jordan Coastal Guard, sometimes called the Jordan Sea Force, comes under the Director of Operations at General Headquarters.

Base

Aqaba

Personnel

(a) 1992: 260 officers and men
(b) Voluntary service

Mercantile Marine

Lloyd's Register of Shipping:
4 vessels of 73 185 tons gross

4 BERTRAM TYPE (COASTAL PATROL CRAFT)

FAYSAL HAN HASAYU MUHAMMED

Displacement, tons: 8 full load
Dimensions, feet (metres): 38 × 13.1 × 1.6 *(11.6 × 4 × 0.5)*
Main machinery: 2 diesels; 600 hp *(441 kW)*; 2 shafts
Speed, knots: 25
Complement: 8
Guns: 1—12.7 mm MG. 1—7.62 mm MG.

Comment: Acquired from Bertram, Miami in 1974. May now be paid off.

1 BERTRAM TYPE (COASTAL PATROL CRAFT)

ALI ABDULLAH

Displacement, tons: 7
Dimensions, feet (metres): 30.4 × 10.8 × 1.6 *(9.2 × 3.3 × 0.5)*
Main machinery: 2 diesels; 430 hp *(316 kW)*; 2 shafts
Speed, knots: 24
Complement: 8
Guns: 1—12.7 mm. 1—7.62 mm.

Comment: Glass fibre hull. Enforcer class built in 1958. May now be paid off.

3 HAWK CLASS (FAST ATTACK CRAFT—GUN)

AL HUSSEIN 101 **AL HUSSAN** 102 **ABDULLAH** 103

Displacement, tons: 124 full load
Dimensions, feet (metres): 100 × 22.5 × 4.9 *(30.5 × 6.9 × 1.5)*
Main machinery: 2 MTU 16V 396 TB 94 diesels; 5800 hp(m) *(4.26 MW)* sustained; 2 shafts
Speed, knots: 32. **Range, miles:** 750 at 15 kts; 1500 at 11 kts
Complement: 16 (3 officers)
Guns: 2 Oerlikon GCM-A03 30 mm (twin). 1 Oerlikon GAM-B01 20 mm. 2—12.5 mm MGs.
Countermeasures: Decoys: 2 Wallop Stockade Chaff launchers.
Combat data systems: Racal Cane 100.
Fire control: Radamec Series 2000 optronic for 30 mm gun.
Radars: Surface search: Kelvin Hughes 1007; I band.

Comment: Ordered from Vosper Thornycroft in December 1987. GRP structure. First one on trials in May 1989 and completed December 1989. Second completed in March 1990 and the third in early 1991. All transported to Aqaba in September 1991.

3 ROTORK CRAFT

AL HASHIM **AL FAISAL** **AL HAMZA**

Displacement, tons: 9 full load
Dimensions, feet (metres): 41.7 × 10.5 × 3 *(12.7 × 3.2 × 0.9)*
Main machinery: 2 diesels; 240 hp *(179 kW)*; 2 shafts
Speed, knots: 28
Military lift: 30 troops
Guns: 1—7.62 mm MG.

Comment: Delivered in late 1990 probably for patrolling the Dead Sea.

AL HUSSAN *7/1990, W. Sartori*

KENYA

Administration

Commander, Kenya Navy:
Major General J R E Kibwana

Diplomatic Representation

Defence Adviser in London:
Colonel F R Nthiggah

Personnel

(a) 1992: 1200 officers and men
(b) Voluntary service

Base

Mombasa

Customs/Police

There are some 20 Customs and Police patrol craft of between 12 and 14 metres. Mostly built by Cheverton, Performance Workboats and Fassmer in the 1980s.

Mercantile Marine

Lloyd's Register of Shipping:
30 vessels of 12 520 tons gross

2 NYAYO CLASS (FAST ATTACK CRAFT—MISSILE)

Name	*No*	*Builders*	*Commissioned*
NYAYO	P 3126	Vosper Thornycroft	23 July 1987
UMOJA	P 3127	Vosper Thornycroft	16 Sep 1987

Displacement, tons: 310 light; 400 full load
Dimensions, feet (metres): 186 × 26.9 × 7.9 *(56.7 × 8.2 × 2.4)*
Main machinery: 4 Paxman Valenta 18CM diesels; 15 000 hp *(11.19 MW)* sustained; 4 shafts; 2 motors (slow speed patrol); 100 hp *(74.6 kW)*
Speed, knots: 40. **Range, miles:** 2000 at 18 kts
Complement: 40

Missiles: SSM: 4 OTO Melara/Matra Otomat Mk 2 (2 twin); active radar homing to 160 km *(86.4 nm)* at 0.9 Mach; warhead 210 kg; sea-skimmer for last 4 km *(2.2 nm)*.
Guns: 1 OTO Melara 3 in *(76 mm)*/62; 85° elevation; 85 rounds/minute to 16 km *(8.7 nm)* anti-surface; 12 km *(6.5 nm)* anti-aircraft; weight of shell 6 kg.
2 Oerlikon/BMARC 30 mm GCM-AO2 (twin); 85° elevation; 650 rounds/minute to 10 km *(5.4 nm)* anti-surface; 3 km *(1.6 nm)* anti-aircraft; weight of shell 0.36 kg.
2 Oerlikon/BMARC 20 mm A41A; 50° elevation; 800 rounds/minute to 2 km; weight of shell 0.24 kg.
Countermeasures: Decoys: 2 Wallop Barricade 18-barrelled launchers; Stockade and Palisade rockets.
ESM: Racal Cutlass; radar warning.
ECM: Racal Cygnus; jammer.
Fire control: CAAIS 450 including Signaal 423; action data automation.
Radars: Surface search: Plessey AWS 4; E/F band; range 101 km *(55 nm)*.
Navigation: Decca AC 1226; I band.
Fire control: Marconi/Ericsson ST802; I band.

Programmes: Ordered in September 1984. Sailed in company from the UK, arriving at Mombasa 30 August 1988. Similar to Omani Province class.
Operational: First live Otomat firing in February 1989. Form Squadron 86.

UMOJA *7/1987, W. Sartori*

1 LARGE PATROL CRAFT

KIONGOZI

Displacement, tons: 55 full load
Dimensions, feet (metres): 73.8 × 17.4 × 5.9 *(22.5 × 5.3 × 1.8)*
Main machinery: 2 Kelvin TAS-6 diesels; 560 hp *(418 kW)*; 2 shafts
Speed, knots: 12
Complement: 4 plus 4 pilots

Comment: Built by Akerboom, Leyden, Netherlands. Delivered early 1983. Primarily intended as pilot craft with a patrol capability. A second of class was probably cancelled.

1 BROOKE MARINE TYPE (FAST ATTACK CRAFT—MISSILE)

Name	*No*	*Builders*	*Commissioned*
MAMBA	P 3100	Brooke Marine, Lowestoft	7 Feb 1974

Displacement, tons: 125 standard; 160 full load
Dimensions, feet (metres): 123 × 22.5 × 5.2 *(37.5 × 6.9 × 1.6)*
Main machinery: 2 Paxman Ventura 16CM diesels; 4000 hp *(2.98 MW)* sustained; 2 shafts
Speed, knots: 25. **Range, miles:** 3300 at 13 kts
Complement: 25 (3 officers)

Missiles: SSM: 4 IAI Gabriel II; active radar or optical guidance; semi-active homing to 36 km *(19.4 nm)* at 0.7 Mach; warhead 75 kg.
Guns: 2 Oerlikon/BMARC 30 mm GCM-A02 (twin); 85° elevation; 650 rounds/minute to 10 km *(5.4 nm)* anti-surface; 3 km *(1.6 nm)* anti-aircraft; weight of shell 0.36 kg.
Radars: Navigation: Decca AC 1226; I band.
Fire control: Selenia RTN 10X; I/J band; range 40 km *(22 nm)*.

Programmes: Laid down 17 February 1972.
Modernisation: In 1982 missiles, new gunnery equipment and an optronic director fitted.
Operational: Arrived Vosper Thornycroft, Portchester on 4 May 1989 for a long refit. Returned to Kenya with *Madaraka* as deck cargo in a transport ship leaving Portsmouth on 7 November 1990.

MAMBA (alongside *Madaraka*) *11/1990, Colin Rossiter*

3 VOSPER TYPE (LARGE PATROL CRAFT)

Name	*No*	*Builders*	*Commissioned*
SIMBA	P 3110	Vosper Ltd, Portsmouth	23 May 1966
CHUI	P 3112	Vosper Ltd, Portsmouth	7 July 1966
NDOVU	P 3117	Vosper Ltd, Portsmouth	27 July 1966

Displacement, tons: 96 standard; 109 full load
Dimensions, feet (metres): 103 × 19.8 × 5.8 *(31.4 × 6 × 1.8)*
Main machinery: 2 Paxman Ventura diesels; 2800 hp *(2.09 MW)*; 2 shafts
Speed, knots: 24. **Range, miles:** 1500 at 16 kts
Complement: 23 (3 officers)
Guns: 2 Bofors 40 mm/60.
Radars: Surface search: Racal Decca 914; I band.

Comment: Previously laid up and apparently derelict, all three were back in operational service in 1991. Form Squadron 66.

3 BROOKE MARINE TYPE (FAST ATTACK CRAFT—MISSILE)

Name	*No*	*Builders*	*Commissioned*
MADARAKA	P 3121	Brooke Marine, Lowestoft	16 June 1975
JAMHURI	P 3122	Brooke Marine, Lowestoft	16 June 1975
HARAMBEE	P 3123	Brooke Marine, Lowestoft	22 Aug 1975

Displacement, tons: 120 standard; 145 full load
Dimensions, feet (metres): 107 × 20 × 5.6 *(32.6 × 6.1 × 1.7)*
Main machinery: 2 Paxman Valenta 16CM diesels; 6650 hp *(4.96 MW)* sustained; 2 shafts
Speed, knots: 25.5. **Range, miles:** 2500 at 12 kts
Complement: 21 (3 officers)

Missiles: SSM: 4 IAI Gabriel II; active radar or optical guidance; semi-active homing to 36 km *(19.4 nm)* at 0.7 Mach; warhead 75 kg.
Guns: 2 Oerlikon/BMARC 30 mm GCM (twin); 85° elevation; 650 rounds/minute to 10 km *(5.4 nm)* anti-surface; 3 km *(1.6 nm)* anti-aircraft; weight of shell 0.36 kg.
Radars: Navigation: Decca AC 1226; I band.
Fire control: Selenia RTN 10X; I/J band; range 40 km *(22 nm)*.

Programmes: Ordered 10 May 1973. *Madaraka* launched 28 January 1975, *Jamhuri* 14 March 1975, *Harambee* 2 May 1975.
Modernisation: *Madaraka* (1981), *Harambee* (1982), *Jamhuri* (1983) all received SSM, new guns and an optronic director.
Operational: *Madaraka* started a long refit at Vosper Thornycroft, Portchester, on 4 May 1989 and completed in August 1990. The other two of the class may be refitted in due course in Mombasa. Form Squadron 76.

MADARAKA *8/1990, Maritime Photographic*

HARAMBEE *6/1991*

1 TUG

NGAMIA

Measurement, tons: 298 grt
Dimensions, feet (metres): 115.8 × 30.5 × 12.8 *(35.3 × 9.3 × 3.9)*
Main machinery: 2 diesels; 1200 hp *(895 kW)*; 1 shaft
Speed, knots: 14

Comment: Tug built in 1969. Acquired from merchant marine in 1982.

KOREA, Democratic People's Republic (North)

Administration

Commander of the Navy:
Vice Admiral Kim Il-Choi

Bases

East coast: Wonsan (main), Mayang-do, Cha-ho (submarines).
Minor bases: Najin, Sanjin-dong, Kimchaek, Yohori, Songjon, Pando, Munchon-up, Namae-ri, Kosong-up.
West coast: Nampo (main), Pipa-got (submarines).
Minor bases: Yogampo-ri, Tasa-ri, Sohae-ri, Chodo, Sunwi-do, Pupo-ri, Sagon-ri.
A number of these bases has underground berthing facilities.

Personnel

(a) 1992: 41 500 officers and men plus 40 000 reserves
(b) 5 years' national service

Strength of the Fleet

Type	*Active*
Submarines—Patrol	24
Submarines—Midgets	48+
Frigates	3
Fast Attack Craft—Missile	33
Fast Attack Craft—Gun/Torpedo	319
Patrol Craft	55
Amphibious Craft	131
Hovercraft (LCP)	52
Minesweepers	29
Depot Ships for Midget Submarines	8
Survey Vessels	4

Mercantile Marine

Lloyd's Register of Shipping:
98 vessels of 511 249 tons gross

Maritime Coastal Security Force

In addition to the Navy there is a Coastal and Port Security Police Force which would be subordinate to the Navy in war. It is reported that the strength of this force is one Sariwon class PGF, 10-15 Chong-Ju patrol craft and 130 patrol boats of the Sin Hung, Kimjin and Yongdo classes.

DELETIONS

Note: Changes to the order of battle represent the most up-to-date information available.

SUBMARINES

20 + 2 Ex-CHINESE and NORTH KOREAN ROMEO CLASS (PATROL TYPE)

Displacement, tons: 1475 surfaced; 1830 dived
Dimensions, feet (metres): 251.3 × 22 × 16.1 *(76.6 × 6.7 × 4.9)*
Main machinery: Diesel-electric; 2 Type 37D diesels; 4000 hp(m) *(2.94 MW)*; 2 motors; 2700 hp(m) *(1.98 MW)*; 2 creep motors; 2 shafts
Speed, knots: 15 surfaced; 13 dived. **Range, miles:** 9000 at 9 kts surfaced
Complement: 54 (10 officers)

Torpedoes: 8—21 in *(533 mm)* tubes (6 bow, 2 stern). 14 probably Soviet Type 53; dual purpose; pattern active/passive homing up to 20 km *(10.8 nm)* at up to 45 kts; warhead 400 kg.
Mines: 28 in lieu of torpedoes.
Radars: Surface search: Snoop Plate; I band.
Sonars: Tamir 5L; hull-mounted; active.
Feniks; hull-mounted; passive.

Programmes: Two transferred from China 1973, two in 1974 and three in 1975. First three of class built in North Korea in 1975. Local building at Mayang-do and Sinpo Shipyards provided two more in 1976. Programme now seems to be running at about one every two years. One reported sunk in February 1985.
Operational: Most are stationed on east coast and occasionally operate in Sea of Japan. Four ex-Chinese units are based on the west coast. By modern standards these are basic attack submarines with virtually no anti-submarine performance or potential.

4 Ex-SOVIET WHISKEY CLASS (PATROL TYPE)

Displacement, tons: 1080 surfaced; 1350 dived
Dimensions, feet (metres): 249.3 × 21.3 × 16.1 *(76 × 6.5 × 4.9)*
Main machinery: Diesel-electric; 2 Type 37D diesels; 4000 hp(m) *(2.94 MW)*; 2 motors; 2700 hp(m) *(1.98 MW)*; 2 shafts
Speed, knots: 18 surfaced; 14 dived. **Range, miles:** 13 000 at 8 kts surfaced
Complement: 54

WHISKEY Class

Torpedoes: 6—21 in *(533 mm)* tubes (4 bow, 2 stern). 12 (or 24 mines) probably obsolescent Soviet types.
Radars: Surface search: Snoop Plate; I band.
Sonars: Herkules; hull-mounted; passive array.

Programmes: Two transferred in 1960, two in 1962. First four were replaced by four more in 1974.

Operational: Stationed on west coast opposite Yellow Sea, probably operate from Pipa-got naval base. Used mostly for training and probably restricted to periscope depth.

MIDGET SUBMARINES

Note: In addition to those listed below there is a single 41 m experimental type built in the late 1970s; this design was not continued. There is also reported to be a 13 m West German design acquired in 1983 via Singapore. There may be up to 30 more commercial types in service including four of 34 metres and two of 32 metres.

48 NORTH KOREAN DESIGN

Displacement, tons: 17 surfaced; 25 dived
Dimensions, feet (metres): 65.6 × 6.6 × 5.2 *(20 × 2 × 1.6)*
Main machinery: Mercedes-Benz diesel, 160 hp(m) *(118 kW)*; 1 shaft
Speed, knots: 10 surfaced; 4 dived
Range, miles: 550 at 10 kts surfaced; 50 at 4 kts dived
Complement: 2 plus 6-7 divers

Comment: Built at Yukdaeso-ri shipyard since early 1960s. Forty-eight confirmed in 1992. Some lost on operations against South Korea. One reported captured by South Korean Navy in 1965 or 1966. Some stationed on Songjong peninsula. Later type imported from Yugoslavia, which began in mid-1970s. Some have two short torpedo tubes. Operate from eight merchant mother ships (see *Service Forces)*.

FRIGATES

1 SOHO CLASS

Displacement, tons: 1600 standard; 1845 full load
Dimensions, feet (metres): 246 × 49.2 × 12.5 *(75 × 15 × 3.8)*
Main machinery: 2 diesels; 15 000 hp(m) *(11.03 MW)*; 2 shafts
Speed, knots: 27
Complement: 190

Missiles: SSM: 4 SS-N-2A Styx; active radar or IR homing to 46 km *(25 nm)* at 0.9 Mach; warhead 513 kg.
Guns: 1—3.9 in *(100 mm)*/56; 40° elevation; 15 rounds/minute to 16 km *(8.6 nm)*; weight of shell 13.5 kg.
4—37 mm/63 (2 twin); 80° elevation; 160 rounds/minute to 9 km *(4.9 nm)*; weight of shell 0.7 kg.
4—25 mm/60 (quad); 85° elevation; 270 rounds/minute to 3 km *(1.6 nm)*; weight of shell 0.34 kg.
A/S mortars: 2 RBU 1200 5-tubed fixed launchers; range 1200 m; warhead 34 kg.

Helicopters: Platform for one medium.

Programmes: Built at Najin Shipyard; laid down 1980; commissioned 1983.
Structure: This is reported as a unique twin hull design with a large helicopter flight deck aft.
Operational: Little time is spent at sea so the design is probably unsuccessful.

2 NAJIN CLASS

Displacement, tons: 1500 full load
Dimensions, feet (metres): 334.6 × 32.8 × 8.9 *(102 × 10 × 2.7)*
Main machinery: 2 diesels; 15 000 hp(m) *(11.03 MW)*; 2 shafts
Speed, knots: 24. **Range, miles:** 4000 at 13 kts
Complement: 180

Missiles: SSM: 2 SS-N-2A Styx ❶; active radar or IR homing to 46 km *(25 nm)* at 0.9 Mach; warhead 513 kg HE. Replaced torpedo tubes on both ships.
Guns: 2—3.9 in *(100 mm)*/56 ❷; 40° elevation; 15 rounds/minute to 16 km *(8.6 nm)*; weight of shell 13.5 kg.
4—57 mm/80 (2 twin) ❸; 85° elevation; 120 rounds/minute to 6 km *(3.2 nm)*; weight of shell 2.8 kg.
8—25 mm/70 (2 quad) ❹; 85° elevation; 270 rounds/minute to 3 km *(1.6 nm)*; weight of shell 0.34 kg.
8—14.5 mm (4 twin) MGs ❺; anti-aircraft.
A/S mortars: 2 RBU 1200 5-tubed fixed launchers ❻; range 1200 m; warhead 34 kg.
Depth charges: 2 projectors; 2 racks.
Mines: 30 (estimated).
Fire control: Optical director ❼.
Radars: Air search: Slim Net ❽; E/F band.
Surface search: Pot Head ❾; I band; range 37 km *(20 nm)*.
Navigation: Pot Drum; H/I band.
Fire control: Drum Tilt ❿; H/I band.
IFF: Ski Pole.
Sonars: One hull-mounted type. One VDS type.

Programmes: Built in North Korea. First completed 1973, second completed 1975.
Structure: There is some resemblance to the obsolete USSR Kola class.

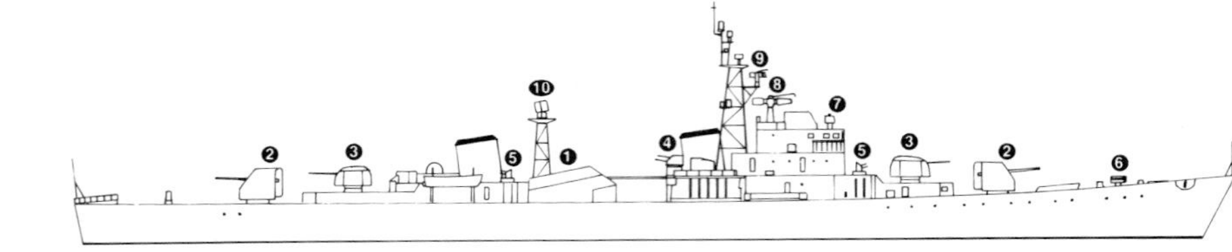

NAJIN Class *(Scale 1 : 900), Ian Sturton*

NAJIN 631 *1990*

NAJIN 531 *1988*

LIGHT FORCES

Note: A few obsolete P4 patrol craft were still active in 1991.

19 SOVIET and NORTH KOREAN SO 1 CLASSES (LARGE PATROL CRAFT)

Displacement, tons: 170 light; 215 normal
Dimensions, feet (metres): 137.8 × 19.7 × 5.9 *(42 × 6 × 1.8)*
Main machinery: 3 Type 40D diesels; 7500 hp(m) *(5.51 MW)*; 3 shafts
Speed, knots: 28. **Range, miles:** 1100 at 13 kts
Complement: 31

Guns: 1—85 mm/52; 85° elevation; 18 rounds/minute to 15 km *(8 nm)*; weight of shell 9.5 kg.
2—37 mm/63 (twin); 80° elevation; 160 rounds/minute to 9 km *(4.9 nm)*; weight of shell 0.7 kg.
4—25 mm/60 (2 twin); 85° elevation; 270 rounds/minute to 3 km *(1.6 nm)*; weight of shell 0.34 kg.
4—14.5 mm/93 MGs.
A/S mortars: 2 RBU 1200 5-tubed launchers; range 1200 m; warhead 34 kg.
Radars: Surface search: Pot Head; I band; range 37 km *(20 nm)*.
Navigation: Don 2; I band.
IFF: Ski Pole or Dead Duck.
Sonars: Tamir 2; hull-mounted; active.

Comment: Eight transferred by the USSR in early 1960s, with RBU 1200 ASW rocket launchers and depth charges instead of the 85 mm and 37 mm guns. Remainder built in North Korea to modified design. Thirteen are fitted out for ASW with sonar and depth charges; the other six are used as gunboats.

11 SOJU CLASS (FAST ATTACK CRAFT—MISSILE)

Displacement, tons: 220 full load
Dimensions, feet (metres): 141 × 24.6 × 5.6 *(43 × 7.5 × 1.7)*
Main machinery: 3 M503A Type diesels; 12 000 hp(m) *(8.82 MW)*; 3 shafts
Speed, knots: 34
Missiles: SSM: 4 SS-N-2 Styx; active radar or IR homing to 46 km *(25 nm)* at 0.9 Mach; warhead 513 kg.
Guns: 4—30 mm AKM-30 (2 twin).
Radars: Surface search: Square Tie; I band.
Fire Control: Drum Tilt; H/I band.

Comment: North Korean built and enlarged version of Osa class. First completed in 1981; building at about one per year.

8 Ex-SOVIET OSA I and 4 Ex-CHINESE HUANGFEN CLASSES (FAST ATTACK CRAFT—MISSILE)

Displacement, tons: 171 standard; 210 full load
Dimensions, feet (metres): 110.2 × 24.9 × 8.9 *(33.6 × 7.6 × 2.7)*
Main machinery: 3 M503A diesels; 12 000 hp(m) *(8.82 MW)*; 3 shafts
Speed, knots: 35. **Range, miles:** 800 at 30 kts
Complement: 30

Missiles: SSM: 4 SS-N-2A Styx; active radar or IR homing to 46 km *(25 nm)* at 0.9 Mach; warhead 513 kg.
Guns: 4—30 mm/65 (2 twin); 85° elevation; 500 rounds/minute to 5 km *(2.7 nm)*; weight of shell 0.54 kg.
Radars: Surface search: Square Tie; I band.
Fire control: Drum Tilt; H/I band.
IFF: High Pole B. Square Head.

Programmes: Twelve Osa I class transferred in 1968 and four more in 1972-83. Eight deleted so far. Four Huangfen class acquired in 1982.

OSA I Class

10 Ex-SOVIET KOMAR and 6 SOHUNG CLASSES (FAST ATTACK CRAFT—MISSILE)

Displacement, tons: 75 standard; 85 full load
Dimensions, feet (metres): 87.9 × 20.3 × 4.9 *(26.8 × 6.2 × 1.5)* (Sohung)
Main machinery: 4 Type M50 diesels; 4800 hp(m) *(3.53 MW)*; 4 shafts
Speed, knots: 40. **Range, miles:** 400 at 30 kts
Complement: 19

Missiles: SSM: 2 SS-N-2A Styx; active radar or IR homing to 46 km *(25 nm)* at 0.9 Mach; warhead 513 kg.
Guns: 2—25 mm/80 (twin); 85° elevation; 270 rounds/minute to 3 km *(1.6 nm)*; weight of shell 0.34 kg.
Radars: Surface search: Square Tie; I band.
IFF: Ski Pole. Dead Duck.

Programmes: Ten Komar class transferred by USSR, all still in service but with wood hulls replaced by steel. The Sohung class is a North Korean copy of the Komar class, first built in 1980-81.

KOMAR Class

3 SARIWON (TRAL) CLASS (LARGE PATROL CRAFT)

Displacement, tons: 600 standard; 650 full load
Dimensions, feet (metres): 203.7 × 23.9 × 7.8 *(62.1 × 7.3 × 2.4)*
Main machinery: 2 diesels; 3000 hp(m) *(2.21 MW)*; 2 shafts
Speed, knots: 21. **Range, miles:** 2700 at 18 kts
Complement: 65-70
Guns: 2—3.9 in *(100 mm)*/56; 40° elevation; 15 rounds/minute to 16 km *(8.6 nm)*; weight of shell 13.5 kg.
12/16—14.5 mm (3/4 quad) MGs (possibly ZPU-4 type).
Depth charges: 2 rails.
Mines: 30.
Radars: Surface search: Skin Head; I band.
Navigation: Don 2; I band.
IFF: Ski Pole.
Sonars: Hull-mounted type.

Comment: Built in North Korea in the mid-1960s. Design similar to that of obsolete Soviet Tral class. Another of the class is the Flagship of the Maritime Coastal Security Forces.

SARIWON Class *1991*

6 Ex-CHINESE HAINAN CLASS (LARGE PATROL CRAFT)

Displacement, tons: 375 standard; 392 full load
Dimensions, feet (metres): 192.8 × 23.6 × 6.6 *(58.8 × 7.2 × 2)*
Main machinery: 4 Kolumna/PCR Type 9-D-8 diesels; 4400 hp(m) *(3.23 MW)*; 4 shafts
Speed, knots: 30.5. **Range, miles:** 1300 at 15 kts
Complement: 69
Guns: 4—57 mm/70 (2 twin); 85° elevation; 120 rounds/minute to 8 km *(4.4 nm)*; weight of shell 2.8 kg.
4—25 mm/80 (2 twin); 85° elevation; 270 rounds/minute to 3 km *(1.6 nm)*; weight of shell 0.34 kg.
A/S mortars: 4 RBU 1200 5-tubed launchers; range 1200 m; warhead 34 kg.
Depth charges: 2 projectors; 2 racks.
Mines: Laying capability.
Radars: Surface search: Pot Head; I band.
Sonars: Hull-mounted; active search and attack; high frequency.

Comment: Transferred in 1975 (2), 1976 (2), 1978 (2).

HAINAN Class *12/1989, G. Jacobs*

1 SOMAN CLASS (LARGE PATROL CRAFT)

Displacement, tons: 190 full load
Dimensions, feet (metres): 91.6 × 19 × 6.2 *(27.9 × 5.8 × 1.9)*
Main machinery: 1 USSR Type 3D-12 diesel; 315 hp(m) *(232 kW)*; 1 shaft
Speed, knots: 10. **Range, miles:** 1200 at 9 kts
Complement: 50 (7 officers)
Guns: 4—25 mm/60 (2 twin); 85° elevation; 270 rounds/minute to 3 km *(1.6 nm)*; weight of shell 0.34 kg.
4—14.5 mm/93 (2 twin) MGs.
Mines: 2 rails for 16.
Radars: Surface search: Skin Head; I band.
IFF: High Pole A; Square Head.

Comment: The only one of its kind possibly used as a command gunboat or may have a secondary role as a minelayer.

8 TAECHONG I and 2 TAECHONG II (MAYANG) CLASSES (LARGE PATROL CRAFT)

Displacement, tons: 385 standard; 410 full load (I); 425 full load (II)
Dimensions, feet (metres): 196.3 (I); 199.5 (II) × 23.6 × 6.6 *(59.8; 60.8 × 7.2 × 2)*
Main machinery: 4 USSR 40-D diesels; 10 000 hp(m) *(7.35 MW)*; 4 shafts
Speed, knots: 30. **Range, miles:** 2000 at 12 kts
Complement: 80
Guns: 1—3.9 in *(100 mm)*/56 (Taechong II); 40° elevation; 15 rounds/minute to 16 km *(8.6 nm)*; weight of shell 13.5 kg.
2—57 mm/70 (twin); 90° elevation; 120 rounds/minute to 8 km *(4.4 nm)*; weight of shell 2.8 kg.
1—37 mm/63 (Taechong I); 85° elevation; 160 rounds/minute to 4 km *(2.2 nm)*; weight of shell 0.7 kg.
4—30 mm/65 (2 twin). 4—14.5 mm/93 (2 twin) MGs.
A/S mortars: 2 RBU 1200 5-tubed fixed launchers; range 1200 m; warhead 34 kg.
Depth charges: 2 racks.
Radars: Surface search: Pot Head; I band; range 37 km *(20 nm)*.
Fire control: Drum Tilt; H/I band.
IFF: High Pole A. Square Head.
Sonars: Stag Ear; hull-mounted; active attack; high frequency.

Comment: North Korean class of mid-1970s design, slightly larger than Hainan class. The first eight are Taechong I class. The last two are slightly longer and are heavily armed for units of this size. Taechong II still building at about one per year and may now be called Mayang class.

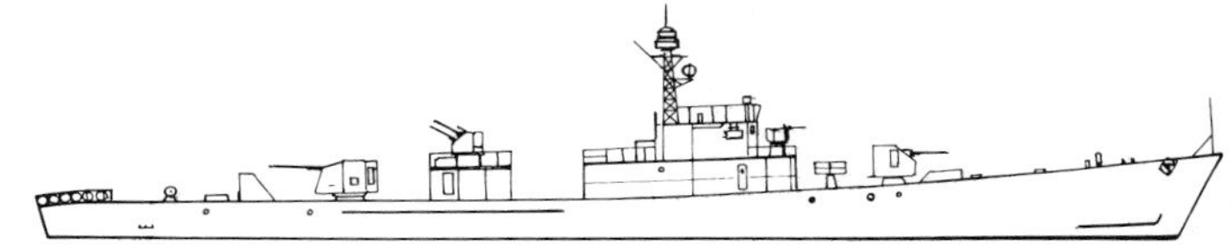

TAECHONG Class *(Not to scale)*

TAECHONG Class *(with Najin)* *1988*

13 SHANGHAI II CLASS (FAST ATTACK CRAFT—GUN)

Displacement, tons: 113 standard; 131 full load
Dimensions, feet (metres): 126.3 × 17.7 × 5.6 *(38.5 × 5.4 × 1.7)*
Main machinery: 2 Type L12-180 diesels; 2400 hp(m) *(1.76 MW)* (forward)
2 Type 12D6 diesels; 1820 hp(m) *(1.34 MW)* (aft); 4 shafts
Speed, knots: 30. **Range, miles:** 700 at 16.5 kts
Complement: 34
Guns: 4—37 mm/63 (2 twin); 80° elevation; 160 rounds/minute to 9 km *(4.9 nm)*; weight of shell 0.7 kg.
4—25 mm/60 (2 twin); 85° elevation; 270 rounds/minute to 3 km *(1.6 nm)*; weight of shell 0.34 kg.
2—3 in *(76 mm)* recoilless rifles.
Depth charges: 8.
Mines: Rails can be fitted for 10 mines.
Radars: Surface search: Pot Head; I band or Skin Head; I band.

Comment: Acquired from China since 1967. One deleted in 1988 and one more in 1990.

SHANGHAI II Class

3 CHODO CLASS (FAST ATTACK CRAFT—GUN)

Displacement, tons: 130 full load
Dimensions, feet (metres): 140 × 19 × 8.5 *(42.7 × 5.8 × 2.6)*
Main machinery: 4 diesels; 6000 hp(m) *(4.41 MW)*; 2 shafts
Speed, knots: 25. **Range, miles:** 2000 at 10 kts
Complement: 40
Guns: 1—3 in *(76 mm)*/66 automatic; 85° elevation; 120 rounds/minute to 15 km *(8 nm)*; weight of shell 7 kg.
2—37 mm/63; 85° elevation; 160 rounds/minute to 4 km *(2.2 nm)*; weight of shell 0.7 kg.
4—25 mm/60 (2 twin); 85° elevation; 270 rounds/minute to 3 km *(1.6 nm)*; weight of shell 0.34 kg.
Radars: Surface search: Skin Head; I band.
IFF: Ski Pole.

Comment: Built in North Korea in mid-1960s.

CHODO Class

62 CHAHO CLASS (FAST ATTACK CRAFT—GUN)

Displacement, tons: 82 full load
Dimensions, feet (metres): 85.3 × 19 × 6.6 *(26 × 5.8 × 2)*
Main machinery: 4 Type M50 diesels; 4800 hp(m) *(3.53 MW)*; 4 shafts
Speed, knots: 40
Complement: 12
Guns: 1 BM 21 multiple rocket launcher. 2 USSR 23 mm/87 (twin). 2—14.5 mm (twin) MGs.
Radars: Surface search: Pot Head; I band.

Comment: Building in North Korea since 1974. Based on P 6 hull. Three transferred to Iran in April 1987. Four deleted in 1990/91.

CHAHO Class *4/1988*

15 IWON CLASS (FAST ATTACK CRAFT—TORPEDO)

Displacement, tons: 25 full load
Dimensions, feet (metres): 66 × 12 × 5 *(20.3 × 3.7 × 1.5)*
Main machinery: 3 Type M50 diesels; 3600 hp(m) *(2.65 MW)*; 3 shafts
Speed, knots: 45
Guns: 4—25 mm (2 twin).
Torpedoes: 2—21 in *(533 mm)* tubes.
Radars: Surface search: Skin Head; I band.
Navigation: One set.
IFF: Dead Duck.

Comment: Built in North Korea in late 1950s. Similar to older Soviet P 2 class design and also to the export Kimjin class.

52 CHONG-JIN and 4 CHONG-JU CLASSES (FAST ATTACK CRAFT—GUN or TORPEDO)

Displacement, tons: 80 full load
Dimensions, feet (metres): 90.9 × 20 × 5.9 *(27.7 × 6.1 × 1.8)*
139.4 × 22.3 × 6.2 *(42.5 × 6.8 × 1.9)* (Chong-Ju class)
Main machinery: 4 Type M50 diesels; 4800 hp(m) *(3.53 MW)*; 4 shafts
Speed, knots: 40
Complement: 12
Guns: 1—85 mm/52; 85° elevation; 18 rounds/minute to 15 km *(8 nm)*; weight of shell 9.5 kg.
4 or 8—14.5 mm (2 or 4 twin) MGs (Chong-Jin). 1 BM 21 MRL and quad 14.5 mm (Chong-Ju).
Radars: Surface search: Pot Head; I band.
IFF: High Pole B; Square Head.

Comment: Particulars similar to Chaho class of which this is an improved version. Building began about 1975. About one third reported to be a hydrofoil development. A further class, Chong-Ju (an enlarged Chong-Jin) started building in 1985; one of these has been converted to fire torpedoes.

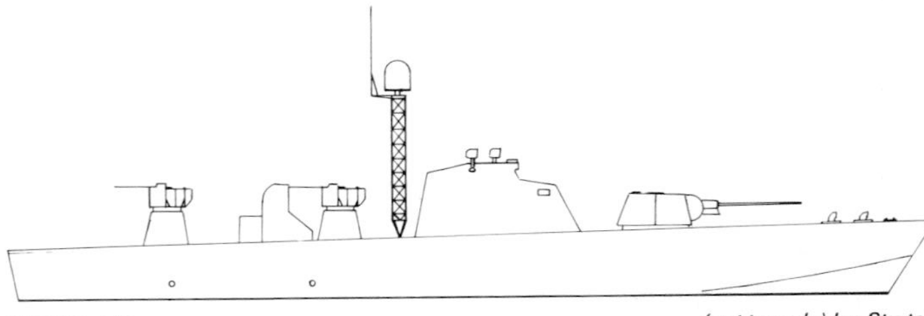

CHONG-JIN *(not to scale) Ian Sturton*

27 SOVIET AND CHINESE P 6 CLASS (FAST ATTACK CRAFT—TORPEDO) and 18 SINPO or SINNAM CLASS (FAST ATTACK CRAFT—GUN)

Displacement, tons: 64 standard; 73 full load
Dimensions, feet (metres): 85.3 × 20 × 4.9 *(26 × 6.1 × 1.5)*
Main machinery: 4 Type M50 F-12 diesels; 3400 hp(m) *(2.5 MW)* sustained; 4 shafts
Speed, knots: 45. **Range, miles:** 450 at 30 kts; 600 at 15 kts
Complement: 15
Guns: 4—25 mm/80 (2 twin) (original). 2—37 mm (others). 6—14.5 mm MGs (Sinpo class).
Torpedoes: 2—21 in *(533 mm)* tubes (in some). Sinpo class has no tubes.
Depth charges: 8 in some.
Radars: Surface search: Skin Head; I band (some have Furuno).
IFF: Dead Duck. High Pole.

Comment: There is a growing number of the Sinpo class with local building programme in hand of a modified form. Originally 27 P 6 class were transferred by the USSR and 15 from China. The Sinpos are replacing the P 6s.

P 6 Class

SINPO Class

88 KU SONG, SIN HUNG and 37 MOD SIN HUNG CLASSES (FAST ATTACK CRAFT—TORPEDO)

Displacement, tons: 40 full load
Dimensions, feet (metres): 72.2 × 11 × 5.5 *(22 × 3.4 × 1.7)*
Main machinery: 2 Type M50 diesels; 2400 hp(m) *(1.76 MW)*; 2 shafts
Speed, knots: 40
Guns: 4—14.5 mm (2 twin) MGs.
Torpedoes: 2—18 in *(457 mm)* or 2—21 in *(533 mm)* tubes (not fitted in all).
Radars: Surface search: Skin Head; I band.
IFF: Dead Duck.

Comment: Ku Song and Sin Hung built in North Korea mid-1950s to 1970. Frequently operated on South Korean border. A modified version of Sin Hung with hydrofoils built from 1981 to 1985.

SIN HUNG Class (no torpedo tubes) *1991*

0 TB 11PA AND 6 TB 40A CLASSES (INSHORE PATROL CRAFT)

isplacement, tons: 8
imensions, feet (metres): 36.7 × 8.6 × 3.3 *(11.2 × 2.7 × 1)*
lain machinery: 2 diesels; 520 hp(m) *(382 kW)*; 2 shafts
peed, knots: 35. **Range, miles:** 200 at 15 kts
omplement: 4
uns: 1—7.62 mm MG.
adars: Surface search/navigation: Radar-24.

omment: New construction high speed patrol boats. Reinforced fibreglass hull. Design closely resembles a number of UK/Western European commercial craft. Twenty ordered by Zaire for delivery in late 1990 but this was probably delayed by lack of funds. Larger hull design, known as 'TB 40A' also building. Both classes being operated by the MSCF.

IGH SPEED INFILTRATION CRAFT

isplacement, tons: 5
imensions, feet (metres): 30.5 × 8.2 × 3.1 *(9.3 × 2.5 × 1)*
lain machinery: 1 V-8 diesel; 260 hp(m) *(191 kW)*; 1 shaft
peed, knots: 35
omplement: 2
uns: 1—7.62 mm MG.
adars: Navigation: Furuno 701; I band.

omment: Large numbers built for Agent infiltration and covert operations. These craft have a very low radar cross section and 'squat' at high speeds.

AMPHIBIOUS FORCES

HANCHON CLASS (LCM)

isplacement, tons: 145 full load
imensions, feet (metres): 117.1 × 25.9 × 3.9 *(35.7 × 7.9 × 1.2)*
lain machinery: 2 Type 3D-12 diesels; 630 hp(m) *(463 kW)* sustained; 2 shafts
peed, knots: 10. **Range, miles:** 600 at 6 kts
omplement: 15 (1 officer)
lilitary lift: 2 tanks or 200 troops
uns: 2—14.5 mm/93 (twin) MG.
adars: Surface search: Skin Head; I band.

omment: Built in North Korea.

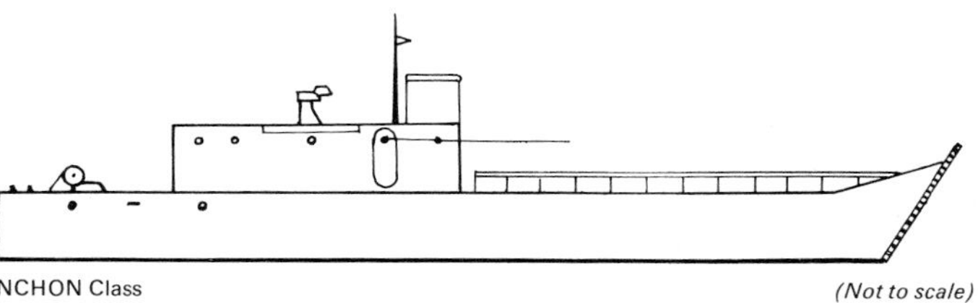

ANCHON Class *(Not to scale)*

00 NAMPO CLASS (LCP)

isplacement, tons: 80 full load
imensions, feet (metres): 84.2 × 20 × 6 *(27.7 × 6.1 × 1.8)*
ain machinery: 4 Type M50 diesels; 4800 hp(m) *(3.53 MW)*; 4 shafts
peed, knots: 40. **Range, miles:** 375 at 40 kts
omplement: 19
ilitary lift: 20-30 troops
uns: 4—14.5 mm (2 twin) MGs.
adars: Surface search: Pot Head; I band.

omment: A class of assault landing craft. Almost identical to the Chong-Jin class but with a smaller forward gun mounting and with retractable ramp in bows. Building began about 1975. Four or five have probably been deleted due to damage. Numbers uncertain. About 20 used for patrol duties with bow doors welded shut.

16 HUNGNAM AND 8 HANTAE CLASSES (LSM)

Comment: Both classes started building in 1980-82 and are capable of taking 4 to 5 medium tanks. Hungnam is slightly larger.

52 + 6 SONGJONG CLASS (LCP—HOVERCRAFT)

Comment: Three types: one Type I, 31 Type II and 20 + 6 Type III. Type III is building at 6-10 per year. Length about 25 m (I) and 18 m (II). A series of high speed air-cushion landing craft first reported in 1987. Use of air-cushion technology is an adoption of commercial technology imported from the UK. Estimated to carry 35 to 55 (or more) light infantry troops. Songjong II may be called the Hwanghae class.

MINESWEEPERS

23 YUKTO I and II CLASSES (COASTAL MINESWEEPERS)

Displacement, tons: 60 full load
Dimensions, feet (metres): 78.7 × 13.1 × 5.6 *(24 × 4 × 1.7)*
Main machinery: 2 diesels; 2 shafts
Speed, knots: 18
Complement: 22 (4 officers)
Guns: 1—37 mm/63 or 2—25 mm/80 (twin). 2—14.5 mm/93 (twin) MGs.
Mines: 2 rails for 4.
Radars: Surface search: Skin Head; I band.

Comment: North Korean design built in the 1980s and replaced the obsolete ex-Soviet KN-14 class. A total of four Yukto IIs were built; they are 3 m shorter (at 21 m length) overall and have no after gun. Wooden construction.

6 PIPA-GOT CLASS (INSHORE MINESWEEPERS)

Comment: A new class of MSI. No details.

SURVEY VESSELS

Note: The Hydrographic Department has four survey ships.

Name	*Displacement*	*Launched*	*Complement*
DONGHAE 101	260 tons	1970	22 (8 officers)
DONGHAE 102	1100 tons	1979	35 (20 officers)
SOHAI 201	260 tons	1972	22 (14 officers)
SOHAI 202	300 tons	1981	26 (16 officers)

SERVICE FORCES

Note: (1) One Kowan class ASR built recently for submarine rescue, possibly catamaran construction. Trawlers operate as AGIs on the South Korean border where several have been sunk over the years. In addition many ocean going commercial vessels are used for carrying weapons and ammunition worldwide in support of international terrorism.
(2) There are also 8 ocean cargo ships adapted as mother ships for midget submarines. Their names are *Soo Gun-Ho, Dong Geon Ae Gook-Ho, Dong Hae-Ho, Choong Seong-Ho Number One, Choong Seong-Ho Number Two, Choong Seong-Ho Number Three, Hae Gum Gang-Ho* and the *Song Rim-Ho*.

KOREA, Republic (South)

eadquarters' Appointments

hief of Naval Operations:
Admiral Kim Chul-Woo
rst Vice Chief Naval Operations:
Vice Admiral Kim Chong Woo
ommandant Marine Corps:
Lieutenant General Cho Ki-Yup
ommandant Naval Academy:
Vice Admiral Baek Sok-Ghee

perational Commands

ommander First Fleet:
Rear Admiral Choe Il Kun
ommander Second Fleet:
Rear Admiral An Pyong-Tae
ommander Third Fleet:
Rear Admiral Kim Man Chong

iplomatic Representation

efence Attaché in London:
Captain S J Kim

rsonnel

) 1992: 35 000 Navy, 25 000 Marine Corps
) 2½ years' (Navy) national service with a proportion of ratings and all marines being volunteers

Bases

Major: Chinhae (Fleet HQ), Pukpyong (1st Fleet)
Minor: Cheju, Mokpo, Mukho, Pohang, Inchon (2nd Fleet), Pusan (3rd Fleet)
Aviation: Pohang, Chinhae

Organisation

In 1986 the Navy was reorganised into three Fleets, each commanded by a Rear Admiral, whereas the Marines retain two Divisions and one brigade plus smaller and support units. From October 1973 the RoK Marine Force was placed directly under the RoK Navy command with a Vice Chief of Naval Operations for Marine Affairs replacing the Commandant of Marine Corps. The Marine Corps was re-established as an independent service on 1 November 1987.

1st Fleet: No 11, 12, 13 DD/FF Sqn; No 101, 102 Coastal Defence Sqn; 181, 191, 111, 121 Coastal Defence Units; 121st Minesweeper Sqn.
2nd Fleet: No 21, 22, 23 DD/FF Sqn; No 201, 202 Coastal Defence Sqn; 211, 212 Coastal Defence Units; 522nd Minesweeper Sqn.
3rd Fleet: 301, 302, 303 DD/FF Sqn; 304, 406th Coastal Defence Units.

Pennant Numbers

Pennant numbers are changed at unspecified intervals. The numbers 0 and 4 are not used as they are unlucky.

Mercantile Marine

Lloyd's Register of Shipping:
2136 vessels of 7 820 532 tons gross

Strength of the Fleet

Type	*Active*	*Building (Proposed)*
Submarines	7	6 (3)
Destroyers	9	—
Frigates	7	1 (9)
Corvettes	26	—
Fast Attack Craft—Missile	11	—
Fast Attack Craft—Patrol	66	—
Minehunters	1	5 (3)
Minesweepers	8	—
LSTs	7	2
LSMs	7	—
LCU/LCM	16	—
Logistic Support Ship	0	1
Salvage Ships	2	1
Tankers	6	—
Tugs	11	—
Survey Ships and Craft	7	—

DELETIONS

Destroyers

1988-89 *Chung Mu, Pusan* (both used for alongside training)

Amphibious Ships

1989 *Tuk Bong*

SUBMARINES

0 + 6 (3) TYPE 209 CLASS (1200)

Displacement, tons: 1100 surfaced; 1285 dived
Dimensions, feet (metres): 183.7 × 20.3 × 18 *(56 × 6.2 × 5.5)*
Main machinery: Diesel-electric; 4 MTU 12V 396 diesels; 3800 hp(m) *(2.8 MW)* sustained; 4 alternators; 1 motor; 4600 hp(m) *(3.38 MW)* sustained; 1 shaft
Speed, knots: 11 surfaced/snorting; 22 dived
Range, miles: 7500 at 8 kts surfaced
Complement: 33 (6 officers)

Torpedoes: 8—21 in *(533 mm)* bow tubes. 14 probably AEG SS4; wire-guided; active/passive homing to 28 km *(15.3 nm)* at 23 kts; 12 km *(6.6 nm)* at 35 kts; warhead 260 kg. Swim-out discharge.
Mines: 28 in lieu of torpedoes.
Countermeasures: ESM: Radar warning.
Fire control: Krupp Atlas ISUS TFCS.
Radars: Navigation: I band.
Sonars: Krupp Atlas CSU 83; hull-mounted; passive/active; medium frequency.

Type 1200 *198*

Programmes: First three ordered in late 1987, one built at Kiel by HDW, and two being assembled at Okpo by Daewoo from material packages transported from Germany. Key Korean personnel have been trained in Germany. Second three ordered in October 1989 to be built at Okpo. The final total could be as many as 18 split between the three fleets and the aim is eventually to be independent of European shipbuilding assistance. First of class is planned to complete in 1992, then one per year thereafter.

Structure: Type 1200 similar to those built for the Turkish Nav with a heavy dependence on Atlas Electronic sensors and AE torpedoes. Air independent propulsion using a Cosworth Arg diesel is an option in some of the later hulls.

4 KSS-1 TOLGORAE and 3 COSMOS CLASSES

Displacement, tons: 150 surfaced; 175 dived (Tolgorae); 70 surfaced (Cosmos)
Torpedoes: 2—406 mm tubes (Tolgorae).
Sonars: Krupp Atlas; hull-mounted; passive search; high frequency.

Comment: First Tolgorae class in service in 1983 and three more in 1988. There are also three or four Cosmos type for a total of six of both classes. Limited endurance, for use only in coastal waters. There is an unconfirmed report that six KSS-1s may have been sold to Saudi Arabia.

TOLGORAE Class *11/1985, G. Jacob*

DESTROYERS

7 Ex-US GEARING (FRAM I and II) CLASS

Name	*No*	*Builders*	*Laid down*	*Launched*	*Commissioned*
CHUNG BUK (ex-USS *Chevalier* DD 805)	DD 915	Bath Iron Works Corporation, Bath, Maine	12 June 1944	29 Oct 1944	9 Jan 1945
JEON BUK (ex-USS *Everett F Larson* DD 830)	DD 916	Bath Iron Works Corporation, Bath, Maine	4 Sep 1944	28 Jan 1945	6 Apr 1945
TAEJON (ex-USS *New* DD 818)	DD 919	Consolidated Steel Corporation	14 Apr 1945	18 Aug 1945	5 Apr 1946
KWANG JU (ex-USS *Richard E Kraus* DD 849)	DD 921	Bath Iron Works Corporation, Bath, Maine	31 July 1945	2 Mar 1946	23 May 1946
KANG WON (ex-USS *William R Rush* DD 714)	DD 922	Federal S B and D D Co, Newark	19 Oct 1944	8 July 1945	21 Sep 1945
KYONG KI (ex-USS *Newman K Perry* DD 883)	DD 923	Consolidated Steel Corporation	10 Oct 1944	17 Mar 1945	26 July 1945
JEON JU (ex-USS *Rogers* DD 876)	DD 925	Consolidated Steel Corporation	3 June 1944	20 Nov 1944	26 Mar 1945

Displacement, tons: 2425 standard; 3470 full load approx
Dimensions, feet (metres): 390.5 × 41.2 × 19 *(119 × 12.6 × 5.8)*
Main machinery: 4 Babcock & Wilcox boilers; 600 psi *(43.3 kg/cm sq)*; 850°F *(454°C)*; 2 GE turbines; 60 000 hp *(45 MW)*; 2 shafts
Speed, knots: 32.5. **Range, miles:** 3275 at 11 kts; 975 at 32 kts
Complement: 280

Missiles: SSM: 8 McDonnell Douglas Harpoon (2 quad) launchers ❶ (all except DD 923 and 925); active radar homing to 130 km *(70 nm)* at 0.9 Mach; warhead 227 kg.
A/S: Honeywell ASROC Mk 112 octuple launcher (DD 923 and 925); inertial guidance to 1.6-10 km *(1-6 nm)*; payload Mk 46 torpedo.
Guns: 4 or 6—5 in *(127 mm)*/38 (2 twin) Mk 38 (3 twin in DD 915-916) ❷; 85° elevation; 15 rounds/minute to 17 km *(9 nm)* anti-surface; 11 km *(5.9 nm)* anti-aircraft; weight of shell 25 kg.
2 USN/Bofors 40 mm/56 (twin) (except DD 915 and 916); 45° elevation; 160 rounds/minute to 11 km *(5.9 nm)* anti-surface; 6 km *(3.3 nm)* anti-aircraft; weight of shell 0.9 kg.
2 General Electric/General Dynamics 20 mm Vulcan Gatling (except DD 923); 3000 rounds/minute combined to 1.5 km.
Torpedoes: 6—324 mm Mk 32 (2 triple) tubes ❸. Honeywell Mk 46; anti-submarine; active/passive homing to 11 km *(5.9 nm)* at 40 kts; warhead 44 kg.
A/S mortars: 2 USN Hedgehog Mk 11 fixed rocket launchers (DD 915-916) ❹; manually loaded; range 350 m; warhead 26 kg; 24 missiles.
Depth charges: 1 Mk IX rack.
Countermeasures: ESM: WLR-1; radar warning. WJ 1140 (DD 916).
ECM: ULQ-6; jammer.
Fire control: 1 Mk 37 GFCS. 1 Mk 51 Mod 2 (except DD 915 and 916) (for 40 mm).
Radars: Air search: Lockheed SPS 40 ❺ (DD 921 has SPS 37); E/F band; range 320 km *(175 nm)*.
Surface search: Raytheon/Sylvania SPS 10 ❻; G band.
Fire control: Western Electric Mk 25 ❼; I/J band.
IFF: UPX 1-12 (DD 919 and 921).
Sonars: SQS 29 (DD 915-916); hull-mounted; active search and attack; high frequency.
Sangamo SQS 23 (remainder); active search and attack; medium frequency.

Helicopters: 1 Aerospatiale SA 316B Alouette III or 1 Westland Super Lynx ❽ (all except DD 923 and 925).

Programmes: First pair on loan on 5 July 1972 and 30 October 1972 respectively and by purchase 31 January 1977. Second pair 23 February 1977 by sale. DD 922 by sale 1 July 1978. Last pair by sale February/March 1981.

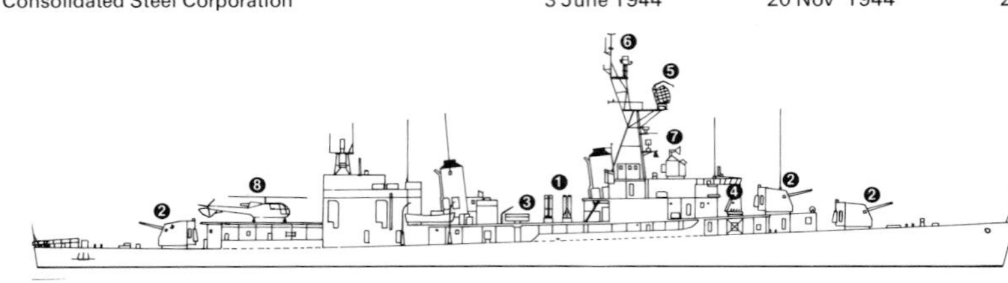
CHUNG BUK *(Scale 1 : 1 200), Ian Sturto*

KANG WON (with Harpoon and Gatling midships plus 40 mm guns forward) *9/198*

CHUNG BUK (with 3 twin 127 mm guns) *9/198*

Modernisation: DD 915 and DD 916 were converted to radar picket destroyers (DDR) in 1949. All subsequently modernised under the US Navy's Fleet Rehabilitation and Modernisation (FRAM) programme—first pair to FRAM II standards, others to FRAM I. Fitted with small helicopter hangar and flight deck. Anti-ship torpedo tubes have been removed. In DD 915 and D 919 the helicopter deck has been strengthened and in 925 tw Vulcan Gatling guns have been positioned at the after end Harpoon fitted in 1979 and some ships may still only carry tw twin launchers. Most are now Tacan and SATCOM fitted.

JEON JU (ASROC and Gatling aft) *1987*

2 Ex-US ALLEN M SUMNER (FRAM II) CLASS

Name	*No*	*Builders*	*Laid down*	*Launched*	*Commissioned*
DAE GU (ex-USS *Wallace L Lind* DD 703)	DD 917	Bath Iron Works Corporation, Bath, Maine	Apr 1944	14 June 1944	8 Sep 1944
INCHON (ex-USS *De Haven* DD 727)	DD 918	Federal S B & D D Co, Kearney, New Jersey	Oct 1943	9 Jan 1944	31 Mar 1944

Displacement, tons: 2200 standard; 3320 full load
Dimensions, feet (metres): 376.5 × 40.9 × 19 *(114.8 × 12.4 × 5.8)*
Main machinery: 4 Babcock & Wilcox boilers; 600 psi *(43.3 kg/cm sq)*; 850°F *(454°C)*; 2 GE turbines; 60 000 hp *(45 MW)*; 2 shafts
Speed, knots: 34. **Range, miles:** 4500 at 16 kts
Complement: 235

Guns: 6 USN 5 in *(127 mm)*/38 (3 twin) Mk 38; 85° elevation; 15 rounds/minute to 17 km *(9 nm)* anti-surface; 11 km *(5.9 nm)* anti-aircraft; weight of shell 25 kg.
2 USN/Bofors 40 mm/56 (twin); 45° elevation; 160 rounds/minute to 11 km *(5.9 nm)* anti-surface; 6 km *(3.3 nm)* anti-aircraft; weight of shell 0.9 kg.
1 General Electric/General Dynamics 20 mm Vulcan Gatling (DD 918); 3000 rounds/minute combined to 1.5 km.
Torpedoes: 6—324 mm Mk 32 (2 triple) tubes. Honeywell Mk 46; anti-submarine; active/passive homing to 11 km *(5.9 nm)* at 40 kts; warhead 44 kg.
A/S mortars: 2 USN Hedgehog Mk 11 fixed rocket launchers; manually loaded; range 350 m; warhead 20 kg; 24 missiles.
Countermeasures: Decoys: 2 Loral-Hycor RBOC 6-barrelled Mk 33 launchers; range 4 km *(2.2 nm)*.
Fire control: USN Mk 37 for 127 mm gunnery. 2 Mk 51 for 40 mm gunnery.
Radars: Air search: Lockheed SPS 40 (DD 917); E/F band; range 320 km *(175 nm)*.
Westinghouse SPS 37 (DD 918); B/C band; range 556 km *(300 nm)*.
Surface search: Raytheon/Sylvania SPS 10; G band.
Fire control: Western Electric Mk 25; I/J band.
IFF: UPX 1-12.
Sonars: Sangamo SQS 23; hull-mounted; active search and attack; medium frequency.
Litton SQA 10; VDS; active/passive search; medium frequency.

Helicopters: 1 Aerospatiale SA 316B Alouette III or 1 Westland Super Lynx.

Programmes: Transferred by sale December 1973.
Modernisation: Both ships were modernised under the US Navy's Fleet Rehabilitation and Modernisation (FRAM II) programme.
Structure: DD 917 fitted with strengthened helicopter deck and hangar.

FRIGATES

1 + (9) KDX-2000 (DW-4000) CLASS

Displacement, tons: 4000 approx
Dimensions, feet (metres): 406.8 × 44 × 12.8 *(124 × 13.4 × 3.9)*
Main machinery: CODOG; 2 GE LM 2500 gas turbines; 2 MTU or SEMT-Pielstick diesels; 2 shafts
Speed, knots: 30. **Range, miles:** 4000 at 18 kts

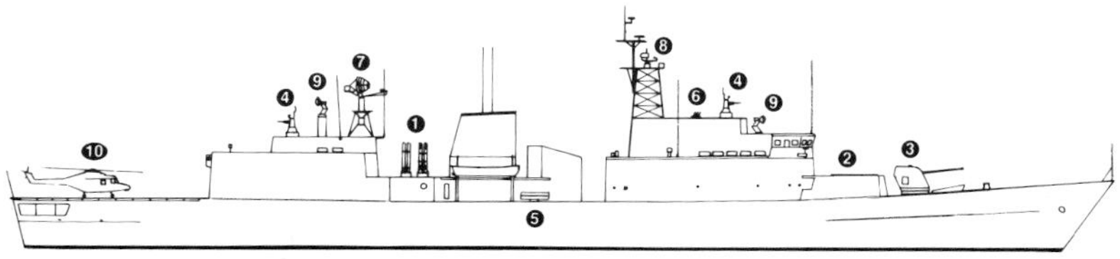

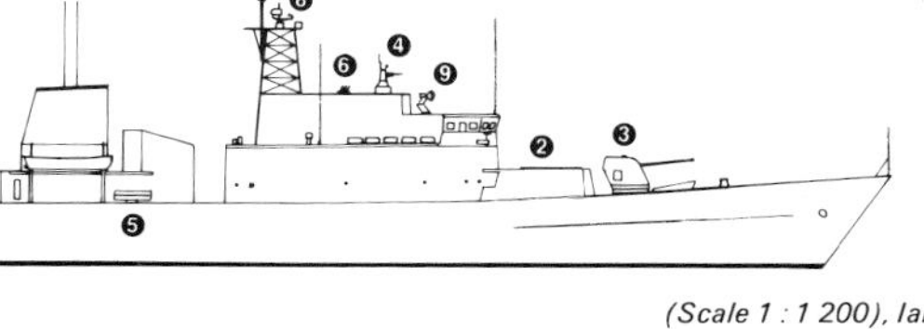

DW-4000 *(Scale 1 : 1 200), Ian Sturton*

Missiles: SSM: 8 McDonnell Douglas Harpoon (2 quad) launchers ❶.
SAM: Raytheon Sea Sparrow Mk 48; VLS launcher ❷.
Guns: 1 FMC 5 in *(127 mm)*/54 or 1 OTO Melara 5 in *(127 mm)*/54 ❸
2 Signaal 30 mm Goalkeeper ❹; 7 barrels per mounting.
Torpedoes: 6—324 mm (2 triple) launchers ❺; Mk 46; anti-submarine.
Countermeasures: Decoys: 2 Chaff launchers ❻. SLQ-25 Nixie towed torpedo decoy.
ESM/ECM: Radar intercept and jammer.
Combat data systems: Dowty-Sema SSCS Mk 7 or Atlas/Contraves COSYS 200. Link 11.

Radars: Air search: Dowty/Signaal or Atlas/Contraves ❼.
Surface search: ❽
Fire control: 2 Signaal or Contraves ❾.
Sonars: Ferranti/Thomson Sintra; hull-mounted active search; medium frequency.

Helicopters: 1 Westland Super Lynx ❿.

Programmes: A much delayed programme which should finally see the first keel laid down in mid-1992 for completion in 1996. Then at least one a year until 1999 although the building rate may be increased. First of class to be built by Daewoo, others by Hyundai.
Structure: Many of the details are unconfirmed and it is reported that some of the eventually chosen systems may be changed in later ships of the class.

7 ULSAN CLASS

Name	No	Builders	Laid down	Launched	Commissioned
ULSAN	FF 951	Hyundai, Ulsan	1979	8 Apr 1980	1 Jan 1981
SEOUL	FF 952	Hyundai, Ulsan	1982	1984	30 June 1985
CHUNG NAM	FF 953	Korean SEC, Pusan	1984	1985	1 June 1986
MASAN	FF 955	Korea Tacoma	1983	26 Oct 1984	20 July 1985
KYONG BUK	FF 956	Daewoo, Okpo	1984	1985	30 May 1986
CHON NAM	FF 957	Hyundai, Ulsan	1986	19 Apr 1988	17 June 1989
CHE JU	FF 958	Daewoo, Okpo	1986	1988	1 Jan 1990

Displacement, tons: 1496 light; 2180 full load (2300 for FF 957-958)
Dimensions, feet (metres): 334.6 × 37.7 × 11.5 *(102 × 11.5 × 3.5)*
Main machinery: CODOG; 2 GE LM 2500 gas turbines; 44 000 hp *(33 MW)* sustained; 2 MTU 16V 538 TB82 diesels; 6000 hp(m) *(4.4 MW)* sustained; 2 shafts; cp props
Speed, knots: 34; 18 on diesels. **Range, miles:** 4000 at 15 kts
Complement: 150 (16 officers)

Missiles: SSM: 8 McDonnell Douglas Harpoon (4 twin) launchers ❶; active radar homing to 130 km *(70 nm)* at 0.9 Mach; warhead 227 kg.
Guns: 2—3 in *(76 mm)*/62 OTO Melara compact ❷; 85° elevation; 85 rounds/minute to 16 km *(8.6 nm)* anti-surface; 12 km *(6.5 nm)* anti-aircraft; weight of shell 6 kg.
8 Emerson Electric 30 mm (4 twin) (FF 951-955) ❸; 6 Breda 40 mm/70 (3 twin) (FF 956-958) ❹.
Torpedoes: 6—324 mm Mk 32 (2 triple) tubes ❺. Honeywell Mk 46 Mod 1; anti-submarine; active/passive homing to 11 km *(5.9 nm)* at 40 kts; warhead 44 kg.
Depth charges: 12.
Countermeasures: Decoys: 4 Loral Hycor SRBOC 6-barrelled Mk 36 launchers ❻; range 4 km *(2.2 nm)*.
Nixie; towed torpedo decoy.
ESM/ECM: Intercept and jammer.
Combat data systems: Samsung/Ferranti WSA 423 action data automation (FF 957-958). Litton systems may be retrofitted to others.
Fire control: 1 Signaal Lirod optronic director (FF 951-956) ❼; 1 Radamec System 2400 optronic director (FF 957-958) ❽.
Radars: Air/surface search: Signaal DA 05 ❾; E/F band.
Surface search: Signaal ZW 06 (FF 951-956) ❿; Marconi S 1810 (FF 957-958) ⓫; I band.
Fire control: Signaal WM 28 (FF 951-956) ⓬; Marconi ST 1802 (FF 957-958) ⓭; I/J band.
Navigation: Raytheon SPS 10C (FF 957-958) ⓮; I band.
Tacan: SRN 15.
Sonars: Signaal PHS 32; hull-mounted; active search and attack; medium frequency.

Structure: Steel hull with aluminium alloy superstructure. There are three versions. The first four ships are the same but *Kyong Buk* has the 4 Emerson Electric twin 30 mm guns replaced by 3 Breda twin 40 mm, and the last two of the class have a built up gun platform aft and a different combination of surface search, target indication and navigation radars. Weapon systems integration caused earlier concern and a Ferranti combat data system has been installed in the last pair; it is reported that a Litton Systems CDS will be retrofitted in the earlier ships of the class. It is possible that *Chon Nam* has pennant number 959.
Operational: *Che Ju* and *Chung Nam* conducted the first ever deployment of South Korean warships to Europe during a four month tour from September 1991 to January 1992. Trainees were embarked.
Sales: Three built for India and four more constructed in India with different armaments and classified as offshore patrol vessels.

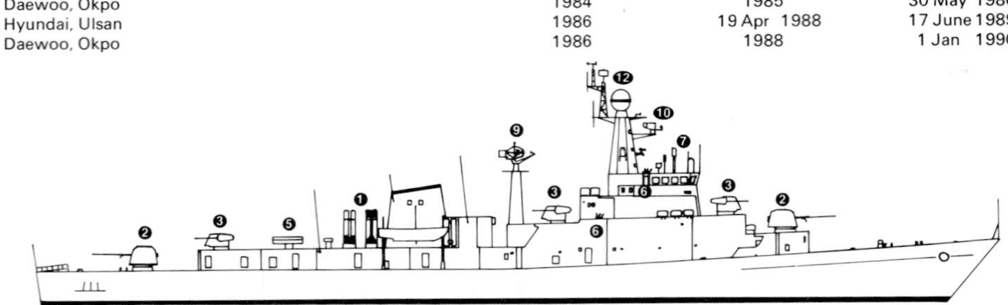

ULSAN (Scale 1 : 900), Ian Sturton

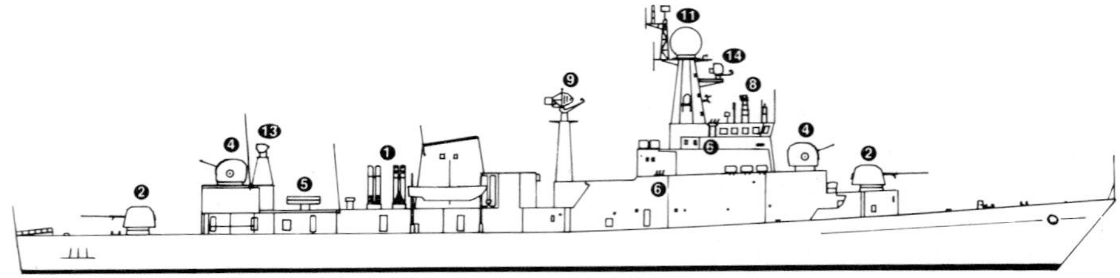

CHE JU (Scale 1 : 900), Ian Sturton

CHE JU (with Marconi FC radar and 40 mm guns) 10/1991, Foto Flite

KYONG BUK (with Signaal FC radar and 40 mm guns) 10/1989

CHUNG NAM (with Signaal FC radar and 30 mm guns) 11/1991, Maritime Photographic

SHIPBORNE AIRCRAFT

Numbers/Type: 12 Westland Super Navy Lynx Mk 99.
Operational speed: 125 kts *(231 km/h)*.
Service ceiling: 12 000 ft *(3660 m)*.
Range: 320 nm *(593 km)*.
Role/Weapon systems: Shipborne ASV helicopter delivered in 1991/92 to replace Alouette III; a further order of six ASW versions is expected in 1992 with 12 more in due course. Sensors: Ferranti Sea Spray Mk 3 radar and Racal ESM. Weapons: 4 BAe Sea Skua missiles. Mk 46 torpedo (in ASW version).

SUPER LYNX *11/1989, Westland*

Numbers/Type: 10 Aerospatiale SA 316B/SA 319B Alouette III.
Operational speed: 113 kts *(210 km/h)*.
Service ceiling: 10 500 ft *(3200 m)*.
Range: 290 nm *(540 km)*.
Role/Weapon systems: Marine support helicopter; operated by RoK Marine Corps. Sensors: None. Weapons: Unarmed.

LAND-BASED MARITIME AIRCRAFT

Numbers/Type: 15 Grumman S-2A/F Tracker.
Operational speed: 130 kts *(241 km/h)*.
Service ceiling: 25 000 ft *(7620 m)*.
Range: 1350 nm *(2500 km)*.
Role/Weapon systems: Maritime surveillance and limited ASW operations; coastal surveillance and EEZ patrol. Sensors: Search radar, ECM. Weapons: ASW; torpedoes, depth bombs and mines. ASV; underwing 127 mm rockets.

Numbers/Type: 8 Lockheed P-3C Orion.
Operational speed: 411 kts *(761 km/h)*.
Service ceiling: 28 300 ft *(8625 m)*.
Range: 4000 nm *(7410 km)*.
Role/Weapon systems: Maritime patrol aircraft ordered in 1991 for delivery in 1995. This is the Update III version.

CORVETTES

22 PO HANG CLASS

Name	*No*	*Builders*	*Commissioned*
PO HANG	756	Korea SEC, Pusan	Dec 1984
KUN SAN	757	Korea Tacoma	Dec 1984
KYONG JU	758	Hyundai	1986
MOK PO	759	Daewoo, Okpo	1986
KIM CHON	761	Korea SEC, Pusan	1987
CHUNG JU	762	Korea Tacoma	1987
JIN JU	763	Hyundai, Ulsan	1988
YO SU	765	Daewoo, Okpo	1988
AN DONG	766	Korea SEC, Pusan	Feb 1989
SUN CHON	767	Korea Tacoma	June1989
YEE REE	768	Hyundai, Ulsan	June1989
WON JU	769	Daewoo, Okpo	1989
JE CHON	771	Korea Tacoma	1989
CHON AN	772	Korea SEC, Pusan	Nov 1989
SONG NAM	773	Daewoo, Okpo	1990
BU CHON	775	Hyundai, Ulsan	1990
DAE CHON	776	Korea Tacoma	1990
JIN HAE	777	Korea SEC, Pusan	1990
SOK CHO	778	Daewoo, Okpo	1991
YONG JU	779	Hyundai, Ulsan	1991
NAM WON	781	Korea Tacoma	1991
KWAN MYONG	782	Korea SEC, Pusan	1991

Displacement, tons: 1180 full load
Dimensions, feet (metres): 289.7 × 32.8 × 9.5 *(88.3 × 10 × 2.9)*
Main machinery: CODOG; 1 GE LM 2500 gas turbine; 23 000 hp *(17.16 MW)* sustained; 2 SEMT-Pielstick 12 PA6 V280 diesels; 4800 hp(m) *(3.53 MW)* sustained; 2 shafts
Speed, knots: 32. **Range, miles:** 4000 at 15 kts
Complement: 95 (10 officers)

Missiles: SSM: 2 Aerospatiale MM 38 Exocet (756-765) ❶; inertial cruise; active radar homing to 42 km *(23 nm)* at 0.9 Mach; warhead 165 kg; sea-skimmer. Not in all.
Guns: 1 or 2 OTO Melara 3 in *(76 mm)*/62 compact ❷; 85° elevation; 85 rounds/minute to 16 km *(8.6 nm)* anti-surface; 12 km *(6.5 nm)* anti-aircraft; weight of shell 6 kg.
4 Emerson Electric 30 mm (2 twin) (756-765) ❸; 2 Breda 40 mm/70 (766 onwards) ❹.
Torpedoes: 6—324 mm Mk 32 (2 triple) tubes (766 onwards) ❺. Honeywell Mk 46; anti-submarine; active/passive homing to 11 km *(5.9 nm)* at 40 kts; warhead 44 kg.
Depth charges: 12 (766 onwards).
Countermeasures: Decoys: 4 MEL Protean fixed launchers; 36 grenades.
2 Loral Hycor SRBOC 6-barrelled Mk 36 launchers (in some); range 4 km *(2.2 nm)*.
ESM/ECM: Intercept/jammer.
Combat data systems: Signaal Sewaco ZK (756-765); Ferranti WSA 423 (766 onwards).
Fire control: Signaal Lirod or Radamec 2400 optronic director ❻.
Radars: Surface search: Marconi 1810 ❼ and/or Raytheon SPS 64 ❽; I band.
Fire control: Signaal WM 28 ❾; I/J band; or Marconi 1802 ❿; I/J band.
Sonars: Signaal PHS 32 (766 onwards); hull-mounted; active search and attack; medium frequency.

Programmes: First laid down early 1983 by Korea SEC. The pennant number/name attribution shown above is uncertain but names and shipbuilders are correct. At least two more of the class were scheduled for completion in 1992 but the status of further orders is uncertain.
Structure: It is probable that there are three groups specialising in surface-to-surface warfare, anti-submarine and, possibly to come, air defence. The first group therefore have no ASW equipment and starting with *An Dong* (766) the second group have no SSM. The second group also have an improved combat data system with Ferranti/Radamec/Marconi fire control systems and radars as in the Ulsan class later versions.

PO HANG *(Scale 1 : 900), Ian Sturton*

AN DONG *(Scale 1 : 900), Ian Sturton*

AN DONG *1989*

CHON AN *1989*

KUN SAN *1987, Korea Tacoma*

4 DONG HAE CLASS

Name	*No*	*Builders*	*Commissioned*
DONG HAE	751	Korea SEC, Pusan	1982
SU WON	752	Korea Tacoma	1983
KANG REUNG	753	Hyundai, Ulsan	1983
AN YANG	755	Daewoo, Okpo	1983

Displacement, tons: 950 full load
Dimensions, feet (metres): 256.2 × 31.5 × 8.5 *(78.1 × 9.6 × 2.6)*
Main machinery: CODOG; 1 GE LM 2500 gas turbine; 23 000 hp *(17.16 MW)* sustained; 2 MTU 12V 956 TB 82 diesels; 6160 hp(m) *(4.53 MW)* sustained; 2 shafts; cp props
Speed, knots: 31. **Range, miles:** 4000 at 15 kts
Complement: 95 (10 officers)

Guns: 1 OTO Melara 3 in *(76 mm)*/62 compact ❶; 85° elevation; 85 rounds/minute to 16 km *(8.6 nm)*; weight of shell 6 kg.
4 Emerson Electric 30 mm (2 twin) ❷. 2 Oerlikon 20 mm (twin) ❸.
Torpedoes: 6—324 mm Mk 32 (2 triple) tubes ❹. Honeywell Mk 46.
Depth charges: 12.
Combat data systems: Signaal Sewaco ZK.
Fire control: Signaal Lirod optronic director ❺.
Radars: Surface search: Raytheon SPS 64 ❻; I band.
Fire control: Signaal WM 28 ❼; I/J band; range 46 km *(25 nm)*.
Sonars: Signaal PHS 32; hull-mounted; active search and attack; medium frequency.

Programmes: This was the first version of the corvette series, with four being ordered in 1980, one each from the four major warship building yards.
Structure: The design was almost certainly too small for the variety of different weapons which were intended to be fitted for different types of warfare and was therefore discontinued in favour of the

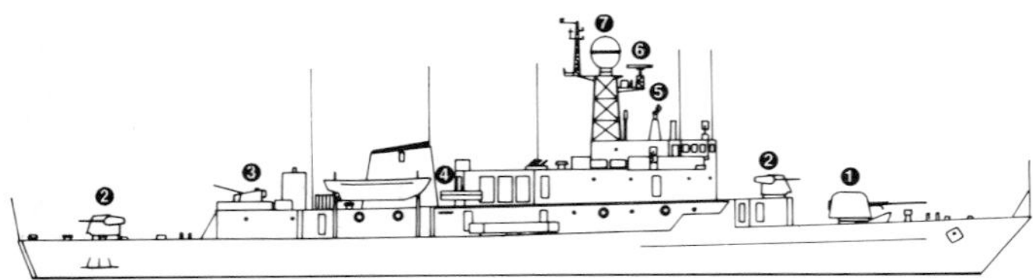

DONG HAE *(Scale 1 : 900), Ian Sturton*

SU WON *1987, Korea Tacoma*

LIGHT FORCES

1 Ex-US ASHEVILLE CLASS (FAST ATTACK CRAFT—MISSILE)

Name	*No*	*Builders*	*Commissioned*
PAE KU 51 (ex-USS *Benicia* PG 96)	PGM 351 (ex-PGM 11, ex-PGM 101)	Tacoma Boatbuilding Co, Tacoma, Wash.	25 Apr 1970

Displacement, tons: 225 standard; 245 full load
Dimensions, feet (metres): 164.5 × 23.9 × 9.5 *(50.1 × 7.3 × 2.9)*
Main machinery: CODOG; 1 GE 7LM-1500 gas turbine; 13 300 hp *(9.92 MW)*; 2 Cummins VT12-875M diesels; 1450 hp *(1.08 MW)*; 2 shafts
Speed, knots: 40; 16 diesels. **Range, miles:** 1700 at 16 kts
Complement: 42 (5 officers)
Missiles: SSM: 2 GDC Standard ARM launchers; anti-radiation homing to 35 km *(18.9 nm)* at 2 Mach; warhead 98 kg; 2 reloads.
Guns: 1 USN 3 in *(76 mm)*/50 Mk 34; 85° elevation; 50 rounds/minute to 12.8 km *(6.9 nm)*; weight of shell 6 kg.
1 Bofors 40 mm/60 Mk 3; 80° elevation; 120 rounds/minute to 10 km *(5.4 nm)* anti-surface; 3 km *(1.6 nm)* anti-aircraft; weight of shell 0.89 kg.
4 Browning 12.7 mm MGs.
Fire control: USN Mk 63 Mod 29 for 76 mm gunnery.
Radars: Surface search: Raytheon 1645; I/J band.
Fire control: Western Electric SPG 50; I/J band.
IFF: APX 72.

Comment: Former US Asheville class patrol gunboat. Launched 20 December 1969; transferred on lease 15 October 1971 and arrived in South Korea in January 1972. Probably paid off in 1991.

PAE KU 51 *9/1988*

8 TACOMA PSMM 5 TYPE (FAST ATTACK CRAFT—MISSILE)

Name	*No*	*Builders*	*Commissioned*
PAE KU 52	PGM 352	Tacoma Boatbuilding Co, Tacoma, Wash.	14 Mar 1975
PAE KU 53	PGM 353	Tacoma Boatbuilding Co, Tacoma, Wash.	14 Mar 1975
PAE KU 55	PGM 355	Tacoma Boatbuilding Co, Tacoma, Wash.	1 Feb 1976
PAE KU 56	PGM 356	Korea Tacoma Marine	1 Feb 1976
PAE KU 57	PGM 357	Korea Tacoma Marine	1977
PAE KU 58	PGM 358	Korea Tacoma Marine	1977
PAE KU 59	PGM 359	Korea Tacoma Marine	1977
PAE KU 61	PGM 361	Korea Tacoma Marine	1978

Displacement, tons: 268 full load
Dimensions, feet (metres): 176.2 × 23.9 × 9.5 *(53.7 × 7.3 × 2.9)*
Main machinery: 6 Avco Lycoming TF 35 gas turbines; 16 800 hp *(12.53 MW)*; 2 shafts; cp props
Speed, knots: 40+. **Range, miles:** 2400 at 18 kts
Complement: 32 (5 officers)

Missiles: SSM: 2 GDC Standard ARM launchers (PGM 352-355); anti-radiation homing to 35 km *(18.9 nm)* at 2 Mach; warhead 98 kg; 2 reloads.
4 McDonnell Douglas Harpoon (PGM 356-361); active radar homing to 130 km *(70 nm)* at 0.9 Mach; warhead 227 kg.
Guns: 1 OTO Melara 3 in *(76 mm)*/62 compact (PGM 356-361); 85° elevation; 85 rounds/minute to 16 km *(8.6 nm)* anti-surface; 12 km *(6.5 nm)* anti-aircraft; weight of shell 6 kg.
1 USN 3 in *(76 mm)*/50 Mk 34 (PGM 352-355); 85° elevation; 50 rounds/minute to 12.8 km *(6.9 nm)*; weight of shell 6 kg.
2 Emerson Electric 30 mm (twin); 80° elevation; 1200 rounds/minute combined to 6 km *(3.2 nm)*; weight of shell 0.35 kg.
2 Browning 12.7 mm MGs.
Countermeasures: Decoys: Loral RBOC 4-barrelled Mk 33 launchers; range 4 km *(2.2 nm)*.
Fire control: Mk 63 GFCS (PGM 352-355). Honeywell H 930 Mod 0 (PGM 356-361).
Radars: Air search: SPS 58; E/F band.
Surface search: Marconi Canada HC 75; I band; range 88 km *(48 nm)*.
Fire control: Western Electric SPG 50 or Westinghouse W-120; I/J band.

Programmes: Tacoma design designation was PSMM for multi-mission patrol ship.
Structure: Aluminium hulls, based on the US Navy's Asheville (PG 84) design, but appearance of Korean built ships' superstructure differs.
Operational: The six TF 35 gas turbines turn two propeller shafts; the Asheville class ships have combination gas turbine-diesel power plants. In the South Korean units one, two, or three turbines can be selected to provide each shaft with a variety of power settings.

PAE KU 53 (with Standard) *3/1987, G. Jacobs*

PAE KU 58 (with Harpoon) *3/1987, G. Jacobs*

32 SEA DOLPHIN CLASS (FAST ATTACK CRAFT—PATROL)

PKM 200 series

Displacement, tons: 170 full load
Dimensions, feet (metres): 108.6 × 22.6 × 8.2 *(33.1 × 6.9 × 2.5)*
Main machinery: 2 MTU 16V 538 TB90 diesels; 6000 hp(m) *(4.41 MW)* sustained; 2 shafts
Speed, knots: 38. **Range, miles:** 700 at 20 kts
Complement: 31
Guns: 2 Emerson Electric 30 mm (twin). 2 GE/GD 20 mm Vulcan Gatlings. 2 Browning 12.7 mm (twin) MGs.

Comment: Built by Korea SEC and Korea Tacoma, Masan. First laid down 1978. Probably some gun armament variations.

SEA DOLPHIN Class *11/1988, van Ginderen Collection*

2 SOUTH KOREAN-BUILT WILDCAT CLASS (FAST ATTACK CRAFT—MISSILE)

PKM 271-272

Displacement, tons: 140 full load
Dimensions, feet (metres): 108.9 × 22.6 × 7.9 *(33.9 × 6.9 × 2.4)*
Main machinery: 2 MTU Mercedes-Benz 20V 672 TY90 (PKM 271); 5800 hp(m) *(4.26 MW)* sustained; 2 shafts
3 MTU 16V 538 TB90 diesels (PKM 272); 9000 hp(m) *(6.61 MW)* sustained; 3 shafts
Speed, knots: 40. **Range, miles:** 800 at 17 kts
Complement: 29 (5 officers)
Missiles: SSM: 2 Aerospatiale MM 38 Exocet; inertial cruise; active radar homing to 42 km *(23 nm)* at 0.9 Mach; warhead 165 kg; sea-skimmer.
Guns: 2 Bofors 40 mm/60; 80° elevation; 120 rounds/minute to 10 km *(5.4 nm)* anti-surface; 3 km *(1.6 nm)* anti-aircraft; weight of shell 0.89 kg.
2 Browning 12.7 mm MGs.
Radars: Surface search: Raytheon 1645; I band.
IFF: UPX 17.

Comment: Built by Korea Tacoma, Masan 1971-72. Steel hull and aluminium superstructure.

WILDCAT Class *12/1985, G. Jacobs*

30 SEA HAWK and 4 SEA FOX CLASS (FAST ATTACK CRAFT—PATROL)

PK 151-189 series

Displacement, tons: 80 full load
Dimensions, feet (metres): 84.3 × 17.7 × 4.9 *(25.7 × 5.4 × 1.5)*
Main machinery: 2 MTU 16V 538 TB90 diesels; 6000 hp(m) *(4.41 MW)* sustained; 2 shafts
Speed, knots: 41. **Range, miles:** 600 at 17 kts; 500 at 20 kts
Complement: 15 (6 officers)
Guns: 4 Oerlikon 20 mm (2 twin). 4 Browning 12.7 mm (2 twin) MGs.

Comment: Built by Korea Tacoma Marine Industries Ltd and Korea SEC between 1975-1978. The term Schoolboy class was also applied to this class. Ordered in three batches: 1973, 1976, 1978. Armament varies amongst boats. Some have a US Bofors 40 mm Mk 3 forward while later boats have a Korean 40 mm mount forward. Some have two MM 38 Exocet.

SEA FOX Class *Korea Tacoma*

MINE WARFARE FORCES

Note: Reported that a Minelayer may be ordered in 1992.

1 + 5 (3) SWALLOW CLASS (MINEHUNTERS)

KAN KEONG

Displacement, tons: 470 standard; 520 full load
Dimensions, feet (metres): 164 × 27.2 × 8.6 *(50 × 8.3 × 2.6)*
Main machinery: 2 MTU diesels; 2040 hp(m) *(1.5 MW)*; 2 shafts; bow thruster
Speed, knots: 15. **Range, miles:** 2000 at 10 kts
Complement: 48
Guns: 1 Oerlikon 20 mm.
Countermeasures: MCM: 2 Gaymarine Pluto remote control submersibles.
Radars: Navigation: Racal Decca; I band.
Sonars: Plessey 193M Mod I; minehunting; high frequency.

Comment: Built to a design similar to the Italian Lerici class by Kangnam Shipyard. GRP hull. Decca/Racal plotting system. First delivered at the end of 1986 for trials. Two more ordered in 1987, three more in 1989. Could lead to a class of 16.

KAN KEONG *1990, Kangnam Corp*

3 Ex-US MSC 268 and 5 289 CLASSES (MINESWEEPERS—COASTAL)

Name	*No*	*Builders*	*Commissioned*
KUM SAN (ex-US *MSC 284*)*	MSC 551	Harbour Boat Building, Terminal Island, Calif	June 1959
KO HUNG (ex-US *MSC 285*)*	MSC 552	Harbour Boat Building, Terminal Island, Calif	Aug 1959
KUM KOK (ex-US *MSC 286*)*	MSC 553	Harbour Boat Building, Terminal Island, Calif	Oct 1959
NAM YANG (ex-US *MSC 295*)	MSC 555	Peterson Builders, Wisconsin	Aug 1963
HA DONG (ex-US *MSC 296*)	MSC 556	Peterson Builders, Wisconsin	Nov 1963
SAM KOK (ex-US *MSC 316*)	MSC 557	Peterson Builders, Wisconsin	July 1968
YONG DONG (ex-US *MSC 320*)	MSC 558	Peterson Builders, Wisconsin	Oct 1975
OK CHEON (ex-US *MSC 321*)	MSC 559	Peterson Builders, Wisconsin	Oct 1975

* MSC 268 class

Displacement, tons: 320 light; 370 full load (268 class) 315 light; 380 full load (289 class)
Dimensions, feet (metres): 141.1 × 26.2 × 8.5 *(43 × 8 × 2.6)* (268 class)
145.4 × 27.2 × 12 (screws) *(44.3 × 8.3 × 2.7)* (289 class)
Main machinery: 2 GM 8-268A diesels; 880 hp *(656 kW)* (268 class); 2 shafts
4 GM 6-71 diesels; 696 hp *(519 kW)* (289 class); 2 shafts
Speed, knots: 14. **Range, miles:** 2500 at 14 kts
Complement: 40
Guns: 2 Oerlikon 20 mm (twin) (268 class); 2 Oerlikon 20 mm (289 class).
3 Browning 12.7 mm MGs.
Radars: Navigation: Decca 45; I band.
Sonars: General Electric UQS 1; hull-mounted; minehunting; high frequency.

Comment: Built by the USA specifically for transfer under the Military Aid Programme with wooden hulls and non-magnetic metal fittings. MSC 551 transferred to South Korea in June 1959, MSC 552 in September 1959, MSC 553 in November 1959, MSC 555 in September 1963, MSC 556 in November 1963, MSC 557 in July 1968, MSC 558 and 559 on 2 October 1975. The last four may be retrofitted with Thomson Sintra mine detection sonars.

KO HUNG *1982, G. Jacobs*

AMPHIBIOUS FORCES

0 + 2 LANDING SHIP TANKS (LST)

Displacement, tons: 4070 full load
Dimensions, feet (metres): 343.8 × 50.5 × 9.8 *(104.8 × 15.4 × 3)*
Main machinery: 2 SEMT-Pielstick 16PA 6V 280; 12 800 hp(m) *(9.41 MW)* sustained; 2 shafts
Speed, knots: 16. **Range, miles:** 10 000 at 12 kts
Complement: 120

Comment: Ordered from Hyundai in June 1990 and being built at Masan by Korea Tacoma. The characteristics listed above are for the later version of the Korean Alligator class but as the only certain facts released about these new ships are the size of the main engines it is possible that larger vessels are being built.

7 Ex-US 1-510 and 511-1152 CLASSES (LSTs)

Name	*No*	*Commissioned*
UN BONG (ex-USS *LST 1010*)	LST 671	25 Apr 1944
BI BONG (ex-USS *LST 218*)	LST 673	12 Aug 1943
KAE BONG (ex-USS *Berkshire County* LST 288)	LST 675	20 Dec 1943
WEE BONG (ex-USS *Johnson County* LST 849)	LST 676	16 Jan 1945
SU YONG (ex-USS *Kane County* LST 853)	LST 677	11 Dec 1945
BUK HAN (ex-USS *Lynn County* LST 900)	LST 678	28 Dec 1944
HWA SAN (ex-USS *Pender County* LST 1080)	LST 679	29 May 1945

Displacement, tons: 1653 standard; 2366 beaching; 4080 full load
Dimensions, feet (metres): 328 × 50 × 14 (screws) *(100 × 15.2 × 4.3)*
Main machinery: 2 GM 12-567A diesels; 1800 hp *(1.34 MW)*; 2 shafts
Speed, knots: 10
Complement: 70
Military lift: 2100 tons including 20 tanks and 2 LCVPs
Guns: 8 Bofors 40 mm (2 twin, 1 quad). 2 Oerlikon 20 mm.

Comment: Former US Navy tank landing ships. Transferred to South Korea between 1955 and 1959. All purchased 15 November 1974.

BUK HAN *1982, G. Jacobs*

7 Ex-US LSM 1 CLASS

Name	*No*
KO MUN (ex-USS *LSM 30*)	LSM 655
PI AN (ex-USS *LSM 96*)	LSM 656
WOL MI (ex-USS *LSM 57*)	LSM 657
KI RIN (ex-USS *LSM 19*)	LSM 658
NUNG RA (ex-USS *LSM 84*)	LSM 659
SIN MI (ex-USS *LSM 316*)	LSM 661
UL RUNG (ex-USS *LSM 17*)	LSM 662

Displacement, tons: 743 beaching; 1095 full load
Dimensions, feet (metres): 203.5 × 34.6 × 8.2 *(62 × 10.5 × 2.5)*
Main machinery: 2 Fairbanks-Morse 38D8-1/8-10 diesels; 3540 hp *(2.64 MW)* sustained; 2 shafts
Speed, knots: 13
Complement: 75
Guns: 2 Bofors 40 mm (twin). 4 Oerlikon 20 mm.

Comment: Former US Navy medium landing ships, built 1944-45. Transferred in 1956. All purchased 15 November 1974. Arrangement of 20 mm guns differs; some ships have two single mounts adjacent to forward 40 mm mount on forecastle; other 20 mm guns along sides of cargo well.

PI AN *3/1987, G. Jacobs*

6 FURSEAL CLASS (LCU)

MULKAE 72, 73, 75, 76, 77, 78

Displacement, tons: 415 full load
Dimensions, feet (metres): 134.8 × 28.8 × 5.9 *(41.1 × 8.8 × 1.8)*
Main machinery: 2 GM 6-71 diesels; 348 hp *(260 kW)* sustained; 2 Kort nozzles
Speed, knots: 13. **Range, miles:** 560 at 11 kts
Complement: 14 (2 officers)
Military lift: 200 tons including battle tanks
Guns: 2 Oerlikon 20 mm.

Comment: In service 1979-81. Built by Korea Tacoma Marine Industries Ltd based on a US design.

FURSEAL 76 *1987, Korea Tacoma*

10 Ex-US LCM 8 CLASS

Displacement, tons: 115 full load
Dimensions, feet (metres): 74.5 × 21 × 4.6 *(22.7 × 6.4 × 1.4)*
Main machinery: 4 GM 6-71 diesels; 696 hp *(519 kW)* sustained; 2 shafts
Speed, knots: 11

Comment: Previously US Army craft. Transferred 1978.

LCVP TYPE

Comment: A considerable number of this US type built of GRP in South Korea.

SERVICE FORCES

Note: The South Korean Navy also operates nine small harbour tugs (designated YTLs). These include one ex-US Navy craft (YTL 550) and five ex-US Army craft. There are also approximately 35 small service craft in addition to the YO-type tankers listed and the harbour tugs. These craft include open lighters, floating cranes, diving tenders, dredgers, ferries, non self-propelled fuel barges, pontoon barges, and sludge removal barges; most are former US Navy craft.

0 + 1 LOGISTIC SUPPORT SHIP

Measurement, tons: 4800 dwt
Dimensions, feet (metres): 426.5 × 58.4 × 21.3 *(130 × 17.8 × 6.5)*
Main machinery: 2 SEMT-Pielstick 12PC2.6V 400; 17 930 hp(m) *(13.17 MW)* sustained; 2 shafts
Speed, knots: 20. **Range, miles:** 4500 at 15 kts
Cargo capacity: 4200 tons liquids; 450 tons solids
Helicopters: 1 medium.

Comment: Ordered in June 1990 and expected to be the first of a class of up to seven. Details listed above are for the Hyundai HDA 8000 design which includes underway replenishment stations on both sides and a helicopter platform and hangar aft. There are three 6 ton lifts.

0 + 1 (2) SUBMARINE SALVAGE SHIP

Comment: One 3000 ton vessel designed by Daewoo and authorised in 1991. Probably similar to the vessel shown in the photograph. Up to 3 may be built in due course.

SALVAGE SHIP *1991, Daewoo*

1 Ex-NORWEGIAN TANKER

Name	*No*	*Builders*	*Launched*
CHUN JI (ex-*Birk*)	51	A/S Berken Mek Verks, Bergen	1951

Displacement, tons: 1400 standard; 4160 full load
Dimensions, feet (metres): 297.6 × 44.6 × 17.7 *(90.7 × 13.6 × 5.4)*
Main machinery: 1 Sulzer 6TD 48 diesel; 1800 hp(m) *(1.32 MW)*; 1 shaft
Speed, knots: 12
Complement: 73
Guns: 1 Bofors 40 mm. 2 Oerlikon 20 mm.

Comment: Transferred to South Korea in September 1953.

1 Ex-US 235-ft YO TYPE (HARBOUR TANKER)

HWA CHON (ex-*Paek Yeon* AO 5 ex-USS *Derrick* YO 59) 52 (ex-*AO 5*)

Displacement, tons: 890 standard; 2700 full load
Dimensions, feet (metres): 235 × 37 × 15 *(71.6 × 11.3 × 4.6)*
Main machinery: 2 Fairbanks-Morse diesels; 1150 hp *(858 kW)*; 1 shaft
Speed, knots: 10.5. **Range, miles:** 4600 at 8 kts
Complement: 46
Cargo capacity: 10 000 barrels petroleum
Guns: Several 20 mm.

Comment: Former US Navy self-propelled fuel barge. Transferred to South Korea on 14 October 1955. The ship has been laid up in reserve since 1974, although purchased on 2 July 1975.

HWA CHON (old number)

2 Ex-US 174-ft YO TYPE (HARBOUR TANKERS)

KU YONG (ex-USS *YO 118)* YO 1 — (ex-USS *YO 179)* YO 6

Displacement, tons: 1400 full load
Dimensions, feet (metres): 174 × 32 × 13.1 *(53 × 9.8 × 4)*
Main machinery: 1 Union diesel; 560 hp *(418 kW)*; 1 shaft
Speed, knots: 7 kts
Complement: 36
Cargo capacity: 900 tons
Guns: Several 20 mm.

Comment: Former US Navy self-propelled fuel barges. Transferred to South Korea on 3 December 1946 and 13 September 1971, respectively.

2 Ex-US DIVER CLASS (SALVAGE SHIPS)

Name	*No*	*Builders*	*Launched*
GUMI (ex-USS *Deliver* ARS 23)	ARS 26	Basalt Rock Co, Napa, Calif.	18 July 1944
CHANG WON (ex-USS *Grasp* ARS 24)	ARS 25	Basalt Rock Co, Napa, Calif.	22 Aug 1944

Displacement, tons: 1530 standard; 1970 full load
Dimensions, feet (metres): 213.5 × 41 × 13 *(65.1 × 12.5 × 4)*
Main machinery: Diesel-electric; 4 Cooper Bessemer GSB8 diesels; 3420 hp *(2.55 MW)*; 4 generators; 2 motors; 3060 hp *(2.28 MW)*; 2 shafts
Speed, knots: 14.8. **Range, miles:** 9000 at 14 kts
Complement: 83
Guns: 2 Oerlikon 20 mm.
Radars: Surface search: Sperry SPS 53; I/J band.
IFF: UPX 12.

Comment: ARS 26 purchased 15 August 1979 and ARS 25 on 31 March 1978. Operated by Service Squadron 51. Equipped for salvage, diver support and towage.

CHANG WON *1982, G. Jacobs*

2 Ex-US SOTOYOMO CLASS (TUGS)

Name	*No*	*Builders*	*Launched*
YONG MUN (ex-USS *Keosanqua* ATA 198)	31 (ex-*ATA 2*)	Levingston S B Co, Orange, Texas	17 Jan 1945
DO BONG (ex-USS *Pinola* ATA 206)	32 (ex-*ATA (S) 3*)	Gulfport Boiler & Welding Works, Port Arthur, Texas	14 Dec 1944

Displacement, tons: 534 standard; 860 full load
Dimensions, feet (metres): 143 × 33.9 × 13 *(43.6 × 10.3 × 4)*
Main machinery: Diesel-electric; 2 GM 12-278A diesels; 2200 hp *(1.64 MW)*; 2 generators; 1 motor; 1500 hp *(1.12 MW)*; 1 shaft
Speed, knots: 13
Complement: 45
Guns: 1 USN 3 in *(76 mm)*/50. 4 Oerlikon 20 mm.

Comment: Former US Navy auxiliary ocean tugs. Both transferred to South Korea in February 1962. 32 modified for salvage work.

DO BONG *1985, G. Jacobs*

2 Ex-US TONTI CLASS (GASOLINE TANKERS)

55 (ex-*Tarland*, ex-USNS *Rincon* T-AOG 77)
56 (ex-*Racoon Bend*, ex-USNS *Petaluma* T-AOG 79)

Displacement, tons: 2100 light; 6047 full load
Dimensions, feet (metres): 325.2 × 48.2 × 19.1 *(99.1 × 14.7 × 5.8)*
Main machinery: 2 Nordberg diesels; 1400 hp *(1.04 MW)*; 1 shaft
Speed, knots: 10. **Range, miles:** 6000 at 10 kts
Complement: 41
Cargo capacity: 31 284 barrels light fuel

Comment: Launched as merchant tankers 9 August 1945 and 5 January 1945 respectively. Transferred 21 February 1982 on lease. Probably armed.

HYDROGRAPHIC SERVICE

Note: The listed craft are operated by the South Korean Hydrographic Service which is responsible to the Ministry of Transport.

7 SURVEY CRAFT

Name	*Displacement, tons*	*Launched*	*Complement*
PUSAN 801	494	1980	15 (8 officers)
PUSAN 802	240	1982	9 (5 officers)
PUSAN 803	125	1979	8 (5 officers)
PUSAN 805	156	1983	5 (5 officers)
CH'UNGNAM 821	65	1981	5 (3 officers)
KANGWON 831	65	1981	5 (3 officers)
PUSAN 806	22	1987	2 (2 officers)

PUSAN 801 *1990, Ships of the World*

COAST GUARD

Note: The South Korean Coast Guard operates a number of small ships and several hundred craft including tugs and rescue craft.

6 SEA DRAGON/WHALE CLASS

PC 501, 502, 503, 505, 506, 507

Displacement, tons: 640 full load
Dimensions, feet (metres): 200.1 × 26.2 × 8.9 *(61 × 8 × 2.7)*
Main machinery: 2 MTU diesels; 9000 hp(m) *(6.61 MW)*; 2 shafts
Speed, knots: 24. **Range, miles:** 6000 at 15 kts
Complement: 40 (7 officers)
Guns: 1 Bofors 40 mm. 2 Oerlikon 20 mm. 2 Browning 12.7 mm MGs.
Radars: Navigation: Two sets.

Comment: Ordered in 1980 from Korea SEC and Korea Tacoma. Fitted with SATNAV. Welded steel hull. Armament varies between ships, one 76 mm gun can be mounted on the forecastle.

SEA DRAGON 507 *1987, Korea Tacoma*

1 MAZINGER CLASS

PC 1001

Displacement, tons: 1200 full load
Dimensions, feet (metres): 264.1 × 32.2 × 11.5 *(80.5 × 9.8 × 3.2)*
Main machinery: 2 Niigata diesels; 10 560 hp(m) *(7.76 MW)*; 2 shafts
Speed, knots: 22. **Range, miles:** 7000 at 18 kts
Complement: 69 (11 officers)
Guns: 1 Bofors 40 mm/70. 4 Oerlikon 20 mm (2 twin).

Comment: Ordered 7 November 1980 from Korea Tacoma and delivered 29 November 1981. All welded mild steel construction. Used for offshore surveillance and general coast guard duties and reported to be the Coast Guard Command ship.

MAZINGER *1987, Korea Tacoma*

6 HAN KANG CLASS

PC 1002-3 PC 1005-8

Displacement, tons: 1180 full load
Dimensions, feet (metres): 289.7 × 32.8 × 9.5 *(88.3 × 10 × 2.9)*
Main machinery: 1 GE LM 2500 gas turbine; 23 000 hp *(17.16 MW)* sustained; 2 MTU 12V 956 TB 82 diesels; 6260 hp(m) *(4.67 MW)* sustained; 3 shafts
Speed, knots: 32. **Range, miles:** 4000 at 15 kts
Complement: 72 (11 officers)
Guns: 1 OTO Melara 76/62 compact. 1 Bofors 40 mm/70. 2 GE/GD 20 mm Vulcan Gatlings.
Fire control: Signaal LIOD optronic director.
Radars: Surface search: Raytheon SPS 64(V); I band.
Fire control: Signaal WM 28; I/J band.

Comment: Built between 1981 and 1988 by Korea SEC. Same hull as Po Hang class but much more lightly armed.

HAN KANG *1989, Ships of the World*

22 SEA WOLF/SHARK CLASS

Displacement, tons: 310 full load
Dimensions, feet (metres): 158.1 × 23.3 × 8.2 *(48.2 × 7.1 × 2.5)*
Main machinery: 2 diesels; 7320 hp(m) *(5.38 MW)*; 2 shafts
Speed, knots: 25. **Range, miles:** 2400 at 15 kts
Complement: 35 (3 officers)
Guns: 4 Oerlikon 20 mm (2 twin or 1 twin, 2 single). Some have a twin Bofors 40 mm/70 vice the twin Oerlikon. 2 Browning 12.7 mm MGs.

Comment: First four ordered in 1979-80 from Korea SEC (Sea Shark), Hyundai and Korea Tacoma (Sea Wolf). Programme terminated in 1988. Pennant numbers in 200 series up to 277.

SEA WOLF Class *1987, Korea Tacoma*

2 + 2 BUKHANSAN CLASS

278 279

Displacement, tons: 371 full load
Dimensions, feet (metres): 164 × 24 × 7.2 *(50 × 7.3 × 2.2)*
Main machinery: 2 MTU diesels; 9000 hp(m) *(6.61 MW)*; 2 shafts
Speed, knots: 28. **Range, miles:** 2500 at 15 kts
Complement: 35 (3 officers)
Guns: 2 Breda 40 mm/70 (twin). 1 MK-1620 mm. 2—12.7 mm MGs.
Fire control: Optronic director.

Comment: Follow on to Sea Wolf class developed by Hyundai in 1987. First two ordered in 1988 and delivered in 1989.

BUKHANSAN Class *1989, Hyundai*

18 SEAGULL CLASS

Displacement, tons: 80 full load
Dimensions, feet (metres): 78.7 × 18 × 6.6 *(24 × 5.5 × 2)*
Main machinery: 2 diesels; 3700 hp(m) *(2.72 MW)*; 2 shafts
Speed, knots: 30. **Range, miles:** 950 at 20 kts
Complement: 18
Guns: 4 Oerlikon 20 mm.

Comment: First ordered in 1971 and 1972 from Korea SEC. Some sold to Kuwait.

INSHORE PATROL CRAFT

Displacement, tons: 47
Dimensions, feet (metres): 69.9 × 17.7 × 4.6 *(21.3 × 5.4 × 1.4)*
Main machinery: 2 diesels; 1800 hp(m) *(1.32 MW)*; 2 shafts
Speed, knots: 22. **Range, miles:** 400 at 12 kts
Complement: 11
Guns: 3—12.7 mm MGs.

Comment: Details are for the latest design of patrol craft. There are large numbers of this type of vessel used for inshore patrol work.

IPC *1991, Kangnam Corp*

KUWAIT

Senior Appointment

Commander of the Navy:
Commodore Qais Al Saleh

Bases

Navy: Al Jilaia
Coast Guard: Shuwaikh, Umm Al-Hainan

Iraq Invasion

In August 1990 Iraq invaded Kuwait. All Naval and Coast Guard ships and aircraft were captured with the exception of two fast attack craft. Subsequently the Iraqi Navy used the captured craft in Operation Desert Storm and all were either sunk or damaged by Allied Forces. In due course some may be recovered and made serviceable again.

Mercantile Marine

Lloyd's Register of Shipping:
197 vessels of 1 372 976 tons gross

DELETIONS (Captured by Iraq in August 1990)

Fast Attack Craft (Missile):	5 Lürssen TNC 45 and 1 Lürssen FPB 57
Patrol Craft:	5 Seagull, 15 Thornycroft, 1 Halter Marine, 7 Magnum Sedan
Landing Craft:	4 Loadmasters, 6 Vosper Singapore Type
Miscellaneous:	10 tugs and launches
Aircraft:	12 Super Puma
Customs:	3 Azimut launches

PATROL FORCES

Note: Reported that eight fast attack craft and three minehunters are to be ordered in 1992. Vosper Thornycroft, Lürssen and Australian Shipbuilding Industries have all offered tenders.

1 TNC 45 TYPE (FAST ATTACK CRAFT—MISSILE)

AL SANBOUK P 4505

Displacement, tons: 255 full load
Dimensions, feet (metres): 147.3 × 23 × 7.5 *(44.9 × 7 × 2.3)*
Main machinery: 4 MTU 16V 538 TB 92 diesels; 13 640 hp(m) *(10 MW)* sustained; 4 shafts
Speed, knots: 41. **Range, miles:** 1800 at 16 kts
Complement: 35 (5 officers)

Missiles: SSM: 4 Aerospatiale MM 40 Exocet; inertial cruise; active radar homing to 70 km *(40 nm)* at 0.9 Mach; warhead 165 kg; sea-skimmer.
Guns: 1 OTO Melara 3 in *(76 mm)*/62 compact; 85° elevation; 85 rounds/minute to 16 km *(8.6 nm)* anti-surface; 12 km *(6.5 nm)* anti-aircraft; weight of shell 6 kg.
2 Breda 40 mm/70 (twin); 85° elevation; 300 rounds/minute to 12.5 km *(6.6 nm)*; weight of shell 0.96 kg.
Countermeasures: Decoys: CSEE Dagaie trainable mounting; automatic dispenser; IR flares and Chaff; H/J band.
ESM: Racal Cutlass; radar intercept.
Fire control: PEAB 9LV 228 system. CSEE Lynx optical sight.
Radars: Surface search: Decca TM 1226C; I band.
Fire control: Philips 9LV 200; J band.

Programmes: Six ordered from Lürssen in 1980 and delivered in 1983/84.
Operational: *Al Sanbouk* escaped to Bahrain when the Iraqis invaded in August 1990, but the rest were taken over by the Iraqi Navy, and either sunk or severely damaged by Allied forces in February 1991.

TNC 45 Type *1984, G. Koop*

0 + 2 (2) ASI 315 CLASS (LARGE PATROL CRAFT)

Displacement, tons: 150 full load
Dimensions, feet (metres): 103.3 × 21.3 × 6.6 *(31.5 × 6.5 × 2)*
Main machinery: 2 diesels; 2 shafts; 1 auxiliary waterjet (centre line)
Speed, knots: 28
Complement: 17 (4 officers)
Guns: 1 Oerlikon 20 mm. 1—12.7 mm MG

Comment: Ordered from Australian Shipbuilding Industries to be delivered in November 1992. Option for two more. Design differs from both Hong Kong patrol craft and Pacific Forum type.

17 COUGAR TYPE (INSHORE PATROL CRAFT)

Comment: Three Cat 900 (32 ft), three Cat 1000 (33 ft) and three Predator 1100 (35 ft) all powered by 2 Yamaha outboards (400 hp(m) *(294 kW)*). Four Type 1200 (38 ft) and four Type 1300 (41 ft) all powered by 2 Sabre diesels (760 hp(m) *(559 kW)*). All based on the high performance planing hull developed for racing, and acquired in 1991.

1 FPB 57 TYPE (FAST ATTACK CRAFT—MISSILE)

ISTIQLAL P 5702

Displacement, tons: 410 full load
Dimensions, feet (metres): 190.6 × 24.9 × 8.9 *(58.1 × 7.6 × 2.7)*
Main machinery: 4 MTU 16V 956 TB 91 diesels; 15 000 hp(m) *(11 MW)* sustained; 4 shafts
Speed, knots: 36. **Range, miles:** 1300 at 30 kts
Complement: 40 (5 officers)

Missiles: SSM: 4 Aerospatiale MM 40 Exocet; inertial cruise; active radar homing to 70 km *(40 nm)* at 0.9 Mach; warhead 165 kg; sea-skimmer.
Guns: 1 OTO Melara 3 in *(76 mm)*/62 compact; 85° elevation; 85 rounds/minute to 16 km *(8.6 nm)* anti-surface; 12 km *(6.5 nm)* anti-aircraft; weight of shell 6 kg.
2 Breda 40 mm/70 (twin); 85° elevation; 300 rounds/minute to 12.5 km *(6.6 nm)*; weight of shell 0.96 kg.
Mines: Fitted for minelaying.
Countermeasures: Decoys: CSEE Dagaie trainable mounting; automatic dispenser; IR flares and Chaff; H/J band.
ESM: Racal Cutlass; radar intercept.
Fire control: PEAB 9LV 228 system. CSEE Lynx optical sight.
Radars: Surface search: Marconi S 810 (after radome); I band; range 43 km *(25 nm)*.
Navigation: Decca TM 1226C; I band.
Fire control: Philips 9LV 200; J band.

Programmes: Two ordered from Lürssen in 1980. In service November 1982 and March 1983.
Operational: *Istiqlal* escaped to Bahrain when the Iraqis invaded in August 1990. The second was captured and sunk in February 1991.

ISTIQLAL *1986*

0 + 5 KOREAN SEAGULL CLASS (LARGE PATROL CRAFT)

Displacement, tons: 80 full load
Dimensions, feet (metres): 78.7 × 18 × 6.6 *(24 × 5.5 × 2)*
Main machinery: 2 diesels; 3700 hp(m) *(2.72 MW)*; 2 shafts
Speed, knots: 30. **Range, miles:** 950 at 20 kts
Complement: 18

Comment: First five ordered 1985-86 from Korea SEC and delivered late 1986. Second five ordered in 1988 but had not been delivered at the time of the invasion in August 1990, when the first five were captured by Iraq and subsequently destroyed by Allied forces in February 1991.

SEAGULL Class *11/1989, Hartmut Ehlers*

LAOS

General

It is reported that the Marine section of the Army has eight patrol craft, four LCMs and four service craft which are used for patrolling the Mekong river. In addition some 40 patrol boats were acquired from the USSR in 1985. Most vessels are probably ex-Soviet types but there may still be a few relics left behind by the US Navy.

Personnel

(a) 1992: 600 officers and men
(b) 18 months' national service

Bases

Luang Prabang, Chinaimo, Savanmma Khet, Pakse

LEBANON

Naval Commander

Rear Admiral Alberto Gorayeb

Personnel

1992: 400 officers and men

Bases

Beirut, Jounieh

General

With Port revenue increasing the Navy is now looking at the requirement for additional patrol craft. The Attacker craft used by the British in Cyprus may be acquired in 1992.

Operational

The Syrian Navy does not patrol off the coast of Lebanon.

Mercantile Marine

Lloyd's Register of Shipping:
164 vessels of 274 288 tons gross

DELETIONS

1990 *Byblos, Sidon, Beyrouth*
1991 *Trablous* (L'Esterel craft), 1 Aztec class

PATROL FORCES

2 FRENCH EDIC CLASS (LANDING CRAFT)

Name	*No*	*Builders*	*Commissioned*
SOUR	21	SFCN, Villeneuve la Garonne	28 Mar 1985
DAMOUR	22	SFCN, Villeneuve la Garonne	28 Mar 1985

Displacement, tons: 670 full load
Dimensions, feet (metres): 193.5 × 39.2 × 4.2 *(59 × 12 × 1.3)*
Main machinery: 2 SACM MGO 175 V12 M1 diesels; 1200 hp(m) *(882 kW)*; 2 shafts
Speed, knots: 10. **Range, miles:** 1800 at 9 kts
Complement: 20 (2 officers)
Military lift: 33 troops; 11 trucks or 5 APCs
Guns: 2 Oerlikon 20 mm (twin). 1—81 mm mortar.

Comment: Both were damaged in early 1990 but repaired in 1991 and are fully operational.

SOUR *11/1985*

5 AZTEC CLASS (COASTAL PATROL CRAFT)

Displacement, tons: 5.2 full load
Dimensions, feet (metres): 29.5 × 8.5 × 1.6 *(9 × 2.6 × 0.5)*
Main machinery: 2 diesels; 320 hp(m) *(235 kW)*; 2 shafts
Speed, knots: 24

Comment: Six supplied by Crestitalia in 1979. GRP hulls. One deleted and five held by Lebanese Customs. All were damaged in 1990, but in 1991 were being repaired by the Navy.

AZTEC Class

2 TRACKER Mk 2 (COASTAL PATROL CRAFT)

Displacement, tons: 31 full load
Dimensions, feet (metres): 63.3 × 16.4 × 4.9 *(19.3 × 5 × 1.5)*
Main machinery: 2 Detroit 12V 71TI diesels; 680 hp *(507 kW)* sustained; 2 shafts
Speed, knots: 25. **Range, miles:** 650 at 20 kts
Complement: 11

Comment: Built in 1980 by Fairey Allday, UK. Both held by the Navy in 1991.

TRACKER 2 *1991, Lebanese Navy*

LIBERIA

General

The Liberian National Coast Guard became the Liberian Navy in 1987. During the civil war the remaining naval vessels were taken over by rebels.

Bases

Elijah Johnson, Monrovia;
Buchanan, Bassa;
Greenville, Sinoe;
Harper, Cape Palmas.

Mercantile Marine

Lloyd's Register of Shipping:
1605 vessels of 52 426 516 tons gross

DELETIONS

1990 *Samuel K Doe, Thomas Quiwonkpa*

1 KOREA TACOMA CRAFT (FAST ATTACK CRAFT—GUN)

FARANDUGU

Displacement, tons: 170 full load
Dimensions, feet (metres): 108.6 × 22.6 × 8.2 *(33.1 × 6.9 × 2.5)*
Main machinery: 2 MTU 16V 538 TB90 diesels; 6000 hp(m) *(4.41 MW)* sustained; 2 shafts
Speed, knots: 38. **Range, miles:** 700 at 20 kts
Complement: 31
Guns: 2 Oerlikon 20 mm. 2—12.7 mm MGs.

Comment: Ordered from Korea Tacoma and delivered in October 1989. Armament is uncertain but the hull is a variation of the South Korean Navy's Sea Dolphin class but less heavily armed. Taken over by the rebels and painted in camouflage colours.

SEA DOLPHIN Class *1989, Korea Tacoma*

1 COASTAL PATROL CRAFT

Name	*No*	*Builders*	*Commissioned*
C G C ALBERT PORTE	CG 8802	Karlskrona Varvet	27 Aug 1980

Displacement, tons: 50
Dimensions, feet (metres): 87.6 × 17.1 × 3.6 *(26.7 × 5.2 × 1.1)*
Main machinery: 2 MTU 8V331 TC82 diesels; 1740 hp(m) *(1.28 MW)* sustained; 2 shafts
Speed, knots: 25. **Range, miles:** 1000 at 18 kts
Complement: 8
Guns: 1 Browning 12.7 mm MG. 2 FN 7.62 mm MGs.
Radars: Navigation: Decca 1226C; I band.

Comment: Aluminium alloy hull. Karlskrona TV 103 design. The survivor of a class of three taken over by the rebels and painted in camouflage colours. The other two of the class were destroyed in 1990.

TV 103 Type *8/1986, van Ginderen Collection*

LIBYA

Headquarters' Appointments

Commander-in-Chief Libyan Armed Forces:
Colonel Abu Bahr Kunis Jabir
Senior Officer, Libyan Navy:
Captain Abdullah Al Latif El Shaksuki

Personnel

(a) 1992: Total 8000 officers and ratings, including Coast Guard
(b) Voluntary service

Bases

Operating Ports at Tripoli, Darnah (Derna) and Benghazi.
Naval bases at Al Khums and Tobruq.
Submarine base at Ras Hilal.
Naval air station at Al Girdabiyah.
Naval infantry battalion at Sidi Bilal.

Strength of the Fleet

Type	*Active*
Submarines	6 (+6 small)
Frigates	3
Corvettes (Missile)	7
Minesweepers—Ocean	8
Fast Attack Craft—Missile	24
Large Patrol Craft	8
Landing Ships	5
LCTs	3
Support Ships	7
Tugs	7
Diving Tender	1
Salvage Ship	1
Floating Docks	2

Camouflage

Photographs of Libyan naval vessels taken in 1991 indicate that some ships have been painted in striped shades of green and black.

General

Specialist teams in unconventional warfare are a threat and almost any Libyan vessel can lay mines, but overall operational effectiveness is not high, not least because of poor maintenance and stores support.

Mercantile Marine

Lloyd's Register of Shipping:
129 vessels of 839 852 tons gross

DELETION

1989 *Tobruk* (training hulk)

SUBMARINES

6 Ex-SOVIET FOXTROT CLASS

AL BADR 311 **AL AHAD** 313 **AL KHYBER** 315
AL FATEH 312 **AL MITRAQA** 314 **AL HUNAIN** 316

Displacement, tons: 1950 surfaced; 2475 dived
Dimensions, feet (metres): 299.5 × 24.6 × 19.7 *(91.3 × 7.5 × 6)*
Main machinery: Diesel-electric; 3 diesels; 5956 hp(m) *(4.3 MW)*; 3 motors; 5400 hp(m) *(3.97 MW)*; 3 shafts
Speed, knots: 16 surfaced; 15 dived. **Range, miles:** 16 000 at 8 kts surfaced
Complement: 75 (8 officers)

Torpedoes: 10—21 in *(533 mm)* (6 bow, 4 stern) tubes. 22 Soviet Type 53; pattern active/passive homing up to 20 km *(10.8 nm)* at up to 45 kts; warhead 400 kg.
Mines: 44 in place of torpedoes.
Countermeasures: ESM: Stop Light; radar warning.
Radars: Surface search: Snoop Tray; I band.
Sonars: Herkules; hull-mounted; active; medium frequency.
Feniks; hull-mounted; passive.

Programmes: Came from a re-activated building line in Leningrad. 311 arrived in Tripoli December 1976; the second boat in February 1978, the third in March 1978, the fourth in February 1982, the fifth in April 1982 and the sixth in February 1983.
Structure: HF masts not fitted.
Operational: Libyan crews trained in the USSR and much of the maintenance is done by Soviet personnel. Only one of the class operational in 1991 with the others in varying stages of refit, two of which may complete by mid-1992. No routine patrols have been seen since 1984.

AL AHAD *9/1988*

6 YUGOSLAV R-2 MALA CLASS

Displacement, tons: 1.4 full load
Dimensions, feet (metres): 16.1 × 4.1 *(4.9 × 1.4)*
Main machinery: 1 motor; 6.2 hp(m) *(4.6 kW)*; 1 shaft
Speed, knots: 4.4
Range, miles: 18 at 4.4 kts; 23 at 3.7 kts
Complement: 2

Mines: Can carry 249 kg of limpet mines and other weapons.

Programmes: Two transferred in 1977, 1981 and 1982 each. A further pair may be on order, possibly of the Una class.
Structure: This is a free-flood craft with the main motor, battery, navigation-pod and electronic equipment housed in separate watertight cylinders. Instrumentation includes aircraft type gyro-compass, magnetic compass, depth gauge (with 0-100 m scale), echo sounder, sonar and two searchlights. Constructed of light aluminium and plexiglass, it is fitted with fore- and after-hydroplanes, the tail being a conventional cruciform with a single rudder abaft the screw. Large perspex windows give a good all-round view.
Operational: Details given are for lead-acid batteries and could be much improved by use of silver-zinc batteries. Operating depth, 60 m max. Passage to the target area can be as pick-a-back on a submarine or as deck cargo on any surface vessel with a 25-ton crane—lacking in all Libyan surface warships. However they could be floated out from *Zeltin's* dock. This class of submarine does not look very suitable for towing. Operational status doubtful in 1991.

R-2 MALA Class (on Swedish submarine) *12/1988, Gilbert Gyssels*

FRIGATES

2 SOVIET KONI CLASS

AL HANI F 212 **AL QIRDABIYAH** F 213

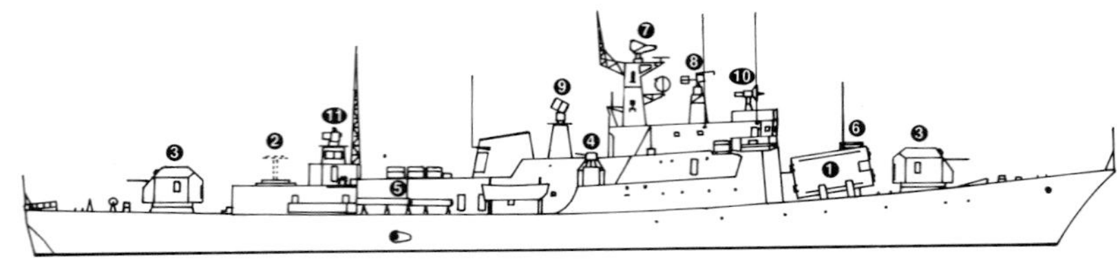

AL HANI (Scale 1 : 900), Ian Sturton

Displacement, tons: 1440 standard; 1900 full load
Dimensions, feet (metres): 316.3 × 41.3 × 11.5
(96.4 × 12.6 × 3.5)
Main machinery: CODAG; 1 SGW, Nikolayev, M8B gas turbine (centre shaft); 18 000 hp(m) *(13.25 MW)* sustained; 2 Russki B-68 diesels; 15 820 hp(m) *(11.63 MW)* sustained; 3 shafts
Speed, knots: 27 on gas; 22 on diesel. **Range, miles:** 1800 at 14 kts
Complement: 120

Missiles: SSM: 4 Soviet SS-N-2C Styx (2 twin) launchers ❶; active radar/IR homing to 83 km *(45 nm)* at 0.9 Mach; warhead 513 kg; sea-skimmer at end of run.
SAM: SA-N-4 Gecko twin launcher ❷; semi-active radar homing to 15 km *(8 nm)* at 2.5 Mach; altitude 9.1-3048 m *(29.5-10 000 ft)*; warhead 50 kg; 20 missiles.
Guns: 4 USSR 3 in *(76 mm)*/60 (2 twin) ❸; 80° elevation; 60 rounds/minute to 15 km *(8 nm)* anti-surface; 14 km *(7.6 nm)* anti-aircraft; weight of shell 16 kg.
4 USSR 30 mm/65 (2 twin) automatic ❹; 85° elevation; 500 rounds/minute to 5 km *(2.7 nm)*; weight of shell 0.54 kg.
Torpedoes: 4—406 mm (2 twin) tubes amidships ❺. Soviet Type 40; anti-submarine; active/passive homing up to 15 km *(8 nm)* at up to 40 kts; warhead 150 kg.
A/S mortars: 1 RBU 6000 12-tubed trainable launcher ❻; automatic loading; range 6000 m; warhead 31 kg.
Depth charges: 2 racks.
Mines: Capacity for 20.
Countermeasures: Decoys: 2—16-barrelled Chaff launchers. Towed torpedo decoys.
ESM: 2 Watch Dog; radar warning.
Radars: Air search: Strut Curve ❼; F band; range 110 km *(60 nm)* for 2 m² target.
Surface search: Plank Shave ❽; I band.
Navigation: Don 2; I band.
Fire control: Drum Tilt ❾; H/I band (for 30 mm).
Hawk Screech ❿; I band; range 27 km *(15 nm)* (for 76 mm).
Pop Group ⓫; F/H/I band (for SAM).
IFF: High Pole B. Square Head.
Sonars: Hull-mounted; active search and attack; medium frequency.

Programmes: Type III Konis built at Zelenodolsk and transferred from the Black Sea. 212 commissioned 28 June 1986 and 213 on 24 October 1987.
Structure: SSMs mounted either side of small deckhouse on forecastle behind gun. A deckhouse amidships contains air-conditioning machinery. Changes to the standard Koni include SSM, four torpedo tubes, only one RBU 6000 and Plank Shave surface search and target indication radar. Camouflage paint applied in 1991.

AL HANI 7/1991, van Ginderen Collection

1 VOSPER THORNYCROFT MARK 7

Name	*No*	*Builders*	*Laid down*	*Launched*	*Commissioned*
DAT ASSAWARI	F 211	Vosper Thornycroft	27 Sep 1968	Sep 1969	1 Feb 1973

DAT ASSAWARI (Scale 1 : 900), Ian Sturton

Displacement, tons: 1360 standard; 1780 full load
Dimensions, feet (metres): 333 × 38.3 × 11.2
(101.5 × 11.7 × 3.4)
Main machinery: CODOG; 2 RR Olympus TM2A gas turbines; 35 400 hp *(26.4 MW)* sustained; 2 Paxman Ventura 16CM diesels; 3800 hp *(2.83 MW)* sustained; 2 shafts; KaMeWa cp props
Speed, knots: 37.5 gas turbines; 17 diesels
Range, miles: 5700 at 17 kts
Complement: 130

Missiles: SSM: 4 OTO Melara/Matra Otomat ❶; active radar homing to 180 km *(100 nm)* at 0.9 Mach; warhead 210 kg.
SAM: 1 Selenia/Elsag Albatros quad launcher ❷; 64 Aspide; semi-active homing to 13 km *(7 nm)* at 2.5 Mach; height envelope 15-5000 m *(49.2-16 405 ft)*; warhead 30 kg.
Guns: 1 Vickers 4.5 in *(114 mm)*/55 Mk 8 ❸; 55° elevation; 25 rounds/minute to 22 km *(11.9 nm)* anti-surface; 6 km *(3.3 nm)* anti-aircraft; warhead 21 kg.
2 Oerlikon GDM-A 35 mm/90 (twin) ❹; 85° elevation; 550 rounds/minute to 6 km *(3.3 nm)* anti-surface; 5 km *(2.7 nm)* anti-aircraft; weight of shell 1.55 kg.
2 Oerlikon A41A 20 mm ❺; 50° elevation; 800 rounds/minute to 2 km; weight of shell 0.24 kg.
Torpedoes: 6—324 mm ILAS 3 (2 triple) tubes ❻. Whitehead Motofides A244; anti-submarine; active/passive homing to 7 km *(3.8 nm)* at 33 kts; warhead 34 kg (shaped charge).
Countermeasures: ESM: Selenia INS-1; radar intercept.
Decca RDS-1. Marconi FH-12 HFD/F.
Combat data systems: Selenia IPN/10 action data automation.
Fire control: 2 Selenia Elsag NA 10 Mod 2 for guns and missiles.
Radars: Air/surface search: Selenia RAN 12 ❼; D/I band; range 82 km *(45 nm)*.
Surface search: Selenia RAN 10S ❽; E/F band; range 155 km *(85 nm)*.
Fire control: Two Selenia RTN 10X ❾; I/J band; range 40 km *(22 nm)*.
Sonars: Thomson Sintra TSM 2310 Diodon; hull-mounted; active search and attack; 11-13 kHz.

DAT ASSAWARI 5/1984, Aldo Fraccaroli

Programmes: Mk 7 Frigate ordered from Vosper Thornycroft on 6 February 1968. Generally similar in design to the two Iranian Mk 5s built by this firm, but larger and with different armament. After trials she carried out work-up at Portland, UK, reaching Tripoli autumn 1973.

Modernisation: In 1979 modernisation of SAM, ASW armament and sensors was started by CNR, Genoa but was interrupted by onboard explosion on 29 October 1980. Completed including trials October 1983. Returned to Italy for major engine repairs in 1984 which completed in 1985.
Operational: In 1990 the ship was non-operational in a partly disarmed state and back in Genoa once again.

SHIPBORNE AIRCRAFT

Numbers/Type: 12 Aerospatiale SA 316B Alouette III.
Operational speed: 113 kts *(210 km/h)*.
Service ceiling: 10 500 ft *(3200 m)*.
Range: 290 nm *(540 km)*.
Role/Weapon systems: Support helicopter; can be operated from amphibious warfare ships. Sensors: None. Weapons: Unarmed.

ALOUETTE III

CORVETTES

Note: *Tobruk* is still used as an alongside training hulk.

3 SOVIET NANUCHKA II CLASS (MISSILE CORVETTES)

TARIQ IBN ZIYAD (ex-*Ean Mara*) 416 **EAN AL GAZALA** 417 **EAN ZARA** 418

Displacement, tons: 850 full load
Dimensions, feet (metres): 194.5 × 38.7 × 8.5 *(59.3 × 11.8 × 2.6)*
Main machinery: 3 Type 507 diesels; 26 000 hp(m) *(19 MW)*; 3 shafts
Speed, knots: 34. **Range, miles:** 2500 at 12 kts; 900 at 31 kts
Complement: 60

Missiles: SSM: 4 Soviet SS-N-2C Styx launchers; auto-pilot; active radar/IR homing to 83 km *(45 nm)* at 0.9 Mach; warhead 513 kg HE; sea-skimmer at end of run.
SAM: SA-N-4 Gecko twin launcher; semi-active radar homing to 15 km *(8 nm)* at 2.5 Mach; altitude 9.1-3048 m *(29.5-10 000 ft)*; warhead 50 kg HE; 20 missiles.
Guns: 2 USSR 57 mm/80 (twin) automatic; 85° elevation; 120 rounds/minute to 6 km *(3.2 nm)*; weight of shell 2.8 kg.
Countermeasures: Decoys: 2 Chaff 16-barrelled launchers.
ESM: Bell Top; radar warning.
Radars: Surface search: Square Tie; I band (Bandstand radome).
Navigation: Don 2; I band.
Fire control: Muff Cob; G/H band.
Pop Group; F/H/I band (for SAM).

Programmes: First reached Libya in October 1981; second in February 1983; third in February 1984; fourth in September 1985.
Structure: Camouflage paint applied in 1991.
Operational: *Ean Zaquit* (419) sunk on 24 March 1986. *Ean Mara* (416) severely damaged on 25 March 1986 by forces of the US Sixth Fleet; repaired in Leningrad and returned to Libya in early 1991 as the *Tariq Ibn Ziyad*.

TARIQ IBN ZIYAD *7/1991, van Ginderen Collection*

4 ASSAD CLASS (MISSILE CORVETTES)

Name	*No*	*Builders*	*Launched*	*Commissioned*
ASSAD AL BIHAR	412	Fincantieri, Muggiano	29 Apr 1977	14 Sep 1979
ASSAD EL TOUGOUR	413	Fincantieri, Muggiano	20 Apr 1978	12 Feb 1980
ASSAD AL KHALI	414	Fincantieri, Muggiano	15 Dec 1978	28 Mar 1981
ASSAD AL HUDUD	415	Fincantieri, Muggiano	21 June 1979	28 Mar 1981

Displacement, tons: 670 full load
Dimensions, feet (metres): 202.4 × 30.5 × 7.2 *(61.7 × 9.3 × 2.2)*
Main machinery: 4 MTU-Bazán 16V 956 TB91 diesels; 15 000 hp(m) *(11 MW)* sustained; 4 shafts
Speed, knots: 34. **Range, miles:** 4400 at 14 kts
Complement: 58

Missiles: SSM: 4 OTO Melara/Matra Otomat Teseo Mk 2 (TG1); active radar homing to 80 km *(43.2 nm)* at 0.9 Mach; warhead 210 kg.
Guns: 1 OTO Melara 3 in *(76 mm)*/62 compact; 85° elevation; 85 rounds/minute to 16 km *(8.6 nm)* anti-surface; 12 km *(6.5 nm)* anti-aircraft; weight of shell 6 kg.
2 Oerlikon GDM-A 35 mm/90 (twin); 85° elevation; 550 rounds/minute to 6 km *(3.3 nm)* anti-surface; 5 km *(2.7 nm)* anti-aircraft.
Torpedoes: 6—324 mm ILAS (2 triple) tubes. Whitehead Motofides A244; anti-submarine; self-adaptive patterns to 7 km *(3.8 nm)* at 33 kts; warhead 34 kg (shaped charge).
Mines: Can lay 16 mines.
Countermeasures: ESM: Selenia INS-1; radar intercept.
Combat data systems: Selenia IPN/10 action data automation.
Fire control: Selenia Elsag NA 10 Mod 2.
Radars: Air/surface search: Selenia RAN 11X; D/I band; range 82 km *(45 nm)*.
Navigation: Decca TM 1226C; I band.
Fire control: Selenia RTN 10X; I/J band; range 40 km *(22 nm)*.
Sonars: Thomson Sintra TSM Diodon; hull-mounted; active search and attack; 11-13 kHz.

Programmes: Ordered in 1974. Previously Wadi class—renamed 1982-83. Similar hull to Ecuador corvettes.
Structure: Fin stabilisers and degaussing equipment fitted.
Operational: At the beginning of 1990 only one was operational with the others cannibalised for spares. Refits in Italy are a possibility.

ASSAD AL HUDUD *1986, W. Magrawa*

LAND-BASED MARITIME AIRCRAFT

Numbers/Type: 6 Aerospatiale SA 321M Super Frelon.
Operational speed: 134 kts *(248 km/h)*.
Service ceiling: 10 000 ft *(3050 m)*.
Range: 440 nm *(815 km)*.
Role/Weapon systems: Obsolescent helicopter; used for naval support tasks but non-operational due to lack of spares. Sensors: None. Weapons: Modified to carry Exocet AM 39.

Numbers/Type: 12 Mil Mi-14 ('Haze A').
Operational speed: 120 kts *(222 km/h)*.
Service ceiling: 15 000 ft *(4570 m)*.
Range: 240 nm *(445 km)*.
Role/Weapon systems: ASW and surface search helicopter with Soviet advisers. Sensors: Search radar, ECM, dipping sonar, MAD. Weapons: ASW; internal torpedoes, depth bombs or mines.

LIGHT FORCES

Note: (i) More than 50 remote control explosive craft acquired from Cyprus. Based on Q-Boats with Q-26 GRP hulls and speed of about 30 kts. Also reported that fifteen 31 ft craft delivered by Storebro, and 60 more built locally are similarly adapted.
(ii) The 1985 order for four Improved Končar class FAC(M) from Yugoslavia was probably cancelled because of contract problems.
(iii) 14 SAR 33 FAC(G) were reported delivered to the Customs Service by Turkey in 1986-87. In fact the order was cancelled.

9 COMBATTANTE II G CLASS (FAST ATTACK CRAFT—MISSILE)

SHARABA (ex-*Beir Grassa*) 518
WAHAG (ex-*Beir Gzir*) 522
SHEHAB (ex-*Beir Gtifa*) 524
SHOUAIAI (ex-*Beir Algandula*) 528
SHOULA (ex-*Beir Ktitat*) 532
SHAFAK (ex-*Beir Alkrarim*) 534
BARK (ex-*Beir Alkardmen*) 536
RAD (ex-*Beir Alkur*) 538
LAHEEB (ex-*Beir Alkuefat*) 542

Displacement, tons: 311 full load
Dimensions, feet (metres): 160.7 × 23.3 × 6.6 *(49 × 7.1 × 2)*
Main machinery: 4 MTU 20V 538 TB 91 diesels; 15 360 hp(m) *(11.29 MW)* sustained; 4 shafts
Speed, knots: 39. **Range, miles:** 1600 at 15 kts
Complement: 27

Missiles: SSM: 4 OTO Melara/Matra Otomat Mk 2 (TG1); active radar homing to 80 km *(43.2 nm)* at 0.9 Mach; warhead 210 kg.
Guns: 1 OTO Melara 3 in *(76 mm)*/62 compact; 85° elevation; 85 rounds/minute to 16 km *(8.6 nm)* anti-surface; 12 km *(6.8 nm)* anti-aircraft; weight of shell 6 kg.
2 Breda 40 mm/70 (twin); 85° elevation; 300 or 450 rounds/minute to 12.5 km *(6.8 nm)* anti-surface; 4 km *(2.2 nm)* anti-aircraft; weight of shell 0.96 kg.
Fire control: CSEE Panda director. Thomson-CSF Vega II system.
Radars: Surface search: Thomson-CSF Triton; G band; range 33 km *(18 nm)* for 2 m² target.
Fire control: Thomson-CSF Castor IIB; I band; range 15 km *(8 nm)* (associated with Vega fire control system).

Programmes: Ordered from CMN Cherbourg in May 1977. 518 completed February 1982; 522 3 April 1982; 524 29 May 1982; 528 5 September 1982; 532 29 October 1982; 534 17 December 1982; 536 11 March 1983; 538 10 May 1983; 542 29 July 1983.
Structure: Steel hull with alloy superstructure.
Operational: In 1983 an unexpected and unexplained change of names took place. *Waheed* (526) sunk on 24 March 1986 and one other severely damaged on 25 March 1986 by forces of the US Sixth Fleet.

RAD *10/1982, van Ginderen Collection*

3 SUSA CLASS (FAST ATTACK CRAFT—MISSILE)

Name	*No*	*Builders*	*Commissioned*
SUSA	512	Vosper Ltd, Portsmouth	23 Jan 1969
SIRTE	514	Vosper Ltd, Portsmouth	23 Jan 1969
SEBHA (ex-*Sokna*)	516	Vosper Ltd, Portsmouth	23 Jan 1969

Displacement, tons: 95 standard; 114 full load
Dimensions, feet (metres): 100 × 25.5 × 7 *(30.5 × 7.8 × 2.1)*
Main machinery: CODOG; 3 RR Proteus gas turbines; 12 750 hp (9.51 MW); 2 GM 6-71 diesels; 348 hp *(260 kW)* sustained; 3 shafts
Speed, knots: 54
Complement: 20

Missiles: SSM: 8 Aerospatiale SS 12M; wire-guided to 5.5 km *(3 nm)* subsonic; warhead 30 kg.
Guns: 2 Bofors 40 mm/70; 90° elevation; 300 rounds/minute to 12 km *(6.5 nm)* anti-surface; 4 km *(2.2 nm)* anti-aircraft; weight of shell 0.96 kg.
Fire control: Aerospatiale/Nord visual director.
Radars: Surface search: Decca 626; I band.

Programmes: The order for these three fast patrol boats was announced on 12 October 1966. They are generally similar to the RN Brave class (now deleted) and the Søløven class designed and built by Vosper for the Royal Danish Navy.
Modernisation: All three overhauled in Italy in 1977 with new electronics. Further Italian refit 1983-84.

SEBHA (all now carry pennant numbers) *Wright and Logan*

12 Ex-SOVIET OSA II CLASS (FAST ATTACK CRAFT—MISSILE)

AL KATUM 511
AL ZUARA 513
AL RUHA 515
AL BAIDA 517
AL NABHA 519
AL SAFHRA 521
AL FIKAH 523
AL SAKAB 525
AL MOSHA 527
AL MATHUR 529
AL BITAR 531
AL SADAD 533

Displacement, tons: 245 full load
Dimensions, feet (metres): 110.2 × 24.9 × 8.8 *(33.6 × 7.6 × 2.7)*
Main machinery: 3 Type M504 diesels; 15 000 hp(m) *(11 MW)* sustained; 3 shafts
Speed, knots: 37. **Range, miles:** 800 at 30 kts; 500 at 35 kts
Complement: 30

Missiles: SSM: 4 Soviet SS-N-2C Styx; active radar or IR homing to 83 km *(45 nm)* at 0.9 Mach; warhead 513 kg HE; sea-skimmer at end of run.
Guns: 4 USSR 30 mm/65 (2 twin) automatic; 85° elevation; 500 rounds/minute to 5 km *(2.7 nm)*; weight of shell 0.54 kg.
Radars: Surface search: Square Tie; I band; range 73 km *(45 nm)*.
Fire control: Drum tilt; H/I band.
IFF: Two Square Head. High Pole.

Programmes: The first craft arrived in October 1976, four more in August-October 1977, a sixth in July 1978, three in September-October 1979, one in April 1980, one in May 1980 (521) and one in July 1980 (529).
Structure: Some have been painted with camouflage stripes in 1991.

AL BAIDA *1986, van Ginderen Collection*

4 GARIAN CLASS (LARGE PATROL CRAFT)

Name	*No*	*Builders*	*Commissioned*
SABRATA	611	Brooke Marine, Lowestoft	early 1970
ZLEITAN (ex-*Garian*)	612	Brooke Marine, Lowestoft	30 Aug 1969
KAWLAN	613	Brooke Marine, Lowestoft	30 Aug 1969
MAROWA	614	Brooke Marine, Lowestoft	early 1970

Displacement, tons: 120 standard; 159 full load
Dimensions, feet (metres): 106 × 21.2 × 5.5 *(32.3 × 6.5 × 1.7)*
Main machinery: 2 Paxman Ventura 12CM diesels; 3000 hp *(2.24 MW)* sustained; 2 shafts
Speed, knots: 24. **Range, miles:** 1500 at 12 kts
Complement: 15-22
Guns: 1 Bofors 40 mm/60. 1 Oerlikon 20 mm.

Comment: At least first pair refitted in Istanbul in 1984. Used for Coast Guard duties. 612 renamed after former MRC became a hulk. At least one has a 144 mm rocket launcher. All non-operational in early 1992.

KHAWLAN *Brooke Marine*

3 THORNYCROFT TYPE (LARGE PATROL CRAFT)

Name	*No*	*Builders*	*Commissioned*
BENINA	CG 3	Vosper Thornycroft	29 Aug 1968
FARWA (ex-*Homs*)	CG 2	Vosper Thornycroft	early 1969
MISURATA	CG 4	Vosper Thornycroft	29 Aug 1968

Displacement, tons: 100
Dimensions, feet (metres): 100 × 21 × 5.5 *(30.5 × 6.4 × 1.7)*
Main machinery: 3 RR DV8TM diesels; 1740 hp *(1.3 MW)*; 3 shafts
Speed, knots: 18. **Range, miles:** 1800 at 14 kts
Complement: 18
Guns: 1 Oerlikon 20 mm.

Comment: Welded steel construction. Two transferred to Malta in 1978. Used for Coast Guard duties.

THORNYCROFT Type *Thornycroft*

1 Ex-SOVIET POLUCHAT CLASS (LARGE PATROL CRAFT)

723

Displacement, tons: 70 standard; 100 full load
Dimensions, feet (metres): 97.1 × 19 × 4.8 *(29.6 × 5.8 × 1.5)*
Main machinery: 2 Type M50F-12 diesels; 1700 hp(m) *(1.25 MW)* sustained; 2 shafts
Speed, knots: 20. **Range, miles:** 1500 at 10 kts
Complement: 15
Guns: 2 (twin) MGs.
Radars: Navigation: Spin Trough; I band.

Comment: Transferred May 1985. Used as Torpedo Recovery Vessel.

MINE WARFARE FORCES

8 Ex-SOVIET NATYA CLASS (OCEAN MINESWEEPERS)

AL ISAR (ex-*Ras El Gelais*) 111
AL TIYAR (ex-*Ras Hadad*) 113
RAS AL HAMMAN 115
RAS AL FULAIJAH 117
RAS AL QULA 119
RAS AL MADWAR 121
RAS AL MASSAD 123
RAS AL HANI 125

Displacement, tons: 770 full load
Dimensions, feet (metres): 200.1 × 31.8 × 8.9 *(61 × 9.7 × 2.7)*
Main machinery: 2 Type M504 diesels; 8000 hp(m) *(5.88 MW)*; 2 shafts
Speed, knots: 19. **Range, miles:** 4000 at 10 kts
Complement: 60

Guns: 4 USSR 30 mm/65 (2 twin) automatic; 85° elevation; 500 rounds/minute to 5 km *(2.7 nm)*; weight of shell 0.54 kg.
4 USSR 25 mm/60 (2 twin); 85° elevation; 270 rounds/minute to 3 km *(1.6 nm)*; weight of shell 0.34 kg.
A/S mortars: 2 RBU 1200 5-tubed fixed launchers; elevating; range 1-2 km; warhead 34 kg.
Mines: 10.
Radars: Surface search: Don 2; I band.
Fire control: Drum Tilt; H/I band.
IFF: Two Square Head. One High Pole B.
Sonars: Hull-mounted; active search; high frequency.

Programmes: First pair transferred February 1981. Second pair arrived February 1983, one in August 1983, the sixth in January 1984 the seventh in January 1985 and the eighth in October 1986.
Structure: At least one of the class painted in green striped camouflage in 1991.
Operational: Capable of magnetic, acoustic and mechanical sweeping.

RAS AL HANI *2/1988*

AMPHIBIOUS FORCES

2 PS 700 CLASS (LSTs)

Name	*No*	*Builders*	*Commissioned*
IBN OUF	132	CNI de la Mediterranée	11 Mar 1977
IBN HARISSA	134	CNI de la Mediterranée	10 Mar 1978

Displacement, tons: 2800 full load
Dimensions, feet (metres): 326.4 × 51.2 × 7.9 *(99.5 × 15.6 × 2.4)*
Main machinery: 2 SEMT-Pielstick 16 PA4V 185 diesels; 5344 hp(m) *(3.93 MW)* sustained; 2 shafts; cp props
Speed, knots: 15.4. **Range, miles:** 4000 at 14 kts
Complement: 35
Military lift: 240 troops; 11 tanks
Guns: 6 Breda 40 mm/70 (3 twin). 1—81 mm mortar.
Fire control: CSEE Panda director.
Radars: Air search: Thomson-CSF Triton; D band.
Surface search: Decca 1226; I band.
Helicopters: 1 Aerospatiale SA 316B Alouette III.

Comment: 132 laid down 1 April 1976 and launched 22 October 1976; 134 laid down 18 April 1977, launched 18 October 1977.

IBN HARISSA *1981*

3 Ex-SOVIET POLNOCHNY D CLASS (LSMs)

IBN AL HADRAMI 112 **IBN UMAYAA** 116 **IBN AL FARAT** 118

Displacement, tons: 1150 full load
Dimensions, feet (metres): 269 × 32.8 × 6.6 *(82 × 10 × 2)*
Main machinery: 2 Type 40D diesels; 5000 hp(m) *(3.68 MW)*; 2 shafts
Speed, knots: 18. **Range, miles:** 900 at 17 kts
Complement: 40
Military lift: 180 troops; 350 tons including 6 tanks
Guns: 4 USSR 30 mm (2 twin). 2—140 mm 18-tubed rocket launchers.
Radars: Surface search: Radwar SRN-745; I band.
Fire control: Drum Tilt; H/I band.
IFF: Salt Pot A. Square Head.

Comment: The first to be transferred arrived in November 1977. On 14 September 1978 *Ibn Qis* (fourth of the class) was burned out during a landing exercise and was a total loss. 118 and 116 delivered June 1978. All are an export variant of the standard Soviet/Polish Polnochny class but with helicopter deck added. Built in Poland. Similar types built for Iraq and India.

IBN AL HADRAMI *12/1987*

IBN UMAYAA *6/1990*

3 TURKISH C 107 CLASS (LCTs)

IBN AL IDRISI 130 **IBN MARWAN** 131 **EL KOBAYAT** 132

Displacement, tons: 280 standard; 600 full load
Dimensions, feet (metres): 183.7 × 37.8 × 3.6 *(56 × 11.6 × 1.1)*
Main machinery: 3 GM 6-71 TI diesels; 900 hp *(671 kW)* sustained; 3 shafts
Speed, knots: 8.5 loaded; 10 max. **Range, miles:** 600 at 10 kts
Complement: 15
Military lift: 100 troops; 350 tons including 5 tanks
Guns: 2—30 mm (twin).

Comment: First two transferred 7 December 1979 (ex-Turkish *C130* and *C131*) from Turkish fleet. Third of class reported in 1991. Previously reported numbers were much exaggerated.

SUPPORT SHIPS

1 LSD TYPE

Name	*No*	*Builders*	*Commissioned*
ZELTIN	711	Vosper Thornycroft, Woolston	23 Jan 1969

Displacement, tons: 2200 standard; 2470 full load
Dimensions, feet (metres): 324 × 48 × 10.2 *(98.8 × 14.6 × 3.1)*; 19 *(5.8)* aft when flooded
Main machinery: 2 Paxman Ventura 16CM diesels; 4000 hp *(2.98 MW)*; 2 shafts
Speed, knots: 15. **Range, miles:** 3000 at 14 kts
Complement: As Senior Officer Ship: 101 (15 officers)

Guns: 2 Bofors 40 mm/70; 90° elevation; 300 rounds/minute to 12 km *(6.5 nm)* anti-surface; 4 km *(2.2 nm)* anti-aircraft; weight of shell 0.96 kg.
Fire control: Vega II-12 for 40 mm guns.
Radars: Surface search: Thomson-CSF Triton; G band; range 33 km *(18 nm)* for 2 m² target (associated with Vega fire control).

Programmes: Ordered in January 1967; launched 29 February 1968.
Structure: Fitted with accommodation for a flag officer or a senior officer and staff. Operational and administrative base of the squadron. Workshops with a total area of approximately 4500 sq ft are situated amidships with ready access to the dock, and there is a 3 ton travelling gantry fitted with outriggers to cover ships berthed alongside up to 200 ft long.
Operational: The ship provides full logistic support, including docking maintenance and repair facilities. Craft up to 120 ft can be docked. Used as tender for Light Forces and is probably no longer capable of going to sea.

ZELTIN *1980, van Ginderen Collection*

6 RO-RO TRANSPORTS

GARYOUNIS (ex-*Mashu*) **EL TEMSAH** + 4

Measurement, tons: 2412 gross
Dimensions, feet (metres): 546.3 × 80.1 × 21.3 *(166.5 × 24.4 × 6.5)*
Main machinery: 2 SEMT-Pielstick diesels; 20 800 hp(m) *(15.29 MW)*; 2 shafts; bow thruster
Speed, knots: 20

Comment: Details are for *Garyounis*, a converted Ro-Ro passenger/car ferry used as a training vessel in 1989. In addition the 117 m *El Temsah* has been refitted and is back in service, and another four Ro-Ro vessels are in regular military service. All have minelaying potential.

SALVAGE SHIP

1 YUGOSLAV SPASILAC CLASS

AL MUNJED (ex-*Zlatica*) 722

Displacement, tons: 1590 full load
Dimensions, feet (metres): 182 × 39.4 × 14.1 *(55.5 × 12 × 4.3)*
Main machinery: 2 diesels; 4340 hp(m) *(3.19 MW)*; 2 shafts; cp props; bow thruster
Speed, knots: 13. **Range, miles:** 4000 at 12 kts
Complement: 50
Guns: 4—12.7 mm MGs. Can also be fitted with 8—20 mm (2 quad) and 2—20 mm.
Radars: Surface search: Racal Decca; I band.

Comment: Transferred in 1982. Fitted for firefighting, towing and submarine rescue—carries recompression chamber. Built at Tito SY, Belgrade.

SPASILAC Class

DIVING TENDER

1 Ex-SOVIET YELVA CLASS

AL MANOUD VM 917

Displacement, tons: 300 full load
Dimensions, feet (metres): 134.2 × 26.2 × 6.6 *(40.9 × 8 × 2)*
Main machinery: 2 Type 3D-12A diesels; 630 hp(m) *(463 kW)*; 2 shafts
Speed, knots: 12.5
Complement: 30
Radars: Navigation: Spin trough; I band.
IFF: High Pole.

Comment: Built in early 1970s. Transferred December 1977. Carries two 1.5 ton cranes and has a portable decompression chamber.

YELVA Class *1973*

FLOATING DOCKS

Comment: One of 5000 tons capacity at Tripoli. One of 3200 tons capacity acquired in April 1985.

TUGS

3 COASTAL TYPE

A 33 **A 34** **A 35**

Measurement, tons: 150 grt
Dimensions, feet (metres): 87.3 × 26 × 8.2 *(26.6 × 7.9 × 2.5)*
Main machinery: 2 diesels; 2 shafts

Comment: Built by Jonker and Stans BV Shipyard, Netherlands. First launched 16 October 1979.

4 COASTAL TYPE

Name	*No*	*Builders*	*Commissioned*
RAS EL HELAL	A 31	Mondego, Portugal	22 Oct 1976
AL AHWEIRIF	A 32	Mondego, Portugal	17 Feb 1977
AL KERIAT	—	Mondego, Portugal	1 July 1977
AL TABKAH	—	Mondego, Portugal	29 July 1978

Measurement, tons: 200 grt
Dimensions, feet (metres): 114 × 29.5 × 13 *(34.8 × 9 × 4)*
Main machinery: 2 diesels; 2300 hp(m) *(1.69 MW)*; 2 shafts
Speed, knots: 14

MADAGASCAR

Personnel

(a) 1992: 515 officers and men (including Marine Company of 120 men)
(b) 18 months' national service

Bases and Ports

Diego-Suarez, Tamatave, Majunga, Tulear, Nossi-Be, Fort Dauphin, Manakara.

Mercantile Marine

Lloyd's Register of Shipping:
86 vessels of 72 803 tons gross

LIGHT FORCES

Note: Five police patrol craft (GC 1-5) were destroyed in 1990.

1 TYPE PR 48 (LARGE PATROL CRAFT)

Name	*No*	*Builders*	*Commissioned*
MALAIKA	—	Chantiers Navals Franco-Belges (SFCN)	Dec 1967

Displacement, tons: 235 light; 250 full load
Dimensions, feet (metres): 155.8 × 23.6 × 8.2 *(47.5 × 7.1 × 2.5)*
Main machinery: 2 SACM V12 CZSHR diesels; 3600 hp(m) *(2.65 MW)* sustained; 2 shafts
Speed, knots: 23. **Range, miles:** 2000 at 15 kts
Complement: 25 (3 officers)
Guns: 2 Bofors 40 mm/60; 90° elevation; 300 rounds/minute to 12 km *(6.5 nm)* anti-surface; 4 km *(2.2 nm)* anti-aircraft; weight of shell 0.89 kg.

Comment: Ordered by the French Navy for delivery to Madagascar. Laid down in November 1966, launched on 22 March 1967. Non-operational in early 1992.

AMPHIBIOUS FORCES

1 Ex-FRENCH EDIC

AINA VAO VAO (ex-*L9082*)

Displacement, tons: 250 standard; 670 full load
Dimensions, feet (metres): 193.5 × 39.2 × 4.5 *(59 × 12 × 1.3)*
Main machinery: 2 MGO diesels; 1000 hp(m) *(753 kW)*; 2 shafts
Speed, knots: 8. **Range, miles:** 1800 at 8 kts
Complement: 17
Guns: 2 Oerlikon 20 mm. 1—81 mm mortar.

Comment: Built in 1964. Transferred 28 September 1985 having been paid off by the French Navy in 1981. This was the only operational ship in the Navy in early 1992.

EDIC Class *1990, J. Y. Robert*

1 BATRAM CLASS

Name	*No*	*Builders*	*Commissioned*
TOKY	—	Arsenal de Diego Suarez	Oct 1974

Displacement, tons: 810
Dimensions, feet (metres): 217.8 × 41 × 6.2 *(66.4 × 12.5 × 1.9)*
Main machinery: 2 MGO diesels; 2400 hp(m) *(1.76 MW)*; 2 shafts
Speed, knots: 13. **Range, miles:** 3000 at 12 kts
Complement: 43
Military lift: 250 tons stores; 30 troops or 120 troops (short range)
Missiles: SSM: 8 Aerospatiale SS 12M; wire-guided to 5.5 km *(3 nm)* subsonic; warhead 30 kg.
Guns: 1 OTO Melara 3 in *(76 mm)*. 2 Oerlikon 20 mm. 1—81 mm mortar.

Comment: Paid for by the French Government as military assistance. Fitted with a bow ramp and similar to, though larger than, the French Edic but smaller than Batral. Non-operational in early 1992.

1 Ex-NORTH KOREAN NAMPO CLASS

Displacement, tons: 82 full load
Dimensions, feet (metres): 84.2 × 20 × 6 *(27.7 × 6.1 × 1.8)*
Main machinery: 4 Type M50 diesels; 4800 hp(m) *(3.53 MW)*; 4 shafts
Speed, knots: 40. **Range, miles:** 375 at 38 kts
Complement: 19
Guns: 4 USSR 14.5 mm (2 twin) MGs. 1—81 mm mortar.

Comment: Assault landing craft based on Soviet P 6 hull. Four transferred February 1979 and June 1979 but three were lost in a typhoon in April 1984. Non-operational in early 1992.

3 LCVP TYPE

FIHERENGA **MAROLA** **SAMBATHRA**

Comment: 14.3 m personnel launches acquired from West Germany in 1988.

TRAINING SHIP

Name	*No*	*Builders*	*Commissioned*
FANANTENANA (ex-*Richelieu*)	—	A G Weser, Bremen	1959

Displacement, tons: 1040 standard; 1200 full load
Dimensions, feet (metres): 206.4 × 30 × 14.8 *(62.9 × 9.2 × 4.5)*
Main machinery: 2 Deutz diesels; 2400 hp(m) *(1.76 MW)*; 1 shaft
Speed, knots: 12
Complement: 45
Guns: 2 Bofors 40 mm/60.

Comment: Trawler (691 tons gross) purchased and converted in 1966-67 for Coast Guard and as training ship/transport. Can accommodate up to 120 people as well as carrying 300 tons of cargo. Occasionally hired out to tourists.

MALAWI

Senior Appointment

Commander of the Navy:
Lieutenant Colonel M M B Gondwe

Base

Monkey Bay, Lake Malawi

Personnel

1992: 220

PATROL FORCES

1 SFCN TYPE

CHIKALA P 703

Displacement, tons: 36 full load
Dimensions, feet (metres): 68.9 × 16.1 × 4.9 *(21 × 4.9 × 1.5)*
Main machinery: 2 Poyaud 520 V12 M2 diesels; 1300 hp(m) *(956 kW)*; 2 shafts
Speed, knots: 22. **Range, miles:** 650 at 15 kts
Complement: 6
Guns: 1 FN 7.62 mm MG.

Comment: Built in prefabricated sections by SFCN Villeneuve-la-Garenne and shipped to Malawi for assembly on 17 December 1984. Commissioned May 1985.

1 NAMACURRA TYPE

Displacement, tons: 5 full load
Dimensions, feet (metres): 29.5 × 9 × 2.8 *(9 × 2.7 × 0.8)*
Main machinery: 2 diesels; 2 shafts
Speed, knots: 32
Complement: 4
Guns: 1—12.7 mm MG. 2—7.62 mm MGs.

Comment: Delivered by South Africa on 29 October 1988.

1 FAIREY MARINE SPEAR CLASS

P 702

Displacement, tons: 4 full load
Dimensions, feet (metres): 29.8 × 9.2 × 2.6 *(9.1 × 2.8 × 0.8)*
Main machinery: 2 Perkins diesels; 290 hp *(216 kW)*; 2 shafts
Speed, knots: 25
Complement: 3
Guns: 2 FN 7.62 mm MGs.

Comment: Acquired late 1976. Three other small patrol boats are deployed on Lake Malawi of which the first was bought in 1968.

2 SURVEY LAUNCHES

Displacement, tons: 70 full load
Dimensions, feet (metres): 68.9 *(21)* length
Main machinery: 2 Baudouin diesels; 2 shafts
Speed, knots: 10.5

Comment: Built by SFCN Villeneuve-la-Garenne and delivered at the end of 1988 for operations on Lake Malawi. There are also two LCVPs.

MALAYSIA

(including Sabah)

Headquarters' Appointments

Chief of the Navy:
Vice Admiral Dato Seri Mohd Shariff Bin Ishak
Deputy Chief of Navy:
Rear Admiral Ahmad Ramli Bin Nor
Fleet Commander:
Rear Admiral Dato Yaacob Bin Haji Daud
Commander Naval Area I (Peninsula):
Commodore Dato Abu Bakar Bin Abdul Jamal
Commander Naval Area II (Sabah and Sarawak):
Commodore Hj Ahmad Bin Haron

Diplomatic Representation

Defence Adviser in London:
Colonel Z Saidi

Personnel

(a) 1992: 12 500 officers and ratings
(b) Voluntary service
(c) RMNVR: Total, 1000 officers and sailors
Divisions at Penang, Selangor and Johore. Target of 7000 in 19 port divisions.

Bases

KD *Malaya,* Lumut HQ Area 1 (West of 109°E); (Telok Muroh) Perak
Fleet Operation Command centre, main fleet base, dockyard and training centre on west coast.
KD *Pelandok,* Lumut (Training Centre)
RMN Barrack Woodlands (Training and Support), Singapore
Kuantan—an advanced base completed in 1981 on east coast
Labuan—(KD *Sri Labuan,* KD *Sri Tawau,* KD *Sri Rejang*) HQ Area 2 (East of 109°E)
Sungei Antu in Sarawak
Sitiawan, Perak; site for planned new naval air station
Kota Kinabalu; site for planned patrol boat base in East Malaysia (1995-96).

Future Plans

It is planned to build 15 small bases around the country with main emphasis on training reserves to man ships taken up in an emergency. Each base will provide a harbour for naval vessels and have up to 400 personnel.

Prefix to Ships' Names

The names of Malaysian warships are prefixed by KD (Kapal Diraja).

Strength of the Fleet

Type	*Active*	*Building (Planned)*
Frigates	2	—
Corvettes	2	(2)
Offshore Patrol Vessels	2	(6)
Logistic Support Vessels	2	—
Fast Attack Craft—Missile	8	—
Fast Attack Craft—Gun	6	—
Patrol Craft	21	(6)
Minehunters	4	—
Diving Tender	1	—
Survey Vessels	1	(1)
LSTs	2	—
Amphibious Craft	198	—
Tugs	17	—

Mercantile Marine

Lloyd's Register of Shipping:
508 vessels of 1 755 279 tons gross

DELETION

1990 *Perantau*

PENNANT LIST

Frigates

24	Rahmat
76	Hang Tuah

Corvettes

25	Kasturi
26	Lekir

Offshore Patrol Vessels

160	Musytari
161	Marikh

Light Forces

34	Kris
36	Sundang
37	Badek
38	Renchong
39	Tombak
40	Lembing
41	Serampang
42	Panah
43	Kerambit
44	Beledau
45	Kelewang
46	Rentaka
47	Sri Perlis
49	Sri Johor
3139	Sri Selangor
3142	Sri Kelantan
3143	Sri Trengganu
3144	Sri Sabah
3145	Sri Sarawak
3146	Sri Negri Sembilan
3147	Sri Melaka
3501	Perdana
3502	Serang
3503	Ganas
3504	Ganyang
3505	Jerong
3506	Todak
3507	Paus
3508	Yu
3509	Baung
3510	Pari
3511	Handalan
3512	Perkasa
3513	Pendekar
3514	Gempita

Mine Warfare Forces

11	Mahamiru
12	Jerai
13	Ledang
14	Kinabalu

Support Forces

152	Mutiara
1109	Duyong
1501	Sri Banggi
1502	Rajah Jarom
1503	Sri Indera Sakti
1504	Mahawangsa

SUBMARINES

Note: Approved in principle in April 1988 to start a submarine squadron with up to two refurbished vessels as training boats while two new ones were to be built. On 28 November 1990 it was announced that the government had approved a naval request to buy two new construction and two second-hand Swedish hulls at a cost of over US$500 million spread over a period of several years. However in 1991 it was reported that the programme had been postponed to 1995 or later.

FRIGATES

1 YARROW TYPE

Name	*No*	*Builders*	*Laid down*	*Launched*	*Commissioned*
RAHMAT (ex-*Hang Jebat*)	24	Yarrow (Shipbuilders)	Feb 1966	18 Dec 1967	31 Aug 1971

Displacement, tons: 1250 standard; 1600 full load
Dimensions, feet (metres): 308 × 34.1 × 14.8 *(93.9 × 10.4 × 4.5)*
Main machinery: CODOG; 1 Bristol Siddeley Olympus TM1B gas turbine; 19 500 hp *(14.5 MW)*; 1 Crossley Pielstick PC 2.2V diesel; 4000 hp *(2.94 MW)* sustained; 2 shafts; cp props
Speed, knots: 26 gas; 16 diesel. **Range, miles:** 6000 at 16 kts; 1000 at 26 kts
Complement: 140

Guns: 1 Vickers 4.5 in *(114 mm)*/45 Mk 5 hand-loaded ❶; 50° elevation; 14 rounds/minute to 17 km *(9.2 nm)* anti-surface; 8 km *(4.4 nm)* anti-aircraft; weight of shell 25 kg. 103 mm rocket for illuminants on each side of mounting.
3 Bofors 40 mm/70 ❷; 90° elevation; 300 rounds/minute to 12 km *(6.5 nm)* anti-surface; 4 km *(2.2 nm)* anti-aircraft; weight of shell 0.96 kg.
A/S mortars: 1 Limbo Mk 10 3-tubed mortar ❸; automatic loading; range 900 m; warhead 92 kg.
Countermeasures: Decoys: 2 UK Mk I rail Chaff launchers.
ESM: UA-3; radar intercept; FH4 HF D/F.
Combat data systems: Signaal Sewaco-MA. Link Y.
Radars: Air search: Signaal LW 02 ❹; D band; range 183 km *(100 nm)*.
Surface search: Decca 626 ❺; I band.
Navigation: Kelvin Hughes MS 32; I band.
Fire control: Signaal M 22 ❻; I/J band; short range.
Sonars: Graseby Type 170B and Type 174; hull-mounted; active search and attack; 15 kHz.

Programmes: Ordered on 11 February 1966. Arrived on station 23 December 1972.
Modernisation: Seacat system removed during refit in 1982-83 and replaced by an additional Bofors gun. A fourth Bofors was mounted (lashed) on the forward part of the flight deck in July 1990 but this appears to have been a temporary arrangement.
Operational: Can land helicopter on MacGregor hatch over Mk 10 well.

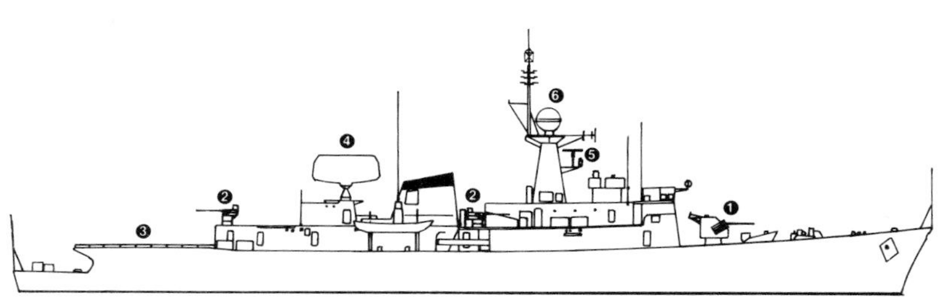

RAHMAT (Scale 1 : 900), Ian Sturton

RAHMAT 2/1991

1 Ex-BRITISH TYPE 41/61

Name	*No*	*Builders*	*Laid down*	*Launched*	*Commissioned*
HANG TUAH (ex-HMS *Mermaid*)	76	Yarrow (Shipbuilders)	1965	29 Dec 1966	16 May 1973

Displacement, tons: 2300 standard; 2520 full load
Dimensions, feet (metres): 339.3 × 40 × 16 (screws) *(103.5 × 12.2 × 4.9)*
Main machinery: 8 VVS ASR 1 diesels; 12 380 hp *(9.2 MW)* sustained; 2 shafts; cp props
Speed, knots: 24. **Range, miles:** 4800 at 15 kts
Complement: 210

Guns: 2 Vickers 4 in *(102 mm)*/45 Mk 19 (twin) ❶; 80° elevation; 16 rounds/minute to 19 km *(10.3 nm)* anti-surface; 13 km *(7 nm)* anti-aircraft; weight of shell 16 kg.
2 Bofors 40 mm/70 ❷; 90° elevation; 300 rounds/minute to 12 km *(6.5 nm)* anti-surface; 4 km *(2.2 nm)* anti-aircraft; weight of shell 0.96 kg.
A/S mortars: 1 RN Limbo 3-tubed Mk 10 mortar ❸; automatic loading; range 1000 m; warhead 92 kg.
Fire control: STD Mk 1 sight for 102 mm gun.
Radars: Air/surface search: Plessey AWS 1 ❹; E/F band; range 110 km *(60 nm)*.
Navigation: Racal Decca 45 ❺; I band.
Sonars: Graseby Type 170B and Type 174; hull-mounted; active search and attack; 15 kHz.

Helicopters: Platform for 1 Westland Wasp HAS 1.

Programmes: Originally built for Ghana as a display ship for ex-President Nkrumah at a cost of £5 million but put up for sale after his departure. She was launched without ceremony on 29 December 1966 and completed in 1968. Commissioned in Royal Navy 16 May 1973, she was based at Singapore 1974-75 returning to the UK early 1976. Transferred to Royal Malaysian Navy May 1977 and refitted by Vosper Thornycroft before sailing for Malaysia in August 1977.
Structure: Similar in hull and machinery to former Leopard and Salisbury classes.
Operational: Refitted in 1991/92 to become a training ship in 1993.

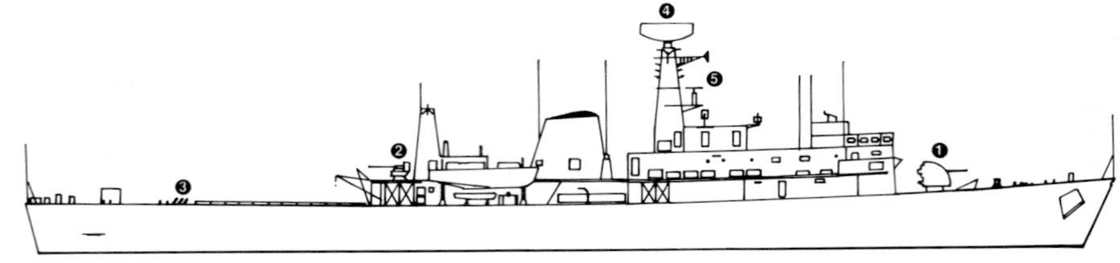
HANG TUAH *(Scale 1 : 900), Ian Sturton*

HANG TUAH *11/1988, Trevor Brown*

OFFSHORE PATROL VESSELS

Note: The new OPV project has taken second priority to the corvettes. The plan is to invite tenders in 1992/93 with the first of class to be built abroad and up to five more in Malaysian shipyards at Lumut and Johore.

2 OFFSHORE PATROL VESSELS

Name	*No*	*Builders*	*Launched*	*Commissioned*
MUSYTARI	160	Korea Shipbuilders, Pusan	20 July 1984	19 Dec 1985
MARIKH	161	Malaysia S B and E Co, Johore	21 Jan 1985	9 Apr 1987

Displacement, tons: 1300 full load
Dimensions, feet (metres): 246 × 35.4 × 12.1 *(75 × 10.8 × 3.7)*
Main machinery: 2 diesels; 12 720 hp(m) *(9.35 MW)*; 2 shafts
Speed, knots: 22. **Range, miles:** 5000 at 15 kts
Complement: 76

Guns: 1 Creusot-Loire 3.9 in *(100 mm)*/55 compact; 80° elevation; 20/45/90 rounds/minute to 17 km *(9.2 nm)* anti-surface; 6 km *(3.2 nm)* anti-aircraft; weight of shell 13.5 kg.
2 Emerson Electric 30 mm (twin); 80° elevation; 1200 rounds/minute combined to 6 km *(3.2 nm)*; weight of shell 0.35 kg.
Fire control: PEAB 9LV 230 optronic system.
Radars: Air/surface search: Signaal DA 05; E/F band; range 137 km *(75 nm)* for 2 m² target.
Navigation: Racal Decca TM 1226; I band.
Fire control: Philips 9LV; J band.

Programmes: Ordered in June 1983. Names translate to Jupiter and Mars.
Structure: Flight deck suitable for Sikorsky S-61A Nari army support helicopter.

MUSYTARI *5/1990, John Mortimer*

CORVETTES

0 + (2) YARROW TYPE

Displacement, tons: 1800 full load
Dimensions, feet (metres): 346 oa; 318.2 wl × 42 × 11.8 *(105.5; 97 × 12.8 × 3.6)*
Main machinery: 4 MTU 20V 1163 TB 93 diesels; 2 shafts; cp props
Speed, knots: 28. **Range, miles:** 5000 at 18 kts
Complement: 146 (19 officers)

Missiles: SSM: 8 Aerospatiale MM 40 Exocet.
SAM: British Aerospace VLS Seawolf; 16 launchers.
Guns: 1 Bofors 57 mm/70 SAK Mk 2; 2 DES 30 mm (twin).
Torpedoes: 6—324 mm (3 triple) tubes; anti-submarine.
Countermeasures: Decoys: 2 Super Barricade 12-barrelled launchers for Chaff.
ESM/ECM: Marconi Mentor/THORN EMI Scimitar; intercept and jammer.
Combat data systems: Marconi Nautis-F; Link Y.
Fire control: 1 Radamec Optronic director.
Radars: Air search: Marconi 1822; E/F band.
Surface search: Marconi 1810; I band.
Fire control: 2 Marconi 1802; I/J band.
Sonars: Thomson Sintra Spherion; hull-mounted active search and attack; medium frequency.

Helicopters: 1 Westland Wasp HAS 1.

YARROW OPV (artist's impression) *1991, Yarrow*

Programmes: Contract being negotiated in early 1992. If it is confirmed work may start at Yarrow in late 1992 with the first ship to be in service in 1996.

Structure: The details listed have not all been confirmed and there may be changes to some of the weapon systems.

2 TYPE FS 1500

Name	*No*	*Builders*	*Laid down*	*Launched*	*Commissioned*
KASTURI	25	Howaldtswerke, Kiel	3 Jan 1983	14 May 1983	15 Aug 1984
LEKIR	26	Howaldtswerke, Kiel	3 Jan 1983	14 May 1983	15 Aug 1984

Displacement, tons: 1500 standard; 1850 full load
Dimensions, feet (metres): 319.1 × 37.1 × 11.5 *(97.3 × 11.3 × 3.5)*
Main machinery: 4 MTU 20V 1163 TB 92 diesels; 23 400 hp(m) *(17.2 MW)* sustained; 2 shafts
Speed, knots: 28; 18 on 2 diesels. **Range, miles:** 3000 at 18 kts; 5000 at 14 kts
Complement: 124 (13 officers)

Missiles: SSM: 4 Aerospatiale MM 38 Exocet ❶; inertial cruise; active radar homing to 42 km *(23 nm)* at 0.9 Mach; warhead 165 kg; sea-skimmer.
Guns: 1 Creusot-Loire 3.9 in *(100 mm)*/55 compact ❷; 80° elevation; 20/45/90 rounds/minute to 17 km *(9.2 nm)* anti-surface; 6 km *(3.2 nm)* anti-aircraft; weight of shell 13.5 kg.
1 Bofors 57 mm/70 ❸; 75° elevation; 200 rounds/minute to 17 km *(9.2 nm)*; weight of shell 2.4 kg. Launchers for illuminants.
4 Emerson Electric 30 mm (2 twin) ❹; 80° elevation; 1200 rounds/minute combined to 6 km *(3.2 nm)*; weight of shell 0.35 kg.
A/S mortars: 1 Bofors 375 mm 6-tubed twin trainable launcher ❺; automatic loading; range 3625 m.
Countermeasures: Decoys: 2 CSEE Dagaie trainable systems; replaceable containers for IR or Chaff.
ESM: Rapids; radar intercept.
ECM: Scimitar; jammer.
Combat data systems: Signaal Sewaco-MA. Link Y.
Fire control: 2 Signaal LIOD optronic directors for gunnery.
Radars: Air/surface search: Signaal DA 08 ❻; F band; range 204 km *(110 nm)* for 2 m² target.
Navigation: Decca TM 1226C; I band.
Fire control: Signaal WM 22 ❼; I/J band; range 46 km *(25 nm)*.
IFF: US Mk 10.
Sonars: Krupp Atlas DSQS 21C; hull-mounted; active search and attack; medium frequency.

Helicopters: Platform for 1 Westland Wasp HAS 1 ❽.

Programmes: First two ordered in February 1981. Fabrication began early 1982. Rated as Corvettes even though they are bigger ships than *Rahmat*.
Modernisation: May be fitted with telescopic hangars in due course.
Structure: Near sisters to the Colombian ships with differing armament.

KASTURI *(Scale 1 : 900), Ian Sturton*

LEKIR *10/1991, John Mortimer*

KASTURI *5/1990, G. Toremans*

SHIPBORNE AIRCRAFT

Numbers/Type: 16 Westland Wasp HAS 1.
Operational speed: 96 kts *(177 km/h)*.
Service ceiling: 12 200 ft *(3720 m)*.
Range: 268 nm *(488 km)*.
Role/Weapon systems: First naval air arm helicopter; six acquired in April 1988, six in 1989-90 and six more in 1991; more modern helicopters (up to a total of 40) planned (either Lynx or Dauphin) but may have to wait for next five year plan. Sensors: None. Weapons: ASW; 1 or 2 Mk 44 torpedoes, depth bombs.

LAND-BASED MARITIME AIRCRAFT

Note: 4 Beechcraft B 200T reported ordered in 1991 for maritime surveillance role.

Numbers/Type: 3 Lockheed C-130H-MP Hercules.
Operational speed: 325 kts *(602 km/h)*.
Service ceiling: 33 000 ft *(10 060 m)*.
Range: 4250 nm *(7880 km)*.
Role/Weapon systems: Long-range MR and SAR tasks; operated by the Air Force. Sensors: Search radar, cameras. Weapons: Unarmed.

LIGHT FORCES

Note: A new class of patrol craft is to be built in batches of six. Design to be decided.

4 SPICA-M CLASS (FAST ATTACK CRAFT—MISSILE)

Name	*No*	*Builders*	*Commissioned*
HANDALAN	3511	Karlskrona Varvet, Sweden	26 Oct 1979
PERKASA	3512	Karlskrona Varvet, Sweden	26 Oct 1979
PENDEKAR	3513	Karlskrona Varvet, Sweden	26 Oct 1979
GEMPITA	3514	Karlskrona Varvet, Sweden	26 Oct 1979

Displacement, tons: 240 full load
Dimensions, feet (metres): 142.6 × 23.3 × 7.4 (screws) *(43.6 × 7.1 × 2.4)*
Main machinery: 3 MTU 16V538 TB91 diesels; 9180 hp(m) *(6.75 MW)* sustained; 3 shafts
Speed, knots: 34.5. **Range, miles:** 1850 at 14 kts
Complement: 40 (6 officers)

Missiles: SSM: 4 Aerospatiale MM 38 Exocet; inertial cruise; active radar homing to 42 km *(23 nm)* at 0.9 Mach; warhead 165 kg; sea-skimmer.
Guns: 1 Bofors 57 mm/70; 75° elevation; 200 rounds/minute to 17 km *(9.2 nm)*; weight of shell 2.4 kg. Illuminant launchers.
1 Bofors 40 mm/70; 90° elevation; 300 rounds/minute to 12 km *(6.5 nm)* anti-surface; 4 km *(2.2 nm)* anti-aircraft; weight of shell 0.96 kg.
Countermeasures: ECM: MEL Susie.
Fire control: 1 PEAB 9LV200 Mk 2 weapon control system with TV tracking. LME anti-aircraft laser and TV rangefinder.
Radars: Surface search: Philips 9GR 600; I band (agile frequency).
Navigation: Decca 616; I band.
Fire control: Philips 9LV 212; J band.
Sonars: Simrad; hull-mounted; active search; high frequency.

Programmes: Ordered 15 October 1976. All named in one ceremony on 11 November 1978, arriving in Port Klang on 26 October 1979.
Structure: Bridge further forward than in Swedish class to accommodate Exocet. Provision has been made for fitting 324 mm torpedo tubes.
Operational: *Handalan* acts as squadron leader.

PENDEKAR *5/1990, John Mortimer*

4 PERDANA CLASS (FAST ATTACK CRAFT—MISSILE)

Name	*No*	*Builders*	*Commissioned*
PERDANA	3501	Constructions Mécaniques de Normandie	21 Dec 1972
SERANG	3502	Constructions Mécaniques de Normandie	31 Jan 1973
GANAS	3503	Constructions Mécaniques de Normandie	28 Feb 1973
GANYANG	3504	Constructions Mécaniques de Normandie	20 Mar 1973

Displacement, tons: 234 standard; 265 full load
Dimensions, feet (metres): 154.2 × 23.1 × 12.8 *(47 × 7 × 3.9)*
Main machinery: 4 Mercedes-Benz MTU 870 diesels; 14 000 hp(m) *(10.3 MW)*; 4 shafts
Speed, knots: 36.5. **Range, miles:** 800 at 25 kts; 1800 at 15 kts
Complement: 30 (4 officers)

Missiles: SSM: 2 Aerospatiale MM 38 Exocet; inertial cruise; active radar homing to 42 km *(23 nm)* at 0.9 Mach; warhead 165 kg; sea-skimmer.
Guns: 1 Bofors 57 mm/70; 75° elevation; 200 rounds/minute to 17 km *(9.2 nm)*; weight of shell 2.4 kg.
1 Bofors 40 mm/70; 90° elevation; 300 rounds/minute to 12 km *(6.5 nm)* anti-surface; 4 km *(2.2 nm)* anti-aircraft; weight of shell 0.96 kg.
Countermeasures: Decoys: 4—57 mm Chaff/flare launchers.
ESM: French type; radar warning.
Fire control: Thomson-CSF Vega optical for guns.
Radars: Air/surface search: Thomson-CSF TH-D 1040 Triton; G band; range 33 km *(18 nm)* for 2 m² target.
Navigation: Racal Decca 616; I band.
Fire control: Thomson-CSF Pollux; I/J band; range 31 km *(17 nm)* for 2 m² target.

Programmes: Left Cherbourg for Malaysia 2 May 1973.
Structure: All of basic La Combattante IID design.

GANAS *5/1991, 92 Wing RAAF*

6 JERONG CLASS (FAST ATTACK CRAFT—GUN)

Name	*No*	*Builders*	*Commissioned*
JERONG	3505	Hong Leong-Lürssen, Butterworth	27 Mar 1976
TODAK	3506	Hong Leong-Lürssen, Butterworth	16 June 1976
PAUS	3507	Hong Leong-Lürssen, Butterworth	16 Aug 1976
YU	3508	Hong Leong-Lürssen, Butterworth	15 Nov 1976
BAUNG	3509	Hong Leong-Lürssen, Butterworth	11 Jan 1977
PARI	3510	Hong Leong-Lürssen, Butterworth	23 Mar 1977

Displacement, tons: 244 full load
Dimensions, feet (metres): 147.3 × 23 × 8.3 *(44.9 × 7 × 2.5)*
Main machinery: 3 MTU/Mercedes-Benz 16V 538 TB90 diesels; 11 250 hp(m) *(8.27 MW)* sustained; 3 shafts
Speed, knots: 32. **Range, miles:** 2000 at 14 kts
Complement: 36 (4 officers)
Guns: 1 Bofors 57 mm/70. 1 Bofors 40 mm/70.
Fire control: CSEE Naja optronic director.
Radars: Surface search: Racal Decca 626; I band.
Navigation: Kelvin Hughes MS 32.
Fire control: Signaal WM 28; I/J band; range 46 km *(25 nm)*.

Comment: Lürssen 45 type. Illuminant launchers on both gun mountings.

PARI *5/1990, John Mortimer*

21 KEDAH, SABAH and KRIS CLASSES (PATROL CRAFT)

Name	*No*	*Builders*	*Commissioned*
SRI SELANGOR	3139	Vosper Ltd, Portsmouth	25 Mar 1963
SRI KELANTAN	3142	Vosper Ltd, Portsmouth	12 Nov 1963
SRI TRENGGANU	3143	Vosper Ltd, Portsmouth	16 Dec 1963
SRI SABAH	3144	Vosper Ltd, Portsmouth	2 Sep 1964
SRI SARAWAK	3145	Vosper Ltd, Portsmouth	30 Sep 1964
SRI NEGRI SEMBILAN	3146	Vosper Ltd, Portsmouth	28 Sep 1964
SRI MELAKA	3147	Vosper Ltd, Portsmouth	2 Nov 1964
KRIS	34	Vosper Ltd, Portsmouth	1 Jan 1966
SUNDANG	36	Vosper Ltd, Portsmouth	29 Nov 1966
BADEK	37	Vosper Ltd, Portsmouth	15 Dec 1966
RENCHONG	38	Vosper Ltd, Portsmouth	17 Jan 1967
TOMBAK	39	Vosper Ltd, Portsmouth	2 Mar 1967
LEMBING	40*	Vosper Ltd, Portsmouth	12 Apr 1967
SERAMPANG	41	Vosper Ltd, Portsmouth	19 May 1967
PANAH	42	Vosper Ltd, Portsmouth	27 July 1967
KERAMBIT	43*	Vosper Ltd, Portsmouth	28 July 1967
BELEDAU	44*	Vosper Ltd, Portsmouth	12 Sep 1967
KELEWANG	45	Vosper Ltd, Portsmouth	4 Oct 1967
RENTAKA	46	Vosper Ltd, Portsmouth	22 Sep 1967
SRI PERLIS	47*	Vosper Ltd, Portsmouth	24 Jan 1968
SRI JOHOR	49*	Vosper Ltd, Portsmouth	14 Feb 1968

* Training

Displacement, tons: 96 standard; 109 full load
Dimensions, feet (metres): 103 × 19.8 × 5.5 *(31.4 × 6 × 1.7)*
Main machinery: 2 Bristol Siddeley/MTU MD 655/18 diesels; 3500 hp(m) *(2.57 MW)*; 2 shafts
Speed, knots: 27. **Range, miles:** 1400 (1660 Sabah class) at 14 kts
Complement: 22 (3 officers)
Guns: 2 Bofors 40 mm/60 (not in 3139, 3142-43).
Radars: Surface search: Racal Decca 616 or 707; I band.

Comment: The first six boats (of which three remain in service), constitute the Kedah class and were ordered in 1961 for delivery in 1963. The four Sabah class were ordered in 1963 for delivery in 1964. The boats of the Kris class were ordered in 1965 for delivery between 1966 and 1968. All are of prefabricated steel construction and are fitted with air-conditioning and Vosper roll damping equipment. The differences between the three classes are minor, the later ones having improved radar, communications, evaporators and engines of MTU, as opposed to Bristol Siddeley construction. *Sri Melaka* (P 3147) is on loan to Sabah. All 21 have been refitted to extend their operational lives. The three Kedah class have had their guns removed.

SRI MELAKA *5/1990, G. Toremans*

KELEWANG *5/1990, John Mortimer*

MINE WARFARE FORCES

Note: Plans for more Lerici class have been shelved in favour of Inshore minehunters in due course.

4 LERICI CLASS (MINEHUNTERS)

Name	*No*	*Builders*	*Commissioned*
MAHAMIRU	11	Intermarine, Italy	11 Dec 1985
JERAI	12	Intermarine, Italy	11 Dec 1985
LEDANG	13	Intermarine, Italy	11 Dec 1985
KINABALU	14	Intermarine, Italy	11 Dec 1985

Displacement, tons: 470 standard; 610 full load
Dimensions, feet (metres): 167.3 × 31.5 × 9.2 *(51 × 9.6 × 2.8)*
Main machinery: 2 MTU 12V 396 TC 82 diesels (passage); 2605 hp(m) *(1.91 MW)* sustained; 2 shafts; KaMeWa cp props; 3 Fincantieri Isotta Fraschini ID 36 SS 6V diesels; 1481 hp(m) *(1.09 MW)* sustained; 2 Riva Calzoni hydraulic thrust jets
Speed, knots: 16 diesels; 7 thrust jet. **Range, miles:** 2000 at 12 kts
Complement: 42 (5 officers)
Guns: 1 Bofors 40 mm/70; 85° elevation; 300 rounds/minute to 12.5 km *(6.8 nm)*; weight of shell 0.96 kg.
Countermeasures: Thomson-CSF IBIS II minehunting system; 2 improved PAP 104 vehicles. Oropesa 'O' MIS-4 mechanical sweep.
Radars: Navigation: Racal Decca 1226; Thomson-CSF Tripartite III; I band.
Sonars: Thomson Sintra TSM 2022 with Display 2060; minehunting; high frequency.

Comment: Ordered on 20 February 1981. First (14) launched 19 March 1983; second (13) 14 July 1983; third (12) 5 January 1984; fourth (11) 23 February 1984. All arrived in Malaysia on 26 March 1986. Heavy GRP construction without frames. Snach active tank stabilisers. Draeger Duocom decompression chamber. Slightly longer than Italian sisters. Endurance, 14 days. Based at Labuan and Lumut to cover both coasts.

JERAI *5/1990, John Mortimer*

LOGISTIC SUPPORT SHIPS

Name	*No*	*Builders*	*Commissioned*
SRI INDERA SAKTI	1503	Bremer Vulkan	24 Oct 1980
MAHAWANGSA	1504	Korea Tacoma	16 May 1983

Displacement, tons: 4300 (1503); 4900 (1504) full load
Dimensions, feet (metres): 328; 337.9 (1504) × 49.2 × 15.7 *(100; 103 × 15 × 4.8)*
Main machinery: 2 Deutz KHD SBV 6M540 diesels; 5865 hp(m) *(4.31 MW)*; 2 shafts; cp props; bow thruster
Speed, knots: 16.5. **Range, miles:** 4000 at 14 kts
Complement: 136 (14 officers) plus accommodation for 215
Military lift: 17 tanks; 600 troops
Cargo capacity: 1300 tons dieso; 200 tons fresh water (plus 48 tons/day distillers)

Guns: 2 Bofors 57 mm Mk 1 (1 only fwd in 1503). 2 Oerlikon 20 mm.
Fire control: 2 CSEE Naja optronic directors (1 only in 1503).
Radars: Navigation: I band.

Helicopters: 1 Sikorsky S-61A Nari (army support) can be carried.

Programmes: Ordered in October 1979 and 1981 respectively.
Modernisation: 100 mm gun included in original design but used for OPVs.
Structure: Fitted with stabilising system, vehicle deck, embarkation ramps port and starboard, recompression chamber and a stern anchor. Large operations room and a conference room are provided. Transfer stations on either beam and aft, light jackstay on both sides and a 15 ton crane for replenishment at sea. 1504 has additional capacity to transport ammunition and the funnel has been removed to enlarge the flight deck.
Operational: Used as training ships for cadets in addition to main roles of long-range support of Light Forces and MCM vessels, command and communications and troop or ammunition transport.

SRI INDERA SAKTI *9/1990, G. Toremans*

MAHAWANGSA *10/1991, John Mortimer*

AMPHIBIOUS FORCES

Note: Some interest shown in LCACs but no orders placed yet.

2 Ex-US 511-1152 CLASS (LSTs)

SRI BANGGI (ex-USS *Henry County* LST 824) 1501
RAJAH JAROM (ex-USS *Sedgewick County* LST 1123) 1502

Displacement, tons: 1653 standard; 2366 beaching; 4080 full load
Dimensions, feet (metres): 328 × 50 × 12 *(100 × 15.3 × 3.7)*
Main machinery: 2 GM 12-567 ATL diesels; 1800 hp(m) *(1.34 MW)*; 2 shafts
Speed, knots: 11.6
Complement: 128 (11 officers)
Military lift: 2100 tons; 500 tons beaching or 125 troops
Guns: 8 Bofors 40 mm (2 twin, 4 single).
Fire control: 2 Mk 51G for guns.
Radars: Surface search: Raytheon SPS 21C (1501); G/H band; range 22 km *(12 nm)*. Sperry SPS 53 (1502); I/J band.

Comment: Built by Missouri Valley BY (1501) and Chicago Bridge Co in 1945. Transferred 1 August 1974, by sale 7 October 1976. Operate as harbour tenders to Light Forces and seldom go to sea.

SRI BANGGI *5/1991, 92 Wing RAAF*

5 LCMs and 15 LCPs

LCM 1-5 **LCP 1-15**

Displacement, tons: 56 (LCM); 18.5 (LCVP) full load
Main machinery: 2 diesels; 330 hp *(246 kW)* (LCM); 400 hp *(298 kW)* (LCVP); 2 shafts
Speed, knots: 10 (LCM); 16 (LCVP)
Military lift: 30 tons (LCM)

Comment: Australian built and transferred 1965-70. LCMs have light armour on sides and some have gun turrets.

LCM 3 (with gun turret) *5/1990, van Ginderen Collection*

9 RCPs and 4 LCUs

RCP 1-9 **LCU 1-4**

Displacement, tons: 30 full load
Main machinery: 2 diesels
Speed, knots: 17
Military lift: 35 troops
Guns: 1 Oerlikon 20 mm.

Comment: Malaysian built. RCPs in service 1974. LCUs in service 1984.

165 DAMEN FAST ASSAULT CRAFT 540

Dimensions, feet (metres): 17.7 × 5.9 × 2 *(5.4 × 1.8 × 0.6)*
Main machinery: 1 outboard; 40 hp(m) *(29.4 kW)*
Speed, knots: 30
Military lift: 10 troops

Comment: First 65 built by Damen Gorinchem, Netherlands in 1986. Remainder built by Limbungan Timor SY. Army assault craft.

DIVING TENDER

Name	*No*	*Builders*	*Commissioned*
DUYONG	1109	Kall Teck (Pte) Ltd, Singapore	5 Jan 1971

Displacement, tons: 120 standard; 140 full load
Dimensions, feet (metres): 110 × 21 × 5.8 *(33.6 × 6.4 × 1.8)*
Main machinery: 2 Cummins diesels; 500 hp *(373 kW)*; 2 shafts
Speed, knots: 12. **Range, miles:** 1000
Complement: 23
Guns: 1 Oerlikon 20 mm (not fitted).

Comment: Launched on 18 August 1970 as TRV. Carries recompression chamber. Can act as support ship for 7-10 commandos.

DUYONG *5/1990, van Ginderen Collection*

SURVEY VESSELS

Note: A replacement survey ship for the deleted *Perantau* is a priority. Negotiations continue for a second-hand ship.

Name	*No*	*Builders*	*Commissioned*
MUTIARA	152	Hong Leong-Lürssen, Butterworth	12 Jan 1978

Displacement, tons: 1905
Dimensions, feet (metres): 232.9 × 42.6 × 13.1 *(71 × 13 × 4)*
Main machinery: 2 Deutz SBA-12M-528 diesels; 4000 hp(m) *(2.94 MW)*; 2 shafts
Speed, knots: 16. **Range, miles:** 4500 at 16 kts
Complement: 155 (14 officers)
Guns: 4 Oerlikon 20 mm (2 twin).
Radars: Navigation: Two Racal Decca; I band.
Helicopters: Platform only.

Comment: Ordered in early 1975. Carries satellite navigation, auto-data system and computerised fixing system. Davits for six survey launches. Painted white. She acted as the Reviewing ship for the Penang Fleet Review in May 1990.

MUTIARA *5/1990, John Mortimer*

MISCELLANEOUS

1 SAIL TRAINING SHIP

TUNAS SAMUDERA

Displacement, tons: 239 full load
Dimensions, feet (metres): 114.8 × 25.6 × 13.1 *(35 × 7.8 × 4)*
Main machinery: 2 Perkins diesels; 370 hp *(272 kW)*; 2 shafts
Speed, knots: 9
Complement: 10

Comment: Ordered from Brooke Yacht, Lowestoft. Laid down 1 December 1988, launched 4 August 1989 and completed 16 October 1989. Two masted brig manned by the Navy but used for training all sea services.

TUNAS SAMUDERA *8/1991, 92 Wing RAAF*

9 COASTAL SUPPLY SHIPS AND TANKERS

LANG HINDEK	**LANG KANGOK**	**LANG SIPUT**
LANG TIRAM	**ENTERPRISE**	**KEPAH**
MELEBAN	**JERNIH**	**TERIJAH**

Comment: Various auxiliaries mostly acquired in the early 1980s.

KEPAH *5/1990, John Mortimer*

12 HARBOUR TUGS AND CRAFT

TUNDA SATU	**KETAM**	**KUPANG**	**SOTONG**
BELAWKAS	**KEMPONG**	**MANGKASA**	**SIPUT**
TEPURUK	**TERITUP**	**PENYU**	**SELAR**

TUNDA SATU *5/1990, van Ginderen Collection*

SABAH SUPPLY SHIPS

Comment: There are a number of Sabah supply ships which are identified by M numbers.

KURAMAH (M 48) *9/1988, van Ginderen Collection*

ROYAL MALAYSIAN POLICE

15 LANG HITAM CLASS

LANG HITAM PZ 1
LANG MALAM PZ 2
LANG LEBAH PZ 3
LANG KUIK PZ 4
BALONG PZ 5
BELIAN PZ 6
KURITA PZ 7
SERANGAN BATU PZ 8
BINTANG PZ 9
KUMBANG PZ 10
BELANG PZ 11
AKAR PZ 12
PERANGAN PZ 13
MERSUJI PZ 14
ALU-ALU PZ 15

Displacement, tons: 230 full load
Dimensions, feet (metres): 126.3 × 22.9 × 5.9 *(38.5 × 7 × 1.8)*
Main machinery: 2 MTU 20V 538 TB92 diesels; 8530 hp(m) *(6.27 MW)* sustained; 2 shafts
Speed, knots: 35. **Range, miles:** 1200 at 15 kts
Complement: 38 (4 officers)
Guns: 1 Bofors 40 mm/70 (in a distinctive plastic turret).
1 Oerlikon 20 mm. 2 FN 7.62 mm MGs.
Radars: Navigation: Kelvin Hughes; I band.

Comment: Ordered from Hong Leong-Lürssen, Butterworth, Malaysia in 1979. First delivered August 1980, last in April 1983.

ALU-ALU *1991, RM Police*

6 BROOKE MARINE 29 METRE CLASS

SANGITAN PX 28
TUMPAT PX 32
SABAHAN PX 29
DUNGUN PX 30
TIOMEN PX 31
SEGAMA PX 33

Displacement, tons: 114
Dimensions, feet (metres): 95.1 × 19.7 × 5.6 *(29 × 6 × 1.7)*
Main machinery: 2 Paxman Valenta 6CM diesels; 2250 hp *(1.68 MW)* sustained; 2 shafts
Speed, knots: 36. **Range, miles:** 1200 at 24 kts
Complement: 18 (4 officers)
Guns: 2 Oerlikon 20 mm.

Comment: Ordered 1979 from Penang Shipbuilding Co First delivery October 1980, last pair completed June 1983. Brooke Marine provided lead yard services.

SANGITAN *1991, RM Police*

9 IMPROVED PX CLASS

ALOR STAR PX 19
KOTA BAHRU PX 20
SRI GAYA PX 25
KUALA TRENGGANU PX 21
JOHORE BAHRU PX 22
SRI KUDAT PX 26
SRI MENANTI PX 23
KUCHING PX 24
SRI TAWAU PX 27

Displacement, tons: 92
Dimensions, feet (metres): 91 × 19 × 4.9 *(27.8 × 5.8 × 1.5)*
Main machinery: 2 MTU 12V 493 TY7 diesels; 2200 hp(m) *(1.62 MW)* sustained; 2 shafts
Speed, knots: 25. **Range, miles:** 900 at 15 kts
Complement: 15
Guns: 2 Oerlikon 20 mm.
Radars: Kelvin Hughes Type 19; I band.

Comment: Built by Vosper Thornycroft (Private) Ltd, Singapore between 1972-73.

SRI MENANTI *1972, Yam Photos, Singapore*

18 PX CLASS

MAHKOTA PX 1
TEMENGGONG PX 2
HULUBALANG PX 3
MAHARAJASETIA PX 4
MAHARAJALELA PX 5
PAHLAWAN PX 6
BENTARA PX 7
PERWIRA PX 8
PERTANDA PX 9
SHAHBANDAR PX 10
SANGSETIA PX 11
LAKSAMANA PX 12
PEKAN PX 13
KELANG PX 14
KUALA KANGSAR PX 15
ARAU PX 16
SRI GUMANTONG PX 17
SRI LABUAN PX 18

Displacement, tons: 86.4 full load
Dimensions, feet (metres): 87.5 × 19 × 4.9 *(26.7 × 5.8 × 1.5)*
Main machinery: 2 Mercedes-Benz MTU 12V 493 TY7 diesels; 2200 hp(m) *(1.62 MW)* sustained; 2 shafts
Speed, knots: 25. **Range, miles:** 550 at 20 kts; 900 at 15 kts
Complement: 15
Guns: 2 Oerlikon 20 mm. 1 FN 7.62 mm MG.
Radars: Kelvin Hughes Type 19; I band; range 117 km *(64 nm)*.

Comment: Built by Vosper Thornycroft (Private) Ltd, Singapore and completed between 1963 and 1970. PX 17 and PX 18 operated by Sabah Government, remainder by Royal Malaysian Police.

BENTARA *1991, RM Police*

99 INSHORE RIVER PATROL CRAFT

Comment: Built in sequence and in several batches and designs since 1964. Some are armed with 7.62 mm MGs. All have PA/PC/PGR or PSC numbers.

PC 2 *1991, RM Police*

6 TRANSPORT VESSELS

PENJAGA PT 1 **MARGHERITA** PT 2
PLC 1-4

Comment: The PLCs are landing craft built in 1980. The two PT craft were built in 1985.

PENJAGA *1991, RM Police*

ROYAL MALAYSIAN CUSTOMS AND EXCISE

6 VOSPER 32 METRE PATROL CRAFT

JUANG K 33 **JERAI** K 35 **BAYU** K 37
PULAI K 34 **PERAK** K 36 **HIJAU** K 38

Displacement, tons: 143 full load
Dimensions, feet (metres): 106.2 × 23.6 × 59 *(32.4 × 7.2 × 1.8)*
Main machinery: 2 Paxman Valenta 16CM diesels; 6650 hp *(5 MW)* sustained; 2 shafts
1 Cummins diesel; 575 hp *(423 kW)* on 1 shaft
Speed, knots: 27; 8 on cruise diesel. **Range, miles:** 2000 at 8 kts
Complement: 26
Guns: 1 Oerlikon 20 mm. 2—7.62 mm MGs.

Comment: Ordered February 1981 from Malaysia Shipyard and Engineering Company with technical support from Vosper Thornycroft (Private) Ltd, Singapore. Two completed 1982, the remainder in 1983-84. Names are preceded by 'Bahtera'.

HIJAU *4/1990, 92 Wing RAAF*

23—13.7 METRE PATROL CRAFT

Comment: Some carry a 7.62 mm machine gun.

13.7m Customs *4/1990, 92 Wing RAAF*

1—18 METRE PATROL CRAFT

KUALA BENGKOKA KA 34

Comment: Built by Mengsina Ltd, Singapore and commissioned on 3 December 1976. Based in Sabah.

KUALA BENGKOKA *9/1988, van Ginderen Collection*

1 + 2 PEMBANTERAS CLASS

Comment: Tenders called for in late 1989 for diesel driven (2400 hp) twin shafted vessels capable of about 28 kts. Being built at Limbungan Timor shipyard, Terengganu. Probable class of 15.

27 PENUMPAS CLASS

Comment: 9 m fast interceptor craft capable of 65 kts. Built in 1991/92.

ROYAL MALAYSIAN FISHERIES DEPARTMENT

Note: Patrol craft have a distinctive diagonal band on the hull and have been mistaken for a Coast Guard.

FISHERIES CRAFT *12/1988, Hartmut Ehlers*

FISHERIES CRAFT *1991, G. Toremans*

MALDIVES

Headquarters' Appointment

Chief of Coast Guard:
Lieutenant Colonel Ibrahim Fulhu

General

All ex-British craft transferred in 1976 have now been scrapped, as have three ex-Taiwanese trawlers.

Personnel

1992: 400

Mercantile Marine

Lloyd's Register of Shipping:
45 vessels of 77 895 tons gross

PATROL FORCES

4 TRACKER II CLASS

11 12 13 14

Displacement, tons: 38 full load
Dimensions, feet (metres): 65.6 × 17.1 × 4.9 *(20 × 5.2 × 1.5)*
Main machinery: 2 Detroit 12V-71TA diesels; 840 hp *(627 kW)* sustained; 2 shafts
Speed, knots: 25. **Range, miles:** 450 at 20 kts
Guns: 2—7.62 mm MGs.

Comment: First one ordered June 1985 from Fairey Marinteknik and commissioned in April 1987. Three more acquired July 1987 ex-UK Customs craft. GRP hulls. Seven days normal endurance. Used for fishery protection and EEZ patrols.

TRACKER II *1989, Maldives CG*

1 CHEVERTON PATROL CRAFT

7

Displacement, tons: 24 full load
Dimensions, feet (metres): 55.8 × 14.8 × 3.9 *(17 × 4.5 × 1.2)*
Main machinery: 2 Detroit 8V-71 TI diesels; 850 hp *(634 kW)* sustained; 2 shafts
Speed, knots: 22. **Range, miles:** 590 at 18 kts
Complement: 9
Guns: 1 FN 7.62 mm MG.

Comment: GRP hull and aluminium superstructure. Originally built for Kiribati and subsequently sold to Maldives in 1984.

CHEVERTON *1989, Maldives CG*

1 LCM

UFULI

Displacement, tons: 108
Dimensions, feet (metres): 85.3 × 26.2 × 3.3 *(26 × 8 × 1)*
Main machinery: 2 Cummins NT 855M diesels; 480 hp *(353 kW)*; 2 shafts
Speed, knots: 8
Complement: 6

Comment: Built by North Shipyard, Singapore and completed in August 1991. Has a bow ramp.

MALI

General

A small river patrol service with three craft operating on headwaters of the Niger with bases at Bamako, Segou, Mopti and Timbuktu. No activity was reported in 1991 so it is possible that all the craft are non-operational.

MALTA

General

A coastal patrol force of small craft was formed in 1971. It is manned by the 2nd Regiment of the Armed Forces of Malta and primarily employed as a Coast Guard. Some patrol craft are in need of replacement and consideration is being given to acquiring two ex-GDR Tarantul class 571 and 573.

Commander, Maritime Squadron

Lieutenant Colonel George Cini, MBE

Personnel

1992: 190

Mercantile Marine

Lloyd's Register of Shipping:
702 vessels of 6 916 325 tons gross

DELETIONS

1989 *C 27, C 29*
1990 *C 25* (old)
1991 *C 20, C 22, C 26* (old)

PATROL FORCES

2 Ex-YUGOSLAV TYPE 131

PRESIDENT TITO (ex-*Cer* 138) C 38
GANNI BONNICI (ex-*Dom Mintoff*, ex-*Durmitor* 139) C 39

Displacement, tons: 85 standard; 120 full load
Dimensions, feet (metres): 91.9 × 14.8 × 8.3 *(28 × 4.5 × 2.5)*
Main machinery: 2 MTU diesels; 2000 hp(m) *(1.47 MW)*; 2 shafts
Speed, knots: 22
Guns: 6—30 mm/70 Hispano Suiza (2 triple).
Radars: Navigation: Kelvin Hughes; I band.

Comment: Built at Trogir Shipyard 1965-68. Transferred 31 March 1982. Need replacements.

TITO and BONNICI *6/1991, van Ginderen Collection*

1 Ex-LIBYAN PATROL CRAFT

C 28 (ex-*Ar Rakib*)

Displacement, tons: 100 full load
Dimensions, feet (metres): 100 × 21 × 5.5 *(30.5 × 6.4 × 1.7)*
Main machinery: 3 RR DV8 TM diesels; 1740 hp *(1.3 MW)*; 3 shafts
Speed, knots: 18. **Range, miles:** 1800 at 14 kts
Complement: 18
Guns: 1 Oerlikon 20 mm.

Comment: Built for Libya by Thornycroft, UK in 1967 and transferred 1979.

C 28 *9/1991, van Ginderen Collection*

2 Ex-US NOAA PATROL CRAFT

C 25 (ex-1255) **C 26** (ex-1257)

Displacement, tons: 35 full load
Dimensions, feet (metres): 59 × 15 × 4 *(18 × 4.6 × 1.2)*
Main machinery: 2 GM 12V-71N diesels; 680 hp *(507 kW)* sustained; 2 shafts
Speed, knots: 20. **Range, miles:** 300 at 15 kts
Complement: 7
Guns: 2—7.62 mm MGs.

Comment: Acquired in 1991.

C 26 *1991, Armed Forces Malta*

2 Ex-US SWIFT CLASS

C 23 (ex-US C 6823) **C 24** (ex-US C 6824)

Displacement, tons: 22.5
Dimensions, feet (metres): 50 × 13 × 4.9 *(15.6 × 4 × 1.5)*
Main machinery: 2 GM 12V-71N diesels; 680 hp *(507 kW)*; 2 shafts
Speed, knots: 25
Complement: 6
Guns: 3—12.7 mm Browning M2 MGs (1 twin, 1 single). 1—81 mm mortar.

Comment: Built by Sewart Seacraft Ltd in 1967. Bought in February 1971. Have an operational endurance of about 24 hours.

C 24 *6/1990, van Ginderen Collection*

1 LCVP

Displacement, tons: 13.5 full load
Dimensions, feet (metres): 36 × 10.5 × 1.1 *(11 × 3.2 × 0.3)*
Main machinery: 1 Detroit 64 HN9 diesel; 225 hp *(168 kW)*; 1 shaft
Speed, knots: 10
Complement: 4

Comment: Built by Gulfstream Co, USA and acquired in January 1987.

LCVP *1989, Armed Forces Malta*

2 PATROL CRAFT

C 27 **C 29**

Comment: Malta built 9.5 m Barberis cabin cruisers acquired in 1989 and used for SAR.

MARSHALL ISLANDS

General

The Marshalls are a group of five main islands which became a self governing republic on 1 May 1979, but with the United States retaining responsibility for defence. Main port is Majuro.

Personnel

1992: 60 (Maritime Authority)

Mercantile Marine

Lloyd's Register of Shipping:
28 vessels of 1 698 051 tons gross

1 PACIFIC FORUM TYPE (LARGE PATROL CRAFT)

Name	*No*	*Builders*	*Commissioned*
—	—	Australian Shipbuilding Industries	29 June 1991

Displacement, tons: 162 full load
Dimensions, feet (metres): 103.3 × 26.6 × 6.9 *(31.5 × 8.1 × 2.1)*
Main machinery: 2 Caterpillar 3516TA diesels; 2820 hp *(2.1 MW)* sustained; 2 shafts
Speed, knots: 20. **Range, miles:** 2500 at 12 kts
Complement: 17 (3 officers)
Radars: Surface search: Furuno 1011; I band.

Comment: The 14th craft to be built in this series for a number of Pacific Island Coast Guards. Ordered in 1989. Capable of mounting a 20 mm gun or 12.7 mm MG.

PACIFIC FORUM Type *1988, Gilbert Gyssels*

1 Ex-USCG CAPE CLASS

Name	*No*	*Builders*	*Commissioned*
IONMETO II (ex-*Cape Small*)	—	CG Yard, Curtis Bay	1953

Displacement, tons: 98 standard; 148 full load
Dimensions, feet (metres): 95 × 20.2 × 6.6 *(28.9 × 6.2 × 2)*
Main machinery: 4 Cummins VT-12 diesels; 2340 hp *(1.75 MW)*; 2 shafts
Speed, knots: 20. **Range, miles:** 2500 at 10 kts
Complement: 15
Guns: Can carry up to 2—12.7 mm MGs.
Radars: Navigation: Raytheon SPS 64(V)1; I band.

Comment: Acquired in 1988.

1 Ex-OFFSHORE SUPPLY SHIP

IONMETO I (ex-*Southern Light*)

Displacement, tons: 110 full load
Dimensions, feet (metres): 100 × — × — *(30.5 × — × —)*
Main machinery: 2 diesels; 2 shafts
Speed, knots: 14
Complement: 12
Guns: Can carry 2—12.7 mm MGs.

Comment: Acquired in 1987 and refitted by Halter Marine for patrol duties in December 1987.

MAURITANIA

Personnel

(a) 1992: 480 (35 officers)
(b) Voluntary service

Bases

Port Etienne, Nouadhibou
Port Friendship, Nouakchott

Future plans

Acquisition of two French Batral LCTs and small number of patrol craft under consideration if finances permit. Another possibility is the FGN Ariadne class with sweep gear removed.

Mercantile Marine

Lloyd's Register of Shipping:
125 vessels of 41 920 tons gross

DELETIONS

1988-89 *Tichitt, Dar El Barka, Im Raq Ni*

LIGHT FORCES

1 PATRA CLASS

Name	*No*	*Builders*	*Commissioned*
EL NASR (ex-*Le Dix Juillet*, ex-*Rapière*)	P 411	Auroux, Arcachon	14 May 1982

Displacement, tons: 147.5 full load
Dimensions, feet (metres): 132.5 × 19.4 × 5.2 *(40.4 × 5.9 × 1.6)*
Main machinery: 2 SACM AGO 195 V12 CZSHR diesels; 4340 hp(m) *(3.2 MW)* sustained; 2 shafts
Speed, knots: 26.3. **Range, miles:** 1750 at 10 kts
Complement: 20 (2 officers)
Guns: 1 Bofors 40 mm/60. 1 Oerlikon 20 mm. 2—12.7 mm Browning MGs.
Radars: Surface search: Racal/Decca 1226; I band.

Comment: Originally built as a private venture by Auroux. Carried out trials with French crew as *Rapière*. Laid down February 1980, launched 3 June 1981, commissioned for trials 1 November 1981. Transferred to Mauritania in 1982. Doubtful operational status.

1 Ex-GERMAN NEUSTADT CLASS

Name	*No*	*Builders*	*Commissioned*
Z'BAR (ex-*Uelzen*)	P 381 (ex-BG 13)	Schlichting, Travemünde	1970

Displacement, tons: 218 full load
Dimensions, feet (metres): 127.1 × 23 × 5 *(38.5 × 7 × 2.2)*
Main machinery: 2 Maybach MTU 16-cyl diesels; 6000 hp(m) *(4.41 MW)*
1 MWM diesel; 685 hp(m) *(503 kW)*; 3 shafts
Speed, knots: 30. **Range, miles:** 450 at 27 kts
Complement: 23 (5 officers)
Guns: 2 Bofors 40 mm/70; 90° elevation; 300 rounds/minute to 12 km *(6.5 nm)* anti-surface; 4 km *(2.2 nm)* anti-aircraft; weight of shell 0.96 kg.

Comment: Ex-West German Coast Guard vessel acquired in March 1990 and recommissioned 29 April 1990. Lürssen design larger but similar to the El Vaiz class.

NEUSTADT Class *1989, Hartmut Ehlers*

1 JURA CLASS

N'MADI (ex-*Criscilla*, ex-*Jura*)

Displacement, tons: 1285 full load
Dimensions, feet (metres): 195.3 × 35 × 14.4 *(59.6 × 10.7 × 4.4)*
Main machinery: 2 British Polar SP 112VS-F diesels; 4200 hp *(3.13 MW)*; 1 shaft
Speed, knots: 15.5
Complement: 28

Comment: Built by Hall Russell, Aberdeen in 1975. Became a Scottish Fishery Protection vessel but was paid off in 1988 and acquired by J Marr Ltd. On lease from July 1989 for Fishery Patrol duties.

3 LÜRSSEN FPB 36 CLASS

Name	*No*	*Builders*	*Commissioned*
EL VAIZ	P 361	Bazan-La Carraca	Oct 1979
EL BEIG	P 362	Bazan-La Carraca	May 1979
EL KINZ	P 363	Bazan-La Carraca	Aug 1982

Displacement, tons: 139 full load
Dimensions, feet (metres): 118.7 × 19 × 6.2 *(36.2 × 5.8 × 1.9)*
Main machinery: 2 MTU 16V538 TB 90 diesels; 7503 hp(m) *(5.51 MW)* sustained; 2 shafts
Speed, knots: 36. **Range, miles:** 1200 at 17 kts
Complement: 19 (3 officers)
Guns: 1 Bofors 40 mm/70. 1 Oerlikon 20 mm. 2—12.7 mm MGs.
Fire control: 1 CSEE Panda optical director (made in Spain).
Radars: Surface search: Raytheon RN 1220/6XB; I band.

Comment: First pair ordered 21 July 1976—third in 1979. Doubtful operational status.

EL BEIG *1980, Bazan*

4 INDIAN PATROL CRAFT

Displacement, tons: 15 full load
Dimensions, feet (metres): 49.2 × 11.8 × 2.6 *(15 × 3.6 × 0.8)*
Main machinery: 2 MWM TBD 232 V12 Marine diesels; 750 hp(m) *(551 kW)*; 2 waterjets
Speed, knots: 24
Complement: 8
Guns: 1—7.62 mm MG.
Radars: Navigation: Furuno FR 8030; I band.

Comment: Built by Garden Reach and delivered in 1990.

LAND-BASED MARITIME AIRCRAFT

Numbers/Type: 2 Piper Cheyenne II.
Operational speed: 283 kts *(524 km/h)*.
Service ceiling: 31 600 ft *(9630 m)*.
Range: 1510 nm *(2796 km)*.
Role/Weapon systems: Coastal surveillance and EEZ protection acquired 1981. Sensors: Bendix 1400 weather radar; cameras. Weapons: Unarmed.

MAURITIUS

Headquarters' Appointments

Commissioner of Police:
Bhimsen Kowlessur MPM, QPM
Commandant Coast Guard:
Commander K N Rao

Base

Port Louis (plus 12 manned CG stations)

Personnel

1992: 500

Mercantile Marine

Lloyd's Register of Shipping:
37 vessels of 82 262 tons gross

PATROL FORCES

Note: In 1991 tenders were invited for a 1000 ton 60 m offshore patrol vessel. Contract expected in late 1992.

1 Ex-INDIAN LARGE PATROL CRAFT

AMAR P 1

Displacement, tons: 120 standard; 151 full load
Dimensions, feet (metres): 117.2 × 20 × 5 *(35.7 × 6.1 × 1.5)*
Main machinery: 2 Paxman diesels; 1000 hp *(746 kW)*; 2 shafts
Speed, knots: 18. **Range, miles:** 500 at 12 kts
Complement: 20
Guns: 1 Bofors 40 mm/60.
Radars: Surface search: Racal Decca 978; I band.

Comment: The last of the old Abhay class built by Garden Reach Workshops Ltd, Calcutta 1969. Transferred April 1974. Retained original name.

AMAR *1991, Mauritius CG*

2 SOVIET ZHUK CLASS

RESCUER **RETRIEVER**

Displacement, tons: 50 full load
Dimensions, feet (metres): 75 × 17 × 6.2 *(23 × 5.2 × 1.9)*
Main machinery: 2 diesels; 2400 hp(m) *(1.76 MW)*; 2 shafts
Speed, knots: 30. **Range, miles:** 1100 at 15 kts
Complement: 17
Guns: 4—14.5 mm (2 twin) MGs.

Comment: Acquired from the Soviet Union in January 1990.

RESCUER (alongside RETRIEVER and AMAR) *1990, Mauritius CG*

9 INDIAN PATROL CRAFT

MARLIN **CASTOR** **SIRIUS** **CAPELLA** **RIGEL**
BARRACUDA **POLARIS** **POLLUX** **CANOPUS**

Displacement, tons: 15 full load
Dimensions, feet (metres): 49.2 × 11.8 × 2.6 *(15 × 3.6 × 0.8)*
Main machinery: 2 MWM TD-232 V12 Marine diesels; 750 hp(m) *(551 kW)*; 2 Hamilton waterjets
Speed, knots: 24
Complement: 8
Guns: 1—7.62 mm MG.
Radars: Navigation: Furuno FR 8030; I band.

Comment: Ordered in 1987 from Mandovi Marine Private Ltd, courtesy of the Indian Government. First two delivered early in 1989; second batch of three with some modifications on 1 May 1990 and the last four at the end of 1990. SATNAV fitted.

MARLIN *1990, Mauritius CG*

32 PATROL BOATS

Comment: Two Rover 663 FPC donated by Australia and 30 Rigid Inflatable craft mostly RHIBS, AVONS and ZODIACS acquired in 1988-89.

LAND-BASED MARITIME AIRCRAFT

Numbers/Type: 1 Dornier 228 (MPCG 01).
Operational speed: 200 kts *(370 km/h)*.
Service ceiling: 28 000 ft *(8535 m)*.
Range: 940 nm *(1740 km)*.
Role/Weapon systems: EEZ surveillance and SAR; acquired from Hindustan Aeronautics in 1990. Sensors: MEL search radar. Weapons: Unarmed.

MEXICO

Headquarters' Appointments

Secretary of the Navy:
Admiral Luis Carlos Ruano Angulo
Under-Secretary of the Navy:
Admiral David Zepeda Torres
Chief of Naval Operations:
Admiral Jorge Mora Perez
Inspector General of the Navy:
Vice Admiral Gregorio Nunez Ehuan
Chief of the Naval Staff:
Vice Admiral Enrique Sangri Namur

Personnel

(a) 1992: Total 36 400 officers and men (including Naval Air Force and 7500 Marines)
(b) Voluntary service

Naval Bases and Commands

Tampico, Veracruz, Guaymas, Manzanillo and Salina Cruz. Light forces bases at Ciudad del Carmen and Acapulco.
The Naval Command is split between the Pacific and Gulf areas each with a Commander-in-Chief with HQs at Veracruz (Gulf) and Acapulco (Pacific). Each area is subdivided into Naval Zones with, in addition, Naval Sectors.

Gulf Area
1st naval zone (state of Tamauilipas); HQ in Ciudad Madero, naval sector HQ in Matamoros
3rd naval zone (state of Veracruz); HQ and naval sector HQs in Tuxpan and Coatzacoalcos
5th naval zone (state of Tabasco); HQ in Frontera
7th naval zone (state of Campeche); HQ in Lerma and naval sector HQs in Ciudad del Carmen and Champoton
9th naval zone (state of Quintana Roo); HQs in Yukalpeten and naval sector HQ in Progreso
11th naval zone; HQ in Chetumal and naval sector HQ in Isla Mujeres and Isla Cozumel

Pacific Area
2nd naval zone (state of Baja California Norte); HQ in Ensenada
4th naval zone (state of Baja California Sur); HQ in La Paz and naval sector HQs in Cortes and Santa Rosalia
6th naval zone (state of Sonora); HQ in Puerto Peñasco, Son
8th naval zone (state of Sinaloa); HQs in Mazatlan and Topolobampo
10th naval zone (state of Nayarit); HQ in San Blas
12th naval zone (state of Jalisco); HQ in Puerto Vallarta
14th naval zone (state of Colima); HQ in Manzanillo and naval sector HQ in Socorro
16th naval zone (state of Michoacan); HQ in Lazaro Cardenas
18th naval zone (state of Guerrero); HQ in Acapulco and naval sector HQ in Ixtapa
20th naval zone (state of Oaxaca); HQ in Salina Cruz and naval sector HQ in Puerto Angel
22nd naval zone (state of Chiapas); HQ in Puerto Madero

Strength of the Fleet

Type	*Active*	*Building (Planned)*
Destroyers	3	—
Frigates	5	—
Patrol Ships	38	2
Large Patrol Craft	35	—
Survey Vessels	3 (1)	—
Coastal and River Patrol Craft	22	—
Support Ships	8	(1)
Tankers-Harbour	2	—
Tugs	6	—
Sail Training Ship	1	—
Repair Ship	1	—
Rescue Ships	2	—
Floating Docks	4	—

Naval Air Force

Naval air bases at Mexico City, Las Bajadas, Puerto Cortes, Isla Mujeres, Ensenada, La Paz. Under consideration are several more CASA transport and logistic support aircraft.

Marine Force

One Marine Paratroop Brigade of two battalions, one Presidential Guard Group (battalion), and 32 independent companies. Three battalion HQs—in Mexico City, Acapulco and Veracruz.

General

One of the persistent problems facing the Mexican Navy is the incursion of foreign fishery poachers, frequently highly organised groups working from the USA. In addition there is a requirement for patrolling the Exclusive Economic Zone including the offshore oil fields. The drug smuggling menace is taking up more and more of the navy's time.

Mercantile Marine

Lloyd's Register of Shipping:
649 vessels of 1 195 517 tons gross

DELETION

1989 *Tehuantepec*

DESTROYERS

2 Ex-US GEARING (FRAM I) CLASS

Name	No	Builders	Laid down	Launched	Commissioned
QUETZALCOATL (ex-USS *Vogelgesang* DD 862)	E 03	Bethlehem, Staten Island	3 Aug 1944	15 Jan 1945	28 Apr 1945
NETZAHUALCOYOTL (ex-USS *Steinaker* DD 863)	E 04	Bethlehem, Staten Island	1 Sep 1944	13 Feb 1945	26 May 1945

Displacement, tons: 2425 standard; 3500 full load
Dimensions, feet (metres): 390.5 × 41.2 × 19 *(119 × 12.6 × 5.8)*
Main machinery: 4 Babcock & Wilcox boilers; 600 psi *(43.3 kg/cm sq)*; 850°F *(454°C)*; 2 GE turbines; 60 000 hp *(45 MW)*; 2 shafts
Speed, knots: 32.5. **Range, miles:** 5800 at 15 kts
Complement: 300

Missiles: A/S: Honeywell ASROC Mk 112 octuple launcher ❶; inertial guidance to 1.6-10 km *(1-5.4 nm)*; payload Mk 46 torpedo.
Guns: 4 USN 5 in *(127 mm)*/38 (2 twin) Mk 38 ❷; 85° elevation; 15 rounds/minute to 17 km *(9.3 nm)* anti-surface; 11 km *(5.9 nm)* anti-aircraft; weight of shell 25 kg.
Torpedoes: 6—324 mm Mk 32 (2 triple) tubes ❸. Honeywell Mk 46; anti-submarine; active/passive homing to 11 km *(5.9 nm)* at 40 kts; warhead 44 kg.
Countermeasures: ESM: WLR-1; radar warning.
Fire control: Mk 37 GFCS.
Radars: Air search: Lockheed SPS 40; E/F band (E 03); range 320 km *(175 nm)*.
Westinghouse SPS 29 ❹; B/C band (E 04); range 457 km *(250 nm)*.
Surface search: Raytheon SPS 10 ❺; G band.
Navigation: Marconi LN 66; I band.
Fire control: Western Electric Mk 25 ❻; I/J band.
Sonars: Sangamo SQS 23; hull-mounted; active search and attack; medium frequency.

Helicopters: 1 MBB BO 105C ❼.

Programmes: Transferred by sale 24 February 1982.
Structure: The devices on top of the funnel are to reduce IR signature.
Operational: E 03 rated as an 'escort vessel'.

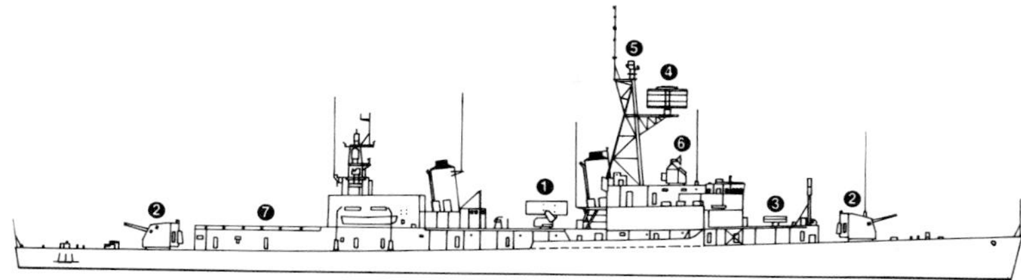

NETZAHUALCOYOTL *(Scale 1 : 1 200), Ian Sturton*

NETZAHUALCOYOTL *1982, Mexican Navy*

1 Ex-US FLETCHER CLASS

Name	No	Builders	Laid down	Launched	Commissioned
CUITLAHUAC (ex-USS *John Rodgers* DD 574)	E 02 (ex-F 2)	Consolidated Steel Corporation	25 July 1941	7 May 1942	9 Feb 1943

Displacement, tons: 2100 standard; 3050 full load
Dimensions, feet (metres): 376.5 × 39.4 × 18 *(114.8 × 12 × 5.5)*
Main machinery: 4 Babcock & Wilcox boilers; 600 psi *(43.3 kg/cm sq)*; 850°F *(454°C)*; 2 GE turbines; 60 000 hp *(45 MW)*; 2 shafts
Speed, knots: 32. **Range, miles:** 5000 at 14 kts
Complement: 197

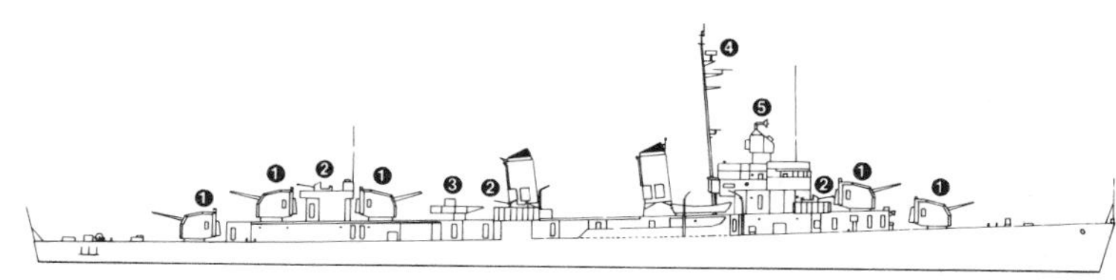

CUITLAHUAC *(Scale 1 : 1 200), Ian Sturton*

Guns: 5 USN 5 in *(127 mm)*/38 Mk 30 ❶; 85° elevation; 15 rounds/minute to 17 km *(9.3 nm)* anti-surface; 8 km *(4.4 nm)* anti-aircraft; weight of shell 25 kg.
10 Bofors 40 mm/60 (5 twin) Mk 2 ❷; 80° elevation; 120 rounds/minute to 10 km *(5.5 nm)*; weight of shell 0.89 kg.
Torpedoes: 5—21 in *(533 mm)* (quin) tubes ❸; anti-surface.
Fire control: Mk 37 GFCS for 127 mm guns. 5 Mk 51 GFCS for 40 mm guns.
Radars: Surface search: Kelvin Hughes 17/9 ❹; I band.
Navigation: Kelvin Hughes 14/9; I band.
Fire control: Western Electric Mk 25 ❺; I/J band.

Programmes: Transferred to the Mexican Navy in August 1970.
Operational: In spite of its age this ship still has a formidable gun armament and is very active in drug enforcement patrols.

CUITLAHUAC (alongside E 03 and E 04) *9/1990*

FRIGATES

1 DURANGO CLASS

Name	No	Builders	Laid down	Launched	Commissioned
DURANGO	B 01 (ex-128)	Union Naval de Levante, Valencia	28 Oct 1933	28 June 1935	14 July 1936

Displacement, tons: 1600 standard; 2000 full load
Dimensions, feet (metres): 256.5 × 36.6 × 10.5 *(78.2 × 11.2 × 3.1)*
Main machinery: Diesel-electric; 2 Enterprise DMR-38 diesels; 5000 hp *(3.73 MW)*; 2 shafts
Speed, knots: 18. **Range, miles:** 3000 at 12 kts
Complement: 149 (24 officers)

Guns: 1—4 in *(102 mm)*. 2—57 mm. 4 Oerlikon 20 mm.

Programmes: Originally designed primarily as an armed transport with accommodation for 20 officers and 450 men. The two Yarrow boilers and Parsons geared turbines of 6500 shp installed when first built were replaced by two 2500 bhp diesels in 1967.
Operational: Became non-operational in the 1970s but has since been refitted as a training ship.

DURANGO *1982, Mexican Navy*

1 Ex-US EDSALL CLASS

Name	*No*	*Builders*	*Laid down*	*Launched*	*Commissioned*
COMODORO MANUEL AZUETA (ex-USS *Hurst* DE 250)	A 06	Brown S B Co, Houston, Texas	27 Jan 1943	14 Apr 1943	30 Aug 1943

Displacement, tons: 1200 standard; 1850 full load
Dimensions, feet (metres): 302.7 × 36.6 × 13 *(92.3 × 11.3 × 4)*
Main machinery: 4 Fairbanks-Morse 38D8-1/8-10 diesels; 7000 hp *(5.3 MW)* sustained; 2 shafts
Speed, knots: 20. **Range, miles:** 13 000 at 12 kts
Complement: 216 (15 officers)

Guns: 3 USN 3 in *(76 mm)*/50 Mk 22; 85° elevation; 20 rounds/minute to 12 km *(6.6 nm)*; weight of shell 6 kg.
8 Bofors 40 mm/60 (1 quad, 2 twin) Mk 2 and Mk 1; 80° elevation; 120 rounds/minute to 10 km *(5.5 nm)*; weight of shell 0.89 kg.
2—37 mm saluting guns.
Fire control: Mk 52 (for 3 in); Mk 51 Mod 2 (for 40 mm).
Radars: Surface search: Kelvin Hughes Type 17; I band.
Navigation: Kelvin Hughes Type 14; I band.
Fire control: RCA/GE Mk 26; I/J band.

Programmes: Transferred to Mexico 1 October 1973.
Operational: Employed as training ship with Gulf Area command. A/S weapons and sensors removed.

COMODORO MANUEL AZUETA *7/1981, Michael D. J. Lennon*

3 Ex-US CHARLES LAWRENCE and CROSLEY CLASSES

Name	*No*	*Builders*	*Laid down*	*Launched*	*Commissioned*
USUMACINTA (ex-USS *Don O Woods* APD 118, ex-*DE 721*)	B 06 (ex-H 6)	Consolidated Steel Corporation	1 Dec 1943	19 Feb 1944	28 May 1945
COAHUILA (ex-USS *Rednour* APD 102, ex-*DE 592*)	B 07	Bethlehem S B Co, Hingham, Mass	9 Jan 1944	1 Mar 1944	15 Mar 1945
CHIHUAHUA (ex-USS *Barber* APD 57, ex-*DE 161*)	B 08	Norfolk Navy Yard, Norfolk, Va	27 Apr 1943	20 May 1943	10 Oct 1943

Displacement, tons: 1400 standard; 2130 full load
Dimensions, feet (metres): 306 × 37 × 11.3 *(93.3 × 11.3 × 3.4)*
Main machinery: Turbo-electric; 2 Foster-Wheeler boilers; 435 psi *(30.6 kg/cm sq)*; 750°F *(399°C)*; 2 GE turbo generators; 12 000 hp *(9 MW)*; 2 motors; 2 shafts
Speed, knots: 20. **Range, miles:** 5000 at 15 kts
Complement: 204 plus 162 troops

Guns: 1 USN 5 in *(127 mm)*/38 Mk 30; 85° elevation; 15 rounds/minute to 17 km *(9.3 nm)*; weight of shell 25 kg.
6 Bofors 40 mm/60 (3 twin) Mk 1. 6 Oerlikon 20 mm/80.
Fire control: 3 Mk 51 GFCS for 40 mm guns.
Radars: Surface search: Kelvin Hughes 14/9; I band.

Programmes: B 06 purchased by Mexico in December 1963, B 07 in June 1969 and B 08 in December 1969. B 07 is the only Charles Lawrence class; the others have a tripod after mast supporting the conspicuous 10 ton boom.

COAHUILA *1982, Mexican Navy*

PATROL SHIPS

2 + 2 AGUILA CLASS

Name	*No*	*Builders*	*Commissioned*
SEBASTIAN JOSE HOLZINGER (ex-*Uxmal*)	C 01 (ex-GA 01)	Tampico	Nov 1991
MITLA	GA 02	Veracruz	1992
PETEN	GA 03	Tampico	1992
ANAHUAC	GA 04	Veracruz	1992

Displacement, tons: 1175 full load
Dimensions, feet (metres): 244.1 × 34.4 × 8.2 *(74.4 × 10.5 × 2.5)*
Main machinery: 2 MTU 20V 956 TB 92 diesels; 11 700 hp(m) *(8.6 MW)* sustained; 2 shafts
Speed, knots: 22. **Range, miles:** 3820 at 18 kts
Complement: 75 (11 officers)

Guns: 1 Bofors 57 mm/70 Mk 2; 75° elevation; 220 rounds/minute to 17 km *(9.3 nm)*; weight of shell 2.4 kg.
Fire control: Elsag NA 18 optronic director.
Radars: Surface search: Raytheon SPS 64(V); I band.
Helicopters: 1 MBB BO 105C.

Programmes: Originally four were ordered from Tampico and Veracruz. First laid down November 1983, second in 1984 but the whole programme has been slowed down by financial problems. An improved variant of the Bazán Halcon class.

ANAHUAC *1/1990*

6 HALCON CLASS (B 119)

Name	*No*	*Builders*	*Laid down*	*Launched*	*Commissioned*
CADETE VIRGILIO URIBE	GH 01	Bazán, San Fernando	1 July 1981	12 Nov 1981	2 June 1982
TENIENTE JOSÉ AZUETA	GH 02	Bazán, San Fernando	7 Sep 1981	12 Dec 1981	30 Aug 1982
CAPITAN de FRAGATA PEDRO SÁINZ de BARANDA	GH 03	Bazán, San Fernando	22 Oct 1981	29 Jan 1982	20 Oct 1982
COMODORO CARLOS CASTILLO BRETÓN	GH 04	Bazán, San Fernando	11 Nov 1981	26 Feb 1982	4 Nov 1982
VICEALMIRANTE OTHÓN P BLANCO	GH 05	Bazán, San Fernando	18 Dec 1981	26 Mar 1982	16 Nov 1982
CONTRAALMIRANTE ANGEL ORTIZ MONASTERIO	GH 06	Bazán, San Fernando	30 Dec 1981	4 May 1982	17 Dec 1982

Displacement, tons: 910 full load
Dimensions, feet (metres): 219.9 × 34.4 × 10.2 *(67 × 10.5 × 3.1)*
Main machinery: 2 MTU-Bazán 16V 956 TB 91 diesels; 7500 hp(m) *(5.52 MW)* sustained; 2 shafts
Speed, knots: 22. **Range, miles:** 5000 at 18 kts
Complement: 46 (7 officers)

Guns: 1 Breda 40 mm/70.
Fire control: Naja optronic director.
Radars: Surface search: Decca AC 1226; I band.
Tacan: SRN 15.

Helicopters: 1 MBB BO 105C.

Programmes: Ordered in 1980. Contracts for a further eight of the class seem to have been shelved.
Operational: Used for EEZ patrol.

VICEALMIRANTE OTHON P. BLANCO *7/1991, Harald Carstens*

CADETE VIRGILIO URIBE *1987, Mexican Navy*

12 Ex-US ADMIRABLE CLASS

Name	*No*	*Name*	*No*
D 01 (ex-USS *Jubilant* AM 255)	ID 01	**D 13** (ex-USS *Knave* AM 256)	ID 13
D 03 (ex-USS *Execute* AM 232)	ID 03	**D 14** (ex-USS *Rebel* AM 284)	ID 14
D 04 (ex-USS *Specter* AM 306)	ID 04	**D 15** (ex-USS *Crag* AM 214)	ID 15
D 05 (ex-USS *Scuffle* AM 298)	ID 05	**D 17** (ex-USS *Diploma* AM 221)	ID 17
D 11 (ex-USS *Device* AM 220)	ID 11	**D 18** (ex-USS *Invade* AM 254)	ID 18
D 12 (ex-USS *Ransom* AM 283)	ID 12	**D 19** (ex-USS *Intrigue* AM 253)	ID 19

Displacement, tons: 650 standard; 900 full load
Dimensions, feet (metres): 184.5 × 33 × 14.4 *(56.3 × 10.1 × 4.4)*
Main machinery: 2 Cooper-Bessemer GSB-8 diesels; 1710 hp *(1.28 MW)*; 2 shafts
Speed, knots: 15. **Range, miles:** 4300 at 10 kts
Complement: 104 (8 officers)
Guns: 1 USN 3 in *(76 mm)*/50 Mk 22; 85° elevation; 20 rounds/minute to 12 km *(6.5 nm)* anti-surface; 9 km *(4.9 nm)* anti-aircraft; weight of shell 6 kg.
2 Bofors 40 mm/70; 90° elevation; 300 rounds/minute to 12 km *(6.5 nm)* anti-surface; 4 km *(2.2 nm)* anti-aircraft; weight of shell 2.4 kg.
6 or 8 Oerlikon 20 mm; 50° elevation; 800 rounds/minute to 2 km; weight of shell 0.24 kg.

Comment: Former US steel hulled fleet minesweepers. All completed in 1943-44. D 20 now fitted for surveying (see *Survey Vessels*). Minesweeping gear removed. Four of the class deleted in 1986 and others are probably non-operational having been cannibalised for spares.

D 13 *1982, Mexican Navy*

17 Ex-US AUK CLASS

Name	*No*
LEANDRO VALLE (ex-USS *Pioneer* MSF 105)	G-01
GUILLERMO PRIETO (ex-USS *Symbol* MSF 123)	G-02
MARIANO ESCOBEDO (ex-USS *Champion* MSF 314)	G-03
MANUEL DOBLADO (ex-USS *Defense* MSF 317)	G-05
SEBASTIAN L DE TEJADA (ex-USS *Devastator* MSF 318)	G-06
SANTOS DEGOLLADO (ex-USS *Gladiator* MSF 319)	G-07
IGNACIO DE LA LLAVE (ex-USS *Spear* MSF 322)	G-08
JUAN N ALVARES (ex-USS *Ardent* MSF 340)	G-09
MANUEL GUTIERREZ ZAMORA (ex-USS *Roselle* MSF 379)	G-10
VALENTIN G FARIAS (ex-USS *Starling* MSF 64)	G-11
IGNACIO MANUEL ALTAMIRANO (ex-USS *Sway* MSF 120)	G-12
FRANCISCO ZARCO (ex-USS *Threat* MSF 124)	G-13
IGNACIO L VALLARTA (ex-USS *Velocity* MSF 128)	G-14
JESUS G ORTEGA (ex-USS *Chief* MSF 315)	G-15
MELCHOR OCAMPO (ex-USS *Scoter* MSF 381)	G-16
JUAN ALDAMA (ex-USS *Piloti* MSF 104)	G-18
HERMENEGILDO GALEANA (ex-USS *Sage* MSF 111)	G-19

Displacement, tons: 1090 standard; 1250 full load
Dimensions, feet (metres): 221.2 × 32.2 × 10.8 *(67.5 × 9.8 × 3.3)*
Main machinery: Diesel-electric; 2 diesels; 2200 hp *(1.64 MW)*; 2 shafts
Speed, knots: 18. **Range, miles:** 4300 at 10 kts
Complement: 105 (9 officers)
Guns: 1 USN 3 in *(76 mm)*/50. 4 Bofors 40 mm/56 (2 twin). 2 Oerlikon 20 mm.
Radars: Surface search: Kelvin Hughes 14/9 (in most); I band.

Comment: Transferred six in February 1973, four in April 1973, nine in September 1973. Employed on patrol duties. All built during Second World War. Variations are visible in the mid-ships section where some have a bulwark running from the break of the fo'c'sle to the quarter-deck. Minesweeping gear removed. There is a variety of diesel engines, radars and even shipbuilders for this class. Starting to be paid off. One used as a survey vessel deleted in 1988.

JUAN N ALVARES *3/1988*

1 PATROL SHIP

Name	*No*	*Builders*	*Commissioned*
GUANAJUATO	C 7	S E C N Ferrol	19 Mar 1936

Displacement, tons: 2000 full load
Dimensions, feet (metres): 301.8 × 37 × 13 *(92 × 11.3 × 4)*
Guns: 1 Vickers 4 in *(102 mm)*/45; 80° elevation; 16 rounds/minute to 19 km *(10.4 nm)*; weight of shell 16 kg.
2 Oerlikon 20 mm; 55° elevation; 800 rounds/minute to 2 km; weight of shell 0.24 kg.

GUANAJUATO *1982, Mexican Navy*

SHIPBORNE AIRCRAFT

Numbers/Type: 12 MBB BO 105C.
Operational speed: 113 kts *(210 km/h)*.
Service ceiling: 9845 ft *(3000 m)*.
Range: 407 nm *(754 km)*.
Role/Weapon systems: Coastal patrol helicopter for patrol, fisheries protection and EEZ protection duties; SAR as secondary role. Sensors: Bendix search radar. Weapons: Unarmed.

BO 105C *1988, Paul Jackson*

LAND-BASED MARITIME AIRCRAFT (FRONT LINE)

Note: A number of confiscated drug-running aircraft are also in service, mostly Cessnas.

Numbers/Type: 9 CASA C-212 Aviocar.
Operational speed: 190 kts *(353 km/h)*.
Service ceiling: 24 000 ft *(7315 m)*.
Range: 1650 nm *(3055 km)*.
Role/Weapon systems: Acquired from 1987 and used for Maritime Surveillance. Have replaced the Albatross and Aravas. Sensors: Search radar; APS 504. Weapons: Unarmed.

LIGHT FORCES

2 Ex-US CAPE CLASS (LARGE PATROL CRAFT)

Name	*No*	*Builders*	*Recommissioned*
JALISCO (ex-*Cape Carter*)	P 42	C G Yard, Curtis Bay	1 Apr 1990
NAYARIT (ex-*Cape Hedge*)	P 43	C G Yard, Curtis Bay	21 Apr 1990

Displacement, tons: 98 standard; 148 full load
Dimensions, feet (metres): 95 × 20.2 × 6.6 *(28.9 × 6.2 × 2)*
Main machinery: 2 GM 16V-149TI diesels; 2070 hp *(1.54 MW)* sustained; 2 shafts
Speed, knots: 20. **Range, miles:** 2500 at 10 kts
Complement: 14 (1 officer)
Guns: 2—12.7 mm MGs.
Radars: Navigation: Raytheon SPS 64; I band

Comment: Built between 1953 and 1959; have been re-engined and extensively modernised. Transferred in 1990 under the FMS programme, having paid off from the US Coast Guard.

JALISCO *4/1990, Mexican Navy*

31 AZTECA CLASS (LARGE PATROL CRAFT)

Name	*No*	*Builders*	*Commissioned*
ANDRES QUINTANA ROO	P 01	Ailsa Shipbuilding Co Ltd	1 Nov 1974
MATIAS DE CORDOVA	P 02	Scott & Sons, Bowling	22 Oct 1974
MIGUEL RAMOS ARIZPE	P 03	Ailsa Shipbuilding Co Ltd	23 Dec 1974
JOSE MARIA IZAZAGA	P 04	Ailsa Shipbuilding Co Ltd	19 Dec 1974
JUAN BAUTISTA MORALES	P 05	Scott & Sons, Bowling	19 Dec 1974
IGNACIO LOPEZ RAYON	P 06	Ailsa Shipbuilding Co Ltd	19 Dec 1974
MANUEL CRESCENCIO REJON	P 07	Ailsa Shipbuilding Co Ltd	4 July 1975
JUAN ANTONIO DE LA FUENTE	P 08	Ailsa Shipbuilding Co Ltd	4 July 1975
LEON GUZMAN	P 09	Scott & Sons, Bowling	7 Apr 1975
IGNACIO RAMIREZ	P 10	Ailsa Shipbuilding Co Ltd	17 July 1975
IGNACIO MARISCAL	P 11	Ailsa Shipbuilding Co Ltd	23 Sep 1975
HERIBERTO JARA CORONA	P 12	Ailsa Shipbuilding Co Ltd	7 Nov 1975
JOSE MARIA MATA	P 13	J Lamont & Co Ltd	13 Oct 1975
FELIX ROMERO	P 14	Scott & Sons, Bowling	23 June 1975
FERNANDO M LIZARDI	P 15	Ailsa Shipbuilding Co Ltd	24 Dec 1975
FRANCISCO J MUJICA	P 16	Ailsa Shipbuilding Co Ltd	21 Nov 1975
PASTOR ROUAIX	P 17	Scott & Sons, Bowling	7 Nov 1975
JOSE MARIA DEL CASTILLO VELASCO	P 18	Lamont & Co Ltd	14 Jan 1975
LUIS MANUEL ROJAS	P 19	Lamont & Co Ltd	3 Apr 1976
JOSE NATIVIDAD MACIAS	P 20	Lamont & Co Ltd	2 Sep 1976
ESTEBAN BACA CALDERON	P 21	Lamont & Co Ltd	18 June 1976
GENERAL IGNACIO ZARAGOZA	P 22	Veracruz	1 June 1976
TAMAULIPAS	P 23	Veracruz	18 May 1977
YUCATAN	P 24	Veracruz	3 July 1977
TABASCO	P 25	Salina Cruz	1 Dec 1978
VERACRUZ	P 26	Veracruz	1 Dec 1978
CAMPECHE	P 27	Veracruz	1 Mar 1980
PUEBLA	P 28	Salina Cruz	1 June 1982
MARGARITA MAZA DE JUAREZ	P 29	Salina Cruz	29 Nov 1976
LEONA VICARIO	P 30	Veracruz	1 May 1977
JOSEFA ORTIZ DE DOMINGUEZ	P 31	Salina Cruz	1 June 1977

Displacement, tons: 148 full load
Dimensions, feet (metres): 111.8 × 28.1 × 6.8 *(34.1 × 8.6 × 2)*
Main machinery: 2 Ruston-Paxman Ventura 12CM diesels; 3000 hp *(2.24 MW)* sustained; 2 shafts
Speed, knots: 24. **Range, miles:** 2500 at 12 kts
Complement: 24 (2 officers)
Guns: 1 Bofors 40 mm/70; 90° elevation; 300 rounds/minute to 12 km *(6.5 nm)* anti-surface; 4 km *(2.2 nm)* anti-aircraft; weight of shell 2.4 kg.
1 Oerlikon 20 mm; 55° elevation; 800 rounds/minute to 2 km; weight of shell 0.24 kg.

Comment: Ordered by Mexico on 27 March 1973 from Associated British Machine Tool Makers Ltd to a design by T T Boat Designs, Bembridge, Isle of Wight. The first 21 were modernised in 1987 in Mexico with spare parts and equipment supplied by ABMTM Marine Division who supervised the work which included engine refurbishment and the fitting of air-conditioning. The refit programme was designed to extend service lives by at least 10 years. Reports that more of the class were to be built were not correct.

ANDRES QUINTANA ROO *1982, Mexican Navy*

2 AZUETA CLASS (COASTAL PATROL CRAFT)

Name	*No*	*Builders*	*Commissioned*
VILLALPANDO	F 06	Astilleros de Tampico	1960
AZUETA	F 07	Astilleros de Tampico	1959

Displacement, tons: 80 full load
Dimensions, feet (metres): 85.3 × 16.4 × 7 *(26 × 5 × 2.1)*
Main machinery: 2 Superior diesels; 600 hp *(448 kW)*; 2 shafts
Speed, knots: 12
Guns: 2—13.2 mm (twin).

Comment: All-steel construction. Were to have paid off in 1988 but have been retained in service.

4 POLIMAR CLASS (COASTAL PATROL CRAFT)

Name	*No*	*Builders*	*Commissioned*
POLIMAR 1	F 01 (ex-G 1)	Astilleros de Tampico	1 Oct 1962
POLIMAR 2	F 02 (ex-G 2)	Icacas Shipyard, Guerrero	1968
POLIMAR 3	F 03 (ex-G 3)	Icacas Shipyard, Guerrero	1968
POLIMAR 4	F 04 (ex-G 4)	Astilleros de Tampico	1971

Displacement, tons: 37 standard; 57 full load
Dimensions, feet (metres): 67.2 × 14.8 × 4.3 *(20.1 × 4.5 × 1.3)*
Main machinery: 2 diesels; 456 hp *(335 kW)*; 2 shafts
Speed, knots: 11
Guns: 1 Oerlikon 20 mm.

Comment: Steel construction.

POLIMAR 3 *1972, Mexican Navy*

5 FLUVIAL CLASS (RIVER PATROL CRAFT)

Name	*No*	*Builders*	*Commissioned*
AM 4	F 14	Vera Cruz	1957
AM 5	F 15	Tampico	1959
AM 6	F 16	Vera Cruz	1959
AM 7	F 17	Tampico	1961
AM 8	F 18	Vera Cruz	1981

Displacement, tons: 37
Dimensions, feet (metres): 56.1 × 16.4 × 8.2 *(17.1 × 5 × 2.5)*
Main machinery: 1 diesel; 1 shaft
Speed, knots: 6

Comment: Steel construction. One already deleted having been replaced by the last of the class which was built 20 years after the others.

AM 4 *1989*

13 OLMECA II CLASS (RIVER PATROL CRAFT)

AM 11-AM 23

Displacement, tons: 18 full load
Dimensions, feet (metres): 54.8 × 14.4 × 7.9 *(16.7 × 4.4 × 2.4)*
Main machinery: 2 Detroit 8V 92TA diesels; 1020 hp *(760 kW)* sustained; 2 shafts
Speed, knots: 20. **Range, miles:** 460 at 15 kts
Complement: 15 (2 officers)
Guns: 1—12.7 mm MG.
Radars: Navigation: Raytheon; I band.

Comment: Built at Acapulco from 1979-83 with GRP hulls. Further group building.

AM 11 *1986, Mexican Navy*

SURVEY VESSELS

Note: Reported that the Auk class *Mariano Matamoros* (H 01) paid off in 1988, may be back in service in 1992.

1 ONJUKU CLASS

ONJUKU H 04

Displacement, tons: 494 full load
Dimensions, feet (metres): 121 × 26.2 × 11.5 *(36.9 × 8 × 3.5)*
Main machinery: 1 Yanmar 6UA-UT diesel; 700 hp(m) *(515 kW)*; 1 shaft
Speed, knots: 12. **Range, miles:** 5645 at 10.5 kts
Complement: 20 (4 officers)
Radars: Navigation: I band.
Sonars: Furuno; hull-mounted; high frequency.

Comment: Launched in 1977 and commissioned in 1980.

ONJUKU *1987, Mexican Navy*

1 Ex-US ROBERT D CONRAD CLASS

Name	*No*	*Builders*	*Commissioned*
ALTAIR (ex-*James M Gilliss* AGOR 4)	H 05	Christy Corp, Wisconsin	5 Nov 1962

Displacement, tons: 1370 full load
Dimensions, feet (metres): 208.9 × 40 × 15.4 *(63.7 × 12.2 × 4.7)*
Main machinery: Diesel-electric; 2 Caterpillar D-378 diesel generators; 1 motor; 1000 hp *(746 kW)*; 1 shaft; bow thruster
Speed, knots: 13.5. **Range, miles:** 12 000 at 12 kts
Complement: 34 (12 officers)
Radars: Navigation: Raytheon TM1600; I band.

Comment: Leased 14 June 1983. Refitted and modernised in Mexico. Recommissioned 27 November 1984. Primarily used for oceanography.

ALTAIR *1989, Mexican Navy*

1 Ex-US ADMIRABLE CLASS

OCEANOGRAFICO (ex-DM 20, ex-USS *Harlequin* AM 365, ex-ID-20) H 02

Comment: Details given in Admirable class under *Patrol Ships*. Now unarmed but has a complement of 62 (12 officers).

OCEANOGRAFICO *1990, Mexican Navy*

SERVICE FORCES

Note: US planned to lease at least one Thomaston class LSD, now in reserve in Mexico, in 1991. No sign of this offer being taken up by early 1992. The ship would be employed in anti-smuggling and anti-drug war duties, which would require formation of a much larger Naval Aviation helicopter wing (UH-1Hs, and so on).

1 Ex-US FABIUS CLASS (LIGHT FORCES TENDER)

Name	*No*	*Builders*	*Commissioned*
VICENTE GUERRERO (ex-USS *Megara* ARVA-6)	A 05	American Bridge Co, Ambridge, Penn	27 June 1945

Displacement, tons: 3284 light; 4100 full load
Dimensions, feet (metres): 328 × 50 × 14 *(100 × 15.3 × 4.3)*
Main machinery: 2 GM 12-567A diesels; 1800 hp *(1.34 MW)*; 2 shafts
Speed, knots: 10.6. **Range, miles:** 6000 at 10 kts
Complement: 250
Guns: 6 Bofors 40 mm (1 quad; 1 twin).
Fire control: 2 Mk 51 Mod 2 GFCS.

Comment: Ex-aircraft repair ship sold to Mexico 1 October 1973. Carries two LCVPs.

VICENTE GUERRERO *7/1991, Harald Carstens*

LCVP (embarked in A 05) *1988*

2 Ex-US 511-1152 CLASS (LSTs)

Name	*No*	*Builders*	*Commissioned*
PANUCO (ex-*Park County*)	A 01	Bethlehem Steel	8 May 1945
MANZANILLO (ex-*Clearwater County*)	A 02	Chicago Bridge & Iron Co	31 Mar 1944

Displacement, tons: 4080 full load
Dimensions, feet (metres): 328 × 50 × 14 *(100 × 15.3 × 4.3)*
Main machinery: 2 GM 12-567A diesels; 1800 hp *(1.34 MW)*; 2 shafts
Speed, knots: 11. **Range, miles:** 6000 at 11 kts
Complement: 13
Guns: 8 Bofors 40 mm (2 twin, 4 single).

Comment: Transferred in 1971-72 and deployed as SAR and disaster relief ships. Were to have paid off when *Huasteco* and *Zapoteco* commissioned but have been retained in service.

PANUCO *7/1991, Harald Carstens*

2 LOGISTIC SUPPORT SHIPS

Name	*No*	*Builders*	*Commissioned*
HUASTECO	A 21	Tampico, Tampa	21 May 1986
ZAPOTECO	A 22	Salina Cruz	1 Sep 1986

Displacement, tons: 2650 full load
Dimensions, feet (metres): 227 × 42 × 18.6 *(69.2 × 12.8 × 5.7)*
Main machinery: 1 diesel; 3600 hp(m) *(2.65 MW)*; 1 shaft
Speed, knots: 16. **Range, miles:** 5500 at 14 kts
Complement: 57 plus 300 passengers
Guns: 1 Bofors 40/60.
Helicopters: 1 MBB BO 105C.

Comment: Can serve as troop transports, supply or hospital ships. Were to have replaced the ex-US LSTs but the latter have been retained in service.

HUASTECO *1988, van Ginderen Collection*

1 LOGISTIC SUPPORT SHIP

Name	*No*	*Builders*	*Commissioned*
TARASCO	A 25	Shipyard AB, Sweden	1 Mar 1990

Comment: Commercial build, taken over in 1990.

TARASCO *1990, Mexican Navy*

1 TRANSPORT VESSEL

Name	*No*	*Builders*	*Commissioned*	*Recommissioned*
IGUALA (ex-*La Paz*)	A 08	Kure Zosencho, Japan	1964	16 Mar 1990

Dimensions, feet (metres): 357.7 × 57.5 × 14.1 *(109 × 17.5 × 4.3)*
Main machinery: 2 Burmeister & Wain diesels; 5600 hp(m) *(4.1 MW)*; 2 shafts
Speed, knots: 17.5

Comment: Former Ro-Ro ferry belonging to the Transport Ministry.

IGUALA *1990, Mexican Navy*

2 Ex-US YOG/YO TYPE (HARBOUR TANKERS)

Name	*No*	*Builders*	*Commissioned*
AGUASCALIENTES (ex-*YOG 6*)	A 03	Geo H Mathis Co Ltd, Camden, NJ	1943
TLAXCALA (ex-*YO 107*)	A 04	Geo Lawley & Son, Neponset, Mass	1943

Displacement, tons: 440 light; 1400 full load
Dimensions, feet (metres): 159.2 × 32.9 × 13.3 *(48.6 × 10 × 4.1)*
Main machinery: 1 Fairbanks-Morse diesel; 500 hp *(373 kW)*; 1 shaft
Speed, knots: 8
Complement: 26 (5 officers)
Cargo capacity: 6570 barrels
Guns: 1 Oerlikon 20 mm.

Comment: Former US self-propelled fuel oil barges. Purchased in August 1964. Entered service in November 1964.

1 LOGISTIC SUPPORT SHIP

Name	*No*	*Builders*	*Commissioned*
MAYA	A 23	Isla Gran Cayman, Ru	1 June 1988

Displacement, tons: 924 full load
Dimensions, feet (metres): 160.1 × 38.7 × 16.1 *(48.8 × 11.8 × 4.9)*
Main machinery: 1 MAN diesel; 1 shaft
Speed, knots: 12
Complement: 15 (8 officers)

Comment: First launched in 1962 and acquired for the navy in 1988. Unarmed.

MAYA *1989, Mexican Navy*

1 SAIL TRAINING SHIP

Name	*No*	*Builders*	*Commissioned*
CUAUHTEMOC	A 07	Astilleros Taleres Calaya, SA, Bilbao	29 July 1982

Displacement, tons: 1800 full load
Dimensions, feet (metres): 296.9 (bowsprit); 257.5 wl × 39.4 × 16.7 *(90.5; 78.5 × 12 × 5.1)*
Main machinery: 1 Detroit 12V-149T diesel; 875 hp *(652 kW)* sustained; 1 shaft
Speed, knots: 11 diesel
Complement: 275 (20 officers, 90 midshipmen)

Comment: Launched January 1982.

CUAUHTEMOC *7/1986, W. Donko*

4 FLOATING DOCKS

— (ex-US ARD 2) — (ex-US ARD 11) **AR 15** (ex-US ARD 15)
— (ex-US AFDL 28)

Comment: ARD 2 (150 × 24.7 m) transferred 1963 and ARD 11 (same size) 1974 by sale. Lift 3550 tons. Two 10 ton cranes and one 100 kW generator. ARD 15 has the same capacity and facilities—transferred 1971 by lease. AFDL 28 built in 1944, transferred 1973. Lift, 1000 tons.

1 TRANSPORT VESSEL

Name	*No*	*Builders*	*Commissioned*
ZACATECAS	B 02	Ulua SY, Veracruz	1960

Displacement, tons: 785 standard
Dimensions, feet (metres): 158 × 27.2 × 10 *(48.2 × 8.3 × 2.7)*
Main machinery: 1 MAN diesel; 560 hp(m) *(412 kW)*; 1 shaft
Speed, knots: 8
Complement: 50 (13 officers)
Cargo capacity: 400 tons

Comment: Cargo ship type employed as a transport. Deleted in error in 1987.

4 Ex-US ABNAKI CLASS (TUGS)

Name	*No*	*Builders*	*Commissioned*
OTOMI (ex-USS *Molala* ATF 106)	A 17	United Eng Co, Alameda, Calif	29 Sep 1943
YAQUI (ex-USS *Abnaki* ATF 96)	A 18	Charleston S B and D D Co	15 Nov 1943
SERI (ex-USS *Cocopa* ATF 101)	A 19	Charleston S B and D D Co	25 Mar 1944
CORA (ex-USS *Hitchiti* ATF 103)	A 20	Charleston S B and D D Co	27 May 1944

Displacement, tons: 1640 full load
Dimensions, feet (metres): 205 × 38.5 × 17 *(62.5 × 11.7 × 5.2)*
Main machinery: Diesel-electric; 4 Busch-Sulzer BS-539 diesels; 6000 hp *(4.48 MW)*; 4 generators; 1 motor; 3000 hp(m) *(2.24 MW)*; 1 shaft
Speed, knots: 15. **Range, miles:** 6500 at 15 kts
Complement: 75
Guns: 1 US 3 in *(76 mm)*/50.
Radars: Navigation: Marconi LN 66; I band.

Comment: *Otomi* transferred 1 August 1978, remainder 30 September 1978. All by sale.

2 Ex-US MARITIME ADMINISTRATION V 4 CLASS (TUGS)

R 2 (ex-*Montauk*) A 12 **R 3** (ex-*Point Vicente*) A 13

Displacement, tons: 1863 full load
Dimensions, feet (metres): 191.3 × 37 × 18 *(58.3 × 11.3 × 5.5)*
Main machinery: 2 Nat Supply 8-cyl diesels; 2250 hp *(1.68 MW)*; 1 Kort nozzle
Speed, knots: 14. **Range, miles:** 9000 at 14 kts
Complement: 90
Guns: 1—3 in *(76 mm)*/50. 2 Oerlikon 20 mm (*R 2*).
Radars: Navigation: Kelvin Hughes 14/9; I band.

Comment: Part of a large class built 1943-45 by US Maritime Administration for civilian use. Not a successful design; most were laid up on completion. In 1968 six were taken from reserve and transferred by sale in June 1969. All originally unarmed—guns fitted in Mexico. *R 2* assigned to Gulf area, *R 3* to Pacific area.

R 3 *1982, Mexican Navy*

MICRONESIA

Headquarters' Appointment

OIC Maritime Surveillance Centre
Mr Lester Ruda

Ports

Kolonia (main base), Kosral, Moen, Takatik.

General

Pacific Islands of the Caroline archipelago comprising the states of Kosral, Pohnpei, Truk and Yep. The Federated States became a self-governing republic on 10 May 1979. The United States maintains responsibility for defence and has leased 3 Cape class Coast Guard patrol craft for anti-narcotics patrols.

Mercantile Marine

Lloyd's Register of Shipping:
17 vessels of 8141 tons gross

PATROL FORCES

2 PACIFIC FORUM TYPE (LARGE PATROL CRAFT)

Name	*No*	*Builders*	*Commissioned*
PALIKIR	FSM 1	Australian Shipbuilding Industries	28 Apr 1990
MICRONESIA	FSM 2	Australian Shipbuilding Industries	3 Nov 1990

Displacement, tons: 162 full load
Dimensions, feet (metres): 103.3 × 26.6 × 6.9 *(31.5 × 8.1 × 2.1)*
Main machinery: 2 Caterpillar 3516TA diesels; 2820 hp *(2.09 MW)* sustained; 2 shafts
Speed, knots: 20. **Range, miles:** 2500 at 12 kts
Complement: 17 (3 officers)
Radars: Surface search: Furuno 1011; I band.

Comment: Ordered in June 1989 from Australian Shipbuilding Industries. Training and support provided by Australia at Port Kolonia.

MICRONESIA *11/1990, Royal Australian Navy*

3 Ex-US CAPE CLASS (LARGE PATROL CRAFT)

Name	*No*	*Builders*	*Commissioned*
— (ex-*Cape George*)	—	Coast Guard Yard, Curtis Bay	15 Mar 1958
— (ex-*Cape Cross*)	—	Coast Guard Yard, Curtis Bay	20 Aug 1958
— (ex-*Cape Corwin*)	—	Coast Guard Yard, Curtis Bay	14 Nov 1958

CAPE GEORGE (in USCG colours) *1990*

Displacement, tons: 148 full load
Dimensions, feet (metres): 95 × 20.2 × 6.6 *(28.9 × 6.2 × 2)*
Main machinery: 2 GM 16V-149 TI diesels; 2070 hp *(1.54 MW)* sustained; 2 shafts
Speed, knots: 20. **Range, miles:** 2500 at 10 kts
Complement: 14
Guns: 2—12.7 mm MGs. 2—40 mm mortars.
Radars: Surface search: Raytheon SPS 64; I band.

Comment: Transferred on loan in early 1991.

MONTSERRAT

Senior Officer

Commissioner of Police:
Sidney Charles MBE, CPM, JP

Base

Plymouth

Mercantile Marine

Lloyd's Register of Shipping:
1 vessel of 711 tons gross

1 HALMATIC M160 CLASS (COASTAL PATROL CRAFT)

SHAMROCK

SHAMROCK *1989, Halmatic*

Displacement, tons: 18 light
Dimensions, feet (metres): 52.5 × 15.4 × 4.6 *(16 × 4.7 × 1.4)*
Main machinery: 2 Detroit 6V-92TA diesels; 520 hp *(388 kW)*; 2 shafts
Speed, knots: 27. **Range, miles:** 500 at 17 kts
Complement: 6
Guns: 1—7.62 mm MG.

Comment: Delivered on 7 January 1990; identical craft acquired by Anguilla and the Turks and Caicos Islands in December 1989.

MOROCCO

Headquarters' Appointment

Inspector of the Navy:
Captain Lahcen Ouhirra

Diplomatic Representation

Defence Attaché in London:
Colonel Mustapha Jabrane

Personnel

(a) 1992: 7000 officers and ratings (including 1500 Marines)
(b) 18 months' national service

Bases

Casablanca, Safi, Agadir, Kenitra, Tangier, Dakhla, Al Hoceima

Mercantile Marine

Lloyd's Register of Shipping:
480 vessels of 483 484 tons gross

DELETION

1989 *Al Bachir*
1991 *Lieutenant Riffi*

FRIGATE

Note: Negotiations have been under way since 1985 for two more frigates. In 1989 credits were asked for to cover purchases of Spanish military equipment which included two lengthened Descubierta class of about 2150 tons with helicopter facilities; to be built by Bazán. Provisional order placed in early 1991.

1 MODIFIED DESCUBIERTA CLASS

Name	*No*	*Builders*	*Laid down*	*Launched*	*Commissioned*
LIEUTENANT COLONEL ERRHAMANI	501	Bazán, Cartagena	20 Mar 1979	26 Feb 1982	28 Mar 1983

Displacement, tons: 1233 standard; 1479 full load
Dimensions, feet (metres): 291.3 × 34 × 12.5 *(88.8 × 10.4 × 3.8)*
Main machinery: 4 MTU-Bazán 16V 956 TB91 diesels; 15 000 hp(m) *(11 MW)* sustained; 2 shafts; cp props
Speed, knots: 25.5. **Range, miles:** 4000 at 18 kts (1 engine)
Complement: 100

Missiles: SSM: 4 Aerospatiale MM 38 Exocet ❶; inertial cruise; active radar homing to 42 km *(23 nm)* at 0.9 Mach; warhead 165 kg; sea-skimmer. Frequently not embarked.
SAM: Selenia/Elsag Albatros octuple launcher ❷; 24 Aspide; semi-active radar homing to 13 km *(8 nm)* at 2.5 Mach; height envelope 15-5000 m *(49.2-16 405 ft)*; warhead 30 kg.
Guns: 1 OTO Melara 3 in *(76 mm)*/62 compact ❸; 85° elevation; 85 rounds/minute to 16 km *(8.6 nm)* anti-surface; 12 km *(6.5 nm)* anti-aircraft; weight of shell 6 kg.
2 Breda Meccanica 40 mm/70 ❹; 85° elevation; 300 rounds/minute to 12.5 km *(6.7 nm)*; weight of shell 0.96 kg.
Torpedoes: 6—324 mm Mk 32 (2 triple) tubes ❺. Honeywell Mk 46 Mod 1; anti-submarine; active/passive homing to 11 km *(5.9 nm)* at 40 kts; warhead 44 kg.
A/S mortars: 1 Bofors SR 375 mm twin trainable launcher ❻; range 3.6 km *(1.9 nm)*; 24 rockets.
Countermeasures: Decoys: 2 CSEE Dagaie double trainable mounting; IR flares and Chaff; H/J band.
ESM/ECM: Elettronica ELT 715; intercept and jammer.
Combat data systems: Signaal SEWACO-MR action data automation.
Radars: Air/surface search: Signaal DA 05 ❼; E/F band; range 137 km *(75 nm)* for 2 m² target.
Surface search: Signaal ZW 06 ❽; I band; range 26 km *(14 nm)*.
Fire control: Signaal WM 25/41 ❾; I/J band; range 46 km *(25 nm)*.
Sonars: Raytheon DE 1160 B; hull-mounted; active/passive; medium range; medium frequency.

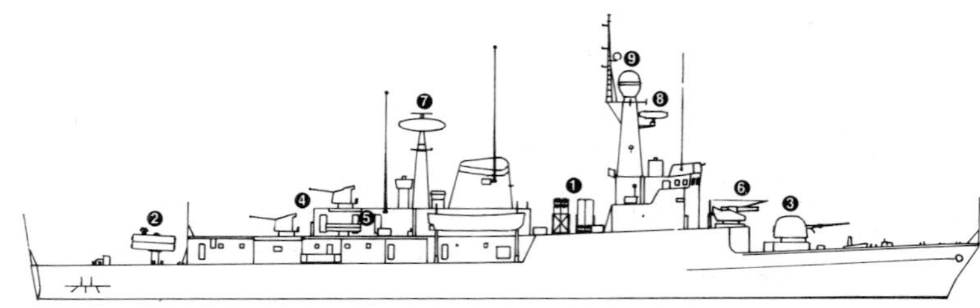

LIEUTENANT COLONEL ERRHAMANI *(Scale: 1 : 900), Ian Sturton*

LIEUTENANT COLONEL ERRHAMANI *1991*

Programmes: Ordered 7 June 1977.

Operational: The ship is fitted to carry Exocet but the missiles are seldom embarked.

LIGHT FORCES

2 FRENCH PR 72 TYPE (FAST ATTACK CRAFT—GUN)

Name	*No*	*Builders*	*Commissioned*
OKBA	302	Soc Française de Construction Navale	16 Dec 1976
TRIKI	303	Soc Française de Construction Navale	12 July 1977

Displacement, tons: 375 standard; 445 full load
Dimensions, feet (metres): 188.8 × 25 × 7.1 *(57.5 × 7.6 × 2.1)*
Main machinery: 4 SACM AGO V16 ASHR diesels; 11 040 hp(m) *(8.11 MW)*; 4 shafts
Speed, knots: 28. **Range, miles:** 2500 at 16 kts
Complement: 53 (5 officers)
Guns: 1 OTO Melara 3 in *(76 mm)*/62 compact; 85° elevation; 85 rounds/minute to 16 km *(8.6 nm)* anti-surface; 12 km *(6.5 nm)* anti-aircraft; weight of shell 6 kg.
1 Bofors 40 mm/70; 85° elevation; 300 rounds/minute to 12.5 km *(6.7 nm)*; weight of shell 0.96 kg.
Fire control: 2 CSEE Panda optical directors.
Radars: Navigation: I band.

Comment: Ordered June 1973. *Okba* launched 10 October 1975, *Triki* 1 February 1976. Can be Exocet fitted (with Vega control system).

TRIKI *1989*

4 LAZAGA CLASS (FAST ATTACK CRAFT—MISSILE)

Name	*No*	*Builders*	*Commissioned*
EL KHATTABI	304	Bazán, San Fernando	26 July 1981
COMMANDANT AZOUGGARH	305	Bazán, San Fernando	2 Aug 1982
COMMANDANT BOUTOUBA	306	Bazán, San Fernando	20 Nov 1981
COMMANDANT EL HARTY	307	Bazán, San Fernando	25 Feb 1982

Displacement, tons: 425 full load
Dimensions, feet (metres): 190.6 × 24.9 × 8.9 *(58.1 × 7.6 × 2.7)*
Main machinery: 2 MTU-Bazán 16V 956 TB91 diesels; 7500 hp(m) *(5.51 MW)* sustained; 2 shafts
Speed, knots: 30. **Range, miles:** 3000 at 15 kts
Complement: 41
Missiles: SSM: 4 Aerospatiale MM 38 Exocet; inertial cruise; active radar homing to 42 km *(23 nm)* at 0.9 Mach; warhead 165 kg; sea-skimmer.
Guns: 1 OTO Melara 3 in *(76 mm)*/62 compact; 85° elevation; 85 rounds/minute to 16 km *(8.6 nm)* anti-surface; 12 km *(6.5 nm)* anti-aircraft; weight of shell 6 kg.
1 Breda Meccanica 40 mm/70; 85° elevation; 300 rounds/minute to 12.5 km *(6.7 nm)*; weight of shell 0.96 kg.
2 Oerlikon 20 mm/90 GAM-BO1; 55° elevation; 800 rounds/minute to 2 km.
Fire control: CSEE Panda optical director.
Radars: Surface search: Signaal ZW 06; I band; range 26 km *(14 nm)*.
Fire control: Signaal WM 25; I/J band; range 46 km *(25 nm)*.

Comment: Ordered from Bazán, San Fernando (Cadiz), Spain 14 June 1977.

COMMANDANT AZOUGGARH *5/1984*

4 OSPREY MK II CLASS (LARGE PATROL CRAFT)

Name	*No*	*Builders*	*Commissioned*
EL HAHIQ	308	Danyard A/S, Frederickshaven	11 Nov 1987
ETTAWFIQ	309	Danyard A/S, Frederickshaven	31 Jan 1988
EL HAMISS	316	Danyard A/S, Frederickshaven	9 Aug 1990
EL KARIB	317	Danyard A/S, Frederickshaven	23 Sep 1990

Displacement, tons: 475 full load
Dimensions, feet (metres): 179.8 × 34 × 8.5 *(54.8 × 10.5 × 2.6)*
Main machinery: 2 MAN Burmeister & Wain Alpha 12V 23/30-DVO diesels; 4440 hp(m) *(3.23 MW)* sustained; 2 waterjets
Speed, knots: 22. **Range, miles:** 4500 at 16 kts
Complement: 15 plus 20 spare berths
Guns: 1 Bofors 40 mm/60. 2 Oerlikon 20 mm.

Comment: First two ordered in September 1986; two more on 30 January 1989 and a third pair in late 1990. First two were for the Customs Service and second pair for the Navy but this may have been reversed. There is a stern ramp with a hinged cover for launching the inspection boat.

ETTAWFIQ *1990, van Ginderen Collection*

6 CORMORAN CLASS (LARGE PATROL CRAFT)

Name	*No*	*Builders*	*Launched*	*Commissioned*
L V RABHI	310	Bázan, San Fernando	23 Sep 1987	16 Sep 1988
ERRACHIQ	311	Bázan, San Fernando	23 Sep 1987	16 Dec 1988
EL AKID	312	Bázan, San Fernando	29 Mar 1988	4 Apr 1989
EL MAHER	313	Bázan, San Fernando	29 Mar 1988	20 June 1989
EL MAJID	314	Bázan, San Fernando	21 Oct 1988	26 Sep 1989
EL BACHIR	315	Bázan, San Fernando	21 Oct 1988	19 Dec 1989

Displacement, tons: 425 full load
Dimensions, feet (metres): 190.6 × 24.9 × 8.9 *(58.1 × 7.6 × 2.7)*
Main machinery: 2 MTU Bazán 16V 956 TB82 diesels; 8340 hp(m) *(6.13 MW)* sustained; 2 shafts
Speed, knots: 22. **Range, miles:** 6100 at 12 kts
Complement: 36 (4 officers)
Guns: 1 Bofors 40 mm/70. 2 Giat 20 mm.
Fire control: Lynx optronic director.

Comment: Three ordered from Bazán, Cadiz in October 1985 as a follow on to the Lazaga class of which these are a slower patrol version with a 10 day endurance. Option on three more taken up. Used for fishery protection.

EL MAHER *6/1989, Bazán*

6 P 32 TYPE (COASTAL PATROL CRAFT)

Name	*No*	*Builders*	*Commissioned*
EL WACIL	203	CMN, Cherbourg	9 Oct 1975
EL JAIL	204	CMN, Cherbourg	3 Dec 1975
EL MIKDAM	205	CMN, Cherbourg	30 Jan 1976
EL KHAFIR	206	CMN, Cherbourg	16 Apr 1976
EL HARIS	207	CMN, Cherbourg	30 June 1976
EL ESSAHIR	208	CMN, Cherbourg	16 July 1976

Displacement, tons: 74 light; 89 full load
Dimensions, feet (metres): 105 × 17.7 × 4.6 *(32 × 5.4 × 1.4)*
Main machinery: 2 SACM MGO 12V BZSHR diesels; 2700 hp(m) *(1.98 MW)*; 2 shafts
Speed, knots: 28. **Range, miles:** 1500 at 15 kts
Complement: 17
Guns: 1 Oerlikon 20 mm.
Radars: Navigation: Decca; I band.

Comment: Ordered in February 1974. In July 1985 a further four of this class were ordered from the same builders but for the Customs Service. Wooden hull sheathed in plastic.

EL WACIL *1988*

AMPHIBIOUS FORCES

3 BATRAL TYPE

Name	*No*	*Builders*	*Commissioned*
DAOUD BEN AICHA	402	Dubigeon, Normandie	28 May 1977
AHMED ES SAKALI	403	Dubigeon, Normandie	Sep 1977
ABOU ABDALLAH EL AYACHI	404	Dubigeon, Normandie	Mar 1978

Displacement, tons: 750 standard; 1409 full load
Dimensions, feet (metres): 262.4 × 42.6 × 7.9 *(80 × 13 × 2.4)*
Main machinery: 2 SACM Type 195 V12 CSHR diesels; 3600 hp(m) *(2.65 MW)* sustained; 2 shafts
Speed, knots: 16. **Range, miles:** 4500 at 13 kts
Complement: 47 (3 officers)
Military lift: 140 troops; 12 vehicles
Guns: 2 Bofors 40 mm/70. 2—81 mm mortars.
Radars: Surface search: Thomson-CSF DRBN 32; I band.
Helicopters: Platform only.

Comment: Two ordered on 12 March 1975. Third ordered 19 August 1975. Of same type as the French *Champlain*. Vehicle-stowage above and below decks.

AHMED ES SAKALI *8/1986, John G. Callis*

1 EDIC CLASS

Name	*No*	*Builders*	*Commissioned*
LIEUTENANT MALGHAGH	401	Chantiers Navales Franco-Belges	1965

Displacement, tons: 250 standard; 670 full load
Dimensions, feet (metres): 193.5 × 39.2 × 4.3 *(59 × 12 × 1.3)*
Main machinery: 2 MGO diesels; 1000 hp(m) *(735 kW)*; 2 shafts
Speed, knots: 8. **Range, miles:** 1800 at 8 kts
Complement: 16 (1 officer)
Military lift: 11 vehicles
Guns: 2 Oerlikon 20 mm. 1—120 mm mortar.

Comment: Ordered early in 1963. Similar to the French landing craft of the Edic type built at the same yard.

LIEUTENANT MALGHAGH (EL KHAFIR alongside) *1989*

SERVICE FORCES

Note: There is also a yacht, *Essaouira*, 60 tons, from Italy in 1967, used as a training vessel for watchkeepers.

2 LOGISTIC SUPPORT SHIPS

AD DAKHLA (ex-*Merc Caribe*) 405
EL AIGH (ex-*Merc Nordia*) 406

Measurement, tons: 1500 grt
Dimensions, feet (metres): 252.6 × 40 × 15.4 *(77 × 12.2 × 4.7)*
Main machinery: 1 Burmeister & Wain diesel; 1250 hp(m) *(919 kW)*; 1 shaft
Speed, knots: 11
Guns: 2—14.5 mm MGs.

Comment: Logistic support vessels with four 5 ton cranes. Former cargo ships built by Fredrickshavn Vaerft in 1973 and acquired in 1981.

EL AIGH *1989*

1 TRANSPORT SHIP

ARRAFIQ (ex-*Thjelvar*, ex-*Gotland*) 407

Measurement, tons: 2990 grt, 784 dwt
Dimensions, feet (metres): 305.8 × 53.8 × 13.8 *(93.2 × 16.4 × 4.2)*
Main machinery: 4 Werkspoor 16V diesels; 8000 hp(m) *(5.88 MW)*; 4 shafts
Speed, knots: 18.5

Comment: Former Ro-Ro ferry converted as a troop transport.

ARRAFIQ *1990*

CUSTOMS/COAST GUARD

4 P 32 TYPE (COASTAL PATROL CRAFT)

Name	*No*	*Builders*	*Commissioned*
ERRAID	209	CMN, Cherbourg	18 Mar 1988
ERRACED	210	CMN, Cherbourg	15 Apr 1988
EL KACED	211	CMN, Cherbourg	17 May 1988
ESSAID	212	CMN, Cherbourg	4 July 1988

Displacement, tons: 89 full load
Dimensions, feet (metres): 105 × 17.7 × 4.6 *(32 × 5.4 × 1.4)*
Main machinery: 2 SACM MGO 12V BZSHR diesels; 2700 hp(m) *(1.98 MW)*; 2 shafts
Speed, knots: 28. **Range, miles:** 1500 at 15 kts
Complement: 17
Guns: 1 Oerlikon 20 mm.
Radars: Navigation: Decca; I band.

Comment: Almost identical to the El Wacil class listed under Light Forces. Ordered in July 1985.

18 ARCOR 46 CLASS (COASTAL PATROL CRAFT)

D01-D18

Displacement, tons: 15 full load
Dimensions, feet (metres): 47.6 × 13 × 3.9 *(14.5 × 4 × 1.2)*
Main machinery: 2 Uni Diesel UD18 V8 M5; 1010 hp(m) *(742 kW)* sustained; 2 shafts
Speed, knots: 32
Complement: 6
Guns: 2 Browning 12.7 mm MGs.

Comment: Ordered from Arcor, La Teste in June 1985. GRP hulls. Delivered in groups of three from April to September 1987. Used for patrolling the Mediterranean coastline.

ARCOR 46 *1987, Arcor*

5 ARCOR 17 (HARBOUR PATROL CRAFT)

Dimensions, feet (metres): 18 × 7.2 × 2.6 *(5.5 × 2.2 × 0.8)*
Speed, knots: 50
Guns: 1—7.62 mm MG.

Comment: Fast patrol boats delivered in 1989-90. More may be ordered.

MOZAMBIQUE

Senior Appointment

Commander of the Navy:
Captain Manuel Gimo Caetano

Personnel

(a) 1992: 1300
(b) Voluntary

General

Apart from one Zhuk class patrol craft at sea in 1991, the whole Navy was in a state of unserviceability by the beginning of 1992. It is not possible to say how many vessels may be recovered when peace is restored.

Bases

Maputo (Naval HQ); Nacala; Beira; Pemba (Porto Amelia); Metangula (Lake Malawi).

Mercantile Marine

Lloyd's Register of Shipping:
114 vessels of 39 143 tons gross

DELETIONS

1988-89 2 Zhuk class, 1 Poluchat class, 2 Bellatrix class, 1 Jupiter class, 1 Alfange class, 2 LDM 100 class

2 Ex-SOVIET SO 1 CLASS (LARGE PATROL CRAFT)

Displacement, tons: 170 standard; 215 full load
Dimensions, feet (metres): 137.8 × 19.7 × 5.9 *(42 × 6 × 1.8)*
Main machinery: 3 Type 40D diesels; 7500 hp(m) *(5.51 MW)*; 3 shafts
Speed, knots: 28. **Range, miles:** 1100 at 13 kts; 350 at 28 kts
Complement: 31
Guns: 4 USSR 25 mm/60 (2 twin); 85° elevation; 270 rounds/minute to 3 km *(1.6 nm)*; weight of shell 0.34 kg.
A/S mortars: 4-5 RBU 1200 tubed fixed/elevating; range 1.2 km; warhead 34 kg.
Depth charges: 2 racks.
Mines: Can carry 18.
Radars: Surface search: Pot Head; I band; range 37 km *(20 nm)*.
Sonars: Tamir II; hull-mounted; active attack; high frequency.

Comment: Transferred in June 1985 by the Ro-Flow ship *Stakhanovets Petrash* which has specialised in carrying out foreign transfers.

3 Ex-SOVIET ZHUK CLASS (COASTAL PATROL CRAFT)

Displacement, tons: 50 full load
Dimensions, feet (metres): 75.4 × 17 × 6.2 *(23 × 5.2 × 1.9)*
Main machinery: 2 M50 F-4 diesels; 2400 hp(m) *(1.76 MW)*; 2 shafts
Speed, knots: 30. **Range, miles:** 1100 at 15 kts
Complement: 17
Guns: 4 USSR 14.5 mm (2 twin) MGs.
Radars: Navigation: Spin Trough; I band.

Comment: Two transferred in February 1979, one in August 1979 and two in October 1980. Only one operational in 1991.

10 INSHORE PATROL CRAFT

Dimensions, feet (metres): 59 × 16.4 × 3.6 *(18 × 5 × 1.1)*
Main machinery: 2 diesels; 1100 hp(m) *(808 kW)*; 2 shafts
Speed, knots: 20

Comment: Ten delivered by Mazagon, Goa by December 1985. Some may have been damaged and replaced in 1990.

2 Ex-PORTUGUESE JUPITER CLASS (COASTAL PATROL CRAFT)

Displacement, tons: 32 standard; 43.5 full load
Dimensions, feet (metres): 69 × 16.5 × 4.3 *(21 × 5 × 1.3)*
Main machinery: 2 Cummins diesels; 1270 hp(m) *(947 kW)*; 2 shafts
Speed, knots: 20
Complement: 8
Guns: 2 Oerlikon 20 mm (twin).

Comment: Survivors of three. Based on Lake Malawi.

2 Ex-SOVIET YEVGENYA CLASS (INSHORE MINESWEEPERS)

Displacement, tons: 77 standard; 90 full load
Dimensions, feet (metres): 80.7 × 18 × 4.9 *(24.6 × 5.5 × 1.5)*
Main machinery: 2 Type 3D 12 diesels; 400 hp(m) *(294 kW)*
Speed, knots: 11. **Range, miles:** 300 at 10 kts
Complement: 10
Guns: 2 USSR 14.5 mm (twin) MGs.
Radars: Surface search: Don 2; I band.
Sonars: Small portable; active minehunting; high frequency.

Comment: Both transferred in 1985. One of them may be the minesweeper PM 525 reported to be called *Graciosa*.

1 SURVEY CRAFT

ALMIRANTE LACARDA

Comment: Ex-Portuguese but no other details available.

BARGES—VARIOUS

Comment: Two built in India in 1984 and four more (two of 200 tons and two of 30 tons) by A C N Chalons-sur-Saône.

NAMIBIA

General

Fishery protection patrols are being carried out by shore-based helicopters but it is reported that United States-supplied patrol craft will become available in due course. The rationale for South Africa to continue holding Walvis Bay is weakening and an opportunity may soon be found to return the port fully to Namibia. A Coast Guard service is being formed.

NATO

Note: The NATO frigate project NFR 90 died a predictable death as participating countries pulled out at the end of 1989. A number of more sensible bilateral projects are now being considered and some of these are taking advantage of the work done on NFR 90.

1 RESEARCH VESSEL

ALLIANCE A1456

Displacement, tons: 2466 standard; 3180 full load
Dimensions, feet (metres): 305.1 × 49.9 × 16.7 *(93 × 15.2 × 5.1)*
Main machinery: Diesel-electric; 2 Fincantieri GMT B230.12 diesels; 6073 hp(m) *(4.46 MW)* sustained; 2 AEG CC 3127 generators; 2 AEG motors; 5100 hp(m) *(3.75 MW)*; 2 shafts; bow thruster
Speed, knots: 16. **Range, miles:** 8000 at 12 kts
Complement: 27 (10 officers) plus 23 scientists

Comment: Built by Fincantieri at Muggiano SY, La Spezia, launched 9 July 1986 and handed over 6 May 1988. NATO's first wholly owned ship is a Public Service vessel of the German Navy with a German, British and Italian crew. Designed for oceanography and acoustic research, replacing the *Maria Paolina*. Based at La Spezia and operated by SACLANT Undersea Research Centre. Facilities include extensive laboratories, position location systems, silent propulsion, and overside deployment equipment. Can tow a 20 ton load at 12 kts. A Kongsberg gas turbine on 02 deck provides silent propulsion power at 1945 hp *(1.43 MW)* up to speeds of 12 kts.

ALLIANCE *1990, van Ginderen Collection*

NETHERLANDS

Headquarters' Appointments

Chief of the Naval Staff:
Vice Admiral N W G Buis
Vice Chief of the Naval Staff:
Rear Admiral C J van der Werf
Director, Material (Navy):
Rear Admiral T J N van der Voort

Commands

Admiral Netherlands Fleet Command:
Vice Admiral F J Haver Droeze
Commander Netherlands Task Group:
Rear Admiral A van der Sande
Commandant General Royal Netherlands Marine Corps:
Major-General R Spiekerman van Weezelenburg
Flag Officer Netherlands Antilles:
Commodore R R Rodrigues
Hydrographer:
Commodore E Bakker

Diplomatic Representation

Naval Attaché in London, Dublin and NLR CINCHAN:
Captain W F L van Leeuwen
Naval Attaché in Madrid:
Captain J G van Ham
Naval Attaché in Paris and Lisbon:
Captain R P Perie
Naval Attaché in Washington and NLR SACLANT:
Rear Admiral J S Tichelman

Bases

Naval HQ: The Hague
Main Base: Den Helder
Minor Bases: Flushing and Curacao
Fleet Air Arm: NAS Valkenburg (LRMP), NAS De Kooy (helicopters)
R Neth Marines: Rotterdam, Doorn and Texel
Training Base (Technical and Logistic): Amsterdam

Personnel

(a) 1992: 15 900 officers and ratings (including the Navy Air Service, 2800 Royal Netherlands Marine Corps and 850 female personnel)
(b) 12 months' national service

Naval Air Force (see *Shipborne Aircraft* section)

Personnel: 1700

Squadron	*Aircraft*	*Task*
7	Lynx (UH-14A)	Utility and Transport/ SAR
320/321	P-3C Orion	LRMP
860	Lynx (SH-14)	Embarked

Royal Netherlands Marine Corps

4 Marine battalions; 1 combat support battalion and 1 logistic battalion. Based at Doorn and in the Netherlands Antilles and Aruba.

Prefix to Ships' Names

Hr Ms

Strength of the Fleet

Type	*Active (Reserve)*	*Building (Projected)*
Submarines (Patrol)	5	2
Frigates	16	6 (2)
Mine Hunters	10 (5)	—
Minesweepers—Coastal	6 (5)	(6)
Submarine Support Ship	1	—
Landing Ship Dock (LPD)	—	(1)
Landing Craft	17	—
Surveying Vessels	3	—
Combat Support Ships	2	1
Training Ships	3	—
Tugs	13	—
Auxiliaries (Major)	10	—

Planned Deployments

All frigates and AOEs are deployed in two approximately equal task groups.
5 Patrol Submarines (6 as from 1994)
13 LRMP Aircraft in 2 squadrons
1 MCM Group operating off Dutch ports
1 MCM Group for Channel command
2 R Neth Marine battalions (arctic trained)
2 R Neth Marine battalions for operations overseas

Mercantile Marine

Lloyd's Register of Shipping:
1249 vessels of 3 872 301 tons gross

DELETIONS

Submarines

1990 *Zeehond* (11 Jan) (trials)
1991 *Tonijn* (Jan) (trials)

Frigates

1989 *Evertsen* (1 Nov) to Indonesia
1990 *Isaac Sweers* (1 Nov) to Indonesia

Minesweeper

1990 *Woerden*

Miscellaneous

1989 Y8016 and Y8017
1990 *Gelderland, Itadda, Eems, L 9520*
1992 *Nautilus* (old), *Hydra* (old)

PENNANT LIST

Submarines

S 802 Walrus
S 803 Zeeleeuw
S 804 Potvis
S 806 Zwaardvis
S 807 Tijgerhaai
S 808 Dolfijn (bldg)
S 810 Bruinvis (bldg)

Frigates

F 801 Tromp
F 806 De Ruyter
F 807 Kortenaer
F 808 Callenburgh
F 809 Van Kinsbergen
F 810 Banckert
F 811 Piet Heyn
F 812 Jacob van Heemskerck
F 813 Witte de With
F 816 Abraham Crijnssen
F 823 Philips van Almonde
F 824 Bloys van Treslong
F 825 Jan van Brakel
F 826 Pieter Florisz
F 827 Karel Doorman
F 828 Van Speijk (new)
F 829 Willem van der Zaan
F 830 Tjerk Hiddes (bldg)
F 831 Van Amstel (bldg)
F 832 Abraham van der Hulst (bldg)
F 833 Van Nes (bldg)
F 834 Van Galen (bldg)

Mine Hunters

M 850 Alkmaar
M 851 Delfzyl
M 852 Dordrecht
M 853 Haarlem
M 854 Harlingen
M 855 Scheveningen
M 856 Maassluis
M 857 Makkum
M 858 Middelburg
M 859 Hellevoetsluis
M 860 Schiedam
M 861 Urk
M 862 Zierikzee
M 863 Vlaardingen
M 864 Willemstad

Coastal Minesweepers

M 802 Hoogezand
M 809 Naaldwijk
M 810 Abcoude
M 812 Drachten
M 813 Ommen
M 815 Giethoorn
M 817 Venlo
M 823 Naarden
M 827 Hoogeveen
M 830 Sittard
M 841 Gemert

Amphibious Forces

L 9512-15
L 9518
L 9530-35
L 9536-41

Auxiliary Ships

A 801 Pelikaan
A 832 Zuiderkruis
A 835 Poolster
A 836 —
A 848 Triton
A 851 Cerberus
A 852 Argus
A 853 Nautilus
A 854 Hydra
A 872 Westgat
A 873 Wielingen
A 874 Linge
A 875 Regge
A 876 Hunze
A 877 Rotte
A 880 Bulgia
A 886 Cornelis Drebbel
A 887 Thetis
A 900 Mercuur
A 903 Zeefakkel
A 904 Buyskes
A 905 Blommendal
A 906 Tydeman
Y 8001 Van Speijk (old)
Y 8018 Breezand
Y 8019 Balgzand
Y 8050 Urania
Y 8055 Schelde
Y 8056 Wierbalg
Y 8057 Malzwin
Y 8058 Zuidwal
Y 8059 Westwal
Y 8500 Tax

SUBMARINES

Note: Flotilla to consist of six boats. Zwaardvis class will serve until 2004 when numbers may reduce to four. The Moray class is a private design by Rotterdam Drydock with the government giving limited financial support on condition that the company collaborates with developers of air independent systems (AIP). The old *Zeehond* hull is being used as a test platform for air independent propulsion by RDM with support from the Navy.

2 + 2 WALRUS CLASS

Name	No	Builders	Laid down	Launched	Commissioned
WALRUS	S 802	Rotterdamse Droogdok Mij, Rotterdam	11 Oct 1979	28 Oct 1985 (13 Sep 1989)	25 Mar 1992
ZEELEEUW	S 803	Rotterdamse Droogdok Mij, Rotterdam	24 Sep 1981	20 June 1987	25 Apr 1990
DOLFIJN	S 808	Rotterdamse Droogdok Mij, Rotterdam	12 June 1986	25 Apr 1990	Dec 1992
BRUINVIS	S 810	Rotterdamse Droogdok Mij, Rotterdam	14 Apr 1988	25 Apr 1992	1993

Displacement, tons: 1900 standard; 2465 surfaced; 2800 dived
Dimensions, feet (metres): 223.1 × 27.6 × 21.6
(67.7 × 8.4 × 6.6)
Main machinery: Diesel-electric; 3 SEMT-Pielstick 12 PA4-200 diesels; 6300 hp(m) *(4.63 MW)*; 3 alternators; 2.94 MW; 1 Holec motor; 6910 hp(m) *(5.1 MW)*; 1 shaft; 7-bladed propeller
Speed, knots: 13 surfaced; 20 dived
Range, miles: 10 000 at 9 kts snorting
Complement: 50 (7 officers)

Missiles: SSM: McDonnell Douglas Sub-Harpoon; active radar homing to 130 km *(70 nm)* at 0.9 Mach; warhead 227 kg.
Torpedoes: 4—21 in *(533 mm)* tubes. Honeywell Mk 48 Mod 4; wire-guided; active/passive homing to 38 km *(20.5 nm)* active at 55 kts; 50 km *(27 nm)* passive at 40 kts; warhead 267 kg and Honeywell NT 37D; wire-guided; active/passive homing to 20 km *(10.8 nm)* at 35 kts; warhead 150 kg; 20 torpedoes or missiles carried. Water-ram discharge gear.
Mines: 40 in lieu of torpedoes.
Countermeasures: ESM: Radar warning.
Fire control: Signaal SEWACO VIII action data automation. Signaal Gipsy data system.
Radars: Surface search: Signaal/Racal ZW 07; I band; range 29 km *(16 nm)* surfaced.
Sonars: Thomson Sintra TSM 2272 Eledone Octopus; hull-mounted; passive/active search and attack; medium frequency.
GEC Avionics Type 2026; towed array; passive search; very low frequency.
Acoustic Telemetry Fenelon; passive ranging.

WALRUS *6/1991, van Ginderen Collection*

Programmes: In the 1975 Navy Estimates money was set aside for design work on this class and a contract for the building of the first was signed 16 June 1979, the second was on 17 December 1979. In 1981 various changes to the design were made which resulted in a delay of 1-2 years. *Dolfijn* and *Bruinvis* ordered 16 August 1985; prefabrication started late 1985. Completion of *Walrus* delayed by serious fire 14 August 1986; hull undamaged but cabling and computers destroyed. *Walrus* re-launched 13 September 1989 and started trials in September 1990. *Dolfijn* starts trials mid-1992. As some equipment ordered for the third and fourth of the class has been diverted to *Walrus* there has been a slight delay in their completion dates.

Structure: These are improved Zwaardvis class with similar dimensions and silhouettes except for X stern. Use of H T steel increases the diving depth by some 50 per cent. New Gipsy fire control and electronic command system fitted and automation reduces the crew from 65 to 50. Diving depth, 300 m *(984 ft)*.

2 ZWAARDVIS CLASS

Name	No	Builders	Laid down	Launched	Commissioned
ZWAARDVIS	S 806	Rotterdamse Droogdok Mij, Rotterdam	14 July 1966	2 July 1970	18 Aug 1972
TIJGERHAAI	S 807	Rotterdamse Droogdok Mij, Rotterdam	14 July 1966	25 May 1971	20 Oct 1972

Displacement, tons: 2350 surfaced; 2640 dived
Dimensions, feet (metres): 216.5 × 27.6 × 23.3
(66 × 8.4 × 7.1)
Main machinery: Diesel-electric; 3 Werkspoor RUB 215X12 diesels; 4200 hp(m) *(3.1 MW)*; 1 motor; 5100 hp(m) *(3.75 MW)*; 1 shaft
Speed, knots: 13 surfaced; 20 dived
Range, miles: 10 000 at 9 kts snorting
Complement: 67 (8 officers)

Missiles: SSM: McDonnell Douglas Sub-Harpoon; fitted for but not with.
Torpedoes: 6—21 in *(533 mm)* bow tubes. Honeywell Mk 48 Mod 4; wire-guided; active/passive homing to 38 km *(20.5 nm)* active at 55 kts; 50 km *(27 nm)* passive at 40 kts; warhead 267 kg and Honeywell NT 37D; wire-guided; active/passive homing to 20 km *(10.8 nm)* at 35 kts; warhead 150 kg; 20 torpedoes or missiles carried. Two torpedoes can be launched simultaneously.
Countermeasures: ESM: Radar warning.
Fire control: Signaal M8 digital system.
Radars: Surface search: RN Type 1001; I band.
Sonars: Thomson Sintra Eledone; hull-mounted; passive/active search and attack; medium frequency.
GEC Avionics Type 2026; towed array; passive search; very low frequency.

TIJGERHAAI *2/1991, van Ginderen Collection*

Programmes: In the 1964 Navy Estimates a first instalment was approved for the construction of two conventionally powered submarines of tear-drop design. Planned to serve until the end of the 1990s.

Modernisation: Mid-life conversion carried out in 1988 *(Tijgerhaai)* and 1989-91 *(Zwaardvis)*. New Thomson Sintra Eledone sonar, Signaal fire control and GEC Avionics Type 2026 towed array plus other minor improvements including a quieter propulsion drive unit and shaft.
Structure: Diving depth, 200 m *(656 ft)*.

1 POTVIS CLASS

Name	No	Builders	Laid down	Launched	Commissioned
POTVIS	S 804	Wilton-Fijenoord, Schiedam	17 Sep 1962	12 Jan 1965	2 Nov 1965

Displacement, tons: 1140 standard; 1520 surfaced; 1831 dived
Dimensions, feet (metres): 260.9 × 25.8 × 15.7
(79.5 × 7.8 × 4.8) (Zeehond); 256.9 × 25.8 × 16.4
(78.3 × 7.8 × 5) (Potvis class)
Main machinery: Diesel-electric; 2 SEMT-Pielstick PA 4 diesels; 3100 hp(m) *(2.28 MW)*; 2 motors; 4400 hp(m) *(3.23 MW)*; 2 shafts
Speed, knots: 14.5 surfaced; 17 dived
Complement: 67 (8 officers)

Torpedoes: 8—21 in *(533 mm)* (4 bow, 4 stern) tubes. 20 Honeywell NT 37D; dual purpose; wire-guided; active/passive homing to 20 km *(10.8 nm)* at 35 kts; warhead 150 kg.
Countermeasures: ESM: Radar warning.
Fire control: Signaal M8 digital system.
Radars: Surface search: RN Type 1001; I band.
Sonars: Hull-mounted; passive search and attack; medium frequency.

POTVIS *4/1990, Wright and Logan*

Programmes: *Potvis*, originally voted for in 1949, but suspended for some years, had several modifications compared with Zeehond class and was officially considered to be a separate class.

Structure: The hull consists of three cylinders arranged in a triangular shape. The upper cylinder accommodates the crew, navigational equipment and armament. The lower two cylinders house the propulsion machinery comprising diesel engines, batteries and electric motors, as well as storerooms. Diving depth, 300 m *(984 ft)*.
Operational: Scheduled to pay off in August 1992.

FRIGATES

Note: It is planned to order two air defence frigates in 1996 possibly in collaboration with German Type 124.

2 TROMP CLASS

Name	*No*	*Builders*	*Laid down*	*Launched*	*Commissioned*
TROMP	F 801	Koninklijke Maatschappij De Schelde, Flushing	4 Aug 1971	2 June 1973	3 Oct 1975
DE RUYTER	F 806	Koninklijke Maatschappij De Schelde, Flushing	22 Dec 1971	9 Mar 1974	3 June 1976

Displacement, tons: 3665 standard; 4308 full load
Dimensions, feet (metres): 454 × 48.6 × 15.1
(138.4 × 14.8 × 4.6)
Main machinery: COGOG; 2 RR Olympus TM3B gas turbines; 43 000 hp *(32 MW)* sustained
2 RR Tyne RM 1C gas turbines; 10 680 hp *(8 MW)* sustained; 2 shafts
Speed, knots: 30. **Range, miles:** 5000 at 18 kts
Complement: 306 (34 officers)

Missiles: SSM: 8 McDonnell Douglas Harpoon (2 quad) launchers ❶; active radar homing to 130 km *(70 nm)* at 0.9 Mach; warhead 227 kg; 16 missiles.
SAM: 40 GDC Pomona Standard SM-1MR; Mk 13 Mod 4 launcher ❷; command guidance; semi-active radar homing to 46 km *(25 nm)* at 2 Mach.
Raytheon Sea Sparrow Mk 29 octuple launcher ❸; semi-active radar homing to 14.6 km *(8 nm)* at 2.5 Mach; warhead 39 kg; 16 missiles.
Guns: 2 Bofors 4.7 in *(120 mm)*/50 (twin) ❹; 85° elevation; 42 rounds/minute to 20 km *(10.8 nm)* anti-surface; 12 km *(6.5 nm)* anti-aircraft; weight of shell 24 kg.
Signaal SGE-30 Goalkeeper with GE 30 mm ❺; 7-barrelled; 4200 rounds/minute combined to 2 km.
2 Oerlikon 20 mm.
Torpedoes: 6—324 mm US Mk 32 (2 triple) tubes ❻. Honeywell Mk 46 Mod 5; anti-submarine; active/passive homing to 11 km *(5.9 nm)* at 40 kts; warhead 44 kg.
Countermeasures: Decoys: 2 Loral Hycor SRBOC ❼; IR flares and Chaff.
ESM/ECM: Ramses; intercept and jammer.
Combat data systems: Signaal SEWACO I action data automation; Links 10 and 11. Scot SATCOM ❽.
Fire control: Signaal WM 25 for guns and missiles.
Radars: Air/surface search: Signaal MTTR/SPS 01 ❾; 3D; F band.
Navigation: Two Decca 1226; I band.
Fire control: Two Raytheon SPG 51C ❿; G/I band.
Signaal WM 25 ⓫; I/J band; range 46 km *(25 nm)*.
Sonars: CWE 610; hull-mounted; active search and attack; medium frequency.

Helicopters: 1 Westland SH-14B Lynx ⓬.

Programmes: First design allowance was voted for in 1967 estimates. The intention is to replace both ships towards the end of the century in collaboration with other European navies needing similar ships in the same timescale.
Modernisation: Modernisation plans cancelled in 1988 as an economy measure but partially resurrected in 1990.
Structure: Goalkeeper is fitted on the starboard side of the hangar roof.
Operational: Fitted as Flagships.

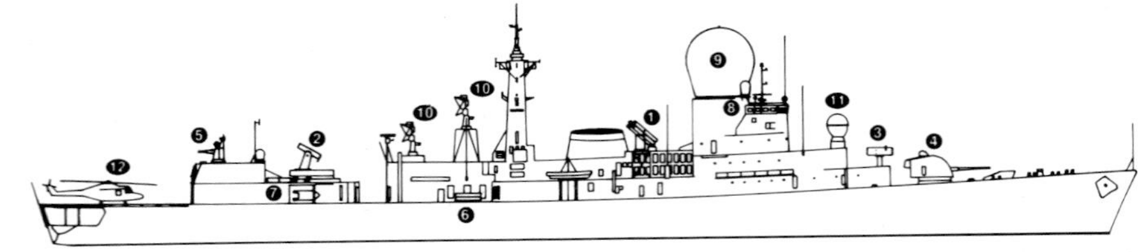

DE RUYTER *(Scale 1 : 1 200), Ian Sturton*

DE RUYTER *7/1991, G. Toremans*

DE RUYTER *5/1991, David Warren*

2 + 6 KAREL DOORMAN CLASS

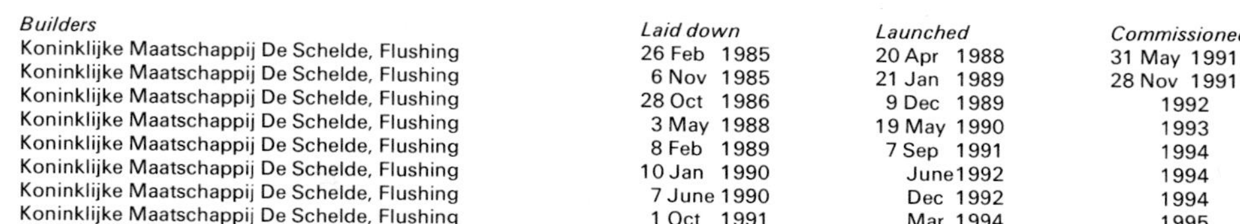

Name	*No*	*Builders*	*Laid down*	*Launched*	*Commissioned*
KAREL DOORMAN	F 827	Koninklijke Maatschappij De Schelde, Flushing	26 Feb 1985	20 Apr 1988	31 May 1991
WILLEM VAN DER ZAAN	F 829	Koninklijke Maatschappij De Schelde, Flushing	6 Nov 1985	21 Jan 1989	28 Nov 1991
TJERK HIDDES	F 830	Koninklijke Maatschappij De Schelde, Flushing	28 Oct 1986	9 Dec 1989	1992
VAN AMSTEL	F 831	Koninklijke Maatschappij De Schelde, Flushing	3 May 1988	19 May 1990	1993
ABRAHAM VAN DER HULST	F 832	Koninklijke Maatschappij De Schelde, Flushing	8 Feb 1989	7 Sep 1991	1994
VAN NES	F 833	Koninklijke Maatschappij De Schelde, Flushing	10 Jan 1990	June 1992	1994
VAN GALEN	F 834	Koninklijke Maatschappij De Schelde, Flushing	7 June 1990	Dec 1992	1994
VAN SPEIJK	F 828	Koninklijke Maatschappij De Schelde, Flushing	1 Oct 1991	Mar 1994	1995

Displacement, tons: 3320 full load
Dimensions, feet (metres): 401.1 × 47.2 × 14.1 *(122.3 × 14.4 × 4.3)*
Main machinery: CODOG; 2 RR Spey SM1C; 41 630 hp *(31 MW)* sustained (early ships of the class will initially only have SM1A gas generators and 29 500 hp *(22 MW)* sustained available); 2 Stork-Wärtsilä 12 SW280 diesels; 8700 hp *(6.4 MW)* sustained; 2 shafts; cp props
Speed, knots: 30 (Speys); 21 (diesels). **Range, miles:** 5000 at 18 kts
Complement: 154 (16 officers) (accommodation for 163)

Missiles: SSM: 8 McDonnell Douglas Harpoon (2 quad) launchers ❶; active radar homing to 130 km *(70 nm)* at 0.9 Mach; warhead 227 kg.
SAM: Raytheon Sea Sparrow Mk 48 vertical launchers ❷; semi-active radar homing to 14.6 km *(8 nm)* at 2.5 Mach; warhead 39 kg; 16 missiles. Canisters mounted on port side of hangar.
Guns: 1—3 in *(76 mm)*/62 OTO Melara compact Mk 100 ❸; 85° elevation; 100 rounds/minute to 16 km *(8.6 nm)* anti-surface; 12 km *(6.5 nm)* anti-aircraft; weight of shell 6 kg. This is the latest version with an improved rate of fire.
1 Signaal SGE-30 Goalkeeper with General Electric 30 mm 7-barrelled ❹; 4200 rounds/minute combined to 2 km.
2 Oerlikon 20 mm; 55° elevation; 800 rounds/minute to 2 km.
Torpedoes: 4—324 mm US Mk 32 (2 twin) tubes (mounted inside the after superstructure) ❺. Honeywell Mk 46 Mod 5; anti-submarine; active/passive homing to 11 km *(5.9 nm)* at 40 kts; warhead 44 kg.
Countermeasures: Decoys: 2 Loral Hycor SRBOC 6-tubed fixed Mk 36 quad launchers; IR flares and Chaff to 4 km *(2.2 nm)*.
ESM/ECM: Ramses; intercept and repeater jammers. Argo APECS II to be fitted in last four ships.
Combat data systems: Signaal SEWACO VII action data automation (upgraded from 1994); Links 11 and 16 in due course. SATCOM.
Radars: Air/surface search: Signaal SMART ❻; 3D; F band.
Air/surface search: Signaal LW 08 ❼; D band.
Surface search: Signaal ZW 06 ❽; I band; range 26 km *(14 nm)*.
Navigation: Racal Decca 1226; I band.
Fire control: Two Signaal STIR ❾; I/J/K band; range 140 km *(76 nm)* for 1 m^2 target.
Sonars: Signaal PHS 36; hull-mounted; active search and attack; medium frequency.
Thomson Sintra Anaconda DSBV 61; towed array; low frequency; to be fitted in last six ships on build and retrofitted to the remainder.

Helicopters: 1 Westland SH-14 Lynx ❿.

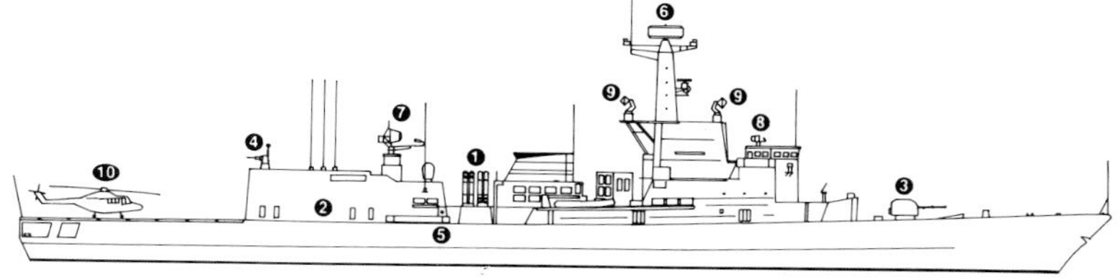

KAREL DOORMAN Class *(Scale 1 : 1 200), Ian Sturton*

WILLEM VAN DER ZAAN *6/1991, Wright and Logan*

Programmes: This class is designed to be inter-operable with the Kortenaer class frigates. Declaration of intent signed on 29 February 1984 although the contract was not signed until 29 June 1985 by which time the design had been completed. A further four ordered 10 April 1986. Because the trials ship *Van Speijk* is still operational, names have been shuffled to make the new *Van Speijk* the last of the class but she has retained her allocated pennant number.

Structure: The VLS SAM is similar to Canadian Halifax and Greek MEKO classes. The ship is designed to reduce radar and IR signatures and has extensive NBCD arrangements. Full automation and roll stabilisation fitted.

Operational: SEWACO VII(A) operational from January 1992.

KAREL DOORMAN *6/1991, Royal Netherlands Navy*

10 KORTENAER CLASS

Name	No	Builders	Laid down	Launched	Commissioned
KORTENAER	F 807	Koninklijke Maatschappij De Schelde, Flushing	8 Apr 1975	18 Dec 1976	26 Oct 1978
CALLENBURGH	F 808	Koninklijke Maatschappij De Schelde, Flushing	30 June 1975	12 Mar 1977	26 July 1979
VAN KINSBERGEN	F 809	Koninklijke Maatschappij De Schelde, Flushing	2 Sep 1975	16 Apr 1977	24 Apr 1980
BANCKERT	F 810	Koninklijke Maatschappij De Schelde, Flushing	25 Feb 1976	13 July 1978	29 Oct 1980
PIET HEYN	F 811	Koninklijke Maatschappij De Schelde, Flushing	28 Apr 1977	3 June 1978	14 Apr 1981
ABRAHAM CRIJNSSEN	F 816	Koninklijke Maatschappij De Schelde, Flushing	25 Oct 1978	16 May 1981	27 Jan 1983
PHILIPS VAN ALMONDE	F 823	Dok en Werfmaatschappij Wilton-Fijenoord	3 Oct 1977	11 Aug 1979	2 Dec 1981
BLOYS VAN TRESLONG	F 824	Dok en Werfmaatschappij Wilton-Fijenoord	27 Apr 1978	15 Nov 1980	25 Nov 1982
JAN VAN BRAKEL	F 825	Koninklijke Maatschappij De Schelde, Flushing	16 Nov 1979	16 May 1981	14 Apr 1983
PIETER FLORISZ (ex-*Willem van der Zaan*)	F 826	Koninklijke Maatschappij De Schelde, Flushing	21 Jan 1981	8 May 1982	1 Oct 1983

Displacement, tons: 3050 standard; 3630 full load
Dimensions, feet (metres): 428 × 47.9 × 14.1; 20.3 (screws) *(130.5 × 14.6 × 4.3; 6.2)*
Main machinery: CODOG; 2 RR Olympus TM3B gas turbines; 43 000 hp *(32 MW)* sustained
2 RR Tyne RM1C gas turbines; 10 680 hp *(8 MW)* sustained; 2 shafts; cp props
Speed, knots: 30. **Range, miles:** 4700 at 16 kts on Tynes
Complement: 176 (18 officers) plus 24 spare berths

Missiles: SSM: 8 McDonnell Douglas Harpoon (2 quad) launchers ❶; active radar homing to 130 km *(70 nm)* at 0.9 Mach; warhead 227 kg.
SAM: Raytheon Sea Sparrow Mk 29 octuple launcher ❷; semi-active radar homing to 14.6 km *(8 nm)* at 2.5 Mach; warhead 39 kg; 24 missiles.
Guns: 1 OTO Melara 3 in *(76 mm)*/62 compact ❸; 85° elevation; 85 rounds/minute to 16 km *(8.6 nm)* anti-surface; 12 km *(6.5 nm)* anti-aircraft; weight of shell 6 kg. New 100 rounds/minute version to be fitted.
Signaal SGE-30 Goalkeeper with General Electric 30 mm ❹; 7-barrelled; 4200 rounds/minute combined to 2 km.
2 Oerlikon 20 mm.
Torpedoes: 4—324 mm US Mk 32 (2 twin) tubes ❺. Honeywell Mk 46 Mod 5; anti-submarine; active/passive homing to 11 km *(5.9 nm)* at 40 kts; warhead 44 kg.
Countermeasures: Decoys: 2 Loral Hycor SRBOC Mk 36 6-tubed launchers ❻; Chaff distraction or centroid modes.
ESM/ECM: Ramses ❼; intercept and jammer.
Combat data systems: Signaal SEWACO II action data automation; Link 11. SATCOM.
Radars: Air search: Signaal LW 08 ❽; D band; range 264 km *(145 nm)* for 2 m² target.
Surface search: Signaal ZW 06 ❾; I band; range 26 km *(14 nm)*.
Fire control: Signaal STIR ❿; I/J band; range 140 km *(76 nm)* for 1 m² target.
Signaal WM 25 ⓫; I/J band; range 46 km *(25 nm)*.
Sonars: Westinghouse SQS 505 (F 807-F 816); SQS 509 (F 823-F 826); bow-mounted; active search and attack; medium frequency.
TACTASS (F 825 and 826 only); passive; very low frequency.

Helicopters: 2 Westland SH-14B Lynx ⓬.

Programmes: First four of class ordered 31 August 1974; second four 28 November 1974; third four 29 December 1976. Complement reduced to 176 by adoption of large amount of automation.
Modernisation: The last six of the 10 were planned to be modernised in 1992-96 (including Signaal SMART 3D radars). The status of this programme is uncertain as six of the class are now to be sold or in reserve, three by 1994 and three more by 1996. During refit in 1985-86 *Pieter Florisz* was adapted for a limited number of female crew (about 25); others similarly converted. Goalkeeper has replaced the 40 mm gun on the hangar roof.
Structure: Although only one Lynx is carried in peacetime there is hangar accommodation for two. TACTASS is not planned except that the last two ships had a temporary fit prior to the completion of the first of the Karel Doorman class. *Jan Van Brakel* had the trials SMART radar fitted on her hangar roof in 1990 with the control room in the hangar.
Sales: Two sold to Greece during construction, mid-1980 and mid-1981.

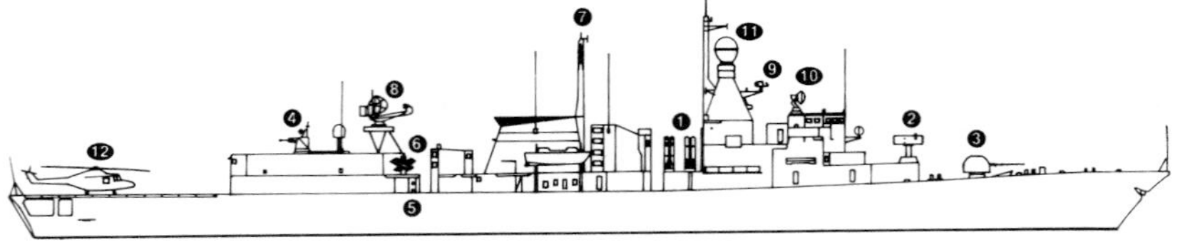

KORTENAER Class *(Scale 1 : 1 200), Ian Sturton*

BANCKERT *8/1991, Giorgio Arra*

JAN VAN BRAKEL *9/1991, Maritime Photographic*

2 JACOB VAN HEEMSKERCK CLASS

Name	*No*	*Builders*	*Laid down*	*Launched*	*Commissioned*
JACOB VAN HEEMSKERCK	F 812	Koninklijke Maatschappij De Schelde, Flushing	21 Jan 1981	5 Nov 1983	15 Jan 1986
WITTE DE WITH	F 813	Koninklijke Maatschappij De Schelde, Flushing	15 Dec 1981	25 Aug 1984	17 Sep 1986

Displacement, tons: 3750 full load approx
Dimensions, feet (metres): 428 × 47.9 × 14.1 (20.3 screws) *(130.5 × 14.6 × 4.3 (6.2))*
Main machinery: COGOG; 2 RR Olympus TM3B gas turbines; 43 000 hp *(32 MW)* sustained
2 RR Tyne RM1C gas turbines; 10 680 hp *(8 MW)* sustained; 2 shafts; cp props
Speed, knots: 30. **Range, miles:** 4700 at 16 kts on Tynes
Complement: 197 (23 officers)

Missiles: SSM: 8 McDonnell Douglas Harpoon (2 quad) launchers ❶; active radar homing to 130 km *(70 nm)* at 0.9 Mach; warhead 227 kg.
SAM: 40 GDC Pomona Standard SM-1MR; Mk 13 Mod 1 launcher ❷; command guidance; semi-active radar homing to 46 km *(25 nm)* at 2 Mach.
Raytheon Sea Sparrow Mk 29 octuple launcher ❸; semi-active radar homing to 14.6 km *(8 nm)* at 2.5 Mach; warhead 39 kg; 24 missiles.
Guns: 1 Signaal SGE-30 Goalkeeper ❹ with General Electric 30 mm 7-barrelled; 4200 rounds/minute combined to 2 km.
2 Oerlikon 20 mm.
Torpedoes: 4—324 mm US Mk 32 (2 twin) tubes ❺. Honeywell Mk 46 Mod 5; anti-submarine; active/passive homing to 11 km *(5.9 nm)* at 40 kts; warhead 44 kg.
Countermeasures: Decoys: 2 Loral Hycor Mk 36 SRBOC 6-tubed fixed quad launchers ❻; IR flares and Chaff to 4 km *(2.2 nm)*.
ESM/ECM: Ramses; intercept and jammer.
Combat data systems: Signaal SEWACO VI action data automation; Link 11. SATCOM.
Radars: Air search: Signaal LW 08 ❼; D band; range 264 km *(145 nm)* for 2 m^2 target.
Air/surface search: Signaal DA 05 ❽; E/F band; range 137 km *(75 nm)* for 2 m^2 target. To be replaced in refit by Signaal Smart; 3D.
Surface search: Signaal ZW 06 ❾; I band; range 26 km *(14 nm)*.
Fire control: Two Signaal STIR 240 ❿; I/J/K band; range 140 km *(76 nm)* for 1 m^2 target.
Signaal STIR 180 ⓫; I/J/K band.
Sonars: Westinghouse SQS 509; hull-mounted; active search and attack; medium frequency.

Programmes: Ordered as replacements for the two Kortenaer class frigates sold to Greece. Same hull and engines.
Operational: Air defence frigates with command facilities for a task group commander and his staff.

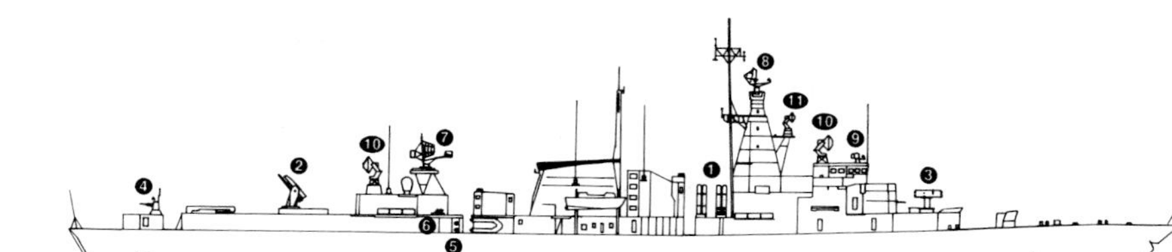

JACOB VAN HEEMSKERCK *(Scale 1 : 1 200), Ian Sturton*

WITTE DE WITH *10/1991, Selim San*

WITTE DE WITH *3/1991, J. L. M. van der Burg*

SHIPBORNE AIRCRAFT

Numbers/Type: 22 Westland Lynx Mks 25/27/81.
Operational speed: 125 kts *(232 km/h)*.
Service ceiling: 12 500 ft *(3810 m)*.
Range: 320 nm *(590 km)*.
Role/Weapon systems: ASW, SAR and utility helicopter series all being converted to 14B type; Mk 25 (UH-14A) is shore-based; Mk 27/81 (SH-14B/C) embarked for ASW duties in escorts. Sensors: Search radar (Mk 25, Mk 28 and Mk 81), Alcatel DUAV-4 dipping sonar (Mk 27), AQS-81, MAD (Mk 81). Weapons: 2 × Mk 46 torpedoes or depth bombs (Mk 27 and Mk 81), unarmed (Mk 25).

LYNX *9/1990, J. L. M. van der Burg*

LAND-BASED MARITIME AIRCRAFT

Numbers/Type: 2 Fokker F27 Maritime.
Operational speed: 250 kts *(463 km/h)*.
Service ceiling: 29 500 ft *(8990 m)*.
Range: 2700 nm *(5000 km)*.
Role/Weapon systems: Netherlands Antilles for ocean surveillance; operated by Air Force with naval observers. Sensors: APS-504 search radar, LAPADS processor. Weapons: ASW; 4 × Mk 46 torpedoes, 6 × underwing points. ASV; has provision for missiles.

Numbers/Type: 13 Lockheed P-3C//Update II Orion.
Operational speed: 410 kts *(760 km/h)*.
Service ceiling: 28 300 ft *(8625 m)*.
Range: 4000 nm *(7410 km)*.
Role/Weapon systems: Long-range MR and NATO area ocean surveillance, particularly for ASW/ASV operations. Sensors: APS-115 radar, AQS-81 MAD, AQA 7 processor, AQS-114 computer, IFF, ECM/ESM, sonobuoys. Weapons: ASW; 8 × Mk 46 torpedoes, depth bombs or mines. Underwing stations for Harpoon missiles for which procurement has been suspended.

MINE WARFARE FORCES

15 ALKMAAR CLASS (TRIPARTITE TYPE) (MINEHUNTERS)

Name	*No*	*Laid down*	*Launched*	*Commissioned*
ALKMAAR	M 850	30 Jan 1979	18 May 1982	28 May 1983
DELFZYL	M 851	29 May 1980	29 Oct 1982	17 Aug 1983
DORDRECHT	M 852	5 Jan 1981	26 Feb 1983	16 Nov 1983
HAARLEM	M 853	16 June 1981	6 May 1983	12 Jan 1984
HARLINGEN	M 854	30 Nov 1981	9 July 1983	12 Apr 1984
SCHEVENINGEN	M 855	24 May 1982	2 Dec 1983	18 July 1984
MAASSLUIS	M 856	7 Nov 1982	5 May 1984	12 Dec 1984
MAKKUM	M 857	25 Feb 1983	27 Sep 1984	13 May 1985
MIDDELBURG	M 858	11 July 1983	23 Feb 1985	10 Dec 1986
HELLEVOETSLUIS	M 859	12 Dec 1983	18 July 1985	20 Feb 1987
SCHIEDAM	M 860	6 May 1984	20 Dec 1985	9 July 1986
URK	M 861	1 Oct 1984	2 May 1986	10 Dec 1986
ZIERIKZEE	M 862	25 Feb 1985	4 Oct 1986	7 May 1987
VLAARDINGEN	M 863	6 May 1986	4 Aug 1988	15 Mar 1989
WILLEMSTAD	M 864	3 Oct 1986	27 Jan 1989	20 Sep 1989

Displacement, tons: 562 standard; 595 full load
Dimensions, feet (metres): 168.9 × 29.2 × 8.5 *(51.5 × 8.9 × 2.6)*
Main machinery: 1 Brons-Werkspoor A-RUB 215X-12 diesel; 1860 hp(m) *(1.35 MW)* sustained; 1 shaft; Lips cp prop; 2 active rudders; 2 motors; 240 hp(m) *(179 kW)*; 2 bow thrusters
Speed, knots: 15 diesel; 7 electric. **Range, miles:** 3000 at 12 kts
Complement: 29-42 depending on task

Guns: 1 GIAT 20 mm (an additional short range missile system may be added for patrol duties).
Countermeasures: MCM: 2 PAP 104 remote-controlled submersibles. Mechanical minesweeping gear and OD 3.
Combat data systems: Signaal Sewaco IX.
Radars: Navigation: Racal Decca TM 1229C; I band.
Sonars: Thomson Sintra DUBM 21A; hull-mounted; minehunting; 100 kHz (± 10 kHz).

Programmes: In 1985 Egypt took an option on M 858 and 859 but financial problems arose and the two have been commissioned in the Royal Netherlands Navy. The two Indonesian ships ordered in 1985 took the place of M 863 and 864 whose laying down was delayed as a result. This class is the Netherlands' part of a tripartite co-operative plan with Belgium and France for GRP hulled minehunters. The whole class built by Van der Giessen-de-Noord-Alblasserdam in a specially constructed 'ship-factory' 143.9 × 43 m *(472 × 141 ft)* which was completed December 1978. Ships were launched virtually ready for trials.
Structure: A 5 ton container can be shipped, stored for varying tasks—research; patrol; extended diving; drone control.
Operational: Endurance, 15 days. Automatic radar navigation system. Automatic data processing and display. EVEC 20. Decca Hi-fix positioning system. Alcatel dynamic positioning system. Five of the class in reserve in 1992.
Sales: Two of a modified design to Indonesia, completed March 1988.

SCHIEDAM *5/1991, Guy Toremans*

11 DOKKUM CLASS (MINESWEEPERS—COASTAL)

HOOGEZAND M 802*
NAALDWIJK M 809
ABCOUDE M 810
DRACHTEN M 812
OMMEN M 813
GIETHOORN M 815*
VENLO M 817*
NAARDEN M 823
HOOGEVEEN M 827*
SITTARD M 830
GEMERT M 841*

*Reserve

Displacement, tons: 373 standard; 453 full load
Dimensions, feet (metres): 152.9 × 28.9 × 7.5 *(46.6 × 8.8 × 2.3)*
Main machinery: 2 Fijenoord MAN V64 diesels; 2500 hp(m) *(1.84 MW)*; 2 shafts
Speed, knots: 16. **Range, miles:** 2500 at 10 kts
Complement: 27-36 depending on task
Guns: 1 or 2 Oerlikon 20 mm (not in all).
Radars: Navigation: Racal Decca TM 1229C; I band.

Comment: 32 Western Union type coastal minesweepers were built in the Netherlands, 18 were under offshore procurement as the Dokkum class, with MAN engines. All launched in 1954-56 and completed in 1955-56. This class was subject to a fleet rehabilitation and modernisation programme completed by 1977 and a 'life prolonging' refit from the mid-1980s to 1991 for six of the class—M 830, 813, 823, 812, 810 and 809. Included in the refit was additional accommodation in the form of a deckhouse. Will be replaced by the new class of MSCs. Five are in reserve stripped of parts and unlikely to go to sea again. The ex-*Dokkum* is a trials ship.

DRACHTEN *3/1991, J. L. M. van der Burg*

0 + (6) NEW MINESWEEPERS

Displacement, tons: 610 approx
Dimensions, feet (metres): 154.2 × 31.5 × 11.8 *(47 × 9.6 × 3.6)*
Speed, knots: 10 (sweeping). **Range, miles:** 3000 at 10 kts
Complement: 25

Comment: Memorandum of Understanding signed 6 April 1989 for a joint Belgium/Netherlands minesweeper project. Design contract awarded November 1990 to Van der Giessen de Noord Marinebouw in a joint venture with Scheepswerf Beliard Polyship to be completed in June 1992 with orders for six vessels for Netherlands expected; first to be laid down in 1995 and to complete by 1999. The requirement is to be able to sweep bottom mines which have sunk so far into the soft sand of the Southern North Sea that they are not detected by hunters.

AMPHIBIOUS FORCES

0 + (1) AMPHIBIOUS TRANSPORT SHIP (LPD)

Displacement, tons: 9500 full load
Dimensions, feet (metres): 492.1 × 82 × 18.4 *(150 × 25 × 5.6)*
Main machinery: 2 diesels; 2 shafts
Speed, knots: 20. **Range, miles:** 6000 at 14 kts
Complement: 115 plus 12 spare
Military lift: 600 troops; 170 APCs or 33 MBTs. 3 LCVP and 2 LCU/LCM or 6 LCVP
Guns: 2 Signaal Goalkeeper 30 mm.
Helicopters: 6 NH 90 or equivalent; or 4 EH 101 or equivalent.

Comment: Collaborative project with Spain. Construction planned to start in 1994 with completion in 1996. Can be used to transport a fully equipped battalion of Marines. Docking facilities for landing craft and a two-spot helicopter flight deck. Alternative employment as an SAR ship for environmental and disaster relief tasks.

5 LCA Mk I

L 9512 **L 9513** **L 9514** **L 9515** **L 9518**

Displacement, tons: 13.6
Dimensions, feet (metres): 47.6 × 12.5 × 4.3 *(14.5 × 3.8 × 1.3)*
Main machinery: 1 RR diesel; 200 hp(m) *(149 kW)*; Schottel prop
Speed, knots: 12
Complement: 3
Military lift: 1 Land Rover or Volvo BV 202E Snowcat
Guns: 1 FN FAL 7.62 mm MG.
Radars: Navigation: Racal Decca 110; I band.

Comment: Landing craft made of polyester, all commissioned in 1962-63. Built by 'Le Conte'.

L 9514 *9/1990, J. L. M. van der Burg*

6 LCA Mk II

L 9530-9535

Displacement, tons: 17.5
Dimensions, feet (metres): 52.5 × 13.9 × 3.5 *(16 × 4.3 × 1.1)*
Main machinery: 1 DAF DKS 1160 M diesel; 272 hp(m) *(200 kW)*; Schottel prop
Speed, knots: 11. **Range, miles:** 220 at 11 kts
Complement: 3
Military lift: 35 troops; 1 Land Rover or BV 202E Snowcat
Guns: 1 FN FAL 7.62 mm MG.
Radars: Navigation: Racal Decca 110; I band.

Comment: L 9530-9541 plus two extra ordered 27 October 1981 from Rijkswerf, Willemsoord and Schottel, Netherlands. First pair completed 1984, next three in 1985, last one in 1986. The rest were cancelled in favour of the Mk III design.

LCA 9531 *5/1989, Ralf Bendfeldt*

6 LCA Mk III

L 9536-9541

Displacement, tons: 30 full load
Dimensions, feet (metres): 55.4 × 15.7 × 3.6 *(16.9 × 4.8 × 1.1)*
Main machinery: 2 diesels; 750 hp(m) *(551 kW)*; 2 shafts
Speed, knots: 14 (full load); 16.5 (light). **Range, miles:** 200 at 12 kts
Complement: 3
Military lift: 34 troops or 7 tons or 2 Land Rovers or 1 Snowcat
Guns: 1—7.62 mm MG.
Radars: Navigation: Racal Decca; I band.

Comment: Ordered from Van der Giessen de Noord 10 December 1988. First one laid down 10 August 1989, commissioned 16 October 1990. Last one commissioned late 1992. These are an improvement over the Mk II type which did not come up to expectations.

LCA 9536 — *1991, Royal Netherlands Navy*

SURVEY SHIPS

Note: There are also four survey boats 8901-8904 completed in 1989-90; dimensions 9.5 × 3.8 m; 1 Volvo Penta diesel of 170 hp(m) *(125 kW)*. The first two are carried by A 904 and A 905 respectively.

1 TYDEMAN CLASS (HYDROGRAPHIC/OCEANOGRAPHIC SHIP)

Name	*No*	*Builders*	*Commissioned*
TYDEMAN	A 906	Scheepswerf en Machine Fabriek 'de Merwede'	10 Nov 1976

Displacement, tons: 2977 full load
Dimensions, feet (metres): 295.9 × 47.2 × 15.7 *(90.2 × 14.4 × 4.8)*
Main machinery: Diesel-electric: 3 Stork-Werkspoor 8-FCHD-240 diesel generators; 3690 hp(m) *(2.71 MW)*; 1 motor; 2730 hp(m) *(2 MW)*; 1 shaft
1 Paxman diesel; 485 hp(m) *(356 kW)*; 1 active rudder; 300 hp(m) *(220 kW)*; bow thruster; 450 hp(m) *(330 kW)*
Speed, knots: 15. **Range, miles:** 15 700 at 10.3 kts; 10 300 at 13.5 kts
Complement: 62 (8 officers) plus 15 scientists
Radars: Navigation: Racal Decca; I band.
Sonars: Atlas-Deco 10 echo-sounders with Edig digitisers. KAe Deso 25 replacements.
Kelvin Hughes; hull-mounted; side-scan. Klein; towed; side-scan.
Elac; bow-mounted; wreck search; trainable in sectors on either bow.
Helicopters: 1 Westland UH-14A Lynx.

Comment: Ordered in October 1974. Laid down 29 April 1975, launched 18 December 1975. Able to operate oceanographic cables down to 7000 m. Has six laboratories and two container spaces each for 20 ft standard container. Has forward working-deck with wet-hall, midships and after working decks, one 10 ton crane, one 4 ton crane and frames. Diving facilities. Passive stabilisation tank. Decca Hi-fix 6; Digital PDP computer; COMPLOT plotting system. Normally operates in the Atlantic and between March 1991 and March 1992 tested a derivative of the Thomson Sintra DUBM 41 towed sonar for the detection of mines buried up to 2 m deep.

TYDEMAN — *10/1989, Gilbert Gyssels*

2 BUYSKES CLASS

Name	*No*	*Builders*	*Commissioned*
BUYSKES	A 904	Boele's Scheepswerven en Machinefabriek BV, Bolnes	9 Mar 1973
BLOMMENDAL	A 905	Boele's Scheepswerven en Machinefabriek BV, Bolnes	22 May 1973

Displacement, tons: 967 standard; 1033 full load
Dimensions, feet (metres): 196.6 × 36.4 × 12 *(60 × 11.1 × 3.7)*
Main machinery: Diesel-electric; 3 Paxman 12 RPH diesel generators; 2100 hp *(1.57 MW)*; 1 motor; 1400 hp(m) *(1.03 MW)*; 1 shaft
Speed, knots: 13.5. **Range, miles:** 3000 at 11.5 kts
Complement: 43 (6 officers)
Radars: Navigation: Racal Decca; I band.
Sonars: Side-scanning and wreck-search.

Comment: Both designed primarily for hydrographic work but have also limited oceanographic and meteorological capability. They operate mainly in the North Sea. A data logging system is installed as part of the automatic handling of hydrographic data. HYDRAUT logging system; wire-drags. Marconi Bathyscan swath sounders. Krupp Atlas Deso 25 echo sounders. They carry two 22 ft survey launches capable of 15 kts and two work-boats normally used for sweeping. Major refits in 1988-89.

BLOMMENDAL — *2/1991, van Ginderen Collection*

SERVICE FORCES

2 POOLSTER CLASS (FAST COMBAT SUPPORT SHIPS)

Name	*No*	*Builders*	*Commissioned*
ZUIDERKRUIS	A 832	Verolme Shipyards, Alblasserdam	27 June 1975
POOLSTER	A 835	Rotterdamse Droogdok Mij	10 Sep 1964

Displacement, tons: 16 800 (16 900, *Zuiderkruis)* full load
Measurement, tons: 10 000 dwt
Dimensions, feet (metres): 552.2 × 66.6 × 26.9 *(168.3 × 20.3 × 8.2) (Poolster)*
556 × 66.6 × 27.6 *(169.6 × 20.3 × 8.4) (Zuiderkruis)*
Main machinery: 2 boilers; 2 turbines; 22 000 hp(m) *(16.2 MW)*; 1 shaft *(Poolster)*
2 Stork-Werkspoor TM 410 diesels; 21 000 hp(m) *(15.4 MW)*; 1 shaft *(Zuiderkruis)*
Speed, knots: 21
Complement: 200 (17 officers) *(Poolster)*; 266 (17 officers) *(Zuiderkruis)*
Cargo capacity: 10 300 tons including 8-9000 tons oil fuel

Guns: 1 Signaal SGE-30 Goalkeeper with GE 30 mm 7-barrelled; 4200 rounds/minute combined to 2 km. Fitted for Gulf deployments in 1990-91.
2 Bofors 40 mm *(Poolster)*. 5 Oerlikon 20 mm *(Zuiderkruis)*.
Countermeasures: Decoys: 2 Loral Hycor SRBOC Mk 36 fixed 6-barrelled launchers; IR flares and Chaff.
ESM: Radar warning.
Radars: Air/surface search: Racal Decca 2459; F/I band.
Navigation: Two Racal Decca TM 1226C *(Zuiderkruis)*; I band.
Racal Decca TM 1229C *(Poolster)*; I band.
Sonars: Signaal CWE 10 *(Poolster)*; hull-mounted; active search; medium frequency.

Helicopters: 1 Westland UH-14A Lynx.

Programmes: *Poolster* laid down on 18 September 1962. Launched on 16 October 1963. *Zuiderkruis* laid down 16 July 1973, launched 15 October 1974, completed refit February 1981.
Structure: Helicopter deck aft. Funnel heightened by 4.5 m *(14.8 ft)*. Additional 20 mm guns and containerised Goalkeeper CIWS fitted for operational deployments.
Operational: Capacity for five helicopters. Both ships carry A/S weapons for helicopters. Two fuelling stations each side for underway replenishment.

POOLSTER — *5/1990, Wright and Logan*

ZUIDERKRUIS — *11/1991, Harald Carstens*

0 + 1 ZUIDERKRUIS TYPE (FAST COMBAT SUPPORT SHIP)

Name	*No*	*Builders*	*Commissioned*
—	A 836	Kon Mij de Schelde	Dec 1994

Displacement, tons: 17 040 full load
Dimensions, feet (metres): 544.6 × 72.2 × 26.2 *(166 × 22 × 8)*
Main machinery: Diesel-electric; 2 diesels; 26 330 hp(m) *(19.36 MW)*; 1 shaft
Speed, knots: 20. **Range, miles:** 13 440 at 20 kts
Complement: 136 plus 24 aircrew plus 20 spare
Cargo capacity: 6700 tons dieso; 1660 tons petrol; 500 tons solids
Guns: 2 Oerlikon 20 mm. 1 Goalkeeper 30 mm CIWS.
Helicopters: 3 Sea King type.

Comment: Replacement for *Poolster* ordered 14 October 1991. Laid down in early 1992. Close co-operation between Dutch Nevesbu and Spanish Bazán has led to this design which has maintenance workshops as well as alongside and Vertrep supply stations. Second of class required to replace *Zuiderkruis* after 2000.

ZUIDERKRUIS Type — *1991, Royal Netherlands Navy*

TRAINING SHIPS

Name	*No*	*Builders*	*Commissioned*
BULGIA	A 880 (ex-P 803)	Rijkswerf, Willemsoord	20 Sep 1954

Displacement, tons: 150 standard; 163 full load
Dimensions, feet (metres): 119.1 × 20.2 × 6.3 *(36.3 × 6.2 × 1.9)*
Main machinery: 2 Werkspoor RUB 612 diesels; 1050 hp(m) *(772 kW)*; 2 shafts
Speed, knots: 15. **Range, miles:** 1000 at 13 kts
Complement: 28
Radars: Navigation: Decca; I band.

Comment: Non-commissioned training tender to the Naval College since November 1986. Armament removed.

BULGIA — *8/1991, van Ginderen Collection*

Name	*No*	*Builders*	*Commissioned*
URANIA (ex-*Tromp*)	Y 8050	Haarlem	23 Apr 1938

Displacement, tons: 76
Dimensions, feet (metres): 78.4 × 17.4 × 10.5 *(23.9 × 5.3 × 3.2)*
Main machinery: 1 diesel; 65 hp(m) *(48 kW)*; 1 shaft
Speed, knots: 5 diesel; 10 sail
Complement: 17

Comment: Schooner used for training in seamanship.

URANIA — *7/1990, Wright and Logan*

Name	*No*	*Builders*	*Commissioned*
ZEEFAKKEL	A 903	J & K Smit, Kinderdijk	16 Mar 1951

Displacement, tons: 355 standard; 384 full load
Dimensions, feet (metres): 149 × 24.6 × 7.2 *(45.4 × 7.5 × 2.2)*
Main machinery: 2 Smit-MAN diesels; 640 hp(m) *(470 kW)*; 2 shafts
Speed, knots: 12
Complement: 26
Radars: Navigation: Racal Decca; I band.

Comment: Laid down 28 November 1949, launched 21 July 1950. Former surveying vessel. Now used as local training ship at Den Helder. Re-engined 1980.

ZEEFAKKEL — *6/1989, J. L. M. van der Burg*

AUXILIARIES

Note: In addition to vessels listed below, non self-propelled craft include Y 8514, floating crane built in 1974 and about 40 others including tank-cleaning vessels, barges, berthing pontoons (Y 8594-8617), diving pontoons (Y 8579-92). Other small craft include general purpose harbour and dockyard craft (Y 8351-2) (Y 8200-03) (Y 8012), four diving craft attached to *Thetis* (Y 8579-82), seven targets (Y 8694-99, Y 8704), four small transports (Y 8343-46) and eight fuel lighters (Y 8347-52, Y 8536, Y 8538).

3 ACCOMMODATION SHIPS

CORNELIS DREBBEL A 886 **THETIS** A 887 **TAX** Y 8500

Displacement, tons: 775 *(Cornelis Drebbel)*; 800 *(Thetis)*
Dimensions, feet (metres): 206.7 × 38.7 × 3.6 *(63 × 11.8 × 1.1) (Cornelis Drebbel)*
223 × 39.4 × 5.3 *(68 × 12 × 1.6) (Thetis)*

Comment: *Cornelis Drebbel* built by Scheepswerf Voorwaarts at Hoogezand in 1971. Serves as accommodation vessel for crews of ships building and refitting at private yards in the Rotterdam area. *Thetis* built by Koninklijke Maatschappij De Schelde, Flushing; completed 14 March 1985 and commissioned 27 June 1985; accommodation for 106. Stationed at Den Oever, she provides harbour training for divers and underwater swimmers. *Tax* built in 1953 as a small cargo ship and converted in 1988.

1 SUBMARINE SUPPORT SHIP and TORPEDO TENDER

Name	*No*	*Builders*	*Commissioned*
MERCUUR	A 900	Kon Mij de Schelde	21 Aug 1987

Displacement, tons: 1400 full load
Dimensions, feet (metres): 212.6 × 39.4 × 14.1 *(64.8 × 12 × 4.3)*
Main machinery: 2 Brons 61-20/27 diesels; 1100 hp(m) *(808 kW)*; 2 shafts; bow thruster
Speed, knots: 14
Complement: 39
Guns: 2 Oerlikon 20 mm.
Torpedoes: 3—324 mm (triple) tubes. 1—21 in *(533 mm)* underwater tube.
Mines: Can lay mines.
Sonars: Hull-mounted; passive search.

Comment: Replacement for previous ship of same name. Ordered 13 June 1984. Laid down 6 November 1985. Floated out 25 October 1986. Can launch training and research torpedoes above and below the waterline. Services, maintains and recovers torpedoes.

MERCUUR — *1990, Audio Visuele Dienst*

1 SUPPORT SHIP

Name	*No*	*Builders*	*Commissioned*
PELIKAAN (ex-*Kilindoni*)	A 801	Vinholmen, Arendal	1984

Displacement, tons: 505 full load
Dimensions, feet (metres): 151.6 × 34.8 × 9.2 *(46.2 × 10.6 × 2.8)*
Main machinery: 2 Caterpillar 3412T diesels; 1080 hp *(806 kW)* sustained; 2 shafts
Speed, knots: 10
Complement: 15
Guns: 2—12.7 mm MGs.

Comment: Ex-oil platform supply ship acquired 28 May 1990 after being refitted in Curaçao. Has taken over from the deleted *Woerden* as tender and transport for marines in the Antilles. Capacity for 40 marines in five accommodation units.

PELIKAAN *11/1990, Hartmut Ehlers*

1 EXPERIMENTAL SHIP

VAN SPEIJK (ex-*Dokkum*) Y 8001

Comment: For data see Dokkum class in Mine Warfare Forces. Weapon systems removed and converted by Wilton Fijenoord, Schiedam in November 1986 for testing fuels. Renamed because there has to be a *Van Speijk* in commission in the Navy.

VAN SPEIJK *6/1987, Hartmut Ehlers*

1 TRITON CLASS (DIVING TENDER)

Name	*No*	*Builders*	*Commissioned*
TRITON	A 848	Rijkswerf, Willemsoord	5 Aug 1964

Displacement, tons: 69 full load
Dimensions, feet (metres): 76 × 16.4 × 4.6 *(23.2 × 5 × 1.4)*
Main machinery: 1 Volvo Penta diesel; 105 hp(m) *(77 kW)*; 1 shaft
Speed, knots: 9
Complement: 8

Comment: Pays off in 1992.

TRITON *9/1985, Hartmut Ehlers*

4 CERBERUS CLASS (DIVING TENDERS)

Name	*No*	*Builders*	*Commissioned*
CERBERUS	A 851	Visser, Den Helder	Dec 1991
ARGUS	A 852	Visser, Den Helder	Feb 1992
NAUTILUS	A 853	Visser, Den Helder	May 1992
HYDRA	A 854	Visser, Den Helder	Aug 1992

Displacement, tons: 180 full load
Dimensions, feet (metres): 89.9 × 27.9 × 4.9 *(27.4 × 8.5 × 1.5)*
Main machinery: 2 Volvo diesels; 380 hp(m) *(279 kW)*; 2 shafts
Speed, knots: 12
Complement: 8

Comment: Ordered 29 November 1990. Replacing Triton class from 1992.

2 SMALL FLOATING DOCKS

Y 8678 **Y 8679**

Comment: Built in 1950 and 1959 at Willemsoord. Of 420 and 450 tons capacity respectively.

TUGS

Name	*No*	*Builders*	*Commissioned*
WESTGAT	A 872	Rijkswerf, Willemsoord	10 Jan 1968
WIELINGEN	A 873	Rijkswerf, Willemsoord	31 May 1968

Displacement, tons: 206
Dimensions, feet (metres): 89.2 × 23 × 7.7 *(27.2 × 7 × 2.3)*
Main machinery: 1 Bolnes diesel; 720 hp(m) *(529 kW)*; 1 shaft
Speed, knots: 12
Complement: 9
Guns: 2 Oerlikon 20 mm (not fitted).

Comment: Equipped with salvage pumps and firefighting equipment. Stationed at Den Helder.

WIELINGEN *5/1990, J. L. M. van der Burg*

Name	*No*	*Builders*	*Commissioned*
LINGE	A 874	Delta SY, Sliedrecht	20 Feb 1987
REGGE	A 875	Delta SY, Sliedrecht	6 May 1987
HUNZE	A 876	Delta SY, Sliedrecht	20 Oct 1987
ROTTE	A 877	Delta SY, Sliedrecht	20 Oct 1987

Displacement, tons: 200 approx
Dimensions, feet (metres): 90.2 × 27.2 × 8.9 *(27.5 × 8.3 × 2.7)*
Main machinery: 2 Stork-Werkspoor diesel; 1600 hp(m) *(1.18 MW)*; 2 shafts
Speed, knots: 11
Complement: 7

Comment: Order placed in 1986. Based at Den Helder.

ROTTE *3/1991, van Ginderen Collection*

7 HARBOUR TUGS

BREEZAND Y 8018
BALGZAND Y 8019
SCHELDE Y 8055
WIERBALG Y 8056
MALZWIN Y 8057
ZUIDWAL Y 8058
WESTWAL Y 8059

Dimensions, feet (metres): 54.2 × 17.5 × 5.9 *(16.5 × 5.3 × 1.8)* (Y 8018/19); 35.4 × 12.5 × 4.3 *(10.8 × 3.8 × 1.3)* (remainder)
Main machinery: 2 diesels; 760 hp(m) *(559 kW)*; 2 shafts (Y 8018/19)
1 DAF diesel; 115 hp(m) *(85 kW)*; 1 shaft (remainder)

Comment: *Breezand* completed December 1989, *Balgzand* January 1990. Remainder completed December 1986 to February 1987. All built by Delta Shipyard.

ROYAL NETHERLANDS ARMY

Note: In addition to the LCT there are three patrol boats and a diving tender RV 50 which commissioned 3 November 1989; all with a limited coastal capability. In addition there are 15 vessels for inland waters.

1 TANK LANDING CRAFT

RV 40

Displacement, tons: 815
Dimensions, feet (metres): 150.3 × 31.2 × 8.2 *(45.8 × 9.5 × 2.5)*
Main machinery: 2 diesels; 654 hp(m) *(481 kW)*; 2 shafts
Speed, knots: 9.4
Complement: 4

Comment: Built by Grave BV and completed 22 November 1979.

RV 40 — *1984, Royal Netherlands Navy*

COAST GUARD (KUSTWACHT)

Note: In 1987 many of the separate maritime services were merged to form a Coast Guard with its own distinctive colours. Included are some of the 70 police craft, 23 customs vessels and over 320 assorted craft of the Ministry of Transport and Public Works. Many of these vessels would come under naval control in an emergency.

BREEVERTIEN — *3/1991, van Ginderen Collection*

RP 20 (Police) — *11/1990, J. L. M. van der Burg*

NEW ZEALAND

Headquarters' Appointments

Chief of Defence Force:
Vice Admiral S F Teagle, ADC
Chief of Naval Staff:
Rear Admiral I Hunter
Deputy Chief of Naval Staff:
Commodore K F Wilson
Commodore Auckland:
Commodore J A B Lewis, OBE

Diplomatic Representation

Head of Defence Liaison Staff, London:
Commodore J G Leonard
Naval Adviser, Canberra:
Captain A J Peck
Defence Attaché, Kuala Lumpur:
Captain J E R Granville
Naval Technical Liaison Officer, London:
Commander K G Black

Personnel

(a) 1992: 2500
(b) Reserve: 450 RNZNVR officers and ratings

Shore Establishments

Naval Staff: HMNZS Wakefield (Wellington)
Fleet Support: HMNZS Philomel (Auckland)
Training: HMNZS Tamaki (Auckland)
Communications: HMNZS Irirangi (Waiouru)
Ship Repair: HMNZ Dockyard (Auckland)

RNZNVR Divisions

Auckland: HMNZS *Ngapona*
Wellington: HMNZS *Olphert*
Christchurch: HMNZS *Pegasus*
Dunedin: HMNZS *Toroa*

Prefix to Ships' Names

HMNZS

Mercantile Marine

Lloyd's Register of Shipping:
142 vessels of 274 849 tons gross

Strength of the Fleet

Type	*Active (Reserve)*	*Building (Projected)*
Frigates	4	2
Inshore Patrol Craft	4	—
Survey Vessels	3	—
Fleet Supply/Logistic Ship	1	(1)
Research Vessel	1	—
Training Craft	1	—
Tugs	2	—
Diving Support Ship	1	—

DELETIONS

Training Ship

1989 *Kuparu* (museum)

Light Forces

1991 *Pukaki, Rotoiti, Taupo, Hawea* (all for sale)

FRIGATES

0 + 2 ANZAC CLASS

Name	*No*	*Builders*	*Laid down*	*Launched*	*Commissioned*
—	—	Amecon	Feb 1993	Mar 1995	Feb 1997
—	—	Amecon	Feb 1995	Jan 1997	Nov 1998

Displacement, tons: 3600 full load
Dimensions, feet (metres): 387.1 oa; 357.6 wl × 48.6 × 14.3 *(118; 109 × 14.8 × 4.4)*
Main machinery: CODOG; 1 GE LM 2500 gas turbine; 23 000 hp *(17.2 MW)* sustained; 2 MTU 12V 1163 TB83 diesels; 8840 hp(m) *(6.5 MW)* sustained; 2 shafts; cp props
Speed, knots: 27. **Range, miles:** 6000 at 18 kts
Complement: 163

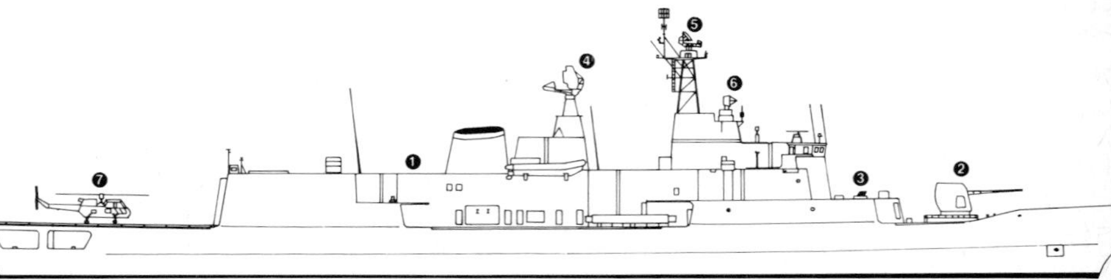

ANZAC — *(Scale 1 : 900), Ian Sturton*

Missiles: SAM: Raytheon Sea Sparrow; Mk 41 Mod 4 octuple vertical launcher ❶.
Guns: 1 FMC 5 in *(127 mm)*/54 Mk 45 Mod 2 ❷.
Countermeasures: Decoys: Loral Hycor SRBOC Mk 36 Chaff launchers ❸ SLQ-25 Nixie towed torpedo decoy (tbd).
ESM: THORN EMI Sceptre A; radar intercept.
Combat data systems: NobelTech (BEAB) 9LV 453 Mk 3. Link 11.
Fire control: NobelTech (BEAB) Sea Viking director. Raytheon CW Mk 73 (for SAM).
Radars: Air search: Raytheon SPS 49(V)8 ANZ ❹; C/D band.
Air/surface search: Ericsson Sea Giraffe 150 HC ❺; G/H band.
Navigation: Krupp Atlas 8600 ARPA; I band.
Fire control: NobelTech (BEAB) 9LV 200 ❻; I/J band.

Sonars: Thomson Sintra Spherion B; hull-mounted; active search and attack; medium frequency.
Provision for Dowty 2031(Z) towed array; passive; very low frequency.

Helicopters: 1 Wasp HAS Mk 1 ❼.

Programmes: Contract signed with Amecon consortium on 19 November 1989 to build eight Blohm & Voss designed MEKO 200 ANZ frigates for Australia and two for New Zealand, which has an option for two more. Modules to be constructed starting in 1992 at Newcastle, Australia and New Zealand, and shipped to Melbourne for final assembly. The two New Zealand ships will be second and fourth of the class to be completed.
Structure: The ships include space and weight provision for considerable enhancement including canister-launched SSM and ESM extensions. Mk 32 torpedo tubes will probably be fitted in New Zealand as soon as the ships are delivered. Signature suppression features are incorporated in the design. All steel construction. Fin stabilisers.

2 LEANDER and 2 BROAD-BEAMED LEANDER CLASSES

Name	*No*	*Builders*	*Laid down*	*Launched*	*Commissioned*
WAIKATO	F 55	Harland & Wolff Ltd, Belfast	10 Jan 1964	18 Feb 1965	16 Sep 1966
WELLINGTON (ex-HMS *Bacchante*)*	F 69	Vickers Armstrong Ltd, Newcastle	27 Oct 1966	29 Feb 1968	17 Oct 1969
SOUTHLAND (ex-HMS *Dido*)	F 104	Yarrow & Co Ltd, Scotstoun	2 Dec 1959	22 Dec 1961	18 Sep 1963
CANTERBURY*	F 421	Yarrow Ltd, Clyde	12 Apr 1969	6 May 1970	22 Oct 1971

* Broad-beamed

Displacement, tons: 2580 standard; 3035 full load
2474 standard; 2945 full load (Broad-beamed)
Dimensions, feet (metres): 372 × 41; 43 (Broad-beamed) × 18 *(113.4 × 12.5; 13.1 × 5.5)*
Main machinery: 2 Babcock & Wilcox boilers; 550 psi *(38.7 kg/cm sq)*; 850°F *(454°C)*; 2 White-English Electric turbines; 30 000 hp *(22.4 MW)*; 2 shafts
Speed, knots: 28. **Range, miles:** 3000 at 15 kts; 5500 at 15 kts *(Wellington)*
Complement: 243 (16 officers) *(Waikato)*; 245 (15 officers) *(Canterbury)*; 257 (19 officers) *(Southland)*; 260 (19 officers) *(Wellington)*

Missiles: SAM: Short Bros Seacat GWS 22 quad launcher (2 quad in *Southland*) ❶; optical/radar guidance to 5 km *(2.7 nm)*; warhead 10 kg; 12 missiles.
A/S: Mod Ikara *(Southland)* ❷; command link/radio/radar guidance to 24 km *(13 nm)* at 0.8 Mach; payload Mk 46 Mod 2.
Guns: 2 Vickers 4.5 in *(114 mm)*/45 Mk 6 (twin) (except *Southland*) ❸; 80° elevation; 20 rounds/minute to 19 km *(10.3 nm)* anti-surface; 6 km *(3.2 nm)* anti-aircraft; weight of shell 25 kg.
4 or 6 Browning 12.7 mm MGs.
2 Bofors 40 mm/60 Mk 9 *(Southland)* ❹; 80° elevation; 120 rounds/minute to 10 km *(5.4 nm)* anti-surface; 3 km *(1.6 nm)* anti-aircraft; weight of shell 0.89 kg.
Torpedoes: 6—324 mm US Mk 32 Mod 5 (2 triple) tubes ❺. Honeywell/Marconi Mk 46 Mod 2; anti-submarine; active/passive homing to 11 km *(5.9 nm)* at 40 kts; warhead 44 kg.
Countermeasures: Decoys: 2 Loral Hycor SRBOC Mk 36 6-barrelled trainable launchers (except *Waikato*). Graseby Type 182; towed torpedo decoy.
ESM: Phoenix (all). PST 1288 HVU (*Canterbury* and *Wellington*). FH5 HF/DF (all).
Combat data systems: ADAWS 5 action data automation; Link 10 (*Southland*). Plessey Nautis F system being fitted in *Wellington* and *Canterbury* in 1992-93.
Fire control: GWS 22 for Seacat. MRS 3 for 114 mm *(Waikato)*. RCA R-76C5 for 114 mm (*Wellington* and *Canterbury*). GWS 46 for Ikara *(Southland)* ❻.
Radars: Air search: Marconi Type 965 AKE-1 *(Waikato)* ❼; A band.
Signaal LW08 *(Canterbury* and *Wellington)*; D band; range 265 km *(145 nm)* for 2 m² target.
Air/surface search: Plessey Type 993 *(Waikato)* ❽ or Plessey Type 994 ❾; E/F band.
Navigation: Kelvin Hughes Type 1006; I band.
Fire control: Plessey Type 904 ❿; I band (for Seacat).
RCA TR 76 (*Wellington* and *Canterbury*) or Plessey 903 ⓫ *(Waikato)* (for 114 mm guns).
Sonars: Kelvin Hughes Type 162M; hull-mounted; bottom classification; 50 kHz.
Graseby Type 750 or Type 177 *(Waikato)*; hull-mounted; active search and attack; medium frequency.
Ferranti FMS 15/2 TACTASS may be fitted in due course.

Helicopters: 1 Westland Wasp HAS 1 ⓬.

Programmes: *Waikato*, ordered on 14 June 1963, arrived in New Zealand in May 1967. *Canterbury* was ordered in August 1968, arrived in New Zealand in August 1972. *Wellington* was transferred on 1 October 1982, arriving in New Zealand December 1982. She immediately paid off into refit to become fully operational in 1986. *Southland* transferred on 18 July 1983. She then had a refit at Vosper Thornycroft, commissioned 21 December, sailing for New Zealand on completion.
Modernisation: *Wellington's* 1984-85 refit programme included: internal rearrangement to provide extra fuel tanks, new RCA gun control system, replacement of A/S mortar by Mk 32 torpedo tubes, improvements to surface radar and new radar intercept system, flight deck enlarged and fitting of SRBOC Chaff launcher. *Canterbury* modernisation in 1988-90 included new RCA gun fire control, new LW08 radar and ESM, fitting of SRBOC and an extension to her flight deck. *Southland* and *Waikato* completed limited refits in 1990 and 1991 respectively. Plessey Nautis combat system and LW08 air search radar fitted in *Wellington* and *Canterbury* in 1991-92.
Structure: Extensions fitted to funnel uptakes on *Waikato* and *Canterbury*.
Operational: *Waikato* has an enlarged hangar for Lynx helicopters. Reported that all ships are to be fitted with MUSL Stingray torpedoes and slimline towed sonar arrays in due course.

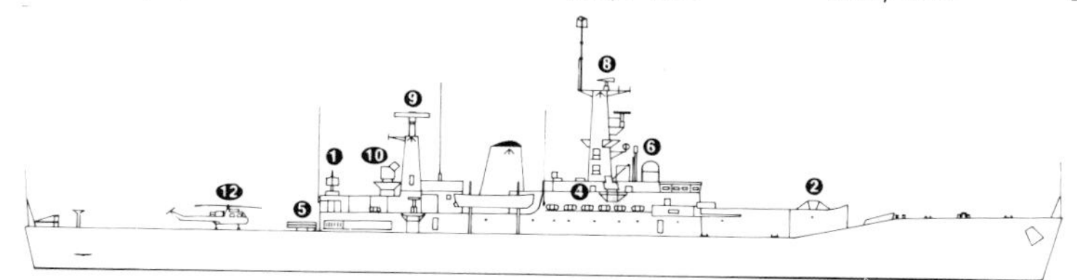

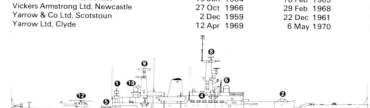

SOUTHLAND *(Scale 1 : 1 200), Ian Sturton*

SOUTHLAND *10/1991, Guy Toremans*

CANTERBURY *10/1991, John Mortimer*

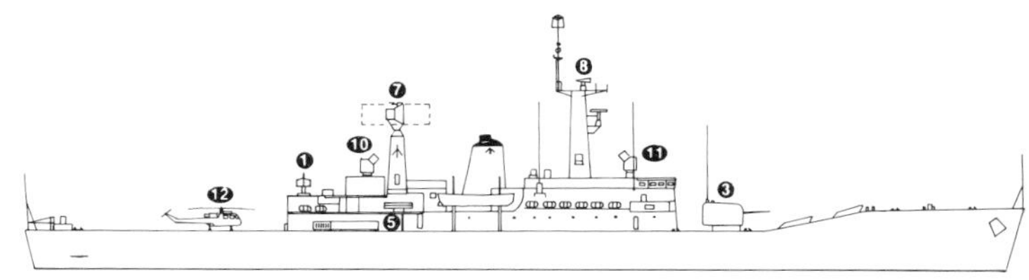

WAIKATO *(Scale 1 : 1 200), Ian Sturton*

WAIKATO *5/1990, 92 Wing RAAF*

SHIPBORNE AIRCRAFT

Numbers/Type: 7 Westland Wasp HAS Mk 1.
Operational speed: 96 kts *(177 km/h)*.
Service ceiling: 12 200 ft *(3720 m)*.
Range: 263 nm *(488 km)*.
Role/Weapon systems: ASW helicopter; low time aircraft procured from UK. Flown by Navy, maintained by Air Force. Were to have been paid off in 1992 but lives extended. Sensors: None. Weapons: ASW; 1 or 2 × Mk 44/46 torpedoes or depth bombs.

WESTLAND WASP *1986, Paul Beaver*

LAND-BASED MARITIME AIRCRAFT

Numbers/Type: 6 Lockheed P-3K Orion.
Operational speed: 410 kts *(760 km/h)*.
Service ceiling: 28 300 ft *(8625 m)*.
Range: 4000 nm *(7410 km)*.
Role/Weapon systems: Long-range surveillance and ASW patrol; update 1981-84 and to Phase II standard 1988-92. Operated by RNZAF. Sensors: APS-134 radar, ASQ-10 MAD, AQH5/AQA1 processor, 3 AYK 14 computers, IFF, ESM, SQ 41/47/SSQ 46 sonobuoys. Weapons: ASW; 8 × torpedoes, depth bombs or mines, 10 × underwing stations for weapons.

LIGHT FORCES

4 MOA CLASS (INSHORE PATROL CRAFT)

Name	*No*	*Builders*	*Commissioned*
MOA	P 3553	Whangarei Engineering and Construction Co Ltd	28 Nov 1983
KIWI	P 3554	Whangarei Engineering and Construction Co Ltd	2 Sep 1984
WAKAKURA	P 3555	Whangarei Engineering and Construction Co Ltd	26 Mar 1985
HINAU	P 3556	Whangarei Engineering and Construction Co Ltd	4 Oct 1985

Displacement, tons: 91.5 standard; 105 full load
Dimensions, feet (metres): 88 × 20 × 7.2 *(26.8 × 6.1 × 2.2)*
Main machinery: 2 Cummins KT-1105M diesels; 710 hp *(530 kW)*; 2 shafts
Speed, knots: 12. **Range, miles:** 1000 at 11 kts
Complement: 18 (5 officers (4 training))
Guns: 1 Browning 12.7 mm MG.
Radars: Surface search: Racal Decca; I band.
Sonars: Sidescan to be fitted in 1991.

Comment: On 11 February 1982 the New Zealand Cabinet approved the construction of four inshore patrol craft. The four IPC are operated by the Reserve Divisions, *Moa* with *Toroa* (Dunedin), *Kiwi* with *Pegasus* (Christchurch), *Wakakura* with *Olphert* (Wellington), *Hinau* with *Ngapona* (Auckland). Same design as Inshore Survey and Training craft *Kahu* but with a modified internal layout.

MOA *10/1991, Guy Toremans*

SURVEY VESSELS

Name	*No*	*Builders*	*Commissioned*
MONOWAI (ex-*Moana Roa*)	A 06	Grangemouth D.Y.	Aug 1960

Displacement, tons: 3903 full load
Dimensions, feet (metres): 298 × 46 × 17 *(90.8 × 14 × 5.2)*
Main machinery: 2 Clark-Sulzer 7-cyl diesels; 3640 hp(m) *(2.68 MW)*; 2 shafts; bow thruster
Speed, knots: 14. **Range, miles:** 12 000 at 12 kts
Complement: 136 (11 officers)
Guns: 2 Oerlikon 20 mm.
Radars: Navigation: Racal Decca 1290A/9; ARPA 1690S; I band.
Helicopters: 1 Wasp HAS Mk 1 (not always embarked).

Comment: Previously owned by the New Zealand Government department of Maori and Island Affairs and employed on the Cook Islands service. Taken over 1974 for conversion by Scott Lithgow which included an up-rating of the engines, provision of a helicopter deck and hangar and fitting of cp propellers. Commissioned into RNZN 4 October 1977. Racal System 960 automated data acquisition and processing with Racal Hadlaps (Hydrographic automated data logging and processing system) fitted in 1991. New radar and communications equipment fitted during 1988 modernisation which included the installation of a reverse osmosis plant and a rigid hull inflatable boat. The ship is white with a yellow funnel. Inmarsat comms fitted.

MONOWAI *10/1991, John Mortimer*

Name	*No*	*Builders*	*Commissioned*
TAKAPU	A 07	Whangarei Engineering and Construction Co Ltd	8 July 1980
TARAPUNGA	A 08	Whangarei Engineering and Construction Co Ltd	9 Apr 1980

Displacement, tons: 91.5 standard; 104.9 full load
Dimensions, feet (metres): 88 × 20 × 7.2 *(26.8 × 6.1 × 2.2)*
Main machinery: 2 Cummins KT-1150M diesels; 710 hp *(530 kW)*; 2 shafts
Speed, knots: 12. **Range, miles:** 1000 at 12 kts
Complement: 11 (2 officers)
Radars: Navigation: Racal Decca; I band.

Comment: Equipment has been specifically designed to work with *Monowai*. Same hull design as Inshore Patrol and Training craft *Kahu* with modified internal layout. Survey equipment: Magnavox MX1102 satellite navigation; Atlas Deso 20 echo-sounders; Del Norte Trisponder position fixing; EG and G 135 (*Tarapunga*) and Klein 531T (*Takapu*) side scan sonars; fitted for but not with Decca Hi-Fix/6. Fitted with two Omega power control gearboxes for slow speed running. Racal System 960 and Racal Hadlaps fitted in 1991.

TARAPUNGA *10/1991, Guy Toremans*

FLEET SUPPLY SHIP

Name	*No*	*Builders*	*Commissioned*
ENDEAVOUR	A 11	Hyundai, South Korea	6 Apr 1988

Displacement, tons: 12 390 full load
Dimensions, feet (metres): 453.1 × 60 × 23 *(138.1 × 18.4 × 7.3)*
Main machinery: 1 MAN-Burmeister & Wain 12V 32/36 diesel; 5780 hp(m) *(4.25 MW)* sustained; 1 shaft
Speed, knots: 14. **Range, miles:** 8000 at 14 kts
Complement: 30 (6 officers)
Cargo capacity: 7500 tons dieso; 100 tons Avcat; 100 tons water
Radars: Navigation: Racal Decca 1290A/9; ARPA 1690S; I band.
Helicopters: 1 Westland Wasp HAS Mk 1.

Comment: Ordered July 1986, laid down April 1987 and launched 14 August 1987. Completion delayed by engine problems but arrived in New Zealand in May 1988. Two abeam RAS rigs (one QRC, one Probe) and one astern refuelling rig. Fitted with Inmarsat. Standard merchant design modified on building to provide a relatively inexpensive replenishment tanker. Still having engine problems in 1991.

ENDEAVOUR *10/1991, John Mortimer*

LOGISTIC SUPPORT SHIP

Comment: Project Definition Study completed in Autumn 1989 for a logistic support ship to carry equipment and stores for the Army's Ready Reaction Force, and is of a design for 'Logistics Over The Shore' (LOTS) operations in island groups. To have a hangar and operate two medium lift helicopters, two LCMs and two LCVPs with a combined Army/Navy complement of approximately 60 plus 200 troops and supporting staff. She would be capable of carrying up to 500 people in an emergency. The design solution produced by British Maritime Technology Defence Services looked like being cancelled but after a second successive disaster in Samoa in 1991, the project may have a new lease of life, perhaps in a more modest form.

LOGISTIC SUPPORT SHIP (model) *1989, BMTDS*

MISCELLANEOUS

Note: In addition to vessels listed below there are four 12 m sail training craft used for seamanship training: *Paea II, Mako II, Mango II, Haku II* (sail nos 6911-6914).

1 TRAINING VESSEL

Name	*No*	*Builders*	*Commissioned*
KAHU (ex-*Manawanui*)	A 04 (ex-A 09)	Whangarei Engineering and Construction Co Ltd	28 May 1979

Displacement, tons: 91.5 standard; 105 full load
Dimensions, feet (metres): 88 × 20 × 7.2 *(26.8 × 6.1 × 2.2)*
Main machinery: 2 Cummins KT-1150M diesels; 710 hp *(530 kW)*; 2 shafts
Speed, knots: 12. **Range, miles:** 1000 at 11 kts
Complement: 16
Radars: Navigation: Racal Decca; I band.

Comment: Same hull design as Inshore Survey Craft and Patrol Craft. Formerly a Diving Tender, now used for navigation and seamanship training. Not permanently manned.

KAHU *10/1991, Guy Toremans*

1 DIVING TENDER

Name	*No*	*Builders*	*Commissioned*
MANAWANUI (ex-*Star Perseus*)	A 09	Cochrane, Selby	May 1979

Displacement, tons: 911 full load
Dimensions, feet (metres): 143 × 31.2 × 10.5 *(43.6 × 9.5 × 3.2)*
Main machinery: 2 Caterpillar diesels; 1130 hp *(843 kW)*; 2 shafts; bow thruster
Speed, knots: 10.7. **Range, miles:** 5000 at 10 kts
Complement: 24 (2 officers)

Comment: North Sea Oil Rig Diving support vessel commissioned into the RNZN on 5 April 1988. Completed conversion in December 1988 and has replaced the previous ship of the same name which proved to be too small for the role. Equipment includes two Phantom HDX remote-controlled submersibles, a decompression chamber (to 250 ft), wet diving bell and 13 ton crane. Fitted with Inmarsat.

MANAWANUI *10/1991, John Mortimer*

RESEARCH VESSEL

Note: Research ship *Rapuhia* does not belong to the RNZN.

Name	*No*	*Builders*	*Commissioned*
TUI (ex-USS *Charles H Davis, T-AGOR 5*)	A 05	Christy Corporation, Sturgeon Bay, Wis.	25 Jan 1963

Displacement, tons: 1050 light; 1380 full load
Dimensions, feet (metres): 208.9 × 40 × 15.3 *(63.7 × 12.2 × 4.7)*
Main machinery: Diesel-electric; 2 Caterpillar D398 V12 diesels; 1500 hp *(1.12 MW)*; 2 generators; 1 twin motor; 1000 hp *(746 kW)*; 1 shaft; bow thruster; 175 hp *(130 kW)*
Speed, knots: 12. **Range, miles:** 12 000 at 12 kts
Complement: 45 (5 officers, 15 scientists)

Comment: Oceanographic research ship. Laid down on 15 June 1961, launched on 30 June 1962. On loan from the USA since 10 August 1970. Commissioned in the RNZN on 11 September 1970. Operates for NZ Defence Scientific Establishment on acoustic research. Port after gallows removed—gallows at stern—cable reels on quarterdeck and amidships—light cable-laying gear over bow. Ferranti FMS 15/2 towed sonar array for trial 1989-91. Fitted with Inmarsat.

TUI *10/1991, John Mortimer*

AUXILIARIES

Note: In addition to the two tugs listed below, there is a floating crane *Hikinui* acquired in 1988. Has a 100 ton lift.

ARATAKI (ex-*Aorangi*) A 10

Displacement, tons: 170 full load
Dimensions, feet (metres): 83 × 25 × 9.9 *(25.3 × 7.6 × 3)*
Main machinery: Ruston 6 ARM diesel; 1100 hp *(821 kW)*; 1 shaft; bow thruster
Speed, knots: 12

Comment: Bollard pull, 16.3 tons. Purchased in November 1984 from Timaru Harbour Board by the RNZFA to replace previous tug of same name. Based at Devonport, Auckland. May be replaced.

ARATAKI *10/1991, John Mortimer*

WAITANGI

Displacement, tons: 410 full load
Dimensions, feet (metres): 105 × 28 × 14.6 *(32 × 8.5 × 4.5)*
Main machinery: 2 Veiten diesels; 1720 hp(m) *(1.3 MW)*; 2 shafts
Speed, knots: 12. **Range, miles:** 2500 at 12 kts
Complement: 4

Comment: Bollard pull, 21 tons. Leased from Northland Harbour Board and still wears NHB colours. Lease renewed in 1991.

WAITANGI *10/1991, van Ginderen Collection*

NICARAGUA

Headquarters' Appointment

Head of Navy:
Major Manuel Rivas Guatemala

Personnel

1992: 1200 officers and men

General

All craft operated by Marina de Guerra Sandinista. Pennant numbers: odd—Atlantic; even—Pacific. Only the Zhuk and Yevgenya classes were operational in 1991.

Ports

Corinto, Puerto Cabezas, El Bluff, San Juan del Sur

Mercantile Marine

Lloyd's Register of Shipping:
25 vessels of 5088 tons gross

DELETIONS

1988 *P 20, P 22, GC 9*
1989 2 Zhuk class, *Yevgenya 503*
1990 2 Kimjin class

3 Ex-SOVIET YEVGENYA CLASS (MINEHUNTERS—INSHORE)

501 508 510

Displacement, tons: 77 standard; 90 full load
Dimensions, feet (metres): 80.7 × 18 × 4.9 *(24.6 × 5.5 × 1.5)*
Main machinery: 2 diesels; 400 hp(m) *(294 kW)*; 2 shafts
Speed, knots: 11. **Range, miles:** 300 at 10 kts
Complement: 10
Guns: 2 USSR 25 mm/80 (twin).
Radars: Surface search/navigation: Don 2; I band.
Sonars: A small sonar is lifted over stern on crane.

Comment: Transferred in 1984 and 1986 via Algeria and Cuba. All four may have refitted in Cuba in 1987-88 but one then sunk in the hurricane of 1989 and was subsequently scrapped. Have GRP hulls. Tripod mast. Used as patrol craft.

YEVGENYA Class *1987*

4 Ex-SOVIET K8 CLASS (MINESWEEPING BOATS)

500 502 504 506

Displacement, tons: 26 full load
Dimensions, feet (metres): 55.4 × 10.5 × 3.9 *(16.9 × 3.2 × 1.2)*
Main machinery: 2 diesels; 300 hp(m) *(220 kW)*; 2 shafts
Speed, knots: 18. **Range, miles:** 300 at 10 kts
Complement: 6
Guns: 2 USSR 14.5 mm (twin) MGs.

Comment: Transferred in 1984. Built in Poland in late 1950s. Non-operational in 1991.

9 Ex-NORTH KOREAN SIN HUNG CLASS

400 402-408 410

Displacement, tons: 40 full load
Dimensions, feet (metres): 72.2 × 11 × 5.5 *(22 × 3.4 × 1.7)*
Main machinery: 2 diesels; 2400 hp(m) *(1.76 MW)*; 2 shafts
Speed, knots: 40
Guns: 4 USSR 14.5 mm (2 twin) MGs.

Comment: Two transferred June 1984, one in August 1988, five in December 1988, and two in 1989. Torpedo tubes have been removed. One deleted so far. Non-operational in 1991.

2 Ex-NORTH KOREAN KIMJIN CLASS

306 308

Displacement, tons: 25 full load
Dimensions, feet (metres): 66.6 × 11 × 5.5 *(20.3 × 3.4 × 1.7)*
Main machinery: 2 diesels; 2400 hp(m) *(1.76 MW)*; 2 shafts
Speed, knots: 42. **Range, miles:** 220 at 20 kts
Complement: 10
Guns: 4 USSR 14.5 mm (2 twin) MGs.

Comment: A smaller version of the Sin Hung class transferred in the early 1980s, causing some confusion over numbers. Non-operational in 1991.

8 Ex-SOVIET ZHUK CLASS

304 305 307 309 311 313 315 317

Displacement, tons: 50 full load
Dimensions, feet (metres): 75.4 × 17 × 6.2 *(23 × 5.2 × 1.9)*
Main machinery: 2 M50 F-4 diesels; 2400 hp(m) *(1.76 MW)*; 2 shafts
Speed, knots: 30. **Range, miles:** 1100 at 15 kts
Complement: 17
Guns: 4 USSR 14.5 mm (2 twin) MGs.
Radars: Surface search: Spin Trough; I band.

Comment: First transferred April 1982, having previously been sent to Algeria in May 1981. Second transferred 24 July 1983, third in 1984, two more early 1986 and three in late 1986/early 1987 via Cuba. Two more of this class were transferred via Cuba in December 1989 to replace two sunk in the hurricane of October 1989.

ZHUK 304 *9/1987*

2 DABUR CLASS

231 235

Displacement, tons: 39 full load
Dimensions, feet (metres): 64.9 × 18 × 5.8 *(19.8 × 5.5 × 1.8)*
Main machinery: 2 GM 12V-71TA; 840 hp *(626 kW)* sustained; 2 shafts
Speed, knots: 19. **Range, miles:** 450 at 13 kts
Complement: 6
Guns: 2 Oerlikon 20 mm. 2 Browning 12.7 mm (twin) MGs.

Comment: Delivered by Israel April 1978 (first pair), May 1978 (second pair). One lost by gunfire in 1985; a second was severely damaged in 1987 and has been deleted. Original armament may have been replaced by Soviet 14.5 mm MGs. Non-operational in 1991.

DABUR Class *5/1989*

2 FRENCH VEDETTE TYPE

300 **302**

Displacement, tons: 57 full load
Dimensions, feet (metres): 92.5 × 17.1 × 5.2 *(28.2 × 5.2 × 1.6)*
Main machinery: 2 Poyaud 520V 12 M25 diesels; 1520 hp(m) *(1.12 MW)*; 2 shafts
Speed, knots: 24. **Range, miles:** 800 at 15 kts
Guns: 2 USSR 14.5 mm (twin) MGs.

Comment: Built by Ch N de l'Esterel. Ordered December 1981 and completed 24 June 1983. Oerlikon 20 mm replaced by Soviet MG. Non-operational in 1991.

VEDETTE 302 *1987*

2 EL TUYACAN CLASS

301 **303**

Comment: 105 ft ex-transport craft taken over and used as Presidential yachts. Fitted with twin 37 mm/63 guns. Probably now hulks without propulsion.

GC 301 *5/1988*

NIGERIA

Headquarters' Appointments

Chief of the Naval Staff:
Vice Admiral Dan-Preston Omatsola
Chief of Personnel:
Commodore S Saidu
Chief of Logistics:
Rear Admiral C O Kaja

Diplomatic Representation

Naval Adviser in Delhi:
Captain W O Arokodare
Naval Adviser in London:
Commander J M Ajayi

Personnel

(a) 1992: 5400 (550 officers)
(b) Voluntary service

Bases

Apapa—Lagos: Western Naval Command; Dockyard (Wilmot Point, Victoria Island, Lagos)
Calabar: Eastern Naval Command (Naval schools at Lagos, Port Harcourt, Apapa (NNS *Quorra*) and Calabar)
Okemimi, Port Harcourt

Prefix to Ships' Names

NNS

Strength of the Fleet (includes Coast Guard which are naval manned and controlled)

Type	*Active*
Frigates	2
Corvettes	3
Fast Attack Craft—Missile	6
Large Patrol Craft	8
Coastal Patrol Craft	41
LSTs	2
Minehunters	2
Survey Ship	1
Training Ship	1
Tugs	8

Port Security Police

A separate force of 1500 officers and men.

Mercantile Marine

Lloyd's Register of Shipping:
259 vessels of 493 288 tons gross

DELETION

Service Forces

1989 *Ribadu*

FRIGATES

1 MEKO TYPE 360

Name	*No*	*Builders*	*Laid down*	*Launched*	*Commissioned*
ARADU (ex-*Republic*)	F 89	Blohm & Voss, Hamburg	1 Dec 1978	25 Jan 1980	20 Feb 1982

Displacement, tons: 3360 full load
Dimensions, feet (metres): 412 × 49.2 × 19 (screws) *(125.6 × 15 × 5.8)*
Main machinery: CODOG; 2 RR Olympus TM3B gas turbines; 43 000 hp *(32 MW)* sustained; 2 MTU 20V 956 TB92 diesels; 10 420 hp(m) *(7.71 MW)* sustained; 2 shafts; 2 KaMeWa cp props
Speed, knots: 30.5. **Range, miles:** 6500 at 15 kts
Complement: 195 (26 officers) plus 35 midshipmen

Missiles: SSM: 8 OTO Melara/Matra Otomat Mk 1 ❶; active radar homing to 80 km *(43.2 nm)* at 0.9 Mach; warhead 210 kg.
SAM: Selenia Elsag Albatros octuple launcher ❷; 24 Aspide; semi-active radar homing to 13 km *(7 nm)* at 2.5 Mach; height envelope 15-5000 m *(49.2-16 405 ft)*; warhead 30 kg.
Guns: 1 OTO Melara 5 in *(127 mm)*/54 ❸; 85° elevation; 45 rounds/minute to 16 km *(8.7 nm)*; weight of shell 32 kg.
8 Breda Bofors 40 mm/70 (4 twin) ❹; 85° elevation; 300 rounds/minute to 12.5 km *(6.8 nm)* anti-surface; weight of shell 0.96 kg.
Torpedoes: 6—324 mm Plessey STWS-1B (2 triple) tubes ❺. 18 Whitehead A244S; anti-submarine; active/passive homing to 7 km *(3.8 nm)* at 33 kts; warhead 34 kg (shaped charge).
Depth charges: 1 rack.
Countermeasures: Decoys: 2 Breda 105 mm SCLAR 20-tubed trainable; Chaff to 5 km *(2.7 nm)*; illuminants to 12 km *(6.6 nm)*.
ESM: Decca RDL-2; intercept.
ECM: RCM-2; jammer.
Combat data systems: Sewaco-BV action data automation.
Fire control: M20 series GFCS. Signaal Vesta ASW.
Radars: Air/surface search: Plessey AWS 5 ❻; E/F band; range 155 km *(85 nm)* for 4 m² target.
Navigation: Racal Decca 1226; I band.
Fire control: Signaal STIR ❼; I/J/K band; range 140 km *(76 nm)* for 1 m² target.
Signaal WM 25 ❽; I/J band; range 46 km *(25 nm)*.
IFF/SIF: Two Decca.
Sonars: Krupp Atlas EA80; hull-mounted; active search and attack; medium frequency.

Helicopters: 1 Lynx Mk 89 ❾.

Programmes: Originally named *Republic*; renamed *Aradu* 1 November 1980.

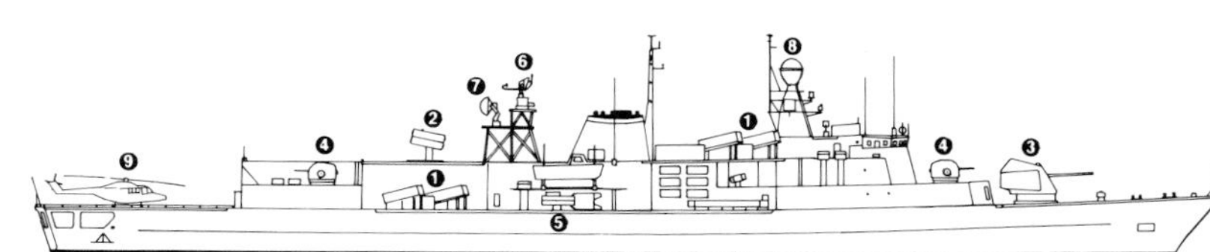

ARADU *(Scale 1 : 1 200), Ian Sturton*

ARADU *9/1987, Hartmut Ehlers*

Modernisation: May be modernised in the early 1990s if funds can be found which in 1992 seems to be unlikely.
Structure: This design shows the flexibility of the modular approach: the Argentinian Meko 360 ships have an all-gas turbine propulsion and two helicopters. This is the first class with containerised armament.
Operational: Had two groundings and a major collision in 1987. Doubtful operational status until refitted.

1 OBUMA CLASS

Name	*No*	*Builders*	*Laid down*	*Launched*	*Commissioned*
OBUMA (ex-*Nigeria*)	F 87	Wilton-Fijenoord NV, Netherlands	9 Apr 1964	12 Apr 1965	16 Sep 1965

Displacement, tons: 1724 standard; 2000 full load
Dimensions, feet (metres): 360.2 × 37 × 11.5 *(109.8 × 11.3 × 3.5)*
Main machinery: 4 MAN Burmeister & Wain V9V24/30B; 16 000 hp(m) *(11.8 MW)* sustained; 2 shafts
Speed, knots: 26. **Range, miles:** 3500 at 15 kts
Complement: 216

Guns: 2 Vickers 4 in *(102 mm)*/45 (twin); 80° elevation; 16 rounds/minute to 19 km *(10.4 nm)*; weight of shell 16 kg.
2 Bofors 40 mm/70 (fitted for but not with).
2 Oerlikon 20 mm.
Fire control: Optical director for 102 mm guns.
Radars: Surface search: Plessey AWS 4; E/F band; range 101 km *(55 nm)*.
Navigation: Decca; I band.

Helicopters: Platform for 1 Lynx Mk 89.

Programmes: Refitted at Birkenhead, 1973. Further refit completed at Schiedam October 1977.
Modernisation: Various plans to improve armament not yet realised. Squid A/S mortar non-operational and sonar removed.
Operational: Used as a training ship. Badly in need of a refit.

OBUMA *6/1983, Hartmut Ehlers*

SHIPBORNE AIRCRAFT

Numbers/Type: 3 Westland Lynx Mk 89.
Operational speed: 125 kts *(232 km/h)*.
Service ceiling: 12 500 ft *(3810 m)*.
Range: 320 nm *(590 km)*.
Role/Weapon systems: Coastal patrol and ASW helicopter; embarked and shore-based for frigate ASW and SAR duties. Sensors: RCA 5000 radar. Weapons: ASW; 2 × 244/S torpedoes. ASV; 1 × 7.62 mm door-mounted machine gun.

LAND-BASED MARITIME AIRCRAFT

Numbers/Type: 6 Dornier Do 128-6MPA.
Operational speed: 165 kts *(305 km/h)*.
Service ceiling: 32 600 ft *(9335 m)*.
Range: 790 nm *(1460 km)*.
Role/Weapon systems: Coastal surveillance and EEZ protection duties; anti-smuggling tasks. Sensors: Weather radar, cameras. Weapons: Unarmed.

Numbers/Type: 4 Fokker F27 Maritime.
Operational speed: 250 kts *(463 km/h)*.
Service ceiling: 25 000 ft *(7620 m)*.
Range: 2700 nm *(5000 km)*.
Role/Weapon systems: Long-range MR and offshore surveillance of vital oil and fishing grounds. Sensors: Search radar, MAD, provision for sonobuoys. Weapons: ASW; 2 × torpedoes, depth bombs or mines. ASV; 4 × 127 mm rockets.

Numbers/Type: 20 MBB BO 105C.
Operational speed: 113 kts *(210 km/h)*.
Service ceiling: 9845 ft *(3000 m)*.
Range: 407 nm *(754 km)*.
Role/Weapon systems: Onshore, coastal and inshore search and rescue helicopter; limited commando assault tasks and other fleet support duties. Sensors: None. Weapons: Unarmed but could be provided with machine gun or cannon pods.

LYNX

CORVETTES

Note: *Dorina* is a training hulk.

2 Mk 9 VOSPER THORNYCROFT TYPE

Name	*No*	*Builders*	*Commissioned*
ERINOMI	F 83	Vosper Thornycroft Ltd	29 Jan 1980
ENYIMIRI	F 84	Vosper Thornycroft Ltd	2 May 1980

Displacement, tons: 680 standard; 780 full load
Dimensions, feet (metres): 226 × 31.5 × 9.8 *(69 × 9.6 × 3)*
Main machinery: 4 MTU 20V 956 TB 92 diesels; 22 140 hp(m) *(16.27 MW)* sustained; 2 shafts; 2 KaMeWa cp props
Speed, knots: 27. **Range, miles:** 2200 at 14 kts
Complement: 90 (including Flag Officer)

Missiles: SAM: Short Bros Seacat triple launcher ❶; optical/radar or TV guidance to 5 km *(2.7 nm)*; warhead 10 kg; 12 missiles.
Guns: 1 OTO Melara 3 in *(76 mm)*/62 Mod 6 compact ❷; 85° elevation; 85 rounds/minute to 16 km *(8.7 nm)*; weight of shell 6 kg.
1 Breda Bofors 40 mm/70 Type 350 ❸; 85° elevation; 300 rounds/minute to 12.5 km *(6.8 nm)*; weight of shell 0.96 kg.
2 Oerlikon 20 mm ❹; 50° elevation; 800 rounds/minute to 2 km.
A/S mortars: 1 Bofors 375 mm twin launcher ❺; range 1600 m or 3600 m (depending on type of projectile).
Countermeasures: ESM: Decca Cutlass; radar warning.
Fire control: Signaal WM 20 series.
Radars: Air/surface search: Plessey AWS 2 ❻; E/F band; range 110 km *(60 nm)*.
Navigation: Racal Decca TM 1226; I band.
Fire control: Signaal WM 24 ❼; I/J band; range 46 km *(25 nm)*.
Sonars: Plessey PMS 26; lightweight; hull-mounted; active search and attack; 10 kHz.

Programmes: Ordered from Vosper Thornycroft 22 April 1975.
Operational: Much of the armament is non-operational.

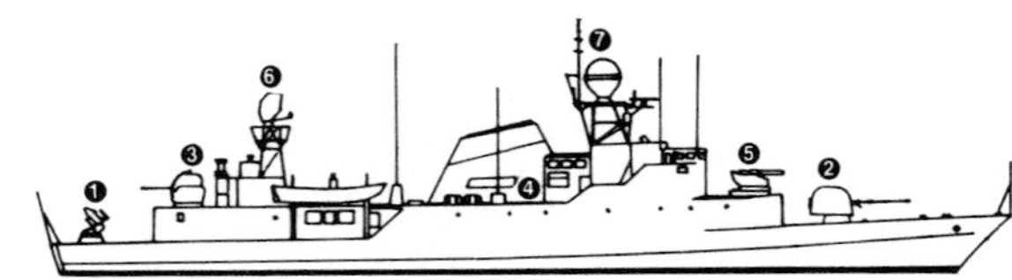

ERINOMI *(Scale 1 : 900), Ian Sturton*

ENYIMIRI *7/1985, Hartmut Ehlers*

1 Mk 3 VOSPER THORNYCROFT TYPE

Name	No	Builders	Commissioned
OTOBO	F 82	Vosper Thornycroft	Nov 1972

Displacement, tons: 580 standard; 660 full load
Dimensions, feet (metres): 202 × 31 × 11.3 *(61.6 × 9.5 × 3.5)*
Main machinery: 2 MAN VSV 24/30-B diesels; 8000 hp(m) *(5.88 MW)*; 2 shafts
Speed, knots: 22. **Range, miles:** 3000 at 14 kts
Complement: 67 (8 officers)

Guns: 1 OTO Melara 76 mm/62 or 1 Bofors 40 mm/70.
2 Bofors 40 mm/70 (aft).
Fire control: Naja optronic director. Selenia 1 PN 10 action data automation.
Radars: Air/surface search: Plessey AWS 1; E/F band; range 110 km *(60 nm)*.
Navigation: Racal Decca TM 1626; I band.

Programmes: Ordered on 28 March 1968. Refitted by Vosper Thornycroft 1975. Arrived Genoa 21 April 1988 for a two year refit by Fincantieri but this has been delayed by difficulties over payments and the ship was still there in early 1992. Originally two of the class but both fell into disrepair and *Dorina* was disarmed in April 1987 (although still exists as a hulk).
Modernisation: Being converted to an OPV for EEZ patrols. Sixty per cent of the hull and 50 per cent of the ship's systems being rebuilt or replaced. New engines. The 102 mm gun is being replaced either by an OTO Melara 76 mm or by one of the after Bofors 40 mm. The radars are also scheduled for renewal.
Structure: Fully air-conditioned.

LIGHT FORCES

Note: Two 21 m fast patrol craft reported ordered in 1990.

3 LÜRSSEN FPB-57 CLASS (FAST ATTACK CRAFT—MISSILE)

Name	No	Builders	Commissioned
EKPE	P 178	Lürssen, Vegesack	Aug 1980
DAMISA	P 179	Lürssen, Vegesack	Apr 1981
AGU	P 180	Lürssen, Vegesack	Apr 1981

Displacement, tons: 444 full load
Dimensions, feet (metres): 190.6 × 24.9 × 10.2 *(58.1 × 7.6 × 3.1)*
Main machinery: 4 MTU 16V 956 TB92 diesels; 17 700 hp(m) *(13 MW)* sustained; 2 shafts
Speed, knots: 42. **Range, miles:** 670 at 36 kts; 2000 at 16 kts
Complement: 40

Missiles: SSM: 4 OTO Melara/Matra Otomat Mk 1; active radar homing to 80 km *(43.2 nm)* at 0.9 Mach; warhead 210 kg.
Guns: 1 OTO Melara 3 in *(76 mm)*/62; 85° elevation; 60 rounds/minute to 16 km *(8.7 nm)*; weight of shell 6 kg.
2 Breda 40 mm/70 (twin); 85° elevation; 300 rounds/minute to 12.5 km *(6.8 nm)*; weight of shell 0.96 kg.
4 Emerson Electric 30 mm (2 twin); 80° elevation; 1200 rounds/minute combined to 6 km *(3.3 nm)*; weight of shell 0.35 kg.
Countermeasures: ESM: Decca RDL; radar intercept.
Radars: Surface search/navigation: Racal Decca TM 1226; I band.
Fire control: Signaal WM 28; I/J band; range 46 km *(25 nm)*.

Programmes: Ordered in late 1977. All three sailed in company for Nigeria on 21 August 1981 and completed major refit at building yard in February 1984.
Operational: Not regular sea-going but two of the class took part in the 1987 fleet exercise 'Odion'.

AGU (alongside DAMISA) *11/1983, G. Koop*

4 BROOKE MARINE TYPE (LARGE PATROL CRAFT)

Name	No	Builders	Commissioned
MAKURDI	P 167	Brooke Marine, Lowestoft	14 Aug 1974
HADEJIA	P 168	Brooke Marine, Lowestoft	14 Aug 1974
JEBBA	P 171	Brooke Marine, Lowestoft	29 Apr 1977
OGUTA	P 172	Brooke Marine, Lowestoft	29 Apr 1977

Displacement, tons: 115 standard; 143 full load
Dimensions, feet (metres): 107 × 20 × 11.5 *(32.6 × 6.1 × 3.5)*
Main machinery: 2 Paxman Ventura 12CM diesels; 3000 hp *(2.24 MW)* sustained; 2 shafts
Speed, knots: 20.5
Complement: 21 (4 officers)
Guns: 4 Emerson Electric 30 mm (2 twin). 2 rocket flare launchers.
Radars: Surface search: Racal Decca TM 1226; I band.

Comment: First pair ordered in 1971. Second pair ordered 30 October 1974. Modifications to *Makurdi* and *Hadejia* were carried out by Brooke Marine in 1981-82. This included provision of new engines and Emerlec guns. The second pair similarly refitted in Nigeria.

HADEJIA *1982, Brooke Marine*

3 COMBATTANTE IIIB CLASS (FAST ATTACK CRAFT—MISSILE)

Name	No	Builders	Commissioned
SIRI	P 181	CMN, Cherbourg	19 Feb 1981
AYAM	P 182	CMN, Cherbourg	11 June 1981
EKUN	P 183	CMN, Cherbourg	18 Sep 1981

Displacement, tons: 385 standard; 430 full load
Dimensions, feet (metres): 184 × 24.9 × 7 *(56.2 × 7.6 × 2.1)*
Main machinery: 4 MTU 16V 956 TB92 diesels; 17 700 hp(m) *(13 MW)* sustained; 2 shafts
Speed, knots: 41. **Range, miles:** 2000 at 15 kts
Complement: 42

Missiles: SSM: 4 Aerospatiale MM 38 Exocet; inertial cruise; active radar homing to 42 km *(23 nm)* at 0.9 Mach; warhead 165 kg; sea-skimmer.
Guns: 1 OTO Melara 3 in *(76 mm)*/62; 85° elevation; 60 rounds/minute to 16 km *(8.7 nm)*; weight of shell 6 kg.
2 Breda 40 mm/70 (twin); 85° elevation; 300 rounds/minute to 12.5 km *(6.8 nm)*; weight of shell 0.96 kg.
4 Emerson Electric 30 mm (2 twin); 80° elevation; 1200 rounds/minute combined to 6 km *(3.3 nm)*; weight of shell 0.35 kg.
Countermeasures: ESM: Decca RDL; radar intercept.
Fire control: Thomson-CSF Vega system. 2 CSEE Panda optical directors.
Radars: Air/surface search: Thomson-CSF Triton (TRS 3033); G band; range 33 km *(18 nm)* for 2 m^2 target.
Navigation: Racal Decca TM 1226; I band.
Fire control: Thomson-CSF Castor II (TRS 3203); I/J band; range 15 km *(8 nm)* for 1 m^2 target.

Programmes: Ordered in late 1977. Finally handed over in February 1982 after delays caused by financial problems.
Modernisation: Major refit and repairs carried out at Cherbourg from March to December 1991.

EKUN (*Siri* behind) *12/1985, Hartmut Ehlers*

4 ABEKING AND RASMUSSEN TYPE (LARGE PATROL CRAFT)

Name	No	Builders	Commissioned
ARGUNGU	P 165	Abeking & Rasmussen	Aug 1973
YOLA	P 166	Abeking & Rasmussen	Aug 1973
BRAS	P 169	Abeking & Rasmussen	Mar 1976
EPE	P 170	Abeking & Rasmussen	Mar 1976

Displacement, tons: 90
Dimensions, feet (metres): 95.1 × 18 × 5.2 *(29 × 5.5 × 1.6)*
Main machinery: 2 MTU diesels; 2200 hp(m) *(1.62 MW)*; 2 shafts
Speed, knots: 20
Complement: 25
Guns: 4 Emerson Electric 30 mm (2 twin).
Radars: Surface search: Racal Decca TM 1229; I band.

Comment: *Yola* and *Bras* rearmed in 1978, the remainder in 1982.

YOLA *8/1983, Hartmut Ehlers*

6 SIMMONEAU 500 TYPE (COASTAL PATROL CRAFT)

P 233 P 234 P 235 P 236 P 237 P 238

Displacement, tons: 22 full load
Dimensions, feet (metres): 51.8 × 15.7 × 5.9 *(15.8 × 4.8 × 1.8)*
Main machinery: 2 MTU 6V 396 TC 82 diesels; 1300 hp(m) *(956 kW)* sustained; 2 shafts
Speed, knots: 33. **Range, miles:** 375 at 25 kts
Complement: 6
Guns: 2—7.62 mm MGs (interchangeable with 20 mm if required).
Radars: Surface search: Racal Decca 976; I band.

Comment: First two commissioned October 1986, remainder by early 1987. Built by Simmoneau Fontenay-le-Comte, France. Aluminium hulls.

P 234 *1987, Simmoneau*

14 INTERMARINE TYPE (COASTAL PATROL CRAFT)

ABEOKUTA P 200
AKURE P 201
BAUCHI P 202
BENIN CITY P 203
ENUGU P 204
IKEJA P 205
ILORIN P 206
JOS P 207
KADUNA P 208
KANO P 209
MAIDUGURI P 210
MINNA P 211
OWERRI P 212
SOKOTO P 214

Displacement, tons: 22 full load
Dimensions, feet (metres): 55.1 × 14.8 × 3.3 *(16.8 × 4.5 × 1)*
Main machinery: 2 MTU 8V331 TC 82 diesels; 1740 hp(m) *(1.28 MW)* sustained; 2 waterjets
Speed, knots: 32. **Range, miles:** 400 at 28 kts
Complement: 6
Guns: 1 Oerlikon 20 mm. 2—7.62 mm (twin) MGs.

Comment: GRP hulls. Last of class delivered April 1982. Built by Intermarine, Sazana, Italy. Most are not operational and are on cradles ashore as in the picture. P 213 sank in 1984.

ENUGU *9/1987, Hartmut Ehlers*

6 DAMEN 1500 TYPE (COASTAL PATROL CRAFT)

P 227 P 228 P 229 P 230 P 231 P 232

Displacement, tons: 16 full load
Dimensions, feet (metres): 49.5 × 14.8 × 4.9 *(15.1 × 4.5 × 1.5)*
Main machinery: 2 MTU diesels; 2250 hp(m) *(1.65 MW)*; 2 shafts
Speed, knots: 34
Complement: 6
Guns: 1—7.62 mm MG.

Comment: Built by Damen, Netherlands. First three completed April 1986, second three June 1986. Aluminium hulls.

5 VAN MILL TYPE (COASTAL PATROL CRAFT)

P 215 P 216 P 217 P 218 P 219

Displacement, tons: 45 full load
Dimensions, feet (metres): 66.3 × 17.4 × 5.9 *(20.2 × 5.3 × 1.8)*
Main machinery: 3 Detroit 12V-71TA diesels; 1260 hp *(939 kW)* sustained; 3 shafts *(P 215-216)*
2 MTU diesels; 2200 hp(m) *(1.61 MW)*; 2 shafts *(P 217-220)*
Speed, knots: 35. **Range, miles:** 950 at 25 kts
Complement: 12 (2 officers)
Guns: 1 Rheinmetall 20 mm. 2—7.62 mm MGs.

Comment: Built by Van Mill, Netherlands. Completed between July 1985 and end 1986. Sixth of class given to Equatorial Guinea in June 1986.

2 WATERCRAFT P-2000 TYPE (COASTAL PATROL CRAFT)

OKRIKA P 225 **ABONNEMA** P 226

Displacement, tons: 49 full load
Dimensions, feet (metres): 68.2 × 19 × 9.8 *(20.8 × 5.8 × 3)*
Main machinery: 2 MTU 8V 396 TB93 diesels; 2180 hp(m) *(1.6 MW)* sustained; 2 shafts
Speed, knots: 33. **Range, miles:** 660 at 22 kts
Guns: 1 Rheinmetall 20 mm. 2—7.62 mm MGs.

Comment: Delayed by Watercraft's insolvency until 1988. GRP hulls.

4 SWIFTSHIPS TYPE (COASTAL PATROL CRAFT)

ISEYIN P 221
ERUWA P 222
AFIKTO P 223
ABA P 224

Displacement, tons: 36 full load
Dimensions, feet (metres): 65.6 × 18.4 × 4.9 *(20 × 5.6 × 1.5)*
Main machinery: 2 MTU 8V 396 TB93 diesels; 2180 hp(m) *(1.6 MW)* sustained; 2 shafts
Speed, knots: 32. **Range, miles:** 500 at 18 kts
Complement: 6
Guns: 1 Rheinmetall 20 mm. 2—7.62 mm MGs.

Comment: Delivered by Swiftships, USA in 1986. Aluminium hulls.

4 ROTORK SEA TRUCKS

P 239 P 240 P 241 P 242

Dimensions, feet (metres): 47.6 × 14.4 × 2.9 *(14.5 × 4.4 × 0.9)*
Main machinery: 2 MTU diesels; 600 hp(m) *(441 kW)*; 2 shafts
Speed, knots: 20
Complement: 8
Guns: 1—7.62 mm MG.

Comment: Delivered in 1986. P 242 used for survey work.

P 242 *12/1985, Hartmut Ehlers*

MINE WARFARE FORCES

2 LERICI CLASS (MINEHUNTERS/SWEEPERS)

Name	*No*	*Builders*	*Commissioned*
OHUE	M 371	Intermarine SY, Italy	28 May 1987
MARABA	M 372	Intermarine SY, Italy	25 Feb 1988

Displacement, tons: 540 full load
Dimensions, feet (metres): 167.3 × 31.5 × 9.2 *(51 × 9.6 × 2.8)*
Main machinery: 2 MTU 12V 396 TB 83 diesels; 3120 hp(m) *(2.3 MW)* sustained; 2 waterjets
Speed, knots: 15.5. **Range, miles:** 2500 at 12 kts
Complement: 50 (5 officers)
Guns: 2 Emerson Electric 30 mm (twin); 80° elevation; 1200 rounds/minute combined to 6 km *(3.3 nm)*; weight of shell 0.35 kg.
2 Oerlikon 20 mm GAM-BO1.
Countermeasures: Fitted with 2 Pluto remote-controlled submersibles, Oropesa 'O' Mis 4 and Ibis V control system.
Radars: Navigation: Racal Decca 1226; I band.
Sonars: Thomson Sintra TSM 2022; hull-mounted; mine detection; high frequency.

Comment: *Ohue* ordered in April 1983 and *Maraba* in January 1986 with an option for a third which has not been taken up. *Ohue* laid down 23 July 1984 and launched 22 November 1985, *Maraba* laid down 11 March 1985, launched 6 June 1986. GRP hulls but, unlike Italian and Malaysian versions they do not have separate hydraulic minehunting propulsion. Carry Galeazzi 2 man decompression chambers. Endurance, 14 days.

OHUE *7/1987, Marina Fraccaroli*

AMPHIBIOUS FORCES

2 FDR TYPE RO-RO 1300 (LSTs)

Name	*No*	*Builders*	*Commissioned*
AMBE	LST 1312	Howaldtswerke, Hamburg	Apr 1979
OFIOM	LST 1313	Howaldtswerke, Hamburg	July 1979

Displacement, tons: 1470 standard; 1860 full load
Dimensions, feet (metres): 285.4 × 45.9 × 7.5 *(87 × 14 × 2.3)*
Main machinery: 2 MTU 16V956 TB92 diesels; 8850 hp(m) *(6.5 MW)* sustained; 2 shafts
Speed, knots: 17. **Range, miles:** 5000 at 10 kts
Complement: 56 (6 officers)
Military lift: 460 tons and 220 troops long haul; 540 troops or 1000 troops seated short haul; can carry 5—40 ton tanks
Guns: 1 Breda 40 mm/70; 85° elevation; 300 rounds/minute to 12.5 km *(6.8 nm)*; weight of shell 0.96 kg.
2 Oerlikon 20 mm.
Radars: Navigation: Racal Decca 1226; I band.

Comment: Ordered September 1976. Built to a design prepared for the FGN. Have a 19 m bow ramp and a 4 m stern ramp. Reported that *Ambe's* bow ramp is welded shut.

AMBE *5/1986, Michael D. J. Lennon*

SURVEY SHIP

Name	*No*	*Builders*	*Commissioned*
LANA	A 498	Brooke Marine, Lowestoft	15 July 1976

Displacement, tons: 800 standard; 1088 full load
Dimensions, feet (metres): 189 × 37.5 × 12 *(57.8 × 11.4 × 3.7)*
Main machinery: 4 Lister-Blackstone ERS-8M diesels; 2640 hp *(1.97 MW)*; 2 shafts
Speed, knots: 16. **Range, miles:** 4500 at 12 kts
Complement: 52 (12 officers)
Guns: 2 Oerlikon 20 mm.
Radars: Navigation: Racal Decca; I band.

Comment: Ordered in late 1973, laid down 5 April 1974, launched 4 March 1976. Sister to Royal Navy Bulldog class.

LANA *8/1983, Hartmut Ehlers*

SERVICE FORCES

Note: Two 46 ft pusher tugs delivered by Damen in 1986 for use in Lagos.

3 TUGS

Displacement, tons: 200
Dimensions, feet (metres): 90.5 × 25.5 × 11.3 *(27.6 × 7.8 × 3.5)*
Main machinery: 2 GM diesels; 2400 hp *(1.79 MW)*; 2 shafts
Speed, knots: 12.5

Comment: Built by Alblas (Krimpen A/D, Rijn). First launched 9 October 1981.

1 TUG

Name	*No*	*Builders*	*Commissioned*
COMMANDER APAYI JOE	A 499	SY de Wiel BV, Asperen, Netherlands	Sep 1983

Displacement, tons: 310 full load
Dimensions, feet (metres): 76.1 × 23.6 × 9.5 *(23.2 × 7.2 × 2.9)*
Main machinery: 2 MAN diesels; 1510 hp(m) *(1.11 MW)*; 2 shafts

Comment: A second of class *Commander Rudolf* was not paid for and therefore not delivered.

COMMANDER APAYI JOE *11/1983, Hartmut Ehlers*

2 TUGS

DOLPHIN MIRA **DOLPHIN RIMA**

Comment: Based at Apapa.

1 TRAINING SHIP

Name	*No*	*Builders*	*Commissioned*
RUWAN YARO (ex-*Ogina Brereton*)	A 497	Van Lent, Netherlands	1976

Displacement, tons: 400 full load
Dimensions, feet (metres): 144.6 × 26.2 × 12.8 *(44.2 × 8 × 3.9)*
Main machinery: 2 Deutz SBA 12M528 diesels; 3000 hp(m) *(2.2 MW)*; 1 shaft; cp prop; bow thruster
Speed, knots: 17. **Range, miles:** 3000 at 15 kts
Complement: 42 (11 midshipmen)
Radars: Navigation: Racal Decca TM 1626; I band.

Comment: Originally built in 1975 as a yacht. Used as navigational training vessel.

RUWAN YARO *12/1983, Hartmut Ehlers*

56 LAUNCHES

Comment: Includes 22 of 7 m, eight of 8 m, two 10 m personnel launches, fifteen 22 ft work boats and five 18 ft work boats, all by Fairey Allday Marine Ltd, UK and four 8.2 m whalers by Cheverton Work-Boats, UK.

POLICE CRAFT

Note: Mostly used to patrol Niger River and Lake Chad. In addition to the craft listed there are some 60 light launches and five small hovercraft, many of which are non-operational.

1 P 1200 TYPE (COASTAL PATROL CRAFT)

Displacement, tons: 9.5
Dimensions, feet (metres): 39 × 13.4 × 3.5 *(11.9 × 4.1 × 1.1)*
Main machinery: 2 Detroit 8V71 TI diesels; 460 hp *(343 kW)* sustained; 2 shafts
Speed, knots: 27. **Range, miles:** 240 at 25 kts

Comment: GRP hull. Delivered February 1981 by Watercraft Ltd, Shoreham, Sussex.

P 1200 Type *Watercraft*

1 FAIREY TRACKER

Displacement, tons: 31
Dimensions, feet (metres): 63.1 × 16.3 × 4.8 *(19.3 × 5 × 1.5)*
Main machinery: 2 diesels; 1290 hp *(962 kW)*; 2 shafts
Speed, knots: 24. **Range, miles:** 650 at 20 kts
Complement: 11
Guns: 1 Oerlikon 20 mm.

Comment: Delivered February 1978 for fishery protection.

8 VOSPER THORNYCROFT TYPE (COASTAL PATROL CRAFT)

Displacement, tons: 15
Dimensions, feet (metres): 34 × 10 × 2.8 *(10.4 × 3.1 × 0.9)*
Main machinery: 2 diesels; 290 hp *(216 kW)*; 2 shafts
Speed, knots: 19
Complement: 6
Guns: 1—12.7 mm MG.

Comment: Ordered for Nigerian Police in March 1971, completed 1971-72. GRP hulls.

NORWAY

Headquarters' Appointments

Inspector General Royal Norwegian Navy:
Rear Admiral K A Prytz
Commander Naval Material Command:
Rear Admiral H F Neegaard
Chief of Naval Staff (Defence HQ):
Commodore R H Christensen
Inspector of Coast Artillery:
Commodore K M Aam
Commodore Coast Fleet and Sea Training:
Commodore H K Svensholt

Diplomatic Representation

Defence Attaché in Bonn:
Lieutenant Colonel Odd I Ruud (A)
Defence Attaché in Helsinki:
Lieutenant Colonel Wegger Strømmen (A)
Defence Attaché in London:
Lieutenant Colonel L H Finstad (A)
Defence Attaché in Moscow:
Lieutenant Colonel Brynjar Nymo (A)
Defence Attaché in Ottawa:
Lieutenant Colonel Jon Reidar Holte
Defence Attaché in Paris:
Lieutenant Colonel Per Harildstad (AF)
Defence Attaché in Stockholm:
Captain Werner Johansen
Defence Attaché in Vienna:
Lieutenant General E Schibbye (AF)
Defence Attaché in Washington:
Major General Olav A Aamoth (AF)

Personnel

(a) 1992: 9000 officers and ratings (including 2000 Coast Artillery)
(b) 12-15 months' national service

Home Guard

Total of 90 000 men and women. The naval section mans some 400 craft including eight Tjeld class and 2 LCTs.

Naval Bases

Karl Johans Vern (Horten)—HQ Eastern District. Haakonsvern (Bergen)—HQ Western District and Major Base
Ramsund (Harstad) and Olavsvern (Tromsø)
Laksevag—Submarine Repair and Maintenance

Air Force Squadrons (see *Shipborne* and *Land-based Aircraft* section)

Aircraft (Squadron)	*Location*	*Duties*
Sea King Mk 43 (330)	Bodø, Banak, Sola, Ørland	SAR
Orion P3B (333)	Andøya	LRMP
Lynx (337)	Coast Guard vessels/ Bardufoss	MP
Bell UH-1D (719 & 720)	Bodø, Rygge	Army Transport

Prefix to Ships' Names

KNM (Naval)
K/V (Coast Guard)

Coast Artillery

Numerous coastal forts—all with co-ordinated radar stations and guns and some with torpedo tubes and/or controlled minefields. Some are also equipped with RB 70 SAM missiles and 120 mm guns.

Coast Guard

Inspector:
Commodore T M Nikoliaisen

Founded April 1977 with operational command held by Norwegian Defence Command. Main bases at Sortland (North) and Haakonsvern (South).

Strength of the Fleet

Type	*Active*	*Building (Projected)*
Submarines—Coastal	12	—
Frigates	5	—
Corvettes	2	—
Fast Attack Craft—Missile	30	(12)
Minelayers	3	—
Minesweepers/Hunters	8	9 (1)
LCTs	5	—
Depot Ship	1	—
Auxiliaries and District Patrol Craft	21	1
Royal Yacht	1	—
Tugs	2	—
Coast Guard Vessels	13	—
Survey Vessels	11	—

Mercantile Marine

Lloyd's Register of Shipping:
2577 vessels of 23 585 661 tons gross

DELETIONS

Submarines

1989 *Kya* (to Denmark)
1991 *Utsira* (old), *Utstein* (old)
1992 *Kaura, Kinn*

Light Forces

1990-91 *Sev, Hval, Laks, Knurr, Skrei, Hai, Lyr, Delfin*
1991-92 *Glimt, Arg, Brann, Tross, Traust, Brott, Odd, Rokk*

Amphibious Forces

1991 *Kvalsund, Raftsund*

Miscellaneous

1990 *Hydrograf*

PENNANT LIST

Note: Ships and craft with three letters preceding their numbers are non-combatant naval district craft.

Submarines

S 300 Ula
S 301 Utsira
S 302 Utstein
S 303 Utvaer
S 304 Uthaug
S 305 Uredd
S 306 Skolpen
S 308 Stord
S 309 Svenner
S 314 Sklinna
S 318 Kobben
S 319 Kunna

Frigates and Corvettes

F 300 Oslo
F 301 Bergen
F 302 Trondheim
F 303 Stavanger
F 304 Narvik
F 310 Sleipner
F 311 Aeger

Minesweepers/Hunter

M 312 Sira
M 313 Tana
M 314 Alta
M 316 Vosso
M 317 Glomma
M 331 Tista
M 332 Kvina
M 334 Utla
M 340 Oksøy
M 341 Karmøy
M 342 Maløy
M 343 Hinnøy
M 350 Alta
M 351 Otra
M 352 Rauma
M 353 Orkla
M 354 Glomma

Minelayers

N 51 Borgen
N 52 Vidar
N 53 Vale

Light Forces

P 358 Hessa
P 359 Vigra
P 961 Blink
P 963 Skjold
P 964 Trygg
P 965 Kjekk
P 966 Djerv
P 967 Skudd
P 969 Steil
P 972 Hvass
P 977 Brask
P 979 Gnist
P 980 Snögg
P 981 Rapp
P 982 Snar
P 983 Rask
P 984 Kvikk
P 985 Kjapp
P 986 Hauk
P 987 Ørn
P 988 Terne
P 989 Tjeld
P 990 Skarv
P 991 Teist
P 992 Jo
P 993 Lom
P 994 Stegg
P 995 Falk
P 996 Ravn
P 997 Gribb
P 998 Geir
P 999 Erle

Amphibious Forces

L 4502 Reinøysund
L 4503 Sørøysund
L 4504 Maursund
L 4505 Rotsund
L 4506 Borgsund

Auxiliaries

A 530 Horten
A 531 Sarpen
A 532 Draug
HSD 15 Krøttøy
N 533 Norge
NSD 35 Rotvaer
ØSD 1 Welding
ØSD 2 Wisting
ØSD 11 Oscarsborg
HSD 12 Garsøy
ØSD 14 Folden
ØSD 15 Nordkep
RSD 20 Foracs II
RSD 21 FKS I
RSD 22 Fjoly
RSD 23 Brimse
RSD 28 Rogin
TRSD 4 Karlsøy
TSD 5 Tautra
VSD 1 Vernøy
VSD 2 Kvarven
VSD 4 Torpen
VSD 7 Samson

Coast Guard

W 300 Nornen
W 301 Farm
W 302 Heimdal
W 313 Malene Østervold
W 314 Stålbas
W 315 Nordsjøbas
W 316 Volstad Jr.
W 317 Lafjord
W 318 Garpeskjaer
W 319 Grimsholm
W 320 Nordkapp
W 321 Senja
W 322 Andenes

SUBMARINES

6 ULA CLASS (TYPE P 6071 (Ex-210))

Name	No	Builders	Laid down	Launched	Commissioned
ULA	S 300	Thyssen Nordseewerke, Emden	29 Jan 1987	28 July 1988	27 Apr 1989
UREDD	S 305	Thyssen Nordseewerke, Emden	23 June 1988	22 Sep 1989	3 May 1990
UTVAER	S 303	Thyssen Nordseewerke, Emden	8 Dec 1988	19 Apr 1990	1 Nov 1990
UTHAUG	S 304	Thyssen Nordseewerke, Emden	15 June 1989	18 Oct 1990	7 May 1991
UTSTEIN	S 302	Thyssen Nordseewerke, Emden	6 Dec 1989	May 1991	14 Nov 1991
UTSIRA	S 301	Thyssen Nordseewerke, Emden	15 June 1990	Nov 1991	May 1992

Displacement, tons: 1040 surfaced; 1150 dived
Dimensions, feet (metres): 193.6 × 17.7 × 15.1 *(59 × 5.4 × 4.6)*
Main machinery: Diesel-electric; 2 MTU 16V 396 SB 83 diesels; 2700 hp(m) *(1.98 MW)* sustained; 1 Siemens motor; 6000 hp(m) *(4.41 MW)*; 1 shaft
Speed, knots: 11 surfaced; 23 dived
Range, miles: 5000 at 8 kts
Complement: 18-20 (3 officers)

Torpedoes: 8—21 in *(533 mm)* bow tubes. 14 AEG DM 2A3 Seeal; dual purpose; wire-guided; active/passive homing to 28 km *(15 nm)* at 23 kts; 13 km *(7 nm)* at 35 kts; warhead 260 kg.
Countermeasures: ESM: Racal Sealion; radar warning.
Fire control: Kongsberg MSI-90(U); command and weapon control system.
Radars: Surface search: Thomson-CSF Calypso III; I band.
Sonars: Krupp Atlas CSU83; active/passive intercept search and attack; medium frequency.
Thomson Sintra; flank array; passive; low frequency.

Programmes: Contract signed on 30 September 1982. This was a joint West German/Norwegian effort known as Project 210 in Germany and is the most expensive ever undertaken by the Norwegian Navy. Although final assembly was at Thyssen a number of pressure hull sections were provided by Norway.

UTHAUG *6/1991, Stefan Terzibaschitsch*

Structure: Diving depth, 250 m *(820 ft)*. The basic command and weapon control systems are Norwegian, the attack sonar is German but the flank array, based on piezoelectric polymer antenna technology, has been developed in France and substantially reduces flow noise. Calzoni Trident modular system of non penetrating masts has been installed.

UTHAUG *6/1991, Antonio Moreno*

6 KOBBEN CLASS (TYPE 207)

Name	No	Builders	Laid down	Launched	Commissioned
SKLINNA	S 314 (ex-S 305)	Rheinstahl-Nordseewerke, Emden	17 Aug 1965	21 Jan 1966	27 May 1966
SKOLPEN	S 306	Rheinstahl-Nordseewerke, Emden	1 Nov 1965	24 Mar 1966	17 Aug 1966
STORD	S 308	Rheinstahl-Nordseewerke, Emden	1 Apr 1966	2 Sep 1966	14 Feb 1967
SVENNER	S 309	Rheinstahl-Nordseewerke, Emden	8 Sep 1966	27 Jan 1967	12 June 1967
KOBBEN	S 318	Rheinstahl-Nordseewerke, Emden	9 Dec 1963	25 Apr 1964	17 Aug 1964
KUNNA	S 319	Rheinstahl-Nordseewerke, Emden	3 Mar 1964	16 July 1964	29 Oct 1964

Displacement, tons: 370; 459 (modernised) standard; 435; 524 (modernised) dived
Dimensions, feet (metres): 148.9 (155.5, modernised) × 15 × 14 *(45.4 (47.4) × 4.6 × 4.3)*
Main machinery: Diesel-electric; 2 MTU 12V 493 AZ80 GA31L diesels; 1200 hp(m) *(880 kW)* sustained; 1 motor; 1800 hp(m) *(1.32 MW)* sustained; 1 shaft
Speed, knots: 12 surfaced; 18 dived. **Range, miles:** 5000 at 8 kts (snorting)
Complement: 18 (17 *Svenner*) (5 officers)

Torpedoes: 8—21 in *(533 mm)* bow tubes. 8 mix of (a) FFV Type 61; anti-surface; wire-guided; passive homing to 25 km *(13.7 nm)* at 45 kts; warhead 240 kg and (b) Honeywell NT37C; dual purpose; wire-guided; active/passive homing to 20 km *(10.8 nm)* at 35 kts; warhead 150 kg.
Countermeasures: ESM: Radar warning.
Fire control: Kongsberg MSI-90(U) TFCS.
Radars: Surface search: Thomson-CSF Calypso II; I band.
Sonars: Krupp Atlas or Simrad; passive search and attack; medium/high frequency.

Programmes: It was announced in July 1959 that the USA and Norway would share equally the cost of these submarines. They are a development of IKL Type 205 (West German U4-U8) with increased diving depth. *Kobben* was the name of the first submarine in the Royal Norwegian Navy. Commissioned on 28 November 1909.
Modernisation: These six modernised at Urivale Shipyard, Bergen, to a similar standard to the three sold to Denmark including lengthening and new communications, navigation and fire control equipment. The remainder phased out with some taken on by the USN for trials. Modernisation completion programme was S 314 January 1989, S 306 October 1989, S 308 August 1990, S 318 May 1991, S 319 December 1991, S 309 April 1992.

KOBBEN *5/1988, W. Sartori*

Structure: Diving depth, 200 m *(650 ft)*. *Svenner*'s second periscope for COs training operations is a metre longer.

Sales: *Utvaer, Uthaug* and *Kya* sold to Denmark and modernised to the same standard as the Norwegian programme. *Kaura* has also been sold to Denmark to be cannibalised to repair *Saelen*, which was flooded after conversion.

FRIGATES

5 OSLO CLASS

Name	No	Builders	Laid down	Launched	Commissioned
OSLO	F 300	Marinens Hovedverft, Horten	1963	17 Jan 1964	29 Jan 1966
BERGEN	F 301	Marinens Hovedverft, Horten	1964	23 Aug 1965	15 June 1967
TRONDHEIM	F 302	Marinens Hovedverft, Horten	1963	4 Sep 1964	2 June 1966
STAVANGER	F 303	Marinens Hovedverft, Horten	1965	4 Feb 1966	1 Dec 1967
NARVIK	F 304	Marinens Hovedverft, Horten	1964	8 Jan 1965	30 Nov 1966

Displacement, tons: 1450 standard; 1745 full load
Dimensions, feet (metres): 317 × 36.8 × 18 (screws) *(96.6 × 11.2 × 5.5)*
Main machinery: 2 Babcock & Wilcox boilers; 600 psi *(42.18 kg/cm sq)*; 850°F *(454°C)*; 1 De Laval Ljungstrom PN20 turbine; 20 000 hp(m) *(14.7 MW)*; 1 shaft
Speed, knots: 25+. **Range, miles:** 4500 at 15 kts
Complement: 150 (11 officers)

Missiles: SSM: 4 Kongsberg Penguin Mk 2 ❶; IR homing to 27 km *(14.6 nm)* at 0.8 Mach; warhead 120 kg.
SAM: Raytheon NATO RIM-7M Sea Sparrow Mk 29 octuple launcher ❷; semi-active radar homing to 14.6 km *(8 nm)* at 2.5 Mach; warhead 39 kg; 24 cell magazine.
Guns: 2 US 3 in *(76 mm)*/50 Mk 33 (twin) ❸; 85° elevation; 50 rounds/minute to 12.8 km *(7 nm)*; weight of shell 6 kg.
1 Bofors 40 mm/70 ❹; 90° elevation; 300 rounds/minute to 12 km *(6.6 nm)*; weight of shell 0.96 kg
2 Rheinmetall 20 mm/20 (not in all); 55° elevation; 1000 rounds/minute to 2 km.
Torpedoes: 6—324 mm US Mk 32 (2 triple) tubes ❺. Marconi Stingray; anti-submarine; active/passive homing to 11 km *(5.9 nm)* at 45 kts; warhead 32 kg (shaped charge); depth to 750 m *(2460 ft)*.
A/S mortars: Kongsberg Terne III 6-tubed trainable ❻; range pattern from 400-5000 m; warhead 70 kg. Automatic reloading in 40 seconds.
Mines: Laying capability.
Countermeasures: Decoys: 2 Chaff launchers.
ESM/ECM: Argo intercept and jammer.
Combat data systems: NFT MSI-3100 action data automation; capability for Link 11 and 14.
Fire control: TVT 300 tracker ❼.
Radars: Air search: Thomson-CSF DRBV 22 ❽; D band; range 366 km *(200 nm)*.
Surface search: Racal Decca TM 1226 ❾; I band.
Fire control: NobelTech 9LV 200 Mk 2 ❿; I band (includes search).
Raytheon Mk 91 ⓫, I/J band (for Sea Sparrow) (may be replaced by Mk 23 TAS).
Navigation: Decca; I band.
Sonars: Thomson Sintra/Simrad TSM 2633; combined hull and VDS; active search and attack; medium frequency.
Simrad Terne III; active attack; high frequency.

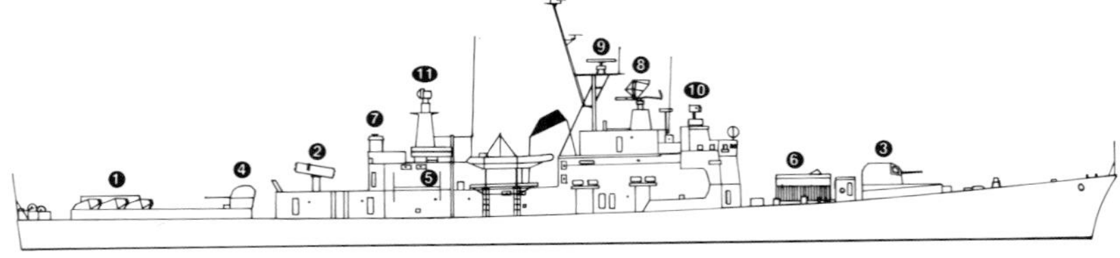
TRONDHEIM *(Scale 1 : 900), Ian Sturton*

BERGEN *11/1991, Antonio Moreno*

Programmes: Built under the five-year naval construction programme approved by the Norwegian Storting (Parliament) late in 1960. Although all the ships of this class were constructed in the Norwegian Naval Dockyard, half the cost was borne by Norway and the other half by the USA. The hull and propulsion design of these ships is based on that of the Dealey class destroyer escorts (now deleted) of the US Navy, but considerably modified to suit Norwegian requirements.

Modernisation: All ships modernised with improvements in weapons control and habitability; new countermeasures equipment includes two Chaff launchers; Spherion TSM-2633 sonar (with VDS) (a joint Thomson Sintra/Simrad-Subsea (Norway) project); the after 76 mm mounting replaced by a Bofors 40 mm/70; and MSI 3100 action data automation. Modernisation completion programme: F 302 30 November 1987, F 304 21 October 1988, F 303 5 June 1989, F 301 4 April 1990, F 300 1 February 1991. A replacement is required for the Mk 91 fire control radar; the preferred option is the Mk 23 TAS.

STAVANGER *3/1991, J. L. M. van der Burg*

CORVETTES

2 SLEIPNER CLASS

Name	*No*	*Builders*	*Laid down*	*Launched*	*Commissioned*
SLEIPNER	F 310	Nylands Verksted Shipyard	1963	9 Nov 1963	29 Apr 1965
AEGER	F 311	Akers, Oslo	1964	24 Sep 1965	31 Mar 1967

Displacement, tons: 600 standard; 780 full load
Dimensions, feet (metres): 227.5 × 27.2 × 9 *(69.4 × 8.3 × 2.7)*
Main machinery: 4 Maybach MTU diesels; 8800 hp(m) *(6.47 MW)*; 2 shafts
Speed, knots: 20+
Complement: 63

Guns: 1 US 3 in *(76 mm)*/50 Mk 34; 85° elevation; 50 rounds/minute to 12.8 km *(7 nm)*; weight of shell 6 kg.
1 Bofors 40 mm/70; 90° elevation; 300 rounds/minute to 12 km *(6.6 nm)*; weight of shell 0.96 kg.
Torpedoes: 6—324 mm US Mk 32 (2 triple) tubes. Honeywell Mk 46; anti-submarine; active/passive homing to 11 km *(5.9 nm)* at 40 kts; warhead 44 kg. May be replaced by Stingray.
A/S mortars: Kongsberg Terne III 6-tubed trainable; range pattern from 400-5000 m; warhead 70 kg. Automatic reloading in 40 seconds.
Mines: Laying capability.
Fire control: 2 TVT-300 optronic GFCS.
Radars: Surface search: Racal Decca TM 1229; I band.
Navigation: Decca 202; I band.
Sonars: Thomson/Simrad TSM 2633 Spherion; hull-mounted; active search and attack; 11, 12 or 13 kHz.
Simrad Terne III; active attack; high frequency.

Programmes: Under the five-year programme only two instead of the originally planned five corvettes were built.
Modernisation: Improved Terne and replacement main sonar; F 310 completed 22 August 1988, F 311 on 2 May 1989.
Operational: Used as training ships.

SLEIPNER *11/1991, Walter Sartori*

SHIPBORNE AIRCRAFT

Numbers/Type: 6 Westland Lynx Mk 86.
Operational speed: 125 kts *(232 km/h)*.
Service ceiling: 12 500 ft *(3810 m)*.
Range: 320 nm *(590 km)*.
Role/Weapon systems: Helicopter, operated by Air Force on behalf of the Coast Guard for fishery protection, offshore oil protection and SAR; embarked in CG vessels and shore-based. Sensors: Search radar, ESM. Weapons: Generally unarmed.

LYNX

LAND-BASED MARITIME AIRCRAFT

Numbers/Type: 2/4 Lockheed P-3B/C Orion.
Operational speed: 410 kts *(760 km/h)*.
Service ceiling: 28 300 ft *(8625 m)*.
Range: 4000 nm *(7410 km)*.
Role/Weapon systems: Long-range MR and oceanic surveillance duties in peacetime, with ASW added as a war role; 4 P-3C on order to replace 4 Orion which may be sold to Spain; remaining 3 to Coast Guard. Sensors: APS-115 radar, ASQ-81 MAD, processor and computer, IFF, ECM/ESM, sonobuoys. Weapons: ASW; 8 MUSL Stingray torpedoes, depth bombs or mines. ASV; possible arming with Penguin missile.

ORION *1990, 333 Squadron*

Numbers/Type: 8/1 Westland Sea King Mk 43/43A/43B.
Operational speed: 125 kts *(232 km/h)*.
Service ceiling: 10 500 ft *(3200 m)*.
Range: 630 nm *(1165 km)*.
Role/Weapon systems: SAR, surface search and surveillance helicopter; supplemented by civil helicopters in wartime. One 43B delivered in June 1992; remainder to be updated to 43B standard. Sensors: MEL search radar; FLIR and dual radar when modernised. Weapons: Generally unarmed.

LIGHT FORCES

Note: 12 new FAC planned by 2000. Air cushion design of 125 tons capable of 52 kts.

14 HAUK CLASS (FAST ATTACK CRAFT—MISSILE)

Name	*No*	*Builders* (see *Programmes*)	*Commissioned*
HAUK	P 986	Bergens Mek Verksteder	17 Aug 1977
ØRN	P 987	Bergens Mek Verksteder	19 Jan 1979
TERNE	P 988	Bergens Mek Verksteder	13 Mar 1979
TJELD	P 989	Bergens Mek Verksteder	25 May 1979
SKARV	P 990	Bergens Mek Verksteder	17 July 1979
TEIST	P 991	Bergens Mek Verksteder	11 Sep 1979
JO	P 992	Bergens Mek Verksteder	1 Nov 1979
LOM	P 993	Bergens Mek Verksteder	15 Jan 1980
STEGG	P 994	Bergens Mek Verksteder	18 Mar 1980
FALK	P 995	Bergens Mek Verksteder	30 Apr 1980
RAVN	P 996	Westamarin A/S, Alta	20 May 1980
GRIBB	P 997	Westamarin A/S, Alta	10 July 1980
GEIR	P 998	Westamarin A/S, Alta	16 Sep 1980
ERLE	P 999	Westamarin A/S, Alta	10 Dec 1980

Displacement, tons: 120 standard; 148 full load
Dimensions, feet (metres): 120 × 20 × 5 *(36.5 × 6.1 × 1.5)*
Main machinery: 2 MTU 16V538 TB92 diesels; 6820 hp(m) *(5 MW)* sustained; 2 shafts
Speed, knots: 32. **Range, miles:** 440 at 30 kts
Complement: 20

Missiles: SSM: 6 Kongsberg Penguin Mk 2; IR homing to 27 km *(14.6 nm)* at 0.8 Mach; warhead 120 kg. At least one boat reported as fitted with Mk 2 Mod 7 Penguin which has a range of 40 km *(21.6 nm)*.
SAM: Twin Simbad launcher for Matra Mistral being fitted from late 1991.
Guns: 1 Bofors 40 mm/70; 90° elevation; 300 rounds/minute to 12 km *(6.6 nm)*; weight of shell 0.96 kg.
1 Rheinmetall 20 mm/20; 55° elevation; 1000 rounds/minute to 2 km.
Torpedoes: 2—21 in *(533 mm)* tubes. FFV Type 61; anti-surface; wire-guided; passive homing to 25 km *(13.7 nm)* at 45 kts; warhead 240 kg.
Fire control: Kongsberg MSI-80S TV optronic tracker and laser rangefinder.
Radars: Surface search/navigation: Two Racal Decca TM 1226; I band.
Sonars: Simrad; active search; high frequency.

Programmes: Ordered 12 June 1975—10 from Bergens Mek Verksteder (Laksevag) (who also built Swedish Hugin class) and four from Westamarin. (Westamarin is the new name for Westermoen (see Storm class)).
Modernisation: Simbad twin launchers for SAM being fitted from late 1991.
Structure: Very similar to Snögg class with improved fire control.

TERNE (firing Penguin) *1989, Royal Norwegian Navy*

10 STORM CLASS (FAST ATTACK CRAFT—MISSILE)

Name	*No*	*Builders*	*Commissioned*
BLINK	P 961	Bergens Mek. Verksteder	18 Dec 1965
SKJOLD	P 963	Westermoen, Mandal	1966
TRYGG	P 964	Bergens Mek Verksteder	1966
KJEKK	P 965	Bergens Mek Verksteder	1966
DJERV	P 966	Westermoen, Mandal	1966
SKUDD	P 967	Bergens Mek Verksteder	1966
STEIL	P 969	Westermoen, Mandal	1967
HVASS	P 972	Westermoen, Mandal	1967
BRASK	P 977	Bergens Mek Verksteder	1967
GNIST	P 979	Bergens Mek Verksteder	1968

Displacement, tons: 100 standard; 135 full load
Dimensions, feet (metres): 120 × 20 × 5 *(36.5 × 6.1 × 1.5)*
Main machinery: 2 Mercedes-Benz MTU 16V 538 TB90 diesels; 6000 hp(m) *(4.41 MW)* sustained; 2 shafts
Speed, knots: 32
Complement: 19 (4 officers)

Missiles: SSM: 6 Kongsberg Penguin Mk 1; IR homing to 20 km *(10.8 nm)* at 0.7 Mach; warhead 120 kg.
Guns: 1 Bofors 3 in *(76 mm)*/50; 30° elevation; 30 rounds/minute to 13 km *(7 nm)* surface fire only; weight of shell 5.9 kg.
1 Bofors 40 mm/70; 90° elevation; 300 rounds/minute to 12 km *(6.6 nm)*; weight of shell 0.96 kg.
Fire control: TVT 300 optronic tracker and laser rangefinder.
Radars: Surface search: Racal Decca TM 1226; I band.
Fire control: Signaal WM 26; I/J band; range 46 km *(25 nm)*.

Programmes: Originally a class of 20. *Storm* (P 960) used as a trials vessel.
Modernisation: The introduction of Penguin surface-to-surface guided missile launchers started in 1970, in addition to originally designed armament, although all boats do not carry full complement at all times. Further modernisation of the surviving 10 of the class is intended and these may in due course also be fitted with Simbad twin launchers for SAM.
Structure: Depth charge rails can still be fitted. The optronic tracker is fitted aft of the mainmast.

STORM Class (old number) — *1989, Royal Norwegian Navy*

6 SNÖGG CLASS (FAST ATTACK CRAFT—MISSILE)

Name	*No*	*Builders*	*Commissioned*
SNÖGG (ex-*Lyr*)	P 980	Båtservice, Mandal	1970
RAPP	P 981	Båtservice, Mandal	1970
SNAR	P 982	Båtservice, Mandal	1970
RASK	P 983	Båtservice, Mandal	1971
KVIKK	P 984	Båtservice, Mandal	1971
KJAPP	P 985	Båtservice, Mandal	1971

Displacement, tons: 100 standard; 135 full load
Dimensions, feet (metres): 120 × 20 × 5 *(36.5 × 6.1 × 1.5)*
Main machinery: 2 MTU 16V 538 TB92 diesels; 6820 hp(m) *(5 MW)* sustained; 2 shafts
Speed, knots: 32
Complement: 19 (3 officers)

Missiles: SSM: 4 Kongsberg Penguin Mk 1; IR homing to 20 km *(10.8 nm)* at 0.7 Mach; warhead 120 kg.
Guns: 1 Bofors 40 mm/70; 90° elevation; 300 rounds/minute to 12 km *(6.6 nm)*; weight of shell 0.96 kg.
Torpedoes: 4—21 in *(533 mm)* tubes. FFV Type 61; anti-surface; wire-guided; passive homing to 25 km *(13.7 nm)* at 45 kts; warhead 240 kg.
Fire control: PEAB TORC1 system.
Radars: Surface search: Racal Decca 1626; I band.

Programmes: Steel hulled fast attack craft, started coming into service in 1970.
Modernisation: Modernisation of fire control and electronics to be done in due course and may include installation of a Simbad SAM twin launcher.
Structure: Hulls are similar to those of the Storm class.

SNAR — *1990, van Ginderen Collection*

NAVAL DISTRICT PATROL CRAFT

Note: As well as the coastal patrol craft below and the transports listed under Miscellaneous, there are auxiliary craft attached to the Rogaland (R) and Oestlandet (O) naval districts. These include: *Oscarsborg* (ØSD 11), *Folden* (ØSD 14), *Nordkep* (ØSD 15), *Rogin* (RSD 28), *FKS I* (RSD 21), and *Foracs II* (RSD 20). Some of them carry a single 12.7 mm MG.

FOLDEN — *1990, Royal Norwegian Navy*

2 COASTAL PATROL CRAFT

Name	*No*	*Builders*	*Commissioned*
BRIMSE (ex-*Tarva*)	RSD 23 (ex-TSD 1)	Fjellstrand Yachts, Omastrand	1 Dec 1974
WELDING	ØSD 1	Fjellstrand Yachts, Omastrand	1 Nov 1974

Displacement, tons: 27.5
Dimensions, feet (metres): 53.3 × 17.3 × 3.8 *(16.3 × 5.3 × 1.2)*
Main machinery: 2 GM diesels; 800 hp *(597 kW)*; 2 shafts
Speed, knots: 15
Complement: 4
Guns: 1 Browning 12.7 mm MG.
Radars: Surface search: Racal Decca; I band.

Comment: All welded aluminium hull. Non-combatant Naval District craft.

BRIMSE — *10/1988, Royal Norwegian Navy*

MINE WARFARE FORCES

1 CONTROLLED MINELAYER

Name	*No*	*Builders*	*Commissioned*
BORGEN	N 51	Marinens Hovedverft, Horten	1961

Displacement, tons: 282 standard
Dimensions, feet (metres): 102.5 × 26.2 × 11 *(31.2 × 8 × 3.4)*
Main machinery: 2 GM 3-71 diesels; 660 hp *(492 kW)*; 2 Voith-Schneider props
Speed, knots: 9
Guns: 1 Rheinmetall 20 mm.
Mines: 2 rails.
Radars: Navigation: I band.

Comment: Launched 29 April 1960. Has two derricks used for mine placement. To be replaced in mid-1994 by a new construction dual purpose amphibious vessel.

BORGEN — *1990, Royal Norwegian Navy*

2 VIDAR CLASS (COASTAL MINELAYERS)

Name	No	Builders	Commissioned
VIDAR	N 52	Mjellem and Karlsen, Bergen	21 Oct 1977
VALE	N 53	Mjellem and Karlsen, Bergen	10 Feb 1978

Displacement, tons: 1500 standard; 1673 full load
Dimensions, feet (metres): 212.6 × 39.4 × 13.1 *(64.8 × 12 × 4)*
Main machinery: 2 Wichmann 7AX diesels; 4200 hp(m) *(3.1 MW)*; 2 shafts; bow thruster; 425 hp(m) *(312 kW)*
Speed, knots: 15
Complement: 50

Guns: 2 Bofors 40 mm/70; 90° elevation; 300 rounds/minute to 12 km *(6.6 nm)*; weight of shell 0.96 kg.
Torpedoes: 6—324 mm US Mk 32 (2 triple) tubes. Probably Honeywell Mk 46; anti-submarine; active/passive homing to 11 km *(5.9 nm)* at 40 kts; warhead 44 kg.
Mines: 300-400 (dependent on type) on 3 decks with an automatic lift between. Loaded through hatches fwd and aft each served by 2 cranes.
Radars: Surface search: Racal Decca TM 1226; I band.
Sonars: Simrad; hull-mounted; search and attack; medium/high frequency.

Programmes: Ordered 11 June 1975.
Operational: Versatile ships that can perform a number of roles in addition to minelaying.

VIDAR *1988, van Ginderen Collection*

0 + 9 (1) OKSØY/ALTA CLASS (MINEHUNTERS/SWEEPERS)

Name	No	Builders	Commissioned
Hunters			
OKSØY	M 340	Kvaerner Mandal	early 1993
KARMØY	M 341	Kvaerner Mandal	end 1993
MALØY	M 342	Kvaerner Mandal	end 1994
HINNØY	M 343	Kvaerner Mandal	mid-1995
Sweepers			
ALTA	M 350	Kvaerner Mandal	early 1994
OTRA	M 351	Kvaerner Mandal	mid-1994
RAUMA	M 352	Kvaerner Mandal	early 1995
ORKLA	M 353	Kvaerner Mandal	end 1995
GLOMMA	M 354	Kvaerner Mandal	mid-1996

Displacement, tons: 367 full load
Dimensions, feet (metres): 181.1 × 44.6 × 7.5 (2.76 cushion) *(55.2 × 13.6 × 2.3 (0.84))*
Main machinery: 2 MTU 12V 396 TE 84 diesels; 3700 hp(m) *(2.72 MW)* sustained; 2 Kvaerner Eureka waterjets; 2 MTU 8V 396 TE 54 diesels; 1740 hp(m) *(1.28 MW/60 Hz)* sustained; lift engines
Speed, knots: 30. **Range, miles:** 1200 at 22 kts
Complement: 37 (14 officers)

Guns: 2 Rheinmetall 20 mm. 2—12.7 mm MGs.

Countermeasures: MCMV: 2 Pluto submersibles (minehunter); mechanical and influence sweeping equipment (minesweepers).
Radars: Navigation: 2 Racal Decca; I band.
Sonars: Thomson Sintra/Simrad TSM 2023N; hull-mounted (minehunters); high frequency. Simrad Subsea SA 950; hull-mounted (minesweepers); high frequency.

Programmes: Orders for nine placed with Kvaerner on 9 November 1989. Four will be minehunters, the remainder minesweepers. There is an option on a tenth of class.
Structure: Design developed by the Navy in Bergen with the Defence Research Institute and Norsk Veritas and uses an air-cushion created by the surface effect between two hulls. The hull is built of Fibre Reinforced Plastics (FRP) in sandwich configuration.
Operational: Simrad Albatross tactical system including mapping; CAST/Del Norte mobile positioning system with GPS. The catamaran design is claimed to give higher transit speeds with lesser installed power than a traditional hull design. Other advantages are lower magnetic and acoustic signatures, more comfortable motion, clearer water for sonar operations, and less susceptibility to shock.
Opinion: There is some scepticism amongst international naval architects as to whether this design will live up to expectations. It is certainly a very bold choice by the Norwegian Navy.

OKSØY Class (model) *1989, Royal Norwegian Navy*

8 Ex-US ADJUTANT/SAUDA CLASS (MSC 60) (MINESWEEPERS—COASTAL)

Name	No	Builders	Commissioned
SIRA	M 312	Hodgeson Bros, Gowdy & Stevens, Maine	28 Nov 1955
TANA (ex-*Roeselare* M 914, ex-*MSC 103*)	M 313	Hodgeson Bros, Gowdy & Stevens, Maine	Sep 1953
ALTA (ex-*Arlon* M 915, ex-*MSC 104*)	M 314	Hodgeson Bros, Gowdy & Stevens, Maine	Oct 1953
VOSSO	M 316	Skaaluren Skibsbyggeri, Rosendal	16 Mar 1955
GLOMMA (ex-*Bastogne* M 916, ex-*MSC 151*)	M 317	Hodgeson Bros, Gowdy & Stevens, Maine	Dec 1953
TISTA	M 331	Forende Båtbyggerier, Risör	27 Apr 1955
KVINA	M 332	Båtservice, Mandal	12 July 1955
UTLA	M 334	Båtservice, Mandal	15 Nov 1955

Displacement, tons: 333 standard; 384 full load
Dimensions, feet (metres): 144 × 28 × 8.5 *(44 × 8.5 × 2.6)*
Main machinery: 2 GM 8-268A diesels; 880 hp *(656 kW)*; 2 shafts
Speed, knots: 13.5. **Range, miles:** 2500 at 10 kts
Complement: 38; 39 *Tana*

Guns: 2 Rheinmetall 20 mm/20; 55° elevation; 1000 rounds/minute to 2 km.
Countermeasures: Thomson-CSF Ibis III minehunting system including 2 PAP 104 (*Tana* only).
Radars: Navigation: Racal Decca TM 1226; I band.
Sonars: UQS-1; hull-mounted; minehunting; high frequency. Plessey 193M (*Tana*).

Programmes: Five coastal minesweepers were built in Norway with US engines. *Alta, Glomma* and *Tana* were taken over from the Royal Belgian Navy in 1966.
Modernisation: *Tana* converted as a minehunter in 1977. All have been given new 20 mm guns.
Operational: Some are in reserve. To be replaced by the Alta class.

KVINA *10/1990, Gilbert Gyssels*

KVINA *11/1990, Antonio Moreno*

AMPHIBIOUS FORCES

Note: Replacements in the late 1990s will have a minelaying capability.

5 REINØYSUND CLASS (LCTs)

Name	No	Builders	Commissioned
REINØYSUND	L 4502	Mjellem & Karlsen, Bergen	Jan 1972
SØRØYSUND	L 4503	Mjellem & Karlsen, Bergen	May 1972
MAURSUND	L 4504	Mjellem & Karlsen, Bergen	Sep 1972
ROTSUND	L 4505	Mjellem & Karlsen, Bergen	Nov 1972
BORGSUND	L 4506	Mjellem & Karlsen, Bergen	Feb 1973

Displacement, tons: 595 full load
Dimensions, feet (metres): 171 × 33.8 × 5.9 *(52.1 × 10.3 × 1.8)*
Main machinery: 2 Maybach MTU diesels; 1350 hp(m) *(992 kW)*; 2 shafts
Speed, knots: 11.5
Complement: 10 (2 officers)
Military lift: 7 tanks; 200 troops
Guns: 3 Rheinmetall 20 mm/20.

Comment: Same design as deleted Kvalsund class.

SØRØYSUND *1985, Royal Norwegian Navy*

DEPOT SHIP

Name	No	Builders	Commissioned
HORTEN	A 530	A/S Horten Verft	Apr 1978

Displacement, tons: 2530
Dimensions, feet (metres): 287 × 42.6 × 16.4 *(87.5 × 13 × 5)*
Main machinery: 2 Wichmann 7AX diesels; 2100 hp(m) *(1.54 MW)*; 2 shafts; bow thruster
Speed, knots: 16.5
Complement: 86
Guns: 2 Bofors 40 mm/70.
Helicopters: Platform only.

Comment: Contract signed 30 March 1976. Laid down 28 January 1977; launched 12 August 1977. To serve both submarines and fast attack craft. Quarters for 45 extra and can cater for 190 extra.

HORTEN — 8/1991, van Ginderen Collection

MISCELLANEOUS

1 RESEARCH SHIP (AGI)

MARJATA

Measurement, tons: 1385 dwt
Dimensions, feet (metres): 193.2 × 36.1 × 15.4 *(58.9 × 11 × 4.7)*
Main machinery: 2 diesels; 2600 hp(m) *(1.91 MW)*; 2 shafts
Speed, knots: 15

Comment: Built by Mjellem and Karlsen in 1976. Has a white superstructure. Used as an AGI and for experimental work.

MARJATA — 4/1980

1 + 1 GARSØY CLASS (COASTAL TRANSPORT)

Name	No	Builders	Commissioned
GARSØY	HSD 12	Eikefjord Marine	19 Aug 1988

Displacement, tons: 195 standard
Dimensions, feet (metres): 111.5 × 23 × 5.9 *(34 × 7 × 1.8)*
Main machinery: 2 MWM TBD 604B V8 diesels; 2313 hp(m) *(1.7 MW)* sustained; 2 waterjets
Speed, knots: 27
Complement: 4
Cargo capacity: 80 passengers

Comment: GRP sandwich hull used as a trials craft for the SES MCMV design. Now used as a personnel transport and patrol craft. Second of class to replace *Tautra* in December 1992.

GARSØY — 8/1990, T. J. Gander

2 DIVING TENDERS

Name	No	Builders	Commissioned
SARPEN	A 531	Nielsen, Harstad	1972
DRAUG	A 532	Nielsen, Harstad	1972

Displacement, tons: 250 full load
Dimensions, feet (metres): 95 × 22 × 8.2 *(29 × 6.8 × 2.5)*
Main machinery: 1 diesel; 530 hp(m) *(389 kW)*; 1 shaft
Speed, knots: 12

Comment: Small depot ships for frogmen and divers.

SARPEN — 4/1987, Ralf Bendfeldt

7 WISTING CLASS (COASTAL TRANSPORTS)

Name	No	Builders	Commissioned
TORPEN	VSD 4	Båtservice Verft, Mandal	15 Dec 1977
WISTING	ØSD 2	Voldnes Skipsverft, Fosnavåg	30 Jan 1978
TAUTRA	TSD 5	Båtservice Verft, Mandal	15 Feb 1978
ROTVAER	NSD 35	Båtservice Verft, Mandal	Mar 1978
FJØLØY	RSD 22 (ex-ØSD 5)	Voldnes Skipsverft, Fosnavåg	Apr 1978
KRØTTØY	HSD 15	Voldnes Skipsverft, Fosnavåg	June 1978
KARLSØY	TRSD 4	P Høivolds Mek Verksted	July 1978

Displacement, tons: 300 full load
Dimensions, feet (metres): 95.1 × 21.6 × 10 *(29 × 6.7 × 3.2)*
Main machinery: 1 MWM TBD 601-6K diesel; 530 hp(m) *(390 kW)*; 1 shaft; cp prop
Speed, knots: 11. **Range, miles:** 1200 at 10 kts
Complement: 6
Cargo capacity: 100 tons; 100 passengers
Guns: 1 Browning 12.7 mm MG.

Comment: Non-combatant Naval District ships. *Tautra* to be deleted in December 1992.

WISTING — 6/1991, van Ginderen Collection

1 TORPEDO RECOVERY VESSEL

Name	No	Builders	Commissioned
VERNØY	VSD 1	Fjellstrand Aluminium Yachts, Omastrand	Oct 1978

Displacement, tons: 100
Dimensions, feet (metres): 102.9 × 22.5 × 6.5 *(31.3 × 6.8 × 2)*
Main machinery: 2 MWM diesels; 2 Schottel rudders
Speed, knots: 10+
Complement: 5

Comment: The vessel is fitted with equipment for oil pollution operations and firefighting. All-welded aluminium hull. Non-combatant Naval District craft.

VERNØY — 1983, Royal Norwegian Navy

2 TRAINING VESSELS

Name	No	Builders	Commissioned
HESSA (ex-*Hitra*, ex-*Marsteinen*)	P 358	Fjellstrand, Omastrand	Jan 1978
VIGRA (ex-*Kvarven*)	P 359	Fjellstrand, Omastrand	July 1978

Displacement, tons: 39
Dimensions, feet (metres): 77 × 16.4 × 3.5 *(23.5 × 5 × 1.1)*
Main machinery: 2 GM diesels; 1800 hp *(1.34 MW)*; 2 shafts
Speed, knots: 20
Complement: 5
Guns: 1—12.7 mm Browning MG.

Comment: The vessels are designed for training students at the Royal Norwegian Naval Academy in navigation, manoeuvring and seamanship. All-welded aluminium hulls. Also equipped with an open bridge and a blind pilotage position below deck. 18 berths.

VIGRA *1983, Royal Norwegian Navy*

ROYAL YACHT

Name	No	Builders	Commissioned
NORGE (ex-*Philante*)	N 533	Camper & Nicholson's Ltd, Southampton	1937

Displacement, tons: 1786
Dimensions, feet (metres): 263 × 38 × 15.2 *(80.2 × 11.6 × 4.6)*
Main machinery: 2 Bergen KRMB-8 diesels; 3520 hp(m) *(2.59 MW)*; 2 shafts
Speed, knots: 17

Comment: Built to the order of T O M Sopwith as an escort and store vessel for the yachts *Endeavour I* and *Endeavour II*. Launched on 17 February 1937. Served in the Royal Navy as an anti-submarine escort during the Second World War, after which she was purchased by the Norwegian people for King Haakon and reconditioned as a Royal Yacht at Southampton. Can accommodate about 50 people in addition to crew. Repaired after serious fire on 7 March 1985.

NORGE *7/1988, Royal Norwegian Navy*

TUGS

SAMSON VSD 7

Displacement, tons: 300
Dimensions, feet (metres): 87.3 × 26.2 × 10.5 *(26.6 × 8 × 3.2)*
Main machinery: 1 MWM diesel; 650 hp(m) *(478 kW)*; 1 shaft
Speed, knots: 10

Comment: Ex-West German built in 1938. Modified in 1978. Non-combatant Naval District craft.

SAMSON *1981, Royal Norwegian Navy*

KVARVEN (ex-*Oscar Tybring*) VSD 2

Displacement, tons: 97
Dimensions, feet (metres): 73.8 × 20.7 × 11.2 *(22.5 × 6.3 × 3.4)*
Main machinery: 1 Detroit V16-149 diesel; 900 hp *(671 kW)*; 1 shaft
Speed, knots: 11

Comment: Built in 1979 by Haugesund Slip. Acquired in 1988.

COAST GUARD

3 NORDKAPP CLASS

Name	No	Builders	Commissioned
NORDKAPP	W 320	Bergens Mek Verksteder	25 Apr 1981
SENJA	W 321	Horten Verft	6 Mar 1981
ANDENES	W 322	Haugesund Mek Verksted	30 Jan 1982

Displacement, tons: 3240 full load
Dimensions, feet (metres): 346 × 47.9 × 16.1 *(105.5 × 14.6 × 4.9)*
Main machinery: 4 Wichmann 9-AXAG diesels; 14 400 hp(m) *(10.6 MW)*; 2 shafts
Speed, knots: 23. **Range, miles:** 7500 at 15 kts
Complement: 52 (6 aircrew)

Missiles: SSM: Fitted for 6 Kongsberg Penguin II but not embarked.
Guns: 1 Bofors 57 mm/70 ❶; 75° elevation; 200 rounds/minute to 17 km *(9.3 nm)*; weight of shell 2.4 kg.
4 Rheinmetall 20 mm/20 ❷; 55° elevation; 1000 rounds/minute to 2 km.
Torpedoes: 6—324 mm US Mk 32 (2 triple) tubes. Probably Honeywell Mk 46; anti-submarine; active/passive homing to 11 km *(5.9 nm)* at 40 kts; warhead 44 kg. Mountings only in peacetime.
Depth charges: 1 rack.
Countermeasures: Decoys: 2 Chaff launchers.
Combat data systems: Navkis action data automation.
Radars: Air/surface search: Plessey AWS 5 ❸; E/F band; range 155 km *(85 nm)* for 4 m² target.
Navigation: Two Racal Decca 1226; I band.
Fire control: Philips 9LV 200 Mk 2 ❹; J band.
Sonars: Simrad SS 105; hull-mounted; active search and attack; 14 kHz.

Helicopters: 1 Westland Lynx Mk 86 ❺.

Programmes: In November 1977 the Coast Guard Budget was cut from 2000 to 1400 million Kronen resulting in a reduction of the immediate building programme from seven to three ships.
Structure: Strengthened for ice. Fitted for firefighting, anti-pollution work, all with two motor cutters and a Gemini-type dinghy.
Operational: Bunks for 109. War complement increases to 76.

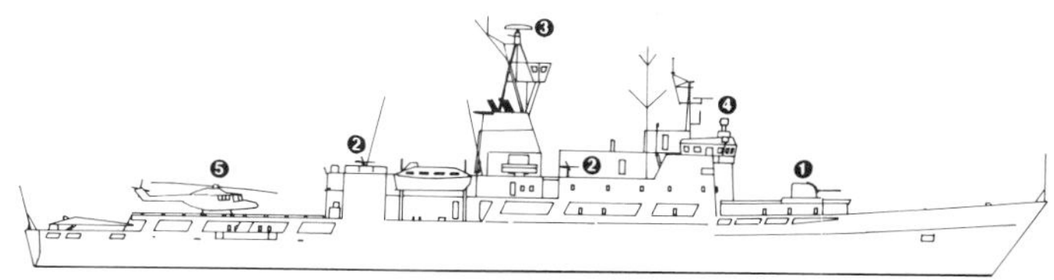

NORDKAPP Class *(Scale 1 : 1 200), Ian Sturton*

ANDENES (with Gulf communications) *1/1991, van Ginderen Collection*

7 CHARTERED SHIPS

Name	No	Tonnage	Completion
MALENE ØSTERVOLD	W 313	1119	1965
STÅLBAS	W 314	498	1955
NORDSJØBAS	W 315	814	1978
VOLSTAD JR.	W 316	598	1950
LAFJORD	W 317	814	1978
GARPESKJAER	W 318	1122	1956
GRIMSHOLM	W 319	1189	1978

Comment: *Stålbas* and *Volstad Jr* chartered in 1977; *Lafjord, Nordsjøbas* and *Grimsholm* in 1980; *Garpeskjaer* in 1986 and *Malene Østervold* in 1987. All armed with one 40 mm/60 gun.

GARPESKJAER *8/1990, T. J. Gander*

Name	No	Builders	Commissioned
NORNEN	W 300	Mjellem & Karlsen, Bergen	1963

Displacement, tons: 1030
Dimensions, feet (metres): 201.8 × 32.8 × 15.8 *(61.5 × 10 × 4.8)*
Main machinery: 4 diesels; 3500 hp(m) *(2.57 MW)*; 1 shaft
Speed, knots: 17
Complement: 32
Guns: 1 Bofors 40 mm/70.

Comment: Launched 20 August 1962. Modernised in 1978 with increased tonnage.

NORNEN *1988, Royal Norwegian Navy*

Name	No	Builders	Commissioned
FARM	W 301	Ankerlokken Verft	1962
HEIMDAL	W 302	Bolsones Verft, Molde	1962

Measurement, tons: 600 gross
Dimensions, feet (metres): 177 × 26.2 × 16.1 *(54.3 × 8.2 × 4.9)*
Main machinery: 2 Wichmann 9ACAT diesels; 2400 hp(m) *(1.76 MW)*; 1 shaft; cp prop
Speed, knots: 16
Complement: 29
Guns: 1 Bofors 40 mm/70.

Comment: *Farm* modernised by Bergens Mekaniske Verksteder in 1979 and *Heimdal* by same firm in 1980.

FARM *6/1991, van Ginderen Collection*

SURVEY VESSELS

Notes: (1) Under control of Ministry of Environment based at Stavanger.
(2) In addition *Sverdrup* and *Sverdrup II* work for the Defence Research Establishment and a new vessel *Minerva* will be in service in late 1993.

Name	Displacement tons	Launched	Officers	Crew
LANCE	960	1978	7	8
SJØVERN	215	1948	3	12
SJØFALK	70	1937	1	4
SJØSKVETT	80	1964	1	4
SJØROKK	75	1964	1	4
SJØDREV	80	1973	1	4
SJØTROLL	80	1976	1	4
OLJEVERN 01	200	1978	2	6
OLJEVERN 02	200	1978	2	6
OLJEVERN 03	200	1978	2	6
OLJEVERN 04	200	1978	2	6

LANCE *10/1988, Gilbert Gyssels*

OMAN

Senior Officers

Commander Royal Navy of Oman:
Rear Admiral (Liwaa Bahry) H H Sayyid Shihab Bin Tarik Bin Taimur Al Said
Chief of Staff:
Commodore (Ameed) Hilal Bin Mohammad Bin Rashid Al Rashdy
Commander Coast Guard:
Captain (Aqeed Bahry) Hamdan Bin Marhoon Al Mamari
Commander Royal Yacht Squadron:
Captain (Aqeed Bahry) J M Knapp

Bases

Qa'Adat Said Bin Sultan Naval Base, Wudam (main base, dockyard and shiplift)
Mina Raysut (advanced naval base), Salalah
Jazirat Ghanam (advanced naval base), Musandam
Muaskar al Murtafa'a (headquarters)

Personnel

(a) 1992: 3400 officers and men
(b) Voluntary service

Future Plans

The main deficiency in this force is in the MCMV category and plans for a limited capability seem to have been postponed. It is intended to replace the Al Waafi and Seeb classes in the 1990s.

Mercantile Marine

Lloyd's Register of Shipping:
27 vessels of 22 578 tons gross

CORVETTES

0 + 2 MUHEET PROJECT TYPE 83

Displacement, tons: 1400 full load
Dimensions, feet (metres): 249.3 wl × 37.7 × 15.4 *(76 × 11.5 × 4.7)*
Main machinery: 4 Pielstick diesels; 2 shafts; cp props
Speed, knots: 30
Complement: 76 (14 officers)

Missiles: SSM: 8 Aerospatiale MM 40 Exocet.
SAM: Thomson CSF Crotale octuple launchers.
Guns: 1 OTO Melara 3 in *(76 mm)*/62 Super Rapid.
2 Oerlikon 20mm.
Countermeasures: Decoys: 2 Barricade Chaff launchers.
ESM/ECM: Radar intercept and jammer.
Combat data systems: Signaal STACOS; SATCOM.
Radars: Air/surface search: Signaal MW 08; G band.
Fire control: Signaal STING; I/J band.
Navigation: Kelvin Hughes 1007; I band.

Helicopters: Platform for 1 medium.

Programmes: Vosper Thornycroft Signed the final contract in March 1992. First delivery expected in 1996.
Structure: Weapon systems listed are not all confirmed. The ship is based on the Vigilance class design.

VOSPER Type 83 (artist's impression) *3/1992, Vosper Thornycroft*

LIGHT FORCES

Note: An invitation to tender for two 45 m attack craft is expected in 1992.

4 PROVINCE CLASS (FAST ATTACK CRAFT—MISSILE)

Name	*No*	*Builders*	*Commissioned*
DHOFAR	B 10	Vosper Thornycroft	7 Aug 1982
AL SHARQIYAH	B 11	Vosper Thornycroft	5 Dec 1983
AL BAT'NAH	B 12	Vosper Thornycroft	18 Jan 1984
MUSSANDAM	B 14	Vosper Thornycroft	31 Mar 1989

Displacement, tons: 311 light; 394 full load
Dimensions, feet (metres): 186 × 26.9 × 7.9 *(56.7 × 8.2 × 2.4)*
Main machinery: 4 Paxman Valenta 18 CM diesels; 15 000 hp *(11.2 MW)* sustained; 4 shafts; auxiliary propulsion; 2 motors; 200 hp *(149 kW)*
Speed, knots: 38. **Range, miles:** 2000 at 18 kts
Complement: 45 (5 officers) plus 14 trainees

Missiles: SSM: 8 or 6 (B 10) Aerospatiale MM 40 Exocet; inertial cruise; active radar homing to 70 km *(40 nm)* at 0.9 Mach; warhead 165 kg; sea-skimmer.
Guns: 1 OTO Melara 3 in *(76 mm)*/62 compact; 85° elevation; 85 rounds/minute to 16 km *(8.7 nm)*; weight of shell 6 kg.
2 Breda 40 mm/70 (twin); 85° elevation; 300 rounds/minute to 12.5 km *(6.8 nm)*; weight of shell 0.96 kg.
2—12.7 mm MGs.
Countermeasures: Decoys: 2 Wallop Barricade fixed triple barrels; 4 modes of fire for Chaff and IR deception.
ESM: Racal Cutlass; radar warning.
ECM: Scorpion; jammer.
Fire control: Sperry Sea Archer (B 10). Philips 9LV 307 (others).
Radars: Air/surface search: Plessey AWS 4 (B 10); E/F band; range 101 km *(55 nm)*.
Racal Decca TM 1226C (remainder); I band.

Programmes: First ordered in 1980, launched 14 October 1981 and sailed from Portsmouth for Oman 21 October 1982. Two more ordered in January 1981 and sailed for Oman on 16 May 1984. Fourth ordered January 1986, launched 19 March 1988 and sailed for Oman 1 May 1989.
Structure: Similar to Kenyan Nyayo class.

DHOFAR (with 6 Exocet and Plessey radar) *1989, Royal Navy of Oman*

MUSSANDAM *5/1989, Maritime Photographic*

4 BROOKE MARINE TYPE (FAST ATTACK CRAFT—GUN)

Name	*No*	*Builders*	*Commissioned*
AL WAAFI	B 4	Brooke Marine, Lowestoft	24 Mar 1977
AL FULK	B 5	Brooke Marine, Lowestoft	24 Mar 1977
AL MUJAHID	B 6	Brooke Marine, Lowestoft	20 July 1977
AL JABBAR	B 7	Brooke Marine, Lowestoft	6 Oct 1977

Displacement, tons: 135 standard; 153 full load
Dimensions, feet (metres): 123 × 22.5 × 6 *(37.5 × 6.9 × 1.8)*
Main machinery: 2 Paxman Ventura 16 CM diesels; 3000 hp *(2.24 MW)* sustained; 2 shafts
Speed, knots: 25. **Range, miles:** 3300 at 15 kts
Complement: 27 (3 officers)
Guns: 1 OTO Melara 3 in *(76 mm)*/62 compact; 85° elevation; 85 rounds/minute to 16 km *(8.7 nm)*; weight of shell 6 kg.
1 Oerlikon 20 mm. 2—7.62 mm MGs.
Fire control: Laurence Scott optical director and Sperry Sea Archer system.
Radars: Surface search/navigation: Racal Decca 1226; Racal Decca 1229; I band.

Comment: Ordered 26 April 1974. To be replaced in the 1990s.

AL FULK *1989, Royal Navy of Oman*

4 VOSPER 25 METRE CLASS (INSHORE PATROL CRAFT)

Name	*No*	*Builders*	*Commissioned*
SEEB	B 20	Vosper Private, Singapore	15 Mar 1981
SHINAS	B 21	Vosper Private, Singapore	15 Mar 1981
SADH	B 22	Vosper Private, Singapore	15 Mar 1981
KHASSAB	B 23	Vosper Private, Singapore	15 Mar 1981

Displacement, tons: 60.7
Dimensions, feet (metres): 82.8 × 19 × 5.2 *(25 × 5.8 × 1.6)*
Main machinery: 2 MTU 12V 331 TC 92 diesels; 2660 hp(m) *(1.96 MW)* sustained; 2 shafts
1 Cummins N855M diesel for slow cruising; 195 hp *(145 kW)* sustained; 1 shaft
Speed, knots: 25; 8 (Cummins diesel). **Range, miles:** 750 at 14 kts
Complement: 13
Guns: 1 Oerlikon 20 mm. 2—7.62 mm (twin) MGs.

Comment: Arrived in Oman on 19 May 1981 having been ordered one month earlier. The craft were built on speculation and completed in 1980.

KHASSAB *1989, Royal Navy of Oman*

TRAINING SHIP/PATROL SHIP

Name	*No*	*Builders*	*Commissioned*
AL MABRUKAH (ex-*Al Said*)	A 1	Brooke Marine, Lowestoft	1971

Displacement, tons: 900 full load
Dimensions, feet (metres): 203.4 × 35.1 × 9.8 *(62 × 10.7 × 3)*
Main machinery: 2 Paxman Valenta 12 CM diesels; 5000 hp *(3.73 MW)* sustained; 2 shafts
Speed, knots: 12
Complement: 39 (7 officers)
Guns: 1 Breda 40 mm/70. 2 Oerlikon 20 mm A41A.
Countermeasures: Decoys: Wallop Barricade 18-barrelled Chaff launcher.
ESM: Radar warning.
Radars: Surface search: Racal Decca TM 1226; I band.
Helicopters: Platform but no hangar.

Comment: Built by Brooke Marine, Lowestoft. Launched 7 April 1970 as a yacht for the Sultan of Oman. Carried on board is one Rotork landing craft. Converted to training ship/patrol ship in 1983 with enlarged helicopter deck.

AL MABRUKAH *1991, van Ginderen Collection*

AMPHIBIOUS FORCES

1 LANDING SHIP—LOGISTIC

Name	*No*	*Builders*	*Commissioned*
NASR AL BAHR	L 2	Brooke Marine, Lowestoft	6 Feb 1985

Displacement, tons: 2500 full load
Dimensions, feet (metres): 305 × 50.8 × 8.5 *(93 × 15.5 × 2.6)*
Main machinery: 2 Paxman Valenta 18 CM diesels; 7500 hp *(5.6 MW)* sustained; 2 shafts
Speed, knots: 16. **Range, miles:** 5000 at 15 kts
Complement: 81 (13 officers)
Military lift: 7 MBT or 400 tons cargo; 240 troops; 2 LCVPs
Guns: 4 Breda 40 mm/70 (2 twin). 2 Oerlikon 20 mm.
Countermeasures: Decoys: Wallop Barricade double layer Chaff launchers.
Fire control: PEAB 9LV 200 GFCS and CSEE Lynx optical sight.
Radars: Surface search/navigation: Two Racal Decca; I band.
Helicopters: Platform for Super Puma.

Comment: Ordered 18 May 1982. Launched 16 May 1984. Carries one 16 ton crane. Bow and stern ramps. Full naval command facilities. The forward ramp is of two sections measuring length 59 ft (when extended) × 16.5 ft breadth *(18 × 5 m)*, and the single section stern ramp measures 14 × 16.5 ft *(4.3 × 5 m)*. Both hatches can support a 60 ton tank. The tank deck side bulkheads extend 7.5 ft *(2.25 m)* above the upper deck between the forecastle and the forward end of the superstructure, and provide two hatch openings to the tank deck below. Positioned between the hatches is a two ton crane with athwartship travel.

NASR AL BAHR *5/1990, John Mortimer*

1 LANDING SHIP—LOGISTIC

Name	*No*	*Builders*	*Commissioned*
AL MUNASSIR	L 1	Brooke Marine, Lowestoft	31 Jan 1979

Displacement, tons: 2000
Dimensions, feet (metres): 276 × 49 × 7.3 *(84.1 × 14.9 × 2.3)*
Main machinery: 2 Mirrlees Blackstone ESL 8MGR diesels; 2440 hp *(1.82 MW)*; 2 shafts
Speed, knots: 12. **Range, miles:** 1000 at 12 kts
Complement: 45 (9 officers)
Military lift: 8 MBTs or 550 tons cargo; 188 troops; 2 Rotork LCPs
Guns: 1 OTO Melara 3 in *(76 mm)*/62. 2 Oerlikon 20 mm.
Countermeasures: Decoys: Wallop Barricade double layer Chaff launchers.
Radars: Navigation: Racal Decca TM 1229; I band.
Helicopters: Platform for 1 medium but no hangar.

Comment: This ship is in reserve but is used for harbour training.

AL MUNASSIR *1986, Royal Navy of Oman*

3 LCMs

Name	*No*	*Builders*	*Commissioned*
SABA AL BAHR	C 8	Vosper Private, Singapore	17 Sep 1981
AL DOGHAS	C 9	Vosper Private, Singapore	10 Jan 1983
AL TEMSAH	C 10	Vosper Private, Singapore	12 Feb 1983

Displacement, tons: 230 full load
Dimensions, feet (metres): 108.2 (83.6, C 8) × 24.3 × 4.3 *(33 (25.5) × 7.4 × 1.3)*
Main machinery: 2 Caterpillar 3408 TA diesels; 1880 hp *(1.4 MW)* sustained; 2 shafts
Speed, knots: 8. **Range, miles:** 1400 at 8 kts
Complement: 11
Military lift: 100 tons

Comment: C 8 launched 30 June 1981. C 9 and C 10, similar but not identical ships, ordered 8 May 1982.

SABA AL BAHR *1988, Royal Navy of Oman*

2 LANDING CRAFT—UTILITY

Name	*No*	*Builders*	*Commissioned*
AL SANSOOR	C 4	Cheverton Ltd, Isle of Wight	Jan 1975
AL NEEMRAN	C 7	Lewis Offshore, Stornoway	1979

Displacement, tons: 130 full load (C 4)
Measurement, tons: 45 (C 4), 85 (C 7) dwt
Dimensions, feet (metres): 60 × 20 × 3.6 *(18.3 × 6.1 × 1.1)* (C 4)
84 × 24 × 6 *(25.5 × 7.4 × 1.8)* (C 7)
Main machinery: 2 diesels; 300 hp *(220 kW)*; 2 shafts
Speed, knots: 7/8

Comment: *Al Sansoor* converted into a Tank Cleaning vessel in 1987 and strictly speaking is no longer an LCU.

AL SANSOOR *1975, Roger Smith*

MISCELLANEOUS

Note: There is a requirement for a 1500 ton Survey Ship similar to the British Roebuck class.

1 SAIL TRAINING SHIP

Name	*No*	*Builders*	*Recommissioned*
SHABAB OMAN (ex-*Captain Scott*)	51	Herd and Mackenzie, Buckie, Scotland	1979

Displacement, tons: 386
Dimensions, feet (metres): 144.3 × 27.9 × 15.1 *(44 × 8.5 × 4.6)*
Main machinery: 2 auxiliary diesels; 1 shaft
Complement: 20 (5 officers) plus 3 officers and 24 trainees

Comment: Topsail schooner taken over from Dulverton Trust in 1977 used for sail training for the young people of Oman.

SHABAB OMAN *12/1991, Giorgio Ghiglione*

Name	*No*	*Builders*	*Commissioned*
FULK AL SALAMAH (ex-*Ghubat Al Salamah*)	L 3	Bremer-Vulkan	3 Apr 1987

Measurement, tons: 10 864 grt; 5186 net
Dimensions, feet (metres): 447.5 × 68.9 × 19.7 *(136.4 × 21 × 6)*
Main machinery: 4 Fincantieri GMT A 420.6 H diesels; 16 800 hp(m) *(12.35 MW)* sustained; 2 shafts
Speed, knots: 19.5
Helicopters: Up to 2 AS 332C Super Puma.

Comment: Support ship and transport with side doors for heavy loading.

FULK AL SALAMAH *8/1990, Maritime Photographic*

1 COASTAL FREIGHTER

Name	*No*	*Builders*	*Commissioned*
AL SULTANA	A 2	G Bijsma, Wartena	4 June 1975

Measurement, tons: 1380 dwt
Dimensions, feet (metres): 215.6 × 35 × 13.5 *(65.7 × 10.7 × 4.2)*
Main machinery: 1 Mirrlees Blackstone diesel; 1120 hp(m) *(835 kW)*; 1 shaft
Speed, knots: 11
Complement: 20

AL SULTANA *1989, Royal Navy of Oman*

1 SURVEY CRAFT

AL RAHMANNIYA H 2

Displacement, tons: 23.6 full load
Dimensions, feet (metres): 50.8 × 13.1 × 4.3 *(15.5 × 4 × 1.3)*
Main machinery: 2 Volvo TMD 120A diesels; 604 hp(m) *(444 kW)* sustained; 2 shafts
Speed, knots: 13.5. **Range, miles:** 500 at 12 kts

Comment: Built by Watercraft, Shoreham, England in 1980.

AL RAHMANNIYA *1988, Royal Navy of Oman*

ROYAL YACHT SQUADRON

Name	*No*	*Builders*	*Commissioned*
AL SAID	—	Picchiotti SpA, Viareggio	1982

Displacement, tons: 3800 full load
Dimensions, feet (metres): 340.5 × 53.2 × 16.4 *(103.8 × 16.2 × 5)*
Main machinery: 2 GMT A 420-6 diesels; 8400 hp(m) *(6.17 MW)* sustained; 2 shafts; cp props; bow thruster
Speed, knots: 18
Complement: 156 (16 officers)
Radars: Navigation: Decca TM 1226C; ACS 1230C; I band.

Comment: This ship is an independent command and not part of the Omani Navy. Fitted with helicopter deck and fin stabilisers. Carries three Puma C service launches and one Rotork beach landing craft.

AL SAID *1991, van Ginderen Collection*

ROYAL OMAN POLICE

Note: In addition to the vessels listed below there are several harbour craft.

3 CG 29 TYPE (COASTAL PATROL CRAFT)

HARAS 7 **HARAS 9** **HARAS 10**

Displacement, tons: 84
Dimensions, feet (metres): 94.8 × 17.7 × 4.3 *(28.9 × 5.4 × 1.3)*
Main machinery: 2 MTU 12V 331 TC 92 diesels; 2660 hp(m) *(1.96 MW)* sustained; 2 shafts
Speed, knots: 25. **Range, miles:** 600 at 15 kts
Complement: 13
Guns: 2 Oerlikon 20 mm.

Comment: Built by Karlskrona Varvet. Commissioned in 1981-82. GRP Sandwich hulls.

HARAS 10 *11/1982, Royal Oman Police*

1 P 2000 TYPE (COASTAL PATROL CRAFT)

DHEEB AL BAHAR I

Displacement, tons: 80
Dimensions, feet (metres): 68.2 × 19 × 5 *(20.8 × 5.8 × 1.5)*
Main machinery: 2 MTU 12V 396 TB93 diesels; 3260 hp(m) *(2.4 MW)* sustained; 2 shafts
Speed, knots: 40. **Range, miles:** 423 at 36 kts; 700 at 18 kts
Guns: 1 Oerlikon 20 mm. 2—7.62 mm MGs.
Radars: Surface search: Furuno 701; I band.

Comment: Delivered January 1985 by Watercraft Ltd, Shoreham, England. GRP hull. Carries SATNAV.

DHEEB AL BAHAR I *1984*

5 VOSPER THORNYCROFT 75 ft TYPE (COASTAL PATROL CRAFT)

HARAS 1-5

Displacement, tons: 50
Dimensions, feet (metres): 75 × 20 × 5.9 *(22.9 × 6.1 × 1.8)*
Main machinery: 2 Caterpillar D348 diesels; 1840 hp *(1.37 MW)*; 2 shafts
Speed, knots: 24.5. **Range, miles:** 600 at 20 kts; 1000 at 11 kts
Complement: 11
Guns: 1 Oerlikon 20 mm.

Comment: First four completed 22 December 1975 by Vosper Thornycroft. GRP hulls. *Haras 5* commissioned November 1978.

VOSPER THORNYCROFT 75 ft Type *1984, N. Overington*

2 D 59116 TYPE (COASTAL PATROL CRAFT)

DHEEB AL BAHAR II and **III**

Displacement, tons: 65
Dimensions, feet (metres): 75.5 × 17.1 × 3.9 *(23 × 5.2 × 1.2)*
Main machinery: 2 MTU 12V 396 TB93 diesels; 3260 hp(m) *(2.4 MW)* sustained; 2 shafts
Speed, knots: 36. **Range, miles:** 420 at 30 kts
Complement: 11
Guns: 1—12.7 mm MG.
Radars: Surface search: Furuno 711-2; Furuno 2400; I band.

Comment: Built by Yokohama Yacht Co, Japan. Commissioned in 1988.

DHEEB AL BAHAR II *1988, Royal Oman Police*

1 P 1903 TYPE (COASTAL PATROL CRAFT)

HARAS 8

Displacement, tons: 26
Dimensions, feet (metres): 63 × 15.7 × 5.2 *(19.2 × 4.8 × 1.6)*
Main machinery: 2 MTU 8V 331 TC 92 diesels; 1770 hp(m) *(1.3 MW)*; 2 shafts
Speed, knots: 30. **Range, miles:** 1650 at 17 kts
Complement: 10
Guns: 2—12.7 mm MGs.

Comment: Built by Le Comte, Netherlands. Commissioned August 1981. Type 1903 Mk III.

HARAS 8 *12/1981, Royal Oman Police*

1 CG 27 TYPE (COASTAL PATROL CRAFT)

HARAS 6

Displacement, tons: 53
Dimensions, feet (metres): 78.7 × 18 × 6.2 *(24 × 5.5 × 1.9)*
Main machinery: 2 MTU 12V 331 TC 92 diesels; 2660 hp(m) *(1.96 MW)* sustained; 2 shafts
Speed, knots: 25
Complement: 11
Guns: 1 Oerlikon 20 mm.

Comment: Completed in 1980 by Karlskrona Varvet. GRP hull.

5 INSHORE PATROL CRAFT

ZAHRA 14 **ZAHRA 15** **ZAHRA 17** **ZAHRA 18** **ZAHRA 21**

Displacement, tons: 16; 18 (*Zahra 18* and *21*)
Dimensions, feet (metres): 45.6 × 14.1 × 4.6 *(13.9 × 4.3 × 1.4)*
52.5 × 13.8 × 7.5 *(16 × 4.2 × 2.3)* (*Zahra 18* and *21*)
Main machinery: 2 Cummins VTA-903-M diesels; 710 hp *(530 kW)*; 2 shafts
Speed, knots: 36. **Range, miles:** 510 at 22 kts
Complement: 5-6
Guns: 1 or 2—7.62 mm MGs.

Comment: Three built by Watercraft, Shoreham, England and completed in 1981. The last two completed by Emsworth S B in 1987.

ZAHRA 15 *1981, Michael D. J. Lennon*

3 LOGISTICS SUPPORT CRAFT

ZAHRA 16 **ZAHRA 20** **ZAHRA 22**

Displacement, tons: 13; 12 (*Zahra 22*)
Dimensions, feet (metres): 59 × 12.4 × 3.6 *(18 × 3.8 × 1.1)*
52.5 × 12.5 × 3.6 *(16 × 3.8 × 1.1)* (*Zahra 22*)
Main machinery: 2 Volvo Penta AQD 70 diesels; 430 hp(m) *(316 kW)* sustained; 2 props
Speed, knots: 20
Complement: 4
Guns: 2—7.62 mm MGs.

Comment: Built by Le Comte, Netherlands. Commissioned 1981-82. Designed as landing craft.

ZAHRA 22 *11/1982, Royal Oman Police*

8 CHEVERTON TYPE

ZAHRA 4-11

Displacement, tons: 3.5
Dimensions, feet (metres): 27 × 9 × 2.8 *(8.2 × 2.7 × 0.8)*
Main machinery: 2 diesels; 2 shafts
Speed, knots: 25

Comment: Purchased April 1975.

PAKISTAN

Headquarters' Appointment

Chief of the Naval Staff:
Admiral Saeed M Khan, HI(M), S Bt

Command Appointment

Commander Pakistan Fleet:
Rear Admiral Khalid Mir, S Bt

Diplomatic Representation

Naval Adviser in London:
Captain S A Malik, TI(M)
Naval Attaché in Paris:
Captain S T Naqvi
Naval Attaché in Washington:
Captain Obaid Sadiq

Personnel

(a) 1992: 18 525 (1455 officers)
(b) Voluntary service

Naval Bases

Karachi, Gwadar (shore base)

Prefix to Ships' Names

PNS

Maritime Security Agency

Set up in 1986 with four Shanghai II class and Fokker reconnaissance aircraft as its assets. Main purpose is to patrol the EEZ in co-operation with the Navy and the Army-manned Coast Guard. The obsolete destroyer *Badr* has been replaced as the HQ ship by *Nazim* (ex-*Tariq*), and four Chinese-built patrol craft have replaced the Shanghai IIs.

Strength of the Fleet

Type	*Active (reserve)*	*Building*
Submarines—Patrol	6	—
Submarines—40 tons	3	—
Destroyers	6	—
Frigates	10	—
Fast Attack Craft—Missile	8	—
Fast Attack Craft—Gun	12	—
Fast Attack Craft—Torpedo	(4)	—
Large Patrol Craft	1	—
Minehunters	0	3
Minesweepers—Coastal	2	—
Survey Vessel	6	—
Tankers	4	—
Tugs	8	—
Repair Ship	1	—
Auxiliaries	7	—
Customs Service	22	—
Coast Guard	5	—
Maritime Security Agency		
Destroyers	1	—
Large Patrol Craft	4	(4)

Mercantile Marine

Lloyd's Register of Shipping:
74 vessels of 358 150 tons gross

DELETIONS

Destroyers

1989 *Tariq* (converted MSA)

Minesweepers

1990 *Mujahid*

Auxiliaries

1991 *Bholu* (old), *Gama* (old)

Maritime Security Agency

1989 *Badr* (old)
1990 *Quetta, Sehwan*
1991 *Larkana, Sahiwal*

PENNANT LIST

Submarines

S 131	Hangor
S 132	Shushuk
S 133	Mangro
S 134	Ghazi
S 135	Hashmat
S 136	Hurmat

Destroyers

C 84	Babur
D 160	Alamgir
D 164	Shahjahan
D 166	Taimur
D 167	Tughril
D 168	Tippu Sultan

Frigates

F 159	Tabuk
F 161	Badr
F 163	Harbah
F 169	Hunain
F 262	Zulfiquar
F 263	Shamsher
F 264	Saif
F 265	Aslat
F 266	Khaibar
F 267	Siqqat

Minesweepers

M 160	Mahmood
M 165	Mukhtar

Light Forces

HDF 01-04	Huchuan class
P 140	Rajshahi
P 142	Lahore
P 143	Mardan
P 144	Gilgit
P 145	Pishin
P 147	Sukkur
P 149	Bahawalpur
P 154	Banum
P 155	Baluchistan
P 156	Kalat
P 159	Sind
P 161	Sarhad
P 197	Punjab
P 301-304	Huangfen class
P 1021	Haibat
P 1022	Jalalat
P 1023	Jurat
P 1024	Shujaat

Maritime Security Agency

D 156	Nazim
P 60	Barkat
P 61	Rehmat
P 62	Nusrat
P 63	Vehdat

Service Forces

A 20	Moawin
A 40	Attock
A 41	Dacca
A 42	Madadgar
A 44	Bholu
A 45	Gama
A 46	Zum Zum
A 47	Nasr
A 49	Gwadar
—	Kalamat
A 260	Orwell

SUBMARINES

Note: Reported that an interest has been shown in acquiring a Chinese Han class SSN and two Chinese Romeo class SSKs.

2 FRENCH AGOSTA CLASS

Name	*No*	*Builders*	*Laid down*	*Launched*	*Commissioned*
HASHMAT (ex-SAS *Astrant*)	S 135	Dubigeon Normandie, Nantes	15 Sep 1976	14 Dec 1977	17 Feb 1979
HURMAT (ex-SAS *Adventurous*)	S 136	Dubigeon Normandie, Nantes	18 Sep 1977	1 Dec 1978	18 Feb 1980

Displacement, tons: 1230 standard; 1490 surfaced; 1740 dived
Dimensions, feet (metres): 221.7 × 22.3 × 17.7 *(67.6 × 6.8 × 5.4)*
Main machinery: Diesel-electric; 2 SEMT-Pielstick 16 PA4 V185 VG diesels; 3600 hp(m) *(2.65 MW)*; 2 Jeumont Schneider alternators; 1.7 MW; 1 motor; 4600 hp(m) *(3.4 MW)*; 1 cruising motor; 32 hp(m) *(23 kW)*; 1 shaft
Speed, knots: 12 surfaced; 20 dived
Range, miles: 8500 at 9 kts snorting; 350 at 3.5 kts dived
Complement: 54 (7 officers)

Missiles: SSM: McDonnell Douglas Sub Harpoon; active radar homing to 130 km *(70 nm)* at 0.9 Mach; warhead 227 kg.
Torpedoes: 4—21 in *(533 mm)* bow tubes. Up to 20 ECAN F17P; wire-guided; active/passive homing to 20 km *(10.8 nm)* at 40 kts; warhead 250 kg; water ram discharge gear.
Countermeasures: ESM: ARUD; intercept and warning.
Radars: Surface search: Thomson-CSF DRUA 33; I band.
Sonars: Thomson Sintra DSUV 2H; passive search; medium frequency.
DUUA 2A/2B; active/passive search and attack; 8 kHz active.
DUUX 2A; hull-mounted; passive ranging.
DUUA 1D; active; high frequency.

Programmes: Purchased in mid-1978 after United Nations' ban on arms sales to South Africa. *Hashmat* arrived Karachi 31 October 1979, *Hurmat* arrived 11 August 1980.
Structure: Diving depth, 300 m *(985 ft)*. Equipped with SSM in 1985.
Operational: Endurance, 45 days.

HASHMAT *1990, G. Jacobs*

4 FRENCH DAPHNE CLASS

Name	No	Builders	Laid down	Launched	Commissioned
HANGOR	S 131	Arsenal de Brest	1 Dec 1967	28 June 1969	12 Jan 1970
SHUSHUK	S 132	C N Ciotat, Le Trait	1 Dec 1967	30 July 1969	12 Jan 1970
MANGRO	S 133	C N Ciotat, Le Trait	8 July 1968	7 Feb 1970	8 Aug 1970
GHAZI (ex-*Cachalote*)	S 134	Dubigeon, Normandie, Nantes	12 May 1967	23 Sep 1968	1 Oct 1969

Displacement, tons: 700 standard; 869 surfaced; 1043 dived
Dimensions, feet (metres): 189.6 × 22.3 × 15.1 *(57.8 × 6.8 × 4.6)*
Main machinery: Diesel-electric; 2 SEMT-Pielstick 12 PA4 V185 diesels; 2450 hp(m) *(1.8 MW)*; 2 Jeumont Schneider alternators; 1.7 MW; 2 motors; 2600 hp(m) *(1.9 MW)*; 2 shafts
Speed, knots: 13 surfaced; 15.5 dived
Range, miles: 4500 at 5 kts
Complement: 45 (5 officers)

Missiles: SSM: McDonnell Douglas Sub Harpoon; active radar homing to 130 km *(70 nm)* at 0.9 Mach; warhead 227 kg.
Torpedoes: 12—21 in *(533 mm)* (8 bow, 4 stern). Probably 12 ECAN L5 Mod 3; dual purpose; active/passive homing to 9.5 km *(5.1 nm)* at 35 kts; warhead 150 kg; depth to 550 m *(1800 ft)*. No reloads.
Countermeasures: ESM: ARUD; intercept and warning.
Radars: Surface search: Thomson-CSF DRUA 31; I band.
Sonars: Thomson Sintra DSUV 1; hull-mounted; passive search; medium frequency.
DUUA 1; active/passive search and attack.

Programmes: The first three are the first submarines built for the Pakistan Navy. The Portuguese Daphne class *Cachalote* was bought by Pakistan in December 1975.
Structure: They are broadly similar to the submarines built in France for Portugal and South Africa and the submarines constructed to the Daphne design in Spain, but slightly modified internally to suit Pakistan requirements and naval conditions. Diving depth 300 m *(985 ft)*. SSM capability added in late 1980s.
Operational: One in collision in late 1990 and badly damaged but back in service in 1992.

GHAZI *10/1991, G. Jacobs*

3 MIDGET SUBMARINES

Displacement, tons: 40 surfaced; 70 dived
Dimensions, feet (metres): 75.5 × 13.1 *(23 × 4)*
Speed, knots: 11 surfaced; 6 dived
Range, miles: 1200 surfaced; 60 dived
Complement: 4

Comment: These are probably SX 756 of Italian design and have replaced the SX 404 which were acquired in 1972. Diving depth of 100 m and can carry eight swimmers with two tons of explosives as well as two SDVs (swimmer delivery vehicles). Similar to the type in service in Colombia.

MIDGET SUBMARINE (Italian design) *10/1990, Hartmut Ehlers*

DESTROYERS

5 Ex-US GEARING (FRAM I) CLASS

Name	No	Builders	Laid down	Launched	Commissioned
ALAMGIR (ex-USS *Cone* DD 866)	D 160	Bethlehem, Staten Island	30 Nov 1944	10 May 1945	18 Aug 1945
SHAHJAHAN (ex-USS *Harold J Ellison* DD 864)	D 164	Bethlehem, Staten Island	3 Oct 1944	14 Mar 1945	23 June 1945
TAIMUR (ex-USS *Epperson* DD 719)	D 166	Todd Pacific Shipyards	20 June 1945	29 Dec 1945	19 Mar 1949
TUGHRIL (ex-USS *Henderson* DD 785)	D 167	Todd Pacific Shipyards	27 Oct 1944	28 May 1945	4 Aug 1945
TIPPU SULTAN (ex-USS *Damato* DD 871)	D 168	Bethlehem, Staten Island	10 May 1945	21 Nov 1945	27 Apr 1946

Displacement, tons: 2425 standard; 3500 full load
Dimensions, feet (metres): 390.5 × 41.2 × 19 *(119 × 12.6 × 5.8)*
Main machinery: 4 Babcock & Wilcox boilers; 600 psi *(43.3 kg/cm sq)*; 850°F *(454°C)*; 2 GE turbines; 60 000 hp *(45 MW)*; 2 shafts
Speed, knots: 32. **Range, miles:** 4500 at 16 kts
Complement: 274 (27 officers)

Missiles: SSM: 6 McDonnell Douglas Harpoon (3 twin) launchers (in *Shahjahan* and may be fitted in others); active radar homing to 130 km *(70 nm)* at 0.9 Mach; warhead 227 kg.
A/S: Honeywell ASROC Mk 112 octuple launcher ❶; 8 reloads; inertial guidance to 1.6-10 km *(1-5.4 nm)*; payload Mk 46 torpedo.
Guns: 2 US 5 in *(127 mm)*/38 (twin) Mk 38 ❷; 85° elevation; 15 rounds/minute to 17 km *(9.3 nm)* anti-surface; 11 km *(5.9 nm)* anti-aircraft; weight of shell 25 kg.
General Electric/General Dynamics 20 mm 6-barrelled Vulcan Phalanx Mk 15 ❸; 3000 rounds/minute combined to 1.5 km.
8—23 mm/87 (2 quad) ❹.
Torpedoes: 6—324 mm US Mk 32 (2 triple) tubes ❺. Probably Honeywell Mk 46; anti-submarine; active/passive homing to 11 km *(5.9 nm)* at 40 kts; warhead 44 kg.
Countermeasures: Decoys: 2 Plessey Shield 6-barrelled fixed launchers; Chaff and IR flares in distraction, decoy or centroid modes.
ESM: WLR 1 or Argo Phoenix II (in some); radar warning.
ECM: Racal; jammer.
Fire control: Mk 37 for 5 in guns. OE 2 SATCOM (in some).
Radars: Air search: Lockheed SPS 40 ❻; E/F band; range 320 km *(175 nm)*.
Surface search: Raytheon/Sylvania ❼; SPS 10; G band.
Navigation: Racal Decca TM 1226; I band.
Fire control: Western Electric Mk 25 ❽; I/J band.
Sonars: Sangamo SQS 23D with Raytheon Solid State transmitters; hull-mounted; active search and attack; medium frequency.

Helicopters: Facilities for 1 SA 319B Alouette III seldom used ❾.

Programmes: First pair transferred 29 April 1977, second pair 30 September 1980. Last two, *Alamgir* on 1 October 1982 and *Shahjahan* on 1 October 1983.

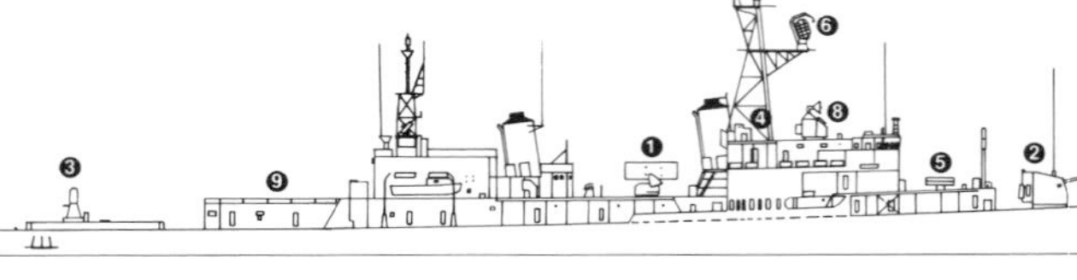

TUGHRIL *(Scale 1 : 1 200), Ian Sturton*

TUGHRIL *10/1988, Gilbert Gyssels*

Modernisation: Most recent improvements include an improved search sonar, Vulcan Phalanx replacing 'Y' gun turret (in D 160, 166 and 167 by 1991) and the addition of two USSR 23 mm quad guns at the base of the foremast. EW equipment has also been updated.

Operational: Form 25 Destroyer Squadron. *Tughril* is able to launch Banshee target drones. *Shahjahan* and *Tippu Sultan* are used as training ships. One of the class *Tariq* (D 165) was converted to an MSA HQ ship in early 1990 (see MSA section). *Shahjahan* may follow her in due course.

1 Ex-BRITISH COUNTY CLASS

Name	*No*	*Builders*	*Laid down*	*Launched*	*Commissioned*
BABUR (ex-HMS *London*)	C 84	Swan Hunter & Wigham Richardson, Wallsend	26 Feb 1960	7 Dec 1961	4 Nov 1963

Displacement, tons: 5440 standard; 6200 full load
Dimensions, feet (metres): 520.5 × 54 × 20.5 *(158.7 × 16.5 × 6.3)*
Main machinery: COSAG; 2 Babcock & Wilcox boilers; 700 psi *(49.2 kg/cm sq)*; 950°F *(510°C)*; 2 AEI turbines; 30 000 hp *(22.4 MW)*; 4 English Electric G6 gas turbines; 30 000 hp *(22.4 MW)*; 2 shafts
Speed, knots: 30
Complement: 470 (36 officers)

Missiles: SAM: 2 Short Bros Seacat GWS 22 quad launchers ❶; non-operational.
Guns: 4 Vickers 4.5 in *(114 mm)*/45 (2 twin) Mk 6 ❷; 80° elevation; 20 rounds/minute to 19 km *(10.4 nm)* anti-surface; 6 km *(3.3 nm)* anti-aircraft; weight of shell 25 kg.
6 China 37 mm/63 (3 twin) ❸; 85° elevation; 180 rounds/minute to 8.5 km *(4.6 nm)*; weight of shell 1.42 kg.
1 GE/GD 20 mm 6-barrelled Vulcan Phalanx Mk 15 ❹; 3000 rounds/minute combined to 1.5 km.
8 ZSU 23 mm (2 quad) ❺; anti-aircraft.
Countermeasures: Decoys: 2 Knebworth Corvus 8-tubed trainable ❻; distraction or centroid Chaff to 1 km.
ESM: Argo Phoenix II; radar warning.
ECM: Racal jammer.
Fire control: MRS 3 for 4.5 in guns.
Radars: Air search: Marconi Type 965M (single aerial) ❼; A band.
Admiralty Type 277M ❽; E band.
Air/surface search: Marconi Type 992Q ❾; E/F band.
Navigation: Decca 978; I band.
Fire control: Sperry/Plessey Type 903 ❿; I band (for 4.5 in guns).
Sonars: Graseby Type 177; hull-mounted; active search and attack; 7-9 kHz.
Type 176; passive search and torpedo warning.
Type 162; active classification and attack.

Helicopters: 2 Sea King Mk 45 ⓫

Programmes: Transferred from Royal Navy after refit 24 March 1982 and sailed for Pakistan May 1982. Officially classed as a cruiser.
Modernisation: Seaslug removed in 1984 and the spaces converted into accommodation and classrooms for trainees. In 1988 the flight deck was extended aft and hangar enlarged to carry Sea King helicopters. At the same time two twin 37 mm guns replaced the Seacat directors (although the launchers remain in place) and a Vulcan Phalanx gun was fitted on the mounting once used by the 901 radar director. A third twin 37 mm is mounted on the quarterdeck and two quadruple 23 mm guns are on new sponsons at bridge level either side of the foremast. A new ESM has been installed at the head of the foremast.
Operational: Primarily used as the midshipmen training ship but retains Flagship capabilities. The Sea King helicopters have no ASW gear but carry Exocet SSM.

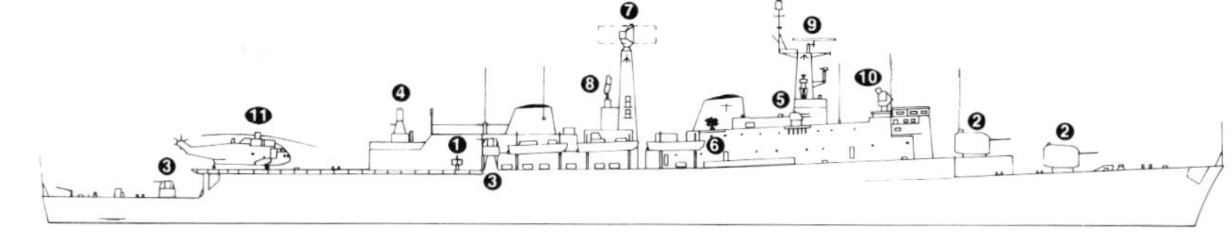

BABUR *(Scale 1 : 1 500), Ian Sturton*

BABUR *1990, Pakistan Navy*

BABUR *1991, Ships of the World*

FRIGATES

2 Ex-BRITISH LEANDER CLASS

Name	No	Builders	Laid down	Launched	Commissioned
ZULFIQUAR (ex-HMS *Apollo*)	F 262	Yarrows, Glasgow	1 May 1969	15 Oct 1970	28 May 1972
SHAMSHER (ex-HMS *Diomede*)	F 263	Yarrows, Glasgow	30 Jan 1968	15 Apr 1969	2 Apr 1971

Displacement, tons: 2500 standard; 2962 full load
Dimensions, feet (metres): 360 wl; 372 oa × 43 × 14.8 (keel); 18 (screws) *(109.7; 113.4 × 13.1 × 4.5; 5.5)*
Main machinery: 2 Babcock & Wilcox boilers; 550 psi *(38.7 kg/cm sq)*; 850°F *(454°C)*; 2 White/English Electric turbines; 30 000 hp *(22.4 MW)*; 2 shafts
Speed, knots: 28. **Range, miles:** 4000 at 15 kts
Complement: 235 (15 officers)

Missiles: SAM: Short Bros Seacat GWS 22 quad launcher ❶; optical/radar guidance to 5 km *(2.7 nm)*; warhead 10 kg.
Guns: 2 Vickers 4.5 in *(114 mm)*/45 Mk 6 (twin) ❷; 80° elevation; 20 rounds/minute to 19 km *(10.3 nm)* anti-surface; 6 km *(3.3 nm)* anti-aircraft; weight of shell 25 kg.
2 Oerlikon 20 mm/70 ❸; 50° elevation; 800 rounds/minute to 2 km; weight of shell 0.24 kg.
1 Oerlikon/BMARC 20 mm GAM-BO1 (on after end of flight deck) ❹; 55° elevation; 1000 rounds/minute to 2 km.
A/S mortars: 3-barrelled UK MoD Mortar Mk 10 ❺; automatic loading; range 1 km; warhead 92 kg.
Countermeasures: Decoys: Graseby Type 182; towed torpedo decoy.
2 Vickers Corvus 8-barrelled trainable launchers ❻; Chaff to 1 km.
ESM: UA-8/9/13; radar warning.
ECM: Type 668; jammer.
Fire control: MRS 3 system for 114 mm guns.
Radars: Air search: Marconi Type 966 ❼; A band; AKE-1; long range.
Surface search: Plessey Type 993 ❽; E/F band.
Navigation: Kelvin Hughes Type 1006; I band.
Fire control: Two Plessey Type 904 (for Seacat and 114 mm guns) ❾; I/J band.
Sonars: Kelvin Hughes Type 162M; hull-mounted; bottom classification; 50 kHz.
Graseby Type 170B; hull-mounted; active search and attack; 15 kHz.
Graseby Type 184P; hull-mounted; active search and attack; 6-9 kHz.

Helicopters: 1 SA 319B Alouette III ❿.

Programmes: Transferred 15 July 1988 (*Shamsher*) and 14 October 1988 (*Zulfiquar*). Both ships are from the Batch 3B broad-beamed group of this class.
Structure: No equipment changes made on transfer except the replacement of the Wasp helicopter by an Alouette III.
Operational: Both ships worked up in UK waters sailing for Pakistan in August and December 1988 respectively.

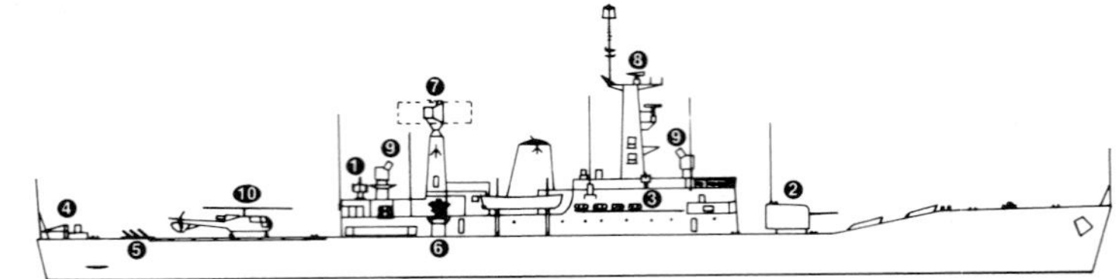

SHAMSHER (Scale 1 : 1 200), Ian Sturton

SHAMSHER 10/1991, G. Jacobs

ZULFIQUAR 11/1988, W. Sartori

4 Ex-US GARCIA CLASS

Name	No	Builders	Laid down	Launched	Commissioned
SAIF (ex-*Garcia*)	F 264 (ex-FF 1040)	Bethlehem Steel, San Francisco	16 Oct 1962	31 Oct 1963	21 Dec 1964
ASLAT (ex-*O'Callaghan*)	F 265 (ex-FF 1051)	Defoe Shipbuilding Co.	19 Feb 1964	20 Oct 1965	13 Jul 1968
KHAIBAR (ex-*Brumby*)	F 266 (ex-FF 1044)	Avondale Shipyard	1 Aug 1963	6 Jun 1964	5 Aug 1965
SIQQAT (ex-*Koelsch*)	F 267 (ex-FF 1049)	Defoe Shipbuilding Co.	19 Feb 1964	8 Jun 1965	10 Jun 1967

Displacement, tons: 2620 standard; 3403 full load
Dimensions, feet (metres): 414.5 × 44.2 × 24 sonar; 14.5 keel *(126.3 × 13.5 × 7.3; 4.4)*
Main machinery: 2 Foster-Wheeler boilers; 1200 psi *(83.4 kg/cm sq)*; 950°F *(510°C)*; 1 GE/Westinghouse turbine; 35 000 hp *(26 MW)*; 1 shaft
Speed, knots: 27.5. **Range, miles:** 4000 at 20 kts
Complement: 270 (18 officers)

Missiles: A/S: Honeywell ASROC Mk 116 octuple launcher ❶; inertial flight to 1.6-10 km *(1-5.5 nm)*; payload Mk 46 torpedo. *Aslat* and *Siqqat* have reload magazines.
Guns: 2 USN 5 in *(127 mm)*/38 Mk 30 ❷; 85° elevation; 15 rounds/minute to 17 km *(9.3 nm)*; weight of shell 25 kg.
GE/GD 20 mm 6-barrelled Vulcan Phalanx Mk 15; to be fitted in all four ships.
Torpedoes: 6—324 mm Mk 32 (2 triple) tubes ❸; 14 Honeywell Mk 46 Mod 5; active/passive homing to 11 km *(6 nm)* at 40 kts; warhead 44 kg.
Countermeasures: Decoys: 2 Loral Hycor Mk 33 RBOC 6-barrelled Chaff launchers. T-Mk 6 Fanfare; torpedo decoy system. Prairie/Masker hull noise/blade rate suppression.
ESM: WLR-6, radar warning.
ECM: ULQ-6, jammer.

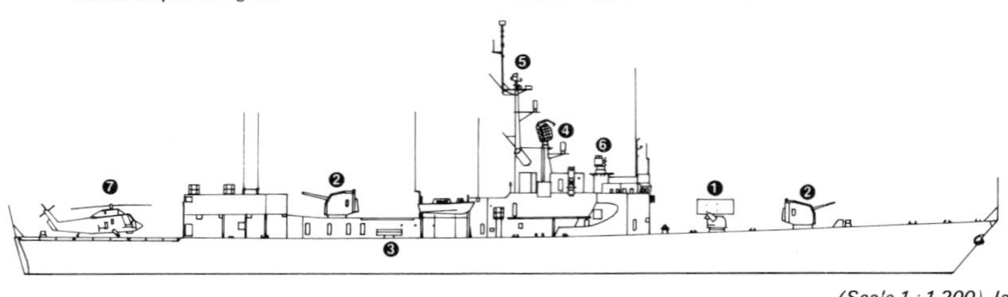

SAIF (Scale 1 : 1 200), Ian Sturton

Fire control: Mk 56 GFCS. Mk 114 ASW FCS. Mk 1 target designation system.
Radars: Air search: Lockheed SPS 40 ❹; E/F band; range 320 km *(175 nm)*
Surface search: Raytheon SPS 10 ❺; G band.
Navigation: Marconi LN 66; I band.
Fire control: General Electric Mk 35 ❻; I/J band.
Tacan: SRN 15.
Sonars: EDO/General Electric SQS 26; bow-mounted; active search and attack; medium frequency.

Helicopters: 1 Seasprite SH-2G Lamps I ❼. May be acquired in due course (see *Shipborne Aircraft*).

Programmes: Four frigates leased from the US. *Saif* transferred 31 January 1989; *Aslat* 8 February 1989; *Khaibar* 31 March 1989 and *Siqqat* on 31 May 1989. All arrived in Pakistan by the end of July 1989.
Modernisation: Vulcan Phalanx CIWS is to be fitted in all of the class in due course.
Structure: In US service *Saif* had a towed array winch on her flight deck which has been removed.

SAIF 1990, Pakistan Navy

4 Ex-US BROOKE CLASS

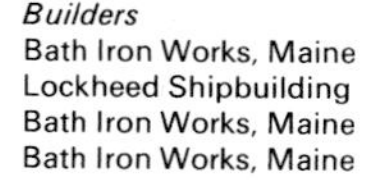

Name	*No*	*Builders*	*Laid down*	*Launched*	*Commissioned*
BADR (ex-*Julius A Furer*)	F 161 (ex-FFG 6)	Bath Iron Works, Maine	12 Jul 1965	22 Jul 1966	11 Nov 1967
HARBAH (ex-*Brooke*)	F 163 (ex-FFG 1)	Lockheed Shipbuilding	10 Dec 1962	19 Jul 1963	3 Jun 1967
TABUK (ex-*Richard L Page*)	F 159 (ex-FFG 5)	Bath Iron Works, Maine	4 Jan 1965	4 Apr 1966	5 Aug 1967
HUNAIN (ex-*Talbot*)	F 169 (ex-FFG 4)	Bath Iron Works, Maine	4 May 1964	6 Jan 1966	22 Apr 1967

Displacement, tons: 2640 standard; 3426 full load
Dimensions, feet (metres): 414.5 × 44.2 × 24.2 sonar; 15 keel *(126.3 × 13.5 × 7.4; 4.6)*
Main machinery: 2 Foster-Wheeler boilers; 1200 psi *(83.4 kg/cm sq)*; 950°F *(510°C)*; 1 GE/Westinghouse turbine; 35 000 hp *(26 MW)*; 1 shaft
Speed, knots: 27.2. **Range, miles:** 4000 at 20 kts
Complement: 277 (17 officers)

Missiles: SAM: 16 GDC Standard MR-SM1 Block IV; Mk 22 Mod 0 launcher ❶; semi-active radar homing to 46 km *(25 nm)* at 2 Mach; height envelope 45.7-18 288 m *(150-60 000 ft)*.
A/S: Honeywell ASROC; Mk 116 octuple launcher ❷; inertial flight to 1.6-10 km *(1-5.5 nm)*; payload Mk 46 torpedo. All except *Harbah* have a reload magazine.
Guns: 1 USN 5 in *(127 mm)*/38 Mk 30 ❸; 85° elevation; 15 rounds/minute to 17 km *(9.3 nm)*; weight of shell 25 kg.
1 GE/GD 20 mm 6-barrelled Vulcan Phalanx Mk 15 *(Badr)*.
Torpedoes: 6—324 mm Mk 32 (2 triple) tubes ❹. 14 Honeywell Mk 46 Mod 5; active/passive homing to 11 km *(6 nm)* at 40 kts; warhead 44 kg.
Countermeasures: Decoys: 4 Loral Hycor SRBOC 6-barrelled fixed Mk 36; IR flares and Chaff to 4 km *(2.2 nm)*.
ESM/ECM: WLR-6, ULQ-6; radar warning and jammers.
Fire control: Mk 74 Mod 6 MFCS. Mk 56 Mod 43 GFCS. Mk 114 ASW FCS. Mk 4 Mod 2 weapon direction system.
Radars: Air search: Hughes SPS 52 ❺; 3D; E/F band; range 439 km *(240 nm)*.
Surface search: Raytheon SPS 10 ❻; G band.
Navigation: Marconi LN 66; I band.
Fire control: Raytheon SPG 51C ❼; G/I band (for SAM).
General Electric Mk 35 ❽; I/J band (for gun).
Tacan: SRN 15.
Sonars: EDO/General Electric SQS 26; bow-mounted; active search and attack; medium frequency.

Helicopters: 1 Seasprite SH-2G Lamps I ❾. May be acquired in due course (see *Shipborne Aircraft*).

Programmes: Four frigates leased from the US. Classified as Destroyers in the Pakistan Navy. *Badr* transferred 31 January 1989; *Harbah* 8 February 1989; *Tabuk* 31 March 1989 and *Hunain* on 31 May 1989. All arrived in Pakistan by the end of July 1989.
Structure: Identical to ex-Garcia class except for the SAM missile system which replaced the second 5 in gun and different electronic equipment. The helicopter hangar is telescopic. In 1990 *Badr* had a Vulcan Phalanx CIWS mounted on her flight deck. This may be a temporary fit until helicopters are available.

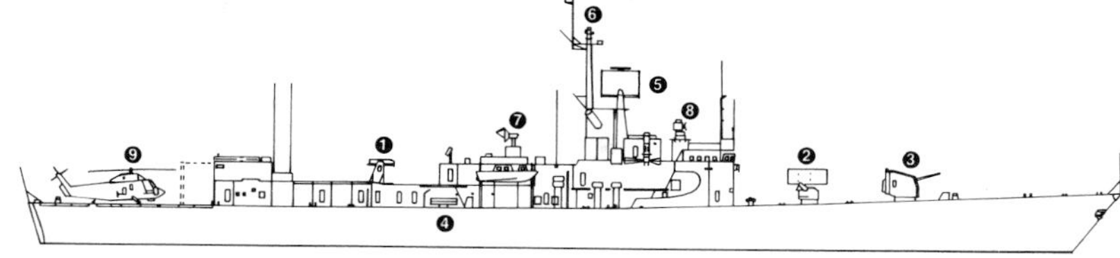

HARBAH *(Scale 1 : 1 200), Ian Sturton*

BADR (with Phalanx) *1990, Pakistan Navy*

HUNAIN *1991*

TABUK *1990, Pakistan Navy*

SHIPBORNE AIRCRAFT

Numbers/Type: 6 Kaman SH-2G Seasprite.
Operational speed: 130 kts *(241 km/h)*.
Service ceiling: 22 500 ft *(6 860 m)*.
Range: 367 nm *(679 km)*
Role/Weapon systems: Surface search and ASW for ex-US Frigates. A contract planned for mid-1990 with FMS funding has been embargoed by Congress until the President of the USA signs an agreement that Pakistan is a 'non-nuclear' country. Other alternatives include Lynx or Dauphin. Sensors: LN-66HP radar; ALR-66 receivers, ASN-123 tactical nav, ASQ-81 MAD, ARR-57 sonobuoy receivers. Weapons: ASW; 2 × Mk 46 torpedoes, 8 × Mk 25 smoke markers.

SEASPRITE

Numbers/Type: 4 Aerospatiale SA 319B Alouette III.
Operational speed: 113 kts *(210 km/h)*.
Service ceiling: 10 500 ft *(3200 m)*.
Range: 290 nm *(540 km)*.
Role/Weapon systems: Reconnaissance helicopter; one embarked in County class DLG and can be carried in the Frigates for reconnaissance, support and SAR. Sensors: Weather/search radar. Weapons: Generally unarmed.

ALOUETTE III — *1989, Paul Jackson*

Numbers/Type: 6 Westland Sea King Mk 45.
Operational speed: 125 kts *(232 km/h)*.
Service ceiling: 10 500 ft *(3200 m)*.
Range: 630 nm *(1165 km)*.
Role/Weapon systems: ASVW helicopter with all ASW gear removed. Sensors: MEL search radar. Weapons: ASW; none. ASV; 1 × AM 39 Exocet missile.

SEA KING — *1990, Pakistan Navy*

LAND-BASED MARITIME AIRCRAFT

Numbers/Type: 4 Breguet Atlantic 1.
Operational speed: 355 kts *(658 km/h)*.
Service ceiling: 32 800 ft *(10 000 m)*.
Range: 4855 nm *(8995 km)*.
Role/Weapon systems: Long-range MR/ASW cover for Arabian Sea; ex-French stock. Sensors: Thomson-CSF radar, ECM/ESM, MAD, sonobuoys. Weapons: ASW; 9 × Mk 46 or 244/S torpedoes, depth bombs, mines. ASV; 2 × AS 12 or AM 39 Exocet missiles.

Numbers/Type: 3 Lockheed P-3C Orion.
Operational speed: 410 kts *(760 km/h)*.
Service ceiling: 28 300 ft *(8625 m)*.
Range: 4000 nm *(7410 km)*.
Role/Weapon systems: Maritime reconnaissance aircraft ordered under US FMS policy for delivery by May 1991 but embargoed for the same reasons as the Seasprite helicopters. Sensors and weapons to include Proteus acoustic processor and possibly air-launched Harpoon.

Numbers/Type: 5 AMD-BA Mirage 5.
Operational speed: 750 kts *(1390 km/h)*.
Service ceiling: 59 055 ft *(18 000 m)*.
Range: 740 nm *(1370 km)*.
Role/Weapon systems: Maritime strike aircraft. Sensors: Thomson-CSF radar. Weapons: ASVW; 2 × AM 39 Exocet; 2 × 30 mm DEFA.

Numbers/Type: 2 Fokker F27 MPA Friendship.
Operational speed: 250 kts *(463 km/h)*.
Service ceiling: 25 000 ft *(7620 m)*.
Range: 2700 nm *(5000 km)*.
Róle/Weapon systems: Visual reconnaissance and coastal surveillance aircraft (ex-Airline) used by the Maritime Security Agency. Sensors: Weather radar and visual means only. Weapons: Limited armament.

LIGHT FORCES

4 Ex-CHINESE HUANGFEN CLASS (FAST ATTACK CRAFT—MISSILE)

P 301-P 304 (ex-*1025-1028*)

Displacement, tons: 171 standard; 205 full load
Dimensions, feet (metres): 110.2 × 24.9 × 8.9 *(33.6 × 7.6 × 2.7)*
Main machinery: 3 M503 diesels; 12 000 hp(m) *(8.8 MW)*; 3 shafts
Speed, knots: 35. **Range, miles:** 800 at 30 kts
Complement: 28
Missiles: SSM: 4 Hai Ying 2; active radar or IR homing to 95 km *(51 nm)* at 0.9 Mach; warhead 513 kg.
Guns: 4 Norinco 25 mm/80 (2 twin); 85° elevation; 270 rounds/minute to 3 km *(1.6 nm)*; weight of shell 0.34 kg.
Radars: Surface search/target indication: Square Tie; I band.

Comment: Transferred April 1984. Chinese version of the Soviet Osa II class.

P 303 (old number) — *1989, Pakistan Navy*

4 Ex-CHINESE HAINAN CLASS (FAST ATTACK CRAFT—GUN)

BALUCHISTAN P 155 **SIND** P 159 **SARHAD** P 161 **PUNJAB** P 197

Displacement, tons: 375 standard; 392 full load
Dimensions, feet (metres): 192.8 × 23.6 × 6 *(58.8 × 7.2 × 2.2)*
Main machinery: 4 PCR/Kolumna Type 9-D diesels; 4400 hp(m) *(3.2 MW)*; 4 shafts
Speed, knots: 30.5. **Range, miles:** 1300 at 15 kts
Complement: 70
Guns: 4 Norinco 57 mm/70 (2 twin); 85° elevation; 120 rounds/minute to 12 km *(6.5 nm)*; weight of shell 6.3 kg.
4 Norinco 25 mm/80 (2 twin); 85° elevation; 270 rounds/minute to 3 km *(1.6 nm)*; weight of shell 0.34 kg.
A/S mortars: 4 RBU 1200 5-tubed fixed; range 1200 m; warhead 34 kg.
Depth charges: 2 projectors; 2 racks.
Mines: Rails fitted.
Radars: Surface search: Pot Head; I band.
Sonars: Hull-mounted; active attack; high frequency.

Comment: First pair transferred mid-1976, second pair in April 1980.

SARHAD — *7/1987*

PUNJAB — *1990, Pakistan Navy*

4 Ex-CHINESE HEGU CLASS (FAST ATTACK CRAFT—MISSILE)

HAIBAT P 1021 **JALALAT** P 1022 **JURAT** P 1023 **SHUJAAT** P 1024

Displacement, tons: 68 standard; 79.2 full load
Dimensions, feet (metres): 88.6 × 20.7 × 4.3 *(27 × 6.3 × 1.3)*
Main machinery: 4 Type L-12V-180 diesels; 4800 hp(m) *(3.53 MW)*; 4 shafts
Speed, knots: 37.5. **Range, miles:** 400 at 30 kts
Complement: 17
Missiles: SSM: 2 Hai Ying 2; active radar or IR homing to 95 km *(51 nm)* at 0.9 Mach; warhead 513 kg.
Guns: 2 Norinco 25 mm/80 (twin); 85° elevation; 270 rounds/minute to 3 km *(1.6 nm)*; weight of shell 0.34 kg.
Radars: Surface search: Pot Head; I band.

Comment: Two transferred in May and two in October 1981. Steel hull version of Komar class.

JALALAT *1983, Pakistan Navy*

8 Ex-CHINESE SHANGHAI II CLASS (FAST ATTACK CRAFT—GUN)

LAHORE P 142 **MARDAN** P 143 **GILGIT** P 144 **PISHIN** P 145 **SUKKUR** P 147 **BAHAWALPUR** P 149 **BANUM** P 154 **KALAT** P 156

Displacement, tons: 113 standard; 131 full load
Dimensions, feet (metres): 127.3 × 17.7 × 5.6 *(38.8 × 5.4 × 1.7)*
Main machinery: 2 Type L12-180 diesels; 2400 hp(m) *(1.76 MW)* (forward); 2 Type 12-D-6 diesels; 1820 hp(m) *(1.34 MW)* (aft); 4 shafts
Speed, knots: 30. **Range, miles:** 700 at 16.5 kts
Complement: 34
Guns: 4—37 mm/63 (2 twin). 4—25 mm/80 (2 twin).
Depth charges: 2 projectors; 8 weapons.
Mines: Fitted with mine rails for approx 10 mines.
Radars: Surface search: Skin Head; I band.

Comment: Acquired between 1972 and 1976. Four were transferred to the Maritime Security Agency in 1986 and scrapped in 1990. Some of the remaining eight are in reserve.

GILGIT *1990, Pakistan Navy*

4 Ex-CHINESE HUCHUAN CLASS (FAST ATTACK HYDROFOIL—TORPEDO)

HDF 01, 02, 03, 04

Displacement, tons: 39 standard; 45.8 full load
Dimensions, feet (metres): 71.5 × 20.7 × 11.8 *(21.8 × 6.3 × 3.6)*
Main machinery: 3 Type M-50-14 diesels; 2550 hp(m) *(1.9 MW)* sustained; 3 shafts
Speed, knots: 50 foilborne. **Range, miles:** 500 at 30 kts
Complement: 11
Guns: 4—14.5 mm (2 twin) MGs.
Torpedoes: 2—21 in *(533 mm)*; anti-surface.
Radars: Surface search: Skin Head; I band.

Comment: Hydrofoil craft transferred by China in 1973. All are kept in reserve but in theory could be made operational quite quickly.

HUCHUAN Class, 03 *1983, Pakistan Navy*

1 TOWN CLASS (LARGE PATROL CRAFT)

Name	*No*	*Builders*	*Commissioned*
RAJSHAHI	P 140	Brooke Marine	1965

Displacement, tons: 115 standard; 143 full load
Dimensions, feet (metres): 107 × 20 × 6.9 *(32.6 × 6.1 × 2.1)*
Main machinery: 2 MTU 12V 538 diesels; 3400 hp(m) *(2.5 MW)*; 2 shafts
Speed, knots: 24
Complement: 19
Guns: 2 Bofors 40 mm/70.

Comment: The last survivor in Pakistan of a class of four built by Brooke Marine in 1965. Steel hull and aluminium superstructure.

RAJSHAHI *1989, Pakistan Navy*

MARITIME SECURITY AGENCY

Note: (i) All ships are painted white with a distinctive diagonal blue band and MSA on each side. (ii) Four Osborne class patrol craft may be acquired in due course.

1 Ex-US GEARING (FRAM 1) CLASS

Name	*No*	*Builders*	*Commissioned*
NAZIM (ex-*Tariq*, ex-*Wiltsie*)	D 156 (ex-D 165, ex-DD 716)	Federal SB & DD Co	12 Jan 1946

Comment: Transferred from the Navy on 25 January 1990 and has replaced the old *Badr* as the MSA Flagship. All details as for the Gearing class (see *Destroyers*) except that ASROC and Torpedo Tubes have been removed and there is a quadruple 14.5 mm gun mounting on each side of the foremast. A second of the class may be similarly converted in due course.

NAZIM *1991, Ships of the World*

4 BARKAT CLASS (LARGE PATROL CRAFT)

Name	*No*	*Builders*	*Commissioned*
BARKAT	P 60	China Shipbuilding Corp	29 Dec 1989
REHMAT	P 61	China Shipbuilding Corp	29 Dec 1989
NUSRAT	P 62	China Shipbuilding Corp	13 June 1990
VEHDAT	P 63	China Shipbuilding Corp	13 June 1990

Displacement, tons: 435 full load
Dimensions, feet (metres): 190.3 × 24.9 × 7.5 *(58 × 7.6 × 2.3)*
Main machinery: 4 MTU 16V 396 TB93 diesels; 8720 hp(m) *(6.4 MW)* sustained; 4 shafts
Speed, knots: 27. **Range, miles:** 1500 at 12 kts
Complement: 42 (6 officers)
Guns: 2—37 mm/63 (twin); 4—25 mm/80 (2 twin).
Radars: Surface search: I band.

Comment: Type P58A patrol craft built in China for the MSA. First two arrived in Karachi at the end of January 1990, second pair in August 1990. There is an option for two more. These vessels replaced four Shanghai II class which have been scrapped.

BARKAT *1990, CSSB*

MINE WARFARE FORCES

Note: There may also be five inshore vessels used for harbour MCM operations. Numbers MSI 01, 02, 06-08.

2 MSC 268 CLASS (MINESWEEPERS—COASTAL)

MAHMOOD (ex-*MSC 267*) M 160 **MUKHTAR** (ex-*MSC 274*) M 165

Displacement, tons: 330 light; 390 full load
Dimensions, feet (metres): 144 × 27.9 × 8.5 *(43.9 × 8.5 × 2.6)*
Main machinery: 2 GM 8-268A diesels; 880 hp *(656 kW)*; 2 shafts
Speed, knots: 13.5. **Range, miles:** 3000 at 10.5 kts
Complement: 39
Guns: 4 USSR 23 mm (quad).
Radars: Navigation: Decca 45; I band.

Comment: Transferred to Pakistan by the USA under MAP. *Mukhtar* on 25 June 1959 and *Mahmood* in May 1957.

MAHMOOD *1991, Pakistan Navy*

0 + 3 ERIDAN CLASS (MINEHUNTERS)

Displacement, tons: 562 standard; 595 full load
Dimensions, feet (metres): 168.9 × 29.2 × 8.2 *(51.5 × 8.9 × 2.5)*
Main machinery: 1 Brons Werkspoor A-RUB 215X-12 diesel; 1860 hp(m) *(1.37 MW)* sustained; 1 shaft; Lips cp prop; Auxiliary propulsion; 2 motors; 240 hp(m) *(179 kW)*; 2 active rudders; 2 bow thrusters
Speed, knots: 15; 7 on auxiliary propulsion. **Range, miles:** 3000 at 12 kts
Complement: 46 (5 officers)
Guns: 1 GIAT 20F2 20 mm; 1—12.7 mm MG.
Countermeasures: MCM; 2 PAP 104 systems; mechanical sweep gear. AP-4 acoustic sweep.
Radars: Navigation: Racal Decca 1229; I band.
Sonars: Thomson Sintra DUBM 21B; hull-mounted; active; high frequency; 100 kHz (±10 kHz).

Comment: Contract signed 17 January 1992. The first is the ex-French *Sagittaire* which is to transfer in August 1992; the second is building at Lorient Dockyard and the third at Karachi.

ERIDAN Class *1991, Bram Risseeuw*

TANKERS

1 FUQING CLASS (AOR)

Name	*No*	*Builders*	*Commissioned*
NASR (ex-*X-350*)	A 47	Dalian Shipyard	27 Aug 1987

Displacement, tons: 7500 standard; 21 750 full load
Dimensions, feet (metres): 561 × 71.5 × 30.8 *(171 × 21.8 × 9.4)*
Main machinery: 1 Sulzer 8RL B66 diesel; 13 000 hp(m) *(9.56 MW)*; 1 shaft
Speed, knots: 18. **Range, miles:** 18 000 at 14 kts
Complement: 130 (during visit to Australia in October 1988 carried 373 (23 officers) including 100 cadets)
Cargo capacity: 10 550 tons fuel; 1000 tons dieso; 200 tons feed water; 200 tons drinking water
Radars: Navigation: Two Decca 1006; I band.
Helicopters: 1 SA 319B Alouette III.

Comment: Similar to Chinese ships of the same class. Two replenishment at sea positions on each side for liquids and one for solids.

1 Ex-US MISSION CLASS (AOR)

Name	*No*	*Builders*	*Commissioned*
DACCA (ex-USNS *Mission Santa Cruz* AO 132)	A 41	Marinship Corp, California	21 June 1944

Displacement, tons: 5730 light; 22 380 full load
Dimensions, feet (metres): 524 × 68 × 31 *(159.7 × 20.7 × 9.5)*
Main machinery: Turbo-electric; 2 Babcock & Wilcox boilers; 2 GE turbo generators; 10 000 hp(m) *(7.46 MW)*; 2 motors; 1 shaft
Speed, knots: 16
Complement: 160 (15 officers)
Cargo capacity: 20 000 tons fuel
Guns: 3 Bofors 40 mm/60.

Comment: Transferred on loan to Pakistan under MDAP. Handed over from the USA on 17 January 1963 after being fitted with underway replenishment rigs on both sides. Purchased 31 May 1974. May be in reserve.

DACCA *1990, Pakistan Navy*

2 HARBOUR TANKERS

Name	*No*	*Builders*	*Commissioned*
GWADAR	A 49	Karachi Shipyard	1984
KALAMAT	—	Karachi Shipyard	1992

Displacement, tons: 831 gross
Dimensions, feet (metres): 206 × 37.1 × 9.8 *(62.8 × 11.3 × 3)*
Main machinery: 1 Sulzer diesel; 550 hp(m) *(404 kW)*; 1 shaft
Speed, knots: 10

Comment: Second of class launched 6 June 1991. One used for oil and one for water.

GWADAR *1987*

OCEANOGRAPHIC SHIP

BEHR PAIMA

Measurement, tons: 1183 gross
Dimensions, feet (metres): 200.1 × 38.7 × 12.1 *(61 × 11.8 × 3.7)*
Main machinery: 2 Daihatsu diesels; 2000 hp(m) *(1.47 MW)*; 2 shafts
Speed, knots: 13.7
Complement: 84 (16 officers)

Comment: Ordered from Ishikawajima, Japan in November 1981. Laid down 16 February 1982, completed 17 December 1982. There is a second survey ship *Jatli* under civilian control.

BEHR PAIMA *1989, G. Jacobs*

NASR *9/1988, John Mortimer*

TUGS

Note: There are three more general purpose tugs plus two harbour tugs *Goga* and *Jhara*.

1 Ex-US CHEROKEE CLASS

Name	*No*	*Builders*	*Commissioned*
MADADGAR (ex-USS *Yuma* ATF 94)	A 42	Commercial Iron Works, Portland, Oregon	31 Aug 1943

Displacement, tons: 1235 standard; 1640 full load
Dimensions, feet (metres): 205 × 38.5 × 17 *(62.5 × 11.7 × 5.2)*
Main machinery: Diesel-electric; 4 GM 12-278 diesels; 4400 hp *(3.28 MW)*; 4 generators; 1 motor; 3000 hp *(2.24 MW)*; 1 shaft
Speed, knots: 16.5. **Range, miles:** 6500 at 16 kts
Complement: 85
Guns: 2 Bofors 40 mm (aft). 1 Oerlikon 20 mm (fwd).
Radars: Navigation: Decca 45; I band.

Comment: Ocean-going salvage tug. Transferred from the US Navy to the Pakistan Navy on 25 March 1959 under MDAP. Fitted with powerful pumps and other salvage equipment. Used for MCMV support and submarine rescue.

2 COASTAL TUGS

Name	*No*	*Builders*	*Commissioned*
BHOLU	A 44	Giessendam Shipyard, Netherlands	Apr 1991
GAMA	A 45	Giessendam Shipyard, Netherlands	Apr 1991

Displacement, tons: 265 full load
Dimensions, feet (metres): 85.3 × 22.3 × 9.5 *(26 × 6.8 × 2.9)*
Main machinery: 2 Cummins KTA-38M diesels; 1900 hp *(1.4 MW)*; 2 shafts
Speed, knots: 12
Complement: 6

Comment: Ordered from Damen in 1990. Have replaced the two old tugs of the same name and pennant numbers.

BHOLU *1991, Pakistan Navy*

AUXILIARIES

1 AJAX CLASS (REPAIR SHIP)

Name	*No*	*Builders*	*Commissioned*
MOAWIN (ex-USS *Hector*)	A 20 (ex-AR 7)	Todd Shipyards, Los Angeles	7 Feb 1944

Displacement, tons: 9140 standard; 16 245 full load
Dimensions, feet (metres): 529.3 × 73.3 × 23.3 *(161.3 × 22.3 × 7.1)*
Main machinery: 4 Babcock & Wilcox boilers; 2 Allis-Chalmers turbines; 11 000 hp *(8.2 MW)*; 2 shafts
Speed, knots: 19.2. **Range, miles:** 18 000 at 12 kts
Complement: 841 (29 officers)
Guns: 4 Oerlikon 20 mm Mk 67.
Radars: Surface search: Raytheon SPS 10 series; G band.

Comment: Ex-US repair ship transferred 20 April 1989 and modernised at Subic Bay, Philippines. Should have recommissioned on 20 January 1990 but this was probably delayed until April 1990. May be moored permanently.

MOAWIN *1990, Pakistan Navy*

2 UTILITY CRAFT

427 **428**

Measurement, tons: 57 gross
Dimensions, feet (metres): 65.6 × 16.4 × 4.9 *(20 × 5 × 1.5)*
Main machinery: 2 Detroit 8V 71 TI diesels; 1360 hp *(1 MW)*; 2 shafts
Speed, knots: 12

Comment: Built by Karachi Shipyard and completed in 1991.

2 WATER BARGES

ZUM ZUM A 46 **ATTOCK** A 40

Displacement, tons: 1200 full load
Dimensions, feet (metres): 177.2 × 32.3 × 15.1 *(54 × 9.8 × 4.6)*
Main machinery: 2 diesels; 800 hp(m) *(276 kW)*; 2 shafts
Speed, knots: 8
Cargo capacity: 550 tons
Guns: 2 Oerlikon 20 mm.

Comment: Built in Italy in 1957 under MDAP.

ATTOCK *1990*

1 DEGAUSSING VESSEL

Displacement, tons: 250
Dimensions, feet (metres): 115.5 × 23 × 7.9 *(35.2 × 7 × 2.4)*
Main machinery: 1 diesel; 375 hp(m) *(276 kW)*; 1 shaft
Speed, knots: 10

Comment: Built at Karachi with French assistance 1981-82.

1 SUPPLY TENDER

ORWELL A 260

Comment: Patrol craft, supply tender and berthing hulk based at Gwadar.

1 OIL BARGE

JANBAZ

Measurement, tons: 282 gross
Dimensions, feet (metres): 114.8 × 30.5 × 11.5 *(35 × 9.3 × 3.5)*
Main machinery: 2 Niigata diesels; 2 shafts

Comment: Built by Karachi Shipyard in 1990.

2 FLOATING DOCKS

PESHAWAR (ex-US *ARD 6*) **FD II**

Comment: *Peshawar* transferred June 1961, 3000 tons lift. *FD II* built 1974, 1200 tons lift.

COAST GUARD AND CUSTOMS SERVICE

Note: Unlike the Maritime Security Agency which comes under the Defence Ministry, the official Coast Guard was set up in 1985 and is manned by the Army and answerable to the Ministry of the Interior.

1 SWALLOW CRAFT

SAIF

Displacement, tons: 30 full load
Dimensions, feet (metres): 65.6 × 14.4 × 4.3 *(20 × 4.4 × 1.3)*
Main machinery: 2 diesels; 1800 hp(m) *(1.3 MW)*; 2 shafts
Speed, knots: 27. **Range, miles:** 500 at 20 kts
Complement: 8
Guns: 2—12.7 mm MGs.

Comment: Built in South Korea in 1986.

22 CRESTITALIA 16.5 METRE CRAFT

P 551-568 (Customs) **SADD** **SHABAZ** **VAQAR** **BURQ**

Displacement, tons: 23
Dimensions, feet (metres): 54.1 × 17.1 × 2.9 *(16.5 × 5.2 × 0.9)*
Main machinery: 2 diesels; 1600 hp(m) *(1.18 MW)*; 2 shafts
Speed, knots: 30. **Range, miles:** 425 at 25 kts
Complement: 5
Guns: 1—14.5 mm MG.

Comment: Acquired 1979-80 from Crestitalia, Italy. The four named craft belong to the Coast Guard.

4 UNIFLITE 10 METRE CRAFT

Displacement, tons: 9
Dimensions, feet (metres): 32.2 × 11.5 × 2.6 *(9.8 × 3.5 × 0.8)*
Main machinery: 2 diesels; 550 hp(m) *(404 kW)*; 2 waterjets
Speed, knots: 30. **Range, miles:** 150 at 25 kts
Complement: 4
Guns: 3—12.7 mm (1 twin, 1 single) MGs.

Comment: Built by Uniflite, Washington in 1983. Customs craft.

PANAMA

Senior Appointment

Major Jose Rosas

General

A force which became a naval service in 1983 and is split between both coasts. Aircraft are all Air Force operated. During the US invasion in December 1989, half the fleet was sunk and most of the others damaged. In 1990 virtually all the officers were dismissed so recovery is going to take time. The US Coast Guard is assisting the re-training and is providing replacement patrol craft and a buoy tender.

Personnel

(a) 1992: 250
(b) Voluntary service

Bases

Balboa, Colon

Mercantile Marine

Lloyd's Register of Shipping:
4953 ships of 44 949 330 tons gross

DELETIONS

1989 *Ligia Elena, Presidente Poras* (sunk), *Zarati* (sunk), *Marte* (sunk), *San Miguel, Bastimento* (sunk)

LIGHT FORCES

Note: In addition to the vessels listed below, there are two Boston Whalers acquired in mid-1991 and one confiscated motor yacht. *San Miguel*, paid off in 1989, may be back in service in 1992.

1 VOSPER TYPE (LARGE PATROL CRAFT)

Name	*No*	*Builders*	*Commissioned*
PANQUIACO	P 301 (ex-GC 10)	Vospers, Portsmouth	Mar 1971

Displacement, tons: 96 standard; 123 full load
Dimensions, feet (metres): 103 × 18.9 × 5.8 *(31.4 × 5.8 × 1.8)*
Main machinery: 2 Paxman Ventura 12 CM diesels; 5000 hp *(3.73 MW)* sustained; 2 shafts
Speed, knots: 24
Complement: 23
Guns: 2 Oerlikon 20 mm.
Radars: Surface search: Decca 916; I band; range 88 km *(48 nm)*.

Comment: Launched on 22 July 1970. Hull of welded mild steel and upperworks of welded or buck-bolted aluminium alloy. Vosper fin stabiliser equipment. Non-operational in 1991.

PANQUIACO *1987*

1 SWIFTSHIPS 65 ft TYPE (COASTAL PATROL CRAFT)

Name	*No*	*Builders*	*Commissioned*
COMANDANTE TORRIJOS	P 201 (ex-GC 16)	Swiftships Inc, USA	July 1982

Displacement, tons: 35 full load
Dimensions, feet (metres): 65 × 18.5 × 6 *(19.8 × 5.6 × 1.8)*
Main machinery: 2 Detroit 12V-71 TA diesels; 840 hp *(627 kW)* sustained; 2 shafts
Speed, knots: 21
Complement: 8
Guns: 1—12.7 mm MG.
Radars: Surface search: Decca 110; I band.

Comment: Aluminium hull.

TORRIJOS and PORAS (Sunk 1989) *1988*

1 + 3 Ex-USCG CAPE CLASS (LARGE PATROL CRAFT)

Displacement, tons: 148 full load
Dimensions, feet (metres): 95 × 20.2 × 6.6 *(28.9 × 6.2 × 2)*
Main machinery: 2 Detroit 16V-149 TI diesels; 2480 hp *(1.85 MW)* sustained; 2 shafts
Speed, knots: 20. **Range, miles:** 2500 at 10 kts
Complement: 18 (2 officers)
Guns: 2—12.7 mm MGs.
Radars: Navigation: Raytheon SPS 64; I band.

Comment: Built at Coast Guard Yard, Maryland in 1957 and modernised in 1980. Transferred in July 1991. It is reported that three more of these vessels may follow in due course.

2 Ex-US LCM 8 CLASS

COIBA CEBACO

Displacement, tons: 118 full load
Dimensions, feet (metres): 73.5 × 21 × 5.2 *(22.4 × 6.4 × 1.6)*
Main machinery: 4 GM 6-71 diesels; 348 hp *(260 kW)* sustained; 2 shafts
Speed, knots: 10
Complement: 6

Comment: Used for patrol and logistic duties with converted superstructure and bows giving increased berthing, thereby extending endurance. Unarmed. Three transferred 1972, one deleted in 1986, two more acquired, two deleted in December 1989.

LCM 8 (converted) *1989*

LAND-BASED MARITIME AIRCRAFT

Numbers/Type: 5 CASA C-212 Aviocar.
Operational speed: 190 kts *(353 km/h)*.
Service ceiling: 24 000 ft *(7315 m)*.
Range: 1650 nm *(3055 km)*.
Role/Weapon systems: Coastal patrol aircraft for EEZ protection and anti-smuggling duties. May be sold in 1991. Sensors: APS-128 radar, limited ESM. Weapons: ASW; 2 × Mk 44/46 torpedoes. ASV; 2 × rocket or machine gun pods.

Numbers/Type: 1 Pilatus Britten-Norman Islander.
Operational speed: 150 kts *(280 km/h)*.
Service ceiling: 18 900 ft *(5760 m)*.
Range: 1500 nm *(2775 km)*.
Role/Weapon systems: Coastal surveillance duties. Sensors: Search radar. Weapons: Unarmed.

PAPUA NEW GUINEA

Senior Officer

Commander Defence Forces:
Brigadier General R I Lokinap, LVO

Personnel

(a) 1992: 420
(b) Voluntary

Bases

Port Moresby (HQ PNGDF and PNGDF Landing Craft Base); Lombrum (Manus) (being improved with Australian assistance) Kieta and Alotau (2 Pacific Forum Patrol Craft at each)

Prefix to Ships' Names

HMPNGS

Mercantile Marine

Lloyd's Register of Shipping:
85 vessels of 36 330 tons gross

DELETIONS

1988 *Ladava, Lae* (both sold)
1989 *Aitape* (used for spares)

4 PACIFIC FORUM TYPE (LARGE PATROL CRAFT)

Name	*No*	*Builders*	*Commissioned*
TARANGAU	01	Australian Shipbuilding Industries	16 May 1987
DREGER	02	Australian Shipbuilding Industries	31 Oct 1987
SEEADLER	03	Australian Shipbuilding Industries	29 Oct 1988
BASILISK	04	Australian Shipbuilding Industries	1 July 1989

Displacement, tons: 162 full load
Dimensions, feet (metres): 103.3 × 26.6 × 6.9 *(31.5 × 8.1 × 2.1)*
Main machinery: 2 Caterpillar 3516 diesels; 2820 hp *(2.1 MW)* sustained; 2 shafts
Speed, knots: 20. **Range, miles:** 2500 at 12 kts
Complement: 17 (3 officers)
Guns: 1 GAM-BO1 20 mm. 2—7.62 mm MGs.
Radars: Surface search: Furuno 1011; I band.

Comment: Contract awarded in 1985 to Australian Shipbuilding Industries (Hamilton Hill, West Australia) under Australian Defence co-operation. These are the first, third, sixth and seventh of the class and the only ones to be armed. Training and support provided by the Australian Navy. Others of the class belong to Vanuatu, Western Samoa, Solomon Islands, Cook Islands, Micronesia, Tonga and Marshall Islands.

DREGER *12/1990, James Goldrick*

1 ATTACK CLASS (LARGE PATROL CRAFT)

Name	*No*	*Builders*	*Commissioned*
MADANG	94	Evans Deakin & Co, Queensland	28 Nov 1968

Displacement, tons: 146 full load
Dimensions, feet (metres): 107.5 × 20 × 7.3 *(32.8 × 6.1 × 2.2)*
Main machinery: 2 Paxman Ventura 16 CM diesels; 4000 hp *(2.98 MW)* sustained; 2 shafts
Speed, knots: 24. **Range, miles:** 1220 at 13 kts
Complement: 18
Guns: 1 Bofors 40 mm/60. 2—7.62 mm MGs.
Radars: Surface search: Racal Decca RM 916; I band.

Comment: Brought out of reserve in 1990 and will continue to be used wherever needed. Sister ship *Aitape* is a hulk used for providing spares.

MADANG *12/1990, James Goldrick*

2 LANDING CRAFT (LCVP)

01 **02**

LCVP 01 *12/1990, James Goldrick*

1 TUG

HTS 503 (ex-RAN *503*)

Displacement, tons: 47.5
Dimensions, feet (metres): 50 × 15 × 3.6 *(15.2 × 4.6 × 1.1)*
Main machinery: 2 GM diesels; 340 hp *(250 kW)*; 2 shafts
Speed, knots: 9
Complement: 8

Comment: Built by Perrin Engineering, Brisbane 1972. Transferred 1974.

2 LANDING CRAFT (LCH)

Name	*No*	*Builders*	*Commissioned*
SALAMAUA	31	Walkers Ltd, Maryborough	19 Oct 1973
BUNA	32	Walkers Ltd, Maryborough	7 Dec 1973

Displacement, tons: 310 light; 503 full load
Dimensions, feet (metres): 146 × 33 × 6.5 *(44.5 × 10.1 × 1.9)*
Main machinery: 2 GM V12 diesels; 2 shafts
Speed, knots: 10. **Range, miles:** 3000 at 10 kts
Complement: 15 (2 officers)
Military lift: 150 tons approx
Guns: 2—12.7 mm MGs.
Radars: Navigation: Racal Decca RM 916; I band.

Comment: Underwent extensive refits 1985-86.

SALAMAUA *12/1990, James Goldrick*

BUNA *1984, PNGDF*

LAND-BASED MARITIME AIRCRAFT

Numbers/Type: 6 GAF N22B Missionmaster.
Operational speed: 168 kts *(311 km/h)*.
Service ceiling: 21 000 ft *(6400 m)*.
Range: 730 nm *(1352 km)*.
Role/Weapon systems: Coastal surveillance and transport duties. Sensors: Search radar. Weapons: Unarmed.

GOVERNMENT CRAFT

1 BUOY TENDER

SEPURA

Displacement, tons: 944
Speed, knots: 12

Comment: Built by Sing Koon Seng Yard, Singapore. Completed 14 December 1982. Government owned, civilian manned.

SEPURA *1990, van Ginderen Collection*

4 LANDING CRAFT

BURTIDE **BURCREST** **BURSEA** **BURWAVE**

Displacement, tons: 725 full load
Dimensions, feet (metres): 122 × 29.5 × 7.9 *(37.2 × 9 × 2.4)*
Main machinery: 2 Deutz MWM BA6 M816 diesels; 930 hp(m) *(684 kW)* sustained; 2 shafts
Speed, knots: 9. **Range, miles:** 1800 at 9 kts
Complement: 18

Comment: Built at Sing Koon Seng Yard, Singapore. Completed April-September 1981. Government owned, civilian manned. Not part of PNGDF, but occasionally used by the Armed Forces. Can carry about 500 tons cargo.

2 PILOT/PATROL CRAFT

DAVARA **NANCY DANIEL**

Comment: Pilot craft of 12 and 8.2 m built by FBM Marine and delivered in March 1989.

PARAGUAY

Headquarters' Appointments

Commander-in-Chief of the Navy:
Vice Admiral Eduardo González Petit
Chief of the Naval Staff:
Rear Admiral Flavio Alcibiades Abadie Gaona

Personnel

(a) 1992: 3664 including Coast Guard and 500 marines (50 per cent conscripts)
(b) 18 months' national service

Training

Specialist training is done with Argentina (Operation Sirena), Brazil (Operation Ninfa) and USA (Operation Unitas).

Bases

Base Naval de Bahia Negra (BNBN) (on upper Paraguay river)
Base Aeronaval de Pozo Hondo (BANPH) (on upper Pilcomayo river)
Base Naval de Saltos del Guaira (BNSG) (on upper Parana river)
Base Naval de Ciudad del Este (BNCE) (on Parana river)
Base Naval de Encarnacion (BNE) (on Parana river)
Base Naval de Ita-Piru (BNIP) (on Parana river)

Marine Corps

BIM 1 (COMIM). BIM 2 (Bahia Negra). BIM 3 (Cuartel Gral del Comando de la Armada). BIM 4 (Prefectura Gral Naval). BIM 5 (BNBN - BANPH - BNIP). BIM 8 (BNSG - BNCE - BNE).

Coast Guard

Prefectura de Puertos (Harbour Guard)

Prefix to Ships' Names

Type designators only used

Mercantile Marine

Lloyd's Register of Shipping:
38 vessels of 35 232 tons gross

PATROL FORCES

2 RIVER DEFENCE VESSELS

Name	*No*	*Builders*	*Commissioned*
PARAGUAY (ex-*Commodor Meza*)	C 1	Odero, Genoa	May 1931
HUMAITA (ex-*Capitan Cabral*)	C 2	Odero, Genoa	May 1931

Displacement, tons: 636 standard; 865 full load
Dimensions, feet (metres): 231 × 35 × 5.3 *(70 × 10.7 × 1.7)*
Main machinery: 2 boilers; 2 Parsons turbines; 3800 hp *(2.83 MW)*; 2 shafts
Speed, knots: 17. **Range, miles:** 1700 at 16 kts
Complement: 86
Guns: 4—4.7 in *(120 mm)*. 3—3 in *(76 mm)*. 2—40 mm. 2—20 mm *(Paraguay* only*)*.
Mines: 6.
Radars: Navigation *(Paraguay)*.

Comment: Both refitted in 1975. Have 0.5 in side armour plating and 0.3 in on deck.

PARAGUAY *5/1991, Paraguay Navy*

1 RORAIMA CLASS (RIVER DEFENCE VESSEL)

Name	*No*	*Builders*	*Commissioned*
ITAIPÚ	P 05 (ex-P 2)	Arsenal de Marinha, Rio de Janeiro	2 Apr 1985

Displacement, tons: 365 full load
Dimensions, feet (metres): 151.9 × 27.9 × 4.6 *(46.3 × 8.5 × 1.4)*
Main machinery: 2 MAN V6V 16/18TL diesels; 1920 hp(m) *(1.41 MW)*; 2 shafts
Speed, knots: 14. **Range, miles:** 6000 at 12 kts
Complement: 40 (9 officers)
Guns: 1 Bofors 40 mm/60. 2—81 mm mortars. 6—12.7 mm MGs.
Helicopters: Platform for 1 HB 350B or equivalent.

Comment: Ordered late 1982. Launched 16 March 1984. Same as Brazilian vessels.

ITAIPÚ *6/1990, Paraguay Navy*

3 BOUCHARD CLASS (PATROL SHIPS)

Name	*No*	*Builders*	*Commissioned*
NANAWA (ex-*Bouchard* M 7)	P 02 (ex-P 01, ex-M 1)	Rio Santiago Naval Yard	27 Jan 1937
CAPITAN MEZA (ex-*Seaver* M 12)	P 03 (ex-P 02, ex-M 2)	Hansen, San Fernando	20 May 1939
TENIENTE FARINA (ex-*Py* M 10)	P 04 (ex-P 03, ex-M 3)	Rio Santiago Naval Yard	1 July 1939

Displacement, tons: 450 standard; 620 normal; 650 full load
Dimensions, feet (metres): 197 × 24 × 8.5 *(60 × 7.3 × 2.6)*
Main machinery: 2 sets MAN 2-stroke diesels; 2000 hp(m) *(1.47 MW)*; 2 shafts
Speed, knots: 16. **Range, miles:** 6000 at 12 kts
Complement: 70
Guns: 4 Bofors 40 mm/60 (2 twin). 2—12.7 mm MGs.
Mines: 1 rail.

Comment: Former Argentinian minesweepers of the Bouchard class. Launched on 20 March 1936, 24 August 1938, 31 March 1938 respectively. Transferred from the Argentinian Navy to the Paraguayan Navy; *Nanawa* commissioned 14 March 1964; *Teniente Farina* and *Capitan Meza*, 6 May 1968.

NANAWA *6/1990, Paraguay Navy*

1 RIVER PATROL CRAFT

Name	*No*	*Builders*	*Commissioned*
CAPITAN CABRAL (ex-*Triunfo*)	P 01 (ex-P 04, ex-A 1)	Werf-Conrad, Haarlem	1908

Displacement, tons: 180 standard; 206 full load
Dimensions, feet (metres): 107.2 × 23.5 × 9.8 *(32.7 × 7.2 × 3)*
Main machinery: 1 boiler; 1 triple expansion reciprocating engine; 300 ihp(m) *(220 kW)*; 1 shaft
Speed, knots: 9
Complement: 47
Guns: 1 Bofors 40 mm/60. 2 Oerlikon 20 mm. 2—12.7 mm MGs.

Comment: Former tug. Launched in 1907. Of wooden construction. Stationed on Upper Paraña River and still in excellent condition although the Vickers guns have been replaced.

CAPITAN CABRAL *6/1990, Paraguay Navy*

5 RIVER PATROL CRAFT

P 07 P 08 P 09 P 10 P 11

Displacement, tons: 18 full load
Dimensions, feet (metres): 48.2 × 10.2 × 4.6 *(14.7 × 3.1 × 1.4)*
Main machinery: 1 diesel; 200 hp(m) *(147 kW)*; 1 shaft
Speed, knots: 12
Complement: 4
Guns: 2—12.7 mm MGs.

Comment: Built by Arsenal de Marina, Paraguay. One launched in 1989, two in 1990 and two in 1991. More may be building.

P 08 *3/1991, Paraguay Navy*

6 TYPE 701 CLASS (RIVER PATROL CRAFT)

P 101 102 103 104 105 106

Displacement, tons: 15 full load
Dimensions, feet (metres): 42.5 × 12.8 × 3 *(13 × 3.9 × 0.9)*
Main machinery: 2 GM diesels; 500 hp *(373 kW)*; 2 shafts
Speed, knots: 20
Complement: 7
Guns: 2—12.7 mm MGs.

Comment: Built by Sewart Inc, Berwick. Transferred by USA, two in December 1967, three in September 1970 and one in March 1971. Some are in poor condition and may be replaced by the P 07 class.

P 104 *5/1991, Paraguay Navy*

Ex-US LSM 1 CLASS (CONVERTED TENDER)

Name	*No*	*Builders*	*Commissioned*
BOQUERON (ex-Argentinian *Corrientes*, ex-US *LSM 86*)	BC 1	Brown S B Co, Houston	13 Oct 1944

Displacement, tons: 1095 full load
Dimensions, feet (metres): 203.5 × 33.8 × 8 *(62 × 10.3 × 2.4)*
Main machinery: 2 Fairbanks-Morse 38D8-1/8-10 diesels; 3540 hp *(2.64 MW)*; 2 shafts
Speed, knots: 13. **Range, miles:** 4100 at 12 kts
Complement: 66
Guns: 2 Bofors 40 mm (twin). 4 Oerlikon 20 mm.
Helicopters: Platform for 1 medium support type.

Comment: Converted at Navyard, Buenos Aires during 1968. Transferred as a gift from Argentina 13 January 1972. Light Forces Tender with helicopter deck added aft.

BOQUERON *1990, Paraguay Navy*

LAND-BASED MARITIME AIRCRAFT (FRONT LINE)

Numbers/Type: 5 Cessna U 206.
Operational speed: 167 kts *(309 km/h)*.
Service ceiling: 20 000 ft *(6100 m)*.
Range: 775 nm *(1435 km)*.
Role/Weapon systems: Fixed-wing MR for short-range operations. Sensors: Visual reconnaissance. Weapons: Unarmed.

Numbers/Type: 2 Helibras HB 350B Esquilo
Operational speed: 125 kts *(232 km/h)*.
Service ceiling: 10 000 ft *(3050 m)*.
Range: 390 nm *(720 km)*.
Role/Weapon systems: Support helicopter for riverine patrol craft. Delivered in July 1985.

AUXILIARIES

1 TRAINING SHIP/TRANSPORT

Name	*No*	*Builders*	*Commissioned*
GUARANI	—	Tomas Ruiz de Velasco, Bilbao	Feb 1968

Measurement, tons: 714 gross; 1047 dwt
Dimensions, feet (metres): 240.3 × 36.3 × 11.9 *(73.6 × 11.1 × 3.7)*
Main machinery: 1 MWM diesel; 1300 hp(m) *(956 kW)*; 1 shaft
Speed, knots: 13
Complement: 21
Cargo capacity: 1000 tons

Comment: Refitted in 1975 after a serious fire in the previous year off the coast of France. Used to spend most of her time acting as a freighter on the Asunción-Europe run, commercially operated for the Paraguayan Navy. Since 1991 she has only been used for river service Asunción-Montevideo.

GUARANI *3/1988, van Ginderen Collection*

5 Ex-US YTL TYPE TUGS

R 2 R 4-R 7

Comment: Harbour tugs transferred under MAP in the 1960s and 1970s. *R 2, R 6* and *R 7* are of 20 tons, *R 4* of 65 tons and *R 5* (ex-YTL 211 first commissioned in 1942) is of 82 tons.

R 6 *1991, Paraguay Navy*

1 RIVER TRANSPORT

TENIENTE HERREROS (ex-*Presidente Stroessner*) T 1

Displacement, tons: 150
Speed, knots: 10
Military lift: 120 tons

Comment: Possibly ex-*Adolfo Riquelme*. Ex-yacht built in 1901 and reconstructed in 1973-75. No armament.

TENIENTE HERREROS *5/1991, Paraguay Navy*

2 Ex-US LCU 501 CLASS

BT 1 (ex-US *YFB 82*) **BT 2** (ex-US *YFB 86*)

Displacement, tons: 309 full load
Main machinery: 3 Gray Marine 64YTL diesels; 675 hp *(504 kW)*; 3 shafts
Speed, knots: 10
Military lift: 120 tons

Comment: Built in 1944 and converted in 1958-60. Leased by the USA in June 1970 and by sale 11 February 1977. Used as ferries.

BT 1 *1991, Paraguay Navy*

1 SURVEY VESSEL

LANCHA ECOGRAFA

Comment: Built in 1957. Displacement 50 tons with a crew of seven.

4 DREDGERS

Name	*No*	*Displacement*	*Launched*	*Officers*	*Crew*
ASUNCIÓN	RP 1	107 tons	1908	1	27
PROGRESO	D 1	140 tons	1907	2	28
DRAGA (ex-*Teniente O C Saguier*)	D 2	110 tons	1957	2	17
—	—	550 tons	1988	2	35

1 FLOATING DOCK

DF 1 (Ex-US *AFDL 26*)

Comment: Built 1944, leased March 1965. Purchased 11 February 1977. Lift 1000 tons.

PERU

Headquarters' Appointments

Commander of the Navy:
Admiral Alfredo Arnaiz Ambrosiani
Chief of the Naval Staff:
Vice Admiral Carlos Martinez Rogas

Command

Chief of Naval Operations:
Vice Admiral Guillerno Zariquiey Alegne
Flag Officer Commanding Marines:
Rear Admiral Luis Monteverde

Personnel

(a) 1992: 25 000 (2500 officers)
(b) 2 years' national service

Bases and Organisation

Three areas:—Pacific Naval Force (HQ Callao), Amazon River Force (HQ Iquitos) and Lake Titicaca Patrol Force (HQ at Puno).
Callao—Main naval base; dockyard with shipbuilding capacity, 1 dry dock, 2 floating docks, 1 floating crane; training schools
Iquitos—River base for Amazon Flotilla; small building yard, repair facilities, floating dock
La Punta (naval academy), San Lorenzo (submarine base), Chimbote, Paita, Talara, Puno (Lake Titicaca), Madre de Dios (river base)

Marines

There is one brigade of 3000 men, armed with amphibious vehicles (twin Oerlikon, 88 mm rocket launchers) and armoured cars. Headquarters at Ancon. First Battalion—Guarnicion de Marina; Second Battalion—Guardia Chalaca.

Strength of the Fleet

Type	*Active*
Submarines—Patrol	10
Cruisers	1 (1)
Destroyers	6
Frigates	4
Fast Attack Craft—Missile	6
Patrol Craft	7
River Gunboats	4
Landing Ships	4
Transports	1
Tankers	9
Survey and Oceanographic Vessels	6
Tugs	11
Water Carriers	2
Hospital Craft	2
Torpedo Recovery Vessel	1
Floating Docks	5
Coast Guard	15

Prefix to Ships' Names

BAP (Buque Armada Peruana). PC (Coastal Patrol). PL (Lake Patrol). PP (Port Patrol). PF (River Patrol).

Coast Guard

A separate service set up in 1975 with a number of light forces transferred from the Navy.

Mercantile Marine

Lloyd's Register of Shipping:
618 vessels of 605 494 tons gross

DELETIONS

Submarine

1990 *Angamos*

Destroyers

1990 *Bolognesi, Castilla*

Auxiliaries

1990 *Rodriguez, Navarro, Chuquito*
1991 *Independencia*

Coast Guard

1990 *Rio Canete, Rio Vitor, Rio Sama, Rio Zarumilla, Rio Reque*

PENNANT LIST

Submarines

SS 31	Casma
SS 32	Antofagasta
SS 33	Pisagua
SS 34	Chipana
SS 35	Islay
SS 36	Arica
SS 41	Dos de Mayo
SS 42	Abtao
SS 44	Iquique
SS 49	La Pedrera

Cruisers

CH 81	Almirante Grau
CH 84	Aguirre

Destroyers

DM 73	Palacios
DM 74	Ferré
DD 76	Quiñones
DD 77	Villar
DD 78	Galvez
DD 79	Diez Canseco

Frigates

FM 51	Meliton Carvajal
FM 52	Manuel Villavicencio
FM 53	Montero
FM 54	Mariategui

Light Forces

CF 401	Marañon
CF 402	Ucayali
CF 403	Amazonas
CF 404	Loreto
CM 21	Velarde
CM 22	Santillana
CM 23	De los Heros
CM 24	Herrera
CM 25	Larrea
CM 26	Sanchez Carrillon
PF 272	Rio Manu
PF 273	Rio Inambari
PF 274	Rio Tambopata
PL 290	Rio Ramis
PL 291	Rio Ilave
PL 292	Rio Azangaro
MP 147	Lagarto

Amphibious Forces

DT 141	Paita
DT 142	Pisco
DT 143	Callao
DT 144	Eten

Auxiliaries

ACA 110	Mantilla
ACA 111	Colayeras
ACP 118	Noguera
ACP 119	Gauden
ARB 120	Mejia
ARB 121	Huerta
ARB 123	Rios
ARB 124	Franco
ARB 126	Duenas
ARB 128	Olaya
ARB 129	Selendon
ATC 131	Ilo
ATP 150	Bayovar
ATP 152	Talara
ATP 156	Parinas
ATP 158	Zorritos
ATP 159	Lobitos
AH 170	Unanue
AH 172	Stiglich
AH 175	Carrillo
AH 176	Melo
ABH 302	Morona
ABH 306	Puno
ART 322	San Lorenzo

Coast Guard

PC 223	Rio Chira
PC 225	Rio Pativilca
PC 227	Rio Locumba
PC 241	Rio Tumbes
PC 242	Rio Piura
PC 243	Rio Nepeña
PC 244	Rio Tambo
PC 245	Rio Ocoña
PC 246	Rio Huarmey
PC 247	Rio Zaña
PP 230	La Punta
PP 232	Rio Santa
PP 233	Rio Majes
PP 235	Rio Viru
PP 236	Rio Lurin

SUBMARINES

1 Ex-US GUPPY 1A CLASS

Name	*No*	*Builders*	*Laid down*	*Launched*	*Commissioned*
LA PEDRERA (ex-*Pabellon de Pica*, ex-USS *Sea Poacher* SS 406)	SS 49	Portsmouth Navy Yard, USA	23 Feb 1944	20 May 1944	31 July 1944

Displacement, tons: 1870 standard; 2440 dived
Dimensions, feet (metres): 308 × 27 × 17 *(93.8 × 8.2 × 5.2)*
Main machinery: Diesel-electric; 4 Fairbanks-Morse 38D8-1/8-10 diesels; 6000 hp *(4.48 MW)*; 2 motors; 5600 hp *(4.2 MW)*; 2 shafts
Speed, knots: 17 surfaced; 15 dived
Range, miles: 8000 at 12 kts
Complement: 85

Torpedoes: 10—21 in *(533 mm)* (6 bow, 4 stern) tubes. Probably Westinghouse Mk 37 Type; typically active/passive homing to 8 km *(4.4 nm)* at 24 kts; warhead 150 kg.
Countermeasures: ESM: Radar warning.
Radars: Surface search: I band.
Sonars: EDO BQR 2B; passive search and attack; medium frequency.
Raytheon/EDO BQS 4; adds an active capability to BQR 2B.

Programmes: Modernised under the 1951 Guppy programme. Purchased by Peru on 1 July 1974. Ex-USS *Tench* (SS 417) purchased for spares in 1976. New batteries shipped in 1982.
Operational: Now used for alongside training. *Pacocha* (SS 48) sunk in 110 ft of water on 2 September 1988 after a surfaced collision with a Japanese fishing boat off Callao. Most of the crew were saved by free ascent. She was salvaged and cannibalised for spares.

GUPPY Class (old number) *1986, Peruvian Navy*

6 TYPE 209 CLASS (TYPE 1200)

Name	*No*	*Builders*	*Laid down*	*Launched*	*Commissioned*
CASMA	SS 31	Howaldtswerke, Kiel	15 July 1977	31 Aug 1979	19 Dec 1980
ANTOFAGASTA	SS 32	Howaldtswerke, Kiel	3 Oct 1977	19 Dec 1979	20 Feb 1981
PISAGUA	SS 33	Howaldtswerke, Kiel	15 Aug 1978	19 Oct 1980	12 July 1983
CHIPANA	SS 34	Howaldtswerke, Kiel	1 Nov 1978	19 May 1981	20 Sep 1982
ISLAY	SS 35	Howaldtswerke, Kiel	15 Mar 1971	11 Oct 1973	29 Aug 1974
ARICA	SS 36	Howaldtswerke, Kiel	1 Nov 1971	5 Apr 1974	21 Jan 1975

Displacement, tons: 1185 surfaced; 1290 dived
Dimensions, feet (metres): 183.7 × 20.3 × 17.9 *(56 × 6.2 × 5.5)*
Main machinery: Diesel-electric; 4 MTU Siemens 12V 493 AZ80 GA31L diesels; 2400 hp(m) *(1.76 MW)* sustained; 4 Siemens alternators; 1.7 MW; 1 Siemens motor; 4600 hp(m) *(3.38 MW)* sustained; 1 shaft
Speed, knots: 11 surfaced/snorting; 21.5 dived
Range, miles: 240 at 8 kts
Complement: 35 (5 officers) *(Islay* and *Arica)*; 31 (others)

Torpedoes: 8—21 in *(533 mm)* tubes. 14 Whitehead A184; dual purpose; wire-guided; active/passive homing to 25 km *(13.7 nm)* at 24 kts; 17 km *(9.2 nm)* at 38 kts; warhead 250 kg. Swim-out discharge.

Countermeasures: ESM: Radar warning.
Fire control: Sepa Mk 3 or Signaal Sinbad M8/24 (*Casma* and *Antofagasta*).
Radars: Surface search: Thomson-CSF Calypso; I band.
Sonars: Krupp Atlas CSU 3; active/passive search and attack; medium/high frequency.
Thomson Sintra DUUX 2C or Krupp Atlas PRS 3; passive ranging.

Programmes: First pair ordered 1969. Two further boats ordered 12 August 1976 and two more ordered 21 March 1977. Designed by Ingenieurkontor, Lübeck for construction by Howaldtswerke, Kiel and sale by Ferrostaal, Essen all acting as a consortium.

Modernisation: Sepa Mk 3 fire control fitted progressively from 1986. A184 torpedoes supplied from 1990.
Structure: A single-hull design with two ballast tanks and forward and after trim tanks. Fitted with snort and remote machinery control. The single screw is slow revving, very high capacity batteries with GRP lead-acid cells and battery cooling—by Wilh Hagen and VARTA. Fitted with two periscopes and Omega receiver. Foreplanes retract. Diving depth, 250 m *(820 ft)*.
Operational: Endurance, 50 days. At least two are in reserve and may be sold.

CASMA *12/1986, G. Jacobs*

3 ABTAO CLASS

Name	*No*	*Builders*	*Laid down*	*Launched*	*Commissioned*
DOS DE MAYO (ex-*Lobo*)	SS 41	General Dynamics (Electric Boat), Groton, Connecticut	12 May 1952	6 Feb 1954	14 June 1954
ABTAO (ex-*Tiburon*)	SS 42	General Dynamics (Electric Boat), Groton, Connecticut	12 May 1952	27 Oct 1953	20 Feb 1954
IQUIQUE (ex-*Merlin*)	SS 44	General Dynamics (Electric Boat), Groton, Connecticut	27 Oct 1955	5 Feb 1957	1 Oct 1957

Displacement, tons: 825 standard; 1400 dived
Dimensions, feet (metres): 243 × 22 × 14 *(74.1 × 6.7 × 4.3)*
Main machinery: Diesel-electric; 2 GM 12-278A diesels; 2400 hp *(1.8 MW)*; 2 motors; 2 shafts
Speed, knots: 16 surfaced; 10 dived
Range, miles: 5000 at 10 kts surfaced
Complement: 40

Guns: 1—5 in *(127 mm)*/25 *(Abtao* and *Dos de Mayo)*; manual control; line of sight range.
Torpedoes: 6—21 in *(533 mm)* (4 bow, 2 stern) tubes. Probably Westinghouse Mk 37 Type; typically active/passive homing to 8 km *(4.4 nm)* at 24 kts; warhead 150 kg.
Countermeasures: ESM: Radar warning.
Radars: Surface search: I band.
Sonars: Thomson Sintra Eledone series; active/passive intercept search and attack; medium frequency.

Programmes: They are of modified US Mackerel class. Refitted at Groton as follows—*Dos de Mayo* and *Abtao* in 1965, *Iquique* in 1968. One deleted in 1990.
Modernisation: New batteries shipped in 1981. Since then engineering and electrical systems have been modernised and Eledone sonar fitted.

ABTAO (with 5 in gun) *1990, Peruvian Navy*

CRUISERS

2 Ex-NETHERLANDS DE RUYTER CLASS

Name	*No*	*Builders*	*Laid down*	*Launched*	*Commissioned*
ALMIRANTE GRAU (ex-HrMs *De Ruyter*)	CH 81	Wilton-Fijenoord, Schiedam	5 Sep 1939	24 Dec 1944	18 Nov 1953
AGUIRRE (ex-HrMs *De Zeven Provincien*)	CH 84	Rotterdamse Droogdok Maatschappij	19 May 1939	22 Aug 1950	17 Dec 1953

Displacement, tons: 9529 standard; 12 165 full load *(Grau)* 9850 standard; 12 250 full load *(Aguirre)*
Dimensions, feet (metres): 609 × 56.7 × 22 *(185.6 × 17.3 × 6.7)* (length 624.5 *(190.3) (Grau))*
Flight deck, feet (metres): 115 × 56 *(35 × 17) (Aguirre)*
Main machinery: 4 Werkspoor-Yarrow boilers; 2 De Schelde-Parsons turbines; 85 000 hp *(62.5 MW)*; 2 shafts
Speed, knots: 32. **Range, miles:** 7000 at 12 kts
Complement: 953 (49 officers)

Missiles: SSM: 8 OTO Melara/Matra Otomat Teseo Mk 2 (*Grau* only) ❶; may be replaced by Exocets from the Daring class.
Guns: 8 Bofors 6 in *(152 mm)*/53 (4 twin) (4 in *Aguirre*) ❷; 60° elevation; 15 rounds/minute to 26 km *(14 nm)*; weight of shell 46 kg.
6 Bofors 57 mm/60 (3 twin) ❸ (these guns removed from *Grau*); 90° elevation; 130 rounds/minute to 14 km *(7.7 nm)*; weight of shell 2.6 kg.
6 Bofors 40 mm/70 (4 in *Aguirre*) ❹; 90° elevation; 300 rounds/minute to 12 km *(6.6 nm)*; weight of shell 0.96 kg. Removed from *Grau* during modernisation—reported still not back at the end of 1991.
Depth charges: 2 racks.
Countermeasures: Decoys: 2 Dagaie and 1 Sagaie Chaff launchers *(Grau)*.
Combat data systems: Signaal Sewaco PE *(Grau)*.
Fire control: 2 Lirod 8 optronic directors *(Grau)* ❺.
Radars: Air search: Signaal LW 08 *(Grau)* ❻; D band. Signaal LW 02 *(Aguirre)* ❼; D band.
Surface search/target indication: Signaal DA 08 *(Grau)* ❽; E/F band. Signaal DA 02 *(Aguirre)* ❾; E/F band.
Navigation: Signaal ZW 03 *(Aguirre)*; I/J band. Racal Decca 1226 *(Grau)*; I band.
Fire control: Signaal WM25 *(Grau)* ❿; I/J band (for 6 in guns); range 46 km *(25 nm)*.
Two M45 *(Aguirre)* ⓫; I/J band. One M25 *(Aguirre)* ⓬; I/J band.
Signaal STIR *(Grau)* ⓭; I/J/K band; range 140 km *(76 nm)* for 1 m² target.
Sonars: CWC 10N; hull-mounted; active search.

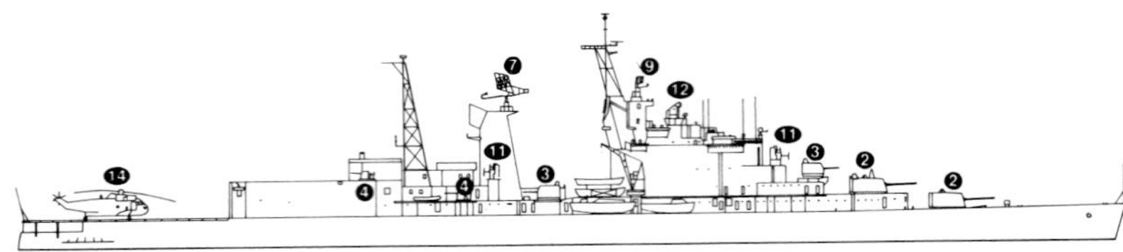
AGUIRRE *(Scale 1 : 1 800), Ian Sturton*

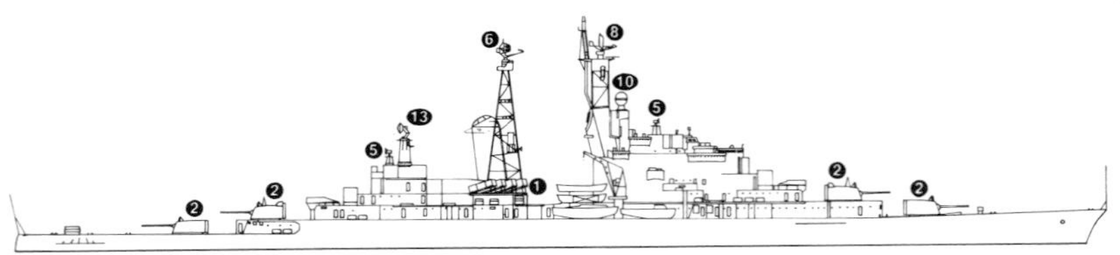
ALMIRANTE GRAU *(Scale 1 : 1 800), Ian Sturton*

Helicopters: 3 Agusta ASH-3D Sea Kings *(Aguirre)* ⓮.

Programmes: *Grau* transferred by purchase 7 March 1973 and *Aguirre* bought August 1976. *Grau* commissioned in Peruvian Navy 23 May 1973. After sale *Aguirre* was taken in hand by her original builders for conversion to a helicopter cruiser. Conversion completed 31 October 1977. In 1986 *Aguirre* assumed the name *Almirante Grau* and the former *Almirante Grau* became *Proyecto 01*, while refitting in Amsterdam. Former names were resumed as soon as *Grau* started sea trials in November 1987.
Modernisation: *Grau* taken in hand for a two and a half year modernisation at Amsterdam Dry Dock Co in March 1985. This was to include reconditioning of mechanical and electrical engineering systems, fitting of SSM and SAM, replacement of electronics and fitting of one CSEE Sagaie and two Dagaie launchers. In 1986 financial constraints limited the work but Otomat missiles were fitted and much has been done to update sensors and fire control equipment. *Grau* sailed for Peru 23 January 1988 without her secondary gun armament, for the work to be completed at Sima Yard, Callao, but lack of funds has so far prevented this and there must be doubts about whether she will go to sea again. The plan in 1992 is to fit the Exocet SSMs from the Daring class. *Aguirre* had her boilers retubed and underwent major refit completing in mid-1986.
Structure: *Aguirre* Terrier missile system replaced by hangar (67 × 54 ft) and flight deck built from midships to the stern. Second landing spot on hangar roof.
Operational: *Aguirre* helicopters carry AM 39 Exocet missiles.

AGUIRRE *1987*

ALMIRANTE GRAU *11/1987, J. L. M. van der Burg*

DESTROYERS

2 Ex-BRITISH DARING CLASS

Name	*No*	*Builders*	*Laid down*	*Launched*	*Commissioned*
PALACIOS (ex-HMS *Diana*)	DM 73	Yarrow, Glasgow	3 Apr 1947	8 May 1952	29 Mar 1954
FERRÉ (ex-HMS *Decoy*)	DM 74	Yarrow, Glasgow	22 Sep 1946	29 Mar 1949	28 Apr 1953

Displacement, tons: 2800 standard; 3600 full load
Dimensions, feet (metres): 390 × 43 × 18 *(118.9 × 13.1 × 5.5)*
Main machinery: 2 Foster-Wheeler boilers; 650 psi *(45.7 kg/cm sq)*; 850°F *(454°C)*; 2 English Electric turbines; 54 000 hp *(40 MW)*; 2 shafts
Speed, knots: 32. **Range, miles:** 3000 at 20 kts
Complement: 297

Missiles: SSM: 8 Aerospatiale MM 38 Exocet ❶; inertial cruise; active radar homing to 42 km *(23 nm)* at 0.9 Mach; warhead 165 kg; sea-skimmer.
Guns: 6 (3 twin) *(Ferré)* ❷ or 4 (2 twin) *(Palacios)* Vickers 4.5 in *(114 mm)*/45 Mk 6; 80° elevation; 20 rounds/minute to 19 km *(10.4 nm)*; weight of shell 25 kg.
4 Breda 40 mm/70 (2 twin) ❸; 85° elevation; 300 rounds/minute to 12.5 km *(6.8 nm)*; weight of shell 0.96 kg.
Radars: Air/surface search: Plessey AWS 1 ❹; E/F band; range 110 km *(60 nm)*.
Navigation: Decca; I band.
Fire control: TSF forward; Signaal aft ❺; I/J band.

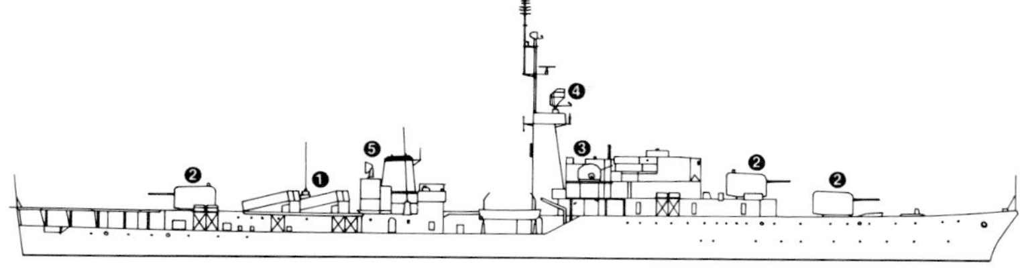
FERRÉ *(Scale 1 : 1 200), Ian Sturton*

Helicopters: Platform only.

Programmes: Purchased by Peru in 1969 and refitted by Cammell Laird (Ship Repairers) Ltd, Birkenhead.

Structure: Two reconstructions took place in the 1970s in which *Palacios* had her X-turret replaced by a helicopter hangar (later removed) and both had helicopter platforms fitted over the quarter deck.
Operational: Both still operational in 1991 but there are plans to sell them without Exocet missiles which may be fitted in *Almirante Grau*.

FERRÉ *2/1988*

4 Ex-NETHERLANDS FRIESLAND CLASS

Name	*No*	*Builders*	*Laid down*	*Launched*	*Commissioned*
QUIÑONES (ex-HrMs *Limburg* DD 814)	DD 76	Koninklijke Maatschappij de Schelde, Flushing	28 Nov 1953	5 Sep 1955	31 Oct 1956
VILLAR (ex-HrMs *Amsterdam* DD 819)	DD 77	Nederlandse Dok en Scheepsbouw Mij, Amsterdam	26 Mar 1955	25 Aug 1956	10 Aug 1958
GALVEZ (ex-HrMs *Groningen* DD 813)	DD 78	Nederlandse Dok en Scheepsbouw Mij, Amsterdam	21 Feb 1952	9 Jan 1954	12 Sep 1956
DIEZ CANSECO (ex-HrMs *Rotterdam* DD 818)	DD 79	Rotterdamse Droogdok Mij, Rotterdam	7 Jan 1954	26 Jan 1956	28 Feb 1957

Displacement, tons: 2497 standard; 3070 full load
Dimensions, feet (metres): 380.5 × 38.5 × 17 *(116 × 11.7 × 5.2)*
Main machinery: 2 Babcock & Wilcox boilers; 550 psi *(38.7 kg/cm sq)*; 850°F *(454°C)*; 2 English Electric/Werkspoor geared turbines; 60 000 hp *(45 MW)*; 2 shafts
Speed, knots: 36. **Range, miles:** 4000 at 15 kts
Complement: 284

Guns: 4 Bofors 4.7 in *(120 mm)*/50 (2 twin) ❶; 85° elevation; 42 rounds/minute to 20 km *(10.8 nm)*; weight of shell 24 kg.
4 Bofors 40 mm/70 ❷; 90° elevation; 300 rounds/minute to 12 km *(6.6 nm)*; weight of shell 2.4 kg.
1—103 mm launcher for illuminants.
A/S mortars: 2 Bofors 375 mm 4-barrelled trainable launchers ❸; range 1600 m or 3600 m depending on weapon.
Depth charges: 2 racks.
Radars: Air search: Signaal LW 03 ❹; D band; range 219 km *(120 nm)* for 2 m² target.
Air/surface search: Signaal DA 05 ❺; E/F band; range 137 km *(75 nm)* for 2 m² target.
Surface search: Signaal ZW 06 ❻; I band.

FRIESLAND Class *(Scale 1 : 1 200), Ian Sturton*

Navigation: Racal Decca TM 1229; I band.
Fire control: Signaal M45 ❼; I/J band.
Sonars: Signaal CWE 10-N, PAE 1-N; hull-mounted; active search and attack; medium frequency.

Programmes: *Quiñones* recommissioned 27 June 1980, *Villar* 23 May 1980, *Galvez* 2 March 1981 and *Diez Canseco* 29 June 1981.

Modernisation: All of this class were to be modernised but plans were rejected as not being cost effective on ships of this age.
Operational: *Quiñones* and *Galvez* were in reserve but recommissioned in 1989. *Bolognesi* and *Castilla* have paid off but are still used for spare parts.

QUINONES *1987*

FRIGATES

4 ITALIAN MODIFIED LUPO CLASS

Name	*No*	*Builders*	*Laid down*	*Launched*	*Commissioned*
MELITON CARVAJAL	FM 51	Fincantieri, Riva Trigoso	8 Aug 1974	17 Nov 1976	5 Feb 1979
MANUEL VILLAVICENCIO	FM 52	Fincantieri, Riva Trigoso	6 Oct 1976	7 Feb 1978	25 June 1979
MONTERO	FM 53	SIMA, Callao	Oct 1978	8 Oct 1982	25 July 1984
MARIATEGUI	FM 54	SIMA, Callao	1979	8 Oct 1984	10 Oct 1987

Displacement, tons: 2208 standard; 2500 full load
Dimensions, feet (metres): 371.3 × 37.1 × 12.1 *(113.2 × 11.3 × 3.7)*
Main machinery: CODOG; 2 GE/Fiat LM 2500 gas turbines; 44 000 hp *(33 MW)* sustained; 2 GMT A 230.2M diesels; 7800 hp(m) *(5.73 MW)*; 2 shafts; cp props
Speed, knots: 35. **Range, miles:** 3450 at 20.5 kts
Complement: 185 (20 officers)

Missiles: SSM: 8 OTO Melara/Matra Otomat Mk 2 (TG 1) ❶; active radar homing to 80 km *(43.2 nm)* at 0.9 Mach; warhead 210 kg; sea-skimmer for last 4 km *(2.2 nm)*.
SAM: Selenia Elsag Albatros octuple launcher ❷; 8 Aspide; semi-active radar homing to 13 km *(7 nm)* at 2.5 Mach; height envelope 15-5000 m *(49.2-16 405 ft)*; warhead 30 kg.
Guns: 1 OTO Melara 5 in *(127 mm)*/54 ❸; 85° elevation; 45 rounds/minute to 16 km *(8.7 nm)*; weight of shell 32 kg.
4 Breda 40 mm/70 (2 twin) ❹; 85° elevation; 300 rounds/minute to 12.5 km *(6.8 nm)*; weight of shell 0.96 kg.
Torpedoes: 6—324 mm ILAS (2 triple) tubes ❺. Probably Whitehead A244; anti-submarine; active/passive homing to 7 km *(3.8 nm)* at 33 kts; warhead 34 kg (shaped charge).
Countermeasures: Decoys: 2 Breda 105 mm SCLAR 20-barrelled trainable launchers ❻; multi-purpose; Chaff to 5 km *(2.7 nm)*; illuminants to 12 km *(6.6 nm)*; HE bombardment.
ESM: Radar intercept.
Combat data systems: Selenia IPN-10 action data automation.
Fire control: 2 Elsag Mk 10 Argo with NA-21 directors. Dardo system for 40 mm.
Radars: Air search: Selenia RAN 10S ❼; E/F band; range 155 km *(85 nm)*.
Surface search: Selenia RAN 11LX ❽; D/I band; range 82 km *(45 nm)*.
Navigation: SMA 3 RM 20R; I band; range 73 km *(40 nm)*.
Fire control: Two RTN 10X ❾; I/J band.
Two RTN 20X ❿; I/J band; range 12.8 km *(7 nm)* (for Dardo).
Sonars: EDO 610E; hull-mounted; active search and attack; medium frequency.

Helicopters: 1 Agusta AB 212ASW ⓫.

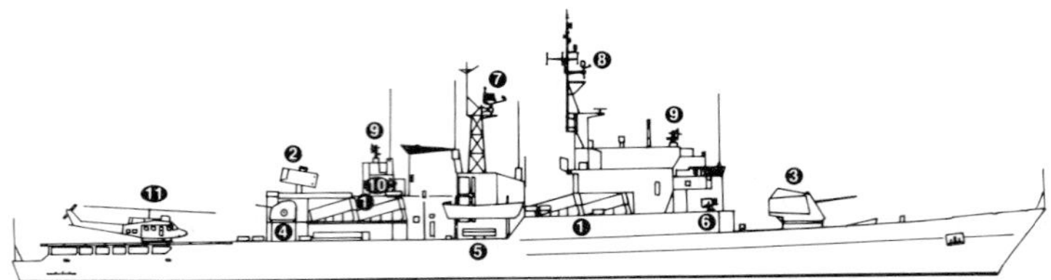

MONTERO *(Scale 1 : 1 200), Ian Sturton*

MONTERO *5/1986, Lieutenant D. M. Stevens RAN*

Programmes: *Montero* and *Mariategui* were the first major warships to be built on the Pacific Coast of South America, although some equipment was provided by Fincantieri.
Structure: In the design for the pair built by Servicios Industriales de la Marina, Callao (SIMA) the two 40 mm guns are mounted higher and reloading of the Albatros is by hand not power. Also the hangar is fixed and the flight deck does not come flush to the stern of the ship.
Operational: Helicopter provides an over-the-horizon targetting capability for SSM. HIFR facilities fitted in 1989 allow refuelling of Sea King helicopters.

SHIPBORNE AIRCRAFT

Note: 4 Agusta AB-412 assault, and 5 Agusta A-109K SAR helicopters to be delivered in 1992.

Numbers/Type: 3 Aerospatiale SA 316B Alouette III.
Operational speed: 113 kts *(210 km/h)*.
Service ceiling: 10 500 ft *(3200 m)*.
Range: 290 nm *(540 km)*.
Role/Weapon systems: ASW helicopter; used for liaison as well. Sensors: None. Weapons: ASW; 2 × Mk 44 torpedoes.

Numbers/Type: 6 Agusta AB 212ASW.
Operational speed: 106 kts *(196 km/h)*.
Service ceiling: 14 200 ft *(4330 m)*.
Range: 230 nm *(425 km)*.
Role/Weapon systems: ASW and surface search helicopter for smaller escorts. Sensors: Selenia search radar, Bendix ASQ-18 dipping sonar, ECM. Weapons: ASW; 2 × Mk 46 or 244/S torpedoes or depth bombs.

Numbers/Type: 8 Agusta-Sikorsky ASH-3D Sea King.
Operational speed: 120 kts *(222 km/h)*.
Service ceiling: 12 200 ft *(3720 m)*.
Range: 630 nm *(1165 km)*.
Role/Weapon systems: ASW helicopter; embarked in larger escorts. Sensors: Selenia search radar, ASQ-18 dipping sonar, sonobuoys. Weapons: ASW; 4 × Mk 46 or 244/S torpedoes or depth bombs or mines. ASV; 2 × AM 39 Exocet missiles.

LAND-BASED MARITIME AIRCRAFT (FRONT LINE)

Numbers/Type: 6 Beechcraft Super King Air 200T.
Operational speed: 282 kts *(523 km/h)*.
Service ceiling: 35 000 ft *(10 670 m)*.
Range: 2030 nm *(3756 km)*.
Role/Weapon systems: Coastal surveillance and EEZ patrol duties. Sensors: Search radar, cameras. Weapons: Unarmed.

Numbers/Type: 7/4 Grumman S-2E/G Tracker.
Operational speed: 130 kts *(241 km/h)*.
Service ceiling: 25 000 ft *(7620 m)*.
Range: 1350 nm *(2500 km)*.
Role/Weapon systems: ASW and coastal MR aircraft with limited ASV role. Sensors: Search radar, MAD, sonobuoys. Weapons: ASW; torpedoes, depth bombs and/or mines. ASV; 6 × 127 mm rockets.

LIGHT FORCES

6 PR-72P CLASS (FAST ATTACK CRAFT—MISSILE)

Name	*No*	*Builders*	*Commissioned*
VELARDE	CM 21	SFCN, France	25 July 1980
SANTILLANA	CM 22	SFCN, France	25 July 1980
DE LOS HEROS	CM 23	SFCN, France	17 Nov 1980
HERRERA	CM 24	SFCN, France	10 Feb 1981
LARREA	CM 25	SFCN, France	16 June 1981
SANCHEZ CARRILLON	CM 26	SFCN, France	14 Sep 1981

Displacement, tons: 470 standard; 560 full load
Dimensions, feet (metres): 210 × 27.4 × 5.2 *(64 × 8.4 × 2.6)*
Main machinery: 4 SACM AGO 240V16 M7 diesels; 22 200 hp(m) *(16.32 MW)* sustained; 4 shafts
Speed, knots: 37. **Range, miles:** 2500 at 16 kts
Complement: 36 (accommodation for 46)

Missiles: SSM: 4 Aerospatiale MM 38 Exocet; inertial cruise; active radar homing to 42 km *(23 nm)* at 0.9 Mach; warhead 165 kg; sea-skimmer.
Guns: 1 OTO Melara 3 in *(76 mm)*/62; 85° elevation; 85 rounds/minute to 16 km *(8.7 nm)*; weight of shell 6 kg.
2 Breda 40 mm/70 (twin); 85° elevation; 300 rounds/minute to 12.5 km *(6.8 nm)*; weight of shell 0.96 kg.
Fire control: CSEE Panda director. Vega system.
Radars: Surface search: Thomson-CSF Triton; G band; range 33 km *(18 nm)* for 2 m² target.
Navigation: Racal Decca 1226; I band.
Fire control: Thomson-CSF/Castor II; I/J band; range 15 km *(8 nm)* for 1 m² target.

Programmes: Ordered late 1976 from SFCN, France. Hulls of *Velarde, De Los Heros, Larrea* sub-contracted to Lorient Naval Yard, the others being built at Villeneuve-la-Garenne. Classified as corvettes by Peruvian Navy. Launched—*Velarde*, 16 Sep 1978; *Santillana*, 11 Sep 1978; *De Los Heros*, 20 May 1979; *Herrera*, 16 Feb 1979; *Larrea*, 12 May 1979; *Sanchez Carrion*, 28 June 1979.

HERRERA *1987, Peruvian Navy*

2 MARAÑON CLASS (RIVER GUNBOATS)

Name	*No*	*Builders*	*Commissioned*
MARAÑON	CF 401 (ex-CF 13)	John I Thornycroft & Co Ltd	July 1951
UCAYALI	CF 402 (ex-CF 14)	John I Thornycroft & Co Ltd	June 1951

Displacement, tons: 365 full load
Dimensions, feet (metres): 154.8 wl × 32 × 4 *(47.2 × 9.7 × 1.2)*
Main machinery: 2 British Polar M 441 diesels; 800 hp *(597 kW)*; 2 shafts
Speed, knots: 12. **Range, miles:** 6000 at 10 kts
Complement: 40 (4 officers)
Guns: 2—3 in *(76 mm)*/50. 1 Bofors 40 mm/60. 4 Oerlikon 20 mm (2 twin).

Comment: Ordered early in 1950 and both laid down in early 1951. Employed on police duties in Upper Amazon. Superstructure of aluminium alloy. Based at Iquitos.

MARAÑON (old number) *1987, Peruvian Navy*

2 LORETO CLASS (RIVER GUNBOATS)

Name	*No*	*Builders*	*Commissioned*
AMAZONAS	CF 403 (ex-CF 11)	Electric Boat Co, Groton	1935
LORETO	CF 404 (ex-CF 12)	Electric Boat Co, Groton	1935

Displacement, tons: 250 standard
Dimensions, feet (metres): 145 × 22 × 4 *(44.2 × 6.7 × 1.2)*
Main machinery: 2 diesels; 750 hp(m) *(551 kW)*; 2 shafts
Speed, knots: 15. **Range, miles:** 4000 at 10 kts
Complement: 35 (5 officers)
Guns: 2—3 in *(76 mm)*. 4 Bofors 40 mm/60. 1 Oerlikon 20 mm.

Comment: Launched in 1934. In Upper Amazon Flotilla.

LORETO (old number) *1987 Peruvian Navy*

3 LAKE PATROL CRAFT

Name	*No*	*Builders*	*Commissioned*
RIO RAMIS	PL 290	American SB&D, Miami	15 Sep 1982
RIO ILAVE	PL 291	American SB&D, Miami	20 Nov 1982
RIO AZANGARO	PL 292	American SB&D, Miami	4 Feb 1983

Displacement, tons: 5
Dimensions, feet (metres): 32.8 × 11.2 × 2.6 *(10 × 3.4 × 0.8)*
Main machinery: 2 Perkins diesels; 480 hp *(358 kW)*; 2 shafts
Speed, knots: 29. **Range, miles:** 450 at 28 kts
Complement: 4
Guns: 1—12.7 mm MG.

Comment: On Lake Titicaca. GRP hulls.

4 RIVER PATROL CRAFT

RIO MANU PF 272 **RIO INAMBARI** PF 273 **RIO TAMBOPATA** PF 274
LAGARTO MP 147

Comment: First three based at Madre de Dios. Commissioned in 1975. Armed with one MG and capable of 18 kts.

AMPHIBIOUS FORCES

Note: Reported that orders may be placed for up to three 300 ft LSLs to be locally built.

4 Ex-US TERREBONNE PARISH CLASS (LSTs)

Name	*No*	*Builders*	*Commissioned*
PAITA (ex-USS *Walworth County* LST 1164)	DT 141	Ingalls SB	26 Oct 1953
PISCO (ex-USS *Waldo County* LST 1163)	DT 142	Ingalls SB	17 Sep 1953
CALLAO (ex-USS *Washoe County* LST 1165)	DT 143	Ingalls SB	30 Nov 1953
ETEN (ex-USS *Traverse County* LST 1160)	DT 144	Bath Iron Works	19 Dec 1953

Displacement, tons: 2590 standard; 5800 full load
Dimensions, feet (metres): 384 × 55 × 17 *(117.1 × 16.8 × 5.2)*
Main machinery: 4 GM 16-278A diesels; 6000 hp *(4.48 MW)*; 2 shafts
Speed, knots: 15. **Range, miles:** 15 000 at 9 kts
Complement: 116
Military lift: 2000 tons; 395 troops
Guns: Fitted for 6—3 in *(76 mm)*/50 (3 twin, 2 fwd and 1 aft) but these have probably been replaced by 6 Oerlikon 20 mm.
Radars: Surface search: Raytheon SPS 10; G band.
Navigation: I band.

Comment: All transferred on loan 7 August 1984, recommissioned 4 March 1985. Have small helicopter platform. *Pisco* is non-operational providing spares for the others. Lease extended to 1994.

PAITA *9/1991, Giorgio Arra*

SERVICE FORCES

Note: All service forces may be used for commercial purposes if not required for naval use.

1 ILO CLASS (TRANSPORT)

Name	*No*	*Builders*	*Commissioned*
ILO	ATC 131	SIMA, Callao	Dec 1971

Displacement, tons: 18 400 full load
Measurement, tons: 13 000 dwt
Dimensions, feet (metres): 507.7 × 67.3 × 27.2 *(154.8 × 20.5 × 8.3)*
Main machinery: 1 Burmeister & Wain 6K47 diesel; 11 600 hp(m) *(8.53 MW)*; 1 shaft
Speed, knots: 15.6
Complement: 60
Cargo capacity: 13 000 tons

Comment: Sister ship *Rimac* is on permanent commercial charter.

ILO *12/1990, Hartmut Ehlers*

1 PIMENTEL CLASS (REPLENISHMENT TANKER)

Name	*No*	*Builders*	*Commissioned*
PARINAS (ex-*Pimentel*)	ATP 156	SIMA, Callao	27 June 1969

Displacement, tons: 3434 light; 13 600 full load
Measurement, tons: 10 000 dwt
Dimensions, feet (metres): 410.9 × 63.1 × 26 *(125.3 × 19.2 × 7.9)*
Main machinery: 1 Burmeister & Wain Type 750 diesel; 5400 hp(m) *(3.97 MW)*; 1 shaft
Speed, knots: 14.5

Comment: Capable of underway replenishment at sea.

PARINAS *5/1986, Surgeon Lieutenant P. J. Buxton RN*

1 FREIGHTING TANKER

Name	*No*	*Builders*	*Commissioned*
BAYOVAR (ex-*Loreto II*, ex-*St Vincent*)	ATP 150	Ch N de la Ciotat	1976

Displacement, tons: 15 175 light; 107 320 full load
Dimensions, feet (metres): 821.9 × 116.5 × 63.7 *(250.5 × 35.5 × 19.4)*
Main machinery: 1 Sulzer 7 RND 90 diesel; 20 300 hp(m) *(14.92 MW)*; 1 shaft
Speed, knots: 16

Comment: Launched in 1976. Acquired by Peruvian Navy from Peruvian civilian company in 1986.

BAYOVAR *1986, Peruvian Navy*

4 HARBOUR TANKERS (FUEL/WATER)

MANTILLA ACA 110 (ex-US *YW 122*)
COLAYERAS ACA 111 (ex-US *YW 128*)
NOGUERA ACP 118 (ex-US *YO 221*)
GAUDEN ACP 119 (ex-US *YO 171*)

Displacement, tons: 1235 full load
Dimensions, feet (metres): 174 × 32 × 13.3 *(52.3 × 9.8 × 4.1)*
Main machinery: 1 GM diesel; 560 hp *(418 kW)*; 1 shaft
Speed, knots: 8
Cargo capacity: 200 000 gal

Comment: *YW 122* transferred to Peru July 1963; *YO 221* January 1975; *YO 171* 20 January 1981; *YW 128* 26 January 1985.

GAUDEN *1988, Peruvian Navy*

2 SECHURA CLASS (SUPPORT TANKERS)

Name	*No*	*Builders*	*Commissioned*
ZORRITOS	ATP 158	SIMA, Callao	1959
LOBITOS	ATP 159	SIMA, Callao	1966

Displacement, tons: 8700 full load
Measurement, tons: 4300 gross; 6000 dwt
Dimensions, feet (metres): 385 × 52 × 21.2 *(117.4 × 15.9 × 6.4)*
Main machinery: 1 Burmeister & Wain 562-VTF-115 diesels; 2400 hp(m) *(1.76 MW)*; 1 shaft
Speed, knots: 12
Radars: Navigation: Decca; I band.

Comment: Alongside at sea refuelling capability. 2 Scotch boilers with Thornycroft oil burners for cargo tank cleaning.

ZORRITOS *5/1986, Surgeon Lieutenant P. J. Buxton RN*

1 TALARA CLASS (REPLENISHMENT TANKER)

Name	*No*	*Builders*	*Commissioned*
TALARA	ATP 152	SIMA, Callao	23 Jan 1978

Displacement, tons: 30 000 full load
Measurement, tons: 25 000 dwt
Dimensions, feet (metres): 561.5 × 82 × 31.2 *(171.2 × 25 × 9.5)*
Main machinery: 2 Burmeister & Wain 6K47EF diesels; 12 000 hp(m) *(8.82 MW)*; 1 shaft
Speed, knots: 15.5
Cargo capacity: 35 662 cu m

Comment: Capable of underway replenishment at sea. *Talara* laid down 1975, launched 9 July 1976. *Bayovar* of this class laid down 9 July 1976, launched 18 July 1977 having been originally ordered by Petroperu (State Oil Company) and transferred to the Navy while building. Sold back to Petroperu in 1979 and renamed *Pavayacu*. A third, *Trompeteros*, of this class has been built for Petroperu.

SURVEY AND OCEANOGRAPHIC VESSELS

Note: Possible second hand purchase may be made in 1992.

1 Ex-US SOTOYOMO CLASS

Name	*No*	*Builders*	*Commissioned*
UNANUE (ex-USS *Wateree* ATA 174)	AH 170	Levingston S B Co, Orange, Texas	20 July 1944

Displacement, tons: 534 standard; 860 full load
Dimensions, feet (metres): 143 × 33.9 × 13 *(43.6 × 10.3 × 4)*
Main machinery: Diesel-electric; 2 GM 12-278A diesels; 2200 hp *(1.64 MW)*; 2 generators; 1 motor; 1500 hp *(1.12 MW)*; 1 shaft
Speed, knots: 13
Complement: 31 (3 officers)

Comment: Former US auxiliary ocean tug. Laid down on 5 October 1943, launched on 18 November 1943. Purchased from the USA in November 1961 under MAP. Refitted in 1985 for operation in the Antarctic.

2 Ex-NETHERLANDS VAN STRAELEN CLASS

CARRILLO (ex-*van Hamel*) AH 175 **MELO** (ex-*van der Wel*) AH 176

Displacement, tons: 169 full load
Dimensions, feet (metres): 99.3 × 18.2 × 5.2 *(30.3 × 5.6 × 1.6)*
Main machinery: 2 Werkspoor diesels; 1100 hp(m) *(808 kW)*; 2 shafts
Speed, knots: 13
Complement: 17 (2 officers)

Comment: Both built as inshore minesweepers in Netherlands in 1960, 1961 respectively. Acquired 23 February 1985.

MELO *1989, Peruvian Navy*

2 INSHORE SURVEY CRAFT

AH 173 **AH 174**

Displacement, tons: 23 *(AH 173)*; 53 *(AH 174)* full load
Dimensions, feet (metres): 64.9 × 17.1 × 3 *(19.8 × 5.2 × 0.9) (AH 174)*
Speed, knots: 13
Complement: 8 (2 officers) *(AH 174)*; 4 (1 officer) *(AH 173)*

Comment: *AH 173* launched in 1979. *AH 174* built at SIMA, Chimbote, commissioned 1982, and has a side scan sonar for plotting bottom contours.

1 INSHORE SURVEY CRAFT

STIGLICH (ex-*Rio Chillón*) AH 172

Displacement, tons: 43 full load
Dimensions, feet (metres): 61 × 17.3 × 5.6 *(18.6 × 5.3 × 1.7)*
Main machinery: 2 Detroit 12V-71 TI diesels; 1120 hp *(836 kW)* sustained; 2 shafts
Speed, knots: 25
Complement: 28 (2 officers)

Comment: Transferred from Coast Guard. Built by McLaren, Niteroi in 1981.

TUGS

1 Ex-US CHEROKEE CLASS

Name	*No*	*Builders*	*Commissioned*
RIOS (ex-USS *Pinto* ATF 90)	ARB 123	USA	1943

Displacement, tons: 1235 standard; 1640 full load
Dimensions, feet (metres): 205 × 38.5 × 17 *(62.5 × 11.7 × 5.2)*
Main machinery: Diesel-electric; 4 GM 12-278 diesels; 4400 hp *(3.28 MW)*; 4 generators; 1 motor; 3000 hp *(2.24 MW)*; 1 shaft
Speed, knots: 16.5. **Range, miles:** 6500 at 16 kts
Complement: 99

Comment: Transferred to Peru on loan in 1960, sold 17 May 1974. Fitted with powerful pumps and other salvage equipment.

Name	*No*	*Builders*	*Commissioned*
OLAYA	ARB 128	Ruhrorter, SW Duisburg	1967
SELENDON	ARB 129	Ruhrorter, SW Duisburg	1967

Measurement, tons: 80 gross
Dimensions, feet (metres): 61.3 × 20.3 × 7.4 *(18.7 × 6.2 × 2.3)*
Main machinery: 1 diesel; 600 hp(m) *(441 kW)*; 1 shaft
Speed, knots: 10

Name	*No*	*Builders*	*Commissioned*
FRANCO (ex-USS *Menewa* YTM 2)	ARB 124	S Bushey, Brooklyn, NY	1939

Displacement, tons: 132
Dimensions, feet (metres): 91 × 23 × 11 *(27.7 × 7 × 3.4)*
Main machinery: 1 diesel; 805 hp(m) *(592 kW)*; 1 shaft

Comment: Transferred March 1947.

7 HARBOUR TUGS

MEJIA ARB 120 **180-181**
HUERTA ARB 121 **185-186**
DUENAS ARB 126

AUXILIARIES

Note: (1) There is also *Duenas* (ex-USS Lapeer) built in 1943 and acquired in 1987.
(2) Names of other miscellaneous craft: *Neptuno, Jupiter, Robles, Tapuina, Sandoval, Andrade, Zambrano, Pucallpa.*

1 TORPEDO RECOVERY VESSEL

SAN LORENZO ART 322

Displacement, tons: 58 standard; 65 full load
Dimensions, feet (metres): 82.7 × 18.4 × 5.6 *(25.2 × 5.6 × 1.7)*
Main machinery: 2 MTU 8V 396 TC82 diesels; 1740 hp(m) *(1.28 MW)* sustained; 2 shafts
Speed, knots: 19. **Range, miles:** 500 at 15 kts
Complement: 9

Comment: Built by Lürssen/Burmeister. Shipped to Peru September 1981. Can carry four long or eight short torpedoes.

SAN LORENZO *1981, Lürssen Werft*

1 LAKE HOSPITAL CRAFT

PUNO (ex-*Yapura*) ABH 306

Comment: Stationed on Lake Titicaca. Commissioned in 1873 at Cammell Laird, Birkenhead. 500 grt and has a diesel engine. Sadly the second of the class was finally paid off in 1990 after 119 years service.

5 FLOATING DOCKS

ADF 106-110

Displacement, tons: 1900 (*106*); 5200 (*107*); 600 (*108*); 18 000 (*109*); 4500 tons (*110*)

Comment: *106* (ex-US *AFDL 33)* transferred 1959; *107* (ex-US *ARD 8)* transferred 1961; *108* built in 1951; *109* built in 1979; *110* built in 1991.

2 WATER CARRIERS

ABA 330 (ex-091) **ABA 332** (ex-113)

Comment: Built in Peru 1972. Attached to Amazon Flotilla. Capacity 800 tons water (330), 300 tons (332).

1 RIVER HOSPITAL CRAFT

Name	*No*	*Builders*	*Commissioned*
MORONA	ABH 302	SIMA, Iquitos	1976

Displacement, tons: 150
Dimensions, feet (metres): 98.4 × 19.6 × 1.5 *(30 × 6 × 0.5)*
Speed, knots: 12

Comment: For service on Peruvian rivers. Two more projected but not built.

MORONA *1989, Peruvian Navy*

COAST GUARD

Note: Six 40 ft river patrol boats are being provided by the United States for drug interdiction patrols. Contract placed in late 1990.

5 LARGE PATROL CRAFT

Name	*No*	*Builders*	*Commissioned*
RIO NEPEÑA	PC 243	SIMA, Chimbote	1 Dec 1981
RIO TAMBO	PC 244	SIMA, Chimbote	1982
RIO OCOÑA	PC 245	SIMA, Chimbote	1983
RIO HUARMEY	PC 246	SIMA, Chimbote	1984
RIO ZAÑA	PC 247	SIMA, Chimbote	12 Feb 1985

Displacement, tons: 300 full load
Dimensions, feet (metres): 164 × 24.8 × 5.6 *(50 × 7.4 × 1.7)*
Main machinery: 4 Bazán MAN V8V diesels; 5640 hp(m) *(4.15 MW)*; 2 shafts
Speed, knots: 25. **Range, miles:** 3050 at 17 kts
Complement: 39
Guns: 1 Bofors 40 mm/60. 1 Oerlikon 20 mm.

Comment: Have aluminium alloy superstructures. The prototype craft was scrapped in 1990.

RIO TAMBO *1989, Peruvian Navy*

2 VOSPER TYPE (LARGE PATROL CRAFT)

Name	*No*	*Builders*	*Commissioned*
RIO PATIVILCA	PC 225	Vosper Ltd, Portsmouth	1965
RIO LOCUMBA	PC 227	Vosper Ltd, Portsmouth	1965

Displacement, tons: 100 standard; 130 full load
Dimensions, feet (metres): 109.7 × 21 × 5.7 *(33.5 × 6.4 × 1.7)*
Main machinery: 2 Napier Deltic T38-37 diesels; 6200 hp *(4.62 MW)*; 2 shafts
Speed, knots: 30. **Range, miles:** 1100 at 15 kts
Complement: 25 (4 officers)
Guns: 2 Bofors 40 mm.

Comment: Of all-welded steel construction with aluminium upperworks. Equipped with Vosper roll damping fins, Decca Type 707 true motion radar, comprehensive radio, up-to-date navigation aids and air-conditioning. A twin rocket projector can be fitted forward instead of gun.

RIO LOCUMBA (old pennant number) *Peruvian Navy*

1 US PGM 71 CLASS (LARGE PATROL CRAFT)

Name	*No*	*Builders*	*Commissioned*
RIO CHIRA (ex-US *PGM 111*)	PC 223 (ex-PC 12)	SIMA, Callao	June 1972

Displacement, tons: 130 standard; 147 full load
Dimensions, feet (metres): 101 × 21 × 6 *(30.8 × 6.4 × 1.8)*
Main machinery: 8 GM 6-71 diesels; 1768 hp *(1.32 MW)*; 2 shafts
Speed, knots: 18.5. **Range, miles:** 1500 at 10 kts
Complement: 15
Guns: 1 Bofors 40 mm. 2 Oerlikon 20 mm. 2—12.7 mm MGs.

5 PORT PATROL CRAFT

LA PUNTA PP 230
RIO SANTA PP 232
RIO MAJES PP 233
RIO VIRU PP 235
RIO LURIN PP 236

Displacement, tons: 43 full load
Dimensions, feet (metres): 61 × 17.3 × 5.6 *(18.6 × 5.3 × 1.7)*
Main machinery: 2 GM 12V-71 TI diesels; 1120 hp *(836 kW)* sustained; 2 shafts
Speed, knots: 25
Guns: 2 Oerlikon 20 mm.

Comment: Built by McLaren, Niteroi in 1980-82. PP 231 transferred to the Navy as a survey craft. PP 234 wrecked in 1990.

2 RIVER PATROL CRAFT

Name	*No*	*Builders*	*Commissioned*
RIO TUMBES	PC 241 (ex-P 251)	Viareggio, Italy	5 Sep 1960
RIO PIURA	PC 242 (ex-P 252)	Viareggio, Italy	5 Sep 1960

Displacement, tons: 37 full load
Dimensions, feet (metres): 65.7 × 17 × 3.2 *(20 × 5.2 × 1)*
Main machinery: 2 GM 8V-71 diesels; 590 hp *(440 kW)* sustained; 2 shafts
Speed, knots: 18
Guns: 2 Bofors 40 mm.

Comment: Ordered in 1959.

RIO PIURA *1975, Peruvian Navy*

PHILIPPINES

Flag Officers

Flag Officer-in-Command:
Rear Admiral Mariano J Dumancas, Jr
Chief of Naval Staff:
Commodore Eduardo Domingo
Commander Fleet:
Commodore Dario T Fajardo
Commandant Coast Guard:
Commodore Carlos L Agustin
Commandant Marines:
Brigadier Eduardo T Cabanlig

Diplomatic Representation

Defence Attaché in London:
Colonel Garcia

Personnel

1992: 23 000 (including 9500 marines and 2000 Coast Guard)

Organisation

The Navy is organised into three major commands: Fleet, Coast Guard and Marines. There are six Naval Districts, Coast Guard has eight Districts, within which there are 40 stations, 13 sub-stations and 140 detachments. Coast Guard units are under operational control of Naval District commanders when conducting counter-insurgency operations. The Navy and the Coast Guard are interchangeable and often share duties.

Marine Corps

Marines comprise ten Infantry Battalions (BNs), deployed as follows: ND II/Subic Command (two); ND IV/Palawan (one); ND VI/Mindanao (seven). Additionally, there are three Navy Construction Brigades and two NC Companies, plus nine Seal Teams deployed in all naval districts.

Naval Bases

Sangley Point/Cavite, Zamboanga, Cebu. Plans for bases at Cagayan de Tawitawi and Taganak.

Prefix to Ships' Names

RPS for Republic of Philippines Ship

New Construction

Plans to acquire six FAC-Missile and six FAC-Gun craft between FY 1991 and FY 1997. First of new gun-armed craft are being built under FY 1991 funds; first of missile-armed craft under FY 1993 funding. New LSM class of six is being funded starting in FY 1991 and an MCM programme of four vessels will begin in FY 1997.

State of the Fleet

There are plans to station five large patrol craft around the archipelago with each one supporting seven fast attack craft. Many older ships have been scrapped so that the remainder can be brought up to an operational standard but the overall age of the 45 patrol and support ships is over 40 years.

Mercantile Marine

Lloyd's Register of Shipping:
1465 vessels of 8 625 561 tons gross

DELETIONS

Frigates

1990 *Datu Siratuna*

Patrol Craft

1989 *Abra, Bukidnon, Tablas, Basilan*
1990 *Katapangan, Nueva Viscaya* (sunk)

Amphibious Ships

1989 *Agusan Del Sur, Mindoro Occidental, Surigao Del Norte, Surigao Del Sur, Maquindanao, Cagayan, Tarlac, Lanao Del Sur, Leyte Del Sur, Davao Oriental, Aurora, Cavite, Cotabato Del Norte, Isabela, Batanes, Western Samar, Oriental Mindoro, Camarines Sur, Sulu, La Union*

Miscellaneous

1989 *Lake Lanao, Tiboli, YD 201, YD 203, Kamagong, Lake Naujan*

FRIGATES

Note: *Rajah Lakandula*, paid off in 1988, is still afloat as an alongside HQ and depot ship where she is planned to remain until the end of the century.

1 Ex-US CANNON CLASS

Name	*No*	*Builders*	*Laid down*	*Launched*	*Commissioned*
RAJAH HUMABON (ex-*Hatsuhi* DE 263, ex-USS *Atherton* DE 169)	PF 78	Norfolk Navy Yard, Portsmouth, Va.	14 Jan 1943	27 May 1943	29 Aug 1943

Displacement, tons: 1390 standard; 1750 full load
Dimensions, feet (metres): 306 × 36.6 × 14 *(93.3 × 11.2 × 4.3)*
Main machinery: Diesel-electric; 4 GM 16-278A diesels; 6000 hp *(4.5 MW)*; 2 shafts
Speed, knots: 18. **Range, miles:** 10 800 at 12 kts
Complement: 165

Guns: 3 US 3 in *(76 mm)*/50 Mk 22 ❶; 85° elevation; 20 rounds/minute to 12 km *(6.6 nm)*; weight of shell 6 kg.
6 US/Bofors 40 mm/56 (3 twin) ❷; 45° elevation; 160 rounds/minute to 11 km *(5.9 nm)*; weight of shell 0.9 kg.
2 Oerlikon 20 mm/70 ❸; 50° elevation; 800 rounds/minute to 2 km.
A/S mortars: 1 manually loaded Hedgehog ❹; range 350 m; warhead 26 kg; 24 rockets.
Depth charges: 8 K-gun Mk 6 projectors ❺; range 160 m; warhead 150 kg; 1 rack.
Fire control: Mk 52 GFCS with Mk 51 rangefinder for 3 in guns. 3 Mk 51 Mod 2 GFCS for 40 mm.
Radars: Surface search: Raytheon SPS 5 ❻; G/H band; range 37 km *(20 nm)*.
Navigation: RCA/GE Mk 26; I band.

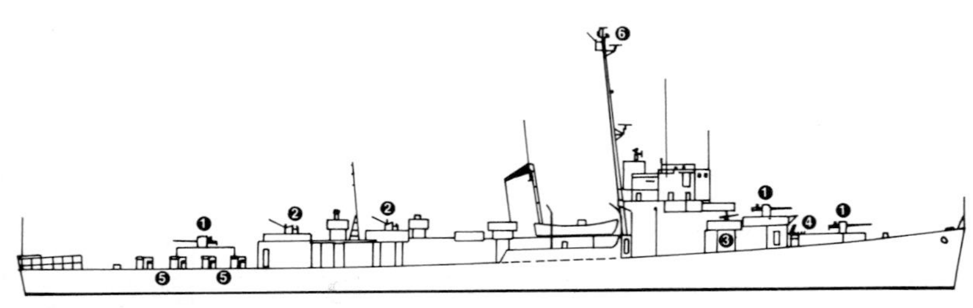

Ex-US CANNON Class *(Scale 1 : 900), Ian Sturton*

Sonars: SQS 17B; hull-mounted; active search and attack; medium/high frequency.

Programmes: *Hatsuhi* originally transferred by the USA to Japan 14 June 1955 and paid off June 1975 reverting to US Navy. Transferred to Philippines 23 December 1978. Towed to South Korea 1979 for overhaul and modernisation. Recommissioned 27 February 1980. A sister ship *Datu Kalantiaw* lost during Typhoon Clara 20 September 1981.

CORVETTES

2 Ex-US AUK CLASS

Name	*No*	*Builders*	*Commissioned*
RIZAL (ex-USS *Murrelet* MSF 372)	PS 69	Savannah Machine & Foundry Co, Georgia	21 Aug 1945
QUEZON (ex-USS *Vigilance* MSF 324)	PS 70	Associated Shipbuilders, Seattle, Washington	28 Feb 1944

Displacement, tons: 1090 standard; 1250 full load
Dimensions, feet (metres): 221.2 × 32.2 × 10.8 *(67.4 × 9.8 × 3.3)*
Main machinery: Diesel-electric; 2 GM 12-278 diesels; 2200 hp *(1.64 MW)*; 2 shafts
Speed, knots: 18. **Range, miles:** 5700 at 16 kts
Complement: 80 (5 officers)

Guns: 1 US 3 in *(76 mm)*/50; 85° elevation; 20 rounds/minute to 12 km *(6.6 nm)*; weight of shell 6 kg.
4 US/Bofors 40 mm/56 (2 twin); 45° elevation; 160 rounds/minute to 11 km *(5.9 nm)*; weight of shell 0.9 kg.
4 Oerlikon 20 mm (2 twin); 50° elevation; 800 rounds/minute to 2 km.
Torpedoes: 3—324 mm US Mk 32 (triple) tubes. Probably Honeywell Mk 44; anti-submarine; active homing to 5.5 km *(3 nm)* at 30 kts; warhead 34 kg.
A/S mortars: 1 manually loaded Hedgehog; range 350 m; warhead 26 kg; 24 rockets.
Depth charges: 2 Mk 9 racks.
Radars: Surface search: Raytheon SPS 5C; G/H band; range 37 km *(20 nm)*.
Navigation: DAS 3; I band.
Sonars: SQS 17B; hull-mounted; active search and attack; high frequency.

Helicopters: Platform only.

Programmes: PS 69 transferred to the Philippines on 18 June 1965 and PS 70 on 19 August 1967.
Structure: Upon transfer the minesweeping gear was removed and a second 3 in gun fitted aft; additional anti-submarine weapons also fitted. PS 70 has bulwarks on iron deck to end of superstructure which PS 69 does not have. Now have helicopter flight deck (but no facilities) in place of after 3 in gun.

QUEZON *1976, Michael D. J. Lennon*

7 Ex-US PCE 827 CLASS

Name	*No*	*Builders*	*Commissioned*
MIGUEL MALVAR (ex-*Ngoc Hoi*, ex-USS *Brattleboro* PCER 852)	PS 19	Pullman Standard Car Co, Chicago	26 May 1944
SULTAN KUDARAT (ex-*Dong Da II*, ex-USS *Crestview* PCER 895)	PS 22	Willamette Iron & Steel Corporation, Portland	30 Oct 1943
DATU MARIKUDO (ex-*Van Kiep II*, ex-USS *Amherst* PCER 853)	PS 23	Pullman Standard Car Co, Chicago	16 June 1944
CEBU (ex-USS *PCE 881*)	PS 28	Albina E and M Works, Portland, Oregon	31 July 1944
NEGROS OCCIDENTAL (ex-USS *PCE 884*)	PS 29	Albina E and M Works, Portland, Oregon	30 Mar 1944
PANGASINAN (ex-USS *PCE 891*)	PS 31	Willamette Iron & Steel Corporation, Portland	15 June 1944
ILOILO (ex-USS *PCE 897*)	PS 32	Willamette Iron & Steel Corporation, Portland	6 Jan 1945

Displacement, tons: 640 standard; 853 full load
Dimensions, feet (metres): 184.5 × 33.1 × 9.5 *(56.3 × 10.1 × 2.9)*
Main machinery: 2 GM 12-278A diesels; 2200 hp *(1.64 MW)*; 2 shafts
Speed, knots: 15. **Range, miles:** 9000 at 12 kts
Complement: 85 (8 officers)

Guns: 1 US 3 in *(76 mm)*/50; 85° elevation; 20 rounds/minute to 12 km *(6.6 nm)*; weight of shell 6 kg.
2 to 6 US/Bofors 40 mm/56 (single or 1-3 twin); 45° elevation; 160 rounds/minute to 11 km *(5.9 nm)*; weight of shell 0.9 kg.
4 Oerlikon 20 mm/70; 50° elevation; 800 rounds/minute to 2 km.
Radars: Surface search: SPS 50 (PS 23). SPS 21D (PS 19). CRM-NIA-75 (PS 29, 31, 32).
Navigation: RCA SPN 18; I/J band.

Programmes: Five transferred to the Philippines in July 1948 (PS 28-32); PS 22 to South Vietnam from US Navy on 29 November 1961, PS 19 on 11 July 1966, and PS 23 in June 1970. PS 19 and 22 to Philippines November 1975 and PS 23 5 April 1976. PS 30 foundered 1979.
Modernisation: PS 19, 22, 31 and 32 refurbished in 1990-91, and two more are in hand in 1992.
Structure: First three were originally fitted as rescue ships (PCER). A/S equipment has now been removed or is inoperable.

PANGASINAN *10/1989, Mel Back*

1 Ex-US ADMIRABLE CLASS

Name	*No*	*Builders*	*Commissioned*
MAGAT SALAMAT (ex-*Chi Lang II*, ex-USS *Gayety* MSF 239)	PS 20	Winslow Marine Railway & S B Co, Seattle, Wash	1944

Displacement, tons: 650 standard; 945 full load
Dimensions, feet (metres): 184.5 × 33 × 9.8 *(56.3 × 10.1 × 3)*
Main machinery: 2 Cooper-Bessemer GSB-8 diesels; 1710 hp *(1.28 MW)*; 2 shafts
Speed, knots: 15. **Range, miles:** 4500 at 14 kts
Complement: 85 (8 officers)

Guns: 1 US 3 in *(76 mm)*/50 Mk 22. 2 US/Bofors 40 mm Mk 3. 6 Oerlikon 20 mm (1 twin, 4 single). 1—81 mm Mk 2 mortar.
Radars: Surface search: Sperry SPS 53A; I/J band.

Programmes: Launched 19 March 1944 and transferred to South Vietnam by US Navy in April 1962. To Philippines November 1975.
Structure: Minesweeping and ASW equipment have been removed.

MAGAT SALAMAT (old name and pennant number) *1962, Vietnamese Navy*

SHIPBORNE AIRCRAFT

Numbers/Type: 11 PADC (MBB) BO 105C.
Operational speed: 145 kts *(270 km/h)*.
Service ceiling: 17 000 ft *(5180 m)*.
Range: 355 nm *(657 km)*.
Role/Weapon systems: Sole shipborne helicopter; some shore-based for SAR; some commando support capability. Being purchased at the rate of one per year. Sensors: Some fitted with search radar. Weapons: Unarmed.

LAND-BASED MARITIME AIRCRAFT

Numbers/Type: 13 PADC (Pilatus Britten-Norman) Islander.
Operational speed: 150 kts *(280 km/h)*.
Service ceiling: 18 900 ft *(5760 m)*.
Range: 1500 nm *(2775 km)*.
Role/Weapon systems: Short-range MR and SAR aircraft. Being purchased at the rate of one per year. Three more belonging to the Air Force are used for coastal surveillance. Sensors: Search radar, cameras. Weapons: Unarmed.

LIGHT FORCES

1 AGUINALDO CLASS (LARGE PATROL CRAFT)

Name	*No*	*Builders*	*Commissioned*
EMILIO AGUINALDO	PG 140	Cavite, Sangley Point	21 Nov 1990

Displacement, tons: 236 full load
Dimensions, feet (metres): 144.4 × 24.3 × 5.2 *(44 × 7.4 × 1.6)*
Main machinery: 4 Detroit 12V 92TA diesels; 2040 hp *(1.52 MW)* sustained; 2 shafts
Speed, knots: 25. **Range, miles:** 1100 at 18 kts
Complement: 58 (6 officers)
Guns: 2 Bofors 40 mm/60. 2 Oerlikon 20 mm. 4—12.7 mm MGs.

Comment: Launched 23 June 1984 but only completed in 1990. Steel hull. The intention is to upgrade the armament in due course to include a SAM and an OTO Melara 76 mm/62 gun.

0 + 3 CORMORAN CLASS (FAST ATTACK CRAFT—MISSILE)

Displacement, tons: 384 full load
Dimensions, feet (metres): 185.7 × 24.7 × 6.5 *(56.6 × 7.5 × 2)*
Main machinery: 3 Bazán-MTU 16V 956 TB91 diesels; 11 250 hp(m) *(8.27 MW)* sustained; 3 shafts
Speed, knots: 34
Complement: 32 (5 officers)
Missiles: SSM: 4 Aerospatiale Exocet MM 40.
Guns: 1 OTO Melara 76 mm/62. 2 Breda 40 mm/70 (twin).
Fire control: Selenia Elsag NA 21.

Comment: Contract signed with Bazán on 30 September 1991. First of class to be built in Spain and delivered in 1994, the other two to be built at Cavite Shipyard. The contract is subject to Spanish Government approval and financial support, as well as credit guarantees from weapon systems manufacturers.

3 KAGITINGAN CLASS (LARGE PATROL CRAFT)

Name	*No*	*Builders*	*Commissioned*
KAGITINGAN	P 101	Hamelin SY, FDR	9 Feb 1979
BAGONG LAKAS	P 102	Hamelin SY, FDR	9 Feb 1979
BAGONG SILANG	P 104	Hamelin SY, FDR	1979

Displacement, tons: 132 full load
Dimensions, feet (metres): 100.3 × 18.6 × 5 *(30.6 × 5.7 × 1.5)*
Main machinery: 2 Mercedes-Benz MTU 12V 493 TZ60 diesels; 1360 hp(m) *(1 MW)* sustained; 2 shafts
Speed, knots: 16
Guns: 4—20 mm (2 twin). 2—12.7 mm MGs.

Comment: Based at Cavite. Operational in 1990. P 103 paid off and used for spares.

0 + 3 (3) LAUNCESTON TYPE (LARGE PATROL CRAFT)

Displacement, tons: 396 full load
Dimensions, feet (metres): 187 × 27 × 8 *(57 × 8.2 × 2.4)*
Main machinery: 3 MTU 16V 956 TB91 diesels; 11 250 hp(m) *(8.27 MW)* sustained; 3 shafts; cp props
Speed, knots: 30. **Range, miles:** 3500 at 18 kts
Guns: 1 OTO Melara 76 mm/62. 2 Breda 40 mm/70 (twin) compact. 2 Oerlikon 25 mm.
Radars: Surface search/fire control: Signaal WM 22.

Comment: Agreement signed in April 1990 with Launceston Marine, Tasmania for six of the class. Negotiations were then taken over by the Australia Submarine Corporation (ASC) which signed a contract on 21 October 1991 to build three of the craft. The contract is subject to Australian Government approval and financial support, as well as credit guarantees from the weapons systems manufacturers. The plan is to build the vessels at ASC Newcastle which is the former Carrington Slipways. The propulsion details have changed since the original CODAG proposals.

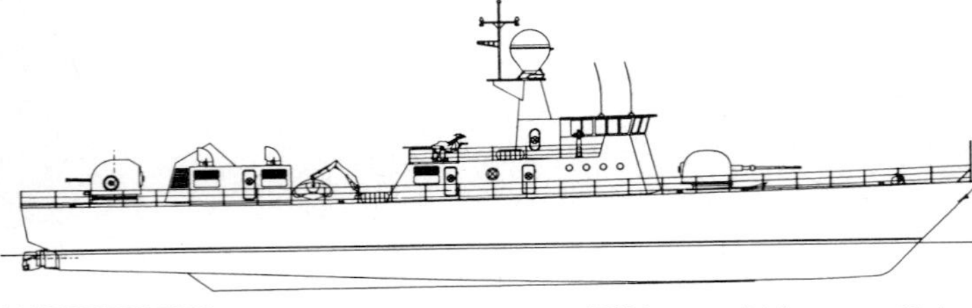

LAUNCESTON TYPE *1990 (not to scale), Launceston Marine*

2 LARGE PATROL CRAFT

Name	*No*	*Builders*	*Commissioned*
BATAAN	SAR 77	Vosper (Private) Ltd, Singapore	Dec 1975
ANG PINUNO	TP 77	Vosper (Private) Ltd, Singapore	Dec 1975

Displacement, tons: 150 full load
Dimensions, feet (metres): 124.3 × 23.6 × 12.5 *(37.9 × 7.2 × 3.8)*
Main machinery: 3 MTU 12V538 TB91 diesels; 4600 hp(m) *(3.38 MW)* sustained; 3 shafts
Speed, knots: 30
Complement: 32

Comment: SAR 77 is used for search and rescue work and belongs to the Coast Guard. TP 77 is a command ship and has been used before 1986 as a presidential yacht.

BATAAN *1984, Gilbert Gyssels*

1 Ex-US PC 461 CLASS (LARGE PATROL CRAFT)

Name	*No*	*Builders*	*Commissioned*
NEGROS ORIENTAL (ex-*E 312*, ex-*L'Inconstant, P 636*, ex-USS *PC 1171*)	PS 26	Leathem D Smith S B Co	15 May 1943

Displacement, tons: 280 standard; 335 full load
Dimensions, feet (metres): 178.8 × 23.1 × 8.5 *(54.5 × 7 × 2.6)*
Main machinery: 2 GM 16-278A diesels; 3000 hp *(2.24 MW)*; 2 shafts
Speed, knots: 20
Complement: 56 (5 officers)
Guns: 1 US 3 in *(76 mm)*/50. Up to 6 Oerlikon 20 mm (single or twin).
Depth charges: 2 racks (PS 80).
Radars: Surface search: RCA CR 104A (SPN 18); I/J band.
Navigation: Decca 202 (PS 80); I band.
Sonars: SQS 17B; hull-mounted; active search and attack; high frequency.

Comment: Acquired by France in 1951, Khmer Republic 1956 and, after transferring to Philippines in 1975, bought December 1976. Converted as escort vessel for planned new fast attack craft in 1987, sea trials in March 1988. Sister ship also converted but sank in a typhoon in October 1990.

4 US PGM-39 CLASS (LARGE PATROL CRAFT)

Name	*No*	*Builders*	*Commissioned*
AGUSAN (ex-*PGM 39*)	PG 61	Tacoma Boatbuilding Co, Washington	Mar 1960
CATANDUANES (ex-*PGM 40*)	PG 62	Tacoma Boatbuilding Co, Washington	Mar 1960
ROMBLON (ex-*PGM 41*)	PG 63	Peterson Builders, Wisconsin	June 1960
PALAWAN (ex-*PGM 42*)	PG 64	Tacoma Boatbuilding Co, Washington	June 1960

Displacement, tons: 133 full load
Dimensions, feet (metres): 100.3 × 18.6 × 6.9 *(30.6 × 5.7 × 2.1)*
Main machinery: 2 Mercedes-Benz MTU 12V 493 TY57 diesels; 2200 hp(m) *(1.6 MW)* sustained; 2 shafts
Speed, knots: 17. **Range, miles:** 1500 at 10 kts
Complement: 26-30
Guns: 2—20 mm. 2—12.7 mm MGs. 1—81 mm mortar.
Radars: Surface search: Raytheon 1500; I/J band.

Comment: Steel-hulled craft built under US military assistance programmes. Assigned US PGM-series numbers while under construction. Transferred upon completion. These craft are lengthened versions of the US Coast Guard 95 ft Cape class patrol boat design. PG 62 serves with the Coast Guard.

CATANDUANES *10/1977, Giorgio Arra*

8 HALTER TYPE (COASTAL PATROL CRAFT)

Displacement, tons: 56 full load
Dimensions, feet (metres): 78 × 20 × 5.8 *(23.8 × 6.1 × 1.8)*
Main machinery: 2 Detroit 16V 92 TA diesels; 1380 hp *(1.03 MW)*; 2 shafts
Speed, knots: 28. **Range, miles:** 1200 at 12 kts
Guns: 2—12.7 mm MGs. 2—7.62 mm MGs.

Comment: First five ordered from Halter Marine in August 1989, a second batch of three in September 1990. Built at Equitable Shipyard, New Orleans. First completed in August 1990, second in December 1990 and then delivered at a rate of one about every three weeks. The aim is for 25 craft divided into five squadrons each based on a support ship and spread through the archipelago. Built to Coast Guard standards with an aluminium hull and superstructure.

HALTER TYPE *8/1990, Trinity Marine*

AMPHIBIOUS FORCES

11 Ex-US 1-511 and 512-1152 CLASSES (LSTs)

Name	*No*	*Commissioned*
ZAMBOANGA DEL SUR (ex-*Cam Ranh*, ex-USS *Marion County* LST 975)	LT 86	3 Feb 1945
COTOBATO DEL SUR (ex-USS *Cayuga County* LST 529)	LT 87	28 Feb 1944
ILOCOS NORTE (ex-USS *Madera County* LST 905)	LT 98	20 Jan 1945
LAGUNA (ex-USNS *T-LST 230*)	LT 501	3 Nov 1943
SAMAR ORIENTAL (ex-USNS *T-LST 287*)	LT 502	15 Dec 1943
LANAO DEL NORTE (ex-USNS *T-LST 566*)	LT 504	29 May 1944
BENGUET (ex-USNS *Davies County* T-LST 692)	LT 507	10 May 1944
SIERRA MADRE (ex-*Dumagat*, ex-*My Tho*, ex-USS *Harnett County, AGP 821*, ex-*LST 821*)	AL 57	14 Jan 1944
SAMAR DEL NORTE (ex-USNS *Nansemond County* T-LST 1064)	LT 510	12 Mar 1945
TAWI-TAWI (ex-USNS *T-LST 1072*)	LT 512	12 Apr 1945
APAYAO (ex-*Can Tho*, ex-USS *Garrett County* AGP 786, ex-LST 786)	AE 516	28 Aug 1944

Displacement, tons: 1620 standard; 2472 beaching; 4080 full load
Dimensions, feet (metres): 328 × 50 × 14 *(100 × 15.2 × 4.3)*
Main machinery: 2 GM 12-567A diesels; 1800 hp *(1.34 MW)*; 2 shafts
Speed, knots: 10
Complement: Varies—approx 60 to 110 (depending upon employment)
Military lift: 2100 tons. 16 tanks or 10 tanks plus 200 troops

Guns: 6 US/Bofors 40 mm (2 twin, 2 single). 4 Oerlikon 20 mm (in refitted ships).

Programmes: LT 98 transferred on 29 November 1969; LT 506 and 510 were transferred to Japan in April 1961 and thence to Philippines in 1975—remainder transferred from US Navy in 1976 with exception of AL 57 and AE 516 which were used as light craft repair ships in South Vietnam and have retained amphibious capability (transferred to Vietnam 1970 and to Philippines 1976, acquired by purchase 5 April 1976). LT 87 and LT 86 transferred (grant aid) 17 November 1975. LT 510 acquired by purchase 24 September 1977. LT 501, 504 and 512 commissioned in Philippine Navy 8 August 1978 and LT 502 and 507 on 18 October 1978. Fourteen of the class scrapped in 1989.
Modernisation: Several have had major refits including replacement of frames and plating as well as engines and electrics and provision for four 20 mm guns.
Structure: Some of the later ships have tripod masts, others have pole masts.
Operational: Many of these ships served as cargo ships in the Western Pacific under the US Military Sealift Command (USNS/T-LST); they were civilian manned by Korean and Japanese crews. The USNS ships lack troop accommodation and other amphibious warfare features. Some are used for general cargo work in Philippine service but in spite of the major clearout in 1989 all in naval service are in urgent need of refit and the first three were taken in hand in 1989.

TAWI-TAWI *6/1988*

3 Ex-US LCU CLASS

Ex US-LCU 1603, 1604, 1606

Displacement, tons: 347 full load
Dimensions, feet (metres): 115 × 34 × 5.3 *(35 × 10.4 × 1.6)*
Main machinery: 3 GM diesels; 680 hp *(507 kW)*; 3 shafts
Speed, knots: 8
Complement: 6
Military lift: 8 troops; 167 tons
Guns: 2 Oerlikon 20 mm.

Comment: Built in Japan for the US Navy in 1954-55. Transferred 17 November 1975. Refitted in Japan in 1979.

9 Ex-US LCM 8 CLASS

LCM 257, 258, 260-266

Displacement, tons: 118 full load
Main machinery: 4 GM 6-71 diesels; 696 hp *(520 kW)* sustained; 2 shafts
Speed, knots: 9
Military lift: 54 tons

Comment: LCM 257 and 258 transferred June 1973, remainder June 1975.

50 Ex-US LCM 6 CLASS

LCM 224-227, 229, 231-234, 237, 239, 240, 249, 255, 256, 259 + 34

Displacement, tons: 56 full load
Main machinery: 2 Gray Marine 64 HN9 diesels; 450 hp *(336 kW)*; 2 shafts
Speed, knots: 10
Military lift: 30 tons

Comment: One transferred in 1955, 13 in 1971-73, 24 in November 1975, remaining 12 in 1973-75.

6 Ex-US LCVP CLASS

LCVP 175, 181 + 4

Comment: Two transferred in 1955-56, one in 1965, two in 1971 and LCVP 175 and 181 in June 1973. One deleted. More of the type reported building at Cavite Naval Yard in mid-1989.

SERVICE FORCES

2 Ex-US ACHELOUS CLASS (REPAIR SHIPS)

Name	*No*	*Commissioned*
NARRA (ex-USS *Krishna* ARL 38, ex-*LST 1149*)	AR 88	3 Dec 1945
YAKAL (ex-USS *Satyr* ARL 23, ex-*LST 852*)	AR 517	20 Nov 1944

Displacement, tons: 4342 full load
Dimensions, feet (metres): 328 × 50 × 14 *(100 × 15.2 × 4.3)*
Main machinery: 2 GM 12-567A diesels; 1800 hp *(1.34 MW)*; 2 shafts
Speed, knots: 11.6
Complement: 220 approx
Guns: 4 US/Bofors 40 mm (quad). 10 Oerlikon 20 mm (5 twin).

Comment: AR 88 transferred to the Philippines on 30 October 1971 and AR 517 on 24 January 1977 by sale. (Originally to South Vietnam 30 September 1971.) Converted during construction. Extensive machine shop, spare parts stowage, supplies, etc.

ACHELOUS Class (old number) *1968, Philippine Navy*

0 + 2 CHINESE LOGISTIC SUPPORT VESSELS (LSVs)

Displacement, tons: 1560 full load
Dimensions, feet (metres): 279.5 × 44 × 15.1 *(85.2 × 13.4 × 4.6)*
Main machinery: 2 diesels; 2 shafts
Speed, knots: 16
Complement: 45 (5 officers)

Comment: Contract signed in September 1991 with China Shipbuilding Corporation. Subject to final approval and with a delivery date for the first in 1994. Both to be built at Guangzhou shipyard. These ships were given a higher priority than two more of the Cormoran class FACs.

SUPPORT SHIPS

1 PRESIDENTIAL YACHT

Name	*No*	*Builders*	*Commissioned*
ANG PANGULO (ex-*The President*, ex-*Roxas*, ex-*Lapu-Lapu*)	TP 777	Ishikawajima, Japan	1959

Displacement, tons: 2239 standard; 2727 full load
Dimensions, feet (metres): 257.6 × 42.6 × 21 *(78.5 × 13 × 6.4)*
Main machinery: 2 Mitsui DE642/VBF diesels; 5000 hp(m) *(3.68 MW)*; 2 shafts
Speed, knots: 18. **Range, miles:** 6900 at 15 kts
Complement: 81 (8 officers)
Guns: 2 Oerlikon 20 mm/70 Mk 4 (twin).
Radars: Navigation: RCA CRMN-1A-75; I band.

Comment: Built as war reparation; launched in 1958. Was used as presidential yacht and command ship with accommodation for 50 passengers. Originally named *Lapu-Lapu* after the chief who killed Magellan; renamed *Roxas* on 9 October 1962 after the late Manuel Roxas, the first President of the Philippines Republic, renamed *The President* in 1967 and *Ang Pangulo* in 1975. One 15 ton crane. In early 1987 she was in Hong Kong with a full crew, having not returned to Cavite since the banishment of ex-President Marcos, and is now for sale.

ANG PANGULO *1982, Ziro Kimata*

1 Ex-US C1-M-AV1 TYPE (SUPPORT SHIP)

Name	*No*	*Builders*	*Commissioned*
MACTAN (ex-USCGC *Kukui* WAK 186, ex-USS *Colquitt* AK 174)	TK 90	Froemming Brothers, Milwaukee	22 Sep 1945

Displacement, tons: 2499 light; 7570 full load
Dimensions, feet (metres): 338.5 × 50 × 18 *(103.2 × 15.2 × 5.5)*
Main machinery: 1 Nordberg TSM-6 diesel; 1700 hp *(1.27 MW)*; 1 shaft
Speed, knots: 11.5
Complement: 85
Guns: 2—12.7 mm Mk 2 MG (twin).
Radars: Navigation: RCA CRMN 1A 75; I band.

Comment: Commissioned in US Navy on 22 September 1945; transferred to the US Coast Guard two days later. Subsequently served as Coast Guard supply ship in Pacific until transferred to Philippines on 1 March 1972 and by purchase 1 August 1980. Used to supply military posts and lighthouses in the Philippine archipelago. Carries one 30 ton, one 20 ton and six 5 ton cranes.

1 Ex-US ADMIRABLE CLASS

Name	*No*	*Builders*	*Commissioned*
MOUNT SAMAT (ex-*Santa Maria*, ex-*Pagasa*, ex-*APO 21*, ex-USS *Quest*, *AM 281*)	TP 21	Gulf Shipbuilding Corporation	25 Oct 1944

Displacement, tons: 650 standard; 945 full load
Dimensions, feet (metres): 184.5 × 33 × 9.8 *(56.3 × 10.1 × 3)*
Main machinery: 2 Cooper-Bessemer GSB8 diesels; 1710 hp *(1.28 MW)*; 2 shafts
Speed, knots: 15. **Range, miles:** 4500 at 14 kts
Complement: 67
Radars: Navigation: RCA CR-104; I/J band.

Comment: Former US Navy minesweeper (AM). Commissioned on 25 October 1944. Transferred to the Philippines in July 1948. Was used as presidential yacht and command ship but now is a humble supply vessel.

MOUNT SAMAT *2/1982, G. Jacobs*

2 Ex-US YW TYPE (WATER CARRIERS)

LAKE BULUAN (ex-US *YW 111*) YW 33
LAKE PAOAY (ex-US *YW 130*) YW 34

Displacement, tons: 1237 full load
Dimensions, feet (metres): 174 × 32.7 × 13.2 *(53 × 10 × 4)*
Main machinery: 2 GM 8-278A diesels; 1500 hp *(1.12 MW)*; 2 shafts
Speed, knots: 7.5
Complement: 29
Cargo capacity: 200 000 gal
Guns: 2 Oerlikon 20 mm.

Comment: Basically similar to YOG type but adapted to carry fresh water. Transferred to the Philippines on 16 July 1975.

1 Ex-US YOG TYPE (TANKER)

Name	*No*	*Commissioned*
LAKE BUHI (ex-US *YOG 73*)	YO 78	1944

Displacement, tons: 447 standard; 1400 full load
Dimensions, feet (metres): 174 × 32.7 × 13.2 *(53 × 10 × 4)*
Main machinery: 2 GM 8-278A diesels; 1500 hp *(1.12 MW)*; 2 shafts
Speed, knots: 8
Complement: 28
Cargo capacity: 6570 barrels dieso and gasoline
Guns: 2 Oerlikon 20 mm/70 Mk 4.

Comment: Former US Navy gasoline tanker. Transferred in July 1967 on loan and by purchase 5 March 1980.

Ex-US YO/YOG Type (old number) *10/1977, Giorgio Arra*

1 LIGHTHOUSE TENDER

PEARL BANK (ex-US Army *LO 4*, ex-Australian *MSL*)

Displacement, tons: 140 standard; 345 full load
Dimensions, feet (metres): 120 × 24.5 × 8 *(36.6 × 7.5 × 2.4)*
Main machinery: 2 Fairbanks-Morse 35F8 diesels; 240 hp *(179 kW)*; 2 shafts
Speed, knots: 7. **Range, miles:** 2200 at 5 kts
Complement: 35

Comment: Originally an Australian motor stores lighter; subsequently transferred to the US Army and then to the Philippines. Employed as a lighthouse tender. Transferred to the Coast Guard.

5 Ex-US YTL 422 CLASS (TUGS)

IGOROT (ex-*YTL 572*) YQ 222
TAGBANUA (ex-*YTL 429*) YQ 223
— (ex-*YTL 750*) —
ILONGOT (ex-*YTL 427*) YQ 225
TASADAY (ex-*YTL 425*) YQ 226

Displacement, tons: 71
Main machinery: 1 diesel; 240 hp *(179 kW)*; 1 shaft
Speed, knots: 10

Comment: Former US Navy 66 ft harbour tugs. Ex-*YTL 750* transferred from Japan—24 September 1976 by sale. *YTL 748* was to be transferred but sank on passage. YQ 225 and 226 acquired by sale 1 August 1980.

4 Ex-US ARMY FS TYPE (BUOY TENDERS)

Name	*No*
CABO BOJEADOR (ex-US Army *FS 203*)	TK 46
LIMASAWA (ex-USCGC *Nettle* WAK 129, ex-US Army *FS 169*)	TK 79
BADJAO (ex-Japanese, ex-US Army *FS 524*)	AS 59
MANGYAN (ex-Japanese, ex-US Army *FS 408*)	AS 71

Displacement, tons: 470 standard; 811 full load
Dimensions, feet (metres): 180 × 32 × 10 *(54.9 × 9.8 × 3)*
Main machinery: 2 GM 6-278A diesels; 1120 hp *(836 kW)*; 2 shafts
Speed, knots: 10
Complement: 50
Cargo capacity: 400 tons
Guns: 12.7 mm (TK 79). 7.62 mm MGs (TK 79).
Radars: Navigation: RCA CRMN 1A 75; I band.

Comment: Former US Army freight and supply ships. Employed as tenders for buoys and lighthouses. Ex-*FS 408* transferred 24 September 1976 by sale. TK 79 acquired by sale 31 August 1978. One 5 ton derrick. Transferred to the Coast Guard. TK 46 paid off in 1988 but was back in service in 1991 after a major overhaul.

LIMASAWA *1977, G. Jacobs*

3 FLOATING DOCKS

YD 200 (ex-*AFDL 24*) **YD 204** (ex-*AFDL 20*) **YD 205** (ex-*ADFL 44*)

Comment: Floating steel dry docks built in the USA; all are former US Navy units with YD 200 transferred in July 1948, YD 204 in October 1961 (sale 1 August 1980) and YD 205 in September 1969.
Capacities: YD 205, 2800 tons; YD 200 and YD 204, 1000 tons. In addition there are two floating cranes, YU 206 and YU 207, built in USA in 1944 and capable of lifting 30 tons.

SURVEY AND RESEARCH SHIPS

Note: (a) Operated by Coast and Geodetic Survey of Ministry of National Defence.
(b) An 83 m hydrographic ship ordered in April 1990 from Japan.

Name	*No*	*Builders*	*Commissioned*
EXPLORER	—	Ishikawajima	9 Feb 1984

Measurement, tons: 500 gross approx
Dimensions, feet (metres): 178.8 × 30.8 × 12.5 *(54.5 × 9.4 × 3.8)*
Main machinery: 2 diesels; 1200 hp(m) *(895 kW)*; 2 shafts
Speed, knots: 12

Comment: Used for research.

Name	*No*	*Builders*	*Commissioned*
ARLUNUYA	—	Walkers, Maryborough, Australia	1964
ARINYA	—	Walkers, Maryborough, Australia	1962

Displacement, tons: 255 full load
Dimensions, feet (metres): 101 × 22 × 8 *(30.8 × 6.7 × 2.4)*
Main machinery: 2 GM 6-71 diesels; 442 hp *(330 kW)* sustained; 2 shafts
Speed, knots: 10
Complement: 33 (6 officers)

Comment: Survey ships of same design as Australian *Banks* and *Bass*.

1 SURVEY SHIP

Name	*No*	*Builders*	*Commissioned*
ATYIMBA	—	Walkers, Maryborough, Australia	1969

Displacement, tons: 611 standard; 686 full load
Dimensions, feet (metres): 161 × 33 × 12 *(49.1 × 10 × 3.7)*
Main machinery: 2 Paxman diesels; 1452 hp *(1.08 MW)*; 2 shafts
Speed, knots: 11. **Range, miles:** 5000 at 8 kts
Complement: 54 (8 officers)
Guns: 2 Oerlikon 20 mm.

Comment: Survey ship similar to HMAS *Flinders* with differences in displacement and use of davits aft instead of cranes. Guns may be removed.

ATYIMBA *1981, van Ginderen Collection*

COAST GUARD

Note: Reported that four 53 m SAR craft were ordered from Japan in April 1990. First to be delivered in 1992. More may be built locally.

1 Ex-US COAST GUARD BALSAM CLASS (TENDER)

Name	*No*	*Builders*	*Commissioned*
KALINGA (ex-USCGC *Redbud, WAGL 398*, ex-USNS *Redbud, T-AKL 398*)	AG 89	Marine Iron & Shipbuilding Co, Duluth	2 May 1944

Displacement, tons: 935 standard; 1025 full load
Dimensions, feet (metres): 180 × 37 × 13 *(54.8 × 11.3 × 4)*
Main machinery: Diesel-electric; 2 Cooper-Bessemer GSB-8 diesels; 1710 hp *(1.28 MW)*; 2 generators; 1 motor; 1200 hp *(895 kW)*; 1 shaft
Speed, knots: 12. **Range, miles:** 3500 at 10 kts
Complement: 53
Guns: 2—12.7 mm MGs.
Radars: Navigation: Sperry SPS 53; I/J band.

Comment: Originally US Coast Guard buoy tender (WAGL 398). Transferred to US Navy on 25 March 1949 as AG 398 and then to the Philippines Navy 1 March 1972. One 20 ton derrick.

KALINGA *10/1977, Giorgio Arra*

1 LARGE PATROL CRAFT (SAR)

Name	*No*	*Builders*	*Commissioned*
TIRAD PASS	SAR 100	Sumidagawa, Japan	1974

Displacement, tons: 279 full load
Dimensions, feet (metres): 144.3 × 24.3 × 4.9 *(44 × 7.4 × 1.5)*
Main machinery: 2 diesels; 800 hp(m) *(588 kW)*; 2 shafts
Speed, knots: 27.5
Complement: 32
Guns: 4—12.7 mm (2 twin) MGs.

Comment: Paid for under Japanese war reparations. More planned but not built. SAR 99 deleted in 1983.

TIRAD PASS *1982, Ziro Kimata*

31 De HAVILLAND SERIES 9209 (COASTAL PATROL CRAFT)

PC 326-331 411-435

Displacement, tons: 15 full load
Dimensions, feet (metres): 45.9 × 14.5 × 3.3 *(14 × 4.4 × 1)*
Main machinery: 2 Cummins diesels; 740 hp *(552 kW)*; 2 shafts
Speed, knots: 25. **Range, miles:** 500 at 12 kts
Complement: 8
Guns: 2—12.7 mm MGs. 1—7.62 mm M60 MG.

Comment: GRP hulls. First six built by De Havilland Marine, Sydney NSW. Completed between 20 November 1974 and 8 February 1975. In August 1975 80 further craft of this design were ordered from Marcelo Yard, Manila to be delivered 1976-78 at the rate of two per month. By the end of 1976, 25 more had been completed but a serious fire in the shipyard destroyed 14 new hulls and halted production.

De HAVILLAND CPC *1977, De Havilland*

25 IMPROVED SWIFT Mk 3 TYPE (COASTAL PATROL CRAFT)

PCF 318-323
PCF 333
PCF 334
PCF 336-352

Displacement, tons: 29 standard; 37 full load
Dimensions, feet (metres): 65 × 16 × 3.4 *(19.8 × 4.9 × 1)*
Main machinery: 3 GM 12V 71 TI diesels; 1680 hp *(1.25 MW)*; 3 shafts
Speed, knots: 25
Complement: 8
Guns: 2—12.7 mm (twin) MGs. 2—7.62 mm MGs.
Radars: Surface search: Marconi Canada LN 66; I band.

Comment: Improved Swift type inshore patrol boats built by Sewart for the Philippine Navy. Delivered 1972-1976. Some are used by the Coast Guard and some by the Navy.

PCF 352 *1984, Gilbert Gyssels*

4 SWIFT Mk 1 and 9 SWIFT Mk 2 TYPE (COASTAL PATROL CRAFT)

PCF 300	**PCF 310**	**PCF 315**
PCF 301	**PCF 311**	**PCF 316**
PCF 306	**PCF 312**	**PCF 317**
PCF 307	**PCF 313**	
PCF 309	**PCF 314**	

Displacement, tons: 22.5 full load
Dimensions, feet (metres): 50 × 13.6 × 4 *(15.2 × 4.1 × 1.2)* (Mk 1) 51.3 × 13.6 × 4 *(15.6 × 4.1 × 1.2)* (Mk 2)
Main machinery: 2 GM 12V 71N diesels; 874 hp *(652 kW)* sustained; 2 shafts
Speed, knots: 28
Complement: 6
Guns: 2—12.7 mm (twin) MGs. 2 M-79 40 mm grenade launchers.
Radars: Surface search: Decca 202; I band.

Comment: Most built in the USA. Built for US military assistance programmes. PCF 300 and 301 transferred to Philippines in March 1966, PCF 306-313 in February 1968, PCF 314-316 in July 1970. PCF 317 built in 1970 in the Philippines (ferro-concrete) with enlarged superstructure.

SWIFT TYPE *10/1977, Giorgio Arra*

7 + 4 COASTAL PATROL CRAFT

Displacement, tons: 24.6
Dimensions, feet (metres): 54.8 × 16.4 × 4.3 *(16.7 × 5 × 1.3)*
Main machinery: 2 MTU diesels; 2400 hp(m) *(1.76 MW)*; 2 shafts
Speed, knots: 36

Comment: Fifty-five originally ordered in 1982 but only four were in service by 1987. Building continues at Cavite Yard, Sangley Point to an improved De Havilland series design, at the rate of one per year, with a new planned total of 11.

POLAND

Headquarters' Appointments

Commander-in-Chief of the Polish Navy:
Vice Admiral Romuald Waga
Chief of the Naval Staff:
Rear Admiral Ryszard Kukasik

Diplomatic Representation

Naval Attaché in London:
Colonel K Cukierski

Personnel

(a) 1992: 19 000 (including 6000 conscripts, 4100 coastal defence)
(b) 18 months by October 1991

Prefix to Ships' Names

ORP, standing for *Okręt Rzeczpospolitej Polskiej*

Bases

Gdynia (3rd Flotilla), Hel (9th Flotilla), Swinoujscie (8th Flotilla), Kolobrzeg, Ustka, Gdansk (Frontier Guard)

Coastal Defence

This branch is formed into several battalions with SS-C-3 missiles and a number of gun batteries covering approaches to naval bases and major commercial ports.

Strength of the Fleet

Type	*Active*	*Building*
Submarines—Patrol	3	—
Destroyer	1	—
Frigates	1	(5)
Corvettes	4	4 (2)
Fast Attack Craft—Missile	8	—
Large Patrol Craft	8	—
Coastal Patrol Craft	11	—
Minesweepers—Ocean	8	—
Minesweepers—Coastal	15	2
LCTs	7	—
LCUs	3	(9)
Surveying and Research Vessels	3 + 2	—
AGIs	2	—
Training Ships	6	—
Salvage Ships and Craft	7	—
Tankers	5	(3)
TRVs	2	—
Tugs	9	—
DGVs	3	—
Icebreaker	1	—

Maritime Frontier Guard (MOSG)

A para-naval force, subordinate to the Minister of the Interior, which could be integrated into the navy in a crisis.

Fast Attack Craft (Gun)	3	—
Large Patrol Craft	7	—
Coastal Patrol Craft	12	—
Inshore Patrol Craft	29	—

Mercantile Marine

Lloyd's Register of Shipping:
673 vessels of 3 348 443 tons gross

DELETIONS

Submarine

1989 *Bielik*

Light Forces

1989 *Gdansk* (Osa I)
1990 *Hel* (Osa I)

Mine Warfare Forces

1990 *Los, Dzik, Rozmak, Foka, Mors, Rys, Zbik, Orlik, Krogulec, Czapla, Jastrzab*
1991 *Bizon, Bobr, Tur* (ex-AGI)

Amphibious Forces

1990 *Brda, San,* 5 Polnochny class, 14 Eichstaden class
1991 14 Polnochny class, 1 Eichstaden class

Support Ships

1991 Z6, Z7, 5 Goliat class (civilian)

Coast Guard

1990 *Orion, PVK 5*
1991 5 Pilica class

SUBMARINES

1 Ex-SOVIET KILO CLASS

ORZEL 291

Displacement, tons: 2325 surfaced; 3076 dived
Dimensions, feet (metres): 243.8 × 32.8 × 21.7 *(74.3 × 10 × 6.6)*
Main machinery: Diesel-electric; 2 diesels; 3650 hp(m) *(2.68 MW)*; 2 generators; 1 motor; 5900 hp(m) *(4.34 MW)*; 1 shaft
Speed, knots: 10 surfaced; 17 dived; 9 snorting
Range, miles: 6000 at 7 kts surfaced; 400 at 3 kts dived
Complement: 45

Torpedoes: 6—21 in *(533 mm)* tubes. 18 Soviet Type 53; dual purpose; pattern active/passive homing up to 20 km *(10.8 nm)* at up to 45 kts; warhead 400 kg.
Mines: 18 in lieu of torpedoes.
Countermeasures: ESM: Brick Group; radar warning; Quad Loop HF D/F.
Radars: Surface search: Snoop Tray; I band.
Sonars: Shark Teeth; hull-mounted; passive search and attack (some active capability); low/medium frequency.
Whale series; passive search; medium frequency.

Programmes: Built in Leningrad (Sudomekh), transferred 21 June 1986. This was the second transfer of this class, the first being to India and others have since gone to Romania and Algeria. It was expected that more than one would be acquired as part of an exchange deal with the USSR for Polish-built amphibious ships, but this class is considered too large for Baltic operations and subsequent transfers have been of the Foxtrot class.
Structure: A SAM system has been fitted in the fin of some of this class. Diving depth, 300 m *(985 ft)*.

ORZEL *6/1990, MoD Bonn*

2 Ex-SOVIET FOXTROT CLASS

WILK 292 **DZIK** 293

Displacement, tons: 1952 surfaced; 2475 dived
Dimensions, feet (metres): 299.5 × 24.6 × 19.7 *(91.3 × 7.5 × 6)*
Main machinery: Diesel-electric; 3 diesels; 5956 hp(m) *(4.3 MW)*; 3 motors; 5400 hp(m) *(3.97 MW)*; 3 shafts
Speed, knots: 16 surfaced; 15 dived; 9 snorting
Range, miles: 22 000 at 8 kts surfaced; 380 at 2 kts dived
Complement: 75

Torpedoes: 10—21 in *(533 mm)* (6 bow, 4 stern) tubes. 22 Type 53; dual purpose; pattern active/passive homing up to 20 km *(10.8 nm)* at up to 45 kts; warhead 400 kg or low yield nuclear.
Mines: 44 in lieu of torpedoes.
Countermeasures: ESM: Stop Light; radar warning.
Radars: Surface search: Snoop Tray; I band.
Sonars: Hull-mounted; passive/active search and attack; high frequency.

Programmes: *Wilk* commissioned 3 November 1987; *Dzik* on 10 December 1988. Both leased from the former USSR.
Structure: Diving depth, 250 m (820 ft).
Operational: The Polish Navy considers that this is about the largest practical size of submarine for Baltic operations. These two submarines may be returned in 1992.

WILK *9/1990*

DESTROYER

1 Ex-SOVIET MODIFIED KASHIN CLASS (DDG)

WARSZAWA (ex-*Smely)* 271

Displacement, tons: 3950 standard; 4900 full load
Dimensions, feet (metres): 482.3 × 51.8 × 15.4 *(147 × 15.8 × 4.7)*
Main machinery: 4 gas turbines; 72 000 hp(m) *(53 MW)*; 2 shafts
Speed, knots: 35. **Range, miles:** 2600 at 30 kts
Complement: 280 (25 officers)

Missiles: SSM: 4 SS-N-2C Styx ❶; active radar or IR homing to 83 km *(45 nm)* at 0.9 Mach; warhead 513 kg; sea-skimmer at end of run; no reloads.
SAM: 2 SA-N-1 Goa twin launchers ❷; command guidance to 31.5 km *(17 nm)* at 2 Mach; warhead 60 kg; 32 missiles. Some SSM capability.
Guns: 4—3 in *(76 mm)*/60 (2 twin) ❸; 80° elevation; 90 rounds/minute to 15 km *(8 nm)*; weight of shell 6.8 kg.
4—30 mm/65; 6 barrels per mounting ❹; 85° elevation; 3000 rounds/minute combined to 2 km.
Torpedoes: 5—21 in *(533 mm)* (quin) tubes ❺. Soviet Type 53; dual purpose; pattern active/passive homing up to 20 km *(10.8 nm)* at up to 45 kts; warhead 400 kg.
A/S mortars: 2 RBU 6000 12-tubed trainable ❻; range 6000 m; warhead 31 kg; 120 rockets.
Countermeasures: Decoys: 4—16-tubed Chaff launchers. 2 towed torpedo decoys.
ESM/ECM: 2 Bell Shroud. 2 Bell Squat.
Radars: Air/surface search: Big Net ❼; C band.
Head Net C; 3D; E band ❽; range 128 km *(70 nm)*.
Navigation: Two Palm Frond; I band.
Fire control: Two Peel Group ❾; H/I band (for SA-N-1). Two Bass Tilt ❿; H/I band (for 30 mm). Two Owl Screech ⓫; G band (for guns).
IFF: High Pole B.
Sonars: Hull-mounted; active search and attack; medium frequency.
VDS; active search; medium frequency.

Helicopters: Platform only.

Programmes: Built at Nikolaev in 1969 and converted in the mid-1970s. Transferred to the Polish Navy on 9 January 1988 at the port of Oksywie after a lengthy refit in Leningrad.

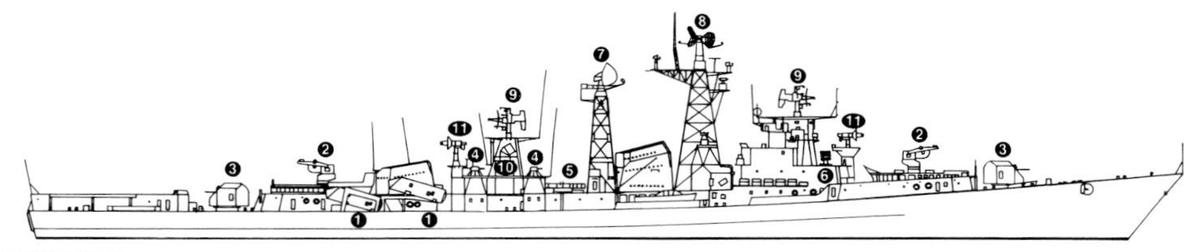
WARSZAWA *(Scale 1 : 1 200), Ian Sturton*

WARSZAWA *5/1989, Marek Twardowski*

Structure: No changes were made to the armament before the transfer.

Operational: The Flagship of the Polish Navy.

WARSZAWA *10/1989, Gilbert Gyssels*

FRIGATE

1 + (5) KASZUB CLASS

Name	*No*	*Builders*	*Laid down*	*Launched*	*Commissioned*
KASZUB	240	Stocznia Polnocna, Gdansk	11 May 1985	4 Oct 1986	23 Nov 1988

Displacement, tons: 1051 standard; 1183 full load
Dimensions, feet (metres): 270 × 32.8 × 10.2 *(82.3 × 10 × 3.1)*
Main machinery: CODAD; 4 diesels; 16 900 hp(m) *(12.42 MW)*; 2 shafts
Speed, knots: 26. **Range, miles:** 2000 at 18 kts
Complement: 87

Missiles: SAM: 2 SA-N-5 quad launchers ❶; IR homing to 10 km *(5.5 nm)* at 1.5 Mach.
Guns: 6 USSR 23 mm (3 twin) ❷. To be replaced by 1—76 mm/60 and 2—30 mm/65 AK 630.
Torpedoes: 2—21 in *(533 mm)* tubes ❸.
A/S mortars: 2 RBU 6000 12-tubed trainable ❹; range 6000 m; warhead 31 kg; 120 rockets.
Depth charges: 2 rails.
Countermeasures: 2 Chaff launchers.
Radars: Air/surface search: Strut Curve ❺; F band.
Surface search: Tamirio RN 231 ❻; I band.
IFF: Square Head.
Sonars: Stern-mounted dipping type mounted on the transom; active; high frequency.

Programmes: Second of class cancelled in 1989 but consideration is now being given to a class of five ASW ships based on the Kaszub hull.
Structure: Design appears to be based on Grisha class but with many alterations. It is reported that the 23 mm gun mountings are being replaced by a single 76 mm and two Gatlings. There is also space for a fire control director on the bridge roof.
Operational: Finally achieved operational status in 1990. Based at Hel with the Border Guard in 1990 but returned to the Navy in 1991.

KASZUB *(Scale 1 : 900), Ian Sturton*

KASZUB *6/1990, MoD Bonn*

CORVETTES

0 + 4 SASSNITZ CLASS

ORKAN PIORUN HURIKAN CYKLON

Displacement, tons: 369 full load
Dimensions, feet (metres): 160.4; 147.6 × 28.5 × 7.2 *(48.9; 45 × 8.7 × 2.2)*
Main machinery: 3 Type M 520 diesels; 14 670 hp(m) *(10.78 MW)*; 3 shafts
Speed, knots: 28. **Range, miles:** 2400 at 20 kts
Complement: 33 (7 officers)

Guns: 1 USSR 3 in *(76 mm)*/66 automatic; 85° elevation; 120 rounds/minute to 15 km *(8 nm)*; weight of shell 7 kg.
1—30 mm/65 ADG; 6 barrels; 3000 rounds/minute combined to 2 km.
Countermeasures: Decoys: 2—16 tubed Chaff launchers.
Radars: Air/surface search: Plank Shave; E band.
Fire control: Bass Tilt; H/I band.
IFF: Square Head; Salt Pot.

Programmes: About 10 of this former GDR Sassnitz class were to be built at Peenewerft for Poland. The future of the programme is uncertain but so far four units have been acquired for completion at Gdynia and more may be built.
Structure: The prototype vessel had two quadruple SSM launchers with an Exocet type (SS-N-25) of missile but this has been removed. The armament listed above is for the German ships and may be changed.

ORKAN and HURIKAN *6/1991, Erik Laursen*

4 + (2) TARANTUL I CLASS

GORNIK 434 **HUTNIK** 435 **METALOWIEC** 436 **ROLNIK** 437

Displacement, tons: 455 full load
Dimensions, feet (metres): 184.1 × 37.7 × 8.2 *(56.1 × 11.5 × 2.5)*
Main machinery: COGOG; 2 Type NK-12MV gas turbines; 24 000 hp(m) *(17.6 MW)*; 2 gas turbines with reversible gearbox; 8000 hp(m) *(5.9 MW)*; 2 shafts
Speed, knots: 35. **Range, miles:** 2300 at 18 kts
Complement: 34 (5 officers)

Missiles: SSM: 4 SS-N-2C Styx (2 twin) launchers; active radar or IR homing to 83 km *(45 nm)* at 0.9 Mach; warhead 513 kg; sea-skimmer in terminal flight.
SAM: SA-N-5 Grail quad launcher; manual aiming; IR homing to 6 km *(3.2 nm)* at 1.5 Mach; warhead 1.5 kg.
Guns: 1—3 in *(76 mm)*/60 automatic; 85° elevation; 120 rounds/minute to 15 km *(8 nm)*; weight of shell 7 kg.
2—30 mm/65 6-barrelled type; 85° elevation; 3000 rounds/minute combined to 2 km.
Countermeasures: Decoys: 2 Chaff launchers.
Radars: Air/surface search: Plank Shave; E band.
Navigation: Krivach; I band.
Fire control: Bass Tilt; H/I band.
IFF: Square Head.

Programmes: Built at Volodyarski Yard. First transferred 28 December 1983, second in April 1984, third in January 1988 and fourth in January 1989. It is possible that two more of the class are to be acquired, the most likely candidates being ex-GDR Nos 574 and 575.

GORNIK *6/1989, Marek Twardowski*

LAND-BASED MARITIME AIRCRAFT (FRONT LINE)

Numbers/Type: 12/2 Mil Mi-14PL/PS Haze A.
Operational speed: 120 kts *(222 km/h)*.
Service ceiling: 15 000 ft *(4570 m)*.
Range: 240 nm *(445 km)*.
Role/Weapon systems: PL for ASW, PS for SAR. PL operates in co-operation with surface units; supported by 12 Mi-2 Hoplite helicopters in same unit. Sensors: Search radar, MAD, sonobuoys. Weapons: ASV; internal torpedoes, depth bombs and mines.

Numbers/Type: 2 PZL Swidnik W-3 Sokol.
Operational speed: 119 kts *(220 km/h)*.
Service ceiling: 16 725 ft *(5100 m)*.
Range: 386 nm *(715 km)*.
Role/Weapon systems: Planned to replace the Haze in due course.

LIGHT FORCES

8 Ex-SOVIET OSA I CLASS (FAST ATTACK CRAFT—MISSILE)

KOLOBRZEG 424 **USTKA** 428 **DARLLOWO** 430 **DZIWNOW** 432
PUCK 427 **OKSYWIE** 429 **SWINOUJSCIE** 431 **WLADYSLAWOWO** 433

Displacement, tons: 171 standard; 210 full load
Dimensions, feet (metres): 110.2 × 24.9 × 8.8 *(33.6 × 7.6 × 2.7)*
Main machinery: 3 Type M503A diesels; 12 000 hp(m) *(8.82 MW)*; 3 shafts
Speed, knots: 35. **Range, miles:** 800 at 30 kts
Complement: 30

Missiles: SSM: 4 SS-N-2A Styx; active radar or IR homing to 46 km *(25 nm)* at 0.9 Mach; warhead 513 kg.
Guns: 4—30 mm/65 (2 twin) automatic; 85° elevation; 500 rounds/minute to 5 km *(2.7 nm)*; weight of shell 0.54 kg.
Radars: Surface search: Square Tie; I band; range 73 km *(40 nm)*.
Fire control: Drum Tilt; H/I band.

Programmes: All date from early to mid-1960s and are running out of operational life.
Structure: Pennant numbers are carried on side-boards on the bridge. By the end of 1991 three (423, 425 and 426) had been converted to Frontier Guard ships with SSM and after gun removed and the forward gun replaced by a twin 25 mm 2M3M. More may be converted.

WLADYSLAWOWO *4/1990, MoD Bonn*

11 PILICA CLASS (COASTAL PATROL CRAFT)

166-176

Displacement, tons: 87 full load
Dimensions, feet (metres): 95.1 × 18.4 × 4.6 *(29 × 5.6 × 1.4)*
Main machinery: 3 diesels; 3600 hp(m) *(2.65 MW)*; 3 shafts
Speed, knots: 30
Complement: 15
Guns: 2—23 mm/87 (twin).
Torpedoes: 2—21 in *(533 mm)* tubes; anti-surface.
Radars: Surface search: Tamirio RN 231; I band.
Sonars: Dipping VDS aft.

Comment: Type 918 built in Poland since 1973. Based at Kolobrzeg and Gdansk. First batch of five, without torpedo tubes, have been deleted. Originally this class was thought to be part of the Frontier Guard but now belongs to the Navy.

PILICA 171 *7/1988, Marek Twardowski*

8 MODIFIED OBLUZE CLASS (LARGE PATROL CRAFT)

GROZNY 351	**ZRECZNY** 353	**ZWROTNY** 355	**NIEUGIETY** 357
WYTRWALY 352	**ZWINNY** 354	**ZAWZIETY** 356	**CZUJNY** 358

Displacement, tons: 237 full load
Dimensions, feet (metres): 135.5 × 20.7 × 6.6 *(41.3 × 6.3 × 2)*
Main machinery: 2 diesels; 4400 hp(m) *(3.23 MW)*; 2 shafts
Speed, knots: 24
Complement: 35
Guns: 4—30 mm/65 (2 twin).
Depth charges: 2 racks.
Radars: Surface search: Tamirio RN 231; I band.
Fire control: Drum Tilt; H/I band.
IFF: Two Square Head. High Pole.
Sonars: Hull-mounted; active attack; high frequency.

Comment: Slightly smaller than original Obluze class. Completed 1969-72.

ZWROTNY *8/1983, Ralf Bendfeldt*

MINE WARFARE FORCES

8 KROGULEC CLASS (MINESWEEPERS—OCEAN)

Name	*No*	*Builders*	*Commissioned*
KORMORAN	616	Stocznia, Gdynia	1963
ALBATROS	618	Stocznia, Gdynia	1964
PELIKAN	619	Stocznia, Gdynia	1965
TUKAN	620	Stocznia, Gdynia	1966
FLAMINGO	621	Stocznia, Gdynia	1966
RYBITWA	622	Stocznia, Gdynia	1966
MEWA	623	Stocznia, Gdynia	1967
CZAJKA	624	Stocznia, Gdynia	1967

Displacement, tons: 474 full load
Dimensions, feet (metres): 190.9 × 26.2 × 6.9 *(58.2 × 8 × 2.1)*
Main machinery: 2 Fiat A-230S diesels; 3750 hp(m) *(2.76 MW)*; 2 shafts
Speed, knots: 18. **Range, miles:** 2000 at 17 kts
Complement: 30 (6 officers)
Guns: 6—25 mm/60 (3 twin) or 4—23 mm (2 twin) and 2—25 mm/60 (twin).
Depth charges: 2 racks.
Mines: 1 rail.
Radars: Surface search: Tamirio RN 231; I band.
Sonars: Hull-mounted; minehunting; high frequency.

Comment: Project 206F. Armament varies with some having 23 mm guns aft instead of the 25 mm guns. Four deleted so far.

TUKAN *10/1989, MoD Bonn*

2 LENIWKA CLASS (MINESWEEPERS—COASTAL)

625 **626**

Displacement, tons: 245 full load
Dimensions, feet (metres): 84.6 × 23.6 × 8.9 *(25.8 × 7.2 × 2.7)*
Main machinery: 1 Puck-Sulzer 6AL 20/24 diesel; 570 hp(m) *(420 kW)*; 1 shaft
Speed, knots: 11. **Range, miles:** 3100 at 8 kts

Comment: Project 410S modified stern trawlers built at Ustka Shipyard in 1982/83. Sweeping is done by using strung-out charges. The ships can carry 40 tons of cargo or 40 people.

LENIWKA Class *3/1991, Erik Laursen*

13 + 2 NOTEC CLASS (MINESWEEPERS—COASTAL)

GOPLO 630	**JAMNO** 634	**RESKO** 637	**NAKLO** 640
GARDNO 631	**MIELNO** 635	**SARBSKO** 638	**DRUZNO** 641
BUKOWO 632	**WICKO** 636	**NECKO** 639	**HANCZA** 642
DABIE 633			

Displacement, tons: 208 standard; 225 full load
Dimensions, feet (metres): 125.7 × 23.6 × 5.9 *(38.3 × 7.2 × 1.8)*
Main machinery: 2 diesels; 1874 hp(m) *(1.38 MW)*; 2 shafts
Speed, knots: 14. **Range, miles:** 1100 at 9 kts
Guns: 2—23 mm (twin).
Radars: Navigation: Tamirio RN 231; I band.

Comment: Project 207 lead ship launched April 1981. 630 is an experimental prototype numbered 207D. Building at about one per year at Gdynia. *642* in service January 1991. The 23 mm guns have replaced the original 25 mm. GRP hulls. Some carry divers for minehunting work.

HANCZA *10/1991, Hartmut Ehlers*

GARDNO *10/1987, MoD Bonn*

AMPHIBIOUS FORCES

Note: The following ships and craft plus a number of civilian Ro-ro ships are planned for use by the 7th Coastal Defence Brigade (ex-Sea Landing Division) (5000 men) based in the Gdansk area.

2 POLNOCHNY CLASS (LCTs)

GLOGOW 809 **GRUNWALD** 811

Displacement, tons: 800 full load (1207 *Grunwald*)
Dimensions, feet (metres): 242.7 × 27.9 × 5.8 *(74 × 8.5 × 1.8)*
269 × 32.8 × 5.8 *(82 × 10 × 1.8) (Grunwald)*
Main machinery: 2 Type 40D diesels; 5000 hp(m) *(3.67 MW)*; 2 shafts
Speed, knots: 19. **Range, miles:** 1000 at 18 kts
Complement: 40
Military lift: 350 tons including 6 tanks; 120 troops
Guns: 2 or 4—30 mm (1 or 2 twin). 2—140 mm rocket launchers.
Radars: Navigation: Don 2; I band.
Fire control: Drum Tilt; H/I band.
IFF: Square Head. High Pole.

Comment: Polish-built in Gdansk between 1964 and 1970. *Glogow* is Group B, *Grunwald* is Group C. All the remainder have been sold for commercial use or scrap.

POLNOCHNY Class *10/1991, Hartmut Ehlers*

5 LUBLIN CLASS (LCT)

LUBLIN 821 **GNIEZNO** 822 **KRAKOW** 823 **POZNAN** 824 **TORUN** 825

Displacement, tons: 1300 standard; 1745 full load
Dimensions, feet (metres): 299.9 × 35.8 × 5.9 *(91.2 × 10.9 × 1.8)*
Main machinery: 3 Cegielski diesels; 5390 hp(m) *(3.96 MW)*; 3 shafts
Speed, knots: 16. **Range, miles:** 2600 at 16 kts
Complement: 60
Military lift: 8 MBT; 135 troops plus equipment
Guns: 8—23 mm (4 twin).
Mines: 50-150.
Radars: Navigation: RN 231; I band.

Comment: Project 767 built at Stocznia Polnocna, Gdansk. *Lublin* started sea trials in August 1989. Designed with a through deck from bow to stern and can be used as minelayers. *Poznan* commissioned 8 March 1991 and *Torun* 24 May 1991.

POZNAN *10/1991, Per Kornefeldt*

POZNAN *10/1991, Hartmut Ehlers*

3 + (9) DEBA CLASS (LCU)

DEBA 851 **852-853**

Displacement, tons: 176 full load
Dimensions, feet (metres): 122 × 23.3 × 5.6 *(37.2 × 7.1 × 1.7)*
Main machinery: 3 Type M401A diesels; 3000 hp(m) *(2.2 MW)*; 3 shafts
Speed, knots: 20. **Range, miles:** 430 at 16 kts
Complement: 10
Military lift: 2 small tanks or 3 vehicles up to 15 tons or 50 troops
Guns: 2—23 mm (twin).

Comment: Project 716 building at Navy Yard, Gdynia. To replace Eichstaden class. First one commissioned 16 June 1988 and the plan was to build 12. By early 1992 only the first three had been built. Can carry up to six launchers for strung-out charges.

INTELLIGENCE VESSELS

2 MOMA CLASS (AGIs)

NAVIGATOR 262 **HYDROGRAF** 263

Displacement, tons: 1580 full load
Dimensions, feet (metres): 240.5 × 36.8 × 12.8 *(73.3 × 11.2 × 3.9)*
Main machinery: 2 Skoda-Sulzer 6TD48 diesels; 3600 hp(m) *(2.65 MW)*; 2 shafts
Speed, knots: 17. **Range, miles:** 9000 at 12 kts
Complement: 65 (10 officers)

Comment: Commissioned June 1975. Much altered in the upperworks and unrecognisable as Momas. The fo'c'sle in *Hydrograf* is longer than in *Navigator* and one deck higher. Both fitted for but not with two twin 25 mm gun mountings. Forward radomes replaced by a cylindrical type and after ones removed on both ships in 1987.

HYDROGRAF *4/1990*

SURVEYING AND RESEARCH VESSELS

Note: There are two Survey Craft KH-121 type of 19 m built in 1988/89.

2 FINIK 2 CLASS

HEWELIUSZ 265 **ARCTOWSKI** 266

Displacement, tons: 1135 full load
Dimensions, feet (metres): 202.1 × 36.7 × 14.8 *(61.6 × 11.2 × 4.5)*
Main machinery: 2 Cegielski-Sulzer 6 AL 25/30 diesels; 1920 hp(m) *(1.4 MW)*; 2 auxiliary motors; 204 hp(m) *(150 kW)*; 2 shafts; cp props; bow thruster
Speed, knots: 14
Complement: 55 (10 officers)

Comment: Built at Stocznia Polnocna, Gdansk and both commissioned 27 November 1982. Sister ships to Soviet class which were built in Poland, except that *Heweliusz* and *Arctowski* have been modified and have no buoy handling equipment. Two sister ships, *Zodiak* and *Planeta*, are civilian operated.

ARCTOWSKI *10/1991, Per Kornefeldt*

1 MOMA CLASS

KOPERNIK 261

Displacement, tons: 1240 standard; 1580 full load
Dimensions, feet (metres): 240.5 × 36.8 × 12.8 *(73.3 × 11.2 × 3.9)*
Main machinery: 2 Skoda-Sulzer 6TD48 diesels; 3600 hp(m) *(2.65 MW)*; 2 shafts
Speed, knots: 17. **Range, miles:** 9000 at 12 kts
Complement: 51 (8 officers)

Comment: Built by Stocznia Polnocna, Gdansk and commissioned 20 February 1971. Forward crane removed in 1983.

KOPERNIK *1982*

TRAINING SHIPS

Note: There is a 498 ton sailing sloop *Iskra II* 253 which was built in 1982 and has a complement of 40 cadets. The larger *Dar Mlodziezy* is civilian owned and operated but also takes naval personnel for training.

ISKRA II *7/1990, Maritime Photographic*

2 WODNIK CLASS

WODNIK 251 **GRYF** 252

Displacement, tons: 1697 standard; 1820 full load
Dimensions, feet (metres): 234.3 × 38.1 × 12.8 *(71.4 × 11.6 × 3.9)*
Main machinery: 2 Cegielski-Sulzer 6TD48 diesels; 3600 hp(m) *(2.65 MW)*; 2 shafts
Speed, knots: 17. **Range, miles:** 7200 at 11 kts
Complement: 75 plus 85 midshipmen
Guns: 4—30 mm (2 twin). 4—23 mm (2 twin) (only in *Gryf*).
Radars: Navigation: Two RN 231; I band.
Fire control: Drum Tilt; H/I band (only in *Gryf*).

Comment: Type 888 built at Gdynia. *Wodnik* launched November 1975, *Gryf* March 1976. Sisters to former GDR *Wilhelm Pieck* and two Soviet ships. *Wodnik* converted to a hospital ship (150 beds) in 1990 for deployment to the Gulf. Armament removed as part of the conversion.

WODNIK *5/1991, Fotoflite*

GRYF *7/1991, Fotoflite*

4 BRYZA CLASS

BRYZA K 18 **PODCHORAZY** 711 **KADET** 712 **ELEW** 713

Displacement, tons: 180 (167, *Bryza*) full load
Dimensions, feet (metres): 98.4 × 22.9 × 6.4 *(30 × 7 × 2)*
Main machinery: 2 Wola diesels; 300 hp(m) *(220 kW)*; 2 shafts
Speed, knots: 10. **Range, miles:** 1100 at 10 kts
Complement: 11 plus 26 cadets
Radars: Navigation: Two RN 231; I band.

Comment: *Podchorazy* commissioned 30 November 1974, *Elew* 5 March 1975 and *Kadet* July 1975. *Bryza* has a lighter superstructure than remainder.

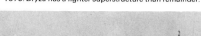

BRYZA *4/1989, Marek Twardowski*

LEW *11/1990, Marek Twardowski*

TANKERS

1 + (3) BALTYK CLASS

Name	*No*	*Builders*	*Commissioned*
BALTYK	Z 1	Naval Shipyard, Gdynia	11 Mar 1991

Displacement, tons: 2918 standard; 2974 full load
Dimensions, feet (metres): 278.2 × 43 × 15.4 *(84.8 × 13.1 × 4.7)*
Main machinery: 2 Cegielski diesels; 4025 hp(m) *(2.96 MW)*; 2 shafts
Speed, knots: 15. **Range, miles:** 4250 at 12 kts
Guns: 2 Wrobel 23 mm.

Comment: Beam replenishment stations, one each side. First of a projected class of four, although the others have so far been victims of budget problems.

3 MOSKIT CLASS

KRAB Z 3 **MEDUSA** Z 8 **SLIMAK** Z 9

Displacement, tons: 1200 full load
Dimensions, feet (metres): 189.3 × 31.2 × 11.2 *(57.7 × 9.5 × 3.4)*
Main machinery: 2 Sulzer diesels; 850 hp(m) *(625 kW)*; 2 shafts
Speed, knots: 10. **Range, miles:** 1200 at 10 kts
Complement: 12
Cargo capacity: 800 tons
Guns: 4—25 mm (2 twin).

Comment: Built in Poland in 1971-72. First two carry oil, the third water. Names are unofficial.

KRAB *10/1991, Per Kornefeldt*

1 TYPE 5

Z 5

Displacement, tons: 625 full load
Dimensions, feet (metres): 144 × 21.3 × 9.8 *(44 × 6.5 × 3.0)*
Main machinery: 1 diesel; 300 hp(m) *(220 kW)*; 1 shaft
Speed, knots: 9. **Range, miles:** 1200 at 9 kts
Complement: 16
Cargo capacity: 280 tons
Guns: 4—25 mm (2 twin).

Comment: Lighter converted into tanker for coastal service. Two others deleted.

Type 5 (old number) *1982*

DEGAUSSING VESSELS

3 MROWKA CLASS

WRONA SD 11 **RYSZ** SD 12 **SD 13**

Displacement, tons: 600 full load
Dimensions, feet (metres): 157.5 × 26.6 × 7.5 *(48 × 8.1 × 2.3)*
Main machinery: 1 diesel; 335 hp(m) *(246 kW)*; 1 shaft
Speed, knots: 9.5
Guns: 1—25 mm (not in all).

Comment: A class of DGVs. First completed in 1972. Names are unofficial.

RYSZ *1978*

TORPEDO RECOVERY VESSELS

2 KORMORAN CLASS

K 8 K 11

Displacement, tons: 130 full load
Dimensions, feet (metres): 124.7 × 19.7 × 5.2 *(38 × 6 × 1.6)*
Main machinery: 2 Type M50 diesels; 1700 hp(m) *(1.25 MW)*; 2 shafts
Speed, knots: 21
Complement: 18
Guns: 2—25 mm (twin).

Comment: Built at Gdynia in 1970.

K II *5/1974*

TUGS

Note: Goliat class sold to civilian use in 1991.

4 BUCHA and 2 H-800 CLASSES

H 3, 4, 5, 7 and H 1, 2

Displacement, tons: 450 *(H 3-7)*
Dimensions, feet (metres): 105 × 27.9 × 11.5 *(32 × 8.5 × 3.5) (H 3-7)*
Main machinery: 1 Cegielski-Sulzer 6AL 20/24H diesel; 760 hp(m) *(559 kW)*; 1 shaft
Speed, knots: 10

Comment: Bucha class (Type 900) first seen in 1981. Have firefighting capability. No details on *H 1, 2* (Type 800).

H 5 *6/1988, Marek Twardowski*

3 MOTYL CLASS

H 12, 19, 20

Displacement, tons: 500 full load
Dimensions, feet (metres): 103.7 × 27.6 × 11.5 *(31.6 × 8.4 × 3.5)*
Main machinery: 1 Sulzer diesel; 1500 hp(m) *(1.1 MW)*; 1 shaft
Speed, knots: 12

Comment: Polish built 1962-63. Type 1500.

MOTYL Class *1973*

SALVAGE SHIPS

2 PIAST CLASS

Name	*No*	*Builders*	*Commissioned*
PIAST	281	Stocznia, Gdansk	26 Jan 1974
LECH	282	Stocznia, Gdansk	30 Nov 1974

Displacement, tons: 1240 standard; 1600 full load
Dimensions, feet (metres): 240.5 × 36.8 × 12.8 *(73.3 × 11.2 × 3.9)*
Main machinery: 2 Cegielski-Sulzer 6TD48 diesels; 3600 hp(m) *(2.65 MW)*; 2 shafts; cp props
Speed, knots: 15. **Range, miles:** 3000 at 12 kts
Guns: 8—25 mm (4 twin) (can be fitted).

Comment: Carry a diving bell. Basically a Moma class hull with towing and firefighting capabilities. Wartime role as hospital ships.

PIAST *5/1991, Fotoflite*

2 ZBYSZKO CLASS

Name	*No*	*Builders*	*Commissioned*
ZBYSZKO	R 14	Uskta Shipyard	Sep 1991
MACKO	R 15	Uskta Shipyard	Dec 1991

Displacement, tons: 380 full load
Dimensions, feet (metres): 114.8 × 26.2 × 9.8 *(35 × 8 × 3)*
Main machinery: 1 Sulzer 6AL 20/24D; 750 hp(m) *(551 kW)*; 1 shaft
Speed, knots: 11. **Range, miles:** 3000 at 10 kts
Radars: Navigation: SRN 402X; I band.

Comment: Type B-823 ordered 30 May 1988. Carries a decompression chamber and two divers. Mobile gantry crane on the stern.

3 PLUSKWA CLASS

Name	*No*	*Builders*	*Commissioned*
GNIEWKO	R 11	Navy Yard, Gdynia	25 July 1981
BOLKO	R 12	Navy Yard, Gdynia	7 Nov 1982
SEMKO	R 13	Navy Yard, Gdynia	9 May 1987

Displacement, tons: 365 full load
Dimensions, feet (metres): 105 × 29.2 × 10.2 *(32 × 8.9 × 3.1)*
Main machinery: 1 Cegielski-Sulzer diesel; 1470 hp(m) *(1.08 MW)*; 1 shaft
Speed, knots: 12. **Range, miles:** 4000 at 7 kts

Comment: Rescue tugs.

GNIEWKO *11/1986, Marek Twardowski*

ICEBREAKER

PERKUN

Measurement, tons: 1152 gross; 272 net
Dimensions, feet (metres): 185 × 46 × — *(56.5 × 14 × —)*
Main machinery: Diesel-electric; 4 diesel generators; 3680 hp(m) *(2.7 MW)*; 4 motors; 3000 hp(m) *(2.2 MW)*; 2 shafts
Speed, knots: 10

Comment: Built by P K Harris and Sons Ltd, Appledore, Devon in 1963. Civilian owned, naval operated and manned.

HARBOUR CRAFT

1 KULIK and 4 R 34 CLASSES

R 23, R 32-33, R 36-37

Comment: *R 23* is MFV type. *R 32-37* are smaller harbour craft. Two scrapped in 1991. Used as Diving craft.

R33 *1986*

9 HARBOUR LIGHTERS AND 8 PATROL LAUNCHES

B 1-2, B 4, B 8, B 10-11, B 13, W 1-2
M 2-3, M 28, M 81-85

Comment: *B 4* is a floating workshop. *B 8* and *B 10* are BST class freighters. *B 11* and *B 13* are oil lighters. *W 1-2* are water lighters. Those with M numbers are patrol launches.

W2 *10/1991, Hartmut Ehlers*

MARITIME FRONTIER GUARD (MOSG)

Note: In addition to the vessels listed there are some 20 K-15 class harbour craft transferred from the navy in 1989.

3 Ex-SOVIET OSA I CLASS (FAST ATTACK CRAFT—GUN)

GDYNIA 301 (ex-423) **SZCZECIN** 302 (ex-425) **ELBLAG** 303 (ex-426)

Comment: Transferred from the Navy in 1991 and more may follow. Details under *Light Forces* except that all armament and fire control radar has been removed leaving only a twin 25 mm 2M3M gun forward.

5 OBLUZE CLASS (LARGE PATROL CRAFT)

FALA 321
SZKWAL 322
ZEFIR 323
ZORZA 324
TECZA 325

Displacement, tons: 250 full load
Dimensions, feet (metres): 143 × 21.3 × 7 *(43.6 × 6.5 × 2.1)*
Main machinery: 2 diesels; 4400 hp(m) *(3.23 MW)*; 2 shafts
Speed, knots: 24
Complement: 34
Guns: 4—30 mm (2 twin). Some have after mounting removed.
Depth charges: 2 internal racks.
Radars: Surface search: Tamirio RN 231; I band.
Sonars: Hull-mounted; active attack; high frequency.

Comment: Built at Oksywie SY in 1965-66.

ZORZA *1974*

14 SZKWAL CLASS (INSHORE PATROL CRAFT)

Dimensions, feet (metres): 38.4 × 15.1 × 3 *(11.7 × 4.6 × 0.9)*
Main machinery: 2 diesels; 2000 hp(m) *(1.47 MW)*; 2 shafts
Speed, knots: 38
Complement: 4
Guns: 1—7.62 mm MG.

Comment: Built at Wisla, Gdansk between 1986 and 1990. Fast pursuit boats.

2 KAPER CLASS (LARGE PATROL CRAFT)

KAPER I **KAPER II**

Displacement, tons: 470 full load
Dimensions, feet (metres): 139.4 × 27.6 × 9.2 *(42.5 × 8.4 × 2.8)*
Main machinery: 2 Sulzer 8ATL 25/30 diesels; 4720 hp(m) *(3.47 MW)*; 2 shafts
Speed, knots: 17. **Range, miles:** 2800 at 14 kts
Complement: 11 plus 7 spare
Radars: Surface search: E/F band.
Navigation: I band.

Comment: *Kaper I* completed at Wisla Yard, Gdansk in January 1991, *Kaper II* in November 1991. Have fish finding sonars fitted. Used for Fishery Protection. More may be built.

12 WISLOKA CLASS (COASTAL PATROL CRAFT)

KP 141-152

Displacement, tons: 45 full load
Dimensions, feet (metres): 69.6 × 12.8 × 4.6 *(21.1 × 3.9 × 1.4)*
Main machinery: 2 Wola ZM diesels; 620 hp(m) *(456 kW)*; 2 shafts
Speed, knots: 13
Complement: 9
Guns: 2—14.5 mm MGs (in some). 1—12.7 mm MG and 1 ZM rocket launcher (in others).

Comment: Type 90 built at Wisla Shipyard, Gdansk between 1973 and 1977.

KP 141 *1982, John Rowe*

PORTUGAL

Headquarters' Appointments

Chief of Naval Staff:
Admiral António Carlos Fuzeta da Ponte
Vice Chief of Naval Staff:
Vice Admiral Fernando Manuel Palla Machado da Silva
Continental Naval Commander:
Vice Admiral Narciso Augusto do Carmo Duro
Azores Naval Commander:
Rear Admiral Pedro Manuel Vasconcelos Caeiro
Madeira Naval Commander:
Captain Raul Trincalhetas Janes Semedo
Marine Corps Commander:
Captain Francisco Isidoro Montes de Oliveira Monteiro

Personnel

(a) 1992: 15 000 (1700 officers) including 2800 marines
(b) 18 months national service

Diplomatic Representation

Defence Attaché in Bonn, Stockholm and Oslo:
Colonel José Francisco Fernandes Nico (Air Force)
Naval Attaché in London:
Commander João Manuel Lopes Pires Neves
Naval Attaché in Paris, Brussels and Hague:
Commander José Manuel de Oliveira Alves Correia
Naval Attaché in Washington, Ottawa and NLR SACLANT:
Captain Adriano Manuel de Sousa Beça Gil
Defence Attaché in Madrid and Athens:
Captain António José Conde Martins

Naval Bases

Main Base: Lisbon—Alfeite
Dockyard: Arsenal do Alfeite
Fleet Support: Porto, Portimão, Funchal, Ponta Delgada

Prefix to Ships' Names

NRP

Mercantile Marine

Lloyd's Register of Shipping:
337 vessels of 890 779 tons gross

DELETIONS

Frigates

1989 *Pereira da Silva, Gago Coutinho, Magalhães Correa*

Patrol Craft

1991 *Atria, Lagoa, Rosario*

PENNANT LIST

Submarines

S 163	Albacora
S 164	Barracuda
S 166	Delfim

Frigates

F 330	Vasco da Gama
F 331	Alvares Cabral
F 332	Corte Real
F 471	Antonio Enes
F 475	João Coutinho
F 476	Jacinto Candido
F 477	Gen Pereira d'Eça
F 480	Comandante João Belo
F 481	Comandante Hermenegildo Capelo
F 482	Comandante Roberto Ivens
F 483	Comandante Sacadura Cabral
F 484	Augusto de Castilho
F 485	Honorio Barreto
F 486	Baptista de Andrade
F 487	João Roby
F 488	Afonso Cerqueira
F 489	Oliveira E Carmo

Light Forces

P 370	Rio Minho
P 1140	Cacine
P 1141	Cunene
P 1142	Mandovi
P 1143	Rovuma
P 1144	Cuanza
P 1145	Geba
P 1146	Zaire
P 1147	Zambeze
P 1148	Dom Aleixo
P 1149	Dom Jeremias
P 1150	Argos
P 1151	Dragão
P 1152	Escorpião
P 1153	Cassiopeia
P 1154	Hidra
P 1160	Limpopo
P 1161	Save
P 1162	Albatroz
P 1163	Açor
P 1164	Andorinha
P 1165	Aguia
P 1167	Cisne
UAM 630	Condor

Patrol Vessels

M 401	São Roque
M 402	Ribeira Grande

Amphibious Forces

LDG 201	Bombarda
LDG 202	Alabarda
LDG 203	Bacamarte
LDM 119-121	
LDM 406, 418, 420-423	

Service Forces

A 520	Sagres
A 521	Schultz Xavier
A 527	Almeida Carvalho
A 5201	Vega
A 5203	Andromeda
A 5204	Polar
A 5205	Auriga
A 5206	São Gabriel
A 5208	São Miguel

SUBMARINES

3 FRENCH DAPHNE CLASS

Name	*No*	*Builders*	*Laid down*	*Launched*	*Commissioned*
ALBACORA	S 163	Dubigeon-Normandie, Nantes	6 Sep 1965	13 Oct 1966	1 Oct 1967
BARRACUDA	S 164	Dubigeon-Normandie, Nantes	19 Oct 1965	24 Apr 1967	4 May 1968
DELFIM	S 166	Dubigeon-Normandie, Nantes	14 May 1967	23 Sep 1968	1 Oct 1969

Displacement, tons: 869 surfaced; 1043 dived
Dimensions, feet (metres): 189.6 × 22.3 × 15.1 *(57.8 × 6.8 × 4.6)*
Main machinery: Diesel-electric; 2 SEMT-Pielstick 12PA4 V185 diesels; 2450 hp(m) *(1.8 MW)*; 2 Jeumont Schneider alternators; 1.7 MW; 2 motors; 2600 hp(m) *(1.9 MW)*; 2 shafts
Speed, knots: 13.5 surfaced; 16 dived
Range, miles: 2710 at 12.5 kts surfaced; 2130 at 10 kts snorting
Complement: 50 (5 officers)

Torpedoes: 12—21.7 in *(550 mm)* (8 bow, 4 stern) tubes. ECAN E14; anti-surface; passive homing to 12 km *(6.6 nm)* at 25 kts; warhead 300 kg or ECAN L3; anti-submarine; active homing to 5.5 km *(3 nm)* at 25 kts; warhead 200 kg. No reloads.
Countermeasures: ESM: ARUR; radar warning.
Fire control: DLT D3 torpedo control.
Radars: Surface search: Thomson-CSF Calypso II; I band; range 31 km *(17 nm)* for 10 m² target.
Sonars: Thomson Sintra DSUV 2; passive search and attack; medium frequency.
DUUA 2; active search and attack; 8.4 kHz.

ALBACORA and BARRACUDA *3/1991, van Ginderen Collection*

Programmes: Basically similar to the French Daphne type, but slightly modified to suit Portuguese requirements. Replacements needed but plans may have to wait at least until 1994.

Modernisation: Similar to French Daphne class.
Structure: Diving depth, 300 m *(984 ft)*. Crushing depth, 575 m *(1885 ft)*.

Sales: *Cachalote* transferred to Pakistan as *Ghazi* in 1975.

FRIGATES

4 COMANDANTE JOÃO BELO CLASS

Name	*No*	*Builders*	*Laid down*	*Launched*	*Commissioned*
COMANDANTE JOÃO BELO	F 480	At et Ch de Nantes	6 Sep 1965	22 Mar 1966	1 July 1967
COMANDANTE HERMENEGILDO CAPELO	F 481	At et Ch de Nantes	13 May 1966	29 Nov 1966	26 Apr 1968
COMANDANTE ROBERTO IVENS	F 482	At et Ch de Nantes	13 Dec 1966	8 Aug 1967	23 Nov 1968
COMANDANTE SACADURA CABRAL	F 483	At et Ch de Nantes	18 Aug 1967	15 Mar 1968	25 July 1969

Displacement, tons: 1750 standard; 2250 full load
Dimensions, feet (metres): 336.9 × 38.4 × 14.4 *(102.7 × 11.7 × 4.4)*
Main machinery: 4 SEMT-Pielstick 12 PC 2.2V 400 diesels; 16 000 hp(m) *(11.8 MW)* sustained; 2 shafts
Speed, knots: 25. **Range, miles:** 7500 at 15 kts
Complement: 201 (15 officers)

Guns: 3 Creusot Loire 3.9 in *(100 mm)*/55 Mod 1953 ❶; 80° elevation; 60 rounds/minute to 17 km *(9 nm)* anti-surface; 8 km *(4.4 nm)* anti-aircraft; weight of shell 13.5 kg.
2 Bofors 40 mm/60 ❷; 90° elevation; 300 rounds/minute to 12 km *(6.6 nm)*; weight of shell 0.89 kg.
Torpedoes: 6—21.7 in *(550 mm)* (2 triple) tubes ❸ or 6—324 mm US Mk 32 Mod 5 (2 triple) tubes (after modernisation); ECAN L3 being replaced by Honeywell Mk 46 Mod 5 (after modernisation).
A/S mortars: 1 Mortier 305 mm 4-barrelled ❹; automatic loading; range 2700 m; warhead 227 kg. May be removed during modernisation.
Countermeasures: Decoys: 2 Loral Hycor Mk 36 SRBOC 6-barrelled Chaff launchers.
SLQ-25 Nixie; towed torpedo decoy.
ESM: ARBR-10 or Argo 700 DF (after modernisation); radar warning.
Radars: Air search: Thomson-CSF DRBV 22A ❺; D band; range 366 km *(200 nm)*.
Surface search: Thomson-CSF DRBV 50 ❻; G band; range 29 km *(16 nm)*.
Navigation: Decca RM 316P; I band.
Fire control: Thomson-CSF DRBC 31D ❼; I band.
Sonars: CDC SQS 510 (after modernisation); hull-mounted; active search and attack; medium frequency.
Thomson Sintra DUBA 3A; hull-mounted; active search; high frequency.

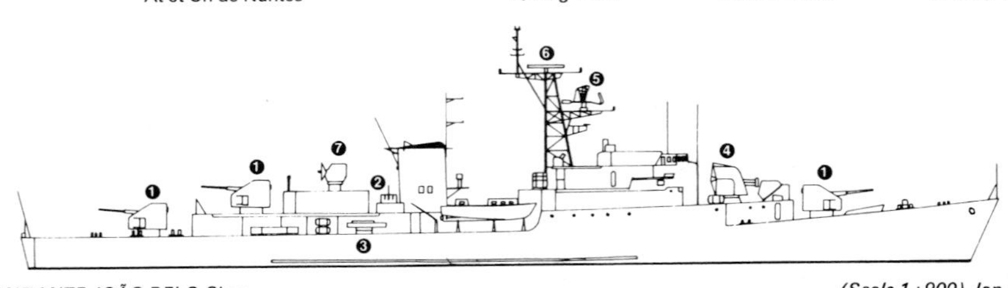
COMMANDANTE JOÃO BELO Class *(Scale 1 : 900), Ian Sturton*

COMMANDANTE ROBERTO IVENS *11/1991, Hartmut Ehlers*

Modernisation: Modernisation of external communications, sensors and electronics completed 1987-90. Chaff launchers installed in 1989. In 1991-96 the hull sonar is being replaced, torpedo tubes updated, the A/S mortar may be removed, towed torpedo decoy installed and ESM equipment changed. It is also planned to add a combat data system compatible with the Vasco da Gama class. The plan to have one or both after guns replaced either by flight deck and hangar for helicopter or by SSM has been shelved.

Structure: They are generally similar to the French Commandant Rivière class.
Operational: Designed for tropical service but being modernised primarily for the ASW role.

3 VASCO DA GAMA CLASS

Name	No	Builders	Laid down	Launched	Commissioned
VASCO DA GAMA	F 330	Blohm & Voss, Hamburg	1 Feb 1989	26 June 1989	18 Jan 1991
ALVARES CABRAL	F 331	Howaldtswerke, Kiel	2 June 1989	6 June 1990	24 May 1991
CORTE REAL	F 332	Howaldtswerke, Kiel	24 Nov 1989	6 June 1990	22 Nov 1991

Displacement, tons: 2700 standard; 3300 full load
Dimensions, feet (metres): 380.3 oa; 357.6 pp × 48.7 × 20 *(115.9; 109 × 14.8 × 6.1)*
Main machinery: CODOG; 2 GE LM 2500 gas turbines; 44 000 hp *(33 MW)* sustained; 2 MTU 12V 1163 TB83 diesels; 8840 hp(m) *(6.5 MW)*; 2 shafts; cp props
Speed, knots: 32 gas; 20 diesel. **Range, miles:** 4900 at 18 kts; 9600 at 12 kts
Complement: 182 (23 officers) plus 16 Flag Staff

Missiles: SSM: 8 McDonnell Douglas Harpoon (2 quad) launchers ❶; active radar homing to 130 km *(70 nm)* at 0.9 Mach; warhead 227 kg.
SAM: Raytheon Sea Sparrow Mk 29 Mod 1 octuple launcher ❷; semi-active radar homing to 14.6 km *(8 nm)* at 2.5 Mach; warhead 39 kg. Space left for VLS Sea Sparrow ❸.
Guns: 1 Creusot Loire 3.9 in *(100 mm)*/55 Mod 68 CADAM ❹; 80° elevation; 60 rounds/minute to 17 km *(9 nm)* anti-surface; 8 km *(4.4 nm)* anti-aircraft; weight of shell 13.5 kg.
1 General Electric/General Dynamics Vulcan Phalanx 20 mm Mk 15 Mod 11 ❺; 6 barrels per mounting; 3000 rounds/minute combined to 1.5 km.
Torpedoes: 6—324 mm US Mk 32 (2 triple) tubes ❻. Honeywell Mk 46 Mod 5; anti-submarine; active/passive homing to 11 km *(5.9 nm)* at 40 kts; warhead 44 kg.
Countermeasures: Decoys: 2 Loral Hycor Mk 36 SRBOC 6-barrelled Chaff launchers ❼.
SLQ 25 Nixie; towed torpedo decoy.
ESM/ECM: Argo AR 700/APECS II; intercept and jammer.
Combat data systems: Signaal SEWACO action data automation with STACOS tactical command; Link 11 and 14. SATCOMs (from 1993).
Fire control: SWG 1A(V) for SSM. Vesta Helo transponder with data link for OTHT.
Radars: Air search: Signaal MW 08 (derived from Smart 3D) ❽; 3D; G band.
Air/surface search: Signaal DA 08 (fitted with IFF Mk 12 Mod 4) ❾; F band.
Navigation: Kelvin Hughes Type 1007; I band.
Fire control: 2 Signaal STIR ❿; I/J/K band; range 140 km *(76 nm)* for 1 m² target.
Sonars: Computing Devices (Canada) SQS 510(V); hull-mounted; active search and attack; medium frequency.

Helicopters: 2 Super Sea Lynx ⓫.

Programmes: The contract for all three was signed on the 26 July 1986. These are Meko 200 type ordered from a consortium of builders. As well as Portugal, which is bearing 40 per cent of the cost, assistance has been given by Germany and NATO with some missile, CIWS and torpedo systems being provided by the USA.
Structure: All steel construction. Stabilisers fitted. Full RAS facilities. Space has been left for a sonar towed array and for VLS Sea Sparrow.
Operational: Designed primarily as ASW ships.

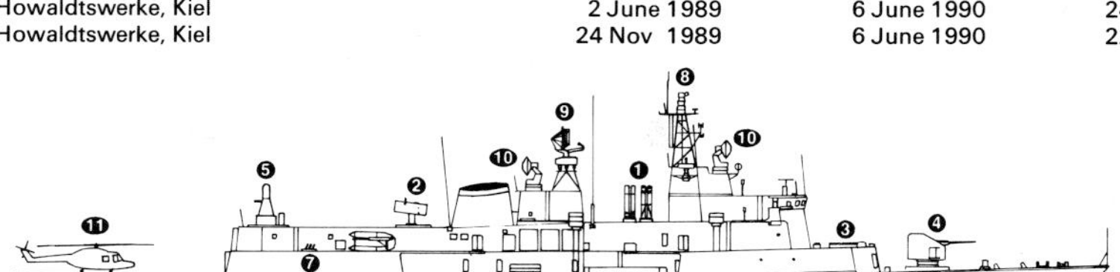

VASCO DA GAMA *(Scale 1 : 1 200), Ian Sturton*

CORTE REAL *12/1991, Stefan Terzibaschitsch*

ALVARES CABRAL *6/1991, Harald Carstens*

4 BAPTISTA DE ANDRADE CLASS

Name	No	Builders	Laid down	Launched	Commissioned
BAPTISTA DE ANDRADE	F 486	Empresa Nacional Bazán, Cartagena	1 Sep 1972	13 Mar 1973	19 Nov 1974
JOÃO ROBY	F 487	Empresa Nacional Bazán, Cartagena	1 Dec 1972	3 June 1973	18 Mar 1975
AFONSO CERQUEIRA	F 488	Empresa Nacional Bazán, Cartagena	10 Mar 1973	6 Oct 1973	26 June 1975
OLIVEIRA E CARMO	F 489	Empresa Nacional Bazán, Cartagena	1 June 1973	22 Feb 1974	28 Oct 1975

Displacement, tons: 1203 standard; 1380 full load
Dimensions, feet (metres): 277.5 × 33.8 × 10.2 *(84.6 × 10.3 × 3.1)*
Main machinery: 2 OEW Pielstick 12 PC 2.2V 400 diesels; 12 000 hp(m) *(8.82 MW)* sustained; 2 shafts
Speed, knots: 22. **Range, miles:** 5900 at 18 kts
Complement: 122 (11 officers) plus marine detachment

Guns: 1 Creusot Loire 3.9 in *(100 mm)*/55 Mod 1968 ❶; 80° elevation; 80 rounds/minute to 17 km *(9 nm)* anti-surface; 8 km *(4.4 nm)* anti-aircraft; weight of shell 13.5 kg.
2 Bofors 40 mm/70 ❷; 90° elevation; 300 rounds/minute to 12 km *(6.6 nm)*; weight of shell 0.96 kg.
Torpedoes: 6—324 mm US Mk 32 (2 triple) tubes ❸. Honeywell Mk 46; anti-submarine; active/passive homing to 11 km *(5.9 nm)* at 40 kts; warhead 44 kg.
Fire control: Vega GFCS.
Radars: Air/surface search: Plessey AWS 2 ❹; E/F band; range 110 km *(60 nm)*.
Navigation: Decca RM 316P; I band.
Fire control: Thomson-CSF Pollux ❺; I/J band; range 31 km *(17 nm)* for 2 m² target.
Sonars: Thomson Sintra Diodon; hull-mounted; active search and attack; 11, 12 or 13 kHz.

Modernisation: Planned programme to include PDMS Sea Sparrow and SSM has been shelved although space and weight allowance is available for two Exocet. Communications equipment updated 1988-91.
Structure: Helicopter platform only.

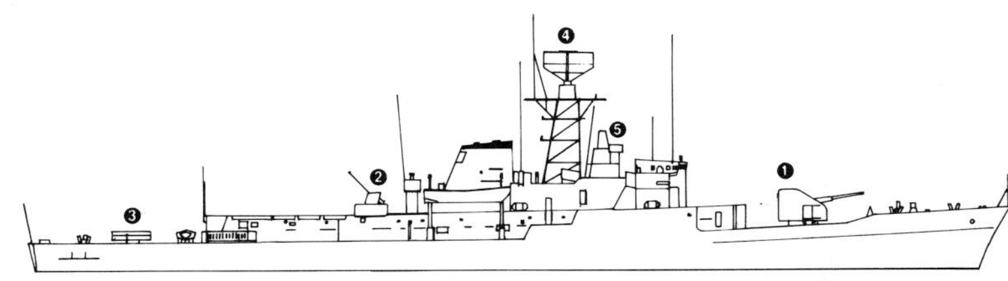

BAPTISTA DE ANDRADE Class *(Scale 1 : 900), Ian Sturton*

JOÃO ROBY *3/1991, van Ginderen Collection*

6 JOÃO COUTINHO CLASS

Name	No	Builders	Laid down	Launched	Commissioned
ANTONIO ENES	F 471	Empresa Nacional Bazán, Cartagena	10 Apr 1968	16 Aug 1969	18 June 1971
JOÃO COUTINHO	F 475	Blohm & Voss AG, Hamburg	24 Dec 1968	2 May 1969	28 Feb 1970
JACINTO CANDIDO	F 476	Blohm & Voss AG, Hamburg	10 Feb 1969	16 June 1969	29 May 1970
GENERAL PEREIRA D'EÇA	F 477	Blohm & Voss AG, Hamburg	21 Apr 1969	26 July 1969	10 Oct 1970
AUGUSTO DE CASTILHO	F 484	Empresa Nacional Bazán, Cartagena	15 Oct 1968	4 July 1969	14 Nov 1970
HONORIO BARRETO	F 485	Empresa Nacional Bazán, Cartagena	20 Feb 1968	11 Apr 1970	15 Apr 1971

Displacement, tons: 1203 standard; 1380 full load
Dimensions, feet (metres): 277.5 × 33.8 × 10.8 *(84.6 × 10.3 × 3.3)*
Main machinery: 2 OEW Pielstick 12 PC 2.2V 400 diesels; 12 000 hp(m) *(8.82 MW)* sustained; 2 shafts
Speed, knots: 22. **Range, miles:** 5900 at 18 kts
Complement: 77 (9 officers)

Guns: 2 US 3 in *(76 mm)*/50 (twin) Mk 33 ❶; 85° elevation; 50 rounds/minute to 12.8 km *(7 nm)*; weight of shell 6 kg.
2 Bofors 40 mm/60 (twin) ❷; 90° elevation; 300 rounds/minute to 12 km *(6.6 nm)*; weight of shell 0.89 kg.
Fire control: Mk 51 GFCS for 40 mm. Mk 63 for 76 mm.
Radars: Air/surface search: Kelvin Hughes ❸; I band.
Navigation: Racal Decca RM 1226C; I band.
Fire control: Western Electric SPG 34 ❹; I/J band.

JOÃO COUTINHO *(Scale 1 : 900), Ian Sturton*

Modernisation: A programme for this class to include SSM and PDMS has been shelved. In 1989-91 the main radar was updated and JATCOMS installed. Also fitted with SIFICAP which is a Fishery Protection data exchange system by satellite to the main database ashore.

Structure: Helicopter platform only.
Operational: A/S equipment no longer operational and laid apart on shore. Crew reduced by 23 as a result.

AUGUSTO DE CASTILHO (new search radar) *1/1991, Harald Carstens*

SHIPBORNE AIRCRAFT

Numbers/Type: 5 Westland Super Navy Lynx Mk 95.
Operational speed: 125 kts *(231 km/h)*.
Service ceiling: 12 000 ft *(3660 m)*.
Range: 320 nm *(593 km)*.
Role/Weapon systems: Ordered 2 November 1990 for MEKO 200 frigates; delivery 1993. Sensors: Bendix 1500 radar; AQS-18 dipping sonar; Racal RNS 252 TDS. Weapons: Mk 46 torpedoes.

SUPER LYNX 11/1989

LAND-BASED MARITIME AIRCRAFT

(All Air Force Manned)

Numbers/Type: 12 Aerospatiale SA 330C Puma.
Operational speed: 151 kts *(280 km/h)*.
Service ceiling: 15 090 ft *(4600 m)*.
Range: 343 nm *(635 km)*.
Role/Weapon systems: For SAR and surface search. Sensors: Omera search radar. Weapons: Unarmed except for pintle-mounted machine guns.

Numbers/Type: 6 CASA C-212 Aviocar.
Operational speed: 190 kts *(353 km/h)*.
Service ceiling: 24 000 ft *(7315 m)*.
Range: 1650 nm *(3055 km)*.
Role/Weapon systems: Short-range SAR support and transport operations. Sensors: Search radar and MAD. Weapons: Unarmed.

Numbers/Type: 5 Lockheed C-130H Hercules.
Operational speed: 325 kts *(602 km/h)*.
Service ceiling: 33 000 ft *(10 060 m)*.
Range: 4250 nm *(7880 km)*.
Role/Weapon systems: MR is a secondary role for the Air Force transport aircraft assigned to NATO. Sensors: Search radar. Weapons: Unarmed.

Numbers/Type: 6 Lockheed P-3B Orion.
Operational speed: 410 kts *(760 km/h)*.
Service ceiling: 28 300 ft *(8625 m)*.
Range: 4000 nm *(7410 km)*.
Role/Weapon systems: Long-range surveillance and ASW patrol aircraft; acquired with NATO funding from RAAF update programme and modernised by Lockheed starting in 1987. Progress is slow. Sensors: APS-115 radar, ASQ-81 MAD, AQS-901 sonobuoy processor, AQS-114 computer, IFF, ECM/ESM. Weapons: ASW; 8 × Mk 46 torpedoes, depth bombs or mines; ASV; 10 × underwing stations for ASMs.

PATROL VESSELS

Note: Up to 12 new OPVs are required. Expected to be ordered in two batches of six from 1992 onwards. Displacement, 1400 tons approx.

2 SÃO ROQUE CLASS

Name	No	Builders	Commissioned
SÃO ROQUE	M 401	CUF Shipyard, Lisbon	6 June 1956
RIBEIRA GRANDE	M 402	CUF Shipyard, Lisbon	8 Feb 1957

Displacement, tons: 394.4 standard; 451.9 full load
Dimensions, feet (metres): 153 × 27.7 × 8.2 *(46.3 × 8.5 × 2.5)*
Main machinery: 2 Mirrlees JVSS-12 diesels; 2500 hp *(1.87 MW)*; 2 shafts
Speed, knots: 15. **Range, miles:** 2400 at 12 kts
Complement: 46 (3 officers)
Guns: 1 Oerlikon 20 mm/65.
Radars: Navigation: I band.

Comment: Same style as British Ton class coastal minesweepers. 40 mm gun removed 1972, as was the minesweeping gear. Neither the equipment nor the trained personnel are available for mine warfare operations. Tenders for replacements may be sought in 1995-97. *São Roque* serves as a Divers support ship, *Ribeira Grande* as a patrol craft. Two others were paid off in 1991.

SÃO ROQUE *3/1991, van Ginderen Collection*

LIGHT FORCES

10 CACINE CLASS (LARGE PATROL CRAFT)

Name	*No*	*Builders*	*Commissioned*
CACINE	P 1140	Arsenal do Alfeite	May 1969
CUNENE	P 1141	Arsenal do Alfeite	June 1969
MANDOVI	P 1142	Arsenal do Alfeite	Sep 1969
ROVUMA	P 1143	Arsenal do Alfeite	Nov 1969
CUANZA	P 1144	Estaleiros Navais do Mondego	May 1969
GEBA	P 1145	Estaleiros Navais do Mondego	May 1970
ZAIRE	P 1146	Estaleiros Navais do Mondego	Nov 1970
ZAMBEZE	P 1147	Estaleiros Navais do Mondego	Jan 1971
LIMPOPO	P 1160	Arsenal do Alfeite	Apr 1973
SAVE	P 1161	Arsenal do Alfeite	May 1973

Displacement, tons: 292.5 standard; 310 full load
Dimensions, feet (metres): 144 × 25.2 × 7.1 *(44 × 7.7 × 2.2)*
Main machinery: 2 MTU 12V 538 TB 80 diesels; 3750 hp(m) *(2.76 MW)* sustained; 2 shafts
Speed, knots: 20. **Range, miles:** 4400 at 12 kts
Complement: 33 (3 officers)
Guns: 1 Bofors 40 mm/60. 1 Oerlikon 20 mm/65.
Radars: Surface search: Kelvin Hughes Type 1007; I/J band.

Comment: Originally mounted a second Bofors aft but most have been removed as has the 37 mm rocket launcher. Have SIFICAP satellite data handling system for Fishery Protection duties.

SAVE *7/1991, van Ginderen Collection*

5 ARGOS CLASS (COASTAL PATROL CRAFT)

Name	*No*	*Builders*	*Commissioned*
ARGOS	P 1150	Arsenal do Alfeite	2 July 1991
DRAGÃO	P 1151	Arsenal do Alfeite	18 Oct 1991
ESCORPIÃO	P 1152	Arsenal do Alfeite	26 Nov 1991
CASSIOPEIA	P 1153	Conafi	11 Nov 1991
HIDRA	P 1154	Conafi	18 Dec 1991

Displacement, tons: 84 standard; 94 full load
Dimensions, feet (metres): 89.2 × 19.4 × 4.6 *(27.2 × 5.9 × 1.4)*
Main machinery: 2 MTU 12V 396 TE 84 diesels; 3700 hp(m) *(2.73 MW)* sustained; 2 shafts
Speed, knots: 28. **Range, miles:** 1350 at 15 kts; 200 at 28 kts
Complement: 9 (1 officer)
Guns: 2—12.7 mm MGs.
Radars: Navigation: Furuno 1505 DA; I band.

Comment: Capable of full speed operation up to sea state 3.

ARGOS *1991, Arsenal do Alfeite*

2 DOM ALEIXO CLASS (COASTAL PATROL CRAFT)

Name	*No*	*Builders*	*Commissioned*
DOM ALEIXO	P 1148	S Jacinto Aveiro	7 Dec 1967
DOM JEREMIAS	P 1149 (ex-A 5202)	S Jacinto Aveiro	22 Dec 1967

Displacement, tons: 62.6 standard; 67.7 full load
Dimensions, feet (metres): 82.1 × 17 × 5.2 *(25 × 5.2 × 1.6)*
Main machinery: 2 Cummins diesels; 1270 hp *(947 kW)*; 2 shafts
Speed, knots: 16
Complement: 10 (2 officers)
Gun: 1 Oerlikon 20 mm/65.
Radars: Surface search: Decca 303; I band.

Comment: *Dom Jeremias* has been used as a survey craft but reverted to being a patrol craft in 1989.

DOM JEREMIAS *3/1991, van Ginderen Collection*

6 ALBATROZ CLASS (COASTAL PATROL CRAFT)

Name	*No*	*Builders*	*Commissioned*
ALBATROZ	P 1162	Arsenal do Alfeite	9 Dec 1974
AÇOR	P 1163	Arsenal do Alfeite	9 Dec 1974
ANDORINHA	P 1164	Arsenal do Alfeite	20 Dec 1974
AGUIA	P 1165	Arsenal do Alfeite	28 Feb 1975
CISNE	P 1167	Arsenal do Alfeite	31 Mar 1976
CONDOR	UAM 630 (ex-P 1166)	Arsenal do Alfeite	23 Apr 1975

Displacement, tons: 45 full load
Dimensions, feet (metres): 77.4 × 18.4 × 5.2 *(23.6 × 5.6 × 1.6)*
Main machinery: 2 Cummins diesels; 1100 hp *(820 kW)*; 2 shafts
Speed, knots: 20. **Range, miles:** 2500 at 12 kts
Complement: 8 (1 officer)
Guns: 1 Oerlikon 20 mm/65. 2—12.7 mm MGs.
Radars: Surface search: Decca RM 316P; I band.

Comment: *Condor* is now used for harbour patrol duties.

AÇOR *1984, Portuguese Navy*

1 RIO MINHO CLASS (RIVER PATROL CRAFT)

Name	*No*	*Builders*	*Commissioned*
RIO MINHO	P 370	Arsenal do Alfeite	1 Aug 1991

Displacement, tons: 70 full load
Dimensions, feet (metres): 73.5 × 19.7 × 2.6 *(22.4 × 6 × 0.8)*
Main machinery: 2 Deutz diesels; 664 hp(m) *(488 kW)*; 2 Schottel pump jets
Speed, knots: 9.5. **Range, miles:** 800 at 9 kts
Complement: 8 (1 officer)
Guns: 1—7.62 mm MG.
Radars: Navigation: Furuno FR 1505; I band.

Comment: New river patrol craft which has replaced *Atria* on the River Minho.

RIO MINHO *1991, Arsenal do Alfeite*

MINE WARFARE FORCES

Note: Planned acquisition of four MCMV is included in the 1995-98 proposed programme. An MoU for a collaborative project definition phase is to be signed in 1992, probably with the Netherlands and Belgium.

AMPHIBIOUS FORCES

3 BOMBARDA CLASS LDG (LCT)

Name	*No*	*Builders*	*Commissioned*
BOMBARDA	LDG 201	Estaleiros Navais do Mondego	1969
ALABARDA	LDG 202	Estaleiros Navais do Mondego	1970
BACAMARTE	LDG 203	Arsenal do Alfeite	1985

Displacement, tons: 652 full load
Dimensions, feet (metres): 184.3 × 38.7 × 6.2 *(56.2 × 11.8 × 1.9)*
Main machinery: 2 Maybach-Mercedes-Benz MTU diesels; 910 hp(m) *(669 kW)*; 2 shafts
Speed, knots: 9.5. **Range, miles:** 2600 at 9 kts
Complement: 21 (3 officers)
Military lift: 350 tons
Guns: 2 Oerlikon 20 mm.
Radars: Navigation: Decca RM 316P; I band.

Comment: Similar to French EDIC.

BOMBARDA *3/1991, van Ginderen Collection*

6 LDM 400 CLASS (LCM)

LDM 406 **LDM 418** **LDM 420** **LDM 421** **LDM 422** **LDM 423**

Displacement, tons: 48 full load
Dimensions, feet (metres): 58.3 × 15.8 × 3.3 *(17.3 × 4.8 × 1)*
Main machinery: 2 Cummins diesels; 400 hp *(298 kW)*; 2 shafts
Speed, knots: 10

Comment: Built 1967-68.

LDM 422 *1990, van Ginderen Collection*

3 LDM 100 CLASS (LCM)

LDM 119 **LDM 120** **LDM 121**

Displacement, tons: 50 full load
Dimensions, feet (metres): 50 × 14.4 × 3.6 *(15.3 × 4.4 × 1.1)*
Main machinery: 2 GM diesels; 450 hp *(336 kW)*; 2 shafts
Speed, knots: 9

Comment: All built at the Estaleiros Navais do Mondego in 1965.

SURVEY SHIPS

Note: A sister ship is needed for *Almeida Carvalho* to aid work on behalf of Portuguese-speaking African countries. An ex-US Robert D Conrad class is a possibility.

1 Ex-US KELLAR CLASS

Name	*No*	*Builders*	*Commissioned*
ALMEIDA CARVALHO (ex-USNS *Kellar, T-AGS 25*)	A 527	Marietta Shipbuilding Co	31 Jan 1969

Displacement, tons: 1297 standard; 1400 full load
Dimensions, feet (metres): 209 × 37.1 × 15.1 *(63.7 × 11.3 × 4.6)*
Main machinery: Diesel-electric; 2 Caterpillar D-378 diesel generators; 1 motor; 1300 hp *(970 kW)*; 1 shaft
Speed, knots: 15. **Range, miles:** 1200 at 14 kts
Complement: 47 (7 officers)
Radars: Surface search: Kelvin Hughes Type 1007; I band.
Navigation: Racal Decca TM 829; I band.

Comment: Leased from the US Navy on 21 January 1972. Transferred finally in 1988.

ALMEIDA CARVALHO *1986, Portuguese Navy*

2 ANDROMEDA CLASS

Name	*No*	*Builders*	*Commissioned*
ANDROMEDA	A 5203	Arsenal do Alfeite	1 Feb 1987
AURIGA	A 5205	Arsenal do Alfeite	1 July 1987

Displacement, tons: 230 full load
Dimensions, feet (metres): 103.3 × 25.4 × 8.2 *(31.5 × 7.7 × 2.5)*
Main machinery: 1 MTU 12V 396 TC62 diesel; 1200 hp(m) *(880 kW)* sustained; 1 shaft
Speed, knots: 12. **Range, miles:** 1980 at 10 kts
Complement: 17 (3 officers)
Radars: Navigation: Decca RM 914C; I band.

Comment: Both ordered in January 1984.

ANDROMEDA *1987, Arsenal do Alfeite*

5 SURVEY CRAFT

CORAL UAM 801
HIDRA UAM 802
ACTINIA UAM 803
SICANDRA UAM 804
FISALIA UAM 805

Comment: 801 and 802 are of 36 tons and were launched in 1980. The other three are converted fishing vessels (803 of 90 tons, 804 of 70 tons) of different designs mostly used as lighthouse tenders.

CORAL *11/1986, Hartmut Ehlers*

SERVICE FORCES

3 HARBOUR TANKERS

ODELEITE UAM 301
ODIVELAS UAM 302
OEIRAS UAM 303 (ex-BC 3, ex-YO 3)

Comment: Cargo capacity: First two, 674 tons; *Oeiras,* 924 tons.

1 REPLENISHMENT TANKER

Name	*No*	*Builders*	*Commissioned*
SÃO GABRIEL	A 5206	Estaleiros de Viana do Castelo	27 Mar 1963

Displacement, tons: 14 200 full load
Measurement, tons: 9854 gross; 9000 dwt
Dimensions, feet (metres): 479 × 59.8 × 26.2 *(146 × 18.2 × 8)*
Main machinery: 2 boilers; 1 Pametrada turbine; 9500 hp *(7.1 MW)*; 1 shaft
Speed, knots: 17. **Range, miles:** 6000 at 15 kts
Complement: 99 (11 officers)
Radars: Air search: Westinghouse SPS 6C; D band.
Navigation: Racal Decca RM 1226C; I band. Racal Decca RMS 1230C; E/F band.

Comment: Two replenishment at sea stations on each side and one Vertrep from helicopter platform aft. Modernisation or replacement is being considered.

SÃO GABRIEL *6/1989, Gilbert Gyssels*

1 LOGISTIC SUPPORT SHIP

Name	*No*	*Builders*	*Commissioned*
SÃO MIGUEL (ex-*Cabo Verde*)	A 5208	Howaldtswerke, Kiel	1962

Displacement, tons: 8290 full load
Measurement, tons: 5456 dwt
Dimensions, feet (metres): 354.6 × 51.2 × 24.7 *(108 × 15.6 × 7.5)*
Main machinery: 1 MAN K62 60/105C diesel; 4000 hp(m) *(2.94 MW)*; 1 shaft
Speed, knots: 15
Complement: 57 (8 officers)
Radars: Navigation: Kelvin Hughes 1600. Kelvin Hughes 18/12; I band.

Comment: Merchant ship purchased and commissioned in the Navy on 8 November 1985. Plans to install helicopter deck and fit facilities for troops and equipment have been shelved. Used to supply allied forces in the Gulf in early 1991. Now used for resupply of Azores and Madeira islands.

SÃO MIGUEL *1/1991, W. Sartori*

1 TRAINING SHIP

Name	*No*	*Builders*	*Commissioned*
SAGRES (ex-*Guanabara*, ex-*Albert Leo Schlageter*)	A 520	Blohm & Voss, Hamburg	10 Feb 1938

Displacement, tons: 1725 standard; 1940 full load
Dimensions, feet (metres): 231 wl; 295.2 oa × 39.4 × 17 *(70.4; 90 × 12 × 5.2)*
Main machinery: 2 MAN auxiliary diesels; 750 hp(m) *(551 kW)*; 1 shaft
Speed, knots: 10.5. **Range, miles:** 5450 at 7.5 kts on diesel
Complement: 162 (12 officers)

Comment: Former German sail training ship launched 30 October 1937. Sister of US Coast Guard training ship *Eagle* (ex-German *Horst Wessel*) and Soviet *Tovarisch* (ex-German *Gorch Fock*). Taken by the USA as a reparation after the Second World War in 1945 and sold to Brazil in 1948. Purchased from Brazil and commissioned in the Portuguese Navy on 2 February 1962 at Rio de Janeiro and renamed *Sagres*. Sail area, 20 793 sq ft. Height of main-mast, 142 ft. Phased refits 1987-88 and again in 1990-91.

SAGRES *6/1990, A. Campenera*

Name	*No*	*Builders*	*Commissioned*
CREOULA	UAM 201	Lisbon Shipyard	1937

Displacement, tons: 818 standard; 1055 full load
Dimensions, feet (metres): 221.1 × 32.5 × 13.8 *(67.4 × 9.9 × 4.2)*
Main machinery: 1 Auxiliary diesel; 480 hp(m) *(353 kW)*; 1 shaft

Comment: Ex-deep sea sail fishing ship used off the coast of Newfoundland for 36 years. Bought by Fishing Department in 1976 to turn into a museum ship but because she was still seaworthy it was decided to convert her to a training ship. Recommissioned in the Navy in 1987. Refit planned for 1992.

CREOULA *9/1991, van Ginderen Collection*

1 OCEAN TUG

Name	*No*	*Builders*	*Commissioned*
SCHULTZ XAVIER	A 521	Alfeite Naval Yard	14 July 1972

Displacement, tons: 900
Dimensions, feet (metres): 184 × 33 × 12.5 *(56 × 10 × 3.8)*
Main machinery: 2 diesels; 2400 hp(m) *(1.76 MW)*; 2 shafts
Speed, knots: 14.5. **Range, miles:** 3000 at 12.5 kts
Complement: 54 (4 officers)

SCHULTZ XAVIER *3/1991, van Ginderen Collection*

1 BUOY TENDER (RIVER)

Name	*No*	*Builders*	*Commissioned*
GUIA	UAM 676	S Jacinto, Aveiro	30 Jan 1985

Displacement, tons: 70
Dimensions, feet (metres): 72.2 × 25.9 × 7.2 *(22 × 7.9 × 2.2)*
Main machinery: 1 Deutz MWM SBA 6M 816 U diesel; 465 hp(m) *(342 kW)* sustained; Schottel Navigator prop
Speed, knots: 8.5 (3.5 on auxiliary engine)

GUIA *3/1991, van Ginderen Collection*

2 TRAINING YACHTS

VEGA (ex-*Arreda*) A 5201 **POLAR** (ex-*Anne Linde*) A 5204

Displacement, tons: 70 (60, *Vega*)
Dimensions, feet (metres): 75 × 16 × 8.2 *(22.9 × 4.9 × 2.5) (Polar)*
65 × 14.1 × 8.2 *(19.8 × 4.3 × 2.5) (Vega)*

HARBOUR PATROL CRAFT

SURRIADA UAM 602
MARETA UAM 605
MARESIA UAM 608
BOLINA UAM 611
BONANCA UAM 612
MAR CHAO UAM 613
LEVANTE UAM 631
— UAM 641

Displacement, tons: 9
Dimensions, feet (metres): 39 × 11.8 × 3.3 *(11.8 × 3.6 × 1)*
Main machinery: 2 Volvo Penta diesels; 426 hp(m) *(313 kW)*; 2 shafts
Speed, knots: 20
Complement: 4

Comment: Large numbers of craft of similar characteristics to those listed. Some have *Marinha* on the side, others of the same type have *Guarda Fiscal*. Two new classes of fast patrol boats are planned for the *Guarda Fiscal* from 1992 onwards. Up to 24 craft are required to assist in controlling drug runners.

BONANCA *3/1991, van Ginderen Collection*

QATAR

Senior Appointment

Commander Naval Force:
Colonel Said Al Suweidi

Personnel

(a) 1992: 700 officers and men (including Marine Police)
(b) Voluntary service

Bases

Doha (main); Halul Island (secondary)

Mercantile Marine

Lloyd's Register of Shipping:
64 vessels of 484 800 tons gross

PATROL FORCES

Note: Funds allocated in 1992 for up to four new FAC(M) of 56 m.

3 COMBATTANTE III M CLASS (FAST ATTACK CRAFT—MISSILE)

Name	*No*	*Builders*	*Commissioned*
DAMSAH	Q 01	CMN, Cherbourg	10 Nov 1982
AL GHARIYAH	Q 02	CMN, Cherbourg	10 Feb 1983
RBIGAH	Q 03	CMN, Cherbourg	11 May 1983

Displacement, tons: 345 standard; 395 full load
Dimensions, feet (metres): 183.7 × 26.9 × 7.2 *(56 × 8.2 × 2.2)*
Main machinery: 4 MTU 20V 538 TB 93 diesels; 15 020 hp(m) *(11 MW)* sustained; 4 shafts
Speed, knots: 38.5. **Range, miles:** 2000 at 15 kts
Complement: 41 (6 officers)

Missiles: SSM: 8 Aerospatiale MM 40 Exocet; inertial cruise; active radar homing to 70 km *(40 nm)* at 0.9 Mach; warhead 165 kg; sea-skimmer.
Guns: 1 OTO Melara 3 in *(76 mm)*/62; 85° elevation; 60 rounds/minute to 16 km *(8.7 nm)*; weight of shell 6 kg.
2 Breda 40 mm/70 (twin); 85° elevation; 300 rounds/minute to 12.5 km *(6.8 nm)*; weight of shell 0.96 kg.
4 Oerlikon 30 mm/75 (2 twin); 85° elevation; 650 rounds/minute to 10 km *(5.5 nm)*; weight of shell 1 kg or 0.36 kg.
Countermeasures: Decoys: CSEE Dagaie trainable single launcher; 6 containers; IR flares and Chaff; H/J band.
ESM/ECM: Racal Cutlass/Cygnus.
Fire control: Vega system. 2 CSEE Naja directors.
Radars: Surface search: Thomson-CSF Triton; G band.
Navigation: Racal Decca 1226; I band.
Fire control: Thomson-CSF Castor II; I/J band; range 15 km *(8 nm)* for 1 m² target.

Programmes: Ordered in 1980 and launched in 1982. All arrived at Doha July 1983.

DAMSAH *1984, N. Overington*

6 DAMEN POLYCAT 1450 CLASS (COASTAL PATROL CRAFT)

Q 31-36

Displacement, tons: 18 full load
Dimensions, feet (metres): 47.6 × 15.4 × 4.9 *(14.5 × 4.7 × 2.1)*
Main machinery: 2 GM 12V 71 TI diesels; 840 hp *(627 kW)* sustained; 2 shafts
Speed, knots: 26
Complement: 11
Guns: 1 Oerlikon 20 mm.
Radars: Navigation: Racal Decca; I band.

Comment: Delivered February-May 1980. May have been transferred to the Marine Police.

Q 33 *3/1980, Damen SY*

6 VOSPER THORNYCROFT TYPE (LARGE PATROL CRAFT)

Name	*No*	*Builders*	*Commissioned*
BARZAN	Q 11	Vosper Thornycroft Ltd	13 Jan 1975
HWAR	Q 12	Vosper Thornycroft Ltd	30 Apr 1975
THAT ASSUARI	Q 13	Vosper Thornycroft Ltd	3 Oct 1975
AL WUSAIL	Q 14	Vosper Thornycroft Ltd	28 Oct 1975
FATEH-AL-KHAIR	Q 15	Vosper Thornycroft Ltd	22 Jan 1976
TARIQ	Q 16	Vosper Thornycroft Ltd	1 Mar 1976

Displacement, tons: 120
Dimensions, feet (metres): 110 × 21 × 5.5 *(33.5 × 6.4 × 1.6)*
Main machinery: 2 Paxman Valenta 16CM diesels; 6703 hp(m) *(5 MW)* sustained; 2 shafts
Speed, knots: 27
Complement: 25
Guns: 4 Oerlikon 30 mm/75 (2 twin).
Radars: Surface search: Racal Decca; I band.

Comment: Ordered in 1972-73. Replacements are needed and funds were allocated in 1992.

AL WUSAIL *1984*

MISCELLANEOUS

Note: A number of amphibious craft are reported to have been delivered including an LCT *Rabha* of 160 ft *(48.8 m)* with a capacity for three tanks and 110 troops, acquired in 1986-87. Also four Rotork craft and 30 Sea Jeeps in 1985. It is not clear how many of these craft are for civilian use.

LAND-BASED MARITIME AIRCRAFT

Numbers/Type: 7 Westland Commando Mk 3.
Operational speed: 125 kts *(230 km/h)*.
Service ceiling: 10 500 ft *(3200 m)*.
Range: 630 nm *(1165 km)*.
Role/Weapon systems: Form No 8 Anti-surface Vessel Squadron for coastal surveillance and anti-shipping operations. Sensors: MEL ARI 5955 radar. Weapons: ASV; 1 × AM 39 Exocet ASM, carried by two helicopters only; general purpose machine guns carried; door-mounted.

MARINE POLICE

2 KEITH NELSON TYPE (COASTAL PATROL CRAFT)

Displacement, tons: 13
Dimensions, feet (metres): 44 × 12.3 × 3.8 *(13.5 × 3.8 × 1.1)*
Main machinery: 2 Caterpillar diesels; 800 hp *(597 kW)*; 2 shafts
Speed, knots: 26
Complement: 6
Guns: 1—12.7 mm MG. 2—7.62 mm MGs.

Comment: The third of this group has been converted into a pilot cutter.

KEITH NELSON TYPE *9/1990*

5 WATERCRAFT P 1200 TYPE (COASTAL PATROL CRAFT)

Displacement, tons: 12.7
Dimensions, feet (metres): 39 × 13.4 × 3.6 *(11.9 × 4.1 × 1.1)*
Main machinery: 2 Wizeman Mercedes 400 diesels; 660 hp(m) *(485 kW)*; 2 shafts
Speed, knots: 29
Complement: 4
Guns: 2—7.62 mm MGs.

Comment: Built by Watercraft, Shoreham, England in 1980. Two have been deleted.

4 CRESTITALIA MV-45 CLASS (COASTAL PATROL CRAFT)

Displacement, tons: 17 full load
Dimensions, feet (metres): 47.6 × 12.5 × 2.6 *(14.5 × 3.8 × 0.8)*
Main machinery: 2 diesels; 1270 hp(m) *(933 kW)*; 2 shafts
Speed, knots: 32. **Range, miles:** 275 at 29 kts
Complement: 6
Guns: 1 Oerlikon 20 mm. 2—7.62 mm MGs.

Comment: Built by Crestitalia and delivered in mid-1989. GRP construction.

MV-45 *1989, Crestitalia*

25 FAIREY MARINE SPEAR CLASS (COASTAL PATROL CRAFT)

Displacement, tons: 4.3
Dimensions, feet (metres): 29.8 × 9 × 2.8 *(9.1 × 2.8 × 0.9)*
Main machinery: 2 diesels; 290 hp *(216 kW)*; 2 shafts
Speed, knots: 26
Complement: 4
Guns: 3—7.62 mm MGs.

Comment: First seven ordered early 1974 and delivered June 1974 to February 1975. Contract for further five signed December 1975. Third contract for three fulfilled with delivery of two on 30 June 1975 and one on 14 July 1975. Fourth order for 10 (four Mk 1, six Mk 2) received October 1976 and delivery effected April 1977.

2 FAIREY MARINE INTERCEPTOR CLASS (ASSAULT CRAFT)

Displacement, tons: 1.25
Dimensions, feet (metres): 25 × 8 × 2.5 *(7.9 × 2.4 × 0.8)*
Main machinery: 2 Johnson outboard motors; 270 hp *(201 kW)*
Speed, knots: 35. **Range, miles:** 150 at 30 kts
Complement: 3
Military lift: 10 troops

Comment: Delivered 28 November 1975. GRP catamaran hull. In rescue role carry a number of life rafts.

ROMANIA

General

Up to the overthrow of President Ceausescu in December 1989 the Fleet was undermanned and seldom went to sea mostly because sailors were used for civilian tasks. At the end of 1990 it was reported that due to financial problems work had stopped on all new construction and major refits, but there was more activity in 1991. It is reported that some of the ships names are to be changed.

Headquarters' Appointments

Commander-in-Chief of the Navy:
Vice Admiral Gheorghe Anghelescu

Diplomatic Representation

Defence Attaché in London:
Colonel G Rotaru (A)

Personnel

1992: 6780 regulars plus 9700 conscripts.

Bases

Black Sea—Mangalia (HQ and Training); Constanta (Coastal Defence and Naval Aviation)
Danube—Giurgiu (HQ), Sulina, Galati, Dulcea

Strength of the Fleet

Type	*Active*
Submarine	1
Destroyer	1
Frigates	5
Corvettes/Monitor	11
Fast Attack Craft (Missile)	6
Fast Attack Craft (Gun and Patrol)	27
Fast Attack Craft (Torpedo)	42
River Patrol Craft	22
Minelayer/MCM Support	3
Minesweepers (Coastal and River)	32
Training Ship	1
Logistic Support Ships	2
Oceanographic Ships	2
Tugs	14
Auxiliaries	13

Mercantile Marine

Lloyd's Register of Shipping:
469 vessels of 3 828 034 tons gross

DELETIONS

Light Forces

1989 4 SM 165 class
1990 2 Kronshtadt class, 9 SM 165 class, 5 SD 200 class,

Minesweepers

1990 6 T 301 class
1991 3 T 301 class

Auxiliaries

1989 Constanta (old)

SUBMARINES

1 Ex-SOVIET KILO CLASS

DELFIN

Displacement, tons: 2325 surfaced; 3076 dived
Dimensions, feet (metres): 243.8 × 32.8 × 21.7 *(74.3 × 10 × 6.6)*
Main machinery: Diesel-electric; 2 diesels; 3650 hp(m) *(2.68 MW)*; 2 generators; 1 motor; 5900 hp(m) *(4.34 MW)*; 1 shaft
Speed, knots: 10 surfaced; 17 dived; 9 snorting
Range, miles: 6000 at 7 kts surfaced; 400 at 3 kts dived
Complement: 45

Torpedoes: 6—21 in *(533 mm)* tubes. 18 Soviet Type 53; pattern active/passive homing up to 20 km *(10.8 nm)* at up to 45 kts; warhead 400 kg.
Mines: 36 in lieu of torpedoes.
Countermeasures: ESM: Brick Group; radar warning. Quad Loop D/F.
Radars: Surface search: Snoop Tray; I band.
Sonars: Shark Teeth; hull-mounted; passive search and attack; medium frequency.
Mouse Roar; active attack; high frequency.

KILO Class *5/1990*

Programmes: Transferred in December 1986. Second one planned but funds not available.

Structure: Diving depth, 240 m *(785 ft)*.
Operational: Very rarely goes to sea.

DESTROYER

MARASESTI (ex-*Muntenia*)

Displacement, tons: 6000 full load
Dimensions, feet (metres): 485.6 × 48.6 × 23 *(148 × 14.8 × 7)*
Main machinery: COGOG; 4 gas turbines; 94 000 hp(m) *(69 MW)*; 2 shafts
Speed, knots: 32

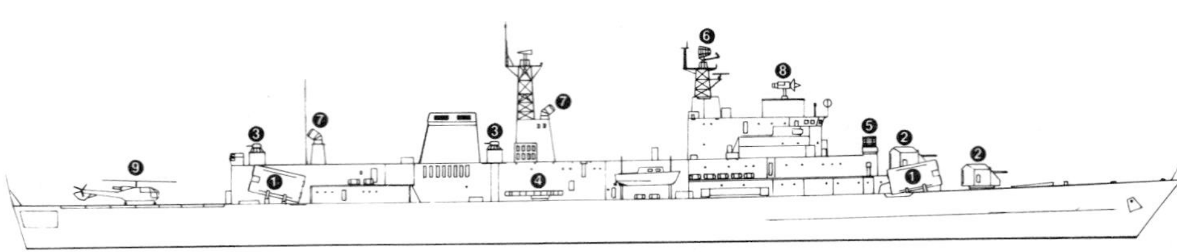

MARASESTI (modernised) *(Scale 1 : 1 200), Ian Sturton*

Missiles: SSM: 8 SS-N-2C Styx ❶; active radar or IR homing to 83 km *(45 nm)* at 0.9 Mach; warhead 513 kg.
Guns: 4 USSR 3 in *(76 mm)*/60 (2 twin) ❷; 80° elevation; 90 rounds/minute to 15 km *(8 nm)*; weight of shell 6.8 kg.
8 USSR 30 mm/65 (4 twin) ❸; 85° elevation; 500 rounds/minute to 4 km *(2.2 nm)*; weight of shell 0.54 kg.
Torpedoes: 6—21 in *(533 mm)* (2 triple) tubes ❹. Probably Soviet Type 53; pattern active/passive homing up to 20 km *(10.8 nm)* at up to 45 kts; warhead 400 kg.
A/S mortars: 2 RBU 6000 ❺; 12 tubed trainable; range 6000 m; warhead 31 kg.
Radars: Air/surface search: Strut Curve ❻; F band; range 110 km *(60 nm)* for 2 m² target.
Fire control: Two Drum Tilt ❼; H/I band.
Hawk Screech ❽; I band; range 27 km *(15 nm)* (for guns).
Navigation: Spin Trough; I band.
IFF: High Pole B.
Sonars: Hull-mounted; active search and attack; medium frequency.

Helicopters: 3 IAR-316 Alouette III type ❾.

Programmes: Built at Mangalia. Launched 1982, commissioned 5 August 1985.

Modernisation: Reported that some attempts have been made to modernise some of the electronic equipment. Also topweight problems are being resolved by reducing the height of the mast structures and the Styx missile launchers have been lowered by one deck. Probably to be fitted with SA-N-5 SAM launchers. RBU 6000 has replaced the RBU 1200.
Structure: A distinctive Romanian design.
Operational: Deactivated in June 1988 due to manpower and fuel shortages but modernisation work in 1990-91 suggests an intention to achieve operational availability in due course.

MARASESTI *1991, Romanian Navy*

FRIGATES

5 TETAL CLASS

260 261 262 263 264

Displacement, tons: 1800 full load
Dimensions, feet (metres): 312 × 37.7 × 9.8 *(95 × 11.5 × 3)*
Main machinery: 2 diesels; 2 shafts
Speed, knots: 25
Complement: 98

TETAL Class *(Scale 1 : 900), Ian Sturton*

Guns: 4 USSR 3 in *(76 mm)*/60 (2 twin) ❶; 80° elevation; 90 rounds/minute to 15 km *(8 nm)*; weight of shell 6.8 kg.
4 USSR 30 mm/65 (2 twin) ❷; 85° elevation; 500 rounds/minute to 4 km *(2.2 nm)*; weight of shell 0.54 kg.
2—14.5 mm MGs.
Torpedoes: 2—21 in *(533 mm)* (twin) tubes ❸. Soviet Type 53; pattern active/passive homing up to 20 km *(10.8 nm)* at up to 45 kts; warhead 400 kg.
A/S mortars: 2 RBU 2500 16-tubed trainable ❹; range 2500 m; warhead 21 kg.
Countermeasures: ESM: 2 Watch Dog; radar warning.

Radars: Air/surface search: Strut Curve ❺; F band.
Fire control: Drum Tilt ❻; H/I band (for 30 mm). Hawk Screech ❼; I band (for 76 mm).
Sonars: Hull-mounted; active search and attack; medium frequency.

Helicopters: Platform only.

Programmes: Built at Mangalia. First commissioned 1983, second in 1984, third in 1985, fourth in 1987 and fifth in 1990. Programme probably continues as there have been unconfirmed reports of frigate building activity at Mangalia. Hawk Screech radars are a comparatively new addition.
Structure: Probably a modified Soviet Koni design.

TETAL 261 *1991, Romanian Navy*

CORVETTES

3 Ex-SOVIET TARANTUL I CLASS

Displacement, tons: 385 standard; 450 full load
Dimensions, feet (metres): 184.1 × 37.7 × 8.2 *(56.1 × 11.5 × 2.5)*
Main machinery: CODOG; 2 Type NK 12 MV gas turbines; 24 000 hp(m) *(17.6 MW)*; 2 diesels; 8000 hp(m) *(5.9 MW)*; 2 shafts
Speed, knots: 36. **Range, miles:** 2000 at 20 kts; 400 at 36 kts
Complement: 41 (5 officers)

Missiles: 4 SS-N-2C Styx (2 twin); active radar or IR homing to 83 km *(45 nm)* at 0.9 Mach; warhead 513 kg.
Guns: 1 USSR 3 in *(76 mm)*/60; 85° elevation; 120 rounds/minute to 15 km *(8 nm)*; weight of shell 7 kg.
2—30 mm/65 AK 630; 6 barrels per mounting; 3000 rounds/minute to 20 km.
Countermeasures: 2—16 barrelled Chaff launchers.
ESM: 2 Watch Dog; radar intercept.
Fire control: Hood Wink optronic director.
Radars: Air/surface search: Plank Shave; E band.
Fire control: Bass Tilt; H/I band.
Navigation: Spin Trough; I band.
IFF: Square Head. High Pole.

Programmes: Built at Petrovsky in 1985. First one transferred in December 1990, two more in February 1992.
Structure: Export version similar to those built for Poland, India, Yemen and former GDR.

TARANTUL I *1991, Stefan Terzibaschitsch*

3 Ex-SOVIET POTI CLASS

31 32 33

Displacement, tons: 400 full load
Dimensions, feet (metres): 196.8 × 26.2 × 6.6 *(60 × 8 × 2)*
Main machinery: CODAG; 2 gas turbines; 30 000 hp(m) *(22 MW)*; 2 M503A diesels; 8000 hp(m) *(5.88 MW)*; 2 shafts
Speed, knots: 38. **Range, miles:** 4500 at 10 kts; 500 at 37 kts
Complement: 78

Guns: 2 USSR 57 mm/80 (twin); 85° elevation; 120 rounds/minute to 6 km *(3.3 nm)*; weight of shell 2.8 kg.
Torpedoes: 2—21 in *(533 mm)* (twin) tubes. Soviet Type 53.
A/S mortars: 2 RBU 2500 16-tubed trainable; range 2500 m; warhead 21 kg.
Radars: Air/surface search: Strut Curve; F band; range 110 km *(60 nm)* for 2 m² target.
Navigation: Spin Trough; I band.
Fire control: Muff Cob; G/H band.
IFF: High Pole B.
Sonars: Hull-mounted; active search and attack; medium/high frequency.

Programmes: Transferred from the USSR in 1970.

4 Ex-GERMAN M 40 CLASS (Ex-MINESWEEPERS)

DEMOCRATIA 13
DESCATUSARIA 14
DESROBIREA 15
DREPTATEA 16

Displacement, tons: 543 standard; 775 full load
Dimensions, feet (metres): 206.5 × 28 × 7.5 *(62.3 × 8.5 × 2.3)*
Main machinery: 2 diesels; 12 400 hp(m) *(9.11 MW)*; 2 shafts
Speed, knots: 17. **Range, miles:** 1200 at 15 kts
Complement: 80
Guns: 4—37 mm (2 twin). 2—12.7 mm MGs.
A/S mortars: 2 RBU 1200 5-tubed fixed; range 1200 m; warhead 34 kg.
Mines: 2 rails.
Radars: Navigation: Don 2; I band.

Comment: German M Boote design—designed as coal-burning minesweepers. Built at Galata. Converted to oil in 1951. The appearance of this class has been changed drastically during recent refits. Referred to locally as Corvettes. All minesweeping gear and the single 37 mm gun removed. A small helicopter platform has been fitted aft.

DREPTATEA *1991, Romanian Navy*

MONITOR

Note: There are unconfirmed reports of up to five Brutar II class in commission.

1 BRUTAR CLASS (RIVER MONITOR)

96

Displacement, tons: 400 full load
Dimensions, feet (metres): 141.1 × 26.2 × 4.9 *(43 × 8 × 1.5)*
Guns: 1—100 mm (in tank turret). 4—14.5 mm (2 twin) MGs. 1—122 mm BM-21 40-barrelled rocket launcher.
Mines: Has laying capability.

Comment: Completed in 1984. Belongs to Danube Flotilla.

SHIPBORNE AIRCRAFT

Numbers/Type: 6 IAR 316 Alouette III.
Operational speed: 113 kts *(210 km/h)*.
Service ceiling: 10 500 ft *(3200 m)*.
Range: 290 nm *(540 km)*.
Role/Weapon systems: ASW helicopter. Status uncertain. Sensors: Nose-mounted search radar(?) Weapons: ASW; 2 × lightweight torpedoes.

LAND-BASED MARITIME AIRCRAFT

Numbers/Type: 6 Mil Mi-14P (Haze A).
Operational speed: 124 kts *(230 km/h)*.
Service ceiling: 15 000 ft *(4570 m)*.
Range: 432 nm *(800 km)*.
Role/Weapon systems: Medium range ASW helicopter; used to support Soviet and coastal naval forces in Black Sea. Sensors: Search radar, dipping sonar, MAD, sonobuoys. Weapons: ASW; internally stored torpedoes, depth mines and bombs.

POTI 33 *1991, Romanian Navy*

LIGHT FORCES

Note: It is reported that one Kronshtadt class patrol craft was still operational in 1991.

6 Ex-SOVIET OSA I CLASS (FAST ATTACK CRAFT—MISSILE)

194-199

Displacement, tons: 171 standard; 210 full load
Dimensions, feet (metres): 110.2 × 24.9 × 8.8 *(33.6 × 7.6 × 2.7)*
Main machinery: 3 Type M503A diesels; 12 000 hp *(11 MW)*; 3 shafts
Speed, knots: 35. **Range, miles:** 400 at 34 kts
Complement: 30

Missiles: SSM: 4 SS-N-2 Styx; active radar or IR homing to 46 km *(25 nm)* at 0.9 Mach; warhead 513 kg.
Guns: 4 USSR 30 mm/65 (2 twin); 85° elevation; 500 rounds/minute to 5 km *(2.7 nm)*; weight of shell 0.54 kg.
Radars: Surface search: Square Tie; I band.
Fire control: Drum Tilt; H/I band.
IFF: High Pole. Square Head.

Programmes: Six transferred by the USSR in 1964. One deleted in error in 1988.

OSA 199 — *1991, Romanian Navy*

27 CHINESE SHANGHAI CLASS (FAST ATTACK CRAFT—GUN and PATROL)

20-40 41-44 VENUS SATURN

Displacement, tons: 113 standard; 131 full load
Dimensions, feet (metres): 127.3 × 17.7 × 5.6 *(38.8 × 5.4 × 1.7)*
Main machinery: 2 L12-180 diesels (forward); 2400 hp(m) *(1.76 MW)*; 2 L12-180Z diesels (aft); 1820 hp(m) *(1.34 MW)*; 4 shafts
Speed, knots: 30. **Range, miles:** 700 at 17 kts
Complement: 34

Guns: 4 China 37 mm/63 (2 twin) (*20-40*); 85° elevation; 180 rounds/minute to 8.5 km *(4.6 nm)*; weight of shell 1.42 kg.
1 China 37 mm/63 (*41-44*). 4—14.5 mm MGs (*41-44*).
A/S mortars: 2 RBU 1200 5-tubed fixed (*41-44*); range 1200 m; warhead 34 kg.
Depth charges: 2 racks (*41-44*).
Radars: Surface search: Don 2; I band.
Sonars: Hull-mounted; active attack; high frequency (*41-44*).

Programmes: Built at Mangalia since 1973 in a programme of about two a year (which is now complete) with the exception of 22, 24 and 25 which were imported from China. V numbers have been removed.
Structure: Three variants of the Shanghai class of which the *41-44* were a new departure and the two named craft differ greatly in their bridge superstructure. The 57 mm gun has been replaced by a second twin 37 mm in the *20-40* type.
Operational: *20-40* serve with Border Guard, *41-44* are used for anti-submarine patrols and *Venus* and *Saturn* are Harbour Security craft. Some may be non-operational.

SHANGHAI 42

SHANGHAI 29 — *1991, Romanian Navy*

29 CHINESE HUCHUAN CLASS (FAST ATTACK CRAFT—TORPEDO)

51-77 MARS JUPITER

Displacement, tons: 39 standard; 45 full load
Dimensions, feet (metres): 71.5 × 20.7 oa; 11.8 hull × 3.3 *(21.8 × 6.3; 3.6 × 1)*
Main machinery: 3 Type M50 diesels; 2550 hp(m) *(1.9 MW)*; 3 shafts
Speed, knots: 50 foilborne. **Range, miles:** 500 at 30 kts
Complement: 11
Guns: 4—14.5 mm (2 twin) MGs.
Torpedoes: 2—21 in *(533 mm)* tubes; anti-surface.

Comment: Hydrofoils of the same class as the Chinese which were started in 1956. Three imported from China. Remainder locally built at Dobreta SY, Turnu in a programme of about two a year which started 1973-74 and is now complete. *Mars* and *Jupiter* have no torpedo tubes and are without foils. V numbers deleted. Some may be non-operational.

HUCHUAN 51 — *1988*

13 EPITROP CLASS (FAST ATTACK CRAFT—TORPEDO)

200-212

Displacement, tons: 215 full load
Dimensions, feet (metres): 120.7 × 24.9 × 5.9 *(36.8 × 7.6 × 1.8)*
Main machinery: 3 Type M503A diesels; 12 000 hp(m) *(8.82 MW)*; 3 shafts
Speed, knots: 36. **Range, miles:** 500 at 35 kts
Guns: 4—30 mm/65 (2 twin).
Torpedoes: 4—21 in *(533 mm)* tubes; anti-surface.
Radars: Surface search: Pot Drum; H/I band.
Fire control: Drum Tilt; H/I band.
IFF: High Pole A.

Comment: First reported in 1981. Built in Mangalia. Based on the Osa class hull.

EPITROP 210 — *1991, Romanian Navy*

18 MONITORS (RIVER PATROL CRAFT)

76-93

Displacement, tons: 85
Dimensions, feet (metres): 105 × 16 × 3 *(32 × 4.8 × 0.9)*
Main machinery: 2 diesels; 1200 hp(m) *(882 kW)*; 2 shafts
Speed, knots: 17
Complement: 25
Guns: 1—85 mm. 4—14.5 mm (2 twin). 2—81 mm mortars.

Comment: Built in Dulcea Shipyard from 1973 in a programme of about two a year. Belong to Danube Flotilla.

RIVER MONITOR 76

4 RIVER PATROL CRAFT

14-17

Displacement, tons: 40
Dimensions, feet (metres): 52.5 × 14.4 × 4 *(16 × 4.4 × 1.2)*
Main machinery: 2—3D12 diesels; 630 hp(m) *(463 kW)*; 2 shafts
Speed, knots: 18
Complement: 10
Guns: 1—20 mm. 1—7.9 mm MG.

Comment: Steel-hulled craft built at Galata in 1954. Belong to Danube Flotilla. Obsolescent and four paid off in 1988.

RIVER PATROL CRAFT 17

MINE WARFARE FORCES

Note: Reported that two Nestin class were ordered from Yugoslavia in 1990.

3 COSAR CLASS (MINELAYER/MCM SUPPORT SHIPS)

271 274 278

Displacement, tons: 1500 full load
Dimensions, feet (metres): 259.1 × 34.8 × 11.8 *(79 × 10.6 × 3.6)*
Main machinery: 2 diesels; 2 shafts
Speed, knots: 18
Complement: 75
Guns: 1—57 mm. 4—30 mm/65 (2 twin). 4—14.5 mm (2 twin) MGs.
A/S mortars: 2 RBU 1200 5-tubed fixed; range 1200 m; warhead 34 kg.
Mines: 200 approx.
Countermeasures: ESM: Watch Dog; radar warning.
Radars: Air/surface search: Strut Curve; F band; range 110 km *(60 nm)* for 2 m² target.
Navigation: Don 2; I band.
Fire control: Muff Cob; G/H band. Drum Tilt; H/I band.
Sonars: Hull-mounted; active search; high frequency.

Comment: Completed in 1980 and 1982. *271* has a helicopter platform, but *274* has a crane on the after deck. There is some doubt about the use of *278* which may be one of the two oceanographic ships.

COSAR 271 — *1991, Romanian Navy*

4 MUSCA CLASS (MINESWEEPERS—COASTAL)

21-24

Displacement, tons: 660 full load
Dimensions, feet (metres): 171.3 × 31.2 × 9.2 *(52.2 × 9.5 × 2.8)*
Main machinery: 2 diesels; 2 shafts
Speed, knots: 14
Guns: 4—30 mm/65 (2 twin). 16—14.5 mm (4 quad).
A/S mortars: 2 RBU 1200 5-tubed fixed; range 1200 m; warhead 34 kg.
Mines: 50.
Radars: Surface search: Krivach; I band.
Fire control: Drum Tilt; H/I band.

Comment: Built at Mangalia at the rate of about one a year from 1986 to 1990.

MUSCA 24 — *1991, Romanian Navy*

3 Ex-SOVIET T 301 CLASS (MINESWEEPERS—INSHORE)

Displacement, tons: 160 full load
Dimensions, feet (metres): 124.7 × 16.7 × 5.2 *(38 × 5.1 × 1.6)*
Main machinery: 3 diesels; 1440 hp(m) *(1.06 MW)*; 3 shafts
Speed, knots: 12. **Range, miles:** 2200 at 9 kts
Complement: 25
Guns: 2—37 mm/63. 4—12.7 mm (2 twin) MGs.

Comment: Transferred in 1956-59. Surviving three will probably be deleted in 1992.

T 301 (old number) — *1988, Romanian Navy*

25 RIVER MINESWEEPERS

VD 141-165

Displacement, tons: 65 full load
Dimensions, feet (metres): 85.3 × 13.1 × 2.6 *(26 × 4 × 0.8)*
Main machinery: 2 Type M50 diesels; 1200 hp(m) *(882 kW)*; 2 shafts
Speed, knots: 18
Guns: 4—14.5 mm (2 twin) MGs.
Mines: Have laying capacity.

Comment: Built in Romania from 1975 onwards and may still be building.

MINESWEEPER 144 — *1979*

OCEANOGRAPHIC SHIPS

2 AGOR

GRIGORE ANTIPA EMIL RACOVITA

Displacement, tons: 1500 full load
Dimensions, feet (metres): 259.1 × 34.8 × 11.8 *(79 × 10.6 × 3.6)*
Main machinery: 2 diesels; 2 shafts
Speed, knots: 18
Complement: 75

Comment: Same hull as Cosar class. First in service in 1980, second in 1984. Large davits aft for launching submersible.

GRIGORE ANTIPA — *1991, Romanian Navy*

TUGS

2 ROSLAVL CLASS

VITEAZUL 101 **VOINICUL** 116

Displacement, tons: 450 full load
Dimensions, feet (metres): 135 × 29.5 × 10.8 *(41.2 × 9 × 3.3)*
Main machinery: Diesel-electric; 2 diesel generators; 1 motor; 1200 hp(m) *(882 kW)*; 1 shaft
Speed, knots: 13
Complement: 28

Comment: Built in Galata shipyard 1953-54.

12 HARBOUR TUGS

SRS 571-573, 576-577, 583-584, 675
MM 132-133, 136-137

AUXILIARIES

1 Ex-FRENCH FRIPONNE CLASS

STIHI (ex-*Mignonne*) 113

Displacement, tons: 440 full load
Dimensions, feet (metres): 200.1 × 23 × 8.2 *(61 × 7 × 2.5)*
Main machinery: 2 Sulzer diesels; 1800 hp(m) *(1.32 MW)*; 2 shafts
Speed, knots: 12. **Range, miles:** 3000 at 10 kts
Complement: 50
Guns: 1—37 mm. 4—14.5 mm (2 twin) MGs.
A/S mortars: 2 RBU 1200 5-tubed fixed; range 1200 m; warhead 34 kg.
Radars: Navigation: Two sets.
Sonars: Hull-mounted; active attack; high frequency.

Comment: Originally built at Brest and Lorient in 1916-17 as a minesweeper. The armament listed above reflects the latest conversion which also included a smoother bridge form. Second of class probably deleted in the late 1980s.

STIHI *1991, Romanian Navy*

3 COASTAL TANKERS

TM 530 **TM 531** **TM 532**

Displacement, tons: 1300 full load
Dimensions, feet (metres): 196.8 × 30.2 × 13.4 *(60 × 9.2 × 4.1)*
Main machinery: 1 diesel; 600 hp(m) *(441 kW)*; 1 shaft
Speed, knots: 10
Cargo capacity: 800 tons
Guns: 1—37 mm. 2—12.7 mm MGs.

Comment: Completed between 1971 and 1973.

6 BRAILA CLASS (RIVER TRANSPORTS)

415-420

Displacement, tons: 240 full load
Dimensions, feet (metres): 124.7 × 28.2 × 3.3 *(38 × 8.6 × 1)*
Main machinery: 2 diesels; 2 shafts
Speed, knots: 4

Comment: Very old and used by civilian as well as naval authorities.

BRAILA 419 *1987*

LOGISTIC SUPPORT SHIPS

2 CROITOR CLASS

CONSTANTA 281 **283**

Displacement, tons: 3500 full load
Dimensions, feet (metres): 354.3 × 44.3 × 12.5 *(108 × 13.5 × 3.8)*
Main machinery: 2 diesels; 2 shafts
Speed, knots: 14
Missiles: SAM: 2 SA-N-5 Grail quad launchers; manual aiming; IR homing to 6 km *(3.2 nm)* at 1.5 Mach; warhead 1.5 kg.
Guns: 2—57 mm/70 (twin). 4—30 mm/65 (2 twin). 4—14.5 mm (2 twin) MGs.
A/S mortars: 2 RBU 1200 5-tubed fixed; range 1200 m; warhead 34 kg.
Radars: Air/surface search: Strut Curve; F band; range 110 km *(60 nm)* for 2 m² target.
Navigation: Krivach; I band.
Fire control: Muff Cob; G/H band. Drum Tilt; H/I band.
Helicopters: 1 IAR-316 Alouette III type.

Comment: Reported in service in 1981 (281) and 1984 (283). These ships are a scaled down version of Soviet Don class. Forward crane for ammunition replenishment. Some ASW escort capability.

CONSTANTA *10/1991, Giorgio Ghiglione*

TRAINING SHIP

Note: *Neptun* belongs to the Merchant Navy.

Name	*No*	*Builders*	*Commissioned*
MIRCEA	—	Blohm & Voss, Hamburg	29 Mar 1939

Displacement, tons: 1604
Dimensions, feet (metres): 206; 266.4 (with bowsprit) × 39.3 × 16.5 *(62.8; 81.2 × 12 × 5.2)*
Main machinery: Auxiliary MAN diesel; 500 hp(m) *(367 kW)*; 1 shaft
Speed, knots: 6
Complement: 83 plus 140 midshipmen for training

Comment: Refitted at Hamburg in 1966. Sail area, 5739 sq m *(18 830 sq ft)*.

MIRCEA *7/1980, Marius Bar*

CONSTANTA *1991, Romanian Navy*

RUSSIA AND ASSOCIATED STATES

Flag Officers

Commander-in-Chief of the Navy and Deputy Minister of Defence:
Admiral of the Fleet V N Chernavin
1st Deputy Commander-in-Chief of the Soviet Navy:
Admiral of the Fleet I M Kapitanets
Chief of Main Naval Staff:
Admiral of the Fleet K V Makarov
1st Deputy Chief of the Main Naval Staff:
Vice Admiral D Komarov
Deputy Commander-in-Chief (Operational Training):
Vice Admiral A A Kuz'min
Deputy Commander-in-Chief (Shipbuilding and Armaments):
Engineer Admiral F I Novoselov
Deputy Commander-in-Chief (Technical Readiness):
Engineer Vice Admiral V V Zaytsev
Deputy Commander-in-Chief (Rear Services):
Admiral V V Sidorov
Deputy Commander-in-Chief (Training Establishments):
Vice Admiral E Semenkov
Commander of Naval Aviation:
Colonel General V P Potapov
1st Deputy Commander Naval Aviation:
Lieutenant General V P Zhitenev
Chief of Staff Naval Aviation:
Lieutenant General V Budeyev
Chief of Personnel (Naval):
Vice Admiral V I Panin
Chief of the Hydrographic Service:
Rear Admiral A P Mikhailovsky

Northern Fleet
Commander:
Admiral F N Gromov
Commander Naval Aviation:
Lieutenant General V Deyneka
Deputy Commander (Rear Services):
Rear Admiral V N Bobushev

Pacific
Commander:
Admiral G A Khvatov
1st Deputy Commander:
Vice Admiral A G Oleynik
Commander Naval Aviation:
Major General V V Akporisov
Deputy Commander (Rear Services):
Rear Admiral A N Loyko

Black Sea
Commander:
Admiral I V Kasatonov
1st Deputy Commander:
Vice Admiral V P Larionov
Chief of Staff:
Vice Admiral G N Gurinov
Commander Naval Aviation:
Major General N N Fadeyev

Baltic
Commander:
Vice Admiral V G Yegorov
Chief of Staff:
Vice Admiral V A Kolmagorov
Commander Naval Aviation:
Lieutenant General P Goncharov
Deputy Commander (Rear Services):
Vice Admiral I I Ryabinin

Caspian Flotilla
Commander:
Rear Admiral B D Zinin

St Petersburg Naval Base
Commander:
Vice Admiral V G Selivanov
Chief of Staff:
Rear Admiral A G Steblyanko
Head of the A A Grechko Naval Academy:
Admiral V P Ivanov
Head of Frunze Naval College:
Rear Admiral Kovalchuk
Deputy Commander (Rear Services):
Rear Admiral V V Anokhin

Personnel

(a) 1992: 410 000 officers and ratings (Afloat, 134 000; Naval Aviation, 75 000; Training, 50 000; Naval Infantry 17 000 (one Brigade for each Fleet); Coastal Defence, 14 000; Shore Support, 120 000; Communications, 4000) plus 23 000 Maritime Border Guard
(b) Approximately 25 per cent volunteers (officers and senior ratings)—remainder two years' national service since 1991 (or three years if volunteered)
(c) Deployed: Northern 103 000, Baltic 85 000, Black Sea 88 000, Pacific 103 000, elsewhere 31 000.

General

The Soviet Union was finally dissolved in December 1991. In early 1992 attempts were being made to form a Commonwealth of Independent States from the Republics of the former Union, but without the Baltic States. The two major Fleets in the North and Pacific are Russian based but the more complicated basing arrangements in the Baltic and Black Seas is going to lead to an allocation of some vessels to the control of the relevant Republics. Whether this will mean, for example, a Ukrainian Coast Guard, or something larger, will take time to resolve.

Main Naval Bases (Russian unless indicated otherwise)

North: Severomorsk (HQ), Motovsky Gulf, Polyarny, Severodvinsk, Gremika
Baltic: Kaliningrad (HQ), St Petersburg, Kronshtadt, Baltiysk, Riga (Latvia), Tallinn (Estonia), Liepaja (Latvia)
Black Sea: Sevastopol (HQ) (Crimea), Tuapse, Poti (Georgia), Balaklava (Crimea), Odessa (Ukraine), Nikolayev (Ukraine), Novorssiysk.
Pacific: Vladivostok (HQ), Sovetskaya Gavan, Magadan, Petropavlovsk, Komsomolsk

Pennant Numbers

The Navy has changes of pennant numbers as a matter of routine every three years and when ships change fleet. The last major overall change of numbers took place in May 1990. Such a list has therefore been omitted in this section as it is of little use identifying ships over any lengthy period.

Building Programme

In early 1992 the building programme was in a state of considerable uncertainty.

Submarines
SSGN—Oscar class at one a year.
SSN—Akula and Sierra classes at about two a year.
SS—Kilo class.
Production in 1991 included three nuclear submarines and three diesel submarines including export models.

Aircraft Carriers
One Kuznetsov class fitting out.
One Ulyanovsk class building.

Cruisers
Fourth Kirov fitting out. Fourth Slava fitting out.

Destroyers
Two Sovremenny class fitting out, four building.
One Udaloy II class fitting out, one building.

Frigates
First Neustrashimy on trials, two building.
Last Krivak III class on trials.
Grisha V class continues.

Light Forces
Tarantul III class continues.
Tarantul class continues for export.
Pauk class continues for export.
Zhuk class coastal patrol craft continue, some for export.
Svetlyak class continues.

Amphibious Forces
Last Ropuchka class fitting out.

Mine Warfare Forces
Natya class continues for export.
Sonya class (MSC) continues including for export.
Lida class (MSI) building.

Air Cushion Vehicles
Pomornik and Tsaplya classes continue.

Auxiliaries
Sorum class ocean tugs continue.
Antonov class cargo ships continue.

Strength of the Fleet

Several types and classes have been revised from new information, not necessarily as new construction.

Type	*Active (Reserve)*	*Building*
Submarines (SSBN)	59	—
Submarines (SSGN)	38	2
Submarines (SSG)	12	—
Submarines (SSN)	62 (5)	7
Submarines (SS)	77 (20)	5
Auxiliary Submarines (SSA(N))	17	—
Aircraft Carriers (CV)	5	2
Helicopter Cruisers (CHG)	2	—
Battle Cruisers (CGN)	3	1
Cruisers (CG)	24	1
Destroyers (DDG)	38	8
Frigates (FFG)	33	1
Frigates (FF)	117	3
Corvettes (Missile)	77	2
Patrol Ships/Radar Pickets	5	—
Fast Attack Craft (Missile)	38	—
Hydrofoils (Missile)	17	—
Fast Attack Craft (Patrol)	157	3
Fast Attack Craft (Hydrofoil)	44	—
Large Patrol Craft	3	—
Coastal Patrol Craft	34	—
River Patrol Craft	142	—
Minelayers	3	—
Minehunters—Ocean	2	—
Minesweepers—Ocean	76	—
Minesweepers—Coastal	99	2
Minesweepers—Inshore	68	6
Minesweeping Boats	15	—
LPDs	3	—
LSTs	41	1
LSMs	32	—
Hovercraft	62	2
Depot, Support and Repair Ships	82	—
Intelligence Collectors (AGI)	58	—
Survey Ships	90 + 42 civilian	—
Oceanographic Research Ships	41 + 66 civilian	—
Missile Range Ships	10	—
Space Associated Ships	0 + 6 civilian	—
Training Ships	12	—
Cable Ships	13	—
Replenishment Tankers	28	—
Support Tankers	25+	—
Special Tankers	13	—
Hospital Ships	5	—
Salvage and Mooring Vessels	54	—
Submarine Rescue Ships	20	—
Transports and Cargo Ships	81+	—
Icebreakers (Nuclear)	0 + 6 civilian	2
Icebreakers	7 + 63 civilian	—

Mercantile Marine

Lloyd's Register of Shipping:
7377 vessels of 26 405 044 tons gross

Approximate Deployments on 1 January 1992

The following figures do not attempt to give an exact deployment of the Navy but offer an approximate apportionment of the totals given above. Traditionally about seven per cent of submarines, cruisers, destroyers, frigates, amphibious forces, depot ships and service forces are deployed 'out of area' — in the Mediterranean, Indian Ocean, West Africa, South China Sea and so on, or on passage. In early 1992 virtually the whole Navy was 'in area'.

Type	*Northern*	*Baltic*	*Black Sea and Caspian*	*Pacific*
SSBN	36	—	—	23
SSGN	21	—	—	17
SSG	4	6	2	—
SSN	48	—	—	14
SS (plus 20 reserve)	27	15	15	20
SSAN, SSA	11	2	2	2
CV	3	—	—	2
CHG	—	—	2	—
CGN	1	1	—	1
CG	9	1	7	7
DDG	14	5	7	12
FFG	6	10	6	11
FF and FFL	40	19	23	35
FAC(M), Missile Corvettes and Hydrofoils (Missile)	22	42	35	33
FAC(P), Patrol Craft	16	125	100	100
MCM Forces	40	67	68	88
LPD	1	—	—	2
LST	8	12	8	13
LSM	6	6	15	5
Hovercraft	7	13	19	23
Depot, Repair and Support Ships	27	11	14	30
Underway Replenishment Ships	7	3	7	11
Support Tankers	10	4	7	4

DELETIONS

Note: Some of the ships listed are still theoretically 'in reserve' but none will go to sea again and a realistic scrapping policy continues with the aim of having 65 per cent of operational ships less than 20 years old. The average age of the ships deleted between 1988 and 1992 is 28 years.

Submarines

1989 1 Echo II (SSGN), 1 Mike (SSN) (sunk), 1 Alfa (SSN), 1 Golf I (SSQ)
1989-90 12 Golf II (SSB), 1 Golf V (SSB), 5 Echo I (SSN), 32 Whiskey (SS), 2 Zulu IV (SS)
1990-91 3 Yankee I (SSBN), 1 Hotel III (SSBN), 1 Papa (SSGN), 1 Charlie (SSGN), 11 Echo II (SSGN), 1 Juliett (SSG), 11 November (SSN), 7 Hotel II (SSN/QN), 34 Whiskey (SS)
1991 1 Yankee I (SSBN), 1 Yankee II (SSBN), 2 Charlie I (SSGN), 3 Echo II (SSGN), 1 Victor I (SSN), 3 Juliett (SSG), 2 Mod Golf (SSQ), 15 Foxtrot (SS), 18 Whiskey (SS)

Cruisers

1989-90 7 Sverdlov (CC and CL)
1990-91 1 Kresta I *(Sevastopol)*, 1 Kynda *(Varyag)*, 3 Sverdlov (CC and CL)
1991 2 Kresta I *(V. A. Drozd, Vladivostok)*

Destroyers

1989 2 Mod Kashin (DDG)
1989-90 3 Mod Kildin (DDG), 4 Kanin (DDG), 7 Sam Kotlin (DDG), 11 Kotlin (DD), 9 Skory (DD)
1990-91 2 Kashin (DDG)
1991 3 Kashin (DDG)

Frigates

1987-88 7 Riga, 3 Petya
1989-90 15 Riga, 5 Mirka, 8 Petya, 1 Koni (to Bulgaria)
1990-91 15 Riga, 3 Mirka, 5 Petya
1991-92 5 Riga, 7 Mirka, 5 Petya

Corvettes (Missile)

1989 1 Nanuchka I

Patrol Ships

1988-89 2 T 58/PGF
1990 1 Purga, 3 T 43/PGR
1991 12 T 58/PGF

Fast Attack Craft

1988-89 1 Slepen, 2 Pchela, 9 Osa
1989 4 Shershen, 1 SO 1
1990-91 25 Osa, 2 Turya, 9 Poti, 6 SO 1, 1 Sarancha
1991-92 8 Osa, 3 Shershen, 29 Poti; 3 SO 1, 5 Stenka

Mine Warfare Vessels

1988-89 1 Yurka, 5 T43, 1 Andryusha, 1 Zhenya, 12 Vanya, 3 Sasha, 1 Olya
1990-91 2 Yurka, 10 Vanya, 1 Sasha, 10 TR 40, 15 K 8, 10 T 43
1991-92 12 Yurka, 10 T 43, 2 Zhenya, 20 Vanya, 3 Ilyusha, 1 Olya

Amphibious Forces

1990-91 7 Polnochny
1991-92 15 SMB 1

Hovercraft

1988-89 2 Gus
1990-91 12 Gus, 1 Aist, 1 Lebed
1991 10 Gus

AGIs

1990-91 3 Okean
1991 4 Mirny, 2 Lentra

Survey Ships

1988-89 1 Samara, 1 Telmovsk, 11 Lentra

Support Ships and Tankers

1988-89 2 Dora
1990-91 2 MP 6, 5 Dnepr, 1 Oskol, *Feolent*
1991 1 Ugra

Space Associated Ships

1990-91 *Kosmonaut Komarov*, 4 Morzhovets
1991 *Nevelsky*, 5 Telnovsk, *Petr Lebedev, Sergey Vavilov, Chukotka*

Transports and Tankers

1988-89 4 Kolomna, 1 Khabarov, 3 Sekstan, 3 Chulyn
1990 2 Komsomol, 2 Muna
1991 *Polyarnik, Sheksna, Indiga, Ural, Ishim*

Icebreaker

1990 Lenin

NAVAL AVIATION

Overall totals: 1950 (some in storage) front-line and training aircraft; 75 000 officers and men.

Tactical deployment: A total of 200 strike/bombers (Badger, Backfire and Blinder), 400 fighter/fighter bombers (Forger, Fencer, Flogger, Fulcrum, Frogfoot and Fitter).
Deployed as follows: Northern 130, Baltic 160, Black Sea 170, Pacific 140.

Tactical support deployment: A total of 180 fixed wing (Badger tankers; Bear D, Badger, Coot, Cub and Blinder reconnaissance and electronic warfare).
Deployed as follows: Northern 60, Baltic 10, Black Sea 30, Pacific 80.
A total of 25 rotary wing (Hormone reconnaissance).
Deployed as follows: Northern 5, Baltic 5, Black Sea 5, Pacific 10.

Anti-submarine warfare deployment: A total of 190 fixed wing (Bear F, May, Mail).
Deployed as follows: Northern 80, Baltic 20, Black Sea 30, Pacific 60.
A total of 240 rotary wing (Helix A, Hormone A, Haze A).
Deployed as follows: Northern 60, Baltic 30, Black Sea 70, Pacific 80.

Mine warfare deployment: A total of 20 (Haze B).

Transport/training deployment: A total of 350 (includes about 15 Flanker B, 10 Fulcrum and 25 Forger).
Deployed as follows: Northern 80, Baltic 90, Black Sea 80, Pacific 100.

Ex-Air Force: In 1990-91 about 680 Air Force aircraft (including Fencers, Floggers, Fulcrums, Fitters and Frogfoots) were transferred to naval air bases. All aircraft that can be embarked in carriers are not subject to CFE restrictions.

TORPEDOES

Note: There are several torpedo types in service. The following table lists broad characteristics.

Type/Designator	*Diameter/Length*	*Role*	*Launch Platform*	*Propulsion*	*Speed/Range*	*Guidance*	*Warhead*	*Remarks*
40	40 cm/4.5 m	ASW	1. Submarine 2. Escorts	Electric	40 kts/15 km (8.1 nm)	Active/passive	100 kg	
45	45 cm/3.9 m	ASW	1. Helicopter 2. SS-N-16	Electric	30 kts/15 km (8.1 nm)	Active/passive	100 kg	
SAET-60	53 cm/7.8 m	Anti-ship	1. Submarine 2. Surface ship	Electric	40 kts/15 km (8.1 nm)	Passive	400 kg	Low yield nuclear variant available
53-65	53 cm/7.8 m	Anti-ship	1. Submarine 2. Surface ship	Turbine	50 kts/25 km (13.8 nm)	Passive/wake	300 kg	Low yield nuclear variant available
ET80-67	53 cm/7.8 m	ASW	1. Submarine 2. Surface ship	Electric	40 kts/15 km (8.1 nm)	Active/passive	300 kg	May be wire-guided
E53-72	53 cm/4.7 m	ASW	1. Aircraft 2. SS-N-14	Electric	40 kts/15 km (8.1 nm)	Active/passive	150 kg	
65	65 cm/10 m	Anti-ship	1. Submarine (Akula, Sierra, Victor III)	Turbine	50 kts/50 km (27.5 nm)	Wake	900 kg	Low yield nuclear variant available

SUBMARINES

Strategic Missile Submarines

Note: The development of Soviet submarine-launched ballistic missiles dates from early trials with German V-2 (A4) missiles. The Lafferentz Project of 1944 was for the launching of V-2 from capsules towed by U-boats. The Soviets probably attempted such operations with the Golem series of missiles without success and then turned to tube launchers.
The deployment of operational missiles dates from the development of the 300 nm surface-launched SS-N-4 missile which was first launched in September 1955. The Zulu V class was converted to carry this missile in two tubes in the fin. All this class now deleted. In 1958 the diesel-propelled Golf class appeared and in 1959 the nuclear Hotel class. Both originally carried the SS-N-4 but from 1962 all the Hotel class and 13 of the Golf class were converted for the SS-N-5 which had the added advantage of dived-launch capability. Both the 4 and 5 missiles carried a megaton head but the apparent lack of an inertial navigation system in the submarines resulted in problems of accuracy. All the Golf and Hotel classes have now been deleted. The SS-N-6 was installed in the Yankee class. In 1971 Mod II and III of SS-N-6, the latter with two MRV warheads, became operational. In the mid-1970s the SS-N-17, with solid propellant, was fitted in one converted Yankee.
In the late 1960s the SS-N-8 was first tested and this was fitted in the Delta I class in 1972 and subsequently the Delta II in 1975. This is a much larger missile than the SS-N-6 and required the increased size of the Delta classes to house it. In the latter half of the 1970s the SS-N-18 appeared in the Delta III class and comes in three versions. Mod 1 and Mod 3 have three and seven MIRV respectively. Mod 2 has a single RV.
In early 1980 a new type of solid-fuelled SLBM, SS-N-20, was tested. This is larger than SS-N-18, carries a seven to ten MIRV head and is in the Typhoon class.
In 1983 testing of SS-N-23 began; this missile is carried in the Delta IV class. Operational in 1986 with seven to ten MIRV. At least two types of new ballistic missiles are being developed and may be retrofitted in existing classes.
With both Delta IV and Typhoon programmes terminated a new class of SSBN is expected in the mid-1990s.
In addition to the ballistic missiles a sea-launched cruise missile (SLCM), the SS-N-21, is operational. Its primary role is nuclear strike against land targets. Its size is compatible with submarine torpedo tubes and it is probably carried in all modern classes of SSN. A larger missile of this type, SS-NX-24, was under test in 1989/90 in a modified Yankee SSN but this programme may have been abandoned or suspended in 1991.

6 TYPHOON CLASS (SSBN)

Displacement, tons: 21 500 surfaced; 26 500 dived
Dimensions, feet (metres): 562.7 oa; 541.3 wl × 80.7 × 42.7 *(171.5; 165 × 24.6 × 13)*
Main machinery: Nuclear; 2 PWR; 320 MW; 2 turbines; 81 600 hp(m) *(60 MW)*; 2 shafts; shrouded props
Speed, knots: 26 dived; 19 surfaced
Complement: 150 (50 officers). 2 crews

Missiles: SLBM: 20 SS-N-20 Sturgeon; three stage solid fuel rocket; stellar inertial guidance to 8300 km *(4500 nm)*; warhead nuclear 6-9 MIRV each of 100 kT; CEP 500 m. 2 missiles fired from the first of class in 15 seconds. May be modified to take an improved version of the Sturgeon.
SAM: There are suggestions that this class may have a SAM capability.
A/S: SS-N-15 fired from 21 in *(533 mm)* tubes; inertial flight to 37 km *(20 nm)*; warhead nuclear 200 kT.
SS-N-16 fired from 25.6 in *(650 mm)* tubes; inertial flight to 120 km *(65 nm)*; payload Type 45 torpedo; active/passive homing to 15 km *(8.1 nm)* at 30 kts; warhead 100 kg. There is also a 16B version with a nuclear warhead.
Torpedoes: 2—21 in *(533 mm)* and 4—25.6 in *(650 mm)* tubes. Type 53; dual purpose; pattern active/passive homing up to 20 km *(10.8 nm)* at up to 45 kts; warhead 400 kg or low yield nuclear and Type 65; anti-surface; pattern active/passive wake homing to 50 km *(27.5 nm)* at 50 kts; warhead 900 kg or low yield nuclear. The weapon load includes a combination of 36 torpedoes and A/S missiles.
Mines: Could be carried in lieu of torpedoes.
Countermeasures: ESM: Rim Hat; radar warning. Park Lamp D/F.
Radars: Surface search: Snoop Pair; I/J band.
Sonars: Shark Gill; hull-mounted; passive/active search and attack; low/medium frequency.
Mouse Roar; hull-mounted; active attack; high frequency.

Programmes: This is the largest type of submarine ever built. The first was begun in 1977 and launched at Severodvinsk in September 1980 (in service 1982) and the second in September 1982 entering service in late 1983. The third was commissioned in late 1984, the fourth followed a year later, the fifth in 1987 and the sixth in 1989. Statements by senior officers indicate disenchantment with these very large submarines and no more of this class are to be completed. One is called *Miskiy Komsomolets*. Reported in Russia as being called the Akula class.
Structure: Two separate 8.5 m diameter hulls covered by a single outer free-flood hull with anechoic Cluster Guard tiles plus separate 6 m diameter pressure-tight compartments in the fin and fore-ends. There is a large separation between the outer and inner hulls along the sides. The unique features of Typhoon are her enormous size and the fact that the missile tubes are mounted forward of the fin. The positioning of the launch tubes means a fully integrated weapons area in the bow section leaving space abaft the fin for the provision of two nuclear reactors, one in each hull—probably needed to achieve a reasonable speed with this huge hull. The fin configuration indicates a designed capability to break through ice cover possibly up to 3 m thick; the retractable forward hydroplanes, the rounded hull and the shape of the fin are all related to under-ice operations. Diving depth, 1000 ft *(300 m)*.
Operational: Strategic targets are within range from anywhere in the world. Two VLF/ELF communication buoys are fitted. VLF navigation system for under-ice operations. Pert Spring SATCOM mast, Cod Eye radiometric sextant and Kremmny 2 IFF. All are based in the Northern Fleet.

TYPHOON *1991, S. Breyer*

TYPHOON

5/1991

TYPHOON *1991, S. Breyer*

TYPHOON *1990*

7 DELTA IV CLASS (SSBN)

Displacement, tons: 10 750 surfaced; 12 150 dived
Dimensions, feet (metres): 544.6 oa; 518.4 wl × 39.4 × 28.5 *(166; 158 × 12 × 8.7)*
Main machinery: Nuclear; 2 PWR; 160 MW; 2 turbines; 37 400 hp(m) *(27.5 MW)* 2 shafts
Speed, knots: 24 dived; 19 surfaced
Complement: 130

Missiles: SLBM: 16 SS-N-23 Skiff; three stage liquid fuel rocket; stellar inertial guidance to 8300 km *(4500 nm)*; warhead nuclear 10 MIRV each of 100 kT; CEP 500 m. Same diameter as SS-N-18 but longer.
Torpedoes: 4—21 in *(533 mm)* and 2—25.6 in *(650 nm)* tubes. Type 53; dual purpose; pattern active/passive homing up to 20 km *(10.8 nm)* at up to 45 kts; warhead 400 kg or low yield nuclear and Type 65; anti-surface; pattern active/passive wake homing to 50 km *(27.5 nm)* at 50 kts; warhead 900 kg or low yield nuclear. Total of 18 weapons.
Countermeasures: ESM: Brick Pulp/Group; radar warning. Park Lamp D/F.
Radars: Surface search: Snoop Tray; I band.
Sonars: Shark Gill; hull-mounted; passive/active search and attack; low/medium frequency.
Mouse Roar; hull-mounted; active attack; high frequency.

Programmes: First of class launched February 1984 and commissioned later that year. All built at Severodvinsk and launched at the rate of about one per year. This programme completed in late 1990. A follow-on class is expected in the mid-1990s.
Structure: A slim fitting is sited on the after fin which is reminiscent of a similar tube in one of the November class in the early 1980s. This may be a form of dispenser for a buoyant communications wire aerial. The other distinguishing feature, apart from the size being greater than Delta III, is the pressure-tight fitting on the after end of the missile tube housing, which may be a TV camera to monitor communications buoy and wire retrieval operations. Also there are two 650 mm torpedo tubes. Diving depth, 1000 ft *(300 m)*. The outer casing has a continuous acoustic coating.
Operational: Two VLF/ELF communication buoys. Navigation systems include SATNAV, SINS, Cod Eye. Pert Spring SATCOM. A modified and more accurate version of SS-N-23 was tested at sea in 1988 bringing the CEP down from 900 m to 500 m. All based in the Northern Fleet.

DELTA IV *8/1991*

14 DELTA III CLASS (SSBN)

Displacement, tons: 10 000 surfaced; 11 700 dived
Dimensions, feet (metres): 524.9 oa; 498.7 wl × 39.4 × 28.5 *(160; 152 × 12 × 8.7)*
Main machinery: Nuclear; 2 PWR; 160 MW; 2 turbines; 37 400 hp(m) *(27.5 MW)*; 2 shafts
Speed, knots: 24 dived; 19 surfaced
Complement: 130

Missiles: SLBM: 16 SS-N-18 Stingray; two stage liquid fuel rocket with post boost vehicle (PBV); stellar inertial guidance; 3 variants:
Mod 1; range 6500 km *(3500 nm)*; warhead nuclear 3 MIRV each of 200 kT; CEP 900 m.
Mod 2; range 8000 km *(4320 nm)*; warhead nuclear 450 kT; CEP 900 m.
Mod 3; range 6500 km *(3500 nm)*; warhead nuclear 7 MIRV 100 kT; CEP 900 m.
Mods 1 and 3 are the first MIRV SLBMs in Soviet service. SS-N-23 retrofitted in some (see Delta IV for details).
Torpedoes: 6—21 in *(533 mm)* tubes. 18 Type 53; dual purpose; pattern active/passive homing up to 20 km *(10.8 nm)* at up to 45 kts; warhead 400 kg or low yield nuclear.
Countermeasures: ESM: Brick Pulp/Group; radar warning. Park Lamp D/F.
Radars: Surface search: Snoop Tray; I band.
Sonars: Shark Teeth; hull-mounted; passive/active search and attack; low/medium frequency.
Mouse Roar; hull-mounted; active attack; high frequency.

Programmes: Built at Severodvinsk 402. Completed 1976-1982.
Modernisation: SS-N-23 Skiff has been retrofitted in some of this class.
Structure: The missile casing is higher than in Delta II class to accommodate SS-N-18 missiles which are longer than the SS-N-8 of the Delta II class. The outer casing has a continuous 'acoustic' coating. Diving depth, 1000 ft *(300 m)*.
Operational: ELF/VLF communications with floating aerial and buoy; UHF and SHF aerials. Navigation equipment includes Cod Eye radiometric sextant, SATNAV, SINS and Omega. Pert Spring SATCOM. Kremmny 2 IFF. Nine of the class are based in the Pacific and five in the Northern Fleet.

DELTA III *9/1991*

DELTA III *1990*

4 DELTA II CLASS (SSBN)

Displacement, tons: 9700 surfaced; 11 300 dived
Dimensions, feet (metres): 508.4 oa; 498.7 wl × 39.4 × 28.5 *(155; 152 × 12 × 8.7)*
Main machinery: Nuclear; 2 PWR; 160 MW; 2 turbines; 37 400 hp(m) *(27.5 MW)*; 2 shafts
Speed, knots: 24 dived; 19 surfaced
Complement: 130

Missiles: SLBM: 16 SS-N-8 Sawfly; 2-stage liquid fuel rocket; stellar inertial guidance; 2 variants:
Mod 1; range 7800 km *(4210 nm)*; warhead nuclear 1.2 MT; CEP 400 m.
Mod 2; range 9100 km *(4910 nm)*; warhead nuclear 2 MIRV each of 800 kT; CEP 400 m.
Torpedoes: 6—21 in *(533 mm)* bow tubes. 18 Type 53; dual purpose; pattern active/passive homing up to 20 km *(10.8 nm)* at up to 45 kts; warhead 400 kg or low yield nuclear.
Countermeasures: ESM: Brick Pulp/Group; radar warning.
Radars: Surface search: Snoop Tray; I band.
Sonars: Shark Teeth; hull-mounted; passive/active search and attack; low/medium frequency.
Mouse Roar; hull-mounted; active attack; high frequency.

Programmes: Building yard—Severodvinsk. First appeared in 1976. Further construction cancelled with the advent of SS-N-18 and the Delta III class.
Structure: A larger edition of Delta I designed to carry four extra missile tubes and suffering a speed reduction as a result. Has a straight run on the after part of the missile casing. The outer casing has a continuous 'acoustic' coating. Diving depth, 1000 ft *(300 m)*.
Operational: ELF/VLF communications with floating aerial and buoy; UHF and SHF aerials. Navigation equipment includes SATNAV, SINS, Omega, Cod Eye radiometric sextant. Pert Spring SATCOM. Kremmny 2 IFF. All based in the Northern Fleet.

DELTA II *8/1991*

18 DELTA I CLASS (SSBN)

Displacement, tons: 8700 surfaced; 10 200 dived
Dimensions, feet (metres): 459.3 oa; 446.2 wl × 39.4 × 28.5 *(140; 136 × 12 × 8.7)*
Main machinery: Nuclear; 2 PWR; 160 MW; 2 turbines; 37 400 hp(m) *(27.5 MW)*; 2 shafts
Speed, knots: 25 dived; 19 surfaced
Complement: 120

Missiles: SLBM: 12—SS-N-8 Sawfly; 2-stage liquid fuel rocket; stellar inertial guidance; 2 variants:
Mod 1; range 7800 km *(4210 nm)*; warhead nuclear 1.2 MT; CEP 400 m.
Mod 2; range 9100 km *(4910 nm)*; warhead nuclear 2 MIRV each of 800 kT; CEP 400 m.
Torpedoes: 6—21 in *(533 mm)* bow tubes. 18 Type 53; dual purpose; pattern active/passive homing up to 20 km *(10.8 nm)* at up to 45 kts; warhead 400 kg or low yield nuclear.
Countermeasures: ESM: Brick Pulp/Group; radar warning. Park Lamp D/F.
Radars: Surface search: Snoop Tray; I band.
Sonars: Shark Teeth; hull-mounted; passive/active search and attack; low/medium frequency.
Mouse Roar; hull-mounted; active attack; high frequency.

Programmes: The first of this class, an advance on the Yankee class SSBNs, was laid down at Severodvinsk in 1969 and completed in 1972. Programme completed 1972-77. Building yards—Severodvinsk 402 (10) and Komsomolsk (8).
Structure: The longer-range SS-N-8 missiles are of greater length than the SS-N-6s and, as this length cannot be accommodated below the keel, they stand several feet proud of the after-casing. At the same time the need to compensate for the additional top-weight would seem to be the reason for the reduction to 12 missiles in this class. The outer casing has a continuous 'acoustic' coating. Diving depth, 1000 ft *(300 m)*.
Operational: ELF/VLF communications with floating aerial and buoy; UHF and SHF aerials. Cod Eye radiometric sextant. Kremmny 2 IFF. In common with all the Delta class variations, this submarine is ill designed for under-ice operations. Nine based in the North, nine in the Pacific.

DELTA I *1990*

10 YANKEE I CLASS (SSBN)

Displacement, tons: 8000 surfaced; 9450 dived
Dimensions, feet (metres): 426.4 × 38 × 26.2 *(130 × 11.6 × 8)*
Main machinery: Nuclear; 2 PWR; 160 MW; 2 turbines; 37 400 hp(m) *(27.5 MW)*; 2 shafts
Speed, knots: 26.5 dived; 20 surfaced
Complement: 120

Missiles: SLBM: 16 SS-N-6 Serb; single-stage liquid fuel rocket; inertial guidance; 2 variants:
Mod 1; range 2400 km *(1300 nm)*; warhead nuclear 1 MT; CEP 1300 m.
Mod 3; range 3000 km *(1620 nm)*; warhead 2 MRV each of 500 kT; CEP 1300 m.
Launch rate for a full salvo is reported as less than 2 minutes.
Torpedoes: 6—21 in *(533 mm)* tubes. 18 Type 53; dual purpose; pattern active/passive homing up to 20 km *(10.8 nm)* at up to 45 kts; warhead 400 kg or low yield nuclear.
Countermeasures: ESM: Brick Group; radar warning. Park Lamp D/F.
Radars: Surface search: Snoop Tray; I band.
Sonars: Shark Teeth; hull-mounted; passive/active search and attack; low/medium frequency.
Mouse Roar; hull-mounted; active attack; high frequency

Programmes: The first of the class was laid down in 1963-64 and delivered late 1967 and the programme then accelerated with output rising to six to eight a year in the period around 1970. The last one was completed in 1974. Construction took place at Severodvinsk 402 (first laid down in 1965) and Komsomolsk. The original deployment of this class was to the eastern seaboard of the US giving a coverage at least as far as the Mississippi. Increase in numbers allowed a Pacific patrol to be established off California in 1971 providing coverage from the western seaboard to the eastern side of the Rockies. Of the total of 34 built, 10 are still fitted with SS-N-6; one (Yankee II) was converted in 1971-76 for 12 SS-N-17. 22 (see entries under SSGN, SSN and SSAN) have had their missile tubes removed (the first in 1978) in order to keep within 62 SSBN and 950 SLBM limit imposed by SALT 1. The future of the others depends on the START treaty and the willingness of the Russian hierarchy to sacrifice more of its 'controlled' seaborne strategic weapons while uncertainty surounds many land-based systems.
Structure: Design is similar to USS *Ethan Allen* (now deleted) with vertical tubes in two rows of eight and fin-mounted fore-planes; the first time the Navy had used this arrangement. The outer casing has a continuous 'acoustic' coating. Diving depth, 1000 ft *(300 m)*.
Operational: Fitted for ELF communications with floating aerial and VLF buoy. VHF and SHF aerials. Navigation equipment includes SATNAV, SINS, Omega and Cod Eye radiometric sextant. Pert Spring SATCOM. Kremmny 2 IFF. One Yankee I sank in Western Atlantic after an internal explosion 6 October 1986 while patrolling 600 miles north of Bermuda. The Yankee II paid off in 1991 as expected.

YANKEE I *1987*

YANKEE I *1990*

Cruise Missile Submarines

Note: The first operational appearance of cruise missiles at sea in submarines was in the Twin-Cylinder variant of the Whiskey class in 1958-60. These carried two SS-N-3C (Shaddock) missiles with a maximum range of approximately 450 nm against shore targets. A capability against ships appears doubtful in view of the targetting problems. The fact that the US Navy had carried out trials with Loon missiles in the submarines *Cusk* and *Carbonero* in 1948-49 and soon afterwards converted several submarines, some to fire and some to guide the 80 ft Regulus cruise missile, shows that at this stage the Navy had lagged far behind. In fact in the Fiscal Year 1956 programme the US Navy included the first nuclear-propelled cruise missile submarine *Halibut*, designed to carry five 560 mile Regulus I missiles. By 1965 the cruise missile programme had been abandoned by the US. Meanwhile the Navy had gone ahead with the production of the first nuclear-propelled cruise missile submarine (Echo I) in the early 1960s with six SS-N-3C, again for use against shore targets. With the advent of the Yankee class in the late 1970s the Echo I class had its missiles removed and was converted to an SSN in the early 1970s. The Echo I was followed very closely by the Echo II nuclears and the conventional Juliett class which were built over the same period (1961-68), armed with eight and four SS-N-3A missiles respectively as a counter to the threat of the US carriers with their nuclear strike capability. The SS-N-3As have so far been replaced by SS-N-12 in about 14 of the Echo II class, seven each in the Northern and Pacific Fleets. By 1968 both production lines had stopped when the first Charlie class appeared with underwater launch capability for its SS-N-7 missiles. The problem which had faced all the earlier boats, that of having to surface to launch, had been overcome. An improved design of Charlie I (Charlie II) and the single unit of the Papa class (since deleted) appeared in the early 1970s with SS-N-9 missiles to be followed by the launch of the giant Oscar in 1980 with 24 SS-N-19 supersonic missiles.

The arrival of SS-N-21, a sea launched land attack cruise missile with an estimated range of 1600 nm and a tube-launch capability for all modern classes of SSN, has already started to change the balance of cruise missile submarines. A larger land attack missile, SS-NX-24 was fitted in a converted Yankee class for trials in 1989/90 but this programme seems to have been abandoned or suspended in 1991.

All these submarines with the exception of Echo II and Juliett classes are coated with Cluster Guard anechoic tiles. All are capable of laying mines from their torpedo tubes.

6 CHARLIE II CLASS (SSGN)

Displacement, tons: 4500 surfaced; 5550 dived
Dimensions, feet (metres): 334.6 oa; 324.8 wl × 32.5 × 25.6 *(102; 99 × 9.9 × 7.8)*
Main machinery: Nuclear; 1 PWR; 65 MW; 1 turbine; 20 000 hp(m) *(15 MW)*; 1 shaft
Speed, knots: 25 dived; 15 surfaced
Complement: 90

Missiles: SSM: 8 SS-N-9 Siren; IR and active radar homing to 110 km *(60 nm)* at 0.9 Mach; warhead nuclear 250 kT or HE 500 kg.
A/S: SS-N-15 fired from 21 in *(533 mm)* tubes; inertial flight to 37 km *(20 nm)*; warhead nuclear 200 kT.
Torpedoes: 6—21 in *(533 mm)* tubes. Type 53; dual purpose; pattern active/passive homing up to 20 km *(10.8 nm)* at up to 45 kts; warhead 400 kg or low yield nuclear. Total of 14 tube-launched weapons.
Countermeasures: ESM: Stop Light and Brick Group; radar warning. Park Lamp D/F.
Radars: Surface search: Snoop Tray; I band.
Sonars: Shark Fin; hull-mounted; passive/active search and attack; low/medium frequency.
Mouse Roar; hull-mounted; active attack; high frequency.

Programmes: Built at Gorky from 1973-80.
Structure: Enlarged Charlie class. The extra length is probably required for the additional fire control equipment for the longer range SS-N-9 missiles. The general remarks for Charlie I apply to this class; the platform on the fin is fitted in the majority of the six boats as well as the platform aft. Diving depth, 1000 ft *(300 m)*.
Operational: VLF communications buoy. Pert Spring SATCOM. Kremmny 2 IFF. All based in the Northern Fleet.

CHARLIE II *1989*

8 CHARLIE I CLASS (SSGN)

Displacement, tons: 4000 surfaced; 5000 dived
Dimensions, feet (metres): 308.3 oa; 295.3 wl × 32.5 × 24.6 *(94; 90 × 9.9 × 7.5)*
Main machinery: Nuclear; 1 PWR; 65 MW; 1 turbine; 15 000 hp(m) *(11 MW)*; 1 shaft; 2 spinners
Speed, knots: 26 dived; 15 surfaced
Complement: 100

Missiles: SSM: 8 SS-N-7; active radar homing to 64 km *(35 nm)* at 0.9 Mach; warhead nuclear 200 kT or HE 500 kg. The 8 SSM tubes are mounted outside the pressure hull with tube doors which hinge upwards.
A/S: SS-N-15 fired from 21 in *(533 mm)* tubes; inertial flight to 37 km *(20 nm)*; warhead nuclear 200 kT.
Torpedoes: 6—21 in *(533 mm)* bow tubes. Type 53; dual purpose; pattern active/passive homing up to 20 km *(10.8 nm)* at up to 45 kts; warhead 400 kg or low yield nuclear. Total of 14 tube-launched weapons.
Countermeasures: ESM: Stop Light and Brick Group; radar warning. Park Lamp D/F.
Radars: Surface search: Snoop Tray; I band.
Sonars: Shark Fin; hull-mounted; passive/active search and attack; low/medium frequency.

Programmes: A class of cruise missile submarines built at Gorky 1967-72.
Structure: The first Soviet SSGNs capable of launching SSMs without having to surface. Although similar in some respects to the Victor class, visible differences include the bulge at the bow, the almost vertical drop of the forward end of the fin, a slightly lower after casing and a different arrangement of free-flood holes in the casing. Some of this class have a raised platform around the forward part of the fin as well as a similar addition around the stern fin. This may be designed to smooth the flow of water in these areas. There is single improved reactor design vice the two in the Victor class resulting in a loss of some five knots. Diving depth, 1000 ft *(300 m)*.
Operational: All are based in the Pacific. One sank off Petropavlovsk in June 1983 and was subsequently salvaged but scrapped in 1987. The class is being paid off.
Sales: One on lease to India in January 1988 and returned for scrapping in January 1991. There are no plans to lease a second.

CHARLIE I *1986*

7 + 3 OSCAR II and 2 OSCAR I CLASSES (SSGN)

Displacement, tons: 10 200 surfaced; 12 500 dived (Oscar I); 10 700 surfaced; 13 500 dived (Oscar II)
Dimensions, feet (metres): 469.2; 505.2 (Oscar II) × 59.7 × 29.5 *(143; 154 × 18.2 × 9)*
Main machinery: Nuclear; 2 PWR; 200 MW; 2 turbines; 75 000 hp(m) *(55 MW)*; 2 shafts; 2 spinners
Speed, knots: 30; 28 (Oscar II) dived; 19 surfaced
Complement: 135

Missiles: SSM: 24 SS-N-19 Shipwreck (improved SS-N-12 with lower flight profile); inertial with command update guidance; active radar homing to 20-550 km *(10.8-300 nm)* at 1.6 Mach; warhead 750 kg HE or nuclear.
A/S: SS-N-15 fired from 21 in *(533 mm)* tubes; inertial flight to 37 km *(20 nm)*; warhead nuclear 200 kT.
SS-N-16 fired from 25.6 in *(650 mm)* tubes; inertial flight to 120 km *(65 nm)*; payload Type 45 torpedo; active passive homing to 15 km *(8.1 nm)* at 40 kts; warhead 100 kg. There is also a 16B version with a nuclear warhead.
Torpedoes: 4—21 in *(533 mm)* and 4—25.6 in *(650 mm)* tubes. Type 53; dual purpose; pattern active/passive homing up to 20 km *(10.8 nm)* at up to 45 kts; warhead 400 kg or low yield nuclear and Type 65; anti-surface; pattern active/passive wake homing to 50 km *(27.5 nm)* at 50 kts; warhead 900 kg or low yield nuclear. Total of 24 weapons including tube-launched A/S missiles.
Countermeasures: ESM: Bald Head/Rim Hat; radar warning. Park Lamp D/F.
Fire control: Punch Bowl for third party targeting.
Radars: Surface search: Snoop Head/Pair; I band.
Sonars: Shark Gill; hull-mounted; passive/active search and attack; low/medium frequency.
Mouse Roar; hull-mounted; active attack; high frequency.

Programmes: First Oscar I class laid down at Severodvinsk in 1978 and launched in Spring 1980. Started trials late 1980. Second completed in 1982. The first Oscar II completed in 1985, a second in 1986, a third in 1988, a fourth in 1989, two more in 1990 and one in 1991. Still building at one a year. Reported in Russia as being called the Plark or Granit class.
Structure: SSM missile tubes are in banks of 12 either side and external to the 8.5 m diameter pressure hull; they are inclined at 40° with one hatch covering each pair, the whole resulting in the very large beam. The position of the missile tubes provides a large gap of some 3 m between the outer and inner hulls. The Oscar II has a hull lengthened by 36.1 ft *(11 m)* and an increased displacement of 1400 tons, presumably as the result of some deficiency found in first of class trials, which could not have been corrected in time to change hull number two. Alternatively it could have something to do with incorporating an SS-N-24 weapon system in due course. Diving depth, 1000 ft *(300 m)*.
Operational: ELF/VLF communications buoy. All but the first of class have a tube on the rudder fin as in Delta IV which may be used for dispensing a VLF floating aerial. Pert Spring SATCOM. Based in both Northern and Pacific Fleets.

OSCAR I  *1989*

OSCAR II *1990*

OSCAR II

1987

14 ECHO II CLASS (SSGN)

Displacement, tons: 4800 surfaced; 5800 dived
Dimensions, feet (metres): 390.4 × 30.2 × 22.6 *(119 × 9.2 × 6.9)*
Main machinery: Nuclear; 2 PWR, 17 500 hp(m) *(13 MW)*; 2 turbines; 30 000 hp(m) *(22 MW)*; 2 shafts
Speed, knots: 24 dived; 18 surfaced
Complement: 90

Missiles: SSM: Either 8 SS-N-12 Sandbox (in 12 of the class); inertial guidance with command update; active radar homing to 550 km *(300 nm)* at 1.7 + Mach; warhead nuclear 350 kT or HE 1000 kg; altitude 10 668 m *(35 000 ft)* or 8 SS-N-3C Shaddock (in 2 of the class); command guidance; active radar or IR homing to 460 km *(250 nm)* at 1.1 Mach; warhead nuclear 350 kT or HE 1000 kg.
Torpedoes: 6—21 in *(533 mm)* bow tubes. Type 53; dual purpose; pattern active/passive homing up to 20 km *(10.8 nm)* at up to 45 kts; warhead 400 kg or low yield nuclear.
4—16 in *(406 mm)* stern tubes. Type 40; anti-submarine; active/passive homing up to 15 km *(8 nm)* at up to 40 kts; warhead 100-150 kg. Total of 20 torpedoes carried.
Countermeasures: ESM: Stop Light and Brick Pulp or Squid Head; radar warning. Quad Loop D/F.
Radars: Surface search: Snoop Tray/Snoop Slab; I band.
Fire control: Front Piece/Front Door; F band (for SS-N-3A mid-course guidance).
Sonars: Hull-mounted; passive/active search and attack; medium frequency.

ECHO II *1990*

Programmes: The decision to produce this class may have been due to the availability of building ways because of a break in SSBN production between the Hotel and Yankee classes in the first half of the 1960s, the development of the SS-N-3A cruise missile with an anti-ship capability and the need to counter the threat from Western strike carriers. Built at Severodvinsk and Komsomolsk between 1961 and 1967.

Structure: SS-N-3A guidance radar is housed in the forward section of fin which opens outward. In SS-N-12 boats a large radome Punch Bowl, used for satellite missile targeting, is housed in the fin and raised like any other mast. At the after end of the fin there is a hinged communications aerial which stows in a depression in the casing. There is no acoustic coating. Diving depth, 650 ft *(200 m)*.

Operational: The submarine needs to be fully surfaced for about 20 minutes to launch all its missiles. After an accident to the reactor primary cooling system in June 1989, it was announced that the H, E and N classes would be prematurely retired. This is happening with great rapidity and the remainder of the class seem likely to be deleted by the end of 1992. Based in the Northern and Pacific Fleets.

1 YANKEE CLASS (conversion) (SSGN)

(see also Yankee Notch class in *Attack Submarine* section)

Displacement, tons: 12 200 dived
Dimensions, feet (metres): 501.8 × 49.2 × 26.2 *(153 × 15 × 8)*
Main machinery: Nuclear; 2 PWR; 160 MW; 2 turbines; 37 400 hp(m) *(27.5 MW)*; 2 shafts
Speed, knots: 22 dived
Complement: 120

Missiles: SLCM: 12 SS-NX-24; inertial guidance; terrain following to 4000 km *(2200 nm)* at 2 Mach; warhead nuclear 1 MT. 6 tubes are sited on either side abaft the fin, inclined and built in outside the pressure hull.
Torpedoes: 6—21 in *(533 mm)* bow tubes. Type 53; dual purpose; pattern active/passive homing up to 20 km *(10.8 nm)* at up to 45 kts; warhead 400 kg or low yield nuclear.
Countermeasures: ESM: Brick Pulp; radar warning.
Radars: Surface search: Snoop Tray; I band.
Sonars: Shark Fin; hull-mounted; passive/active search and attack; low/medium frequency.

Programmes: Completed conversion in 1983 as the trials submarine for SSN-X-24, a new long-range SLCM which may be incorporated in an Oscar variant or retrofitted into existing Oscar IIs. Trials are taking longer than expected and may even have been suspended or abandoned. Others of the Yankee class ex-SSBNs have been modified as SSNs and to carry SS-N-21 torpedo tube-launched SLCMs, and also as SSANs.
Structure: A lengthened section of some 23 m added in place of original SLBM tubes. The configuration of the SLCM launchers has also increased the beam dimensions and the fin is rounder in appearance. Diving depth, 1000 ft *(300 m)*.

12 JULIETT CLASS (SSG)

Displacement, tons: 3150 surfaced; 3850 dived
Dimensions, feet (metres): 285.4 × 32.8 × 23 *(87 × 10 × 7)*
Main machinery: Direct drive or diesel-electric; 2 Type D43 diesels; 4000 hp(m) *(3 MW)*; 2 motors; 4000 hp(m) *(3 MW)*; 2 shafts
Speed, knots: 19 surfaced; 11 dived; 8 snorting
Range, miles: 9000 at 8 kts snorting
Complement: 79

Missiles: SSM: 4 SS-N-12 Sandbox; inertial guidance with command update; active radar homing to 550 km *(300 nm)* at 1.7 Mach; warhead nuclear 350 kT or HE 1000 kg; altitude 10 668 m *(35 000 ft)* or 4 SS-N-3C Shaddock; command guidance; active radar or IR homing to 460 km *(250 nm)* at 1.1 Mach; warhead nuclear 350 kT or HE 1000 kg. The tubes elevate to 20°.
Torpedoes: 6—21 in *(533 mm)* bow tubes. 18 Type 53; dual purpose; pattern active/passive homing up to 20 km *(10.8 nm)* at up to 45 kts; warhead 400 kg or low yield nuclear.
4—15.7 in *(400 mm)* stern tubes; 4 Type 40; active/passive homing to 15 km *(8.1 nm)* at 40 kts; warhead 100 kg.
Countermeasures: ESM: Stop Light; radar warning. Quad Loop D/F.
Radars: Surface search: Snoop Slab; I band.
Fire control: Front Door; F band (for SSM mid-course guidance).
Sonars: Pike Jaw; hull-mounted; passive/active search and attack; medium/high frequency.

Programmes: Completed between 1961 and 1968 at Gorky and was the logical continuation of the Whiskey class conversions.
Structure: The massive casing and four missile launchers either end of the long, fairly low fin make this an unmistakable class. At least one has the large Punch Bowl radome in the fin similar to Echo II. This is a receiver for satellite targeting information for an SS-N-12 retrofit. Diving depth, 650 ft *(200 m)*.
Operational: There are suggestions that silver zinc batteries are installed. This would give an increased dived endurance. In 1980-81 three were transferred from the Northern Fleet to the Baltic Fleet, probably establishing a pattern of patrols in that area. Two more were transferred in 1989 but operational patrols have now stopped and the class began paying off in 1990.

JULIETT *1988*

JULIETT *10/1991*

Attack Submarines

Note: The use of nuclear power for marine propulsion was developed from 1950 onwards, the first submarine reactor being put in hand in 1953 probably about the same time as a larger reactor for the icebreaker *Lenin* was under construction. The latter commissioned in September 1959, a year after the first of the November class entered service. These submarines, of which 14 were built between 1958-63, had a very long hull, and this long form was also used in the Hotel and Echo I designs. It was a new concept designed to take full advantage of the available horsepower and, in the November class, was fitted with a small streamlined fin.

No prototype was produced before series production of the November class began and this was also true for the Victor class which followed after a four year pause in 1967. Since the early November class provided sea-experience of this new form of submarine some years of redesign were therefore available before the first Victor was laid down. The ability to produce hydrodynamically advanced hull forms was further proved by the efficiency of the Victor and her near sister the Charlie. Five years after the first Victor came the Victor II, an enlarged edition whose increase in size may be due to the fitting of the new tube-launched ASW system, SS-N-15, probably similar to the Subroc of the US Navy. This again was followed six years later by the Victor III, slightly longer than the Victor II.

The Alfa class was a new concept of attack submarine built in 1970-83 with a length/beam ratio very different from its predecessors, much improved propulsion plant with high speeds and a very deep diving depth. This was probably an extended research and development project with a limited production run. Some of this technology was reflected in the Mike and Sierra classes which appeared in 1983. The Akula class which is a more traditional design successor of the Victor III class, appeared first in 1984. The single Mike was sunk in an accident in April 1989 and subsequent Soviet official statements indicated a diving depth of 1000 m with a titanium reinforced hull and the use of explosive charges to blow main ballast tanks at great depths. An attempt is being made to salvage the Mike but by 1992 there were problems with funding the operation.

A significant change in the capability of the fleet submarines has resulted from the introduction of SS-N-21, a tube-launched land attack cruise missile with a 1600 nm range. The stern pod on the rudder of the Victor III, Sierra, Akula and one converted Yankee is a towed array dispenser which has taken several years to become operational, and may not be very effective.

The last of the November class paid off in mid-1991. All Fleet submarines are coated with Cluster Guard anechoic tiles. All submarines are capable of laying mines from their torpedo tubes. Newer classes are increasingly being fitted with environmental sensors for measuring discontinuities caused by the passage of a submarine in deep water.

9 + 4 AKULA CLASS (SSN)

Displacement, tons: 7500 surfaced; 9100 dived
Dimensions, feet (metres): 360.1 oa; 337.9 wl × 45.9 × 34.1 *(110; 103 × 14 × 10.4)*
Main machinery: Nuclear; 2 PWR; 200 MW; 2 turbines; 47 600 hp(m) *(35 MW)*; 1 shaft; 2 spinners
Speed, knots: 32 dived; 18 surfaced
Complement: 90 approx

Missiles: SLCM: SS-N-21 Sampson fired from 21 in *(533 mm)* tubes; land-attack; inertial/terrain following to 3000 km *(1620 nm)* at 0.7 Mach; warhead nuclear 200 kT. CEP 150 m. Probably flies at a height of about 200 m.
A/S: SS-N-15 fired from 21 in *(533 mm)* tubes; inertial flight to 37 km *(20 nm)*; warhead nuclear 200 kT.
SS-N-16 fired from 25.6 in *(650 mm)* tubes; inertial flight to 120 km *(65 nm)*; payload Type 45 torpedo; warhead 100 kg. There is also a 16B version with a nuclear warhead.
Torpedoes: 4—21 in *(533 mm)* and 4—25.6 in *(650 mm)* tubes. Type 53; dual purpose; pattern active/passive homing up to 20 km *(10.8 nm)* at up to 45 kts; warhead 400 kg or low yield nuclear and Type 65; anti-surface; pattern active/passive wake homing to 50 km *(27.5 nm)* at 50 kts; warhead 900 kg or low yield nuclear.
Countermeasures: ESM: Rim Hat; radar warning. Park Lamp D/F.
Radars: Surface search: Snoop Pair with back-to-back aerials on same mast as ESM.
Sonars: Shark Gill; hull-mounted; passive/active search and attack; low/medium frequency.
Mouse Roar; hull-mounted; active attack; high frequency.

Programmes: First of class launched July 1984 at Komsomolsk and operational at the end of 1985. The class is in series production at both Komsomolsk and Severodvinsk with a construction rate of one or two per year. As this is obviously the favoured design a modified version is due shortly if the Victor precedent is followed. Russian name may be Bars class.
Structure: The very long fin is particularly notable. Has the same broad hull as Sierra and has reduced radiated noise levels by comparison with Victor III of which she is the traditional follow-on design. A number of prominent water environment sensors have begun to appear on the fin leading edge and on the forward casing. These are similar to devices tested on a Hotel II class from the early 1980s. The engineering standards around the bridge and casing are noticeably to a higher quality than other classes. Diving depth, 1300 ft *(400 m)*.
Operational: A multi-role SSN following the Victor III class. Pert Spring SATCOM. Based in both Northern and Pacific Fleets.

AKULA *1989*

AKULA *1989*

1 + 3 SIERRA II CLASS (SSN)

Displacement, tons: 7200 surfaced; 8200 dived
Dimensions, feet (metres): 364.2 × 46.6 × 28.9 *(111 × 14.2 × 8.8)*
Main machinery: Nuclear; 2 PWR; 200 MW; 2 turbo alternators; 95 000 hp(m) *(70 MW)*; 1 shaft; 2 spinners
Speed, knots: 32 dived; 18 surfaced
Complement: 100 approx

Missiles: SLCM: SS-N-21 Sampson fired from 21 in *(533 mm)* tubes; land-attack; inertial/terrain following to 3000 km *(1620 nm)* at 0.7 Mach; warhead nuclear 200 kT. CEP 150 m. Probably flies at a height of about 200 m.
A/S: SS-N-15 fired from 21 in *(533 mm)* tubes; inertial flight to 37 km *(20 nm)*; warhead nuclear 200 kT.
SS-N-16 fired from 25.6 in *(650 mm)* tubes; inertial flight to 120 km *(65 nm)*; payload Type 45 torpedo; warhead 100 kg. There is also a 16B version with a nuclear warhead.
Torpedoes: 8—25.6 in *(650 mm)* tubes. Type 53; dual purpose; pattern active/passive homing up to 20 km *(10.8 nm)* at up to 45 kts; warhead 400 kg or low yield nuclear and Type 65; anti-surface; pattern active/passive wake homing to 50 km *(27.5 nm)* at 50 kts; warhead 900 kg or low yield nuclear. Tube liners are used for 21 in *(533 mm)* weapons. A typical load might include 10 Type 53 and 12 Type 65. Carrying missiles would reduce this torpedo load.
Mines: Up to 50 or 60 in lieu of torpedoes.
Countermeasures: ESM: Rim Hat; radar warning. Park Lamp D/F.
Radars: Surface search: Snoop Pair with back-to-back ESM aerial.
Sonars: Shark Gill; hull-mounted; passive/active search and attack; low/medium frequency.
Mouse Roar; hull-mounted; active attack; high frequency.

Programmes: First launched in July 1989 and on trials in 1990. In series production and building at about one every two and a bit years.
Structure: A follow-on class to the Sierra I. Apart from larger overall dimensions the Sierra II has a longer fin by some 16.5 ft *(5 m)* and an almost flat surface at the leading edge. The towed communications buoy has been recessed. A ten point environmental sensor is fitted at the front end of the fin. The stand-off distance between hulls is considerable and has obvious advantages for radiated noise reduction and damage resistance. Diving depth, 2100 ft *(650 ft)*.
Operational: Pert Spring SATCOM.

SIERRA II *5/1991*

SIERRA II *5/1991*

2 SIERRA I CLASS (SSN)

Displacement, tons: 7000 surfaced; 7900 dived
Dimensions, feet (metres): 351 × 41 × 28.9 *(107 × 12.5 × 8.8)*
Main machinery: Nuclear; 2 PWR; 200 MW; 2 turbo alternators; 95 000 hp(m) *(70 MW)*; 1 shaft; 2 spinners
Speed, knots: 34 dived; 18 surfaced
Complement: 100 approx

Missiles: SLCM: SS-N-21 Sampson fired from 21 in *(533 mm)* tubes; land-attack; inertial/terrain following to 3000 km *(1620 nm)* at 0.7 Mach; warhead nuclear 200 kT. CEP 150 m. Probably flies at a height of about 200 m.
A/S: SS-N-15 fired from 21 in *(533 mm)* tubes; inertial flight to 37 km *(20 nm)*; warhead nuclear 200 kT.
SS-N-16 fired from 25.6 in *(650 mm)* tubes; inertial flight to 120 km *(65 nm)*; payload Type 45 torpedo; warhead 100 kg. There is also a 16B version with a nuclear warhead.
Torpedoes: 8—25.6 in *(650 mm)* tubes. Type 53; dual purpose; pattern active/passive homing up to 20 km *(10.8 nm)* at up to 45 kts; warhead 400 kg or low yield nuclear and Type 65; anti-surface; pattern active/passive wake homing to 50 km *(27.5 nm)* at 50 kts; warhead 900 kg or low yield nuclear. Tube liners are used for 21 in *(533 mm)* weapons. A typical load might include 10 Type 53 and 12 Type 65. Carrying missiles would reduce this torpedo load.
Mines: Up to 50 or 60 in lieu of torpedoes.
Countermeasures: ESM: Rim Hat; radar warning. Park Lamp D/F.
Radars: Surface search: Snoop Pair with back-to-back ESM aerial.
Sonars: Shark Gill; hull-mounted; passive/active search and attack; low/medium frequency.
Mouse Roar; hull-mounted; active attack; high frequency.

SIERRA I (Unit 2) *1989*

Programmes: First launched in July 1983 at Gorky, and fitted out at Severodvinsk. In service for trials in late 1984. Second launched July 1986 and on trials in early 1987. Russian name is Barakuda class.
Structure: Probably similar to the late Mike in having a strengthened hull which would make it much more expensive than Akula and a logical successor to the Alfa class. The pod on the after fin is larger than that in Victor III. The stand-off distance between hulls is considerable and has obvious advantages for radiated noise reduction and damage resistance. The second unit picture shows the V-shaped casing on the port side of the fin which covers the releasable escape chamber. This submarine also has a bulbous casing at the after end of the fin for a towed communications buoy. Diving depth, 2100 ft *(650 m)*.
Operational: Pert Spring SATCOM.

SIERRA I (Unit 1) *1984*

5 ALFA CLASS (SSN)

Displacement, tons: 2700 surfaced; 3600 dived
Dimensions, feet (metres): 267.4 oa; 246.1 wl × 31.2 × 24.6 *(81.5; 75 × 9.5 × 7.5)*
Main machinery: Nuclear; 2 PWR; 170 MW; 2 turbo alternators; 50 000 hp(m) *(37 MW)*; 1 shaft; 2 spinners
Speed, knots: 40 dived; 20 surfaced
Complement: 40

Missiles: A/S: SS-N-15 fired from 21 in *(533 mm)* tubes; inertial flight to 37 km *(20 nm)*; warhead nuclear 200 kT.
Torpedoes: 6—21 in *(533 mm)* fwd tubes. Type 53; dual purpose; pattern active/passive homing up to 20 km *(10.8 nm)* at up to 45 kts; warhead 400 kg or low yield nuclear. Can carry 20 torpedoes or a mixed equivalent load.
Mines: Up to 40 in lieu of torpedoes.
Countermeasures: ESM: Bald Head and Brick Group; radar warning. Park Lamp D/F.
Radars: Surface search: Snoop Head (on same mast as ESM); I band.
Sonars: Shark Gill; hull-mounted; passive/active search and attack; low/medium frequency.
Mouse Roar; hull-mounted; active attack; high frequency.

Programmes: The first of this class was laid down in mid-1960s and completed in 1970 at Sudomekh, Leningrad. The building time was very long in comparison with normal programmes and it seems most likely that this was a prototype. This boat was scrapped in 1974. Six more were then built between 1979 and 1983 at Sudomekh and Severodvinsk.
Structure: The reduction of the length combined with the high speed indicates considerable progress in hydrodynamic design and laminar flow techniques. A greater diving depth, down to 2500 ft *(700 m)* has been achieved by use of titanium alloy for the hull. This also results in a much reduced magnetic signature. The sound profile of this class is, however, high, reflecting the fact that this is a design now over 25 years old. All these submarines may have minor variations, possibly to study future designs now at sea in the Sierra class and to be incorporated in future classes.
Operational: Small complement indicates a high level of automation. Navigation systems include SINS, SATNAV, Loran and Omega. High levels of speed dependent noise, much quieter when slow. One was reported as scrapped in 1988 and a second recommissioned in late 1989 as a trials boat, having been in refit for five years. It is also reported that most of the class may be in reserve as an economy measure.

ALFA *5/1990*

26 VICTOR III CLASS (SSN)

Displacement, tons: 4850 surfaced; 6000 dived
Dimensions, feet (metres): 351.1 × 34.8 × 24.3 *(107 × 10.6 × 7.4)*
Main machinery: Nuclear; 2 PWR; 130 MW; 2 turbines; 30 000 hp(m) *(22 MW)*; 1 shaft; 2 spinners
Speed, knots: 30 dived; 18 surfaced
Complement: 70 (17 officers)

Missiles: SLCM: SS-N-21 Sampson fired from 21 in *(533 mm)* tubes; land-attack; inertial/terrain following to 3000 km *(1620 nm)* at 0.7 Mach; warhead nuclear 200 kT. CEP 150 m. Probably flies at a height of about 200 m.
A/S: SS-N-15 fired from 21 in *(533 mm)* tubes; inertial flight to 37 km *(20 nm)*; warhead nuclear 200 kT.
SS-N-16 A/B fired from 25.6 in *(650 mm)* tubes; inertial flight to 120 km *(65 nm)*; payload Type 45 torpedo; warhead 100 kg. There is also a 16B version with a nuclear warhead.
Torpedoes: 2—21 in *(533 mm)* and 4—25.6 in *(650 mm)* tubes. Type 53; dual purpose; pattern active/passive homing up to 20 km *(10.8 nm)* at up to 45 kts; warhead 400 kg or low yield nuclear and Type 65; anti-surface; pattern active/passive wake homing to 50 km *(27.5 nm)* at 50 kts; warhead 900 kg or low yield nuclear. Can carry up to 24 torpedoes.
Mines: Can carry 36 in lieu of torpedoes.
Countermeasures: ESM: Brick Group (Brick Spit and Brick Pulp); radar warning. Park Lamp D/F.
Radars: Surface search: Snoop Tray; I band.
Sonars: Shark Gill; hull-mounted; passive/active search and attack; low/medium frequency.
Mouse Roar; hull-mounted; active attack; high frequency.

Programmes: An improvement on Victor II, the first of class being completed at Komsomolsk in 1978. With construction also being carried out at Admiralty Yard, Leningrad, there was a very rapid building programme up to the end of 1984. Since then construction continued only at Leningrad and at a rate of about one per year which terminated in 1991.
Structure: The streamlined pod on the stern fin is now described as a towed sonar array dispenser. Water environment sensors are being mounted at the front of the fin and on the forward casing as in the Akula and Sierra classes. One of the class, sometimes called the Victor IV, has the trials SS-N-21 SLCM mounted on the forward casing. Diving depth, 1000 ft *(300 m)*.
Operational: VLF communications buoy. VHF/UHF aerials. Navigation equipment includes SINS and SATNAV. Pert Spring SATCOM. Kremmny 2 IFF. Much improved acoustic quietening puts the radiated noise levels at the upper limits of the USN Los Angeles class. Based in Northern and Pacific Fleets.

VICTOR III (with SS-N-21 trials capsule) *1990*

VICTOR III (with sensors at front of the fin) *1990*

VICTOR III *1990*

7 VICTOR II CLASS (SSN)

Displacement, tons: 4700 surfaced; 5800 dived
Dimensions, feet (metres): 337.9 oa; 315 wl × 34.8 × 24.3 *(103; 96 × 10.6 × 7.4)*
Main machinery: Nuclear; 2 PWR; 130 MW; 2 turbines; 30 000 hp(m) *(22 MW)*; 1 shaft; 2 spinners
Speed, knots: 30 dived; 18 surfaced
Complement: 70 (17 officers)

Missiles: A/S: SS-N-15 fired from 21 in *(533 mm)* tubes; inertial flight to 37 km *(20 nm)*; warhead nuclear 200 kT.
SS-N-16 A/B fired from 25.6 in *(650 mm)* tubes; inertial flight to 120 km *(65 nm)*; payload Type 45 torpedo; warhead 100 kg. There is also a 16B version with a nuclear warhead.
Torpedoes: 2—21 in *(533 mm)* and 4—25.6 in *(650 mm)* tubes. Type 53; dual purpose; pattern active/passive homing up to 20 km *(10.8 nm)* at up to 45 kts; warhead 400 kg or low yield nuclear and Type 65; anti-surface; pattern active/passive wake homing to 50 km *(27.5 nm)* at 50 kts; warhead 900 kg or low yield nuclear. Can carry up to 24 torpedoes.
Mines: Up to 48 in lieu of torpedoes.
Countermeasures: ESM: Brick Group (Brick Spit and Brick Pulp); radar warning. Park Lamp D/F.
Radars: Surface search: Snoop Tray; I band.
Sonars: Shark Teeth; hull-mounted; passive/active search and attack; low/medium frequency.
Mouse Roar; hull-mounted; active attack; high frequency.

Programmes: First appeared in 1972, class completed 1978. Built at Admiralty Yard, Leningrad and Gorky.

VICTOR II *1990*

Structure: An enlarged Victor I design, 9 m longer to provide more space for torpedo stowage. Diving depth, 1000 ft *(300 m)* approx.

Operational: VLF communications buoy. VHF and UHF aerials. Navigation equipment includes SINS and SATNAV. Kremmny 2 IFF. All based in the Northern Fleet.

VICTOR II *1990, S. S. Breyer*

14 VICTOR I CLASS (SSN)

Displacement, tons: 4400 surfaced; 5300 dived
Dimensions, feet (metres): 308.4 oa; 282.2 wl × 34.4 × 24 *(94; 86 × 10.5 × 7.3)*
Main machinery: Nuclear; 2 PWR; 130 MW; 2 turbines; 30 000 hp(m) *(22 MW)*; 1 shaft; 2 spinners
Speed, knots: 32 dived; 18 surfaced
Complement: 70 (17 officers)

Missiles: A/S: SS-N-15 fired from 21 in *(533 mm)* tubes; inertial flight to 37 km *(20 nm)*; warhead nuclear 200 kT.
Torpedoes: 6—21 in *(533 mm)* bow tubes. Type 53; dual purpose; pattern active/passive homing up to 20 km *(10.8 nm)* at up to 45 kts; warhead 400 kg or low yield nuclear. Can carry up to 24 torpedoes.
Mines: In lieu of torpedoes.
Countermeasures: ESM: Brick Group; radar warning. Park Lamp D/F.
Radars: Surface search: Snoop Tray; I band.
Sonars: Shark Teeth; hull-mounted; passive/active search and attack; low/medium frequency.
Mouse Roar; hull-mounted; active attack; high frequency.

Programmes: The first of class laid down in 1965 entering service in 1967-68—class completed 1974 at a building rate of two per year. Superseded by the Victor II programme. Built at Admiralty Yard, Leningrad.
Structure: This was the first Soviet submarine with an Albacore hull-form and a new reactor system, a new generation design shared by the Charlie class. Is of double-hulled form but, unlike Charlie, has two reactors giving an enhanced speed. Diving depth, 1000 ft *(300 m)* approx.

VICTOR I *1990*

Operational: The majority is deployed with the Northern Fleet, although some have joined the Pacific Fleet. Becoming unreliable and of the original 16 units at least two have been withdrawn from service, one as a result of a reactor refuelling accident.

3 YANKEE NOTCH CLASS (SSN, ex-SSBN)

Displacement, tons: 8500 surfaced; 10 300 dived
Dimensions, feet (metres): 464.2 × 38.1 × 26.6 *(141.5 × 11.6 × 8.1)*
Main machinery: Nuclear; 2 PWR; 160 MW; 2 turbines; 37 400 hp(m) *(27.5 MW)*; 2 shafts
Speed, knots: 26 dived; 16 surfaced
Complement: 120

Missiles: SLCM: 35 approx SS-N-21 Sampson fired from 21 in *(533 mm)* tubes; land attack; inertial/terrain following to 3000 km *(1620 nm)* at 0.7 Mach; warhead nuclear 200 kT. CEP 150 m. Probably flies at a height of about 200 m.
Torpedoes: 6—21 in *(533 mm)* tubes; Type 53; dual purpose; pattern active/passive homing up to 20 km *(10.8 nm)* at up to 45 kts; warhead 400 kg or low yield nuclear.
Countermeasures: ESM: Brick Group; radar warning. Park Lamp D/F.
Radars: Surface search: Snoop Tray; I band.
Sonars: Shark Gill; hull-mounted; passive/active search and attack; low/medium frequency.
Mouse Roar; hull-mounted; active attack; high frequency.

Programmes: The SALT limits of 62 SSBNs and 950 SLBMs have been adhered to by the Soviet Navy and this has resulted in the conversion of Yankee class as well as the deleted Hotel and Golf classes. The Yankee conversion to SSN was first seen in 1983. The conversion takes about two years and it seemed to be the intention to convert about 10 of the class until the programme fell victim to financial cuts in 1989-90. See also *Auxiliary Submarine* section.

YANKEE NOTCH *1990*

Structure: In spite of the removal of the ballistic missile section the overall length of the hull has increased by 39.4 ft *(12 m)* with the insertion of a 'notch waisted' central section. This new section houses three tubes amidships on each side and it is likely that the magazine holds up to 20 SS-N-21s or additional torpedoes and mines. There may also have been a rearrangement of torpedo tubes to include some at 26.5 in *(650 mm)*. Diving depth, 1000 ft *(300 m)*.

Patrol Submarines

Note: When the time came to rebuild the Soviet Navy after the Revolution the first major new construction programme was that for submarines. By 1941 this force numbered about 220. At the end of the war new German designs and concepts became available to the USSR. This knowledge was incorporated in a 1948 plan to build 1200 submarines between 1950 and 1965 at an initial rate of 78 a year, increasing to 100. This programme was probably split into three sections, representing the three zones of defence—200 long-range boats (Zulu and, later, Foxtrot classes), 900 medium-range boats (Whiskey and, later, Romeo classes) and 100 coastal boats of the Quebec class, the last being fitted with either Walter turbines or closed-cycle diesels. These last were German designs as were the hull-forms of the submarines, being similar to the German Type XXI.

This plan was largely amended with the post-Stalin readjustments and the successful experiments with nuclear power plants. Of the projected boats only 28 out of 40 Zulu class were built, 60 out of 160 Foxtrot class, 240 out of 340 Whiskey class (albeit in seven years), 20 out of 560 Romeo class and 40 out of 100 Quebec class. After the arrival of the nuclears, diesel submarine design has concentrated since the early 1960s on long-range attack types with the exception of the Golf class SSBs and the Juliett class SSGs. The Foxtrot class was built from 1958-71 with 62 completed for the Soviet Navy, and a further 17, last in 1983, for client countries. In 1972 came the Tango class, produced at the rate of two a year. The Kilo class, built at Komsomolsk, appeared in the late 1970s and was initially produced at the rate of one a year. This rate has increased with production at Gorky and Leningrad. The latter two yards are most concerned with exports, the first clients being Poland, Romania, India and Algeria. Iran and Syria are expected to join this club in 1992/93. Non-nuclear submarine construction will continue, probably with a follow-on to the Kilo class as its 1970s technology has severe limitations by modern Western standards. In addition certain specialised submarines have been built—the four Bravo class target boats in the late 1960s, the India class rescue submarines and the Lima research submarine in the late 1970s, Beluga class in 1987 and others.

Kilo and Tango classes are coated with Cluster Guard anechoic tiles and both have a minelaying capability from their torpedo tubes. As well as the submarines listed there were a further 20 Foxtrot and Whiskey class in reserve and waiting to be scrapped at the beginning of 1992.

19 + 5 KILO CLASS (SS)

Displacement, tons: 2325 surfaced; 3076 dived
Dimensions, feet (metres): 243.8 × 32.8 × 21.7 *(74.3 × 10 × 6.6)*
Main machinery: Diesel-electric; 2 diesels; 3500 hp(m) *(2.58 MW)*; 2 generators; 1 motor; 5900 hp(m) *(4.34 MW)*; 1 shaft
Speed, knots: 17 dived; 10 surfaced
Range, miles: 6000 at 7 kts surfaced; 400 at 3 kts dived.
Complement: 45

Torpedoes: 6—21 in *(533 mm)* tubes. 18 Type 53; dual purpose; pattern active/passive homing up to 20 km *(10.8 nm)* at up to 45 kts; warhead 400 kg or low yield nuclear.
Mines: In lieu of torpedoes.
Countermeasures: ESM: Squid Head or Brick Pulp; radar warning. Quad Loop D/F.
Radars: Surface search: Snoop Tray; I band.
Sonars: Shark Teeth; hull-mounted; passive/active search and attack; medium frequency.
Mouse Roar; hull-mounted; active attack; high frequency.

Programmes: First launched in 1979 at Komsomolsk. Construction is taking place in Gorky and Leningrad as well as at Komsomolsk. The building rate at the beginning of 1992 was still about four a year, Soviet numbers depending on the export rate.
Structure: Has a better hull form than the Foxtrot or Tango but is still fairly basic by comparison with modern Western designs. Diving depth, 1000 ft *(300 m)*.
Operational: There is evidence of trials being carried out with a SAM launcher fitted on the fin. Probably SA-N-8; IR homing from 600 m to 6000 m; warhead 2 kg.

KILO *6/1991*

Sales: The Kilo programme replaced the Foxtrot export stream and the class has so far been exported to Poland (1), Romania (1), India (8) and Algeria (2). Further transfers are expected to Iran and Syria and also as replacements for ageing Romeos and Foxtrots in other countries as well as more for India.

18 TANGO CLASS (SS)

Displacement, tons: 3000 surfaced; 3800 dived
Dimensions, feet (metres): 298.6 × 29.9 × 23.6 *(91 × 9.1 × 7.2)*
Main machinery: Diesel-electric; 3 diesels; 5475 hp(m) *(4 MW)*; 3 motors; 6256 hp(m) *(4.6 MW)*; 3 shafts
Speed, knots: 13 surfaced; 16 dived
Complement: 62

Torpedoes: 8—21 in *(533 mm)* (6 bow, 2 stern) tubes. Type 53; dual purpose; pattern active/passive homing up to 20 km *(10.8 nm)* at up to 45 kts; warhead 400 kg or low yield nuclear.
Mines: In lieu of torpedoes.
Countermeasures: ESM: Squid Head or Stop Light; radar warning. Quad Loop D/F.
Radars: Surface search: Snoop Tray; I band.
Sonars: Shark Teeth; hull-mounted; passive/active search and attack; medium frequency. There is a large array mounted above the torpedo tubes as well as a bow-mounted dome.

Programmes: This class was first seen at the Sevastopol Review in July 1973 and, immediately succeeding the Foxtrot class, showed a continuing commitment to non-nuclear-propelled boats. The building rate rose to two a year at Gorky and the programme finished in 1982.
Structure: There is a marked increase in the internal capacity of the hull which has most likely been used to improve battery capacity, habitability and weapon load compared with Foxtrot. Diving depth, 1000 ft *(300 m)*. The casing and fin have a continuous acoustic coating.
Operational: Long-range operational capability as shown by deployments to the Mediterranean and to West Africa. All except one is based in the Northern Fleet with refits at Kronshtadt in the Baltic. One of the class is in the Black Sea.

TANGO *5/1991*

TANGO *1990*

40 FOXTROT CLASS (SS)

Displacement, tons: 1952 surfaced; 2475 dived
Dimensions, feet (metres): 299.5 × 24.6 × 19.7 *(91.3 × 7.5 × 6)*
Main machinery: Diesel-electric; 3 diesels; 5956 hp(m) *(4.3 MW)*; 3 motors; 5400 hp(m) *(3.97 MW)*; 3 shafts
Speed, knots: 16 surfaced; 15 dived; 9 snorting
Range, miles: 20 000 at 8 kts surfaced; 380 at 2 kts dived
Complement: 75

Torpedoes: 10—21 in *(533 mm)* (6 bow, 4 stern) tubes. 22 Type 53; dual purpose; pattern active/passive homing up to 20 km *(10.8 nm)* at up to 45 kts; warhead 400 kg or low yield nuclear.
Mines: 44 in lieu of torpedoes.
Countermeasures: ESM: Stop Light; radar warning. Quad Loop D/F.
Radars: Surface search: Snoop Tray or Snoop Plate; I band.
Sonars: Herkules/Feniks; hull-mounted; passive/active search and attack; high frequency.

Programmes: Built between 1958 and 1971 at Sudomekh. Production continued until 1984 for transfer to other countries ie Cuba, India, Libya. A follow-on of the Zulu class. Only 60 out of a total programme of 160 were completed as the changeover to nuclear boats took effect. A most successful class which has been deployed worldwide, forming the bulk of the submarine force in the Mediterranean in the 1960s and 1970s.
Operational: This class is now progressively being withdrawn from front-line service, with Northern Fleet units being redeployed to the Baltic and Black Sea. Diving depth was 820 ft *(250 m)* but this is reducing with age.
Sales: All new construction (except those for Poland): Cuba: One in February 1979, one in March 1980, one in February 1984. India: One in April 1968, one in March 1969, one in November 1969, one in February 1970, one in November 1973, one in December 1973, one in October 1974, one in February 1975. Libya: One in December 1976, two in February 1978, one in February 1981, one in January 1982 and one in February 1983. One to Poland in 1987 and a second in 1988.

FOXTROT *1990*

Auxiliary Submarines

Note: In addition to those listed there is also an Alfa class SSN used for trials, and an elderly Romeo class diesel submarine with two large experimental torpedo type tubes fitted on the casing at the bow.

2 YANKEE CLASS (SSAN, ex-SSBN)

Displacement, tons: 9800 surfaced
Dimensions, feet (metres): 440.6 × 38 × 26.6 *(134.3 × 11.6 × 8.1)*
Main machinery: Nuclear; 2 PWR; 160 MW; 2 turbines; 37 400 hp(m) *(27.5 MW)*; 2 shafts
Speed, knots: 26 dived; 20 surfaced
Complement: 120

Comment: As well as the Yankee SSGN and Yankee Notch SSN conversions, two other hulls have been converted for research and development roles. The dimensions given are for the so-called Yankee Pod which has been used as a trials platform for the towed array pod on the stern since about 1984. There are also two prominent bulges either side of the fin. The other conversion is a Yankee Stretch which has a lengthened central section extending the hull to some 525 ft *(160 m)* and is used for unspecified underwater research which may include submarine rescue operations. The Yankee Pod probably has the same torpedo armament as the standard Yankee class. Based in the Northern Fleet.

YANKEE POD *1989*

2 UNIFORM CLASS AND 1 PALTUS CLASS (SSAN)

Displacement, tons: 1750 surfaced; 2100 dived
Dimensions, feet (metres): 240 × 23 × 17 *(73 × 7 × 5.2)*
Speed, knots: 10 dived

Comment: Appear to be research and development nuclear powered submarines. Details given are for the Uniform class, the first of which was launched at Sudomekh in 1982, the second in 1988. Paltus is about 20 m less in length and was launched at Sudomekh in April 1991; it is probably nuclear powered. Both classes are deep diving and are based in the Northern Fleet.

1 LIMA CLASS (SSA)

Displacement, tons: 1700 surfaced; 2100 dived
Dimensions, feet (metres): 282.2 × 25.9 × 23 *(86 × 7.9 × 7)*
Main machinery: Diesel-electric; 2 diesels; 1 motor; 2500 hp(m) *(1.8 MW)*; 1 shaft
Speed, knots: 12 surfaced; 12 dived
Complement: 70
Radars: Navigation: Snoop Tray; I band.
Sonars: Hull-mounted; passive/active search and attack; high frequency.

Comment: Built at Sudomekh Yard and launched in August 1978. A bulge at the forward end of the fin is similar to that used for the German Balkon sonar in the early 1940s but could be a tower for exit/re-entry trials. The most conspicuous feature is that some of the masts are non-retractable. Returned to St Petersburg from the Black Sea in 1990, possibly to refit.

LIMA *1989*

1 BELUGA CLASS (SSA)

Displacement, tons: 1900 dived
Dimensions, feet (metres): 213.3 × 28.5 × 19.7 *(65 × 8.7 × 6)*
Main machinery: Diesel-electric; 2 diesels; 1 motor; 5440 hp *(4 MW)*; 1 shaft
Speed, knots: 10 surfaced; 22 dived

Comment: Built at Leningrad and completed in February 1987. A single experimental unit with a fin similar to the Alfa class. Propulsion referred to as the 'Oxygen System' and is therefore likely to be an air independent prototype. Stated by the Russians to be for marine and biological research. There are probably six torpedo tubes and standard Snoop Tray radar, Brick Group ESM and Shark Teeth and Mouse Roar sonars. Based in the Black Sea and may be a prototype for the follow-on to the Kilo class.

BELUGA *10/1991*

1 X-RAY CLASS AND 1 LOSOS CLASS (SSA)

Displacement, tons: 520 dived
Dimensions, feet (metres): 154.2 × 13.1 × 13.1 *(47 × 4 × 4)*

Comment: Details given are for the X-Ray which is a very small research submarine built at Sudomekh Yard, St Petersburg in 1984. Originally thought to be nuclear powered. Based in the Northern Fleet and probably associated with deep diving seabed operations. Losos is a 25 m experimental submarine built at St Petersburg and associated with air independent propulsion. Based in the Baltic.

2 INDIA CLASS (SSA)

Displacement, tons: 4000 surfaced; 4800 dived
Dimensions, feet (metres): 354.3 oa; 344.5 wl × 32.8 × 23 *(108; 105 × 10 × 7)*
Main machinery: 2 diesels; 3800 hp(m) *(2.79 MW)*; 2 motors; 3000 hp *(2 MW)*; 2 shafts; bow thruster
Speed, knots: 15 surfaced; 10 dived

Countermeasures: ESM: Stop Light/Squid Head; radar warning. Quad Loop D/F.
Radars: Navigation: Snoop Tray; I band.
Sonars: Hull-mounted; passive/active search; high frequency.

Programmes: Built at Komsomolsk. First launched in 1975, second in 1979.
Structure: Designed for rescue work and carry two 12.1 m DSRVs on the after casing. The overall silhouette is similar to Delta class SSBNs. Both DSRVs have access hatches in the hull and probably have an operating depth of about 2000 m, although this would be reduced to 600-700 m for actual submarine rescue operations. It seems unlikely that these submarines carry any armament.
Operational: One is in service in the Pacific and one in the Northern Fleet but it is possible that at least one may be replaced by a Yankee Stretch SSAN.

INDIA with DSRVs *1984, Sem and Stenersen*

4 BRAVO CLASS (TARGET SUBMARINES)

Displacement, tons: 2250 surfaced; 2750 dived
Dimensions, feet (metres): 239.5 oa; 219.8 wl × 32.1 × 26.2 *(73; 67 × 9.8 × 8)*
Main machinery: Diesel-electric; 2 diesels; 3970 hp(m) *(2.9 MW)*; 2 generators; 1 motor; 5900 hp(m) *(4.34 MW)*; 1 shaft
Speed, knots: 14 dived
Complement: 60

Torpedoes: 6—21 in *(533 mm)* bow tubes. Type 53; dual purpose; pattern active/passive homing up to 20 km *(10.8 nm)* at up to 45 kts; warhead 400 kg or low yield nuclear.
Countermeasures: ESM: Brick Group; radar warning.
Radars: Navigation: Snoop Tray; I band.
Sonars: Hull-mounted; passive; medium frequency and active search and attack; high frequency.

Programmes: Completed at Komsomolsk 1967-70.
Structure: The beam-to-length ratio is larger than normal in a diesel submarine which would account in part for the large displacement for a comparatively short hull. Diving depth 1000 ft *(300 m)*.
Operational: These four submarines are in the Northern, Black Sea and Pacific fleets and act as 'padded targets' for ASW exercises and weapon firings.

BRAVO

AIRCRAFT CARRIERS

1 MODIFIED KIEV CLASS (CV)

Name	*Builders*	*Laid down*	*Launched*	*Commissioned*
ADMIRAL GORSHKOV (ex-*Baku*)	Nikolayev South (Nosenko, 444)	Dec 1978	17 Apr 1982	Jan 1987

Displacement, tons: 40 500 full load
Dimensions, feet (metres): 899 oa; 818.6 wl × 167.3 oa; 107.3 wl × 32.8 (screws) *(274; 249.5 × 51; 32.7 × 10)*
Flight deck, feet (metres): 640 × 68 *(195 × 20.7)*
Main machinery: 8 boilers; 4 turbines; 200 000 hp(m) *(147 MW)*; 4 shafts
Speed, knots: 32. **Range, miles:** 13 500 at 18 kts; 4000 at 31 kts
Complement: 1200 plus aircrew

Missiles: SSM: 12 SS-N-12 Sandbox (6 twin) launchers ❶; inertial guidance with command update; active radar homing to 550 km *(300 nm)* at 1.7 Mach; warhead nuclear 350 kT or HE 1000 kg; 24 reloads.
SAM: 4 SA-N-9 sextuple vertical launchers ❷; command guidance; active radar homing to 12 km *(6.6 nm)* at 2 Mach; warhead 15 kg; altitude 3.4-12 192 m *(10-40 000 ft)*; 24 magazines; 192 missiles.
Guns: 2—3.9 in *(100 mm)*/70 ❸; 80° elevation; 80 rounds/minute to 15 km *(8.2 nm)*; weight of shell 16 kg.
8—30 mm/65 ❹; 6 barrels per mounting; 85° elevation; 3000 rounds/minute combined to 2 km.
A/S mortars: 2 RBU 12 000 ❺; 10 tubes per launcher; range 12 000 m; warhead 80 kg.
Countermeasures: Decoys: 2 twin Chaff launchers. Towed torpedo decoy.
ESM/ECM: 4 Wine Flask; 8 Foot Ball; 4 Bell Nip; 4 Bell Thump. 2 Cage Pot.
Fire control: 3 Tin Man optronic trackers ❻. 2 Punch Bowl SATCOM for SSM data link. 2 Low Ball SATNAV. 1 Bob Tail.
Radars: Air search: Sky Watch; 4 Planar phased array ❼; 3D.
Air/surface search: Plate Steer ❽; E band.
Surface search: Two Strut Pair ❾; F band.
Navigation: Three Palm Frond; I band.
Fire control: Trap Door (for SS-N-12) ❿. Kite Screech ⓫; H/I/K band (for 100 mm). Four Bass Tilt ⓬; H/I band (for Gatlings). Four Cross Sword ⓭ (for SA-N-9).
Aircraft control: Fly Trap; G/H band. Cake Stand ⓮.
IFF: 2 Salt Pot A and B. 1 Long Head.
Sonars: Horse Jaw; hull-mounted; active search and attack; low/medium frequency.
Horse Tail; VDS; active search; medium frequency.

Fixed wing aircraft: 12 Yak-38 Forger A VSTOL ⓯; (see *Operational*).
Helicopters: 19 Ka-27 Helix A ⓰; 3 Ka-25 Hormone B (OTHT).

Programmes: The fourth and last of the Kiev class much delayed by the planar radar development. Full name is *Admiral Flota Sovietskogo Sojuza Gorshkov*.
Structure: Major differences with *Kiev* include 12 SSMs, 2—100 mm guns, 24 SA-N-9 magazines, planar 3D radar and a 30.5 × 19.7 ft *(9 × 6 m)* cupola at the top of the mast. The *Kiev's* torpedo armament has been removed. Many of these innovations have been incorporated in *Kuznetsov*.

ADMIRAL GORSHKOV *11/1990*

Operational: *Gorshkov* is based in the Northern Fleet. The Sky Watch radar should allow full control of the air battle when it finally becomes operational. As with the Kiev class, the impending withdrawal of Forger aircraft from service in 1992 will effectively reduce the ship to a Helicopter Carrier unless Freestyle development continues.

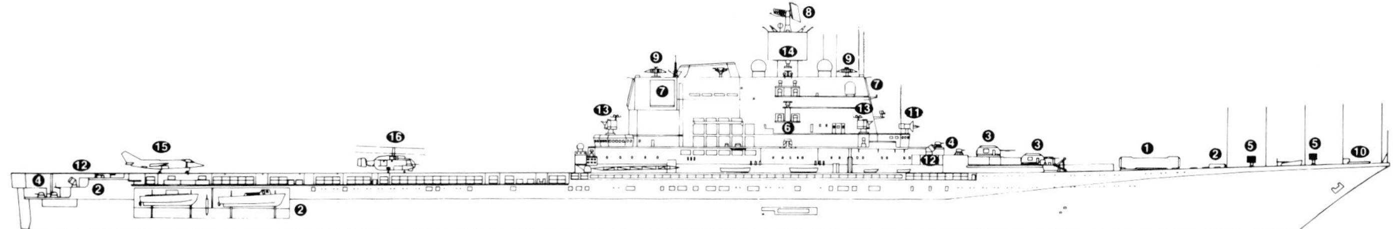
ADMIRAL GORSHKOV *(Scale 1 : 1 500), Ian Sturton*

ADMIRAL GORSHKOV *6/1989*

3 KIEV CLASS (CV)

Name	*Builders*	*Laid down*	*Launched*	*Commissioned*
KIEV	Nikolayev South (Nosenko, 444)	July 1970	27 Dec 1972	May 1975
MINSK	Nikolayev South (Nosenko, 444)	26 Dec 1972	3 Oct 1975	Feb 1978
NOVOROSSIYSK	Nikolayev South (Nosenko, 444)	Oct 1975	4 Dec 1978	Aug 1982

Displacement, tons: 40 500 full load
Dimensions, feet (metres): 899 oa; 818.6 wl × 154.8 oa; 107.3 wl × 32.8 (screws) *(274; 249.5 × 47.2; 32.7 × 10)*
Flight deck, feet (metres): 620 × 68 *(189 × 20.7)*
Main machinery: 8 boilers; 4 turbines; 200 000 hp(m) *(147 MW)*; 4 shafts
Speed, knots: 32. **Range, miles:** 13 500 at 18 kts; 4000 at 31 kts
Complement: 1200 plus aircrew

Missiles: SSM: 8 SS-N-12 Sandbox (4 twin) launchers ❶; inertial guidance with command update; active radar homing to 550 km *(300 nm)* at 1.7 Mach; warhead nuclear 350 kT or HE 1000 kg; 16 reloads.
SAM: 2 SA-N-3B Goblet twin launchers ❷; semi-active radar homing to 55 km *(30 nm)* at 2.5 Mach; warhead 80 kg; altitude 91.4-22 860 m *(300-75 000 ft)*; 72 missiles.
2 SA-N-4 Gecko twin launchers *(Kiev* and *Minsk)* ❸; semi-active radar homing to 15 km *(8 nm)* at 2.5 Mach; warhead 50 kg; altitude 9.1-3048 m *(30-10 000 ft)*; 40 missiles.
4 SA-N-9 sextuple vertical launchers (*Novorossiysk*); command guidance; active radar homing to 12 km *(6.6 nm)* at 2 Mach; warhead 15 kg; altitude 3.4-12 192 m *(10-40 000 ft)*; 96 missiles.
A/S: SUW-N-1 twin launcher ❹; FRAS-1; inertial flight to 29 km *(16 nm)*; warhead nuclear 5 kT.
Guns: 4—3 in *(76 mm)*/60 (2 twin) ❺; 80° elevation; 90 rounds/minute to 15 km *(8 nm)*; weight of shell 6.8 kg.
8—30 mm/65 ❻; 6 barrels per mounting; 85° elevation; 3000 rounds/minute combined to 2 km.
Torpedoes: 10—21 in *(533 mm)* (2 quin). Type 53; dual purpose; pattern active/passive homing up to 20 km *(10.8 nm)* at up to 45 kts; warhead 400 kg or low yield nuclear.
A/S mortars: 2 RBU 6000 12-tubed trainable ❼; range 6000 m; warhead 31 kg.
Countermeasures: Decoys: 2 twin Chaff launchers. Towed torpedo decoy.
ESM/ECM: 8 Side Globe (*Kiev* and *Minsk*). 4 Rum Tub. 2 Bell Bash. 4 Bell Nip *(Novorossiysk)*. 2 Cage Pot (*Kiev* and *Minsk*).
Fire control: 4 Tin Man optronic trackers (5 in *Novorossiysk*). Punch Bowl SATCOM for SSM data link. *Novorossiysk* has more VHF systems.
Radars: Air search: Top Sail ❽; 3D; D band; range 555 km *(300 nm)*.
Two Strut Pair (*Novorossiysk*); F band.
Air/surface search: Top Steer ❾; 3D; D/E band.
Navigation: Don Kay; I band. Two Palm Frond (three in *Novorossiysk*); I band. Shot Dome; I band.
Fire control: Trap Door (for SS-N-12) ❿. Two Head Light C ⓫; E band (for SA-N-3). Two Pop Group (*Kiev* and *Minsk*) ⓬; F/H/I band (for SA-N-4). Two Owl Screech ⓭; G band (for 76 mm). Four Bass Tilt ⓮; H/I band (for Gatlings). Four Cross Sword (for SA-N-9) (*Novorossiysk*).
Aircraft control: Top Knot; G/H band.
IFF: High Pole A and B (*Kiev* and *Minsk*). Salt Pot A and B (*Novorossiysk*). Square Head.
Sonars: Moose Jaw and Bull Horn or Horse Jaw *(Novorossiysk)*; hull-mounted; active search and attack; low/medium frequency. Mare Tail or Horse Tail; VDS; active search; medium frequency.

Fixed wing aircraft: 12 Yak-36 Forger A VSTOL ⓯; (see *Operational*).
Helicopters: 19 Ka-25 Hormone A or Ka-27 Helix (ASW); 2 Ka-25 Hormone B (OTHT) ⓰.

Programmes: The first post-war sign of acceptance of the need for organic air defence was the appearance of *Moskva* and *Leningrad* in 1967-68 (see Moskva class later). This class was the first to be built with a surface warfare capability as well as being ASW ships. They carried the embarked helicopter concept a long stage further than the cruisers with a single aircraft. It is most probable that a much larger number of ships was projected but cancelled because of the growing realisation of the important part its Navy could play in overseas affairs and the need for organic air defence. The prototype of the first VTOL aircraft, the Yakovlev 'Freehand' first appeared in public in 1967 and its capabilities were known at least a year before that. This was 10 years before *Kiev* became operational, a reasonable lead time for designers and constructors. Although originally classified as *protivolodochny kreyser* meaning anti-submarine cruiser, this class is now classified as *takticheskoye avianosny kreyser* meaning tactical aircraft-carrying cruiser. The fourth member of the class has sufficient modifications to justify a separate entry.
Structure: Flight deck has a 4¼ degree angle and two lifts, one larger one abaft the island and a smaller one amidships abreast the bridge. Six spots are provided with a seventh at the forward tip of the flight deck. A larger spot amidships aft is apparently for VSTOL. The layout varies in *Novorossiysk*. Problems with SA-N-9 meant that the system was still not operational in *Novorossiysk* and the Cross Sword fire control radars were still not fitted by early 1992.
Operational: The ageing Forger appears to be about to be withdrawn from service in 1992 which means no fixed wing capability, unless Freestyle development continues. The task of this class is primarily to act as the focus for task group operations making use of the excellent command, control and communications equipment. The inclusion of SS-N-12, ASW systems, and a gun armament as well as both SAM and Point Defence suggest an acknowledgement of the need for general purpose ships at the expense of a greater number of aircraft which could otherwise be carried. The ships have an unusually low freeboard for aircraft carriers and the stern tends to squat at high speeds. *Kiev* is based in the Northern Fleet, the other two in the Pacific. *Minsk* has engine problems and was alongside in Vladivostok from March 1989 until at least early 1992.

MINSK *4/1991, van Ginderen Collection*

KIEV *1988*

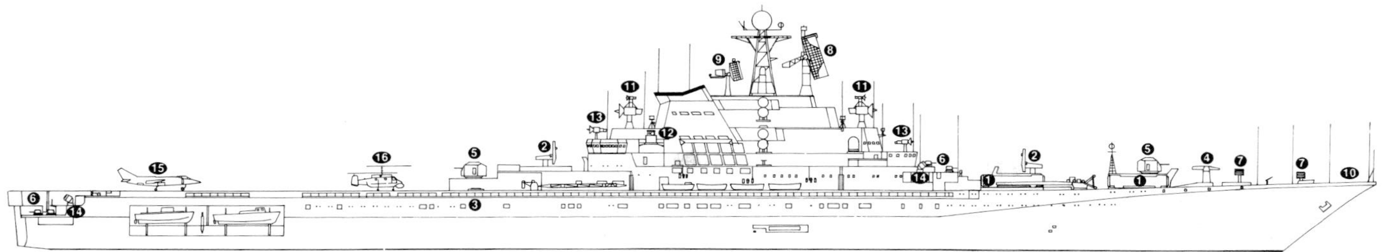

KIEV

(Scale 1 : 1 500), Ian Sturton

KIEV

1987

MINSK

4/1991, Ships of the World

MINSK

4/1991, Ships of the World

0 + 1 (1) ULYANOVSK CLASS (CVN)

Name	*Builders*	*Laid down*	*Launched*	*Commissioned*
ULYANOVSK	Nikolayev South	Dec 1988	1992	1996

Displacement, tons: 75 000
Dimensions, feet (metres): 1050 × — × — *(320 × — × —)*
Main machinery: Nuclear; 2 PWR; 3 turbines; 3 shafts

Programmes: First of a new class. Original intention was to build four, but the future is now very uncertain and this ship may not be completed in spite of being quite far advanced by early 1992.

Structure: According to a Russian Admiral the ship will have steam catapults for Flanker aircraft as opposed to the ski jump of *Kuznetsov* (ex-*Tbilisi*).

1 + 1 KUZNETSOV CLASS (CV)

Name	*Builders*	*Laid down*	*Launched*	*Commissioned*
ADMIRAL KUZNETSOV (ex-*Tbilisi*, ex-*Leonid Brezhnev*)	Nikolayev South	Jan 1983	5 Dec 1985	21 Jan 1991
VARYAG (ex-*Riga*)	Nikolayev South	Dec 1985	28 Nov 1988	1992-93

Displacement, tons: 67 500 full load
Dimensions, feet (metres): 999 oa; 918.6 wl × 229.7 oa; 121.4 wl × 34.4 *(304.5; 280 × 70; 37 × 10.5)*
Flight deck, feet (metres): 999 × 229.7 *(304.5 × 70)*
Main machinery: 8 boilers; 4 turbines; 200 000 hp(m) *(147 MW)*; 4 shafts
Speed, knots: 30
Complement: 1700 (200 officers)

Missiles: SSM: 12 SS-N-19 Shipwreck launchers (flush mounted) ❶; inertial guidance with command update; active radar homing to 20-450 km *(10.8-243 nm)* at Mach 1.6; warhead nuclear or 750 kg HE.
SAM: 4 SA-N-9 sextuple vertical launchers (192 missiles) ❷; command guidance and active radar homing to 12 km *(6.6 nm)* at 2 Mach; warhead 15 kg.
SAM/Guns: 8 CADS-N-1 ❸; each has a twin 30 mm Gatling combined with 8 SA-N-11 and Hot Flash fire control radar. Laser beam riding guidance for missiles to 8 km *(4.4 nm)*.
Guns: 6—30 mm/65 ❹; 6 barrels per mounting; 85° elevation; 3000 rounds/minute combined to 2 km.
A/S mortars: 2 RBU 12 000 ❺; range 12 000 m; warhead 80 kg.
Countermeasures: Decoys: Chaff launchers.
ESM/ECM: 2 Bell Crown. 2 Bell Push. 8 Foot Ball. 2 Wine Flask. 2 Flat Track.
Fire control: 4 Tin Man optronic trackers. 2 Punch Bowl SATCOM data link ❻. 2 Low Ball SATNAV ❼.
Radars: Air search: Sky Watch; four Planar phased arrays ❽; 3D.
Air/surface search: Top Plate ❾; D/E band.
Surface search: Two Strut Pair ❿; F band.
Navigation: Three Palm Frond; I band.
Fire control: Four Cross Sword (for SAM) ⓫; Four Bass Tilt (for guns); H/I bands.
Aircraft control: Fly Trap B; G/H band. Cake Stand ⓬.
Sonars: Horse Jaw; hull-mounted; active search and attack; medium/low frequency.

Fixed wing aircraft: 12 Su-27B2 Flanker; 12 MiG-29 Fulcrum or 12 Su-25 Frogfoot or 12 Yak-38 Forger (see *Shipborne Aircraft* section).
Helicopters: 15 Ka-27 Helix. 3 Ka-29 Helix AEW.

ADMIRAL KUZNETSOV *6/1991*

Programmes: The building of the first ship, a logical continuation of the Kiev class and a basic component of a task force including the nuclear-propelled Kirov class battle cruisers, was reported as acknowledged by Admiral Gorshkov in 1979. Sea trials of first ship started in late 1989 and the second should follow in 1992 having been nearly fully completed by the end of 1991. Names were changed in 1990 because the Navy was unhappy about ships being called after the cities of dissident republics. The full name of *Kuznetsov* is *Admiral Flota Sovietskogo Sojuza Kuznetsov*.
Structure: The hangar is approximately 610 × 98 × 25 ft and can hold up to 18 Flanker or 25 Fulcrum aircraft. There are two starboard side lifts, a ski-jump of 12° and an angled deck of 7°. There are four arrester wires. The SSM system is in the centre of the flight deck forward with flush deck covers. The class has some 16.5 m of freeboard (13 m in *Kiev*).
Operational: AEW, ASW and reconnaissance tasks undertaken by Helix helicopters. Three varieties of fixed wing aircraft (Su-27 Flanker, Su-25 Frogfoot and MiG-29 Fulcrum) have conducted extensive deck landing trials. The aircraft complement listed is based on the number which might be embarked for peacetime operations but the Russians claim a top limit of sixty. With Forger being taken out of service, it looks as though the preferred fixed wing aircraft is to be the Flanker. Sky Watch radar was still non-operational when *Kuznetsov* sailed for the Northern Fleet in December 1991. Hokum helicopters may supplement Helix in due course.
Opinion: This design is part of a natural progression in naval aviation development from a helicopter carrier to full fixed-wing capabilities, including catapults, which may be fitted in *Ulyanovsk*. Once the composition of the air wing has been established, naval air power projection out of range of Russian shore-based airfields will become one of many available options.

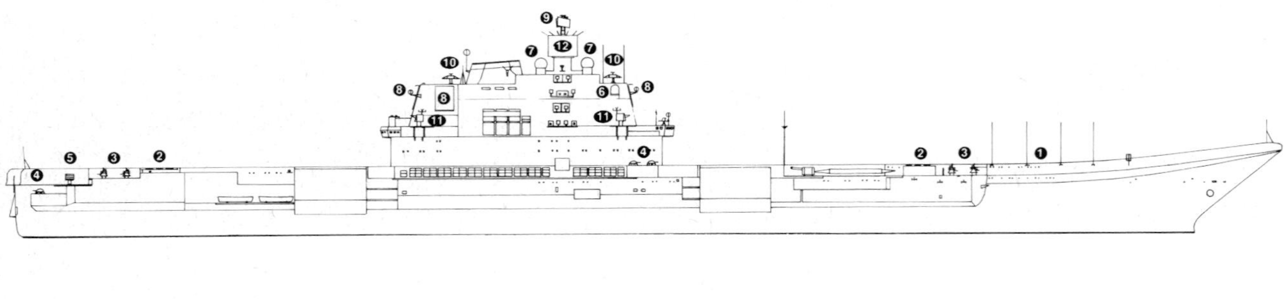

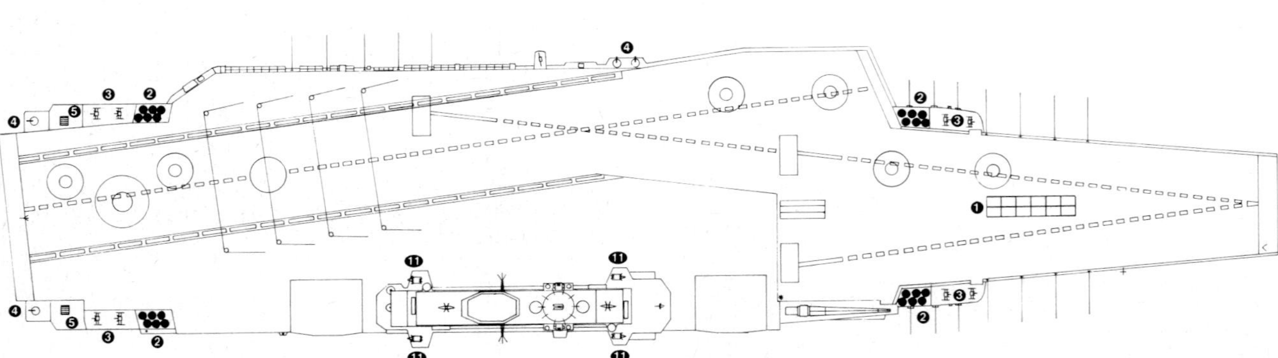

ADMIRAL KUZNETSOV *(Scale 1 : 1 800), Ian Sturton*

ADMIRAL KUZNETSOV

12/1991

ADMIRAL KUZNETSOV

1990, TASS

BATTLE CRUISERS

3 + 1 KIROV CLASS

Name	*Builders*	*Laid down*	*Launched*	*Commissioned*
KIROV	Baltic Yard 189, Leningrad	June1973	26 Dec 1977	July 1980
FRUNZE	Baltic Yard 189, Leningrad	26 Dec 1977	23 May 1981	Nov 1983
KALININ	Baltic Yard 189, Leningrad	May 1983	26 Apr 1986	Oct 1988
YURI ANDROPOV	Baltic Yard 189, St Petersburg	Apr 1986	29 Apr 1989	1992

Displacement, tons: 19 000 standard; 24 300 full load
Dimensions, feet (metres): 826.8; 754.6 wl × 93.5 × 29.5 *(252; 230 × 28.5 × 9.1)*
Main machinery: Nuclear; 2 PWR; 2 oil-fired boilers; 2 turbines; 108 800 hp(m) *(80 MW)*; 2 shafts
Speed, knots: 30. **Range, miles:** 14 000 at 33 kts
Complement: 692 (82 officers)

Missiles: SSM: 20 SS-N-19 Shipwreck (improved SS-N-12 with lower flight profile) (1); inertial guidance with command update; active radar homing to 20-450 km *(10.8-243 nm)* at 1.6 Mach; warhead nuclear or 750 kg HE; no reloads.
SAM: 12 SA-N-6 Grumble vertical launchers (2); 8 rounds per launcher; command guidance; semi-active radar homing to 100 km *(54 nm)*; warhead 90 kg (or nuclear?); altitude 27 432 m *(90 000 ft)*.
2 SA-N-4 twin launchers (3); semi-active radar homing to 15 km *(8 nm)* at 2.5 Mach; warhead 50 kg; altitude 9.1-3048 m *(30-10 000 ft)*; 40 missiles.
2 SA-N-9 octuple vertical launchers (not in *Kirov*) (4); command guidance; active radar homing to 12 km *(6.6 nm)* at 2 Mach; warhead 15 kg; altitude 3.4-12 192 m *(10-40 000 ft)*; 128 missiles.
SAM/Guns: 6 CADS-N-1 (*Kalinin*) (7); each has a twin 30 mm Gatling combined with 8 SA-N-11 and Hot Flash fire control radar. Laser beam riding guidance for missiles to 8 km *(4.4 nm)*.
A/S: 1 twin SS-N-14 Silex launcher *(Kirov)* (4); command guidance to 55 km *(30 nm)* at 0.95 Mach; payload nuclear or Type E53 torpedo; active/passive homing to 15 km *(8.1 nm)* at 40 kts; warhead 150 kg; 14 missiles. SSM version; range 35 km *(19 nm)*; warhead 500 kg.
Guns: 2—3.9 in *(100 mm)*/70 *(Kirov)* (5); 80° elevation; 80 rounds/minute to 15 km *(8.2 nm)*; weight of shell 16 kg.
2—130 mm/70 (twin) (not in *Kirov*) (5); 85° elevation; 35/45 rounds/minute to 29 km *(16 nm)*; weight of shell 27 kg.
8—30 mm/65 (*Kirov* and *Frunze*) (6); 6 barrels per mounting; 85° elevation; 3000 rounds/minute combined to 2 km.

Torpedoes: 10—21 in *(533 mm)* (2 quin). Type 53; dual purpose; pattern active/passive homing up to 20 km *(10.8 nm)* at up to 45 kts; warhead 400 kg or low yield nuclear. Mounted in the hull adjacent to the RBU 1000s on both quarters.
A/S mortars: 1 RBU 6000 12-tubed trainable fwd (*Kirov* and *Frunze*) (8); range 6000 m; warhead 31 kg.
1 RBU 12 000 (*Kalinin*) (9); 10 tubes per launcher; range 12 000 m; warhead 80 kg.
2 RBU 1000 6-tubed aft (10); range 1000 m; warhead 55 kg.
Countermeasures: Decoys: 2 twin 150 mm Chaff launchers. Towed torpedo decoy.
ESM/ECM: 8 Side Globe (*Kirov*). 8 Foot Ball (not in *Kirov*). 4 Rum Tub (*Kirov*). 4 Wine Flask (not in *Kirov*). 8 Bell Bash. 4 Bell Nip.
Fire control: 4 Tin Man optronic trackers. 2 Punch Bowl SATCOM (11). 4 Low Ball SATNAV.
Radars: Air search: Top Pair (Top Sail + Big Net) (12); 3D; C/D band; range 366 km *(200 nm)* for bomber, 183 km *(100 nm)* for 2 m² target.
Air/surface search: Top Steer (13) (Top Plate in *Kalinin* (14)); 3D; D/E band.
Navigation: Three Palm Frond; I band.
Fire control: Two Eye Bowl (*Kirov* only) (15); F band (for SS-N-14). Cross Sword (not in *Kirov*) (16); E/F band (for SA-N-9). Two Top Dome (17); J band (for SA-N-6). Two Pop Group, F/H/I band (for SA-N-4) (18). Kite Screech (19); H/I/K band (for main guns). Four Bass Tilt (20); H/I band (for Gatlings (not in *Kalinin*)).
Aircraft control: Flyscreen A *(Kirov)* or B; I band.
IFF: Salt Pot A and B.
Tacan: 2 Round House B.
Sonars: Horse Jaw; hull-mounted; active search and attack; low/medium frequency.
Horse Tail; VDS; active search; medium frequency. Depth to 150-200 m *(492.1-656.2 ft)* depending on speed.

Helicopters: 3 Ka-25 Hormone (21) or Ka-27 Helix (22).

Programmes: Type name is *atomny raketny kreyser* meaning nuclear-powered missile cruiser. In 1989-90 Baltic Yard started to build eight Kronshtadt Ro Ro ships for civilian use, which confirms statements that only four Kirovs are to be built. Some may be re-named in 1992.
Structure: The first surface warships with nuclear propulsion. In addition to the nuclear plant a unique maritime combination with an auxiliary oil-fuelled system has been installed. This provides a superheat capability, boosting the normal steam output by some 50 per cent. The SS-N-19 tubes are set at an angle of about 45 degrees. *Frunze* and subsequent ships of the class have a modified superstructure and armament although the SS-N-19 and SA-N-6 missile fits are the same. *Frunze* has an SA-N-9 octuple launcher in place of *Kirov's* SS-N-14 and another one aft in place of 4—30 mm guns which have been moved to a lengthened after deckhouse. *Kalinin* has CADS-N-1 with a central fire control radar on six mountings, each of which has two cannon and eight missile launchers. Two are mounted either side of the SS-N-19 forward and four on the after superstructure. These ships are reported as carrying about 500 SAM of different types.
Operational: The CIWS in *Kalinin* is an attempt further to improve inadequate hard-kill air defences in *Kirov*, following the installation of SA-N-9 in *Frunze*. Over-the-horizon targeting for SS-N-19 provided by SATCOM or Hormone B helicopter. *Kirov* and *Kalinin* are in the Northern Fleet, *Frunze* in the Pacific and *Andropov* may start sea trials in the Baltic in 1992. As the support for a strike carrier or as the focus of a task force including the Kiev, Slava, Kara, Krivak and Ivan Rogov classes with support from *Berezina* or *Boris Chilikin*, they would form a formidable intervention force, with VTOL and helicopter aircraft as well as a full outfit of missiles and guns.

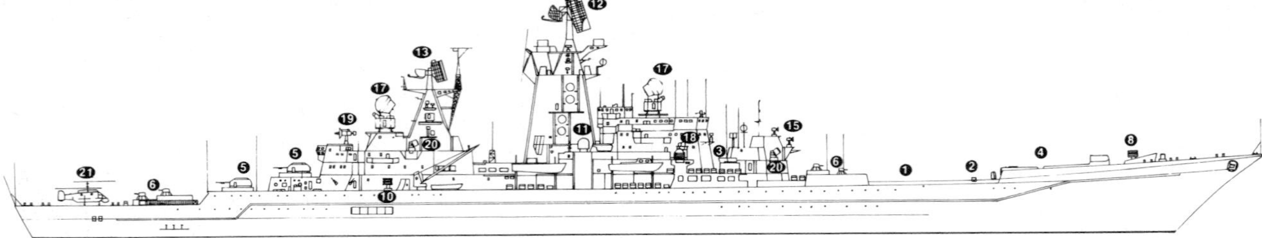

KIROV *(Scale 1 : 1 500), Ian Sturton*

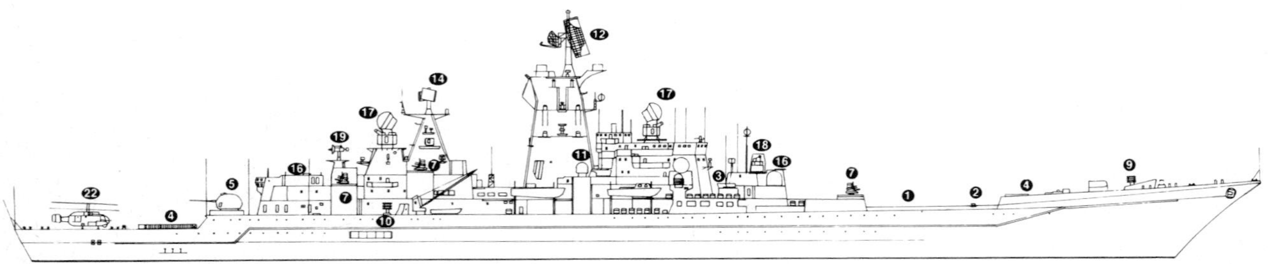

KALININ *(Scale 1 : 1 500), Ian Sturton*

KALININ 6/1991

KALININ 5/1990

KALININ 5/1990

KIROV 6/1990

HELICOPTER CRUISERS

2 MOSKVA CLASS (CHG)

Name	*Builders*	*Laid down*	*Launched*	*Commissioned*
MOSKVA	Nikolayev South	1963	1965	May 1967
LENINGRAD	Nikolayev South	1965	1967	late 1968

Displacement, tons: 14 900 standard; 17 500 full load
Dimensions, feet (metres): 626.6 oa; 587.3 wl × 115.5 oa; 75.5 wl × 28.5 *(191 oa; 179 wl × 34; 23 × 8.7)*
Flight deck, feet (metres): 265.7 × 111.5 *(81 × 34)*
Main machinery: 4 boilers; 2 turbines; 100 000 hp(m) *(73.5 MW)*; 2 shafts
Speed, knots: 31. **Range, miles:** 9000 at 18 kts; 4500 at 29 kts
Complement: 840 plus aircrew

Missiles: SAM: 2 SA-N-3 Goblet twin launchers ❶; semi-active radar homing to 55 km *(30 nm)* at 2.5 Mach; warhead 80 kg; altitude 91.4-22 860 m *(300-75 000 ft)*; 48 missiles.
A/S: SUW-N-1 twin launcher ❷; 18 Fras 1A or 1B; inertial flight to 29 km *(16 nm)*; warhead nuclear 5 kT or Type 45 torpedo.
Guns: 4—57 mm/80 (2 twin) ❸; 85° elevation; 120 rounds/minute to 6 km *(3.3 nm)*; weight of shell 2.8 kg.
Torpedoes: Tubes removed in both ships.
A/S mortars: 2 RBU 6000 12-tubed trainable ❹; range 6000 m; warhead 31 kg.
Countermeasures: Decoys: 2 twin Chaff launchers.
ESM/ECM: 8 Side Globe. 2 Bell Clout. 2 Bell Slam. 2 Bell Tap. 2 Top Hat
Fire control: 2 Tee Plinth and 3 Tilt Pot optronic directors.
Radars: Air search: Top Sail ❺; 3D; D band; range 555 km *(300 nm)*.
Head Net C ❻; E band; range 128 km *(70 nm)*.
Surface search: Two Don 2; I band.
Fire control: Two Head Light A ❼; F/G/H band (for SA-N-3). Two Muff Cob ❽; G/H band (for 57 mm).
IFF: 2 High Pole *(Moskva)*. 2 Salt Pot *(Leningrad)*.
Sonars: Moose Jaw; hull-mounted; active search and attack; medium/low frequency.
Mare Tail; VDS ❾; active search; medium frequency.

Helicopters: 14 Ka-25 Hormone A ASW ❿.

Programmes: Type name is *protivolodochny kreyser* meaning anti-submarine cruiser. This class represented a radical change of thought. The design must have been completed while the November class submarines were building and the heavy A/S armament and sensors (helicopters and VDS) suggest an ambitious attempt to cope with nuclear submarines.
Structure: In early 1973 *Moskva* was seen with a landing pad on the after end of the flight deck for flight tests of VTOL aircraft. Since removed. Main hangar, 67 × 25 m *(219.8 × 82 ft)*. There is also a small hangar 41 × 12 m *(134.5 × 39.4 ft)* in the superstructure. Two 10 ton lifts. Has Bell Crown data link antennas.

LENINGRAD *5/1990*

Operational: General purpose capability including command, air defence and ASW. These ships have poor sea-keeping qualities and although *Moskva* is still in good condition, both may soon be put in reserve or even scrapped as an economy measure. Based in the Black Sea.

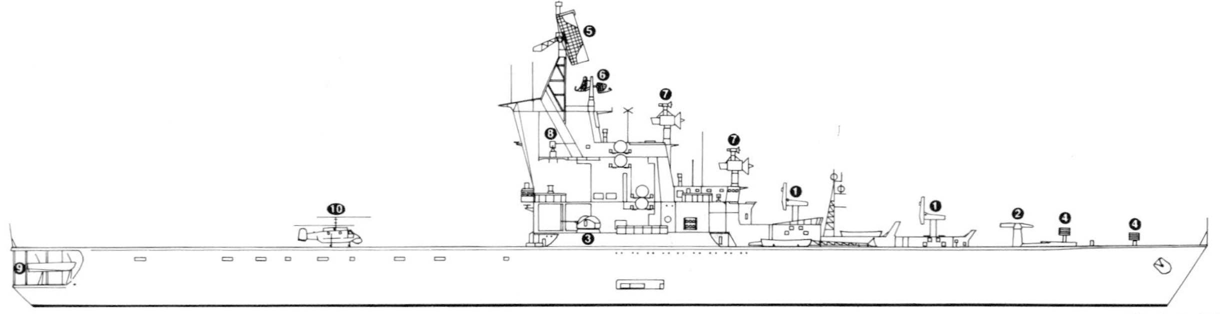

MOSKVA *(Scale 1 : 1 200), Ian Sturton*

MOSKVA *9/1991, TASS*

CRUISERS

3 + 1 SLAVA CLASS (CG)

Name	*Builders*	*Laid down*	*Launched*	*Commissioned*
SLAVA	Nikolayev North (61 Kommuna)	1976	1979	Aug 1982
MARSHAL USTINOV	Nikolayev North (61 Kommuna)	1978	1982	Apr 1986
CHERVONA UKRAINA	Nikolayev North (61 Kommuna)	1979	1983	Jan 1990
ADMIRAL LOBOV	Nikolayev North (61 Kommuna)	1984	Aug 1990	1994

Displacement, tons: 9800 standard; 11 200 full load
Dimensions, feet (metres): 610.2 × 68.2 × 24.9 *(186 × 20.8 × 7.6)*
Main machinery: COGAG; 4 gas turbines; 108 800 hp(m) *(80 MW)*; 2 gas turbines; 13 600 hp(m) *(10 MW)*; 2 shafts
Speed, knots: 32. **Range, miles:** 2500 at 30 kts; 6000 at 15 kts
Complement: 454 (38 officers)

Missiles: SSM: 16 SS-N-12 (8 twin) launchers ❶; inertial guidance with command update; active radar homing to 550 km *(300 nm)* at 1.7 Mach; warhead nuclear 350 kT or HE 1000 kg.
SAM: 8 SA-N-6 Grumble vertical launchers ❷; 8 rounds per launcher; command guidance; semi-active radar homing to 100 km *(54 nm)*; warhead 90 kg (or nuclear?); altitude 27 432 m *(90 000 ft)*.
2 SA-N-4 Gecko twin launchers ❸; semi-active radar homing to 15 km *(8 nm)* at 2.5 Mach; warhead 50 kg; altitude 9.1-3048 m *(30-10 000 ft)*; 40 missiles.
Guns: 2—130 mm/70 (twin) ❹; 35/45 rounds/minute to 29 km *(16 nm)*; weight of shell 27 kg.
6—30 mm/65; 6 barrels per mounting; 85° elevation; 3000 rounds/minute to 2 km.
Torpedoes: 10—21 in *(533 mm)* (2 quin) ❺. Type 53; dual purpose; pattern active/passive homing up to 20 km *(10.8 nm)* at up to 45 kts; warhead 400 kg or low yield nuclear.
A/S mortars: 2 RBU 6000 12-tubed trainable ❻; range 6000 m; warhead 31 kg.
Countermeasures: Decoys: 2 twin 12-tubed Chaff launchers.
ESM/ECM: 8 Side Globe. 4 Rum Tub. Bell series. IR surveillance.
Fire control: 2 Tee Plinth and 3 Tilt Pot optronic directors. 2 Punch Bowl satellite data receiving/targeting systems.
Radars: Air search: Top Pair (Top Sail + Big Net) ❼; 3D; C/D band; range 366 km *(200 nm)* for bomber, 183 km *(100 nm)* for 2 m² target.
Air/surface search: Top Steer ❽ or Top Plate *(Ukraina)*; 3D; D/E band.
Navigation: Three Palm Frond; I band.
Fire control: Front Door ❾; F band (for SS-N-12). Top Dome ❿; J band (for SA-N-6). Two Pop Group ⓫; F/H/I band (for SA-N-4). Three Bass Tilt ⓬; H/I band (for Gatlings). Kite Screech ⓭; H/I/K band (for 130 mm).
IFF: Salt Pot A and B. 2 Long Head.
Sonars: Bull Horn; hull-mounted; active search and attack; low/medium frequency.
Mare Tail; VDS; active search; medium frequency.

Helicopters: 1 Ka-25 Hormone B ⓮.

Programmes: Building at the same yard that built the Kara class but at a rate of one every four years. This is a smaller edition of the dual-purpose surface warfare/ASW *Kirov*, designed as a conventionally powered back-up for that class. *Admiral Lobov* is the last of the class and may not be completed.
Structure: The notable gap abaft the twin funnels (SA-N-6 area) is traversed by a large crane which stows between the funnels. The hangar is recessed below the flight deck with an inclined ramp. The torpedo tubes are behind shutters in the hull below the Top Dome radar director aft.
Operational: The SA-N-6 system effectiveness is diminished by having only one radar director. Over-the-horizon targeting for SS-N-12 provided by Hormone or SATCOM. *Slava* is based in the Black Sea Fleet, *Marshal Ustinov* deployed to the Northern Fleet on a permanent basis in March 1987. *Chervona Ukraina* started sea trials in August 1989 and transferred to the Pacific in October 1990.

MARSHAL USTINOV — *7/1991, Giorgio Arra*

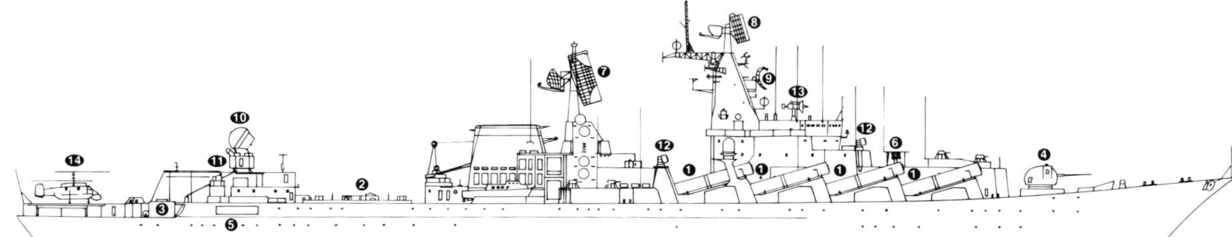

SLAVA — *(Scale 1 : 1 200), Ian Sturton*

CHERVONA UKRAINA (with Top Plate) — *10/1990, 92 Wing RAAF*

7 KARA CLASS (CG)

Name	*Builders*	*Laid down*	*Launched*	*Commissioned*
NIKOLAYEV	Nikolayev North (61 Kommuna)	Jan 1969	Feb 1970	Sep 1971
OCHAKOV	Nikolayev North (61 Kommuna)	Mar 1970	June 1971	Mar 1973
KERCH	Nikolayev North (61 Kommuna)	June 1971	July 1972	Sep 1974
AZOV	Nikolayev North (61 Kommuna)	Aug 1972	Sep 1973	Nov 1975
PETROPAVLOVSK	Nikolayev North (61 Kommuna)	Nov 1973	Dec 1974	Nov 1976
TASHKENT	Nikolayev North (61 Kommuna)	Jan 1975	Oct 1975	Nov 1977
VLADIVOSTOK (ex-*Tallinn*)	Nikolayev North (61 Kommuna)	Dec 1975	Mar 1977	Apr 1980

Displacement, tons: 8000 standard; 9900 full load
Dimensions, feet (metres): 568 × 61 × 22 *(173.2 × 18.6 × 6.7)*
Main machinery: COGAG; 4 gas turbines; 108 800 hp(m) *(80 MW)*; 2 gas turbines; 13 600 hp(m) *(10 MW)*; 2 shafts
Speed, knots: 34. **Range, miles:** 9000 at 15 kts cruising turbines; 3000 at 32 kts
Complement: 540 (30 officers)

Missiles: SAM: 2 SA-N-3 Goblet twin launchers (1 launcher in *Azov*) ❶; semi-active radar homing to 55 km *(30 nm)* at 2.5 Mach; warhead 80 kg; altitude 91.4-22 860 m *(300-75 000 ft)*; 72 missiles.
6 SA-N-6 Grumble vertical launchers (*Azov* only); 4 rounds per launcher; command guidance; semi-active radar homing to 100 km *(54 nm)*; warhead 90 kg (or nuclear?); altitude 27 432 m *(90 000 ft)*.
2 SA-N-4 Gecko twin launchers (twin either side of mast) ❷; semi-active radar homing to 15 km *(8 nm)* at 2.5 Mach; warhead 50 kg; altitude 9.1-3048 m *(30-10 000 ft)*; 40 missiles.
A/S: 2 SS-N-14 Silex quad launchers ❸; command guidance to 55 km *(30 nm)* at 0.95 Mach; payload nuclear or Type E53 torpedo; active/passive homing to 15 km *(8.1 nm)* at 40 kts; warhead 150 kg. SSM version; range 35 km *(19 nm)*; warhead 500 kg.
In addition to the Kresta II armament of eight tubes for the SS-N-14 A/S system (probably with a surface-to-surface capability) and the pair of twin launchers for SA-N-3 system with Goblet missiles, Kara class mounts the SA-N-4 system in 2 silos, either side of the mast. The SA-N-3 system has only 2 loading doors per launcher and a larger launching arm. This might indicate an SSM capability for the SA-N-3. *Azov* was the trials ship for the new SA-N-6 SAM system designed for subsequent classes. This replaces the after SA-N-3, after RBUs and torpedo tubes of a standard Kara.
Guns: 4—3 in *(76 mm)*/60 (2 twin) ❹; 80° elevation; 90 rounds/minute to 15 km *(8 nm)*; weight of shell 6.8 kg.
4—30 mm/65 ❺; 6 barrels per mounting; 85° elevation; 3000 rounds/minute combined to 2 km.
The siting of both main and secondary armament on either beams in the waist follows the precedent of both Kresta classes, although the weight of the main armament is increased.
Torpedoes: 10 or 4—21 in *(533 mm)* (2 quin) (2 twin in *Azov*) ❻. Type 53; dual purpose; pattern active/passive homing up to 20 km *(10.8 nm)* at up to 45 kts; warhead 400 kg or low yield nuclear.
A/S mortars: 2 RBU 6000 12-tubed trainable ❼; range 6000 m; warhead 31 kg.
2 RBU 1000 6-tubed (aft) (not in *Petropavlovsk*) ❽; range 1000 m; warhead 55 kg.
Countermeasures: Decoys: 2 twin Chaff launchers. 1 BAT-1 torpedo decoy.
ESM/ECM: 8 Side Globe. 2 Bell Slam. 1 Bell Clout and 2 Bell Tap (in *Nikolayev* and *Ochakov*). 4 Rum Tub (fitted on mainmast in *Kerch*).

KERCH (with Flat Screen) *3/1990*

Fire control: 2 Tee Plinth (*Azov*) and 4 Tilt Pot optronic directors.
Radars: Air search: Top Sail ❾; 3D; D band; or Flat Screen; E/F band.
Air/surface search: Head Net C ❿; 3D; E band; range 128 km *(70 nm)*.
Navigation: Two Don Kay (not in *Nikolayev*); I band. Two Palm Frond (*Nikolayev* only); I band. Don 2 (not in *Azov*); I band.
Fire control: Two Head Light B or C (one in *Azov*) ⓫; F/G/H band (for SA-N-3 and SS-N-14). Two Pop Group ⓬; F/H/I band (for SA-N-4). Top Dome (aft in *Azov* in place of one Head Light C); J band (for SA-N-6). Two Owl Screech ⓭; G band (for 76 mm). Two Bass Tilt ⓮; H/I band (for 30 mm).
Tacan: Fly Screen A (not in all). Two Round House (*Petropavlovsk*).
IFF: High Pole A. High Pole B. Salt Pot/Square Head (*Nikolayev*).
Sonars: Bull Nose; hull-mounted; active search and attack; low/medium frequency.
Mare Tail; VDS ⓯; active search; medium frequency.

Helicopters: 1 Ka-25 Hormone A ⓰.

Programmes: Apart from the specialised Moskva class this was the first class of large cruisers to join the Soviet Navy since the Sverdlov class—designed specifically for ASW. *Nikolayev* although commissioned in 1971 was first seen out of area when she entered the Mediterranean from the Black Sea on 2 March 1973. Type name is *bolshoy protivolodochny korabl*, meaning large anti-submarine ship.
Modernisation: The Flat Screen air search radar, first seen in *Kerch*, is expected to be retrofitted in all of the class.
Structure: *Azov* is of a modified design as the SA-N-6 trials ship and emerged from the Black Sea only in June 1986. All are fitted with stabilisers. *Petropavlovsk* has a higher hangar with two Round House Tacan on each side. The helicopter is raised to flight deck level by a lift in all of the class.

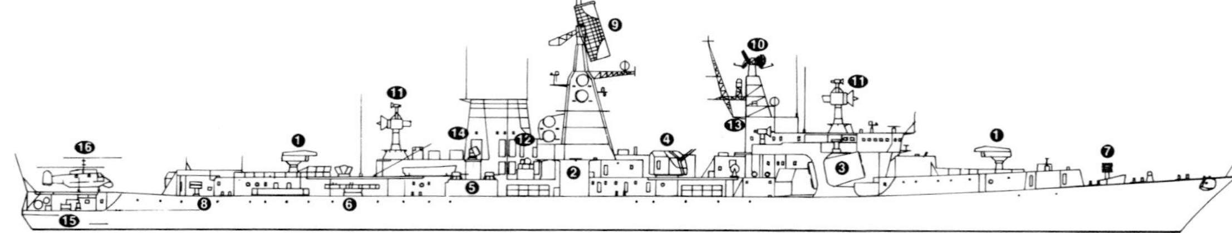
KARA Class *(Scale 1 : 1 200), Ian Sturton*

AZOV (with Top Dome and one Head Light) *6/1990*

10 KRESTA II CLASS (CG)

Name	*Builders*	*Laid down*	*Launched*	*Commissioned*
KRONSHTADT	Zhdanov, Leningrad	June 1966	Feb 1968	Sep 1969
ADMIRAL ISAKOV	Zhdanov, Leningrad	June 1966	Dec 1968	Sep 1970
ADMIRAL NAKHIMOV	Zhdanov, Leningrad	May 1967	Apr 1969	Aug 1971
ADMIRAL MAKAROV	Zhdanov, Leningrad	Mar 1968	Apr 1970	June 1972
KHABAROVSK (ex-*Marshal Voroshilov*)	Zhdanov, Leningrad	Jan 1969	Nov 1970	May 1973
ADMIRAL OKTYABRSKY	Zhdanov, Leningrad	May 1969	June 1971	Sep 1973
ADMIRAL ISACHENKOV	Zhdanov, Leningrad	Feb 1970	Mar 1972	Aug 1974
MARSHAL TIMOSHENKO	Zhdanov, Leningrad	June 1971	Oct 1973	Aug 1975
VASILY CHAPAYEV	Zhdanov, Leningrad	Feb 1972	Jan 1975	Sep 1976
ADMIRAL YUMASHEV	Zhdanov, Leningrad	Nov 1973	Oct 1976	Oct 1977

Displacement, tons: 6400 standard; 7850 full load
Dimensions, feet (metres): 519.9 × 55.4 × 19.7 *(158.5 × 16.9 × 6)*
Main machinery: 4 boilers; 2 turbines; 110 000 hp(m) *(80.85 MW)*; 2 shafts
Speed, knots: 35. **Range, miles:** 10 500 at 14 kts; 2400 at 32 kts
Complement: 400

Missiles: SAM: 2 SA-N-3 Goblet twin launchers ❶; semi-active radar homing to 55 km *(30 nm)* at 2.5 Mach; warhead 80 kg; altitude 91.4-22 860 m *(300-75 000 ft)*; 48 missiles.
A/S: 2 SS-N-14 Silex quad launchers ❷; command guidance to 55 km *(30 nm)* at 0.95 Mach; payload nuclear or Type E53 torpedo; active/passive homing to 15 km *(8.1 nm)* at 40 kts; warhead 150 kg. SSM version; range 35 km *(19 nm)*; warhead 500 kg.
Guns: 4—57 mm/80 (2 twin) ❸; 85° elevation; 120 rounds/minute to 6 km *(3.3 nm)*; weight of shell 2.8 kg.
4—30 mm/65 ❹; 6 barrels per mounting; 85° elevation; 3000 rounds/minute combined to 2 km.
Torpedoes: 10—21 in *(533 mm)* (2 quin) ❺. Type 53; dual purpose; pattern active/passive homing up to 20 km *(10.8 nm)* at up to 45 kts; warhead 400 kg or low yield nuclear.
A/S mortars: 2 RBU 6000 12-tubed trainable ❻; range 6000 m; warhead 31 kg.
2 RBU 1000 6-tubed ❼; range 1000 m; warhead 55 kg.
Countermeasures: Decoys: 2 twin Chaff launchers.
ESM/ECM: 8 Side Globe. 2 Bell Slam. 1 Bell Clout. 2 Bell Tap. 2 Bell Crown.
Fire control: 2 Tee Plinth optronic directors.
Radars: Air search: Top Sail ❽; 3D; D band; range 555 km *(300 nm)*.
Air/surface search: Head Net C ❾; 3D; E band; range 128 km *(70 nm)*.
Navigation: Two Don Kay; I band or Two Palm Frond; I band.
Fire control: Two Head Light A (aft), B (forward) or C ❿; F/G/H band (for SA-N-3 and SS-N-14). Two Muff Cob ⓫; G/H band (for 57 mm). Two Bass Tilt (not in hulls 1-4) ⓬; H/I band (for 30 mm).
IFF: High Pole A and B.
Sonars: Bull Nose; hull-mounted; active search and attack; medium frequency.

Helicopters: 1 Ka-25 Hormone A ⓭.

Programmes: Type name is *bolshoy protivolodochny korabl*, meaning large anti-submarine ship.
Structure: The design was developed from that of the Kresta I class, but with the SS-N-14 replacing the SS-N-3 the role has been changed from that of surface warfare for Kresta I to ASW for Kresta II although the SS-N-14 probably has an anti-surface ship capability. At the same time the substitution of SA-N-3 for SA-N-1 improved Kresta II class's air defence capability. Fin stabilisers. Hulls 8-10 have an additional deck-house abaft the bridge and between the four 30 mm mounts. The helicopter is raised to flight deck level by a lift.

ADMIRAL MAKAROV *6/1989*

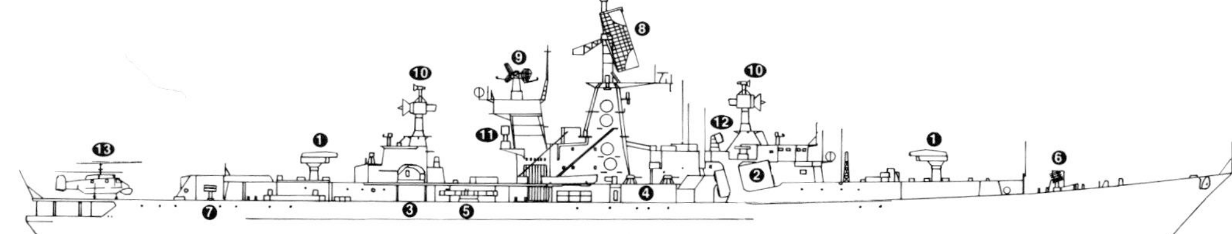
KRESTA II Class *(Scale 1 : 1 200), Ian Sturton*

ADMIRAL NAKHIMOV *5/1990*

1 KRESTA I CLASS (CG)

Name	*Builders*	*Laid down*	*Launched*	*Commissioned*
ADMIRAL ZOZULYA	Zhdanov, Leningrad	Sep 1964	Oct 1965	Mar 1967

Displacement, tons: 6140 standard; 7700 full load
Dimensions, feet (metres): 510 × 55.7 × 19.7 *(155.5 × 17 × 6)*
Main machinery: 4 boilers; 2 turbines; 110 000 hp(m) *(80.85 MW)*; 2 shafts
Speed, knots: 35. **Range, miles:** 10 500 at 14 kts; 2400 at 32 kts
Complement: 360

Missiles: SSM: 4 SS-N-3B Sepal (2 twin) launchers ❶; command guidance; active radar homing to 460 km *(250 nm)* at 1.1 Mach; warhead nuclear 350 kT or HE 1000 kg; no reloads.
SAM: 2 SA-N-1 Goa twin launchers ❷; command guidance to 31.5 km *(17 nm)* at 2 Mach; warhead 60 kg; altitude 91.4-22 860 m *(300-75 000 ft)*; 32 missiles.
Guns: 4—57 mm/80 (2 twin) ❸; 85° elevation; 120 rounds/minute to 6 km *(3.3 nm)*; weight of shell 2.8 kg.
4—30 mm/65 AK 630 ❹; 6 barrels per mounting; 3000 rounds/minute to 2 km.
Torpedoes: 10—21 in *(533 mm)* (2 quin) ❺. Type 53; dual purpose; pattern active/passive homing up to 20 km *(10.8 nm)* at up to 45 kts; warhead 400 kg or low yield nuclear.
A/S mortars: 2 RBU 6000 12-tubed trainable ❻; range 6000 m; warhead 31 kg.
2 RBU 1000 6-tubed ❼; range 1000 m; warhead 55 kg.
Countermeasures: Decoys: 2 twin Chaff launchers.
ESM/ECM: 8 Side Globe. Bell Clout. 2 Bell Slam. 2 Bell Tap. 2 Bell Strike. 2 Bell Crown.
Fire control: 2 Tee Plinth optronic directors ❽.
Radars: Air search: Big Net ❾; C band; range 183 km *(100 nm)* for 2 m² target.
Air/surface search; Head Net C ❿; 3D; E band; range 128 km *(70 nm)*.
Navigation: Two Palm Frond; I band.
Fire control: Scoop Pair ⓫; E band (for SS-N-3). Two Peel Group ⓬; H/I band (for SA-N-1). Two Muff Cob ⓭; G/H band (for 57 mm). Two Bass Tilt ⓮; H/I band (for 30 mm).
IFF: High Pole B.
Sonars: Herkules; hull-mounted; active search and attack; medium frequency.

Helicopters: 1 Ka-25 Hormone B ⓯.

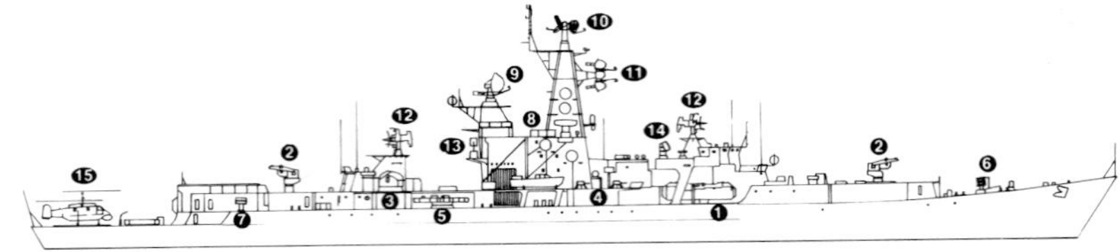
KRESTA I Class *(Scale 1 : 1 500), Ian Sturton*

KRESTA I Class *6/1986*

Programmes: Designed for surface warfare, the successor to the Kynda class. Type name *bolshoy protivolodochny korabl*, meaning large anti-submarine ship. Changed in 1977-78 to *raketny kreyser*, meaning missile cruiser.
Modernisation: The addition of the 30 mm guns and fire control radars is assumed following the changes made during a similar long refit to *Admiral Drozd* (since deleted). Armament not yet confirmed.
Structure: Provided with a helicopter landing deck and hangar aft. This gives an enhanced carried-on-board target-location facility for the SS-N-3B system. The Kresta I was therefore the first missile cruiser free to operate alone and without targeting assistance from shore-based aircraft.
Operational: In refit at Kronshtadt from 1985 and against expectations emerged in November 1991 to start sea trials and probably become the Baltic Fleet Flagship. The remainder of the class have been paid off.

3 KYNDA CLASS (CG)

Name	*Builders*	*Laid down*	*Launched*	*Commissioned*
GROZNY	Zhdanov, Leningrad	June 1960	Apr 1961	May 1962
ADMIRAL FOKIN	Zhdanov, Leningrad	Dec 1960	Nov 1961	May 1963
ADMIRAL GOLOVKO	Zhdanov, Leningrad	Dec 1961	Nov 1962	June 1963

Displacement, tons: 4400 standard; 5550 full load
Dimensions, feet (metres): 465.8 × 51.8 × 17.4 *(142 × 15.8 × 5.3)*
Main machinery: 4 boilers; 2 turbines; 110 000 hp(m) *(80.85 MW)*; 2 shafts
Speed, knots: 34. **Range, miles:** 6000 at 14.5 kts; 1500 at 34 kts
Complement: 329 (25 officers)

Missiles: SSM: 8 SS-N-3B Sepal (2 quad) launchers ❶; inertial guidance; active radar homing to 460 km *(250 nm)* at 1.1 Mach; warhead nuclear 350 kT or HE 1000 kg; 8 reloads.
SAM: SA-N-1 Goa twin launcher ❷; command guidance to 31.5 km *(17 nm)* at 2 Mach; warhead 60 kg; altitude 91.4-22 860 m *(300-75 000 ft)*; 16 missiles. Some SSM capability.
Guns: 4—3 in *(76 mm)*/60 (2 twin) ❸; 80° elevation; 90 rounds/minute to 15 km *(8 nm)*; weight of shell 6.8 kg.
4—30 mm/65 ❹; 6 barrels per mounting; 85° elevation; 3000 rounds/minute combined to 2 km.
Torpedoes: 6—21 in *(533 mm)* (2 triple) ❺. Type 53; dual purpose; pattern active/passive homing up to 20 km *(10.8 nm)* at up to 45 kts; warhead 400 kg or low yield nuclear.
A/S mortars: 2 RBU 6000 12-tubed trainable ❻; range 6000 m; warhead 31 kg.
Countermeasures: ESM/ECM: 4 Top Hat. Bell Clout. Bell Tap. Bell Slam.
Fire control: 2 Tee Plinth (not *Grozny*); 2 Plinth Net ❼ (not *Admiral Golovko*) optronic directors.
Radars: Air search: Two Head Net A ❽ (*Grozny* and *Admiral Golovko*) or Head Net A and Head Net C (*Admiral Fokin*); E band.
Surface search and Navigation: Two Don 2; I band.
Fire control: Two Scoop Pair ❾; E band (for SS-N-3B). Peel Group ❿; H/I band (for SS-N-1). Owl Screech ⓫; G band (for 76 mm). Two Bass Tilt ⓬; H/I band (for 30 mm).
IFF: High Pole B.
Sonars: Herkules; hull-mounted; active search and attack; medium frequency.

Helicopters: Platform only.

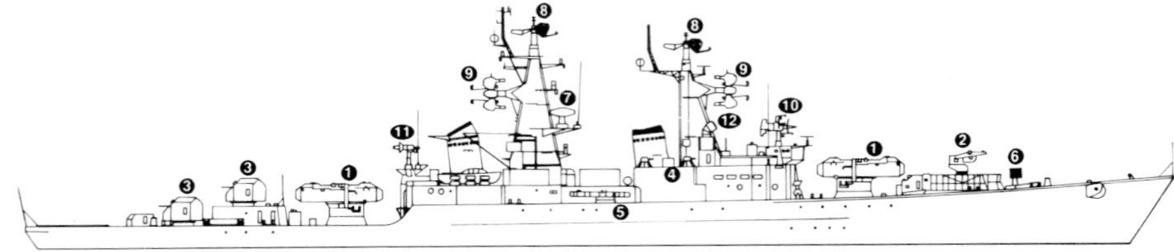
GROZNY *(Scale 1 : 1 200), Ian Sturton*

Programmes: This class was designed for surface warfare and was the first class of missile cruisers built. The role made it the successor of the Sverdlov class. Type name is *raketny kreyser* meaning missile cruiser.
Modernisation: All were modernised in the early 1980s, including the installation of a Head Net C radar in place of Head Net A (*Fokin*), the four 30 mm Gatling mounts with two associated Bass Tilt radars and a twin level deckhouse abaft the forward funnel.
Operational: This class showed at an early stage the Soviet ability to match radar availability to weapons systems. The duplicated aerials provide not only a capability for separate target engagement but also provide a reserve in the event of damage. *Fokin* based in the Pacific, *Grozny* in the Baltic and *Golovko* in the Black Sea. One deleted in 1990 and the remainder are unlikely to go to sea again.

GROZNY *7/1985*

DESTROYERS

0 + 2 UDALOY II CLASS (DDG)

Name	*Builders*	*Laid down*	*Launched*	*Commissioned*
—	Yantar, Kaliningrad 820	1989	1992	1993

Displacement, tons: 8900 full load
Dimensions, feet (metres): 536.4 × 63.3 × 24.6 *(163.5 × 19.3 × 7.5)*
Main machinery: COGAG; 4 gas turbines; 2 shafts
Speed, knots: 30. **Range, miles:** 6000 at 20 kts
Complement: 250

Missiles: SSM: 4 SS-N-22 Sunburn.
SAM: 8 SA-N-9 vertical launchers.
SAM/Guns: 2 CADS-N-1; each with twin 30 mm Gatling; combined with 8 SA-N-11.
Guns: 4—130 mm/70 (2 twin).
Torpedoes: 8—21 in *(533 mm)* (2 quad tubes).
A/S mortars: 2 RBU 6000.

Programmes: Follow-on class from the Udaloys. Inevitably there is uncertainty over build-rates and dates of completion because of the funding problems of the shipyards in early 1992.
Structure: Similar size to the Udaloy and probably has the same propulsion machinery. Improved combination of weapon systems owing something to both the Sovremenny and the Neustrashimy classes.

12 UDALOY CLASS (DDG)

Name	*Builders*	*Laid down*	*Launched*	*Commissioned*
UDALOY	Yantar, Kaliningrad 820	1978	Feb 1980	Nov 1980
VITSE-ADMIRAL KULAKOV	Zhdanov Yard, Leningrad 190	1978	Apr 1980	Sep 1981
MARSHAL VASILEVSKY	Zhdanov Yard, Leningrad 190	1979	Jan 1982	June 1983
ADMIRAL ZAKHAROV	Yantar, Kaliningrad 820	1979	Nov 1982	Oct 1983
ADMIRAL SPIRIDONOV	Yantar, Kaliningrad 820	1981	Nov 1983	Sep 1984
ADMIRAL TRIBUTS	Zhdanov Yard, Leningrad 190	1980	Apr 1983	Aug 1985
MARSHAL SHAPOSHNIKOV	Yantar, Kaliningrad 820	1983	Jan 1985	Oct 1985
SIMFEROPOL (ex-*Marshal Buokenny*)	Yantar, Kaliningrad 820	1983	Feb 1985	Dec 1986
ADMIRAL LEVCHENKO	Zhdanov Yard, Leningrad 190	1982	Mar 1985	Jan 1988
ADMIRAL VINOGRADOV	Yantar, Kaliningrad 820	1985	June 1987	Oct 1988
ADMIRAL KHARLAMOV	Yantar, Kaliningrad 820	1985	June 1988	Sep 1989
ADMIRAL PANTELEYEV	Yantar, Kaliningrad 820	1987	Feb 1990	July 1991

Displacement, tons: 6700 standard; 8700 full load
Dimensions, feet (metres): 536.4 × 63.3 × 24.6 *(163.5 × 19.3 × 7.5)*
Flight deck, feet (metres): 65.6 × 59 *(20 × 18)*
Main machinery: COGAG; 2 gas turbines; 55 500 hp(m) *(40.8 MW)*; 2 gas turbines; 13 600 hp(m) *(10 MW)*; 2 shafts
Speed, knots: 30. **Range, miles:** 2600 at 30 kts; 6000 at 20 kts
Complement: 249 (29 officers)

Missiles: SAM: 8 SA-N-9 vertical launchers ❶; command guidance; active radar homing to 12 km *(6.6 nm)* at 2 Mach; warhead 15 kg; altitude 3.4-12 192 m *(10-40 000 ft)*; 64 missiles. Probably 4 channels of fire.
The launchers are set into the ships' structures with 6 ft diameter cover plates—four on the fo'c'sle, two between the torpedo tubes and two at the forward end of the after deckhouse between the RBUs.
A/S: 2 SS-N-14 Silex quad launchers ❷; command guidance to 55 km *(30 nm)* at 0.95 Mach; payload nuclear or Type E53 torpedo; active/passive homing to 15 km *(8.1 nm)* at 40 kts; warhead 150 kg. SSM version; range 35 km *(19 nm)*; warhead 500 kg.
Guns: 2—3.9 in *(100 mm)*/70 ❸; 80° elevation; 80 rounds/minute to 15 km *(8.2 nm)*; weight of shell 16 kg.
4—30 mm/65 ❹; 6 barrels per mounting; 85° elevation; 3000 rounds/minute combined to 2 km.
Torpedoes: 8—21 in *(533 mm)* (2 quad) tubes ❺. Type 53; dual purpose; pattern active/passive homing up to 20 km *(10.8 nm)* at up to 45 kts; warhead 400 kg or low yield nuclear.
A/S mortars: 2 RBU 6000 12-tubed trainable ❻; range 6000 m; warhead 31 kg.
Mines: Rails for 30 mines.
Countermeasures: Decoys; 8 ten-barrelled Chaff launchers. US Masker type noise reduction.
ESM/ECM: 2 Bell Shroud. 2 Bell Squat. 4 Foot Ball (not in all).

ADMIRAL PANTELEYEV *7/1991, MoD Bonn*

Radars: Air search: One or two (*Udaloy* and *Kulakov*) Strut Pair ❼; F band.
Top Plate (not *Udaloy* and *Kulakov*) ❽; 3D; D/E band.
Surface search: Three Palm Frond ❾; I band.
Fire Control: Two Eye Bowl ❿; F band (for SS-N-14). Two Cross Sword ⓫ (for SA-N-9). Kite Screech ⓬; H/I/K band (for 100 mm guns). Two Bass Tilt ⓭; H/I/K band (for 30 mm guns).
IFF: Salt Pot A and B.
Tacan: Two Round House.
CCA: Fly Screen B (by starboard hangar) ⓮.
Sonars: Horse Jaw; hull-mounted; active search and attack; low/medium frequency.
Horse Tail; VDS; active search; medium frequency.

Helicopters: 2 Ka-27 Helix A ⓯.

Programmes: Successor to Kresta II class but based on Krivak class design. Type name is *bolshoy protivolodochny korabl* meaning large anti-submarine ship.

Structure: The two hangars are set side by side with inclined elevating ramps to the flight deck. Has pre-wetting NBCD equipment and replenishment at sea gear. Initially SA-N-9 was not operational and the first three of the class commissioned without the Cross Sword fire control radars. There also seemed to be a shortage of Strut Pair radars and numbers three to seven initially had no air search radar on their foremasts on commissioning. These deficiencies are slowly being made good. Active stabilisers are fitted. The Chaff launchers are fitted on both sides of the foremast and inboard of the torpedo tubes.
Operational: A general purpose ship with the emphasis on ASW and complementary to Sovremenny class. Good sea-keeping and endurance have been reported. Based as follows: Northern Fleet—*Udaloy, Kulakov, Vasilevsky, Simferopol* and *Levchenko*; Pacific Fleet—*Zakharov, Spiridonov, Tributs, Shaposhnikov,* and *Vinogradov*. *Kharlamov* returned to the Baltic from the Northern Fleet in 1991 and *Panteleyev* was on sea trials also in the Baltic.

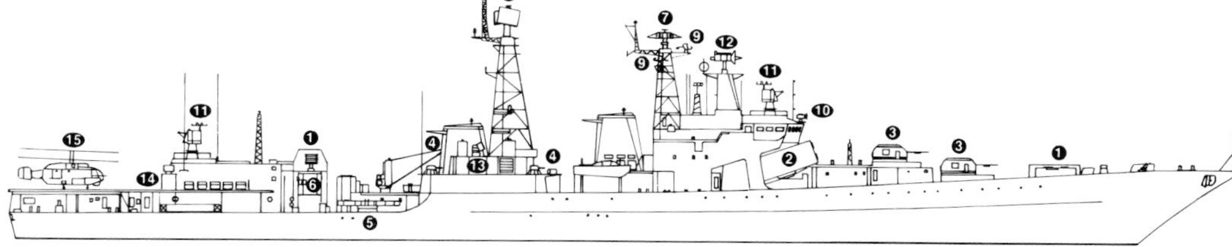
ADMIRAL SPIRIDONOV *(Scale 1 : 1 200), Ian Sturton*

MARSHAL SHAPOSHNIKOV *7/1991, 92 Wing RAAF*

15 + 6 SOVREMENNY CLASS (DDG)

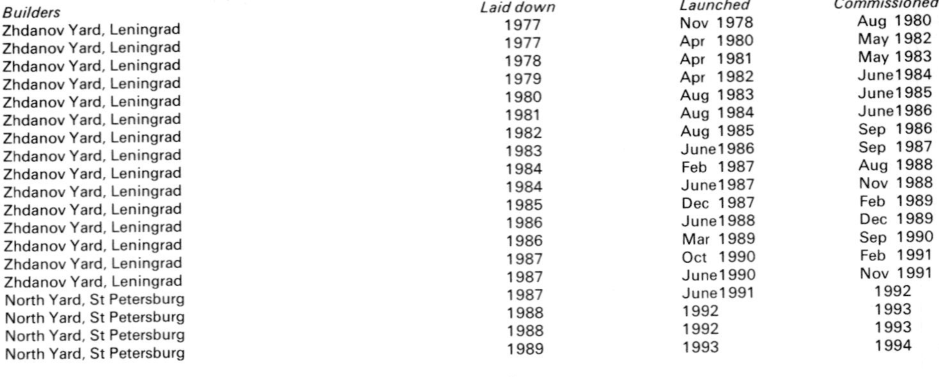

Name	*Builders*	*Laid down*	*Launched*	*Commissioned*
SOVREMENNY	Zhdanov Yard, Leningrad	1977	Nov 1978	Aug 1980
OTCHYANNY	Zhdanov Yard, Leningrad	1977	Apr 1980	May 1982
OTLICHNNY	Zhdanov Yard, Leningrad	1978	Apr 1981	May 1983
OSMOTRITELNY	Zhdanov Yard, Leningrad	1979	Apr 1982	June 1984
BEZUPRECHNY	Zhdanov Yard, Leningrad	1980	Aug 1983	June 1985
BOYEVOY	Zhdanov Yard, Leningrad	1981	Aug 1984	June 1986
STOYKY	Zhdanov Yard, Leningrad	1982	Aug 1985	Sep 1986
OKRYLENNY	Zhdanov Yard, Leningrad	1983	June 1986	Sep 1987
BURNY	Zhdanov Yard, Leningrad	1984	Feb 1987	Aug 1988
GREMYASHCHY	Zhdanov Yard, Leningrad	1984	June 1987	Nov 1988
BYSTRY	Zhdanov Yard, Leningrad	1985	Dec 1987	Feb 1989
RASTOROPNY	Zhdanov Yard, Leningrad	1986	June 1988	Dec 1989
BEZBOYAZNENNY	Zhdanov Yard, Leningrad	1986	Mar 1989	Sep 1990
BEZUDERZHNY	Zhdanov Yard, Leningrad	1987	Oct 1990	Feb 1991
BESPOKOINY	Zhdanov Yard, Leningrad	1987	June 1990	Nov 1991
—	North Yard, St Petersburg	1987	June 1991	1992
—	North Yard, St Petersburg	1988	1992	1993
—	North Yard, St Petersburg	1988	1992	1993
—	North Yard, St Petersburg	1989	1993	1994

Displacement, tons: 6500 standard; 7300 full load
Dimensions, feet (metres): 511.8 × 56.8 × 21.3 *(156 × 17.3 × 6.5)*
Main machinery: 4 boilers; 2 turbines; 102 000 hp(m) *(75 MW)*; 2 shafts; bow thruster
Speed, knots: 32. **Range, miles:** 2400 at 32 kts; 6500 at 20 kts; 14 000 at 14 kts
Complement: 296 (25 officers)

Missiles: SSM: 8 SS-N-22 Sunburn (2 quad) launchers (1); active radar homing to 110 km *(60 nm)* at 2.5 Mach; warhead nuclear or HE; sea-skimmer. Modified missile has a range of 160 km *(87 nm)*.
SAM: 2 SA-N-7 Gadfly (2); command/semi-active radar and IR homing to 28 km *(15 nm)* at 3 Mach; warhead 54 kg; altitude 30.4-14 020 *(100-46 000 ft)*; 44 missiles. Multiple channels of fire.
Guns: 4—130 mm/70 (2 twin) (3); 85° elevation; 35/45 rounds/minute to 29.5 km *(16 nm)*; weight of shell 27 kg.
4—30 mm/65 ADG 630 (4); 6 barrels per mounting; 85° elevation; 3000 rounds/minute combined to 2 km.
Torpedoes: 4—21 in *(533 mm)* (2 twin) tubes (5). Type 53; dual purpose; pattern active/passive homing up to 20 km *(10.8 nm)* at up to 45 kts; warhead 400 kg or low yield nuclear.
A/S mortars: 2 RBU 1000 6-barrelled (6); range 1000 m; warhead 55 kg; 120 rockets carried.
Mines: Have mine rails for up to 40.
Countermeasures: Decoys: 8 ten-barrelled Chaff launchers.
ESM/ECM: 4 Foot Ball (some variations including 2 Bell Shroud and 2 Bell Squat).
Fire control: 1 Squeeze Box optronic director and laser rangefinder (7). 2 Shot Dome.
Radars: Air search: Top Steer (in first three). Plate Steer (in 4th and 5th ships). Top Plate (remainder) (8); 3D; D/E band.
Surface search: Three Palm Frond (9); I band.
Fire control: Band Stand (10); D/E/F band (for SS-N-22). Six Front Dome (11); F band (for SA-N-7). Kite Screech (12); H/I/K band (for 30 mm guns). Two Bass Tilt (13); H/I band (for 30 mm guns).
IFF: Salt Pot A and B. High Pole A and B. Long Head.
Tacan: Two Light Bulb.
Sonars: Bull Horn and Steer Hide; hull-mounted; active search and attack; medium frequency.

Helicopters: 1 Ka-25 Hormone B or Ka-27 Helix (14).

Programmes: Built at the same yard as the Kresta II class. Zhdanov was renamed North Yard in 1989. Type name is *eskadrenny minonosets* meaning destroyer. Still building at the rate of about two a year.

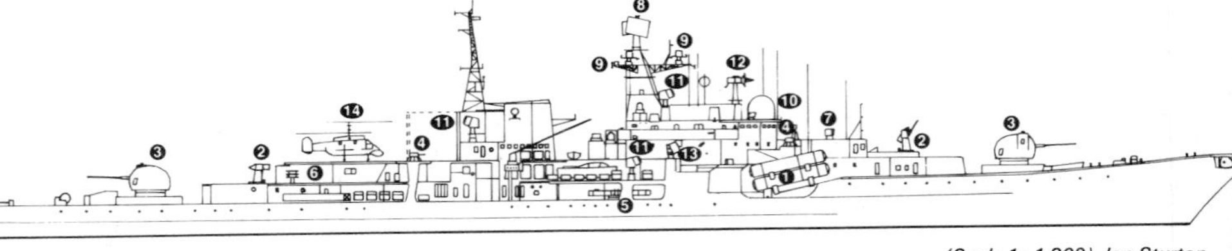

BOYEVOY *(Scale 1 : 1 200), Ian Sturton*

BEZBOYAZNENNY (with Top Plate) *6/1991, Guy Toremans*

Structure: Telescopic hangar. The fully automatic 130 mm gun was first seen in 1976. Chaff launchers are fitted on both sides of the foremast and either side of the after SAM launcher.
Operational: A specialist surface warfare ship complementing the ASW-capable Udaloy class. Based as follows: Northern Fleet—*Sovremenny, Otchyanny, Otlichnny, Bezuprechny, Okrylenny, Gremyashchy, Rastoropny* and *Bezuderzhny*. Pacific Fleet—*Osmotritelny, Boyevoy, Stoyky, Burny, Bystry* and *Bezboyaznenny*. *Bespokoiny* was on trials in the Baltic in 1992.

BEZUPRECHNY (with Plate Steer) *7/1990, W. Sartori*

9 KASHIN and 2 MODIFIED KASHIN CLASSES (DDG)

KOMSOMOLETS UKRAINY	**OBRAZTSOVY**	**SDERZHANNY***	**SMYSHLENNY***
KRASNY-KAVKAZ	**RESHITELNY**	**SKORY**	**SPOSOBNY**
KRASNY-KRYM	**ODARENNY**	**SMETLIVY**	

* Modified

Displacement, tons: 3500 standard; 4750 full load (Kashin)
3950 standard; 4900 full load (mod Kashin)
Dimensions, feet (metres): 472.4 (482.3 mod) × 51.8 × 15.4 *(144 (147) × 15.8 × 4.7)*
Main machinery: COGAG; 4 gas turbines; 72 000 hp(m) *(52.9 MW)*; 2 shafts
Speed, knots: 35. **Range, miles:** 4000 at 20 kts; 2600 at 30 kts
Complement: 280 (20 officers, unmodified), (25 officers, modified).

Missiles: SSM: 4 SS-N-2C Styx (modified ships) ❶; active radar or IR homing to 83 km *(45 nm)* at 0.9 Mach; warhead 513 kg; sea-skimmer at end of run; no reloads.
SAM: 2 SA-N-1 Goa twin launchers ❷; command guidance to 31.5 km *(17 nm)* at 2 Mach; warhead 60 kg; altitude 91.4-22 860 m *(300-75 000 ft)*; 32 missiles. Some SSM capability.
Guns: 4—3 in *(76 mm)*/60 (2 twin) ❸; 80° elevation; 90 rounds/minute to 15 km *(8 nm)*; weight of shell 6.8 kg.
4—30 mm/65 (modified ships) ❹; 6 barrels per mounting; 85° elevation; 3000 rounds/minute combined to 2 km.
Torpedoes: 5—21 in *(533 mm)* (quin) tubes ❺. Type 53; dual purpose; pattern active/passive homing up to 20 km *(10.8 nm)* at up to 45 kts; warhead 400 kg or low yield nuclear.
A/S mortars: 2 RBU 6000 12-tubed trainable ❻; range 6000 m; warhead 31 kg; 120 rockets.
2 RBU 1000 6-tubed (not in modified ships) ❼; range 1000 m; warhead 55 kg.
Mines: Laying capability (unmodified only) for up to 20.
Countermeasures: Decoys: 4—16-tubed Chaff launchers (modified ships). 2 towed torpedo decoys.
ESM/ECM: 2 Bell Shroud. 2 Bell Squat (modified ships). 2 Watch Dog (remainder).
Fire control: 3 Tee Plinth and 4 Tilt Pot optronic directors.
Radars: Air/surface search: Head Net C ❽; 3D; E band; (except *Komsomolets Ukrainy* and *Obraztsovy*).
Big Net ❾; C band (except *Komsomolets Ukrainy* and *Obraztsovy*).
Two Head Net A ❿; E band. (*Komsomolets Ukrainy* and *Obraztsovy*).
Navigation: Two Don 2/Don Kay/Palm Frond; I band.
Fire control: Two Peel Group ⓫; H/I band (for SA-N-1). Two Owl Screech ⓬; G band (for guns). Two Bass Tilt (modified ships) ⓭; H/I band (for 30 mm).
IFF: High Pole B (Modified ships).
Sonars: Bull Horn or Bull Nose; hull-mounted; active search and attack; medium frequency.
Mare Tail; VDS (modified ships plus *Smetlivy* and *Sposobny*); search; medium frequency.

Helicopters: Platform only ⓮.

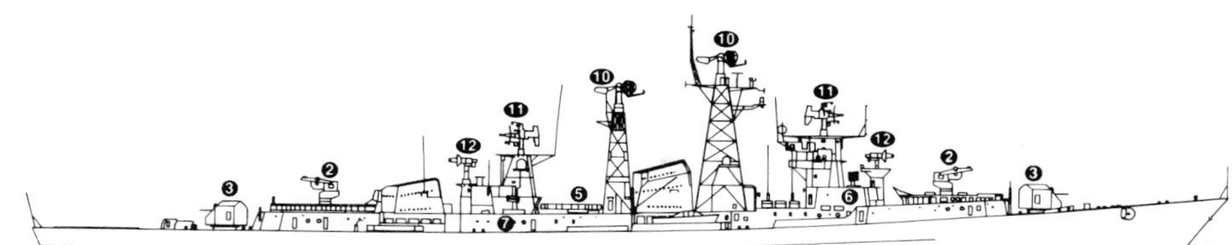
KOMSOMOLETS UKRAINY *(Scale 1 : 1 200), Ian Sturton*

KRASNY-KRYM *6/1991, van Ginderen Collection*

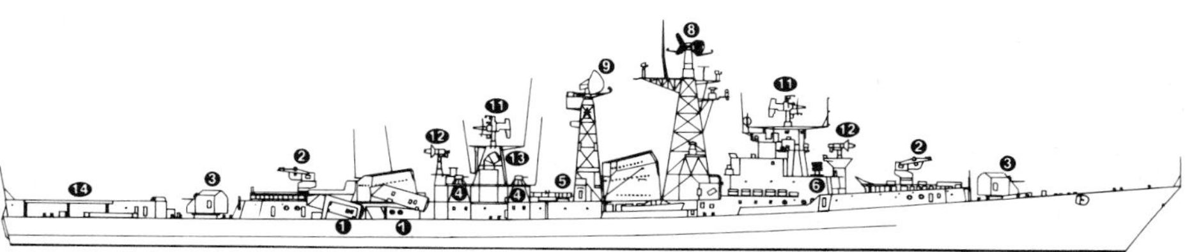
SMYSHLENNY *(Scale 1 : 1 200), Ian Sturton*

Programmes: The first class of warships in the world to rely entirely on gas-turbine propulsion. These ships were delivered from 1962 to 1972 from the Zhdanov Yard, Leningrad (*Obraztsovy* and *Odarenny*) (1965-67) and the remainder from the 61 Kommuna (North) Yard, Nikolayev (1962-72). *Sderzhanny*, last of the class, was the only one to be built to the modified design, *Smyshlenny* was converted after completion. Type name is *bolshoy protivolodochny korabl*, meaning large anti-submarine ship.
Modernisation: In order to bring this class up-to-date with SSM and VDS a conversion programme was started in 1972 to the same pattern as set in *Sderzhanny*. This conversion consisted of lengthening the hull by 10 ft *(3 m)*, shipping four SS-N-2 (C) launchers (SSM), four Gatling close range weapons, a VDS under a new stern helicopter platform and removing the after RBUs. By 1976 four had been so converted. The fifth and last conversion was completed in 1980. In the mid-1970s *Provorny* was converted to carry out trials of the new SA-N-7 SAM system for new construction ships. Two more of the class *Smetlivy* and *Sposobny* have been equipped with VDS since 1987. All but two of the modified ships have been paid off.
Operational: One sank in the Black Sea in 1974. The class is now being paid off at the rate of about three a year.
Sales: Additional ships of a modified design built for India. First transferred September 1980, the second in June 1982, the third in 1983, the fourth in August 1986 and the fifth and last in January 1988. All are fitted with helicopter hangars. *Smely* transferred to Poland 9 January 1988.

SMYSHLENNY (modified) *10/1988*

FRIGATES

1 + 1 NEUSTRASHIMY CLASS (FFG)

Name	*Builders*	*Laid down*	*Launched*	*Commissioned*
NEUSTRASHIMY	Yantar, Kaliningrad	Apr 1986	May 1988	1992
—	Yantar, Kaliningrad	May 1988	May 1991	1993

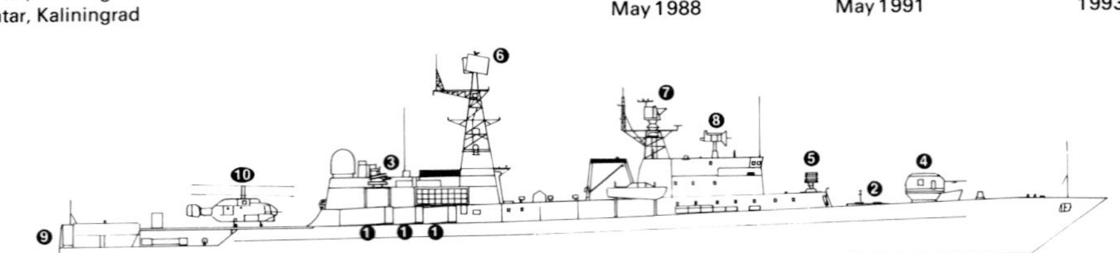

NEUSTRASHIMY (Scale 1 : 1 200), *Ian Sturton*

Displacement, tons: 4100 full load
Dimensions, feet (metres): 423.2 oa; 403.5 wl × 50.9 × 15.7 *(129; 123 × 15.5 × 4.8)*
Main machinery: COGAG; 4 gas turbines; 68 000 hp(m) *(50 MW)*; 2 shafts
Speed, knots: 32
Complement: 200

Missiles: SSM: A/S: SS-N-16 type ❶; inertial flight to 120 km *(65 nm)*; payload Type 45 torpedo or nuclear warhead; fired from torpedo tubes. SS-N-25 may be fitted in due course.
SAM: 4 SA-N-9 sextuple vertical launchers ❷; command guidance; active radar homing to 12 km *(6.6 nm)* at 2 Mach; warhead 15 kg.
SAM/Guns: 2 CADS-N-1 ❸; each has a twin 30 mm Gatling combined with 8 SA-N-11 and Hot Flash fire control radar. Laser beam guidance for missiles to 8 km *(4.4 nm)*.
Guns: 1—3.9 in *(100 mm)*/70 ❹; 80° elevation; 80 rounds/minute to 15 km *(8.2 nm)*; weight of shell 16 kg.
Torpedoes: 6 tubes combined with SSM launcher ❶; can fire SS-N-16 type missiles or anti-submarine torpedoes.
A/S mortars: 1 RBU 12 000 ❺; 10-tubed trainable; range 12 000 m; warhead 80 kg.
Mines: 2 rails.
Countermeasures: Decoys: 2—10-barrelled Chaff launchers.
ESM/ECM: Intercept and jammers. 2 Bell Crown; 2 Foot Ball; 2 Half Hat; 3 Cage Flask.
Radars: Air/surface search: Top Plate ❻; 3D; D/E band.
Navigation: 2 Palm Frond; I band.
Fire control: Cross Sword ❼ (for SAM). Kite Screech ❽ (for SSM and guns); I band.
IFF: 2 Salt Pot.
Sonars: Bull Nose; hull-mounted; active search and attack.
Steer Hide VDS ❾ or towed sonar array.

Helicopters: 1 Ka-27 Helix ❿.

Programmes: The last naval (as opposed to Border Guard) Krivak class frigate commissioned in 1981 and a follow-on class has been expected for some time. The first of class started sea trials in the Baltic in December 1990. Build rate may rise to two per year by mid-1990s if a second shipyard is made available but the programme has been badly affected by funding problems and construction is very slow.
Structure: This ship is slightly larger than the Krivak and has a helicopter which is a standard part of the armament of modern Western frigates. There are three horizontal angled launchers at main deck level on each side of the ship. These appear to double up for a combined SSM and A/S missile of the submarine-launched SS-N-16 type plus normal torpedoes, although this analysis is still uncertain. The dome next to the CADS-N-1 mountings is the same as that in *Kalinin* which is also adjacent to the combined SAM/gun close-in weapon system. The helicopter deck extends across the full width of the ship. The after funnel is unusually flush decked. There is space for SS-N-25 aft of the forward funnel.

NEUSTRASHIMY (VDS streamed) *2/1991, MoD Bonn*

NEUSTRASHIMY *12/1990, MoD Bonn*

NEUSTRASHIMY *12/1990, MoD Bonn*

15 GRISHA I, 12 GRISHA II, 30 GRISHA III and 26 + 3 GRISHA V CLASSES (FFL)

AMETYST, BRILLIANT, IZUMRUD, PREDANNY RUBIN, SAPFIR, ZHEMCHUG, PROVORNY
(All Grisha II class (Border Guard))

Displacement, tons: 950 standard; 1200 full load
Dimensions, feet (metres): 236.2 × 32.8 × 12.1 *(72 × 10 × 3.7)*
Main machinery: CODAG; 1 gas turbine; 15 000 hp(m) *(11 MW)*; 2 diesels; 16 000 hp(m) *(11.8 MW)*; 3 shafts
Speed, knots: 30. **Range, miles:** 4500 at 10 kts; 1750 at 22 kts diesels; 950 at 27 kts
Complement: 70 (Grisha III); 60 (Grisha I)

Missiles: SAM: SA-N-4 Gecko twin launcher (Grisha I, III and V classes) ❶; semi-active radar homing to 15 km *(8 nm)* at 2.5 Mach; warhead 50 kg; altitude 9.1-3048 m *(30-10 000 ft)*; 20 missiles (see *Structure* for SA-N-9).
Guns: 2—57 mm/80 (twin) (2 twin in Grisha II class) ❷; 85° elevation; 120 rounds/minute to 6 km *(3.3 nm)*; weight of shell 2.8 kg.
1—3 in *(76 mm)*/60 (Grisha V) ❸; 85° elevation; 120 rounds/minute to 15 km *(8 nm)*; weight of shell 7 kg.
1—30 mm/65 (Grisha III and V classes) ❹; 6 barrels; 85° elevation; 3000 rounds/minute combined to 2 km.
Torpedoes: 4—21 in *(533 mm)* (2 twin) tubes ❺. Type 53; dual purpose; pattern active/passive homing up to 20 km *(10.8 nm)* at up to 45 kts; warhead 400 kg or low yield nuclear.
A/S mortars: 2 RBU 6000 12-tubed trainable ❻; range 6000 m; warhead 31 kg. (Only 1 in Grisha Vs).
Depth charges: 2 racks (12).
Mines: Capacity for 18 in lieu of depth charges.
Countermeasures: ESM: 2 Watch Dog. 1—10-barrelled Chaff launcher (Grisha V).
Radars: Air/surface search: Strut Curve (Strut Pair in early Grisha Vs) ❼; F band; range 110 km *(60 nm)* for 2 m² target.
Half Plate Bravo (in later Grisha Vs); E/F band.
Navigation: Don 2; I band.
Fire control: Pop Group (Grisha I, III and V) ❽; F/H/I band (for SA-N-4). Muff Cob (except in Grisha III and V) ❾; G/H band (for 57 mm). Bass Tilt (Grisha III and V) ❿; H/I band (for 57/76 mm and 30 mm).
IFF: High Pole A or B. Square Head. Salt Pot.
Sonars: Hull-mounted; active search and attack; high/medium frequency.
VDS ⓫; active search; high frequency. Similar to Hormone helicopter dipping sonar.

Programmes: Grisha I series production 1968-75; Grisha II 1973-84; Grisha III 1973-85; Grisha V 1982 onwards. All were built or are building at Kiev, Kharbarovsk and Zelenodolsk except Grisha II which were only built at Zelenodolsk. Type name is *maly protivolodochny korabl* meaning small anti-submarine ship (Grisha I, III and V) or *pogranichny storozhevoy korabl* meaning border patrol ship (Grisha II).
Structure: SA-N-4 launcher mounted on the fo'c'sle in all but Grisha II. This is replaced by a second twin 57 mm in Grisha II class. Grisha III class has Muff Cob radar removed, Bass Tilt and 30 mm ADG (fitted aft), and Rad-haz screen removed from abaft funnel as a result of removal of Muff Cob. Grisha V is similar to Grisha III with the after twin 57 mm mounting replaced by a single Tarantul type 76 mm gun. One Grisha III in the Black Sea was modified as the trials unit for the SA-N-9/Cross Swords SAM system in the early 1980s and is sometimes known as Grisha IV.

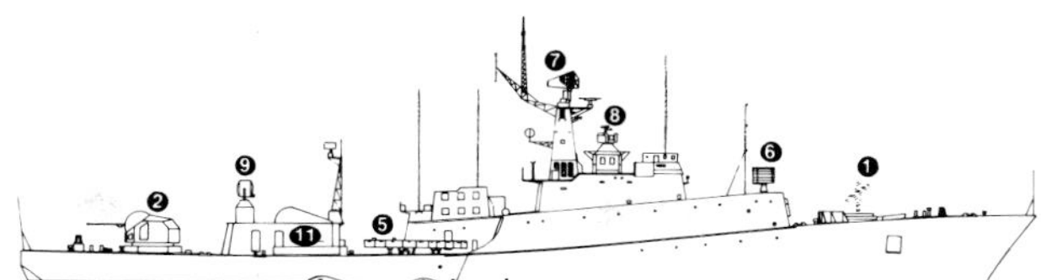
GRISHA I
(Scale 1 : 900), Ian Sturton

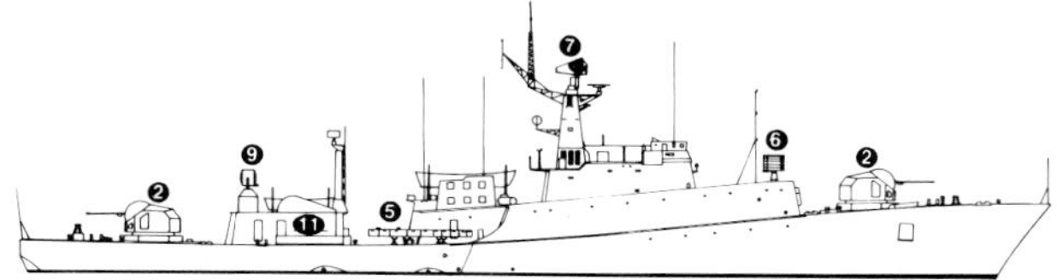
GRISHA II
(Scale 1 : 900), Ian Sturton

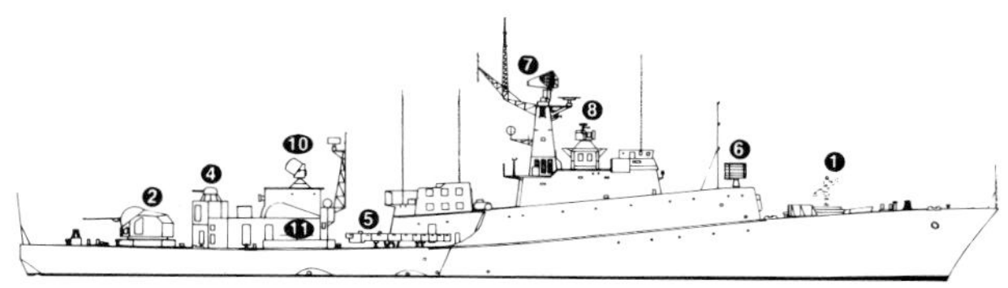
GRISHA III
(Scale 1 : 900), Ian Sturton

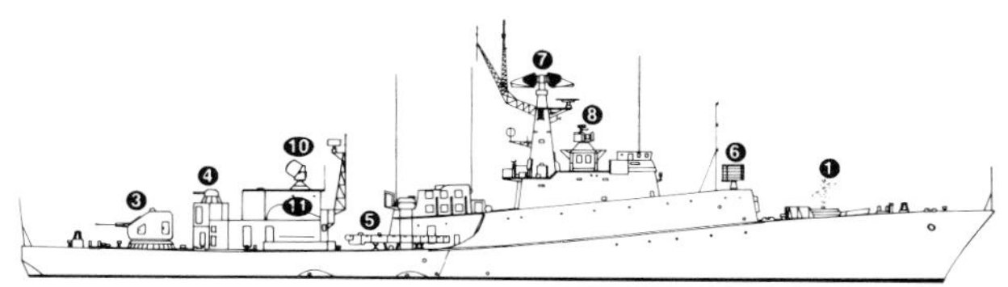
GRISHA V
(Scale 1 : 900), Ian Sturton

Operational: Grisha II and six Grisha III are Border Guard ships and have names. Some Grisha IIIs and Vs may have 2 SA-N-5 launchers.

GRISHA I *5/1990*

GRISHA II *5/1990*

GRISHA III *7/1991*

GRISHA V *6/1991, 92 Wing RAAF*

21 KRIVAK I (FFG), 11 KRIVAK II (FFG) and 8 KRIVAK III CLASSES (FF)

KRIVAK I (Kaliningrad)

BDITELNY
BODRY
DRUZHNY
RAZUMNY
RAZYASHCHY
SILNY
STOROZHEVOY
SVIREPY

KRIVAK I (Zhdanov, Leningrad*) (Kamysh-Burun (Kerch))

LENINGRADSKY KOMSOMOLETS*
LETUCHY*
PYLKY*
RETIVY*
ZADORNY*
ZHARKY*
BEZZAVETNY
BÉZUKORIZNENNY
DOSTOYNY
DOBLESTNY
DEYATELNY
LADNY
PORYVISTY

KRIVAK II (Kaliningrad)

BESSMENNY
GORDELIVY
GROMKY
GROZYASHCHY
NEUKROTIMY (ex-*Komsomolets Litvii*)
PYTLIVY
RAZITELNY
REVNOSTNY
REZKY
REZVY
RYANNY

KRIVAK III (Zaliv (Kerch))

MENZHINSKY
DZERZHINSKY
IMENI XXVII SEZDA KPSS
IMENI LXX LETIYA VCHK-KGB
IMENI LXX LETIYA POGRANVOYSK
KEDROV
VOROVSKY
+1

Displacement, tons: 3100 standard; 3600 full load
Dimensions, feet (metres): 405.2 × 46.9 × 16.4 (*123.5 × 14.3 × 5*)
Main machinery: COGAG; 2 gas turbines; 55 500 hp(m) (*40.8 MW*); 2 gas turbines; 13 600 hp(m) (*10 MW*); 2 shafts
Speed, knots: 32. **Range, miles:** 4600 at 20 kts; 1600 at 30 kts
Complement: 180 (18 officers)

Missiles: SSM: 8 SS-N-25 (2 quad) (1); (Krivak I after modernisation); radar homing to 150 km (*76.5 nm*) at 0.9 Mach; warhead 250 kg; sea-skimmer.
SAM: 2 SA-N-4 Gecko twin launchers (1 in Krivak III) (2); semi-active radar homing to 15 km (*8 nm*) at 2.5 Mach; warhead 50 kg; altitude 9.1-3048 m (*30-10 000 ft*); 40 missiles (20 in Krivak III). The launcher retracts into the mounting for stowage and protection, rising to fire and retracting to reload. The two mountings are forward of the bridge and abaft the funnel.
A/S: SS-N-14 Silex quad launcher (not in Krivak III) (3); command guidance to 55 km (*30 nm*) at 0.95 Mach; payload nuclear or Type E53 torpedo; active/passive homing to 15 km (*8.1 nm*) at 40 kts; warhead 150 kg. SSM version; range 35 km (*19 nm*); warhead 500 kg.
Guns: 4—3 in (*76 mm*)/60 (2 twin) (Krivak I) (4); 80° elevation; 90 rounds/minute to 15 km (*8 nm*); weight of shell 6.8 kg.
2—3.9 in (*100 mm*)/70 (Krivak II) (1 in Krivak III) (5); 80° elevation; 80 rounds/minute to 15 km (*8.2 nm*); weight of shell 16 kg.
2—30 mm/65 (Krivak III) (6); 6 barrels per mounting; 3000 rounds/minute combined to 2 km.
Torpedoes: 8—21 in (*533 mm*) (2 quad) tubes (7). Type 53; dual purpose; pattern active/passive homing up to 20 km (*10.8 nm*) at up to 45 kts; warhead 400 kg or low yield nuclear.
A/S mortars: 2 RBU 6000 12-tubed trainable (8); (not in modernised Krivak I); range 6000 m; warhead 31 kg.
Mines: Capacity for 20.
Countermeasures: Decoys: 4 Chaff launchers (16 tubes per launcher) or 10 (10 tubes per launcher). Towed torpedo decoy.
ESM/ECM: 2 Bell Shroud. 2 Bell Squat.
Radars: Air search: Head Net C (9); 3D; E band; range 128 km (*70 nm*). Top Plate (*Imeni XXVII* and later and some Krivak I after modernisation) (10).
Surface search: Don Kay or Palm Frond or Don 2 or Spin Trough (11); I band.
Peel Cone (12); I band (Krivak III).
Fire control: Two Eye Bowl (not in Krivak III) (13); F band (for SS-N-14). Two Pop Group (one in Krivak III) (14); F/H/I band (for SA-N-4). Owl Screech (Krivak I) (15); G band. Kite Screech (Krivak II and III) (16); H/I/K band. Bass Tilt (Krivak III) (17); H/I band.
IFF: High Pole B. Salt Pot (Krivak III).
Sonars: Bull Nose; hull-mounted; active search and attack; medium frequency.
Mare Tail or Steer Hide (*Zharky, Bditelny, Leningradsky Komsomolets* and other Krivak Is after modernisation); VDS (18); active search; medium frequency.

Helicopters: 1 Ka-25 Hormone or Ka-27 Helix (Krivak III) (19).

Programmes: The Krivak I class built from 1969-1981, Krivak II from 1976-81 and Krivak III from 1984-1992. Type name was originally *bolshoy protivolodochny korabl*, meaning large anti-submarine ship. Changed in 1977-78 to *storozhevoy korabl* meaning escort ship. Some of the Krivak III names seem certain to be changed.
Modernisation: Krivak I are being modernised with SS-N-25 quadruple launchers replacing RBU mountings forward of the bridge. Top Plate radar is replacing Head Net and a more modern VDS is also being fitted.

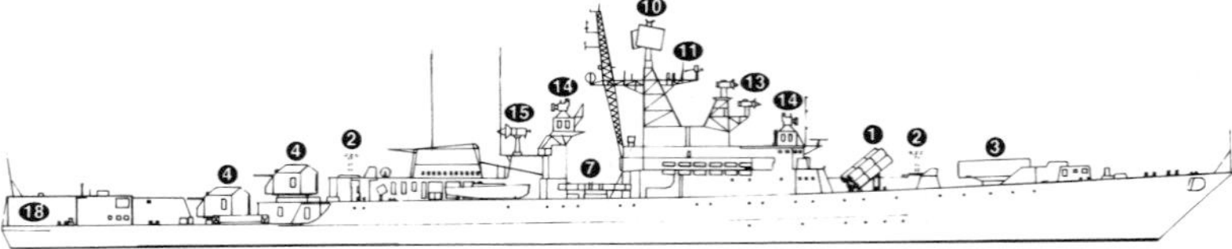

KRIVAK I (mod) *(Scale 1 : 1 200), Ian Sturton*

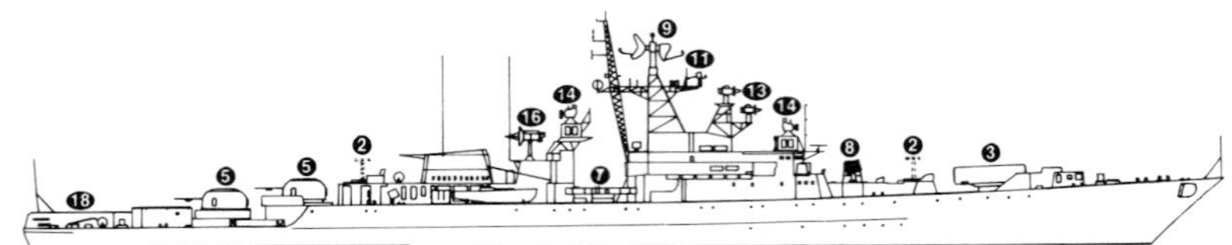
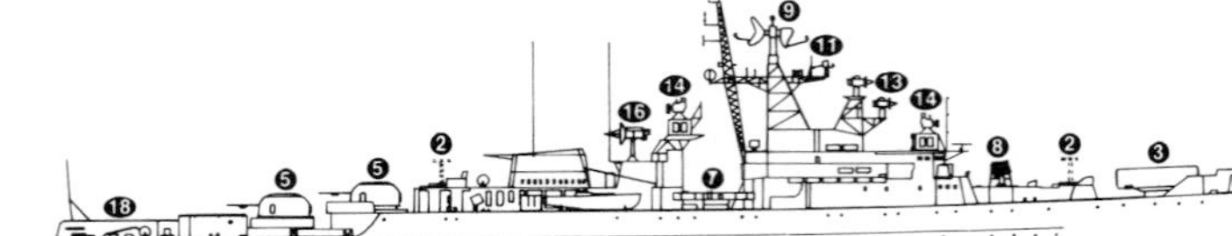

KRIVAK II *(Scale 1 : 1 200), Ian Sturton*

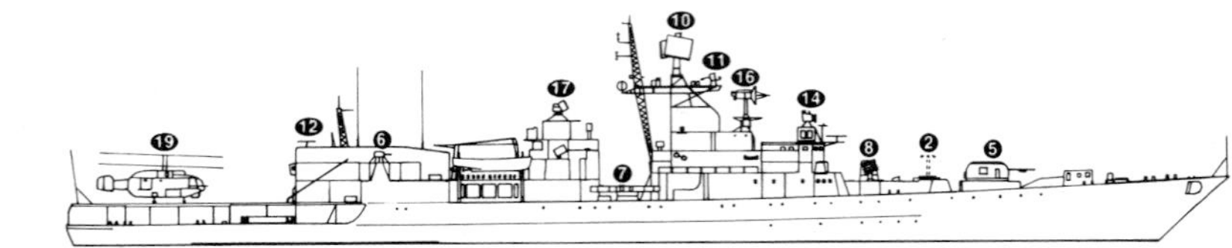

KRIVAK III *(Scale 1 : 1 200), Ian Sturton*

NEUKROTIMY (II) *6/1991, Harald Carstens*

Structure: Krivak II class has X-gun mounted higher and the break to the quarter-deck further aft apart from other variations noted. Krivak III class built for the former KGB but now under naval control. The removal of SS-N-14 and one SA-N-4 mounting compensates for the addition of a hangar and flight deck.

ZHARKY (I) (with Steer Hide VDS) *6/1991*

LENINGRADSKIY KOMSOMOLETS (I) (with SS-N-25 rails, Top Plate radar and Steer Hide VDS) *10/1991*

BDITELNY (I) (with Head Net radar and Mare Tail VDS) *6/1991, Guy Toremans*

GROMKY (II) *9/1991*

VOROVSKY (III) (with Top Plate) *9/1991, 92 Wing RAAF*

5 RIGA CLASS (FF)

Displacement, tons: 1260 standard; 1510 full load
Dimensions, feet (metres): 300.1 × 33.1 × 10.5 *(91.5 × 10.1 × 3.2)*
Main machinery: 2 boilers; 2 geared turbines; 20 000 hp(m) *(14.7 MW)*; 2 shafts
Speed, knots: 30. **Range, miles:** 2000 at 13 kts; 700 at 27 kts
Complement: 175

Guns: 3—3.9 in *(100 mm)*/56; 40° elevation; 15 rounds/minute to 16 km *(8.8 nm)*; weight of shell 13.5 kg.
4—37 mm/63 (2 twin); 80° elevation; 160 rounds/minute to 9 km *(5 nm)*; weight of shell 0.7 kg.
4—25 mm/80 (2 twin) (in some); 85° elevation; 270 rounds/minute to 3 km *(1.6 nm)*; weight of shell 0.34 kg.
Torpedoes: 2 or 3—21 in *(533 mm)* (twin or triple) tubes. Type 53; dual purpose; pattern active/passive homing up to 20 km *(10.8 nm)* at up to 45 kts; warhead 400 kg or low yield nuclear.
A/S mortars: 2 RBU 2500 16-tubed trainable; range 2500 m; warhead 21 kg.
Depth charges: 4 projectors; 2 racks.
Mines: Capacity for 28.
Countermeasures: ESM: 2 Watch Dog.
Radars: Surface search: Slim Net; E/F band.
Navigation: Don 2/Neptun; I band.
Fire control: Sun Visor B; G/H/I band. Wasp Head; H band.
IFF: Two Square Head. One High Pole.
Sonars: Hull-mounted; active search and attack; high frequency.
VDS (in some); active search; high frequency.

Programmes: Built from 1952 to 1959 at several yards. Successors to the Kola class escorts (now deleted) of which they are lighter and less heavily armed but improved versions. Type name is *storozhevoy korabl* meaning escort ship.
Modernisation: A small number of this class has been improved. Some have a twin 25 mm gun mounting on either side of the funnel and a dipping sonar abreast of the bridge.

RIGA *1990, van Ginderen Collection*

Operational: Seven deleted by early 1989 and 15 sold abroad for scrap in 1989. All the remainder except five deleted by early 1992. Of the survivors four are in the Northern Fleet and one in the Caspian Flotilla.

Sales: Three to Bulgaria (1957-58 and 1985), four to East Germany (1956-59), two to Finland (1964), eight to Indonesia (1962-65). All but one of the Bulgarian ships have been scrapped.

12 PARCHIM II CLASS (FFL)

Displacement, tons: 769 standard; 1200 full load
Dimensions, feet (metres): 246.7 × 32.2 × 14.4 *(75.2 × 9.8 × 4.4)*
Main machinery: 3 diesels; 13 200 hp(m) *(9.7 MW)*; 3 shafts
Speed, knots: 28
Complement: 60

Missiles: SAM: 2 SA-N-5 Grail quad launchers ❶; manual aiming; IR homing to 6 km *(3.2 nm)* at 1.5 Mach; altitude to 2500 m *(8000 ft)*; warhead 1.5 kg.
Guns: 1—3 in *(76 mm)*/66 ❷; 85° elevation; 120 rounds/minute to 15 km *(8 nm)*; weight of shell 7 kg.
1—30 mm/65 ❸; 6 barrels; 85° elevation; 3000 rounds/minute combined to 2 km.
Torpedoes: 4—21 in *(533 mm)* (2 twin) tubes ❹. Type 53; dual purpose.
A/S mortars: 2 RBU 6000 12-tubed trainable ❺; range 6000 m; warhead 31 kg.
Depth charges: 2 racks.
Mines: Rails fitted.
Countermeasures: Decoys: 2—16 barrelled Chaff launchers.
ESM: 2 Watch Dog.
Radars: Air/surface search: Positive E ❻; E/F band.
Navigation: TSR 333; I band.
Fire control: Bass Tilt ❼; H/I band.

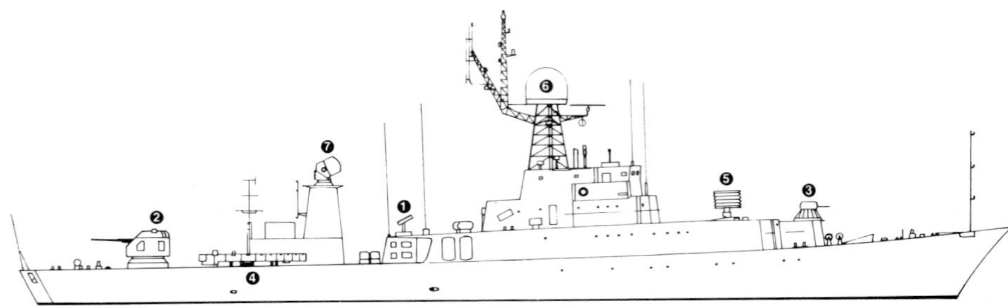

PARCHIM II *(Scale 1 : 600), Ian Sturton*

Sonars: Hull-mounted; active search and attack; medium frequency.
Helicopter type VDS; high frequency.

Programmes: Built in the GDR at Peenewerft, Wolgast for the Soviet Navy. First unit launched 29 August 1985 and delivered in 1986, three in 1987, three in 1988 and the remainder in 1989-90. The last unit was launched 20 January 1989.
Structure: Similar design to the ex-GDR Parchim I class but some armament differences.
Operational: All operate in the Baltic replacing the ageing Potis.

PARCHIM II *10/1991, Per Kornefeldt*

3 MIRKA II CLASS (FFL)

Displacement, tons: 950 standard; 1150 full load
Dimensions, feet (metres): 270.3 × 29.9 × 9.8 *(82.4 × 9.1 × 3)*
Main machinery: CODAG; 2 gas turbines; 25 000 hp(m) *(18.4 MW)*; 2 diesels; 12 000 hp(m) *(8.8 MW)*; 2 shafts
Speed, knots: 32; 20 diesels. **Range, miles:** 4800 at 10 kts; 500 at 30 kts
Complement: 96

Guns: 4—3 in *(76 mm)*/60 (2 twin); 80° elevation; 90 rounds/minute to 15 km *(8 nm)*; weight of shell 6.8 kg.
Torpedoes: 10—16 in *(406 mm)* (2 quin) tubes. Type 40; anti-submarine; active/passive homing to 15 km *(8.1 nm)* at 40 kts; warhead 100 kg.
A/S mortars: 2 RBU 6000 12-tubed trainable; range 6000 m; warhead 31 kg.
Countermeasures: ESM: 2 Watch Dog.
Radars: Air/surface search: Slim Net; E/F band or Strut Curve; F band.
Navigation: Don 2; I band.
Fire control: Hawk Screech; I band; range 27 km *(15 nm)*.
IFF: Two Square Head. High Pole B.
Sonars: Hull-mounted; active search and attack; high/medium frequency.
Dipping sonar is also fitted in some ships in the transom, and in others abreast the bridge.

Programmes: This class of ships was completed at Kaliningrad in 1963-66 as variation on Petya class. Type name was originally *maly protivolodochny korabl* meaning small anti-submarine ship. Changed in 1977-78 to *storozhevoy korabl* meaning escort.
Structure: While the hull is basically the same as that of Petya the housing in the stern for the two gas turbines results in a very distinctive silhouette. This arrangement calls for only two shafts as opposed to the three in Petya with the gas turbines driving twin compressors which feed into thrust tubes around the propellers. The gas turbine exhausts in the transom presumably provide additional thrust.
Operational: Five deleted in 1989, three in 1990, seven in 1991. The last three are in the Baltic and may be scrapped in 1992.

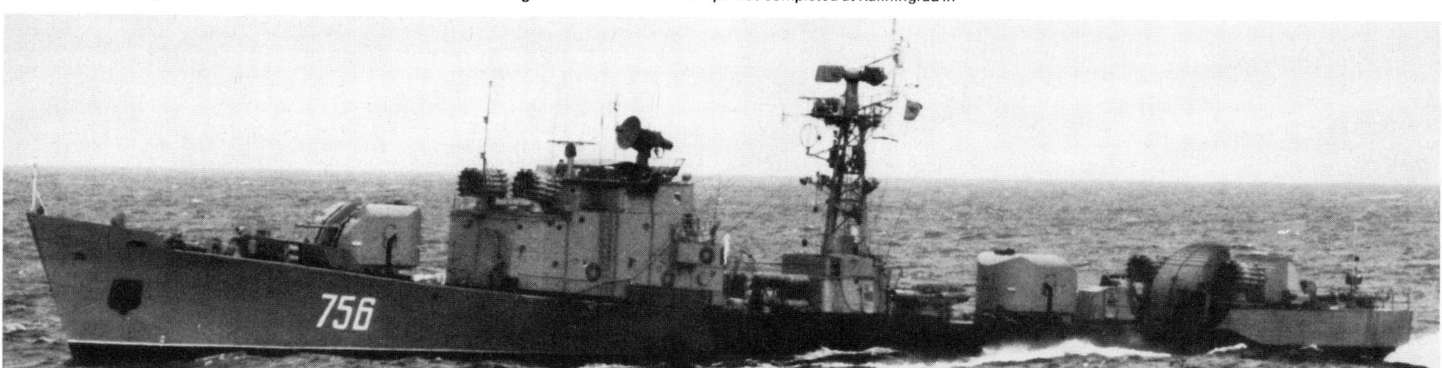

MIRKA *2/1989, MoD Bonn*

1 PETYA I, 4 MODIFIED PETYA I, 8 PETYA II and 1 MODIFIED PETYA II CLASSES (FFL)

Displacement, tons: 950 standard; 1180 full load
Dimensions, feet (metres): 268.3 (270.6, Mod Petya II) × 29.9 × 9.5 *(81.8 (82.5) × 9.1 × 2.9)*
Main machinery: CODAG; 2 gas turbines; 30 000 hp(m) *(22 MW)*; 1 Type 61V-3 diesel; 6000 hp(m) *(4.4 MW)* (centre shaft); 3 shafts
Speed, knots: 32. **Range, miles:** 4870 at 10 kts; 450 at 29 kts
Complement: 98

Guns: 4—3 in *(76 mm)*/60 (2 twin); (1 twin in some Mod Petya I); 80° elevation; 90 rounds/minute to 15 km *(8 nm)*; weight of shell 6.8 kg.
Torpedoes: 10 (Petya II) or 5 (remainder) 16 in *(406 mm)* (2 or 1 quin) tubes. Type 40; anti-submarine; active/passive homing to 15 km *(8.1 nm)* at 40 kts; warhead 100 kg.
A/S mortars: 4 (Petya I) or 2 (Mod Petya I) RBU 2500 16-tubed trainable; range 2500 m; warhead 21 kg.
2 RBU 6000 12-tubed trainable (Petya II and Mod Petya II); range 6000 m; warhead 31 kg.
Depth charges: 2 racks (not in Mod Petya II and some Mod Petya I).
Mines: Capacity for 22 (not in Mod Petya I).
Countermeasures: ESM: 2 Watch Dog; radar warning.
Radars: Air/surface search: Slim Net (Petya I); E/F band.
Strut Curve (Petya II); F band; range 110 km *(60 nm)* for 2 m² target.
Navigation: Neptun or Don 2 (Petya I); I band. Don 2 (Mod Petya I and II); I band.
Fire control: Hawk Screech; I band; range 27 km *(15 nm)*.
IFF: Two Square Head (Petya I). High Pole B (Petya I and II).
Sonars: Hull-mounted; active search and attack; high/medium frequency.
VDS (in some); active search; high frequency.

Programmes: The first ship was built in 1960-61 at Kaliningrad. Construction continued there and at Komsomolsk until about 1970.
Structure: Petya I—the basic hull and armament.
Mod Petya I—carry towed sonar in a deckhouse on the stern. One has a towed acoustic sensor in the open with no deckhouse. One has a deckhouse abaft the funnel replacing the quintuple torpedo tube mounting and a reel and winch on the stern similar to a towed array, while another has a deckhouse smaller than the remainder on the stern.
Petya II—extra quin torpedo tubes vice after RBUs.
Mod Petya II—first seen in 1978. After torpedo tubes removed and with a deckhouse built abaft the after 3 in *(76 mm)* gun to contain the towed trials equipment. There is a space either side for mine rails.
Operational: Numbers represent operational hulls in early 1992. More are being scrapped.
Sales: Petya III (sales version)—ten to India, two to Syria and two to Vietnam December 1978. Some of these have been deleted including one Indian ship which sank in 1990. These export versions are on Petya II hulls but fitted with one triple 21 in *(533 mm)* torpedo tube mounting in place of the two 16 in *(406 mm)* mountings and four RBU 2500s in place of two RBU 6000s. In addition other Petya II of Soviet type have been transferred: to Ethiopia—one in July 1983, second in March 1984, and to Vietnam—two in December 1983 and one in December 1984.

PETYA II *9/1991*

Mod PETYA I *6/1989*

PETYA II *9/1991*

SHIPBORNE AIRCRAFT

Numbers/Type: 120 Kamov Ka-25 Hormone.
Operational speed: 119 kts *(220 km/h)*.
Service ceiling: 11 500 ft *(3500 m)*.
Range: 350 nm *(650 km)*.
Role/Weapon systems: First Soviet successful shipborne ASW helicopter (being replaced by 'Helix'); 'A' version for ASW, 'B' for recce (called REB) and 'C' for utility; 30 Ka-25B versions reported. Sensors: Puff Ball search radar, dipping sonar, sonobuoys, MAD, ECM (A), EW equipment and Big Bulge search radar (B), Radar only (C). Weapons: ASW; 2 × torpedoes, nuclear or conventional depth bombs (A). ASV; 2 or 4 × missiles or rocket launchers (A).

HORMONE *1986, US Navy*

Numbers/Type: 150 Kamov Ka-27/Ka-29 Helix A/B.
Operational speed: 135 kts *(250 km/h)*.
Service ceiling: 19 685 ft *(6000 m)*.
Range: 432 nm *(800 km)*.
Role/Weapon systems: ASW helicopter; successor to 'Hormone' with greater ASW potential; three versions—'A' for ASW, 'B' for assault, 'C' for SAR/utility; deployed to surface ships and some shore stations. Sensors: Search radar, dipping sonar, sonobuoys, MAD, ECM. Weapons: ASW; 3 × torpedoes, nuclear or conventional depth bombs or mines. Assault type: 2 UV-57 rocket pods (2 × 32).

HELIX *9/1991*

Numbers/Type: 2 Kamov Ka-34 Hokum.
Operational speed: 189 kts *(350 km/h)*.
Service ceiling: 20 175 ft *(6150 m)*.
Range: 135 nm *(250 km)*.
Role/Weapon systems: Possible amphibious assault role still being evaluated. Full production started in 1991.

Numbers/Type: 15/5 Sukhoi Su-27 Flanker B/D.
Operational speed: 1345 kts *(2500 km/h)*.
Service ceiling: 59 000 ft *(18 000 m)*.
Range: 2160 + nm *(4000 km)*.
Role/Weapon systems: Fleet air defence fighter. Sensors: Track-while-scan pulse Doppler radar, IR scanner. Weapons: 1 × 30 mm cannon, 10 × AAMs (AA-10, AA-11, AA-8, AA-9).

FLANKER D *8/1991*

Numbers/Type: 50 Sukhoi Su-25UD Frogfoot B.
Operational speed: 526 kts *(975 km/h)*.
Service ceiling: 22 965 ft *(7000 m)*.
Range: 675 nm *(1250 km)*.
Role/Weapon systems: Two seater ground attack aircraft used for deck trials in the carrier *Kuznetsov* but not considered a likely candidate for the normal air wing complement.

Numbers/Type: 10 Mikoyan MiG-29 Fulcrum D.
Operational speed: 1320 kts *(2450 km/h)*.
Service ceiling: 56 000 ft *(17 000 m)*.
Range: 1130 nm *(2100 km)*.
Role/Weapon systems: Fleet air defence fighter or ground attack. Sensors: pulse Doppler radar, IR scanner, laser rangefinder. Weapons: 1 × 30 mm cannon, 6 × AA-10 and/or AA-11.

FULCRUM (on board *Kuznetsov*) *11/1989, TASS*

Numbers/Type: 30 Mil Mi-14BT Haze B.
Operational speed: 124 kts *(230 km/h)*.
Service ceiling: 15 000 ft *(4570 m)*.
Range: 432 nm *(800 km)*.
Role/Weapon systems: Minesweeping and possible minelaying helicopter; seen in action in Red Sea in 1985. Sensors: Search radar, sweep gear. Weapons: Unarmed.

HAZE *6/1989*

Numbers/Type: 30/25 Yakovlev Yak-38 Forger A/B.
Operational speed: 545 kts *(1009 km/h)*.
Service ceiling: 39 375 ft *(12 000 m)*.
Range: 200 nm *(370 km)*.
Role/Weapon systems: First Soviet shipborne fighter; limited air defence but primarily attack; STOVL operation. Being phased out of operational service. Sensors: RWR, ECM. Weapons: ASV; 2 × 'Kerry' ASM, 3.6 tons of 'iron' bombs. AD; 4 × 'Aphid' AAM and gun pods.

FORGER *1986, US Navy*

Numbers/Type: 1 Yakovlev Yak-41 Freestyle.
Operational speed: 984 kts *(1800 km/h)*.
Service ceiling: 49 200 ft *(15 000 m)*.
Range: 1150 nm *(2100 km)*.
Role/Weapon systems: Follow-on to the Forger. STOVL development which has run into problems and may even be cancelled. Much may depend on the future of the Russian aircraft carriers.

FREESTYLE *8/1991*

LAND-BASED MARITIME AIRCRAFT (FRONT LINE)

Note: The numbers listed below do not include some 680 Fencer, Flogger, Fitter, Fulcrum and Frogfoot aircraft transferred from the Air Force in 1989-91 to naval bases apparently to place them outside CFE arms reduction negotiations.

Numbers/Type: 100 Beriev Be-12 Mail.
Operational speed: 328 kts *(608 km/h)*.
Service ceiling: 37 000 ft *(11 280 m)*.
Range: 4050 nm *(7500 km)*.
Role/Weapon systems: Long-range ASW/MR amphibian in arctic waters, Baltic and Black Sea areas; to be replaced by mid-1990s. Sensors: Search/weather radar, sonobuoys, MAD, EW. Weapons: ASW; 5 tons of depth bombs, mines or torpedoes, nuclear-capable. ASV; limited missile and rocket armament.

Numbers/Type: 3 Ilyushin Il-20 Coot A.
Operational speed: 364 kts *(675 km/h)*.
Service ceiling: 32 800 ft *(10 000 m)*.
Range: 3508 nm *(6500 km)*.
Role/Weapon systems: Long-range Elint and MR for naval forces' intelligence gathering, especially in European waters. Sensors: SLAR, weather radar, cameras, Elint equipment. Weapons: Unarmed.

Numbers/Type: 50 Ilyushin Il-38 May.
Operational speed: 347 kts *(645 km/h)*.
Service ceiling: 32 800 ft *(10 000 m)*.
Range: 3887 nm *(7200 km)*.
Role/Weapon systems: Long-range MR and ASW over Atlantic, Indian and Mediterranean Sea areas. Sensors: Wet Eye search/weather radar, MAD, sonobuoys. Weapons: ASW; internal storage for 6 tons weapons.

Numbers/Type: 8 Antonov An-12 Cub ('Cub B/C/D') ('Cub C/D' ECM/ASW).
Operational speed: 419 kts *(777 km/h)*.
Service ceiling: 33 500 ft *(10 200 m)*.
Range: 3075 nm *(5700 km)*.
Role/Weapon systems: Used either for intelligence gathering (B) or electronic warfare (C, D); is versatile with long range; operated by and for all Soviet Fleets and in support of client states. Sensors: Search/weather radar, 3 × EW blisters (B), tail-mounted EW/Elint equipment in addition (C/D). Weapons: Self-defence; 2 × 23 mm cannon (B and D only).

Numbers/Type: 45 Mil Mi-8 Hip.
Operational speed: 140 kts *(260 km/h)*.
Service ceiling: 18 700 ft *(5700 m)*.
Range: 270 nm *(500 km)*.
Role/Weapon systems: Transport, Assault, ECM and Support helicopter for naval assault and limited ASV support duties. Sensors: None. Weapons: ASV; up to 192 rockets, machine guns or cannon pods, guided weapons with 5 nm range.

Numbers/Type: 125 Mil Mi-14PL/BT/PS Haze A/C.
Operational speed: 124 kts *(230 km/h)*.
Service ceiling: 15 000 ft *(4570 m)*.
Range: 432 nm *(800 km)*.
Role/Weapon systems: ASW (A) and assault (C) helicopters for medium-range operations. Sensors: Search radar, dipping sonar, sonobuoys, MAD, EW (A only). Weapons: ASW; 4 × torpedoes, nuclear or conventional depth bombs or mines (A); self-defence weapons (B).

Numbers/Type: 110 Sukhoi Su-17 Fitter C/D.
Operational speed: Mach 2.09.
Service ceiling: 59 050 ft *(18 000 m)*.
Range: 700 nm *(1300 km)*.
Role/Weapon systems: Anti-ship and support strike aircraft. Sensors: Attack radar, ECM. Weapons: ASV; 2 × 30 mm cannon and 3.5 tons of underwing stores, including rockets and missiles. Self-defence; can mount AAMs.

Numbers/Type: 310 Tupolev Tu-16 Badger.
Operational speed: 535 kts *(992 km/h)*.
Service ceiling: 40 350 ft *(12 300 m)*.
Range: 2605 nm *(4800 km)*.
Role/Weapon systems: Medium-range operations over most oceans in the strike/attack role. Other variants include reconnaissance, tanker and electronic warfare support role. Sensors: Puff Ball or Short Horn search/weather radar, EW. Weapons: Self-defence; 2 × 23 mm cannon. ASV; 2 × 'Kangaroo' or 'Kitchen' ASMs or 9 tons of nuclear/conventional bombs.

Numbers/Type: 25 Tupolev Tu-22 Blinder.
Operational speed: 800 kts *(1480 km/h)*.
Service ceiling: 60 000 ft *(18 300 m)*.
Range: 3100 nm *(5740 km)*.
Role/Weapon systems: Limited number in service for Fleet reconnaissance, intelligence gathering and EW tasks, especially from Kola bases. Sensors: Short Horn search/attack radar, EW, cameras. Weapons: ASV; 'iron' bombs or stand-off weapons. Self-defence; 1 × 23 mm cannon.

Numbers/Type: 150 Tupolev Tu-22 M Backfire B/C.
Operational speed: Mach 2.0.
Service ceiling: 60 000 ft *(18 300 m)*.
Range: 5000 nm *(9260 km)*.
Role/Weapon systems: Medium-range nuclear/conventional strike against CVBG and other groups; reconnaissance in peacetime. Sensors: Down Beat search/Fan Tail attack radars, EW. Weapons: ASV; 12 tons of 'iron' bombs or stand-off missiles including 'Kitchen'. Self-defence; 2 × 23 mm cannon.

Numbers/Type: 120 Tupolev Tu-95/Tu-142 Bear D/F/J.
Operational speed: 500 kts *(925 km/h)*.
Service ceiling: 60 000 ft *(18 300 m)*.
Range: 6775 nm *(12 550 km)*.
Role/Weapon systems: Multi-mission long-range aircraft (reconnaissance, ASW and communications variants); seen over all oceans of the world, in increased numbers. Sensors: Big Bulge and Short Horn search radars, ECM (D); search radar, sonobuoys, ECM, MAD (F), ELINT systems (J). Weapons: ASW; various torpedoes, depth bombs and/or mines (F). ASV; none (D), (J). Self-defence; some have 2 × 23 mm or more cannon.

Numbers/Type: 65 Sukhoi Su-24 Fencer E.
Operational speed: Mach 1.15.
Service ceiling: 57 400 ft *(17 500 m)*.
Range: 650 nm *(1050 km)*.
Role/Weapon systems: Maritime reconnaissance and strike. Sensors: Radar and ECM. Weapons: 30 mm Gatling gun; various ASM missiles and bombs; some have 23 mm cannon.

Numbers/Type: 2 Beriev Be-42 Albatross.
Operational speed: 431 kts *(800 km/h)*.
Service ceiling: 42 980 ft *(13 100 m)*
Range: 2700 nm *(5000 km)*.
Role/Weapon systems: Multi-role amphibian capable of nine hour patrols. Not yet at production stage but could replace the Mail in due course.

LIGHT MISSILE FORCES

1 DERGACH CLASS (FAST ATTACK CRAFT —MISSILE AIR CUSHION VESSEL)

SIVUCH

Displacement, tons: 750 full load
Dimensions, feet (metres): 211.6 × 55.8 × 7.9 *(64.5 × 17 × 2.4)*
Main machinery: 2 gas turbines; 2 diesels; 2 props on retractable pods
Speed, knots: 40+
Range, miles: 2000 (hull), 500 (air cushion)
Complement: 60

Missiles: SSM: 8 SS-N-22 (2 quad) Sunburn launchers ❶; active radar homing to 110 km *(60 nm)* at 2.5 Mach; warhead nuclear or HE; sea-skimmer.
SAM: SA-N-4 Gecko twin launcher ❷; semi-active radar homing to 15 km *(8 nm)* at 2.5 Mach; warhead 50 kg; 20 missiles.
Guns: 1—3 in *(76 mm)*/60 ❸; 85° elevation; 120 rounds/minute to 7 km *(3.8 nm)*; weight of shell 16 kg.
2—30 mm/65 AK 630 ❹; 6 barrels per mounting; 3000 rounds/minute combined to 2 km.
Countermeasures: Decoys: 2—10-barrelled launchers.
ESM/ECM: 2 Foot Ball A.
Fire control: 2 Light Bulb data link ❺.
Radars: Air/surface search: Band Stand ❻; D/E/F band.
Surface search: Positive E ❼; E band.
Fire control: Bass Tilt ❽; H/I band (for guns).
Pop Group ❾; F/H/I band (for SAM).
IFF: Square Head. Salt Pot.

Programmes: Built at Kerch and launched in 1987. Classified as a PGGA (Guided Missile Patrol Air Cushion Vessel). A single prototype so far.
Structure: Twin hulled surface effect design.
Operational: Based in the Black Sea at Sevastopol.

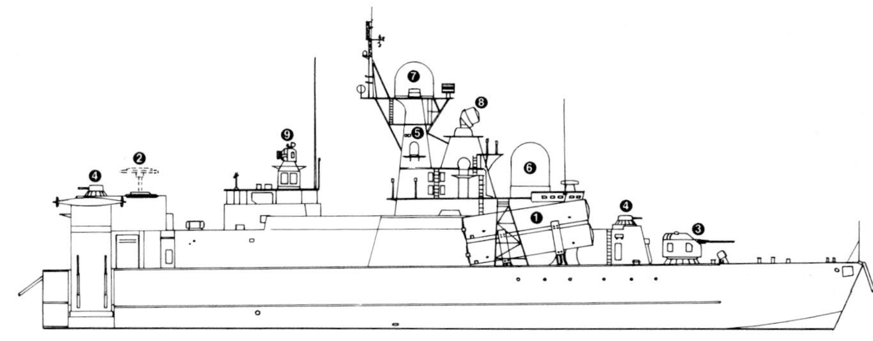

SIVUCH *(Scale 1 : 600), Ian Sturton*

SIVUCH *5/1990*

16 NANUCHKA I, 18 NANUCHKA III and 1 NANUCHKA IV CLASSES (MISSILE CORVETTES)

Nanuchka I: GRAD RADUGA SUVAL STORM TAIFUN ZYKLON METL ZARNITSA GROM MOLNIJA MUSSON +5
Nanuchka III: METEOR ZYB TUCHA PRILIV BURUN URAGAN LIVEN +11

Displacement, tons: 850 full load
Dimensions, feet (metres): 194.5 × 38.7 × 8.5 *(59.3 × 11.8 × 2.6)*
Main machinery: 3 Type M 507 diesels; 26 000 hp(m) *(19 MW)*; 3 shafts
Speed, knots: 36. **Range, miles:** 2500 at 12 kts; 900 at 31 kts
Complement: 42 (7 officers)

Missiles: SSM: 6 SS-N-9 Siren (2 triple) launchers ❶; command guidance and IR and active radar homing to 110 km *(60 nm)* at 0.9 Mach; warhead nuclear 250 kT or HE 500 kg. Nanuchka IV has 2 sextuple launchers for a possible improved version of SS-N-9 or a new longer range missile.
SAM: SA-N-4 Gecko twin launcher ❷; semi-active radar homing to 15 km *(8 nm)* at 2.5 Mach; warhead 50 kg; altitude 9.1-3048 m *(30-10 000 ft)*; 20 missiles. Some anti-surface capability.
Guns: 2—57 mm/80 (twin) (Nanuchka I) ❸; 85° elevation; 120 rounds/minute to 6 km *(3.3 nm)*; weight of shell 2.8 kg.
1—3 in *(76 mm)*/60 (Nanuchka III and IV) ❹; 85° elevation; 120 rounds/minute to 7 km *(3.8 nm)*; weight of shell 7 kg.
1—30 mm/65 (Nanuchka III and IV) ❺; 6 barrels; 3000 rounds/minute combined to 2 km.
Countermeasures: Decoys: 2—16 or 10 (Nanuchka III) barrelled Chaff launchers ❻.
ESM: Bell Tap or other Bell series. 4 radomes.
Fire control: Two Fish Bowl or Light Bulb (data links).
Radars: Air/surface search: Band Stand (also associated with SS-N-9 fire control) ❼; D/E/F band. Plank Shave in later Nanuchka III units.
Surface search: Peel Pair ❽; I band (in early units).
Fire control: Muff Cob (Nanuchka I) ❾; G/H band. Bass Tilt (Nanuchka III) ❿; H/I band. Pop Group ⓫; F/H/I band (for SA-N-4).
IFF: High Pole. Square Head. Spar Stump.

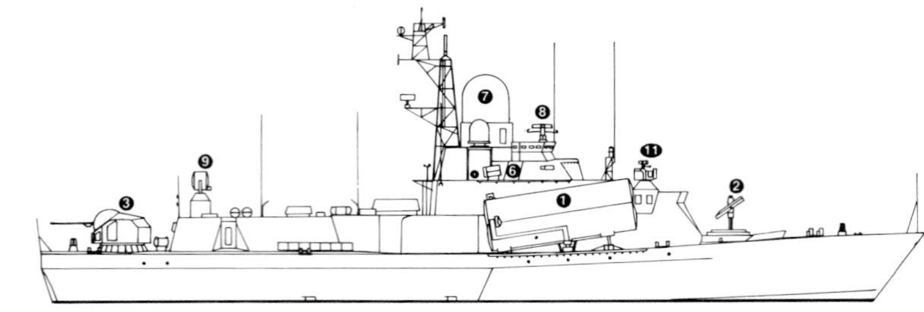

NANUCHKA I (Scale 1 : 600), Ian Sturton

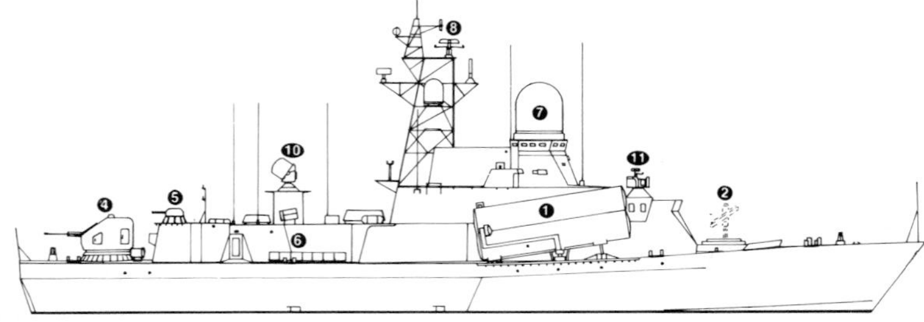

NANUCHKA III (Scale 1 : 600), Ian Sturton

Programmes: Built from 1969 onwards at Petrovsky, Leningrad and in the Pacific (Nanuchka III only). Nanuchka III, first seen in 1978. Nanuchka IV completed in 1987 as a trials ship. Programme terminated when *Liven* was commissioned in November 1991. A follow-on class is expected. Type name is *maly raketny korabl* meaning small missile ship.
Structure: The Nanuchka IV is similar in detail to Nanuchka III except that she is the trials vehicle for a possible 300 km range version of SS-N-9 or its successor.
Operational: Probably mainly intended for deployment in coastal waters although formerly deployed in the Mediterranean (in groups of two or three), North Sea and Pacific. One more Nanuchka I in reserve.
Sales: Three of a modified version of Nanuchka I (Nanuchka II) with four SS-N-2B missiles have been supplied to India in 1977-78, three to Algeria in 1980-82, one to Libya in 1981, a second in February 1983, a third in February 1984 and a fourth in September 1985.

NANUCHKA III *5/1991*

NANUCHKA I *2/1989, MoD Bonn*

NANUCHKA IV (2 sextuple launchers) *5/1990*

2 TARANTUL I, 18 TARANTUL II and 22 + 2 TARANTUL III CLASSES (MISSILE CORVETTES)

Displacement, tons: 385 standard; 455 full load
Dimensions, feet (metres): 184.1 × 37.7 × 8.2 *(56.1 × 11.5 × 2.5)*
Main machinery: COGOG; 2 Type NK-12MV gas turbines; 24 000 hp(m) *(17.6 MW)*; 2 gas turbines with reversible gearbox; 8000 hp(m) *(5.9 MW)*; 2 shafts or CODOG with 2 diesels; 8000 hp(m) *(5.9 MW)*; replacing second pair of gas turbines
Speed, knots: 36. **Range, miles:** 400 at 36 kts; 2000 at 20 kts
Complement: 34 (5 officers)

Missiles: SSM: 4 SS-N-2C Styx (2 twin) launchers (Tarantul I and Tarantul II); active radar or IR homing to 83 km *(45 nm)* at 0.9 Mach; warhead 513 kg; sea-skimmer at end of run.
4 SS-N-22 (2 twin) launchers (Tarantul III); active radar homing to 110 km *(60 nm)* at 2.5 Mach; warhead nuclear or HE; sea-skimmer. Modified version in one of the class.
SAM: SA-N-5 Grail quad launcher; manual aiming; IR homing to 6 km *(3.2 nm)* at 1.5 Mach; altitude to 2500 m *(8000 ft)*; warhead 1.5 kg.
SAM/Guns: 1 CADS-N-1 (one Tarantul II only); twin 30 mm gun combined with 8 SA-N-11 and Hot Flash fire control radar; range 8 km *(4.4 nm)*.
Guns: 1—3 in *(76 mm)*/60; 85° elevation; 120 rounds/minute to 15 km *(8 nm)*; weight of shell 7 kg.
2—30 mm/65; 6 barrels per mounting; 3000 rounds/minute to 2 km.
Countermeasures: Decoys: 2—16 or 10 (Tarantul III) barrelled Chaff launchers.
ESM: 2 Foot Ball, 2 Half Hat (in some).
Fire control: Hood Wink optronic director. Light Bulb data link.
Radars: Air/surface search: Plank Shave (Tarantul I); E band. Band Stand (with Plank Shave) (Tarantul II and III); E band.
Navigation: Spin Trough; I band.
Fire control: Bass Tilt; H/I band.
IFF: Square Head. High Pole.

Programmes: The first Tarantul I was completed in 1978 at Petrovsky, Leningrad. A single experimental Tarantul III with four SS-N-22 was completed at Petrovsky in 1981. Tarantul II were built at Kolpino, Petrovsky, Leningrad and in the Pacific in 1980-86. A second Tarantul I without Band Stand is retained to train foreign crews. Current production is of Tarantul III class for Russia and Tarantul I for export. Type name is *raketny kater* meaning missile cutter.
Modernisation: One Tarantul III is serving as a trials platform for a modified version of SS-N-22 possibly with a longer range; the missile is distinguished by end caps on the launcher doors. A Tarantul II is also serving as a trials platform for the CADS-N-1 air defence system in the Black Sea.
Structure: Basically same hull as Pauk class without 2 m extension for sonar.
Sales: Tarantul I class—one to Poland 28 December 1983, second in April 1984 and third in March 1988. One to GDR in September 1984, second in December 1984, third in September 1985, fourth in January 1986 and fifth in November 1986 (all deleted or sold including one which is doing trials with the US Navy in 1991/92). One to India in April 1987, second in January 1988, third in December 1988, fourth in November 1989 and fifth in January 1990. Two to Yemen in November 1990 and January 1991. One to Romania in December 1990. One Tarantul II to Bulgaria in March 1990.

TARANTUL I — *3/1991, van Ginderen Collection*

TARANTUL II — *5/1991*

TARANTUL III — *10/1991, van Ginderen Collection*

16 MATKA CLASS (FAST ATTACK CRAFT—MISSILE HYDROFOIL)

Displacement, tons: 225 standard; 260 full load
Dimensions, feet (metres): 129.9 × 24.9 (41 over foils) × 6.9 (13.1 over foils) *(39.6 × 7.6 (12.5) × 2.1 (4))*
Main machinery: 3 diesels; 15 000 hp(m) *(11 MW)*; 3 shafts
Speed, knots: 40. **Range, miles:** 600 at 35 kts foilborne; 1500 at 14 kts hullborne
Complement: 33

Missiles: SSM: 2 SS-N-2C Styx; active radar or IR homing to 83 km *(45 nm)* at 0.9 Mach; warhead 513 kg; sea-skimmer at end of run.
8 SS-N-25 (in one of the class); radar homing to 150 km *(80 nm)* at 0.9 Mach; warhead 250 kg.
Guns: 1—3 in *(76 mm)*/60; 85° elevation; 120 rounds/minute to 15 km *(8 nm)*; weight of shell 7 kg.
1—30 mm/65 AK 630; 6 barrels per mounting; 3000 rounds/minute to 2 km.
Countermeasures: Decoys: 2—16-barrelled Chaff launchers.
ESM: Radar warning.
Radars: Air/surface search: Plank Shave; E band.
Navigation: Cheese Cake; I band.
Fire control: Bass Tilt; H/I band.
IFF: High Pole B or Salt Pot B and Square Head.

Programmes: In early 1978 the first of class was seen. Built at Kolpino Yard, Leningrad. Production stopped in 1983 being superseded by Tarantul class. Type name is *raketny kater* meaning missile cutter.
Structure: Similar hull to the Osa class with similar single hydrofoil system to Turya class. The combination has produced a better sea-boat than the Osa class. One of the class is the trials craft for the SS-N-25 first seen in 1988 in the German prototype Sassnitz class but removed when the GDR was reunited with Germany. Also being fitted in modernised Krivak Is.
Operational: Based in the Baltic and Black Seas. Some may be fitted with quadruple SA-N-5 systems.

MATKA — *4/1989, MoD Bonn*

18 OSA I and 20 OSA II CLASSES (FAST ATTACK CRAFT—MISSILE)

Displacement, tons: 210 (245, Osa II) full load
Dimensions, feet (metres): 110.2 × 24.9 × 8.8 *(33.6 × 7.6 × 2.7)*
Main machinery: 3 M503A diesels; 12 000 hp(m) *(8.8 MW)*; 3 shafts (Osa I)
3 M504 diesels; 15 000 hp(m) *(11 MW)*; 3 shafts (Osa II)
Speed, knots: 35 (Osa I); 37 (Osa II). **Range, miles:** 400 at 34 kts (Osa I); 500 at 35 kts (Osa II)
Complement: 30

Missiles: SSM: 4 SS-N-2A/B (Osa I); 4 SS-N-2B/C (Osa II); active radar or IR homing to 46 km *(25 nm)* at 0.9 Mach; warhead 513 kg. C has a range of 83 km *(45 nm)* and is a sea-skimmer at end of run.
SAM: SA-N-5 Grail quad launcher (some Osa II); manual aiming; IR homing to 6 km *(3.2 nm)* at 1.5 Mach; altitude to 2500 m *(8000 ft)*; warhead 1.5 kg.
Guns: 4—30 mm/65 (2 twin); 85° elevation; 500 rounds/minute to 5 km *(2.7 nm)*; weight of shell 0.54 kg.
Radars: Surface search/fire control: Square Tie; I band.
Fire control: Drum Tilt; H/I band.
IFF: High Pole A or B. Square Head.

Programmes: Osa I class built in first half of the 1960s and Osa II class in the latter half at a number of yards. Type name is *raketny kater* meaning missile cutter.
Structure: This class was a revolution in naval shipbuilding leading to a whole generation of fast missile patrol craft being built worldwide.
Operational: Although confined by their size and range to coastal operations the lethality and accuracy of the Styx missile were first proved by the sinking of the Israeli destroyer *Eilat* on 21 October 1967 by an Egyptian Komar class vessel. Nine deleted in 1988-89, 25 in 1990 and eight more in 1991.
Sales: Osa I: Algeria (3), Bulgaria (3), Cuba (5), Egypt (12—8 remaining), East Germany (15), India (8), Iraq (4), North Korea (8), Poland (14), Romania (6), Syria (6), Yugoslavia (10).
Osa II: Algeria (9), Angola (6), Bulgaria (3), Cuba (13), Ethiopia (4), Finland (4), India (8), Iraq (8), Libya (12), Somalia (2), Syria (10—six remaining), North Yemen (2) (subsequently returned), South Yemen (8), Vietnam (8). Many of both types have been deleted.

OSA I — *1983, US Navy*

OSA II — *1987, G. Jacobs*

PATROL SHIPS

2/3 T 58 PGF/PGR CLASS

Displacement, tons: 790 standard; 860 full load
Dimensions, feet (metres): 229.9 × 29.5 × 7.9 *(70.1 × 9 × 2.4)*
Main machinery: 2 diesels; 4000 hp(m) *(2.94 MW)*; 2 shafts
Speed, knots: 17. **Range, miles:** 2500 at 13 kts
Complement: 82

Guns: 4—57 mm/70 (2 twin); 90° elevation; 120 rounds/minute to 8 km *(4.4 nm)*; weight of shell 2.8 kg.
4—25 mm/80 (2 twin) (in some); 85° elevation; 270 rounds/minute to 3 km *(1.6 nm)*; weight of shell 0.34 kg.
A/S mortars: 2 RBU 1200 5-tubed fixed; range 1200 m; warhead 34 kg (in PGF type).
Depth charges: 2 projectors.
Countermeasures: ESM: 2 Watch Dog.
Radars: Air search: Big Net; C band (PGR type).
Surface search: Spin Trough or Strut Curve; I band.
Navigation: One or two Don 2; I band.
Fire control: Muff Cob; G/H band.
IFF: Two Square Head. High Pole A or B.
Sonars: Tamir II; hull-mounted; active search and attack; high frequency.

Programmes: Built from 1957 to 1963, conversion to patrol ships in about 1975 with sweep winches, magnetic sweep cable reel and stern davit retained but without associated minesweeping gear. Originally fleet minesweepers with steel hulls. Of this class 16 were completed as submarine rescue ships with armament and sweeping gear removed, see later page (Valday class).
Modernisation: Three converted to radar pickets with Big Net radar in late 1970s and early 1980s. These ships had the A/S systems removed and have two SA-N-5 quad launchers fitted.
Operational: From a total of 18 in 1988, these are the survivors in 1992.

T 58/PGR *5/1990*

LIGHT FORCES

32 PAUK I CLASS (FAST ATTACK CRAFT—PATROL)

Displacement, tons: 440 full load
Dimensions, feet (metres): 195.2 × 33.5 × 10.8 *(59.5 × 10.2 × 3.3)*
Main machinery: 2 diesels; 21 000 hp(m) *(15.4 MW)*; 2 shafts
Speed, knots: 32. **Range, miles:** 2200 at 18 kts
Complement: 32

Missiles: SAM: SA-N-5 Grail quad launcher; manual aiming; IR homing to 6 km *(3.2 nm)* at 1.5 Mach; altitude to 2500 m *(8000 ft)*; warhead 1.5 kg; 8 missiles.
Guns: 1—3 in *(76 mm)*/60; 85° elevation; 120 rounds/minute to 15 km *(8 nm)*; weight of shell 7 kg.
1—30 mm/65 AK 630; 6 barrels; 3000 rounds/minute combined to 2 km.
Torpedoes: 4—16 in *(406 mm)* tubes. Type 40; anti-submarine; active/passive homing up to 15 km *(8 nm)* at up to 40 kts; warhead 100-150 kg.
A/S mortars: 2 RBU 1200 5-tubed fixed; range 1200 m; warhead 34 kg.
Depth charges: 2 racks (12).
Countermeasures: Decoys: 2—16-barrelled Chaff launchers.
ESM: Radar warning.
Radars: Air/surface search: Peel Cone; E band.
Surface search: Kivach; I band.
Fire control: Bass Tilt; H/I band.
Sonars: Rat Tail; VDS (mounted on transom); active attack; high frequency.

Programmes: First laid down in 1977 and completed in 1979. Replacement for Poti class. In series production at Yaroslavl in the Black Sea and at Vladivostok until 1988 when the Sveltyak class took over. Type name is *maly protivolodochny korabl* meaning small anti-submarine ship. Overall numbers slightly reduced from previous assessments.
Structure: This appears to be an ASW version of the Tarantul class having the same hull form with a 1.8 m extension for dipping sonar. First three of class have a lower bridge than successors.
Operational: 25 of the craft are operated by the Border Guard.
Sales: A modified version (Pauk II) with a longer superstructure, two twin 533 mm torpedo tubes and a radome similar to the Parchim class is building for export. First one to India in March 1989, second in January 1990, third in December 1990, fourth in February 1991 and fifth in February 1992. One Pauk I to Bulgaria in September 1989.

PAUK I *4/1989, MoD Bonn*

PAUK I *5/1991, Erik Laursen*

2 MUKHA CLASS (FAST ATTACK CRAFT—PATROL HYDROFOIL)

Displacement, tons: 400 full load
Dimensions, feet (metres): 164 × 27.9 × 9.2 *(50 × 8.5 × 2.8)*
Main machinery: 2 gas turbines; 2 shafts
Speed, knots: 45
Complement: 45

Guns: 1—3 in *(76 mm)*/60; 85° elevation; 120 rounds/minute to 7 km *(3.8 nm)*; weight of shell 16 kg.
1—30 mm/65 AK 630; 6 barrels; 3000 rounds/minute combined to 2 km.
Torpedoes: 8—16 in *(406 mm)* tubes (2 quad); Type 40; anti-submarine; active/passive homing up to 15 km *(8 nm)* at up to 40 kts; warhead 100-150 kg.
Radars: Surface search: Peel Cone; E band.
Fire control: Bass Tilt; H/I band.
IFF: High Pole B. Square Head.

Programmes: Built at Feodosiya and first seen in 1987. Only two of the class completed and there may be no series production.
Structure: Looks like a development of *Babochka* with two sets of torpedo tubes mounted aft.
Operational: Based in the Black Sea.

MUKHA *1990, S. Breyer*

29 TURYA CLASS (FAST ATTACK CRAFT—TORPEDO HYDROFOIL)

Displacement, tons: 190 standard; 250 full load
Dimensions, feet (metres): 129.9 × 24.9 (41 over foils) × 5.9 (13.1 over foils) *(39.6 × 7.6 (12.5) × 1.8 (4))*
Main machinery: 3 M504 diesels; 15 000 hp(m) *(11 MW)*; 3 shafts
Speed, knots: 40 foilborne. **Range, miles:** 600 at 35 kts foilborne; 1450 at 14 kts hullborne
Complement: 30

Guns: 2—57 mm/80 (twin, aft); 85° elevation; 120 rounds/minute to 6 km *(3.3 nm)*; weight of shell 2.8 kg.
2—25 mm/80 (twin, fwd); 85° elevation; 270 rounds/minute to 3 km *(1.6 nm)*; weight of shell 0.34 kg.
1—14.5 mm MG.
Torpedoes: 4—21 in *(533 mm)* tubes. Type 53; dual purpose; pattern active/passive homing up to 20 km *(10.8 nm)* at up to 45 kts; warhead 400 kg or low yield nuclear.
Depth charges: 1 rack.
Radars: Surface search: Pot Drum; H/I band.
Fire control: Muff Cob; G/H band.
IFF: High Pole B. Square Head.
Sonars: VDS; active search and attack; high frequency. Similar to Hormone dipping sonar. This sonar is not fitted in most export versions.

Programmes: The second class of hydrofoil with single foil forward (after Matka class). Has a naval orientation rather than the earlier Pchela class of the Border Guard. Entered service from 1972 to 1978—built at Petrovsky, Kolpino, Leningrad and Vladivostok. Basically Osa hull. Type name is *torpedny kater* meaning torpedo cutter. Production ended in 1987.
Sales: Two to Cuba 9 February 1979, two in February 1980, two in February 1981, two in January 1983 and one in November 1983; one to Ethiopia in early 1985 and one in March 1986; one to Kampuchea in mid-1984 and one in early 1985; one to Seychelles in April 1986 (no tubes or sonar); two to Vietnam in mid-1984, one in late 1984 and two in early 1986.

TURYA *8/1988, van Ginderen Collection*

6 POTI CLASS (FAST ATTACK CRAFT—PATROL)

Displacement, tons: 600 full load
Dimensions, feet (metres): 193.6 × 26.2 × 6.6 *(59 × 8 × 2)*
Main machinery: CODOG; 2 gas turbines; 30 000 hp(m) *(22.4 MW)*; 2 Type M503A diesels; 8000 hp(m) *(5.9 MW)*; 2 shafts
Speed, knots: 38. **Range, miles:** 4500 at 10 kts; 500 at 37 kts
Complement: 80

Guns: 2—57 mm/80 (twin); 85° elevation; 120 rounds/minute to 6 km *(3.3 nm)*; weight of shell 2.8 kg.
Torpedoes: 4—16 in *(406 mm)* tubes. Type 40; anti-submarine; active/passive homing up to 15 km *(8 nm)* at up to 40 kts; warhead 100-150 kg.
A/S mortars: 2 RBU 6000 12-tubed trainable; range 6000 m; warhead 31 kg.
Countermeasures: ESM: 2 Watch Dog.
Radars: Air search: Strut Curve; F band; range 110 km *(60 nm)* for 2 m² target.
Surface search: Spin Trough; I band.
Fire control: Muff Cob; G/H band.
IFF: High Pole B.
Sonars: VDS; active attack; high frequency; dipping sonar.

Programmes: This class of ship was under series construction from 1961 to 1968 at Zelenodolsk and Khabarov and is now being replaced by the Pauk and Parchim II classes. Soviet type name is *maly protivolodochny korabl* meaning small anti-submarine ship. Eleven deleted in 1988-89, nine in 1990 and another 29 in 1991.
Sales: Three to Bulgaria (mid-1970s), one in 1980s and two in 1990. Three to Romania (late 1960s).

POTI *6/1991, Hartmut Ehlers*

1 BABOCHKA CLASS (FAST ATTACK CRAFT—PATROL HYDROFOIL)

Displacement, tons: 400 full load
Dimensions, feet (metres): 164 × 27.9 (33.5 over foils) × 13.1 (19.4 foils) *(50 × 8.5 (10.2.) × 4 (5.9))*
Main machinery: CODOG; 3 Type NK-12 gas turbines; 30 000 hp(m) *(22.4 MW)*; 2 diesels; 3 shafts
Speed, knots: 45
Complement: 45

Guns: 1—3 in *(76 mm)*/60 (in one only); 85° elevation; 120 rounds/minute to 15 km *(8 nm)*; weight of shell 7 kg.
2—30 mm/65 AK 630; 6 barrels per mounting; 3000 rounds/minute combined to 2 km.
Torpedoes: 8—16 in *(406 mm)* (2 quad) tubes. Type 40; anti-submarine; active/passive homing up to 15 km *(8 nm)* at up to 40 kts; warhead 100-150 kg.
Countermeasures: Decoys: 2—16-barrelled Chaff launchers.
ESM: Radar warning.
Radars: Surface search: Peel Cone; E band.
Navigation: Don 2; I band.
Fire control: Bass Tilt; H/I band.
Sonars: Dipping sonar.

Programmes: First sighted 1977 in the Black Sea. Probably used for research and development. Only one built, reports of a second of class were not correct.
Structure: Features include a hydrofoil arrangement with a single fixed foil forward, large gas turbine exhausts aft, and trainable torpedo mountings forward.

BABOCHKA *1991*

14 MURAVEY CLASS (FAST ATTACK CRAFT—PATROL HYDROFOIL)

Displacement, tons: 180 standard; 230 full load
Dimensions, feet (metres): 126.6 × 24.9 × 6.2; 14.4 (foils) *(38.6 × 7.6 × 1.9; 4.4)*
Main machinery: 2 gas turbines; 8000 hp(m) *(5.9 MW)*; 2 shafts
Speed, knots: 40. **Range, miles:** 950 at 28 kts
Guns: 1—3 in *(76 mm)*/60; 85° elevation; 120 rounds/minute to 15 km *(8 nm)*; weight of shell 7 kg.
1—30 mm/65 AK 630; 6 barrels; 3000 rounds/minute combined to 2 km.
Torpedoes: 2—16 in *(406 mm)* tubes; Type 40; anti-submarine; active/passive homing up to 15 km *(8 nm)* at up to 40 kts; warhead 100-150 kg.
Depth charges: 6.
Radars: Surface search: Peel Cone; E band.
Fire control: Bass Tilt; H/I band.
IFF: High Pole B; Square Head.
Sonars: VDS: active attack; high frequency; dipping sonar.

Comment: Built at Feodosya. First seen in 1983. Programme terminated in 1988 in favour of the Mukha class. Assigned to Border Guard.

MURAVEY *1/1989, MoD Bonn*

7 + 3 SVETLYAK CLASS (FAST ATTACK CRAFT—PATROL)

Displacement, tons: 450 full load
Dimensions, feet (metres): 164 × 29.5 × 11.5 *(50 × 9 × 3.5)*
Main machinery: 2 diesels; 20 000 hp(m) *(14.7 MW)*; 2 shafts
Speed, knots: 30
Complement: 55
Missiles: SAM: SA-N-5 Grail quad launcher; manual aiming; IR homing to 6 km *(3.2 nm)* at 1.5 Mach; warhead 1.5 kg.
Guns: 1—3 in *(76 mm)*/60; 85° elevation; 120 rounds/minute to 15 km *(8 nm)*; weight of shell 7 kg.
1—30 mm/65 AK 630; 6 barrels; 3000 rounds/minute combined to 2 km.
Torpedoes: 2—16 in *(406 mm)* tubes; Type 40; anti-submarine; active/passive homing up to 15 km *(8 nm)* at up to 40 kts; warhead 100-150 kg.
Radars: Air/surface search: Peel Cone; E band.
Fire control: Bass Tilt; H/I band.
IFF: High Pole B; Square Head.

Comment: A class of attack craft for the Border Guard building at Vladivostok. It complements the Pauks in the Pacific in place of the less seaworthy Muravey class. Series production after first of class trials in 1989, expected to rise to about three a year. Also building in a Baltic yard by 1990.

SVETLYAK *12/1989, G. Jacobs*

3 SO 1 CLASS (LARGE PATROL CRAFT)

Displacement, tons: 170 standard; 215 full load
Dimensions, feet (metres): 137.8 × 19.7 × 5.9 *(42 × 6 × 1.8)*
Main machinery: 3 diesels; 7500 hp(m) *(5.5 MW)*; 3 shafts
Speed, knots: 28. **Range, miles:** 1100 at 13 kts; 350 at 28 kts
Complement: 31
Guns: 4—25 mm/80 (2 twin).
A/S mortars: 4 RBU 1200.
Depth charges: 2 racks.
Mines: Can carry 10.
Radars: Surface search: Pot Head; I band; range 37 km *(20 nm)*.
IFF: High Pole A or B. Dead Duck.
Sonars: Tamir 2; hull-mounted; active attack; high frequency.

Comment: Built between 1957 and late 1960s at Zelenodolsk and Khabarov—total about 150. Steel hulled. Some have one 57 mm and two 25 mm guns. A few have been modernised with two 16 in anti-submarine torpedo tubes and only two 25 mm guns. This class is being phased out of service. Transfers include: Algeria (6), Bulgaria (6), Cuba (12), Egypt (12), East Germany (12—all now scrapped), Iraq (3), North Korea (15), Mozambique (2 in mid-1985), Vietnam (13, of which 5 have been lost), South Yemen (2). Many of these have been deleted.

SO 1 *1980*

110 STENKA CLASS (FAST ATTACK CRAFT—PATROL)

Displacement, tons: 170 standard; 210 full load
Dimensions, feet (metres): 127.9 × 25.6 × 5.9 *(39 × 7.8 × 1.8)*
Main machinery: 3 Type M503A diesels; 12 000 hp(m) *(8.8 MW)*; 3 shafts
Speed, knots: 36. **Range, miles:** 800 at 24 kts; 500 at 35 kts
Complement: 30
Guns: 4—30 mm/65 (2 twin).
Torpedoes: 4—16 in *(406 mm)* tubes.
Depth charges: 2 racks.
Radars: Surface search: Pot Drum or Peel Cone; H/I or E band.
Fire control: Drum Tilt; H/I band.
IFF: High Pole. 2 Square Head.
Sonars: VDS; high frequency; Hormone type dipping sonar.

Comment: Based on the hull design of the Osa class. Construction started in 1967 and continued at a rate of about five a year at Petrovsky, Leningrad and Vladivostok for the Border Guard. Programme terminated in 1989 at a total of 133 hulls. Type name is *pogranichny storozhevoy korabl* meaning border patrol ship. Some are beginning to be paid off.
Transfers include: Cuba, two in February 1985 and one in August 1985. Four to Cambodia in October 1985 and November 1987.

STENKA — *8/1989, MoD Bonn*

34 ZHUK CLASS (COASTAL PATROL CRAFT)

Displacement, tons: 50 full load
Dimensions, feet (metres): 75.4 × 17 × 6.2 *(23 × 5.2 × 1.9)*
Main machinery: 2 diesels; 2400 hp(m) *(1.76 MW)*; 2 shafts
Speed, knots: 30. **Range, miles:** 1100 at 15 kts
Complement: 17
Guns: 2—14.5 mm (twin, fwd) MGs. 1—12.7 mm (aft) MG.
Radars: Surface search: Spin Trough; I band.

Comment: Under construction since 1970. Building at three to eight a year mostly for export. Manned by the Border Guard. Export versions have twin (over/under) 14.5 mm aft.
Transfers: Algeria (one in 1981), Angola (one in 1977), Benin (four in 1978-80), Bulgaria (five in 1977), Cape Verde (one in 1980), Cuba (40 in 1971-88), Equatorial Guinea (three in 1974-75), Ethiopia (two in October 1982 and two in June 1990), Guinea (two in July 1987), Iraq (five in 1974-75), Kampuchea (three in 1985-87), Mauritius (two in January 1990), Mozambique (five in 1978-80), Nicaragua (eight in 1982-86), Seychelles (one in 1981, one in October 1982), Somalia (one in 1974), Syria (six in 1981-84), Vietnam (nine in 1978-88 (at least one passed on to Cambodia), five in 1990), North Yemen (five in 1978-87), South Yemen (two in 1975). Some have been deleted.

ZHUK — *5/1991*

21 YAZ CLASS

Displacement, tons: 400 full load
Dimensions, feet (metres): 180.4 × 29.5 × 4.9 *(55 × 9 × 1.5)*
Main machinery: 2 diesels; 2 shafts
Speed, knots: 15. **Range, miles:** 1000 at 10 kts
Complement: 60
Guns: 2—115 mm tank guns (TB 62). Twin barrel rocket launcher on after deckhouse. 2—30 mm/65 AK 630; 6 barrels per mounting.
Mines: Laying capability.
Radars: Surface search: Square Tie; I band.
Fire control: Bass Tilt; H/I band.
Navigation: Don 2; I band.
IFF: High Pole B. Square Head.

Comment: First entered service in Amur Flotilla 1978. Building on Pacific coast until 1987.

YAZ — *1990*

96 SHMEL CLASS

Displacement, tons: 85 full load
Dimensions, feet (metres): 91.8 × 14.1 × 3.6 *(28 × 4.3 × 1.1)*
Main machinery: 2 diesels; 2400 hp(m) *(1.76 MW)*; 2 shafts
Speed, knots: 22. **Range, miles:** 600 at 12 kts
Complement: 12
Guns: 1—3 in *(76 mm)*/48 (tank turret). 2—25 mm/70 (twin) (later ships). 2—14.5 mm (twin) MGs (earlier ships). 5—7.62 mm MGs. 1 BP 6 rocket launcher; 18 barrels.
Mines: Can lay 9.
Radars: Surface search: Spin Trough; I band.

Comment: Completed at Kerch and Khabarovsk 1967-74. Some of the later ships also mount one or two multi-barrelled rocket launchers amidships. The 7.62 mm guns fire through embrasures in the superstructure with one mounted on the 76 mm. Probably more than half of this class is in reserve. Can be carried on land transport. Type name is *artillerisky kater* meaning artillery cutter.
Transfers: Four to Cambodia (1984-85).

SHMEL CLASS — *1991*

6 TR 40 CLASS

Displacement, tons: 70 full load
Dimensions, feet (metres): 91.2 × 13.1 × 3.6 *(27.8 × 4 × 1.1)*
Main machinery: 2 diesels; 600 hp(m) *(440 kW)*; 2 shafts
Speed, knots: 17. **Range, miles:** 500 at 10 kts
Guns: 2—25 mm/70 (twin). 2—14.5 mm (twin) MGs.

Comment: Numbers are uncertain.

TR 40 — *1990*

RIVER PATROL CRAFT

Note: Attached to Black Sea and Pacific Fleets for operations on the Danube, Amur and Usuri Rivers, and to the Caspian Flotilla. Belong to the Maritime Border Guard.

8 PIYAVKA CLASS

Displacement, tons: 150 full load
Dimensions, feet (metres): 126.3 × 20.7 × 2.9 *(38.5 × 6.3 × 0.9)*
Main machinery: 2 diesels; 2 shafts
Speed, knots: 14
Guns: 1—30 mm/65 AK 630; 6 barrels.

Comment: Built at Khabarovsk from 1979 to 1984. Amur Flotilla.

10 VOSH CLASS

Displacement, tons: 190 full load
Dimensions, feet (metres): 140.1 × 20.7 × 3.3 *(42 × 6.3 × 1)*
Main machinery: 2 diesels; 2 shafts
Speed, knots: 18
Guns: 1—3 in *(76 mm)*/48 (tank turret). 1—30 mm/65 AK 630.
Countermeasures: 1 twin barrel decoy launcher.

Comment: Building started in Pacific yards in 1980.

1 COMMAND SHIP

SSV-10

Displacement, tons: 340 full load
Dimensions, feet (metres): 160.8 × 32.8 × 4.9 *(49 × 10 × 1.5)*
Speed, knots: 12
Guns: 2—40 mm saluting guns. 2—14.5 mm MGs (1 twin).

Comment: Support ship on the Danube for the river patrols.

SSV-10 *4/1985, Erwin Sieche*

MINE WARFARE FORCES

Note: Some 40-50 craft of various dimensions, some with cable reels, some self-propelled and unmanned, some towed and unmanned are reported including the 8 m Kater and Volga unmanned mine-clearance craft. Some are attached to the Polnochny (MCM) ships, others may be used for wide deployment of magnetic sweeps. Both Mi-8 'Hip' and Mi-14 'Haze B' helicopters have carried out what may be acoustic and magnetic sweeping with small craft of the Volga type towed by a cable.

MINE CLEARANCE SWEEPS *1990*

3 ALESHA CLASS (MINELAYERS)

PRIPYAT **VYCHEGDA** **PECHORA**

Displacement, tons: 3860 full load
Dimensions, feet (metres): 324.8 × 44.3 × 17.7 *(99 × 13.5 × 5.4)*
Main machinery: 4 diesels; 30 000 hp(m) *(22.4 MW)*; 2 shafts
Speed, knots: 24. **Range, miles:** 4000 at 16 kts
Complement: 150
Guns: 4—45 mm/70 (quad, fwd).
Mines: 400.
Radars: Surface search: Strut Curve; F band.
Navigation: Don 2; I band.
Fire control: Muff Cob; G/H band.
IFF: High Pole B.

Comment: In service since 1967. Fitted with four mine tracks to provide stern launchings. Also have a capability in general support role. Can act as netlayers. Type name is *zagraditel minny* meaning minelayer and the Russian name is the Alyosha Popovich class. One in each of the Northern, Pacific and Black Sea fleets. *Vychegda* sighted in the Pacific in 1991 with Elint vans fitted forward of the bridge. Fitted with Army surplus guns.

VYCHEGDA *12/1989, G. Jacobs*

4 POLNOCHNY A and B CLASSES

Comment: Four of this class of LSMs (see *Amphibious Warfare* section for details) have been converted to carry large counter-mining charges on long chutes discharging over the stern on either side. These charges are laid in lines using a radio-controlled MCM craft to tow the charges into position before detonation. In one case these craft are carried on davits amidships and the remainder carry them on chutes aft.

POLNOCHNY B (MCM) *1984, JMSDF*

35 NATYA I and 1 NATYA II CLASSES (MINESWEEPERS—OCEAN)

DIZELIST	**MINER**	**STARSHKIY**	**SNAYPR**
ELEKTRIK	**MOTORIST**	**SIGNALSHIK**	**TURBINIST**
POLEMETCHIZ	**RULEVOY**	**ZAPAL**	**ZENITCHIK**
RADIST	**DOBROTAY**	**ZARYAD**	**+ 21**

Displacement, tons: 770 full load
Dimensions, feet (metres): 200.1 × 31.8 × 8.9 *(61 × 9.7 × 2.7)*
Main machinery: 2 diesels; 8000 hp(m) *(5.88 MW)*; 2 shafts
Speed, knots: 19. **Range, miles:** 4000 at 10 kts
Complement: 65

Missiles: SAM: 2 SA-N-5 Grail quad launchers (in some); manual aiming; IR homing to 6 km *(3.2 nm)* at 1.5 Mach; altitude to 2500 m *(8000 ft)*; warhead 1.5 kg; 16 missiles.
Guns: 4—30 mm/65 (2 twin); 85° elevation; 500 rounds/minute to 5 km *(2.7 nm)*; weight of shell 0.54 kg or 2—30 mm/65 AK 630; 6 barrels per mounting; 3000 rounds/minute combined to 2 km. 4—25 mm/80 (2 twin) (Natya I); 85° elevation; 270 rounds/minute to 3 km *(1.6 nm)*; weight of shell 0.34 kg.
A/S mortars: 2 RBU 1200 5-tubed fixed (Natya I); range 1200 m; warhead 34 kg.
Mines: 10.
Countermeasures: MCM: Capable of magnetic, acoustic and mechanical sweeping.
Radars: Surface search: Don 2 or Low Trough; I band.
Fire control: Drum Tilt; H/I band (not in all).
IFF: Two Square Head. High Pole B.
Sonars: Hull-mounted; active minehunting; high frequency.

Programmes: First reported in 1970, as successor to the Yurka class. Built at Kolpino and Khabarovsk. Construction for Soviet Navy ended in 1980 with Natya II although Natya I building continues for export. Type name is *morskoy tralshchik* meaning seagoing minesweeper.
Structure: Some have hydraulic gantries aft. Have aluminium/steel alloy hulls. Natya II was built without minesweeping gear to make way for a lengthened superstructure, the transom has been cut away amidships to take a 5 ft sheave. This is believed to be a minehunting version for research and development. Some have Gatling 30 mm guns and a different radar configuration without Drum Tilt.
Operational: Usually operate in home waters but have deployed to the Mediterranean, Indian Ocean and West Africa.
Sales: India (two in 1978, two in 1979, two in 1980, one in August 1986, two in 1987, three in 1988). Libya (two in 1981, two in February 1983, one in August 1983, one in January 1984, one in January 1985, one in October 1986). Syria (one in 1985). Yemen (two in 1991).

NATYA I (without Drum Tilt radar) *6/1991, 92 Wing RAAF*

NATYA I *7/1991*

NATYA II *5/1986, US Navy*

2 GORYA CLASS (MINEHUNTERS—OCEAN)

ZHELEZNYAKOV + 1

Displacement, tons: 1130 full load
Dimensions, feet (metres): 216.5 oa; 200.1 wl × 36.1 × 10.8 *(66; 61 × 11 × 3.3)*
Main machinery: 2 diesels; 5000 hp(m) *(3.7 MW)*; 2 shafts
Speed, knots: 17
Complement: 80

Missiles: 2 SA-N-5 Grail quad launchers; IR homing to 6 km *(3.2 nm)* at 1.5 Mach; warhead 1.5 kg.
Guns: 1—3 in *(76 mm)*/60; 85° elevation; 120 rounds/minute to 15 km *(8 nm)*; weight of shell 7 kg.
1—30 mm/65 AK 630; 6 barrels; 3000 rounds/minute to 2 km.
Countermeasures: Decoys: 2—16-barrelled Chaff launchers.
ESM: Cross Loop; Long Fold.
Radars: Surface search: Palm Frond; I band.
Navigation: Nayada; I band.
Fire control: Bass Tilt; H/I band.
IFF: Salt Pot C. 2 Square Head.
Sonars: Hull-mounted; active search; high frequency.

Programmes: First one completed at Kolpino Yard, Leningrad in late 1986 and transferred to the Black Sea in 1989. Second completed in 1991.
Structure: Appears to carry mechanical, magnetic and acoustic sweep gear and may have accurate positional fixing equipment. A remote-controlled submersible is housed behind the sliding doors in the superstructure below the ADG gun mounting.
Operational: *Zheleznyakov* is conducting trials and training in the Black Sea. The second of class undergoing sea trials in the Baltic in 1992.

GORYA *8/1989*

30 YURKA CLASS (MINESWEEPERS—OCEAN)

GAFEL	**EVGENIY NIKONOV**	**MAZLOV**
NAVODCHIK	**SEMEN ROSAL**	+ 25

Displacement, tons: 460 full load
Dimensions, feet (metres): 171.9 × 30.8 × 8.5 *(52.4 × 9.4 × 2.6)*
Main machinery: 2 diesels; 5500 hp(m) *(4 MW)*; 2 shafts
Speed, knots: 17. **Range, miles:** 1500 at 12 kts
Complement: 60

Missiles: SAM: 2 SA-N-5 Grail quad launchers (in some); manual aiming; IR homing to 6 km *(3.2 nm)* at 1.5 Mach; altitude to 2500 m *(8000 ft)*; warhead 1.5 kg; 16 missiles.
Guns: 4—30 mm/65 (2 twin); 85° elevation; 500 rounds/minute to 5 km *(2.7 nm)*; weight of shell 0.54 kg.
Mines: 10.
Countermeasures: Fitted for wire, magnetic and acoustic sweeping.
ESM: Watch Dog.
Radars: Surface search: Don 2 or Spin Trough; I band.
Fire control: Drum Tilt; H/I band.
IFF: Two Square Head. High Pole B.
Sonars: Hull-mounted; active minehunting; high frequency.

Programmes: A class of medium fleet minesweepers with aluminium/steel alloy hull. Completed from 1963 to 1972 at Kolpino and Khabarovsk. Type name is *morskoy tralshchik* meaning seagoing minesweeper.
Operational: One sank in the Black Sea after an explosion in August 1989. Being scrapped at about 10 per year.
Sales: Four to Egypt (1969), two to Vietnam (1979).

YURKA *5/1990*

10 T 43 CLASS (MINESWEEPERS—OCEAN)

Displacement, tons: 500 standard; 580 (600 for 60 m ships) full load
Dimensions, feet (metres): 190.2 × 27.6 × 6.9 *(58 × 8.4 × 2.1)* (older units)
196.8 × 27.6 × 7.5 *(60 × 8.4 × 2.3)* (in later ships)
Main machinery: 2 Type 9-D-8 diesels; 2200 hp(m) *(1.6 MW)*; 2 shafts
Speed, knots: 15. **Range, miles:** 3000 at 10 kts; 2000 at 14 kts
Complement: 65

Guns: 4—37 mm/63 (2 twin); 85° elevation; 160 rounds/minute to 9 km *(5 nm)*; weight of shell 0.7 kg.
2 or 4—14.5 mm (1 or 2 twin) MGs.
Depth charges: 2 projectors.
Mines: 16.
Radars: Surface search: Ball End; E/F band.
Navigation: Don 2 or Spin Trough; I band.
IFF: Square Head. High Pole A.
Sonars: Hull-mounted; active minehunting; high frequency.

Programmes: Built in 1948-57 in shipyards throughout the Soviet Union. A number of this class was converted into radar pickets. Of the 200+ hulls built a number were also used as diving ships, tenders and so on as well as a number employed as patrol ships. Type name is *morskoy tralshchik* meaning seagoing minesweeper.
Structure: Steel hulls. The later version (*60 m* long) carries the additional four 25 mm guns and has a double-level bridge instead of the straight-up type in earlier ships.
Operational: Being paid off at about 10 per year.
Sales: Algeria (2), Albania (2), Bulgaria (3), China (2), Egypt (7), Indonesia (6), Iraq (2), Syria (2), 12 built in Poland for Polish Navy; one converted to a radar picket in late 1970s. Many of these had the 58 m hull and double-level bridges.

T 43 *1981, MoD*

2 ANDRYUSHA CLASS (MINESWEEPERS—COASTAL SPECIAL)

ALTAYSKIY **ESTONIY**

Displacement, tons: 380 full load
Dimensions, feet (metres): 154.2 × 27.9 × 6.5 *(47 × 8.5 × 2)*
Main machinery: 2 diesels; 2200 hp(m) *(1.6 MW)*; 2 shafts
Speed, knots: 15. **Range, miles:** 3000 at 10 kts
Complement: 40
Guns: None.
Radars: Surface search: Spin Trough or Don 2; I band.
IFF: High Pole B.

Comment: First entered service in 1975. Probably built at Kolpino. Specially designed, possibly with GRP hulls, for deep water magnetic sweeping. Possibly carry a gas turbine generator. May be trials ships as no more have been built and one has been paid off.

ANDRYUSHA *9/1984, G. Jacobs*

1 BALTIKA CLASS (MINESWEEPER—COASTAL)

Displacement, tons: 210 full load
Dimensions, feet (metres): 83.3 × 22.3 × 10.8 *(25.4 × 6.8 × 3.3)*
Main machinery: 1 ChlSP 18/22 diesel; 300 hp(m) *(220 kW)*; 1 shaft; cp prop
Speed, knots: 9. **Range, miles:** 1400 at 9 kts
Complement: 10
Guns: 2—14.5 mm MGs (twin).
Radars: Navigation: Spin Trough; I band.

Comment: A trawler acquired in 1980 and converted for some form of MCM operations probably to test the feasibility of rapid conversion of trawlers to the minesweeping role.

2 PELIKAN CLASS ACV (MINESWEEPER—INSHORE)

Displacement, tons: 115
Dimensions, feet (metres): 98.4 × 42.7 *(30 × 13)*
Speed, knots: 55
Guns: 1—30 mm/65 AK 630.
Radars: Navigation: Shot Dome; I band.
IFF: Salt Pot.

Comment: Air cushion vehicles built at Feodosiya and commissioned in 1985-86. Experimental craft to investigate the application of hovercraft for the mine countermeasures role. The programme is reported as unsuccessful and no more are to be built. One of the pair may have been wrecked in 1990.

72 + 2 SONYA CLASS (MINESWEEPERS—HUNTERS/COASTAL)

Displacement, tons: 400 full load
Dimensions, feet (metres): 157.4 × 28.9 × 6.6 *(48 × 8.8 × 2)*
Main machinery: 2 diesels; 2000 hp(m) *(1.47 MW)*; 2 shafts
Speed, knots: 15. **Range, miles:** 3000 at 10 kts
Complement: 43
Missiles: SAM: 2 quad SA-N-5 launchers (in some).
Guns: 2—30 mm/65 AK 630 or 2—30 mm/65 (twin) and 2—25 mm/80 (twin).
Mines: 8.
Radars: Surface search: Don 2; I band.
IFF: Two Square Head. High Pole B.

Comment: Wooden hull with GRP sheath. Still in series production at about two a year in western yards and at Ulis (Pacific). First reported 1973. Type name is *bazovy tralshchik* meaning base minesweeper. Some have two twin 30 mm Gatling guns, others one 30 mm/65 (twin) plus one 25 mm (twin).
Transfers: Bulgaria, four in 1981-85. Cuba, four in 1980-85. Syria, one in 1986. Vietnam, one in February 1987, one in February 1988, one in July 1989 and one in February 1990. Yemen, one in February 1991.

SONYA (new guns) *5/1990, MoD Bonn*

SONYA (old guns) *1991, Ships of the World*

45 YEVGENYA CLASS (MINEHUNTERS—INSHORE)

Displacement, tons: 77 standard; 90 full load
Dimensions, feet (metres): 80.7 × 18 × 4.9 *(24.6 × 5.5 × 1.5)*
Main machinery: 2 diesels; 400 hp(m) *(294 kW)*; 2 shafts
Speed, knots: 11. **Range, miles:** 300 at 10 kts
Complement: 10
Guns: 2—14.5 mm (twin) MGs or 2—25 mm/80 (twin) (in some later ships).
Radars: Surface search: Spin Trough; I band.
IFF: High Pole.
Sonars: A small sonar is lifted over stern on crane; a TV system may also be used.

Comment: GRP hulls. Production started in late 1960s and completed in 1988 at Kolpino. Type name is *reydny tralshchik* meaning roadstead minesweeper.
Transfers: Two to Angola (September 1987), three to Bulgaria (1976-77), 10 to Cuba (1977-82), six to India (1983-84), three to Iraq (1975), three to Mozambique (1985-86), eight to Nicaragua (1984-88), five to Syria (1978-86), three to North Yemen (May 1982-November 1987), three to Vietnam (December 1986-November 1987), three to South Yemen in March 1990.

YEVGENYA *1991*

20 VANYA and 3 MODIFIED VANYA CLASSES (MINESWEEPERS—HUNTERS/COASTAL)

Displacement, tons: 250 full load
Dimensions, feet (metres): 131.2 × 23.9 × 5.9 *(40 × 7.3 × 1.8)*
Main machinery: 2 Type 9-D-8 diesels; 2200 hp(m) *(1.6 MW)*; 2 shafts
Speed, knots: 16. **Range, miles:** 1400 at 14 kts; 2400 at 10 kts
Complement: 30
Guns: 2—30 mm/65 (twin). 2—25 mm/80 (twin) (in conversions in place of 30 mm).
Mines: 8 (12 in Vanya II).
Radars: Surface search: Don 2. Don Kay (in conversions).
IFF: Square Head (unmodified). High Pole B.

Comment: A coastal class with wooden hulls of a type suitable for series production built from 1961-73. The normal Vanya class can act as minehunters. Three have been modified with superstructure extended forward, with 25 mm mounting on fo'c'sle in place of 30 mm, lattice mast at break amidships and two boats stowed on quarterdeck. Guidance ships for Ilyusha class. Type name is *bazovy tralshchik* meaning base minesweeper. Twelve deleted in 1988-89, ten in 1990 and twenty more in 1991.
Transfers: Six to Bulgaria (1970-85), two to Syria (1973) and one to Vietnam (November 1986).

VANYA *1980*

1 SASHA CLASS (MINESWEEPERS—COASTAL)

Displacement, tons: 250 standard; 280 full load
Dimensions, feet (metres): 147.9 × 20 × 6.6 *(45.1 × 6.1 × 2)*
Main machinery: 2 diesels; 2200 hp(m) *(1.6 MW)*; 2 shafts
Speed, knots: 19. **Range, miles:** 1300 at 18 kts; 2000 at 12 kts
Complement: 25
Guns: 1—57 mm/70 or 45 mm/85. 4—25 mm/80 (2 twin).
Mines: 12.
Radars: Surface search: Ball End; E/F band.
IFF: High Pole. Dead Duck.

Comment: Of steel construction. Built between 1956-63. Now phasing out with two more in reserve. Type name is *reydny tralshchik* meaning roadstead minesweeper. Based in the Baltic.

SASHA *1980*

8 + 4 LIDA CLASS (MINEHUNTERS—INSHORE)

Displacement, tons: 110 full load
Dimensions, feet (metres): 101.7 × 20.3 × 5.2 *(31 × 6.2 × 1.6)*
Main machinery: 2 diesels; 400 hp(m) *(294 kW)*; 2 shafts
Speed, knots: 11
Complement: 10
Guns: 2—25 mm/80 (twin).
Radars: Surface search: I band.

Comment: A follow-on to the Yevgenya class started construction in 1989 at Kolpino Yard, Leningrad. Similar in appearance to Yevgenya. Building rate is about four a year.

LIDA *1991*

7 ILYUSHA CLASS (MINESWEEPERS—INSHORE)

Displacement, tons: 85 full load
Dimensions, feet (metres): 86.6 × 19.4 × 4.6 *(26.4 × 5.9 × 1.4)*
Main machinery: 2 diesels; 500 hp(m) *(367 kW)*; 2 shafts
Speed, knots: 12. **Range, miles:** 300 at 10 kts
Complement: 10
Radars: Navigation: Spin Trough; I band.

Comment: First reported in 1966. Large foremast carrying electronic arrays. Capable of operating unmanned and radio controlled. (See Vanya class.) Three left in the Baltic and four in the Black Sea; the remainder scrapped.

ILYUSHA *1980*

3 + 2 TANYA CLASS (MINESWEEPERS—INSHORE)

Displacement, tons: 73 full load
Dimensions, feet (metres): 87 × 13 × 5 *(26.5 × 4 × 1.5)*
Main machinery: 1 diesel; 270 hp(m) *(200 kW)*; 1 shaft
Speed, knots: 10
Radars: Surface search: Spin Trough; I band.

Comment: Built at Kolpino Yard. First operational in 1987, second and third in 1989/90. Probably replacing the Ilyusha class as radio-controlled drones.

TANYA *1990, S. Breyer*

3 OLYA CLASS (MINESWEEPERS—INSHORE)

Displacement, tons: 66 full load
Dimensions, feet (metres): 74.8 × 14.8 × 4.6 *(22.8 × 4.5 × 1.4)*
Main machinery: 2 diesels; 400 hp(m) *(294 kW)*; 2 shafts
Speed, knots: 12. **Range, miles:** 500 at 10 kts
Complement: 15
Guns: 2—25 mm/80 (twin).
Radars: Surface search: Spin Trough; I band.

Comment: Built in mid-1970s. Type name is *reydny tralshchik* meaning roadstead minesweeper. One deleted in 1988-89 and one in 1991. Remainder based in the Baltic. Two to Bulgaria in mid-1970s.

OLYA *1990*

15 K 8 CLASS (MINESWEEPING BOATS)

Displacement, tons: 26 full load
Dimensions, feet (metres): 55.4 × 10.5 × 3.9 *(16.9 × 3.2 × 1.2)*
Main machinery: 2 Type 3-D-6 diesels; 316 hp(m) *(232 kW)*; 2 shafts
Speed, knots: 18. **Range, miles:** 300 at 10 kts
Complement: 6
Guns: 2—14.5 mm (twin) MGs.

Comment: Built in Poland between 1954-59. Being deleted. Over half in reserve.
Transfers: Two to Egypt (late 1960s), four to Nicaragua (1984), five to Vietnam (October 1980).

K 8

AMPHIBIOUS FORCES

14 ALLIGATOR CLASS (LSTs)

Type 1
KRIMSKY KOMSOMOLETS
TOMSKY KOMSOMOLETS
VORONEZHSKY KOMSOMOLETS
KOMSOMOLETS KARELY

Type 2
SERGEY LAZO
+ 1

Type 3
ALEKSANDR TORTSEV
DONETSKY SHAKHTER
KRASNAYA PRESNYA
PETR ILICHEV
50 LET SHEFTSVA VLKSM
ILYA AZAROV

Type 4
NIKOLAY FILCHENKOV
NIKOLAY VILKOV

Displacement, tons: 3400 standard; 4700 full load
Dimensions, feet (metres): 370.7 × 50.8 × 14.7 *(113 × 15.5 × 4.5)*

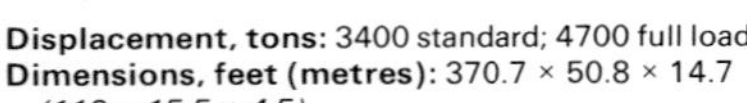

Main machinery: 2 diesels; 9000 hp(m) *(6.6 MW)*; 2 shafts
Speed, knots: 18. **Range, miles:** 10 000 at 15 kts
Complement: 100
Military lift: 300 troops; 1700 tons including about 20 tanks and various trucks; 40 AFVs

Missiles: SAM: 3 SA-N-5 Grail twin launchers with 24 missiles in all ships except *Komsomolets Karely, Sergey Lazo* and *Donetsky Shakhter*.
2 SA-N-5 Grail twin launchers *(Petr Ilichev)*; manual aiming; IR homing to 6 km *(3.2 nm)* at 1.5 Mach; altitude to 2500 m *(8000 ft)*; warhead 1.5 kg; 16 missiles.
Guns: 2—57 mm/70 (twin); 85° elevation; 120 rounds/minute to 8 km *(4.4 nm)*; weight of shell 2.8 kg.
4—25 mm/80 (2 twin) (Type 4); 85° elevation; 270 rounds/minute to 3 km *(1.6 nm)*; weight of shell 0.34 kg.
1—122 mm BM-21; 2 × 20-barrelled rocket launchers (in last seven); range 9 km *(5 nm)*.
Fire control: 1 Squeeze Box optronic director (Types 3 and 4).
Radars: Surface search: Two Don 2 or Don 2 and Spin Trough (in two Type 1); I band.
Don 2 *(Krimsky Komsomolets)*; I band.

NIKOLAY FILCHENKOV *7/1991*

Programmes: First ship commissioned in 1966 at Kaliningrad. Last of class completed in 1976. Type name is *bolshoy desantny korabl* meaning large landing ship. One Type 2 has no name.
Structure: These ships have ramps on the bow and stern. There are four variations of rig. In Type 1 two cranes are carried—other types have only one crane. In Type 3 the bridge structure has been raised and a forward deck house has been added to accommodate shore bombardment rocket launchers. Type 4 is similar to Type 3 with the addition of two twin 25 mm gun mountings on centre-line abaft the bridge superstructure. As well as a tank deck 300 ft long stretching right across the hull there are two smaller deck areas and a hold.
Operational: In the 1980s the class operated regularly off West Africa, in the Mediterranean and in the Indian Ocean, usually with Naval Infantry units embarked.

3 IVAN ROGOV CLASS (LPDs)

IVAN ROGOV **ALEKSANDR NIKOLAEV** **MITROFAN MOSKALENKO**

Displacement, tons: 12 600 full load
Dimensions, feet (metres): 518.2 × 80.2 × 21.2 (27.8 flooded) *(158 × 24.5 × 6.5 (8.5))*
Main machinery: 2 gas turbines; 48 000 hp(m) *(35.3 MW)*; 2 shafts
Speed, knots: 25. **Range, miles:** 4000 at 18 kts
Complement: 250
Military lift: 522 troops (battalion); 20 tanks or equivalent weight of APCs and trucks; 2 Lebed class ACVs and 1 Ondatra class LCM in docking bay

Missiles: SAM: SA-N-4 Gecko twin launcher ❶; semi-active radar homing to 15 km *(8 nm)* at 2.5 Mach; warhead 50 kg; altitude 9.1-3048 m *(30-10 000 ft)*; 20 missiles.
2 SA-N-5 Grail quad launchers; manual aiming; IR homing to 6 km *(3.2 nm)* at 1.5 Mach; warhead 1.5 kg.
Guns: 2—3 in *(76 mm)*/60 (twin) ❷; 80° elevation; 60 rounds/minute to 15 km *(8 nm)*; weight of shell 6.8 kg.
1—122 mm BM-21 (naval); 2 × 20-barrelled rocket launcher; range 9 km *(5 nm)*.
4—30 mm/65 AK 630 ❸; 6 barrels per mounting; 3000 rounds/minute combined to 2 km.
Countermeasures: Decoys: 4—10-barrelled Chaff launchers.
ESM: 2 Bell Squat. 2 Bell Shroud.
Fire control: 2 Squeeze Box optronic directors ❹.
Radars: Air/surface search: Head Net C (first two); Half Plate (third) ❺; 3D; E band.
Navigation: 2 Don Kay or 2 Palm Frond; I band.
Fire control: Owl Screech ❻; G band (for 76 mm). Two Bass Tilt ❼; H/I band (for 30 mm). Pop Group ❽; F/H/I band (for SA-N-4).
CCA: Fly Screen ❾; I band.
IFF: High Pole B. Salt Pot B.
Tacan: 2 Round House ❿.

Helicopters: 4 Ka-29 Helix B ⓫.

Programmes: First launched in July 1977 having been built at Kaliningrad. Second launched April 1982; third launched in July 1989 and completed trials in March 1991. No more are to be built. Type name is *bolshoy desantny korabl* meaning large landing ship.
Structure: Has bow ramp with beaching capability leading from a tank deck 200 ft long and 45 ft wide. Stern doors open into a docking bay 250 ft long and 45 ft wide. A helicopter spot forward has a flying-control station and the after helicopter deck and hangar is similarly fitted. Helicopters can enter the hangar from both front and rear. Positions arranged on main superstructure for replenishment of both fuel and solids.

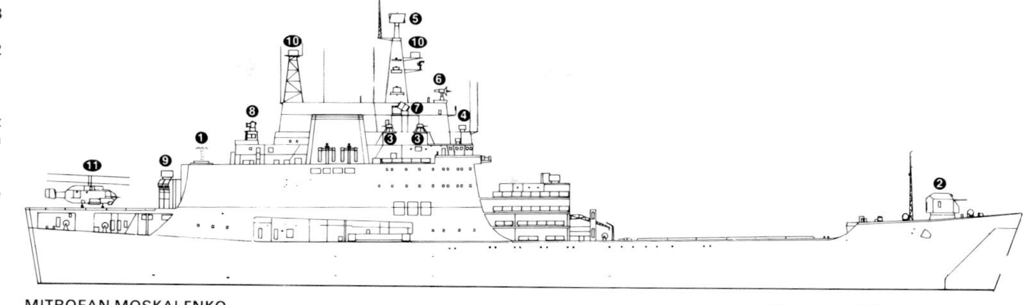
MITROFAN MOSKALENKO *(Scale 1 : 1 200), Ian Sturton*

MITROFAN MOSKALENKO *2/1991*

Operational: The first long-range, long endurance assault capability acquired by the Soviet Navy. First two are based in the Pacific and the last one in the Northern Fleet.

25 ROPUCHKA I and 2 + 1 ROPUCHKA II CLASSES (LSTs)

ALEKSANDR SHABALIN **CONSTANTIN OLSHANSKIY** **TSESAR KUNIKOV** **BOBRUISK**

Displacement, tons: 3800 full load
Dimensions, feet (metres): 370.7 × 50.9 × 16.7 *(113 × 15.5 × 5.1)*
Main machinery: 2 diesels; 9000 hp(m) *(6.6 MW)*; 2 shafts
Speed, knots: 18. **Range, miles:** 3500 at 16 kts; 6000 at 12 kts
Complement: 90
Military lift: 450 tons; 225 troops; 24 AFVs

Missiles: SAM: 4 SA-N-5 Grail quad launchers (in at least two ships); manual aiming; IR homing to 6 km *(3.2 nm)* at 1.5 Mach; altitude to 2500 m *(8000 ft)*; warhead 1.5 kg; 32 missiles.
Guns: 4—57 mm/80 (2 twin) (Ropuchka I); 85° elevation; 120 rounds/minute to 6 km *(3.3 nm)*; weight of shell 2.8 kg.
1—76 mm/60 (Ropuchka II); 2—30 mm/65 AK 630 (Ropuchka II).
2—122 mm BM-21 (naval) (in some). 2 × 20-barrelled rocket launchers; range 9 km *(5 nm)*.
Radars: Air/surface search: Strut Curve or Positive E; F band.
Navigation: Don 2 or Kivach; I band.
Fire control: Muff Cob (Ropuchka I); G/H band.
Bass Tilt (Ropuchka II): H/I band.
IFF: Two High Pole A or Salt Pot A.

Programmes: Ropuchka Is completed at Gdansk, Poland in two spells from 1974-78 (12 ships) and 1980-88. Ropuchka IIs started building in 1987 with the first one commissioning in May 1990. The third and last of the class was still in Gdansk in early 1992. Type name is *bolshoy desantny korabl* meaning large landing ship.

ROPUCHKA II (with 76 mm gun and 30 mm ADGs) *10/1991, Foto Flite*

Structure: A 'roll-on-roll-off' design with a tank deck running the whole length of the ship. All have very minor differences in appearance. These ships have a higher troop-to-vehicle ratio than the Alligator class. At least five of the class have rocket launchers at the after end of the forecastle. The second type have a 76 mm gun forward in place of one twin 57 mm and an ADG aft instead of the second. Radar and EW suites are also different. The after mast has been replaced by a solid extension to the superstructure. One Ropuchka II has a masthead radome possibly with a Positive E radar underneath it.
Operational: Distributed between the four Fleets. Only four appear to show names.
Sales: One to South Yemen in 1979.

ROPUCHKA I (with 57 mm guns) *9/1991, van Ginderen Collection*

32 POLNOCHNY CLASS (13 GROUP A, 16 GROUP B, 3 GROUP C) (LSMs)

Displacement, tons: 750 standard; 800 full load (Group A)
760 standard; 860 full load (Group B)
1120 standard; 1150 full load (Group C)
Dimensions, feet (metres): 239.5 × 27.9 × 5.8
(73 × 8.5 × 1.8) (Group A)
242.7 × 27.9 × 5.8 *(74 × 8.5 × 1.8)* (Group B)
269 × 32.8 × 6.6 *(82 × 10 × 2)* (Group C)
Main machinery: 2 Type 40D diesels; 5000 hp(m) *(3.67 MW)*; 2 shafts
Speed, knots: 19; 18 (Group C). **Range, miles:** 1000 at 18 kts (Groups A and B); 900 at 17 kts (Group C); 2000 at 12 kts (Group C)
Complement: 40-42
Military lift: 180 troops; 350 tons including 6 tanks

Missiles: SAM: 2 SA-N-5 Grail quad launchers (Group A); manual aiming; IR homing to 6 km *(3.2 nm)* at 1.5 Mach; altitude to 2500 m *(8000 ft)*; warhead 1.5 kg; 16 missiles.
4 SA-N-5 Grail quad launchers (Groups B and C); manual aiming; IR homing to 6 km *(3.2 nm)* at 1.5 Mach; altitude to 2500 m *(8000 ft)*; warhead 1.5 kg; 32 missiles.
Guns: 2—30 mm (twin) (in one ship) (Group A).
2 or 4—30 mm (1 or 2 twin) (Group B). 4—30 mm (2 twin) (Group C).
2—140 mm rocket launchers (Groups A, B and C); 18 barrels.
Fire control: PED-1 system.
Radars: Surface search: Spin Trough; I band.
Fire control: Drum Tilt; H/I band (for 30 mm guns).
IFF: High Pole A. Square Head.

POLNOCHNY C *1/1991*

Programmes: All Soviet ships built in Poland, Group A in 1963-68, Group B in 1968-70 and Group C in 1970-74. Many of Group A are unarmed. Group D are export models for Iraq, Libya and India built later than the others. Soviet type name is *stredny desantny korabl* meaning medium landing ship. Another four of the class (probably from Group B) have been converted for MCM operations (see *Mine Warfare* section).

Structure: Have bow ramps only. Tank decks vary considerably in size between groups—Group A, 36.9 × 5.2 m *(120 × 17 ft)*; Group B, 45.7 × 5.2 m *(150 × 17 ft)*; Group C, 53.3 × 6.7 m *(175 × 22 ft)*. Group D have a helicopter landing platform amidships.
Operational: Many of the earlier units are being paid off.

Sales: From Navy: Algeria (1), Angola (3), Bulgaria (2), Cuba (2), Egypt (3), Ethiopia (2), Somalia (1), Syria (3), Vietnam (3), Yemen (3). All Type A or B. From Poland: India (8), Indonesia (1), Iraq (4), Libya (4). All Type D. Of these some have been deleted. In addition 23 built for the Polish Navy, most of which have been scrapped.

9 VYDRA CLASS (LCUs)

Displacement, tons: 550 full load
Dimensions, feet (metres): 179.7 × 25.3 × 6.6 *(54.8 × 7.7 × 2)*
Main machinery: 2 Type 3-D-12 diesels; 630 hp(m) *(463 kW)*; 2 shafts
Speed, knots: 12. **Range, miles:** 2500 at 10 kts
Complement: 20
Military lift: 3 MBTs or 200 tons or 100 troops
Radars: Navigation: Don 2; I band.

Comment: Built from 1967-69 to a German MFP design. No armament. Transfers: 19 to Bulgaria, 10 to Egypt. Some employed as YF transports.

VYDRA *8/1980, MoD*

14 ONDATRA CLASS (LCMs)

Displacement, tons: 145 full load
Dimensions, feet (metres): 78.7 × 16.4 × 4.9 *(24 × 5 × 1.5)*
Main machinery: 1 diesel; 315 hp(m) *(231 kW)*
Speed, knots: 10. **Range, miles:** 500 at 5 kts
Military lift: 1 MBT

Comment: First completed in 1979—associated with *Ivan Rogov*. Tank deck of 45 × 13 ft.

ONDATRA *4/1979, MoD*

AMPHIBIOUS CRAFT (AIR CUSHION VEHICLES)

Note: (a) Fuller details appear in the latest edition of *Jane's High-Speed Marine Craft and Air-Cushion Vehicles*.
(b) Pelikan class are included under *Mine Warfare Forces*.

7 + 2 TSAPLYA CLASS

Displacement, tons: 115 full load
Dimensions, feet (metres): 102.4 × 42.6 *(31.2 × 13)*
Main machinery: 2 gas turbines; 8000 hp(m) *(5.9 MW)*; 2 shafts
Speed, knots: 70
Complement: 6
Military lift: 1 MBT plus 80 troops or 25 tons plus 160 troops
Guns: 2—30 mm/65 AK 630. 8—14.5 mm MGs (4 twin).

Comment: Prototype built at Feodosiya entered service in 1982, second in 1987, and now at about one a year. Follow-on to the Lebed class and to replace the Gus class. Embarked in Ivan Rogov class.

TSAPLYA *1989*

6 POMORNIK CLASS

Displacement, tons: 370 full load
Dimensions, feet (metres): 189 × 70.5 *(57.6 × 21.5)*
Main machinery: 5 Type NK-12 gas turbines (2 for lift, 24 000 hp(m) *(17.6 MW)*; 3 for drive, 36 000 hp(m) *(26.5 MW)*)
Speed, knots: 70
Complement: 40
Military lift: 100 tons; 1 MBT plus 80 troops or 25 tons stores plus 160 troops
Missiles: SAM: 2 SA-N-5 Grail quad launchers; manual aiming; IR homing to 6 km *(3.2 nm)* at 1.5 Mach; altitude to 2500 m *(8000 ft)*; warhead 1.5 kg.
Guns: 2—30 mm/65 AK 630; 6 barrels per mounting; 3000 rounds/minute combined to 2 km. 2 retractable 122 mm rocket launchers (not in first of class).
Fire control: Quad Look (modified Squeeze Box) optronic director.
Radars: Air/surface search: Kivach II or Shot Dome; I band.
Fire control: Bass Tilt; H/I band.
IFF: Salt Pot A/B; High Pole A.

Comment: First of class delivered 1986. Produced at Almaz, Leningrad and at Feodosiya and Tochka-Werft. Probable total of six only unless more are ordered for export. Bow and stern ramps for ro-ro working. Black Sea units have a different radar.

POMORNIK *8/1989, MoD Bonn*

18 AIST CLASS

Displacement, tons: 275 full load
Dimensions, feet (metres): 155.2 × 58.4 *(47.3 × 17.8)*
Main machinery: 2 gas turbines driving four axial lift fans and four propeller units for propulsion; 24 000 hp(m) *(17.6 MW)*
Speed, knots: 70. **Range, miles:** 120 at 50 kts
Complement: 10
Military lift: 80 tons or 4 light tanks plus 50 troops or 2 medium tanks plus 200 troops or 3 APCs plus 100 troops
Guns: 4—30 mm/65 (2 twin) AK 630; 6 barrels per mounting; 3000 rounds/minute combined to 2 km.
Radars: Surface search: Kivach; I band.
Fire control: Drum Tilt; H/I band.
IFF: High Pole B. Square Head.

Comment: First produced at Leningrad in 1970, subsequent production at rate of about six every four years. The first large hovercraft for naval use. Similar to British SR.N4. Type name is *maly desantny korabl na vozdushnoy podushke* meaning small ACV. Modifications have been done to the original engines and some units have been reported carrying two SA-N-5 quadruple SAM systems and Chaff launchers. One scrapped in the Baltic in 1988.

AIST *1987*

19 LEBED CLASS

Displacement, tons: 87 full load
Dimensions, feet (metres): 80.1 × 36.7 *(24.4 × 11.2)*
Main machinery: 2 AI-20K gas turbines for lift and propulsion; 8300 hp(m) *(6.1 MW)*
Speed, knots: 50. **Range, miles:** 100 at 50 kts
Complement: 6 (2 officers)
Military lift: 2 light tanks or 40 tons cargo or 120 troops
Guns: 2—14.5 mm (twin) MGs.
Radars: Navigation: Kivach; I band.

Comment: First entered service 1975. At least two can be carried in Ivan Rogov class. Have a bow ramp with gun on starboard side and the bridge to port.

LEBED *9/1991*

2 UTENOK CLASS

Displacement, tons: 70 full load
Dimensions, feet (metres): 75.4 × 36.1 *(23 × 11)*
Main machinery: 1 gas turbine; 530 hp(m) *(390 kW)*; 2 airscrews
Speed, knots: 65
Military lift: 1 MBT or 24 tons.
Guns: 2—30 mm/65 (twin).

Comment: Completed at Feodosiya in 1980-81.

10 GUS CLASS

Displacement, tons: 27 full load
Dimensions, feet (metres): 67.6 × 24 *(20.6 × 7.3)*
Main machinery: 2 TVD 10 marine gas turbines; 1560 hp(m) *(1.15 MW)* (propulsion); 1 TVD 10 marine gas turbine; 780 hp(m) *(573 kW)* (lift)
Speed, knots: 60. **Range, miles:** 230 at 43 kts; 185 at 50 kts
Complement: 6
Military lift: 70 tons or 25 troops and equipment

Comment: Completed 1969-1974. This is a naval version of a passenger carrying design *(Skate)*. Built for Naval Infantry. Deployed to all fleets except Northern. Rapidly being scrapped.

GUS *9/1981, Royal Danish Navy*

1 UTKA and 3 ORLAN CLASSES (WING-IN-GROUND EFFECT CRAFT)

Displacement, tons: 125 full load
Dimensions, feet (metres): 190.3 × 103.3 *(58 × 31.5)*
Main machinery: 1 NK-12 gas turbine; 12 000 hp(m) *(8.82 MW)* (propulsion); 2 NK-8 gas turbines (lift)
Speed, knots: 250. **Range, miles:** 1200 at 250 kts
Complement: 5
Military lift: 28 tons or 150 troops with equipment

Comment: Details given are for the Orlan class which is an amphibious transporter. This type of craft takes advantage of the lift created between a wide wing and the ground at low altitude. On take-off the forward engines are angled down to generate initial lift. The first experimental craft dates back to the 1960s followed by two prototypes completed in 1982. *Utka* is 229.7 ft *(70 m)* in length and has a wing span of 131.2 ft *(40 m)*. Weight is 350 tons and it is thought to have an operational radius of 1000 nm flying at an altitude of 5 m. There are eight turbofan engines and the craft is armed with six SS-N-22 anti-ship missiles. This was an ambitious programme which is reported to have failed mainly because of corrosion problems associated with flying so close to the sea. All these craft are probably for sale. At least one crashed during testing.

ORLAN *1990*

SUPPORT AND DEPOT SHIPS

6 UGRA CLASS (SUBMARINE DEPOT SHIPS)

IVAN KOLYSHKIN	IVAN VAKHRAMEEV	VOLGA
IVAN KUCHERENKO	TOBOL	LENTRA

Displacement, tons: 6750 standard; 9650 full load
Dimensions, feet (metres): 462.6 × 57.7 × 23 *(141 × 17.6 × 7)*
Main machinery: Diesel-electric; 4 Kolumna Type 2-D-42 diesel generators; 2 motors; 8000 hp(m) *(5.88 MW)*; 2 shafts
Speed, knots: 17. **Range, miles:** 21 000 at 10 kts; 9500 at 16 kts
Complement: 450

Missiles: SAM: 2 SA-N-5 Grail quad launchers; manual aiming; IR homing to 6 km *(3.2 nm)* at 1.5 Mach; altitude to 2500 m *(8000 ft)*; warhead 1.5 kg; 16 missiles (in some ships).
Guns: 8—57 mm/70 (4 twin).
Countermeasures: ESM: 2 Watch Dog.
Radars: Air/surface search: Strut Curve; F band.
Navigation: Two Don 2; I band.
Fire control: Two Muff Cob; G/H band.
IFF: Two Square Head. High Pole B.

Helicopters: Platform (hangar in *Ivan Kolyshkin)*.

Programmes: Built at Nikolayev from 1962 to 1970. Type name is *plavuchaya baza* meaning floating base.
Structure: Improved versions of the Don class with the superstructure stretching aft to the funnel. Equipped with workshops. Provided with a helicopter platform and, in *Ivan Kolyshkin* (last of class), a hangar. Has mooring points in hull about 100 ft apart, and has baggage ports for coastal craft and submarines. Two 10 ton and two 5 ton cranes. *Volga* and some others have lattice mainmast with Vee Cone HF antenna.

IVAN KOLYSHKIN (with hangar) *1988*

Operational: One scrapped in 1991. The last pair of this class were completed as training ships (*Borodino* and *Gangut*).
Sales: *Amba*, (sixth of class) which has 76 mm guns, was transferred to India in 1969.

6 DON CLASS (SUBMARINE DEPOT SHIPS)

DMITRY GALKIN
FEDOR VIDYAYEV
KAMCHATSKY KOMSOMOLETS (ex-*Mikhail Tukhachevsky*)
MAGADANSKY KOMSOMOLETS
MAGOMET GADZHIEV
VIKTOR KOTELNIKOV

Displacement, tons: 5100 standard; 6850 full load
Dimensions, feet (metres): 459.3 × 57.7 × 17.7 *(140 × 17.6 × 5.4)*
Main machinery: Diesel-electric; 4 diesel generators; 2 motors; 8000 hp(m) *(5.88 MW)*; 2 shafts
Speed, knots: 17. **Range, miles:** 21 000 at 10 kts; 9500 at 16 kts
Complement: 300 plus 450 submariners

Guns: 4—3.9 in *(100 mm)*/56 (2 in *Viktor Kotelnikov*, none mounted in *Magadansky Komsomolets*).
8—57 mm/70 (4 twin).
8—25 mm/80 (4 twin) (mounted in *K. Komsomolets* and *Fedor Vidyayev*).
Countermeasures: ESM: 2 Watch Dog.
Radars: Surface search: Slim Net; E/F band. Strut Curve (in some); F band.
Navigation: Two Don 2; I band. Snoop Plate (in some); I band.
Fire control: Two Hawk Screech (not in *M. Komsomolets*); I band.
IFF: Two Square Head. High Pole A.

Helicopters: Platform *(Magadansky Komsomolets* and *Viktor Kotelnikov)*.

Programmes: Originally seven ships were built in 1957 to 1962, all in Nikolayev. Type name is *plavuchaya baza* meaning floating base.
Structure: Have a 100 ton bow lift and two 10 ton and two 5 ton cranes.
Operational: Used as Flagships. Vee Cone fitted in *Dmitry Galkin* and *Fedor Vidyayev* for long-range communications.
Sales: One to Indonesia in 1962.

VIKTOR KOTELNIKOV *11/1990*

1 ALEKSANDR BRYKIN CLASS (MISSILE SUPPORT SHIP)

ALEKSANDR BRYKIN

Displacement, tons: 14 350 full load
Dimensions, feet (metres): 511.8 × 76.1 × 26.2 *(156 × 23.2 × 8)*
Main machinery: Diesel-electric; 2 diesel generators; 1 motor; 26 000 hp(m) *(19 MW)*; 1 shaft; bow thruster
Speed, knots: 16
Complement: 140
Missiles: SAM: 4 SA-N-5 Grail quad launchers; manual aiming; IR homing to 6 km *(3.2 nm)* at 1.5 Mach; altitude to 2500 m *(8000 ft)*; warhead 1.5 kg.
Guns: 4—30 mm/65 AK 630.
Countermeasures: ESM: 2 Bell Shroud; 2 Bell Squat.
Radars: Surface search: Half Plate Alpha; E/F band.
Navigation: 2 Nayhda; I band.
Fire control: Two Bass Tilt; H/I band.
IFF: Salt Pot. Longhead.

Comment: Completed in Leningrad in 1986. A missile supply ship for submarine ballistic missiles including SS-N-20, carried in the Typhoon class. A 75 ton crane plumbs 16 vertical storage holds forward of the funnel. Transferred to Northern Fleet in 1987.

ALEKSANDR BRYKIN *5/1987*

3 AMGA CLASS (MISSILE SUPPORT SHIPS)

AMGA **VETLUGA** **DAUGAVA**

Displacement, tons: 5750 *(Amga)*, 6100 *(Vetluga)*, 6400 *(Daugava)* full load
Dimensions, feet (metres): 334.6 × 59 × 14.8 *(102 × 18 × 4.5)* (*Amga*) (see *Comment*)
Main machinery: 2 diesels; 9000 hp(m) *(6.6 MW)*; 2 shafts
Speed, knots: 16. **Range, miles:** 4500 at 14 kts
Complement: 210
Guns: 4—25 mm/80 (2 twin).
Radars: Surface search: Strut Curve; F band; range 110 km *(60 nm)* for 2 m² target.
Navigation: Don 2; I band.
IFF: High Pole B.

Comment: Built at Gorkiy. Ships with similar duties to the Lama class. Fitted with a large 55 ton crane forward and thus capable of handling much larger missiles than their predecessors. Each ship has a different length and type of crane to handle later types of missiles. Designed for servicing submarines, particularly those armed with SS-N-6, 8 and 18 missiles. First appeared in December 1972, the second *Vetluga* (6 m longer than *Amga*) in 1976 and third *Daugava* (11 m longer than *Amga*) in 1981. *Amga* in the North, *Vetluga* and *Daugava* in the Pacific.

DAUGAVA *10/1981, MoD*

3 MALINA CLASS (NUCLEAR SUBMARINE SUPPORT SHIPS)

PM 63 PM 74 PM 12

Displacement, tons: 10 500 full load
Dimensions, feet (metres): 449.5 × 68.9 × 18.4 *(137 × 21 × 5.6)*
Main machinery: 4 gas turbines; 60 000 hp(m) *(44 MW)*; 2 shafts
Speed, knots: 17
Complement: 260
Radars: Navigation: Two Palm Frond; I band.

Comment: Built at Nikolayev. First deployed to the Northern Fleet in October 1984, second to Pacific in 1986, and third to the Northern Fleet in 1991. Designed to support nuclear-powered submarines and surface ships. Carry two 15 ton cranes.

PM 12 *4/1991*

2 PINEGA CLASS (NUCLEAR SUBMARINE SUPPORT SHIPS)

AMUR PINEGA

Displacement, tons: 6500 full load
Dimensions, feet (metres): 393.7 × 55.8 × 18 *(120 × 17 × 5.5)*
Main machinery: 2 diesels; 6800 hp(m) *(5 MW)*; 2 shafts
Speed, knots: 16
Complement: 100

Comment: Built at Vyborg. *Amur* completed in 1986 and went to the Northern Fleet. *Pinega* completed in 1987 and transferred to the Pacific in 1989.

PINEGA *10/1991, G. Jacobs*

2 MODIFIED ANDIZHAN CLASS (MISSILE SUPPORT SHIPS)

VENTA VILYUY

Displacement, tons: 6700 full load
Dimensions, feet (metres): 341.1 × 47.2 × 21.6 *(104 × 14.4 × 6.6)*
Main machinery: 2 diesels; 2500 hp(m) *(1.84 MW)*; 2 shafts
Speed, knots: 14. **Range, miles:** 6000 at 13 kts
Complement: 60
Radars: Navigation: Don 2; I band.
IFF: Square Head. High Pole.

Comment: Cargo ships built in late 1950s at Rostock. Converted to support ships 1974-75. Have one main crane forward, two smaller cranes aft and a helicopter platform. Can carry 10 SS-N-9 missiles as well as 20 SA-N-3. Type name is *voyenny transport* meaning military transport. *Venta* in the Pacific, *Vilyuy* in the Black Sea.

VENTA *1980*

7 LAMA CLASS (MISSILE SUPPORT SHIPS)

GENERAL RYABAKOV	**VORONESH**	**PM 44**	**PM 93**
PM 131	**PM 150**	**PM 154**	

Displacement, tons: 4600 full load
Dimensions, feet (metres): 370 × 49.2 × 14.4 *(112.8 × 15 × 4.4)*
Main machinery: 2 diesels; 4800 hp(m) *(3 MW)*; 2 shafts
Speed, knots: 14. **Range, miles:** 6000 at 10 kts
Complement: 200
Missiles: SAM: 4 SA-N-5 Grail quad launchers (*General Ryabakov, Voronesh, PM 131* and *PM 154*); manual aiming; IR homing to 6 km *(3.2 nm)* at 1.5 Mach; altitude to 2500 m *(8000 ft)*; warhead 1.5 kg.
Guns: 4 or 8—57 mm/70 (quad, on the fo'c'sle or 2 or 4 twin) (*PM 44* and *PM 131*).
4—25 mm/80 (*PM 44* and *PM 131*).
Radars: Surface search: Slim Net; E/F band (*Voronesh, PM 44* and *PM 154*) or Strut Curve (remainder); F band.
Navigation: Don 2; I band.
Fire control: Two Hawk Screech or Owl Screech (*PM 44*); I band or Muff Cob; G/H band.
IFF: Two Square Head. High Pole A.

Comment: Built between 1963 and 1972 at Nikolayev with seventh ship in 1979. The engines are sited aft to allow for a very large and high hangar or hold amidships for carrying missiles or weapons' spares for submarines, surface ships and missile craft. This is about 12 ft high above the main deck. There are doors at the forward end with rails leading in and a raised turntable gantry or 20 ton travelling cranes for armament supply. Variations in armament may reflect differences in missile stowage. The well deck is about 40 ft long, enough for most missiles to fit horizontally before being lifted for loading. There are several differences in midships superstructure in these ships, those specifically designed for missile craft having a longer missile store, two 10 ton cranes and a shorter forward well-deck. Type name is *plavuchaya masterskaya* meaning floating workshop except for *General Ryabakov* and *PM 150*. The two named ships and *PM 154* are based in the Black Sea, *PM 93* and *PM 150* in the Pacific, and *PM 44* and *PM 131* in the Northern Fleet.

LAMA Class *6/1989*

24 AMUR I and 5 AMUR II CLASS (REPAIR SHIPS)

AMUR I
PM 9, PM 10, PM 15, PM 37, PM 49, PM 52, PM 56, PM 75, PM 94, PM 138, PM 161, PM 163
5, 30, 34, 40, 64, 73, 81, 82, 129, 139, 140, 156
AMUR II
59, 69, 86, 92, 97

Displacement, tons: 5500 full load
Dimensions, feet (metres): 400.3 × 55.8 × 16.7 *(122 × 17 × 5.1)*
Main machinery: 1 diesel; 3000 hp(m) *(2.2 MW)*; 1 shaft
Speed, knots: 12. **Range, miles:** 13 000 at 8 kts
Complement: 145
Radars: Navigation: Don 2; I band.

Comment: Amur I class general purpose depot and repair ships completed 1968-83 in Szczecin, Poland. Successors to the Oskol class. Carry two 5 ton cranes and have accommodation for 200 from ships alongside. Amur II class similar in design. First unit completed at Szczecin in 1986.

PM 15 (Amur I) *9/1991, G. Jacobs*

PM 97 (Amur II) *9/1991, G. Jacobs*

11 OSKOL CLASS (REPAIR SHIPS)

PM 2, PM 24, PM 26, PM 42, PM 147, PM 148
20, 21, 51, 68, 146

Displacement, tons: 2550 (3500, Oskol IV) full load
Dimensions, feet (metres): 300.1 × 40 × 13.1 *(91.5 × 12.2 × 4)*
Main machinery: 2 diesels; 2500 hp(m) *(1.84 MW)*; 1 shaft
Speed, knots: 12. **Range, miles:** 8000 at 10 kts
Complement: 100
Radars: Navigation: Don 2; I band.
IFF: High Pole.

Comment: Four series: Oskol I class, well-decked hull, no armament; Oskol II class, well-decked hull, open promenade deck aft and twin 14.5 mm MGs forward; Oskol III class, well-decked hull, armed with two 57 mm guns (one twin forward) and four 25 mm guns (2 twin aft); Oskol IV class, flush-decked hull with no armament and a bridge one deck higher than other types. General purpose tenders and repair ships with one or two 3.5 ton cranes. Built from 1963 to 1970 in Poland. Type name is *plavuchaya masterskaya* meaning floating workshop. *PM 21* to South Yemen in 1988 but may have been returned, in which case there are 12 in the class.

OSKOL III (with twin 57 mm gun) *4/1991*

4 TOMBA CLASS (SUPPORT SHIPS)

244, 254, 348, 357

Displacement, tons: 5200 full load
Dimensions, feet (metres): 351 × 55.8 × 16.4 *(107 × 17 × 5)*
Main machinery: Diesel-electric; 3 diesel generators; 1 motor; 5500 hp(m) *(4 MW)*; 1 shaft
Speed, knots: 18. **Range, miles:** 7000 at 14 kts
Complement: 50
Radars: Navigation: Don 2 and Spin Trough; I band.
IFF: High Pole B.

Comment: First completed 1974. *244* and *254* deployed in Northern Fleet and *348* and *357* in the Pacific. There is a donkey funnel on fo'c'sle. Two 3 ton cranes. Type name is *elektrostantsiye nalivatelnoye sudno* meaning electricity supply ship.

TOMBA *10/1982*

8 VYTEGRALES CLASS

APSHERON (ex-*Vagales*)
BASKUNCHAK (ex-*Kirishi*)
DAURIYA (ex-*Vyborgles*)
DIKSON (ex-*Vostok 3*)
DONBAS (ex-*Vostok 4*)
SEVAN (ex-*Siverles*)
TAMAN (ex-*Suzdal*)
YAMAL (ex-*Tosnoles*)

Displacement, tons: 6150 full load
Dimensions, feet (metres): 400.3 × 55.1 × 22.3 *(122.1 × 16.8 × 6.8)*
Main machinery: 1 Burmeister & Wain 950 VTBF diesel; 5200 hp(m) *(3.82 MW)*; 1 shaft
Speed, knots: 15
Complement: 150
Radars: Air search: Big Net; C band (*Donbas* only).
Navigation: Two Don 2; I band.
Helicopters: 1 Ka-25 'Hormone C'.

Comment: Standard timber carriers of a class of 27. These eight ships were modified for naval use in 1966-68 with helicopter flight deck. Built at Zhdanov Yard, Leningrad between 1963 and 1966. *Sevan* and *Taman* fitted as squadron Flagships in support of Indian Ocean detachments. Variations exist between ships of this class; *Baskunchak* and *Dauriya* have a deckhouse over the aft hold and *Donbas* has a large air-search radar aerial on the central mast. All have two Vee Cone communications aerials. The first of class, completed in 1962, was originally *Vytegrales*, but this was later changed to *Kosmonaut Pavel Belyayev* and, with three other ships of this class, converted to Space Support Ships. Four others (*Borovichi* etc) received a different conversion for the same purpose. The eight civilian-manned ships together with these eight naval ships are often incorrectly called Vostok or Baskunchak class.

TAMAN (with helo) *8/1991, 92 Wing RAAF*

BARRACKS SHIPS

8 BOLVA 1, 30 BOLVA 2 and 10 BOLVA 3 CLASSES

Displacement, tons: 6500
Dimensions, feet (metres): 560.9 × 45.9 × 9.8 *(110 × 14 × 3)*
Cargo capacity: 350-400 tons

Comment: All built by Valmet Oy, Helsinki between 1960-74. Used for accommodation of ships' companies during refit etc. The Bolva 2 and 3 have a helicopter pad. Have alongside berthing facilities for about 400. Have no means of propulsion but can be steered. In addition there are several other types of Barracks Ships including five ex-Atrek class depot ships as well as converted merchant ships and large barges.

INTELLIGENCE COLLECTORS (AGIs)

Notes: (a) About three quarters of the AGIs are fitted with SA-N-5 (Grail).
(b) SSV in pennant numbers of some AGIs is a contraction of *sudno svyazy* meaning communications vessel.
(c) GS in pennant numbers of some AGIs is a contraction of *gidrograficheskoye sudno* meaning survey ship.
(d) One Keyla class *(Ritsa)* converted to AGI in 1987. Details under Keyla class.
(e) Activity in 1991 was reduced to less than half the normal level of the 1980s.

7 VISHNYA CLASS

SSV 169, SSV 175, SSV 201, SSV 208, SSV 231, SSV 520, SSV 535

Displacement, tons: 3800 full load
Dimensions, feet (metres): 305.1 × 47.6 × 18.4 *(93 × 14.5 × 5.6)*
Main machinery: 2 diesels; 8300 hp(m) *(6.1 MW)*; 2 shafts
Speed, knots: 18
Complement: 160
Missiles: SAM: 2 SA-N-5 Grail quad launchers; manual aiming; IR homing to 6 km *(3.2 nm)* at 1.5 Mach; altitude to 2500 m *(8000 ft)*; warhead 1.5 kg.
Guns: 2—30 mm/65 AK 630; 6 barrels per mounting.

Comment: Built in Poland for Soviet Navy. First of class entered service in July 1986, the last had completed by July 1988. *SSV 169, 231* and *520* based in the Baltic, *SSV 175* and *201* in the Black Sea and *SSV 208* and *535* in the Pacific.

SSV 231 *6/1991, Foto Flite*

4 BALZAM CLASS

SSV 80 SSV 493 SSV 516 SSV 571

Displacement, tons: 4000 standard; 5400 full load
Dimensions, feet (metres): 344.5 × 50.9 × 16.4 *(105 × 15.5 × 5)*
Main machinery: 2 diesels; 18 000 hp(m) *(13.2 MW)*; 2 shafts
Speed, knots: 20. **Range, miles:** 7000 at 16 kts
Complement: 200
Missiles: SAM: 2 SA-N-5 Grail quad launchers; manual aiming; IR homing to 6 km *(3.2 nm)* at 1.5 Mach; altitude to 2500 m *(8000 ft)*; warhead 1.5 kg; 16 missiles.
Guns: 1—30 mm/65 AK 630; 6 barrels per mounting.

Comment: All built at Kaliningrad. First of class completed in 1980, second in 1981, third in 1984 and last in 1987. Notable for twin radomes. The first class of AGI to be armed. *SSV 493* based in Pacific, remainder in the Northern Fleet.

SSV 493 *10/1991, G. Jacobs*

6 PRIMORYE CLASS

ZABAYKALYE SSV 464
PRIMORYE SSV 465
ZAPOROZHYE SSV 501
ZAKARPATYE SSV 502
KRYM SSV 590
KAVKAZ SSV 591

Displacement, tons: 3400 standard; 5000 full load
Dimensions, feet (metres): 278 × 46 × 23 *(84.7 × 14 × 7)*
Main machinery: 2 diesels; 2000 hp(m) *(1.47 MW)*; 2 shafts
Speed, knots: 12. **Range, miles:** 10 000 at 10 kts
Complement: 120
Missiles: SAM: 2 SA-N-5 Grail quad launchers (SSV 464, 501 and 591); manual aiming; IR homing to 6 km *(3.2 nm)* at 1.5 Mach; altitude to 2500 m *(8000 ft)*; warhead 1.5 kg; 16 missiles. SSV 590 has 1 launcher.

Comment: The first custom-built class of AGIs and the first to have an onboard analysis capability. First unit built 1968-70 to the same hull design as the Mayakovsky class of stern trawlers. Mast arrangements and electronic fits vary between ships. SSV 464 and 465 in the Pacific, 501 and 502 in the North and 590 and 591 in the Black Sea. SSV 501 has a Mad Hack active phased array radar for the collection of missile related data and telemetry.

KAVKAZ *11/1989*

ZAKARPATYE *1986, US Navy*

ZAPOROZHYE *4/1991*

ZABAYKALYE *10/1990, G. Jacobs*

8 MAYAK CLASS

KHERSONES
KURS
KURSOGRAF
LADOGA
GS 239
GS 242
GIRORULEVOY
ANEROID

Displacement, tons: 914 full load
Dimensions, feet (metres): 178.1 × 30.5 × 11.8 *(54.3 × 9.3 × 3.6)*
Main machinery: 1 SKL 8NVD 48 2U diesel; 880 hp(m) *(647 kW)* sustained; 1 shaft
Speed, knots: 16. **Range, miles:** 9500 at 7.5 kts
Complement: 75
Missiles: SAM: 2 SA-N-5 Grail quad launchers (in all except *GS 239, Girorulevoy* and *Khersones*); manual aiming; IR homing to 6 km *(3.2 nm)* at 1.5 Mach; altitude to 2500 m *(8000 ft)*; warhead 1.5 kg; 16 missiles.
Guns: 4—14.5 mm (2 twin) MGs (*Kursograf* only).

Comment: Built in the USSR from 1965. All ships except *Aneroid* have had additional accommodation built on the well-deck. The port side of the superstructure is enclosed while the starboard is open. *Kursograf* and *Aneroid* are in the Pacific, *GS 239, Kurs* and *Ladoga* in the Black Sea and remainder in the Baltic. More ships of the class are in the *Transports* section.

KHERSONES *8/1991*

KURS *5/1990*

GS 242 *5/1991*

3 NIKOLAY ZUBOV CLASS

GAVRIL SARYCHEV (mod) SSV 468
SEMEN CHELYUSKIN SSV 469
KHARITON LAPTEV (mod) SSV 503

Displacement, tons: 2674 standard; 3021 full load
Dimensions, feet (metres): 294.2 × 42.7 × 15 *(89.7 × 13 × 4.6)*
Main machinery: 2 Skoda 8TD48 diesels; 4400 hp(m) *(3.23 MW)* sustained; 2 shafts
Speed, knots: 16.5. **Range, miles:** 11 000 at 14 kts
Complement: 85
Missiles: SAM: 3 SA-N-5 Grail quad launchers (SSV 468 and 469); manual aiming; IR homing to 6 km *(3.2 nm)* at 1.5 Mach; altitude to 2500 m *(8000 ft)*; warhead 1.5 kg; 24 missiles.

Comment: Built in Poland. Similar class operates as research ships. SSV 468 and SSV 503 now have additional superstructure and a flush deck from bow to stern. Operational in 1965. SSV 468 and 469 in the Pacific, 503 in the Northern Fleet.

SEMEN CHELYUSKIN *8/1991, G. Jacobs*

1 MODIFIED PAMIR CLASS

PELENG (ex-*Arban*) SSV 477

Displacement, tons: 1443 standard; 2240 full load
Dimensions, feet (metres): 256 × 42 × 13.5 *(78 × 12.8 × 4.1)*
Main machinery: 2 MAN Giot 40/60 diesels; 4200 hp(m) *(3.1 MW)*; 2 shafts; cp props
Speed, knots: 18. **Range, miles:** 21 000 at 12 kts
Complement: 60
Missiles: SAM: 3 SA-N-5 Grail quad launchers; manual aiming; IR homing to 6 km *(3.2 nm)* at 1.5 Mach; altitude to 2500 m *(8000 ft)*; warhead 1.5 kg; 24 missiles.

Comment: Built in Sweden 1959-60. Originally a salvage tug and has higher deckhouse abaft bridge than other ships of class. Converted to AGI by 1965. Based in the Pacific.

PELENG *1985*

9 MOMA CLASS

EKVATOR
YUPITER (mod)
KILDIN (mod)
SSV 472 (ex-*Ilmen*) (mod)
SSV 474 (ex-*Vega*) (mod)
SSV 506 (ex-*Nakhodka*)
SSV 509 (ex-*Pelorus*) (mod)
SSV 512 (ex-*Arkhipelag*) (mod)
SSV 514 (ex-*Seliger*) (mod)

Displacement, tons: 1240 standard; 1600 full load
Dimensions, feet (metres): 240.5 × 36.8 × 12.8 *(73.3 × 11.2 × 3.9)*
Main machinery: 2 Skoda-Sulzer 6TD48 diesels; 3300 hp(m) *(2.43 MW)* sustained; 2 shafts
Speed, knots: 17. **Range, miles:** 9000 at 11 kts
Complement: 85
Missiles: SAM: 2 SA-N-5 Grail quad launchers (*SSV 472, 474, 514, Kildin* and *Yupiter*); manual aiming; IR homing to 6 km *(3.2 nm)* at 1.5 Mach; altitude to 2500 m *(8000 ft)*; warhead 1.5 kg; 16 missiles.

Comment: The six modernised versions have a new foremast in the fore well-deck and a new, low superstructure before the bridge. Non-modernised ships retain their cranes in the forward well-deck. Similar class operates as survey ships. Built at Gdansk, Poland between 1968-72. *SSV 472* and *474* in the Pacific, named ships in the Black Sea, remainder Northern Fleet.

SSV 512 *10/1990*

YUPITER *1986, US Navy*

EKVATOR *5/1991*

4 ALPINIST CLASS

GS 7 (mod) **GS 8** **GS 19** (mod) **GS 39** (mod)

Displacement, tons: 1260 full load
Dimensions, feet (metres): 177.1 × 34.4 × 13.1 *(54 × 10.5 × 4)*
Main machinery: 1 SKL 8NVD 48 A2U diesel; 1320 hp(m) *(970 kW)*; 1 shaft; bow thruster
Speed, knots: 13. **Range, miles:** 7000 at 13 kts
Complement: 50
Missiles: SAM: 1 SA-N-5 Grail quad launcher *(GS 39)*; manual aiming; IR homing to 6 km *(3.2 nm)* at 1.5 Mach; altitude to 2500 m *(8000 ft)*; warhead 1.5 kg.

Comment: Similar to Alpinist stern-trawlers which have been built at about 10 a year at the Leninskaya Kuznitsa yard at Kiev and at the Volvograd shipyard. These AGIs could come from either yard. In 1987 and 1988 *GS 7, GS 39* and *GS 19* forecastle was extended further aft and the electronics fit upgraded. *GS 7* and *GS 8* in the Pacific, the other two in the Baltic.

GS 19 *6/1990, Foto Flite*

GS 39 *5/1989, Hartmut Ehlers*

12 OKEAN CLASS

ALIDADA*	**KRENOMETR**	**REPITER**
BAROGRAF	**LINZA** (mod)*	**TEODOLIT**
DEFLEKTOR	**LOTLIN** (mod)*	**TRAVERZ**
EKHOLOT	**REDUKTOR** (mod)*	**ZOND** (mod)*

* No missiles

Displacement, tons: 750 full load
Dimensions, feet (metres): 167.3 × 28.9 × 12.1 *(51 × 8.8 × 3.7)*
Main machinery: 1 diesel; 540 hp(m) *(397 kW)*; 1 shaft
Speed, knots: 13. **Range, miles:** 7900 at 11 kts
Complement: 70
Missiles: SAM: 2 SA-N-5 Grail quad launchers (in some ships); manual aiming; IR homing to 6 km *(3.2 nm)* at 1.5 Mach; altitude to 2500 m *(8000 ft)*; warhead 1.5 kg; 16 missiles.

Comment: Built in East Germany from 1959 to mid-1960s. Have the same unbalanced superstructure with the port side closed in and the starboard side open as in the Mayak class, although there are many variations. Modified ships have additional accommodation on the well-deck. Three of the class scrapped in 1990-91. *Alidada* in the Black Sea, *Barograf* and *Deflektor* in the Pacific, *Lotlin, Reduktor* and *Zond* in the Baltic, and the remainder in Northern Fleet.

LOTLIN (mod) *1988*

EKHOLOT *1987*

LINZA (mod) *5/1989*

REDUKTOR (mod) *10/1991, Per Kornefeldt*

4 LENTRA CLASS

GS 41 **GS 43** (mod) **GS 55** **GS 59**

Displacement, tons: 250 standard; 480 (600, *GS 43* and *55*) full load
Dimensions, feet (metres): 128.6 × 24.3 × 9.2 *(39.2 × 7.4 × 2.8)*
141.7 × 24.9 × 9.5 *(43.2 × 7.6 × 2.9) (GS 43* and *55)*
Main machinery: 1 diesel; 330 hp(m) *(243 kW)* (450 hp(m) *(331 kW)* in *GS 43* and *55*); 1 shaft
Speed, knots: 11. **Range, miles:** 6000 at 9 kts
Complement: 35; 45 (*GS 43* and *55*)

Comment: Built in USSR and East Germany *(GS 59)* 1957-63. Mainly employed in-area in the Pacific Fleet *(GS 59)*, the remainder in the Black Sea. Two of the class deleted in 1991.

LENTRA Class *3/1988*

NAVAL RESEARCH SHIPS

Note: (a) Research submarines are listed at the end of the Submarine section.
(b) *Sibiriyakov* is a new type of AGOR built in Poland in 1990.

SIBIRIYAKOV *8/1990*

6 AKADEMIK KRYLOV CLASS

ADMIRAL VLADIMIRSKY	**IVAN KRUZENSHTERN**	**LEONID DEMIN**
AKADEMIK KRYLOV	**LEONID SOBOLEV**	**MIKHAIL KRUPSKY**

Displacement, tons: 9100 full load
Dimensions, feet (metres): 482.3 × 60.7 × 20.3 *(147 × 18.5 × 6.2)*
Main machinery: 2 diesels; 14 500 hp(m) *(10.7 MW)*; 2 shafts
Speed, knots: 20. **Range, miles:** 23 000 at 15 kts
Complement: 90
Radars: Navigation: Two Don 2; I band.
Helicopters: 1 Hormone.

Comment: Built in Szczecin 1974-79. Carry two survey launches and have 26 laboratories. *Krupsky* has a large radome abaft the foremast.

ADMIRAL VLADIMIRSKY *11/1990*

4 ABKHAZIYA CLASS

ABKHAZIYA **ADZHARIYA** **BASHKIRIYA** **MOLDAVIA**

Displacement, tons: 7500 full load
Dimensions, feet (metres): 409.2 × 56 × 21.1 *(124.8 × 17.1 × 6.4)*
Main machinery: 2 MAN K62 57/80 diesels; 10 500 hp(m) *(7.72 MW)*; 2 shafts; 2 bow thrusters
Speed, knots: 17. **Range, miles:** 20 000 at 16 kts
Complement: 105
Helicopters: 1 Hormone (not normally carried).

Comment: Built by Mathias Thesen Werft at Wismar. A modified Akademik Kurchatov class. Fitted telescopic hangar aft. Completed: 1971, *Abkhaziya;* 1972, *Adzhariya;* 1973, other two. Two survey launches are usually embarked. Vee Cone communications. Endurance, 60 days.

ADZHARIYA *3/1990*

3 POLYUS CLASS (KOVEL TYPE)

BAYKAL (mod) **BALKHASH** (mod) **POLYUS**

Displacement, tons: 6700 full load
Measurement, tons: 3897 gross; 1195 net
Dimensions, feet (metres): 365.8 × 46.2 × 20.7 *(111.6 × 14.1 × 6.3)*
Main machinery: Diesel-electric; 4 diesel generators; 1 motor; 3000 hp(m) *(2.2 MW) (Polyus)*, 3700 hp(m) *(2.72 MW)* (remainder); 1 shaft
Speed, knots: 14. **Range, miles:** 25 000 at 12 kts
Complement: 120

Comment: These ships are a part of the Andizhan class of some 45 ships. They were converted while building by Schiffswerft Neptun of Rostock. *Polyus* in 1962 and the other two in 1964. Oceanographic research ships. First two ships have modified superstructure with two king-posts on the fo'c'sle and several A-frame davits down each side.

BAYKAL *7/1989, G. Jacobs*

8 NIKOLAY ZUBOV CLASS

ALEKSEY CHIRIKOV
ANDREY VILKITSKY
BORIS DAVIDOV
FADDEY BELLINSGAUSEN
FEDOR LITKE
NIKOLAY ZUBOV
SEMEN DEZHNEV
VASILY GOLOVNIN

Displacement, tons: 2674 standard; 3021 full load
Dimensions, feet (metres): 294.2 × 42.7 × 15 *(89.7 × 13 × 4.6)*
Main machinery: 2 Skoda-Sulzer 8TD48 diesels; 4400 hp(m) *(3.23 MW)* sustained; 2 shafts
Speed, knots: 16.5. **Range, miles:** 11 000 at 14 kts
Complement: 50

Comment: Oceanographic research ships built at Szczecin Shipyard, Poland in 1964-68. Also employed on navigational, sonar and radar trials. Have nine laboratories and small deck aft for hydromet-balloon work. Carry two to four survey launches. Ships of same class act as AGIs. The whole class varies marginally in appearance from ship to ship.

NIKOLAY ZUBOV *6/1991, van Ginderen Collection*

1 MODIFIED DOBRYNYA NIKITICH CLASS

VLADIMIR KAVRAYSKY

Displacement, tons: 3900 full load
Dimensions, feet (metres): 239.4 × 59.4 × 20 *(73 × 18.1 × 6.1)*
Main machinery: Diesel-electric; 3 Type 13-D-100 diesel generators; 2 motors; 5400 hp(m) *(3.97 MW)*; 2 shafts
Speed, knots: 14. **Range, miles:** 8000 at 13 kts
Complement: 60

Comment: One of a numerous class of icebreakers built at Leningrad since the early 1960s and built for polar research in 1970. Has helicopter deck aft, 8 ton crane on the after well-deck and two 3 ton derricks. Carries a survey launch. Has nine laboratories.

VLADIMIR KAVRAYSKY *1982*

18 YUG CLASS

V ADM VORONTSOV (ex-*Briz*)	**MANGYSHLAK**	**PLUTON**	**TAYGA**
DONUZLAV	**MARSHAL GELOVANI**	**SENEZH**	**VIZIR**
GALS	**NIKOLAY MATUSEVICH**	**STRELETS**	**ZODIAK**
GIDROLOG	**PEGAS**	**STVOR**	**704** (ex-*SSV*...)
GORIZONT	**PERSEY**		

Displacement, tons: 2500 full load
Dimensions, feet (metres): 270.6 × 44.3 × 12.8 *(82.5 × 13.5 × 3.9)*
Main machinery: 2 Skoda-Sulzer Type 6TD 48 diesels; 3300 hp(m) *(2.43 MW)* sustained; 2 shafts; bow thruster
Speed, knots: 15. **Range, miles:** 11 000 at 12 kts
Complement: 66
Guns: 6—25 mm/80 (3 twin) (fitted for but not with).

Comment: Built at Gdansk 1978-83. Have a 4 ton davit at the stern and two survey craft. *Zodiak* has a large gantry aft. Others have minor variations around the stern area. *704* was converted in 1989 and her role is now uncertain—serves in the Northern Fleet, possibly as an AGI.

SENEZH *6/1990*

1 MOD SORUM CLASS

OS 572

Displacement, tons: 1660 full load
Dimensions, feet (metres): 190.2 × 41.3 × 15.1 *(58 × 12.6 × 4.6)*
Main machinery: Diesel-electric; 2 type 5-2 DW2 diesel generators; 1 motor; 2000 hp(m) *(1.47 MW)*; 1 shaft
Speed, knots: 14. **Range, miles:** 6750 at 13 kts
Complement: 35
Radars: Navigation: Two Nayada; I band.

Comment: A Sorum class tug built in 1987 and converted for acoustic trials. The built-up stern houses a winch and cable drum for a lengthy acoustic array which is deployed through the stern doors.

OS 572 *1988, CHOD Norway*

NAVAL SURVEY SHIPS

Note: There are plans to lease out some of these ships to commercial organisations in 1992.

20 MOMA CLASS (+9 AGIs)

ALTAIR	**ARKTIKA**	**KOLGUEV** (mod)	**OKEAN**
ANADYR	**ASKOLD**	**KRILON**	**RYBACHI** (mod)
ANDROMEDA	**BEREZAN**	**LIMAN**	**SEVER**
ANTARES	**CHELEKEN**	**MARS**	**TAYMYR**
ANTARKTYDA	**ELTON**	**MORZHOVETS**	**ZAPOLYARYE**

Displacement, tons: 1550 full load
Dimensions, feet (metres): 240.5 × 36.8 × 12.8 *(73.3 × 11.2 × 3.9)*
Main machinery: 2 Skoda-Sulzer 6TD48 diesels; 3300 hp(m) *(2.43 MW)* sustained; 2 shafts; cp props
Speed, knots: 17. **Range, miles:** 9000 at 11 kts
Complement: 55
Radars: Navigation: Two Don 2; I band.
IFF: High Pole A.

Comment: Built in Poland from 1967 to 1972. Some of the class are particularly active in ASW research associated operations. Four laboratories. One survey launch and a 7 ton crane. *Rybachi* has no crane but has an additional deckhouse forward and is classed as an experimental auxiliary. She also carries two twin 12.7 mm MG mountings and two SA-N-5 launchers. Ships of this class serve in the Bulgarian, Polish and Yugoslav navies.

BEREZAN *3/1990*

KOLGUEV *6/1989*

13 SAMARA CLASS

AZIMUT	**GLUBOMER**	**TROPIK**
DEVIATOR	**GRADUS**	**VOSTOK**
GIGROMETR	**KOMPAS**	**VAYGACH** (mod)
MOSKOVSKY UNIVERSITET (ex-*Gorizont*) (mod)	**PAMYAT MERKURYIA**	**ZENIT**
	RUMB	

Displacement, tons: 1000 standard; 1270 full load
Dimensions, feet (metres): 193.5 × 34.4 × 12.5 *(59 × 10.5 × 3.8)*
Main machinery: 2 Skoda-Sulzer STD48 diesels; 3300 hp(m) *(2.43 MW)*; 2 shafts; cp props
Speed, knots: 15. **Range, miles:** 6200 at 10 kts
Complement: 45

Comment: Built at Gdansk, Poland 1962-64 for hydrographic surveying and research. Have laboratories and one survey launch and a 5 ton crane. *Vaygach* has additional accommodation around the base of the crane. *Moskovsky Universitet* is subordinated to the Academy of Sciences and has an extended superstructure forward and no crane.

VAYGACH *6/1991*

24 FINIK CLASS

GS 44, 47, 84, 86, 87, 260, 265, 270, 272, 278, 296, 297, 301, 388, 392, 397-405

Displacement, tons: 1100 full load
Dimensions, feet (metres): 201.7 × 33.5 × 9.8 *(61.5 × 10.2 × 3)*
Main machinery: 2 Cegielski-Sulzer 6AL 25/30 diesels; 1920 hp(m) *(1.4 MW)*; 2 shafts; cp props
Auxiliary propulsion; 2 motors; 204 hp(m) *(150 kW)*
Speed, knots: 13
Complement: 30 (5 officers)

Comment: Improved Biya class. Built in Poland 1978-82. Fitted with 7 ton crane for buoy handling. Can carry three small landing craft on well-deck. Ships of same class serve in the Polish Navy.

265 *1991*

14 BIYA CLASS

GS 182, 193, 194, 198, 200, 202, 204, 206, 210, 212, 214, 271, 273, 275

Displacement, tons: 750 full load
Dimensions, feet (metres): 180.4 × 32.1 × 8.5 *(55 × 9.8 × 2.6)*
Main machinery: 2 diesels; 1200 hp(m) *(882 kW)*; 2 shafts; cp props
Speed, knots: 13. **Range, miles:** 4700 at 11 kts
Complement: 25
Radars: Navigation: Don 2; I band.

Comment: Built in Poland 1972-76. With laboratory and one survey launch and a 5 ton crane. Transfers: One to Cuba in November 1980 (from Poland); one to Cape Verde in 1979.

GS 271 *3/1991, van Ginderen Collection*

12 KAMENKA CLASS

GS 66, 74, 78, 82, 107, 108 (ex-*Vernier*), **113** (ex-*Belbeck*), **118, 199** (ex-*Sima*), **207, 211, ASTRONOM** (mod)

Displacement, tons: 700 full load
Dimensions, feet (metres): 175.5 × 29.8 × 8.5 *(53.5 × 9.1 × 2.6)*
Main machinery: 2 diesels; 1800 hp(m) *(1.32 MW)*; 2 shafts; cp props
Speed, knots: 14. **Range, miles:** 4000 at 10 kts
Complement: 25
Radars: Navigation: Don 2; I band.
IFF: High Pole.

Comment: Built in Poland 1968-72. A 5 ton crane forward. They do not carry a survey launch but have facilities for handling and stowing buoys. In *Astronom* the deckhouse below the crane is twice the length of that in other ships of the class.

GS 107 *6/1984*

2 VINOGRAD CLASS

GS 525 **GS 526**

Displacement, tons: 1000
Dimensions, feet (metres): 164 × 34.4 × 6.6 *(50 × 10.5 × 2)*
Main machinery: 2 diesels; 2 motors; 1200 hp(m) *(882 kW)*; 2 trainable props
Speed, knots: 11.5
Complement: 30

Comment: Built by Rauma-Repola 1985-87 as hydrographic research ships.

5 MELITOPOL CLASS

MAYAK **NIVELIR** **PRIZMA** **INDIGURKA** (mod) **SHEVCHENOKO** (mod)

Displacement, tons: 1200 full load
Dimensions, feet (metres): 189 × 29.5 × 14.1 *(57.6 × 9 × 4.3)*
Main machinery: 1 Type 6DR 30/40 diesel; 600 hp(m) *(441 kW)*; 1 shaft
Speed, knots: 11. **Range, miles:** 2500 at 10 kts
Complement: 50
Radars: Navigation: Low Trough; I band.

Comment: Built in the USSR 1952-55. Converted merchant ships carrying one survey launch. Two have been modified to carry armaments for resupply.

MAYAK *7/1967, MoD*

NYRYAT 1 and 2 CLASSES

Comment: A number of these 120 and 55 ton classes (see *Auxiliaries* section for details) were built for inshore survey work using Nyryat hull and machinery. They carry GPB pennant numbers which are also used in the 7 ton survey launches carried in the larger ships.

CIVILIAN RESEARCH SHIPS

Notes: (a) There are some 200 ships ranging downward from 3200 tons engaged on fishery research world-wide. The larger ships are of the Mayakovsky, Tropik, Atlantik, Leskov and Luchegorsk classes of 3200-2400 tons. Two of the Mayakovsky class carry submersibles.
Research ships (also tugs, cargo ships, training ships) operating on behalf of the fishery ministries carry a form of pennant number. This usually consists of two letters followed by four numbers. The first letter indicates the port or area where the vessel is based, the second, the type of vessel and the numerals indicate a specific ship and are usually allocated consecutively to a particular class.
(b) In addition to the classes listed below there are several more, although some are converted trawler designs. New classes include Iscatel II and Svetlomar which are for civilian use.
(c) Some classes are not included because they are associated only with geophysical research. These include Bavenit, Tropik, Pulkovsky Meridian, Agat, Akademik Orbeli and Zarya.

Known letter allocations:

1st Letter		*2nd Letter*	
A/M	Murmansk	A	Fish factory
B	Novorossiysk	B/b	Large ST/FF
K	Kaliningrad	H	Tanker
L	Klaypeda	M	Fish factory-mother ship
M	Vladivostok	R	Fish carrier (small)
R	Riga	T	Fish carrier (large)
Q	Kerch/Sevastopol	Y	Tugs, rescue ship, icebreakers
C	Korsakov	X	Cargo ship
		G	Large stern trawler
		W	Tuna factory ship

3 VITYAZ CLASS

AKADEMIK ALEKSANDR NESMEYANOV **VITYAZ**
AKADEMIK ALEKSANDR VINOGRADOV

Displacement, tons: 6000 full load
Dimensions, feet (metres): 364.1 × 54.5 × 18.7 *(111 × 16.6 × 5.7)*
Main machinery: 2 Skoda-Sulzer 6ZL140/48 diesels; 6500 hp(m) *(4.78 MW)*; 2 shafts; cp props
Speed, knots: 17. **Range, miles:** 16 000 at 16 kts
Complement: 60 plus 65 scientists

Comment: Built in Poland. First completed in 1981, second in 1982 and third in 1983. Operate for Academy of Scientists. Capabilities for a wide range of oceanographical and meteorological studies and have excellent diver support facilities. Carry Argus submersible; 8 tons displacement; diving to 600 m *(1968.6 ft)* with endurance of eight hours; has a complement of three. *Vityaz* based at Novorossiysk, *A A Nesmeyanov* and *A A Vinogradov* at Vladivostok.

AKADEMIK ALEXANDR VINOGRADOV *12/1991, 92 Wing RAAF*

1 A A KRYLOV and 2 A N ANDREYEV CLASSES

AKADEMIK ALEKSEY KRYLOV **AKADEMIK NIKOLAY ANDREYEV**
AKADEMIK BORIS KONSTANTINOV

Displacement, tons: 9920 full load
Dimensions, feet (metres): 406.7 × 55.8 × 23 *(124 × 17 × 7)*
Main machinery: 2 Type 58D-6R diesels; 9000 hp(m) *(6.6 MW)*; 2 shafts; cp props
Speed, knots: 16. **Range, miles:** 10 000 at 16 kts
Complement: 117 plus 32 scientists *(Krylov)*; 90 plus 40 scientists (remainder)

Comment: Built at Nikolayev, *Krylov* for the Institute of Shipbuilding, *Andreyev* and *Konstantinov* for the Institute of Acoustics. *Krylov* carries a submersible in an internal compartment with doors in the port side and sailed on her maiden voyage in December 1982. *Andreyev* entered service in October 1986 and *Konstantinov* in March 1989; they have a different superstructure shape from *Krylov*. *Konstantinov* has a large stern door for streaming towed devices and with *Andreyev* has replaced the two Lebedev class ships for oceanographic acoustic research.

AKADEMIK ALEKSEY KRYLOV *1/1991*

AKADEMIK ALEKSEY KRYLOV (Research Submarine) *9/1990, Harald Carstens*

2 AKADEMIK SERGEI VAVILOV CLASS

AKADEMIK SERGEI VAVILOV **AKADEMIK IOFFE**

Displacement, tons: 6600 full load
Dimensions, feet (metres): 383.9 × 59.7 × 19.4 *(117 × 18.2 × 5.9)*
Main machinery: 2 SEMT-Pielstick diesels; 7000 hp(m) *(15.15 MW)*; 2 shafts; cp props; bow thruster
Speed, knots: 15. **Range, miles:** 20 000 at 14 kts
Complement: 128

Comment: Built by Hollming, Rauma, Finland for hydrophysical/biological/chemical research. *Vavilov* launched on 16 December 1986 and completed 17 February 1988; *Ioffe* launched on 29 August 1987 and completed sea trials in February 1989. Low speed manoeuvrability is achieved by an Aquamatic propulsion unit aft and bow thruster forward. *Ioffe* has two rigid sails which stow horizontally on the superstructure. The sails minimise self noise during acoustic research operations. Both have extensive acoustic trials equipment including multi-beam echo sounders and low frequency sidescan sonars. Sonar transducers are compact and ice resistant. It was reported in 1991 that *Ioffe* is to be converted to a ferry.

AKADEMIK IOFFE *7/1989, van Ginderen Collection*

AKADEMIK SERGEI VAVILOV *5/1990*

1 AKADEMIK M KELDYSH CLASS

AKADEMIK MSTISLAV KELDYSH

Displacement, tons: 5500
Dimensions, feet (metres): 400.2 × 59 × 19.7 *(122 × 18 × 6)*
Main machinery: 4 Wärtsilä Vasa 824 TS diesels; 5820 hp(m) *(3.88 MW)*; 2 shafts; bow thruster
Speed, knots: 16
Complement: 50 plus 80 scientists

Comment: Built by Hollming Yard, Rauma, Finland. Commissioned December 1980. One of the most sophisticated oceanographic research ships in the world. Under the Academy of Sciences. Has 17 laboratories and can carry two MIR manned submersibles which can dive to 6000 m *(19 686 ft)*. Two garage structures have been added aft of the funnel. Fitted with a rotatable stern propulser. Based at Kaliningrad.

AKADEMIK MSTISLAV KELDYSH *8/1988, Gilbert Gyssels*

1 AKADEMIK FEDOROV CLASS

AKADEMIK FEDOROV

Measurement, tons: 7600 dwt; 10 000 gross
Dimensions, feet (metres): 462.6 × 77 × 28 (141 × *23.5 × 8.5)*
Main machinery: Diesel-electric; 2 Wärtsilä diesel generators; 18 700 hp(m) *(13.74 MW)*; 1 motor; 1 shaft
Speed, knots: 16
Complement: 90 plus 160 scientists
Helicopters: 1 Mi-8 Hip.

Comment: Built by Rauma-Repola, Finland and completed 10 September 1987 as a Polar Research and Support Ship. Comes under the Arctic and Antarctic Research Institute and is used for servicing Antarctic bases. Ice strengthened and has a transverse omni-thruster. To replace *Mikhail Somov*.

AKADEMIK FEDOROV *8/1991, Peter Humphries*

1 KOLOMNA CLASS

MIKHAIL LOMONOSOV

Displacement, tons: 5470 full load
Measurement, tons: 3897 gross; 1195 net
Dimensions, feet (metres): 336 × 47.2 × 22 *(102.5 × 14.4 × 6.7)*
Main machinery: 1 Liebknecht reciprocating engine; 2450 ihp(m) *(1.8 MW)*; 1 shaft
Speed, knots: 13

Comment: Built by Neptun, Rostock, in 1957 from the hull of a freighter of the Kolomna class. Operated for the Academy of Sciences by Ukraine Institute of Oceanology, Black Sea. Equipped with 16 laboratories.

MIKHAIL LOMONOSOV *9/1986, van Ginderen Collection*

1 AMGUEMA CLASS

MIKHAIL SOMOV

Displacement, tons: 15 100 full load
Measurement, tons: 8445 dwt; 7714 gross; 3113 net
Dimensions, feet (metres): 436.4 × 62.3 × 28.2 *(133 × 19 × 8.6)*
Main machinery: Diesel-electric; 4 diesel generators; 2 motors; 7200 hp(m) *(5.3 MW)*; 2 shafts
Speed, knots: 15
Complement: 58
Radars: Navigation: Two Don 2; I band.
Helicopters: Platform only.

Comment: Built at Kherson SY 1975. Ice strengthened. Operates under Arctic and Antarctic Research Institute for research duties and Antarctic support. To be replaced by *Akademik Fedorov* in due course.

MIKHAIL SOMOV *6/1990, Harald Carstens*

7 AKADEMIK KURCHATOV CLASS

AKADEMIK KOROLEV
AKADEMIK KURCHATOV
AKADEMIK SHIRSHOV
AKADEMIK VERNADSKY
DMITRY MENDELEYEV
PROFESSOR ZUBOV
PROFESSOR VIEZE

Displacement, tons: 6681 full load
Measurement, tons: 1986 dwt; 5460 gross; 1387 net
Dimensions, feet (metres): 400.3-406.8 × 56.1 × 15 *(122.1-124.1 × 17.1 × 4.6)*
Main machinery: 2 Halberstadt-MAN 6KZ 57/60 diesels; 8000 hp(m) *(5.88 MW)*; 2 shafts; 2 bow thrusters; 360 hp(m) *(264 kW)*
Speed, knots: 20. **Range, miles:** 20 000 at 18 kts

Comment: All built by Mathias Thesen Werft at Wismar, East Germany between 1966 and 1968. All have a hull of the same design as the Mikhail Kalinin class of merchant vessels. There are variations in mast and aerial rig. *Professor Vieze* is similar to *A Shirshov* while *A Kurchatov, A Vernadsky* and *D Mendeleyev* are the same. *Kurchatov* and *Mendeleyev* have launched submersibles from a specially fitted crane.
Employment: Hydromet (Vladivostok): *A Korolev, A Shirshov*. Institute of Oceanology (Baltic): *A Kurchatov*. Institute of Oceanology (Vladivostok): *D Mendeleyev*. Ukraine Institute of Oceanology: *A Vernadsky*. Hydromet (Baltic): *P Vieze, P Zubov*.

PROFESSOR VIEZE *8/1991, Peter Humphries*

IZUMRUD

Displacement, tons: 5170 full load
Measurement, tons: 3862 gross; 465 net
Dimensions, feet (metres): 326 × 46 × 15.5 *(99.4 × 14 × 4.7)*
Main machinery: Diesel-electric; 4 diesel generators; 1 motor; 1 shaft
Speed, knots: 13.8

Comment: A research ship built in 1970 at Nikolayev. Used for structural and material tests. Owned by Ministry of Shipping. Operated by Naval Institute of Shipbuilding, Black Sea.

IZUMRUD *10/1991, van Ginderen Collection*

9 PASSAT CLASS (B 88 TYPE)

ERNST KRENKEL (ex-*Vikhr)*
GEORGY USHAKOV (ex-*Schkval*)
MUSSON
OKEAN
PASSAT
PRIBOY
PRILIV
VIKTOR BUGAYEV (ex-*Poriv*)
VOLNA

Displacement, tons: 4145 full load
Measurement, tons: 3280 (3311, *E Krenkel* and *V Bugayev*) gross
Dimensions, feet (metres): 318.5 × 45.6 × 15.4 *(97.1 × 13.9 × 4.7)*
328 × 48.5 × 15.4 *(100 × 14.8 × 4.7) (E Krenkel* and *V Bugayev)*
Main machinery: 2 Sulzer Cegielski diesels; 4800 hp(m) *(3.53 MW)*; 2 shafts
Speed, knots: 16
Complement: 110

Comment: Hydromet ships built at Szczecin, Poland. 1968: *Musson, Passat, Volna;* 1969: *Okean, Priboy;* 1970: *Priliv;* 1971: *G Ushakov, E Krenkel, V Bugayev*. Most are based in the Black Sea but *Okean, Priboy,* and *Priliv* are at Vladivostok.

PRIBOY *5/1990, van Ginderen Collection*

9 AKADEMIK FERSMAN CLASS (B 93 TYPE)

AKADEMIK FERSMAN
AKADEMIK SHATSKY
AKADEMIK SELSKIY
AKADEMIK LAZAREV
AKADEMIK GUBKIN
AKADEMIK NALIVKIN
AKADEMIK NAMYOTKIN
AKADEMIK KREPS
AKADEMIK NEMCHINOV

Displacement, tons: 3500 full load
Dimensions, feet (metres): 269 × 49.2 × 16.4 *(82 × 15 × 5)*
Main machinery: 1 Sulzer diesel; 4200 hp(m) *(3.1 MW)*; 1 Kort nozzle
Speed, knots: 15. **Range, miles:** 12 000 at 15 kts
Complement: 65

Comment: First pair completed at Szczecin, Poland in 1986, next five in 1987 and last two in 1988. Three more ordered in August 1988 but may not have been completed. Fitted for gravimetric and geophysical research with towed seismic array and bow thruster. Ice strengthened. *Shatsky* and *Nemchinov* were working under contract for Western companies in 1990/91. *Shatsky* has a helo deck aft.

AKADEMIK SHATSKY *7/1991*

AKADEMIK FERSMAN *7/1991*

OTTO SCHMIDT

Displacement, tons: 3650 full load
Dimensions, feet (metres): 239.4 × 59.4 × 20 *(73 × 18.1 × 6.1)*
Main machinery: Diesel-electric; 3 Type 13-D-100 diesel generators; 2 motors; 5400 hp(m) *(4 MW)*; 2 shafts
Speed, knots: 14. **Range, miles:** 11 000 at 14 kts

Comment: Built at Admiralty Yard, Leningrad. Launched 27 December 1978. Commissioned 17 July 1979. Icebreaker/polar research ship.

OTTO SCHMIDT *2/1989, G. Jacobs*

1 MODIFIED MAYAKOVSKY CLASS

ALEKSANDR IVANOVITCH VOEYKOV

Displacement, tons: 3260 full load
Dimensions, feet (metres): 277.9 × 45.9 × 18 *(84.7 × 14 × 5.5)*
Main machinery: 1 diesel; 2040 hp(m) *(1.5 MW)*; 1 shaft
Speed, knots: 14
Complement: 50

Comment: Operated by Hydromet Service, Vladivostok. Due for deletion soon.

A I VOEYKOV *1/1987, van Ginderen Collection*

3 MODIFIED ALPINIST CLASS

GIDROBIOLOG, GIDRONAVT, RIFT

Displacement, tons: 1140 full load
Dimensions, feet (metres): 177.1 × 34.4 × 13.1 *(54 × 10.5 × 4)*
Main machinery: 1 SKL 8NVD 48 A-2U diesel; 1320 hp(m) *(970 kW)*; 1 shaft; cp prop
Speed, knots: 13. **Range, miles:** 7000 at 13 kts
Complement: 26 plus 12 scientists

Comment: Of the same stern-trawler design as the Alpinist AGIs. Modified to carry and operate a manned submersible (*Rift*—Pisces; others—Argus) from the gantry crane. Completed 1982-83.

RIFT *1987*

10 AKADEMIK SHULEYKIN CLASS

AKADEMIK GAMBURTSEV*	**PROFESSOR GOLITSYN***
AKADEMIK SHULEYKIN	**PROFESSOR KHROMOV**
AKADEMIK SHOKALSKY	**PROFESSOR PAVEL MOLCHANOV**
ARNOLD VEIMER	**PROFESSOR MULTANOVSKY**
GEOLOG DIMITRI NALIVKIN*	**PROFESSOR POLSHOV***

* Second group

Displacement, tons: 2000 (first five); 2554 (second five)
Dimensions, feet (metres): 236.2 × 42.6 × 15.4 *(72 × 13 × 4.7)* (first five)
244.3 × 48.3 × 14.8 *(74.5 × 14.7 × 4.5)* (second five)
Main machinery: 2 Gorkiy G-74 diesels; 3060 hp(m) *(2.25 MW)*; 2 shafts (first five)
2 SEMT-Pielstick 6 PC2.5 L400 diesels; 7020 hp(m) *(5.16 MW)*; 2 shafts (second five)
Speed, knots: 14
Complement: 70 (including scientists)

Comment: Built by Laivateollisuus, Turku, Finland. Ice strengthened. First two entered service in 1982, next three in 1983. *A Shuleykin* based at Leningrad, *A Shokalsky* at Vladivostok, *Professor P Molchanov* at Murmansk, *Professor Khromov* in Pacific, *Professor Multanovsky* at Leningrad. All hydromet ships work for Hydromet Service. Four more built for Academy of Sciences and Ministry of Geology. Completion December 1983 to October 1984. *Arnold Veimer* belongs to the Estonia Academy and is painted dark blue. *Nalivkin* has a Qubit TRAC IV integrated navigation and data logging system for work in the Norwegian Sea.

PROFESSOR MOLCHANOV *6/1990*

ARNOLD VEIMER *3/1989, van Ginderen Collection*

7 VADIM POPOV CLASS

VADIM POPOV	**VASILIY LOMINADZE**
VIKTOR BUINITSKIY	**IGOR MAKSIMOV**
PAVEL GORDIYENKO	**VLADIMIR PARSHIN**
	IVAN PETROV

Displacement, tons: 927 full load
Dimensions, feet (metres): 164 × 33 × 12 *(49.9 × 10 × 3.6)*
Main machinery: 1 diesel; 1340 hp(m) *(985 kW)*; 1 shaft
Speed, knots: 13
Complement: 35

Comment: Small hydromet ships built at Laivateollisuus, Turku, the first of which entered service 6 October 1986. *Buinitskiy* is based at Murmansk, *Lominadze* in the Caspian, and three others are based in the Pacific. *Ivan Petrov* to commission in 1991.

VLADIMIR PARSHIN *9/1989*

4 AKADEMIK BORIS PETROV CLASS

AKADEMIK BORIS PETROV	**AKADEMIK M A LAVRENTYEV**
AKADEMIK N STRAKHOV	**AKADEMIK OPARIN**

Displacement, tons: 2550 full load
Dimensions, feet (metres): 247.6 × 48.2 × 15.4 *(75.5 × 14.7 × 4.7)*
Main machinery: 2 SEMT-Pielstick Russkiy 6 PC2.5 L400 diesels; 7020 hp(m) *(5.16 MW)*; 1 shaft; cp prop
Speed, knots: 15
Complement: 74
Radars: Navigation: Okean; I band. Don; I band.

Comment: Built by Hollming, Finland. Data similar to second group of Akademik Shuleykin class. *Petrov* and *Lavrentyev* completed June and October 1984, *Strakhov* on 14 May 1985 and *Oparin* launched 1 February 1985. May be used for sea-bed coring as part of programme of geophysical and hydrophysical research for Academy of Sciences.

AKADEMIK N STRAKHOV *7/1988, Gilbert Gyssels*

22 VALERIAN URYVAYEV CLASS

CHAYVO	**POISK**
DALNIE ZELENTSY	**PROFESSOR FEDYINSKY**
ELM	**RUDOLF SAMOYLOVICH***
GEOFIZIK	**VALERIAN URYVAYEV***
ISKATEL	**VEKTOR**
VLADIMIR OBRUCHEV	**ISSLEDOVATEL**
VSEVOLOD BEREZKIN*	**LEV TITOV***
VULKANOLOG	**MODUL**
VYACHESLAV FROLOV*	**MORSKOY GEOFIZIK**
YAKOV GAKKEL*	**ZOND**
KERN	**PROFESSOR GAGARINSKY**

* Hydromet ships.

Displacement, tons: 1050 full load
Measurement, tons: 350 dwt; 697 gross; 85 net
Dimensions, feet (metres): 180.1 × 31.2 × 13.1 *(54.9 × 9.5 × 4)*
Main machinery: 1 Deutz diesel; 850 hp(m) *(625 kW)*; 1 shaft
Speed, knots: 12
Complement: 40 plus 12 scientists

Comment: Built at Khabarovsk between 1974 and 1990.
Bases: Murmansk; *V Berezkin, D Zelentsy, Chayvo, Geofizik, Kern*. Baltic; *L Titov, R Samoylovich*. Black Sea; *Modul, Vektor, Issledovatel, Y Gakkel*. Caspian; *Elm*. Pacific; Remainder.
Tasks: Hydromet; *D Zelentsy, Elm,* Marine Biology; *Modul, Vektor,* Hydro-acoustics; *Issledovatel,* General Oceanography; Remainder, geology and geophysics.

VEKTOR *10/1990*

LEV TITOV *1/1991, van Ginderen Collection*

3 ALEKSEY MARYSHEV CLASS

ALEKSEY MARYSHEV **GRIGORY MIKHEYEV** **PETR KOTSOV**

Comment: Built by Hollming, Rauma, Finland in 1990/91. Ice strengthened, designed for survey work on the Arctic Coast and in the Siberian Rivers. Subordination not yet known, but they may, like the Dmitry Ovstyn class, be owned by the Ministry of Merchant Marine.

ALEKSEY MARYSHEV *5/1991, Foto Flite*

19 DMITRY OVSTYN CLASS

DMITRY LAPTEV
DMITRY OVSTYN
DMITRY STERLEGOV
E TOLL
FEDOR MATISEN
GEORGY MAKSIMOV
IVAN KIREYEV
NIKOLAI KOLOMEYTSEV
NIKOLAI YEVGENOV
PAVEL BASHMAKOV
PROFESSOR BOGOROV
PROFESSOR KURENTSOV
PROFESSOR SHTOKMAN
PROFESSOR VODYANITSKY
SERGEY KRAKOV
STEFAN MALYGIN
VALERIAN ALBANOV
V SUKHOTSKY
YAKOV SMIRNITSKY

Displacement, tons: 1800 full load
Dimensions, feet (metres): 220 × 39 × 15 *(67.1 × 11.9 × 4.6)*
Main machinery: 1 Deutz RBV6M 358 diesel; 2200 hp(m) *(1.62 MW)*; 1 shaft; bow thruster
Speed, knots: 16. **Range, miles:** 9000 at 13.5 kts
Complement: 52 (including 20 scientists)
Radars: Navigation: Okean or Don 2 or Decca 626; I band.

Comment: Built by Laivateollisuus, Åbo, Finland except *P Bogorov* at Turku, Finland. Fitted with eight laboratories. Employed largely on geological research oceanographic work and survey in the Arctic. Completed between 1974 and 1978. Average time from launch to completion, seven months. Owned by Ministry of Merchant Marine except for the four Professors which are subordinated to the Academy of Sciences. Have ice-strengthened bows.

GEORGY MAKSIMOV *8/1991, Bryan Hird*

NAVAL MISSILE RANGE SHIPS

Note: A Vytegrales class converted merchant ship *Yablonya* has been used for R & D work since 1989.

2 DESNA CLASS

CHAZHMA (ex-*Dangara*) **CHUMIKAN** (ex-*Dolgeschtschelje*)

Displacement, tons: 5300 light; 13 600 full load
Dimensions, feet (metres): 457.7 × 59 × 25.9 *(139.6 × 18 × 7.9)*
Main machinery: 1 MAN diesel; 5200 hp(m) *(3.8 MW)*; 1 shaft
Speed, knots: 15. **Range, miles:** 20 000 at 13 kts
Complement: 240
Countermeasures: ESM: 2 Watch Dog; radar warning.
Radars: Missile tracker: Ship Globe.
Air search: Head Net B; E band.
Navigation: Don 2; I band.
Helicopters: 1 Ka-25 'Hormone C'.

Comment: Formerly bulk ore-carriers of the Dshankoy class (7265 tons gross) built at Warnemunde. Range Instrumentation Ships. Active since 1963. Based in the Pacific. Two Vee Cone communications aerials.

CHAZHMA *7/1989, G. Jacobs*

2 SIBIR CLASS

SAKHALIN **SPASSK** (ex-*Suchan*)

Displacement, tons: 7400 full load
Dimensions, feet (metres): 354 × 49.2 × 20 *(108 × 15 × 6.1)*
Main machinery: 2 boilers; Compound reciprocating engine; 2500 ihp(m) *(1.84 MW)*; 1 shaft
Speed, knots: 12. **Range, miles:** 9800 at 12 kts
Complement: 200
Radars: Air search: Head Net C; E band.
Three smaller trackers forward of the bridge.
Navigation: Two Don 2; I band.
Helicopters: 1 Ka-25 'Hormone C' (no hangar).

Comment: Converted bulk ore carriers employed as Missile Range Ships in the Pacific. *Sakhalin* has three radomes forward and aft. Launched in 1957-59. Formerly freighters of the Polish B 31 type (Donbas class). One of the class *Sibir* deleted in 1990 and *Chukotka* in 1991.

SIBIR Class *1/1991, 92 Wing RAAF*

1 KAMCHATKA CLASS (AG)

KAMCHATKA SSV 391

Displacement, tons: 6000 full load
Dimensions, feet (metres): 350.1 × 52.5 × 19.7 *(106.7 × 16 × 6)*
Main machinery: 2 diesels; 6100 hp(m) *(4.5 MW)*; 2 shafts
Speed, knots: 16
Complement: 178
Missiles: SAM: 2 SA-N-5 Grail quad launchers; manual aiming; IR homing to 6 km *(3.2 nm)* at 1.5 Mach; altitude to 2500 m *(8000 ft)*; warhead 1.5 kg.
Guns: 2—30 mm/65 AK 630. 6 barrels per mounting.
Radars: Navigation: 3 Palm Frond; 2 Shot Dome; I band.
CCA: Fly Screen; I band.
Tacan: 2 Round House.
Helicopters: 2 Ka-25 'Hormone C'.

Comment: Launched at Nikolayev in August 1985, started trials in the Black Sea in September 1987 and then sailed for the Pacific at the end of the year. AGE stands for Auxiliary General Experimental. Pennant number indicates intelligence collection and as the large tower could house an acoustic device for lowering below the hull, this ship is most probably involved in VLF bi-static sonar trials similar to the type being tested in major Western navies. A second or consort vessel is expected to complete in 1991 and will join her in the Pacific.

KAMCHATKA *11/1987*

MARSHAL KRYLOV *6/1990, 92 Wing RAAF*

1 KAPUSTA CLASS

URAL SSV 33

Displacement, tons: 36 000 full load
Dimensions, feet (metres): 866.1 × 98.1 × 31.5 *(264 × 29.9 × 9.6)*
Main machinery: CONAS; nuclear; 2 PWR; 2 boilers; 4 turbines; 75 000 hp(m) *(55 MW)*; 4 shafts
Speed, knots: 27
Complement: 940
Missiles: SAM: 4 SA-N-10 mountings each with 4 IR-guided missiles derived from SA-16.
Guns: 2—3 in *(76 mm)*/60. 4—30 mm/65 AK 630. 8—14.5 mm (4 twin) MGs.
Countermeasures: ESM: Trawl Net; 2 Soup Cup; Cage Box; Cake Tin.
Fire control: 4 Tin Man and 4 Spot Pot optronic directors.
Radars: Air search: Top Plate; 3D; D/E band.
Air/surface search: 4 Mad Hack planar arrays.
Navigation: 3 Palm Frond; I band.
Fire control: Two Bass Tilt. Six Owl Perch (missile telemetry and tracking).
CCA: Fly Screen B.
Tacan: Two Round House.
IFF: 1 Long Head; 2 Salt Pot.
Sonars: Hull-mounted active/passive sonar; medium frequency.
Helicopters: 1 or 2 Ka-27 'Helix D'.

Comment: Laid down in May 1981 and launched in May 1983 at Baltic Yard, Leningrad. Did trials in the Baltic in 1987 and 1988, commissioning in August 1989 and sailing for the Pacific in September 1989. Has an extensive space associated electronic fit including Ship Globe (satellite tracking) and 1 Quad Leaf, 2 Low Ball and Punch Bowl for SATCOMs. Naval manned and heavily armed, the official description is *sudno suyazyy* meaning communications ship. As well as being a missile range control ship and having an intelligence gathering role monitoring other countries' missile tests, it also has obvious potential as a Flagship. The fourth planar array is mounted horizontally on the deck aft and to starboard of the midship's mast. Probable Kirov class hull. There is some doubt about the name.

URAL *9/1989, 92 Wing RAAF*

URAL *8/1989*

3 MARSHAL NEDELIN CLASS

MARSHAL NEDELIN **MARSHAL KRYLOV** **AKADEMIK NICOLAI PILYUGIN**

Displacement, tons: 24 000 full load
Dimensions, feet (metres): 695.5 × 88.9 × 25.3 *(212 × 27.1 × 7.7)*
Main machinery: 2 gas turbines; 54 000 hp(m) *(40 MW)*; 2 shafts
Speed, knots: 20. **Range, miles:** 22 000 at 16 kts
Complement: 500
Radars: Air search: Strut Pair *(Nedelin)*; Top Plate *(Krylov)*.
Navigation: Three Palm Frond; I band.
Helicopter control: Fly Screen B; I band.
Space trackers: End Tray (balloons). Quad Leaf. Three Quad Wedge. Four smaller aerials.
Tacan: Two Round House.
Helicopters: 2-4 Ka-32 'Helix C'.

Comment: First completed at Admiralty Yard, Leningrad in 1983, second in 1989 and third in 1992. Fitted with a variety of space and missile associated electronic systems. Fitted for but not with six twin 30 mm/65 ADG guns and three Bass Tilt fire control radars. Naval subordinated, the task is probably the monitoring of missile tests with a war time role of command ship. The Ship Globe radome is for SATCOM. The third ship of the class may work for the Academy of Sciences under civilian control.

CIVILIAN SPACE ASSOCIATED SHIPS

1 KOROLEV CLASS

AKADEMIK SERGEY KOROLEV

Displacement, tons: 21 250
Measurement, tons: 17 114 gross; 2158 net
Dimensions, feet (metres): 596.6 × 82 × 25.9 *(181.9 × 25 × 7.9)*
Main machinery: 1 Bryansk Burmeister & Wain diesel; 12 000 hp(m) *(8.8 MW)*; 1 shaft
Speed, knots: 17
Radars: Navigation: Two Don Kay; I band.

Comment: Built at Chernomorsky Shipyard, Nikolayev in 1970, completing in 1971. Space associated communications include four Quad Rings, two Ship Bowl and one Ship Globe. Based in the Pacific Fleet.

AKADEMIK SERGEY KOROLEV *3/1989*

1 GAGARIN CLASS

KOSMONAUT YURY GAGARIN

Displacement, tons: 53 500
Measurement, tons: 32 291 gross; 5247 net
Dimensions, feet (metres): 760 × 101.7 × 30.2 *(232 × 31 × 9.2)*
Main machinery: 2 boilers; 2 turbines; 19 000 hp(m) *(14 MW)*; 1 shaft; bow and stern thrusters
Speed, knots: 17
Radars: Navigation: Don Kay and Okean; I band.

Comment: Design based on the Sofia or Akhtyuba (ex-Hanoi) class steam tanker. Built at Leningrad by Baltic SB & Eng Works in 1970, completed in 1971. Used for investigation into conditions in the upper atmosphere, and the control of space vehicles. She is the largest research vessel. Communications fit includes two Ship Shell (the largest dishes), two Ship Bowl, four Quad Ring and two Vee Cone (alongside funnel). With all four aerials vertical and facing forward she experiences a loss in speed of 2 kts. Based in Black Sea.

KOSMONAUT YURY GAGARIN *8/1989*

4 KOSMONAUT VLADISLAV VOLKOV CLASS

KOSMONAUT VLADISLAV VOLKOV
KOSMONAUT GEORGY DOBROVOLSKY
KOSMONAUT PAVEL BELYAYEV
KOSMONAUT VIKTOR PATSAYEV

Displacement, tons: 8920 full load
Dimensions, feet (metres): 400.3 × 55.1 × 22.3 *(122.1 × 16.8 × 6.8)*
Main machinery: 1 Bryansk Burmeister & Wain diesel; 5200 hp(m) *(3.82 MW)*; 1 shaft
Speed, knots: 15
Radars: Navigation: Don 2; I band.

Comment: Former freighters of Vytegrales class rebuilt as space associated research ships at Leningrad 1977-78. Space associated communications include one Quad Spring and three smaller aerials. Have Kite Screech fire control radars.

KOSMONAUT VLADISLAV VOLKOV *11/1990, Harald Carstens*

TRAINING SHIPS

Notes: In addition to the naval training ships listed here a considerable fleet of other training ships, mainly mercantile marine, may be encountered. These are mainly in the 300-400 ft bracket. Names: *Equator, Gorizont, Meridian, Professor Anichkov, P Khlyustin, P Kudrevich, P Minyayev, P Pavlenko, P Rybaltovsky, P Shchyogolev, P Ukhov, P Yushchenko.*

2 UGRA II CLASS (AXT)

BORODINO **GANGUT**

Displacement, tons: 6750 standard; 7000 full load
Dimensions, feet (metres): 462.6 × 57.7 × 23 *(141 × 17.6 × 7)*
Main machinery: Diesel-electric; 4 Kolumna Type 2-D-42 diesel generators; 2 motors; 8000 hp(m) *(5.88 MW)*; 2 shafts
Speed, knots: 17. **Range, miles:** 21 000 at 10 kts; 9500 at 16 kts
Complement: 250 plus 400 instructors and trainees
Missiles: SAM: 2 SA-N-5 Grail quad launchers; manual aiming; IR homing to 6 km *(3.2 nm)* at 1.5 Mach; altitude to 2500 m *(8000 ft)*; warhead 1.5 kg.
Guns: 8—57 mm/70 (4 twin).
Radars: Air/surface search: Strut Curve; F band; range 110 km *(60 nm)* for 2 m² target.
Navigation: Three Don 2; I band.
Fire control: Two Muff Cob; G/H band.
IFF: Two Square Head. One High Pole B.
Sonars: Hull-mounted; active search; medium frequency (for training).

Comment: These are the last two of this class built, the remainder being submarine depot ships. Built at Nikolayev in 1971-72. Have large deckhouse aft in place of helicopter deck. No bow lift. One 10 ton and two 3.2 ton cranes.

GANGUT *7/1991, Foto Flite*

3 SMOLNY CLASS (AXT)

KHASAN **PEREKOP** **SMOLNY**

Displacement, tons: 9150 full load
Dimensions, feet (metres): 452.8 × 53.1 × 21.3 *(138 × 16.2 × 6.5)*
Main machinery: 2 diesels; 15 000 hp(m) *(11 MW)*; 2 shafts
Speed, knots: 20. **Range, miles:** 12 000 at 15 kts
Complement: 150 plus 350 cadets
Guns: 4—3 in *(76 mm)*/60 (2 twin). 4—30 mm/65 (2 twin).
A/S mortars: 2 RBU 2500.
Countermeasures: ESM: 2 Watch Dog; radar warning.
Radars: Air/surface search: Head Net C; 3D; E band; range 128 km *(70 nm)*.
Navigation: Four Don 2; I band. Don Kay *(Perekop)*; I band.
Fire control: Owl Screech; G band. Drum Tilt; H/I band.
IFF: Two High Pole A. Square Head.
Sonars: Hull-mounted; active search and attack; medium frequency.

Comment: Built at Szczecin, Poland. *Smolny* completed in 1976, *Perekop* in 1977 and *Khasan* in 1978. Have considerable combatant potential. *Khasan* collided with and sank a Turkish Kartal class FAC in the Bosphorus in October 1985.

PEREKOP *6/1991, van Ginderen Collection*

2 WODNIK II CLASS (AXT)

LUGA **OKA**

Displacement, tons: 1820 full load
Dimensions, feet (metres): 234.3 × 38.1 × 13.8 *(71.4 × 11.6 × 4.2)*
Main machinery: 2 Skoda-Sulzer 6TD48 diesels; 3300 hp(m) *(2.43 MW)* sustained; 2 shafts; cp props
Speed, knots: 17. **Range, miles:** 7200 at 11 kts
Complement: 60 plus 100 instructors and cadets
Radars: Navigation: Two Don 2; I band.
IFF: High Pole A.

Comment: Built at Gdansk, Poland in 1976-77. Of same general design as Polish ships with an extra deck in the bridge and a larger superstructure. No armament.

OKA *1984*

5 SAIL TRAINING SHIPS

MIR **DRUZJBA** **KHERSONES** **PALLADA** +1

Measurement, tons: 2996 gross
Dimensions, feet (metres): 346.1 × 45.9 × 19.7 *(105.5 × 14 × 6)*
Main machinery: 1 Sulzer 8AL-20/24 diesel; 1500 hp(m) *(1.1 MW)*; 1 shaft
Speed, knots: 17
Complement: 55 plus 144 cadets

Comment: Three masted ship rig. Ordered from Stocznia Gdansk in July 1985. First launched 30 December 1986, second 31 March 1987, third 10 June 1988, fourth 30 July 1989. One more building. Not all are naval manned.

KHERSONES *1/1991, Harald Carstens*

CABLE SHIPS

8 KLASMA CLASS

DONETS	INGUL*	INGURI	KATUN
TAVDA	TSNA	YANA*	ZEYA

*Type I

Displacement, tons: 6000 standard; 6900 full load
Measurement, tons: 3400 dwt; 5786 gross
Dimensions, feet (metres): 427.8 × 52.5 × 19 *(130.5 × 16 × 5.8)*
Main machinery: Diesel-electric; 5 Wärtsilä Sulzer 624TS diesel generators (4 in *Ingul* and *Yana*); 5000 hp(m) *(3.68 MW)*; 2 motors; 2150 hp(m) *(1.58 MW)*; 2 shafts
Speed, knots: 14. **Range, miles:** 12 000 at 14 kts
Complement: 85
Radars: Navigation: Two Don 2; I band.

Comment: *Ingul* and *Yana* were built by Wärtsilä, Helsingforsvarvet, Finland in 1962; *Donets* and *Tsna* at the Wärtsilä, Åbovarvet in 1968-69; *Zeya* in 1970. *Donets, Tsna* and *Zeya* are of slightly modified design. *Tavda* completed 1977; *Inguri* in 1978. All are ice strengthened and can carry 1650 miles of cable. Type II can be distinguished by gantry right aft.

TAVDA *12/1990, G. Jacobs*

TSNA *5/1987*

3 EMBA I and 2 EMBA II CLASSES

Group I: **EMBA, NEPRYADVA, SETUN**
Group II: **BIRIUSA, KEMJ**

Displacement, tons: 2050 full load (Group I); 2400 (Group II)
Dimensions, feet (metres): 249 × 41.3 × 9.8 *(75.9 × 12.6 × 3)* (Group I)
282.4 × 41.3 × 9.9 *(86.1 × 12.6 × 3)* (Group II)
Main machinery: Diesel-electric; 2 Wärtsilä Vasa 6R 22 diesel generators; 2 motors; 1360 hp(m) *(1 MW)*; 2 shafts (Group I)
2 Wärtsilä Vasa 8 R 22 diesel generators; 2 motors; 2180 hp(m) *(1.6 MW)*; 2 shafts (Group II)
The two turnable propulsion units can be inclined to the ship's path giving, with a bow thruster, improved turning movement
Speed, knots: 11
Complement: 40
Radars: Navigation: Two Spin Trough; I band.

Comment: *Emba* completed by Wärtsilä in 1980, second pair in 1981. Designed for shallow water cable-laying. Carry 380 tons of cable. Order placed with Wärtsilä in January 1985 for two larger (Group II) ships; *Biriusa* delivered 4 July 1986 and *Kemj* on 23 October 1986. Can lay about 600 tons of cable. Designed for use off Vladivostok but also capable of operations in inland waterways.

SETUN (Emba I) *1981, Wärtsilä*

KEMJ (Emba II) *1986, Wärtsilä*

SERVICE FORCES

1 BEREZINA CLASS (REPLENISHMENT SHIP)

BEREZINA

Displacement, tons: 35 000 full load
Dimensions, feet (metres): 695.5 × 85.3 × 38.7 *(212 × 26 × 11.8)*
Main machinery: 2 diesels; 47 500 hp(m) *(35 MW)*; 2 shafts
Speed, knots: 22. **Range, miles:** 15 000 at 16 kts
Complement: 600
Cargo capacity: Approx 16 000 tons fuel (including Avgas); 2000 tons provisions; 500 tons fresh water

Missiles: SAM: SA-N-4 Gecko twin launcher (abaft funnel); semi-active radar homing to 15 km *(8 nm)* at 2.5 Mach; warhead 50 kg; altitude 9.1-3048 m *(30-10 000 ft)*; 20 missiles.
Guns: 4—57 mm/80 (2 twin); 85° elevation; 120 rounds/minute to 6 km *(3.3 nm)*; weight of shell 2.8 kg.
4—30 mm/65; 6 barrels per mounting; 3000 rounds/minute combined to 2 km.
A/S mortars: 2 RBU 1000 6-tubed; range 1000 m; warhead 55 kg
Countermeasures: Decoys: 2—16-barrelled Chaff launchers.
ESM: 2 Bell series.
Radars: Air/surface search: Strut Curve; F band; range 110 km *(60 nm)* for 2 m² target.
Navigation: Two Don Kay; I band. Two Don 2; I band.
Fire control: Pop Group; F/H/I band (for SA-N-4). Muff Cob; G/H band (for 57 mm). Two Bass Tilt; H/I band (for 30 mm).
IFF: Two High Pole B. Two Square Head.
Sonars: Hull-mounted; active search and attack; medium frequency.

Helicopters: 2 Ka-25 'Hormone C'.

Programmes: Laid down in 1973; launched in 1975. Built at Nikolayev (61 Kommuna) and completed in 1977.
Structure: Two storing gantries (apparently with moving high-points); four 10 ton cranes and one other; liquid fuelling gantry (amidships); stern refuelling. The weight of her armament is notable in comparison with Western practice. This is the first replenishment ship to be fitted with SAM missiles and Gatling guns as well as carrying helicopters and mounting RBUs. This gives her a considerable AA capability and, if the helicopters have an ASW as well as Vertrep role, some self-sufficiency in anti-submarine operations. This is the only ship to site the RBU 1000 forward of the bridge.
Operational: Can replenish two ships at a time or refuel three. Based in the Black Sea and rarely deploys even to the Mediterranean.

BEREZINA *8/1991*

6 BORIS CHILIKIN CLASS (REPLENISHMENT SHIPS)

BORIS BUTOMA **GENRICH GASANOV**
BORIS CHILIKIN **IVAN BUBNOV**
DNESTR **VLADIMIR KOLECHITSKY**

Displacement, tons: 23 400 full load
Dimensions, feet (metres): 531.5 × 70.2 × 33.8 *(162.1 × 21.4 × 10.3)*
Main machinery: 1 diesel; 9600 hp(m) *(7 MW)*; 1 shaft
Speed, knots: 17. **Range, miles:** 10 000 at 16 kts
Complement: 75 (without armament)
Cargo capacity: 13 000 tons oil fuel and dieso; 400 tons ammunition; 400 tons spares; 400 tons victualling stores; 500 tons fresh water

Guns: 4—57 mm/80 (2 twin). Most are fitted for but not with the guns.
Radars: Air/surface search/fire control: Strut Curve (fitted for but not with).
Muff Cob (fitted for but not with).
Navigation: Two Don Kay (plus Don 2 in *V Kolechitsky*); I band.
IFF: High Pole B.

Programmes: Based on the Veliky Oktyabr merchant ship tanker design, *Boris Chilikin* was built at the Baltic Yard, Leningrad completing in 1971. Last of class *Boris Butoma* completed in 1978.
Structure: This is the only class of purpose-built underway fleet replenishment ships for the supply of both liquids and solids. The removal of both fire control radar and armament is in contrast to the considerable weight of such items carried in *Berezina*. Although most operate in merchant navy paint schemes, all wear naval ensigns.
Operational: Earlier ships can supply solids on both sides forward. Later ships supply solids to starboard, liquids to port forward. All can supply liquids either side aft and astern.

DNESTR *7/1991*

4 DUBNA CLASS (REPLENISHMENT TANKERS)

DUBNA **PECHENGA**
IRKUT **SVENTA**

Displacement, tons: 11 500 full load
Dimensions, feet (metres): 426.4 × 65.6 × 23.6 *(130 × 20 × 7.2)*
Main machinery: 1 Russkiy 8DRPH 23/230 diesel; 6000 hp(m) *(4.4 MW)*; 1 shaft
Speed, knots: 16. **Range, miles:** 7000 at 16 kts
Complement: 70
Cargo capacity: 7000 tons fuel; 300 tons fresh water; 1500 tons stores

Radars: Navigation: One or two Don 2; I band.

Programmes: *Dubna* completed 1974, *Irkut* December 1975, both at Rauma-Repola, Finland. *Pechenga* commissioned end 1978, *Sventa* completed April 1979.
Structure: Have 1 ton replenishment stations forward. Normally painted in merchant navy colours.
Operational: Can refuel on either beam and astern.

IRKUT *8/1991, 92 Wing RAAF*

5 UDA CLASS (REPLENISHMENT TANKERS)

DUNAY (mod) **KOIDA** **LENA** (mod) **TEREK** (mod) **VISHERA**

Displacement, tons: 5500 standard; 7110 full load
Dimensions, feet (metres): 400.3 × 51.8 × 20.3 *(122.1 × 15.8 × 6.2)*
Main machinery: 2 diesels; 9000 hp(m) *(6.6 MW)*; 2 shafts
Speed, knots: 17. **Range, miles:** 4000 at 15 kts
Complement: 85
Cargo capacity: 3000 tons oil fuel
Guns: Positions for 8—57 mm/70 (2 quad); 6—25 mm/80 (3 twin) (landed in peacetime).
Radars: Navigation: Two Don 2; I band.
Fire control: Two Muff Cob (when guns are fitted); G/H band.
IFF: High Pole A.

Comment: All have a beam replenishment capability. May retain fitting for a quadruple 57 mm or three twin 25 mm guns. Built in 1961-67. *Koida* was first Soviet ship refitted in Greek Orion shipyard. Modified ships have a second A-frame amidships thus providing two alongside refuelling positions. One deleted in 1991. Three transferred to Indonesia 1963-64 and since deleted.

LENA *6/1991*

6 MOD ALTAY CLASS (REPLENISHMENT TANKERS)

ELNYA **ILIM** **IZHORA** **KOLA** **PRUT** **YEGORLIK**

Displacement, tons: 7250 full load
Dimensions, feet (metres): 348 × 51 × 22 *(106.2 × 15.5 × 6.7)*
Main machinery: 1 Burmeister & Wain BM-550VTBN-110 diesel; 3200 hp(m) *(2.35 MW)*; 1 shaft
Speed, knots: 14. **Range, miles:** 8600 at 12 kts
Complement: 60
Cargo capacity: 4400 tons oil fuel
Radars: Navigation: Two Don 2; I band.

Comment: Built from 1967-72 by Rauma-Repola, Finland. All modified for alongside replenishment. This class is part of 38 ships, being the third group of Rauma types built in Finland in 1967. Some have armament fittings similar to the Uda class with 25 mm guns.

IZHORA *11/1991, G. Jacobs*

3 OLEKMA CLASS (REPLENISHMENT TANKERS)

OLEKMA (mod) **IMAN** **ZOLOTOY ROG**

Displacement, tons: 4000 standard; 6700 full load
Dimensions, feet (metres): 344.5 × 47.9 × 22 *(105.1 × 14.6 × 6.7)*
Main machinery: 1 Burmeister & Wain diesel; 2900 hp(m) *(2.13 MW)*; 1 shaft
Speed, knots: 14. **Range, miles:** 8000 at 14 kts
Complement: 40
Cargo capacity: 4500 tons oil fuel
Radars: Navigation: Don 2 and Spin Trough; I band.

Comment: Part of the second group of 34 tankers built by Rauma-Repola, Finland between 1960 and 1966. *Olekma* is modified for replenishment with refuelling rig abaft the bridge as well as astern refuelling. The other two can only refuel astern. *Zolotoy Rog* has a square sided funnel.

ZOLOTOY ROG (alongside DON Class) *11/1989*

2 KALININGRADNEFT CLASS (SUPPORT TANKERS)

ARGUN **VYAZMA**

Displacement, tons: 8600 full load
Dimensions, feet (metres): 380.5 × 56 × 21 *(116 × 17 × 6.5)*
Main machinery: 1 Russkiy-Burmeister & Wain 5DKRP 50/110-2 diesel; 3850 hp(m) *(2.83 MW)*; 1 shaft
Speed, knots: 14. **Range, miles:** 5000 at 14 kts
Complement: 32
Cargo capacity: 5400 tons oil fuel and other liquids
Radars: Navigation: Okean; I band.

Comment: Built by Rauma-Repola, Finland in 1982. Can refuel alongside or astern. At least an additional 20 of this class operate with the fishing fleets.

ARGUN *11/1991, G. Jacobs*

1 SOFYA CLASS (SUPPORT TANKER)

AKHTYUBA (ex-*Hanoi*)

Displacement, tons: 62 600 full load
Dimensions, feet (metres): 757.9 × 100.4 × 38 *(231.2 × 30.6 × 11.6)*
Main machinery: 2 boilers; 1 turbine; 21 000 hp(m) *(15.4 MW)*; 1 shaft
Speed, knots: 17. **Range, miles:** 10 000 at 17 kts
Complement: 75
Cargo capacity: 45 000 tons oil fuel.
Radars: Navigation: Two Don 2; I band.

Comment: Built as the merchant tanker *Hanoi* in 1963 at Leningrad, she was taken over by the Navy in 1969 and renamed *Akhtyuba*. The hull type was used in the construction of the space associated ship *Kosmonaut Yury Gagarin*. Astern refuelling. Active in the South China Sea.

AKHTYUBA *9/1991, 92 Wing RAAF*

3 MOD KAZBEK CLASS (REPLENISHMENT TANKERS)

ALATYR **DESNA** **VOLKHOV**

Displacement, tons: 16 250 full load
Measurement, tons: 12 000 dwt; 8230 gross; 3942 net
Dimensions, feet (metres): 477.2 × 62.9 × 26.9 *(145.5 × 19.2 × 8.2)*
Main machinery: 1 Russkiy Dizel diesel; 4000 hp(m) *(2.94 MW)*; 1 shaft
Speed, knots: 15. **Range, miles:** 18 000 at 12 kts
Complement: 46
Cargo capacity: 10 500 tons oil fuel
Radars: Navigation: Two Don 2; I band.
IFF: High Pole A.

Comment: Former Leningrad class merchant fleet tankers taken over by the Navy. Built at Leningrad and Nikolayev from 1951 to 1961. Eight others—*Karl Marx, Kazbek, Dzerzhinsk, Grodno, Cheboksary, Liepaya, Zhitomir* and *Buguzuslan*—have acted in support of naval operations. The original class numbered 64. All three now modified for alongside replenishment. The naval ships of this class can be distinguished by the A-frame before the bridge, the two forward kingposts and the cat-walks. Due to be scrapped.

VOLKHOV *1981*

2 NERCHA CLASS (SUPPORT TANKERS)

NARA **NERCHA**

Displacement, tons: 1850 full load
Dimensions, feet (metres): 208.3 × 33 × 14.1 *(63.5 × 10.1 × 4.3)*
Main machinery: 1 diesel; 1000 hp(m) *(735 kW)*; 1 shaft
Speed, knots: 11. **Range, miles:** 2000 at 10 kts
Complement: 25
Cargo capacity: 700 tons oil fuel
Radars: Navigation: Don 2; I band.

Comment: Built in Finland 1952-55 as part of class of 12. Renamed in naval service. Have astern refuelling capability. Strengthened for ice.

13 KHOBI CLASS (SUPPORT TANKERS)

CHEREMSHAN	**ORSHA**	**SHELON**	**TARTU**
KHOBI	**SEIMA**	**SOSVA**	**TITAN**
LOVAT	**SHACHA**	**SYSOLA**	**TUNGUSKA**
METAN			

Displacement, tons: 700 light; 1500 full load
Dimensions, feet (metres): 206.6 × 33 × 14.8 *(63 × 10.1 × 4.5)*
Main machinery: 2 diesels; 1600 hp(m) *(1.18 MW)*; 2 shafts
Speed, knots: 13. **Range, miles:** 2500 at 12 kts
Complement: 35 (4 officers)
Cargo capacity: 500 tons oil fuel
Radars: Navigation: Don 2 and Spin Trough; I band.

Comment: Built from 1957 to 1959. Part of a class of 25. Can refuel while being towed. Now being deleted. Transfers: Two to Albania; one to Hungary (deleted); three to Indonesia (two deleted).

2 BASKUNCHAK CLASS (SUPPORT TANKERS)

IVAN GOLUBETS **SOVIETSKY POGRANICHNIK**

Displacement, tons: 2280 full load
Dimensions, feet (metres): 272.6 × 39.4 × 15.7 *(83.1 × 12 × 4.8)*
Main machinery: 1 Type 8DR 34/61 VI diesel; 2000 hp(m) *(1.47 MW)*; 1 shaft
Speed, knots: 13. **Range, miles:** 5000 at 12 kts
Complement: 30
Cargo capacity: 1500 tons oil fuel

Comment: Last of a large class. These two support Border Guard units in the Pacific.

SOVIETSKY POGRANICHNIK *11/1991, G. Jacobs*

4 KONDA CLASS (SUPPORT TANKERS)

KONDA **ROSSOSH** **SOYANA** **YAKHROMA**

Displacement, tons: 2090 full load
Dimensions, feet (metres): 226.3 × 33 × 14.1 *(69 × 10.1 × 4.3)*
Main machinery: 1 diesel; 1600 hp(m) *(1.18 MW)*; 1 shaft
Speed, knots: 12. **Range, miles:** 2200 at 11.5 kts
Complement: 36
Cargo capacity: 1000 tons oil fuel
Radars: Navigation: Don 2; I band. Spin Trough; I band.

Comment: Originally of the Iskra class of merchant tankers built in 1955. Have a stern refuelling capability. Icebreaker bow.

KONDA *5/1990*

1 IRTYSH CLASS (SUPPORT TANKER)

NARVA

Displacement, tons: 1700 full load
Dimensions, feet (metres): 224.7 × 34.1 × 14.1 *(68.5 × 10.4 × 4.3)*
Main machinery: 1 diesel; 880 hp(m) *(647 kW)*; 1 shaft
Speed, knots: 12. **Range, miles:** 2000 at 10 kts
Complement: 40
Cargo capacity: 1170 tons oil fuel
Radars: Navigation: Neptun or Spin Trough; I band.

NARVA *11/1985, van Ginderen Collection*

TOPLIVO SERIES (HARBOUR TANKERS)

Comment: There are three versions under this name. Toplivo 1, built in Poland, are of 420 tons full load and 34.4 m long. Toplivo 2, some of which were built in Egypt but the majority in the USSR, are of 1200 tons full load and 53 m long. Toplivo 3, built in the USSR, are of 1300 tons full load and 52.7 m long with a very different appearance from Toplivo 2. These ships are used in many bases for the transport of all forms of liquids.

TOPLIVO 1 *3/1991, Erik Laursen*

TOPLIVO 3 *6/1991*

6 LUZA CLASS (SPECIAL TANKERS)

ALAMBAI **ARAGVI** **BARGUZIN** **DON** **KAMA** **SELENGA**

Displacement, tons: 1900 full load
Dimensions, feet (metres): 205 × 35.1 × 14.1 *(62.5 × 10.7 × 4.3)*
Main machinery: 1 diesel; 1000 hp(m) *(735 kW)*; 1 shaft
Speed, knots: 12. **Range, miles:** 2000 at 11 kts
Complement: 60
Radars: Navigation: Don 2; I band. Spin Trough; I band.
IFF: High Pole B.

Comment: Completed at Kolpino 1962-70. Used for transporting special liquids such as missile fuel.

DON *8/1991, van Ginderen Collection*

7 VALA CLASS (SPECIAL TANKERS)

VALA **TNT 11** **TNT 27** **12** **19** **25** **29**

Displacement, tons: 2030 full load
Dimensions, feet (metres): 239.8 × 42.3 × 15.7 *(73.1 × 12.9 × 4.8)*
Main machinery: 1 diesel; 1000 hp(m) *(735 kW)*; 1 shaft
Speed, knots: 14. **Range, miles:** 2000 at 11 kts
Complement: 30
Guns: 4—14.5 mm (2 twin) MGs (in some).
Radars: Navigation: Spin Trough; I band.

Comment: Completed 1964-71. Used for transporting radiological liquids and nuclear waste.

VALA Class *9/1978, MoD*

HOSPITAL SHIPS

Note: The 9885 ton passenger liner *Mikhail Bulgakov* (ex-*Mikhail Suslov*) was converted to a hospital ship in a Polish shipyard in mid-1989.

4 OB CLASS (AH)

OB **YENISEI** **SVIR** **IRTYSH**

Displacement, tons: 9700 full load
Dimensions, feet (metres): 492.1 × 60.7 × 19.7 *(150 × 18.5 × 6)*
Main machinery: 4 diesels; 14 000 hp(m) *(10.3 MW)*; 2 shafts; bow thruster
Speed, knots: 20. **Range, miles:** 20 000 at 18 kts
Complement: 85 plus 200 medical staff
Radars: Navigation: Three Don 2; I band.
IFF: High Pole A.
Helicopters: 1 Ka-25 'Hormone C'.

Comment: Built at Szczecin, Poland. *Ob* completed in 1980 and transferred to the Pacific in September 1980. *Yenisei* completed 1981 and is based in the Black Sea. *Svir* completed in early 1989 and transferred to the Northern Fleet in September 1989. *Irtysh* completed in June 1990 and was stationed in the Gulf in 1990-91. A fifth of the class was cancelled. Have 100 beds and seven operating theatres. The first purpose-built hospital ships in the Navy, a programme which may have been prompted by the use of several merchant ships off Angola for Cuban casualties in the 'war of liberation.'

YENISEI *11/1989*

SALVAGE, RESCUE AND MOORING VESSELS

4 MIKHAIL RUDNITSKY CLASS (ARS)

MIKHAIL RUDNITSKY **GEORGY KOZMIN** **GEORGY TITOV** **SAYANY**

Displacement, tons: 10 700 full load
Dimensions, feet (metres): 427.4 × 56.7 × 23.9 *(130.3 × 17.3 × 7.3)*
Main machinery: 1 S5DKRN 62/140-3 diesel; 6100 hp(m) *(4.48 MW)*; 1 shaft
Speed, knots: 16. **Range, miles:** 12 000 at 15.5 kts
Complement: 70
Radars: Navigation: Palm Frond; Nayada; I band.

Comment: Built at Vyborg, based on Moskva Pionier class merchant ship hull. First completed 1979, second in 1980, third in 1983 and fourth in 1984. Fly flag of Salvage and Rescue Service. Have two 40 ton and one 20 ton lift with cable fairleads forward and aft. This lift capability would be adequate for handling small submersibles, one of which is carried in the centre hold. *Sayany* is also described as a research ship. *Rudnitsky* based in the Black Sea, *Titov* in the Northern Fleet and the other two in the Pacific.

MIKHAIL RUDNITSKY *6/1989*

2 PAMIR CLASS

AGATAN **ALDAN**

Displacement, tons: 2050 full load
Dimensions, feet (metres): 256 × 42 × 13.5 *(78 × 12.8 × 4.1)*
Main machinery: 2 MAN G10V 40/60 diesels; 4200 hp(m) *(3.1 MW)*; 2 shafts; cp props
Speed, knots: 17. **Range, miles:** 15 000 at 17 kts
Complement: 77
Radars: Navigation: Two Don 2; I band.
IFF: High Pole A.

Comment: Salvage tugs built at AB Gävle Varv, Sweden in 1959-60. Equipped with one 10 ton and two 1.5 ton derricks, powerful pumps, air compressors, diving gear, recompression chambers, firefighting apparatus and electric generators. Have rather less cluttered bridge area than the two of this class converted to AGIs.

ALDAN *2/1983, MoD*

10 SURA CLASS (BUOY TENDERS)

KIL 1, 2, 21, 22, 25, 27, 29, 31, 32, 33

Displacement, tons: 2370 standard; 3150 full load
Dimensions, feet (metres): 285.4 × 48.6 × 16.4 *(87 × 14.8 × 5)*
Main machinery: Diesel-electric; 4 diesel generators; 2 motors; 2240 hp(m) *(1.65 MW)*; 2 shafts
Speed, knots: 12. **Range, miles:** 2000 at 11 kts
Complement: 40
Cargo capacity: 900 tons cargo; 300 tons fuel for transfer
Radars: Navigation: Two Don 2; I band.

Comment: Heavy lift ships built as mooring and buoy tenders between 1965 and 1978 in East Germany, 65 ton and 5 ton lifts with stern cage. Have been seen to carry 12 m DSRVs.

KIL 1 *3/1991, Per Kornefeldt*

4 INGUL CLASS

PAMIR **MASHUK** **ALATAU** **KARABAKH**

Displacement, tons: 4050 full load
Dimensions, feet (metres): 304.4 × 50.5 × 19 *(92.8 × 15.4 × 5.8)*
Main machinery: 2 Type 58D-4R diesels; 9000 hp(m) *(6.6 MW)*; 2 shafts; cp props
Speed, knots: 20. **Range, miles:** 9000 at 19 kts
Complement: 35 plus salvage party of 18
Guns: Positions for 2—57 mm/70 (twin) and 4—25 mm/80 (2 twin) (not fitted).
Radars: Navigation: Two Palm Frond; I band.
IFF: High Pole. Square Head.

Comment: Built at Admiralty Yard, Leningrad in 1975-84. NATO class-name the same as one of the Klasma class cable-ships. Naval manned arctic salvage and rescue tugs. Two more, *Yaguar* (Murmansk) and *Bars* (Vladivostok), operate with the merchant fleet. Carry salvage pumps, diving and firefighting gear as well as a high-line for transfer of personnel. *Pamir* and *Karabakh* in the North, the other pair in the Pacific.

MASHUK *4/1990, Ships of the World*

4 SLIVA CLASS

SB 406 **SB 408** **SB 921** **SHAKHTER** SB 922

Displacement, tons: 3050 full load
Dimensions, feet (metres): 227 × 50.5 × 16.7 *(69.2 × 15.4 × 5.1)*
Main machinery: 2 SEMT-Pielstick-Russkiy 6PC 2.5 L400 diesels; 7020 hp(m) *(5.2 MW)*; 2 shafts; cp props; bow thruster
Speed, knots: 16
Complement: 43 plus 10 salvage party
Radars: Navigation: Nayada; I band.

Comment: Built at Rauma-Repola, Finland. *SB 406* completed 20 February 1984. *SB 408* completed 5 June 1984. Second pair ordered 1984 *SB 921* completed 5 July 1985 and *SB 922* on 20 December 1985. *SB 922* named *Shakhter* in 1989.

SB 406 (alongside *Karabakh*) *9/1991*

8 KASHTAN CLASS (BUOY TENDERS)

KIL 926 **KIL 143** **KIL 164** **KIL 498**
KIL 927 **KIL 158** **KIL 140** **KIL 168**

Displacement, tons: 4600 full load
Dimensions, feet (metres): 313.3 × 56.4 × 16.4 *(95.5 × 17.2 × 5)*
Main machinery: 4 Wärtsilä diesels; 29 000 hp(m) *(2.31 MW)*; 2 shafts
Speed, knots: 13
Complement: 51 plus 20 spare berths
Radars: Navigation: Nayada; I band.

Comment: Enlarged Sura class built at the Neptun Shipyard, Rostock. Ordered 29 August 1986; *926* handed over in June 1988 and is in the Baltic; *927* to the Pacific in July 1989; *143* to the North in July 1989; *158* to the Black Sea in November 1989; *164* to the North in January 1990; *140* to the Baltic in May 1990; *498* to the Pacific in November 1990 and *168* to the Pacific in mid-1991. Lifting capacity is 130 tons.

KIL 143 *6/1990*

2 OREL CLASS (SALVAGE TUGS)

SB 38 **SB 43**

Displacement, tons: 1750 full load
Dimensions, feet (metres): 201.2 × 39.2 × 14.8 *(61.4 × 12 × 4.5)*
Main machinery: 1 MAN G5Z 52/70 diesel; 1700 hp(m) *(1.25 MW)*; 1 shaft
Speed, knots: 15. **Range, miles:** 14 000 at 13.5 kts
Complement: 40
Radars: Navigation: Two Don 2; I band.

Comment: Class of salvage and rescue tugs normally operated by Ministry of Fisheries with the fishing fleets. Naval manned with sick bay and recompression chamber. Built in Finland in late 1950s and early 1960s. Ice strengthened.

SB 38 *10/1988*

9 KATUN I and 2 KATUN II CLASSES (SALVAGE AND RESCUE TUGS)

Katun I: **PZHS 96, 98, 123, 124, 209, 273, 279, 282, 551**
Katun II: **PZHS 64, 92**

Displacement, tons: 920 full load
Dimensions, feet (metres): 205.3 × 33.1 × 11.5 *(62 × 10.1 × 3.5)* (Katun I)
Main machinery: 2 diesels; 5000 hp(m) *(3.68 MW)*; 2 shafts
Speed, knots: 17. **Range, miles:** 2000 at 17 kts
Complement: 30
Radars: Navigation: Spin Trough or Kivach (Katun II); I band.
IFF: High Pole A.

Comment: Katun I built in USSR 1970-78. Equipped for firefighting and rescue. PZHS 64 and 92, both Katun II, were completed in 1982—3 m *(9.8 ft)* longer than Katun I with an extra bridge level and lattice masts. Some may have a PDS prefix to their pennant numbers.

KATUN I Class *1970*

9 NEPTUN CLASS

KIL 3, 6, 7, 9, 11, 13, 15, 17, 18

Displacement, tons: 1240 full load
Dimensions, feet (metres): 187.9 × 37.4 × 10.8 *(57.3 × 11.4 × 3.3)*
Main machinery: 2 boilers; 2 steam reciprocating engines; 1000 ihp(m) *(735 kW)*; 2 shafts
Speed, knots: 12. **Range, miles:** 1000 at 10 kts
Complement: 28

Comment: Mooring tenders similar to Western boom defence vessels. Built in 1957-60 by Neptun, Rostock. Have a crane of 75 tons lifting capacity on the bow. Several of the class scrapped in 1989-90.

NEPTUN Class *1973*

SUBMARINE RESCUE SHIPS

2 ELBRUS CLASS

ELBRUS **ALAGEZ**

Displacement, tons: 19 000 standard; 22 500 full load
Dimensions, feet (metres): 562.7 × 80.4 × 27.9 *(171.5 × 24.5 × 8.5)*
Main machinery: Diesel-electric; 4 diesel generators; 2 motors; 24 500 hp(m) *(18 MW)*; 2 shafts
Speed, knots: 17. **Range, miles:** 14 500 at 15 kts
Complement: 420
Guns: 4—30 mm/65 (2 twin).
Radars: Navigation: Don 2 and two Don Kay; I band.
Helicopters: 1 Ka-25 Hormone C.

Comment: Very large submarine rescue and salvage ships with icebreaking capability, possibly in view of under-ice capability of some SSBNs. Built at Nikolayev. First seen 1981. Second one completed 1989. Can carry two submersibles in store abaft the funnel which are launched from telescopic gantries. *Elbrus* is based in the Black Sea, *Alagez* in the Pacific.

ALAGEZ *9/1991, G. Jacobs*

1 NEPA CLASS

KARPATY

Displacement, tons: 6100 full load
Dimensions, feet (metres): 424.9 × 62 × 21 *(129.5 × 18.9 × 6.4)*
Main machinery: Diesel-electric; 4 diesel generators; 2 motors; 8000 hp(m) *(5.88 MW)*; 2 shafts
Speed, knots: 16. **Range, miles:** 8000 at 14 kts
Complement: 270
Radars: Navigation: Two Don 2; I band.
IFF: High Pole B.

Comment: Completed 1968 at Nikolayev. Submarine rescue and salvage ship with a special high stern which extends out over the water for rescue manoeuvres. Has two 750 ton lifts which can work in tandem. Also one 100 ton lift, one 60 ton derrick and two 10 ton derricks. Carries a rescue bell, two submersibles and a number of recompression chambers. Based in the Baltic since November 1988.

KARPATY *1972, A. Nubert*

7 PRUT CLASS

ALTAY **BESHTAU** **VLADIMIR TREFOLEV** **ZHIGULI**
SS 21 **EPRON** (ex-*SS 26*) **SS 83**

Displacement, tons: 2120 standard; 2800 full load
Dimensions, feet (metres): 295.9 × 46.9 × 18 *(90.2 × 14.3 × 5.5)*
Main machinery: Diesel-electric; 4 diesel generators; 2 motors; 10 000 hp(m) *(7.35 MW)*; 2 shafts
Speed, knots: 20. **Range, miles:** 9000 at 16 kts
Complement: 130
Guns: 4—57 mm/70 (2 quad) (not fitted).
Radars: Navigation: Two Don 2; I band.
Sonars: Tamir; hull-mounted; active search; high frequency.

Comment: Large rescue vessels. Built 1960-66. Carry two heavy duty derricks, submersible recompression chambers, rescue chambers and bells. Four marker buoys stowed abaft mainmast. All except *Altay* and *Zhiguli* have been modernised with quadruped foremasts and smaller marker buoys. One scrapped in 1987.

EPRON *6/1991, van Ginderen Collection*

10 VALDAY CLASS (Ex-T 58 CLASS)

KAZBEK KHIBINY VALDAY ZANGEZUR PULKOVO (ex-*SS 38*)
SS 30, 35, 40, 47, 50

Displacement, tons: 725 standard; 930 full load
Dimensions, feet (metres): 236.2 × 29.5 × 9.9 *(72 × 9 × 3)*
Main machinery: 2 diesels; 4000 hp(m) *(2.94 MW)*; 2 shafts
Speed, knots: 17. **Range, miles:** 2500 at 12 kts
Complement: 100
Radars: Navigation: Don; I band.
IFF: High Pole, Square Head or Dead Duck.
Sonars: Tamir; hull-mounted; active search; high frequency.

Comment: Basically of similar design to that of the T 58 class fleet minesweepers, but they were completed as emergency salvage vessels and submarine rescue ships at Leningrad in 1961-62. Equipped with diving bell, recompression chamber and emergency medical ward. Have stern lift of 10 tons and rescue chamber aft. One transferred to India (*Nistar* ex-SS 48) in 1971. Two scrapped in 1990.

VALDAY Class *1973*

TRANSPORTS

Notes: (a) In addition to the following some 30 other cargo ships/transports have naval connections.
(b) First of a new class of offshore supply ships seen in 1991, the *Marina Tsvetayeva* is based in the Pacific Fleet.

MARINA TSVETAYEVA *7/1991, 92 Wing RAAF*

1 ANADYR CLASS

ANADYR

Displacement, tons: 27 000 full load
Dimensions, feet (metres): 741.5 × 98.4 × 21.3 *(226 × 30 × 6.5)*
Main machinery: 4 Wärtsilä Vasa 16V 32D diesels; 32 200 hp(m) *(23.7 MW)* sustained; 2 shafts
Speed, knots: 20
Complement: 70
Cargo capacity: 10 500 tons
Radars: Navigation: Two Spin Trough; I band.
Helicopters: 2 medium.

Comment: Ro-flo ship built at Wärtsilä, Finland and completed in 1988. Handed over to the Navy and transferred to the Pacific via the Northern Sea route in August 1990. The ship's well-deck is 150 m in length.

ANADYR *10/1991, G. Jacobs*

1 ANGARA CLASS

ANGARA (ex-*Hela*)

Displacement, tons: 2520 full load
Dimensions, feet (metres): 327.4 × 41.7 × 13.5 *(99.8 × 12.7 × 4.1)*
Main machinery: 2 MAN diesels; 8360 hp(m) *(6.14 MW)*; 2 shafts
Speed, knots: 19. **Range, miles:** 2000 at 15 kts
Complement: 224
Radars: Navigation: Spin Trough; I band

Comment: Acts as a yacht for the Commander-in-Chief of the Navy. Stationed in the Black Sea. Built by Stülcken of Hamburg and launched 29 December 1938. Passed to USSR as partial reparation. Refit in Greece in 1983. Little change seen except improved electronics.

ANGARA *5/1990, S. Breyer*

1 AMGUEMA CLASS

YAUZA

Displacement, tons: 15 000 full load
Dimensions, feet (metres): 436.4 × 62.3 × 29.7 *(133 × 19 × 9)*
Main machinery: Diesel-electric; 4 diesel generators; 1 motor; 7200 hp(m) *(5.29 MW)*; 1 shaft
Speed, knots: 16. **Range, miles:** 7000 at 15 kts
Cargo capacity: 6500 tons
Radars: Navigation: Two Don 2; I band.

Comment: Built in Kherson in 1974. Ice strengthened. Similar class operates in merchant fleet. Based in the Northern Fleet.

YAUZA *1985*

2 ANDIZAN CLASS

ONDA POSYET

Displacement, tons: 6550 full load
Dimensions, feet (metres): 341.1 × 47.6 × 21.7 *(104 × 14.5 × 6.6)*
Main machinery: 2 diesels; 2500 hp(m) *(1.84 MW)*; 1 shaft
Speed, knots: 14. **Range, miles:** 6000 at 13 kts
Complement: 43
Cargo capacity: 4000 tons
Radars: Navigation: Don 2; I band.

Comment: Part of a class of about 50 merchant ships, built at Neptun, Rostock 1960-61.

ONDA *7/1987*

1 CHULYM CLASS

SEVERODONETSK

Displacement, tons: 4900 full load
Dimensions, feet (metres): 310.6 × 44.3 × 19.7 *(94.7 × 13.5 × 6)*
Main machinery: 2 boilers; 1 Compound reciprocating engine with LP turbine; 1650 ihp(m) *(1.2 MW)*; 1 shaft
Speed, knots: 12. **Range, miles:** 8500 at 11 kts
Complement: 40
Cargo capacity: 2300 tons

Comment: Built by Stocznia Szczecinska, Poland in 1956. Three were paid off in 1988-89. Thirteen others of this B 32 Type operate with the merchant navy. Based in the Northern Fleet.

1 KALININ CLASS

KUBAN (ex-*Nadeshda-Krupskaya*)

Displacement, tons: 6400 full load
Dimensions, feet (metres): 401 × 52.5 × 16.4 *(122.2 × 16 × 5)*
Main machinery: 2 MAN diesels; 8000 hp(m) *(5.88 MW)*; 2 shafts
Speed, knots: 17. **Range, miles:** 8200 at 17 kts
Complement: 120 plus 350 passengers
Cargo capacity: 1000 tons
Radars: Navigation: Two Don 2; I band.

Comment: Built in 1958 by Mathias Thesen Werft, Wismar, East Germany. Part of Mikhail Kalinin class of merchant ships originally to have been 24 ships of which only 19 were completed 1958-64. Name changed on transfer to naval service. Employed under naval command as personnel support ship for the Mediterranean Squadron.

KUBAN *1987, Selçuk Emre*

11 ANTONOV CLASS

NEON ANTONOV
IVAN LEDNEV
IVAN ODTEJEV
DVINA
IRBIT
NIKOLAY SIPYAGIN
VICTOR DENISON
MIKHAIL KONOVALOV
NICOLAY STARSHINOV
IVAN SUDTSOV
SERGEY SUDETSKY

Displacement, tons: 5600 full load
Dimensions, feet (metres): 311.7 × 48.2 × 21.3 *(95 × 14.7 × 6.5)*
Main machinery: 2 diesels; 7000 hp(m) *(5.15 MW)*; 2 shafts
Speed, knots: 17. **Range, miles:** 8500 at 13 kts
Complement: 40
Capacity: 2500 tons
Missiles: SAM: 2 SA-N-5 Grail twin launchers; manual aiming; IR homing to 6 km *(3.2 nm)* at 1.5 Mach; altitude to 2500 m *(8000 ft)*; warhead 1.5 kg.
Guns: 2—30 mm/65 (twin). 4—14.5 mm (2 twin) MGs.
Radars: Navigation: Don Kay; Spin Trough; I band.

Comment: Built at Nikolayev in 1975-early 1980s. All but *Irbit* (Pacific Fleet) and *Dvina* (Northern Fleet) operated by the Border Guard in the Pacific. Have two small landing craft aft. Armament is not normally mounted.

SERGEY SUDETSKY *1/1992, van Ginderen Collection*

4 PARTIZAN CLASS

PECHORA **TURGAY** **UFA** **V ADM FOMIN** (ex-*Pinega*) (mod)

Displacement, tons: 2150 full load
Dimensions, feet (metres): 291.3 × 42.3 × 16.4 *(88.8 × 12.9 × 5)*
Main machinery: 1 Sulzer diesel; 2080 hp(m) *(1.53 MW)*; 1 shaft
Speed, knots: 13. **Range, miles:** 4000 at 12 kts
Complement: 35
Cargo capacity: 3150 tons
Radars: Navigation: Don 2 or Palm Frond; I band.

Comment: Built at Turnu Severin SY, Romania 1975-76. Have two 10 ton and one 20 ton derricks. Basically small container ships with 20 similar in merchant fleet. *Fomin* is an ammunition transport and is armed with SA-N-5 missiles and two twin MG mountings.

PECHORA *9/1988*

10 KEYLA CLASS

MEZEN
RITSA (AGI)
TVERTSA
YERUSLAN
ONEGA
TERIBERKA
UNZA
PONOI
TULOMA
USSURY

Displacement, tons: 2440 full load
Dimensions, feet (metres): 257.5 × 34.8 × 14.8 *(78.5 × 10.6 × 4.5)*
Main machinery: 1 diesel; 1000 hp(m) *(735 kW)*; 1 shaft
Speed, knots: 14. **Range, miles:** 3000 at 11 kts
Complement: 26
Cargo capacity: 1195 tons
Radars: Navigation: Spin Trough or Neptun (plus Don 2 in some); I band.

Comment: Built 1959-61 in Budapest. Cargo ships. *Ritsa* has a deckhouse forward of the bridge, several communications type aerials, and has been used for intelligence gathering. *Teriberka* and *Ussury*, of original design, have one 15 ton and six 2.5 ton derricks. The remainder have one 10 ton and six 5 ton derricks.

PONOI *9/1991, G. Jacobs*

13 MUNA CLASS

VTR 28, 48, 81-86, 91-94, 148

Displacement, tons: 690 full load
Dimensions, feet (metres): 165 × 26.9 × 9.5 *(50.3 × 8.2 × 2.9)*
Main machinery: 1 diesel; 300 hp(m) *(220 kW)*; 1 shaft
Speed, knots: 10. **Range, miles:** 3000 at 10 kts
Complement: 40
Radars: Navigation: Two Spin Trough; I band.

Comment: Torpedo and ammunition transports with large crane amidships. Most have VTR prefix to their pennant numbers. Some act as experimental ships.

MUNA *8/1991, G. Jacobs*

8 MAYAK CLASS

BUZULUK, ISHIM, LAMA, MIUS, NEMAN, RIONI, ULMA, VYTEGRA

Displacement, tons: 920 full load
Dimensions, feet (metres): 178.1 × 30.5 × 11.8 *(54.3 × 9.3 × 3.6)*
Main machinery: 1 diesel; 1000 hp(m) *(735 kW)*; 1 shaft
Speed, knots: 12. **Range, miles:** 11 000 at 11 kts
Cargo capacity: 240 tons refrigerated stores
Radars: Navigation: Spin Trough; I Band.

Comment: Converted trawlers. Refrigerated stores ships.

MIUS *7/1987*

10 LENTRA CLASS

ALMA, KACHA, UFA, UGRA, VTR 1, 28, 32, 143-145

Comment: Victualling transports. Details under AGIs. Being phased out.

2 MP 4 CLASS

VTR 294 **VTR 295**

Displacement, tons: 790 full load
Dimensions, feet (metres): 183.7 × 26.2 × 9.2 *(56 × 8 × 2.8)*
Main machinery: 1 diesel; 650 hp(m) *(478 kW)*; 1 shaft
Speed, knots: 10. **Range, miles:** 1500 at 8 kts
Complement: 40
Guns: 4—25 mm/80 (2 twin).
Radars: Navigation: Don 2; I band.
IFF: High Pole A.

Comment: Ex-amphibious craft with four 3 ton derricks. Based in the Northern Fleet.

MP 4 Class *1979, USN*

5 MP 6 CLASS

BIRA **VOLOGDA** **+3**

Displacement, tons: 2130 full load
Dimensions, feet (metres): 246 × 37.1 × 14.4 *(75 × 11.3 × 4.4)*
Main machinery: 2 diesels; 800 hp(m) *(588 kW)*; 2 shafts
Speed, knots: 11. **Range, miles:** 3000 at 10 kts
Cargo capacity: 1000 tons
Guns: 6—37 mm/63 (3 twin) (not always fitted).
Radars: Navigation: Don 2 and Spin Trough; I band.

Comment: Ex-amphibious craft. Bow doors now welded shut. One 10 ton derrick on some; six 2.5 ton derricks in all. Two of the class are used as ammunition transports.

BIRA *9/1991, Reinhard Kramer*

7 KHABAROV CLASS

VTR 8, 13, 15, 25 **+3**

Displacement, tons: 650 full load
Dimensions, feet (metres): 152.5 × 26.2 × 9.2 *(46.5 × 8 × 2.8)*
Main machinery: 2 diesels; 650 hp(m) *(480 kW)*; 2 shafts
Speed, knots: 10. **Range, miles:** 1130 at 10 kts
Complement: 40
Cargo capacity: 400 tons
Guns: 2—14.5 mm (twin) MGs.
Radars: Navigation: Don 2 or Spin Trough; I band.

Comment: Built in USSR in 1950s and similar to the Shalanda class. Four 1.5 ton derricks. Three of the class used by the Border Guard in the Pacific. One deleted in 1989.

KHABAROV *3/1991, Erik Laursen*

4 TELNOVSK CLASS

BUROVESTNIK, LAG, VTR 73, VTR 74 (ex-*Jan Kreuks*)

Displacement, tons: 1680 full load
Dimensions, feet (metres): 229.6 × 32.8 × 13.1 *(70 × 10 × 4)*
Main machinery: 2 diesels; 800 hp(m) *(588 kW)*; 2 shafts
Speed, knots: 11. **Range, miles:** 3000 at 10 kts
Complement: 28
Cargo capacity: 1000 tons
Radars: Navigation: Don 2; I band.

Comment: Light freighters built at Budapest 1949-57. Some operate with the Border Guard in the Pacific. Six sister ships serve as naval survey vessels. Two 10 ton and four 2 ton derricks.

TORPEDO OPERATING/PATROL AND TARGET CRAFT

4 POTOK CLASS (TORPEDO EXPERIMENTAL SHIPS)

OS-100 **OS-138** **OS-145** **OS-225**

Displacement, tons: 850 full load
Dimensions, feet (metres): 236.5 × 30.8 × 8.2 *(72.1 × 9.4 × 2.5)*
Main machinery: 2 diesels; 4000 hp(m) *(2.94 MW)*; 2 shafts
Speed, knots: 17. **Range, miles:** 2500 at 12 kts
Torpedoes: 1—21 in *(533 mm)* tube. 1—16 in *(406 mm)* tube.

Comment: Used for torpedo trials in Black Sea. Torpedo tubes fitted on fo'c'sle with large recovery crane aft. Built since 1977. Type name is *opytnoye sudno* meaning experimental ship. Two scrapped in 1988-89.

OS-225 *1978*

90 POLUCHAT I, II and III CLASSES

Displacement, tons: 70 standard; 100 full load
Dimensions, feet (metres): 97.1 × 19 × 4.8 *(29.6 × 5.8 × 1.5)*
Main machinery: 2 diesels; 1700 hp(m) *(1.25 MW)*; 2 shafts
Speed, knots: 20. **Range, miles:** 1500 at 10 kts
Complement: 15
Guns: 2—14.5 mm (twin) MGs (in some).
Radars: Navigation: Spin Trough; I band.

Comment: Employed as specialised or dual purpose torpedo recovery vessels and/or patrol boats. They have a stern slipway. Several exported as patrol craft. Some used by the Border Guard. Transfers: Algeria, Angola, Congo (3), Ethiopia (1), Guinea-Bissau, India, Indonesia (3), Iraq (2), Mozambique, Somalia (6), Syria, Tanzania, Vietnam (5), North Yemen (2), South Yemen. Many deleted.

POLUCHAT III *6/1989*

20 SHELON CLASS

Displacement, tons: 340 full load
Dimensions, feet (metres): 160.8 × 29.9 × 6.6 *(49 × 9.1 × 2)*
Main machinery: 2 diesels; 10 000 hp(m) *(7.35 MW)*; 2 shafts
Speed, knots: 26
Complement: 20
Radars: Navigation: Spin Trough or Kivach; I band.

Comment: Built since 1978. Built-in weapon recovery ramp aft.

SHELON *8/1991*

20 OSA I CLASS

Comment: Details as in Light Forces (Osa) but with no armament. Half used as control craft and remainder as target vessels. Control craft use Square Tie radar while the targets carry radar reflectors and heat generators. In addition there is a large number of immobile target barges fitted with infra-red sources and radar reflectors as well as a number of P 6 class.

OSA Target *5/1990*

BARGE Target *5/1990*

AUXILIARIES

Note: Large numbers of assorted types and classes are employed on experimental work.

4 KOMANDOR CLASS

KOMANDOR **SHKIPER GYEK** **HERLUF BIDSTRUP** +1

Displacement, tons: 2435 full load
Dimensions, feet (metres): 289.7 × 44.6 × 15.4 *(88.3 × 13.6 × 4.7)*
Main machinery: 2 Russkiy SEMT-Pielstick 6 PC 2.5 L 400 diesels; 7020 hp(m) *(5.2 MW)*; 1 shaft; bow thruster; 1500 hp(m) *(1.1 MW)*
Speed, knots: 19. **Range, miles:** 7000 at 19 kts
Complement: 42
Radars: Navigation: Furuno; I band.
Helicopters: 2 Helix type for SAR.

Comment: Built by Danyard A/S for the Ministry of Fisheries. Contract signed in December 1987 and the ships were completed between August 1989 and April 1990. The hull is ice strengthened. The helicopter deck has a lift serving the double hangar below. There are considerable command and control facilities and these vessels have obvious military potential.

14 ONEGA CLASS

GKS 52	**SFP 95**	**SFP 224**	**SFP 240**	**SFP 283**	**GKS 286**	**SFP 295**
SFP 322	**SFP 340**	**SFP 173**	**SFP 511**	**SFP 542**	**SFP 562**	**SFP 177**

Displacement, tons: 2150 full load
Dimensions, feet (metres): 265.7 × 36 × 13.7 *(81 × 11 × 4.2)*
Main machinery: 2 gas turbines; 8000 hp(m) *(5.9 MW)*; 1 shaft
Speed, knots: 20
Complement: 45
Radars: Navigation: Neptun or Spin Trough; I band.

Comment: First seen in September 1973. Helicopter platform but no hangar in earlier ships of the class but in later hulls the space is taken up with more laboratory accommodation. Used as hydroacoustic monitoring ships.

SFP 173 *5/1991*

15 T 43 CLASS

GKS 11, 12, 14-24, 26, 45

Comment: Details under *Mine Warfare Forces*. Fitted with davits aft for laying hydroacoustic buoys for measuring ships' noise signatures. Unarmed but can carry one 37 mm/63 on fo'c'sle.

GKS 21 *3/1990, MoD Bonn*

PO 2 and NYRYAT 2 CLASSES

Displacement, tons: 56 full load
Dimensions, feet (metres): 70.5 × 11.5 × 3.3 *(21.5 × 3.5 × 1)*
Main machinery: 1 Type 3-D-12 diesel; 315 hp(m) *(231 kW)*; 1 shaft
Speed, knots: 12
Complement: 8
Guns: Some carry 1—12.7 mm MG on the fo'c'sle.

Comment: This 1950s design of hull and machinery has been used for a wide and diverse number of adaptations. Steel hull. Nyryat 2 have the same characteristics but are used as diving tenders and inshore survey craft.
Transfers: Albania, Bulgaria, Cuba, Guinea, Iraq. Many deleted.

NYRYAT 1 CLASS

Displacement, tons: 120 full load
Dimensions, feet (metres): 93 × 18 × 5.5 *(28.4 × 5.5 × 1.7)*
Main machinery: 1 diesel; 450 hp(m) *(331 kW)*; 1 shaft
Speed, knots: 12.5. **Range, miles:** 1500 at 10 kts
Complement: 15
Guns: 1—12.7 mm MG (in some).

Comment: Built from 1955. Can operate as patrol craft or diving tenders with recompression chamber. Similar hull and propulsion used for inshore survey craft. Some have BGK, VM or GBP numbers.
Transfers: Albania, Algeria, Cuba, Egypt, Iraq, North Yemen. Many deleted.

NYRYAT 1

1 PETRUSHKA CLASS

MIERNYK

Displacement, tons: 350 full load
Dimensions, feet (metres): 131.2 × 26.2 × 8.5 *(40 × 8 × 2.6)*
Main machinery: 2 diesels; 2 shafts
Speed, knots: 11

Comment: Training vessel built in Poland and commissioned in 1989. May be more of the class to follow.

MIERNYK *1989, MoD Bonn*

1 DALDYN CLASS

DALDYN

Displacement, tons: 360
Dimensions, feet (metres): 103.6 × 23.9 × 9.2 *(31.7 × 7.3 × 2.8)*
Main machinery: 1 SKL 6 VD 36/24-1U diesel; 305 hp(m) *(224 kW)* sustained; 1 shaft
Speed, knots: 9
Complement: 13

Comment: First seen in May 1973. Of Kareliya class trawler design with a high bridge. Used for MCM trials.

DALDYN *1973*

12 YELVA CLASS

VM 143, 146, 154, 266, 268, 413, 414, 416, 420, 425, 907, 909

Displacement, tons: 300 full load
Dimensions, feet (metres): 134.2 × 26.2 × 6.6 *(40.9 × 8 × 2)*
Main machinery: 2 Type 3-D-12A diesels; 630 hp(m) *(463 kW)* sustained; 2 shafts
Speed, knots: 12.5
Complement: 30
Radars: Navigation: Spin Trough; I band.

Comment: Diving tenders built in early 1970s. Carry a 1 ton crane and diving bell. Some have submersible recompression chamber. Ice strengthened. One to Cuba 1973, one to Libya 1977.

YELVA *1990, G. Jacobs*

FIRE/PATROL CRAFT

Note: In addition there are many specialised firefighting vessels.

9 IVA CLASS

PZHK 415, 1514, 1544, 1547, 1859 +4

Displacement, tons: 320 full load
Dimensions, feet (metres): 119.8 × 25.6 × 7.2 *(36.5 × 7.8 × 2.2)*
Main machinery: 2 diesels; 1040 hp(m) *(764 kW)*; 2 shafts
Speed, knots: 12.5
Complement: 20

Comment: Carry four water monitors. Completed in 1984-86, Can be used for patrol/towage.

IVA 415 *5/1990*

15 VIKHR CLASS

Displacement, tons: 1500
Dimensions, feet (metres): 237.2 × — × — *(72.3 × — × —)*

Comment: Completed at Gdansk Shipyard in 1986-87.

VIKHR 4 *1988*

40 POZHARNY I CLASS

Displacement, tons: 180 full load
Dimensions, feet (metres): 114.5 × 20 × 6 *(34.9 × 6.1 × 1.8)*
Main machinery: 2 Type M50-F1 diesels; 1800 hp(m) *(1.32 MW)*; 2 shafts
Speed, knots: 10
Guns: 4—12.7 mm (2 twin) MGs (in some).

Comment: Built in the mid-1950s. Harbour fire boats but can be used for patrol duties. One transferred to Iraq.

POZHARNY I *7/1991*

WATER CARRIERS

14 VODA CLASS

ABAKAN, SURA
MVT 6, 9, 10, 16, 17, 18, 20, 21, 24, 134, 135, 138

Displacement, tons: 3000 full load
Dimensions, feet (metres): 267.3 × 37.7 × 13.2 *(81.5 × 11.5 × 4)*
Main machinery: 2 diesels; 1600 hp(m) *(1.18 MW)*; 2 shafts
Speed, knots: 12. **Range, miles:** 3000 at 10 kts
Complement: 40
Cargo capacity: 1500 tons
Radars: Navigation: Don 2; Spin Trough; I band.
IFF: High Pole A.

Comment: Built in 1956 onwards. No armament. Some lack the catwalk forward of the bridge. Astern replenishment only.

SURA *10/1991, van Ginderen Collection*

2 MANYCH CLASS (WATER TANKERS)

MANYCH **TAGIL**

Displacement, tons: 7700 full load
Dimensions, feet (metres): 380.5 × 51.5 × 23 *(116 × 15.7 × 7)*
Main machinery: 2 diesels; 9000 hp(m) *(6.6 MW)*; 2 shafts
Speed, knots: 18. **Range, miles:** 7500 at 16 kts
Complement: 90
Cargo capacity: 4400 tons
Guns: 4—57 mm/70 (2 twin) (not normally fitted).
Radars: Air/surface search: Strut Curve; F band.
Navigation: Two Don Kay; I band.
Fire control: Two Muff Cob (not in *Tagil*); G/H band.
IFF: High Pole B.

Comment: Completed 1972 and 1976 in Vyborg. The high point on the single gantry is very similar to that on *Boris Chilikin*'s third gantry. Both ships in use as distilled water-carriers with armament removed. Have underway abeam replenishment capability.

MANYCH *2/1990*

DEGAUSSING SHIPS (YDG)

21 PELYM CLASS

SR 70	**SR 111**	**SR 179**	**SR 180**	**SR 191**	**SR 203**	**SR 215**	**SR 218**
SR 221	**SR 222**	**SR 233**	**SR 241**	**SR 276**	**SR 280**	**SR 281**	**SR 407**
SR 409	**SR 455**	+3					

Displacement, tons: 1370 full load
Dimensions, feet (metres): 214.8 × 38 × 11.2 *(65.5 × 11.6 × 3.4)*
Main machinery: 2 diesels; 2400 hp(m) *(1.76 MW)*; 2 shafts
Speed, knots: 14. **Range, miles:** 4500 at 13 kts
Complement: 70

Comment: First completed in 1971. Earlier ships have stump mast on funnel, later ships a tripod main mast and a platform deck extending to the stern. Type name is *sudno razmagnichivanya* meaning degaussing ship. One to Cuba 1982.

PELYM Class *5/1979*

5 KHABAROV CLASS

KHABAROV **SR 164** +3

Displacement, tons: 650 full load
Dimensions, feet (metres): 152.5 × 26.2 × 9.2 *(46.5 × 8 × 2.8)*
Main machinery: 2 diesels; 650 hp(m) *(480 kW)*; 2 shafts
Speed, knots: 10. **Range, miles:** 1130 at 10 kts
Complement: 30

Comment: Steel-hulled built in USSR in 1950s. Prominent deckhouse and stern anchors. Same class listed under *Transports*.

31 SEKSTAN CLASS

Displacement, tons: 528 full load
Dimensions, feet (metres): 136.2 × 29.9 × 9.8 *(41.5 × 9.1 × 3)*
Main machinery: 1 diesel; 400 hp(m) *(300 kW)*; 1 shaft
Speed, knots: 10

Comment: Most have SR numbers in the 100 series.

17 BEREZA CLASS

SR 28	**SR 59**	**SR 74**	**SR 120**	**SR 137**	**SR 188**	**SR 216**
SR 370	**SR 478**	**SR 479**	**SR 541**	**SR 548**	**SR 568**	**SR 569**
SR 570	**SR 936**	**SR 939**				

Displacement, tons: 2000 full load
Dimensions, feet (metres): 229.6 × 40.7 × 10.8 *(70 × 12.4 × 3.3)*
Main machinery: 2 Skoda-Sulzer 8TD 48 diesels; 3000 hp(m) *(2.2 MW)*; 2 shafts; cp props
Speed, knots: 15
Complement: 70
Radars: Navigation: Kivach; I band.

Comment: First completed in Poland in 1984. One transferred to Bulgaria in 1988. Still building in Poland.

SR 936 *3/1991, Per Kornefeldt*

KORALL CLASS

Displacement, tons: 620 full load
Dimensions, feet (metres): 140.4 × 29.9 × 11.4 *(42.8 × 9.1 × 3.5)*
Main machinery: 1 diesel; 400 hp(m) *(300 kW)*; 1 shaft
Speed, knots: 10

Comment: Modified schooners fitted with deperming equipment. Numbers not known.

ICEBREAKERS

Notes: All these ships are operated by Ministry of Merchant Marine and civilian manned except for the seven Dobrynya Nikitich class shown as being naval manned. All are an indispensable part of many naval operations not only in the Baltic, Northern and Pacific Fleet areas but also on rivers, lakes and canals.

3 MUDYUG CLASS

Name	*Builders*	*Commissioned*
MUDYUG	Wärtsilä, Helsinki	29 Oct 1982
MAGADAN	Wärtsilä, Helsinki	29 Dec 1982
DIKSON	Wärtsilä, Helsinki	17 Mar 1983

Displacement, tons: 6210; 7775 *(Mudyug)*
Dimensions, feet (metres): 290.7 × 69.6 × 19.7 *(88.6 × 21.2 × 6)*
365.5 × 72.8 × 21.3 *(111.4 × 22.2 × 6.5) (Mudyug)*
Main machinery: 4 Wärtsilä Vasa 8 R 32 diesels; 16 100 hp(m) *(11.83 MW)* sustained; 2 shafts; cp props
Speed, knots: 16.5. **Range, miles:** 15 000 at 16 kts
Complement: 43
Radars: Navigation: Okean and Nyada; I band.

Comment: Ordered on 3 April 1980 and all launched 16 April 1982. For use in Barents Sea, the Baltic and the Sea of Okhotsk. Fitted with Wärtsilä bubbling gear. *Mudyug* fitted with a new ice-breaking bow and longer stern by Thyssen-Nordseewerke, Emden. This means a power saving of about 65 per cent when breaking ice. Completed 30 October 1986.

MUDYUG (conversion) *1987, Thyssen-Nordseewerke*

DIKSON *8/1989*

2 TAMYR CLASS

TAMYR **VAYGACH**

Displacement, tons: 23 500 full load
Dimensions, feet (metres): 492 × 93.8 × 26.2 *(150 × 28.6 × 8)*
Main machinery: Nuclear; 2 PWR; 3 turbines; 52 000 hp(m) *(38 MW)*; 3 shafts
Speed, knots: 18.5
Complement: 138 plus 12 spare bunks
Radars: Navigation: 3 Okean; I band.
Helicopters: 1 Ka-32 Helix C.

Comment: Ordered from Wärtsilä, Helsinki 12 November 1984; first launched 10 April 1987, second 26 February 1988. *Tamyr* handed over 7 April 1988 and *Vaygach* 8 March 1989. Both ships had to spend over a year in the Baltic Yard, Leningrad for installation of nuclear reactors. The design is a combined Finnish/Soviet effort, the requirement being for comparatively shallow draught ships to operate in Siberian estuaries in temperatures down to −50°C. *Tamyr* joined the Northern Fleet in July 1989, *Vaygach* in late 1990.

TAMYR *8/1991, Bryan Hird*

4 + 2 ARKTIKA CLASS

Name	*Builders*	*Commissioned*
ARKTIKA	Baltic Yard, Leningrad	Dec 1974
SIBIR	Baltic Yard, Leningrad	Nov 1977
ROSSIYA	Baltic Yard, Leningrad	Feb 1986
SOVETSKIY SOYUZ	Baltic Yard, Leningrad	Jan 1990
OKTYABRYSKAYA REVOLUTSIYA	Baltic Yard, Leningrad	1992
URAL	Baltic Yard, Leningrad	1996

Displacement, tons: 19 300 standard; 23 460 full load
Dimensions, feet (metres): 485.4 × 98.4 × 36.4 *(148 × 30 × 11.1)*
Main machinery: Nuclear; 2 PWR; 3 turbines; 67 500 hp(m) *(49.6 MW)*; 3 shafts
Speed, knots: 22
Complement: 144 (49 officers)
Guns: 4—3 in *(76 mm)*/60 (2 twin) (fitted for but not with). 2—30 mm/65 AK 630.
Radars: Air/surface search: Head Net C (first two); Flat Screen (remainder); 3D; E band.
Navigation: Don 2 or Palm Frond; I band.
Helicopters: 2 Ka-32 Helix C.

Comment: *Arktika* launched 1972, *Sibir* 1976, *Rossiya* November 1983, *Sovetskiy Soyuz* 31 October 1986, *Oktyabryskaya Revolutsiya* October 1989 and should complete in 1992. *Ural* laid down in October 1989. *Arktika* was renamed *L I Brezhnev* in 1982 but reverted to original name in 1986. Can be fitted with guns and fire control radars. Some superstructure differences between the first two and the newer ships. The purpose of these ships is to extend the Arctic passage navigational season beyond the present June to October period, but according to a former Captain of *Arktika* the ships would need twice the power to achieve this aim, and it is reported that *Ural* may have an increased power output of 90 000 bhp. 2.3 m ice can be broken at 3 kts and ridges up to 8 m have been broken. Double hull construction with water ballast. The outer hull is 55 mm thick at ice levels, with the cast steel prow 2 m thick at its strongest point.

SOVETSKIY SOYUZ *5/1990*

SIBIR *6/1989*

3 YERMAK CLASS

Name	*Builders*	*Commissioned*
YERMAK	Wärtsilä, Helsinki	30 June 1974
ADMIRAL MAKAROV	Wärtsilä, Helsinki	2 June 1975
KRASIN	Wärtsilä, Helsinki	28 Apr 1976

Displacement, tons: 20 241 full load
Dimensions, feet (metres): 442.8 × 85.3 × 36.1 *(135 × 26 × 11)*
Main machinery: Diesel-electric; 9 Wärtsilä-Sulzer 12 ZH 40/48 diesels; 41 400 hp(m) *(30.4 MW)*; 9 Oy Strömberg Ab generators; 3 Strömberg motors; 36 000 hp(m) *(26.5 MW)*; 3 shafts
Speed, knots: 19.5. **Range, miles:** 40 000 at 15 kts
Complement: 118 plus 28 spare berths
Radars: Navigation: Okean and Don 2; I band.
Helicopters: Platform only.

Comment: Ordered on 29 April 1970 from Wärtsilä Shipyard, Helsinki, for delivery in 1974, 1975 and 1976. These are the first vessels to be fitted with Wärtsilä mixed-flow air-bubbling system to decrease friction between hull and ice. *Yermak* launched 7 September 1973. *A Makarov* launched 26 April 1974. *Krasin* launched 18 April 1975. Can maintain 2 kts in 6 ft ice.
There is also a former icebreaker built in 1917 called *Krasin* which is still afloat and occasionally goes to sea.

ADMIRAL MAKAROV *1985*

5 MOSKVA CLASS

Name	*Builders*	*Commissioned*
KIEV	Wärtsilä, Helsinki	Dec 1965
LENINGRAD	Wärtsilä, Helsinki	1960
MOSKVA	Wärtsilä, Helsinki	1959
MURMANSK	Wärtsilä, Helsinki	May 1968
VLADIVOSTOK	Wärtsilä, Helsinki	Apr 1969

Displacement, tons: 13 290 standard; 15 360 full load
Dimensions, feet (metres): 400.7 × 80.3 × 34.5 *(122.2 × 24.5 × 10.5)*
Main machinery: Diesel-electric; 8 Wärtsila-Sulzer 9 MH 51 diesels; 8 generators; 26 000 hp(m) *(19.1 MW)* (*Murmansk* and *Vladivostok*); 22 000 hp(m) *(16.2 MW)* (remainder); 1 motor (centre shaft); 11 000 hp(m) *(8.1 MW)*; 2 motors (wing shafts); 5500 hp(m) *(4 MW)*; 3 shafts
Speed, knots: 18. **Range, miles:** 20 000 at 14 kts
Complement: 100
Helicopters: 2 Ka-32 Helix C.

Comment: Built by Wärtsilä Shipyard, Helsinki. *Moskva* was launched on 10 January 1959; *Leningrad* on 24 October 1959; *Murmansk* on 14 July 1967 and *Vladivostok* on 28 May 1968. Designed to stay at sea for a year without returning to base. The concave embrasure in the ship's stern is a housing for the bow of a following vessel when additional power is required. *Moskva* has four pumps which can move 480 tons of water from one side to the other in two minutes to rock the icebreaker and wrench her free of thick ice. Becoming increasingly unreliable and may soon start to be scrapped.

LENINGRAD *1988*

3 KAPITAN BELOUSOV CLASS

Name	*Builders*	*Commissioned*
KAPITAN BELOUSOV	Wärtsilä, Helsinki	1955
KAPITAN MELEKHOV	Wärtsilä, Helsinki	1957
KAPITAN VORONIN	Wärtsilä, Helsinki	1956

Displacement, tons: 4375-4415 standard; 5350 full load
Dimensions, feet (metres): 273 × 63.7 × 23 *(83.3 × 19.4 × 7)*
Main machinery: Diesel-electric; 6 Polar diesel generators; 4 motors; 10 500 hp(m) *(7.72 MW)*; 4 shafts (2 fwd, 2 aft)
Speed, knots: 14.9. **Range, miles:** 10 000 at 14 kts
Complement: 75

Comment: *K Belousov* launched 1954, *K Voronin* 1955 and *K Melekhov* 19 October 1956. Used for harbour ice clearance.

KAPITAN BELOUSOV *1970, Michael D. J. Lennon*

4 KAPITAN SOROKIN CLASS

Name	*Builders*	*Commissioned*
KAPITAN SOROKIN (mod)	Wärtsilä, Helsinki	14 July 1977
KAPITAN NIKOLAYEV	Wärtsilä, Helsinki	31 Jan 1978
KAPITAN DRANITSYN	Wärtsilä, Helsinki	2 Dec 1980
KAPITAN KHLEBNIKOV	Wärtsilä, Helsinki	1 Dec 1981

Displacement, tons: 14 917 full load; 17 150 (conversion) full load
Dimensions, feet (metres): 424.5; 463.9 (conversion) × 86.9; 102 (conversion) × 27.9 *(129.4; 141.4 × 26.5; 31.1 × 8.5)*
Main machinery: Diesel-electric; 6 Wärtsilä-Sulzer 9 ZL 40/48 diesels; 24 800 hp(m) *(18.2 MW)*; 6 alternators; 22 000 hp(m) *(16.2 MW)*; 3 motors; 3 shafts
Speed, knots: 19. **Range, miles:** 10 500 at 16 kts
Complement: 76 (16 spare berths)
Helicopters: Platform only.

Comment: Shallow draught polar icebreakers fitted with Wärtsilä bubbling system. Fitted with single cabins (except spare berths), sauna, swimming pool, gymnasium, library, cinema and hospital. They are used for North Siberian operations in shallow deltas at ambient temperatures down to −50°C. As a result of *Mudyug's* successful conversion, the first two of this class are being given similar treatment with major extensions to bow and stern. *Sorokin* completed 18 November 1990 at Thyssen-Nordseewerke, Emden. *Nikolayev* is planned to be similarly converted in due course. After conversion the hull is 17 per cent wider, has an increased displacement of 15 per cent and, as well as cutting a wider channel, has an icebreaking performance increased by 48 per cent to 2.15 m thick.

KAPITAN SOROKIN (modified) *11/1990, Thyssen Nordseewerke*

KAPITAN DRANITSYN *1989, van Ginderen Collection*

6 KAPITAN CHECHKIN CLASS

Name	*Builders*	*Commissioned*
KAPITAN CHECHKIN	Wärtsilä, Helsinki	6 Nov 1977
KAPITAN PLAKHIN	Wärtsilä, Helsinki	30 Dec 1977
KAPITAN CHADAYEV	Wärtsilä, Helsinki	7 Apr 1978
KAPITAN KRUTOV	Wärtsilä, Helsinki	6 June 1978
KAPITAN BUKAYEV	Wärtsilä, Helsinki	29 Sep 1978
KAPITAN ZARUBIN	Wärtsilä, Helsinki	10 Nov 1978

Displacement, tons: 2240 full load
Dimensions, feet (metres): 254.5 × 53.5 × 10.7 *(77.6 × 16.3 × 3.3)*
Main machinery: Diesel-electric; 3 Wärtsilä Vasa 12V22 diesel generators; 6.3 MW sustained; 3 motors; 3877 hp(m) *(2.85 MW)*; 3 shafts
Speed, knots: 14
Complement: 28

Comment: Ordered 16 May 1975. *K Chechkin* launched 29 April 1977; *K Plakhin*, 8 August 1977; *K Chadayev*, 13 October 1977; *K Krutov*, 11 January 1978; *K Bukayev*, in 1978. Designed for service on Volga-Baltic waterways and Siberian rivers. Fitted with three rudders, air-bubbling system and an automatic lowering system for masts, radar and aerials.

KAPITAN CHADAYEV (operating bubbling equipment) *1978, Wärtsilä*

21 DOBRYNYA NIKITICH CLASS

AFANASY NIKITIN (ex-*Ledokol 2*) (1962)
BURAN (1966)*
DOBRYNYA NIKITICH (1960)*
FEDOR LITKE (1970)
GEORGY SEDOV (1967)**
ILYA MUROMETS (1966)*
IVAN MOSKVITIN (1971)
IVAN KRUZENSHTERN (ex-*Ledokol 6*) (1964)
KHARITON LAPTEV (ex-*Ledokol 3*) (1962)
P PAKHTUSOV (1966)**
PERESVET (1969)*
YURY LISYANSKY (ex-*Ledokol 9*) (1965)
PURGA (1961)*
SADKO (1968)*
SEMEN CHELYUSKIN (ex-*Ledokol 8*) (1965)
SEMEN DEZHNEV (1971)
VASILY POYARKOV (ex-*Ledokol 4*) (1963)
VLADIMIR RUSANOV (ex-*Ledokol 7*) (1964)
VYUGA (1961)*
(ex-*Ledokol 5*) (1963)
YEROFEI KHABAROV
PLUG (1961)

* Naval manned.
** Occasionally used for hydrographic work in the Arctic.

Displacement, tons: 2995 full load
Measurement, tons: 2254 gross; 1118 dwt; 50 net
Dimensions, feet (metres): 222.1 × 59.4 × 20 *(67.7 × 18.1 × 6.1)*
Main machinery: Diesel-electric; 3 Type 13D100 diesel generators; 3 motors; 5400 hp(m) *(4 MW)*; 3 shafts (1 fwd, 2 aft)
Speed, knots: 14.5. **Range, miles:** 5500 at 12 kts
Complement: 45
Guns: 2—57 mm/70 (twin). 2—37 mm/63 (fitted for but not with in *Dobrynya Nikitich* and *Vyuga*). 2—25 mm/80 (twin) *(Sadko)* (fitted for but not with in remainder). Non-naval ships unarmed.
Radars: Navigation: Two Don 2; I band.

Comment: All built at Admiralty Yard, Leningrad between 1960 (first ship, *Dobrynya Nikitich*) and 1971 (last ship, *Semen Dezhnev*). Divided between the Baltic, Black Sea and Pacific. One scrapped in 1989.

AFANASY NIKITIN *6/1991, Harald Carstens*

8 KAPITAN YEVDOKIMOV CLASS

Name	*Builders*	*Commissioned*
KAPITAN YEVDOKIMOV	Wärtsilä, Helsinki	31 Mar 1983
KAPITAN BABICHEV	Wärtsilä, Helsinki	30 June 1983
KAPITAN CHUDINOV	Wärtsilä, Helsinki	9 Sep 1983
KAPITAN BORODKIN	Wärtsilä, Helsinki	18 Nov 1983
AVRAMIY ZAVENYAGIN (ex-*Kapitan Krylov*)	Wärtsilä, Helsinki	1 Dec 1983
KAPITAN METSAYK	Wärtsilä, Helsinki	21 Aug 1984
KAPITAN DEMIDOV	Wärtsilä, Helsinki	22 Nov 1984
KAPITAN MOSHKIN	Wärtsilä, Helsinki	14 May 1986

Displacement, tons: 2150 full load
Dimensions, feet (metres): 250.9 × 54.4 × 8.2 *(76.5 × 16.6 × 2.5)*
Main machinery: Diesel-electric; 3 Wärtsilä Vasa 12V 22B diesel generators; 6.3 MW sustained; 4 Strömberg motors; 5170 hp(m) *(3.8 MW)*; 4 shafts
Speed, knots: 13.5
Complement: 25

Comment: Contract for first seven signed in December 1980 for completion by 1984. One more ordered in 1983. This design is unique, having a draught shallower than any previous icebreaker. Designed for service in temperatures of −50°C on Siberian rivers and deltas.

KAPITAN YEVDOKIMOV *1990, van Ginderen Collection*

3 KAPITAN IZMAYLOV CLASS

Name	*Builders*	*Commissioned*
KAPITAN M IZMAYLOV	Wärtsilä, Helsinki	15 June 1976
KAPITAN KOSOLAPOV	Wärtsilä, Helsinki	14 July 1976
KAPITAN A RADZABOV	Wärtsilä, Helsinki	5 Oct 1976

Displacement, tons: 2045 full load
Dimensions, feet (metres): 185.3 × 51.5 × 13.8 *(56.5 × 15.7 × 4.2)*
Main machinery: Diesel-electric; 4 Wärtsilä Vasa 824 TS diesel generators; 4100 hp(m) *(3 MW)*; 2 Strömberg motors; 3400 hp(m) *(2.5 MW)*; 2 shafts
Speed, knots: 13. **Range, miles:** 5000 at 12 kts
Complement: 25
Radars: Navigation: Low Trough; I band.

Comment: Contract signed with Wärtsilä, Helsinki on 22 March 1974 for the building of these three icebreakers for delivery in 1976. All fitted with Wärtsilä air-bubbling system. *K Izmaylov* launched 11 December 1975; *K Kosolapov*, 13 February 1976; *K Radzabov*, 9 March 1976.

KAPITAN A RADZABOV *7/1986, Ralf Bendfeldt*

7 STROPTIVY CLASS

Name	*Builders*	*Commissioned*
STROPTIVY	Wärtsilä, Helsinki	30 Nov 1979
STAKHANOVETS	Wärtsilä, Helsinki	29 Feb 1980
SIBIRSKY	Wärtsilä, Helsinki	2 July 1980
SPRAVEDLIVY	Wärtsilä, Helsinki	1982
SUVOROVETS	Wärtsilä, Helsinki	1982
FOBOS	Wärtsilä, Helsinki	29 Apr 1983
DEYMOS	Wärtsilä, Helsinki	31 May 1983

Displacement, tons: 4200 full load
Dimensions, feet (metres): 238.5 × 59 × 21.3 *(72.7 × 18 × 6.5)*
Main machinery: 2 Wärtsilä-SEMT-Pielstick 6 PC 2.5 L400 diesels; 7020 hp(m) *(5.2 MW)*; 2 shafts; cp props; bow thruster
Speed, knots: 15
Complement: 40 plus 12 spare berths

Comment: Designed as icebreaking salvage vessels, serving in support of Arctic fishing fleets. Can carry out repair, firefighting, salvage and towing. Have two 5 ton and two 3 ton cranes, four foam generators, a diving centre with oxy-acetylene equipment, TV monitors and a hospital.

STAKHANOVETS *10/1991, van Ginderen Collection*

ARMED ICEBREAKERS

8 IVAN SUSANIN CLASS

AISBERG
DUNAY
IMENI XXVI SYEZDA KPSS
IVAN SUSANIN
NEVA
RUSLAN
VOLGA
IMENI XXV SYEZDA KPSS

Displacement, tons: 2720 full load
Dimensions, feet (metres): 229.7 × 59.4 × 21 *(70 × 18.1 × 6.4)*
Main machinery: Diesel-electric; 3 Type 13-D-150 diesel generators; 3 motors; 5400 hp(m) *(4 MW)*; 3 shafts (1 fwd, 2 aft)
Speed, knots: 14.5. **Range, miles:** 5500 at 12.5 kts
Guns: 2—3 in *(76 mm)*/60 (twin). 2—30 mm/65 AK 630 (not in all).
Radars: Surface search: Strut Curve; F band.
Navigation: 2 Don Kay; I band.
Fire control: Hawk Screech; I band.
Helicopters: Platform only.

Comment: Generally similar to Dobrynya Nikitich class though larger with a tripod mast and different superstructure. Operated by the Border Guard. Armament sometimes removed.

AISBERG *8/1991, Bryan Hird*

TUGS

Note: SB means *Spasatelny Buksir* or Salvage Tug. MB means *Morskoy Buksir* or Seagoing Tug.

2 BAKLAZHAN CLASS

NIKOLAI CHIKER SB 131 **SB 135**

Displacement, tons: 7000
Dimensions, feet (metres): 324.8 × 64 × 23.6 *(99 × 19.5 × 7.2)*
Main machinery: 4 Wärtsilä Vasa 12V32 diesels; 24 160 hp(m) *(17.76 MW)*; 2 shafts; bow thruster; 1360 hp(m) *(1 MW)*
Speed, knots: 18. **Range, miles:** 11 000 at 16 kts
Complement: 51 plus 20 spare berths
Radars: Navigation: Nyada; I band.

Comment: Built by Hollming (Rauma), Helsinki and completed 12 April 1989 and 30 June 1989 respectively. These are the largest salvage tugs in the world with a 250 ton bollard pull on each of two towing winches with a third 60 ton winch. The crew includes two divers and there are two decompression chambers. Four firefighting foam/water guns are fitted on the bridge/mast. Designed to operate in extreme temperatures.

NIKOLAI CHIKER *10/1991*

4 NEFTEGAZ CLASS

ALEKSEY KORTUNOV **ILGA** **UMKA** **KALAR**

Displacement, tons: 2800 full load
Dimensions, feet (metres): 267.4 × 53.5 × 14.8 *(81.5 × 16.3 × 4.5)*
Main machinery: 2 Sulzer diesels; 7200 hp(m) *(5.29 MW)*; 2 shafts; bow thruster
Speed, knots: 15
Complement: 25

Comment: Built by Warski, Szczecin in 1983. Can carry 600 tons cargo or be used as a tug or for firefighting. These naval units are mostly used in a range monitoring role.

UMKA *2/1990, van Ginderen Collection*

13 GORYN CLASS

MB 15	**MB 119**
MB 18	**SB 365** (ex-*MB 29*)
MB 32	**SB 521** (ex-*MB 61*)
MB 35	**SB 522** (ex-*MB 62)*
MB 36	**SB 523** (ex-*MB 64*)
MB 38	**SB 524** (ex-*MB 108*)
MB 105	

Displacement, tons: 2240 standard; 2600 full load
Dimensions, feet (metres): 208.3 × 46.9 × 16.7 *(63.5 × 14.3 × 5.1)*
Main machinery: 2 Russkiy SEMT-Pielstick 6PC 2.5 L400 diesels; 7020 hp(m) *(5.2 MW)*; 2 shafts; cp props; bow thruster
Speed, knots: 15
Complement: 43 plus 16 spare berths
Radars: Navigation: Two Don 2; I band.

Comment: Built by Rauma-Repola 1977-83. Have sick-bay. First ships have goal-post mast with 10 ton and 5 ton derricks and bollard pull of 35 tons. Remainder have an A-frame mast with a 15 ton crane and bollard pull of 45 tons. SB number indicates a 'rescue' tug.

MB 15 (with goalposts) *5/1990*

SB 523 (with 'A' frame) *4/1991*

39 SORUM CLASS

AMUR	**PRIMORYE**	**MB 4**	**MB 31**	**MB 147**
BREST	**SAKHALIN**	**MB 6**	**MB 37**	**MB 148**
BUG	**URAL**	**MB 13**	**MB 56**	**MB 196**
BURYA	**VICTOR KINGSIEPP**	**MB 19**	**MB 58**	**MB 236**
CHUKOTKA	**YAN BERZIN**	**MB 25**	**MB 61**	**MB 304**
KAMCHATKA	**YENISEY**	**MB 26**	**MB 76**	**MB 307**
KARELIA	**ZABAYKALYE**	**MB 28**	**MB 99**	
LADOGA	**ZAPOLARYE**	**MB 30**	**MB 110**	
NEMAN				

Displacement, tons: 1660 full load
Dimensions, feet (metres): 190.2 × 41.3 × 15.1 *(58 × 12.6 × 4.6)*
Main machinery: Diesel-electric; 2 Type 5-2DW2 diesels; 2900 hp(m) *(2.13 MW)* 1 motor; 2000 hp(m) *(1.47 MW)*; 1 shaft
Speed, knots: 14. **Range, miles:** 3500 at 13 kts
Complement: 35
Guns: 4—30 mm/65 (2 twin) (all fitted for, but only Border Guard ships carry them).
Radars: Navigation: Two Don 2 or Nayada; I band.
IFF: High Pole B.

Comment: A class of ocean tugs with firefighting and diving capability. Named ships are used as patrol vessels and are Border Guard operated. Built in Yaroslavl and Oktyabskoye since 1973 to a similar design used for Ministry of Fisheries rescue tugs.

SORUM *1991*

50 OKHTENSKY CLASS

LOKSA	**ORION**	**SATURN**
NEPTUN	**POCHETNY**	**TYULEN**

Displacement, tons: 930 full load
Dimensions, feet (metres): 156.1 × 34 × 13.4 *(47.6 × 10.4 × 4.1)*
Main machinery: Diesel-electric; 2 BM diesels; 1 motor; 1500 hp(m) *(1.1 MW)*; 1 shaft
Speed, knots: 13. **Range, miles:** 8000 at 7 kts; 6000 at 13 kts
Complement: 40
Guns: 2—57 mm/70 (twin) or 2—25 mm/80 (twin) (Border Guard only).
Radars: Navigation: One or two Don 2 or Spin Trough; I band.
IFF: High Pole B.

Comment: Oceangoing salvage and rescue tugs. First completed 1958. Fitted with powerful pumps and other apparatus for salvage. The six named ships are manned by the Border Guard and are armed; others have either SB or MB numbers.

LOKSA *1991*

16 ZENIT CLASS

Displacement, tons: 800 full load
Dimensions, feet (metres): 157.1 × 32.8 × 15.3 *(47.9 × 10 × 4.3)*
Main machinery: 2 boilers; 1 steam reciprocating engine; 800 ihp(m) *(588 kW)*; 1 shaft
Speed, knots: 11. **Range, miles:** 10 000 at 8 kts
Complement: 25
Radars: Navigation: Don 2; I band.

Comment: Have icebreaking capability. Survivors in the navy of a large class of naval and merchant tugs built by Wärtsilä in 1950s.

BERTHING TUGS

Displacement, tons: 350 full load
Dimensions, feet (metres): 114.1 × 27.9 × 9.2 *(34.8 × 8.5 × 2.8)*
Main machinery: 1 diesel; 1 shaft
Speed, knots: 11

Comment: Large numbers built in 1970s by Edgar Andre, Magdeburg, East Germany. All originally numbered MB 70 et seq. Some renamed.

10 ROSLAVL CLASS

MB 50, MB 94, MB 95, MB 102, MB 125, MB 145-147, SB 41, SB 46

Displacement, tons: 750 full load
Dimensions, feet (metres): 146 × 31.2 × 10.8 *(44.5 × 9.5 × 3.3)*
Main machinery: Diesel-electric; 2 diesel generators; 1 motor; 1200 hp(m) *(882 kW)*; 1 shaft
Speed, knots: 12. **Range, miles:** 6000 at 11 kts
Complement: 30
Radars: Navigation: Don 2; I band.

Comment: First completed in 1953. Some of the same class are in the merchant fleet.

MB 94 *7/1991, Erik Laursen*

SCHOLLE CLASS (HARBOUR TUGS)

Displacement, tons: 189 full load
Dimensions, feet (metres): 98.4 × 21.3 × 9.8 *(30 × 6.5 × 3)*
Main machinery: 1 RGDV 148 K10 diesel; 1 shaft
Speed, knots: 10

Comment: Very numerous class built in East Germany in 1964.

TUGUR CLASS (HARBOUR TUGS)

Displacement, tons: 300 full load
Dimensions, feet (metres): 100.7 × 25.3 × 7.5 *(30.7 × 7.7 × 2.3)*
Main machinery: 2 boilers; 1 steam reciprocating engine; 500 ihp(m) *(367 kW)*; 1 shaft
Speed, knots: 10

Comment: Numerous class (over 200 built) with tall funnel built in 1950s in Finland. Two transferred to Albania.

TUGUR *3/1991, Erik Laursen*

50 SIDEHOLE 1 and 2 CLASSES (HARBOUR TUGS)

Displacement, tons: 183 (Sidehole 1); 197 (Sidehole 2)
Dimensions, feet (metres): 80 × 23 × 6.9 *(24.4 × 7 × 2.1)*
Main machinery: 2 diesels; 600 hp(m) *(441 kW)* (Sidehole 1), 900 hp(m) *(661 kW)* (Sidehole 2); 2 shafts
Speed, knots: 9 (Sidehole 1); 10 (Sidehole 2)
Complement: 12
Radars: Navigation: Spin Trough; I band.

Comment: Built at Leningrad in 1960s (Sidehole 1) and 1970s (Sidehole 2). About 20 are Sidehole 2s. There are a large number of other tugs in naval and commercial service.

SIDEHOLE 2 *1990*

FLOATING DOCKS and ANCILLARIES

Note: In addition to the docks there are also numerous floating cranes—the largest having a lift of 1500 tons—and many floating workshops, either purpose built or converted.

2 LARGE FLOATING DOCKS

PD 41 **PD 50**

Displacement, tons: 80 000
Dimensions, feet (metres): 1082.4 × 232.9 (inertial beam) × 49.2 (over blocks) *(330 × 71 × 15) (PD 41)*
1000.4 × 226.3 (inertial beam) × 49.2 (over blocks) *(305 × 69 × 15) (PD 50)*
Complement: 175

Comment: Amongst the largest independently supported dry docks in the world. *PD 41* built by Ishikawajima Heavy Industries, Japan and towed to Vladivostok in October 1978. *PD 50* built by Götaverken Arendal, Sweden. Two 30 ton cranes *(PD 41)* and two 50 ton *(PD 50)*.

FLOATING DOCK (with ARKTIKA (ex-*L. Brezhnev*)) *1989, S. S. Breyer*

150 FLOATING DOCKS

Comment: There is a dock of some 35-40 000 tons capacity in Vladivostok in addition to the 80 000 ton dock above. At least six of 30 000 tons capacity have been built in Yugoslavia and another six of about 28 000 tons capacity have been delivered from Sweden. The 20 or so various types of docks which are in use throughout the Soviet naval bases may total about 150 of which about half have a capacity of 5000 tons to 25 000 tons.

FLOATING DOCK *10/1989*

MARITIME BORDER GUARD

Note: The Border Guard operates a considerable fleet of warships which would be integrated with naval operations in a crisis. Formerly run by the KGB, the force came under the Ministry of Defence in October 1991 and some of the vessels will be devolved to the individual Republics with coastal regions. The OOB of this group on 1 January 1992 is listed here for convenience—details of the classes are listed in the sections preceding.

Frigates
7 Krivak III class
12 Grisha II class
6 Grisha III class

Light Forces
112 Stenka class
15 Muravey class
30 Zhuk class
6 Svetlyak class
20 Sorum class
5 Okhtensky class

Patrol Ships
25 Pauk class

River Monitors
10 Piyavka class
8 Vosh class
20 Yaz class
96 Schmel class

Armed Icebreakers
8 Ivan Susanin class

Support Forces
8 Antonov class
3 Khabarov class
1 Telnovsk class
2 Baskunchak class

HARBOUR CRAFT *5/1990, Marko Enquist*

ST KITTS-NEVIS

Senior Appointments

Commissioner of Police:
Stanley V Franks
Commanding Officer:
Inspector Ivor Blake

Base

Basseterre

Personnel

1992: 35

Mercantile Marine

Lloyd's Register of Shipping:
1 vessel of 300 tons

1 SWIFTSHIPS 110 ft PATROL CRAFT

STALWART C 253

Displacement, tons: 99.1 normal
Dimensions, feet (metres): 116.5 × 25 × 7 *(35.5 × 7.6 × 2.1)*
Main machinery: 4 Detroit 12V 71 TA diesels; 1680 hp *(1.25 MW)* sustained; 4 shafts
Speed, knots: 21. **Range, miles:** 1800 at 15 kts
Complement: 11
Guns: 2—12.7 mm MGs. 2—7.62 mm MGs.

Comment: Built by Swiftships, Morgan City, and delivered August 1985. Aluminium alloy hull and superstructure.

STALWART *1990, St Kitts-Nevis Police*

1 FAIREY MARINE SPEAR CLASS

RANGER I

Displacement, tons: 4.3
Dimensions, feet (metres): 29.8 × 9.5 × 2.8 *(9.1 × 2.8 × 0.9)*
Main machinery: 2 Ford Mermaid diesels; 360 hp *(268 kW)*; 2 shafts
Speed, knots: 30
Complement: 2
Guns: Mountings for 2—7.62 mm MGs.

Comment: Ordered for the police in June 1974—delivered 10 September 1974. Refitted 1986.

RANGER II

Dimensions, feet (metres): 27 × 9.7 × 3 *(8.2 × 2.95 × 0.9)*
Main machinery: 1 Johnson outboard; 180 hp *(134 kW)*
Speed, knots: 19. **Range, miles:** 105 at 16 kts
Complement: 2

RANGER II *1990 St Kitts-Nevis Police*

ST LUCIA

Senior Appointments

Comptroller of Customs and Excise:
M J Scholar
Coast Guard Commander:
Lieutenant Commander Mike Critchley RN

Base

Castries

Personnel

1992: 10

Mercantile Marine

Lloyd's Register of Shipping:
7 vessels of 1891 tons gross

DELETION

1990 *Vigilant I*

1 SWIFT 65 ft CLASS

DEFENDER P02

Displacement, tons: 42 full load
Dimensions, feet (metres): 64.9 × 18.4 × 6.6 *(19.8 × 5.6 × 2)*
Main machinery: 2 Detroit 12V 71 diesels; 680 hp *(507 kW)* sustained; 2 shafts
Speed, knots: 22. **Range, miles:** 1200 at 18 kts
Complement: 5

Comment: Ordered from Swiftships, Morgan City in November 1983. Completed 1985. Similar to craft supplied to Antigua and Dominica.

DEFENDER *1/1992, A. Sheldon Duplaix*

2 BOSTON WHALERS

P 03 **P 04**

Displacement, tons: 3
Dimensions, feet (metres): 22 × 6.8 × 2 *(6.7 × 2 × 0.6)*
Main machinery: 1 V6-2500CC Johnson outboard
Speed, knots: 36

Comment: Acquired in July 1988.

1 PATROL CRAFT

VIGILANT II P 06

Displacement, tons: 5 full load
Dimensions, feet (metres): 29 × 10 × 2.4 *(8.8 × 3.1 × 0.7)*
Main machinery: 2 Volvo Turbo diesels; 400 hp(m) *(294 kW)*; 2 shafts
Speed, knots: 30

Comment: Completed in May 1990 by Phoenix Marine Enterprises, Hialeah, Florida. Has replaced *Vigilant I*.

VIGILANT II *1990 St Lucia CG*

ST VINCENT AND THE GRENADINES

Senior Appointments

Commissioner of Police:
Leopold Stoddard
Coast Guard Commander:
Lieutenant Commander C E Jagger, RN

Base

Calliaqua

Personnel

1992: 40

Mercantile Marine

Lloyd's Register of Shipping:
698 vessels of 2 709 794 tons gross

1 SWIFTSHIPS 120 ft PATROL CRAFT

CAPTAIN MULZAC SVG 01

Displacement, tons: 101
Dimensions, feet (metres): 120 × 25 × 7 *(36.6 × 7.6 × 2.1)*
Main machinery: 4 Detroit 12V 71 TA diesels; 1360 hp *(1.01 MW)* sustained; 4 shafts
Speed, knots: 21. **Range, miles:** 1800 at 15 kts
Complement: 13
Guns: 2—12.7 mm MGs. 2—7.62 mm MGs.
Radars: Surface search: Furuno 1411; I/J band.

Comment: Built by Swiftships, Morgan City and delivered in June 1987.

CAPTAIN MULZAC *1/1992, A. Sheldon Duplaix*

1 VOSPER THORNYCROFT 75 ft PATROL CRAFT

GEORGE McINTOSH SVG 05

Displacement, tons: 70
Dimensions, feet (metres): 75 × 19.5 × 8 *(22.9 × 6 × 2.4)*
Main machinery: 2 Caterpillar 12V D 348 TA diesels; 1840 hp *(1.37 MW)*; 2 shafts
Speed, knots: 24.5. **Range, miles:** 1000 at 11 kts; 600 at 20 kts
Complement: 11
Guns: 1 Oerlikon 20 mm.

Comment: Handed over 23 March 1981. GRP hull.

GEORGE McINTOSH *1987, St Vincent Coastguard*

2 BUHLER TYPE (PATROL CRAFT)

LARIKAI SVG 06 **BRIGHTON** SVG 07

Displacement, tons: 6 full load
Dimensions, feet (metres): 27 × 6.8 × 2.4 *(8.2 × 2.1 × .73)*
Main machinery: 2 outboard engines; 2 props
Speed, knots: 23

Comment: Locally built by Buhler's Yachts Ltd. Converted to outboard engines in 1990-91.

BRIGHTON *1991, St Vincent Coastguard*

SAUDI ARABIA

Senior Appointments

Chief of Naval Staff:
Vice Admiral Talal Salem Al Mofadhi
Director of Coast Guard:
Captain Al Jumayha

Diplomatic Representation

Naval Attaché in London:
Commander A Al Fozan

Personnel

(a) 1992: 10 800 officers and men (including 1200 marines)
(b) Voluntary service

Bases

Naval HQ: Riyadh
Main bases: Jiddah, Jubail, Ruwais (Coast Guard), Aziziyah (Coast Guard)
Minor bases (Naval and Coast Guard): Ras Tanura, Al Dammam, Yanbo, Ras al-Mishab, Al Wajh, Al Qatif, Haqi, Al Sharmah, Qizan

Strength of the Fleet

Type	*Active*	*Building*
Frigates	4	(3)
Corvettes—Missile	4	—
Fast Attack Craft—Missile	9	—
Fast Attack Craft—Torpedo	2 (1)	—
Patrol Craft	20	(20)
Minehunters	1	2 (3)
Minesweepers—Coastal	4	—
Replenishment Tankers	2	—
LCMs	4	—
LCUs	4	—
Tugs	14	—
Royal Yacht	1	—
Hydrofoil	1	—
Coast Guard		
Patrol Craft	500 approx	—
Miscellaneous	35	—

Command and Control

The United States is providing an update of C^3 capabilities during the period 1991-95, including a commercial datalink to improve interoperability.

Coast Guard

Part of the Frontier Force under the Minister of the Interior. 5200 officers and men in January 1992.

Mercantile Marine

Lloyd's Register of Shipping:
309 vessels of 1 321 464 tons gross

DELETION

1990 *Riyadh*

SUBMARINES

Note: France has emerged as the front runner for sales of up to six patrol submarines with a training programme in Lorient and the use of the Daphne class *Flore* as a training boat. Orders are unlikely until mid-1990s. It has also been reported that up to two midget submarines of 225 tons and six KSS-1 class are to be acquired from South Korea in an Agreement reached in July 1989. Advice is also being given by Pakistan.

FRIGATES

0 + (3) IMPROVED LA FAYETTE CLASS

Displacement, tons: 3700 full load
Dimensions, feet (metres): 423.2 × 50.5 × 13.5 *(129 × 15.4 × 4.1)*
Main machinery: 4 SEMT-Pielstick 16 PA6 280 BTC diesels; 38 400 hp(m) *(28 MW)* sustained; 2 shafts
Speed, knots: 28
Complement: 160

Missiles: SSM: 8 Aerospatiale MM 40 Exocet ❶.
SAM: 16 Aster 15 SAAM VLS ❷ or Crotale NG octuple launcher. 2 Matra Sadral sextuple launchers ❸; Mistral.
Guns: 1 Creusot Loire 3.9 in *(100 mm)*/55 compact ❹. 2 Emerlec 30 mm (twin) ❺.
Torpedoes: 4 fixed 324 mm tubes (2 twin) ❻; Murene.
Countermeasures: Decoys: 2 Dagaie Mk 2 launchers ❼; Chaff and IR flares.
ESM/ECM: Intercept and jammer.
Combat data systems: Thomson-CSF TAVITAC. Syracuse SATCOM ❽.
Fire control: Vega system; NAJIR optronic director ❾.
Radars: Air/surface search: Thomson-CSF DRBV 26C ❿; D band.

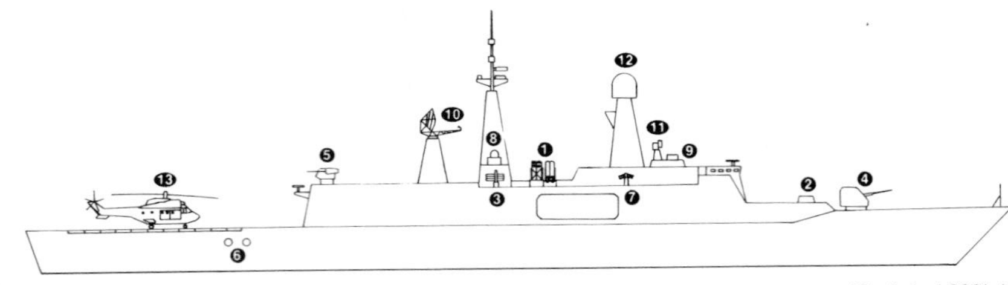

IMPROVED LA FAYETTE Class *(Scale 1 : 1 200), Ian Sturton*

Fire control: Castor II ⓫; I band.
Arabel ⓬ for SAAM.
Navigation: 2 Racal Decca (one for helo control); I band.
Sonars: Thomson Sintra Spherion; hull-mounted active search and attack; medium frequency.

Helicopters: 2 SA 365F Dauphin 2 ⓭

Programmes: An outline agreement (accord cadre) was signed on 11 June 1989 for three French *La Fayette* type frigates to be built at Lorient Naval Yard. The plan is for the first of class to start sea trials in 1995 with the others following at 18 month intervals.
Structure: Details shown above represent the outline plan provided by DCN and there will probably be some changes.
Operational: Main role is air defence.

4 TYPE F 2000S

Name	*No*	*Builders*	*Laid down*	*Launched*	*Commissioned*
MADINA	702	Lorient (DTCN)	15 Oct 1981	23 Apr 1983	4 Jan 1985
HOFOUF	704	CNIM, Seyne-sur-Mer	14 June 1982	24 June 1983	31 Oct 1985
ABHA	706	CNIM, Seyne-sur-Mer	7 Dec 1982	23 Dec 1983	4 Apr 1986
TAIF	708	CNIM, Seyne-sur-Mer	1 Mar 1983	25 May 1984	29 Aug 1986

Displacement, tons: 2000 standard; 2870 full load
Dimensions, feet (metres): 377.3 × 41 × 16 (sonar) *(115 × 12.5 × 4.9)*
Main machinery: 4 SEMT-Pielstick 16 PA6 280 BTC diesels; 38 400 hp(m) *(28 MW)* sustained; 2 shafts
Speed, knots: 30. **Range, miles:** 8000 at 15 kts; 6500 at 18 kts
Complement: 179 (15 officers)

Missiles: SSM: 8 OTO Melara/Matra Otomat Mk 2 (2 quad) ❶; active radar homing to 160 km *(86.4 nm)* at 0.9 Mach; warhead 210 kg; sea-skimmer for last 4 km *(2.2 nm)*. ERATO system allows mid-course guidance by ship's helicopter.
SAM: Thomson-CSF Crotale Navale octuple launcher ❷; radar guidance; IR homing to 13 km *(7 nm)* at 2.4 Mach; warhead 14 kg; 26 missiles.
Guns: 1 Creusot Loire 3.9 in *(100 mm)*/55 compact ❸; 80° elevation; 20/45/90 rounds/minute to 17 km *(9.3 nm)* anti-surface; 6 km *(3.3 nm)* anti-aircraft; weight of shell 13.5 kg. 4 Breda 40 mm/70 (2 twin) ❹; 85° elevation; 300 rounds/minute to 12.5 km *(6.8 nm)*; weight of shell 0.96 kg.
Torpedoes: 4—21 in *(533 mm)* tubes ❺. ECAN F17P; anti-submarine; wire-guided; active/passive homing to 20 km *(10.8 nm)* at 40 kts; warhead 250 kg.
Countermeasures: Decoys: CSEE Dagaie double trainable mounting ❻; IR flares and Chaff; H/J band.
ESM: Thomson-CSF DR 4000; intercept; HF/DF.
ECM: Janet; jammer.
Combat data systems: Thomson-CSF TAVITAC (Senit 6) action data automation; capability for Link 11.
Fire control: Vega system. 3 CSEE Naja optronic directors. DLT for torpedoes.
Radars: Air/surface search/IFF: Thomson-CSF Sea Tiger (DRBV 15) ❼; E/F band; range 110 km *(60 nm)* for 2 m² target.
Navigation: Racal Decca TM 1226; I band.
Fire control: Thomson-CSF Castor IIB ❽; I/J band; range 15 km *(8 nm)* for 1 m² target.
Thomson-CSF DRBC 32 ❾; I/J band (for SAM).
Sonars: Thomson Sintra Diodon TSM 2630; hull-mounted; active search and attack with integrated Sorel VDS ❿; 11, 12 or 13 kHz.

Helicopters: 1 SA 365F Dauphin 2 ⓫.

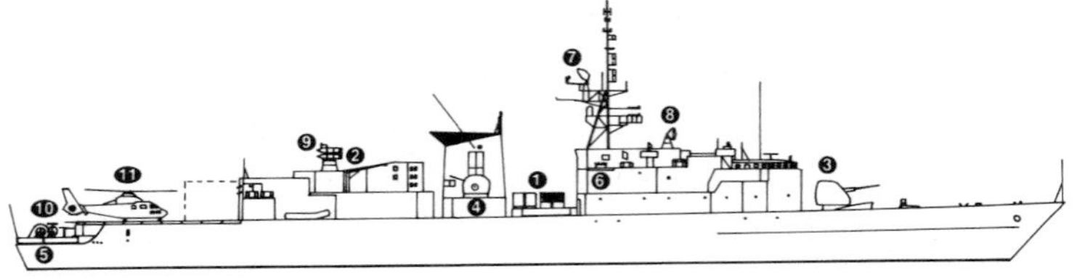

MADINA *(Scale 1 : 1 200), Ian Sturton*

ABHA *4/1988, A. Sheldon Duplaix*

Programmes: Ordered in 1980, the major part of the Sawari contract. Agreement for France to provide supplies and technical help.

Structure: Fitted with Snach/Saphir folding fin stabilisers.
Operational: Navigation: CSEE Sylosat. Helicopter can provide mid-course guidance for SSM. All based in the Red Sea.

TAIF *9/1989, G. Jacobs*

CORVETTES

4 MISSILE CORVETTES

Name	*No*	*Builders*	*Laid down*	*Launched*	*Commissioned*
BADR	612	Tacoma Boatbuilding Co, Tacoma	6 Oct 1979	26 Jan 1980	30 Nov 1980
AL YARMOOK	614	Tacoma Boatbuilding Co, Tacoma	3 Jan 1980	13 May 1980	18 May 1981
HITTEEN	616	Tacoma Boatbuilding Co, Tacoma	19 May 1980	5 Sep 1980	3 Oct 1981
TABUK	618	Tacoma Boatbuilding Co, Tacoma	22 Sep 1980	18 June 1981	10 Jan 1983

Displacement, tons: 870 standard; 1038 full load
Dimensions, feet (metres): 245 × 31.5 × 8.9 *(74.7 × 9.6 × 2.7)*
Main machinery: CODOG; 1 GE LM2500 gas turbine; 23 000 hp *(17.2 MW)* sustained; 2 MTU 12V652 TB91 diesels; 3470 hp(m) *(2.55 MW)* sustained; 2 shafts; cp props
Speed, knots: 30 gas; 20 diesels. **Range, miles:** 4000 at 20 kts
Complement: 58 (7 officers)

Missiles: SSM: 8 McDonnell Douglas Harpoon (2 quad) launchers ❶; active radar homing to 130 km *(70 nm)* at 0.9 Mach; warhead 227 kg.
Guns: 1 FMC/OTO Melara 3 in *(76 mm)*/62 Mk 75 Mod 0 ❷; 85° elevation; 85 rounds/minute to 16 km *(8.7 nm)*; weight of shell 6 kg.
1 General Electric/General Dynamics 20 mm 6-barrelled Vulcan Phalanx ❸; 3000 rounds/minute combined to 2 km.
2 Oerlikon 20 mm/80 ❹; 55° elevation; 800 rounds/minute to 2 km anti-aircraft.
1—81 mm mortar. 2—40 mm Mk 19 grenade launchers.
Torpedoes: 6—324 mm US Mk 32 (2 triple) tubes ❺. Honeywell Mk 46; anti-submarine; active/passive homing to 11 km *(5.9 nm)* at 40 kts; warhead 44 kg.
Countermeasures: Decoys: 2 Loral Hycor SRBOC 6-barrelled fixed Mk 36 ❻; IR flares and Chaff to 4 km *(2.2 nm)*.
ESM: SLQ 32(V)1 ❼; intercept.
Fire control: Mk 24 optical director ❽. Mk 309 for torpedoes.
Radars: Air search: Lockheed SPS 40B ❾; E/F band; range 320 km *(175 nm)*.
Surface search: ISC Cardion SPS 55 ❿; I/J band.
Fire control: Sperry Mk 92 ⓫; I/J band.
Sonars: Raytheon SQS 56 (DE 1164); hull-mounted; active search and attack; medium frequency.

Modernisation: A five year programme started in 1988.
Structure: Fitted with fin stabilisers.
Operational: All based at Jubail on the east coast.

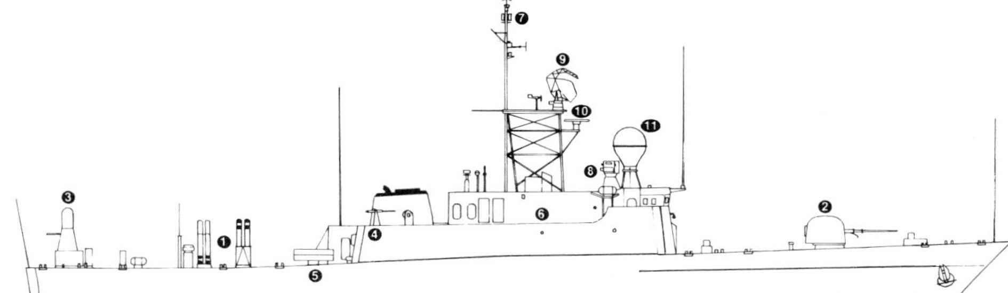

BADR *(Scale 1 : 600), Ian Sturton*

BADR *1989, van Ginderen Collection*

SHIPBORNE AIRCRAFT

Numbers/Type: 20 Aerospatiale SA 365F Dauphin 2.
Operational speed: 140 kts *(260 km/h)*.
Service ceiling: 15 000 ft *(4575 m)*.
Range: 410 nm *(758 km)*.
Role/Weapon systems: ASV/ASW helicopter; procured for initial embarked naval aviation force; systems developed jointly with France; surface search/attack is the primary role. Sensors: Thomson-CSF Agrion 15, Crouzet MAD. Weapons: ASV; 4 × AS/15TT missiles or 2 Mk 46 torpedoes.

LAND-BASED MARITIME AIRCRAFT

Note: 6 P3C Orion may be acquired in 1992.

Numbers/Type: 30 Aerospatiale AS 332SC Super Puma.
Operational speed: 150 kts *(280 km/h)*.
Service ceiling: 15 090 ft *(4600 m)*.
Range: 335 nm *(620 km)*.
Role/Weapon systems: Six have coast guard quick reaction role and six have anti-shipping capability. Two delivered in August 1989 then one per month to a total of 30 by the end of 1990. Sensors: Six, none; some have Omera for Exocet. Weapons: Some have GIAT 20 mm cannon; others have AM39 Exocet ASM.

Numbers/Type: 4 Aerospatiale SA 365N Dauphin 2.
Operational speed: 140 kts *(260 km/h)*.
Service ceiling: 15 000 ft *(4575 m)*.
Range: 410 nm *(758 km)*.
Role/Weapon systems: Overwater SAR and limited surface search helicopter. Sensors: Omera ORB 32 search radar. Weapons: Unarmed.

LIGHT FORCES

Note: Reported that 52 fast patrol boats of 35 ft were ordered from the USA in 1991.

17 HALTER TYPE (COASTAL PATROL CRAFT)

Displacement, tons: 56 full load
Dimensions, feet (metres): 78 × 20 × 5.8 *(23.8 × 6.1 × 1.8)*
Main machinery: 2 Detroit 16V 92 TA diesels; 1380 hp *(1.03 MW)*; 2 shafts
Speed, knots: 28. **Range, miles:** 1200 at 12 kts
Guns: 2—12.7 mm MGs. 2—7.62 mm MGs

Comment: Ordered from Halter Marine 17 February 1991. Last to be delivered in 1992. Same type for Philippines.

9 FAST ATTACK CRAFT (MISSILE)

Name	*No*	*Builders*	*Commissioned*
AL SIDDIQ	511	Peterson Builders, Wisconsin	15 Dec 1980
AL FAROUQ	513	Peterson Builders, Wisconsin	22 June 1981
ABDUL AZIZ	515	Peterson Builders, Wisconsin	3 Sep 1981
FAISAL	517	Peterson Builders, Wisconsin	23 Nov 1981
KAHLID	519	Peterson Builders, Wisconsin	11 Jan 1982
AMYR	521	Peterson Builders, Wisconsin	21 June 1982
TARIQ	523	Peterson Builders, Wisconsin	11 Aug 1982
OQBAH	525	Peterson Builders, Wisconsin	18 Oct 1982
ABU OBAIDAH	527	Peterson Builders, Wisconsin	6 Dec 1982

Displacement, tons: 425 standard; 478 full load
Dimensions, feet (metres): 190.5 × 26.5 × 6.6 *(58.1 × 8.1 × 2)*
Main machinery: CODOG; 1 GE LM2500 gas turbine; 23 000 hp *(17.2 MW)* sustained; 2 MTU 12V652 TB91 diesels; 3470 hp(m) *(2.55 MW)* sustained; 2 shafts; cp props
Speed, knots: 38 gas; 25 diesel. **Range, miles:** 2900 at 14 kts
Complement: 38 (5 officers)

Missiles: SSM: 4 McDonnell Douglas Harpoon (2 twin) launchers; active radar homing to 130 km *(70 nm)* at 0.9 Mach; warhead 227 kg.
Guns: 1 FMC/OTO Melara 3 in *(76 mm)*/62 Mk 75 Mod 0; 85° elevation; 85 rounds/minute to 16 km *(8.7 nm)*; weight of shell 6 kg.
1 General Electric/General Dynamics 20 mm 6-barrelled Vulcan Phalanx; 3000 rounds/minute combined to 2 km.
2 Oerlikon 20 mm/80; 55° elevation; 800 rounds/minute to 2 km anti-aircraft.
2—81 mm mortars. 2—40 mm Mk 19 grenade launchers.
Countermeasures: Decoys: 2 Loral Hycor SRBOC 6-barrelled fixed Mk 36; IR flares and Chaff to 4 km *(2.2 nm)*.
ESM: SLQ 32(V)1; intercept.
Fire control: Mk 92 mod 5 GFCS.
Radars: Surface search: ISC Cardion SPS 55; I/J band.
Fire control: Sperry Mk 92; I/J band.

Modernisation: There is a planned modernisation programme but the Gulf conflict caused it to be postponed.
Operational: Two operate from the west coast, the remainder are based at Jubail.

OQBAH *1983, Giorgio Arra*

3 FDR JAGUAR CLASS (FAST ATTACK CRAFT—TORPEDO)

Name	No	Builders	Commissioned
DAMMAM	190	Lürssen, Vegesack	1969
KHABAR	192	Lürssen, Vegesack	1969
MACCAH	194	Lürssen, Vegesack	1969

Displacement, tons: 160 standard; 190 full load
Dimensions, feet (metres): 139.4 × 23 × 7.9 *(42.5 × 7 × 2.4)*
Main machinery: 4 Maybach 16-cyl diesels; 12 000 hp(m) *(8.82 MW)*; 4 shafts
Speed, knots: 42. **Range, miles:** 1000 at 30 kts
Complement: 33 (3 officers)
Guns: 2 Bofors 40 mm/70; 90° elevation; 300 rounds/minute to 12 km *(6.6 nm)*; weight of shell 0.96 kg.
Torpedoes: 4—21 in *(533 mm)* tubes; anti-surface.

Comment: Refitted by Lürssen Werft, West Germany in 1976. Two are used for training, mostly alongside, and one is in reserve.

JAGUAR Class *1974, Reiner Nerlich*

20 SIMMONEAU TYPE (INSHORE PATROL CRAFT)

Displacement, tons: 22
Dimensions, feet (metres): 51.8 × 15.7 × 5.9 *(15.8 × 4.8 × 1.8)*
Main machinery: 2 diesels; 2400 hp(m) *(1.76 MW)*; 2 shafts
Speed, knots: 33. **Range, miles:** 375 at 25 kts
Guns: 1 GIAT 20 mm. 2—7.62 mm MGs.
Radars: Surface search: Furuno; I band.

Comment: Ordered in June 1988 and delivered in 1989-90. Used by naval commandos. These craft were also reported as Panhards. A second batch of 20 may be ordered.

SIMMONEAU TYPE *1989, Simmoneau Marine*

MINE WARFARE FORCES

4 MSC 322 CLASS (MINESWEEPERS/HUNTERS—COASTAL)

Name	No	Builders	Commissioned
ADDRIYAH	MSC 412	Peterson Builders, Wisconsin	6 July 1978
AL QUYSUMAH	MSC 414	Peterson Builders, Wisconsin	15 Aug 1978
AL WADEEAH	MSC 416	Peterson Builders, Wisconsin	7 Sep 1979
SAFWA	MSC 418	Peterson Builders, Wisconsin	2 Oct 1979

Displacement, tons: 320 standard; 407 full load
Dimensions, feet (metres): 153 × 26.9 × 8.2 *(46.6 × 8.2 × 2.5)*
Main machinery: 2 Waukesha L1616 diesels; 1200 hp *(895 kW)*; 2 shafts
Speed, knots: 13
Complement: 39 (4 officers)
Guns: 1 Oerlikon 20 mm.
Radars: Surface warning: ISC Cardion SPS 55; I/J band.
Sonars: GE SQQ 14; VDS; active minehunting; high frequency.

Comment: Ordered on 30 September 1975 under the International Logistics Programme. Wooden structure.
Fitted with fin stabilisers, wire and magnetic sweeps and also for minehunting.

SAFWA *1984, van Ginderen Collection*

1 + 2 (3) SANDOWN CLASS (MINEHUNTERS—COASTAL)

Name	No	Builders	Launched	Commissioned
AL JAWF	420	Vosper Thornycroft	2 Aug 1989	12 Dec 1991
SHAQRA	422	Vosper Thornycroft	15 May 1991	1992
AL KHARJ	424	Vosper Thornycroft	1992	1993

Displacement, tons: 450 standard; 480 full load
Dimensions, feet (metres): 172.9 × 34.4 × 6.9 *(52.7 × 10.5 × 2.1)*
Main machinery: 2 Paxman Valenta 6-RP 200E diesels; 1500 hp *(1.12 MW)* sustained; Voith-Schneider propulsion; 2 shafts; 2 Schottel bow thrusters
Speed, knots: 13 diesels; 6 electric drive. **Range, miles:** 3000 at 12 kts
Complement: 34 (7 officers) plus 6 spare berths
Guns: 2 Emmerson Electric 30 mm (twin); 80° elevation; 1200 rounds/minute combined to 6 km *(3.3 nm)*; weight of shell 0.35 kg.
Countermeasures: MCM: ECA mine disposal system; 2 PAP 104 Mk 5.
Combat data systems: Plessey Nautis M action data automation.
Fire control: Contraves TMEO optronic director.
Radars: Navigation: Kelvin Hughes Type 1007; I band.
Sonars: Plessey/MUSL Type 2093; VDS; high frequency.

Comment: Three ordered 2 November 1988 from Vosper Thornycroft with option for three more. *Al Kharj* laid down September 1990. GRP hull. Combines vectored thrust units with bow thrusters and Remote Controlled Mine Disposal System (RCMDS). Some of the hulls have been reallocated from the RN production line. Up to three more to be ordered in 1992.

AL JAWF *12/1991, H. M. Steele*

SHAQRA *5/1991, Vosper Thornycroft*

AMPHIBIOUS FORCES

4 Ex-US LCU 1610 TYPE

AL QIAQ (ex-*SA 310*) 212
AL SULAYEL (ex-*SA 311*) 214
AL ULA (ex-*SA 312*) 216
AFIF (ex-*SA 313*) 218

Displacement, tons: 200 light; 375 full load
Dimensions, feet (metres): 134.9 × 29 × 6.1 *(41.1 × 8.8 × 1.9)*
Main machinery: 4 GM diesels; 1000 hp *(746 kW)*; 2 Kort nozzles
Speed, knots: 11. **Range, miles:** 1200 at 8 kts
Complement: 14 (2 officers)
Military lift: 170 tons; 20 troops
Guns: 2—12.7 mm MGs.
Radars: Surface search: Marconi LN 66; I band.

Comment: Built by Newport Shipyard, Rhode Island. Transferred June/July 1976. Two may be in reserve.

4 US LCM 6 TYPE

DHEBA 220
UMLUS 222
AL LEETH 224
AL QUONFETHA 226

Displacement, tons: 62 full load
Dimensions, feet (metres): 56.2 × 14 × 3.9 *(17.1 × 4.3 × 1.2)*
Main machinery: 2 GM diesels; 450 hp *(336 kW)*; 2 shafts
Speed, knots: 9. **Range, miles:** 130 at 9 kts
Complement: 5
Military lift: 34 tons or 80 troops
Guns: 2—40 mm grenade launchers.

Comment: Four transferred July 1977 and four in July 1980. The first four have been cannibalised for spares.

SERVICE FORCES

2 MOD DURANCE CLASS (REPLENISHMENT SHIPS)

Name	*No*	*Builders*	*Commissioned*
BORAIDA	902	C du N et de la Méditerranée, La Ciotat	29 Feb 1984
YUNBOU	904	C du N et de la Méditerranée, La Ciotat	29 Aug 1985

Displacement, tons: 10 500
Dimensions, feet (metres): 442.9 × 61.3 × 22.9 *(135 × 18.7 × 7)*
Main machinery: 2 SEMT-Pielstick 14 PC 2.5 V400 diesels; 18 200 hp(m) *(13.4 MW)* sustained; 2 shafts; cp props
Speed, knots: 20.5. **Range, miles:** 7000 at 15 kts
Complement: 129 plus 11 trainees
Cargo capacity: 4350 tons diesel; 350 tons AVCAT; 140 tons fresh water; 100 tons victuals; 100 tons ammunition; 70 tons spares

Guns: 4 Breda Bofors 40 mm/70 (2 twin); 85° elevation; 300 rounds/minute to 12.5 km *(6.8 nm)*; weight of shell 0.96 kg.
Fire control: 2 CSEE Naja optronic directors. 2 CSEE Lynx optical sights.
Radars: Navigation: Two sets; I band.

Helicopters: 2 SA 365 F Dauphin.

Programmes: Contract signed October 1980 as part of Sawari programme.
Structure: Refuelling positions: Two alongside, one astern.
Operational: Also serve as training ships and as depot and maintenance ships. Helicopters can have ASM or ASW armament.

BORAIDA *11/1987, G. Toremans*

1 SALVAGE TUG

JIDDAH 13

Displacement, tons: 350
Dimensions, feet (metres): 112.8 × — × — *(34.4 × — × —)*
Main machinery: 2 diesels; 800 hp(m) *(588 kW)*; 2 shafts
Speed, knots: 12

Comment: Built at Hayashikane, Shimonoseki. Laid down 19 August 1977.

3 OCEAN TUGS

RADHWA 12, 16, 17

Displacement, tons: 680
Dimensions, feet (metres): 142.7 × 44.9 × 18.4 *(43.5 × 13.7 × 5.6)*
Main machinery: 2 Fuji diesels; 5600 hp(m) *(4.12 MW)*; 2 shafts
Range, miles: 12

Comment: First launched 16 October 1982, second 17 May 1983 and third 24 June 1983.

8 HARBOUR TUGS

RADHWA 1-6, 14-15

Measurement, tons: 350 gross
Dimensions, feet (metres): 118 × 42 × 15 *(35.9 × 12.8 × 4.6)*
Main machinery: 2 Fuji 8L 32X diesels; 5600 hp(m) *(4.12 MW)* sustained; 2 shafts
Speed, knots: 15

Comment: Builders Hitachi Robin DY, Singapore (for 1-3), Jonker and Stans, Netherlands (4-6) and Damen, Netherlands (14-15). All commissioned between 1981 and 1983.

2 Ex-US YTB TYPE (HARBOUR TUGS)

TUWAIG (ex-*YTB 837*) EN 111 **DAREEN** (ex-*YTB 838*) EN 112

Displacement, tons: 350 full load
Dimensions, feet (metres): 109 × 30 × 13.8 *(31.1 × 9.8 × 4.5)*
Main machinery: 2 diesels; 2000 hp *(1.49 MW)*; 2 shafts
Speed, knots: 12
Complement: 12
Guns: 2 Oerlikon 20 mm.

Comment: Transferred by US Navy 15 October 1975. Used mostly to aid weapons firing exercises.

ROYAL YACHT SQUADRON

1 ROYAL YACHT

Name	*No*	*Builders*	*Commissioned*
AL RIYADH	—	Van Lent (de Kaag), Netherlands	Jan 1978

Displacement, tons: 650
Dimensions, feet (metres): 228 × 34.4 × 10.8 *(69.5 × 10.5 × 3.3)*
Main machinery: 2 MTU 16V 956 TB91 diesels; 7500 hp(m) *(5.51 MW)* sustained; 2 shafts; bow thruster
Speed, knots: 26
Complement: 26 (accommodation for 18 passengers)

Comment: Ordered 12 December 1975. Laid down 6 May 1976. Launched 17 December 1977. Fittings include helicopter pad, sauna, swimming pool, hospital with intensive care unit.

1 PEGASUS CLASS (HYDROFOIL)

Displacement, tons: 115 full load
Dimensions, feet (metres): 89.9 × 29.9 × 6.2 *(27.4 × 9.1 × 1.9)*
Main machinery: 2 Allison 501-KF20A gas turbines; 8660 hp *(6.46 MW)* sustained; 2 waterjets (foilborne); 2 Detroit 8V92 diesels; 606 hp *(452 kW)* sustained; 2 shafts (hullborne)
Speed, knots: 46. **Range, miles:** 890 at 42 kts
Guns: 2 General Electric 20 mm Sea Vulcan.

Comment: Ordered in 1984 from Boeing, Seattle; delivered in August 1985. Mostly used as a tender to the Royal Yacht.

COAST GUARD

4 LARGE PATROL CRAFT

AL JOUF 351 **TURAIF** 352 **HAIL** 353 **NAJRAN** 354

Displacement, tons: 210 full load
Dimensions, feet (metres): 126.6 × 26.2 × 6.2 *(38.6 × 8 × 1.9)*
Main machinery: 3 MTU 16 V 538 TB 93 diesels; 11 265 hp(m) *(8.28 MW)* sustained; 3 shafts
Speed, knots: 38. **Range, miles:** 1700 at 15 kts
Complement: 20
Guns: 2 Oerlikon GAM-BO1 20 mm. 2—12.7 mm MGs.
Radars: Surface search: ARPA 1690; I band.
Navigation: Racal RM 1290A; I band.

Comment: Ordered on 18 October 1987 from Blohm & Voss. First two completed 15 June 1989; second pair 20 August 1989. Steel hulls with aluminium superstructure. Two based at Jiddah in the Red Sea and two at Damman in the Arabian Gulf.

AL JOUF *6/1989, Blohm & Voss*

2 LARGE PATROL CRAFT

AL JUBAIL **SALWA**

Displacement, tons: 95 full load
Dimensions, feet (metres): 86 × 19 × 5.6 *(26.2 × 5.8 × 1.7)*
Main machinery: 2 MTU 16V 396 TB 94 diesels; 5800 hp(m) *(4.26 MW)* sustained; 2 shafts
Speed, knots: 42. **Range, miles:** 1100 at 25 kts
Complement: 10
Guns: 1 Oerlikon 20 mm. 2—7.62 mm MGs.

Comment: Built by Abeking & Rasmussen, completed in April 1987. Smaller version of Turkish SAR 33 Type.

AL JUBAIL *1987, Abeking and Rasmussen*

15 SKORPION CLASS (COASTAL PATROL CRAFT)

139-153

Displacement, tons: 33 full load
Dimensions, feet (metres): 55.8 × 16.1 × 4.6 *(17 × 4.9 × 1.4)*
Main machinery: 2 GM 12V 71 TA diesels; 840 hp *(627 kW)* sustained; 2 shafts
Speed, knots: 25. **Range, miles:** 200 at 20 kts
Complement: 7
Guns: 2—7.62 mm MGs.

Comment: Twenty built by Bayerische SY, Erlenbach am Main. 139-148 shipped to Jiddah in October 1979. Last 10 completed February 1981. Remainder built by Arminias Werft, Bodenwerder in 1979. Ten deleted so far.

SKORPION 144 — *10/1979, van Ginderen Collection*

12 RAPIER CLASS (COASTAL PATROL CRAFT)

127-138

Displacement, tons: 26
Dimensions, feet (metres): 50 × 15.1 × 4.6 *(15.2 × 4.6 × 1.4)*
Main machinery: 2 GM 12V 71 TA diesels; 840 hp *(627 kW)* sustained; 2 shafts
Speed, knots: 28
Complement: 9 (1 officer)
Guns: 2—7.62 mm MGs.

Comment: Three completed 1976, remainder in 1977 by Halter Marine, New Orleans.

8 SR N6 HOVERCRAFT

Displacement, tons: 10.9 full load
Dimensions, feet (metres): 48.5 × 23 × 3.9 (skirt) *(14.8 × 7 × 1.2)*
Main machinery: 1 Rolls-Royce Gnome 1050 gas turbine; 1050 hp *(783 kW)*
Speed, knots: 60. **Range, miles:** 170 at 54 kts
Complement: 3
Military lift: 20 troops plus 5 tons equipment
Guns: 1—7.62 mm MG.

Comment: First eight acquired from British Hovercraft Corporation Ltd, between February and December 1970. Eight more ordered in 1980 of which two delivered in 1981, four in 1982 and two in 1983. First eight have been scrapped.

SR N6 Hovercraft — *11/1981, G. S. Long*

1 TRAINING SHIP

TABBOUK

Displacement, tons: 350
Dimensions, feet (metres): 196.8 × 32.8 × 5.8 *(60 × 10 × 1.8)*
Main machinery: 2 MTU 16V 538 TB 80 diesels; 5000 hp(m) *(3.68 MW)* sustained; 2 shafts
Speed, knots: 20. **Range, miles:** 3500 at 12 kts
Complement: 24 plus 36 trainees
Guns: 1 Oerlikon GAM-BO1 20 mm.
Radars: Navigation: Racal Decca TM 1226; I band.

Comment: Built by Bayerischen Schiffbau, Germany and commissioned 1 December 1977. Based at Jiddah.

10 SLINGSBY SAH 2200 HOVERCRAFT

Dimensions, feet (metres): 34.8 × 13.8 *(10.6 × 4.2)*
Main machinery: 1 Deutz BF 6L 913C diesel; 190 hp(m) *(140 kW)* sustained; lift and propulsion
Speed, knots: 40. **Range, miles:** 500 at 40 kts
Military lift: 2.2 tons or 24 troops
Guns: 1—7.62 mm MG.

Comment: First three supplied in 1990. Final total could be up to 30 for coastal defence and oil rig protection. Have Kevlar armour.

SLINGSBY 2200 — *1991*

1 ROYAL YACHT (COAST GUARD)

Name	*No*	*Builders*	*Commissioned*
ABDUL AZIZ	—	Halsingør Waerft, Denmark	12 June 1984

Displacement, tons: 5000 full load
Measurement, tons: 1450 dwt
Dimensions, feet (metres): 482.2 × 59.2 × 16.1 *(147 × 18 × 4.9)*
Main machinery: 2 Lindholmen-Pielstick 12 PC 2.5V diesels; 15 600 hp(m) *(11.47 MW)* sustained; 2 shafts
Speed, knots: 22.5
Complement: 65 plus 4 Royal berths and 60 spare
Helicopters: 1 Bell 206B JetRanger type.

Comment: Completed March 1983 for subsequent fitting out at Vosper's Ship Repairers, Southampton. Helicopter hangar set in hull forward of bridge—covers extend laterally to form pad. Swimming pool. Stern ramp leading to garage.

ABDUL AZIZ — *6/1984, W. Sartori*

300 INSHORE PATROL CRAFT

Comment: There are 200 of 16.7 ft *(5.1 m)* with a 40 hp Q-17 engine and 100 of 13.8 ft *(4.2 m)* with a 20 hp engine.

3 SMALL TANKERS

AL FORAT, DAJLAH +1

Comment: Of 88.6 ft *(27 m)*. Named ships in Red Sea.

3 FIREFIGHTING CRAFT

JUBAIL, JIDDAH, DAMMAM

Comment: Built by Vosper Private Ltd, Singapore.

1 FIREFIGHTING/ANTI-POLLUTION CRAFT

Comment: Of 52 m with three MTU diesels. Ordered from Damen, Netherlands in March 1983.

MISCELLANEOUS

Comment: Two yachts *(Al Deriyah* and *Promineut)*, five barges and four motor dhows (1192, 1193, 1353, 1474).

135 COASTAL PATROL CRAFT

Number/Type	*Length*	*Comment*
7 84-5, 88-91, 569	68.9 ft *(21 m)*	Steel hulls. 569 in Gulf; remainder in Red Sea.
33 92, 97-105, 107-114, 116-7, 120-3, 125-6, 565, 570-71, 574-77	44.3 ft *(13.5 m)*	Steel hulls. 500 series in Gulf; remainder in Red Sea.
4 Brooke Marine	82 ft *(25 m)*	Built in 1979.
2 Brooke Marine	52.5 ft *(16 m)*	Built in 1979.
8 Japanese; 11-18	32.5 ft *(9.9 m)*	2 General Motors diesels; 280 hp. 11 and 12 in Gulf; remainder in Red Sea.
29 Whittingham and Mitchell UK	45 ft *(13.7 m)*	2 diesels; 362 hp. One 12.7 mm MG.
41 Northshore Yard UK; C80 class	29.3 ft *(8.9 m)*	1 diesel (pumpjet); 210 hp. GRP hull. One 7.62 mm MG. Delivered 1975.
10 Fairey Marine Huntress; 1-5, 229, 233-36.	23 ft *(7 m)*	1 diesel; 180 hp. Endurance, 150 miles at 20 kts. Delivered 1976. 1-5 in Gulf; remainder in Red Sea.

SENEGAL

Political

On 1 February 1982 the two countries of Senegal and The Gambia united to form the confederation of Senegambia, which included merging the armed forces. Confederation was cancelled on 30 September 1989 and the forces again became national and independent of each other.

Head of Navy:
Captain Alexandre Diam

Personnel

(a) 1992: 700 officers and men
(b) 2 years' conscript service

Bases

Dakar, Casamance

Mercantile Marine

Lloyd's Register of Shipping:
167 vessels of 54 862 tons gross

LIGHT FORCES

1 IMPROVED OSPREY 55 CLASS

Name	*No*	*Builders*	*Commissioned*
FOUTA	—	Danyard A/S, Fredrikshavn	1 June 1987

Displacement, tons: 470 full load
Dimensions, feet (metres): 180.5 × 33.8 × 8.5 *(55 × 10.3 × 2.6)*
Main machinery: 2 MAN Burmeister & Wain Alpha 12V 23/30-DVO diesels; 4400 hp(m) *(3.23 MW)* sustained; 2 shafts; cp props
Speed, knots: 20. **Range, miles:** 4000 at 16 kts
Complement: 38 (4 officers) plus 8 spare berths
Guns: 2 Hispano Suiza 30 mm.
Radars: Surface search: Furuno FR 1411; I band.
Navigation: Furuno FR 1221; I band.

Comment: Ordered in 1985. Intended for patrolling the EEZ rather than as a warship, hence the modest armament. A 25 knot rigid inflatable boat can be launched from a stern ramp which has a protective hinged door. Similar vessels built for Morocco and Greece.

FOUTA (without guns) *1987, Danyard A/S*

3 INTERCEPTOR CLASS (COASTAL PATROL CRAFT)

Name	*No*	*Builders*	*Commissioned*
SÉNÉGAL II	—	Les Bateaux Turbec Ltd, Sainte Catherine, Canada	Feb 1979
SINE-SALOUM II	—	Les Bateaux Turbec Ltd, Sainte Catherine, Canada	16 Nov 1979
CASAMANCE II	—	Les Bateaux Turbec Ltd, Sainte Catherine, Canada	Aug 1979

Displacement, tons: 62 full load
Dimensions, feet (metres): 86.9 × 19.3 × 5.2 *(26.5 × 5.8 × 1.6)*
Main machinery: 2 diesels; 2700 hp *(2.01 MW)*; 2 shafts
Speed, knots: 32.5
Guns: 2 Oerlikon 20 mm.

Comment: Used for EEZ patrol. Doubtful operational status.

CASAMANCE II *9/1979, van Ginderen Collection*

1 PR 72M CLASS

Name	*No*	*Builders*	*Commissioned*
NJAMBUUR	P 773	SFCN, Villeneuve-la-Garenne	1983

Displacement, tons: 375 standard; 451 full load
Dimensions, feet (metres): 192.5 × 24.9 × 7.2 *(58.7 × 7.6 × 2.2)*
Main machinery: 4 SACM AGO 195 V16 RVR diesels; 11 760 hp(m) *(8.64 MW)* sustained; 4 shafts
Speed, knots: 29. **Range, miles:** 2500 at 16 kts
Complement: 39 plus 7 passengers
Guns: 2 OTO Melara 3 in *(76 mm)* compact.
2 Oerlikon 20 mm F2.
Fire control: 2 CSEE Naja optronic directors.
Radars: Surface search: Racal Decca 1226; I band

Comment: Ordered in 1979. Completed September 1981 for shipping of armament at Lorient.

NJAMBUUR *1983*

3 P 48 CLASS (LARGE PATROL CRAFT)

Name	*No*	*Builders*	*Commissioned*
SAINT LOUIS	—	Ch Navales Franco-Belges	1 Mar 1971
POPENGUINE	—	Soc Française de Constructions Navales	10 Aug 1974
PODOR	—	Soc Française de Constructions Navales	13 July 1977

Displacement, tons: 250 full load
Dimensions, feet (metres): 156 × 23.3 × 8.1 *(47.5 × 7.1 × 2.5)*
Main machinery: 2 SACM AGO V12 CZSHR diesels; 4340 hp(m) *(3.2 MW)*; 2 shafts
Speed, knots: 23. **Range, miles:** 2000 at 16 kts
Complement: 33 (3 officers)
Guns: 2 Bofors 40 mm/70.

Comment: Ordered by Senegal. Sisters to *Malaika* of Madagascar, *Le Vigilant* and *Le Valeureux* of Ivory Coast and Bizerte class of Tunisian Navy. *Podor* ordered August 1975.

P 48 Class *1972*

2 FAIREY MARINE TRACKER 2 CLASS (COASTAL PATROL CRAFT)

Name	*No*	*Builders*	*Commissioned*
CHALLENGE	P 3	Fairey Marine, UK	1978
CHAMPION	P 4	Fairey Marine, UK	1978

Displacement, tons: 34
Dimensions, feet (metres): 65.7 × 17 × 4.8 *(20 × 5.2 × 1.5)*
Main machinery: 2 GM 12V 71 TI diesels; 820 hp *(612 kW)* sustained; 2 shafts
Speed, knots: 24. **Range, miles:** 650 at 20 kts
Complement: 11
Guns: 1 Oerlikon 20 mm. 2—7.62 mm MGs.
Radars: Surface search: Racal Decca; I band.

Comment: Hull and superstructure of GRP. Air-conditioned accommodation. The third of the class belongs to the Gambia.

TRACKER 2 Class (Gambia number) *1/1990, E. Grove*

LAND-BASED MARITIME AIRCRAFT

Numbers/Type: 1 de Havilland Canada DHC-6 Twin Otter.
Operational speed: 168 kts *(311 km/h)*.
Service ceiling: 23 200 ft *(7070 m)*.
Range: 1460 nm *(2705 km)*.
Role/Weapon systems: MR for coastal surveillance but effectiveness limited. Backed up by a French Navy Breguet Atlantique based at Dakar. Sensors: Search radar. Weapons: Unarmed.

Numbers/Type: 1 Embraer EMB-111 Bandeirante.
Operational speed: 194 kts *(360 km/h)*.
Service ceiling: 25 500 ft *(7770 m)*.
Range: 1590 nm *(2945 km)*.
Role/Weapon systems: Armed reconnaissance and surface search. Sensors: Litton APS-128 radar. Weapons: ASV; 70 mm and 127 mm rockets only.

AMPHIBIOUS FORCES

1 FRENCH TYPE 700 EDIC (LCT)

Name	*No*	*Builders*	*Commissioned*
KARABANE	841	SFCN, Villeneuve-la-Garenne	30 Jan 1987

Displacement, tons: 730 full load
Dimensions, feet (metres): 193.5 × 39 × 5.6 *(59 × 11.9 × 1.7)*
Main machinery: 2 SACM MGO 175 V12 ASH diesels; 1200 hp(m) *(882 kW)* sustained; 2 shafts
Speed, knots: 12. **Range, miles:** 1800 at 10 kts
Complement: 18 (33 spare billets)
Military lift: 12 trucks; 340 tons equipment
Guns: Fitted for 2 Oerlikon 20 mm.

Comment: Ordered May 1985, delivered 23 June 1986. Replaced similar LCT *Damour*.

1 Ex-FRENCH EDIC (LCT)

LA FALENCE (ex-9095)

Displacement, tons: 250 standard; 670 full load
Dimensions, feet (metres): 193.5 × 39.2 × 4.5 *(59 × 12 × 1.3)*
Main machinery: 2 SACM MGO diesels; 1000 hp(m) *(735 kW)*; 2 shafts
Speed, knots: 8
Complement: 16
Military lift: 10 trucks or 5 LCPs
Guns: 2 Oerlikon 20 mm.

Comment: Launched 7 April 1958. Transferred to Senegal 1 July 1974.

2 Ex-US LCM 6 CLASS

DIOU LOULOU (ex-6723) **DIOMBOS** (ex-6733)

Displacement, tons: 62 full load
Dimensions, feet (metres): 56.2 × 14 × 3.9 *(17.1 × 4.3 × 1.2)*
Main machinery: 2 Gray Marine 64 HN9 diesels; 330 hp *(264 kW)*; 2 shafts
Speed, knots: 10
Military lift: 34 tons or 80 troops

Comment: Transferred to Senegal July 1968.

MISCELLANEOUS

1 TENDER

CRAME JEAN (ex-*Raymond Sarr*)

Comment: An 18 ton fishing boat used as training craft since 1979.

2 TUGS

IBIS **AIGRETTE**

Displacement, tons: 56
Dimensions, feet (metres): 60.4 × 18.7 × 8.2 *(18.4 × 5.7 × 2.5)*
Main machinery: 1 SACM Poyaud diesel; 250 hp(m) *(184 kW)*; 1 shaft
Speed, knots: 9. **Range, miles:** 1700 at 9 kts

Comment: Lent by France.

CUSTOMS SERVICE

2 TYPE DS-01 (COASTAL PATROL CRAFT)

Displacement, tons: 22
Dimensions, feet (metres): 52.5 × 15.1 × 7.5 *(16 × 4.6 × 2.3)*
Main machinery: 2 GM diesels; 970 hp *(724 kW)*; 2 shafts
Speed, knots: 20
Complement: 8
Guns: 1—12.7 mm MG.

Comment: Ordered A T Celaya, Bilbao March 1981. Delivered 9 February 1982.

4 LVI 85 S CLASS

DJIBRIL **N'DIAYE** **GORÉE** **DJILOR**

Displacement, tons: 3.4
Speed, knots: 18

Comment: Ordered from Aresa, Barcelona and delivered in mid-1987 after long delays.

ARESA patrol craft *1980, Aresa*

SEYCHELLES

Senior Appointment

Commander of the Navy:
Major Paul Hodoul

Base

Port Victoria, Mahé

Personnel

1992: 200 officers and men

Mercantile Marine

Lloyd's Register of Shipping:
8 vessels of 3886 tons gross

PATROL CRAFT

1 Ex-SOVIET TURYA CLASS

ZOROASTER

Displacement, tons: 190 standard; 250 full load
Dimensions, feet (metres): 129.9 × 24.9 × 5.9 *(39.6 × 7.6 × 1.8)*
Main machinery: 3 Type M504 diesels; 15 000 hp *(11 MW)*; 3 shafts
Speed, knots: 18. **Range, miles:** 1450 at 14 kts
Complement: 30
Guns: 2—57 mm/70 (twin). 2—25 mm/80 (twin).
Depth charges: 1 rack.
Radars: Surface search: Pot Drum; H/I band.
Fire control: Muff Cob; G/H band.
Sonars: Helicopter type VDS; active search and attack; high frequency.

Comment: Craft presented by USSR 21 June 1986. Same as Turya class except torpedo tubes and hydrofoils removed. Seychelles crew trained in USSR. Russian Commanding Officer and Executive Officer returned to USSR in August 1986. The retention of the sonar is unusual in the export version as is the removal of the hydrofoils.

ZOROASTER *1988, PDFS*

1 TYPE FPB 42 (LARGE PATROL CRAFT)

Name	*No*	*Builders*	*Commissioned*
ANDROMACHE	— (ex-605)	Picchiotti, Viareggio	10 Jan 1983

Displacement, tons: 268 full load
Dimensions, feet (metres): 137.8 × 26 × 8.2 *(41.8 × 8 × 2.5)*
Main machinery: 2 Paxman Valenta 16 CM diesels; 6650 hp *(5 MW)* sustained; 2 shafts
Speed, knots: 26. **Range, miles:** 3000 at 16 kts
Complement: 22 (3 officers)
Guns: 1 Oerlikon 25 mm. 2—7.62 mm MGs.
Radars: Navigation: Furuno; I band.

Comment: Ordered from Inma, La Spezia in November 1981. Pennant numbers no longer worn. A second of class reported ordered in 1991.

ANDROMACHE *1988, PDFS*

1 Ex-FRENCH SIRIUS CLASS (LARGE PATROL CRAFT)

TOPAZ (ex-*Croix du Sud*)

Displacement, tons: 440 full load
Dimensions, feet (metres): 152 × 28 × 8.2 *(46.4 × 8.6 × 2.5)*
Main machinery: 2 SEMT-Pielstick diesels; 2000 hp(m) *(1.47 MW)*; 2 shafts
Speed, knots: 15. **Range, miles:** 3000 at 10 kts
Complement: 38
Guns: 1 Bofors 40 mm/60. 1 Oerlikon 20 mm.

Comment: Ex-French minesweeper built in 1956 and transferred without sweep gear in January 1979. Paid off in 1987 but brought back into service in late 1990. Not in good repair.

2 Ex-SOVIET ZHUK CLASS (COASTAL PATROL CRAFT)

CONSTANT **FORTUNE**

Displacement, tons: 50 full load
Dimensions, feet (metres): 75.4 × 17 × 6.2 *(23 × 5.2 × 1.9)*
Main machinery: 2 M50 diesels; 2400 hp *(1.76 MW)*; 2 shafts
Speed, knots: 30. **Range, miles:** 1100 at 15 kts
Complement: 17
Guns: 4—14.5 mm (2 twin) MGs.
Radars: Surface search: Furuno; I band.

Comment: Transferred from Black Sea on 11 October 1981 and 6 November 1982.

FORTUNE *3/1990*

1 COASTAL PATROL CRAFT

JUNON

Displacement, tons: 40 approx
Dimensions, feet (metres): 60 × — × — *(18.3 × — × —)*
Main machinery: 2 GM diesels; 1040 hp *(746 kW)*; 2 shafts
Speed, knots: 26. **Range, miles:** 1000 at 22 kts

Comment: Built by Tyler, UK in 1980.

JUNON *1989, PDFS*

1 LANDING CRAFT (TANK)

Name	*No*	*Builders*	*Commissioned*
CINQ JUIN	—	La Perrière, France	11 Jan 1979

Displacement, tons: 855 full load
Dimensions, feet (metres): 186.8 × 38 × 6 *(56.9 × 11.6 × 1.9)*
Main machinery: 2 Poyaud A12 150M diesels; 880 hp(m) *(647 kW)*; 2 shafts
Speed, knots: 9. **Range, miles:** 2000 at 8 kts
Military lift: 300 tons plus 1 LCP

Comment: Ordered 12 December 1977. Although government-owned, this ship is commercially operated except for occasional exercises.

CINQ JUIN *1986, PDFS*

LAND-BASED MARITIME AIRCRAFT

Numbers/Type: 1 Fairchild Merlin IIIB.
Operational speed: 309 kts *(571 km/h)*.
Service ceiling: 31 400 ft *(9570 m)*.
Range: 2468 nm *(4574 km)*.
Role/Weapon systems: Reconnaissance aircraft for coastal patrol. Sensors: Search radar. Weapons: Unarmed.

Numbers/Type: 2 HAL (Aerospatiale) Chetak (Alouette III).
Operational speed: 113 kts *(210 km/h)*.
Service ceiling: 10 500 ft *(3200 m)*.
Range: 290 nm *(540 km)*.
Role/Weapon systems: Support helicopter; used for police and anti-smuggler patrols. Sensors: None. Weapons: 2 × 7.62 mm machine guns can be fitted.

Numbers/Type: 1 Pilatus Britten-Norman Maritime Defender.
Operational speed: 150 kts *(280 km/h)*.
Service ceiling: 18 900 ft *(5760 m)*.
Range: 1500 nm *(2775 km)*.
Role/Weapon systems: Coastal surveillance and surface search aircraft. Sensors: Search radar. Weapons: Provision for rockets or guns.

SIERRA LEONE

Senior Appointment

Commander of Navy:
Lieutenant Commander Alimany Sasay

Personnel

(a) 1992: 158 officers and men
(b) Voluntary service

Base

Freetown

Mercantile Marine

Lloyd's Register of Shipping:
59 vessels of 20 733 tons gross

PATROL FORCES

Note: In addition to the naval ships there is a vessel, *Maritime Protector* (ex-*Arctic Prowler*), chartered by the government from Maritime Protection Services to enforce Fishery Protection laws. This is a 46 m ship built in Canada in 1959 and formerly used by the Canadian Department of Fisheries and Oceans.

2 SHANGHAI II CLASS (FAST ATTACK CRAFT—GUN)

MOA NAIMBANA

Displacement, tons: 113 standard; 131 full load
Dimensions, feet (metres): 127.3 × 17.7 × 5.6 *(38.8 × 5.4 × 1.7)*
Main machinery: 2 Type L12-180 diesels; 2400 hp(m) *(1.76 MW)* (forward); 2 Type L12-180Z diesels; 1820 hp(m) *(1.34 MW)* (aft); 4 shafts
Speed, knots: 30. **Range, miles:** 700 at 16.5 kts
Complement: 34
Guns: 2 China 37 mm/63 (twin); 85° elevation; 180 rounds/minute to 8.5 km *(4.6 nm)*; weight of shell 1.42 kg.
4 USSR 25 mm/60 (2 twin); 85° elevation; 270 rounds/minute to 3 km *(1.6 nm)* anti-aircraft; weight of shell 0.34 kg.
Mines: Mine rails can be fitted for 10 mines.
Radars: Surface search: Skin Head or Pot Head; I band.

Comment: Delivered in March 1987. Chinese technicians were loaned for maintenance work and training. These craft only have one twin 37 mm gun (forward) vice two in Chinese craft. Only one was serviceable in early 1992.

1 SWIFT 105 FT CLASS (LARGE PATROL CRAFT)

FARANDUGU

Displacement, tons: 103 full load
Dimensions, feet (metres): 105 × 22 × 7 *(31.5 × 6.7 × 2.1)*
Main machinery: 4 MTU 12V 331 TC 92 diesels; 5320 hp(m) *(3.92 MW)* sustained; 4 shafts
Speed, knots: 25. **Range, miles:** 1200 at 12 kts
Complement: 19
Guns: 2—12.7 mm MGs. 2—7.62 mm MGs.

Comment: Laid down under FMS funding by Swiftships in October 1987 and apparently delivered in December 1989 although this is not confirmed.

1 HALMATIC CLASS (INSHORE PATROL CRAFT)

Displacement, tons: 13.5 full load
Dimensions, feet (metres): 40.3 × 11.2 × 3.3 *(12.3 × 3.4 × 1)*
Main machinery: 2 Volvo Penta TAMD 70E diesels; 530 hp *(386 kW)*; 2 shafts
Speed, knots: 23
Guns: Can carry 1—7.62 mm MG.

Comment: Built by Halmatic, UK in 1987. Used mainly for Pilot duties.

2 CAT 900S CLASS (INSHORE PATROL CRAFT)

Displacement, tons: 7.4 full load
Dimensions, feet (metres): 34.1 × 9.5 × 2.6 *(10.4 × 2.9 × 0.8)*
Main machinery: 2 Volvo Penta TAMD 41A diesels; 400 hp(m) *(294 kW)* sustained; 2 shafts
Speed, knots: 30
Complement: 4

Comment: Built by Cougar Holdings Ltd, Hamble and completed in May 1988. Catamaran hulls. Both unserviceable in early 1992.

3 LANDING CRAFT (LCU)

POMPOLI GULAMA KAILONDO

Displacement, tons: 634 full load
Dimensions, feet (metres): 180.4 × 38.1 × 4.9 *(55 × 11.6 × 1.5)*
Main machinery: 1 Yanmer diesel; 1 shaft
Speed, knots: 13. **Range, miles:** 1540 at 12 kts
Complement: 13 (6 officers)
Military lift: 262 troops; 31 small vehicles

Comment: Built by Shikoku (first pair) and Kegoya, Japan. Delivered 14 May 1980. Flush deck construction; bow and stern ramps; used as troop transports in protected waters.

SINGAPORE

Headquarters' Appointment

Chief of the Navy:
Commodore Teo Chee Hean

Personnel

(a) 1992: 4500 officers and men including 1800 conscripts
(b) National Service: 2½ years for Corporals and above; 2 years for the remainder
(c) 4500 reservists

Base

Pulau Brani, Tuas (Jurong) (by 1994)

Prefix to Ships' Names

RSS

Organisation

Missile Corvettes (188)
Missile Boat Squadron (185)
Patrol Craft Squadron (182)
Coastal Patrol Craft Squadron (183/186)
Landing Ship Squadron (191)
Support Ship Squadron (194)

Maritime Air

The navy has no separate air arm but the Air Force has Grumman E 2C Hawkeyes (see *Land-based Maritime Aircraft* section) and several reconnaissance aircraft. In addition the Air Force has more than 50 A4 Skyhawks, (possibly with Harpoon when modernised), and eight F16 A/B. There is a requirement for up to eight maritime patrol aircraft.

Mercantile Marine

Lloyd's Register of Shipping:
854 vessels of 8 488 172 tons gross

Strength of the Fleet

Type	*Active*	*Building (Projected)*
Missile Corvettes	6	—
Fast Attack Craft—Missile	6	—
Fast Attack Craft—Gun	6	(6)
Coastal Patrol Craft	12	—
Inshore Patrol Craft	12	—
Minesweepers—Coastal	1	4
LSTs	4 (1)	—
LCMs	8	—
LHC	1	—
Training Ships	1	—
Diving Support Vessel	1	—

DELETIONS

1988-89 *Brani, Berlayer*
1990 *Utara, Jupiter* (old)
1991 *Panglima*

MISSILE CORVETTES

6 VICTORY CLASS

Name	No	Builders	Launched	Commissioned
VICTORY	P 88	Lürssen Werft, Bremen	8 June 1988	18 Aug 1990
VALOUR	P 89	Singapore SB and Marine	10 Dec 1988	18 Aug 1990
VIGILANCE	P 90	Singapore SB and Marine	27 Apr 1989	18 Aug 1990
VALIANT	P 91	Singapore SB and Marine	22 July 1989	25 May 1991
VIGOUR	P 92	Singapore SB and Marine	1 Dec 1989	25 May 1991
VENGEANCE	P 93	Singapore SB and Marine	23 Feb 1990	25 May 1991

Displacement, tons: 550 full load
Dimensions, feet (metres): 204.4 × 27.9 × 8.5 *(62.3 × 8.5 × 2.6)*
Main machinery: 4 MTU 16V 538 TB93 diesels; 15 020 hp(m) *(11 MW)* sustained; 4 shafts
Speed, knots: 35. **Range, miles:** 4000 at 18 kts
Complement: 49 (8 officers)

Missiles: SSM: 8 McDonnell Douglas Harpoon; active radar homing to 130 km *(70 nm)* at 0.9 Mach; warhead 227 kg.
SAM: Rafael Barak I to be fitted.
Guns: 1 OTO Melara 3 in *(76 mm)*/62 Super Rapid; 85° elevation; 120 rounds/minute to 16 km *(8.7 nm)*; weight of shell 6 kg.
Torpedoes: 6—324 mm Whitehead B 515 (2 triple) tubes. Whitehead A 244; anti-submarine; active/passive homing to 7 km *(3.8 nm)* at 33 kts; warhead 34 kg (shaped charge).
Countermeasures: Decoys: Plessey Shield Chaff launcher.
ESM/ECM: Rafael RAN 1101 intercept and jammer.
Fire control: BEAB 9LV 200 Mk 3
Radars: Surface search: Ericsson/Radamec Sea Giraffe; G/H band.
Navigation: Racal Decca; I band.
Fire control: Bofors Electronic 9LV 200; I/J band.
Sonars: EDO 780; VDS; active search and attack; 13, 7 or 5 kHz.

Programmes: Ordered in June 1986 to a Lürssen MGB 62 design similar to Bahrain and UAE vessels.
Structure: Close range armament is to include Barak I CIWS which may start being installed in 1992. Reported but not confirmed that a Sewaco combat data system is fitted. Trials are being done on stabilisers to try and improve roll characteristics.
Operational: Form Squadron 188.

VIGOUR *10/1991, John Mortimer*

LIGHT FORCES

6 LÜRSSEN FPB 45 CLASS (FAST ATTACK CRAFT—MISSILE)

Name	No	Builders	Commissioned
SEA WOLF	P 76	Lürssen Werft, Vegesack	1972
SEA LION	P 77	Lürssen Werft, Vegesack	1972
SEA DRAGON	P 78	Singapore SBEC	1974
SEA TIGER	P 79	Singapore SBEC	1974
SEA HAWK	P 80	Singapore SBEC	1975
SEA SCORPION	P 81	Singapore SBEC	29 Feb 1976

Displacement, tons: 226 standard; 254 full load
Dimensions, feet (metres): 147.3 × 23 × 7.5 *(44.9 × 7 × 2.3)*
Main machinery: 4 MTU 16V 538 TB92 diesels; 13 640 hp(m) *(10 MW)* sustained; 4 shafts
Speed, knots: 38. **Range, miles:** 950 at 30 kts; 1800 at 15 kts
Complement: 36 (6 officers)

Missiles: SSM: 4 McDonnell Douglas Harpoon (2 twin); active radar homing to 130 km *(70 nm)* at 0.9 Mach; warhead 227 kg.
2 IAI Gabriel I launchers; radar or optical guidance; semi-active radar homing to 20 km *(10.8 nm)* at 0.7 Mach; warhead 75 kg.
Guns: 1 Bofors 57 mm/70 (not in all); 75° elevation; 200 rounds/minute to 17 km *(9.3 nm)*; weight of shell 2.4 kg.
1 Bofors 40 mm/70; 90° elevation; 300 rounds/minute to 12 km *(6.6 nm)*; weight of shell 0.96 kg.
Countermeasures: ESM/ECM: Racal intercept and jammer.
Radars: Surface search: Racal Decca; I band.
Fire control: Signaal WM 28/5; I/J band; range 46 km *(25 nm)*.

Programmes: Designed by Lürssen Werft which built the first pair.
Modernisation: *Sea Hawk* was the first to complete refit in January 1988 with two sets of twin Harpoon launchers replacing the triple Gabriel launcher. The remainder were converted by December 1990 with the exception of *Sea Wolf* which finished refit in Spring 1991. ECM equipment has also been fitted on a taller mast.

SEA HAWK *4/1990, 92 Wing RAAF*

3 VOSPER TYPE A (FAST ATTACK CRAFT—GUN)

Name	No	Builders	Commissioned
INDEPENDENCE	P 69	Vosper Thornycroft Ltd, Gosport	8 July 1970
FREEDOM	P 70	Vosper Thornycroft Private Ltd, Singapore	11 Jan 1971
JUSTICE	P 72	Vosper Thornycroft Private Ltd, Singapore	23 Apr 1971

Displacement, tons: 112 standard; 142 full load
Dimensions, feet (metres): 109.6 × 21 × 5.6 *(33.5 × 6.4 × 1.8)*
Main machinery: 2 Maybach MTU 16V 538 TB 90 diesels; 3580 hp(m) *(2.63 MW)* sustained; 2 shafts
Speed, knots: 32. **Range, miles:** 1100 at 14 kts
Complement: 19-22 (3 officers)
Guns: 1 Bofors 40 mm/70 fwd; 90° elevation; 300 rounds/minute to 12 km *(6.6 nm)*; weight of shell 0.96 kg.
1 Oerlikon 20 mm/80 aft; 55° elevation; 800 rounds/minute to 2 km.
Radars: Surface search: Racal Decca; I band.
Navigation: Decca 626; I band.

Comment: Ordered on 21 May 1968. Two sub-types, the first of each *(Independence* and *Sovereignty)* built in UK, the remainder in Singapore.

JUSTICE *4/1990, 92 Wing RAAF*

FREEDOM *1989, Singapore Navy*

3 VOSPER TYPE B (FAST ATTACK CRAFT—GUN)

Name	*No*	*Builders*	*Commissioned*
SOVEREIGNTY	P 71	Vosper Thornycroft Ltd, Gosport	Feb 1971
DARING	P 73	Vosper Thornycroft Private Ltd, Singapore	18 Sep 1971
DAUNTLESS	P 74	Vosper Thornycroft Private Ltd, Singapore	July 1971

Displacement, tons: 112 standard; 142 full load
Dimensions, feet (metres): 109.6 × 21 × 5.6 *(33.5 × 6.4 × 1.8)*
Main machinery: 2 Maybach MTU 16V 538 TB 90 diesels; 3580 hp(m) *(2.63 MW)* sustained; 2 shafts
Speed, knots: 32. **Range, miles:** 1000 at 14 kts
Complement: 19 (3 officers)
Guns: 1 Bofors 3 in *(76 mm)*/50; 30° elevation; 30 rounds/minute to 13 km *(7 nm)* surface fire only; weight of shell 5.9 kg.
1 Oerlikon 20 mm/80; 55° elevation; 800 rounds/minute to 2 km.
Radars: Surface search: Racal Decca; I band.
Fire control: Signaal WM 26; I/J band; range 46 km *(25 nm)*.

Comment: Steel hulls of round bilge form. Aluminium alloy superstructure.

DARING *3/1991, 92 Wing RAAF*

12 SWIFT CLASS (COASTAL PATROL CRAFT)

SWIFT KNIGHT P 11
SWIFT LANCER P 12
SWIFT SWORDSMAN P 14
SWIFT WARRIOR P 15
SWIFT ARCHER P 16
SWIFT WARLORD P 17
SWIFT COMBATANT P 18
SWIFT CHALLENGER P 19
SWIFT CAVALIER P 20
SWIFT CONQUEROR P 21
SWIFT CENTURION P 22
SWIFT CHIEFTAIN P 23

Displacement, tons: 45.7 full load
Dimensions, feet (metres): 74.5 × 20.3 × 5.2 *(22.7 × 6.2 × 1.6)*
Main machinery: 2 Deutz 816 diesels; 2660 hp(m) *(1.96 MW)*; 2 shafts
Speed, knots: 32. **Range, miles:** 550 at 20 kts; 900 at 10 kts
Complement: 12 (3 officers)
Guns: 1 Oerlikon 20 mm. 2—7.62 mm MGs.
Radars: Surface search: Decca 1226; I band.

Comment: Delivered by Singapore SBEC 20 October 1981. Fitted for but not with two Gabriel SSMs.

SWIFT LANCER *9/1991, 92 Wing RAAF*

12 INSHORE PATROL CRAFT

Displacement, tons: 20 full load
Dimensions, feet (metres): 47.6 × 13.5 × 3.6 *(14.5 × 4.1 × 1.1)*
Main machinery: 2 MTU 12V 183 TC 91 diesels; 1200 hp(m) *(882 kW)*; 2 shafts
Speed, knots: 30
Complement: 4
Guns: 1—7.62 mm MG.
Radars: Surface search: Racal Decca; I band.

Comment: Built by Singapore SBEC and delivered in 1990/91. Based at Brani.

FB 32 *1991, Singapore Navy*

LAND-BASED MARITIME AIRCRAFT

Note: A squadron of four Fokker F50 Maritime Enforcer II aircraft will be formed in 1994.

Numbers/Type: 4 Grumman E-2C Hawkeye.
Operational speed: 323 kts *(598 km/h)*.
Service ceiling: 30 800 ft *(9390 m)*.
Range: 1000 nm *(1850 km)*.
Role/Weapon systems: Delivered in 1987 for surveillance of shipping in sea areas around Singapore and South China Sea; understood to have priority assistance from US Government. Sensors: APS-125 radar; data link for SSM targeting; later aircraft will have APS-138 radar. Weapons: Unarmed.

MINE WARFARE FORCES

0 + 4 LANDSORT CLASS (MINEHUNTERS)

Displacement, tons: 360 full load
Dimensions, feet (metres): 155.8 × 31.5 × 7.3 *(47.5 × 9.6 × 2.2)*
Main machinery: 4 diesels; 2 shafts
Speed, knots: 15. **Range, miles:** 2000 at 12 kts
Complement: 26

Comment: Kockums/Karlskrona design selected in 1991. To be fitted with TSM 2061 tactical system and TSM 2022 minehunting sonar plus 2 PAP ROVs. All to be delivered by 1995. First one is to be built in Sweden; the remainder will be fitted out by Singapore SBEC.

1 Ex-US BLUEBIRD CLASS (MINESWEEPER—COASTAL)

Name	*No*	*Builders*	*Commissioned*
MERCURY (ex-USS *Whippoorwill* MSC 207)	M 102	Bellingham S Y	20 Oct 1955

Displacement, tons: 365 standard; 408 full load
Dimensions, feet (metres): 144 × 28 × 8.2 *(43.9 × 8.5 × 2.5)*
Main machinery: 2 GM 8-268A diesels; 880 hp *(656 kW)*; 2 shafts
Speed, knots: 12. **Range, miles:** 2500 at 10 kts
Complement: 39 (4 officers)
Guns: 1 Oerlikon 20 mm (not always fitted).
Radars: Surface search: Raytheon SPS 5; G/H band; range 37 km *(20 nm)*.
Sonars: UQS 1; hull-mounted; active minehunting; high frequency.

Comment: Transferred by sale 5 December 1975. Wooden hull. Minesweeping gear was removed as being inappropriate for the tasks in Singapore approaches but has now been replaced and the ship also acts as a platform for diving and salvage operations.

MERCURY *1976, Singapore Navy*

AMPHIBIOUS FORCES

4 AYER CHAWAN CLASS (LCM)

AYER CHAWAN RPL 54 **AYER MERBAN** RPL 55 **RPL 56** **RPL 57**

Displacement, tons: 60 light; 150 full load
Dimensions, feet (metres): 88.5 × 22 × 4 *(27 × 6.9 × 1.2)*
Main machinery: 2 diesels; 650 hp(m) *(478 kW)*; 2 shafts
Speed, knots: 10. **Range, miles:** 300 at 10 kts
Complement: 9
Military lift: 40 tons general or 20 tons fuel or 1 medium tank.

Comment: Built by Vosper Thornycroft Private Ltd, Singapore 1968-69.

AYER CHAWAN *1/1989, Hartmut Ehlers*

5 Ex-US 511-1152 CLASS (LSTs)

Name	*No*	*Builders*	*Commissioned*
ENDURANCE (ex-USS *Holmes County* LST 836)	L 201 (ex-A 82)	American Bridge Co	25 Nov 1944
EXCELLENCE (ex-US *LST 629*)	L 202 (ex-A 81)	Chicago Bridge & Iron Co	28 July 1944
INTREPID (ex-US *LST 579*)	L 203 (ex-A 83)	Missouri Valley B and I Co	21 July 1944
RESOLUTION (ex-US *LST 649*)	L 204 (ex-A 84)	Chicago Bridge & Iron Co	26 Oct 1944
PERSISTENCE (ex-US *LST 613*)	L 205 (ex-A 85)	Chicago Bridge & Iron Co	19 May 1944

Displacement, tons: 1653 light; 4100-4150 full load (modernised)
Dimensions, feet (metres): 328 × 50 × 14 *(100 × 15.2 × 4.3)*
Main machinery: 2 General Motors 12-567ATL diesels; 1800 hp *(1.34 MW)*; 2 shafts
Speed, knots: 11.6. **Range, miles:** 19 000 at 10.5 kts
Complement: 120 (15 officers)
Military lift: 1500 tons general; 500 tons beaching; 440 m² tank deck; 500 m² main deck storage; can carry 125 troops on long haul; 2—5 ton cranes; 2 LCVPs on davits

Guns: Up to 3 Bofors 40 mm/60; 80° elevation; 120 rounds/minute to 10 km *(5.5 nm)*; weight of shell 0.89 kg.
2—7.62 mm MGs.
Radars: Navigation: Decca 626; I band.
IFF: UPX 12.

Helicopters: Platform only.

Programmes: *Endurance* loaned from the US Navy on 1 July 1971 and bought on 5 December 1975. Remainder transferred 4 June 1976. One of the class *Perseverence* has been cannibalised for spares.
Modernisation: This class has been modernised since 1977. This includes new electrics, new communications, an enclosed bridge and updated command facilities. A goal-post derrick has been fitted forward of the bridge (except in *Endurance*) and the lattice mast replaced by a pole mast. *Excellence* has a helicopter pad aft, others have a landing spot amidships. Most have been re-engined.
Operational: Used as Command ships and in support of the Army. *Resolution* is in reserve.

PERSISTENCE *10/1991, van Ginderen Collection*

EXCELLENCE (with helo platform aft) *5/1990, G. Toremans*

4 RPL TYPE (LCM)

RPL 60 **RPL 61** **RPL 62** **RPL 63**

Displacement, tons: 151
Dimensions, feet (metres): 120.4 × 28 × 5.9 *(36.7 × 8.5 × 1.8)*
Main machinery: 2 MAN D2540 MLE diesels; 860 hp(m) *(632 kW)*; 2 Schottel props
Speed, knots: 10.7
Complement: 6
Military lift: 2 tanks or 450 troops or 110 tons cargo (fuel or stores)

Comment: First pair built at North Shipyard Point, second pair by Singapore SBEC. First two launched August 1985, next two in October 1985. Cargo deck 86.9 × 21.6 ft *(26.5 × 6.6 m)*. Bow ramp suitable for beaching.

RPL 61 *1/1989, Hartmut Ehlers*

450 ASSAULT CRAFT

Dimensions, feet (metres): 17.4 × 5.9 × 2.3 *(5.3 × 1.8 × 0.7)*
Main machinery: 1 outboard; 50 hp(m) *(37 kW)*
Speed, knots: 12
Military lift: 12 troops

Comment: Built by Singapore SBEC. Manportable craft which can carry a section of troops in the rivers and creeks surrounding Singapore island.

LANDING CRAFT (LCVP)

EP series

Comment: Fast Craft, Equipment and Personnel (FCEP) are used to transport troops around the Singapore archipelago. They have a single bow ramp, twin diesel and can carry a rifle platoon. May be Army manned. More than 100 are in service.

EP 04 *1/1989, Hartmut Ehlers*

1 TIGER 40 HOVERCRAFT (LHC)

Displacement, tons: 12
Dimensions, feet (metres): 54.1 × 19.7 *(16.5 × 6)*
Main machinery: 4 Deutz diesels; 760 hp(m) *(559 kW)* (for lift and propulsion)
Speed, knots: 35. **Range, miles:** 175 at 35 kts
Military lift: 30 troops or 2.6 tons equipment
Guns: 2—12.7 mm MGs.

Comment: Delivered by Singapore SBEC in 1987 for trials as a logistic support craft. More may be ordered.

TIGER 40 Class *3/1987, Singapore Shipbuilding and Engineering Co Ltd*

SUPPORT SHIPS

1 DIVING SUPPORT VESSEL

Name	*No*	*Builders*	*Commissioned*
JUPITER	A 102	Singapore SBEC	June 1990

Displacement, tons: 170 full load
Dimensions, feet (metres): 117.5 × 23.3 × 7.5 *(35.8 × 7.1 × 2.3)*
Main machinery: 2 Deutz MWM TBD 234 V12 diesels; 1360 hp(m) *(1 MW)* sustained; 2 shafts; bow thruster
Speed, knots: 14. **Range, miles:** 200 at 14 kts
Complement: 33 (5 officers)
Guns: 1 Oerlikon 20 mm.
Radars: Navigation: Racal Decca; I band.

Comment: Designed for underwater search and salvage operations and built to German naval standards. Secondary role of surveying. Equipped with a precise navigation system, towed sidescan sonar, and a remotely operated vehicle (ROV). The ship's diving support equipment comprises two high pressure compressors, a two-man decompression chamber, a rubber dinghy with 40 hp outboard motor and a 1.5 ton SWL crane.

JUPITER *9/1991, Guy Toremans*

TRAINING SHIP

Name	*No*	*Builders*	*Commissioned*
ENDEAVOUR	P 75	Schiffswerft Oberwinter, Germany	30 Sep 1970

Displacement, tons: 250 full load
Dimensions, feet (metres): 135 × 25 × 8 *(40.9 × 7.6 × 2.4)*
Main machinery: 2 Maybach diesels; 2600 hp(m) *(1.91 MW)*; 2 shafts
Speed, knots: 20. **Range, miles:** 800 at 8 kts
Complement: 24
Guns: 2 Oerlikon 20 mm.
Radars: Navigation: Racal Decca; I band.

Comment: Training ship for divers.

ENDEAVOUR *1976, Singapore Navy*

POLICE PATROL CRAFT

24 PATROL CRAFT

PX 10-33

Displacement, tons: 11
Dimensions, feet (metres): 37 × 10.5 × 1.6 *(11 × 3.2 × 0.5)*
Main machinery: 2 MTU diesels; 770 hp(m) *(566 kW)*; 2 shafts
Speed, knots: 30

Comment: Completed 1981 by Sembawang SY.

PX 14 *6/1990, F. Sadek*

23 PATROL CRAFT

PT 1-23

Displacement, tons: 20
Dimensions, feet (metres): 48.6 × 13.8 × 3.9 *(14.8 × 4.2 × 1.2)*
Main machinery: 2 MAN D2542 MLE or MTU 12V 183 TC 91 diesels; 1076 hp(m) *(791 kW)* or 1200 hp(m) *(882 kW)*; 2 shafts
Speed, knots: 30. **Range, miles:** 310 at 22 kts
Complement: 4 plus 8 spare berths
Guns: 1—7.62 mm MG.

Comment: First 13 completed by Singapore SBEC between January and August 1984, two more completed February 1987 and eight more (including two Command Boats) in 1989. Of aluminium construction. Four more operated by Customs and Excise. There are differences in the deck houses between earlier and later vessels.

PT 1 *9/1988, van Ginderen Collection*

34 PATROL CRAFT

PC 32-51 **PC 52-65**

Comment: First 20 were of 21.3 ft *(6.5 m)*, 35 kt craft from Vosper Thornycroft Private Ltd, built in 1978-79. Second series is still building with some used by the Navy. All have twin Johnson outboard engines.

PC 61 *4/1990, F. Sadek*

PILOT and CUSTOMS CRAFT

Note: Customs Craft include CE 1-4 and CE 5-8, the latter being sisters to PT 1 Police Craft. Pilot craft have GP numbers and include GP 40-57 built in 1989-90 by Cheoy Lee, Kowloon.

CE 2 *1/1989, Hartmut Ehlers*

SOLOMON ISLANDS

Control

Tulagi is operated by the Department of Fisheries. SIPV *Lata* and *Savo* are operated by the maritime wing of the Royal Solomon Islands Police Force.

Senior Officer

Commissioner of Police:
F Soaks

Personnel

1992: 30 (6 officers)

Prefix to Ships' Names

RSIPV

Mercantile Marine

Lloyd's Register of Shipping:
35 vessels of 8214 tons gross

DELETION

1989 1 LCU

PATROL FORCES

2 PACIFIC FORUM TYPE

Name	*No*	*Builders*	*Commissioned*
LATA	03	Australian Shipbuilding Industries	3 Sep 1988
AUKI	04	Australian Shipbuilding Industries	2 Nov 1991

Displacement, tons: 162 full load
Dimensions, feet (metres): 103.3 × 26.6 × 6.9 *(31.5 × 8.1 × 2.1)*
Main machinery: 2 Caterpillar 3516 TA diesels; 2820 hp *(2.1 MW)* sustained; 2 shafts
Speed, knots: 20. **Range, miles:** 2500 at 12 kts
Complement: 14 (1 officer)
Guns: 3—12.7 mm MGs (not always mounted).
Radars: Surface search: Furuno 1011; I band.

Comment: Built under the Australian Defence Co-operation Programme. Training, operational and technical assistance provided by the Royal Australian Navy. Aluminium construction. Nominal endurance of 10 days.

AUKI *12/1991, RAN*

2 LANDING CRAFT

LIGOMO 3 **ULUSAGE**

Measurement, tons: 105 dwt
Main machinery: 2 diesels; 2 shafts
Speed, knots: 9

Comment: Built by Carpenter BY, Suva in 1981. 27 m in length.

2 TUGS

SOLOMAN ATU **SOLOMAN KARIQUA**

Comment: Acquired in 1981. 140 tons and capable of 9 kts.

1 PATROL CRAFT

SAVO 02

Dimensions, feet (metres): 82 × 25.8 × 6.2 *(25 × 7.9 × 1.9)*
Main machinery: 2 Caterpillar 3412 TA diesels; 2000 hp *(1.49 MW)* sustained; 2 shafts
Speed, knots: 36. **Range, miles:** 3000 at 12 kts

Comment: Built by ASI, Western Australia in 1984 as a prototype for the Pacific Forum class which eventually finished 21 ft *(6.3 m)* longer.

SAVO *6/1991, van Ginderen Collection*

1 CARPENTARIA CLASS

TULAGI 01

Displacement, tons: 27 full load
Dimensions, feet (metres): 51.5 × 15.7 × 4.3 *(15.7 × 4.8 × 1.3)*
Main machinery: 2 GM 12V71 TI diesels; 840 hp *(626 kW)* sustained; 2 shafts
Speed, knots: 28. **Range, miles:** 950 at 18 kts
Complement: 10
Guns: 1—7.62 mm MG.
Radars: Surface search: Racal Decca; I band.

Comment: Built by De Havilland Marine, Homebush Bay, Australia. Launched December 1978. Arrived Solomon Islands 4 May 1979.

TULAGI *1984, van Ginderen Collection*

SOMALIA

General

After the revolution in January 1991, the Navy effectively ceased to exist. The only vessels which were not sunk were 1 Polnochny LST and 4 Mol class attack craft. All were ransacked with every fixture and fitting removed by mid-1991.

Bases

Berbera, Mogadishu and Kismayu

Mercantile Marine

Lloyd's Register of Shipping:
27 vessels of 17 011 tons gross

SOUTH AFRICA

Headquarters' Appointments

Chief of Defence Force Staff:
Vice Admiral M A Bekker
Chief of the Navy:
Vice Admiral L J Woodburne, DVR
Chief of Naval Support:
Rear Admiral R C Simpson-Anderson
Chief of Naval Operations:
Rear Admiral P R Viljoen

Personnel

(a) 1992: 4500
(b) Voluntary service plus 12 months' compulsory national service and 720 days' camps
(c) There are two intakes per year for Indian volunteers. This is due to the considerable response from this group of 800 000 who are not subject to conscription.

Prefix to Ships' Names

SAS (South African Ship/Suid Afrikaanse Skip)

Naval Bases

Pretoria: Headquarters and Command Centre
Durban: Attack Craft
Simonstown: Remainder of the Fleet
Saldanha Bay, Gordon's Bay, Walvis Bay (Namibia): minor bases.

Marine Corps

The Marine Branch was re-established in 1979 after its earlier stand-down in 1957. Disbanded again in 1990 as part of the defence cuts.

Strength of the Fleet

Type	*Active*
Submarines (Patrol)	3
Fast Attack Craft—Missile	9
Minesweepers (Coastal)	4
Minehunters (Coastal)	4
Survey Vessel	1
Fleet Replenishment Ships	2
TRV	1
Tugs	3
Harbour Patrol Launches	33
SAR Launches	2

Future Construction

The Navy plans to build six offshore patrol vessels of 2000 tons at Dorbyl, Durban by the end of the decade.

Mercantile Marine

Lloyd's Register of Shipping:
231 vessels of 340 148 tons gross

DELETIONS

Frigates

1990 *President Pretorius* (reserve), *President Steyn* (sunk)

Miscellaneous

1988 *Navigator, P 1552*

PENNANT LIST

Submarines

S 97	Maria Van Riebeeck
S 98	Emily Hobhouse
S 99	Johanna Van der Merwe

Light Forces

P 1561	Jan Smuts
P 1562	P W Botha
P 1563	Frederic Cresswell
P 1564	Jim Fouché
P 1565	Frans Erasmus
P 1566	Oswald Pirow
P 1567	Hendrik Mentz
P 1568	Kobie Coetsee
P 1569	Magnus Malan
P 3148	Fleur (TRV)

Mine Warfare Forces

M 1210	Kimberley
M 1214	Walvisbaai
M 1215	East London
M 1498	Windhoek
—	Umkomaas
—	Umhloti
—	Umzimkulu
—	Umgeni

Service Forces

A 243	Tafelberg
A 301	Drakensberg
A 324	Protea

SUBMARINES

3 FRENCH DAPHNE CLASS

Name	*No*	*Builders*	*Laid down*	*Launched*	*Commissioned*
MARIA VAN RIEBEECK	S 97	Dubigeon—Normandie, Nantes-Chantenay	14 Mar 1968	18 Mar 1969	22 June 1970
EMILY HOBHOUSE	S 98	Dubigeon—Normandie, Nantes-Chantenay	18 Nov 1968	24 Oct 1969	25 Jan 1971
JOHANNA VAN DER MERWE	S 99	Dubigeon—Normandie, Nantes-Chantenay	24 Apr 1969	21 July 1970	21 July 1971

Displacement, tons: 869 surfaced; 1043 dived
Dimensions, feet (metres): 189.6 × 22.3 × 15.1 *(57.8 × 6.8 × 4.6)*
Main machinery: Diesel-electric; 2 SEMT-Pielstick 12 PA4 V185 diesels; 2450 hp(m) *(1.8 MW)*; 2 Jeumont Schneider alternators; 1.7 MW; 2 motors; 2600 hp(m) *(1.9 MW)*; 2 shafts
Speed, knots: 13.5 surfaced; 16 dived
Range, miles: 4500 at 5 kts snorting; 2700 at 12.5 kts surfaced
Complement: 47 (6 officers)

Torpedoes: 12—21.7 in *(550 mm)* (8 bow, 4 stern) tubes. ECAN E15; dual purpose; passive homing to 12 km *(6.6 nm)* at 25 kts; warhead 300 kg; or ECAN L4/L5 to 9.5 km *(5.1 nm)*. No reloads.
Countermeasures: ESM: ARUD; radar warning.
Fire control: Trivetts-UEC weapon control system.
Radars: Surface search: Thomson-CSF Calypso II; I band; range 31 km *(17 nm)* for 10 m² target.
Sonars: Thomson Sintra DUUA 2; hull-mounted; active/passive search and attack; 8.4 kHz active.
Thomson Sintra DUUX 2; passive range finding.
Thomson Sintra DSUV 2; passive search; medium frequency.

Programmes: First submarines ordered for the South African Navy. Armscor are conducting a feasibility study into the local construction of additional submarines by Dorbyl Shipbuilders, Durban. Design would be similar to German S 209 class.
Modernisation: Weapon systems upgrading (including sonar) as well as improved habitability as part of a mid-life improvement programme. *Emily Hobhouse* completed in July 1988, *Van der Merwe* in late 1990.
Structure: French Daphne design, similar to those built in France for that country, Pakistan and Portugal and also built in Spain. Diving depth, 300 m *(985 ft)*.
Operational: In common with all small submarines, this class can be used for the deployment of underwater swimmers and chariots.

MARIA VAN RIEBEECK *10/1987, van Ginderen Collection*

LIGHT FORCES

9 MINISTER CLASS (FAST ATTACK CRAFT—MISSILE)

Name	*No*	*Builders*	*Commissioned*
JAN SMUTS	P 1561	Haifa Shipyard	18 July 1977
P W BOTHA	P 1562	Haifa Shipyard	2 Dec 1977
FREDERIC CRESSWELL	P 1563	Haifa Shipyard	6 Apr 1978
JIM FOUCHÉ	P 1564	Sandock Austral, Durban	22 Dec 1978
FRANS ERASMUS	P 1565	Sandock Austral, Durban	27 July 1979
OSWALD PIROW	P 1566	Sandock Austral, Durban	4 Mar 1980
HENDRIK MENTZ	P 1567	Sandock Austral, Durban	11 Feb 1983
KOBIE COETSEE	P 1568	Sandock Austral, Durban	11 Feb 1983
— (ex-*Magnus Malan*)	P 1569	Sandock Austral, Durban	4 July 1986

OSWALD PIROW *11/1991, Peter Humphries*

Displacement, tons: 430 full load
Dimensions, feet (metres): 204 × 25 × 8 *(62.2 × 7.8 × 2.4)*
Main machinery: 4 Maybach MTU 16V 965 TB 91 diesels; 15 000 hp(m) *(11 MW)* sustained; 4 shafts
Speed, knots: 32. **Range, miles:** 1500 at 30 kts; 3600+ at economical speed
Complement: 47 (7 officers)

Missiles: SSM: 8 Skerpioen; active radar or optical guidance; semi-active radar homing to 36 km *(19.4 nm)* at 0.7 Mach; warhead 75 kg. Another pair may be mounted. Skerpioen is an Israeli Gabriel II built under licence in South Africa.
Guns: 2 OTO Melara 3 in *(76 mm)*/62 compact; 85° elevation; 85 rounds/minute to 16 km *(8.7 nm)*; weight of shell 6 kg; 500 rounds per gun.
2 Oerlikon 20 mm. 2—12.7 mm MGs.
Countermeasures: Decoys: 4 launchers for Chaff.
ESM: Elta; radar warning.
Combat data systems: Mini action data automation with Link.
Radars: Air/surface search: Thomson-CSF Triton; G band; range 33 km *(18 nm)* for 2 m² target.
Fire control: Selenia RTN 10X; I/J band; range 40 km *(22 nm)*.

Programmes: Contract signed with Israel in late 1974 for this class, similar to Saar 4 class. Three built in Haifa and reached South Africa in July 1978. The ninth craft launched late March 1986. Three more improved vessels of this class were ordered but subsequently cancelled. The last of the class is known as P 1569.
Modernisation: *P W Botha* recommissioned 3 November 1986 after modernisation; *Kobie Coetsee* in July 1988; *Oswald Pirow* in May 1989.
Operational: Three were in reserve in early 1991. Seakeeping qualities are barely adequate and larger corvettes are required to replace them.

SHIPBORNE AIRCRAFT

Note: Super Frelon and Wasp helicopters paid off in 1990.

Numbers/Type: 10 Aerospatiale SA 330E/H/J Puma.
Operational speed: 139 kts *(258 km/h)*.
Service ceiling: 15 750 ft *(4800 m)*.
Range: 297 nm *(550 km)*.
Role/Weapon systems: Support helicopter; allocated by SAAF for naval duties and can be embarked in both AORs and in *Agulhas*. Sensors: Doppler navigation, some with search radar. Weapons: Unarmed but can mount Armscor 30 mm Ratler.

LAND-BASED MARITIME AIRCRAFT

Note: Albatross aircraft were withdrawn from service in 1990.

Numbers/Type: 20 Douglas Turbodaks.
Operational speed: 161 kts *(298 km/h)*.
Service ceiling: 24 000 ft *(7315 m)*.
Range: 1390 nm *(2575 km)*.
Role/Weapon systems: With replacement of Shackleton impossible a number of Dakotas are being converted for MR/SAR and other tasks. Additional fuel tanks extend the range to 2620 nm *(4800 km)*. Sensors: Search radar and navigation aids. Weapons: Unarmed.

MINE WARFARE FORCES

4 BRITISH TON CLASS (MINESWEEPERS)

Name	*No*	*Builders*	*Commissioned*
KIMBERLEY (ex-HMS *Stratton*)	M 1210	Dorset Yacht Co	1958
WALVISBAAI (ex-HMS *Packington*)	M 1214	Harland & Wolff, Belfast	1959
EAST LONDON (ex-HMS *Chilton*)	M 1215	Cook Welton and Gemmell	1958
WINDHOEK	M 1498	Thornycroft, Southampton	1959

Displacement, tons: 360 standard; 440 full load
Dimensions, feet (metres): 153 × 28.9 × 8.2 *(46.6 × 8.8 × 2.5)*
Main machinery: 2 Paxman Deltic 18A-7A diesels; 3000 hp *(2.24 MW)*; 2 shafts
Speed, knots: 15. **Range, miles:** 2300 at 13 kts
Complement: 27

Guns: 1 Bofors 40 mm/60; 80° elevation; 120 rounds/minute to 10 km *(5.5 nm)*; weight of shell 0.89 kg.
2 Oerlikon 20 mm. 2—7.62 mm MGs.
Countermeasures: 2 PAP 104 submersibles and diver support facilities for minehunting *(Kimberley* only).
Radars: Navigation: Racal Decca; I band.

Programmes: The last four survivors of a class of 10. Six were paid off in 1987 because of a shortage of trained personnel.
Structure: *Kimberley* converted to minehunter 1977-78 but has now reverted to Minesweeping duties.

WALVISBAAI *1989, van Ginderen Collection*

4 RIVER CLASS (COASTAL MINEHUNTERS)

UMKOMAAS UMHLOTI UMZIMKULU UMGENI

Displacement, tons: 380 full load
Dimensions, feet (metres): 157.5 × 27.9 × 7.5 *(48 × 8.5 × 2.3)*
Main machinery: 2 MTU diesels; 4500 hp(m) *(3.3 MW)*; 2 shafts
Speed, knots: 15
Complement: 37 (7 officers)
Guns: 1 Oerlikon 20 mm. 2—12.7 mm MGs.
Countermeasures: MCM: 2 PAP remote-controlled submersibles.
Radars: Navigation: Decca; I band.
Sonars: Klein VDS; sidescan; high frequency.

Comment: Completed by Sandock Austral, Durban. The design derived from the German Schütze class. Commissioned 1986-87. Wooden hulls. Minehunting gear was mostly taken from the deleted Ton class. Reported that DUBM 21 hull-mounted sonar was fitted on build but this is apparently incorrect. Four more are to be built in due course to replace the surviving Ton class and construction may have started in 1991.

UMKOMAAS *5/1987, Shiphoto International*

TORPEDO RECOVERY VESSEL

Name	*No*	*Builders*	*Commissioned*
FLEUR	P 3148	Dorman Long, Durban	3 Dec 1969

Displacement, tons: 220 standard; 257 full load
Dimensions, feet (metres): 121.5 × 27.5 × 11.1 *(37 × 8.4 × 3.4)*
Main machinery: 2 Paxman Ventura 6 CM diesels; 1400 hp *(1.04 MW)* sustained; 2 shafts
Speed, knots: 14
Complement: 22 (4 officers)

Comment: Combined torpedo recovery vessel and diving tender with recompression chamber.

FLEUR *12/1981, South African Navy*

SURVEY SHIP

Name	*No*	*Builders*	*Commissioned*
PROTEA	A 324	Yarrow (Shipbuilders) Ltd	23 May 1972

Displacement, tons: 2733 full load
Dimensions, feet (metres): 260.1 × 49.1 × 15.6 *(79.3 × 15 × 4.7)*
Main machinery: Diesel-electric; 3 Paxman Ventura 12 CM diesel generators; 3840 hp *(2.68 MW)*; 1 motor; 2000 hp *(1.49 MW)*; 1 shaft; cp prop; bow thruster
Speed, knots: 14. **Range, miles:** 12 000 at 11 kts
Complement: 114 (10 officers)
Helicopters: 1 Alouette III.

Comment: Laid down 20 July 1970. Launched 14 July 1971. RN Hecla class equipped for hydrographic survey with limited facilities for the collection of oceanographical data and for this purpose fitted with special communications equipment, naval surveying gear, survey launches and facilities for helicopter operations. Hull strengthened for navigation in ice and fitted with a passive roll stabilisation system.

PROTEA *12/1990*

FLEET REPLENISHMENT SHIPS

Name	*No*	*Builders*	*Commissioned*
TAFELBERG (ex-*Annam*)	A 243	Nakskovs Skibsvaerft, Denmark	1959

Displacement, tons: 27 000 full load
Measurement, tons: 12 500 gross; 18 980 dwt
Dimensions, feet (metres): 559.8 × 72.1 × 30.2 *(170.6 × 21.9 × 9.2)*
Main machinery: 1 Burmeister & Wain diesel; 8420 hp(m) *(6.19 MW)*; 1 shaft
Speed, knots: 15.5
Complement: 100
Military lift: 1000 troops plus 6 Delta 80 LCUs
Guns: 2 Bofors 40 mm. 2 Oerlikon 20 mm.
Helicopters: 2 SA 330H/J Puma.

Comment: Built as Danish East Asiatic Co tanker. Launched on 20 June 1958. Purchased by the Navy in 1965. Accommodation rehabilitated by Barens Shipbuilding & Engineering Co, Durban with extra accommodation, air-conditioning, re-wiring for additional equipment, new upper RAS (replenishment at sea) deck to contain gantries, re-fuelling pipes. Remainder of conversion by James Brown & Hamer, Durban. A helicopter flight deck was added aft during refit in 1975. One fuel and one stores replenishment station each side. During a major refit 1983-84 armament was added and the flight deck, hangar and sick-bay were enlarged with additional accommodation. Can now act as rescue vessel. Life expectancy increased by 10 years. Refitted again in 1991.

TAFELBERG *1989, van Ginderen Collection*

Name	*No*	*Builders*	*Commissioned*
DRAKENSBERG	A 301	Sandock Austral, Durban	11 Nov 1987

Displacement, tons: 6000 light; 12 500 full load
Dimensions, feet (metres): 482.3 × 64 × 25.9 *(147 × 19.5 × 7.9)*
Main machinery: 2 diesels; 16 320 hp(m) *(12 MW)*; 1 shaft; cp prop; bow thruster
Speed, knots: 20+
Complement: 96 (10 officers)
Cargo capacity: 5500 tons fuel; 750 tons ammunition and dry stores; 2 Delta 80 LCUs
Guns: 4 Oerlikon 20 mm.
Helicopters: 2 SA 330H/J Puma.

Comment: The largest ship ever built in South Africa and the first naval vessel to be completely designed in that country. In addition to her replenishment role she is employed on SAR, patrol and surveillance with a considerable potential for disaster relief. Laid down in August 1984 and launched 24 April 1986. Two abeam positions and astern fuelling, jackstay and vertrep. Two helicopter landing spots. Has obvious potential as a mother ship for small craft and for troop transport and commando insertion operations.

DRAKENSBERG *7/1990*

HARBOUR PATROL VESSELS

3 TYPE T 2212 COASTGUARD CRAFT

Displacement, tons: 23 full load
Dimensions, feet (metres): 72.2 × 23 × 3 *(22 × 7 × 0.9)*
Main machinery: 2 ADE 444 TI 12V diesels; 2000 hp *(1.5 MW)*; 2 Castoldi waterjets
Speed, knots: 37. **Range, miles:** 530 at 30 kts
Complement: 4 (1 officer)
Guns: 1 MG-151 20 mm. 6—107 mm mortars.
Fire control: Hesis optical director.
Radars: Surface search: I band.

Comment: GRP sandwich construction with a hydrofoil hull. Built by T Craft International, Cape Town. Capable of carrying up to 15 people. First three ordered in mid-1991.

COASTGUARD Class *1991, T Craft International*

30 NAMACURRA TYPE

Y 1501-1530

Displacement, tons: 5 full load
Dimensions, feet (metres): 29.5 × 9 × 2.8 *(9 × 2.7 × 0.8)*
Complement: 4
Guns: 1—12.7 mm MG. 2—7.62 mm MGs.
Depth charges: 1 rack.

Comment: Built in South Africa in 1980-81. Can be transported by road.

NAMACURRA Type *12/1981, South African Navy*

AIR SEA RESCUE LAUNCHES

1 FAIREY MARINE TRACKER CLASS

P 1555

Displacement, tons: 26
Dimensions, feet (metres): 64 × 16 × 5 *(19.5 × 4.9 × 1.5)*
Main machinery: 2 GM diesels; 1120 hp *(836 kW)*; 2 shafts
Speed, knots: 28. **Range, miles:** 650 at 18 kts
Complement: 11

Comment: Built by Groves and Gutteridge, Cowes and commissioned in 1973.

1 KRÖGERWERFT TYPE

P 1551

Displacement, tons: 82 full load
Dimensions, feet (metres): 96 × 19 × 4 *(29.3 × 5.8 × 1.2)*
Main machinery: 2 Maybach diesels; 4480 hp(m) *(3.29 MW)*; 2 shafts
Speed, knots: 30. **Range, miles:** 1000 at 30 kts
Complement: 12

Comment: Built by Krögerwerft, Rendsburg and commissioned in 1961. Can carry a 12.7 mm MG. Sister ship was wrecked in Saldanha Bay in 1988.

P 1551 *12/1981, South African Navy*

TUGS

DE MIST

Displacement, tons: 275
Dimensions, feet (metres): 111.5 × 29.5 × 9.8 *(34 × 9 × 3)*
Main machinery: 2 Lister-Blackstone diesels; 2400 hp *(1.79 MW)*; 2 Voith-Schneider props
Speed, knots: 12

Comment: Completed by Dorman Long, Durban in December 1978.

DE NEYS

Displacement, tons: 170
Dimensions, feet (metres): 94 × 26.5 × 15.7 *(28.7 × 8.7 × 4.8)*
Main machinery: 2 Lister-Blackstone diesels; 1216 hp *(907 kW)*; 2 Voith-Schneider props
Speed, knots: 9
Complement: 10

Comment: Built by Globe Engineering, Cape Town and commissioned 23 July 1969.

DE NOORDE

Displacement, tons: 180
Dimensions, feet (metres): 104.5 × 25 × 15 *(31.9 × 7.6 × 4.6)*
Main machinery: 2 Lister-Blackstone diesels; 1216 hp *(907 kW)*; 2 Voith-Schneider props
Speed, knots: 8
Complement: 10

Comment: Built by Globe Engineering, Cape Town and commissioned in December 1961.

DEPARTMENT OF TRANSPORT

1 ANTARCTIC SURVEY AND SUPPLY VESSEL

S A AGULHAS

Measurement, tons: 3050 dwt
Dimensions, feet (metres): 358.3 × 59 × 19 *(109.2 × 18 × 5.8)*
Main machinery: 2 Mirrlees-Blackstone K6 major diesels; 6000 hp *(4.48 MW)*; 1 shaft
Speed, knots: 14. **Range, miles:** 8200 at 14 kts
Complement: 40 plus 92 spare berths
Radars: Navigation: Racal Decca; I band.
Helicopters: 2 SA 330J Puma.

Comment: Built by Mitsubishi, Shimonoseki and commissioned 31 January 1978. Red hull and white superstructure. Civilian manned. Has a new crane on the forecastle.

S A AGULHAS (with Christmas tree) *12/1991, Peter Humphries*

SPAIN

Headquarters' Appointments

Chief of the Defence Staff:
Admiral Gonzalo Rodriguez Martin-Granizo
Chief of the Naval Staff:
Admiral Carlos Vila Miranda
Second Chief of the Naval Staff:
Vice Admiral Eduardo Liberal Lucini
Chief of Fleet Support:
Admiral José Maria Gurucharri Martinez

Commands

Commander-in-Chief of the Fleet:
Admiral Pedro Regalado Aznar
Commander-in-Chief, Cantabrian Zone:
Admiral Francisco J Lopez de Arenosa Diaz
Commander-in-Chief, Straits Zone:
Vice Admiral José Antonio Serrano Punyed
Commander-in-Chief, Mediterranean Zone:
Admiral Miguel J Garcia de Lomas Ristori
Commander-in-Chief, Canarias Zone:
Vice Admiral José E Delgado Manzanares
Commander-in-Chief, Central Zone:
Vice Admiral Luis Carrero-Blanco Pichot
Commandant General, Marines:
Major General José Manuel Estévez Ons

Diplomatic Representation

Naval Attaché in Bonn:
Commander Miguel Angel Castillo Cuervo-Arango
Naval Attaché in Brasilia:
Commander José Luis Gamboa Ballester
Naval Attaché in Buenos Aires:
Commander Francisco J Fontán Suances
Naval Attaché in Lisbon:
Commander José Maria Molina Saenz-Diez
Naval Attaché in London:
Captain José Maria Pascual del Río
Naval Attaché in Paris:
Commander Antonio M Ugarte de la Azuela
Naval Attaché in Rome:
Commander José Manuel Veiga García
Naval Attaché in Santiago:
Captain Santiago Gibert Crespo
Naval Attaché in Washington:
Captain Manuel Fernández Rivera
Naval Attaché in The Hague:
Captain Carlos Rodriguez Casau
Naval Attaché in Morocco:
Commander Carlos de Solinis y Lecuona
Naval Attaché in Saudi Arabia and UAE:
Commander Guillermo Carrero González

Personnel

(a) 1992: 25 000 (2900 officers) plus 9300 civilians
Marine Corps: 6200 (470 officers)
(b) 12 months' national service

Bases

Ferrol: Cantabrian Zone HQ—Ferrol arsenal, support centre at La Graña, naval school at Marín, Pontevedra, electronics school at Vigo, Pontevedra
Cadiz: Straits Zone HQ—La Carraca arsenal, fleet command HQ and naval air base at Rota, amphibious base at Puntales, Tarifa small ships' base
Cartagena: Mediterranean Zone HQ—Cartagena arsenal, underwater weapons and divers school at La Algameca; support base at Mahón, Minorca and at Porto Pi, Majorca, submarine weapons schools at La Algameca and Porto Pi base, Majorca
Las Palmas: Canaries Zone HQ—Las Palmas arsenal

Naval Air Service (see *Shipborne Aircraft* section)

Type	*Escuadrilla*
AB 212ASW (with AS-12 missiles)	3
Twin Comanche Cessna Citation	4
Sikorsky SH-3D/G Sea King (with AS-12 missiles) Sikorsky SH-3E Sea King (AEW)	5
Hughes 500M (Training)	6
Matador AV-8A (Harrier) Matador TAV-8A (Harrier)	8
EAV-8B Bravo	9
Sikorsky SH-60B Seahawk	10

Marine Corps

This consists of four 'Tercios' (intermediate between a Regiment and a Brigade) based at Ferrol, Cartagena and Cádiz (two). Two Groups (intermediate between a Battalion and a Regiment) are based in Madrid and Las Palmas (Canary Islands). These Tercios and Groups are charged with the protection of their naval bases and establishments.
The Tercio de Armada is based at San Fernando, Cádiz and is the landing force available for immediate embarkation. The Tercio de Armada, brigade-sized, consists of two landing battalions plus a special operations unit (UOE) of 170 men, a support logistic battalion, a communications company, a tank company (with 17 M-48E and one M-88 recovery vehicle, plus 17 Scorpion light tanks), one amphibious tractors company (19 LVT-7 in three versions, possibly to be replaced by the VMA Pegaso 8331), one artillery battalion (six M109A2 with six M-992 ammunition vehicles, 12 towed OTO Melara 105 mm L14 howitzers), one anti-tank company with 12 TOW and 16/18 Dragon missile launchers. Infantry support weapons include 106 mm M40 recoilless rifles, 120, 81 and 60 mm ECIA mortars, Instalaza 90 mm and LAWS 72 mm anti-tank rocket launchers, Rasura infantry locating radars. Also armoured Pegaso BLR-400 infantry carriers (not in Tercio de Armada) and Pegaso 3550 three ton amphibious trucks.
There are plans for a Fuerza de Intervencion Rápida (FIR). This would include Marines and Group Delta amphibious ships.

Guardia Civil del Mar

Started operations in 1992. For details, see end of section.

Fleet Deployment

1. Flota
   (a) Grupo Aeronaval Alfa: (based at Rota)
   Principe de Asturias with appropriate escorts
   (b) Escuadrillas de Escoltas:
   21st Squadron; 6 Descubierta class (based at Cartagena)
   31st Squadron; 5 Baleares class (based at Ferrol)
   41st Squadron; 4 Santa Maria class (based at Rota)
   (c) Grupo Anfibio Delta: (based at Puntales, Cádiz)
   All Amphibious Forces
   (d) Fuerza de Medidas contra Minas: (based at Cartagena from September 1990)
   8 MSCs and 4 MSOs
   (e) Flotilla de Submarinos: (based at Cartagena)
   All submarines
2. Support units, Cantabrian Zone:
   1 Ocean Tug, 2 Water-boats, 8 Tugs, 4 Patrol Ships, 5 Large Patrol Craft, 7 Coastal Patrol Craft, 10 Inshore Patrol Craft, 1 Inshore/River Patrol Launch, 3 Sail Training Ships, 5 Training Craft
3. Support units, Straits Zone:
   6 Oceanographic Ships, 1 Sail Training Ship, 8 Fast Attack Craft, 1 Transport, 1 Ocean Tug, 7 Tugs, 2 Water-boats, 13 Coastal Patrol Craft, 6 Inshore Patrol Craft
4. Support units, Mediterranean Zone:
   4 Fast Attack Craft, 1 Boom Defence Vessel, 1 Water-boat, 1 Large Patrol Craft, 2 Inshore/River Patrol Launch, 11 Coastal Patrol Craft, 14 Inshore Patrol Craft, 7 Tugs, 1 Frogman Support Ship
5. Support units, Canaries Zone:
   1 Water-boat, 2 Ocean Tugs, 4 Large Patrol Craft, 7 Coastal Patrol Craft, 2 Tugs

Strength of the Fleet

Type	*Active*	*Building (Planned)*
Submarines—Patrol	8	(4)
Aircraft Carrier	1	—
Frigates	15	2 (4)
Corvettes	4	—
Offshore Patrol Vessels	4	—
Fast Attack Craft—Missile/Gun	13	(1)
Large Patrol Craft	13	—
Coastal Patrol Craft	37	—
Inshore Patrol Craft	30	—
Attack Transports	2	—
LSTs	2	(1)
LCTs	3	—
LCU/LCM/LCP	55	—
Hovercraft	1	—
Minesweepers	12	(4)
Minehunters	—	(4)
Survey Ships	7	—
Replenishment Tankers	1	1
Harbour Tankers	12	—
Transport	1	—
Training Ships	9	—
Tugs (Ocean, Coastal and Harbour)	41	—

New Construction

'Alta Mar' plan envisages the building of two more FFGs for a total of six Santa Maria class ships, plus four F 100 class and five F 110 class frigates; eight minehunters and four sweepers; four patrol cutters; an LPD, a logistic support ship, EAV-8B Plus Harrier aircraft, and Seahawk LAMPS III helicopters. It is eventually planned that the Navy should be centred on two carrier groups, and replacement Amphibious Ships and FAC(M) will also be required.

Mercantile Marine

Lloyd's Register of Shipping:
2305 vessels of 3 617 151 tons gross

DELETIONS

Aircraft Carriers

1989 *Dédalo* (museum ship in New Orleans)

Destroyers

1989 *Churruca* (sunk)
1991 *Gravina, Blas de Lezo*
1992 *Méndez Núñez, Lángara*

Offshore Patrol Vessels

1991 *Princesa, Nautilus*
1992 *Atrevida, Villa de Bilbao*

Amphibious Forces

1990 *Conde del Venadito*

Light Forces

1990 *Sálvora, P 103, P 126, P 236-237*

Support Ships

1990 *Azor*
1991 *Y 234* (tanker)

PENNANT LIST

Submarines

S 61	Delfin
S 62	Tonina
S 63	Marsopa
S 64	Narval
S 71	Galerna
S 72	Siroco
S 73	Mistral
S 74	Tramontana

Aircraft Carriers

R 11	Principe de Asturias

Frigates/Corvettes

F 31	Descubierta
F 32	Diana
F 33	Infanta Elena
F 34	Infanta Cristina
F 35	Cazadora
F 36	Vencedora
F 71	Baleares
F 72	Andalucia
F 73	Cataluña
F 74	Asturias
F 75	Extremadura
F 81	Santa Maria
F 82	Victoria
F 83	Numancia
F 84	Reina Sofía
F 85	— (bldg)
F 86	— (bldg)

Offshore Patrol Vessels

P 71	Serviola
P 72	Centinela
P 73	Vigia
P 74	Atalaya

Light Forces

P 01	Lazaga
P 02	Alsedo
P 03	Cadarso
P 04	Villamil
P 05	Bonifaz
P 06	Recalde
P 11	Barceló
P 12	Laya
P 13	Javier Quiroga
P 14	Ordóñez
P 15	Acevedo
P 16	Cándido Pérez
P 21	Anaga
P 22	Tagomago
P 23	Marola
P 24	Mouro
P 25	Grosa
P 26	Medas
P 27	Izaro
P 28	Tabarca
P 29	Deva
P 30	Bergantin
P 31	Conejera
P 32	Dragonera
P 33	Espalmador
P 34	Alcanada
P 41	Cormoran
P 51	Nalón
P 52	Ulla
P 54	Turia
P 81	Toralla
P 82	Formentor
P 201	Cabo Fradera

Amphibious Forces

L 11	Velasco
L 12	Martin Alvarez
L 21	Castilla
L 22	Aragón

Mine Warfare Forces

M 21	Júcar
M 22	Ebro
M 23	Duero
M 24	Tajo
M 25	Genil
M 26	Odiel
M 27	Sil
M 28	Miño
M 41	Guadalete
M 42	Guadalmedina
M 43	Guadalquivir
M 44	Guadiana

Survey Ships

A 21	Castor
A 22	Pollux

Survey Ships

A 23 Antares
A 24 Rigel
A 31 Malaspina
A 32 Tofiño
A 33 Hesperides

Service Forces

A 01 Contramaestre Casado
A 11 Mar del Norte
A 12 Poseidón
A 13 Ciclope
A 41 Cartagena
A 42 Cádiz
A 43 Ferrol
A 51 Mahón
A 52 Las Palmas
A 61 Contramaestre Castelló
A 62 Maquinista Mácias
A 63 Torpedista Hernández
A 64 Fogonero Bañobre
A 65 Marinero Jarana
A 66 Condestable Zaragoza
A 71 Juan Sebastian de Elcano
A 72 Arosa
A 73 Hispania
A 74 La Graciosa
A 81 Guardiamarina Barrutia
A 82 Guardiamarina Salas
A 83 Guardiamarina Godínez
A 84 Guardiamarina Rull
A 85 Guardiamarina Chereguini
A 101 Mar Caribe
A 102 Mar Rojo
Y 381 Sanson
Y 562 Nereida
Y 563 Proserpina

SUBMARINES

Note: Four S80 Delfin class replacements are planned to start building in 1998.

4 TYPE S 70 CLASS (FRENCH AGOSTA CLASS)

Name	*No*	*Builders*	*Laid down*	*Launched*	*Commissioned*
GALERNA	S 71	Bazán, Cartagena	5 Sep 1977	5 Dec 1981	22 Jan 1983
SIROCO	S 72	Bazán, Cartagena	27 Nov 1978	13 Nov 1982	5 Dec 1983
MISTRAL	S 73	Bazán, Cartagena	30 May 1980	14 Nov 1983	5 June 1985
TRAMONTANA	S 74	Bazán, Cartagena	10 Dec 1981	30 Nov 1984	27 Jan 1986

Displacement, tons: 1490 surfaced; 1740 dived
Dimensions, feet (metres): 221.7 × 22.3 × 17.7 *(67.6 × 6.8 × 5.4)*
Main machinery: Diesel-electric; 2 SEMT-Pielstick 16 PA4 V185 VG diesels; 3600 hp(m) *(2.7 MW)*; 2 Jeumont Schneider alternators; 1.7 MW; 1 motor; 4600 hp(m) *(3.4 MW)*; 1 cruising motor; 32 hp(m) *(23 kW)*; 1 shaft
Speed, knots: 12 surfaced; 20 dived; 17.5 sustained
Range, miles: 8500 snorting at 9 kts; 350 dived on cruising motor at 3.5 kts
Complement: 54 (6 officers)

Missiles: SSM: Probably Aerospatiale SM 39 Exocet; active radar homing to 50 km *(27 nm)* at 0.9 Mach; warhead 165 kg. Each missile carried in lieu of 1 torpedo.
Torpedoes: 4—21 in *(533 mm)* tubes. 20 combination of (a) ECAN L5 Mod 3/4; dual purpose; active/passive homing to 9.5 km *(5.1 nm)* at 35 kts; warhead 150 kg; depth to 550 m *(1800 ft)*.
(b) ECAN F17 Mod 2; wire-guided; active/passive homing to 20 km *(10.8 nm)* at 40 kts; warhead 250 kg; depth 600 m *(1970 ft)*.
Mines: 19 can be carried if torpedo load is reduced to 9.
Countermeasures: ESM: THORN EMI Manta; radar warning.
Radars: Surface search: Thomson-CSF DRUA 33C; I band.
Sonars: Thomson Sintra DSUV 22; passive search and attack; medium frequency.
Thomson Sintra DUUA 2A/2B; active search and attack; 8 or 8.4 kHz active.
DUUX 2A (S 71-72) or DUUX-5 (S 73-74); passive; range finding. Eledone; intercept.
Thomson Sintra DSUV-62 towed passive array (S 72-73); trials in 1991.

Programmes: First two ordered 9 May 1975 and second pair 29 June 1977. Built with some French advice. About 67 per cent of equipment and structure from Spanish sources.
Modernisation: All to be modernised by the mid-1990s with new attack periscopes, towed array sonars, new ESM and IR enhanced periscopes. New main batteries to be installed with central control monitoring. *Galerna* will be the first to start the update in 1993.

SIROCO *7/1991, Antonio Moreno*

Structure: Diving depth, 300 m *(984 ft)*.

Operational: Endurance, 45 days.

4 TYPE S 60 CLASS (FRENCH DAPHNE CLASS)

Name	*No*	*Builders*	*Laid down*	*Launched*	*Commissioned*
DELFIN	S 61	Bazán, Cartagena	13 Aug 1968	25 Mar 1972	3 May 1973
TONINA	S 62	Bazán, Cartagena	2 Mar 1970	3 Oct 1972	10 July 1973
MARSOPA	S 63	Bazán, Cartagena	19 Mar 1971	15 Mar 1974	12 Apr 1975
NARVAL	S 64	Bazán, Cartagena	24 Apr 1972	14 Dec 1974	22 Nov 1975

Displacement, tons: 869 surfaced; 1043 dived
Dimensions, feet (metres): 189.6 × 22.3 × 15.1 *(57.8 × 6.8 × 4.6)*
Main machinery: Diesel-electric; 2 SEMT-Pielstick 12 PA4 V185 diesels; 2450 hp(m) *(1.8 MW)*; 2 Jeumont Schneider alternators; 1.7 MW; 2 motors; 2600 hp(m) *(1.9 MW)*; 2 shafts
Speed, knots: 13.2 surfaced; 15.5 dived
Range, miles: 4300 snorting at 7.5 kts; 2710 surfaced at 12.5 kts
Complement: 47 (6 officers)

Torpedoes: 12—21.7 in *(550 mm)* (8 bow, 4 stern) tubes. 12 combination of (a) ECAN L5 Mod 3/4; dual purpose; active/passive homing to 9.5 km *(5.1 nm)* at 35 kts; warhead 150 kg; depth to 550 m *(1800 ft)*.
(b) ECAN F17 Mod 2; wire-guided; active/passive homing to 20 km *(10.8 nm)* at 40 kts; warhead 250 kg; depth 600 m *(1970 ft)*.
Mines: 12 in lieu of torpedoes.
Countermeasures: ESM: THORN EMI Manta; radar warning.
Radars: Surface search: Thomson-CSF DRUA 31 or 33A; I band.
Sonars: Thomson Sintra DSUV 22; passive search and attack; medium frequency.
Thomson Sintra DUUA 2A; active search and attack; 8 or 8.4 kHz active.

Programmes: First pair ordered 26 December 1966 and second pair in March 1970. Identical to the French Daphne class and built with extensive French assistance.
Modernisation: The class has been taken in hand since 1983 for modernisation of sonar (DUUA 2A for DUUA 1), updating of fire control and torpedo handling. It is possible that torpedo tubes were also linered to 21 in *(533 mm)*. Last one completed at the end of 1988. ESM updated in 1990-91.
Structure: Modernised submarines have a bulbous sonar dome on forward casing. Diving depth, 300 m *(984 ft)*.

DELFIN *7/1991, Antonio Moreno*

AIRCRAFT CARRIER

Name	*No*	*Builders*	*Laid down*	*Launched*	*Commissioned*
PRINCIPE DE ASTURIAS (ex-*Almirante Carrero Blanco*)	R 11	Bazán, Ferrol	8 Oct 1979	22 May 1982	30 May 1988

Displacement, tons: 16 700 full load
Dimensions, feet (metres): 642.7 oa; 615.2 pp × 79.7 × 30.8 *(195.9; 187.5 × 24.3 × 9.4)*
Flight deck, feet (metres): 575.1 × 95.1 *(175.3 × 29)*
Main machinery: 2 GE LM 2500 gas turbines; 44 000 hp *(33 MW)* sustained; 1 shaft; cp prop; 2 motors; 1600 hp(m) *(1.18 MW)*; retractable prop
Speed, knots: 26 (4.5 on motors). **Range, miles:** 6500 at 20 kts
Complement: 555 (90 officers) plus 208 (Flag Staff (7 officers) and Air Group)

Guns: 4 Bazán Meroka 12-barrelled 20 mm/120 ❶; 85° elevation; 3600 rounds/minute combined to 2 km.
2 Rheinmetall 37 mm saluting guns.
Countermeasures: Decoys: 4 Loral Hycor SRBOC 6-barrelled fixed Mk 36; IR flares and Chaff to 4 km *(2.2 nm)*.
SLQ 25 Nixie; towed torpedo decoy.
US Prairie/Masker; hull noise/blade rate suppression.
ESM/ECM: Elettronica Nettunel; intercept and jammers.
Combat data systems: Tritan Digital Command and Control System NTDS; Links 11 and 14. Saturn SATCOM ❷.
Fire control: Four Selenia directors (for Meroka). Radamec 2000 series.
Radars: Air search: Hughes SPS 52 C/D ❸; 3D; E/F band; range 439 km *(240 nm)*.
Surface search: ISC Cardion SPS 55 ❹; I/J band.
Aircraft control: ITT SPN 35 A ❺; J band.
Fire control: Four VPS 2 ❻; I/J band (for Meroka).
RTN 11L/X; I/J band; missile warning.

Fixed wing aircraft: 6-12 AV 8B Bravo (see *Shipborne Aircraft* section).
Helicopters: 6-10 SH-3 Sea Kings; 2-4 AB 212ASW; 2 SH-60B Seahawks.

PRINCIPE DE ASTURIAS *1991, Camil Busquets i Vilanova*

Programmes: Ordered on 29 June 1977. Associated US firms were Gibbs and Cox, Dixencast, Bath Iron Works and Sperry SM. Commissioning delays caused by changes to command and control systems and the addition of a Flag Bridge.
Modernisation: After two years service some modifications have been made to the port after side of the island, to improve briefing rooms and provide sheltered parking space for FD vehicles. Also improved accommodation has been added on for six officers and 50 specialist ratings.
Structure: Based on US Navy Sea Control Ship design. 12 degree ski-jump. Two flight deck lifts, one right aft. Two LCVPs carried. Two pairs of fin stabilisers. The hangar is 24 748 sq ft *(2300 m²)*. The Battle Group Commander occupies the lower bridge. Two saluting guns have been mounted on the port quarter.
Operational: Three Sea Kings have Searchwater AEW radar. Aircraft complement could be increased to 37 (parking on deck) in an emergency but maximum operational number is 24. A typical air wing includes 10 Matador IIs and 10 Sea Kings (including two AEW). Ship is based at Rota.

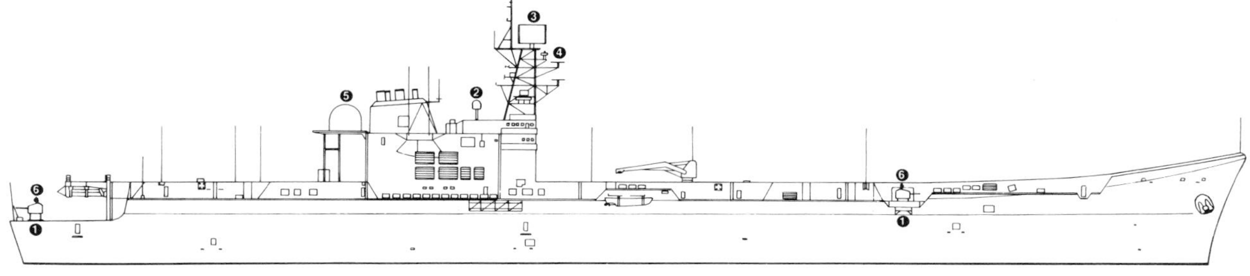
PRINCIPE DE ASTURIAS *(Scale 1 : 1 200), Ian Sturton*

PRINCIPE DE ASTURIAS *9/1990, F. Gámez*

FRIGATES

Note: Four F 100 class frigates are at the design stage, following the demise of NATO NFR 90. The plan was to place orders in 1993 with the first laid down in December 1993 and the last completed by 2000. This programme is unlikely to be met. Stealth features will be an important part of the design which will have a vertical launch air defence weapon system with four channels of fire. Collaboration is being sought for ships of about 3800 tons.

4 + 2 SANTA MARÍA CLASS

Name	*No*	*Builders*	*Laid down*	*Launched*	*Commissioned*
SANTA MARÍA	F 81	Bazán, Ferrol	23 May 1982	24 Nov 1984	12 Oct 1986
VICTORIA	F 82	Bazán, Ferrol	16 Aug 1983	23 July 1986	11 Nov 1987
NUMANCIA	F 83	Bazán, Ferrol	8 Jan 1986	30 Jan 1987	8 Nov 1988
REINA SOFÍA (ex-*América*)	F 84	Bazán, Ferrol	12 Dec 1987	19 July 1989	18 Oct 1990
—	F 85	Bazán, Ferrol	15 Apr 1991	Nov 1992	Apr 1994
—	F 86	Bazán, Ferrol	Feb 1992	Aug 1993	May 1995

Displacement, tons: 3610 standard; 4017 full load
Dimensions, feet (metres): 451.2 × 46.9 × 24.6 *(137.7 × 14.3 × 7.5)*
Main machinery: 2 GE LM 2500 gas turbines; 44 000 hp *(33 MW)* sustained; 1 shaft; cp prop; 2 motors; 1600 hp(m) *(1.18 MW)*; 1 retractable prop
Speed, knots: 29; 4.5 on auxiliary. **Range, miles:** 4500 at 20 kts
Complement: 223 (13 officers)

Missiles: SSM: 8 McDonnell Douglas Harpoon; active radar homing to 130 km *(70 nm)* at 0.9 Mach; warhead 227 kg.
SAM: 32 GDC Pomona Standard SM-1MR; Mk 13 Mod 4 launcher ❶; command guidance; semi-active radar homing to 46 km *(25 nm)* at 2 Mach.
Both missile systems share a common magazine.
Guns: 1 OTO Melara 3 in *(76 mm)*/62 ❷; 85° elevation; 85 rounds/minute to 16 km *(8.7 nm)*; weight of shell 6 kg.
1 Bazán 20 mm/120 12-barrelled Meroka ❸; 85° elevation; 3600 rounds/minute combined to 2 km.
Torpedoes: 6—324 mm US Mk 32 (2 triple) tubes ❹. Honeywell Mk 46 Mod 5; anti-submarine; active/passive homing to 11 km *(5.9 nm)* at 40 kts; warhead 44 kg.
Countermeasures: Decoys: 2 Loral Hycor SRBOC 6-barrelled fixed Mk 36 ❺; IR flares and Chaff to 4 km *(2.2 nm)*.
Prairie/Masker: hull noise/blade rate suppression.
SLQ 25 Nixie; torpedo decoy.
ESM/ECM: Elettronica Nettunel; intercept and jammer.
Combat data systems: IPN 10 action data automation; Link 11. SSQ 28 LAMPS III helo data link. Saturn SATCOM ❻.
Fire control: Mk 92 Mod 2 (Mod 6 with CORT in F 85 and 86).
Radars: Air search: Raytheon SPS 49 ❼; C/D band; range 457 km *(250 nm)*.
Surface search: Raytheon SPS 55 ❽; I band.
Navigation: Raytheon VPS 2; I/J band.
Fire control: RCA Mk 92 Mod 2/6 ❾; I/J band. Signaal STIR ❿; I/J band.
Selenia RAN 12L ⓫; I band (for Meroka). Sperry VPS 2 ⓬ (for Meroka).
Tacan: URN-25.
Sonars: Raytheon SQS 56 (DE 1160); hull-mounted; active search and attack; medium frequency.
Gould SQR 19; tactical towed array (TACTASS); passive; very low frequency.

Helicopters: 2 Sikorsky S-70L Seahawk ⓭ (only one normally embarked).

Programmes: Three ordered 29 June 1977. The execution of this programme was delayed due to the emphasis placed on the carrier construction. The fourth ship was ordered on 19 June 1986, and numbers five and six on 26 December 1989. The original plan to build four more has been shelved and the last two have been delayed by lack of timely payments to the shipyard.

Structure: Based on the US FFG 7 Oliver Perry class although broader in the beam and therefore able to carry more topweight. Fin stabilisers fitted. RAST helicopter handling system. Numbers five and six are to have an indigenous combat data system thereby increasing national inputs to 75 per cent.

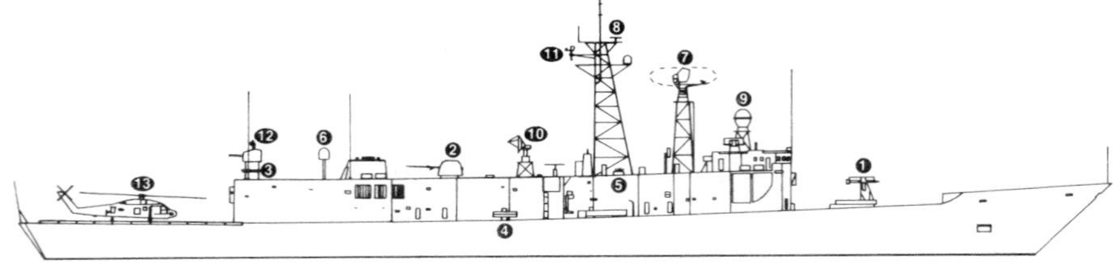
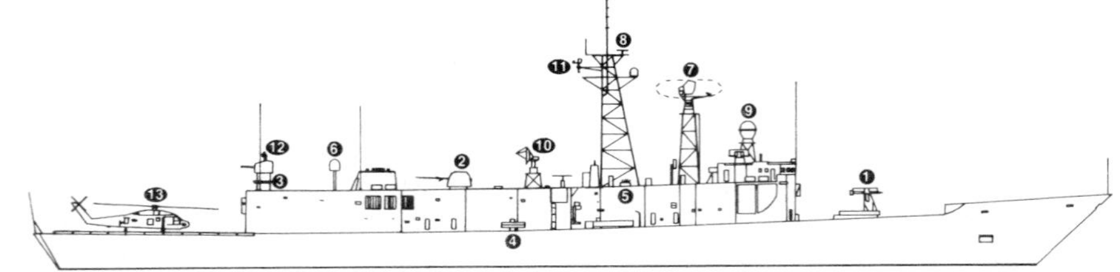

SANTA MARIA *(Scale 1 : 1 200), Ian Sturton*

SANTA MARIA *11/1991, Antonio Moreno*

NUMANCIA *10/1989, Wright & Logan*

5 BALEARES (F 70) CLASS

Name	No	Builders	Laid down	Launched	Commissioned
BALEARES	F 71	Bazán, Ferrol	31 Oct 1968	20 Aug 1970	24 Sep 1973
ANDALUCÍA	F 72	Bazán, Ferrol	2 July 1969	30 Mar 1971	23 May 1974
CATALUÑA	F 73	Bazán, Ferrol	20 Aug 1970	3 Nov 1971	16 Jan 1975
ASTURIAS	F 74	Bazán, Ferrol	30 Mar 1971	13 May 1972	2 Dec 1975
EXTREMADURA	F 75	Bazán, Ferrol	3 Nov 1971	21 Nov 1972	10 Nov 1976

Displacement, tons: 3015 standard; 4177 full load
Dimensions, feet (metres): 438 × 46.9 × 15.4; 25.6 (sonar) *(133.6 × 14.3 × 4.7; 7.8)*
Main machinery: 2 Combustion Engineering V2M boilers; 1200 psi *(84.4 kg/cm sq)*; 950°F *(510°C)*; 1 Westinghouse turbine; 35 000 hp(m) *(25.7 MW)*; 1 shaft
Speed, knots: 28. **Range, miles:** 4500 at 20 kts
Complement: 256 (15 officers)

Missiles: SSM: 8 McDonnell Douglas Harpoon (4 normally carried) ❶; active radar homing to 130 km *(70 nm)* at 0.9 Mach; warhead 227 kg.
SAM: 16 GDC Pomona Standard SM-1MR; Mk 22 Mod 0 launcher ❷; command guidance; semi-active radar homing to 46 km *(25 nm)* at 2 Mach.
A/S: Honeywell ASROC Mk 112 octuple launcher ❸; 8 reloads; inertial guidance to 1.6-10 km *(1-5.4 nm)*; payload Mk 46 torpedo.
Guns: 1 FMC 5 in *(127 mm)*/54 Mk 42 Mod 9 ❹; dual purpose; 85° elevation; 20-40 rounds/minute to 24 km *(13 nm)* anti-surface; 14 km *(7.7 nm)* anti-aircraft; weight of shell 32 kg; 600 rounds in magazine.
2 Bazán 20 mm/120 12-barrelled Meroka ❺; 85° elevation; 3600 rounds/minute combined to 2 km.
Torpedoes: 4—324 mm US Mk 32 fixed tubes (fitted internally and angled at 45 degrees) ❻. Honeywell Mk 46 Mod 5; anti-submarine; active/passive homing to 11 km *(5.9 nm)* at 40 kts; warhead 44 kg.
2—484 mm US Mk 25 stern tubes ❼. Westinghouse Mk 37; anti-submarine; wire-guided; active/passive homing to 8 km *(4.4 nm)* at 24 kts; warhead 150 kg. Total of 41 torpedoes of all types carried.
Countermeasures: Decoys: 4 Loral Hycor SRBOC Mk 36 6-barrelled Chaff launchers.
ESM: Ceselsa Deneb; intercept.
ECM: Ceselsa Canopus; jammer.
Combat data systems: Tritan 1 action data automation; Link 11. Saturn SATCOM ❽.
Fire control: Mk 68 GFCS (2 channels of fire). Mk 74 missile system with Mk 73 director. Mk 114 torpedo control.
Radars: Air search: Hughes SPS 52A ❾; 3D; E/F band; range 439 km *(240 nm)*.
Surface search: Raytheon SPS 10 ❿; G band.
Navigation: Raytheon Marine Pathfinder; I/J band.
Fire control: Western Electric SPG 53B ⓫; I/J band (for Mk 68). Raytheon SPG 51C ⓬; G/I band (for Mk 73).
Selenia RAN 12L ⓭; I band (for Meroka). 2 Sperry VPS 2 ⓮ (for Meroka).
Tacan: SRN 15A.
Sonars: Raytheon SQS 56 (DE 1160); hull-mounted; active search and attack; medium frequency.
EDO SQS 35V; VDS; active search and attack; medium frequency.

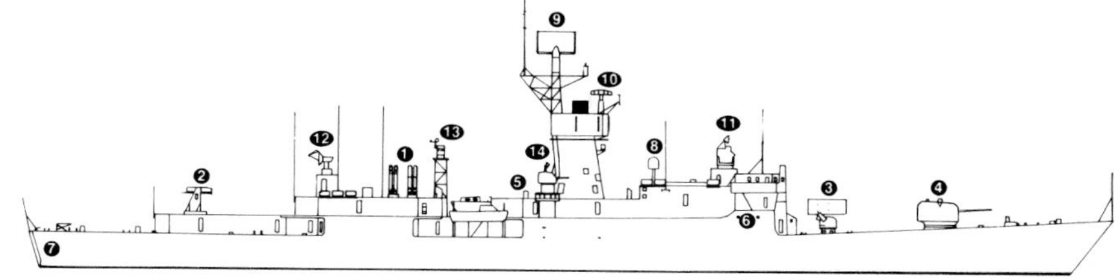

BALEARES *(Scale 1 : 1 200), Ian Sturton*

CATALUÑA *7/1991, Guy Toremans*

Programmes: This class resulted from a very close co-operation between Spain and the USA. Programme was approved 17 November 1964, technical support agreement with USA being signed 31 March 1966. US Navy supplied weapons and sensors. Major hull sections, turbines and gearboxes made at El Ferrol, superstructures at Alicante, boilers, distilling plants and propellers at Cadiz.
Modernisation: The mid-life update programme was done in two stages; all had completed the first stage by the end of 1987 and *Asturias* was the first to be fully modernised in 1988; *Extremadura* completed in May 1989, *Cataluña* in early 1990, *Baleares* in July 1990 and *Andalucía* in February 1991. Changes included the fitting of two Meroka 20 mm CIWS, Link 11, Tritan data control, Deneb passive EW systems, four Mk 36 SRBOC Chaff launchers and replacing SQS 23 with DE 1160 sonar.
Structure: Generally similar to US Navy's Knox class although they differ in the missile system, Mk 25 torpedo tubes and lack of helicopter facilities.

EXTREMADURA *5/1991, H. M. Steele*

6 DESCUBIERTA CLASS

Name	*No*	*Builders*	*Laid down*	*Launched*	*Commissioned*
DESCUBIERTA	F 31	Bazán, Cartagena	16 Nov 1974	8 July 1975	18 Nov 1978
DIANA	F 32	Bazán, Cartagena	8 July 1975	26 Jan 1976	30 June 1979
INFANTA ELENA	F 33	Bazán, Cartagena	26 Jan 1976	14 Sep 1976	12 Apr 1980
INFANTA CRISTINA	F 34	Bazán, Cartagena	11 Sep 1976	25 Apr 1977	24 Nov 1980
CAZADORA	F 35	Bazán, Ferrol	14 Dec 1977	17 Oct 1978	20 July 1982
VENCEDORA	F 36	Bazán, Ferrol	1 June 1978	27 Apr 1979	18 Mar 1983

Displacement, tons: 1233 standard; 1482 full load
Dimensions, feet (metres): 291.3 × 34 × 12.5 *(88.8 × 10.4 × 3.8)*
Main machinery: 4 MTU-Bazán 16V 956 TB 91 diesels; 15 000 hp(m) *(11 MW)* sustained; 2 shafts; cp props
Speed, knots: 25. **Range, miles:** 4000 at 18 kts; 7500 at 12 kts
Complement: 118 (10 officers) plus 30 marines

Missiles: SSM: 8 McDonnell Douglas Harpoon (2 quad) launchers ❶; active radar homing to 130 km *(70 nm)* at 0.9 Mach; warhead 227 kg. Normally only 2 pairs are embarked.
SAM: Selenia Albatros octuple launcher ❷; 24 Raytheon Sea Sparrow; semi-active radar homing to 14.6 km *(8 nm)* at 2.5 Mach; height envelope 15-5000 m *(49.2-16 405 ft)*; warhead 39 kg.
Guns: 1 OTO Melara 3 in *(76 mm)*/62 compact ❸; 85° elevation; 85 rounds/minute to 16 km *(8.7 nm)*; weight of shell 6 kg.
1 or 2 Bofors 40 mm/70 ❹; 85° elevation; 300 rounds/minute to 12.5 km *(6.8 nm)*; weight of shell 0.96 kg.
1 Bazán 20 mm/120 12-barrelled Meroka; 85° elevation; 3600 rounds/minute combined to 2 km. Replacing one 40 mm gun in due course.
Torpedoes: 6—324 mm US Mk 32 (2 triple) tubes ❺. Honeywell Mk 46 Mod 5; anti-submarine; active/passive homing to 11 km *(5.9 nm)* at 40 kts; warhead 44 kg.
A/S mortars: 1 Bofors 375 mm twin-barrelled trainable ❻; automatic loading; range 3600 m.
Countermeasures: Decoys: 2 Loral Hycor SRBOC 6-barrelled Mk 36 for Chaff and IR flares.
US Prairie Masker; blade rate suppression.
ESM/ECM: Elettronica SpA 'Beta'; intercept and jammer.
Combat data systems: SEWACO action data automation; Link 11 being fitted. Saturn SATCOM ❼.
Fire control: Signaal WM 22/41 or WM 25; GM 101.
Radars: Air/surface search: Signaal DA 05/2 ❽; E/F band; range 137 km *(75 nm)* for 2 m² target.
Navigation: Signaal ZW 06 ❾; I band.
Fire control: Signaal WM 22/41 or WM 25 system ❿; I/J band; range 46 km *(25 nm)*.
Selenia RAN 12L; I band and Sperry VPS 2 (to be fitted with Meroka).
Sonars: Raytheon 1160B; hull-mounted; active search and attack; medium frequency. VDS may be added.

Programmes: Officially rated as Corvettes. *Diana* (tenth of the name) originates with the galley *Diana* of 1570. Infanta Elena and Cristina are the daughters of King Juan Carlos. Approval for second four ships given on 21 May 1976. First four ordered 7 December 1973 (83 per cent Spanish ship construction components) and four more from Bazán, Ferrol on 25 May 1976.
Modernisation: The 40 mm gun aft of the mainmast is planned to be replaced by Meroka with associated fire control radars. SRBOC Chaff launchers fitted and EW equipment updated. Link 11 added. WM 25 fire control system being updated in four of the class by 1995.

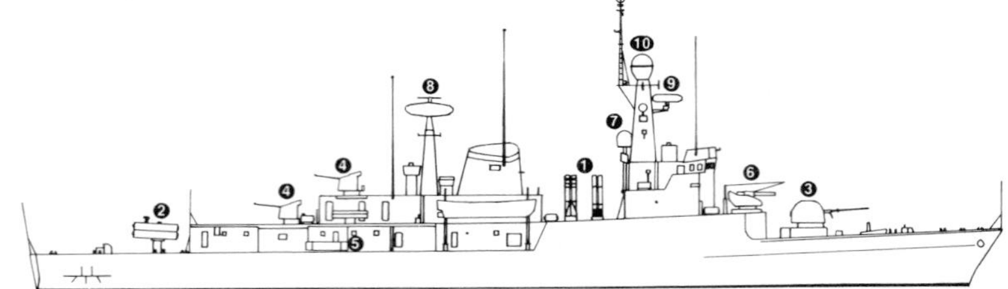

DESCUBIERTA *(Scale 1 : 900), Ian Sturton*

INFANTA CRISTINA *5/1991, Camil Busquets i Vilanova*

Structure: Original Portuguese 'João Coutinho' design by Comodoro de Oliveira PN developed by Blohm & Voss and considerably modified by Bazán including use of Y-shaped funnel. Harpoon fitted between bridge and funnel. Noise reduction measures include Masker fitted to shafts, propellers (five types tested) under trial for four years, auxiliary gas turbine generator fitted on upper deck for use during passive sonar search, all main and auxiliary diesels sound-mounted. Fully stabilised. Automatic computerised engine and alternator control; two independent engine rooms; normal running on two diesels.
Sales: F 37 and F 38 sold to Egypt prior to completion. One to Morocco in 1983.

OFFSHORE PATROL VESSELS

4 SERVIOLA CLASS

Name	*No*	*Builders*	*Laid down*	*Launched*	*Commissioned*
SERVIOLA	P 71	Bazán, Ferrol	17 Oct 1989	10 May 1990	22 Mar 1991
CENTINELA	P 72	Bazán, Ferrol	12 Dec 1989	30 Mar 1990	24 Sep 1991
VIGIA	P 73	Bazán, Ferrol	30 Oct 1990	12 Apr 1991	Mar 1992
ATALAYA	P 74	Bazán, Ferrol	14 Dec 1990	22 Nov 1991	June 1992

Displacement, tons: 836 standard; 1106 full load
Dimensions, feet (metres): 225.4; 206.7 pp × 34 × 11 *(68.7; 63 × 10.4 × 3.4)*
Main machinery: 2 MTU-Bazán 16V 956 TB 91 diesels; 7500 hp(m) *(5.5 MW)* sustained; 2 shafts
Speed, knots: 19. **Range, miles:** 8000 at 12 kts
Complement: 42 (8 officers) plus 6 spare berths

Guns: 1 US 3 in *(76 mm)*/50 Mk 26; 85° elevation; 20 rounds/minute to 12 km *(6.6 nm)*; weight of shell 6 kg (see *Structure*).
2—12.7 mm MGs.
Fire control: Bazán Alcor optronic director. Hispano mini combat system.
Radars: Surface search: Racal Decca 2459; I band.

Helicopters: 1 AB-212.

Programmes: Project B215 ordered from Bazán, Ferrol in late 1988. Patrulleros de Altura have replaced the Atrevida class. The larger Milano design was rejected as being too expensive.
Structure: A modified Halcón class design similar to ships produced for Argentina and Mexico. Full helicopter facilities enabling operation in up to Sea State 4 using non-retractable stabilisers. Three firefighting pumps. The guns are old stock refurbished but could be replaced by an OTO Melara 76 mm/62 or a Bofors 40 mm/70 Model 600. Other equipment fits could include four Harpoon SSM, Meroka CIWS, Sea Sparrow SAM or a Bofors 375 mm ASW rocket launcher.
Operational: For EEZ patrol only. May carry some female crew. The ships are based at Cadiz, Ferrol and Las Palmas.

CENTINELA *1991, Bazán*

SHIPBORNE AIRCRAFT

Numbers/Type: 10 Agusta AB 212ASW.
Operational speed: 106 kts *(196 km/h)*.
Service ceiling: 14 200 ft *(4330 m)*.
Range: 230 nm *(426 km)*.
Role/Weapon systems: ASW and surface search; four are equipped for Fleet ECM support and six for Assault operations with the Amphibious Brigade. Sensors: Selenia search radar, Bendix dipping sonar, Elmer ECM. Weapons: ASW; 2 × Mk 46 torpedoes or 4 × depth bombs. ASV; 4 × Aerospatiale AS 12 wire-guided missiles.

AB 212 *9/1989, Stefan Terzibaschitsch*

Numbers/Type: 11 BAe/McDonnell Douglas EAV-8B Bravo.
Operational speed: 562 kts *(1041 km/h)*.
Service ceiling: Not available.
Range: 480 nm *(889 km)*.
Role/Weapon systems: Delivered in 1987-88 for the new aircraft carrier. The plan is to update them to AV-8B Harrier Plus standard with APG-65 radar plus FLIR by 1994-95. Sensors: No radar (a letter of intent for the APG-65 multi-mode radar was signed in 1988). ECM: ALQ 164. Weapons: Strike; 2 × 25 mm GAU-12/U cannon, 2 or 4 × AIM-9L Sidewinder, 2 or 4 × AGM-65E Maverick; up to 16 GP bombs.

BRAVO *6/1991, Camil Busquets i Vilanova*

Numbers/Type: 7 BAe/McDonnell Douglas AV-8S Matador (Harrier).
Operational speed: 640 kts *(1186 km/h)*.
Service ceiling: 51 200 ft *(15 600 m)*.
Range: 800 nm *(1480 km)*.
Role/Weapon systems: AV-8S supplied via US and formed for strike/reconnaissance role with one squadron. Sensors: None. Weapons: Strike; 2 × 30 mm Aden cannon, 2 × AIM-9 Sidewinder or 20 mm/127 mm rockets and 'iron' bombs.

MATADOR *1991, Camil Busquets i Vilanova*

Numbers/Type: 9 Sikorsky SH-3D/G Sea King.
Operational speed: 118 kts *(219 km/h)*.
Service ceiling: 14 700 ft *(4480 m)*.
Range: 542 nm *(1005 km)*.
Role/Weapon systems: Medium ASW helicopter from aircraft carrier; surface search and SAR are secondary roles. Modernisation in 1989 included new sonars, Doppler radars and IFF. Sensors: APS-124 search radar, Bendix AQS-13F dipping sonar, sonobuoys. Weapons: ASW; 4 × Mk 46 torpedoes or depth bombs. ASV; 4 Aerospatiale AS 12 wire-guided missiles.

SEA KING *11/1990, F. Gámez*

Numbers/Type: 10 Hughes 500MD/ASW.
Operational speed: 110 kts *(204 km/h)*.
Service ceiling: 10 000 ft *(3050 m)*.
Range: 203 nm *(376 km)*.
Role/Weapon systems: Weapons carrier helicopter for ASW operations, with MAD detection capability; used for training; secondary role is SAR and surface search. Sensors: Some have search radar, MAD. Weapons: ASW; 1 × Mk 46 torpedo or depth bomb.

HUGHES 500 *9/1990, F. Gámez*

Numbers/Type: 3 Sikorsky SH-3D AEW Sea King.
Operational speed: 110 kts *(204 km/h)*.
Service ceiling: 14 700 ft *(4480 m)*.
Range: 542 nm *(1005 km)*.
Role/Weapon systems: Three Sea King helicopters were taken in hand in 1986 for conversion to AEW role to provide organic cover; first entered service August 1987. Three more may be converted in due course. Sensors: Thorn-EMI Searchwater radar, ESM. Weapons: Unarmed.

SEA KING AEW *9/1989, F. Gámez*

Numbers/Type: 6 Sikorsky S-70L Seahawk (LAMPS III).
Operational speed: 135 kts *(249 km/h)*.
Service ceiling: 10 000 ft *(3050 m)*.
Range: 600 nm *(1110 km)*.
Role/Weapon systems: ASW helicopter; delivery in 1988-89 for new FFG 7 frigates. Four more to be acquired in due course. Sensors: Search radar, sonobuoys, ECM/ESM. Weapons: ASW; 2 × Mk 46 torpedoes or depth bombs.

SEAHAWK *11/1991, Antonio Moreno*

LAND-BASED MARITIME AIRCRAFT (FRONT LINE)

Numbers/Type: 10 Aerospatiale AS 332M Super Puma.
Operational speed: 151 kts *(279 km/h)*.
Service ceiling: 15 090 ft *(4600 m)*.
Range: 335 nm *(620 km)*.
Role/Weapon systems: Limited search and SAR helicopter operated by Air Force. Sensors: Search radar. Weapons: Unarmed.

Numbers/Type: 7 CASA C-212 Aviocar.
Operational speed: 190 kts *(353 km/h)*.
Service ceiling: 24 000 ft *(7315 m)*.
Range: 1650 nm *(3055 km)*.
Role/Weapon systems: Mediterranean and Atlantic surveillance is carried out by detached flights for the Air Force; SAR is secondary role. Sensors: APS-128 radar, MAD, sonobuoys and ESM. Weapons: ASW; Mk 46 torpedoes or depth bombs. ASV; 2 × rockets or machine gun pods.

Numbers/Type: 6 CASA/Nurtanio CN-235
Operational speed: 240 kts *(445 km/h)*.
Service ceiling: 26 600 ft *(8110 m)*.
Range: 669 nm *(1240 km)*.
Role/Weapon systems: Air Force operated; 21 of the type used for transport tasks. Programme to be completed by 1993. Medium-range maritime patrol for surface surveillance and possible ASV/ASW; Sensors: Search radar: Litton AN/APS 504; MAD; acoustic processors; sonobuoys. Weapons suite to be selected.

Numbers/Type: 3 Fokker F27 Maritime.
Operational speed: 250 kts *(463 km/h)*.
Service ceiling: 29 500 ft *(8990 m)*.
Range: 2700 nm *(5000 km)*.
Role/Weapon systems: Canaries and offshore patrol by Air Force. Sensors: APS-504 search radar, cameras. Weapons: ASW; torpedoes or depth bombs. ASV; possible conversion for missiles under consideration.

Numbers/Type: 2/5 Lockheed P-3A/B Orion.
Operational speed: 410 kts *(760 km/h)*.
Service ceiling: 28 300 ft *(8625 m)*.
Range: 4000 nm *(7410 km)*.
Role/Weapon systems: Air Force operation for long-range MR/ASW; P-3A supplemented in 1988 by P-3B Orions from Norway after Lockheed modernisation. All to be further upgraded with APS 134 radar, FLIR, ALR 66 V(3) ESM and AQS 81 MAD by 1995. Sensors: Search radar, MAD, ECM/ESM, 87 × sonobuoys. Weapons: ASW; 8 × torpedoes or depth bombs internally; 10 × underwing stations. ASV; 4 × Harpoon or 127 mm rockets.

LIGHT FORCES

Note: The plan to build six Fishery Protection craft (P 50-P 55) has been shelved.

6 LAZAGA CLASS (FAST ATTACK CRAFT—MISSILE)

Name	*No*	*Builders*	*Commissioned*
LAZAGA	P 01	Lürssen, Vegesack	16 July 1975
ALSEDO	P 02	Bazán, La Carraca	28 Feb 1977
CADARSO	P 03	Bazán, La Carraca	10 July 1976
VILLAMIL	P 04	Bazán, La Carraca	26 Apr 1977
BONIFAZ	P 05	Bazán, La Carraca	11 July 1977
RECALDE	P 06	Bazán, La Carraca	17 Dec 1977

Displacement, tons: 275 standard; 393 full load
Dimensions, feet (metres): 190.6 × 24.9 × 8.5 *(58.1 × 7.6 × 2.6)*
Main machinery: 2 MTU-Bazán 16V 965 TB 91 diesels; 7500 hp(m) *(5.5 MW)* sustained; 2 shafts
Speed, knots: 28. **Range, miles:** 6100 at 17 kts
Complement: 30 (4 officers)

Missiles: SSM: Possibly to be fitted with McDonnell Douglas Harpoon or Israeli Penguin.
Guns: 1 OTO Melara 3 in *(76 mm)*/62 compact; 85° elevation; 85 rounds/minute to 16 km *(8.7 nm)*; weight of shell 6 kg.
1 Breda 40 mm/70; 85° elevation; 300 rounds/minute to 12.5 km *(6.8 nm)*; weight of shell 0.96 kg.
2 Oerlikon 20 mm/85; 55° elevation; 800 rounds/minute to 2 km.
Torpedoes: Fitted for but not with 6—324 mm US Mk 31 (2 triple) tubes.
Depth charges: Fitted for 2 racks.
Countermeasures: ESM: Radar intercept.
Fire control: CSEE optical director.
Radars: Surface search/fire control: Signaal WM 22/41; I/J band.
Navigation: Raytheon TM 1620/6X; I/J band.
Sonars: Fitted for—hull-mounted; active attack; high frequency.

Programmes: Ordered in 1972, primarily for Fishery Protection duties. Although all are operated by the Navy half the cost is being borne by the Ministry of Commerce.
Modernisation: Fire control radars to be modernised by Signaal by 1995.
Structure: Of similar hull form to Israeli Reshef class and to S-143 class of West Germany and of basic Lürssen Type 57 design but with only two engines. A mast which is abaft and higher than the radome has been fitted in some of the class, probably for ESM. The plan was to fit SSMs but this is unlikely to happen.
Operational: Meroka CIWS trials were carried out in P 03. At least one of the class may be fitted with the ASW equipment. Portable containers with EW equipment are sometimes embarked.

VILLAMIL *5/1989, Stefan Terzibaschitsch*

0 + (1) BES-50 CLASS (SURFACE EFFECT SHIP—MISSILE)

Displacement, tons: 360 full load
Dimensions, feet (metres): 180.4 oa; 158.1 pp × 47.6 × 3.9 (with lift) *(55; 48.2 × 14.5 × 1.2)*
Main machinery: 2 Allison 570 KF gas turbines (for propulsion); 12 700 hp *(9.47 MW)* sustained; 2 KaMeWa waterjets
4 MTU 6V 396 TB 83 diesels (for lift); 3120 hp(m) *(2.3 MW)* sustained
Speed, knots: 50. **Range, miles:** 800 at 50 kts; 2000 at 12 kts
Complement: 30 (6 officers)
Missiles: SSM: 8 McDonnell Douglas Harpoon.
Guns: 2 Bazán/Bofors 40 mm/70.
Countermeasures: Decoys: 1 Chaff launcher. ESM.
Fire control: 2 optronic directors.
Radars: Air/surface search.
Navigation.
Helicopters: 1 S-70L Seahawk.

Comment: Surface effect ship planned to be built by Bazán-Chaconsa based on the experimental BES-16 platform which started trials in June 1988. If the Navy decides to go ahead the first ship should be in service in the mid-1990s and 6000 million pesetas have been allocated for research and development between 1989 and 1993. The programme has been held up by budget problems in 1991. BES-16 has a displacement of 14 tons; dimensions, 55.1 × 17.7 × 2.5 ft (lifted) *(16.8 × 5.4 × 0.75 m)*; two Isotta Fraschini diesels generating 900 hp(m) *(662 kW)* and two Macchi-Castoldi waterjets. The cushion is generated by two MWM diesels (220 hp(m) *(162 kW)*) and the craft has a speed of 38 kts. BES (*Buque de Efecto de Superficie*).

BES-50 (model) *1989, Bazán*

BES-16 *10/1991, Diego Quevedo*

1 CORMORAN CLASS (FAST ATTACK CRAFT—GUN)

Name	*No*	*Builders*	*Commissioned*
CORMORAN	P 41 (ex-*P 53*)	Bazán, San Fernando	27 Oct 1989

Displacement, tons: 374 full load
Dimensions, feet (metres): 185.7 × 24.7 × 6.5 *(56.6 × 7.5 × 2)*
Main machinery: 3 MTU-Bazán 16V 956 TB 91 diesels; 11 250 hp(m) *(8.27 MW)* sustained; 3 shafts
Speed, knots: 34
Complement: 32 (5 officers)
Guns: 1 Bofors 40/70 SP 48; 1 Oerlikon 20 mm.
Fire control: Alcor C modular system.
Radars: Surface search: I band.

Comment: Launched as a private venture and demonstrator in October 1985; taken over by the Navy in October 1989 but not purchased, and may be reclaimed by Bazán if a buyer is found. The design is able to carry SSMs and a 76 mm/62 gun but has commissioned with a second-hand Bofors taken from a deleted ship. Based at Cadiz and is used as a testbed as well as for Straits patrols. More being built for sale.

CORMORAN *1991, Royal Spanish Navy*

6 BARCELÓ CLASS (FAST ATTACK CRAFT—GUN)

Name	No	Builders	Commissioned
BARCELÓ	P 11	Lürssen, Vegesack	20 Mar 1976
LAYA	P 12	Bazán, La Carraca	23 Dec 1976
JAVIER QUIROGA	P 13	Bazán, La Carraca	4 Apr 1977
ORDÓÑEZ	P 14	Bazán, La Carraca	7 June 1977
ACEVEDO	P 15	Bazán, La Carraca	14 July 1977
CÁNDIDO PÉREZ	P 16	Bazán, La Carraca	25 Nov 1977

Displacement, tons: 134 full load
Dimensions, feet (metres): 118.7 × 19 × 6.2 *(36.2 × 5.8 × 1.9)*
Main machinery: 2 MTU-Bazán MD-16V 538 TB 90 diesels; 6000 hp(m) *(4.41 MW)* sustained; 2 shafts
Speed, knots: 36. **Range, miles:** 1200 at 17 kts
Complement: 19 (3 officers)
Guns: 1 Breda 40 mm/70. 1 Oerlikon 20 mm/85. 2—12.7 mm MGs.
Torpedoes: Fitted for 2—21 in *(533 mm)* tubes.
Fire control: CSEE optical director.
Radars: Surface search: Raytheon 1220/6XB; I/J band.

Comment: Ordered 5 December 1973. All manned by the Navy although the cost is being borne by the Ministry of Commerce. Of Lürssen TNC 36 design. Reported as able to take two or four surface-to-surface missiles instead of 20 mm gun and torpedo tubes.

LAYA *5/1989, Camil Busquets i Vilanova*

3 ADJUTANT CLASS (LARGE PATROL CRAFT)

Name	No	Builders	Commissioned
NALÓN (ex-*MSC 139*)	P 51	S Coast SY, Calif	16 Feb 1954
ULLA (ex-*MSC 265*)	P 52	Adams YY, Mass	24 July 1956
TURIA (ex-*MSC 130*)	P 54	Hildebrand DD, NY	1 June 1959

Comment: These ships were transferred from the Mine Warfare Forces in 1980 for patrol duties. Details given under Adjutant class in *Mine Warfare Forces* section.

NALÓN *7/1990, Maritime Photographic*

10 ANAGA CLASS (LARGE PATROL CRAFT)

Name	No	Builders	Commissioned
ANAGA	P 21	Bazán, La Carraca	14 Oct 1980
TAGOMAGO	P 22	Bazán, La Carraca	30 Jan 1981
MAROLA	P 23	Bazán, La Carraca	4 June 1981
MOURO	P 24	Bazán, La Carraca	14 July 1981
GROSA	P 25	Bazán, La Carraca	15 Sep 1981
MEDAS	P 26	Bazán, La Carraca	16 Oct 1981
IZARO	P 27	Bazán, La Carraca	9 Dec 1981
TABARCA	P 28	Bazán, La Carraca	30 Dec 1981
DEVA	P 29	Bazán, La Carraca	3 June 1982
BERGANTIN	P 30	Bazán, La Carraca	28 July 1982

Displacement, tons: 296.5 standard; 350 full load
Dimensions, feet (metres): 145.6 × 21.6 × 8.2 *(44.4 × 6.6 × 2.5)*
Main machinery: 1 MTU-Bazán 16V 956 SB 90 diesel; 4000 hp(m) *(2.94 MW)* sustained; 1 shaft; cp prop
Speed, knots: 22. **Range, miles:** 4000 at 13 kts
Complement: 25 (3 officers)
Guns: 1 FMC 3 in *(76 mm)*/50 Mk 22. 1 Oerlikon 20 mm Mk 10. 2—7.62 mm MGs.
Radars: Surface search: 2 Racal Decca 1226; I band.

Comment: Ordered from Bazán, Cádiz on 22 July 1978. For fishery and EEZ patrol duties. Rescue and firefighting capability.

IZARO *6/1991, A. Campanera i Rovira*

4 CONEJERA CLASS (COASTAL PATROL CRAFT)

Name	No	Builders	Commissioned
CONEJERA	P 31	Bazán, Ferrol	31 Dec 1981
DRAGONERA	P 32	Bazán, Ferrol	31 Dec 1981
ESPALMADOR	P 33	Bazán, Ferrol	10 May 1982
ALCANADA	P 34	Bazán, Ferrol	10 May 1982

Displacement, tons: 85 full load
Dimensions, feet (metres): 106.6 × 17.4 × 4.6 *(32.2 × 5.3 × 1.4)*
Main machinery: 2 MTU-Bazán MA 16V 362 SB 80 diesels; 2450 hp(m) *(1.8 MW)*; 2 shafts
Speed, knots: 25. **Range, miles:** 1200 at 15 kts
Complement: 12
Guns: 1 Oerlikon 20 mm Mk 10. 1—12.7 mm MG.

Comment: Ordered in 1978, funded jointly by the Navy and the Ministry of Commerce. Naval manned.

ESPALMADOR *10/1991, Diego Quevedo*

2 TORALLA CLASS (COASTAL PATROL CRAFT)

Name	No	Builders	Commissioned
TORALLA	P 81	Viudes, Barcelona	27 Feb 1987
FORMENTOR	P 82	Viudes, Barcelona	23 June 1988

Displacement, tons: 56 standard; 77 full load
Dimensions, feet (metres): 93.5 × 21.3 × 5.9 *(28.5 × 6.5 × 1.8)*
Main machinery: 2 MTU-Bazán 396 TB 93 diesels; 2180 hp(m) *(1.6 MW)* sustained; 2 shafts
Speed, knots: 20. **Range, miles:** 1000 at 12 kts
Complement: 13
Guns: 1 Browning 12.7 mm MG.
Radars: Surface search: Racal Decca RM 1070; I band.
Navigation: Racal Decca RM 270; I band.

Comment: Wooden hull with GRP sheath. It is possible that a third of the class is to be built for Angola.

FORMENTOR *7/1991, Antonio Moreno*

3 USCG TYPE (COASTAL PATROL CRAFT)

No	Builders	Commissioned
P 311 (ex-*PAS 11*, ex-*LAS 1*, ex- *LAS 10*)	Bazán, Cartagena	26 Apr 1965
P 312 (ex-*PAS 12*, ex-*LAS 2*, ex- *LAS 20*)	Bazán, Cartagena	4 May 1965
P 313 (ex-*PAS 13*, ex-*LAS 3*, ex- *LAS 30*)	Bazán, Cartagena	3 Sep 1965

Displacement, tons: 49 standard; 62 full load
Dimensions, feet (metres): 83.3 × 14.8 × 6.6 *(25.4 × 4.5 × 2)*
Main machinery: 2 diesels; 800 hp(m) *(588 kW)*; 2 shafts
Speed, knots: 15
Complement: 10
Guns: 1 Oerlikon 20 mm. 2—7.62 mm MGs.
Radars: Navigation: Decca; I band.

Comment: All launched 1964. Of wooden hull construction. Former anti-submarine craft which have had all ASW equipment removed.

P 311 *5/1991, Camil Busquets i Vilanova*

22 P 101 CLASS (COASTAL PATROL CRAFT)

P 101-102 P 104-123

Displacement, tons: 18.5 standard; 20.8 full load
Dimensions, feet (metres): 44.9 × 14.4 × 4.3 *(13.7 × 4.4 × 1.3)*
Main machinery: 2 Baudouin-Interdiesel DNP-350; 768 hp(m) *(564 kW)*; 2 shafts
Speed, knots: 23.3. **Range, miles:** 430 at 18 kts
Complement: 6
Guns: 1—12.7 mm MG.
Radars: Surface search: Decca 110; I band.

Comment: Ordered under the programme agreed 13 May 1977, funded jointly by the Navy and the Ministry of Commerce. Built to the Aresa LVC 160 design by Aresa, Arenys de Mar, Barcelona. GRP hull. All completed by early 1980 except *P 121* in February 1981 and *P 122* and *123* in 1983. *P 122* and *123* have supercharged engines giving a 25 per cent increase in power and a speed of 27 kts. *P 103* deleted in 1990. *P 115* may be scrapped in 1992 after a fire.

P 114 — *6/1991, Antonio Moreno*

1 COASTAL PATROL CRAFT

P 124 (ex-*PVC 21*, ex-*V 33*)

Displacement, tons: 23 full load
Dimensions, feet (metres): 52.5 × 14.1 × 3.3 *(16 × 4.3 × 1)*
Main machinery: 2 MAN D 2542 MTE diesels; 1100 hp(m) *(808 kW)*; 2 shafts
Speed, knots: 24. **Range, miles:** 700 at 18 kts
Complement: 6
Guns: 1 Browning 12.7 mm MG.
Radars: Surface search: Decca 110; I band.

Comment: Built by Viudes, Barcelona to Bazán 16 m design with GRP hull in 1977.

P 124 — *6/1988, Camil Busquets i Vilanova*

5 P 231 CLASS (COASTAL PATROL CRAFT)

P 231-235

Displacement, tons: 18 full load
Dimensions, feet (metres): 46 × 15.4 × 3.3 *(14 × 4.7 × 1)*
Main machinery: 2 Gray Marine diesels; 450 hp *(336 kW)*; 2 shafts
Speed, knots: 13
Complement: 8
Guns: 2—7.62 mm (twin) MGs.

Comment: Laid down 1964 by Bazán, La Carraca. Wooden hulled. Originally LPI-1 etc. All completed February-March 1965 to USCG design.

P 233 — *9/1987, Camil Busquets i Vilanova*

1 INSHORE/RIVER PATROL LAUNCH

Name	*No*	*Builders*	*Commissioned*
CABO FRADERA	P 201	Bazán, La Carraca	25 Feb 1963

Displacement, tons: 21
Dimensions, feet (metres): 58.3 × 13.8 × 3 *(17.8 × 4.2 × 0.9)*
Speed, knots: 10
Complement: 9
Guns: 1—7.62 mm MG

Comment: Based at Tuy on River Minho for border patrol with Portugal.

CABO FRADERA — *1987, Royal Spanish Navy*

29 P 202 CLASS (INSHORE PATROL CRAFT)

P 202-230 (ex-*PVI 1-18* and ex-*PVI 110-130*)

Displacement, tons: 4.8 full load
Dimensions, feet (metres): 29.2 × 10.2 × 2.3 *(8.9 × 3.1 × 0.7)*
Main machinery: 2 Ebro MH 58 diesels; 180 hp(m) *(132 kW)* sustained; 2 shafts
Speed, knots: 18. **Range, miles:** 120 at 18 kts
Complement: 4
Guns: 1—7.62 mm MG.
Radars: Navigation: Decca 60 for 10 craft based in northern ports.

Comment: A class of 30 craft ordered from Rodman, Vigo under the programme agreed 13 May 1977, funded jointly by the Navy and the Ministry of Commerce. All completed 1978-79. GRP hull. Ex-PVI 19 destroyed by terrorists in 1984 in San Sebastian (before new pennant number system was introduced). *P 205* attacked in August 1990 and another one in February 1991 but both are probably repairable.

P 209 — *7/1991, Camil Busquets i Vilanova*

AMPHIBIOUS FORCES

0 + (1) AMPHIBIOUS TRANSPORT SHIP (ATS)

Displacement, tons: 9500 full load
Dimensions, feet (metres): 492.1 × 82 × 18.4 *(150 × 25 × 5.6)*
Main machinery: 2 diesels, 2 shafts
Speed, knots: 20. **Range, miles:** 6000 at 14 kts
Complement: 115 plus 12 spare
Military lift: 600 fully equipped troops or 170 APCs or 33 MBTs. 3 LCVPs and 2 LCUs/LCMs or 6 LCVPs in docking well
Guns: 2 Meroka CIWS.
Helicopters: 6 NH-90 or 4 EH-101.

Comment: Originally started as a national project by the Netherlands. In 1990 the ATS was seen as a possible solution to fulfil the requirements for a new LPD. Joint project definition study announced in July 1991. The ship will be able to transport a fully equipped battalion of 600 marines providing a built-in dock for landing craft and a helicopter flight deck for debarkation in offshore conditions. Alternatively the ship can also be used as a general logistic support ship for both military and civil operations, including environmental and disaster relief tasks. Construction is planned to start in 1994.

2 Ex-US PAUL REVERE CLASS (ATTACK TRANSPORTS)

Name	*No*	*Builders*	*Commissioned*
CASTILLA (ex-*Diamond Mariner*, ex-USS *Paul Revere* LPA 248)	L 21 (ex-TA 12)	New York SB	3 Sep 1958
ARAGÓN (ex-*Prairie Mariner*, ex-USS *Francis Marion* LPA 249)	L 22	New York SB	6 July 1961

Displacement, tons: 10 709 light; 16 315 (L 21), 16 573 (L 22) full load
Dimensions, feet (metres): 563.5 × 76 × 27 *(171.8 × 23.1 × 8.2)*
Main machinery: 2 Foster-Wheeler boilers; 600 psi *(42.3 kg/cm sq)*; 870°F *(467°C)*; 1 GE turbine; 22 000 hp *(16.4 MW)*; 1 shaft
Speed, knots: 22. **Range, miles:** 17 000 at 14 kts
Complement: 610 (L 21), 660 (L 22) (35 officers)
Military lift: 1657 troops; 7 LCM 6s (161-167 for L 21 and 261-267 for L 22); 5 LCVPs; 3 LCPs

Guns: 8 US 3 in *(76 mm)*/50 (4 twin); 85° elevation; 50 rounds/minute to 12.8 km *(7 nm)*; weight of shell 6 kg.
Countermeasures: Decoys: Loral Hycor SRBOC Mk 36 Chaff launcher.
ESM: WLR1; radar intercept. ECM: ULQ 6; jammer.
Radars: Air search: RCA SPS 12 (L 21); D band; range 119 km *(65 nm)*.
Lockheed SPS 40 (L 22); E/F band; range 320 km *(175 nm)*.
Surface search: Raytheon SPS 10; G band.
Fire control: Four SPG 50 or SPG 34; I/J band.

Helicopters: Platform for 1 AS 332 Super Puma type.

Programmes: Originally C4-S-1 cargo vessels converted to APAs. L 21 by Todd Shipyard, San Pedro and L 22 by Bethlehem, Baltimore. Designated LPAs in 1969. L 21 transferred 17 January 1980 by sale, L 22 11 July 1980.
Operational: *Aragón* is the Flagship for Amphibious Command.

ARAGÓN *6/1990, Camil Busquets i Vilanova*

2 Ex-US TERREBONNE PARISH CLASS (LSTs)

Name	*No*	*Builders*	*Commissioned*
VELASCO (ex-USS *Terrebonne Parish* LST 1156)	L 11	Bath Iron Works	21 Nov 1952
MARTIN ALVAREZ (ex-USS *Wexford County* LST 1168)	L 12	Christy Corporation	15 June 1954

Displacement, tons: 2590 standard; 5800 full load
Dimensions, feet (metres): 384 × 55 × 17 *(117.1 × 16.8 × 5.2)*
Main machinery: 4 General Motors 16-278A diesels; 6000 hp *(4.48 MW)*; 2 shafts
Speed, knots: 15. **Range, miles:** 15 000 at 9 kts
Complement: 153 (395 troops)
Military lift: 395 troops; 10 Mk 48 tanks or 17 LVTPs; 3 LCVPs; 1 LCP

Guns: 6 US 3 in *(76 mm)*/50 (3 twin).
Fire control: 2 Mk 63 GFCS.
Radars: Surface search: Racal Decca TM 1229; I band.
Navigation: Decca; I band.
Fire control: Two Western Electric SPG 34; I/J band.

Programmes: Both transferred on 29 October 1971. Purchased on 17 May 1978.

VELASCO *1990, van Ginderen Collection*

3 SPANISH LCTs

A 06-A 08

Displacement, tons: 279 standard; 665 full load
Dimensions, feet (metres): 193.5 × 39 × 4.3 *(59 × 11.9 × 1.3)*
Main machinery: 2 MTU-Bazán MA6 R362 SB 70 diesels; 1100 hp(m) *(808 kW)*; 2 shafts
Speed, knots: 9.5. **Range, miles:** 1500 at 9 kts
Complement: 23
Military lift: 300 tons; 35 troops
Guns: 2—12.7 mm MGs. 1—81 mm mortar.
Radars: Navigation: Decca; I band.

Comment: Built by Bazán, La Carraca and commissioned in December 1966. Rated as logistic craft.

A 06 *1987, Royal Spanish Navy*

2 Ex-US LCUs

L 71 (ex-*LCU 11*, ex-*LCU 1*, ex-*LCU 1471*)
L 72 (ex-*LCU 12*, ex-*LCU 2*, ex-*LCU 1491*)

Displacement, tons: 354 full load
Dimensions, feet (metres): 119.7 × 31.5 × 5.2 *(36.5 × 9.6 × 1.6)*
Main machinery: 3 Gray Marine 64 YTL diesels; 675 hp *(504 kW)*; 3 shafts
Speed, knots: 7.6
Complement: 14
Military lift: 160 tons

Comment: Transferred June 1972. Purchased August 1976.

L 71 *1990, Royal Spanish Navy*

8 LCM 8

L 81-86 (ex-*LCM 81-86*, ex-*E 81-86*) **L 87-88**

Displacement, tons: 113 full load
Dimensions, feet (metres): 74.5 × 21.7 × 5.9 *(22.7 × 6.6 × 1.8)*
Main machinery: 4 GM 6-71 diesels; 696 hp *(519 kW)* sustained; 2 shafts
Speed, knots: 11
Complement: 5

Comment: First six ordered from Oxnard, California in 1974. Assembled in Spain. Commissioned in July-September 1975. Two more built by Bazán, San Fernando, and completed in early 1989.

L 82 *10/1989, Camil Busquets i Vilanova*

43 LANDING CRAFT

Comment: Apart from those used for divers there are 14 LCM 6, 20 LCVP and 9 LCP. Ten of the LCM 6, eight of the LCVPs and most of the LCPs were built in Spanish Shipyards 1986-88.

LCP over LCVP (on L11) *5/1985, X. Taibo*

1 HOVERCRAFT

VCA 36

Displacement, tons: 36 full load
Dimensions, feet (metres): 82.7 × 37.4 × 31.2 (height) *(25.2 × 11.4 × 9.5)*
Main machinery: 2 Textron-Lycoming TF25 gas turbines; 5000 hp *(3.73 MW)* sustained
Speed, knots: 60. **Range, miles:** 145 at 45 kts
Complement: 3
Military lift: 14 tons or 70 troops and 3 Land Rovers or 1 Scorpion light tank
Sonars: French helicopter type for trials; VDS; high frequency.

Comment: Built by Chaconsa, Mercia as an evolution of the VCA 3 design. Operational in 1988. More may be ordered in due course.

VCA 36 *6/1988, Camil Busquets i Vilanova*

MINE WARFARE FORCES

0 + (4) MODIFIED SANDOWN CLASS (MINEHUNTERS)

Displacement, tons: 480 full load
Dimensions, feet (metres): 177.2 × 32.8 × 7.2 *(54 × 10 × 2.2)*
Main machinery: 2 MTU-Bazán diesels; 1523 hp(m) *(1.12 MW)*; 2 shafts
Speed, knots: 14
Complement: 40 (7 officers)

Comment: On 4 July 1989 a technology transfer contract was signed with Vosper Thornycroft to allow Bazán to design a new MCM vessel based on the Sandown class. Previously planned programme has been delayed and the first is unlikely to be completed before 1996. Minehunting system will be by FABA-Bazán with Inisel. The ships will have an SAES ROV and either the British 2093 sonar or the SQQ 32 developed for the US Osprey class. Final requirement is for eight of the class.

4 Ex-US AGGRESSIVE CLASS (MINESWEEPERS—OCEAN)

Name	*No*	*Builders*	*Commissioned*
GUADALETE (ex-USS *Dynamic* MSO 432)	M 41	Colbert BW, Stockton, Calif	15 Dec 1953
GUADALMEDINA (ex-USS *Pivot* MSO 463)	M 42	Wilmington BW, Calif	12 July 1954
GUADALQUIVIR (ex-USS *Persistant* MSO 491)	M 43	Tacoma, Washington	3 Feb 1956
GUADIANA (ex-USS *Vigor* MSO 473)	M 44	Burgess Boat Co, Manitowoc	8 Nov 1954

Displacement, tons: 804-840 full load
Dimensions, feet (metres): 172.5 × 35 × 14.1 *(52.6 × 10.7 × 4.3)*
Main machinery: 4 Packard diesels; 2280 hp *(1.7 MW)*; 2 shafts; cp props
Speed, knots: 14. **Range, miles:** 3000 at 10 kts
Complement: 74 (6 officers)

Guns: 2 Oerlikon 20 mm (twin).
Countermeasures: Pluto ROVs in some.
Radars: Surface search: Raytheon SPS 5C; G/H band; range 37 km *(20 nm)*.
Navigation: Decca; I band.
Sonars: General Electric SQQ 14; VDS; active minehunting; high frequency.

Programmes: The first three were transferred and commissioned on 1 July 1971. The fourth ship was delivered 4 April 1972. All purchased August 1974. To be paid off when new MCMVs commission.
Modernisation: Completed in 1984-86 to extend service lives to 1992. At least 2 Pluto ROVs acquired in 1989 in order to gain experience while the new MCMVs are being built.

GUADIANA *9/1991, F. Gámez*

8 Ex-US ADJUTANT, REDWING and MSC 268 CLASSES (MINESWEEPERS—COASTAL)

Name	*No*	*Builders*	*Commissioned*
JÚCAR (ex-*MSC 220*)	M 21	Bellingham SY	22 June 1956
EBRO (ex-*MSC 269*)	M 22	Bellingham SY	19 Dec 1958
DUERO (ex-*Spoonbill* MSC 202)	M 23	Tampa Marine Corporation	16 June 1959
TAJO (ex-*MSC 287*)	M 24	Tampa Marine Corporation	9 July 1959
GENIL (ex-*MSC 279*)	M 25	Tacoma, Seattle	11 Sep 1959
ODIEL (ex-*MSC 288*)	M 26	Tampa Marine Corporation	9 Oct 1959
SIL (ex-*Redwing* MSC 200)	M 27	Tampa Marine Corporation	16 Jan 1959
MIÑO (ex-*MSC 266*)	M 28	Adams YY, Mass	25 Oct 1956

Displacement, tons: 355 standard; 384 full load
Dimensions, feet (metres): 144 × 28 × 8.2 *(43.9 × 8.5 × 2.5)*
Main machinery: 2 GM 8-268A diesels; 880 hp *(656 kW)*; 2 shafts
Speed, knots: 14. **Range, miles:** 2700 at 10 kts
Complement: 39 (3 officers)

Guns: 2 Oerlikon 20 mm (twin).
Radars: Navigation: Decca TM 626 or RM 914; I band.
Sonars: UQS 1; active minehunting; high frequency.

Comment: Wooden hulled. Two sub-types: M 22, M 24, M 25 and M 26 with no mainmast but crane abreast the funnel. M 21, M 23, M 27 and M 28 have derrick on mainmast. Three others of the class transferred to Patrol Ship duties in 1980.

EBRO *8/1990, Antonio Moreno*

MIÑO *8/1991, Camil Busquets i Vilanova*

SURVEY AND RESEARCH SHIPS

4 CASTOR CLASS

Name	*No*	*Builders*	*Commissioned*
CASTOR	A 21 (ex-H 4)	Bazán, La Carraca	10 Nov 1966
POLLUX	A 22 (ex-H 5)	Bazán, La Carraca	6 Dec 1966
ANTARES	A 23	Bazán, La Carraca	21 Nov 1974
RIGEL	A 24	Bazán, La Carraca	21 Nov 1974

Displacement, tons: 327 standard; 355 full load
Dimensions, feet (metres): 125.9 × 24.9 × 10.2 *(38.4 × 7.6 × 3.1)*
Main machinery: 1 Sulzer 4TD-36 diesel; 720 hp(m) *(530 kW)*; 1 shaft
Speed, knots: 11.5. **Range, miles:** 3620 at 8 kts
Complement: 36 (4 officers)
Radars: Navigation: Raytheon 1620; I/J band.

Comment: Fitted with Raydist, Omega and digital presentation of data. A 21 and 22 have gaps in the gunwhale aft for Oropesa sweep. In A 23 and 24 this is a full run to the stern.

ANTARES *1991, Camil Busquets i Vilanova*

1 RESEARCH SHIP

Name	*No*	*Builders*	*Commissioned*
HESPÉRIDES (ex-*Mar Antártico*)	A 33	Bazán, Cartagena	16 May 1991

Displacement, tons: 2738 full load
Dimensions, feet (metres): 270.7; 255.2 × 46.9 × 14.8 *(82.5; 77.8 × 14.3 × 4.5)*
Main machinery: Diesel-electric; 4 MAN-Bazán 14V 20/27 diesels; 6860 hp(m) *(5 MW)* sustained; 4 generators; 2 AEG motors; 3800 hp(m) *(2.8 MW)*; 1 shaft; bow and stern thrusters; 350 hp(m) *(257 kW)* each
Speed, knots: 15. **Range, miles:** 12 000 at 13 kts
Complement: 39 (9 officers) plus 30 scientists
Helicopters: AB 212 or similar.

Comment: Ordered in July 1988 from Bazán, Cartagena, by the Ministry of Education and Science. Laid down in 1989, launched 12 March 1990. Has 330 sq m of laboratories, Simbad ice sonar, navigation radars and GPS. Ice strengthened hull capable of breaking first year ice up to 45 cm at 5 kts. The main task is to support the Spanish base at Livingston Island, Antarctica replacing the tug *Las Palmas*. Manned and operated by the Navy. Has a red hull, foremast and funnels and a telescopic hangar.

HESPÉRIDES *1991, Royal Spanish Navy*

2 MALASPINA CLASS (OCEANOGRAPHIC SHIPS)

Name	*No*	*Builders*	*Commissioned*
MALASPINA	A 31	Bazán, La Carraca	21 Feb 1975
TOFIÑO	A 32	Bazán, La Carraca	23 Apr 1975

Displacement, tons: 820 standard; 1090 full load
Dimensions, feet (metres): 188.9 × 38.4 × 12.8 *(57.6 × 11.7 × 3.9)*
Main machinery: 2 San Carlos MWM TbRHS-345-61 diesels; 3600 hp(m) *(2.64 MW)*; 2 shafts; cp props
Speed, knots: 15. **Range, miles:** 4000 at 12 kts; 3140 at 14.5 kts
Complement: 63 (9 officers)
Guns: 2 Oerlikon 20 mm.
Radars: Navigation: Raytheon 1220/6XB; I/J band.

Comment: Ordered mid-1972. Both named after their immediate predecessors. Developed from British Bulldog class. Fitted with two Atlas DESO-10 AN 1021 (280-1400 m) echo-sounders, retractable Burnett 538-2 sonar for deep sounding, Egg Mark B side-scan sonar, Raydist DR-S navigation system, Hewlett Packard 2100A computer inserted into Magnavox Transit satellite navigation system, active rudder with fixed pitch auxiliary propeller. *Malaspina* used for a NATO evaluation of a Ship's Laser Inertial Navigation System (SLINS) produced by British Aerospace.

TOFIÑO *1991, Camil Busquets i Vilanova*

SERVICE FORCES

Note: Until the new tanker and logistic ships are in service, tanker requirements are being met by civilian leased ships. Two chartered as required and fitted for one beam and one stern RAS station. Their names are *Campéon* and *Camponubla*; 14 900 grt, 166 m in length and with a top speed of 14.5 kts.

0 + 1 ZUIDERKRUIS TYPE (FLEET LOGISTIC TANKER)

Name	*No*	*Builders*	*Commissioned*
MAR DEL SUR	—	Bazán, Ferrol	Apr 1995

Displacement, tons: 17 040 full load
Dimensions, feet (metres): 544.6 × 72.2 × 26.2 *(166 × 22 × 8)*
Main machinery: Diesel-electric; 2 diesels; 26 330 hp(m) *(19.36 MW)*; 1 motor; 1 shaft
Speed, knots: 20. **Range, miles:** 13 440 at 20 kts
Complement: 136 plus 24 aircrew plus 20 spare
Cargo capacity: 6700 tons dieso; 1660 tons petrol; 500 tons solids
Guns: 2 Bazán 20 mm/120 Meroka CIWS. 2 Oerlikon 20 mm/90.
Countermeasures: ESM/ECM/Chaff/Nixie.
Radars: 2 Navigation; I band.
Helicopters: 3 SH-3D Sea King size.

Comment: The Bazán design AP 21 was rejected in favour of this joint Netherlands/Spain design based on *Zuiderkruis*. Finally ordered on 26 December 1991. To be laid down in May 1993 which is two years later than planned. She will replace the discarded *Teide* as a carrier group support ship. Two Vertrep supply stations and workshops for aircraft maintenance. Medical facilities. Accommodation for up to 50 female crew members.

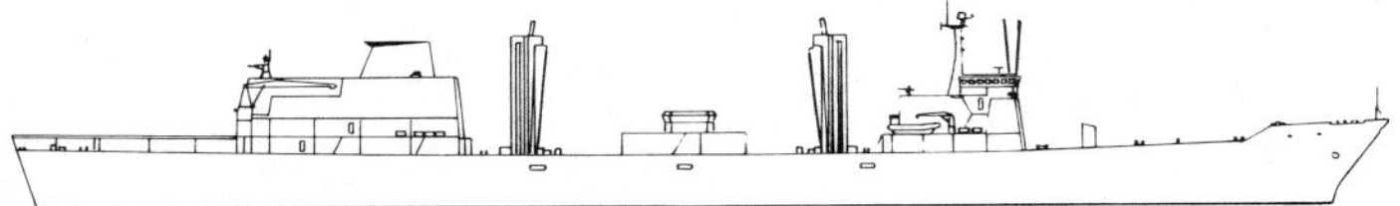

MAR DEL SUR *(not to scale), Ian Sturton*

1 TRANSPORT

Name	*No*	*Builders*	*Commissioned*
CONTRAMAESTRE CASADO (ex-*Thanasis-K*, ex-*Fortuna Reefer*, ex-*Bonzo*, ex-*Bajamar*, ex-*Leeward Islands*)	A 01	Eriksberg-Göteborg, Sweden	15 Dec 1982

Displacement, tons: 5300 full load
Dimensions, feet (metres): 343.4 × 46.9 × 29.2 *(104.7 × 14.3 × 8.9)*
Main machinery: 1 Burmeister & Wain diesel; 3600 hp(m) *(2.65 MW)*; 1 shaft
Speed, knots: 16. **Range, miles:** 8000 at 15 kts
Complement: 72
Guns: 2 Oerlikon 20 mm.

Comment: Built in the 1950s. Impounded as smuggler. Delivered after conversion 6 December 1983. Has a helicopter deck.

CONTRAMAESTRE CASADO *1987, Royal Spanish Navy*

1 FLEET TANKER

Name	*No*	*Builders*	*Commissioned*
MAR DEL NORTE	A 11	Bazán, Ferrol	3 June 1991

Displacement, tons: 13 247 full load
Dimensions, feet (metres): 403.9 oa; 377.3 wl × 64 × 25.9 *(123.1; 115 × 19.5 × 7.9)*
Main machinery: 1 MAN-Bazán 18V 40/54A; 18 000 hp(m) *(13.23 MW)* sustained; 1 shaft
Speed, knots: 16. **Range, miles:** 10 000 at 15 kts
Complement: 80 (11 officers)
Cargo capacity: 7498 tons dieso; 1746 tons JP-5; 120 tons deck cargo
Guns: 2—12.7 mm MGs.
Radars: Air/surface search. Navigation.
Helicopters: 1 AB 212 or similar.

Comment: Ordered 30 December 1988. Laid down 16 November 1989 and launched 3 October 1990. The deletion of the *Teide* has left a serious deficiency in the Fleet's at sea replenishment capability which is to be restored in due course by the new Zuiderkruis type of logistic tanker. In addition, and as a stop gap, this tanker is being built at one third of the cost of the larger support ship. It will have two Vertrep stations and a platform for a Sea King size helicopter. Replenishment stations on both sides and one astern. Provision for Meroka CIWS behind the bridge and four Chaff launchers. Has a small hospital.

MAR DEL NORTE *6/1991, A. Companera i Rovira*

11 HARBOUR TANKERS

No	*Displacement, tons*	*Dimensions metres*	*Builders*	*Commissioned*
Y 231	524	34 × 7 × 2.9	Bazán, Cádiz	1981
Y 232	830	42.8 × 8.4 × 3.1	Bazán, Cádiz	1981
Y 233	510	37.8 × 6.6 × 3	Bazán, Ferrol	1959
Y 235	510	37.8 × 6.6 × 3	Bazán, Ferrol	1959
Y 236	200	28 × 5.2 × 1.9	Bazán, Ferrol	1959
Y 237	344	34.3 × 6.2 × 2.5	Bazán, Cádiz	1965
Y 251	200	28 × 5.2 × 1.9	Bazán, Ferrol	1959
Y 252	337	34.3 × 6.2 × 2.5	Bazán, Cádiz	1965
Y 253	337	34.3 × 6.2 × 2.5	Bazán, Cádiz	1965
Y 254	214.7	24.5 × 5.5 × 2.2	Bazán, Cádiz	1981
Y 255	524	34 × 7 × 2.9	Bazán, Cádiz	1981

Y 231 (old number) *6/1985, X. Taibo*

TRAINING SHIPS

4 SAIL TRAINING SHIPS

Name	*No*	*Builders*	*Commissioned*
JUAN SEBASTIÁN DE ELCANO	A 71	Echevarrieta, Cadiz	28 Feb 1928
AROSA	A 72	—	1 Apr 1981
HISPANIA	A 73	Barracuda SY, Palma	25 July 1988
LA GRACIOSA (ex-*Dejá Vu*)	A 74	—	30 June 1988

Displacement, tons: 3420 standard; 3656 full load
Dimensions, feet (metres): 269.2 pp; 308.5 oa × 43.3 × 24.6 *(82; 94.1 × 13.2 × 7.5)*
Main machinery: 1 Sulzer diesel; 1500 hp(m) *(1.1 MW)*; 1 shaft
Speed, knots: 8.5. **Range, miles:** 10 000 at 9.5 kts
Complement: 332
Guns: 2—37 mm saluting guns.
Radars: Navigation: Two Decca TM 626; I band.

Comment: Details are for A 71 which is a four masted top-sail schooner—near sister of Chilean *Esmeralda*. Named after the first circumnavigator of the world (1519-22) who succeeded to the command of the expedition led by Magellan after the latter's death. Laid down 24 November 1925. Launched on 5 March 1927. Carries 230 tons oil fuel. She may be kept in service until 2027. The other three are a ketch (A 72) and two schooners (38 tons and 24.5 m in length) used by the Naval School.

JUAN SEBASTIAN DE ELCANO *1990, Royal Spanish Navy*

5 TRAINING CRAFT

Name	*No*	*Builders*	*Commissioned*
GUARDIAMARINA BARRUTIA	A 81	Cartagena	14 Sep 1982
GUARDIAMARINA SALAS	A 82	Cartagena	10 May 1983
GUARDIAMARINA GODINEZ	A 83	Cartagena	4 July 1984
GUARDIAMARINA RULL	A 84	Cartagena	11 June 1984
GUARDIAMARINA CHEREGUINI	A 85	Cartagena	11 June 1984

Displacement, tons: 56
Dimensions, feet (metres): 62 × 16.7 × 5.2 *(18.9 × 5.1 × 1.6)*
Speed, knots: 13
Complement: 15; 22 (A 81)
Radars: Navigation: Halcon 948; I band.

Comment: Tenders to Naval School. A 81 has an operations centre.

GUARDIAMARINA BARRUTIA *1987, Royal Spanish Navy*

BOOM DEFENCE VESSELS

Y 611 (ex-*YBPN 01*)

Displacement, tons: 51.1
Dimensions, feet (metres): 73.1 × 28.5 × 2.6 *(22.3 × 8.7 × 0.8)*

Comment: Gate Vessel. Delivered 1960. Unpropelled. Four other vessels include Y 361-362 net laying barges, Y 364 tug for gate vessel and barges, and Y 365.

Name	*No*	*Builders*	*Commissioned*
CÍCLOPE	A 13 (*ex-AC 01*, ex-*CR 1*, ex-*G 6*)	Penhoët, France	29 July 1955

Displacement, tons: 750.5 full load
Dimensions, feet (metres): 151.9 × 33.5 × 13.8 *(46.3 × 10.2 × 4.2)*
Main machinery: Diesel-electric; 2 diesel generators; 1 motor; 1600 hp(m) *(1.18 MW)*; 1 shaft
Speed, knots: 14. **Range, miles:** 5200 at 12 kts
Complement: 40
Guns: 1 Bofors 40 mm/60. 4 Oerlikon 20 mm.

Comment: US off-shore order. Transferred from the USA in 1955 under MDAP. Sister ship of French Cigale class (deleted). Based at Cartagena.

CICLOPE *1987, Royal Spanish Navy*

TUGS

2 LOGISTIC SUPPORT TUGS

Name	*No*	*Builders*	*Commissioned*
MAR CARIBE (ex-*Amatista*)	A 101	Duro Felguera, Gijon	24 Mar 1975
MAR ROJO (ex-*Amapola*)	A 102	Duro Felguera, Gijon	24 Mar 1975

Displacement, tons: 1860 full load
Dimensions, feet (metres): 176.4 × 38.8 × 14.8 *(53.8 × 11.8 × 4.5)*
Main machinery: 2 Echevarria-Burmeister & Wain 18V 23 HU diesels; 4860 hp(m) *(3.57 MW)*; 2 shafts; bow thruster
Speed, knots: 13.5. **Range, miles:** 6000 at 10 kts
Complement: 44

Comment: Two offshore oil rig support tugs were acquired and commissioned into the Navy 14 December 1988. Bollard pull, 80 tons. *Mar Rojo* converted as a diver support vessel completing in January 1991. A Vosma submergence vehicle is to be replaced by a DSRV. She has a dynamic positioning system and carries a sidescan mine detection high frequency sonar. *Mar Caribe* works with Amphibious Forces.

MAR ROJO *7/1991, Antonio Moreno*

2 OCEAN TUGS

Name	*No*	*Builders*	*Commissioned*
MAHÓN	A 51	Astilleros Atlántico, Santander	1978
LAS PALMAS	A 52	Astilleros Atlántico, Santander	1978

Displacement, tons: 1437 full load
Dimensions, feet (metres): 134.5 × 38.1 × 18 *(41 × 11.6 × 5.5)*
Main machinery: 2 AESA/Sulzer 16 ASV25-30 diesels; 7744 hp(m) *(5.69 MW)*; 2 shafts
Speed, knots: 13. **Range, miles:** 27 000 at 12 kts (A 52)
Complement: 33 (8 officers) plus 45 scientists
Guns: 2—12.7 mm MGs.

Comment: Built for Compania Hispano Americana de Offshore SA as *Circos* (A 51) and *Somiedo*. Commissioned in the Navy 30 July 1981. *Las Palmas* converted in 1988 for Polar Research Ship duties in Antarctica with an ice strengthened bow, an enlarged bridge and two containers aft for laboratories. With the commissioning of *Hesperides*, the ship might be sold or continue to operate in tandem.

MAHÓN *1987, Royal Spanish Navy*

4 OCEAN TUGS

Name	*No*	*Builders*	*Commissioned*
POSEIDÓN	A 12 (ex-*AS 01*, ex-*RA 6*)	Bazán, La Carraca	8 Aug 1964
CARTAGENA (ex-*Valen*)	A 41 (ex-*RA 1*)	Bazán, Cartagena	9 July 1955
CÁDIZ	A 42 (ex-*AR 44*, ex-*RA 4*)	Bazán, La Carraca	25 Mar 1964
FERROL	A 43 (ex-*AR 45*, ex-*RA 5*)	Bazán, La Carraca	11 Apr 1964

Displacement, tons: 951 standard; 1069 full load
Dimensions, feet (metres): 183.5 × 32.8 × 13.1 *(55.9 × 10 × 4)*
Main machinery: 2 Sulzer diesels; 3200 hp *(2.53 MW)*; 1 shaft; cp prop
Speed, knots: 15. **Range, miles:** 4640 at 14 kts
Complement: 49; 60 (A 12)
Guns: 2 or 4 Oerlikon 20 mm (twin).
Radars: Navigation: Decca TM 626; I band.

Comment: A 12 acts as a frogman support ship and submarine SAR vessel at Cartagena and carries a 300 m/6 hr bathyscaphe.

POSEIDON *1991, Camil Busquets i Vilanova*

CARTAGENA *1991, Camil Busquets i Vilanova*

2 COASTAL TUGS

Y 116 (ex-*YRR 21*, ex-*71*) **Y 117** (ex-*YRR 22*, ex-*72*)

Displacement, tons: 422 full load
Dimensions, feet (metres): 91.8 × 26.2 × 12.5 *(28 × 8 × 3.8)*
Main machinery: 1 diesel; 1500 hp *(1.1 MW)*; 1 shaft
Speed, knots: 12.4. **Range, miles:** 3000 at 10 kts

Comment: Built by Bazán, Ferrol. Commissioned 10 April and 1 June 1981 respectively.

31 COASTAL and HARBOUR TUGS

No	*Displacement tonnes (full load)*	*HP/speed*	*Commissioned*
Y 111, Y 114	227	800/10	1963
Y 112	222	800/10	1963
Y 113	217	1400/12	1965
Y 115	216	1500/12	1967
Y 118, Y 121-123	236	1560/14	1989-91
Y 119 (ex-*Punta Amer*)	260	1750/12	1973
Y 120 (ex-*Punta Roca*)	260	1750/12	1973
Y 131-140	70	200/8	1965-67
Y 141-142	229	800/11	1981
Y 143	133	600/10	1961
Y 144-145	195	2030/11	1983
Y 146	173	829/10	1983
Y 147	87	400/10	1987
Y 171-173	10	440/11	1982 (171) 1985 (172-3)

Comment: Y 143 has a troop carrying capability. Y 171-173 are pusher tugs for submarines. Y 118, Y 119-123 have Voith Schneider propulsion.

Y 118 *1988, Bazán*

WATER CARRIERS

CONTRAMAESTRE CASTELLÓ A 61 (ex-*AA 06*, ex-*A 6*)

Displacement, tons: 1811 full load
Dimensions, feet (metres): 210.3 × 31.5 × 15.7 *(64.1 × 9.6 × 4.8)*
Main machinery: 1 boiler; 1 reciprocating engine; 800 ihp(m) *(588 kW)*; 1 shaft
Speed, knots: 9
Complement: 27
Cargo capacity: 1000 tons
Guns: 2—12.7 mm MGs.

Comment: Commissioned 30 January 1952. Ocean-going.

CONTRAMAESTRE CASTELLÓ *1987, Royal Spanish Navy*

MAQUINISTA MACÍAS A 62 (ex-*AA 21*, ex-*A 9*)
TORPEDISTA HERNÁNDEZ A 63 (ex-*AA 22*, ex-*A 10*)
FOGONERO BAÑOBRE A 64 (ex-*AA 23*, ex-*A 11*)

Displacement, tons: 575 full load
Dimensions, feet (metres): 146.9 × 24.9 × 9.8 *(44.8 × 7.6 × 3)*
Main machinery: 1 diesel; 700 hp(m) *(514 kW)*; 1 shaft
Speed, knots: 9. **Range, miles:** 1000 at 8 kts
Complement: 17
Cargo capacity: 350 tons

Comment: Built at Bazán, La Carraca. Commissioned 24 January 1963. All ocean-going.

MAQUINISTA MACÍAS *1987, Royal Spanish Navy*

MARINERO JARANA A 65 (ex-*AA 31*)

Displacement, tons: 527 full load
Dimensions, feet (metres): 123 × 23 × 9.8 *(37.5 × 7 × 3)*
Main machinery: 1 diesel; 600 hp(m) *(441 kW)*; 1 shaft
Speed, knots: 10.8
Complement: 13
Cargo capacity: 300 tons

Comment: Built by Bazán, Cádiz. Similar to Y 231 and Y 255 (harbour tankers). Commissioned 16 March 1981.

MARINERO JARANA *1987, Royal Spanish Navy*

CONDESTABLE ZARAGOZA A 66 (ex-*AA 41*)

Displacement, tons: 892 full load
Dimensions, feet (metres): 152.2 × 27.6 × 11.2 *(46.4 × 8.4 × 3.4)*
Main machinery: 1 diesel; 700 hp(m) *(515 kW)*; 1 shaft
Speed, knots: 10.8
Complement: 16
Cargo capacity: 600 tons

Comment: Built by Bazán, Cádiz. Commissioned 16 October 1981.

CONDESTABLE ZARAGOZA *1990, Royal Spanish Navy*

Y 271-273 (ex-*YA 01-03*, ex-*AB 01-03*)

Displacement, tons: 320 (Y 271-2); 344 (Y 273)
Dimensions, feet (metres): 112.5 × 20.3 × 8.2 *(34.3 × 6.2 × 2.5)*
Main machinery: 1 diesel; 280 hp(m) *(206 kW)*; 1 shaft
Speed, knots: 9.7
Complement: 8
Cargo capacity: 200 tons

Comment: Harbour water-boats. Commissioned 1959. Similar to tankers Y 237, 252 and 253.

DIVING CRAFT

NEREIDA Y 562 (ex-*YBZ 11*) **PROSERPINA** Y 563 (ex-*YBZ 12*) **Y 561** (ex-*YBZ 01*) **Y 564** (ex-*YBZ 32*) **Y 565** (ex-*YBZ 31*)

Displacement, tons: 103.5
Dimensions, feet (metres): 70.5 × 19.2 × 9.5 *(21.5 × 5.9 × 2.9)*
Main machinery: 1 Sulzer diesel; 200 hp(m) *(147 kW)*; 1 shaft
Speed, knots: 9

Comment: Built by Bazán, Cartagena. Frogmen support craft.

PROSERPINA *6/1988, Camil Busquets i Vilanova*

Y 571-Y 584

Displacement, tons: 8-13.7
Dimensions, feet (metres): 35.8 × 12.8 × 2.6 *(10.9 × 3.9 × 0.8)*
Speed, knots: 7-12

Comment: *Y 579* deleted in 1991.

MISCELLANEOUS

1 MINE TRANSPORT CRAFT

YTM 352

Displacement, tons: 178 full load
Dimensions, feet (metres): 101.4 × 21.7 × 9.8 *(30.9 × 6.6 × 3)*
Speed, knots: 7
Complement: 8
Mines: 50.

Comment: Built by Bazán 1961. Transports torpedoes and mines and, in emergency, can act as a minelayer.

5 FLOATING CRANES

SANSÓN Y 381 **Y 382-384** **Y 385**

Displacement, tons: 589 (Y 381); 490 (Y 384); 470 (Y 382-3); 272 (Y 385-6)
Dimensions, feet (metres): 102.4 × 54.1 × 10.5 *(31.2 × 16.5 × 3.2)* (Y 381)
73.8 × 45.9 × 9.8 *(22.5 × 14 × 3)* (Y 382-4)
62.3 × 38.4 × 7.9 *(19 × 11.7 × 2.4)* (Y 385-6)
Military lift: 100 tons (Y 381); 30 tons (Y 382-4); 15 tons (Y 385-6)

Comment: Based at Cartagena, Ferrol and La Carraca. Completed 1929 (Y 381), 1953-56 remainder. Y 386 deleted in 1990.

1 SUCTION DREDGER

Y 441 (ex-*YDR 11*)

Comment: Can dredge to 8 m. Built in 1981 by IHC, Netherlands. Operates at La Carraca.

1 BARRACK SHIP

Y 601 (ex-*YCFN 01*)

Comment: Former US LSM of 1094 tons. Built in 1944. Based at Ferrol.

23 HARBOUR LAUNCHES

Y 501-513 **Y 517-518**
Y 531-535 **Y 538-540**

Comment: Can carry up to 40 people at 17 kts (*531-535*). Remainder, 10 kts.

39 BARGES

Comment: Have Y numbers. 200 series carry fuel, 300 for ammunition and general stores. 400 for anti-pollution. Four deleted in 1991 and replaced by Y 421-425.

Y 423 *7/1991, Antonio Moreno*

GUARDIA CIVIL DEL MAR

Note: Formed in 1992 with bases initially at La Coruña, Cartagena and Barcelona. Personnel strength 1526 (39 officers). The force takes over the anti-terrorist role as a peacetime paramilitary organisation coming under the Ministry of Defence in war. Order of battle to include:
(a) 11 Coastal Patrol Craft of 50 tons, 30 kts and a complement of 12
(b) 37 Inshore Patrol Craft of 25 tons, 35 kts and a complement of 7
(c) 39 Harbour Patrol Craft of 8 tons, 40 kts and a complement of 4.
All vessels are to be armed. Full strength will take about 5 years to achieve.

GUARDIA CIVIL Craft *2/1992, Diego Quevedo*

CUSTOMS SERVICE

Note: All carry ADUANAS on ships' sides. There are 41 craft of all types painted black with a white diagonal stripe in 1990/91. Most recent additions are 70 kt interceptor craft IPP 1-3 and IMP 1-2. Some of the larger vessels are armed with machine guns. There are also four CASA C-212 maritime patrol aircraft and four helicopters.

CONDOR III (ex-*Smit-Lloyd Cairo*)

Displacement, tons: 1600 full load
Dimensions, feet (metres): 196.2 × 37.1 × 14.1 *(59.8 × 11.3 × 4.3)*
Main machinery: 2 MAN Alpha diesels; 2700 hp(m) *(1.98 MW)*; 2 shafts
Speed, knots: 14
Complement: 12

Comment: Acquired in 1991 and is based in Corunna. Serves as a depot ship for Interceptor craft.

Name	*Displacement tons (full load)*	*HP/speed*	*Commissioned*
ÁGUILA	80	2700/29	1974
ALBATROS 1 and **3**	83	2700/29	1964-69
ALCA 1-3	22	2000/45	1987-88
ALCAVARÁN 1-5	85	3920/28	1984-87
ALCOTÁN 2	95	3200/23	—
CÁRABO	60	1350/16	1977
COLIMBO	36	850/20	—
GAVILÁN 1, AGUILUCHO	63	2700/28	1975-76
GAVILÁN 2	65	3200/30	1983
GAVILÁN 3	65	3920/28	1987
HALCÓN 2-3	68	3200/28	1980-83
HJ 1, HJ 3-13	20	2000/50	1986
VA 2-5	23	1400/27	1985
CORMORÁN	20	2970/65	1990

ALCAVARAN V *6/1991, A. Campanera i Rovira*

SRI LANKA

Headquarters' Appointment

Commander of the Navy:
Vice Admiral W W E C Fernando

Formation

The Royal Ceylon Navy was formed on 9 December 1950 when the Navy Act was proclaimed. Called the Sri Lanka Navy since Republic Day 22 May 1972.

Personnel

(a) 1992: 9150 (650 officers)
(b) Voluntary service
(c) SLVNF: 870 (70 officers)
(d) Naval reservists: 102 (12 officers)

General

The Tamil insurgency in Sri Lanka had a major impact on the naval programme. The main area of maritime importance is the Palk Strait between India and the primarily Tamil area of northern Sri Lanka. This area has many small creeks—the main requirement is the support of shallow draught fast craft, a very different task from EEZ patrols.

Naval Bases

Naval Base at Trincomalee was expanded in 1988-89 programme. Minor bases at Karainagar, Colombo, Welisara, Tangalle, and Kalpitiya.
There are three Area Commands—North, East and West.

Prefix to Ships' Names

SLNS. Pennant numbers changed on 1 November 1987.

Strength of the Fleet

Type	*Active*
Command Ships/Tenders	4
Fast Attack Craft—Gun	23
Offshore Patrol Vessels	2
Coastal Patrol Craft	19
Inshore Patrol Craft	30
Landing Craft	4
FPCs	2

Mercantile Marine

Lloyd's Register of Shipping:
78 vessels of 332 978 tons gross

DELETIONS

1989 P 203
1990 P 236
1991 *Balawatha*, P 150

COMMAND SHIPS

Name	*No*	*Builders*	*Commissioned*
ABHEETHA (ex-*Carinia*)	P 714	Chung Wah SB & Eng Co Ltd	9 Aug 1984
EDITHARA (ex-*Francesca*)	P 715	Singapore Slipway Co	9 Aug 1984
WICKRAMA (ex-*Delicia*)	P 716	Chung Wah SB & Eng Co Ltd	9 Aug 1984

Displacement, tons: 2628 full load
Dimensions, feet (metres): 249.7 × 56.1 × 12.5 *(76.1 × 17.1 × 3.8)*
Main machinery: 2 Deutz SBA 12M 525 diesels; 3000 hp(m) *(2.2 MW)*; 2 shafts
Speed, knots: 12. **Range, miles:** 6000 at 10 kts
Complement: 50
Guns: 2 China 25 mm/60 (twin) Type 61; 85° elevation; 270 rounds/minute to 3 km *(1.6 nm)*; weight of shell 0.34 kg.
8 China 14.5 mm/93 (4 twin) MGs.
Radars: Surface search: Selesmar/Selescan; I band.
Navigation: Furuno; I band.

Comment: Former Ro-Ro ships built 1976-77 and used as command and HQ ships for Light Forces. Classified as Surveillance Command Ships. Dates given are commissioning dates in the Navy. Have a 30 ton crane.

WICKRAMA *1984, Sri Lanka Navy*

A 526 (ex-*Kota Rukun*, ex-*Mercury Cove*, ex-*Tjimanuk*)

Displacement, tons: 6300 full load
Dimensions, feet (metres): 326.4 × 51.2 × 22.6 *(99.5 × 15.6 × 6.9)*
Main machinery: 1 NV Werkspoor 6-cyl diesel; 3600 hp(m) *(2.64 MW)*; 1 shaft
Speed, knots: 13. **Range, miles:** 12 000 at 8 kts
Complement: 50
Guns: 1—12.7 mm MG.
Radars: Surface search: Decca 110; I band.
Navigation: Furuno FR 1011; I band.

Comment: Launched in 1959 at Gorinchem Shipyard and acquired from Pacific International Lines in 1986. 3350 grt. Classified as a Command Tender.

A 526 *1986, Sri Lanka Navy*

LIGHT FORCES

2 OFFSHORE PATROL VESSELS (OPV)

Name	*No*	*Builders*	*Commissioned*
JAYESAGARA	P 601	Colombo Dockyard	9 Dec 1983
SAGARAWARDENE	P 602	Colombo Dockyard	6 Apr 1984

Displacement, tons: 330 full load
Dimensions, feet (metres): 130.5 × 23 × 7 *(39.8 × 7 × 2.1)*
Main machinery: 2 MAN 8L 20/27 diesels; 2180 hp(m) *(1.6 MW)* sustained; 2 shafts
Speed, knots: 15. **Range, miles:** 3000 at 11 kts
Complement: 52 (4 officers)
Guns: 2 China 25 mm/80 (twin). 2 China 14.5 mm (twin) MGs.

Comment: Ordered from Colombo Dockyard on 31 December 1981. P 601 launched 26 May 1983, P 602 launched 20 November 1983.

JAYESAGARA *5/1990, John Mortimer*

5 SOORAYA CLASS (FAST ATTACK CRAFT—GUN)

SOORAYA P 310 (ex-P 3140)
WEERAYA P 311 (ex-P 3141)
RANAKAMEE P 312 (ex-P 3142)
JAGATHA P 315 (ex-P 3145)
RAKSHAKA P 316 (ex-P 3146)

Displacement, tons: 113 standard; 131 full load
Dimensions, feet (metres): 127.3 × 17.7 × 5.2 *(38.8 × 5.4 × 1.6)*
Main machinery: 2 Type L12-180 diesels; 2400 hp(m) *(1.76 MW)* (forward); 2 Type L12-180Z; 1820 hp(m) *(1.34 MW)* (aft); 4 shafts
Speed, knots: 29. **Range, miles:** 700 at 16 kts
Complement: 34
Guns: 2 China 37 mm/63 (twin). 4 China 25 mm/80 (2 twin abaft the bridge).
Depth charges: 8.
Radars: Surface search: Skin Head; I band; range 37 km *(20 nm)*.
Navigation: Furuno 825 D; I band.

Comment: Ex-Shanghai II class, the first pair transferred by China in February 1972, the second pair in July 1972, one in December 1972 and two more on 30 November 1980. One deleted in 1991.

SOORAYA (old number) *1987, Sri Lanka Navy*

3 RANA CLASS (FAST ATTACK CRAFT—GUN)

RANASURU P 320 **RANAWIRU** P 321 **RANARISI** P 322

Displacement, tons: 150 full load
Dimensions, feet (metres): 134.5 × 17.7 × 5.2 *(41 × 5.4 × 1.6)*
Main machinery: 4 diesels; 4800 hp(m) *(3.53 MW)*; 4 shafts
Speed, knots: 29. **Range, miles:** 750 at 16 kts
Complement: 28 (4 officers)
Guns: 2 China 37 mm/63 (twin) Type 76. 4 China 14.5 mm (twin) Type 69.
Radars: Surface search: Racal Decca; I band.

Comment: Modified Shanghai II class acquired from China in September 1991 and commissioned in November 1991. More powerful engines than the Sooraya class; automatic guns and improved habitability.

RANA Class *11/1991, Sri Lanka Navy*

12 ISRAELI DVORA CLASS (FAST ATTACK CRAFT—GUN)

P 453-458, P463-468

Displacement, tons: 47 full load
Dimensions, feet (metres): 70.8 (73.5, 463-8) × 18 × 5.8 *(21.6 (22.4) × 5.5 × 1.8)*
Main machinery: 2 MTU 12V 331 TC 81 diesels; 2605 hp(m) *(1.91 MW)* sustained; 2 shafts *(P 453-458)*
2 MTU 12V 396 TB 93 diesels; 3260 hp(m) *(2.4 MW)* sustained; 2 shafts *(P 463-468)*
Speed, knots: 36 (42 *(P 463-468)*). **Range, miles:** 1200 at 17 kts
Complement: 12
Guns: 2 Oerlikon 20 mm. 2—12.7 mm MGs.
Radars: Surface search: Decca 926; I band.

Comment: First pair transferred early 1984, next four in October 1986 with a further six ordered at that time. Of the second batch two were delivered in November 1987 and the remainder in early 1988. All were built by Israeli Aircraft Industries. The second batch of six have more powerful engines and are slightly lighter and faster than similar craft in the Israeli Navy.

P 464 *1988, Sri Lanka Navy*

3 SOUTH KOREAN KILLER CLASS (FAST ATTACK CRAFT—GUN)

P 473-475

Displacement, tons: 56 full load
Dimensions, feet (metres): 75.5 × 17.7 × 5.9 *(23 × 5.4 × 1.8)*
Main machinery: 2 MTU 396 TB 93 diesels; 3260 hp(m) *(2.4 MW)* sustained; 2 shafts
Speed, knots: 40
Complement: 12
Guns: 2 Oerlikon 20 mm. 2—12.7 mm MGs.
Radars: Surface search: Racal Decca; I band.

Comment: Built by Korea SB and Eng, Buson. All commissioned February 1988.

P 474 *1988, Sri Lanka Navy*

10 COASTAL PATROL CRAFT

P 231-235, P241-245

Displacement, tons: 40
Dimensions, feet (metres): 66 × 18 × 7 *(20 × 5.5 × 2.1)*
Main machinery: 2 GM 12V 71 VTI diesels; 840 hp *(626 kW)* sustained; 2 shafts
Speed, knots: 22. **Range, miles:** 1500 at 14 kts
Complement: 10
Guns: 2 Oerlikon 20 mm (24 series). 2—12.7 mm MGs (23 series).

Comment: Ordered from Colombo DY June 1976 (first pair). First six commissioned 1980-81, last five in 1982-83. All craft refitted 1988-89 except *P 236* which was deleted in June 1990.

P 231 Class *1987, Sri Lanka Navy*

4 COASTAL PATROL CRAFT

P 201, 202, 204, 211

Displacement, tons: 21 full load
Dimensions, feet (metres): 46.6 × 12.8 × 3.3 *(14.2 × 3.9 × 1)*
Main machinery: 2 GM 8V71 TI diesels; 460 hp *(343 kW)*; 2 shafts
Speed, knots: 20. **Range, miles:** 450 at 14 kts
Complement: 6
Guns: 2—12.7 mm MGs.

Comment: Built by Colombo DY and commissioned in 1982-83 (P 201-204) and June 1986 (P 211). P 203 sunk in 1989.

P 201 Class *1986, Sri Lanka Navy*

5 COASTAL PATROL CRAFT

P 221-225 (ex-*P 421-425*)

Displacement, tons: 22 full load
Dimensions, feet (metres): 55.9 × 14.8 × 3.9 *(17 × 4.5 × 1.2)*
Main machinery: 2 GM 8V71 TI diesels; 460 hp *(343 kW)*; 2 shafts
Speed, knots: 23. **Range, miles:** 1000 at 12 kts
Complement: 7
Guns: 1—12.7 mm MG.

Comment: Used for general patrol duties. Built by Cheverton Workboats, UK and commissioned in 1977.

P 223 (old number) *1983, Sri Lanka Navy*

9 INSHORE PATROL CRAFT

P 111-119

Displacement, tons: 5
Dimensions, feet (metres): 44 × 9.8 × 1.6 *(13.4 × 3 × 0.5)*
Main machinery: 2 Yamaha D 343 K diesels; 324 hp(m) *(238 kW)*; 2 shafts
Speed, knots: 26
Complement: 5
Guns: 1—12.7 mm MG.

Comment: Built by Consolidated Marine Engineers, Sri Lanka. All delivered in 1988. Operate from Command Ships.

P 112 *1988, Sri Lanka Navy*

9 COUGAR CLASS (INSHORE PATROL CRAFT)

P 101-109

Displacement, tons: 7.4 full load
Dimensions, feet (metres): 34.1 × 9.5 × 2.6 *(10.4 × 2.9 × 0.8)*
Main machinery: 2 Sabre diesels; 500 hp *(373 kW)*; 2 shafts
Speed, knots: 30
Complement: 4
Guns: 1—12.7 mm MG.

Comment: First ordered in 1984 for trials, order for remainder placed in 1985. Operate from Command Ships.

COUGAR Class *1987, Sri Lanka Navy*

2 + (10) INSHORE PATROL CRAFT

P 151-152

Displacement, tons: 9
Dimensions, feet (metres): 9.8 × 12.1 × 1.6 *(3 × 3.7 × 0.5)*
Main machinery: 2 Cummins 6 BTA 5.9M2; 600 hp *(448 kW)*; 2 waterjets
Speed, knots: 33. **Range, miles:** 330 at 25 kts
Complement: 5
Guns: 1—12.7 mm MG.

Comment: Built by TAOS Yacht Company, Colombo, and delivered in 1991. Ten more may be acquired.

P 151 *1991, Sri Lanka Navy*

10 INSHORE PATROL CRAFT

P 140-149

Displacement, tons: 3.5
Dimensions, feet (metres): 42 × 8 × 1.6 *(12.8 × 2.4 × 0.5)*
Main machinery: 2 outboard motors; 280 hp *(209 kW)*
Speed, knots: 30
Complement: 4

Comment: Acquired in 1988. Similar to *P 111* but with outboard engines. *P 150* was mined and sunk in August 1991.

P150 *1989, Sri Lanka Navy*

AMPHIBIOUS FORCES

Note: There are plans for an assault force of Marines in due course.

3 LANDING CRAFT (LCM)

Name	*No*	*Builders*	*Commissioned*
KANDULA	L 837 (ex-A 537)	Vospers, Singapore	21 Dec 1987
PABBATHA	L 838 (ex-A 538)	Vospers, Singapore	21 Dec 1987
GAJASINGHA	L 839	Colombo Dockyard	15 Nov 1991

Displacement, tons: 268 full load
Dimensions, feet (metres): 108.3 × 26 × 4.9 *(33 × 8 × 1.5)*
Main machinery: 2 Caterpillar diesels; 1524 hp *(1.14 MW)*; 2 shafts
Speed, knots: 8. **Range, miles:** 1800 at 8 kts
Complement: 12 (2 officers)
Guns: 2 Oerlikon 20 mm. 2—12.7 mm MGs.

Comment: First pair built in 1983 and acquired in October 1985. Third of the class taken over by the Navy in September 1991.

GAJASINGHA *10/1991, Sri Lanka Navy*

2 FAST PERSONNEL CARRIERS (FPC)

Name	*No*	*Builders*	*Commissioned*
HANSAYA	A 540 (ex-*Offshore Pioneer*)	Sing Koon Seng, Singapore	20 Dec 1987
LIHINIYA	A 541 (ex-*Offshore Pride*)	Sing Koon Seng, Singapore	20 Dec 1987

Displacement, tons: 154 full load
Dimensions, feet (metres): 98.4 × 36.8 × 7.7 *(30 × 11.2 × 2.3)*
Main machinery: 2 MTU diesels; 2 shafts
Speed, knots: 30
Complement: 12 (2 officers)
Cargo capacity: 60 tons; 120 troops
Guns: 1 Oerlikon 20 mm. 2—12.7 mm MGs.

Comment: Acquired in January 1986 from Aluminium Shipbuilders. Catamaran hulls used for fast transport.

HANSAYA *1988*

1 CHINESE YUNNAN CLASS (LCU)

L 820

Displacement, tons: 128 full load
Dimensions, feet (metres): 93.8 × 17.7 × 4.6 *(28.6 × 5.4 × 1.4)*
Main machinery: 2 diesels; 600 hp(m) *(441 kW)*; 2 shafts
Speed, knots: 12. **Range, miles:** 500 at 10 kts
Complement: 12 (2 officers)
Military lift: 46 tons
Guns: 2—12.7 mm MGs.

Comment: Acquired from China in May 1991.

L 820 *6/1991, Sri Lanka Navy*

SUDAN

Headquarters' Appointment

Commander-in-Chief and Commander (Navy):
Brigadier Said El Hussein Abdel Kariem

Diplomatic Representation

Defence Attaché in London:
Brigadier M O Idris

Personnel

(a) 1992: 500 officers and men
(b) Voluntary service

Establishment

The Navy was established in 1962 to operate on the Red Sea coast and on the River Nile.

Bases

Flamingo Bay for Red Sea operations with a separate riverine unit on the Nile based at Khartoum.

Mercantile Marine

Lloyd's Register of Shipping:
16 vessels of 45 445 tons gross

General

The overall standard of operational efficiency has suffered from lack of maintenance and spare parts and auxiliaries have drifted into total disrepair. Also reported are an ex-Tanker used for training, a Water Tanker (PB 6) and an unarmed Survey Ship (PB 35). Some of the craft listed under Deletions are non-operational but have not yet been scrapped. More patrol craft may be acquired from China or Iran.

DELETIONS

1987-88 *El Fasher, Fashoda, Tienga, Baraka, Shaab, Gihad, Horriya, Istiqlal, Sheikan, Khartoum*

LIGHT FORCES

2 Ex-IRANIAN COASTAL PATROL CRAFT

KADIR (ex-*Shahpar*) 129 **KARARI** (ex-*Shahram*) 130

Displacement, tons: 70 full load
Dimensions, feet (metres): 75.2 × 16.5 × 6 *(22.9 × 5 × 1.8)*
Main machinery: 2 MTU diesels; 2200 hp(m) *(1.62 MW)*; 2 shafts
Speed, knots: 27
Complement: 19 (3 officers)
Guns: 1 Oerlikon 20 mm.

Comment: Built for Iran by Abeking & Rasmussen in 1970. Transferred to Iranian Coast Guard 1975 and to Sudan later that year. *Sheikan* has been cannibalised for spares.

KADIR *2/1990*

4 Ex-IRANIAN SEWART PATROL CRAFT

MAROUB 1161 **FIJAB** 1162 **SALAK** 1163 **HALOTE** 1164

Displacement, tons: 9.1 full load
Dimensions, feet (metres): 40 × 12.1 × 3.3 *(12.2 × 3.7 × 1)*
Main machinery: 2 GM diesels; 348 hp *(260 kW)*; 2 shafts
Speed, knots: 31
Complement: 6
Guns: 1—12.7 mm MG.

Comment: Transferred by Iranian Coast Guard in 1975. At least two were operational in 1990.

4 YUGOSLAV TYPE 15 (INSHORE PATROL CRAFT)

KURMUK 502 **QAYSAN** 503 **RUMBEK** 504 **MAYOM** 505

Displacement, tons: 19.5 full load
Dimensions, feet (metres): 55.4 × 12.8 × 2.3 *(16.9 × 3.9 × 0.7)*
Main machinery: 2 diesels; 330 hp(m) *(243 kW)*; 2 shafts
Speed, knots: 16. **Range, miles:** 160 at 12 kts
Complement: 6
Guns: 1 Oerlikon 20 mm; 2—7.62 mm MGs.
Radars: Surface search: I band.

Comment: Delivered by Yugoslavia on 18 May 1989 for operations on the White Nile.

KURMUK *1989, G. Jacobs*

LAND-BASED MARITIME AIRCRAFT

Numbers/Type: 2 CASA C-212 Aviocar.
Operational speed: 190 kts *(353 km/h)*.
Service ceiling: 24 000 ft *(7315 m)*.
Range: 1650 nm *(3055 km)*.
Role/Weapon systems: Limited capability over the Red Sea; no real combat role. Sensors: Search radar. Weapons: Unarmed.

AMPHIBIOUS FORCES

2 Ex-YUGOSLAV DTM 221 CLASS (LCUs)

SOBAT 221 **DINDER** 222

Displacement, tons: 410
Dimensions, feet (metres): 155.1 × 21 × 7.5 *(47.3 × 6.4 × 2.3)*
Speed, knots: 9
Complement: 15
Guns: 1 Oerlikon 20 mm. 2—12.7 mm MGs.

Comment: Transferred during 1969.

SURINAM

Personnel

1992: 230 officers and men

Base

Paramaribo

Mercantile Marine

Lloyd's Register of Shipping:
24 vessels of 12 876 tons gross

LIGHT FORCES

2 COASTAL PATROL CRAFT

C 301 **C 303**

Displacement, tons: 65
Dimensions, feet (metres): 72.2 × 15.5 × 7.6 *(22 × 4.7 × 2.3)*
Main machinery: 2 Dorman 8 JT diesels; 560 hp *(418 kW)*; 2 shafts
Speed, knots: 13.5. **Range, miles:** 650 at 13 kts
Complement: 8
Guns: 1—12.7 mm MG. 2—7.62 mm MGs.
Radars: Surface search: Decca 110; I band.

Comment: Three ordered April 1975 from Schottel, Netherlands. Commissioned in 1976. *C 302* cannibalised for spares.

C 301 *1980, Surinam Ministry*

3 RIVER PATROL CRAFT

Name	*No*	*Builders*	*Commissioned*
BAHADOER	RP 201	Schottel, Netherlands	Dec 1975
FAJABLOW	RP 202	Schottel, Netherlands	Dec 1975
KORANGON	RP 203	Schottel, Netherlands	Feb 1976

Displacement, tons: 15
Dimensions, feet (metres): 41.4 × 12.5 × 3.6 *(12.6 × 3.8 × 1.1)*
Main machinery: 1 Dorman 8 JT diesel; 280 hp *(209 kW)*; 1 shaft
Speed, knots: 14. **Range, miles:** 350 at 10 kts
Complement: 4
Guns: 1—12.7 mm MG.

Comment: Ordered December 1974.

KORANGON *1980, Surinam Ministry*

2 SURVEY CRAFT

COEROENI LITANI

Comment: *Coeroeni* of 80 tons launched in 1962; *Litani* of 70 tons launched in 1958. Both craft are owned by the Ministry of Economic Affairs and manned by the Navy.

3 LARGE PATROL CRAFT

P 401-403 (ex-*S 401-403*)

Displacement, tons: 140 full load
Dimensions, feet (metres): 105 × 21.3 × 5.5 *(32 × 6.5 × 1.7)*
Main machinery: 2 Paxman 12 YHCM diesels; 2110 hp *(1.57 MW)*; 2 shafts
Speed, knots: 17.5. **Range, miles:** 1200 at 13.5 kts
Complement: 15
Guns: 2 Bofors 40 mm. 2—7.62 mm MGs.
Radars: Surface search: Decca 110; I band.

Comment: Built by De Vries, Aalsmeer, Netherlands and commissioned in 1976-77. This design has far greater speed and armament potential but Surinam apparently opted for the scaled-down version.

S 403 (old number) *1980, Surinam Ministry*

LAND-BASED MARITIME AIRCRAFT

Numbers/Type: 4 Pilatus Britten-Norman BN-2A Maritime Defender.
Operational speed: 150 kts *(280 km/h)*.
Service ceiling: 18 900 ft *(5760 m)*.
Range: 1500 nm *(2775 km)*.
Role/Weapon systems: Flown by Air Force for coastal patrol. Sensors: Lightweight search radar. Weapons: Unarmed.

SWEDEN

Headquarters' Appointments

Chief of the Defence Staff:
General Bengt Gustafsson
Commander-in-Chief:
Vice Admiral Dick Börjesson
Chief of Naval Material Department:
Rear Admiral Torbjorn Hultman

Senior Command

Commander-in-Chief of Coastal Fleet:
Rear Admiral Sten Swedlund

Diplomatic Representation

Defence Attaché in London:
Commodore Jan Bring
Naval Attaché in Moscow:
Captain Lennart Stenberg
Naval Attaché in Washington:
Captain Christer Hägg
Defence Attaché in Canberra:
Commander Nils Bruzelius
Naval Attaché in Bonn:
Captain Lars Norrsell

Pennant Numbers

Numbers are not displayed on major patrol craft.

Coastal Artillery

Being re-organised into six amphibious battalions of 800 men in each. Each battalion to have 24 Combatboat 90, 7 Combatboat 90E, 13 Trossbät, 1 mine support vessel, 27 section vessels and 56 canoes. The plan is to form one battalion per year from 1991. All Coastal Artillery vessels are fully integrated with the Navy and are therefore not shown as a separate section.

Personnel

(a) 1992: 9150 officers and men of Navy and Coastal Artillery made up of 3100 regulars and 6050 national servicemen
(b) 10-17½ months' national service

Bases

Musko (Stockholm), Karlskrona.
Minor bases at Härnösand and Göteborg.

Strength of the Fleet

Type	*Active (Reserve)*	*Building (Planned)*
Submarines—Patrol	12	3
Missile Corvettes	6	—
Fast Attack Craft—Missile	28	—
Coastal Patrol Craft	12	—
Inshore Patrol Craft	21	—
Experimental Patrol Craft	1	—
Minelayers	3	—
MCM Support Ship	1	—
Minelayers—Coastal	9	—
Minelayers—Small	22	—
Minesweepers/Hunters—Coastal	9	1
Minesweepers—Inshore	14	—
LCMs	26	—
LCUs	79	—
LCAs	38	(63)
Mine Transports	2	—
Survey Ships	3	—
Electronic Surveillance Ship	1	—
Transport Ships	1	—
Tankers—Support	2	—
Divers Support Ship	1	—
Tugs	20	—
Salvage Ship	1	—
Sonobuoy Tenders	4	—
Sail Training Ships	2	—
Icebreakers	7	—
TRVs	3	—
Water Boats	2	—
Coast Guard	130 (approx)	—

Mercantile Marine

Lloyd's Register of Shipping:
684 vessels of 3 174 274 tons gross

DELETIONS

Submarines

1989-90 *Delfinen, Nordkaparen* (museum ship), *Springaren, Vargen*

Light Forces

1989 *Spica, Capella, Vega, Virgo, Skanör, Smyge, Tärno*
1990 *Tjurko*

Mine Warfare Forces

1989 *Sparö, Styrsö, Hasslö, M 17-18, M 23, M 26*
1990 *Skaftö*
1992 *Fårösund*

Miscellaneous

1989 *Oden, Thule*

PENNANT LIST

Corvettes

K 11	Stockholm
K 12	Malmö
K 21	Göteborg
K 22	Gälve
K 23	Kalmar
K 24	Sundsvall

Light Forces

P 151	Hugin
P 152	Munin
P 153	Magne
P 154	Mode
P 155	Vale
P 156	Vidar
P 157	Mjölner
P 158	Mysing
P 159	Kaparen
P 160	Väktaren
P 161	Snapphanen
P 162	Spejaren
P 163	Styrbjörn
P 164	Starkodder
P 165	Tordön
P 166	Tirfing
R 131	Norrköping
R 132	Nynäshamn
R 133	Norrtälje
R 134	Varberg
R 135	Västerås
R 136	Västervik
R 137	Umeå
R 138	Piteå
R 139	Luleå
R 140	Halmstad
R 141	Strömstad
R 142	Ystad
V 03	Arild
V 04	Viken
V 05	Öregrund
V 06	Slite
V 07	Marstrand
V 08	Lysekil
V 09	Dalarö
V 10	Sandhamn
V 11	Östhammar
50	Rörö
V 55	Ornö
V 150	Jägaren
61-77	CPC
SVK 1	Svärdet
SVK 2	Spjutet
SVK 3	Pilen
SVK 4	Bågen

Amphibious Forces

324	Ane
325	Balder
326	Loke
327	Ring
333	Skagul
335	Sleipner
210-288	LCUs
331-354	LCAs
603-604	LCMs
606-612	LCMs
651-658	LCMs
801	Helge
802	Helga

Mine Warfare Forces

M 02	Älvsborg
M 03	Visborg
M 04	Carlskrona
M 21-22	IMS
M 24-25	IMS
M 31	Gåssten
M 32	Norsten
M 33	Viksten
M 43	Hisingen
M 44	Blackan
M 45	Dämman
M 46	Galten
M 47	Gillöga
M 48	Rödlöga
M 49	Svartlöga
M 57	Arkö
M 67	Nämdö
M 68	Blidö
M 71	Landsort
M 72	Arholma
M 73	Koster
M 74	Kullen
M 75	Vinga
M 76	Ven
M 77	Ulvön (bldg)
MUL 11	Kalvsund
MUL 12	Arkösund
MUL 13	Kalmarsund
MUL 14	Alnösund
MUL 15	Grundsund
MUL 17	Skramsösund
MUL 18	Öresund
MUL 19	Barösund
MUL 20	Furusund
501-516	Small Minelayers
1879-1884	Small Minelayers

Service Forces

A 201	Orion
A 211	Belos
A 217	Fryken
A 228	Brännaren
A 229	Eldaren
A 236	Fällaren
A 237	Minören
A 241	Urd
A 242	Skuld
A 246	Hägern
A 247	Pelikanen
A 248	Pingvinen
A 251	Achilles
A 252	Ajax
A 253	Hermes
A 256	Sigrun
A 262	Skredsvik
A 313	Meranda
A 322	Heros
A 323	Hercules
A 324	Hera
A 326	Hebe
A 327	Passopp
A 330	Atlas
A 341	ATB 1
A 342	ATB 2
A 701-705	Tugs
A 751-756	Tugs
S 01	Gladan
S 02	Falken

SUBMARINES

Notes: (a) A rescue vehicle, *Urf (Ubats Räddnings Farkost)* of 52 tons with a diving depth of 1500 ft *(460 m)* was launched 17 April 1978. Similar to US Navy DSRV she has a capacity for 25 men on each dive.
(b) R-2 (Mala class) acquired from Yugoslavia in 1985. This is a two-man craft with a laden weight of 1400 kg, 4.9 × 1.4 m, and a 4.5 kW electric motor. With a lead-acid battery the performance is 4.4 kts for 18 n miles and 3.7 kts for 23 n miles. Has aluminium and plexiglass hull. Can carry 250 kg of limpet mines. With a silver-zinc battery the performance is much improved. Diving depth 30 m normal, 60 m maximum. R-1 deleted in 1990.
(c) A midget submarine *Spiggen II* was launched on 19 June 1990. Displacing 14 tons dived she has Volvo Penta diesel, a submerged speed of 5 kts, and a diving depth of 100 m. Dimensions, 11 × 1.7 × 1.4 m. She is to be used as a 'target' for ASW training and has an endurance of 14 days submerged.

SPIGGEN II *1991, Royal Swedish Navy*

0 + 3 (2) GÖTLAND (A 19) CLASS

Name	*No*	*Builders*	*Laid down*	*Launched*	*Commissioned*
GÖTLAND	—	Kockums, Malmö	1992	1995	1997
UPPLAND	—	Kockums, Malmö	1993	1996	1998
HALLAND	—	Kockums, Malmö	1994	1997	1999

Displacement, tons: 1240 surfaced; 1400 dived
Dimensions, feet (metres): 170.6 × 20.3 × 18.4 *(52 × 6.2 × 5.6)*
Main machinery: Diesel-electric; 2 Hedemora diesels; 1 Kockums/MAN Stirling engine; 1 motor; 1 shaft
Speed, knots: 11 surfaced; 20 dived
Complement: 25

Torpedoes: 6—21 in *(533 mm)* tubes; 12 FFV Type 613.
3—15.75 in *(400 mm)* tubes; 6 Swedish Ordnance Type 432.
Mines: Capability for 22 mines in external containers.
Countermeasures: ESM: Radar warning.
Fire control: NobelTech data automation.
Radars: Navigation: I band.
Sonars: Krupp Atlas; hull-mounted.

Programmes: In October 1986 a research contract was awarded to Kockums for a design to replace the A 12 class in the mid-1990s. The first three were ordered on 28 March 1990. There is an option for two more.
Structure: The design has been developed on the basis of the Type A 17 series but this class will be the first to be built with Air Independent propulsion as part of the design. Kockums/MAN Technologies are developing a 600 kW V-12 version of the Stirling engine.

GÖTLAND (model) *1991, Kockums*

4 VÄSTERGÖTLAND (A 17) CLASS

Name	No	Builders	Laid down	Launched	Commissioned
VÄSTERGÖTLAND	—	Kockums, Malmö	10 Jan 1983	17 Sep 1986	27 Nov 1987
HÄLSINGLAND	—	Kockums, Malmö	1 Jan 1984	31 Aug 1987	20 Oct 1988
SÖDERMANLAND	—	Kockums, Malmö	1985	12 Apr 1988	21 Apr 1989
ÖSTERGÖTLAND	—	Kockums, Malmö	1986	9 Dec 1988	10 Jan 1990

Displacement, tons: 1070 surfaced; 1143 dived
Dimensions, feet (metres): 159.1 × 20 × 18.4 *(48.5 × 6.1 × 5.6)*
Main machinery: Diesel-electric; 2 Hedemora V12A/15 diesels; 2200 hp(m) *(1.62 MW)*; 1 Jeumont Schneider motor; 1800 hp(m) *(1.32 MW)*; 1 shaft
Speed, knots: 11 surfaced; 20 dived
Complement: 21

Torpedoes: 6—21 in *(533 mm)* tubes. 12 FFV Type 613; anti-surface; wire-guided; passive homing to 15 km *(8.2 nm)* at 45 kts; warhead 240 kg. Swim-out discharge.
3—15.75 in *(400 mm)* tubes. 6 FFV Type 431; anti-submarine; wire-guided; active/passive homing to 20 km *(10.8 nm)* at 25 kts; warhead 45 kg shaped charge or a small charge anti-intruder version is available.
Mines: Capability for 22 mines in removable containers fitted externally.
Countermeasures: ESM: Argo; radar warning.
Fire control: Ericsson IPS-17 data automation.
Radars: Navigation: Terma; I band.
Sonars: Krupp Atlas CSU83; hull-mounted; passive search and attack; medium frequency.

Programmes: Design contract awarded to Kockums, Malmö on 17 April 1978. Contract for construction of these boats signed 8 December 1981. Kockums built midship section and carried out final assembly while Karlskrona built bow and stern sections. Have replaced the Draken class.

ÖSTERGÖTLAND *4/1991, Antonio Moreno*

Structure: Single hulled with an X type rudder/after hydroplane design. Reported that SSM were considered but rejected as non-cost-effective weapons in the context of submarine operations in the Baltic. May be back fitted with Stirling engines in due course.

3 NÄCKEN (A 14) CLASS

Name	No	Builders	Laid down	Launched	Commissioned
NÄCKEN	—	Kockums, Malmö	Nov 1972	17 Apr 1978	25 Apr 1980
NAJAD	—	Kockums, Malmö/Karlskronavarvet	Sep 1973	6 Dec 1978	26 June 1981
NEPTUN	—	Kockums, Malmö	Mar 1974	13 Aug 1979	5 Dec 1980

Displacement, tons: 1015 surfaced; 1085 dived
Dimensions, feet (metres): 162.4 (182.1, *Näcken*) × 18.7 × 18 *(49.5 (55.5) × 5.7 × 5.5)*
Main machinery: Diesel-electric; 1 MTU 16V 652 MB80 diesel; 1730 hp(m) *(1.27 MW)*; 2 Stirling V4-275R engines (*Näcken*); 150 kW; 1 Jeumont Schneider motor; 1800 hp(m) *(1.32 MW)*; 1 shaft
Speed, knots: 12 surfaced; 20 dived
Complement: 19 (5 officers)

Torpedoes: 6—21 in *(533 mm)* tubes. 8 FFV Type 613; anti-surface; wire-guided; passive homing to 15 km *(8.2 nm)* at 45 kts; warhead 250 kg.
2—15.75 in *(400 mm)* tubes. 4 FFV Type 431; anti-submarine; wire-guided; active/passive homing to 20 km *(10.8 nm)* at 25 kts; warhead 45 kg shaped charge.
Mines: Minelaying capability including an external girdle.
Countermeasures: ESM: Argo; radar warning.
Fire control: Ericsson A1 with 2 Censor 932 computers for data processing.
Radars: Navigation: Terma; I band.
Sonars: Krupp Atlas CSU83; hull-mounted; passive search and attack; medium frequency.

NÄCKEN *6/1991, Erik Laursen*

Modernisation: *Näcken* was taken in hand by Kockums in November 1987 for the installation of a closed-circuit Tillma Stirling diesel which provides non-nuclear propulsion without requiring access to the atmosphere. This involved the ship being lengthened by 6 m and she was relaunched on 6 September 1988. The new section which is neutrally buoyant contains the Stirling generators, two LOX supply tanks and control systems. The other two of the class will not be similarly modified. There are plans to update all of the class with new fire control systems, torpedo tube automation and new sonars, to extend service lives into the next century.
Structure: The very high beam to length ratio is notable in this hull design. Has large bow-mounted sonar. Main accommodation space is abaft the control room with machinery spaces right aft. A central computer provides both attack information and data on main machinery. Single periscope. Diving depth 300 m *(984 ft)*.
Operational: The Stirling engine is primarily for slow submerged speed patrolling without much use of battery power. Liquid oxygen (LOX) provides the combustible air. Exhaust products dissolve in water. It is claimed that fully submerged endurance is possible up to 14 days. Trials started on 23 November 1988 and the submarine returned to operational service on 11 April 1989.

5 SJÖORMEN (A 12) CLASS

Name	No	Builders	Laid down	Launched	Commissioned
SJÖORMEN	—	Kockums, Malmö	1965	25 Jan 1967	31 July 1968
SJÖLEJONET	—	Kockums, Malmö	1966	29 June 1967	16 Dec 1968
SJÖHUNDEN	—	Kockums, Malmö	1966	21 Mar 1968	25 June 1969
SJÖBJÖRNEN	—	Karlskronavarvet	1967	6 Aug 1968	28 Feb 1969
SJÖHÄSTEN	—	Karlskronavarvet	1966	9 Jan 1968	15 Sep 1969

Displacement, tons: 1130 surfaced; 1210 dived
Dimensions, feet (metres): 167.3 × 20 × 19 *(51 × 6.1 × 5.8)*
Main machinery: Diesel-electric; 2 Hedemora-Pielstick V12A/A2/15 diesels; 2200 hp(m) *(1.62 MW)*; 1 ASEA motor; 1500 hp(m) *(1.1 MW)*; 1 shaft
Speed, knots: 12 surfaced; 20 dived
Complement: 23 (7 officers)

Torpedoes: 4—21 in *(533 mm)* bow tubes. 10 FFV Type 61; anti-surface; wire-guided; passive homing to 15 km *(8.2 nm)* at 45 kts; warhead 240 kg.
2—15.75 in *(400 mm)* tubes. 4 FFV Type 431; anti-submarine; wire-guided; active/passive homing to 20 km *(10.8 nm)* at 25 kts; warhead 45 kg shaped charge.
Mines: Minelaying capability including an external girdle.
Fire control: Ericsson A1 system.
Radars: Navigation: Terma; I band.
Sonars: Plessey Hydra; hull-mounted; passive search and attack; medium frequency.

Modernisation: *Sjölejonet* and *Sjöhunden* modernised with Näcken type electronics to extend life into the late 1990s. All of the class are being given Plessey sonars (replacing Krupp Atlas CSU 3) which are similar to RN Type 2074.

SJÖHÄSTEN *6/1991, Erik Laursen*

Structure: Albacore hull. Twin-decked. Diving depth, 150 m *(492 ft)*.

Operational: Endurance, three weeks. The three unmodernised boats will be replaced in the late 1990s by the A 19 class.

MISSILE CORVETTES

2 STOCKHOLM CLASS

Name	No	Builders	Laid down	Launched	Commissioned
STOCKHOLM	K 11	Karlskronavarvet	1 Aug 1982	24 Aug 1984	22 Feb 1985
MALMÖ	K 12	Karlskronavarvet	14 Mar 1983	22 Mar 1985	10 May 1985

Displacement, tons: 310 standard; 335 full load
Dimensions, feet (metres): 164 × 22.3 × 6.2 *(50 × 6.8 × 1.9)*
Main machinery: CODAG; 1 GM/Allison 570KF gas turbine; 6350 hp(m) *(4.74 MW)* sustained; 2 MTU 16V 396 TB93 diesels; 4200 hp(m) *(3.1 MW)* sustained; 3 shafts
Speed, knots: 32 gas; 20 diesel
Complement: 40

Missiles: SSM: 8 Saab RBS 15 (4 twin) launchers (1); inertial guidance; active radar homing to 70 km *(37.8 nm)* at 0.8 Mach; warhead 150 kg.
Guns: 1 Bofors 57 mm/70 Mk 2 (2); 75° elevation; 220 rounds/minute to 17 km *(9.3 nm)*; weight of shell 2.4 kg.
1 Bofors 40 mm/70 (3); 85° elevation; 300 rounds/minute to 12.5 km *(6.8 nm)*; weight of shell 0.96 kg.
Torpedoes: 2—21 in *(533 mm)* tubes (4). FFV Type 613; wire-guided; passive homing to 15 km *(8.2 nm)* at 45 kts; warhead 240 kg.
A/S mortars: 4 Saab Elma LLS-920 9-tubed launchers; range 300 m; warhead 4.2 kg shaped charge. IR/Chaff decoys.
Depth charges: 2 racks.
Mines: Minelaying capability.

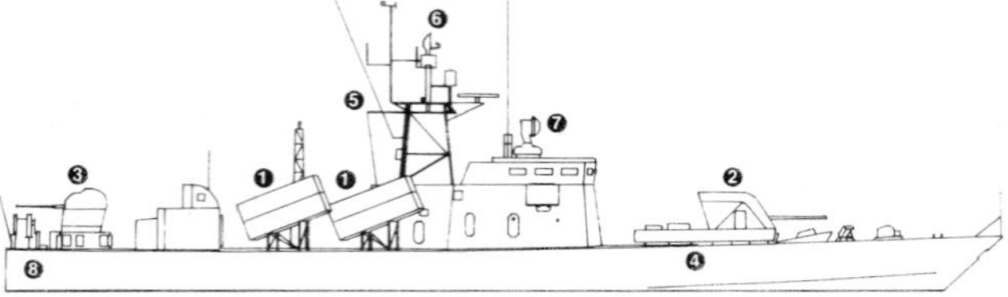

STOCKHOLM *(Scale 1 : 600), Ian Sturton*

Countermeasures: Decoys: 2 Philips Philax fixed launchers; 4 magazines each holding 36 IR/Chaff grenades; fired in groups of nine. A/S mortars have also been adapted to fire IR/Chaff decoys.
ESM: Saab-Scania EWS 905; radar intercept.
Fire control: Ericsson Maril system. Philips 9LV 300 GFCS including a 9LV 100 optronic director (5).
Radars: Air/surface search: Ericsson Sea Giraffe 50 (6); G band.
Navigation: Terma PN 612; I band.
Fire control: Philips 9LV 200 Mk 3 (7); J band.

Sonars: Simrad SS 304; hull-mounted; active attack; 34 kHz.
Thomson Sintra TSM 2642 Salmon (8); VDS; search; medium frequency.

Programmes: Orders placed in September 1981. Developed from Spica II class.
Operational: Some flexibility in weapon fit depending on mission. Trials have been done with a Plessey COMTASS towed passive sonar array. The Elma LLS-920 system is designed not to sink a submarine but to make it surface.

STOCKHOLM *4/1991, Antonio Moreno*

4 GÖTEBORG CLASS

Name	No	Builders	Laid down	Launched	Commissioned
GÖTEBORG	K 21	Karlskronavarvet	10 Feb 1986	14 Apr 1989	15 Feb 1990
GÄLVE	K 22	Karlskronavarvet	Sep 1988	23 Mar 1990	1 Feb 1991
KALMAR	K 23	Karlskronavarvet	Sep 1988	1 Nov 1990	1 Sep 1991
SUNDSVALL	K 24	Karlskronavarvet	Mar 1989	29 Nov 1991	July 1992

Displacement, tons: 300 standard; 399 full load
Dimensions, feet (metres): 187 × 26.2 × 6.6 *(57 × 8 × 2)*
Main machinery: 3 MTU 16V 396 TB 94 diesels; 8700 hp(m) *(6.4 MW)* sustained; KaMeWa 80562-6 waterjets
Speed, knots: 32+
Complement: 36 (7 officers) plus 4 spare berths

Missiles: SSM: 8 Saab RBS 15 (4 twin) launchers (1); inertial guidance; active radar homing to 70 km *(37.8 nm)* at 0.8 Mach; warhead 150 kg.
Guns: 1 Bofors 57 mm/70 Mk 2 (2); 75° elevation; 220 rounds/minute to 17 km *(9.3 nm)*; weight of shell 2.4 kg.
1 Bofors 40 mm/70 (3); 85° elevation; 330 rounds/minute to 12.5 km *(6.8 nm)*; weight of shell 0.96 kg.
Torpedoes: 2—21 in *(533 mm)* or 4—15.75 in *(400 mm)* tubes (4). FFV Type 613; anti-surface; wire-guided; passive homing to 15 km *(8.2 nm)* at 45 kts; warhead 240 kg or Swedish Ordnance Type 432; anti-submarine.
A/S mortars: 4 Saab Elma LLS-920 9-tubed launchers (5); range 300 m; warhead 4.2 kg shaped charge. IR/Chaff decoys.
Mines: Minelaying capability.
Countermeasures: Decoys: 4 Philips Philax fixed launchers; IR flares and Chaff grenades. A/S mortars have also been adapted to fire IR/Chaff decoys.
ESM/ECM: Argo Carol/Sceptre XL; intercept and jammer.
Fire control: Two Bofors Electronics 9LV 200 Mk 3 Sea Viking optronic directors (7). Bofors Electronics 9LV 450 GFCS. RC1-400 MFCS. 9AU-300 ASW control system. Bofors 9EW 400 EW control.
Radars: Air/surface search: Ericsson Sea Giraffe 150 HC (6); G band.
Navigation: Terma PN 612; I-band.
Fire control: Two Bofors Electronics 9GR 400 (7); I/J band.
Sonars: Thomson Sintra TSM 2643 Salmon (8); VDS; active search; medium frequency.
Simrad S 304; hull-mounted; active attack; 34 kHz.

Programmes: Ordered 1 December 1985 as replacements for Spica I class.
Structure: Efforts have been made to reduce radar and IR signatures. Fixed torpedo tubes are positioned on the starboard side firing forward or aft. A Bofors Sea Trinity gun is to replace the 40 mm/70 in one of the class for trials in 1992.

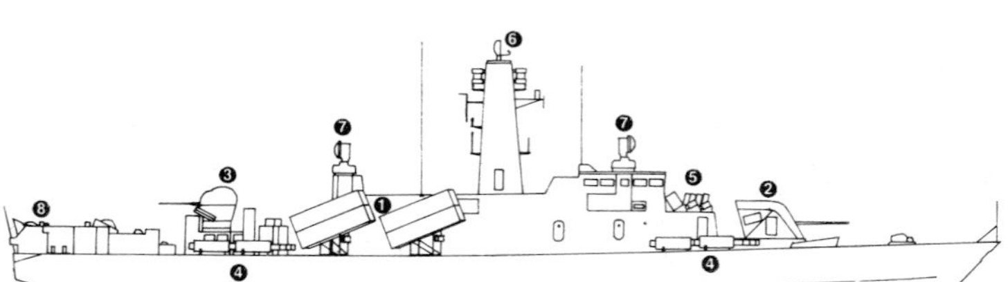

GÖTEBORG *(Scale 1 : 600), Ian Sturton*

GÖTEBORG *8/1990, Gilbert Gyssels*

LAND-BASED MARITIME AIRCRAFT

Numbers/Type: 10 Agusta-Bell 206A JetRanger (HKP-6B).
Operational speed: 115 kts *(213 km/h)*.
Service ceiling: 13 500 ft *(4115 m)*.
Range: 368 nm *(682 km)*.
Role/Weapon systems: Primarily operated in a liaison and training role and for secondary ASW, SAR and surface search helicopter operations. Weapons: ASW; 4 × Type 11 or 45 depth bombs.

Numbers/Type: 7 Boeing 107-II-5/7 Kawasaki KV 107-II. All to HKP-4B/C standard.
Operational speed: 137 kts *(254 km/h)*.
Service ceiling: 8500 ft *(2590 m)*.
Range: 180 nm *(338 km)*.
Role/Weapon systems: ASW and surface search helicopter; primary ASW role in approaches to naval installations and SAR (taken over from the air force in 1990); updated with new avionics, TM2D engines, BEAB Omera radar PS 864, data link for SSM targeting, MARIL 920 combat information system, updated Thomson Sintra DUAV-4 dipping sonar; life prolonged until 2000. Sensors: BEAB Omera radar, DUAV-4 dipping sonar. Weapons: ASW; 6 × Type 11/51 depth bombs and/or 2 × Type 42 or Type 43 torpedoes.

Numbers/Type: 24 Saab-Scania SH 37 Viggen.
Operational speed: 726 kts *(1345 km/h)*.
Service ceiling: 50 000 ft *(15 240 m)*.
Range: 1080 nm *(1975 km)*.
Role/Weapon systems: Operated by Air Force; to cover the Baltic approaches; peacetime EEZ surveillance assisted by air data camera. Sensors: Ericsson UAP-1023 radar, 1 × recce pod, 1 × camera pod, 1 × ECM pod, 1 × Chaff/jammer pod. Weapons: Attack; 2 × Saab RB04 + 2 × Saab RB05 ASV missiles. MR; 2 × RB24 air-to-air missiles. Total warload is 6 tons.

Numbers/Type: 1 CASA C-212 Aviocar.
Operational speed: 190 kts *(353 km/h)*.
Service ceiling: 24 000 ft *(7315 m)*.
Range: 1650 nm *(3055 km)*.
Role/Weapon systems: For ASW and surface surveillance. Sensors: Omera radar, Sonobuoys/Lofar, FLIR, data link, computer devices AN/UYS-503 processors. Coastguard variants also in service. Weapons: ASW; depth charges.

LIGHT FORCES

12 NORRKÖPING CLASS (FAST ATTACK CRAFT—MISSILE)

Name	*No*	*Builders*	*Commissioned*
NORRKÖPING	R 131	Karlskronavarvet	11 May 1973
NYNÄSHAMN	R 132	Karlskronavarvet	28 Sep 1973
NORRTÄLJE	R 133	Karlskronavarvet	1 Feb 1974
VARBERG	R 134	Karlskronavarvet	14 June 1974
VÄSTERÅS	R 135	Karlskronavarvet	25 Oct 1974
VÄSTERVIK	R 136	Karlskronavarvet	15 Jan 1975
UMEÅ	R 137	Karlskronavarvet	7 May 1975
PITEÅ	R 138	Karlskronavarvet	12 Sep 1975
LULEÅ	R 139	Karlskronavarvet	28 Nov 1975
HALMSTAD	R 140	Karlskronavarvet	9 Apr 1976
STRÖMSTAD	R 141	Karlskronavarvet	24 Sep 1976
YSTAD	R 142	Karlskronavarvet	10 Jan 1976

Displacement, tons: 190 standard; 230 full load
Dimensions, feet (metres): 143 × 23.3 × 7.4 *(43.6 × 7.1 × 2.4)*
Main machinery: 3 RR Proteus gas turbines; 12 900 hp *(9.62 MW)*; 3 shafts
Speed, knots: 40.5
Complement: 27 (7 officers)

Missiles: SSM: 8 Saab RBS 15; active radar homing to 70 km *(37.8 nm)* at 0.8 Mach; warhead 150 kg.
Guns: 1 Bofors 57 mm/70 Mk 1; 75° elevation; 200 rounds/minute to 17 km *(9.3 nm)*; weight of shell 2.4 kg. 8 launchers for 57 mm illuminants on side of mounting.
Torpedoes: 6—21 in *(533 mm)* tubes. Type 61 (2-6 can be fitted at the expense of missile armament).
A/S mortars: 4 Saab Elma 9-tubed launchers (not fitted in all); range 300 m; warhead 4.2 kg shaped charge. IR/Chaff decoys.
Mines: Minelaying capability.
Countermeasures: Decoys: 2 Philips Philax fixed launchers; IR flares and Chaff. A/S mortars can also fire Chaff/IR decoys.
ESM: Saab Scania EWS 905; radar intercept.
Combat data systems: MARIL 880 data link.
Radars: Air/surface search: Ericsson Sea Giraffe 50; G band.
Fire control: Philips 9LV 200; J band.

Modernisation: Programme included missile launchers, new fire control equipment, modernised electronics and new 57 mm guns. All completed by late 1984.
Structure: Similar to the original Spica class from which they were developed.
Operational: Six of the craft may be fitted with GEC Avionics AQS 924 or the more modern AQS 928 sonobuoy processing equipment.

STRÖMSTAD (with 4 SSM and 2 Torpedoes) *8/1990, Gilbert Gyssels*

UMEÅ (with 2 SSM and 4 Torpedoes) *4/1989, Antonio Moreno*

VÄSTERVIK *10/1991, van Ginderen Collection*

16 HUGIN CLASS (FAST ATTACK CRAFT—MISSILE)

Name	*No*	*Builders*	*Commissioned*
HUGIN	P 151	Bergens MV, Norway	3 July 1978
MUNIN	P 152	Bergens MV, Norway	3 July 1978
MAGNE	P 153	Bergens MV, Norway	12 Oct 1978
MODE	P 154	Westamarin, Norway	12 Jan 1979
VALE	P 155	Westamarin, Norway	26 Apr 1979
VIDAR	P 156	Westamarin, Norway	10 Aug 1979
MJÖLNER	P 157	Westamarin, Norway	25 Oct 1979
MYSING	P 158	Westamarin, Norway	14 Feb 1980
KAPAREN	P 159	Bergens MV, Norway	7 Aug 1980
VÄKTAREN	P 160	Bergens MV, Norway	19 Sep 1980
SNAPPHANEN	P 161	Bergens MV, Norway	14 Jan 1980
SPEJAREN	P 162	Bergens MV, Norway	21 Mar 1980
STYRBJÖRN	P 163	Bergens MV, Norway	15 June 1980
STARKODDER	P 164	Bergens MV, Norway	24 Aug 1981
TORDÖN	P 165	Bergens MV, Norway	26 Oct 1981
TIRFING	P 166	Bergens MV, Norway	23 Jan 1982

Displacement, tons: 120 standard; 150 full load
Dimensions, feet (metres): 120 × 20.7 × 5.6 *(36.6 × 6.3 × 1.7)*
Main machinery: 2 MTU MB20V 672 TY90 diesels; 5800 hp(m) *(4.26 MW)* sustained; 2 shafts
Speed, knots: 36
Complement: 22 (3 officers)

Missiles: SSM: 6 Kongsberg Penguin Mk 2; IR homing to 27 km *(14.6 nm)* at 0.8 Mach; warhead 120 kg.
Guns: 1 Bofors 57 mm/70 Mk 1; 75° elevation; 200 rounds/minute to 17 km *(9.3 nm)*; weight of shell 2.4 kg. 103 mm illuminant launchers on either side of mounting.
A/S mortars: 4 Saab Elma 9-tubed launchers; range 300 m; warhead 4.2 kg shaped charge.
Depth charges: 2 racks.
Mines: 24. Mine-rails extend from after end of bridge superstructure with an extension over the stern. Use of these would mean the removal of any missiles.
Countermeasures: Decoys: 2 Philips Philax fixed launchers; IR flares and Chaff grenades. The A/S mortars can also fire IR/Chaff decoys.
ESM: Saab Scania EWS 905; radar intercept.
Radars: Surface search: Skanter 16 in Mk 009; I band.
Fire control: Philips 9LV 200 Mk 2; J band.
Sonars: Simrad SQ 3D/SF; hull-mounted; active attack; high frequency.
VDS (in most); active; high frequency.

Programmes: In the early 1970s it was decided to build fast attack craft similar to the Norwegian Hauk class. Prototype *Jägaren* underwent extensive trials and, on 15 May 1975, an order for a further 11 was placed.
Modernisation: Most ships of the class are fitted with VDS, a modified helicopter version lowered on a gantry over the stern. Half-life modernisation being done from 1990-95 to include new sonar, low speed machinery and better action data automation, air defence and ASW weapons systems. One of the class has been used for trials of an RBS-70 SAM launcher mounted aft of the superstructure. The launcher carries four missile canisters and has an optronic sensor. Main engines from deleted Plejad class, refitted and up-rated by MTU.

SNAPPHANEN (with VDS) *4/1991, Hartmut Ehlers*

1 JÄGAREN CLASS (COASTAL PATROL CRAFT)

Name	*No*	*Builders*	*Commissioned*
JÄGAREN	V 150	Bergens MV, Norway	24 Nov 1972

Displacement, tons: 120 standard; 150 full load
Dimensions, feet (metres): 120 × 20.7 × 5.6 *(36.6 × 6.3 × 1.7)*
Main machinery: 2 Cummins KTA 50-M; 2500 hp *(1.87 MW)* sustained; 2 shafts
Speed, knots: 20
Complement: 15
Guns: 1 Bofors 40 mm/70.
Mines: Minelaying capability.
Radars: Surface search.

Comment: The prototype for the Hugin class but was not fitted with missiles, and up to 1988 was used for training and testing. In 1988 new engines were installed and the craft recommissioned for patrol duties. Has no torpedo tubes, fire control radar, ESM or sonar.

JÄGAREN *8/1991, Maritime Photographic*

1 HANÖ CLASS (COASTAL PATROL CRAFT)

Name	*No*	*Builders*	*Commissioned*
ORNÖ	V 55	Karlskronavarvet	14 Sep 1953

Displacement, tons: 280 standard
Dimensions, feet (metres): 137.8 × 23 × 9.9 *(42 × 7 × 3)*
Main machinery: 2 Nohab diesels; 910 hp(m) *(669 kW)*; 2 shafts
Speed, knots: 13
Complement: 25
Guns: 2 Bofors 40 mm/70.

Comment: Former minesweeper with steel hull. Converted for patrol duties—reclassified 1 January 1979. The last survivor of the class.

ORNÖ *7/1991, Erik Laursen*

1 RÖRÖ CLASS (COASTAL PATROL CRAFT)

RÖRÖ (ex-*Astrida II*) 50

Displacement, tons: 177 full load
Dimensions, feet (metres): 89.9 × 25.6 × 10.5 *(27.4 × 7.8 × 3.2)*
Main machinery: 1 diesel; 460 hp(m) *(338 kW)*; 1 shaft
Speed, knots: 9
Guns: 1 Oerlikon 20 mm.

Comment: Former fishing vessel used as a patrol craft.

RORO *11/1991, van Ginderen Collection*

3 DALARÖ CLASS (COASTAL PATROL CRAFT)

Name	*No*	*Builders*	*Commissioned*
DALARÖ	V 09	Djupviksvarvet	21 Sep 1984
SANDHAMN	V 10	Djupviksvarvet	5 Dec 1984
ÖSTHAMMAR	V 11	Djupviksvarvet	1 Mar 1985

Displacement, tons: 50
Dimensions, feet (metres): 76.8 × 16.7 × 3.6 *(23.4 × 5.1 × 1.1)*
Main machinery: 2 MTU 8V 396 TB83 diesels; 2100 hp(m) *(1.54 MW)* sustained; 2 shafts
Speed, knots: 30
Complement: 7 (3 officers)
Guns: 1 Bofors 40 mm/70. 2—7.62 mm MGs.
Mines: Rails fitted.
Radars: Surface search: Terma 610; I band.

Comment: Ordered 28 February 1983 for anti-intruder patrols instead of conversion of further Skanör class.

DALARÖ *1987, Royal Swedish Navy*

6 SKANÖR CLASS (COASTAL PATROL CRAFT)

Name	*No*	*Builders*	*Recommissioned*
ARILD	V 03 (ex-T 45)	Kockums, Malmö	1977
VIKEN	V 04 (ex-T 44)	Kockums, Malmö	1977
ÖREGRUND	V 05 (ex-T 47)	Naval Dockyard, Stockholm	1 Feb 1983
SLITE	V 06 (ex-T 48)	Naval Dockyard, Stockholm	15 Apr 1983
MARSTRAND	V 07 (ex-T 50)	Naval Dockyard, Stockholm	16 May 1983
LYSEKIL	V 08 (ex-T 52)	Naval Dockyard, Stockholm	13 June 1983

Displacement, tons: 25 standard
Dimensions, feet (metres): 75.5 × 19.4 × 3.9 *(23 × 5.9 × 1.2)*
Main machinery: 2 MTU 8V396 TB83 diesels; 2100 hp(m) *(1.54 MW)* sustained; 2 shafts
Speed, knots: 25
Complement: 12
Guns: 1 Bofors 40 mm/70. 1—12 rail 57 mm illuminant launcher.
Mines: Up to 10 (or depth charges).
Radars: Surface search: Skanter 009; I band.

Comment: These craft were originally eight of the T 42 class which first commissioned in 1957-59. First four reconstructed at Karlskrona having their torpedo tubes removed and their petrol engines replaced by diesels. Last four similarly converted at Djupviksvarvet. First two deleted in early 1989.

SLITE *5/1990, Hartmut Ehlers*

LYSEKIL *8/1989, Erik Laursen*

17 INSHORE PATROL CRAFT (COASTAL ARTILLERY)

61-67 **68-77**

Displacement, tons: 30 full load
Dimensions, feet (metres): 69.2 × 15 × 4.3 *(21.1 × 4.6 × 1.3)*
Main machinery: 3 diesels; 3 shafts
Speed, knots: 18 *(61-67)*; 22 *(68-77)*
Guns: 1 Oerlikon 20 mm.
Depth charges: Carried in all of the class.
Radars: Navigation: Decca RM 914; I band.

Comment: These are operated by the Coastal Artillery. The 60 series launched in 1960-61 and 70 series in 1966-67. Modernised in the 1980s with a tripod mast and radar mounted over the bridge. Now called Type 72.

73 (older type) *8/1990, Gilbert Gyssels*

71 (after conversion) *8/1990, Gilbert Gyssels*

4 SVK CLASS (INSHORE PATROL CRAFT)

SVÄRDET SVK 1 (ex-*TV 228)*
SPJUTET SVK 2 (ex-*TV 226)*
PILEN SVK 3 (ex-*TV 230)*
BÅGEN SVK 4 (ex-*TV 234)*

Displacement, tons: 12
Dimensions, feet (metres): 45.9 × 11.1 × 3.3 *(14 × 3.4 × 1)*
Speed, knots: 10
Guns: 1 Oerlikon 20 mm (not always carried).

Comment: *Svärdet, Spjutet* and *Pilen* completed 1954-57. *Bågen* completed 1960 is slightly larger at 15.2 × 3.6 × 1.2 m. All belong to Sjövärnskåren (SVK) which is the Swedish Naval Reserve Association and are used for navigational training.

SVÄRDET *1989, Royal Swedish Navy*

1 EXPERIMENTAL PATROL CRAFT (SES)

SMYGE

Displacement, tons: 140 full load
Dimensions, feet (metres): 99.7 oa; 88.6 wl × 37.4 × 6.2; 2.3 on cushion *(30.4; 27 × 11.4 × 1.9; 0.7)*
Main machinery: 2 MTU 16V 396 TB 94 diesels (drive); 5080 hp(m) *(3.73 MW)* sustained; 2 KaMeWa waterjets
2 Scania DSI 14 diesels (lift); 947 hp(m) *(696 kW)* sustained
Speed, knots: 40+
Complement: 14 (6 officers)
Missiles: SSM: 2 RBS 15 retractable mountings.
Guns: 1 Sea Trinity 40 mm CIWS; stealth cupola.
Torpedoes: Type 42; anti-submarine; wire-guided from covered stern tubes.
Mines: Rails or mine countermeasure equipment.
Radars: Air/surface search: Elevating mast.
Sonars: VDS or light towed array.

Comment: A surface effect experimental craft launched 14 March 1991 incorporating a high degree of stealth technology. GRP sandwich construction with Kevlar protection. Evaluation and trials in the period 1991-93 as a basis for the design of future attack craft.

SMYGE *1991, Royal Swedish Navy*

MINE WARFARE FORCES

2 ÄLVSBORG CLASS (MINELAYERS)

Name	*No*	*Builders*	*Commissioned*
ÄLVSBORG	M 02	Karlskronavarvet	6 Apr 1971
VISBORG	M 03	Karlskronavarvet	6 Feb 1976

Displacement, tons: 2500 standard; 2660 full load (*Älvsborg*)
2400 standard; 2650 full load (*Visborg*)
Dimensions, feet (metres): 303.1 × 48.2 × 13.2 *(92.4 × 14.7 × 4)*
Main machinery: 2 Nohab-Polar diesels; 4200 hp(m) *(3.1 MW)*; 1 shaft
Speed, knots: 16
Complement: 95 (accommodation for 205 submariners in *Älvsborg*—158 Admiral's staff in *Visborg*)
Guns: 3 Bofors 40 mm/70. 6—103 mm (2 triple) launchers for illuminants.
Mines: 300.
Countermeasures: 2 Philips Philax Chaff/IR launchers.
Radars: Surface search: Raytheon; E/F band.
Fire control: Philips 9LV 200; I/J band.
Helicopters: Platform only.

Comment: *Älvsborg* was ordered in 1968 and launched on 11 November 1969; acts as a submarine depot ship. *Visborg*, laid down on 16 October 1973 and launched 22 January 1975 also acts as Command Ship for C-in-C Coastal Fleet. A Bofors Sea Trinity CIWS is to replace one of the 40 mm/70 guns for trials in *Älvsborg*.

ÄLVSBORG *1990, van Ginderen Collection*

VISBORG *4/1991, Antonio Moreno*

1 CARLSKRONA CLASS (MINELAYER)

Name	*No*	*Builders*	*Commissioned*
CARLSKRONA	M 04	Karlskronavarvet	11 Jan 1982

Displacement, tons: 3300 standard; 3550 full load
Dimensions, feet (metres): 346.7 × 49.9 × 13.1 *(105.7 × 15.2 × 4)*
Main machinery: 4 Nohab F212 D825 diesels; 10 560 hp(m) *(7.76 MW)*; 2 shafts; cp props
Speed, knots: 20
Complement: 50 plus 136 trainees. Requires 118 as operational minelayer
Guns: 2 Bofors 57 mm/70. 2 Bofors 40 mm/70. 6—103 mm (2 triple) launchers for illuminants.
Mines: Can lay 105.
Countermeasures: 2 Philips Philax Chaff/IR launchers.
Radars: Air/surface search: Ericsson Sea Giraffe 50; G band.
Surface search: Raytheon; E/F band.
Fire control: Two Philips 9LV 200; I/J band.
Sonars: Simrad SQ 3D/SF; hull-mounted; active search; high frequency.
Helicopters: Platform only.

Comment: Ordered 25 November 1977, laid down in sections late 1979 and launched 28 June 1980 at the same time as Karlskrona celebrated its tercentenary. Midshipmen's Training Ship as well as a minelayer; also a 'padded' target for exercise torpedoes. Name is an older form of Karlskrona.

CARLSKRONA *1/1990, van Ginderen Collection*

1 MCM SUPPORT SHIP

Name	*No*	*Builders*	*Commissioned*
UTÖ (ex-*Smit Manila*, ex-*Seaford* ex-*Seaforth Challenger*)	—	Drypool, Selby	1974

Displacement, tons: 1100 full load
Dimensions, feet (metres): 182.1 × 40.4 × 14.1 *(55.5 × 12.3 × 4.3)*
Main machinery: 1 diesel; 5000 hp(m) *(3.68 MW)*; 1 shaft
Speed, knots: 12
Complement: 32
Guns: 2 Oerlikon 20 mm.

Comment: Ex-supply ship converted by Pan United Ltd, Singapore and recommissioned in April 1989 replacing *Thule*.

UTO *6/1989, van Ginderen Collection*

1 FURUSUND CLASS (COASTAL MINELAYER)

FURUSUND MUL 20

Displacement, tons: 155 standard; 216 full load
Dimensions, feet (metres): 106.9 × 26.9 × 7.5 *(32.6 × 8.2 × 2.3)*
Main machinery: Diesel-electric; 2 Scania GAS 1 diesel generators; 2 motors; 416 hp(m) *(306 kW)*; 2 shafts
Speed, knots: 11.5
Complement: 24
Guns: 1 Oerlikon 20 mm. 2—7.62 mm MGs.
Mines: 22 tons.
Radars: Navigation: Racal Decca 1226; I band.

Comment: Built for Coastal Artillery by ASI Verken, Åmål. *Furusund* launched 16 December 1982, completed 10 October 1983. Plans for three more abandoned.

FURUSUND *1984, Royal Swedish Navy*

7 ARKOSUND CLASS (COASTAL MINELAYERS)

ARKOSUND MUL 12 **KALMARSUND** MUL 13 **ALNÖSUND** MUL 14 **GRUNDSUND** MUL 15 **SKRAMSÖSUND** MUL 17 **ÖRESUND** MUL 18 **BARÖSUND** MUL 19

Displacement, tons: 200 standard; 245 full load
Dimensions, feet (metres): 102.3 × 24.3 × 10.2 *(31.2 × 7.4 × 3.1)*
Main machinery: Diesel-electric; 2 Nohab/Scania diesel generators; 2 motors; 460 hp(m) *(338 kW)*; 2 shafts
Speed, knots: 10.5
Guns: 1 Bofors 40 mm/60; on platform aft of the funnel.
Mines: 26 tons.
Radars: Navigation: Racal Decca 1226; I band.

Comment: All completed by 1954-1957. Operated by Coastal Artillery. One scrapped in 1992 and *Skramsösund* is to be reclassified as an auxiliary.

ALNÖSUND *6/1989, T. J. Gander*

1 COASTAL MINELAYER

KALVSUND MUL 11

Displacement, tons: 200 full load
Dimensions, feet (metres): 98.4 × 23.6 × 11.8 *(30 × 7.2 × 3.6)*
Main machinery: 2 MAN Atlas diesels; 300 hp(m) *(221 kW)*; 2 shafts
Speed, knots: 10
Guns: 2 Oerlikon 20 mm.
Mines: 21 tons.

Comment: Commissioned in 1947. Operated by Coastal Artillery.

KALVSUND *11/1991, van Ginderen Collection*

16 SMALL MINELAYERS

501-516

Displacement, tons: 15
Dimensions, feet (metres): 47.9 × 13.8 × 2.9 *(14.6 × 4.2 × 0.9)*
Main machinery: 2 diesels; 2 shafts
Speed, knots: 14
Complement: 7
Mines: 12.

Comment: Ordered in 1969. Mines are laid from single traps on either beam. Operated by Coastal Artillery.

510 *9/1990, van Ginderen Collection*

6 SMALL MINELAYERS

1879-1884

Displacement, tons: 2.5
Speed, knots: 20

Comment: Ordered from Farösünd on 27 November 1982. Completed July 1983-January 1984 for Coastal Artillery. Waterjet propulsion.

6 + 1 LANDSORT CLASS (MINEHUNTERS)

Name	No	Builders	Commissioned
LANDSORT	M 71	Karlskronavarvet	19 Apr 1984
ARHOLMA	M 72	Karlskronavarvet	23 Nov 1984
KOSTER	M 73	Karlskronavarvet	30 May 1986
KULLEN	M 74	Karlskronavarvet	28 Nov 1986
VINGA	M 75	Karlskronavarvet	27 Nov 1987
VEN	M 76	Karlskronavarvet	12 Dec 1988
ULVÖN	M 77	Karlskronavarvet	1992

Displacement, tons: 270 standard; 360 full load
Dimensions, feet (metres): 155.8 × 31.5 × 7.3 *(47.5 × 9.6 × 2.2)*
Main machinery: 4 Saab-Scania DSI 14 diesels; 1516 hp(m) *(1.11 MW)* sustained; coupled in pairs to 2 Voith Schneider props
Speed, knots: 15. **Range, miles:** 2000 at 12 kts
Complement: 26 (12 officers) plus 13 spare berths

Guns: 1 Bofors 40 mm/70 Mod 48; 85° elevation; 300 rounds/minute to 12.5 km *(6.8 nm)*; weight of shell 0.96 kg. Bofors Sea Trinity CIWS trial being carried out in *Vinga* (fitted in place of 40 mm/70). 2—7.62 mm MGs.
A/S mortars: 4 Saab Elma 9-tubed launchers; range 300 m; warhead 4.2 kg shaped charge.
Countermeasures: Decoys: 2 Philips Philax fixed launchers with 4 magazines each holding 36 grenades; IR/Chaff.
MCM: This class is fitted for mechanical sweeps for moored mines as well as magnetic and acoustic sweeps. In addition it is possible to operate 2—15 ton unmanned catamaran magnetic and acoustic sweepers (59 × 20 ft *(18 × 6 m)*); these have SAM numbers. Fitted with 2 Sutec Sea Owl remote controlled units.
Fire control: Philips 9LV 100 optronic director. Philips 9 MJ 400 minehunting system.
Radars: Navigation: Thomson-CSF Terma; I band.
Sonars: Thomson-CSF TSM-2022; Racal Decca 'Mains' control system; hull-mounted; minehunting; high frequency.

Programmes: The first two of this class ordered in early 1981. Second four in 1984 and the seventh in 1989. *Landsort* launched 2 November 1982, *Arholma* 2 August 1984, *Koster* 16 January 1986, *Kullen* 15 August 1986, *Vinga* 14 August 1987, *Ven* 10 August 1988, and *Ulvön* in 1992. The projected eighth of the class has been cancelled.
Structure: The GRP mould for the hull has been available for several years and has been used for the Coast Guard Kbv 171 class.
Operational: The integrated navigation and action data automation system has been developed by Philips and Racal Decca.
Sales: SAM 3 and SAM 5 leased to the United States Navy in February 1991.

ARHOLMA *10/1990, Per Kornefeldt*

SAM 02 *1990, van Ginderen Collection*

2 MINE TRANSPORTS

FÄLLAREN A 236 **MINÖREN** A 237

Displacement, tons: 170 full load
Dimensions, feet (metres): 97 × 20.3 × 7.2 *(31.8 × 6.2 × 2.2)*
Main machinery: 2 diesels; 240 hp(m) *(176 kW)*; 2 shafts
Speed, knots: 9
Mines: Have minelaying capability.

Comment: Built in 1941 and 1940 respectively. Mahogany hulls.

FÄLLAREN *1987, Royal Swedish Navy*

3 ARKÖ CLASS (MINESWEEPERS—COASTAL)

Name	No	Builders	Commissioned
ARKÖ	M 57	Karlskronavarvet	1958
NÄMDÖ	M 67	Karlskronavarvet	1964
BLIDÖ	M 68	Hälsingborg	1964

Displacement, tons: 285 standard; 300 full load
Dimensions, feet (metres): 145.6 × 24.6 × 9.9 *(44.4 × 7.5 × 3)*
Main machinery: 2 Mercedes-Benz MTU 12V 493 TZ60 diesels; 1360 hp(m) *(1 MW)* sustained; 2 shafts
Speed, knots: 14
Complement: 25
Missiles: SAM: Saab RBS 70 (in some) (sited above sweep winch); IR homing to 6 km *(3.2 nm)*.
Guns: 1 Bofors 40 mm/70 Mod 48.

Comment: Of wooden construction. There is a small difference in the deck-line between *Arkö* and the remainder.

NÄMDÖ *8/1990, Gilbert Gyssels*

3 GILLÖGA CLASS (MINESWEEPERS—INSHORE)

GILLÖGA M 47 **RÖDLÖGA** M 48 **SVARTLÖGA** M 49

Displacement, tons: 110 standard; 135 full load
Dimensions, feet (metres): 72.2 × 21.3 × 11.5 *(22 × 6.5 × 3.5)*
Main machinery: 1 diesel; 380 hp(m) *(279 kW)*; 1 shaft
Speed, knots: 9
Guns: 1 Oerlikon 20 mm.

Comment: Built in 1964. Trawler type.

SVARTLÖGA *9/1985, Gilbert Gyssels*

4 HISINGEN CLASS (MINESWEEPERS—INSHORE)

HISINGEN M 43 **BLACKAN** M 44
DÄMMAN M 45 **GALTEN** M 46

Displacement, tons: 130 standard; 150 full load
Dimensions, feet (metres): 78.7 × 21.3 × 11.5 *(24 × 6.5 × 3.5)*
Main machinery: 1 diesel; 380 hp(m) *(279 kW)*; 1 shaft
Speed, knots: 9
Guns: 1 Oerlikon 20 mm.

Comment: Built in 1960. Trawler type.

GALTEN *8/1987, Gilbert Gyssels*

3 GÅSSTEN CLASS (MINESWEEPERS—INSHORE)

Name	*No*	*Builders*	*Commissioned*
GÅSSTEN	M 31	Knippla Skeppsvarv	16 Nov 1973
NORSTEN	M 32	Hellevikstrands Skeppsvarv	12 Oct 1973
VIKSTEN	M 33	Karlskronavarvet	20 June 1974

Displacement, tons: 120 standard; 135 full load
Dimensions, feet (metres): 78.7 × 21.3 × 11.5 *(24 × 6.5 × 3.5)*
Main machinery: 1 diesel; 460 hp(m) *(338 kW)*; 1 shaft
Speed, knots: 11
Guns: 1 Oerlikon 20 mm.

Comment: Ordered 1972. *Viksten* built of GRP, as a forerunner to new minehunters building at Karlskrona. Others have wooden hulls. These are repeat Hisingen class.

NORSTEN *8/1985, Gunnar Olsen*

4 M 15 CLASS (MINESWEEPERS—INSHORE)

M 21 **M 22** **M 24** **M 25**

Displacement, tons: 70 standard
Dimensions, feet (metres): 90.9 × 16.5 × 4.6 *(27.7 × 5 × 1.4)*
Main machinery: 2 diesels; 320 hp(m) *(235 kW)* sustained; 2 shafts
Speed, knots: 12
Complement: 10

Comment: All launched in 1941 and now used as platforms for mine clearance divers. M 20 of this class was re-rated as tender and renamed *Skuld* (see *Tenders* section). Four deleted in 1989.

M 15 Class *8/1985, Gunnar Olsen*

AMPHIBIOUS FORCES

3 LCMs

Name	*No*	*Builders*	*Commissioned*
BORE	—	Åsigeverken	1967
GRIM	—	Åsigeverken	1961
HEIMDAL	—	Åsigeverken	1967

Displacement, tons: 340 full load
Dimensions, feet (metres): 124 × 28.2 × 8.5 *(37.8 × 8.6 × 2.6)*
Main machinery: 2 diesels; 800 hp(m) *(588 kW)*; 2 shafts
Speed, knots: 12
Military lift: 325 troops
Guns: 2 Oerlikon 20 mm.

Comment: Launched in 1961 *(Grim)* and other two in 1966. Operated by Coastal Artillery and used to transport guns.

BORE *5/1990, Hartmut Ehlers*

24 LCAs

Displacement, tons: 6 full load
Dimensions, feet (metres): 30.8 × 10.5 × 1.6 *(9.4 × 3.2 × 0.5)*
Speed, knots: 20-25

Comment: Built between 1965 and 1973. Operated by Coastal Artillery.

LCA 352 *8/1990, Gilbert Gyssels*

14 + 63 (30) COMBATBOAT 90H RAIDING CRAFT

HELGE 801 **HELGA** 802 803-814

Displacement, tons: 17 full load
Dimensions, feet (metres): 48.9 × 12.5 × 2.6 *(14.9 × 3.8 × 0.8)*
Main machinery: 2 SAAB Scania DSI 14 diesels; 1100 hp(m) *(808 kW)* (801); 1250 hp(m) *(919 kW)* (802); 2 Alumina Waterjets
Speed, knots: 30
Complement: 3
Military lift: 20 troops plus equipment or 2.8 tons
Missiles: SSM: Rockwell RBS 17 Hellfire; semi-active laser guidance to 5 km *(3 nm)* at 1.0 Mach; warhead 8 kg.
Guns: 1 Aden 30 mm; 1500 rounds/minute to 0.8 km.
1—12.7 mm MG.
Mines: 4 (or 6 depth charges).
Radars: Navigation: Decca; RD 360 (801); Furuno 8050 (802); I band.

Comment: The first two are prototypes built at Dockstavarvet in 1989. 12 more building in 1991/92. 63 more ordered from Dockstavarvet and Gotlands Varv in mid-January 1992, with an option for 30 more. The building period for the ordered boats will take up to 1995. This craft has a large hatch forward to aid disembarkation. 801 has a 20° deadrise and 802 has 26°. All carry four 6-man inflatable rafts.

COMBATBOAT 90H *1989, Royal Swedish Navy*

COMBATBOAT 90H *1992, Royal Swedish Navy*

2 LCMs

Name	*No*	*Builders*	*Commissioned*
SKAGUL	333	Hammarbyverken	1960
SLEIPNER	335	Hammarbyverken	1960

Displacement, tons: 275 standard
Dimensions, feet (metres): 116.4 × 27.9 × 9.5 *(35.5 × 8.5 × 2.9)*
Main machinery: 2 diesels; 640 hp(m) *(470 kW)*; 2 shafts
Speed, knots: 10
Military lift: 100 tons

SKAGUL *1981, Royal Swedish Navy*

4 ANE CLASS (LCMs)

ANE 324 **BALDER** 325 **LOKE** 326 **RING** 327

Displacement, tons: 135 standard
Dimensions, feet (metres): 91.9 × 26.2 × 3.9 *(28 × 8 × 1.2)*
Main machinery: 2 diesels; 2 shafts
Speed, knots: 8.5
Guns: 1 Oerlikon 20 mm. 1—7.62 mm MG.

Comment: Built in 1943-45. Operated by Coastal Artillery.

LOKE *7/1987, van Ginderen Collection*

17 LCMs

603, 604, 606-612, 651-658

Displacement, tons: 55 full load
Dimensions, feet (metres): 68.9 × 19.7 × 4.9 *(21 × 6 × 1.5)*
Main machinery: 2 diesels; 340 hp(m) *(250 kW)*; 2 shafts
Speed, knots: 10
Military lift: 30 tons

Comment: Operated by Navy and Coastal Artillery. Completed from 1980-88. Equipped with Schottel system. Classified as Trossbåt (support boat). Built by Djupviksvarvet.

LCM 604 *5/1990, Hartmut Ehlers*

79 LCUs

210-288

Displacement, tons: 31 full load
Dimensions, feet (metres): 70.2 × 13.8 × 4.2 *(21.4 × 4.2 × 1.3)*
Main machinery: 3 diesels; 600 hp(m) *(441 kW)*; 3 shafts
Speed, knots: 18
Military lift: 40 tons; 40 troops
Guns: 3 to 8—6.5 mm MGs (277-279). 1 Oerlikon 20 mm (remainder).
Mines: Minelaying capability (280-288 only).

Comment: 210-276 completed 1960-76; 277-279 in 1976, 280-284 in 1976-77 and 285-288 in 1986-87.

LCU 211 *8/1990, Gilbert Gyssels*

ICEBREAKERS

1 ODEN CLASS

Name	*No*	*Builders*	*Commissioned*
ODEN	—	Gotaverken Arendal, Göteborg	29 Jan 1989

Displacement, tons: 12 900 full load
Dimensions, feet (metres): 352.4 × 102 × 27.9 *(107.4 × 31.1 × 8.5)*
Main machinery: 4 Sulzer ZAL40S 8L diesels; 23 940 hp(m) *(17.6 MW)* sustained; 2 shafts; cp props
Speed, knots: 17. **Range, miles:** 30 000 at 13 kts
Complement: 32 plus 17 spare berths
Guns: 4 Bofors 40 mm/70 can be fitted.

Comment: Ordered in February 1987, laid down 19 October 1987, launched 25 August 1988. Can break 1.8 m thick ice at 3 kts. Towing winch aft with a pull of 150 tons. Helicopter platform 73.5 × 57.4 ft *(22.4 × 17.5 m)*. The main hull is only 25 m wide but the full width is at the bow. Also equipped as a minelayer. Second of class may be ordered in due course and is to be called *Thule*.

ODEN *5/1989, van Ginderen Collection*

Name	*No*	*Builders*	*Commissioned*
TOR	—	Wärtsilä, Crichton-Vulcan Yard, Turku	31 Jan 1964

Displacement, tons: 5290 full load
Dimensions, feet (metres): 277.2 × 66.9 × 20.3 *(84.5 × 20.4 × 6.2)*
Main machinery: Diesel-electric; 4 Wärtsilä diesel generators; 4 motors; 12 000 hp(m) *(8.82 MW)*; 4 shafts (2 fwd, 2 aft)
Speed, knots: 18
Guns: 4 Bofors 40 mm/70 (not all always embarked).
Helicopters: 1 light.

Comment: Towed to Sandvikens Skeppsdocka, Helsingfors, for completion. A near sister to *Tarmo* built for Finland.

TOR *1986, Royal Swedish Navy*

3 ATLE CLASS

Name	*No*	*Builders*	*Commissioned*
ATLE	—	Wärtsilä, Helsinki	21 Oct 1974
FREJ	—	Wärtsilä, Helsinki	30 Sep 1975
YMER	—	Wärtsilä, Helsinki	25 Oct 1977

Displacement, tons: 7900 standard; 9500 full load
Dimensions, feet (metres): 343.1 × 78.1 × 23.9 *(104.6 × 23.8 × 7.3)*
Main machinery: 5 Wärtsilä-Pielstick diesels; 22 000 hp(m) *(16.2 MW)*; 4 Strömberg motors; 22 000 hp(m) *(16.2 MW)*; 4 shafts (2 fwd, 2 aft)
Speed, knots: 19
Complement: 54 (16 officers)
Guns: 4 Bofors 40 mm/70 (not all always embarked).
Helicopters: 2 light.

Comment: Similar to Finnish Urho class.

FREJ *4/1990, van Ginderen Collection*

Name	*No*	*Builders*	*Commissioned*
NJORD	—	Wärtsilä, Helsinki	8 Oct 1969

Displacement, tons: 5150 standard; 5686 full load
Dimensions, feet (metres): 283.8 × 69.5 × 22.6 *(86.5 × 21.2 × 6.9)*
Main machinery: Diesel-electric; 4 Wärtsilä diesel generators; 4 motors; 12 000 hp(m) *(8.82 MW)*; 4 shafts (2 fwd, 2 aft)
Speed, knots: 18
Guns: 4 Bofors 40 mm/70 (not all always embarked).
Helicopters: 1 light.

Comment: Near sister ship of *Tor*.

NJORD *6/1988, A. Sheldon Duplaix*

Name	*No*	*Builders*	*Commissioned*
ALE	—	Wärtsilä, Helsinki	19 Dec 1973

Displacement, tons: 1550
Dimensions, feet (metres): 154.2 × 42.6 × 16.4 *(47 × 13 × 5)*
Main machinery: 2 diesels; 4750 hp(m) *(3.49 MW)*; 2 shafts
Speed, knots: 14
Complement: 32 (8 officers)
Guns: 1 Bofors 40 mm/70 (not embarked).

Comment: Built for operations on Lake Vänern. Also used for surveying.

ALE *7/1990, A. Sheldon Duplaix*

SURVEY SHIPS

Notes: (1) All are owned by the National Maritime Administration but manned and operated by the Navy.
(2) There is also a research ship *Argos* which is civilian manned and owned by the National Board of Fisheries.

JOHAN NORDENANKAR

Displacement, tons: 2000
Dimensions, feet (metres): 239.5 × 45.9 × 12.5 *(73 × 14 × 3.8)*
Main machinery: 2 diesels; 4000 hp(m) *(2.94 MW)*; 1 shaft
Speed, knots: 15
Complement: 64 (14 officers)
Helicopters: Platform only.

Comment: Ordered from Falkenbergsvarvet in 1977. Commissioned 1 July 1980. Carries eight survey boats.

JOHAN NORDENANKAR *1980, Maritime Defence*

NILS STRÖMCRONA

Displacement, tons: 175 standard
Dimensions, feet (metres): 95.1 × 32.8 × 5.2 *(29 × 10 × 1.6)*
Main machinery: 4 Saab Scania DSI 14 diesels; 1516 hp(m) *(1.11 MW)* sustained; 2 shafts
Speed, knots: 12
Complement: 14 (5 officers)

Comment: Completed 28 June 1985. Of catamaran construction—each hull of 3.9 m made of aluminium.

NILS STRÖMCRONA *1986, Ove Hagström*

JACOB HÄGG

Displacement, tons: 131 standard; 160 full load
Dimensions, feet (metres): 119.8 × 24.6 × 5.6 *(36.5 × 7.5 × 1.7)*
Main machinery: 4 Saab Scania DSI 14 diesels; 1516 hp(m) *(1.11 MW)* sustained; 2 shafts
Speed, knots: 16
Complement: 13 (5 officers)

Comment: Laid down April 1982. Launched 12 March 1983. Completed 16 May 1983. Aluminium hull.

JACOB HÄGG *1988, Royal Swedish Navy*

SERVICE FORCES

Note: There is also a general purpose auxiliary named *Ardal* of 450 tons, 50 × 11 × 3.5 m and capable of 12 kts.

1 TRANSPORT SHIP

FEEDERCHIEF (ex-*Modo Gorthon*)

Measurement, tons: 3592 dwt; 1813 grt
Dimensions, feet (metres): 387.8 × 51.2 × 16.4 *(118.2 × 15.6 × 5)*
Main machinery: 1 MAK diesel; 3990 hp(m) *(2.93 MW)*; 1 shaft
Speed, knots: 13.5

Comment: Built by Paul Lindenau, Kiel in 1975. Acquired by the Navy in 1991. A Ro-Ro cargo vessel design.

1 ELECTRONIC SURVEILLANCE SHIP

Name	*No*	*Builders*	*Commissioned*
ORION	A 201	Karlskronavarvet	7 June 1984

Displacement, tons: 1400 full load
Dimensions, feet (metres): 201.1 × 32.8 × 9.8 *(61.3 × 10 × 3)*
Main machinery: 2 Hedemora V8A diesels; 1800 hp(m) *(1.32 MW)* sustained; 2 shafts; cp props
Speed, knots: 15
Complement: 35

Comment: Ordered 23 April 1982. Laid down 28 June 1982. Launched 30 November 1983.

ORION *10/1990, van Ginderen Collection*

1 DIVER SUPPORT SHIP

SKREDSVIK (ex-*Kbv 172*) A 262 (ex-M 20)

Comment: Details as for Kbv 171 in *Coast Guard* section. Transferred from the Coast Guard in 1991 and is to be used as a Diver Support ship after a refit planned for Autumn 1992. Armament not decided. Will be employed for Command and Control in war.

SKREDSVIK (old number) *6/1991, Erik Laursen*

1 OIL TANKER

Name	*No*	*Builders*	*Commissioned*
BRÄNNAREN	A 228	West Germany	1965

Displacement, tons: 655 standard; 857 full load
Dimensions, feet (metres): 203.4 × 28.2 × 12.1 *(62 × 8.6 × 3.7)*
Main machinery: 1 MAN 6MU 51 diesel; 800 hp(m) *(588 kW)*; 1 shaft
Speed, knots: 11
Cargo capacity: 777 tons oil fuel

Comment: Ex-West German merchant tanker *Indio* purchased early 1972.

BRÄNNAREN *1991, Royal Swedish Navy*

2 BUOY TENDERS

BALTICA **SCANDICA**

Displacement, tons: 450
Dimensions, feet (metres): 177.1 × 39.4 × 16.4 *(54 × 12 × 5)*
Speed, knots: 15

Comment: Completed in 1982-83.

1 SALVAGE SHIP

Name	*No*	*Builders*	*Commissioned*
BELOS	A 211	—	29 May 1963

Displacement, tons: 965 standard; 1000 full load
Dimensions, feet (metres): 190.2 × 37 × 12 *(58 × 11.2 × 3.8)*
Main machinery: 2 diesels; 1200 hp(m) *(882 kW)*; 2 shafts
Speed, knots: 13
Helicopters: Platform only.

Comment: Equipped with decompression chamber. Reported that she underwent a major refit from late 1985.

BELOS *6/1991, Erik Laursen*

2 SAIL TRAINING SHIPS

Name	*No*	*Builders*	*Commissioned*
GLADAN	S 01	Naval Dockyard, Stockholm	1947
FALKEN	S 02	Naval Dockyard, Stockholm	1947

Displacement, tons: 225 standard
Dimensions, feet (metres): 112.8 × 23.6 × 13.8 *(34.4 × 7.2 × 4.2)*
Main machinery: 1 diesel; 120 hp(m) *(88 kW)*; 1 shaft

Comment: Sail training ships. Two masted schooners. Sail area, 512 sq m. Both have had major overhauls in 1986-88 in which all technical systems have been replaced.

FALKEN *7/1990, Maritime Photographic*

2 TORPEDO AND MISSILE RECOVERY VESSELS

Name	*No*	*Builders*	*Commissioned*
PELIKANEN	A 247	Djupviksvarvet	26 Sep 1963
PINGVINEN	A 248	Lundevarv-Ooverkstads	14 Mar 1975

Displacement, tons: 191 full load
Dimensions, feet (metres): 108.2 × 19 × 7.2 *(33 × 5.8 × 2.2)*
Main machinery: 2 Mercedes-Benz diesels; 1040 hp(m) *(764 kW)*; 2 shafts
Speed, knots: 14

Comment: Torpedo recovery and rocket trials vessels. A 247 has her bridge superstructure forward instead of aft and only has one mast which is abaft the bridge.

PINGVINEN *11/1991, van Ginderen Collection*

1 TORPEDO TRANSPORT

HÄGERN A 246

Displacement, tons: 50 standard; 58 full load
Dimensions, feet (metres): 95.1 × 16.4 × 5.9 *(29 × 5 × 1.8)*
Main machinery: 2 diesels; 480 hp(m) *(353 kW)*; 2 shafts
Speed, knots: 10

Comment: Launched in 1951.

HÄGERN *8/1990, Gilbert Gyssels*

1 COASTAL ARTILLERY SUPPORT VESSEL (TROSSBÄT)

Displacement, tons: 45 full load
Dimensions, feet (metres): 75.5 × 17.7 × 4.6 *(23 × 5.4 × 1.4)*
Main machinery: 2 Scania DSI 14 diesels; 1516 hp(m) *(1.11 MW)* sustained; 2 Alumina waterjets
Speed, knots: 15
Complement: 3
Guns: 1 — 12.7 mm MG

Comment: Prototype Trossbät built at Holms Shipyard and capable of carrying 15 tons of deck cargo and 9 tons internal cargo or 17 troops plus mines. The aim is to build up to 25 of these craft but no contract had been given by early 1992. Aluminium hull with a bow ramp. Some ice capability.

TROSSBÄT *5/1991, Per Kornefeldt*

3 TENDERS

SIGRUN A 256

Displacement, tons: 256 standard
Dimensions, feet (metres): 105 × 22.3 × 10.5 *(32 × 6.8 × 3.2)*
Main machinery: 1 diesel; 320 hp(m) *(235 kW)*; 1 shaft
Speed, knots: 11

Comment: Launched in 1961. Laundry ship.

URD (ex-*Capella*) A 241

Displacement, tons: 63 standard; 90 full load
Dimensions, feet (metres): 73.8 × 18.3 × 9.2 *(22.5 × 5.6 × 2.8)*
Main machinery: 1 diesel; 200 hp(m) *(147 kW)*; 1 shaft
Speed, knots: 8

Comment: Experimental vessel added to the official list in 1970. Launched in 1929.

SKULD (ex-*M 20*) A 242

Displacement, tons: 70 standard
Dimensions, feet (metres): 90.9 × 16.5 × 4.6 *(27.7 × 5 × 1.4)*
Main machinery: 2 diesels; 410 hp(m) *(301 kW)*; 2 shafts
Speed, knots: 12

Comment: Former inshore minesweeper of the M 15 class. Launched in 1941.

SKULD *8/1990, Gilbert Gyssels*

2 AMMUNITION TRANSPORTS

ATB 1 A 341 **ATB 2** A 342

Displacement, tons: 70
Dimensions, feet (metres): 99.7 × 19.7 × 6.6 *(30.4 × 6 × 2)*
Speed, knots: 10
Cargo capacity: 100 tons

ATB 1 *8/1986, van Ginderen Collection*

4 SONOBUOY TENDERS

EJDERN B 01
KRICKAN B 02
SVÄRTEN B 03
VIGGEN B 04

Displacement, tons: 36 full load
Dimensions, feet (metres): 65.6 × 15.7 × 4.3 *(20 × 4.8 × 1.3)*
Main machinery: 2 Volvo Penta TAMD 122 diesels; 775 hp(m) *(570 kW)*; 2 shafts
Speed, knots: 15
Complement: 9
Guns: 1—12.7 mm MG.

Comment: Built by Djupviks Varvet and completed in 1991. GRP hulls.

TUGS

ACHILLES A 251 **AJAX** A 252

Displacement, tons: 450
Dimensions, feet (metres): 108.2 × 28.9 × 15.1 *(33 × 8.8 × 4.6)*
Main machinery: 1 diesel; 1650 hp(m) *(1.2 MW)*; 1 shaft
Speed, knots: 12

Comment: *Achilles* was launched in 1962 and *Ajax* in 1963. Both are icebreaking tugs.

ACHILLES *4/1991, Hartmut Ehlers*

HERMES A 253 **HEROS** A 322

Displacement, tons: 185 standard; 215 full load
Dimensions, feet (metres): 80.5 × 22.6 × 13.1 *(24.5 × 6.9 × 4)*
Main machinery: 1 diesel; 600 hp(m) *(441 kW)*; 1 shaft
Speed, knots: 11

Comment: Launched 1953-57. Icebreaking tugs.

HERMES *1990, van Ginderen Collection*

HERCULES A 323 **HERA** A 324

Displacement, tons: 127 full load
Dimensions, feet (metres): 65.3 × 21.3 × 12.5 *(19.9 × 6.5 × 3.8)*
Main machinery: 1 diesel; 615 hp(m) *(452 kW)*; 1 shaft
Speed, knots: 10.5

Comment: Launched 1969 and 1971. Icebreaking tugs.

HERA *8/1990, Gilbert Gyssels*

A 701-705, 751-756

Displacement, tons: 42 full load
Dimensions, feet (metres): 50.9 × 16.4 × 8.9 *(15.5 × 5 × 2.7)*
Main machinery: 1 diesel; 1 shaft
Speed, knots: 9.5

Comment: Can carry 40 people. Icebreaking tugs. 701-703 used by Coast Artillery.

A 755 *8/1990, Gilbert Gyssels*

HEBE A 326 **PASSOPP** A 327 **ATLAS** A 330

Displacement, tons: 35; 25 *(Passopp)*
Speed, knots: 9

Comment: *Passopp* built in 1957; *Hebe* in 1969; *Atlas* in 1975.

WATER CARRIERS

1 WATER TANKER

Name	*No*	*Builders*	*Commissioned*
ELDAREN (ex-*Brotank*)	A 229	Asiverken, Åmål	1959

Measurement, tons: 320 dwt
Dimensions, feet (metres): 122 × 21.3 × 9.5 *(37.2 × 6.5 × 2.9)*
Main machinery: 1 Volvo-Penta diesel; 300 hp(m) *(220 kW)*; 1 shaft
Speed, knots: 9
Cargo capacity: 300 tons oil fuel; 10 tons water

Comment: Civilian tanker purchased from A F Karlsson in 1980.

ELDAREN (camouflaged) *7/1991, Erik Laursen*

FRYKEN A 217 **MERANDA** A 313

Displacement, tons: 307 standard
Dimensions, feet (metres): 111.5 × 19.7 × 9.5 *(34 × 6 × 2.9)*
Main machinery: 1 diesel; 370 hp(m) *(272 kW)*; 1 shaft
Speed, knots: 10
Cargo capacity: 200 tons

Comment: Naval construction water carriers built in 1960-61.

FRYKEN *1976, Royal Swedish Navy*

COAST GUARD
(KUSTBEVAKNING)

Establishment: Established in 1638, and for 350 years was a part of the Swedish Customs administration. From 1 July 1988 the Coast Guard became an independent civilian authority with a Board supervised by the Ministry of Defence. Organised in four regions with a central Headquarters.

Duties: Responsible for civilian surveillance of Swedish waters, fishery zone and continental shelf. Supervises and enforces fishing regulations, customs, dumping and pollution regulations, environmental protection and traffic regulations. Also concerned with prevention of drug running and forms part of the Swedish search and rescue organisation.

Headquarters Appointments

Director General:
Leif H Sjöström
Chief of Operations:
Staffan Kvarnström

Personnel: 1992: 580

Aircraft: One Cessna 402C. Two CASA 212.

Ships: Tv pennant numbers replaced by Kbv in 1988 but the Kbv is not displayed. Vessels are unarmed and have a distinctive yellow diagonal stripe on blue painted hulls. Superstructures are painted white.

Deletion

1991 *Kbv 172* (sold to Navy)

1 KBV 181 CLASS

Kbv 181

Displacement, tons: 800 approx
Dimensions, feet (metres): 183.7 × 33.5 × 15.1 *(56 × 10.2 × 4.6)*
Main machinery: 2 diesels; 3755 hp(m) *(2.76 MW)*; 2 shafts
Speed, knots: 16
Complement: 12
Guns: 1 Oerlikon 20 mm (if required).
Radars: Navigation: 2 Racal Decca; I band.
Sonars: Simrad Subsea; active search; high frequency.

Comment: Ordered from Rauma Shipyards in August 1989 and built at Uusikaupunki. Commissioned 30 November 1990. Unarmed in peacetime. Equipped as a Command vessel for SAR and anti-pollution operations. All-steel construction similar to Finnish *Tursas*. Has replaced *Kbv 172*.

Kbv 181 *11/1990, Swedish Coast Guard*

1 KBV 171 CLASS

Kbv 171

Displacement, tons: 335 standard; 375 full load
Dimensions, feet (metres): 164 × 27.9 × 7.9 *(50 × 8.5 × 2.4)*
Main machinery: 2 Hedemora V16A diesels; 4500 hp(m) *(3.3 MW)*; 2 shafts
Speed, knots: 20. **Range, miles:** 3000 at 12 kts
Complement: 9
Gun: 1 Oerlikon 20 mm (if required).
Mines: Has mining capability.
Radars: Navigation: Two Racal Decca; I band.
Sonars: Simrad Subsea; active search; high frequency.
Helicopters: Platform for 1 light.

Comment: Ordered from Karlskronavarvet in 1978 and completed in 1980. GRP hull identical to Landsort class for the Navy. Sister ship *Kbv 172* replaced by *181* and sold to the Navy as a Diver support ship.

Kbv 171 *6/1991, Erik Laursen*

5 KBV 101 CLASS

Kbv 101-105

Displacement, tons: 50-53 full load
Dimensions, feet (metres): 87.6 × 16.4 × 3.6 *(26.7 × 5 × 1.1)*
Main machinery: 2 Cummins KTA 38 M diesels; 2120 hp *(1.56 MW)*; 2 shafts
Speed, knots: 20. **Range, miles:** 1000 at 15 kts
Complement: 8 (accommodation for 16)
Sonars: Hull-mounted; active search; high frequency.

Comment: Built 1969-73 at Djupviksvarvet. Class A cutters. All-welded aluminium hull and upperworks. Equipped for salvage divers. Modernised with new diesels, a new bridge and new electronics completed in 1988.

Kbv 103 *4/1991, Erik Laursen*

10 KBV 281 CLASS (CLASS B)

Kbv 281-290

Displacement, tons: 36-39 full load
Dimensions, feet (metres): 68.9 × 16.4 × 3 *(21 × 5 × 0.9)*
Main machinery: 2 Cummins KTA 38 M diesels; 2120 hp *(1.56 MW)*; 2 shafts
Speed, knots: 27
Complement: 5

Comment: Built by Djupviksvarvet and delivered at one a year from 1979. Last one commissioned 6 December 1990. Aluminium hulls.

Kbv 283 (317 alongside) *5/1990, Hartmut Ehlers*

8 KBV 271 CLASS (CLASS C)

Kbv 271-278

Displacement, tons: 18-20 full load
Dimensions, feet (metres): 63 × 13.1 × 4.3 *(19.2 × 4 × 1.3)*
Main machinery: 2 Volvo Penta TAMD 120 A diesels; 700 hp(m) *(515 kW)*; 2 shafts
Speed, knots: 22
Complement: 5

Comment: Built 1974-77. Aluminium hulls.

COAST GUARD PATROL CRAFT (SMALL)

Number	*Comment*
Kbv 238, 240-250, 255-261	17 ton aluminium hulls built 1961-72. Class D.
Kbv 314, 317-8, 321, 341, 365-6, 368-9, 371-3, 381-5, 389, 391-4	Fast patrol craft built 1962-88.
Kbv 602, 661-2, 644-5	'Gemini' type built 1971-88.
Kbv 801, 804-8	Ice craft built 1965-72.

Kbv 256 *5/1990, Hartmut Ehlers*

POLLUTION CONTROL CRAFT

Number	Displacement (tons)	Comment
Kbv 041-4	70-76	Steel hulled. Class B sea trucks built
045-51	235-340	1972-1983 by Lunde SY. Complement includes salvage divers.
Kbv 02-03	190-300	Steel hulled support ships. Class A built 1971-76 by Lunde SY. Complement includes salvage divers. Kbv 02 is an older modernised vessel.
Kbv 04	450	Built by Lunde SY in 1978. Carries salvage divers
Kbv 010	400	15 kts. Built by Lunde SY 1985. Sea Truck.
Kbv 020-23	30 (60 Kbv 020)	Aluminium catamaran hulls. Class D.
Kbv 0701-0712	6	Skerry boats. Class E built since 1979.
Kbv 081-099	1	Work boats. GRP on aluminium hulls. Class K built 1971-79.

Kbv 044 *9/1990, van Ginderen Collection*

Kbv 02 *5/1990, Hartmut Ehlers*

Kbv 048 *5/1990, Hartmut Ehlers*

SWITZERLAND

Diplomatic Representation

Defence Attaché in London:
Major General G de Loës

General

The patrol boats are manned by the Army and split between Lakes Constance, Geneva and Maggiore; one company to each.

Mercantile Marine

Lloyd's Register of Shipping:
21 vessels of 285 653 tons gross

11 AQUARIUS CLASS (Patrouillenboot 80)

ANTARES, AQUARIUS, CASTOR, MARS, ORION, PERSEUS, POLLUX, SATURN, SIRIUS, URANUS, VENUS

Displacement, tons: 5.2
Dimensions, feet (metres): 35.1 × 10.8 × 3 *(10.7 × 3.3 × 0.9)*
Main machinery: 2 Volvo-Penta AQ 260A petrol engines; 520 hp(m) *(382 kW)* sustained; 2 shafts
Speed, knots: 32.5
Complement: 8
Guns: 2—12.7 mm MGs.
Radars: Surface search: I band.

Comment: Builders Müller AG, Spiez. GRP hulls, wooden superstructure. *Aquarius* commissioned in 1978, *Pollux* in 1984, the remainder in 1981.

MARS *1991, Aldo Fraccaroli*

6 RELIANCE TYPE

Comment: Standard 11 m craft ordered in March 1991 for the Police. Being built by Reliance Workboats, Laverstock.

SYRIA

Headquarters' Appointments

Commander-in-Chief Navy:
Vice Admiral Tayyara
Chief of Staff:
Vice Admiral Kassiem Mahummed Baydoun
Director of Naval Operations:
Commodore Muhammad Hamud

Personnel

(a) 1992: 4000 officers and men (2500 reserves)
(b) 18 months' national service

Pennant Numbers

Side numbers are not displayed.

Bases

Latakia, Tartous, Al-Mina-al-Bayda, Baniyas

Mercantile Marine

Lloyd's Register of Shipping:
79 vessels of 109 452 tons gross

DELETIONS

1990 2 Osa Is

SUBMARINES

Note: There continue to be rumours of impending Kilo class replacements for the Romeos.

3 Ex-SOVIET ROMEO CLASS

Displacement, tons: 1475 surfaced; 1830 dived
Dimensions, feet (metres): 251.3 × 22 × 16.1 *(76.6 × 6.7 × 4.9)*
Main machinery: Diesel-electric; 2 diesels; 4000 hp(m) *(2.94 MW)*; 2 motors; 2700 hp(m) *(1.98 MW)*; 2 creep motors; 2 shafts
Speed, knots: 16 surfaced; 13 dived
Range, miles: 9000 at 9 kts surfaced
Complement: 54

Torpedoes: 8—21 in *(533 mm)* (6 bow, 2 stern) tubes. 14 Type 53; dual purpose; pattern active/passive homing up to 20 km *(10.8 nm)* at up to 45 kts; warhead 400 kg.
Mines: 28 in lieu of torpedoes.
Countermeasures: ESM: Stop Light; radar warning.
Radars: Surface search: Snoop Tray; I band.
Sonars: Hercules/Feniks; hull-mounted; passive/active search and attack; medium/high frequency.

Programmes: First pair sailed for Tartous in November 1985 under Soviet flag and transferred to Syrian flag after training period in July 1986. Third transferred December 1986. These are unlikely to be new construction and would therefore have been completed about 1961 and badly need replacements.
Operational: One ex-Soviet Whiskey class submarine transferred from the Black Sea in November 1985 and acts as an alongside charging platform. All based at Tartous.

ROMEO Class *1987*

FRIGATES

2 Ex-SOVIET PETYA III CLASS

1/508 (ex-*12*) **AL HIRASA** 2/508 (ex-14)

Displacement, tons: 950 standard; 1180 full load
Dimensions, feet (metres): 268.3 × 29.9 × 9.5 *(81.8 × 9.1 × 2.9)*
Main machinery: CODAG; 2 gas turbines; 30 000 hp(m) *(22 MW)*; 1 Type 61V-3 diesel; 6000 hp(m) *(4.4 MW)* (centre shaft); 3 shafts
Speed, knots: 32. **Range, miles:** 4870 at 10 kts; 450 at 29 kts
Complement: 98 (8 officers)

Guns: 4—3 in *(76 mm)*/60 (2 twin) ❶; 80° elevation; 90 rounds/minute to 15 km *(8 nm)*; weight of shell 6.8 kg.
Torpedoes: 3—21 in *(533 mm)* (triple) tubes ❷. Soviet Type 53; dual purpose; pattern active/passive homing up to 20 km *(10.8 nm)* at up to 45 kts; warhead 400 kg or low yield nuclear.
A/S mortars: 4 RBU 2500 16-tubed trainable ❸; range 2500 m; warhead 21 kg.
Depth charges: 2 racks.
Mines: Can carry 22.
Radars: Surface search: Slim Net ❹; E/F band.
Navigation: Don 2; I band.
Fire control: Hawk Screech ❺; I band; range 27 km *(15 nm)*.
IFF: High Pole B. Two Square Head.
Sonars: Hull-mounted; active search and attack; high frequency.

Programmes: Transferred by the USSR in July 1975 and March 1975.
Operational: Based at Tartous.

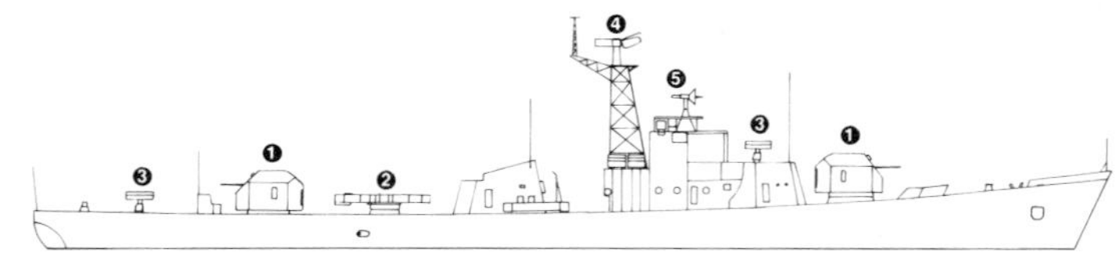

PETYA Class *(Scale 1 : 900), Ian Sturton*

AL HIRASA *7/1975, MoD*

LAND-BASED MARITIME AIRCRAFT

Numbers/Type: 20 Mil Mi-14P Haze A.
Operational speed: 124 kts *(230 km/h)*.
Service ceiling: 15 000 ft *(4570 m)*.
Range: 432 nm *(800 km)*.
Role/Weapon systems: Medium-range ASW helicopter. Sensors: Search radar, dipping sonar, MAD, sonobuoys. Weapons: ASW; internally stored torpedoes, depth mines and bombs.

Numbers/Type: 4 Kamov Ka-27 Helix.
Operational speed: 135 kts *(250 km/h)*.
Service ceiling: 19 685 ft *(6000 m)*.
Range: 432 nm *(800 km)*.
Role/Weapon systems: ASW helicopter. All delivered in February 1990. Sensors: Search radar, dipping sonar, sonobuoys, MAD, ECM. Weapons: ASW; 3 torpedoes, depth bombs, mines.

MINE WARFARE FORCES

1 Ex-SOVIET NATYA CLASS

642

Displacement, tons: 770 full load
Dimensions, feet (metres): 200.1 × 31.8 × 8.9 *(61 × 9.7 × 2.7)*
Main machinery: 2 diesels; 8000 hp(m) *(5.88 MW)*; 2 shafts
Speed, knots: 19. **Range, miles:** 4000 at 10 kts
Complement: 65
Missiles: SAM: 2 SA-N-5 Grail quad launchers; manual aiming; IR homing to 6 km *(3.2 nm)* at 1.5 Mach; altitude to 2500 m *(8000 ft)*; warhead 1.5 kg; 16 missiles.
Guns: 4—30 mm/65 (2 twin). 4—25 mm/80 (2 twin).
A/S mortars: 2 RBU 1200 5-tubed fixed; range 1200 m; warhead 34 kg.
Mines: 10.
Radars: Surface search: Don 2; I band.
Fire control: Drum Tilt; H/I band.

Comment: Arrived in Tartous January 1985. Has had sweeping gear removed and acts as a patrol ship. Based at Tartous.

NATYA Class (old number) *1991*

1 Ex-SOVIET T 43 CLASS (MINESWEEPER—OCEAN)

HITTIN 504

Displacement, tons: 500 standard; 580 full load
Dimensions, feet (metres): 190.2 × 27.6 × 6.9 *(58 × 8.4 × 2.1)*
Main machinery: 2 diesels; 2200 hp(m) *(1.6 MW)*; 2 shafts
Speed, knots: 15. **Range, miles:** 3000 at 10 kts
Complement: 65
Guns: 2—37 mm/63 (twin). 8—14.5 mm MGs (4 twin).
Mines: Can carry 16.
Radars: Surface search: Ball End; E/F band.
Navigation: Don 2; I band.
IFF: Square Head. High Pole A.

Comment: Two transferred in 1959. The second of this class was sunk in the Israeli October 1973 war.

T 43 Class (old number) *1985, van Ginderen Collection*

1 Ex-SOVIET SONYA CLASS

532

Displacement, tons: 400 full load
Dimensions, feet (metres): 157.4 × 28.9 × 6.6 *(48 × 8.8 × 2)*
Main machinery: 2 diesels; 2000 hp(m) *(1.47 MW)*; 2 shafts
Speed, knots: 15. **Range, miles:** 3000 at 10 kts
Complement: 43
Guns: 2—30 mm/65 (twin). 2—25 mm/80 (twin).
Mines: 5.
Radars: Surface search: Don 2; I band.
IFF: Two Square Head. One High Pole B.

Comment: Wooden hull. Made passage from Black Sea in December 1985, transferred January 1986. Based at Tartous.

2 Ex-SOVIET VANYA CLASS (MINESWEEPERS—COASTAL)

KADISIA 775 **YARMUK** 776

Displacement, tons: 200 standard; 250 full load
Dimensions, feet (metres): 131.2 × 23.9 × 5.9 *(40 × 7.3 × 1.8)*
Main machinery: 2 diesels; 2200 bhp; 2 shafts
Speed, knots: 16. **Range, miles:** 1400 at 14 kts
Complement: 30
Guns: 2—30 mm/65 (twin).
Mines: Can carry 8.
Radars: Surface search: Don 2; I band.
IFF: Square Head. High Pole B.

Comment: Transferred January 1973. Probably only one is still operational. Based at Tartous.

5 Ex-SOVIET YEVGENYA CLASS (MINESWEEPERS—INSHORE)

4/507-8/507

Displacement, tons: 77 standard; 90 full load
Dimensions, feet (metres): 80.7 × 18 × 4.9 *(24.6 × 5.5 × 1.5)*
Main machinery: 2 diesels; 400 hp(m) *(294 kW)*; 2 shafts
Speed, knots: 11. **Range, miles:** 300 at 10 kts
Complement: 10
Guns: 2—14.5 mm (twin) MGs (first pair). 2—25 mm/80 (twin) (second pair).
Radars: Surface search: Spin Trough; I band.
IFF: High Pole.

Comment: First transferred 1978, two in 1985 and two in 1986. Second pair by Ro-flow from Baltic in February 1985 being new construction with tripod mast. The first two may be non-operational. All based at Tartous.

YEVGENYA Class (old number) *1991*

AMPHIBIOUS FORCES

3 Ex-SOVIET POLNOCHNY B CLASS (LSM)

1/114 **2/114** **3/114**

Displacement, tons: 760 standard; 800 full load
Dimensions, feet (metres): 242.7 × 27.9 × 5.8 *(74 × 8.5 × 1.8)*
Main machinery: 2 Type 40D diesels; 5000 hp(m) *(3.67 MW)*; 2 shafts
Speed, knots: 19. **Range, miles:** 1500 at 15 kts
Complement: 40
Military lift: 180 troops; 350 tons cargo
Guns: 4—30 mm/65 (2 twin); 85° elevation; 500 rounds/minute to 5 km *(2.7 nm)*; weight of shell 0.54 kg.
2—140 mm rocket launchers; 18 barrels per launcher; range 9 km *(5 nm)*.
Radars: Surface search: Spin Trough; I band.
Fire control: Drum Tilt; H/I band.

Comment: First transferred January 1984, two in February 1985 from Black Sea. All based at Tartous.

LIGHT FORCES

Note: (a) There is still one ex-Soviet P6 class (No 75) based at Tartous and two Hamelin class 37 m patrol craft based at Latakia.
(b) Second-hand purchase of Nanuchka class is a possibility in due course.

4 Ex-SOVIET OSA I and 10 OSA II CLASSES (FAST ATTACK CRAFT—MISSILE)

23-26 (Osa I); **31-40** (Osa II)

Displacement, tons: 210 (245 Osa II) full load
Dimensions, feet (metres): 110.2 × 24.9 × 8.8 *(33.6 × 7.6 × 2.7)*
Main machinery: 3 M503A diesels; 12 000 hp(m) *(8.8 MW)*; 3 shafts (Osa I)
3 M504 diesels; 15 000 hp(m) *(11 MW)*; 3 shafts (Osa II)
Speed, knots: 35 (Osa I); 37 (Osa II). **Range, miles:** 400 at 34 kts (Osa I); 500 at 35 kts (Osa II)
Complement: 30

Missiles: SSM: 4 SS-N-2A Styx (Osa I); active radar or IR homing to 46 km *(25 nm)* at 0.9 Mach; warhead 513 kg.
4 SS-N-2C (Osa II); active radar or IR homing to 83 km *(43 nm)* at 0.9 Mach; warhead 513 kg; sea-skimmer at end of run.
Guns: 4—30 mm/65 (2 twin, 1 fwd, 1 aft); 85° elevation; 500 rounds/minute to 5 km *(2.7 nm)*; weight of shell 0.54 kg.
Radars: Surface search: Square Tie; I band; range 73 km *(40 nm)* or limits of radar horizon.
Fire control: Drum Tilt; H/I band.
IFF: Two Square Head. High Pole A or B.

Programmes: Osa I class delivered as follows: December 1972 (2), October 1973 (3), November 1973 (1), December 1973 (3). Osa II class delivered: September 1978 (1), October 1978 (1), October 1979 (2), November 1979 (2), August 1982 (1), September 1982 (1) and May 1984 (2). Some have already been deleted; more may follow soon.

OSA Class *1987*

Structure: Two of the Osa IIs are modified (Nos 39 and 40).

Operational: Osa Is based at Tartous; Osa IIs at Latakia.

5 Ex-SOVIET KOMAR CLASS (FAST ATTACK CRAFT—MISSILE)

42-46

Displacement, tons: 85 full load
Dimensions, feet (metres): 88.6 × 20.7 × 4.3 *(27 × 6.3 × 1.3)*
Main machinery: 4 Type M50 diesels; 4800 hp(m) *(3.53 MW)*; 4 shafts
Speed, knots: 37. **Range, miles:** 400 at 30 kts
Complement: 19

Missiles: SSM: 2 SSN-2A Styx; active radar or IR homing to 46 km *(25 nm)* at 0.9 Mach; warhead 513 kg.
Guns: 2—25 mm/80 (twin); 85° elevation; 270 rounds/minute to 3 km *(1.6 nm)*; weight of shell 0.34 kg.
Radars: Surface search: Square Tie; I band.
Fire control: Drum Tilt; H/I band.

Programmes: Acquired in May 1974. Laid up in 1987 but refitted and operational again in 1990.
Operational: Based at Al-Mina-al-Bayda.

8 Ex-SOVIET ZHUK CLASS (COASTAL PATROL CRAFT)

1-8

Displacement, tons: 50 full load
Dimensions, feet (metres): 75.4 × 17 × 6.2 *(23 × 5.2 × 1.9)*
Main machinery: 2 diesels; 2400 hp(m) *(1.76 MW)*; 2 shafts
Speed, knots: 30. **Range, miles:** 1100 at 15 kts
Complement: 17
Guns: 4—14.5 mm (2 twin) MGs.
Radars: Surface search: Spin Trough; I band.

Comment: Three transferred from Black Sea in August 1981, three on 25 December 1984 and two more in the late 1980s. All based at Tartous.

SUPPORT SHIPS

1 Ex-SOVIET SEKSTAN CLASS

SR 153

Displacement, tons: 400 full load
Dimensions, feet (metres): 133.8 × 30.5 × 14.1 *(40.8 × 9.3 × 4.3)*
Main machinery: 1 diesel; 400 hp(m) *(2.94 MW)*; 1 shaft
Speed, knots: 11. **Range, miles:** 1000 at 11 kts
Complement: 24
Cargo capacity: 115 tons

Comment: Initially probably belonged to and was used by the Soviet Mediterranean Squadron. At some stage transferred to the Syrian Navy.

3 SURVEY LAUNCHES

Dimensions, feet (metres): 32.2 × 11.2 × 3 *(9.8 × 3.4 × 0.9)*
Main machinery: 2 Volvo Penta diesels; 310 hp(m) *(228 kW)*; 2 shafts
Speed, knots: 25
Complement: 4

Comment: Completed 1986 at Arcor, La Teste, France. GRP hulls.

1 TRAINING SHIP

AL ASSAD

Displacement, tons: 3500 full load
Dimensions, feet (metres): 344.5 × 56.4 × 13.1 *(105 × 17.2 × 4)*
Main machinery: 2 diesels; 2 shafts
Speed, knots: 16. **Range, miles:** 12 500 at 15 kts
Complement: 56 plus 140 cadets

Comment: Built in Polnocny Shipyard, Gdansk and launched 18 February 1987. Delivered in late 1988. Ro-Ro design used as a naval training ship. Unarmed. Based at Latakia.

AL ASSAD *6/1990, Selçuk Emre*

1 Ex-SOVIET POLUCHAT CLASS

Displacement, tons: 70 standard; 100 full load
Dimensions, feet (metres): 97.1 × 19 × 4.8 *(29.6 × 5.8 × 1.5)*
Main machinery: 2 diesels; 1700 hp(m) *(1.25 MW)*; 2 shafts
Speed, knots: 20. **Range, miles:** 1500 at 10 kts
Complement: 15
Guns: 2—14.5 mm (twin) MGs.
Radars: Surface search: Spin Trough; I band.

Comment: Used as divers' base-ship. Transferred September 1967. Based at Al-Mina-al-Bayda.

7 ROTORK SEA TRUCKS

Dimensions, feet (metres): 47.6 × 14.4 × 2.9 *(14.5 × 4.4 × 0.9)*
Main machinery: 2 diesels; 600 hp(m) *(441 kW)*; 2 shafts
Speed, knots: 20
Complement: 8
Guns: 1—7.62 mm MG.

Comment: Light logistic craft delivered in 1980.

TAIWAN

Headquarters' Appointment

Chief of the General Staff:
Admiral Ho-Chien Liu

Senior Flag Officers

Commander-in-Chief:
Admiral Yeh Chang Tung
Deputy Commanders-in-Chief:
Vice Admiral Chun-Lien Ku
Vice Admiral Ming-Kao Lee
Commandant of Marine Corps:
Lieutenant General Y H Tu
Fleet Commander:
Vice Admiral Li-Chung Cheng
Amphibious Forces Commander:
Vice Admiral Tse-Fong Wu
Director of Political Warfare:
Vice Admiral Wei Ouyang
Director of Logistics:
Vice Admiral Te-An Han

Personnel

(a) 1992: 30 000 (and 32 500 reserves) in Navy, 35 000 (and 35 000 reserves) in Marine Corps
(b) 2 years' conscript service

Bases

Tsoying: HQ First Naval District (Southern Taiwan, Pratas and Spratly). Main Base, HQ of Fleet Command, Naval Aviation Group and Marine Corps. Base of southern patrol and transport squadrons. Officers and ratings training, Naval Academy, Naval Shipyard.
Kao-hsiung; Naval Shipyard.
Makung (Pescadores): HQ Second Naval District (Pescadores, Quemoy and Wu Ch'iu). Base for attack squadrons. Naval Shipyard and Training facilities.
Keelung: HQ Third Naval District (Northern Taiwan and Matsu group). Base of northern patrol and transport squadrons. Naval Shipyard.
Minor bases at Suao, Hualien, Tamshui, Hsinchu, Wuchi, Anping and Kenting.

Commands

Fleet Commander commands the Amphibious Forces (two landing ship squadrons and other elements), two destroyer squadrons, a patrol squadron, a mine warfare squadron and a logistic squadron. Tactical control of the 33rd and 34th ASW Squadrons (Tracker aircraft) of the RoCAF, also comes under the Fleet Commander. CTF 62 commands the northern and southern patrol and transport squadrons and the attack squadron.

Marine Corps

Two divisions, the 66th and 99th. Equipped with M-116, M-733, LARC-5, LVTP5 personnel carriers and LVTH6 armour tractors. Based at Tsoying and in southern Taiwan with detachments at Pratas and Spratley Islands in the South China Sea.

Strength of the Fleet

Type	*Active*	*Building (Planned)*
Submarines	4	(16)
Destroyers	24	—
Frigates	10	6 (26)
Corvettes	3	(10)
Fast Attack Craft (Missile)	52	(12)
Coastal Patrol Craft	70	6
Coastal Minesweepers/Hunters	17	(8)
Minesweeping Boats	9	—
LSD	1	—
Landing Ships (LST and LSM)	25	—
LCUs	52	—
LCMs	250	—
Minor Landing Craft	120	—
Combat Support Ship	1	—
Repair Ship	1	—
Transports	9	1
Salvage Ship	1	—
Survey Vessels	3	—
Support Tankers	4	—
AGI	1	—
Tugs	12	—
Floating Docks	5	—
Customs	13+	9

Maritime Security Police

Comes under the Minister of the Interior but its numerous patrol boats are integrated with the Navy for operational purposes.

Pennant Numbers

Pennant numbers were changed in early 1987.

Mercantile Marine

Lloyd's Register of Shipping:
644 vessels of 5 888 100 tons gross

DELETIONS

Light Forces

1990 PTC 35-36

Amphibious Forces

1990 *Chung Cheng*

Miscellaneous

1989 *Chiu Hua* (sunk as target), *Ta Wan* (sunk as target)

PENNANT LIST

Submarines

736	Hai Shih
793	Hai Lung
795	Hai Hu
791	Hai Pao

Destroyers

902	Heng Yang
903	Hua Yang
905	Yuen Yang
906	Huei Yang
907	Fu Yang
908	Kwei Yang
909	Chiang Yang
911	Dang Yang
912	Chien Yang
914	Lo Yang
915	Han Yang
917	Nan Yang
918	An Yang
919	Kun Yang
920	Lai Yang
921	Liao Yang
923	Chen Yang
924	Kai Yang
925	Te Yang
926	Shao Yang
927	Yun Yang
928	Cheng Yang
929	Chao Yang
930	Lao Yang

Frigates

815	Tien Shan
827	Tai Yuan
832	Yu Shan
833	Hua Shan
834	Wen Shan
835	Fu Shan
836	Lu Shan
837	Shou Shan
838	Tai Shan
843	Chung Shan
1101	Cheng Kung (bldg)
1103	Cheng Ho (bldg)
1105	Chi Kuang (bldg)
1106	Yueh Fei (bldg)
1107	Tzu-I (bldg)
1108	Pan Chao (bldg)
1109	Chang Chien (planned)
1110	Tien Tan (planned)

Corvettes

867	Ping Jin
884	Wu Sheng
896	Chu Yung

Light Forces

601	Lung Chiang
602	Sui Chang

Amphibious Forces

192	Cheng Hai
201	Chung Hai
203	Chung Ting
204	Chung Hsing
205	Chung Chien
206	Chung Chi
208	Chung Shun
209	Chung Lien
210	Chung Yung
216	Chung Kuang
217	Chung Suo
219	Kao Hsiung
221	Chung Chuan
222	Chung Sheng
223	Chung Fu
225	Chung Chiang
226	Chung Chih
227	Chung Ming
228	Chung Shu
229	Chung Wan
230	Chung Pang
231	Chung Yeh
401	Ho Chi
402	Ho Huei
403	Ho Yao
404	Ho Deng
405	Ho Feng
406	Ho Chao
407	Ho Teng
481	Ho Shun
482	Ho Tsung
484	Ho Chung
485	Ho Chang
486	Ho Cheng
488	Ho Shan
489	Ho Chuan
490	Ho Seng
491	Ho Meng
492	Ho Mou
493	Ho Shou
494	Ho Chun
495	Ho Yung
496	Ho Chien
637	Mei Lo
649	Mei Chin
659	Mei Ping
694	Mei Sung
SB 1	Ho Chie

Mine Warfare Forces

423	Yung Chou
432	Yung Ching
441	Yung Cheng
449	Yung An
457	Yung Ju
462	Yung Sui
469	Yung Lo
476	Yung Shan
479	Yung Nien
482	Yung Fu
485	Yung Jen
488	Yung Hsin
497	Yung Chi

Survey Ships

AGS 563	Chiu Lien
AGSC 466	Lien Chang

Service Forces

324	Ta Hu
514	Chang Pei
515	Lung Chuan
516	Hsin Lung
518	Yun Tai
521	Yu Tai
522	Tai Hu
523	Yuen Feng
525	Wu Kang
530	Wu Yi
AKL 359	Yung Kang
AP 520	Tai Wu
AOG 512	Wan Shou

Tugs

AFDL 1	Hay Tan
AFDL 2	Kim Men
AFDL 3	Han Jih
ARD 5	Fo Wu 5
ARD 6	Fo Wu 6
ATA 357	Ta Sueh
ATA 367	Ta Teng
ATA 395	Ta Peng
ATF 542	Ta Han
ATF 548	Ta Tung

SUBMARINES

Note: (a) Up to 16 patrol submarines are to be acquired in the 1990s. Builders in Argentina, Germany and the Netherlands are most frequently mentioned with indications that the first six are to be ordered in 1992. In February 1992 the Netherlands Government refused permission to build in Dutch shipyards.
(b) A Maschinebau Gabler, German-built Tows 64 DGK/300 class midget submarine was acquired in the early 1980s. Weight, 14 tons; length, 22.6 ft *(6.9 m)*; speed, 3 kts submerged and a diving depth of 300 m. Further craft based on this commercial prototype may have been built locally for military purposes although this is not confirmed.

2 NETHERLANDS HAI LUNG CLASS

Name	*No*	*Builders*	*Laid down*	*Launched*	*Commissioned*
HAI LUNG	793	Wilton Fijenoord	1982	6 Oct 1986	9 Oct 1987
HAI HU	795	Wilton Fijenoord	1982	20 Dec 1986	9 Apr 1988

Displacement, tons: 2376 surfaced; 2660 dived
Dimensions, feet (metres): 219.6 × 27.6 × 22 *(66.9 × 8.4 × 6.7)*
Main machinery: Diesel-electric; 3 Bronswerk D-RUB 215-12 diesels; 4050 hp(m) *(3 MW)*; 3 alternators; 2.7 MW; 1 Holec motor; 5100 hp(m) *(3.74 MW)*; 1 shaft
Speed, knots: 12 surfaced; 20 dived
Range, miles: 10 000 at 9 kts surfaced
Complement: 67 (8 officers)

Torpedoes: 6—21 in *(533 mm)* bow tubes. 28 AEG SUT; dual purpose; wire-guided; active/passive homing to 12 km *(6.6 nm)* at 35 kts; warhead 250 kg.
Countermeasures: ESM: Signaal Rapids; radar warning.
Fire control: Sinbads M Combat System.
Radars: Surface search: Signaal ZW 06; I band.
Sonars: Signaal SIASS-Z; hull-mounted; passive/active intercept search and attack; low/medium frequency.
Fitted for but not with towed passive array.

Programmes: Order signed with Wilton Fijenoord in September 1981 for these submarines with variations from the standard Zwaardvis design. Construction was delayed by the financial difficulties of the builders but was resumed in 1983. Sea trials of *Hai Lung* in March 1987 and *Hai Hu* in January 1988 and both submarines were shipped out on board a heavy dock vessel. The names mean *Sea Dragon* and *Sea Tiger*.

HAI LUNG *4/1991, DTM*

Structure: Two 196-cell batteries. The four horns on the forward casing are Signaal sonar intercept transducers. Torpedoes manufactured under licence in Indonesia.

Operational: Hsiung Feng 2 submerged launch SSMs are planned to be part of the weapons load but a torpedo-launched version has not yet been developed.

2 Ex-US GUPPY II TYPE

Name	*No*	*Builders*	*Laid down*	*Launched*	*Commissioned*
HAI SHIH (ex-USS *Cutlass* SS 478)	736 (ex-SS 91)	Portsmouth Navy Yard	22 July 1944	5 Nov 1944	17 Mar 1945
HAI PAO (ex-USS *Tusk* SS 426)	791 (ex-SS 92)	Federal S B & D D Co, Kearney, New Jersey	23 Aug 1943	8 July 1945	11 Apr 1946

Displacement, tons: 1870 standard; 2420 dived
Dimensions, feet (metres): 307.5 × 27.2 × 18 *(93.7 × 8.3 × 5.5)*
Main machinery: Diesel-electric; 3 Fairbanks-Morse diesels; 4500 hp *(3.3 MW)*; 2 Elliott motors; 5400 hp *(4 MW)*; 2 shafts
Speed, knots: 18 surfaced; 15 dived
Range, miles: 8000 at 12 kts surfaced
Complement: 75 (7 officers)

Torpedoes: 10—21 in *(533 mm)* (6 fwd, 4 aft) tubes. Probably US Mk 37 or AEG SUT; dual purpose.
Countermeasures: ESM: WLR-1/3; radar warning.
Radars: Surface search: US SS 2; I band.
Sonars: EDO BQR 2B; hull-mounted; passive search and attack; medium frequency.
Raytheon/EDO BQS 4C; adds active capability to BQR 2B.
Thomson Sintra DUUG 1B; passive ranging.

HAI PAO *8/1990, DTM*

Programmes: Originally fleet-type submarines of the US Navy's Tench class; extensively modernised under the Guppy II programme. *Hai Shih* transferred in April 1973 and *Hai Pao* in October the same year.

Structure: Four 126-cell batteries. After 45 years in service diving depth will be very limited. The submarine torpedo tubes, 'sealed' by the US Navy were 'unsealed' in Taiwan.
Operational: Used for anti-submarine training exercises.

DESTROYERS

6 Ex-US GEARING (WU CHIN I and II CONVERSIONS) (FRAM I and II) CLASS

Name	*No*	*Builders*	*Laid down*	*Launched*	*Commissioned*
***FU YANG** (ex-USS *Ernest G Small* DD 838) (FRAM II)	907	Bath Iron Works Corporation	30 Jan 1945	14 June 1945	21 Aug 1945
****DANG YANG** (ex-USS *Lloyd Thomas* DD 764) (FRAM II)	911	Bethlehem Steel, San Francisco	26 Mar 1944	5 Oct 1945	21 Mar 1947
****HAN YANG** (ex-USS *Herbert J Thomas* DD 833)	915	Bath Iron Works Corporation	30 Oct 1944	25 Mar 1945	29 May 1945
****LAI YANG** (ex-USS *Leonard F Mason* DD 852)	920	Bethlehem (Quincy)	8 June 1945	4 Jan 1946	28 June 1946
****KAI YANG** (ex-USS *Richard B Anderson* DD 786)	924	Todd Pacific SY, Seattle, Washington	1 Dec 1944	7 July 1945	26 Oct 1945
***SHAO YANG** (ex-USS *Hawkins* DD 873)	926	Consolidated Steel Corporation	14 May 1944	7 Oct 1944	10 Feb 1945

* Wu Chin I ** Wu Chin II

Displacement, tons: 2425 standard; 3500 approx full load
Dimensions, feet (metres): 390.5 × 41.2 × 19 *(119 × 12.6 × 5.8)*
Main machinery: 4 Babcock & Wilcox boilers; 600 psi *(43.3 kg/cm sq)*; 850°F *(454°C)*; 2 GE turbines; 60 000 hp *(45 MW)*; 2 shafts
Speed, knots: 32.5. **Range, miles:** 5800 at 15 kts
Complement: 275 approx

Missiles: SSM: 5 Hsiung Feng I or II (1 triple ❶, 2 single ❷); radar or optical guidance (HFI); inertial guidance and active radar or IR homing (HF II) to 36 km *(19.4 nm)* (I) or 60 km *(32.4 nm)* (II) at 0.7 Mach (I) and 0.85 Mach (II); warhead 75 kg.
1 Sea Chapparal quad launcher ❸; Sidewinder missile; IR homing to 3 km *(1.6 nm)* supersonic; warhead 5 kg; 16 reloads.
A/S: Honeywell ASROC Mk 112 octuple launcher ❹ *(Shao Yang)*; inertial guidance to 1.6-10 km *(1-5.4 nm)*; payload Mk 46 torpedo.

Guns: 2 or 4 USN 5 in *(127 mm)*/38 (1 or 2 twin) Mk 38 ❺; 85° elevation; 15 rounds/minute to 17 km *(9.3 nm)*; weight of shell 25 kg.
1 OTO Melara 3 in *(76 mm)*/62 ❻; 85° elevation; 85 rounds/minute to 16 km *(8.7 nm)*; weight of shell 6 kg.
2 or 4 Bofors 40 mm/70 (2 single or 2 twin) ❼. 4 or 6—12.7 mm MGs.
Torpedoes: 6—324 mm US Mk 32 (2 triple) tubes ❽. Honeywell Mk 46; anti-submarine; active/passive homing to 11 km *(5.9 nm)* at 40 kts; warhead 44 kg.
Countermeasures: Decoys: 4 Kung Fen 6 16-tubed Chaff launchers.
Mk T-6 Fanfare torpedo decoy.
ESM/ECM: ULQ-6 jammers and WLR-1 and WLR-3 passive warning receivers or Chang Feng II combined intercept and jammers.
Combat data systems: Elbit; action data automation (Wu Chin II).
Fire control: Honeywell H 930 with 2 RCA HR 76 directors for SSM. Mk 37 GFCS with Kollmorgen electro-optical sight ❾ for 127 mm or IAI Galileo optronic director Mk 114 system (for ASROC).
Radars: Air search: Lockheed SPS 40 ❿; E/F band or Westinghouse SPS 29 ⓫; B/C band.
Surface search: Raytheon SPS 10/SPS 58 ⓬; G band or Israeli Elta 1040 ⓭ (Wu Chin II).
Fire control: Western Electric Mk 25 ⓮ or Selenia RTN-10X ⓯ (Wu Chin II); I/J band.
Two RCA HR 76 ⓰; I/J band (for SSM and guns).
Tacan: SRN 15.
Sonars: Krupp Atlas DSQS-21CZ *(Fu Yang* and *Dang Yang)* or Raytheon SQS 23H; hull-mounted; active search and attack; medium frequency.

Helicopters: 1 McDonnell Douglas 500MD ⓱.

Programmes: *Fu Yang* transferred 5 February 1971; *Dang Yang*, 12 October 1972; *Han Yang*, 6 May 1974; *Lai Yang*, 20 April 1973; *Kai Yang*, 10 June 1977 by sale; *Shao Yang*, 10 March 1978.
Modernisation: All ships have been modernised:
(a) Wu Chin I: Installation of SSM and Honeywell H 930 Mod 1 fire control system with twin lattice masts topped by HR 76 directors in *Fu Yang* and *Shao Yang*. Developed by Honeywell and Chung-Shan Institute. Can track 8 targets simultaneously and attack 3 with a 20 second response time.
(b) Wu Chin II: *Han Yang*, *Lai Yang*, *Kai Yang* and *Dang Yang* separately upgraded with the Elbit Naval Tactical Command and Control System. Developed by IAI, Israel and Chung-Shan Institute. Can track up to 12 targets simultaneously and attack 3 with a 20 second response time. Each ship also received an OTO Melara 76 mm gun, two Bofors 40 mm/70 single mounts, a quad Sea Chapparal SAM launcher and five (two single and one triple) Hsiung Feng I missile launchers. An RTN-10X on a lattice mast and an Officine Galileo optronic director replaced the Mk 37 fire control director on the bridge. The SPS-10 surface search radar was replaced by an Elta EL-1040. *Dang Yang* is unique in having her OTO Melara in 'A' position, triple Hsiung Fengs in 'B' position and a twin 5 in mount aft. All the others have a twin 5 in, in 'A', OTO Melara in 'B' and triple Hsiung Fengs aft.
Operational: *Fu Yang* is the Fleet Flagship.

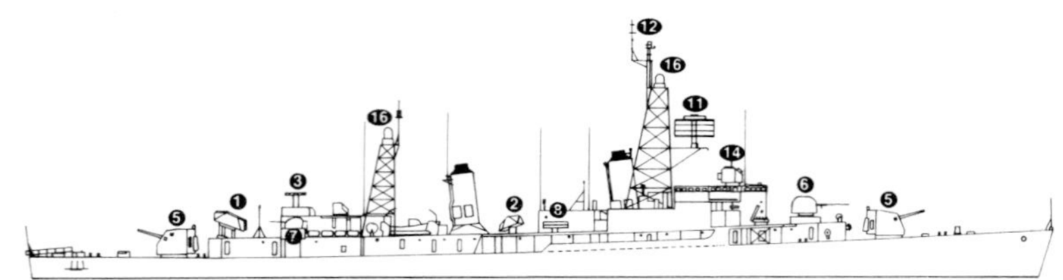

FU YANG *(Scale 1 : 1 200), Ian Sturton*

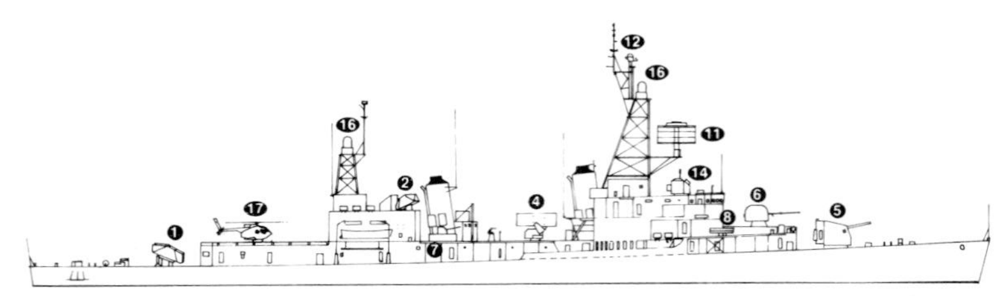

SHAO YANG *(Scale 1 : 1 200), Ian Sturton*

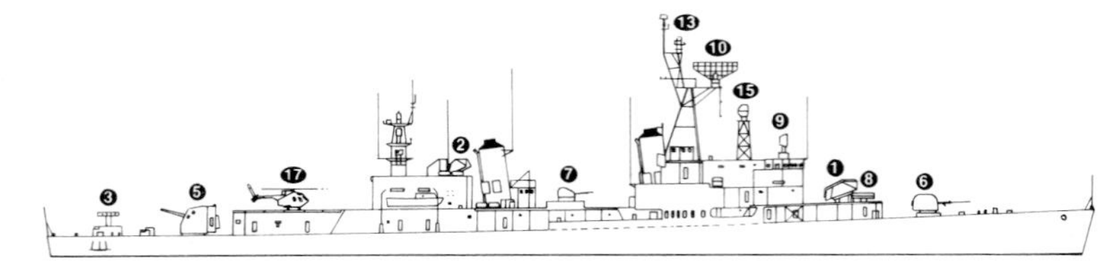

DANG YANG *(Scale 1 : 1 200), Ian Sturton*

DANG YANG (Wu Chin II) *6/1985, DTM (Raymond Cheung)*

SHAO YANG (Wu Chin I) *6/1989, van Ginderen Collection*

8 Ex-US GEARING (WU CHIN III CONVERSION) (FRAM I) CLASS

Name	No	Builders	Laid down	Launched	Commissioned
CHIEN YANG (ex-USS *James E Kyes* DD 787)	912	Todd Pacific SY, Seattle, Washington	27 Dec 1944	4 Aug 1945	8 Feb 1946
LIAO YANG (ex-USS *Hanson* DD 832)	921	Bath Iron Works Corporation	7 Oct 1944	11 Mar 1945	11 May 1945
CHEN YANG (ex-USS *Hollister* DD 788)	923	Todd Pacific SY, Seattle, Washington	18 Jan 1945	9 Oct 1945	26 Mar 1946
TE YANG (ex-USS *Sarsfield* DD 837)	925	Bath Iron Works Corporation	15 Jan 1945	27 May 1945	31 July 1945
YUN YANG (ex-USS *Johnston* DD 821)	927	Consolidated Steel Corporation	6 May 1945	19 Oct 1945	10 Oct 1946
SHEN YANG (ex-USS *Power* DD 839)	928	Bath Iron Works Corporation	26 Feb 1945	30 June 1945	13 Sep 1945
CHAO YANG (ex-USS *Hamner* DD 718)	929	Federal S B and D D Co	5 Apr 1945	24 Nov 1945	11 July 1946
LAO YANG (ex-USS *Shelton* DD 790)	930	Todd Pacific SY, Seattle, Washington	31 May 1945	8 Mar 1946	21 June 1946

Displacement, tons: 2425 standard; 3500 approx full load
Dimensions, feet (metres): 390.5 × 41.2 × 19 *(119 × 12.6 × 5.8)*
Main machinery: 4 Babcock & Wilcox boilers; 600 psi *(43.3 kg/cm sq)*; 850°F *(454°C)*; 2 GE turbines; 60 000 hp *(45 MW)*; 2 shafts
Speed, knots: 32.5. **Range, miles:** 5800 at 15 kts
Complement: 275 approx

Missiles: SAM: 10 General Dynamics Standard SM1-MR (2 triple ❶; 2 twin ❷); command guidance; semi-active radar homing to 46 km *(25 nm)* at 2 Mach.
A/S: Honeywell ASROC Mk 112 octuple launcher ❸; inertial guidance to 1.6-10 km *(1-5.4 nm)*; payload Mk 46 torpedo.
Guns: 1 OTO Melara 3 in *(76 mm)*/62 ❹; 85° elevation; 85 rounds/minute to 16 km *(8.7 nm)*; weight of shell 6 kg.
1 GE/GD 20 mm Vulcan Phalanx Block 1 6-barrelled Mk 15 ❺; 3000 rounds/minute combined to 1.5 km.
4 Bofors 40 mm/70 (2 single or 2 twin) ❻. 4 or 6—12.7 mm MGs.
Torpedoes: 6—324 mm US Mk 32 (2 triple) tubes ❼. Honeywell Mk 46; anti-submarine; active/passive homing to 11 km *(5.9 nm)* at 40 kts; warhead 44 kg.
Countermeasures: Decoys: 4 Kung Fen 6 16-tubed Chaff launchers.
Mk T-6 Fanfare torpedo decoy.
ESM/ECM: Chang Feng III (Hughes SLQ 17) intercept and jammers.
Fire control: Honeywell H 930 MFCS Mk 114 system (for ASROC).
Radars: Air search: Signaal DA-08 (with DA 05 aerial) ❽; E/F band.
Surface search: Raytheon SPS 10/SPS 58 ❾; G band.
Fire control: Signaal STIR ❿; I/J band (for Standard and 76 mm).
Westinghouse W-160 ⓫; I band (for Bofors).
Tacan: SRN 15.
Sonars: Raytheon SQS 23 H; hull-mounted; active search and attack; medium frequency.

Helicopters: 1 McDonnell Douglas 500MD ⓬.

Programmes: *Chien Yang* transferred 18 April 1973; *Liao Yang*, 18 April 1973; *Te Yang* and *Chen Yang*, 1 October 1977 by sale; *Yun Yang*, December 1980; *Shen Yang* by sale 27 February 1981; *Chao Yang* and *Lao Yang* by sale 3 March 1983.
Modernisation: All ships converted to area air defence ships under the Wu Chin III programme. This upgrade involved the installation of the H 930 Modular Combat System (MCS) with a Signaal DA-08 air search radar (employing a lightweight DA-05 antenna) and a Signaal STIR missile control radar directing 10 box-launched Standard SM-1 surface-to-air missiles (two twin in 'B' position, two triple facing either beam aft). The system can track 24 targets simultaneously and attack 4 with an 8 second response time. An OTO Melara 76 mm is fitted to 'A' position, one Bofors 40 mm/70 is mounted forward of the seaboat on the starboard side, one abaft the ASROC magazine on the port side and a Mk 15 Block 1 Phalanx CIWS is aft between two banks of Standard launchers. A Westinghouse W-160 is mounted on a lattice mast on the hangar to control the Bofors. The amidships ASROC launcher is retained, its Mk 114 fire control system is integrated with the H 930 MCS via a digital-analogue interface. The SQS-23 sonar has also been upgraded to the H standard using a Raytheon solid-state transmitter. The Chang Feng III EW system was developed jointly by Taiwan's Chung-Shan Institute of Science and Technology (CSIST) with the assistance of Hughes. The Chang Feng III employs phased-array antennas which resemble those of the Hughes SLQ-17, it is capable of both deception and noise jamming.

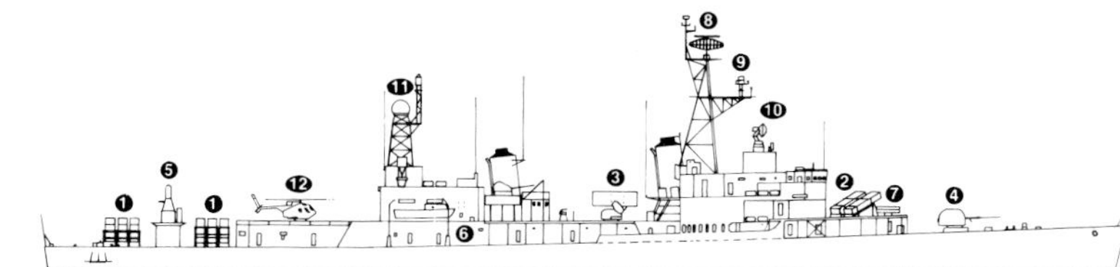

LIAO YANG (Wu Chin III) *(Scale 1 : 1 200), Ian Sturton*

LIAO YANG *1989*

LIAO YANG *1991*

LIAO YANG *1989, IDR*

4 Ex-US ALLEN M SUMNER CLASS

Name	*No*	*Builders*	*Laid down*	*Launched*	*Commissioned*
HENG YANG (ex-USS *Samuel N Moore* DD 747)	902	Bethlehem Steel, Staten Island	30 Sep 1943	23 Feb 1944	24 June 1944
HUA YANG (ex-USS *Bristol* DD 857)	903	Bethlehem Steel, San Pedro	5 May 1944	29 Oct 1944	17 Mar 1945
***YUEN YANG** (ex-USS *Haynsworth* DD 700)	905	Federal S B & D D Co	16 Dec 1943	15 Apr 1944	22 June 1944
***HUEI YANG** (ex-USS *English* DD 696)	906	Federal S B & D D Co	19 Oct 1943	27 Feb 1944	4 May 1944

* Wu Chin I

Displacement, tons: 2200 standard; 3320 full load
Dimensions, feet (metres): 376.6 × 40.9 × 19 *(114.8 × 12.4 × 5.8)*
Main machinery: 4 Babcock & Wilcox boilers; 600 psi *(43.3 kg/cm sq)*; 850°F *(454°C)*; 2 GE or Westinghouse turbines; 60 000 hp *(45 MW)*; 2 shafts
Speed, knots: 34. **Range, miles:** 1000 at 32 kts
Complement: 275

Missiles: SSM: 5 or 6 Hsiung Feng I (2 triple or 1 triple, 2 single in *Huei Yang* and *Yuen Yang*) ❶; radar or optical guidance to 36 km *(19.4 nm)* at 0.7 Mach; warhead 75 kg.
SAM: 1 Sea Chapparal quad launcher ❷; Sidewinder missile; IR homing to 3 km *(1.6 nm)* supersonic; warhead 5 kg; 16 reloads.
Guns: 4 USN 5 in *(127 mm)*/38 (2 twin) Mk 38 ❸; 85° elevation; 15 rounds/minute to 17 km *(9.3 nm)*; weight of shell 25 kg.
1 OTO Melara 3 in *(76 mm)*/62 ❹ *(Huei Yang* and *Yuen Yang)*.
4 Bofors 40 mm/70 (2 twin) ❺.
Several 20 mm and 12.7 mm MGs. Secondary armament varies.
Torpedoes: 6—324 mm US Mk 32 (2 triple) tubes ❻. Honeywell Mk 46; anti-submarine; active/passive homing to 11 km *(5.9 nm)* at 40 kts; warhead 44 kg.
A/S mortars: 2 Mk 10 24-tubed fixed Hedgehogs ❼; range 350 m; warhead 26 kg.
Depth charges: 1 rack in some ships; 9 weapons.
Countermeasures: Decoys: 4 Kung Fen 6 16-barrelled Chaff launchers.
ECM/ESM: Argo 680/681; intercept and jammer.
Fire control: Galileo optronic director or Honeywell H 930 with two RCA HR 76 directors *(Huei Yang* and *Yuen Yang)*.
Radars: Air search: Lockheed SPS 40 ❽; D band; range 146 km *(80 nm)* against fighter aircraft.
Surface search: Raytheon SPS 10 ❾; G band.
Fire control: Selenia RTN 10X ❿; I/J band or two RCA HR 76 *(Huei Yang* and *Yuen Yang)* ⓫; I/J band.
Sonars: EDO SQS 29; hull-mounted; active search and attack; medium frequency.

Programmes: *Heng Yang* transferred February 1970; *Hua Yang*, 9 December 1969; *Yuen Yang*, 12 May 1970; *Huei Yang*, 11 August 1970. Two others *Hsiang Yang* and *Po Yang* used for spares.
Modernisation: Unmodified on transfer. *Heng Yang* and *Hua Yang* had most of their weapons and sensors updated under the Tien Shi (Angel) modification programme. This included the addition of Hsiung Feng SSM and Sea Chapparal SAM. *Huei Yang* and *Yuen Yang* were modified under the Wu Chin I programme and have 76 mm OTO Melara guns fitted in 'B' position.
Operational: Both *Heng Yang* and *Yuen Yang* are probably in reserve and are soon to be scrapped.

HENG YANG *(Scale 1 : 900), Ian Sturton*

HENG YANG *1987, DTM*

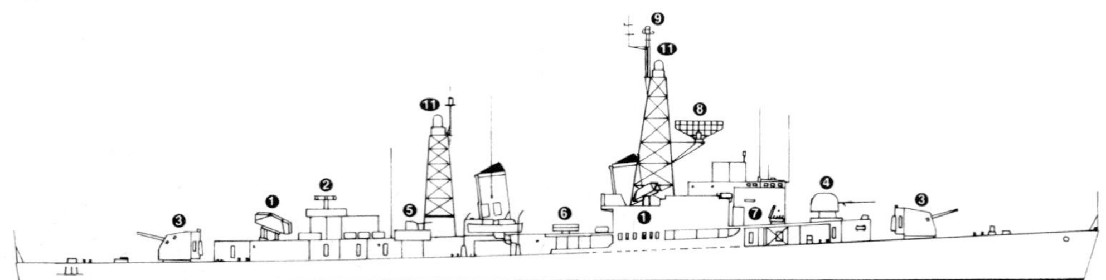

HUEI YANG *(Scale 1 : 900), Ian Sturton*

HUEI YANG *1990, Ships of the World*

2 Ex-US ALLEN M SUMNER (FRAM II) CLASS

Name	*No*	*Builders*	*Laid down*	*Launched*	*Commissioned*
LO YANG (ex-USS *Taussing* DD 746)	914	Bethlehem Steel, Staten Island	30 Aug 1943	25 Jan 1944	20 May 1944
NAN YANG (ex-USS *John W Thomas* DD 760)	917	Bethlehem Steel, San Francisco	21 Nov 1944	30 Sep 1944	11 Oct 1945

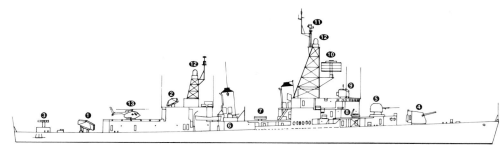

Displacement, tons: 2200 standard; 3320 full load
Dimensions, feet (metres): 376.6 × 40.9 × 19 *(114.8 × 12.4 × 5.8)*
Main machinery: 4 Babcock & Wilcox boilers; 600 psi *(43.3 kg/cm sq)*; 850°F *(454°C)*; 2 GE or Westinghouse geared turbines; 60 000 hp *(45 MW)*; 2 shafts
Speed, knots: 34. **Range, miles:** 1000 at 32 kts
Complement: 275 approx

Missiles: SSM: 5 Hsiung Feng I (1 triple ❶ and 2 single ❷); radar or optical guidance to 36 km *(19.4 nm)* at 0.7 Mach; warhead 75 kg.
SAM: 1 Sea Chaparral quad launcher ❸; Sidewinder missile; IR homing to 3 km *(1.6 nm)* supersonic; warhead 5 kg; 16 reloads.
Guns: 2 USN 5 in *(127 mm)*/38 (twin) Mk 38 ❹; 85° elevation; 15 rounds/minute to 17 km *(9.3 nm)*; weight of shell 25 kg.
1 OTO Melara 3 in *(76 mm)*/62 ❺; 85° elevation; 85 rounds/minute to 16 km *(8.7 nm)*; weight of shell 6 kg.
2 Bofors 40 mm/70 ❻. 4—12.7 mm MGs.
Torpedoes: 6—324 mm US Mk 32 (2 triple) tubes ❼. Honeywell Mk 46; anti-submarine; active/passive homing to 11 km *(5.9 nm)* at 40 kts; warhead 44 kg.
A/S mortars: 2 Mk 10 24-tubed fixed Hedgehogs ❽; range 350 m; warhead 26 kg.
Countermeasures: Decoys: 4 Kung Fen 6 16-barrelled Chaff launchers.
ESM/ECM: Argo AR 680/681; intercept and jammer.
Fire control: Honeywell H 930 for SSM. Mk 37 GFCS with Kollmorgen electro-optical sight ❾ for 127 mm.
Radars: Air search: Westinghouse SPS 29 or SPS 37 ❿; B/C band; range 457 km *(250 nm)*.
Air/surface search: Raytheon SPS 10/SPS 58 ⓫; D band.
Fire control: Two RCA HR 76 ⓬; I/J band (for SSM and guns).
Tacan: SRN-15.
Sonars: EDO SQS 29; hull-mounted; active search and attack; medium frequency.

Helicopters: 1 McDonnell Douglas 500MD ⓭.

Programmes: Both ships transferred 6 May 1974.
Modernisation: Under the Wu Chin I modification programme the same weapon system changes were made as in the Gearing class.
Structure: Both ships have latticed masts. *Lo Yang* has the single SSM launchers on the signal deck on either side of the foremast; its Starboard Bofors abreast the forward funnel and the Port Bofors abreast the after funnel. *Nan Yang* has both Bofors abreast the after funnel.

NAN YANG *(Scale 1 : 900), Ian Sturton*

NAN YANG *1985, DTM (Raymond Cheung)*

4 Ex-US FLETCHER CLASS

Name	*No*	*Builders*	*Laid down*	*Launched*	*Commissioned*
KWEI YANG (ex-USS *Twining* DD 540)	908	Bethlehem Steel, San Francisco	20 Nov 1942	11 July 1943	1 Dec 1943
CHIANG YANG (ex-USS *Mullany* DD 528)	909	Bethlehem Steel, San Francisco	15 Jan 1942	12 Oct 1942	23 Apr 1943
AN YANG (ex-USS *Kimberly* DD 521)	918	Bethlehem Steel, Staten Island	27 July 1942	4 Feb 1943	22 May 1943
KUN YANG (ex-USS *Yarnall* DD 541)	919	Bethlehem Steel, San Francisco	5 Dec 1942	25 July 1943	30 Dec 1943

Displacement, tons: 2100 standard; 3050 full load
Dimensions, feet (metres): 376.5 × 39.5 × 18 *(114.8 × 12 × 5.5)*
Main machinery: 4 Babcock & Wilcox boilers; 600 psi *(43.3 kg/cm sq)*; 850°F *(454°C)*; 2 GE/Allis Chalmers/Westinghouse turbines; 60 000 hp *(45 MW)*; 2 shafts
Speed, knots: 35. **Range, miles:** 3750 at 14 kts
Complement: 261 *(Kwei Yang)*; 279 *(Chiang Yang)*; 270 (remainder)

Missiles: SSM: 5 Hsiung Feng I (1 triple ❶ and 2 single ❷); radar or optical guidance to 36 km *(19.4 nm)* at 0.7 Mach; warhead 75 kg.
SAM: 1 Sea Chaparral quad launcher ❸; Sidewinder missile; IR homing to 3 km *(1.6 nm)* supersonic; warhead 5 kg; 16 reloads.
Guns: 2 USN 5 in *(127 mm)*/38 Mk 30 ❹; 85° elevation; 15 rounds/minute to 17 km *(9.3 nm)*; weight of shell 25 kg. Some may still have 3—5 in *(127 mm)* instead of the 76 mm.
1 OTO Melara 3 in *(76 mm)*/62 ❺; 85° elevation; 85 rounds/minute to 16 km *(8.8 nm)*; weight of shell 6 kg.
Torpedoes: 6—324 mm US Mk 32 (2 triple) tubes ❻. Honeywell Mk 46; anti-submarine; active/passive homing to 11 km *(5.9 nm)* at 40 kts; warhead 44 kg.
A/S mortars: 2 Mk 10 24-tubed fixed Hedgehogs ❼; range 350 m; warhead 26 kg.
Depth charges: 1 rack.
Mines: 1 rail.
Countermeasures: Decoys: 4 Kung Fen 6 16-barrelled Chaff launchers.
ESM/ECM: Argo 680/681; intercept and jammer.
Fire control: Honeywell H 930 for SSM. Mk 37 GFCS with Kollmorgen electro-optical sight ❽ for 127 mm.
Radars: Air search: Lockheed SPS 40 ❾; E/F band.
Air/surface search: Westinghouse SPS 58 ❿; D band.
Fire control: Two RCA HR 76 ⓫; I/J band (for SSM and guns).
Sonars: Krupp Atlas DSQS-21CZ; hull-mounted; active search and attack; medium frequency.

Programmes: *Kwei Yang* transferred 16 August 1971 (sale); *Chiang Yang*, 6 October 1971 (sale); *An Yang*, 2 June 1967; *Kun Yang*, 10 June 1968. *Kun Yang* and *An Yang* purchased 25 January 1974.
Modernisation: Armaments modernised under the Wu Chin I programme. *Kun Yang* can act as a minelayer.
Operational: Because of the state of the hulls, time spent at sea is very limited.

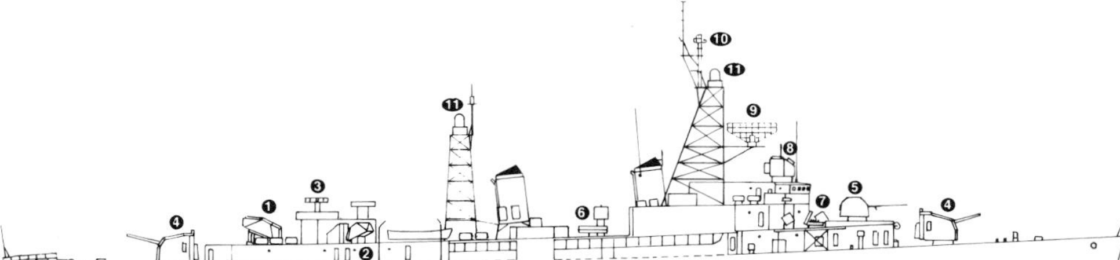

KWEI YANG *(Scale 1 : 900), Ian Sturton*

CHIANG YANG *4/1991, DTM*

FRIGATES

Notes: (a) In September 1991 the French Government authorised negotiations by Thomson-CSF for the sale of up to 16 La Fayette class frigates. The plan is for DCAN Lorient to deliver outfitted sections for the first six hulls to the China Shipbuilding Corporation, who will complete and arm the ships. The first delivery is scheduled for 1994. In 1990 France withdrew from a similar contract due to pressure from China.

(b) Up to eight ex-USN Knox class may be leased to Taiwan in late 1992 to replace some of the elderly Fletcher and Sumner class destroyers which have reached the end of their useful lives.

1 RUDDEROW, 3 Ex-US CHARLES LAWRENCE and 6 CROSLEY CLASSES

Name	*No*	*Builders*	*Laid down*	*Launched*	*Commissioned*
TIEN SHAN (ex-USS *Kleinsmith* APD 134/DE 718)	815 (ex-615)	Defoe S B Co, Bay City, Michigan	1944	27 Jan 1945	12 June 1945
****TAI YUAN** (ex-USS *Ridley* DE 579)	827 (ex-959)	Bethlehem S B Co, Higham, Mass	1943	29 Dec 1943	13 Mar 1944
YU SHAN (ex-USS *Kinzer* APD 91/DE 232)	832 (ex-826)	Charleston Navy Yard, South Carolina	1943	9 Dec 1943	1 Nov 1944
HUA SHAN (ex-USS *Donald W Wolf* APD 129/DE 713)	833 (ex-854)	Defoe S B Co, Bay City, Michigan	1944	22 July 1944	13 Apr 1945
***WEN SHAN** (ex-USS *Gantner* APD 42/DE 60)	834	Bethlehem S B Co, Higham, Mass	1942	17 Apr 1943	23 July 1943
FU SHAN (ex-USS *Truxton* APD 98/DE 282)	835 (ex-838)	Charleston Navy Yard, South Carolina	1943	9 Mar 1944	9 July 1944
***LU SHAN** (ex-USS *Bull* APD 78/DE 693)	836 (ex-821)	Defoe S B Co, Bay City, Michigan	1942	25 Mar 1943	12 Aug 1943
SHOU SHAN (ex-USS *Kline* APD 120/DE 687)	837 (ex-893)	Bethlehem, Quincy, Mass	1944	27 June 1944	18 Oct 1944
TAI SHAN (ex-USS *Register* APD 92/DE 233)	838 (ex-878)	Charleston Navy Yard, South Carolina	1943	20 Jan 1944	11 Jan 1945
***CHUNG SHAN** (ex-USS *Blessman* APD 48/DE 69)	843 (ex-845)	Bethlehem S B Co, Higham, Mass	1943	19 June 1943	19 Sep 1943

* Charles Lawrence class ** Rudderow class

Displacement, tons: 1680 standard; 2130 full load
Dimensions, feet (metres): 306 × 37 × 12.6 *(93.3 × 11.3 × 3.8)*
Main machinery: Turbo-electric; 2 Foster-Wheeler boilers; 435 psi *(30.6 kg/cm sq)*; 750°F *(399°C)*; 2 GE turbo generators; 12 000 hp *(9 MW)*; 2 motors; 2 shafts
Speed, knots: 23.6. **Range, miles:** 5000 at 15 kts
Complement: 200
Military lift: 160 troops, commandos or frogmen

Guns: 2 USN 5 in *(127 mm)*/38 Mk 30; 85° elevation; 15 rounds/minute to 17 km *(9.3 nm)*; weight of shell 25 kg (see *Operational*).
4 or 6 Bofors 40 mm/56 (2 or 3 twin); 45° elevation; 160 rounds/minute to 11 km *(5.9 nm)*; weight of shell 0.9 kg.
4—20 mm (2 twin) (4 twin in *Hua Shan*).
Fire control: Mk 51 GFCS.
Radars: Surface search: Raytheon SPS 5 (in most); G/H band; SPS 6C (in *Tai Yuan*); D band.
Navigation: Decca 707 (in some); I band.
Fire control: RCA/GE Mk 26; I/J band.
Sonars: Hull-mounted; active attack; high frequency.

Programmes: *Yu Shan* transferred April 1962; *Hua Shan*, May 1965; *Wen Shan*, May 1966; *Fu Shan*, March 1966; *Lu Shan*, August 1966; *Shou Shan*, March 1966; *Tai Shan*, October 1966; *Chung Shan*, July 1967; *Tien Shan*, June 1967; *Tai Yuan* July 1968. All began as destroyer escorts (DE), but converted during construction or after completion to high-speed transports.
Modernisation: All ships were refitted with a second 5 in gun aft. One twin 40 mm gun mount forward of bridge and two twin mounts amidships.
Structure: Charles Lawrence (APD 37-86) class has high bridge; Crosley class (APD 87 and above) has low bridge. Radars and fire control equipment vary. Davits amidships can hold four LCVP-type landing craft but ships usually carry only one each. Rudderow class (*Tai Yuan*) has a tripod mast and platforms below the bridge for 20 mm guns.
Operational: In 1990 five vessels were transferred to the Customs Service with light armament only. They returned to the Navy and were rearmed again in 1991. All of the class remains operational into 1992. *Shou Shan* and *Chung Shan* have been employed again on Customs work but under naval control. Armaments tend to be changed depending on tasks, with lighter guns being fitted for Fishery Patrols and Customs work.

HUA SHAN *1986*

0 + 6 CHENG KUNG CLASS (KWANG HUA PROJECT) (FLIGHT I)

Name	*No*	*Builders*	*Laid down*	*Launched*	*Commissioned*
CHENG KUNG	1101	China SB Corporation, Keelung	7 Jan 1990	5 Oct 1991	Apr 1993
CHENG HO	1103	China SB Corporation, Keelung	21 Dec 1990	1993	1994
CHI KUANG	1105	China SB Corporation, Keelung	1992	1994	1995
YUEH FEI	1106	China SB Corporation, Keelung	1992	1995	1996
TZU-I	1107	China SB Corporation, Keelung	1993	1996	1997
PAN CHAO	1108	China SB Corporation, Keelung	1994	1997	1998

Displacement, tons: 2750 light; 4105 full load
Dimensions, feet (metres): 453 × 45 × 14.8; 24.5 (sonar) *(138.1 × 13.7 × 4.5; 7.5)*
Main machinery: 2 GE LM 2500 gas turbines; 44 000 hp *(33 MW)* sustained; 1 shaft; cp prop
2 auxiliary retractable props; 650 hp *(484 kW)*
Speed, knots: 29. **Range, miles:** 4500 at 20 kts
Complement: 206 (13 officers) including 19 aircrew

Missiles: SSM: 8 Hsiung Feng II ❶ (2 quad); inertial guidance; active radar or IR homing to 60 km *(32.4 nm)* at 0.85 Mach; warhead 75 kg.
SAM: 40 GDC Standard SM1-MR; Mk 13 launcher ❷; command guidance; semi-active radar homing to 46 km *(25 nm)* at 2 Mach.
Guns: 1 OTO Melara 76 mm/62 Mk 75 ❸; 85° elevation; 85 rounds/minute to 16 km *(8.7 nm)*; weight of shell 6 kg.
2 Bofors 40 mm/70 ❹. 4—12.7 mm MGs.
1 GE/GD 20 mm/76 Vulcan Phalanx 6-barrelled Mk 15 ❺; 3000 rounds/minute combined to 1.5 km.
Torpedoes: 6—324 mm Mk 32 (2 triple) tubes ❻. Honeywell Mk 46; anti-submarine; active/passive homing to 11 km *(5.9 nm)* at 40 kts; warhead 44 kg.
Countermeasures: Decoys: 4 Kung Fen 6 Chaff launchers or locally produced version of RBOC (114 mm).
ESM/ECM: Chang Feng IV (locally produced version of SLQ 32(V)2 with Sidekick); combined radar warning and jammers.
Combat data systems: SYS-2(V)2 action data automation with UYK 43 computer. Ta Chen link (from *Chi Kuang* onwards).

CHENG KUNG *(Scale 1 : 1 200), Ian Sturton*

Fire control: Mk 92 Mod 6. Mk 13 Mod 4 weapon direction system. 2 Mk 24 optical directors. Mk 309 TFCS.
Radars: Air search: Raytheon SPS 49(V)2 ❼; C/D band.
Surface search: ISC Cardion SPS 55 ❽ or Raytheon Chang Bai; I/J band.
Fire control: USN UD 417 STIR ❾; I/J band.
Signaal WM 28 ❿; I/J band.
Sonars: Raytheon SQS 56; hull-mounted; active search and attack; medium frequency.
SQR 18A; passive towed array (from *Chi Kuang* onwards).

Helicopters: 2 Sikorsky S-70C(M) ⓫ (only 1 to be embarked).

Programmes: First two ordered 8 May 1989. The first six of the class are known as Flight I. Named after Chinese generals and warriors. There are unconfirmed reports that the first planned Flight II ship *Chang Chien* may become a seventh Flight I. Decision to be taken in 1992.
Structure: Similar to the USS *Ingraham*. RAST helicopter haul down. The area between the mast had to be strengthened to take the Hsiung Feng II missiles.

0 + (10) PFG-2 CLASS (KWANG HUA PROJECT) (FLIGHT II)

Name	No	Builders	Laid down	Launched	Commissioned
CHANG CHIEN	1109	China SB Corporation, Keelung	1995	1998	1999
TIEN TAN	1110	China SB Corporation, Keelung	1996	1999	2000

Displacement, tons: 4300 full load
Dimensions, feet (metres): 470 × 45 × 14.8; 24.5 (sonar) *(143.3 × 13.7 × 4.5; 7.5)*
Main machinery: 2 GE LM 2500 gas turbines; 44 000 hp *(33 MW)*; 1 shaft; cp prop; 2 auxiliary props
Speed, knots: 29

Missiles: SSM: 8 Hsiung Feng II (2 quad) ❶.
SAM: Mk 41 VLS ❷; Tien Kung or Standard SM-2 (32 cells).
Guns: 1 OTO Melara 76 mm/62 Mk 75 ❸.
2 GE/GD 20 mm/76 6-barrelled Vulcan Phalanx ❹.
Torpedoes: 6—324 mm Mk 32 (2 triple) tubes ❺; Honeywell Mk 46.
Radars: Air search: GE/ADAR or Raytheon C-MAR; phased arrays ❻.
Fire control: 2 USN UD 417 STIR ❼.

Helicopters: 1 Sikorsky S-70 ❽ or SH-60B.

Programmes: Flight II of the PFG-2 class project. If more time is needed because of revised instructions to potential contractors, *Chang Chien* may become the seventh Flight I ship.
Structure: Several design and equipment options are not yet finalised and the details listed could change. Modifications to Flight I include adding 17 ft to the hull forward of the bridge. The 76 mm gun mounted in 'A' position. A 32-cell Mk 41 VLS will replace the Mk 13 launcher and a second Phalanx will be added on a step forward of the bridge. The starboard hangar may be replaced by four Mk 41 VLS cells sub-divided into 16 with the Martin Marrietta Quad-pack. The superstructure will be cut down amidships, the CIC will be moved from the superstructure down into the hull. There will be a backup CIC aft of the main CIC as survivability measure (made possible by the modular nature of the combat system). A phased array radar system similar to the SPY-1 will be fitted, the two competing are the GE/RCA ADAR-2N and the Raytheon C-MAR. Two STIRs will provide target illumination. Hughes is offering the MCS-2000 combat data system while Raytheon has a licensed produced version of the Plessey Nautis-F. In the break in the superstructure amidships, eight Hsiung Feng II launchers will be fitted with options for either Bofors guns or ASW missiles.

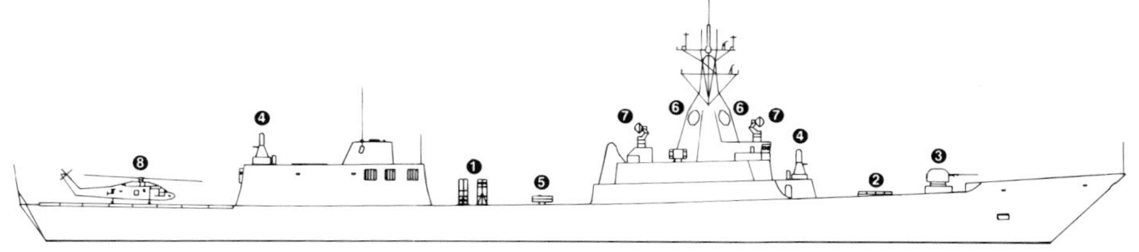
PFG-2 (FLIGHT II) *(Scale 1 : 1 200), Ian Sturton*

SHIPBORNE AIRCRAFT

Numbers/Type: 10 Hughes 500MD/ASW.
Operational speed: 110 kts *(204 km/h)*.
Service ceiling: 16 000 ft *(4880 m)*.
Range: 203 nm *(376 km)*.
Role/Weapon systems: Short-range ASW helicopter with limited surface search capability. Sensors: Search radar, Texas Instruments MAD. Weapons: ASW; 1 × Mk 46 torpedo or 2 × depth bombs. ASV; Could carry machine gun pods.

HUGHES 500 MD *1990, Dr Chien Chung*

Numbers/Type: 10 Sikorsky S-70C(M)1.
Operational speed: 145 kts *(269 km/h)*.
Service ceiling: 19 000 ft *(5790 m)*.
Range: 324 nm *(600 km)*.
Role/Weapon systems: Delivered in 1991. This is a variant of the SH-60B and will become seaborne with the first Cheng Kung class frigates. Another 14 S-70B/C SAR and assault aircraft belong to the Air Force. Sensors: APS 143 search radar; ALR 606 ESM; ARR 84 sonobuoy receiver with ASN 150 data link; dipping sonar. Weapons: ASW; 2 × Mk 46 torpedoes or 2 × Mk 64 depth bombs. ASV; Could carry ASM.

SIKORSKY 70 C(M) *1991, Youth Daily News*

LAND-BASED MARITIME AIRCRAFT

Note: Albatross aircraft replaced by Air Force Sikorsky S-70B/C for SAR.

Numbers/Type: 32 Grumman S-2E/T (Turbo) Trackers.
Operational speed: 130 kts *(241 km/h)*.
Service ceiling: 25 000 ft *(7620 m)*.
Range: 1350 nm *(2500 km)*.
Role/Weapon systems: Patrol and ASW tasks undertaken by Air Force-manned Trackers, which come under naval control; being updated with turboprop engines and new sensors. Seeking P-3C Orion as replacement. Sensors: APS 504 search radar, ESM, MAD, AAS 40 FLIR, SSQ-41B, SSQ-47B sonobuoys; AQS 902F sonobuoy processor; ASN 150 data link. Weapons: ASW; 4 × Mk 44 torpedoes, Mk 54 depth charges or Mk 64 depth bombs or mines. ASV; 6 × 127 mm rockets.

TRACKER *1991, Dr Chien Chung*

CORVETTES

Note: Ten 1250 ton corvettes are planned for ASW patrols. First pair to be acquired from a European shipbuilder and the remainder constructed locally.

3 Ex-US AUK CLASS

Name	No	Builders	Commissioned
PING JIN (ex-USS *Steady* MSF 118)	867	American S B Co, Cleveland, Ohio	16 Nov 1942
WU SHENG (ex-USS *Redstart* MSF 378)	884	Savannah Machine & Foundry Co, Georgia	4 Apr 1945
CHU YUNG (ex-USS *Waxwing* MSF 389)	896	American S B Co, Cleveland, Ohio	6 Aug 1945

Displacement, tons: 890 standard; 1250 full load
Dimensions, feet (metres): 221.2 × 32.2 × 10.8 *(67.4 × 9.8 × 3.3)*
Main machinery: Diesel-electric; 2 GM 12-278A diesels; 2200 hp *(1.64 MW)*; 2 shafts
Speed, knots: 18
Complement: 80

Guns: 2 USN 3 in *(76 mm)*/50; 85° elevation; 20 rounds/minute to 12 km *(6.6 nm)*; weight of shell 6 kg.
4 Bofors 40 mm/56 (2 twin). 4 Oerlikon 20 mm (2 twin).
Torpedoes: 3—324 mm US Mk 32 (triple) tubes.
A/S mortars: 1 Mk 10 Hedgehog.
Depth charges: 2 racks.
Mines: Rails fitted in *Chu Yung* (1975).
Radars: Surface search: Raytheon SPS 5; G/H band; range 37 km *(20 nm)*.
Sonars: SQS 17; hull-mounted; active attack; high frequency.

Programmes: *Wu Sheng* transferred July 1965; *Chu Yung*, November 1965; *Ping Jin*, March 1968.
Structure: Minesweeping equipment removed and second 3 in gun fitted aft in Taiwan service.
Operational: All have reached the limit of hull life and are only used for Fishery protection and counter-insurgency patrols.

WU SHENG (old pennant number)

LIGHT FORCES

Note: Twelve 300 ton craft are planned. First two to be acquired from European shipbuilders and remainder constructed locally.

2 LUNG CHIANG CLASS (FAST ATTACK CRAFT—MISSILE)

Name	*No*	*Builders*	*Commissioned*
LUNG CHIANG	601 (ex-PGG 581)	Tacoma Boatbuilding, Wa	15 May 1978
SUI CHIANG	602 (ex-PGG 582)	China Shipbuilding Corp, Kaohsiung	1982

Displacement, tons: 218 standard; 250 full load
Dimensions, feet (metres): 164.5 × 23.1 × 7.5 *(50.2 × 7.3 × 2.3)*
Main machinery: CODAG; 3 Avco Lycoming TF 40A gas turbines; 12 000 hp *(8.95 MW)* sustained; 3 GM 12V 149TI diesels; 2736 hp *(2.04 MW)* sustained; 3 shafts; cp props
Speed, knots: 20 kts diesels; 40 kts gas. **Range, miles:** 2700 at 12 kts on 1 diesel; 1900 at 20 kts; 700 at 40 kts
Complement: 34 (5 officers)

Missiles: SSM: 4 Hsiung Feng I; radar or optical guidance to 36 km *(19.4 nm)* at 0.7 Mach; warhead 75 kg.
Guns: 1 OTO Melara 3 in *(76 mm)*/62; 85° elevation; 60 rounds/minute to 16 km *(8.7 nm)*; weight of shell 6 kg.
2 Emerlec 30 mm (twin). 2—12.7 mm MGs.
Countermeasures: Decoys: 4 Chaff launchers.
Combat data systems: IPN 10 action data automation.
Fire control: NA 10 Mod 0 GFCS. Honeywell H 930 Mod 2 MFCS (602).
Radars: Surface/air search: Selenia RAN 11 L/X; D/I band; range 82 km *(45 nm)*.
Fire control: RCA HR 76; I/J band (for SSM) (602).
Navigation: SPS 58(A); I band.

Programmes: Similar to the US Patrol Ship Multi-Mission Mk 5 (PSMM Mk 5). Second of class was built to an improved design. A much larger number of this class was intended, all to be armed with Harpoon. However, the US ban on export of Harpoon to Taiwan coupled with the high cost and doubts about seaworthiness caused the cancellation of this programme.
Structure: Fin stabilisers were fitted to help correct the poor sea keeping qualities of the design. Hsiung Feng missiles are mounted aft. *Sui Chiang* has a large lattice mast for the HR 76 radar. Both have had engine room fires caused by overheating in GT gearboxes.

PSMM Mk 5

50 HAI OU CLASS (FAST ATTACK CRAFT—MISSILE)

FABG 1-50

Displacement, tons: 47 full load
Dimensions, feet (metres): 70.8 × 18 × 3.3 *(21.6 × 5.5 × 1)*
Main machinery: 2 MTU 12V 331 TC82 diesels; 2605 hp(m) *(1.92 MW)* sustained; 2 shafts
Speed, knots: 36. **Range, miles:** 700 at 32 kts
Complement: 10

Missiles: SSM: 2 Hsiung Feng I; radar or optical guidance to 36 km *(19.4 nm)* at 0.7 Mach; warhead 75 kg.
Guns: 1 Oerlikon 20 mm. 2—12.7 mm MGs.
Countermeasures: Decoys: 4 Israeli AV2 Chaff launchers.
Fire control: Kollmorgen Mk 35 optical director.
Radars: Surface search: Marconi LN 66; I band.
Fire control: RCA R76 C5; I band; range 40 km *(22 nm)* for 1 m² target.

Programmes: This design was developed by Sun Yat Sen Scientific Research Institute from the basic Israeli Dvora plans. Built by China Shipbuilding Corporation (Tsoying SY), Kaohsiung.
Structure: Aluminium alloy hulls. The first series had a solid mast and the missiles were nearer the stern. Second series changed to a lattice mast and moved the missiles further forward allowing room for 1—20 mm gun right aft.
Operational: The prototype reached 45 kts on trials (probably without 20 mm gun). These craft often carry shoulder launched SAMs. Based at Makung, Pescadores where they form the Hai Chiao squadron. One task is to provide exercise high speed targets in shallow waters.

HAI OU Class *1983*

FABG 47 *4/1991, DTM*

22 PCL TYPE (COASTAL PATROL CRAFT)

Displacement, tons: 143 full load
Dimensions, feet (metres): 105 × 29.5 × 5.9 *(32 × 9 × 1.8)*
Main machinery: 3 MTU 12V 396 TB 93 diesels; 4890 hp(m) *(3.6 MW)* sustained; 3 shafts
Speed, knots: 40
Complement: 16 (3 officers)
Guns: 1 Bofors 40 mm/60. 2—12.7 mm MGs.
Depth charges: 2 racks.
Radars: Surface search: Decca; I band.
Sonars: Hull-mounted; active search and attack; high frequency.

Comment: Built to Vosper QAF design by China Shipbuilding, Kaohsiung in 1987-90. Pennant numbers in PCL series. They are used mainly for harbour defence against midget submarines and frogmen and also for Fishery protection tasks.

PCL *1990, DTM*

7 PBC 5501 TYPE (COASTAL PATROL CRAFT)

PBC 5501-5507

Displacement, tons: 100 full load
Dimensions, feet (metres): 90 × 28.6 × 6 *(27.4 × 8.7 × 1.8)*
Main machinery: 2 diesels; 2 shafts
Speed, knots: 30
Guns: 2—12.7 mm MGs (aft).
Radars: Surface search: Decca; I band.

Comment: Built by China Shipbuilding, Kaohsiung 1989-91. For Fishery patrol and counter-insurgency tasks.

PBC 5506 and 5507 *1/1992, Dr Chien Chung*

10 + 6 PBC 3521 TYPE (COASTAL PATROL CRAFT)

PBC 3521 series

Displacement, tons: 55 full load
Dimensions, feet (metres): 68.9 × 15.7 × 3.3 *(21 × 4.8 × 1)*
Main machinery: 2 Detroit 16V-92TA diesels; 1380 hp *(1.03 MW)*; 2 shafts
Speed, knots: 35
Complement: 8
Guns: 2—12.7 mm MGs.
Radars: Surface search: Decca; I band.

Comment: Building at Kaohsiung Shipyard from 1990 after the first of class had been constructed in Singapore by Vosper QAF. Form the bulk of the Coastal Patrol Squadron for Fishery protection.

PBC 3521 *1991, Dr Chien Chung*

16 COASTAL PATROL CRAFT

Displacement, tons: 30 approx
Main machinery: 2 diesels; 2 waterjets
Speed, knots: 25
Guns: 1 Bofors 40 mm/60.

Comment: Small patrol boats designated PB. Constructed in Taiwan with the first of a reported 10 craft completed about 1971. These are believed the first warships of indigenous Taiwan construction.

PB 1

15 TYPE 42 (COASTAL PATROL CRAFT)

PB 60-74

Displacement, tons: 10.5
Main machinery: 2 diesels; 2 shafts
Speed, knots: 40
Guns: 1 Bofors 40 mm/60.

Comment: Built in late 1960s and early 1970s in Taiwan.

AMPHIBIOUS FORCES

20 Ex-US LST 1-510 and 511-1152 CLASSES

Name	*No*
CHUNG HAI (ex-USS *LST 755*)	201 (ex-697)
CHUNG TING (ex-USS *LST 537*)	203 (ex-673)
CHUNG HSING (ex-USS *LST 557*)	204 (ex-684)
CHUNG CHIEN (ex-USS *LST 716*)	205 (ex-679)
CHUNG CHI (ex-USS *LST 1017*)	206 (ex-626)
CHUNG SHUN (ex-USS *LST 732*)	208 (ex-624)
CHUNG LIEN (ex-USS *LST 1050*)	209 (ex-691)
CHUNG YUNG (ex-USS *LST 574*)	210 (ex-657)
CHUNG KUANG (ex-USS *LST 503*)	216 (ex-646)
CHUNG SUO (ex-USS *Bradley County* LST 400)	217 (ex-667)
CHUNG CHUAN (ex-*LST 1030*)	221 (ex-651)
CHUNG SHENG (ex-*LST 211*, ex-USS *LSTH 1033*)	222 (ex-686)
CHUNG FU (ex-USS *Iron County* LST 840)	223 (ex-619)
CHUNG CHIANG (ex-USS *San Bernardino County* LST 1110)	225 (ex-635)
CHUNG CHIH (ex-USS *Sagadahoc County* LST 1091)	226 (ex-655)
CHUNG MING (ex-USS *Sweetwater County* LST 1152)	227 (ex-681)
CHUNG SHU (ex-USS *LST 520*)	228 (ex-642)
CHUNG WAN (ex-USS *LST 535*)	229 (ex-654)
CHUNG PANG (ex-USS *LST 578*)	230 (ex-629)
CHUNG YEH (ex-USS *Sublette County* LST 1144)	231 (ex-699)

Displacement, tons: 1653 standard; 4080 (3640, 1-510 class) full load
Dimensions, feet (metres): 328 × 50 × 14 *(100 × 15.2 × 4.3)*
Main machinery: 2 GM 12-567A diesels; 1800 hp *(1.34 MW)*; 2 shafts
Speed, knots: 11.6. **Range, miles:** 15 000 at 10 kts
Complement: Varies—100-125 in most ships
Guns: Varies—up to 10 Bofors 40 mm/56 (2 twin, 6 single) with some modernised ships rearmed with 2 USN 3 in *(76 mm)*/50 and 6—40 mm (3 twin).
Several Oerlikon 20 mm (twin or single).
Radars: Navigation: US SO 1, 2 or 8; I band.

Comment: Constructed between 1943 and 1945. These ships have been rebuilt in Taiwan. Six transferred 1946; two in 1947; one in 1948; eight in 1958; one in 1959; two in 1960; one in 1961. Some have davits forward and aft. Pennant numbers have reverted to those used in the 1960s. One deleted in 1990. The midships deck is occasionally used as a helicopter platform.

CHUNG YUNG *1990, Dr Chien Chung*

1 Ex-US CABILDO CLASS (LSD)

Name	*No*	*Builders*	*Commissioned*
CHENG HAI (ex-USS *Fort Marion* LSD 22)	192 (ex-618)	Gulf S B Co, Chickasaw, Alabama	29 Jan 1946

Displacement, tons: 4790 standard; 9078 full load
Dimensions, feet (metres): 457.8 × 72.2 × 18 *(139.6 × 22 × 5.5)*
Main machinery: 2 boilers; 435 psi *(30.6 kg/cm sq)*; 740°F *(393°C)*; 2 turbines; 7000 hp *(5.22 MW)*; 2 shafts
Speed, knots: 15.4. **Range, miles:** 8000 at 15 kts
Complement: 316
Military lift: 3 LCUs or 18 LCMs or 32 LVTs in docking well
Missiles: SAM: 1 Sea Chaparral quadruple launcher.
Guns: 12 Bofors 40 mm/56 (2 quad, 2 twin).
Fire control: US Mk 26 Mod 4.
Radars: Surface search: Raytheon SPS 5; G/H band.
Navigation: Marconi LN 66; I band.

Comment: Launched on 22 May 1945, modernised in 1960 and transferred to Taiwan on 15 April 1977. Docking well is 392 × 44 ft with a redundant helicopter platform over well. SAM system fitted forward in 1989.

CHENG HAI *2/1988*

1 Ex-US LST 511-1152 CLASS (FLAGSHIP) (AGC)

Name	*No*	*Builders*	*Commissioned*
KAO HSIUNG (ex-*Chung Hai*, ex-USS *Dukes County* LST 735)	219 (ex-663)	Dravo Corporation, Neville Island, Penn	26 Apr 1944

Displacement, tons: 1653 standard; 3675 full load
Dimensions, feet (metres): 328 × 50 × 14 *(100 × 15.2 × 4.3)*
Main machinery: 2 GM 12-567A diesels; 1800 hp *(1.34 MW)*; 2 shafts
Speed, knots: 11.6. **Range, miles:** 11 200 at 10 kts
Complement: 195
Guns: 10 Bofors 40 mm/56 (5 twin).
Radars: Air search: RCA SPS 12; D band; range 119 km *(65 nm)*.
Surface search: Raytheon SPS 10; G band.

Comment: Launched on 11 March 1944. Transferred to Taiwan in May 1957 for service as an LST. Converted to a flagship for amphibious operations and renamed and redesignated (AGC) in 1964. Purchased November 1974. Note lattice mast above bridge structure, modified bridge levels, and antenna mountings on main deck. Operational status doubtful.

KAO HSIUNG (old pennant number) *1968*

4 Ex-US LSM 1 CLASS

Name	*No*
MEI LO (ex-USS *LSM 362*)	637 (ex-*LSM 356*)
MEI CHIN (ex-USS *LSM 155*)	649 (ex-*LSM 341*)
MEI PING (ex-USS *LSM 471*)	659 (ex-*LSM 353*)
MEI SUNG (ex-USS *LSM 431*)	694 (ex-*LSM 347*)

Displacement, tons: 1095 full load
Dimensions, feet (metres): 203.5 × 34.2 × 8.3 *(62.1 × 10.4 × 2.5)*
Main machinery: 2 Fairbanks Morse 38D8-1/8-10 diesels; 3540 hp *(2.64 MW)* (637 and 659); 4 GM 16-278A diesels; 3000 hp *(2.24 MW)* (649 and 694); 2 shafts
Speed, knots: 13. **Range, miles:** 2500 at 12 kts
Complement: 65-75
Guns: 2 Bofors 40 mm/56 (twin). 4 or 8 Oerlikon 20 mm (4 single or 4 twin).
Radars: Surface search: SO 8; I band.

Comment: All built in 1945. *Mei Chin* and *Mei Sung* transferred 1946, *Mei Ping* in 1956 and *Mei Lo* in 1962. Rebuilt in Taiwan and bear little resemblance to 1970s photographs.

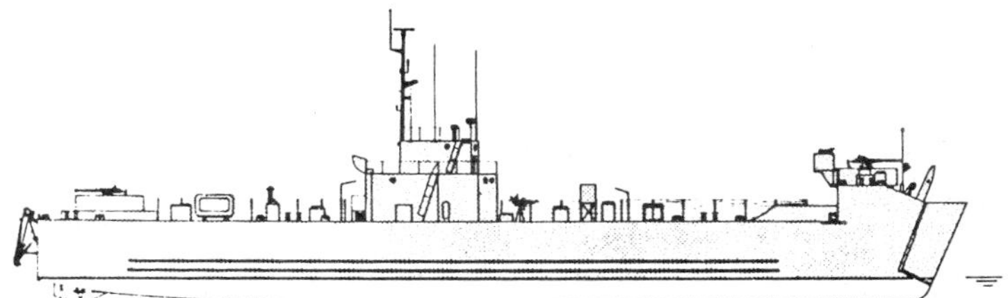

LSM 1 Class (modernised) *1988*

22 Ex-US LCU 501 and LCU 1466 CLASSES

Name	No	Name	No
HO CHI (ex-*LCU 1212*)	401	**HO CHENG** (ex-*LCU 1145*)	486
HO HUEI (ex-*LCU 1218*)	402	**HO SHAN** (ex-*LCU 1596*)	488
HO YAO (ex-*LCU 1244*)	403	**HO CHUAN** (ex-*LCU 1597*)	489
HO DENG (ex-*LCU 1367*)	404	**HO SENG** (ex-*LCU 1598*)	490
HO FENG (ex-*LCU 1397*)	405	**HO MENG** (ex-*LCU 1599*)	491
HO CHAO (ex-*LCU 1429*)	406	**HO MOU** (ex-*LCU 1600*)	492
HO TENG (ex-*LCU 1452*)	407	**HO SHOU** (ex-*LCU 1601*)	493
HO SHUN (ex-*LCU 892*)	481	**HO CHUN** (ex-*LCU 1225*)	494
HO TSUNG (ex-*LCU 1213*)	482	**HO YUNG** (ex-*LCU 1271*)	495
HO CHUNG (ex-*LCU 849*)	484	**HO CHIEN** (ex-*LCU 1278*)	496
HO CHANG (ex-*LCU 512*)	485	**HO CHIE** (ex-*LCU 700*)	SB 1

LCU 501 Class (401-486, 494-496, SB 1)

Displacement, tons: 158 light; 309 full load
Dimensions, feet (metres): 119 × 32.7 × 5 *(36.3 × 10 × 1.5)*
Main machinery: 3 GM 6-71 diesels; 522 hp *(390 kW)* sustained; 3 shafts
Speed, knots: 10
Complement: 10-25
Guns: 2 Oerlikon 20 mm. Some also may have 2—12.7 mm MGs.

LCU 1466 Class (488-493)

Displacement, tons: 180 light; 360 full load
Dimensions, feet (metres): 119 × 34 × 6 *(36.3 × 10.4 × 1.8)*
Main machinery: 3 Gray Marine 64 YTL diesels; 675 hp *(504 kW)*; 3 shafts
Speed, knots: 10
Complement: 15-25
Guns: 3 Oerlikon 20 mm. Some may also have 2—12.7 mm MGs.

Comment: The LCU 501 series were built in the USA during the Second World War; initially designated LCT(6) series. The six of LCU 1466 series built by Ishikawajima Heavy Industries Co, Tokyo, Japan, for transfer to Taiwan; completed in March 1955. All originally numbered in 200-series; subsequently changed to 400-series.
Transfers: 401-407: November/December 1959 (acquired outright 3 April 1978). SB1, 494-496: January/February 1958. Remainder: 1946-48.

LCU 489 *1991*

250 US LCM(6) CLASS

Displacement, tons: 57 full load
Dimensions, feet (metres): 56.4 × 13.8 × 3.9 *(17.2 × 4.2 × 1.2)*
Main machinery: 2 diesels; 450 hp *(336 kW)*; 2 shafts
Speed, knots: 9
Military lift: 34 tons
Guns: 1—12.7 mm MG.

Comment: Some built in the US, some in Taiwan.

120 Ex-US LCVPs

Displacement, tons: 13 full load
Speed, knots: 9
Military lift: 4 tons
Guns: 2—7.62 mm MGs.

30 TAIWAN TYPE 272 (LCU)

Displacement, tons: 5 full load
Guns: 2—7.62 mm MGs.

Comment: Some have radar. Used as reconnaissance and beach landing craft. Built in 1970s.

TYPE 272 *1989, DTM (Raymond Cheung)*

MINE WARFARE FORCES

8 MINESWEEPING LAUNCHES

MSML 1	**MSML 5**	**MSML 7**	**MSML 11**
MSML 3	**MSML 6**	**MSML 8**	**MSML 12**

Comment: These 50 ft minesweeping launches originally built in the USA as personnel transports in 1944-45 were transferred to Taiwan in March 1961. Have wooden hulls and must be near the end of their lives.

4 + (8) MWV 50 CLASS (MINEHUNTERS—COASTAL)

Displacement, tons: 500 full load
Dimensions, feet (metres): 163.1 × 28.5 × 10.2 *(49.7 × 8.7 × 3.1)*
Main machinery: 2 MTU 8V 396 TB93 diesels; 2180 hp(m) *(1.6 MW)* sustained; 2 shafts
Speed, knots: 14
Complement: 45 (5 officers)
Guns: 1 Bofors 40 mm/60 or Oerlikon 20 mm.
Radars: Navigation: I band.
Sonars: Simrad SA 950; hull-mounted; active minehunting; high frequency.

Comment: Built for the Chinese Petroleum Corporation by Abeking & Rasmussen at Lemwerder, Germany. First four delivered in 1991 under cover of being offshore oil rig support ships and then converted for minehunting in Taiwan. Armament is uncertain. It is reported that Thomson-CSF MCM system is fitted and that a Pluto ROV is carried. Up to eight more of the class may be built.

MWV 50 *1990, van Ginderen Collection*

13 US ADJUTANT and MSC 268 CLASSES (MINESWEEPERS—COASTAL)

Name	No	Builders	Commissioned
YUNG CHOU (ex-US *MSC 278*)	423	USA	July 1959
YUNG CHING (ex-*Eeklo*, ex-US *MSC 101*)	432	USA	May 1953
YUNG CHENG (ex-*Maaseik*, ex-US *MSC 78*)	441	USA	July 1953
YUNG AN (ex-US *MSC 123*)	449	USA	June 1955
YUNG JU (ex-US *MSC 300*)	457	USA	Apr 1965
YUNG SUI (ex-*Diksmuiden*, ex-US *MSC 65*)	462	USA	Feb 1954
YUNG LO (ex-US *MSC 306*)	469	USA	Apr 1966
YUNG SHAN (ex-*Lier*, ex-US *MSC 63*)	476	USA	July 1953
YUNG NIEN (ex-US *MSC 277*)	479	USA	May 1959
YUNG FU (ex-*Diest*, ex-USS *Macaw* MSC 77)	482	USA	May 1953
YUNG JEN (ex-*St Niklaas*, ex-US *MSC 64*)	485	USA	Feb 1954
YUNG HSIN (ex-US *MSC 302*)	488	USA	Mar 1965
YUNG CHI (ex-*Charleroi*, ex-US *MSC 152*)	497	USA	Feb 1954

Displacement, tons: 375 full load
Dimensions, feet (metres): 144 × 27.9 × 8 *(43.9 × 8.5 × 2.4)*
Main machinery: 2 GM 8-268A diesels; 880 hp *(656 kW)*; 2 shafts
Speed, knots: 13. **Range, miles:** 2500 at 12 kts
Complement: 35
Guns: 2 Oerlikon 20 mm (twin).
Radars: Navigation: Decca 707; I band.
Sonars: UQS 1; hull-mounted; minehunting; high frequency.

Comment: Non-magnetic, wood-hulled minesweepers built in the USA specifically for transfer to allied navies. Seven originally built for Belgium and transferred to Taiwan November 1969. The remainder transferred directly from USA on completion. All are of similar design; the ex-Belgian ships have a small boom aft on a pole mast. All refitted 1984-86. Reported that only four of the class have operational sonars.

YUNG CHI (pole mast aft) (old pennant number) *1972*

YUNG CHOU (no pole mast aft) (old pennant number)

1 MINESWEEPING BOAT

MSB 12 (ex-US *MSB 4*)

Displacement, tons: 39 full load
Dimensions, feet (metres): 57.1 × 15.1 × 3.9 *(17.4 × 4.6 × 1.2)*
Main engines: 2 diesels; 1200 hp *(895 kW)*; 2 shafts
Speed, knots: 12
Complement: 6

Comment: Former US Army minesweeping boat; assigned hull number MSB 4 in US Navy and transferred to Taiwan in December 1961.

SURVEY AND RESEARCH SHIPS

1 Ex-US LSIL 351 CLASS

Name	No	Builders	Commissioned
LIEN CHANG (ex-USS *LSIL 1017*)	AGSC 466	Albina Engineering & Machinery Works, Portland, Oregon	12 Apr 1944

Displacement, tons: 387 full load
Dimensions, feet (metres): 157 × 23.6 × 5.6 *(47.9 × 7.2 × 1.7)*
Main machinery: 2 GM diesels; 1320 hp *(985 kW)*; 2 shafts
Speed, knots: 14
Complement: 40
Guns: 2 Bofors 40 mm/56 (twin). 4 Oerlikon 20 mm.

Comment: Launched on 14 March 1944. Transferred to Taiwan in March 1958. Employed as surveying ship; retains basic LSIL appearance.

1 STERN TRAWLER TYPE

Name	No	Builders	Commissioned
BIEN DOU	—	Flekkefjord	20 June 1985

Displacement, tons: 1050 full load
Dimensions, feet (metres): 164 × 33.8 × 16.7 *(50 × 10.3 × 5.1)*
Main machinery: 1 diesel; 1680 hp(m) *(1.23 MW)*; 1 shaft
Speed, knots: 14.2
Complement: 34

Comment: Stern trawler type in use for fishery, seismic and oceanographic research for naval and civilian authorities.

1 Ex-US SOTOYOMO CLASS

Name	No	Builders	Commissioned
CHIU LIEN (ex-USS *Geronimo* ATA 207)	AGS 563	Gulfport Boiler & Welding Works, Port Arthur, Texas	1 Mar 1945

Displacement, tons: 860 full load
Dimensions, feet (metres): 143 × 33.9 × 13 *(43.6 × 10.3 × 4)*
Main machinery: Diesel-electric; 2 GM 12-278A diesels; 2200 hp *(1.64 MW)*; 2 generators; 1 motor; 1500 hp *(1.19 MW)*; 1 shaft
Speed, knots: 13
Complement: 45

Comment: Former US Navy auxiliary tug. Launched 4 January 1945. Transferred to Taiwan in February 1969 and converted to surveying ship. Acquired by sale 1 February 1976. Currently employed as research ship for the Institute of Oceanology. Civilian manned. Painted white.

CHIU LIEN *2/1988*

SERVICE FORCES

1 Ex-US DIVER CLASS (SALVAGE SHIP)

Name	No	Builders	Commissioned
TA HU (ex-USS *Grapple* ARS 7)	324	Basalt Rock Co, USA	16 Dec 1943

Displacement, tons: 1557 standard; 1745 full load
Dimensions, feet (metres): 213.5 × 39 × 15 *(65.1 × 11.9 × 4.6)*
Main machinery: Diesel-electric; 4 Cooper Bessemer GSB-8 diesels; 3420 hp *(2.55 MW)*; 2 generators; 2 motors; 2 shafts
Speed, knots: 14. **Range, miles:** 8500 at 13 kts
Complement: 85
Guns: 2 Oerlikon 20 mm.
Radars: Navigation: SPS-53; I band.

Comment: Fitted for salvage, towing and compressed-air diving. Transferred 1 December 1977 by sale.

1 COMBAT SUPPORT SHIP (AOE)

Name	No	Builders	Launched	Commissioned
WU YI	530	China SB Corporation, Keelung	4 Mar 1989	23 June 1990

Displacement, tons: 7700 light; 17 000 full load
Dimensions, feet (metres): 531.8 × 72.2 × 28 *(162.1 × 22 × 8.6)*
Main machinery: 2 MAN 14-cyl diesels; 25 000 hp(m) *(18.37 MW)*; 2 shafts
Speed, knots: 21. **Range, miles:** 9200 at 10 kts
Cargo capacity: 9300 tons
Missiles: SAM: 1 Sea Chaparral quad launcher.
Guns: 2 Bofors 40 mm/70. 2 Oerlikon 20 mm GAM-CO1.
Countermeasures: Decoys: 2 Chaff launchers.
ESM: Radar warning.
Radars: 2 navigation; I band.
Helicopters: Platform for 2 CH-47 or 2 S-70C(M)1.

Comment: Largest unit built so far for the Taiwanese Navy. Design assisted by the United Shipping Design Center in the USA. Beam replenishment rigs on both sides. SAM system on forecastle, 40 mm guns aft of the funnels. Helicopter deck at the stern. Although this is a major step forward in fleet support at sea, more than one of these ships will be needed.

WU YI *12/1991, Dr Chien Chung*

1 Ex-US AMPHION CLASS (REPAIR SHIP)

Name	No	Builders	Commissioned
YU TAI (ex-USS *Cadmus* AR 14)	521	Tampa Shipbuilding Co, Tampa, Florida	23 Apr 1946

Displacement, tons: 7826 standard; 14 490 full load
Dimensions, feet (metres): 492 × 70 × 27.5 *(150.1 × 21.3 × 8.4)*
Main machinery: 2 Foster-Wheeler boilers; 435 psi *(30.6 kg/cm sq)*; 720°F *(382°C)*; 2 Westinghouse turbines; 8560 hp *(6.4 MW)*; 1 shaft
Speed, knots: 16.5
Complement: 920
Guns: 1 USN 5 in *(127 mm)*/38. 6 Bofors 40 mm/56 (3 twin).
Radars: Surface search: Raytheon SPS 5; G/H band; range 37 km *(20 nm)*.

Comment: Transferred to Taiwan on 31 January 1974. Fitted with SATCOM and carries up to three LCVPs.

YU TAI *6/1989, van Ginderen Collection*

1 Ex-US ACHELOUS CLASS (TRANSPORT)

Name	No	Builders	Commissioned
TAI WU (ex-*Sung Shan* ARL 336, ex-USS *Agenor* ARL 3, ex-*LST 490*)	AP 520	Kaiser Co, Vancouver, Washington	20 Aug 1943

Displacement, tons: 1625 light; 4100 full load
Dimensions, feet (metres): 328 × 50 × 14 *(100 × 15.2 × 4.3)*
Main machinery: 2 GM 12-567A diesels; 1800 hp *(1.34 MW)*; 2 shafts
Speed, knots: 11.6
Complement: 100
Military lift: 600 troops
Guns: 8 Bofors 40 mm/56 (2 quad).

Comment: Begun for the US Navy as an LST, completed as a repair ship for landing craft (ARL). Launched on 3 April 1943. Transferred to France in 1951 for service in Indo-China; subsequently returned to USA and retransferred to Taiwan on 15 September 1957. Employed as a repair ship (ARL 336, subsequently ARL 236) until converted in Japan in 1973-74 to troop transport. Fully air-conditioned.

TAI WU (as repair ship) (old pennant number)

2 YUEN FENG CLASS (ATTACK TRANSPORTS)

Name	No	Builders	Commissioned
YUEN FENG	523	Taiwan Shipbuilding Co, Keelung	1983
—	524	Taiwan Shipbuilding Co, Keelung	1984

Displacement, tons: 4500 full load
Dimensions, feet (metres): 360.9 × 59.1 × 18 *(110 × 18 × 5.5)*
Main machinery: 1 diesel; 1 shaft
Speed, knots: 18
Guns: 1 Bofors 40 mm/70. 2 Oerlikon 20 mm.

Comment: Can carry between 500 and 800 troops in air-conditioned accommodation.

YUEN FENG *7/1985, L. J. Lamb*

4 + 1 WU KANG CLASS (ATTACK TRANSPORTS)

Name	No	Builders	Commissioned
WU KANG	525	China Shipbuilding Corp, Keelung	Feb 1985
—	526	China Shipbuilding Corp, Keelung	1987
—	527	China Shipbuilding Corp, Keelung	1989
—	528	China Shipbuilding Corp, Keelung	1991
—	529	China Shipbuilding Corp, Keelung	1993

Displacement, tons: 3040 full load
Dimensions, feet (metres): 331.3 × 55.8 × 16.4 *(101 × 17 × 5)*
Main machinery: 2 diesels; 2 shafts; bow thruster
Speed, knots: 20
Guns: 3 Bofors 40 mm/70.

Comment: With a helicopter platform, stern docking facility and davits for 4 LCVP, the design resembles an LPD. Used mostly for supplying garrisons in offshore islands, and on the Spratley and Pratas islands in the South China Sea.

WU KANG *1985, DTM*

2 TAI HU CLASS (TRANSPORTS)

Name	No	Builders	Commissioned
TAI HU (ex-*Ling Yuen*)	522	Taiwan Shipbuilding Co, Keelung	15 Aug 1975
YUN TAI	518	Taiwan Shipbuilding Co, Keelung	1985

Measurement, tons: 2510 dwt; 3040 gross
Dimensions, feet (metres): 328.7 × 47.9 × 16.4 *(100.2 × 14.6 × 5)*
Main machinery: 1—6-cyl diesel; 1 shaft
Complement: 55
Military lift: 500 troops
Guns: 2 Oerlikon 20 mm. 2—12.7 mm MGs.

Comment: Designed by Chinese First Naval Shipyard at Tsoying. *Tai Hu* launched 27 January 1975.

YUN TAI *7/1985, L. J. Lamb*

1 JAPANESE TYPE (SUPPORT TANKER)

Name	No	Builders	Commissioned
WAN SHOU	AOG 512	Ujina Shipbuilding Co, Hiroshima, Japan	1 Nov 1969

Displacement, tons: 1049 light; 4150 full load
Dimensions, feet (metres): 283.8 × 54 × 18 *(86.5 × 16.5 × 5.5)*
Main machinery: 1 diesel; 2100 hp(m) *(1.54 MW)*; 1 shaft
Speed, knots: 13
Complement: 70
Cargo capacity: 73 600 gal fuel; 62 000 gal water
Guns: 2 Bofors 40 mm/56. 2 Oerlikon 20 mm.

Comment: Employed in resupply of offshore islands.

WAN SHOU *1984, L. J. Lamb*

3 Ex-US PATAPSCO CLASS (SUPPORT TANKERS)

Name	No	Builders	Commissioned
CHANG PEI (ex-USS *Pecatonica* AOG 57)	514	Cargill, Inc, Savage Minnesota	28 Nov 1945
LUNG CHUAN (ex-HMNZS *Endeavour*, ex-USS *Namakagon* AOG 53)	515	Cargill, Inc, Savage, Minnesota	10 May 1945
HSIN LUNG (ex-USS *Elkhorn* AOG 7)	516	Cargill, Inc, Savage, Minnesota	12 Feb 1944

Displacement, tons: 1850 light; 4335 full load
Dimensions, feet (metres): 310.8 × 48.5 × 15.7 *(94.8 × 14.8 × 4.8)*
Main machinery: 2 GM 16-278A diesels; 3000 hp *(2.24 MW)*; 2 shafts
Speed, knots: 14. **Range, miles:** 7000 at 12 kts
Complement: 124
Cargo capacity: 2000 tons
Guns: 1 USN 3 in *(76 mm)*/50. 2 Bofors 40 mm/60.
Radars: Surface search: Raytheon SPS 21 *(Chang Pei)*; G/H band.

Comment: *Chang Pei* was launched on 17 March 1945 and transferred to Taiwan on 24 April 1961. The ex-USS *Namakagon* was launched on 4 November 1944 and transferred to New Zealand on 5 October 1962 for use as an Antarctic resupply ship; strengthened for polar operations and renamed *Endeavour;* returned to the US Navy on 29 June 1971 and retransferred to Taiwan the same date. *Hsin Lung* was launched on 15 May 1943 and was transferred to Taiwan on 1 July 1972. All three transferred by sale 19 May 1976.

LUNG CHUAN *2/1988*

1 Ex-US MARK CLASS (AGI)

Name	No	Builders	Commissioned
YUNG KANG (ex-USS *Mark* AKL 12, ex-*AG 143*, ex-US Army *FS 214*)	AKL 359	Higgins	21 Dec 1944

Displacement, tons: 900 full load
Dimensions, feet (metres): 180.1 × 32.2 × 10.2 *(54.9 × 9.8 × 3.1)*
Main machinery: 2 GM 6-278A diesels; 1120 hp *(836 kW)*; 2 shafts
Speed, knots: 12. **Range, miles:** 4000 at 11 kts
Complement: 37
Guns: 2 Oerlikon 20 mm.

Comment: Built as a small cargo ship (freight and supply) for the US Army. Transferred to US Navy on 30 September 1947; operated in South-east Asia from 1963 until transferred to Taiwan on 1 June 1971 and by sale 19 May 1976. Acts as AGI.

TUGS

4 Ex-US ARMY TUGS

YTL 9 (ex-US Army *ST 2004*)
YTL 11 (ex-USN *YTL 454*)
YTL 12 (ex-USN *YTL 584*)
YTL 14 (ex-USN *YTL 585*)

Comment: One diesel and 8 kts.

5 Ex-US CHEROKEE CLASS

Name	No	Builders	Commissioned
TA HAN (ex-USS *Tawakoni)*	ATF 542	United Engineering Co	14 Sep 1944
TA TUNG (ex-USS *Chickasaw)*	ATF 548	United Engineering Co	4 Feb 1943
— (ex-USS *Shakori)*	ATF 563	Charleston S B & D D	20 Dec 1945
— (ex-USS *Wenatchee)*	—	Charleston S B & D D	7 Sep 1944
— (ex-USS *Achomawi)*	—	United Engineering Co	10 Sep 1944

Three more transferred in 1990.

Displacement, tons: 1235 standard; 1731 full load
Dimensions, feet (metres): 205 × 38.5 × 17 *(62.5 × 11.7 × 5.2)*
Main machinery: Diesel-electric; 4 GM 12-278 diesels; 4400 hp *(3.28 MW)*; 4 generators; 1 motor; 3000 hp *(2.24 MW)*; 1 shaft
Speed, knots: 15. **Range, miles:** 6000 at 14 kts
Complement: 85
Guns: 1 USN 3 in *(76 mm)*/50. Several 12.7 mm MGs.

Comment: *Ta Tung* transferred to Taiwan in January 1966 and by sale 19 May 1976, *Ta Han* by sale 1 August 1978 and ex-*Shakori* by sale 29 August 1980. Three more transferred in 1990 but one was immediately cannibalised for spares. *Ta Wan* was sunk as a target in 1988.

3 Ex-US SOTOYOMO CLASS

Name	No	Builders	Commissioned
TA SUEH (ex-USS *Tonkawa* ATA 176)	ATA 357	Levingston S B Co, Orange, Texas	19 Aug 1944
TA TENG (ex-USS *Cahokia* ATA 186)	ATA 367	Levingston S B Co, Orange, Texas	24 Nov 1944
TA PENG (ex-USS *Mahopac* ATA 196)	ATA 395	Levingston S B Co, Orange, Texas	21 Dec 1944

Displacement, tons: 435 standard; 860 full load
Dimensions, feet (metres): 143 × 33.9 × 13 *(43.6 × 10.3 × 4)*
Main machinery: Diesel-electric; 2 GM 12-278A diesels; 2200 hp *(1.64 MW)*; 2 generators; 1 motor; 1500 hp *(1.12 MW)*; 1 shaft
Speed, knots: 13
Guns: 1 USN 3 in *(76 mm)*/50. Several 12.7 mm MGs.

Comment: *Ta Sueh* transferred to Taiwan in April 1962. *Ta Teng* assigned briefly to US Air Force in 1971 until transferred to Taiwan on 14 April 1972. *Ta Peng* transferred on 1 July 1971. Latter two by sale 19 May 1976. A fourth tug of this class serves as a surveying ship.

5 Ex-US FLOATING DOCKS

HAY TAN (ex-USN *AFDL 36*) AFDL 1
KIM MEN (ex-USN *AFDL 5*) AFDL 2
HAN JIH (ex-USN *AFDL 34*) AFDL 3
FO WU 5 (ex-USN *ARD 9*) ARD 5
FO WU 6 (ex-USS *Windsor* ARD 22) ARD 6

Comment: Former US Navy floating dry docks. *Hay Tan* transferred in March 1947, *Kim Men* in January 1948, *Han Jih* in July 1959, *Fo Wu 5* in June 1971, *Fo Wu 6* in June 1971. *Fo Wu 6* by sale 19 May 1976 and *Fo Wu 5* on 12 January 1977.

CUSTOMS SERVICE

Note: (a) In 1990 a total of 16 naval units (including five Shan class frigates) were partially disarmed and transferred from the Navy to the Customs Service of Taiwan, an agency of the Ministry of Finance. In 1991 the five frigates were returned to the Navy and rearmed leaving only the 11 smaller units all of 1940s vintage.
(b) The nine patrol vessels (one of 800 tons and eight of 500 tons) ordered in 1990 for the Maritime Patrol Bureau will probably now be given to the Customs Service.
(c) There is also a Fishery Protection Service under the Ministry of Fishery and Agriculture. Two 380 ton vessels *Yu Jian 1* and *2* were acquired 24 November 1989. All vessels are tasked with patrolling the EEZ.

2 TACOMA TYPE (LARGE PATROL CRAFT)

TEH HSING + 1

Displacement, tons: 1795 full load
Dimensions, feet (metres): 270 × 38.1 × 13.1 *(82.3 × 11.6 × 4)*
Main machinery: 2 MTU 16V 1163 TB 93 diesels; 13 310 hp(m) *(9.78 MW)* sustained; 2 shafts
Speed, knots: 22. **Range, miles:** 7000 at 16 kts
Complement: 80 (18 officers)

Comment: Built by the China SB Corporation, Keelung, to a Tacoma design. Four high speed interceptor boats are carried on individual davits.

2 PAO HSING CLASS (COASTAL PATROL CRAFT)

PAO HSING **CHIN HSING**

Displacement, tons: 550 full load
Dimensions, feet (metres): 189.6 × 25.6 × 6.9 *(57.8 × 7.8 × 2.1)*
Main machinery: 2 MAN 12V 25/30 diesels; 7183 hp(m) *(5.28 MW)* sustained; 2 shafts
Speed, knots: 24
Complement: 40 approx
Guns: 1 Bofors 40 mm/56. 2 Oerlikon 20 mm.

Comment: First delivered 20 May 1980; second 23 May 1985. Built by Kaohsiung yard of China SB Corporation.

CHIN HSING *2/1988*

2 COASTAL PATROL CRAFT

MOU HSING **FU HSING**

Displacement, tons: 850 full load
Dimensions, feet (metres): 214.6 × 31.5 × 10.5 *(65.4 × 9.6 × 3.2)*
Main machinery: 2 MTU 16V 538 TB 93 diesels; 7510 hp(m) *(5.52 MW)* sustained; 2 shafts
Speed, knots: 28
Complement: 54

Comment: Ordered from Wilton Fijenoord in September 1986, and commissioned 14 June 1988.

MOU HSING *5/1988, Wilton Fijenoord*

1 YUN HSING CLASS (COASTAL PATROL CRAFT)

YUN HSING

Displacement, tons: 900 full load
Dimensions, feet (metres): 213.3 × 32.8 × 9.5 *(65 × 10 × 2.9)*
Main machinery: 1 Sulzer 12V AT 25 diesel; 2640 hp(m) *(1.94 MW)* sustained; 1 shaft

Comment: Built by China SB Corporation and delivered 28 December 1987.

YUN HSING *6/1988*

1 HSUN HSING CLASS (COASTAL PATROL CRAFT)

HSUN HSING

Displacement, tons: 239 full load
Dimensions, feet (metres): 146 × 24.6 × 5.8 *(44.5 × 7.5 × 1.7)*
Main machinery: 3 MTU 16V 396 TB 93 diesels; 6540 hp(m) *(4.81 MW)* sustained; 3 shafts

Comment: Built by China SB Corporation and delivered 15 December 1986.

3 HAI PING CLASS (INSHORE PATROL CRAFT)

HAI PING **HAI AN** **HAI CHENG**

Displacement, tons: 63 full load
Dimensions, feet (metres): 85.3 × 18.4 × 3.6 *(26 × 5.6 × 1.1)*
Main machinery: 2 MTU 8V 331 TC 81 diesels; 1740 hp(m) *(1.28 MW)* sustained; 2 shafts

Comment: Built by China SB Corporation, Kaohsiung and delivered 28 February, 18 April and 8 June 1979 respectively.

HAI PING *1989*

2 HALTER TYPE (INSHORE PATROL CRAFT)

Displacement, tons: 70
Dimensions, feet (metres): 78.7 × 18.4 × 4.9 *(24 × 5.6 × 1.5)*
Main machinery: 2 GM 12V 71 TI diesels; 840 hp *(627 kW)* sustained; 2 shafts
Speed, knots: 19

Comment: Purchased in 1977. Aluminium hulls.

MARITIME SECURITY POLICE

Note: Set up in early 1990 with three Squadrons based at Tamshui, Hsinchu and Kaohsing. Main duties are anti-smuggling and the prevention of illegal immigration. Some naval patrol boats are reported to have been transferred. The planned Maritime Patrol Bureau which was to have augmented Police and Customs services was abandoned in mid-1991. There are two main types of patrol craft, both still building: 60 ft (601 series) and 50 (501 series). All are armed with 12.7 mm or 6.72 mm MGs. There are also some unarmed river boats (301 series).

POLICE 601 *1989, DTM*

TANZANIA

Senior Appointment

Chief of Navy:
Brigadier Ligate G Sande

Personnel

(a) 1992: 800
(b) Voluntary service

Mercantile Marine

Lloyd's Register of Shipping:
38 vessels of 39 389 tons gross

General

No naval vessels have been operational since January 1990. There is a small Coastguard Service (KMKM), based on Zanzibar, which uses small boats for anti-smuggling patrols.

Bases

Dar Es Salaam, Zanzibar, Mwanza (Lake Victoria). Mtwara (Lake Victoria).

DELETIONS

1990 *Araka, Salaam*
1991 *Utafiti, Rafiki, Uhuru*

PATROL FORCES

6 Ex-CHINESE SHANGHAI II CLASS (FAST ATTACK CRAFT—GUN)

JW 9861-6

Displacement, tons: 131 full load
Dimensions, feet (metres): 127.3 × 17.7 × 5.6 *(38.8 × 5.4 × 1.7)*
Main machinery: 2 Type L12-180 diesels; 2400 hp(m) *(1.76 MW)* (forward); 2 Type 12D6 diesels; 1820 hp(m) *(1.34 MW)* (aft); 4 shafts
Speed, knots: 30. **Range, miles:** 700 at 16.5 kts
Complement: 34
Guns: 4—37 mm/63 (2 twin). 4—25 mm/80 (2 twin).
Radars: Surface search: Skin Head; I band.

Comment: Transferred by the People's Republic of China in 1971-72. Non-operational in early 1992.

JW 9864 *1984, van Ginderen Collection*

4 Ex-CHINESE YULIN CLASS (LAKE PATROL CRAFT)

Displacement, tons: 9.8 full load
Dimensions, feet (metres): 42.6 × 9.5 × 3.5 *(13 × 2.9 × 1.1)*
Main machinery: 1 PRC Type 12150 diesel; 300 hp(m) *(221 kW)*; 1 shaft
Speed, knots: 24
Complement: 10
Guns: 2—14.5 mm (twin) MGs. 2—12.7 mm (twin) MGs.

Comment: Transferred late 1966. Based on Victoria Nyanza. Non-operational in early 1992.

2 Ex-NORTH KOREAN KIMJIN CLASS (COASTAL PATROL CRAFT)

YU CHAI **SCHALBE**

Displacement, tons: 25 full load
Dimensions, feet (metres): 66.6 × 11 × 5.5 *(20.3 × 3.4 × 1.7)*
Main machinery: 2 diesels; 2400 hp(m) *(1.76 MW)*; 2 shafts
Speed, knots: 42. **Range, miles:** 220 at 20 kts
Complement: 10
Guns: 4—14.5 mm (2 twin) MGs.

Comment: Two delivered in September 1987. Same type to Nicaragua. Three more ordered but not delivered. Non-operational in early 1992.

4 Ex-CHINESE HUCHUAN CLASS (FAST ATTACK CRAFT—TORPEDO)

JW 9841-4

Displacement, tons: 39 standard; 45.8 full load
Dimensions, feet (metres): 71.5 × 20.7 oa × 11.8 (hullborne) *(21.8 × 6.3 × 3.6)*
Main machinery: 3 Type M50-12 diesels; 2550 hp(m) *(1.9 MW)*; 3 shafts
Speed, knots: 50. **Range, miles:** 500 at 20 kts
Complement: 11
Guns: 2—14.5 mm (twin) MGs.
Torpedoes: 2—21 in *(533 mm)* tubes. Probably Soviet Type 53.
Radars: Surface search: Skin Head; I band.

Comment: Transferred 1975. Non-operational in early 1992.

HUCHUAN Class *1990*

4 VOSPER THORNYCROFT 75ft TYPE (COASTAL PATROL CRAFT)

Displacement, tons: 70 full load
Dimensions, feet (metres): 75 × 19.5 × 8 *(22.9 × 6 × 2.4)*
Main machinery: 2 diesels; 1840 hp *(1.37 MW)*; 2 shafts
Speed, knots: 24.5. **Range, miles:** 800 at 20 kts
Complement: 11
Guns: 2 Oerlikon 20 mm

Comment: First pair delivered 6 July 1973, second pair 1974.

VOSPER THORNYCROFT 75ft Type *1984, N. Overington*

THAILAND

Headquarters' Appointments

Commander-in-Chief of the Navy:
Admiral Vichet Karunyavanij
Deputy Commander-in-Chief:
Admiral Thawatchai Kosolnawin
Assistant Commander-in-Chief:
Admiral Pravit Sivaraks
Chief of Staff (RTN):
Admiral Surawut Maharom
Deputy Chief-of-Staff (RTN):
Vice Admiral Matra Ampaipast
Commander-in-Chief, Fleet:
Admiral Prachume Kruawal
Deputy Fleet Commander:
Vice Admiral Santiparb Moo-Ming
Chief of Staff, Fleet:
Vice Admiral Prachet Siridej

Diplomatic Representation

Naval Attaché in London:
Captain Suchart Kolasastraseni
Naval Attaché in Washington:
Captain Suvatchai Kasemsook
Naval Attaché in Bonn:
Captain Daweesak Somabha
Naval Attaché in Paris:
Captain Roongrat Boonyaratapan
Naval Attaché in Canberra:
Captain Kiat Korbsook
Naval Attaché in Madrid:
Captain Rangsan Temiyaves
Naval Attaché in Tokyo:
Captain Thaworn Pradabwit

Personnel

(a) 1992: Navy, 66 000 including Naval Air Arm, Marines and Coastal Defence Command
(b) 2 years' national service

Organisation

First naval area command (East Thai Gulf)
Second naval area command (West Thai Gulf)
Third naval area command (Andaman Sea)
First air wing (U-Tapao)
Second air wing (Songkhla)

Bases

Bangkok, Sattahip, Songkhla, Paknam, Phang-Nga (west coast)

Prefix to Ships' Names

HTMS

Strength of the Fleet

Type	*Active*	*Building (Projected)*
Frigates	10	2
Corvettes	5	—
Fast Attack Craft (Missile)	6	—
Fast Attack Craft (Gun)	3	—
Large Patrol Craft	21	—
Coastal Patrol Craft	35	—
River Patrol Craft	41 +	—
MCM Support Ship	1	—
Minehunters	2	—
Coastal Minesweepers	4	—
MSBs	5	—
Helicopter Support Ship	—	(1)
LSTs	6	—
LSMs	2	—
LCG	1	—
LSIL	1	—
Hovercraft	3	—
LCUs	9	—
Landing Craft	40	—
Survey Vessels	5	—
Oil Tankers	5	—
Water Tanker	1	—
Tugs	4	—
Training Ships	2	—
Marine Police Craft	134	1

Marine Corps

Currently consists of two Divisions including an amphibious assault battalion. In 1992 personnel strength is about 20 000, although the establishment figure is 25 000.

Coast Guard

A trial coastal unit of 1 frigate, 8 patrol craft and 4 aircraft was established on 1 April 1989. It is intended to set up a permanent Coast Guard Squadron in due course. Armed Sea Rangers in converted Fishing Vessels are being used to counter pirates.

Coastal Defence Command

This unit has been rapidly expanded to the 1992 two Division level after the government charged the RTN with the responsibility of defending the entire Eastern Seaboard Development Project on the east coast of the Gulf of Thailand in 1988. Equipment includes 155 mm and 130 mm guns for coastal defence, 76 mm, 40 mm, 37 mm, 20 mm guns and PL-9B SAM for air defence.

Marine Police

Acts as a Coast Guard in inshore waters with some 72 armed patrol craft and another 62 equipped with small arms only.

Future Plans

Plans to acquire submarines still under consideration although a Replenishment Ship and a Helicopter Support Ship have a higher priority. Potential submarine officers are being trained in the Netherlands. A new support facility is planned for light forces including a 50 m synchrolift.

Mercantile Marine

Lloyd's Register of Shipping:
333 vessels of 724 648 tons gross

DELETIONS

Amphibious Ship

1990 *Phai*

Service Forces

1990 *Prong, Kled Keo*

FRIGATES

0 + 2 NARESUAN CLASS (TYPE 25T) (FFG)

Name	*No*	*Builders*	*Laid down*	*Launched*	*Commissioned*
NARESUAN	621	Zhonghua SY, Shanghai	1991	Dec 1992	1994
TAKSIN	622	Zhonghua SY, Shanghai	1991	Oct 1993	1994

Displacement, tons: 2500 standard; 2980 full load
Dimensions, feet (metres): 393.7 × 42.7 × 12.5 *(120 × 13 × 3.8)*
Main machinery: CODOG; 2 GE LM 2500 gas turbines; 44 000 hp *(33 MW)* sustained; 2 MTU 20 V 1163 TB 83 diesels; 14 720 hp(m) *(10.8 MW)* sustained; 2 shafts; cp props
Speed, knots: 32. **Range, miles:** 4000 at 18 kts
Complement: 150

Missiles: SSM: 8 McDonnell Douglas Harpoon (2 quad) launchers ❶.
SAM: Mk 41 LCHR 8 cell VLS launcher ❷ Sea Sparrow missiles.
Guns: 1 FMC 5 in *(127 mm)*/54 Mk 45 Mod 2 ❸.
4 China 37 mm/76 (2 twin) H/PJ 76 A ❹.
Torpedoes: 6—324 mm Mk 32 Mod 5 (2 triple) tubes ❺. Honeywell Mk 46.
Countermeasures: Decoys: China Type 945 GPJ 26-barrelled launchers ❻; Chaff and IR.
ESM/ECM: Mirage EW System.
Fire control: 1 JM-83H Optical Director ❼.
Radars: Air search: Signaal LW 08 ❽; D band.
Surface search: China Type 360 ❾.

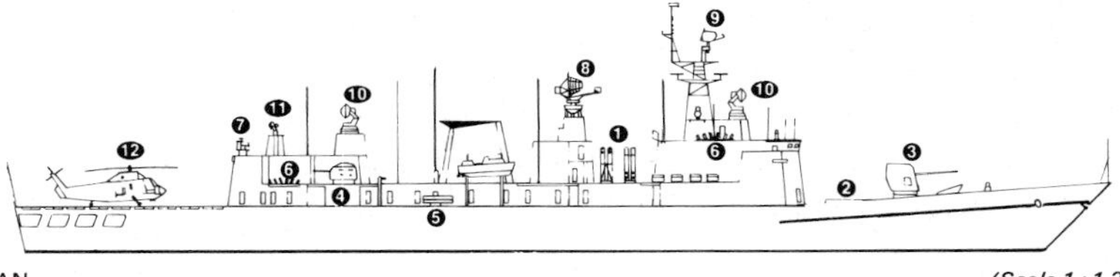

NARESUAN *(Scale 1 : 1 200), Ian Sturton*

Navigation: Two Raytheon SPS 64(V)5; I band.
Fire control: Two Signaal STIR ❿; I/J/K band (for SSM and 127 mm).
China 374 G ⓫ (for 37 mm).
Sonars: China SJD-7; hull-mounted; active search and attack; medium frequency.

Helicopters: 1 Kamen SH-2F Seasprite ⓬.

Programmes: Contract signed 21 September 1989 for construction of two ships by the China SB Corporation. US and European weapon systems are to be fitted after delivery in Thailand.
Structure: Jointly designed by the Royal Thai Navy and China State Shipbuilding Corporation (CSSC). This is a new design incorporating much Western machinery and equipment and will be more formidable than the four Type 053 class. The combat data system details are still uncertain.

NARESUAN (artist's impression) *1991, Royal Thai Navy*

4 CHAO PHRAYA CLASS (TYPES 053 HT and 053 HT (H)) (FFG)

Name	*No*	*Builders*	*Laid down*	*Launched*	*Commissioned*
CHAO PHRAYA	455	Hudong SY, Shanghai	1989	24 June 1990	5 Apr 1991
BANGPAKONG	456	Hudong SY, Shanghai	1989	25 July 1990	20 July 1991
KRABURI	457	Hudong SY, Shanghai	1990	28 Dec 1990	10 Jan 1992
SAIBURI	458	Hudong SY, Shanghai	1990	27 Aug 1991	July 1992

Displacement, tons: 1676 standard; 1924 full load
Dimensions, feet (metres): 338.5 × 37.1 × 10.2 *(103.2 × 11.3 × 3.1)*
Main machinery: 4 MTU 20V 1163 TB 83 diesels; 29 440 hp(m) *(21.6 MW)* sustained; 2 shafts; cp props
Speed, knots: 30. **Range, miles:** 3500 at 18 kts
Complement: 168 (22 officers)

Missiles: SSM: 8 Ying Ji (Eagle Strike) ❶; active radar/IR homing to 40 km *(22 nm)* at 0.9 Mach; warhead 165 kg; sea-skimmer.
Guns: 2 (457 and 458) or 4 China 100 mm/56 (1 or 2 twin) ❷; 85° elevation; 25 rounds/minute to 22 km *(12 nm)*; weight of shell 15.9 kg.
8 China 37 mm/76 (4 twin) H/PJ 76 A ❸; 85° elevation; 180 rounds/minute to 8.5 km *(4.6 nm)* anti-aircraft; weight of shell 1.42 kg.
A/S mortars: 2 RBU 1200 (China Type 86) 5-tubed fixed launchers ❹.
Depth charges: 2 BMB racks.
Countermeasures: Decoys: 2 China Type 945 GPJ 26-barrelled Chaff launchers.
ESM: China Type 923(1); intercept.
ECM: China Type 981(3); jammer.
Combat data systems: China Type 2KJ-3 action data automation.
Radars: Air/surface search: China Type 354 Eye Shield ❺; E band.
Surface search/fire control: China Type 352C Square Tie ❻; I band (for SSM).
Fire control: China Type 343 Sun Visor ❼; I band (for 100 mm).
China Type 341 Rice Lamp ❽; I band (for 37 mm).
Navigation: Racal Decca 1290; I band.
IFF: Type 651.
Sonars: China Type SJD-5A; hull-mounted; active search and attack; medium frequency.

Helicopters: 1 Kamen SH-2F Seasprite (457 and 458) ❾, or Z-9A Dauphin 2.

Programmes: Contract signed 18 July 1988 for four modified Jianghu class ships to be built by the China SB Corporation.
Structure: Thailand would have preferred only the hulls but China insisted on full armament. Two of the ships are the Type III variant with 100 mm guns, fore and aft, and the other two are a variation of the Type II with a helicopter platform replacing the after 100 mm gun. German communication equipment fitted.
Opinion: Some early concern was expressed about shipbuilding standards, in particular welding and damage control, but this has not delayed the programme.

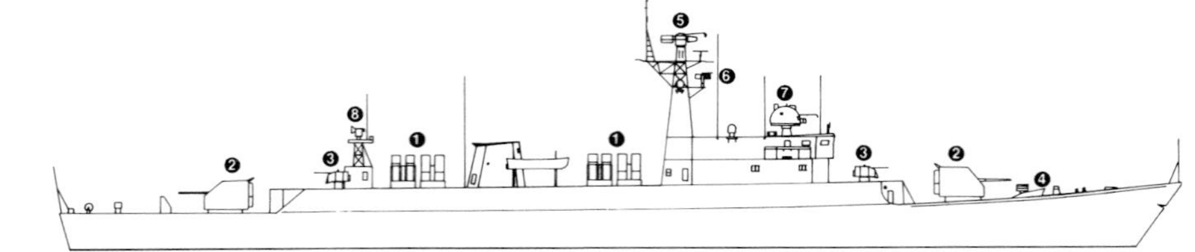

CHAO PHRAYA *(Scale 1: 900), Ian Sturton*

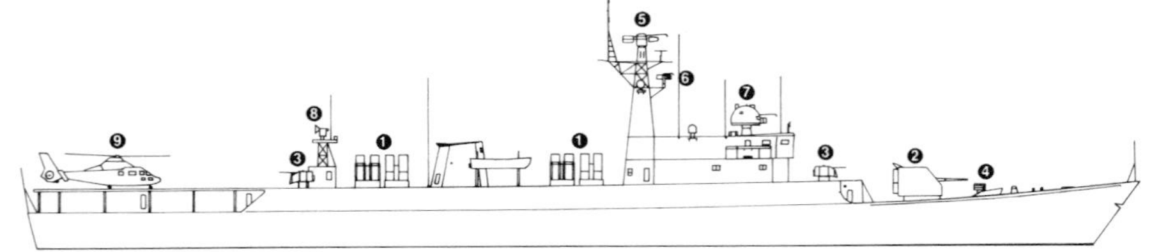

KRABURI *(Scale 1: 900), Ian Sturton*

CHAO PHRAYA *1991, Royal Thai Navy*

BANGPAKONG *1991, Royal Thai Navy*

BANGPAKONG *1992, Royal Thai Navy*

1 YARROW TYPE (FF)

Name	No	Builders	Laid down	Launched	Commissioned
MAKUT RAJAKUMARN	7	Yarrow (Shipbuilders)	11 Jan 1970	18 Nov 1971	7 May 1973

Displacement, tons: 1650 standard; 1900 full load
Dimensions, feet (metres): 320 × 36 × 18.1 *(97.6 × 11 × 5.5)*
Main machinery: CODOG; 1 RR Olympus TBM 3B gas turbine; 21 500 hp *(16 MW)* sustained; 1 Crossley-Pielstick 12PC 2.2 V400 diesel; 6000 hp(m) *(4.4 MW)* sustained; 2 shafts
Speed, knots: 26 gas; 18 diesel. **Range, miles:** 5000 at 18 kts; 1200 at 26 kts
Complement: 140 (16 officers)

Guns: 2 Vickers 4.5 in *(114 mm)*/55 Mk 8 ❶; 55° elevation; 25 rounds/minute to 22 km *(12 nm)* anti-surface; 6 km *(3.3 nm)* anti-aircraft; weight of shell 21 kg.
2 Bofors 40 mm/60 ❷; 80° elevation; 120 rounds/minute to 10 km *(5.5 nm)*; weight of shell 0.89 kg.
Depth charges: 1 rack.
Countermeasures: ESM: Racal; radar warning. D/F.
Combat data systems: Signaal Sewaco TH action data automation.
Radars: Air/surface search: Signaal DA 05 ❸; E/F band; range 137 km *(75 nm)* for 2 m² target.
Navigation: Signaal ZW 06; I band.
Fire control: Signaal WM 22 series ❹; I/J band; range 46 km *(25 nm)*.
Sonars: Krupp Atlas DSQS 21C; hull-mounted; active search and attack; medium frequency.

Programmes: Ordered on 21 August 1969 as a general purpose frigate.
Modernisation: A severe fire in February 1984 resulted in extensive work including replacement of the Olympus gas turbine, a new ER control room and central electric switchboard. Further modifications included the removal of Limbo mortar, Seacat SAM system and the installation of new electronics. Plans to fit SSM, Sea Sparrow SAM system or CIWS, and torpedo tubes, have been shelved.
Operational: The ship is largely automated with a consequent saving in complement, and has been most successful in service. Will lose its Flagship role to one of the Chinese-built frigates and will then become a training ship.

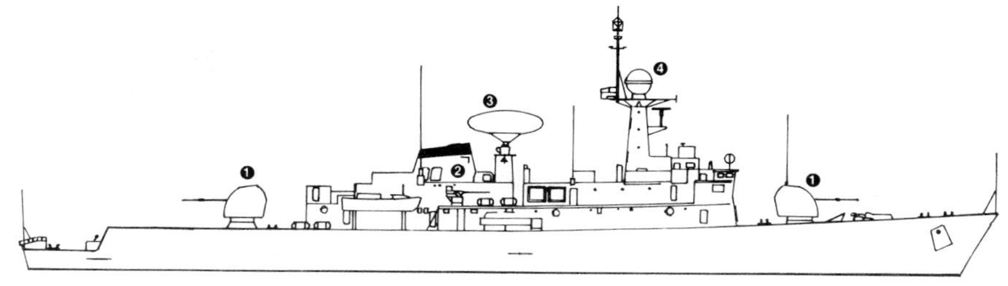

MAKUT RAJAKUMARN *(Scale 1: 900), Ian Sturton*

MAKUT RAJAKUMARN *1991, Royal Thai Navy*

2 US PF 103 CLASS

Name	No	Builders	Laid down	Launched	Commissioned
TAPI	5	American S B Co, Toledo, Ohio	1 Apr 1970	17 Oct 1970	1 Nov 1971
KHIRIRAT	6	Norfolk S B & D D Co	18 Feb 1972	2 June 1973	10 Aug 1974

Displacement, tons: 885 standard; 1172 full load
Dimensions, feet (metres): 275 × 33 × 10; 14.1 (sonar) *(83.8 × 10 × 3; 4.3)*
Main machinery: 2 Fairbanks-Morse 38 TD8-1/8-9 diesels; 5250 hp *(3.9 MW)* sustained; 2 shafts
Speed, knots: 20. **Range, miles:** 2400 at 18 kts
Complement: 135 (15 officers)

Guns: 1 OTO Melara 3 in *(76 mm)*/62 compact ❶; 85° elevation; 85 rounds/minute to 16 km *(8.7 nm)* anti-surface; 12 km *(6.6 nm)* anti-aircraft; weight of shell 6 kg.
1 Bofors 40 mm/70 ❷; 85° elevation; 300 rounds/minute to 12.5 km *(6.8 nm)*; weight of shell 0.96 kg.
2 Oerlikon 20 mm ❸. 2—12.7 mm MGs.
Torpedoes: 6—324 mm US Mk 32 (2 triple) tubes ❹. Honeywell Mk 46; anti-submarine; active/passive homing to 11 km *(5.9 nm)* at 40 kts; warhead 44 kg.
Depth charges: 1 rack.
Combat data systems: Signaal Sewaco TH.
Radars: Air/surface search: Signaal DA 05 ❺; E/F band; range 137 km *(75 nm)* for 2 m² target.
Surface search: Raytheon ❻; I band.
Fire control: Signaal WM 25 ❼; I/J band; range 46 km *(25 nm)*.

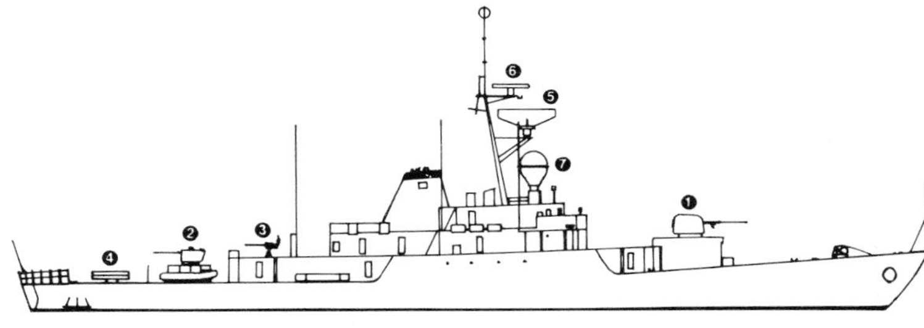

TAPI *(Scale 1 : 900), Ian Sturton*

Sonars: Krupp Atlas DSQS 21C; hull-mounted; active search and attack; medium frequency.

Programmes: *Tapi* was ordered on 27 June 1969. *Khirirat* was ordered on 25 June 1971.

Modernisation: *Tapi* completed 1983 and *Khirirat* in 1987. This included new gunnery and radars and a slight heightening of the funnel. Further modernisation in 1988-89 mainly to external and internal communications.
Structure: Of similar design to the Iranian ships of the Bayandor class.

KHIRIRAT *5/1990, John Mortimer*

1 Ex-US CANNON CLASS

Name	No	Builders	Laid down	Launched	Commissioned
PIN KLAO (ex-USS *Hemminger* DE 746)	3 (ex-1)	Western Pipe & Steel Co	1943	12 Sep 1943	30 May 1944

Displacement, tons: 1240 standard; 1930 full load
Dimensions, feet (metres): 306 × 36.7 × 14 *(93.3 × 11.2 × 4.3)*
Main machinery: Diesel-electric; 4 GM 16-278A diesels; 6000 hp *(4.5 MW)*; 2 shafts
Speed, knots: 20. **Range, miles:** 10 800 at 12 kts; 6700 at 19 kts
Complement: 192 (14 officers)

Guns: 3 USN 3 in *(76 mm)*/50 Mk 22; 85° elevation; 20 rounds/minute to 12 km *(6.6 nm)*; weight of shell 6 kg.
6 Bofors 40 mm/60 (3 twin); 80° elevation; 120 rounds/minute to 10 km *(5.5 nm)*; weight of shell 0.89 kg.
Torpedoes: 6—324 mm US Mk 32 (2 triple) tubes; anti-submarine.
A/S mortars: 1 Mk 10 multi-barrelled fixed Hedgehog; range 350 m; warhead 26 kg; 24 rockets.
Depth charges: 8 projectors; 2 racks.
Countermeasures: ESM: WLR-1; radar warning.
Fire control: Mk 52 radar GFCS for 3 in guns. Mk 63 radar GFCS for aft gun only. 2 Mk 51 optical GFCS for 40 mm.
Radars: Air/surface search: Raytheon SPS 5; G/H band.
Navigation: Raytheon SPS 21; G/H band.
Fire control: Western Electric Mk 34; I/J band.
RCA/General Electric Mk 26; I/J band.
IFF: SLR 1.
Sonars: SQS 11; hull-mounted; active attack; high frequency.

Programmes: Transferred from US Navy to Royal Thai Navy at New York Navy Shipyard in July 1959 under MDAP and by sale 6 June 1975.
Modernisation: The three 21 in torpedo tubes were removed and the four 20 mm guns were replaced by four 40 mm. The six A/S torpedo tubes were fitted in 1966.
Operational: Used mostly as an alongside training ship.

PIN KLAO *3/1991, 92 Wing RAAF*

2 Ex-US TACOMA CLASS

Name	No	Builders	Laid down	Launched	Commissioned
TACHIN (ex-USS *Glendale* PF 36)	1	Consolidated Steel Corporation, Los Angeles	6 Apr 1943	28 May 1943	1 Oct 1943
PRASAE (ex-USS *Gallup* PF 47)	2	Consolidated Steel Corporation, Los Angeles	18 Aug 1943	17 Sep 1943	29 Feb 1944

Displacement, tons: 1430 standard; 2454 full load
Dimensions, feet (metres): 304 × 37.5 × 12.5 *(92.7 × 11.4 × 4.1)*
Main machinery: 2 boilers; 2 reciprocating engines; 5500 ihp *(4.1 MW)*; 2 shafts
Speed, knots: 18. **Range, miles:** 7200 at 12 kts; 5400 at 15 kts
Complement: 214 (13 officers)

Guns: 3 USN 3 in *(76 mm)*/50; 85° elevation; 20 rounds/minute to 12 km *(6.6 nm)*; weight of shell 6 kg.
2 Bofors 40 mm/60; 80° elevation; 120 rounds/minute to 10 km *(5.5 nm)*; weight of shell 0.89 kg.
9 Oerlikon 20 mm/70; 800 rounds/minute to 2 km.
Torpedoes: 6—324 mm US Mk 32 (2 triple) tubes; anti-submarine.
A/S mortars: 1 Mk 10 multi-barrelled fixed Hedgehog; range 350 m; warhead 26 kg; 24 rockets.
Depth charges: 8 projectors; 2 racks.
Radars: Air search: Westinghouse SPS 6; D band; range 146 km *(80 nm)* against fighter aircraft.
Surface search: Raytheon SPS 5 *(Tachin)*; G/H band. Raytheon SPS 10 *(Prasae)*; G/H band.
Navigation: Decca; I band.
Fire control: Mk 51; I/J band.
IFF: UPX 12B.
Sonars: EDO SQS 17B; hull-mounted; active search and attack; medium/high frequency.

PRASAE *1/1991, Royal Thai Navy*

Programmes: Delivered to the Royal Thai Navy on 29 October 1951. The last active survivors of the US equivalent of the British and Canadian River class.

Operational: Used in Training Squadron but one may have been transferred to Coastguard duties.

CORVETTES

3 KHAMRONSIN CLASS (ASW CORVETTES)

Name	No	Builders	Laid down	Launched	Commissioned
KHAMRONSIN	2	Ital Thai Marine, Bangkok	15 Mar 1988	15 Aug 1989	1992
THAYANCHON	3	Ital Thai Marine, Bangkok	20 Apr 1988	7 Dec 1989	1992
LONGLOM	1	Bangkok Naval Dockyard	15 Mar 1988	8 Aug 1989	1992

Displacement, tons: 475 half load
Dimensions, feet (metres): 203.4 oa; 186 wl × 26.9 × 8.2 *(62; 56.7 × 8.2 × 2.5)*
Main machinery: 2 MTU 12V 1163 TB 93; 9980 hp(m) *(7.34 MW)* sustained; 2 KaMeWa cp props
Speed, knots: 25. **Range, miles:** 2500 at 15 kts
Complement: 57 (6 officers)

Guns: 1 OTO Melara 76 mm/62 Mod 7; 85° elevation; 60 rounds/minute to 16 km *(8.7 nm)*; weight of shell 6 kg.
2 Breda 30 mm/70 (twin); 85° elevation; 800 rounds/minute to 12.5 km *(6.8 nm)*; weight of shell 0.37 kg.
Torpedoes: 6 Plessey PMW 49A (2 triple) launchers; MUSL Stingray; active/passive homing to 11 km *(6 nm)* at 45 kts; warhead 35 kg shaped charge.
Combat data systems: Plessey Nautis P action data automation.
Fire control: British Aerospace Sea Archer 1A Mod 2 optronic GFCS.
Radars: Air/surface search: Plessey AWS 4; E/F band; range 101 km *(55 nm)*.
Sonars: Krupp Atlas DSQS-21C; hull-mounted; active search and attack; medium/high frequency.

Programmes: Contract signed on 29 September 1987 with Ital Thai Marine of Bangkok for the construction of two ASW corvettes and for technical assistance with a third to be built in Bangkok Naval Dockyard. A fourth of the class with a different superstructure and less armament was ordered by the Police in September 1989.

LONGLOM *1991, Royal Thai Navy*

Structure: The vessels are based on a Vosper Thornycroft Province class 56 m design stretched by increasing the frame spacing along the whole length of the hull. Depth charge racks and mine rails may be added.

2 RATTANAKOSIN CLASS (MISSILE CORVETTES)

Name	*No*	*Builders*	*Laid down*	*Launched*	*Commissioned*
RATTANAKOSIN	1	Tacoma Boatbuilders, Washington	6 Feb 1984	11 Mar 1986	26 Sep 1986
SUKHOTHAI	2	Tacoma Boatbuilders, Washington	26 Mar 1984	20 July 1986	10 June 1987

Displacement, tons: 960 full load
Dimensions, feet (metres): 252 × 31.5 × 8 *(76.8 × 9.6 × 2.4)*
Main machinery: 2 MTU 20V1163 TB83 diesels; 14 730 hp(m) *(10.83 MW)* sustained; 2 shafts
Speed, knots: 26. **Range, miles:** 3000 at 16 kts
Complement: 87 (15 officers) plus Flag Staff

Missiles: SSM: 8 McDonnell Douglas Harpoon (2 quad) launchers ❶; active radar homing to 130 km *(70 nm)* at 0.9 Mach; warhead 227 kg (84A) or 258 kg (84B/C).
SAM: Selenia Elsag Albatros octuple launcher ❷; 24 Aspide; semi-active radar homing to 13 km *(7 nm)* at 2.5 Mach; height envelope 15-5000 m *(49.2-16 405 ft)*; warhead 30 kg.
Guns: 1 OTO Melara 3 in *(76 mm)*/62 ❸; 85° elevation; 60 rounds/minute to 16 km *(8.7 nm)*; weight of shell 6 kg.
2 Breda 40 mm/70 (twin) ❹; 85° elevation; 300 rounds/minute to 12.5 km *(6.8 nm)*; weight of shell 0.96 kg.
2 Oerlikon 20 mm ❺; 55° elevation; 800 rounds/minute to 2 km.
Torpedoes: 6—324 mm US Mk 32 (2 triple) tubes ❻. MUSL Stingray; active/passive homing to 11 km *(5.9 nm)* at 45 kts; warhead 35 kg (shaped charge); depth to 750 m *(2460 ft)*.
Countermeasures: Decoys: CSEE Dagaie 6 or 10-tubed trainable; IR flares and Chaff; H-J band.
ESM: Elettronica; intercept.
Fire control: Signaal Sewaco TH action data automation. Lirod 8 optronic director ❼.
Radars: Air/surface search: Signaal DA 05 ❽; E/F band; range 137 km *(75 nm)* for 2 m² target.
Surface search: Signaal ZW 06 ❾; I band.
Navigation: Decca 1226; I band.
Fire control: Signaal WM 25/41 ❿; I/J band; range 46 km *(25 nm)*.
Sonars: Krupp Atlas DSQS 21C; hull-mounted; active attack; high frequency.

Programmes: Contract signed with Tacoma on 9 May 1983. Intentions to build a third were overtaken by the Vosper corvettes. First laid down 6 February 1984, launched 11 March 1986; second laid down 26 March 1984, launched 20 July 1986.
Structure: Similar design to missile corvettes built for Saudi Arabia five years earlier. Space for Phalanx aft of the Harpoon launchers.

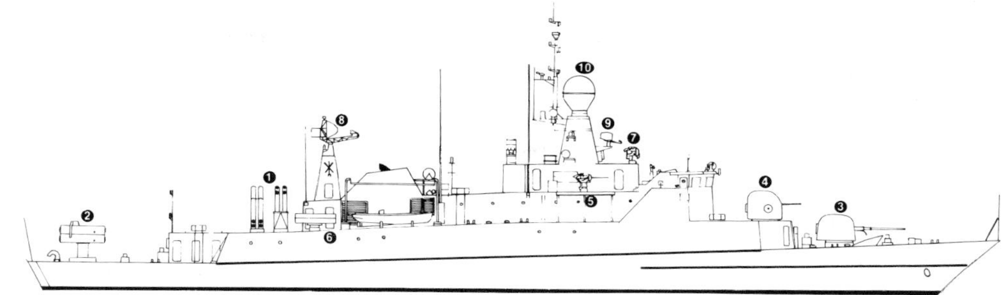

RATTANAKOSIN *(Scale 1 : 600), Ian Sturton*

SUKHOTHAI *1991, Royal Thai Navy*

SHIPBORNE AIRCRAFT

Note: Six Kamen Seasprite to be ordered. Reported that up to 9 Harbin Z-9A Haitun (Dauphin 2) may be acquired first.

Numbers/Type: 8 Bell 212.
Operational speed: 100 kts *(185 km/h)*.
Service ceiling: 13 200 ft *(4025 m)*.
Range: 200 nm *(370 km)*.
Role/Weapon systems: Commando assault and general support, based ashore but operate from Normed class. Weapons: Pintle-mounted M60 machine guns.

LAND-BASED MARITIME AIRCRAFT (FRONT LINE)

Note: Three P-3B Orion (with Harpoon) may be acquired in 1992. There are also plans for up to 30 A7-E Corsair aircraft to be delivered from the US Navy starting in late 1992.

Numbers/Type: 5 Bell 214ST.
Operational speed: 130 kts *(241 km/h)*.
Service ceiling: 10 000 ft *(3050 m)*.
Range: 450 nm *(834 km)*.
Role/Weapon systems: VIP and general support duties. Weapons: Pintle-mounted M60 machine guns.

Numbers/Type: 3/2 Fokker F27 Maritime 200/400.
Operational speed: 250 kts *(463 km/h)*.
Service ceiling: 2500 ft *(7620 m)*.
Range: 2700 nm *(5000 km)*.
Role/Weapon systems: Increased coastal surveillance and response is provided, including ASW and ASV action. Sensors: APS-504 search radar, Bendix weather radar, ESM and MAD equipment. Weapons: ASW; 4 × Mk 46 or Stingray torpedoes or depth bombs or mines. ASV; 2 × Harpoon ASM.

Numbers/Type: 5 GAF Searchmaster B (Nomad).
Operational speed: 168 kts *(311 km/h)*.
Service ceiling: 21 000 ft *(6400 m)*.
Range: 730 nm *(1352 km)*.
Role/Weapon systems: Short-range MR for EEZ protection and anti-smuggling operations. Sensors: Search radar, cameras. Weapons: Unarmed.

Numbers/Type: 9 Grumman S-2F Tracker.
Operational speed: 130 kts *(241 km/h)*.
Service ceiling: 25 000 ft *(7620 m)*.
Range: 1350 nm *(2500 km)*.
Role/Weapon systems: MR and ASW operations, with limited ASV capability; now being supplemented by F27. Turbo conversion being considered but is unlikely because of airframe condition. Sensors: Search radar, ESM, MAD. Weapons: ASW; 4 × Mk 46 torpedoes, depth bombs, mines. ASV; 6 × 127 mm rockets.

Numbers/Type: 3 Dornier 228.
Operational speed: 200 kts *(370 km/h)*.
Service ceiling: 28 000 ft *(8535 m)*.
Range: 940 nm *(1740 km)*.
Role/Weapon systems: Coastal surveillance and EEZ protection. Acquired in 1991.

LIGHT FORCES

Note: In 1992 there is a total of 151 small patrol boats belonging to the Naval Riverine Squadron.

3 RATCHARIT CLASS (FAST ATTACK CRAFT—MISSILE)

Name	*No*	*Builders*	*Commissioned*
RATCHARIT	4	C N Breda (Venezia)	10 Aug 1979
WITTHAYAKHOM	5	C N Breda (Venezia)	12 Nov 1979
UDOMDET	6	C N Breda (Venezia)	21 Feb 1980

Displacement, tons: 235 standard; 270 full load
Dimensions, feet (metres): 163.4 × 24.6 × 7.5 *(49.8 × 7.5 × 2.3)*
Main machinery: 3 MTU MD20 V538 TB91 diesels; 11 520 hp(m) *(8.47 MW)* sustained; 3 shafts
Speed, knots: 37. **Range, miles:** 2000 at 15 kts
Complement: 45 (7 officers)

Missiles: SSM: 4 Aerospatiale MM 38 Exocet; inertial cruise; active radar homing to 42 km *(23 nm)* at 0.9 Mach; warhead 165 kg; sea-skimmer.
Guns: 1 OTO Melara 3 in *(76 mm)*/62 compact; 85° elevation; 85 rounds/minute to 16 km *(8.7 nm)* anti-surface; 12 km *(6.6 nm)* anti-aircraft; weight of shell 6 kg.
1 Bofors 40 mm/70; 85° elevation; 300 rounds/minute to 12.5 km *(6.8 nm)*; weight of shell 0.96 kg.
Countermeasures: ESM: Radar warning.
Radars: Surface search: Decca; I band.
Fire control: Signaal WM 25; I/J band; range 46 km *(25 nm)*.

Programmes: Ordered June 1976. *Ratcharit* launched 30 July 1978, *Witthayakhom* 2 September 1978 and *Udomdet* 28 September 1978.
Structure: Standard Breda BMB 230 design.

WITTHAYAKHOM *1/1991*

3 PRABPARAPAK CLASS (FAST ATTACK CRAFT—MISSILE)

Name	No	Builders	Commissioned
PRABPARAPAK	1	Singapore SBEC	28 July 1976
HANHAK SATTRU	2	Singapore SBEC	6 Nov 1976
SUPHAIRIN	3	Singapore SBEC	1 Feb 1977

Displacement, tons: 224 standard; 268 full load
Dimensions, feet (metres): 149 × 24.3 × 7.5 *(45.4 × 7.4 × 2.3)*
Main machinery: 4 MTU 16V 538 TB92 diesels; 13 640 hp(m) *(10 MW)* sustained; 4 shafts
Speed, knots: 40. **Range, miles:** 2000 at 15 kts; 750 at 37 kts
Complement: 41 (5 officers)

Missiles: SSM: 5 IAI Gabriel I (1 triple, 2 single) launchers; radar or optical guidance; semi-active radar homing to 20 km *(10.8 nm)* at 0.7 Mach; warhead 75 kg.
Guns: 1 Bofors 57 mm/70; 75° elevation; 200 rounds/minute to 17 km *(9.3 nm)*; weight of shell 2.4 kg. 8 rocket illuminant launchers on either side of 57 mm gun.
1 Bofors 40 mm/70; 90° elevation; 300 rounds/minute to 12 km *(6.6 nm)*; weight of shell 2.4 kg.
Countermeasures: ESM: Radar intercept.
Radars: Surface search: Kelvin Hughes Type 17; I band.
Fire control: Signaal WM 28/5 series; I/J band.

Programmes: Ordered June 1973. Built under licence from Lürssen. Launch dates—*Prabparapak* 29 July 1975, *Hanhak Sattru* 28 October 1975, *Suphairin* 20 February 1976.
Structure: Same design as Lürssen standard 45 m class built for Singapore.

PRABPARAPAK *1/1991, Royal Thai Navy*

SUPHAIRIN *9/1991, Royal Thai Navy*

3 CHON BURI CLASS (FAST ATTACK CRAFT—GUN)

Name	No	Builders	Commissioned
CHON BURI	1	C N Breda (Venezia) Mestre	22 Feb 1983
SONGKHLA	2	C N Breda (Venezia) Mestre	15 July 1983
PHUKET	3	C N Breda (Venezia) Mestre	13 Jan 1984

Displacement, tons: 450 full load
Dimensions, feet (metres): 198 × 29 × 15 *(60.4 × 8.8 × 4.5)*
Main machinery: 3 MTU 20V 538 TB92 diesels; 12 795 hp(m) *(9.4 MW)* sustained; 3 shafts; cp props
Speed, knots: 30. **Range, miles:** 2500 at 18 kts; 900 at 30 kts
Complement: 41 (6 officers)
Guns: 2 OTO Melara 3 in *(76 mm)*/62. 2 Breda 40 mm/70 (twin).
Countermeasures: Decoys: 4 Hycor Mk 135 Chaff launchers.
ESM: Radar intercept.
Fire control: Lirod 8 optronic director.
Radars: Surface search: Signaal ZW 06; I band.
Fire control: Signaal WM 22/61; I/J band; range 46 km *(25 nm)*.

Comment: Ordered in 1979 (first pair) and 1981. Laid down—*Chon Buri* 15 August 1981 (launched 29 November 1982), *Songkhla* 15 September 1981, *Phuket* 15 December 1981 (launched 3 February 1983). Steel hulls, alloy superstructure. Can be adapted to carry surface-to-surface missiles.

CHON BURI *1/1991*

6 SATTAHIP CLASS (LARGE PATROL CRAFT)

Name	No	Builders	Commissioned
SATTAHIP	4	Ital Thai (Samutprakarn) Ltd	16 Sep 1983
KLONGYAI	5	Ital Thai (Samutprakarn) Ltd	7 May 1984
TAKBAI	6	Ital Thai (Samutprakarn) Ltd	18 July 1984
KANTANG	7	Ital Thai (Samutprakarn) Ltd	14 Oct 1985
THEPHA	8	Ital Thai (Samutprakarn) Ltd	17 Apr 1986
TAIMUANG	9	Ital Thai (Samutprakarn) Ltd	17 Apr 1986

Displacement, tons: 270 standard; 300 full load
Dimensions, feet (metres): 164.5 × 23.9 × 5.9 *(50.1 × 7.3 × 1.8)*
Main machinery: 2 MTU 16V 538 TB92 diesels; 6820 hp(m) *(5 MW)* sustained; 2 shafts
Speed, knots: 22. **Range, miles:** 2500 at 15 kts
Complement: 56
Guns: 1 USN 3 in *(76 mm)*/50 Mk 26 (in 3 of the class). 1 OTO Melara 3 in *(76 mm)*/62 (in 3 of the class). 1 Bofors 40 mm/70. 2 Oerlikon 20 mm. 2—12.7 mm MGs.
Fire control: NA 18 optronic director (in 3 ships).
Radars: Surface search: Decca; I band.

Comment: First four ordered 9 September 1981, *Thepha* on 27 December 1983 and *Taimuang* on 31 August 1984.

TAKBAI *1/1991, Royal Thai Navy*

5 Ex-US PC 461 CLASS (LARGE PATROL CRAFT)

SARASIN (ex-PC *495*) PC 1
PHALI (ex-PC *1185*) PC 4
SUKRIP (ex-PC *1218*) PC 5
TONGPLIU (ex-PC *616*) PC 6
LIULOM (ex-PC *1253*) PC 7

Displacement, tons: 280 standard; 450 full load
Dimensions, feet (metres): 173.7 × 23 × 8.9 *(52.9 × 7 × 2.7)*
Main machinery: 2 diesels; 2880 hp *(2.15 MW) (Tongpliu* and *Liulom)*, 2560 hp *(1.91 MW)* (remainder); 2 shafts
Speed, knots: 20. **Range, miles:** 5000 at 10 kts
Complement: 62-71
Guns: 1 USN 3 in *(76 mm)*/50. 1 Bofors 40 mm/60. 5 Oerlikon 20 mm.
Torpedoes: 2—324 mm US Mk 32 tubes (except *Sarasin*); anti-submarine.

Comment: Launched in 1941-43 as US PCs. All transferred between March 1947 and December 1952. Two may be in reserve.

SUKRIP *8/1991*

10 Ex-US PGM 71 CLASS (LARGE PATROL CRAFT)

T 11-19 **T 110**

Displacement, tons: 130 standard; 147 full load
Dimensions, feet (metres): 101 × 21 × 6 *(30.8 × 6.4 × 1.9)*
Main machinery: 2 GM diesels; 1800 hp *(1.34 MW)*; 2 shafts
Speed, knots: 18.5. **Range, miles:** 1500 at 10 kts
Complement: 30
Guns: 1 Bofors 40 mm/60. 1 Oerlikon 20 mm. 2—12.7 mm MGs.
In some craft the 20 mm gun has been replaced by an 81 mm mortar/12.7 mm combined mounting aft.

Comment: Built by Peterson Inc between 1966 and 1970. Deleted in error in 1990.

T 14 *1980, Royal Thai Navy*

9 T 91 CLASS (COASTAL PATROL CRAFT)

T 91-99

Displacement, tons: 87.5 (T 91), 130 (remainder) standard
Dimensions, feet (metres): 104.3 × 17.5 × 5.5 *(31.8 × 5.3 × 1.7)* (T 91)
118 × 18.7 × 4.9 *(36 × 5.7 × 1.5)* (remainder)
Main machinery: 2 MTU 12V 538 TB 81/82 diesels; 3300 hp(m) *(2.43 MW)*/4430 hp(m) *(3.26 MW)* sustained; 2 shafts
Speed, knots: 25. **Range, miles:** 700 at 21 kts
Complement: 21; 23 (T 93-94); 25 (T 99)
Guns: 2 Bofors 40 mm/60. 1—12.7 mm MG (see *Comment*).
Fire control: Sea Archer 1A optronic director (T 99 only).

Comment: Built by Royal Thai Naval Dockyard, Bangkok. T 91 commissioned in 1965; T 92-93 in 1973; T 94-98 between 1981 and 1984; T 99 in 1987. T 91 has an extended upperworks and a 20 mm gun in place of the after 40 mm. T 99 has a single Bofors 40/70, one Oerlikon 20 mm and two MGs. There may be other armament variations in the group T 94-98. Major refits from 1983-86 for earlier vessels of the class.

T 97 — *5/1991, Royal Thai Navy*

12 Ex-US SWIFT CLASS (COASTAL PATROL CRAFT)

T 21-29 T 210-212

Displacement, tons: 20 standard; 22 full load
Dimensions, feet (metres): 50 × 13 × 3.5 *(15.2 × 4 × 1.1)*
Main machinery: 2 diesels; 480 hp *(358 kW)*; 2 shafts
Speed, knots: 25
Complement: 5
Guns: 2—81 mm mortars. 2—12.7 mm MGs.

Comment: Transferred from US Navy from 1967 to 1975.

T 27 — *10/1989, S. Tabusa*

14 T 213 CLASS (COASTAL PATROL CRAFT)

T 213-226 T 227-230

Displacement, tons: 35 standard
Dimensions, feet (metres): 64 × 17.5 × 5 *(19.5 × 5.3 × 1.5)*
Main machinery: 2 MTU diesels; 715 hp(m) *(526 kW)*; 2 shafts
Speed, knots: 25
Complement: 8
Guns: 1 Oerlikon 20 mm. 1—81 mm mortar with 12.7 mm MG.

Comment: Built by Ital Thai Marine Ltd. Commissioned—T 213-215, 29 August 1980; T 216-218, 26 March 1981; T 219-223, 16 September 1981; T 224, 19 November 1982; T 225 and T 226, 28 March 1984; T 227-230 in 1990/91. Of alloy construction. Used for fishery patrol and coastal control duties.

T 220, 221 — *1983, Royal Thai Navy*

37 Ex-US PBR Mk II (RIVER PATROL CRAFT)

11-19, 110-132 +5

Displacement, tons: 8 full load
Dimensions, feet (metres): 32.1 × 11.5 × 2.3 *(9.8 × 3.5 × 0.7)*
Main machinery: 2 Detroit diesels; 430 hp *(321 kW)*; 2 Jacuzzi waterjets
Speed, knots: 25. **Range, miles:** 150 at 23 kts
Complement: 4
Guns: 2—12.7 mm (twin) MGs. 2—6.72 mm MGs. 1—60 mm mortar.

Comment: Transferred from 1967-73. Employed on Mekong River. Reported to be getting old and maximum speed has been virtually halved. All belong to the Riverine Squadron.

PBR Mk II — *1991, Royal Thai Navy*

1 HYSUCAT 18 HYDROFOIL (RIVER PATROL CRAFT)

T 231

Displacement, tons: 39
Dimensions, feet (metres): 60 × 21.6 (hull) × 5.9 *(18.3 × 6.6 × 1.6)*
Main machinery: 2 MWM Type diesels; 1640 hp(m) *(1.2 MW)*; 2 shafts
Speed, knots: 36
Complement: 10
Guns: 1 Oerlikon 20 mm.

Comment: Designed by Technautic in association with Lürssen. Ordered in 1984 and started trials in December 1986. GRP hull for hydrofoil-supported catamarans. Reported that the Thai Navy was not happy with the trials results and the plan for a class of 12 was cancelled. Gatling gun replaced in 1988 and the associated fire control equipment removed.

HYSUCAT 231 — *11/1988, Trevor Brown*

3 Ex-US RPC CLASS (RIVER PATROL CRAFT)

Displacement, tons: 13 full load
Dimensions, feet (metres): 35.8 × 10.5 × 3.3 *(10.9 × 3.2 × 1)*
Main machinery: 2 Gray diesels; 450 hp *(335 kW)*; 2 shafts
Speed, knots: 14
Complement: 6
Guns: 4—12.7 mm MGs.

Comment: Transferred in 1967. Employed on Mekong River.

RPC Class — *1989*

100 + ASSAULT BOATS (AB)

Displacement, tons: 0.4 full load
Dimensions, feet (metres): 16.4 × 6.2 × 1.3 *(5 × 1.9 × 0.4)*
Speed, knots: 24
Guns: 1—7.62 mm MG.

Comment: Part of the Riverine Squadron with the PBRs and 2 PCFs.

ASSAULT BOAT — *1991, Royal Thai Navy*

MINE WARFARE FORCES

Note: Purchase of further Lürssen types is uncertain because of cost and reported problems with the minehunting system. Acquisition of inshore minehunters is being considered; possibly eight Chinese Type 312 drones which can be controlled from shore.

1 MCM SUPPORT SHIP

Name	*No*	*Builders*	*Commissioned*
THALANG	1	Bangkok Dock Co Ltd	4 Aug 1980

Displacement, tons: 1000 standard
Dimensions, feet (metres): 185.5 × 33 × 10 *(55.7 × 10 × 3.1)*
Main machinery: 2 MTU diesels; 1310 hp(m) *(963 kW)*; 2 shafts
Speed, knots: 12
Complement: 77
Guns: 1 Bofors 40 mm/70. 2 Oerlikon 20 mm. 2—12.7 mm MGs.
Radars: Surface search: Racal Decca 1226; I band.

Comment: Has minesweeping capability. Two 3 ton cranes provided for change of minesweeping gear in MSCs—four sets carried. Design by Ferrostaal, Essen.

THALANG *1981, Royal Thai Navy*

2 BANG RACHAN CLASS (MINEHUNTERS/SWEEPERS)

Name	*No*	*Builders*	*Commissioned*
BANG RACHAN	2	Lürssen Vegesack	29 Apr 1987
NONGSARAI	3	Lürssen Vegesack	17 Nov 1987

Displacement, tons: 444 full load
Dimensions, feet (metres): 161.1 × 30.5 × 8.2 *(49.1 × 9.3 × 2.5)*
Main machinery: 2 MTU 12V 396 TB 83 diesels; 3120 hp(m) *(2.3 MW)* sustained; 2 shafts; KaMeWa cp props
Auxiliary propulsion; 1 motor
Speed, knots: 17; 7 (electric motor). **Range, miles:** 3100 at 12 kts
Complement: 30
Guns: 3 Oerlikon GAM-BO1 20 mm.
Countermeasures: MCM: MWS 80R minehunting system. Acoustic, magnetic and mechanical sweeps.
2 Gaymarine Pluto 15 remote controlled submersibles.
Radars: Navigation: 2 Krupp Atlas 8600 ARPA; I band.
Sonars: Krupp Atlas DSQS-11H or 11M; hull-mounted; minehunting; high frequency.

Comment: First ordered from Lürssen late 1984, arrived Bangkok 22 October 1987. Second ordered 5 August 1985 and arrived in Bangkok May 1988. Option on four more. There have been reports of problems with the minehunting systems and the 11H sonar may be replaced by 11M. Amagnetic steel frames and deckhouses, wooden hull. Motorola Miniranger MRS III precise navigation system. Draeger decompression chamber.

NONGSARAI *1/1991*

5 Ex-US MSBs

MLMS 6-10

Displacement, tons: 25 full load
Dimensions, feet (metres): 50.2 × 13.1 × 3 *(15.3 × 4 × 0.9)*
Main machinery: 1 Gray Marine 64 HN9 diesel; 165 hp *(123 kW)*; 1 shaft
Speed, knots: 8
Complement: 10
Guns: 2—7.62 mm MGs.

Comment: Three transferred in October 1963 and two in 1964. Wooden hulled, converted from small motor launches. Operated on Chao Phraya river.

4 US BLUEBIRD CLASS (MINESWEEPERS—COASTAL)

Name	*No*	*Builders*	*Commissioned*
LADYA (ex-US *MSC 297*)	5	Peterson Builders Inc, Sturgeon Bay, Wisconsin	14 Dec 1963
BANGKEO (ex-US *MSC 303*)	6	Dorchester S B Corporation, Camden	9 July 1965
TADINDENG (ex-US *MSC 301*)	7	Tacoma Boatbuilding Co, Tacoma, Washington	26 Aug 1965
DONCHEDI (ex-US *MSC 313*)	8	Peterson Builders Inc, Sturgeon Bay, Wisconsin	17 Sep 1965

Displacement, tons: 317 standard; 384 full load
Dimensions, feet (metres): 145.3 × 27 × 8.5 *(44.3 × 8.2 × 2.6)*
Main machinery: 4 GM 12-278 diesels; 4400 hp *(3.28 MW)*; 2 shafts
Speed, knots: 13. **Range, miles:** 2750 at 12 kts
Complement: 43 (7 officers)
Guns: 2 Oerlikon 20 mm/80 (twin).
Countermeasures: MCM: US Mk 4 (V). Mk 6. US Type Q2 magnetic.
Radars: Navigation: Decca TM 707; I band.
IFF: UPX 5 *(Ladya)*. UPX 12 (rest).
Sonars: UQS 1; hull-mounted; minehunting; high frequency.

Comment: Constructed for Thailand. *Ladya, Bangkeo* and *Tadindeng* in reserve for a time but all are now in limited operational service.

DONCHEDI *1/1991*

AMPHIBIOUS FORCES

0 + (1) HELICOPTER SUPPORT SHIP

Displacement, tons: 9500 full load (minimum)
Dimensions, feet (metres): 557.7 × 85.3 × 24.6 *(170 × 26 × 7.5)*
Main machinery: CODOG; 2 LM 2500 gas turbines; 2 MTU 16V 1163 TB 83 diesels; 2 shafts
Speed, knots: 26; 16 (diesels). **Range, miles:** 10 000 at 12 kts
Complement: 455 (62 officers) including air crew; plus 4 (Royal family)
Guns: 4 CIWS. 2—30 mm.
Countermeasures: Decoys: 4 Chaff launchers.
Helicopters: 10 Sea King size.

Comment: Bremer Vulcan contract for a 7800 ton ship was cancelled on 22 July 1991 because of doubts about costs and delays in obtaining German Government approval. Negotiations had already started with Bazán in February 1991 and they must be the favourite alternative shipbuilder. Invitations to tender issued 30 December 1991, with a decision expected in late 1992. Details include five landing spots, a future complement of 600 with a fixed wing Air Group and accommodation for a Flag Officer and four members of the Royal family.

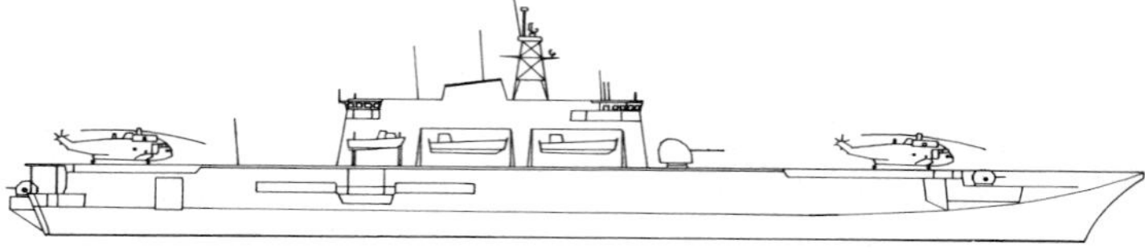

HELICOPTER SUPPORT SHIP *(not to scale), Ian Sturton*

2 NORMED CLASS (LSTs)

Name	*No*	*Builders*	*Commissioned*
SICHANG	LST 6	Ital Thai	9 Oct 1987
SURIN	LST 7	Bangkok Dock Co	16 Dec 1988

Displacement, tons: 3540 standard; 4235 full load
Dimensions, feet (metres): 337.8 × 51.5 × 11.5 *(103 × 15.7 × 3.5)*
Main machinery: 2 MTU 20V 1163 TB 82 diesels; 11 000 hp(m) *(8.1 MW)* sustained; 2 shafts
Speed, knots: 16. **Range, miles:** 7000 at 12 kts
Complement: 129
Military lift: 348 troops; 14 tanks or 12 APCs or 850 tons cargo; 3 LCVP; 1 LCPL
Guns: 1 Bofors 40 mm/70. 2 Oerlikon GAM-CO1 20 mm. 2—12.7 mm MGs. 1—81 mm mortar.
Fire control: 2 Sea Archer Mk 1A optronic directors.
Radars: Navigation: Decca; I band.
Helicopters: Platform for 2 Bell 212.

Comment: First ordered 31 August 1984 to a Chantier du Nord (Normed) design. Second ordered from Bangkok Dock Co Ltd, to a modified design (possibly 31.2 ft *(9.5 m)* longer and with MWM diesels). The largest naval ships yet built in Thailand. First launched in April 1987, second in early 1988. Have bow doors and a 17 m ramp.

SICHANG *1/1991*

4 Ex-US 511-1152 CLASS (LSTs)

Name	No	Builders	Commissioned
CHANG (ex-USS *Lincoln County* LST 898)	LST 2	Dravo Corporation	29 Dec 1944
PANGAN (ex-USS *Stark County* LST 1134)	LST 3	Chicago Bridge and Iron Co, Ill.	7 Apr 1945
LANTA (ex-USS *Stone County* LST 1141)	LST 4	Chicago Bridge and Iron Co, Ill.	9 May 1945
PRATHONG (ex-USS *Dodge County* LST 722)	LST 5	Jefferson B & M Co, Ind.	13 Sep 1944

Displacement, tons: 1650 standard; 3640/4145 full load
Dimensions, feet (metres): 328 × 50 × 14 *(100 × 15.2 × 4.4)*
Main machinery: 2 GM 12-567A diesels; 1800 hp *(1.34 MW)*; 2 shafts
Speed, knots: 11.5. **Range, miles:** 9500 at 9 kts
Complement: 80; 157 (war)
Military lift: 1230 tons max; 815 tons beaching
Guns: 8 Bofors 40 mm/60 (2 twin, 4 single). 2—12.7 mm MGs *(Chang)*. 2 Oerlikon 20 mm/80 (others).
Fire control: 2 Mk 51 GFCS. 2 optical systems.
Radars: Surface search: Raytheon SPS 10 *(Pangan)*; G band.
Navigation: Raytheon; I/J band.

Comment: *Chang,* transferred to Thailand in August 1962. *Pangan* was transferred on 16 May 1966, *Lanta* on 15 August 1973 (by sale 1 March 1979) and *Prathong* on 17 December 1975. *Chang* has a reinforced bow and waterline. *Lanta, Prathong* and *Chang* have mobile crane on well deck. All have tripod mast.

PRATHONG 1/1991

2 Ex-US LSM 1 CLASS

Name	No	Builders	Commissioned
KUT (ex-USS *LSM 338*)	LSM 1	Pullman Std Car Co, Chicago	10 Jan 1945
KRAM (ex-USS *LSM 469*)	LSM 3	Brown S B Co, Houston, Texas	17 Mar 1945

Displacement, tons: 743 standard; 1107 full load
Dimensions, feet (metres): 203.5 × 34.5 × 9.9 *(62 × 10.5 × 3)*
Main machinery: 2 Fairbanks-Morse 38D8-1/8-10 diesels; 3540 hp *(2.64 MW)*; 2 shafts
Speed, knots: 12.5. **Range, miles:** 4500 at 12.5 kts
Complement: 91 (6 officers)
Military lift: 452 tons beaching; 50 troops with vehicles
Guns: 2 Bofors 40 mm/60 Mk 3 (twin). 4 Oerlikon 20 mm/70.
Fire control: Mk 51 Mod 2 optical director *(Kram)*.
Radars: Surface search: Raytheon SPS 5 *(Kram)*; G/H band.
Navigation: Raytheon 1500 B; I band.

Comment: Former US landing ships of the LCM, later LSM (Medium Landing Ship) type. *Kram* was transferred to Thailand under MAP at Seattle, Washington, on 25 May 1962, *Kut* in October 1946. One deleted in 1990.

KUT 1/1991

2 Ex-US LSIL 351 CLASS

PRAB LSIL 1
SATAKUT (ex-*LSIL 739*) LSIL 2

Displacement, tons: 230 standard; 399 full load
Dimensions, feet (metres): 157 × 23 × 6 *(47.9 × 7 × 1.8)*
Main machinery: 4 General Motors 6051-71 diesels; 2320 bhp; 2 shafts
Speed, knots: 15. **Range, miles:** 5600 at 12.5 kts
Complement: 49 (7 officers)
Military lift: 101 tons or 76 troops
Guns: 1 Bofors 40 mm/60. 4 Oerlikon 20 mm/70.

Comment: Built in 1944-45—transferred May 1947. *Prab* has been refitted and is back in commission.

PRAB 8/1991

1 Ex-US LCG TYPE

NAKHA (ex-USS *LSSL 102*) LSSL 3

Displacement, tons: 233 standard; 393 full load
Dimensions, feet (metres): 158.1 × 23.6 × 6.2 *(48.2 × 7.2 × 1.9)*
Main machinery: 2 GM diesels; 1320 hp *(985 kW)*; 2 shafts
Speed, knots: 15. **Range, miles:** 5000 at 6 kts
Complement: 60
Guns: 1 USN 3 in *(76 mm)*/50. 4 Bofors 40 mm/60 (2 twin). 4 Oerlikon 20 mm/70 (2 twin). 6—81 mm mortars. 2—12.7 mm MGs.
Radars: Navigation: Raytheon 1500 B; I band.

Comment: Built by Commercial Ironworks, Oregon in 1945. Transferred in 1966. Acquired when Japan returned her to the USA.

NAKHA

4 THONG KAEO CLASS (LCUs)

Name	No	Builders	Commissioned
THONG KAEO	7	Bangkok Dock Co Ltd	23 Dec 1982
THONG LANG	8	Bangkok Dock Co Ltd	19 Apr 1983
WANG NOK	9	Bangkok Dock Co Ltd	16 Sep 1983
WANG NAI	10	Bangkok Dock Co Ltd	11 Nov 1983

Displacement, tons: 193 standard; 396 full load
Dimensions, feet (metres): 134.5 × 29.5 × 6.9 *(41 × 9 × 2.1)*
Main machinery: 2 GM 16V-71N diesels; 1400 hp *(1.04 MW)*; 2 shafts
Speed, knots: 10. **Range, miles:** 1200 at 10 kts
Complement: 31 (3 officers)
Military lift: 3 lorries; 150 tons equipment
Guns: 2 Oerlikon 20 mm. 2—7.62 mm MGs.

Comment: Ordered in 1980. A fifth ship of the class was abandoned.

WANG NOK 1/1991, Royal Thai Navy

3 GRIFFON 1000 TD HOVERCRAFT

Dimensions, feet (metres): 27.6 × 12.5 *(8.4 × 3.8)*
Main machinery: 1 Deutz BF 6L913C diesel; 190 hp(m) *(140 kW)*
Speed, knots: 33. **Range, miles:** 200 at 27 kts
Cargo capacity: 1000 kg plus 9 troops

Comment: Acquired in mid-1990 from Griffon Hovercraft. Although having an obvious amphibious capability they are also to be used for rescue and flood control.

GRIFFON HOVERCRAFT 1990, Griffon

5 Ex-US 501 CLASS (LCUs)

MATAPHON LCU 1
RAWI LCU 2
ADANG LCU 3
PHETRA LCU 4
TALIBONG LCU 6

Displacement, tons: 145 standard; 330 full load
Dimensions, feet (metres): 120.4 × 32 × 4 *(36.7 × 9.8 × 1.2)*
Main machinery: 3 Gray Marine 65 diesels; 675 hp *(503 kW)*; 3 shafts
Speed, knots: 10. **Range, miles:** 650 at 8 kts
Complement: 13
Military lift: 150 tons or 3-4 tanks or 250 troops
Guns: 2 Oerlikon 20 mm/80.

Comment: Transferred 1946-47. Employed as transport ferries.

TALIBONG *8/1991*

24 Ex-US LCM 6

14-16, 61-68, 71-78, 81-82, 85-87

Displacement, tons: 56 full load
Main machinery: 2 Gray Marine 64HN 9 diesels; 330 hp *(264 kW)*; 2 shafts
Speed, knots: 9
Complement: 5
Military lift: 34 tons

Comment: First 21 delivered 1965-69.

12 Ex-US LCVP

L 51-59, 510-512

Displacement, tons: 12
Main machinery: 1 diesel; 225 hp *(168 kW)*; 1 shaft
Speed, knots: 9
Military lift: 40 troops

Comment: Six transferred in 1953, remainder in 1963.

4 LCAs

L 40-43

Displacement, tons: 10 full load
Dimensions, feet (metres): 39.4 × 9.8 × 3.3 *(12 × 3 × 1)*
Main machinery: 2 Chrysler diesels; 2 Castoldi Mod 06 waterjets
Speed, knots: 25
Military lift: 35 troops

Comment: Built in Thailand in 1984. Fibreglass hull with bow ramp.

TRAINING SHIPS

1 Ex-BRITISH ALGERINE CLASS

Name	*No*	*Builders*	*Commissioned*
PHOSAMTON (ex-HMS *Minstrel*)	MSF 1	Redfern Construction Co	1945

Displacement, tons: 1040 standard; 1335 full load
Dimensions, feet (metres): 225 × 35.5 × 11.5 *(68.6 × 10.8 × 3.5)*
Main machinery: 2 boilers; 2 reciprocating engines; 2000 ihp *(1.49 MW)*; 2 shafts
Speed, knots: 16. **Range, miles:** 4000 at 10 kts
Complement: 103
Guns: 1 Vickers 4 in *(102 mm)*/45. 1 Bofors 40 mm/60. 2 Oerlikon 20 mm.
Radars: Navigation: Decca; I band.

Comment: Transferred in April 1947. Received engineering overhaul in 1984. Minesweeping gear replaced by a deckhouse to increase training space.

PHOSAMTON *1/1991, Royal Thai Navy*

Name	*No*	*Builders*	*Commissioned*
MAEKLONG	3	Uraga Dock Co, Japan	June 1937

Displacement, tons: 1400 standard; 2000 full load
Dimensions, feet (metres): 269 × 34 × 10.5 *(82 × 10.4 × 3.2)*
Main machinery: 2 boilers; 2 reciprocating engines; 2500 ihp *(1.87 MW)*; 2 shafts
Speed, knots: 14. **Range, miles:** 8000 at 12 kts
Complement: 155 as training ship
Guns: 4 USN 3 in *(76 mm)*/50. 3 Bofors 40 mm/60. 3 Oerlikon 20 mm.

Comment: The four 18 in torpedo tubes were removed to provide more training space.

MAEKLONG *3/1991, 92 Wing RAAF*

OCEANOGRAPHIC AND SURVEY SHIPS

Note: There is also a civilian research vessel *Chulab Horn* which completed in 1986.

Name	*No*	*Builders*	*Commissioned*
SUK	—	Bangkok Dock Co Ltd	3 Mar 1982

Displacement, tons: 1450 standard; 1526 full load
Dimensions, feet (metres): 206.3 × 36.1 × 13.4 *(62.9 × 11 × 4.1)*
Main machinery: 2 MTU diesels; 2400 hp(m) *(1.76 MW)*; 2 shafts
Speed, knots: 15
Complement: 86 (20 officers)
Guns: 2 Oerlikon 20 mm. 2—7.62 mm MGs.

Comment: Laid down 27 August 1979, launched 8 September 1981. Designed for oceanographic and survey duties.

SUK *5/1988, van Ginderen Collection*

Name	*No*	*Builders*	*Commissioned*
CHANTHARA	AGS 11	Lürssen Werft	1961

Displacement, tons: 870 standard; 996 full load
Dimensions, feet (metres): 229.2 × 34.5 × 10 *(69.9 × 10.5 × 3)*
Main machinery: 2 Klöckner-Humboldt-Deutz diesels; 1090 hp(m) *(801 kW)*; 2 shafts
Speed, knots: 13.25. **Range, miles:** 10 000 at 10 kts
Complement: 68 (8 officers)
Guns: 1 Bofors 40 mm/60. 1 Oerlikon 20 mm.

Comment: Laid down on 27 September 1960. Launched on 17 December 1960.

CHANTHARA *1/1991*

Name	*No*	*Builders*	*Commissioned*
SURIYA	—	Bangkok Dock Co Ltd	14 May 1979

Displacement, tons: 690 full load
Dimensions, feet (metres): 177.8 × 33.5 × 10.2 *(54.2 × 10.2 × 3.1)*
Main machinery: 2 MTU diesels; 1310 hp(m) *(963 kW)*; 2 shafts; bow thruster; 135 hp(m) *(99 kW)*
Speed, knots: 12
Complement: 60 (12 officers)
Guns: 2 Oerlikon 20 mm.

Comment: Mostly used to service navigational aids.

SURIYA *5/1990, 92 Wing RAAF*

2 OCEANOGRAPHIC VESSELS

II **III**

Displacement, tons: 90 full load
Dimensions, feet (metres): 91.9 × 18 × 4.9 *(28 × 5.5 × 1.5)*
Main machinery: 1 diesel; 1 shaft
Speed, knots: 12
Complement: 11 (2 officers)

Comment: *II* launched in 1955 by Lürssen, Vegesack and *III* in 1972.

SERVICE FORCES

3 HARBOUR TANKERS

PROET YO 9 **CHIK** YO 10 **SAMED** YO 11

Displacement, tons: 360 standard; 485 full load
Dimensions, feet (metres): 122.7 × 19.7 × 8.7 *(37.4 × 6 × 2.7)*
Main machinery: 1 diesel; 500 hp(m) *(368 kW)*; 1 shaft
Speed, knots: 9
Cargo capacity: 210 tons

Comment: Built by Bangkok Naval Dockyard in 1970. All three vessels are identical.

PROET *8/1991*

1 HARBOUR TANKER

SAMUI (ex-USS *YOG 60*) YO 4

Displacement, tons: 422 standard
Dimensions, feet (metres): 174.5 × 32 × 15 *(53.2 × 9.7 × 4.6)*
Main machinery: 2 diesels; 600 hp *(448 kW)*; 2 shafts
Speed, knots: 8
Complement: 29

Comment: Deleted in error in 1990.

SAMUI (alongside CHANG) *8/1991*

1 REPLENISHMENT TANKER

CHULA 2

Displacement, tons: 2000 full load
Measurement, tons: 960 dwt
Dimensions, feet (metres): 219.8 × 31.2 × 14.4 *(67 × 9.5 × 4.4)*
Main machinery: 2 MTU 12V 396 TC62 diesels; 2400 hp(m) *(1.76 MW)* sustained; 2 shafts
Speed, knots: 14
Complement: 39 (7 officers)
Cargo capacity: 800 tons oil fuel
Guns: 2 Oerlikon 20 mm.
Radars: Navigation: Decca; I band.

Comment: Launched on 24 September 1980 by Singapore Slipway and Engineering Company. Fitted with SATNAV. Replenishment is done by a hose handling crane boom.

CHULA (alongside SURIN) *8/1991*

1 WATER CARRIER

Name	*No*	*Builders*	*Commissioned*
CHUANG	YW 5	Royal Thai Naval Dockyard, Bangkok	1965

Displacement, tons: 305 standard; 485 full load
Dimensions, feet (metres): 136 × 24.6 × 10 *(42 × 7.5 × 3.1)*
Main machinery: 1 GM diesel; 500 hp *(373 kW)*; 1 shaft
Speed, knots: 11
Complement: 29

Comment: Launched on 14 January 1965.

CHUANG *8/1991*

MISCELLANEOUS

VISUD SAKORN

Comment: Naval manned and looks like a VIP yacht. Training Ship which is run by the Ministry of Communications.

VISUD SAKORN *10/1987*

TUGS

RIN ATA 5 **RANG** ATA 6

Displacement, tons: 350 standard
Dimensions, feet (metres): 106 × 29.7 × 15.2 *(32.3 × 9 × 4.6)*
Main machinery: 1 MWM TBD 441V/12K diesel; 2100 hp(m) *(1.54 MW)*; 1 shaft
Speed, knots: 12. **Range, miles:** 1000 at 10 kts
Complement: 19

Comment: Launched 12 and 14 June 1980 at Singapore Marine Shipyard. Both commissioned 5 March 1981.

RANG *1988, Trevor Brown*

2 Ex-US YTL 422 CLASS

KLUENG BADEN YTL 2 **MARN VICHAI** YTL 3

Displacement, tons: 63 standard
Dimensions, feet (metres): 64.7 × 16.5 × 6 *(19.7 × 5 × 1.8)*
Main machinery: 1 diesel; 240 hp *(179 kW)*; 1 shaft
Speed, knots: 8

Comment: Bought from Canada 1953.

KLUENG BADEN *8/1991*

ROYAL THAI MARINE POLICE

2 HAMELN TYPE (LARGE PATROL CRAFT)

DAMRONG RACHANUPHAT 1802 **LOPBURI RAMAS** 1803

Displacement, tons: 430 full load
Dimensions, feet (metres): 186 × 26.6 × 8 *(56.7 × 8.1 × 2.4)*
Main machinery: 2 MTU diesels; 4400 hp(m) *(3.23 MW)*; 2 shafts
Speed, knots: 23
Guns: 1 USN 3 in *(76 mm)*/50. 2 Oerlikon 20 mm (twin).

Comment: Delivered by Schiffwerft Hameln, Germany.

DAMRONG RACHANUPHAT *1990, Marine Police*

0 + 1 VOSPER THORNYCROFT TYPE (LARGE PATROL CRAFT)

Displacement, tons: 450 full load
Dimensions, feet (metres): 203.4 × 26.9 × 8.2 *(62 × 8.2 × 2.5)*
Main machinery: 2 Deutz/MWM BV 16M 628 diesels; 9524 hp(m) *(7 MW)* sustained; 2 shafts; KaMeWa cp props
Speed, knots: 25. **Range, miles:** 2500 at 15 kts
Complement: 57
Guns: 1 Oerlikon 30 mm. 2 Oerlikon 20 mm (twin).

Comment: Ordered in September 1989 from Ital Thai Marine. Same hull as the Khamronsin class corvettes for the Navy but much more lightly armed. To be delivered in 1992.

2 SUMIDAGAWA TYPE (COASTAL PATROL CRAFT)

CHASANYABADEE 1101 **PHROMYOTHEE** 1103

Displacement, tons: 130 full load
Dimensions, feet (metres): 111.5 × 19 × 9.1 *(34 × 5.8 × 2.8)*
Main machinery: 3 Ikegai diesels; 4050 hp(m) *(2.98 MW)*; 3 shafts
Speed, knots: 32
Guns: 2—12.7 mm MGs.

PHROMYOTHEE *1990, Marine Police*

1 YOKOHAMA TYPE (COASTAL PATROL CRAFT)

CHAWENGSAK SONGKRAM 1102

Displacement, tons: 190 full load
Dimensions, feet (metres): 116.5 × 23 × 11.5 *(35.5 × 7 × 3.5)*
Main machinery: 4 Ikegai diesels; 5400 hp(m) *(3.79 MW)*; 2 shafts
Speed, knots: 32
Guns: 2 Oerlikon 20 mm.

Comment: Built in 1975.

CHAWENGSAK SONGKRAM *1990, Marine Police*

1 ITAL THAI MARINE TYPE (COASTAL PATROL CRAFT)

SRIYANONT 901

Displacement, tons: 52 full load
Dimensions, feet (metres): 90 × 16 × 6.5 *(27.4 × 4.9 × 2)*
Main machinery: 2 Deutz BA 16M 816 diesels; 2680 hp(m) *(1.97 MW)* sustained; 2 shafts
Speed, knots: 23
Guns: 1 Oerlikon 20 mm. 2—7.62 mm MGs.

SRIYANONT *1990, Marine Police*

3 HALTER TYPE (COASTAL PATROL CRAFT)

PHRAONGKAMROP 807 **PICHARNPHOLAKIT** 808 **RAM INTHRA** 809

Displacement, tons: 34 full load
Dimensions, feet (metres): 65 × 17 × 8.3 *(19.8 × 5.2 × 2.5)*
Main machinery: 3 Detroit 12V-71TA diesels; 1020 hp(m) *(761 kW)* sustained; 3 shafts
Speed, knots: 25
Guns: 1 Oerlikon 20 mm. 2—7.62 mm MGs.

Comment: Delivered by Halter Marine, New Orleans in 1978. Aluminium hulls.

PICHARNPHOLAKIT *1990, Marine Police*

3 TECHNAUTIC TYPE (COASTAL PATROL CRAFT)

810-812

Displacement, tons: 50 full load
Dimensions, feet (metres): 88.6 × 19.4 × 6.2 *(27 × 5.9 × 1.9)*
Main machinery: 3 Isotta Fraschini diesels; 2500 hp(m) *(1.84 MW)*; 3 hydrojets
Speed, knots: 27
Guns: 1 Oerlikon 20 mm. 2—7.62 mm MGs.

Comment: Delivered by Technautic, Bangkok in 1984.

812 *1990, Marine Police*

5 ITAL THAI MARINE TYPE (COASTAL PATROL CRAFT)

625-629

Displacement, tons: 42 full load
Dimensions, feet (metres): 64 × 17.5 × 5 *(19.5 × 5.3 × 1.5)*
Main machinery: 2 MAN D2842LE diesels; 1520 hp(m) *(1.12 MW)* sustained; 2 shafts
Speed, knots: 27
Guns: 1—12.7 mm MG.

Comment: Built in Bangkok 1987-90. Aluminium hulls.

ITAL THAI 625 *1990, Marine Police*

17 TECHNAUTIC TYPE (COASTAL PATROL CRAFT)

608-624

Displacement, tons: 30 full load
Dimensions, feet (metres): 60 × 16 × 2.9 *(18.3 × 4.9 × 0.9)*
Main machinery: 2 Isotta Fraschini ID 36 SS 8V diesels; 1760 hp(m) *(1.29 MW)* sustained; 2 hydrojets
Speed, knots: 27
Guns: 1—12.7 mm MG.

Comment: Built from 1983 to 1987 in Bangkok.

TECHNAUTIC 614 *1990, Marine Police*

2 MARSUN TYPE

539-540

Displacement, tons: 30 full load
Dimensions, feet (metres): 57 × 16 × 3 *(17.4 × 4.9 × 0.9)*
Main machinery: 2 Detroit 12V-71TA diesels; 840 hp *(627 kW)* sustained; 2 shafts
Speed, knots: 25
Guns: 1—12.7 mm MG.

Comment: Built in Thailand.

MARSUN 540 *1990, Marine Police*

26 SUMIDAGAWA TYPE (RIVER PATROL CRAFT)

513-538

Displacement, tons: 18 full load
Dimensions, feet (metres): 54.1 × 12.5 × 2.3 *(16.5 × 3.8 × 0.7)*
Main machinery: 2 Cummins diesels; 800 hp *(597 kW)*; 2 shafts
Speed, knots: 23
Guns: 1—12.7 mm MG.

Comment: First 21 built by Sumidagawa, last five by Captain Co, Thailand 1978-79.

SUMIDAGAWA 530 *1990, Marine Police*

24 CAMCRAFT TYPE (RIVER PATROL CRAFT)

415-440

Displacement, tons: 13 full load
Dimensions, feet (metres): 40 × 12 × 3.2 *(12.2 × 3.7 × 1)*
Main machinery: 2 Detroit diesels; 540 hp *(403 kW)*; 2 shafts
Speed, knots: 25

Comment: Delivered by Camcraft, Louisiana. Aluminium hulls.

CAMCRAFT 434 *1990, Marine Police*

38 RIVER PATROL CRAFT

Displacement, tons: 5 full load
Dimensions, feet (metres): 37 × 11 × 6 *(11.3 × 3.4 × 1.8)*
Speed, knots: 25

Comment: Numbers in the 300 series.

RIVER PATROL CRAFT 339 *1990, Marine Police*

22 TYPHOON BOATS

Comment: Rigid inflatables being acquired from Task Force Boats plc in 1990-91. Two Johnson outboard motors, 450 hp *(336 kW)*; speed 50 kts light or 40 kts with 12 men embarked.

TOGO

Senior Officer

Commanding Officer, Navy:
Commander Lucien Laval

Personnel

(a) 1992: 115
(b) Voluntary service

Base

Lome

Mercantile Marine

Lloyd's Register of Shipping:
8 vessels of 21 852 tons gross

PATROL FORCES

2 COASTAL PATROL CRAFT

Name	*No*	*Builders*	*Commissioned*
KARA	P 761	Chantiers Navals de l'Esterel, Cannes	1976
MONO	P 762	Chantiers Navals de l'Esterel, Cannes	1976

Displacement, tons: 80 full load
Dimensions, feet (metres): 105 × 19 × 5.3 *(32 × 5.8 × 1.6)*
Main machinery: 2 MTU MB 12V 493 TY60 diesels; 2000 hp(m) *(1.47 MW)* sustained; 2 shafts
Speed, knots: 30. **Range, miles:** 1500 at 15 kts
Complement: 17 (1 officer)
Missiles: SSM: Aerospatiale SS 12M; wire-guided to 5 km *(3 nm)* subsonic; warhead 30 kg.
Guns: 1 Bofors 40 mm/70 (aft). 1 Oerlikon 20 mm.
Radars: Surface search: Decca 916; I band; range 88 km *(48 nm)*.

Comment: Both craft in good condition at the beginning of 1992.

KARA *1990*

TONGA

Headquarters' Appointments

Commander Tongan Defence Services
Lieutenant Colonel F Tupou

Base

Touliki Base, Nuku'alofa

Mercantile Marine

Lloyd's Register of Shipping:
17 vessels of 39 596 tons gross

PATROL FORCES

3 PACIFIC FORUM TYPE (LARGE PATROL CRAFT)

Name	*No*	*Builders*	*Commissioned*
NEIAFU	P 201	Australian Shipbuilding Industries	28 Oct 1989
PANGAI	P 202	Australian Shipbuilding Industries	30 June 1990
SAVEA	P 203	Australian Shipbuilding Industries	23 Mar 1991

Displacement, tons: 162 full load
Dimensions, feet (metres): 103.3 × 26.6 × 6.9 *(31.5 × 8.1 × 2.1)*
Main machinery: 2 Caterpillar 3516 diesels; 2820 hp *(2.1 MW)* sustained; 2 shafts
Speed, knots: 20. **Range, miles:** 2500 at 12 kts
Complement: 17 (3 officers)
Radars: Surface search: Furuno 1101; I band.

Comment: Part of the Pacific Forum Australia Defence co-operation. First laid down 30 January 1989, second 2 October 1989, third February 1990. Capable of mounting a 20 mm gun or MGs.

SAVEA *10/1991, John Mortimer*

2 COASTAL PATROL CRAFT

Name	*No*	*Builders*	*Commissioned*
NGAHAU KOULA	P 101	Brooke Marine, Lowestoft	10 Mar 1973
NGAHAU SILIVA	P 102	Brooke Marine, Lowestoft	10 May 1976

Displacement, tons: 15 full load
Dimensions, feet (metres): 45 × 13 × 3.8 *(13.7 × 4 × 1.2)*
Main machinery: 2 Cummins KT 2300 M diesels; 700 hp *(522 kW)*; 2 shafts
Speed, knots: 21. **Range, miles:** 1000 at 18 kts
Complement: 7
Guns: 2 Browning 12.7 mm MGs.
Radars: Surface search: Koden MD 306; I band.

Comment: DF and echo-sounder (Ferrograph), Codan HF 6294 radio communications. Manned by volunteers from the Maritime Defence Division Tongan Defence Service. *Ngahau Siliva* was completed 2 February 1976 and commissioned by HM Queen Halaevalu Mata'aho in May 1976. Names mean Golden and Silver Arrow respectively.

NGAHAU KOULA *1986*

1 LCM

Name	*No*	*Builders*	*Commissioned*
LATE (ex-Australian Army LCM 8 *1057)*	C 315	North Queensland Eng Ltd, Cairns	1 Sep 1982

Displacement, tons: 116 full load
Dimensions, feet (metres): 73.5 × 21 × 3.3 *(22.4 × 6.4 × 1)*
Main machinery: 2 Detroit 12V-71 diesels; 680 hp *(507 kW)* sustained; 2 shafts
Speed, knots: 10. **Range, miles:** 480 at 10 kts
Military lift: 60 tons
Radars: Surface search: Koden MD 305; I band.

Comment: Acquired from the Australian Army.

LATE *1986*

1 Ex-GERMAN MANNHEIM 59 CLASS (LCM)

Name	*No*	*Builders*	*Commissioned*
TUFOU	—	Schiffs und Motorenwerke AG, Mannheim	1960

Displacement, tons: 89 standard
Dimensions, feet (metres): 89.9 × 23.6 × 3.9 *(27.4 × 7.2 × 1.2)*
Main machinery: 2 MWM RMS 518A diesels; 432 hp(m) *(317 kW)*; 2 shafts
Speed, knots: 9
Complement: 9
Military lift: 70 tons

Comment: Acquired in 1989 and refitted in Fiji in 1990.

2 LOGISTIC SUPPORT CRAFT

Name	*No*	*Builders*	*Commissioned*
FANGAILIFUKA	PBF 512	Rotork Marine, UK	29 Sep 1983
'ALO-I-TALAU	LSC 512	Rotork Marine, UK	25 Mar 1985

Displacement, tons: 5.4
Dimensions, feet (metres): 41.5 × 7.5 × 3.3 *(12.7 × 2.3 × 1)*
Main machinery: 2 Volvo Penta AQAD 40; 220 hp(m) *(162 kW)* sustained; Aquamatic jets
Speed, knots: 25. **Range, miles:** 85 at 25 kts
Complement: 3
Radars: Navigation: Decca 060; I band.

Comment: Fitted with Codan HF 6924 communications.

FANGAILIFUKA *1986*

1 ROYAL YACHT

TITILUPE

Comment: 34 ft *(10.4 m)* long and has a speed of 8 kts. GRP displacement hull. Also used as auxiliary patrol craft.

TITILUPE *1982, J. Cox, RAN*

TRINIDAD AND TOBAGO

COAST GUARD

Headquarters' Appointments

Chief of Defence Staff:
Brigadier Ralph Brown, ED
Commanding Officer, Coast Guard:
Captain Richard Kelshall, MOM, ED, MN

General

On 30 June 1989 all former Police craft were handed over to the Coast Guard and re-named. After a review in 1991 some may be returned to the Police.

Aircraft

The Coast Guard operates a single Cessna 402B for surveillance. This aircraft can be backed by Air Division helicopters when necessary.

Personnel

(a) 1992: 645 (45 officers)
(b) Voluntary service

Bases

Staubles Bay (HQ)
Hart's Cut, Tobago, Port Fortin (all established in 1989)
Piarco (Air station)

Prefix to Ship's Names

T.T.S.

Mercantile Marine

Lloyd's Register of Shipping:
48 vessels of 22 230 tons gross

DELETIONS

1990 *Mathura*
1991 *Fort Chacon*

PATROL FORCES

2 TYPE CG 40 (LARGE PATROL CRAFT)

Name	No	Builders	Commissioned
BARRACUDA	CG 5	Karlskronavarvet	15 June 1980
CASCADURA	CG 6	Karlskronavarvet	15 June 1980

Displacement, tons: 210 full load
Dimensions, feet (metres): 133.2 × 21.9 × 5.2 *(40.6 × 6.7 × 1.6)*
Main machinery: 2 Paxman Valenta 16 CM diesels; 6700 hp *(5 MW)* sustained; 2 shafts
Speed, knots: 30. **Range, miles:** 3000 at 15 kts
Complement: 25
Guns: 1 Bofors 40 mm/70. 1 Oerlikon 20 mm.
Radars: Surface search: Racal Decca 1226; I band.

Comment: Ordered in Sweden mid-1978. Laid down early 1979. Fitted with foam-cannon oil pollution equipment and for oceanographic and hydrographic work. Nine spare berths. The hull is similar to Swedish Spica class but with the bridge amidships. One refitted in 1988, the other in 1989.

CASCADURA *1990, Trinidad and Tobago Coast Guard*

1 VOSPER TYPE (LARGE PATROL CRAFT)

Name	No	Builders	Commissioned
BUCCOO REEF	CG 4	Vosper Ltd, Portsmouth	18 Mar 1972

Displacement, tons: 100 standard; 125 full load
Dimensions, feet (metres): 103 × 19.8 × 5.8 *(31.5 × 5.9 × 1.8)*
Main machinery: 2 Paxman Ventura 12 YJCM diesels; 3000 hp *(2.24 MW)* sustained; 2 shafts
Speed, knots: 24. **Range, miles:** 2000 at 13 kts
Complement: 19 (3 officers)
Guns: 1 Hispano Suiza 20 mm/20.

Comment: Fitted with air-conditioning and roll-damping. Commissioned at Portsmouth, England. In spite of her age is still giving good service.

BUCCOO REEF *1985, Trinidad and Tobago Coast Guard*

4 SOUTER WASP 17 METRE CLASS (COASTAL PATROL CRAFT)

Name	No	Builders	Commissioned
PLYMOUTH	CG 27	W A Souter and Sons Ltd	27 Aug 1982
CARONI	CG 28	W A Souter and Sons Ltd	27 Aug 1982
GALEOTA	CG 29	W A Souter and Sons Ltd	27 Aug 1982
MORUGA	CG 30	W A Souter and Sons Ltd	27 Aug 1982

Displacement, tons: 19.3
Dimensions, feet (metres): 55.1 × 13.8 × 4.6 *(16.8 × 4.2 × 1.4)*
Main machinery: 2 GM Stewart and Stevenson 8V92 MTI diesels; 1300 hp *(970 kW)*; 2 shafts
Speed, knots: 32. **Range, miles:** 500 at 18 kts
Complement: 7 (2 officers)
Guns: 1—7.62 mm MG.
Radars: Surface search: Decca 150; I band.

Comment: GRP hulls. There have been reliability problems.

MORUGA *1985, Trinidad and Tobago Coast Guard*

2 WASP 20 METRE CLASS (COASTAL PATROL CRAFT)

Name	No	Builders	Commissioned
KAIRI (ex-*Sea Bird*)	CG 31	W A Souter, Cowes	Dec 1982
MORIAH (ex-*Sea Dog*)	CG 32	W A Souter, Cowes	Dec 1982

Displacement, tons: 32 full load
Dimensions, feet (metres): 65.8 × 16.5 × 5 *(20.1 × 5 × 1.5)*
Main machinery: 2 GM Stewart and Stevenson diesels; 2400 hp *(1.79 MW)*; 2 shafts
Speed, knots: 30. **Range, miles:** 450 at 30 kts
Complement: 6 (2 officers)
Guns: 2—7.62 mm MGs.
Radars: Navigation: Decca 150; I band.

Comment: Ordered late 1981. Aluminium alloy hull. Transferred from the Police in June 1989.

MORIAH *1989, Trinidad and Tobago Coast Guard*

1 WASP 17 METRE CLASS (COASTAL PATROL CRAFT)

Name	No	Builders	Commissioned
CEDROS (ex-*Sea Erne*)	CG 35	W A Souter, Cowes	1984

Displacement, tons: 19.3 full load
Dimensions, feet (metres): 55.1 × 13.8 × 4.6 *(16.8 × 4.2 × 1.4)*
Main machinery: 2 GM Stewart and Stevenson 8V-92MTI diesels; 1300 hp *(970 kW)*; 2 shafts
Speed, knots: 25
Complement: 7
Radars: Navigation: Decca 150; I band.

Comment: Transferred from Police in June 1989.

CEDROS *1989, Trinidad and Tobago Coast Guard*

1 SWORD CLASS (COASTAL PATROL CRAFT)

Name	No	Builders	Commissioned
MATELOT (ex-*Sea Skorpion*)	CG 33	Sea Ark Marine	May 1979

Displacement, tons: 15.5 full load
Dimensions, feet (metres): 44.9 × 13.4 × 4.3 *(13.7 × 4.1 × 1.3)*
Main machinery: 2 GM diesels; 850 hp *(634 kW)*; 2 shafts
Speed, knots: 28. **Range, miles:** 500 at 20 kts
Complement: 6
Guns: 1—7.62 mm MG.

Comment: Two transferred from the Police in June 1989, one scrapped in 1990.

MATELOT *1989, Trinidad and Tobago Coast Guard*

1 COASTAL PATROL CRAFT

Name	*No*	*Builders*	*Commissioned*
CARENAGE (ex-*Sea Dragon*)	CG 37	Watercraft, Shoreham	1980

Displacement, tons: 14.9 full load
Dimensions, feet (metres): 45 × 14.1 × 4 *(13.7 × 4.3 × 1.2)*
Main machinery: 2 GM 8V-92 diesels; 606 hp *(452 kW)* sustained; 2 shafts
Speed, knots: 23.5. **Range, miles:** 360 at 18 kts
Complement: 4
Guns: 2—7.62 mm MGs.

Comment: GRP hull. Transferred from Police in June 1989.

CARENAGE *1989, Trinidad and Tobago Coast Guard*

1 COASTAL SUPPORT CRAFT

SPEYSIDE (ex-*Sea Hawk*) CG 36

Displacement, tons: 12 full load
Dimensions, feet (metres): 36 × 13 × 4 *(10.9 × 3.9 × 1.2)*
Main machinery: 2 GM diesels; 460 hp *(343 kW)*; 2 shafts
Speed, knots: 22. **Range, miles:** 400 at 20 kts

Comment: Built by Tugs and Lighters Ltd, Port of Spain. Transferred from Police in June 1989.

1 SURVEY CRAFT

MERIDAN

Comment: 75 tons displacement craft launched in 1985. Has a complement of 5 (2 officers).

2 BOWEN CLASS (FAST INTERCEPTOR CRAFT)

CG 001 **CG 002**

Comment: 31 ft fast patrol boats acquired with US funds in May 1991. Capable of 40 kts.

CG 001 *1991, Trinidad and Tobago Coast Guard*

8 AUXILIARY VESSELS

NAPARIMA (ex-*CG 26)* A 01
EL TUCUCHE (ex-*CG 25)* A 02
REFORM A 04
REHAB A 05
REDEEM (ex-*Cocrico*) A 06
RECOVER (ex-*Semp*) A 07
RELAY A 08
REVIEW (ex-*Egret*) A 09

Comment: A variety of craft some of which transferred from Police duties in June 1989 and used for Port Services.

TUNISIA

Headquarters' Appointment

Chief of Naval Staff:
Capitaine Chadli Cherif

Bases

Sfax, Bizerte, La Goulette, Kelibia

Personnel

(a) 1992: 4500 officers and men (including 700 conscripts)
(b) 1 year's national service

Mercantile Marine

Lloyd's Register of Shipping:
71 vessels of 276 447 tons gross

DELETIONS

1989 *Hannibal, Sousse* (both in reserve)

FRIGATE

1 Ex-US SAVAGE CLASS

Name	*No*	*Builders*	*Laid down*	*Launched*	*Commissioned*
INKADH (ex-*Président Bourguiba*, ex-USS *Thomas J Gary* DER 326, ex-*DE 326*)	E 7	Consolidated Steel Corporation, Texas	15 June 1943	21 Aug 1943	27 Nov 1943

Displacement, tons: 1200 standard; 1490 full load
Dimensions, feet (metres): 306 × 35 × 14 *(93.3 × 10.7 × 4.3)*
Main machinery: 4 Fairbanks-Morse 38D8-1/8-10 diesels; 7000 hp *(5.2 MW)* sustained; 2 shafts
Speed, knots: 19. **Range, miles:** 12 000 at 11 kts
Complement: 169

Guns: 2—3 in *(76 mm)*/50; 85° elevation; 20 rounds/minute to 12 km *(6.6 nm)*; weight of shell 6 kg.
2 Oerlikon 20 mm/80; 800 rounds/minute to 2 km.
Torpedoes: 6—324 mm US Mk 32 (2 triple) tubes. Honeywell Mk 44; anti-submarine; active homing to 5.5 km *(3 nm)* at 30 kts; warhead 34 kg.
Fire control: Mk 63 GFCS. Mk 51 Mod 2 GFCS.
Radars: Air search: Westinghouse SPS 29; B/C band; range 457 km *(250 nm)*.
Surface search: Raytheon SPS 10; G band.
Fire control: Western Electric Mk 34; I/J band.
Sonars: EDO SQS 29; hull-mounted; active search and attack; medium/high frequency.

Programmes: Completed as Edsall class DE. Converted to Radar Picket Savage class in 1958. Transferred 27 October 1973.
Operational: Still used for training but non-operational as a warship and a replacement is still being sought.

INKADH *7/1989, van Ginderen Collection*

LIGHT FORCES

Note: Six 55 m FAC(M) were out to tender in late 1988 but shortage of funds has impeded further progress so far.

3 COMBATTANTE III M CLASS (FAST ATTACK CRAFT—MISSILE)

Name	*No*	*Builders*	*Commissioned*
LA GALITÉ	501	CMN, Cherbourg	27 Feb 1985
TUNIS	502	CMN, Cherbourg	27 Mar 1985
CARTHAGE	503	CMN, Cherbourg	29 Apr 1985

Displacement, tons: 345 standard; 425 full load
Dimensions, feet (metres): 183.7 × 26.9 × 7.2 *(56 × 8.2 × 2.2)*
Main engines: 4 MTU 20V538 TB93 diesels; 18 740 hp(m) *(13.8 MW)* sustained; 4 shafts
Speed, knots: 38.5. **Range, miles:** 700 at 33 kts; 2800 at 10 kts
Complement: 35

Missiles: SSM: 8 Aerospatiale MM 40 Exocet (2 quad) launchers; inertial cruise; active radar homing to 70 km *(40 nm)* at 0.9 Mach; warhead 165 kg; sea-skimmer.
Guns: 1 OTO Melara 3 in *(76 mm)*/62; 85° elevation; 55-65 rounds/minute to 16 km *(8.7 nm)*; weight of shell 6 kg.
2 Breda 40 mm/70 (twin); 85° elevation; 300 rounds/minute to 12.5 km *(6.8 nm)*; weight of shell 0.96 kg.
4 Oerlikon 30 mm/75 (2 twin); 85° elevation; 650 rounds/minute to 10 km *(5.5 nm)*; weight of shell 1 kg or 0.36 kg.
Countermeasures: Decoys: 1 CSEE Dagaie trainable launcher; IR flares and Chaff.
ESM: Radar warning.
Combat data systems: Tavitac action data automation.
Fire control: 2 CSEE Naja optronic directors for 30 mm. Thomson-CSF Vega II for SSM, 76 mm and 40 mm.
Radars: Air/surface search: Thomson-CSF Triton S; G band; range 33 km *(18 nm)* for 2 m² target.
Fire control: Thomson-CSF Castor II; I/J band; range 31 km *(17 nm)* for 2 m² target.

Programmes: Ordered in 1981.
Operational: One CSEE Sylosat navigation system.

CARTHAGE *8/1991, Giorgio Ghiglione*

2 Ex-CHINESE SHANGHAI II CLASS (FAST ATTACK CRAFT—GUN)

GAFSAH P 305 **AMILCAR** P 306

Displacement, tons: 113 standard; 131 full load
Dimensions, feet (metres): 127.3 × 17.7 × 5.6 *(38.8 × 5.4 × 1.7)*
Main machinery: 4 MTU 8V331 TC92 diesels; 3540 hp(m) *(2.6 MW)* sustained; 4 shafts
Speed, knots: 30. **Range, miles:** 700 at 16.5 kts
Complement: 34
Guns: 4—37 mm/63 (2 twin). 4—25 mm/80 (2 twin).
Radars: Surface search: Skin Head; I band; range 37 km *(20 nm)*.

Comment: Transferred 2 April 1977. Two others transferred in 1973, since deleted. Engine change completed December 1984 by the Navy at Socomena shipyards, Bizerte.

SHANGHAI II Class

4 COASTAL PATROL CRAFT

Comment: Built by Aresa, Spain in 1981 (first pair). Two more ordered in 1982. Of 75.4 ft *(23 m)*. Possibly for Fishery Protection.

2 VOSPER THORNYCROFT TYPE (FAST ATTACK CRAFT—PATROL)

Name	*No*	*Builders*	*Commissioned*
TAZARKA	P 205	Vosper Thornycroft	27 Oct 1977
MENZEL BOURGUIBA	P 206	Vosper Thornycroft	27 Oct 1977

Displacement, tons: 125 full load
Dimensions, feet (metres): 103 × 19.5 × 5.5 *(31.4 × 5.9 × 1.7)*
Main machinery: 2 MTU diesels; 4000 hp(m) *(2.94 MW)*; 2 shafts
Speed, knots: 27. **Range, miles:** 1500 at 15 kts
Complement: 24
Guns: 2 Oerlikon 20 mm.
Radars: Surface search: Decca 916; I band; range 88 km *(48 nm)*.

Comment: Ordered 9 September 1975. *Tazarka* laid down 23 March 1976 and launched 19 July

MENZEL BOURGUIBA *1989*

3 P 48 CLASS (LARGE PATROL CRAFT)

Name	*No*	*Builders*	*Commissioned*
BIZERTE	P 301	Ch Franco-Belges (Villeneuve, la Garenne)	10 July 1970
HORRIA (ex-*Liberté*)	P 302	Ch Franco-Belges (Villeneuve, la Garenne)	Oct 1970
MONASTIR	P 304	Soc Française Constructions Navale	25 Mar 1975

Displacement, tons: 250 full load
Dimensions, feet (metres): 157.5 × 23.3 × 7.5 *(48 × 7.1 × 2.3)*
Main machinery: 2 MTU 16V 652 TB81 diesels; 4600 hp(m) *(3.4 MW)* sustained; 2 shafts
Speed, knots: 20. **Range, miles:** 2000 at 16 kts
Complement: 34 (4 officers)
Missiles: SSM: 8 Aerospatiale SS 12M; wire-guided to 5.5 km *(3 nm)* subsonic; warhead 30 kg.
Guns: 2 Bofors 40 mm/70. 2—12.7 mm MGs.
Radars: Surface search: Thomson-CSF DRBN 31; I band.

Comment: First pair ordered in 1968, third in August 1973.

BIZERTE *7/1989, van Ginderen Collection*

4 COASTAL PATROL CRAFT

Name	*No*	*Builders*	*Commissioned*
ISTIKLAL (ex-*VC 11, P 761*)	P 201	Ch Navals de l'Esterel	Apr 1957
JOUMHOURIA	P 202	Ch Navals de l'Esterel	Jan 1961
AL JALA	P 203	Ch Navals de l'Esterel	Nov 1963
REMADA	P 204	Ch Navals de l'Esterel	July 1967

Displacement, tons: 60 standard; 80 full load
Dimensions, feet (metres): 104 × 19 × 5.3 *(31.5 × 5.8 × 1.6)*
Main machinery: 2 MTU MB 12V 493 TY70 diesels; 2200 hp(m) *(1.62 MW)* sustained; 2 shafts
Speed, knots: 30. **Range, miles:** 1500 at 15 kts
Complement: 17 (3 officers)
Guns: 2 Oerlikon 20 mm.

Comment: *Istiklal* transferred from France March 1959. Wooden hulls. Doubtful operational status.

ISTIKLAL *3/1981, R. van Bree*

6 COASTAL PATROL CRAFT

V 101-106

Displacement, tons: 38 full load
Dimensions, feet (metres): 83 × 15.6 × 4.2 *(25 × 4.8 × 1.3)*
Main machinery: 2 Detroit 12V-71TI diesels; 840 hp *(627 kW)* sustained; 2 shafts
Speed, knots: 23. **Range, miles:** 900 at 15 kts
Complement: 11
Guns: 1 Oerlikon 20 mm.

Comment: Built by Chantiers Navals de l'Esterel and commissioned in 1961-63. Two further craft of the same design *(Sabaq el Bahr* T 2 and *Jaouel el Bahr* T 1) but unarmed were transferred to the Fisheries Administration in 1971—same builders.

V 101 *10/1984, van Ginderen Collection*

10 COASTAL PATROL CRAFT (CUSTOMS)

ASSAD BIN FOURAT +9

Displacement, tons: 32 full load
Dimensions, feet (metres): 67.3 × 15.4 × 4.3 *(20.5 × 4.7 × 1.3)*
Main machinery: 2 diesels; 1000 hp(m) *(735 kW)*; 2 shafts
Speed, knots: 28. **Range, miles:** 500 at 20 kts
Complement: 8
Guns: 1—12.7 mm MG.

Comment: First one built by Socomena, Bizerte with assistance from South Korea, and completed March 1986. Nine more building in 1991 for Customs.

TUG

Name	*No*	*Builders*	*Commissioned*
RAS ADAR (ex-*Zeeland*, ex-*Pan America*, ex-*Ocean Pride*, ex-HMS *Oriana*, BAT 1)	—	Gulfport Boilerworks & Eng Co	13 Dec 1942

Displacement, tons: 534 standard; 860 full load
Dimensions, feet (metres): 143 × 33.9 × 13 *(43.6 × 10.3 × 4)*
Main machinery: 2 GM 12-278A diesels; 2200 hp *(1.64 MW)*; 2 shafts
Speed, knots: 13
Complement: 45

Comment: Built in 1942 of Sotoyomo class with enlarged upperworks. Leased to the Royal Navy in that year as BAT 1 HMS *Oriana*, returned and sold in 1946 as *Ocean Pride*, then *Pan America* in 1947, then *Zeeland* in 1956. Transferred 1968.

TURKEY

Headquarters' Appointments

Commander-in-Chief, Turkish Naval Forces:
Admiral Irfan Tinaz
(Admiral Vural Bayazit from Sep 1992)
Chief of Naval Staff:
Vice Admiral Turhan Özer

Senior Commands

Fleet Commander (Gölcük):
Admiral Vural Bayazit
Comsarnorth (Istanbul):
Vice Admiral Mustafa Turunçoğlu
Comsarsouth (Izmir):
Vice Admiral Guven Erkaya
Combosphorus (Istanbul):
Admiral Bülent Alpkaya
Comdardanel (Çanakkale):
Admiral Aykut Uras
Combasetraining (Karamürsel):
Admiral Çetin Ersari
Comeageanzone (Izmir):
Rear Admiral Altac Atilan
Commedzone (Mersin):
Rear Admiral Tanzar Dinçer
Comebaseiskenderun (Iskenderun):
Rear Admiral Aytekin Ersan
Combasegölcük (Gölcük):
Rear Admiral Niyazi Ulusoy
Comblackzone (Ereğli):
Rear Admiral Hüseyin Saglam
Comseaguard (Coast Guard) (Ankara):
Rear Admiral Ekmel Totrakan
Comsuracgrup (Gölcük):
Rear Admiral Aydan Erol
Comsabğrup (Gölcük):
Rear Admiral Dogan Haçipoglu
Comminesgrup (Gölcük):
Rear Admiral Kani Kanbak
Comamphibigrup (Foça-Izmir):
Rear Admiral Özman Erkmen
Comfastgrup (Istanbul):
Rear Admiral Saim Ergun

Diplomatic Representation

Naval Attaché in Athens:
Commander Irfan Bilgin
Naval Attaché in Bonn:
Commander Levent Gungor
Naval Attaché in Islamabad:
Captain Vedat Ersin
Naval Attaché in London:
Captain Ramis Akdemir
Naval Attaché in Moscow:
Rear Admiral Erol Adayener
Naval Attaché in Paris:
Commander Reha Erzi
Naval Attaché in Rome:
Lieutenant Commander Baha Eren
Naval Attaché in Tokyo:
Commander Tekin Kiyar
Naval Attaché in Washington:
Captain Eser Sahan

Personnel

(a) 1992: 59 400 officers and ratings including 900 Naval Air Arm (reserves 70 000) (see additional Marines)
(b) 18 months' national service

Naval Bases

Headquarters: Ankara
Main Naval Base: Gölcük
Istanbul, Izmir, Foça, Erdek
Ereğli, Büyükdere, Aksas, Karamürsel (Training), Çanakkale, Iskenderun, Mersin
Dockyards: Gölcük, Taşkizak (Istanbul)

Strength of the Fleet (including Coast Guard)

Type	*Active*	*Building (Planned)*
Submarines—Patrol	15	2 (4)
Destroyers	12	—
Frigates	8	2
Fast Attack Craft—Missile	16	2 (6)
Fast Attack Craft—Gun	1	—
Fast Attack Craft—Torpedo	2	—
Large Patrol Craft	23	—
Coastal Patrol Craft	5	—
Minelayer—Large	1	—
Minelayers—Coastal	4	—
Minelayers—Tenders	2	—
Minesweepers—Coastal	22	(6)
Minesweepers—Inshore	4	—
Minehunting Tenders	8	—
LSTs	7	1
LCTs	34	3
LCUs	5	—
LCMs	23	—
Survey Vessels	4	—
Depot/Training Ships	5	—
Fleet Replenishment Tanker	1	—
Support Tankers	5	—
Harbour Tankers	3	—
Water Tankers	10	—
Repair Ships	2	—
Transports—Large and small	42	—
Salvage Ships	3	—
Boom Defence Vessels	4	—
Net Vessels	1 (6)	—
Tugs—Ocean/Coastal	10	—
Tugs—Harbour	42	—
Floating Docks/Cranes	11	—
Coast Guard	55	(24)

Marines

Total: 4000
One brigade of HQ company, three infantry battalions, one artillery battalion, support units.

Coast Guard (Sahil Güvenlik)

Formed in July 1982 from the naval wing of the Jandarma. Prefix J replaced by SG and paint scheme is very light grey with a diagonal stripe forward. About 1000 officers and men.

Mercantile Marine

Lloyd's Register of Shipping:
880 vessels of 4 107 075 tons gross

DELETIONS

Mine Warfare Forces

1990 *Dalgiç 1*

Amphibious Forces

1991 4 EDIC, 8 LCM 8, 7 LCUs

Service Forces

1990 *Mehmet Kaptan*

PENNANT LIST

Submarines

S 333	Ikinci Inönü
S 335	Burakreis
S 336	Muratreis
S 338	Uluçalireis
S 340	Çerbe
S 341	Çanakkale
S 342	Hizirreis
S 343	Pirireis
S 346	Birinci Inönü
S 347	Atilay
S 348	Saldiray
S 349	Batiray
S 350	Yildiray
S 351	Doğanay
S 352	Dolunay
S 353	Preveze
S 354	Sakarya

Destroyers

D 345	Yücetepe
D 346	Alcitepe
D 347	Anittepe
D 348	Savaştepe
D 349	Kiliç Ali Paşa
D 350	Piyale Paşa
D 351	M Fevzi Çakmak
D 352	Gayret
D 353	Adatepe
D 354	Kocatepe
D 356	Zafer
DM 357	Muavenet

Frigates

D 358	Berk
D 359	Peyk
D 360	Gelibolu
D 361	Gemlik
F 240	Yavuz
F 241	Turgutreis
F 242	Fatih
F 243	Yildirim
F 244	Barbaros
F 245	Orucreis

Mine Warfare Forces (Layers)

N 101	Mordogan
N 104	Mersin
N 105	Mürefte
N 110	Nusret
N 115	Mehmetcik

Mine Warfare Forces (Sweepers)

M 500	Foça
M 501	Fethiye
M 502	Fatsa
M 503	Finike
M 507	Seymen
M 508	Selçuk
M 509	Seyhan
M 510	Samsun
M 511	Sinop
M 512	Surmene
M 513	Seddülbahir
M 514	Silifke
M 515	Saros
M 516	Sigacik
M 517	Sapanca
M 518	Sariyer
M 520	Karamürsel
M 521	Kerempe
M 522	Kilimli
M 523	Kozlu
M 524	Kuşadasi
M 525	Kemer
P 530	Trabzon
P 531	Terme
P 532	Tirebolu
A 601	Tekirdağ
P 312-19	MTB 2-9

Amphibious Forces

L 401	Ertuğrul
L 402	Serdar
NL 120	Bayraktar
NL 121	Sancaktar
NL 122	Çakabey
NL 123	Sarucabey
NL 124	Karamürselbey
NL 125	Osman Gazi

Light Forces

P 111	Sultanhisar
P 112	Demirhisar
P 113	Yarhisar
P 114	Akhisar
P 115	Sivrihisar
P 116	Koçhisar
P 140	Girne
P 145	Caner Gönyeli
P 321	Denizkusu
P 322	Atmaca
P 323	Sahin
P 324	Kartal
P 326	Pelikan
P 327	Albatros
P 328	Şimşek
P 329	Kasirga
P 333	Mizrak
P 335	Kalkan
P 339	Bora
P 340	Dogan
P 341	Marti
P 342	Tayfun
P 343	Volkan
P 344	Rüzgar
P 345	Poyraz
P 346	Gurbet
P 347	Firtina
P 348	Yildiz
P 349	Karayel
P 121-136	AB 21-36
P 141-144	LS 9-12

Service Forces

A 570	Taşkizak
A 571	Yüzbaşi Tolunay
A 572	Albay Hakki Burak
A 573	Binbasi Saadettin Gürçan
A 575	Inebolu
A 576	Derya
A 577	Sokullu Mehmet Paşa
A 579	Cezayirli Gazi Hasan Paşa
A 580	Akar
A 581	Onaran
A 582	Basaran
A 584	Kurtaran
A 585	Akin
A 586	Ülkü
A 587	Gazal
A 588	Umur Bey
A 589	Işin
A 590	Yunus
A 594	Çubuklu
A 597	Van
A 598	Ulubat
A 599	Sögüt
A 600	Kavak
P 301	AG 1 (BDV)
P 304	AG 4 (BDV)
P 305	AG 5 (BDV)
P 306	AG 6 (BDV)

Auxiliaries

All have Y numbers (4 figure numbers reduced to 3 in 1991)

SUBMARINES

Note: (1) Reported that ex-USN Barbel class may be acquired to replace the Guppys.
(2) In addition to those listed below, three old submarines are moored at Gölcük as accommodation ships.

0 + 2 + (4) TYPE 209 CLASS (TYPE 1400)

Name	*No*	*Builders*	*Laid down*	*Launched*	*Commissioned*
PREVEZE	S 353	Gölcük/Kocaeli	12 Sep 1989	1993	1994
SAKARYA	S 354	Gölcük/Kocaeli	1 Feb 1990	1994	1995

Displacement, tons: 1454 surfaced; 1586 dived
Dimensions, feet (metres): 203.4 × 20.3 × 18 *(62 × 6.2 × 5.5)*
Main machinery: Diesel-electric; 4 MTU 12V 396 SB83 diesels; 3800 hp(m) *(2.8 MW)* sustained; 4 alternators; 1 Siemens motor; 4000 hp(m) *(3.38 MW)* sustained; 1 shaft
Speed, knots: 15 surfaced/snorting; 21.5 dived. **Range, miles:** 8200 at 8 kts surfaced; 400 at 4 kts dived
Complement: 30

Missiles: SSM: McDonnell Douglas Sub Harpoon.
Torpedoes: 8—21 in *(533 mm)* bow tubes. MUSL Tigerfish Mk 24 Mod 2. Total of 14 torpedoes and missiles.
Countermeasures: ESM: Racal Porpoise; radar warning.
Fire control: Atlas Elektronik system.
Radars: Surface search; I band.
Sonars: Atlas Elektronik; passive/active search and attack; medium/high frequency.

Programmes: Order for first two signed in Ankara on 17 November 1987. Being built with HDW assistance. Prefabrication started in March 1989.
Structure: Diving depth, 280 m *(820 ft)*. Kollmorgen masts.
Operational: Endurance, 50 days.

6 TYPE 209 CLASS (TYPE 1200)

Name	*No*	*Builders*	*Laid down*	*Launched*	*Commissioned*
ATILAY	S 347	Howaldtswerke, Kiel	1 Dec 1972	23 Oct 1974	23 July 1975
SALDIRAY	S 348	Howaldtswerke, Kiel	2 Jan 1973	14 Feb 1975	21 Oct 1976
BATIRAY	S 349	Howaldtswerke, Kiel	1 June 1975	24 Oct 1977	20 July 1978
YILDIRAY	S 350	Gölcük, Izmit	1 May 1976	20 July 1979	20 July 1981
DOĞANAY	S 351	Gölcük, Izmit	21 Mar 1980	16 Nov 1983	16 Nov 1985
DOLUNAY	S 352	Gölcük, Izmit	9 Mar 1981	22 July 1988	21 July 1989

Displacement, tons: 980 surfaced; 1185 dived
Dimensions, feet (metres): 200.8 × 20.3 × 17.9 *(61.2 × 6.2 × 5.5)*
Main machinery: Diesel-electric; 4 MTU 12V493 AZ80 GA 31L diesels; 2400 hp(m) *(1.76 MW)* sustained; 4 alternators; 1.7 MW; 1 Siemens motor; 4600 hp(m) *(3.38 MW)* sustained; 1 shaft
Speed, knots: 11 surfaced; 22 dived. **Range, miles:** 7500 at 8 kts surfaced
Complement: 33 (6 officers)

Torpedoes: 8—21 in *(533 mm)* tubes. 14 AEG SST 4; wire-guided; active/passive homing to 28 km *(15.3 nm)* at 23 kts; 12 km *(6.6 nm)* at 35 kts; warhead 260 kg. Swim-out discharge.
Countermeasures: ESM: Thomson-CSF DR 2000; radar warning.
Fire control: Signaal M8 (S 347-348). Sinbads (remainder).
Radars: Surface search: S 63B; I band.
Sonars: Krupp Atlas CSU 3; hull-mounted; passive/active search and attack; medium/high frequency.

Programmes: Designed by Ingenieurkontor, Lübeck for construction by Howaldtswerke, Kiel and sale by Ferrostaal, Essen, all acting as a consortium. Last three built in Turkey with assistance given by Howaldtswerke.

Modernisation: Fire control system to be updated starting with the first pair. Possibly by Atlas Elektronik to Preveze class standards.
Structure: A single-hull design with two ballast tanks and forward and after trim tanks. Fitted with snort and remote machinery control. The single screw is slow revving. Very high capacity batteries with GRP lead-acid cells and battery cooling—by Wilh Hagen. Active and passive sonar, sonar detection equipment, sound ranging gear and underwater telephone. Fitted with two periscopes, radar and Omega receiver. Fore-planes retract. Diving depth, 250 m *(820 ft)*.
Operational: Endurance, 50 days.

SALDIRAY *10/1991, Selim San*

2 Ex-US GUPPY III CLASS

Name	No	Builders	Laid down	Launched	Commissioned
ÇANAKKALE (ex-USS *Cobbler* SS 344)	S 341	Electric Boat Co	3 Apr 1944	1 Apr 1945	8 Aug 1945
IKINCI INÖNÜ (ex-USS *Corporal* SS 346)	S 333	Electric Boat Co	27 Apr 1944	10 June 1945	9 Nov 1945

Displacement, tons: 1975 standard; 2450 dived
Dimensions, feet (metres): 326.5 × 27 × 17 *(99.5 × 8.2 × 5.2)*
Main machinery: Diesel-electric; 4 GM 16-278A diesels; 6000 hp *(4.41 MW)*; 2 motors; 5600 hp *(4.2 MW)*; 2 shafts
Speed, knots: 17.5 surfaced; 15 dived. **Range, miles:** 10 000 at 10 kts surfaced
Complement: 86 (8 officers)

Torpedoes: 10—21 in *(533 mm)* (6 bow, 4 stern) tubes; 24 US Mk 37 torpedoes.
Mines: 40 in lieu of torpedoes.
Radars: Surface search: SS 2A; I band.
Sonars: EDO BQR 2B; hull-mounted; passive search and attack; medium frequency.
Sperry/Raytheon BQG 4; passive ranging.

Programmes: Transferred 21 November 1973.
Operational: Diving probably restricted to periscope depth.

IKINCI INÖNÜ *10/1987, Selim San*

5 Ex-US GUPPY IIA CLASS

Name	No	Builders	Laid down	Launched	Commissioned
BURAKREIS (ex-USS *Seafox* SS 402)	S 335	Portsmouth Navy Yard	2 Nov 1943	28 Mar 1944	13 June 1944
MURATREIS (ex-USS *Razorback* SS 394)	S 336	Portsmouth Navy Yard	9 Sep 1943	27 Jan 1944	3 Apr 1944
ULUÇALIREIS (ex-USS *Thornback* SS 418)	S 338	Portsmouth Navy Yard	5 Apr 1944	7 July 1944	13 Oct 1944
ÇERBE (ex-USS *Trutta* SS 421)	S 340	Portsmouth Navy Yard	22 Dec 1943	22 May 1944	16 Nov 1944
BIRINCI INÖNÜ (ex-USS *Threadfin* SS 410)	S 346	Portsmouth Navy Yard	18 Mar 1944	26 June 1944	30 Aug 1944

Displacement, tons: 1848 surfaced; 2440 dived
Dimensions, feet (metres): 306 × 27 × 17 *(93.2 × 8.2 × 5.2)*
Main machinery: Diesel-electric; 3 Fairbanks-Morse 38D8-1/8-10 diesels; 4500 hp *(3.4 MW)*; 2 motors; 4800 hp *(3.6 MW)*; 2 shafts
Speed, knots: 17 surfaced; 14-15 dived. **Range, miles:** 12 000 at 10 kts surfaced
Complement: 82 (8 officers)

Torpedoes: 10—21 in *(533 mm)* (6 bow, 4 stern) tubes; 24 US Mk 37 torpedoes.
Mines: 40 in lieu of torpedoes.
Fire control: Mk 106 TFCS.
Radars: Surface search: SS 2A; I band.
Sonars: EDO BQR 2B; hull-mounted; passive search and attack; medium frequency.
EDO BQS 4; adds active capability to BQR 2B.
Sperry/Raytheon BQG 3; passive ranging.

ÇERBE *10/1985, Selim San*

Programmes: Transfers: S 335 December 1970, S 336 17 November 1970, S 340 June 1972, S 338 24 August 1973 and S 346 15 August 1973.

Structure: *Çerbe* is the only Guppy class submarine still in commission to retain the original low bridge which becomes unpleasantly wet during surface passages in heavy seas.
Operational: Diving probably restricted to periscope depth.

ULUÇALIREIS *6/1990, Selim San*

2 Ex-US TANG CLASS

Name	No	Builders	Laid down	Launched	Commissioned
HIZIRREIS (ex-USS *Gudgeon* SS 567)	S 342	Portsmouth Navy Yard	20 May 1950	11 June 1952	21 Nov 1952
PIRIREIS (ex-USS *Tang* SS 563)	S 343	Portsmouth Navy Yard	18 Apr 1949	Apr 1951	25 Oct 1951

Displacement, tons: 2100 surfaced; 2700 dived
Dimensions, feet (metres): 287 × 27.3 × 19 *(87.4 × 8.3 × 5.8)*
Main machinery: Diesel-electric; 3 Fairbanks-Morse 38D8-1/8-10 diesels; 4500 hp *(3.4 MW)*; 2 motors; 5600 hp *(4.2 MW)*; 2 shafts
Speed, knots: 16 surfaced; 16 dived. **Range, miles:** 7600 at 15 kts surfaced
Complement: 87 (8 officers)

Torpedoes: 8—21 in *(533 mm)* (6 fwd, 2 aft) tubes. Mixed load including Westinghouse Mk 37 (aft tubes); active/passive homing to 8 km *(4.4 nm)* at 24 kts; warhead 150 kg.
Mines: In lieu of torpedoes.
Fire control: Mk 106 torpedo FCS.
Radars: Surface search: Fairchild BPS 12; I band.
Sonars: EDO BQR 2B; hull-mounted; passive search and attack; medium frequency.
EDO BQS 4; adds active capability to BQR 2B.
Sperry/Raytheon BQG 4; passive ranging.

Programmes: S 343 transferred by lease January 1980—commissioned 21 March 1980. S 342 transferred by lease 30 September 1983. Both finally purchased in June 1987.

PIRIREIS *7/1989, Selçuk Emre*

DESTROYERS

8 Ex-US GEARING (FRAM I and II) CLASS

Name	No	Builders	Laid down	Launched	Commissioned
YÜCETEPE (ex-USS *Orleck* DD 886)	D 345	Consolidated Steel Corporation	28 Nov 1944	12 May 1945	15 Sep 1945
SAVAŞTEPE (ex-USS *Meredith* DD 890)	D 348	Consolidated Steel Corporation	27 Jan 1945	28 June 1945	31 Dec 1945
KILIÇ ALI PAŞA (ex-USS *Robert H. McCard* DD 822)	D 349	Consolidated Steel Corporation	26 June 1945	9 Nov 1945	26 Oct 1946
PIYALE PAŞA (ex-USS *Fiske* DD 842)	D 350	Bath Iron Works	9 Apr 1945	8 Sep 1945	28 Nov 1945
M FEVZI ÇAKMAK (ex-USS *Charles H Roan* DD 853)	D 351	Bethlehem Steel Corporation, Quincy	27 Sep 1944	15 May 1945	12 Sep 1946
GAYRET (ex-USS *Eversole* DD 789)	D 352	Todd Pacific Shipyard	28 Feb 1945	8 Jan 1946	10 July 1946
ADATEPE (ex-USS *Forrest Royal* DD 872)	D 353	Bethlehem, Staten Island	6 Aug 1945	17 Jan 1946	28 June 1946
***KOCATEPE** (ex-USS *Norris* DD 859)	D 354	Bethlehem Steel Corporation, San Pedro	29 June 1944	25 Feb 1945	9 June 1945

* FRAM II conversion

Displacement, tons: 2425 standard; 3500 full load
Dimensions, feet (metres): 390.5 × 41.2 × 19 *(119 × 12.6 × 5.8)*
Main machinery: 4 Babcock & Wilcox boilers; 600 psi *(43.3 kg/cm sq)*; 850°F *(454°C)*; 2 GE turbines; 60 000 hp *(45 MW)*; 2 shafts
Speed, knots: 32.5. **Range, miles:** 5800 at 15 kts; 2400 at 25 kts
Complement: 275 (15 officers)

Missiles: SSM: McDonnell Douglas Harpoon (1) (DD 351-352); active radar homing to 130 km *(70 nm)* at 0.9 Mach; warhead 227 kg.
A/S: Honeywell ASROC Mk 112 octuple launcher (FRAM I) (2); inertial guidance to 1.6-10 km *(1-5.4 nm)*; payload Mk 46 torpedo.
Guns: 4 USN 5 in *(127 mm)*/38 (2 twin) Mk 38 (3); 85° elevation; 15 rounds/minute to 17 km *(9.3 nm)*; weight of shell 25 kg. In A and Y positions in all except D 348 which has them in A and B.
2 or 4 Bofors 40 mm/56 (1 twin mounting fwd in D 353, 2 twin mountings midships in D 354, none in D 345) (4); 45° elevation; 160 rounds/minute to 11 km *(5.9 nm)*; weight of shell 0.9 kg.
2 or 4 Oerlikon 35 mm/90 (twin) (5) (2 twin in D 351-352); 85° elevation; 550 rounds/minute to 6 km *(3.3 nm)*; weight of shell 1.55 kg. In B and X positions in D 351-352; remainder have a single mounting in X position except D 348 which has it in Y and D 345 in B.
Torpedoes: 6—324 mm US Mk 32 (2 triple) tubes (6). Honeywell Mk 46; anti-submarine; active/passive homing to 11 km *(5.9 nm)* at 40 kts; warhead 44 kg.
A/S mortars: 1 Mk 15 Hedgehog 24-rocket launcher (FRAM II) (7); range 350 m; warhead 26 kg.
Depth charges: 1 rack (9).
Countermeasures: Decoys: 2 or 4 20-barrelled Breda 105 mm SCLAR Mk 2 or SRBOC Chaff launchers.
ESM: WLR-1 and WLR-3; radar warning.
ECM: ULQ 6; jammer.
Fire control: GFCS Mk 37 for 127 mm. 1 or 2 Mk 51 for 40 mm.
Radars: Air search: Lockheed SPS 40 (8); E/F band; range 320 km *(175 nm)*.
Surface search: Raytheon SPS 10 (9); G band.
Navigation: Racal Decca; I band.
Fire control: Western Electric Mk 25 (10); I/J band.
Sonars: Sangamo SQS 23; hull-mounted; active search and attack; medium frequency.

Programmes: D 354 is FRAM II conversion—remainder FRAM I. Transfers to Turkey took place on 27 March 1971 (D 353), 11 July 1973 (D 352) and 21 September 1973 (D 351). D 353 purchased 15 February 1973 and D 354 7 July 1974. D 349 and D 350 leased 5 June 1980, D 348 commissioned in the Turkish Navy on 20 July 1981. D 345 commissioned 30 March 1983. Ex-USS *McKean* DD 784 purchased for spares 25 November 1982. D 345, 349 and 350 purchased outright in June 1987.
Modernisation: Plans to install SAM systems in some of the class have been cancelled but *Kocatepe* may be fitted with Sea Zenith CIWS in due course.
Structure: All were built with a DASH helicopter platform and hangar but only D 345 and D 348 retain a flight deck uncluttered by guns.

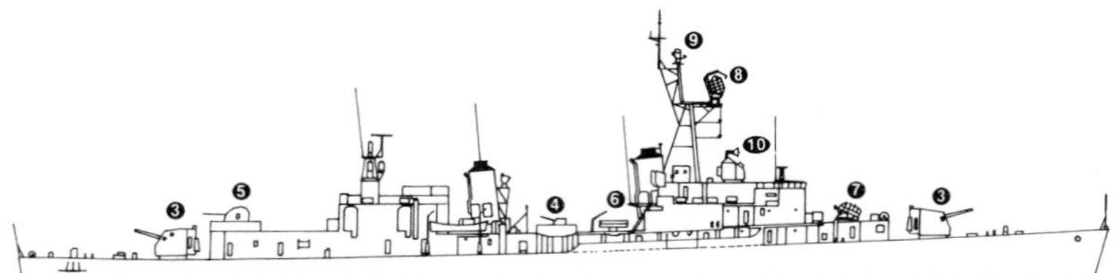

KOCATEPE — *(Scale 1 : 1 200), Ian Sturton*

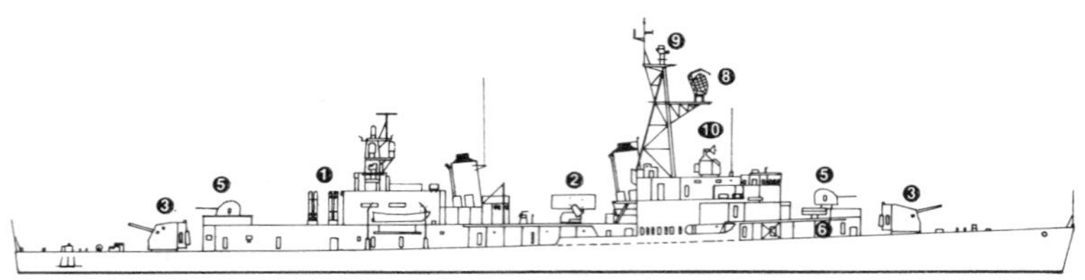

GAYRET — *(Scale 1 : 1 200), Ian Sturton*

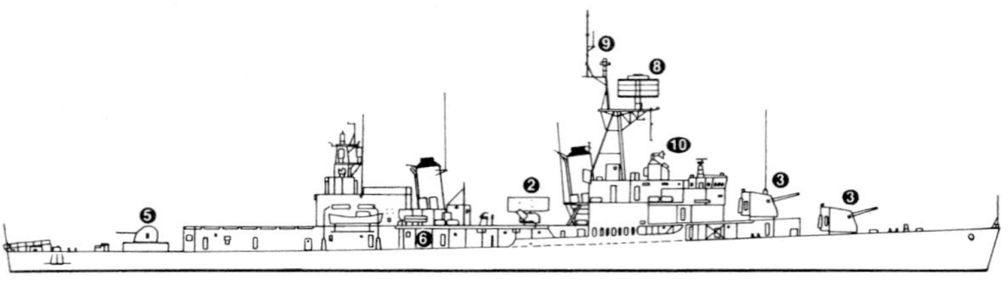

SAVASTEPE — *(Scale 1 : 1 200), Ian Sturton*

KOCATEPE — *10/1991, Selim San*

KILIÇ ALI PASA — *10/1991, C. D. Yaylali*

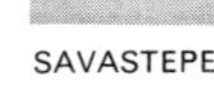
SAVASTEPE
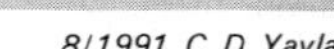
8/1991, C. D. Yaylali

YÜCETEPE (with EW van on flight deck and 35 mm gun forward) — *4/1989, O. W. Borgeld*

2 Ex-US CARPENTER (FRAM I) CLASS

Name	No	Builders	Laid down	Launched	Commissioned
ALCITEPE (ex-USS *Robert A Owens* DD 827)	D 346	Bath Iron Works, Maine	29 Oct 1945	15 July 1946	5 Nov 1949
ANITTEPE (ex-USS *Carpenter* DD 825)	D 347	Consolidated Steel, Texas	30 July 1945	30 Dec 1945	15 Dec 1949

Displacement, tons: 2425 standard; 3540 full load
Dimensions, feet (metres): 390.5 × 41 × 20.9 *(119 × 12.5 × 6.4)*
Main machinery: 4 Babcock & Wilcox boilers; 600 psi *(43.3 kg/cm sq)*; 850°F *(454°C)*; 2 GE turbines; 60 000 hp *(45 MW)*; 2 shafts
Speed, knots: 33. **Range, miles:** 6000 at 12 kts
Complement: 275 (15 officers)

Missiles: A/S: Honeywell ASROC Mk 112 octuple launcher ❶; inertial guidance to 1.6-10 km *(1-5.4 nm)*; payload Mk 46 torpedo.
Guns: 2—5 in *(127 mm)*/38 (twin) Mk 38 ❷; 85° elevation; 15 rounds/minute to 17 km *(9.3 nm)*; weight of shell 25 kg.
2—3 in *(76 mm)*/50 twin ❸; 85° elevation; 50 rounds/minute to 12.8 km *(7 nm)*; weight of shell 6 kg.
2 Oerlikon 35 mm/90 (twin) ❹; 85° elevation; 550 rounds/minute to 6 km *(3.3 nm)*; weight of shell 1.55 kg.
Torpedoes: 6—324 mm US Mk 32 (2 triple) tubes ❺. Honeywell Mk 46; anti-submarine; active/passive homing to 11 km *(5.9 nm)* at 40 kts; warhead 44 kg.
Depth charges: 1 rack (9).
Countermeasures: ESM: WLR-1; radar warning.
ECM: ULQ-6; jammer.
Fire control: Mk 56 GFCS. Mk 114 ASW FCS. Mk 1 target designation system.
Radars: Air search: Lockheed SPS 40 ❻; E/F band; range 320 km *(175 nm)*.
Surface search: Raytheon SPS 10 ❼; G band.
Fire control: General Electric Mk 35 ❽; I/J band.
Sonars: Sangamo SQS 23; hull-mounted; active search and attack; medium frequency.

Helicopters: 1 AB 212ASW ❾.

Programmes: D 347 transferred 1981, D 346 in 1982. Both purchased outright in June 1987.
Modernisation: Plans to fit a SAM system have been suspended.
Structure: A Gearing design with an ASW bias. Can handle but not house AB 212ASW helicopters.

ALCITEPE *(Scale 1 : 1 200), Ian Sturton*

ANITTEPE *1990, Camil Busquets i Vilanova*

1 Ex-US ALLEN M SUMNER (FRAM II) CLASS

Name	No	Builders	Laid down	Launched	Commissioned
ZAFER (ex-USS *Hugh Purvis* DD 709)	D 356	Federal S B and D D Co	23 May 1944	17 Dec 1944	1 Mar 1945

Displacement, tons: 2200 standard; 3320 full load
Dimensions, feet (metres): 376.5 × 40.9 × 19 *(114.8 × 12.5 × 5.8)*
Main machinery: 4 Babcock & Wilcox boilers; 600 psi *(43.3 kg/cm sq)*; 850°F *(454°C)*; 2 GE turbines; 60 000 hp *(45 MW)*; 2 shafts
Speed, knots: 34. **Range, miles:** 4600 at 15 kts
Complement: 275 (15 officers)

Guns: 6 USN 5 in *(127 mm)*/38 (3 twin) Mk 38 ❶; 85° elevation; 15 rounds/minute to 17 km *(9.3 nm)*; weight of shell 25 kg.
4 Bofors 40 mm/56 (2 twin) ❷; 45° elevation; 160 rounds/minute to 11 km *(5.9 nm)*; weight of shell 0.9 kg.
2 Oerlikon 35 mm/90 (twin) ❸; 85° elevation; 550 rounds/minute to 6 km *(3.3 nm)*; weight of shell 1.55 kg.
Torpedoes: 6—324 mm US Mk 32 (2 triple) tubes ❹. Honeywell Mk 46; anti-submarine; active/passive homing to 11 km *(5.9 nm)* at 40 kts; warhead 44 kg.
A/S mortars: 2 Mk 15 Hedgehog 24-rocket launchers ❺; range 350 m; warhead 26 kg.
Depth charges: 1 rack (9).
Countermeasures: Decoys: 2 multi-barrelled Chaff launchers.
ESM: WLR 1; radar warning. ECM: ULQ 6; jammer.
Fire control: Mk 37 GFCS for 127 mm. 2 Mk 51 GFCS for 40 mm.

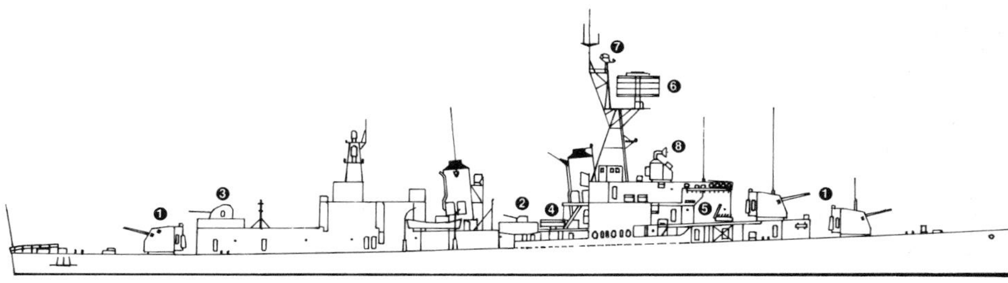

ZAFER *(Scale 1 : 900), Ian Sturton*

Radars: Air search: Westinghouse SPS 37 ❻; B/C band; range 556 km *(300 nm)*.
Surface search: Raytheon SPS 10 ❼; G band.
Fire control: Western Electric Mk 25 ❽; I/J band.
Sonars: Sangamo SQS 29 series; hull-mounted; active search and attack; high frequency.

Programmes: Allen M Sumner class of modified FRAM II having been used as a US Navy trials ship for planar passive sonar. Purchased 15 February 1973.
Structure: 35 mm gun mounting on former helicopter platform. There is an extra deckhouse in X position.

ZAFER *8/1988, Jasper Mortimer*

1 Ex-US ROBERT H SMITH CLASS

Name	*No*	*Builders*	*Laid down*	*Launched*	*Commissioned*
MUAVENET (ex-USS *Gwin*, ex-*MMD 33*, ex-*DM 33*, ex-*DD 772*)	DM 357	Bethlehem Steel Corporation, San Pedro	31 Oct 1943	9 Apr 1944	30 Sep 1944

Displacement, tons: 2250 standard; 3375 full load
Dimensions, feet (metres): 376.5 × 40.9 × 19 *(114.8 × 12.5 × 5.8)*
Main machinery: 4 Babcock & Wilcox boilers; 600 psi *(43.3 kg/cm sq)*; 850°F *(454°C)*; 2 GE turbines; 60 000 hp *(45 MW)*; 2 shafts
Speed, knots: 34. **Range, miles:** 4600 at 15 kts
Complement: 274

Guns: 6 USN 5 in *(127 mm)*/38 (3 twin) Mk 38 ❶; 85° elevation; 15 rounds/minute to 17 km *(9.3 nm)*; weight of shell 25 kg.
2 USN 3 in *(76 mm)*/50 (twin) Mk 33 ❷; 85° elevation; 50 rounds/minute to 12.8 km *(7 nm)*; weight of shell 6 kg.
12 Bofors 40 mm/56 (2 quad Mk 2 ❸, 2 twin Mk 1 ❹); 45° elevation; 160 rounds/minute to 11 km *(5.9 nm)*; weight of shell 0.9 kg.
Torpedoes: 6—324 mm US Mk 32 (2 triple) tubes ❺. Honeywell Mk 46; anti-submarine; active/passive homing to 11 km *(5.9 nm)* at 40 kts; warhead 44 kg.
A/S mortars: 2 Mk 10 Hedgehog 24-rocket launchers ❻; range 350 m; warhead 26 kg.
Depth charges: 1 rack (9).
Mines: 80.
Countermeasures: Decoys: 4 multi-barrelled Chaff launchers.
ESM: WLR 1; radar warning. ECM: Jammer.
Fire control: 1 Mk 37 GFCS for 127 mm. 2 Mk 51 GFCS for 40 mm. 1 Mk 63 GFCS for 76 mm.
Radars: Air search: Lockheed SPS 40 ❼; E/F band; range 320 km *(175 nm)*.
Surface search: Raytheon SPS 10 ❽; G band.
Fire control: Western Electric Mk 25 ❾; I/J band.
Western Electric Mk 34; I/J band.
Sonars: QCU or QHB; hull-mounted; active search and attack; high frequency.

Programmes: Modified Allen M Sumner class converted for minelaying. After modernisation at Philadelphia she was transferred on 22 October 1971.
Modernisation: Improved air defence armament, ECM and radar fitted in 1983.

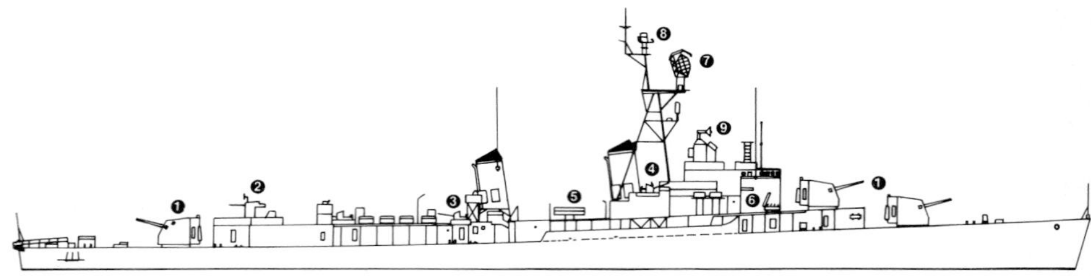
MUAVENET (Scale 1 : 900), *Ian Sturton*

MUAVENET *10/1991, Selim San*

FRIGATES

2 BERK CLASS

Name	*No*	*Builders*	*Laid down*	*Launched*	*Commissioned*
BERK	D 358	Gölcük Naval Yard	9 Mar 1967	25 June 1971	12 July 1972
PEYK	D 359	Gölcük Naval Yard	18 Jan 1968	7 June 1972	24 July 1975

Displacement, tons: 1450 standard; 1950 full load
Dimensions, feet (metres): 311.7 × 38.7 × 18.1 *(95 × 11.8 × 5.5)*
Main machinery: 4 Fiat-Tosi Type 3-016-RSS diesels; 24 000 hp(m) *(17.7 MW)*; 1 shaft
Speed, knots: 25

Guns: 4 USN 3 in *(76 mm)*/50 (2 twin) ❶; 85° elevation; 50 rounds/minute to 12.8 km *(7 nm)*; weight of shell 6 kg.
Torpedoes: 6—324 mm US Mk 32 (2 triple) tubes ❷. Honeywell Mk 46; anti-submarine; active/passive homing to 11 km *(5.9 nm)* at 40 kts; warhead 44 kg.
A/S mortars: 2 Mk 11 Hedgehog 24-rocket launchers ❸; range 350 m; warhead 26 kg.
Depth charges: 1 rack.
Countermeasures: ESM: WLR 1; radar warning.
Fire control: 2 Mk 63 GFCS.
Radars: Air search: Lockheed SPS 40 ❹; E/F band; range 320 km *(175 nm)*.
Surface search: Raytheon SPS 10 ❺; G band.
Navigation: Racal Decca; I band.
Fire control: Two Western Electric Mk 34 ❻; I/J band (for guns).

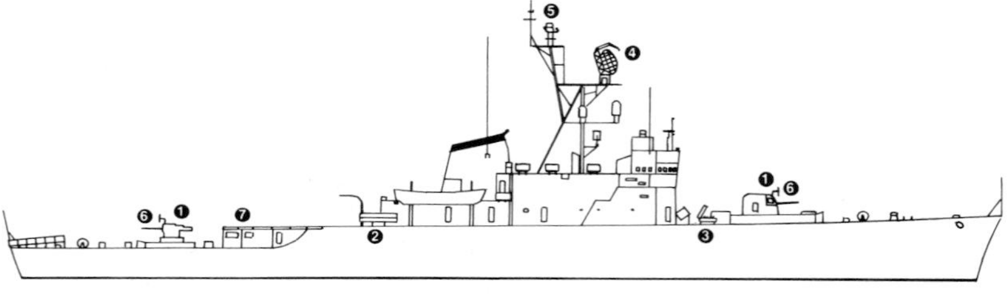
BERK (Scale 1 : 900), *Ian Sturton*

Sonars: Sangamo SQS 29/31 series; hull-mounted; active search and attack; high frequency.

Helicopters: Platform only for AB 212ASW ❼.

Programmes: First major warships built in Turkey. Both are named after famous ships of the Ottoman Navy.
Structure: Of modified US Claud Jones design (now Indonesian Samadikun class).

BERK *1/1989, Hartmut Ehlers*

4 YAVUZ CLASS (MEKO 200 TYPE)

Name	*No*	*Builders*	*Laid down*	*Launched*	*Commissioned*
YAVUZ	F 240	Blohm & Voss, Hamburg	30 May 1985	7 Nov 1985	17 July 1987
TURGUTREIS (ex-*Turgut*)	F 241	Howaldtswerke, Kiel	20 May 1985	30 May 1986	4 Feb 1988
FATIH	F 242	Gölcük, Izmit	1 Jan 1986	24 Apr 1987	22 July 1988
YILDIRIM	F 243	Gölcük, Izmit	24 Apr 1987	22 July 1988	21 July 1989

Displacement, tons: 2500 standard; 2784 full load
Dimensions, feet (metres): 362.4 × 46.6 × 13.5 *(110.5 × 14.2 × 4.1)*
Main machinery: CODAD; 4 MTU 20V 1163 TB93 diesels; 33 300 hp(m) *(24.5 MW)* sustained; 2 shafts; cp props
Speed, knots: 27. **Range, miles:** 4100 at 18 kts
Complement: 180 (24 officers)

Missiles: SSM: 8 McDonnell Douglas Harpoon (2 quad) launchers ❶; active radar homing to 130 km *(70 nm)* at 0.9 Mach; warhead 227 kg.
SAM: Raytheon Sea Sparrow Mk 29 octuple launcher ❷; 24 Selenia Elsag Aspide; semi-active radar homing to 13 km *(7 nm)* at 2.5 Mach; warhead 39 kg.
Guns: 1 FMC 5 in *(127 mm)*/54 Mk 45 Mod 1 ❸; 65° elevation; 20 rounds/minute to 23 km *(12.6 nm)* anti-surface; 15 km *(8.2 nm)* anti-aircraft; weight of shell 32 kg.
3 Oerlikon-Contraves 25 mm Sea Zenith ❹; 4 barrels per mounting; 127° elevation; 3400 rounds/minute combined to 2 km.
Torpedoes: 6—324 mm Mk 32 (2 triple) tubes ❺. Honeywell Mk 46; anti-submarine; active/passive homing to 11 km *(5.9 nm)* at 40 kts; warhead 44 kg.
Countermeasures: Decoys: 2 Loral Hycor 6-tubed fixed Mk 36 Mod 1 SRBOC ❻; IR flares and Chaff to 4 km *(2.2 nm)*.
Nixie SLQ 25; towed torpedo decoy.
ESM/ECM: Signaal Rapids/Ramses; intercept and jammer.
Combat data systems: Signaal STACOS-TU; action data automation; Link 11. WSC 3V(7) SATCOMs.
Fire control: 2 Siemens Albis optronic directors.
Radars: Air search: Signaal DA 08 ❼; F band.
Air/surface search: Plessey AWS 6 Dolphin ❽; G band.
Fire control: Signaal STIR ❾; I/J/K band (for SAM); range 140 km *(76 nm)* for 1 m² target.
Signaal WM 25 ❿; I/J band (for SSM and 127 mm); range 46 km *(25 nm)*.
Two Contraves Seaguard ⓫; I/J band (for 25 mm).
Tacan: URN 25. IFF Mk XII.
Sonars: Raytheon SQS 56 (DE 1160); hull-mounted; active search and attack; medium frequency.

Helicopters: 1 AB 212ASW ⓬.

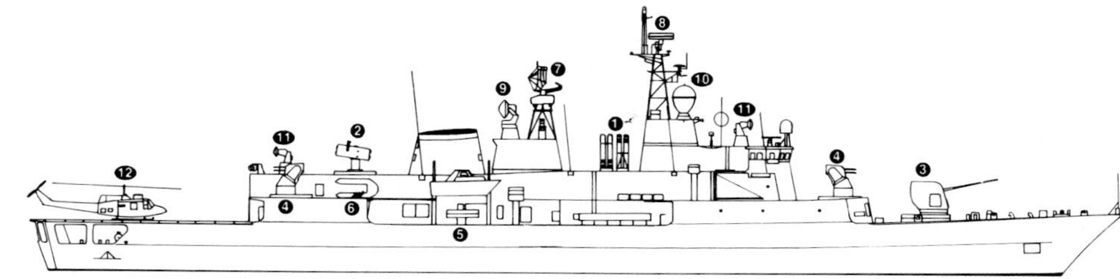

YAVUZ *(Scale 1 : 900), Ian Sturton*

FATIH *9/1991, van Ginderen Collection*

Programmes: Ordered 29 December 1982 with builders and Thyssen Rheinstahl Technik of Dusseldorf. Meko 200 type similar to Portuguese frigates. *Turgutreis* was renamed on 14 February 1988. A second batch of two ships are sufficiently different to merit a separate entry.
Operational: Helicopter has Sea Skua anti-ship missiles.

YILDIRIM *10/1991, Selim San*

TURGUTREIS *5/1990, John Mortimer*

0 + 2 BARBAROS CLASS (MODIFIED MEKO 200 TYPE)

Name	*No*	*Builders*	*Laid down*	*Launched*	*Commissioned*
BARBAROS	F 244	Blohm & Voss, Hamburg	Apr 1993	May 1994	Mar 1995
ORUCREIS	F 245	Gölcük, Kocaeli	Apr 1994	Nov 1995	Sep 1995

Displacement, tons: 3350 full load
Dimensions, feet (metres): 383.5 × 48.6 × 14.1 *(116.9 × 14.8 × 4.3)*
Main machinery: CODOG; 2 GE LM 2500 gas turbines; 44 000 hp *(33 MW)* sustained; 2 MTU 16V 1163 TB83 diesels; 11 780 hp(m) *(8.7 MW)* sustained; 2 shafts; cp props
Speed, knots: 32. **Range, miles:** 4100 at 18 kts
Complement: 180 (24 officers)

Missiles: SSM: 8 McDonnell Douglas Harpoon (2 quad) launchers ❶; active radar homing to 130 km *(70 nm)* at 0.9 Mach; warhead 227 kg.
SAM: Raytheon Sea Sparrow Mk 29 octuple launcher ❷; 24 Selenia Elsag Aspide; semi-active radar homing to 13 km *(7 nm)* at 2.5 Mach; warhead 39 kg. To be fitted for but not with VLS.
Guns: 1 FMC 5 in *(127 mm)*/54 Mk 45 Mod 2 ❸; 65° elevation; 20 rounds/minute to 23 km *(12.6 nm)* anti-surface; 15 km *(8.2 nm)* anti-aircraft; weight of shell 32 kg.
3 Oerlikon-Contraves 25 mm Sea Zenith ❹; 4 barrels per mounting; 127° elevation; 3400 rounds/minute combined to 2 km.
Torpedoes: 6—324 mm Mk 32 (2 triple) tubes ❺. Honeywell Mk 46; anti-submarine; active/passive homing to 11 km *(5.9 nm)* at 40 kts; warhead 44 kg.
Countermeasures: Decoys: 2 Loral Hycor 6-tubed fixed Mk 36 Mod 1 SRBOC ❻; IR flares and Chaff to 4 km *(2.2 nm)*.
Nixie SLQ 25; towed torpedo decoy.
ESM/ECM: Racal Cutlass/Cygnus; intercept and jammer.
Combat data systems: Atlas/Siemens/Contraves; action data automation; Link 11. WSC 3V(7) SATCOMs.

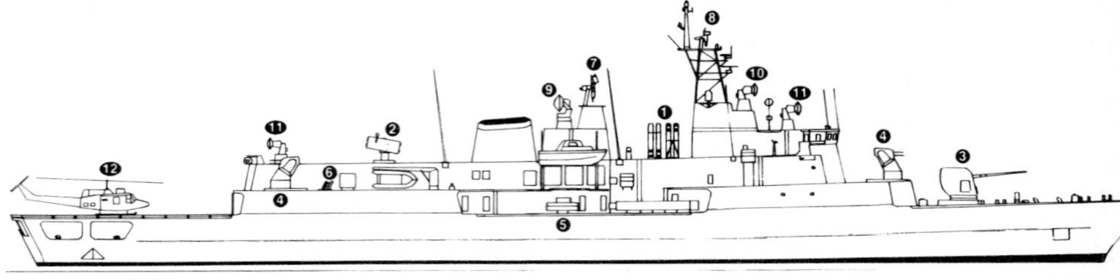

BARBAROS (Scale 1 : 900), *Ian Sturton*

Fire control: 2 Siemens Albis optronic directors.
Radars: Air search: Siemens/Plessey AWS 9 ❼; 3D; E/F band.
Air/surface search: Plessey AWS 6 Dolphin ❽; G band.
Fire control: Signaal STIR ❾; I/J/K band (for SAM); range 140 km *(76 nm)* for 1 m² target.
Contraves TMX ❿; I/J band (for SSM and 127 mm).
Two Contraves Seaguard ⓫; I/J band (for 25 mm).
Tacan: URN 25. IFF Mk XII.
Sonars: Raytheon SQS 56 (DE 1160); hull-mounted; active search and attack; medium frequency.

Helicopters: 1 AB 212ASW ⓬.

Programmes: Ordered 19 January 1990. Programme started 5 November 1991 with construction commencing in June 1992 in Germany and about mid-1993 in Turkey. Total may finally reach four as a result of the cancellation of the plan to buy Garcia class from the USN.
Structure: An improvement on the Yavuz class which will retain Mk 29 Sea Sparrow launchers but will be fitted for but not with VLS. The ships will be 5 m longer and have CODOG propulsion for a higher top speed. Other differences include a full command system, improved radars, better NBCD and air-conditioning.
Operational: Helicopter has Sea Skua anti-ship missiles. Both ships will probably be used as Flagships.

BARBAROS (artist's impression) *1991, Blohm & Voss*

2 KÖLN CLASS

Name	*No*	*Builders*	*Laid down*	*Launched*	*Commissioned*
GELIBOLU (ex-*Gazi Osman Pasa*) (ex-*Karlsruhe* F 223)	D 360	H C Stulcken Sohn, Hamburg	15 Dec 1958	24 Oct 1959	15 Dec 1962
GEMLIK (ex-*Emden* F 221)	D 361	H C Stulcken Sohn, Hamburg	15 Apr 1958	21 Mar 1959	24 Oct 1961

Displacement, tons: 2100 standard; 2700 full load
Dimensions, feet (metres): 360.5 × 36.1 × 16.7 (sonar) *(109.9 × 11 × 5.1)*
Main machinery: CODAG; 2 Brown Boveri gas turbines; 24 000 hp(m) *(17.7 MW)*; 4 MAN 16-cyl diesels; 12 000 hp(m) *(8.8 MW)*; 2 shafts; cp props
Speed, knots: 28; 18 diesels. **Range, miles:** 920 at 28 kts; 3000 at 18 kts
Complement: 210 (17 officers)

Guns: 2 Creusot Loire 3.9 in *(100 mm)*/55 Mod 53 ❶; 80° elevation; 60-80 rounds/minute to 17 km *(9.3 nm)*; weight of shell 13.5 kg.
6 Bofors 40 mm/70 (2 twin ❷, 2 single ❸); 85° elevation to 12 km *(6.6 nm)*; weight of shell 0.96 kg.
Torpedoes: 4—21 in *(533 mm)* tubes ❹; anti-submarine.
A/S mortars: 2 Bofors 375 mm 4-tubed trainable ❺; range 1600 m or 3600 m depending on weapon; 72 carried.
Depth charges: 2 racks (12).
Mines: Can carry 80.
Countermeasures: Decoys: 2 multi-barrelled Chaff launchers.
ESM: Radar intercept.
Radars: Air/surface search: Signaal DA 08 ❻; F band; range 204 km *(110 nm)* for 2 m² target.
Navigation: Kelvin Hughes; I band.
Fire control: Two Signaal M 44 ❼; I/J band (for 100 mm).
Signaal M 45 ❽; I/J band (for 40 mm).
Sonars: PAE/CWE; hull-mounted; active search and attack; high/medium frequency.

Programmes: First two transferred by West German Navy. *Gelibolu* commissioned 28 March 1983; *Gemlik*, 23 September 1983. The last two of this class, ex-FGN *Lübeck* and *Braunschweig* were also bought in December 1988 and June 1989 respectively to be used to provide spares for the other two.
Operational: An engine fire in *Gemlik* in 1989 led to speculation that she might be replaced by one of the others, but this did not happen.

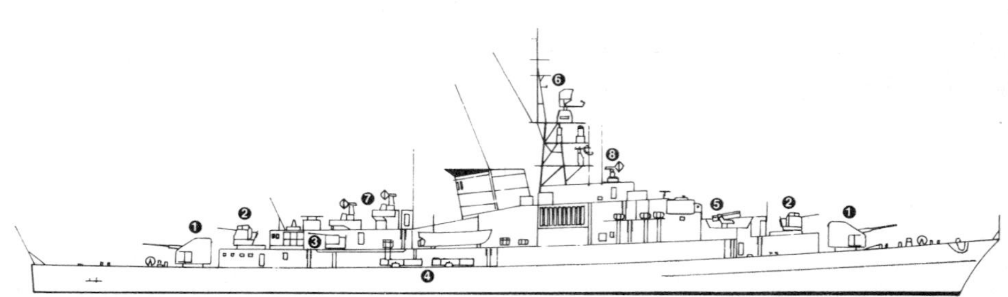

GELIBOLU (Scale 1 : 1 200), *Ian Sturton*

GELIBOLU *1989, Turkish Navy*

SHIPBORNE AIRCRAFT

Numbers/Type: 12 Agusta AB 212ASW.
Operational speed: 106 kts *(196 km/h)*.
Service ceiling: 14 200 ft *(4330 m)*.
Range: 230 nm *(426 km)*.
Role/Weapon systems: ASV/ASW helicopter with recently updated systems. Sensors: Ferranti Sea Spray Mk 3 radar, ECM/ESM, MAD, Bendix ASQ-18 dipping sonar. Weapons: ASW; 2 × Mk 46 or 244/S torpedoes. AVS; 2 × Sea Skua missiles.

LAND-BASED MARITIME AIRCRAFT

Numbers/Type: 8/15/18 Grumman S-2A/2E/2F Tracker.
Operational speed: 130 kts *(241 km/h)*.
Service ceiling: 2500 ft *(7620 m)*.
Range: 1350 nm *(2500 km)*.
Role/Weapon systems: Air Force manned for ASW and MR operations in Black and Mediterranean Seas; 18 updated in past but in need of replacement. Sensors: Search radar, ESM, MAD. Weapons: ASW; 4 × Mk 46 torpedoes, depth bombs or mines. ASV; 6 × 127 mm rockets.

LIGHT FORCES

0 + 2 (6) YILDIZ CLASS (FAST ATTACK CRAFT—MISSILE)

Name	*No*	*Builders*	*Commissioned*
YILDIZ	P 348	Taskizak Yard, Istanbul	1994
KARAYEL	P 349	Taskizak Yard, Istanbul	1995

Displacement, tons: 436 full load
Dimensions, feet (metres): 190.6 × 25 × 8.8 *(58.1 × 7.6 × 2.7)*
Main machinery: 4 MTU 16 V956 TB92 diesels; 17 700 hp(m) *(13 MW)* sustained; 4 shafts
Speed, knots: 38. **Range, miles:** 1050 at 30 kts
Complement: 45 (6 officers)

Missiles: SSM: 8 McDonnell Douglas Harpoon (2 quad) launchers; active radar homing to 130 km *(70 nm)* at 0.9 Mach; warhead 227 kg.
Guns: 1 OTO Melara 3 in *(76 mm)*/62 compact; 85° elevation; 85 rounds/minute to 16 km *(8.7 nm)* anti-surface; 12 km *(6.6 nm)* anti-aircraft; weight of shell 6 kg.
2 Oerlikon 35 mm/90 (twin); 85° elevation; 550 rounds/minute to 6 km *(3.3 nm)*; weight of shell 1.55 kg.
Countermeasures: Decoys: 2 SRBOC Chaff launchers.
ESM/ECM: Racal Cutlass.
Combat data systems: Signaal STACOS Mod IV.
Fire control: LIOD optronic director; Vesta helo data link.
Radars: Surface search: Plessey Dolphin; I band.
Fire control: Contraves TMX; I/J band.

Programmes: Ordered in June 1991. Final total may be up to eight.
Structure: Dogan class hull with much improved weapon systems.

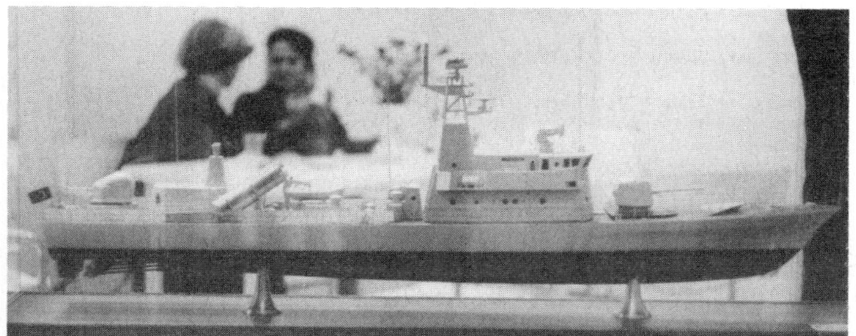

YILDIZ (model) *1991, C. D. Yaylali*

8 DOGAN CLASS (FAST ATTACK CRAFT—MISSILE)

Name	*No*	*Builders*	*Commissioned*
DOĞAN	P 340	Lürssen, Vegesack	15 June 1977
MARTI	P 341	Taşkizak Yard, Istanbul	28 July 1978
TAYFUN	P 342	Taşkizak Yard, Istanbul	19 July 1979
VOLKAN	P 343	Taşkizak Yard, Istanbul	25 July 1980
RÜZGAR	P 344	Taşkizak Yard, Istanbul	17 Dec 1984
POYRAZ	P 345	Taşkizak Yard, Istanbul	7 Feb 1986
GURBET	P 346	Taşkizak Yard, Istanbul	22 July 1988
FIRTINA	P 347	Taşkizak Yard, Istanbul	23 Oct 1988

Displacement, tons: 436 full load
Dimensions, feet (metres): 190.6 × 25 × 8.8 *(58.1 × 7.6 × 2.7)*
Main machinery: 4 MTU 16 V956 TB92 diesels; 17 700 hp(m) *(13 MW)* sustained; 4 shafts
Speed, knots: 38. **Range, miles:** 1050 at 30 kts
Complement: 38 (5 officers)

Missiles: SSM: 8 McDonnell Douglas Harpoon (2 quad) launchers; active radar homing to 130 km *(70 nm)* at 0.9 Mach; warhead 227 kg.
Guns: 1 OTO Melara 3 in *(76 mm)*/62 compact; 85° elevation; 85 rounds/minute to 16 km *(8.7 nm)* anti-surface; 12 km *(6.6 nm)* anti-aircraft; weight of shell 6 kg.
2 Oerlikon 35 mm/90 (twin); 85° elevation; 550 rounds/minute to 6 km *(3.3 nm)*; weight of shell 1.55 kg.
Countermeasures: Decoys: 2 multi-barrelled Chaff launchers.
ESM: MEL Susie; radar warning.
Radars: Surface search: Racal Decca 1226; I band.
Fire control: Signaal WM 28/41; I/J band; range 46 km *(25 nm)*.

Programmes: First ordered 3 August 1973 to a Lürssen FPB 57 design. Successor class being built using the same hull and propulsion.
Structure: Aluminium superstructure; steel hulls.

GURBET *6/1990, Selim San*

8 KARTAL CLASS (FAST ATTACK CRAFT—MISSILE)

Name	*No*	*Builders*	*Commissioned*
DENIZKUSU	P 321 (ex-*P 336*)	Lürssen, Vegesack	1967
ATMACA	P 322 (ex-*P 335*)	Lürssen, Vegesack	1967
SAHIN	P 323 (ex-*P 334*)	Lürssen, Vegesack	1967
KARTAL	P 324 (ex-*P 333*)	Lürssen, Vegesack	1967
PELIKAN	P 326	Lürssen, Vegesack	1968
ALBATROS	P 327 (ex-*P 325*)	Lürssen, Vegesack	1968
ŞIMŞEK	P 328 (ex-*P 332*)	Lürssen, Vegesack	1968
KASIRGA	P 329 (ex-*P 338*)	Lürssen, Vegesack	1967

Displacement, tons: 160 standard; 190 full load
Dimensions, feet (metres): 139.4 × 23 × 7.9 *(42.5 × 7 × 2.4)*
Main machinery: 4 Maybach MTU 16V 538 TB90 diesels; 12 000 hp(m) *(8.82 MW)* sustained; 4 shafts
Speed, knots: 42. **Range, miles:** 500 at 40 kts
Complement: 39

Missiles: SSM: 2 or 4 Kongsberg Penguin Mk 2; IR homing to 27 km *(14.6 nm)* at 0.8 Mach; warhead 120 kg.
Guns: 2 Bofors 40 mm/70; 90° elevation; 300 rounds/minute to 12 km *(6.6 nm)*; weight of shell 0.96 kg.
Torpedoes: 2—21 in *(533 mm)* tubes; anti-surface.
Mines: Can carry 4.
Radars: Surface search: Racal Decca 1226; I band.

Structure: Similar design to the Jaguar class.
Operational: *Meltem* sunk in collision with Soviet naval training ship *Khasan* in Bosphorus in 1985. Subsequently salvaged but beyond repair.

ALBATROS *1/1989, Hartmut Ehlers*

12 LARGE PATROL CRAFT

AB 25-AB 36 P 125-P 136 (ex-P 1225-P 1236)

Displacement, tons: 170 full load
Dimensions, feet (metres): 132 × 21 × 5.5 *(40.2 × 6.4 × 1.7)*
Main machinery: 4 SACM-AGO V16CSHR diesels; 9600 hp(m) *(7.06 MW)*
2 cruise diesels; 300 hp(m) *(220 kW)*; 2 shafts
Speed, knots: 22
Guns: 1 or 2 Bofors 40 mm/70 (in some).
1 Oerlikon 20 mm (in those with 1—40 mm). 2—12.7 mm MGs.
A/S mortars: 1 Mk 20 Mousetrap 4-rocket launcher; range 200 m; warhead 50 kg.
Depth charges: 1 rack.
Sonars: Hull-mounted; active search and attack; high frequency.

Comment: Built at Taşkizak Naval Yard and commissioned between 1967 and 1970. Pennant numbers changed in 1991.

AB 28 *12/1991, C. D. Yaylali*

2 Ex-GERMAN JAGUAR CLASS (FAST ATTACK CRAFT—TORPEDO)

Name	No	Builders	Commissioned
MIZRAK (ex-*Häher* P 6087)	P 333	Lürssen, Vegesack	1962
KALKAN (ex-*Wolf* P 6062)	P 335	Lürssen, Vegesack	1959

Displacement, tons: 160 standard; 190 full load
Dimensions, feet (metres): 139.4 × 23 × 7.9 *(42.5 × 7 × 2.4)*
Main machinery: 4 MTU 16V 538 TB90 diesels; 12 000 hp *(8.82 MW)* sustained; 4 shafts
Speed, knots: 42. **Range, miles:** 500 at 40 kts
Complement: 39
Guns: 2 Bofors 40 mm/70; 90° elevation; 300 rounds/minute to 12 km *(6.6 nm)*; weight of shell 0.96 kg.
Torpedoes: 4—21 in *(533 mm)* tubes (2 tubes can be removed to embark 4 mines).
Mines: Up to 4.

Comment: In late 1975-early 1976 seven Jaguar class were transferred by West Germany to Turkey. In addition three more were transferred for spare parts. Two deleted 1982, one in 1987 and two in 1988.

MIZRAK *1/1989, Hartmut Ehlers*

1 GIRNE CLASS (FAST ATTACK CRAFT—GUN)

Name	No	Builders	Commissioned
GIRNE	P 140	Taşkizak Naval Yard	30 July 1976

Displacement, tons: 341 standard; 399 full load
Dimensions, feet (metres): 190.6 × 24.9 × 9.2 *(58.1 × 7.6 × 2.8)*
Main machinery: 2 MTU 16V 956 SB90 diesels; 8000 hp(m) *(5.9 MW)* sustained; 2 shafts
Speed, knots: 36. **Range, miles:** 4200 at 16 kts
Complement: 30 (3 officers)
Guns: 2 Bofors 40 mm/70. 2 Oerlikon 20 mm.
A/S mortars: 2 Mk 20 Mousetrap 4-rocket launchers; range 200 m; warhead 50 kg.
Depth charges: 2 projectors; 2 racks.
Fire control: CSEE Naja optronic director.
Radars: Surface search: Racal Decca; I band.
Sonars: MS 25; hull-mounted; active attack; high frequency.

Comment: Unsuccessful prototype of an ASW patrol boat on a Lürssen 57 hull.

GIRNE *1988, Turkish Navy*

1 Ex-US ASHEVILLE CLASS (LARGE PATROL CRAFT)

Name	No	Builders	Commissioned
BORA (ex-USS *Surprise* PG 97)	P 339	Petersons, Wisconsin	17 Oct 1969

Displacement, tons: 225 standard; 245 full load
Dimensions, feet (metres): 164.5 × 23.8 × 9.5 *(50.1 × 7.3 × 2.9)*
Main machinery: CODAG; 1 GE LM 1500 gas turbine; 13 300 hp *(9.92 MW)*; 2 Cummins VT12-875M diesels; 1450 hp *(1.08 MW)*; 2 shafts
Speed, knots: 40 gas; 16 diesels. **Range, miles:** 320 at 38 kts
Complement: 25
Guns: 1 USN 3 in *(76 mm)*/50 Mk 34; 85° elevation; 50 rounds/minute to 12.8 km *(7 nm)*; weight of shell 6 kg.
1 Bofors 40 mm/56 Mk 10. 4—12.7 mm (2 twin) MGs.
Fire control: Mk 63 GFCS.
Radars: Surface search: Sperry SPS 53; I/J band.
Fire control: Western Electric SPG 50; I/J band.

Comment: This vessel belongs to the largest Patrol Type built by the US Navy since the Second World War and the first of that Navy to have gas turbines. Transferred to Turkey on 28 February 1973 on loan and purchased outright in June 1987.

BORA *8/1988, Selçuk Emre*

6 Ex-US PC 1638 CLASS (LARGE PATROL CRAFT)

Name	No	Builders	Commissioned
SULTANHISAR (ex-*PC 1638*)	P 111	Gunderson Bros Engineering Co, Portland, Oregon	May 1964
DEMIRHISAR (ex-*PC 1639*)	P 112	Gunderson Bros Engineering Co, Portland, Oregon	Apr 1965
YARHISAR (ex-*PC 1640*)	P 113	Gunderson Bros Engineering Co, Portland, Oregon	Sep 1964
AKHISAR (ex-*PC 1641*)	P 114	Gunderson Bros Engineering Co, Portland, Oregon	Dec 1964
SIVRIHISAR (ex-*PC 1642*)	P 115	Gunderson Bros Engineering Co, Portland, Oregon	June 1965
KOÇHISAR (ex-*PC 1643*)	P 116	Gölcük Dockyard, Turkey	July 1965

Displacement, tons: 325 standard; 477 full load
Dimensions, feet (metres): 173.7 × 23 × 10.2 *(53 × 7 × 3.1)*
Main machinery: 2 Fairbanks-Morse diesels; 2800 hp *(2.09 MW)*; 2 shafts
Speed, knots: 19. **Range, miles:** 6000 at 10 kts
Complement: 65 (5 officers)
Guns: 1 Bofors 40 mm/60. 4 Oerlikon 20 mm (2 twin).
A/S mortars: 1 Mk 15 trainable Hedgehog 24-rocket launcher; range 350 m; warhead 26 kg.
Depth charges: 4 projectors; 1 rack (9).
Radars: Surface search: Decca 707; I band.
Sonars: EDO SQS 17A; hull-mounted; active attack; high frequency.

YARHISAR *1/1990, Selim San*

4 US PGM 71 CLASS (LARGE PATROL CRAFT)

AB 21-AB 24 (ex-*PGM 104-PGM 108*) P 121-P 124 (ex-P 1221-P 1224)

Displacement, tons: 130 standard; 147 full load
Dimensions, feet (metres): 101 × 21 × 7 *(30.8 × 6.4 × 2.1)*
Main machinery: 8 GM 6-71 diesels; 1392 hp *(1.04 MW)* sustained; 2 shafts
Speed, knots: 18.5. **Range, miles:** 1500 at 10 kts
Complement: 15
Guns: 1 Bofors 40 mm/60. 4 Oerlikon 20 mm (2 twin). 1—7.62 mm MG.
A/S mortars: 2 Mk 22 Mousetrap 8-rocket launchers; range 200 m; warhead 50 kg.
Depth charges: 2 racks (4).
Radars: Surface search: Raytheon; I band.
Sonars: EDO SQS 17A; hull-mounted; active attack; high frequency.

Comment: Built by Peterson, Sturgeon Bay and commissioned 1967-68. Transferred almost immediately after completion. Pennant numbers changed in 1991.

AB 23 (old number) *5/1990, A. Sheldon Duplaix*

4 Ex-US COAST GUARD TYPE (COASTAL PATROL CRAFT)

LS 9-LS 12 P 141-P 144 (ex-P 1209-P 1212)

Displacement, tons: 63 standard
Dimensions, feet (metres): 83 × 14 × 5 *(25.3 × 4.3 × 1.6)*
Main machinery: 2 Cummins diesels; 1100 hp *(820 kW)*; 2 shafts
Speed, knots: 20
Complement: 15
Guns: 1 Oerlikon 20 mm.
A/S mortars: 2 Mk 20 Mousetrap 8-rocket launchers; range 200 m; warhead 50 kg.
Radars: Surface search: I band.
Sonars: Hull-mounted; active attack; high frequency.

Comment: Transferred on 25 June 1953. All built by US Coast Guard Yard, Curtis Bay, Maryland. Pennant numbers changed in 1991.

LS 12 (old number) *1986, Selçuk Emre*

1 COASTAL PATROL CRAFT

CANER GÖNYELI P 145

Displacement, tons: 56 full load
Dimensions, feet (metres): 87.6 × 15.4 × 5.6 *(26.7 × 4.7 × 1.7)*
Main machinery: 2 diesels; 1250 hp(m) *(918 kW)*; 2 shafts
Speed, knots: 19
Guns: 2 Oerlikon 20 mm.

Comment: Based at Girne in North Cyprus.

CANER GÖNYELI *1990 Turkish Navy*

MINE WARFARE FORCES

Note: (a) Options for new construction include a Tripartite type for local production under protocol arrangement with the Netherlands or an Abeking & Rasmussen design. Four Simrad Subsea minehunting sonars acquired in 1989. The plan is to order six with eight more to follow in due course. The operational requirement is to be able to classify and neutralise all ground and moored mines to a depth of 200 m. Tenders called for in April 1991 from Germany, UK, France, Italy and South Korea. Bids submitted in October 1991.
(b) Minelayers: see *Bayraktar, Sancaktar, Çakabey, Sarucabey* and *Karamürselbey* under Amphibious Forces

1 MINELAYER

Name	*No*	*Builders*	*Commissioned*
NUSRET	N 110 (ex-N 108)	Frederikshavn Dockyard, Denmark	16 Sep 1964

Displacement, tons: 1880 standard
Dimensions, feet (metres): 252.7 × 41 × 11 *(77 × 12.6 × 3.4)*
Main machinery: 2 GM 16-567 diesels; 2800 hp *(2.1 MW)*; 2 shafts; cp props
Speed, knots: 18
Complement: 146
Guns: 4 USN 3 in *(76 mm)* (2 twin) Mk 33; 85° elevation; 50 rounds/minute to 12.8 km *(7 nm)*; weight of shell 6 kg.
Mines: 400.
Fire control: 2 Mk 63 GFCS.
Radars: Air/surface search: Selenia RAN 7S; E/F band; range 165 km *(90 nm)*.
Navigation: I band.
Fire control: Western Electric Mk 34; I/J band.

Comment: Laid down in 1962, launched in 1964. Similar to Danish Falster class.

NUSRET *1986, Selçuk Emre*

3 Ex-US MODIFIED LSM 1 CLASS (COASTAL MINELAYERS)

Name	*No*	*Builders*	*Commissioned*
MORDOĞAN (ex-US *LSM 484*, ex-*MMC 11*)	N 101	Brown S B Co, Texas	15 Apr 1945
MERSIN (ex-US *LSM 494*, ex-*MMC 13*)	N 104	Brown S B Co, Texas	8 May 1945
MÜREFTE (ex-US *LSM 492*, ex-*MMC 14*)	N 105	Brown S B Co, Texas	1 May 1945

Displacement, tons: 743 standard; 1100 full load
Dimensions, feet (metres): 203.2 × 34.5 × 8.5 *(61.9 × 10.5 × 2.6)*
Main machinery: 2 GM 16-278A diesels; 3000 hp *(2.24 MW)*; 2 shafts
Speed, knots: 12. **Range, miles:** 2500 at 12 kts
Complement: 89
Guns: 6 Bofors 40 mm/60 (3 twin). 6 Oerlikon 20 mm.
Mines: 400.

Comment: Ex-US Landing Ships Medium. All launched in 1945, converted into coastal minelayers by the US Navy in 1952 and taken over by the Turkish Navy (LSM 484 and 490) and the Norwegian Navy (LSM 492) in October 1952 under MAP. LSM 492 *(Vale)* was retransferred to the Turkish Navy on 1 November 1960 at Bergen, Norway.

MORDOGAN *5/1990, A. Sheldon Duplaix*

1 Ex-US YMP TYPE (COASTAL MINELAYER)

Name	*No*	*Builders*	*Commissioned*
MEHMETCIK (ex-US *YMP 3*)	N 115	Higgins Inc, New Orleans	1958

Displacement, tons: 540 full load
Dimensions, feet (metres): 130 × 35 × 6 *(39.6 × 10.7 × 1.9)*
Main machinery: 2 GM 6-71 diesels; 348 hp *(260 kW)* sustained; 2 shafts
Speed, knots: 10
Complement: 22

Comment: Former US motor mine planter. Steel hulled. Transferred under MAP in 1958. For harbour defence. Soon to be deleted.

MEHMETCIK *9/1991, Erik Laursen*

2 MINELAYER TENDERS

SAMANDIRA 1 Y 131 (ex-Y 1148) **SAMANDIRA 2** Y 132 (ex-Y 1149)

Displacement, tons: 72 full load
Dimensions, feet (metres): 64.3 × 18.7 × 5.9 *(19.6 × 5.7 × 1.8)*
Main machinery: 1 Gray Marine 64 HN 9 diesel; 225 hp *(168 kW)*; 1 shaft
Speed, knots: 10
Complement: 8

Comment: Acquired in 1959. Used for laying and recovering mine distribution boxes.

SAMANDIRA 2 *9/1991, Erik Laursen*

12 Ex-US ADJUTANT, MSC 268 and MSC 294 CLASSES (MINESWEEPERS—COASTAL)

SEYMEN (ex-*MSC 131*) M 507
SELÇUK (ex-*MSC 124*) M 508
SEYHAN (ex-*MSC 142*) M 509
SAMSUN (ex-USS *MSC 268*) M 510
SINOP (ex-USS *MSC 270*) M 511
SURMENE (ex-USS *MSC 271*) M 512
SEDDULBAHIR (ex-*MSC 272*) M 513
SILIFKE (ex-USS *MSC 304*) M 514
SAROS (ex-USS *MSC 305*) M 515
SIGACIK (ex-USS *MSC 311*) M 516
SAPANCA (ex-USS *MSC 312*) M 517
SARIYER (ex-USS *MSC 315*) M 518

Displacement, tons: 320 standard; 370 full load
Dimensions, feet (metres): 141 × 26 × 8.3 *(43 × 8 × 2.6)*
Main machinery: 4 GM 6-71 diesels; 880 hp *(656 kW)*; 2 shafts (MSC 268 class)
2 Waukesha L 1616 diesels; 1200 hp *(895 kW)*; 2 shafts (MSC 294 class)
Speed, knots: 14. **Range, miles:** 2500 at 10 kts
Complement: 38 (4 officers)
Guns: 2 Oerlikon 20 mm (twin).
Radars: Navigation: Decca; I band.
Sonars: UQS-1D; hull-mounted mine search; high frequency.

Comment: Built 1955-59 (M 507-M 513) and 1965-67 (M 514-M 518). Transferred on 19 November 1970, 24 March 1970, 24 March 1970, 30 September 1958, February 1959, 27 March 1959, May 1959, September 1965, February 1966, June 1965, 26 July 1965, 8 September 1967, respectively. M 508 and M 509 were transferred from France (via the USA) and M 507 from Belgium (via the USA). Height of funnels and bridge arrangements vary.

SELÇUK *7/1991, Selim San*

4 Ex-CANADIAN MCB TYPE (MINESWEEPERS—COASTAL)

TRABZON (ex-HMCS *Gaspe*) P 530 (ex-M 530)
TERME (ex-HMCS *Trinity*) P 531 (ex-M 531)
TIREBOLU (ex-HMCS *Comax*) P 532 (ex-M 532)
TEKIRDAG (ex-HMCS *Ungava*) A 601 (ex-M 533)

Displacement, tons: 370 standard; 470 full load
Dimensions, feet (metres): 164 × 30.2 × 9.2 *(50 × 9.2 × 2.8)*
Main machinery: 2 GM 12-278A diesels; 2200 hp *(1.64 MW)*; 2 shafts
Speed, knots: 15. **Range, miles:** 4500 at 11 kts
Complement: 35 (4 officers)
Guns: 1 Bofors 40 mm/60. 2—12.7 mm MGs.

Comment: Sailed from Sydney, Nova Scotia, to Turkey on 19 May 1958. Built by Davie S B Co 1951-53. Of similar type to British Ton class. *Tekirdag* has been fitted with ECM pods abaft mast. Pennant numbers changed in 1991 suggesting use of three as patrol ships and one as an auxiliary.

TERME (old number) *10/1989, Hartmut Ehlers*

6 Ex-GERMAN VEGESACK CLASS (MINESWEEPERS—COASTAL)

Name	No	Builders	Commissioned
KARAMÜRSEL (ex-*Worms* M 1253)	M 520	Amiot, Cherbourg	30 Apr 1960
KEREMPE (ex-*Detmold* M 1252)	M 521	Amiot, Cherbourg	20 Feb 1960
KILIMLI (ex-*Siegen* M 1254)	M 522	Amiot, Cherbourg	9 July 1960
KOZLU (ex-*Hameln* M 1251)	M 523	Amiot, Cherbourg	15 Oct 1959
KUŞADASI (ex-*Vegesack* M 1250)	M 524	Amiot, Cherbourg	19 Sep 1959
KEMER (ex-*Passau* M 1255)	M 525	Amiot, Cherbourg	15 Oct 1960

Displacement, tons: 362 standard; 378 full load
Dimensions, feet (metres): 155.1 × 28.2 × 9.5 *(47.3 × 8.6 × 2.9)*
Main machinery: 2 Mercedes-Benz MTU diesels; 1500 hp(m) *(1.1 MW)*; 2 shafts; cp props
Speed, knots: 15
Complement: 40
Guns: 2 Oerlikon 20 mm (twin).
Radars: Navigation: Decca; I band.

Comment: Of similar class to French *Mercure*. M 520-524 transferred by West Germany to Turkey late 1975-early 1976. M 525 transferred 1979 and refitted 1980 at Taşkizak. M 520 converted for trials July 1986-1987.

KILIMLI *9/1990, Selim San*

4 Ex-US CAPE CLASS (MINESWEEPERS—INSHORE)

Name	No	Builders	Commissioned
FOÇA (ex-*MSI 15*)	M 500	Peterson, Wisconsin	Aug 1967
FETHIYE (ex-*MSI 16*)	M 501	Peterson, Wisconsin	Aug 1967
FATSA (ex-*MSI 17*)	M 502	Peterson, Wisconsin	Sep 1967
FINIKE (ex-*MSI 18*)	M 503	Peterson, Wisconsin	Nov 1967

Displacement, tons: 180 standard; 235 full load
Dimensions, feet (metres): 111.9 × 23.5 × 7.9 *(34 × 7.1 × 2.4)*
Main machinery: 4 GM 6-71 diesels; 880 hp *(656 kW)*; 2 shafts
Speed, knots: 13. **Range, miles:** 900 at 11 kts
Complement: 30
Guns: 1—12.7 mm MG.

Comment: Built in USA and transferred under MAP at Boston, Massachusetts, August-December 1967.

FATSA *9/1990, Selim San*

8 MINEHUNTING TENDERS

DALGIÇ 2 (ex-*MTB 2*) P 312
MTB 3 P 313
MTB 4 P 314
MTB 5 P 315
MTB 6 P 316
MTB 7 P 317
MTB 8 P 318
MTB 9 P 319

Displacement, tons: 70 standard
Dimensions, feet (metres): 71.5 × 13.8 × 8.5 *(21.8 × 4.2 × 2.6)*
Main machinery: 2 diesels; 2000 hp(m) *(1.47 MW)*; 2 shafts
Speed, knots: 20
Guns: 1 Oerlikon 20 mm or 1—12.7 mm MG (aft) (in some).

Comment: All launched in 1942. Now employed as minehunting base ships (P 313-319) and diver support craft (P 312).

MTB 9 *9/1991, Erik Laursen*

AMPHIBIOUS FORCES

Note: The prefix 'Ç' for smaller amphibious vessels stands for 'Çikartma Gemisi' (landing vessel) and indicates that the craft are earmarked for national rather than NATO control.

0 + 1 OSMAN GAZI CLASS (LST)

Name	No	Builders	Commissioned
OSMAN GAZI	NL 125	Taşkizak Yard, Istanbul	July 1993

Displacement, tons: 3773 full load
Dimensions, feet (metres): 344.5 × 52.8 × 15.7 *(105 × 16.1 × 4.8)*
Main machinery: 2 MTU 12V 1163 TB73 diesels; 8800 hp(m) *(6.47 MW)*; 2 shafts
Speed, knots: 17. **Range, miles:** 4000 at 15 kts
Military lift: 900 troops; 15 tanks; 4 LCVPs
Guns: 3 Bofors 40 mm/70; 2 Oerlikon 35 mm/90 (twin).
Helicopters: Platform for one large.

Comment: Laid down 7 July 1989, launched 20 July 1990. Full NBCD protection. Equipped with a support weapons co-ordination centre to control amphibious operations. The ship has about a 50 per cent increase in military lift capacity compared with the Sarucabey class. Second of class cancelled in 1991.

OSMAN GAZI *9/1991, Erik Laursen*

2 Ex-US 512-1152 CLASS (LSTs)

Name	No	Commissioned
BAYRAKTAR (ex-FDR *Bottrop*, ex-USS *Saline County* LST 1101)	NL 120 (ex-N-111, ex-A 579, ex-L 403)	26 Jan 1945
SANCAKTAR (ex-FDR *Bochum*, ex-USS *Rice County* LST 1089)	NL 121 (ex-N-112, ex-A 580, ex-L 404)	14 Mar 1945

Displacement, tons: 1653 standard; 4080 full load
Dimensions, feet (metres): 328 × 50 × 14 *(100 × 15.2 × 4.3)*
Main machinery: 2 GM 12-567A diesels; 1800 hp *(1.34 MW)*; 2 shafts; cp props
Speed, knots: 11. **Range, miles:** 15 000 at 9 kts
Complement: 125
Guns: 6 Bofors 40 mm/70 (2 twin, 2 single).
Mines: 4 rails.
Radars: Navigation: Kelvin Hughes; I band.

Comment: Transferred to West Germany in 1961 and thence to Turkey on 13 December 1972. Converted into minelayers in West Germany 1962-64. Minelaying gear removed 1974-75 and replaced in 1979. Now dual purpose ships.

BAYRAKTAR *1990, Turkish Navy*

2 Ex-US TERREBONNE PARISH CLASS (LSTs)

Name	*No*	*Builders*	*Commissioned*
ERTUĞRUL (ex-USS *Windham County* LST 1170)	L 401	Christy Corporation	15 Dec 1954
SERDAR (ex-USS *Westchester County* LST 1167)	L 402	Christy Corporation	10 Mar 1954

Displacement, tons: 2590 light; 5800 full load
Dimensions, feet (metres): 384 × 55 × 17 *(117.1 × 16.8 × 5.2)*
Main machinery: 4 GM 12-268A diesels; 6000 hp *(4.48 MW)*; 2 shafts; cp props
Speed, knots: 15
Complement: 116
Military lift: 395 troops; 2200 tons cargo; 4 LCVPs
Guns: 6 USN 3 in *(76 mm)*/50 (3 twin).
Fire control: 2 Mk 63 GFCS.
Radars: Surface search: Raytheon SPS 21; G/H band; range 22 km *(12 nm)*.
Fire control: Two Western Electric Mk 34; I/J band.

Comment: Transferred by USA June 1973 (L 401) and 27 August 1974 (L 402) on loan. Purchased outright in 1988.

ERTUĞRUL *1990, Turkish Navy*

1 ÇAKABEY CLASS (LST)

Name	*No*	*Builders*	*Commissioned*
ÇAKABEY	NL 122 (ex-L 405)	Taşkizak Naval Yard	25 July 1980

Displacement, tons: 1600
Dimensions, feet (metres): 253.5 × 39.4 × 7.5 *(77.3 × 12 × 2.3)*
Main machinery: 3 diesels; 4320 hp *(3.2 MW)*; 3 shafts
Speed, knots: 14
Military lift: 400 troops; 9 tanks; 10 jeeps; 2 LCVPs
Guns: 4 Bofors 40 mm/60 (2 twin). 4 Oerlikon 20 mm (2 twin).
Mines: 150 in lieu of amphibious load.
Radars: Navigation: Racal Decca; I band.
Helicopters: Platform only.

Comment: Launched 30 June 1977. Dual purpose minelayer.

ÇAKABEY *2/1987, Selçuk Emre*

2 SARUCABEY CLASS (LSTs)

Name	*No*	*Builders*	*Commissioned*
SARUCABEY	NL 123	Taşkizak Naval Yard	26 July 1984
KARAMÜRSELBEY	NL 124	Taşkizak Naval Yard	27 July 1985

Displacement, tons: 2600 full load
Dimensions, feet (metres): 301.8 × 45.9 × 7.5 *(92 × 14 × 2.3)*
Main machinery: 3 diesels; 4320 hp *(3.2 MW)*; 3 shafts
Speed, knots: 14
Military lift: 600 troops; 11 tanks; 12 jeeps; 2 LCVPs
Guns: 3 Bofors 40 mm/70. 4 Oerlikon 20 mm (2 twin).
Mines: 150 in lieu of amphibious lift.
Radars: Navigation: Racal Decca; I band.
Helicopters: Platform only.

Comment: *Sarucabey* is an enlarged Çakabey design more suitable for naval requirements. First one launched 30 July 1981, second 26 July 1984. Dual purpose minelayers.

KARAMÜRSELBEY *1989, Selçuk Emre*

8 EDIC TYPE (LCTs)

Ç 108, 110, 112-114, 116-118

Displacement, tons: 580 full load
Dimensions, feet (metres): 186.9 × 39.4 × 4.6 *(57 × 12 × 1.4)*
Main machinery: 3 GM 6-71 diesels; 522 hp *(390 kW)* sustained; 3 shafts
Speed, knots: 8.5. **Range, miles:** 600 at 10 kts
Complement: 15
Military lift: 100 troops; up to 5 tanks
Guns: 2 Oerlikon 20 mm. 2—12.7 mm MGs.

Comment: Built at Gölcük Naval Shipyard 1966-73. French EDIC type. 4 scrapped in 1991.

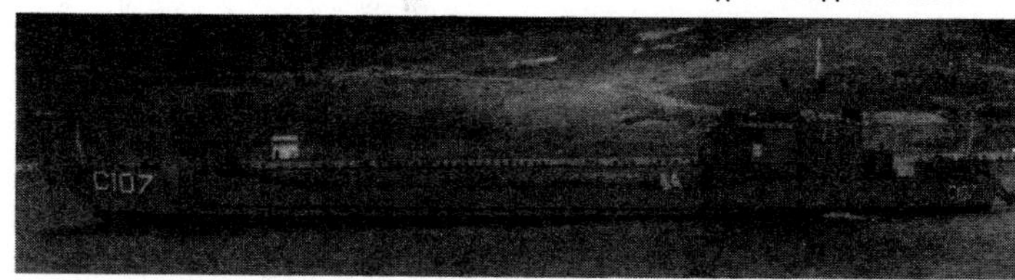

EDIC Type (old number) *1987*

26 + 3 LCTs

Ç 119-129, 132-135, 137-147

Displacement, tons: 600 full load
Dimensions, feet (metres): 195.5 × 38 × 4.6 *(59.6 × 11.6 × 1.4)*
Main machinery: 3 GM 6-71 diesels; 522 hp *(390 kW)* sustained; 3 shafts (119-138) or 3 MTU diesels; 900 hp(m) *(662 kW)*; 3 shafts (139-147)
Speed, knots: 8.5. **Range, miles:** 600 at 8 kts
Complement: 15
Military lift: 100 troops; 5 tanks
Guns: 2 Oerlikon 20 mm. 2—12.7 mm MGs.

Comment: Follow-on to the Ç 107 type started building in 1977. Ç 130 and Ç 131 transferred to Libya January 1980 and Ç 136 sunk in 1985. The delivery rate was about two per year from the Taşkizak and Gölcük yards until 1987. Two more launched in July 1987 and commissioned in mid-1991. More may be building. Dimensions given are for Ç 139 onwards, earlier craft are 3.6 m shorter and have less freeboard.

Ç 120 *10/1991, Harald Carstens*

Ç 141 *6/1986, Hartmut Ehlers*

5 LCUs

Ç 205-207, 213-214

Displacement, tons: 320 light; 405 full load
Dimensions, feet (metres): 142 × 28 × 5.7 *(43.3 × 8.5 × 1.7)*
Main machinery: 2 GM 6-71 diesels; 348 hp *(260 kW)* sustained; 2 shafts
Speed, knots: 10
Guns: 2 Oerlikon 20 mm.

Comment: Built by Taşkizak, Istanbul 1965-66. Seven scrapped in 1991.

Ç 206 *9/1988, Selçuk Emre*

23 LCM 8 TYPE

Ç 301-303, 305, 308-309, 312-314, 316, 318-319, 321-331

Displacement, tons: 58 light; 113 full load
Dimensions, feet (metres): 72 × 20.5 × 4.8 *(22 × 6.3 × 1.4)*
Main machinery: 2 GM 6-71 diesels; 348 hp *(260 kW)* sustained; 2 shafts
Speed, knots: 9.5
Complement: 9
Guns: 1—12.7 mm MG.

Comment: Built by Taşkizak, Istanbul in 1965-66. Eight scrapped in 1991.

Ç 308 — *10/1989, Hartmut Ehlers*

SURVEY SHIPS

Name	*No*	*Builders*	*Commissioned*
YUNUS (ex-*Alster*, ex-*Mellum*)	A 590 (ex-A 50)	Unterweser, Bremen	21 Mar 1961

Displacement, tons: 1497 full load
Dimensions, feet (metres): 275.5 × 34.4 × 18.4 *(84 × 10.5 × 5.6)*
Main machinery: 1 Deutz diesel; 1800 hp(m) *(1.32 MW)*; 1 shaft
Speed, knots: 15
Complement: 90

Comment: Ex-trawler, purchased by West German Navy in 1965. Conversion at Blohm & Voss and commissioned for naval service on 19 October 1971. Transferred in February 1989. Continues to be used as an AGI.

YUNUS — *10/1991, Selim San*

Name	*No*	*Builders*	*Commissioned*
ÇUBUKLU (ex-*Y 1251*)	A 594	Gölcük	July 1984

Displacement, tons: 680 full load
Dimensions, feet (metres): 132.8 × 31.5 × 10.5 *(40.5 × 9.6 × 3.2)*
Main machinery: 1 MWM diesel; 820 hp(m) *(603 kW)*; 1 shaft; cp prop
Speed, knots: 11
Complement: 31 (5 officers)
Guns: 2 Oerlikon 20 mm.

Comment: Launched 17 November 1983. Qubit advanced integrated navigation and data processing system being fitted in 1991.

ÇUBUKLU — *7/1990, Selçuk Emre*

MESAHA 1 Y 35 (ex-Y 1221) **MESAHA 2** Y 36 (ex-Y 1222)

Displacement, tons: 45 full load
Dimensions, feet (metres): 52.2 × 14.8 × 4.3 *(15.9 × 4.5 × 1.3)*
Main machinery: 2 GM diesels; 330 hp *(246 kW)*; 2 shafts
Speed, knots: 10. **Range, miles:** 600 at 10 kts
Complement: 8

Comment: Built in 1966. Former US Sounding Boats. Similar to Brazil Paraibano class. Pennant numbers changed in 1991.

MESAHA 1 — *10/1991, Harald Carstens*

SERVICE FORCES

1 Ex-US DIXIE CLASS (DEPOT SHIP)

Name	*No*	*Builders*	*Commissioned*
DERYA (ex-USS *Piedmont* AD 17)	A 576	Tampa Shipbuilding Co	5 Jan 1944

Displacement, tons: 9450 standard; 18 000 full load
Dimensions, feet (metres): 530.5 × 73.2 × 25.6 *(161.7 × 22.3 × 7.8)*
Main machinery: 4 Babcock & Wilcox boilers; 400 psi *(28.4 kg/cm sq)*; 720°F *(382°C)*; 2 Allis Chalmers turbines; 12 000 hp *(8.95 MW)*; 2 shafts
Speed, knots: 18.2. **Range, miles:** 12 000 at 12 kts
Complement: 120
Guns: 3 Bofors 40 mm/70. 8 Oerlikon 20 mm.
Radars: Surface search: Raytheon SPS 10; G band.
Helicopters: Platform only.

Comment: Modernised to service destroyers with ASROC, helicopters and modern electronics. Transferred on loan at Norfolk, Virginia October 1982. Commissioned in Turkish Navy 28 March 1983. Purchased outright in June 1987.

DERYA — *3/1988, Hartmut Ehlers*

2 Ex-GERMAN RHEIN CLASS (TRAINING SHIPS)

Name	*No*	*Builders*	*Commissioned*
SOKULLU MEHMET PAŞA (ex-*Isar*)	A 577	Blohm & Voss	25 Jan 1964
CEZAYIRLI GAZI HASAN PAŞA (ex-*Ruhr*)	A 579	Schliekerwerft, Hamburg	2 May 1964

Displacement, tons: 2370 standard; 2940 full load
Dimensions, feet (metres): 322.1 × 38.8 × 14.4 *(98.2 × 11.8 × 4.4)*
Main machinery: 6 Maybach diesels; 14 400 hp(m) *(10.58 MW)*; 2 shafts
Speed, knots: 20.5. **Range, miles:** 1625 at 15 kts
Complement: 110/125 (accommodation for 200)
Guns: 2 Creusot Loire 3.9 in *(100 mm)*/55. 4 Bofors 40 mm/60.
Radars: Surface search: Signaal DA 02; E/F band.
Fire control: Two Signaal M 45; I/J band.

Comment: A 579, transferred 18 July 1975, commissioned in Turkish Navy 16 January 1977 after major refit. A 577 transferred 30 September 1982, commissioned 28 March 1983.

CEZAYIRLI GAZI HASAN PAŞA — *6/1990, Selim San*

2 Ex-GERMAN ANGELN CLASS (DEPOT SHIPS)

Name	*No*	*Builders*	*Commissioned*
ÜLKÜ (ex-*Angeln*)	A 586	A C de Bretagne	20 Jan 1955
UMUR BEY (ex-*Dithmarschen*)	A 588	A C de Bretagne	17 Nov 1955

Displacement, tons: 4190 full load
Dimensions, feet (metres): 296.9 × 43.6 × 20.3 *(90.5 × 13.3 × 6.2)*
Main machinery: 2 SEMT-Pielstick diesels; 3000 hp(m) *(2.2 MW)*; 1 shaft
Speed, knots: 17. **Range, miles:** 3660 at 15 kts
Complement: 57
Cargo capacity: 2670 tons
Guns: 2 Bofors 40 mm/60 (aft). 2 Oerlikon 20 mm.

Comment: Ex-cargo ships bought by West Germany in 1959. Transferred 22 March 1972 and December 1975. A 588 employed as submarine depot ship and A 586 as light forces depot ship.

UMUR BEY — *4/1986, Hartmut Ehlers*

1 FLEET REPLENISHMENT TANKER

Name	*No*	*Builders*	*Commissioned*
AKAR	A 580	Gölcük Naval DY	24 Apr 1987

Displacement, tons: 19 350 full load
Dimensions, feet (metres): 475.9 × 74.8 × 27.6 *(145.1 × 22.8 × 8.4)*
Main machinery: 1 diesel; 6500 hp(m) *(4.78 MW)*; 1 shaft
Speed, knots: 15
Complement: 329
Cargo capacity: 6000 tons oil fuel
Guns: 2—3 in *(76 mm)*/50 (twin). 2 Bofors 40 mm/70.
Fire control: Mk 63; GFCS.
Helicopters: Platform only.

Comment: Launched 17 November 1983. Helicopter flight deck aft. There is a requirement for a second ship.

AKAR — *9/1991, van Ginderen Collection*

1 SUPPORT TANKER

Name	*No*	*Builders*	*Commissioned*
TAŞKIZAK	A 570	Taşkizak Naval DY, Istanbul	25 July 1984

Displacement, tons: 1440
Dimensions, feet (metres): 211.9 × 30.8 × 11.5 *(64.6 × 9.4 × 3.5)*
Main machinery: 1 diesel; 1400 hp(m) *(1.03 MW)*; 1 shaft
Speed, knots: 13
Complement: 57
Cargo capacity: 800 tons
Guns: 1 Bofors 40 mm/70. 2 Oerlikon 20 mm.

Comment: Laid down 20 July 1983.

TAŞKIZAK (Dogan Class in background) — *5/1990, A. Sheldon Duplaix*

1 SUPPORT TANKER

Name	*No*	*Builders*	*Commissioned*
YÜZBAŞI TOLUNAY	A 571	Taşkizak Naval DY, Istanbul	1951

Displacement, tons: 2500 standard; 3500 full load
Dimensions, feet (metres): 260 × 41 × 19.5 *(79 × 12.4 × 5.9)*
Main machinery: 2 Atlas-Polar diesels; 1920 hp(m) *(1.41 MW)*; 2 shafts
Speed, knots: 14
Guns: 2 Bofors 40 mm/70 (not always embarked).

Comment: Launched on 22 August 1950. Beam and stern replenishment facilities.

YÜZBAŞI TOLUNAY — *5/1987, Selçuk Emre*

1 SUPPORT TANKER

Name	*No*	*Builders*	*Commissioned*
ALBAY HAKKI BURAK	A 572	Gölcük Naval DY	1965

Displacement, tons: 3800 full load
Dimensions, feet (metres): 274.7 × 40.2 × 18 *(83.7 × 12.3 × 5.5)*
Main machinery: Diesel-electric; 4 GM 16-567A diesels; 5600 hp *(4.12 MW)*; 4 generators; 2 motors; 4400 hp *(3.28 MW)*; 2 shafts
Speed, knots: 16
Complement: 88
Cargo capacity: 1900 tons oil fuel approx
Guns: 2 Bofors 40 mm/60 (not always fitted).

ALBAY HAKKI BURAK — *3/1988, Hartmut Ehlers*

1 SUPPORT TANKER

Name	*No*	*Builders*	*Commissioned*
BINBAŞI SAADETTIN GÜRÇAN	A 573	Taşkizak Naval DY, Istanbul	1970

Displacement, tons: 1505 standard; 4460 full load
Dimensions, feet (metres): 294.2 × 38.7 × 17.7 *(89.7 × 11.8 × 5.4)*
Main machinery: Diesel-electric; 4 GM 16-567A diesels; 5600 hp *(4.12 MW)*; 4 generators; 2 motors; 4400 hp *(3.28 MW)*; 2 shafts
Speed, knots: 16
Guns: 1—3 in *(76 mm)*/62. 2 Oerlikon 20 mm.

BINBAŞI SAADETTIN GÜRÇAN — *1987, Selçuk Emre*

3 HARBOUR TANKERS

H 500, H 501, H 502 (ex-Y 1231-1233)

Displacement, tons: 300
Dimensions, feet (metres): 110.2 × 27.9 × 5.9 *(33.6 × 8.5 × 1.8)*
Main machinery: 1 diesel; 225 hp(m) *(165 kW)*; 1 shaft
Speed, knots: 11
Cargo capacity: 150 tons

Comment: Sisters of water tankers of Pinar series. Built at Taşkizak in early 1970s. Pennant numbers changed in 1991.

H 501 (old number) — *3/1990, Selim San*

1 Ex-GERMAN SUPPORT TANKER

Name	No	Builders	Commissioned
INEBOLU (ex-*Bodensee* A 1406, ex-*Unkas*)	A 575	Lindenau, Kiel	26 Mar 1959

Displacement, tons: 1840 full load
Measurement, tons: 1238 dwt
Dimensions, feet (metres): 219.8 × 32.1 × 14.1 *(67 × 9.8 × 4.3)*
Main machinery: 1 MAK diesel; 1050 hp(m) *(772 kW)*; 1 shaft
Speed, knots: 12
Complement: 26
Cargo capacity: 1230 tons
Guns: 2 Oerlikon 20 mm (on bridge).

Comment: Launched 19 November 1955. Of Bodensee class. Transferred September 1977 at Wilhelmshavn, under West German military aid programme. Has replenishment capability.

INEBOLU *4/1986, Hartmut Ehlers*

2 Ex-US REPAIR SHIPS

Name	No	Builders	Commissioned
ONARAN (ex-*Alecto* AGP 14, ex-*LST 558*)	A 581	Missouri Valley Bridge & Iron Co	8 Feb 1945
BAŞARAN (ex-*Patroclus* ARL 19, ex-*LST 955*)	A 582	Bethlehem Hingham Shipyard	13 Nov 1944

Displacement, tons: 1625 standard; 4080 full load
Dimensions, feet (metres): 328 × 50 × 14 *(100 × 15.2 × 4.4)*
Main machinery: 2 GM 12-278A diesels; 2200 hp *(1.64 MW)*; 2 shafts
Speed, knots: 11. **Range, miles:** 9000 at 9 kts
Complement: 80
Guns: 8 Bofors 40 mm/60 (2 quad). 8 Oerlikon 20 mm.

Comment: Former US repair ship and MTB tender, respectively, of the LST type. A 582 was launched on 22 October 1944, A 581 on 14 April 1944. Acquired from the USA in November 1952 and May 1948, respectively.

BAŞARAN *1986, Selçuk Emre*

1 Ex-US DIVER CLASS (SALVAGE SHIP)

Name	No	Builders	Commissioned
IŞIN (ex-USS *Safeguard* ARS 25)	A 589	Basalt Rock Co, Napa, California	31 Oct 1944

Displacement, tons: 1530 standard; 1970 full load
Dimensions, feet (metres): 213.5 × 41 × 13 *(65.1 × 12.5 × 4)*
Main machinery: Diesel-electric; 4 Cooper-Bessemer GSB-8 diesels; 3420 hp *(2.55 MW)*; 4 generators; 2 motors; 2 shafts
Speed, knots: 14.8
Complement: 110
Guns: 2 Oerlikon 20 mm.

Comment: Transferred 28 September 1979 and purchased outright in June 1987.

IŞIN *5/1990, A. Sheldon Duplaix*

1 Ex-US CHANTICLEER CLASS (SUBMARINE RESCUE SHIP)

Name	No	Builders	Commissioned
AKIN (ex-USS *Greenlet* ASR 10)	A 585	Moore S B & D D Co	29 May 1943

Displacement, tons: 1653 standard; 2321 full load
Dimensions, feet (metres): 251.5 × 44 × 16 *(76.7 × 13.4 × 4.9)*
Main machinery: Diesel-electric; 4 Alco 539 diesels; 3532 hp *(2.63 MW)*; 4 generators; 1 motor; 1 shaft
Speed, knots: 15
Complement: 85
Guns: 1 Bofors 40 mm/60. 4 Oerlikon 20 mm (twin).

Comment: Transferred 12 June 1970 and purchased 15 February 1973. Carries a Diving Bell.

AKIN *4/1986, Hartmut Ehlers*

1 Ex-US BLUEBIRD CLASS (SUBMARINE RESCUE SHIP)

KURTARAN (ex-USS *Bluebird* ASR 19, ex-*Yurak* AT 165) A 584

Displacement, tons: 1294 standard; 1675 full load
Dimensions, feet (metres): 205 × 38.5 × 11 *(62.5 × 12.2 × 3.5)*
Main machinery: Diesel-electric; 4 GM 12-278A diesels; 4400 hp *(3.28 MW)*; 4 generators; 1 motor; 3000 hp *(2.24 MW)*; 1 shaft
Speed, knots: 16
Complement: 100
Guns: 1 USN 3 in *(76 mm)*/50. 2 Oerlikon 20 mm.

Comment: Former salvage tug adapted as a submarine rescue vessel in 1947. Transferred from the US Navy on 15 August 1950. Carries a Diving Bell.

KURTARAN *5/1990, A. Sheldon Duplaix*

4 TRANSPORTS

KANARYA (ex-Y 1155) **SARKÖY** (ex-Y 1156) **KARADENIZ EREĞLISI** (ex-Y 1157)
ECEABAT (ex-Y 1165)

Displacement, tons: 820 full load
Dimensions, feet (metres): 166.3 × 26.2 × 9.2 *(50.7 × 8 × 2.8)*
Main machinery: 1 diesel; 1440 hp *(1.06 MW)*; 1 shaft
Speed, knots: 10
Cargo capacity: 300 tons
Guns: 1 Oerlikon 20 mm.

Comment: Funnel-aft coaster type. *Sarköy* has a wireless mast at after end of the superstructure. Pennant numbers changed in 1991.

KANARYA (old number) *12/1987, Selçuk Emre*

3 AMMUNITION TRANSPORTS

CEPHANE 2 and **3** (ex-Y 1195 and 1197) **BEKIRDERE** (ex-Y 1196)

Comment: Pennant numbers changed in 1991.

BEKIRDERE (old number) *1980, Stüdyo Oskar, Gölcük*

2 BARRACK SHIPS

NAŞIT ÖNGEREN (ex-US *APL 47*) (ex-Y 1204)
BINBAŞI NETIN SÜLÜS (ex-US *APL 53*) (ex-Y 1205)

Comment: Ex-US barrack ships transferred on lease: Y 1204 in October 1972 and Y 1205 on 6 December 1974. Y 1204 based at Ereğli and Y 1205 at Gölcük. Purchased outright June 1987. Pennant numbers changed in 1991.

35 SMALL TRANSPORTS

SALOPA 1-15 (ex-Y 1031-1045)
LAYTER 1-6 (ex-Y 1011-1015)
AZIZIYE (ex-Y 1016)
PONTON 1-7 (ex-Y 1061-1067)
GONCA (ex-Y 1099)
ISCI TASITI 1-4 (ex-Y 1096, Y 1097, Y 1110, Y 1102)
ARSLAN (ex-Y 1112)

Comment: Of varying size and appearance. Pennant numbers changed in 1991.

SALOPA *9/1991, Erik Laursen*

2 WATER TANKERS

SÖGÜT (ex-FGR *FW 2*) A 599 (ex-Y 1217) **KAVAK** (ex-German *FW 4*) A 600

Displacement, tons: 626 full load
Dimensions, feet (metres): 144.4 × 25.6 × 8.2 *(44.1 × 7.8 × 2.5)*
Main machinery: 1 MWM diesel; 230 hp(m) *(169 kW)*; 1 shaft
Speed, knots: 9.5
Cargo capacity: 340 tons

Comment: *Sögüt* transferred by West Germany 3 December 1975. Pennant number changed in 1991. *Kavak* transferred from Germany 12 April 1991.

SÖGÜT (old number) *11/1985, Bernd Langensiepen*

2 WATER TANKERS

VAN A 597 (ex-Y 1208) **ULUBAT** A 598 (ex-Y 1209)

Displacement, tons: 1200 full load
Dimensions, feet (metres): 174.2 × 29.5 × 9.8 *(53.1 × 9 × 3)*
Main machinery: 1 diesel; 650 hp(m) *(478 kW)*; 1 shaft
Speed, knots: 14
Cargo capacity: 700 tons
Guns: 1 Oerlikon 20 mm.

Comment: Two small tankers built in 1968-70 at Gölcük Dockyard. Pennant numbers changed in 1991.

VAN *9/1991, Selim San*

6 WATER TANKERS

PINAR 1-6 Y 111-Y 116 (ex-Y 1211-Y 1216)

Displacement, tons: 300
Dimensions, feet (metres): 110.2 × 27.9 × 5.9 *(33.6 × 8.5 × 1.8)*
Main machinery: 1 GM diesel; 225 hp *(168 kW)*; 1 shaft
Speed, knots: 11
Cargo capacity: 150 tons

Comment: Built by Taşkizak Naval Yard. Details given for last four, sisters to harbour tankers H 500-502. First pair differ from these particulars and are individually different. *Pinar 1* (launched 1938) of 490 tons displacement with one 240 hp *(179 kW)* diesel, and *Pinar 2* built in 1958 of 1300 tons full load, 167.3 × 27.9 ft *(51 × 8.5 m)*.

PINAR 5 (old number) *10/1988, Selim San*

BOOM DEFENCE VESSELS

Name	*No*	*Builders*	*Commissioned*
AG 6 (ex-USS *AN 93*, ex-Netherlands *Cerberus* A 895)	P 306	Bethlehem Steel Corporation, Staten Island	10 Nov 1952

Displacement, tons: 780 standard; 855 full load
Dimensions, feet (metres): 165 × 33 × 10 *(50.3 × 10.1 × 3)*
Main machinery: Diesel-electric; 2 GM 8-268A diesels; 880 hp *(656 kW)*; 2 generators; 1 motor; 1 shaft
Speed, knots: 12.8. **Range, miles:** 5200 at 12 kts
Complement: 48
Guns: 1 USN 3 in *(76 mm)*/50. 4 Oerlikon 20 mm.

Comment: Netlayer. Transferred from USA to Netherlands in December 1952. Used first as a boom defence vessel and latterly as salvage and diving tender since 1961 but retained her netlaying capacity. Handed back to US Navy on 17 September 1970 but immediately turned over to the Turkish Navy under grant aid.

AG 6 *5/1990, A. Sheldon Duplaix*

Name	*No*	*Builders*	*Commissioned*
AG 5 (ex-*AN 104*)	P 305	Kröger, Rendsburg	5 Feb 1961

Displacement, tons: 680 standard; 960 full load
Dimensions, feet (metres): 173.8 × 35 × 13.5 *(53 × 10.7 × 4.1)*
Main machinery: 1 MAN G7V 40/60 diesel; 1470 hp(m) *(1.08 MW)*; 1 shaft
Speed, knots: 12. **Range, miles:** 6500 at 11 kts
Complement: 49
Guns: 1 Bofors 40 mm/60. 3 Oerlikon 20 mm.

Comment: Netlayer P 305 built in US off-shore programme for Turkey.

AG 5 *5/1987, van Ginderen Collection*

Name	*No*	*Builders*	*Commissioned*
AG 4 (ex-USS *Larch*, ex-*AN 21*)	P 304	American S B Co, Cleveland	13 Dec 1941

Displacement, tons: 560 standard; 805 full load
Dimensions, feet (metres): 163 × 30.5 × 10.5 *(49.7 × 9.3 × 3.2)*
Main machinery: Diesel-electric; 2 diesels; 800 hp *(597 kW)*; 2 generators; 1 motor; 1 shaft
Speed, knots: 12
Complement: 48
Guns: 1—3 in *(76 mm)*. 4 Oerlikon 20 mm.

Comment: Former US netlayer of the Aloe class. Acquired in May 1946.

AG 4 *5/1982, Hartmut Ehlers*

1 BAR CLASS

Name	*No*	*Builders*	*Commissioned*
AG 1 (ex-HMS *Barbarian*)	P 301	Blyth S B Co	16 Apr 1938

Displacement, tons: 750 standard; 1000 full load
Dimensions, feet (metres): 173.8 × 32.2 × 9.5 *(52.9 × 9.8 × 2.9)*
Main machinery: 1 diesel; 1 shaft
Speed, knots: 11.5. **Range, miles:** 3100 at 10 kts
Complement: 32
Guns: 4 Oerlikon 20 mm.

Comment: Former British boom defence vessel. Re-engined in 1960s.

AG 1 *6/1980, Selçuk Emre*

7 NET TENDERS/DAN LAYERS

ŞAMANDIRA MOTORU 1-7 (ex-Y 1141-1147)

Comment: Six of the class laid up in reserve.

TUGS

1 Ex-US CHEROKEE CLASS

GAZAL (ex-USS *Sioux* ATF 75) A 587

Displacement, tons: 1235 standard; 1675 full load
Dimensions, feet (metres): 205 × 38.5 × 17 *(62.5 × 11.7 × 5.2)*
Main machinery: Diesel-electric; 4 GM 12-278 diesels; 4400 hp *(3.28 MW)*; 4 generators; 1 motor; 3000 hp *(2.24 MW)*; 1 shaft
Speed, knots: 16. **Range, miles:** 15 000 at 8 kts
Complement: 85
Guns: 1 USN 3 in *(76 mm)*/50. 2 Oerlikon 20 mm.

Comment: Transferred 30 October 1972. Purchased 15 August 1973. Can be used for salvage.

GAZAL *3/1988, Hartmut Ehlers*

1 Ex-US ARMY TYPE

AKBAŞ (ex-Y 1119)

Displacement, tons: 971
Dimensions, feet (metres): 146.6 × 33.5 × 14.1 *(44.7 × 10.2 × 4.3)*
Speed, knots: 12
Guns: 2 Oerlikon 20 mm.

Comment: Based at Gölcük. Pennant number changed in 1991.

AKBAS (old number) *1990, Turkish Navy*

1 OCEAN TUG

DARICA (ex-Y 1125)

Displacement, tons: 750 full load
Dimensions, feet (metres): 134.2 × 32.2 × 12.8 *(40.9 × 9.8 × 3.9)*
Main machinery: 2 ABC diesels; 4000 hp *(2.94 MW)*; 2 shafts
Speed, knots: 14. **Range, miles:** 2500 at 14 kts

Comment: Built at Taşkizak Naval Yard and commissioned 20 July 1990. Equipped for firefighting and as a torpedo tender. Pennant number changed in 1991.

DARICA (old number) *1987, Selçuk Emre*

2 COASTAL TUGS

ÖNCÜ (ex-Y 1120) **ÖNDER** (ex-Y 1124)

Displacement, tons: 500
Dimensions, feet (metres): 131.2 × 29.9 × 13.1 *(40 × 9.1 × 4)*
Main machinery: 1 diesel; 1 shaft
Speed, knots: 12
Guns: 2 Oerlikon 20 mm (twin).

Comment: Transferred by USA under MAP. Y 1124 based at Ereğli supporting submarines operating in the Black Sea and towing targets. Y 1120 at Izmir.

ÖNDER (old number) *10/1989, Hartmut Ehlers*

9 COASTAL/HARBOUR TUGS

Name	*No*	*Displacement, tons/ Speed, knots*	*Commissioned*
SÖNDÜREN	(ex-Y 1117)	128/12	1954
YEDEKCI	(ex-Y 1121)	128/12	1955
KUVVET	(ex-Y 1122)	390/10	1962
DOGANARSLAN	(ex-Y 1123)	—	1985
ÖZGEN	(ex-Y 1128)	—	1987
GÜVEN	(ex-Y 1130)	300/10	1962
ATIL	(ex-Y 1132)	300/10	1962
ERSEN BAYRAK	(ex-Y 1134)	30/9	1946
KUDRET	(ex-Y 1229)	128/12	1957

DOGANARSLAN (old number) *10/1989, Hartmut Ehlers*

38 PUSHER TUGS

KATIR 1-38

Comment: From Katir 36, new design.

KATIR 38 *10/1989, Hartmut Ehlers*

FLOATING DOCKS/CRANES

(ex-*Y 1081*) 16 000 tons lift.	(ex-*Y 1082*) 12 000 tons lift.	(ex-*Y 1083*) (ex-US *AFDL*) 2500 tons lift.
(ex-*Y 1084*) 4500 tons lift.	(ex-*Y 1085*) 400 tons lift.	(ex-*Y 1086*) 3000 tons lift.

HAVUZ 7 (ex-*Y 1087*) (ex-US *ARD 12*)
3500 tons lift.

Comment: *Havuz* transferred November 1971 by lease; purchased outright in June 1987. A new 700 ton dock was launched in July 1989 at Gölcük Yard and completed in 1990.

3 Ex-US FLOATING CRANES

ALGARNA 1 (ex-Y 1021) **LEVENT** (ex-Y 1022) **TURGUT ALP** (ex-Y 1024)

AUXILIARIES

1 NAVAL DREDGER

TARAK (ex-Y 1029)

Displacement, tons: 200

14 UTILITY CRAFT

MAVNA 1-4 (ex-Y 1181-1184) **MAVNA 7-13** (ex-Y 1187-1193)
MAVNA 14-16 (ex-Y 1198-1200)

MAVNA 9 (old number) *10/1989, Hartmut Ehlers*

1 Ex-GERMAN TORPEDO RETRIEVER (TRV)

Ex-TF 107 (ex-Y 873)

Comment: Transferred 4 September 1989. Built in 1966 of approximately 56 tons.

TRV (old number) *7/1987, Gilbert Gyssels*

3 TORPEDO RETRIEVERS (TRV)

TORPITO TENDERI (ex-Y 1051) **TAKIP** (ex-Y 1052) **AHMET ERSOY** (ex-Y 1102)

TAKIP (old number) *6/1986, Selçuk Emre*

3 FLAG OFFICERS' YACHTS

HALAS (ex-Y 1089) **ACAR** (ex-Y 1092) **GÜL** (ex-Y 1103)

Comment: Pennant numbers not displayed.

ACAR *6/1983, F. Örgünsür*

COAST GUARD (SAHIL GÜVENLIK)

Notes: (a) Tenders out in May 1990 for ten 250 ton craft and fourteen 70 ton craft. Orders expected in 1992.
(b) Previous reports of Lürssen 45 craft building in 1987-89 were not correct.

8 KW 15 CLASS (LARGE PATROL CRAFT)

SG 12-16, 18-20

Displacement, tons: 70 full load
Dimensions, feet (metres): 94.8 × 15.4 × 4.6 *(28.9 × 4.7 × 1.4)*
Main machinery: 2 MTU diesels; 2000 hp(m) *(1.47 MW)*; 2 shafts
Speed, knots: 25. **Range, miles:** 1500 at 19 kts
Complement: 15
Guns: 1 Bofors 40 mm/60. 2 Oerlikon 20 mm.

Comment: Built by Schweers, Bardenfleth. Commissioned 1961-62.

SG 14 *10/1991, Harald Carstens*

14 LARGE PATROL CRAFT

SG 21-34

Displacement, tons: 170 full load
Dimensions, feet (metres): 132 × 21 × 5.5 *(40.2 × 6.4 × 1.7)*
131.2 × 21.3 × 4.9 *(40 × 6.5 × 1.5)* (SG 30-34)
Main machinery: 2 SACM AGO 195 V16 CSHR diesels; 4800 hp(m) *(3.53 MW)*
2 cruise diesels; 300 hp(m) *(220 kW)*; 2 shafts
Speed, knots: 22
Guns: 1 or 2 Bofors 40 mm/60. 2—12.7 mm MGs.

Comment: SG 21 and 22 built by Gölcük Naval Yard, remainder by Taşkizak Naval Yard. SG 34 commissioned in 1977, remainder 1968-71. SG 30-34 have minor modifications—knuckle at bow, radar stirrup on bridge and MG on superstructure sponsons. These are similar craft to the 12 listed under Light Forces for the Navy.

SG 22 *9/1990, Selçuk Emre*

10 SAR 33 TYPE (LARGE PATROL CRAFT)

SG 61-70

Displacement, tons: 140 standard; 170 full load
Dimensions, feet (metres): 108.3 × 28.3 × 9.7 *(33 × 8.6 × 3)*
Main machinery: 3 SACM AGO 195 V16 CSHR diesels; 7200 hp(m) *(5.29 MW)*; 3 shafts; cp props
Speed, knots: 40. **Range, miles:** 450 at 35 kts; 1000 at 20 kts
Complement: 24
Guns: 1 Bofors 40 mm/60. 2—7.62 mm MGs.
Radars: Surface search: Racal Decca; I band.

Comment: Prototype ordered from Abeking & Rasmussen, Lemwerder in May 1976. The remainder were built at Taşkizak Naval Yard, Istanbul between 1979 and 1981. Fourteen of this class were to have been transferred to Libya but the order was cancelled.

SG 61 *1990, Turkish CG*

4 SAR 35 TYPE (LARGE PATROL CRAFT)

SG 71-74

Displacement, tons: 210 full load
Dimensions, feet (metres): 120 × 28.3 × 6.2 *(36.6 × 8.6 × 1.9)*
Main machinery: 3 SACM AGO 195 V16 CSHR diesels; 7200 hp(m) *(5.29 MW)*; 3 shafts
Speed, knots: 40. **Range, miles:** 450 at 35 kts; 1000 at 20 kts
Complement: 24
Guns: 1 Bofors 40 mm/70. 2—7.62 mm MGs.
Radars: Surface search: Racal Decca; I band.

Comment: A slightly enlarged version of SAR 33 Type built by Taşkizak Shipyard between 1985 and 1987.

SG 74 *10/1989, Hartmut Ehlers*

9 COASTAL PATROL CRAFT

SG 41-47, 49, 50

Displacement, tons: 19 full load
Dimensions, feet (metres): 45.9 × 13.8 × 3.6 *(14 × 4.2 × 1.1)*
Main machinery: 2 diesels; 450 hp *(335 kW)*; 2 shafts
Speed, knots: 13
Complement: 5
Guns: 2—7.62 mm (twin) MGs.

Comment: Transferred in the 1950s. Former US Mk 5 45 ft craft built in Second World War. Some have radar on forward edge of bridge, whilst SG 41 has circular scuttles in place of square ports. Similar to Spanish P 231-P 235.

SG 44 *6/1991, Mike Foster*

6 COASTAL PATROL CRAFT

SG 51-56

Displacement, tons: 25 full load
Dimensions, feet (metres): 47.9 × 11.5 × 3.6 *(14.6 × 3.5 × 1.1)*
Main machinery: 2 diesels; 700 hp(m) *(514 kW)*; 2 shafts
Speed, knots: 18
Complement: 6
Guns: 1—12.7 mm MG.

Comment: First three built at Taşkizak Shipyard and commissioned 20 July 1990. Three more laid down in mid-1990 and commissioned in 1991. Two more of the class were built for North Cyprus and handed over in August 1990 and July 1991.

SG 52 *1991, Turkish Navy*

2 TRANSPORT CRAFT

SG 104-105

Comment: Small utility craft which sometimes carry two 12.7 mm MGs.

SG 104 *10/1989, Hartmut Ehlers*

2 HARBOUR PATROL CRAFT

SG 1-2

Comment: High speed patrol boats for anti-smuggling duties.

SG 2 *7/1991, Selim San*

TURKS AND CAICOS

General

An Island Police Force funded by the UK Government.

Mercantile Marine

Lloyd's Register of Shipping:
13 vessels of 4573 tons gross

1 DAGGER CLASS (PATROL CRAFT)

Displacement, tons: 8
Dimensions, feet (metres): 39.7 × 11.2 × 3.6 *(12.1 × 3.4 × 1.1)*
Main machinery: 2 Perkins T 6.3544 diesels; 290 hp *(216 kW)*; 2 shafts
Speed, knots: 24. **Range, miles:** 540 at 20 kts
Guns: 1—7.62 mm MG.

Comment: Completed by Fairey Marine in June 1986. GRP hull.

1 HALMATIC M160 CLASS (PATROL CRAFT)

SEA QUEST

Displacement, tons: 18.5 light
Dimensions, feet (metres): 52.5 × 15.4 × 4.6 *(16 × 4.7 × 1.4)*
Main machinery: 2 Detroit 6V 92 TA diesels; 520 hp *(388 kW)* sustained; 2 shafts
Speed, knots: 27. **Range, miles:** 500 at 17 kts
Complement: 8

Comment: Built by Halmatic, Havant and delivered on 22 December 1989. Similar craft acquired by the Virgin Islands, Montserrat and Anguilla. Has a rigid inflatable boat on the stern launched by a gravity davit.

SEA QUEST *9/1989, Gilbert Gyssels*

UGANDA

General

Small patrol craft manned by the Army for use on Lake Victoria.

Mercantile Marine

Lloyd's Register of Shipping:
3 vessels of 5091 tons gross

PATROL FORCES

6 YUGOSLAV AL8K TYPE

Displacement, tons: 6.3 full load
Dimensions, feet (metres): 36.6 × 12.3 × 1.5 *(11.2 × 3.7 × 0.5)*
Main machinery: 2 diesels; 300 hp(m) *(220 kW)*; 2 shafts
Speed, knots: 25
Guns: 1—12.7 mm MG.

Comment: Acquired in September 1988. Aluminium hulls. Designed for patrol work on rivers and lakes.

LAKE PATROL CRAFT *1989*

UNITED ARAB EMIRATES

Headquarters' Appointments

Commander, Naval Forces:
Brigadier Hazaa Sultan Al Darmaki
Commander, Coast Guard:
Brigadier Saif Al Shaafar

General

This federation of the former Trucial States (Abu Dhabi, Ajman, Dubai, Fujairah, Ras al Khaimah, Sharjah, Umm al Qaiwan) was formed under a provisional constitution in 1971 with a new constitution coming into effect on 2 December 1976.
Following a decision of the UAE Supreme Defence Council on 6 May 1976 the armed forces of the member states were unified and the organisation of the UAE Armed Forces was furthered by decisions taken on 1 February 1978.

Future Plans

In common with some of its neighbours it would seem probable that future construction will include more FAC as well as hovercraft. Intentions are to acquire three minehunters.

Personnel

(a) 1992: 1900 (130 officers)
(b) Voluntary service

Ports

Taweela (main base) between Abu Dhabi and Dubai.
Dalma and Mina Zayed (Abu Dhabi),
Mina Rashid and Mina Jebel Ali (Dubai),
Mina Saqr (Ras al Khaimah), Mina Sultan (Sharjah),
Khor Fakkan (Sharjah-East Coast).

Mercantile Marine

Lloyd's Register of Shipping:
279 vessels of 888 893 tons gross

MISSILE CORVETTES

2 LÜRSSEN 62 TYPE

Name	*No*	*Builders*	*Commissioned*
MURAY JIP	P 6501	Lürssen, Bremen	Nov 1990
DAS	P 6502	Lürssen, Bremen	Jan 1991

Displacement, tons: 630 full load
Dimensions, feet (metres): 206.7 × 30.5 × 8.2 *(63 × 9.3 × 2.5)*
Main machinery: 4 MTU 16V 538 TB92 diesels; 13 640 hp(m) *(10 MW)* sustained; 4 shafts
Speed, knots: 32. **Range, miles:** 4000 at 16 kts
Complement: 43

Missiles: SSM: 4 Aerospatiale MM 40 Exocet; inertial cruise; active radar homing to 70 km *(40 nm)* at 0.9 Mach; warhead 165 kg; sea-skimmer.
SAM: Thomson-CSF modified Crotale Navale octuple launcher; radar guidance; IR homing to 13 km *(7 nm)* at 2.4 Mach; warhead 14 kg.
Guns: 1 OTO Melara 3 in *(76 mm)*/62 Super Rapid; 85° elevation; 120 rounds/minute to 16 km *(8.7 nm)*; weight of shell 6 kg.
1 Signaal Goalkeeper with GE 30 mm 7-barrelled; 4200 rounds/minute combined to 2 km.
Countermeasures: Decoys: Dagaie launcher; IR flares and Chaff.
ESM/ECM: Racal Cutlass/Cygnus; intercept/jammer.
Radars: Air/surface search: Bofors Electronic Sea Giraffe; G band.
Navigation: Racal Decca 1226; I band.
Fire control: Bofors Electronic 9LV 331; J band (for gun and SSM).
Thomson-CSF DRBV 51C; J band (for Crotale).

Helicopters: 1 Aerospatiale Alouette SA 316.

Programmes: Ordered in late 1986. Similar vessels to Bahrain craft. Delivery in late 1991.
Structure: Lürssen design adapted for the particular conditions of the Gulf. This class has good air defence and a considerable anti-ship capability if the helicopter also carries anti-surface missiles.

MURAY JIP *6/1990, van Ginderen Collection*

DAS *4/1991, Harald Carstens*

LIGHT FORCES

2 MUBARRAZ CLASS (FAST ATTACK CRAFT—MISSILE)

Name	*No*	*Builders*	*Commissioned*
MUBARRAZ	P 4401	Lürssen, Bremen	Aug 1990
MAKASIB	P 4402	Lürssen, Bremen	Aug 1990

Displacement, tons: 260 full load
Dimensions, feet (metres): 147.3 × 23 × 7.2 *(44.9 × 7 × 2.2)*
Main machinery: 2 MTU 20V 538 TB93 diesels; 9370 hp(m) *(6.9 MW)* sustained; 2 shafts
Speed, knots: 40. **Range, miles:** 500 at 38 kts
Complement: 40 (5 officers)

Missiles: SSM: 4 Aerospatiale MM 40 Exocet; inertial cruise; active radar homing to 70 km *(40 nm)* at 0.9 Mach; warhead 165 kg; sea-skimmer.
SAM: 1 Matra Sadral sextuple launcher; Mistral; IR homing to 4 km *(2.2 nm)*; warhead 3 kg.
Guns: 1 OTO Melara 3 in *(76 mm)*/62 Super Rapid; 85° elevation; 120 rounds/minute to 16 km *(8.7 nm)*; weight of shell 6 kg.
Countermeasures: Decoys: Dagaie launchers; IR flares and Chaff.
ESM/ECM: Racal Cutlass/Cygnus; intercept/jammer.
Fire control: CSEE Najir optronic director (for SAM).
Radars: Air/surface search: Bofors Electronic Sea Giraffe; G band.
Navigation: Racal Decca 1226; I band.
Fire control: Bofors Electronic 9LV 331; J band (for gun and SSM).

Programmes: Ordered in late 1986 from Lürssen Werft at the same time as the two Type 62 vessels.
Structure: This is a modified FPB 38 design, with the first export version of Matra Sadral.

MAKASIB *9/1990, Foto Flite*

6 VOSPER THORNYCROFT TYPE (LARGE PATROL CRAFT)

Name	*No*	*Builders*	*Commissioned*
ARDHANA	P 1101	Vosper Thornycroft	24 June 1975
ZURARA	P 1102	Vosper Thornycroft	14 Aug 1975
MURBAN	P 1103	Vosper Thornycroft	16 Sep 1975
AL GHULLAN	P 1104	Vosper Thornycroft	16 Sep 1975
RADOOM	P 1105	Vosper Thornycroft	1 July 1976
GHANADHAH	P 1106	Vosper Thornycroft	1 July 1976

Displacement, tons: 110 standard; 175 full load
Dimensions, feet (metres): 110 × 21 × 6.6 *(33.5 × 6.4 × 2)*
Main machinery: 2 Paxman Valenta 12 CM diesels; 5000 hp *(3.73 MW)* sustained; 2 shafts
Speed, knots: 30. **Range, miles:** 1800 at 14 kts
Complement: 26
Guns: 2 Oerlikon/BMARC 30 mm/75 A32 (twin); 85° elevation; 650 rounds/minute to 10 km *(5.5 nm)*; weight of shell 1 kg or 0.36 kg.
1 Oerlikon/BMARC 20 mm/80 A41A; 800 rounds/minute to 2 km.
2—51 mm projectors for illuminants.
Radars: Surface search: Racal Decca TM 1626; I band.

Comment: A class of round bilge steel hull craft. P 1101-2 and P 1105-6 transported by heavy-lift ships. P 1103 and P 1104 were sailed out. Originally operated by Abu Dhabi.

AL GHULLAN *11/1987*

6 LÜRSSEN TNC 45 CLASS (FAST ATTACK CRAFT—MISSILE)

Name	No	Builders	Commissioned
BAN YAS	P 4501	Lürssen Vegesack	Nov 1980
MARBAN	P 4502	Lürssen Vegesack	Nov 1980
RODQM	P 4503	Lürssen Vegesack	July 1981
SHAHEEN	P 4504	Lürssen Vegesack	July 1981
SAGAR	P 4505	Lürssen Vegesack	Sep 1981
TARIF	P 4506	Lürssen Vegesack	Sep 1981

Displacement, tons: 260 full load
Dimensions, feet (metres): 147.3 × 23 × 8.2 *(44.9 × 7 × 2.5)*
Main machinery: 4 MTU 16V538 TB 92 diesels; 13 640 hp(m) *(10 MW)* sustained; 4 shafts
Speed, knots: 40. **Range, miles:** 500 at 38 kts
Complement: 40 (5 officers)

Missiles: SSM: 4 Aerospatiale MM 40 Exocet; inertial cruise; active radar homing to 70 km *(40 nm)* at 0.9 Mach; warhead 165 kg; sea-skimmer.
Guns: 1 OTO Melara 3 in *(76 mm)*/62; 85° elevation; 60 rounds/minute to 16 km *(8.7 nm)*; weight of shell 6 kg.
2 Breda 40 mm/70 (twin); 85° elevation; 300 rounds/minute to 12.5 km *(6.8 nm)*; weight of shell 0.96 kg.
2—7.62 mm MGs.
Countermeasures: Decoys: 1 CSEE trainable Dagaie; IR flares and Chaff; H-J band.
ESM/ECM: Racal Cutlass/Cygnus; intercept/jammer.
Fire control: 1 CSEE Panda director for 40 mm. PEAB low light USFA IR and TV tracker.
Radars: Surface search: Racal Decca TM 1226; I band.
Fire control: Philips 9LV 200 Mk 2; J band.

Programmes: Ordered in late 1977. First two shipped in September 1980 and four more in Summer 1981. This class was the first to be fitted with MM40.
Structure: Modified FPB 38 design.

SAGAR *5/1987*

3 KEITH NELSON TYPE (COASTAL PATROL CRAFT)

Name	No	Builders	Commissioned
KAWKAB	P 561	Keith Nelson, Bembridge	7 Mar 1969
THOABAN	P 562	Keith Nelson, Bembridge	7 Mar 1969
BANI YAS	P 563	Keith Nelson, Bembridge	27 Dec 1969

Displacement, tons: 32 standard; 38 full load
Dimensions, feet (metres): 57 × 16.5 × 4.5 *(17.4 × 5 × 1.4)*
Main machinery: 2 Caterpillar diesels; 750 hp *(560 kW)*; 2 shafts
Speed, knots: 19. **Range, miles:** 445 at 15 kts
Complement: 11 (2 officers)
Guns: 2 Oerlikon 20 mm.
Radars: Surface search: Racal Decca TM 1626; I band.

Comment: Of glass fibre hull construction. Originally operated by Abu Dhabi.

BANI YAS *11/1976, UAE Armed Forces*

SERVICE FORCES

2 CHEVERTON TYPE (TENDERS)

A 271 **A 272**

Displacement, tons: 3.3
Dimensions, feet (metres): 27 × 9 × 2.7 *(8.2 × 2.7 × 0.8)*
Main machinery: 1 Lister RMW3 diesel; 150 hp *(112 kW)*; 1 shaft
Speed, knots: 8

Comment: Built of GRP. Acquired from Chevertons, Cowes, Isle of Wight in 1975 by Abu Dhabi. A272 has a 2 ton hoist.

2 + 2 VOSPER QAF TYPE LANDING CRAFT (LCT)

JANANAH **DAYYINAH**

Measurement, tons: 350 dwt
Dimensions, feet (metres): 177.2 × — × — *(54 × — × —)*

Comment: Built by Argos Shipyard, Singapore. Both completed December 1988. Can carry four medium tanks. Two more reported ordered in June 1990.

1 LSL

AL FEYI

Displacement, tons: 650 full load
Dimensions, feet (metres): 164 × 36.1 × 9.2 *(50 × 11 × 2.8)*
Main machinery: 2 diesels; 1248 hp *(931 kW)*; 2 shafts
Speed, knots: 11. **Range, miles:** 1800 at 11 kts
Complement: 10

Comment: Built by Siong Huat, Singapore; completed 4 August 1987.

1 LCM

GHAGHA II

Displacement, tons: 100 full load
Dimensions, feet (metres): 131.2 × 32.8 × 3.3 *(40 × 10 × 1)*
Main machinery: 2 diesels; 730 hp *(544 kW)*; 2 shafts
Speed, knots: 9
Complement: 6

Comment: Built by Siong Huat, Singapore; launched 17 April 1987.

1 SUPPORT CRAFT

BARACUDA

Displacement, tons: 1400 full load
Dimensions, feet (metres): 190 × 39.4 × 13.1 *(57.9 × 12 × 4)*
Main machinery: 2 Ruston RKCM diesels; 6000 hp *(4.48 MW)* sustained; 2 shafts
Speed, knots: 12

Comment: Completed June 1983 by Singapore Slipway Co.

1 M/V 100 TYPE DIVING TENDER

D 1051

Displacement, tons: 100 full load
Dimensions, feet (metres): 103 × 22.6 × 3.6 *(31.4 × 6.9 × 1.1)*
Main machinery: 2 MTU 12V 396 TB 93 diesels; 3260 hp(m) *(2.4 MW)* sustained; 2 waterjets
Speed, knots: 26. **Range, miles:** 390 at 24 kts
Complement: 6

Comment: Ordered from Crestitalia end 1985 for Abu Dhabi and delivered in July 1987. GRP hull. Used primarily for mine clearance but also for diving training, salvage and SAR. Fitted with a decompression chamber and diving bell. Reports of a second of class are not confirmed. Lengthened version of Italian *Alcide Pedretti*.

D 1051 *1987, Crestitalia*

1 TUG

ANNAD A 3501

Displacement, tons: 795 full load
Dimensions, feet (metres): 114.8 × 32.2 × 13.8 *(35 × 9.8 × 4.2)*
Main machinery: 2 Caterpillar 3606TA diesels; 4180 hp *(3.12 MW)* sustained; 2 shafts; bow thruster
Speed, knots: 14. **Range, miles:** 2500 at 14 kts
Complement: 14 (3 officers)

Comment: Built by Dunston, Hessle, and completed in April 1989. Bollard pull, 55 tons. Equipped for SAR.

SHIPBORNE AIRCRAFT

Numbers/Type: 7 Aerospatiale SA 316/319S Alouette.
Operational speed: 113 kts *(210 km/h)*.
Service ceiling: 10 500 ft *(3200 m)*.
Range: 290 nm *(540 km)*.
Role/Weapon systems: Reconnaissance and general purpose helicopters. Sensors: radar. Weapons: To be fitted with ASV weapons.

LAND-BASED MARITIME AIRCRAFT

Numbers/Type: 4 Aerospatiale AS 332F Super Puma.
Operational speed: 150 kts *(280 km/h)*.
Service ceiling: 15 090 ft *(4600 m)*.
Range: 335 nm *(620 km)*.
Role/Weapon systems: Anti-ship and transport helicopter with limited ASV role; utility role widely used. Sensors: Omera ORB 30 radar. Weapons: ASV; 1 × AM 39 Exocet. ASM; depth bombs.

Numbers/Type: 2 Pilatus Britten-Norman Maritime Defender.
Operational speed: 150 kts *(280 km/h)*.
Service ceiling: 18 900 ft *(5760 m)*.
Range: 1500 nm *(2775 km)*.
Role/Weapon systems: Coastal patrol and surveillance aircraft. Sensors: Nose-mounted search radar, underwing searchlight. Weapons: Underwing rocket and gun pods.

COAST GUARD CRAFT

Note: Under control of Minister of Interior. In addition to the vessels listed below there are a number of Customs and Police launches including three Swedish Boghammar 13 m craft of the same type used by Iran and delivered in 1985, about 10 elderly Dhafeer and Spear class of 12 and 9 m respectively, and two Halmatic Arun class Pilot craft delivered in 1990/91; some of these launches carry light machine guns.

5 CAMCRAFT 77 ft (COASTAL PATROL CRAFT)

753-757

Displacement, tons: 70 full load
Dimensions, feet (metres): 76.8 × 18 × 4.9 *(23.4 × 5.5 × 1.5)*
Main machinery: 2 GM 12V 71TA diesels; 840 hp *(627 kW)* sustained; 2 shafts
Speed, knots: 25
Guns: 2 Lawrence Scott 20 mm (not always embarked).

Comment: Completed 1975 by Camcraft, New Orleans.

CAMCRAFT 757 *6/1990*

16 CAMCRAFT 65 ft (COASTAL PATROL CRAFT)

Displacement, tons: 50
Dimensions, feet (metres): 65 × 18 × 5 *(19.8 × 5.5 × 1.5)*
Main machinery: 2 MTU 6V 396 TB93 diesels; 1630 hp(m) *(1.2 MW)* sustained; 2 shafts (in 14) 2 Detroit 8V-92TA diesels; 700 hp *(522 kW)* sustained; 2 shafts (in 2)
Speed, knots: 25
Guns: 1 Oerlikon 20 mm.

Comment: Ordered in 1978.

CAMCRAFT 65 ft *1987, UAE Coast Guard*

1 POSILIPO (COASTAL PATROL CRAFT)

Displacement, tons: 35.5 full load
Dimensions, feet (metres): 64.9 × 19.68 × 3.9 *(19.8 × 6 × 1.2)*
Main machinery: 2 MTU 6V 396 TB93 diesels; 1630 hp(m) *(1.2 MW)* sustained; 2 shafts
Speed, knots: 24
Gun: 1 Oerlikon 20 mm.

Comment: Built by Posilipo, Italy and commissioned on 24 November 1984 in the Abu Dhabi Coast Guard. GRP hull.

6 BAGLIETTO GC 23 TYPE (COASTAL PATROL CRAFT)

758 +5

Displacement, tons: 50.7 full load
Dimensions, feet (metres): 78.7 × 18 × 3 *(24 × 5.5 × 0.9)*
Main machinery: 2 MTU 12V 396 TB93 diesels; 3260 hp(m) *(2.4 MW)* sustained; 2 KaMeWa waterjets
Speed, knots: 43. **Range, miles:** 700 at 20 kts
Complement: 9
Guns: 1 Oerlikon 20 mm. 2—7.62 mm MGs.

Comment: Built by Baglietto, Varazze. First two completed in March and May 1986, second pair in July 1987 and two more in 1988. All were delivered to UAE Coast Guard in Dubai.

BAGLIETTO *1987, UAE Coast Guard*

2 BAGLIETTO 13 FC TYPE (COASTAL PATROL CRAFT)

Displacement, tons: 11 full load
Dimensions, feet (metres): 43 × 10.8 × 2.5 *(13.1 × 3.3 × 0.8)*
Main machinery: 2 MAN D 2848 LE turbo diesels; 760 hp(m) *(550 kW)* sustained; 2 shafts
Speed, knots: 43. **Range, miles:** 180 at 30 kts
Complement: 4
Guns: 2—7.62 mm MGs.

Comment: Built by Baglietto, Varazze for Abu Dhabi police. Delivered in October 1988.

10 WATERCRAFT 45 ft (COASTAL PATROL CRAFT)

Displacement, tons: 25 full load
Dimensions, feet (metres): 45 × 14.1 × 4.6 *(13.7 × 4.3 × 1.4)*
Main machinery: 2 MAN 2542 diesels; 1300 hp(m) *(956 kW)*; 2 shafts
Speed, knots: 26. **Range, miles:** 380 at 18 kts
Complement: 5
Guns: Mounts for 2—7.62 mm MGs.

Comment: Ordered from Watercraft, UK in February 1982. Delivery in early 1983.

WATERCRAFT 45 ft *1984, UAE Coast Guard*

16 BARACUDA 30 ft and 23 FPB 22 ft (HARBOUR PATROL CRAFT)

Comment: Powered by twin Yamaha outboard engines of 200 hp(m) *(147 kW)* each. All can carry one 7.62 mm MG.

2 DIVING TENDERS

Displacement, tons: 8.8
Main machinery: 2 Volvo Penta diesels; 2 shafts
Speed, knots: 11

Comment: FPB 512 Rotork design. Completed May 1981 for Abu Dhabi.

UNITED KINGDOM

Admiralty Board

Chief of the Naval Staff and First Sea Lord:
Admiral Sir Julian Oswald, GCB, ADC
Chief of Naval Personnel and Second Sea Lord:
Admiral Sir Michael Livesay, KCB
Controller of the Navy:
Vice Admiral Sir Kenneth Eaton, KCB
Chief of Fleet Support:
Vice Admiral Sir Neville Purvis, KCB
Assistant Chief of the Naval Staff:
Rear Admiral P C Abbott

Commanders-in-Chief

Commander-in-Chief, Fleet:
Admiral Sir Jock Slater, KCB, LVO
Commander-in-Chief, Naval Home Command:
Admiral Sir John Kerr, KCB

Flag Officers

Flag Officer, Submarines:
Rear Admiral R T Frere
Flag Officer, Surface Flotilla:
Vice Admiral Sir Nicholas Hill-Norton, KCB
Flag Officer, Naval Aviation:
Rear Admiral C H D Cooke Priest
Commander, UK Task Group:
Rear Admiral J R Brigstock
Flag Officer, Sea Training:
Rear Admiral M C Boyce, OBE
Commander British Forces, Gibraltar:
Rear Admiral S E Saunders
Flag Officer, Plymouth:
Vice Admiral R T Newman, CB
Flag Officer, Portsmouth:
Rear Admiral D K Bawtree
Flag Officer, Scotland and Northern Ireland:
Vice Admiral Sir Hugo White, KCB, CBE
Hydrographer of the Navy:
Rear Admiral J A L Myers
Commodore Minor War Vessels Flotilla:
Commodore C J Freeman

Royal Marines Headquarters

Commandant-General, Royal Marines:
Lieutenant General Sir Henry Beverley, KCB, OBE
Chief of Staff to Commandant-General, Royal Marines:
Major General A M Keeling
Major General Commando Forces, Royal Marines:
Major General R J Ross, OBE
Commander Training and Reserve Forces, Royal Marines:
Brigadier J S Chester, OBE

Fleet Disposition

Submarine Flotilla
1st Squadron (*Dolphin*, Portsmouth) 6 Patrol submarines
2nd Squadron (*Defiance*, Devonport) 9 Fleet submarines
3rd Squadron (*Neptune*, Faslane) 4 Fleet submarines, 1 Patrol submarine
10th Squadron (*Neptune*, Faslane) 4 Strategic submarines
Note: The 1st Squadron will be disbanded by December 1993.

Surface Flotilla
1st Frigate Squadron (Devonport) Type 22 Batch 2
2nd Frigate Squadron (Devonport) Type 22 Batch 1
3rd Destroyer Squadron (Portsmouth) Type 42
4th Frigate Squadron (Devonport) Type 21
5th Destroyer Squadron (Portsmouth) Type 42
7th Frigate Squadron (Devonport/Portsmouth) Leander
8th Frigate Squadron (Devonport) Type 22 Batch 3
9th Frigate Squadron (Devonport) Type 23

MCM Flotilla
1st Squadron (Rosyth), 2nd Squadron (Portsmouth)
3rd Squadron (Rosyth), 4th Squadron (Rosyth)
Fishery Protection Squadron (Rosyth), 10th Squadron (RNR)

Surveying Flotilla (Devonport)
2 Ocean and 4 Coastal Survey Ships

Diplomatic Representation

Naval Attaché in Athens:
Captain J J Pearson
Naval Attaché in Beijing:
Commander A B P Armstrong
Naval Attaché in Bonn:
Captain J McLees
Naval Attaché in Brasilia:
Captain J R Luard
Naval Adviser in Bridgetown:
Commander H M Humphreys
Naval Attaché in Cairo:
Commander P G Blanchford
Defence Adviser in Canberra:
Commodore A C G Wolstenholme
Defence Attaché in Caracas (and Santo Domingo):
Captain W R McLaren
Defence Attaché in Copenhagen:
Commander R Kirkwood
Naval Attaché in The Hague:
Captain M Bickley
Naval Attaché in Islamabad:
Commander D A Scott
Assistant Defence Adviser in Kuala Lumpur:
Lieutenant Commander C C Williams
Defence Attaché in Lisbon:
Commander P M Jones
Naval Attaché in Madrid:
Captain S N G Sloot, LVO
Defence Attaché in Manila:
Colonel J P Clough, RM
Defence Attaché in Montevideo:
Captain R A Highton
Naval Attaché in Moscow:
Captain J M Dobson
Naval Attaché, Muscat:
Commander K A Harris, OBE
Naval Adviser in Nassau (and Georgetown and Port of Spain):
Captain A J S Taylor
Naval Adviser in New Delhi:
Captain J P Cardale
Naval Attaché in Oslo:
Commander G S Pearson, OBE
Naval Adviser in Ottawa:
Captain P J Bootherstone, DSC
Naval Attaché in Paris:
Captain J G F Cooke, OBE
Naval Attaché in Riyadh:
Commander T Waddington
Naval Attaché in Rome:
Captain W C McKnight, LVO
Defence Attaché in Santiago:
Captain R A Rowley, OBE
Naval Attaché in Stockholm:
Commander J J M Curtis
Naval Attaché in Tokyo:
Captain C M C Crawford
Naval Attaché in Washington:
Rear Admiral A P Hoddinott, OBE

Royal Marines Operational Units

HQ 3 Commando Brigade RM; 29 Commando Regiment RA (Army); 59 Independent Commando Squadron RE (Army); 40 Commando RM; 42 Commando RM; 45 Commando RM; Commando Logistic Regiment RM (RN/RM/Army); 3 Commando Brigade HQ and Signal Squadron RM including Air Defence Troop RM (Javelin), EW Troop RM, Tactical Air Control Parties RM (3 regular, 1 reserve); 3 Commando Brigade Air Squadron RM (Helicopters); 539 Assault Squadron RM (Landing Craft); Special Boat Service RM; Comacchio Group RM (Security); 2 Raiding Troop RMR (Raiding Craft); T Company RMR; 289 Commando Battery RA (Volunteers); 131 Independent Commando Squadron RE (Volunteers).

Bases

Northwood (*Warrior*); C-in-C Fleet; FO Submarines
Portsmouth; C-in-C Navhome; FO Portsmouth; FO Surface Flotilla
Devonport; FO Plymouth
Rosyth; FO Scotland and Northern Ireland
Portland; FO Sea Training
Faslane (*Neptune*); Commodore Clyde
Gibraltar; CBF Gibraltar
Hong Kong (*Tamar*); Captain-in-Charge

Personnel (including Royal Marines)

(a) 1 January 1992: 62 400 (RN 54 850; RM 7410)
(b) Volunteer Reserves: RN 5750; RM 1240
(c) Regular Reserves: RN 16 000; RM 2275
(d) RNXS: 2000

Strength of the Fleet—1 May 1992

Type	*Active (Reserve)*	*Building (Projected)*
SSBNs	4	3 (1)
Submarines—Attack	13	(1)
Submarines—Patrol	6	1
A/S Carriers	2 (1)	—
Destroyers	12 (1)	—
Frigates	30	7 (10)
Assault Ships (LPDs)	1 (1)	(2)
Helicopter Carrier (LPH)	—	(1)
LSLs	5	—
LCLs	2	—
LCRs	9	—
LCVPs	21	(4)
LCUs	15	—
RPLs	3	—
Offshore Patrol Vessels	10	—
Patrol Craft/Training Craft	6/14	—
Minehunters	21	2 (4)
Minesweepers—Coastal	10 (2)	—
Repair/Maintenance Ships	1	—
Survey Ships	2	—
Coastal Survey Ships	4	—
Antarctic Patrol Ship	1	—
Training Ships	3	—
Royal Yacht	1	—
Large Fleet Tankers	3	—
Support Tankers	4	—
Small Fleet Tankers	4	—
Coastal Tankers	5	—
Aviation Training Ship	1	—
Fleet Replenishment Ships	4	2 (2)
SMVs and PMLs	8	—
Trials Ships	2 (1)	—
TRVs	5	—
Armament Carriers	1 (1)	—
Water Carriers	6	—
Ocean Tugs	3	—
Harbour Tugs	49	—
Range Support Vessels	15	—
Submarine Support Vessels	3	1
Aviation Support Craft	13	—
Tenders	53	—
RNXS Craft	14	—
DG Vessels	1 (1)	—
Sea Cadet Corps Vessels	8	—
Target Vessels	3	—
Floating Docks	2	—
Royal Corps of Transport	24	—

Mercantile Marine

Lloyd's Register of Shipping:
1998 vessels of 6 716 325 tons gross

Fleet Air Arm Squadron (see *Shipborne Aircraft* section)

F/W Aircraft	*Role*	*Deployment*	*Squadron no.*
Sea Harrier	FRS	*Invincible*	800
Sea Harrier	FRS	*Ark Royal*	801
Sea Harrier	Aircrew Training	Yeovilton, *Heron*	899
Jetstream	Aircrew Training	Culdrose, *Seahawk*	750

Helicopters	*Role*	*Deployment*	*Squadron no.*
Sea King AEW 2	Aircrew Training	Culdrose	849 HQ
Sea King AEW 2	AEW	*Invincible*	849 A flight
Sea King AEW 2	AEW	*Ark Royal*	849 B flight
Sea King HAS 5	ASW	*Invincible*	814
Sea King HAS 5	ASW	*Ark Royal*	820
Sea King HAS 5	ASW	RFAs	826
Sea King HAS 6	ASW	Prestwick, *Gannet*	819
Sea King HAS 5	Aircrew Training	Culdrose, *Seahawk*	810
Sea King HAS 5	Aircrew Training	Culdrose, *Seahawk*	706
Sea King HC 4	Commando Assault	Yeovilton, *Heron*	845
Sea King HC 4	Commando Assault	Yeovilton, *Heron*	846
Sea King HC 4	Aircrew Training	Yeovilton, *Heron*	707
Sea King HAS 5	SAR	Culdrose, *Seahawk*	771
Sea King HC 4	SAR	Portland, *Osprey*	772
Lynx HAS 3	ASUW/ASW	Portland (T21, T42) *Osprey*	815
Lynx HAS 3	ASUW/ASW	Portland (Leander, T22) *Osprey*	829
Lynx HAS 3	Aircrew Training	Portland, *Osprey*	702
Gazelle HT 2	Aircrew Training	Culdrose, *Seahawk*	705

Note: Training and Liaison aircraft not listed under the *Shipborne* or *Land-based Aircraft* sections include five Sea Harrier T4N/T4, 31 Gazelle HT 2, 20 Jetstream, 16 Chipmunk, five Canberra, 26 Hunter, 16 Falcon 20 (under contract).

DELETIONS

Note: Disposal List following

Submarines

1989 *Olympus* (sold to Canada)
1991 *Onyx* (sold), *Odin* (sold), *Onslaught* (sold)

Frigates

1989 *Leander* (sunk), *Falmouth* (bu), *Euryalus* (sold), *Londonderry* (sunk)
1990 *Plymouth* (museum), *Achilles* (sold to Chile), *Naiad* (sunk)
1991 *Danae* (sold to Ecuador), *Penelope* (sold to Ecuador), *Arethusa* (sunk)

MCM Vessels

1989 *Bossington* (bu), *Portisham* (bu), *Maxton* (bu), *Stubbington* (bu)
1990 *Walkerton* (sold)
1991 *Gavinton* (sold), *Kirkliston* (sold), *Upton* (sold)

Fast Attack Craft etc

1991 *Sandpiper* (sold), *Peterel* (sold), *Cormorant* (sold), *Hart* (sold)

Amphibious Forces

1989 *Sir Lancelot* (sold)

Survey Ship and Craft

1990 *Fox* (sold)
1991 *Fawn* (sold), *Yarmouth Navigator* (sold)

Service Forces

1989 *Pintail* (sold), *Kinloss*, *Endeavour* (sold), *Datchet*, *Cartmel Appleleaf* (to Australia)
1990 *Dolwen* (sold), *Engadine* (sold)
1991 *Bembridge* (sold), *Lofoten* (sold), *Stalker* (sold), *Garganey* (sold), *Goldeneye* (sold), *Green Rover* (sold to Indonesia), *AFD 58* and *59* (sold)
1992 *Throsk* (sold), *Waterside* (sold) (both to Ecuador)

Tugs

1989 *Typhoon* (sold), *Daisy*, *Charlotte*, *Christine*, *Doris*
1991 *Dorothy* (sold)

DISPOSAL LIST

Note: The following ships already deleted from the Navy List are not on the Active or Reserve list and are held pending disposal by sale or scrap in which event they are transferred to Deletions above.

Submarines

Dreadnought, *Warspite*, *Conqueror*, *Churchill*, *Otus*, *Ocelot*, *Otter*, *Courageous*, *Osiris*, *Swiftsure*

Destroyers

Kent, *Bristol*

Frigates

Phoebe, *Charybdis*, *Cleopatra*, *Ariadne*, *Minerva*, *Jupiter*, *Hermione*

Minesweepers—Coastal

Bronington (Manchester museum), *Hubberston*, *Brereton*, *Cuxton*, *Soberton*, *Kedleston*

Target Ships

Droxford, *Eskimo*, *Woodlark* (all in Pembroke)

Patrol Vessels

Attacker, *Hunter*, *Striker*, *Fencer*, *Chaser*, *Endurance*, *Manly*, *Mentor*, *Millbrook*

Survey Ships

Echo, *Egeria* (both on loan to Marine Society), *Hecate*

Service Forces

Mandarin, *Kinbrace*, *Oilfield*, *Crystal*, *Torrid*, *Denmead*

Support Vessels

Rame Head (RM Training Ship), *Challenger*, *Tidespring*

Immobile Tenders

Kent or *Bristol* (Portsmouth, Training)
Orpheus (*Dolphin*, Training)

PENNANT LIST

Note: Numbers are not displayed on Submarines or some RMAS craft.

Aircraft Carriers

R 05	Invincible
R 06	Illustrious
R 07	Ark Royal

Destroyers

D 86	Birmingham
D 87	Newcastle
D 88	Glasgow
D 89	Exeter
D 90	Southampton
D 91	Nottingham
D 92	Liverpool
D 95	Manchester
D 96	Gloucester
D 97	Edinburgh
D 98	York
D 108	Cardiff

Frigates

F 40	Sirius
F 52	Juno (training)
F 56	Argonaut
F 57	Andromeda
F 71	Scylla
F 85	Cumberland
F 86	Campbeltown
F 87	Chatham
F 88	Broadsword
F 89	Battleaxe
F 90	Brilliant
F 91	Brazen
F 92	Boxer
F 93	Beaver
F 94	Brave
F 95	London
F 96	Sheffield
F 98	Coventry
F 99	Cornwall
F 169	Amazon
F 171	Active
F 172	Ambuscade
F 173	Arrow
F 174	Alacrity
F 185	Avenger
F 229	Lancaster
F 230	Norfolk
F 231	Argyll
F 233	Marlborough
F 234	Iron Duke
F 235	Monmouth
F 236	Montrose
F 237	Westminster
F 238	Northumberland
F 239	Richmond
F 240	Somerset
F 241	Grafton
F 242	Sutherland

Assault Ships

L 10	Fearless
L 11	Intrepid

Logistic Landing Ships and LCTs

L 105	Arromanches
L 106	Antwerp
L 107	Andalsnes
L 108	Abbeville
L 109	Akyab
L 110	Aachen
L 111	Arezzo
L 112	Agheila
L 113	Audemer
L 3004	Sir Bedivere
L 3005	Sir Galahad
L 3027	Sir Geraint
L 3036	Sir Percivale
L 3505	Sir Tristram
L 4001	Ardennes
L 4003	Arakan

LCMs (RCT)

RPL 05	Eden
RPL 06	Forth
RPL 12	Medway

Minesweepers/Minehunters

M 29	Brecon
M 30	Ledbury
M 31	Cattistock
M 32	Cottesmore
M 33	Brocklesby
M 34	Middleton
M 35	Dulverton
M 36	Bicester
M 37	Chiddingfold
M 38	Atherstone
M 39	Hurworth
M 40	Berkeley
M 41	Quorn
M 101	Sandown
M 102	Inverness
M 103	Cromer
M 104	Walney
M 105	Bridport
M 1114	Brinton
M 1116	Wilton (training)
M 1151	Iveston
M 1154	Kellington
M 1166	Nurton
M 1181	Sheraton
M 2003	Waveney
M 2004	Carron
M 2005	Dovey
M 2006	Helford
M 2007	Humber
M 2008	Blackwater
M 2009	Itchen
M 2010	Helmsdale
M 2011	Orwell
M 2012	Ribble
M 2013	Spey
M 2014	Arun

Light Forces/Patrol Ships

P 239	Peacock
P 240	Plover
P 241	Starling
P 246	Sentinel
P 258	Leeds Castle
P 259	Redpole
P 260	Kingfisher
P 261	Cygnet
P 264	Archer
P 265	Dumbarton Castle
P 270	Biter
P 272	Smiter
P 273	Pursuer
P 277	Anglesey
P 278	Alderney
P 279	Blazer
P 280	Dasher
P 291	Puncher
P 292	Charger
P 293	Ranger
P 294	Trumpeter
P 295	Jersey
P 297	Guernsey
P 298	Shetland
P 299	Orkney
P 300	Lindisfarne

Support Ships and Auxiliaries

A 00	Britannia
A 72	Cameron
A 81	Brambleleaf
A 83	Melton
A 84	Menai
A 86	Gleaner
A 87	Meon
A 91	Milford
A 100	Beddgelert
A 103	Sultan Venturer
A 106	Alsatian
A 107	Messina
A 109	Bayleaf
A 110	Orangeleaf
A 111	Oakleaf
A 112	Felicity
A 114	Magnet
A 115	Lodestone
A 122	Olwen
A 123	Olna
A 124	Olmeda
A 126	Cairn
A 127	Torrent
A 129	Dalmatian
A 130	Roebuck
A 132	Diligence
A 133	Hecla
A 135	Argus
A 138	Herald
A 140	Tornado
A 141	Torch
A 142	Tormentor
A 143	Toreador
A 146	Waterman
A 147	Frances
A 148	Fiona
A 149	Florence
A 150	Genevieve
A 152	Georgina
A 153	Example
A 154	Explorer
A 155	Deerhound
A 156	Daphne
A 157	Loyal Helper
A 158	Supporter
A 159	Loyal Watcher
A 160	Loyal Volunteer
A 161	Loyal Mediator
A 162	Elkhound
A 163	Express
A 164	Goosander
A 165	Pochard
A 166	Kathleen
A 167	Exploit
A 168	Labrador
A 170	Kitty
A 172	Lesley
A 174	Lilah
A 175	Mary
A 176	Polar Circle
A 177	Edith
A 178	Husky
A 180	Mastiff
A 181	Irene
A 182	Saluki
A 183	Isabel
A 185	Salmoor
A 186	Salmaster
A 187	Salmaid
A 188	Pointer
A 189	Setter
A 190	Joan
A 193	Joyce
A 196	Gwendoline
A 197	Sealyham
A 198	Helen
A 199	Myrtle
A 201	Spaniel

Support Ships and Auxiliaries

No	Name
A 202	Nancy
A 205	Norah
A 207	Llandovery
A 208	Lamlash
A 211	Lechlade
A 216	Bee
A 220	Loyal Moderator
A 221	Forceful
A 222	Nimble
A 223	Powerful
A 224	Adept
A 225	Bustler
A 226	Capable
A 227	Careful
A 228	Faithful
A 229	Cricket
A 230	Cockchafer
A 231	Dexterous
A 239	Gnat
A 250	Sheepdog
A 251	Lydford
A 253	Ladybird
A 254	Meavy
A 263	Cicala
A 269	Grey Rover
A 270	Blue Rover
A 271	Gold Rover
A 272	Scarab
A 273	Black Rover
A 274	Ettrick
A 277	Elsing
A 285	Auricula
A 308	Ilchester
A 309	Instow
A 311	Ironbridge
A 317	Bulldog
A 318	Ixworth
A 319	Beagle
A 326	Foxhound
A 327	Basset
A 328	Collie
A 330	Corgi
A 341	Fotherby
A 348	Felsted
A 353	Elkstone
A 354	Froxfield
A 355	Epworth
A 361	Roysterer
A 364	Whitehead
A 365	Fulbeck
A 366	Robust
A 367	Newton
A 368	Warden
A 378	Kinterbury
A 381	Cricklade
A 382	Arrochar
A 383	Appleby (SCC)
A 385	Fort Grange
A 386	Fort Austin
A 387	Fort Victoria
A 388	Fort George
A 389	Clovelly
A 391	Criccieth
A 392	Glencoe
A 393	Dunster
A 394	Fintry
A 402	Grasmere
A 480	Resource
A 486	Regent
A 488	Cromarty
A 490	Dornoch
A 502	Rollicker
A 1766	Headcorn
A 1767	Hever
A 1768	Harlech
A 1769	Hambledon
A 1770	Loyal Chancellor
A 1771	Loyal Proctor
A 1772	Holmwood
A 1773	Horning

Auxiliaries

No	Name
Y 01	Petard
Y 02	Falconet
Y 10	Aberdovey (SCC)
Y 11	Abinger (SCC)
Y 13	Alnmouth (SCC)
Y 17	Waterfall
Y 18	Watershed
Y 19	Waterspout
Y 21	Oilpress
Y 22	Oilstone
Y 23	Oilwell
Y 25	Oilbird
Y 26	Oilman
Y 30	Watercourse
Y 31	Waterfowl
Y 32	Moorhen
Y 33	Moorfowl

SUBMARINES

Strategic Missile Submarines (SSBN)

0 + 3 + (1) VANGUARD CLASS (SSBN)

Name	*No*	*Builders*	*Laid down*	*Launched*	*Commissioned*
VANGUARD	05	Vickers Shipbuilding and Engineering	3 Sep 1986	4 Mar 1992	1993
VICTORIOUS	06	Vickers Shipbuilding and Engineering	3 Dec 1987	1992	1994
VIGILANT	07	Vickers Shipbuilding and Engineering	16 Feb 1991	1994	1995
—	08	Vickers Shipbuilding and Engineering	—	—	—

Displacement, tons: 15 000 dived
Dimensions, feet (metres): 491.8 × 42 × 39.4 *(149.9 × 12.8 × 12)*
Main machinery: Nuclear; 1 RR PWR 2; 2 turbines; 27 500 hp *(20.5 MW)*; 1 shaft; pump jet propulsor; 1 auxiliary retractable propulsion motor; 2 diesel alternators; 2700 hp *(2 MW)*
Speed, knots: 25 dived approx
Complement: 135 (2 crews)

Missiles: SLBM: 16 Lockheed Trident 2 (D5) three stage solid fuel rocket; stellar inertial guidance to 12 000 km *(6500 nm)*; thermonuclear warhead of 8 MIRV of 150 kT; cep 90 m. The D5 can carry up to 12 MIRV but will be restricted to 7 or 8 (of UK manufacture).
Torpedoes: 4—21 in *(533 mm)* tubes. Marconi Spearfish; dual purpose; wire-guided; active/passive homing to 65 km *(35 nm)* at 60 kts; warhead directed energy. Marconi Tigerfish Mk 24 Mod 2; wire-guided; active/passive homing to 13 km *(7 nm)* at 35 kts active; 29 km *(15.7 nm)* at 24 kts passive; warhead 134 kg.
Countermeasures: Decoys: 2 SSDE Mk 10 launchers.
ESM: Racal UAP 3; passive intercept.
Combat data systems: Dowty Sema SMCS.
Fire control: Dowty tactical control system.
Radars: Navigation: Kelvin Hughes Type 1007; I band.
Sonars: Marconi/Plessey Type 2054 composite multi-frequency hull-mounted sonar suite plus Marconi/Ferranti Type 2046 towed array.

Programmes: On 15 July 1980 the government announced its intention to procure from the United States the Trident I weapon system, comprising the C4 ballistic missile and supporting systems for a force of new British missile launching submarines to replace the present Polaris-equipped force in the 1990s. On 11 March 1982 it was announced that the government had opted to procure the improved Trident II weapon system, with the D5 missile, to be deployed in a force of four submarines, in the mid-1990s. *Vanguard* ordered 30 April 1986; *Victorious* 6 October 1987; *Vigilant* 13 November 1990. The original programme anticipated ordering one per year for the first three years so there has been much stretching out of the building programme. The fourth ship to be ordered in 1992.
Structure: Refit and recore interval is anticipated at eight to nine years. The outer surface of the submarine is covered with conformal anechoic noise reduction coatings. An optronic mast is a new feature.

VANGUARD 3/1992

Operational: After some early problems there were three successful submerged launched firings of the D5 missile from USS *Tennessee* in December 1989 and the missile was first deployed operationally in April 1990. *Vanguard* is planned to start sea trials in late 1992; first operational patrol December 1994.
Opinion: Because the funding for Trident has come mainly from the naval share of the defence budget, it is having a detrimental effect on the equipment programmes for the rest of the Fleet. Annual expenditure peaked in 1989-90 and remains at a high level until at least the mid-1990s. The stretching out of the building programme and the extended development programme of the follow-on SSN to the Trafalgar class, means an inevitable increase in estimated costs, although money has been saved on the dollar exchange rate for the missiles.

VANGUARD 3/1992

4 RESOLUTION CLASS (SSBN)

Name	*No*	*Builders*	*Laid down*	*Launched*	*Commissioned*
RESOLUTION	S 22	Vickers (Shipbuilding), Barrow-in-Furness	26 Feb 1964	15 Sep 1966	2 Oct 1967
REPULSE	S 23	Vickers (Shipbuilding), Barrow-in-Furness	12 Mar 1965	4 Nov 1967	28 Sep 1968
RENOWN	S 26	Cammell Laird & Co, Birkenhead	25 June 1964	25 Feb 1967	15 Nov 1968
REVENGE	S 27	Cammell Laird & Co, Birkenhead	19 May 1965	15 Mar 1968	4 Dec 1969

Displacement, tons: 7600 surfaced; 8500 dived
Dimensions, feet (metres): 425 × 33 × 30 *(129.5 × 10.1 × 9.1)*
Main machinery: Nuclear; 1 RR PWR 1; 2 English Electric turbines; 15 000 hp *(11.2 MW)*; 1 shaft; 2 diesel alternators; 2200 hp *(1.64 MW)*; 1 motor for emergency drive; 1 auxiliary retractable prop
Speed, knots: 20 surfaced; 25 dived
Complement: 143 (13 officers) (2 crews)

Missiles: SLBM: 16 Lockheed Polaris A3 two stage solid fuel rocket; inertial guidance to 4630 km *(2500 nm)*; each missile carries 3 MRV heads each of 200 kT; Chevaline nuclear warheads (fitted in *Renown* 1982, *Resolution* 1984, *Repulse* 1986, *Revenge* 1988); cep 900 m.
Torpedoes: 6—21 in *(533 mm)* bow tubes. Marconi Tigerfish Mk 24 Mod 2; wire-guided; active/passive homing to 13 km *(7 nm)* at 35 kts active; 29 km *(15.7 nm)* at 24 kts passive; warhead 134 kg.
Countermeasures: Decoys: 2 SSDE launchers.
ESM: MEL UA 11/12; passive intercept.
Combat data systems: Gresham/Dowty DCB data handling system.
Fire control: Dowty tactical control system.
Radars: Navigation: Kelvin Hughes Type 1006; I band.
Sonars: Plessey Type 2001; hull-mounted; active/passive; low frequency.
BAe Type 2007; hull-mounted; flank array; passive; long range; low frequency.
Ferranti Type 2046; towed array; passive search; very low frequency.
Thomson Sintra Type 2019 PARIS (to be replaced by Type 2082); passive intercept and ranging.

Programmes: In February 1963 it was stated that it was intended to order four or five 7000 ton nuclear powered submarines, each to carry 16 Polaris missiles, and it was planned that the first would be on patrol in 1968. Their hulls and machinery would be of British design. As well as building two submarines Vickers (Shipbuilding) would give lead yard service to the builder of the other two. Four Polaris submarines were in fact ordered in May 1963. The plan to build a fifth Polaris submarine was cancelled on 15 February 1965. Britain's first SSBN, *Resolution*, put to sea on 22 June 1967.
Modernisation: The Chevaline warheads were substituted for the original Polaris missile payloads in a rolling programme between 1982 and 1988. The warhead is similar but it is supported by 'a variety of penetration aids' to overcome anti-ballistic missile (ABM) defences.
Operational: Since early 1969 there has been at least one of these submarines at immediate readiness to fire its inter-continental ballistic missiles. Each submarine, which has accommodation for 19 officers and 135 ratings, is manned on a two-crew basis, in order to get maximum operational time at sea. It has been reported that the Polaris stockpile is some 70 missiles with 45-50 warheads. First one of the class to pay off in 1993 then sequentially as the Vanguard class commissions.

RESOLUTION *8/1989*

RENOWN *11/1985, MoD(N)*

Attack Submarines (SSN)

Notes: (1) In early 1987 Vickers SEL was given a contract to carry out design work for the W class (SSN 20) with the aim of ordering the first of the new class in 1990. Four years later in August 1991 Vickers were again invited to tender but this time for a studies contract for a design "based on the development, with minimum change, of the existing Trafalgar class", the last of which was ordered on 3 January 1986. The first of this Batch 2 Trafalgar class is unlikely to be ordered until 1994 with an in-service date of 2001, which means a gap of 10 years between the commissioning of the last of the Trafalgars and the first of its successors.

(2) As pennant numbers are never displayed and rarely used class lists are in order of completion.

7 TRAFALGAR CLASS (SSN)

Name	*No*	*Builders*	*Laid down*	*Launched*	*Commissioned*
TRAFALGAR	S 107	Vickers Shipbuilding & Engineering Ltd, Barrow-in-Furness	1979	1 July 1981	27 May 1983
TURBULENT	S 87	Vickers Shipbuilding & Engineering Ltd, Barrow-in-Furness	1980	1 Dec 1982	28 Apr 1984
TIRELESS	S 88	Vickers Shipbuilding & Engineering Ltd, Barrow-in-Furness	1981	17 Mar 1984	5 Oct 1985
TORBAY	S 90	Vickers Shipbuilding & Engineering Ltd, Barrow-in-Furness	1982	8 Mar 1985	7 Feb 1987
TRENCHANT	S 91	Vickers Shipbuilding & Engineering Ltd, Barrow-in-Furness	1984	3 Nov 1986	14 Jan 1989
TALENT	S 92	Vickers Shipbuilding & Engineering Ltd, Barrow-in-Furness	1986	15 Apr 1988	12 May 1990
TRIUMPH	S 93	Vickers Shipbuilding & Engineering Ltd, Barrow-in-Furness	1987	16 Feb 1991	12 Oct 1991

Displacement, tons: 4700 surfaced; 5208 dived
Dimensions, feet (metres): 280.1 × 32.1 × 31.2 *(85.4 × 9.8 × 9.5)*
Main machinery: Nuclear; 1 RR PWR 1; 2 GEC turbines; 15 000 hp *(11.2 MW)*; 1 shaft; pump jet propulsor; 2 Paxman diesel alternators; 2800 hp *(2.09 MW)*; 1 motor for emergency drive; 1 auxiliary retractable prop
Speed, knots: 32 dived
Complement: 97 (12 officers)

Missiles: SSM: McDonnell Douglas UGM-84B Sub-Harpoon; active radar homing to 130 km *(70 nm)* at 0.9 Mach; warhead 227 kg.
Torpedoes: 5—21 in *(533 mm)* bow tubes. Marconi Spearfish; wire-guided; active/passive homing to 65 km *(35 nm)* at 60 kts; warhead directed energy. Marconi Tigerfish Mk 24 Mod 2; wire-guided; active/passive homing to 13 km *(7 nm)* at 35 kts active; 29 km *(15.7 nm)* at 24 kts passive; warhead 134 kg; 20 reloads.
Mines: Can be carried in lieu of torpedoes.
Countermeasures: Decoys: 2 SSDE Mk 8 launchers.
ESM: Racal UAC/CXA (being upgraded to UAP); passive intercept.
Combat data systems: Gresham/Dowty DCB tactical data handling system. Dowty Sema SMCS after refit.
Fire control: Dowty tactical control system.
Radars: Navigation: Kelvin Hughes Type 1006 or Type 1007; I band.
Sonars: BAe Type 2007 AC or Marconi 2072; hull-mounted; flank array; passive; low frequency.
Plessey Type 2020 or Marconi/Plessey 2074; hull-mounted; passive/active search and attack; low frequency.
GEC Avionics Type 2026 or Ferranti Type 2046 or Marconi/Plessey 2057; towed array; passive search; very low frequency.
Thomson Sintra Type 2019 PARIS; passive intercept and ranging (to be replaced by 2082 in due course).

Programmes: The first of an improved class of Fleet Submarines was ordered in September 1977. *Turbulent* ordered 28 July 1978; *Tireless* 5 July 1979; *Torbay* 26 June 1981; *Trenchant* 22 March 1983; *Talent* 10 September 1984; *Triumph* 3 January 1986.
Modernisation: Trials have been done on Sonar Type 2057 which has a reelable wet end for the towed array sonar. *Turbulent* has a hump on the after casing under which there is a small winch. Type 1006 radar is to be replaced by Type 1007. All to be updated with Type 2076 sonar system and integrated countermeasures. 2076 includes Type 2074 and Type 2046.
Structure: Designed to be considerably quieter than previous submarines. The pressure hull and outer surfaces are covered with conformal anechoic noise reduction coatings. Other improvements include speed and endurance. Retractable forward hydroplanes and strengthened fins for under ice operations. Diving depth in excess of 300 m *(985 ft)*.

TRAFALGAR Class *1991*

Operational: *Trafalgar* is the trials submarine for Spearfish which started full production in 1992. All of the class belong to the Second Submarine Squadron.

TALENT *9/1991, Giorgio Arra*

5 SWIFTSURE CLASS (SSN)

Name	*No*	*Builders*	*Laid down*	*Launched*	*Commissioned*
SOVEREIGN	S 108	Vickers (Shipbuilding) Ltd, Barrow-in-Furness	18 Sep 1970	17 Feb 1973	11 July 1974
SUPERB	S 109	Vickers (Shipbuilding) Ltd, Barrow-in-Furness	16 Mar 1972	30 Nov 1974	13 Nov 1976
SCEPTRE	S 104	Vickers (Shipbuilding) Ltd, Barrow-in-Furness	19 Feb 1974	20 Nov 1976	14 Feb 1978
SPARTAN	S 105	Vickers (Shipbuilding) Ltd, Barrow-in-Furness	26 Apr 1976	7 Apr 1978	22 Sep 1979
SPLENDID	S 106	Vickers (Shipbuilding) Ltd, Barrow-in-Furness	23 Nov 1977	5 Oct 1979	21 Mar 1981

Displacement, tons: 4000 light; 4400 standard; 4900 dived
Dimensions, feet (metres): 272 × 32.3 × 28 *(82.9 × 9.8 × 8.5)*
Main machinery: Nuclear; 1 RR PWR 1; 2 GEC turbines; 15 000 hp *(11.2 MW)*; 1 shaft; pump jet propulsor; 1 Paxman diesel alternator; 1900 hp *(1.42 MW)*; 1 motor for emergency drive; 1 auxiliary retractable prop
Speed, knots: 30+ dived
Complement: 116 (13 officers)

Missiles: SSM: McDonnell Douglas UGM-84B Sub-Harpoon; active radar homing to 130 km *(70 nm)* at 0.9 Mach; warhead 227 kg.
Torpedoes: 5—21 in *(533 mm)* bow tubes. Marconi Tigerfish Mk 24 Mod 2; wire-guided; active/passive homing to 13 km *(7 nm)* at 35 kts active; 29 km *(15.7 nm)* at 24 kts passive; warhead 134 kg; 20 reloads. Individual reloading of torpedoes in 15 seconds. To be replaced by Spearfish in mid-1990s.
Mines: Can be carried in lieu of torpedoes.
Countermeasures: Decoys: 2 SSDE Mk 6 launchers.
ESM: Racal UAC (being upgraded to UAP); passive intercept.
Combat data systems: Gresham/Dowty DCB/DCG tactical data handling system. Dowty Sema SMCS after refit.
Radars: Navigation: Kelvin Hughes Type 1006; I band.
Sonars: AUWE Type 2001 or Plessey Type 2020 or Marconi/Plessey Type 2074; hull-mounted; active/passive search and attack; low frequency.
BAC Type 2007; hull-mounted; flank array; passive; low frequency.
Ferranti Type 2046; towed array; passive search; very low frequency.
Thomson Sintra Type 2019 PARIS; passive intercept and ranging (to be replaced by 2082 in due course).

Programmes: *Sovereign* ordered 16 May 1969; *Superb*, 20 May 1970; *Sceptre*, 1 Nov 1971; *Spartan*, 7 Feb 1973; *Splendid*, 26 May 1976.
Modernisation: *Sceptre* finished refit in 1987, *Spartan* in 1989, and *Splendid* in 1992, each fitted with a PWR 1 Core Z giving a 12 year life cycle although refits/refuel cycles will remain at eight to nine year intervals. Other improvements included acoustic elastomeric tiles, new sonar 2020 processing equipment and improved decoys. Others of the class to follow some with Marconi/Plessey 2074 sonar instead of 2020 to replace Type 2001. Spearfish torpedoes will also be fitted in the mid-1990s.
Structure: Compared with the Valiant class submarines these are slightly shorter with a fuller form, the fore-planes set further forward, one less torpedo tube and with a deeper diving depth and faster. The pressure hull in the Swiftsure class maintains its diameter for much greater length than previous classes. Control gear by MacTaggart, Scott & Co Ltd for: attack and search periscopes, snort induction and exhaust, radar and ESM masts, ALK buoy. The forward hydroplanes house within the casing.
Operational: All either have moved, or will move on completion of refit, to the Third Submarine Squadron. As a result of budget cuts *Swiftsure* paid off in 1992 after less than 20 years' service.

SWIFTSURE *3/1989, van Ginderen Collection*

SCEPTRE *4/1988, Giorgio Arra*

SOVEREIGN *10/1988, W. Sartori*

1 VALIANT CLASS (SSN)

Name	No	Builders	Laid down	Launched	Commissioned
VALIANT	S 102	Vickers (Shipbuilding) Ltd, Barrow-in-Furness	22 Jan 1962	3 Dec 1963	18 July 1966

Displacement, tons: 4000 light; 4300 standard; 4800 dived
Dimensions, feet (metres): 285 × 33.2 × 27.5 *(86.9 × 10.1 × 8.4)*
Main machinery: Nuclear; 1 RR PWR 1; 2 English Electric turbines; 15 000 hp *(11.2 MW)*; 1 shaft; 2 diesel alternators; 2200 hp *(1.64 MW)*; 1 motor for emergency drive; 1 auxiliary retractable prop
Speed, knots: 28 dived
Complement: 116 (13 officers)

Missiles: SSM: McDonnell Douglas UGM-84B Sub-Harpoon; active radar homing to 130 km *(70 nm)* at 0.9 Mach; warhead 227 kg.
Torpedoes: 6—21 in *(533 mm)* bow tubes. Marconi Tigerfish Mk 24 Mod 2; wire-guided; active/passive homing to 13 km *(7 nm)* at 35 kts active; 29 km *(15.7 nm)* at 24 kts passive; warhead 134 kg; 26 reloads. Individual reloading in 15 seconds.
Mines: Can be carried in lieu of torpedoes.
Countermeasures: ESM: Type UAL; radar warning.
Combat data systems: Gresham/Dowty DCB/DCG tactical data handling system.
Radars: Navigation: Kelvin Hughes Type 1006; I band.

VALIANT *7/1991, D & B Teague*

Sonars: Plessey Type 2020; hull-mounted; active/passive search and attack; low frequency.
Ferranti Type 2046; towed array; passive search: very low frequency.
Thomson Sintra Type 2019 PARIS; passive intercept and ranging.

Operational: The first of a class of five and the last to survive the cutbacks in overall SSN numbers. Employed primarily for trials and evaluations possibly until 1994.

Patrol Submarines (SS)

3 + 1 UPHOLDER CLASS (TYPE 2400) (SS)

Name	No	Builders	Start date	Launched	Commissioned
UPHOLDER	S 40	Vickers Shipbuilding and Engineering Ltd, Barrow-in-Furness	Nov 1983	2 Dec 1986	9 June 1990
UNSEEN	S 41	Cammell Laird, Birkenhead (VSEL)	Jan 1986	14 Nov 1989	7 June 1991
URSULA	S 42	Cammell Laird, Birkenhead (VSEL)	Aug 1987	28 Feb 1991	8 May 1992
UNICORN	S 43	Cammell Laird, Birkenhead (VSEL)	Feb 1989	16 Apr 1992	1993

Displacement, tons: 2168 surfaced; 2455 dived
Dimensions, feet (metres): 230.6 × 25 × 17.7 *(70.3 × 7.6 × 5.5)*
Main machinery: Diesel-electric; 2 Paxman Valenta 1600 RPA-200 SZ diesels; 4000 hp *(2.98 MW)*; 2 GEC alternators; 2.8 MW; 1 GEC motor; 5400 hp *(4 MW)*; 1 shaft
Speed, knots: 12 surfaced; 20 dived; 12 snorting.
Range, miles: 8000 at 8 kts snorting
Complement: 47 (7 officers)

Missiles: SSM: McDonnell Douglas UGM-84B Sub-Harpoon; active radar homing to 130 km *(70 nm)* at 0.9 Mach; warhead 227 kg.
Torpedoes: 6—21 in *(533 mm)* bow tubes. Marconi Tigerfish Mk 24 Mod 2; wire-guided; active/passive homing to 13 km *(7 nm)* at 35 kts active; 29 km *(15.7 nm)* at 24 kts passive; warhead 134 kg; 12 reloads. Spearfish in due course. Air turbine pump discharge.
Mines: M Mk 5 carried in lieu of torpedoes.
Countermeasures: Decoys: 2 SSDE launchers.
ESM: Racal Type UAC (being updated to UAP); passive intercept.
Combat data systems: Ferranti-Gresham-Lion DCC tactical data handling system.
Radars: Navigation: Kelvin Hughes Type 1007; I band.
Sonars: Thomson Sintra Type 2040; hull-mounted; passive search; medium frequency.
BAe Type 2007; flank array; passive; low frequency.
GEC Avionics Type 2026 or Type 2046; towed array; passive search; very low frequency.
Thomson Sintra Type 2019 PARIS; intercept and passive ranging (to be replaced by Type 2082 in due course).

Programmes: The need for the provision of a new class of non-nuclear submarines was acknowledged in the late 1970s and in 1979 the Type 2400 design was first revealed. First boat ordered from Vickers SEL, 2 November 1983. Further three ordered on 2 January 1986. Plans for four more were dropped in 1990 as part of a cost cutting exercise designed to reduce the diesel submarine strength to four by the mid-1990s. Refit interval is anticipated at seven and a half years.
Modernisation: Sonar suite Type 2076 may be fitted in due course in place of the cancelled Type 2075.
Structure: Single skinned NQ1 high tensile steel hull, tear dropped shape 9:1 ratio, five man lock-out chamber in fin. This is the first time that the Valenta diesel has been fitted in submarines. Fitted with elastomeric acoustic tiles. Diving depth, greater than 200 m *(650 ft)*.
Operational: Endurance, 49 days stores and 90 hours at 3 kts dived. Problems with the torpedo tube discharge system are being rectified; *Upholder* in 1992, *Unseen* and *Ursula* in 1993, *Unicorn* before commissioning.

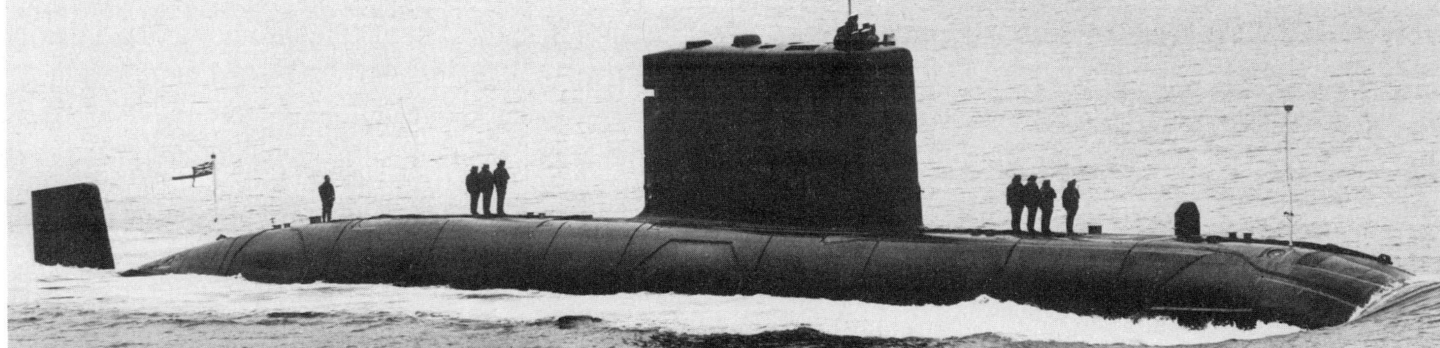

UNSEEN *7/1991, W. Sartori*

3 OBERON CLASS (SS)

Name	No	Builders	Laid down	Launched	Commissioned
ORACLE	S 16	Cammell Laird & Co Ltd, Birkenhead	26 Apr 1960	26 Sep 1961	14 Feb 1963
OPOSSUM	S 19	Cammell Laird & Co Ltd, Birkenhead	21 Dec 1961	23 May 1963	5 June 1964
OPPORTUNE	S 20	Scotts (Shipbuilding) Co Ltd, Greenock	26 Oct 1962	14 Feb 1964	29 Dec 1964

Displacement, tons: 1610 standard; 2030 surfaced; 2410 dived
Dimensions, feet (metres): 295.2 × 26.5 × 18 *(90 × 8.1 × 5.5)*
Main machinery: Diesel-electric; 2 ASR 16 VVS-ASR1 diesels; 3680 hp *(2.74 MW)*; 2 AEI motors; 6000 hp *(4.48 MW)*; 2 shafts
Speed, knots: 12 surfaced; 17 dived; 10 snorting.
Range, miles: 9000 at 12 kts surfaced
Complement: 69 (7 officers)

Torpedoes: 6—21 in *(533 mm)* bow tubes. Marconi Tigerfish Mk 24 Mod 2; wire-guided; active/passive homing to 13 km *(7 nm)* at 35 kts active; 29 km *(15.7 nm)* at 24 kts passive; warhead 134 kg; 20 torpedoes. Stern tubes have either been removed or are no longer operational.
Mines: Can be carried in lieu of torpedoes.
Countermeasures: Decoys: 2 SSDE Mk 4.
ESM: MEL Manta UAL; radar warning.
Fire control: Ferranti DCH tactical data handling system. Dual channel fire control.
Radars: Navigation: Kelvin Hughes Type 1006; I band.
Sonars: Plessey Type 2051; hull-mounted; passive/active search and attack; medium frequency.
BAC Type 2007; hull-mounted; flank array; passive; long-range; low frequency.
US Type 2024; clip-on towed array.

OPPORTUNE *10/1991, Wright & Logan*

Modernisation: The Triton sonar modernisation programme was completed in 1989. *Otus* (now deleted) did trials to establish the feasibility of fitting Sub-Harpoon but there are no plans to retrofit the class.
Structure: Before and abaft the bridge the superstructure is mainly of glass fibre laminate. Diving depth, 200 m *(650 ft)*.

Operational: All are planned to pay off by 1993 as part of a cost cutting exercise designed to reduce diesel submarine strength to four boats. *Orpheus* is used as a training hulk in *Dolphin*.
Sales: A total of 14 of this class were sold abroad, six to Australia, three to Canada, three to Brazil and two to Chile. *Olympus* to Canada in 1989 as a training hulk.

AIRCRAFT CARRIERS

3 LIGHT AIRCRAFT CARRIERS (CVSG)

Name	*No*	*Builders*	*Laid down*	*Launched*	*Commissioned*
INVINCIBLE	R 05	Vickers (Shipbuilding), Barrow-in-Furness	20 July 1973	3 May 1977	11 July 1980
ILLUSTRIOUS	R 06	Swan Hunter Shipbuilders, Wallsend	7 Oct 1976	1 Dec 1978	20 June 1982
ARK ROYAL	R 07	Swan Hunter Shipbuilders, Wallsend	14 Dec 1978	2 June 1981	1 Nov 1985

Displacement, tons: 19 500 (R 05, 06), 20 600 (R 07) full load
Dimensions, feet (metres): 677 oa; 632 wl × 105 oa; 90 wl × 21 keel; 27.9 screws (R 05, 06)
(206.3; 192.6 × 31.9; 27.5 × 6.4; 8.5)
685.8 oa; 632 wl × 118 oa; 90 wl × 21 keel; 26 screws (R 07)
(209.1; 192.6 × 36; 27.5 × 6.4; 8)
Flight deck, feet (metres): 550 × 44.3 *(167.8 × 13.5)*
Main machinery: COGAG; 4 RR Olympus TM3B gas turbines; 86 000 hp *(64 MW)* sustained; 2 shafts
Speed, knots: 28. **Range, miles:** 5000 at 18 kts
Complement: 666 (57 officers) plus 366 (80 officers) aircrew
685 (60 officers) plus 376 (90 officers) aircrew (R 07)

Missiles: SAM: British Aerospace Sea Dart twin launcher ❶; radar/semi-active radar guidance to 40 km *(21.5 nm)* at Mach 2; height envelope 100-18 300 m *(328-60 042 ft)*; 36 missiles; limited anti-ship capability.
Guns: 3 General Electric/General Dynamics 20 mm Mk 15 Vulcan Phalanx (R 07) ❷; 6 barrels per launcher; 3000 rounds/minute combined to 1.5 km.
3 Signaal/General Electric 30 mm 7-barrelled Gatling Goalkeeper (R 05 and R 06) ❸; 4200 rounds/minute to 1.5 km.
2 Oerlikon/BMARC 20 mm GAM-BO1 ❹; 55° elevation; 1000 rounds/minute to 2 km.
Countermeasures: Decoys: 2 Vickers Corvus 8-tubed trainable launchers (not in R 05); Chaff to 1 km.
2 Loral Hycor SRBOC 6-tubed fixed Mk 36 launchers ❺; IR flares and Chaff to 4 km *(2.2 nm)* max.
2 THORN EMI Sea Gnat dispensers. Prairie Masker noise suppression system.
ESM: MEL UAA 2; intercept.
ECM: THORN EMI Type 675(2); jammer.
Combat data systems: ADAWS 10 action data automation; Links 10, 11 and 14. US OE-82 VHF SATCOM. SCOT communications ❻; Link 16 in due course. Marisat.
Fire control: GWS 30 for SAM.
Radars: Air search: Marconi/Signaal Type 1022 ❼; D band; range 265 km *(145 nm)*.
Surface search: Marconi Type 992R ❽; or Plessey Type 996(2) ❾ (R 05); E/F band.
Navigation: Two Kelvin Hughes Type 1006; I band.
Fire control: Two Marconi Type 909 ❿; I/J band.
Sonars: Plessey Type 2016; hull-mounted; active search and attack.

Fixed wing aircraft: 9 British Aerospace Sea Harrier FRS 1 (see *Shipborne Aircraft* section) ⓫.
Helicopters: Up to 9 Westland Sea King HAS 6 ⓬; 3 Westland Sea King AEW 2.

Programmes: The first of class, the result of many compromises, was ordered from Vickers on 17 April 1973. The order for the second ship was placed on 14 May 1976, the third in December 1978.
Modernisation: In January 1989 R 05 completed a 27 month modernisation which included a 12° ski ramp, space and support facilities for at least 21 aircraft (Sea Harriers, Sea King AEW and ASW helicopters), three Goalkeeper systems, Sonar 2016, Seagnat decoys, 996 radar, Flag and Command facilities to R 07 standards and accommodation for an additional 120 aircrew and Flag Staff. In August 1991 R 06 started a similar 30 month modernisation to bring her to the same standard, but with additional command and weapon system improvements to those listed for R 05. Plans to fit four lightweight Seawolf launchers were cancelled as an economy measure in 1991. Contract placed in early 1991 to redesign the flight deck lifts.
Structure: The design allows for an open fo'c'sle head and a slightly angled deck which allows the Sea Dart launcher to be set almost amidships. In 1976-77 an amendment was incorporated to allow for the transport and landing of an RM Commando. The forward end of the flight deck (ski-ramp of 12°) allows STOVL aircraft of greater all-up weight to operate more efficiently.
Operational: The role of this class, apart from its primary task of providing a command, control and communications facility, is the operation of both helicopters and STOVL aircraft. Provision has been made for sufficiently large lifts and hangars to accommodate the next generation of both these aircraft. Only two of the class are in commission at any one time, the third either being in refit or stand-by.

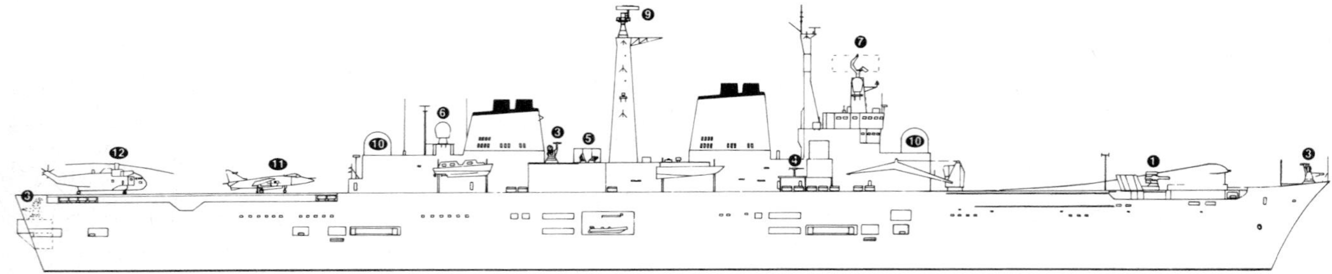

INVINCIBLE *(Scale 1 : 1 200), Ian Sturton*

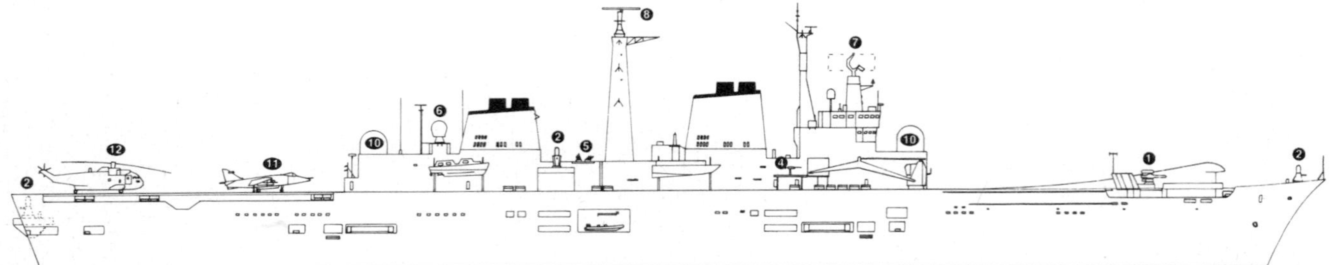

ARK ROYAL *(Scale 1 : 1 200), Ian Sturton*

ARK ROYAL *9/1991, Giorgio Arra*

ARK ROYAL *2/1991*

INVINCIBLE *8/1991*

INVINCIBLE *2/1992, Maritime Photographic*

INVINCIBLE *8/1991*

DESTROYERS

Notes: (a) There is a requirement for a Type 42 Air Defence ship replacement. Such a ship must have a local area missile system (LAMS). The requirement is to be advanced in the future frigate programme for which a 'joint statement of need' was signed with the French Navy on 1 March 1991. Whether the project remains collaborative or not, the plan is to start project definition in 1993, with the first of class to be ordered in 1996 and in service by 2002.
(b) *Bristol* (D 23) may replace *Kent* as an immobile tender used for training in Portsmouth Harbour.

12 TYPE 42

Batch 1

Name	*No*	*Builders*	*Laid down*	*Launched*	*Commissioned*
BIRMINGHAM	D 86	Cammell Laird & Co Ltd, Birkenhead	28 Mar 1972	30 July 1973	3 Dec 1976
NEWCASTLE	D 87	Swan Hunter Ltd, Wallsend-on-Tyne	21 Feb 1973	24 Apr 1975	23 Mar 1978
GLASGOW	D 88	Swan Hunter Ltd, Wallsend-on-Tyne	16 Apr 1974	14 Apr 1976	24 May 1979
CARDIFF	D 108	Vickers (Shipbuilding) Ltd, Barrow-in-Furness	6 Nov 1972	22 Feb 1974	24 Sep 1979

Batch 2

Name	*No*	*Builders*	*Laid down*	*Launched*	*Commissioned*
EXETER	D 89	Swan Hunter Ltd, Wallsend-on-Tyne	22 July 1976	25 Apr 1978	19 Sep 1980
SOUTHAMPTON	D 90	Vosper Thornycroft Ltd	21 Oct 1976	29 Jan 1979	31 Oct 1981
NOTTINGHAM	D 91	Vosper Thornycroft Ltd	6 Feb 1978	18 Feb 1980	14 Apr 1983
LIVERPOOL	D 92	Cammell Laird & Co Ltd, Birkenhead	5 July 1978	25 Sep 1980	1 July 1982

Displacement, tons: 3500 standard; 4100 full load
Dimensions, feet (metres): 392 wl; 412 oa × 47 × 19 (screws); 13.9 (keel) *(119.5; 125 × 14.3 × 5.8; 4.2)*
Main machinery: COGOG; 2 RR Olympus TM3B gas turbines; 43 000 hp *(32 MW)* sustained; 2 RR Tyne RM1C gas turbines (cruising); 10 680 hp *(8 MW)* sustained; 2 shafts; cp props
Speed, knots: 29. **Range, miles:** 4000 at 18 kts
Complement: 253 (24 officers) (accommodation for 312)

Missiles: SAM: British Aerospace Sea Dart twin launcher ❶; radar/semi-active radar guidance to 40 km *(21.5 nm)* at 2 Mach; height envelope 100-18 300 m *(328-60 042 ft)*; 22 missiles; limited anti-ship capability.
Guns: 1 Vickers 4.5 in *(114 mm)*/55 Mk 8 ❷; 55° elevation; 25 rounds/minute to 22 km *(11.9 nm)* anti-surface; 6 km *(3.3 nm)* anti-aircraft; weight of shell 21 kg.
2 or 4 Oerlikon/BMARC 20 mm GAM-BO1 ❸; 55° elevation; 1000 rounds/minute to 2 km.
2 Oerlikon 20 mm Mk 7A ❹ (in some); 50° elevation; 800 rounds/minute to 2 km; weight of shell 0.24 kg.
2 General Electric/General Dynamics 20 mm Vulcan Phalanx Mk 15 ❺; 6 barrels per launcher; 3000 rounds/minute combined to 1.5 km.
Torpedoes: 6—324 mm Plessey STWS Mk 3 (2 triple) tubes ❻ (to be fitted from 1993 in some). Marconi Stingray; active/passive homing to 11 km *(5.9 nm)* at 45 kts; warhead 35 kg (shaped charge); depth to 750 m *(2460 ft)* (see *Modernisation*).
Countermeasures: Decoys: 2 Vickers Corvus 8-tubed trainable launchers or 2 Marconi Sea Gnat ❼; Chaff and IR flares.
2 Loral Hycor SRBOC 6-tubed fixed Mk 36 launchers ❽; (in some); IR flares and Chaff to 4 km *(2.2 nm)*.
Graseby Type 182; towed torpedo decoy.
ESM: MEL UAA-2; intercept.
ECM: Type 670; being replaced by Type 675(2) (Batch 2); jammer.
Combat data systems: ADAWS 7 action data automation. 2 Marconi SCOT SATCOMs ❾; Links 10, 11 and 14. Marisat.
Fire control: GWS 30 Mod 2 (for SAM); GSA 1 secondary system. Radamec 2000 series optronic surveillance system.
Radars: Air search: Marconi/Signaal Type 1022 ❿; D band; range 265 km *(145 nm)*.
Surface search: Plessey Type 996 ⓫; E/F band.
Navigation: Kelvin Hughes Type 1006; I band.
Fire control: Two Marconi Type 909 ⓬; or 9091; I/J band.
Sonars: Ferranti Type 2050 or Plessey Type 2016; hull-mounted; active search and attack; medium frequency.
Kelvin Hughes Type 162M; hull-mounted; bottom classification; 50 kHz.

Helicopters: 1 Westland Lynx HAS 3 ⓭.

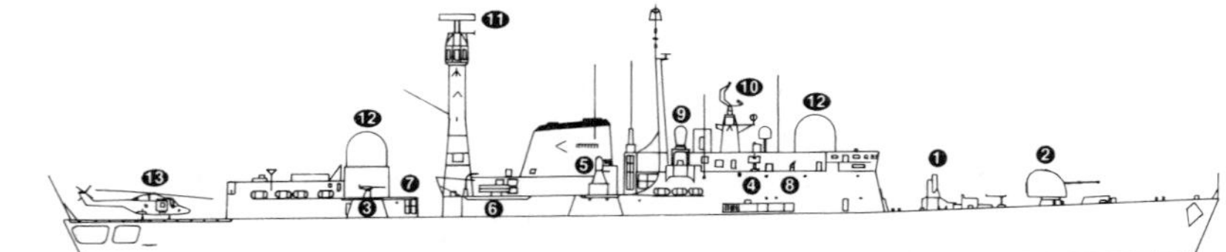

EXETER (Batch 2) *(Scale 1 : 1 200), Ian Sturton*

GLASGOW (with Satcom and Marisat) *5/1991, Maritime Photographic*

NOTTINGHAM *10/1991, W. Sartori*

Batch 3

Name	*No*	*Builders*	*Laid down*	*Launched*	*Commissioned*
MANCHESTER	D 95	Vickers (Shipbuilding) Ltd, Barrow-in-Furness	19 May 1978	24 Nov 1980	16 Dec 1982
GLOUCESTER	D 96	Vosper Thornycroft Ltd	29 Oct 1979	2 Nov 1982	11 Sep 1985
EDINBURGH	D 97	Cammell Laird & Co Ltd, Birkenhead	8 Sep 1980	14 Apr 1983	17 Dec 1985
YORK	D 98	Swan Hunter Ltd, Wallsend-on-Tyne	18 Jan 1980	21 June 1982	9 Aug 1985

Displacement, tons: 3500 standard; 4775 full load
Dimensions, feet (metres): 434 wl; 462.8 oa × 49 × 19 (screws) *(132.3; 141.1 × 14.9 × 5.8)*
Main machinery: COGOG; 2 RR Olympus TM3B gas turbines; 43 000 hp *(32 MW)* sustained; 2 RR Tyne RM1C gas turbines (cruising); 10 680 hp *(8 MW)* sustained; 2 shafts; cp props
Speed, knots: 30+. **Range, miles:** 4000 at 18 kts
Complement: 301 (26 officers)

Missiles: SAM: British Aerospace Sea Dart twin launcher ❶; radar/semi-active radar guidance to 40 km *(21 nm)*; warhead HE; 22 missiles; limited anti-ship capability.
Guns: 1 Vickers 4.5 in *(114 mm)*/55 Mk 8 ❷; 55° elevation; 25 rounds/minute to 22 km *(11.9 nm)* anti-surface; 6 km *(3.3 nm)* anti-aircraft; weight of shell 21 kg.
2 Oerlikon/BMARC 20 mm GAM-BO1 ❸; 55° elevation; 1000 rounds/minute to 2 km.
2 Oerlikon 20 mm Mk 7A ❹; 50° elevation; 800 rounds/minute to 2 km; weight of shell 0.24 kg.
2 BMARC 30 mm ❺ (temporary mountings in D 97).
1 or 2 General Electric/General Dynamics 20 mm Vulcan Phalanx Mk 15 ❻; 6 barrels per launcher; 3000 rounds/minute combined to 1.5 km. See *Modernisation* comment.
Torpedoes: 6—324 mm STWS Mk 2 (2 triple) tubes ❼. Marconi Stingray; active/passive homing to 11 km *(5.9 nm)* at 45 kts; warhead 35 kg.
Countermeasures: Decoys: 2 Vickers Corvus 8-tubed trainable launchers or 2 Marconi Sea Gnat ❽; Chaff and IR flares.
2 Loral Hycor SRBOC 6-tubed fixed Mk 36 launchers; IR flares and Chaff to 4 km *(2.2 nm)* (in some).
Graseby Type 182; towed torpedo decoy.
ESM: MEL UAA-2; intercept.
ECM: Type 670 being replaced by Type 675(2); jammer.
Combat data systems: ADAWS 8 (with ADIMP) action data automation. 2 Marconi SCOT SATCOMs ❾; Links 10, 11 and 14. Marisat.
Fire control: GWS 30 Mod 2 (for SAM); GSA 1 secondary system. Radamec 2000 series optronic surveillance system.
Radars: Air search: Marconi/Signaal Type 1022 ❿; D band; range 265 km *(145 nm)*.
Air/surface search: Marconi Type 992R or Plessey Type 996 ⓫; E/F band.
Navigation: Kelvin Hughes Type 1006; I band.
Fire control: Two Marconi Type 909 ⓬ or 909 Mod 1; I/J band.
Sonars: Ferranti Type 2050 or Plessey Type 2016; hull-mounted; active search and attack.
Kelvin Hughes Type 162M; hull-mounted; bottom classification; 50 kHz.

Helicopters: 1 Westland Lynx HAS 3 ⓭.

Batches 1, 2 and 3

Programmes: Designed to provide area air defence for a task force. In order to provide space for improved weapon systems and to improve speed and seakeeping a radical change was made to this class. The completion of later ships was delayed to allow for some modifications resulting from experience in the Falklands' campaign (1982).
Modernisation: Vulcan Phalanx replaced 30 mm guns 1987-89. All are receiving Plessey Type 996 radar in place of Type 992, and Type 909(1) fire control radars with improved Tx/Rx circuits. STWS Mk 3 is replacing the obsolete Mk 1 in Batch 2 and may then be retrofitted to Batches 1 and 3. D 97 had a partial conversion completing in 1990 with the Phalanx moved forward and a protective visor fitted around the bow of the ship. As a temporary measure 30 mm guns were placed where Seawolf launchers would have been fitted. That modification was cancelled in 1991 and D 97 will revert to the standard armament in due course. All Batch 3 ships are having a command system update starting with D 95 in 1992.
Structure: All have two pairs of stabilisers and twin rudders. Advantages of gas turbine propulsion include ability to reach maximum speed with great rapidity, reduction in space and weight and 25 per cent reduction in technical manpower. The stretched Batch 3 have been fitted with a strengthening beam on each side which increases displacement by 150 tons and width by 2 feet.
Operational: The helicopter carries the Sea Skua air-to-surface weapon for use against lightly defended surface ship targets. Ships may be fitted with DEC laser dazzle sight and additional decoy flare launchers on operational deployments.

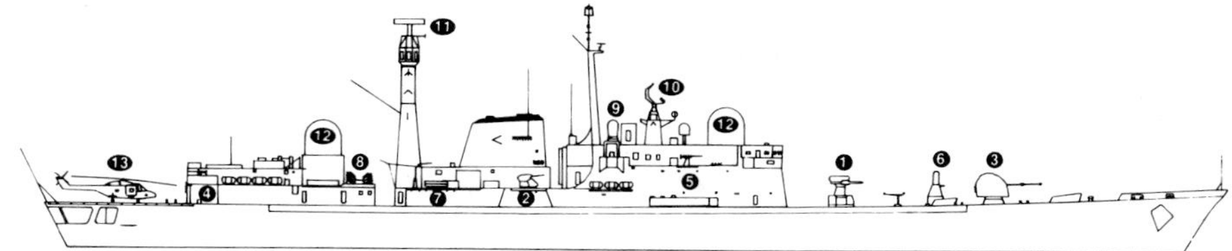

EDINBURGH *(Scale 1 : 1 200), Ian Sturton*

EDINBURGH *3/1991*

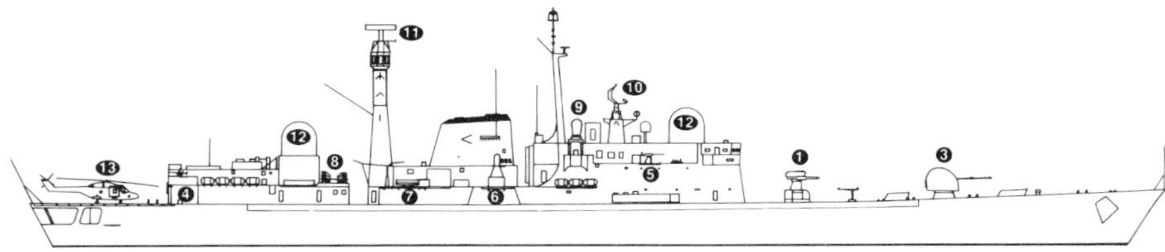

GLOUCESTER *(Scale 1 : 1 200), Ian Sturton*

YORK *6/1991, H. M. Steele*

FRIGATES

14 BROADSWORD CLASS (TYPE 22)

Batch 1

Name	*No*	*Builders*	*Laid down*	*Launched*	*Commissioned*
BROADSWORD	F 88	Yarrow (Shipbuilders), Glasgow	7 Feb 1975	12 May 1976	3 May 1979
BATTLEAXE	F 89	Yarrow (Shipbuilders), Glasgow	4 Feb 1976	18 May 1977	28 Mar 1980
BRILLIANT	F 90	Yarrow (Shipbuilders), Glasgow	25 Mar 1977	15 Dec 1978	15 May 1981
BRAZEN	F 91	Yarrow (Shipbuilders), Glasgow	18 Aug 1978	4 Mar 1980	2 July 1982

Batch 2

Name	*No*	*Builders*	*Laid down*	*Launched*	*Commissioned*
BOXER	F 92	Yarrow (Shipbuilders), Glasgow	1 Nov 1979	17 June 1981	14 Jan 1984
BEAVER	F 93	Yarrow (Shipbuilders), Glasgow	20 June 1980	8 May 1982	18 Dec 1984
BRAVE	F 94	Yarrow (Shipbuilders), Glasgow	24 May 1982	19 Nov 1983	4 July 1986
LONDON (ex-*Bloodhound*)	F 95	Yarrow (Shipbuilders), Glasgow	7 Feb 1983	27 Oct 1984	5 June 1987
SHEFFIELD	F 96	Swan Hunter (Shipbuilders), Wallsend	29 Mar 1984	26 Mar 1986	26 July 1988
COVENTRY	F 98	Swan Hunter (Shipbuilders), Wallsend	29 Mar 1984	8 Apr 1986	14 Oct 1988

Displacement, tons: 3500 standard; 4400 full load (Batch 1)
4100 standard; 4800 full load (Batch 2)
Dimensions, feet (metres): 410 wl; 430 oa × 48.5 × 19.9 (screws) *(125; 131.2 × 14.8 × 6)* (Batch 1)
485.8 oa × 48.5 × 21 (screws) *(145 × 14.8 × 6.4)* (F 92-93)
480.5 × 48.5 × 21 *(146.5 × 14.8 × 6.4)* (F 94-96 and 98)
Main machinery: COGOG; 2 RR Olympus TM3B gas turbines; 43 000 hp *(32 MW)* sustained or 2 RR Spey SM1C (F 94); 41 630 hp *(31 MW)* sustained; 2 RR Tyne RM1C gas turbines; 10 680 hp *(8 MW)* sustained; 2 shafts; cp props
Speed, knots: 30; 18 on Tynes. **Range, miles:** 4500 at 18 kts on Tynes
Complement: 222 (17 officers) (accommodation for 249) (Batch 1)
273 (30 officers) (accommodation for 296) (Batch 2)

Missiles: SSM: 4 Aerospatiale MM 38 Exocet ❶; inertial cruise; active radar homing to 42 km *(23 nm)* at 0.9 Mach; warhead 165 kg; sea-skimmer.
SAM: 2 British Aerospace 6-barrelled Seawolf GWS 25 Mod 0 or Mod 4 (except F 94-96 and 98) ❷; command line of sight (CLOS) TV/radar tracking to 5 km *(2.7 nm)* at 2+ Mach; warhead 14 kg; 32 rounds. Being upgraded to Mod 4 with improved radar and optronics.
2 British Aerospace Seawolf GWS 25 Mod 3 (F 94-96 and 98) ❷; has a Type 911 tracker with a second radar channel instead of TV.
Guns: 4 Oerlikon/BMARC GCM-A03 30 mm/75 (2 twin) ❸; 80° elevation; 650 rounds/minute to 10 km *(5.5 nm)*; weight of shell 0.36 kg.
2 Oerlikon/BMARC 20 mm GAM-BO1 ❹; 55° elevation; 1000 rounds/minute to 2 km.
Torpedoes: 6—324 mm Plessey STWS Mk 2 (2 triple) tubes ❺. Marconi Stingray; active/passive homing to 11 km *(5.9 nm)* at 45 kts; warhead 35 kg.
Countermeasures: Decoys: 2 Plessey Shield 12-tubed launchers ❻; IR flares and Chaff to 4 km *(2.2 nm)*.
2 Loral Hycor SRBOC 6-tubed fixed Mk 36 launchers; IR flares and Chaff to 4 km *(2.2 nm)*.
Graseby Type 182; towed torpedo decoy.
ESM: MEL UAA-1; intercept.
ECM: 2 Type 670; to be replaced by Type 675(2); jammers.
Combat data systems: Ferranti CACS 1 (Batch 2); Links 11 and 14; CAAIS (Batch 1); Links 10 and 14 (receive); action data automation. Marconi SCOT SATCOM ❼. Marisat.
Fire control: GWS 25 Mod 0 or 4 (for SAM) (except F 94-96 and 98); GWS 25 Mod 3 (for SAM) (F 94-96 and 98); GWS 50.
Radars: Air/surface search: Marconi Type 967/968 (Type 967M in F 94) ❽; D/E band.
Navigation: Kelvin Hughes Type 1006; I band.
Fire control: Two Marconi Type 911 or Type 910 (in Mod 0 ships) ❾; I/Ku band (for Seawolf).
Sonars: Plessey Type 2016 or Ferranti/Thomson Sintra Type 2050; hull-mounted; search and attack.
Dowty Type 2031Z (Batch 2 only); towed array; passive search; very low frequency.

Helicopters: 2 Westland Lynx HAS 3 (in all) ❿; or 1 Westland Sea King HAS 5 (or EH 101 Merlin) (F 94-96 and 98).

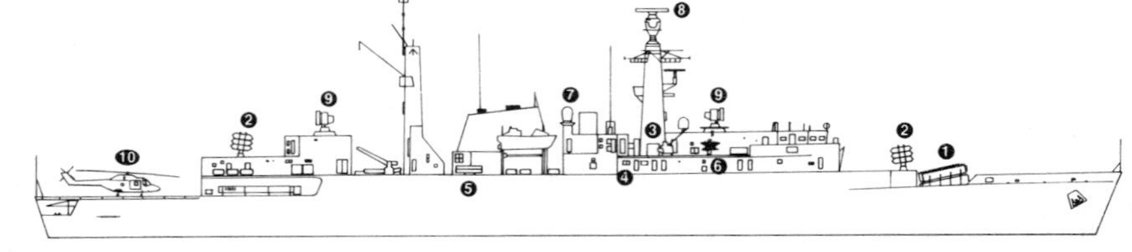

TYPE 22 (Batch 1) *(Scale 1 : 1 200), Ian Sturton*

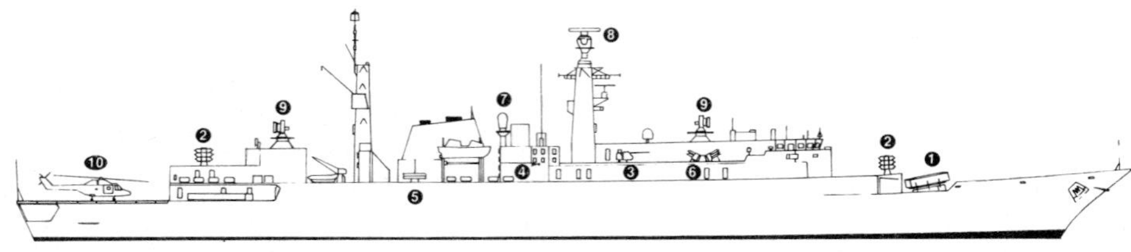

TYPE 22 (Batch 2) *(Scale 1 : 1 200), Ian Sturton*

BATTLEAXE *6/1991, Wright & Logan*

SHEFFIELD *6/1991, David Warren*

Batch 3

Name	*No*	*Builders*	*Laid down*	*Launched*	*Commissioned*
CORNWALL	F 99	Yarrow (Shipbuilders), Glasgow	14 Dec 1983	14 Oct 1985	23 Apr 1988
CUMBERLAND	F 85	Yarrow (Shipbuilders), Glasgow	12 Oct 1984	21 June 1986	10 June 1989
CAMPBELTOWN	F 86	Cammell Laird (Shipbuilders), Birkenhead	4 Dec 1985	7 Oct 1987	27 May 1989
CHATHAM	F 87	Swan Hunter (Shipbuilders), Wallsend	12 May 1986	20 Jan 1988	4 May 1990

Displacement, tons: 4200 standard; 4900 full load
Dimensions, feet (metres): 485.9 × 48.5 × 21 *(148.1 × 14.8 × 6.4)*
Main machinery: COGOG; 2 RR Spey SM1A gas turbines; 29 500 hp *(22 MW)* sustained; 2 RR Tyne RM1C gas turbines; 10 680 hp *(8 MW)* sustained; 2 shafts; cp props
Speed, knots: 30; 18 on Tynes. **Range, miles:** 4500 at 18 kts on Tynes
Complement: 250 (31 officers) (accommodation for 301)

Missiles: SSM: 8 McDonnell Douglas Harpoon Block 1C (2 quad) launchers ❶; pre-programmed; active radar homing to 130 km *(70 nm)* at 0.9 Mach; warhead 227 kg.
SAM: 2 British Aerospace Seawolf GWS 25 Mod 3 ❷; command line of sight (CLOS) with 2 channel radar tracking to 5 km *(2.7 nm)* at 2+ Mach; warhead 14 kg.
Guns: 1 Vickers 4.5 in *(114 mm)*/55 Mk 8 ❸; 55° elevation; 25 rounds/minute to 22 km *(11.9 nm)* anti-surface; 6 km *(3.3 nm)* anti-aircraft; weight of shell 21 kg.
1 Signaal/General Electric 30 mm 7-barrelled Goalkeeper ❹; 4200 rounds/minute combined to 1.5 km.
2 DES/Oerlikon 30 mm/75 ❺; 80° elevation; 650 rounds/minute to 10 km *(5.5 nm)*; weight of shell 0.36 kg.
Torpedoes: 6—324 mm Plessey STWS Mk 2 (2 triple) tubes ❻. Marconi Stingray; active/passive homing to 11 km *(5.9 nm)* at 45 kts; warhead 35 kg.
Countermeasures: Decoys: 4 Marconi Sea Gnat 6-barrelled fixed launchers ❼; electronic decoy with jammer.
Graseby Type 182; towed torpedo decoy.
ESM: MEL UAA-1; intercept.
ECM: Type 675(2); jammer.
Combat data systems: CACS 5 action data automation; Links 11 and 14. 2 Marconi SCOT SATCOMs ❽. ICS-3 integrated comms. Marisat.
Fire control: 2 BAe GSA 8A Sea Archer optronic directors with TV and IR imaging and laser rangefinders ❾. GWS 60. GWS 25 Mod 3 (for SAM).
Radars: Air/surface search: Marconi Type 967/968 ❿; D/E band.
Navigation: Kelvin Hughes Type 1006; I band.
Fire control: Two Marconi Type 911 ⓫; I/Ku band (for Seawolf).
Sonars: Plessey Type 2016; hull-mounted; active search and attack. Being replaced by Ferranti Type 2050.
Dowty Type 2031; towed array; passive search; very low frequency.

Helicopters: 2 Westland Lynx HAS 3; or 1 Westland Sea King HAS 5 ⓬ (or EH 101 Merlin).

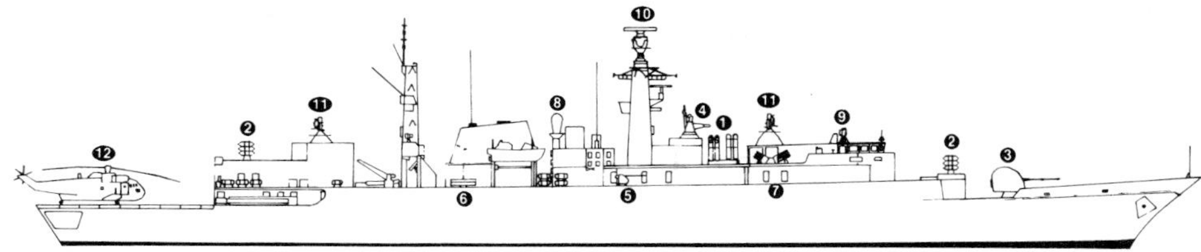

TYPE 22 (Batch 3) *(Scale 1 : 1 200), Ian Sturton*

CHATHAM *11/1991, Maritime Photographic*

Batches 1, 2 and 3

Programmes: Originally planned as successors to the Leander class. Order for the first of class, *Broadsword*, was placed on 8 February 1974.
Modernisation: Rolls Royce Spey SM1C engines (operational in F 94 in early 1990) give greater power and may be back fitted in due course. Seawolf GWS 25 will be progressively upgraded to Mod 4 standard in all Mod 0 ships. Sonar 2016 is being replaced by Sonar 2050 and Bofors 40 mm/60 in Batch 1 and 2 have been replaced by Oerlikon 30 mm guns. EW fit is being updated. CAAIS combat data system in Batch 1 is overdue for replacement.
Structure: Funnel in *Brilliant* and later ships was smoother, slimmer and shorter than in first two in build but *Broadsword* and *Battleaxe* have been modified and are now the same. Last four Batch 2 and all Batch 3 have enlarged flight decks to take Sea King or EH 101 Merlin helicopters.
Operational: This class is primarily designed for ASW operations and is capable of acting as OTC. Batch 3 have facilities for Flag and staff. One Lynx normally embarked for peacetime operations. Ships may be fitted with DEC laser dazzle device on operational deployments. Batch 2: 1st Frigate Squadron. Batch 1: 2nd Frigate Squadron. Batch 3: 8th Frigate Squadron.

CUMBERLAND *6/1991, H. M. Steele*

6 + 7 + (10) DUKE CLASS (TYPE 23)

Name	No	Builders	Laid down	Launched	Commissioned
NORFOLK	F 230	Yarrow (Shipbuilders), Glasgow	14 Dec 1985	10 July 1987	1 June 1990
ARGYLL	F 231	Yarrow (Shipbuilders), Glasgow	20 Mar 1987	8 Apr 1989	31 May 1991
LANCASTER	F 229 (ex-F 232)	Yarrow (Shipbuilders), Glasgow	18 Dec 1987	24 May 1990	May 1992
MARLBOROUGH	F 233	Swan Hunter Shipbuilders, Wallsend	22 Oct 1987	21 Jan 1989	14 June 1991
IRON DUKE	F 234	Yarrow (Shipbuilders), Glasgow	12 Dec 1988	2 Mar 1991	Mar 1993
MONMOUTH	F 235	Yarrow (Shipbuilders), Glasgow	1 June 1989	23 Nov 1991	Oct 1993
MONTROSE	F 236	Yarrow (Shipbuilders), Glasgow	1 Nov 1989	Sep 1992	May 1994
WESTMINSTER	F 237	Swan Hunter Shipbuilders, Wallsend	18 Jan 1991	4 Feb 1992	Dec 1993
NORTHUMBERLAND	F 238	Swan Hunter Shipbuilders, Wallsend	4 Apr 1991	4 Apr 1992	May 1994
RICHMOND	F 239	Swan Hunter Shipbuilders, Wallsend	16 Feb 1992	Jan 1993	Dec 1994
SOMERSET	F 240	Yarrow (Shipbuilders), Glasgow	1993	1995	1996
GRAFTON	F 241	Yarrow (Shipbuilders), Glasgow	1993	1995	1997
SUTHERLAND	F 242	Yarrow (Shipbuilders), Glasgow	1994	1996	1997

Displacement, tons: 3500 standard; 4200 full load
Dimensions, feet (metres): 436.2 × 52.8 × 18 (screws); 24 (sonar) *(133 × 16.1 × 5.5; 7.3)*
Main machinery: CODLAG; 2 RR Spey SM1A (F 229-F 236) or SM1C (F 237 onwards) gas turbines; 29 500 hp *(22 MW)* sustained (1A) or 41 630 hp *(31 MW)* sustained (1C); 4 Paxman Valenta 12 CM diesels; 8100 hp *(6 MW)*; 2 GEC motors; 4000 hp *(3 MW)*; 2 shafts
Speed, knots: 28; 15 on diesel-electric. **Range, miles:** 7800 miles at 15 kts
Complement: 169 (12 officers) (accommodation for 185 (16 officers))

Missiles: SSM: 8 McDonnell Douglas Harpoon (2 quad) launchers ❶; active radar homing to 130 km *(70 nm)* at 0.9 Mach; warhead 227 kg (84C).
SAM: British Aerospace Seawolf GWS 26 Mod 1 VLS ❷; command line of sight (CLOS) radar/TV tracking to 6 km *(3.3 nm)* at 2.5 Mach; warhead 14 kg; 32 canisters.
Guns: 1 Vickers 4.5 in *(114 mm)*/55 Mk 8 ❸; 55° elevation; 25 rounds/minute to 22 km *(11.9 nm)* anti-surface; 6 km *(3.3 nm)* anti-aircraft; weight of shell 21 kg.
2 Oerlikon/DES 30 mm/75 Mk 1 ❹; 80° elevation; 650 rounds/minute to 10 km *(5.4 nm)* anti-surface; 3 km *(1.6 nm)* anti-aircraft; weight of shell 0.36 kg.
Torpedoes: 4 J & S Marine 324 mm fixed (2 twin) tubes ❺. Marconi Stingray; active/passive homing to 11 km *(5.9 nm)* at 45 kts; warhead 35 kg (shaped charge); depth to 750 m *(2460 ft)*. Automatic reload in 9 minutes.
Countermeasures: Decoys: 4 Marconi Sea Gnat 6-barrelled fixed launchers ❻; for Chaff and IR flares.
Type 182; towed torpedo decoy.
ESM: Racal UAF-1 Cutlass ❼; intercept. THORN EMI UAT (F 237 onwards and then retrofit).
ECM: Type 675(2) or Racal Cygnus; jammer.
Combat data systems: Dowty Sema SSCS action data automation (see *Structure* comment); Links 11, 14 and 16 in due course. Marconi SCOT 1D SATCOMs ❽.
Fire control: BAe GSA 8B/GPEOD optronic director ❾. GWS 60 (for SSM). GWS 26 (for SAM).
Radars: Air/surface search: Plessey Type 996(I) ❿; 3D; E/F band.
Navigation: Kelvin Hughes Type 1007; I band.
Fire control: Two Marconi Type 911 ⓫; I/Ku band.
Sonars: Ferranti/Thomson Sintra Type 2050; bow-mounted; active search and attack.
Dowty Type 2031Z; towed array; passive search; very low frequency. To be replaced by Marconi/Plessey 2057 in due course.

Helicopters: 1 Westland Lynx HAS 3 (1 EH 101 Merlin, later) ⓬.

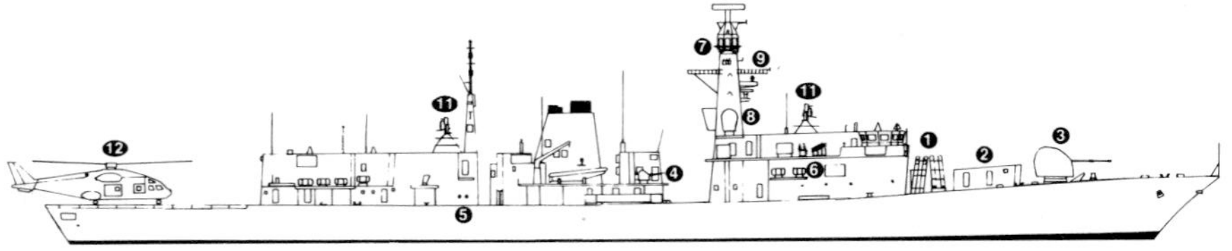
NORFOLK (Scale 1 : 1 200), Ian Sturton

ARGYLL 7/1991, H. M. Steele

Programmes: The first of this class was ordered from Yarrows on 29 October 1984. Next three in September 1986, with four more out to tender in October 1987 but only three ordered in July 1988. Again four out to tender in late 1988 and only three ordered 19 December 1989. Long lead items for another six ordered in 1990 but contracts were not placed until 23 January 1992 when three more were ordered. Planned final total is 23 at the present rate of less than two per year. F 229 pennant number changed because 232 was considered unlucky as it is the RN report form number for collisions and groundings.

Structure: Incorporates stealth technology to minimise acoustic, magnetic, radar and IR signatures. The design includes a 7° slope to all vertical surfaces, rounded edges, reduction of IR emissions and a hull bubble system to reduce radiated noise. The combined diesel electric and GT propulsion system provides quiet motive power during towed sonar operations. A CIWS gun is not fitted but a possible extension by 7 m at some stage in the building programme would allow one or two Goalkeeper to be carried and increase Seawolf magazine capacity. The early Type 23s will lack fully automated co-ordination of all weapons and sensors until about 1993-94 when the SSCS system is installed.

Operational: The ship is capable of carrying out all weapon systems functions without the SSCS Combat Data System. The problem is that in multi-threat situations command speed of response will in theory be much slower. F 233 carrying out a trial of a Dowty track management system (TMS) which uses a form of artificial intelligence.

MARLBOROUGH 6/1991

6 AMAZON CLASS (TYPE 21)

Name	*No*	*Builders*	*Laid down*	*Launched*	*Commissioned*
AMAZON	F 169	Vosper Thornycroft Ltd, Woolston	6 Nov 1969	26 Apr 1971	11 May 1974
ACTIVE	F 171	Vosper Thornycroft Ltd, Woolston	23 July 1971	23 Nov 1972	17 June 1977
AMBUSCADE	F 172	Yarrow (Shipbuilders) Ltd, Glasgow	1 Sep 1971	18 Jan 1973	5 Sep 1975
ARROW	F 173	Yarrow (Shipbuilders) Ltd, Glasgow	28 Sep 1972	5 Feb 1974	29 July 1976
ALACRITY	F 174	Yarrow (Shipbuilders) Ltd, Glasgow	5 Mar 1973	18 Sep 1974	2 July 1977
AVENGER	F 185	Yarrow (Shipbuilders) Ltd, Glasgow	30 Oct 1974	20 Nov 1975	19 July 1978

Displacement, tons: 3100 standard; 3600 full load
Dimensions, feet (metres): 360 wl; 384 oa × 41.7 × 19.5 (screws) *(109.7; 117 × 12.7 × 5.9)*
Main machinery: COGOG; 2 RR Olympus TM3B gas turbines; 43 000 hp *(32 MW)* sustained; 2 RR Tyne RM1C gas turbines (cruising); 10 680 hp *(8 MW)* sustained; 2 shafts; cp props
Speed, knots: 30; 18 on Tynes. **Range, miles:** 4000 at 17 kts; 1200 at 30 kts
Complement: 175 (13 officers) (accommodation for 192)

Missiles: SSM: 4 Aerospatiale MM 38 Exocet ❶; inertial cruise; active radar homing to 42 km *(23 nm)* at 0.9 Mach; warhead 165 kg; sea-skimmer.
SAM: Short Bros Seacat GWS 24 quad launcher ❷; optical/radar guidance to 5 km *(2.7 nm)*; warhead 10 kg; sea-skimmer modification.
Guns: 1 Vickers 4.5 in *(114 mm)*/55 Mk 8 ❸; 55° elevation; 25 rounds/minute to 22 km *(11.9 nm)* anti-surface; 6 km *(3.3 nm)* anti-aircraft; weight of shell 21 kg.
2 or 4 Oerlikon 20 mm Mk 7A ❹; 50° elevation; 800 rounds/minute to 2 km; weight of shell 0.24 kg.
Torpedoes: 6—324 mm Plessey STWS Mk 2 (2 triple) tubes ❺. Marconi Stingray; active/passive homing to 11 km *(5.9 nm)* at 45 kts; warhead 35 kg (shaped charge); depth to 750 m *(2460 ft)*. Only in *Alacrity* and *Active*; the others have a second pair of 20 mm guns in lieu.
Countermeasures: Decoys: Graseby Type 182; towed torpedo decoy.
2 Vickers Corvus 8-tubed trainable launchers ❻; Chaff to 1 km.
ESM: MEL UAA-1; intercept.
Combat data systems: CAAIS combat data system with Ferranti FM 1600B computers. Marconi SCOT SATCOMs ❼; Links 10 and 14 (receive).
Fire control: Ferranti WSA-4 digital fire control system for gun and Seacat. GWS 50.
Radars: Air/surface search: Marconi Type 992R ❽; E/F band.
Navigation: Kelvin Hughes Type 1006; I band.
Fire control: Two Selenia Type 912 ❾; I/J band; range 40 km *(22 nm)*.
Sonars: Graseby Type 184P; hull-mounted; active search and attack.
Kelvin Hughes Type 162M; hull-mounted; bottom classification; 50 kHz.

Helicopters: 1 Westland Lynx HAS 3 ❿.

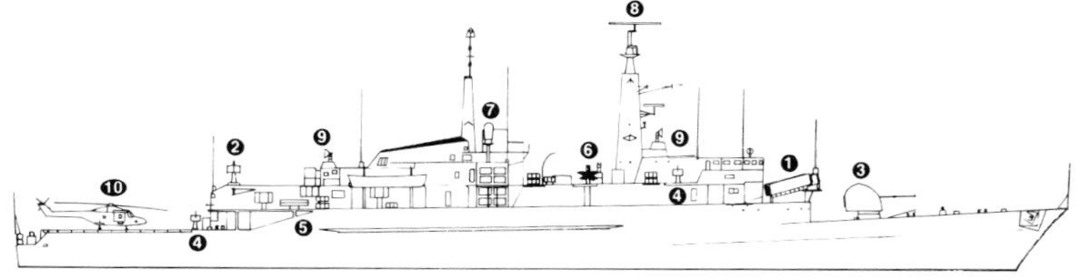

ALACRITY *(Scale 1 : 1 200), Ian Sturton*

AVENGER *7/1991, W. Sartori*

Programmes: A contract was awarded to Vosper Thornycroft on 27 February 1968 for the design of a patrol frigate to be prepared in full collaboration with Yarrow Ltd. This was the first custom built gas turbine frigate (designed and constructed as such from the keel up, as opposed to conversion) and the first RN warship designed by commercial firms for many years.
Modernisation: During service life, GWS 50 Exocet, SCOT, STWS Mk 1 and Lynx helicopter facilities added. With the removal from service of all STWS Mk 1, only two of the class have been fitted with Mk 2 in lieu.
Structure: Due to severe cracking in the upper deck structure large strengthening pieces have been fixed to the ships' side at the top of the steel hull as shown in the illustration. The addition of permanent ballast to improve stability has increased displacement by about 350 tons. Further hull modifications to reduce noise and vibration started in 1988 and completed in 1992.
Operational: Form 4th Frigate Squadron (leader, *Active*).

ACTIVE (with STWS) *6/1991, Wright & Logan*

4 LEANDER CLASS

EXOCET GROUP (Batch 2)

Name	*No*	*Builders*	*Laid down*	*Launched*	*Commissioned*	*Conversion completed*
SIRIUS	F 40	HM Dockyard, Portsmouth	9 Aug 1963	22 Sep 1964	15 June 1966	Oct 1977
ARGONAUT	F 56	Hawthorn Leslie, Hebburn-on-Tyne	27 Nov 1964	8 Feb 1966	17 Aug 1967	Mar 1980

Displacement, tons: 2450 standard; 3200 full load
Dimensions, feet (metres): 360 wl; 372 oa × 41 × 14.8 (keel); 19 (screws) *(109.7; 113.4 × 12.5 × 4.5; 5.8)*
Main machinery: 2 Babcock & Wilcox boilers; 550 psi *(38.7 kg/cm sq)*; 850°F *(454°C)*; 2 White/English Electric turbines; 30 000 hp *(22.4 MW)*; 2 shafts
Speed, knots: 28. **Range, miles:** 4000 at 15 kts
Complement: 266 (18 officers)

Missiles: SSM: 4 Aerospatiale MM 38 Exocet ❶; inertial cruise; active radar homing to 42 km *(23 nm)* at 0.9 Mach; warhead 165 kg; sea-skimmer.
SAM: 2 Short Bros Seacat GWS 22 quad launchers ❷; optical/radar guidance to 5 km *(2.7 nm)*; warhead 10 kg; sea-skimmer modification.
Guns: 2 Oerlikon 20 mm Mk 7A ❸; 50° elevation; 800 rounds/minute to 2 km; weight of shell 0.24 kg.
Countermeasures: Decoys: Graseby Type 182; towed torpedo decoy.
2 Vickers Corvus 8-barrelled trainable launchers ❹; Chaff to 1 km.
1 Loral Hycor SRBOC 6-tubed fixed Mk 36 launcher; IR flares and Chaff to 4 km *(2.2 nm)*.
ESM: UA-8/9/13; radar warning.
ECM: Type 667/668; jammer.
Combat data systems: CAAIS action data automation. SCOT SATCOM in some ❺; Link 10 and Link 14 (receive).
Radars: Air/surface search: Plessey Type 994 ❻; E/F band.
Navigation: Kelvin Hughes Type 1006; I band.
Fire control: Plessey Type 903/904; I band (for Seacat) ❼.
IFF: Type 1010 ❽
Sonars: Graseby Type 184P; hull-mounted; active search and attack.
Waverley Type 2031 ❾; towed array; passive search; very low frequency.
Kelvin Hughes Type 162M; hull-mounted; bottom classification; 50 kHz.

Helicopters: 1 Westland Lynx HAS 3 (F 28 has no flight) ❿.

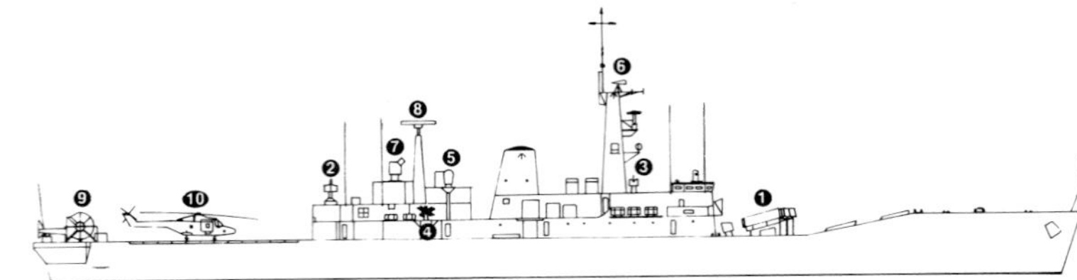
ARGONAUT *(Scale 1 : 1 200), Ian Sturton*

SIRIUS *10/1991, Maritime Photographic*

BROAD-BEAMED GROUP (Batch 3A)

Name	*No*	*Builders*	*Laid down*	*Launched*	*Commissioned*	*Conversion completed*
ANDROMEDA	F 57	HM Dockyard, Portsmouth	25 May 1966	24 May 1967	2 Dec 1968	Dec 1980
SCYLLA	F 71	HM Dockyard, Devonport	17 May 1967	8 Aug 1968	12 Feb 1970	7 Dec 1984

Displacement, tons: 2500 standard; 2962 full load
Dimensions, feet (metres): 360 wl; 372 oa × 43 × 14.8 (keel); 18 (screws) *(109.7; 113.4 × 13.1 × 4.5; 5.5)*
Main machinery: 2 Babcock & Wilcox boilers; 550 psi *(38.7 kg/cm sq)*; 850°F *(454°C)*; 2 White/English Electric turbines; 30 000 hp *(22.4 MW)*; 2 shafts
Speed, knots: 28. **Range, miles:** 4000 at 15 kts
Complement: 260 (19 officers)

Missiles: SSM: 4 Aerospatiale MM 38 Exocet ❶; inertial cruise; active radar homing to 42 km *(23 nm)* at 0.9 Mach; warhead 165 kg.
SAM: British Aerospace 6-barrelled Seawolf GWS 25 Mod 0 ❷; command line of sight (CLOS) radar/TV tracking to 5 km *(2.7 nm)* at 2+ Mach; warhead 14 kg; 32 canisters.
Guns: 2 Oerlikon/BMARC 20 mm GAM-BO1 ❸; 50° elevation; 800 rounds/minute to 2 km; weight of shell 0.24 kg.
2 Oerlikon 20 mm Mk 7A; 50° elevation; 800 rounds/minute to 2 km; weight of shell 0.24 kg.
Torpedoes: 6—324 mm Mk 32 STWS 2 (2 triple) tubes ❹. Marconi Stingray; active/passive homing to 11 km *(5.9 nm)* at 45 kts; warhead 35 kg.
Countermeasures: Decoys: Graseby Type 182; towed torpedo decoy.
2 Vickers Corvus 8-barrelled trainable launchers ❺; Chaff to 1 km.
ESM: UAA-1; intercept.
ECM: Type 670; jammer.
Combat data systems: CAAIS action data automation. SCOT SATCOM in some ❻; Link 10 and 14 (receive).

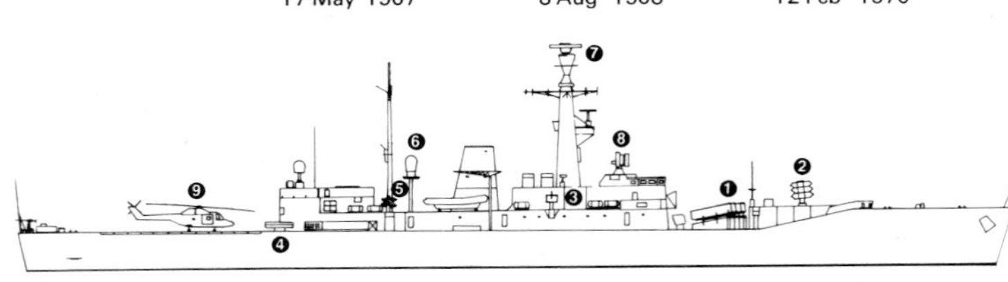
ANDROMEDA *(Scale 1 : 1 200), Ian Sturton*

Fire control: GWS 50.
Radars: Air/surface search: Marconi Type 967/968 ❼; D/E band.
Navigation: Kelvin Hughes Type 1006; I band.
Fire control: Marconi Type 910 ❽; I/J band (for Seawolf).
Sonars: Plessey Type 2016; hull-mounted; active search and attack; medium frequency.
Kelvin Hughes Type 162M; hull-mounted; bottom classification; 50 kHz.

Helicopters: 1 Westland Lynx HAS 3 ❾.

Programmes: The last survivors of an original class of 26 ships. In addition *Juno* (F 52) is still in commission in 1992 as a navigation and engineering training ship, stripped of most weapons and sensors (see *Training Ship* section).
Modernisation: Batch 3 conversion included the provision of four Exocet launchers, the Seawolf SAM system, improved sonar, Lynx helicopter, modern EW equipment and STWS torpedo tubes. At the same time the 114 mm turret, Seacat and Limbo were removed. A further conversion of Batch 2 included the installation of a towed array on the quarter-deck. As a result of this extra 70 tons of top-weight the forward Seacat has been removed, the bridge 40 mm guns replaced by 20 mm, the Exocet mountings have been lowered, boats have been replaced by a Pacific 22 craft and small crane, the Type 965 radar aerial removed and the STWS torpedo tubes first moved down a deck and then removed when STWS 1 tubes were made obsolete. Marconi SCOT SATCOM fitted to some. Close range gun armament refits vary between ships in same Batch. *Sirius* is a trials ship.
Sales: *Bacchante* and *Dido* to New Zealand, the former on 1 October 1982 and *Dido* on 18 July 1983. *Apollo* and *Diomede* to Pakistan in 1988. *Achilles* to Chile in September 1990 probably to be followed by *Ariadne* and possibly *Minerva* in 1992. *Danae* and *Penelope* to Ecuador in 1991.

SCYLLA *5/1991, Wright & Logan*

SHIPBORNE AIRCRAFT

Numbers/Type: 39 British Aerospace Sea Harrier FRS 1.
Operational speed: 640 kts *(1186 km/h)*.
Service ceiling: 51 200 ft *(15 600 m)*.
Range: 800 nm *(1480 km)*.
Role/Weapon systems: Strike, reconnaissance and local air defence duties; update for 29 aircraft by 1994 to FRS 2 Standard (including Blue Vixen radar and AIM 120 AAM) plus 10 new FRS 2 aircraft. Sensors: Blue Fox radar, RWR, cameras. Weapons: ASV; 2 × Sea Eagle missiles. Strike; 2 × 30 mm cannon and 'iron' bombs. AD; 4 × AIM-9L Sidewinder + 2 × 30 mm Aden cannon.

SEA HARRIER *5/1990, H. M. Steele*

Numbers/Type: 80 Westland Lynx HAS 3.
Operational speed: 120 kts *(222 km/h)*.
Service ceiling: 10 000 ft *(3048 m)*.
Range: 320 nm *(593 km)*.
Role/Weapon systems: Primarily ASV helicopter with short-range ASW capability; embarked in all modern RN escorts; Royal Marines operate anti-armour/reconnaissance version (Lynx AH 1); planned update with centralised tactical system Racal 4000 radar, Sea Owl passive identification system and MAD (Lynx HAS 8) to be fitted from 1994. Sensors: Ferranti Sea Spray Mk 1 radar, 'Orange Crop' ESM, Chaff and flare dispenser. Weapons: ASW; 2 × Stingray torpedoes or Mk 11 depth bombs or 1 × WE 177 nuclear depth bomb. ASV; 4 × Sea Skua missiles; 2—12.7 mm MG pods.

LYNX *10/1990*

Numbers/Type: 76 Westland Sea King HAS 5/6.
Operational speed: 112 kts *(207 km/h)*.
Service ceiling: 10 000 ft *(3050 m)*.
Range: 500 nm *(925 km)*.
Role/Weapon systems: Embarked and shore-based medium ASW helicopter in front-line and training squadron service; used as active/passive screen force and provides RN's principal airborne ASW assets; Mk 6 entered service in June 1989. Sensors: MEL Sea Searcher radar, 'Orange Crop' ESM, Ferranti 2069 (HAS 6) replacing Type 195M dipping sonar, AQS-902C sonobuoy processor, combined sonar processor AQS 902G-DS to replace 902C. Weapons: ASW; 4 × Stingray torpedoes or Mk 11 depth bombs or 1 × WE 177 nuclear depth bomb.

SEA KING 5 *8/1990, Maritime Photographic*

Numbers/Type: 10 Westland Sea King AEW 2.
Operational speed: 110 kts *(204 km/h)*.
Service ceiling: 10 000 ft *(3050 m)*.
Range: 660 nm *(1220 km)*.
Role/Weapon systems: Primarily used for airborne early warning organic to the Fleet, with EW, surface search and OTHT secondary roles; modified from ASW version. Sensors: Searchwater AEW radar, 'Orange Crop' ESM, 'Jubilee Guardsmen' IFF. Weapons: Unarmed.

SEA KING AEW 2 *5/1988, N. Overington*

Numbers/Type: 35 Westland Sea King HC4.
Operational speed: 112 kts *(208 km/h)*.
Service ceiling: 5000 ft *(1525 m)*.
Range: 664 nm *(1230 km)*.
Role/Weapon systems: Commando support and re-supply helicopter; capable of carrying most RM Commando Force equipment underslung. Sensors: None. Weapons: Can fit 7.62 mm GPMG or similar, missile armament abandoned.

SEA KING HC4 *1990*

Numbers/Type: 12 Westland Gazelle AH Mk 1.
Operational speed: 142 kts *(264 km/h)*.
Service ceiling: 9350 ft *(2850 m)*.
Range: 361 nm *(670 km)*.
Role/Weapon systems: Observation with 3 Commando Brigade Air Squadron, Royal Marines. Sensors: None. Weapons: Normally unarmed.

GAZELLE *1989*

Numbers/Type: 6 Westland Lynx AH Mk 1.
Operational speed: 140 kts *(259 km/h)*.
Service ceiling: 10 600 ft *(3230 m)*.
Range: 340 nm *(630 km)*.
Role/Weapon systems: Military general purpose and anti-tank with 3 Commando Brigade Air Squadron, Royal Marines. Sensors: None. Weapons: Up to 8 Hughes TOW anti-tank missiles.

LYNX AH Mk 1 *1989*

Numbers/Type: 1 Westland/Agusta EH 101 Merlin.
Operational speed: 160 kts *(296 km/h)*.
Service ceiling: —
Range: 550 nm *(1019 km)*.
Role/Weapon systems: Primary anti-submarine role with secondary anti-surface and troop carrying capabilities. Contract for 44 signed 9 October 1991. Sensors: Ferranti Blue Kestrel radar, Ferranti Flash dipping sonar, sonobuoy acoustic processor AQS-903, Racal Orange Reaper ESM, ECM. Weapons: ASW; 4 Stingray torpedoes or Mk 11 depth bombs. ASV; 4 Sea Skua or replacement, capability for guidance of ship-launched SSM.

MERLIN *1991*

LAND-BASED MARITIME AIRCRAFT (FRONT LINE)

Numbers/Type: 25 British Aerospace Buccaneer S2.
Operational speed: Mach 0.85.
Service ceiling: 60 000 ft *(18 290 m)*.
Range: 3000 nm *(5486 km)*.
Role/Weapon systems: Maritime strike with in-flight refuelling capability. Being phased out. Sensors: Ferranti search/attack radar, ECM. Weapons: ASV; 4 × Sea Eagle or 7.3 tons of 'iron' bombs, 4 × Martel (S2B/S2D).

Numbers/Type: 26 Hawker Siddeley Nimrod MR 2/2P.
Operational speed: 500 kts *(926 km/h)*.
Service ceiling: 42 000 ft *(12 800 m)*.
Range: 5000 nm *(9265 km)*.
Role/Weapon systems: Primarily ASW but with ASV, OTHT and control potential at long range from shore bases; peacetime duties include SAR, EEZ protection, maritime surveillance. Sensors: THORN EMI Searchwater radar, ECM, ESM, cameras, MAD, sonobuoys, AQS-901 processor. Weapons: ASW; 6.1 tons of Mk 44/46 or Stingray torpedoes or depth bombs or mines, provision for B57 or Mk 101 nuclear depth bombs. ASV; 4 × Harpoon missiles. Self-defence; 4 × AIM-9L Sidewinder.

Numbers/Type: 7 Boeing E-3D Sentry AWAC.
Operational speed: 460 kts *(853 km/h)*.
Service ceiling: 30 000 ft *(9145 m)*.
Range: 870 nm *(1610 km)*.
Role/Weapon systems: Air defence early warning aircraft with secondary role to provide coastal AEW for the Fleet; six hours endurance at the range given above. Sensors: Westinghouse APY-2 surveillance radar, Bendix weather radar, Mk XII IFF, Yellow Gate, ESM, ECM. Weapons: Unarmed.

MINE WARFARE FORCES

13 HUNT CLASS (MINESWEEPERS/MINEHUNTERS—COASTAL)

Name	*No*	*Builders*	*Commissioned*
BRECON	M 29	Vosper Thornycroft Ltd	21 Mar 1980
LEDBURY	M 30	Vosper Thornycroft Ltd	11 June 1981
CATTISTOCK	M 31	Vosper Thornycroft Ltd	16 June 1982
COTTESMORE	M 32	Yarrow, Glasgow	24 June 1983
BROCKLESBY	M 33	Vosper Thornycroft Ltd	3 Feb 1983
MIDDLETON	M 34	Yarrow, Glasgow	15 Aug 1984
DULVERTON	M 35	Vosper Thornycroft Ltd	4 Nov 1983
BICESTER	M 36	Vosper Thornycroft Ltd	20 Mar 1986
CHIDDINGFOLD	M 37	Vosper Thornycroft Ltd	10 Aug 1984
ATHERSTONE	M 38	Vosper Thornycroft Ltd	30 Jan 1987
HURWORTH	M 39	Vosper Thornycroft Ltd	2 July 1985
BERKELEY	M 40	Vosper Thornycroft Ltd	14 Jan 1988
QUORN	M 41	Vosper Thornycroft Ltd	21 Apr 1989

Displacement, tons: 615 light; 750 full load
Dimensions, feet (metres): 187 wl; 197 oa × 32.8 × 9.5 (keel); 11.2 (screws) *(57; 60 × 10 × 2.9; 3.4)*
Main machinery: 2 Ruston-Paxman 9-59K Deltic diesels; 1900 hp *(1.42 MW)*; 1 Deltic Type 9-55B diesel for pulse generator and auxiliary drive; 780 hp *(582 kW)*; 2 shafts; bow thruster
Speed, knots: 15 diesels; 8 hydraulic drive. **Range, miles:** 1500 at 12 kts
Complement: 45 (6 officers)

Guns: 1 Oerlikon/BMARC 30 mm/75 DS 30B; 65° elevation; 650 rounds/minute to 10 km *(5.4 nm)* anti-surface; 3 km *(1.6 nm)* anti-aircraft; weight of shell 0.36 kg. Replaced Bofors 40 mm.
2 Oerlikon/BMARC 20 mm GAM-CO1 (enhancement); 55° elevation; 900 rounds/minute to 2 km.
2—7.62 mm MGs.
Countermeasures: Decoys: 2 Wallop Barricade (enhancement); 6 sets of triple barrels.
2 Irvin Replica RF; passive decoys.
ESM: MEL Matilda E (enhancement); Marconi Mentor A (in some).
Combat data systems: CAAIS DBA 4 action data automation.
Radars: Navigation: Kelvin Hughes Type 1006; I band.
Sonars: Plessey Type 193M or 193M Mod 1; hull-mounted; minehunting; 100/300 kHz.
Mil Cross mine avoidance sonar; hull-mounted; active; high frequency.
Type 2059 addition to track PAP 104/105.

Programmes: A class of MCM Vessels combining both hunting and sweeping capabilities.
Modernisation: Ten PAP 105 were acquired in 1988-89 to replace the 104s. They have a range of 600 m *(1968 ft)* down to 300 m *(984 ft)* depth and a speed of 6 kts; weight 700 kg. 30 mm gun has replaced the Bofors 40 mm. Racal Mk 53 navigation system ordered in August 1990 for all ships. Mid-life update being planned.
Structure: Hulls of GRP.
Operational: Two PAP 104/105 remotely controlled submersibles, MS 14 magnetic loop, Sperry MSSA Mk 1 Towed Acoustic Generator and conventional Mk 8 Oropesa sweeps. For operational deployments fitted with enhanced weapons systems, Inmarsat SATCOMs and some have the SCARAB remote control floating mine towing device which helps the safe destruction of moored mines once they have been cut from their moorings. Allocation: 30, 33, 35 and 36 to 4th MCM Squadron. 34, 37, 40, 41 to 1st MCM Squadron. 29, 31, 32, 38, 39 to 2nd MCM Squadron.

HURWORTH *4/1991, W. Sartori*

12 RIVER CLASS (MINESWEEPERS—COASTAL)

Name	*No*	*Builders*	*Commissioned*
WAVENEY	M 2003	Richards Ltd (L)	12 July 1984
CARRON	M 2004	Richards Ltd (GY)	29 Sep 1984
DOVEY	M 2005	Richards Ltd (GY)	30 Mar 1985
HELFORD	M 2006	Richards Ltd (GY)	May 1985
HUMBER	M 2007	Richards Ltd (L)	7 June 1985
BLACKWATER	M 2008	Richards Ltd (GY)	5 July 1985
ITCHEN	M 2009	Richards Ltd (L)	12 Oct 1985
HELMSDALE	M 2010	Richards Ltd (L)	1 Mar 1986
ORWELL	M 2011	Richards Ltd (GY)	27 Nov 1985
RIBBLE	M 2012	Richards Ltd (GY)	19 Feb 1986
SPEY	M 2013	Richards Ltd (L)	4 Apr 1986
ARUN	M 2014	Richards Ltd (L)	29 Aug 1986

Displacement, tons: 890 full load
Dimensions, feet (metres): 156 × 34.5 × 9.5 *(47.5 × 10.5 × 2.9)*
Main machinery: 2 Ruston 6-RKCM diesels; 3100 hp *(2.3 MW)* sustained; 2 shafts
Speed, knots: 14. **Range, miles:** 4500 at 10 kts
Complement: 30 (7 officers)

Guns: 1 Bofors 40 mm/60 Mk 3; 80° elevation; 120 rounds/minute to 10 km *(5.4 nm)* anti-surface; 3 km *(1.6 nm)* anti-aircraft; weight of shell 0.89 kg.
Radars: Navigation: Two Racal Decca TM 1226C; I band.

Programmes: First four ordered 23 September 1982. All built at Lowestoft and Great Yarmouth. Three more planned to be built for Fishery Protection Squadron to replace Ton class but the requirement was cancelled in 1990.
Structure: Steel hulled for deep team sweeping. There have been problems with upper-deck corrosion in some ships. 40 mm guns may be replaced by 30 mm.
Operational: BAJ Wire Sweep Mk 9 EDATS fitted. RNR 10th MCM Squadron: *Waveney* (South Wales); *Carron* (Severn); *Dovey* (Clyde); *Helford* (Ulster); *Itchen* (Solent); *Orwell* (Tyne); *Humber* (Mersey); *Spey* (Forth); *Arun* (Sussex); *Blackwater* (Coastal Division RN); *Helmsdale* and *Ribble* in reserve in early 1992. London Division is having to share with other RNR sea training centres.

WAVENEY *5/1991, H. M. Steele*

5 TON CLASS (COASTAL MINEHUNTERS)

Name	No	Builders	Commissioned
BRINTON	M 1114	Cook Welton and Gemmell	4 Mar 1954
IVESTON	M 1151	Philip & Sons Ltd, Dartmouth	29 June 1955
KELLINGTON	M 1154	William Pickersgill & Son	4 Nov 1955
NURTON	M 1166	Harland & Wolff Ltd, Belfast	21 Aug 1957
SHERATON	M 1181	White's Shipyard Ltd, Southampton	24 Aug 1956

Displacement, tons: 360 standard; 440 full load
Dimensions, feet (metres): 153 × 28.9 × 8.2 *(46.6 × 8.8 × 2.5)*
Main machinery: 2 Paxman Deltic 18A-7A diesels; 3000 hp *(2.24 MW)*; 2 shafts
Speed, knots: 15. **Range, miles:** 2500 at 12 kts
Complement: 38 (5 officers)

Guns: 1 Bofors 40 mm/60 Mk 3; 80° elevation; 120 rounds/minute to 10 km *(5.4 nm)* anti-surface; 3 km *(1.6 nm)* anti-aircraft; weight of shell 0.89 kg.
3 FN 7.62 mm MGs.
2 Oerlikon 20 mm (on deployment); 50° elevation; 800 rounds/minute to 2 km; weight of shell 0.24 kg.
Countermeasures: Decoys: Plessey Shield 12-tubed Chaff launcher.
Radars: Navigation: Kelvin Hughes Type 1006; I band.
Sonars: Plessey Type 193M; hull-mounted; minehunting; 100/300 kHz.

Programmes: The survivors of a class of 118 built between 1953 and 1960, largely as a result of lessons from the Korean War. John I Thornycroft & Co Ltd, Southampton was the lead yard.
Modernisation: The majority has been fitted with 'Cascover' nylon in place of copper sheathing. In 1983-84 *Iveston* had an extensive refit to prolong her life, *Nurton* completed a similar refit in 1989.
Structure: These ships have double mahogany hull on aluminium frames and incorporate a considerable amount of non-magnetic material. All have active rudders.
Operational: Allocation: M 1181, 1154, 1114, 1151 to 3rd MCM Squadron. All are used for Fishery Protection except M 1166 which is in Northern Ireland.
Sales: Argentina (six in 1968), Australia (six in 1962), Ghana (one in 1964), India (four in 1956), Ireland (three in 1971), Malaysia (seven in 1960-68), South Africa (ten in 1958-59). Many deleted.

IVESTON *6/1991, Maritime Photographic*

3 + 2 + (11) SANDOWN CLASS (MINEHUNTERS)

Name	No	Builders	Launched	Commissioned
SANDOWN	M 101	Vosper Thornycroft, Woolston	16 Apr 1988	9 June 1989
INVERNESS	M 102	Vosper Thornycroft, Woolston	27 Feb 1990	24 Jan 1991
CROMER	M 103	Vosper Thornycroft, Woolston	6 Oct 1990	7 Apr 1992
WALNEY	M 104	Vosper Thornycroft, Woolston	25 Nov 1991	Dec 1992
BRIDPORT	M 105	Vosper Thornycroft, Woolston	July 1992	Sept 1993

Displacement, tons: 450 standard; 484 full load
Dimensions, feet (metres): 172.2 × 34.4 × 7.5 *(52.5 × 10.5 × 2.3)*
Main machinery: 2 Paxman Valenta 6-RP 200E diesels; 1500 hp *(1.12 MW)* sustained; Voith-Schneider propulsion; 2 shafts; 2 Schottel bow thrusters
Speed, knots: 13 diesels; 6.5 electric drive. **Range, miles:** 3000 at 12 kts
Complement: 34 (7 officers) plus 6 spare berths

Guns: 1 Oerlikon/DES 30 mm/75 DS 30B; 65° elevation; 650 rounds/minute to 10 km *(5.4 nm)* anti-surface; 3 km *(1.6 nm)* anti-aircraft; weight of shell 0.36 kg.
Countermeasures: Decoys: 2 Wallop Barricade (to be fitted for deployment).
Combat data systems: Plessey Nautis M action data automation.
Radars: Navigation: Kelvin Hughes Type 1007; I band.
Sonars: Marconi/Plessey Type 2093; VDS; VLF-VHF multi-function with five arrays; mine search and classification.

Programmes: A class designed for hunting and destroying mines and for operating in deep and exposed waters. Complements the Hunt and River classes. On 9 January 1984 the Vosper Thornycroft design for this class was approved. First one ordered August 1985, laid down 2 February 1987. Four further ships ordered 23 July 1987. A second batch were to have been ordered in 1990 but these were re-allocated to the Saudi Arabian Navy which is now being given precedence over RN orders, which were again deferred in 1991.
Structure: GRP hull. Combines vectored thrust units with bow thrusters and Remote Control Mine Disposal System (RCMDS). The sonar is deployed from a well in the hull.
Operational: ECA mine disposal system, two PAP 104 Mk 5. These craft can carry two mine wire cutters, a charge of 100 kg and a manipulator with TV/projector. Control cables are either 1000 m (high capacity) or 2000 m (low capacity) and the craft can dive to 300 m at 6 kts with an endurance of 5 × 20 minute missions. Racal Hyperfix. Decca Navigation Mk 21. Allocation: 101, 102, 103 to 3rd MCM Squadron.
Sales: Three plus an option of three more to Saudi Arabia.

CROMER *11/1991, Maritime Photographic*

AMPHIBIOUS WARFARE FORCES

Note: Further amphibious ships and craft covered in RFA and RCT sections. These include a Helicopter Support Ship, 5 LSLs, 2 LCLs and 9 LCTs.

0 + (1) HELICOPTER CARRIER (LPH)

Displacement, tons: 17 000 full load
Dimensions, feet (metres): 623.4 × 111.5 × 23 *(190 × 34 × 7)*
Flight deck, feet (metres): 590 × 111.5 *(180 × 34)*
Main machinery: 2 diesels; 2 shafts
Speed, knots: 18. **Range, miles:** 20 000 at 18 kts
Complement: 300 plus 170 aircrew plus 480 Marines

Guns: Oerlikon/BMARC 30 mm/75 GCM.
Oerlikon/BMARC 20 mm GAM.
Countermeasures: ESM/ECM.
Radars: Air/surface search.

Helicopters: 12 Sea King or equivalent.

Programmes: In 1987 five joint venture consortia were invited to prepare tenders. Three tenders submitted in July 1989 by Swan Hunter/Ferranti International Signal/CAP, Tyne Shiprepairers/Sea Containers/Racal Marine Systems; and Vickers Shipbuilding and Engineering/Cammel Laird with Three Keys Marine. These tenders were then allowed to lapse and a further invitation for designs was issued in early 1992 with the aim of placing an order for the ship in 1994.
Structure: The details listed are illustrative of the sort of size of vessel required either as a new construction or a merchant conversion. The deck would be strong enough to take Chinook helicopters. Six landing and six parking spots are required for the aircraft. Armament to consist of light guns only.
Operational: The LPH is to provide a helicopter lift and assault capability. The prime role of the vessel will be embarking, supporting and operating a squadron of helicopters (currently Westland Sea King HC4) and carrying most of a Royal Marine Commando including vehicles, arms and ammunition. A second of class is preferred to meet the operational requirement but linkage with the new LPDs gives a single unit more credibility than it would have without the LPDs.

LPH (artist's impression) *1987, BAe*

2 ASSAULT SHIPS (LPD)

Name	*No*	*Builders*	*Laid down*	*Launched*	*Commissioned*
FEARLESS	L 10	Harland & Wolff Ltd, Belfast	25 July 1962	19 Dec 1963	25 Nov 1965
INTREPID	L 11	John Brown & Co (Clydebank) Ltd	19 Dec 1962	25 June 1964	11 Mar 1967

Displacement, tons: 11 060 standard; 12 120 full load; 16 950 dock flooded
Dimensions, feet (metres): 500 wl; 520 oa × 80 × 20.5 (32 flooded) *(152.4; 158.5 × 24.4 × 6.2 (9.8))*
Main machinery: 2 Babcock & Wilcox boilers; 550 psi *(38.66 kg/cm sq)*; 850°F *(454°C)*; 2 English Electric turbines; 22 000 hp *(16.4 MW)*; 2 shafts
Speed, knots: 21. **Range, miles:** 5000 at 20 kts
Complement: 550 (50 officers) plus 22 (3 officers) air group plus 88 (3 officers) RM
Military lift: 380-400 troops; overload 1000 troops; 15 MBTs; 7—3 ton trucks; 20½ ton trucks (specimen load)
Landing craft: 4 LCU Mk 9 (dock); 4 LCVP Mk 3 (davits)

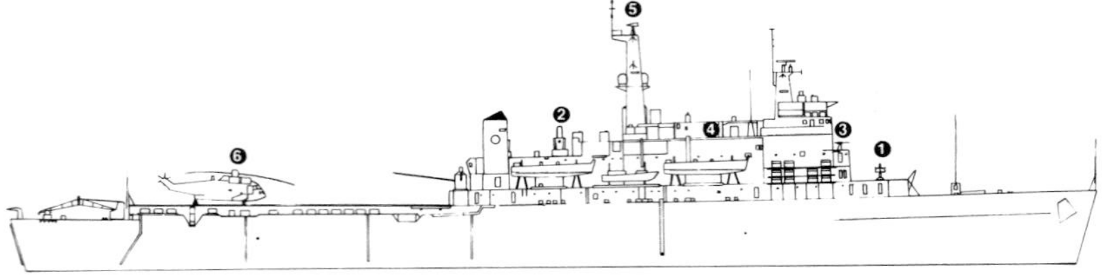

FEARLESS *(Scale 1 : 1 500), Ian Sturton*

Missiles: SAM: 2 Shorts Seacat GWS 20 quad launchers ❶; optical guidance to 5 km *(2.7 nm)*.
Guns: 2 GE/GD 20 mm Mk 15 Vulcan Phalanx (L10) ❷; 6 barrels per launcher; 3000 rounds/minute combined to 1.5 km.
4 Oerlikon/BMARC 30 mm/75 GCM-AO3 (2 twin) (L 11); 80° elevation; 650 rounds/minute to 10 km *(5.4 nm)* anti-surface; 3 km *(1.6 nm)* anti-aircraft; weight of shell 0.36 kg.
2 Oerlikon/BMARC 20 mm GAM-BO1 ❸; 55° elevation; 1000 rounds/minute to 2 km.
Countermeasures: Decoys: 2 Vickers Corvus 8-tubed trainable launchers (L 11) or 4 Sea Gnat 6-barrelled fixed launchers for Chaff and IR flares (L 10) ❹.
ESM: Marconi Mentor A; radar warning.
Combat data systems: Plessey Nautis M (L 10).
Fire control: GWS 20 optical directors for Seacat.

Radars: Surface search: Plessey Type 994 ❺; E/F band.
Navigation: Kelvin Hughes Type 1006; I band.

Helicopters: Platform for up to 4 Westland Sea King HC 4 ❻.

Programmes: In 1981 their impending deletion was announced—*Intrepid* in 1982 and *Fearless* in 1984. In February 1982 it was reported that they were to be reprieved, a fortunate decision in view of the vital part played by both in the 1982 Falklands' campaign.
Modernisation: *Intrepid* refitted 1984-85. *Fearless* completed a two year refit in November 1990 and has been fitted with two Vulcan Phalanx 20 mm gun mountings and new decoy launchers. Masthead height has been increased by 12 ft.

Structure: The two funnels are staggered across the beam of the ship. Landing craft are floated through the open stern by flooding compartments of the ship and lowering her in the water. They are able to deploy tanks, vehicles and men and have seakeeping qualities much superior to those of tank landing ships as well as greater speed and range. The helicopter platform is also the deckhead of the dock and has two landing spots.
Operational: Each ship is fitted out as a Naval Assault Group/Brigade Headquarters with an Assault Operations Room from which naval and military personnel can mount and control the progress of an assault operation. *Intrepid* is in reserve until her planned replacement commissions when she will be scrapped.

FEARLESS *12/1990, Wright & Logan*

0 + (2) ASSAULT SHIPS (LPD)

Displacement, tons: 15 000 full load
Dimensions, feet (metres): 524.9 × 85.3 × 36.1 *(160 × 26 × 11)*
Main machinery: Diesel or diesel-electric; 2 shafts
Speed, knots: 18
Complement: 350
Military lift: 400 troops; overload 1100 troops; 80 support vehicles
Landing craft: 4 LCU (dock); 4 LCVP (davits)

Missiles: SAM: 2 lightweight Seawolf launchers.
Guns: CIWS supported by portable close range weapons.
Countermeasures: Decoys and ESM/ECM.
Combat data systems: Action data automation.
Radars: Air/surface search. Fire control.

Helicopters: Platform for 4.

Programmes: After surveys had shown that *Intrepid* could not again be refurbished, a decision was taken in mid-1991 to replace both existing LPDs by similar ships. If there are no further delays, project definition studies by YARD Ltd should complete in late 1992 for an invitation to tender in 1993.
Structure: The illustrative design shown in the picture dates back to 1987 and probably shows a more complex ship than the one which is likely to emerge from project definition. Two helicopter landing spots. Substantial command and control facilities will be included.

LPD (artist's impression) *1987*

15 LCU Mk 9

L 3508 L 700-702 L 704-711 L 713-715

Displacement, tons: 89 light; 160 full load
Dimensions, feet (metres): 90.2 × 21.5 × 5 *(27.5 × 6.8 × 1.6)*
Main machinery: 2 Paxman or Dorman diesels; 474 hp *(354 kW)* sustained; 2 shafts; Kort nozzles
Speed, knots: 10
Military lift: 1 MBT or 70 tons of vehicles/stores

Comment: Operated by the Royal Marines. Four in each LPD. To be replaced by a new generation LCA probably of a hovercraft design.

LCU Mk 9 *5/1991, Wright & Logan*

17 LCVP Mk 4 (+ 4 ARMY)

LCVPs 8031, 8401, 8403-8408, 8410-8418

Displacement, tons: 9.7 light; 16 full load
Dimensions, feet (metres): 43.8 × 10.9 × 2.8 *(13.4 × 3.3 × 0.8)*
Main machinery: 2 Perkins T6.3544 diesels; 290 hp *(216 kW)*; 2 shafts
Speed, knots: 16 (light)
Complement: 3
Military lift: 20 Arctic equipped troops or 4 tons

Comment: Built by Souters and McTays. Introduced into service in 1986 as a replacement for the LCVP Mk 3. Fitted with removable arctic canopies across welldeck. Operated by the Royal Marines. LCVPs 8402, 8409, 8619 and 8620 built for the Royal Corps of Transport. These serve in rotation between the Falklands and UK.

LCVP Mk 4 *1991, van Ginderen Collection*

0 + (4) LCA (HOVERCRAFT)

Dimensions, feet (metres): 27.6 × 12.5 *(8.4 × 3.8)*
Main machinery: 1 diesel; 195 hp *(145 kW)*
Speed, knots: 40. **Range, miles:** 500 at 40 kts
Military lift: 16 troops plus equipment or 2 tons

Comment: Reported as out to tender in 1991 with an order expected in 1993. Capable of being embarked in an LCU.

3 TYPES OF SMALL CRAFT

Rigid Inflatable Boat Osborne Arctic 22

Comment: Of 1.4 tons and 7.2 m *(23.5 ft)*; twin 140 hp *(104 kW)* or Suzuki outboard motors; 40+ kts; range 30 nm (normal tanks); carry 15 troops or 2475 lbs stores. GRP hull, deck and command console with 20 in diameter neoprene tube.

Rigid Inflatable Boat Osborne Pacific 22

Comment: 1.75 tons and 6.8 m *(22.2 ft)*; Ford Mermaid 4-cyl; turbocharged diesel 140 hp *(104 kW)* max; 26 kts; range 85 nm; carry 15 troops or 2475 lbs stores. Construction similar to Arctic 22.

Rigid raiding craft

Comment: 0.87 tons and 5.2 m *(17.2 ft)*; powered by 140 hp *(104 kW)* or Suzuki outboard; 30+ kts fully laden; range 50 nm; carry coxswain plus 8 troops or 2000 lbs. GRP cathedral hull.

RIB Arctic 22 *1986, Royal Marines*

RRC *1989, Royal Marines*

ROYAL YACHT

Name	*No*	*Builders*	*Laid down*	*Launched*	*Commissioned*
BRITANNIA	A 00	John Brown & Co Ltd, Clydebank	July 1952	16 Apr 1953	14 Jan 1954

Displacement, tons: 3990 light; 4961 full load
Measurement, tons: 5769 gross
Dimensions, feet (metres): 412.2 × 55 × 17 *(125.7 × 16.8 × 5.2)*
Main machinery: 2 boilers; 2 turbines; 12 000 hp *(8.95 MW)*; 2 shafts
Speed, knots: 21; 22.5 trials. **Range, miles:** 2800 at 20 kts; 3200 at 18 kts; 3675 at 14 kts
Complement: 277 (21 officers)
Radars: Navigation: Two Kelvin Hughes Type 1006; I band.

Comment: Designed for use by Her Majesty The Queen in peacetime as the Royal Yacht but can be converted as a medium sized naval hospital ship. Construction conformed to mercantile practice. Fitted with Denny-Brown single fin stabilisers to reduce roll in bad weather from 20 to 6 degrees. To pass under the bridges of the St. Lawrence Seaway when she visited Canada, the top 20 ft of her mainmast and the radio aerial on her foremast were hinged in November 1958 so that they could be lowered as required. 1984 refit included conversion to diesel fuel. SATNAV fitted. Further refit carried out at Devonport 1986-87 which has extended her life by 10-15 years. Oil fuel, 330 tons (510 with auxiliary fuel tanks). Ranges given are without auxiliary fuel tanks.

BRITANNIA *7/1991, H. M. Steele*

PATROL SHIPS

1 ANTARCTIC PATROL SHIP

Name	*No*	*Builders*	*Commissioned*
POLAR CIRCLE	A 176	Ulstein Hatlo, Norway	21 Nov 1991

Displacement, tons: 6500 full load
Dimensions, feet (metres): 298.6 × 57.4 × 21.3 *(91 × 17.9 × 6.5)*
Main machinery: 2 Bergen BRM8 diesels, 8160 hp(m) *(6 MW)* sustained; 1 shaft; cp prop; bow and stern thrusters
Speed, knots: 15. **Range, miles:** 6500 at 12 kts
Complement: 112 (15 officers) plus 14 Royal Marines
Radars: Surface search: Furuno; E/F band.
Navigation: 2 Furuno; I band.
Helicopters: 2 Westland Lynx HAS 3.

Comment: Leased initially in late 1991 and then bought outright in early 1992 to replace *Endurance* as support ship and guard vessel for the British Antarctic Survey. Hull is painted red. Flight deck can take up to Super Puma sized aircraft. Inmarsat and SATCOM fitted. Main machinery is resiliently mounted. Ice strengthened hull capable of breaking one metre thick ice at 3 kts. Accommodation is to standards previously unknown in the Royal Navy.

POLAR CIRCLE *11/1991, W. Sartori*

POLAR CIRCLE *11/1991, Maritime Photographic*

2 CASTLE CLASS (OFFSHORE PATROL VESSELS Mk 2)

Name	*No*	*Builders*	*Commissioned*
LEEDS CASTLE	P 258	Hall Russell & Co Ltd	27 Oct 1981
DUMBARTON CASTLE	P 265	Hall Russell & Co Ltd	26 Mar 1982

Displacement, tons: 1427 full load
Dimensions, feet (metres): 265.7 × 37.7 × 11.8 *(81 × 11.5 × 3.6)*
Main machinery: 2 Ruston 12RKCM diesels; 5640 hp *(4.21 MW)* sustained; 2 shafts; cp props
Speed, knots: 19.5. **Range, miles:** 10 000 at 12 kts
Complement: 45 (6 officers) plus austerity accommodation for 25 Royal Marines
Guns: 1 DES/Lawrence Scott Mk 1 30 mm/75; 80° elevation; 650 rounds/minute to 10 km *(5.4 nm)*; weight of shell 0.36 kg.
Mines: Can lay mines.
Countermeasures: Decoys: 2 Plessey Shield Chaff launchers.
Combat data systems: Racal CANE DEA-3 action data automation.
Fire control: Radamec 2000 series optronic director.
Radars: Surface search: Plessey Type 944 (P 265); E/F band.
Navigation: Kelvin Hughes Type 1006; I band.
Helicopters: Platform for operating Westland Sea King.

Comment: Started as a private venture. Ordered 8 August 1980. *Leeds Castle* launched 29 October 1980; *Dumbarton Castle* 3 June 1981. Design includes an ability to lay mines. Inmarsat commercial SATCOM terminals fitted. 2 Avon Sea Rider high speed craft are embarked. P 265 is the South Atlantic patrol ship until 1994. P 258 belongs to the Fishery Protection Squadron Offshore Division.

DUMBARTON CASTLE *8/1990, Maritime Photographic*

7 ISLAND CLASS (OFFSHORE PATROL VESSELS)

Name	*No*	*Builders*	*Commissioned*
ANGLESEY	P 277	Hall Russell & Co Ltd	1 June 1979
ALDERNEY	P 278	Hall Russell & Co Ltd	6 Oct 1979
JERSEY	P 295	Hall Russell & Co Ltd	15 Oct 1976
GUERNSEY	P 297	Hall Russell & Co Ltd	28 Oct 1977
SHETLAND	P 298	Hall Russell & Co Ltd	14 July 1977
ORKNEY	P 299	Hall Russell & Co Ltd	25 Feb 1977
LINDISFARNE	P 300	Hall Russell & Co Ltd	3 Mar 1978

Displacement, tons: 925 standard; 1260 full load
Dimensions, feet (metres): 176 wl; 195.3 oa × 36 × 15 *(53.7; 59.5 × 11 × 4.5)*
Main machinery: 2 Ruston RKCM diesels; 5640 hp *(4.21 MW)* sustained; 1 shaft
Speed, knots: 16.5. **Range, miles:** 7000 at 12 kts
Complement: 39

Guns: 1 Bofors 40 mm Mk 3. 1 DES/Oerlikon 30 mm/75 Mk 1 (P 297). 2 FN 7.62 mm MGs.
Countermeasures: ESM: Orange Crop; intercept.
Combat data systems: Racal CANE DEA-1 action data automation.
Radars: Navigation: Kelvin Hughes Type 1006; I band.

Programmes: Order for first five announced 11 February 1975. Order placed 2 July 1975. Two more of class ordered 21 October 1977.
Structure: The earlier ships of this class were retrofitted and the remainder built with enlarged bilge keels to damp down their motion in heavy weather. Fitted with stabilisers and water ballast arrangement.
Operational: Operate as the Offshore Division of the Fishery Protection Squadron. Can carry small RM detachment and two Avon Sea Rider semi-rigid craft with 85 hp motor, for boarding.

LINDISFARNE *11/1991, Maritime Photographic*

LINDISFARNE *3/1991, Bram Risseeuw*

1 OFFSHORE PATROL VESSEL

Name	*No*	*Builders*	*Commissioned*
SENTINEL (ex-*Seaforth Warrior*)	P 246	Husumwerft, Husum	1975

Displacement, tons: 1710 standard
Measurement, tons: 934 gross; 324 net; 745 dwt
Dimensions, feet (metres): 198.4 × 43.7 × 14.8 *(60.5 × 13.3 × 4.5)*
Main machinery: 2 Atlas MAK 12V diesels; 7700 hp(m) *(5.66 MW)*; 2 shafts; cp props; bow thruster
Speed, knots: 14
Complement: 32
Guns: 3 FN 7.62 mm MGs.
Countermeasures: Decoys: 2 Loral Hycor SRBOC Mk 36.
Radars: Navigation: Kelvin Hughes Type 1006; I band.

Comment: Acquired 1983. Commissioned in Royal Navy 14 January 1984 for Falkland Islands patrol duties. Previous owners British Linen Bank Ltd, managed by Seaforth Maritime. Ice strengthened. Converted by Tyne Ship Repair Co. Refitted at Rosyth in 1987 prior to replacing *Wakeful* as Clyde patrol ship monitoring AGI activity in the North West approaches and support ship for submarines on work-up. Was to have been paid off in 1991 but retained in service in 1992.

SENTINEL *5/1990, Foto Flite*

TRAINING SHIPS

1 LEANDER CLASS

Name	*No*	*Builders*	*Commissioned*
JUNO	F 52	John I Thornycroft, Woolston	18 July 1967

Comment: Details under Leander class in *Frigates* section. All armament removed leaving only surface search and navigation radars. Used as a training ship for navigation and engineering and may be paid off at the end of 1992.

JUNO *6/1991, Maritime Photographic*

1 DARTMOUTH TRAINING SHIP

Name	*No*	*Builders*	*Commissioned*
WILTON	M 1116	Vosper Thornycroft, Woolston	14 July 1973

Displacement, tons: 450 full load
Dimensions, feet (metres): 145 wl; 153 oa × 29.2 × 8.5 *(44.2; 46.3 × 8.9 × 2.5)*
Main machinery: 2 Napier Deltic 18-7A diesels; 3000 hp *(2.24 MW)*; 2 shafts
Speed, knots: 16. **Range, miles:** 2300 at 13 kts
Complement: 37 (5 officers)
Guns: 1 Bofors 40 mm/70 Mk 7; 90° elevation; 300 rounds/minute to 12 km *(6.5 nm)* anti-surface; 4 km *(2.2 nm)* anti-aircraft; weight of shell 0.96 kg.
Radars: Navigation: Kelvin Hughes Type 975; I/J band.
Sonars: Plessey Type 193M; hull-mounted; high frequency.

Comment: The world's first GRP warship. Laid down 7 August 1970 and launched on 18 January 1972. Similar to the Ton class minesweepers and fitted with reconditioned machinery and equipment from the scrapped *Derriton*. Twin active rudders. Used for seamanship and navigation training at the Naval College, Dartmouth. All minesweeping gear removed and a classroom has been built on the stern.

WILTON *6/1991, BRNC*

1 NAVIGATION TRAINING VESSEL

NORTHELLA

Comment: Having been taken up from trade in April 1982 to act as an auxiliary minesweeper in Falklands campaign (with four others) she was returned to her owners then taken up from trade again in October 1983 to act as target vessel. In 1985 became navigational training ship. Based at Portsmouth and now painted grey. She flies a Blue Ensign and is on charter until 1994.

NORTHELLA *3/1991, Wright & Logan*

LIGHT FORCES

2 BIRD and 1 SEAL CLASS (LARGE PATROL CRAFT)

Name	*No*	*Builders*	*Commissioned*
REDPOLE (ex-*Sea Otter*)	P 259	Brooke Marine Ltd, Lowestoft	4 Aug 1967
KINGFISHER	P 260	R Dunston Ltd, Hessle	8 Oct 1975
CYGNET	P 261	R Dunston Ltd, Hessle	8 July 1976

Displacement, tons: 194 (218, P 259) full load
Dimensions, feet (metres): 120 × 23.6 × 6.5 *(36.6 × 7.2 × 2)*
Main machinery: 2 Paxman 16YJCM diesels; 4200 hp *(3.13 MW)*; 2 shafts
Speed, knots: 21. **Range, miles:** 2000 at 14 kts
Complement: 28 (3 officers, 10 RM)
Guns: 2 FN 7.62 mm MGs.

Comment: *Kingfisher* launched 20 September 1974; *Cygnet* 6 October 1975; *Redpole* transferred by RAF March 1985. *Kingfisher* and *Redpole* completed extended refits in 1986; *Cygnet* in 1987. Bird class based on the Seal class RAF rescue launches with some improvement to sea-keeping qualities by cutting down topweight. All deployed to Northern Ireland.

CYGNET *1991*

14 ARCHER CLASS (TRAINING and PATROL CRAFT)

ARCHER P 264
BITER P 270
SMITER P 272
PURSUER P 273
BLAZER P 279
DASHER P 280
PUNCHER P 291
CHARGER P 292
RANGER P 293
TRUMPETER P 294
EXAMPLE A153 (RNXS)
EXPLORER A 154 (RNXS)
EXPRESS A 163 (RNXS)
EXPLOIT A 167 (RNXS)

Displacement, tons: 49 full load
Dimensions, feet (metres): 68.2 × 19 × 5.9 *(20.8 × 5.8 × 1.8)*
Main machinery: 2 RR CV 12 M800T; 1590 hp *(1.19 MW)*; 2 shafts
Speed, knots: 22. **Range, miles:** 550 at 15 kts
Complement: 10-14
Guns: 1 Oerlikon 20 mm (can be fitted).
Radars: Navigation: Racal Decca 1216; I band.

Comment: Ordered from Watercraft Ltd, Shoreham. Commissioning dates: *Archer*, August 1985; *Example*, September 1985; *Explorer*, January 1986; *Biter* and *Smiter*, February 1986. The remaining nine were incomplete when Watercraft went into liquidation in 1986 and were towed to Portsmouth for completion by Vosper Thornycroft. Commissioning dates (all 1988): *Pursuer*, February; *Blazer*, March; *Express* and *Dasher*, May; *Charger*, June; *Puncher*, July; *Exploit*, August; *Ranger* and *Trumpeter*, September. Initially allocated for RNR training but under used in that role and now employed: *Ranger* and *Trumpeter* as Gibraltar guard ships; remainder University Naval Units (URNU)—*Puncher* (London), *Blazer* (Southampton), *Smiter* (Glasgow), *Charger* (Liverpool), *Dasher* (Bristol), *Archer* (Aberdeen), *Pursuer* (Sussex) and *Biter* (Manchester and Salford).

BLAZER *9/1991, Maritime Photographic*

EXPLORER (RNXS) *11/1991, Maritime Photographic*

3 PEACOCK CLASS (LARGE PATROL CRAFT)

Name	*No*	*Builders*	*Commissioned*
PEACOCK	P 239	Hall Russell, Aberdeen	14 July 1984
PLOVER	P 240	Hall Russell, Aberdeen	20 July 1984
STARLING	P 241	Hall Russell, Aberdeen	10 Aug 1984

Displacement, tons: 690 full load
Dimensions, feet (metres): 204.1 × 32.8 × 8.9 *(62.6 × 10 × 2.7)*
Main machinery: 2 Crossley Pielstick 18 PA6V 280 diesels; 14 000 hp(m) *(10.6 MW)* sustained; 2 shafts; 1 retractable Schottel prop; 181 hp *(135 kW)*
Speed, knots: 25. **Range, miles:** 2500 at 17 kts
Complement: 31 (6 officers) plus 7 spare berths
Guns: 1—3 in *(76 mm)*/62 OTO Melara compact; 85° elevation; 85 rounds/minute to 16 km *(8.6 nm)* anti-surface; 12 km *(6.5 nm)* anti-aircraft; weight of shell 6 kg.
4 FN 7.62 mm MGs.
Fire control: British Aerospace Sea Archer for 76 mm gun.
Radars: Navigation: Kelvin Hughes Type 1006; I band.

Comment: This class replaced the elderly Ton class in Hong Kong, the colony's government paying 75 per cent of the cost. All ordered 30 June 1981. *Peacock* launched 1 December 1982, *Plover* on 12 April 1983, *Starling* on 11 September 1983. All sailed for Hong Kong September 1984-July 1985. Carry two Sea Riders and a Fast Pursuit craft. Have telescopic cranes, loiter drive and replenishment at sea equipment. *Swallow* and *Swift* sold to Ireland 21 November 1988. The remainder are planned to remain in Hong Kong until 1997.

PEACOCK *1987, Giorgio Arra*

SURVEY SHIPS

Note: In addition to the ships listed below some work is done by chartered vessels with Naval Parties embarked. These include *Proud Seahorse* (of MFV type) which operates for the Hydrographer with Naval Party 1016 embarked and *British Enterprise IV* on charter until 1993 with Naval Party 1008.

1 IMPROVED HECLA CLASS

Name	*No*	*Builders*	*Commissioned*
HERALD	A 138	Robb Caledon, Leith	31 Oct 1974

Displacement, tons: 2000 standard; 2945 full load
Dimensions, feet (metres): 259.1 × 49.2 × 16 *(79 × 15.4 × 4.9)*
Main machinery: Diesel-electric; 3 Paxman Ventura 12 CZ diesels; 3780 hp *(2.82 MW)* sustained; 3 generators; 1 motor; 2000 hp *(1.49 MW)*; 1 shaft; bow thruster
Speed, knots: 14. **Range, miles:** 12 000 at 11 kts
Complement: 128 (12 officers)
Guns: 2 Oerlikon 20 mm (can be fitted).
Radars: Navigation: Kelvin Hughes Type 1006; I band.
Helicopters: 1 Westland Lynx HAS 3.

Comment: A later version of the Hecla class design. Laid down 9 November 1972. Launched 4 October 1973. Fitted with Hydroplot Satellite navigation system, computerised data logging, gravimeter, magnetometer, sonars, echo-sounders, an oceanographic winch, passive stabilisation tank and two 35 ft surveying motor-boats. Completed refit in January 1988 with a strengthened and extended flight deck for Lynx. Conducted trials of Scarab remote controlled mine clearance device. Works in the North Norwegian Sea when not required as an MCM support ship.

HERALD *3/1991, David Warren*

1 HECLA CLASS

Name	*No*	*Builders*	*Commissioned*
HECLA	A 133	Yarrow & Co, Blythswood	9 June 1965

Displacement, tons: 1915 light; 2733 full load
Measurement, tons: 2898 gross
Dimensions, feet (metres): 260.1 × 49.1 × 15.4 *(79.3 × 15 × 4.7)*
Main machinery: Diesel-electric; 3 Paxman Ventura 12 CZ diesels; 3780 hp *(2.82 MW)* sustained; 3 generators; 1 motor; 2000 hp *(1.49 MW)*; 1 shaft; bow thruster
Speed, knots: 14. **Range, miles:** 12 000 at 11 kts
Complement: 115 (13 officers) plus 6 scientists
Guns: 2 Oerlikon 20 mm (can be fitted).
Radars: Navigation: Kelvin Hughes Type 1006; I band.
Helicopters: 1 Westland Lynx HAS 3.

Comment: The first Royal Navy ship to be designed with a combined oceanographical and hydrographic role. Of merchant ship design and similar in many respects to the Royal Research ship *Discovery*. The fore end of the superstructure incorporates a Land Rover garage and the after end a helicopter hangar with adjacent flight deck. Equipped with chartroom, drawing office and photographic studio; two laboratories, dry and wet; electrical, engineering and shipwright workshops, large storerooms, two 9 m surveying motor-boats and an oceanographic winch. Air-conditioned throughout. Converted in 1990/91 to the same standard as *Herald* for MCM support ship duties with an extended flight deck and a recompression chamber for clearance divers. One of the class sold to Indonesia in 1986, a second for disposal in 1990.

HECLA *10/1991, D & B Teague*

COASTAL SURVEY VESSELS

1 ROEBUCK CLASS

Name	*No*	*Builders*	*Commissioned*
ROEBUCK	A 130	Brooke Marine Ltd, Lowestoft	3 Oct 1986

Displacement, tons: 1059 light, 1431 full load
Dimensions, feet (metres): 210 × 42.6 × 13 *(63.9 × 13 × 4)*
Main machinery: 4 Mirrlees Blackstone ES 8 Mk 1 diesels; 3040 hp *(2.27 MW)*; 2 shafts; cp props
Speed, knots: 15. **Range, miles:** 4000 at 10 kts
Complement: 46 (6 officers)

Comment: Designed for hydrographic surveys to full modern standards on UK continental shelf. Passive tank stabiliser; Hyperfix and transponder position fixing systems; Type 2033BB hull mounted, high definition, sector scanning sonar. Qubit SIPS I integrated navigation and survey system. Air-conditioned. Carries two 9 m surveying motor boats and one 4.5 m RIB.

ROEBUCK (with survey craft on davits) *5/1990, Gilbert Gyssels*

Name	*No*	*Builders*	*Commissioned*
GLEANER	A 86	Emsworth Shipyard	5 Dec 1983

Displacement, tons: 22 full load
Dimensions, feet (metres): 48.6 × 15.4 × 4.3 *(14.8 × 4.7 × 1.3)*
Main machinery: 2 RR diesels; 524 hp *(391 kW)*; 1 Perkins 4-236 diesel; 72 hp *(54 kW)*; 3 shafts
Speed, knots: 14 diesels; 7 centre shaft only
Complement: 5 plus 1 spare bunk

Comment: This craft is prefixed HMSML—HM Survey Motor Launch.

GLEANER *10/1987, W. Sartori*

2 BULLDOG CLASS

Name	*No*	*Builders*	*Commissioned*
BULLDOG	A 317	Brooke Marine Ltd, Lowestoft	21 Mar 1968
BEAGLE	A 319	Brooke Marine Ltd, Lowestoft	9 May 1968

Displacement, tons: 800 standard; 1088 full load
Dimensions, feet (metres): 189 × 36.8 × 12 *(57.6 × 11.2 × 3.7)*
Main machinery: 4 Lister-Blackstone ERS8M diesels; 2640 hp *(1.97 MW)*; 2 shafts; cp props
Speed, knots: 15. **Range, miles:** 4500 at 12 kts
Complement: 39 (5 officers)
Guns: Fitted for 2 Oerlikon 20 mm.

Comment: Originally designed for duty overseas, working in pairs although normally now employed in home waters. Built to commercial standards. Fitted with passive tank stabiliser, precision ranging radar, Hyper Fix system, automatic steering. Qubit SIPS II integrated navigation and survey system being fitted in 1990. This allows chart processing in real time as the data is acquired. Air-conditioned throughout. Carry 9 m surveying motor-boat. *Bulldog* completed refit including new radar and UHF in early 1985. *Fox* sold in early 1989 and *Fawn* in 1991.

BEAGLE (with 20 mm gun) *11/1990, van Ginderen Collection*

ROYAL FLEET AUXILIARY SERVICE

Headquarters Appointment

Commodore and Chief Marine Superintendent, RFA:
Commodore R M Thorn

Personnel

1992: 2430 UK personnel; 32 Hong Kong Chinese

General

The Royal Fleet Auxiliary Service is a civilian manned fleet owned and operated by the Ministry of Defence. Its main task is to supply warships at sea with fuel, food, stores and ammunition. It also provides aviation platforms, amphibious support for the Navy and Marines and sea transport for Army units. An additional and continuing role is manning the forward repair ship *Diligence*. All ships take part in operational sea training. An order in council on 30 November 1989 changed the status of the RFA service to government-owned vessels on non-commercial service and they therefore no longer come under the Merchant Shipping Act.

Ships taken up from Trade (1 April 1992)

The following ships taken up from trade: *Proud Seahorse* and *British Enterprise IV* operate in home waters under the Hydrographer; *Northella* in service for navigational training. *Oil Mariner* (supply), *St Brendan* (ferry), *Indomitable* (tug), all operate in the Falkland Islands; *Maersk Ascension* and *Maersk Gannet* as tankers to Ascension Island; *St Angus* as Gulf supply ship.

LARGE FLEET TANKERS (AO)

3 OL CLASS (AO)

Name	*No*	*Builders*	*Launched*	*Commissioned*
OLWEN	A 122	Hawthorn Leslie, Hebburn	10 July 1964	21 June 1965
OLNA	A 123	Hawthorn Leslie, Hebburn	28 July 1965	1 Apr 1966
OLMEDA	A 124	Swan Hunter, Wallsend	19 Nov 1964	18 Oct 1965

Displacement, tons: 10 890 light; 36 000 full load
Measurement, tons: 25 100 dwt; 18 600 gross
Dimensions, feet (metres): 648 × 84 × 36.4 *(197.5 × 25.6 × 11.1)*
Main machinery: 2 Babcock & Wilcox boilers; 750 psi *(52.75 kg/cm sq)*; 950°F *(510°C)*; Pametrada turbines; 26 500 hp *(19.77 MW)*; 1 shaft
Speed, knots: 20

Complement: 95 RFA (accommodation for 40 RN)
Cargo capacity: 16 000 tons diesel; 125 tons lub oil; 2750 tons Avcat; 375 tons fresh water
Guns: 3 Oerlikon 20 mm. 2—7.62 mm MGs.
Countermeasures: 2 Corvus Chaff launchers.
Radars: Surface search and Navigation: 2 Racal Decca; I band.
Helicopters: 2 Westland Sea King HAS 5.

Comment: Designed for underway replenishment both alongside and astern (fuel only) or by helicopter. Specially strengthened for operations in ice, fully air-conditioned. *Olna* has a transverse bow thrust unit for improved manoeuvrability in confined waters and an improved design of replenishment-at-sea systems. Inmarsat SATCOM system fitted. Hangar accommodation for two helicopters port side of funnel.

OLMEDA *5/1991, Wright & Logan*

SUPPORT TANKERS (AOT)

Name	No	Builders	Commissioned	Recommissioned
OAKLEAF (ex-*Oktania*)	A 111	Uddevalla, Sweden	1981	14 Aug 1986

Displacement, tons: 49 310 full load
Measurement, tons: 34 800 dwt
Dimensions, feet (metres): 570 × 105.6 × 33.5 *(173.7 × 32.2 × 10.2)*
Main machinery: 1 Burmeister & Wain 4L 80MCE diesel; 12 000 hp(m) *(8.82 MW)*; 1 shaft; cp prop; bow and stern thrusters
Speed, knots: 15
Complement: 36
Cargo capacity: 40 000 cu m fuel
Guns: 2 Oerlikon 20 mm. 2—7.62 mm MGs.
Countermeasures: 2 Plessey Shield Chaff launchers.

Comment: Acquired in July 1985 and converted by Falmouth Ship Repairers to include full RAS rig and extra accommodation. Handed over on completion and renamed. Ice strengthened hull. Marisat fitted.

OAKLEAF *8/1991, Giorgio Arra*

3 APPLELEAF CLASS (AOT)

Name	No	Builders	Launched	Commissioned
BRAMBLELEAF (ex-*Hudson Cavalier*)	A 81	Cammell Laird & Co, Birkenhead	22 Jan 1976	3 Mar 1980
BAYLEAF	A 109	Cammell Laird & Co, Birkenhead	27 Oct 1981	26 Mar 1982
ORANGELEAF (ex-*Balder London*, ex-*Hudson Progress*)	A 110	Cammell Laird & Co, Birkenhead	—	2 May 1984

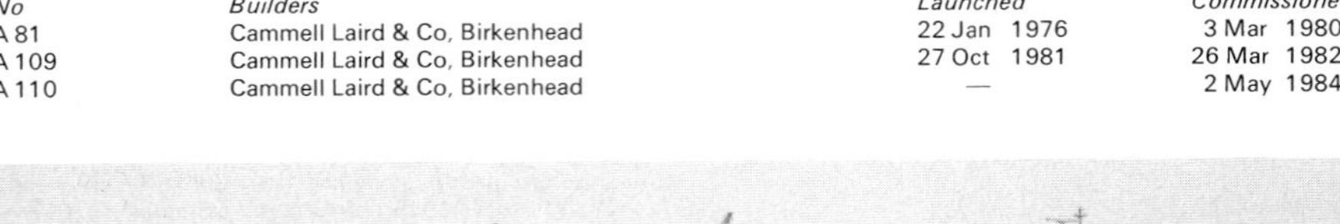

Displacement, tons: 37 747 full load (A 109-110); 40 870 (A 81)
Measurement, tons: 20 761 gross; 10 851 net; 33 595 dwt
Dimensions, feet (metres): 560 × 85 × 38.9 *(170.7 × 25.9 × 11.9)*
Main machinery: 2 Pielstick 14 PC 2.2 V400 diesels; 14 000 hp(m) *(10.29 MW)* sustained; 1 shaft
Speed, knots: 15.5; 16.3 (A 109)
Complement: 60 (20 officers)
Cargo capacity: 22 000 cu m dieso; 3800 cu m Avcat
Guns: 2 Oerlikon 20 mm (amidships in *Orangeleaf*).
Countermeasures: Decoys: 2 Vickers Corvus launchers or 2 Plessey Shield launchers.

Comment: *Brambleleaf* chartered in 1979-80 and converted, completing Autumn 1979. Part of a four-ship order cancelled by Hudson Fuel and Shipping Co, but completed by the shipbuilders, being the only mercantile order then in hand. *Bayleaf* built under commercial contract to be chartered by MoD. *Orangeleaf* started major refit September 1985 to fit full RAS capability and extra accommodation. *Appleleaf* leased to Australia in September 1989 for five years.

ORANGELEAF *9/1991, Maritime Photographic*

SMALL FLEET TANKERS (AOL)

4 ROVER CLASS

Name	No	Builders	Commissioned
GREY ROVER	A 269	Swan Hunter, Hebburn-on-Tyne	10 Apr 1970
BLUE ROVER	A 270	Swan Hunter, Hebburn-on-Tyne	15 July 1970
GOLD ROVER	A 271	Swan Hunter, Wallsend-on-Tyne	22 Mar 1974
BLACK ROVER	A 273	Swan Hunter, Wallsend-on-Tyne	23 Aug 1974

Displacement, tons: 4700 light; 11 522 full load
Measurement, tons: 6692 (A 271, 273), 6822 (remainder) dwt; 7510 gross; 3185 net
Dimensions, feet (metres): 461 × 63 × 24 *(140.6 × 19.2 × 7.3)*
Main machinery: 2 SEMT-Pielstick 16PA4 185 diesels; 5344 hp(m) *(3.93 MW)*; 1 shaft; cp prop; bow thruster
Speed, knots: 19. **Range, miles:** 15 000 at 15 kts
Complement: 49 (A 268, 269-270); 54 (A 271, 273)
Cargo capacity: 6600 tons fuel
Guns: 2 Oerlikon 20 mm.
Countermeasures: Decoys: 2 Vickers Corvus launchers. 2 Plessey Shield launchers.
1 Graseby Type 182; towed torpedo decoy.
Radars: Navigation: Kelvin Hughes Type 1006; I band.
Helicopters: Platform for Westland Sea King HAS 5 or HC 4.

Comment: Small fleet tankers designed to replenish HM ships at sea with fuel, fresh water, limited dry cargo and refrigerated stores under all conditions while under way. No hangar but helicopter landing platform is served by a stores lift, to enable stores to be transferred at sea by 'vertical lift'. Capable of HIFR. Siting of SATCOM aerial varies. First two re-engined 1973-74. *Gold Rover* employed on training duties at Portland. *Green Rover* sold in 1991 to Indonesia.

BLUE ROVER *12/1990, Gilbert Gyssels*

FLEET REPLENISHMENT SHIPS

0 + 2 FORT VICTORIA CLASS

Name	*No*	*Builders*	*Laid down*	*Launched*	*Commissioned*
FORT VICTORIA	A 387	Harland & Wolff	4 Apr 1988	12 June 1990	Oct 1992
FORT GEORGE	A 388	Swan Hunter Shipbuilders, Wallsend	9 Mar 1989	1 Mar 1991	Nov 1992

Displacement, tons: 32 300 full load
Dimensions, feet (metres): 667.7 oa; 607 wl × 99.7 × 32 *(203.5; 185 × 30.4 × 9.8)*
Main machinery: 2 Crossley SEMT-Pielstick PC 2.6 V400 diesels; 23 904 hp(m) *(17.57 MW)* sustained; 2 shafts
Speed, knots: 20
Complement: 126 (34 officers) RFA plus 32 (1 officer) RN plus 122 (29 officers) aircrew
Cargo capacity: 12 505 cu m liquids; 6234 cu m solids

Missiles: SAM: British Aerospace Seawolf GWS 26 Mod 1 VLS; command line of sight (CLOS) radar/TV tracking to 6 km *(3.3 nm)* at 2.5 Mach; warhead 14 kg; 32 canisters.
Guns: 4 Lawrence Scott 30 mm/75 Mk 1.
Countermeasures: Decoys: 4 Plessey Shield 6-barrelled Chaff/IR launchers. Graseby Type 182; towed torpedo decoy.
ESM: Marconi UAG Mentor; intercept.
Combat data systems: Dowty Sema SSCS; Scot SATCOM.
Radars: Air search: Plessey Type 996; 3D; E/F band.
Fire control: Two Marconi Type 911; I/Ku band.
Navigation: Kelvin Hughes Type 1007; I band.

Helicopters: 3 Westland Sea King/Merlin helicopters.

Programmes: The requirement for these ships is to provide fuel and stores support to the Fleet at sea. *Fort Victoria* ordered 23 April 1986 and *Fort George* on 18 December 1987. *Fort Victoria* delayed by damage during building. The original plan was for six of this class. In view of the cost this now seems unlikely and unarmed variants will be built instead.

FORT GEORGE *1/1992, Swan Hunter*

Structure: Four dual purpose abeam replenishment rigs for simultaneous transfer of liquids and solids. Stern refuelling. Repair facilities for Merlin helicopters.

Operational: Two helicopter spots. There is a requirement to provide an emergency landing facility for Sea Harriers.

2 FORT GRANGE CLASS (AFS(H))

Name	*No*	*Builders*	*Launched*	*Commissioned*
FORT GRANGE	A 385	Scott-Lithgow, Greenock	9 Dec 1976	6 Apr 1978
FORT AUSTIN	A 386	Scott-Lithgow, Greenock	9 Mar 1978	11 May 1979

Displacement, tons: 23 384 full load
Measurement, tons: 8300 dwt
Dimensions, feet (metres): 603 × 79 × 28.2 *(183.9 × 24.1 × 8.6)*
Main machinery: 1 Sulzer RND90 diesel; 23 200 hp(m) *(17.05 MW)*; 1 shaft; bow thruster
Speed, knots: 22. **Range, miles:** 10 000 at 20 kts
Complement: 127 RFA plus 45 RN plus 36 RNSTS (civilian supply staff)
Cargo capacity: 3500 tons armament, naval and victualling stores in 4 holds of 12 800 cu m
Guns: 4 Oerlikon GAM-BO3 20 mm.
Countermeasures: 2 Vickers Corvus 8-barrelled launchers (upper bridge).
Radars: Navigation: Kelvin Hughes Type 1006; I band.
Helicopters: 4 Westland Sea King.

Comment: Ordered in November 1971. Fitted with a helicopter flight-deck and hangar, thus allowing not only for vertical replenishment but also a base for Force ASW helicopters. ASW stores for helicopters carried on board. Emergency flight deck on the hangar roof. There are six cranes, three of 10 tons lift and three of 5 tons.

FORT GRANGE *1991*

2 REGENT CLASS (AFS(H))

Name	*No*	*Builders*	*Launched*	*Commissioned*
RESOURCE	A 480	Scotts Shipbuilding & Eng Co, Greenock	11 Feb 1966	16 May 1967
REGENT	A 486	Harland & Wolff, Belfast	9 Mar 1966	6 June 1967

Displacement, tons: 13 590 light; 22 890 full load
Measurement, tons: 18 029 gross; 9300 dwt
Dimensions, feet (metres): 640 × 77.2 × 28.5 *(195.1 × 23.5 × 8.7)*
Main machinery: 2 Foster-Wheeler boilers; 2 AEI turbines; 20 000 hp *(14.92 MW)*; 2 shafts
Speed, knots: 20. **Range, miles:** 12 000 at 18 kts
Complement: 134 RFA plus 37 RNSTS
Guns: 2 Oerlikon 20 mm (can be fitted)
Radars: Navigation: Two Kelvin Hughes; I band.

Comment: Ordered on 24 January 1963. They have lifts for armaments and stores, seven advanced replenishment rigs and helicopter platforms for transferring loads at sea. A number of the seven holds are temperature controlled to increase cargo storage life. Helicopter not carried but hangar and full flight deck facilities are fitted although the hangar is not big enough for Sea King sized aircraft. Designed from the outset as Fleet Replenishment Ships. Air-conditioned. *Resource* was in reserve in early 1992 pending a decision to give her a service life extension refit.

REGENT *6/1990, van Ginderen Collection*

REPAIR/MAINTENANCE SHIP

1 STENA TYPE (FORWARD REPAIR SHIP)

Name	*No*	*Builders*	*Commissioned*
DILIGENCE (ex-*Stena Inspector*)	A 132	Oresundsvarvet AB, Landskrona, Sweden	1981

Displacement, tons: 10 765 full load
Measurement, tons: 6550 gross; 4860 dwt
Dimensions, feet (metres): 367.5 × 67.3 × 27.2 *(112 × 20.5 × 8.3)*
Flight deck, feet (metres): 83 × 83 *(25.4 × 25.4)*
Main machinery: Diesel-electric; 5 V16 Nohab-Polar diesel generators; 2650 kW; 4 NEBB motors; 6000 hp(m) *(4.41 MW)*; 1 shaft; KaMeWa cp prop; 2 KaMeWa bow tunnel thrusters; 3000 hp(m) *(2.2 MW)*; 2 azimuth thrusters (aft); 3000 hp(m) *(2.2 MW)*
Speed, knots: 14. **Range, miles:** 5000 at 12 kts
Complement: 31 RFA plus 90 RN (accommodation for 147 plus 55 temporary)
Cargo capacity: Long-jib crane SWL 5 tons; max lift, 40 tons

Guns: 4 Oerlikon 20 mm; 50° elevation; 800 rounds/minute to 2 km; weight of shell 0.24 kg.
Countermeasures: Decoys: 4 Plessey Shield 6-tubed launchers.

Helicopters: Facilities for up to Boeing Chinook HC 1 (medium lift) size.

DILIGENCE — *1/1990, W. Sartori*

Programmes: *Stena Inspector* was designed originally as a Multipurpose Support Vessel for North Sea oil operations, and completed in January 1981. Chartered on 25 May 1982 for use as a fleet repair ship during the Falklands' campaign. Purchased from Stena (UK) Line in October 1983, and converted for use as Forward Repair Ship in the South Atlantic (Falkland Islands). Conversion by Clyde Dock Engineering Ltd, Govan from 12 November 1983 to 29 February 1984; accepted into RFA service on 12 March 1984. Naval Party 2010 embarked.
Modernisation: Following items added during conversion: large workshop for hull and machinery repairs (in well-deck); accommodation for naval Junior Rates (new accommodation block); accommodation for crew of conventional submarine (in place of Saturation Diving System); extensive craneage facilities; overside supply of electrical power, water, fuel, steam, air, to ships alongside; large naval store (in place of cement tanks); armament and magazines; Naval Communications System; decompression chamber.
Structure: Four 5 ton anchors for 4-point mooring system. Strengthened for operations in ice (Ice Class 1A). Köngsberg Albatross Positioning System has been retained in full. Uses bow and stern thrusters and main propeller to maintain a selected position to within a few metres, up to Beaufort Force 9. Controlled by Kongsberg KS 500 computers.
Operational: Deployed to the Gulf in August 1987, back on station in the Falkland Islands in 1989 and returned to the Gulf in September 1990.

AVIATION TRAINING SHIP

Name	*No*	*Builders*	*Commissioned*	*Recommissioned*
ARGUS (ex-*Contender Bezant*)	A 135	CNR Breda, Venice, Italy	1981	1 June 1988

Displacement, tons: 18 280 standard; 28 480 full load
Measurement, tons: 10 200 dwt
Dimensions, feet (metres): 574.5 × 99.7 × 27 *(175.1 × 30.4 × 8.2)*
Main machinery: 2 Lindholmen SEMT-Pielstick 18PC2.5V 400 diesels; 23 400 hp(m) *(17.2 MW)* sustained; 2 shafts
Speed, knots: 18. **Range, miles:** 20 000 at 19 kts
Complement: 79 RFA plus 39 permanent RN plus 137 RN aircrew
Cargo capacity: 3300 tons dieso; 1100 tons aviation fuel

Guns: 4 Oerlikon/DES 30 mm Mk 1.
Countermeasures: Decoys: 2 Sea Gnat Chaff launchers. Graseby Type 182; torpedo decoy.
ESM: THORN EMI Guardian; radar warning.
Combat data systems: Racal CANE DEB-1 data automation. Inmarsat SATCOM communications. Marisat.
Radars: Air search: Type 994 MTI; E/F band.
Air/surface search: Kelvin Hughes Type 1006; I band.
Navigation: Racal Decca Type 994; I band.

Fixed wing aircraft: Provision to transport 12 British Aerospace Sea Harrier FRS 1.
Helicopters: 6 Westland Sea King HAS 5 or similar.

ARGUS — *4/1991, W. Sartori*

Programmes: Ro-ro container ship whose conversion for her new task was begun by Harland and Wolff in March 1984 and completed on 3 March 1988. Purchase price approx £18 million; conversion approx £45 million which included full contractor responsibility for equipment, trials and setting to work. Relieved *Engadine* in early 1989.
Structure: Uses former ro-ro deck as hangar with four sliding WT doors able to operate at a speed of 10 m per minute. Can replenish other ships underway. One lift port midships, one abaft funnel. Domestic facilities are very limited if she is to be used in the Command support role. Flight deck is 372.4 ft *(113.5 m)* long and has a 5 ft thick concrete layer on its lower side. First RFA to be fitted with a command system.
Operational: Not as heavily armed as *Fort Victoria* but similar 'advantage' is being taken of the cost effectiveness of mixed civilian and naval manning. Deployed to the Gulf in 1990/91 as a Primary Casualty Receiving Ship (PCRS) with the hangar converted into hospital accommodation.

LOGISTIC LANDING SHIPS (LSLs)

Name	*No*	*Builders*	*Laid down*	*Launched*	*Commissioned*
SIR GALAHAD	L 3005	Swan Hunter Shipbuilders, Wallsend	12 May 1985	13 Dec 1986	25 Nov 1987

Displacement, tons: 8585 full load
Measurement, tons: 3080 dwt
Dimensions, feet (metres): 461 × 64 × 14.1 *(140.5 × 19.5 × 4.3)*
Main machinery: 2 Mirrlees Blackstone diesels; 13 320 hp *(9.94 MW)*; 2 shafts; cp props
Speed, knots: 18. **Range, miles:** 13 000 at 15 kts
Complement: 49 (17 officers)
Military lift: 343 troops (537 hard-lying); 18 MBT; 20 mixed vehicles; ammunition, fuel and stores
Guns: 2 Bofors 40 mm. 3 Oerlikon 20 mm GAM-BO3.
Countermeasures: Decoys: 4 Plessey Shield launchers.
Combat data systems: Racal CANE data automation.
Radars: Navigation: Kelvin Hughes Type 1006; I band.
Helicopters: 1 Westland Sea King HC 4.

Comment: Ordered on 6 September 1984 as a replacement for *Sir Galahad*, sunk as a war grave after air attack at Bluff Cove, Falkland Islands on 8 June 1982. Has bow and stern ramps with a visor bow gate. One 25 ton crane and three smaller ones. Mexeflote pontoons can be attached on both sides of the hull superstructure.

SIR GALAHAD — *11/1991, Maritime Photographic*

Name	*No*	*Builders*	*Laid down*	*Launched*	*Commissioned*
SIR BEDIVERE	L 3004	Hawthorn Leslie, Hebburn-on-Tyne	Oct 1965	20 July 1966	18 May 1967
SIR GERAINT	L 3027	Alex Stephen, Glasgow	June 1965	26 Jan 1967	12 July 1967
SIR PERCIVALE	L 3036	Hawthorn Leslie, Hebburn-on-Tyne	Apr 1966	4 Oct 1967	23 Mar 1968
SIR TRISTRAM	L 3505	Hawthorn Leslie, Hebburn-on-Tyne	Feb 1966	12 Dec 1966	14 Sep 1967

Displacement, tons: 3270 light; 5674 full load 5800 full load *(Sir Tristram)*
Dimensions, feet (metres): 412.1; 441.1 *(Sir Tristram)* × 59.8 × 13 *(125.6; 134.4 × 18.2 × 4)*
Main machinery: 2 Mirrlees 10-ALSSDM diesels; 9400 hp *(7.01 MW)*; 2 shafts; bow thruster
Speed, knots: 17. **Range, miles:** 8000 at 15 kts
Complement: 65 (21 officers); 50 *(Sir Tristram)*
Military lift: 340 troops (534 hard lying); 16 MBTs; 34 mixed vehicles; 120 tons POL; 30 tons ammunition; 1—20 ton crane; 2—4.5 ton cranes. *Sir Tristram* has increased capacity for 20 helicopters (11 tank deck and 9 vehicle deck)
Guns: 4 Oerlikon 20 mm.
Radars: Navigation: Kelvin Hughes Type 1006; I band.
Helicopters: Platforms to operate Gazelle AH 1 or Lynx AH 1/7.

Comment: Fitted for bow and stern loading with drive-through facilities and deck-to-deck ramps. Facilities provided for onboard maintenance of vehicles and for laying out pontoon equipment. Mexeflote self-propelled floating platforms can be strapped one on each side. Carries 850 tons oil fuel. On 8 June 1982 *Sir Tristram* was severely damaged off the Falkland Islands. Tyne Shiprepairers were given a contract to repair and modify her. This included lengthening by 29 ft, an enlarged flight deck capable of taking Chinooks and a new bridge. The aluminium superstructure was replaced by steel and the provision of new communications, an EMR, SATCOM, new navigation systems and helicopter control radar greatly increase her effectiveness. Completed 9 October 1985. The first three are to be modernised to the same standard as *Sir Tristram* with SLEPs in the 1990s. All deployed to the Gulf in 1991 with additional 20 mm guns, decoy systems and navigation equipment.

SIR BEDIVERE *8/1991, Wright & Logan*

ROYAL MARITIME AUXILIARY SERVICE

SALVAGE AND MOORING VESSELS

Note: *Scarab* (Insect class tender) with bow sheave acts as mooring vessel at Pembroke Dock. *Cricket* (no bow sheave) acts as mooring vessel in the Clyde.

3 SAL CLASS

Name	*No*	*Builders*	*Commissioned*
SALMOOR	A 185	Hall Russell, Aberdeen	12 Nov 1985
SALMASTER	A 186	Hall Russell, Aberdeen	10 Apr 1986
SALMAID	A 187	Hall Russell, Aberdeen	28 Oct 1986

Displacement, tons: 1605 light; 2225 full load
Dimensions, feet (metres): 253 × 48.9 × 12.5 *(77 × 14.9 × 3.8)*
Main machinery: 2 Ruston 8-RKCM diesels; 4000 hp *(2.98 MW)* sustained; 1 shaft
Speed, knots: 15
Complement: 17 (4 officers) plus 27 spare billets

Comment: Ordered on 23 January 1984. *Salmoor* on Clyde, *Salmaster* at Rosyth, *Salmaid* at Devonport. Lift, 400 tons; 200 tons on horns. Can carry submersibles including LR 5.

SALMOOR *6/1991, Maritime Photographic*

2 WILD DUCK CLASS

Name	*No*	*Builders*	*Commissioned*
GOOSANDER	A 164	Robb Caledon Ltd	10 Sep 1973
POCHARD	A 165	Robb Caledon Ltd	11 Dec 1973

Displacement, tons: 692 light; 1648 full load
Dimensions, feet (metres): 197.6 × 40.5 × 13.8 *(60.2 × 12.2 × 4.2)*
Main machinery: 1 Davey Paxman diesel; 750 hp *(560 kW)*; 1 shaft; cp prop
Speed, knots: 10. **Range, miles:** 3000 at 10 kts
Complement: 23

Comment: Capable of laying out and servicing the heaviest moorings used by the Fleet and also maintaining booms for harbour defence. Heavy lifting equipment enables a wide range of salvage operations to be performed, especially in harbour clearance work. The special heavy winches have an ability for tidal lifts over the apron of 200 tons. *Goosander* is based on the Clyde; *Pochard* in reserve at Portsmouth.

GOOSANDER *1991, RMAS*

3 MOORHEN CLASS

Name	*No*	*Builders*	*Commissioned*
MOORHEN	Y 32	McTay, Bromborough	Apr 1989
MOORFOWL	Y 33	McTay, Bromborough	May 1989
CAMERON	A 72	Dunston, Hessle	Sep 1991

Displacement, tons: 530 full load
Dimensions, feet (metres): 106 × 37.7 × 6.6 *(32.3 × 11.5 × 2)*
Main machinery: 2 Cummins KT 19M diesels; 730 hp *(545 kW)* sustained; 2 Aquamasters
Speed, knots: 8
Complement: 10 (2 officers)

Comment: Classified as powered mooring lighters. The whole ship can be worked from a 'flying bridge' which is constructed over a through deck. Day mess for five divers. *Moorhen* at Portsmouth, *Moorfowl* at Devonport. *Cameron* works for DRA (Maritime) and is modified as a trials support vessel.

MOORHEN *6/1991, Maritime Photographic*

COASTAL TANKERS

5 OILPRESS CLASS

Name	*No*	*Builders*	*Commissioned*
OILPRESS	Y 21	Appledore Ferguson S.B.	1969
OILSTONE	Y 22	Appledore Ferguson S.B.	1969
OILWELL	Y 23	Appledore Ferguson S.B.	1969
OILBIRD	Y 25	Appledore Ferguson S.B.	1969
OILMAN	Y 26	Appledore Ferguson S.B.	1969

Displacement, tons: 280 standard; 530 full load
Dimensions, feet (metres): 139.5 × 30 × 8.3 *(42.5 × 9 × 2.5)*
Main machinery: 1 Lister-Blackstone ES6 diesel; 405 hp *(302 kW)*; 1 shaft
Speed, knots: 9
Complement: 8
Cargo capacity: 250 tons dieso

Comment: Ordered on 10 May 1967. One deleted in 1992.

OILPRESS *2/1986, A. Denholm*

TRIALS SHIPS

Notes: A Shock Trials Vessel, *STV 02*, was completed 14 June 1981 by Scotts, Greenock.

Name	*No*	*Builders*	*Commissioned*
NEWTON	A 367	Scott Lithgow Ltd	17 June 1976

Displacement, tons: 3140 light; 4652 full load
Dimensions, feet (metres): 323.5 × 53 × 18.5 *(98.6 × 16 × 5.7)*
Main machinery: Diesel-electric; 3 Mirrlees-Blackstone diesel generators; 4350 hp *(3.25 MW)*; 1 GEC motor; 2040 hp *(1.52 MW)*; Kort nozzle; bow thruster
Speed, knots: 14. **Range, miles:** 5000 at 14 kts
Complement: 64 including 12 scientists

Comment: Passive tank stabilisation. Prime duty sonar propagation trials. Can serve as cable-layer with large cable tanks. Special winch system. Low noise level electric propulsion system. Based at Plymouth.

NEWTON *1990, van Ginderen Collection*

Name	*No*	*Builders*	*Commissioned*
WHITEHEAD	A 364	Scotts Shipbuilding Co Ltd, Greenock	30 Mar 1971

Displacement, tons: 3040 full load
Dimensions, feet (metres): 319 × 48 × 17 *(97.3 × 14.6 × 5.2)*
Main machinery: 2 Paxman 12 YLCM diesels; 3000 hp *(2.24 MW)* sustained; 2 shafts
Speed, knots: 15.5. **Range, miles:** 4000 at 12 kts
Complement: 50 plus 15 trials and scientific staff
Torpedoes: 1—21 in *(533 mm)* bow tube (submerged). 3—324 mm Mk 32 (triple) tube.

Comment: Designed to provide mobile preparation, firing and control facilities for weapons and research vehicles. Named after Robert Whitehead, the torpedo development pioneer and engineer. Fitted with equipment for tracking weapons and target and for analysing the results of trials. Based at Plymouth and in reserve awaiting decision on future.

WHITEHEAD *7/1989, John Callis*

Name	*No*	*Builders*	*Commissioned*
AURICULA	A 285	Appledore Ferguson S.B.	6 Nov 1980

Displacement, tons: 940 light; 1118 full load
Dimensions, feet (metres): 170.5 × 36 × 11.8 *(52 × 11 × 3.6)*
Main machinery: 2 Mirrlees-Blackstone diesels; 1300 hp *(970 kW)*; 2 shafts; bow thruster
Speed, knots: 12
Complement: 32 (7 officers, 10 trials party)

Comment: Sonar trials and experimental ship. Based at Portland.

AURICULA *7/1988, W. Sartori*

TORPEDO RECOVERY VESSELS

4 TORNADO CLASS

TORNADO A 140
TORCH A 141
TORMENTOR A 142
TOREADOR A 143

Displacement, tons: 698 full load
Dimensions, feet (metres): 154.5 × 31.3 × 11.3 *(47.1 × 9.6 × 3.4)*
Main machinery: 2 Mirrlees-Blackstone ESL8 MCR diesels; 2200 hp *(1.64 MW)*; 2 shafts
Speed, knots: 14. **Range, miles:** 3000 at 14 kts
Complement: 14

Comment: Ordered from Hall Russell, Aberdeen on 1 July 1977 and launched in 1979-80. *Torch* based at Portland, *Tormentor* at Plymouth, others in the Clyde.

TORCH *8/1991, Wright & Logan*

Name	*No*	*Builders*	*Commissioned*
TORRENT	A 127	Cleland S B Co, Wallsend	10 Sep 1971

Displacement, tons: 550 gross
Dimensions, feet (metres): 162 × 31 × 11.5 *(49.4 × 9.5 × 3.5)*
Main machinery: 2 Paxman diesels; 700 hp *(522 kW)*; 2 shafts
Speed, knots: 10
Complement: 18

Comment: Has a stern ramp for torpedo recovery—can carry 22 torpedoes in hold and 10 on deck. Based at Kyle of Loch Alsh.

TORRENT *1991, RMAS*

ARMAMENT STORE CARRIERS (AKF and ASL)

Name	No	Builders	Commissioned
KINTERBURY	A 378	Appledore Ferguson S.B.	Nov 1980
ARROCHAR (ex-*St George*)	A 382	Appledore Ferguson S.B.	July 1981

Displacement, tons: 2207 full load
Measurement, tons: 1150 dwt
Dimensions, feet (metres): 231.2 × 39 × 15 *(70.5 × 11.9 × 4.6)*
Main machinery: 2 Mirrlees-Blackstone diesels; 3000 hp *(2.24 MW)*; 1 shaft
Speed, knots: 14.5. **Range, miles:** 4000 at 11 kts
Complement: 24 (8 officers)

Comment: Carry armament stores in two holds. Internal arrangements of *Arrochar* differ and she is classified as an Armament Ship Logistic (ASL). Twin cranes in the well-deck. *Arrochar* transferred from the RCT on 7 November 1988. *Arrochar* and *Kinterbury* alternate in reserve at Portsmouth.

ARROCHAR *8/1991, Maritime Photographic*

WATER CARRIERS

6 WATER CLASS

Name	No	Builders	Commissioned
WATERFALL	Y 17	Drypool Engineering & Drydock Co, Hull	1967
WATERSHED	Y 18	Drypool Engineering & Drydock Co, Hull	1967
WATERSPOUT	Y 19	Drypool Engineering & Drydock Co, Hull	1967
WATERCOURSE	Y 30	Drypool Engineering & Drydock Co, Hull	1974
WATERFOWL	Y 31	Drypool Engineering & Drydock Co, Hull	1974
WATERMAN	A 146	R Dunston (Hessle) Ltd	1978

Measurement, tons: 285 gross
Dimensions, feet (metres): 131.5 × 24.8 × 8 *(40.1 × 7.5 × 2.4)*
Main machinery: 1 Lister-Blackstone ERS 8 MCR diesel; 660 hp *(492 kW)*; 1 shaft
Speed, knots: 11
Complement: 8

Comment: Y 19 after deckhouse extended forward. A 146 is a modified ship, having a store-carrying capability and, like Y 31 has a deckhouse forward of the bridge. *Waterfall* based in the Clyde and used as a Salvage Training Vessel. One deleted in 1991.

WATERSHED *10/1990, Maritime Photographic*

TUGS

Note: Appearance of RMAS tugs—black hull with white line, buff upperworks, buff funnel with black top. The blue band on the funnel varies between ports.

3 OCEAN TUGS

Name	No	Builders	Commissioned
ROYSTERER	A 361	C D Holmes, Beverley, Humberside	26 Apr 1972
ROBUST	A 366	C D Holmes, Beverley, Humberside	6 Apr 1974
ROLLICKER	A 502	C D Holmes, Beverley, Humberside	6 Mar 1973

Displacement, tons: 1630 full load
Dimensions, feet (metres): 178 × 40.3 × 21 *(54.3 × 12.3 × 6.4)*
Main machinery: 2 Mirrlees KMR 6 diesels; 4500 hp *(3.36 MW)*; 2 shafts; cp props
Speed, knots: 15. **Range, miles:** 12 500 at 12 kts
Complement: 28 (salvage party—10 RN officers and ratings)

Comment: Nominal bollard pull, 50 tons. Designed principally for salvage and long-range towage but can be used for general harbour duties, which *Robust* undertakes at Devonport. *Roysterer* based on Clyde, *Rollicker* at Portsmouth.

ROBUST *12/1988, W. Sartori*

9 ADEPT CLASS (TUTT)

FORCEFUL A 221
NIMBLE A 222
POWERFUL A 223
ADEPT A 224
BUSTLER A 225
CAPABLE A 226
CAREFUL A 227
FAITHFUL A 228
DEXTEROUS A 231

Displacement, tons: 450
Dimensions, feet (metres): 127.3 × 30.8 × 11.2 *(38.8 × 9.4 × 3.4)*
Main machinery: 2 Ruston 6 RKCM diesels; 3000 hp *(2.24 MW)* sustained; 2 Voith-Schneider props
Speed, knots: 12
Complement: 10

Comment: 'Twin unit tractor tugs' (TUTT). First four ordered from Richard Dunston (Hessle) on 22 February 1979 and next five on 8 February 1984. Primarily for harbour work with coastal towing capability. Nominal bollard pull, 27.5 tons. *Adept* accepted 28 October 1980, *Bustler* 15 April 1981, *Capable* 11 September 1981, *Careful* 12 March 1982, *Forceful* 18 March 1985, *Nimble* 25 June 1985, *Powerful* 30 October 1985, *Faithful* 21 December 1985, *Dexterous* 23 April 1986. *Adept* at Portland, *Powerful* and *Bustler* at Portsmouth, *Forceful*, *Faithful* and *Careful* at Plymouth, *Nimble* and *Dexterous* at Rosyth, *Capable* at Gibraltar.

BUSTLER *11/1991, Maritime Photographic*

18 DOG CLASS (16 TUGS + 2 RANGE TRIALS VESSELS)

ALSATIAN A 106
CAIRN A 126
DALMATIAN A 129
DEERHOUND A 155
ELKHOUND A 162
LABRADOR A 168
HUSKY A 178
MASTIFF A 180
SALUKI A 182
POINTER A 188
SETTER A 189
SEALYHAM A 197
SPANIEL A 201
SHEEPDOG A 250
FOXHOUND (ex-*Boxer*) A 326
BASSET (ex-*Beagle*) A 327
COLLIE A 328
CORGI A 330

Displacement, tons: 248 full load
Dimensions, feet (metres): 94 × 24.5 × 12 *(28.7 × 7.5 × 3.7)*
Main machinery: 2 Lister-Blackstone ERS 8 MCR diesels; 1320 hp *(985 kW)*; 2 shafts
Speed, knots: 10. **Range, miles:** 2236 at 10 kts
Complement: 7

Comment: Harbour berthing tugs. *Sealyham* at Gibraltar. Nominal bollard pull, 17.5 tons. Completed 1962-72. *Cairn* and *Collie* operate at Kyle of Loch Alsh as Range trials vessels and have had towing gear removed. Appearance varies considerably, some with mast, some with curved upper-bridge work, some with flat monkey-island. The class needs replacing as a priority.

FOXHOUND *6/1991, Maritime Photographic*

2 MODIFIED GIRL CLASS

DAPHNE A 156 **EDITH** A 177

Displacement, tons: 138 standard
Dimensions, feet (metres): 61 × 16.4 × 7.2 *(18.6 × 5 × 2.2)*
Main machinery: 1 diesel; 495 hp *(396 kW)*; 1 shaft
Speed, knots: 10
Complement: 6

Comment: *Edith* at Gibraltar. Both built by Dunstons. Completed 1971-72. Nominal bollard pull, 6.5 tons.

Modified GIRL Class *4/1986, Michael D. J. Lennon*

12 TRITON CLASS

KATHLEEN A 166
KITTY A 170
LESLEY A 172
LILAH A 174
MARY A 175
IRENE A 181
ISABEL A 183
JOAN A 190
JOYCE A 193
MYRTLE A 199
NANCY A 202
NORAH A 205

Displacement, tons: 107.5 standard
Dimensions, feet (metres): 57.7 × 18 × 7.9 *(17.6 × 5.5 × 2.4)*
Main machinery: 1 diesel; 330 hp *(264 kW)*; 1 shaft
Speed, knots: 7.5
Complement: 4

Comment: All completed by August 1974 by Dunstons. 'Water-tractors' with small wheelhouse and adjoining funnel. Later vessels have masts stepped abaft wheelhouse. Voith-Schneider vertical axis propellers. Nominal bollard pull, 3 tons. Order for two more in 1990 was cancelled.

KITTY *11/1991, W. Sartori*

8 FELICITY CLASS

FELICITY A 112
FRANCES A 147
FIONA A 148
FLORENCE A 149
GENEVIEVE A 150
GEORGINA A 152
GWENDOLINE A 196
HELEN A 198

Displacement, tons: 144 full load
Dimensions, feet (metres): 70 × 21 × 9.8 *(21.5 × 6.4 × 3)*
Main machinery: 1 Mirrlees-Blackstone ESM 8 diesel; 615 hp *(459 kW)*; 1 Voith-Schneider cp prop
Speed, knots: 10
Complement: 4

Comment: First five completed 1973. A 112 built by Dunstons and remainder by Hancocks. A 147, 149 and 150 ordered early 1979 from Richard Dunston (Thorne) and completed by end 1980. Nominal bollard pull, 5.7 tons.

HELEN *7/1987, Michael D. J. Lennon*

RANGE SUPPORT VESSELS

WARDEN A 368

Displacement, tons: 900 full load
Dimensions, feet (metres): 159.4 × 34.4 × 8.2 *(48.6 × 10.5 × 2.5)*
Main machinery: 2 Ruston 8 RKCM diesels; 4000 hp *(2.98 MW)* sustained; 1 shaft
Speed, knots: 15
Complement: 11 (4 officers)
Radars: Navigation: Racal Decca RM 1250; I band.
Sonars: Dowty 2053; high frequency.

Comment: Built by Richards, Lowestoft and completed in January 1990. In service at Pembroke Dock.

WARDEN *1990, RMAS*

FALCONET (ex-*Alfred Herring V C*) Y 02 (ex-Y 497)
PETARD (ex-*Michael Murphy V C*) Y 01 (ex-519)

Displacement, tons: 70 full load
Dimensions, feet (metres): 77.7 × 18 × 4.9 *(23.7 × 5.5 × 1.5)*
Main engines: 2 Paxman 8 CM diesels; 2000 hp *(1.49 MW)* sustained; 2 shafts
Speed, knots: 20

Comment: Range Safety Craft built by James and Stone, Brightlingsea. Similar design to Spitfire class. Transferred from the RCT on 30 September 1988. *Falconet* commissioned 1978 serves at the Royal Artillery missile range in the Outer Hebrides; *Petard* commissioned 1983 serves at Pendine range, South Wales.

PETARD *9/1987, Michael D. J. Lennon*

RSC 7713 (ex-*Samuel Morley V C*)
RSC 7821 (ex-*Joseph Hughes G C*)
RSC 8125 (ex-*Sir Paul Travers*)
RSC 8126 (ex-*Sir Cecil Smith*)
RSC 8124 (ex-*Sir John Potter*)
RSC 8487 (ex-*Geoffrey Rackman G C*)
RSC 8489 (ex-*Sir Evan Gibb*)
RSC 7820 (ex-*Richard Masters V C*)
RSC 7822 (ex-*James Dalton V C*)
RSC 8128 (ex-*Sir Reginald Kerr*)
RSC 8129 (ex-*Sir Humfrey Gale*)
RSC 8488 (ex-*Walter Cleal G C*)

Displacement, tons: 20.2
Dimensions, feet (metres): 49.2 × 14.9 × 4.3 *(15 × 4.6 × 1.3)*
Main machinery: 2 RR C8M 410 diesels; 820 hp *(612 kW)*; 2 shafts
Speed, knots: 22. **Range, miles:** 300 at 20 kts
Complement: 3

Comment: Range Safety Craft of the Honours and Sirs classes, built by Fairey Marine, A R P Whitstable and Halmatic. All completed 1982-86. Transferred from the RCT on 30 September 1988. A 13th vessel *Sir William Roe* is based in Cyprus and has remained with the RCT. Based at Whitehaven, Pembroke Dock, Hebrides, Dover and Portland. Now known only by their pennant numbers.

RSC 7820 *6/1991, Maritime Photographic*

SUBMARINE SUPPORT VESSELS

3 TOWED ARRAY TENDERS

Dimensions, feet (metres): 65.9 × 19.7 × 7.9 *(20.1 × 6 × 2.4)*
Main machinery: 2 Perkins diesels; 400 hp *(298 kW)*; 2 Kort nozzles
Speed, knots: 12
Complement: 8

Comment: Used for transporting clip-on towed arrays from submarine bases at Faslane, Portsmouth and Devonport.

TARV *7/1988, W. Sartori*

0 + 1 SUBMARINE TENDER

Dimensions, feet (metres): 101 × 25.6 × 3.6 *(30.8 × 7.8 × 1.1)*
Main machinery: 2 diesels; 2 waterjets
Speed, knots: 23
Comment: Twin-hulled support ship ordered in 1991 from FBM Marine, Cowes. To be delivered in November 1992 and probably to be used for personnel and stores transfers in the Firth of Clyde.

AVIATION SUPPORT CRAFT

Note: On 1 February 1991 vessels of the Royal Air Force Maritime Section were transferred to the RMAS. Operation by James Fisher & Son will continue until the expiration of the current contract. The vessels are based at Plymouth, Invergordon, Holyhead and Great Yarmouth.

2 SEAL CLASS (LRRSC)

Name	*No*	*Builders*	*Commissioned*
SEAL	5000	Brooke Marine, Lowestoft	Aug 1967
SEAGULL	5001	Fairmile Construction, Berwick-on-Tweed	1970

Displacement, tons: 159 full load
Dimensions, feet (metres): 120.3 × 23.5 × 6.5 *(36.6 × 7.2 × 2)*
Main machinery: 2 Paxman 16 CM diesels; 4000 hp *(2.98 MW)* sustained; 2 shafts
Speed, knots: 21
Complement: 9

Comment: Long range recovery and support craft (LRRSC). All welded steel hull. Aluminium alloy superstructure. Used for weapon recovery, target towing, search and rescue. Both at Invergordon.

SEAL *8/1984, Michael D. J. Lennon*

6 SPITFIRE CLASS (RTTL Mk 3)

Name	*No*	*Builders*	*Commissioned*
SPITFIRE	4000	James and Stone, Brightlingsea	1972
HALIFAX	4003	James and Stone, Brightlingsea	1977
HAMPDEN	4004	James and Stone, Brightlingsea	1980
HURRICANE	4005	James and Stone, Brightlingsea	1980
LANCASTER	4006	James and Stone, Brightlingsea	1981
WELLINGTON	4007	James and Stone, Brightlingsea	1981

Displacement, tons: 70.2 full load
Dimensions, feet (metres): 78.7 × 18 × 4.9 *(24.1 × 5.5 × 1.5)*
Main machinery: 2 Paxman 8 CM diesels; 2000 hp *(1.49 MW)* sustained; 2 shafts
Speed, knots: 22
Complement: 6

Comment: Rescue target towing launches (RTTL). All welded steel hulls; aluminium alloy superstructure. *Spitfire* has twin funnels, remainder none. Invergordon, *Hurricane*; Great Yarmouth, *Hampden, Lancaster, Wellington;* Plymouth, *Spitfire, Halifax*.

HAMPDEN *8/1987, Michael D. J. Lennon*

5 PINNACES 1300 SERIES

1374, 1387, 1389, 1390, 1392

Displacement, tons: 28.3
Dimensions, feet (metres): 63 × 15.5 × 5 *(19.2 × 4.7 × 1.5)*
Main machinery: 2 RR C6 diesels; 190 hp *(142 kW)*; 2 shafts
Speed, knots: 13
Complement: 5

Comment: Hard chine, wooden hulls. Built by Groves and Gutteridge, Robertsons (Dunoon) and Dorset Yacht Co (Poole) in 1955-65. Of 5 ton cargo capacity. Two in storage at Plymouth (1387 and 1390); 1392, 1374 at Holyhead; 1389 at Plymouth.

1300 Series *8/1982, Michael D. J. Lennon*

FLEET TENDERS

7 INSECT CLASS

BEE A 216
CICALA A 263
COCKCHAFER A 230
CRICKET A 229
GNAT A 239
LADYBIRD A 253
SCARAB A 272

Displacement, tons: 475 full load
Dimensions, feet (metres): 111.8 × 28 × 11 *(34.1 × 8.5 × 3.4)*
Main machinery: 1 Lister-Blackstone ERS 8 MCR diesel; 660 hp *(492 kW)*; 1 shaft
Speed, knots: 11.3. **Range, miles:** 3000 at 10 kts
Complement: 7

Comment: First three built as stores carriers, three as armament carriers and *Scarab* as mooring vessel capable of lifting 10 tons over the bows. All commissioned between 1970 and 1973. *Cricket* acts as a mooring vessel in the Clyde while *Gnat* and *Ladybird* operate as armament carriers with a red funnel band. *Bee* and *Cicala* have an armament capability. Of 200 ton cargo capacity and 2 ton crane.

BEE *9/1990, Maritime Photographic*

8 LOYAL CLASS (RNXS)

LOYAL HELPER A 157
SUPPORTER (ex-*Loyal Supporter*) A 158
LOYAL WATCHER A 159
LOYAL VOLUNTEER A 160
LOYAL MEDIATOR A 161
LOYAL MODERATOR A 220
LOYAL CHANCELLOR A 1770
LOYAL PROCTOR A 1771

Displacement, tons: 143
Dimensions, feet (metres): 80 × 21 × 6.6 *(24.1 × 6.4 × 2)*
Main machinery: 1 Lister-Blackstone ERS 4 MCR diesel; 320 hp *(239 kW)*; 1 shaft
Speed, knots: 10.5
Complement: 6 (1 officer)

Comment: *Loyal Helper* completed 10 February 1978 and last four later in 1978. (See also Coastal Training Craft). Bases: Portsmouth Command: *Loyal Mediator*. Plymouth Command: *Loyal Moderator* (Pembroke Dock), *Loyal Watcher* (Birkenhead), *Loyal Chancellor* (Plymouth). Scotland Command: *Loyal Volunteer, Loyal Proctor, Supporter* (Belfast), *Loyal Helper* (Rosyth).

LOYAL HELPER *7/1990, Gilbert Gyssels*

4 DIVING TENDERS

ILCHESTER A 308
INSTOW A 309
IRONBRIDGE* A 311
IXWORTH* A 318
*RN manned

Displacement, tons: 143
Dimensions, feet (metres): 80 × 21 × 6.6 *(24.1 × 6.4 × 2)*
Main machinery: 2 Gray Marine diesels; 450 hp *(336 kW)*; 2 shafts
Speed, knots: 12
Complement: 6

Comment: Similar to Clovelly class. Built by Gregson Ltd, Blyth and commissioned in 1974.

INSTOW *8/1989, Wright & Logan*

28 CLOVELLY CLASS

CLOVELLY A 389
CRICCIETH A 391
CRICKLADE A 381
CROMARTY A 488
DORNOCH A 490
DUNSTER A 393
ELKSTONE A 353
ELSING* A 277
EPWORTH A 355
ETTRICK* A 274
FELSTED A 348
FINTRY A 394
FOTHERBY A 341
FROXFIELD A 354
FULBECK A 365
GLENCOE** A 392
GRASMERE A 402
HAMBLEDON A 1769
HARLECH A 1768
HEADCORN A 1766
HEVER A 1767
HOLMWOOD A 1772
HORNING A 1773
LAMLASH A 208
LECHLADE A 211
LLANDOVERY A 207
LYDFORD (ex-*Loyal Governor*, ex-*Alert*) A 251
MEAVY (ex-*Loyal Factor*, ex-*Vigilant*) A 254
**RNXS *RN

Displacement, tons: 143 full load
Dimensions, feet (metres): 80 × 21 × 6.6 *(24.4 × 6.4 × 2)*
Main machinery: 1 Lister-Blackstone ERS 4 MCR diesel; 320 hp *(239 kW)*; 1 shaft
Speed, knots: 10.3. **Range, miles:** 600 at 10 kts
Complement: 4
Cargo capacity: 36 tons

Comment: All fleet tenders of an improved Aberdovey class commissioned 1970-74. *Elsing* and *Ettrick* at Gibraltar (Royal Navy manned), used for patrol duties. Three based at Falmouth operating with Culdrose helicopters *(Clovelly, Hever, Headcorn)*. Can be used for varying tasks—cargo, passenger, training, diving *(Dornoch* and *Fotherby)*. *Meavy* in Clyde, *Lydford* at Portland. Listed in alphabetical order.

HAMBLEDON *11/1991, Maritime Photographic*

5 MANLY CLASS

MELTON A 83
MENAI A 84
MEON A 87
MILFORD A 91
MESSINA A 107

Displacement, tons: 143 full load
Dimensions, feet (metres): 80 × 21 × 6.6 *(24.4 × 6.4 × 2)*
Main machinery: 1 Lister-Blackstone ESR 4 MCR diesel; 320 hp *(239 kW)*; 1 shaft
Speed, knots: 10
Complement: 6 (1 officer)

Comment: All built by Richard Dunston, Hessle. Details similar to Clovelly class but with larger deck-house. All completed by early 1983. *Messina*, attached to Royal Marines, Poole for navigational training and remainder RMAS. Three of the class used for training at *Raleigh* have been paid off.

MEON *6/1990, van Ginderen Collection*

1 FBM CATAMARAN CLASS

Displacement, tons: 21 full load
Dimensions, feet (metres): 51.8 × 18 × 4.9 *(15.8 × 5.5 × 1.5)*
Main machinery: 2 Mermaid Turbo 4 diesels; 280 hp *(209 kW)*; 2 shafts
Speed, knots: 13. **Range, miles:** 400 at 10 kts
Complement: 2

Comment: Built by FBM Marine. Can carry 30 passengers or 2 tons stores. First of a new construction type designed to replace some of the older harbour launches.

FBM Type *9/1990, Maritime Photographic*

TARGET VESSELS

BULLSEYE (ex-*Tokio*), **MAGPIE** (ex-*Hondo*), **TARGE** (ex-*Erimo*)

Measurement, tons: 273 gross; 91 net
Dimensions, feet (metres): 117.8 × 25.3 × 12.1 *(35.9 × 7.7 × 3.7)*
Main machinery: 1 Mirrlees diesel; 700 hp *(522 kW)*; 1 shaft
Speed, knots: 12
Complement: 2 (on passage only)

Comment: Built by Goole Shipbuilding Co in 1961-62. Side trawlers acquired in June 1982 and January 1984 *(Targe)*. These are employed as radio controlled targets at Portland.

MAGPIE *7/1987, Michael D. J. Lennon*

DEGAUSSING VESSELS

2 MAGNET CLASS

MAGNET A 114
LODESTONE A 115

Displacement, tons: 955 full load
Dimensions, feet (metres): 179.7 × 37.4 × 9.8 *(54.8 × 11.4 × 3)*
Main machinery: 2 Mirrlees-Blackstone ESL-6 MCR diesels; 1650 hp *(1.23 MW)*; 2 shafts
Speed, knots: 14. **Range, miles:** 1750 at 12 kts
Complement: 15

Comment: The pair replaced the three Ham class, *Magnet* based at Portsmouth (in reserve) and *Lodestone* at Greenock. Built by Cleland S B Co Ltd, Wallsend 1979-80.

MAGNET *7/1990, A. Sheldon Duplaix*

AUXILIARY TRAINING VESSELS

6 ABERDOVEY CLASS

APPLEBY A 383 **SULTAN VENTURER** (ex-*Bibury*) A 103 **ABERDOVEY** Y 10
ALNMOUTH Y 13 **ABINGER** Y 11 **BEDDGELERT** A 100

Displacement, tons: 117.5 full load
Dimensions, feet (metres): 79.8 × 18 × 5.5 *(24 × 5.5 × 1.7)*
Main machinery: 1 Lister-Blackstone ERS 4 MCR diesel; 320 hp *(239 kW)*; 1 shaft
Speed, knots: 10.5. **Range, miles:** 700 at 10 kts
Complement: 3

Comment: Commissioned in the mid-1960s as multi-purpose stores carriers (25 tons) or passengers (200). Four of the class have been modified with Sampson posts removed and improved accommodation. These are allocated to Sea Cadet Corps: *Aberdovey* (southern area based at Portsmouth); *Abinger* (eastern area based at Grimsby); *Appleby* (south-west area based at Bristol); *Alnmouth* (north-west area based at Liverpool). *Sultan Venturer* is a tender to *Sultan* at Gosport, and *Beddgelert* to *Caroline* at Belfast.

ABINGER *8/1991, Maurice Ball*

4 SEA CADET CORPS VESSELS

Comment: As well as the Aberdovey class above, there are three MFVs and one ex-IMS used by the SCC: MFV 15 (northern area based at Rosyth); MFV 96 (London); MFV 816 (Gravesend); IMS *Pagham* (Stranraer). All these vessels are in constant use.

MFV *9/1991, Maritime Photographic*

OLIVER TWIST **URIAH HEEP**

Comment: Ex-RCT General Service Launches of 20 tons. Two RNR tenders—*Oliver Twist* (London); *Uriah Heep* (Bristol).

FLOATING DOCKS

AFD 26

Dimensions, feet (metres): 380 × 92 oa; 50 clear inside width × 19 max draught of ship docked *(115.8 × 28; 15.2 × 5.8)*

Comment: 2750 ton lift. Built Bombay 1944. At Rosyth since 1984.

AFD 60

Dimensions, feet (metres): 492 × 92 oa; 54 clear × 35 *(150 × 28; 16.5 × 10.7)*

Comment: 13 500 ton lift. Built Portsmouth DY 1967. At Faslane for nuclear submarines.

SCOTTISH FISHERY PROTECTION AGENCY

Notes: (1) In addition to the ships listed below *Scotia* is used for research by the Department of Fisheries.
(2) Two Cessna Caravan II aircraft with Seaspray 2000 radars ordered in 1991.

SKUA **OSPREY**

Displacement, tons: 6 full load
Dimensions, feet (metres): 38 × 12.1 × 3.9 *(11.6 × 3.7 × 1.2)*
Main machinery: 2 Sabre 212 diesels; 424 hp *(316 kW)*; 2 shafts
Speed, knots: 28
Complement: 3

Comment: Pacific 38 class built by Osborne Marine in 1987-88. Dimensions given include the inflatable flotation collar.

SULISKER **VIGILANT** **NORNA**

Displacement, tons: 1652 full load
Dimensions, feet (metres): 233.9 × 38 × 15.7 *(71.3 × 11.6 × 4.8)*
Main machinery: 2 Ruston 12 RKC (6AT 350 in *Norna*) diesels; 6000 hp *(4.48 MW)* sustained; 2 shafts; cp props; bow thruster; 450 hp *(336 kW)*
Speed, knots: 18. **Range, miles:** 7000 at 14 kts
Complement: 26 (7 officers) plus 6 spare bunks

Comment: Built by Appledore Ferguson S B Fitted with 450 bhp bow thruster and helicopter platform. *Sulisker* completed 1981, *Vigilant* completed June 1982. Third ship of this class (although not identical) launched 11 September 1987 by Richards, Lowestoft and completed in June 1988. *Corystes* of this class was built for the Ministry of Agriculture and Fisheries in London.

SULISKER *6/1987, A. Denholm*

WESTRA

Displacement, tons: 778 light; 1285 full load
Measurement, tons: 942 gross
Dimensions, feet (metres): 195.3 × 35 × 14.4 *(59.6 × 10.7 × 4.4)*
Main machinery: 2 British Polar SP112VS-F diesels; 4200 hp *(3.13 MW)*; 1 shaft
Speed, knots: 15.5
Complement: 28

Comment: Built in 1975 by Hall Russell, Aberdeen. Near sister to RN Island class.

WESTRA *7/1982, van Ginderen Collection*

MOIDART **MORVEN**

Displacement, tons: 44 full load
Dimensions, feet (metres): 65 *(19.8)* long
Main machinery: 3 Detroit 8V 92TA diesels; 1050 hp *(783 kW)* sustained; 3 shafts
Speed, knots: 20
Complement: 5

Comment: Cheverton patrol craft completed April 1983. GRP hull.

MOIDART *1/1984, A. Denholm*

ROYAL CORPS OF TRANSPORT

4 LCVP 4

8402 **8409** **8619** **8620**

Displacement, tons: 9.7 light; 16 full load
Dimensions, feet (metres): 43.8 × 10.9 × 2.8 *(13.4 × 3.3 × 8)*
Main machinery: 2 Perkins diesels; 440 hp *(328 kW)*; 2 shafts
Speed, knots: 14
Complement: 3
Military lift: 35 troops or 5.5 tons vehicle/stores

Comment: One in Belize, one in Falklands and two in UK.

2 LOGISTIC LANDING CRAFT (LCLs) (HMAV)

Name	No	Builders	Commissioned
ARDENNES	L 4001	Brooke Marine, Lowestoft	1977
ARAKAN	L 4003	Brooke Marine, Lowestoft	1978

Displacement, tons: 1146 light; 1733 full load
Dimensions, feet (metres): 236.8 × 49.3 × 15 *(72.2 × 15 × 4.6)*
Main machinery: 2 Mirrlees-Blackstone ESL8 MCR diesels; 2200 hp *(1.64 MW)*; 2 shafts
Speed, knots: 10.3. **Range, miles:** 4000 at 10 kts
Complement: 35 (4 officers) plus 34 troops
Military lift: 350 tons stores or 36 ISO containers; 5 MBTs or 11—8 ton trucks

Comment: Both ordered in October 1974. 150 tons dieso fuel.

ARDENNES *5/1989, Gilbert Gyssels*

9 RAMPED CRAFT, LOGISTIC (RCLs)

Name	No	Builders	Commissioned
ARROMANCHES	L 105	Brooke Marine	31 July 1981
ANTWERP	L 106	Brooke Marine	14 Aug 1981
ANDALSNES	L 107	James and Stone, Brightlingsea	22 May 1984
ABBEVILLE	L 108	James and Stone, Brightlingsea	9 Nov 1984
AKYAB	L 109	James and Stone, Brightlingsea	15 Dec 1984
AACHEN	L 110	James and Stone, Brightlingsea	12 Feb 1987
AREZZO	L 111	James and Stone, Brightlingsea	26 Mar 1987
AGHEILA	L 112	James and Stone, Brightlingsea	12 June 1987
AUDEMER	L 113	James and Stone, Brightlingsea	21 Aug 1987

Displacement, tons: 290 full load
Dimensions, feet (metres): 109.2 × 27.2 × 4.9 *(33.3 × 8.3 × 1.5)*
Main machinery: 2 Dorman 8JTC WM diesels; 504 hp *(376 kW)* sustained; 2 shafts
Speed, knots: 10
Complement: 6 (2 NCOs)

Comment: *Arromanches* and *Antwerp* based in Cyprus; *Andalsnes, Abbeville* and *Akyab* in Hong Kong.

AACHEN *6/1991, Maritime Photographic*

3 AVON CLASS

EDEN RPL 05 **FORTH** RPL 06 **MEDWAY** RPL 12

Displacement, tons: 100 full load approx
Dimensions, feet (metres): 72.2 × 20.5 × 5.5 *(22 × 6.2 × 1.7)*
Main machinery: 2 diesels; 870 hp *(649 kW)*; 2 shafts
Speed, knots: 9
Complement: 6

Comment: Ramped Powered Lighters (RPL) manned by RCT and available for short coastal hauls. Built by White and Saunders-Roe, Isle of Wight in 1961-67. All assigned to Belize (one normally in refit in UK).

EDEN *3/1987, Michael D. J. Lennon*

1—15 METRE RANGE SAFETY CRAFT

SIR WILLIAM ROE 8127

Comment: Built by Halmatic in 1985. Details under RMAS 'Range Support Vessels'. The sole RCT survivor of a class of 13 of which 12 were transferred to the RMAS on 30 Septmeber 1988. Based in Cyprus.

4 WORK BOATS Mk II

BREAM WB 03 **PERCH** WB 06
ROACH WB 05 **MILL REEF** WB 08

Displacement, tons: 19
Dimensions, feet (metres): 47 *(14.3)* long
Speed, knots: 8

Comment: First three built 1966-71; last one built in 1987. Can be handled by LSLs.

PERCH *6/1987, Michael D. J. Lennon*

HM CUSTOMS

Note: The Customs and Excise (Marine Branch) of HM Treasury operates a considerable number of craft around the UK: two Brooke Marine 33 m craft *(Searcher, Seeker)*; three FBM Marine 26 m craft *(Vigilant, Valiant* and *Venturous)* two Fairey Marine 20 m craft *(Safeguard* and *Swift)*; five Cheverton 8.2 m craft *(Avocet, Bittern, Courser, Diver* and *Egret)*; plus 59 small craft ranging from 4 m Seariders to 10 m harbour launches. None of these vessels is armed.

VENTUROUS *8/1990, Maritime Photographic*

SEEKER *2/1992, Maritime Photographic*

TRINITY HOUSE

Note: A number of vessels of varying types—offshore support craft and lighthouse tenders—may be met throughout the waters of the UK.

THV PATRICIA *7/1990, Wright & Logan*

UNITED STATES OF AMERICA

Headquarters' Appointments

Chief of Naval Operations:
Admiral Frank B Kelso II
Vice Chief of Naval Operations:
Admiral Jerome L Johnson
Director, Naval Nuclear Propulsion Programme, Naval Sea Systems Command:
Admiral Bruce DeMars
US Representative to the NATO Military Committee:
Admiral William D Smith
Commander, Military Sealift Command:
Vice Admiral Francis R Donovan
Commander, Naval Air Systems Command:
Vice Admiral William C Bowes
Commander, Naval Sea Systems Command:
Vice Admiral Kenneth C Malley
Commander, Space and Naval Warfare Systems Command:
Rear Admiral Robert H Ailes

Commanders-in-Chief

Commander-in-Chief, US Atlantic Command and Supreme Allied Commander, Atlantic:
Admiral Paul D Miller
Commander-in-Chief, US Pacific Command:
Admiral Charles R Larson
Commander-in-Chief, US Atlantic Fleet:
Admiral Henry H Mauz Jr
Commander-in-Chief, US Pacific Fleet:
Admiral Robert J Kelly
Commander-in-Chief, US Naval Forces, Europe, and Allied Forces, Southern Europe:
Admiral Jeremy M Boorda

Flag Officers (Central Area)

Commander, US Naval Forces, Central Command and Middle East Force:
Rear Admiral Raynor A K Taylor
Commander, US Naval Forces, Central Command (Rear):
Rear Admiral David N Rogers

Flag Officers (Atlantic Area)

Commander, Second Fleet, US Atlantic Fleet and Striking Fleet, Atlantic:
Vice Admiral William J Flanagan Jr
Commander, Naval Surface Force, US Atlantic Fleet:
Vice Admiral Joseph P Reason
Commander, Sixth Fleet and Strike Force, South, Allied Naval Forces South:
Vice Admiral William A Owens
Commander, Submarine Force, US Atlantic Fleet and Submarine Allied Command, Atlantic:
Vice Admiral Henry G Chiles Jnr
Deputy Commander-in-Chief, US Naval Forces, Europe:
Vice Admiral Edward W Clexton Jnr
Commander, Naval Air Force, US Atlantic Fleet:
Vice Admiral Anthony A Less
Commander, Fleet Air, Keflavik and US Defense Force, Iceland:
Rear Admiral Thomas F Hall
Commander, South Atlantic Force, US Atlantic Fleet:
Rear Admiral Theodore C Lockhart
Commander, Mine Warfare Command:
Rear Admiral John D Pearson
Commander, Joint Task Force Four:
Rear Admiral George N Gee

Flag Officers (Pacific Area)

Commander, Seventh Fleet, US Pacific Fleet:
Vice Admiral Stanley R Arthur
Commander, Naval Surface Force, US Pacific Fleet:
Vice Admiral David M Bennett
Commander, Third Fleet, US Pacific Fleet:
Vice Admiral Jerry L Unruh
Commander, Naval Air Force, US Pacific Fleet:
Vice Admiral Edwin R Kohn Jnr
Commander, US Naval Forces, Japan:
Rear Admiral Jesse J Hernandez
Commander, Submarine Force, US Pacific Fleet:
Rear Admiral Henry C McKinney
Commander, US Naval Forces, Korea:
Rear Admiral William W Mathis

Marine Corps

Commandant:
General Carl E Mundy Jnr
Assistant Commandant:
General John R Dailey
Commander, Fleet Marine Force, Atlantic:
Lieutenant General William M Keys
Commander, Fleet Marine Force, Pacific:
Lieutenant General Royal N Moore Jnr

Territorial Seas

On 27 December 1988, the United States claimed territorial seas were extended from three to 12 nautical miles. The USA now exercises sovereignty over waters, seabed and airspace out to 12 nautical miles. This extension also applies to the Commonwealth of Puerto Rico, Guam, American Samoa, the US Virgin Islands, the Commonwealth of the Northern Mariana Islands and any other territory or possession over which the USA exercises sovereignty. The USA continues to recognise the right of all ships to conduct innocent passage and, in the case of international straits, the right of all ships and aircraft to conduct transit passage through its territorial sea.

Personnel

	1 Jan 1990	*31 Jan 1991*	*1 Jan 1992*
Navy			
Officers	74 374	76 894	72 392
Midshipmen	4557	4368	4273
Enlisted	529 925	532 516	505 174
Marine Corps			
Officers	20 099	20 605	19 753
Enlisted	176 857	179 643	174 287

Mercantile Marine

Lloyd's Register of Shipping:
6175 vessels of 18 583 989 tons gross

Strength of the Fleet (1992)

Type	*Active (NRF)*	*Building (Projected) or Conversion/SLEP*
SHIPS OF THE FLEET		
Strategic Missile Submarines		
SSBN (Ballistic Missile Submarines) (nuclear-powered)	25	6
Attack Submarines		
SSN Submarines (nuclear-powered)	83	14
Aircraft Carriers		
CVN Multi-purpose Aircraft Carriers (nuclear-powered)	6	3
CV Multi-purpose Aircraft Carriers (conventionally powered)	6	1
Cruisers		
CGN Guided Missile Cruisers (nuclear-powered)	9	—
CG Guided Missile Cruisers	40	5
Destroyers		
DDG Guided Missile Destroyers	9	12 (9)
DD Destroyers	31	—
Frigates		
FFG Guided Missile Frigates	35 (16)	—
FF Frigates	21 (8)	—
Light Forces		
PHM Guided Missile Patrol Combatants	6	—
PC Coastal Patrol Craft	—	13
Amphibious Warfare Ships		
LCC Amphibious Command Ships	2	—
LHA Amphibious Assault Ships (general purpose)	5	—
LHD Amphibious Assault Ships (multi-purpose)	1	4 (1)
LKA Amphibious Cargo Ships	5	—
LPD Amphibious Transport Docks	11	—
LPH Amphibious Assault Ships (helicopter)	7	—
LSD Dock Landing Ships	13	3
LST Tank Landing Ships	16 (3)	—
Mine Warfare Ships		
MCM Mine Countermeasures Ships	8	6
MSO Minesweepers (Ocean)	(9)	—
MHC Minehunters (Coastal)	—	7 (3)
Auxiliary Ships		
AD Destroyer Tenders	9	—
AE Ammunition Ships	12	—
AFS Combat Stores Ships	7	—
AGF Miscellaneous Command Ships	2	—
AGSS Auxiliary Research Submarine	1	—
AO Oilers	5	—
AOE Fast Combat Support Ships	4	4
AOR Replenishment Oilers	7	—
AR Repair Ships	1	—
ARL Repair Ship Small	1	—
ARS Salvage Ships	8 (3)	—
AS Submarine Tenders	11	—
ASR Submarine Rescue Ships	4	—
ATF Fleet Tugs	2	—
ATS Salvage and Rescue Ships	3	—
AVT Training Carrier	1	—
NAVAL RESERVE FORCE		
FF Frigates	8	—
FFG Guided Missile Frigates	16	—
LST Tank Landing Ships	3	—
MSO Minesweepers (Ocean)	9	—
ARS Salvage Ships	3	—
MILITARY SEALIFT COMMAND INVENTORY		
STRATEGIC SEALIFT (Active)		
Ocean Transportation Ships		
TAO/TAOT Oilers, Tankers	13	—
Ro-Ro, Freighters, Tankers	As required	—
Prepositioning Ships		
TAK/TAKB/TAKF Cargo Ships	7	—
TAOT Tankers	2	—
TAK Maritime Prepositioning Ships (MPS)	13	—
Naval Fleet Auxiliary Force		
TAO Oilers	13	8
TAFS Combat Stores Ships	3	—
TATF Fleet Ocean Tugs	7	—
TAGOS Ocean Surveillance Ships	20	4 (3)
TAK-FBM Fleet Ballistic Missile Ships	2	—
TAF Fleet Stores Ship	1	—
TAE Ammunition Ship	1	—
STRATEGIC SEALIFT (Reserve)		
Fast Sealift Ships		
TAKR Fast Sealift Ships (MPS)	8	—
Aviation Support Ships		
TAVB Aviation Support Ships (MPS)	2	—
Hospital Ships		
TAH Hospital Ships	2	—
Ready Reserve Force		
TAK, TAKR Cargo Ships	74	—
TAK Seatrain Ships	2	—
TAOT Tankers	8	—
TAOG Gasoline Tankers	3	—
TACS Auxiliary Crane Ships (MPS)	9	—
TAP Troop Ship	2	—

Type	Active (NRF)	Building (Projected) or Conversion/SLEP
SPECIAL MISSION SUPPORT SHIPS		
TAGFF Frigate Research Ship	1	—
TAGM/TAGDS Missile Range Instrumentation Ships	4	—
TAGOR Oceanographic Research Ships	2 (6 loan)	(1)
TAGS Surveying Ships	10	3
TAG Navigation Support Ship	1	—
TAG Acoustic Research Ship	1	—
TARC/TAK Cable Repairing Ships	2	—

Special Notes

To provide similar information to that included in other major navies' Deployment Tables the fleet assignment (abbreviated 'F/S') status of each ship in the US Navy has been included. The assignment appears in a column immediately to the right of the commissioning date. In the case of the Floating Dry Dock section this system is not used. The following abbreviations are used to indicate fleet assignments:

AA	active Atlantic Fleet
Active	active under charter with MSC
AR	in reserve Out of Commission, Atlantic Fleet
ASA	active In Service, Atlantic Fleet
ASR	in reserve Out of Service, Atlantic Fleet
Bldg	building
CONV	ship undergoing conversion
LOAN	ship or craft loaned to another government, or non-government agency, but US Navy retains title and the ship or craft is on the NVR
MAR	in reserve Out of Commission, Atlantic Fleet and laid up in the temporary custody of the Maritime Administration
MPR	same as 'MAR', but applies to the Pacific Fleet
NRF	assigned to the Naval Reserve Force (ships so assigned are listed in a special table for major warships and amphibious ships)
Ord	the contract for the construction of the ship has been let, but actual construction has not yet begun
PA	active Pacific Fleet
PR	in reserve Out of Commission, Pacific Fleet
Proj	the ship is scheduled for construction at some time in the immediate future
PSA	active In Service, Pacific Fleet
PSR	in reserve Out of Service, Pacific Fleet
ROS	reduced Operating Status
TAA	active Military Sealift Command, Atlantic Fleet
TAR	in Ready Reserve, Military Sealift Command, Atlantic Fleet
TPA	active Military Sealift Command, Pacific Fleet
TPR	in Ready Reserve, Military Sealift Command, Pacific Fleet
TWWR	active Military Sealift Command, World-wide Routes

Ship Status Definitions

In Commission: as a rule any ship, except a Service Craft, that is active, is in commission. The ship has a Commanding Officer and flies a commissioning pennant. 'Commissioning date' as used in this section means the date of being 'in commission' rather than 'completion' or 'acceptance into service' as used in some other navies.
In Service: all service craft (dry docks and with classifications that start with 'Y'), with the exception of *Constitution*, that are active, are 'in service'. The ship has an Officer-in-Charge and does not fly a commissioning pennant.
Ships 'in reserve, out of commission' or 'in reserve, out of service' are put in a state of preservation for future service. Depending on the size of the ship or craft, a ship in 'mothballs' usually takes from 30 days to nearly a year to restore to full operational service.
The above status definitions do not apply to the Military Sealift Command.

Approved Fiscal Year 1991 Programme

Shipbuilding	Appropriations (US$ million)
1 Ohio class SSBN (SSBN 743)	1298.0
1 Seawolf class SSN (SSN 22)	1781.7
4 Arleigh Burke class DDG (DDG 64-67)	3145.1
1 Wasp class LHD (LHD 51)	958.1
1 Whidbey Island CV class LSD (LSD 51)	245.0
2 Osprey class MHC (MHC 56-57)	203.8
12 Landing Craft, Air Cushion	267.5
Sealift	900.0

Approved Fiscal Year 1992 Programme

Shipbuilding	Appropriations (US$ million)
1 Seawolf class SSN (SSN 23)	1903.2
5 Arleigh Burke class DDG (DDG 68-72)	4107.7
3 Osprey class MHC (MHC 58-60)	341.0
1 Supply class AOE (AOE 9)	500.0
1 TAGOS Surtass Ship (TAGOS 24)	149.0
2 AGOR/TAGS Oceanographic Research Ships	99.8
24 Landing Craft, Air Cushion	504.0
Sealift	600.0
1 Whidbey Island CV class (LSD 52) authorised but not funded	

Note: SSN 22 and 23 cancelled in 1992.

Proposed Fiscal Year 1993 Programme

Shipbuilding	Appropriations (US$ million)
4 Arleigh Burke class DDG (DDG 73-76)	3369.6
2 Osprey class MHC (MHC 61-62)	246.2
Carrier Replacement Programme (Advance Procurement)	832.2
Sealift	1201.4

Note: The Sealift account is being established in FY 1993, with the sum above being the request for FY 1993. It also will be augmented by the $1875.1 million appropriated in prior years. The latter funds will be transferred from the Ship Construction, Navy (SCN) account, into which those dollars initially were assigned. It is to be augmented by leasing of DOD assets and the sale and scrapping of current Sealift assets as they reach the end of their service lives.

Provisional Shipbuilding Programme FY 1994-97

	94	95	96	97
CVN	—	1	—	—
DDG 51	3	4	4	4
MHC(V)	—	1	—	2
LHD	—	—	1	—
LX	—	1	—	1
AR	—	—	1	—
TAGOS	1	2	—	1
TAGS/AGOR	2	—	—	—

Naval Aviation

US Naval Aviation is scaling down to an active inventory of 5100 aircraft, with approximately 25 per cent of these being operated by the Marine Corps. The principal naval aviation organisations are 11 carrier air wings, 19 maritime patrol squadrons, and three Marine aircraft wings. In addition the Naval Reserve and the Marine Corps Reserve operate 11 fighter squadrons, two attack squadrons, and 11 maritime patrol squadrons, plus various electronic warfare, tanker, helicopter and transport units.

Fighter Attack: 23 Naval and 13 Marine Corps squadrons with F/A-18 Hornets. 22 Navy Squadrons for F-14 Tomcats.
Attack: 14 Navy and 2 Marine squadrons with A-6E Intruders. 8 Marine squadrons with AV-8B Harriers.
Airborne Early Warning: 12 Navy squadrons with E-2C Hawkeye aircraft.
Electronic Warfare: 13 Navy and 3 Marine squadrons with EA-6B Prowler aircraft.
Anti-Submarine: 11 Navy squadrons with S-3A/B Viking aircraft.
Maritime Patrol: 19 Navy squadrons with P-3B/C Orion aircraft.
Helicopter Anti-Submarine: 23 Navy squadrons with SH-3G/H Sea King, SH-2 LAMPS I, SH-60B and SH-60F LAMPS III helicopters.
Helicopter Mine Countermeasures: 3 Navy squadrons with MH-53E Sea Dragons.
Helicopter Support: 7 Navy squadrons with UH-46D/E Sea Knight and CH-53E Super Stallion helicopters.
Electronic Reconnaissance: 2 Navy squadrons with EP-3E Orion and 2 with ES-3A aircraft.
Communications Relay: 2 Navy squadrons with E-6A aircraft.
Helicopter Gunship: 6 Marine Corps squadrons with AH-1T/W SuperCobra and UH-1N Twin Huey helicopters.
Helicopter Transport: 24 Marine squadrons with CH-46D/E Sea Knight, and CH-53D Sea Stallion/CH-53E Super Stallion helicopters.

Aircraft Procurement Plan FY 1992-95

	92	93	94	95
AV8B	6	—	—	—
EA-6B	—	3	9	9
F/A-18C	48	48	39	45
CH/MH-53E	16	20	20	—
AH-1W	14	12	12	12
SH-60B	13	12	12	12
SH-60F	12	12	12	12
E-2C	6	—	—	—
T-45TS	12	12	36	48
HH-60H	—	7	8	9

Naval Special Warfare

SEAL (Sea Air Land) teams are manned at a nominal 10 platoons per team, with 30 platoons on each coast based at Coronado and Norfolk, Virginia. Assigned directly to CinC US Special Operations Command, platoons are allocated to theatre commanders during operational deployments.

Bases

Naval Air Stations and Air Facilities

NAS Adak, AK; NAS Alameda, CA; NAF China Lake, CA; NAF El Centro, CA; NAS Los Alamitos, CA; NAS Miramar; NAS Lemoore, CA; NAS Moffett Field (San Jose), CA; NAS Point Mugu, CA; NAS North Island (San Diego), CA; NAF Andrews, Washington DC; NAS Cecil Field (Jacksonville), FL; NAS Jacksonville, FL; NAS Key West, FL; NAS Whiting Field (Milton), FL; NAS Saufley Field (Pensacola), FL; NAS Pensacola, FL; NAS Mayport, FL; NAS Atlanta (Marietta), GA; NAS Glenview, Ill; NAS Barbers Point (Oahu), HI; NAS New Orleans, LA; NAS Brunswick, ME; NAS Patuxent River, MD; NAS South Weymouth, MA; NAF Detroit, MI; NAS Meridian, MS; NAS Fallon, NV; NAS Lakehurst, NJ; NAF Warminster, PA; NAS Willow Grove, PA; NAS Memphis (Millington), TN; NAS Chase Field (Beeville), TX; NAS Corpus Christi, TX; NAS Dallas, TX; NAS Kingsville, TX; NAS Norfolk, VA; NAS Oceana, VA; NAS Whidbey Island (Oak Harbor), WA; NAF Lajes, Azores; NAS Bermuda; NAS Guantanamo Bay, Cuba; NAF Naples, NAS Sigonella (Sicily), Italy; NAF Atsugi, Japan; NAS Agana, Guam; NAF Okinawa; NAS Diego Garcia.

Naval Stations and Naval Bases (24)

Yokosuka, Japan; Subic Bay, Philippines; Midway Is; Adak, AK; Pearl Harbor, HI; Treasure Is, San Francisco, CA; San Diego, CA; Coronado, San Diego, CA (Amphibs); Long Beach, CA; Mayport, FL; Roosevelt Roads, Puerto Rico; Guantanamo Bay, Cuba; Charleston, SC; Norfolk, VA; Little Creek, Norfolk, VA (Amphibs); Philadelphia, PA; Brooklyn, NY; New London, CT (Submarines); Newport, RI; Argentia, Newfoundland; Keflavik, Iceland; Rota, Spain; Naples, Italy; Staten Island, NY.

Strategic Missile Submarine Bases (3)

Charleston, SC; Bangor, WA (West Coast Trident base); Kings Bay, GA (East Coast Trident base)

Navy Yard (1)

Washington, DC (MSC Headquarters) (administration and historical activities).

Naval Shipyards (8)

Pearl Harbor, HI; Puget Sound, Bremerton, WA; Mare Is, Vallejo, CA; Charleston, SC; Norfolk, VA; Philadelphia, PA; Portsmouth, NH (located in Kittery, ME); Long Beach, CA.

Naval Ship Repair Facilities (3)

Yokosuka, Japan; Apra Harbor, Guam; Lumut, Singapore.

Marine Corps Air Stations and Helicopter Facilities (10)

MCAS: Beaufort, SC; El Toro (Santa Ana), CA; Yuma, AZ; Kaneohe Bay, Oahu, HI; Quantico, VA; Cherry Point, NC; Iwakuni, Honshu, Japan; New River (Jacksonville), NC.
MCHF: Tustin, CA; Futema, Okinawa.

Marine Corps Bases (5)

Camp Pendleton, CA; Twentynine Palms, CA; Camp H M Smith (Oahu), HI; Camp Lejeune, NC; Camp Smedley D Butler (Kawasaki), Okinawa, Japan.

CLASSIFICATION OF NAVAL SHIPS AND SERVICE CRAFT

COMBATANT SHIPS

WARSHIPS

Aircraft Carriers:

Aircraft Carrier	CV
Aircraft Carrier (nuclear propulsion)	CVN
Aircraft Carrier (for anti-submarine warfare)	CVS

Surface Combatants:

Battleship	BB
Gun Cruiser	CA
Guided Missile Cruiser	CG
Guided Missile Cruiser (nuclear propulsion)	CGN
Destroyer	DD
Guided Missile Destroyer	DDG
Frigate	FF
Guided Missile Frigate	FFG

Patrol Combatants:

Patrol Combatant	PG
Patrol Combatant Missile (hydrofoil)	PHM

Submarines:

Submarine	SS
Auxiliary Submarine	SSAG
Guided Missile Submarine	SSG
Attack Submarine (nuclear propulsion)	SSN
Ballistic Missile Submarine (nuclear propulsion)	SSBN

AMPHIBIOUS WARFARE SHIPS

Amphibious Command Ship	LCC
Amphibious Assault Ship (multi-purpose)	LHA/LHD
Amphibious Cargo Ship	LKA
Amphibious Transport	LPA
Amphibious Transport Dock	LPD
Amphibious Assault Ship (helicopter)	LPH
Dock Landing Ship	LSD
Tank Landing Ship	LST

MINE WARFARE SHIPS

Mine Countermeasures Ship	MCM
Minehunter Coastal	MHC
Minesweeper Ocean	MSO
Minesweeping Boats	MSB

COMBATANT CRAFT

AMPHIBIOUS WARFARE CRAFT

Amphibious Assault Landing Craft	AALC
Landing Craft, Air Cushion	LCAC
Landing Craft, Mechanised	LCM
Landing Craft, Personnel, Large	LCPL
Landing Craft, Utility	LCU
Landing Craft, Vehicle, Personnel	LCVP
Light Seal Support Craft	LSSC
Amphibious Warping Tug	LWT
Medium Seal Support Craft	MSSC
Swimmer Delivery Vehicle	SDV
Side Loading Warping Tug	SLWT
Special Warfare Craft, Light	SWCL
Special Warfare Craft, Medium	SWCM

MINE WARFARE CRAFT

Minesweeping Boat	MSB
Minesweeping, Drone	MSD
Minesweeper, Inshore	MSI
Minesweeper, River (converted LCM-6)	MSM
Minesweeper, Patrol	MSR

PATROL CRAFT

Mini-Armored Troop Carrier	ATC
Patrol Boat (Coastal)	PB(C)
River Patrol Boat	PBR
Patrol Craft (fast)	PCF
Patrol Gunboat (hydrofoil)	PGH
Fast Patrol Craft	PTF

AUXILIARY SHIPS

Destroyer Tender	AD
Ammunition Ship	AE
Store Ship	AF
Combat Store Ship	AFS
Miscellaneous	AG
Deep Submergence Support Ship	AGDS
Hydrofoil Research Ship	AGEH
Miscellaneous Command Ship	AGF
Frigate Research Ship	AGFF
Missile Range Instrumentation Ship	AGM
Oceanographic Research Ship	AGOR
Ocean Surveillance Ship	AGOS
Patrol Craft Tender	AGP
Surveying Ship	AGS
Auxiliary Research Submarine	AGSS
Hospital Ship	AH
Cargo Ship	AK
Vehicle Cargo Ship	AKR
Auxiliary Lighter	ALS
Oiler	AO
Fast Combat Support Ship	AOE
Gasoline Tanker	AOG
Replenishment Oiler	AOR
Transport Oiler	AOT
Transport	AP
Self-Propelled Barracks Ship	APB
Repair Ship	AR
Cable Repairing Ship	ARC
Repair Ship, Small	ARL
Salvage Ship	ARS
Submarine Tender	AS
Submarine Rescue Ship	ASR
Auxiliary Ocean Tug	ATA
Fleet Ocean Tug	ATF
Salvage and Rescue Ship	ATS
Guided Missile Ship	AVM
Auxiliary Aircraft Landing Training Ship	AVT

SERVICE CRAFT

Large Auxiliary Floating Dry Dock (non self-propelled)	AFDB
Small Auxiliary Floating Dry Dock (non self-propelled)	AFDL
Medium Auxiliary Floating Dry Dock (non self-propelled)	AFDM
Barracks Craft (non self-propelled)	APL
Auxiliary Repair Dry Dock (non self-propelled)	ARD
Medium Auxiliary Repair Dry Dock (non self-propelled)	ARDM
Deep Submergence Rescue Vehicle	DSRV
Deep Submergence Vehicle	DSV
Unclassified Miscellaneous	IX
Submersible Research Vehicle	NR
Miscellaneous Auxiliary (self-propelled)	YAG
Open Lighter (non self-propelled)	YC
Car Float (non self-propelled)	YCF
Aircraft Transportation Lighter (non self-propelled)	YCV
Floating Crane (non self-propelled)	YD
Diving Tender (non self-propelled)	YDT
Covered Lighter (self-propelled)	YF
Ferry Boat or Launch (self-propelled)	YFB
Yard Floating Dry Dock (non self-propelled)	YFD
Covered Lighter (non self-propelled)	YFN
Large Covered Lighter (non self-propelled)	YFNB
Dry Dock Companion Craft (non self-propelled)	YFND
Lighter (special purpose) (non self-propelled)	YFNX
Floating Power Barge (non self-propelled)	YFP
Refrigerated Covered Lighter (self propelled)	YFR
Refrigerated Covered Lighter (non self-propelled)	YFRN
Covered Lighter (range tender) (self-propelled)	YFRT
Harbor Utility Craft (self-propelled)	YFU
Garbage Lighter (self-propelled)	YG
Garbage Lighter (non self-propelled)	YGN
Salvage Lift Craft, Heavy (non self-propelled)	YHLC
Dredge (self-propelled)	YM
Salvage Lift Craft, Medium (non self-propelled)	YMLC
Gate Craft (non self-propelled)	YNG
Fuel Oil Barge (self-propelled)	YO
Gasoline Barge (self-propelled)	YOG
Gasoline Barge (non self-propelled)	YOGN
Fuel Oil Barge (non self-propelled)	YON
Oil Storage Barge (non self-propelled)	YOS
Patrol Craft (self-propelled)	YP
Floating Pile Driver (non self-propelled)	YPD
Floating Workshop (non self-propelled)	YR
Repair and Berthing Barge (non self-propelled)	YRB
Repair, Berthing and Messing Barge (non self-propelled)	YRBM
Floating Dry Dock Workshop (hull) (non self-propelled)	YRDH
Floating Dry Dock Workshop (machine) (non self-propelled)	YRDM
Radiological Repair Barge (non self-propelled)	YRR
Salvage Craft Tender (non self-propelled)	YRST
Seaplane Wrecking Derrick (self-propelled)	YSD
Sludge Removal Barge (non self-propelled)	YSR
Large Harbour Tug	YTB
Small Harbour Tug	YTL
Medium Harbour Tug	YTM
Water Barge (self-propelled)	YW
Water Barge (non self-propelled)	YWN

Letter prefixes to classification symbols may be added for further identification. E: prototype ship in an experimental or developmental status. T: assigned to Military Sealift Command. F: being built for a foreign government. X: often added to existing classifications to indicate a new class whose characteristics have not been defined. N: denotes nuclear propulsion when used as last letter of ship symbol.

Classification Of Maritime Administration Ship Designs

The US Maritime Administration is a Division of the US Department of Transportation. All US flag merchant vessels are built under the jurisdiction of the US Maritime Administration and are assigned Maritime Administration design classifications. These classifications consist of three groups of letters and numbers.

A number of US Naval Auxiliaries were originally built to Maritime Administration specifications and were acquired during construction or after the ship was completed. It should be noted that the Maritime Administration acts as a 'ship broker' for the US Government and does not build ships for itself. The Maritime Administration generally oversees the operation and administration of the US Merchant Marine.

Merchant Ship Design Classifications

	Length in feet at load water line			
Type	1	2	3	4
C Cargo	'400	400-450	450-500	500-550
P Passenger	'500	500-600	600-700	700-800
N Coastal Cargo	'200	200-250	250-300	300-350
R Refrigerated Cargo	'400	400-450	450-500	500-550
S Special (Navy)	'200	200-300	300-400	400-500
T Tanker	'450	450-500	500-550	550-600

Type of propulsion; number of propellers and passengers

	Single screw		*Twin screw*	
Passengers	1/12	13+	1/12	13+
Power				
Steam	S	S1	ST	S2
Motor (Diesel)	M	M1	MT	M2
Turbo-Electric	SE	SE1	SET	SE2

Example: C4-S-B1. C4: Cargo Ship between 500 and 550 ft long; S: steam powered; B1: 1st variation ('1') of the original design ('B'). If the third group of letters and numbers read BV1 instead of B1, the translation of the code would be, the 1st variation ('1') of the 22nd modification ('V') of the original design ('B').

Electronic Equipment Classification

The 'AN' nomenclature was designed so that a common designation could be used for Army, Navy and Air Force equipment. The system indicator 'AN' does not mean that the Army, Navy and Air Force use the equipment, but means that the type number was assigned in the 'AN' system.

'AN' nomenclature is assigned to complete sets of equipment and major components of military design; groups of articles of either commercial or military design which are grouped for military purposes; major articles of military design which are not part of or used with a set; and commercial articles when nomenclature will not facilitate military identification and/or procedures.

'AN' nomenclature is not assigned to articles catalogued commercially except as stated above; minor components of military design for which other adequate means of identification are available; small parts such as capacitors and resistors; and articles having other adequate identification in joint military specifications. Nomenclature assignments remain unchanged regardless of later installation and/or application.

Installation

A	Airborne (installed and operated in aircraft).
B	Underwater mobile, submarine.
C	Air transportable (inactivated, do not use).
D	Pilotless carrier.
F	Fixed.
G	Ground, general ground use (includes two or more ground-type installations).
K	Amphibious.
M	Ground, mobile (installed as operating unit in a vehicle which has no function other than transporting the equipment).
P	Pack or portable (animal or man).
S	Water surface craft.
T	Ground, transportable.
U	General utility (includes two or more general installation classes, airborne, shipboard, and ground).
V	Ground, vehicular (installed in vehicle designed for functions other than carrying electronic equipment, etc, such as tanks).
W	Water surface and underwater.

Type of Equipment

A Invisible light, heat radiation.
B Pigeon.
C Carrier.
D Radiac.
E Nupac.
F Photographic.
G Telegraph or teletype.
I Interphone and public address.
J Electromechanical or inertial wire covered.
K Telemetering.
L Countermeasures.
M Meteorological.
N Sound in air.
P Radar.
Q Sonar and underwater sound.
R Radio.
S Special types, magnetic, etc, or combinations of types.
T Telephone (wire).
V Visual and visible light.
W Armament (peculiar to armament, not otherwise covered).
X Facsimile or television.
Y Data processing.

Purpose

A Auxiliary assemblies (not complete operating sets used with or part of two or more sets or sets series).
B Bombing.
C Communications (receiving and transmitting).
D Direction finder, reconnaissance and/or surveillance.
E Ejection and/or release.
G Fire-control or searchlight directing.
H Recording and/or reproducing (graphic meteorological and sound).
K Computing.
L Searchlight control (inactivated, use G).
M Maintenance and test assemblies (including tools).
N Navigational aids (including altimeters, beacons, compasses, racons, depth sounding, approach, and landing).
P Reproducing (inactivated, do not use).
Q Special, or combination of purposes.
R Receiving, passive detecting.
S Detecting and/or range and bearing, search.
T Transmitting.
W Automatic flight or remote control.
X Identification and recognition.

Example: AN/URD-4A. AN: 'AN' System; U: General Utility; R: Radio; D: Direction Finder, Reconnaissance, and/or Surveillance; 4: Model Number; A: Modification Letter.

Major Commercial Shipyards

Avondale Industries, New Orleans, Louisiana
Avondale Gulfport, Gulfport, Mississippi
Bath Iron Works, Bath, Maine
Bethlehem Steel, Sparrows Point, Maryland
Bollinger Machine Shop and Shipyard, Lockport, Louisiana
Derecktor Shipyards, Middletown, Rhode Island
General Dynamics Corporation, Electric Boat Division, Groton, Connecticut
Halter Marine Inc, Moss Point, Mississippi
Ingalls Shipbuilding, Pascagoula, Mississippi
Intermarine USA, Savannah, Georgia
Marinette Marine, Marinette, Wisconsin
McDermott Shipyards, Morgan City, Louisiana
National Steel & Shipbuilding Company, San Diego, California
Newport News Shipbuilding Company, Newport News, Virginia
Peterson Builders Incorporated, Sturgeon Bay, Wisconsin
Tampa Shipyards, Tampa, Florida
Textron Marine Systems, New Orleans, Louisiana
Todd Shipyards Corporation, Galveston, Texas

Note: All the above yards have engaged in naval shipbuilding, overhaul, or modernisation except for the General Dynamics/ Electric Boat yard which is engaged only in submarine work. Newport News is the only US shipyard capable of building nuclear-powered aircraft carriers.

Ships Scheduled for Delivery during FY 1992 (22)

Fleet Ballistic Missile Submarine: *Maryland* (SSBN 738).
Attack Submarines: *Jefferson City* (SSN 759), *Annapolis* (SSN 760).
Aircraft Carrier: *George Washington* (CVN 73).
Cruisers: *Shiloh* (CG 67), *Anzio* (CG 68).
Guided Missile Destroyer: *John Barry* (DDG 52).
Amphibious Assault Ship: *Essex* (LHD 2).
Dock Landing Ship: *Ashland* (LSD 48).
Mine Countermeasures Ship: *Pioneer* (MCM 9).
Coastal Minehunter: *Osprey* (MHC 51).
Coastal Hydrographic Survey Ships: *John McDonnell* (TAGS 51), *Littlehales* (TAGS 52).
Oilers: *Isherwood* (TAO 191), *Kanawha* (TAO 196), *Big Horn* (TAO 198), *Guadalupe* (TAO 200).
Ocean Surveillance Ships (SWATH): *Able* (TAGOS 20), *Effective* (TAGOS 21).

CONVERSIONS:
Fleet Oilers (Jumbo): *Monongahela* (AO(J) 178), *Cimarron* (AO(J) 177).
Acoustic Research Ship: *Hayes* (TAG 195).

Ships Scheduled for Delivery during FY 1993 (19)

Attack Submarines: *Springfield* (SSN 761), *Columbus* (SSN 762).
Cruisers: *Vicksburg* (CG 69), *Cape St George* (CG 71).
Guided Missile Destroyers: *John Paul Jones* (DDG 53), *Curtis Wilbur* (DDG 54).
Amphibious Assault Ship: *Kearsage* (LHD 3).
Mine Countermeasures Ships: *Warrior* (MCM 10), *Gladiator* (MCM 11), *Ardent* (MCM 12).
Coastal Minehunter: *Heron* (MHC 52).
Oceanographic Survey Ship: *Waters* (TAGS 45).
Oilers: *Henry Eckford* (TAO 192), *Tippecanoe* (TAO 199), *Patuxent* (TAO 201), *Yukon* (TAO 202).
Ocean Surveillance Ship: *Loyal* (TAGOS 22).

CONVERSIONS:
Aircraft Carrier: *Constellation* (CV 64).
Fleet Oiler (Jumbo): *Platte* (AO(J) 186).

Major Warships Taken Out of Service mid-1989 to mid-1992

SSBN
1989 *John Adams, Andrew Jackson*
1990 *James Monroe, Henry Clay, Lafayette, Daniel Webster* (training ship)
1991 *Lewis and Clark, George C Marshall*
1992 *Alexander Hamilton, Woodrow Wilson, Tecumseh, Ulysses S Grant, George Washington Carver, Will Rodgers, James Madison*

SSN
1989 *Glenard P Lipscomb, Pollack, Skipjack, Skulpin*
1990 *Plunger, Dace, Shark, Queenfish, Sea Devil, Sam Houston, Barb, Jack*
1991 *Permit, Tinosa, Guardfish, Haddo, Lapon, Guitarro, Flasher, Greenling*
1992 *John Marshall, Gato, Haddock*

SS
1989 *Bonefish, Darter*
1990 *Barbel, Blueback*

CV
1990 *Coral Sea*
1991 *Midway, Lexington*

BB
1990 *Iowa, New Jersey*
1991 *Wisconsin*
1992 *Missouri*

DDG
1989 *Farragut, Coontz, Henry B Wilson, Sellers, Claude V Ricketts*
1990 *Joseph Strauss, John King, Lawrence, Byrd, Barney, Towers, Conyngham, Cochrane*
1991 *Dewey, Luce, King, Charles F Adams, Sampson, Hoel, Tattnall, William V Pratt, Preble, Lynde McCormick, Robison, Buchanan, Semmes, Goldsborough, Benjamin Stoddert, Waddell*

FF
1990 *Bronstein, McCloy, Glover* (to MSC)
1991/92 *Knox, Roark, Gray, Hepburn, Rathburne, Meyerkord, W S Sims, Lang, Patterson, Whipple, Bagley, Badger, Blakely, Brewton, Barbey, Miller, Valdez*

LSD/LPD/LST
1989 *Spiegel Grove, Hermitage* (Brazil)
1990 *Alamo* (Brazil)
1991 *Raleigh*
1992 *Vancouver, Barbour County*

MSO
1989 *Fidelity*
1990 *Fearless, Illusive, Inflict, Pluck*
1991 *Adroit, Engage, Enhance, Esteem, Exultant, Impervious, Leader*

Auxiliaries
1990 *Robert D Conrad* (AGOR), *Mispillion* (AO)
1991 *Vulcan* (AR), *Fulton* (AS), *Petrel* (ASR), *Florikan* (ASR), *Lynch* (AGOR), *H H Hess* (AGS), *Mississinewa* (AO), *Hassayampa* (AO), *Truckee* (AO), *Navasota* (AO), *Passumpsic* (AO), *Pawcatuck* (AO), *Waccamaw* (AO), *Neptune* (ARC)

HULL NUMBERS

Note: Ships in reserve not included.

SUBMARINES

Ballistic Missile Submarines

James Madison class
SSBN 629 Daniel Boone
SSBN 630 John C Calhoun
SSBN 632 Von Steuben
SSBN 633 Casimir Pulaski
SSBN 634 Stonewall Jackson

Benjamin Franklin class
SSBN 640 Benjamin Franklin
SSBN 641 Simon Bolivar
SSBN 642 Kamehameha
SSBN 643 George Bancroft
SSBN 645 James K Polk
SSBN 655 Henry L Stimson
SSBN 657 Francis Scott Key
SSBN 658 Mariano G Vallejo

Ohio class
SSBN 726 Ohio
SSBN 727 Michigan
SSBN 728 Florida
SSBN 729 Georgia
SSBN 730 Henry M Jackson
SSBN 731 Alabama
SSBN 732 Alaska
SSBN 733 Nevada
SSBN 734 Tennessee
SSBN 735 Pennsylvania
SSBN 736 West Virginia
SSBN 737 Kentucky
SSBN 738 Maryland
SSBN 739 Nebraska
SSBN 740 Rhode Island
SSBN 741 Maine
SSBN 742 Wyoming

Attack Submarines

Seawolf class
SSN 21 Seawolf

Sturgeon class
SSN 637 Sturgeon
SSN 638 Whale
SSN 639 Tautog
SSN 646 Grayling
SSN 647 Pogy
SSN 648 Aspro
SSN 649 Sunfish
SSN 650 Pargo
SSN 652 Puffer
SSN 653 Ray
SSN 660 Sand Lance
SSN 662 Gurnard
SSN 663 Hammerhead
SSN 666 Hawkbill
SSN 667 Bergall
SSN 668 Spadefish
SSN 669 Seahorse
SSN 670 Finback
SSN 672 Pintado
SSN 673 Flying Fish
SSN 674 Trepang
SSN 675 Bluefish
SSN 676 Billfish
SSN 677 Drum
SSN 678 Archerfish
SSN 679 Silversides
SSN 680 William H Bates
SSN 681 Batfish
SSN 682 Tunny
SSN 683 Parche
SSN 684 Cavalla
SSN 686 L Mendel Rivers
SSN 687 Richard B Russell

Narwhal class
SSN 671 Narwhal

Los Angeles class
SSN 688 Los Angeles
SSN 689 Baton Rouge
SSN 690 Philadelphia
SSN 691 Memphis
SSN 692 Omaha
SSN 693 Cincinnati
SSN 694 Groton
SSN 695 Birmingham
SSN 696 New York City
SSN 697 Indianapolis
SSN 698 Bremerton
SSN 699 Jacksonville
SSN 700 Dallas
SSN 701 La Jolla
SSN 702 Phoenix
SSN 703 Boston
SSN 704 Baltimore
SSN 705 City of Corpus Christi
SSN 706 Albuquerque
SSN 707 Portsmouth
SSN 708 Minneapolis—Saint Paul
SSN 709 Hyman G Rickover
SSN 710 Augusta
SSN 711 San Francisco
SSN 712 Atlanta
SSN 713 Houston
SSN 714 Norfolk
SSN 715 Buffalo
SSN 716 Salt Lake City
SSN 717 Olympia
SSN 718 Honolulu
SSN 719 Providence
SSN 720 Pittsburgh
SSN 721 Chicago
SSN 722 Key West
SSN 723 Oklahoma City
SSN 724 Louisville
SSN 725 Helena
SSN 750 Newport News

Attack Submarines

SSN 751 San Juan
SSN 752 Pasadena
SSN 753 Albany
SSN 754 Topeka
SSN 755 Miami
SSN 756 Scranton
SSN 757 Alexandria
SSN 758 Asheville
SSN 759 Jefferson City
SSN 760 Annapolis
SSN 761 Springfield
SSN 762 Columbus
SSN 763 Santa Fe
SSN 764 Boise
SSN 765 Montpelier
SSN 766 Charlotte
SSN 767 Hampton
SSN 768 Hartford
SSN 769 Toledo
SSN 770 Tucson
SSN 771 Columbia
SSN 772 Greeneville
SSN 773 Cheyenne

SURFACE COMBATANTS

Aircraft Carriers

Forrestal class
AVT 59 Forrestal
CV 60 Saratoga
CV 61 Ranger
CV 62 Independence

Kitty Hawk class
CV 63 Kitty Hawk
CV 64 Constellation
CV 66 America

John F Kennedy class
CV 67 John F Kennedy

Enterprise class
CVN 65 Enterprise

Nimitz class
CVN 68 Nimitz
CVN 69 Dwight D Eisenhower
CVN 70 Carl Vinson
CVN 71 Theodore Roosevelt
CVN 72 Abraham Lincoln
CVN 73 George Washington
CVN 74 John C Stennis
CVN 75 United States

Cruisers

Leahy class
CG 16 Leahy
CG 17 Harry E Yarnell
CG 18 Worden
CG 19 Dale
CG 20 Richmond K Turner
CG 21 Gridley
CG 22 England
CG 23 Halsey
CG 24 Reeves

Belknap class
CG 26 Belknap
CG 27 Josephus Daniels
CG 28 Wainwright
CG 29 Jouett
CG 30 Horne
CG 31 Sterett
CG 32 William H Standley
CG 33 Fox
CG 34 Biddle

Ticonderoga class
CG 47 Ticonderoga
CG 48 Yorktown
CG 49 Vincennes
CG 50 Valley Forge
CG 51 Thomas S Gates
CG 52 Bunker Hill
CG 53 Mobile Bay
CG 54 Antietam
CG 55 Leyte Gulf
CG 56 San Jacinto
CG 57 Lake Champlain
CG 58 Philippine Sea
CG 59 Princeton
CG 60 Normandy
CG 61 Monterey
CG 62 Chancellorsville
CG 63 Cowpens
CG 64 Gettysburg
CG 65 Chosin
CG 66 Hue City
CG 67 Shiloh
CG 68 Anzio
CG 69 Vicksburg
CG 70 Lake Erie
CG 71 Cape St George
CG 72 Vella Gulf
CG 73 Port Royal

Long Beach class
CGN 9 Long Beach

Bainbridge class
CGN 25 Bainbridge

Truxtun class
CGN 35 Truxtun

California class
CGN 36 California
CGN 37 South Carolina

Virginia class
CGN 38 Virginia
CGN 39 Texas
CGN 40 Mississippi
CGN 41 Arkansas

Destroyers

Spruance class
DD 963 Spruance
DD 964 Paul F Foster
DD 965 Kinkaid
DD 966 Hewitt
DD 967 Elliott
DD 968 Arthur W Radford
DD 969 Peterson
DD 970 Caron
DD 971 David R Ray
DD 972 Oldendorf
DD 973 John Young
DD 974 Comte de Grasse
DD 975 O'Brien
DD 976 Merrill
DD 977 Briscoe
DD 978 Stump
DD 979 Conolly
DD 980 Moosbrugger
DD 981 John Hancock
DD 982 Nicholson
DD 983 John Rodgers
DD 984 Leftwich
DD 985 Cushing
DD 986 Harry W Hill
DD 987 O'Bannon
DD 988 Thorn
DD 989 Deyo
DD 990 Ingersoll
DD 991 Fife
DD 992 Fletcher
DD 997 Hayler

Charles F Adams class
DDG 15 Berkeley

Coontz class
DDG 39 MacDonough
DDG 42 Mahan
DDG 43 Dahlgren

Arleigh Burke class
DDG 51 Arleigh Burke
DDG 52 Barry
DDG 53 John Paul Jones
DDG 54 Curtis Wilbur
DDG 55 Stout
DDG 56 John S McCain
DDG 57 Mitscher
DDG 58 Laboon
DDG 59 Russell
DDG 60 Paul Hamilton
DDG 61 Ramage
DDG 62 Fitzgerald
DDG 63 Stethem
DDG 64 Carney
DDG 65 Benfold
DDG 66 Gonzalez
DDG 67 Cole

Kidd class
DDG 993 Kidd
DDG 994 Callaghan
DDG 995 Scott
DDG 996 Chandler

Frigates

Knox class
FF 1056 Connole
FF 1063 Reasoner
FF 1064 Lockwood
FF 1065 Stein
FF 1066 Marvin Shields
FF 1067 Francis Hammond
FF 1068 Vreeland
FF 1070 Downes
FF 1073 Robert E Peary
FF 1074 Harold E Holt
FF 1075 Trippe
FF 1076 Fanning
FF 1077 Ouellet
FF 1078 Joseph Hewes
FF 1079 Bowen
FF 1080 Paul
FF 1081 Aylwin
FF 1082 Elmer Montgomery
FF 1083 Cook
FF 1084 McCandless
FF 1085 Donald B Beary
FF 1087 Kirk
FF 1089 Jesse L Brown
FF 1090 Ainsworth
FF 1092 Thomas C Hart
FF 1093 Capodanno
FF 1094 Pharris
FF 1095 Truett
FF 1097 Moinester

Oliver Hazard Perry class
FFG 7 Oliver Hazard Perry
FFG 8 McInerney
FFG 9 Wadsworth
FFG 10 Duncan
FFG 11 Clark
FFG 12 George Philip
FFG 13 Samuel Eliot Morison
FFG 14 John H Sides
FFG 15 Estocin
FFG 16 Clifton Sprague
FFG 19 John A Moore
FFG 20 Antrim
FFG 21 Flatley
FFG 22 Fahrion
FFG 23 Lewis B Puller
FFG 24 Jack Williams
FFG 25 Copeland
FFG 26 Gallery
FFG 27 Mahlon S Tisdale
FFG 28 Boone
FFG 29 Stephen W Groves
FFG 30 Reid
FFG 31 Stark
FFG 32 John L Hall
FFG 33 Jarrett
FFG 34 Aubrey Fitch
FFG 36 Underwood
FFG 37 Crommelin
FFG 38 Curts
FFG 39 Doyle
FFG 40 Halyburton
FFG 41 McClusky
FFG 42 Klakring
FFG 43 Thach
FFG 45 De Wert
FFG 46 Rentz
FFG 47 Nicholas
FFG 48 Vandegrift
FFG 49 Robert G Bradley
FFG 50 Taylor
FFG 51 Gary
FFG 52 Carr
FFG 53 Hawes
FFG 54 Ford
FFG 55 Elrod
FFG 56 Simpson
FFG 57 Reuben James
FFG 58 Samuel B Roberts
FFG 59 Kauffman
FFG 60 Rodney M Davis
FFG 61 Ingraham

Hydrofoil Missile Ships

Pegasus class
PHM 1 Pegasus
PHM 2 Hercules
PHM 3 Taurus
PHM 4 Aquila
PHM 5 Aries
PHM 6 Gemini

AMPHIBIOUS WARFARE SHIPS

Amphibious Assault Ships

Wasp class
LHD 1 Wasp
LHD 2 Essex
LHD 3 Kearsage
LHD 4 Boxer
LHD 5 Bataan

Tarawa class
LHA 1 Tarawa
LHA 2 Saipan
LHA 3 Belleau Wood
LHA 4 Nassau
LHA 5 Peleliu

Iwo Jima class
LPH 2 Iwo Jima
LPH 3 Okinawa
LPH 7 Guadalcanal
LPH 9 Guam
LPH 10 Tripoli
LPH 11 New Orleans
LPH 12 Inchon

Amphibious Transport Docks

Austin class
LPD 4 Austin
LPD 5 Ogden
LPD 6 Duluth
LPD 7 Cleveland
LPD 8 Dubuque
LPD 9 Denver
LPD 10 Juneau
LPD 12 Shreveport
LPD 13 Nashville
LPD 14 Trenton
LPD 15 Ponce

Amphibious Cargo Ships

Charleston class
LKA 113 Charleston
LKA 114 Durham
LKA 115 Mobile
LKA 116 Saint Louis
LKA 117 El Paso

Anchorage class
LSD 36 Anchorage
LSD 37 Portland
LSD 38 Pensacola
LSD 39 Mount Vernon
LSD 40 Fort Fisher

Whidbey Island class
LSD 41 Whidbey Island
LSD 42 Germantown
LSD 43 Fort McHenry
LSD 44 Gunston Hall
LSD 45 Comstock
LSD 46 Tortuga
LSD 47 Rushmore
LSD 48 Ashland
LSD 49 Harpers Ferry
LSD 50 Carter Hall
LSD 51 Oak Hill

Tank Landing Ships

Newport class
LST 1179 Newport
LST 1180 Manitowoc
LST 1181 Sumter
LST 1182 Fresno
LST 1183 Peoria
LST 1184 Frederick
LST 1185 Schenectady
LST 1186 Cayuga
LST 1187 Tuscaloosa
LST 1188 Saginaw
LST 1189 San Bernardino
LST 1190 Boulder
LST 1191 Racine
LST 1192 Spartanburg County
LST 1193 Fairfax County
LST 1194 La Moure County
LST 1196 Harlan County
LST 1197 Barnstable County
LST 1198 Bristol County

Amphibious Command Ships

Blue Ridge class
LCC 19 Blue Ridge
LCC 20 Mount Whitney

MINE WARFARE SHIPS

Ocean Minesweepers

Aggressive class
MSO 427 Constant
MSO 439 Excel
MSO 440 Exploit
MSO 446 Fortify
MSO 455 Implicit
MSO 488 Conquest
MSO 489 Gallant
MSO 492 Pledge

Acme class
MSO 511 Affray

Mine Countermeasures Ships

Avenger class
MCM 1 Avenger
MCM 2 Defender
MCM 3 Sentry
MCM 4 Champion
MCM 5 Guardian
MCM 6 Devastator
MCM 7 Patriot
MCM 8 Scout
MCM 9 Pioneer
MCM 10 Warrior
MCM 11 Gladiator
MCM 12 Ardent
MCM 13 Dextrous
MCM 14 Chief

Osprey class
MHC 51 Osprey
MHC 52 Heron
MHC 53 Pelican
MHC 54 Robin
MHC 55 Oriole
MHC 56 Kingfisher
MHC 57 Cormorant

UNDERWAY REPLENISHMENT SHIPS

Ammunition Ships

Suribachi class
AE 21 Suribachi
AE 22 Mauna Kea

Nitro class
AE 23 Nitro
AE 24 Pyro
AE 25 Haleakala

Kilauea class
AE 27 Butte
AE 28 Santa Barbara
AE 29 Mount Hood
AE 32 Flint
AE 33 Shasta
AE 34 Mount Baker
AE 35 Kiska

Combat Stores Ships

Mars class
AFS 1 Mars
AFS 2 Sylvania

Combat Stores Ships

AFS 3 Niagara Falls
AFS 4 White Plains
AFS 5 Concord
AFS 6 San Diego
AFS 7 San Jose

Fleet Oilers

Cimarron class
AO 177 Cimarron
AO 178 Monongahela
AO 179 Merrimack
AO 180 Willamette
AO 186 Platte

Fast Combat Support Ships

Sacramento class
AOE 1 Sacramento
AOE 2 Camden
AOE 3 Seattle
AOE 4 Detroit

Supply class
AOE 6 Supply
AOE 7 Rainier
AOE 8 Arctic

Replenishment Oilers

Wichita class
AOR 1 Wichita
AOR 2 Milwaukee
AOR 3 Kansas City
AOR 4 Savannah
AOR 5 Wabash
AOR 6 Kalamazoo
AOR 7 Roanoke

MATERIAL SUPPORT SHIPS

Destroyer Tenders

Dixie class
AD 15 Prairie
AD 18 Sierra
AD 19 Yosemite

Samuel Gompers class
AD 37 Samuel Gompers
AD 38 Puget Sound

Yellowstone class
AD 41 Yellowstone
AD 42 Acadia
AD 43 Cape Cod
AD 44 Shenandoah

Repair Ship

Vulcan class
AR 8 Jason

Submarine Tenders

Fulton class
AS 18 Orion

Proteus class
AS 19 Proteus

Hunley class
AS 31 Hunley
AS 32 Holland

Simon Lake class
AS 33 Simon Lake
AS 34 Canopus

Spear class
AS 36 L Y Spear
AS 37 Dixon

Emory S Land class
AS 39 Emory S Land
AS 40 Frank Cable
AS 41 McKee

Salvage Ships

Bolster class
ARS 8 Preserver
ARS 38 Bolster
ARS 39 Conserver
ARS 40 Hoist
ARS 41 Opportune
ARS 42 Reclaimer
ARS 43 Recovery

Safeguard class
ARS 50 Safeguard
ARS 51 Grasp
ARS 52 Salvor
ARS 53 Grapple

Edenton class
ATS 1 Edenton
ATS 2 Beaufort
ATS 3 Brunswick

Submarine Rescue Ships

Chanticleer class
ASR 13 Kittiwake
ASR 15 Sunbird

Pigeon class
ASR 21 Pigeon
ASR 22 Ortolan

Fleet Ocean Tugs

Abnaki class
ATF 159 Paiute
ATF 160 Papago

SHIPS WITH MISCELLANEOUS MISSIONS

Miscellaneous Flagships

Raleigh and Austin classes
AGF 3 La Salle
AGF 11 Coronado

Auxiliary Research Submarine

Dolphin class
AGSS 555 Dolphin

SHIPS OF THE MILITARY SEALIFT COMMAND

(These ships, when operational, are manned by civilian crews, and carry the prefix 'T' before their normal Hull Numbers)

NAVAL FLEET AUXILIARY FORCE

Fleet Ballistic Missile Support Ships

TAK 282 Marshfield
TAK 286 Vega

Ammunition Ship

TAE 26 Kilauea

Fleet Stores Ship

TAF 58 Rigel

Combat Stores Ships

TAFS 8 Sirius
TAFS 9 Spica
TAFS 10 Saturn

Oilers

Neosho class
TAO 143 Neosho
TAO 146 Kawishiwi
TAO 148 Ponchatoula

Henry J Kaiser class
TAO 187 Henry J Kaiser
TAO 188 Joshua Humphreys
TAO 189 John Lenthall
TAO 190 Andrew J Higgins
TAO 191 Benjamin Isherwood
TAO 192 Henry Eckford
TAO 193 Walter S Diehl
TAO 194 John Ericsson
TAO 195 Leroy Grumman
TAO 196 Kanawha
TAO 197 Pecos
TAO 198 Big Horn
TAO 199 Tippicanoe
TAO 200 Guadaloupe
TAO 201 Patuxent
TAO 202 Yukon
TAO 203 Laramie
TAO 204 Rappahannock

Fleet Ocean Tugs

Powhatan class
TATF 166 Powhatan
TATF 167 Narragansett
TATF 168 Catawba
TATF 169 Navajo
TATF 170 Mohawk
TATF 171 Sioux
TATF 172 Apache

Ocean Surveillance Ships

TAGOS 1 Stalwart
TAGOS 2 Contender
TAGOS 3 Vindicator
TAGOS 4 Triumph
TAGOS 5 Assurance
TAGOS 6 Persistent
TAGOS 7 Indomitable
TAGOS 8 Prevail
TAGOS 9 Assertive
TAGOS 10 Invincible
TAGOS 11 Audacious
TAGOS 12 Bold
TAGOS 13 Adventurous
TAGOS 14 Worthy
TAGOS 15 Titan
TAGOS 16 Capable
TAGOS 17 Intrepid
TAGOS 18 Relentless

Ocean Surveillance Ships (SWATH)

TAGOS 19 Victorious
TAGOS 20 Able
TAGOS 21 Effective
TAGOS 22 Loyal
TAGOS 23 Impeccable

STRATEGIC SEALIFT (Active)

Maritime Prepositioning Ships (MPS)

(These 13 ships are divided into three squadrons and are almost constantly underway. Each squadron contains the equipment and 30 days of supplies for a marine amphibious brigade.)

TAK 3000 Cpl Louis J Hauge Jr
TAK 3001 Pfc William B Baugh
TAK 3002 Pfc James Anderson Jr
TAK 3003 1st Lt Alexander Bonnyman Jr
TAK 3004 Pvt Harry Fisher
TAK 3005 Sgt Matej Kocak
TAK 3006 Pfc Eugene A Obregon
TAK 3007 Maj Stephen W Pless
TAK 3008 2nd Lt John P Bobo
TAK 3009 Pfc Dewayne T Williams
TAK 3010 1st Lt Baldomero Lopez
TAK 3011 1st Lt Jack Lummus
TAK 3012 Staff Sgt William R Button

Prepositioning (PREPO) Ships

Lash

TAK 1015 Green Island
TAK 2043 American Kestrel
TAK 2046 Austral Rainbow
TAK 2064 Green Harbour

Freighters

TAK 5076 Noble Star
TAK 2040 Advantage
TAK 2062 American Cormorant

Tankers

TAOT 170 Sealift China Sea
TAOT 181 Potomac

Ocean Transportation Ships

In addition to the ships listed, there were 40 merchant ships under charter in early 1992. No numbers are allocated and ships come and go as needed to meet MSC commitments. Types of vessel include Ro-Ro, Freighters, Tankers and Combination ships.

Tankers

TAOT 168 Sealift Pacific
TAOT 169 Sealift Arabian Sea
TAOT 171 Sealift Indian Ocean
TAOT 172 Sealift Atlantic
TAOT 173 Sealift Mediterranean
TAOT 174 Sealift Caribbean
TAOT 175 Sealift Arctic
TAOT 176 Sealift Antarctic
TAOT 1121 Gus W Darnell
TAOT 1122 Paul Buck
TAOT 1123 Samuel L Cobb
TAOT 1124 Richard G Matthieson
TAOT 1125 Lawrence H Gianella

STRATEGIC SEALIFT (Reserve)

Fast Sealift Ships

(These ships are maintained in a high state of readiness for deployment with equipment for a full Army division, but have only skeleton crews except when assigned to specific missions.)

TAKR 287 Algol
TAKR 288 Bellatrix
TAKR 289 Denebola
TAKR 290 Pollux
TAKR 291 Altair
TAKR 292 Regulus
TAKR 293 Capella
TAKR 294 Antares

Aviation Support Ships

TAVB 3 Wright
TAVB 4 Curtiss

Hospital Ships

TAH 19 Mercy
TAH 20 Comfort

SPECIAL MISSION SUPPORT SHIPS

Frigate Research Ship

T-AGFF1 Glover

Missile Range Instrumentation Ships

TAGM 20 Redstone
TAGM 22 Range Sentinel
TAGM 23 Observation Island

Oceanographic Research Ships

TAGOR 10 Thomas Washington (loan)
TAGOR 12 De Steigeur
TAGOR 13 Bartlett
TAGOR 14 Melville (loan)
TAGOR 15 Knorr (loan)
TAGOR 21 Gyre (loan)
TAGOR 22 Moana Wave (loan)
TAGOR 23 Thomas G Thompson (loan)
TAG 195 Hayes

Surveying Ships

TAGS 26 Silas Bent
TAGS 27 Kane
TAGS 29 Chauvenet
TAGS 32 Harkness
TAGS 33 Wilkes
TAGS 34 Wyman
TAGS 39 Maury
TAGS 40 Tanner
TAGS 45 Waters
TAGS 51 John McDonnell
TAGS 52 Littlehales
TAGS 60 Pathfinder
TAGS 61 Sumner

Navigation Test Support Ship

TAG 194 Vanguard

Cable Repair Ships

TARC 6 Albert J Myer
TARC 7 Zeus

Deep Submergence Support Ship

TAGDS 2 Point Loma

Ready Reserve Force (RRF)

(See page 791)

SUBMARINES

Strategic Missile Submarines (SSBN)

Notes: The current SSBN force provides the principle US strategic deterrent. Land and air based systems have been sharply reduced since 1991. All SSBNs built before the Ohio class are over 25 years old. As a result of the decline of the threat from the former Soviet Union, Poseidon fitted submarines ceased operational patrols in October 1991 and all except two have been withdrawn from service. The whole force comes under the US Strategic Command Headquarters at Offut Air Force Base, Nebraska.

Strategic Cruise Missiles: There is a canister version of the Tomahawk SLCM which can be carried in submarines. This is an underwater-launched weapon with ram-jet propulsion which can deliver nuclear warheads to a range of approximately 2500 km *(1400 nm)*. A shorter-range version of the weapon with a conventional warhead has a land attack capability to 900 km *(485 nm)* which is increased by more than 30 per cent in the Block III version approved for production in early 1992. The strategic cruise missile has a low-level, terrain-following flight path over land, much like that of a manned bomber in contrast to the ballistic trajectory of a Polaris/Poseidon/Trident missile. In September 1991 all nuclear capable Tomahawks were removed from both submarines and surface ships.

Names: When the Polaris submarine programme was initiated, ballistic missile submarines were named after 'distinguished Americans who were known for their devotion to freedom'. Included as 'Americans' were Latin American and Hawaiian leaders, and several Europeans who supported the American fight for independence. In 1976 the SSBN name source was changed to States of the Union, although an exception was made in September 1983 when the selected name of SSBN 730 was changed from *Rhode Island* to *Henry M Jackson*. Jackson was a long time Senator from the State of Washington, a presidential candidate in 1976 and one of the most vigorous and outspoken advocates of a strong national defence.

12 + 6 OHIO CLASS (SSBN)

Name	*No*	*Builders*	*Launched*	*Commissioned*	*F/S*
OHIO	SSBN 726	General Dynamics (Electric Boat Div)	7 Apr 1979	11 Nov 1981	PA
MICHIGAN	SSBN 727	General Dynamics (Electric Boat Div)	26 Apr 1980	11 Sep 1982	PA
FLORIDA	SSBN 728	General Dynamics (Electric Boat Div)	14 Nov 1981	18 June 1983	PA
GEORGIA	SSBN 729	General Dynamics (Electric Boat Div)	6 Nov 1982	11 Feb 1984	PA
HENRY M JACKSON	SSBN 730	General Dynamics (Electric Boat Div)	15 Oct 1983	6 Oct 1984	PA
ALABAMA	SSBN 731	General Dynamics (Electric Boat Div)	19 May 1984	25 May 1985	PA
ALASKA	SSBN 732	General Dynamics (Electric Boat Div)	12 Jan 1985	25 Jan 1986	PA
NEVADA	SSBN 733	General Dynamics (Electric Boat Div)	14 Sep 1985	16 Aug 1986	PA
TENNESSEE	SSBN 734	General Dynamics (Electric Boat Div)	13 Dec 1986	17 Dec 1988	AA
PENNSYLVANIA	SSBN 735	General Dynamics (Electric Boat Div)	23 Apr 1988	9 Sep 1989	AA
WEST VIRGINIA	SSBN 736	General Dynamics (Electric Boat Div)	14 Oct 1989	20 Oct 1990	AA
KENTUCKY	SSBN 737	General Dynamics (Electric Boat Div)	11 Aug 1990	13 July 1991	AA
MARYLAND	SSBN 738	General Dynamics (Electric Boat Div)	10 Aug 1991	June 1992	Bldg/AA
NEBRASKA	SSBN 739	General Dynamics (Electric Boat Div)	Aug 1992	Aug 1993	Bldg/AA
RHODE ISLAND	SSBN 740	General Dynamics (Electric Boat Div)	July 1993	Aug 1994	Bldg
MAINE	SSBN 741	General Dynamics (Electric Boat Div)	July 1994	Aug 1995	Bldg
WYOMING	SSBN 742	General Dynamics (Electric Boat Div)	July 1995	Aug 1996	Bldg
—	SSBN 743	General Dynamics (Electric Boat Div)	July 1996	Aug 1997	Bldg

Displacement, tons: 16 600 surfaced; 18 750 dived
Dimensions, feet (metres): 560 × 42 × 36.4 *(170.7 × 12.8 × 11.1)*
Main machinery: Nuclear; 1 GE PWR S8G; 2 turbines; 60 000 hp *(44.8 MW)*; 1 shaft; 1 Magnetek auxiliary prop motor; 325 hp *(242 kW)*
Speed, knots: 20+ dived
Complement: 155 (14 officers in first 6, 15 in remainder)

Missiles: SLBM: 24 Lockheed Trident 1 (C4) (726-733); stellar inertial guidance to 7400 km *(4000 nm)*; thermonuclear warhead of 8 MIRV of 100 kT or 6 MARV of 100 kT; CEP 450 m. The Mk 500 MARV (Manoeuvring Re-entry Vehicle) is under development to demonstrate its compatibility with the Trident I missile. This re-entry vehicle is intended to evade ABM interceptor missiles.
24 Lockheed Trident 2 (D5) (734 onwards); stellar inertial guidance to 12 000 km *(6500 nm)*; thermonuclear warhead of 12 MIRV of 150 kT or 7 MARV of 300-475 kT; CEP 90 m.
Torpedoes: 4—21 in *(533 mm)* Mk 68 bow tubes. Gould Mk 48; wire-guided (option); active/passive homing to 50 km *(27 nm)*/38 km *(21 nm)* at 40/55 kts; warhead 267 kg; depth to 900 m *(2950 ft)*.
Countermeasures: Decoys: 8 launchers for Emerson Electric Mk 2; torpedo decoy.
ESM: WLR-8(V)5; intercept.
Combat data systems: CCS Mk 2 Mod 3 with UYK 43/UYK 44 computers.
Fire control: Mk 118 digital torpedo fire control system. Mk 98 missile control system.
Radars: Surface search/navigation/fire control: BPS 15A; I/J band.
Sonars: IBM BQQ 6; passive search.
Raytheon BQS 13; spherical array for BQQ 6.
Ametek BQS 15; active/passive for close contacts; high frequency.
Western Electric BQR 15 (with BQQ 9 signal processor); passive towed array.
Raytheon BQR 19; active for navigation; high frequency.

Programmes: The 'date laid down' column has been deleted in this case as being irrelevant because there is a great amount of pre-fabrication before the various sections are joined on the building ways. The lead submarine was contracted to the Electric Boat Division of the General Dynamics Corp (Groton, Connecticut) on 25 July 1974. Newport News Shipbuilding failed in its bid to win a contract for construction of the FY 1987 ship and has not bid on later ships.
Structure: The size of the Trident submarine is dictated primarily by the 24 vertically launched Trident missiles and the larger reactor plant to drive the ship. The reactor has a nuclear core life of about nine years between refuellings. Diving depth is 300 m *(984 ft)*.
Operational: The Extremely Low Frequency (ELF) communications system became operational in 1986 at Michigan and in 1991 at Wisconsin enabling SSBNs to receive signals at greater depths and higher speeds than before although the data rate of ELF is much less than VLF. Each submarine has two Mk 2 Ship's Inertial Navigation Systems.
Pacific Fleet units with C4 missiles are based at Bangor, Washington, while the D5 submarines in the Atlantic Fleet are based at King's Bay, Georgia. The base structure permits bringing in ships of the Ohio class after 70 days at sea, accomplishing necessary, and sometimes very significant, voyage repairs, and sending them back to sea in 25 days. That schedule allows keeping these ships at sea, from commissioning to decommissioning, 66% of the time, including shipyard overhauls. The latter will be at nine year intervals. After two failed tests of the D-5 missile at sea early in 1989, modifications were made leading to eight successful tests from *Tennessee* and her first operational deployment started in March 1990. The original plan to retrofit D-5 missiles into the first eight of the class will not go ahead unless the threat posed by Russian strategic forces is revived.

WEST VIRGINIA *10/1991, Giorgio Arra*

WEST VIRGINIA *10/1991, Giorgio Arra*

13 BENJAMIN FRANKLIN and JAMES MADISON CLASSES (SSBN)

Name	*No*	*Builders*	*Laid down*	*Launched*	*Commissioned*	*F/S*
DANIEL BOONE	SSBN 629	Mare Island Naval Shipyard	6 Feb 1962	22 June 1963	23 Apr 1964	AA
JOHN C CALHOUN	SSBN 630	Newport News Shipbuilding & D D Co	4 June 1962	22 June 1963	15 Sep 1964	AA
VON STEUBEN	SSBN 632	Newport News Shipbuilding & D D Co	4 Sep 1962	18 Oct 1963	30 Sep 1964	AA
CASIMIR PULASKI	SSBN 633	General Dynamics (Electric Boat Div)	12 Jan 1963	1 Feb 1964	14 Aug 1964	AA
STONEWALL JACKSON	SSBN 634	Mare Island Naval Shipyard	4 July 1962	30 Nov 1963	26 Aug 1964	AA
BENJAMIN FRANKLIN	SSBN 640	General Dynamics (Electric Boat Div)	25 May 1963	5 Dec 1964	22 Oct 1965	AA
SIMON BOLIVAR	SSBN 641	Newport News Shipbuilding & D D Co	17 Apr 1963	22 Aug 1964	29 Oct 1965	AA
KAMEHAMEHA*	SSBN 642	Mare Island Naval Shipyard	2 May 1963	16 Jan 1965	10 Dec 1965	AA
GEORGE BANCROFT	SSBN 643	General Dynamics (Electric Boat Div)	24 Aug 1963	20 Mar 1965	22 Jan 1966	AA
JAMES K POLK*	SSBN 645	General Dynamics (Electric Boat Div)	23 Nov 1963	22 May 1965	16 Apr 1966	AA
HENRY L STIMSON	SSBN 655	General Dynamics (Electric Boat Div)	4 Apr 1964	13 Nov 1965	20 Aug 1966	AA
FRANCIS SCOTT KEY	SSBN 657	General Dynamics (Electric Boat Div)	5 Dec 1964	23 Apr 1966	3 Dec 1966	AA
MARIANO G VALLEJO	SSBN 658	Mare Island Naval Shipyard	7 July 1964	23 Oct 1965	16 Dec 1966	AA

* not Trident

Displacement, tons: 7330 surfaced; 8250 dived
Dimensions, feet (metres): 425 × 33 × 31.5 *(129.5 × 10.1 × 9.6)*
Main machinery: Nuclear; 1 Westinghouse PWR S5W; 2 turbines; 15 000 hp *(11.2 MW)*; 1 shaft; 1 Magnetek auxiliary prop motor; 325 hp *(242 kW)*
Speed, knots: 18 surfaced; 25 dived
Complement: 143 (13 officers)

Missiles: SLBM: 16 Lockheed Trident 1 (C4) (in 12 of the class); stellar inertial guidance to 7400 km *(4000 nm)*; thermonuclear warhead of 8 MIRV of 100 kT or 6 MARV of 100 kT; CEP 450 m. 16 Lockheed Poseidon (C3) (in SSBN 642 and 645); stellar inertial guidance to 4630 km *(2500 nm)*; thermonuclear warhead of 14 MIRV of 40 kT or 10 MIRV of 100 kT; CEP 450 m.
Torpedoes: 4—21 in *(533 mm)* Mk 65 bow tubes. Gould Mk 48; wire-guided (option); active/passive homing to 50 km *(27 nm)*/38 km *(21 nm)* at 40/55 kts; warhead 267 kg; depth to 900 m *(2950 ft)*.
Countermeasures: Decoys: Emerson Electric Mk 2; torpedo decoy.
ESM: WLR-8; intercept.
Fire control: Mk 113 Mod 9 torpedo fire control system. Mk 88 missile control system.
Radars: Surface search/navigation/fire control: BPS 11A or BPS 15; I/J band.
Sonars: EDO BQR 7; passive search.
Western Electric; BQR 15; passive towed array.
Raytheon BQR 19; active for navigation; high frequency.
Honeywell BQR 21 (Dimus); passive array.
Raytheon BQS 4; active search and classification.

JOHN C CALHOUN — *2/1991, Giorgio Arra*

Programmes: In early 1986, on commissioning of *Alaska* SSBN 732, *Sam Rayburn* had her missile tubes plugged in order to keep within limits of the SALT agreement and has converted to a 'moored nuclear reactor training submarine'. Since then the earlier ships of the class have started to be decommissioned at the rate of two to three per year, a process which rapidly accelerated in 1991/92 with all Poseidon submarines withdrawn from operational patrols. *Daniel Webster* has joined *Sam Rayburn* as a second moored training ship. *Kamehameha* and *James K Polk* are to be converted for non-strategic missions.
Modernisation: The first eight submarines of this class were fitted with the Polaris A-2 missile (1500 nm range) and the next 23 with the Polaris A-3 missile (2500 nm range). All were then fitted with Poseidon between 1970 and 1977. Between 24 September 1978 and 10 December 1982 twelve were converted to launch Trident I missiles. The conversion included minor modifications to the launcher and to the ballasting of the submarine to accommodate the greater weight of the Trident missile as well as extensive modifications to the installed fire control, instrumentation and missile checkout subsystems to support the increased sophistication of the longer range missile. *Francis Scott Key* served as a sea-going testbed for the testing phase. She completed her trials role and returned to her deterrent mission on 20 October 1979 as the first SSBN to deploy with the Trident I missile.
Structure: *Benjamin Franklin* and subsequent submarines of this class have been fitted with quieter machinery and are considered as a separate class. All SSBNs have diesel-electric stand-by machinery, snorts, and 'outboard' auxiliary propeller for emergency use. Diving depth is approx 300 m *(984 ft)*.
Operational: Three Mk 2 Mod 4 Ship's Inertial Navigation Systems (SINS) are fitted. Navigation data produced by SINS can be provided to each missile's guidance package until the instant the missile is fired. All fitted with navigational satellite receivers. Most of the class have two alternating crews designated 'Blue' and 'Gold'. Each crew does a 70 day patrol and partially assists during the intermediate 30 day refit alongside a tender. A 22-23 month refit is required every six years. Trident fitted SSBNs of this class are based at King's Bay, Georgia. Submarines fitted with Poseidon missiles ceased operational patrols on 1 October 1991 and all except two of the Poseidon boats which are to be converted for non-strategic missions, have now been withdrawn from service.

HENRY L STIMSON — *3/1991, Giorgio Arra*

Attack Submarines (SSN)

Building programme: The attack submarine force is entirely nuclear. The last remaining diesel-electric submarine paid off in May 1990. The current SSN building programme has been thrown into disarray by the proposal to terminate the Seawolf programme at one hull, and to advance the design work on the follow-on Centurion class. In early 1992 the Navy was seeking to rescind funding for the second and third of the Seawolf class. With the last of the Los Angeles hulls scheduled for completion in 1995 and the last Trident submarine in 1997, there is obvious concern over the possible loss of one of the two nuclear submarine building yards. The Centurion design is based on a capability of about 75% of Seawolf. Studies have included a modular concept with common propulsion and different weapon systems sections to be decided on build.

Ancillary programmes: These include thin-line towed arrays with greatly enhanced detection capability, special hull treatments which improve detection capability against quieter targets, the Mk 48 advanced capability (ADCAP) torpedo, Tomahawk missiles, offboard sensors and decoys.

Deep submergence vehicles: The Deep Submergence Vehicles (DSV), including the nuclear-propelled *NR-1*, are rated as Service Craft and are listed at the end of the 'Special Vessels' section following the MSC section.

Swimmer-Seal Delivery Vehicles (SDVs): About 15 two-man and six-man mini submarines have been built for naval commando units. Three more ordered in December 1990. These SDVs have a speed of six kts and can be carried by suitably modified SSNs.

Unmanned Undersea Vehicles (UUVs): Two prototype vessels started tests in Spring 1990 and a third in late 1991. The prototype is 36 ft long and has a diameter of 3 ft 8 in, while the second has a titanium hull. The mission payload is housed in an internal pressure hull. The propulsion motor is free flooding and develops about 12 hp from two battery sections. The first set of operational trials are expected to complete in about mid-1993 followed by launch and control experiments using *Memphis* (SSN 691) as the mother ship. The UUV is capable of remote-control from either submarine or surface ship. Roles are limitless but remote sensing and acoustic deception are two obvious front runners.

Autonomous Undersea Vehicles (AUVs): Early research work is being done with the aim of producing torpedo-launched remote-controlled vehicles for a range of tasks including surveillance, communications and mine warfare.

Permit Class. The last of the class is scheduled to pay off in late 1992.

0 + 1 SEAWOLF CLASS (SSN)

Name	*No*	*Builders*	*Start date*	*Launched*	*Commissioned*
SEAWOLF	SSN 21	General Dynamics (Electric Boat Div)	28 Oct 1989	Jan 1995	May 1996

Displacement, tons: 7460 surfaced; 9150 dived
Dimensions, feet (metres): 326.1 × 42.3 × 35.8 *(99.4 × 12.9 × 10.9)*
Main machinery: Nuclear; 1 GE PWR S6W; 2 turbines; 52 000 hp *(38.8 MW)*; 1 shaft; pumpjet propulsor
Speed, knots: 35 dived
Complement: 133 (12 officers)

Missiles: SLCM: 12 GDC Tomahawk.
SSM: Tomahawk; Harpoon.
Torpedoes: 8—26 in *(660 mm)* tubes (external measurement is 30 in *(762 mm)*); Mk 48 ADCAP (added capability). Total of about 50 tube-launched missiles and torpedoes.
Mines: In lieu of torpedoes.
Countermeasures: Decoys: torpedo decoys.
ESM: WLQ-4(V)1; intercept.
Combat data systems: General Electric BSY-1 system with UYK 44 computers.
Fire control: Raytheon Mk 2 FCS
Sonars: BQQ 5D suite; TB-16 and TB-23 towed arrays. One surveillance; one tactical.

SEAWOLF (artist's impression) *1989, General Dynamics*

Programmes: First of class ordered on 9 January 1989. Second of class funded in FY 1991, third in FY 1992. In January 1992 it was proposed that funding for the second and third would be rescinded although some of the money would be spent on development of the Centurion class. Delays in *Seawolf* construction programme have been caused by pressure hull welding problems.
Structure: The modular design has more weapons, a higher tactical speed, better sonars and an ASW mission effectiveness 'three times better than the improved Los Angeles class' according to the Navy. It is estimated that over a billion dollars has been allocated for research and development including $365 million for the S6W reactor system. Full acoustic cladding will be fitted. There are no external weapons (as in the improved Los Angeles class). Emphasis has been put on sub-ice capabilities including retractable bow planes. Diving depth, 2000 ft *(610 m)* approx.
Operational: A quoted 'silent' speed of 20 kts. If there is only to be one of the class it may become an R&D submarine.
Opinion: This submarine was intended to restore the level of acoustic advantage (in the one to one nuclear submarine engagement against the Russians) which the USN has enjoyed for the last three decades. At the same time the larger capacity of the magazine will enhance overall effectiveness in a number of other roles. The decision to discontinue building this one very expensive design has happened sooner than expected but was the inevitable result of falling defence budgets, technical problems and a perception of a diminishing Russian threat.

SEAWOLF (model) *1989, David Merriman, D & E Miniatures*

49 + 13 LOS ANGELES CLASS (SSN)

Name	*No*	*Builders*	*Laid down*	*Launched*	*Commissioned*	*F/S*
LOS ANGELES	SSN 688	Newport News S B & D D Co	8 Jan 1972	6 Apr 1974	13 Nov 1976	PA
BATON ROUGE	SSN 689	Newport News S B & D D Co	18 Nov 1972	26 Apr 1975	25 June 1977	AA
PHILADELPHIA	SSN 690	General Dynamics (Electric Boat Div)	12 Aug 1972	19 Oct 1974	25 June 1977	AA
MEMPHIS	SSN 691	Newport News S B & D D Co	23 June 1973	3 Apr 1976	17 Dec 1977	AA
OMAHA	SSN 692	General Dynamics (Electric Boat Div)	27 Jan 1973	21 Feb 1976	11 Mar 1978	PA
CINCINNATI	SSN 693	Newport News S B & D D Co	6 Apr 1974	19 Feb 1977	10 June 1978	AA
GROTON	SSN 694	General Dynamics (Electric Boat Div)	3 Aug 1973	9 Oct 1976	8 July 1978	AA
BIRMINGHAM	SSN 695	Newport News S B & D D Co	26 Apr 1975	29 Oct 1977	16 Dec 1978	AA
NEW YORK CITY	SSN 696	General Dynamics (Electric Boat Div)	15 Dec 1973	18 June 1977	3 Mar 1979	PA
INDIANAPOLIS	SSN 697	General Dynamics (Electric Boat Div)	19 Oct 1974	30 July 1977	5 Jan 1980	PA
BREMERTON	SSN 698	General Dynamics (Electric Boat Div)	8 May 1976	22 July 1978	14 Mar 1981	PA
JACKSONVILLE	SSN 699	General Dynamics (Electric Boat Div)	21 Feb 1976	18 Nov 1978	16 May 1981	AA
DALLAS	SSN 700	General Dynamics (Electric Boat Div)	9 Oct 1976	28 Apr 1979	18 July 1981	AA
LA JOLLA	SSN 701	General Dynamics (Electric Boat Div)	16 Oct 1976	11 Aug 1979	24 Oct 1981	PA
PHOENIX	SSN 702	General Dynamics (Electric Boat Div)	30 July 1977	8 Dec 1979	19 Dec 1981	AA
BOSTON	SSN 703	General Dynamics (Electric Boat Div)	11 Aug 1978	19 Apr 1980	30 Jan 1982	AA
BALTIMORE	SSN 704	General Dynamics (Electric Boat Div)	21 May 1979	13 Dec 1980	24 July 1982	AA
CITY OF CORPUS CHRISTI	SSN 705	General Dynamics (Electric Boat Div)	4 Sep 1979	25 Apr 1981	8 Jan 1983	AA
ALBUQUERQUE	SSN 706	General Dynamics (Electric Boat Div)	27 Dec 1979	13 Mar 1982	21 May 1983	AA
PORTSMOUTH	SSN 707	General Dynamics (Electric Boat Div)	8 May 1980	18 Sep 1982	1 Oct 1983	AA
MINNEAPOLIS-SAINT PAUL	SSN 708	General Dynamics (Electric Boat Div)	30 Jan 1981	19 Mar 1983	10 Mar 1984	AA
HYMAN G RICKOVER	SSN 709	General Dynamics (Electric Boat Div)	24 July 1981	27 Aug 1983	21 July 1984	AA
AUGUSTA	SSN 710	General Dynamics (Electric Boat Div)	1 Apr 1982	21 Jan 1984	19 Jan 1985	AA
SAN FRANCISCO	SSN 711	Newport News S B and D D Co	26 May 1977	27 Oct 1979	24 Apr 1981	PA
ATLANTA	SSN 712	Newport News S B and D D Co	17 Aug 1978	16 Aug 1980	6 Mar 1982	AA
HOUSTON	SSN 713	Newport News S B and D D Co	29 Jan 1979	21 Mar 1981	25 Sep 1982	PA
NORFOLK	SSN 714	Newport News S B and D D Co	1 Aug 1979	31 Oct 1981	21 May 1983	AA
BUFFALO	SSN 715	Newport News S B and D D Co	25 Jan 1980	8 May 1982	5 Nov 1983	PA
SALT LAKE CITY	SSN 716	Newport News S B and D D Co	26 Aug 1980	16 Oct 1982	12 May 1984	AA
OLYMPIA	SSN 717	Newport News S B and D D Co	31 Mar 1981	30 Apr 1983	17 Nov 1984	PA
HONOLULU	SSN 718	Newport News S B and D D Co	10 Nov 1981	24 Sep 1983	6 July 1985	PA
PROVIDENCE	SSN 719	General Dynamics (Electric Boat Div)	14 Oct 1982	4 Aug 1984	27 Aug 1985	AA
PITTSBURGH	SSN 720	General Dynamics (Electric Boat Div)	15 Apr 1983	8 Dec 1984	23 Nov 1985	AA
CHICAGO	SSN 721	Newport News S B & D D Co	5 Jan 1983	13 Oct 1984	27 Sep 1986	PA
KEY WEST	SSN 722	Newport News S B & D D Co	6 July 1983	20 July 1985	12 Sep 1987	AA
OKLAHOMA CITY	SSN 723	Newport News S B & D D Co	4 Jan 1984	2 Nov 1985	9 June 1988	AA
LOUISVILLE	SSN 724	General Dynamics (Electric Boat Div)	16 Sep 1984	14 Dec 1985	8 Nov 1986	AA
HELENA	SSN 725	General Dynamics (Electric Boat Div)	28 Mar 1985	28 June 1986	11 July 1987	PA
NEWPORT NEWS	SSN 750	Newport News S B & D D Co	3 Mar 1984	15 Mar 1986	3 June 1989	AA
SAN JUAN	SSN 751	General Dynamics (Electric Boat Div)	16 Aug 1985	6 Dec 1986	6 Aug 1988	AA
PASADENA	SSN 752	General Dynamics (Electric Boat Div)	20 Dec 1985	12 Sep 1987	11 Feb 1989	PA
ALBANY	SSN 753	Newport News S B & D D Co	22 Apr 1985	13 June 1987	7 Apr 1990	AA
TOPEKA	SSN 754	General Dynamics (Electric Boat Div)	13 May 1986	23 Jan 1988	21 Oct 1989	AA
MIAMI	SSN 755	General Dynamics (Electric Boat Div)	24 Oct 1986	12 Nov 1988	30 June 1990	AA
SCRANTON	SSN 756	Newport News S B & D D Co	29 June 1986	3 July 1989	26 Jan 1991	AA
ALEXANDRIA	SSN 757	General Dynamics (Electric Boat Div)	19 June 1987	23 June 1990	29 June 1991	AA
ASHEVILLE	SSN 758	Newport News S B & D D Co	1 Jan 1987	24 Feb 1990	28 Sep 1991	PA
JEFFERSON CITY	SSN 759	Newport News S B & D D Co	21 Sep 1987	17 Aug 1990	30 Jan 1992	AA
ANNAPOLIS	SSN 760	General Dynamics (Electric Boat Div)	15 June 1988	18 May 1991	Apr 1992	AA
SPRINGFIELD	SSN 761	General Dynamics (Electric Boat Div)	29 Jan 1990	4 Jan 1992	Nov 1992	Bldg
COLUMBUS	SSN 762	General Dynamics (Electric Boat Div)	7 Jan 1991	June 1992	June 1993	Bldg
SANTA FE	SSN 763	General Dynamics (Electric Boat Div)	9 July 1991	Dec 1992	Jan 1994	Bldg
BOISE	SSN 764	Newport News S B & D D Co	25 Aug 1988	23 Mar 1991	July 1992	Bldg
MONTPELIER	SSN 765	Newport News S B & D D Co	19 May 1989	23 Aug 1991	Nov 1992	Bldg
CHARLOTTE	SSN 766	Newport News S B & D D Co	31 July 1990	July 1992	Jan 1994	Bldg
HAMPTON	SSN 767	Newport News S B & D D Co	2 Mar 1990	29 Feb 1992	Aug 1993	Bldg
HARTFORD	SSN 768	General Dynamics (Electric Boat Div)	22 Feb 1992	Oct 1993	Sep 1994	Bldg
TOLEDO	SSN 769	Newport News S B & D D Co	8 Apr 1991	Dec 1992	June 1994	Bldg
TUCSON	SSN 770	Newport News S B & D D Co	30 Sep 1991	May 1993	Nov 1994	Bldg
COLUMBIA	SSN 771	General Dynamics (Electric Boat Div)	Aug 1992	Feb 1994	Mar 1995	Bldg
GREENEVILLE	SSN 772	Newport News S B & D D Co	31 Jan 1992	Oct 1993	Apr 1995	Bldg
CHEYENNE	SSN 773	Newport News S B & D D Co	Aug 1992	Dec 1994	Mar 1996	Bldg

Displacement, tons: 6080 standard; 6927 dived
Dimensions, feet (metres): 362 × 33 × 32.3 *(110.3 × 10.1 × 9.9)*
Main machinery: Nuclear; 1 GE PWR S6G; 2 turbines; 35 000 hp *(26 MW)*; 1 shaft; 1 Magnetek auxiliary prop motor; 325 hp *(242 kW)*
Speed, knots: 32 dived
Complement: 133 (13 officers)

Missiles: SLCM: GDC Tomahawk (TLAM-N); land attack; Tercom aided inertial navigation system (TAINS) to 2500 km *(1400 nm)* at 0.7 Mach; altitude 15-100 m; nuclear warhead 200 kT; CEP 80 m. There are also two versions (TLAM-C/D) with either a single 454 kg HE warhead or a single warhead with submunitions; range 900 km *(485 nm)*; CEP 10 m.
Nuclear warheads are not normally carried. Block III missiles, approved for production in 1992, increases TLAM-C ranges by more than 30%.
SSM: GDC Tomahawk (TASM); anti-ship; inertial guidance; active radar/anti-radiation homing to 460 km *(250 nm)* at 0.7 Mach; warhead 454 kg.
From SSN 719 onwards all are equipped with the Vertical Launch System, which places 12 launch tubes external to the pressure hull behind the BQQ 5 spherical array forward.
McDonnell Douglas Harpoon; active radar homing to 130 km *(70 nm)* at 0.9 Mach; warhead 227 kg.
Torpedoes: 4—21 in *(533 mm)* tubes midships. Gould Mk 48; wire-guided (option); active/passive homing to 50 km *(27 nm)*/38 km *(21 nm)* at 40/55 kts; warhead 267 kg; depth to 900 m *(2950 ft)*. ADCAP first carried in 1990. Air Turbine Pump discharge.
Total of 26 weapons can be tube-launched, for example—8 Tomahawk, 4 Harpoon, 14 torpedoes.
Mines: Can lay Mk 67 Mobile and Mk 60 Captor mines.
Countermeasures: Decoys: Emerson Electric Mk 2; torpedo decoy.
ESM: BRD-7; direction finding. WLR-12; radar warning. WLR-9A; intercept. WLR-1H (in 771-773).
Combat data systems: CCS Mk 1 (being replaced by Mk 2) (688-750) with UYK 7 computers; IBM BSY-1 (751-773) with UYK 43/UYK 44 computers.
Fire control: Mk 113 Mod 10 torpedo fire control system fitted in SSN 688-699 (being replaced by Mk 117) and Mk 117 in later submarines.
Radars: Surface search/navigation/fire control: Sperry BPS 15 A; I/J band.
Sonars: IBM BQQ 5A(V)1 (being updated to BQQ 5D/E); passive/active search and attack; low frequency.
BQR 23/25 (being replaced by TB-23/29 thin line array during overhauls); passive towed array.

ALBANY *9/1991, Giorgio Arra*

Ametek BQS 15; active close-range including ice detection; high frequency.
MIDAS (mine and ice detection avoidance system) (SSN 751 onwards); high frequency.
Raytheon SADS-TG active detection system (being retrofitted).

Programmes: Various major improvement programmes and updating design changes have caused programme delays in the late 1980s, not helped by a long strike at the Electric Boat Division. Future commissioning dates are very speculative. From SSN 751 onwards the class is prefixed by an 'I' for 'improved'. Programme terminates at 62 hulls.
Modernisation: Mk 117 TFCS is being back fitted in earlier submarines of the class.
Structure: Every effort has been made to improve sound quieting and from SSN 751 onwards the class have acoustic tile cladding to augment the 'mammalian' skin which up to then had been the standard USN outer casing coating. Also from SSN 751 the forward hydro planes are fitted forward instead of on the fin. The planes are retractable mainly for surfacing through ice. The S6G reactor is a modified version of the D2G type fitted in *Bainbridge* and *Truxtun*. The towed sonar array is stowed in a blister on the side of the casing. Reactor core life between refuellings is estimated at 10 years. Diving depth is 450 m *(1475 ft)*. *Memphis* was withdrawn from active service in late 1989 to become an interim research platform for advanced submarine technology. Up to now these trials have not involved major changes to the submarine but tests started in September 1990 for optronic non-hull penetrating masts and a major overhaul in 1993 will include installation of a large diameter tube for testing UUVs and large torpedoes. Subsequently an after casing hangar will be fitted for housing larger UUVs and towed arrays. *Augusta* is the trials platform for the BQG-5D wide aperture array passive sonar system which may be built into the last three and retrofitted in others of the class. Various staged design improvements have added some 220 tons to the class displacement between 668 and 771.
Operational: The growing emphasis on the ability to operate under the Arctic ice has led to improvements in ice detection sensors, navigation and communications equipment as well as strengthening the sail and placing the sailplanes forward in later units of the class. *Norfolk* fired the first ADCAP torpedo on 23 July 1988 and sank the destroyer *Jonas K Ingram*. Nine of the class took part in the war with Iraq in 1991 and two fired Tomahawk from the eastern Mediterranean. Normally eight Tomahawk missiles are carried internally (in addition to the external tubes in 719 onwards) but this load can be increased depending on the mission. Subroc phased out in 1990.

NEWPORT NEWS *9/1991, Giorgio Arra*

MIAMI *9/1991, Giorgio Arra*

LOUISVILLE *3/1991, Scott Connolly, RAN*

33 STURGEON CLASS (SSN)

Name	No	Builders	Laid down	Launched	Commissioned	F/S
STURGEON	SSN 637	General Dynamics (Electric Boat Div)	10 Aug 1963	26 Feb 1966	3 Mar 1967	AA
WHALE	SSN 638	General Dynamics (Quincy)	27 May 1964	14 Oct 1966	12 Oct 1968	AA
TAUTOG	SSN 639	Ingalls Shipbuilding Corp	27 Jan 1964	15 Apr 1967	17 Aug 1968	PA
GRAYLING	SSN 646	Portsmouth Naval Shipyard	12 May 1964	22 June 1967	11 Oct 1969	AA
POGY	SSN 647	Ingalls Shipbuilding Corp	4 May 1964	3 June 1967	15 May 1971	PA
ASPRO	SSN 648	Ingalls Shipbuilding Corp	23 Nov 1964	29 Nov 1967	20 Feb 1969	PA
SUNFISH	SSN 649	General Dynamics (Quincy)	15 Jan 1965	14 Oct 1966	15 Mar 1969	AA
PARGO	SSN 650	General Dynamics (Electric Boat Div)	3 June 1964	17 Sep 1966	5 Jan 1968	AA
PUFFER	SSN 652	Ingalls Shipbuilding Corp	8 Feb 1965	30 Mar 1968	9 Aug 1969	PA
RAY	SSN 653	Newport News S B & D D Co	1 Apr 1965	21 June 1966	12 Apr 1967	AA
SAND LANCE	SSN 660	Portsmouth Naval Shipyard	15 Jan 1965	11 Nov 1969	25 Sep 1971	AA
GURNARD	SSN 662	San Francisco NSY (Mare Island)	22 Dec 1964	20 May 1967	6 Dec 1968	PA
HAMMERHEAD	SSN 663	Newport News S B & D D Co	29 Nov 1965	14 Apr 1967	28 June 1968	AA
HAWKBILL	SSN 666	San Francisco NSY (Mare Island)	12 Sep 1966	12 Apr 1969	4 Feb 1971	PA
BERGALL	SSN 667	General Dynamics (Electric Boat Div)	16 Apr 1966	17 Feb 1968	13 June 1969	AA
SPADEFISH	SSN 668	Newport News S B & D D Co	21 Dec 1966	15 May 1968	14 Aug 1969	AA
SEAHORSE	SSN 669	General Dynamics (Electric Boat Div)	13 Aug 1966	15 June 1968	19 Sep 1969	AA
FINBACK	SSN 670	Newport News S B & D D Co	26 June 1967	7 Dec 1968	4 Feb 1970	AA
PINTADO	SSN 672	San Francisco NSY (Mare Island)	27 Oct 1967	16 Aug 1969	11 Sep 1971	PA
FLYING FISH	SSN 673	General Dynamics (Electric Boat Div)	30 June 1967	17 May 1969	29 Apr 1970	AA
TREPANG	SSN 674	General Dynamics (Electric Boat Div)	28 Oct 1967	27 Sep 1969	14 Aug 1970	AA
BLUEFISH	SSN 675	General Dynamics (Electric Boat Div)	13 Mar 1968	10 Jan 1970	8 Jan 1971	AA
BILLFISH	SSN 676	General Dynamics (Electric Boat Div)	20 Sep 1968	1 May 1970	12 Mar 1971	AA
DRUM	SSN 677	San Francisco NSY (Mare Island)	20 Aug 1968	23 May 1970	15 Apr 1972	PA
ARCHERFISH	SSN 678	General Dynamics (Electric Boat Div)	19 June 1969	16 Jan 1971	17 Dec 1971	AA
SILVERSIDES	SSN 679	General Dynamics (Electric Boat Div)	13 Oct 1969	4 June 1971	5 May 1972	AA
WILLIAM H BATES (ex-*Redfish*)	SSN 680	Ingalls Shipbuilding (Litton)	4 Aug 1969	11 Dec 1971	5 May 1973	PA
BATFISH	SSN 681	General Dynamics (Electric Boat Div)	9 Feb 1970	9 Oct 1971	1 Sep 1972	AA
TUNNY	SSN 682	Ingalls Shipbuilding (Litton)	22 May 1970	10 June 1972	26 Jan 1974	PA
PARCHE	SSN 683	Ingalls Shipbuilding (Litton)	10 Dec 1970	13 Jan 1973	17 Aug 1974	PA
CAVALLA	SSN 684	General Dynamics (Electric Boat Div)	4 June 1970	19 Feb 1972	9 Feb 1973	PA
L MENDEL RIVERS	SSN 686	Newport News S B & D D Co	26 June 1971	2 June 1973	1 Feb 1975	AA
RICHARD B RUSSELL	SSN 687	Newport News S B & D D Co	19 Oct 1971	12 Jan 1974	16 Aug 1975	PA

Displacement, tons: 4250; 4460 standard; 4780; 4960 dived (see *Structure*)
Dimensions, feet (metres): 302.2; 292 × 31.8 × 28.9 *(92.1; 89 × 9.7 × 8.8)* (see *Structure*)
Main machinery: Nuclear; 1 Westinghouse PWR S5W; 2 turbines; 15 000 hp *(11.2 MW)*; 1 shaft
Speed, knots: 15 surfaced; 30 dived
Complement: 107 (12 officers)

Missiles: SLCM: GDC Tomahawk (TLAM-N); land attack; Tercom aided inertial navigation system (TAINS) to 2500 km *(1400 nm)* at 0.7 Mach; altitude 15-100 m; nuclear warhead 200 kT; CEP 80 m. There are also two versions (TLAM-C/D) with either a single 454 kg HE warhead or a single warhead with submunitions; range 900 km *(485 nm)*; CEP 10 m.
Nuclear warheads are not normally carried. TLAM-C Block III missiles with increased ranges of more than 30% may be embarked in due course.
SSM: GDC Tomahawk (TASM); anti-ship; inertial guidance; active radar/anti-radiation homing to 460 km *(250 nm)* at 0.7 Mach; warhead 454 kg.
McDonnell Douglas Harpoon; active radar homing to 130 km *(70 nm)* at 0.9 Mach; warhead 227 kg (84A) or 258 kg (84B/C).
Torpedoes: 4—21 in *(533 mm)* Mk 63 tubes midships. Gould Mk 48; wire-guided (option); active/passive homing to 50 km *(27 nm)*/38 km *(21 nm)* at 40/55 kts; warhead 267 kg; depth to 900 m *(2950 ft)*.
Total of 23 weapons, for example 4 Harpoon, 4 Tomahawk and 15 torpedoes. Up to 8 Tomahawk can be carried in most of the class in place of other weapons.
Mines: Mk 67 Mobile and Mk 60 Captor can be carried.
Countermeasures: Decoys: Emerson Electric Mk 2; torpedo decoy.
ESM: WLQ-4; radar warning.
Fire control: Mk 117 torpedo fire control system.
Radars: Surface search/navigation/fire control: Sperry BPS 15 or Raytheon BPS 14; I/J band.
Sonars: IBM BQQ 5 (SSN 678 onwards) or Raytheon BQQ 2; passive/active search and attack; low frequency.
EDO BQS 8 or Raytheon BQS 14A; ice detection; high frequency.
Raytheon BQS 13; active/passive array.
BQR 15; towed array; passive search; very low frequency.

Structure: These submarines are slightly larger than the Permit class and can be identified by their taller sail structure and the lower position of their diving planes on the sail (to improve control at periscope depth). Sail height is 20 ft 6 in above deck. Sail-mounted diving planes rotate to vertical for breaking through ice when surfacing in arctic regions. SSN 678-684, 686 and 687 are 10 ft longer than remainder of class to accommodate BQQ 5 sonar and electronic gear. Under FY 1982 programme *Cavalla* was converted at Pearl Harbor in August-December 1982 to have a secondary amphibious assault role by carrying a Swimmer Delivery Vehicle (SDV). *Archerfish, Silversides, Tunny* and *L Mendel Rivers* are similarly equipped. *William H Bates, Hawkbill, Pintado, Richard B Russell* and others have been modified to carry and support the Navy's Deep Submergence Rescue Vehicles (DSRV). See section on Deep Submergence Vehicles for additional DSRV details. *Silversides* and *Richard B Russell* carry Bustle prototype communications buoy in container abaft the sail. Diving depth is 400 m *(1320 ft)*. Acoustic tiles are fitted and some of the class are getting anechoic coatings.
Operational: Operational life was expected to be 30 years but many more are expected to decommission early. Subroc phased out in 1990.

RICHARD B RUSSELL (with DSRV and Bustle) *1987, Giorgio Arra*

SILVERSIDES (with Bustle) *10/1990*

ARCHERFISH *3/1991, Giorgio Arra*

BILLFISH *6/1991, Giorgio Arra*

1 NARWHAL CLASS (SSN)

Name	*No*	*Builders*	*Laid down*	*Launched*	*Commissioned*	*F/S*
NARWHAL	SSN 671	General Dynamics (Electric Boat Div)	17 Jan 1966	9 Sep 1967	12 July 1969	AA

Displacement, tons: 5284 standard; 5830 dived
Dimensions, feet (metres): 314.6 × 37.7 × 27 *(95.9 × 11.5 × 8.2)*
Main machinery: Nuclear; 1 GE PWR S5G; 2 turbines; 17 000 hp *(12.7 MW)*; 1 shaft
Speed, knots: 20 surfaced; 25 dived
Complement: 129 (13 officers)

Missiles: SSM: 8 GDC Tomahawk (TASM); anti-ship; inertial guidance; active radar/anti-radiation homing to 460 km *(250 nm)* at 0.7 Mach; warhead 454 kg. 4 McDonnell Douglas Harpoon; active radar homing to 130 km *(70 nm)* at 0.9 Mach; warhead 227 kg.

Torpedoes: 4—21 in *(533 mm)* tubes midships. Gould Mk 48; wire-guided (option); active/passive homing to 50 km *(27 nm)*/38 km *(21 nm)* at 40/55 kts; warhead 227 kg; depth to 900 m *(2950 ft)*.

Countermeasures: Decoys: Emerson Electric Mk 2; torpedo decoy.
ESM: WLQ-4; radar warning.

Fire control: Mk 117 torpedo fire control system. Fitted with WSC-3 satellite communications transceiver.

Radars: Surface search/navigation/fire control: Raytheon BPS 14; I/J band.

Sonars: IBM BQQ 5; passive/active search and attack; low frequency.
EDO BQS 8; upward-looking for ice detection; high frequency.

Programmes: Authorised in FY 1964.
Structure: *Narwhal* is similar to the Sturgeon class submarines in hull design but is fitted with the prototype sea-going S5G natural circulation reactor plant. The natural circulation reactor 'offers promise of increased reactor plant reliability, simplicity, and noise reduction due to the elimination of the need for large reactor coolant pumps and associated electrical and control equipment by taking maximum advantage of natural convection to circulate the reactor coolant.'

NARWHAL *3/1987, Michael D. J. Lennon*

1 DOLPHIN CLASS (AGSS)

Name	*No*	*Builders*	*Laid down*	*Launched*	*Commissioned*	*F/S*
DOLPHIN	AGSS 555	Portsmouth Naval Shipyard	9 Nov 1962	8 June 1968	17 Aug 1968	PA

Displacement, tons: 800 standard; 930 full load
Dimensions, feet (metres): 152 × 19.3 × 18 *(46.3 × 5.9 × 5.5)*
Main machinery: Diesel-electric; 2 Detroit 12 V71 diesels; 1650 hp *(1.23 MW)*; 1 motor; 1 shaft
Fitted with 330 cell silver-zinc battery
Speed, knots: 15+ dived
Complement: 37 (4 officers) plus 4-7 scientists

Torpedoes: Single tube removed.
Radars: Navigation: Sperry SPS 53 portable; I/J band.
Sonars: Ametek BQS 15; active close-range detection; high frequency.
EDO BQR 2; passive search; low frequency.
Acoustic arrays towed at up to 4000 ft astern.

Programmes: Authorised in FY 1961 but delayed because of changes in mission and equipment coupled with higher priorities being given to other submarine projects.
Structure: Has a constant diameter cylindrical pressure hull approximately 15 ft in outer diameter closed at both ends with hemispherical heads. Pressure hull fabricated of HY-80 steel with aluminium and fibreglass used in secondary structures to reduce weight. No conventional hydroplanes are mounted, improved rudder design and other features provide manoeuvring control and hovering capability. Fitted for deep-ocean sonar and oceanographic research. She is highly automated and has three computer-operated systems, a safety system, hovering system, and one that is classified. The digital-computer submarine safety system monitors equipment and provides data on closed-circuit television screens; malfunctions in equipment set off an alarm and if they are not corrected within the prescribed time the system, unless overridden by an operator, automatically brings the submarine to the surface. There are several research stations for scientists and she is fitted to take water samples down to her operating depth. Underwater endurance is limited (endurance and habitability were considered of secondary importance in design).
Operational: Assigned to Submarine Development Group 1 at San Diego. Designed for deep diving operations. Submerged endurance is approximately 24 hours with an at-sea endurance of 14 days.

DOLPHIN *9/1985, Giorgio Arra*

AIRCRAFT CARRIERS

Ships: In the first half of 1992 there were 14 carriers, including two in SLEP/overhaul and one training ship. In addition one more was due to commission in July 1992, two are building and another is projected to start building in 1995. If overall numbers are to be cut, *Enterprise* in SLEP is a candidate for reserve status.

Air Wings: Air wing composition depends on the operational task, but is based on a normal complement of two fighter squadrons of 20 F-14s, two light attack squadrons of 20 F/A-18s, two medium attack squadrons of 20 A-6E Intruders (including some tanker KA-6D aircraft depending on availability), one ASW squadron of 10 S-3A Viking aircraft, one detachment of five EA-6B Prowler electronic-warfare aircraft, five E-2C Hawkeye early-warning/control aircraft and one ASW squadron of six SH-60F which are replacing the SH-3G/H helicopters. Budget constraints and shortages of aircraft may limit numbers embarked. See *Shipborne Aircraft* section for details of aircraft.

Service Life Extension Programme (SLEP): The SLEP programme was initiated in 1979. *Saratoga, Forrestal, Independence* and *Kitty Hawk* have completed and *Constellation* is planned to finish in December 1992. The principal objective of SLEP is to extend the service life of aircraft carriers an additional 15 years, providing a reliable, logistically supportable platform capable of operating all current and future fleet aircraft. While the major thrust of SLEP is repair and life enhancement, warfighting improvements are incorporated to keep pace with the aircraft carrier modernisation baseline. SLEP includes complete overhaul of propulsion, auxiliary, and launch systems; upgrade of aircraft recovery equipment; extensive structure, tank, and piping repair, and installation of updated sensors, weapons systems, and electronic suites. On earlier SLEP ships this included installation of Vulcan Phalanx close-in weapons system (CIWS), NATO Sea Sparrow missile system, SPS 49 radar, and F/A-18 Hornet capability. Future SLEP ships, if already equipped with these systems, will receive modernisation to current standards incorporating improved NTDS, SPS 48E, TAS Mk 23 radar, new ASW systems and Raytheon SLQ-32(V)4 combined EW intercept and jammer.

6 + 2 + (1) NIMITZ CLASS (CVN)

Name	*No*	*Builders*	*Laid down*	*Launched*	*Commissioned*	*F/S*
NIMITZ	CVN 68	Newport News Shipbuilding & Dry Dock Co	22 June 1968	13 May 1972	3 May 1975	PA
DWIGHT D EISENHOWER	CVN 69	Newport News Shipbuilding & Dry Dock Co	15 Aug 1970	11 Oct 1975	18 Oct 1977	AA
CARL VINSON	CVN 70	Newport News Shipbuilding & Dry Dock Co	11 Oct 1975	15 Mar 1980	13 Mar 1982	PA
THEODORE ROOSEVELT	CVN 71	Newport News Shipbuilding & Dry Dock Co	13 Oct 1981	27 Oct 1984	25 Oct 1986	AA
ABRAHAM LINCOLN	CVN 72	Newport News Shipbuilding & Dry Dock Co	3 Nov 1984	13 Feb 1988	11 Nov 1989	PA
GEORGE WASHINGTON	CVN 73	Newport News Shipbuilding & Dry Dock Co	25 Aug 1986	21 July 1990	4 July 1992	AA
JOHN C STENNIS	CVN 74	Newport News Shipbuilding & Dry Dock Co	13 Mar 1991	Nov 1993	Dec 1995	Bldg
UNITED STATES	CVN 75	Newport News Shipbuilding & Dry Dock Co	Aug 1992	Mar 1996	Dec 1997	Bldg

Displacement, tons: 72 916 (CVN 68-70), 73 973 (CVN 71) light; 91 487 (CVN 68-70), 96 386 (CVN 71), 102 000 (CVN 72-73) full load
Dimensions, feet (metres): 1040 pp; 1092 × 134 × 37 (CVN 68-70); 38.7 (CVN 71); 39 (CVN 72-73) *(317; 332.9 × 40.8 × 11.3; 11.8; 11.9)*
Flight deck, feet (metres): 1092; 779.8 (angled) × 252 *(332.9; 237.7 × 76.8)*
Main machinery: Nuclear; 2 GE PWR A4W/A1G; 4 turbines; 260 000 hp *(194 MW)*; 4 emergency diesels; 10 720 hp *(8 MW)*; 4 shafts
Speed, knots: 30+
Complement: 3184 (203 officers); 2800 aircrew (366 officers); Flag 70 (25 officers)

Missiles: SAM: 3 Raytheon GMLS Mk 29 octuple launchers; NATO Sea Sparrow; semi-active radar homing to 14.6 km *(8 nm)* at 2.5 Mach; warhead 39 kg.
Guns: 4 General Electric/General Dynamics 20 mm Vulcan Phalanx 6-barrelled Mk 15 (3 in CVN 68 and 69); 3000 rounds/minute (or 4500 in Block 1) combined to 1.5 km.
Countermeasures: Decoys: 4 Loral Hycor SRBOC 6-barrelled fixed Mk 36; IR flares and Chaff to 4 km *(2.2 nm)*. SSTDS (torpedo defence system). SLQ 36 Nixie (Phase I).
ESM/ECM: SLQ 29 (WLR 8 radar warning and SLQ 17AV jammer and deception system). To be replaced by SLQ-32(V)4 in retrofit.
Combat data systems: NTDS/ACDS naval tactical and advanced combat direction systems; Links 4A, 11 and 14. Link 16 in due course. JOTS, POST, CVIC, TESS UMM-1(V)1, SSQ-82. SATCOMS SRR-1, WSC-3 (UHF), WSC-6 (SHF), USC-38 (EHF) (from 1992).
Fire control: 3 Mk 91 Mod 1 MFCS directors (part of the NSSMS Mk 57 SAM system).
Radars: Air search: ITT SPS 48E; 3D; E/F band; range 402 km *(220 nm)*.
Raytheon SPS 49(V)5; C/D band; range 457 km *(250 nm)*.
Hughes Mk 23 TAS; D band.
Surface search: Norden SPS 67V; G band.
CCA: SPN 41, 2 SPN 42 (CVN 68-70), SPN 43B, SPN 44, 2 SPN 46 (CVN 71-73); J/K/E/F band.
Navigation: Raytheon SPS 64(V)9; I/J band.
Fire control: Six Mk 95; I/J band (for SAM).
Tacan: URN 25.

Fixed wing aircraft: Notional air wing including: 20 F14 Tomcat; 20 F/A-18 Hornet; 6 EA-6B Prowler; 20 A-6E Intruders (includes some KA-6D tankers); 5 E-2C Hawkeye; 10 S-3A/B Viking. See *Shipborne Aircraft* section.
Helicopters: 6 SH-3G/H/SH 60F Sea King.

DWIGHT D EISENHOWER *4/1991, Giorgio Arra*

Programmes: *Nimitz* was authorised in FY 1967, *Dwight D Eisenhower* in FY 1970, *Carl Vinson* in FY 1974, *Theodore Roosevelt* in FY 1980 and *Abraham Lincoln* and *George Washington* in FY 1983. Construction contracts for the last two were awarded in June 1988. The builder is the only US shipyard now capable of constructing large, nuclear-propelled surface warships. The FY 1993 ship construction budget shows $832.2 million for lead items for CVN 76 which is expected to be included in the FY 1995 programme.
Structure: Damage control measures include sides with system of full and empty compartments (full compartments can contain aviation fuel), approximately 2.5 in Kevlar plating over certain areas of side shell, box protection over magazine and machinery spaces. Aviation facilities include four lifts, two at the forward end of the flight deck, one to starboard abaft the island and one to port at the stern. There are four steam catapults (C13-1) and four (or three) Mk 7 Mod 3 arrester wires. Launch rate is one every 20 seconds. The hangar can hold less than half the full aircraft complement, deckhead is 25.6 ft. Aviation fuel, 9000 tons. Tactical Flag Command Centre for Flagship role.
Operational: Multi-mission role of 'attack/ASW'. From CVN 70 onwards ships have an A/S control centre and A/S facilities; CVN 68 and 69 will be back fitted.
Endurance of 16 days for aviation fuel (steady flying). 13 years' theoretical life for nuclear reactors (CVN 68-70); 15 years' (CVN 71-73); 800 000 to 1 million miles between refuelling.

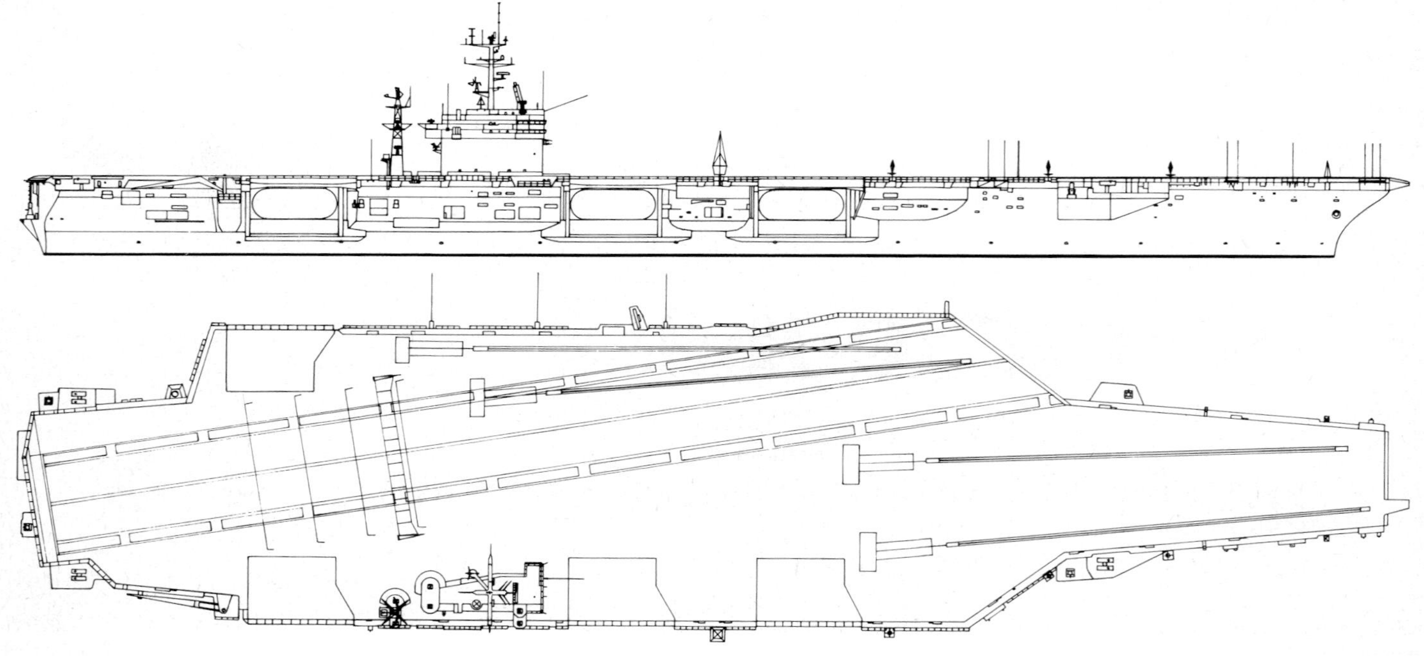
CARL VINSON *(Scale 1 : 1 800), Ian Sturton*

NIMITZ *10/1991, Giorgio Arra*

DWIGHT D EISENHOWER *4/1991, Giorgio Arra*

DWIGHT D EISENHOWER *4/1991, Giorgio Arra*

ABRAHAM LINCOLN *7/1991, 92 Wing RAAF*

4 KITTY HAWK and JOHN F KENNEDY CLASSES (CV)

Name	*No*	*Builders*	*Laid down*	*Launched*	*Commissioned*	*F/S*
KITTY HAWK	CV 63	New York Shipbuilding Corp, Camden, NJ	27 Dec 1956	21 May 1960	29 Apr 1961	PA
CONSTELLATION	CV 64	New York Naval Shipyard	14 Sep 1957	8 Oct 1960	27 Oct 1961	SLEP/PA
AMERICA	CV 66	Newport News Shipbuilding & Dry Dock Co	9 Jan 1961	1 Feb 1964	23 Jan 1965	AA
JOHN F KENNEDY	CV 67	Newport News Shipbuilding & Dry Dock Co	22 Oct 1964	27 May 1967	7 Sep 1968	AA

Displacement, tons: 60 100 standard; 81 123 full load (CV 63)
60 100 standard; 81 773 full load (CV 64)
60 300 standard; 79 724 full load (CV 66)
61 000 standard; 80 941 full load (CV 67)
Dimensions, feet (metres): 1062.5 (CV 63); 1072.5 (CV 64); 1047.5 (CV 66); 1052 (CV 67) × 130 × 37.4
(323.6; 326.9; 319.3; 320.6 × 39.6 × 11.4)
Flight deck, feet (metres): 1046 × 252 *(318.8 × 76.8)*
Main machinery: 8 Foster-Wheeler boilers; 1200 psi *(83.4 kg/cm sq)*; 950°F *(510°C)*; 4 Westinghouse turbines; 280 000 hp *(209 MW)*; 4 shafts
Speed, knots: 32. **Range, miles:** 4000 at 30 kts; 12 000 at 20 kts
Complement: 2930 (155 officers); aircrew 2480 (320 officers) (except CV 67); aircrew 2279 (329 officers) (CV 67); Flag 70 (25 officers)

Missiles: SAM: 3 Raytheon GMLS Mk 29 octuple launchers; NATO Sea Sparrow; semi-active radar homing to 14.6 km *(8 nm)* at 2.5 Mach; warhead 39 kg.
Guns: 3 General Electric/General Dynamics 20 mm Vulcan Phalanx 6-barrelled Mk 15; 3000 rounds/minute (or 4500 in Block 1) combined to 1.5 km.
Countermeasures: Decoys: 4 Loral Hycor SRBOC 6-barrelled fixed Mk 36; IR flares and Chaff to 4 km *(2.2 nm)*. SSTDS (Surface Ship Torpedo Defence System). SLQ-36 Nixie (Phase I).
ESM/ECM: SLQ-32(V)4 (in CV 63 and 64) to be retrofitted in all. SLQ 29 (WLR 8 and SLQ 17) in CV 66; SLQ 17 and SLQ 26 in CV 67; WLR 3, WLR 11; combined radar warning, jammer and deception system.
Combat data systems: NTDS/ACDS naval tactical and advanced combat direction systems; Links 4A, 11 and 14. Link 16 in due course. JOTS, POST, CVIC, TESS UMM-1(V)1, SSQ-82. SATCOMS SRR-1, WSC-3 (UHF), WSC-6 (SHF), USC-38 (EHF) (from 1992).
Fire control: 3 Mk 91 MFCS directors (part of NSSMS Mk 57 SAM system).
Radars: Air search: ITT SPS 48C/E; 3D; E/F band; range 402 km *(220 nm)*.
Raytheon SPS 49(V)5; C/D band; range 457 km *(250 nm)*.
Hughes Mk 23 TAS; D band.
Surface search: Raytheon SPS 10F or Norden SPS 67; G band.
CCA: SPN 41, SPN 43A; SPN 44; 2 SPN 46; J/K/E/F band.
Navigation: Raytheon SPN 64(V)9; I band.
Fire control: 6 Mk 95; I/J band (for SAM).
Tacan: URN 25.
Sonars: Fitted for SQS 23 (CV 66-67).

Fixed wing aircraft: Notional air wing including: 20 F14 Tomcat; 20 FA-18 Hornet; 4 EA-6B Prowler; 14 A-6E Intruders (includes some KA-6D tankers); 4 E-2C Hawkeye; 10 S-3A/B Viking. See *Shipborne Aircraft* section.
Helicopters: 6 SH-3G/H/SH 60F Sea King.

Programmes: *Kitty Hawk* was authorised in FY 1956, *Constellation* in FY 1957, *America* in FY 1961, and *John F Kennedy* in FY 1963.
Modernisation: Service Life Extension Programme (SLEP): *Kitty Hawk* completed in February 1991 and *Constellation* is scheduled to complete in December 1992. $113 million was funded in the FY 1991 budget for procurement of materials to be used in the 'complex overhaul' of *Kennedy*, which is scheduled to start in late 1992, subject to budget cuts.
Structure: These ships were built to an improved Forrestal design and are easily recognised by their island structure being set farther aft than the superstructure in the four Forrestal class ships. They have two deck-edge lifts forward of the superstructure, a third lift aft of the structure, and the port-side lift on the after quarter. This arrangement considerably improves flight deck operations. Four C13 steam catapults (with one C13-1 in *America* and *Kennedy*) and four arrester wires. *John F Kennedy* and *America* have stern anchors as well as bow anchors because of their planned bow sonar domes. All have a small radar mast abaft the island. The island is painted black between flight deck and bridge to mask jet exhaust stains. Aviation fuel of 5882 tons are carried.

KENNEDY *3/1991, Giorgio Arra*

KENNEDY *6/1991, Giorgio Arra*

AMERICA *10/1991, H. M. Steele*

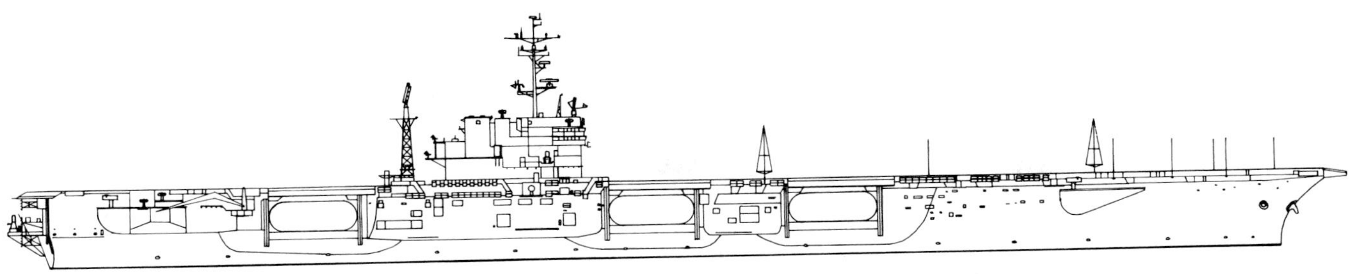

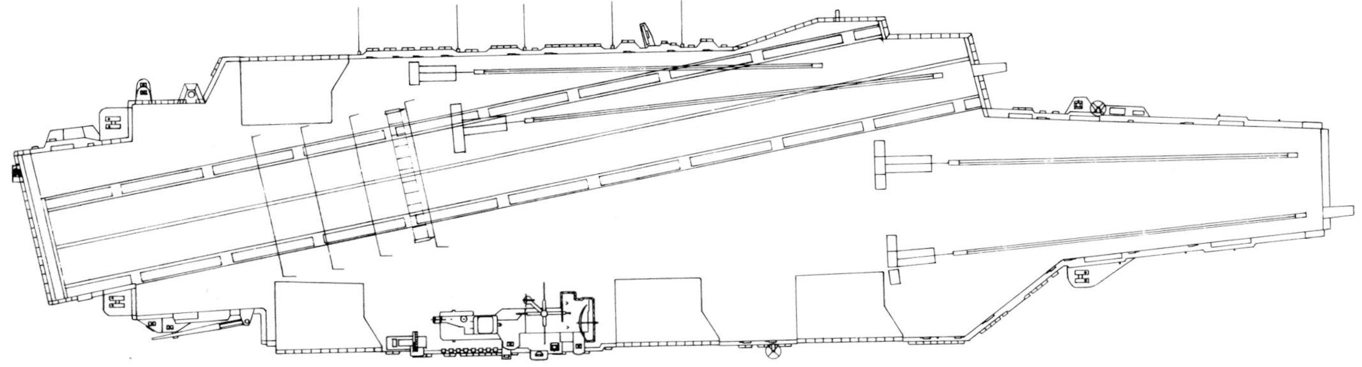

AMERICA (Scale 1 : 1 800), Ian Sturton

AMERICA 9/1991, Maritime Photographic

AMERICA 10/1991, H. M. Steele

4 FORRESTAL CLASS (3 CV and 1 AVT)

Name	No	Builders	Laid down	Launched	Commissioned	F/S
FORRESTAL	AVT 59	Newport News S B & D D Co	14 July 1952	11 Dec 1954	1 Oct 1955	AA
SARATOGA	CV 60	New York Naval Shipyard	16 Dec 1952	8 Oct 1955	14 Apr 1956	AA
RANGER	CV 61	Newport News S B & D D Co	2 Aug 1954	29 Sep 1956	10 Aug 1957	PA
INDEPENDENCE	CV 62	New York Naval Shipyard	1 July 1955	6 June 1958	10 Jan 1959	PA

Displacement, tons: 59 060 (AVT 59 and CV 60), 60 000 (CV 61-62) standard;
79 250 (AVT 59), 80 383 (CV 60), 81 163 (CV 61), 80 643 (CV 62) full load
Dimensions, feet (metres): 1086 (AVT 59); 1063 (CV 60); 1071 (CV 61-62) × 130 × 37 *(331; 324; 326.4 × 39.6 × 11.3)*
Flight deck, feet (metres): 1047 × 250.3 (AVT 59 and CV 60); 270 (CV 61-62) *(319.1 × 76.3; 82.3)*
Main machinery: 8 Babcock & Wilcox boilers; 600 psi *(41.7 kg/cm sq)* (AVT 59); 1200 psi *(83.4 kg/cm sq)* (remainder); 950°F *(510°C)*; 4 Westinghouse turbines; 260 000 hp *(194 MW)* (AVT 59); 280 000 hp *(209 MW)* (remainder); 4 shafts
Speed, knots: 33. **Range, miles:** 8000 at 20 kts; 4000 at 30 kts
Complement: 2900 (154 officers); aircrew 2279 (329 officers); Flag 70 (25 officers)

Missiles: SAM: 2 (AVT 59 and CV 61) or 3 Raytheon GMLS Mk 29 octuple launchers; NATO Sea Sparrow; semi-active radar homing to 14.6 km *(8 nm)* at 2.5 Mach; warhead 39 kg.
Guns: 3 General Electric/General Dynamics 20 mm Vulcan Phalanx 6-barrelled Mk 15; 3000 rounds/minute (or 4500 in Block 1) combined to 1.5 km.
Countermeasures: Decoys: 4 Loral Hycor SRBOC 6-barrelled fixed Mk 36; IR flares and Chaff to 4 km *(2.2 nm)*. SSTDS (Surface Ship Torpedo Defence System). SLQ-36 Nixie (Phase I).
ESM/ECM: SLQ-32(V)3 (CV 62). SLQ-32(V)4 (AVT 59 and CV 60).
WLR 1, WLR 3, WLR 11, SLQ 26 (in CV 61); combined radar warning, jammer and deception systems.
Combat data systems: NTDS/ACDS naval tactical and advanced combat direction systems; Links 4A, 11 and 14. Link 16 in due course. JOTS, POST, CVIC, TESS UMM-1(V)1, SSQ-82. SATCOMS SRR-1, WSC-3 (UHF), WSC-6 (SHF), USC-38 (EHF) (from 1992).
Fire control: 2 or 3 Mk 91 Mod 3 MFCS directors (part of NSSMS Mk 57 SAM system).
Radars: Air search: ITT SPS 48C; 3D; E/F band; range 402 km *(220 nm)*.
Raytheon SPS 49(V)5; C/D band; range 457 km *(250 nm)*.
Hughes Mk 23 TAS; D band.
Surface search: Norden SPS 67; G band.
CCA: SPN 41, 2 SPN 42, SPN 43A, SPN 44; J/K/E/F band.
Navigation: Raytheon SPN 64(V)9; I band.
Fire control: 4 or 6 Mk 95 (for SAM); I/J band.
Tacan: URN 25.

Fixed wing aircraft: Notional air wing (not in AVT 59) including: 20 F-14; 20 F/A 18; 20 A-6E (includes some KA-6D tankers); 4 EA-6B; 10 S-3A/B; 4 E-2C. See *Shipborne Aircraft* section.
Helicopters: 6 SH-3H/SH 60F Sea King.

Programmes: *Forrestal* was the world's first aircraft carrier built after the Second World War. The *Forrestal* design drew heavily from the aircraft carrier *United States* (CVA 58) which was cancelled immediately after being laid down in April 1949. *Forrestal* was authorised in FY 1952, *Saratoga* followed in FY 1953, *Ranger* in FY 1954 and *Independence* in FY 1955.

FORRESTAL (as AVT) *2/1992, Giorgio Arra*

Modernisation: Service Life Extension Programme (SLEP): The Navy's aircraft carrier Service Life Extension Programme (SLEP) began with three ships of the *Forrestal* class. *Saratoga* from October 1980 to February 1983, *Forrestal* January 1983 to 20 May 1985, and *Independence* April 1985 to May 1988. The four after 5 in guns were removed from *Forrestal* late in 1967 and a single BPDMS launcher for Sea Sparrow missiles was installed forward on the starboard side. Two Mk 25 BPDMS launchers fitted in *Independence* in 1973 with the subsequent removal of all 5 in guns, *Saratoga* in 1974, *Forrestal* in 1976. These have been replaced by three Mk 29 GMLS launchers during SLEP and they have also been fitted in *Ranger*.
Structure: The Forrestal class ships were the first aircraft carriers designed and built specifically to operate jet-propelled aircraft. *Forrestal* was redesigned early in construction to incorporate British-developed angled flight deck and steam catapults. These were the first US aircraft carriers built with an enclosed bow area to improve seaworthiness. Other features include armoured flight deck and advanced underwater protection and internal compartmentation to reduce effects of conventional and nuclear attack. Mast configurations differ. Funnel height of *Forrestal* and *Independence* increased by 10 ft in 1980. Aviation facilities include four 72 × 50 ft *(21.9 × 15.2 m)* lifts with capacity of 99 000 lb (45 tons), four steam catapults (2 C7 and 2 C 11 in AVT 59 and CV 60, 4 C7 in CV 61 and 4 C 13 in CV 62) and four arrester wires. During SLEP the port forward elevator in *Independence* was moved to the port quarter. Aviation fuel, 5500 tons.
Operational: *Independence* is based in Yukosuka, Japan. *Forrestal* was reclassified as the training carrier (AVT) in February 1992. *Ranger* is to be paid off in 1993, *Saratoga* in 1995.

INDEPENDENCE *11/1990, 92 Wing RAAF*

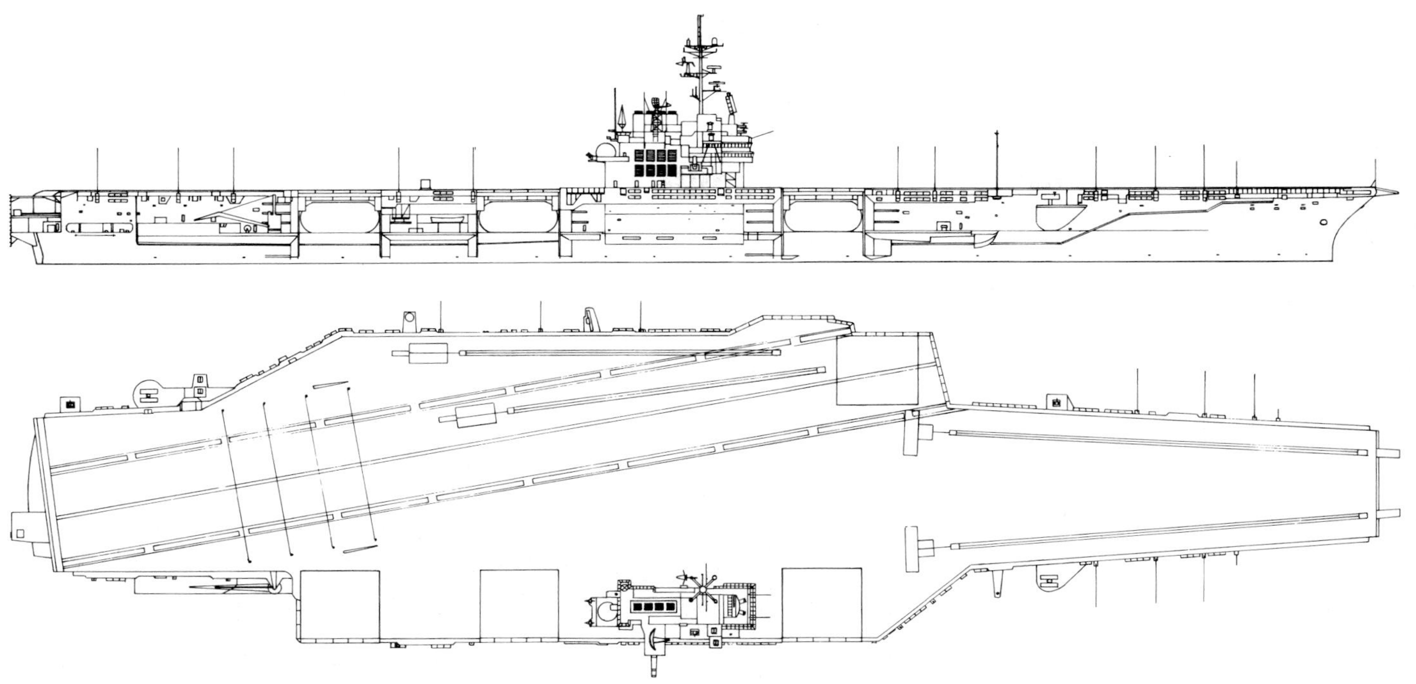

FORRESTAL

(Scale 1 : 1 800), Ian Sturton

INDEPENDENCE

11/1990, 92 Wing RAAF

SARATOGA

3/1991, Giorgio Arra

1 ENTERPRISE CLASS (CVN)

Name	*No*	*Builders*	*Laid down*	*Launched*	*Commissioned*	*F/S*
ENTERPRISE	CVN 65	Newport News Shipbuilding & Dry Dock Co	4 Feb 1958	24 Sep 1960	25 Nov 1961	Conv

Displacement, tons: 73 502 light; 75 700 standard; 93 970 full load
Dimensions, feet (metres): 1123 × 133 × 39 *(342.3 × 40.5 × 11.9)*
Flight deck, feet (metres): 1088 × 252 *(331.6 × 76.8)*
Main machinery: Nuclear; 8 Westinghouse PWR A2W; 4 Westinghouse turbines; 280 000 hp *(209 MW)*; 4 emergency diesels; 10 720 hp *(8 MW)*; 4 shafts
Speed, knots: 33
Complement: 3215 (171 officers); 2480 aircrew (358 officers); Flag 70 (25 officers)

Missiles: SAM: 3 Raytheon GMLS Mk 29 octuple launchers; NATO Sea Sparrow; semi-active radar homing to 14.6 km *(8 nm)* at 2.5 Mach; warhead 39 kg.
Guns: 3 General Electric/General Dynamics 20 mm Vulcan Phalanx 6-barrelled Mk 15; 3000 rounds/minute (or 4500 in Block 1) combined to 1.5 km.
Countermeasures: Decoys: 4 Loral Hycor SRBOC 6-barrelled fixed Mk 36; IR flares and Chaff to 4 km *(2.2 nm)*. SSTDS (Surface Ship Torpedo Defence System). SLQ-36 Nixie (Phase I).
ESM/ECM: SLQ 32(V)4; radar warning; jammer and deception system.
Combat data systems: NTDS/ACDS naval tactical and advanced combat direction systems; Links 4A, 11 and 14. Link 16 in due course. JOTS, POST, CVIC, TESS UMM-1(V)1, SSQ-82. SATCOMS SRR-1, WSC-3 (UHF), WSC-6 (SHF), USC-38 (EHF).
Fire control: 3 Mk 91 Mod 1 MFCS directors (part of NSSMS Mk 57 SAM system).
Radars: Air search: ITT SPS 48E; 3D; E/F band; range 402 km *(220 nm)*.
Raytheon SPS 49(V)5; C/D band; range 457 km *(250 nm)*.
Hughes Mk 23 TAS; D band.
Surface search: Norden SPS 67; G band.
CCA: SPN 41, SPN 43A; SPN 44; 2 SPN 46; J/K/E/F band.
Navigation: Raytheon SPS 64(V)9; I/J band.
Fire control: Six Mk 95; I/J band (for SAM).
Tacan: URN 25.

Fixed wing aircraft: Notional air wing including: 20 F14 Tomcat; 20 F/A-18 Hornet; 5 EA-6B Prowler; 20 A-6E Intruders (includes some KA-6D tankers); 5 E-2C Hawkeye; 10 S-3A/B Viking. See *Shipborne Aircraft* section.
Helicopters: 6 SH-3G/H/SH 60F Sea King.

ENTERPRISE *3/1990, Giorgio Arra*

ENTERPRISE *3/1990, Giorgio Arra*

Programmes: Authorised in FY 1958 and launched only 31 months after her keel was laid down. Underwent a refit/overhaul at Puget Sound Naval SY, Bremerton, Washington from January 1979 to March 1982. $1.4 billion provided in FY 1990 budget for a 42 month 'complex overhaul' including refuelling, which is the CVN equivalent of SLEP. This started at Newport News in early 1991 and is scheduled to complete in May 1994.
Modernisation: *Enterprise* was completed without any armament in an effort to hold down construction costs. Space for Terrier missile system was provided. Mk 25 Sea Sparrow BPDMS subsequently was installed in later 1967 and this has been replaced by first two and then three Mk 29 and supplemented with three 20 mm Mk 15 CIWS. A re-shaping of the island took place in her 1979-82 refit. This included the removal of the mast and dome (which carried obsolete ECM gear) which were replaced with a mast similar to that of the Nimitz class. The 'billboards' of the SPS 32 and 33 radars were removed and replaced by the antennas of SPS 48C and 49 radars on the new mast. Planned improvements during current overhaul include SPS 48E and Mk 23 TAS air search radars, SPN 46 (vice SPN 42) precision approach and landing radar and improved C^3 and EW systems.
Structure: Built to a modified Forrestal class design. *Enterprise* was the world's second nuclear powered warship (the cruiser *Long Beach* was completed a few months earlier). The first of the eight reactors installed achieved initial criticality on 2 December 1960, shortly after the carrier was launched. After three years of operation during which she steamed more than 207 000 miles, *Enterprise* was refuelled from November 1964 to July 1965. Her second set of cores provided about 300 000 miles steaming. The eight cores initially installed cost $64 million; the second set cost about $20 million. Refuelled again in 1970 the third set of cores lasted for eight years until replaced in 1979-82 overhaul. There are two reactors for each of the ship's four shafts. The eight reactors feed 32 heat exchangers. Aviation facilities include four deck edge lifts, two forward and one each side abaft the island. There are four 295 ft C 13 Mod 1 catapults. Hangars cover 216 000 sq ft with 25 ft deck head. Aviation fuel, 8500 tons.
Operational: 12 days' aviation fuel for intensive flying.

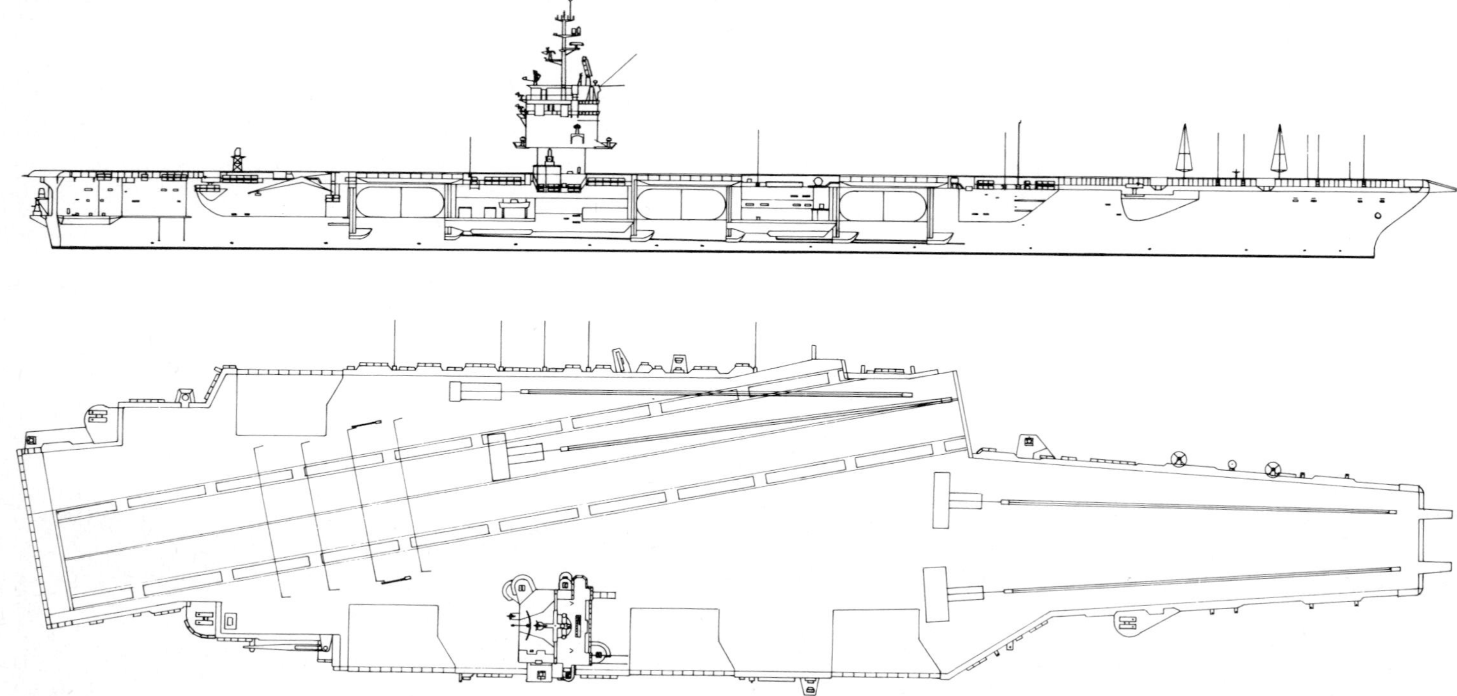
ENTERPRISE *(Scale 1 : 1 800), Ian Sturton*

CRUISERS

Notes: (a) The Virginia, California, Belknap and Leahy class cruisers, and Kidd class destroyers, have either received or are receiving the New Threat Upgrade (NTU) modernisation. This includes Standard SM-2 missiles where appropriate, updated air/surface search and fire control radars, improved weapons direction and missile fire control systems and the SYS-2 Integrated Automatic Target Detection and Tracking system (IADT). Where appropriate Mk 10 and Mk 26 missile launchers are also being converted from analog to digital systems. The original timetable for these changes ran from FY 1986 to FY 1991, but budget constraints have delayed completion of the work into FY 1996 at least.

(b) Navstar GPS (SRN-24) is being fitted in all major warships. As well as being an incomparable aid to navigation, this system has marked implications in combat data exchange and third party targeting for long-range weapon systems.

4 VIRGINIA CLASS: GUIDED MISSILE CRUISERS (CGN)

Name	*No*	*Builders*	*Laid down*	*Launched*	*Commissioned*	*F/S*
VIRGINIA	CGN 38	Newport News S B and D D Co	19 Aug 1972	14 Dec 1974	11 Sep 1976	AA
TEXAS	CGN 39	Newport News S B and D D Co	18 Aug 1973	9 Aug 1975	10 Sep 1977	PA
MISSISSIPPI	CGN 40	Newport News S B and D D Co	22 Feb 1975	31 July 1976	5 Aug 1978	AA
ARKANSAS	CGN 41	Newport News S B and D D Co	17 Jan 1977	21 Oct 1978	18 Oct 1980	PA

Displacement, tons: 8623 light; 11 300 full load
Dimensions, feet (metres): 585 × 63 × 31.5 (sonar) *(178.3 × 19.2 × 9.6)*
Main machinery: Nuclear; 2 GE PWR D2G; 2 turbines; 70 000 hp *(52 MW)*; 2 shafts
Speed, knots: 30+
Complement: 558-624 (38-45 officers)

Missiles: SLCM/SSM: 8 GDC Tomahawk (2 quad) ❶; combination of (a) land attack; TAINS (Tercom aided navigation system) to 2500 km *(1400 nm)* at 0.7 Mach; altitude 15-100 m *(49.2-328.1 ft)*; warhead nuclear 200 kT (TLAM-N); CEP 80 m; or warhead 454 kg (TLAM-C) or submunitions (TLAM-D); range 1300 km *(700 nm)*; CEP 10 m. Nuclear warheads are not normally carried. Range increased by over 30% in TLAM-C Batch III which started production in 1992.
(b) anti-ship (TASM); inertial guidance; active radar and anti-radiation homing to 460 km *(250 nm)* at 0.7 Mach; warhead 454 kg.
8 McDonnell Douglas Harpoon (2 quad) ❷; active radar homing to 130 km *(70 nm)* at 0.9 Mach; warhead 227 kg.
SAM: GDC Standard SM-2MR; command/inertial guidance; semi-active radar homing to 73 km *(40 nm)* at 2 Mach.
A/S: Honeywell ASROC; inertial guidance to 1.6-10 km *(1-5.4 nm)*; payload Mk 46 Mod 5 Neartip or Mk 50 in due course.
SAM and A/S missiles are fired from 2 twin GMLS Mk 26 launchers supplied by a total of 68 weapons ❸.
Guns: 2 FMC 5 in *(127 mm)*/54 Mk 45 Mod 0 ❹; 65° elevation; 20 rounds/minute to 23 km *(12.6 nm)* anti-surface; 15 km *(8.2 nm)* anti-aircraft; weight of shell 32 kg.
2 General Electric/General Dynamics 20 mm Vulcan Phalanx 6-barrelled Mk 15 ❺; 3000 rounds/minute (or 4500 in Block 1) combined to 1.5 kg.
4—12.7 mm MGs.
Torpedoes: 6—324 mm Mk 32 (2 triple) tubes ❻. Honeywell Mk 46 Mod 5; anti-submarine; active/passive homing to 11 km *(5.9 nm)* at 40 kts; warhead 44 kg. To be replaced by Mk 50 in due course.
Countermeasures: Decoys: 4 Loral Hycor SRBOC 6-barrelled fixed Mk 36 ❼; IR flares and Chaff to 4 km *(2.2 nm)*. T Mk 6 Fanfare or SLQ-26 Nixie; torpedo decoy system.
ESM/ECM: SLQ 32V(3); combined radar warning, jammer and deception system. OUTBOARD II (CGN 38 only).
Combat data systems: NTDS with Links 4A, 11, 14 and 16 in due course. SATCOM ❽ SRR-1; WSC-3 (UHF); USC 38 (EHF) (from 1992).
Fire control: SWG-2 Tomahawk WCS. SWG-1A Harpoon LCS. 1 Mk 74 MFCS. 1 digital Mk 116 ASW FCS. 1 Mk 86 Mod 5 GFCS for forward missile channel and gun fire. SYS-2(V)1 IADT.
Radars: Air search: ITT SPS 48C or 48D/E (NTU) ❾; 3D; E/F band; range 402 km *(220 nm)*.
Lockheed SPS 40B ❿ or Raytheon SPS 49(V)5 (NTU); C/D band.
Surface search: ISC Cardion SPS 55 ⓫; I/J band.
Navigation: Raytheon SPS 64(V)9; I/J band.
Fire control: Two SPG 51D ⓬; G/I band.
SPG 60D ⓭; I/J band. SPQ 9A ⓮; I/J band.
Tacan: URN 25. IFF Mk XII AIMS UPX 29.

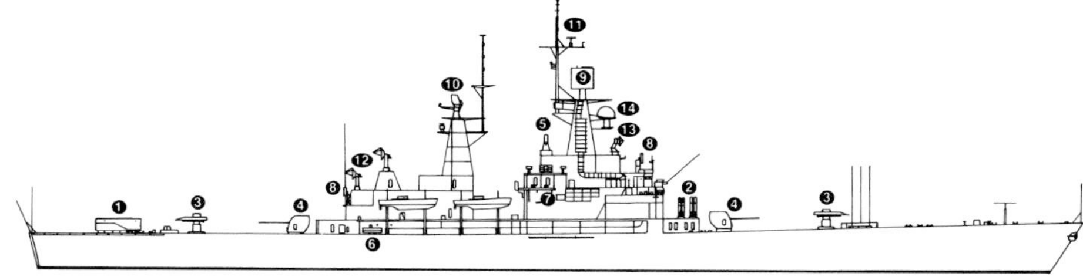

VIRGINIA *(Scale 1 : 1 500), Ian Sturton*

MISSISSIPPI *3/1991, Giorgio Arra*

Sonars: EDO/GE SQS 53A; bow-mounted; active search and attack; medium frequency. Based on SQS 26 but with digital computers.

Programmes: *Virginia* was authorised in FY 1970, *Texas* in FY 1971, *Mississippi* in FY 1972, and *Arkansas* in FY 1975. Originally classified as guided missile frigates (DLGN); subsequently reclassified as guided missile cruisers (CGN) on 30 June 1975.
Modernisation: Standard SM-1MR replaced by SM-2MR using Block II missiles to counter current and projected anti-ship cruise missile threats at extended ranges in the presence of severe enemy electronic countermeasures. Production systems were deployed in all guided missile cruisers and in DDG 993 class destroyers in FY 1988. The initial phase of fleet introduction of SM-2 in a Tartar ship was completed in May 1986 in *Virginia*. Tomahawk fitted in two armoured box launchers in all of the class at the expense of the helicopter capability. *Mississippi* and *Arkansas* have completed NTU; *Texas* scheduled in FY 1992, and *Virginia* in FY 1994. This includes upgrading the Mk 74 MFCS and SPG 51D radars, improving the Mk 26 launchers, replacing SPS 40B radar by Raytheon SPS 49 and improving SPS 48, plus IADT SYS-2(V)2 (Integrated Automatic Detection and Track). The programme may be delayed by cuts in the defence budget.
Structure: The principal differences between the Virginia and California classes are the provision of improvements to anti-air warfare capability, electronic warfare equipment, and anti-submarine fire control system. The deletion of the separate ASROC Mk 16 launcher permitted the Virginia class to be 11 ft shorter.

ARKANSAS *10/1991, Scott Connolly, RAN*

2 CALIFORNIA CLASS: GUIDED MISSILE CRUISERS (CGN)

Name	*No*	*Builders*	*Laid down*	*Launched*	*Commissioned*	*F/S*
CALIFORNIA	CGN 36	Newport News S B and D D Co	23 Jan 1970	22 Sep 1971	16 Feb 1974	PA
SOUTH CAROLINA	CGN 37	Newport News S B and D D Co	1 Dec 1970	1 July 1972	25 Jan 1975	AA

Displacement, tons: 8706 light; 9561 standard; 10 450 full load (9473, CGN 37)
Dimensions, feet (metres): 596 × 61 × 31.5 (sonar) *(181.7 × 18.6 × 9.6)*
Main machinery: Nuclear; 2 GE PWR D2G; 2 turbines; 70 000 hp *(52 MW)*; 2 shafts
Speed, knots: 30+
Complement: 603 (44 officers)

Missiles: SSM: 8 McDonnell Douglas Harpoon (2 quad) launchers ❶; active radar homing to 130 km *(70 nm)* at 0.9 Mach; warhead 227 kg.
SAM: 80 GDC Standard SM-2MR; 2 Mk 13 Mod 7 launchers ❷; command/inertial guidance; semi-active radar homing to 73 km *(40 nm)* at 2 Mach.
A/S: Honeywell ASROC Mk 16 octuple launcher ❸; inertial guidance to 1.6-10 km *(1-5.4 nm)*; Mk 46 Mod 5 Neartip/Mk 50; 24 weapons carried.
Guns: 2 FMC 5 in *(127 mm)*/54 Mk 45 Mod 0 ❹; 65° elevation; 20 rounds/minute to 23 km *(12.6 nm)* anti-surface; 15 km *(8.2 nm)* anti-aircraft; weight of shell 32 kg.
2 General Electric/General Dynamics 20 mm Vulcan Phalanx 6-barrelled Mk 15 ❺; 3000 rounds/minute (or 4500 in Block 1) combined to 1.5 km.
4—12.7 mm MGs.
Torpedoes: 4—324 mm Mk 32 (2 twin) fixed tubes. Honeywell Mk 46 Mod 5; anti-submarine; active/passive homing to 11 km *(5.9 nm)* at 40 kts; warhead 44 kg. To be replaced by Mk 50 in due course.
Countermeasures: Decoys: 4 Loral Hycor SRBOC 6-barrelled fixed Mk 36; IR flares and Chaff to 4 km *(2.2 nm)*. SLQ-25; torpedo decoy system.
ESM/ECM: SLQ 32(V)3; combined radar warning, jammer and deception system. OUTBOARD.
Combat data systems: NTDS with Links 4A, 11, 14 and 16 in due course. SATCOM SRR-1, WSC-3 (UHF), USC 38 (EHF) (from 1992).
Fire control: SWG-1A Harpoon LCS. 2 Mk 74 MFCS Mod 2. 1 Mk 86 Mod 3 GFCS. 1 Mk 14 weapon direction system. 1 Mk 114 ASW FCS. SYS-2(V)2 IADT.
Radars: Air search: ITT SPS 48E ❻; 3D; E/F band; range 402 km *(220 nm)*.
Raytheon SPS 49(V)5 ❼; C/D band.
Surface search: Norden SPS 67 ❽; G band.
Navigation: Marconi LN 66; I/J band.
Fire control: Four SPG 51D ❾; G/I band.
SPG 60D ❿; I/J band. SPQ 9A ⓫; I/J band.
Tacan: URN 25.
Sonars: EDO/GE SQS 26 CX; bow-mounted; active search and attack; medium frequency.

Helicopters: Platform only.

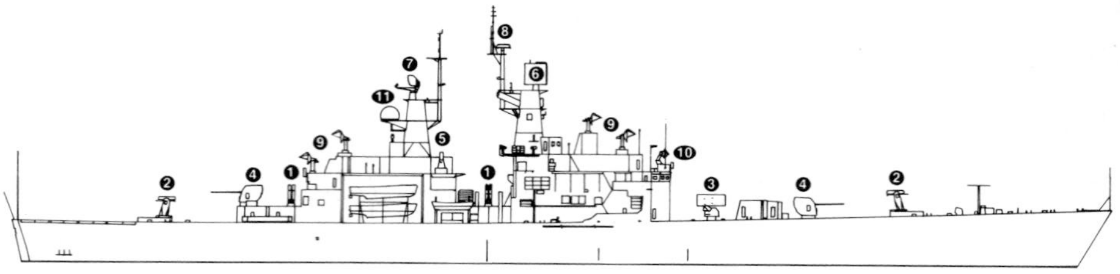

CALIFORNIA *(Scale 1 : 1 500), Ian Sturton*

SOUTH CAROLINA *6/1987, Giorgio Arra*

Programmes: *California* was authorised in FY 1967 and *South Carolina* in FY 1968. Originally classified as guided missile destroyers (DLGN); subsequently reclassified as guided missile cruisers (CGN) on 30 June 1975.
Modernisation: It was planned to fit Tomahawk missiles but the project was cancelled due to topweight constraints. Both have completed the New Threat Upgrade modernisation. This included Standard SM-2 missiles, upgrading the Mk 74 MFCS and SPG 51D radars, replacing SPS 40B radar by SPS 49, upgrading SPS 48 radar, fitting the Mk 14 weapon direction system and the SYS(V)2 IADT.
Structure: Harpoon missiles are in two quadruple sets with the midships launcher facing to starboard and the aft launcher to port.

SOUTH CAROLINA *3/1991, Giorgio Arra*

1 TRUXTUN CLASS: GUIDED MISSILE CRUISER (CGN)

Name	*No*	*Builders*	*Laid down*	*Launched*	*Commissioned*	*F/S*
TRUXTUN	CGN 35	New York SB Corp (Camden, New Jersey)	17 June 1963	19 Dec 1964	27 May 1967	PA

Displacement, tons: 8322 light; 9127 full load
Dimensions, feet (metres): 564 × 58 × 31 (sonar) *(171.9 × 17.7 × 9.4)*
Main machinery: Nuclear; 2 GE PWR D2G; 2 turbines; 70 000 hp *(52 MW)*; 2 shafts
Speed, knots: 30
Complement: 561 (39 officers); Flag 18 (6 officers)

Missiles: SSM: 8 McDonnell Douglas Harpoon (2 quad) launchers ❶; active radar homing to 130 km *(70 nm)* at 0.9 Mach; warhead 227 kg.
SAM: 40 GDC Standard SM-2ER Block 2; command/inertial guidance; semi-active radar homing to 137 km *(75 nm)* at 2.5 Mach.
A/S: 20 Honeywell ASROC; inertial guidance to 1.6-10 km *(1-5.4 nm)*; payload Mk 46 Mod 5 Neartip. 1 twin Mk 10 Mod 16 launcher for SAM and ASROC ❷.
Guns: 1 FMC 5 in *(127 mm)*/54 Mk 42 Mod 10 ❸; 85° elevation; 20-40 rounds/minute to 24 km *(13.1 nm)* anti-surface; 14 km *(7.7 nm)* anti-aircraft; weight of shell 32 kg.
2 General Electric/General Dynamics 20 mm Vulcan Phalanx 6-barrelled Mk 15 ❹; 3000 rounds/minute (or 4500 in Block 1) combined to 1.5 km.
4—12.7 mm MGs.
Torpedoes: 4—324 mm Mk 32 (2 twin) fixed tubes. Honeywell Mk 46 Mod 5; anti-submarine; active/passive homing to 11 km *(5.9 nm)* at 40 kts; warhead 44 kg.
Countermeasures: Decoys: 4 Loral Hycor SRBOC 6-barrelled fixed Mk 36; IR flares and Chaff to 4 km *(2.2 nm)*. SLQ-25 Nixie; towed torpedo decoy.
ESM/ECM: SLQ 32(V)3; combined radar warning, jammer and deception system. WLR-1; radar warning.
Combat data systems: NTDS with Links 4A, 11 and 14. SATCOM SRR-1, WSC-3 (UHF).
Fire control: SWG-1A Harpoon LCS. 2 Mk 76 Mod 6 MFCS. 1 Mk 68 GFCS. 1 Mk 14 weapon direction system. Mk 111 ASW FCS. SYS-2(V)2 IADT.
Radars: Air search: ITT SPS 48E ❺; 3D; E/F band; range 402 km *(220 nm)*.
Raytheon SPS 49(V)5 ❻; C/D band; range 457 km *(250 nm)*.
Surface search: Norden SPS 67 ❼; G band.
Navigation: Marconi LN 66; I band.
Fire control: SPG 53F ❽; I/J band. Two SPG 55C ❾; G/H band.
Tacan: URN 25. IFF Mk 12 AIMS.
Sonars: EDO/GE SQS 26 AXR; bow-mounted; active search and attack; medium frequency.

Helicopters: 1 SH-2F Sea Sprite ❿.

Programmes: *Truxtun* was the US Navy's fourth nuclear-powered surface warship. The Navy had requested seven oil-burning frigates in the FY 1962 shipbuilding programme; Congress authorised seven ships, but stipulated that one ship must be nuclear-powered. Originally classified as a guided missile frigate (DLGN); subsequently reclassified as a guided missile cruiser (CGN) on 30 June 1975. *Truxtun* is the fifth ship to be named after Commodore Thomas Truxtun *(sic)* who commanded the frigate *Constellation* (38 guns) in her successful encounter with the French frigate *L'Insurgente* (44) in 1799.

Structure: Although the *Truxtun* design is adapted from the Belknap class, the nuclear ship's gun-missile launcher arrangement is reversed from the non-nuclear ships.
Operational: Now planned to be paid off in FY 1994; this is the first nuclear powered surface ship to be decommissioned.

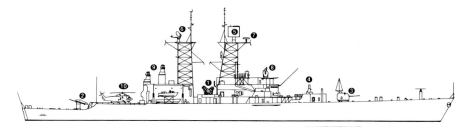

TRUXTUN *(Scale 1 : 1 500), Ian Sturton*

TRUXTUN *6/1990, G. Salmeri, RAN*

1 BAINBRIDGE CLASS: GUIDED MISSILE CRUISER (CGN)

Name	*No*	*Builders*	*Laid down*	*Launched*	*Commissioned*	*F/S*
BAINBRIDGE	CGN 25	Bethlehem Steel Co, Quincy, Mass	15 May 1959	15 Apr 1961	6 Oct 1962	AA

Displacement, tons: 7804 light; 8592 full load
Dimensions, feet (metres): 565 × 57.9 × 31.2 (sonar) *(172.3 × 17.6 × 9.5)*
Main machinery: Nuclear; 2 GE PWR D2G; 2 turbines; 70 000 hp *(52 MW)*; 2 shafts
Speed, knots: 30
Complement: 558 (42 officers); Flag 18 (6 officers)

Missiles: SSM: 8 McDonnell Douglas Harpoon (2 quad) launchers ❶; active radar homing to 130 km *(70 nm)* at 0.9 Mach; warhead 227 kg.
SAM: 80 GDC Standard SM-2ER; 2 twin Mk 10 launchers (Mod 13 fwd, Mod 14 aft) ❷; command/inertial guidance; semi-active radar homing to 137 km *(75 nm)* at 2.5 Mach.
A/S: Honeywell ASROC Mk 16 octuple launcher ❸; inertial guidance to 1.6-10 km *(1-5.4 nm)*; payload Mk 46 Mod 5 Neartip.
Guns: 2 General Electric/General Dynamics 20 mm Vulcan Phalanx 6-barrelled Mk 15 ❹; 3000 rounds/minute (or 4500 in Block 1) combined to 1.5 km.
4—12.7 mm MGs.
Torpedoes: 6—324 mm Mk 32 (2 triple) tubes ❺. Honeywell Mk 46; anti-submarine; active/passive homing to 11 km *(5.9 nm)* at 40 kts; warhead 44 kg.
Countermeasures: Decoys: 4 Loral Hycor SRBOC 6-barrelled fixed Mk 36; IR flares and Chaff to 4 km *(2.2 nm)*. T-Mk 6-Fanfare; towed torpedo decoy.
ESM/ECM: SLQ 32V(3); combined radar warning, jammer and deception system. WLR-1; radar warning.
Combat data systems: NTDS with Links 4A, 11 and 14. SATCOM SRR-1, WSC-3 (UHF).
Fire control: SWG-1A Harpoon LCS. 2 Mk 76 MFCS. 1 Mk 14 weapons direction system. Mk 111 ASW FCS.
Radars: Air search: ITT SPS 48C ❻; 3D; E/F band; range 402 km *(220 nm)*.
Raytheon SPS 49(V)5 ❼; C/D band; range 457 km *(250 nm)*.
Surface search: Norden SPS 67 ❽; G band.
Fire control: Four Sperry SPG 55C ❾; G/H band; range 51 km *(28 nm)*.
Navigation: Raytheon SPS 64(V)9; I band.
Tacan: URN 25. IFF Mk XV.
Sonars: Sperry SQQ 23; bow-mounted; active search and attack; medium frequency.
BQR-20A sonar receiver.

Helicopters: Platform for Sea King but no hangar.

Programmes: *Bainbridge* was the US Navy's third nuclear powered surface warship (after the cruiser *Long Beach* and the aircraft carrier *Enterprise*). Authorised in FY 1959. Originally classified as a guided missile frigate (DLGN); reclassified as a guided missile cruiser (CGN) on 30 June 1975.
Modernisation: *Bainbridge* underwent an Anti-Air Warfare (AAW) modernisation at the Puget Sound Naval Shipyard from 30 June 1974 to 24 September 1976. The ship was fitted with the Naval Tactical Data System (NTDS) and improved guidance capability for missiles. Four 3 in twin gun mountings were removed. Further improvements during 1983/85 refit, including Phalanx 20 mm, upgrading of SAM, SRBOC fit and replacement radars and ESM.
Operational: Now planned to be paid off in FY 1995 although she may cease to be operational some time before then.

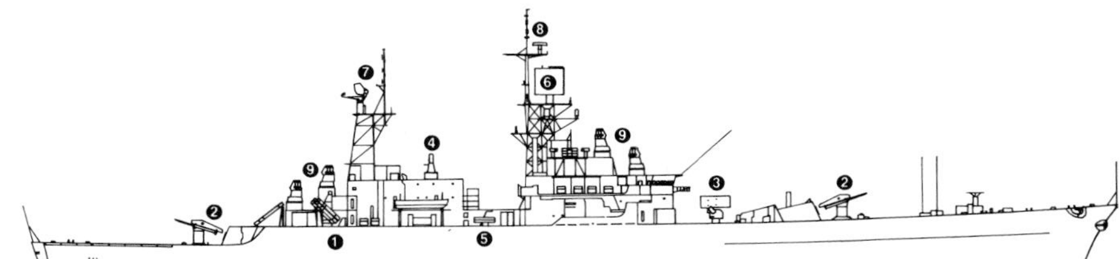

BAINBRIDGE *(Scale 1 : 1 500), Ian Sturton*

BAINBRIDGE *9/1990, W. Sartori*

22 + 5 TICONDEROGA CLASS GUIDED MISSILE CRUISERS (CG—AEGIS)

Name	*No*	*Builder/Programme*	*Laid down*	*Launched*	*Commissioned*	*F/S*
TICONDEROGA	CG 47 (ex-DDG 47)	Ingalls Shipbuilding	21 Jan 1980	25 Apr 1981	22 Jan 1983	AA
YORKTOWN	CG 48	Ingalls Shipbuilding	19 Oct 1981	17 Jan 1983	4 July 1984	AA
VINCENNES	CG 49	Ingalls Shipbuilding	20 Oct 1982	14 Jan 1984	6 July 1985	PA
VALLEY FORGE	CG 50	Ingalls Shipbuilding	14 Apr 1983	23 June 1984	18 Jan 1986	PA
THOMAS S GATES	CG 51	Bath Iron Works	31 Aug 1984	14 Dec 1985	22 Aug 1987	PA
BUNKER HILL	CG 52	Ingalls Shipbuilding	11 Jan 1984	11 Mar 1985	20 Sep 1986	PA
MOBILE BAY	CG 53	Ingalls Shipbuilding	6 June 1984	22 Aug 1985	21 Feb 1987	PA
ANTIETAM	CG 54	Ingalls Shipbuilding	15 Nov 1984	14 Feb 1986	6 June 1987	PA
LEYTE GULF	CG 55	Ingalls Shipbuilding	18 Mar 1985	20 June 1986	26 Sep 1987	AA
SAN JACINTO	CG 56	Ingalls Shipbuilding	24 July 1985	14 Nov 1986	23 Jan 1988	AA
LAKE CHAMPLAIN	CG 57	Ingalls Shipbuilding	3 Mar 1986	3 Apr 1987	12 Aug 1988	PA
PHILIPPINE SEA	CG 58	Bath Iron Works	8 May 1986	12 July 1987	18 Mar 1989	AA
PRINCETON	CG 59	Ingalls Shipbuilding	15 Oct 1986	2 Oct 1987	11 Feb 1989	PA
NORMANDY	CG 60	Bath Iron Works	7 Apr 1987	19 Mar 1988	9 Dec 1989	PA
MONTEREY	CG 61	Bath Iron Works	19 Aug 1987	23 Oct 1988	16 June 1990	AA
CHANCELLORSVILLE	CG 62	Ingalls Shipbuilding	24 June 1987	15 July 1988	4 Nov 1989	PA
COWPENS	CG 63	Bath Iron Works	23 Dec 1987	11 Mar 1989	9 Mar 1991	PA
GETTYSBURG	CG 64	Bath Iron Works	17 Aug 1988	22 July 1989	22 June 1991	AA
CHOSIN	CG 65	Ingalls Shipbuilding	22 July 1988	1 Sep 1989	12 Jan 1991	PA
HUE CITY	CG 66	Ingalls Shipbuilding	20 Feb 1989	1 June 1990	14 Sep 1991	AA
SHILOH	CG 67	Bath Iron Works	1 Aug 1989	8 Sep 1990	July 1992	Bldg/PA
ANZIO	CG 68	Ingalls Shipbuilding	21 Aug 1989	2 Nov 1990	2 May 1992	AA
VICKSBURG	CG 69	Ingalls Shipbuilding	30 May 1990	2 Aug 1991	Jan 1993	Bldg
LAKE ERIE	CG 70	Bath Iron Works	6 Mar 1990	13 July 1991	Mar 1993	Bldg
CAPE ST GEORGE	CG 71	Ingalls Shipbuilding	19 Nov 1990	10 Jan 1992	Apr 1993	Bldg
VELLA GULF	CG 72	Ingalls Shipbuilding	22 Apr 1991	May 1992	Sep 1993	Bldg
PORT ROYAL	CG 73	Ingalls Shipbuilding	20 Nov 1991	Nov 1992	Feb 1994	Bldg

Displacement, tons: 7015 light; 9590 (CG 47-48); 9407 (CG 49-51); 9466 (remainder) full load
Dimensions, feet (metres): 567 × 55 × 31 (sonar) *(172.8 × 16.8 × 9.5)*
Main machinery: 4 GE LM 2500 gas turbines; 88 000 hp *(66 MW)* sustained; 2 shafts; cp props
Speed, knots: 30+. **Range, miles:** 6000 at 20 kts
Complement: 358 (24 officers); accommodation for 405 total

Missiles: SLCM/SSM: GDC Tomahawk (CG 52 onwards); combination of (a) land attack; TAINS (Tercom aided navigation system) to 2500 km *(1400 nm)* at 0.7 Mach; altitude 15-100 m *(49.2-328.1 ft)*; warhead nuclear 200 kT (TLAM-N); CEP 80 m; or warhead 454 kg (TLAM-C) or submunitions (TLAM-D); range 1300 km *(700 nm)*; CEP 10 m. Nuclear warheads are not normally carried. Range increased by 30% in TLAM-C Block III which started production in 1992.
(b) anti-ship (TASM); inertial guidance; active radar and anti-radiation homing to 460 km *(250 nm)* at 0.7 Mach; warhead 454 kg.
8 McDonnell Douglas Harpoon (2 quad) ❶; active radar homing to 130 km *(70 nm)* at 0.9 Mach; warhead 227 kg. Extended range SLAM can be fired from modified Harpoon canisters.
SAM: 68 (CG 47-51); 122 (CG 52 onwards) GDC Standard SM-2MR; command/inertial guidance; semi-active radar homing to 73 km *(40 nm)* at 2 Mach.
A/S: 20 Honeywell ASROC; inertial guidance to 1.6-10 km *(1-5.4 nm)*; payload Mk 46 Mod 5 Neartip/Mk 50.
SAM and A/S missiles are fired from 2 twin Mk 26 Mod 5 launchers ❷ (CG 47-51) and 2 Mk 41 Mod 0 vertical launchers ❸ (61 missiles per launcher) (CG 52 onwards). Tomahawk is carried in CG 52 onwards with 8 missiles in each VLS launcher and 12 in the magazines. Operational evaluation of VLS continues in conjunction with operational evaluation of Tomahawk. Vertical launch ASROC will be back fitted when available.
Guns: 2 FMC 5 in *(127 mm)*/54 Mk 45 (Mod 0 (CG 47-50); Mod 1 (CG 51 onwards)) ❹; 65° elevation; 20 rounds/minute to 23 km *(12.6 nm)* anti-surface; weight of shell 32 kg.
2 General Electric/General Dynamics 20 mm/76 Vulcan Phalanx 6-barrelled Mk 15 ❺; 3000 rounds/minute (4500 in Block 1) combined to 1.5 km.
4—12.7 mm MGs.
Torpedoes: 6—324 mm Mk 32 (2 triple) tubes (fitted in the ship's side aft) ❻. 36 Honeywell Mk 46 Mod 5; anti-submarine; active/passive homing to 11 km *(5.9 nm)* at 40 kts; warhead 44 kg. To be replaced by Mk 50 in due course.
Countermeasures: Decoys: 4 or 6 Loral Hycor SRBOC 6-barrelled fixed Mk 36 ❼; IR flares and Chaff to 4 km *(2.2 nm)*. SLQ-25 Nixie; towed torpedo decoy.
ESM/ECM: SLQ 32V(3) ❽; combined radar warning, jammer and deception system.
Combat data systems: NTDS with Links 4A, 11, 14 and 16 in due course. SATCOM SRR-1, WSC-3 (UHF), USC-38 (EHF) (from 1992). UYK 7 and 20 computers (CG 47-58); UYK 43/44 (CG 59 onwards). SQQ 28 for LAMPS sonobuoy data link ❾.
Fire control: SWG-3 Tomahawk WCS. SWG-1A Harpoon LCS. Aegis Mk 7 Mod 2 multi-target tracking with Mk 99 MFCS (includes 4 Mk 80 illuminator directors); has at least 12 channels of fire. Mk 116 Mod 6 (53B) or 7 (53C) FCS for ASW. Mk 86 Mod 9 GFCS.
Radars: Air search/fire control: RCA SPY 1A phased arrays ❿; 3D; E/F band (CG 47-58).
Raytheon SPY 1B phased arrays ⓫; 3D; E/F band (CG 59 on).
Air search: Raytheon SPS 49(V)7 ⓬; C/D band; range 457 km *(250 nm)*.
Surface search: ISC Cardion SPS 55 ⓭; I/J band.
Navigation: Marconi LN 66 (CG 47-48); I band.
Raytheon SPS 64(V)9 (remainder); I band.
Fire control: Lockheed SPQ 9A ⓮; I/J band; range 37 km *(20 nm)*.
Four Raytheon/RCA SPG 62 ⓯; I/J band.
Tacan: URN 25. IFF Mk XII AIMS UPX-29.
Sonars: General Electric/Hughes SQS 53A/B (CG 47-55); bow-mounted; active search and attack; medium frequency.
Gould SQR 19 (CG 54-55); passive towed array (TACTAS).
Gould/Raytheon SQQ 89(V)3 (CG 56 onwards); combines hull-mounted active SQS 53B (CG 56-67) or SQS 53C (CG 68-73) and passive towed array SQR 19.

Helicopters: 2 SH-60B Seahawk LAMPS III ⓰; 2 SH-2F LAMPS I (CG 47-48) ⓱.

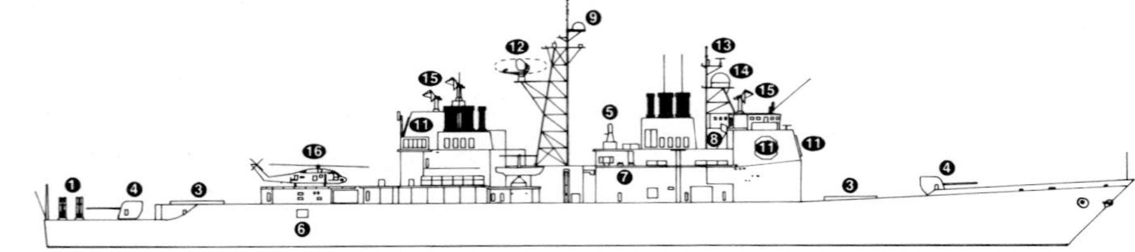

BUNKER HILL *(Scale 1 : 1 500), Ian Sturton*

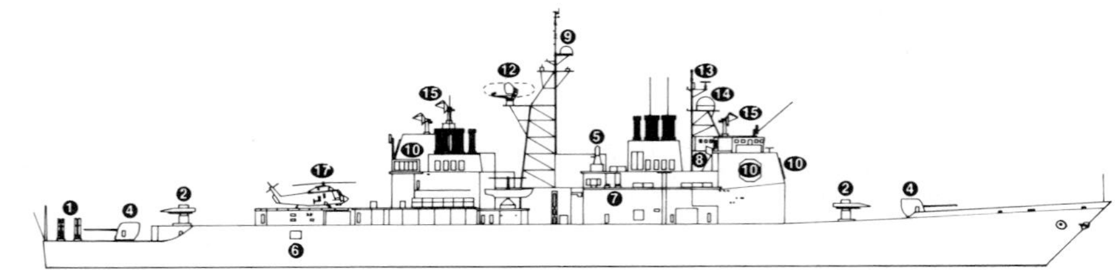

TICONDEROGA *(Scale 1 : 1 500), Ian Sturton*

Programmes: Three ships were funded in each of FYs 1985, 1986 and 1987. However, the FY 1987 request originally was for two, but Congress took the unusual action of deleting one of three Burke class DDG 51s being requested and adding a third CG 47 class ship. In finally approving the FY 1988 ship construction budget, Congress elected to authorise and fund the remaining five cruisers in the 27-ship programme. That decision stemmed from the delays being encountered in the construction of DDG 51 by Bath Iron Works, and the realisation that the Navy was in no position at that time to award further contracts for construction of more DDG 51s. There have been delays in the six ships of the class being built by Bath Iron Works.
Modernisation: Long Range Improvement Programme: In order to include the latest in technology in these ships, four baselines were planned and five have evolved. *Ticonderoga*, equipped with LAMPS I, represents Baseline O. Baseline I starts with *Vincennes* equipped with LAMPS III, RAST haul down flight deck system and Block 2 Standard missiles. Baseline II, beginning with *Bunker Hill*, adds Tomahawk, and the Vertical Launch System. Baseline III starting with *San Jacinto* adds the SQQ 89 sonar. Baseline IV, beginning with *Princeton* (CG 59), incorporates the advanced AN/SPY 1B radar on UYQ-21 displays and includes the upgraded computers UYK-43/44. According to the Navy, this method of upgrading ship capabilities provides the best available combat system to the fleet while reducing operation and support costs. *Lake Champlain* fired the first SLAM missile from a Harpoon canister in June 1990; the extended range SSM was controlled in terminal flight by a LAMPS III helicopter.
Structure: The Ticonderoga class design is a modification of the Spruance class. The same basic hull is used, with the same gas turbine propulsion plant although the overall length is slightly increased. The design includes Kevlar armour to protect vital spaces. No stabilisers. *Vincennes* and later ships have a lighter tripod mainmast vice the square quadruped of the first two.
Operational: *Yorktown* provided the air-intercept support for Navy fighters intercepting the Egyptian airliner carrying the hijackers of the cruise ship *Achille Lauro* from Egypt to Tunisia. In March and April of 1986, *Yorktown* and *Vincennes* were focal points of the successful operations in the Gulf of Sidra which led to the sinking of two Libyan patrol boats and of the strike by carrier-based Navy aircraft and shore-based F-111s against Libyan missile sites and other targets. *Vincennes* was again in the news with the misidentification and shooting down of an airliner during a surface engagement with Iranian gunboats in 1988. The report of that incident describes the Aegis system as having performed as designed, and the sensor data collected was accurate but 'it should be appreciated that Aegis is not capable of identifying the type of aircraft being tracked. Ships of the class were again active in directing the air defence of the northern Gulf during the Iraq war in early 1991. *Princeton* was damaged by a mine; repairs were completed in December 1991. Seven of the class fired Tomahawk missiles. Aegis's major advantages are the extended range of its sensors, its fast reaction time, the capacity to track many targets at once, its ability to send this information automatically to other units, and its data displays which combine sensor information with other inputs. Because of its long-range radar, it gives operators additional time to react, to gather data, and to make considered judgements. Operating close to land, these advantages can be eroded. Two of the class are based at Yukosuka, Japan.

HUE CITY *4/1991, Ingalls Shipbuilding*

VINCENNES *6/1990, Vic Jeffery, RAN*

THOMAS S GATES *6/1991, Giorgio Arra*

SAN JACINTO *8/1991, Giorgio Arra*

HUE CITY *6/1991, Ingalls Shipbuilding*

CHANCELLORSVILLE *10/1991, Giorgio Arra*

1 LONG BEACH CLASS: GUIDED MISSILE CRUISER (CGN)

Name	*No*	*Builders*	*Laid down*	*Launched*	*Commissioned*	*F/S*
LONG BEACH	CGN 9 (ex-CGN 160, CLGN 160)	Bethlehem Steel Co, Quincy, Mass	2 Dec 1957	14 July 1959	9 Sep 1961	PA

Displacement, tons: 15 540 light; 17 525 full load
Dimensions, feet (metres): 721.2 × 73.2 × 29.7 (sonar) *(219.9 × 22.3 × 9.1)*
Main machinery: Nuclear; 2 Westinghouse PWR C1W; 2 GE turbines; 80 000 hp *(60 MW)*; 2 shafts
Speed, knots: 30
Complement: 958 (65 officers); Flag 68 (10 officers); marines 45 (1 officer)

Missiles: SLCM/SSM: 8 GDC Tomahawk (2 quad) ❶; combination of (a) land attack; TAINS (Tercom aided navigation system) to 2500 km *(1400 nm)* at 0.7 Mach; altitude 15-100 m *(49.2-328.1 ft)*; warhead nuclear 200 kT (TLAM-N); CEP 80 m; or warhead 454 kg (TLAM-C) or submunitions (TLAM-D); range 1300 km *(700 nm)*; CEP 10 m. Nuclear warheads are not normally carried. Range increased by 30% in TLAM-C Block III which started production in 1992.
(b) anti-ship (TASM); inertial guidance; active radar and anti-radiation homing to 460 km *(250 nm)* at 0.7 Mach; warhead 454 kg.
8 McDonnell Douglas Harpoon (2 quad) ❷; active radar homing to 130 km *(70 nm)* at 0.9 Mach; warhead 227 kg.
SAM: 120 GDC Standard SM-2ER; 2 twin Mk 10 launchers (Mod 11 forward, Mod 12 aft) ❸; command/inertial guidance; semi-active radar homing to 137 km *(75 nm)* at 2.5 Mach.
A/S: Honeywell ASROC Mk 16 octuple launcher ❹; inertial guidance to 1.6-10 km *(1-5.4 nm)*; payload Mk 46 Mod 5 Neartip/Mk 50.
Guns: 2 USN 5 in *(127 mm)*/38 Mk 30 ❺; 85° elevation; 15 rounds/minute to 17 km *(9.3 nm)* anti-surface; 11 km *(5.9 nm)* anti-aircraft; weight of shell 25 kg. Completed with an all-missile armament. 2 single 5 in mounts were fitted during 1962-63.
2 General Electric/General Dynamics 20 mm Vulcan Phalanx 6-barrelled Mk 15 ❻; 3000 rounds/minute (or 4500 in Block 1) combined to 1.5 km.
4—12.7 mm MGs.
Torpedoes: 6—324 mm Mk 32 (2 triple) tubes ❼. Honeywell Mk 46; anti-submarine; active/passive homing to 11 km *(5.9 nm)* at 40 kts; warhead 44 kg. To be replaced by Mk 50 in due course.

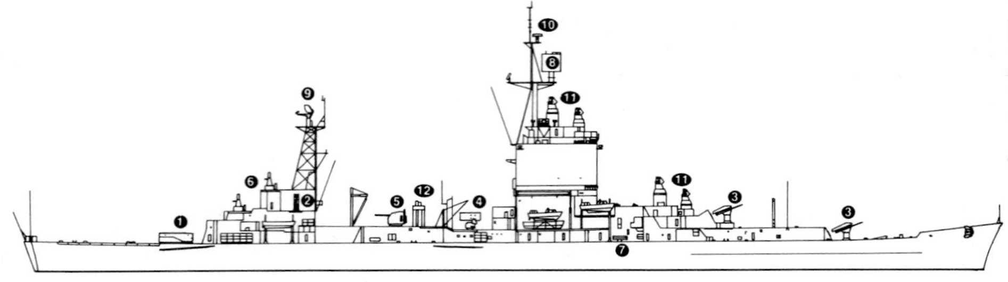
LONG BEACH *(Scale 1 : 1 800), Ian Sturton*

Countermeasures: Decoys: 4 Loral Hycor SRBOC 6-barrelled fixed Mk 36; IR flares and Chaff to 4 km *(2.2 nm)*. SLQ-25 Nixie; towed torpedo decoy.
ESM/ECM: SLQ 32V(3); combined radar warning, jammer and deception system. OUTBOARD I. SAR-8 IRSDT (Infra-Red Search, Detection and Track) in due course.
Combat data systems: NTDS with Links 4A, 11 14 and 16 in due course. SATCOM SRR-1, WSC-3 (UHF), USC-38 (EHF) (from 1993).
Fire control: SWG-2 Tomahawk WCS. SWG-1 Harpoon LCS. 4 Mk 76 Mod 2 MFCS. 2 Mk 56 GFCS. 1 Mk 14 weapon direction system. Mk 111 ASW. SYS 1(V)1 IADT.
Radars: Air search: ITT SPS 48C ❽; 3D; E/F band; range 402 km *(220 nm)*.
Raytheon SPS 49(V)3 ❾; C/D band; range 457 km *(250 nm)*.
Surface search: Norden SPS 67 ❿; G band.
Navigation: Marconi LN 66; I band.
Fire control: Four SPG 55D ⓫; G/H band.
Two General Electric Mk 35 Mod 2 ⓬; I/J band.
Tacan: URN 25. IFF Mk XII AIMS UPX-29.
Sonars: Sperry SQQ 23B pair; hull-mounted; active search and attack; medium frequency.

Helicopters: Platform but no facilities.

Programmes: *Long Beach* was the first ship to be designed as a cruiser for the USA since the end of the Second World War. She is the world's first nuclear powered surface warship and the first warship to have a guided missile main battery. Authorised in FY 1957 and first got underway on nuclear power on 5 July 1961. Ordered as a guided missile light cruiser (CLGN 160) reclassified as a guided missile cruiser (CGN 160) early in 1957 and renumbered (CGN 9) on 1 July 1957. The original plan was to install Polaris missiles.
Modernisation: As a result of the 1976 cancellation of the planned fitting of AEGIS *Long Beach* underwent a mid-life modernisation 1980-83. This included updating of missile systems, restoration of the missile radars, the SPS 32 and 33 air search replaced by SPS 48 and 49 systems, replacement of the ship's computer and modernisation of the communications system. Tomahawk box launchers have since been added. New Threat Update, planned to start in 1993, has probably been shelved and the ship will be paid off in 1994.
Structure: Initially planned at about 7800 tons (standard) to test the feasibility of a nuclear powered surface warship. Early in 1956 her displacement was increased to 11 000 tons and a second SAM missile launcher was added. A Talos missile launcher (now removed) was also added which, with other features, further increased the displacement.

LONG BEACH *10/1991, 92 Wing RAAF*

9 BELKNAP CLASS: GUIDED MISSILE CRUISERS (CG)

Name	*No*	*Builders*	*Laid down*	*Launched*	*Commissioned*	*F/S*
BELKNAP	CG 26	Bath Iron Works Corporation	5 Feb 1962	20 July 1963	7 Nov 1964	AA
JOSEPHUS DANIELS	CG 27	Bath Iron Works Corporation	23 Apr 1962	2 Dec 1963	8 May 1965	AA
WAINWRIGHT	CG 28	Bath Iron Works Corporation	2 July 1962	25 Apr 1964	8 Jan 1966	AA
JOUETT	CG 29	Puget Sound Naval Shipyard	25 Sep 1962	30 June 1964	3 Dec 1966	PA
HORNE	CG 30	San Francisco Naval Shipyard	12 Dec 1962	30 Oct 1964	15 Apr 1967	PA
STERETT	CG 31	Puget Sound Naval Shipyard	25 Sep 1962	30 June 1964	8 Apr 1967	PA
WILLIAM H STANDLEY	CG 32	Bath Iron Works Corporation	29 July 1963	19 Dec 1964	9 July 1966	PA
FOX	CG 33	Todd Shipyard Corporation	15 Jan 1963	21 Nov 1964	8 May 1966	PA
BIDDLE	CG 34	Bath Iron Works Corporation	9 Dec 1963	2 July 1965	21 Jan 1967	AA

Displacement, tons: 6570 standard; 8200 full load (CG 27-28); 8065 (CG 29-33); 8250 (CG 34); 8575 (CG 26)
Dimensions, feet (metres): 547 × 54.8 × 28.8 (sonar) *(166.7 × 16.7 × 8.8)*
Main machinery: 4 Babcock & Wilcox/Combustion Engineering boilers; 1200 psi *(84.4 kg/cm sq)*; 950°F *(510°C)*; 2 GE/De Laval/Allis Chalmers turbines; 85 000 hp *(63 MW)*; 2 shafts
Speed, knots: 32.5. **Range, miles:** 8000 at 14 kts; 2500 at 30 kts
Complement: 479 (26 officers); Flag 18 (6 officers); Flag 111 (30 officers) (CG 26)

Missiles: SSM: 8 McDonnell Douglas Harpoon (2 quad) launchers ❶; active radar homing to 130 km *(70 nm)* at 0.9 Mach; warhead 227 kg.
SAM: 40 GDC Standard SM-2ER; combined/inertial guidance; semi-active radar homing to 137 km *(75 nm)* at 2.5 Mach.
A/S: 20 Honeywell ASROC; inertial guidance to 1.6-10 km *(1-5.4 nm)*; payload Mk 46 Mod 5 Neartip/Mk 50. 1 twin Mk 10 Mod 15 launcher for SAM and ASROC ❷.
Guns: 1 FMC 5 in *(127 mm)*/54 Mk 42 Mod 10 ❸; 85° elevation; 20-40 rounds/minute to 24 km *(13.1 nm)* anti-surface; 14 km *(7.7 nm)* anti-aircraft; weight of shell 32 kg.
2 General Electric/General Dynamics 20 mm Vulcan Phalanx 6-barrelled Mk 15 ❹; 3000 rounds/minute (4500 in Block 1) combined to 1.5 km.
Torpedoes: 6—324 mm Mk 32 (2 triple) tubes ❺. 18 Honeywell Mk 46 Mod 5; anti-submarine; active/passive homing to 11 km *(5.9 nm)* at 40 kts; warhead 44 kg. To be replaced by Mk 50 in due course.
Countermeasures: Decoys: 4 Loral Hycor SRBOC 6-barrelled fixed Mk 36; IR flares and Chaff to 4 km *(2.2 nm)*. SLQ 25 Nixie; torpedo decoy.
ESM/ECM: SLQ 32(V)3; combined radar warning, jammer and deception system. OUTBOARD II (CG 27-29 and 32-34).
Combat data systems: NTDS with Links 4A, 11, 14 and 16 in due course. SATCOM SRR-1, WSC-3 (UHF); WSC-6 (SHF) (CG 26), USC-38 (EHF) (from 1992).
Fire control: SWG-1 Harpoon LCS. 2 Mk 76 Mod 9 MFCS. Mk 68 GFCS. Mk 14 weapon direction system (Mk 7 in CG26). Mk 114 ASW fire control system (Mk 116 in CG 26). SYS 2(V)1/2 IADT.
Radars: Air search: ITT SPS 48E (C in CG26) ❻; 3D; E/F band; range 402 km *(220 nm)*.
Raytheon SPS 49(V)3/5 ❼; C/D band.
Surface search: Norden SPS 67 ❽; G band.
Navigation: Marconi LN 66; I band.
Fire control: Western Electric SPG 53F ❾; I/J band.
Two Sperry/RCA SPG 55D ❿; G/H band; range 51 km *(28 nm)* (for Standard).
Tacan: URN 25. IFF Mk XII AIMS UPX-29.
Sonars: EDO SQS 26BX; General Electric/Hughes SQS 53C (CG 26); bow-mounted; active search and attack; medium/low frequency.

Helicopters: 1 SH-2F LAMPS I ⓫ (no hangar in *Belknap*).

Programmes: Authorised as guided missile frigates; first three in FY 1961, remainder in FY 1962. Reclassified as CGs on 30 June 1975.
Modernisation: *Belknap* was severely damaged in a collision with the carrier *John F Kennedy* (CV 67) on 22 November 1975 near Sicily. Repair and modernisation began 9 January 1978. Included Flag accommodation in front of the bridge and the hangar converted for additional accommodation. Recommissioned 10 May 1980. *Belknap, Wainwright, Horne* and *Sterett* all had the Tactical Flag Command Centre fitted in 1983-85. All except *Belknap* have received the New Threat Upgrade modernisation which includes SPS 48E radar, Mk 14 WDS and SYS 2 automated action data system, integrated with SPS 49 radar.
Structure: Distinctive in having their single missile launcher forward and 5 in gun mount aft. This arrangement allowed missile stowage in the larger bow section and provided space aft of the superstructure for a helicopter hangar and platform. Harpoon is forward of Phalanx on the port side, with this arrangement reversed on the starboard side.
Operational: *Belknap* is 6th Fleet Flagship. *Wainwright* was the SM-2ER trials ship.

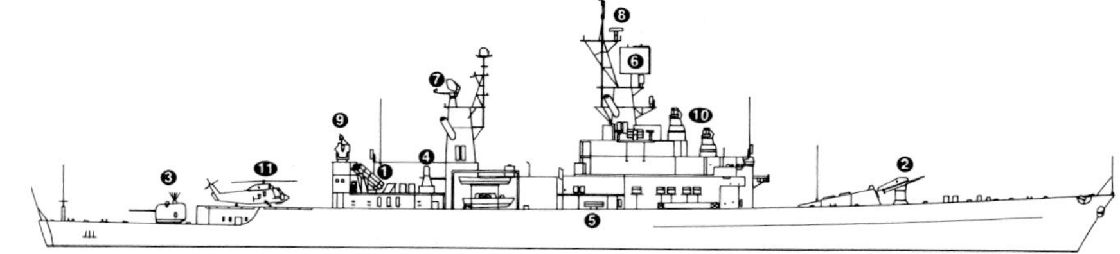

BIDDLE (Scale 1 : 1 500), *Ian Sturton*

JOUETT *10/1991, Giorgio Arra*

HORNE *7/1991, van Ginderen Collection*

BIDDLE *3/1991, Giorgio Arra*

BELKNAP *10/1991, C. D. Yaylali*

9 LEAHY CLASS: GUIDED MISSILE CRUISERS (CG)

Name	*No*	*Builders*	*Laid down*	*Launched*	*Commissioned*	*F/S*
LEAHY	CG 16	Bath Iron Works Corporation	3 Dec 1959	1 July 1961	4 Aug 1962	PA
HARRY E YARNELL	CG 17	Bath Iron Works Corporation	31 May 1960	9 Dec 1961	2 Feb 1963	AA
WORDEN	CG 18	Bath Iron Works Corporation	19 Sep 1960	2 June 1962	3 Aug 1963	PA
DALE	CG 19	New York S B Corporation	6 Sep 1960	28 July 1962	23 Nov 1963	AA
RICHMOND K TURNER	CG 20	New York S B Corporation	9 Jan 1961	6 Apr 1963	13 June 1964	AA
GRIDLEY	CG 21	Puget Sound Bridge & Dry Dock Co	15 July 1960	31 July 1961	25 May 1963	PA
ENGLAND	CG 22	Todd Shipyards Corporation	4 Oct 1960	6 Mar 1962	7 Dec 1963	PA
HALSEY	CG 23	San Francisco Naval Shipyard	26 Aug 1960	15 Jan 1962	20 July 1963	PA
REEVES	CG 24	Puget Sound Naval Shipyard	1 July 1960	12 May 1962	15 May 1964	PA

Displacement, tons: 4650 light; 5670 standard; 8203 full load
Dimensions, feet (metres): 533 × 54.9 × 24.8 (sonar) *(162.5 × 16.6 × 7.6)*
Main machinery: 4 boilers (Babcock & Wilcox in CG 16-20, Foster-Wheeler in CG 21-24); 1200 psi *(84.4 kg/cm sq)*; 950°F *(510°C)*; 2 GE/De Laval/Allis Chalmers turbines; 85 000 hp *(63 MW)*; 2 shafts
Speed, knots: 32.7. **Range, miles:** 8000 at 20 kts; 2500 at 30 kts
Complement: 423 (26 officers); Flag 18 (6 officers)

Missiles: SSM: 8 McDonnell Douglas Harpoon (2 quad) launchers ❶; active radar homing to 130 km *(70 nm)* at 0.9 Mach; warhead 227 kg.
SAM: 80 GDC Standard SM-2ER; 2 twin Mk 10 launchers (Mod 13 fwd, Mod 14 aft) ❷; command/inertial guidance; semi-active radar homing to 137 km *(75 nm)* at 2.5 Mach.
A/S: Honeywell ASROC Mk 16 octuple launcher ❸; inertial guidance to 1.6-10 km *(1-5.4 nm)*; payload Mk 46 Mod 5 Neartip/Mk 50.
Guns: 2 General Electric/General Dynamics 20 mm Vulcan Phalanx 6-barrelled Mk 15 ❹; 3000 rounds/minute (4500 in Block 1) combined to 1.5 km.
4—12.7 mm MGs.
Torpedoes: 6—324 mm Mk 32 (2 triple) tubes ❺. Honeywell Mk 46 Mod 5; anti-submarine; active/passive homing to 11 km *(5.9 nm)* at 40 kts; warhead 44 kg. To be replaced by Mk 50 in due course.
Countermeasures: Decoys: 6 Loral Hycor SRBOC 6-barrelled fixed Mk 36; IR flares and Chaff to 4 km *(2.2 nm)*. T-Mk 6 Fanfare/SLQ 25 Nixie; towed torpedo decoy. NATO Sea Gnat. SSQ-95 AEB. SLQ 39/49 Chaff buoy/expendables.
ESM/ECM: SLQ 32(V)3; combined radar warning, jammer and deception system.
Combat data systems: NTDS with Links 4A, 11, 14 and 16 in due course. SATCOM SRR-1, WSC-3 (UHF), USC-38 (EHF) (from 1992).
Fire control: SWG-1A Harpoon LCS. Mk 76 MFCS. Mk 14 weapon direction system. Mk 114 ASW FCS. SYS-2(V)2 IADT.
Radars: Air search: ITT SPS 48 E ❻; 3D; E/F band; range 402 km *(220 nm)*.
Raytheon SPS 49(V)3/5 ❼; C/D band; range 457 km *(250 nm)*.
Surface search: Raytheon SPS 10F or Norden SPS 67 ❽; G band.
Navigation: Raytheon SPS 64(V)9; I band.
Fire control: Four Sperry/RCA SPG 55C ❾; G/H band; range 51 km *(28 nm)*.
Tacan: URN 25. IFF Mk XV.
Sonars: Sperry SQQ 23 pair (CG 17); bow-mounted; active search and attack; medium frequency.
Sangamo SQS 23B (remainder); active search and attack; medium frequency.

Helicopters: Platform only with limited facilities.

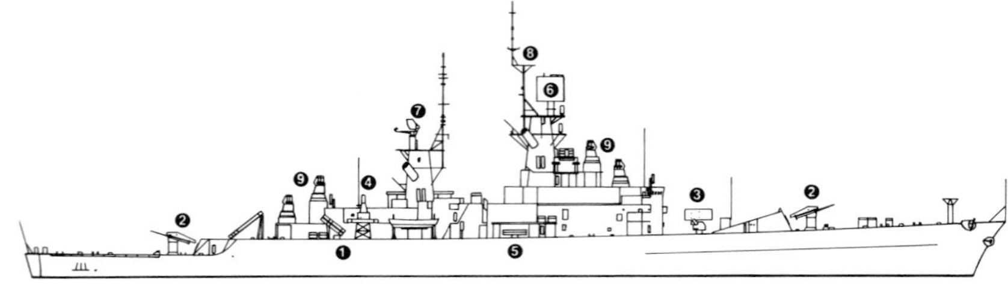
LEAHY *(Scale 1 : 1500), Ian Sturton*

HARRY E YARNELL *6/1991, Stefan Terzibaschitsch*

Programmes: First three authorised in FY 1958 and remainder in FY 1959. Reclassified as guided missile cruisers (CG) on 30 June 1975.
Modernisation: Modernised between 1967 and 1972 to improve their Anti-Air Warfare (AAW) capabilities. 76 mm guns were removed and superstructure enlarged to provide space for additional electronic equipment, including NTDS; improved Tacan fitted and improved guidance system for SAM missiles installed, and larger ship's service turbo generators provided. New Threat Upgrade modernisation completed in all of the class 1987-91; this included SPS 48E radar, updating the Mk 10 launchers and Mk 76 MFCS and improving the SPG 55 fire control radars.
Structure: Distinctive in having twin missile launchers forward and aft with ASROC launcher between the forward missile launcher and bridge on main deck level.
Operational: 'Double-end' missile cruisers especially designed to screen fast carrier task forces.

RICHMOND K TURNER *3/1990, Giorgio Arra*

DESTROYERS

1 + 12 + 5 (4) ARLEIGH BURKE CLASS GUIDED MISSILE DESTROYERS (AEGIS) (DDG)

Name	*No*	*Builders*	*Laid down*	*Launched*	*Commissioned*	*F/S*
ARLEIGH BURKE	DDG 51	Bath Iron Works, Maine	6 Dec 1988	16 Sep 1989	4 July 1991	AA
JOHN BARRY	DDG 52	Ingalls Shipbuilding	26 Feb 1990	10 May 1991	Nov 1992	Bldg
JOHN PAUL JONES	DDG 53	Bath Iron Works, Maine	8 Aug 1990	26 Oct 1991	July 1993	Bldg
CURTIS WILBUR	DDG 54	Bath Iron Works, Maine	12 Mar 1992	May 1992	Oct 1993	Bldg
STOUT	DDG 55	Ingalls Shipbuilding	13 Sep 1991	Oct 1992	Feb 1994	Bldg
JOHN S McCAIN	DDG 56	Bath Iron Works, Maine	12 Aug 1991	Sep 1992	Mar 1994	Bldg
MITSCHER	DDG 57	Ingalls Shipbuilding	10 Feb 1992	Apr 1993	July 1994	Bldg
LABOON	DDG 58	Bath Iron Works, Maine	24 Mar 1992	Feb 1993	Aug 1994	Bldg
RUSSELL	DDG 59	Ingalls Shipbuilding	July 1992	Aug 1993	Oct 1994	Bldg
PAUL HAMILTON	DDG 60	Bath Iron Works, Maine	Aug 1992	July 1993	Dec 1994	Bldg
RAMAGE	DDG 61	Ingalls Shipbuilding	Nov 1992	Dec 1993	Jan 1995	Bldg
FITZGERALD	DDG 62	Bath Iron Works, Maine	Feb 1993	Dec 1993	Apr 1995	Bldg
STETHEM	DDG 63	Ingalls Shipbuilding	Mar 1993	Apr 1994	July 1995	Bldg
CARNEY	DDG 64	Bath Iron Works, Maine	Aug 1993	June 1994	Sep 1995	Ord
BENFOLD	DDG 65	Ingalls Shipbuilding	Aug 1993	Oct 1994	Nov 1995	Ord
GONZALEZ	DDG 66	Ingalls Shipbuilding	Jan 1994	Nov 1994	Mar 1996	Ord
COLE	DDG 67	Bath Iron Works, Maine	Feb 1994	Mar 1995	May 1996	Ord
—	DDG 68-72	Authorised FY 1992	—	—	—	Proj

Displacement, tons: 6625 light; 8315 full load
Dimensions, feet (metres): 504.5 × 66.9 × 20.7; 32.7 (sonar) *(153.8 × 20.4 × 6.3; 9.9)*
Main machinery: 4 GE LM 2500-30 gas turbines; 92 000 hp *(69 MW)* sustained; 2 shafts; cp props
Speed, knots: 32. **Range, miles:** 4400 at 20 kts
Complement: 303 (23 officers) plus 38 spare

Missiles: SLCM/SSM: 56 GDC Tomahawk; combination of (a) land attack; TAINS (Tercom aided navigation system) to 2500 km *(1400 nm)* at 0.7 Mach; altitude 15-100 m *(49.2-328.1 ft)*; warhead nuclear 200 kT (TLAM-N); CEP 80 m; or warhead 454 kg (TLAM-C) or submunitions (TLAM-D); range 1300 km *(700 nm)*; CEP 10 m. Nuclear warheads not normally carried. Range increased by 30% in TLAM-C Block III which started production in 1992.
(b) anti-ship (TASM); inertial guidance; active radar and anti-radiation; homing to 460 km *(250 nm)* at 0.7 Mach; warhead 454 kg.
8 McDonnell Douglas Harpoon (2 quad) ❶; active radar homing to 130 km *(70 nm)* at 0.9 Mach; warhead 227 kg.
SAM: GDC Standard SM-2MR Block 4; command/inertial guidance; semi-active radar homing to 73 km *(40 nm)* at 2 Mach.
A/S: Honeywell ASROC; inertial guidance to 1.6-10 km *(1-5.4 nm)*; payload Mk 46 Mod 5 Neartip/Mk 50.
2 Martin Marietta Mk 41 (Mod 0 forward, Mod 1 aft) Vertical Launch Systems (VLS) for Tomahawk, Standard and ASROC ❷; 2 magazines; 29 missiles fwd, 61 aft. Mod 2 from DDG 59 onwards.
Guns: 1 FMC 5 in *(127 mm)*/54 Mk 45 Mod 1 or 2 ❸; 65° elevation; 20 rounds/minute to 23 km *(12.6 nm)*; weight of shell 32 kg. No anti-aircraft capability.
2 General Electric/General Dynamics 20 mm Vulcan Phalanx 6-barrelled Mk 15 ❹; 3000 rounds/minute (4500 in Block 1) combined to 1.5 km.
Torpedoes: 6—324 mm Mk 32 Mod 14 (2 triple) tubes ❺. Honeywell Mk 46 Mod 5; anti-submarine; active/passive homing to 11 km *(5.9 nm)* at 40 kts; warhead 44 kg. To be replaced by Mk 50 in due course.
Countermeasures: Decoys: 2 Loral Hycor SRBOC 6-barrelled fixed Mk 36 Mod 12 ❻; IR flares and Chaff to 4 km *(2.2 nm)*. SLQ 25 Nixie; torpedo decoy. NATO Sea Gnat. SLQ-95 AEB. SLQ-39 Chaff buoy.
ESM/ECM: Raytheon SLQ 32(V)2 ❼ ((V)3 from DDG 59 onwards); radar warning. Sidekick modification adds jammer and deception system.
Combat data systems: NTDS Mod 5 with Links 4A, 11, 14 and 16 in due course. SATCOM SRR-1, WSC-3 (UHF), USC-38 (EHF) (from 1992). SQQ 28 for LAMPS processor data link.
Fire control: SWG-3 Tomahawk WCS. SWG-1A Harpoon LCS. Aegis multi-target tracking with Mk 99 Mod 3 MFCS and three Mk 80 illuminators. Mk 160 Mod 4 GFCS (includes Kollmorgen optronic sight). Singer Librascope Mk 116 Mod 7 FCS for ASW. SAR-8 IR surveillance system to be fitted in due course.
Radars: Air search/fire control: RCA SPY 1D phased arrays ❽; 3D; E/F band.
Surface search: Norden SPS 67(V)3 ❾; G band.
Navigation: Raytheon SPS 64(V)9; I band.
Fire control: Three Raytheon/RCA SPG 62 ❿; I/J band.
Tacan: URN 25 ⓫. IFF Mk XII AIMS UPX-29.
Sonars: Gould/Raytheon/GE SQQ 89(V)6; combines SQS 53C; hull-mounted; active search and attack with SQR 19 passive towed array (TACTAS) and SRQ-4 LAMPS III shipboard terminal); medium frequency.

Helicopters: Platform and facilities to fuel and rearm LAMPS III SH 60B/F helicopters ⓬.

Programmes: Designed as replacements for the Adams and Coontz classes of guided missile destroyers. First ship authorised in FY 1985. Order rate is four to five per year. The first 17 or 18 are Flight 1 and the next 11 are planned to be Flight II or IIA.
Structure: The ship, except for the aluminium funnels, is constructed of steel. 70 tons of Kevlar armour provided to protect vital spaces. This is the first class of US Navy warship designed with a 'collective protection system for defense against the fallout associated with NBC Warfare'. The ship's crew are protected by double air-locked hatches, fewer accesses to the weatherdecks and positive pressurisation of the interior of the ship to keep out contaminants. All incoming air is filtered and more reliance placed on recirculating air inside the ship. All accommodation compartments have sprinkler systems. Stealth technology includes angled surfaces and rounded edges to reduce radar signature and IR signature suppression. The Ops room is below the waterline and electronics are EMP hardened. The original upright mast design has been changed possibly to increase separation between electronic systems and the forward funnel. Electric propulsion will not be fitted. Structural differences in Flight II were still being reviewed in early 1992 but proposals included a cheaper Flight IIA version with a helicopter hangar but no Harpoon, Phalanx or Towed Array sonar.
Opinion: The obvious deficiency in a ship of this size is the lack of its own helicopter and this has been recognised in the bringing forward of modifications proposed for later ships of the class. Regardless of attempts at role specialisation the modern warship's usage over its full life means that the ubiquitous helicopter receives more operational tasking than any other weapon system.

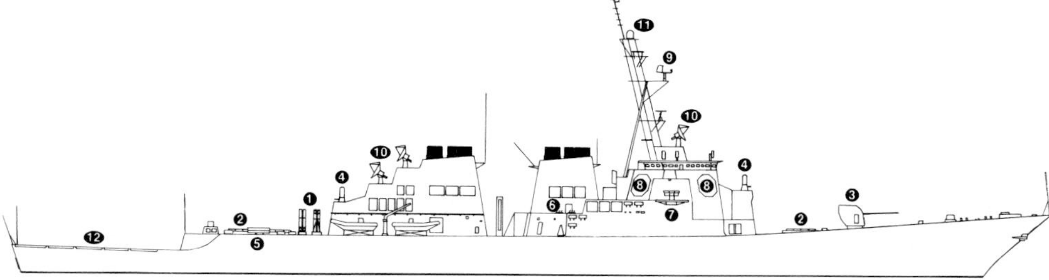
ARLEIGH BURKE (Scale 1 : 1 200), *Ian Sturton*

ARLEIGH BURKE *2/1992, Giorgio Arra*

ARLEIGH BURKE *2/1992, Giorgio Arra*

ARLEIGH BURKE *8/1991, Giorgio Arra*

4 KIDD CLASS GUIDED MISSILE DESTROYERS (DDG)

Name	*No*	*Builders*	*Laid down*	*Launched*	*Commissioned*	*F/S*
KIDD (ex-Iranian *Kouroosh*)	DDG 993 (ex-US DD 993)	Ingalls Shipbuilding Corp	26 June 1978	11 Aug 1979	27 June 1981	AA
CALLAGHAN (ex-Iranian *Daryush*)	DDG 994 (ex-US DD 994)	Ingalls Shipbuilding Corp	23 Oct 1978	1 Dec 1979	29 Aug 1981	PA
SCOTT (ex-Iranian *Nader*)	DDG 995 (ex-US DD 995, ex-US DD 996)	Ingalls Shipbuilding Corp	12 Feb 1979	1 Mar 1980	24 Oct 1981	AA
CHANDLER (ex-Iranian *Anoushirvan*)	DDG 996 (ex-US DD 996, ex-US DD 998)	Ingalls Shipbuilding Corp	7 May 1979	24 May 1980	13 Mar 1982	PA

Displacement, tons: 6950 light; 9574 full load
Dimensions, feet (metres): 563.3 × 55 × 20; 33 sonar *(171.7 × 16.8 × 6.2; 10)*
Main machinery: 4 GE LM 2500 gas turbines; 88 000 hp *(66 MW)* sustained; 2 shafts
Speed, knots: 33. **Range, miles:** 3300 at 30 kts; 6000 at 20 kts; 8000 at 17 kts
Complement: 339 (20 officers)

Missiles: SSM: 8 McDonnell Douglas Harpoon (2 quad) launchers ❶; active radar homing to 130 km *(70 nm)* at 0.9 Mach; warhead 227 kg.
SAM: 52 GDC Standard SM-2MR; command/inertial guidance; semi-active radar homing to 73 km *(40 nm)* at 2 Mach.
A/S: 16 Honeywell ASROC; inertial guidance to 1.6-10 km *(1-5.4 nm)*; payload Mk 46 Mod 5 Neartip/Mk 50. 2 twin Mk 26 (Mod 3 and Mod 4) launchers for Standard and ASROC ❷; missiles are split between 2 magazines.
Guns: 2 FMC 5 in *(127 mm)*/54 Mk 45 Mod 0 ❸; 65° elevation; 20 rounds/minute to 23 km *(12.6 nm)*; weight of shell 32 kg plus SALGP (Semi-Active Laser-Guided Projectiles).
2 General Electric/General Dynamics 20 mm Vulcan Phalanx 6-barrelled Mk 15 ❹; 3000 rounds/minute (4500 in Block 1) combined to 1.5 km.
4—12.7 mm MGs.
Torpedoes: 6—324 mm Mk 32 (2 triple) tubes ❺. Honeywell Mk 46; anti-submarine; active/passive homing to 11 km *(5.9 nm)* at 40 kts; warhead 44 kg. To be replaced by Mk 50 in due course. Torpedoes fired from inside the hull under the hangar.
Countermeasures: Decoys: 4 Loral Hycor SRBOC 6-barrelled fixed Mk 36; IR flares and Chaff to 4 km *(2.2 nm)*. SLQ 25 Nixie; torpedo decoy.
ESM/ECM: SLQ 32(V)2; radar warning. Sidekick modification adds jammer and deception system.
Combat data systems: NTDS with Links 4A, 11, 14 and 16 in due course. SATCOM SRR-1, WSC-3 (UHF); USC-38 (EHF) (from 1992).
Fire control: SWG-1A Harpoon LCS. 2 Mk 74 MFCS. Mk 86 Mod 5 GFCS. Mk 116 FCS for ASW. Mk 14 WDS. SYS 2(V)2 IADT. SRQ-4 for LAMPS III. 4 SYR 3393 for SAM mid-course guidance.
Radars: Air search: ITT SPS 48E ❻; 3D; E/F band; range 402 km *(220 nm)*.
Raytheon SPS 49(V)5 ❼; C/D band.
Surface search: ISC Cardion SPS 55 ❽; I/J band.
Navigation: Raytheon SPS 64; I/J band.
Fire control: Two SPG 51D ❾, 1 SPG 60 ❿, 1 SPQ 9A ⓫; G/I/J band.
Tacan: URN 25. IFF Mk XII AIMS UPX-29.
Sonars: General Electric/Hughes SQS 53A; bow-mounted; search and attack; medium frequency. To receive SQS 53C on completion of evaluation.
Gould SQR 19 (TACTAS); passive towed array (may be fitted).

Helicopters: 2 SH-2F LAMPS I ⓬ or 1 SH-60 LAMPS III.

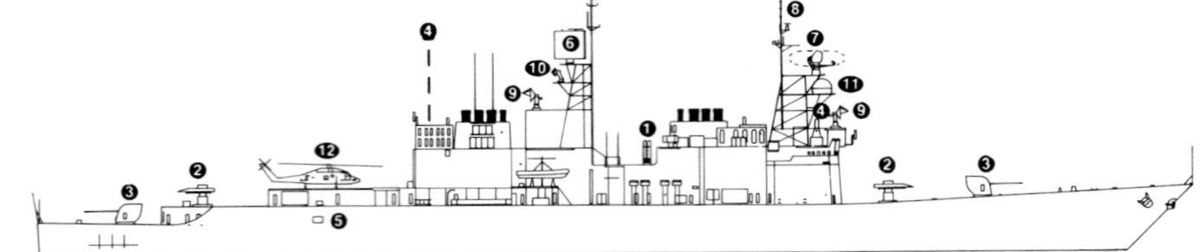

SCOTT *(Scale 1 : 1 500), Ian Sturton*

SCOTT *9/1990, Giorgio Arra*

Programmes: On 25 July 1979 the US Navy took over the contracts of four destroyers originally ordered by the Iranian Government in 1974.
Modernisation: Between 1988 and 1990 all received the New Threat Upgrade modernisation with updated Mk 74 MFCS for SM-2MR and SPG 51D radars, SPS 49(V)5 and Mk 14 weapon direction system.
Structure: The modular concept has been used extensively to facilitate construction and modernisation. Displacement could be up to 1000 tons over design because of the addition of Kevlar armour. Excellent air conditioning because of original Iranian requirements. NTU has led to a rearrangement of the mainmast and repositioning of SPS 48 and the SPG 60 aerials, in order to make room for the SPS 49. Originally, it had been planned to build the entire Spruance class to this design, but because of 'costs' the design was altered to the current plan.
Operational: These ships are optimised for general warfare instead of anti-submarine warfare as are the Spruance class, and the ability to fire SM-2MR allows them to support Aegis cruisers, if necessary allowing Aegis to control the missiles. The addition of SPS 49 markedly improves air picture compilation capability. They are the most powerful destroyers in the fleet.

KIDD *4/1990, Giorgio Arra*

3 COONTZ CLASS: GUIDED MISSILE DESTROYERS (DDG)

Name	*No*	*Builders*	*Laid down*	*Launched*	*Commissioned*	*F/S*
MACDONOUGH	DDG 39 (ex-DLG 8)	Bethlehem Co, Quincy, Mass	15 Apr 1958	9 July 1959	4 Nov 1961	AA
MAHAN	DDG 42 (ex-DLG 11)	San Francisco Naval Shipyard	31 July 1957	7 Oct 1959	25 Aug 1960	AA
DAHLGREN	DDG 43 (ex-DLG 12)	Philadelphia Naval Shipyard	1 Mar 1958	16 Mar 1960	8 Apr 1961	AA

Displacement, tons: 4150/4580 standard; 6150 full load
Dimensions, feet (metres): 512.5 × 52.5 × 15; 23.4 sonar *(156.3 × 16 × 4.6; 7.1)*
Main machinery: 4 Foster-Wheeler/Babcock & Wilcox boilers; 1200 psi *(84.4 kg/cm sq)*; 950°F *(510°C)*; 2 De Laval/Allis Chalmers turbines; 85 000 hp *(63 MW)*; 2 shafts
Speed, knots: 33. **Range, miles:** 5000 at 20 kts; 1500 at 30 kts
Complement: 402 (25 officers)

Missiles: SSM: 8 McDonnell Douglas Harpoon (2 quad) launchers ❶; active radar homing to 130 km *(70 nm)* at 0.9 Mach; warhead 227 kg.
SAM: 40 GDC Standard SM-2ER; twin Mk 10 Mod 0 launcher ❷; command/inertial guidance; semi-active radar homing to 137 km *(75 nm)* at 2.5 Mach.
A/S: Honeywell ASROC Mk 16 octuple launcher ❸; inertial guidance to 1.6-10 km *(1-5.4 nm)*; payload Mk 46 Mod 5 Neartip.
Guns: 1 FMC 5 in *(127 mm)*/54 Mk 42 Mod 10 ❹; 85° elevation; 20-40 rounds/minute to 24 km *(13 nm)*; weight of shell 32 kg.
4—12.7 mm MGs.
Torpedoes: 6—324 mm Mk 32 (2 triple) tubes ❺. Honeywell Mk 46; anti-submarine; active/passive homing to 11 km *(5.9 nm)* at 40 kts; warhead 44 kg.
Countermeasures: Decoys: 4 Loral Hycor SRBOC 6-barrelled fixed Mk 36; IR flares and Chaff to 4 km *(2.2 nm)*. T Mk 6 Fanfare; torpedo decoy.
ESM/ECM: SLQ 32(V)3; combined radar warning, jammer and deception system.
Combat data systems: NTDS with Links 11 and 14 (receive only). SATCOM SRR-1, WSC-3 (UHF).
Fire control: SWG-1 Harpoon LCS. 1 Mk 76 MFCS. Mk 68 GFCS. Mk 11 WDS (Mk 14 in DDG 42). Mk 111 ASW FCS. SYS-2(V)2 IADT (DDG 42).
Radars: Air search: ITT SPS 48C (48E in DDG 42) ❻; 3D; E/F band; range 402 km *(220 nm)*.
Raytheon SPS 49(V)2 ❼ ((V)5 in DDG 42); C/D band; range 457 km *(250 nm)*.
Surface search: Raytheon SPS 10B ❽; G band.
Navigation: Marconi LN 66; I/J band.
Fire control: Western Electric SPG 53A ❾; I/J band.
Two Sperry/RCA SPG 55B ❿; G/H band; range 51 km *(28 nm)* (for Standard).
Tacan: URN 25/SRN 6. IFF Mk XII AIMS UPX-29.
Sonars: Sperry SQQ 23A PAIR; hull-mounted; active search and attack; medium frequency.

Helicopters: Platform and limited support capability only.

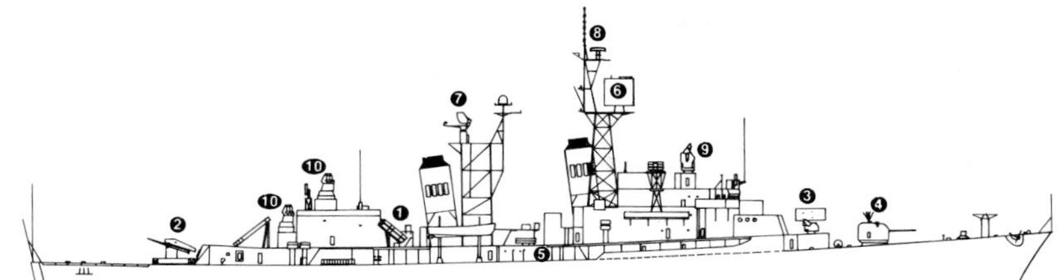

MAHAN *(Scale 1 : 1 500), Ian Sturton*

MAHAN *2/1990, Giorgio Arra*

Modernisation: These ships have been modernised to improve their Anti-Air Warfare (AAW) capabilities. Superstructure enlarged to provide space for additional electronic equipment, including NTDS; improved Tacan installed, improved guidance system for Standard missiles (SPG 55 fire control radar), and larger ship's service turbo generators fitted. *Mahan* was trials ship for the New Threat Upgrade (NTU) system which includes SPS 48E (3D radar), SPS 49(V)5 (2D radar), SYS 2 computerised AIO system and Standard SM-2ER missiles. The SM-2 missiles are now in most of the remaining ships of the class.
Operational: *Dahlgren* is scheduled to pay off in late 1992, *MacDonough* in late 1993.

1 CHARLES F ADAMS CLASS: GUIDED MISSILE DESTROYER (DDG)

Name	*No*	*Builders*	*Laid down*	*Launched*	*Commissioned*	*F/S*
BERKELEY	DDG 15	New York Shipbuilding Corporation	1 June 1960	29 July 1961	15 Dec 1962	PA

Displacement, tons: 3370 standard; 4825 full load
Dimensions, feet (metres): 437 × 47 × 15.6; 21 (sonar) *(133.2 × 14.3 × 4.8; 6.4)*
Main machinery: 4 Combustion Engineering boilers; 1200 psi *(84.4 kg/cm sq)*; 950°F *(510°C)*; 2 GE turbines; 70 000 hp *(52 MW)*; 2 shafts
Speed, knots: 30. **Range, miles:** 6000 at 15 kts; 1600 at 30 kts
Complement: 360 (20 officers)

Missiles: SSM: 6 McDonnell Douglas Harpoon; active radar homing to 130 km *(70 nm)* at 0.9 Mach; warhead 227 kg.
SAM: 36 GDC Standard SM-1MR; Mk 13 launcher ❶; command guidance; semi-active radar homing to 46 km *(25 nm)* at 2 Mach; height 150-60 000 ft *(45.7-18 288 m)*. Harpoon is fired from the same launcher.
A/S: Honeywell ASROC Mk 16 octuple launcher ❷; inertial guidance to 1.6-10 km *(1-5.4 nm)*; payload Mk 46 Mod 5 Neartip.
Guns: 2 FMC 5 in *(127 mm)*/54 Mk 42 ❸; 85° elevation; 20-40 rounds/minute to 24 km *(13 nm)*; weight of shell 32 kg.
4—12.7 mm MGs.
Torpedoes: 6—324 mm Mk 32 (2 triple) tubes ❹. Honeywell Mk 46; anti-submarine; active/passive homing to 11 km *(5.9 nm)* at 40 kts; warhead 44 kg.
Countermeasures: Decoys: 4 Loral Hycor SRBOC 6-barrelled fixed Mk 36; IR flares and Chaff to 4 km *(2.2 nm)*.
T—Mk-6 Fanfare; torpedo decoy.
ESM/ECM: SLQ 32V(2); radar warning. WLR-11.
Combat data systems: Link 14 receive only. SATCOM SRR-1, WSC-3 (UHF).
Fire control: Mk 68 GFCS. Mk 4 WDS. Mk 70 MFCS. Mk 111 FCS ASW. SYS-1 IADT.
Radars: Air search: Hughes SPS 52B/C ❺; 3D; E/F band; range 439 km *(240 nm)*.
Lockheed SPS 40B/D ❻; E/F band; range 320 km *(175 nm)*.
Surface search: Raytheon SPS 10D/F ❼; G band.
Navigation: Marconi LN 66; I band.
Fire control: Two Raytheon SPG 51D ❽; G/I band.
Lockheed SPG 53A ❾; K band.
Tacan: URN 25/SRN 6. IFF Mk XII AIMS UPX-29.
Sonars: Sangamo SQS 23D; hull-mounted; active search and attack; medium frequency.

Structure: Built to an improved Forrest Sherman class design with aluminium superstructure.
Operational: This last survivor of a class of 23 ships is scheduled to pay off in 1993.
Sales: Three to Australia and three to West Germany; all new construction. Four to Greece in 1991/92 as part of a deal which includes US bases in Greece.

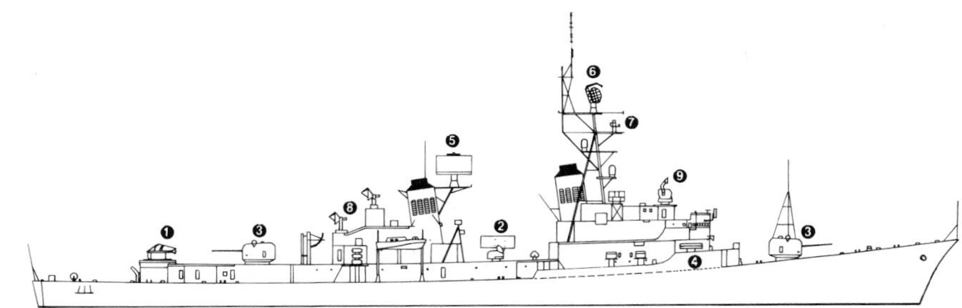

BERKELEY *(Scale 1 : 1 200), Ian Sturton*

BERKELEY *10/1991, Giorgio Arra*

31 SPRUANCE CLASS: DESTROYERS (DD)

Name	*No*	*Builders*	*Laid down*	*Launched*	*Commissioned*	*F/S*
SPRUANCE	DD 963	Ingalls Shipbuilding Corporation	17 Nov 1972	10 Nov 1973	20 Sep 1975	AA
PAUL F FOSTER	DD 964	Ingalls Shipbuilding Corporation	6 Feb 1973	23 Feb 1974	21 Feb 1976	PA
KINKAID	DD 965	Ingalls Shipbuilding Corporation	19 Apr 1973	25 May 1974	10 July 1976	PA
HEWITT	DD 966	Ingalls Shipbuilding Corporation	23 July 1973	24 Aug 1974	25 Sep 1976	PA
ELLIOTT	DD 967	Ingalls Shipbuilding Corporation	15 Oct 1973	19 Dec 1974	22 Jan 1976	PA
ARTHUR W RADFORD	DD 968	Ingalls Shipbuilding Corporation	14 Jan 1974	1 Mar 1975	16 Apr 1977	AA
PETERSON	DD 969	Ingalls Shipbuilding Corporation	29 Apr 1974	21 June 1975	9 July 1977	AA
CARON	DD 970	Ingalls Shipbuilding Corporation	1 July 1974	24 June 1975	1 Oct 1977	AA
DAVID R RAY	DD 971	Ingalls Shipbuilding Corporation	23 Sep 1974	23 Aug 1975	19 Nov 1977	PA
OLDENDORF	DD 972	Ingalls Shipbuilding Corporation	27 Dec 1974	21 Oct 1975	4 Mar 1978	PA
JOHN YOUNG	DD 973	Ingalls Shipbuilding Corporation	17 Feb 1975	7 Feb 1976	20 May 1978	PA
COMTE DE GRASSE	DD 974	Ingalls Shipbuilding Corporation	4 Apr 1975	26 Mar 1976	5 Aug 1978	AA
O'BRIEN	DD 975	Ingalls Shipbuilding Corporation	9 May 1975	8 July 1976	3 Dec 1977	PA
MERRILL	DD 976	Ingalls Shipbuilding Corporation	16 June 1975	1 Sep 1976	11 Mar 1978	PA
BRISCOE	DD 977	Ingalls Shipbuilding Corporation	21 July 1975	15 Dec 1976	3 June 1978	AA
STUMP	DD 978	Ingalls Shipbuilding Corporation	25 Aug 1975	29 Jan 1977	19 Aug 1978	AA
CONOLLY	DD 979	Ingalls Shipbuilding Corporation	29 Sep 1975	19 Feb 1977	14 Oct 1978	AA
MOOSBRUGGER	DD 980	Ingalls Shipbuilding Corporation	3 Nov 1975	23 July 1977	16 Dec 1978	AA
JOHN HANCOCK	DD 981	Ingalls Shipbuilding Corporation	16 Jan 1976	29 Oct 1977	1 Mar 1979	AA
NICHOLSON	DD 982	Ingalls Shipbuilding Corporation	20 Feb 1976	11 Nov 1977	12 May 1979	AA
JOHN RODGERS	DD 983	Ingalls Shipbuilding Corporation	12 Aug 1976	25 Feb 1978	14 July 1979	AA
LEFTWICH	DD 984	Ingalls Shipbuilding Corporation	12 Nov 1976	8 Apr 1978	25 Aug 1979	PA
CUSHING	DD 985	Ingalls Shipbuilding Corporation	27 Dec 1976	17 June 1978	21 Sep 1979	PA
HARRY W HILL	DD 986	Ingalls Shipbuilding Corporation	3 Jan 1977	10 Aug 1978	17 Nov 1979	PA
O'BANNON	DD 987	Ingalls Shipbuilding Corporation	21 Feb 1977	25 Sep 1978	15 Dec 1979	AA
THORN	DD 988	Ingalls Shipbuilding Corporation	29 Aug 1977	14 Nov 1978	16 Feb 1980	AA
DEYO	DD 989	Ingalls Shipbuilding Corporation	14 Oct 1977	27 Jan 1979	22 Mar 1980	AA
INGERSOLL	DD 990	Ingalls Shipbuilding Corporation	5 Dec 1977	10 Mar 1979	12 Apr 1980	PA
FIFE	DD 991	Ingalls Shipbuilding Corporation	6 Mar 1978	1 May 1979	31 May 1980	PA
FLETCHER	DD 992	Ingalls Shipbuilding Corporation	24 Apr 1978	16 June 1979	12 July 1980	PA
HAYLER	DD 997	Ingalls Shipbuilding Corporation	20 Oct 1980	27 Mar 1982	5 Mar 1983	AA

Displacement, tons: 5770 light; 8040 full load
Dimensions, feet (metres): 563.2 × 55.1 × 19; 29 (sonar) *(171.7 × 16.8 × 5.8; 8.8)*
Main machinery: 4 GE LM 2500 gas turbines; 88 000 hp *(66 MW)* sustained; 2 shafts; cp props
Speed, knots: 33. **Range, miles:** 6000 at 20 kts
Complement: 319-339 (20 officers)

Missiles: SLCM/SSM: GDC Tomahawk ❶; combination of (a) land attack; TAINS (Tercom aided navigational system) to 2500 km *(1400 nm)* at 0.7 Mach; altitude 15-100 m *(49.2-328.1 ft)*; warhead nuclear 200 kT (TLAM-N); CEP 80 m; or warhead 454 kg (TLAM-C) or submunitions (TLAM-D); range 1300 km *(700 nm)*; CEP 10 m. Nuclear warheads not normally carried. Range increased by 30% in TLAM-C Batch III which started production in 1992.
(b) anti-ship (TASM); active radar/anti-radiation homing to 460 km *(250 nm)* at 0.7 Mach; warhead 454 kg.
8 fitted on the forecastle in 2 Mk 44 armoured box launchers in DD 974, 976, 979, 983-984, 989-990. Remainder being fitted with the Mk 41 Mod 0 VLS ❷ with one 61 missile magazine combining 45 Tomahawk and ultimately ASROC.
8 McDonnell Douglas Harpoon (2 quad) ❸; active radar homing to 130 km *(70 nm)* at 0.9 Mach; warhead 227 kg.
SAM: Raytheon GMLS Mk 29 octuple launcher ❹; 24 Sea Sparrow; semi-active radar homing to 14.6 km *(8 nm)* at 2.5 Mach; warhead 39 kg.
GDC RAM (DD 971); passive IR/anti-radiation homing to 9.6 km *(5.2 nm)* at 2 Mach; warhead 9.1 kg. May be fitted in others in early 1990s.
A/S: 24 Honeywell ASROC Mk 16 octuple launcher with Mk 112 reload system ❺ (not in VLS fitted ships); inertial guidance to 1.6-10 km *(1-5.5 nm)*; payload Mk 46 Mod 5 Neartip/Mk 50.

Guns: 2 FMC 5 in *(127 mm)*/54 Mk 45 Mod 0/1 ❻; 65° elevation; 20 rounds/minute to 23 km *(12.6 nm)* anti-surface; 15 km *(8.2 nm)* anti-aircraft; weight of shell 32 kg. SALGP (Semi-Active Laser-Guided Projectile).
2 General Electric/General Dynamics 20 mm/76 6-barrelled Mk 15 Vulcan Phalanx ❼; 3000 rounds/minute (4500 in Batch 1) combined to 1.5 km.
4—12.7 mm MGs.
Torpedoes: 6—324 mm Mk 32 (2 triple) tubes ❽. 14 Honeywell Mk 46; anti-submarine; active/passive homing to 11 km *(5.9 nm)* at 40 kts; warhead 44 kg. To be replaced by Mk 50 in due course. The tubes are inside the superstructure to facilitate maintenance and reloading. Torpedoes are fired through side ports.
Countermeasures: Decoys: 4 Loral Hycor SRBOC 6-barrelled fixed Mk 36 ❾; IR flares and Chaff to 4 km *(2.2 nm)*.
SLQ 25 Nixie; torpedo decoy. Prairie/Masker hull/blade rate noise suppression system.
ESM/ECM: SLQ 32(V)2 ❿; radar warning. Sidekick modification adds jammer and deception system. WLR-1 (in some). OUTBOARD (in some).
Combat data systems: NTDS with Links 11 and 14. SATCOMS ⓫ SRR-1, WSC-3 (UHF), USC-38 (EHF) (in DD 971; others to be fitted from 1992). SQQ 28 for LAMPS data link.
Fire control: SWG-3 Tomahawk WCS. SWG-1A Harpoon LCS. Mk 116 Mod 7 FCS ASW. Mk 86 Mod 3 GFCS. Mk 91 MFCS. SRQ-4 LAMPS III. SAR-8 IR director (DD 965).
Radars: Air search: Lockheed SPS 40B/C/D (not in DD 997) ⓬; E/F band; range 320 km *(175 nm)*.
Raytheon SPS 49V (DD 997); C/D band; range 457 km *(250 nm)*.
Hughes Mk 23 TAS; D band.
Surface search: ISC Cardion SPS 55 ⓭; I/J band.
Navigation: Marconi LN 66 or SPS 53; I band. Raytheon SPS 64(V)9 to be fitted.
Fire control: Lockheed SPG 60 ⓮; I/J band.
Lockheed SPQ 9A ⓯; I/J band; range 37 km *(20 nm)*.
Raytheon Mk 91 ⓰; I/J band (for SAM).
Tacan: URN 20 or URN 25 (D 997). IFF Mk XII AIMS UPX-25.
Sonars: SQQ 89(V)6 including GE/Hughes SQS 53B/C; bow-mounted; active search and attack; medium frequency; and Gould SQR 19 (TACTAS); passive towed array. Some ships still have SQR 15 but these are being replaced. All except DDs 988-990 will have the full SQQ 89 system by 1994.

Helicopters: 1 SH-60B LAMPS III ⓱ or 1 SH-2F LAMPS I.

Programmes: Funds approved between FY 1970 and FY 1978.
Modernisation: Beginning with FY 1986 overhauls, major improvements have been made. These include the installation of VLS, upgrading of EW to SLQ 32V(2) plus sidekick; LAMPS III and the recovery, assist, secure and traverse system (RAST), the Halon 1301 firefighting system and anti-missile and target acquisition systems. VLS Mk 41 ships are capable of launching Standard SM-2MR for control by Aegis fitted vessels. Eleven of the class converted to VLS by mid-1992 and the programme continues at one 'plus' a year. One of the class is being used to test the development model of RAIDS (rapid anti-ship missile integrated defence system).
Structure: Extensive use of the modular concept has been used to facilitate construction and block modernisation. There is a high level of automation. These were the first large US warships to employ gas turbine propulsion and advanced self-noise reduction features. Kevlar internal coating in all vital spaces.
Operational: Two of the class are based at Yukosuka, Japan. Eleven took part in the war with Iraq in 1991. *Fife* with 58 firings was the most prolific launcher of Tomahawk missiles.

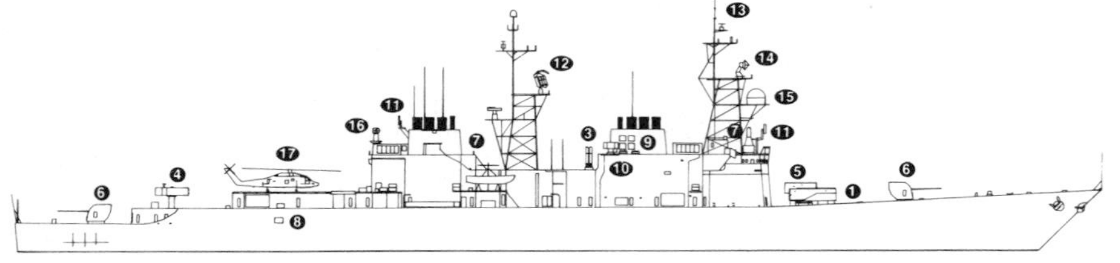
MERRILL *(Scale 1 : 1 500), Ian Sturton*

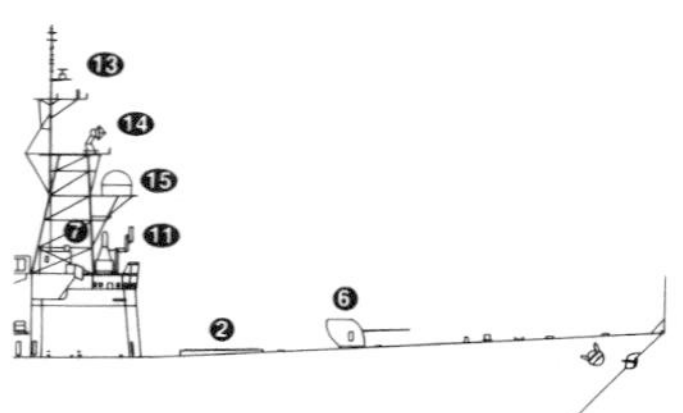
SPRUANCE *(Scale 1 : 1 500), Ian Sturton*

MERRILL (with box Tomahawk) *7/1991, 92 Wing RAAF*

O'BRIEN (with VLS)

10/1991, Giorgio Arra

OLDENDORF

8/1989, John Mortimer

FRIGATES

Note: Frigates could be supplemented in the ocean escort role by the 12 Hamilton class high-endurance cutters operated by the Coast Guard.

51 OLIVER HAZARD PERRY CLASS: GUIDED MISSILE FRIGATES (FFG)

Name	*No*	*Builders*	*Laid down*	*Launched*	*Commissioned*	*F/S*
OLIVER HAZARD PERRY	FFG 7 (ex-PF 109)	Bath Iron Works, Bath, Maine	12 June 1975	25 Sep 1976	17 Dec 1977	NRF
McINERNEY	FFG 8	Bath Iron Works, Bath, Maine	7 Nov 1977	4 Nov 1978	19 Nov 1979	AA
WADSWORTH	FFG 9	Todd Shipyards Corporation, San Pedro	13 July 1977	29 July 1978	28 Feb 1980	NRF
DUNCAN	FFG 10	Todd Shipyards Corporation, Seattle	29 Apr 1977	1 Mar 1978	15 May 1980	NRF
CLARK	FFG 11	Bath Iron Works, Bath, Maine	17 July 1978	24 Mar 1979	9 May 1980	NRF
GEORGE PHILIP	FFG 12	Todd Shipyards Corporation, San Pedro	14 Dec 1977	16 Dec 1978	10 Oct 1980	NRF
SAMUEL ELIOT MORISON	FFG 13	Bath Iron Works, Bath, Maine	4 Dec 1978	14 July 1979	11 Oct 1980	NRF
JOHN H SIDES	FFG 14	Todd Shipyards Corporation, San Pedro	7 Aug 1978	19 May 1979	30 May 1981	NRF
ESTOCIN	FFG 15	Bath Iron Works, Bath, Maine	2 Apr 1979	3 Nov 1979	10 Jan 1981	NRF
CLIFTON SPRAGUE	FFG 16	Bath Iron Works, Bath, Maine	30 Sep 1979	16 Feb 1980	21 Mar 1981	NRF
JOHN A MOORE	FFG 19	Todd Shipyards Corporation, San Pedro	19 Dec 1978	20 Oct 1979	14 Nov 1981	NRF
ANTRIM	FFG 20	Todd Shipyards Corporation, Seattle	21 June 1978	27 Mar 1979	26 Sep 1981	NRF
FLATLEY	FFG 21	Bath Iron Works, Bath, Maine	13 Nov 1979	15 May 1980	20 June 1981	NRF
FAHRION	FFG 22	Todd Shipyards Corporation, Seattle	1 Dec 1978	24 Aug 1979	16 Jan 1982	NRF
LEWIS B PULLER	FFG 23	Todd Shipyards Corporation, San Pedro	23 May 1979	15 Mar 1980	17 Apr 1982	NRF
JACK WILLIAMS	FFG 24	Bath Iron Works, Bath, Maine	25 Feb 1980	30 Aug 1980	19 Sep 1981	AA
COPELAND	FFG 25	Todd Shipyards Corporation, San Pedro	24 Oct 1979	26 July 1980	7 Aug 1982	NRF
GALLERY	FFG 26	Bath Iron Works, Bath, Maine	17 May 1980	20 Dec 1980	5 Dec 1981	AA
MAHLON S TISDALE	FFG 27	Todd Shipyards Corporation, San Pedro	19 Mar 1980	7 Feb 1981	27 Nov 1982	NRF
BOONE	FFG 28	Todd Shipyards Corporation, Seattle	27 Mar 1979	16 Jan 1980	15 May 1982	AA
STEPHEN W GROVES	FFG 29	Bath Iron Works, Bath, Maine	16 Sep 1980	4 Apr 1981	17 Apr 1982	AA
REID	FFG 30	Todd Shipyards Corporation, San Pedro	8 Oct 1980	27 June 1981	19 Feb 1983	PA
STARK	FFG 31	Todd Shipyards Corporation, Seattle	24 Aug 1979	30 May 1980	23 Oct 1982	AA
JOHN L HALL	FFG 32	Bath Iron Works, Bath, Maine	5 Jan 1981	24 July 1981	26 June 1982	AA
JARRETT	FFG 33	Todd Shipyards Corporation, San Pedro	11 Feb 1981	17 Oct 1981	2 July 1983	PA
AUBREY FITCH	FFG 34	Bath Iron Works, Bath, Maine	10 Apr 1981	17 Oct 1981	9 Oct 1982	AA
UNDERWOOD	FFG 36	Bath Iron Works, Bath, Maine	3 Aug 1981	6 Feb 1982	29 Jan 1983	AA
CROMMELIN	FFG 37	Todd Shipyards Corporation, Seattle	30 May 1980	1 July 1981	18 June 1983	PA
CURTS	FFG 38	Todd Shipyards Corporation, San Pedro	1 July 1981	6 Mar 1982	8 Oct 1983	PA
DOYLE	FFG 39	Bath Iron Works, Bath, Maine	16 Nov 1981	22 May 1982	21 May 1983	AA
HALYBURTON	FFG 40	Todd Shipyards Corporation, Seattle	26 Sep 1980	15 Oct 1981	7 Jan 1984	AA
McCLUSKY	FFG 41	Todd Shipyards Corporation, San Pedro	21 Oct 1981	18 Sep 1982	10 Dec 1983	PA
KLAKRING	FFG 42	Bath Iron Works, Bath, Maine	19 Feb 1982	18 Sep 1982	20 Aug 1983	AA
THACH	FFG 43	Todd Shipyards Corporation, San Pedro	10 Mar 1982	18 Dec 1982	17 Mar 1984	PA
De WERT	FFG 45	Bath Iron Works, Bath, Maine	14 June 1982	18 Dec 1982	19 Nov 1983	AA
RENTZ	FFG 46	Todd Shipyards Corporation, San Pedro	18 Sep 1982	16 July 1983	30 June 1984	PA
NICHOLAS	FFG 47	Bath Iron Works, Bath, Maine	27 Sep 1982	23 Apr 1983	10 Mar 1984	AA
VANDEGRIFT	FFG 48	Todd Shipyards Corporation, Seattle	13 Oct 1981	15 Oct 1982	24 Nov 1984	PA
ROBERT G BRADLEY	FFG 49	Bath Iron Works, Bath, Maine	28 Dec 1982	13 Aug 1983	11 Aug 1984	AA
TAYLOR	FFG 50	Bath Iron Works, Bath, Maine	5 May 1983	5 Nov 1983	1 Dec 1984	AA
GARY	FFG 51	Todd Shipyards Corporation, San Pedro	18 Dec 1982	19 Nov 1983	17 Nov 1984	PA
CARR	FFG 52	Todd Shipyards Corporation, Seattle	26 Mar 1982	26 Feb 1983	27 July 1985	AA
HAWES	FFG 53	Bath Iron Works, Bath, Maine	22 Aug 1983	18 Feb 1984	9 Feb 1985	AA
FORD	FFG 54	Todd Shipyards Corporation, San Pedro	16 July 1983	23 June 1984	29 June 1985	PA
ELROD	FFG 55	Bath Iron Works, Bath, Maine	21 Nov 1983	12 May 1984	18 May 1985	AA
SIMPSON	FFG 56	Bath Iron Works, Bath, Maine	27 Feb 1984	21 Aug 1984	10 Aug 1985	AA
REUBEN JAMES	FFG 57	Todd Shipyards Corporation, San Pedro	19 Nov 1983	8 Feb 1985	22 Mar 1986	PA
SAMUEL B ROBERTS	FFG 58	Bath Iron Works, Bath, Maine	21 May 1984	8 Dec 1984	12 Apr 1986	AA
KAUFFMAN	FFG 59	Bath Iron Works, Bath, Maine	8 Apr 1985	29 Mar 1986	28 Feb 1987	AA
RODNEY M DAVIS	FFG 60	Todd Shipyards Corporation, San Pedro	8 Feb 1985	11 Jan 1986	9 May 1987	PA
INGRAHAM	FFG 61	Todd Shipyards Corporation, San Pedro	30 Mar 1987	25 June 1988	5 Aug 1989	PA

Displacement, tons: 2750 light; 3638; 4100 (FFG 8, 36-61) full load

Dimensions, feet (metres): 445; 453 (FFG 8, 36-61) × 45 × 14.8; 24.5 (sonar) *(135.6; 138.1 × 13.7 × 4.5; 7.5)*

Main machinery: 2 GE LM 2500 gas turbines; 44 000 hp *(33 MW)* sustained; 1 shaft; cp prop
2 auxiliary retractable props; 650 hp *(484 kW)*

Speed, knots: 29. **Range, miles:** 4500 at 20 kts

Complement: 206 (13 officers) including 19 aircrew

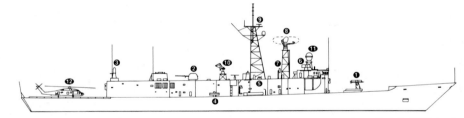

FFG 7 Class (modified) *(Scale 1 : 1 200), Ian Sturton*

Missiles: SSM: 4 McDonnell Douglas Harpoon; active radar homing to 130 km *(70 nm)* at 0.9 Mach; warhead 227 kg.
SAM: 36 GDC Standard SM-1MR; command guidance; semi-active radar homing to 46 km *(25 nm)* at 2 Mach.
1 Mk 13 Mod 4 launcher for both SSM and SAM missiles ❶.

Guns: 1 OTO Melara 3 in *(76 mm)*/62 Mk 75 ❷; 85° elevation; 85 rounds/minute to 16 km *(8.7 nm)* anti-surface; 12 km *(6.6 nm)* anti-aircraft; weight of shell 6 kg.
1 General Electric/General Dynamics 20 mm/76 6-barrelled Mk 15 Vulcan Phalanx ❸; 3000 rounds/minute (4500 in Block 1) combined to 1.5 km.
4—12.7 mm MGs.

Torpedoes: 6—324 mm Mk 32 (2 triple) tubes ❹. 24 Honeywell Mk 46; anti-submarine; active/passive homing to 11 km *(5.9 nm)* at 40 kts; warhead 44 kg. To be replaced by Mk 50 in due course.

Countermeasures: Decoys: 2 Loral Hycor SRBOC 6-barrelled fixed Mk 36 ❺; IR flares and Chaff to 4 km *(2.2 nm)*.
T—Mk-6 Fanfare/SLQ-25 Nixie; torpedo decoy.
ESM/ECM: SLQ 32(V)2 ❻; radar warning. Sidekick modification adds jammer and deception system.

Combat data systems: NTDS with Link 11 and 14. Link 14 only (NRF ships). SATCOM ❼ SRR-1, WSC-3 (UHF). SQQ 28 for LAMPS data link.

Fire control: SWG-1 Harpoon LCS. Mk 92 (Mod 4 or Mod 6 (FFG 61 and during modernisation in others of the class)), WCS with CAS (Combined Antenna System). The Mk 92 is the US version of the Signaal WM-28 system. Mk 13 weapon direction system. 2 Mk 24 optical directors. SYS 2(V)2 IADT (FFG 61 and during modernisation in others of the class). SRQ-4 for LAMPS III, SKR-4A for LAMPS I.

Radars: Air search: Raytheon SPS 49(V)4 or 5 (FFG 61 and during modernisation of others) ❽; C/D band; range 457 km *(250 nm)*.
Surface search: ISC Cardion SPS 55 ❾; I band.
Fire control: Lockheed STIR (modified SPG 60) ❿; I/J band; range 110 km *(60 nm)*.
Sperry Mk 92 (Signaal WM 28) ⓫; I/J band.
Tacan: URN 25. IFF Mk XII AIMS UPX-29.

Sonars: Raytheon SQS 56 or SQS 53B; hull-mounted; active search and attack; medium frequency.
Gould SQR 19; passive towed array. A few SQR 18A still fitted to ships assigned to the NRF.
SQQ 89(V)2 (SQS 53B and SQR 19) (in FFG 36-61 and retrofitted in all except 14 of the class by 1994).

ANTRIM *5/1991, Giorgio Arra*

Helicopters: 2 SH-2F LAMPS I or 2 SH-60B LAMPS III ⓬ (FFG 8, 36-61). 3 Canadair CL 227 (FFG 39) (see *Operational*).

Programmes: They are follow-on ships to the large number of frigates (formerly DE) built in the 1960s and early 1970s, with the later ships emphasising anti-ship/aircraft/missile capabilities while the previous classes were oriented primarily against submarines (eg, larger SQS 26 sonar and ASROC). The lead ship (FFG 7) was authorised in FY 1973. On 31 January 1984 the first of this class transferred to the Naval Reserve Force. Since then 15 more have transferred. NRF ships have about 75 reservists in their complement.

Modernisation: To accommodate the helicopter landing system (RAST), the overall length of the ship was increased by 8 ft *(2.4 m)* by increasing the angle of the ship's transom, between the waterline and the fantail, from virtually straight up to a 45° angle outwards. LAMPS III support facilities and RAST were fitted in all ships authorised from FFG 36 onwards, during construction. Thirty three of this class are able to operate, land and maintain LAMPS III while the remainder can operate this aircraft without landing facilities. *Ingraham* has much improved Combat Data and Fire Control equipment which was retrofitted in *Taylor* in 1991 and thereafter in four ships per year up to a total of at least 12.

Structure: The original single hangar has been changed to two adjacent hangars. Provided with 19 mm Kevlar armour protection over vital spaces.

Operational: Ships of this class were the first Navy experience in implementing a design-to-cost acquisition concept. Many of their limitations were manifest during the intense fires which resulted from *Stark* (FFG 31) being struck by two Exocet missiles in the Persian Gulf 17 May 1987. Since then there have been many improvements in firefighting and damage control doctrine and procedures and equipment to deal with residual missile propellant-induced fires. *Stark* was once again operational in August 1988. On 14 April 1988, *Samuel B Roberts* (FFG 58), was mined in the Gulf. *Roberts* was able to reach Bahrain using the auxiliary propulsion motor and was then transported to the United States, where she was repaired at Bath Iron Works returning to the fleet in November 1989. Fourteen ships of the class were active in the war with Iraq in 1991. *Doyle* is the trials ship for the Sentinel MAVUS unmanned rotary wing air vehicle. This machine can carry either TV or IR cameras, or an ECM decoy system or a communications relay. Other payloads include synthetic aperture radar or Elint and Sigint equipment.

Sales: Australia has bought four of the class and has built two more. Spain has four completed and is building two more. Taiwan is building eight.

DOYLE

11/1991, Antonio Moreno

GARY

10/1991, 92 Wing RAAF

29 KNOX CLASS: FRIGATES (FF)

Name	*No*	*Builders*	*Laid down*	*Launched*	*Commissioned*	*F/S*
CONNOLE	FF 1056	Avondale Shipyards	23 Mar 1967	20 July 1968	30 Aug 1969	AA
REASONER	FF 1063	Lockheed S B & Construction Co	6 Jan 1969	1 Aug 1970	31 July 1971	PA
LOCKWOOD	FF 1064	Todd Shipyards, Seattle	3 Nov 1967	5 Sep 1968	5 Dec 1970	PA
STEIN	FF 1065	Lockheed S B & Construction Co	1 June 1970	19 Dec 1970	8 Jan 1972	PA
MARVIN SHIELDS	FF 1066	Todd Shipyards, Seattle	12 Apr 1968	23 Oct 1969	10 Apr 1971	PA
FRANCIS HAMMOND	FF 1067	Todd Shipyards, San Pedro	15 July 1967	11 May 1968	25 July 1970	PA
VREELAND	FF 1068	Avondale Shipyards	20 Mar 1968	14 June 1969	13 June 1970	AA
DOWNES	FF 1070	Todd Shipyards, Seattle	5 Sep 1968	13 Dec 1969	28 Aug 1971	PA
ROBERT E PEARY	FF 1073	Lockheed S B & Construction Co	20 Dec 1970	23 June 1971	23 Sep 1972	PA
HAROLD E HOLT	FF 1074	Todd Shipyards, San Pedro	11 May 1968	3 May 1969	26 Mar 1971	PA
TRIPPE	FF 1075	Avondale Shipyards	29 July 1968	1 Nov 1969	19 Sep 1970	AA
FANNING	FF 1076	Todd Shipyards, San Pedro	7 Dec 1968	24 Jan 1970	23 July 1971	PA
OUELLET	FF 1077	Avondale Shipyards	15 Jan 1969	17 Jan 1970	12 Dec 1970	PA
JOSEPH HEWES	FF 1078	Avondale Shipyards	15 May 1969	7 Mar 1970	24 Apr 1971	NRF
BOWEN	FF 1079	Avondale Shipyards	11 July 1969	2 May 1970	22 May 1971	NRF
PAUL	FF 1080	Avondale Shipyards	12 Sep 1969	20 June 1970	14 Aug 1971	AA
AYLWIN	FF 1081	Avondale Shipyards	13 Nov 1969	29 Aug 1970	18 Sep 1971	AA
ELMER MONTGOMERY	FF 1082	Avondale Shipyards	23 Jan 1970	21 Nov 1970	30 Oct 1971	AA
COOK	FF 1083	Avondale Shipyards	20 Mar 1970	23 Jan 1971	18 Dec 1971	PA
McCANDLESS	FF 1084	Avondale Shipyards	4 June 1970	20 Mar 1971	18 Mar 1972	NRF
DONALD B BEARY	FF 1085	Avondale Shipyards	24 July 1970	22 May 1971	22 July 1972	NRF
KIRK	FF 1087	Avondale Shipyards	4 Dec 1970	25 Sep 1971	9 Sep 1972	PA
JESSE L BROWN	FF 1089	Avondale Shipyards	8 Apr 1971	18 Mar 1972	17 Feb 1973	NRF
AINSWORTH	FF 1090	Avondale Shipyards	11 June 1971	15 Apr 1972	31 Mar 1973	NRF
THOMAS C HART	FF 1092	Avondale Shipyards	8 Oct 1971	12 Aug 1972	28 July 1973	AA
CAPODANNO	FF 1093	Avondale Shipyards	12 Oct 1971	21 Oct 1972	17 Nov 1973	AA
PHARRIS	FF 1094	Avondale Shipyards	11 Feb 1972	16 Dec 1972	26 Jan 1974	AA
TRUETT	FF 1095	Avondale Shipyards	27 Apr 1972	3 Feb 1973	1 June 1974	NRF
MOINESTER	FF 1097	Avondale Shipyards	25 Aug 1972	12 May 1973	2 Nov 1974	NRF

Displacement, tons: 3011 standard; 3877 (FF 1052-1077), 4260 (remainder) full load
Dimensions, feet (metres): 439.6 × 46.8 × 15; 24.8 (sonar) *(134 × 14.3 × 4.6; 7.8)*
Main machinery: 2 Combustion Engineering/Babcock & Wilcox boilers; 1200 psi *(84.4 kg/cm sq)*; 950°F *(510°C)*; 1 turbine; 35 000 hp *(26 MW)*; 1 shaft
Speed, knots: 27. **Range, miles:** 4000 at 22 kts on 1 boiler
Complement: 288 (17 officers)

Missiles: SSM: 8 McDonnell Douglas Harpoon; active radar homing to 130 km *(70 nm)* at 0.9 Mach; warhead 227 kg.
A/S: Honeywell ASROC Mk 16 octuple launcher with reload system (has 2 cells modified to fire Harpoon) ❶; inertial guidance to 1.6-10 km *(1-5.4 nm)*; payload Mk 46 Mod 5 Neartip/Mk 50.
Guns: 1 FMC 5 in *(127 mm)*/54 Mk 42 Mod 9 ❷; 85° elevation; 20-40 rounds/minute to 24 km *(13 nm)* anti-surface; 14 km *(7.7 nm)* anti-aircraft; weight of shell 32 kg.
1 General Electric/General Dynamics 20 mm/76 6-barrelled Mk 15 Vulcan Phalanx ❸; 3000 rounds/minute combined to 1.5 km.
Torpedoes: 4—324 mm Mk 32 (2 twin) fixed tubes ❹. 22 Honeywell Mk 46 Mod 5; anti-submarine; active/passive homing to 11 km *(5.9 nm)* at 40 kts; warhead 44 kg.
Countermeasures: Decoys: 2 Loral Hycor SRBOC 6-barrelled fixed Mk 36 ❺; IR flares and Chaff to 4 km *(2.2 nm)*. T Mk-6 Fanfare/SLQ-25 Nixie; torpedo decoy. Prairie Masker hull and blade rate noise suppression.
ESM/ECM: SLQ 32(V)2 ❻; radar warning. Sidekick modification adds jammer and deception system.
Combat data systems: Link 14 receive only. SATCOM ❼ SRR-1, WSC-3 (UHF). FFISTS (Frigate Integrated Shipboard Tactical Systems) (see *Modernisation*).
Fire control: SWG-1A Harpoon LCS. Mk 68 GFCS. Mk 114 ASW FCS. Mk 1 target designation system. MMS target acquisition sight (for mines, small craft and low flying aircraft). SRQ-4 for LAMPS I.
Radars: Air search: Lockheed SPS 40B ❽; E/F band; range 320 km *(175 nm)*.
Surface search: Raytheon SPS 10 or Norden SPS 67 ❾; G band.
Navigation: Marconi LN 66; I band.
Fire control: Western Electric SPG 53A/D/F ❿; I/J band.
Tacan: SRN 15. IFF: UPX-12.
Sonars: EDO/General Electric SQS 26 CX; bow-mounted; active search and attack; medium frequency.
EDO SQS 35; independent VDS.
EDO SQR 18A(V)1; passive towed array.

Helicopters: 1 SH-2F LAMPS I ⓫.

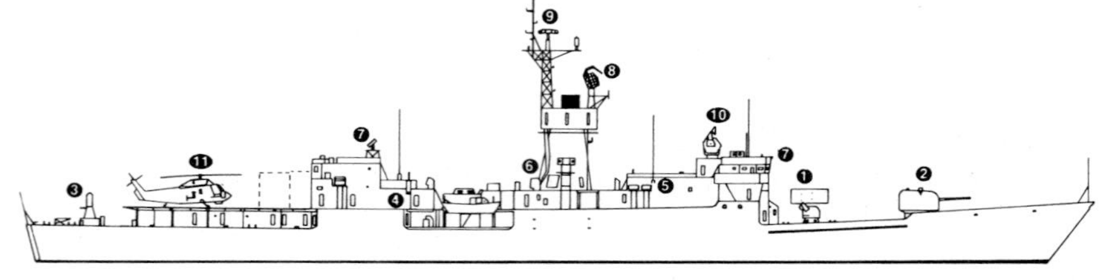

KNOX Class *(Scale 1 : 1 200), Ian Sturton*

CONNOLE *6/1991, G. Toremans*

Modernisation: Designed to operate the now-discarded DASH unmanned helicopter. From FY 1972 to FY 1976 they were modified to accommodate the Light Airborne Multi-Purpose System (LAMPS) and the SH-2F Seasprite anti-submarine helicopter; hangar and flight deck are enlarged. In 1979 a programme was initiated to fit 3.5 ft bow bulwarks and spray strakes to all ships of the class adding 9.1 tons to the displacement. Sea Sparrow SAM replaced by Phalanx 1982-88. FFISTS is a poor man's combat system using desktop computers to integrate ASW data from Link and from ships' sonars.
Structure: Improved ASROC-torpedo reloading capability (note slanting face of bridge structure immediately behind ASROC). Four Mk 32 torpedo tubes are fixed in the midships structure, two to a side, angled out at 45 degrees. The arrangement provides improved loading capability over exposed triple Mk 32 torpedo tubes. A 4000 lb lightweight anchor is fitted on the port side and an 8000 lb anchor fits into the after section of the sonar dome.
Operational: Apart from the eight Naval Reserve Force Training ships, all are scheduled to be paid off to reserve by the end of 1993. Each NRF ship has been designated as a training platform (FFT) for its own selected reserve crew and four additional crews designated as the nucleus of reactivation crews for the decommissioned ships of the class. In theory the laid up ships can be reactivated within 180 days.
Sales: FF 1056, 1068 and 1075 to Greece in late 1992/early 1993.

PHARRIS *4/1991, W. Sartori*

Major Combatant Naval Reserve Force Training Ships

Name/Hull No	*NRF Homeport*	*Assignment*
OLIVER HAZARD PERRY (FFG 7)	Philadelphia, PA	May 1984
WADSWORTH (FFG 9)	San Diego, CA	June 1985
DUNCAN (FFG 10)	Long Beach, CA	Jan 1984
CLARK (FFG 11)	Boston, MA	Sep 1985
GEORGE PHILIP (FFG 12)	Long Beach, CA	Jan 1986
SAMUEL ELIOT MORISON (FFG 13)	Charleston, SC	June 1986
JOHN H SIDES (FFG 14)	Long Beach, CA	Aug 1986
ESTOCIN (FFG 15)	Philadelphia, PA	Sep 1986
CLIFTON SPRAGUE (FFG 16)	Philadelphia, PA	Aug 1984
JOHN A MOORE (FFG 19)	Long Beach, CA	Jan 1987
ANTRIM (FFG 20)	Mayport, FL	Jan 1987
FLATLEY (FFG 21)	Mayport, FL	Nov 1987
FAHRION (FFG 22)	Charleston, SC	Sep 1988
LEWIS B PULLER (FFG 23)	Long Beach, CA	June 1987
COPELAND (FFG 25)	San Diego, CA	July 1988
MAHLON S TISDALE (FFG 27)	San Diego, CA	July 1988
JOSEPH HEWES (FF 1078)	Staten Island, NY	1992
BOWEN (FF 1079)	Staten Island, NY	1992
McCANDLESS (FF 1084)	Ingleside, TX	1992
DONALD B BEARY (FF 1085)	Staten Island, NY	1992
JESSE L BROWN (FF 1089)	Mobile, AL	1992
AINSWORTH (FF 1090)	Staten Island, NY	1992
TRUETT (FF 1095)	Ingleside, TX	1992
MOINESTER (FF 1097)	Mobile, AL	1992

SHIPBORNE AIRCRAFT (FRONT LINE)

Note: Development aircraft types which have been cancelled include the General Dynamics A-12 stealth advanced tactical aircraft (ATA), and the Lockheed P-7A MPA. The Boeing MV-22A Osprey tilt rotor aircraft has so far survived several attempts at cancellation and continues development into 1992.

Numbers/Type: 375/60/43 Grumman F-14A/A Plus/D Tomcat.
Operational speed: 1342 kts *(2485 km/h)*.
Service ceiling: 56 000 ft *(17 070 m)*.
Range: 1735 nm *(3220 km)*.
Role/Weapon systems: Standard fleet fighter aircraft for long-range air defence of task groups; undergoing phased improvements; F-14D flew in early 1988 with in service date of 1990. Sensors: AWG-9 or APG-71 (D type) radar, ALQ-126 or 165 (D type) jammers, ASN-92 nav or ASN-139 (D type), ALR-45 or ALR-67 (D type) RWR; IRST and JTIDS (D type). Weapons: AD; 1 × 20 mm cannon, 6 × AIM-54 Phoenix; HARM and Harpoon to be added. CAP; 1 × 20 mm cannon, 4 × Phoenix, 2 × AIM-7M, 2 × AIM-9M. Recce; 1 × 20 mm cannon, 2 × AIM-7M, 2 × AIM-9M.

TOMCAT *1991, US Navy*

TOMCAT *1989*

Numbers/Type: 335/38/242/79 McDonnell Douglas F/A-18A/B/C/D Hornet.
Operational speed: 1032 kts *(1910 km/h)*.
Service ceiling: 50 000 ft *(15 240 m)*.
Range: 1000 nm *(1850 km)*.
Role/Weapon systems: Strike interdictor for USN/USMC air groups; total procurement of at least 800 expected. Some are used for EW support with ALQ-167 jammers. Sensors: ESM: ALQ 165 ASPJ (18C/D), APG-65 radar, AAS-38 FLIR, ASQ-173 tracker. Weapons: ASV; 4 × Harpoon missiles. Strike; up to 7.7 tons of 'iron' bombs. AD; 1 × 20 mm Vulcan cannon, 9 × AIM-7/AIM-9 missiles. Typical ASV load might include 20 mm gun, 7.7 ton bombs, 2 AIM-9 missiles. Typical AAW load might include 20 mm gun, 4 AIM-7, 2 AIM-9 missiles. 18C/D includes AMRAAM and Maverick capability.

HORNET *8/1989, W. Donko*

Numbers/Type: 59/335 Grumman KA-6D/A-6E Intruder.
Operational speed: 560 kts *(1037 km/h)*.
Service ceiling: 42 400 ft *(12 925 m)*.
Range: 2818 nm *(5222 km)*.
Role/Weapon systems: All weather strike and armed reconnaissance role; 290 aircraft are being progressively updated. KA-6D is the tanker version. Sensors: APQ-148 or 156 search/attack radar, RWR, ECM. Weapons: ASV; 24 × Harpoon and nuclear weapons, 12 × Mk 36 mines. Strike; up to 8.2 tons of underwing stores. Self-defence; 4 × AIM-9 Sidewinder or 2 AIM-120 AMRAAM or 2 AIM-7M Sparrow. Systems Weapons Improvements Programme (SWIP) planned to include Harpoon, HARM, Maverick and Skipper missiles.

INTRUDER *1990, US Navy*

Numbers/Type: 190/1/24 McDonnell Douglas/British Aerospace AV-8B/AV-8B Plus/TAV-8B Harrier II.
Operational speed: 562 kts *(1041 km/h)*.
Service ceiling: 50 000 ft *(15 240 m)*.
Range: 800 nm *(1480 km)*.
Role/Weapon systems: Close support for USMC operational from 1985; planned numbers up to 207 (14 TAV trainers). A total of 28 AV-8B Plus delivery scheduled to start in June 1993. Sensors: FLIR, laser designator and ECM; APG-65 radar (AV-8B Plus). Weapons: Strike; up to 4.2 tons of 'iron' bombs or Paveway II LGM, AGM-62 Walleye or AGM-65 Maverick. Self-defence; 1 × GAU-12/U 25 mm cannon and 4 × AIM-9L Sidewinder.

HARRIER II *1/1991, Ingalls Shipbuilding*

Numbers/Type: 80 McDonnell Douglas A-4M Skyhawk.
Operational speed: 560 kts *(1038 km/h)*.
Service ceiling: 45 000 ft *(13 780 m)*.
Range: 1060 nm *(1963 km)*.
Role/Weapon systems: Ageing but important strike potential for USMC maintained for reserves; about 150 training versions in service. Sensors: Attack radar, ECM. Weapons: Strike; up to 1.6 tons fuselage and 3 tons underwing. AD; 2 × 20 mm cannon, 4 × AIM-7 or 9s.

SKYHAWK *1989, Hughes Aircraft*

Numbers/Type: 157 Lockheed S-3A/3B Viking.
Operational speed: 450 kts *(834 km/h)*.
Service ceiling: 35 000 ft *(10 670 m)*.
Range: 2000 nm *(3706 km)*.
Role/Weapon systems: Standard ASW aircraft; works in concert with towed array escorts; possible replacement from 1996 by Osprey tilt-rotor; first S-3B flew in 1987; conversion to B type at the rate of about 30 a year to complete in 1994; 16 being converted to ELINT configuration. Link 11 fitted. Sensors: APS-137(V)1 radar; APN-200 radar, FLIR, MAD, ASQ-81(V)1, 60 × sonobuoys; ESM: ALR-76; ECM ALE 47; ALE 39 Chaff. Weapons: ASW; 4 × Mk 54 depth charges, 4 × Mk 46 (or Mk 50) torpedoes. ASV; 2 × Harpoon Block 1C; mines.

VIKING *1987, US Navy*

Numbers/Type: 132 Grumman EA-6B Prowler.
Operational speed: 566 kts *(1048 km/h)*.
Service ceiling: 41 200 ft *(12 550 m)*.
Range: 955 nm *(1769 km)*.
Role/Weapon systems: EW and jamming aircraft to accompanying strikes and armed reconnaissance; being uprated to ADVCAP with new engines and ECM. Sensors: APS-130 radar; ALQ-99F, ALQ-149 (ADVCAP) jammers. Weapons: HARM anti-radiation missile capable.

PROWLER *10/1990, US Navy*

Numbers/Type: 113 Grumman E-2C Hawkeye.
Operational speed: 323 kts *(598 km/h)*.
Service ceiling: 30 800 ft *(9390 m)*.
Range: 1000 nm *(1850 km)*.
Role/Weapon systems: Used for direction of AD and strike operations; being ordered at about six a year to a planned total of 147. Sensors: ESM: ALR-73 PDS, ALQ-108; Airborne tactical data system with Links 4A and 11, APS-125 radar, later aircraft have APS-138/139 radar. Weapons: Unarmed.

HAWKEYE *1989, US Navy*

Numbers/Type: 142/48 Sikorsky SH-60B/F Seahawk (LAMPS III).
Operational speed: 135 kts *(250 km/h)*.
Service ceiling: 10 000 ft *(3050 m)*.
Range: 600 nm *(1110 km)*.
Role/Weapon systems: LAMPS III air vehicle for medium-range ASW and for ASV; total of 204 (60B) and 175 (60F) planned at a rate of about 12 each per year; operated from DDH and FFH class escorts; non-autonomous; SH-60F is derived model to replace Sea King; entered service 1989; Link 11 fitted. Sensors: APS-124 search radar, FLIR, ASQ-811 (V) MAD, 25 sonobuoys (Difar or Dicass (60F)), LLTV. AQS-13F dipping sonar (60F) (to be replaced by ALFS in due course); ALQ-142/156 ESM, ALQ-144 ECM. ALE-39 Chaff and flare dispenser. Weapons: ASW; 2/3 × Mk 46/Mk 50 torpedoes or depth bombs. ASV; 1 × Penguin Mk 2 Mod 7 missile (in 28 aircraft for Oliver Perry frigates from 1992); 1—7.62 mm MG M60.

SEAHAWK *1990, Karl Webb, RN*

Numbers/Type: 90/20 Kaman SH-2F/G Seasprite (LAMPS I).
Operational speed: 130 kts *(241 km/h)*.
Service ceiling: 22 500 ft *(6860 m)*.
Range: 367 nm *(679 km)*.
Role/Weapon systems: ASW and OTHT helicopter; second production run ended in 1987; in LAMPS I programme, acts as ASW information relay for surface ships. Six SH-2G were new build, 14 more converted by 1993 with improved engines, avionics and sensor processing. 30 more to be converted in due course. Sensors: LN-66HP radar, ALR-66 ESM, ASN-123 tactical nav, ASQ-81(V)2 MAD, AAQ-16 night vision system; ARR-57 sonobuoy receivers; 15 sonobuoys. For the Gulf War in 1991, additional EW equipment included AAQ-34 FLIR, ALE-37 Chaff, ALQ 144 IR counter, plus DLQ 3B video data link. A DEMON mine detection system was also fitted. Weapons: ASW; 2 × Mk 46 (or Mk 50) torpedoes, 8 × Mk 25 smoke markers, 1 depth bomb. ASV: 1 Penguin; 1—7.62 mm MG M60.

SEASPRITE *1991, Kaman*

Numbers/Type: 35/113 Sikorsky SH-3G/H Sea King.
Operational speed: 144 kts *(267 km/h)*.
Service ceiling: 12 200 ft *(3720 m)*.
Range: 630 nm *(1166 km)*.
Role/Weapon systems: Carrier battle group inner zone ASW; also used for liaison and SAR tasks. Being replaced by SH-60F. Sensors: AN/APS-24 search radar, Bendix AQS-13 dipping sonar, Texas Instruments ASQ-81(V)2 MAD, 25 sonobuoys. Weapons: ASW; 2 × Mk 46/Mk 50 torpedoes or depth bombs or mines.

SEA KING *5/1986, US Navy*

Numbers/Type: 345 Boeing HH-46D/E, CH-46D/E and UH-46D/E Sea Knight.
Operational speed: 137 kts *(254 km/h)*.
Service ceiling: 8500 ft *(2590 m)*.
Range: 180 nm *(338 km)*.
Role/Weapon systems: Support/assault (USMC) for 18 Marines and re-supply (USN) helicopter respectively. Can lift 1.3 tons or 4.5 tons in a cargo net or sling. Sensors: None. Weapons: Unarmed.

SEA KNIGHT *7/1991, G. Toremans*

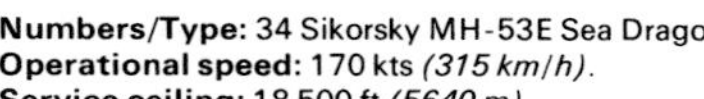

Numbers/Type: 78 Sikorsky CH-53D Sea Stallion.
Operational speed: 150 kts *(278 km/h)*.
Service ceiling: 21 000 ft *(6400 m)*.
Range: 540 nm *(1000 km)*.
Role/Weapon systems: Assault, support and transport helicopters; can carry 38 Marines. Sensors: None. Weapons: Up to 3 × 12.7 mm machine guns.

SEA STALLION *1986, US Navy*

Numbers/Type: 125 Sikorsky CH-53E Super Stallion.
Operational speed: 170 kts *(315 km/h)*.
Service ceiling: 18 500 ft *(5640 m)*.
Range: 230 nm *(425 km)*.
Role/Weapon systems: Uprated, three-engined version of Sea Stallion with support (USN) and transport (USMC) roles. Total of about 200 aircraft planned. Carries 56 Marines. Sensors: None. Weapons: Up to 3 × 12.7 mm machine guns.

SUPER STALLION *1990, US Navy*

Numbers/Type: 34 Sikorsky MH-53E Sea Dragon.
Operational speed: 170 kts *(315 km/h)*.
Service ceiling: 18 500 ft *(5640 m)*.
Range: 1000 nm *(1850 km)*.
Role/Weapon systems: Three-engined AMCM helicopter similar to Super Stallion; total of about 60 planned; tows ALQ-166 MCM sweep equipment; self-deployed if necessary. Sensors: AQS-14 or AQS-20 dipping sonar being fitted. Weapons: 2 × 12.7 mm guns for self-defence.

SEA DRAGON *1991*

Numbers/Type: 105 Bell AH-1W Super Cobra.
Operational speed: 149 kts *(277 km/h)*.
Service ceiling: 12 200 ft *(3718 m)*.
Range: 317 nm *(587 km)*.
Role/Weapon systems: Close support helicopter; uprated and improved version, with own air defence capability; being procured at about 12 a year. Sensors: NTS (laser and FLIR nightsight) to be retrofitted from 1993 at the rate of 24 aircraft per year. Weapons: Strike/assault; 1 or 3 × 20 mm cannon, 8 × TOW or Hellfire missiles, gun and grenade pods. Self-defence; 2 × AIM-9L Sidewinder missiles.

SUPER COBRA *1984, Bell Helicopters*

Numbers/Type: 118 Bell UH-1N Iroquois. Twin Huey
Operational speed: 110 kts *(204 km/h)*.
Service ceiling: 15 000 ft *(4570 m)*.
Range: 250 nm *(463 km)*.
Role/Weapon systems: Support and logistics helicopter for USMC operations afloat and ashore. Can carry 16 Marines. Sensors: None. Weapons: Can be armed with 7.62 mm machine guns.

TWIN HUEY *1990, Bell Helicopters*

LAND-BASED MARITIME AIRCRAFT (FRONT LINE)

Numbers/Type: 253 Lockheed P-3C Orion.
Operational speed: 411 kts *(761 km/h)*.
Service ceiling: 28 300 ft *(8625 m)*.
Range: 4000 nm *(7410 km)*.
Role/Weapon systems: Deployed worldwide in support of US Naval operations; primarily ASW; update III conversions to 113 airframes; update IV with tactical ESM for the remainder, first delivered in 1990. Remainder of P-3Bs have been allocated to the Naval Reserves. Sensors: APS-115 search radar, ASQ-81 MAD, up to 100 × sonobuoys, FLIR, cameras, AXR-13 LLTV, ALR 66 or ALQ 78 ESM. Weapons: ASW; 4 × Mk 44/46 torpedoes or 2 × Mk 101 nuclear depth bombs. ASV; 4 × Harpoon (P-3C). ML; 6 × Mk 55/56 mines.

Numbers/Type: 17 Lockheed EP-3E Orion.
Operational speed: 411 kts *(761 km/h)*.
Service ceiling: 28 300 ft *(8625 m)*.
Range: 4000 nm *(7410 km)*.
Role/Weapon systems: Electronic warfare and intelligence gathering aircraft. Sensors: EW equipment including AN/ALR-60, AN/ALQ-76, AN/ALQ-78, AN/ALQ-108 and AN/ASQ-114. Weapons: Unarmed.

Numbers/Type: 14 Boeing E-6A Hermes/TACAMO.
Operational speed: 455 kts *(842 km/h)*.
Service ceiling: 42 000 ft *(12 800 m)*.
Range: 6350 nm *(11 760 km/h)*.
Role/Weapon systems: First flew in February 1987 and has replaced EC-130Q. EMP hardened against nuclear bursts. Sensors: Supports Trident Fleet radio communications. Weapons: Unarmed.

TACAMO *1989, Boeing*

AMPHIBIOUS WARFARE FORCES

Note: In early 1992, the Navy had an amphibious lift capacity of 60 vessels. The five ships of the Wasp class are designed to supplement and ultimately replace the Iwo Jima class of LPHs, which are scheduled to be retired in the late 1990s. The construction of the LX, which is the planned replacement for LPDs, LSTs, LKAs, and older class LSDs, is expected to start in the mid-1990s. The projected total of 18 LXs will provide a lift capability of 2.5 Marine Expeditionary Brigades, far short of the Marine Corps goal of being able to lift two Marine Expeditionary Forces simultaneously.

Additional capacity is provided by the 13 maritime pre-positioning ships (see listing at end of *Military Sealift Command* section) which are either new construction (5) or conversions of relatively new commercial ships. One squadron is maintained on station in the Atlantic, a second at Guam, and a third at Diego Garcia. Each carries equipment for a Marine Expeditionary Brigade. Ships of the latter two squadrons were the first to arrive at Saudi Arabian ports after the build-up of US forces in the Middle East was ordered in late 1990. In addition, 43 fleet amphibious ships were involved in the war with Iraq in 1991.

Amphibious units took part in five other operations in 1990-91. These were the six month long deployment off Liberia to evacuate US and foreign nationals and to protect the embassy during the civil war; the rescue of US and foreign nationals from the Somalian capital of Mogadishu; assistance to Kurdish refugees in northern Iraq; SAR operations after a typhoon devastated Bangladesh, and assistance in cleaning up the Subic Bay naval base in the Philippines after the eruption of Mt Pinatubo.

Minesweeping: Several of the larger amphibious ships have been used as operating bases for minesweeping helicopters in the absence of a 'mother ship' for such aircraft. *Tripoli* (LPH 10) was serving in that capacity in February 1991 when she was severely damaged by an Iraqi mine in the Persian Gulf.

2 BLUE RIDGE CLASS: AMPHIBIOUS COMMAND SHIPS (LCC)

Name	*No*	*Builders*	*Laid down*	*Launched*	*Commissioned*	*F/S*
BLUE RIDGE	LCC 19	Philadelphia Naval Shipyard	27 Feb 1967	4 Jan 1969	14 Nov 1970	PA
MOUNT WHITNEY	LCC 20	Newport News Shipbuilding & Dry Dock Co.	8 Jan 1969	8 Jan 1970	16 Jan 1971	AA

Displacement, tons: 16 790 light; 18 372 full load *(Blue Ridge)* 16 100 light; 18 646 full load *(Mount Whitney)*
Dimensions, feet (metres): 636.5 × 107.9 × 28.9 *(194 × 32.9 × 8.8)*
Main machinery: 2 Foster-Wheeler boilers; 600 psi *(42.3 kg/cm sq)*; 870°F *(467°C)*; 1 GE turbine; 22 000 hp *(16.4 MW)*; 1 shaft
Speed, knots: 23. **Range, miles:** 13 000 at 16 kts
Complement: 821 (43 officers); Flag 170-190.
Military lift: 700 troops; 3 LCPs; 2 LCVPs

Missiles: SAM: 2 Raytheon GMLS Mk 25 Mod 1 octuple launchers ❶; 16 Sea Sparrow; semi-active radar homing to 14.6 km *(8 nm)* at 2.5 Mach; warhead 39 kg.
Guns: 4 USN 3 in *(76 mm)*/50 (2 twin) Mk 33 ❷; 85° elevation; 50 rounds/minute to 12.8 km *(7 nm)*; weight of shell 6 kg. Antennas and their supports severely restrict firing arcs of guns. 2 General Electric/General Dynamics 20 mm/76 6-barrelled Vulcan Phalanx Mk 15 ❸; 3000 rounds/minute (4500 in Block 1) combined to 1.5 km.
Countermeasures: Decoys: 4 Loral Hycor SRBOC 6-barrelled fixed Mk 36; IR flares and Chaff to 4 km *(2.2 nm)*. SLQ-25 Nixie; torpedo decoy.
ESM/ECM: SLQ 32(V)3; combined radar intercept, jammer and deception system.
Combat data systems: NTDS with Links 4A, 11, 14 and 16 in due course. Amphibious Command Information System (ACIS), and Naval Intelligence Processing System (NIPS). SATCOMS ❹ SSR-1, WSC-3 (UHF), WSC-6 (SHF), USC-38 (EHF) (from 1992), SMQ-6 receiver.
Fire control: 2 Mk 115 MFCS. No GFCS.
Radars: Air search: ITT SPS 48C ❺; 3D; E/F band; range 402 km *(220 nm)*.
Lockheed SPS 40C ❻; E/F band; range 320 km *(175 nm)*.
Hughes Mk 23 TAS; D band (to be fitted).
Surface search: Raytheon SPS 65(V)1 ❼; G band.
Navigation: Marconi LN 66; Raytheon SPS 64(V)9; I band.
Fire control: Two Mk 115; I/J band (for SAM).
Tacan: URN 20/25. IFF: Mk XII AIMS UPX-29.

Helicopters: 1 utility can be carried.

Programmes: Authorised in FY 1965 and 1966. Originally designated Amphibious Force Flagships (AGC); redesignated Amphibious Command Ships (LCC) on 1 January 1969.
Modernisation: Modernisation completed FY 1987 although the Mk 23 TAS radar may be fitted in due course.
Structure: General hull design and machinery arrangement are similar to the Iwo Jima class assault ships.

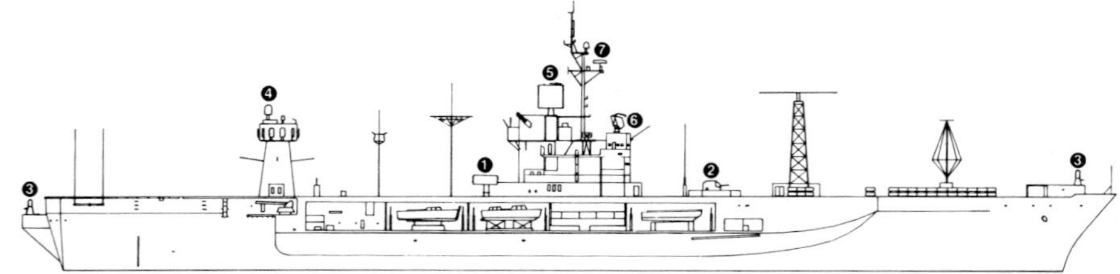
BLUE RIDGE (Scale 1 : 1 800), *Ian Sturton*

MOUNT WHITNEY 9/1991, *Maritime Photographic*

Operational: These are large amphibious force command ships of post-Second World War design. They can provide integrated command and control facilities for sea, air and land commanders in amphibious operations. *Blue Ridge* is the Seventh Fleet flagship, based at Yokosuka, Japan. *Mount Whitney* serves as flagship Second Fleet, based at Norfolk, Virginia. *Blue Ridge* deployed to the Gulf during the war with Iraq in 1991.

5 CHARLESTON CLASS: AMPHIBIOUS CARGO SHIPS (LKA)

Name	*No*	*Builders*	*Commissioned*	*F/S*
CHARLESTON	LKA 113	Newport News SB & DD Co	14 Dec 1968	AA
DURHAM	LKA 114	Newport News SB & DD Co	24 May 1969	PA
MOBILE	LKA 115	Newport News SB & DD Co	29 Sep 1969	PA
SAINT LOUIS	LKA 116	Newport News SB & DD Co	22 Nov 1969	PA
EL PASO	LKA 117	Newport News SB & DD Co	17 Jan 1970	AA

Displacement, tons: 10 000 light; 20 700 full load
Dimensions, feet (metres): 575.5 × 62 × 25.5 *(175.4 × 18.9 × 7.7)*
Main machinery: 2 Combustion Engineering boilers; 600 psi *(42.3 kg/cm sq)*; 870°F *(467°C)*; 1 Westinghouse turbine; 19 250 hp *(14.4 MW)*; 1 shaft
Speed, knots: 20. **Range, miles:** 9600 at 16 kts
Complement: 356 (22 officers)
Military lift: 362 troops (25 officers). 4 LCM 8, 5 LCM 6, 2 LCPL

Guns: 2 or 6 USN 3 in *(76 mm)*/50 (1 or 3 twin) Mk 33; 85° elevation; 50 rounds/minute to 12.8 km *(7 nm)*; weight of shell 6 kg. Local control only.
2 General Electric/General Dynamics 20 mm Vulcan Phalanx Mk 15 (instead of 2 twin 76 mm).
Countermeasures: Decoys: 2 MBA Loral Hycor SRBOC 6-barrelled fixed Mk 36; IR flares and Chaff to 4 km *(2.2 nm)*.
ESM: SLQ 32(V)1; intercept. May be upgraded to (V)2.
Combat data systems: SATCOM SRR-1, WSC-3 (UHF).
Radars: Surface search: Raytheon SPS 10F; G band.
SPS 67 (fitted in FY 1989-92).
Navigation: Marconi LN 66 (in addition CRP 2900 Pathfinder in LKA 113); I band.
Tacan: IFF: Mk XII.

Helicopters: Platform only.

Programmes: Originally designated Attack Cargo Ship (AKA), *Charleston* redesignated Amphibious Cargo Ship (LKA) on 14 December 1968; others to LKA on 1 January 1969.

DURHAM 3/1991, *92 Wing RAAF*

Structure: Designed specifically for the attack cargo ship role for amphibious operations. Design includes two heavy-lift cranes with a 78.4 ton capacity, two 40 ton capacity booms, and eight 15 ton capacity booms. These are among the first US Navy ships with a fully automated main propulsion plant. Control of plant is from bridge or central machinery space console. This automation permitted a 45 man reduction in complement. Phalanx have replaced two of the 76 mm guns in some of the class.
Operational: *Saint Louis* is based at Sasebo, Japan.

1 + 4 + (1) WASP CLASS: AMPHIBIOUS ASSAULT SHIP (multi-purpose) (LHD)

Name	No	Builders	Laid down	Launched	Commissioned	F/S
WASP	LHD 1	Ingalls Shipbuilding	30 May 1985	4 Aug 1987	29 July 1989	AA
ESSEX	LHD 2	Ingalls Shipbuilding	20 Mar 1989	4 Jan 1991	July 1992	Bldg/PA
KEARSAGE	LHD 3	Ingalls Shipbuilding	6 Feb 1990	Apr 1992	May 1993	Bldg/AA
BOXER	LHD 4	Ingalls Shipbuilding	8 Apr 1991	Apr 1993	Dec 1994	Bldg/PA
BATAAN	LHD 5	Ingalls Shipbuilding	May 1992	June1994	Dec 1996	Ord

Displacement, tons: 28 233 light; 40 532 full load
Dimensions, feet (metres): 844 × 140.1 × 26.6 *(257.3 × 42.7 × 8.1)*
Flight deck, feet (metres): 820 × 106 *(249.9 × 32.3)*
Main machinery: 2 Combustion Engineering boilers; 600 psi *(42.3 kg/cm sq)*; 900°F *(482°C)*; 2 Westinghouse turbines; 70 000 hp *(52.2 MW)*; 2 shafts
Speed, knots: 22. **Range, miles:** 9500 at 18 kts
Complement: 1077 (98 officers)
Military lift: 2074 troops; 12 LCM 6s or 3 LCACs; 1232 tons aviation fuel; 4 LCPL

Missiles: SAM: 2 Raytheon GMLS Mk 29 octuple launchers ❶; 16 Sea Sparrow; semi-active radar homing to 14.6 km *(8 nm)* at 2.5 Mach; warhead 39 kg. 1 launcher located aft, on a specially-built transom that overhangs the stern, and a second on a raised deck forward of the superstructure.
Guns: 3 General Electric/General Dynamics 20 mm 6-barrelled Vulcan Phalanx Mk 15 ❷; 3000 rounds/minute (4500 in Batch 1) combined to 1.5 km. One fitted on each quarter and one aft of the NSSMS launcher on the island.
8—12.7 mm MGs.
Countermeasures: Decoys: 4 or 6 Loral Hycor SRBOC 6-barrelled fixed Mk 36; IR flares and Chaff to 4 km *(2.2 nm)*.
SLQ 25 Nixie; acoustic torpedo decoy system. NATO Sea Gnat. SLQ-49 Chaff buoys. AEB SSQ-95.
ESM/ECM: SLQ 32(V)3; combined radar warning, jammer and deception system.
Combat data systems: Integrated Tactical Amphibious Warfare Data System (ITAWDS) and Marine Tactical Amphibious C² System (MTACCS). Links 4A, 11 (modified), 14 and 16 in due course. SATCOMS ❸ SSR-1, WSC-3 (UHF), USC-38 (EHF) (from 1992). SMQ-11 Metsat.
Fire control: 2 Mk 91 MFCS. SYS-2(V)3 IADT.
Radars: Air search: Hughes SPS 52C ❹ (LHD 1); 3D; E/F band; range 439 km *(240 nm)*.
ITT SPS 48E (except LHD 1); 3D; E/F band; range 402 km *(220 nm)*.
Raytheon SPS 49(V)9 ❺; C/D band; range 457 km *(250 nm)*.
Hughes Mk 23 TAS ❻; D band.
Surface search: Norden SPS 67 ❼; G band.
Navigation: SPS 64(V)9; I band.
CCA: SPN 35A and SPN 43B.
Fire control: 2 Mk 95; I/J band.
Tacan: URN 25. IFF: CIS Mk XV UPX-29.

Fixed wing aircraft: 6-8 AV-8B Harriers or up to 20 in secondary role.
Helicopters: Capacity for 42 CH-46E Sea Knight but has the capability to support: AH-1W Super Cobra, CH-53E Super Stallion, CH-53D Sea Stallion, UH-1N Twin Huey, AH-1T Sea Cobra, and SH-60B Seahawk helicopters.

Programmes: Fifth of the class ordered 20 December 1991. One more projected in FY 1996 probably as a result of Marine Corps leaders' concern that five were insufficient to meet the operational lift requirement.
Structure: Two aircraft elevators, one to starboard and aft of the 'island' and one to port amidships. The well deck is 50 ft *(15.2 m)* wide and can accommodate up to three Amphibious Air-Cushion Vehicles (LCAC). The flight deck has nine helicopter landing spots. Cargo capacity is 101 000 cu ft total with an additional 20 000 sq ft to accommodate vehicles. The bridge is two decks lower than that of an LHA, command, control and communication spaces having been moved inside the hull to avoid 'cheap kill' damage. Fitted with a 600-bed capacity hospital and six operating rooms. HY-100 steel covers the flight deck.
Operational: A typical complement of aircraft would be a mix of 30 helicopters and six to eight Harriers (AV-8B). In the secondary role as a sea control ship the most likely mix is 20 AV-8B Harriers and four to six SH-60B Seahawk helicopters.

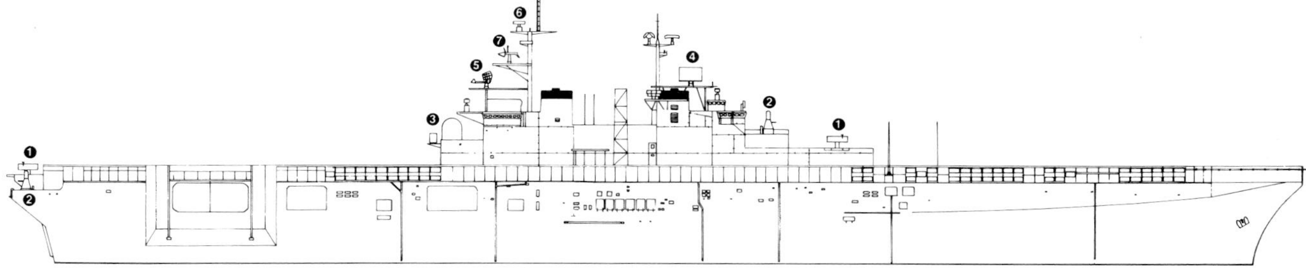

WASP (Scale 1 : 1 500), *Ian Sturton*

WASP *7/1991, G. Toremans*

WASP *2/1990, Giorgio Arra*

WASP *7/1991, G. Toremans*

5 TARAWA CLASS: AMPHIBIOUS ASSAULT SHIPS (multi-purpose) (LHA)

Name	No	Builders	Erection of First Module	Launched	Commissioned	F/S
TARAWA	LHA 1	Ingalls Shipbuilding	15 Nov 1971	1 Dec 1973	29 May 1976	PA
SAIPAN	LHA 2	Ingalls Shipbuilding	21 July 1972	18 July 1974	15 Oct 1977	AA
BELLEAU WOOD	LHA 3	Ingalls Shipbuilding	5 Mar 1973	11 Apr 1977	23 Sep 1978	PA
NASSAU	LHA 4	Ingalls Shipbuilding	13 Aug 1973	21 Jan 1978	28 July 1979	AA
PELELIU (ex-*Da Nang*)	LHA 5	Ingalls Shipbuilding	12 Nov 1976	25 Nov 1978	3 May 1980	PA

Displacement, tons: 39 967 full load
Dimensions, feet (metres): 834 × 131.9 × 25.9 *(254.2 × 40.2 × 7.9)*
Flight deck, feet (metres): 820 × 118.1 *(250 × 36)*
Main machinery: 2 Combustion Engineering boilers; 600 psi *(42.3 kg/cm sq)*; 900°F *(482°C)*; 2 Westinghouse turbines; 70 000 hp *(52.2 MW)*; 2 shafts; bow thruster; 900 hp *(670 kW)*
Speed, knots: 24. **Range, miles:** 10 000 at 20 kts
Complement: 930 (56 officers)
Military lift: 1703 troops; 4 LCU 1610 type or 2 LCU and 2 LCM 8 or 17 LCM 6 or 45 LVT tractors; 1200 tons aviation fuel. 1 LCAC may be embarked. 4 LCPL

Guns: 2 FMC 5 in *(127 mm)*/54 Mk 45 Mod 1 ❶; 65° elevation; 20 rounds/minute to 23 km *(12.6 nm)* anti-surface; 15 km *(8.2 nm)* anti-aircraft; weight of shell 32 kg.
6 Mk 242 25 mm automatic cannons.
2 General Electric/General Dynamics 20 mm/76 6-barrelled Vulcan Phalanx Mk 16 ❷; 3000 rounds/minute (4500 in Block 1) combined to 1.5 km.
Countermeasures: Decoys: 4 Loral Hycor SRBOC 6-barrelled fixed Mk 36; IR flares and Chaff to 4 km *(2.2 nm)*.
SLQ 25 Nixie; acoustic torpedo decoy system. NATO Sea Gnat. SLQ-49 Chaff buoys. AEB SSQ-95.
ESM/ECM: SLQ 32V(3); combined radar intercept, jammer and deception system.
Combat data systems: Integrated Tactical Amphibious Warfare Data System (ITAWDS) to provide computerised support in control of helicopters and aircraft, shipboard weapons and sensors, navigation, landing craft control, and electronic warfare. Links 4A, 11, 14 and 16 in due course. SATCOM SRR-1, WSC-3 (UHF), USC-38 (EHF) (LHA 2 and 4). SMQ-11 Metsat.
Fire control: Mk 86 Mod 4 GFCS. 2 optronic directors.
Radars: Air search: Hughes SPS 52C ❸; 3D; E/F band; range 439 km *(240 nm)*.
Lockheed SPS 40B/C/D ❹; E/F band; range 320 km *(175 nm)*.
Surface search: Raytheon SPS 67 ❺; G band.
Navigation: Raytheon SPS 64(V)9; I band.

NASSAU — *3/1991, van Ginderen Collection*

CCA: SPN 35A; SPN 43B.
Fire control: Lockheed SPG 60 ❻; I/J band.
Lockheed SPQ 9A ❼; I/J band; range 37 km *(20 nm)*.
Tacan: URN 25. IFF: CIS Mk XV.

Fixed wing aircraft: Harrier AV-8B VSTOL aircraft in place of some helicopters as required.
Helicopters: 19 CH-53D Sea Stallion or 26 CH-46D/E Sea Knight.

Programmes: Originally intended to be a class of nine ships. LHA1 was authorised in FY 1969, LHA 2 and LHA 3 in FY 1970 and LHA 4 and LHA 5 in FY 1971.
Modernisation: Two Vulcan Phalanx CIWS replaced the GMLS Mk 25 Sea Sparrow launchers. Programme completed in early 1991.
Structure: Beneath the full-length flight deck are two half-length hangar decks, the two being connected by an elevator amidships on the port side and a stern lift; beneath the after elevator is a floodable docking well measuring 268 ft in length and 78 ft in width which is capable of accommodating four LCU 1610 type landing craft. Also included is a large garage for trucks and AFVs and troop berthing for a reinforced battalion. 33 730 sq ft available for vehicles and 116 900 cu ft for palletted stores. Extensive medical facilities including operating rooms, X-ray room, hospital ward, isolation ward, laboratories, pharmacy, dental operating room and medical store rooms.
Operational: The flight deck can operate a maximum of nine CH-53D Sea Stallion or 12 CH-46D/E Sea Knight helicopters or a mix of these and other helicopters. With some additional modifications, ships of this class can effectively operate AV-8B aircraft. The normal mix of aircraft allows for six AV-8Bs. The optimum aircraft configuration for this class is dependent upon assigned missions. Unmanned Reconnaissance Vehicles (URVs) can be operated. LHA 3 is based at Sasebo, Nagasaki. Three of the class were involved in the war with Iraq in 1991.

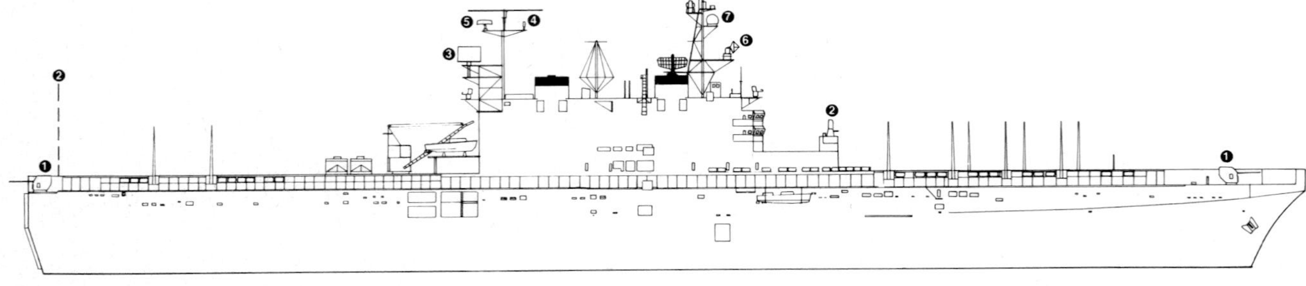
TARAWA — *(Scale 1 : 1 500), Ian Sturton*

TARAWA — *6/1991, 92 Wing RAAF*

7 IWO JIMA CLASS: AMPHIBIOUS ASSAULT SHIPS (LPH)

Name	No	Builders	Laid down	Launched	Commissioned	F/S
IWO JIMA	LPH 2	Puget Sound Naval Shipyard	2 Apr 1959	17 Sep 1960	26 Aug 1961	AA
OKINAWA	LPH 3	Philadelphia Naval Shipyard	1 Apr 1960	14 Aug 1961	14 Apr 1962	PA
GUADALCANAL	LPH 7	Philadelphia Naval Shipyard	1 Sep 1961	16 Mar 1963	20 July 1963	AA
GUAM	LPH 9	Philadelphia Naval Shipyard	15 Nov 1962	22 Aug 1964	16 Jan 1965	AA
TRIPOLI	LPH 10	Ingalls Shipbuilding Corp	15 June 1964	31 July 1965	6 Aug 1966	PA
NEW ORLEANS	LPH 11	Philadelphia Naval Shipyard	1 Mar 1966	3 Feb 1968	16 Nov 1968	PA
INCHON	LPH 12	Ingalls Shipbuilding Corp	8 Apr 1968	24 May 1969	20 June 1970	AA

Displacement, tons: 11 250 light; 18 300 full load
Dimensions, feet (metres): 602.3 × 104 × 31.7 *(183.7 × 31.7 × 9.7)*
Flight deck, feet (metres): 602.3 × 104 *(183.7 × 31.7)*
Main machinery: 2 Babcock & Wilcox/Combustion Engineering boilers; 600 psi *(42.3 kg/cm sq)*; 900°F *(482°C)*; 1 De Laval/GE/Westinghouse turbine; 23 000 hp *(17.2 MW)*; 1 shaft
Speed, knots: 23. **Range, miles:** 10 000 at 20 kts
Complement: 686 (48 officers)
Military lift: 1746 troops (144 officers); 1500 tons aviation fuel; 2 LCPL

Missiles: SAM: 2 Raytheon GMLS Mk 25 octuple launchers ❶; Sea Sparrow; semi-active radar homing to 14.6 km *(8 nm)* at 2.5 Mach; warhead 39 kg. 1 launcher forward of island structure and 1 on the port quarter.
Guns: 4 USN 3 in *(76 mm)*/50 (2 twin) Mk 33 ❷; 85° elevation; 50 rounds/minute to 12.8 km *(7 nm)*; weight of shell 6 kg.
2 General Electric/General Dynamics 20 mm 6-barrelled Vulcan Phalanx Mk 15 ❸; 3000 rounds/minute (4500 in Batch 1) combined to 1.5 km.
Up to 8—12.7 mm MGs.
Countermeasures: Decoys: 4 Loral Hycor SRBOC 6-barrelled fixed Mk 36; IR flares and Chaff to 4 km *(2.2 nm)*.
ESM/ECM: SLQ 32(V)3; combined radar warning, jammer and deception system.
Combat data systems: SATCOM ❹ SRR-1, WSC-3 (UHF).
Fire control: 2 Mk 71 directors.
Radars: Air search: Westinghouse SPS 58 ❺; 3D; D band.
Lockheed SPS 40 ❻; E/F band; range 320 km *(175 nm)*.
Surface search: Raytheon SPS 10 ❼; G band.
CCA: SPN 35 and SPN 43.
Navigation: Marconi LN 66; I band.
Fire control: Two Mk 115; I/J band.
Tacan: URN 25. IFF: Mk XII UPX-29.

Fixed wing aircraft: 4 AV-8B Harriers in place of some helicopters.
Helicopters: Capacity for 20 CH-46D/E Sea Knight or 11 CH-53D Sea Stallion.

Programmes: *Iwo Jima* was authorised in FY 1958. *Guam* was modified late in 1971 and began operations in January 1972 as an interim sea control ship; she reverted to the amphibious role in 1974 but kept 12 AV-8As on board. All seven will be replaced by the Wasp class in due course.
Structure: *Iwo Jima* was the world's first ship designed specifically to operate helicopters. Two deck-edge lifts, one to port opposite the bridge and one to starboard aft of island. Full hangars are provided; no arresting wires or catapults. Two small elevators carry cargo from holds to flight deck. Stowage of 4300 sq ft for vehicles and 37 400 cu ft for palletted stores. Fitted with extensive medical facilities including operating room, X-ray room, hospital ward, isolation ward, laboratory, pharmacy, dental operating room, and medical store rooms.
Operational: The flight decks provide for simultaneous take off or landing of seven CH-46 Sea Knight or four CH-53 Sea Stallion helicopters during normal operations. Can operate AV-8Bs following modifications to refine day/night capability. Each LPH can carry a Marine battalion landing team, its guns, vehicles, and equipment, plus a reinforced squadron of transport helicopters and various support personnel. All have been used on many occasions as platforms for airborne minesweeping operations. Six of the class were involved in the war with Iraq in 1991. *Tripoli* was damaged by a mine but was operational again within a few weeks.

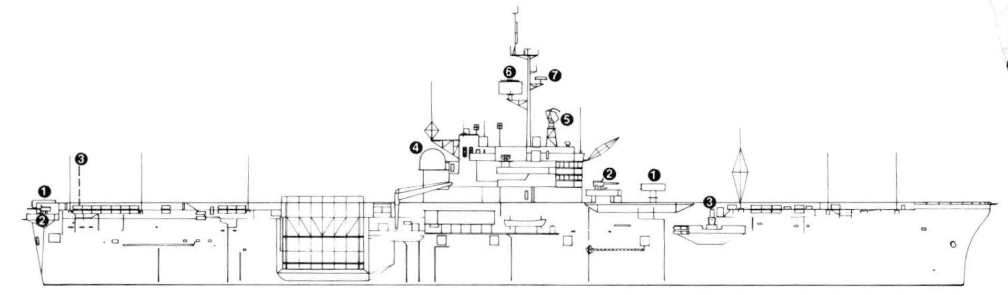

IWO JIMA — *(Scale 1 : 1 500), Ian Sturton*

TRIPOLI — *10/1991, Giorgio Arra*

INCHON — *3/1991, Giorgio Arra*

11 AUSTIN CLASS: AMPHIBIOUS TRANSPORT DOCKS (LPD)

Name	*No*	*Builders*	*Laid down*	*Launched*	*Commissioned*	*F/S*
AUSTIN	LPD 4	New York Naval Shipyard	4 Feb 1963	27 June 1964	6 Feb 1965	AA
OGDEN	LPD 5	New York Naval Shipyard	4 Feb 1963	27 June 1964	19 June 1965	PA
DULUTH	LPD 6	New York Naval Shipyard	18 Dec 1963	14 Aug 1965	18 Dec 1965	PA
CLEVELAND	LPD 7	Ingalls Shipbuilding Corp	30 Nov 1964	7 May 1966	21 Apr 1967	PA
DUBUQUE	LPD 8	Ingalls Shipbuilding Corp	25 Jan 1965	6 Aug 1966	1 Sep 1967	PA
DENVER	LPD 9	Lockheed SB & Construction Co	7 Feb 1964	23 Jan 1965	26 Oct 1968	PA
JUNEAU	LPD 10	Lockheed SB & Construction Co	23 Jan 1965	12 Feb 1966	12 July 1969	PA
SHREVEPORT	LPD 12	Lockheed SB & Construction Co	27 Dec 1965	25 Oct 1966	12 Dec 1970	AA
NASHVILLE	LPD 13	Lockheed SB & Construction Co	14 Mar 1966	7 Oct 1967	14 Feb 1970	AA
TRENTON	LPD 14	Lockheed SB & Construction Co	8 Aug 1966	3 Aug 1968	6 Mar 1971	AA
PONCE	LPD 15	Lockheed SB & Construction Co	31 Oct 1966	20 May 1970	10 July 1971	AA

Displacement, tons: 9130 light; 16 500-17 244 full load
Dimensions, feet (metres): 570 × 100 (84 hull) × 23 *(173.8 × 30.5 (25.6) × 7)*
Main machinery: 2 Foster-Wheeler boilers (Babcock & Wilcox in LPD 5 and 12); 600 psi *(42.3 kg/cm sq)*; 870°F *(467°C)*; 2 De Laval turbines; 24 000 hp *(18 MW)*; 2 shafts
Speed, knots: 21. **Range, miles:** 7700 at 20 kts.
Complement: 420 (24 officers); Flag 90 (in LPD 7-13)
Military lift: 930 troops (840 only in LPD 7-13); 9 LCM 6s or 4 LCM 8s or 2 LCAC or 20 LVTs. 4 LCPL/LCVP

Guns: 2 or 4 USN 3 in *(76 mm)*/50 (1 or 2 twin) Mk 33 ❶; 85° elevation; 50 rounds/minute to 12.8 km *(7 nm)*; weight of shell 6 kg. Local control only.
2 General Electric/General Dynamics 20 mm/76 6-barrelled Vulcan Phalanx Mk 15 ❷; 3000 rounds/minute (4500 in Block 1) combined to 1.5 km. Being fitted in FY 1988-93 during maintenance periods.
Countermeasures: Decoys: 4 Loral Hycor SRBOC 6-barrelled Mk 36; IR flares and Chaff to 4 km *(2.2 nm)*.
ESM: SLQ 32(V)1; intercept. May be updated to (V)2.
Combat data systems: SATCOM SRR-1, WSC-3 (UHF).
Radars: Air search: Lockheed SPS 40B/C ❸; E/F band; range 320 km *(175 nm)*.
Surface search: Raytheon SPS 10F or Norden SPS 67 ❹; G band.
Navigation: Marconi LN 66; I band.
Tacan: URN 25. IFF: Mk XII UPX-29.

Helicopters: Up to 6 CH-46D/E Sea Knight can be carried. Hangar for only 1 light (not in LPD 4).

Programmes: LPD 4-6 were authorised in the FY 1962 new construction programme, LPD 7-10 in FY 1963, LPD 12 and 13 in FY 1964, LPD 14 and LPD 15 in FY 1965. LPD 16 was cancelled.
Modernisation: Planned SLEPs cancelled. Modernisation being carried out in normal maintenance periods from FY 1987. This includes fitting two Phalanx, SPS 67 radar replacing SPS 10 and updating EW capability.
Structure: Enlarged versions of the earlier Raleigh class (now paid off). LPD 7-13 have an additional bridge and are fitted as flagships. One small telescopic hangar. There are structural variations in the positions of guns and electronic equipment in different ships of the class. Flight deck is 168 ft *(51.2 m)* in length. Well deck 394 × 50 ft *(120.1 × 15.2 m)*. This design is the model for the LX class to start building in the mid-1990s.
Operational: A typical operational load might include one Seahawk, two Sea Knight, two Twin Huey, four Sea Cobra helicopters and one patrol boat armed with two 20 mm guns. Eight of the class were involved in the war with Iraq in 1991.

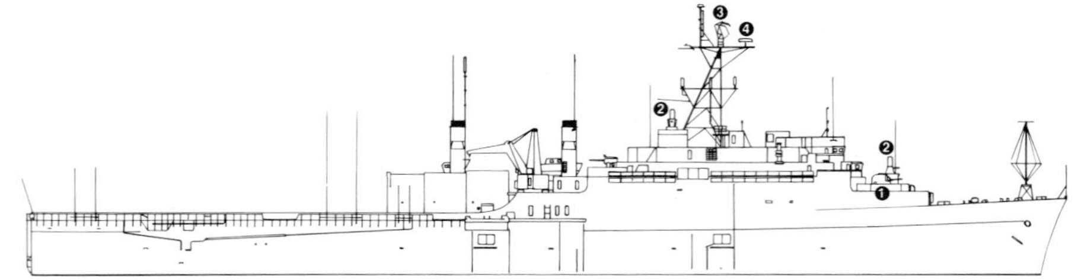

NASHVILLE *(Scale 1 : 1 500), Ian Sturton*

PONCE (low bridge) *7/1991, Guy Toremans*

CLEVELAND (flag bridge, Phalanx not fitted) *10/1991, 92 Wing RAAF*

8 WHIDBEY ISLAND and 0 + 3 HARPERS FERRY CLASSES: DOCK LANDING SHIPS (LSD and LSD-CV)

Name	*No*	*Builders*	*Laid down*	*Launched*	*Commissioned*	*F/S*
WHIDBEY ISLAND	LSD 41	Lockheed SB & Construction Co	4 Aug 1981	10 June 1983	9 Feb 1985	AA
GERMANTOWN	LSD 42	Lockheed SB & Construction Co	5 Aug 1982	29 June 1984	8 Feb 1986	PA
FORT McHENRY	LSD 43	Lockheed SB & Construction Co	10 June 1983	1 Feb 1986	8 Aug 1987	PA
GUNSTON HALL	LSD 44	Avondale Industries	26 May 1986	27 June 1987	22 Apr 1989	AA
COMSTOCK	LSD 45	Avondale Industries	27 Oct 1986	16 Jan 1988	3 Feb 1990	PA
TORTUGA	LSD 46	Avondale Industries	23 Mar 1987	15 Sep 1988	17 Nov 1990	AA
RUSHMORE	LSD 47	Avondale Industries	9 Nov 1987	6 May 1989	1 June 1991	PA
ASHLAND	LSD 48	Avondale Industries	4 Apr 1988	11 Nov 1989	May 1992	AA
HARPERS FERRY	LSD 49	Avondale Industries	15 Apr 1991	June 1992	June 1994	Bldg
CARTER HALL	LSD 50	Avondale Industries	11 Nov 1991	Apr 1993	Dec 1994	Bldg
OAK HILL	LSD 51	Avondale Industries	Sep 1992	Oct 1993	June 1995	Bldg

Displacement, tons: 11 125 light; 15 726 (LSD 41-48), 16 740 (LSD 49 onwards) full load
Dimensions, feet (metres): 609 × 84 × 20.5 *(185.6 × 25.6 × 6.3)*
Main machinery: 4 Colt-Pielstick 16PC2.5V 400 diesels; 41 600 hp(m) *(31 MW)* sustained; 2 shafts; cp props
Speed, knots: 22. **Range, miles:** 8000 at 18 kts
Complement: 340 (21 officers)
Military lift: 450 troops; 2 (CV) or 4 LCACs (Amphibious Air Cushion Vehicles), or 9 (CV) or 21 LCM 6, or 1 (CV) or 3 LCUs, or 64 LVTs. 2 LCPL
Cargo capacity: 5000 cu ft for marine cargo, 12 500 sq ft for vehicles (including four preloaded LCACs in the well deck). The 'cargo version' has 67 600 cu ft for marine cargo, 20 200 sq ft for vehicles but only two LCACs. Aviation fuel, 90 tons.

Guns: 2 General Electric/General Dynamics 20 mm/76 6-barrelled Vulcan Phalanx Mk 15 ❶; 3000 rounds/minute (4500 in Block 1) combined to 1.5 km.
2 Mk 68 Mod 1 20 mm. 8—12.7 mm MGs. 2 Mk 88 25 mm Bushmaster (LSD 47 and 48 vice the 20 mm guns).
Countermeasures: Decoys: 4 Loral Hycor SRBOC 6-barrelled Mk 36; IR flares and Chaff to 4 km *(2.2 nm)*.
ESM: SLQ 32(V)1; intercept. May be updated to (V)2.
Combat data systems: SATCOM SRR-1, WSC-3 (UHF).
Radars: Air search: Raytheon SPS 49V ❷; C/D band.
Surface search: Norden SPS 67V ❸; G band.
Navigation: Raytheon SPS 64(V)9; I/J band.
Tacan: URN 25. IFF: Mk XII UPX-29.

Helicopters: Platform only for 2 CH-53 series Stallion.

Programmes: Originally it was planned to construct six ships of this class as replacements for the Thomaston class LSDs. Eventually, the level of Whidbey Island class ships was established at eight, with five additional cargo-carrying variants of that class to be built to provide increased cargo-carrying capability. The first cargo variant, LSD 49, was authorised and funded in the FY 1988 budget; LSD 50 in FY 1989 and LSD 51 in FY 1991. The fourth was authorised in FY 1992 but Congress failed to provide funds. It seems likely that the programme has terminated.

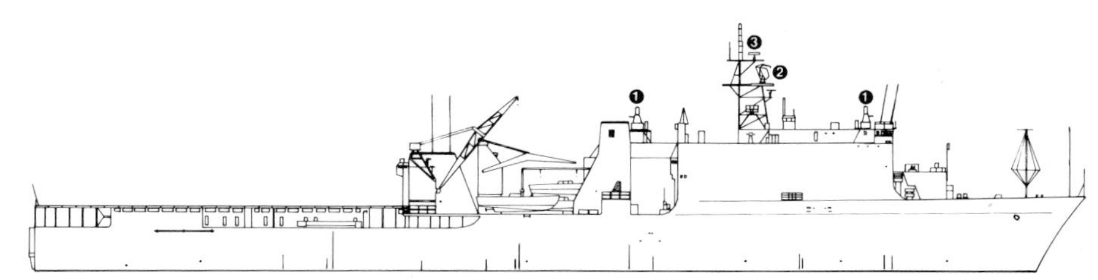

WHIDBEY ISLAND *(Scale 1 : 1 500), Ian Sturton*

GUNSTON HALL *4/1991, Giorgio Arra*

Structure: Based on the earlier Anchorage class. One 60 and one 20 ton crane. Well deck measures 440 × 50 ft *(134.1 × 15.2 m)* in the LSD but is shorter in the Cargo Variant (CV). The cargo version is a minimum modification to the LSD 41 design. Changes in that design include additional air-conditioning, piping and hull structure; the forward Phalanx is lower down and there is only one crane. There is approximately 90% commonality between the two ships.
Operational: The first four of the class took part in the war with Iraq in 1991.

RUSHMORE *10/1991, Avondale*

5 ANCHORAGE CLASS: DOCK LANDING SHIPS (LSD)

Name	No	Builders	Laid down	Launched	Commissioned	F/S
ANCHORAGE	LSD 36	Ingalls Shipbuilding Corp	13 Mar 1967	5 May 1968	15 Mar 1969	PA
PORTLAND	LSD 37	General Dynamics, Quincy, Mass	21 Sep 1967	20 Dec 1969	3 Oct 1970	AA
PENSACOLA	LSD 38	General Dynamics, Quincy, Mass	12 Mar 1969	11 July 1970	27 Mar 1971	AA
MOUNT VERNON	LSD 39	General Dynamics, Quincy, Mass	29 Jan 1970	17 Apr 1971	13 May 1972	PA
FORT FISHER	LSD 40	General Dynamics, Quincy, Mass	15 July 1970	22 Apr 1972	9 Dec 1972	PA

Displacement, tons: 8600 light; 13 700 full load
Dimensions, feet (metres): 553.3 × 84 × 20 *(168.6 × 25.6 × 6)*
Main machinery: 2 Foster-Wheeler boilers (Combustion Engineering in LSD 36); 600 psi *(42.3 kg/cm sq)*; 870°F *(467°C)*; 2 De Laval turbines; 24 000 hp *(18 MW)*; 2 shafts
Speed, knots: 22. **Range, miles:** 14 800 at 12 kts
Complement: 374 (24 officers)
Military lift: 366 troops (18 officers); 3 LCUs or 3 LCACs or 18 LCM 6 or 9 LCM 8 or 50 LVTs; 1 LCM 6 on deck; 2 LCPLs and 1 LCVP on davits. Aviation fuel, 90 tons

Guns: 4 USN 3 in *(76 mm)*/50 (2 twin) Mk 33 ❶; 85° elevation; 50 rounds/minute to 12.8 km *(7 nm)*; weight of shell 6 kg. Local control only.
2 General Electric/General Dynamics 20 mm/76 6-barrelled Vulcan Phalanx Mk 15 ❷; 3000 rounds/minute combined to 1.5 km.
Countermeasures: Decoys: 4 Loral Hycor SRBOC 6-barrelled Mk 36; IR flares and Chaff to 4 km *(2.2 nm)*.
ESM: SLQ 32(V)1; intercept. May be updated to (V)2.

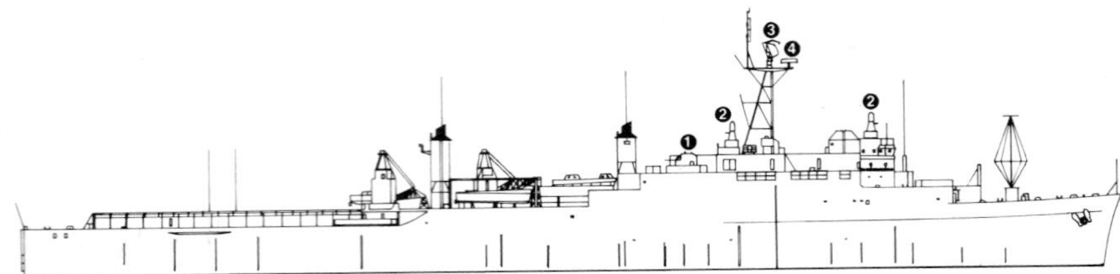

ANCHORAGE *(Scale 1 : 1 500), Ian Sturton*

Combat data systems: SATCOM SRR-1, WSC-3 (UHF).
Radars: Air search: Lockheed SPS 40 ❸; E/F band; range 320 km *(175 nm)*.
Surface search: Raytheon SPS 10 ❹; G band.
Navigation: Marconi LN 66; I band.

Helicopters: Platform only.

Structure: Helicopter platform aft with docking well partially open; helicopter platform can be removed. Docking well approximately 430 × 50 ft *(131.1 × 15.2 m)*. Two 50 ton capacity cranes.
Operational: Four of the class were involved in the war with Iraq in 1991.

PENSACOLA *8/1988, Giorgio Arra*

19 NEWPORT CLASS: TANK LANDING SHIPS (LST)

Name	No	Builders	Laid down	Launched	Commissioned	F/S
NEWPORT	LST 1179	Philadelphia Naval Shipyard	1 Nov 1966	3 Feb 1968	7 June 1969	AA
MANITOWOC	LST 1180	Philadelphia Naval Shipyard	1 Feb 1967	4 June 1969	24 Jan 1970	AA
SUMTER	LST 1181	Philadelphia Naval Shipyard	14 Nov 1967	13 Dec 1969	20 June 1970	AA
FRESNO	LST 1182	National Steel & SB Co, San Diego, California	16 Dec 1967	28 Sep 1968	22 Nov 1969	NRF
PEORIA	LST 1183	National Steel & SB Co, San Diego, California	22 Feb 1968	23 Nov 1968	21 Feb 1970	PA
FREDERICK	LST 1184	National Steel & SB Co, San Diego, California	13 Apr 1968	8 Mar 1969	11 Apr 1970	PA
SCHENECTADY	LST 1185	National Steel & SB Co, San Diego, California	2 Aug 1968	24 May 1969	13 June 1970	PA
CAYUGA	LST 1186	National Steel & SB Co, San Diego, California	28 Sep 1968	12 July 1969	8 Aug 1970	PA
TUSCALOOSA	LST 1187	National Steel & SB Co, San Diego, California	23 Nov 1968	6 Sep 1969	24 Oct 1970	PA
SAGINAW	LST 1188	National Steel & SB Co, San Diego, California	24 May 1969	7 Feb 1970	23 Jan 1971	AA
SAN BERNARDINO	LST 1189	National Steel & SB Co, San Diego, California	12 July 1969	28 Mar 1970	27 Mar 1971	PA
BOULDER	LST 1190	National Steel & SB Co, San Diego, California	6 Sep 1969	22 May 1970	4 June 1971	NRF
RACINE	LST 1191	National Steel & SB Co, San Diego, California	13 Dec 1969	15 Aug 1970	9 July 1971	NRF
SPARTANBURG COUNTY	LST 1192	National Steel & SB Co, San Diego, California	7 Feb 1970	11 Nov 1970	1 Sep 1971	AA
FAIRFAX COUNTY	LST 1193	National Steel & SB Co, San Diego, California	28 Mar 1970	19 Dec 1970	16 Oct 1971	AA
LA MOURE COUNTY	LST 1194	National Steel & SB Co, San Diego, California	22 May 1970	13 Feb 1971	18 Dec 1971	AA
HARLAN COUNTY	LST 1196	National Steel & SB Co, San Diego, California	7 Nov 1970	24 July 1971	8 Apr 1972	AA
BARNSTABLE COUNTY	LST 1197	National Steel & SB Co, San Diego, California	19 Dec 1970	2 Oct 1971	27 May 1972	AA
BRISTOL COUNTY	LST 1198	National Steel & SB Co, San Diego, California	13 Feb 1971	4 Dec 1971	5 Aug 1972	PA

Displacement, tons: 4975 light; 8450 full load
Dimensions, feet (metres): 522.3 (hull) × 69.5 × 17.5 (aft) *(159.2 × 21.2 × 5.3)*
Main machinery: 6 GM 16-645-E5 diesels (in LST 1179-1181) or ARCO 16-251 diesels (in others); 16 500 hp *(12.3 MW)*; 2 shafts; cp props; bow thruster
Speed, knots: 20. **Range, miles:** 2500 at 14 kts
Complement: 257 (13 officers)
Military lift: 400 troops (20 officers); 500 tons vehicles; 3 LCVPs and 1 LCPL on davits

Guns: 4 USN 3 in *(76 mm)*/50 (2 twin) Mk 33; 85° elevation; 50 rounds/minute to 12.8 km *(7 nm)*; weight of shell 6 kg. Local control only.
1 General Electric/General Dynamics 20 mm Vulcan Phalanx Mk 15 (being fitted on bridge roof).
Combat data systems: SATCOM SRR-1, WSC-3 (UHF).
Radars: Surface search: Raytheon SPS 10F; G band. To be replaced by SPS 67 in FY 1990-93.
Navigation: Marconi LN 66 (LST 1179-81, 1183, 1184, 1186, 1187, 1196, 1197); I band.
Raytheon CRP 3100 Pathfinder (LST 1188, 1192-94); I/J band.

Helicopters: Platform only.

Programmes: *Newport* was authorised in FY 1965. *Boulder* (LST 1190) was assigned to the NRF on 1 December 1980, *Racine* (LST 1191) on 15 January 1981 and *Fresno* (LST 1182) on 30 September 1990.

BOULDER *4/1991, Giorgio Arra*

Modernisation: Phalanx CIWS is being fitted on the bridge roof in some of the class.
Structure: The hull form required to achieve 20 kts would not permit bow doors, thus these ships unload by a 112 ft ramp over their bow. The ramp is supported by twin derrick arms. A ramp just forward of the superstructure connects the lower tank deck with the main deck and a vehicle passage through the superstructure provides access to the parking area amidships. A stern gate to the tank deck permits unloading of amphibious tractors into the water, or unloading of other vehicles into an LCU or on to a pier. Vehicle stowage covers 19 000 sq ft. Length over derrick arms is 562 ft *(171.3 m)*; full load draught is 11.5 ft forward and 17.5 ft aft. Bow thruster fitted to hold position offshore while unloading amphibious tractors.
Operational: They operate with 20 knot amphibious squadrons to transport tanks, other heavy vehicles, engineering equipment, and supplies which cannot be readily landed by helicopters or landing craft. ESM equipment fitted in some. Fourteen of the class were involved in the war with Iraq in 1991. One deleted in early 1992. *San Bernardino* is based at Sasebo, Japan.

LANDING CRAFT

48 + 48 LANDING CRAFT AIR-CUSHION (LCAC)

Displacement, tons: 87.2 light; 170-182 full load
Dimensions, feet (metres): 88 oa (on cushion) (81 between hard structures) × 47 beam (on cushion) (43 beam hard structure) × 2.9 draught (off cushion) *(26.8 (24.7) × 14.3 (13.1) × 0.9)*
Main machinery: 4 Avco-Lycoming TF40B gas turbines; 2 for propulsion and 2 for lift; 16 000 hp *(12 MW)* sustained; 2 shrouded reversible pitch airscrews (propulsion); 4 double entry fans, centrifugal or mixed flow (lift)
Speed, knots: 40 (loaded). **Range, miles:** 300 at 35 kts; 200 at 40 kts
Complement: 5
Military lift: 24 troops; 1 MBT or 60-75 tons

Guns: 2—12.7 mm MGs.
Radars: Navigation: Marconi LN 66; I band.

Programmes: Being built by Textron Marine Systems and Avondale Gulfport, the latter yard having been purchased from Lockheed Shipbuilding. 33 funded FY 1982-86, 15 in FY 1989, 12 in each of FY 1990 and 1991. In FY 1992 Congress authorised 12 but then provided funds for 24 which terminates the programme.
Structure: Incorporates the best attributes of the JEFF(A) and JEFF(B) learned from over five years of testing the two prototypes. Bow ramp 28.8 ft, stern ramp 15 ft. Cargo space capacity is 1809 sq ft. Noise and dust levels are high and if disabled the craft is not easy to tow. Spray suppressors have been added to the skirt to reduce interference with the driver's vision.
Operational: Ship classes capable of carrying the LCAC are Wasp (three), Tarawa (one), Anchorage (four), Austin (two), Whidbey (four) and Modified Whidbey (two). MCMV role is still being evaluated as a secondary priority to the amphibious commitment. According to the USMC the craft can cross 70 per cent of the world's coastlines compared to about 15 per cent for conventional landing craft. Some limitations in very rough seas. Shore bases on each coast at Little Creek, Virginia and Camp Pendleton, California. Some were used in the Gulf in 1991 to recapture an Iraq-held island which belonged to Kuwait. They were also used for relief operations in Bangladesh.

LCAC 7 — *4/1991, Giorgio Arra*

LCAC 26 — *6/1991, Camil Busquets i Vilanova*

5 LSV 1 CLASS: LOGISTIC SUPPORT VESSELS (LSV-ARMY)

Name	*No*	*Builders*	*Completed*
GENERAL FRANK S BESSON JR	LSV 1	Moss Point Marine, Mississippi	18 Dec 1987
CW 3 HAROLD C CLINGER	LSV 2	Moss Point Marine, Mississippi	20 Feb 1988
GENERAL BREHON B SOMERVELL	LSV 3	Moss Point Marine, Mississippi	2 Apr 1988
LT GENERAL WILLIAM B BUNKER	LSV 4	Moss Point Marine, Mississippi	18 May 1988
MAJOR GENERAL CHARLES P GROSS	LSV 5	Moss Point Marine, Mississippi	30 Apr 1991

Displacement, tons: 4265 full load
Dimensions, feet (metres): 272.8 × 60 × 12 *(83.1 × 18.3 × 3.7)*
Main machinery: 2 GM EMD 16-645-E2 diesels; 3900 hp *(2.9 MW)* sustained; 2 shafts
Speed, knots: 11.6. **Range, miles:** 6500 at 11 kts
Complement: 30 (6 officers)
Military lift: 2000 tons of vehicles, containers or general cargo

Comment: Army owned Ro-ro design with 10 500 sq ft of deck space for cargo. Capable of beaching with 4 ft over the ramp or a 1:30 offshore gradient with a payload of 900 tons of cargo.

GENERAL BESSON — *5/1988, Giorgio Arra*

18 + 22 LCU 2001 CLASS: UTILITY LANDING CRAFT (LCU-ARMY)

LCU 2001-2018

Displacement, tons: 1013 full load
Dimensions, feet (metres): 173.8 × 42 × 8.5 *(53 × 12.8 × 2.6)*
Main machinery: 2 Cummins KTA-50M diesels; 2500 hp *(1.87 MW)* sustained; 2 shafts; bow thruster
Speed, knots: 11.5. **Range, miles:** 4500 at 11.5 kts
Complement: 13 (2 officers)
Military lift: 350 tons
Radars: Navigation: Two Raytheon SPS 64; I band.

Comment: Order placed with Avondale by US Army 11 June 1986 for 25 craft with an option on 15 more. First laid down at leased area of Thunderbolt Marine, Savannah on 8 December 1986. Moss Point Marine is building 35. First one completed 10 September 1987. Building rate about six a year. The 2001 series have names.

LCU 2006 — *7/1990, Giorgio Arra*

32 LCU 1600 CLASS: UTILITY LANDING CRAFT (LCU-ARMY and NAVY)

LCU 1616-17	**LCU 1619**	**LCU 1621**	**LCU 1623-24**
LCU 1627-35	**LCU 1643-46**	**LCU 1667-79 (Army)**	

Displacement, tons: 200 light; 375 (437, LCU 1680-81) full load
Dimensions, feet (metres): 134.9 × 29 × 6.1 *(41.1 × 8.8 × 1.9)*
Main machinery: 4 Detroit 6-71 diesels; 696 hp *(519 kW)* sustained; 2 shafts; Kort nozzles
2 Detroit 12V-71 diesels (LCU 1621, 1680-1681); 680 hp *(508 kW)* sustained; 2 shafts; Kort nozzles
Speed, knots: 11. **Range, miles:** 1200 at 8 kts
Complement: 14 (2 officers)
Military lift: 170 tons; 3 M103 (64 tons) or M48 (48 tons) tanks or 350 troops
Guns: 2—12.7 mm MGs.
Radars: Navigation: LN 66 or SPS-53; I band.

Comment: Improved steel hulled landing craft, larger than previous series; LCU 1616-1619, 1623, 1624 built by Gunderson Bros Engineering Corp, Portland, Oregon; LCU 1621, 1626, 1629, 1630 built by Southern Shipbuilding Corp, Slidell, Louisiana; LCU 1627, 1628, 1631-1635 built by General Ship and Engine Works (last five units completed in 1968); LCU 1643-1645 built by Marinette Marine Corp, Marinette, Wisconsin (completed 1969-70); LCU 1646-1666 built by Defoe Shipbuilding Co, Bay City, Michigan (completed 1970-71). LCU 1667-1670 built by General Ship & Engine Works, East Boston, in 1973-74; LCU 1671-1679 built by Marinette Marine Corp, 1974-76. LCU 1680, 1681 in FY 1985 estimates for NRF Orange and Buffalo and ordered from Moss Point Marine, Escatawpa, Mississippi. LCU 1667-1679 under operational control of the Army with LCU 1486 reclassified as YFU 50. At least three converted as ASDV 1-3, 1 and 3 based in San Diego and 2 in Little Creek. LCU 1641 carries a chute over a cutaway stern and is apparently used as a mine recovery tender at Charleston, South Carolina.

LCU 1644 — *9/1991, Giorgio Arra*

ASDV I — *5/1989, Giorgio Arra*

87 MECHANISED LANDING CRAFT: LCM 8 TYPE

Displacement, tons: 125 full load (steel) or 105 full load (aluminium)
Dimensions, feet (metres): 73.7 × 21 × 5.2 *(22.5 × 6.4 × 1.6)*
Main machinery: 2 Detroit 6-71 diesels; 348 hp *(260 kW)* sustained or 2 Detroit 12V-71 diesels; 680 hp *(508 kW)* sustained; 2 shafts
Speed, knots: 9 (steel) or 12 (aluminium). **Range, miles:** 190 at 9 kts full load
Complement: 5
Military lift: 60 tons (steel) or 180 tons (aluminium) or 1 M48 or 1 M60 tank or 200 troops

Comment: Constructed of welded-steel or (later units) aluminium. Also operated in large numbers by the US Army. Many of the older type deleted but more are being built by Swiftships.

LCM 8 — *9/1991, Giorgio Arra*

99 MECHANISED LANDING CRAFT: LCM 6 TYPE

Displacement, tons: 64 full load
Dimensions, feet (metres): 56.2 × 14 × 3.9 *(17.1 × 4.3 × 1.2)*
Main machinery: 2 Detroit 6V-71 diesels; 348 hp *(260 kW)* sustained or 2 Detroit 8V-71 diesels; 460 hp *(344 kW)* sustained; 2 shafts
Speed, knots: 9. **Range, miles:** 130 at 9 kts
Complement: 5
Military lift: 34 tons or 80 troops

Comment: Welded-steel construction. 74 are used as LCMs and 25 as workboats.

LCM 6 — *9/1986, Giorgio Arra*

63 LANDING CRAFT VEHICLE AND PERSONNEL (LCVP)

Displacement, tons: 13.3 full load
Dimensions, feet (metres): 35.8 × 10.5 × 3.5 *(10.9 × 3.2 × 1.1)*
Main machinery: 1 Gray Marine 64HN9 diesel; 165 hp *(123 kW)* sustained; 1 shaft
Speed, knots: 10. **Range, miles:** 110 at 10 kts full load
Military lift: 3.6 tons or 36 troops

Comment: Constructed of GRP. Fitted with 30-calibre machine guns when in combat areas. A slightly larger version capable of 19 kts is being built. First one (pennant number 9001) in service in early 1991.

8 LCPL Mk 13 CLASS

Displacement, tons: 11 full load
Dimensions, feet (metres): 36 × 12.1 × 3.8 *(11 × 3.7 × 1.2)*
Main machinery: 1 GM 8V 71 TI diesel; 425 hp *(317 kW)* sustained; 1 shaft
Speed, knots: 20. **Range, miles:** 150 at 20 kts
Complement: 3
Military lift: 17 troops

Comment: GRP construction. Ordered from Bollinger Shipyard in FY 1989 and delivered in 1991. For use as control craft and carried aboard LHA, LPD, LSD and LST classes.

LCPL — *4/1991, Bollinger*

NAVAL RESERVE FORCE AMPHIBIOUS WARFARE TRAINING SHIPS

Name/Hull No	*NRF Homeport*	*Assignment*
BOULDER (LST 1190)	Little Creek, VA	1 Dec 1980
RACINE (LST 1191)	San Diego, CA	15 Jan 1981
FRESNO (LST 1182)	Long Beach, CA	30 Sep 1990

MINE WARFARE FORCES

Note: (1) The use of LCACs for MCM duties is being evaluated.
(2) There are no surface minelayers. Mining is done by carrier-based aircraft, land-based patrol aircraft and submarines. US Air Force B-52s also have a minelaying capability.
(3) NRF ships are manned by composite active/reserve crews.
(4) Two SAM unmanned sweepers (*Gerry* (SAM 03) and *Peggy* (SAM 05)) were acquired from Sweden in February 1991. Details under Swedish Landsort class.
(5) MH-53E Sea Stallion helicopters are deployed in aircraft carriers and large amphibious ships for mine countermeasures operations.

0 + 7 + 3 (2) OSPREY CLASS (MINEHUNTERS COASTAL) (MHC)

Name	*No*	*Builders*	*Launched*	*Commissioned*	*F/S*
OSPREY	MHC 51	Intermarine, Savannah	23 Mar 1991	Sep 1992	Bldg
HERON	MHC 52	Intermarine, Savannah	21 Mar 1992	Mar 1993	Bldg
PELICAN	MHC 53	Avondale Industries	Oct 1992	Mar 1994	Bldg
ROBIN	MHC 54	Avondale Industries	May 1993	Oct 1994	Bldg
ORIOLE	MHC 55	Intermarine, Savannah	Feb 1993	Sep 1994	Bldg
KINGFISHER	MHC 56	Avondale Industries	Dec 1993	Mar 1995	Bldg
CORMORANT	MHC 57	Avondale Industries	July 1994	July 1995	Bldg
—	MHC 58-60	Approved FY 1992 programme	—	—	Ord
—	MHC 61-62	Proposed FY 1992 programme	—	—	Proj

Displacement, tons: 895 full load
Dimensions, feet (metres): 188 × 34.8 × 8.9 *(57.3 × 10.6 × 2.7)*
Main machinery: 2 Isotta Fraschini ID 36 SS-8V AM diesels; 1600 hp(m) *(1.18 MW)* sustained; 2 Voith Schneider props
Speed, knots: 12. **Range, miles:** 1500 at 12 kts
Complement: 51 (4 officers)

Guns: 2—12.7 mm MGs.
Countermeasures: MCM: Both mechanical and modular influence sweep systems being developed independently of ship construction programme. SLQ-48 ROV mine neutralisation system.
Combat data systems: Unisys integrated control system.
Radars: Navigation: Raytheon SPS 64; I band.
Sonars: Raytheon/Thomson Sintra SQQ 32; VDS; active minehunting; high frequency.

Programmes: A project to construct 17 MSH was cancelled in mid-1986 because the design, based on a surface effect ship, failed shock testing. A design contract for Lerici class minehunters was then awarded in August 1986 followed by a construction contract in May 1987 for the lead ship of the class. Intermarine Sarzana established Intermarine USA and purchased Sayler Marine Corporation in Savannah, Georgia. On 2 October 1989 Avondale Gulfport was named as the second construction source. Twelve of the class are to be built followed by a lengthened MHC(V) version (the first in FY 1995).
Structure: Construction is of heavy GRP throughout hull, decks and bulkheads, with frames eliminated. Main machinery is mounted on vibration dampers.

OSPREY — *1991, Intermarine*

8 + 6 AVENGER CLASS: MINE COUNTERMEASURES VESSELS (MCM)

Name	No	Builders	Laid down	Launched	Commissioned	F/S
AVENGER	MCM 1	Peterson Builders Inc, Sturgeon Bay, Wisc	3 June 1983	16 June 1985	12 Sep 1987	AA
DEFENDER	MCM 2	Marinette Marine Corp, Marinette, Wisc	1 Dec 1983	4 Apr 1987	30 Sep 1989	AA
SENTRY	MCM 3	Peterson Builders Inc, Sturgeon Bay, Wisc	8 Oct 1984	20 Sep 1986	2 Sep 1989	PA
CHAMPION	MCM 4	Marinette Marine Corp, Marinette, Wisc	28 June 1984	15 Apr 1989	27 July 1991	PA
GUARDIAN	MCM 5	Peterson Builders Inc, Sturgeon Bay, Wisc	8 May 1985	20 June 1987	6 Dec 1989	PA
DEVASTATOR	MCM 6	Peterson Builders Inc, Sturgeon Bay, Wisc	9 Feb 1987	11 June 1988	6 Oct 1990	AA
PATRIOT	MCM 7	Marinette Marine Corp, Marinette, Wisc	31 Mar 1987	15 May 1990	18 Oct 1991	AA
SCOUT	MCM 8	Peterson Builders Inc, Sturgeon Bay, Wisc	8 June 1987	20 May 1989	15 Dec 1990	AA
PIONEER	MCM 9	Peterson Builders Inc, Sturgeon Bay, Wisc	20 Mar 1989	25 Aug 1990	Aug 1992	Bldg
WARRIOR	MCM 10	Peterson Builders Inc, Sturgeon Bay, Wisc	25 Sep 1989	8 Dec 1990	Oct 1992	Bldg
GLADIATOR	MCM 11	Peterson Builders Inc, Sturgeon Bay, Wisc	5 July 1990	29 June 1991	July 1993	Bldg
ARDENT	MCM 12	Peterson Builders Inc, Sturgeon Bay, Wisc	22 Oct 1990	16 Nov 1991	Sep 1993	Bldg
DEXTEROUS	MCM 13	Peterson Builders Inc, Sturgeon Bay, Wisc	11 Mar 1991	May 1992	Nov 1993	Bldg
CHIEF	MCM 14	Peterson Builders Inc, Sturgeon Bay, Wisc	19 Aug 1991	Oct 1992	Aug 1994	Bldg

Displacement, tons: 1312 full load
Dimensions, feet (metres): 224 × 39 × 12.2 *(68.3 × 11.9 × 3.7)*
Main machinery: 4 Waukesha L-1616 diesels (MCM 1-2); 2400 hp(m) *(1.76 MW)* sustained; 2 shafts; bow thruster; 350 hp *(257 kW)*
4 Isotta Fraschini ID 36 SS 6VAM diesels (MCM 3 onwards); 2400 hp(m) *(1.76 MW)* sustained; 2 motors; 400 hp(m) *(294 kW)* for hovering; 2 shafts; bow thruster; 350 hp *(257 kW)*
Speed, knots: 13.5
Complement: 81 (6 officers)

Guns: 2—12.7 mm Mk 26 MGs.
Countermeasures: MCM: 2 SLQ-48; ROV mine neutralisation system (1500 m cable with cutter and countermining charge). SLQ 37(V)2; magnetic/acoustic influence sweep equipment. Oropesa Type 0 Size 1; mechanical sweep. EDO ALQ 166 magnetic minesweeping vehicle to be provided when available.
Combat data systems: SATCOM SRR-1; WSC-3 (UHF). May be fitted with Nautis-M or equivalent in due course.
Radars: Surface search: ISC Cardion SPS 55; I/J band.
Sonars: General Electric SQQ 30 or SQQ 32 (Raytheon/Thomson Sintra SQQ 32 in MCM 10 onwards and being retrofitted); VDS; active minehunting; high frequency.

Programmes: The contract for the prototype MCM was awarded in June 1982; MCM 2 in May 1983; MCM 3-5 in December 1983; MCM 6-8 in August 1986. MCM 9 was funded in the FY 1985 programme and MCM 10-11 in the FY 1986 programme; however, contracts for their construction were not awarded until January 1989. The last three were funded in FY 1990.
Structure: The hull is constructed of oak, Douglas fir and Alaskan cedar, with a thin coating of fibreglass on the outside, to permit taking advantage of wood's low magnetic signature. A problem of engine rotation on the Waukesha diesels in MCM 1-2 was resolved; however, those engines have been replaced in the rest of the class by low magnetic engines manufactured by Isotta-Fraschini of Milan, Italy. Fitted with SSN2(V) precise integrated navigation system (PINS).
Operational: *Avenger* fitted with the SQQ 32 for Gulf operations in 1991. The plan is for all of the class to be based at Ingleside, Texas, but this may prove to be too expensive an option.

GUARDIAN *3/1991, Giorgio Arra*

8 AGGRESSIVE CLASS: OCEAN MINESWEEPERS (MSO)

Name	No	Launched	Commissioned	F/S
CONSTANT*	MSO 427	14 Feb 1952	8 Sep 1954	NRF
EXCEL	MSO 439	25 Sep 1953	24 Feb 1955	NRF
EXPLOIT	MSO 440	10 Apr 1953	31 Mar 1954	NRF
FORTIFY*	MSO 446	14 Feb 1953	16 July 1954	NRF
IMPLICIT	MSO 455	1 Aug 1953	10 Mar 1954	NRF
CONQUEST*	MSO 488	20 May 1954	20 July 1955	NRF
GALLANT	MSO 489	4 June 1954	14 Sep 1955	NRF
PLEDGE	MSO 492	20 July 1955	20 Apr 1956	NRF

* Modernised

Displacement, tons: 720 standard; 780 full load
Dimensions, feet (metres): 172.5 × 35.1 × 14.1 *(52.6 × 10.7 × 4.3)*
Main machinery: 4 Packard ID-1700 diesels (Waukesha in modernised ships); 2280 hp *(1.7 MW)*; 2 shafts; cp props
Speed, knots: 14. **Range, miles:** 3000 at 10 kts
Complement: 86 (7 officers); 39 (3 officers) plus 47 (4 officers) reserves in NRF ships

Guns: 2—12.7 mm MGs.
Combat data systems: SATCOM SRR-1.
Radars: Navigation: Sperry SPS 53L; I/J band.
Sonars: General Electric SQQ 14; VDS; active minehunting; high frequency.

Programmes: Built on the basis of mine warfare experience in the Korean War (1950-53); 58 built for US service and 35 transferred on completion to NATO navies. All surviving ships were built in private shipyards. Initially designated as minesweepers (AM); reclassified as ocean minesweepers (MSO) in February 1955. Originally fitted with UQS 1 mine detecting sonar.
Modernisation: Some MSOs were modernised during the mid-1960s. The modernisation provided improvements in mine detection, engines, communications, and habitability: four Waukesha Motor Co diesel engines installed (plus two or three diesel generators for sweep gear), SQQ 14 sonar with mine classification as well as detection capability provided, guns removed, habitability improved, and advanced communications equipment fitted; bridge structure in modernised ships extended around mast and aft to funnel.
Structure: Wooden hulls. Diesel engines are fabricated of non-magnetic stainless steel alloy.
Operational: Many have paid off; the remainder will decommission by 1996.
Sales: Ships of this class were transferred to the navies of Belgium, France, Italy, Netherlands and Spain; many of them have been deleted.

FORTIFY *9/1991, Giorgio Arra*

AGGRESSIVE Class (old number) *1991, Giorgio Arra*

1 ACME CLASS: OCEAN MINESWEEPER (MSO)

Name	*No*	*Launched*	*Commissioned*	*F/S*
AFFRAY	MSO 511	18 Dec 1956	8 Dec 1958	NRF

Displacement, tons: 633 light; 924 full load
Dimensions, feet (metres): 173 × 35 × 14 *(52.7 × 10.7 × 4.3)*
Main machinery: 4 Packard ID-1700 diesels; 2280 hp *(1.7 MW)*; 2 shafts; cp props
Speed, knots: 15. **Range, miles:** 3000 at 10 kts
Complement: 44 (7 officers) plus 37 (4 officers) reserves
Countermeasures: MCM: Acoustic; A Mk 2, Mk 4, Mk 6. Magnetic; M Mk 5, Mk 6, Mk 7. Wire; Orepesa No 1.
Radars: Navigation: Sperry SPS 53L; I/J band.
Sonars: General Electric SQQ 14; VDS; active minehunting; high frequency

Comment: Built by Frank L Sample, Jr, Inc, Boothbay Harbor, Maine.

ACME Class (old number) *6/1989, Giorgio Arra*

HARBOUR DEFENCE PROJECT (COOP)

11 YP 654 CLASS

Displacement, tons: 68 full load
Dimensions, feet (metres): 80.4 × 18.8 × 5.3 *(24.5 × 5.7 × 1.6)*
Main machinery: 4 GM diesels; 660 hp *(492 kW)*; 2 shafts
Speed, knots: 13. **Range, miles:** 400 at 12 kts
Complement: 9

Radars: Navigation: Raytheon 1220; I band.

Programmes: The Craft of Opportunity Programme (COOP) was planned to consist of:
(a) YP craft no longer required by the US Naval Academy. Eleven of the YP 654 have been converted by adding extra ballast and removing the after deckhouse to give space for MCM equipment.
(b) Converted fishing trawlers.
(c) Local craft earmarked in peacetime.
These craft, fitted with Dowty 3010/T side-scanning sonar, probably up to a total of 88 in wartime, were planned to form a widely dispersed auxiliary MCM force in 22 ports. The permanent force to consist of five converted fishing vessels on the west coast and 11 YPs on the east coast. The programme has been delayed by lack of funds and is unlikely to be completed.
Operational: One craft assigned to each of the following ports: Savannah, GA; Kings Bay, GA; Galveston, TX; Puget Sound, WA; Portland, OR; Long Beach, CA; New London, CT; Sunny Point, NC; Pensacola, FL; New York, NY; Earle, NJ; Delaware Bay, DE; Morehead City, NC; Boston, MA; Baltimore, MD; Honolulu, HI; Gulfport, MS. There are four crews to each vessel with a total of nine reservists in each crew.

CT 6 *4/1991, Giorgio Arra*

7 MINESWEEPING BOATS (MSB)

MSB 15 **MSB 16** **MSB 25** **MSB 28** **MSB 29** **MSB 41** **MSB 51**

Displacement, tons: 30 light; 44 (80, MSB 29) full load
Dimensions, feet (metres): 57.2 × 15.5 × 4 *(17.4 × 4.7 × 1.2)*
87 × 19 × 5.5 *(26.5 × 5.8 × 1.7) (MSB 29)*
Main machinery: 2 Packard 2D850 geared diesels; 600 hp *(448 kW)*; 2 shafts
Speed, knots: 12
Complement: 6; 11 *(MSB 29)*
Guns: Several 12.7 mm MGs.
Radars: Navigation: Raytheon 1900; I band.
Sonars: Hydroscan Mk 24; high frequency active.

Comment: Wooden hull minesweepers intended to be carried to theatre of operations by large assault ships. From 1966 to 1972 they were used extensively in Vietnam for river minesweeping operations. A total of 49 were built. *MSB 29* to an enlarged design by John Trumpy & Sons, Annapolis, Maryland, in an effort to improve seakeeping ability.

MSB 41 *4/1988, Giorgio Arra*

LIGHT FORCES

Note: One ex-GDR Tarantul class is on loan from the German Navy for trials in 1991/92.

0 + 13 CYCLONE CLASS (COASTAL PATROL CRAFT) (PC)

CYCLONE PC 1
TEMPEST PC 2
HURRICANE PC 3
MONSOON PC 4
TYPHOON PC 5
SIROCCO PC 6
SQUALL PC 7
ZEPHYR PC 8
WILLIWAW PC 9
CHINOOK PC 10
TORRENT PC 11
LIGHTNING PC 12
THUNDERBOLT PC 13

Displacement, tons: 320 full load
Dimensions, feet (metres): 170.6 × 24.9 × 7.2 *(52 × 7.6 × 2.2)*
Main machinery: 4 Paxman Valenta 16RP200 diesels; 13 400 hp *(10 MW)*; 4 shafts
Speed, knots: 35. **Range, miles:** 2000 at 12 kts
Complement: 39 (3 officers) including Marines or SEALs
Guns: 2—25 mm Mk 38. 2—12.7 mm MGs. 2—40 mm Mk 19 grenade launchers (MG and grenade launchers are interchangeable).
Countermeasures: ESM and FLIR Mk 52 Chaff.
Fire control: Marconi VISTAR IM 405 IR system.
Radars: Surface search and navigation: I band.

Comment: Contract awarded for eight in August 1990 and five more in July 1991. Building at Bollinger Shipyard, Louisiana. The design is based on the Vosper Thornycroft Ramadan class modified to meet US Navy requirements. Stinger SAM may be carried. The craft have a slow speed loiter capability. First one to be delivered in June 1992 and then one every two months thereafter to a required total of 13. The names would best be described as 'challenging'.

CYCLONE Class (model) *1990, Tony Nichols*

18 PATROL BOATS—Mk III (15) and Mk IV (3) Series (PB)

Displacement, tons: 31.5 light; 41.25 full load
Dimensions, feet (metres): 65 × 18 × 5.9 *(19.8 × 5.5 × 1.8)*
Main machinery: 3 Detroit 8V 71 diesels; 690 hp *(515 kW)* sustained (Mk III); 3 Detroit 8V 92; 909 hp *(670 kW)* sustained (Mk IV); 3 shafts
Speed, knots: 28. **Range, miles:** 450 at 26 kts
Complement: 9 (1 officer)
Guns: 2—25 mm Mk 38. 2—12.7 mm MGs. 1—81 mm mortar. 1—40 mm Mk 19 grenade launcher.

Comment: The PB series was developed as replacements for the Swift type inshore patrol craft (PCF). Mk III built by Peterson, Wisconsin in the mid-1970s and Mk IV by Atlantic Marine, Florida in 1985-86. The Mk III design has the pilot house offset to starboard to provide space on port side for installation of additional weapons. Armaments can vary with combinations of guns, MGs and mortars. Used by the Special Boat Units. Active in the Gulf, one of them being involved with the capture of the *Iran Ajr* minelayer on 22 September 1987. Two delivered to Columbia in 1990. The three Mk IV are extended by 3 ft in length and are based in Panama.

PB Mk III *4/1991, Giorgio Arra*

6 PATROL COMBATANTS MISSILE (HYDROFOIL) (PHM)

Name	*No*	*Builders*	*Commissioned*	*F/S*
PEGASUS	PHM 1	Boeing Co, Seattle	9 July 1977	AA
HERCULES	PHM 2	Boeing Co, Seattle	15 Jan 1983	AA
TAURUS	PHM 3	Boeing Co, Seattle	10 Oct 1981	AA
AQUILA	PHM 4	Boeing Co, Seattle	26 June 1982	AA
ARIES	PHM 5	Boeing Co, Seattle	11 Sep 1982	AA
GEMINI	PHM 6	Boeing Co, Seattle	13 Nov 1982	AA

Displacement, tons: 239.6 full load
Dimensions, feet (metres): 132.9 oa × 28.2 hull; 47.5 (foils) × 23.2 (foils extended) *(40.5 × 8.6; 14.5 × 7.1)*
145.3 oa × 28.2 hull × 7.5 (foils retracted) *(44.3 × 8.6 × 2.3)*
Main machinery: 1 GE LM 2500 gas turbine (foilborne); 18 000 hp *(13.4 MW)* sustained; 2 Aerojet waterjets
2 MTU 8V 331 TC81 diesels (hullborne); 1600 hp(m) *(1.18 MW)* sustained; 2 waterjets
Speed, knots: 40 foils; 10 hullborne. **Range, miles:** 1700 at 9 kts; 700 at 40 kts
Complement: 25 (5 officers) plus 5 (1 officer) Coast Guard for drug patrols

Missiles: SSM: 8 McDonnell Douglas Harpoon; active radar homing to 130 km *(70 nm)* at 0.9 Mach; warhead 227 kg.
Guns: 1 OTO Melara 3 in *(76 mm)*/62 Mk 75; 85° elevation; 85 rounds/minute to 16 km *(8.7 nm)*; weight of shell 6 kg.
Countermeasures: Decoys: 2 Loral Hycor RBOC Mk 34; IR flares and Chaff to 4 km *(2.2 nm)*.
ESM/ECM: TAC Mk 105 (ALR 66 in PHM 6).
Combat data systems: SATCOM SSR-1; WSC-3 (UHF).
Fire control: SWG-1A(V)4 ship command launch and control systems replacing SWG-1(V)4.
Radars: Surface search: Raytheon SPS 64; I band (PHM 2 has APS-137).
Fire control: Signaal WM 28 *(Pegasus)*; Mk 92 (remainder); I/J band.

Programmes: *Pegasus* made her first foilborne trip on 25 February 1975 but the programme was cancelled in February 1977 leaving only *Pegasus* to serve as a High Speed Test Vehicle. In August 1977 after heavy Congressional pressure, the Secretary of Defense released the funds appropriated to complete the six ship programme. The designation PHM originally was for Patrol Hydrofoil-Missile; reclassified Patrol Combatant Missile (Hydrofoil) on 30 June 1975.
Structure: The PHM design was developed in conjunction with the Italian and West German navies in an effort to produce a small combatant that would be universally acceptable to NATO navies with minor modifications.
Operational: All based at Key West. Operations are conducted off the Yucatan peninsula and off bases at Guantanamo Bay (Cuba) and Roosevelt Roads (Puerto Rico).

AQUILA *10/1990, Giorgio Arra*

PEGASUS *5/1991, Giorgio Arra*

31 RIVER PATROL BOATS Mk II Series (PBR)

Displacement, tons: 8.9 full load
Dimensions, feet (metres): 32 × 11 × 2.6 *(9.8 × 3.4 × 0.8)*
Main machinery: 2 GM 6V-53N diesels; 296 hp *(221 kW)*; 2 Jacuzzi waterjets
Speed, knots: 24. **Range, miles:** 150 at 22 kts
Complement: 4 or 5
Guns: 3—12.7 mm MGs (twin mount fwd, single aft). 1—40 mm Mk 19 grenade launcher. 1—60 mm mortar (in some boats).
Radars: Navigation: Raytheon 1900; I band.

Comment: Fibreglass hull river patrol boats. Approximately 500 built 1967-73; most transferred to South Vietnam and some to Thailand. Used for Reserve training.

PBR Mk II *1988, Giorgio Arra*

6 STINGER CLASS (RIVER PATROL BOATS)

Displacement, tons: 7.4 full load
Dimensions, feet (metres): 35 × 9.3 × 2.2 *(10.6 × 2.8 × 0.6)*
Main machinery: 2 Cummins 6B TA5.9-M2 diesels; 600 hp *(448 kW)*; 2 Hamilton waterjets
Speed, knots: 38. **Range, miles:** 250 at 26 kts
Complement: 4
Military lift: 10 troops
Guns: 2 or 4—12.7 mm MGs (2 single or 2 twin) or 2—40 mm Mk 19 grenade launchers; 2—7.62 mm MGs.
Radars: Navigation: Raytheon 1900; I band.

Comment: Riverine assault craft ordered for the Marines from SeaArk Marine 5 May 1990 and delivered less than three months later on 1 August 1990. Aluminium hulls which can be transported by road each on its own trailer. Being evaluated in transport, fire support and reconnaissance roles.

STINGER Class *7/1990, SeaArk*

22 MINI ARMOURED TROOP CARRIERS (ATC)

Displacement, tons: 14.8 full load
Dimensions, feet (metres): 36 × 12.7 × 3.5 *(11 × 3.9 × 1.1)*
Main machinery: 2 GM 8V 53N diesels; 566 hp *(422 kW)*; 2 Jacuzzi 14YS waterjets
Speed, knots: 28. **Range, miles:** 37 at 28 kts
Complement: 2
Military lift: 20 troops
Guns: 4—12.7 mm MGs. 1—40 mm Mk 19 grenade launcher.

Comment: Built by Sewart, Louisiana 1972-73. A small troop carrier for riverine and SEAL operations; aluminium hull; ceramic armour. Draught 1 ft when underway at high speed. Used by Special Boat Forces of the NRF.

MINI ATC *1987, Giorgio Arra*

85 PORT SECURITY CRAFT

Displacement, tons: 3.9 full load
Dimensions, feet (metres): 24 × 8 × 3.3 *(7.3 × 2.4 × 1)*
Main machinery: 1 Volvo Penta AQAD 41A diesel; 165 hp(m) *(123 kW)*; Type 290 outdrive
Speed, knots: 22
Complement: 2
Guns: 1—7.62 mm MG.

Comment: Built by Peterson, Wisconsin and delivered between 29 February 1988 and 12 May 1989 in batches of 50, 25 and 10. Used for protecting naval installations, ports, harbours and anchorages. In addition there are large numbers of other small craft used in similar roles.

PORT SECURITY CRAFT *1/1988, Peterson*

SEAFOX CLASS (RIVER PATROL BOATS)

Displacement, tons: 11.3 full load
Dimensions, feet (metres): 36.1 × 9.7 × 2.7 *(11 × 3 × 0.8)*
Main machinery: 2 GM 6V 92TA diesels; 510 hp *(380 kW)* sustained; 2 shafts
Speed, knots: 30
Complement: 3
Guns: 2—12.7 mm MGs. 2—7.62 mm MGs.

Comment: 31 of the class built by Uniflite, Washington 1980-84. GRP construction. Used for Swimmer Delivery operations. Being withdrawn from service; the last one will be paid off in early 1993.

SEAFOX — *5/1989, Giorgio Arra*

AUXILIARY SHIPS

Notes: (1) The Auxiliary Ships of the US Navy are usually divided into two broad categories, underway replenishment ships (UNREP) and fleet support ships. UNREP ships carry out the direct support of deployed forces in the forward area of operations.
Most US Navy replenishment ships are fitted with helicopter platforms to allow the transfer of supplies by vertical replenishment (VERTREP). Helicopters are carried specifically for this purpose by the ammunition ships (AE), the combat store ships (AFS), the fast combat support ships (AOE), and replenishment oilers (AOR). Carrier-based helicopters are sometimes employed in this role.
Planned UNREP ship force levels provide a wartime capability to support deployed carrier and amphibious task groups in up to four or five locations simultaneously. This plan is based on the availability of some storage depots on foreign territory, and the use of Military Sealift Ships to carry fuels, munitions, and the stores from the USA or overseas sources for transfer to UNREP ships in overseas areas.
Some 16 to 18 UNREP ships are normally forward deployed in the Mediterranean, Western Pacific and Indian Ocean areas in support of the 6th and 7th Fleets, respectively. During the build up to the war with Iraq in 1991, more than 30 ships were involved.
Fleet support ships provide primarily maintenance and related towing and salvage services at advanced bases and at ports in the USA. These ships normally do not provide fuel, munitions, or other supplies except when ships are alongside for maintenance.
Most fleet support ships operate from bases in the USA. The four Poseidon/Trident submarine tenders (AS) are based at Bangor, Washington; Kings Bay, Georgia; Charleston, South Carolina and Norfolk, Virginia. In addition, one AS is forward deployed in the Mediterranean and another in the Pacific.
Many underway replenishment ships and fleet support ships are Navy manned and armed, but an increasing number are being operated by the Military Sealift Command (MSC) with civilian crews and unarmed. The latter ships have T-prefix before their designations and are listed in the next section.
A new class of ammunition ship AE 36, first planned for authorisation in FY 1986, remains beyond the five year shipbuilding programme. There are also plans for a 'one stop' AOE(V) which in due course would replace all AE, AFS, AOE and AORs. In early 1992 the five year shipbuilding programme included one AR repair ship (in FY 1996) and no other auxiliaries.
(2) The *S P Lee* (ex-AG 192) was transferred to the Geological Survey on loan in 1974. The ship is unlikely to return to the Navy.

6 YELLOWSTONE and SAMUEL GOMPERS CLASSES: DESTROYER TENDERS (AD)

Name	*No*	*Builders*	*Commissioned*	*F/S*
SAMUEL GOMPERS	AD 37	Puget Sound SY, Bremerton	1 July 1967	PA
PUGET SOUND	AD 38	Puget Sound SY, Bremerton	27 Apr 1968	AA
YELLOWSTONE	AD 41	National Steel, San Diego	31 May 1980	AA
ACADIA	AD 42	National Steel, San Diego	6 June 1981	PA
CAPE COD	AD 43	National Steel, San Diego	17 Apr 1982	PA
SHENANDOAH	AD 44	National Steel, San Diego	17 Dec 1983	AA

Displacement, tons: 20 500 (20 224, AD 41-44) full load
Dimensions, feet (metres): 644 × 85 × 22.5 *(196.3 × 25.9 × 6.9)* (AD 37-38)
641.8 × 85 × 22.5 *(195.6 × 25.9 × 6.9)* (AD 41-44)
Main machinery: 2 Combustion Engineering boilers; 620 psi *(43.6 kg/cm sq)*; 860°F *(462°C)*; 1 De Laval turbine; 20 000 hp *(14.9 MW)*; 1 shaft
Speed, knots: 20
Complement: 1681 including 4 officers and 96 enlisted women
Guns: 4—20 mm Mk 67 (AD 37-38). 2—20 mm Mk 67 (AD 41-44).
2—40 mm Mk 14 MGs. 2—40 mm saluting guns (AD 37-38).
Radars: Surface search: Raytheon SPS 10; G band.
Navigation: Marconi LN 66; I band.
Helicopters: Platform for 1 utility.

Comment: The first US destroyer tenders of post-Second World War design. Also have facilities for servicing nuclear power plants. Services can be provided simultaneously to six guided-missile destroyers moored alongside. Basic hull design similar to L Y Spear and Simon Lake submarine tenders. Two 30 ton capacity cranes. *Puget Sound* has a hangar. All have WSC-3 (UHF) SATCOM. Four of the class were involved in the war with Iraq in 1991.

CAPE COD — *10/1991, Giorgio Arra*

3 DIXIE CLASS: DESTROYER TENDERS (AD)

Name	*No*	*Builders*	*Commissioned*	*F/S*
PRAIRIE	AD 15	NY Shipbuilding Corp, NJ	5 Aug 1940	PA
SIERRA	AD 18	Tampa Shipbuilding Co, Florida	20 Mar 1944	AA
YOSEMITE	AD 19	Tampa Shipbuilding Co, Florida	25 Mar 1944	AA

Displacement, tons: 9876 light; 17 430-18 400 full load
Dimensions, feet (metres): 530.5 × 73.3 × 25.5 *(161.7 × 22.3 × 7.8)*
Main machinery: 4 Babcock & Wilcox boilers; 400 psi *(28.4 kg/cm sq)*; 720°F *(382°C)*; 2 Allis Chalmers turbines; 12 000 hp *(8.95 MW)*; 2 shafts
Speed, knots: 18.2. **Range, miles:** 12 200 at 12 kts
Complement: 872 (32 officers)
Guns: 4—20 mm Mk 67. 2—40 mm saluting guns.
Radars: Surface search: Raytheon SPS 10 series; G band.
Navigation: Marconi LN 66; I band.
Helicopters: Platform only.

Comment: All fitted as flagships. All modernised under the FRAM II programme to service destroyers fitted with ASROC, improved electronics, helicopters, etc. Two or three 5 in guns and eight 40 mm guns removed during modernisation. Two 20 ton cranes. One of the class is in service with the Turkish Navy.

YOSEMITE — *3/1991, Giorgio Arra*

7 KILAUEA CLASS: AMMUNITION SHIPS (AE)

Name	*No*	*Builders*	*Commissioned*	*F/S*
BUTTE	AE 27	General Dynamics Corp, Quincy, Mass	14 Dec 1968	AA
SANTA BARBARA	AE 28	Bethlehem Steel Corp, Sparrows Pt, Md	11 July 1970	AA
MOUNT HOOD	AE 29	Bethlehem Steel Corp, Sparrows Pt, Md	1 May 1971	PA
FLINT	AE 32	Ingalls SB Corp, Pascagoula, Miss	20 Nov 1971	PA
SHASTA	AE 33	Ingalls SB Corp, Pascagoula, Miss	26 Feb 1972	PA
MOUNT BAKER	AE 34	Ingalls SB Corp, Pascagoula, Miss	22 July 1972	AA
KISKA	AE 35	Ingalls SB Corp, Pascagoula, Miss	16 Dec 1972	PA

Displacement, tons: 9340 light; 19 940 full load
Dimensions, feet (metres): 564 × 81 × 28 *(171.9 × 24.7 × 8.5)*
Main machinery: 3 Foster-Wheeler boilers; 600 psi *(42.3 kg/cm sq)*; 870°F *(467°C)*; 1 GE turbine; 22 000 hp *(16.4 MW)*; 1 shaft
Speed, knots: 20. **Range, miles:** 10 000 at 18 kts
Complement: 383 (17 officers)
Guns: 4 USN 3 in *(76 mm)*/50 (2 twin) Mk 33. Twin closed mounts forward and twin open mounts aft, between funnel and after booms. Local control only.
2 General Electric/General Dynamics 20 mm Vulcan Phalanx.
Countermeasures: Decoys: 2 Loral Hycor SRBOC 6-barrelled Mk 36; IR flares and Chaff.
ESM: SLQ 32(V)1; intercept.
Radars: Surface search: Raytheon SPS 10F; G band.
Navigation: Marconi LN 66; I band.
Tacan: URN 25.
Helicopters: 2 UH-46E Sea Knight (cargo normally embarked).

Comment: FAST replenishment system. Vulcan Phalanx is now fitted in all. Another of the class, *Kilauea*, disarmed and transferred to MSC 1 October 1980 and is renumbered TAE 26. Five of the class involved in the war with Iraq in 1991.

FLINT — *3/1991, Scott Connolly, RAN*

5 SURIBACHI and NITRO CLASSES: AMMUNITION SHIPS (AE)

Name	No	Builders	Commissioned	F/S
SURIBACHI	AE 21	Bethlehem Steel Corp, Sparrows Pt, Md	17 Nov 1956	AA
MAUNA KEA	AE 22	Bethlehem Steel Corp, Sparrows Pt, Md	30 Mar 1957	PA
NITRO	AE 23	Bethlehem Steel Corp, Sparrows Pt, Md	1 May 1959	AA
PYRO	AE 24	Bethlehem Steel Corp, Sparrows Pt, Md	24 July 1959	PA
HALEAKALA	AE 25	Bethlehem Steel Corp, Sparrows Pt, Md	3 Nov 1959	PA

Displacement, tons: 7470 light; 10 000 standard; 15 500 full load (AE 21-22) 15 900 standard; 16 083 full load (remainder)
Dimensions, feet (metres): 502 × 72 × 29 *(153 × 21.9 × 8.8)* (AE 21-22)
512 × 72 × 29 *(156.1 × 21.9 × 8.8)* (remainder)
Main machinery: 2 Combustion Engineering boilers; 625 psi *(43.9 kg/cm sq)*; 850°F *(454°C)*; 1 Bethlehem turbine; 16 000 hp *(11.9 MW)*; 1 shaft
Speed, knots: 20.6; 18 (AE 21-22)
Complement: 312 (18 officers)
Guns: 4 USN 3 in *(76 mm)*/50 (2 twin) Mk 33. Local control only.
Countermeasures: Decoys: 2 Loral Hycor SRBOC 6-barrelled Mk 36; IR flares and Chaff (not in all).
ESM: SLQ 32(V)1; intercept (not in all).
Radars: Surface search: Raytheon SPS 10; G band.
Navigation: Marconi LN 66; I band.
Helicopters: Platform only.

Comment: All five ships were modernised in 1960s, being fitted with high-speed transfer equipment, three holds configured for stowage of missiles and helicopter platform fitted aft (two after twin 3 in gun mounts removed). Arrangements of twin 3 in gun mounts differ, some ships have them in tandem and others side-by-side. *Mauna Kea* fitted with mine rails for trials in 1984. *Mauna Kea* to NRF 1 October 1979 and *Pyro* 1 September 1980. Both returned to active fleet on 1 January 1982 and 1 June 1982 respectively. No plans for replacement reflected in five year shipbuilding forecast. Three of the class involved in the war with Iraq in 1991.

MAUNA KEA *6/1990, Vic Jeffery*

7 MARS CLASS: COMBAT STORE SHIPS (AFS)

Name	No	Builders	Commissioned	F/S
MARS	AFS 1	National Steel and SB Co, San Diego	21 Dec 1963	PA
SYLVANIA	AFS 2	National Steel and SB Co, San Diego	11 July 1964	AA
NIAGARA FALLS	AFS 3	National Steel and SB Co, San Diego	29 Apr 1967	PA
WHITE PLAINS	AFS 4	National Steel and SB Co, San Diego	23 Nov 1968	PA
CONCORD	AFS 5	National Steel and SB Co, San Diego	27 Nov 1968	PA
SAN DIEGO	AFS 6	National Steel and SB Co, San Diego	24 May 1969	AA
SAN JOSE	AFS 7	National Steel and SB Co, San Diego	23 Oct 1970	AA

Displacement, tons: 9200 light; 15 900-18 663 full load
Dimensions, feet (metres): 581 × 79 × 24 *(177.1 × 24.1 × 7.3)*
Main machinery: 3 Babcock & Wilcox boilers; 580 psi *(40.8 kg/cm sq)*; 825°F *(440°C)*; 1 De Laval turbine (Westinghouse in AFS 6); 22 000 hp *(16.4 MW)*; 1 shaft
Speed, knots: 20. **Range, miles:** 10 000 at 18 kts
Complement: 428 (25 officers)
Cargo capacity: 2625 tons dry stores; 1300 tons refrigerated stores (varies with specific loadings)
Guns: 4 USN 3 in *(76 mm)*/50 (2 twin) Mk 33. Local control only.
2 General Electric/General Dynamics 20 mm Vulcan Phalanx Mk 15.
Countermeasures: Decoys: 2 Loral Hycor SRBOC 6-barrelled Mk 36; IR flares and Chaff to 4 km *(2.2 nm)*.
ESM: SLQ 32(V)1; intercept.
Radars: Surface search: Raytheon SPS 10 series; G band.
Navigation: Marconi LN 66.
Tacan: URN 25.
Helicopters: 2 UH-46E Sea Knight normally assigned.

Comment: 'M' frames replace conventional king posts and booms, which are equipped with automatic tensioning devices. Armament has been modified. As well as the provisions listed above these ships carry comprehensive inventories of aviation and spare parts of all types for the Fleet. Phalanx placements vary in different ships of the class. All took part in support of the war with Iraq in 1991. In late 1992 one is to be paid off and the others transferred to MSC.

SAN JOSE *3/1991, 92 Wing RAAF*

1 CONVERTED RALEIGH CLASS: MISCELLANEOUS COMMAND SHIP (AGF)

Name	No	Builders	Commissioned	F/S
LA SALLE	AGF 3 (ex-LPD 3)	New York Naval Shipyard	22 Feb 1964	AA

Displacement, tons: 9670 light; 14 650 full load
Dimensions, feet (metres): 519.7 × 84 × 21 *(158.4 × 25.6 × 6.4)*
Main machinery: 2 Babcock & Wilcox boilers; 600 psi *(42.2 kg/cm sq)*; 870°F *(467°C)*; 2 De Laval turbines; 24 000 hp *(17.9 MW)*; 2 shafts
Speed, knots: 20. **Range, miles:** 9600 at 16 kts
Complement: 440 (25 officers) plus 59 Flag Staff (12 officers)
Guns: 4 USN 3 in *(76 mm)*/50 (2 twin) Mk 33. Local control only.
2 General Electric/General Dynamics 20 mm Vulcan Phalanx Mk 15.
2—40 mm saluting guns.
Countermeasures: Decoys: 4 Loral Hycor SRBOC Mk 36; Chaff and IR flares.
ESM: SLQ 32(V)2; WLR-1; intercept.
Radars: Air search: Lockheed SPS 40; E/F band; range 320 km *(175 nm)*.
Surface search: Raytheon SPS 10D; G band.
Navigation: Marconi LN 66; I band.
Tacan: URN 25.
Helicopters: 1 light.

Comment: A former amphibious transport dock (LPD) of the Raleigh class. Authorised in FY 1961. She served as an amphibious ship until 1972 and still retains an amphibious assault capability. Converted in 1972 at Philadelphia Navy Yard. Flag command and communications facilities installed; additional air-conditioning fitted; painted white to help retard heat of Persian Gulf area. Helicopter hangar installed on the port side of the flight deck. Deck landing spots for heavy helicopters. Reclassified as a flagship and designated AGF 3 on 1 July 1972 keeping previous '3' hull number. Serves as flagship for the US Commander, Middle East Force, operating in the Persian Gulf, Arabian Sea and Indian Ocean. A comprehensive communications fit includes WSC-6.

LA SALLE *1983, Giorgio Arra*

5 NEW CIMARRON CLASS: OILERS (AO)

Name	No	Builders	Commissioned	F/S
CIMARRON	AO 177	Avondale SY	10 Jan 1981	PA
MONONGAHELA	AO 178	Avondale SY	5 Sep 1981	AA
MERRIMACK	AO 179	Avondale SY	14 Nov 1981	AA
WILLAMETTE	AO 180	Avondale SY	18 Dec 1982	PA
PLATTE	AO 186	Avondale SY	16 Apr 1983	AA

Displacement, tons: 8210 light; 37 870 full load
Dimensions, feet (metres): 708.5 × 88 × 35 *(216 × 26.8 × 10.7)*
Main machinery: 2 Combustion Engineering boilers; 600 psi *(42.2 kg/cm sq)*; 850°F *(454°C)*; 1 turbine; 24 000 hp *(17.9 MW)*; 1 shaft
Speed, knots: 19
Complement: 135 (12 officers) plus 90 spare berths
Cargo capacity: 180 000 barrels of fuel
Guns: 2 General Electric/General Dynamics 20 mm Vulcan Phalanx Mk 15.
Countermeasures: Decoys: Loral Hycor SRBOC 6-barrelled Mk 36; IR flares and Chaff to 4 km *(2.2 nm)*.
SLQ Nixie; towed torpedo decoy.
ESM: SLQ 32(V)1; intercept.
Radars: Surface search: ISC Cardion SPS 55 (AO 177-179); I/J band.
Raytheon SPS 10B (AO 180 and 186); G band.
Navigation: Marconi LN 66; I band.
Helicopters: Platform only.

Comment: Significantly smaller than the previous Neosho class (now in MSC), these ships were originally 'sized' to provide two complete refuellings of a fossil-fuelled aircraft carrier and six to eight accompanying destroyers. All five ships of the class are being 'jumboised', thus increasing their capacities from 120 000 bbls to 180 000 bbls and improving underway replenishment capabilities. Funding for the first 'jumboisation' was provided in FY 1987, second in FY 1988, third and fourth in FY 1989, and fifth in FY 1990. All to complete with new mid-body sections by the end of 1992. The class may be transferred to the MSC in due course.

CIMARRON *11/1990, 92 Wing RAAF*

1 CONVERTED AUSTIN CLASS: MISCELLANEOUS COMMAND SHIP (AGF)

Name	No	Builders	Commissioned	F/S
CORONADO	AGF 11 (ex-LPD 11)	Lockheed SB & Construction Co	23 May 1970	PA

Displacement, tons: 11 482 light; 16 912 full load
Dimensions, feet (metres): 570 × 100 × 23 *(173.8 × 30.5 × 7)*
Main machinery: 2 Foster-Wheeler boilers; 600 psi *(42.2 kg/cm sq)*; 870°F *(467°C)*; 2 De Laval turbines; 24 000 hp *(17.9 MW)*; 2 shafts
Speed, knots: 21. **Range, miles:** 7700 at 20 kts
Complement: 516 (25 officers) plus 120 Flag Staff
Guns: 2 USN 3 in *(76 mm)*/50 (twin) Mk 33. Local control only.
2 General Electric/General Dynamics 20 mm Vulcan Phalanx Mk 15. 2—12.7 mm MGs.
Countermeasures: Decoys: 4 Loral Hycor SRBOC 6-barrelled Mk 36; IR flares and Chaff.
ESM: SLQ 32V(2); WLR-1; intercept.
Radars: Air search: Lockheed SPS 40C; E/F band; range 320 km *(175 nm)*.
Surface search: Raytheon SPS 10F; G band.
Navigation: Marconi LN 66; I band.
Tacan: URN 25.
Helicopters: 2 Light.

Comment: A former LPD of the Austin class. Authorised in FY 1964. She retains an amphibious assault capability. Converted in late 1980 as a temporary replacement for *La Salle* (AGF 3), as flagship, US Commander, Middle East Force, so *La Salle* could be overhauled. When *Coronado* was relieved by *La Salle* in early 1983, it was planned for her to be reconverted back to an LPD. Due to the shortage of fleet flagships, however, she will continue in the flagship role for the foreseeable future. When relieved by *Belknap* as Sixth Fleet flagship in July 1986, she returned to Philadelphia and in November 1986 deployed to the Pacific to become the flagship of the Third Fleet in Hawaii. Comprehensive communications fit includes WSC-6 on a lattice mast fitted in 1987. At the same time a sponson built out over the port side increased the overall width of the ship by some 15 ft.

CORONADO *1988, Giorgio Arra*

4 SACRAMENTO CLASS: FAST COMBAT SUPPORT SHIPS (AOE)

Name	No	Builders	Commissioned	F/S
SACRAMENTO	AOE 1	Puget Sound SY	14 Mar 1964	PA
CAMDEN	AOE 2	New York SB, Camden	1 Apr 1967	PA
SEATTLE	AOE 3	Puget Sound SY	5 Apr 1969	AA
DETROIT	AOE 4	Puget Sound SY	28 Mar 1970	AA

Displacement, tons: 19 200 light; 51 400-53 600 full load
Dimensions, feet (metres): 793 × 107 × 39.3 *(241.7 × 32.6 × 12)*
Main machinery: 4 Combustion Engineering boilers; 600 psi *(42.2 kg/cm sq)*; 900°F *(480°C)*; 2 GE turbines; 100 000 hp *(76.4 MW)*; 2 shafts
Speed, knots: 26. **Range, miles:** 6000 at 25 kts; 10 000 at 17 kts
Complement: 601 (24 officers)
Cargo capacity: 177 000 barrels of fuel; 2150 tons munitions; 500 tons dry stores; 250 tons refrigerated stores
Missiles: SAM: Raytheon NATO Sea Sparrow Mk 29 octuple launcher.
Guns: 2 General Electric/General Dynamics 20 mm Vulcan Phalanx Mk 15. 4—12.7 mm MGs.
Countermeasures: Decoys: Loral Hycor SRBOC 6-barrelled Mk 36; IR flares and Chaff to 4 km *(2.2 nm)*.
ESM/ECM: SLQ 32(V)3; combined intercept and jammer.
Fire control: Mk 91 Mod 1 MFCS.
Radars: Air search: Lockheed SPS 40 series, Westinghouse SPS 58A (AOE 1 and 2), SPS 58A only (AOE 4); E/F and D band (SPS 58). Hughes Mk 23 TAS (AOE 3); D band.
Surface search: Raytheon SPS 10F; G band.
Navigation: Marconi LN 66; I band.
Fire control: 2 Raytheon Mk 95; I/J band (for SAM).
Tacan: URN 25.
Helicopters: 2 UH-46E Sea Knight normally assigned.

Comment: Designed to provide rapid replenishment at sea of petroleum, munitions, provisions, and fleet freight. Fitted with large hangar for vertical replenishment operations (VERTREP). These ships can be distinguished from the smaller Wichita class replenishment oilers by their larger superstructures and funnel, helicopter deck at lower level, and hangar structure aft of funnel. *Camden* is being used as the trials ship for improved replenishment at sea equipment. Three of the class were involved in the war with Iraq in 1991.

DETROIT *1989, Gilbert Gyssels*

0 + 4 SUPPLY CLASS: FAST COMBAT SUPPORT SHIPS (AOE)

Name	No	Builders	Commissioned
SUPPLY	AOE 6	National Steel & SB	May 1993
RAINIER (ex-*Paul Hamilton*)	AOE 7	National Steel & SB	Mar 1994
ARCTIC	AOE 8	National Steel & SB	Sep 1994
—	AOE 9	Approved in FY 1992	1995

Displacement, tons: 19 700 light; 48 800 full load
Dimensions, feet (metres): 754 × 107 × 38 *(229.8 × 32.6 × 11.6)*
Main machinery: 4 GE LM 2500 gas turbines; 92 000 hp *(68.6 MW)* sustained; 2 shafts
Speed, knots: 25
Complement: Accommodation for 660 (35 officers)
Cargo capacity: 156 000 barrels of fuel; 1800 tons ammunition; 400 tons refrigerated cargo; 250 tons general cargo
Missiles: SAM: Raytheon GMLS Mk 29 octuple launcher; NATO Sea Sparrow.
Guns: 2 General Electric/General Dynamics 20 mm Vulcan Phalanx Mk 15.
2 Hughes 25 mm Mk 88. 4—12.7 mm MGs.
Countermeasures: Decoys: 4 Loral Hycor SRBOC 6-barrelled Mk 36; IR flares and Chaff.
ESM/ECM: SLQ 32(V)3; combined intercept and jammer.
Fire control: Mk 91 MFCS.
Radars: Air search: Hughes Mk 23 TAS; D band.
Air/surface search: Norden SPS 67; G band.
Navigation: Raytheon SPS 64(V)9; I band.
Fire control: 2 Raytheon Mk 95; I/J band.
Tacan: URN 25.
Helicopters: 3 UH-46E Sea Knight.

Comment: To augment underway replenishment capability. Construction of *Supply* started in June 1988 and the second and third in August 1989 and July 1990 respectively. The aim was one ship per carrier air group but after the fourth there are no more in the five year shipbuilding programme. The long term plan is for an AOE(V) 'one stop' follow on class which would provide fuel, stores and ammunitions from one platform (see Note under *Auxiliary Ships*). *Supply* was launched on 6 October 1990 and should start sea trials in February 1993.

SUPPLY *7/1991, van Ginderen Collection*

SUPPLY (model) *1988, (US Navy)*

1 VULCAN CLASS: REPAIR SHIP (AR)

Name	No	Builders	Commissioned	F/S
JASON	AR 8 (ex-ARH 1)	Los Angeles SB & DD Corp	19 June 1944	PA

Displacement, tons: 9140 standard; 16 380 full load
Dimensions, feet (metres): 529.3 × 73.3 × 23.3 *(161.3 × 22.3 × 7.1)*
Main machinery: 4 Babcock & Wilcox boilers; 400 psi *(28.2 kg/cm sq)*; 720°F *(382°C)*; 2 Allis Chalmers turbines; 11 535 hp *(8.6 MW)*; 2 shafts
Speed, knots: 19.2. **Range, miles:** 18 000 at 12 kts
Complement: 841 (29 officers)
Guns: 4 Oerlikon 20 mm Mk 67.
Radars: Surface search: Raytheon SPS 10 series; G band.
Navigation: Marconi LN 66; I band.

Comment: Carry equipment to undertake repairs of every description. *Jason*, originally designated ARH 1 and rated as heavy hull repair ship, was reclassified AR 8 on 9 September 1957. Deployed to the Gulf for the war with Iraq in 1991. AR 7 transferred to Pakistan in 1989.

VULCAN Class (old number) *2/1990, Giorgio Arra*

7 WICHITA CLASS: REPLENISHMENT OILERS (AOR)

Name	No	Builders	Commissioned	F/S
WICHITA	AOR 1	General Dynamics, Quincy	7 June 1969	PA
MILWAUKEE	AOR 2	General Dynamics, Quincy	1 Nov 1969	AA
KANSAS CITY	AOR 3	General Dynamics, Quincy	6 June 1970	PA
SAVANNAH	AOR 4	General Dynamics, Quincy	5 Dec 1970	AA
WABASH	AOR 5	General Dynamics, Quincy	20 Nov 1971	PA
KALAMAZOO	AOR 6	General Dynamics, Quincy	11 Aug 1973	AA
ROANOKE	AOR 7	National Steel & SB, San Diego	30 Oct 1976	PA

Displacement, tons: 13 000 light; 41 350 full load
Dimensions, feet (metres): 659 × 96 × 33.3 *(200.9 × 29.3 × 10.2)*
Main machinery: 3 Foster-Wheeler boilers; 615 psi *(43.3 kg/cm sq)*; 851°F *(454°C)*; 2 GE turbines; 32 000 hp *(23.9 MW)*; 2 shafts
Speed, knots: 20. **Range, miles:** 6500 at 19 kts; 10 000 at 16 kts
Complement: 454 (20 officers)
Cargo capacity: 160 000 barrels of fuel; 600 tons munitions; 200 tons dry stores; 100 tons refrigerated stores
Missiles: SAM: Raytheon NATO Sea Sparrow Mk 29 octuple launcher (AOR 2-7).
Guns: 2 General Electric/General Dynamics 20 mm Vulcan Phalanx Mk 15. 2 or 4 Oerlikon 20 mm may also be carried.
Countermeasures: Decoys: 4 Loral Hycor SRBOC 6-barrelled Mk 36; IR flares and Chaff to 4 km *(2.2 nm)*.
ESM/ECM: SLQ 32(V)3 (being fitted to replace WLR 6).
Fire control: 1 Mk 91 MFCS (AOR 2-7).
Radars: Air search: Hughes Mk 23 TAS; D band (AOR 2-7).
Surface search: Raytheon SPS 10F; G band.
Navigation: Marconi LN 66; I band.
Fire control: 2 Mk 76; I/J band.
Tacan: URN 25 or SRN 15.
Helicopters: 2 UH-46E Sea Knight can be embarked.

Comment: Designed to provide rapid replenishment at sea of petroleum and munitions with a limited capacity for provision and fleet freight. Fitted with helicopter platform and internal arrangement for vertical replenishment operations (VERTREP). Hangars were added after the main gun armament was removed. Three of the class were involved in the war with Iraq in 1991.

ROANOKE *7/1991, 92 Wing RAAF*

4 SAFEGUARD CLASS: SALVAGE SHIPS (ARS)

Name	No	Builders	Commissioned	F/S
SAFEGUARD	ARS 50	Peterson Builders Inc, Sturgeon Bay, Wisc	16 Aug 1985	PA
GRASP	ARS 51	Peterson Builders Inc, Sturgeon Bay, Wisc	14 Dec 1985	AA
SALVOR	ARS 52	Peterson Builders Inc, Sturgeon Bay, Wisc	14 June 1986	PA
GRAPPLE	ARS 53	Peterson Builders Inc, Sturgeon Bay, Wisc	15 Nov 1986	AA

Displacement, tons: 2880 full load
Dimensions, feet (metres): 255 × 51 × 17 *(77.7 × 15.5 × 5.2)*
Main machinery: 4 Caterpillar diesels; 4200 hp *(3.13 MW)*; 2 shafts; cp Kort nozzle props; bow thruster; 500 hp *(373 kW)*
Speed, knots: 14. **Range, miles:** 8000 at 12 kts
Complement: 90 (6 officers)
Guns: 2 Oerlikon 20 mm Mk 67.
Radars: Navigation: ISC Cardion SPS 55; I/J band.

Comment: Prototype approved in FY 1981, two in FY 1982 and one in FY 1983. The procurement of the fifth ARS was dropped on instructions from Congress. *Safeguard* launched 12 November 1983, *Grasp* 21 April 1984, *Salvor* 28 July 1984 and *Grapple* 8 December 1984. This class is essentially an updated Bolster class ARS which required only a moderate amount of development effort, primarily to satisfy new standards of habitability, galley, messing, medical and storeroom areas. The design follows conventional commercial and Navy design criteria. Equipped with recompression chamber. Bollard pull, 65.5 tons. Using beach extraction equipment the pull increases to 360 tons. 150 ton deadlift.

GRAPPLE *5/1991, W. Sartori*

7 BOLSTER CLASS: SALVAGE SHIPS (ARS)

Name	No	Builders	Commissioned	F/S
PRESERVER	ARS 8	Basalt Rock Co, Napa, Calif	11 Nov 1944	NRF
BOLSTER	ARS 38	Basalt Rock Co, Napa, Calif	1 May 1945	NRF
CONSERVER	ARS 39	Basalt Rock Co, Napa, Calif	9 June 1945	PA
HOIST	ARS 40	Basalt Rock Co, Napa, Calif	21 July 1945	AA
OPPORTUNE	ARS 41	Basalt Rock Co, Napa, Calif	5 Oct 1945	AA
RECLAIMER	ARS 42	Basalt Rock Co, Napa, Calif	20 Dec 1945	NRF
RECOVERY	ARS 43	Basalt Rock Co, Napa, Calif	15 May 1946	AA

Displacement, tons: 1530 standard; 2045 full load
Dimensions, feet (metres): 213.5 × 44 (41, ARS 38) × 13 *(65.1 × 13.4 (12.5) × 4)*
Main machinery: Diesel-electric; 4 Cooper-Bessemer GSB-8 diesels (Caterpillar D399 in ARS 38, 39, 42); 2736 hp *(2.04 MW)* sustained; 2 shafts
Speed, knots: 14.8. **Range, miles:** 9000 at 14 kts; 20 000 at 7 kts
Complement: 103 (6 officers)
Guns: 2 Oerlikon 20 mm Mk 68 (Mk 67 in ARS 39 and 41).
Radars: Surface search: Raytheon SPS 10; G band or Sperry SPS 53; I/J band.
Navigation: Marconi LN 66; I band.

Comment: Equipped with compressed air diving equipment and 10 ton and 20 ton booms. Bollard pull 30 tons. *Bolster* transferred to Naval Reserve Force on 1 June 1983, *Hoist* and *Reclaimer* on 30 September 1986, and *Preserver* in June 1989. *Hoist* transferred back to the active fleet in 1989. All have SATCOM receivers.

RECOVERY *4/1991, Giorgio Arra*

5 L Y SPEAR and EMORY S LAND CLASS: SUBMARINE TENDERS (AS)

Name	No	Builders	Commissioned	F/S
L Y SPEAR	AS 36	General Dynamics Corp, Quincy	28 Feb 1970	AA
DIXON	AS 37	General Dynamics Corp, Quincy	7 Aug 1971	PA
EMORY S LAND	AS 39	Lockheed SB & Cons Co, Seattle	7 July 1979	AA
FRANK CABLE	AS 40	Lockheed SB & Cons Co, Seattle	5 Feb 1980	AA
McKEE	AS 41	Lockheed SB & Cons Co, Seattle	15 Aug 1981	PA

Displacement, tons: 13 000 standard (13 840, later ships); 22 640 (AS 36 and AS 37); 23 493 (AS 39-41) full load
Dimensions, feet (metres): 643.8 × 85 × 28.5 *(196.2 × 25.9 × 8.7)*
Main machinery: 2 Foster-Wheeler boilers; 620 psi *(43.6 kg/cm sq)*; 860°F *(462°C)*; 1 GE turbine; 20 000 hp *(14.9 MW)*; 1 shaft
Speed, knots: 20. **Range, miles:** 10 000 at 12 kts
Complement: 535 (52 officers) plus Flag Staff 69 (25 officers) (AS 39-41)
Guns: 4 Oerlikon 20 mm Mk 67.
Radars: Navigation: Raytheon SPS 10 (AS 36, 37); G band.
ISC Cardion SPS 55 (others); I/J band.
Helicopters: Platform only.

Comment: The first US submarine tenders designed specifically for servicing nuclear-propelled attack submarines. Basic hull design similar to Samuel Gompers and Simon Lake classes tenders. Each ship can simultaneously provide services to four submarines moored alongside. AS 39 and later ships (Emory S Land class) are especially configured to support SSN 688 class submarines. Carry one 30 ton crane and two 5-ton mobile cranes. Have a 23 bed sick bay. *McKee* was involved in the war with Iraq in 1991.

McKEE *5/1991, 92 Wing RAAF*

2 SIMON LAKE CLASS: SUBMARINE TENDERS (AS)

Name	No	Builders	Commissioned	F/S
SIMON LAKE	AS 33	Puget Sound Naval Shipyard	7 Nov 1964	AA
CANOPUS	AS 34	Ingalls SB Co, Pascagoula	4 Nov 1965	AA

Displacement, tons: 19 934 (AS 33); 21 089 (AS 34) full load
Dimensions, feet (metres): 643.7 × 85 × 30 *(196.2 × 25.9 × 9.1)*
Main machinery: 2 Combustion Engineering boilers; 620 psi *(43.6 kg/cm sq)*; 860°F *(462°C)*; 1 De Laval turbine; 20 000 hp *(14.9 MW)*; 1 shaft
Speed, knots: 20. **Range, miles:** 7600 at 18 kts
Complement: 915 (58 officers) (AS 33); 660 (56 officers) (AS 34)
Guns: 4 USN 3 in *(76 mm)*/50 (twin) Mk 33. Local control only.
Radars: Surface search: Raytheon SPS 10; G band.
Navigation: Marconi LN 66; I band.
Helicopters: Platform only.

Comment: Designed to service fleet ballistic missile submarines (SSBN), with three submarines alongside being supported simultaneously. Carry two 30 ton cranes and four 5 ton mobile cranes. Conversions for Poseidon C-3 missile handling and repairing and support of related systems carried out 1970-71. Retrofitting for support of Trident C-4 missiles carried out in *Simon Lake* in FY 1978. *Canopus* similarly converted in FY 1984.

SIMON LAKE *6/1990, van Ginderen Collection*

2 HUNLEY CLASS: SUBMARINE TENDERS (AS)

Name	No	Builders	Commissioned	F/S
HUNLEY	AS 31	Newport News SB & DD Co	16 June 1962	AA
HOLLAND	AS 32	Ingalls SB Co, Pascagoula	7 Sep 1963	AA

Displacement, tons: 10 500 standard; 19 820 full load
Dimensions, feet (metres): 599 × 83 × 27 *(182.6 × 25.3 × 8.2)*
Main machinery: Diesel-electric; 6 Fairbanks-Morse 38D-1/8-12 diesel generators; 8.7 MW sustained; 1 motor; 1 shaft
Speed, knots: 19. **Range, miles:** 10 000 at 12 kts
Complement: 612/658 (54 officers)
Guns: 4 Oerlikon 20 mm.
Radars: Surface search: Raytheon SPS 10; G band.
Navigation: Marconi LN 66; I band.
Helicopters: Platform only.

Comment: The first US submarine tenders of post-Second World War construction; they are designed to provide repair and supply services to fleet ballistic missile submarines (SSBN). Have 52 separate workshops to provide complete support. Both ships originally fitted with a 32 ton capacity hammerhead crane; subsequently refitted with two amidships cranes as in Simon Lake class. Conversions to provide for Poseidon C-3 missile handling and repairing and support of related systems carried out in 1974/75.

HOLLAND *5/1991, Louis Amsterdam*

2 CHANTICLEER CLASS: SUBMARINE RESCUE SHIPS (ASR)

Name	No	Builders	Commissioned	F/S
KITTIWAKE	ASR 13	Savannah Machine & Foundry Co	18 July 1946	AA
SUNBIRD	ASR 15	Savannah Machine & Foundry Co	28 Jan 1947	AA

Displacement, tons: 1653 standard; 2320 full load
Dimensions, feet (metres): 251.5 × 44 × 16 *(76.7 × 13.4 × 4.9)*
Main machinery: Diesel-electric; 4 Alco 539 diesels (ASR 15); 3532 hp *(2.6 MW)*; 4 GM diesels (ASR 13); 3000 hp *(2.24 MW)*; 4 generators; 1 motor; 1 shaft
Speed, knots: 15
Complement: 103 (7 officers)
Guns: 2 Oerlikon 20 mm Mk 68.
Radars: Surface search: Sperry SPS 53; I/J band.

Comment: Equipped with powerful pumps, heavy air compressors, and rescue chambers for submarine salvage and rescue operations. Fitted for helium-oxygen diving. Underwater communications equipped. Former US Navy submarine rescue ships serve in the navies of Brazil and Turkey.

KITTIWAKE *4/1991, Giorgio Arra*

2 FULTON and PROTEUS CLASSES: SUBMARINE TENDERS (AS)

Name	No	Builders	Commissioned	F/S
ORION	AS 18	Moore SB & DD Co, Oakland	30 Sep 1943	AA
PROTEUS	AS 19	Moore SB & DD Co, Oakland	31 Jan 1944	PA

Displacement, tons: 9734 standard; 16 230-17 020 (19 200, AS 19) full load
Dimensions, feet (metres): 530.5 (574.5, AS 19) × 73.3 × 25.5 *(161.7 (175.1) × 22.3 × 7.8)*
Main machinery: Diesel-electric; 8 GM 16-248 diesels; 11 200 hp *(8.36 MW)*; 2 shafts
Speed, knots: 15.4. **Range, miles:** 32 000 at 15 kts
Complement: 677 (53 officers) (AS 19); 746 (56 officers) (AS 18); 575 (53 officers) (AS 11)
Guns: 4 Oerlikon 20 mm Mk 67.
Radars: Surface search: Raytheon SPS 10; G band.
Navigation: Marconi LN 66; I band.

Comment: These venerable ships are contemporaries of the similar-design Dixie class destroyer tenders and the Vulcan class repair ships. As built, they carried the then-standard large auxiliary armament of four 5 in guns plus eight 40 mm guns (twin). *Proteus* was converted under the FY 1959 programme, to service nuclear-powered fleet ballistic missile submarines SSBNs. Conversion was begun on 19 January 1959 and she was recommissioned on 8 July 1960. She was lengthened by adding a 44 ft section amidships, and the bare hull weight of this six-deck high insertion was approximately 500 tons. Three 5 in guns were removed and her upper decks extended aft to provide additional workshops. Storage tubes for Polaris missiles were installed with a bridge crane to handle the missiles. *Orion* has undergone FRAM II modernisation to service nuclear-powered attack submarines. Additional maintenance shops provided to service nuclear plant components and advanced electronic equipment and weapons.

ORION *9/1991, van Ginderen Collection*

2 PIGEON CLASS: SUBMARINE RESCUE SHIPS (ASR)

Name	No	Builders	Commissioned	F/S
PIGEON	ASR 21	Alabama DD & SB Co, Mobile	28 Apr 1973	PA
ORTOLAN	ASR 22	Alabama DD & SB Co, Mobile	14 July 1973	AA

Displacement, tons: 3411 standard; 4570 full load
Dimensions, feet (metres): 251 × 86 (see *Comment*) × 21.3 *(76.5 × 26.2 × 6.5)*
Main machinery: 4 Alco diesels; 6000 hp *(4.48 MW)*; 2 shafts; 2 bow thrusters to be fitted
Speed, knots: 15. **Range, miles:** 8500 at 13 kts
Complement: 195 (9 officers); includes 24 (4 officers) for the submersibles; Flag 14 (4 officers)
Guns: 2 Oerlikon 20 mm Mk 68.
Radars: Surface search: Sperry SPS 53; I/J band.
Navigation: Marconi LN 66; I band.
Sonars: SQQ-25; hull-mounted; precision 3D system for tracking submersibles; high frequency.
Helicopters: Platform only.

Comment: Tasks include (1) surface support for the Deep Submergence Rescue Vehicles (DSRV), (2) rescue employing the existing McCann rescue chamber, (3) major deep-sea diving support and (4) operational control for salvage operations. Each ASR is capable of transporting, servicing, lowering, and raising two Deep Submergence Rescue Vehicles (DSRV) (see section on Deep Submergence Vehicles). Designed with catamaran hulls, the first ocean-going catamaran ships to be built for the US Navy with the exception of TAG *Hayes* of the MSC, since Robert Fulton's steam gunboat *Demologos* of 1812. Each of the twin hulls is 251 ft long and 26 ft wide. The well between the hulls is 34 ft across, giving the ASR a maximum beam of 86 ft. The Mk II Deep Diving System supports conventional or saturation divers operating at depths to 850 ft. The system consists of two recompression chambers and two personnel transfer capsules to transport divers between the ship and ocean floor. Fitted for helium-oxygen diving.

ORTOLAN *6/1990, Giorgio Arra*

2 ACHOMAWI CLASS: FLEET TUGS (ATF)

Name	*No*	*Builders*	*Commissioned*	*F/S*
PAIUTE	ATF 159	Charleston SB & DD Co, SC	27 Aug 1945	AA
PAPAGO	ATF 160	Charleston SB & DD Co, SC	3 Oct 1945	AA

Displacement, tons: 1235 standard; 1640 full load
Dimensions, feet (metres): 205 × 38.5 × 17 *(62.5 × 11.7 × 5.2)*
Main machinery: Diesel-electric drive; 4 Caterpillar D399 diesels; 4 generators; 1 motor; 3000 hp *(2.24 MW)*; 1 shaft
Speed, knots: 15. **Range, miles:** 6500 at 15 kts; 15 000 at 8 kts
Complement: 99 (6 officers)
Radars: Navigation: Sperry SPS 53; I/J band.

Comment: Large ocean tugs fitted with powerful pumps and other salvage equipment. Both recommissioned 30 September 1988. Three others are in reserve but are unlikely ever to be reactivated. Ships of this class (or similar Abnaki class) serve with Argentina, Chile, Colombia, Dominican Republic, Ecuador, Indonesia, Mexico, Pakistan, Peru, Taiwan, Turkey and Venezuela and with the US Coast Guard.

PAPAGO *4/1991, Giorgio Arra*

3 EDENTON CLASS: SALVAGE AND RESCUE SHIPS (ATS)

Name	*No*	*Builders*	*Commissioned*	*F/S*
EDENTON	ATS 1	Brooke Marine, Lowestoft, England	23 Jan 1971	AA
BEAUFORT	ATS 2	Brooke Marine, Lowestoft, England	22 Jan 1972	PA
BRUNSWICK	ATS 3	Brooke Marine, Lowestoft, England	19 Dec 1972	PA

Displacement, tons: 2929 full load
Dimensions, feet (metres): 282.6 × 50 × 15.1 *(86.1 × 15.2 × 4.6)*
Main machinery: 4 Paxman Ventura 12CM diesels; 6000 hp *(4.48 MW)* sustained; 2 shafts; cp props; bow thruster
Speed, knots: 16. **Range, miles:** 10 000 at 13 kts
Complement: 129 (7 officers)
Guns: 2 Oerlikon 20 mm Mk 68 (ATS 2 and 3). 2 Oerlikon 20 mm (twin) Mk 24 (ATS 1).
Radars: Navigation: Sperry SPS 53; I/J band.

Comment: Capable of (1) ocean towing, (2) supporting diver operations to depths of 850 ft, (3) lifting submerged objects weighing as much as 600 000 lb from a depth of 120 ft by static tidal lift or 30 000 lb by dynamic lift, (4) fighting ship fires. Fitted with 10 ton capacity crane forward and 20 ton capacity crane aft. ATS 1 was authorised in FY 1966; ATS 2 and ATS 3 in FY 1967. Three follow-on ships of this class were cancelled. Classification changed from salvage tug (ATS) to salvage and rescue ship (ATS) on 16 February 1971. Can carry the air-transportable Mk 1 Deep Diving System which can support four divers working in two-man shifts at depths to 850 ft. The system consists of a double-chamber recompression chamber and a personnel transfer capsule to transport divers between the ship and ocean floor. The ships' organic diving capability is compressed air only.

BEAUFORT *6/1991, 92 Wing RAAF*

NAVAL RESERVE AUXILIARY SHIPS

Name/Hull No.	*NR Homeport*	*Date Entered NRF*
BOLSTER (ARS 38)	Long Beach, CA	June 1983
RECLAIMER (ARS 42)	Pearl Harbor, HI	Sep 1986
PRESERVER (ARS 8)	Little Creek, VA	June 1989

FLOATING DRY DOCKS

Note: The US Navy operates a number of floating dry docks to supplement dry dock facilities at major naval activities, to support fleet ballistic missile submarines (SSBN) at advanced bases, and to provide repair capabilities in forward combat areas.
The larger floating dry docks are made sectional to facilitate movement overseas and to render them self docking. The ARD-type docks have the forward end of their docking well closed by a structure resembling the bow of a ship to facilitate towing. Berthing facilities, repair shops, and machinery are housed in sides of larger docks. None is self-propelled.
Each section of the AFDB docks has a lifting capacity of about 10 000 tons and is 256 ft long, 80 ft in width, with wing walls 83 ft high; the wing walls, which contain compartments, fold down when the sections are towed.
There are plans to seek funding for large floating docks in FY 1993, 95 and 97.

LARGE AUXILIARY FLOATING DRY DOCKS (AFDB)

Name/No	*Completed*	*Capacity (tons)*	*Construction**	*Status*
ARTISAN (AFDB 1)	1943	90 000	Steel (4)	Navy Reserve, Pearl Harbor (B-E)
AFDB 2	1944	90 000	Steel (10)	Navy Reserve, Pearl Harbor (C, D, H and I)
MACHINIST (AFDB 8)	1979	25 000	Steel (1)	Subic Bay

* Figures in brackets indicate the number of sections of each dock remaining.

AFDB *6/1990, van Ginderen Collection*

MEDIUM AUXILIARY FLOATING DRY DOCKS (AFDM)

Name/No	*Completed*	*Capacity (tons)*	*Construction*	*Status*
AFDM 2 (ex-YFD 4)	1942	15 000	Steel (3)	Marad Reserve
AFDM 3 (ex-YFD 6)	1943	15 000	Steel (3)	Commercial lease, Todd SY, New Orleans
RESOURCEFUL (AFDM 5) (ex-YFD 21)	1943	15 000	Steel (3)	Active, Subic Bay, Philippines
COMPETENT (AFDM 6) (ex-YFD 62)	1944	15 000	Steel (3)	Active, Pearl Harbor
SUSTAIN (AFDM 7) (ex-YFD 63)	1945	15 000	Steel (3)	Active, Norfolk, Va. Two sections in reserve at James River
RICHLAND (AFDM 8) (ex-YFD 64)	1944	15 000	Steel (3)	Active, Guam, Marianas
RESOLUTE (AFDM 10)	1945	15 000	Steel (3)	Active, Norfolk, Va
STEADFAST (AFDM 14) (ex-YFD 71)	1945	14 000	Steel (3)	Active, San Diego

STEADFAST (with MARVIN SHIELDS) *4/1988, Giorgio Arra*

SMALL AUXILIARY FLOATING DRY DOCKS (AFDL)

Name/No	*Completed*	*Capacity (tons)*	*Construction*	*Status*
DYNAMIC (AFDL 6)	1944	1000	Steel	Little Creek, Virginia
ADEPT (AFDL 23)	1944	1900	Steel	Subic Bay, Philippines
UNDAUNTED (AFDL 25)	1944	499	Steel	Guantanamo Bay, Cuba
RELIANCE (AFDL 47)	1946	6500	Steel	Commercial lease, Deytens, South Carolina, 15 May 1991
DILIGENCE (AFDL 48)	—	—	Concrete	Commercial lease, South West Marine, San Diego

Sales: AFDL 1 to Dominican Republic; 4, Brazil; 5, Taiwan; 11, Kampuchea; 20, Philippines; 22, Vietnam; 24, Philippines; 26, Paraguay; 28, Mexico; 33, Peru; 34 and 36, Taiwan; 39, Brazil; 44, Philippines.

DYNAMIC *6/1986, Giorgio Arra*

AUXILIARY REPAIR DRY DOCKS and MEDIUM AUXILIARY REPAIR DRY DOCKS (ARD and ARDM)

Name/No	*Completed*	*Capacity (tons)*	*Construction*	*Status*
WATERFORD (ARD 5)	1942	3500	Steel	New London, Connecticut
WEST MILTON (ARD 7)	1943	3500	Steel	Maritime Reserve, James River (from 30 June 1981)
SAN ONOFRE (ARD 30)	1944	3500	Steel	San Diego, Calif
OAK RIDGE (ARDM 1) (ex-ARD 19)	1944	8000	Steel	Kings Bay, Georgia
ALAMAGORDO (ARDM 2) (ex-ARD 26)	1944	8000	Steel	Charleston, South Carolina
ENDURANCE (ARDM 3) (ex-ARD 18)	1944	8000	Steel	Charleston, South Carolina
SHIPPINGPORT (ARDM 4)	1979	10 000	Steel	New London, Connecticut
ARCO (ARDM 5)	1986	7800	Steel	San Diego Naval Station

Sales: ARD 2 to Mexico; 6, Pakistan; 8, Peru; 9, Taiwan; 11, Mexico; 12, Turkey; 13, Venezuela; 14, Brazil; 15, Mexico; 17, Ecuador; 22 *(Windsor)*, Taiwan; 23, Argentina; 24, Ecuador; 25, Chile; 28, Colombia; 29, Iran; 32, Chile.

ARCO (with BLUEBACK) *7/1987, W. Donko*

YARD FLOATING DRY DOCKS (YFD)

Name/No	*Completed*	*Capacity (tons)*	*Construction*	*Status*
YFD 54	1943	5000	Wood	Commercial lease, Todd Pacific SY, Seattle
YFD 68	1945	14 000	Steel (3)	Commercial lease, Todd Pacific SY, San Pedro
YFD 69	1945	14 000	Steel (3)	Commercial lease, Port of Portland, Oregon
YFD 70	1945	14 000	Steel (3)	Commercial lease, Todd Pacific SY, Seattle
YFD 83 (ex-AFDL 31)	1943	1000	Steel	US Coast Guard loan since Jan 1947

UNCLASSIFIED MISCELLANEOUS (IX)

Notes: (i) In addition to the vessels listed below it is planned to use one of the ex-Forrest Sherman class, *Decatur* as a platform for high energy laser trials in 1992-93.
(ii) Ex-*Thomas G Thompson* (AGOR 9) is expected to become IX 517 when relieved by the new AGOR 23 in 1992.

Name	*No*	*Builders*	*Commissioned*	*F/S*
MERCER	IX 502 (ex-APB 39, ex-APL 39)	Boston Navy Yard	19 Sep 1945	PSA
NUECES	IX 503 (ex-APB 40, ex-APL 40)	Boston Navy Yard	30 Nov 1945	PSA
ECHOLS	IX 504 (ex-APB 37, ex-APL 37)	Boston Navy Yard	1 Jan 1947	ASA

Displacement, tons: 4080 full load
Dimensions, feet (metres): 328 × 50 × 14.1 *(100 × 15.2 × 4.3)*
Main machinery: 2 GM 12-267 ATL diesels; 1800 hp *(1.34 MW)*; 2 shafts
Speed, knots: 12
Complement: 193 (13 officers) as APB
Military lift: 1226 troops (26 officers) as APB

Comment: Originally built as self-propelled barracks ships (APB) to provide support and accommodation for small craft and riverine forces. Launched on 30 July 1945, 17 November 1944, 6 May 1945, respectively. All ex-LST type ships of the same basic characteristics. *Mercer* and *Nueces* recommissioned in 1968 for service in Vietnam; decommissioned in 1969-71 as US riverine forces in South Vietnam were reduced. *Mercer* and *Nueces* again reactivated in 1974 to serve as barrack ships for ships in overhaul at Bremerton, Washington. *Echols* reactivated in 1976 to provide berthing for crews of Trident missile submarines being built by General Dynamics Electric Boat Division in Groton, Connecticut. Each APB has troop berthing and messing facilities, evaporators which produce up to 40 000 gallons of fresh water per day, a 16-bed hospital, X-ray room, dental room, bacteriological laboratory, pharmacy, laundry, library, and tailor shop; living and most working spaces are air-conditioned.

MERCER *10/1986, Giorgio Arra*

Name	*No*	*Under Way*	*F/S*
CONSTITUTION	— (ex-IX 21)	22 July 1798	AA

Displacement, tons: 2200
Dimensions, feet (metres): 175.2 × 45 × 20 *(53.4 × 13.7 × 6.1)*
Speed, knots: 12 under sail
Complement: 49 (2 officers)

Comment: The oldest ship remaining on the Navy List. *Constitution* is one of the six frigates authorised by act of Congress on 27 March 1794. After rehabilitation was formerly placed in commission 1 July 1931. Served as Flagship of the First Naval District until 1 October 1977 when she was transferred to the control of the Director of Naval History, Department of the Navy. Every year she is taken out into Boston Harbor and 'turned around' so her masts and spars will weather evenly. Overhauled at the former Boston Naval Shipyard from April 1973 to early 1975 to 'spruce her up' for the American Bicentennial. A hull survey is scheduled for 1992. The sailing ship *Constellation*, which survives under private ownership at Baltimore, Maryland, is apparently the last sailing man-of-war built for the US Navy; she was constructed at the Norfolk (Virginia) Navy Yard in 1853-54, built in part with material from the earlier frigate *Constellation* (launched 1797).

CONSTITUTION *7/1987, A. Sheldon Duplaix*

IX 506 (ex-YFU 82)

Displacement, tons: 375 full load
Dimensions, feet (metres): 119 × 34 × 6 *(36.3 × 10.4 × 1.8)*
Main machinery: 4 GM 6-71 diesels; 696 hp *(519 kW)* sustained; 2 shafts
Speed, knots: 10
Complement: 12 (2 officers)

Comment: Reclassified 1 April 1978 for Naval Oceanographic Systems Center and fitted with a triple 324 mm torpedo tube mounting in the bows.

IX 506 *5/1986, Giorgio Arra*

Name	*No*	*Commissioned*	*F/S*
GENERAL HUGH J GAFFEY	IX 507	Sep 1944	PSA
(ex-General William O Darby)	IX 510	Sep 1945	ASA

Displacement, tons: 22 574 full load
Dimensions, feet (metres): 609 × 76 × 29 *(185.6 × 23.2 × 8.8)*
Main machinery: Turbo-electric; 2 GE gas turbine alternators; 18 000 hp *(13.43 MW)*; 2 motors; 2 shafts
Speed, knots: 20
Complement: Accommodation for 2076 (499 officers)

Comment: Troop transports now used as barracks ships. Converted Admiral W S Benson class.

IX 510 *7/1988, W. Donko*

Name	*No*	*Builders*	*Commissioned*	*F/S*
ORCA	IX 508 (ex-LCU 1618)	Gunderson Bros, Portland	1959	PSA

Comment: For general characteristics, see under LCU 1610 class in the *Amphibious Warfare* section. Conversion and overhaul in 1977 included installation of a bow thruster, a bridge and pilot house, and a hangar type enclosed storage area in the well deck, for the support of the Center's recovery vehicles CURV I and CURV II and installation of a crane. Reclassified as IX on 1 December 1979. Assigned to the Naval Ocean Systems Center, San Diego, California for trials with NAVSTAR GPS.

ORCA *4/1988, Giorgio Arra*

Name	*Builders*	*Commissioned*	*F/S*
IX 509 (ex-Underwater Explosive Barge *No 1)*	Norfolk SY	1942	ASA

Displacement, tons: 3000
Dimensions, feet (metres): 184 × — × 12.1 *(56.1 × — × 3.7)*

Comment: Put on the Naval Vessel Register on 1 December 1979 as *IX 509*. Has a 60 ton capacity crane. Based at David W Taylor Naval Ship Research and Development Center.

IX 509 *8/1988, van Ginderen Collection*

Name	*No*	*Builders*	*Operational*	*F/S*
EMPRESS II	IX 513	EG & G Inc	31 July 1990	ASA

Displacement, tons: 3845 maximum
Dimensions, feet (metres): 120 × 90 × 15.5 *(36.5 × 27.4 × 4.7)*
Complement: 13

Comment: A radiation trials barge ordered in July 1984. In spite of its unusual appearance the barge has accommodation and work spaces. Used to simulate EMP (electromagnetic pulse) by means of a 7 MV pulse generator. The barge is capable of being towed at 8 kts. Trials are carried out in the Gulf of Mexico. The first ship tested was the Spruance class destroyer *Deyo* in July 1990.

EMPRESS II *1990, EG & G Inc.*

Name	*Builders*	*Commissioned*	*F/S*
IX 516 (ex-*Matthew*)	Sea Train, New York	1976	ASA

Comment: Ex-barge converted and brought into service as a Trident missile training simulator at Kings Bay, Georgia in April 1988.

Name	*Commissioned*	*F/S*
IX 512 (ex-US Army *BD 6651*)	1954	PSA

Displacement, tons: 1000 full load
Dimensions, feet (metres): 142.1 × 58.1 × 5.2 *(43.3 × 17.7 × 1.6)*

Comment: Acquired and placed on Naval Vessel Register 1 September 1983. Non self-propelled. Used as Trident II missile firing simulator to test system integration. Has a 52 ton crane and a Trident D 5 launch tube.

IX 512 *1987, Giorgio Arra*

Name	*Builders*	*Commissioned*
IX 514 (ex-*YFU 79*)	Pacific Coast Eng, Alameda	1968

Displacement, tons: 380 full load
Dimensions, feet (metres): 125 × 36 × 7.5 *(38.1 × 10.9 × 2.3)*
Main machinery: 4 GM 6-71 diesels; 696 hp *(519 kW)* sustained; 2 shafts
Speed, knots: 8

Comment: Harbour utility craft converted in 1986 with a flight deck covering two thirds of the vessel and a new bridge and flight control position at the forward end. Used for basic helicopter flight training at Pensacola, Florida.

1 SURFACE EFFECT SHIP (SES)

Name	*Builders*	*Commissioned*
IX 515 (ex-SES-200, ex-USCG *Dorado*)	Bell Halter, New Orleans	Feb 1979

Displacement, tons: 243 full load
Dimensions, feet (metres): 159.1 × 42.6 × 6; 3 on cushion *(48.5 × 13 × 1.8; 0.9)*
Main machinery: 2 MTU 16V 396 TB 94 diesels (propulsion); 5800 hp(m) *(4.26 MW)* sustained; 2 KaMeWa waterjets
2 MTU 6V 396 TB 83 diesels (lift); 1630 hp(m) *(1.2 MW)* sustained
Speed, knots: 45. **Range, miles:** 2950 at 30 kts
Complement: 22 (2 officers)

Comment: Transferred to Coast Guard operational control for joint Navy/Coast Guard trials, she was commissioned as USCG *Dorado* (WSES 1). After the conclusion of successful trials, which led to the Coast Guard ordering three more for duty in the Caribbean Sea (see Coast Guard Sea Bird class for details), she was decommissioned on 15 December 1981 and returned to the Navy. After 10 months (December 1981 to August 1982) modification at the Bell-Halter yard, New Orleans, which included the addition of a 50 ft *(15.2 m)* mid-section, she was returned to service 24 September 1982. The mid-section was added to increase the cushion length-to-beam ratio which leads to higher speeds. From January-June 1986, IX 515, which is an afloat component of the David Taylor Naval Ship Research and Development Center, carried out a series of trials in European waters in conjunction with NATO navies and in August-September 1986 in Canadian waters. In 1990 she was fitted with more powerful MTU diesels driving KaMeWa waterjets and new lift engines.
The IX 515 is a water-borne, air-supported craft with catamaran-style rigid sidewalls. It uses a cushion of air trapped between the sidewalls and flexible bow and stern seals to lift a large part of the hull clear of the water to reduce drag. A portion of the sidewall remains in the water to aid in stability and manoeuvrability. To relieve pressure within the sidewalls and bow and stern seals a Ride Control System (RCS) was fitted on the main deck amidships in mid-1983. This allows for the venting of wave pressure. Carries 10 tons fuel which could be increased to 60 with minor modifications. Based at Patuxent River Naval Air Station, Maryland.

IX 515 *2/1990, Giorgio Arra*

SERVICE CRAFT

Note: As of January 1992, the US Navy had about 900 service craft, primarily small craft, on the US Naval Vessel Register. A majority of them provide services to the fleet in various harbours and ports. Other are ocean going ships such as *Elk River* that provide services to the fleet in the research area. Only the self-propelled craft and relics are listed in the Register. The non self-propelled craft, such as floating cranes and dredgers are not included. Most of the service craft are rated as 'active, in service', but a few are rated as 'in commission'. In addition there are over 3000 craft rated as 'floating equipment'.

6 FERRYBOATS (YFB)

Comment: 390 ton ferryboats built in the late 1960s and used to transport personnel and vehicles in large harbours; self-propelled; YFB 83 and 87-91. YFB 88-91 are the former LCU 1636, 1638-1640, all reclassified on 1 September 1969.

Name	*No*	*Builders*	*Commissioned*	*F/S*
MONOB I	YAG 61 (ex-IX 309, ex-YW 87)	Zenith Dredge Co	Nov 1943	ASA

Displacement, tons: 440 light; 1390 full load
Dimensions, feet (metres): 191.9 × 33.1 × 15.7 *(58.5 × 10.1 × 4.8)*
Main machinery: 1 Caterpillar D 398 diesel; 850 hp *(634 kW)*; 1 shaft
Speed, knots: 9

Comment: *Monob I* is a mobile listening barge converted from a self-propelled water barge. Built in 1943 and completed conversion for acoustic research in May 1969. Conducts research for the Naval Mine Defence Laboratory, Panama City, Florida. Designation changed from IX 309 to YAG 61 on 1 July 1970. Planned to be replaced by Hayes (TAG 195) in 1992.

MONOB I *7/1988, Giorgio Arra*

Name	*No*	*Builders*	*Commissioned*	*F/S*
DEER ISLAND	YAG 62	Halter Marine	1962	ASA

Displacement, tons: 400 full load
Dimensions, feet (metres): 120.1 × 27.9 × 6.9 *(36.6 × 8.5 × 2.1)*
Speed, knots: 10
Complement: 20

Comment: Acquired for use in tests in sound quieting for surface vessels. Based at Port Everglades, Florida. Put on the Naval Vessel Register on 15 March 1982.

DEER ISLAND *6/1991, Giorgio Arra*

11 DIVING TENDERS (YDT)

Comment: Tenders used to support shallow-water diving operations. Of 1940s vintage are *Phoebus* YDT 14 (ex-YF 294), and *Suitland* YDT 15 (ex-YF 336). There is also a non self-propelled vessel *Tom O'Malley* YDT 16 (ex-YFNB 43). More recent acquisitions include eight Peterson Dive Boats with portable standardised diving systems delivered between November 1989 and August 1990. The craft are 50 ft in length, displace some 42 tons and are capable of 9 knots on two diesels. The Diving Module has its own diesel generator.

DIVING TENDER *11/1990, Peterson Builders*

5 HARBOUR UTILITY CRAFT LCU TYPE (YFU)

YFU 83
YFU 91 (ex-LCU 1608)
YFU 100 (ex-LCU 1610)
YFU 102 (ex-LCU 1462)
LCU 1647

Comment: Former utility landing craft of the LCU 1466 and 1610 classes employed primarily as harbour and coastal cargo craft (see section on Landing Craft for basic characteristics). *LCU 1647* has replaced *YFU 97* which was transferred to the Bahamas.
Several YFUs were loaned to the US Army in 1970 for use in Vietnam after withdrawal of US Navy riverine and coastal forces.

YFU 91 *7/1991, Giorgio Arra*

LCU 1647 *5/1991, Giorgio Arra*

10 FUEL OIL BARGES (YO)

YO 129, 203, 220, 223-225, 230—active
YO 47, 153, 228—reserve

Comment: Small liquid fuel carriers intended to fuel ships where no pierside fuelling facilities are available, self-propelled; seven active, three in reserve. In addition there are 51 non self-propelled (YON).

YO 203 *1987, Giorgio Arra*

5 GASOLINE BARGES (YOG)

YOG 78, 88, 196—active
YOG 68, 93—reserve

Comment: Similar to the fuel barges (YO), but carry about 950 tons of gasoline and aviation fuels; self-propelled; three are active and two in reserve. In addition there are 18 non self-propelled (YOGN).

YOG 88 *4/1988, Giorgio Arra*

26 PATROL CRAFT (YP)

YP 676-702

Displacement, tons: 167 full load
Dimensions, feet (metres): 108 × 24 × 5.9 *(32.9 × 7.3 × 1.8)*
Main machinery: 2 Detroit 12V-71N diesels; 680 hp *(507 kW)* sustained; 2 shafts
Speed, knots: 13.3. **Range, miles:** 1500 at 12 kts
Complement: 6 (2 officers) plus 24 midshipmen

Comment: First seven completed by Peterson Builders on 19 September 1984 under the FY 1982 programme. Six more ordered 25 May 1983 from Peterson and the remainder from Marinette Marine Corp, Wisconsin in 1984-85. Last of the Series YP 702 completed 2 September 1988. Used for instruction in seamanship and navigation at the Naval Academy, Annapolis, Maryland; Naval Officer Candidate School, Newport, Rhode Island; and Surface Warfare Officers School at Newport. Fitted with surface search radar, fathometer, gyro compass, and UHF and MF radio. Eleven earlier versions of the same type of craft converted for MCM work under the COOP project (see *Mine Warfare Forces*).

YP 689 — *4/1991, Giorgio Arra*

4 TORPEDO TRIALS CRAFT (YTT)

CAPE FLATTERY YTT 9
BATTLE POINT YTT 10
DISCOVERY BAY YTT 11
AGATE PASS YTT 12

Displacement, tons: 1168 full load
Dimensions, feet (metres): 186.5 × 40 × 10.5 *(56.9 × 12.2 × 3.2)*
Main machinery: 1 Cummins KTA 50 M diesel; 1213 hp *(905 kW)* sustained; 1 shaft; 1 bow thruster; 400 hp *(298 kW)*; 2 stern thrusters; 600 hp *(448 kW)*
Speed, knots: 11. **Range, miles:** 1000 at 10 kts
Complement: 31 plus 9 spare berths

Comment: Built by McDermott Shipyard, Morgan City, and delivered in 1990-91. Fitted with two 21 in Mk 59 and three (one triple) 12.75 in Mk 32 Mod 5 torpedo tubes. These vessels have replaced the YFRT covered lighters for torpedo trials and development. Underwater recovery vessels SORD 4, TROV and CURV.

CAPE FLATTERY — *1990, McDermott Shipyard*

80 LARGE HARBOUR TUGS (YTB)

EDENSHAW	YTB 752
MARIN	YTB 753
PONTIAC	YTB 756
OSHKOSH	YTB 757
PADUCAH	YTB 758
BOGALUSA	YTB 759
NATICK	YTB 760
OTTUMWA	YTB 761
TUSCUMBIA	YTB 762
MUSKEGON	YTB 763
MISHAWAKA	YTB 764
OKMULGEE	YTB 765
WAPAKONETA	YTB 766
APALACHICOLA	YTB 767
ARCATA	YTB 768
CHESANING	YTB 769
DAHLONEGA	YTB 770
KEOKUK	YTB 771
NASHUA	YTB 774
WAUWATOSA	YTB 775
WEEHAWKEN	YTB 776
NOGALES	YTB 777
APOPKA	YTB 778
MANHATTAN	YTB 779
SAUGUS	YTB 780
NIANTIC	YTB 781
MANISTEE	YTB 782
REDWING	YTB 783
KALISPELL	YTB 784
WINNEMUCCA	YTB 785
TONKAWA	YTB 786
KITTANNING	YTB 787
WAPATO	YTB 788
TOMAHAWK	YTB 789
MENOMINEE	YTB 790
MARINETTE	YTB 791
ANTIGO	YTB 792
PIQUA	YTB 793
MANDAN	YTB 794
KETCHIKAN	YTB 795
SACO	YTB 796
TAMAQUA	YTB 797
OPELIKA	YTB 798
NATCHITOCHES	YTB 799
EUFAULA	YTB 800
PALATKA	YTB 801
CHERAW	YTB 802
NANTICOKE	YTB 803
AHOSKIE	YTB 804
OCALA	YTB 805
TUSKEGEE	YTB 806
MASSAPEQUA	YTB 807
WENATCHEE	YTB 808
AGAWAN	YTB 809
ANOKA	YTB 810
HOUMA	YTB 811
ACCONAC	YTB 812
POUGHKEEPSIE	YTB 813
WAXAHATCHIE	YTB 814
NEODESHA	YTB 815
CAMPTI	YTB 816
HYANNIS	YTB 817
MECOSTA	YTB 818
IUKA	YTB 819
WANAMASSA	YTB 820
TONTOGANY	YTB 821
PAWHUSKA	YTB 822
CANONCHET	YTB 823
SANTAQUIN	YTB 824
WATHENA	YTB 825
WASHTUCNA	YTB 826
CHETEK	YTB 827
CATAHECASSA	YTB 828
METACOM	YTB 829
PUSHMATAHA	YTB 830
DEKANAWIDA	YTB 831
PETALESHARO	YTB 832
SHABONEE	YTB 833
NEWGAGON	YTB 834
SKENANDOA	YTB 835
POKAGON	YTB 836

Displacement, tons: 356 full load
Dimensions, feet (metres): 109 × 30 × 13.8 *(33.2 × 9.1 × 4.2)*
Main machinery: 2 Fairbanks-Morse 38D8-1/8-12 diesels; 4248 hp *(3.17 MW)* sustained; 2 shafts
Speed, knots: 12. **Range, miles:** 2000 at 12 kts
Complement: 10-12

Comment: Large harbour tugs; 80 are in active service. First six are Edenshaw class, remainder Natick class. YTB 752 completed in 1959, YTB 753 in 1960, YTB 756-762 in 1961, YTB 763-766 in 1963, YTB 770 and YTB 771 in 1964, YTB 767-769, 776 in 1965, YTB 774, 775, 777-789 in 1966, YTB 790-793 in 1967, YTB 794 and 795 in 1968, YTB 796-803 in 1969, and YTB 804-815 completed in 1970-72, YTB 816-827 completed 1972-73, YTB 828-836 completed 1974-75. YTB 837 and YTB 838 transferred upon completion in late 1975 to Saudi Arabia. In future tugs will be provided by contractors.

YTB 832 — *8/1991, Giorgio Arra*

25 TORPEDO RETRIEVERS (TR and TWR)

Comment: Four different types spread around the Fleet bases and at AUTEC.

TWR 3 — *4/1991, Giorgio Arra*

TWR 1 — *6/1989, Giorgio Arra*

RESEARCH AND EXPERIMENTAL SHIPS

3 ASHEVILLE CLASS

ATHENA (ex-*Chehalis*) **ATHENA II** (ex-*Grand Rapids*) **LAUREN** (ex-*Douglas*)

Displacement, tons: 245 full load
Dimensions, feet (metres): 164.5 × 23.8 × 9.5 *(50.1 × 7.3 × 2.9)*
Main machinery: CODOG; 1 GE LM 1500 gas turbine; 12 500 hp *(9.3 MW)*; 2 Cummins VT 12-875 diesels; 1450 hp *(1.07 MW)*; 2 shafts
Speed, knots: 16. **Range, miles:** 1700 at 16 kts
Complement: 22

Comment: All built 1969-71. Work for the Ships Research and Development centre, Carderock. Disarmed except *Lauren* which has maintained its military appearance.

ATHENA *4/1991, Giorgio Arra*

LAUREN *11/1991, Giorgio Arra*

Note: There are many naval associated research vessels which are civilian manned and not carried on the US Naval Vessel Register. In addition civilian ships are leased for short periods to support a particular research project or trial.

RSB-1 (missile retriever) *9/1991, Giorgio Arra*

MILITARY SEALIFT COMMAND (MSC)

Notes: (1) The US Navy's Military Sealift Command has the responsibility for providing sealift for all components of the Department of Defense. In 1990-91, the US response to the Iraqi invasion of Kuwait resulted in MSC having to use almost all of its available and usable sealift and support ship assets to move military equipment to the Middle East and to provide maintenance and medical support to US forces transported to that area.

This mobilisation and supply effort included the activation of all eight fast sealift ships (former SL-7s) and 79 of the 96 ships in the Ready Reserve Force at the time of the invasion, including all 17 Ro-Ros in the RRF. It required the movement of two Maritime Prepositioning Ship squadrons (nine ships loaded with equipment for two Marine Expeditionary Brigades) from Guam and Diego Garcia to Saudi Arabia and of the Afloat Prepositioning Force (12 ships loaded with equipment for the Army and the Air Force). Later the third Maritime Prepositioning Ship squadron was moved from the Atlantic to the combat area. The two hospital ships were sailed immediately to the Middle East, as were the two aviation support ships. With usable MSC assets exhausted, MSC began chartering ships, both US flag and foreign, and by the end of 1991 a total of 127 US flag and 293 foreign ships had been chartered. At the start of the war with Iraq on 17 January 1991, MSC had delivered 1.7 million short tons of cargo to Saudi Arabia, had another half million tons underway, and had delivered 3.9 million tons of POL. In all, more than 2.5 million short tons of cargo and 6.1 million tons of POL were moved to the Middle East.

To meet manning requirements for all of the ships activated more than 3000 merchant seamen were hired by the Maritime Administration at MSC's request. Difficulties were encountered in finding enough qualified personnel to man the steam propulsion plants which were predominant in the RRF.

At the end of the war, millions of tons of supplies had to be returned to the United States and Europe, and at the end of 1991 a total of 199 ships, including 84 foreign and 44 US flag charters, were still involved.

This operation focused attention on a number of basic US sealift problems:
(a) There was a shortage of Ro-Ros, the types of ships most needed to handle military rolling stock. Only 17 were available within the RRF and another six from US flag operators.
(b) Over the years, insufficient funds had been made available to properly maintain RRF ships and have them ready for emergencies. As a consequence, many could not be activated.
(c) There are not enough fast sealift ships available. The United States only has eight, and seven of these (one broke down on its initial voyage) were operated at a tempo that caused maintenance problems. Those seven ships carried nine per cent of the cargo moved to the Middle East.

(2) In January 1992 a Mobility Requirements Study was submitted to Congress. The report advocated a national defence sealift fund initially capitalised in FY 1993 navy funds which will be added to $1.9 billion in previous sealift acquisition funds. The acquisition plan calls for the DoD to acquire (through new construction or conversion) the equivalent of 20 large, medium-speed roll-on/roll-off ships. These are defined as having 35 302 m² of total capacity, with 27 870 m² available for prepositioning. The ships should also be able to achieve a sustained speed of 24 kts. In addition at least two container ships (holding 2000 containers each) are to be leased for prepositioning.

Although the exact size and number of ships will be determined during acquisition, the estimated schedule calls for acquisition to be completed by FY 1998; including nine prepositioning ships, 11 fast sealift ships and two container ships. In the near term chartered prepositioning ships will be used as a supplement.

(3) Other MSC ships such as ocean surveillance vessels, research ships, and scientific support ships continue their routine operations. At the beginning of 1992 a total of 22 ships was assigned to special mission support, and 47 to MSC's fleet auxiliary force.
(4) MSC headquarters are in the Washington Navy Yard. The organisation is commanded by a vice admiral, and its four principal area commands by captains.
(5) No ship of the Military Sealift Command is armed in peacetime.
(6) Military Sealift Command nucleus ships are assigned standard US Navy hull designations with the added prefix 'T'.
(7) On 1 October 1987, the transportation elements of the three services were merged into the US Transportation Command, a unified command with headquarters at Scott AFB, Illinois, and reporting directly to the Joint Chiefs of Staff. It is commanded by an Air Force general, with a Navy vice admiral as deputy. The three components of USTRANSCOM (Military Sealift Command, Military Airlift Command, and Military Traffic Management Command) exercise operational control of their respective forces.

1 KILAUEA CLASS: AMMUNITION SHIP (AE)

Name	*No*	*Commissioned*	*F/S*
KILAUEA	T-AE 26	10 Aug 1968	TPA

Comment: Transferred to MSC for activation and operation 1 October 1980. Ship underwent a civilian modification (CIVMOD) overhaul during which extensive superstructure work was accomplished in the living spaces. All gear from station seven was removed. Main armament was taken out. *Kilauea* has 7 UNREP stations operational: 4 port, 3 stbd and has been outfitted with a commercial type satellite navigation equipment. For particulars refer to Kilauea class in Auxiliaries section. Complement is 120 civilians and 67 naval personnel (for communications equipment and helicopter handling).

KILAUEA *10/1989, L/S P. Steele RAN*

1 CONVERTED MISSION CLASS: MISCELLANEOUS (AG)

Name	*No*	*Builders*	*Delivered*	*F/S*
VANGUARD (ex-*Muscle Shoals*, ex-*Mission San Fernando*)	T-AG 194 (ex-AGM 19, ex-AO 122)	Marine Ship Corp, Sausalito, Calif	29 Feb 1944	TAA

Comment: In 1980, USNS *Vanguard* was modified as test ship for Fleet Ballistic Missile guidance and ship navigation systems. Under operational control of Commander Submarine Force, Atlantic Fleet. Complement of 160 (86 civil service crew, 40 technicians and 34 naval officers and men). For characteristics see Converted Mission class AGM. Reclassified as AG 194 on 30 September 1980.

VANGUARD *2/1991, Giorgio Arra*

1 RIGEL CLASS: STORE SHIP (AF)

Name	*No*	*Builders*	*Commissioned*	*F/S*
RIGEL	T-AF 58	Ingalls, Pascagoula	2 Sep 1955	TAA

Displacement, tons: 7950 light; 15 540 full load
Dimensions, feet (metres): 502 × 72 × 27 *(153 × 22 × 8.2)*
Main machinery: 2 Combustion Engineering boilers; 600 psi *(42.3 kg/cm sq)*; 875°F *(467°C)*; 1 GE turbine; 16 000 hp *(11.94 MW)*; 1 shaft
Speed, knots: 16. **Range, miles:** 15 000 at 15 kts
Complement: 133 (16 officers) comprises 17 naval party plus 116 civilians
Cargo capacity: 5975 cu m dry; 5400 cu m frozen
Radars: Surface search: Raytheon SPS 10; G band.
Navigation: CAS 1650/6X; I band.
Helicopters: Platform only.

Comment: R3-S-A4 type. Fitted with SATCOMs. Assigned to Military Sealift Command on 23 June 1975 (guns removed). Operates in the Mediterranean.

RIGEL *7/1986, Gilbert Gyssels*

3 Ex-BRITISH LYNESS CLASS: COMBAT STORES SHIP (AFS)

Name	*No*	*Builders*	*Commissioned*	*F/S*
SIRIUS (ex-RFA *Lyness*)	T-AFS 8	Swan Hunter & Wigham Richardson Ltd, Wallsend-on-Tyne	22 Dec 1966	TAA
SPICA (ex-RFA *Tarbatness*)	T-AFS 9	Swan Hunter & Wigham Richardson Ltd, Wallsend-on-Tyne	21 Mar 1967	TPA
SATURN (ex-RFA *Stromness*)	T-AFS 10	Swan Hunter & Wigham Richardson Ltd, Wallsend-on-Tyne	10 Aug 1967	TAA

Displacement, tons: 9010 light; 16 792 full load
Measurement, tons: 7782 dwt; 12 359 gross; 4744 net
Dimensions, feet (metres): 524 × 72 × 22 *(159.7 × 22 × 6.7)*
Main machinery: 1 Wallsend-Sulzer 8RD-76 diesel; 11 520 hp *(8.59 MW)*; 1 shaft
Speed, knots: 18. **Range, miles:** 12 000 at 16 kts
Complement: 116 (with a Navy contingent of 18 (1 officer))
Cargo capacity: 8313 cu m dry; 3921 cu m frozen
Helicopters: 2 UH-46E Sea Knight.

Comment: Lifts and mobile appliances for handling stores internally, and a new replenishment at sea system and a helicopter landing platform for transferring loads at sea. A feature of the ship is the use of closed-circuit television to monitor the movement of stores. Air-conditioned. After a period of charter *Sirius* was purchased on 1 March 1982, *Spica* on 30 September 1982 and *Saturn* on 1 October 1983. Two of the class were involved in the war with Iraq in 1991.

SATURN *7/1991, Guy Toremans*

1 HAYES CLASS: ACOUSTIC RESEARCH SHIP (AG)

Name	*No*	*Builders*	*Completed*	*F/S*
HAYES	T-AG 195 (ex-AGOR 16)	Todd Shipyards, Seattle	21 July 1971	TAA

Displacement, tons: 4037 full load
Dimensions, feet (metres): 256.5 × 75 (see *Comment*) × 22 *(78.2 × 22.9 × 6.7)*
Main machinery: Diesel-electric; 2 Caterpillar 3516 diesels; 2820 hp *(2.1 MW)* sustained; 2 Westinghouse motors; 2400 hp *(1.79 MW)*; 2 auxiliary diesels (for creep speed); 330 hp *(246 kW)*; 2 shafts; cp props
Speed, knots: 10. **Range, miles:** 2000 at 10 kts
Complement: 74 (10 officers) including scientists
Radars: Navigation: Raytheon TM 1650/6X and TM 1660/12S; I band.

Comment: *Hayes* is one of two classes of US naval ships to have a catamaran hull, the other being the ASR 21 class submarine rescue ships. Laid down 12 November 1969; launched 2 July 1970. To Ready Reserve 10 June 1983 and transferred to James River (Maritime Administration) for lay-up in 1984 having been too costly to operate. Under FY 1986 programme being converted to Acoustic Research Ship (AG) in place of *Monob I* (YAG 61); reclassified T-AG 195 and completed in early 1992 after five years work in two shipyards. Mission is to transport, deploy and retrieve acoustic arrays, to conduct acoustic surveys in support of the submarine noise reduction programme and to carry out acoustic testing. Catamaran hull design provides large deck working area, centre well for operating equipment at great depths, and removes laboratory areas from main propulsion machinery. Each hull is 246 ft long and 24 ft wide (maximum). There are three 36 in diameter instrument wells in addition to the main centre well.

HAYES *2/1992, A. Denholm*

1 CONVERTED AKD CLASS: MISSILE RANGE INSTRUMENTATION SHIP/DEEP SUBMERGENCE SUPPORT SHIP (AGDS)

Name	*No*	*Builders*	*Commissioned*	*F/S*
POINT LOMA (ex-*Point Barrow*)	T-AGDS 2 (ex-T-AKD1)	Maryland Shipbuilding and Drydock Company, Baltimore MD	28 Feb 1958	TPA

Displacement, tons: 7609 light; 12 430 full load
Dimensions, feet (metres): 492.1 × 74 × 20 *(150 × 22.6 × 6.1)*
Main machinery: 2 Foster-Wheeler boilers; 450 psi *(32 kg/cm sq)*; 750°F *(400°C)*; 2 Westinghouse turbines; 6000 hp *(4.48 MW)*; 2 shafts
Speed, knots: 12. **Range, miles:** 8800 at 10 kts
Complement: 73 civilian (12 officers, 29 technicians); 18 naval (6 officers)

Comment: Former 'AKD' *Point Barrow* converted to deep-submergence support-ship in 1974 by Fellows and Stuart Shipyard, Long Beach, CA and renamed *Point Loma* (AGDS 2). Conversion for a secondary mission to support the Trident missile test programme was accomplished in 1982 by Mare Island Naval Shipyard, Vallejo, CA. On 30 September 1986, the *Point Loma* was turned over to MSC for operation for continued support of the Trident missile test programme as the Pacific Launch Area Support Ship. The deep-submergence support-ship mission is available on a contingency basis only.

POINT LOMA *7/1990, van Ginderen Collection*

1 GLOVER CLASS: FRIGATE RESEARCH SHIP (AGFF)

Name	*No*	*Builders*	*Commissioned*
GLOVER	T-AGFF 1 (ex-FF 1098, ex-AGFF 1, ex-AGDE 1, ex-AG 163)	Bath Iron Works, Bath, Maine	13 Nov 1965

Displacement, tons: 2643 standard; 3615 full load
Dimensions, feet (metres): 414.5 × 44.2 × 14.5; 24 (sonar) *(126.3 × 13.5 × 4.4; 7.3)*
Main machinery: 2 Foster-Wheeler boilers; 1200 psi *(84.3 kg/cm sq)*; 950°F *(510°C)*; 1 Westinghouse turbine; 35 000 hp *(26 MW)*; 1 shaft
Speed, knots: 27. **Range, miles:** 4000 at 20 kts
Complement: 79 civilians; 21 naval
Radars: Air search: Lockheed SPS 40; E/F band.
Surface search: Raytheon SPS 10; G band.
Navigation: Marconi LN 66; I band.
Sonars: EDO/General Electric SQS 26 AXR; bow-mounted; active search and attack; medium frequency.
EDO SQS 35; Independent Variable Depth Sonar (IVDS); active search; medium frequency.

Comment: Built to test a pump jet propulsor system. She was classed as a miscellaneous auxiliary (AG 163) but retained a full combat capability and was completed as an escort research ship (AGDE 1). Subsequently changed to frigate research ship (AGFF) on 30 June 1975, reclassified as a regular frigate on 1 October 1979 and transferred to the MSC on 11 June 1990. Now used as a testbed for sonars, radars and electronics as part of the Special Mission Ship Force. Armament deactivated.

GLOVER *2/1991, Giorgio Arra*

1 CONVERTED HASKELL CLASS: MISSILE RANGE INSTRUMENTATION SHIP (AGM)

Name	*No*	*Builders*	*Commissioned*	*F/S*
RANGE SENTINEL (ex-*Sherburne*)	T-AGM 22 (ex-APA 205)	Permanente Metals Corp, Richmond, Calif	20 Sep 1944	TAA

Displacement, tons: 8853 light; 12 170 full load
Dimensions, feet (metres): 455 × 62 × 26 *(138.7 × 18.9 × 7.9)*
Main machinery: 2 Combustion Engineering boilers; 525 psi *(37 kg/cm sq)*; 750°F *(399°C)*; 1 Westinghouse turbine; 8500 hp *(6.34 MW)*; 1 shaft
Speed, knots: 17.7. **Range, miles:** 12 000 at 15 kts
Complement: 81 civilian (15 officers, 12 technical personnel); 43 naval (3 officers)
Radars: Navigation: Raytheon TM 1650/6X and TM 1660/12S; I band.

Comment: Former attack transport (APA) converted specifically to serve as a range instrumentation ship in support of the Fleet Ballistic Missile (FBM) programme. Maritime Administration VC2-S-AP5 type. Reclassified AGM 22 on 16 April 1969 and renamed *Range Sentinel* on 26 April 1971. In Maritime Administration reserve from 1 October 1958 until 22 October 1969. Converted from October 1969 to October 1971; placed in service as T-AGM 22 on 14 October 1971. Has telemetry and missile tracking equipment.

RANGE SENTINEL *11/1989, Giorgio Arra*

1 CONVERTED MISSION CLASS: MISSILE RANGE INSTRUMENTATION SHIP (AGM)

Name	*No*	*Builders*	*Completed*	*F/S*
REDSTONE (ex-*Johnstown*, ex-*Mission de Pala*)	T-AGM 20 (ex-AO 114)	Marine Ship Corp, Sausalito, Calif	22 Apr 1944	TAA

Displacement, tons: 13 882 light; 24 710 full load
Dimensions, feet (metres): 595 × 75 × 25 *(181.4 × 22.9 × 7.6)*
Main machinery: Turbo-electric; 2 Babcock & Wilcox boilers; 600 psi *(42.3 kg/cm sq)*; 825°F *(440°C)*; Westinghouse turbo-generators; 10 000 hp *(7.46 MW)*; 1 motor; 1 shaft
Speed, knots: 14. **Range, miles:** 25 000 at 13 kts
Complement: 165 civilian (20 officers, 80 technical personnel)
Radars: Navigation: Raytheon TM 1650/9X and TM 1660/12S; I band.

Comment: Maritime Administration T2-SE-A2 type. Converted in 1964-66 to serve as mid-ocean communications and tracking ship in support of the Apollo manned lunar flights.
Converted to range instrumentation ship by General Dynamics Corp, Quincy Division, Massachusetts; was cut in half and a 72 ft mid-section was inserted, increasing length, beam, and displacement; approximately 450 tons of electronic equipment installed for support of lunar flight operations, including communications and tracking systems; balloon hangar and platform fitted aft. Operated for the US Air Force Eastern Space Missile Center, Patrick Air Force Base, Florida.

REDSTONE *1/1990, Giorgio Arra*

2 GYRE CLASS: OCEANOGRAPHIC RESEARCH SHIPS (AGOR)

Name	*No*	*Builders*	*Completed*	*F/S*
GYRE	T-AGOR 21	Halter Marine Service, New Orleans	14 Nov 1973	Loan
MOANA WAVE	T-AGOR 22	Halter Marine Service, New Orleans	16 Jan 1974	Loan

Displacement, tons: 1427 (AGOR 21), 1853 (AGOR 22) full load
Dimensions, feet (metres): 174 × 36 × 13 *(53 × 11 × 4)* (AGOR 21)
210 × 36 × 13 *(64 × 11 × 4)* (AGOR 22)
Main machinery: 2 Caterpillar diesels; 1700 hp *(1.27 MW)*; 2 shafts; cp props; bow thruster; 150 hp *(112 kW)*
Speed, knots: 11.5. **Range, miles:** 12 000 at 10 kts
Complement: 13 plus 19 scientists

Comment: Based on a commercial ship design. Open deck aft provides space for equipment vans to permit rapid change of mission capabilities. Single hard-chine hulls. *Moana Wave* was lengthened in 1984 and fitted with a laboratory at the stern. They are assigned for operation to Texas A & M University and the University of Hawaii, respectively.

MOANA WAVE *1991, van Ginderen Collection*

1 CONVERTED COMPASS ISLAND CLASS: MISSILE RANGE INSTRUMENTATION SHIP (AGM)

Name	*No*	*Builders*	*Commissioned*	*F/S*
OBSERVATION ISLAND (ex-*Empire State Mariner*)	T-AGM 23 (ex-AG 154, ex-YAG 57)	New York SB Corp, NJ	5 Dec 1958	TPA

Displacement, tons: 13 060 light; 17 015 full load
Dimensions, feet (metres): 564 × 76 × 25 *(171.6 × 23.2 × 7.6)*
Main machinery: 2 Foster-Wheeler boilers; 600 psi *(42.3 kg/cm sq)*; 875°F *(467°C)*; 1 GE turbine; 19 250 hp *(14.36 MW)*; 1 shaft
Speed, knots: 20. **Range, miles:** 17 000 at 15 kts
Complement: 143 civilian (20 officers, 60-65 technicians)
Missiles: SLBM: She fired the first ship-launched Polaris missile at sea on 27 August 1959. Refitted to fire the improved Poseidon missile in 1969 and launched the first Poseidon test missile fired afloat on 16 December 1969.
Radars: Navigation: Raytheon 1650/9X and 1660/12S; I band.

Comment: Built as a Mariner class merchant ship (C4-S-A1 type); launched on 15 August 1953; acquired by the Navy on 10 September 1956 for use as a Fleet Ballistic Missile (FBM) test ship. Converted at Norfolk Naval Shipyard. In reserve from September 1972. On 18 August 1977, *Observation Island* was re-acquired by the US Navy from the Maritime Administration and transferred to the Military Sealift Command. Converted to Missile Range Instrumentation Ship from July 1979-April 1981 at Maryland SB and DD Co, Baltimore, Maryland. Reclassified AGM 23 on 1 May 1979. Converted again in 1980-81 to carry an Air Force shipborne phased-array radar system (Cobra Judy) for collection of data on foreign ballistic missile tests. Operated for the US Air Force Eastern Space Missile Center, Patrick Air Force Base, Florida, US Navy retaining title.

OBSERVATION ISLAND *1986, van Ginderen Collection*

1 + (1) OCEANOGRAPHIC RESEARCH SHIPS (AGOR)

Name	*No*	*Builders*	*In Service*	*F/S*
THOMAS G THOMPSON (ex-*Ewing*)	AGOR-23	Halter Marine, Moss Point	July 1992	Loan

Displacement, tons: 3251 full load
Dimensions, feet (metres): 274 oa; 246.8 wl × 52.5 × 19 *(83.5; 75.2 × 16 × 5.6)*
Main machinery: Diesel-electric; 6 diesel generators; 6.65 MW (3 × 1.5 MW and 3 × 715 kW); 2 motors; 2 shafts; bow thruster; 1140 hp *(850 kW)*
Speed, knots: 15. **Range, miles:** 8000 at 12 kts
Complement: 20 plus 30 scientists plus 20 spare berths
Sonars: Krupp Atlas Hydrographic.

Comment: *Thomas G Thompson* is the first of a new class of oceanographic research vessels capable of operating worldwide in all seasons and suitable for use by navy laboratories, contractors and academic institutions; laid down 23 March 1989, launched 27 July 1990 and delivered 8 July 1991. Dynamic positioning system enables station to be held within 300 ft of a point. 4000 sq ft of laboratories. Loaned to the University of Washington and sponsored by the Chief of Naval Research. Ships in this series may be of different hull designs and will be able to meet changing oceanographic requirements for general, year-round, worldwide research. This will include launching, towing and recovering a variety of equipment. The ships will also be involved in hydrographic data collection. The next ship of the class authorised in FY 1992.

THOMAS G THOMPSON *7/1991, Halter Marine*

3 ROBERT D CONRAD CLASS: OCEANOGRAPHIC RESEARCH SHIPS (AGOR)

Name	No	Builders	Completed	F/S
THOMAS WASHINGTON	AGOR 10	Marinette Marine Corp, Wisc	27 Sep 1965	Loan
DE STEIGUER	T-AGOR 12	Northwest Marine Iron Works, Portland, Oregon	28 Feb 1969	TPA
BARTLETT	T-AGOR 13	Northwest Marine Iron Works, Portland, Oregon	31 Mar 1969	TAA

Displacement, tons: 950-1200 light; 1362-1370 full load
Dimensions, feet (metres): 208.9 × 40 × 15.3 *(63.7 × 12.2 × 4.7)*
Main machinery: Diesel-electric; 2 Cummins diesel generators; 1 motor; 1000 hp *(746 kW)*; 1 shaft; bow thruster (AGOR 12 and 13)
Speed, knots: 13.5. **Range, miles:** 12 000 at 12 kts
Complement: 41 (9 officers, 15 scientists)
Radars: Navigation: TM 1650/6X (*Lynch* and *De Steiguer*); I band.
TM 1660/12S (*Lynch*, *De Steiguer* and *Bartlett*); I band.

Comment: *Thomas Washington* operated by Scripps Institution of Oceanography (University of California) under technical control of the Chief of Naval Research.
De Steiguer and *Bartlett* operated by Military Sealift Command under the technical control of the Naval Oceanographic Command.
This is the first class of ships designed and built by the US Navy for oceanographic research. Fitted with instrumentation and laboratories to measure gravity and magnetism, water temperature, sound transmission in water, and the profile of the ocean floor. Special features include 10 ton capacity boom and winches for handling over-the-side equipment; bow thruster; 620 hp gas turbine (housed in funnel structure) for providing 'quiet' power when conducting experiments; can propel the ship at 6.5 kts. There are variations in types of mast (some lattice, some pole) and in their positions on the superstructure.
Ships of this class are in service with Brazil *(Sands)*, Mexico *(James M Gilliss)*, New Zealand *(Charles H Davies)* and the US Geological Survey *(S P Lee)*. Ex-AGOR 9 was relieved by *Thomas G Thompson* in 1991 and was scheduled to become IX 517. *Lynch* placed in reserve.

BARTLETT *10/1991, Giorgio Arra*

2 MELVILLE CLASS: OCEANOGRAPHIC RESEARCH SHIPS (AGOR)

Name	No	Builders	Completed	F/S
MELVILLE	T-AGOR 14	Defoe SB Co, Bay City, Mich	27 Aug 1969	Loan
KNORR	T-AGOR 15	Defoe SB Co, Bay City, Mich	14 Jan 1970	Loan

Displacement, tons: 2670 full load
Dimensions, feet (metres): 278.9 × 46.3 × 15.1 *(85 × 14.1 × 4.6)*
Main machinery: Diesel-electric; 4 diesel generators; 3 motors; 3000 hp *(2.24 MW)*; 3 shafts (2 aft, 1 fwd)
Speed, knots: 14. **Range, miles:** 12 000 at 12 kts
Complement: 58 (9 officers) plus 33 scientists

Comment: *Melville* operated by Scripps Institution of Oceanography and *Knorr* by Woods Hole Oceanography Institution for the Office of Naval Research, under technical control of the Oceanographer of the Navy. Fitted with internal wells for lowering equipment, underwater lights and observation ports. Facilities for handling small research submersibles. Problems with the propulsion system have led to major modifications including electric drive (vice the original mechanical) and the insertion of a 34 ft central section increasing the displacement from the original 1915 tons and allowing better accommodation and improved laboratory spaces. The forward propeller is retractable. These ships are highly manoeuvrable for precise position keeping.

MELVILLE (before conversion) *1986, Giorgio Arra*

0 + 2 PATHFINDER CLASS: SURVEYING SHIPS (AGS)

Name	No	Builders	Commissioned
PATHFINDER	T-AGS 60	Halter Marine	Jan 1994
SUMNER	T-AGS 61	Halter Marine	July 1994

Displacement, tons: 4762 full load
Dimensions, feet (metres): 328.5 × 58 × 18 *(100.1 × 17.7 × 5.5)*
Main machinery: Diesel-electric; 6 diesel generators; 2 motors; 6000 hp *(4.48 MW)*; 2 shafts; bow thruster
Speed, knots: 16. **Range, miles:** 12 000 at 12 kts
Complement: 60

Comment: Contract awarded in January 1991 for two ships with an option for a third. Replacements for *De Steiguer* and *Bartlett*. *Sumner* may be equipped for Arctic operations.

2 JOHN McDONNELL CLASS: SURVEYING SHIPS (AGS)

Name	No	Builders	In Service	F/S
JOHN McDONNELL	T-AGS 51	Halter Marine	Nov 1992	TAA
LITTLEHALES	T-AGS 52	Halter Marine	Jan 1993	PAA

Displacement, tons: 2054 full load
Dimensions, feet (metres): 205 × 45 × 14 *(62.5 × 13.7 × 4.3)*
Main machinery: 1 Caterpillar EMD 12 645 E6 diesel; 2550 hp *(1.9 MW)* sustained; 1 shaft
Speed, knots: 12. **Range, miles:** 13 800 at 12 kts
Complement: 22 plus 11 scientists

Comment: Laid down on 3 August 1989 and 25 October 1989 respectively. *McDonnell* launched 15 August 1990 and delivered 16 December 1991; *Littlehales* launched 14 February 1991 and delivered 10 January 1992. Planned to replace *Chauvenet* and *Harkness*. Carry 34 ft survey launches for data collection in coastal regions with depths between 10 and 600 m and in deep water to 4000 m. A small diesel is used for propulsion at towing speeds of up to 6 kts.

JOHN McDONNELL *1/1992, Halter Marine*

2 MAURY CLASS: SURVEYING SHIPS (AGS)

Name	No	Builders	Commissioned	F/S
MAURY	T-AGS 39	Bethlehem, Sparrows Point, Md	31 Mar 1989	TAA
TANNER	T-AGS 40	Bethlehem, Sparrows Point, Md	27 Aug 1990	TAA

Displacement, tons: 16 074 full load
Dimensions, feet (metres): 500; 462.1 wl × 72 × 30 *(152.4; 140.8 × 22 × 9.1)*
Main machinery: 2 Transamerica De Laval R5-V16 Enterprise diesels; 24 740 hp *(18.46 MW)*; 1 shaft
Speed, knots: 20. **Range, miles:** 12 000 at 20 kts
Complement: 108 (56 civilian, 52 Navy) plus 20 scientists

Comment: The first such ships to be constructed in many years. Both ordered 25 June 1985. *Maury* laid down 29 July 1986 and *Tanner* 22 October 1986. They have replaced *Bowditch* (T-AGS 21) and *Dutton* (T-AGS 22) and are operated by MSC for the Oceanographer of the Navy under technical control of the Naval Oceanographic office. Fitted with SQN-17 bottom topography survey system and other acoustic systems including 2 BQN-3 narrow-beam for surveying purposes. In-service dates delayed by main machinery installation problems. Almost half the displacement is water ballast to provide sufficient draft for the sonar.

TANNER *12/1990, Harald Carstens*

0 + 1 WATERS CLASS: SURVEYING SHIP (AGS)

Name	No	Builders	Commissioned	F/S
WATERS	T-AGS 45	Avondale Industries	Mar 1993	Bldg/TPA

Displacement, tons: 12 208 full load
Dimensions, feet (metres): 455 × 68.9 × 21 *(138.7 × 21 × 6.4)*
Main machinery: Diesel-electric; 5 GM EMD diesels; 2 Westinghouse motors; 6800 hp *(15.07 MW)*; 2 shafts
Speed, knots: 13. **Range, miles:** 6500 at 12 kts
Complement: 89 (37 officers) plus 6 spare

Comment: Ordered 4 April 1990. Laid down 16 May 1991. To support the Integrated Underwater Surveillance System. Planned to conduct oceanographic and acoustic surveys. The ship will carry a remote-controlled submersible.

WATERS (artist's impression) *1990, Avondale*

2 CHAUVENET CLASS: SURVEYING SHIPS (AGS)

Name	No	Builders	Completed	F/S
CHAUVENET	T-AGS 29	Upper Clyde Shipbuilders, Glasgow	13 Nov 1970	TPA
HARKNESS	T-AGS 32	Upper Clyde Shipbuilders, Glasgow	29 Jan 1971	TPA

Displacement, tons: 3035 light; 4330 full load
Dimensions, feet (metres): 393.2 × 54 × 16 *(119.8 × 16.5 × 4.9)*
Main machinery: Diesel-electric; 2 Alco diesel generators; 1 Westinghouse motor; 3600 hp *(2.69 MW)*; 1 shaft
Speed, knots: 15. **Range, miles:** 15 000 at 12 kts
Complement: 125 (69 civilian, 55 Navy) plus 12 scientists
Radars: Navigation: TM 1650/6X; I band. TM 1660/12S (*Chauvenet*); I band.
Tacan: URN-25.
Helicopters: 2 Seasprite.

Comment: These ships are operated for the Oceanographer of the Navy with Navy and USMC detachments on board and are under technical control of the Naval Oceanographic office. Capable of extensive military hydrographic and oceanographic surveys, supporting coastal surveying craft, amphibious survey teams and helicopters. To be replaced by *John McDonnell* and *Littlehales* in late 1992 and early 1993.

HARKNESS *1/1989, Hartmut Ehlers*

4 SILAS BENT and WILKES CLASSES: SURVEYING SHIPS (AGS)

Name	No	Builders	Completed	F/S
SILAS BENT	T-AGS 26	American SB Co, Lorain	23 July 1965	TPA
KANE	T-AGS 27	Christy Corp, Sturgeon Bay	19 May 1967	TAA
WILKES	T-AGS 33	Defoe SB Co, Bay City, Mich	28 June 1971	TAA
WYMAN	T-AGS 34	Defoe SB Co, Bay City, Mich	3 Nov 1971	TAA

Displacement, tons: 2550-2843 full load
Dimensions, feet (metres): 285.3 × 48 × 15.1 *(87 × 14.6 × 4.6)*
Main machinery: Diesel-electric; 2 Alco diesel generators; 1 Westinghouse/GE motor; 3600 hp *(2.69 MW)*; 1 shaft; bow thruster; 350 hp *(261 kW)*
Speed, knots: 15. **Range, miles:** 8000 at 13 kts
Complement: 37 (12 officers) plus 28 scientists
Radars: Navigation: RM 1650/9X and TM 1660/12S *(Silas Bent)*; I band.

Comment: Designed specifically for surveying operations. Bow propulsion unit for precise manoeuvrability and station keeping. All ships in commission operated for the Oceanographer of the Navy under technical control of the Naval Oceanographic office.

WYMAN *3/1991, Giorgio Arra*

2 MERCY CLASS: HOSPITAL SHIPS (AH)

Name	No	Builders	Completed	F/S
MERCY (ex-SS *Worth*)	T-AH 19	National Steel and SB Co, San Diego	1976	ROS
COMFORT (ex-SS *Rose City*)	T-AH 20	National Steel and SB Co, San Diego	1976	ROS

Displacement, tons: 69 360 full load
Measurement, tons: 54 367 gross; 35 958 net
Dimensions, feet (metres): 894 × 105.6 × 32.8 *(272.6 × 32.2 × 10)*
Main machinery: 2 boilers; 2 GE turbines; 24 500 hp *(18.3 MW)*; 2 shafts
Speed, knots: 16.5. **Range, miles:** 12 500 at 15 kts
Complement: 68 civilian crew; 820 naval medical staff; 372 naval support staff; 15 naval communications staff
Radars: Navigation: SPS 67; I band.
Tacan: URN 25.
Helicopters: Platform only.

Comment: Plans to convert SS *United States* were dropped in favour of converting these two San Clemente class tankers. Contracts awarded to National Steel & Shipbuilding in 1983. Conversion of T-AH 19 was begun in 1984 and that of T-AH 20 in 1985. *Mercy* was commissioned 19 December 1986; *Comfort* on 30 November 1987. *Mercy* berthed at Oakland, CA, in a reduced operating status; *Comfort* at Baltimore. Each ship has 1000 beds, 12 operating theatres, laboratories, pharmacies, dental, radiology and optometry departments, physical-therapy and burn-care units and radiological services. Both deployed in the Gulf in 1990-91 with full medical staffs mostly drawn from naval hospitals on both US Coasts.

MERCY *3/1991, 92 Wing RAAF*

2 + 2 VICTORIOUS CLASS: OCEAN SURVEILLANCE SHIPS (AGOS)

Name	No	Builders	Commissioned	F/S
VICTORIOUS	T-AGOS 19	McDermott Marine	5 Sep 1991	TPA
ABLE	T-AGOS 20	McDermott Marine	Mar 1992	TAA
EFFECTIVE	T-AGOS 21	McDermott Marine	Oct 1992	Bldg/TPA
LOYAL	T-AGOS 22	McDermott Marine	Apr 1993	Bldg/TAA

Displacement, tons: 3396 full load
Dimensions, feet (metres): 234.5 × 93.6 × 24.8 *(71.5 × 28.5 × 7.6)*
Main machinery: Diesel-electric; 4 Caterpillar 3512-TA diesels; 5120 hp *(3.82 MW)* sustained; 2 GE motors; 3200 hp *(2.39 MW)*; 2 shafts; 2 bow thrusters; 2400 hp *(1.79 MW)*
Speed, knots: 16; 3 when towing
Complement: 34 (22 civilian, 12 Navy)
Radars: Navigation: Two Raytheon; I band.
Sonars: UQQ 2 SURTASS; towed array; passive surveillance.

Comment: All of SWATH design because of its greater stability at slow speeds in high latitudes under adverse weather conditions. A contract for the first SWATH ship, T-AGOS 19, was awarded in November 1986, and options for the next three were exercised in October 1988. Same WSC-6 communications, links and operating procedures as the Stalwart class. *Victorious* launched 5 May 1990, *Able* 7 February 1991.

VICTORIOUS *1991, McDermott Marine*

0 + 2 (3) IMPECCABLE CLASS: OCEAN SURVEILLANCE SHIPS (AGOS)

Name	No	Builders	Completed	F/S
IMPECCABLE	T-AGOS 23	Tampa Shipyard	May 1994	Bldg
—	T-AGOS 24	Tampa Shipyard	1995	Ord

Displacement, tons: 5370 full load
Dimensions, feet (metres): 281.5 × 95.8 × 26 *(85.8 × 29.2 × 7.9)*
Main machinery: Diesel-electric; 3 EMD 12-645 F7B diesel generators; 2 Westinghouse motors; 5000 hp *(3.73 MW)*; 2 shafts; 2 bow thrusters; 1800 hp *(1.34 MW)*
Speed, knots: 12; 3 when towing
Complement: 45 (26 civilian, 19 Navy)

Comment: Hull form based on that of *Victorious*. Acoustic systems may include an active towed array. First of the class included in FY 1990 budget but a contract was not awarded until March 1991. A second of class was funded in FY 1992 and three more are projected in the five year shipbuilding programme.

IMPECCABLE (artist's impression) *1991, Tampa Shipyard*

18 STALWART CLASS: OCEAN SURVEILLANCE SHIPS (AGOS)

Name	*No*	*Laid down*	*Commissioned*	*F/S*
STALWART	T-AGOS 1	3 Nov 1982	9 Apr 1984	TAA
CONTENDER	T-AGOS 2	10 Jan 1983	29 July 1984	TPA
VINDICATOR	T-AGOS 3	14 Apr 1983	20 Nov 1984	TAA
TRIUMPH	T-AGOS 4	3 Jan 1984	19 Feb 1985	TPA
ASSURANCE	T-AGOS 5	16 Apr 1984	1 May 1985	TPA
PERSISTENT	T-AGOS 6	22 Oct 1984	14 Aug 1985	TAA
INDOMITABLE	T-AGOS 7	26 Jan 1985	1 Dec 1985	TPA
PREVAIL	T-AGOS 8	13 Mar 1985	5 Mar 1986	TAA
ASSERTIVE	T-AGOS 9	30 July 1985	12 Sep 1986	TPA
INVINCIBLE	T-AGOS 10	8 Nov 1985	30 Jan 1987	TAA
AUDACIOUS (ex-*Dauntless*)	T-AGOS 11	29 Feb 1986	18 June 1989	TPA
BOLD (ex-*Vigorous*)	T-AGOS 12	13 June 1988	20 Oct 1989	TAA
ADVENTUROUS	T-AGOS 13	19 Dec 1985	19 Aug 1988	TPA
WORTHY	T-AGOS 14	3 Apr 1986	7 Apr 1989	TAA
TITAN	T-AGOS 15	30 Oct 1986	8 Mar 1989	TPA
CAPABLE	T-AGOS 16	17 Oct 1987	8 July 1989	TAA
TENACIOUS (ex-*Intrepid*)	T-AGOS 17	26 Feb 1988	8 Nov 1989	TPA
RELENTLESS	T-AGOS 18	22 Apr 1988	8 Mar 1990	TAA

Displacement, tons: 2262 full load
Dimensions, feet (metres): 224 × 43 × 14.9 *(68.3 × 13.1 × 4.5)*
Main machinery: Diesel-electric; 4 Caterpillar 398 diesel generators; 2 motors; 1600 hp *(1.2 MW)*; 2 shafts; bow thruster; 550 hp *(410 kW)*
Speed, knots: 11; 3 when towing. **Range, miles:** 4000 at 11 kts; 6450 at 3 kts
Complement: 30-33 (9 officers) (21 civilian manning, 9-12 Navy contingent)
Radars: Navigation: Two Raytheon; I band.
Sonars: UQQ2 SURTASS; towed array; passive surveillance.

Comment: This programme has been completed after several rocky years stemming from the financial difficulties of Tacoma Boatbuilding Co, which built the first eight ships but initially was unable to complete T-AGOS 9-12 before filing for bankruptcy. Halter Marine built T-AGOS 13-18. The ships are operated and maintained by civilian contractors. SURTASS is a linear array of 8575 ft *(2614 m)* deployed on a 6000 ft *(1829 m)* tow cable and neutrally buoyant. The array can operate at depths between 500 and 1500 ft. Information from the array is relayed via WSC-6 (SHF) SATCOM link to shore. Patrols are of 60-90 days duration which even with passive tank stabilisation is a long time to wallow around at 3 kts. Many of the COs are retired USN Captains.
Because of the diminished operational requirement, the whole class may be decommissioned at the rate of three per year. It is reported that *Capable* and *Adventurous* may transfer to NOAA and *Tenacious* to SPAWARSYSCOM in 1992.

RELENTLESS *5/1990, Giorgio Arra*

PERSISTENT *8/1989, Giorgio Arra*

1 CONVERTED C3-S-33a TYPE: CARGO SHIP (AK)

Name	*No*	*Completed*	*F/S*
VEGA (ex-SS *Bay*, ex-*Mormacbay*)	T-AK 286	14 Oct 1960	TAA

Displacement, tons: 15 404 full load
Measurement, tons: 6590 gross
Dimensions, feet (metres): 483.3 × 68 × 28.5 *(147.2 × 20.7 × 8.7)*
Main machinery: 2 Combustion Engineering boilers; 615 psi *(43.3 kg/cm sq)*; 850°F *(457°C)*; 1 GE turbine; 12 100 hp *(9 MW)*; 1 shaft
Speed, knots: 19. **Range, miles:** 14 000 at 18 kts
Complement: 67 plus 7 man naval contingent

Comment: Built by Sun Shipbuilding and Drydock Co, Chester, Pennsylvania for the Moore-McCormack Lines. *Vega* was acquired in October 1981 and was converted to an FBM Support Ship. Capable of carrying 16 Trident missiles; equipped with eight 10-ton capacity booms, four 5-ton capacity booms and one 75-ton capacity boom. Deployed with MSC Atlantic Fleet in July 1983.

VEGA *1986, Giorgio Arra*

1 NORWALK CLASS: CARGO SHIP (AK)

Name	*No*	*F/S*
MARSHFIELD (ex-*Marshfield Victory*)	T-AK 282	TAA

Displacement, tons: 5469 light; 11 277 full load
Dimensions, feet (metres): 455.25 × 62 × 22 *(138.8 × 18.9 × 6.7)*
Main machinery: 2 Combustion Engineering boilers; 525 psi *(37 kg/cm sq)*; 750°F *(399°C)*; 1 turbine; 8500 hp *(6.34 MW)*; 1 shaft
Speed, knots: 17. **Range, miles:** 20 000 at 16 kts
Complement: 70 (14 officers) plus 7 Navy personnel
Cargo capacity: 355 000 gal (US) diesel oil; 430 000 gal (US) fuel oil
Radars: Navigation: TM/RM 1650/6X and TM 1660/12S; I band.

Comment: Former merchant ship of the VC2-S-AP3 Victory type built during the Second World War. Converted to a supply tender for Fleet Ballistic Missile (FBM) submarines by Boland Machine & Manufacturing Co, and accepted on 28 May 1970. Fitted to carry torpedoes, spare parts, packaged petroleum products, bottled gas, black oil and diesel fuel, frozen and dry provisions, and general cargo as well as missiles. No 3 hold converted to carry Polaris missiles and subsequently modified to carry Poseidon missiles. Operated by the Military Sealift Command with a civilian operating crew; a small Navy detachment provides security and technical services. Second of class *Furman* (T-AK 280) is in reserve.

MARSHFIELD *8/1984, Giorgio Arra*

3 NEOSHO CLASS: OILERS (AO)

Name	*No*	*Builders*	*Commissioned*	*F/S*
NEOSHO	T-AO 143	Bethlehem Steel, Quincy	24 Sep 1954	TAA
KAWISHIWI	T-AO 146	New York SB, Camden	6 July 1955	TPA
PONCHATOULA	T-AO 148	New York SB, Camden	12 Jan 1956	TPA

Displacement, tons: 19 533 light; 36 840 full load
Dimensions, feet (metres): 655 × 86 × 35 *(199.6 × 26.2 × 10.7)*
Main machinery: 2 Babcock & Wilcox boilers; 600 psi *(42.2 kg/cm sq)*; 675°F *(357°C)*; 2 GE turbines; 28 000 hp *(21 MW)*; 2 shafts
Speed, knots: 20
Complement: 107 civilian (19 officers); 21 naval (1 officer)
Cargo capacity: 180 000 barrels of fuel oil
Radars: Navigation: Raytheon SPS 10; G band; RM 1650/12X or TM 1650/6X; I band.
Helicopters: Platform only (T-AO 143, 144, 147).

Comment: Two twin 3 in gun mounts removed from *Neosho* which also has a helicopter platform installed and additional superstructure. All fitted to carry a service force commander and staff (12 officers).
Neosho assigned to Military Sealift Command on 25 May 1978, *Kawishiwi* on 10 October 1979 and *Ponchatoula* on 5 September 1980. Being replaced by Henry J Kaiser class.

PONCHATOULA *7/1991, 92 Wing RAAF*

PECOS *5/1990, Avondale*

10 + 8 HENRY J KAISER CLASS: OILERS (AO)

Name	*No*	*Builders*	*Laid down*	*Completed*	*F/S*
HENRY J KAISER	T-AO 187	Avondale	22 Aug 1984	19 Dec 1986	TAA
JOSHUA HUMPHREYS	T-AO 188	Avondale	17 Dec 1984	2 Apr 1987	TAA
JOHN LENTHALL	T-AO 189	Avondale	15 July 1985	2 June 1987	TAA
ANDREW J HIGGINS	T-AO 190	Avondale	21 Nov 1985	20 Oct 1987	TPA
BENJAMIN ISHERWOOD	T-AO 191	Penn Ship/ Tampa	12 July 1986	May 1992	TPA
HENRY ECKFORD	T-AO 192	Penn Ship/ Tampa	22 Jan 1987	Dec 1992	Bldg/TAA
WALTER S DIEHL	T-AO 193	Avondale	8 July 1986	13 Sep 1988	TPA
JOHN ERICSSON	T-AO 194	Avondale	15 Mar 1989	25 Jan 1991	TPA
LEROY GRUMMAN	T-AO 195	Avondale	7 June 1987	2 Aug 1989	TAA
KANAWHA	T-AO 196	Avondale	13 July 1989	11 June 1991	TAA
PECOS	T-AO 197	Avondale	17 Feb 1988	6 July 1990	TPA
BIG HORN	T-AO 198	Avondale	9 Oct 1989	Oct 1992	TAA
TIPPECANOE	T-AO 199	Avondale	19 Nov 1990	Mar 1993	Bldg/TPA
GUADALUPE	T-AO 200	Avondale	9 July 1990	Aug 1992	Bldg/TPA
PATUXENT	T-AO 201	Avondale	21 Oct 1991	Jan 1994	Bldg/TAA
YUKON	T-AO 202	Avondale	13 May 1991	Aug 1993	Bldg/TPA
LARAMIE	T-AO 203	Avondale	Nov 1992	Nov 1994	Bldg/TAA
RAPPAHANNOCK	T-AO 204	Avondale	Mar 1992	June1994	Bldg/TPA

Displacement, tons: 40 700 full load
Dimensions, feet (metres): 677.5 × 97.5 × 35 *(206.5 × 29.7 × 10.7)*
Main machinery: 2 Colt-Pielstick 10 PC4.2V 570 diesels; 39 600 hp(m) *(29.11 MW)* sustained; 2 shafts
Speed, knots: 20. **Range, miles:** 6000 at 18 kts
Complement: 95 civilian (20 officers); 21 naval (1 officer)
Cargo capacity: 180 000 barrels of fuel oil
Guns: 1 Vulcan Phalanx CIWS (fitted for).
Countermeasures: Decoys: SLQ-25 Nixie; towed torpedo decoy.
Helicopters: Platform only.

Comment: Construction of the class was delayed initially by design difficulties, and by excessive vibration at high speeds and other problems encountered in the first ship of the class. The two ships being constructed by Penn Ship are being completed by Tampa Shipyards after Penn Ship went bankrupt and shut down. As the ships had sat idle for months, much refurbishing was necessary. Funding for the final five ships in the programme was provided in FY 1989. The ships are fitted for Vulcan Phalanx CIWS. There are stations on both sides for underway replenishment of fuel and solids. Fitted with integrated electrical auxiliary propulsion.

5—T 5 TYPE: TRANSPORT OILERS (AOT)

Name	*No*	*Builders*	*Commissioned*
GUS W DARNELL	T-AOT 1121	American SB Co, Tampa, Fla	11 Sep 1985
PAUL BUCK	T-AOT 1122	American SB Co, Tampa, Fla	11 Sep 1985
SAMUEL L COBB	T-AOT 1123	American SB Co, Tampa, Fla	15 Nov 1985
RICHARD G MATTHIESON	T-AOT 1124	American SB Co, Tampa, Fla	18 Feb 1986
LAWRENCE H GIANELLA	T-AOT 1125	American SB Co, Tampa, Fla	22 Apr 1986

Displacement, tons: 39 000 full load
Dimensions, feet (metres): 615 × 90 × 34 *(187.5 × 27.4 × 10.4)*
Main machinery: 1 Sulzer 5 RTA-76 diesel; 18 400 hp(m) *(13.52 MW)* sustained; 1 shaft
Speed, knots: 16. **Range, miles:** 12 000 at 16 kts
Complement: 23 (9 officers)
Cargo capacity: 238 400 barrels of oil fuel

Comment: Built for Ocean Carriers Inc, Houston, Texas specifically for long term time charter to the Military Sealift Command (20 years) as Ocean Transportation ships. The last two are able to rig underway replenishment gear.

SAMUEL L COBB *3/1988, Giorgio Arra*

9 SEALIFT CLASS: TRANSPORT OILERS (AOT, ex-AO)

Name	*No*	*Builders*	*Completed*	*F/S*
SEALIFT PACIFIC	T-AOT 168	Todd Shipyards	14 Aug 1974	TWWR
SEALIFT ARABIAN SEA	T-AOT 169	Todd Shipyards	6 May 1975	TWWR
SEALIFT CHINA SEA	T-AOT 170	Todd Shipyards	9 May 1975	TWWR
SEALIFT INDIAN OCEAN	T-AOT 171	Todd Shipyards	29 Aug 1975	TWWR
SEALIFT ATLANTIC	T-AOT 172	Bath Iron Works	26 Aug 1974	TWWR
SEALIFT MEDITERRANEAN	T-AOT 173	Bath Iron Works	6 Nov 1974	TWWR
SEALIFT CARIBBEAN	T-AOT 174	Bath Iron Works	10 Feb 1975	TWWR
SEALIFT ARCTIC	T-AOT 175	Bath Iron Works	22 May 1975	TWWR
SEALIFT ANTARCTIC	T-AOT 176	Bath Iron Works	1 Aug 1975	TWWR

Displacement, tons: 34 100 full load
Measurement, tons: 27 300 dwt
Dimensions, feet (metres): 587 × 84 × 34.6 *(178.9 × 25.6 × 10.6)*
Main machinery: 2 Colt-Pielstick 14 PC-2V400 diesels; 14 000 hp(m) *(10.3 MW)* sustained; 1 shaft; cp prop; bow thruster
Speed, knots: 16. **Range, miles:** 7500 at 16 kts
Complement: 24 (9 officers) plus 2 Maritime Academy cadets
Cargo capacity: 185 000 barrels of oil fuel

Comment: Built specially for long term-charter by the Military Sealift Command. Operated for MSC as Ocean Transportation Ships under charter by Marine Transport Lines Inc. Automated engine room. All reclassified T-AOT on 30 September 1978. One of the class serves as a PREPO ship (*China Sea* in 1992).

SEALIFT CHINA SEA *2/1991, Giorgio Arra*

MISCELLANEOUS OCEAN TRANSPORTATION SHIPS

Comment: In addition to the AOTs listed in the Sealift and T Type classes, there were 40 plus ships of varying types under charter to the MSC in early 1992. Numbers and names are constantly changing and many of these will be released as soon as all equipment has been returned from Saudi Arabia.

MERCURY (MSC charter for the Gulf) *8/1991, 92 Wing RAAF*

1 ZEUS CLASS CABLE REPAIRING SHIP (ARC)

Name	*No*	*Builders*	*Completed*	*F/S*
ZEUS	T-ARC 7	National Steel and SB Co, San Diego	19 Mar 1984	TPA

Displacement, tons: 8370 light; 14 157 full load
Dimensions, feet (metres): 502.5 × 73 × 25 *(153.2 × 22.3 × 7.6)*
Main machinery: Diesel-electric; 5 GM EMD 20-645 F7B diesel generators; 14.32 MW sustained; 2 motors; 2 shafts; cp props; bow thrusters (forward and aft)
Speed, knots: 15.8. **Range, miles:** 10 000 at 15 kts
Complement: 126 (88 civilians, 6 Navy, 32 scientists)

Comment: Ordered 7 August 1979. Remotely manned engineering room controlled from the bridge. Painted white.

ZEUS *4/1991, Giorgio Arra*

1 NEPTUNE CLASS: CABLE REPAIRING SHIP (ARC)

Name	*No*	*Builders*	*Commissioned*	*F/S*
ALBERT J MYER	T-ARC 6	Pusey & Jones Corp, Wilmington, Del	13 May 1963	TPA

Displacement, tons: 8500 full load
Dimensions, feet (metres): 369 × 47 × 27 *(112.5 × 14.3 × 8.2)*
Main machinery: Diesel-electric; 4 GE diesel generators; 2 motors; 4000 hp *(2.98 MW)*; 2 shafts
Speed, knots: 14. **Range, miles:** 10 000 at 13 kts
Complement: 92 civilian (16 officers, 18 scientists)
Radars: Navigation: RM 1650/6X *(Myer)*; I band.

Comment: Built as an S3-S2-BP1 type cable ship for the Maritime Administration. *Albert J Myer* acquired from US Army on 18 September 1963. Fitted with electric cable handling machinery (in place of steam equipment) and precision navigation equipment. Rebuilt at Bethlehem Steel Co, Key Highway Division, Baltimore from March 1978 to May 1980. Modernisation included stripping the superstructure down to the main deck, gutting the hull, replacing the entire propulsion system, the wiring and piping and replacing the decks and superstructure with aluminium where possible. Sister ship *Neptune* in reserve from October 1991.

ALBERT J MYER *4/1990, Giorgio Arra*

7 POWHATAN CLASS: FLEET OCEAN TUGS (ATF)

Name	*No*	*Laid down*	*Completed*	*F/S*
POWHATAN	T-ATF 166	30 Sep 1976	15 June 1979	TAA
NARRAGANSETT	T-ATF 167	5 May 1977	9 Nov 1979	TPA
CATAWBA	T-ATF 168	14 Dec 1977	28 May 1980	TPA
NAVAJO	T-ATF 169	14 Dec 1977	13 June 1980	TPA
MOHAWK	T-ATF 170	22 Mar 1979	16 Oct 1980	TAA
SIOUX	T-ATF 171	22 Mar 1979	1 May 1981	TPA
APACHE	T-ATF 172	22 Mar 1979	30 July 1981	TAA

Displacement, tons: 2260 full load
Dimensions, feet (metres): 240.2 × 42 × 15 *(73.2 × 12.8 × 4.6)*
Main machinery: 2 GM EMD 20-645 F7B diesels; 7200 hp *(5.37 MW)* sustained; 2 shafts; Kort nozzles (except in *Powhatan* and one other); cp props; bow thruster; 300 hp *(224 kW)*
Speed, knots: 14.5. **Range, miles:** 10 000 at 13 kts
Complement: 23 (17 civilians, 6 naval communications technicians)
Guns: Space provided to fit 2—20 mm and 2—12.7 mm MGs in war.

Comment: Built at Marinette Marine Corp, Wisconsin patterned after commercial off-shore supply ship design. Originally intended as successors to the Cherokee and Abnaki class ATFs. However, procurement was halted at seven ships with no more planned. All transferred to MSC upon completion. 10 ton capacity crane and a bollard pull of at least 54 tons. A 'deck grid' is fitted aft which contains 1 in bolt receptacles spaced 24 in apart. This allows for the bolting down of a wide variety of portable equipment. There are two GPH fire-pumps supplying three fire monitors with up to 2200 gallons of foam per minute. A deep module can be embarked to support naval salvage teams.

POWHATAN *6/1991, Giorgio Arra*

AUXILIARY SEALIFT SHIPS: READY RESERVE FORCE (RRF)

Note: Due to the lack of sealift capability within the US Navy and US Merchant Marine, a programme was initiated in the 1980s to establish a Ready Reserve Force (RRF) of ships that could be made available for military sealift operations without disrupting routine commerce. Included are roll-on/roll-off, break bulk, LASH, and combination cargo ships, oilers, troop transports, and auxiliary crane ships. Most of these are normally maintained in a laid-up status at three principal main sites: James River, VA (East); Beaumont, TX (Gulf); and Suisun Bay, CA (West). Several are maintained and operated in other ports including Quonset Point, RI; San Pedro, CA; and Portland, OR. The responsibility for their maintenance and upkeep was transferred from the Military Sealift Command to the Maritime Administration in FY 1989, but they remain under the operational control of MSC. 79 RRF ships were activated for the war with Iraq and at the beginning of 1992 many were still involved in returning equipment. MSC hopes to be able to increase the numbers of Ro-Ros by purchasing such ships through MARAD. MARAD's first attempt in 1992 ended in failure when prices for several Ro-Ros were deemed too high and were rejected. The long-range ship goal for the RRF was 142 by FY 1999, but this seems likely to be cut back.

RRF ships have red, white and blue funnel markings and all have additional navigation and communications equipment fitted.

JAMES RIVER, VIRGINIA (EAST)

Freighters

TAK 285	Southern Cross
TAK 1014	Cape Nome
TAK 5005	Adventurer
TAK 5006	Aide
TAK 5007	Ambassador
TAK 5008	Banner
TAK 5009	Cape Ann
TAK 5010	Cape Alexander
TAK 5011	Cape Archway
TAK 5012	Cape Alava
TAK 5013	Cape Avinof
TAK 5015	Agent
TAK 5016	Lake
TAK 5017	Pride
TAK 5018	Scan
TAK 5019	Courier
TAK 5037	Cape Canso
TAK 5040	Cape Canaveral
TAK 5042	Cape Carthage
TAK 5043	Cape Catoche
TAK 5075	Cape Johnson
TAK 5077	Cape Juby
TAKR 1001	Admiral Callaghan
TAKR 5052	Cape Douglas
TAKR 5053	Cape Domingo
TAKR 5054	Cape Decision
TAKR 5055	Cape Diamond
TAKR 5065	Cape Mohican
TAKR 5066	Cape Hudson
TAKR 5067	Cape Henry
TAKR 5077	Cape Lambert
TAKR 5078	Cape Lobos

Crane Ships

TACS 1	Keystone State
TACS 4	Gopher State
TACS 5	Flickertail State
TACS 6	Cornhusker State
TACS 9	Green Mountain State

Transport

TAP 1000	Patriot State
TAP 1001	Empire State

BEAUMONT, TEXAS (GULF)

Seatrain Ships

TAK 5020	Washington
TAK 5021	Maine

Tankers

TAOT 165	American Explorer
TAOT 169	Mount Washington
TAOT 181	Potomac
TAOT 1012	Mission Buenaventura
TAOT 5005	Mission Capistrano
TAOT 5075	American Osprey
TAOT 5083	Mount Vernon

Crane Ships

TACS 7	Diamond State
TACS 8	Equality State

Freighters

TAK 2016	Pioneer Commander
TAK 2018	Pioneer Contractor
TAK 2019	Pioneer Crusader
TAK 2033	Buyer
TAK 2035	Gulf Shipper
TAK 2036	Gulf Trader
TAK 5022	Santa Ana
TAK 5026	Del Viento
TAK 5036	Cape Chalmers
TAK 5038	Cape Charles
TAK 5039	Cape Clear
TAK 5041	Cape Cod
TAK 5044	Gulf Banker

BEAUMONT, TEXAS (GULF)

Freighters

TAK 5045	Gulf Farmer
TAK 5046	Gulf Merchant
TAK 5049	Del Monte
TAK 5050	Del Valle
TAK 5063	Cape May
TAK 5064	Cape Mendocino
TAK 5070	Cape Flattery
TAK 5071	Cape Florida
TAK 5073	Cape Farewell
TAK 5074	Cape Catawba
TAK 5076	Cape Inscription

SUISUN BAY (WEST)

Tanker

TAOT 151	Shoshone

Gasoline Tankers

TAOG 78	Nodaway
TAOG 81	Alatna
TAOG 82	Chattahoochee

Crane Ships

TACS 2	Gem State
TACS 3	Grand Canyon State

Freighters

TAKR 7	Comet
TAKR 9	Meteor
TAKR 11	Jupiter
TAKR 284	Northern Light
TAK 5029	California
TAK 2039	Cape Girardeau
TAK 5051	Cape Gibson
TAK 5057	Cape Bover
TAK 5058	Cape Borda
TAK 5059	Cape Bon
TAK 5060	Cape Blanco
TAK 5061	Austral Lightning
TAK 5084	Chesapeake
TAKR 5051	Cape Ducato
TAKR 5056	Cape Breton
TAKR 5062	Cape Isabel
TAKR 5068	Cape Horn
TAKR 5069	Cape Edmont

AIDE *7/1991, 92 Wing RAAF*

CAPE MOHICAN *1/1991, van Ginderen Collection*

WASHINGTON *8/1990, Giorgio Arra*

CAPE DECISION *1/1992, 92 Wing RAAF*

AFLOAT PREPOSITIONING FORCE

Note: In order to improve US capability to deploy its forces rapidly to any area of conflict, and especially to South-West Asia, and to enhance the readiness of existing forces, the Carter Administration created a force comprising elements of all three services and named it the Rapid Deployment Joint Task Force (RDJTF). Initially composed of seven Military Sealift Command ships, it was first deployed to Diego Garcia in July 1980. For a time it was expanded to 17 ships; it carried tactical equipment, ammunition, POL, and supplies to sustain combat operations until reinforcements could be shipped from the USA. Thirteen ships were converted or built as part of the Maritime Prepositioning Ship programme (MPS) (see following section), and one five-ship squadron of MPS ships was based at Diego Garcia in 1985. On 7 August 1990, the PREPO force consisted of 11 ships. All 11 of these were deployed to Saudi Arabia when the military reinforcement began and were among the first arrivals in the build-up of American forces. Several are also being used in other roles in 1992 to enable MSC to meet its worldwide sealift responsibilities.

PREPOSITIONING SHIPS (PREPO)

Note: As of January 1992, the following PREPO ships were deployed:

Green Island (TAK 1015)	*Potomac* (TAOT 181)
American Cormorant (TAK 2062)	*Green Harbour* (TAK 2064)
American Kestrel (TAK 2043)	*Austral Rainbow* (TAK 2046)
MV Advantage (TAK 2040)	*MV Noble Star* (TAK 5076)

Comment: The PREPO ships carry Army, Navy and Air Force equipment and supplies. Commander, Maritime Prepositioning Ships Squadron Two controls the MPS and PREPO ships at Diego Garcia and Commander, MSC, South East Asia, controls MPS ships at Subic Bay. Commander, MSC, Mediterranean controls the PREPO ship *Advantage*. *Noble Star* carries a fleet hospital. In addition a number of tankers shuttle in and out of the force and are therefore not listed. In early 1992 these included *Patriot* and *Richard Gianella*, and *Sealift China Sea* from the MSC.

2 LASH TYPE: CARGO SHIPS, BARGE (AKB)

Name	*No*	*Builders*	*Completed*	*F/S*
GREEN ISLAND	T-AK 1015	Avondale Shipyards	Feb 1975	PREPO
GREEN HARBOUR	T-AK 2064	Avondale Shipyards	Feb 1974	PREPO

Displacement, tons: 62 314 full load
Measurement, tons: 32 278 gross; 46 152 dwt
Dimensions, feet (metres): 893.3 × 100 × 60 *(272.3 × 30.5 × 18.3)*
Main machinery: 2 Combustion Engineering boilers; 1100 psi *(77.3 kg/cm sq)*; 2 De Laval turbines; 32 000 hp *(23.9 MW)*; 1 shaft
Speed, knots: 22. **Range, miles:** 15 000 at 20 kts
Complement: 32
Cargo capacity: 1 691 500 cu ft (in 85 bales)

Comment: *Green Island* acquired on 17 September 1982 and *Green Harbour* 20 October 1985 for assignment in APF. Stationed at Diego Garcia. Owned and operated by Central Gulf Lines.

GREEN ISLAND *7/1991, van Ginderen Collection*

2 LASH TYPE: CARGO SHIPS, BARGE (AKB)

Name	*No*	*Builders*	*Completed*	*F/S*
AUSTRAL RAINBOW (ex-*American Veteran*)	TAK 2046	Avondale Shipyards	1972	PREPO
AMERICAN KESTREL	TAK 2043	Avondale Shipyards	1974	PREPO

Measurement, tons: 26 406 gross; 39 277 dwt
Dimensions, feet (metres): 820 × 100 × 40.7 *(249.9 × 30.4 × 12.4)*
Speed, knots: 19+
Complement: 33
Cargo capacity: 1 663 248 cu ft (77 bales)

Comment: *Austral Rainbow* re-acquired 26 May 1987 for assignment to PREPO force. Owned and operated by Farrell Lines and stationed at Diego Garcia. *American Kestrel* acquired 20 June 1988 and assigned to PREPO force in December 1988. Owned by American Automar and operated by Pacific Gulf Marine. Stationed at Diego Garcia.

1 FLOAT-ON/FLOAT-OFF TYPE CARGO SHIP, SEMI-SUBMERSIBLE (AKF)

Name	*No*	*Builders*	*Completed*	*F/S*
AMERICAN CORMORANT (ex-*Ferncarrier*)	T-AK 2062	Eriksbergs Mekaniska Verkstads AB	Sep 1974	PREPO

Displacement, tons: 69 555 full load
Measurement, tons: 10 196 gross; 47 230 dwt
Dimensions, feet (metres): 738 × 135 × 35.1 *(225 × 41.1 × 10.7)*
Main machinery: 1 Eriksberg/Burmeister & Wain 10K84 EF diesel; 19 900 hp(m) *(14.6 MW)*; 1 shaft; 2 thrusters; 3000 hp(m) *(2.2 MW)*
Speed, knots: 16. **Range, miles:** 23 700 at 13 kts
Complement: 21
Cargo capacity: 10 000 barrels of fuel; 44 000 tons deck cargo

Comment: Converted in 1982. Acquired on time charter 25 November 1985 and assigned to Diego Garcia Maritime PREPO ship squadron two. Owned by American Automar and operated by Pacific Gulf Marine. Cargo includes Army watercraft and port support equipment. Rated as a heavy lift ship.

AMERICAN CORMORANT *8/1989, W. Sartori*

1 TANKER TYPE: TRANSPORT OILER (AOT)

Name	*No*	*Builders*	*Commissioned*	*F/S*
POTOMAC	TAOT 181	Sun Shipbuilding	Jan 1957	PREPO

Displacement, tons: 34 700 full load
Dimensions, feet (metres): 614.5 × 83.5 × 33.7 *(187.3 × 25.5 × 10.3)*
Main machinery: 2 boilers; 2 turbines; 20 460 hp *(15.3 MW)*; 2 shafts
Speed, knots: 18
Complement: 49
Cargo capacity: 1 069 700 cu ft liquids; 30 400 cu ft solids

Comment: Acquired in 1991.

1 C5 NOMINAL TYPE: CARGO SHIP (AK)

Name	*No*	*Builders*	*Completed*	*F/S*
MV ADVANTAGE	T-AK 2040	Nippon Kokan, TSU, Shipyard	1977	PREPO

Measurement, tons: 18 998 gross; 27 807 dwt
Dimensions, feet (metres): 561.1 × 86.2 × 38.3 *(171 × 26.3 × 11.5)*
Main machinery: 1 AHJ/Sulzer diesel, 12 600 hp(m) *(9.26 MW)*; 1 shaft
Speed, knots: 17
Complement: 22

Comment: *MV Advantage* acquired on time charter in October 1988 and assigned to PREPO force in November 1988. Stationed in the Mediterranean. Owned by American Automar in conjunction with Red Rivers Carriers, Inc.

1 FLEET HOSPITAL CARGO SHIP (AK)

Name	*No*	*Builders*	*Completed*	*F/S*
MV NOBLE STAR	T-AK 5076	Kaldnes, Norway	1977	PREPO

Displacement, tons: 32 403 full load
Dimensions, feet (metres): 562 × 83 × 32 *(171.3 × 25.3 × 9.7)*
Main machinery: 1 diesel; 1 shaft
Speed, knots: 18. **Range, miles:** 28 000 at 16 kts
Complement: 22
Cargo capacity: 1 085 403 cu ft

Comment: Time chartered from Sealift Inc. Stationed at Diego Garcia from late 1989.

1 TRANSPORT OILER (AOT)

Comment: The Military Sealift Command regularly assigns one Sealift class oiler to the PREPO force on a rotating basis. USNS *Sealift China Sea* (TAOT 170) was assigned in 1992. Ships of this class are operated by a civilian contractor. Details in MSC section.

MARITIME PREPOSITIONING SHIP (MPS) PROGRAMME

Note: (a) The Navy has been able to achieve a notable increase in its lift capability by the construction of five ships and the conversion of eight others. These are now divided into three squadrons, each of which contains the equipment for one Marine Expeditionary Brigade (MEB). Lift capability also can be augmented by the eight Algol class fast logistics ships. These amphibious elements are supported by two maintenance aviation support ships, nine crane ships and two hospital ships. The maintenance aviation support ships and the hospital ships are maintained in a reduced operating status and the crane ships as a part of the Ready Reserve Force. All but four crane ships were activated for the war with Iraq.
(b) MPS Squadron 1 supports No 6 Marine Expeditionary Brigade in Eastern Atlantic and Squadron 2 supports No 7 MEB at Diego Garcia. Squadron 3 supports No 1 MEB in the Central Pacific. Permanent squadron staff of 57 officers and 133 men. MPS Squadrons 2 and 3 were the first ships to arrive in Saudi Arabia in the build up to the war with Iraq in 1991. Squadron 1 joined in later.

3 SGT MATEJ KOCAK CLASS: VEHICLE CARGO SHIPS (T-AK)

Name	*No*	*Builders*	*Completed*	*F/S*
SGT MATEJ KOCAK (ex-SS *John B Waterman*)	T-AK 3005	Pennsylvania SB Co, Chester, Pa	Mar 1981	Sqn 1
PFC EUGENE A OBREGON (ex-SS *Thomas Heywood*)	T-AK 3006	Pennsylvania SB Co, Chester, Pa	Nov 1982	Sqn 1
MAJ STEPHEN W PLESS (ex-SS *Charles Carroll*)	T-AK 3007	General Dynamics Corp, Quincy, Mass	Mar 1983	Sqn 1

Displacement, tons: 48 754 full load
Dimensions, feet (metres): 821 × 105.6 × 32.3 *(250.2 × 32.2 × 9.8)*
Main machinery: 2 boilers; 2 GE turbines; 30 000 hp *(22.4 MW)*; 1 shaft
Speed, knots: 20. **Range, miles:** 13 000 at 20 kts
Complement: 39 plus 25 technicians
Cargo capacity: Containers, 532; Ro-ro, 152 236 sq ft; JP-5 bbls, 20 290; DF-2 bbls, 12 355; Mogas bbls, 3717; stable water, 2189; cranes, 2 twin 50 ton and 1—30 ton gantry
Helicopters: Platform only.

Comment: Converted from three Waterman Line ships by National Steel and Shipbuilding, San Diego. Delivery dates T-AK 3005, 1 October 1984; T-AK 3006, 16 January 1985; T-AK 3007, 15 May 1985. Conversion work included the addition of 157 ft *(47.9 m)* amidships.

MATEJ KOCAK *6/1991, Giorgio Arra*

8 ALGOL CLASS: VEHICLE CARGO SHIPS (T-AKR)

Name	*No*	*Builders*	*Delivered*
ALGOL (ex-SS *Sea-Land Exchange*)	T-AKR 287	Rotterdamsche DD Mij NV, Rotterdam	7 May 1973
BELLATRIX (ex-SS *Sea-Land Trade*)	T-AKR 288	Rheinstahl Nordseewerke, Emden, West Germany	6 Apr 1973
DENEBOLA (ex-SS *Sea-Land Resource*)	T-AKR 289	Rotterdamsche DD Mij NV, Rotterdam	4 Dec 1973
POLLUX (ex-SS *Sea-Land Market*)	T-AKR 290	A G Weser, Bremen, West Germany	20 Sep 1973
ALTAIR (ex-SS *Sea-Land Finance*)	T-AKR 291	Rheinstahl Nordseewerke, Emden, West Germany	17 Sep 1973
REGULUS (ex-SS *Sea-Land Commerce*)	T-AKR 292	A G Weser, Bremen, West Germany	30 Mar 1973
CAPELLA (ex-SS *Sea-Land McLean*)	T-AKR 293	Rotterdamsche DD Mij NV, Rotterdam	4 Oct 1972
ANTARES (ex-SS *Sea-Land Galloway*)	T-AKR 294	A G Weser, Bremen, West Germany	27 Sep 1972

Displacement, tons: 55 355 full load
Measurement, tons: 25 389 net; 27 051-28 095 dwt
Dimensions, feet (metres): 946.2 × 106 × 34.8 *(288.4 × 32.3 × 10.6)*
Main machinery: 2 Foster-Wheeler boilers; 875 psi *(61.6 kg/cm sq)*; 950°F *(510°C)*; 2 GE MST-19 steam turbines; 120 000 hp *(89.5 MW)*; 2 shafts
Speed, knots: 30. **Range, miles:** 12 200 at 27 kts
Complement: 42 (as merchant ship); 24 (minimum)
Helicopters: Platform only.

Comment: All originally built as container-ships for Sea-Land Services Inc, Port Elizabeth, New Jersey but reported as using too much fuel to be cost effective as merchant ships. Six ships of this class were approved for acquisition in FY 1981 and the remaining two in FY 1982. The purchase price included 4000 containers and 800 container chassis for use in container ship configuration. All eight converted to Vehicle Cargo Ships (AKR). Conversion included the addition of roll-on/roll-off features. The area between the forward and after superstructures allows for a helicopter flight deck and hangar. The capacities are as follows: (square feet) enclosed roll-on/roll-off and helo hangar 114 000—128 000, flight deck 32 000 and light vehicle roll-on/roll-off aft 17 500. In addition to one roll-on/roll-off ramp port and starboard, twin 35-ton pedestal cranes are installed between the deckhouses and twin 50-ton cranes are installed aft to facilitate lift-on/lift-off cargo operations. 93 per cent of an army mechanised division can be lifted using all eight ships.
Seven of the class (*Antares* broke down) moved some 13 per cent of all cargo transported between the US and Saudi Arabia for the war with Iraq in 1991, at an average speed of 26 kts. All are based in Atlantic and Gulf of Mexico ports. They will probably be augmented by 25 kt diesel propelled ships which will be cheaper to build and maintain.

BELLATRIX *8/1991, Foto Flite*

5 CPL LOUIS J HAUGE, JR CLASS: VEHICLE CARGO SHIPS (T-AK)

Name	*No*	*Builders*	*Completed*	*F/S*
CPL LOUIS J HAUGE, JR (ex-MV *Estelle Maersk*)	T-AK 3000	Odense Staalskibsvaerft A/S, Lindo	Oct 1979	Sqn 2
PFC WILLIAM B BAUGH (ex-MV *Eleo Maersk*)	T-AK 3001	Odense Staalskibsvaerft A/S, Lindo	Apr 1979	Sqn 2
PFC JAMES ANDERSON, JR (ex-MV *Emma Maersk*)	T-AK 3002	Odense Staalskibsvaerft A/S, Lindo	July 1979	Sqn 2
1st LT ALEX BONNYMAN (ex-MV *Emilie Maersk*)	T-AK 3003	Odense Staalskibsvaerft A/S, Lindo	Jan 1980	Sqn 2
PVT HARRY FISHER (ex-MV *Evelyn Maersk*)	T-AK 3004	Odense Staalskibsvaerft A/S, Lindo	Apr 1980	Sqn 2

Displacement, tons: 46 552 full load
Dimensions, feet (metres): 755 × 90 × 37.1 *(230 × 27.4 × 11.3)*
Main machinery: 1 Sulzer 7RND 76M diesel; 16 800 hp(m) *(12.35 MW)*; 1 shaft
Speed, knots: 17.5. **Range, miles:** 10 800 at 16 kts
Complement: 27 plus 30 technicians
Cargo capacity: Containers, 361; Ro-ro, 121 595 sq ft; JP-5 bbls, 17 128; DF-2 bbls, 10 642; Mogas bbls, 3865; stable water, 2022; cranes, 3 twin 30 ton; 92 831 cu ft breakbulk
Helicopters: Platform only.

Comment: Converted from five Maersk Line ships by Bethlehem Steel, Sparrow Point, MD; T-AK 3000, 3002 and 3004 delivered 7 September 1984, 26 March 1985 and 24 September 1985 respectively and by Bethlehem Steel, Beaumont, TX; T-AK 3001 and 3003 delivered 12 September 1985 and 30 October 1985 respectively. Conversion work included the addition of 157 ft *(47.9 m)* amidships.

LOUIS J HAUGE *1/1991, van Ginderen Collection*

5 2nd LT JOHN P BOBO CLASS: VEHICLE CARGO SHIPS (T-AK)

Name	*No*	*Builders*	*Completed*	*F/S*
2nd LT JOHN P BOBO	T-AK 3008	General Dynamics Corp, Quincy, Mass	14 Feb 1985	Sqn 1
PFC DEWAYNE T WILLIAMS	T-AK 3009	General Dynamics Corp, Quincy, Mass	6 June 1985	Sqn 3
1st LT BALDOMERO LOPEZ	T-AK 3010	General Dynamics Corp, Quincy, Mass	20 Nov 1985	Sqn 3
1st LT JACK LUMMUS	T-AK 3011	General Dynamics Corp, Quincy, Mass	6 Mar 1986	Sqn 3
SGT WILLIAM R BUTTON	T-AK 3012	General Dynamics Corp, Quincy, Mass	27 May 1986	Sqn 3

Displacement, tons: 44 330 full load
Dimensions, feet (metres): 675.2 × 105.5 × 29.6 *(205.8 × 32.2 × 9)*
Main machinery: 2 Stork Werkspoor 16 TM 410 diesels; 27 000 hp(m) *(19.84 MW)* sustained; 1 shaft; bow thruster; 1000 hp *(746 kW)*
Speed, knots: 18. **Range, miles:** 12 840 at 18 kts
Complement: 30 plus 25 technicians
Cargo capacity: Containers, 530; Ro-ro, 152 185 sq ft; JP-5 bbls, 20 776; DF-2 bbls, 13 334; Mogas bbls, 4880; stable water, 2357; cranes, 1 single and 2 twin 39 ton
Helicopters: Platform only.

Comment: Operated by American Overseas Marine on a long charter. Each ship is capable of carrying 25 per cent of the equipment needed to support a Marine Expeditionary Brigade.

JACK LUMMUS *9/1991, Giorgio Arra*

2 T-AVB 3 CLASS: MAINTENANCE AVIATION/SUPPORT SHIPS (T-AVB)

Name	*No*	*Builders*	*Completed*
WRIGHT (ex-SS *Young America*)	T-AVB 3	Ingalls SB Corp, Pascagoula, Miss	1970
CURTISS (ex-SS *Great Republic*)	T-AVB 4	Ingalls SB Corp, Pascagoula, Miss	1969

Displacement, tons: 23 872 full load
Measurement, tons: 11 757 gross; 6850 net; 15 946 dwt
Dimensions, feet (metres): 602 × 90.2 × 29.8 *(183.5 × 27.5 × 9.1)*
Main machinery: 2 Combustion Engineering boilers; 2 GE turbines; 30 000 hp *(22.4 MW)*; 1 shaft
Speed, knots: 23. **Range, miles:** 9000 at 22 kts
Complement: 41 crew and 1 Aircraft Maintenance Detachment totalling 366 men

Comment: To further reinforce the capabilities of the Maritime Prepositioning Ship programme, conversion of two ro-ro ships into maintenance aviation support ships was approved in FY 1985 and FY 1986. *Wright* was completed 14 May 1986, *Curtiss* 18 August 1987. Both conversions took place at Todd Shipyards, Galveston, Texas. Each ship has side ports and three decks aft of the bridge superstructure and has the capability to load the vans and equipment of a Marine Aviation Intermediate Maintenance Activity. The ships' mission is to service aircraft until their containerised units can be offloaded. They can then revert to a standard sealift role if required. Maritime Administration hull design is C5-S-78a.

WRIGHT *10/1991, 92 Wing RAAF*

9 KEYSTONE STATE CLASS: AUXILIARY CRANE SHIPS (T-ACS)

Name	*No*	*Builders*	*Conversion Completed*
KEYSTONE STATE (ex-SS *President Harrison*)	T-ACS 1	Defoe SB Co, Bay City	1984
GEM STATE (ex-SS *President Monroe*)	T-ACS 2	Defoe SB Co, Bay City	1985
GRAND CANYON STATE (ex-SS *President Polk*)	T-ACS 3	Dillingham S R, Portland	1986
GOPHER STATE (ex-*Export Leader*)	T-ACS 4	Norshipco, Norfolk	Oct 1987
FLICKERTAIL STATE (ex-*Export Lightning*)	T-ACS 5	Norshipco, Norfolk	Dec 1987
CORNHUSKER STATE (ex-*Staghound*)	T-ACS 6	Norshipco, Norfolk	Mar 1988
DIAMOND STATE (ex-*President Truman*)	T-ACS 7	Tampa SY	Jan 1989
EQUALITY STATE (ex-*American Banker*)	T-ACS 8	Tampa SY	May 1989
GREEN MOUNTAIN STATE (ex-*American Altair*)	T-ACS 9	Norshipco, Norfolk	Sep 1990

Displacement, tons: 31 500 full load
Dimensions, feet (metres): 668.6 × 76.1 × 33.5 *(203.8 × 23.2 × 10.2)*
Main machinery: 2 boilers; 2 GE turbines; 19 250 hp *(14.4 MW)*; 1 shaft
Speed, knots: 20. **Range, miles:** 13 000 at 20 kts
Complement: 89
Cargo capacity: 300+ standard containers

Comment: Auxiliary crane ships are container ships to which have been added up to three twin boom pedestal cranes which will lift containerised or other cargo from itself or adjacent vessels and deposit it on a pier or into lighterage. Since a significant portion of the US merchant fleet is composed of non-self sustaining container ships lacking integral cranes, thus needing a fully developed port to unload, a requirement exists for crane ships that can unload others in areas of the world which have very simple, damaged or no developed port facilities. Funds provided in the FY 1988 budget for conversion of T-ACS 9 and 10 were transferred to other Navy SCN accounts. Funding for T-ACS 9 was then taken from Maritime Administration budgets. The 10th ship was cancelled in 1991. There are minor dimensional differences between some of the class. Five of the ships were deployed to the Gulf in 1990-91 but the excellent Saudi harbour facilities meant that dockside cranes were available to unload cargoes, so their particular talents were not required other than as standard cargo ships.

DIAMOND STATE *5/1991, 92 Wing RAAF*

DEEP SUBMERGENCE VEHICLES

(Included in US Naval Vessel Register)

Note: The US Navy acquired its first deep submergence vehicle with the purchase in 1958 of the bathyscope *Trieste*, designed and constructed by Professor Auguste Piccard.

Trieste reached a record depth of 35 800 ft *(10 910 m)* in the Challenger Deep off the Marianas on 23 January 1960, being piloted by Lieutenant Don Walsh, USN, and Jacques Piccard (son of Auguste). Rebuilt and designated *Trieste II*. Transferred to Naval museum of Underwater Warfare, Keyport Washington.
After the loss of *Thresher* (SSN 593) in 1963 the US Navy initiated an extensive deep submergence programme that led to construction of two Deep Submergence Rescue Vehicles (DSRV). Several of these deep submergence vehicles and other craft and support ships are operated by Submarine Development Group One at San Diego, California. The Group is a major operational command that includes advanced diving equipment; divers trained in 'saturation' techniques; the DSVs *Turtle, Sea Cliff*, DSRV-1, DSRV-2; the submarine *Dolphin* (AGSS 555); several submarine rescue ships. Two unmanned vessels CURV (Cable Controlled Underwater Remote Vehicle) and ATV (Advanced Tethered Vehicle) made test dives to 20 000 ft *(1800 m)* in late 1990.

1 NUCLEAR-POWERED OCEAN ENGINEERING AND RESEARCH VEHICLE

Name	*Builders*	*Commissioned*	*F/S*
NR 1	General Dynamics (Electric Boat Div)	27 Oct 1969	ASA

Displacement, tons: 372 surfaced; 700 dived
Dimensions, feet (metres): 136.4 × 12.4 × 14.6 *(41.6 × 3.8 × 4.5)*
Main machinery: Nuclear; 1 PWR; 1 turbo-alternator; 2 motors (external to the hull); 2 props; 4 ducted thrusters (2 vertical, 2 horizontal)
Complement: 7 (2 officers, 2 scientists)

Comment: NR 1 was built primarily to serve as a test platform for a small nuclear propulsion plant; however, the craft additionally provides an advanced deep submergence ocean engineering and research capability. She was the only Naval deep submergence vehicle to be used in the recovery of the wreckage of the space shuttle *Challenger* January-April 1986.
Laid down on 10 June 1967; launched on 25 January 1969. Commanded by an officer-in-charge vice commanding officer. First nuclear-propelled service craft. Being refitted with a new bow which will extend her length by about 10ft, and new sonars and cameras.
The NR 1 is fitted with wheels beneath the hull to permit 'bottom crawling' and she is fitted with external lights, external television cameras, a remote-controlled manipulator, and various recovery devices. No periscopes, but fixed television mast. Diving depth, 2600 ft *(800 m)*. A surface 'mother' ship is required to support her.

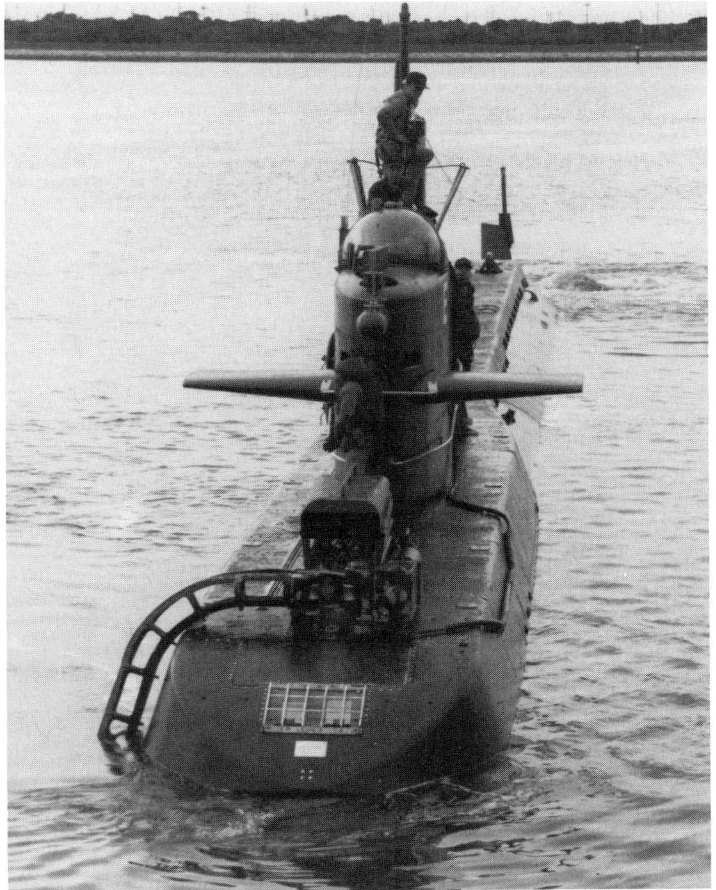

NR 1 — *1986, US Navy*

1 DEEP SUBMERGENCE VEHICLE: ALVIN TYPE

Name	*No*	*Builders*	*F/S*
ALVIN	DSV 2	General Mills Inc, Minneapolis, Minn	PSA

Displacement, tons: 18
Dimensions, feet (metres): 22.5 × 8.5 *(6.9 × 2.6)*
Main machinery: 6 brushless DC motors; 6 thrusters; 2 vertical-motion thrusters (located near the centre of gravity); 2 horizontally (near stern) (1 directed athwartships, 1 directed longitudinally); 2 on rotatable shaft near stern for vertical or longitudinal motion
Speed, knots: 1.5. **Range, miles:** 6-10 at 1 kt
Complement: 3 (1 pilot, 2 observers)

Comment: *Alvin* was built for operation by the Woods Hole Oceanographic Institution for the Office of Naval Research. Original configuration had an operating depth of 6000 ft. Named for Allyn C Vine of Woods Hole Oceanographic Institution. *Alvin* accidentally sank in 5051 ft of water on 16 October 1968; subsequently raised in August 1969; refurbished 1970-71 in original configuration. Placed in service on Navy List 1 June 1971. Subsequently refitted with titanium pressure sphere to provide increased depth capability and again operational in November 1973. Currently leased to Wood's Hole. She has three banks of lead acid batteries, 120 and 30 volt DC systems with 72 KHW capacity. Operating depth, 4000 m *(13 120 ft)*.

2 DEEP SUBMERGENCE RESCUE VEHICLES

Name	*No*	*Builders*	*Commissioned*	*F/S*
MYSTIC	DSRV 1	Lockheed Missiles and Space Co,	7 Aug 1971	PSA
AVALON	DSRV 2	Sunnyvale, Calif	28 July 1972	ASA

Displacement, tons: 30 surfaced; 38 dived
Dimensions, feet (metres): 49.2 × 8 *(15 × 2.4)*
Main machinery: Electric motors; silver/zinc batteries; 1 prop (movable control shroud); 4 ducted thrusters (2 fwd, 2 aft)
Speed, knots: 4. **Range, miles:** 24 at 3 kts
Complement: 4 (pilot, co-pilot, 2 rescue sphere operators) plus 24 rescued men
Sonars: Search and navigational sonar, and closed-circuit television (supplemented by optical devices) are installed in the DSRV to determine the exact location of a disabled submarine within a given area and for pinpointing the submarine's escape hatches. Side-looking sonar can be fitted for search missions.

Comment: The DSRV is intended to provide a quick-reaction world-wide, all-weather capability for the rescue of survivors in a disabled submarine. Transportable by road, aircraft (in C141 and C 5 jet cargo aircraft), surface ship (on Pigeon ASR 21 class submarine rescue ships), and specially modified SSNs.
The carrying submarine will launch and recover the DSRV while submerged and, if necessary, while under ice. A total of six DSRVs were planned, but only two were funded. They alternate their duties every two months.
The outer hull is constructed of formed fibreglass. Within this outer hull are three interconnected spheres which form the main pressure capsule. Each sphere is 7.5 ft in diameter and is constructed of HY-140 steel. The forward sphere contains the vehicle's control equipment and is manned by the pilot and co-pilot, the centre and after spheres accommodate 24 passengers and a third crewman. Under the DSRV's centre sphere is a hemispherical protrusion or 'skirt' which seals over the disabled submarine's hatch. During the mating operation the skirt is pumped dry to enable personnel to transfer. Operating depth, 1525 m *(5000 ft)*. Names are not 'official'. Both are due to receive more modern electronics and navigation systems.

AVALON — *12/1985, Giorgio Arra*

2 DEEP SUBMERGENCE VEHICLES: MODIFIED ALVIN TYPE

Name	*No*	*Builders*	*F/S*
TURTLE (ex-*Autec II*)	DSV 3	General Dynamics (Electric Boat Div)	PA
SEA CLIFF (ex-*Autec I*)	DSV 4	General Dynamics (Electric Boat Div)	PSA

Displacement, tons: 25 (DSV 3); 30 (DSV 4)
Dimensions, feet (metres): 26 × 10 *(7.9 × 3.1)* (DSV 3); 31 × 12 *(9.5 × 3.7)* (DSV 4)
Main machinery: Electric motors; 1 prop (trainable); 2 thrusters (trainable)
Speed, knots: 2.5. **Range, miles:** 24 at 2 kts
Complement: 3 (pilot, co-pilot, observer)

Comment: Intended for deep submergence research and work tasks. Launched on 11 December 1968 and commissioned on 1 June 1971. In 1979-80 *Turtle* was overhauled and upgraded for operations to 10 000 feet. In 1983-84 *Sea Cliff* provided with titanium sphere giving a depth capability of 20 000 feet. *Sea Cliff* reached a depth of 20 000 feet 10 March 1985. Three pressure spheres were fabricated for the Alvin submersible programme, one for installation in *Alvin*, a spare, and one for testing. The second and third spheres subsequently were allocated to these later submersibles. Twin-arm manipulator fitted. Silver/zinc batteries. Operating depth 3050 m *(10 000 ft)* for DSV 3 and 6100 m *(20 000 ft)* for DSV 4. Mother ship is the *Laney Chouest*.

TURTLE — *7/1988, W. Donko*

LANEY CHOUEST (tender) — *5/1991, Stefan Terzibaschitsch*

COAST GUARD

Senior Officers

Commandant:
Admiral J William Kime
Vice-Commandant:
Vice Admiral Martin H Daniell
Chief of Staff:
Rear Admiral Robert T Nelson
Commander, Atlantic Area:
Vice Admiral Paul A Welling
Commander, Pacific Area:
Vice Admiral A Bruce Beran

Establishment

The United States Coast Guard was established by an Act of Congress approved 28 January 1915, which consolidated the Revenue Cutter Service (founded in 1790) and the Life Saving Service (founded in 1848). The act of establishment stated the Coast Guard "shall be a military service and a branch of the armed forces of the USA at all times. The Coast Guard shall be a service in the Treasury Department except when operating as a service in the Navy".
Congress further legislated that in time of national emergency or when the President so directs, the Coast Guard operates as a part of the Navy. Some ships of the Coast Guard did operate as a part of the Navy during the First and Second World Wars and the Vietnam War.
The Lighthouse Service (founded in 1789) was transferred to the Coast Guard on 1 July 1939 and the Bureau of Navigation and Steamboat Inspection on 28 February 1942.
The Coast Guard was transferred to the newly established Department of Transportation on 1 April 1967.

Missions

The current missions of the Coast Guard are to (1) enforce or assist in the enforcement of applicable Federal laws upon the high seas and waters subject to the jurisdiction of the USA including environmental protection; (2) administer all Federal laws regarding safety of life and property on the high seas and on waters subject to the jurisdiction of the USA, except those laws specifically entrusted to other Federal agencies; (3) develop, establish, maintain, operate, and conduct aids to maritime navigation, ocean stations, icebreaking activities, oceanographic research, and rescue facilities; and (4) maintain a state of readiness to function as a specialised service in the Navy when so directed by the President.

Personnel

1 Jan 1992: 5522 officers, 1501 warrant officers, 29 583 enlisted men, 921 cadets, 165 Public Health Service personnel, 11 857 reserves (1623 officers).

Cutter Strength

All Coast Guard vessels over 65 ft in length and that have adequate crew accommodation are referred to as 'cutters'. All names are preceded by USCG. The first two digits of the hull number for all Coast Guard vessels under 100 ft in length indicates the approximate length overall.
Approximately 2000 standard and non-standard boats are in service ranging in size from 11 ft skiffs to 55 ft aids-to-navigation craft.

Category/Classification		*Active*	*Building*
Cutters			
WHEC	High Endurance Cutters	12	—
WMEC	Medium Endurance Cutters	34	—
Icebreakers			
WAGB	Icebreakers	3	(1)
WTGB	Icebreaking Tugs	9	—
Patrol Craft			
WSES	Surface Effect Craft	3	—
WPB	Patrol Craft, Large	90	—
Training Cutter			
WIX	Training Cutter	1	—
Buoy Tenders			
WLB	Buoy Tenders, Seagoing	27	(1)
WLM	Buoy Tenders, Coastal	11	(1)
WLI	Buoy Tenders, Inland	6	—
WLR	Buoy Tenders, River	18	—
Construction Tenders			
WLIC	Construction Tenders, Inland	16	—
Harbour Tugs			
WYTL	Harbour Tugs, Small	14	—
SAR Craft		2000+	—

DELETIONS

Medium Endurance Cutters

1990 *Clover, Evergreen, Citrus*
1991 *Chilula, Cherokee*

Icebreakers

1989 *Northwind*

Patrol Craft

1989 *Cape Upright, Cape Knox, Cape Henelopen* (Costa Rica), *Cape York, Cape Current, Cape Morgan* (Bahamas), *Cape Romain, Cape Fox* (Bahamas), *Cape Hedge* (Mexico)
1990 *Cape Cross* (Micronesia), *Cape George* (Micronesia), *Cape Carter* (Mexico), *Cape Higgon* (Uruguay), *Cape Horn* (Uruguay)
1991 *Cape Hatteras, Cape Corwin* (Micronesia), *Point Hope, Point Verde, Point Thatcher, Point Herron, Point Roberts, Point Baker, Point Judith, Point Barrow, Point Charles, Point Brown, Point Knoll, Point Harris*

Tenders

1990 *Mesquite, Dogwood, Lantana*
1991 *Fir, Salvia*

HIGH ENDURANCE CUTTERS

12 HAMILTON and HERO CLASSES (WHEC)

Name	*No*	*Builders*	*Laid down*	*Launched*	*Commissioned*	*F/S*
HAMILTON	WHEC 715	Avondale Shipyards Inc, New Orleans, Louisiana	Jan 1965	18 Dec 1965	20 Feb 1967	PA
DALLAS	WHEC 716	Avondale Shipyards Inc, New Orleans, Louisiana	7 Feb 1966	1 Oct 1966	1 Oct 1967	PA
MELLON	WHEC 717	Avondale Shipyards Inc, New Orleans, Louisiana	25 July 1966	11 Feb 1967	22 Dec 1967	PA
CHASE	WHEC 718	Avondale Shipyards Inc, New Orleans, Louisiana	27 Oct 1966	20 May 1967	1 Mar 1968	PA
BOUTWELL	WHEC 719	Avondale Shipyards Inc, New Orleans, Louisiana	5 Dec 1966	17 June 1967	14 June 1968	PA
SHERMAN	WHEC 720	Avondale Shipyards Inc, New Orleans, Louisiana	23 Jan 1967	23 Sep 1967	23 Aug 1968	PA
GALLATIN	WHEC 721	Avondale Shipyards Inc, New Orleans, Louisiana	27 Feb 1967	18 Nov 1967	20 Dec 1968	AA
MORGENTHAU	WHEC 722	Avondale Shipyards Inc, New Orleans, Louisiana	17 July 1967	10 Feb 1968	14 Feb 1969	PA
RUSH	WHEC 723	Avondale Shipyards Inc, New Orleans, Louisiana	23 Oct 1967	16 Nov 1968	3 July 1969	PA
MUNRO	WHEC 724	Avondale Shipyards Inc, New Orleans, Louisiana	18 Feb 1970	5 Dec 1970	10 Sep 1971	PA
JARVIS	WHEC 725	Avondale Shipyards Inc, New Orleans, Louisiana	9 Sep 1970	24 Apr 1971	30 Dec 1971	PA
MIDGETT	WHEC 726	Avondale Shipyards Inc, New Orleans, Louisiana	5 Apr 1971	4 Sep 1971	17 Mar 1972	PA

Displacement, tons: 3050 full load
Dimensions, feet (metres): 378 × 42.8 × 20 (sonar) *(115.2 × 13.1 × 6.1)*
Flight deck, feet (metres): 88 × 40 *(26.8 × 12.2)*
Main machinery: CODOG; 2 Pratt & Whitney FT-4A6 gas turbines; 36 000 hp *(26.86 MW)*; 2 Fairbanks-Morse 38TD8-1/8-12 diesels; 7000 hp *(5.22 MW)* sustained; 2 shafts; cp props; retractable bow propulsor; 350 hp *(261 kW)*
Speed, knots: 29. **Range, miles:** 14 000 at 11 kts diesels; 2400 at 29 kts gas
Complement: 179 (21 officers)

Missiles: SSM: 8 McDonnell Douglas Harpoon ❶; active radar homing to 130 km (70 nm) at 0.9 mach; warhead 227 kg. Not in all.
Guns: 1 OTO Melara 3 in *(76 mm)*/62 Mk 75 Compact ❷; 85° elevation; 85 rounds/minute to 16 km *(8.7 nm)* anti-surface; 12 km *(6.6 nm)* anti-aircraft; weight of shell 6 kg.
2 Aerospace 20 mm/80 Mk 67; 800 rounds/minute to 3 km *(1.6 nm)*. 4—12.7 mm MGs.
1 GE/GD 20 mm Vulcan Phalanx 6 barrelled Mk 15 ❸; 3000 rounds/minute combined to 1.5 km. Not in all.
Torpedoes: 6—324 mm Mk 32 (2 triple) tubes ❹. Honeywell Mk 46; anti-submarine; active/passive homing to 11 km *(5.9 nm)* at 40 kts; warhead 44 kg.
Countermeasures: Decoys: 2 Loral Hycor SRBOC 6-barrelled fixed Mk 36; IR flares and Chaff.
ESM: WLR-1C, WLR-3; radar warning.
Fire control: Mk 92 Mod 1 GFCS. Mk 309 ASW.
Radars: Air search: Lockheed SPS 40B ❺; D/E band.
Surface search: Raytheon SPS 64(V)6 ❻; I band.
Fire control: Sperry Mk 92 ❼; I/J band.
Tacan: URN 25.
Sonars: EDO SQS 38; hull-mounted; active search and attack; medium frequency.

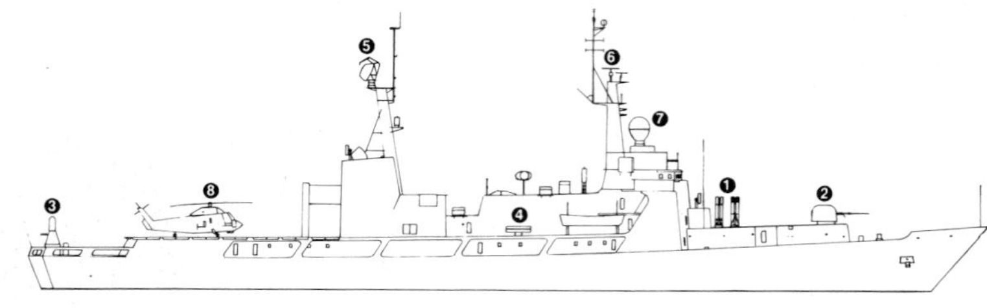

HAMILTON *(Scale 1 : 1 200), Ian Sturton*

Helicopters: 1 HH-65A or LAMPS I ❽.

Programmes: In the autumn of 1977 *Gallatin* and *Morgenthau* were the first of the Coast Guard ships to have women assigned as permanent members of the crew.

Modernisation: FRAM programme for all 12 ships in this class from October 1985 to October 1992. Work included standardising the engineering plants, improving the clutching systems, replacing SPS 29 air-search radar with SPS 40 radar and replacing the Mk 56 fire control system and 5 in/38 gun mount with the Mk 92 system and a single 76 mm OTO Melara Compact gun. In addition Harpoon and Phalanx CIWS fitted to five of the class by 1992 but shortage of funds may limit final numbers to be equipped. The flight deck and other aircraft facilities upgraded to handle the LAMPS I helicopter including a telescopic hangar. URN 25 Tacan added along with the SQR 4 and SQR 17 sonobuoy receiving set and passive acoustic analysis systems. SRBOC Chaff launchers are also fitted but not improved ESM which has been shelved along with towed array sonar. Last pair started post-FRAM trials in April, to be ready for operations in October 1992.

Structure: These ships have clipper bows, twin funnels enclosing a helicopter hangar, helicopter platform aft. All are fitted with elaborate communications equipment. Superstructure is largely of aluminium construction. Bridge control of manoeuvring is by aircraft-type joy-stick rather than wheel. Engine and propeller pitch consoles are located in wheelhouse and at bridge wing stations as well as engine room control booth.

Operational: *Mellon* fired the first Harpoon missile to be fitted in this class on 16 January 1990. Four Atlantic based ships transferred to the Pacific in 1991, leaving only one on the East Coast.

HAMILTON 2/1991, Giorgio Arra

MEDIUM ENDURANCE CUTTERS

13 FAMOUS CUTTER CLASS (WMEC)

Name	No	Builders	Laid down	Launched	Commissioned	F/S
BEAR	WMEC 901	Tacoma Boatbuilding Co, Tacoma	23 Aug 1979	25 Sep 1980	4 Feb 1983	AA
TAMPA	WMEC 902	Tacoma Boatbuilding Co, Tacoma	3 Apr 1980	19 Mar 1981	18 Dec 1983	AA
HARRIET LANE	WMEC 903	Tacoma Boatbuilding Co, Tacoma	15 Oct 1980	6 Feb 1982	20 Sep 1984	AA
NORTHLAND	WMEC 904	Tacoma Boatbuilding Co, Tacoma	9 Apr 1981	7 May 1982	15 July 1984	AA
SPENCER	WMEC 905	Robert E Derecktor Corp, Middletown, RI	26 June 1982	17 Apr 1984	28 June 1986	AA
SENECA	WMEC 906	Robert E Derecktor Corp, Middletown, RI	16 Sep 1982	17 Apr 1984	15 Jul 1986	AA
ESCANABA	WMEC 907	Robert E Derecktor Corp, Middletown, RI	1 Apr 1983	6 Feb 1985	3 Feb 1987	AA
TAHOMA	WMEC 908	Robert E Derecktor Corp, Middletown, RI	28 June 1983	6 Feb 1985	1 Sep 1987	AA
CAMPBELL	WMEC 909	Robert E Derecktor Corp, Middletown, RI	10 Aug 1984	29 Apr 1986	3 Jan 1988	AA
THETIS	WMEC 910	Robert E Derecktor Corp, Middletown, RI	24 Aug 1984	29 Apr 1986	2 June 1988	AA
FORWARD	WMEC 911	Robert E Derecktor Corp, Middletown, RI	11 July 1986	22 Aug 1987	8 May 1989	AA
LEGARE	WMEC 912	Robert E Derecktor Corp, Middletown, RI	11 July 1986	22 Aug 1987	1 Dec 1989	AA
MOHAWK	WMEC 913	Robert E Derecktor Corp, Middletown, RI	15 Mar 1987	5 May 1988	23 Aug 1990	AA

Displacement, tons: 1780 full load
Dimensions, feet (metres): 270 × 38 × 13.5 *(82.3 × 11.6 × 4.1)*
Main machinery: 2 Alco 18V-251 diesels; 7290 hp *(5.44 MW)* sustained; 2 shafts; cp props
Speed, knots: 19.5. **Range, miles:** 9500 at 13 kts, 3850 at 19.5 kts
Complement: 100 (12 officers) plus 16 aircrew when LAMPS is embarked

Guns: 1 OTO Melara 3 in *(76 mm)*/62 Mk 75 ❶; 85° elevation; 85 rounds/minute to 16 km *(8.7 nm)* anti-surface; 12 km *(6.6 nm)* anti-aircraft; weight of shell 6 kg.
2—12.7 mm MGs and/or 2—40 mm Mk 19 grenade launchers ❷.
Countermeasures: Decoys: 2 Loral Hycor SRBOC 6-barrelled fixed Mk 36; IR flares and Chaff.
ESM/ECM: SLQ 32(V)2; radar intercept.
Combat data systems: Sperry COMDAC.
Radars: Surface search: Raytheon SPS 64(V) ❸; I/K/F band.
Fire control: Sperry Mk 92 Mod 1 ❹; I/J band.
Tacan: URN 25.

Helicopters: 1 HH-65A ❺ or LAMPS I or 1 LAMPS III.

Programmes: This class has replaced the Campbell class and other medium and high endurance cutters. The contract for construction of WMEC 905-913 was originally awarded to Tacoma Boatbuilding Co on 29 August 1980. However, under lawsuit from the Robert E Derecktor Corp, Middletown, Rhode Island, the contract to Tacoma was determined by a US District Court to be invalid and was awarded to Robert E Derecktor Corp on 15 January 1981. WMEC 901-902 were authorised in FY 1977, WMEC 903-904 in FY 1978, WMEC 905-906 in FY 1979, WMEC 907-909 in FY 1980, WMEC 910 in FY 1981, and WMEC 911-913 in FY 1982.
Structure: They are the only medium endurance cutters with a helicopter hangar (which is telescopic) and the first cutters with automated command and control centre. Fin stabilisers fitted. *Thetis* has been fitted with the French DCN Talon landing and hold down helicopter system, which in due course is to be retrofitted to all helicopter capable cutters. Plans to fit SSM and/or CIWS have been abandoned as has towed array sonar.
Operational: No A/S weapons other than those carried by helicopter. Bases are at Portsmouth, New Bedford, Key West and Boston. Reported to be very lively in heavy seas perhaps because the length to beam ratio is unusually small for ships required to operate in Atlantic conditions.

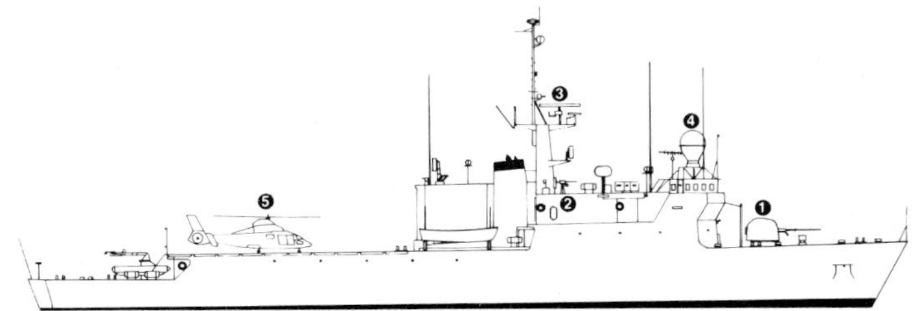

BEAR *(Scale 1 : 900), Ian Sturton*

TAHOMA *7/1991, Giorgio Arra*

16 RELIANCE CLASS (WMEC)

Name	*No*	*Builders*	*Commissioned*	*MMA completion*	*F/S*
RELIANCE	WMEC 615	Todd Shipyards	20 June 1964	Jan 1989	AA (Newcastle)
DILIGENCE	WMEC 616	Todd Shipyards	26 Aug 1964	Mar 1992	AA (Wilmington)
VIGILANT	WMEC 617	Todd Shipyards	3 Oct 1964	Aug 1990	AA (Cape Canaveral)
ACTIVE	WMEC 618	Christy Corp	17 Sep 1966	Feb 1987	PA (Port Angeles)
CONFIDENCE	WMEC 619	Coast Guard Yard, Baltimore	19 Feb 1966	June 1988	AA (Cape Canaveral)
RESOLUTE	WMEC 620	Coast Guard Yard, Baltimore	8 Dec 1966	Nov 1995	PA (New London)
VALIANT	WMEC 621	American Shipbuilding Co	28 Oct 1967	May 1993	AA (Miami)
COURAGEOUS	WMEC 622	American Shipbuilding Co	10 Apr 1968	Mar 1990	AA (Panama City)
STEADFAST	WMEC 623	American Shipbuilding Co	25 Sep 1968	Nov 1993	AA (Astoria)
DAUNTLESS	WMEC 624	American Shipbuilding Co	10 June 1968	Nov 1994	AA (Galveston)
VENTUROUS	WMEC 625	American Shipbuilding Co	16 Aug 1968	May 1995	PA (St Petersburg)
DEPENDABLE	WMEC 626	American Shipbuilding Co	22 Nov 1968	May 1996	AA (Corpus Christi)
VIGOROUS	WMEC 627	American Shipbuilding Co	2 May 1969	Nov 1992	AA (Cape May)
DURABLE	WMEC 628	Coast Guard Yard, Baltimore	8 Dec 1967	Jan 1989	AA (St Petersburg)
DECISIVE	WMEC 629	Coast Guard Yard, Baltimore	23 Aug 1968	Nov 1996	AA (Panama City)
ALERT	WMEC 630	Coast Guard Yard, Baltimore	4 Aug 1969	May 1994	AA (Astoria)

Displacement, tons: 950 standard; 1007 (1129 after MMA) full load (WMEC 620-630)
970 (1110 after MMA) full load (WMEC 618, 619)
Dimensions, feet (metres): 210.5 × 34 × 10.5 *(64.2 × 10.4 × 3.2)*
Main machinery: 2 Alco 16V-251 diesels; 6480 hp *(4.83 MW)* sustained; 2 shafts; cp props
Speed, knots: 18. **Range, miles:** 6100 at 14 kts; 2700 at 18 kts
Complement: 71 (8 officers)

Guns: 1 USN 3 in *(76 mm)*/50; 85° elevation; 20 rounds/minute to 12 km *(6.6 nm)*; weight of shell 6 kg.
1—25 mm Mk 38 being fitted. 2—12.7 mm MGs.
Radars: Surface search: 2 Raytheon SPS 64(V); I band.

Helicopters: 1 HH-65A embarked as required.

Modernisation: All 16 cutters have undergone or will undergo a Major Maintenance Availability (MMA) which takes approximately 18 months. The exhausts for main engines, ship service generators and boilers are run in a new vertical funnel which reduces flight deck size. Scheduled completion dates are listed above but future dates are at best only estimates.
Structure: Designed for search and rescue duties. Design features include 360 degree visibility from bridge; helicopter flight deck (no hangar); and engine exhaust vent at stern in place of conventional funnel which is being built during MMA. Capable of towing ships up to 10 000 tons. Air-conditioned throughout except engine room; high degree of habitability.
Operational: Normally operate within 500 miles of the coast. All these cutters are active with the exception of those decommissioned for an MMA. Primary roles are SAR, law-enforcement and defence operations. Vessels up to 10 000 tons can be towed.

VALIANT *11/1991, Giorgio Arra*

COURAGEOUS (after MMA) *4/1991, Giorgio Arra*

1 CHEROKEE CLASS (WMEC)

Name	*No*	*Builders*	*USN Comm.*	*F/S*
TAMAROA (ex-*Zuni*)	WMEC 166 (ex-WAT 166, ATF 95)	Commercial Iron Works, Portland, Oregon	9 Oct 1943	AA

Displacement, tons: 1731 full load
Dimensions, feet (metres): 205 × 38.5 × 17 *(62.5 × 11.7 × 5.2)*
Main machinery: Diesel-electric; 4 GM 12-278A diesels; 4400 hp *(3.28 MW)*; 4 generators; 1 motor; 3000 hp *(2.24 MW)*; 1 shaft
Speed, knots: 16.2. **Range, miles:** 6500 at 16 kts
Complement: 72 (7 officers)
Guns: 1 USN 3 in *(76 mm)*/50 (not carried).
Radars: Navigation: Raytheon SPS 64; I band.

Comment: The one remaining cutter of this class was transferred from the Navy to the Coast Guard on loan in 1946 and permanently transferred in 1969. Classification was changed to WMEC in 1968. The 3 in gun has been landed.

CHEROKEE Class (old number) *6/1990, Giorgio Arra*

3 DIVER CLASS (WMEC)

Name	*No*	*Builders*	*USN Comm.*	*F/S*
ACUSHNET (ex-USS *Shackle*)	WMEC 167 (ex-WAGO 167, ex-WAT 167, ex-ARS 9)	Basalt Rock Co, Napa, California	5 Feb 1944	AA
YOCONA (ex-USS *Seize*)	WMEC 168 (ex-WAT 168, ex-ARS 26)	Basalt Rock Co, Napa, California	3 Nov 1944	PA
ESCAPE	WMEC 6 (ex-ARS 6)	Basalt Rock Co, Napa, California	20 Nov 1943	AA

Displacement, tons: 1557 standard; 1745 full load
Dimensions, feet (metres): 213.5 × 39 × 15 *(65.1 × 11.9 × 4.6)*
Main machinery: 4 Cooper-Bessemer GSB-8 *(Yocona)*, 4 CAT D399 *(Escape)*, 4 Fairbanks-Morse *(Acushnet)* diesels; 3000 hp *(2.24 MW)*; 2 shafts
Speed, knots: 15.5. **Range, miles:** 9000 at 15 kts
Complement: 64 (7 officers) *(Acushnet)*; 72 (7 officers) *(Yocona)*
Radars: Navigation: 2 Raytheon SPS 64; I band.

Comment: Large, steel-hulled salvage ships transferred from the Navy to the Coast Guard and employed in tug and oceanographic duties. *Acushnet* modified for handling environmental data buoys and reclassified WAGO in 1968 and reclassified WMEC in 1980; *Yocona* reverted to WMEC in 1968. *Escape* transferred on loan from USN on 4 December 1980. Refitted at Curtis Bay Yard in 1980-81. Major renovation work completed on *Acushnet* in 1983 will enable her to continue operating through 1995. Plans to replace *Yocona* have been delayed.

ACUSHNET *5/1989, Giorgio Arra*

ESCAPE (twin masts) *7/1990, Giorgio Arra*

1 STORIS CLASS (WMEC)

Name	*No*	*Builders*	*Commissioned*	*F/S*
STORIS (ex-*Eskimo*)	WMEC 38 (ex-WAGB 38, ex-WAGL 38)	Toledo Shipbuilding Co, Ohio	30 Sep 1942	PA

Displacement, tons: 1715 standard; 1925 full load
Dimensions, feet (metres): 230 × 43 × 15 *(70.1 × 13.1 × 4.6)*
Main machinery: Diesel-electric; 3 EMD diesel generators; 1 motor; 3000 hp *(2.24 MW)*; 1 shaft
Speed, knots: 14. **Range, miles:** 22 000 at 8 kts; 12 000 at 14 kts
Complement: 106 (10 officers)
Guns: 1 USN 3 in *(76 mm)*/50.
Radars: Navigation: Raytheon SPS 64; I band.

Comment: Laid down on 14 July 1941; launched on 4 April 1942 as ice patrol tender. Strengthened for ice navigation and sometimes employed as icebreaker. Employed in Alaskan service for search, rescue and law enforcement. *Storis* completed a major maintenance availability in June 1986, during which her main engines were replaced with EMD diesels and her living quarters expanded. Despite her advanced age, there are no plans to decommission her until 1995.

STORIS *1983, USCG*

5 AEROSTAT SHIPS

Name	*Builders*	*Completed*	*F/S*
ATLANTIC SENTRY	Steiner Marine, Alabama	1986	AA (Key West)
CARIBBEAN SENTRY	Halter Marine, Louisiana	1987	AA (Key West)
GULF SENTRY	Halter Marine, Louisiana	1984	AA (Miami)
PACIFIC SENTRY	Halter Marine, Louisiana	1983	AA (Miami)
WINDWARD SENTRY	McDermott, Louisiana	1979	AA (Key West)

Displacement, tons: 2140 full load
Dimensions, feet (metres): 192 × 44 × 15.1 *(58.5 × 13.4 × 4.6)*
Main machinery: 2 GM EMD 16-645E6 diesels; 3900 hp *(2.91 MW)*; 2 shafts
Speed, knots: 12. **Range, miles:** 7000 at 10 kts
Complement: 10 civilian plus 9 CG

Comment: There are some minor differences between these ships which have been either purchased or leased between April 1987 and November 1989. Each consists of a Mobile Aerostat Platform (MAP) with installed mooring system, a helium-filled aerostat with APS-143(V)2 or APS 128 attached radar, and radar, communications, and computer consoles in the MAP operations centre. Their mission is to provide continuous traffic-surveillance information to other law-enforcement units for the purpose of interdicting drug-trafficking and alien vessels. SBAs normally work in conjunction with Coast Guard cutters and patrol boats but successful operations have also been conducted with other US and foreign naval resources. They are operated throughout the Caribbean Sea, the Gulf of Mexico, and the Straits of Florida, and particularly in choke points between major islands where target vessels must pass. The aerostats are 109 ft long and 37 ft in diameter; their operational altitude is zero to 2500 ft. The first system was first tested and evaluated in 1984. Four of the five systems are operational at any given time. At sea endurance is 31 days.

CARIBBEAN SENTRY with AEROSTAT *1/1990, Giorgio Arra*

CARIBBEAN SENTRY with AEROSTAT *1/1990, Giorgio Arra*

SHIPBORNE AIRCRAFT

Numbers/Type: 96 Aerospatiale HH 65A Dolphin.
Operational speed: 140 kts *(260 km/h)*.
Service ceiling: 11 810 ft *(3600 m)*.
Range: 460 nm *(855 km)*.
Role/Weapon systems: Short-range rescue and recovery (SRR) helicopter. 80 aircraft are operational. Sensors: Bendix RDR 1500 radar and Collins mission management system. Weapons: Unarmed.

DOLPHIN *1989, USCG*

LAND-BASED MARITIME AIRCRAFT (FRONT LINE)

Note: In February 1992 there were in addition 3 CH-3Es on loan from the Air Force and two RG-8A single-engined reconnaissance aircraft. Naval E-2Cs have been returned.

Numbers/Type: 41 AMD-BA HU-25A/B/D Guardian Falcon.
Operational speed: 465 kts *(862 km/h)*.
Service ceiling: 42 000 ft *(12 800 m)*.
Range: 1810 nm *(3350 km)*.
Role/Weapon systems: Medium-range maritime reconnaissance role. 31 are operational. Sensors: Weather/search radar. Weapons: Unarmed.

Numbers/Type: 31 Lockheed HC-130H/V.
Operational speed: 325 kts *(602 km/h)*.
Service ceiling: 33 000 ft *(10 060 m)*.
Range: 4250 nm *(7876 km)*.
Role/Weapon systems: Long-range maritime reconnaissance role; further orders expected. 28 are operational. Sensors: Weather/search radar: GE APS 125 (in V conversion). Weapons: Unarmed.

Numbers/Type: 20 Sikorsky HH-3F Pelican.
Operational speed: 125 kts *(232 km/h)*.
Service ceiling: 11 100 ft *(3385 m)*.
Range: 404 nm *(748 km)*.
Role/Weapon systems: Medium rescue and recovery (MRR) helicopter for all-weather operations. Being replaced by HH-60J. Phasing out to complete in 1994. Sensors: Weather/search radar. Weapons: Unarmed.

Numbers/Type: 19 Sikorsky HH-60J Rescue Hawk.
Operational speed: 162 kts *(300 km/h)*.
Service ceiling: 17 200 ft *(5240 m)*.
Range: 297 nm *(550 km)*.
Role/Weapon systems: First flew in 1988, replacing HH-3F in MRR role. Total of 38 ordered, all to be delivered by April 1994. Sensors: Bendix weather/search radar. Weapons: Unarmed.

ICEBREAKERS

0 + (1) NEWCON TYPE (WAGB)

HEALY

Displacement, tons: 17 710 full load
Dimensions, feet (metres): 459.6 oa; 401.2 wl × 94.5 × 31.2 *(140.1; 122.3 × 28.8 × 9.5)*
Main machinery: Diesel electric; 4 Colt-Pielstick diesel generators; 2 motors; 30 000 hp(m) *(22.4 MW)*; 2 shafts; bow thruster; 2000 hp *(1.49 MW)*
Speed, knots: 13. **Range, miles:** 34 500 at 12.5 kts
Complement: 137 (17 officers) plus 30 scientists
Guns: 2—12.7 mm MGs.
Radars: Navigation: I band.
Helicopters: 2 HH-65A.

Comment: In response to the 1984 interagency Polar Icebreaker Requirements Study and Congressional mandate, a design has been approved for a replacement for the two aged Wind class icebreakers, both of which were decommissioned in 1988 because of severe reductions in the Coast Guard operating budget. The Coast Guard also studied the possibility of leasing an icebreaker if one were built by a source outside the government. However, no action was taken to provide funds until Congress surprisingly appropriated $329 million for inclusion in the Navy's shipbuilding budget for construction of one icebreaker. A construction contract is still expected in 1992 with an in service date of 1996. A total of three ships are required. Design includes standard icebreaking hull capable of breaking 4.6 ft of ice at 3 kts or 8 ft by ramming. Five research laboratories equipped for Arctic research.

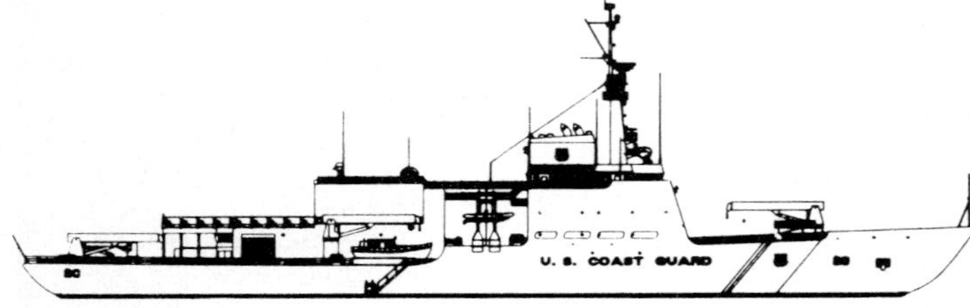

HEALY (not to scale) *1991, USCG*

1 MACKINAW CLASS (WAGB)

Name	*No*	*Builders*	*Commissioned*	*F/S*
MACKINAW	WAGB 83	Toledo Shipbuilding Co, Ohio	20 Dec 1944	GLA

Displacement, tons: 5252
Dimensions, feet (metres): 290 × 74 × 19 *(88.4 × 22.6 × 5.8)*
Main machinery: Diesel-electric; 6 Fairbanks-Morse 38D8-1/8-12 diesel generators; 8.7 MW sustained; Elliot electric drive; 10 000 hp *(7.46 MW)*; 3 shafts (1 fwd, 2 aft)
Speed, knots: 18.7. **Range, miles:** 41 000 at 11.5 kts; 10 000 at 18.7 kts
Complement: 74 (8 officers)
Radars: Navigation: Raytheon SPS 64; I band.
Helicopters: Platform only.

Comment: Specially designed and constructed for service as icebreaker on the Great Lakes. Equipped with two 5 ton capacity cranes. Clear area for helicopter is provided on the quarterdeck, the aircraft being called for from shore Coast Guard station. Scheduled to be paid off in FY 1988 as a means of helping the Coast Guard cope with severe budget cuts but pressure from members of Congress from states bordering the Great Lakes, where *Mackinaw* operates, resulted in her being placed in an 'In Commission, Special' status in April 1988. Operational again in Spring 1989 and received a safety and survivability overhaul in 1990.

MACKINAW *1983, USCG*

2 POLAR STAR CLASS (WAGB)

Name	*No*	*Builders*	*Commissioned*	*F/S*
POLAR STAR	WAGB 10	Lockheed Shipbuilding Co, Seattle, Washington	19 Jan 1976	PA
POLAR SEA	WAGB 11	Lockheed Shipbuilding Co, Seattle, Washington	23 Feb 1978	PA

Displacement, tons: 12 087 full load
Dimensions, feet (metres): 399 × 86 × 31 *(121.6 × 26.2 × 9.5)*
Main machinery: CODOG; 3 Pratt & Whitney FT4A-12 gas turbines; 60 000 hp *(44.76 MW)*; 6 Alco 16V-251 diesels; 19 440 hp *(14.5 MW)* sustained; 3 shafts; cp props
Speed, knots: 18. **Range, miles:** 28 000 at 13 kts
Complement: 140 (14 officers) plus 20 scientists and 14 aircrew
Guns: 2—12.7 mm MGs.
Radars: Navigation: Raytheon SPS 64; I band.
Helicopters: 2 HH-65A.

Comment: These ships are the first icebreakers built for US service since *Glacier* was constructed two decades earlier. *Polar Star* based at Seattle. These are the largest ships operated by the US Coast Guard. At a continuous speed of 3 kts they can break ice 6 ft thick and by riding on the ice they can break 21 ft pack. Conventional icebreaker hull form with cutaway bow configuration and well rounded body sections to prevent being trapped in ice. Two 15 ton capacity cranes fitted aft; research laboratories provided for arctic and oceanographic research. *Polar Star* science facilities upgraded in 1990-91. Similar work on *Polar Sea* should complete in 1993.

POLAR STAR *9/1991, W. Sartori*

9 KATMAI BAY CLASS (TUGS—WGTB)

Name	*No*	*Laid down*	*Commissioned*	*F/S*
KATMAI BAY	WTGB 101	7 Nov 1977	8 Jan 1979	GLA
BRISTOL BAY	WTGB 102	13 Feb 1978	5 Apr 1979	GLA
MOBILE BAY	WTGB 103	13 Feb 1978	6 May 1979	GLA
BISCAYNE BAY	WTGB 104	29 Aug 1978	8 Dec 1979	GLA
NEAH BAY	WTGB 105	6 Aug 1979	18 Aug 1980	GLA
MORRO BAY	WTGB 106	6 Aug 1979	25 Jan 1981	AA
PENOBSCOT BAY	WTGB 107	24 July 1983	4 Sep 1984	AA
THUNDER BAY	WTGB 108	20 July 1984	29 Dec 1985	AA
STURGEON BAY	WTGB 109	9 July 1986	20 Aug 1988	AA

Displacement, tons: 662 full load
Dimensions, feet (metres): 140 × 37.6 × 12.5 *(42.7 × 11.4 × 3.8)*
Main machinery: Diesel-electric; 2 Fairbanks-Morse 38D8-1/8-10 diesel generators; 2.4 MW sustained; Westinghouse electric drive; 2500 hp *(1.87 MW)*; 1 shaft
Speed, knots: 14.7. **Range, miles:** 4000 at 12 kts
Complement: 17 (3 officers)
Radars: Navigation: Raytheon SPS 64; I band.

Comment: This class has replaced the 110 ft class WYTMs. Originally classified as WYTMs. Reclassified WTGBs on 5 February 1979. The size, manoeuvrability and other operational characteristics of these vessels are tailored for operations in harbours and other restricted waters and for fulfilling present and anticipated multi-mission requirements. All units are ice strengthened for operation on the Great Lakes, coastal waters and in rivers and can break 24 in of ice continuously and up to 8 ft by ramming. A self contained portable bubbler van and system reduces hull friction. First six built at Tacoma Boatbuilding, Tacoma. WTGB 107-109 built in Tacoma by Bay City Marine, San Diego.

PENOBSCOT BAY *6/1991, Giorgio Arra*

PATROL CRAFT

Note: Heritage class programme cancelled on 25 November 1991. The first of class *Leopold* is unlikely to be completed. The cause of the cancellation was attributed to changing requirements and availability of more ships as a result of Soviet decline. It was also reported that there were concerns about the design. A smaller patrol craft is now being considered.

49 ISLAND CLASS (WPB)

Name	*No*	*Home Port*	*Commissioned*
FARALLON	WPB 1301	Miami, FL	15 Nov 1985
MANITOU	WPB 1302	Miami, FL	24 Jan 1986
MATAGORDA	WPB 1303	Miami, FL	28 Feb 1986
MAUI	WPB 1304	Miami, FL	24 Mar 1986
MONHEGAN	WPB 1305	Roosevelt Roads, OR	11 Apr 1986
NUNIVAK	WPB 1306	Roosevelt Roads, OR	2 May 1986
OCRACOKE	WPB 1307	Roosevelt Roads, OR	23 May 1986
VASHON	WPB 1308	Roosevelt Roads, OR	13 June 1986
AQUIDNECK	WPB 1309	Portsmouth, VA	25 July 1986
MUSTANG	WPB 1310	Seward, AK	29 Aug 1986
NAUSHON	WPB 1311	Ketchikan, AK	3 Oct 1986
SANIBEL	WPB 1312	Rockland, ME	14 Nov 1986
EDISTO	WPB 1313	Crescent City, CA	7 Jan 1987
SAPELO	WPB 1314	Eureka, CA	24 Feb 1987
MATINICUS	WPB 1315	Cape May, NJ	16 Apr 1987
NANTUCKET	WPB 1316	Roosevelt Roads, OR	4 June 1987
ATTU	WPB 1317	Roosevelt Roads, OR	6 Feb 1988
BARANOF	WPB 1318	Miami, FL	12 Mar 1988
CHANDELEUR	WPB 1319	Miami, FL	16 Apr 1988
CHINCOTEAGUE	WPB 1320	Mobile, AL	21 May 1988
CUSHING	WPB 1321	Mobile, AL	25 June 1988
CUTTYHUNK	WPB 1322	Port Angeles, WA	30 July 1988
DRUMMOND	WPB 1323	Port Canaveral, FL	3 Sep 1988
KEY LARGO	WPB 1324	Savannah, GA	8 Oct 1988
METOMPKIN	WPB 1325	Charleston, SC	12 Nov 1988
MONOMOY	WPB 1326	Woods Hole, MA	17 Dec 1988
ORCAS	WPB 1327	Coos Bay, OR	21 Jan 1989
PADRE	WPB 1328	Key West, FL	25 Feb 1989
SITKINAK	WPB 1329	Key West, FL	1 Apr 1989
TYBEE	WPB 1330	San Diego, CA	5 May 1989
WASHINGTON	WPB 1331	Honolulu, HI	9 June 1989
WRANGELL	WPB 1332	Sandy Hook, NJ	9 July 1989
ADAK	WPB 1333	Sandy Hook, NJ	18 Aug 1989
LIBERTY	WPB 1334	Auke Bay, AK	22 Sep 1989
ANACAPA	WPB 1335	Petersburg, AK	27 Oct 1989
KISKA	WPB 1336	Hilo, HI	1 Dec 1989
ASSATEAGUE	WPB 1337	Honolulu, HI	5 Jan 1990
GRAND ISLE	WPB 1338	Gloucester, MA	19 Feb 1991
KEY BISCAYNE	WPB 1339	Corpus Christi, TX	12 Mar 1991
JEFFERSON	WPB 1340	South Portland, ME	9 Apr 1991
KODIAK	WPB 1341	Panama City, FL	14 May 1991
LONG	WPB 1342	Monterey, CA	18 June 1991
BAINBRIDGE	WPB 1343	Sandy Hook, NJ	16 July 1991
BLOCK	WPB 1344	Atlantic Beach, NC	27 Aug 1991
STATEN	WPB 1345	Atlantic Beach, NC	1 Oct 1991
ROANOKE	WPB 1346	Homer, AK	5 Nov 1991
PEA	WPB 1347	Mayport, FL	10 Dec 1991
KNIGHT	WPB 1348	Freeport, TX	14 Jan 1992
GALVESTON	WPB 1349	Apra Harbor, Guam	25 Feb 1992

Displacement, tons: 162 full load
Dimensions, feet (metres): 110 × 21 × 7.3 *(33.5 × 6.4 × 2.2)*
Main machinery: 2 Paxman Valenta diesels (A and B series); 5800 hp *(4.3 MW)*; 2 Caterpillar diesels (C series); 6800 hp *(5.1 MW)*; 2 shafts
Speed, knots: 29. **Range, miles:** 3600 at 12 kts
Complement: 16 (2 officers)
Guns: 1 Oerlikon 20 mm or 1—25 mm Mk 38. 2—7.62 mm M60 MGs.
Radars: Navigation: Raytheon SPS 64V; I band.

Comment: All built by the Bollinger Machine Shop and Shipyard at Lockport, Louisiana. The design is based upon the 110 ft patrol craft built by Vosper Thornycroft, UK, which are currently serving in Venezuela, Qatar, Abu Dhabi and Singapore, but modified to meet Coast Guard needs. Vosper Thornycroft supplied design support, stabilisers, propellers, and steering gear. All are having 25 mm Mk 38 guns installed. Batches: A 1301-1316, B 1317-1337, C 1338-1349. Names mostly have 'Island' after them. Batch C had their allocated names changed prior to completion in 1991/92.

ADAK ISLAND *6/1991, Giorgio Arra*

ORCAS *6/1990, van Ginderen Collection*

3 SEA BIRD CLASS (SURFACE EFFECT SHIPS—WSES)

Name	*No*	*Builders*	*Commissioned*	*F/S*
SEA HAWK	WSES 2	Bell Halter Inc, New Orleans, La	16 Oct 1982	AA
SHEARWATER	WSES 3	Bell Halter Inc, New Orleans, La	16 Oct 1982	AA
PETREL	WSES 4	Bell Halter Inc, New Orleans, La	17 June 1983	AA

Displacement, tons: 150 full load
Dimensions, feet (metres): 110 × 39 × 8.3 *(33.5 × 11.9 × 2.5)*
Main machinery: 2 GM 16V 149 TI diesels (propulsion); 2790 hp *(2.08 MW)* sustained; 2 shafts; cp prop; 2 GM 8V-92 TA diesels (lift); 750 hp *(560 kW)* sustained; 2 centrifugal fans (lift); 736 hp *(549 kW)*
Speed, knots: 30+. **Range, miles:** 1500 at 23 kts
Complement: 17 (1 officer)
Guns: 2—12.7 mm MGs.
Radars: Navigation: 2 Decca 914; I band.

Comment: Modified units of the surface effect ship constructed in the late 1970s which in 1981, after extensive testing by the Navy, was transferred to the Coast Guard and became the *Dorado* (WSES 1). All three are based in Key West and their high speed and shallow draft make them ideal for drug-interdiction and law-enforcement missions in the Caribbean basin. Designed primarily for law-enforcement and search and rescue missions. Design includes welded marine aluminium alloy 5086 hull with a catamaran configuration that consists of two side hulls with a connecting deck. The bow and stern have flexible seals to contain an air cushion. Each craft is supported by cushion lift as well as hydrostatic and hydrodynamic lift on the sidewalls. The bow seal consists of eight fingers, each of which is attached to the underside of the centre hull. The stern seal consists of three inflated lobes. During the early years of operation, vibration was a major concern; however, that problem has been corrected and they have become sufficiently reliable to exceed by far their planned operating hours. There are no plans to build more of them.

SEA HAWK *4/1990, Giorgio Arra*

41 POINT CLASS (WPB)

Name	*No*	*F/S*	*Name*	*No*	*F/S*
A Series			**POINT HANNON**	82355	AA
POINT SWIFT	82312	AA	**POINT FRANCIS**	82356	AA
			POINT HURON	82357	AA
C Series			**POINT STUART**	82358	PA
POINT HIGHLAND	82333	AA	**POINT STEELE**	82359	AA
POINT LEDGE	82334	PA	**POINT WINSLOW**	82360	PA
POINT COUNTESS	82335	PA	**POINT NOWELL**	82363	AA
POINT GLASS	82336	PA	**POINT WHITEHORN**	82364	AA
POINT DIVIDE	82337	PA	**POINT TURNER**	82365	AA
POINT BRIDGE	82338	PA	**POINT LOBOS**	82366	AA
POINT CHICO	82339	PA	**POINT WARDE**	82368	AA
POINT BATAN	82340	AA	**POINT HEYER**	82369	PA
POINT LOOKOUT	82341	AA	**POINT RICHMOND**	82370	AA
POINT WELLS	82343	AA			
POINT ESTERO	82344	AA	D Series		
POINT ARENA	82346	AA	**POINT BARNES**	82371	AA
POINT BONITA	82347	AA	**POINT BROWER**	82372	PA
POINT SPENCER	82349	AA	**POINT CAMDEN**	82373	PA
POINT FRANKLIN	82350	AA	**POINT CARREW**	82374	PA
POINT BENNETT	82351	PA	**POINT DORAN**	82375	PA
POINT SAL	82352	AA	**POINT HOBART**	82377	PA
POINT MONROE	82353	AA	**POINT JACKSON**	82378	AA
POINT EVANS	82354	PA	**POINT MARTIN**	82379	AA

Displacement, tons: 67 (A series); 66 (C series); 69 (D series) full load
Dimensions, feet (metres): 83 × 17.2 × 5.8 *(25.3 × 5.2 × 1.8)*
Main machinery: 2 Cummins or Caterpillar diesels; 1600 hp *(1.19 MW)*; 2 shafts
Speed, knots: 23.5; 22.6 (D series). **Range, miles:** 1500 at 8 kts; 1200 at 8 kts (D series)
Complement: 10 (1 officer)
Guns: 2—12.7 mm MGs.
Radars: Navigation: Raytheon SPS 64; I band.

Comment: Steel-hulled craft with aluminium superstructures designed for patrol and search and rescue. A series built 1960-61; C series in 1961-67, and D series in 1970. Some of the cutters operate with an officer assigned, the rest with all-enlisted crews. Twenty-six of the 'A' and 'B' series were transferred to South Vietnam in 1969-70. Some of the remaining cutters are being re-engined with Caterpillar engines. Being replaced by Island class patrol boats. One C series to Venezuela in 1992.

POINT BROWER *10/1991, Giorgio Arra*

SEAGOING TENDERS

Note: Contracts given in May 1991 for three shipbuilders to submit designs for a new ocean going buoy tender. Possible contract in late 1992.

27 BALSAM CLASS (BUOY TENDERS—WLB)

Name	*No*	*Launched*	*F/S*	*Name*	*No*	*Launched*	*F/S*
A Series				**BITTERSWEET**	WLB 389	1944	AA
COWSLIP	WLB 277	1942	AA	**BLACKHAW**	WLB 390	1944	PA
GENTIAN	WLB 290	1942	AA	**BRAMBLE**	WLB 392	1944	GLA
LAUREL	WLB 291	1942	AA	**FIREBUSH**	WLB 393	1944	PA
SORREL	WLB 296	1943	AA	**HORNBEAM**	WLB 394	1944	AA
CONIFER	WLB 301	1943	PA	**IRIS**	WLB 395	1944	PA
MADRONA	WLB 302	1943	AA	**MALLOW**	WLB 396	1944	PA
				MARIPOSA	WLB 397	1944	GLA
B Series				**SASSAFRAS**	WLB 401	1944	PA
IRONWOOD	WLB 297	1943	PA	**SEDGE**	WLB 402	1944	PA
BUTTONWOOD	WLB 306	1943	AA	**SPAR**	WLB 403	1944	AA
PLANETREE	WLB 307	1943	PA	**SUNDEW**	WLB 404	1944	GLA
PAPAW	WLB 308	1943	AR	**SWEETBRIER**	WLB 405	1944	PA
SWEETGUM	WLB 309	1943	AR	**ACACIA**	WLB 406	1944	GLA
				WOODRUSH	WLB 407	1944	PA
C Series							
BASSWOOD	WLB 388	1944	AA				

Displacement, tons: 935 standard; 1 025 full load
Dimensions, feet (metres): 180 × 37 × 13 *(54.9 × 11.3 × 4)*
Main machinery: Diesel-electric; 2 diesels; 1710 hp *(1.28 MW)*; 1 motor; 1200 hp *(895 kW)*; 1 shaft; bow thruster
Speed, knots: 13
Complement: 53 (6 officers)
Guns: 2 Oerlikon 20 mm guns (in *Ironwood, Bittersweet, Sassafras, Sedge* and *Sweetbrier*). 2—12.7 mm MGs (in remainder except *Bramble, Mariposa, Acacia* and *Sundew*).
Radars: Navigation: Raytheon SPS 64; I band.

Comment: Seagoing buoy tenders. *Ironwood* built by Coast Guard Yard at Curtis Bay, Maryland; others by Marine Iron & Shipbuilding Co, Duluth, Minnesota, or Zenith Dredge Co, Duluth, Minnesota. Completed 1943-45. All have 20 ton capacity booms.
Modernisation and Service Life Extension Programmes: *Cowslip, Gentian, Conifer, Sorrel, Madrona, Laurel, Papaw* and *Sweetgum* have completed an 18 month SLEP. *Buttonwood* is to be the last SLEP and is planned to complete in January 1993. Work includes replacement of main engines, improvement of electronics, navigation and weight-handling systems, and improved habitability. *Ironwood, Bittersweet, Bramble, Firebush, Hornbeam, Mariposa, Sassafras, Sedge, Spar, Sundew, Sweetbrier, Acacia* and *Woodrush* all underwent major renovation in the mid- to late 1970s which was not as extensive as the current SLEPs. However, all of these cutters have received in the 1988-91 period new main engines which are the same as those installed in cutters receiving SLEP.

LAUREL *8/1991, Giorgio Arra*

COASTAL TENDERS

5 RED CLASS (BUOY TENDERS—WLM)

Name	*No*	*Launched*	*F/S*	*Name*	*No*	*Launched*	*F/S*
RED WOOD	WLM 685	1964	AA	**RED CEDAR**	WLM 688	1970	AA
RED BEECH	WLM 686	1964	AA	**RED OAK**	WLM 689	1971	AA
RED BIRCH	WLM 687	1965	AA				

Displacement, tons: 471 standard; 536 full load
Dimensions, feet (metres): 157 × 33 × 6 *(47.9 × 10.1 × 1.8)*
Main machinery: 2 diesels; 1800 hp *(1.34 MW)*; 2 shafts; cp props; bow thruster
Speed, knots: 12.8. **Range, miles:** 2248 at 11.6 kts
Complement: 31 (4 officers)

Comment: All built by Coast Guard Yard, Curtis Bay, Maryland. Steel hulls strengthened for light icebreaking. Steering and engine controls on each bridge wing as well as in pilot house. Living spaces are air-conditioned. Fitted with 10 ton capacity boom.

RED OAK *8/1987, van Ginderen Collection*

6 WHITE SUMAC CLASS (BUOY TENDERS—WLM)

Name	*No*	*F/S*	*Name*	*No*	*F/S*
WHITE SUMAC	WLM 540	AA	**WHITE HEATH**	WLM 545	AA
WHITE LUPINE	WLM 546	AA	**WHITE HOLLY**	WLM 543	AA
WHITE PINE	WLM 547	AA	**WHITE SAGE**	WLM 544	AA

Displacement, tons: 435 standard; 485 full load
Dimensions, feet (metres): 133 × 31 × 9 *(40.5 × 9.5 × 2.7)*
Main machinery: 2 Caterpillar diesels; 600 hp *(448 kW)*; 2 shafts
Speed, knots: 9.8
Complement: 24 (1 officer)

Comment: All launched in 1943. All six ships are former US Navy YFs, adapted for the Coast Guard. Fitted with 10 ton capacity boom.

WHITE SUMAC *1/1992, Giorgio Arra*

BUOY-TENDERS (INLAND—WLI)

Name	*No*	*F/S*
BLUEBELL	WLI 313	PA
BUCKTHORN	WLI 642	GLA

Displacement, tons: 226 (174 *Bluebell*) full load
Dimensions, feet (metres): 100 × 24 × 5 *(30.5 × 7.3 × 1.5)* (*Buckthorn* draught 4 *(1.2)*)
Main machinery: 2 Caterpillar diesels; 600 hp *(448 kW)*; 2 shafts
Speed, knots: 11.9; 10.5 *(Bluebell)*
Complement: 14 (1 officer); 15 *(Bluebell)*

Comment: *Bluebell* completed 1945, and *Buckthorn* in 1963.

BUCKTHORN *2/1989, van Ginderen Collection*

Name	*No*	*F/S*
BLACKBERRY	WLI 65303	AA
CHOKEBERRY	WLI 65304	AA
BAYBERRY	WLI 65400	PA
ELDERBERRY	WLI 65401	PA

Displacement, tons: 68 full load
Dimensions, feet (metres): 65 × 17 × 4 *(19.8 × 5.2 × 1.2)*
Main machinery: 2 GM diesels (various); 2 shafts
Speed, knots: 11
Complement: 5

Comment: First two completed in 1946, second two in 1954.

BAYBERRY *1983, USCG*

BUOY TENDERS (RIVER) (WLR)

Notes: (1) All are based on rivers of USA especially the Mississippi and the Missouri and its tributaries.
(2) Two ATON (aids to navigation) barges completed in 1991/92 by Marinette Marine. For use on the Great Lakes in conjunction with icebreaker tugs.

ATON I and Buoy Tender *1991, Marinette Marine*

KANKAKEE WLR 75500 **GREENBRIAR** WLR 75501

Displacement, tons: 161 full load
Dimensions, feet (metres): 75.1 × 24 × 4.9 *(22.9 × 7.3 × 1.5)*
Main machinery: 2 Caterpillar 3412T diesels; 1006 hp *(750 kW)* sustained; 2 shafts
Speed, knots: 12. **Range, miles:** 600 at 12 kts
Complement: 13

Comment: *Kankakee* completed by Avondale 27 February 1990, and *Greenbriar* 12 April 1990. Have replaced *Dogwood* and *Lantana*. More of the class are planned.

SUMAC WLR 311

Displacement, tons: 423 full load
Dimensions, feet (metres): 115 × 30 × 6 *(35.1 × 9.1 × 1.8)*
Main machinery: 3 Caterpillar D-379 diesels; 1250 hp *(932 kW)*; 3 shafts
Speed, knots: 10.6
Complement: 22

Comment: Built in 1943. Scheduled for replacement in 1993.

GASCONADE	WLR 75401	**KICKAPOO**	WLR 75406
MUSKINGUM	WLR 75402	**KANAWHA**	WLR 75407
WYACONDA	WLR 75403	**PATOKA**	WLR 75408
CHIPPEWA	WLR 75404	**CHENA**	WLR 75409
CHEYENNE	WLR 75405		

Displacement, tons: 150 full load
Dimensions, feet (metres): 75 × 22 × 4 *(22.9 × 6.7 × 1.2)*
Main machinery: 2 Caterpillar diesels; 660 hp *(492 kW)*; 2 shafts
Speed, knots: 10.8
Complement: 12

Comment: Built 1964-71.

Buoy Tender *6/1991, Giorgio Arra*

OUACHITA	WLR 65501	**SCIOTO**	WLR 65504
CIMARRON	WLR 65502	**OSAGE**	WLR 65505
OBION	WLR 65503	**SANGAMON**	WLR 65506

Displacement, tons: 146 full load
Dimensions, feet (metres): 65.6 × 21 × 5 *(20 × 6.4 × 1.5)*
Main machinery: 2 Caterpillar diesels; 660 hp *(492 kW)*; 2 shafts
Speed, knots: 12.5
Complement: 10

Comment: Built in 1960-62.

SAIL TRAINING CUTTER

1 EAGLE CLASS (WIX)

Name	*No*	*Builders*	*F/S*
EAGLE (ex-*Horst Wessel*)	WIX 327	Blohm & Voss, Hamburg	AA

Displacement, tons: 1784 full load
Dimensions, feet (metres): 231 wl; 293.6 oa × 39.4 × 16.1 *(70.4; 89.5 × 12 × 4.9)*
Main machinery: 1 Caterpillar D-399 auxiliary diesel; 750 hp *(560 kW)*; 1 shaft
Speed, knots: 10.5; 18 sail. **Range, miles:** 5450 at 7.5 kts diesel only
Complement: 245 (19 officers, 180 cadets)
Radars: Navigation: Raytheon SPS 64; I band.

Comment: Former German training ship. Launched on 13 June 1936. Taken by the USA as part of reparations after the Second World War for employment in US Coast Guard Practice Squadron. Taken over at Bremerhaven in January 1946; arrived at home port of New London, Connecticut, in July 1946. (Sister ship *Albert Leo Schlageter* was also taken by the USA in 1945 but was sold to Brazil in 1948 and re-sold to Portugal in 1962. Another ship of similar design, *Gorch Fock*, transferred to the USSR in 1946 and survives as *Tovarisch*). *Eagle* was extensively overhauled 1981-82. When the Coast Guard added the orange-and-blue marking stripes to cutters in the 1960s *Eagle* was exempted because of their effect on her graceful lines; however, in early 1976 the stripes and words 'Coast Guard' were added in time for the July 1976 Operation Sail in New York harbour. During the Coast Guard's year-long bicentennial celebration, which ended 4 August 1990, *Eagle* visited each of the 10 ports where the original revenue cutters were homeported: Baltimore, MD; New London, CT; Washington, NC; Savannah, GA; Philadelphia, PA; Newburyport, MA; Portsmouth, NH; Charleston, SC; New York, NY; and Hampton, VA.
Fore and main masts 150.3 ft *(45.8 m)*; mizzen 132 ft *(40.2 m)*; sail area, 25 351 sq ft.

EAGLE and CONDOR (the old and the new) *1991*

CONSTRUCTION TENDERS (INLAND) (WLIC)

Notes: All, although operating on inland waters, are administered by the Atlantic Area.

4 PAMLICO CLASS

Name	*No*	*F/S*	*Name*	*No*	*F/S*
PAMLICO	WLIC 800	AA	**KENNEBEC**	WLIC 802	AA
HUDSON	WLIC 801	AA	**SAGINAW**	WLIC 803	AA

Displacement, tons: 459 full load
Dimensions, feet (metres): 160.9 × 30 × 4 *(49 × 9.1 × 1.2)*
Main machinery: 2 Caterpillar diesels; 1000 hp *(746 kW)*; 2 shafts
Speed, knots: 11.5

HUDSON *12/1989, Giorgio Arra*

3 COSMOS CLASS

Name	*No*	*F/S*
RAMBLER	WLIC 298	AA
SMILAX	WLIC 315	AA
PRIMROSE	WLIC 316	AA

Displacement, tons: 178 full load
Dimensions, feet (metres): 100 × 24 × 5 *(30.5 × 7.3 × 1.5)*
Main machinery: 2 Caterpillar D353 diesels; 600 hp *(448 kW)*; 2 shafts
Speed, knots: 10.5

PRIMROSE *7/1990, van Ginderen Collection*

9 ANVIL/CLAMP CLASSES

Name	*No*	*F/S*	*Name*	*No*	*F/S*	*Name*	*No*	*F/S*
ANVIL	WLIC 75301	AA	**MALLET**	WLIC 75304	AA	**WEDGE**	WLIC 75307	AA
HAMMER	WLIC 75302	AA	**VISE**	WLIC 75305	AA	**HATCHET**	WLIC 75309	AA
SLEDGE	WLIC 75303	AA	**CLAMP**	WLIC 75306	AA	**AXE**	WLIC 75310	AA

Displacement, tons: 140 full load
Dimensions, feet (metres): 75 (76—WLIC 75306-75310) × 22 × 4 *(22.9 (23.2) × 6.7 × 1.2)*
Main machinery: 2 Caterpillar diesels; 660 hp *(492 kW)*; 2 shafts
Speed, knots: 10
Complement: 13 (1 officer in *Mallet, Sledge* and *Vise)*

Comment: Completed 1962-65.

SLEDGE *7/1988, W. Donko*

HARBOUR TUGS

14 65 ft CLASS (WYTL)

CAPSTAN WYTL 65601
CHOCK WYTL 65602
SWIVEL WYTL 65603
TACKLE WYTL 65604
TOWLINE WYTL 65605
CATENARY WYTL 65606
BRIDLE WYTL 65607
PENDANT WYTL 65608
SHACKLE WYTL 65609
HAWSER WYTL 65610
LINE WYTL 65611
WIRE WYTL 65612
BOLLARD WYTL 65614
CLEAT WYTL 65615

Displacement, tons: 72 full load
Dimensions, feet (metres): 65 × 19 × 7 *(19.8 × 5.8 × 2.1)*
Main machinery: 1 diesel; 400 hp *(298 kW)*; 1 shaft
Speed, knots: 10
Complement: 10

Comment: Built from 1961 to 1967. All active in the Atlantic Fleet.

HAWSER *6/1991, Giorgio Arra*

2000 + RESCUE AND UTILITY CRAFT

Note: A new class of self-righting lifeboat 4720 is being built by Textron, New Orleans. Six ordered by early 1992, the first having completed trials in mid-1991. About 100 may eventually be acquired to replace existing classes.

Type 41 SAR Craft *7/1991, Giorgio Arra*

21 NAPCO SEA RAIDER TYPE

Displacement, tons: 1.3 full load
Dimensions, feet (metres): 22.3 × 7.4 × 1.2 *(6.7 × 2.3 × 0.4)*
Main machinery: 2 outboards; 310 hp *(231 kW)*
Speed, knots: 40. **Range, miles:** 167 at 25 kts
Complement: 3
Guns: 2—12.7 mm MGs.

Comment: Boston Whaler Hull built by NAPCO International. Can carry more than 2100 lbs of equipment. Transportable by trailer, helicopter sling or C-130 aircraft. Normally used on the Great Lakes to train CG reserves but 18 were deployed to the Gulf in 1990/91 where they were used for Port Security and other duties. All returned to the Great Lakes by 1992.

NAPCO Raider *1989, NAPCO International*

NATIONAL OCEANIC AND ATMOSPHERIC ADMINISTRATION

Command

Director, NOAA Corps Operations:
Rear Admiral Sigmund R Petersen
Director, Charting and Geodetic Services:
Rear Admiral J Austin Yeager
Deputy Director, NOAA Corps Operations:
Rear Admiral Christian Andreasen
Director, Atlantic Marine Center:
Rear Admiral Freddie L Jeffries
Director, Pacific Marine Center:
Rear Admiral Raymond L Speer
Director Aircraft Operations Center:
Rear Admiral Francis D Moran

Establishment

The Survey of the Coast was established by an act of the US Congress on February 10, 1807. In 1834 the organisation was renamed the US Coast Survey, and in 1878, the Coast and Geodetic Survey. In 1917 the Commissioned Officer Corps was established to provide a pool of sea-going scientists and engineers to command and operate the vessels of the Coast and Geodetic Survey, lead field parties, and manage research and engineering programs. The Coast and Geodetic Survey was made a component of the Environmental Science Services Administration in the US Department of Commerce on July 13, 1965. In October 1970, the Environmental Science Services Administration was reorganised and renamed the National Oceanic and Atmospheric Administration (NOAA). The Coast and Geodetic Survey was incorporated into NOAA as the National Ocean Survey, with its jurisdiction expanded to include functions of the US Lake Survey (formerly a part of the US Army Corps of Engineers), the US Coast Guard's national Data Buoy Development Project, and the US Navy's National Oceanographic Instrumentation Center. The Commissioned Officer Corps was renamed the NOAA Corps.

Missions

The office of NOAA Corps Operations is responsible to the US Department of Commerce. NOAA's research vessels conduct operations in hydrography, bathymetry, oceanography, atmospheric research, fisheries surveys and research, and related programmes in living and non-living marine resources. Larger research vessels operate in international waters; smaller vessels operate primarily in Atlantic and Pacific coastal waters, in the Gulfs of Mexico and Alaska, and in the US Lakes. The Office of NOAA also conducts diving operations and operates fixed-wing and rotary-wing aircraft for reconnaissance, oceanographic and atmospheric research, and to support aerial mapping and charting. NOAA is the largest component of the US Department of Commerce, with a diverse set of responsibilities in environmental science. These responsibilities include the Office of NOAA Corps Operations, the National Ocean Service, the National Weather Service, the National Marine Fisheries Service, the National Environmental Satellite, Data, and Information Service, and the Office of Oceanic and Atmospheric Research.

Ships

The following ships may be met with at sea. All are painted white with two-tone blue bands on the funnels and buff masts.
Oceanographic Survey Ships: *Researcher, Oceanographer, Surveyor, Malcolm Baldrige.*
Hydrographic Survey Ships: *Fairweather, Rainier, Mt. Mitchell.*
Coastal Survey Ships: *McArthur, Davidson, Whiting, Pierce.*
Coastal Vessels: *Rude, Heck, Ferrel.*
Fisheries Assessment: *Millar Freeman, Oregon II, Chapman, Albatros IV, Townsend Cromwell, David Jorden, Delaware II, John N Cobb, Murre II*
Two Stalwart class TAGOS ships may be taken on in 1992.

Personnel

The National Ocean Survey has approximately 400 commissioned officers and 12 000 civil service personnel. NOAA commissioned officers frequently serve with the military and may be transferred for hostilities.

Bases

Major: Norfolk, Va and Seattle, Wa.
Minor: Woods Hole, Mass; Pascagoula, Miss; Miami, Fla; La Jolla, Calif; Honolulu, Haw.

MALCOLM BALDRIGE *1989, NOAA*

PIERCE *1989, NOAA*

DELAWARE II *9/1989, van Ginderen Collection*

URUGUAY

Headquarters' Appointment

Commander-in-Chief of the Navy:
Vice Admiral James Coates

Diplomatic Representation

Naval Attaché in London:
Captain R H Medina

Personnel

(a) 1992: 5400 (including Marines, Air Arm and Prefectura)
(b) Voluntary service

Prefectura Naval (PNN)

Established in 1981 primarily for harbour security and coastline guard duties. In 1991 it was integrated with the Navy.

Base

Montevideo: Main naval base with two dry docks and a slipway
La Paloma: Naval station Ernesto Motto

Marines

Cuerpo de Fusileros' Navales consisting of 550 men in three units of 150 plus command company of 100.

Prefix to Ships' Names

ROU

Mercantile Marine

Lloyd's Register of Shipping:
91 vessels of 105 078 tons gross

DELETIONS

Frigate

1990 *Uruguay* (old)
1991 *18 de Julio*

Patrol Craft

1990 *Rio Negro* (old)

Support Ship

1991 *Vanguardia* (old)

FRIGATES

3 Ex-FRENCH COMMANDANT RIVIÈRE CLASS

Name	*No*	*Builders*	*Laid down*	*Launched*	*Commissioned*	*Recommissioned*
GENERAL ARTIGAS (ex-*Victor Schoelcher*)	2	Lorient Naval Dockyard	Oct 1957	11 Oct 1958	15 Oct 1962	9 Jan 1989
URUGUAY (ex-*Commandant Bourdais*)	1	Lorient Naval Dockyard	Apr 1959	15 Apr 1961	10 Mar 1962	20 Aug 1990
MONTEVIDEO (ex-*Amiral Charner*)	4	Lorient Naval Dockyard	Nov 1958	12 Mar 1960	14 Dec 1962	28 Jan 1991

Displacement, tons: 1750 standard; 2250 full load
Dimensions, feet (metres): 336.9 × 38.4 × 14.1 *(102.7 × 11.7 × 4.3)*
Main machinery: 4 SEMT-Pielstick 12PC series diesels; 16 000 hp(m) *(11.8 MW)*; 2 shafts
Speed, knots: 25. **Range, miles:** 7500 at 15 kts
Complement: 159 (9 officers)

Guns: 2 DCN 3.9 in *(100 mm)*/55 Mod 1953 automatic ❶; dual purpose; 80° elevation; 60 rounds/minute to 17 km *(9 nm)* anti-surface; 8 km *(4.4 nm)* anti-aircraft; weight of shell 13.5 kg. 2 Hispano Suiza 30 mm/70 ❷; 83° elevation; 600 rounds/minute to 8.5 km *(4.8 nm)* anti-aircraft.
Torpedoes: 6—21.7 in *(550 mm)* (2 triple) tubes ❸ ECAN L3; anti-submarine; active homing to 5.5 km *(3 nm)* at 25 kts; warhead 200 kg; depth to 300 m *(985 ft)*.
A/S mortars: 1 Mortier 305 mm 4-barrelled launcher ❹; automatic loading; range 2700 m; warhead 227 kg.
Countermeasures: ESM: ARBR 16; radar warning.
Radars: Air/surface search: Thomson-CSF DRBV 22A ❺; D band.
Navigation: Racal Decca 1226 ❻; I band.
Fire control: DRBC 32C ❼; I band.

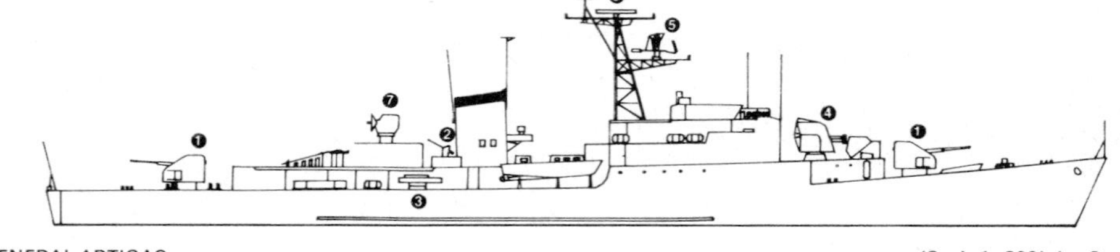

GENERAL ARTIGAS *(Scale 1 : 900), Ian Sturton*

Sonars: EDO SQS 17; hull-mounted; active search; medium frequency.
Thomson Sintra DUBA 3; active attack; high frequency.

Programmes: First one bought through SOFMA on 30 September 1988, second pair 14 March 1990. All refitted before transfer.

Structure: Exocet and Dagaie removed before transfer but SSM casings have been retained.
Operational: Can carry a Flag Officer and staff. In French service this class sometimes embarked up to 80 soldiers and two LCPs.

GENERAL ARTIGAS *12/1991, Peter Humphries*

LAND-BASED MARITIME AIRCRAFT (FRONT LINE)

Note: In addition there are also four helicopters (one Sikorsky CH-34A, one Bell 47G and two Westland Wessex) and nine fixed wing aircraft (5 T-28F, 3 Cessna C-182 and 1 Piper Seneca).

Numbers/Type: 4 Beechcraft Super King Air T34B/C.
Operational speed: 282 kts *(523 km/h)*.
Service ceiling: 35 000 ft *(10 670 m)*.
Range: 2030 nm *(3756 km)*.
Role/Weapon systems: Used for coastal patrol and protection operations, as well as transport. Sensors: Search radar. Weapons: Unarmed.

Numbers/Type: 3 Grumman S-3G Tracker.
Operational speed: 130 kts *(241 km/h)*.
Service ceiling: 25 000 ft *(7620 m)*.
Range: 1350 nm *(2500 km)*.
Role/Weapon systems: ASW and surface search with recently improved systems. Sensors: Search radar, MAD, sonobuoys. Weapons: ASW; torpedoes, depth bombs or mines. ASV; rockets underwing.

LIGHT FORCES

1 COASTAL PATROL CRAFT

Name	*No*	*Builders*	*Commissioned*
PAYSANDU	12 (ex-PR 12)	Sewart, USA	1968

Displacement, tons: 60 full load
Dimensions, feet (metres): 83 × 18 × 6 *(25.3 × 5.5 × 1.8)*
Main machinery: 2 GM 16V 71N diesels; 1400 hp *(1.04 MW)*; 2 shafts
Speed, knots: 22. **Range, miles:** 800 at 20 kts
Complement: 8
Guns: 3—12.7 mm MGs.
Radars: Surface search: Raytheon 1500B; I band.

Comment: Formerly incorrectly listed under Coast Guard.

3 VIGILANTE CLASS (LARGE PATROL CRAFT)

Name	*No*	*Builders*	*Commissioned*
25 de AGOSTO	5	CMN, Cherbourg	25 Mar 1981
15 de NOVIEMBRE	6	CMN, Cherbourg	25 Mar 1981
COMODORO COÉ	7	CMN, Cherbourg	25 Mar 1981

Displacement, tons: 190 full load
Dimensions, feet (metres): 137 × 22.4 × 5.2 *(41.8 × 6.8 × 1.6)*
Main machinery: 2 MTU 12 V538 TB91 diesels; 4600 hp(m) *(3.4 MW)* sustained; 2 shafts
Speed, knots: 28. **Range, miles:** 2400 at 15 kts
Complement: 28 (5 officers)
Gun: 1 Bofors 40 mm/70.
Fire control: CSEE Naja optronic director.
Radars: Surface search: Racal Decca TM 1226C; I band.

Comment: Ordered in 1979. Steel hull. First launched 16 October 1980, second 11 December 1980 and third 27 January 1981.

COMODORO COÉ *1981, CMN, Cherbourg*

1 LARGE PATROL CRAFT

Name	*No*	*Builders*	*Commissioned*
SALTO	14 (ex-GS 24, ex-PR 2)	Cantieri Navali Riuniti, Ancona	1936

Displacement, tons: 150 standard; 180 full load
Dimensions, feet (metres): 137 × 18 × 10 *(41.8 × 5.5 × 3.1)*
Main machinery: 2 GM diesels; 1000 hp *(746 kW)*; 2 shafts
Speed, knots: 17. **Range, miles:** 4000 at 10 kts
Complement: 26
Guns: 1 Bofors 40 mm/70.

Comment: She also acts as a survey vessel.

SALTO *1988, Uruguayan Navy*

2 Ex-US CAPE CLASS (LARGE PATROL CRAFT)

Name	*No*	*Builders*	*Commissioned*
COLONIA (ex-*Cape Higgon*)	10	Coast Guard Yard, Curtis Bay	14 Oct 1953
RIO NEGRO (ex-*Cape Horn*)	11	Coast Guard Yard, Curtis Bay	3 Sep 1958

Displacement, tons: 98 standard; 148 full load
Dimensions, feet (metres): 95 × 20.2 × 6.6 *(28.9 × 6.2 × 2)*
Main machinery: 2 GM 16V 149 TI diesels; 2070 hp *(1.54 MW)* sustained; 2 shafts
Speed, knots: 20. **Range, miles:** 2500 at 10 kts
Complement: 14 (1 officer)
Guns: 2—12.7 mm MGs.
Radars: Navigation: Raytheon SPS 64; I band

Comment: Designed for port security and search and rescue. Steel hulled. During modernisation in 1974 received new engines, electronics, and deck equipment, had superstructure modified or replaced, and had habitability improved. Transferred from the US Coast Guard in January 1990.

COLONIA *1/1990, Giorgio Arra*

MINE WARFARE FORCES

4 Ex-GERMAN KONDOR II CLASS (MINESWEEPERS—COASTAL)

Name	*No*	*Builders*	*Recommissioned*
TEMERARIO (ex-*Riesa*)	31	Peenewerft, Wolgast	11 Oct 1991
VALIENTE (ex-*Eilenburg*)	32	Peenewerft, Wolgast	11 Oct 1991
FORTUNA (ex-*Bernau*)	33	Peenewerft, Wolgast	11 Oct 1991
AUDAZ (ex-*Eisleben*)	34	Peenewerft, Wolgast	11 Oct 1991

Displacement, tons: 414 standard
Dimensions, feet (metres): 186 × 24.6 × 7.9 *(56.7 × 7.5 × 2.4)*
Main machinery: 2 Type 40D diesels; 5000 hp(m) *(3.68 MW)*; 2 shafts; cp props
Speed, knots: 21
Complement: 40
Guns: Twin 25 mm guns removed on transfer. To be replaced by 40 mm.
Mines: 2 rails.
Radars: Surface search: TSR 333; I band.

Comment: Built between 1970 and 1978 and belonged to the former GDR Navy. Transferred in October 1991 without armament. Possibly more to follow in due course.

AUDAZ *11/1991, van Ginderen Collection*

RESEARCH VESSEL

1 Ex-US AUK CLASS

Name	*No*	*Builders*	*Commissioned*
COMANDANTE PEDRO CAMPBELL (ex-USS *Chickadee*, MSF 59)	24 (ex-4, ex-MS 31, ex-MSF 1)	Defoe B & M Works	9 Nov 1942

Displacement, tons: 1090 standard; 1250 full load
Dimensions, feet (metres): 221.2 × 32.2 × 10.8 *(67.5 × 9.8 × 3.3)*
Main machinery: Diesel-electric; 4 Alco 539 diesels; 3532 hp *(2.63 MW)*; 2 motors; 2 shafts
Speed, knots: 18. **Range, miles:** 4300 at 10 kts
Complement: 105

Comment: Former US fleet minesweeper. Launched on 20 July 1942. Transferred on loan and commissioned at San Diego on 18 August 1966. Purchased 15 August 1976. Sweeping gear removed and classified as a corvette. Refitted again at Montevideo naval yard in 1988-89 and then recommissioned for Antarctic service without armament. Now classified as a 'Buque Cientifico' and has a red hull.

COMANDANTE PEDRO CAMPBELL (guns now removed) *1987, Uruguayan Navy*

SAIL TRAINING SHIP

Name	*No*	*Builders*	*Commissioned*
CAPITAN MIRANDA	20 (ex-GS 10)	Sociedad Espanola de Construccion Naval, Matagorda, Cadiz	1930

Displacement, tons: 516 standard; 527 full load
Dimensions, feet (metres): 179 × 26 × 10.5 *(54.6 × 7.9 × 3.2)*
Main machinery: 1 GM diesel; 600 hp *(448 kW)*; 1 shaft
Speed, knots: 11
Complement: 49

Comment: Originally a diesel-driven survey ship with pronounced clipper bow. Converted for service as a three-masted schooner, commissioning as cadet training ship in 1978.

CAPITAN MIRANDA *8/1990, van Ginderen Collection*

SALVAGE VESSELS

1 Ex-GERMAN PIAST CLASS

Name	*No*	*Builders*	*Commissioned*
VANGUARDIA (ex-*Otto Von Guericke*)	26 (ex-A 441)	Danzig, Poland	1977

Displacement, tons: 1732 full load
Dimensions, feet (metres): 240 × 39.4 × 13.1 *(73.2 × 12 × 4)*
Main machinery: 2 Skoda diesels; 3800 hp(m) *(2.79 MW)*; 2 shafts
Speed, knots: 16. **Range, miles:** 3000 at 12 kts
Radars: Navigation: TSR 333; I band.

Comment: Acquired from Germany in October 1991 and sailed from Rostock in January 1992 after a refit at Neptun-Warnow Werft. Carries extensive towing and firefighting equipment plus a diving bell forward of the bridge. Armed with four 25 mm twin guns when in service with the former GDR Navy.

VANGUARDIA *10/1991, Reinhard Kramer*

1 Ex-US COHOES CLASS

Name	*No*	*Builders*	*Commissioned*
HURACAN (ex-USS *Nahant* AN 83)	25 (ex-AM 25, ex-BT 30)	Commercial Ironworks, Portland, Oregon	24 Aug 1945

Displacement, tons: 650 standard; 855 full load
Dimensions, feet (metres): 168.5 × 33.8 × 11.7 *(51.4 × 10.3 × 3.6)*
Main machinery: Diesel-electric; 2 Busch-Sulzer 539 diesels; 1500 hp *(1.12 MW)*; 1 motor; 1 shaft
Speed, knots: 11.5
Complement: 48
Guns: 3 Oerlikon 20 mm.

Comment: Former US netlayer, transferred 15 October 1968 for salvage services carrying divers and underwater swimmers. In 1954 diving equipment and a recompression chamber were installed. Commissioned in Uruguayan Navy 7 April 1969.

HURACAN *1987, Uruguayan Navy*

AMPHIBIOUS CRAFT

2 LCM 6 CLASS

40 41

Displacement, tons: 24 light; 57 full load
Dimensions, feet (metres): 56.1 × 14.1 × 3.9 *(17.1 × 4.3 × 1.2)*
Main machinery: 2 Gray Marine 64 HN9 diesels; 330 hp *(264 kW)*; 2 shafts
Speed, knots: 9. **Range, miles:** 130 at 9 kts
Complement: 5
Military lift: 30 tons

Comment: Transferred on lease October 1972.

LCM 41 *1988, Uruguayan Navy*

2 LCVPs

42 45

Displacement, tons: 15 full load
Dimensions, feet (metres): 46.5 × 11.6 × 2.7 *(14.1 × 3.5 × 0.8)*
Main machinery: 1 GM 4-71 diesel; 115 hp *(86 kW)* sustained; 1 shaft
Speed, knots: 9. **Range, miles:** 580 at 9 kts
Military lift: 10 tons

Comment: Details given are for *45* which was built at Naval Shipyard, Montevideo and completed 1981. *42* is slightly smaller at 12 tons and has two Bedford diesels and two shafts. Two deleted in 1991.

TANKERS

Name	*No*	*Builders*	*Commissioned*
PRESIDENTE RIVERA (ex-M/V *Viking Harrier*)	—	Uddevallavarvet AB	2 July 1981

Measurement, tons: 42 235 gross; 87 325 dwt
Dimensions, feet (metres): 750 × 139.1 × 44.3 *(228.6 × 42.4 × 13.5)*
Main machinery: 1 MAN Burmeister & Wain diesel; 15 800 hp(m) *(11.6 MW)*; 1 shaft
Speed, knots: 15

Comment: Purchased in September 1987 and handed over in January 1988. Chartered to ANCAP (state oil company).

PRESIDENTE RIVERA *2/1991, van Ginderen Collection*

SUPPORT SHIPS

1 SOTOYOMO CLASS

Name	*No*	*Builders*	*Commissioned*
SAN JOSE (ex-*Lautaro*)	22 (ex-USS ATA 122, ex-62)	Levingstone SB Co	10 June 1943

Displacement, tons: 860 full load
Dimensions, feet (metres): 143 × 33.9 × 13 *(43.6 × 10.3 × 4)*
Main machinery: Diesel-electric; 2 GM 12-278A diesels; 2200 hp *(1.64 MW)*; 2 generators; 1 motor; 1500 hp *(1.12 MW)*; 1 shaft
Speed, knots: 13. **Range, miles:** 16 500 at 12 kts
Complement: 49 (3 officers)
Guns: 1 USN 3 in *(76 mm)*/50 Mk 26. 2 Oerlikon 20 mm.
Radars: Navigation: Decca 505; I band.

Comment: Originally an ocean rescue tug in USN service but was reclassified as a patrol vessel on transfer to the Chilean Navy. Paid off in 1990 and recommissioned in the Uruguay Navy on 17 May 1991.

SAN JOSE (old number) *1983*

SIRIUS 21

Displacement, tons: 290 full load
Dimensions, feet (metres): 115.1 × 32.8 × 5.9 *(35.1 × 10 × 1.8)*
Main machinery: 2 Detroit 12 V-71 TA diesels; 820 hp *(612 kW)* sustained; 2 shafts
Speed, knots: 11
Complement: 15

Comment: Buoy tender built at Montevideo Naval Yard and completed in 1988. Endurance, 5 days.

SIRIUS *1988, Uruguayan Navy*

BANCO ORTIZ (ex-*Zingst*, ex-*Elbe*) 7 (ex-Y 1655)

Displacement, tons: 261 full load

Comment: Ex-GDR Type 270 coastal tug acquired in October 1991.

BANCO ORTIZ *11/1991, Hartmut Ehlers*

VANUATU

Senior Officer

Commissioner of Police:
W D Saul

General

Originally the New Hebrides. Achieved independence on 30 July 1980, having previously been under Franco-British condominium. The Marine Police are based at Vita (capital) on Efate Island.

Mercantile Marine

Lloyd's Register of Shipping:
287 vessels of 2 172 621 tons gross

PATROL FORCES

1 PACIFIC FORUM PATROL CRAFT

Name	*No*	*Builders*	*Commissioned*
TUKORO	—	Australian Shipbuilding Industries	13 June 1987

Displacement, tons: 165 full load
Dimensions, feet (metres): 103.3 × 26.6 × 6.9 *(31.5 × 8.1 × 2.1)*
Main machinery: 2 Caterpillar 3516TA diesels; 2820 hp *(2.1 MW)* sustained; 2 shafts
Speed, knots: 18. **Range, miles:** 2500 at 12 kts
Complement: 18 (3 officers)
Guns: Can carry 1—20 mm and 2—12.7 mm MGs, but will probably remain unarmed.
Radars: Navigation: Furuno 1011; I band.

Comment: Under the Defence Co-operation Programme Australia has provided one Patrol Craft to the Vanuatu Government. Training and operational and technical assistance is also given by the Royal Australian Navy. Ordered 13 September 1985.

TUKORO *10/1991, Guy Toremans*

VENEZUELA

Headquarters' Appointments

Commander General of the Navy (Chief of Naval Operations):
Vice Admiral Ignacio Peña Cimarro
Deputy Chief of Naval Operations:
Vice Admiral Julian Mauco Quinta
Chief of Naval Staff:
Rear Admiral Hector Gerardo Pacheco Moreno

Diplomatic Representation

Naval Attaché in London:
Rear Admiral Jose H Tavio Gonzalez

Personnel

(a) 1992: 14 200 officers and men including 5200 Marine Corps
(b) 2 years national service

Marines

Two operational Commands—Western and Eastern. The Marines consist of four Battalion Groups—UTC 1 *Libertador Simón Bolívar,* at Maiquetía; UTC 2 *General Rafael Urdaneta,* at Puerto Cabello; UTC 3 *Mariscal José Antonio de Sucre,* at Carúpano and UTC 4 *General Francisco de Miranda,* at Punto Fijo—the existing battalions having been re-designated 'Unidades Tácticas de Combate'; an Amphibious Vehicles Unit—the Unidad de Tanques Anfíbios *Capitán de Corbeta Miguel Ponce Lugo,* equipped with nine LVTP7 amphibious APCs, one LVTC7 command vehicle and one LVTR7 recovery vehicle plus six EE-9 Cascavel armoured cars, 30 EE-11 APCs and eight EE-3 Jararacá scout cars; a Mixed Artillery Group (with twelve OTO Melara Model 56 105 mm howitzers, 16 Thomson-Brandt 120 mm mortars, one battery of Sea Cat SAMs and twelve M-42A1 S/P A/A guns); an Engineer Unit; a Signals Unit; a Transport Unit and one regiment of Naval Police. There is also the Comando Ribereno de Infantería de Marina *General Frank Rísquez Irribaren,* a paracommando unit and a unit of frogmen commandos.

Coast Guard

Formed in August 1982 as a para-naval force under the command of a Rear Admiral. With headquarters at La Guaira its primary task is the surveillance of the 200 mile Exclusive Economic Zone. Naval control.

National Guard

The Fuerzas Armadas de Cooperacion, generally known as the National Guard, is a paramilitary organisation, 10 000 strong. It is concerned, among other things, with customs and internal security—the Maritime Wing operates Coastal Patrol Craft.

Bases

Caracas: Main HQ. La Carlota Naval Air Station.
Puerto Cabello: Contralmirante Agustin Armario Main Naval Base, Naval Air Station Command, Naval Schools and Dockyard.
Punto Fijo: Mariscal Falcón Base for Fast Attack Craft.
La Guaira: Small Naval Base (Naval Academy).
Maracaibo: Teniente de Navio Pedro Lucas Urribarri Base for Coast Guard Squadron.
La Banquilla: Secondary Coast Guard Base.
La Tortuga, Los Testigos Islands and Aves de Sotavento: Minor Coast Guard Bases.
Ciudad Bolivar (Orinoco River): HQ Fluvial Command.

Fleet Organisation

The fleet is split into 'Type' squadrons—all the frigates together (except GC 11 and 12) and the same for submarines, light and amphibious forces. Service Craft Squadron composed of T 44 and BE 11, and Coast Guard Squadron includes GC 11 and 12, RA 33 and BO 11. The Fast Attack Squadron of the Constitución class is again subordinate to the Fleet Command. There is also a River Forces (Fluvial) Command subordinate to the Marines.

New Construction

Long term plans include two further submarines, four MCM vessels, two LSMs and a replenishment tanker. Current financial problems may continue to cause delays in construction.

Mercantile Marine

Lloyd's Register of Shipping:
278 vessels of 970 311 tons gross

Strength of the Fleet

Type	*Active*	*Building (Planned)*
Submarines, Patrol	2	—
Frigates	6	—
Fast Attack Craft—Missile/Gun	6	—
LSTs	5	—
LCUs	2	—
LCVPs	12	—
Transport	1	—
Survey Vessels	3	—
Coast Guard Craft	26	(4)
Sail Training Ship	1	—
National Guard CPC	100 approx	—

DELETIONS

1989 *Puerto Santo*
1990 *Picua, Felipe Larrazabal, Fernando Gomez*

PENNANT LIST

Submarines

S 31	Sabalo
S 32	Caribe

Frigates

GC 11	Almirante Clemente
GC 12	General Moran
F 21	Mariscal Sucre
F 22	Almirante Brión
F 23	General Urdaneta
F 24	General Soublette
F 25	General Salom
F 26	Almirante Garcia

Light Forces

PC 11	Constitución
PC 12	Federación
PC 13	Independencia
PC 14	Libertad
PC 15	Patria
PC 16	Victoria

Amphibious Forces

T 51	Amazonas
T 61	Capana
T 62	Esequibo
T 63	Goajira
T 64	Los Llanos
T 71	Margarita
T 72	La Orchila

Survey Ships

BO 11	Punta Brava
LH 11	Peninsula De Araya
LH 12	Peninsula De Paraguana

Auxiliaries

BE 11	Simon Bolivar
RA 33	Miguel Rodriguez
T 44	Puerto Cabello

SUBMARINES

Note: The Guppy II *Picua* is used for harbour training. Plans to acquire an ex-USN Barbel class have probably been shelved.

2 TYPE 209 CLASS (TYPE 1300)

Name	*No*	*Builders*	*Laid down*	*Launched*	*Commissioned*
SABALO	S 31 (ex-S 21)	Howaldtswerke, Kiel	2 May 1973	1 July 1975	6 Aug 1976
CARIBE	S 32 (ex-S 22)	Howaldtswerke, Kiel	1 Aug 1973	6 Nov 1975	11 Mar 1977

Displacement, tons: 1285 surfaced; 1600 dived
Dimensions, feet (metres): 200.1 × 20.3 × 18 *(61.2 × 6.2 × 5.5)*
Main machinery: Diesel-electric; 4 MTU 12V 493 AZ80 GA31L diesels; 2400 hp(m) *(1.76 MW)* sustained; 4 alternators; 1.7 MW; 1 Siemens motor; 4600 hp(m) *(3.38 MW)* sustained; 1 shaft
Speed, knots: 10 surfaced; 22 dived
Range, miles: 7500 at 10 kts surfaced
Complement: 33 (5 officers)

Torpedoes: 8—21 in *(533 mm)* bow tubes. Combination of (a) AEG SST 4; anti-surface; wire-guided; active/passive homing to 12 km *(6.6 nm)* at 35 kts or 28 km *(15.3 nm)* at 23 kts; warhead 260 kg and (b) Westinghouse Mk 37; anti-submarine; wire-guided; active/passive homing to 8 km *(4.4 nm)* at 24 kts; warhead 150 kg. 14 torpedoes carried. Swim-out discharge. May be replaced by Marconi Tigerfish.
Countermeasures: ESM: Radar warning.
Fire control: Krupp-Atlas TFCS.
Radars: Surface search: Thomson-CSF Calypso C61/63; I band; range 31 km *(17 nm)* for 10 m² target.
Sonars: Krupp Atlas; hull-mounted; passive/active search and attack; medium frequency.
Thomson Sintra DUUX 2; passive ranging.

Programmes: Type 209, IK81 designed by Ingenieurkontor Lübeck for construction by Howaldtswerke, Kiel and sale by Ferrostaal, Essen, all acting as a consortium. Both refitted at Kiel in 1981 and 1984 respectively. There are plans for two more of the class.
Modernisation: Being carried out by HDW at Kiel. *Sabalo* started in April 1990 and completed March 1992; *Caribe* started in June 1991. The hull is slightly lengthened and new engines, fire control, sonar and attack periscopes fitted.

SABALO *1990, HDW*

Structure: A single-hull design with two main ballast tanks and forward and after trim tanks. The additional length is due to the new sonar dome similar to German Type 206 system. Fitted with snort and remote machinery control. Slow revving single screw. Very high capacity batteries with GRP lead-acid cells and battery-cooling. Diving depth 250 m *(820 ft)*.
Operational: Endurance, 50 days patrol.

FRIGATES

6 MODIFIED LUPO CLASS

Name	No	Builders	Laid down	Launched	Commissioned
MARISCAL SUCRE	F 21	Fincantieri, Riva Trigoso	19 Nov 1976	28 Sep 1978	10 May 1980
ALMIRANTE BRIÓN	F 22	Fincantieri, Riva Trigoso	June 1977	22 Feb 1979	7 Mar 1981
GENERAL URDANETA	F 23	Fincantieri, Riva Trigoso	23 Jan 1978	23 Mar 1979	8 Aug 1981
GENERAL SOUBLETTE	F 24	Fincantieri, Riva Trigoso	26 Aug 1978	4 Jan 1980	5 Dec 1981
GENERAL SALOM	F 25	Fincantieri, Riva Trigoso	7 Nov 1978	13 Jan 1980	3 Apr 1982
ALMIRANTE GARCIA (ex-*José Felix Ribas*)	F 26	Fincantieri, Riva Trigoso	21 Aug 1979	4 Oct 1980	30 July 1982

Displacement, tons: 2208 standard; 2520 full load
Dimensions, feet (metres): 371.3 × 37.1 × 12.1 *(113.2 × 11.3 × 3.7)*
Main engines: CODOG; 2 Fiat/GE LM 2500 gas turbines; 44 000 hp *(32.8 MW)*; 2 GMT A230.20M diesels; 7800 hp(m) *(5.7 MW)*; 2 shafts; cp props
Speed, knots: 35; 21 on diesels. **Range, miles:** 5000 at 15 kts
Complement: 185

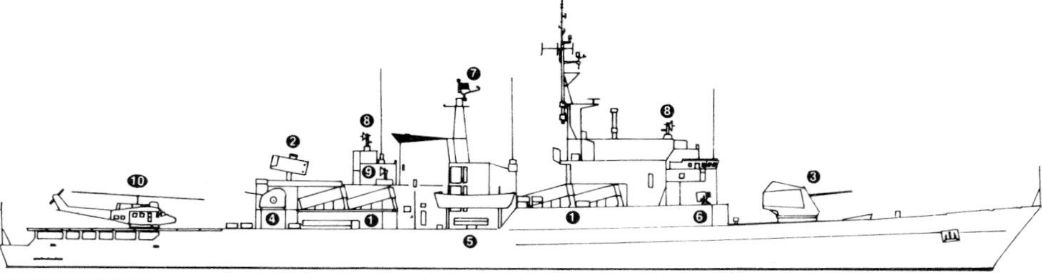

MARISCAL SUCRE *(Scale 1 : 900), Ian Sturton*

Missiles: SSM: 8 OTO Melara/Matra Otomat Teseo Mk 2 TG1 ❶; active radar homing to 80 km *(43.2 nm)* at 0.9 Mach; warhead 210 kg; sea-skimmer for last 4 km *(2.2 nm)*.
SAM: Selenia Elsag Albatros octuple launcher ❷; 8 Aspide; semi-active radar homing to 13 km *(7 nm)* at 2.5 Mach; height envelope 15-5000 m *(49.2-16 405 ft)*; warhead 30 kg.
Guns: 1 OTO Melara 5 in *(127 mm)*/54 ❸; 85° elevation; 45 rounds/minute to 16 km *(8.7 nm)*; weight of shell 32 kg.
4 Breda 40 mm/70 (2 twin) ❹; 85° elevation; 300 rounds/minute to 12.5 km *(6.8 nm)*; weight of shell 0.96 kg.
Torpedoes: 6—324 mm ILAS 3 (2 triple) tubes ❺. Whitehead A 244S; anti-submarine; active/passive homing to 7 km *(3.8 nm)* at 33 kts; warhead 34 kg (shaped charge).
Countermeasures: Decoys: 2 Breda 105 mm SCLAR 20-barrelled trainable ❻; Chaff to 5 km *(2.7 nm)*; illuminants to 12 km *(6.6 nm)*. Can be used for HE bombardment.
ESM: Sperry Marine Guardian Star; intercept.

Fire control: Selenia IPN 10 action data automation. 2 Elsag NA 10 MFCS. 2 Dardo GFCS for 40 mm.
Radars: Air/surface search: Selenia RAN 10S ❼; E/F band; range 155 km *(85 nm)*.
Surface search: SMA SPQ/2F; I band; range 73 km *(40 nm)*.
Fire control: Two Selenia Orion 10XP ❽; I/J band.
Two Selenia RTN 20X ❾; I/J band; range 15 km *(8 nm)* (for Dardo).
Tacan: SRN 15A.
Sonars: EDO SQS 29 (Mod 610E); hull-mounted; active search and attack; medium frequency.

Helicopters: 1 AB 212ASW ❿.

Programmes: All ordered on 24 October 1975. Similar to ships in the Italian and Peruvian navies.
Modernisation: Tenders invited in 1991 for a contract to update two of the class starting in 1992. New communications, EW and data link equipment to be fitted. The helicopter is also to be upgraded.
Structure: Fixed hangar means no space for Aspide reloads. Fully stabilised.

ALMIRANTE BRIÓN *7/1989*

SHIPBORNE AIRCRAFT

Numbers/Type: 5 Agusta AB 212ASW.
Operational speed: 106 kts *(196 km/h)*.
Service ceiling: 14 200 ft *(4330 m)*.
Range: 230 nm *(426 km)*.
Role/Weapon systems: ASW helicopter with secondary ASV role; has ECM/EW potential. Sensors: APS-705 search radar, Bendix ASQ-18A dipping sonar. Weapons: ASW; 2 × Mk 46 or A244/S torpedoes or depth bombs. ASV, 2 × Marte anti-ship missiles.

LAND-BASED MARITIME AIRCRAFT

Numbers/Type: 1 CASA C-212 S 3 Aviocar.
Operational speed: 190 kts *(353 km/h)*.
Service ceiling: 24 000 ft *(7315 m)*.
Range: 1650 nm *(3055 km)*.
Role/Weapon systems: Medium-range MR and coastal protection aircraft; limited armed action. Eight additional aircraft reported ordered in mid-1990 to replace the Trackers and to provide two Communications aircraft. Sensors: APS-128 radar. Weapons: ASW; depth bombs. ASV; gun and rocket pods.

Numbers/Type: 6 Grumman S-2E Tracker.
Operational speed: 130 kts *(241 km/h)*.
Service ceiling: 25 000 ft *(7620 m)*.
Range: 1350 nm *(2500 km)*.
Role/Weapon systems: ASW, surface search and armed MR in Caribbean Sea. Plans to update engines have been abandoned. Sensors: Search radar, MAD, 32 × sonobuoys. Weapons: ASW; internally carried torpedoes, depth bombs and/or mines. ASV; 6 × 127 mm rockets.

Numbers/Type: 3 Agusta ASH-3H Sea King.
Operational speed: 120 kts *(222 km/h)*.
Service ceiling: 12 200 ft *(3720 m)*.
Range: 630 nm *(1165 km)*.
Role/Weapon systems: Medium ASW support. Sensors: Selenia MM/APS-705 chin-mounted search radar, limited ESM. Weapons: ASW, 4 × Mk 46 or A244/S torpedoes or 4 × depth bombs, or combination. ASV; 2 × Marte anti-ship missiles.

AMPHIBIOUS FORCES

Note: In addition there are 11 LCVPs built in 1976.

4 CAPANA CLASS (TANK LANDING SHIPS)

Name	No	Builders	Commissioned
CAPANA	T 61	Korea Tacoma Marine	24 July 1984
ESEQUIBO	T 62	Korea Tacoma Marine	24 July 1984
GOAJIRA	T 63	Korea Tacoma Marine	20 Nov 1984
LOS LLANOS	T 64	Korea Tacoma Marine	20 Nov 1984

Displacement, tons: 4070 full load
Dimensions, feet (metres): 343.8 × 50.5 × 9.8 *(104.8 × 15.4 × 3)*
Main machinery: 2 diesels; 7200 hp(m) *(5.3 MW)*; 2 shafts
Speed, knots: 14. **Range, miles:** 5600 at 11 kts
Complement: 117 (13 officers)
Cargo capacity: 202 troops; 1600 tons cargo; 4 LCVPs
Guns: 2 Breda 40 mm/70 (twin). 2 Oerlikon 20 mm GAM-BO1.
Fire control: Selenia NA 18/V; optronic director.
Helicopters: Platform only.

Comment: Ordered in August 1982. Version III of Korea Tacoma Alligator type. Each has a 50 ton tank turntable and a lift between decks. Similar to Indonesian LSTs.

CAPANA *1990*

1 Ex-US TERREBONNE PARISH CLASS (LST)

Name	*No*	*Builders*	*Commissioned*
AMAZONAS (ex-USS *Vernon County* LST 1161)	T 51 (ex-T 21)	Ingalls Shipbuilding Corp	1953

Displacement, tons: 2590 light; 5800 full load
Dimensions, feet (metres): 384 oa × 55 × 17 *(117.4 × 16.8 × 3.7)*
Main machinery: 4 GM 16-278A diesels; 6000 hp *(4.48 MW)*; 2 shafts; cp props
Speed, knots: 15. **Range, miles:** 6000 at 12 kts
Complement: 116
Military lift: 395 troops; 2000 tons cargo; 4 LCVPs
Guns: 6 USN 3 in *(76 mm)*/50 (3 twin).
Fire control: 2 Mk 63 GFCS.
Radars: Surface search: Racal Decca; I band.
Fire control: Two Western Electric Mk 34; I/J band.

Comment: Built 1952-53. Transferred on loan 29 June 1973. Purchased 1977. Recommissioned following repairs after grounding 6 August 1980.

AMAZONAS *1990, van Ginderen Collection*

2 LCUs

Name	*No*	*Builders*	*Commissioned*
MARGARITA	T 71	Swiftships Inc, Morgan City	Jan 1984
LA ORCHILA	T 72	Swiftships Inc, Morgan City	May 1984

Displacement, tons: 390 full load
Dimensions, feet (metres): 129.9 × 36.1 × 5.9 *(39.6 × 11 × 1.8)*
Main machinery: 2 Detroit 16V-149 diesels; 1800 hp *(1.34 MW)* sustained; 2 shafts
Speed, knots: 13. **Range, miles:** 1500 at 10 kts
Complement: 26 (4 officers)
Military lift: 150 tons cargo; 100 tons fuel
Guns: 3—12.7 mm MGs.

Comment: Both serve in River Command. Reported that four or more are planned in due course. Have a 15 ton crane.

MARGARITA (with MANAURE alongside) *1989, Venezuelan Navy*

LIGHT FORCES

Note: Plans for new patrol craft have been delayed by priority being given to modernisation programme. Tenders were called for in mid-1990 for up to four 800 ton offshore patrol vessels for the Coast Guard.

6 VOSPER THORNYCROFT 121 ft CLASS (FAST ATTACK CRAFT—MISSILE AND GUN)

Name	*No*	*Builders*	*Laid down*	*Launched*	*Commissioned*
CONSTITUCIÓN	PC 11	Vosper Thornycroft	Jan 1973	1 June 1973	16 Aug 1974
FEDERACIÓN	PC 12	Vosper Thornycroft	Aug 1973	26 Feb 1974	25 Mar 1975
INDEPENDENCIA	PC 13	Vosper Thornycroft	Feb 1973	24 July 1973	20 Sep 1974
LIBERTAD	PC 14	Vosper Thornycroft	Sep 1973	5 Mar 1974	12 June 1975
PATRIA	PC 15	Vosper Thornycroft	Mar 1973	27 Sep 1973	9 Jan 1975
VICTORIA	PC 16	Vosper Thornycroft	Mar 1974	3 Sep 1974	22 Sep 1975

Displacement, tons: 170 full load
Dimensions, feet (metres): 121 × 23.3 × 6 *(36.9 × 7.1 × 1.8)*
Main machinery: 2 MTU MD 16V538 TB90 diesels; 6000 hp(m) *(4.4 MW)* sustained; 2 shafts
Speed, knots: 31. **Range, miles:** 1350 at 16 kts
Complement: 20 (4 officers)

Missiles: SSM: 2 OTO Melara/Matra Otomat Teseo Mk 2 TG1 *(Federación, Libertad* and *Victoria)*; active radar homing to 80 km *(43.2 nm)* at 0.9 Mach; warhead 210 kg; sea-skimmer.
Guns: 1 OTO Melara 3 in *(76 mm)*/62 compact *(Constitución, Independencia* and *Patria)*; 85° elevation; 85 rounds/minute to 16 km *(8.7 nm)*; weight of shell 6 kg.
1 Breda 40 mm/70 *(Federación, Libertad* and *Victoria)*; may be replaced by 30 mm guns which may also be fitted in the other three of the class.
Fire control: Elsag NA 10 Mod 1 GFCS.
Radars: Surface search: SPQ 2D.
Fire control: Selenia RTN 10X (in 76 mm ships); I/J band.

Programmes: Transferred from the Navy in 1983 to the Coast Guard but now back again with Fleet Command.
Modernisation: All were to have been modernised with the three gun FACs being fitted with Harpoon SSM in place of the 76 mm and Harpoon replacing Otomat in the other three. It is possible that this may not now happen if the Harpoon missiles are to be used for shore-based coastal defence. Single Breda 30 mm guns were acquired in 1989 and may replace the other 40 mm as well as being fitted in the missile craft.

FEDERACIÓN (with Otomat) *7/1990, Venezuelan Navy*

CONSTITUCIÓN *7/1990 Venezuelan Navy*

SERVICE FORCES

Note: (1) A fleet tanker is to be acquired as soon as possible.
(2) A Torpedo Recovery Vessel was ordered from Maracaibo in 1989.

1 LOGISTIC SUPPORT SHIP

Name	*No*	*Builders*	*Commissioned*
PUERTO CABELLO (ex-M/V *Sierra Nevada*)	T 44	Drammen Slip & Verk, Drammen	1972

Displacement, tons: 13 500 full load
Measurement, tons: 6682 gross; 9218 dwt
Dimensions, feet (metres): 461.3 × 59 × 29.5 *(140.6 × 18 × 9)*
Main machinery: 1 Sulzer diesel; 13 200 hp(m) *(9.7 MW)*; 1 shaft
Speed, knots: 22.5

Comment: Commissioned in the Navy 22 May 1986. Former refrigerated cargo ship.

PUERTO CABELLO *5/1991, Giorgio Arra*

SAIL TRAINING SHIP

Name	*No*	*Builders*	*Commissioned*
SIMON BOLIVAR	BE 11	A T Celaya, Bilbao	6 Aug 1980

Displacement, tons: 1260 full load
Measurement, tons: 934 gross
Dimensions, feet (metres): 270.6 × 34.8 × 14.4 *(82.5 × 10.6 × 4.4)*
Main machinery: 1 Detroit 12V-149T diesel; 875 hp *(652 kW)* sustained; 1 shaft
Speed, knots: 10
Complement: 195 (17 officers, 76 ratings, 18 midshipwomen, 84 midshipmen)

Comment: Ordered in 1978. Launched 21 November 1979. Three-masted barque; near sister to *Guayas* (Ecuador). Sail area (23 sails), 1650 m². Highest mast, 131.2 ft *(40 m)*.

SIMON BOLIVAR *5/1988, Giorgio Arra*

SURVEY VESSELS

Name	*No*	*Builders*	*Commissioned*
PUNTA BRAVA	BO 11	Bazán, Cartagena	14 Mar 1991

Displacement, tons: 1170 full load
Dimensions, feet (metres): 202.4 × 39 × 12.1 *(61.7 × 11.9 × 3.7)*
Main machinery: 2 Bazán-MAN 7L 20/27 diesels; 2500 hp(m) *(1.84 MW)*; 2 shafts
Speed, knots: 13. **Range, miles:** 8000 at 13 kts
Complement: 49 (6 officers) plus 6 scientists
Radars: Navigation: ARPA; I band.

Comment: Ordered in September 1988 and launched 9 March 1990. Developed from the Spanish Malaspina class. A multi-purpose ship for oceanography, marine resource evaluation, geophysical and biological research. Equipped with Qubit hydrographic system. Carries two survey launches. EW equipment is to be fitted.

PUNTA BRAVA *1991, Bazán*

Name	*No*	*Builders*	*Commissioned*
PENINSULA DE ARAYA (ex-*Gabriela*)	LH 11 (ex-P 119)	Abeking & Rasmussen, Lemwerder	5 Feb 1974
PENINSULA DE PARAGUANA (ex-*Lely*)	LH 12 (ex-P 121)	Abeking & Rasmussen, Lemwerder	7 Feb 1974

Displacement, tons: 90 full load
Dimensions, feet (metres): 88.6 × 18.4 × 4.9 *(27 × 5.6 × 1.5)*
Main machinery: 2 MTU diesels; 2300 hp(m) *(1.69 MW)*; 2 shafts
Speed, knots: 20
Complement: 9 (1 officer)

Comment: LH 12 laid down 28 May 1973, launched 12 December 1973 and LH 11 laid down 10 March 1973, launched 29 November 1973. Acquired in September 1986 from the Instituto de Canalizaciones.

COAST GUARD

2 ALMIRANTE CLEMENTE CLASS

Name	*No*	*Builders*	*Commissioned*
ALMIRANTE CLEMENTE	GC 11	Ansaldo, Leghorn	1956
GENERAL MORAN	GC 12	Ansaldo, Leghorn	1956

Displacement, tons: 1300 standard; 1500 full load
Dimensions, feet (metres): 325.1 × 35.5 × 12.2 *(99.1 × 10.8 × 3.7)*
Main machinery: 2 GMT 16-645E7C diesels; 6080 hp(m) *(4.47 MW)* sustained; 2 shafts
Speed, knots: 22. **Range, miles:** 3500 at 15 kts
Complement: 162 (12 officers)

Guns: 2 OTO Melara 3 in *(76 mm)*/62 compact; 85° elevation; 85 rounds/minute to 16 km *(8.7 nm)*; weight of shell 6 kg.
2 Breda 40 mm/70 (twin); 85° elevation; 300 rounds/minute to 12.5 km *(6.8 nm)*; weight of shell 0.96 kg.
Torpedoes: 6—324 mm ILAS 3 (2 triple) tubes. Whitehead A 244S; anti-submarine; active/passive homing to 7 km *(3.8 nm)* at 33 kts; warhead 34 kg (shaped charge).
Fire control: Elsag NA 10 GFCS.
Radars: Air search: Plessey AWS 4; D band.
Surface search: Racal Decca 1226; I band.
Fire control: Selenia RTN 10X; I/J band; range 40 km *(22 nm)*.
Sonars: Plessey PMS 26; hull-mounted; active search and attack; 10 kHz.

Programmes: Survivors of a class of six ordered in 1953. Both laid down 5 May 1954 and launched 12 December 1954.
Modernisation: Both ships were refitted by Cammell Laird/Plessey group in April 1968. 4 in guns replaced by 76 mm OTO Melara compact. Both refitted again in Italy in 1983-85, prior to transfer to Coast Guard duties.
Structure: Fitted with Denny-Brown fin stabilisers and air-conditioned throughout the living and command spaces.
Operational: Navigation, SATNAV fitted. Oil fuel, 350 tons.

ALMIRANTE CLEMENTE *1989, Venezuelan Navy*

1 Ex-US CHEROKEE CLASS

Name	*No*	*Builders*	*Commissioned*
MIGUEL RODRIGUEZ (ex-USS *Salinan* ATF 161)	RA 33 (ex-R 23)	Charleston SB and DD Co	9 Nov 1945

Displacement, tons: 1235 standard; 1675 full load
Dimensions, feet (metres): 205 × 38.5 × 17 *(62.5 × 11.7 × 5.2)*
Main machinery: Diesel-electric; 4 GM 16-278A diesels; 4400 hp *(3.28 MW)*; 4 generators; 1 motor; 3000 hp *(2.24 MW)*; 1 shaft
Speed, knots: 15. **Range, miles:** 7000 at 15 kts.
Complement: 85
Guns: 1 USN 3 in *(76 mm)*/50 *(Felipe Larrazábal)*.
Radars: Navigation: Sperry SPS 53; I/J band.

Comment: Acquired on 1 September 1978. Last of a class of three.

MIGUEL RODRIGUEZ *7/1990, Venezuelan Navy*

1 Ex-US POINT CLASS

PETREL (ex-*Point Knoll*) **PG 31** (ex-WPB 82367)

Displacement, tons: 66 full load
Dimensions, feet (metres): 83 × 17.2 × 5.8 *(25.3 × 5.2 × 1.8)*
Main machinery: 2 Caterpillar diesels; 1600 hp *(1.19 MW)*; 2 shafts
Speed, knots: 23.5. **Range, miles:** 1500 at 8 kts
Complement: 10 (1 officer)

Comment: Transferred in early 1992. The 12.7 mm MGs in US service may be upgraded. More of the class may be acquired.

2 UTILITY CRAFT

LOS TAQUES LG 11 **LOS CAYOS** LG 12

Comment: Former trawlers; displacement, 300 tons. Commissioned 15 May 1981 and 17 July 1984 respectively. Used for salvage and SAR tasks.

LOS CAYOS *1989, Venezuelan Navy*

8 RIVER PATROL CRAFT

Name	*No*	*Displacement (tons)*	*Speed (kts)*
MANAURE	PF 21	18	15
MARA	PF 22	18	15
GUAICAIPURO	PF 23	14	15
TAMANACO	PF 24	14	15
TEREPAIMA	PF 31	3	45
TIUNA	PF 32	3	45
YARACUY	PF 33	3	45
SOROCAIMA	PF 34	3	45

Comment: All have a complement of five and are armed with one 12.7 mm MG. See picture of *Margarita* with *Manaure* alongside (p 812).

6 RIVER CRAFT

ANACOCO LF 11 **ATURES** LF 13 **EL AMPARO** LA 01
MANAIPO LF 12 **MAIPURES** LF 14 **YOPITO** LC 01

Comment: *El Amparo* is an ambulance launch similar to PF 31.

7 INSHORE PATROL CRAFT

POLARIS LG 21 **RIGEL** LG 23 **ANTARES** LG 25 **ALTAIR** LG 27
SPICA LG 22 **ALDEBARAN** LG 24 **CANOPUS** LG 26

Displacement, tons: 5 full load
Dimensions, feet (metres): 32.8 × 8.5 × 2.6 *(10 × 2.6 × 0.8)*
Main machinery: 2 diesels; 400 hp(m) *(294 kW)*; 2 shafts
Speed, knots: 45. **Range, miles:** 140 at 45 kts
Complement: 4

Comment: Acquired in 1987 from Cougar Marine, Hamble.

NATIONAL GUARD

(FUERZAS ARMADAS DE COOPERACION)

Note: Up to about 100 patrol craft in total including River Launches and undecked District Craft.

22 ITALIAN TYPE A (COASTAL PATROL CRAFT)

Name	*No*	*Name*	*No*
RIO ORINOCO	A 7414	**RIO CAPANAPARO**	A 7425
RIO CUYUNI	A 7415	**RIO YURUARI**	A 7426
RIO VENTUARI	A 7416	**RIO CAURA**	A 7427
RIO CAPARO	A 7417	**RIO MOTATAN**	A 7628
RIO TOCUYO	A 7418	**RIO GRITA**	A 7629
RIO VENAMO	A 7419	**RIO YURUAN**	A 7630
RIO LIMON	A 7420	**RIO BOCONO**	A 7631
RIO SAN JUAN	A 7421	**RIO NEVERI**	A 7632
RIO TURBIO	A 7422	**RIO CARONI**	A 7633
RIO TORBES	A 7423	**RIO GUANARE**	A 7634
RIO ESCALANTE	A 7424	**RIO GUAINIA**	A 7635

Italian built (A 7414, A 7416-A 7424)

Displacement, tons: 48 full load
Dimensions, feet (metres): 75.4 × 19 × 8.5 *(23 × 5.8 × 2.6)*
Main machinery: 2 MTU 12V 493 TY70 diesels; 2200 hp(m) *(1.62 MW)* sustained; 2 shafts
Speed, knots: 30. **Range, miles:** 500 at 25 kts
Complement: 8
Guns: 1—12.7 mm MG.
Radars: Navigation: FR 24; I band.

Comment: First ordered in May 1973 from INMA, La Spezia and delivered from 1974 onwards.

Venezuelan built (A 7415, A 7425-A 7635)

Displacement, tons: 43 full load
Dimensions, feet (metres): 76.8 × 16.1 × 10.2 *(23.4 × 4.9 × 3.1)*
Main machinery: 2 GM 12V 92 TI diesels; 2040 hp *(1.52 kW)* sustained; 2 shafts
Speed, knots: 30. **Range, miles:** 1000 at 25 kts
Complement: 12
Guns: 1—12.7 mm MG.
Radars: Navigation: FR 711; I band.

Comment: Ordered from Dianca, Puerto Cabello.

RIO GUANARE *1989*

2 VENEZUELAN TYPE

RIO ALTAGRACIA A 6704 **RIO MANZANARES** A 6705

Dimensions, feet (metres): 49.2 × 12.5 × 6.2 *(15 × 3.8 × 1.9)*
Main machinery: 1 Type 4B-316 diesel; 1 shaft
Speed, knots: 12. **Range, miles:** 140 at 12 kts
Complement: 6
Radars: Navigation: FR 10; I band.

12 PUNTA CLASS

Name	*No*	*Name*	*No*
PUNTA BARIMA	A 8201	**PUNTA MACOYA**	A 8307
PUNTA MOSQUITO	A 8202	**PUNTA MORON**	A 8308
PUNTA MULATOS	A 8203	**PUNTA UNARE**	A 8309
PUNTA PERRET	A 8204	**PUNTA BALLENA**	A 8310
PUNTA CARDON	A 8205	**PUNTA MACURO**	A 8311
PUNTA PLAYA	A 8206	**PUNTA MARIUSA**	A 8312

Displacement, tons: 15 full load
Dimensions, feet (metres): 43 × 13.4 × 3.9 *(13.1 × 4.1 × 1.2)*
Main machinery: 2 Detroit 12V-92TA diesels; 1020 hp *(761 kW)* sustained; 2 shafts
Speed, knots: 28. **Range, miles:** 390 at 25 kts
Complement: 4
Guns: 2—12.7 mm MGs.
Radars: Navigation: Raytheon; I band.

Comment: Ordered 24 January 1984. Built by Bertram Yacht, Miami, Florida. Aluminium hulls. Completed from July-December 1984.

PUNTA Class (alongside RIO GUANARE) *1989*

12 PROTECTOR CLASS

Name	No	Name	No
RIO ARAUCA II	B 8421	**RIO SARARE**	B 8427
RIO CATATUMBO II	B 8422	**RIO URIBANTE**	B 8428
RIO APURE II	B 8423	**RIO SINARUCO**	B 8429
RIO NEGRO II	B 8424	**RIO ICABARU**	B 8430
RIO META II	B 8425	**RIO GUARICO II**	B 8431
RIO PORTUGUESA II	B 8426	**RIO YARACUY**	B 8432

Displacement, tons: 15 full load
Dimensions, feet (metres): 43.6 × 14.8 × 3.9 *(13.3 × 4.5 × 1.2)*
Main machinery: 2 Detroit 8V 92TA diesels; 750 hp *(560 kW)* sustained; 2 shafts
Speed, knots: 28. **Range, miles:** 600 at 25 kts
Complement: 4
Guns: 3—12.7 mm MGs.

Comment: Built by SeaArk Marine, Monticello and commissioned in 1987.

RIO META II and others *1987, SeaArk*

10 LAGO CLASS (RIVER PATROL CRAFT)

Name	No	Name	No
LAGO 1	A 6901	**RIO CHAMA**	A 7919
LAGO 2	A 6902	**RIO CARIBE**	A 7920
LAGO 3	A 6903	**RIO TUY**	A 7921
LAGO 4	A 6904	**MANATI**	A 7929
RIO CABRIALES	A 7918	**GOAIGOAZA**	A 8223

Displacement, tons: 1.5 full load
Dimensions, feet (metres): 20.7 × 7.9 × 1 *(6.3 × 2.4 × 0.3)*
Main machinery: 2 Evinrude outboard petrol engines; 230 hp *(172 kW)*
Speed, knots: 30. **Range, miles:** 120 at 15 kts
Complement: 4
Guns: 1—12.7 mm MG.
Radars: Navigation: FR 10.

Comment: Built by SeaArk Marine, Monticello. All delivered 6 August 1984. The last pair are classified as Yachts.

15 SEA ARK TYPE (RIVER PATROL CRAFT)

Displacement, tons: 0.5
Dimensions, feet (metres): 18 × 6.9 × 0.7 *(5.5 × 2.1 × 0.2)*
Main machinery: 1 OMC outboard
Speed, knots: 30. **Range, miles:** 75 at 15 kts
Complement: 4
Guns: 1—12.7 mm MG.

Comment: Ordered from SeaArk Marine, Monticello. Completed May-August 1984. Aluminium hull.

VIETNAM

Headquarters' Appointment

Chief of Naval Forces:
Vice Admiral Hoang Hau Thai

Personnel

(a) 1992: 9000 regulars
(b) Additional conscripts on three to four year term (about 3000)
(c) 27 000 naval infantry

Strength of the Fleet

From 1978 to 1990 the USSR transferred a number of ships and craft as well as providing fuel in return for the use of Cam-Ranh Bay naval base. From 1 January 1991 the relationship became formal with further transfers only available at market prices. Many of the ex-US naval ships have now been deleted either by sale or scrap. The resultant order of battle is now composed of vessels most of which can lay some claim to operational availability. There are many others still alongside in naval bases either as hulks or providing spares for the operational units.

Bases

Cam Ranh Bay, Cân Tho, Hai Phong, Hue, Da Nang, Hanoi.

Pennant numbers

Appear to change frequently.

Mercantile Marine

Lloyd's Register of Shipping:
230 vessels of 574 023 tons gross

FRIGATES

5 Ex-SOVIET PETYA CLASS

HQ 09, 11 (Type III) **HQ 13, 15, 17 (Type II)**

Displacement, tons: 950 standard; 1180 full load
Dimensions, feet (metres): 268.3 × 29.9 × 9.5 *(81.8 × 9.1 × 2.9)*
Main machinery: CODAG; 2 gas turbines; 30 000 hp(m) *(22 MW)*; 1 diesel; 6000 hp(m) *(4.4 MW)*; 3 shafts
Speed, knots: 32. **Range, miles:** 4870 at 10 kts; 450 at 29 kts
Complement: 98

Guns: 4 USSR 3 in *(76 mm)*/60 (2 twin); 80° elevation; 90 rounds/minute to 15 km *(8 nm)*; weight of shell 6.8 kg.
Torpedoes: 3—21 in *(533 mm)* (triple) tubes (Petya III). Soviet Type 53; dual purpose; pattern active/passive homing up to 20 km *(10.8 nm)* at up to 45 kts; warhead 400 kg.
10—16 in *(406 mm)* (2 quin) tubes (Petya II). Soviet Type 40; anti-submarine; active/passive homing up to 15 km *(8 nm)* at up to 40 kts; warhead 100-150 kg.
A/S mortars: 4 RBU 6000 12-tubed trainable (Petya II); range 6000 m; warhead 31 kg.
4 RBU 2500 16-tubed trainable (Petya III); range 2500 m; warhead 21 kg.
Depth charges: 2 racks.
Mines: Can carry 22.
Countermeasures: ESM: 2 Watch Dog; radar warning.
Radars: Air/surface search: Strut Curve; F band; range 110 km *(60 nm)* for 2 m^2 target.
Navigation: Don 2; I band.
Fire control: Hawk Screech; I band.
IFF: High Pole B. Two Square Head.
Sonars: Hull-mounted; active attack; high frequency.

Programmes: Two Petya III (export version) transferred in December 1978 and three Petya IIs, two in December 1983 and one in December 1984.
Structure: The Petya IIIs have the same hulls as the Petya IIs but are fitted with one triple 21 in *(533 mm)* torpedo launcher in place of the two 16 in *(406 mm)* quintuple tubes and have four RBU 2500s in place of two RBU 6000s.

PETYA II *1989*

1 Ex-US SAVAGE CLASS

Name	No	Builders	Commissioned
DAI KY (ex-*Tran Khanh Du*, ex-USS *Forster* DER 334)	HQ 03	Consolidated Steel Corporation, Orange, Texas	25 Jan 1944

Displacement, tons: 1590 standard; 1850 full load
Dimensions, feet (metres): 306 × 36.6 × 14 *(93.3 × 11.2 × 4.3)*
Main machinery: 4 Fairbanks-Morse 38D8-1/8-10 diesels; 7080 hp *(5.28 MW)* sustained; 2 shafts
Speed, knots: 21. **Range, miles:** 10 000 at 15 kts
Complement: 170 approx

Missiles: SAM: 2 SA-N-5 Grail quad launchers; manual aiming; IR homing to 6 km *(3.2 nm)* at 1.5 Mach; altitude to 2500 m *(8000 ft)*; warhead 1.5 kg.
Guns: 2 USN 3 in *(76 mm)*/50; 85° elevation; 20 rounds/minute to 12 km *(6.6 nm)*; weight of shell 6 kg.
Torpedoes: 6—324 mm US Mk 32 (2 triple) tubes.
A/S mortars: 1 Mk 15 Hedgehog.
Depth charges: 1 rack.
Fire control: Mk 63 GFCS (fwd). Mk 51 GFCS (aft).
Radars: Air search: Westinghouse SPS 28; B/C band.
Surface search: Raytheon SPS 10; G band.
Fire control: Western Electric Mk 34; I/J band.
Sonars: SQS 29; hull-mounted; active attack; high frequency.

Programmes: Former US Navy destroyer escort of the FMR design group. Transferred to South Vietnamese Navy on 25 September 1971. Was in overhaul at time of occupation of South Vietnam and was written off by the USN as 'Transferred to Vietnam' 30 April 1975.
Operational: Used as a training ship.

DAI KY *1983*

1 Ex-US BARNEGAT CLASS

Name	*No*	*Builders*	*Commissioned*
PHAM NGU LAO (ex-USCG *Absecon WHEC 374*, ex-*WAVP 23)*	HQ 01	Lake Washington S.Y.	28 Jan 1943

Displacement, tons: 1766 standard; 2800 full load
Dimensions, feet (metres): 310.8 × 41.1 × 13.5 *(94.7 × 12.5 × 4.1)*
Main machinery: 2 Fairbanks-Morse 38D8-1/8-10 diesels; 3540 hp *(2.64 MW)* sustained; 2 shafts
Speed, knots: 18. **Range, miles:** 20 000 at 12 kts
Complement: 200 approx

Missiles: SSM: 2 SS-N-2A Styx; active radar or IR homing to 46 km *(25 nm)* at 0.9 Mach; warhead 513 kg.
SAM: 2 SA-N-5 Grail quad launchers; manual aiming; IR homing to 6 km *(3.2 nm)* at 1.5 Mach; altitude to 2500 m *(8000 ft)*; warhead 1.5 kg.
Guns: 1 USN 5 in *(127 mm)*/38; 85° elevation; 15 rounds/minute to 17 km *(9.3 nm)*; weight of shell 25 kg.
3—37 mm/63. 4—25 mm (2 twin).
2—81 mm mortars.
Radars: Surface search: Raytheon SPS 21; G/H band; range 22 km *(12 nm)*.
Fire control: RCA/GE Mk 26; I/J band.

Programmes: Last of a group built as seaplane tenders for the US Navy. Transferred to US Coast Guard in 1948, initially on loan designated WAVP and then on permanent transfer, subsequently redesignated as high endurance cutter (WHEC). Transferred from US Coast Guard to South Vietnamese Navy in 1971.
Modernisation: SSMs mounted aft and close range armament fitted in the mid-1980s.

CORVETTES

2 Ex-US ADMIRABLE CLASS

Name	*No*	*Launched*
— (ex-USS *Prowess* IX 305, ex-MSF 280, ex-*Ha Hoi*)	HQ 07	17 Feb 1944
— (ex-USS *Sentry*, ex-MSF 299)	HQ 13	30 May 1944

Displacement, tons: 650 standard; 945 full load
Dimensions, feet (metres): 184.5 × 33 × 9.75 *(56.3 × 10 × 3)*
Main machinery: 2 Cooper-Bessemer GSB-8 diesels; 1710 hp *(1.28 MW)*; 2 shafts
Speed, knots: 14
Complement: 80 approx
Guns: 2 China 57 mm/70 (twin). 2—37 mm/63. Up to 8 Oerlikon 20 mm (4 twin).
Radars: Surface search: Sperry SPS 53; I band.

Comment: Former US Navy minesweepers of the Admirable class (originally designated AM). Built by Gulf SB Corp, Chicasaw, Alabama. Transferred to South Vietnam in 1970. Minesweeping equipment has been removed. Written off by the USN as 'Transferred to Vietnam' 30 April 1975. One employed in patrol and escort roles. Second ship probably non-operational.

LAND-BASED MARITIME AIRCRAFT

Numbers/Type: 6 Mil Mi-4 Hound B.
Operational speed: 113 kts *(210 km/h)*.
Service ceiling: 18 000 ft *(5500 m)*.
Range: 216 nm *(400 km)*.
Role/Weapon systems: Limited value ASW helicopter with primary support and assault roles. Sensors: Possible search radar and sonobuoys. Weapons: 4 × torpedoes or mines, light machine guns.

Numbers/Type: 5 Kamov Ka-27/Ka-29 Helix A.
Operational speed: 135 kts *(250 km/h)*.
Service ceiling: 19 685 ft *(6000 m)*.
Range: 432 nm *(800 km)*.
Role/Weapon systems: ASW helicopter; successor to Hormone with greater ASW potential. Sensors: Search radar, dipping sonar, MAD, ECM. Weapons: ASW; 3 × torpedoes, depth bombs or mines.

Numbers/Type: 10 Kamov Ka-25 Hormone A.
Operational speed: 119 kts *(220 km/h)*.
Service ceiling: 11 500 ft *(3500 m)*.
Range: 350 nm *(650 km)*.
Role/Weapon systems: Sensors: Search radar, dipping sonar, MAD, ECM, EW equipment and search radar. Weapons: ASW; 2 × torpedoes, depth bombs. ASV; 2 or 4 × missiles or rocket launchers.

Numbers/Type: 4 Beriev Be-12 Mail.
Operational speed: 328 kts *(608 km/h)*.
Service ceiling: 37 000 ft *(11 280 m)*.
Range: 4050 nm *(7500 km)*.
Role/Weapon systems: Long-range ASW/MR amphibian. Sensors: Search/weather radar, MAD, EW. Weapons: ASW; 5 tons of depth bombs, mines or torpedoes. ASV; limited missile and rocket armament.

LIGHT FORCES

Note: In addition to the craft listed below there are eight ex-Chinese Shanghai II class and 14 ex-Chinese Shantou class of doubtful operational status.

8 Ex-SOVIET OSA II CLASS (FAST ATTACK CRAFT—MISSILE)

Displacement, tons: 245 full load
Dimensions, feet (metres): 110.2 × 24.9 × 8.8 *(33.6 × 7.6 × 2.7)*
Main machinery: 3 diesels; 15 000 hp(m) *(11 MW)*; 3 shafts
Speed, knots: 37. **Range, miles:** 500 at 35 kts
Complement: 30
Missiles: SSM: 4 SS-N-2B Styx; active radar or IR homing to 46 km *(25 nm)* at 0.9 Mach; warhead 513 kg.
Guns: 4 USSR 30 mm/65 (2 twin); 85° elevation; 500 rounds/minute to 5 km *(2.7 nm)*; weight of shell 0.54 kg.
Radars: Surface search: Square Tie; I band.
Fire control: Drum Tilt; H/I band.
IFF: High Pole. Two Square Head.

Comment: Transferred: two in October 1979, two in September 1980, two in November 1980 and two in February 1981.

OSA II Class (Soviet number) *1987, G. Jacobs*

5 Ex-SOVIET TURYA CLASS (FAST ATTACK CRAFT—TORPEDO, HYDROFOIL)

Displacement, tons: 190 standard; 250 full load
Dimensions, feet (metres): 129.9 × 29.9 (41 over foils) × 5.9 (13.1 over foils) *(39.6 × 7.6 (12.5) × 1.8 (4))*
Main machinery: 3 diesels; 15 000 hp(m) *(11 MW)*; 3 shafts
Speed, knots: 40. **Range, miles:** 600 at 35 kts foilborne; 1450 at 14 kts hullborne
Complement: 30
Guns: 2 USSR 57 mm/70 (twin, aft); 90° elevation; 120 rounds/minute to 8 km *(4.4 nm)*; weight of shell 2.8 kg.
2 USSR 25 mm/80 (twin, fwd); 85° elevation; 270 rounds/minute to 3 km *(1.6 nm)*; weight of shell 0.34 kg.
Torpedoes: 4—21 in *(533 mm)* tubes (not in all). Soviet Type 53.
Depth charges: 2 racks.
Radars: Surface search: Pot Drum; H/I band.
Fire control: Muff Cob; G/H band.
IFF: High Pole B. Square Head.
Sonars: Helicopter (not in all); VDS; high frequency.

Comment: Transferred: two in mid-1984, one in late 1984 and two in January 1986. Two of the five do not have torpedo tubes or sonar.

TURYA Class (without torpedo tubes) *1988*

16 Ex-SOVIET SHERSHEN CLASS (FAST ATTACK CRAFT—TORPEDO)

Displacement, tons: 145 standard; 170 full load
Dimensions, feet (metres): 113.8 × 22 × 4.9 *(34.7 × 6.7 × 1.5)*
Main machinery: 3 diesels; 12 000 hp(m) *(8.8 MW)*; 3 shafts
Speed, knots: 45. **Range, miles:** 850 at 30 kts; 460 at 42 kts
Complement: 23
Missiles: SAM: 1 SA-N-5 Grail quad launcher; manual aiming; IR homing to 6 km *(3.2 nm)* at 1.5 Mach; altitude to 2500 m *(8000 ft)*; warhead 1.5 kg.
Guns: 4 USSR 30 mm/65 (2 twin); 85° elevation; 500 rounds/minute to 5 km *(2.7 nm)*; weight of shell 0.54 kg.
Torpedoes: 4—21 in *(533 mm)* tubes (not in all). Soviet Type 53.
Depth charges: 2 racks (12).
Mines: Can carry 6.
Radars: Surface search: Pot Drum; H/I band.
Fire control: Drum Tilt; H/I band.
IFF: High Pole A. Square Head.

Comment: Transferred: two in 1973, two in April 1979 (without torpedo tubes), two in September 1979, two in August 1980, two in October 1980, two in January 1983 and four in June 1983.

SHERSHEN Class *1987*

8 Ex-SOVIET SO 1 CLASS (LARGE PATROL CRAFT)

Displacement, tons: 170 standard; 215 full load
Dimensions, feet (metres): 137.8 × 19.7 × 5.9 *(42 × 6 × 1.8)*
Main machinery: 3 diesels; 7500 hp(m) *(5.5 MW)*; 3 shafts
Speed, knots: 28. **Range, miles:** 1100 at 13 kts; 350 at 28 kts
Complement: 31
Guns: 4 USSR 25 mm/80 (2 twin); 85° elevation; 270 rounds/minute to 3 km *(1.6 nm)*; weight of shell 0.34 kg.
A/S mortars: 4 RBU 1200 5-tubed fixed; range 1200 m; warhead 34 kg.
Depth charges: 2 racks (24).
Mines: 10.
Radars: Surface search: Pot Head; I band.
IFF: High Pole A. Dead Duck.

Comment: Transferred: two in March 1980, two in September 1980, two in May 1981, and two in September 1983. Four more of this class were transferred in 1960-63 but have been deleted.

SO 1 *1984*

3 Ex-US PGM 71 CLASS (LARGE PATROL CRAFT)

Displacement, tons: 142 full load
Dimensions, feet (metres): 101 × 21.3 × 7.5 *(30.8 × 6.5 × 2.3)*
Main machinery: 2 GM 6-71 diesels; 1392 hp *(1.04 MW)* sustained; 2 shafts
Speed, knots: 17. **Range, miles:** 1000 at 17 kts
Complement: 30
Guns: 1 Bofors 40 mm/56. 4 Oerlikon 20 mm.

Comment: Ten transferred to South Vietnam 1963-67. Three deleted in 1988-89, four more in 1990-91.

11 Ex-SOVIET ZHUK CLASS (FAST ATTACK CRAFT—PATROL)

Displacement, tons: 50 full load
Dimensions, feet (metres): 75.4 × 17 × 6.2 *(23 × 5.2 × 1.9)*
Main machinery: 2 diesels; 2400 hp(m) *(1.76 MW)*; 2 shafts
Speed, knots: 30. **Range, miles:** 1100 at 15 kts
Complement: 17
Guns: 4—14.5 mm (2 twin) MGs.

Comment: Transferred: three in 1978, three in November 1979, three in February 1986, two in January 1990 and three in August 1990. So far three have been deleted, a further four are of doubtful operational status.

2 Ex-SOVIET PO 2 CLASS (COASTAL PATROL CRAFT)

Displacement, tons: 55 full load
Dimensions, feet (metres): 82 × 16.7 × 5.6 *(25 × 5.1 × 1.7)*
Main machinery: 1 diesel; 300 hp(m) *(220 kW)*; 1 shaft
Speed, knots: 12
Complement: 8
Guns: 2 USSR 25 mm/80.

Comment: Two transferred in 1977, two in February 1980, one in October 1981, one in 1982 and four in 1983. Four deleted 1983-84, four more in 1986-87.

2 Ex-SOVIET POLUCHAT CLASS (COASTAL PATROL CRAFT)

Displacement, tons: 100 full load
Dimensions, feet (metres): 97.1 × 19 × 4.8 *(29.6 × 5.8 × 1.5)*
Main machinery: 2 diesels; 1700 hp(m) *(1.25 MW)*; 2 shafts
Speed, knots: 20. **Range, miles:** 1500 at 10 kts
Complement: 15
Guns: 2—12.7 mm MGs.
Radars: Navigation: Spin Trough; I band.

Comment: Both transferred in January 1990. Can be used as torpedo recovery vessels.

POLUCHAT *1987*

AMPHIBIOUS FORCES

3 Ex-SOVIET POLNOCHNY B CLASS (LSM)

HQ 511 **HQ 512** **HQ 513**

Displacement, tons: 760 standard; 800 full load
Dimensions, feet (metres): 242.7 × 27.9 × 5.8 *(74 × 8.5 × 1.8)*
Main machinery: 2 diesels; 5000 hp(m) *(3.67 MW)*; 2 shafts
Speed, knots: 19
Complement: 40
Guns: 2 or 4 USSR 30 mm/65 (1 or 2 twin). 2—140 mm rocket launchers.
Radars: Surface search: Don 2 or Spin Trough; I band.
Fire control: Drum Tilt; H/I band.

Comment: Transfers: one in May 1979 (B), one in November 1979 (A) and one in February 1980 (B). Details as for Polnochny B class.

1 Ex-US LST 1-510 and 2 Ex-US LST 511-1152 CLASSES

QUI NONH (ex-USS *Bulloch County* LST 509) HQ 502
VUNG TAU (ex-USS *Cochino County* LST 603) HQ 503
DA NANG (ex-USS *Maricopa County* LST 938) HQ 505

Displacement, tons: 2366 beaching; 4080 full load
Dimensions, feet (metres): 328 × 50 × 14 *(100 × 15.2 × 4.3)*
Main machinery: 2 GM 12-567A diesels; 1800 hp *(1.34 MW)*; 2 shafts
Speed, knots: 11. **Range, miles:** 6000 at 10 kts
Complement: 110

Comment: Built in 1943-44. Transferred to South Vietnam in mid-1960s.

DA NANG *1988, G. Jacobs*

3 Ex-US LSM 1 CLASS

ex-**LSM 85**, ex-**LSM 276**, ex-**LSM 313**

Displacement, tons: 1100 full load
Dimensions, feet (metres): 203.4 × 34.4 × 8.2 *(62 × 10.5 × 2.5)*
Main machinery: 2 GM 16-278A diesels; 3000 hp *(2.24 MW)*; 2 shafts
Speed, knots: 12
Complement: 70
Guns: 2 Bofors 40 mm/56. 4 Oerlikon 20 mm. 4—12.7 mm MGs.

Comment: Transferred 1955 (one to France) to 1965. Written off 'Transferred to Vietnam' by USN on 30 April 1975. Two reported to be non-operational in 1990.

12 Ex-SOVIET T 4 CLASS (LCUs)

Displacement, tons: 93 full load
Dimensions, feet (metres): 65.3 × 18.4 × 4.6 *(19.9 × 5.6 × 1.4)*
Main machinery: 2 diesels; 316 hp(m) *(232 kW)*; 2 shafts
Speed, knots: 10
Complement: 4

Comment: Transfers: ten in 1967, five in 1969, all of which were probably sunk. Twelve more in 1979.

24 Ex-US LANDING CRAFT (LCM and LCU)

Comment: It is reported that at the beginning of 1992 there were still some seven LCUs, 14 LCM 8 and LCM 6, and three LCVPs remaining of the 180 minor landing craft left behind by the US in 1975.

MINE WARFARE FORCES

2 LIENYUN CLASS (MINESWEEPERS—COASTAL)

Displacement, tons: 400 full load
Dimensions, feet (metres): 131.2 × 26.2 × 11.5 *(40 × 8 × 3.5)*
Main machinery: 1 diesel; 400 hp(m) *(294 kW)*; 1 shaft
Speed, knots: 8
Guns: 2—12.7 mm MGs.

Comment: Acquired from China. Trawler type with a minesweeping winch and davits aft.

2 Ex-SOVIET YURKA CLASS (MINESWEEPER—OCEAN)

HQ 851 **HQ 852**

Displacement, tons: 460 full load
Dimensions, feet (metres): 171.9 × 30.8 × 8.5 *(52.4 × 9.4 × 2.6)*
Main machinery: 2 diesels; 5500 hp(m) *(4 MW)*; 2 shafts
Speed, knots: 17. **Range, miles:** 1500 at 12 kts
Complement: 60
Guns: 4 USSR 30 mm/65 (2 twin); 500 rounds/minute to 5 km *(2.7 nm)*; weight of shell 0.54 kg.
Mines: 10.
Radars: Surface search: Don 2; I band.
Fire control: Drum Tilt; H/I band.
Sonars: Hull-mounted; active minehunting; high frequency.

Comment: Transferred December 1979. Steel-hulled, built in early 1970s.

YURKA 852 *1988, G. Jacobs*

4 SOVIET SONYA CLASS (MINESWEEPER/HUNTER—COASTAL)

Displacement, tons: 400 full load
Dimensions, feet (metres): 157.4 × 28.9 × 6.6 *(48 × 8.8 × 2)*
Main machinery: 2 diesels; 2000 hp(m) *(1.47 MW)*; 2 shafts
Speed, knots: 15. **Range, miles:** 3000 at 10 kts
Complement: 43
Guns: 2 USSR 30 mm/65 AK 630. 2—25 mm/80 (twin).
Mines: 5.
Radars: Surface search: Don 2; I band.

Comment: First one transferred 16 February 1987, second in February 1988, third in July 1989, fourth in March 1990.

SONYA *11/1991, G. Jacobs*

2 YEVGENYA CLASS (MINEHUNTER—INSHORE)

Displacement, tons: 90 full load
Dimensions, feet (metres): 80.7 × 18 × 4.9 *(24.6 × 5.5 × 1.5)*
Main machinery: 2 diesels; 400 hp(m) *(294 kW)*; 2 shafts
Speed, knots: 11. **Range, miles:** 300 at 10 kts
Complement: 10
Guns: 2 USSR 25 mm/80 (twin).
Radars: Surface search: Spin Trough; I band.

Comment: First transferred in October 1979; two in December 1986. One deleted in 1990.

5 Ex-SOVIET K 8 CLASS (MINESWEEPING BOATS)

Displacement, tons: 26 full load
Dimensions, feet (metres): 55.4 × 10.5 × 2.6 *(16.9 × 3.2 × 0.8)*
Main machinery: 2 diesels; 300 hp(m) *(220 kW)*; 2 shafts
Speed, knots: 18
Complement: 6
Guns: 2—14.5 mm (twin) MGs.

Comment: Transferred in October 1980.

MISCELLANEOUS

Note: (a) In addition to the vessels listed below there are two YOG 5 fuel lighters, two floating cranes and two ex-Soviet unarmed Nyryat 2 diving tenders.
(b) Small numbers of ex-US Riverine craft have been refitted with Soviet engines and are still operational with Soviet weapons.
(c) A diving support vessel *(Hai Son)* of 881 tons and 50 m in length was completed by Korea Tacoma, Masan in March 1990. This ship may not be naval.

1 Ex-SOVIET KAMENKA CLASS (SURVEY SHIP)

Displacement, tons: 705 full load
Dimensions, feet (metres): 175.5 × 29.8 × 8.5 *(53.5 × 9.1 × 2.6)*
Main machinery: 2 diesels; 1800 hp(m) *(1.32 MW)*; 2 shafts; cp props
Speed, knots: 14. **Range, miles:** 4000 at 10 kts
Complement: 25
Radars: Navigation: Don 2; I band.

Comment: Transferred December 1979 having been built in Poland in 1971.

2 Ex-SOVIET FLOATING DOCKS

Comment: One has a lift capacity of 8500 tons. Transferred August 1983. Second one *(Khersson)* has a lift capacity of 4500 tons and was supplied in 1988.

12 Ex-CHINESE SL CLASS TRANSPORTS AND 4 TANKERS

Comment: These are ships of between 200 and 550 tons used for coastal transport having been left over from the Vietnam war. Most were delivered in the late 1960s. The tankers have a cargo capacity of 400 tons of fuel oil. All are armed with 12.7 mm MGs.

HQ 671 (SL Class) *12/1988, G. Jacobs*

VIRGIN ISLANDS

Administration

Commissioner of Police:
J B Rutherford

Base

Road Town, Tortola

Mercantile Marine

Lloyd's Register of Shipping:
2 vessels of 339 tons gross

1 HALMATIC M 140 PATROL CRAFT

ST URSULA

Displacement, tons: 17 full load
Dimensions, feet (metres): 50.6 × 12.8 × 3.9 *(15.4 × 3.9 × 1.2)*
Main machinery: 2 Detroit 6V 92TA diesels; 520 hp *(388 kW)* sustained; 2 shafts
Speed, knots: 27. **Range, miles:** 300 at 20 kts
Complement: 6
Guns: 1—7.62 mm MG.

Comment: Built by Halmatic with funds provided by the UK and commissioned 4 July 1988. Large davit aft for rapid launch and recovery of a rigid inflatable boat.

2 SEA RIDER DINGHIES

Comment: Model SR5M, built by Avon, with 70 hp *(52 kW)* Evinrude outboard engines. Acquired in 1986.

ST URSULA *1988, Halmatic*

WESTERN SAMOA

General

After 48 years of New Zealand occupation, mandate and trusteeship, Western Samoa achieved independence in 1962.

Base

Apia

Mercantile Marine

Lloyd's Register of Shipping:
7 vessels of 6253 tons gross

1 PACIFIC FORUM PATROL CRAFT

NAFANUA

Displacement, tons: 165 full load
Dimensions, feet (metres): 103.3 × 26.6 × 6.9 *(31.5 × 8.1 × 2.1)*
Main machinery: 2 Caterpillar 3516TA diesels; 2820 hp *(2.1 MW)* sustained; 2 shafts
Speed, knots: 20. **Range, miles:** 2500 at 12 kts
Complement: 17 (3 officers)
Guns: Can carry 1 Oerlikon 20 mm and 2—7.62 mm MGs.
Radars: Surface search: Furuno 1011; I band.

Comment: Under the Defence Co-operation Programme Australia has provided an Australian Shipbuilding Industries (ASI) 315 Patrol Boat to the Western Samoan Government. Training, operational and technical assistance is being provided by the Royal Australian Navy. Ordered 3 October 1985, commissioned 5 March 1988.

NAFANUA *10/1991, John Mortimer*

1 LCU

LADY SAMOA II

Comment: Built by Yokohama Yacht Co and launched 28 July 1988.

YEMEN

General

In May 1990 the north and south Yemen republics were again reunited. Many ships of the Ethiopian Navy took refuge in Yemeni ports during 1991 and some of the larger units may have been retained by the Yemen Navy.

Headquarters' Appointment

Commander Naval Forces:
Colonel Ali Qasim Talib
Chief of Staff
Lieutenant Colonel Abdul Karim Muharram

Bases

Main: Aden, Hodeida
Secondary: Mukalla, Perim, Socotra

Ministerial

Minister of Defence:
Brigadier Haytham Qasim Tahir

Personnel

(a) 1992: 2500 (including 500 Marines)
(b) 2 years' national service

Mercantile Marine

Lloyd's Register of Shipping:
39 vessels of 16 716 tons gross

LIGHT FORCES

Note: (a) Two ex-Soviet Mol class occasionally reported, but both belong to Ethiopia.
(b) Two ex-Soviet SO 1 class (*402* and *619*) may still be just operational.

2 SOVIET TARANTUL I CLASS (MISSILE CORVETTE)

971 976

Displacement, tons: 385 standard; 580 full load
Dimensions, feet (metres): 184.1 × 37.7 × 8.2 *(56.1 × 11.5 × 2.5)*
Main machinery: COGOG; 2 NK-12MV gas turbines; 24 000 hp(m) *(17.6 MW)*; 2 gas turbines with reversible gearbox; 8000 hp(m) *(5.9 MW)*; 2 shafts
Speed, knots: 36. **Range, miles:** 400 at 36 kts; 2000 at 20 kts
Complement: 50

Missiles: SSM: 4 SS-N-2C Styx (2 twin) launchers; active radar or IR homing to 83 km *(45 nm)* at 0.9 Mach; warhead 513 kg; sea-skimmer at end of run.
SAM: SA-N-5 Grail quad launcher; manual aiming; IR homing to 10 km *(5.4 nm)* at 1.5 Mach; altitude to 2500 m *(8000 ft)*; warhead 1.1 kg.
Guns: 1—3 in *(76 mm)*/60; 85° elevation; 120 rounds/minute to 7 km *(3.8 nm)*; weight of shell 7 kg.
2—30 mm/65 AK 630; 6 barrels per mounting; 3000 rounds/minute to 2 km.
Countermeasures: Decoys: 2—16-barrelled Chaff launchers.
ESM: 2 receivers.
Fire control: Hood Wink optronic director.
Radars: Air/surface search: Plank Shave (also for missile control); E band.
Navigation: Spin Trough; I band.
Fire control: Bass Tilt; H/I band.
IFF: Square Head. High Pole.

Programmes: First one delivered in November 1990, second in January 1991. This is the standard export version.

TARANTUL 971 *1991, US Navy*

6 Ex-SOVIET OSA II CLASS (FAST ATTACK CRAFT—MISSILE)

116-121

Displacement, tons: 245 full load
Dimensions, feet (metres): 110.2 × 24.9 × 8.8 *(33.6 × 7.6 × 2.7)*
Main machinery: 3 M504 diesels; 15 000 hp(m) *(11 MW)*; 3 shafts
Speed, knots: 37. **Range, miles:** 500 at 35 kts
Complement: 30
Missiles: SSM: 4 SS-N-2B Styx; active radar or IR homing to 46 km *(25 nm)* at 0.9 Mach; warhead 513 kg.
Guns: 4 USSR 30 mm/65 (2 twin); 85° elevation; 500 rounds/minute to 5 km *(2.7 nm)*; weight of shell 0.54 kg.
Radars: Surface search: Square Tie; I band.
Fire control: Drum Tilt; H/I band.

Comment: Transferred: one in February 1979, one in March 1979, two in January 1980, one in December 1980, one in January 1982, one on 24 February 1983 and one in September 1983. Two (*122* and *123*) were sunk in 1987.

OSA 121 *1990*

3 BROADSWORD CLASS (COASTAL PATROL CRAFT)

26 SEPTEMBER 141 **RAMADAN** 142 **SANA'A** 143

Displacement, tons: 90.5 standard; 110 full load
Dimensions, feet (metres): 105 × 20.4 × 6.3 *(32 × 6.2 × 1.9)*
Main machinery: 2 GM 16V-149TI diesels; 2880 hp *(2.15 MW)* sustained; 2 shafts
Speed, knots: 32
Complement: 14
Guns: 2 USSR 25 mm/80 (twin). 2—14.5 mm (twin) MGs. 2—12.7 mm MGs.
Radars: Surface search: Decca 914; I band.

Comment: Acquired in 1978 from Halter Marine, New Orleans. Guns added after delivery. Still used for offshore patrol but in poor repair.

5 Ex-SOVIET ZHUK CLASS (FAST ATTACK CRAFT—PATROL)

400 500 600 700 800

Displacement, tons: 50 full load
Dimensions, feet (metres): 75.4 × 17 × 6.2 *(23 × 5.2 × 1.9)*
Main machinery: 2 diesels; 2400 hp(m) *(1.76 MW)*; 2 shafts
Speed, knots: 30. **Range, miles:** 1100 at 15 kts
Complement: 17
Guns: 4—14.5 mm (2 twin) MGs.
Radars: Surface search: Spin Trough; I band.

Comment: Two delivered in December 1984 and three in January 1987. Earlier transfers have been deleted.

ZHUK *3/1990*

AMPHIBIOUS FORCES

1 ROPUCHKA I CLASS (LST)

139

Displacement, tons: 3800 full load
Dimensions, feet (metres): 370.7 × 50.9 × 16.4 *(113 × 15.5 × 5)*
Main machinery: 2 diesels; 9000 hp(m) *(6.6 MW)*; 2 shafts
Speed, knots: 18. **Range, miles:** 3500 at 16 kts; 6000 at 12 kts
Complement: 90
Military lift: 225 troops; 450 tons equipment
Guns: 4 USSR 57 mm/80 (2 twin).
Radars: Surface search: Kivach; I band.
Fire control: Muff Cob; G/H band.

Comment: Built at Gdansk, Poland after 1975. Transferred June 1979. As this ship was sighted in the English Channel in October 1991 it is possible that it was always part of the Soviet Indian Ocean Squadron and has now been recalled to Russia.

ROPUCHKA 139 *10/1991, Foto Flite*

2 Ex-SOVIET POLNOCHNY A CLASS (LCT)

AL WUDIA 136 **SIRA** 137

Displacement, tons: 750 standard; 800 full load
Dimensions, feet (metres): 239.3 × 27.9 × 5.8 *(73 × 8.5 × 1.8)*
Main machinery: 2 diesels; 5000 hp(m) *(3.67 MW)*; 2 shafts
Speed, knots: 19. **Range, miles:** 1000 at 18 kts
Complement: 40
Military lift: 100 troops; 6 tanks
Guns: 2 USSR 30 mm/65 (twin). 2—18-barrelled 140 mm rocket launchers.

Comment: Transferred in August 1973 (two) and July 1977. *138* burnt out in March 1986.

SIRA *7/1986, van Ginderen Collection*

2 Ex-SOVIET ONDATRA CLASS (LCUs)

13 14

Displacement, tons: 145 full load
Dimensions, feet (metres): 78.7 × 16.4 × 4.9 *(24 × 5 × 1.5)*
Main machinery: 1 diesel; 300 hp(m) *(221 kW)*; 1 shaft
Speed, knots: 10. **Range, miles:** 500 at 5 kts
Complement: 4
Military lift: 1 MBT

Comment: Transferred January 1983.

ONDATRA Class *1989, S. S. Breyer*

2 Ex-SOVIET T 4 CLASS (LCVP)

134 135

Displacement, tons: 70 full load
Dimensions, feet (metres): 62.3 × 14 × 3.3 *(19 × 4.3 × 1)*
Main machinery: 2 diesels; 316 hp(m) *(232 kW)*; 2 shafts
Speed, knots: 10. **Range, miles:** 1500 at 10 kts
Complement: 4

Comment: Three transferred in November 1970 and two in December 1981. First three deleted.

MINE WARFARE FORCES

2 SOVIET NATYA CLASS (MINESWEEPERS—OCEAN)

634 641

Displacement, tons: 770 full load
Dimensions, feet (metres): 200.1 × 31.8 × 8.9 *(61 × 9.7 × 2.7)*
Main machinery: 2 diesels; 8000 hp(m) *(5.88 MW)*; 2 shafts
Speed, knots: 19. **Range, miles:** 4000 at 10 kts
Complement: 65
Guns: 4—30 mm/65 (2 twin); 85° elevation; 500 rounds/minute to 5 km *(2.7 nm)*; weight of shell 0.54 kg.
4—25 mm/80 (2 twin); 270 rounds/minute to 3 km *(1.6 nm)*; weight of shell 0.34 kg.
A/S mortars: 2 RBU 1200 five-tubed fixed launchers; range 1200 m; warhead 34 kg.
Mines: 10
Radars: Surface search: Don 2; I band.
Sonars: Hull-mounted; active minehunting; high frequency.

Comment: First one transferred in February 1991, second in October 1991.

NATYA 634 *10/1991, Foto Flite*

6 Ex-SOVIET YEVGENYA CLASS (MINEHUNTERS—INSHORE)

11 12 15 +3

Displacement, tons: 77 standard; 90 full load
Dimensions, feet (metres): 80.7 × 18 × 4.9 *(24.6 × 5.5 × 1.5)*
Main machinery: 2 diesels; 400 hp(m) *(294 kW)*; 2 shafts
Speed, knots: 11. **Range, miles:** 300 at 10 kts
Complement: 10
Guns: 2—25 mm/80 (twin) or 2—14.5 mm (twin) MGs.
Radars: Navigation: Spin Trough; I band.
IFF: High Pole.
Sonars: Small transducer lifted over stern on crane.

Comment: GRP hulls. Two transferred in May 1982, third in November 1987, and three more in March 1990.

1 SOVIET SONYA CLASS (MINESWEEPER—COASTAL)

441

Displacement, tons: 400 full load
Dimensions, feet (metres): 157.4 × 28.9 × 6.6 *(48 × 8.8 × 2)*
Main machinery: 2 diesels; 2000 hp(m) *(1.47 MW)*; 2 shafts
Speed, knots: 15. **Range, miles:** 3000 at 10 kts
Complement: 43

Guns: 2—30 mm/65 (twin); 85° elevation; 500 rounds/minute to 5 km *(2.7 nm)*; weight of shell 0.54 kg.
2—25 mm/80 (twin); 85° elevation; 270 rounds/minute to 3 km *(1.6 nm)*.
Mines: 8.
Radars: Surface search: Don 2; I band.

Programmes: Delivered in January 1991. There was some early confusion as to whether this ship had been delivered to Ethiopia or Yemen.

SONYA (Russian number) *1991, Ships of the World*

SERVICE FORCES

Note: (a) A 4500 ton Floating Dock has been provided by the USSR.
(b) A 14 m Hydrographic craft acquired from Cougar Marine in 1988.

1 DELYANKA OSKOL II CLASS (REPAIR SHIP)

Displacement, tons: 2550 full load
Dimensions, feet (metres): 300.1 × 40 × 13.1 *(91.5 × 12.2 × 4)*
Main machinery: 2 diesels; 2500 hp(m) *(1.84 MW)*; 2 shafts
Speed, knots: 12. **Range, miles:** 8000 at 10 kts
Complement: 100
Guns: 2—12.7 mm MGs (twin).
Radars: Navigation: Don 2; I band.

Comment: Transferred in 1988 and was probably used more by the former Soviet Navy than the local flotilla. This is a general purpose tender and repair ship with two 3.5 ton cranes. May have returned to Russia in late 1991.

2 TOPLIVO CLASS

135 140

Displacement, tons: 1300
Dimensions, feet (metres): 172.9 × 27.2 × 12.5 *(52.7 × 8.3 × 3.8)*
Main machinery: 2 diesels; 2 shafts
Speed, knots: 10

Comment: Two small harbour tankers acquired in the early 1980s. *135* carries water, *140* oil.

TOPLIVO 140 *1990*

CUSTOMS SERVICE

1 FAIREY MARINE TRACKER 2 CLASS (COASTAL PATROL CRAFT)

1034

Displacement, tons: 31 full load
Dimensions, feet (metres): 63.1 × 16.3 × 4.8 *(19.3 × 5 × 1.5)*
Main machinery: 2 MTU 8V 331 TC 92 diesels; 1770 hp(m) *(1.3 MW)* sustained; 2 shafts
Speed, knots: 29. **Range, miles:** 650 at 22 kts
Complement: 11
Gun: 1 Oerlikon 20 mm.

Comment: Delivered 1979. Four destroyed in the civil war in January 1986.

3 FAIREY MARINE SPEAR CLASS (COASTAL PATROL CRAFT)

Displacement, tons: 4.5 full load
Dimensions, feet (metres): 29.8 × 9.2 × 2.6 *(9.1 × 2.8 × 0.8)*
Main machinery: 2 Perkins diesels; 290 hp *(216 kW)*; 2 shafts
Speed, knots: 25
Guns: 3—7.62 mm MGs.

Comment: Three delivered 30 September 1975, one in 1978. One acts as Navy Commander's barge; one deleted in 1986.

2 SHABWAH CLASS (TUGS)

SHABWAH AL MAHRAH

Comment: 225 grt; built by McTay Marine, Bromborough and launched 14 November 1986 and 6 January 1987. Both delivered in May 1987.

YUGOSLAVIA AND CROATIA

Yugoslavia

Flag Officers

Navy Section Chief and Deputy of General Staff (Navy):
Vice Admiral Vjekoslav Culić
Commander-in-Chief:
Vice Admiral Mile Kandic
Deputy Commander:
Rear Admiral Jovan Popovic
Chief of Staff:
Vice Admiral Fridrih Moreti
Commander Adriatic Fleet:
Rear Admiral Nikola Ercegovic
Commander Sibenik Naval Sector:
Vice Admiral Djuro Pojer
Commander Kotor Naval Sector:
Vice Admiral Miodrag Jokic
Commander Danube Flotilla:
Captain Dmitrije Kostic

Croatia

Flag Officers

Commander Navy:
Vice Admiral Sveto Letica
Deputy Commander:
Vice Admiral Bodizar Grubisic

Personnel

(a) 1992: 13 000 (1500 officers) (about half belong to Croatian Navy)
(b) 12 months' national service

Croatia and Slovenia

In early 1992 the permanent division of the former Yugoslav Navy seemed inevitable. For convenience all ships are retained in this section until the picture becomes clearer next year. Vessels known to belong to Croatia are listed separately in the Strength of the Fleet table. About half of all naval personnel have joined the Croatian flotilla which may mean that Yugoslavia cannot man all its ships and, in particular, the submarines. The Yugoslavs have retained all the Styx SSMs but none of the RBS 15s. Slovenia has two unidentified patrol craft. The major shipbuilding yards are in Croatia. Some ship names are being changed.

Strength of the Fleet

Type	*Yugoslavia*	*Croatia*
Submarines—Patrol	5	—
Midget Submarines	6	—
Frigates	4	—
Corvettes	2	— (4)
Fast Attack Craft—Missile	13	3
Fast Attack Craft—Torpedo	10	4
Fast Attack Craft—Patrol	8	2
Large Patrol Craft	7	—
River Patrol Craft	11	—
Minehunters/sweepers	4	—
Minesweepers—Inshore	4	—
River Minesweepers	16	—
LCTs/Minelayers	16	1
LCUs/LCVPs	33	4
Training Ships	2	—
Survey Vessels	7	1
HQ Ships	2 + 2	—
Salvage Vessel	1	—
Tankers	2	1
Transports	10	—
Tugs	12	1
Water Carrier	1	—

Bases and Organisation

Headquarters: Kumbor (Yugoslavia); Split (Croatia).
Main bases: Tivat, Boka Kotorska Gulf (Yugoslavia); Sibenik, Split (Croatia).

Naval Air Arm

ASW helicopter squadron (Divulje) was formed in 1974-75 and has Ka-25 'Hormones' and Ka-28 'Helix'.
There is also an air liaison detachment (Divulje) composed of a few Mi-8 and Aerospatiale/Soko SA 341 Gazelle helicopters.
The Air Force has a 'Naval Air Brigade'. This includes 20 RJ-1 Jastreb, 18 RT 33 surveillance, 24 MiG-21 'Fishbed' fighter-interceptors, 18 Jastreb/Orao-B fighter-bombers, and four Canadian CL-215 amphibians. The Yugoslav Air Force may also use some of its MiG-29 'Fulcrum' fighter-bombers for the support of naval forces.

Mercantile Marine

Lloyd's Register of Shipping:
462 vessels of 3 293 447 tons gross

DELETIONS

Light Forces

1989 *Proleter* 524
1990 *Marijan*
1991 *Mukos* (sunk)

Auxiliaries

1989 PT 61, PT 62

Minesweepers

1989 5 M 301 class

PENNANT LIST

Submarines

821	Heroj
822	Junak
823	Uskok
831	Sava
832	Drava
911	Una
912	Tisa
913	Zeta
914	Soca
915	Kupa
916	Vardar

Frigates

VPB 31	Split
VPB 32	Kopar
VPB 33	Kotor
VPB 34	Pula

Corvettes

PBR 551	Mornar
PBR 552	Borač

Light Forces

PC 132	Kalnik
PC 133	Velebit
PC 134	Graničar
PC 135	Rudnik
PC 136	Romanija
PC 137	Kamenar
PC 140	Kozuf
PC 171	Biokovo
PC 172	Pohorje
PC 173	Koprivnik
PC 174	Učka
PC 175	Grmeč
PC 177	Fruška Gora
PC 178	Kosmaj
PC 179	Zelengora
PC 180	Cer
PC 181	Kozolo
TC 211	Pionir
TC 212	Partizan
TC 213	Proleter
TC 214	Topcider
TC 215	Ivan
TC 216	Jadran
TC 217	Kornat
TC 218	Biokovak
TC 219	Streljko
TC 220	Crvena Zvezda
TC 221	Partizan II
TC 222	Partizan III
TC 223	Napredak
TC 224	Pionir II
RČ 301	Mitar Acev
RČ 302	Vlado Bagat
RČ 303	Petar Drapšin
RČ 304	Stevan Filipovič
RČ 305	Žikica Jovanovič-Španac
RČ 306	Nikola Martinovič
RČ 307	Josip Mazar Soša
RČ 308	Karlo Rojc
RČ 309	Franc Rozman-Stane
RČ 310	Velimir Škorpik
RT 401	Rade Končar
RT 402	Sibenic
RT 403	Ramiz Sadiku
RT 404	Hasan Zahirovič-Laca
RT 405	Orce Nikolov
RT 406	Ante Banina

Mine Warfare Forces

M 141	Mlj
M 142	Brseč
M 143	Olib
M 144	Iž
M 151	Vukov Klanac
M 152	Podgora
M 153	Blitvenica
M 161	Gradac
M 331	Neštin
M 332	Motajica
M 333	Belegiš
M 334	Bosut
M 335	Vučedol
M 336	Djerdap
M 337	Panonsko More

Miscellaneous

PB 25	Vis
PB 30	Kozara
M 11	Galeb
PH 33	Andrija Mohorovičič
PT 71	Meduza
PT 72	Jastog
PV 17	Alga

SUBMARINES

Note: (1) The Lora class of locally designed 900 ton patrol submarines has been cancelled. One of the Sutjeska class is still used for alongside training.
(2) Reported that the majority of submariners are Croatian, which may mean the Yugoslavs are having difficulty manning the flotilla.

2 SAVA CLASS (PATROL SUBMARINES)

Name	*No*	*Builders*	*Laid down*	*Launched*	*Commissioned*
SAVA	831	S and DE Factory, Split	1975	1977	1978
DRAVA	832	S and DE Factory, Split	1978	1980	1981

Displacement, tons: 830 surfaced; 960 dived
Dimensions, feet (metres): 182.7 × 23.6 × 16.7 *(55.7 × 7.2 × 5.1)*
Main machinery: Diesel-electric; 2 Sulzer diesels; 1600 hp(m) *(1.18 MW)*; 2 generators; 1 MW; 1 motor; 1560 hp(m) *(1.15 MW)*; 1 shaft
Speed, knots: 10 surfaced; 16 dived
Complement: 27

Torpedoes: 6—21 in *(533 mm)* bow tubes. 10 Soviet Type 53 or Swedish TP 61.
Mines: 20 in lieu of torpedoes.
Countermeasures: ESM: Stop Light; radar warning.
Radars: Surface search: Snoop Group; I band.
Sonars: Krupp Atlas PRS3; hull-mounted; passive ranging; medium frequency.

Structure: An improved version of the Heroj class. Diving depth, 300 m *(980 ft)*. Probably built with Soviet electronic equipment and armament. Possible Thomson Sintra active/passive sonar and unconfirmed reports of Swedish torpedoes.

DRAVA *1988, Yugoslav Navy*

3 HEROJ CLASS (PATROL SUBMARINES)

Name	*No*	*Builders*	*Laid down*	*Launched*	*Commissioned*
HEROJ	821	Uljanik Shipyard, Pula	1964	1967	1968
JUNAK	822	S and DE Factory, Split	1965	1968	1969
USKOK	823	Uljanik Shipyard, Pula	1966	1969	1970

Displacement, tons: 1170 surfaced; 1350 dived
Dimensions, feet (metres): 210 × 23.6 × 16.7 *(64 × 7.2 × 5.1)*
Main machinery: Diesel-electric; 2 Sulzer diesels; 1600 hp(m) *(1.18 MW)*; 2 generators; 1 MW; 1 motor; 1560 hp(m) *(1.15 MW)*; 1 shaft
Speed, knots: 10 surfaced; 16 dived
Range, miles: 4100 at 10 kts dived and snorting
Complement: 35

Torpedoes: 6—21 in *(533 mm)* bow tubes. 10 Soviet Type 53.
Mines: 20 in lieu of torpedoes.
Countermeasures: ESM: Stop Light; radar warning.
Radars: Surface search: Snoop Group; I band.
Sonars: Krupp Atlas PRS3; hull-mounted; passive ranging; medium frequency.

Structure: Have mainly Soviet electronic equipment and armament. Diving depth 300 m *(980 ft)*.

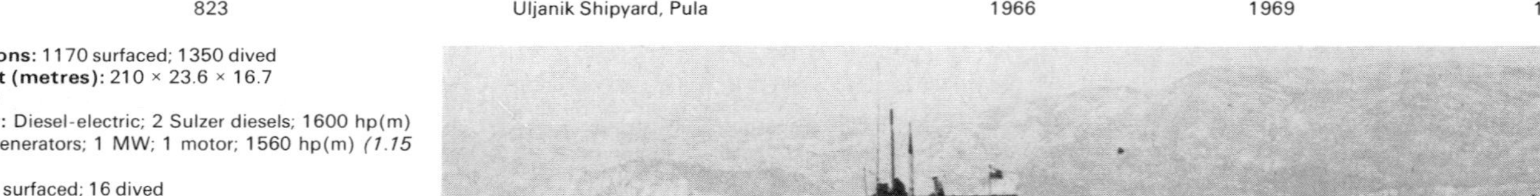

HEROJ *1982*

6 M 100-D CLASS (MIDGET SUBMARINES)

TISA 911 **UNA** 912 **ZETA** 913
SOCA 914 **KUPA** 915 **VARDAR** 916

Displacement, tons: 76 surfaced; 88 dived
Dimensions, feet (metres): 61.7 × 9 × 8.2 *(18.8 × 2.7 × 2.5)*
Main machinery: 2 motors; 68 hp(m) *(50 kW)*; 1 shaft
Speed, knots: 6 surfaced; 8 dived
Range, miles: 200 at 4 kts
Complement: 6
Sonars: Krupp Atlas; passive/active search; high frequency.

Programmes: Building yard, Split. First of class commissioned May 1985; last two in 1989. More may be built.
Structure: Exit/re-entry capability with mining capacity. Can carry six combat swimmers, plus four Swimmer Delivery Vehicles (SDV) and limpet mines. Diving depth: 105 m *(345 ft)*. Batteries can only be charged from shore or from a depot ship.

UNA *1987*

4 R-2 MALA CLASS (TWO-MAN SWIMMER DELIVERY VEHICLES)

Displacement, tons: 1.4
Dimensions, feet (metres): 16.1 × 4.6 × 4.3 *(4.9 × 1.4 × 1.3)*
Main machinery: 1 motor; 4.5 hp(m) *(3.3 kW)*; 1 shaft
Speed, knots: 4.4
Range, miles: 18 at 4.4 kts; 23 at 3.7 kts
Complement: 2

Mines: 250 kg of limpet mines.

Structure: This is a free-flood craft with the main motor, battery, navigation-pod and electronic equipment housed in separate watertight cylinders. Instrumentation includes aircraft type gyro-compass, magnetic compass, depth gauge (with 0-100 m scale), echo sounder, sonar and two searchlights. Constructed of light aluminium and plexiglass, it is fitted with fore and after-hydroplanes, the tail being a conventional cruciform with a single rudder abaft the screw. Large perspex windows give a good all-round view. Operating depth, 60 m *(196.9 ft)*, maximum.

Operational: Performance figures given are for lead-acid batteries and could be much improved by use of silver-zinc batteries.

Sales: It is reported that a number of these craft have been sold to Russia. Six transferred to Libya. Sweden has also taken delivery of both two and one-man versions of this type.

Note: Yugoslavia also reported to operate a number of R-1 'wet chariots'. Can be transported in submarine torpedo tubes. Crewed by one man. Propulsion 1 kW electric motor; 24 v silver-zinc batteries. Normal operating depth 60 m *(196.9 ft)*. Range 6 nm at 3 kts. Weight 145 kg. Dimensions 12.2 × 3.45 × 0.8 ft *(3.72 × 1.05 × 0.26 m)*.

R-2 with Swedish NACKEN — *12/1988, Gilbert Gyssels*

FRIGATES

2 SPLIT and 2 KOTOR CLASSES

SPLIT VPB 31	**KOTOR** VPB 33
KOPAR VPB 32	**PULA** VPB 34

Displacement, tons: 1700 standard; 1900 full load
Dimensions, feet (metres): 317.3 × 42 × 13.7 *(96.7 × 12.8 × 4.2)*
Main machinery: CODAG; 1 gas turbine; 18 000 hp(m) *(13.2 MW)*; 2 Russki B-68 diesels; 15 820 hp(m) *(11.63 MW)* sustained (*Split* and *Kopar*); 2 SEMT-Pielstick 12 PA6 280 diesels; 9600 hp(m) *(7.1 MW)* sustained (*Kotor* and *Pula*); 3 shafts
Speed, knots: 27 gas; 22 diesel. **Range, miles:** 1800 at 14 kts
Complement: 110

Missiles: SSM: 4 SS-N-2C Styx ❶; active radar or IR homing to 83 km *(45 nm)* at 0.9 Mach; warhead 513 kg; sea-skimmer at end of run. May be replaced by RBS-15 in due course.
SAM: SA-N-4 Gecko twin launcher ❷; semi-active radar homing to 15 km *(8 nm)* at 2.5 Mach; height envelope 9-3048 m *(29.5-10 000 ft)*; warhead 50 kg.
Guns: 4 USSR 3 in *(76 mm)*/60 (2 twin) (1 mounting only in VPB 33 and 34) ❸; 80° elevation; 90 rounds/minute to 15 km *(8 nm)*; weight of shell 6.8 kg.
4 USSR 30 mm/65 (2 twin) ❹; 85° elevation; 500 rounds/minute to 5 km *(2.7 nm)*; weight of shell 0.54 kg.
Torpedoes: 6—324 mm (2 triple) tubes ❺ (VPB 33 and 34 only). Whitehead A 244; anti-submarine; active passive homing to 6 km *(3.3 nm)* at 30 kts; warhead 34 kg.
A/S mortars: 2 RBU 6000 12-barrelled trainable ❻; range 6000 m; warhead 31 kg.
Mines: Can lay mines.
Countermeasures: Decoys: 2 Wallop Barricade double layer Chaff launchers.
Radars: Air/surface search: Strut Curve ❼; F band; range 110 km *(60 nm)* for 2 m² target.
Navigation: Don 2 (VPB 31 and 32); I band. Palm Frond (VPB 33 and 34); I band.
Fire control: Owl Screech ❽; G band (VPB 31 and 32). PEAB 9LV200 ❾; I band (VPB 33 and 34) (for 76 mm and SSM).
Drum Tilt ❿; H/I band (for 30 mm).
Pop Group ⓫; F/H/I band (for SAM).
IFF: High Pole; two Square Head.
Sonars: Hull-mounted; active search and attack; medium frequency.

Programmes: First two transferred from the USSR 10 March 1980 and 5 December 1982. *Split* was fourth Koni hull and *Kopar* the eighth. Both Batch 1 type. *Kotor* and *Pula* built under licence in Uljanic and Tito SYs, respectively. Both completed in mid-1988. Type name, VPB (Veliki Patrolni Brod).

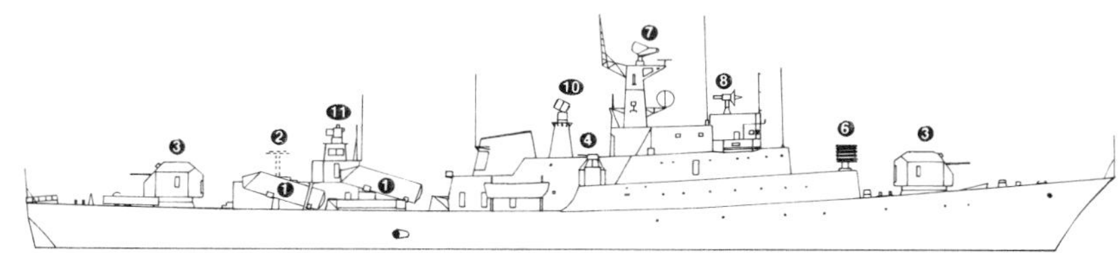
SPLIT — *(Scale 1 : 900), Ian Sturton*

KOPAR — *1989, Yugoslav Navy*

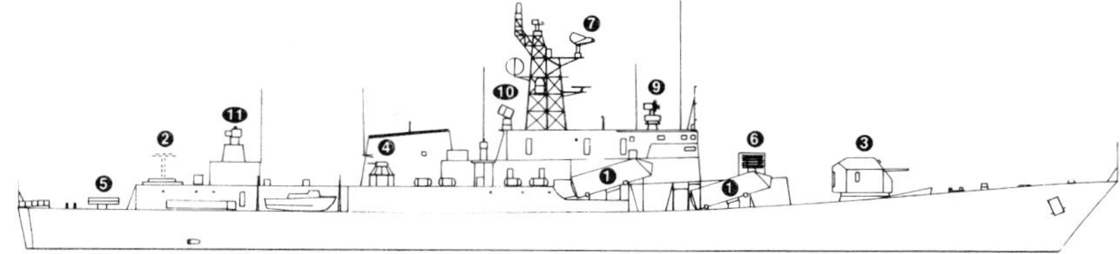
KOTOR — *(Scale 1 : 900), Ian Sturton*

Structure: Although the hulls are identical to the Koni class there are some equipment, and considerable structural differences between the Soviet and Yugoslav built ships. The two ex-Soviet ships have the SS-N-2C missiles aft of midships and facing aft; *Kotor* and *Pula* have the same missiles level with the forward end of the bridge facing forward. The Yugoslav built ships probably have the same gas turbine engines as the other pair but there are different diesels. Two triple torpedo tubes replace the after 76 mm gun mounting and there is a different arrangement of the bridge superstructure which is similar to the training frigates sold to Iraq and Indonesia.

KOTOR — *1989, Yugoslav Navy*

CORVETTES

0 + 4 KOBRA CLASS (TYPE 400)

Displacement, tons: 450 full load
Dimensions, feet (metres): 169 × 27.9 × 10.5 *(51.5 × 8.5 × 3.2)*
Main machinery: 4 MTU diesels; 14 400 hp(m) *(10.6 MW)*; 2 shafts
Speed, knots: 29. **Range, miles:** 2500 at 15 kts
Complement: 41

Missiles: SSM: 4 Saab RBS 15; active radar homing to 70 km *(37.8 nm)* at 0.8 Mach; warhead 150 kg.
Guns: 1 Bofors 57 mm/70. 1—30 mm/65 AK 630. 2 Oerlikon 20 mm.
Fire control: Saab optronic director.
Radars: Surface search: E/F band.
Fire control: BEAB 9LV Mk 2; I/J band.

Comment: The building of this class was officially announced as 'suspended' in 1989 but may have been restarted with the first launched in 1991 at Kaljevika Shipyard. Reported that two of the class, without engines or missiles, were in Croatian hands in early 1992.

KOBRA (artist's impression) *1990, Yugoslav Navy*

2 MORNAR CLASS

Name	No	Builders	Commissioned
MORNAR	PBR 551	Tito SY, Kraljevica	10 Sep 1959
BORAČ	PBR 552	Tito SY, Kraljevica	1965

Displacement, tons: 330 standard; 430 full load
Dimensions, feet (metres): 174.8 × 23 × 6.6 *(53.3 × 7 × 2)*
Main machinery: 4 SEMT-Pielstick PA1 175 diesels; 3240 hp(m) *(2.38 MW)*; 2 shafts
Speed, knots: 20. **Range, miles:** 3000 at 12 kts; 2000 at 15 kts
Complement: 60

Guns: 2 Bofors 40 mm/60. 2 Hispano 20 mm.
A/S mortars: 4 RBU 1200.
Depth charges: 2 projectors; 2 racks.
Countermeasures: 2 Wallop Barricade double layer Chaff launchers.
Radars: Surface search: Decca 45; I band.
Sonars: Hull-mounted; active attack; high frequency.

Comment: The design is an improved version of that of *Udarnik*. Type name, Patrolni Brod. Modernised in 1970-73 at Naval repair yard, Sava Kovacevic, Tivat, Gulf of Cattaro.

MORNAR *10/1990, Eric Grove*

LAND-BASED MARITIME AIRCRAFT

Numbers/Type: 12 Kamov Ka-25 Hormone A.
Operational speed: 104 kts *(193 km/h)*.
Service ceiling: 11 500 ft *(3500 m)*.
Range: 217 nm *(400 km)*.
Role/Weapon systems: ASW within Yugoslavian waters in support of submarine flotilla. Sensors: Search radar, MAD, dipping sonar, sonobuoys. Weapons: ASW; 2 × torpedoes or depth bombs. ASV; 4 × locally produced wire-guided missiles.

Numbers/Type: 15 Mil Mi-8 Hip C.
Operational speed: 112 kts *(225 km/h)*.
Service ceiling: 14 760 ft *(4500 m)*.
Range: 251 nm *(465 km)*.
Role/Weapon systems: Coastal patrol and support helicopter for harbour protection and coastal patrol; supported by air force Aerospatiale SA 341/2 Gazelles from time to time. Sensors: Cameras only. Weapons: Self-defence; 1 × 27 mm cannon. Strike; up to 192 × 68 mm rockets or gun pods, 6 × locally produced wire-guided missiles.

Numbers/Type: 5 Kamov Ka-28 Helix A.
Operational speed: 110 kts *(204 km/h)*.
Service ceiling: 12 000 ft *(3658 m)*.
Range: 270 nm *(500 km)*.
Role/Weapon systems: ASW within territorial waters, to supplement and replace Ka-25. Sensors: Search radar, MAD, dipping sonar, sonobuoys. Weapons: ASW only; 2 × torpedoes or depth bombs.

LIGHT FORCES

6 KONČAR CLASS (TYPE 240) (FAST ATTACK CRAFT—MISSILE)

Name	No	Builders	Commissioned
RADE KONČAR	RT 401	Tito SY, Kraljevica	Apr 1977
SIBENIC (ex-*Vlado Cetkovič*)	RT 402	Tito SY, Kraljevica	Mar 1978
RAMIZ SADIKU	RT 403	Tito SY, Kraljevica	Aug 1978
HASAN ZAHIROVIČ-LACA	RT 404	Tito SY, Kraljevica	Dec 1978
ORCE NIKOLOV	RT 405	Tito SY, Kraljevica	Aug 1979
ANTE BANINA	RT 406	Tito SY, Kraljevica	Nov 1980

Displacement, tons: 242 full load
Dimensions, feet (metres): 147.6 × 27.6 × 8.2 *(45 × 8.4 × 2.5)*
Main machinery: CODAG; 2 RR Proteus gas turbines; 11 600 hp *(8.65 MW)*; 2 MTU 20V538 TB92 diesels; 8530 hp(m) *(6.27 MW)* sustained; 4 shafts
Speed, knots: 39. **Range, miles:** 500 at 35 kts; 880 at 23 kts (diesels)
Complement: 30 (5 officers)

Missiles: SSM: 2 SS-N-2B Styx; active radar or IR homing to 46 km *(25 nm)* at 0.9 Mach; warhead 513 kg. May be replaced by RBS-15 in due course.
Guns: 1 or 2 Bofors 57 mm/70; 75° elevation; 200 rounds/minute to 17 km *(9.3 nm)*; weight of shell 2.4 kg.
128 mm rocket launcher for illuminants.
2—30 mm/65 (twin) may be fitted in place of the after 57 mm.
Countermeasures: Wallop Barricade double layer Chaff launcher.
Fire control: PEAB 9LV 200 GFCS.
Radars: Surface search: Decca 1226; I band.
Fire control: Philips TAB; I/J band.

Programmes: Type name, Raketna Topovnjaca. There are probably four additional hulls, without engines or weapons, which belonged to a cancelled Libyan order.
Structure: Aluminium superstructure. Designed by the Naval Shipping Institute in Zagreb based on Swedish Spica class with bridge amidships like Malaysian boats. The after 57 mm gun is being replaced by a twin 30 mm mounting.
Operational: RT 402 held by Croatia in early 1992 and one other may have been sunk or damaged.

RADE KONČAR *1986*

SIBENIC (with 30 mm gun) *1992, S. S. Breyer*

10 Ex-SOVIET OSA I CLASS (FAST ATTACK CRAFT—MISSILE)

MITAR ACEV RČ 301
VLADO BAGAT RČ 302
PETAR DRAPŠIN RČ 303
STEVAN FILIPOVIĆ RČ 304
ŽIKICA JOVANOVIĆ-ŠPANAC RČ 305
NIKOLA MARTINOVIĆ RČ 306
JOSIP MAŽAR SOSA RČ 307
KARLO ROJC RČ 308
FRANČ ROZMAN-STANE RČ 309
VELIMIR ŠKORPIK RČ 310

Displacement, tons: 171 standard; 210 full load
Dimensions, feet (metres): 110.2 × 24.9 × 8.8 *(33.6 × 7.6 × 2.7)*
Main machinery: 3 diesels; 12 000 hp(m) *(8.82 MW)*; 3 shafts
Speed, knots: 35. **Range, miles:** 400 at 34 kts
Complement: 30 (4 officers)

Missiles: SSM: 4 SS-N-2A Styx; active radar or IR homing to 46 km *(25 nm)* at 0.9 Mach; warhead 513 kg.
Guns: 4 USSR 30 mm/65 (2 twin); 85° elevation; 500 rounds/minute to 5 km *(2.7 nm)*; weight of shell 0.54 kg.
Radars: Surface search: Square Tie; I band.
Fire control: Drum Tilt; H/I band.
IFF: High Pole. 2 Square Head.

Programmes: Transferred in 1965 (1), 1966 (1), 1967 (1), 1968 (4), 1969 (3). Named after war heroes. Type name, Raketni Čamac.
Operational: Two of the class held by Croatia in early 1992 and one other may have been sunk.

FRANČ ROZMAN-STANE *1982, Yugoslav Navy*

14 Ex-SOVIET SHERSHEN CLASS (TYPE 201) (FAST ATTACK CRAFT—TORPEDO)

PIONIR TČ 211	**BIOKOVAK** TČ 218
PARTIZAN TČ 212	**STRELJKO** TČ 219
PROLETER TČ 213	**CRVENA ZVEZDA** TČ 220
TOPCIDER TČ 214	**PARTIZAN II** TČ 221
IVAN TČ 215	**PARTIZAN III** TČ 222
JADRAN TČ 216	**NAPREDAK** TČ 223
KORNAT TČ 217	**PIONIR II** TČ 224

Displacement, tons: 145 standard; 170 full load
Dimensions, feet (metres): 113.8 × 22.3 × 4.9 *(34.7 × 6.7 × 1.5)*
Main machinery: 3 diesels; 12 000 hp *(8.82 MW)*; 3 shafts
Speed, knots: 45. **Range, miles:** 850 at 30 kts
Complement: 23
Guns: 4 USSR 30 mm/65 (2 twin); 85° elevation; 500 rounds/minute to 5 km *(2.7 nm)*; weight of shell 0.54 kg.
Torpedoes: 4—21 in *(533 mm)* tubes. Soviet Type 53.
Mines: 6.
Radars: Surface search: Pot Head; I band.
Fire control: Drum Tilt; H/I band.
IFF: High Pole. Square Head

Comment: Three craft *(Topcider, Ivan,* and *Jadran)* acquired from USSR. Remainder built under licence by Tito Shipyard, Kraljevica between 1966 and 1971. Named after partisan craft of the Second World War. Type name, Torpedni Čamac. First one deleted in 1988. Four probably held by Croatia in early 1992.

JADRAN *1982, Yugoslav Navy*

10 MIRNA CLASS (TYPE 140) (FAST ATTACK CRAFT—PATROL)

BIOKOVO 171	**GRMEČ** 175	**ZELENGORA** 179
POHORJE 172	**FRUŠKA GORA** 177	**CER** 180
KOPRIVNIK 173	**KOSMAJ** 178	**KOZOLO** 181
UČKA 174		

Displacement, tons: 120 full load
Dimensions, feet (metres): 104.9 × 22 × 7.5 *(32 × 6.7 × 2.3)*
Main machinery: 2 SEMT-Pielstick 12 PA4 200 VGDS diesels; 5292 hp(m) *(3.89 MW)* sustained; 2 shafts
Speed, knots: 30. **Range, miles:** 400 at 20 kts
Complement: 19 (3 officers)
Missiles: SAM: 1 SA-N-5 Grail quad mounting; manual aiming; IR homing to 6 km *(3.2 nm)* at 1.5 Mach; altitude to 2500 m *(8000 ft)*; warhead 1.5 kg.
Guns: 1 Bofors 40 mm/70. 1 Oerlikon 20 mm. 2—128 mm illuminant launchers.
Depth charges: 8 rails.

Comment: Builders, Kraljevica Yard. Commissioned 1981-85. A most unusual feature of this design is the fitting of an electric outboard motor giving a speed of up to 6 kts. One sunk possibly by a limpet mine in November 1991. At least two probably held by Croatia in early 1992.

POHORJE *1988, Yugoslav Navy*

7 TYPE 131 (LARGE PATROL CRAFT)

KALNIK PC 132	**ROMANIJA** PC 136
VELEBIT PC 133	**KAMENAR** PC 137
GRANIČAR PC 134	**KOZUF** PC 140
RUDNIK PC 135	

Displacement, tons: 85 standard; 120 full load
Dimensions, feet (metres): 91.9 × 14.8 × 8.3 *(28 × 4.5 × 2.5)*
Main machinery: 2 MTU MB 12V 493 TY7 diesels; 2200 hp(m) *(1.62 MW)* sustained; 2 shafts
Speed, knots: 22
Guns: 6 Hispano-Suiza 20 mm (2 triple).
Radars: Surface search: Kelvin Hughes; I band.

Comment: Built at Trogir SY between 1965 and 1968. Type name, Patrolni Čamac. *Durmitor* and *Cer* sold to Malta in March 1982.

RUDNIK *1982, Yugoslav Navy*

6 TYPE 20 (RIVER PATROL CRAFT)

PC 211-216

Displacement, tons: 55 standard
Dimensions, feet (metres): 71.5 × 17 × 3.9 *(21.8 × 5.3 × 1.2)*
Main machinery: 2 diesels; 1156 hp(m) *(850 kW)*; 2 shafts
Speed, knots: 16. **Range, miles:** 200 at 15 kts
Complement: 10
Guns: 2 Oerlikon 20 mm.
Radars: Surface search: Decca 110; I band.

Comment: Completed since 1984. Steel hull with GRP superstructure.

PC 215 *1988, Yugoslav Navy*

5 BOTICA CLASS (TYPE 16) (RIVER PATROL CRAFT)

PC 301-304, 306

Displacement, tons: 23 full load
Dimensions, feet (metres): 55.8 × 11.8 × 2.8 *(17 × 3.6 × 0.8)*
Main machinery: 2 diesels; 464 hp(m) *(340 kW)*; 2 shafts
Speed, knots: 15
Complement: 7
Military lift: 3 tons
Guns: 1 Oerlikon 20 mm. 7—7.62 mm MGs.
Radars: Surface search: Decca 110; I band.

Comment: Can carry up to 30 troops. May be in reserve.

12 TYPE 15 (RIVER PATROL CRAFT)

Displacement, tons: 19.5 full load
Dimensions, feet (metres): 55.4 × 12.8 × 2.3 *(16.9 × 3.9 × 0.7)*
Main machinery: 2 diesels; 330 hp(m) *(242 kW)*; 2 shafts
Speed, knots: 16. **Range, miles:** 160 at 12 kts
Complement: 6
Guns: 1 Oerlikon 20 mm; 2—7.62 mm MGs.
Radars: Surface search: Racal Decca 110; I band.

Comment: Built in Yugoslavia in the late 1980s for use in shallow water. Steel hulls with GRP superstructure. Four air conditioned craft were delivered to Sudan on 18 May 1989.

PC 15 Type *1989, Yugoslav Navy*

MINE WARFARE FORCES

4 VUKOV KLANAC CLASS (MINESWEEPERS/HUNTERS)

Name	No	Builders	Commissioned
VUKOV KLANAC* (ex-*Hrabri*)	M 151 (ex-D 25)	A Normand, France	Sep 1957
PODGORA (ex-*Smeli*)	M 152 (ex-D 26)	A Normand, France	Sep 1957
BLITVENICA* (ex-*Slobodni*)	M 153 (ex-D 27)	A Normand, France	Sep 1957
GRADAC (ex-*Snazni*)	M 161	Mali Losinj SY, Yugoslavia	1960

*Hunters

Displacement, tons: 365 standard; 424 full load
Dimensions, feet (metres): 152 × 28 × 8.2 *(46.4 × 8.6 × 2.5)*
Main machinery: 2 SEMT-Pielstick PA1-175 diesels; 1620 hp(m) *(1.19 MW)*; 2 shafts
Speed, knots: 15. **Range, miles:** 3000 at 10 kts
Complement: 40
Guns: 2 Oerlikon 20 mm.
Countermeasures: MCMV: PAP 104 (minehunters); remote controlled submersibles.
Radars: Navigation: Thomson-CSF DRBN 30; I band.
Sonars: Plessey Type 193M (minehunters); hull-mounted; active minehunting; high frequency.

Comment: The first three were built as US 'off-shore' orders. *Gradac* (ex-*Snazni*) was built in Yugoslavia in 1960 with French assistance. Two converted to minehunters in 1980-81. Decca Hi-fix. *Vukov Klanac* had her upper deck extensively damaged in November 1991 and may be scrapped.

VUKOV KLANAC *10/1990, Eric Grove*

4 BRITISH HAM CLASS (MINESWEEPERS—INSHORE)

MLJ M 141 **BRSEČ** M 142 **OLIB** M 143 **IZ** M 144

Displacement, tons: 120 standard; 159 full load
Dimensions, feet (metres): 106.5 × 21.3 × 5.5 *(32.5 × 6.5 × 1.7)*
Main machinery: 2 Paxman YHAXM diesels; 1100 hp *(821 kW)*; 2 shafts
Speed, knots: 14. **Range, miles:** 2000 at 9 kts
Complement: 22
Guns: 2 Oerlikon 20 mm (twin).

Comment: Built in Yugoslavia 1964-66 under the US Military Aid Programme. Wooden hulls.

BRSEČ *1968, Yugoslav Navy*

6 TYPE M 117 CLASS (MINESWEEPERS—INSHORE)

M 117-122

Displacement, tons: 131 full load
Dimensions, feet (metres): 98.4 × 18 × 4.9 *(30 × 5.5 × 1.5)*
Main machinery: 2 GM diesels; 1000 hp *(746 kW)*; 2 shafts
Speed, knots: 12
Complement: 25
Guns: 1 Bofors 40 mm/60. 2—12.7 mm MGs.

Comment: Built in Yugoslavia 1966-68. M 117 used for surveying.

9 TYPE M 301 CLASS (RIVER MINESWEEPERS)

M 314, 317-324

Displacement, tons: 38
Speed, knots: 12
Guns: 2 Oerlikon 20 mm.
Radars: Surface search: Racal Decca; I band.

Comment: All launched in 1951-53. Serve on the Danube. Have minelaying capability. Being paid off.

M 301 Class *1982, Yugoslav Navy*

7 NESTIN CLASS (RIVER MINESWEEPERS)

Name	No	Builders	Commissioned
NESTIN	M 331	Brodotehnika, Belgrade	20 Dec 1975
MOTAJICA	M 332	Brodotehnika, Belgrade	18 Dec 1976
BELEGIŠ	M 333	Brodotehnika, Belgrade	1976
BOSUT	M 334	Brodotehnika, Belgrade	1979
VUČEDOL	M 335	Brodotehnika, Belgrade	1979
DJERDAP	M 336	Brodotehnika, Belgrade	1980
PANONSKO MORE	M 337	Brodotehnika, Belgrade	1980

Displacement, tons: 65 full load
Dimensions, feet (metres): 88.6 × 21.7 × 5.2 *(27 × 6.3 × 1.6)*
Main machinery: 2 diesels; 520 hp(m) *(382 kW)*; 2 shafts
Speed, knots: 15. **Range, miles:** 860 at 11 kts
Complement: 17
Guns: 5 Hispano 20 mm (triple fwd, 2 single aft).
Mines: 24 can be carried.
Countermeasures: MCMV: Magnetic, acoustic and explosive sweeping gear.
Radars: Surface search: Racal Decca 1226; I band.

Comment: Eight transferred to Hungary and three to Iraq.

MOTAJICA *1982, Yugoslav Navy*

AMPHIBIOUS FORCES

1 SILBA CLASS (LCT/MINELAYER)

DBM 241

Displacement, tons: 880 full load
Measurement, tons: 160.8 oa; 144 wl × 33.5 × 8.5 *(49; 43.9 × 10.2 × 2.6)*
Main machinery: 2 diesels; 3100 hp(m) *(2.28 MW)* sustained; 2 shafts; cp props
Speed, knots: 12. **Range, miles:** 360 at 12 kts
Complement: 39
Military lift: 460 tons or 4 medium tanks or 7 APCs or 300 troops with equipment
Guns: 4—30 mm/65 (2 twin) AK 230.
4—20 mm M75 (quad). 2—128 mm illuminant launchers.
Radars: Surface search: I band.

Comment: Commissioned in 1990. Ro-Ro design with bow and stern ramps. Can be used for minelaying.

DBM 241 *1990, Yugoslav Navy*

14 MFPD-3 TYPE + 3 DSM 501 TYPE (LCTs/MINELAYERS)

DTM 213, 215, 217, 219, 221-223, 226, 228, 229, 232-234, 237
DSM 509, 513, 514

Displacement, tons: 410 full load
Dimensions, feet (metres): 155.1 × 21 × 7.5 *(47.3 × 6.4 × 2.3)*
Main machinery: 3 Gray Marine 64HN9 diesels; 495 hp *(369 kW)*; 3 shafts
Speed, knots: 9
Complement: 15
Military lift: 200 troops or 3 heavy tanks
Guns: 2—12.7 mm MGs.
Mines: Can carry 100.

Comment: Unlike other tank landing craft in that the centre part of the bow drops to form a ramp down which the tanks go ashore, the vertical section of the bow being articulated to form outer end of ramp. Built in Yugoslavia. Can also act as minelayers. Two sold to Sudan in 1969. DTM (Desantni Tenkonosac/Minopolagac means landing ship tank/minelayer). DTM 217 is named *Jastreb*. DTM 217 held by Croatia in early 1992.

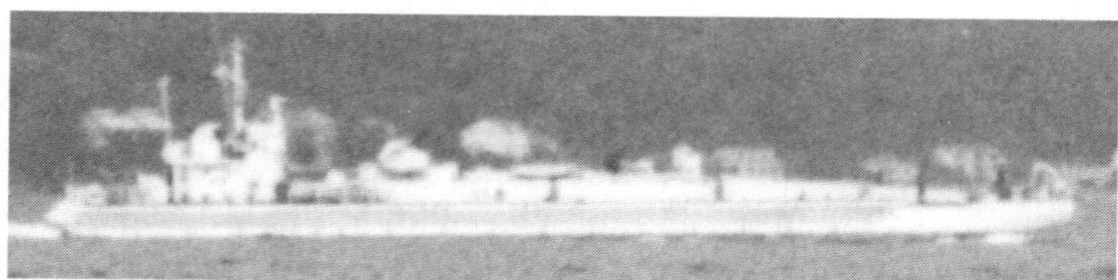

DTM 217 *10/1990, Eric Grove*

10 TYPE 22 (LCUs)

DJC 623-632

Displacement, tons: 48 full load
Dimensions, feet (metres): 73.2 × 15.7 × 3.3 *(22.3 × 4.8 × 1)*
Main engines: 2 MTU diesels; 1740 hp(m) *(1.28 MW)*; 2 waterjets
Speed, knots: 35. **Range, miles:** 320 at 22 kts
Complement: 8
Military lift: 40 troops or 15 tons cargo
Guns: 2—20 mm M71.
Radars: Navigation: Decca 101; I band.

Comment: Built of polyester and glass fibre. Last one completed in 1987.

12 TYPE 21 (LCUs)

DJC 601-631 series

Displacement, tons: 32 full load
Dimensions, feet (metres): 69.9 × 15.7 × 5.2 *(21.3 × 4.8 × 1.6)*
Main machinery: 1 diesel; 1450 hp(m) *(1.07 MW)*; 1 shaft
Speed, knots: 23. **Range, miles:** 320 at 22 kts
Complement: 6
Military lift: 6 tons
Guns: 1—20 mm M71.

Comment: The survivors of a class of 30 built between 1976 and 1979. At least four held by Croatia in early 1992.

DJC 627 — *1989, Yugoslav Navy*

DJC 607 — *1989, Yugoslav Navy*

15 TYPE 11 (LCVP)

Displacement, tons: 10 full load
Dimensions, feet (metres): 37 × 10.2 × 1.6 *(11.3 × 3.1 × 0.5)*
Main machinery: 2 diesels; 2 waterjets
Speed, knots: 23. **Range, miles:** 100 at 15 kts
Complement: 2
Military lift: 4.8 tons of equipment or troops
Guns: 1—7.62 mm MG.
Radars: Navigation: I band.

Comment: GRP construction building since 1986.

LCVP Type II — *1990, Yugsolav Navy*

TRAINING SHIPS

JADRAN (ex-*Marco Polo*)

Displacement, tons: 720
Dimensions, feet (metres): 190 × 29.2 × 13.8 *(58 × 8.9 × 4.2)*
Main machinery: 1 Linke-Hofmann diesel; 375 hp(m) *(276 kW)*; 1 shaft
Speed, knots: 8 diesel; 14 sail
Complement: 150

Comment: Topsail schooner. Sail area, 8600 sq ft *(800 sq m)*. Built by H C Stülcken, Hamburg. Served in Italian Navy during the Second World War *(Marco Polo)*. Launched in 1932.

JADRAN — *1982, Yugoslav Navy*

1 GALEB CLASS

Name	*No*	*Builders*	*Commissioned*
GALEB (ex-*Kuchuk*, ex-*Ramb III*, ex-German *Kiebitz*)	M 11	Ansaldo, Genoa	1939

Displacement, tons: 5182 standard
Measurement, tons: 3667 gross
Dimensions, feet (metres): 384.8 × 51.2 × 18.4 *(117.3 × 15.6 × 5.6)*
Main machinery: 2 Burmeister & Wain diesels; 7200 hp(m) *(5.29 MW)*; 2 shafts
Speed, knots: 17. **Range, miles:** 20 000 at 16 kts
Guns: 4—40 mm/56.
Mines: Capacity not known.

Comment: Ex-Italian. Launched 6 March 1938. Sunk as an auxiliary cruiser in 1944, refloated and reconstructed in 1952. Serves as Fleet Flagship, Presidential Yacht and training ship. Former armament was four 3.5 in, four 40 mm and 24—20 mm (six quadruple) guns but these guns were landed in the mid-1960s and replacements only mounted several years later. Classified as a minelayer.

GALEB — *7/1989, A Sheldon-Duplaix*

HEADQUARTERS SHIPS

Note: (1) Previously reported *Sabac* is not part of the Yugoslav Navy.
(2) Two Presidential yachts are manned by the Navy.

2 Presidential Yachts — *1990, Florian Jentsch*

KOZARA PB 30

Displacement, tons: 695 full load
Dimensions, feet (metres): 219.8 × 31.2 × 4.6 *(67 × 9.5 × 1.4)*
Main machinery: 2 Deutz RV 6M 545 diesels; 800 hp(m) *(588 kW)*; 2 shafts
Speed, knots: 12

Comment: Former Presidential Yacht on Danube. Built in Austria in 1940. Now acts as Flagship of the river flotilla.

KOZARA *1982, Yugoslav Navy*

VIS PB 25

Displacement, tons: 680 full load
Dimensions, feet (metres): 187 × 27.9 × 11.5 *(57 × 8.5 × 3.5)*
Main machinery: 2 diesels; 2000 hp(m) *(1.47 MW)*; 2 shafts
Speed, knots: 17
Guns: 1 Bofors 40 mm/60. 2 Oerlikon 20 mm.

Comment: Built in 1956. Serves as HQ ship of the Adriatic Fleet.

VIS *1987*

SURVEY SHIPS

Name	*No*	*Builders*	*Commissioned*
ANDRIJA MOHOROVIČIĆ	PH 33	Gdansk Shipyard, Poland	1972

Displacement, tons: 1200 standard; 1475 full load
Dimensions, feet (metres): 240.5 × 33.5 × 12.8 *(73.3 × 10.2 × 3.9)*
Main machinery: 2 Skoda Sulzer 6TD48 diesels; 3600 hp(m) *(2.65 MW)*; 2 shafts; cp props
Speed, knots: 15. **Range, miles:** 9000 at 12 kts
Complement: 37 (4 officers)
Radars: Navigation: Don 2; I band.

Comment: Built in 1971 at the shipyard in Gdansk, Poland, and added to the Yugoslav Navy List in 1972. Soviet Moma class type. Held by Croatia in early 1992.

ANDRIJA MOHOROVIČIĆ *1982, Yugoslav Navy*

7 SURVEY CRAFT

Comment: *PH 123* of 115 tons and a complement of 21; *BH 11* and *BH 12* of 70 tons, complement 12; and *BH 1* and *BH 2* of 30 tons, complement 5; *CH 1* and *CH 2* of 4.5 tons, complement 3.

PH 123 *1991, van Ginderen Collection*

SALVAGE VESSEL

SPASILAC PS 12

Displacement, tons: 1590 full load
Dimensions, feet (metres): 182 × 39.4 × 14.1 *(55.5 × 12 × 4.3)*
Main engines: 2 diesels; 4340 hp(m) *(3.19 MW)*; 2 shafts; Kort nozzle props; bow thruster
Speed, knots: 13. **Range, miles:** 4000 at 12 kts
Complement: 53 plus 19 spare berths

Comment: Built at Tito SY, Belgrade. In service 10 September 1976. Fitted for firefighting and fully equipped for salvage work. Decompression chamber, and can support a manned rescue submersible. Can be fitted with two quadruple M 75 and two single M 71 20 mm guns. Sister ship in Libyan Navy. Held by Croatia in early 1992.

SPASILAC *1988, Yugoslav Navy*

SERVICE FORCES

3 LUBIN CLASS (AKL)

LUBIN PO 91 **UGOR** PO 92 **KIT** PO 93

Displacement, tons: 860 full load
Dimensions, feet (metres): 190.9 × 36 × 9.2 *(58.2 × 11 × 2.8)*
Main machinery: 2 diesels; 3500 hp(m) *(2.57 MW)*; 2 shafts; cp props
Speed, knots: 16. **Range, miles:** 1500 at 16 kts.
Complement: 43
Military lift: 150 troops; 6 tanks
Guns: 1 Bofors 40 mm/70. 4—20 mm M75 (quad). 128 mm rocket launcher for illuminants.

Comment: Fitted with bow doors and two upper-deck cranes. Roll-on/roll-off cargo ships built in the 1950s and employed by the Navy usually as ammunition transports. PO (Pomocni Oruzar or auxiliary ammunition ship).

KIT *1987, Yugoslav Navy*

4 PT 82 CLASS (AKL)

PT 82 **PT 83** **PT 86** **PT 87**

Displacement, tons: 58 full load
Dimensions, feet (metres): 67.3 × 14.8 × 3.7 *(20.5 × 4.5 × 1.4)*
Main machinery: 2 diesels; 304 hp(m) *(223 kW)*; 2 shafts
Speed, knots: 12. **Range, miles:** 400 at 10 kts
Complement: 6
Cargo capacity: 15 tons or 70 troops with equipment
Guns: 2—20 mm M71 (can be fitted).

Comment: Completed in 1987. General purpose transport craft.

PT 83 *1989, Yugoslav Navy*

2 PT 71 TYPE

MEDUZA PT 71 **JASTOG** PT 72

Displacement, tons: 310 standard; 428 full load
Dimensions, feet (metres): 152.2 × 23.6 × 17.1 *(46.4 × 7.2 × 5.2)*
Main machinery: 1 Burmeister & Wain diesel; 300 hp(m) *(220 kW)*; 1 shaft
Speed, knots: 7

Comment: Built in 1953.

JASTOG *1982, Yugoslav Navy*

1 PO TYPE (AMMUNITION TRANSPORT)

PO 51

Displacement, tons: 700
Main machinery: 2 Burmeister and Wain diesels; 600 hp(m) *(440 kW)*; 2 shafts
Speed, knots: 16
Complement: 43
Cargo capacity: 150 troops plus all types of ammunition

Comment: Built at Split in 1950s.

1 WATER CARRIER

ALGA PV 17

Displacement, tons: 600 full load
Dimensions, feet (metres): 144.4 × 25.6 × 10.5 *(44 × 7.8 × 3.2)*
Main machinery: 1 diesel; 350 hp(m) *(257 kW)*; 1 shaft
Speed, knots: 8
Cargo capacity: 380 tons
Guns: 1 Bofors 40 mm/60. 1—20 mm M71.

Comment: Used to supply off-shore islands. Four names were deleted from this class in 1986-87. As their role is vital to the inhabitants of the islands it seems most likely that these have been either transferred to civil operations or been replaced by civilian craft.

ALGA *10/1990, Eric Grove*

3 HARBOUR TANKERS

PN 20 **PN 21** **PN 25**

Displacement, tons: 430 full load
Dimensions, feet (metres): 151 × 23.6 × 10.2 *(46 × 7.2 × 3.1)*
Main machinery: 1 diesel; 300 hp(m) *(220 kW)*; 1 shaft
Speed, knots: 7

Comment: Built at Split in mid-1950s. The last surviving three of the class. PN 25 held by Croatia in early 1992.

4 COASTAL TUGS

PR 36-39

Displacement, tons: 550 full load
Dimensions, feet (metres): 105 × 26.2 × 16.4 *(32 × 8 × 5)*
Speed, knots: 11

Comment: Built at Split in 1950s. Type name, PR (Pomorski Remorker). One held by Croatia in early 1992.

COASTAL TUG *1988, Yugoslav Navy*

9 HARBOUR TUGS

LR 71-79

Displacement, tons: 130

Comment: Built at Split in 1960s. Type name, LR (Lučki Remorker). Four may be civilian manned.

1 DEGAUSSING VESSEL

36

Displacement, tons: 110 standard
Dimensions, feet (metres): 105.6 × 23.3 × 3.9 *(32.2 × 7.1 × 1.2)*
Main machinery: 1 diesel; 528 hp(m) *(388 kW)*; 1 shaft
Speed, knots: 10. **Range, miles:** 660 at 10 kts
Complement: 20
Guns: 2—20 mm M71.

Comment: Used to degauss River vessels up to a length of 50 m.

36 *1987, Yugoslav Navy*

TENDERS

Displacement, tons: 51 full load
Dimensions, feet (metres): 69 × 14.8 × 4.6 *(21 × 4.5 × 1.4)*
Main machinery: 2 diesels; 304 hp(m) *(224 kW)*; 2 shafts
Speed, knots: 12
Guns: 2—20 mm M71 can be carried.
Radars: Navigation: Decca; I band.

Comment: A number of tenders which, as transports, can carry 130 people or 15 tons of cargo and also act as diving tenders.

TENDER *10/1990, Eric Grove*

ZAIRE

General

With a civil war in prospect and the local currency virtually destroyed, it is difficult to establish the state of the Navy in 1992.

Personnel

(a) 1992: 2300 officers and men (including 600 marines)
(b) Voluntary service

Bases

Kalemie, Kinshasa, Banana

Mercantile Marine

Lloyd's Register of Shipping:
30 vessels of 56 393 tons gross

DELETIONS

1990 2 Shanghai II class, 1 Swift class

PATROL FORCES

Note: Several North Korean patrols were ordered in 1989 but none was delivered due to lack of funds.

2 Ex-CHINESE SHANGHAI II CLASS (FAST ATTACK CRAFT—GUN)

106 +1

Displacement, tons: 113 standard; 131 full load
Dimensions, feet (metres): 127.3 × 17.7 × 5.6 *(38.8 × 5.4 × 1.7)*
Main machinery: 2 Type L12-180 diesels; 2400 hp(m) *(1.76 MW)* forward; 2 Type L12-180Z diesels; 1820 hp(m) *(1.34 MW)* aft; 4 shafts
Speed, knots: 30. **Range, miles:** 700 at 17 kts
Complement: 34
Guns: 4—37 mm/65 (2 twin). 4—25 mm/80 (2 twin).

Comment: First four delivered in 1976-78. All were thought to be beyond repair by 1985 but two of the four were patched up and two replacements were delivered in February 1987. Two sunk at moorings in mid-1990.

SHANGHAI II 106 *1988, Gilbert Gyssels*

4 SWIFTSHIPS (COASTAL PATROL CRAFT)

KIALA **LUADIA** **KANITSHA** **MBOKO**

Displacement, tons: 19 full load
Dimensions, feet (metres): 51.2 × 13.5 × 3.6 *(15.6 × 4.1 × 1.1)*
Main machinery: 2 GM 12V-71N diesels; 680 hp *(507 kW)* sustained; 2 shafts
Speed, knots: 25. **Range, miles:** 400 at 24 kts
Complement: 12
Guns: 6—12.7 mm MGs.

Comment: Built by Swiftships, Morgan City, in 1971. Doubtful operational status and two have already been deleted.

8 ARCOA 25 CLASS (PATROL CRAFT)

Displacement, tons: 2 full load
Dimensions, feet (metres): 24.6 × 9.8 × 2.6 *(7.5 × 3 × 0.8)*
Main machinery: 2 Baudouin diesels; 320 hp(m) *(235 kW)*; 2 shafts
Speed, knots: 30

Comment: Twenty-nine ordered in 1974 in France and delivered by Arcoa. MG mountings forward and aft. Fourteen more delivered 1980-81. Eight were still serviceable at the end of 1990.

Indexes

COUNTRY ABBREVIATIONS

Alb	Albania
Alg	Algeria
Ana	Anguilla
Ang	Angola
Ant	Antigua and Barbuda
Arg	Argentina
Aus	Austria
Aust	Australia
Ban	Bangladesh
Bar	Barbados
Bel	Belgium
Ben	Benin
Bhm	Bahamas
Bhr	Bahrain
Blz	Belize
Bmd	Bermuda
Bol	Bolivia
Bru	Brunei
Brz	Brazil
Bul	Bulgaria
Bur	Burma
Cam	Cameroon
Can	Canada
Chi	Chile
Cmb	Cambodia
Col	Colombia
Com	Comoro Islands
Con	Congo
CI	Cook Islands
CPR	China, People's Republic
CpV	Cape Verde
CR	Costa Rica
Cub	Cuba
Cypr	Cyprus (Republic)
Cyp T	Cyprus (Turkish)
Cz	Czechoslovakia
Den	Denmark
Dji	Djibouti
Dom	Dominica
DPRK	Korea, Democratic People's Republic (North)
DR	Dominican Republic
Ecu	Ecuador
Egy	Egypt
EIS	El Salvador
EqG	Equatorial Guinea
Eth	Ethiopia
Fae	Faeroes
Fiji	Fiji
FI	Falkland Islands
Fin	Finland
Fra	France
Gab	Gabon
Gam	The Gambia
GB	Guinea-Bissau
Ger	Germany
Gha	Ghana
Gn	Guinea
Gra	Grenada
Gre	Greece
Gua	Guatemala
Guy	Guyana
Hai	Haiti
HK	Hong Kong
Hon	Honduras
Hun	Hungary
IC	Ivory Coast
Ice	Iceland
Ind	India
Indo	Indonesia
Iran	Iran
Iraq	Iraq
Ire	Ireland
Isr	Israel
Ita	Italy
Jam	Jamaica
Jor	Jordan
Jpn	Japan
Ken	Kenya
Kwt	Kuwait
Lbr	Liberia
Lby	Libya
Leb	Lebanon
Mad	Madagascar
Mex	Mexico
MI	Marshall Islands
Mic	Micronesia
Mld	Maldive Islands
Mlt	Malta
Mlw	Malawi
Mly	Malaysia
Mnt	Montserrat
Mor	Morocco
Moz	Mozambique
Mrt	Mauritius
Mtn	Mauritania
NATO	NATO
Nic	Nicaragua
Nig	Nigeria
Nld	Netherlands
Nor	Norway
NZ	New Zealand
Omn	Oman
Pak	Pakistan
Pan	Panama
Par	Paraguay
Per	Peru
Plp	Philippines
PNG	Papua New Guinea
Pol	Poland
Port	Portugal
Qat	Qatar
RoC	Taiwan
RoK	Korea, Republic (South)
Rom	Romania
Rus	Russia and Associated States
SA	South Africa
Sab	Sabah
SAr	Saudi Arabia
Sen	Senegal
Sey	Seychelles
Sin	Singapore
SL	Sierra Leone
Sol	Solomon Islands
Spn	Spain
Sri	Sri Lanka
StK	St Kitts
StL	St Lucia
StV	St Vincent and the Grenadines
Sud	Sudan
Sur	Surinam
Swe	Sweden
Swi	Switzerland
Syr	Syria
Tan	Tanzania
TC	Turks and Caicos
Tld	Thailand
Tog	Togo
Ton	Tonga
TT	Trinidad and Tobago
Tun	Tunisia
Tur	Turkey
UAE	United Arab Emirates
Uga	Uganda
UK	United Kingdom
Uru	Uruguay
USA	United States of America
Van	Vanuatu
Ven	Venezuela
VI	Virgin Islands
Vtn	Vietnam
WS	Western Samoa
Yem	Yemen
Yug	Yugoslavia
Zai	Zaire

Named Ships

† denotes secondary reference is in text or note.

B

C

D

E

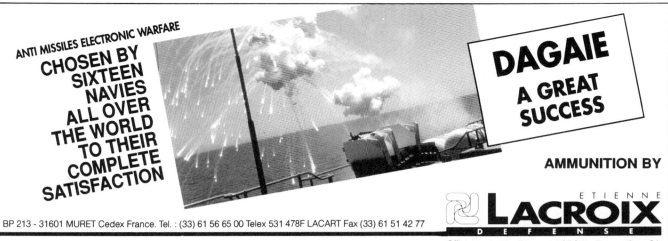

H

I

N

O

Q

R

S

T

U

V

Classes

† denotes reference is in text or note.

H

I

J

K

L

M

N

O

P

Q

R

S

T

U

Aircraft By Countries

Printed and bound in Great Britain by
Butler & Tanner Ltd, Frome and London

YOUR NAVAL DATA NEEDS

Every year there is a range of new systems and upgrades - missiles, guns and control systems for surface warships and submarines - and modernisation plans are announced. To keep pace with every development, complete information on the navies of the World, their capabilities, and available naval warfare systems is essential.

This data is supplied in Jane's Fighting Ships, Jane's Naval Weapon Systems and Jane's Underwater Warfare Systems. Together these three titles cover data on all warships and their capabilities and include detailed descriptions of weapon systems, combat, command and control systems, and full specifications of underwater systems.

They form an essential source for manufacturers who want to be up-to-date on their competitors and the latest technology, for procurement officers who need to compare and contrast equipment for new programmes, and for operators who must be fully equipped to recognise warships and their capabilities.

To place your order or ask for more information please contact:

Jane's
INFORMATION GROUP

FOR ORDERS FROM:
EUROPE/ASIA/AFRICA/AUSTRALASIA

Department DSM,
Sentinel House,
163 Brighton Road,
Coulsdon, Surrey CR5 2NH,
United Kingdom

FOR ORDERS FROM:
CANADA/USA/S.AMERICA/CARIBBEAN

Department DSM,
1340 Braddock Place,
Suite 300,
Alexandria VA 22314 – 1651
USA

JANE'S FIGHTING SHIPS 1992-93

Accurate and clearly-presented data on over 8000 warships, auxiliaries and armed vessels owned by over 150 nations in one easy-to-use volume.

80% of individual entries have updated information.

Publication date: May 1992
Price: £135 US$225

JANE'S UNDERWATER WARFARE SYSTEMS 1992-93

Details of over 600 different systems for underwater warfare - shipborne, submarine borne or airborne - from 168 manufacturers around the world.

70% of individual entries contain updated information.

Publication date: May 1992
Price: £135 US$225

JANE'S NAVAL WEAPON SYSTEMS

Jane's Naval Weapon Systems is an updatable information service (in loose-leaf binder) on weapon, command, control and associated systems for warships.

First year of subscription: binder + three updates
Subsequent years: three updates per year
New annual subscription price: £250; Renewals £200
US$395; Renewals US$335

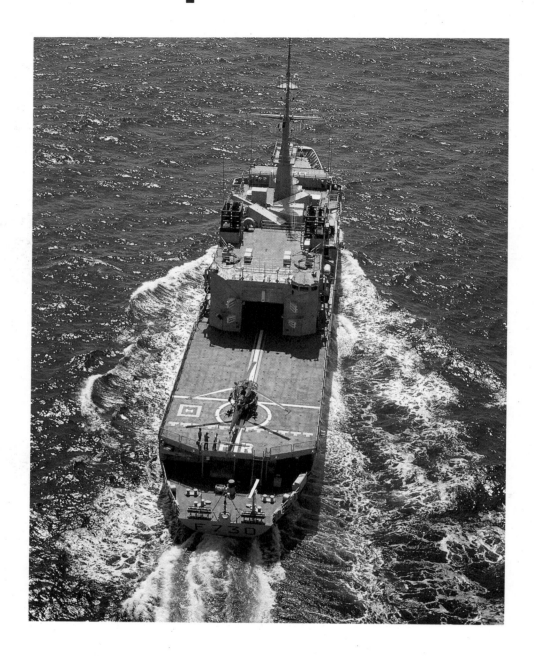